TRAVELING WITH YOUR PET
THE AAA PETBOOK®

The AAA guide to more than 15,000 pet-friendly, AAA Approved® hotels, restaurants and campgrounds across the United States and Canada.

17th Edition

AAA PUBLISHING

AAA thanks the following organization for its assistance:
Veterinary Emergency & Critical Care Society

Cover Photos

Front: Editors' Pick - Lyric at Camp Gone to the Dogs, Stowe, Vermont
Submitted by owner Carrie Neri
Back: 1st place Photo Contest Winner: Casey at Mokelumne River, Lodi, California
Submitted by owner Ruth Clark
Spine: 2nd place Photo Contest Winner: Murphy at Mt. Hood National Forest, Oregon
Submitted by owner Tracey Vukovich

Published by AAA Publishing
1000 AAA Drive, Heathrow, Florida 32746

Seventeenth Edition Copyright © 2015 AAA Publishing. All rights reserved.
ISBN: 978-1-59508-568-9 Stock Number 552215
Printed in the USA by Quad/Graphics, Inc.

This book was printed on third-party certified sustainably forested paper.

ABOUT THIS BOOK

Welcome to the 17th edition of **Traveling With Your Pet: The AAA PetBook®**, an indispensable, easy-to-use resource for travelers with pets. This comprehensive book provides all the information needed to take a four-legged friend on the road, from activity planning to trip preparation to finding a place to stay.

Recreational Resources

- Dog parks where you and your furry friends can play, exercise or just relax.
- A roundup of attractions that allow pets or offer kennel service.
- Recreation information for U.S. and Canadian national public lands that allow pets.

Practical Considerations

- An extensive list of emergency animal clinics for unexpected situations en route and at your destination, compiled by the Veterinary Emergency & Critical Care Society.
- Procedures and tips for crossing the U.S./Canadian border in either direction with pets.
- Policies pertaining to service animals.

Detailed Listings

- Specific pet policy details: deposits and fees (rounded to the nearest dollar), size restrictions, housekeeping and pet care services, designated rooms and other stipulations.
- More than 13,000 AAA Approved hotels which include AAA's trustworthy Diamond Ratings, the traveler's assurance of quality accommodations and reliable decision making information, plus facility details including rates, highway directions, amenities, recreation, dining and accessibility.
- About 1,000 AAA Approved restaurants that allow pets in outside dining areas.
- More than 800 top-rated campgrounds, including pet policies, facility details and AAA member discounts.

About the AAA PetBook Photo Contest

Have some great pictures from traveling with your pet? The annual AAA PetBook Photo Contest sponsored by Best Western gives you a chance to win great prizes and see your pet pictured on a cover of the next edition. Turn the page to read about the current contest winners, and turn to the photo gallery insert to see some irresistible photos of finalists. For contest requirements and an entry form, visit AAA.com/PetBook.

Picture Your Pet as the Next AAA PetBook® Cover Model!

For a chance to see your pet on or in the next **AAA PetBook**, enter the AAA PetBook Photo Contest sponsored by Best Western, open yearly from May 1 to Nov. 30. Visit **AAA.com/PetBook** for rules, entry forms, prize listings and photos of previous winners and finalists.

Editors' Pick — Lyric

Every so often, we get an entry that's so compelling our editors decide to use it on the book's front cover — separate from the placements designated for our first- and second-place contest winners. This year the honor was awarded to Lyric, a travel-loving Australian shepherd from Connecticut.

Lyric is shown here on a scenic trail teeming with cairns during a walk at Camp Gone to the Dogs in Stowe, Vermont. For Lyric's owner and her dogs, who spend much of the year performing semi-professionally in canine musical freestyle and Frisbee events, time to hang out and bond is a special treat on their annual getaway.

1st place winner — Casey

Casey, an enthusiastic Maltese, is pictured kayaking down the Mokelumne River in Lodi, California. His family's favorite outdoor vacation destination is Lake Tahoe, where they rent a cabin every year and take Casey along on bike rides, kayaking trips and strolls through the local farmer's market.

2nd place winner — Murphy

Murphy, a Pembroke Welsh corgi, poses near Trillium Lake in Oregon's Mount Hood National Forest. His family enjoys the priceless sparkle outdoor activities put in their dogs' eyes. Their favorite spot is Lincoln City, on Oregon's coast, because of the many pet-friendly businesses, trails and miles of uninterrupted beach.

Turn to Page p. 353 to view a sampling of more highlights from the last photo contest.

TABLE OF CONTENTS

AAA PetBook® Photo Contest

Traveling With Pets

Pet-Friendly Places

Pet-Friendly Hotels, Restaurants & Campgrounds

U.S. Hotels

Canadian Hotels

Restaurants

Campgrounds

Many people view their pets as full-fledged members of the family. Spot and Snowball often have their own beds, premium-quality foods, a basketful of toys and a special place in their humans' hearts.

Until it's time to go on vacation, that is. Then the family dog or cat is consigned to "watching the fort" at home while everyone else experiences the joy of traveling. Many animal lovers hesitate to take their pet with them because they don't think they'll be able to find accommodations that accept four-legged guests. Others aren't sure how — or if — their furry friends will adapt.

The truth is, including a pet in the family vacation is fairly easy, so long as you plan ahead. Most pets respond well to travel, a fact that isn't lost on the tourism industry. More than 15,000 AAA Approved hotels, restaurants and campgrounds from coast to coast are pet-friendly, and airline bookings for pet passengers are on the rise. Great companions at home, pets are earning their stripes on the road, too.

So if you've been longing to hit the trail with a canine or feline companion, read the tips on the following pages. You may find that a getaway can be far more enjoyable with than without your pet.

Should Your Pet Travel?

❧ **Rule 1: Pets who are very young, very old, pregnant, sick, injured, prone to biting or excessive vocalizing, or who cannot follow basic obedience commands should not travel.**

Before you make reservations, determine if your pet is able to travel. Most animals can and do make the most of the experience, but a small percentage simply are not cut out for traveling. Illness, physical condition and temperament are important factors, as is your pet's ability to adjust to such stresses as changes to his environment and routine. When in doubt, check with your veterinarian. If you feel your pet isn't up to the trip, it's better for everyone if he stays home.

❧ **Rule 2: If your pet can't actively participate in the trip, she should stay home.**

Even if Spot and Snowball are seasoned travelers, take into account the type of vacation and activities you have planned. No pet is going to be happy (or safe) cooped up in a car or hotel room. Likewise, the family dog may love camping and hiking, but the family cat may not. Putting a little thought toward your animal's needs and safety will pay off in a more enjoyable vacation for everyone.

❧ **Rule 3: Be specific when making travel plans that include your pet. Nobody wants unpleasant surprises on vacation.**

Most of the information in this book pertains to cats and dogs. If you own a bird, hamster, pig, ferret, lizard or other exotic creature, remember that unusual animals are not always accepted as readily as more conventional pets. Always specify the type of pet you have when making arrangements. Check if the municipalities you are traveling through and staying within have breed-specific regulations, i.e. certain dogs not allowed on the premises or even in the municipality. City or county resources should be referenced, as establishments may be unaware of their local restrictions.

Also check states' animal policies. **Hawaii** imposes a 120-day quarantine for all imported dogs, cats and other carnivores to prevent the importation of rabies. In some cases, the quarantine period may be reduced to 5 days or less if a pet meets various pre- and post-arrival requirements. Guide dogs and service dogs are exempt from the quarantine provided they have: a standard health certificate issued within 30 days prior to arrival; a current rabies vaccination with documentation of the product name, lot number and lot expiration date; a successful result of an OIE-FAVN rabies blood test conducted after 1 year of age; and an electronic identification microchip implanted and operational. Upon arrival, guide dogs and service dogs still must be examined for external parasites. For additional details, obtain the Hawaii Rabies Quarantine Information Brochure from the Hawaii Department of Agriculture, Animal Quarantine Station, 99-951 Halawa Valley St., Aiea, HI 96701-5602; phone (808) 483-7151, e-mail rabiesfree@hawaii.gov. Further information also is available from the department's web site: www.hdoa.hawaii.gov/ai/aqs.

North Carolina has stringent restrictions regarding pets in hotels. Make certain you understand an accommodation's specific policies before making reservations.

❧ **Rule 4: Never leave your pet with someone you don't trust.**

If Spot and Snowball stay behind, leave them in good hands while you're gone. **Family, friends and neighbors** make good sitters (provided they're willing), especially if they know your pet and can care for him in your home. Provide detailed instructions for feeding, exercise and medication, as well as phone numbers for your destination, your veterinarian and your local animal emergency clinic.

Professional pet sitters offer a range of services, from feeding and walking your pet daily to full-time house sitting while you are gone. Interview several candidates, and always check credentials and references. For additional information, contact the National Association of Professional Pet Sitters or Pet Sitters International. *(See sidebars on p. 8 and p. 9.)*

Kennels board many animals simultaneously and generally are run by professionals who will provide food and exercise according to your instructions. Pets usually are kept in a run (dogs) or cage (cats and small dogs) and may not get the same level of human interaction as at home. Veterinary clinics also board pets and may be the best choice if yours is sick, injured or needs special medical care.

Veterinarians, fellow pet owners and professional associations are a good source of referrals for sitters and kennels.

Travelers Who Have Disabilities

Individuals with disabilities who own service animals to assist them with everyday activities undoubtedly face challenges, but traveling should not be one of them. Service animals (the accepted term for animals trained to help people with disabilities) are not pets and thus are not subject to many of the laws or policies pertaining to pets.

The Americans With Disabilities Act (ADA) defines a service animal as "any guide dog, signal dog or other animal individually trained to provide assistance to an individual with a disability." ADA regulations stipulate that public accommodations are required to modify policies, practices and procedures to permit the use of a service animal by an individual with a disability.

The purpose of these regulations is to provide equal access opportunities for people with disabilities and to ensure that they are not separated from their service animals. A tow truck operator, for example, must allow a service animal to ride in the truck with her owner rather than in the towed vehicle.

Public accommodations may charge a fee or deposit to an individual who has a disability — provided that fee or

CHOOSING A PET SITTER

Before hiring a pet sitter, ask:
- Is he or she insured (for commercial liability) and bonded?
- What is included in the fee?
- Does the sitter require that your pet have a current vaccination?
- What kind of animals does the sitter typically care for?
- How will a medical, weather or home emergency be handled?
- Does he or she fully understand your pet's medical or dietary needs?
- How much time will be spent with your pet?

The pet sitter should:
- Have a polished, professional attitude.
- Provide references.
- Have a standard contract outlining terms of service.
- Have experience in caring for animals.
- Insist on current vaccinations.
- Ask about your pet's health, temperament, schedule and needs.
- Visit and interact with your pet before you leave.
- Devote time and attention to your pet.
- Be affiliated with pet care organizations.

Be sure you:
- Explain your pet's personality — favorite toys, good and bad habits, hiding spots, general health, etc.
- Leave care instructions, keys, food and water dishes, extra supplies (food, medication, etc.), and phone numbers for your veterinarian and an emergency contact.
- Bring pets inside before leaving.

CHOOSING A KENNEL

Before reserving a kennel, ask:
- What is included in the fee?
- Are current vaccinations required?
- What kind of animals do they board?
- How will a medical or weather emergency be handled?
- Will your pet be kept in a cage or run?
- Will your pet receive daily exercise?
- Does the kennel fully understand your pet's medical or dietary needs?
- How and how often will staff interact with your pet?

The kennel should:
- Require proof of current vaccinations.
- Be clean, well-ventilated and offer adequate protection from the elements.
- Have separate areas for dogs, cats and other animals, with secure fencing and caging.
- Clean and disinfect facilities daily.
- Give your pet his regular food on his regular schedule.
- Provide soft bedding in runs/cages.
- Understand your pet's medical needs.
- Provide or obtain veterinary care if necessary.
- Offer sufficient supervision.
- Have a friendly, animal-loving staff.

Be sure you:
- Notify staff of behavior quirks (dislike of other animals, children, etc.).
- Provide food and medication.
- Leave a familiar object with your pet.
- Leave phone numbers for your veterinarian and an emergency contact.
- Spend time with your pet before boarding him.

deposit is required of all customers — but no fees or deposits may be charged for the service animal, even those normally charged for pets.

The handler/owner is responsible for the animal's care and behavior; if the dog creates an altercation or poses a direct threat, the handler may be required to remove it from the premises and pay for any resulting damages.

Pet Partners, an organization devoted to companion and service animals, has information about laws that affect people and service animals in public accommodations. Phone (425) 679-5500 for more information, or visit www.petpartners.org.

Preparing Your Pet for Travel

Happily, many vacations can be planned to include fun activities for pets. Trips to parks, nature trails, the ocean or lakes offer exposure to the world beyond the window or fence at home, as well as the chance to explore new sights and sounds. Even the streets of an unfamiliar city can provide a smorgasbord of discoveries for your animal friend to enjoy.

Once you decide Spot and Snowball are ready to hit the road, plan accordingly:

❧ **Get a clean bill of health from the veterinarian.** Update your pet's vaccinations, check his general physical condition and obtain a health certificate showing proof of up-to-date inoculations, particularly rabies, distemper and kennel cough. Such documentation will be necessary if you cross state or country lines, and also may come in handy in the unlikely event your pet gets lost and must be retrieved from the local shelter. Don't forget to ask the doctor about potential health risks at your destination (Lyme disease, heartworm infection) and the necessary preventive measures.

If your pet is taking prescribed medicine, pack a sufficient supply plus a few days' extra. Also take the prescription in case you need a refill. Be prepared for emergencies by getting the names and numbers of clinics or doctors at your destination from your veterinarian or the American Animal Hospital Association. **Hint:** Obtain these references before you leave and keep them handy throughout the trip.

Make sure your pet is in good physical shape overall, especially if you are planning an active vacation. If your animal is primarily sedentary or overweight, he may not be up to lengthy hikes through the woods.

Note: Some owners believe a sedated animal will travel more easily than one that is fully aware, but this is rarely the case. In fact, tranquilizing an animal can make travel much more stressful. Always consult a veterinarian about what is best for your pet, and administer sedatives only under the doctor's direction. In addition, never give an animal medication that is specifically prescribed for humans. The dosage may be too high for an animal's

much smaller body mass, or may cause dangerous side effects.

❧ **Acclimate your pet to car travel.** Even if you're flying, your pet will have to ride in the car to get to the airport or terminal, and you don't want any unpleasant surprises before departure.

Some animals are used to riding in the car and even enjoy it. But most associate the inside of the carrier or the car with one thing only: the annual visit to the V-E-T. Considering that these visits usually end with a jab from a sharp needle, it's no wonder that some pets forget

---

CONTACT INFORMATION

The following organizations offer information, tips, brochures and other travel materials designed to help you and your pet enjoy a happy and safe vacation.

American Animal Hospital Association
12575 W. Bayaud Ave., Lakewood, CO 80228
(303) 986-2800 — www.aaha.org

American Society for the Prevention of Cruelty to Animals
424 E. 92nd St., New York, NY 10128-6804
(212) 876-7700 — www.aspca.org

American Veterinary Medical Association
1931 N. Meacham Rd., Suite 100
Schaumburg, IL 60173-4360
(800) 248-2862 — www.avma.org

The Humane Society of the United States
2100 L St. N.W., Washington, DC 20037
(202) 452-1100 — www.humanesociety.org

National Association of Professional Pet Sitters
1120 Rte. 73, Suite 200
Mt. Laurel, NJ 08054
(856) 439-0324 — www.petsitters.org

Pet Sitters International
201 E. King St., King, NC 27021
(336) 983-9222 — www.petsit.com

USDA-APHIS-Center for Animal Welfare
Beacon Facility, Mailstop 1180
Kansas City, MO 64131
(816) 737-4200 —

www.aphis.usda.gov/wps/portal/aphis

their training and act up in the car. If this is your situation, you will have to re-train your animal to view a drive as a reward, not a punishment.

Begin by allowing your pet to become used to the car without actually going anywhere. Then take short trips to places that are fun for animals, such as the park or the drive-through window at a fast-food restaurant. (Keep those indulgent snacks to a minimum!) Be sure to praise her for good behavior with words, petting and healthy treats. It shouldn't take long before you and your furry friend are enjoying leisurely drives without incident. *(See Traveling by Car, p. 12.)*

❧ **Brush up on behavior.** Will Snowball make a good travel companion? Or will he be an absolute terror on the road? Don't wait until the vacation is already under way to find out; review general behavioral guidelines with respect to your animal, keeping in mind that the unfamiliarity of travel situations may test the temperament of even the most well-behaved pet.

It's a good idea to socialize Spot by exposing her to other people and animals (especially if she normally stays inside). You're likely to encounter both on your trip, and it is important that she learns to behave properly in the company of strangers. Make her introduction to the outside world gradual, such as a walk in a new neighborhood or taking her along while you run errands. Exposure to new situations will help reduce fear of the unknown and result in more socially acceptable behavior.

Is your pet housebroken? How is he around children? Does he obey vocal commands? Be honest about your animal's ability to cope in unfamiliar surroundings. Depending on the length and nature of the trip and your pet's level of command response, an obedience refresher course might be a good idea.

❧ **Learn about your destination.** Check into quarantines or other restrictions well in advance, and make follow-up calls as your departure date approaches. Find out what types of documentation will be required — not just en route, but on the way home as well.

Be aware of potential safety or health risks where you're going, and plan accordingly. For example, the southeastern United States — particularly Florida — is home to alligators and heartworm-carrying mosquitoes, and many mountainous and wooded areas may harbor ticks that transmit Lyme disease.

Confirm all travel plans within a few days of your departure, especially with hotels and airlines; their policies may have changed after you made the reservations. If you plan to visit state parks or attractions that accept pets on the premises, obtain their animal regulations in advance.

❧ **Determine the best mode of transportation.** Most people traveling with pets drive. Many airlines do accept animals in the passenger cabin or cargo hold, and as more people choose to fly with their pet airlines are becoming more pet-conscious. Restrictions vary as to the type and number of pets an airline will carry, however, so

WHAT TO TAKE

- ❑ Carrier or crate. *(See Selecting a Carrier or Crate, p. 11, for specifications.)*
- ❑ Nylon or leather collar or harness, license tag, ID tag(s) and leash. All should be sturdy and should fit your pet properly.
- ❑ Food and water dishes.
- ❑ Can opener and spoon (for canned food).
- ❑ An ample supply of food, plus a few days' extra.
- ❑ Bottled water from home. (Many animals are finicky about their drinking water.)
- ❑ Cooler with ice.
- ❑ Healthy treats.
- ❑ Medications, if necessary.
- ❑ Health certificate and other required documents.
- ❑ A blanket or other bedding. (If your pet is used to sleeping on the furniture, bring an old blanket or sheet to place on top of the hotel's bedding.)
- ❑ Litter supplies (for cats or other small animals), a scooper and plastic bags (for dogs).
- ❑ Favorite toys.
- ❑ Carpet deodorizer.
- ❑ Chewing preventative.

- ❑ A recent photograph and a written description including name, breed, gender, height, weight, coloring and distinctive markings.
- ❑ Grooming supplies:
  comb/brush
  nail clippers
  shampoo
  cloth and paper towels
  cotton balls/tissues
- ❑ First-aid kit:
  gauze, bandages and adhesive tape
  hydrogen peroxide
  rubbing alcohol
  ointment
  muzzle
  scissors
  tweezers (for removing ticks, burrs, splinters, etc.)
  local emergency phone numbers
  first-aid guide (such as *Pet First Aid: Cats & Dogs*, published by The Humane Society of the United States and the American Red Cross)

inquire about animal shipping and welfare policies before making reservations. If your pet must travel in the cargo hold, heed the cautionary advice in the Traveling by Air section. *(See p. 13.)*

Flying is really the only major alternative to car travel. Amtrak, as well as Greyhound and other interstate bus lines, do not accept pets. **Note:** Seeing-eye dogs and other service animals are exempt from the regulations prohibiting pets on Amtrak and interstate bus lines. Local rail and bus companies may allow pets in small carriers, but this is an exception rather than a rule.

The only cruise ship that currently permits pets is the Cunard Line's *Queen Mary 2* (on trans-Atlantic crossings only); kennels are provided, but animals are accepted on a very limited basis. Some small charter and sightseeing boat companies permit pets onboard, however.

A word of advice: Never try to sneak your pet onto any mode of public transportation where she is not permitted. You may face legal action or fines, and the animal may be confiscated if discovered.

✤ **Pack as carefully for your pet as you do for yourself.** *(See What To Take, p. 10.)* Make sure she has a collar with a license tag and ID tag(s) listing her name and yours, along with your address and phone number. As an added precaution, some owners outfit their dog with a second tag listing the name and number of a contact person at home. Popular backup identification methods are to have your animal tattooed with an ID number (usually a social security number) or to implant a microchip under her skin.

If your pet requires medication, make sure that is specified on his tag. This helps others understand your animal's needs and also may prevent people from keeping a found pet or from stealing one to sell.

Note: Choke chains, collars that tighten when they are pulled, may be useful during training sessions, but they do not make good full-time collars. If the chain catches on something, your pet could choke herself trying to pull free. For regular wear, use a harness or a conventional collar made of nylon or leather.

Selecting a Carrier or Crate

This is one of the most important steps in ensuring your pet's safety when traveling. A good-quality carrier not only contains your pet during transit, it also gives him a safe, reassuring place to stay when confinement is necessary at your destination. Acclimate the animal before the trip so he views the crate as a cozy den, not a place of exile.

If you plan to travel by car, a carrier will confine your pet en route, and also may come in handy if Spot or Snowball must stay in the room unsupervised. A secured crate will prevent your pet from escaping from the room when the cleaning staff arrives, or at night if camping in the open. *(See At Your Destination, p. 15.)*

Some airlines allow small pets to travel in the passenger cabin as carry-on luggage. There are no laws dictating the type of carrier to use, but remember that it must be small enough to fit under a standard airplane seat and should not exceed 45 linear inches (length + width + height), or roughly **22 by 14 by 9 inches.** Depending on the airline, carrier size limits may be even smaller. If your pet will be flying in the cargo hold, you must use a carrier that meets U.S. Department of Agriculture Animal and Plant Health Inspection Service (USDA-APHIS) specifications. *(See Traveling by Air, p. 13.)*

Crates are available at pet supply stores; some airlines also sell carriers. Soft-sided travel bags are handy for flyers with small pets. Before you make the investment, make sure your carrier is airline-approved.

Even if you never take to the skies, these common-sense guidelines provide a good rule of thumb in selecting a crate for other uses. USDA-APHIS rules stipulate the following:

✤ The crate must be enclosed, but with ventilation openings occupying at least 14 percent of total wall space, at least one-third of which must be located on the top half of the kennel. A three-quarter-inch lip or rim must surround the exterior to prevent air holes from being blocked.

✤ The crate must open easily, but must be sufficiently strong to hold up during normal cargo transit procedures (loading, unloading, etc.).

✤ The floor must be solid and leakproof, and must be covered with an absorbent lining or material (such as an old towel or litter).

✤ The crate must be just large enough to allow the animal to turn freely while standing, and to have a full range of normal movement while standing or lying down.

✤ The crate must offer exterior grips or handles so that handlers do not have to place their hands or fingers inside.

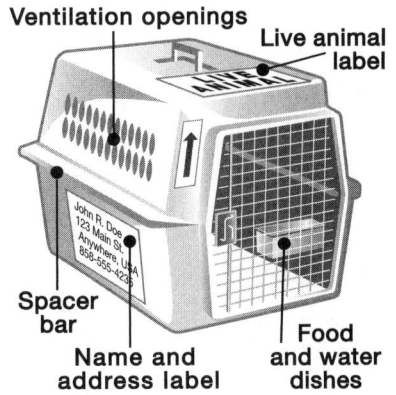

Ventilation openings

Live animal label

Spacer bar

Name and address label

Food and water dishes

HEATSTROKE AND HYPOTHERMIA

The best way to treat heatstroke or hypothermia is to prevent it. Do not leave pets unattended in a car, even if only for a few minutes. Also heed airlines' restrictions on pet travel, and carefully investigate animal welfare policies to make certain the airline has safeguards to protect your pet from both conditions.

Other preventive measures are to avoid strenuous exercise — including such activities as hiking and "fetch" — when the sun is strongest (10 a.m.-2 p.m.), and to provide your pet access to clean, fresh drinking water at all times.

Following are the warning signs and basic first aid for heatstroke and hypothermia. Always be alert to your pet's physical condition and watch for symptoms — immediate attention to the situation may mean the difference between life and death. If your pet is struck with either disorder, take him to an animal hospital or veterinarian as fast as safely possible.

HEATSTROKE

Symptoms
- rapid, shallow breathing
- excessive salivation
- heavy panting
- hot to the touch
- glazed eyes
- unsteadiness, dizziness
- deep red or purple tongue or gums
- vomiting
- body temperature of 104 F or higher

First Aid
- place pet in the shade
- quickly dampen with cool water, especially on the head and neck
- give small amounts of water

HYPOTHERMIA

Symptoms
- shivering
- weakness
- lethargy
- cold to the touch
- body temperature of 95 F or lower

First Aid
- place in a warm area
- wrap in towels or a blanket
- quickly warm by gently massaging the head, chest and extremities

☙ Food and water dishes must be securely attached and accessible without opening the kennel.

☙ If the carrier has wheels, they must be removed or immobilized prior to loading.

☙ One-inch lettering stating "Live Animals" must be placed visibly on the exterior and must be accompanied by directional arrows showing the crate's proper orientation. It also is a good idea to label the crate with your name, home address and home phone number, as well as an address and phone number where you can be reached during the trip. **Hint:** Use an adhesive label or an indelible marker and write directly on the crate, as paper may be ripped off accidentally in transit.

☙ Attach a list of care instructions (feeding, watering, etc.) for a 24-hour period to the exterior of the carrier. This will help airport workers care for your pet if he is sent to the wrong destination.

☙ If you are traveling with multiple pets, note that crates may contain only one animal whose weight exceeds 20 pounds. Smaller animals may travel together under the following guidelines: one species to a crate, except compatible dogs and cats of similar size; two puppies or kittens under 6 months of age; 15 guinea pigs or rabbits; 50 hamsters. **Note:** These are federal limits; airlines may impose more stringent regulations.

Traveling by Car

The first step in ensuring your pet's well-being during a vacation is to train her to ride in the car. AAA recommends that you restrain your pet in the back seat of the vehicle to avoid distractions as well as to protect the animal and other passengers in the event of a collision. The front airbag can be deadly to a pet during a crash, even if the pet is restrained. Options for restraints include harnesses and crates that can be strapped down. Visit AAA.com/PetBook for additional information about traveling safely with your pet.

To help prevent car sickness, feed your pet a light meal 4 to 6 hours before departing. Do not give an animal food or water in a moving vehicle.

Never allow your pet to ride in the bed of a pickup truck. It's illegal in some states; he also can jump out or be thrown, endangering himself and others on the road. Harnessing or leashing him to the truck bed is not advisable either: If he tries to jump out, he could be dragged along the road or the restraint could become a noose. Avoid placing animals in campers or trailers as well. **If your pet cannot ride in the car with you, leave him at home.**

Don't let your dog stick her head out the window, no matter how enjoyable it seems. Road debris and other flying objects can injure delicate eyes and ears, and the animal is at greater risk for severe injury if the vehicle should stop suddenly or be struck. If it is hot outside, run the air conditioner instead of opening the windows, and be sure that the air flow is reaching your pet.

AAA recommends that drivers stop every 2 hours to stretch their legs and take a quick break from driving. Your pet will appreciate the same break. Plan to visit a rest stop every 4 hours or so to let him have a drink and a chance to answer the call of nature. (Cat owners should bring along a litter box; dog owners should clean up afterward.)

Be sure your pet is leashed before opening the car door. This is not merely a courtesy to fellow travelers; it will prevent her from unexpectedly breaking free and running away. Keep in mind that even the most obedient pet may become disoriented during travel or in strange places and set off for home. **Hint:** If your pet is not used to traveling, use a harness instead of a collar; it is more difficult for an animal to wriggle out of a harness.

NEVER leave an animal in a parked car, even if the windows are partially open. Even on pleasant days the temperature inside a car can soar to well over 100 degrees in less than 10 minutes, placing your pet at risk for heatstroke and possibly death. On very cold days, hypothermia is a risk. Also, animals left unattended in parked cars can be stolen.

Traveling by Air

(Service animals are normally exempt from most of the regulations and fees specified in this section. Check policies with the airline when making reservations.)

Opinion is divided as to whether air travel is truly safe for pets. Statistically, it is less dangerous than being a passenger in a car, but some experts warn of potentially deadly conditions for animals. The truth lies somewhere in between: Most pets arrive at their destination in fine condition, but death or injury is always a possibility. Before you decide to fly, know the risk factors and the necessary precautions to keep your pet safe.

❧ **Determine whether your pet is fit to fly.** The Animal Welfare Act (AWA), administered by USDA-APHIS, specifies that dogs and cats must be at least 8 weeks old and weaned at least 5 days before air travel. Animals that are very young, very old, pregnant, ill or injured should not fly at all. Cats, snub-nosed dogs (pugs, boxers, etc.) and long-nosed dogs (shelties, collies, etc.) are prone to severe respiratory difficulties in an airplane's poorly ventilated cargo hold and should travel only in the passenger cabin (if size allows) with their owner. Some airlines will not accept snub-nosed breeds if the temperature exceeds 75 degrees anywhere in the routing. A few airlines may not allow snub-nosed breeds in the cargo hold at any time of year.

❧ **Decide where your pet will fly.** Most animals fly in the hold as checked baggage when traveling with their owners, or as cargo when they are unaccompanied. The AWA was enacted to ensure animals traveling in this manner are treated humanely and are not subjected to dangerous or life-threatening conditions. For specific requirements pertaining to your animal, check with the airline in advance, as policies vary. Some airlines will not ship dogs as checked baggage, and others will only accept dogs shipped as cargo from "known shippers"; i.e., commercial shippers or licensed pet breeders.

Items classified as "dangerous goods" (dry ice or toxic chemicals, for example) must be transported in a different part of the hold from where live animals are carried. Some planes are designed to have separate hold areas, but so-called "people mover" airlines that are primarily interested in getting human passengers from one point to another as quickly as possible may not give priority to this feature. Check your airline's specific baggage policies so you know exactly where in the hold your pet will be traveling.

Small pets may be taken into the passenger cabin with you as carry-on luggage on most airlines. This places the animal's welfare squarely in your hands but is feasible only if he is very well-behaved and fits comfortably in a container that meets standard carry-on regulations. *(See Selecting a Carrier or Crate, p. 11.)* Keep in mind that

PET INSURANCE

Just like their owners, pets can experience major medical problems at some point in their lifetime — even those that live indoors. And if illness strikes while you're on the road, it may be necessary to obtain care quickly. As a result, more and more people who travel with their devoted companion are considering pet health insurance.

Insurance plans run the gamut from basic coverage and routine care for illness and injury to comprehensive health maintenance, vaccinations and exams. Annual premiums range from less than $100 to more than $700, depending on the type of pet and plan. When choosing your plan, consider the following:

- What are the enrollment guidelines (age, breed, specific restrictions, etc.)?

- Which expenses are covered and which are excluded?

- What is the plan's policy concerning existing health problems?

- Does the plan allow you to use your own veterinarian?

- How are veterinary fees paid?

- Is a multiple pet discount offered?

the carrier — with the animal inside — must be kept under the seat in front of you throughout the flight. Most airlines charge a fee (anywhere from $75-$250 each way) for carry-on pets. **Note:** AWA regulations do not apply to animals traveling in the cabin.

❀ **Do your homework.** Investigate the airline's animal transport and welfare policies, especially if you are flying with a small or commuter airline. All airlines are subject to basic AWA regulations, but specific standards of care vary greatly from one company to another. Do your research well in advance and confirm the information 24-48 hours before departing.

The more information an airline provides, the better care your pet is likely to receive. Beware of companies that have vague animal welfare guidelines, or none at all. All major airlines provide information about pet transport on their Web sites. Also talk to fellow travelers and pet owners about their experiences. Finally, keep in mind that airlines are not required to transport live animals and can refuse to carry them for any reason.

❀ **Protect your investment.** Most people think of their pets as part of the family, but the legal system assigns them the same value as a piece of luggage. Inquire about insurance — an airline that won't insure animals in its care may not be the right one for your pet. (Always read the fine print before purchasing any insurance policy.) Also ask if the airline's workers are trained to handle animals. Few are, but it doesn't hurt to check.

AIRLINE CONTACT INFORMATION

Following is a list of the major North American airlines and their toll-free reservation numbers.

Web site addresses include information about flying with animals. **Hint:** Look under links for baggage, cargo or special travel needs, or do a site search for "pets."

Air Canada . . . .(888) 247-2262
www.aircanada.com

Alaska Airlines . . . .(800) 252-7522
www.alaskaair.com

American Airlines . . . .(800) 433-7300
www.aa.com

Delta Air Lines . . . .(800) 221-1212
www.delta.com

JetBlue Airways . . . .(800) 538-2583
www.jetblue.com

Southwest Airlines . . . .(800) 435-9792
www.southwest.com

United Airlines . . . .(800) 864-8331
www.united.com

Remember, it's up to you to choose an airline that values pets and will treat yours with care.

❀ **Understand the potential hazards.** Because a plane's cargo hold is neither cooled nor heated until take-off, the most dangerous time for your pet is that spent on the ground in this unventilated compartment. In summer the space absorbs heat while the plane sits on the tarmac; the reverse is true in winter, when it is no warmer inside the hold than outside. Both instances expose pets to the possibility of serious injury or death from heatstroke or hypothermia. **Note:** The latter also may be a concern during flight if the hold's heater is disabled or turned off, allowing the temperature to drop to near-freezing levels.

To minimize these risks, USDA-APHIS rules prohibit animals from being kept in the hold or on the tarmac for more than 45 minutes when temperatures are above 85 F or below 45 F. Some airlines impose even tighter temperature restrictions and may not permit animals to fly on planes going to cities where the ground temperatures may exceed these limits during certain months of the year. (Exceptions may be made for animals whose veterinarians certify they are acclimated to colder temperatures, but never warmer.)

❀ **Make stress-free travel arrangements.** Once you decide to fly, reserve space for Spot or Snowball when you arrange your own tickets, preferably well in advance of your travel date. Airlines accept only a limited number of animals per flight — usually two to four in the passenger cabin and one pet per passenger — on a first-come, first-served basis. More animals are generally allowed in the cargo hold.

Prepare to pay a fee each way; the cost is often greater for large animals traveling on a flight without their owner. Always reconfirm your reservations and flight information 24-48 hours before departure.

If your pet will be flying in the hold, travel on the same plane and reserve a nonstop flight. This not only reduces the danger of heatstroke or hypothermia during layovers, it also eliminates the possibility that she will be placed on the wrong connecting flight. In summer, fly during the early morning or late evening when temperatures are cooler. Because of large crowds and the chance of heavy air traffic causing delays, avoid holiday travel whenever possible.

Additional precautions may be necessary when traveling outside the United States and Canada. Other countries may impose lengthy quarantines, and airline workers outside North America may not be bound by animal welfare laws. *(See International Travel, p. 17.)*

❀ **Play an active role in your pet's well-being.** Flying safely with your pet requires careful planning and attention to his welfare. See the veterinarian within 10 days of departure for a health certificate (required by most airlines) and a pre-flight check-up.

Address any concerns you have about your pet traveling by air, especially if you are considering tranquilization. Sedation usually is not recommended for cats and dogs, regardless of whether they fly in the cabin or in the hold. Exposure to increased altitude pressure can create respiratory and cardiovascular problems; animals with short, wide heads are particularly susceptible to disorientation and possible injury. Sedation should never be administered without your veterinarian's approval.

Obtain an airline-approved carrier and acclimate your pet to its presence by leaving it open with a familiar object inside. A sturdy, well-ventilated crate adds an additional measure of protection.

Because animals are classified as luggage, they may be loaded on the plane via conveyor belt. If the crate falls off the belt, your pet could be injured or released. Ask that she be hand-carried on and off the plane, and that you be permitted to watch both procedures. Also ask about "counter-to-counter" shipping, in which the animal is loaded immediately before departure and unloaded immediately after arrival. There usually is an additional fee for this service.

Make sure you will have access to your pet if there is a lengthy layover or delay. Think twice about flying on an airline that won't allow you to check on your animal under such circumstances.

❧ **Prepare for the flight.** Keep in mind that traveling with an animal will require additional pre-flight time and preparation on your part. Exercise your pet before the flight, and arrive at least 2 but not more than 4 hours before departure. If he is traveling as carry-on luggage, check-in is normally at the passenger terminal; if he is traveling as checked baggage or as cargo in the cargo hold, proceed to the airline's cargo terminal, which is often in a different location. Find this out when making reservations and again when confirming flight information.

Make sure your animal's crate is properly labeled and secured, but do not lock it in case airline personnel have to provide emergency care. Include an ice pack for extra comfort on a hot day or a hot water bottle on a cold day. **Hint:** Wrap in a towel to prevent leaking.

Do not feed your pet less than 4 hours before departure, but provide water up until boarding. **Hint:** Freeze water in the bowl so that it melts throughout the trip, providing a constant drinking source.

Spot or Snowball should wear a sturdy collar (breakaway collars are recommended for cats) and two identification tags marked with your name, home address and phone number, and travel address and phone number. It's also a good idea to clip your pet's nails before departure so they won't accidentally get caught on any part of the carrier.

Note: You may be required to take your pet out of the carrier as you pass through security on your way to the gate. Make sure the animal is wearing a collar and leash or harness.

Attach food and water dishes inside the carrier so that airline workers can reach them without opening the door. If the trip will take longer than 12 hours, also attach a plastic bag with at least one meal's worth of dry food. Animals under 16 weeks of age must be fed every 12 hours, adult animals every 24 hours. Water must be provided at least every 12 hours, regardless of the animal's age.

Allow your pet to answer the call of nature before boarding, but do not take her out of the carrier while in the terminal. As a courtesy, wait until you are outside and away from fellow travelers. Keep her leash with you — do not leave it inside or attached to the kennel.

If your pet is traveling as carry-on luggage, let the passenger sitting next to you know. Someone with allergies may want to change seats.

Perhaps the most important precaution is to alert the flight crew and the captain that your pet is aboard. The pilot must activate the heater for the cargo hold; make sure this is done once you are in the air. If there are layovers or delays, ask the flight crew to be sure your pet has adequate shelter and/or ventilation; better yet, ask them to allow you to check in-person.

If you have arranged to watch your pet being unloaded, ask a flight attendant to call the baggage handlers and let them know you are on the way. Above all, do not hesitate to voice any concerns you have for your pet's welfare — it is your responsibility to do so.

❧ **Be prepared for emergencies.** In the unlikely event your pet gets lost en route, contact the airline, local humane shelters, animal control agencies or USDA-APHIS. Many airlines can trace a pet that was transferred to the wrong flight. If your pet is injured in transit, proceed to the nearest animal hospital; register any complaints with USDA-APHIS. **Hint:** Carry a list of emergency contact numbers and a current photograph of your pet in your wallet or purse, just in case.

At Your Destination

How well you and your companion behave on the road directly affects the way future furry travelers will be treated. Always clean up after your pet and keep him under your control. This is not only a courtesy to fellow human travelers; it's the surest way to enjoy a safe and happy vacation.

Inquire about pet policies before making hotel reservations. Properties may impose restrictions on the type or size of pet allowed, or they may designate only certain rooms, such as smoking rooms, for travelers with animals. If you have a dog, get a room on the first floor with direct access outside, preferably near a walking area; keep her leashed on any excursion.

Hotels may have supervision policies requiring that pets be crated when unattended or that they may not be left alone at all. Allow your pet only in designated exercise or animal-approved areas; never take him into such off-limits places as the lobby, pool area, patio or restaurant. Prepare to receive limited housekeeping service, or none at all.

Expect to pay some type of additional charge, which may be per room or per pet and may include any of the following: refundable deposit, non-refundable deposit, daily fee, weekly fee.

If staying with friends or relatives, make certain your pet is a welcome guest. Know and respect their "house rules," especially if they have small children or pets of their own.

Once in the room, check for such hazards as chemically treated toilet water, hiding spaces and electrical cords before freeing your pet. Give her time to adjust to her new surroundings under your supervision.

Above all, practice good "petiquette":

❧ Try not to leave your pet alone, but if you must, crate or otherwise confine her.

❧ Crate at night as well.

❧ To keep your pet and the housekeeper from having an unexpected encounter, leave the "Do Not Disturb" sign on the door when you go out without him.

❧ Barking dogs make poor hotel neighbors — keep your pet quiet.

❧ Don't allow your pet on the furniture. If she insists on sleeping on the bed, bring a bedspread or sheet from home and place that on top of the hotel bedding.

❧ Clean up after your pet immediately — inside the room and out — and leave no trace of him behind when checking out.

❧ Dispose of litter and other "accidents" properly — check with housekeeping.

❧ Notify the management immediately if something is damaged, and be ready to pay for repairs.

❧ Add a little extra to the housekeeping tip.

❧ When you take your pet out of the room, keep her leashed, especially in wilderness areas and around small children. No matter how obedient she is at home, new stimuli and distractions may cause her to forget or ignore vocal commands. Know and obey animal policies at parks, beaches and other public areas. Check before arriving to make certain animals still are welcome, even if you've been there before — the rules may have changed.

❧ Look for outdoor cafes when selecting restaurants. For health reasons, pets are not permitted inside eating establishments, but many restaurants allow animals to sit quietly with their owners at outdoor tables *(see Pet-Friendly Restaurants, p. 612).* Drive-through restaurants are another alternative.

In Case of Emergency

Be prepared for any turn of events by knowing how to get to the nearest animal hospital. *(See Emergency Animal Clinics, p. 54.)* Also have the name and number of a local animal shelter and a local veterinarian handy — ask your veterinarian for a recommendation. Take first-aid supplies with you and know how to use them. An animal in pain may become aggressive, so exercise caution at all times.

Emergency evacuation shelters do not accept pets, and domesticated animals do not fare well if left to weather an emergency on their own, especially when far from home. Avert a potential tragedy by planning in advance where you will go with your pet in case of evacuation. Use the listings in this book to find other hotels willing to take you and your pet. Above all, don't wait for disaster to strike. Leave as soon as the evacuation order is announced, and take your animal with you.

The Great Outdoors

Travelers planning an active or camping vacation should make some additional preparations. Check in advance to be sure your pet is permitted at campgrounds, parks, beaches, trails and anywhere else you will be visiting. If there are restrictions — and there usually are — follow them. Remember that pets other than service animals usually are not allowed in public buildings.

Note: It is not advisable to take animals other than dogs into wilderness areas. For example, bringing a pet is not recommended at some national parks in Alaska. Also keep in mind that rural areas often have few veterinarians and even fewer boarding kennels.

Use common sense. Clean up after your pet, do not allow excessive vocalizing and keep her under your control. If the property requires your pet to be leashed or crated at all times, do so. Few parks or natural areas will allow a pet to be unattended, even when chained — the risk of disagreeable encounters with other travelers or wildlife is too great. The National Park Service may confiscate pets that harm wildlife or other visitors.

If camping, crate your pet at night to protect him from the elements and predators. (Chaining confines the animal but won't keep him from becoming a midnight snack.)

When hiking, stick to the trail and keep your pet on a short leash. It is all too easy for an unleashed pet to wander off and get lost or fall prey to a larger animal.

Keep an eye out for such wildlife as alligators, bears, big cats, porcupines and skunks, and avoid other dogs and small children. Be aware of indigenous poisonous plants, such as English ivy and oleander, or those causing physical injury, such as cactus, poison ivy or stinging nettle. Your veterinarian or local poison control center should be able to give you a full list of hazardous flora.

Before setting out on the trail, make sure both of you are in good physical shape. An animal that rarely exercises at home will not suddenly be ready for a 10-mile trek across uneven terrain. Plan a hike well within the limits of your pet's endurance, and don't push — remember, if Spot gets too tired to make it back on her own, you'll have to carry her.

Carry basic first-aid supplies, including a first-aid guide. *(See What To Take, p. 10.)* Also carry fresh drinking water for both of you — "found" water may contain harmful germs or toxins. Drink often, not just when thirst strikes, and have your pet do the same. Watch for signs of dehydration, leg or foot injuries, heat exhaustion or heatstroke. Stop immediately and return home or to camp if any of these occur.

Note: Dogs can carry their own backpacks (check your local pet store for specially designed packs), but should never carry more than one-third of their body weight. Train the dog to accept the pack beforehand, and only use it with a strong, healthy animal in excellent physical condition.

No matter where or how you spend your vacation, visit the veterinarian when you return home to check for injuries, parasites and general health.

Traveling Between the United States and Canada

Traveling across the international border with your pet — either from the United States into Canada or from Canada into the United States — should prove largely hassle-free, although some basic regulations need to be kept in mind. All U.S. and Canadian citizens traveling between the United States and Canada are required to show a passport or other accepted secure document. For additional information about secure documents visit www.travel.state.gov or phone (877) 487-2778.

U.S. citizens taking pet cats and dogs 3 months of age and older into Canada must carry a rabies vaccination certificate signed by a licensed veterinarian that describes the animal, provides proof of rabies vaccination and includes documentation of the product name, lot number and lot expiration date. Collar tags are not sufficient proof of immunization. The certificate also is needed to bring a pet dog back into the United States; make sure the vaccination doesn't expire while you're in Canada. **Note:** Pit bulls are not permitted to be taken into Ontario.

Service animals are exempt from import restrictions. Also exempt are puppies and kittens under 3 months old; obtain a certificate of health from your veterinarian indicating that the animal is too young to vaccinate. **Note:** For details on pet imports, contact the Canadian Embassy; 501 Pennsylvania Ave. N.W., Washington, DC 20001; phone (202) 682-1740. The Web site address is http://can-am.gc.ca/washington.

The Canadian Food Inspection Agency (CFIA) provides additional pet information; phone (800) 442-2342 or visit the Web site at www.inspection.gc.ca. If you need assistance while in Canada, contact the U.S. Embassy, P.O. Box 866/Station B, Ottawa, ON, Canada K1P 5T1; phone (613) 688-5335.

Canadian travelers may take pet cats and dogs into the United States with no restrictions, but U.S. Customs requires that dogs have proof of rabies vaccination no less than 30 days before arrival. For additional information on U.S. regulations, contact the USDA-APHIS National Center for Import & Export, (301) 734-8364.

International Travel

If you plan to travel abroad with Spot or Snowball, prepare for a lengthy flight and at least a short quarantine period. Be aware that airline and animal workers in other countries may not be bound by the same animal welfare laws that exist in the United States and Canada. Contact the embassy or consulate at your destination for information about documentation and quarantine requirements, animal control laws and animal welfare regulations.

As with any trip, have your pet checked by your regular veterinarian within 10 days of departure to obtain a health certificate showing proof of rabies and other inoculations. If you are traveling with an animal other than a domesticated dog or cat, check with USDA-APHIS for restrictions or additional documentation required.

The booklet "Bringing Pets and Wildlife into the United States: Licensing and Health Requirements" has general information about traveling abroad with animals; visit www.cbp.gov.

Note: Island nations such as Australia and the United Kingdom, which are rabies-free, have adopted the Pet Travel Scheme (PETS) to allow entry for dogs, cats and ferrets from the U.S. and Canada without the usual 6-month quarantine. Pets must be tested and vaccinated for rabies at least 21 days prior to travel, be implanted with microchip identification and receive a certificate of treatment from an official government veterinarian. For information, visit the U.K. Web site for the Department for Environment, Food & Rural Affairs (DEFRA) at www.defra.gov.uk. Hawaii, which has a standard 120-day quarantine for all imported animals except guide dogs, has adopted a similar expedited program of 5 days or less; a pet must have been vaccinated at least *twice* for rabies in its lifetime.

Loss Prevention Tips

Searching the woods or an unfamiliar town for a missing pet is easily prevented by following these helpful tips:

🐾 Have your pet wear a sturdy nylon or leather collar with current ID and rabies tags firmly attached. Be sure the ID tag includes the phone number of an emergency contact. Consider having your pet implanted with microchip identification; it's a simple procedure similar to a vaccination.

🐾 Keep your pet on a leash or harness. Even trained animals can become agitated or disoriented in unfamiliar surroundings and fail to obey vocal commands.

🐾 Attach the leash or harness while your pet is still inside the closed car or crate.

🐾 Do not leave your pet unattended at any time, anywhere. A stolen pet is extremely difficult to recover.

🐾 Escape-proof your hotel room by crating your pet and asking hotel management to make certain no one enters your room while you are gone. (Inform the property that you're traveling with an animal when making reservations.)

🐾 Take along a recent picture and a detailed written description of your pet.

If your pet gets lost these steps will improve your chances of recovery:

🐾 If your pet is lost in transit, contact the airline immediately. Ask to trace the animal via the airline's automated baggage tracking system.

🐾 Contact local police, animal control, animal shelters, humane organizations and veterinary clinics with a description and a recent photograph. Stay in contact until your pet is found, and provide your home and destination phone numbers.

🐾 Post signs and place an ad in the local newspaper so that anyone who comes across your pet knows she is lost and how to reach you.

The Last Word

You are ultimately responsible for your pet's welfare and behavior while traveling. Since animals cannot speak for themselves, it is up to you to focus on your pet's well-being every step of the way. It also is important to make sure he conducts himself properly so that other pets will be welcome visitors in the future. Following the common-sense information in this book will help ensure that both you and your animal companion have a safe and happy trip.

Pet-Friendly
Places

in the United States and Canada

Dog Parks
Attractions
National Public Lands
Emergency Animal Clinics

DOG PARKS

A dog park is a place where people and their dogs can play together. These places offer dogs an area to play, exercise and socialize with other dogs while their owners enjoy the park-like setting. Dog park size and features vary greatly from location to location, from several hundred square feet in urban areas to several hundred acres in the suburbs and rural locations. Dog owners should remember to always keep their animal leashed until they reach the dog park entrance, to maintain voice control of their animal at all times, to bring their own supply of bags for picking up after their pet (and to be diligent in doing so), and to always have fresh water available for their dog. Please observe all dog park rules. The dog parks listed here welcome people who travel with their dogs; private parks or parks requiring local residency are not included. **Note:** Fence types and heights vary, and some areas have no fencing at all, requiring that the dog be under firm voice control.

United States

ALABAMA

Cahaba Beach Dog Park - Birmingham
www.cbdogpark.com, (205) 397-3647
3555 Cahaba Beach Rd., 35242.
Daily 8-8, May-Oct.; 8-6, rest of year.
Fenced, 2.5 acres, trees, trails, streams, dog beach, staffed, separate areas for large and small dogs.

Loch Haven Dog Park - Hoover
www.hooveralabama.gov/index.aspx?nid=667,
(205) 444-7500
3469 Loch Haven Dr., 35216.
Daily dawn-dusk.
Fenced, obstacle course, .4-mile walking track, picnic area.

Moss Rock Preserve - Hoover
www.hooveralabama.gov/index.aspx?nid=214,
(205) 823-1641
616 Preserve Pkwy., 35226.
Daily dawn-dusk.
Fenced, rocks for climbing, trees, trails. Dogs must be leashed.

ARIZONA

Echo Mountain Off-Leash Area - Phoenix
www.phoenix.gov/parks/parks/dog-parks, (602) 262-6696
17447 N. 20th St., 85022.
Daily dawn-dusk.
Fenced, 2.3 acres, grass surface, separate areas for large and small dogs, disposal bags and trash cans, drinking fountains in both areas, double-gated entryways.

Hance Dog Park - Phoenix
www.friendsofhancedogpark.com, (623) 850-4716
323 W. Culver St., 85003.
Daily 6:30 a.m.-9 p.m.
Fenced, 1 acre, drinking fountains with integrated water bowls, benches, sound buffer, trees.

Petsmart Dog Park at Washington Park - Phoenix
www.phoenix.gov/parks/parks/dog-parks, (602) 262-6971
6503 N. 21st Ave., 85015.
Daily 6:30 a.m.-10 p.m.
Fenced, 2.65 acres, separate areas for large and small dogs, two double-gated entryways, grass surface, drinking fountains, benches, disposal bags and trash cans.

RJ Dog Park at Pecos Park - Phoenix
www.phoenix.gov/parks/parks/dog-parks/pecos-dog-park,
(602) 534-5252
17010 48th St., 85048.
Daily 6 a.m.-11 p.m.
Fenced, 2 acres, separate areas for large and small dogs, double-gated entryways, drinking fountain, lighted, disposal bags and trash cans.

Rose Mofford Sports Complex Dog Park - Phoenix
www.phoenix.gov/parks/parks/dog-parks/mofford-dog-park,
(602) 261-8011
9833 N. 25th Ave., 85021.
Daily 6:30 a.m.-10 p.m.
Fenced, 2.5 acres, separate areas for large and small dogs, double-gated entryways, drinking fountains, benches, trees, disposal bags and trash cans.

Steele Indian School Park - Phoenix
www.phoenix.gov/parks/parks/dog-parks/steele-dog-park,
(602) 495-0739
300 E. Indian School Rd., 85012.
Daily 6 a.m.-10 p.m.
Fenced, 1.63 acres, separate areas for large and small dogs, double-gated entryways, drinking fountain, cement pathways, grass surface.

Christopher Columbus Park - Tucson
cms3.tucsonaz.gov/parksandrec/offleash, (520) 791-5909
4600 N. Silverbell Rd., 85745.
Daily dawn-dusk.
Fenced, less than 1 acre, lighted, drinking fountain, agility equipment, shade, covered pavilion, disposal scoop and trash cans.

Jacobs Park - Tucson
cms3.tucsonaz.gov/parksandrec/offleash, (520) 791-5909
3300 N. Fairview Ave., 85705.
Daily dawn-dusk.
Fenced, less than 1 acre, grass and cement surface, picnic area, disposal bags and trash cans.

Miko's Corner Playground at Reid Park - Tucson
cms3.tucsonaz.gov/parksandrec/offleash, (520) 791-4873
900 S. Randolph Way, 85716.
Daily 7 a.m.-10 p.m.
Fenced, 2 acres, double-gated entryway, lighted, separate areas for large and small dogs, drinking fountain, covered pavilion with picnic area.

Palo Verde Park - Tucson
cms3.tucsonaz.gov/parksandrec/offleash, (520) 791-5930
300 S. Mann Ave., 85710.
Daily 6 a.m.-10:30 p.m.
Fenced, less than 1 acre, separate areas for large and small dogs, lighted, picnic areas, double-gated entryway, disposal scoops and trash cans, drinking fountains.

Purple Heart Park - Tucson
cms3.tucsonaz.gov/parksandrec/offleash, (520) 791-4873
10050 E. Rita Rd., 85747.
Daily 7 a.m.-10 p.m.
Fenced, 1 acre, separate areas for large and small dogs, double-gated entryway, walking path, drinking fountains, trees, benches, granite gravel surface, lighted.

Sixth Avenue Dog Park - Tucson
cms3.tucsonaz.gov/parksandrec/offleash, (520) 791-5909
2075 N. 6th Ave., 85705.
Daily dawn-dusk.
Fenced, grass and gravel surface, covered pavilion, dog
wash area, picnic area, double-gated entryway.

Udall Park - Tucson
cms3.tucsonaz.gov/parksandrec/offleash, (520) 791-4931
7290 E. Tanque Verde Rd., 85715.
Daily 6 a.m.-10 p.m.
Fenced, less than 1 acre, gravel and artificial turf surface,
benches, drinking fountains.

CALIFORNIA
Wildcatters Dog Park - Brea
www.ci.brea.ca.us, (714) 671-4437
3450 E. Santa Fe Rd., 92821.
Fri.-Wed. 7 a.m.-dusk, Thurs. noon-dusk.
Benches, dog water fountains, picnic tables, double-entry
gates, grass turf, separate areas for large and small dogs,
dog waste clean-up stations.

Fullerton Pooch Park - Fullerton
www.fullertondogparkfoundation.org, (714) 738-6575
210 S. Basque Ave., 92832.
Thurs.-Tues. 7 a.m.-8 p.m.
Fenced, three areas for large and small dogs, grass, wood
chip surface, disposal bags and trash cans.

Huntington Dog Beach - Huntington Beach
www.dogbeach.org, (714) 841-8644
100 Goldenwest St., 92648.
Daily 5 a.m.-10 p.m. Parking: $1.50/hour.
One-mile stretch of beach, disposal bags and trash cans,
restrooms, lifeguard station.

Laguna Beach Dog Park - Laguna Beach
www.lagunabeachdogpark.com, (949) 910-9947
20672 Laguna Canyon Rd., 92651.
Thurs.-Tues. dawn-dusk.
Fenced, 2 acres, grass, separate areas for large and small
dogs, drinking fountains, benches, shade.

Arroyo Seco Dog Park at Hermon Park - Los Angeles
www.laparks.org, (323) 255-0370
5568 Via Marisol, 90042.
Daily dawn-dusk.
Fenced, 1.3 acres, benches, drinking fountains, restrooms,
separate areas for large and small dogs, lighted.

Barrington Dog Park - Los Angeles
www.fobdp.org/index2.html, (310) 476-4866
333 S. Barrington Ave., 90049.
Wed.-Mon. 5 a.m.-10:30 p.m., Tues. 10 a.m.-10:30 p.m.
Fenced, 1.5 acres, separate areas for large and small dogs,
benches, drinking fountain, three-dog limit, mulch surface.

Griffith Dog Park - Los Angeles
www.laparks.org/dos/parks/facility/dogparks/
griffithParkDogPk.htm, (323) 913-4688
4701 Zoo Dr., 90027.
Daily dawn-dusk.
Fenced, 1.5 acres, separate areas for large and small or
timid dogs, picnic tables, drinking troughs, drinking fountain,
restrooms.

Laurel Canyon Dog Park - Los Angeles
www.laparks.org/info/dogparks.htm, (818) 769-4415
8260 Mulholland Dr., 90046.
Sat.-Thurs. 6 a.m.-dusk, Fri. 11-dusk.
Fenced, 3 acres, separate areas for large and small or timid
dogs, grass, wash station, restrooms.

Runyon Canyon Dog Park - Los Angeles
www.laparks.org, (323) 666-5046
2000 N. Fuller Ave., 90046.
Daily dawn-dusk.
Fenced, 90 acres, hiking and walking trails.

Silverlake Dog Park - Los Angeles
www.laparks.org, (323) 644-3946
1850 W. Silver Lake Dr., 90026.
Thurs.-Tues. 6 a.m.-10 p.m., Wed. 8:30 a.m.-10 p.m.
Fenced, 1.25 acres, separate areas for large and small
dogs, gravel surface, lighted.

Canine Commons at Alston Park - Napa
www.cityofnapa.org, (707) 257-9529
2099 Dry Creek Rd., 94558.
Daily dawn-dusk.
8 acres, agility equipment, dog water fountain, double-gated
entry, disposal bags.

Whitnall Off-Leash Dog Park - North Hollywood
www.laparks.org, (818) 756-8190
5801 Whitnall Hwy., 91601.
Daily dawn-dusk.
Fenced, 3 acres, separate areas for large and small dogs,
grass, drinking fountains, lighted, disposal bags and trash
cans, water bowls, common tennis balls.

Alice Frost Kennedy Dog Park - Pasadena
www.pasadenapooch.org, (626) 577-8738
3026 E. Orange Grove Blvd., 91107.
Daily 6 a.m.-10 p.m.
Fenced, 2.5-acre grassy area, separate areas for large dogs
and small and special-needs dogs, trees, benches, drinking
fountains.

Cadman Community Park - San Diego
www.sandiego.gov/park-and-recreation/parks/dogs/
leashfree.shtml, (619) 525-8213
4280 Avati Dr., 92117.
Daily 7-9:30, 5-7. Phone ahead to confirm schedule.
Fenced, trees, shade, grass surface, restrooms.

Capehart Park - San Diego
www.sandiego.gov/park-and-recreation/parks/dogs/
leashfree.shtml, (619) 221-8901
4747 Soledad Mountain Rd., 92109.
The dog park is open daily 24 hours.
Fenced, 1 acre, separate areas for large and small dogs,
drinking fountains, picnic tables, benches.

Doyle Community Park - San Diego
www.sandiego.gov/park-and-recreation/parks/dogs/
leashfree.shtml, (619) 525-8213
8175 Regents Rd., 92122.
The dog park is open daily 24 hours.
Fenced, separate areas for large and small dogs, drinking
fountains, grass surface.

Kearny Mesa Community Park - San Diego
www.sandiego.gov/park-and-recreation/parks/dogs/
leashfree.shtml, (619) 525-8212
3170 Armstrong St., 92111.
Daily 6:30 a.m.-10 p.m.
Fenced, 1 acre, lighted, drinking fountains, separate areas
for large and small dogs, disposal bags and trash cans,
restrooms, trees.

Maddox Neighborhood Park - San Diego
www.sandiego.gov/park-and-recreation/parks/dogs/
leashfree.shtml, (619) 525-8213
7815 Flanders St., 92126.
Daily dawn-dusk.
Fenced, less than 1 acre, artificial turf surface, drinking
fountain.

Nate's Point Dog Park at Balboa Park - San Diego
www.npdog.org/park.html, (619) 325-5620
2500 Balboa Dr., 92103.
The dog park is open daily 24 hours.
Fenced, trees, benches, picnic area, disposal bags and trash cans, drinking fountains, grass surface.

Rancho Peñasquitos Park - San Diego
www.sandiego.gov/park-and-recreation/parks/dogs/leashfree.shtml, (619) 525-8213
13292 Salmon River Rd., 92129.
Daily dawn-dusk.
Fenced, double-gated entryway, separate areas for large and small dogs, benches, drinking fountains, artificial turf surface.

Alamo Square Dog Play Area - San Francisco
www.sfrecpark.org/destination/alamo-square/alamo-square-dog-play-area, (415) 218-0259
1012 Hayes St., 94117.
Daily dawn-dusk.
10 acres, open grass field, shaded slopes, bushes, city views, picnic tables, dog play area.

Alta Plaza Park - San Francisco
www.sfrecpark.org/destination/alta-plaza-park/alta-plaza-dog-play-areas, (415) 292-2012
Jackson & Steiner sts., 94115.
Daily dawn-dusk.
Fenced, less than 1 acre, grass surface, restrooms, paved pathways.

Bernal Heights Dog Park - San Francisco
www.sfdogparks.com/Bernal_Heights.html, (415) 831-2084
3458 Folsom St., 94110.
Daily dawn-dusk.
39 acres, city views, disposal bags and trash cans, gravel trails, drinking fountains, benches.

Buena Vista Park - San Francisco
www.sfdogparks.com/Buena_Vista.html, (415) 831-2084
1106 Haight St., 94117.
Daily dawn-dusk.
35 acres, paved and dirt paths, trees, shade, bench, grass.

Corona Heights Dog Play Area - San Francisco
www.sfrecpark.org/destination/corona-heights-park/corona-heights-dog-play-area, (415) 819-2699
Roosevelt & Museum Way, 94114.
Daily dawn-dusk.
Fenced, double-gated entryway, drinking fountains, mulch surface.

Douglass Dog Play Area - San Francisco
www.sfrecpark.org/destination/douglass-playground/douglass-dog-play-area, (415) 970-8063
26th & Douglass sts., 94131.
Daily dawn-dusk.
Fenced, 1.6 acres, hills, drinking fountains, benches, trees, disposal bags and trash cans, walking path.

Eureka Valley Dog Play Area - San Francisco
www.sfrecpark.org/destination/eureka-valley-rec-center/eureka-valley-dog-play-area, (415) 831-6810
100 Collingwood St., 94114.
Fenced, less than 1 acre, trash cans, shade, benches, double-gated entryway, sand surface.

Head & Brotherhood Dog Play Area - San Francisco
www.sfrecpark.org/destination/head-brotherood-mini-park/headbrotherhood-dog-play-area, (415) 831-2700
Head St. & Brotherhood Way, 94122.
Daily dawn-dusk.
Less than 1 acre, grass surface, trees, disposal bags and trash cans.

Lafayette Park Dog Play Area - San Francisco
www.sfrecpark.org/destination/lafayette-park/lafayette-park-dog-play-area, (415) 831-2700
Washington & Laguna sts., 94109.
Daily dawn-dusk.
Fenced, less than 1 acre, drinking fountains, disposal bags and trash cans, mulch surface, restrooms, picnic area.

McKinley Square - San Francisco
www.sfrecpark.org/destination/mckinley-square, (415) 831-6358
2301 20th St., 94107.
Daily dawn-dusk.
Less than 1 acre, grass surface, walking trails.

Mission Dolores Park Dog Play Areas - San Francisco
www.sfrecpark.org/destination/mission-dolores-park/mission-dolores-park-dog-play-area, (415) 831-2700
568 Dolores St., 94110.
Daily dawn-dusk.
Grass surface, two off-leash play areas, hills, benches, covered pavilions.

St. Mary's Dog Park - San Francisco
www.sfrecpark.org/destination/st-marys-rec-center, (415) 695-5006
95 Justin Dr., 94112.
Daily dawn-dusk.
Fenced, trees, grass surface, shade, benches, drinking fountains.

Roy M. Butcher Dog Park - San Jose
www.sanjoseca.gov/facilities/Facility/Details/19, (408) 535-3500
3950 Camden Ave., 95109.
Daily dawn-1 hour after dusk.
Fenced, 10 acres, separate areas for large and small dogs, benches, restrooms.

Selma Olinder Park - San Jose
www.sanjoseca.gov/facilities/Facility/Details/123, (408) 535-3500
848 E. Williams St., 95116.
Daily dawn-1 hour after dusk.
Fenced, separate areas for large and small dogs, mulch surface, double-gated entryway, drinking fountain, shade, benches.

Sepulveda Basin Off-Leash Dog Park - Van Nuys
www.laparks.org/info/dogparks.htm, (818) 756-7667
17550 Victory Blvd., 91406.
Daily dawn-dusk.
Fenced, 5 acres, separate areas for large and small or timid dogs, grass, shade, drinking fountains with water bowls, picnic tables.

Westminster Dog Park - Venice
www.laparks.org/dos/parks/facility/dogparks/westminsterDogPk.htm, (310) 396-1615
1234 Pacific Ave., 90291.
Daily 6 a.m.-10 p.m.
Fenced, less than 1 acre, separate areas for large and small dogs, mulch.

COLORADO

Cheyenne Meadows Dog Park - Colorado Springs
(719) 385-5940
1560 Charmwood Dr., 80906.
Daily dawn-dusk.
Fenced, grass, benches, disposal bags.

Garden of the Gods Dog Run - Colorado Springs
www.gardenofgods.com/parkinfo/index_109.cfm,
(719) 634-6666
1805 N. 30th St., 80904.
Daily 5 a.m.-11 p.m., May-Oct.; 5 a.m.-9 p.m., rest of year.
Less than 1 acre, benches, walking and hiking trails, trash
cans.

Palmer Park Ute Crest Dog Run - Colorado Springs
parks.coloradosprings.gov/explore-play/explore/parks/
dog-parks, (719) 385-5940
3650 Maizeland Rd., 80909.
Daily 5 a.m.-11 p.m., May-Oct.; 5 a.m.-9 p.m., rest of year.
Fenced area for small dogs, picnic area, walking and
hiking trails.

Rampart Dog Park - Colorado Springs
parks.coloradosprings.gov/explore-play/explore/parks/
dog-parks, (719) 385-5940
8270 Lexington Dr., 80920.
Daily 5 a.m.-11 p.m., May-Oct.; 5 a.m.-9 p.m., rest of year.
Fenced, drinking fountains, water bowls, benches, shade,
agility course, trash can.

Red Rock Canyon Open Space - Colorado Springs
www.redrockcanyonopenspace.org/recreation/maps,
(719) 385-5940
3550 W. High St., 80904.
Daily 5 a.m.-11 p.m., May-Oct.; 5 a.m.-9 p.m., rest of year.
Two off-leash areas, 5/8 mile in length, walking and hiking
trails.

**Chatfield State Park Dog Off-Leash Area (DOLA) -
Littleton**
www.cpw.state.co.us/placestogo/parks/Chatfield/Pages/
DogOff-LeashArea.aspx, (303) 791-7275
11500 N. Roxborough Park Rd., 80125.
Daily 5 a.m.-10 p.m. $2.
69 acres, paved and unpaved trails, two ponds.

DISTRICT OF COLUMBIA

Gage-Eckington Dog Park - Washington, D.C.
www.dpr.dc.gov/page/dog-parks, (202) 673-7647
286 V St. N.W., 20001.
Daily dawn-dusk.
Fenced, less than 1 acre, grass surface, disposal bags and
trash cans.

Guy Mason Dog Park - Washington, D.C.
www.dogsofguymason.wordpress.com, (202) 673-7647
3600 Calvert St. N.W., 20008.
Mon.-Fri. 9 a.m.-10 p.m., Sat. 9-5.
Fenced, double-gated entryway, drinking fountain, disposal
bags and trash cans, benches, shade, restrooms.

Langdon Dog Park - Washington, D.C.
www.langdondogpark.org, (202) 673-7647
2901 20th St. N.E., 20018.
Daily dawn-dusk.
Fenced, gravel surface, drinking fountains, separate areas
for large and small dogs, disposal bags and trash cans.

Newark Street Dog Park - Washington, D.C.
www.newarkstdogpark.wordpress.com, (202) 673-7647
3878 Newark St. N.W., 20008.
Mon.-Fri. 7-dusk, Sat.-Sun. 8-dusk.
Fenced, double-gated entryway, benches, shade, covered
pavilion, granite gravel surface, separate areas for large and
small dogs, disposal bags and trash cans, common tennis
balls.

Shaw Dog Park - Washington, D.C.
www.shawdogs.org, (330) 737-1364
1673 11th St. N.W., 20001.
Mon.-Fri. 7 a.m.-10 p.m., Sat.-Sun. 8 a.m.-10 p.m.
Fenced, separate areas for large and small or senior dogs,
common water and water bowls, gravel surface, lighted.

S Street Dog Park - Washington, D.C.
www.dpr.dc.gov/page/dog-parks, (202) 673-7647
1706 S St. N.W., 20009.
Mon.-Fri. 7 a.m.-8 p.m., Sat.-Sun. 8-8.
Fenced, double-gated entryway, artificial turf surface,
drinking fountain, benches, trees, shade.

Upshur Dog Park - Washington, D.C.
www.dpr.dc.gov/page/dog-parks, (202) 576-6842
4300 Arkansas Ave. N.W., 20011.
Mon.-Fri. 7 a.m.-9 p.m., Sat.-Sun. 8 a.m.-9 p.m.
Fenced, double-gated entryway, disposal bags and trash
cans, drinking fountains, gravel surface.

Walter Pierce Dog Park - Washington, D.C.
www.walterpiercepark.org, (202) 588-7332
2630 Adams Mill Rd. N.W., 20009.
Daily dawn-dusk.
Fenced, double-gated entryway, sand surface, trees, shade.

FLORIDA

Crest Lake Dog Park - Clearwater
www.clearwater-fl.com/gov/depts/parksrec, (727) 562-4800
201 S. Glenwood Ave., 33755.
Daily 6 a.m.-9 p.m.
Fenced, 1.75 acres, double-gated entryway, benches,
disposal bags and trash cans, drinking fountains, water
bowls, leash holders, wash station.

Enterprise Dog Park - Clearwater
www.myclearwater.com, (727) 562-4800
2671 Enterprise Rd. E., 33761.
Daily dawn-dusk.
Fenced, drinking fountains, dog wash station, agility
equipment, benches, disposal bags and trash cans, covered
picnic areas.

Manatee Island Dog Park - Daytona Beach
(386) 671-3400
325 N. Beach St., 32114.
Daily dawn-dusk.
1 acre, separate fenced areas for large and small dogs,
double-entry gate, time-out pen, water fountain, benches,
restrooms.

Gemini Springs Dog Park - Debary
www.daytonabeach.com/listings/Gemini-Springs-Park-and-
Gemini-Springs-Dog-Park/962, (386) 668-3810
37 Dirksen Dr., 32713.
Daily dawn-dusk.
Fenced, 4.5 acres, separate areas for larger dogs (over 25
lbs.) and smaller dogs, shaded areas, dog wash stations,
water fountains, benches.

Canine Beach - Fort Lauderdale
www.fortlauderdale.gov/citydogs/dogs.htm, (954) 564-4521
3109 E. Sunrise Blvd., 33304.
Fri.-Sun. 3-7, Nov.-Feb.; Fri.-Sun. 5-9, rest of year.
Park ranger on duty, disposal bags and trash cans, beach
showers, drinking fountains.

Snyder Park - Fort Lauderdale
www.fortlauderdale.gov/citydogs/dogs.htm, (954) 847-3428
3299 S.W. 4th Ave., 33315.
Fri.-Wed. 7-7, Thurs. 11-7. Sat.-Sun. $5 per day, $1 per
hour; Mon.-Fri. free.
Fenced, separate areas for large and small dogs, agility
course, drinking fountains, disposal bags and trash cans,
benches, trees, dog beach.

Riviera Oaks Dog Park - Holly Hill
(832) 596-4048
980 Alabama Ave., 32117.
Daily dawn-dusk.
Benches, covered pavilion, separate areas for large and
small dogs, water stations, restrooms.

Confederate Park Dog Park - Jacksonville
www.visitjacksonville.com/directory/confederate-park-dog-park,
(904) 630-2489
956 Hubbard St., 32206.
Mon.-Fri. 8 a.m.-10 p.m.
Fenced, 3 acres, disposal bags and trash cans, covered
pavilions, drinking fountain.

Higgs Beach Dog Park - Key West
www.monroecounty-fl.gov, (305) 295-4385
Atlantic Blvd., 33040.
Daily 6 a.m.-11 p.m.
Separate areas for large and small dogs, water fountains,
picnic tables, disposal bags.

Amelia Earhart Bark Park - Miami
www.miamidade.gov/parks, (305) 685-8389
401 E. 65th St., 33138.
Daily dawn-dusk. Parking: $4 per private vehicle.
Fenced, 5 acres, separate areas for large and small dogs,
shade, cement and grass surfaces, benches, picnic areas,
drinking fountains, disposal bags and trash cans.

Blanche Park - Miami
www.miamigov.com, (305) 960-2946
3045 Shipping Ave., 33133.
Daily dawn-dusk.
Fenced, turf and grass surfaces, trees, shade, drinking
fountains, disposal bags and trash cans, benches.

Perrine Wayside Park - Miami
www.palmettobay-fl.gov/node/95, (305) 259-1234
16425 S. Dixie Hwy., 33157.
Daily 8-8.
Fenced, 3 acres, separate areas for large and small dogs,
disposal bags and trash cans, dog pond, grass, walking
trails, wash station, drinking fountains, trees, benches, picnic
tables, two entrances.

West Kendall District Park - Miami
www.miamidade.gov/parks/facilities-dog-parks.asp,
(305) 386-0227
11255 S.W. 157th Ave., 33196.
Daily 9-6.
Fenced, 6.5 acres, agility courses, separate areas for large
and small dogs, drinking fountain, water sprays, shade,
picnic areas, disposal bags and trash cans, benches,
restrooms.

Flamingo Bark Park - Miami Beach
web.miamibeachfl.gov/parksandrecreation, (305) 673-7766
1200 Meridian Ave., 33139.
Daily 7 a.m.-9 p.m.
Fenced, less than 1 acre, double-gated entrance, benches,
shade, separate areas for large and small dogs, grass,
drinking fountains, disposal bags and trash cans.

North Shore Open Space Park - Miami Beach
web.miamibeachfl.gov/parksandrecreation, (305) 861-3616
8101 Collins Ave., 33141.
Daily dawn-dusk.
Fenced, 1 acre, double-gated entrance, separate areas for
large and small dogs, drinking fountains, dog bowls, walking
paths, benches, disposal bags and trash cans, beach
access.

Pinetree Bark Park - Miami Beach
web.miamibeachfl.gov/parksandrecreation, (305) 673-7730
4400 Pinetree Dr., 33140.
Daily dawn-dusk.
Double-gated entry, grass, benches, drinking fountains,
disposal bags and trash cans.

South Pointe Park - Miami Beach
web.miamibeachfl.gov/parksandrecreation, (305) 673-7766
1 Washington Ave., 33109.
Daily dawn-7 p.m.
Fenced, less than 1 acre, double-gated entrance, drinking
fountains, picnic tables, benches.

Washington Avenue Bark Park - Miami Beach
web.miamibeachfl.gov/parksandrecreation, (305) 673-7766
201 2nd St., 33139.
Daily dawn-dusk.
Fenced, disposal bags and trash cans, trees, double-gated
entry, shade, grass surface, drinking fountains, wash station,
benches.

East Greynolds Dog Park - North Miami Beach
www.miamidade.gov/parks/facilities-dog-parks.asp,
(305) 945-3425
16700 Biscayne Blvd., 33160.
Daily dawn-dusk. Parking: $1 per hour (Mon.-Fri.), $6
(Sat.-Sun. and major holidays).
Fenced, 2 acres, separate areas for large and small
dogs, drinking fountains, wash stations, walkways, shade,
grass.

Barber Park - Orlando
www.ocfl.net/CultureParks/DogParks.aspx, (407) 254-6860
3701 Gatlin Ave., 32812.
Daily 8-6.
Fenced, shade, covered pavilion, drinking fountain, common
water bowls, grass and cement surface, disposal bags and
trash cans, benches, separate areas for large and small
dogs.

Barnett Park - Orlando
www.ocfl.net/CultureParks/DogParks.aspx, (407) 836-6248
4801 W. Colonial Dr., 32808.
Daily 8-8.
Fenced, benches, grass surface, disposal bags and trash
cans.

Downey Dog Park - Orlando
www.ocfl.net/CultureParks/DogParks.aspx, (407) 254-9180
10107 Flowers Ave., 32825.
Daily 8-8.
Fenced, benches, separate areas for large and small dogs,
grass surface, wash station.

Dr. Phillips Dog Park - Orlando
www.ocfl.net/CultureParks/DogParks.aspx, (407) 254-9045
8249 Buenavista Woods Blvd., 32836.
Daily 8-8.
Fenced, separate areas for large and small dogs, grass and
mulch surface, splash area, benches, trees, disposal bags
and trash cans.

Meadow Woods Dog Park - Orlando
www.ocfl.net/CultureParks/DogParks.aspx, (407) 858-4725
1751 Rhode Island Woods Cir., 32824.
Daily 8-8.
Fenced, separate areas for large and small dogs, benches,
grass, drinking fountains, walking paths.

Yucatan Park - Orlando
www.ocfl.net/CultureParks/DogParks.aspx, (407) 254-9160
6400 Yucatan Dr., 32807.
Daily 8-8.
Fenced, separate areas for large and small dogs, benches,
trees, covered pavilion, drinking fountain.

Veterans Park Dog Park - Saint Johns
www.co.st-johns.fl.us/recreation/parks/Veterans.aspx,
(904) 209-0655
1332 Veterans Pkwy., 32259.
Daily dawn-dusk.
Fenced, 3 acres, separate areas for large and small dogs,
drinking fountains, picnic areas, disposal bags and trash
cans.

Paws Dog Park at Treaty Park - St. Augustine
www.co.st-johns.fl.us/Recreation/Parks/TreatyDogPark.aspx,
(904) 209-0655
1595 Wildwood Dr., 32086.
Daily dawn-dusk.
Fenced, drinking fountain, separate areas for large and
small dogs, shade, benches.

Coquina Key Dog Park - St. Petersburg
www.stpeteparksrec.org, (727) 893-7441
3595 Locust St. S.E., 33705.
Daily dawn-dusk.
Fenced, drinking fountains, shade, trees, agility equipment,
disposal bags and trash cans, wash station.

Crescent Lake Dog Park - St. Petersburg
www.stpeteparksrec.org, (727) 893-7335
1320 5th St. N., 33704.
Daily dawn-dusk.
Fenced, double-gated entryway, separate areas for large
and small dogs, grass and gravel surface, benches, drinking
fountain, disposal bags and trash cans.

Kenwood Dog Park - St. Petersburg
www.stpeteparksrec.org/dog-parks.html, (727) 893-7441
401 20th St. N., 33713.
Daily dawn-dusk.
Fenced, 3 acres, dog wash area, double-gated entryway,
separate areas for large and small dogs, grass surface,
trees, picnic area, benches.

Lake Vista Dog Park - St. Petersburg
www.stpeteparksrec.org/dog-parks.html, (727) 893-7441
1401 62nd Ave. S., 33705.
Daily dawn-dusk.
Fenced, double-gated entryway, separate areas for large
and small dogs, gravel and grass surfaces, trees, benches.

North Shore Dog Park - St. Petersburg
www.stpeteparksrec.org/dog-parks.html, (727) 893-7335
901 N. Shore Dr. N.E., 33701.
Daily dawn-dusk.
Fenced, separate areas for large and small dogs, trees,
shade, benches, wash station, disposal bags and trash
cans.

Walter Fuller Dog Park - St. Petersburg
www.stpeteparksrec.org/dog-parks.html, (727) 893-7441
7891 26th Ave. N., 33710.
Daily dawn-dusk.
Fenced, double-gated entryway, separate areas for large
and small dogs, gravel and grass surfaces, drinking fountain.

Curtis Hixon Waterfront Dog Park - Tampa
www.tampagov.net/parks-and-recreation, (813) 274-8211
600 N. Ashley Dr., 33602.
Daily dawn-10 p.m. Parking: $5.
Fenced, drinking fountains, artificial turf surface, separate
areas for large and small dogs, lighted.

Davis Islands Dog Beach - Tampa
www.tampagov.net/parks-and-recreation, (813) 274-8615
1002 Severn Ave., 33606.
Daily dawn-dusk.
Beach access, wash station, picnic areas, trees, disposal
bags and trash cans.

Gadsden Dog Park - Tampa
www.tampagov.net/parks-and-recreation, (813) 274-8211
6901 S. MacDill Ave., 33611.
Daily dawn-dusk.
Fenced, double-gated entryway, separate areas for large
and small dogs, shade, benches, trees, disposal bags and
trash cans.

Giddens Dog Park - Tampa
www.tampagov.net/parks-and-recreation, (813) 231-5284
5202 N. 12th St., 33603.
Daily dawn-dusk.
Fenced, grass surface, shade, benches, trees.

James Urbanski Dog Park at Al Lopez Park - Tampa
www.tampagov.net/parks-and-recreation, (813) 274-8211
4810 N. Himes Ave., 33614.
Daily dawn-dusk.
Fenced, 1.5 acres, separate areas for large and small dogs,
drinking fountains, benches, picnic area, grass surface,
disposal bags and trash cans, trees.

Palma Ceia Dog Park - Tampa
www.tampagov.net/parks-and-recreation, (813) 274-8615
2200 S. Marti St., 33629.
Mon.-Fri. 8-dusk, Sat.-Sun. 9-dusk.
Fenced, less than 1 acre, drinking fountains, shade, trees,
grass surface.

Rowlett Dog Park - Tampa
www.tampagov.net/parks-and-recreation, (813) 274-8211
2501 E. River Hills Dr., 33604.
Daily dawn-dusk.
Fenced, trees, covered pavilions, separate areas for large
and small dogs, grass surface, agility equipment.

Washington Street Dog Park - Tampa
www.tampagov.net/parks-and-recreation, (813) 274-8211
118 N. 12th St., 33602.
Daily dawn-dusk.
Fenced, artificial turf surface, shade, trees, benches, drinking
fountain, covered pavilion.

Vero Beach Dog Park - Vero Beach
www.verodogpark.org, (772) 234-2824
3449 Indian River Dr. E., 32963.
Daily dawn-dusk.
Fenced, 5 acres, separate areas for large and small dogs,
grass, shade, drinking fountains, benches, dog wash area,
covered pavilion, double-gated entryway, restrooms, disposal
bags and trash cans.

West Orange Park - Winter Garden
www.ocfl.net/CultureParks/DogParks.aspx, (407) 656-3299
12400 Marshall Farms Road, 34787.
Daily dawn-dusk.
Fenced, separate areas for large and small dogs, mulch and
concrete surface, trees, drinking fountains, disposal bags
and trash cans, benches, picnic tables.

Lake Baldwin Dog Park - Winter Park
www.ffpp.org, (407) 599-3399
2000 S. Lakemont Ave., 32789.
Daily dawn-dusk.
Fenced, lake access, dog beach, trees, trails, wash stations,
drinking stations, disposal bags and trash cans, water bowls,
picnic tables.

GEORGIA

Piedmont Park - Atlanta
www.piedmontpark.org, (404) 875-7275
1320 Monroe Dr. N.E., 30306.
Daily 6 a.m.-11 p.m.
Fenced, 3 acres, separate areas for large and small dogs,
benches, restrooms.

South Bend Park - Atlanta
www.atlantaga.gov, (404) 546-6788
1955 Compton Dr. S.E., 30315.
Daily 6 a.m.-11 p.m.
Fenced, 74 acres, trees, shade.

HAWAII

Hawaii Kai Dog Park - Honolulu
www.hui-ilio.org, (808) 396-5225
234 Keahole St., 96825.
Wed.-Mon. dawn-dusk, Tues. noon-dusk.
Fenced, separate areas for large and small dogs, benches, drinking fountain, trees, picnic tables.

Moanalua Dog Park - Honolulu
www.moanaluadogpark.org, (808) 768-4385
2900 Moanalua Park Rd., 96819.
Wed.-Mon. dawn-dusk; Tues. noon-dusk.
Fenced, drinking fountain, picnic tables, restrooms, shade.

Mililani Dog Park - Mililani
www.hawaiianhumane.org/Dog-Friendly-Parks.html,
(808) 946-2187
95-1069 Ukuwai St., 96789.
Daily dawn-dusk.
Fenced, drinking fountain with water bowls, trees, disposal bags and trash cans.

ILLINOIS

Grant Bark Park - Chicago
www.southloopdogpac.org/south-loop-dog-parks/
grant-bark-park, (312) 742-3918
900 S. Columbus Dr., 60605.
Fenced, less than 1 acre, drinking fountain, disposal bags and trash cans, asphalt, pea gravel.

Montrose Dog Beach - Chicago
www.chicagoparkdistrict.com/facilities/dog-friendly-areas,
(312) 742-5121
4400 N. Lake Shore Dr., 60640.
Daily dawn-9 p.m.
Separate fenced area, 4 acres, dog beach, boat launch, trash cans.

Noethling Playlot Park ("Wiggly Field") - Chicago
www.chicagoparkdistrict.com/parks/Noethling-Playlot-Park,
(312) 742-7816
2645 N. Sheffield Ave., 60614.
Daily 6 a.m.-11 p.m.
Fenced, less than 1 acre, drinking fountain.

Pottawattomie Park - Chicago
www.chicagoparkdistrict.com/parks/Pottawattomie-Park,
(773) 262-5835
7403-27 N. Wolcott, 60626.
Daily 6 a.m.-11 p.m.
Less than 1 acre, separate areas for large and small dogs, drinking fountain.

Puptown at Margate Park Fieldhouse - Chicago
www.chicagoparkdistrict.com/facilities/dog-friendly-areas,
(312) 742-7522
4900 N. Marine Dr., 60640.
Daily 6 a.m.-11 p.m.
Fenced, less than 1 acre, asphalt, pea gravel, disposal bags and trash cans, dog water fountain.

INDIANA

Smock Dog Park - Greenwood
www.indy.gov, (317) 888-0070
4200 E. County Line Rd., 46143.
Daily dawn-dusk. $5.
Fenced, 4 acres, benches.

Broad Ripple Park - Indianapolis
www.broadripplepark.org, (317) 327-7161
1550 Broad Ripple Ave., 46220.
Mon.-Thurs. 9-9, Fri. 9-5, Sat. 9-1. $5.
Fenced, grass, drinking fountain, disposal bags and trash cans, restrooms, benches.

Eagle Creek Bark Park - Indianapolis
www.eaglecreekpark.org/park/park_bark_park.htm,
(317) 327-7116
6515 Delong Rd., 46278.
Daily 8-7. $5.
Fenced, grass and gravel surface.

Paul Ruster Bark Park - Indianapolis
www.indy.gov, (317) 327-0143
11300 E. Prospect St., 46239.
Daily 7 a.m.-8 p.m. $5.
Fenced, grass and gravel surfaces, disposal bags and trash cans, benches.

KANSAS

Shawnee Mission Park Off-Leash Dog Park - Shawnee
www.jcprd.com/parks_facilities/shawnee_mission.cfm,
(913) 888-4713
7900 Renner Rd., 66219.
Daily 5 a.m.-11 p.m., Mar.-Oct.; 6 a.m.-8 p.m., rest of year.
53 acres, wood chip surface, trails, restrooms, dog beach, disposal bags and trash cans, drinking fountains.

KENTUCKY

The Barklands of Floyds Fork - Louisville
www.louisvilledogs.com, (502) 584-0350
1310 S. Beckley Station Rd., 40245.
Daily dawn-dusk.
Fenced, 4 acres, divided into three areas for resting, small and all dogs. Email info@louisvilledogs.com before visiting and bring a copy of vaccination records for entrance to the park.

Champions Dog Run at Champions Park - Louisville
www.louisvilledogs.com, (502) 456-8100
2930 River Rd., 40206.
Fenced, 3.6 acres, separate area for small dogs, drinking fountain. Email info@louisvilledogs.com before visiting and bring a copy of vaccination records for entrance to the park.

Cochran Hill Dog Run at Cherokee Park - Louisville
www.louisvilledogs.com, (502) 456-8100
745 Cochran Hill Rd., 40206.
Daily dawn-dusk.
Fenced, 2 acres, separate areas for large and small dogs, disposal bags and trash cans, benches, trees, shade. Email info@louisvilledogs.com before visiting and bring a copy of vaccination records for entrance to the park.

Sawyer Dog Park at E.P. "Tom" Sawyer State Park - Louisville
www.louisvilledogs.com, (502) 429-3280
3111 Freys Hill Rd., 40241.
Daily dawn-dusk.
Fenced, 6 acres, separate area for small dogs, shade, benches, drinking fountains, walking paths, common toys and tennis balls, dog pool, disposal bags and trash cans.

Vettiner Dog Run - Louisville
www.louisvilledogs.com, (502) 456-8100
5550 Charlie Vettiner Park Rd., 40299.
Daily dawn-dusk.
Fenced, 2 acres, gated, separate areas for large and small dogs. Email info@louisvilledogs.com before visiting and bring a copy of vaccination records for entrance to the park.

LOUISIANA

Bonnabel Boat Launch BarkPark - Metairie
www.bonnabelboatlaunch.com/barkpark-dog-park-bonnabel-metairie-la.htm, (504) 658-4000
1599 Bonnabel Blvd., 70005.
Daily dawn-dusk.
Fenced, double-gated entryway, agility courses, grass surface, disposal bags and trash cans, drinking fountain. Maximum of two dogs per person.

NOLA City Bark - New Orleans
www.nolacitybark.org, (504) 483-9377
30 Zachary Taylor Dr., 70124.
Wed.-Mon. 5:30 a.m.-9 p.m., Tues. 1-9. $10 (three-day permit).
Fenced, 4.6 acres, .25-mi. walking trail, separate areas for large and small dogs, restrooms, drinking fountain, splash area, disposal bags and trash cans. Purchase permits online or in person Mon.-Fri. between 8 a.m. and 5 p.m.

MARYLAND

Canton Dog Park - Baltimore
www.cantoncommunity.org, (410) 342-0900
1285 S. Bouldin St., 21224.
Daily dawn-dusk.
Fenced, separate areas for large and small or older dogs, shade, parking, water source, disposal bags.

Locust Point Dog Park - Baltimore
www.locustpointdogpark.org, (410) 396-7900
1627 E. Fort Ave., 21230.
Daily dawn-dusk.
Fenced, trees, benches, hours for small and older dogs in the morning and afternoon, water station, artificial turf surface, water slide.

Patterson Dog Park - Baltimore
www.pattersondogpark.org, (410) 276-3676
27 S. Patterson Park Ave., 21231.
Daily dawn-dusk.
Fenced, trees, benches, rocks for climbing, drinking fountain and hose bibb, disposal stations, artificial turf surface.

MASSACHUSETTS

Peters Park Dog Run - Boston
www.peterspark.org, (617) 635-4500
1277 Washington St., 02118.
Daily dawn-dusk.
Fenced, less than 1 acre, separate areas for large and small dogs, benches.

Danehy Park - Cambridge
www.cambridgema.gov/CDD/parks/osplanning/offleash.aspx, (617) 349-4800
168 New St., 02238.
Daily dawn-dusk.
Fenced, separate areas for large and small dogs, gravel surface, drinking water, disposal bags, benches.

Fresh Pond Reservation - Cambridge
www.cambridgema.gov/Water/freshpondreservation.aspx, (617) 349-4770
250 Fresh Pond Pkwy., 02138.
Daily dawn-dusk.
Partially fenced, trees, shade, trash cans, beach, disposal bags.

Falmouth Dog Park - Falmouth
www.falmouthdogpark.com, (508) 331-2929
257 Brick Kiln Rd., 02541.
Daily dawn-dusk.
Fenced, 1.6 acres, separate areas for large and small dogs, benches, water fountains, waste disposal cans.

MINNESOTA

Franklin Terrace Off-Leash Recreation Area - Minneapolis
www.minneapolisparks.org, (612) 230-6400
925 Franklin Terr., 55406.
Daily 6 a.m.-10 p.m. $5.
Fenced, 1.37 acres, double-gated entryway, mulch surface, disposal bags and trash cans, trees, shade.

Lake of the Isles Off-Leash Recreation Area - Minneapolis
www.minneapolisparks.org, (612) 230-6400
2845 Lake of the Isles Pkwy. W., 55405.
Daily 6 a.m.-10 p.m. $5.
Fenced 1.87 acres, separate areas for large and small dogs, mulch surface, water bowls, benches.

Loring Park Off-Leash Dog Park - Minneapolis
www.minneapolisparks.org, (612) 230-6400
1382 Willow St., 55403.
Daily 6 a.m.-10 p.m. $5.
Fenced, less than 1 acre, agility course, grass, double-gated entryway, water bowls, gravel surface.

Lyndale Farmstead Off-Leash Recreation Area - Minneapolis
www.minneapolisparks.org, (612) 230-6400
3845 Dupont Ave. S., 55409.
Daily 6 a.m.-10 p.m. $5.
Fenced, less than 1 acre, crushed granite surface, benches, covered pavilion.

Minnehaha Off-Leash Recreation Area - Minneapolis
www.minneapolisparks.org, (612) 230-6400
5399 S. Minnehaha Park Dr., 55417.
Daily 6 a.m.-10 p.m. $5.
Fenced, 6.58 acres, walking trails, woods, river access, dog beach.

St. Anthony Parkway Off-Leash Recreation Area - Minneapolis
www.minneapolisparks.org, (612) 230-6400
700 St. Anthony Pkwy., 55418.
Daily 6 a.m.-10 p.m. $5.
Fenced, 2.17 acres, mulch surface, disposal bags and trash cans.

Victory Prairie Off-Leash Recreation Area - Minneapolis
www.minneapolisparks.org, (612) 230-6400
4701 Russell Ave. N., 55412.
Daily 6 a.m.-10 p.m. $5.
Fenced, 2.62 acres, grass, common tennis balls, disposal bags and trash cans, water bowls.

MISSOURI

Elmo & Rosalea Marrs Memorial Dog Park at Stockstill Park - Branson
www.bransonparksandrecreation.com, (417) 335-2368
524 Stockstill Ln., 65615.
Daily dawn-dusk. $5 day pass, $2 each additional dog.
Fenced, 1.5 acres, separate areas for large and small dogs, pavilion, picnic tables, benches, play equipment. Maximum of two dogs per person.

Penn Valley Off-Leash Dog Park - Kansas City
www.kcparks.org/parks/dog-park, (816) 513-7500
2927 Wyandotte St., 64111.
Daily dawn-dusk.
Fenced, 2.7 acres, separate areas for large and small dogs, drinking fountains, disposal bags and trash cans.

Swope Park Off-Leash Dog Park - Kansas City
www.kcparks.org/parks/dog-park, (816) 513-7500
4701 E. Gregory Blvd., 64132.
Daily dawn-one hour after dusk.
Fenced, 5 acres, separate areas for large and small dogs, drinking fountains, trees.

Wayside Waifs Bark Park - Kansas City
(816) 761-8151
3901 Martha Truman Rd., 64137.
The park is open daily 24 hours. $3.
Fenced, 5 acres, separate areas for large and small dogs, trees, shade, covered pavilions, park benches, lighted, time-out kennels, drinking fountains, restrooms.

DuSable Dog Park - St. Charles
www.stcharlesparks.com, (636) 949-3372
2301 N. Main St., 63301.
Daily dawn-10 p.m.
Fenced, 2.5 acres, separate areas for large and small dogs, covered pavilion, shade, trees, grass surface, restrooms.

Lister Dog Park - St. Louis
www.apamo.org/DogParks.aspx, (314) 289-5300
4597 Olive St., 63108.
Daily dawn-dusk.
Fenced, 2.5 acres, mulch surface.

NEVADA

All American Park - Las Vegas
www.lasvegasnevada.gov/Find/parks_facilities.htm,
(702) 229-6011
1309 S. Buffalo Dr., 89117.
Daily dawn-dusk.
Fenced, restrooms, picnic areas.

Barkin' Basin Park - Las Vegas
www.lasvegasnevada.gov/Find/parks_facilities.htm,
(702) 229-6011
7351 W. Alexander Blvd., 89129.
Daily dawn-9 p.m.
Fenced, 7.75 acres, separate areas for large and small dogs, shaded benches, drinking fountains, water stations, lighted walking trails, grass, restrooms.

Centennial Hills Park - Las Vegas
www.lasvegasnevada.gov/Find/parks_facilities.htm,
(702) 229-6718
7101 N. Buffalo Dr., 89131.
Mon.-Wed. and Fri.-Sun. dawn-dusk, Thurs. 3-dusk.
Fenced, separate areas for large and small dogs, grass, benches, shade, covered pavilion, disposal bags and trash cans.

Charlie Kellogg and Joe Zaher Sports Complex - Las Vegas
www.lasvegasnevada.gov/Find/parks_facilities.htm,
(702) 229-2100
7901 W. Washington Ave., 89128.
Fri.-Wed. dawn-dusk, Thurs. 3-dusk.
Fenced, separate areas for large and small dogs, drinking fountain, walking trails, disposal bags and trash cans, benches, restrooms, shade.

Children's Memorial Park Dog Park - Las Vegas
www.lasvegasnevada.gov/Find/parks_facilities.htm,
(702) 229-6718
6601 W. Gowan Rd., 89108.
Daily dawn-dusk.
Fenced, less than 1 acre, separate areas for large and small dogs, drinking fountains, shade trees.

Justice Myron E. Leavitt Family Park - Las Vegas
www.lasvegasnevada.gov/Find/parks_facilities.htm,
(702) 229-6718
2329 S. Eastern Ave., 89104.
Daily dawn-dusk.
Fenced, separate areas for large and small dogs, picnic areas, walking trails, drinking fountain, agility course, disposal bags and trash cans.

Police Memorial Park - Las Vegas
www.lasvegasnevada.gov/Find/parks_facilities.htm,
(702) 229-6011
3250 Metro Academy Way, 89129.
Daily dawn-dusk.
Fenced, separate areas for large and small dogs, shade, drinking fountain, disposal bags and trash cans.

Woofter Dog Park - Las Vegas
www.lasvegasnevada.gov/Find/parks_facilities.htm,
(702) 229-2330
1682 N. Rock Springs Dr., 89128.
Daily dawn-dusk.
Fenced, separate areas for large and small dogs, benches, trees, restrooms.

Whitaker Dog Park - Reno
www.reno.gov/government/departments/parks-recreation-community-services/parks-trails/dogs-dog-parks,
(775) 334-2270
550 University Terr., 89503.
Fenced, less than 1 acre, double-gated entries, shade, disposal bags.

NEW MEXICO

Coronado Dog Park - Albuquerque
www.cabq.gov/parksandrecreation/parks/dog-parks,
(505) 768-5300
301 McKnight Ave. N.W., 87102.
Daily 6 a.m.-10 p.m.
Fenced, picnic areas, benches, trees, disposal bags and trash cans.

North Domingo Baca Dog Park - Albuquerque
www.cabq.gov/parksandrecreation/parks/dog-parks,
(505) 768-5305
7520 Corona Ave. N.E., 87113.
Daily 6 a.m.-10 p.m.
Fenced, separate areas for large and small dogs, disposal bags and trash cans, two levels, covered picnic areas, benches, mulch surface.

Skyline Dog Park - Albuquerque
www.cabq.gov/parksandrecreation/parks/dog-parks,
(505) 768-5300
12700 Montgomery Blvd. N.E., 87111.
Daily 6 a.m.-10 p.m.
Fenced, sand surface, disposal bags and trash cans.

Frank Ortiz Park Off-Leash Area - Santa Fe
www.santafenm.gov, (505) 955-2100
160 Camino Las Crucitas, 87501.
Daily dawn-dusk.
Walking trails, water bowls, disposal bags and trash cans, sand surface.

Salvador Perez Park - Santa Fe
www.santafe.com/directory/salvador-perez-park,
(505) 955-2510
601 Alta Vista St., 87505.
Daily 6 a.m.-8 p.m.
Fenced, grass surface, drinking fountain, disposal bags and trash cans, benches.

NEW YORK

Amherst Paw Park - Amherst
www.amherst.ny.us, (716) 631-7000
500 Smith Rd., 14051.
Daily dawn-dusk.
Fenced, separate areas for large and small dogs, grass surface, disposal bags and trash cans.

The Barkyard - Buffalo
www.thebarkyard.org, (716) 218-0303
D A R Ave., 14202.
Daily dawn-dusk.
Fenced, 1.6 acres, separate areas for large and small dogs, double-gated entryway, lighted, drinking fountains, benches, covered pavilions.

Madison Square Park Dog Run - New York
www.madisonsquarepark.org/things-to-do/dog-run,
(212) 538-1884
2 E. 23rd St., 10010.
Daily dawn-midnight.
Fenced, double-gated entryway, benches, disposal bags and trash cans, separate areas for large and small dogs, wash station, drinking fountain, gravel surface.

Peter Detmold Park Dog Run - New York
www.nycgovparks.org/parks/peterdetmoldpark,
(212) 639-9675
454 E. 51st St., 10022.
Daily dawn-midnight.
Fenced, brick surface, disposal bags and trash cans, common tennis balls and toys, lighted, trees, shade, picnic area.

Sir William's Dog Run at Ft. Tryon Park - New York
www.nycgovparks.org/parks/fort-tryon-park, (212) 795-1388
689 Fort Washington Ave., 10032.
Daily dawn-dusk.
Fenced, 1.5 acres, shade, benches, separate areas for timid and friendly dogs, mulch and grass surfaces.

Union Square Dog Run - New York
www.nycgovparks.org/parks/union-square-park,
(212) 639-9675
40 E. 14th St., 10003.
Daily 6 p.m.-midnight.
Fenced, double-gated entryway, trees, benches, disposal bags and trash cans.

Washington Square Park Dog Run - New York
www.nycgovparks.org/parks/washington-square-park,
(212) 639-9675
1 Washington Square E., 10011.
Daily dawn-midnight. Free.
Fenced, separate areas for large and small dogs, drinking fountain, lighted, benches, trees, shade, dog splash area, common toys and tennis balls.

NORTH CAROLINA

Barkingham Park at Reedy Creek Park - Charlotte
www.charmeck.org/mecklenburg/county/ParkandRec/Parks/
DogParks/Pages/default.aspx, (704) 336-3854
2900 Rocky River Rd., 28215.
Daily 7:30 a.m.-dusk.
Fenced, 4 acres, grass, trees, shade, benches.

Davie Dog Park - Charlotte
www.charmeck.org/mecklenburg/county/ParkandRec/Parks/
DogParks/Pages/default.aspx, (704) 554-0402
4635 Pineville-Matthews Rd., 28277.
Daily 7:30 a.m.-dusk.
Fenced, 5 acres, separate areas for large and small dogs, trails, dog pool, benches, disposal bags and trash cans, drinking fountain.

Frazier Park - Charlotte
www.charmeck.org/mecklenburg/county/ParkandRec/Parks/
DogParks/Pages/default.aspx, (704) 432-4280
1201 W. 4th St., 28202.
Daily 7:30 a.m.-dusk.
Fenced, 1.3 acres, separate areas for large and small dogs, drinking fountains.

Ray's Fetching Meadow - Charlotte
www.charmeck.org/mecklenburg/county/ParkandRec/Parks/
DogParks/Pages/default.aspx, (704) 643-5725
8711 Monroe Rd., 28212.
Daily 7:30 a.m.-dusk.
Fenced, 1 acre, walking trails.

Shuffletown Park - Charlotte
www.charmeck.org/mecklenburg/county/ParkandRec/Parks/
DogParks/Pages/default.aspx, (704) 336-8869
9500 Bellhaven Blvd., 28214.
Daily 7:30 a.m.-dusk.
Fenced, separate areas for large and small dogs, walking path, disposal bags and trash cans, water stations, trees, benches.

Swaney Pointe K-9 Park - Cornelius
www.charmeck.org/mecklenburg/county/ParkandRec/Parks/
DogParks/Pages/default.aspx, (704) 336-8869
18441 Nantz Rd., 28078.
Daily 7:30 a.m.-dusk.
Fenced, 4 acres, separate areas for large and small dogs, picnic area.

OHIO

Mt. Airy Forest Dog Park - Cincinnati
www.cincinnatiparks.com/mt-airy-forest, (513) 352-4080
3006 Westwood Northern Blvd., 45211.
Daily 6 a.m.-10 p.m.
Fenced, 2 acres, separate areas for large and small dogs, trees, drinking fountain, benches, obstacle course, wash station. No disposal bags available.

Otto Armleder Dog Park - Cincinnati
www.hamiltoncountyparks.org, (513) 521-7275
5057 Wooster Pike, 45226.
Daily 6 a.m.-10 p.m.
Fenced, 10 acres, separate areas for large and small dogs, grass, drinking fountains, wash station, disposal bags and trash cans.

Washington Park - Cincinnati
www.washingtonpark.org, (513) 621-4400
1230 Elm St., 45202.
Daily 6:00 a.m.-11:00 p.m.
Fenced, less than 1 acre, climbing rocks, benches, drinking fountain, splash area, artificial turf surface, pea gravel.

Clark Field Dog Park - Cleveland
www.clevelanddogparks.com, (216) 575-0920
1095 Clark Ave., 44113.
Daily 8 a.m.-9 p.m.
Separate areas for large and small dogs, gravel, drinking fountain, trees, disposal bags and trash cans, hand sanitizer, benches.

Lakewood Dog Park - Cleveland
www.lakewooddogpark.com, (216) 364-7274
1699 Valley Pkwy., 44107.
Daily 8 a.m.-9 p.m.
Gravel and grass surfaces, trees, shade, drinking fountain, toys, water bowls, disposal bags and trash cans, 50-foot gated area for smaller or less-social dogs.

Big Walnut Dog Park - Columbus
www.columbus.gov/recreationandparks/dog-parks/
All-Dog-Parks, (614) 645-3300
5000 E. Livingston Ave., 43227.
Daily 7 a.m.-11 p.m.
Fenced, 3 acres, two entrances, lighted, pond access, separate areas for large and small dogs.

Godown Dog Park - Columbus
www.worthingtondogpark.com, (614) 349-6630
6099 Godown Rd., 43235.
Daily dawn-dusk.
Fenced, 4.5-acre large dog area, 1-acre small dog area, two entrances, paved pathways, wash station, disposal bags and trash cans, information pavilion, hills, trees, benches, drinking fountains.

Three Creeks Dog Park - Columbus
www.columbus.gov/recreationandparks/dog-parks/
All-Dog-Parks, (614) 645-3300
2648 Spangler Rd., 43207.
Daily 8 a.m.-dusk.
Fenced, 5 acres, separate areas for large and small dogs,
walking trails, drinking fountains.

Wheeler Dog Park - Columbus
www.columbus.gov/recreationandparks/dog-parks/
All-Dog-Parks, (614) 645-3300
725 Thurber Dr. W., 43215.
Daily 7 a.m.-11 p.m.
Fenced, 1.5 acres, benches, disposal bags and trash cans,
close to neighboring parks, lighted, walking paths, drinking
fountain.

Woodland Dog Park - Eastlake
www.eastlakeohio.com, (440) 951-1416
35576 Lake Shore Blvd., 44095.
Daily dawn-dusk.
Fenced, less than 1 acre, picnic tables, shade, water bowls,
disposal bags and trash cans.

Memorial Dog Park - Medina
www.medinaoh.org/government/departments/parks/
memorial-park, (330) 721-6950
349 E. Homestead St., 44256.
Daily dawn-dusk.
Fenced, less than 1 acre, separate areas for large and
small dogs, benches, grass, trees, disposal bags and trash
cans, drinking fountain.

OKLAHOMA

Joe Barnes Dog Park - Oklahoma City
www.midwestcityok.org, (405) 732-2281
2516 N. Towry Dr., 73110.
Daily 5 a.m.-11 p.m.
Fenced, splash pond, benches, lighted, common toys and
tennis balls, disposal bags and trash cans, covered
pavilions, separate areas for large and small dogs.

Paw Park at Lake Hefner - Oklahoma City
www.pawok.com, (405) 949-7293
3303 N.W. Grand Blvd., 73116.
Daily dawn-dusk.
Fenced, 2 acres, separate areas for large and small dogs,
double-gated entryway, drinking fountains, swimming pond,
benches, shade, disposal bags and trash cans. Children
under 10 are not allowed in the dog park.

Biscuit Acres Dog Park - Tulsa
www.biscuitacres.com, (918) 596-7275
5804 E. 91st St., 74137.
Daily 5 a.m.-9 p.m.
Fenced, 2.5 acres, separate areas for large and small dogs,
drinking fountains, fire hydrant, shade, disposal bags and
trash cans, double-gated entryways.

Joe Station Dog Park - Tulsa
www.cityoftulsa.org/culture--recreation/tulsa-parks.aspx,
(918) 596-2100
2279 Charles Page Blvd., 74127.
Daily 5 a.m.-11 p.m.
Fenced, grass surface, drinking fountain, separate areas for
large and small dogs, lighted.

OREGON

L.L. Stub Stewart State Park - Buxton
www.oregonstateparks.org/park_255.php, (503) 986-0707
30380 N.W. Hwy. 47, 97109.
Daily dawn-dusk.
Fenced, less than 1 acre, double-gated entryway, drinking
fountain, disposal bags and trash cans, benches.

Alberta Park - Portland
www.portlandpooch.com/dogparks/alberta.htm,
(503) 823-3647
2187 N.E. Killingsworth St., 97211.
Daily 5 a.m.-midnight.
1.32 acres, trees, disposal bags and trash cans, drinking
fountains, restrooms.

Brentwood Park Off-Leash Area - Portland
www.portlandoregon.gov/parks/article/91310, (503) 823-3647
6100 S.E. Duke St., 97206.
Daily 5 a.m.-midnight.
Fenced, drinking fountain, benches, disposal bags and trash
cans.

Chimney Park - Portland
www.portlandpooch.com/dogparks/chimney.htm,
(503) 823-7529
9360 N. Columbia Blvd., 97203.
Daily 5 a.m.-midnight.
Fenced, 5.52 acres, disposal bags and trash cans, trees,
grass surface, double-gated entryway, common water bowls,
drinking fountains.

Couch Park - Portland
www.portlandoregon.gov/parks, (503) 823-3647
2004 N.W. Glisan St., 97209.
Daily 5 a.m.-midnight.
Less than 1 acre, disposal bags and trash cans, trees,
grass surface, drinking fountain.

Delta Park - Portland
www.portlandparks.org, (503) 823-3647
10774 N. Union Ct., 97217.
Daily 5 a.m.-midnight.
Fenced, 1.81 acres, trees, picnic area, trash cans.

East Holladay Park - Portland
www.portlandparks.org, (503) 823-3647
12999 N.E. Holladay St., 97230.
Daily 8 a.m.-9 p.m., June 15-Sept. 1; Mon.-Fri. 6-7:30 a.m.
and 4-9 p.m., Sat.-Sun. 8 a.m.-9 p.m., rest of year.
Fenced, 5.59 acres, grass surface, walking paths, trees.

Gabriel Park - Portland
www.portlandparks.org, (503) 823-2525
6820 S.W. 45th Ave., 97219.
Daily 5 a.m.-midnight.
Fenced, 1.75 acres, grass surface, walking trails, drinking
fountains, trees, disposal bags and trash cans, benches.

Lynchwood Park - Portland
www.portlandpooch.com/dogparks/lynchwood.htm,
(503) 823-7529
16982 S.E. Haig St., 97236.
Daily 5 a.m.-midnight.
Fenced, 1.18 acres, grass surface, picnic areas, benches,
trees.

Mt. Tabor Park - Portland
www.portlandpooch.com/dogparks/mttabor.htm,
(503) 823-3647
1204 S.E. 60th Ave., 97215.
Daily 7 a.m.-9 p.m.
Partially fenced, 4.19 acres, three double-gated entryways,
trees, drinking fountains, trash cans.

Normandale Park - Portland
www.portlandpooch.com/dogparks/normandale.htm,
(503) 823-7529
1282 N.E. 57th Ave., 97213.
Daily 5 a.m.-midnight.
Fenced, 1.62 acres, separate areas for large and small
dogs, trees, drinking fountains, disposal bags and trash
cans.

Wallace Park - Portland
www.portlandoregon.gov/parks/article/91385, (503) 823-3647
2595 N.W. Raleigh St., 97210.
Daily 5 a.m.-midnight.
Fenced, less than 1 acre, drinking fountain, trash cans, trees, shade.

Potso Dog Park - Tigard
www.tigard-or.gov/community/parks/potso_dog_park.asp, (503) 639-2931
13200 S.W. Wall St., 97223.
Daily dawn-dusk.
Fenced, 1.55 acres, drinking fountain, disposal bags and trash cans, covered picnic area, walking path, separate areas for large and small dogs, grass surface.

Summerlake Park Dog Park - Tigard
www.tigard-or.gov/community/parks/
summerlake_dog_park.asp, (503) 639-2931
11450 S.W. Winterlake Dr., 97223.
Daily dawn-dusk.
Fenced, less than 1 acre, drinking fountains, disposal bags and trash cans, covered picnic areas, trees, double-gated entryway.

PENNSYLVANIA

Grove Park Dog Run - Abington
www.thephillydog.com/dog-parks, (215) 576-5213
1436 Easton Rd., 19001.
Daily dawn-dusk.
Fenced, 2 acres, separate areas for large and small dogs, grass surface, trees, benches, drinking fountains, disposal bags and trash cans.

Curtis Dog Park - Elkins Park
www.cheltenhamtownship.org, (215) 887-6200
1250 W. Church Rd., 19027.
Daily dawn-dusk.
Fenced, more than 1 acre, trees, benches, mulch surface, separate areas for large and small dogs, disposal bags and trash cans.

Horsham Dog Park - Horsham
www.horshamdogpark.com, (215) 290-1917
1013 Horsham Rd., 19044.
Daily dawn-dusk.
Fenced, 1.5 acres, separate areas for large and small dogs, benches, grass surface, disposal bags and trash cans, restrooms, trees, water bowls.

MonDaug Bark Park - Philadelphia
www.upperdublin.net/departments/parks/dogpark.aspx, (215) 643-1600
1130 Camphill Rd., 19034.
Daily dawn-dusk.
Fenced, 1 acre, separate areas for large and small dogs, three double-gated entryways, walking trails, disposal bags and trash cans, grass surface.

Passyunk Square Dog Park - Philadelphia
www.thephillydog.com/dog-parks, (215) 685-1890
1200 Wharton St., 19147.
Daily 7 a.m.-9 p.m.
Fenced, trees, agility equipment, benches, wash station, common toys and water bowls, gravel surface.

Schuylkill River Dog Run - Philadelphia
www.phillyfido.net, (215) 686-1776
2500 Lombard St., 19103.
Daily dawn-dusk.
Fenced, separate areas for large and small dogs, gravel, artificial turf and brick surface, trees, benches, drinking fountain, water bowls, wash station.

Seger Dog Run - Philadelphia
www.segerdogrun.org, (215) 686-1780
1020 Lombard St., 19105.
Daily dawn-dusk. Donations.
Fenced, 2 acres, double-gated entryway, drinking fountain, disposal bags and trash cans, mulch surface, benches.

Allegheny Commons Park - Pittsburgh
www.alleghenycommons.org, (412) 330-2569
11 Children's Way, 15212.
Daily 6 a.m.-11 p.m.
Grass surface, trees, benches, pond access, walking paths.

Bernard Dog Run - Pittsburgh
www.bernarddogrun.org, (412) 255-2539
3 Rivers Heritage Trail System, 15201.
Daily dawn-dusk.
Fenced, drinking fountains, separate areas for large and small dogs, disposal bags and trash cans, common water bowls, trees.

Frick Park Dog Park - Pittsburgh
www.pittsburghparks.org/frick-dogs, (412) 682-7275
6750 Forbes Ave., 15221.
Daily 6 a.m.-11 p.m.
Fenced, drinking fountains, disposal bags and trash cans, pond access, benches, two separate play areas.

Riverview Park Dog Park - Pittsburgh
www.pittsburghpa.gov/citiparks/off-leash-areas, (412) 255-2539
1 Riverview Ave., 15214.
Daily dawn-dusk.
Fenced, separate areas for large and small dogs, grass and mulch surface.

RHODE ISLAND

Dexter Training Ground Dog Park - Providence
www.providenceri.com/provconnex, (401) 421-2489
73 Dexter St., 02909.
Daily dawn-dusk.
Fenced, mulch surface, separate areas for large and small dogs.

Gano Street Dog Park - Providence
www.providenceri.com/parks-and-rec, (401) 785-9450
123 Gano St., 02906.
Daily dawn-dusk.
Fenced, separate areas for large and small dogs, double-gated entryway, benches, disposal bags and trash cans, gravel surface, common water bowls.

SOUTH CAROLINA

James Island County Park - Charleston
www.ccprc.com, (843) 795-7275
871 Riverland Dr., 29412.
Daily 8-dusk, Mar.-Apr. and day after Labor Day-Oct. 31; 8-8, May-Labor Day; 8-5, rest of year.
Fenced, separate areas for large and small dogs, dog beach, benches, shade, restrooms.

Sesquicentennial State Park - Columbia
www.southcarolinaparks.com/sesqui/introduction.aspx, (803) 788-2706
9564 Two Notch Rd., 29223.
Daily 8 a.m.-6 p.m. $4.
Fenced, 2 acres, lake access, grass surface, disposal bags and trash cans.

Mount Pleasant Palmetto Islands County Park - Mount Pleasant
www.ccprc.com, (843) 884-0832
444 Needlerush Pkwy., 29464.
Daily dawn-dusk.
Fenced, separate areas for large and small dogs, benches, shade, restrooms, picnic areas.

North Charleston Wannamaker County Park - North Charleston
www.ccprc.com, (843) 572-7275
8888 University Blvd., 29406.
Daily dawn-dusk. $1.
Fenced, separate areas for large and small dogs, benches, shade, restrooms, drinking fountain, dog wash station.

TENNESSEE

Nutro Dog Park - Brentwood
www.brentwood-tn.org, (615) 371-0060
1 Heritage Way, 37027.
Daily 8 a.m.-dusk.
Fenced, 1.5 acres, separate areas for large and small dogs, benches, fire hydrants, trees, shade, drinking fountains.

Freedom Run Dog Park at Liberty Park - Franklin
www.franklintn.gov/government/parks/facilities-and-parks/dogs-dog-parks, (615) 791-3217
2098 Turning Wheel Ln., 37067.
Daily dawn-dusk.
Fenced, 1 acre, separate areas for large and small dogs, shade, disposal bags and trash cans. Dogs must be older than 4 months.

K-9 Korral Dog Park - Franklin
www.franklintn.gov/government/parks/facilities-and-parks/dogs-dog-parks, (615) 550-6948
239 Franklin Rd., 37064.
Daily dawn-dusk.
Fenced, double-gated entryway, disposal bags and trash cans, grass surface, common tennis balls and toys.

The Outback at Shelby Farms Park - Memphis
www.shelbyfarmspark.org, (901) 767-7275
500 N. Pine Lake Dr., 38134.
Daily 6 a.m.-8 p.m., Mar. 15-Oct. 31; 6-6, Nov. 15-Mar. 14.
More than 100 acres, separate areas for large and small dogs, disposal bags and trash cans, benches, lakes for swimming, drinking fountains, wash station.

Centennial Dog Park - Nashville
www.nashville.gov/Parks-and-Recreation/Parks/Dog-Parks.aspx, (615) 862-8400
2500 West End Ave., 37210.
Daily dawn-8 p.m.
Fenced, double-gated entryway, separate areas for large and small dogs, grass and mulch surfaces, drinking fountain, benches, picnic tables, common tennis balls and toys, disposal bags and trash cans.

Shelby Dog Park - Nashville
www.nashville.gov/Parks-and-Recreation/Parks/Dog-Parks.aspx, (615) 862-8750
2001 Boscobel St., 37206.
Daily dawn-8 p.m.
Fenced, grass surface, drinking fountain, common tennis balls, disposal bags and trash cans, benches.

Warner Dog Park - Nashville
www.nashville.gov/Parks-and-Recreation/Parks/Dog-Parks.aspx, (615) 862-8750
50 Vaughn Rd., 37221.
Daily dawn-dusk.
Fenced, double-gated entryway, grass surface, trees, common tennis balls, drinking fountain, benches.

TEXAS

Red Bud Isle Dog Park - Austin
www.friendsofredbudisle.org, (512) 477-1566
3401 Red Bud Tr., 78703.
Daily dawn-dusk.
13 acres, loop trail, several swimming areas.

Bark Park Central in Deep Ellum Park - Dallas
www.dallasparks.org/Facilities, (214) 670-4100
2530 Commerce St., 75226.
Tues.-Sun. 5 a.m.-midnight.
Fenced, 1.2 acres, drinking fountains, disposal bags and trash cans, grass, benches, tennis balls, vending machines with pet items, canine artwork.

NorthBark Dog Park - Dallas
www.dallasparks.org/Facilities, (214) 670-1923
4899 Gramercy Oaks Dr., 75287.
Wed.-Mon. dawn-dusk.
Fenced, 21 acres, lawn, walking trails, pavilion, dog beach, benches, drinking fountain, shade, separate areas for large and small dogs, wash station.

Wagging Tail Dog Park - Dallas
www.waggingtaildogpark.org, (214) 670-1589
5841 Keller Springs Rd., 75248.
Tues.-Sat. dawn-dusk.
Fenced, 7 acres, separate areas for large and small dogs, .25-mi. walking trail, drinking fountains, benches.

White Rock Dog Park - Dallas
www.whiterockdogpark.org, (214) 670-4100
8000 Mockingbird Ln., 75218.
Daily 5 a.m.-11 p.m.
Fenced, swimming pool, separate areas for large and small dogs, benches, drinking fountain, picnic tables.

Ervan Chew - Houston
www.houstontx.gov/parks/dogparks.html, (832) 395-7000
4502 Dunlavy St., 77006.
Daily dawn-dusk.
Fenced, less than 1 acre, shade, benches, dog splash area, 2 dog per person limit.

Levy Park - Houston
www.houstontx.gov/parks/dogparks.html, (713) 524-8000
3801 Eastside St., 77098.
Daily dawn-dusk.
Fenced, trees, benches, picnic tables, designated dog run.

Maxey Park - Houston
www.houstontx.gov/parks/dogparks.html, (713) 837-0311
601 Maxey Rd., 77013.
Daily dawn-dusk.
Fenced, 12 acres, drinking fountains, separate areas for large and small dogs, wash station, disposal bags and trash cans, benches, trees.

Tanglewood Park - Houston
www.houstontx.gov/parks/dogparks.html, (832) 395-7000
5801 Woodway Dr., 77057.
Daily dawn-dusk.
Fenced, less than 1 acre, picnic tables, drinking fountain, lighted, benches, mulch surface, tennis balls, trash cans.

T.C. Jester Park - Houston
www.houstontx.gov/parks/dogparks.html, (832) 395-7000
4201 W. T.C. Jester Blvd., 77018.
Daily 6 a.m.-11 p.m.
Fenced, 1 acre, separate areas for large and small dogs, benches, drinking fountains, disposal bags and trash cans, dog pool.

West Webster Park - Houston
www.houstontx.gov/parks/dogparks.html, (832) 395-7000
1502 W. Webster St., 77019.
Daily dawn-dusk.
Fenced, less than 1 acre, drinking fountain, wash station, disposal bags and trash cans, trees.

Madison Square Park Dog Park - San Antonio
www.sanantonio.gov/parksandrec/dog_parks.aspx,
(210) 207-8480
400 Lexington Ave., 78215.
Daily 5 a.m.-11 p.m.
Fenced, less than 1 acre, disposal bags and trash cans,
drinking fountain, benches.

McAllister Park Dog Park - San Antonio
www.sanantonio.gov/parksandrec/dog_parks.aspx,
(210) 207-8480
13102 Jones Maltsberger Rd., 78247.
Daily 5 a.m.-11 p.m.
Fenced, 1.5 acres, exercise equipment, picnic area,
benches, walking trail.

Pearsall Dog Park - San Antonio
www.sanantonio.gov/parksandrec/dog_parks.aspx,
(210) 207-8480
4700 Old Pearsall Rd., 78242.
Daily 5 a.m.-11 p.m.
Fenced, 1.5 acres, picnic areas, trash cans, agility
equipment.

Phil Hardberger Park Dog Park - San Antonio
www.sanantonio.gov/parksandrec/dog_parks.aspx,
(210) 207-8480
13203 Blanco Rd., 78216.
Daily 7:30 a.m.-dusk.
Fenced, 1.8 acres, separate areas for large and small dogs,
dog playhouse, grass surface.

Phil Hardberger Park West Dog Park - San Antonio
www.sanantonio.gov/parksandrec/dog_parks.aspx,
(210) 207-8480
8400 N.W. Military Hwy., 78231.
Daily 7:30 a.m.-dusk.
Fenced, 1.5 acres, agility equipment, separate areas for
large and small dogs.

Tom Slick Dog Park - San Antonio
www.sanantonio.gov/parksandrec/dog_parks.aspx,
(210) 207-8480
7400 Hwy. 151, 78227.
Daily 5 a.m.-11 p.m.
Fenced, 1 acre, separate areas for large and small dogs,
benches, picnic area, drinking fountain, dog wash area,
shade.

UTAH

Millrace Park - Salt Lake City
www.taylorsvilleut.gov/parks_rec.dogpark.html,
(385) 468-1800
1150 W. 5400 S., 84123.
Mon. and Wed.-Fri. 8-7, Sat. 8-4, Sun. 4-7. $10.
Fenced.

West Jordan Off-Leash Dog Park - West Jordan
www.slco.org/recreation/parks/WestJordanDog/index.html,
(385) 468-1800
5982 W. New Bingham Hwy., 84081.
Daily dawn-dusk.
Fenced, 3.77 acres, separate areas for large and small
dogs, drinking fountains.

VIRGINIA

Shirlington Park - Arlington
parks.arlingtonva.us/parksfacilities/dog-parks,
(703) 228-6525
2601 S. Arlington Mill Dr., 22206.
Daily 6 a.m.-8 p.m.
Fenced, double-gated entryway, splash area, trees,
separate areas for large and small dogs, dog wash area.

Barker Field at Byrd Park - Richmond
www.friendsofbarkerfield.org, (804) 646-5733
600 S. Boulevard, 23220.
Daily dawn-dusk.
Fenced, double-gated entryway, benches, grass surface,
shade, trees, disposal bags and trash cans.

Church Hill Dog Park - Richmond
www.richmondgov.com/parks/parkChimborazo.aspx,
(804) 447-6205
3200 E. Broad St., 23223.
Daily dawn-dusk.
Fenced, separate areas for large and small dogs, drinking
fountains.

Waller Mill Dog Park - Williamsburg
www.williamsburgva.gov/index.aspx?page=353,
(757) 259-3778
Route 645, Airport Rd., 23185.
$2 per dog.
Fenced, 1.5 acres, separate areas for large and small dogs.

WASHINGTON

Blue Dog Pond - Seattle
www.seattle.gov/parks, (206) 684-4075
1520 26th Ave. S., 98144.
Daily 4 a.m.-11:30 p.m.
Fenced, less than 1 acre, drinking fountains.

Denny Park - Seattle
www.seattle.gov/parks, (206) 684-4075
100 Dexter Ave. N., 98109.
Daily 4:30 a.m.-11:30 p.m.
Fenced, trees, benches, lighted, double-gated entryway,
grass and gravel surface.

Dr. Jose Rizal Park - Seattle
www.seattle.gov/parks, (206) 684-4075
1008 12th Ave. S., 98144.
Daily 4 a.m.-11:30 p.m.
Fenced, 4 acres, drinking fountains, gravel surface.

Genesee Park and Playfield - Seattle
www.seattle.gov/parks, (206) 684-4075
4316 S. Genesee St., 98118.
Daily 4 a.m.-11:30 p.m.
Fenced, 2.5 acres, double-gated entryway, gravel surface,
drinking fountain.

Golden Gardens Park - Seattle
www.seattle.gov/parks, (206) 684-4075
8498 Seaview Pl. N.W., 98117.
Daily 6 a.m.-11:30 p.m.
Less than 1 acre, mulch surface, trees, picnic areas,
covered pavilion, restrooms.

Kinnear Park - Seattle
www.seattle.gov/parks, (206) 684-4075
899 W. Olympic Pl., 98119.
Daily 6 a.m.-dusk.
Fenced, double-gated entry way, less than 1 acre, mulch
surface, agility equipment, benches, trees, shade.

Magnolia Manor Park - Seattle
www.seattle.gov/parks, (206) 684-4075
3430 27th Ave. W., 98199.
Daily 4 a.m.-11:30 p.m.
Fenced, less than 1 acre, drinking fountain, agility
equipment, picnic areas, benches, walking paths.

Northacres Park - Seattle
www.seattle.gov/parks, (206) 684-4075
12718 1st Ave. N.E., 98125.
Daily 6 a.m.-10 p.m.
Fenced, less than 1 acre, trails, shade, trees, benches,
restrooms, picnic areas.

Regrade Park - Seattle
www.seattle.gov/parks, (206) 684-4075
2251 3rd Ave., 98121.
Daily 6 a.m.-10 p.m.
Fenced, less than 1 acre, double-gated entryway, drinking fountains.

Warren G. Magnuson Park - Seattle
www.seattle.gov/parks/Magnuson, (206) 684-4946
7400 Sand Point Way N.E., 98115.
Daily 4 a.m.-11:30 p.m.
Fenced, 9 acres, drinking fountains, trails, gravel surface, separate areas for large and small or shy dogs.

Westcrest Park - Seattle
www.seattle.gov/parks, (206) 684-4075
9000 8th Ave. S.W., 98106.
Daily 6 a.m.-10 p.m.
Fenced, 4 acres, walking paths, drinking fountain, shade, trees, benches, restrooms, picnic areas, lighted, separate areas for large and small or shy dogs.

Woodland Park - Seattle
www.seattle.gov/parks, (206) 684-4075
1000 N. 50th St., 98103.
Daily 4 a.m.-11:30 p.m.
Fenced, less than 1 acre, benches, drinking fountain.

Sequim Dog Park - Sequim
www.sequimdogparks.org, (360) 681-5373
202 N. Blake Rd., 98382.
Double-gated entry, separate areas for large and small dogs, agility equipment.

Kane Memorial Dog Park - Vancouver
www.cityofvancouver.us/parksrec/page/leash-dog-parks, (888) 899-0025
10910 N.E. 172nd Ave., 98682.
Daily dawn-dusk.
Fenced, 2.5 acres, double-gated entryway, walking trail, drinking fountains.

Lucky Memorial Dog Park (Brush Prairie) - Vancouver
www.clarkdogpaw.org, (888) 899-0025
10102 N.E. 149th St., 98662.
Daily dawn-dusk.
Fenced, 7.5 acres, separate areas for large and small dogs, walking path, double-gated entryways, agility course, water available, disposal bags and trash cans.

Northeast Vancouver Dakota Dog Park - Vancouver
www.clarkdogpaw.org/dog-parks, (888) 899-0025
1502 N.E. 164th Ave., 98684.
Daily dawn-dusk.
Fenced, 8 acres, separate areas for large and small dogs, double-gated entryway, mulch walking path, grass surface, drinking fountains, agility area, trees and shade, benches.

Ross Off-Leash Dog Recreation Area - Vancouver
www.clarkdogpaw.org, (888) 899-0025
5274 N.E. 18th Ave., 98663.
Daily dawn-dusk.
Fenced, 8 acres, separate areas for large and small dogs, double-gated entryway, walking trails, benches.

WISCONSIN

Currie Park - Milwaukee
www.milwaukeedogparks.org, (414) 464-8400
3535 N. Mayfair Rd., 53222.
Daily 5 a.m.-10 p.m. $5.
Fenced, 1.5 acres, trees, benches, dog bowls, grass and mulch surfaces.

Estabrook Park - Milwaukee
www.milwaukeedogparks.org, (414) 964-0064
4400 N. Estabrook Ln., 53211.
Daily 5 a.m.-10 p.m. Parking: $5.
Fenced, 3 acres, separate areas for large and small dogs, trees, benches, picnic area, restrooms.

Granville Park - Milwaukee
www.milwaukeedogparks.org/dog-exercise-areas/granville, (414) 257-7275
11718 W. Good Hope Pl., 53224.
Daily 5 a.m.-10 p.m. $5.
10 acres, hills, woods, grass, river access, walking trails, disposal bags and trash cans.

Warnimont Dog Exercise Area - Milwaukee
www.milwaukeedogparks.org, (414) 678-9364
5400 S. Lake Dr., 53217.
Daily 5 a.m.-10 p.m. $5.
Fenced, 5 acres, woods, trails, separate areas for large and small dogs, restrooms, benches, disposal bags and trash cans.

Runway Dog Exercise Area - Oak Creek
www.county.milwaukee.gov/Dogs9203/DogExerciseAreas.htm, (414) 762-1550
1214 E. Rawson Ave., 53154.
Daily 5 a.m.-10 p.m. $5.
Fenced, 26 acres, separate areas for large and small dogs, wood-chipped walking trails, covered pavilion with picnic tables, water bowls, disposal bags and trash cans.

Canada

ALBERTA

Bowmont Off-Leash Area - Calgary
www.calgary.ca/CSPS/Parks/Pages/Locations/
Off-leash-area-locations.aspx, (403) 268-2489
85th St. N.W. & 48th Ave. N.W., T3L 1S4.
Daily dawn-dusk.
Fenced, disposal bags and trash cans, grass surface, benches, trees.

Edworthy Off-Leash Area - Calgary
www.calgary.ca/CSPS/Parks/Pages/Locations/SW-parks/
Edworthy-Park.aspx, (403) 268-3800
5050 Spruce Dr. S.W., T3C 3B2.
Daily 5 a.m.-11 p.m.
Trees, grass surface, benches, walking paths, disposal bags and trash cans, hills.

River Park - Calgary
www.calgary.ca/CSPS/Parks/Pages/Locations/
Off-leash-area-locations.aspx, (403) 268-2489
5139 14th St. S.W., T3E 1P1.
Daily dawn-dusk.
Trees, shade, grass surface, river, beach access, disposal bags and trash cans.

Tom Campbell's Hill - Calgary
www.calgary.ca/CSPS/Parks/Pages/Locations/
Off-leash-area-locations.aspx, (403) 268-2489
25 St. Georges Dr. N.E., T2E 5E4.
Daily 5 a.m.-11 p.m.
Trees, hills, shade, grass surface.

Jackie Parker Recreation Area - Edmonton
www.edmonton.ca/activities_parks_recreation/
parks_rivervalley/jackie-parker-park.aspx, (780) 442-5311
4540 50th St. N.W., T6L 6B6.
Daily 5 a.m.-11 p.m.
Walking paths, river access, trees, shade, restrooms, disposal bags and trash cans.

Terwillegar Park - Edmonton
www.edmonton.ca/attractions_recreation/parks_rivervalley/
terwillegar-park.aspx, (780) 442-5311
10 Rabbit Hill Rd. N.W., T6R 0J3.
Daily 5 a.m.-11 p.m.
Trees, benches, picnic area, walking trails, river access, disposal bags and trash cans, restrooms.

BRITISH COLUMBIA

Andy Livingstone Dog Park - Vancouver
www.vancouver.ca/parks-recreation-culture/
dog-off-leash-areas.aspx, (604) 257-8400
89 Expo Blvd., V6B 1R1.
Daily 6 a.m.-10 p.m.
Fenced, grass surface.

Charleson Dog Park - Vancouver
www.vancouver.ca/parks-recreation-culture/
dog-off-leash-areas.aspx, (604) 257-8400
999 Charleson St., V5Z 4A2.
Daily 6 a.m.-10 p.m.
Fenced, splash area, benches, grass surface, disposal bags and trash cans.

Coopers Park Dog Park - Vancouver
www.vancouver.ca/parks-recreation-culture/
coopers-park-dog-park.aspx, (604) 873-7000
1020 Marinaside Cres., V6Z 2W9.
Daily 6 a.m.-10 p.m.
Grass surface, trees, hedges, disposal bags and trash cans, benches.

Devonian Harbour Park Dog Park - Vancouver
www.vancouver.ca/parks-recreation-culture/
devonian-harbour-park-dog-park.aspx, (604) 873-7000
1929 W. Georgia St., V6G 2W9.
Daily 6 a.m.-10 p.m.
Fenced, grass surface, benches, lake access, walking paths, trees, shade.

Dusty Greenwell Park Dog Park - Vancouver
www.vancouver.ca/parks-recreation-culture/
dusty-greenwell-park-dog-park.aspx, (604) 873-7000
2799 Wall St., V5K 1A9.
Daily 5-10 and 5-10.
Grass surface, benches, disposal bags and trash cans, walking paths, hills, trees, shade.

Emery Barnes Park Dog Park - Vancouver
www.vancouver.ca/parks-recreation-culture/
emery-barnes-park-dog-park.aspx, (604) 873-7000
1188 Seymour St., V6B 3M7.
Daily 6 a.m.-10 p.m.
Fenced, benches, picnic areas, gravel surface, drinking fountains, restrooms, disposal bags and trash cans.

Fraserview Dog Park - Vancouver
www.vancouver.ca/parks-recreation-culture/
fraserview-golf-course-dog-park.aspx, (604) 873-7000
8101 Kerr St., V5S 2C8.
Daily 5-10 and 5-10.
Partially fenced, walking trails, trees, hills, shade, disposal bags and trash cans, grass and mulch surface.

Hadden Park Dog Park - Vancouver
www.vancouver.ca/parks-recreation-culture/
hadden-park-dog-park.aspx, (604) 873-7000
1905 Ogden Ave., V6J 1A3.
Daily 6 a.m.-10 p.m., Oct.-Apr.; 6-10 and 5-10, rest of year.
Beach access, disposal bags and trash cans, trees.

Portside Dog Park at Crab Park - Vancouver
www.vancouver.ca/parks-recreation-culture/
crab-park-at-portside-dog-park.aspx, (604) 873-7000
101 E. Waterfront Rd., V6A 4K3.
Daily 6-10 and 5-10.
Grass surface, benches, trees, hedges, disposal bags and trash cans.

ONTARIO

Niagara Falls Dog Park in Fireman's Park - Niagara Falls
www.niagarafalls.ca/city-hall/recreation/parks/dog-park.aspx,
(905) 356-7521
2275 Dorchester Rd., L2J 4L6.
Daily dawn-dusk.
Separate areas for large and small dogs, disposal bags, benches, shade.

Jack Purcell Dog Park - Ottawa
www.ottawa.ca/en/residents/parks-and-recreation,
(613) 564-1050
320 Jack Purcell Ln., K2P 2J5.
The dog park is open daily 24 hours.
Fenced, gravel and grass surface, drinking fountain, separate areas for large and small dogs.

Bickford Park - Toronto
(416) 338-5058
400 Grace St., M6G 3A8.
Daily dawn-dusk.
Grass surface, trees, water bowls, benches, hills, lighted.

Carlaw Parkette - Toronto
www1.toronto.ca/parks/prd/facilities/complex/50,
(416) 338-5058
855 Gerrard St. E., M4M 1Y7.
Daily dawn-dusk.
Fenced, mulch surface, drinking fountain, disposal bags and
trash cans.

Coronation Dog Park - Toronto
(416) 338-5058
711 Lake Shore Blvd. W., M5V 3T7.
Daily dawn-dusk.
Fenced, trees, double-gated entryway, walking paths,
disposal bags and trash cans.

High Park Off-Leash Area - Toronto
(416) 392-2489
1873 Bloor St. W., M6P 3K7.
Daily 8 a.m.-dusk.
Walking trails, grass surface, disposal bags and trash cans,
trees, shade, drinking fountains, restrooms.

Orphan's Greenspace Dog Park - Toronto
www.toronto.ca/parks, (416) 338-5058
51 Power St., M5A 3Y7.
Daily dawn-dusk.
Fenced, double-gated entryway, picnic areas, benches,
mulch surface, trees.

Riverdale Park West - Toronto
www.toronto.ca/parks, (416) 338-5058
500 Gerrard St. E., M5A 3P7.
Daily dawn-dusk.
Grass surface, hills, walking trails, trees, shade, benches,
drinking fountains.

QUEBEC

Parc Lafontaine - Montréal
www.montreal.com/parks/lafontaine.html, (514) 872-6381
3933 Avenue du Parc La Fontaine, H2L 3A8.
Daily 6 a.m.-7 p.m.
Fenced, splash area, grass surface, disposal bags and
trash cans.

Pente Douce Dog Park - Québec
www.pets.ca/dogs/dog-parks/quebec/quebec-city,
(418) 641-6010
600 Avenue Belvedere, G1N 2J7.
Daily 8:00 a.m.-11 p.m.
Fenced, gravel surface, picnic areas, trees.

Pointe-aux-Lievres Dog Park - Québec
www.ville.quebec.qc.ca, (418) 641-6345
25 Rue de la Pointe-aux-Lievres, G1K 2L1.
Daily 8 a.m.-11 p.m.
Fenced, benches, double-gated entryway, gravel surface,
disposal bags and trash cans.

ATTRACTIONS
United States

CALIFORNIA

Disneyland Resort

(714) 781-4400, 1313 Harbor Blvd., is off I-5 Disneyland Dr. and Disney Way exits at 1313 Harbor Blvd., Anaheim Disneyland® Resort consists of two family-oriented theme parks—Disneyland® Park and Disney California Adventure® Park—and the shops, restaurants and entertainment of Downtown Disney® District. Indoor kennel facilities are available on a first-come, first-served basis at Disneyland Kennel Club, located to the right of the main entrance of Disneyland® park; overnight boarding is not available. Pets are permitted to ride on Disneyland Resort trams but are not permitted on buses running to and from Toy Story Parking Lot. Both theme parks are open daily with extended hours during the summer, on some holidays and on weekends. Cost: One-day, one-park ticket $99; $93 (ages 3-9). Two-day $185; $172 (ages 3-9). Three-day $235; $224 (ages 3-9). Four-day $260; $245 (ages 3-9). Five-day $275; $259 (ages 3-9). One-day Park Hopper ticket $155; $149 (ages 3-9). Two-day $225; $212 (ages 3-9). Three-day $275; $264 (ages 3-9). Four-day $300; $285 (ages 3-9). Five-day $315; $299 (ages 3-9). Validity periods for Park Hopper tickets vary according to ticket type. Select theme park tickets are available at participating AAA/CAA Travel offices. Parking: $17 (autos or motorcycles); $22 (RVs or oversized vehicles). Disneyland.com

Mendocino Coast Botanical Gardens

(707) 964-4352, 18220 N. SR 1, 1 mi. s. on SR 1, Fort Bragg
This 47-acre facility is one of the few gardens located directly on an ocean shore. Pathways wind past succulents, camellias, rhododendrons, rose and dahlia gardens, and a coastal forest of pines, magnolias and ferns that leads to bluffs overlooking the Pacific. Pets on leash are permitted. Daily 9-5, Mar.-Oct.; 9-4, rest of year. Closed first Sat. in Aug., the Sat. after Labor Day, Thanksgiving and Christmas. Cost: $14; $10 (ages 65+); $5 (ages 5-17). Electric carts are available for a fee. www.gardenbythesea.org

SeaWorld San Diego

(800) 257-4268, 500 SeaWorld Dr., 500 SeaWorld Dr., off I-5 on Mission Bay's south shore, San Diego
SeaWorld San Diego offers animal shows, rides and exhibits featuring marine creatures from around the world, including killer whales, sharks, penguins and sea lions. Talented dolphins, pilot whales, birds and humans perform in the Blue Horizons show. Outdoor kennel facilities are available for a fee on a first-come, first-served basis; overnight boarding is not available. Opens daily at 9 or 10; closing times vary. Hours vary and may be extended during summer and holiday periods. Phone ahead for show schedules. Cost: $84; $78 (ages 3-9). Rates may vary; phone ahead. Parking: $16; $11 (motorcycles); $21 (RVs and preferred). seaworldparks.com/en/seaworld-sandiego

Six Flags Magic Mountain

(661) 255-4111, 26101 Magic Mountain Pkwy., 26101 Magic Mountain Pkwy., Valencia
This 260-acre theme park boasts 18 roller coasters and more than 100 other rides, games and attractions for all ages. Free kennel facilities are available in the main parking lot. Opens daily at 10:30, late Mar.-Labor Day; Fri.-Sun. at 10:30, day after Labor Day-Oct. 31; Sat.-Sun. and holidays at 10:30, rest of year. Closing times vary. Cost: $69.99; $43.99 (under 48 inches tall); free (ages 0-2). Prices may vary; phone ahead. Parking: $20. www.sixflags.com

Universal Studios Hollywood

(800) 864-8377, 100 Universal Dr., 100 Universal City Plaza. For guests arriving by Metro, a free shuttle across the street from the station provides transportation to the park's front gate, Universal City
In addition to thrill rides and attractions, Universal Studios gives visitors a behind-the-scenes look at the workings of a major film and TV studio. Free indoor kennel facilities are available; inquire at Will Call. Overnight boarding is not available. Park generally opens daily at 9 or 10; closing times vary. It opens at 8 on select peak dates. The Studio Tour is offered continuously; last tour departs 2 hours, 45 minutes before closing during summer. Cost: $84.99; $76.99 (under 48 inches tall). Front of Line passes are available; details are available at participating AAA offices. Rates and availability of attractions may vary; phone ahead. Parking: $15 (per private vehicle); $10 (per private vehicle after 3 p.m.); $20 (RVs); $25 (preferred); $30 (front gate parking). www.universalstudios.com

DISTRICT OF COLUMBIA

Washington Monument

(202) 426-6841, 15th St. & Constitution Ave. N.W., near the center of the National Mall; the grounds extend from 14th to 17th sts. and from Constitution to Independence aves. N.W., Washington, D.C.
This instantly recognizable 555-foot marble obelisk commemorates our nation's first president and is surrounded by expansive grounds. Pets on leash permitted. Daily 9-5 (also 5-10, mid-May through Labor Day). Last elevator tour to the observation room begins 15 minutes before closing. Cost: Advance ticket reservations $2 per ticket. www.nps.gov/wamo

FLORIDA

 Busch Gardens Tampa

(888) 800-5447, 3000 E. Busch Blvd., 3000 E. Busch Blvd. (SR 580), 2 mi. e. of jct. I-275 exit 50 or 2 mi. w. of I-75 exit 265, Tampa
This family entertainment park combines world-class thrill rides, live entertainment and one of North America's largest zoos, providing an adventure for the entire family. Indoor kennel facilities are available for a fee on a first-come, first-served basis; overnight boarding is not available. Proof of current vaccinations is required. Generally opens daily between 9 and 10; closing times vary. Cost: $95; $90 (ages 3-9). Admission includes a second visit within 7 days of first visit. There is an additional fee for the Serengeti Safari Tour. Discounted tickets are available in advance at participating AAA offices. Parking: $15; $20 (RVs and preferred).
www.buschgardens.com

 Kennedy Space Center Visitor Complex

(321) 449-4444, SR 405 & SR 3, 11 mi. e. of I-95 on SR 405, Kennedy Space Center
Built in 1967, the modern facility explores the past, present and future of the U.S. space program. Free kennel facilities are available. Complex open daily at 9; closing times vary. Bus tours depart daily every 15 minutes beginning at 10; last tour departs at 2:30. Cost: (includes all shows, exhibits, IMAX films, KSC bus tour, Shuttle Launch Experience and U.S. Astronaut Hall of Fame) $50; $40 (ages 3-11). Phone ahead to verify prices. Parking: $10; $5 (motorcycle); $15 (RV).
www.kennedyspacecenter.com

 LEGOLAND Florida

(877) 350-5346, One LEGOLAND Way, 4 mi. w. on SR 540 at jct. US 27 and SR 540 at 1 LEGOLAND Way, Winter Haven
More than 50 family-oriented shows, attractions and rides—including four rollercoasters—cover 10 themed zones. Free kennels are located west of the front gate area; phone ahead to confirm availability in 2015. Opens daily at 10, mid-Mar. to late Apr. and late May-late Aug.; Thurs.-Mon. at 10, rest of year.
Closing times vary; phone ahead to confirm schedule. Cost: $84; $77 (ages 3-12 and 60+). Combination ticket with LEGOLAND Florida Water Park $99; $92 (ages 3-12 and 60+); $3 (ages 0-2). Parking: $14.
florida.legoland.com

 SeaWorld Orlando

(888) 800-5447, 7007 SeaWorld Dr., at jct. I-4 and SR 528 (Beachline Expwy.), Orlando
This marine life adventure park has themed shows; up-close animal encounters; attractions; and rides, including the face-down flying coaster Manta, the floorless coaster Kraken and the water coaster Journey to Atlantis. Air-conditioned kennels are available for a fee on a first-come, first-served basis. Proof of current vaccinations is required. Opens daily at 9; closing times vary. Cost: $95; $90 (ages 3-9). For an additional $15 per ticket, guests can enjoy a second visit within 7 days of their first visit; stop at the Information and Reservations Center during your first visit for details. Fourteen-day combination ticket with Aquatica $135; $130 (ages 3-9). Fourteen-day combination ticket with Aquatica and Busch Gardens Tampa $165; $160 (ages 3-9). There is an additional fee for VIP tours. AAA members save on the Dine with Shamu experience. Dine with Shamu reservations are required; visit Guest Relations for details. Discounted theme park tickets are available in advance at participating AAA offices. Parking: $17 (private vehicles and motorcycles); $22 (RVs, trailers, semitrucks and preferred); $35 (valet).
www.seaworld.com/orlando

 Universal Orlando Resort

(407) 363-8000, 1000 Universal Studios Plaza, off I-4 exit 75A (eastbound) or 74B (westbound), following signs to the parking garages at 6000 Universal Blvd., Orlando
At Universal Orlando you can "ride the movies" at the Universal Studios® theme park, cavort with superheroes and cartoon characters at Universal's Islands of Adventure® theme park, or visit the specialty shops, themed restaurants and entertainment venues at Universal CityWalk®. Kennel facilities are available for a fee on a first-come, first-served basis. Proof of current vaccinations is required. Follow signs to RV and Camper parking lot for kennel access. The theme parks generally open daily at 9; closing times vary by season. Universal CityWalk is open daily 11 a.m.-2 a.m. Theme park and CityWalk hours may vary; phone ahead. Cost: A 1-Day Park to Park ticket, which allows same-day access to both Universal Studios Florida and Universal's Islands of Adventure, is $147; $142 (ages 3-9). A 2-Day Park to Park ticket, which allows same-day access to both parks over two days, is $195.99; $185.99 (ages 3-9). A 3-Day Park to Park ticket, which allows same-day access to both parks over three days, is $205.99; $194.99 (ages 3-9). All multi-day park tickets include admission to select live entertainment venues at Universal CityWalk. Special advance purchase discount tickets are available at participating AAA/CAA offices. Members who pre-purchase admission through their AAA/CAA branch will receive discounts at select restaurant and merchandise locations within the resort (excludes purchases at food or merchandise carts and purchases of alcohol, tobacco, candy, film, collectibles, sundry items, tattoos and services). Parking: $17; $5 (6-10 p.m.); free (after 10 p.m.). Valet parking $15-$40.
www.universalorlando.com

Walt Disney World Resort

(407) 824-4321, 3111 World Dr., accessible from Florida's Tpke., US 192, Osceola Pkwy. and several exits off I-4 s. of Orlando, Lake Buena Vista

The sprawling complex includes Magic Kingdom® Park, Epcot®, Disney's Hollywood Studios™, Disney's Animal Kingdom® Theme Park, family water parks and numerous entertainment, shopping and dining facilities.

With the exception of service dogs for guests with disabilities, pets are not permitted in the Theme Parks or Disney Resort hotels, or on Disney buses. Best Friends Pet Care boarding facility offers air-conditioned accommodations for pets across from Disney's Port Orleans Resort at 2510 Bonnet Creek Pkwy.

Reservations at Best Friends Pet Care are not required but are suggested. Disney Resort hotel reservations do not guarantee space for pets. Proof of current vaccinations is required. Phone (877) 4 WDW-PETS for information and reservations.

Theme parks open daily generally at 9, with earlier openings for guests staying at a Disney resort hotel; closing times vary. Cost: One-day ticket for Magic Kingdom Park $105; $99 (ages 3-9). One-day ticket for Epcot or Disney's Hollywood Studios or Disney's Animal Kingdom Theme Park $97; $91 (ages 3-9). Ticket options for additional fees include admission to other entertainment areas and "hopping" between theme parks. Select theme park tickets are available at participating AAA/CAA Travel offices. Parking: $17; $18 (camper or trailer); free (Disney resort guests with valid resort ID). The fee allows parking at any of the theme parks for that entire day. Disneyworld.com

GEORGIA

 Six Flags Over Georgia

(770) 948-9290, 275 Riverside Pkwy., 275 Riverside Pkwy. S.W., Austell

Six Flags offers rides, attractions and live shows. Kennel facilities are available for a fee. Proof of current vaccinations is required. Opens daily at 10:30, late May-early Aug.; Sat.-Sun. at 10:30, early Mar.-late May and early Aug.-late Sept. Closing times vary. The park also is open select days in Oct. for Fright Fest. Cost: All-inclusive 1-day (including Hurricane Harbor) $61.99; $41.99 (children under 48 inches tall); free (ages 0-2). Prices may vary; phone ahead. AAA members save on select services and merchandise. See Guest Relations for details. Parking: $20. www.sixflags.com/overgeorgia

IOWA

 Pella Historical Village

(641) 620-9463, jct. E. First and Franklin sts., Pella

A country store, log cabin, grist mill, windmill, smithy and other buildings (including Wyatt Earp's boyhood home) are reminders of this town's Dutch heritage. Leashed pets are permitted but are not allowed in the windmill. Mon.-Sat. 9-5, mid-Mar. through Dec. 31. Early closing some holidays; phone ahead. Cost: $10; $6 (ages 12+ and college students with ID); $2 (ages 5-11); free (military with ID). www.pellahistorical.org

MASSACHUSETTS

 Bunker Hill Monument

(617) 242-5641, Address not available, in Monument Square in Charlestown, Boston

Part of Boston National Historical Park, this 221-foot-tall granite obelisk commemorates the site of the Battle of Bunker Hill, which occurred on June 17, 1775. Leashed pets are permitted on the grounds but not inside the monument. Daily 9-6, July-Aug.; 9-5, rest of year. Last admission 30 minutes before closing. Cost: Free. www.nps.gov/bost/historyculture/bhm.htm

MISSOURI

 The Gateway Arch

(314) 982-1410, Memorial Dr. and Market St. within Jefferson National Expansion Memorial park, St. Louis

This curved, stainless steel monument soars 630 feet high and symbolizes the gateway to the West. A tram ride takes visitors to an observation deck. Pets on leashes are permitted on the grounds. Ticket center open daily 8 a.m.-10 p.m., tram departures daily 8:15 a.m.-9:10 p.m., Memorial Day-Labor Day; Ticket center 9-6, tram departures 9:50-4:50, rest of year. Cost: $3 (ages 16+). Tram ride $10; $5 (ages 3-15). Individual movie admission $7; $2.50 (ages 3-15). www.nps.gov/jeff

 Six Flags St. Louis

(636) 938-5300, I-44 & Allenton Rd., off I-44 at 4900 Six Flags Rd., Eureka

Themed areas showcase a variety of shows, rides and attractions; kids will have a ball exploring Bugs Bunny National Park. Free kennel facilities are available in the parking lot; see toll plaza attendant for details. Pets cannot be kept overnight and must have current vaccinations and registration tags. Park open early Apr.-late Oct.; days and hours vary. Hurricane Harbor open Memorial Day weekend-Labor Day; days and hours vary. Cost: (Includes Hurricane Harbor) $59.99; $44.99 (children under 48 inches tall); free (ages 0-2). Prices may vary; phone ahead. AAA members save on select services and merchandise. See guest relations for details. Parking: $20. www.sixflags.com/stlouis

NORTH CAROLINA

 Carowinds Amusement and Water Park

(704) 588-2600, 14523 Carowinds Blvd., 10 mi. s. on I-77 to exit 90, is on the North Carolina/South Carolina border at 14523 Carowinds Blvd., Charlotte
Covering 398 acres, the park features more than 50 rides, shows and attractions, including 13 roller coasters—Intimidator is the tallest, fastest and longest in the Southeast. Climate-controlled kennels are available for a fee on a first-come, first-served basis. Overnight boarding is not available. Park opens daily at 10, late May to mid-Aug.; Sat.-Sun. at 10, late Mar.-late May and mid-Aug. to early Sept.; closing times vary but are either 8 or 10 p.m. The park is also open Sat.-Sun., early Sept.-late Oct.; phone for hours. Cost: $57.99; $39.99 (ages 62+ and under 48 inches tall); $29.99 (after 4 p.m. and all day for the physically impaired); free (ages 0-2). Season passes also are available. Parking: $15. www.carowinds.com

OHIO

 Kings Island

(513) 754-5700, 6300 Kings Island Dr., 6300 Kings Island Dr., Mason
This family entertainment park offers more than 100 rides, shows and attractions, including more than a dozen thrill rides. A day-use pet kennel is available for a fee. Park opens daily at 10 a.m., late May-late Aug.; Fri.-Sun. at 11, in Oct.; Sat.-Sun. at 10 a.m., late Apr. to late May and first weekend in Sept. Closing times vary. Soak City Waterpark daily 11-8, late May-late Aug. Cost: (includes Soak City Waterpark) $43.99; $36.99 (ages 3-6, ages 62+ and children under 48 inches tall). Dinosaurs Alive! $6. Prices vary throughout the season; phone ahead to confirm. Parking: $12. www.visitkingsisland.com

PENNSYLVANIA

 Hersheypark

(800) 437-7439, 100 W. Hersheypark Dr., just off SR 743 and US 422, Hershey
Hersheypark has more than 65 rides and attractions—including 11 roller coasters—plus live entertainment. Day-use kennels are available mid-May to mid-Sept. for a fee on a first come, first-served basis. Proof of current vaccinations is required. Open daily at 10, Memorial Day-Labor Day; Sat.-Sun. at 10, in May; Sat.-Sun. at 10, select weekends in Sept. after Labor Day. Closing times vary; phone ahead. Phone for Springtime and Halloween schedules. Cost: (includes ZooAmerica North American Wildlife Park) $56.95; $35.95 (ages 3-8 and 55-69); $22.95 (ages 70+). Sunset admission (after 3 when park closes at 6, after 4 when park closes at 8, after 5 when park closes at 10 and 11) $28.95; $24.95 (ages 3-8 and 55-69); $17.95 (ages 70+). Other admission packages, including multiday options, are available. www.hersheypark.com

TEXAS

 SeaWorld San Antonio

(800) 700-7786, 10500 SeaWorld Dr., 10500 SeaWorld Dr., San Antonio
This 250-acre marine life adventure park entertains and educates with shows, up-close animal encounters, attractions and rides. Free outdoor kennel facilities are available; overnight boarding is not available. Opens daily at 9 or 10, late May-late Aug.; days and hours vary rest of year. Cost: $65; $55 (ages 3-9). Combination ticket with Aquatica, SeaWorld's Waterpark $90; $80 (ages 3-9). Admission and parking prices may vary; phone ahead. Parking: $17; $25 (preferred). seaworldparks.com/en/seaworld-sanantonio

 Six Flags Fiesta Texas

(210) 697-5050, 17000 I-10W, 17000 I-10W, San Antonio
Housed in a former rock quarry, the park celebrates Texas and the Southwest with thrill and family-style rides, live entertainment and themed areas. Kennel facilities are located to the right of the main entrance. Pets cannot be kept overnight and must have current vaccinations and registration tags. Park open daily, late May-late Aug. (also in mid-Mar. for spring break); open Sat.-Sun. and some weekdays, late Apr.-late May; open Sat.-Sun., Mar. 1 to mid-Mar. and late Mar.-late Apr.; open select days, Sept. 1-early Jan. Water park open daily, early June-late Aug. Park and water park hours vary. Cost: $66.99; $51.99 (under 48 inches tall); free (ages 0-2). Rates may vary; phone ahead. AAA members save on select services and merchandise. See guest relations for details. Parking: $20. www.sixflags.com

 Six Flags Over Texas

(817) 530-6000, 2201 Road to Six Flags, 2201 Road to Six Flags, Arlington
The 205-acre theme park depicts Texas under the flags of France, Mexico, the Republic of Texas, the Old South, Spain and the United States. Air-conditioned kennels are available. Daily, late May-early Aug.; Sat.-Sun., Mar. 1-late May, mid-Aug. through Oct. 31 and day after Thanksgiving-Dec. 31. Hours vary. Cost: $64.99; $49.99 (under 48 inches tall); free (ages 0-2). Rates may vary; phone ahead. AAA members save on select services and merchandise. See guest relations for details. Parking: $20. www.sixflags.com

VIRGINIA

 Busch Gardens Williamsburg

(800) 343-7946, 1 Busch Gardens Blvd., 1 Busch Gardens Blvd., Williamsburg
This 100-acre adventure park features thrill rides, animal attractions and shows, and shops and eateries set amid various European-themed villages. Kennel facilities are available for a fee and are located in the England parking lot. Open Mar.-Dec.; days and hours vary. Cost: $75; $65 (ages 3-9). Multiday and combination tickets with Water Country USA are available. Parking: $15. www.buschgardens.com/bgw/default.aspx

Kings Dominion

(804) 876-5000, 16000 Theme Park Dr., .5 mi. e. off I-95 exit 98 on SR 30, Doswell

A 300-foot replica of the Eiffel Tower stands at the gates to this 400-acre theme park, which features live shows, thrill and family rides, and a water park. Kennels are available for a fee; overnight boarding is not allowed. Parks open daily, Memorial Day-Labor Day. Schedules vary rest of year; phone ahead. Cost: (includes WaterWorks in season) $64; $41 (ages 62+ and under 48 inches tall); free (ages 0-2). Dinosaurs Alive! additional $6. Prices may vary. Parking: $15. www.kingsdominion.com

WASHINGTON

Hovander Homestead Park

(360) 384-3444, 1 mi. s. via Hovander Rd. to 5299 Nielsen Ave., Ferndale

This restored house, dating from 1903 and furnished with antiques, is within a large park encompassing gardens, picnic sites and a children's farm area. Dogs are allowed in on-leash areas of the park. Grounds open daily 8 a.m.-dusk. House open Fri.-Sun. 12:30-4:30, Memorial Day-Labor Day. The house is not always open during scheduled times; phone ahead to confirm. The boardwalk may be closed during designated hunting season. Cost: House $1; 50c (ages 0-12). www.co.whatcom.wa.us/parks/hovander/index.jsp

Canada

ONTARIO

Canada's Wonderland

(905) 832-7000, off Hwy. 400, Rutherford Rd. exit northbound or Major MacKenzie Dr. E. exit southbound at 9580 Jane St., Vaughan

This 121-hectare (365-acre) theme park has more than 200 attractions and 65 rides, in addition to a water park and participative play areas for children. Air-conditioned kennels are available for a fee. Daily 10-10, late July-Aug. 31; Sat.-Sun. and Labour Day 10-8, in Sept.; Sat.-Sun. 10-5, Oct. 1-Nov. 1. Hours are subject to change without notice; phone to verify schedule and admission prices. Cost: Passport for grounds and most rides $59.99; $34.99 (ages 3-6 and 60+). Concerts are available at an extra charge. Height restrictions apply to some rides. Parking: $15. www.canadaswonderland.com

Upper Canada Village

(613) 543-4328, 13740 CR 2, 11 km (7 mi.) e. on CR 2 off Hwy. 401, Morrisburg

Upper Canada Village re-creates life during the 1860s through a working community of artisans and costumed interpreters who perform chores typical of the era. Guide dogs and other service animals are welcome. All other pets must be kept on a leash and may not enter historic buildings. Daily 9:30-5, Victoria Day weekend-Labour Day; Wed.-Sun. 9:30-5, day after Labour Day-Thanksgiving. Cost: Village $18; $16 (ages 65+); $12 (ages 6-12); free (ages 0-5). Rates may vary; phone ahead. www.uppercanadavillage.com

NATIONAL PUBLIC LANDS

The National Public Lands listed below permit pets on a leash. Keep in mind that animals may be prohibited from entering public buildings and even some areas outdoors, particularly those that are ecologically sensitive. Where swimming is permitted, there are usually no lifeguards on duty; people and pets swim at their own risk. Specific pet policies vary from park to park and are subject to change. Always check in advance regarding any applicable regulations and to confirm that pets are still permitted where you are going.

Be aware of dangers to your pet in natural areas, including snakes, ticks and fast-moving currents in rivers and streams. An unleashed dog may chase after a wild animal and become separated from its owner, increasing the risk of loss or injury. Never leave your pet unattended. Keep him leashed or crated at all times. Follow park guidelines faithfully, and monitor your pet's behavior; the National Park Service may confiscate pets that harm wildlife or other visitors. *For additional information on outdoor vacations, see The Great Outdoors, p. 16.*

United States

ALABAMA

Conecuh National Forest
On the Alabama-Florida border.
(334) 222-2555
🚲 🅰 🥾 ⛱ 🏊

Horseshoe Bend National Military Park
12 mi. n. of Dadeville on SR 49.
(256) 234-7111
🥾 ⛱ 🏊 👥

Talladega National Forest
In central Alabama.
(256) 362-2909
🚲 🅰 🥾 ⛱ 🏊

Tuskegee National Forest
Northeast of Tuskegee.
(334) 727-2652
🚲 🅰 🥾 ⛱

William B. Bankhead National Forest
In northwestern Alabama.
(205) 489-5111
🚲 🅰 🥾 ⛱ 🏊

ALASKA

Chugach National Forest
Along the Gulf of Alaska from Cape Suckling to Seward.
(907) 743-9500
🚲 🅰 🥾 ⛱ 👥

Denali National Park and Preserve
In south-central Alaska.
(907) 683-2294
🅰 🥾 ⛱ 👥 🍴

Glacier Bay National Park and Preserve
North of Cross Sound to the Canadian border.
(907) 697-2230
🅰 🥾 👥 🍴

Kenai Fjords National Park
Southeastern side of the Kenai Peninsula.
(907) 224-7500 or (907) 224-2132
🅰 🥾 ⛱ 👥

Lake Clark National Park and Preserve
In southern Alaska.
(907) 644-3626
🅰 👥

Tongass National Forest
In southeastern Alaska.
(907) 228-6220
🅰 🥾 ⛱ 👥

Wrangell-St. Elias National Park and Preserve
In southeastern Alaska, northwest of Tongass National Forest.
(907) 822-7250
🅰 🥾 ⛱ 👥

ARIZONA

Apache-Sitgreaves National Forests
In east-central Arizona.
(928) 333-4301
🚲 🅰 🥾 ⛱ 👥 🍴

Coconino National Forest
In north-central Arizona.
(928) 527-3600
🚲 🅰 🥾 ⛱ 🏊 🍴

Coronado National Forest
In southeastern Arizona and southwestern New Mexico.
(520) 388-8300
🚲 🅰 🥾 ⛱ 👥

Glen Canyon National Recreation Area
In northern Arizona and Southern Utah.
(928) 608-6200
🚲 🅰 🥾 ⛱ 🏊 👥 🍴

Grand Canyon National Park
In northwestern Arizona.
(928) 638-2901
🅰 🥾 ⛱ 👥 🍴

Kaibab National Forest
In north-central Arizona.
(928) 643-7298
🚲 🅰 🥾 ⛱ 👥 🍴

🚲 Bicycling Trails   🅰 Camping   🥾 Hiking Trails   ⛱ Picnic Facilities
🏊 Swimming   👥 Visitor Center   🍴 Food Service

Petrified Forest National Park
In east-central Arizona, east of Holbrook.
(928) 524-6228
⬚ ⬚ ⬚ ⬚

Prescott National Forest
In central Arizona.
(928) 443-8000
⬚ ⬚ ⬚ ⬚

Saguaro National Park
Two districts, 15 mi. east and west of Tucson.
(520) 733-5153
⬚ ⬚ ⬚ ⬚ ⬚

Tonto National Forest
In central Arizona.
(602) 225-5200
⬚ ⬚ ⬚ ⬚ ⬚ ⬚

ARKANSAS
Buffalo National River
In northwestern Arkansas.
(870) 439-2502
⬚ ⬚ ⬚ ⬚ ⬚ ⬚

Hot Springs National Park
In western Arkansas.
(501) 620-6715
⬚ ⬚ ⬚ ⬚

Ouachita National Forest
In west-central Arkansas and southeastern Oklahoma.
(501) 321-5202
⬚ ⬚ ⬚ ⬚ ⬚ ⬚

Ozark National Forest
In northwestern Arkansas.
(479) 964-7200
⬚ ⬚ ⬚ ⬚ ⬚ ⬚

St. Francis National Forest
In east-central Arkansas.
(479) 964-7200
⬚ ⬚ ⬚ ⬚ ⬚

CALIFORNIA
Angeles National Forest
In southern California.
(626) 574-5200
⬚ ⬚ ⬚ ⬚ ⬚ ⬚ ⬚

Cleveland National Forest
In southwestern California.
(858) 673-6180
⬚ ⬚ ⬚ ⬚ ⬚ ⬚

Death Valley National Park
Along the Nevada border in east-central California.
(760) 786-3200
⬚ ⬚ ⬚ ⬚ ⬚ ⬚

Eldorado National Forest
In central California.
(530) 644-6048
⬚ ⬚ ⬚ ⬚ ⬚ ⬚ ⬚

Golden Gate National Recreation Area
North of the Golden Gate Bridge and in northern and western San Francisco.
(415) 561-4700
⬚ ⬚ ⬚ ⬚ ⬚ ⬚ ⬚

Inyo National Forest
In east-central California.
(760) 873-2400
⬚ ⬚ ⬚ ⬚ ⬚ ⬚ ⬚

Joshua Tree National Park
East of Desert Hot Springs.
(760) 367-5500
⬚ ⬚ ⬚ ⬚

King Range National Conservation Area
In northwestern California.
(707) 825-2300
⬚ ⬚ ⬚ ⬚ ⬚ ⬚ ⬚

Klamath National Forest
In northern California.
(530) 842-6131
⬚ ⬚ ⬚ ⬚ ⬚ ⬚

Lassen National Forest
In northeastern California.
(530) 257-2151
⬚ ⬚ ⬚ ⬚ ⬚ ⬚ ⬚

Lassen Volcanic National Park
In northeastern California.
(530) 595-4444
⬚ ⬚ ⬚ ⬚ ⬚ ⬚

Los Padres National Forest
In southern California.
(805) 968-6640
⬚ ⬚ ⬚ ⬚ ⬚ ⬚

Mendocino National Forest
In northwestern California.
(530) 934-2350
⬚ ⬚ ⬚ ⬚ ⬚ ⬚ ⬚

Modoc National Forest
In northeastern California.
(530) 233-5811
⬚ ⬚ ⬚ ⬚ ⬚ ⬚

Mojave National Preserve
Between I-15 and I-40 in southeastern California.
(760) 252-6108
⬚ ⬚ ⬚ ⬚ ⬚

Plumas National Forest
In northern California.
(530) 283-2050
⬚ ⬚ ⬚ ⬚ ⬚ ⬚ ⬚

Point Reyes National Seashore
Along the California coast just north of San Francisco.
(415) 464-5100
⬚ ⬚ ⬚ ⬚ ⬚ ⬚

Redwood National and State Parks
On the northern California coast.
(707) 465-7765
⑤ Ⓐ Ⓜ Ⓟ ⓈⒽ ⓕ

San Bernardino National Forest
In southern California.
(909) 382-2600
⑤ Ⓐ Ⓜ Ⓟ ⓈⒽ ⓕ

Santa Monica Mountains National Recreation Area
West from Griffith Park in Los Angeles past the Ventura County line.
(805) 370-2301
⑤ Ⓐ Ⓜ Ⓟ ⓈⒽ ⓕ

Sequoia and Kings Canyon National Parks
In east-central California.
(559) 565-3341
Ⓐ Ⓜ Ⓟ Ⓗ

Sequoia National Forest
In south-central California.
(559) 784-1500
⑤ Ⓐ Ⓜ Ⓟ ⓈⒽ ⓕ

Shasta-Trinity National Forests
In northern California.
(530) 226-2500
⑤ Ⓐ Ⓜ Ⓟ ⓈⒽ ⓕ

Sierra National Forest
In central California.
(559) 297-0706
⑤ Ⓐ Ⓜ Ⓟ ⓈⒽ ⓕ

Six Rivers National Forest
In northwestern California.
(707) 442-1721
⑤ Ⓐ Ⓜ Ⓟ ⓈⒽ ⓕ

Smith River National Recreation Area
Within Six Rivers National Forest in northwestern California.
(707) 457-3131
⑤ Ⓐ Ⓜ Ⓟ Ⓢ

Stanislaus National Forest
Within Six Rivers National Forest in northwestern California.
(707) 457-3131
⑤ Ⓐ Ⓜ Ⓟ Ⓢ ⓕ

Tahoe National Forest
In north-central California.
(530) 265-4531
Ⓐ Ⓜ Ⓟ Ⓢ Ⓗ ⓕ

Whiskeytown-Shasta-Trinity National Recreation Area
North and west of Redding.
(530) 242-3400
⑤ Ⓐ Ⓜ Ⓟ ⓈⒽ ⓕ

Yosemite National Park
In central California.
(209) 372-0200
⑤ Ⓐ Ⓜ Ⓟ ⓈⒽ ⓕ

COLORADO

Arapaho and Roosevelt National Forests and Pawnee National Grassland
In north-central Colorado.
(970) 295-6700
⑤ Ⓐ Ⓜ Ⓟ Ⓢ Ⓗ

Arapaho National Recreation Area
In north-central Colorado.
(970) 887-4100
⑤ Ⓐ Ⓜ Ⓟ Ⓢ Ⓗ

Black Canyon of The Gunnison National Park
In western Colorado.
(970) 249-1914
Ⓐ Ⓜ Ⓟ Ⓗ

Curecanti National Recreation Area
In south-central Colorado between Gunnison and Montrose, paralleling US 50.
(970) 641-2337
Ⓐ Ⓜ Ⓟ Ⓢ Ⓗ ⓕ

Dinosaur National Monument
In northeast Utah and northwest Colorado.
(435) 781-7700
⑤ Ⓐ Ⓜ Ⓟ Ⓗ

Grand Mesa—Uncompahgre—Gunnison National Forests
In west-central Colorado.
(970) 874-6600
⑤ Ⓐ Ⓜ Ⓟ Ⓗ ⓕ

Great Sand Dunes National Park and Preserve
Northeast of Alamosa.
(719) 378-6399
Ⓐ Ⓜ Ⓟ Ⓗ

Mesa Verde National Park
In southwestern Colorado.
(970) 529-4465
Ⓐ Ⓜ Ⓟ Ⓗ

Pikes Peak and Pike National Forest
In south-central Colorado.
(719) 553-1400
⑤ Ⓐ Ⓜ Ⓟ Ⓗ ⓕ

Rio Grande National Forest
In south-central Colorado.
(719) 852-5941
⑤ Ⓐ Ⓜ Ⓟ Ⓢ Ⓗ

Rocky Mountain National Park
In north-central Colorado.
(970) 586-1206
Ⓐ Ⓜ Ⓟ Ⓗ

---

⑤ Bicycling Trails   Ⓐ Camping   Ⓜ Hiking Trails   Ⓟ Picnic Facilities
Ⓢ Swimming   Ⓗ Visitor Center   ⓕ Food Service

Routt National Forest
In northwestern Colorado.
(970) 638-4516
♿ ⛺ 🚵 ⛏ 🏊 🚶

San Isabel National Forest
In central Colorado.
(719) 553-1400
♿ ⛺ 🚵 ⛏ 🚶 🍴

San Juan National Forest
In southwestern Colorado.
(970) 247-4874
♿ ⛺ 🚵 ⛏ 🚶 🍴

White River National Forest
In west-central Colorado.
(970) 945-2521
♿ ⛺ 🚵 ⛏ 🏊 🚶 🍴

FLORIDA
Apalachicola National Forest
In northwestern Florida.
(850) 926-3561
♿ ⛺ 🚵 ⛏ 🏊

Biscayne National Park
In southeast Florida.
(305) 230-7275
⛺ 🚵 ⛏ 🏊 🚶

Ocala National Forest
In north-central Florida.
(352) 236-0288
♿ ⛺ 🚵 ⛏ 🏊 🚶 🍴

Ocala National Forest (Alexander Springs Recreation Area)
13 mi. n.e. of Umatilla via SR 19 and CR 445.
(352) 669-3522
♿ ⛺ 🚵 ⛏ 🏊 🍴

Ocala National Forest (Juniper Springs Recreation Area)
28 mi. e. of Ocala on SR 40.
(352) 625-3147
♿ ⛺ 🚵 ⛏ 🏊 🚶 🍴

Ocala National Forest (Lake Dorr Recreation Area)
5 mi. n. of Umatilla on SR 19.
(352) 236-0288
⛺ ⛏ 🚶

Osceola National Forest
Near the Georgia border.
(386) 752-2577
♿ ⛺ 🚵 ⛏ 🏊

Osceola National Forest (Olustee Beach Recreation Area)
.25 mi. n. of Olustee on CR 231 (Pine Street).
(904) 487-1462
♿ 🚵 ⛏ 🏊

GEORGIA
Chattahoochee and Oconee National Forests
In central and northern Georgia.
(770) 297-3000
♿ ⛺ 🚵 ⛏ 🏊 🚶

Chattahoochee River National Recreation Area
North of Atlanta.
(678) 538-1200
♿ 🚵 ⛏ 🏊 🚶

IDAHO
Boise National Forest
In southwestern Idaho.
(208) 373-4007
♿ ⛺ 🚵 ⛏ 🏊 🚶

Caribou-Targhee National Forest
In southeastern Idaho.
(208) 524-7500
♿ ⛺ 🚵 ⛏ 🏊 🚶

Clearwater National Forest
In northeastern Idaho.
(208) 476-4541
♿ ⛺ 🚵 ⛏ 🏊 🚶

Idaho Panhandle National Forests
In northern and northwestern Idaho.
(208) 765-7223
♿ ⛺ 🚵 ⛏ 🏊 🚶

Nez Perce National Forest
In northwestern Idaho.
(208) 983-1950
♿ ⛺ 🚵 ⛏ 🏊 🚶

Payette National Forest
In west-central Idaho.
(208) 634-0700
♿ ⛺ 🚵 ⛏ 🏊 🚶 🍴

Salmon-Challis National Forest
In east-central Idaho.
(208) 756-5100
♿ ⛺ 🚵 ⛏ 🏊 🚶

Sawtooth National Forest
In south-central Idaho.
(208) 737-3200
♿ ⛺ 🚵 ⛏ 🏊 🚶

Sawtooth National Recreation Area
In south-central Idaho.
(208) 727-5013
♿ ⛺ 🚵 ⛏ 🏊 🚶 🍴

ILLINOIS
Shawnee National Forest
In southern Illinois.
(618) 253-7114
⛺ 🚵 ⛏ 🏊 🚶

INDIANA
Hoosier National Forest
In southern Indiana.
(812) 275-5987
♿ ⛺ 🚵 ⛏ 🏊

Indiana Dunes National Lakeshore
On the southern shore of Lake Michigan.
(219) 926-7561
⛺ 🚵 ⛏ 🏊 🚶

KENTUCKY

Daniel Boone National Forest
Five districts in eastern and southeastern Kentucky.
(859) 745-3100
🚲 🛖 🥾 ⛩ 🏠 🍴

Daniel Boone National Forest (Laurel River Lake)
Off I-75 west of Corbin.
(606) 864-4163
🚲 🛖 🥾 ⛩ ⚓

Daniel Boone National Forest (Red River Gorge Geological Area)
Off SR 15.
(606) 663-8100
🛖 🥾 ⛩ 🏠

Daniel Boone National Forest (Rockcastle)
22 mi. southwest of London via SR 192/3497.
(606) 864-4163
🛖 🥾 ⛩ ⚓

Daniel Boone National Forest (Sawyer)
5 mi. west of Cumberland Falls on SR 90, then 7 mi. north on SR 896 following signs.
(606) 376-5323
🛖 🥾 ⛩

Daniel Boone National Forest (S-Tree)
.5 mi. west of McKee on US 421, 3 mi. south on SR 89, 1 mi. west on FR 43, then south on FR 20 following signs.
(606) 864-4163
🛖 🥾 ⛩

Daniel Boone National Forest (Turkey Foot)
3 mi. north of McKee on SR 89, then east on FR 4 following signs for 3 mi.
(606) 864-4163
🛖 🥾 ⛩

Land Between The Lakes National Recreation Area
In western Kentucky and Tennessee.
(270) 924-2000
🚲 🛖 🥾 ⛩ ⚓ 🏠

Mammoth Cave National Park
In south-central Kentucky 10 mi. west of Cave City.
(270) 758-2180
🚲 🛖 🥾 ⛩ 🏠

LOUISIANA

Bayou Sauvage National Wildlife Refuge
Within the New Orleans city limits.
(985) 882-2000
🚲 🥾 ⛩

Kisatchie National Forest
In central and northern Louisiana.
(318) 473-7160
🚲 🛖 🥾 ⛩ ⚓

Sabine National Wildlife Refuge
In southwestern Louisiana.
(337) 762-3816
🥾

MAINE

Acadia National Park
Along the Atlantic coast southeast of Bangor.
(207) 288-3338
🚲 🛖 🥾 ⛩ ⚓ 🏠 🍴

MICHIGAN

Hiawatha National Forest
In Michigan's Upper Peninsula.
(906) 786-4062
🚲 🛖 🥾 ⛩ ⚓ 🏠

Huron-Manistee National Forests
In the northern part of the Lower Peninsula.
(231) 775-2421
🚲 🛖 🥾 ⛩ ⚓ 🏠

Ottawa National Forest
In Michigan's Upper Peninsula.
(906) 932-1330
🚲 🛖 🥾 ⛩ ⚓ 🏠

Pictured Rocks National Lakeshore
Along Lake Superior in Michigan's Upper Peninsula.
906-387-3700
🛖 🥾 ⛩ ⚓ 🏠

Sleeping Bear Dunes National Lakeshore
Along Lake Michigan in the northwestern part of the Lower Peninsula.
(231) 326-5134
🛖 🥾 ⛩ ⚓ 🏠

MINNESOTA

Chippewa National Forest
In north-central Minnesota.
(218) 335-8600
🚲 🛖 🥾 ⛩ ⚓ 🏠 🍴

Superior National Forest
In northeastern Minnesota.
(218) 626-4300
🚲 🛖 🥾 ⛩ ⚓ 🏠 🍴

MISSISSIPPI

Bienville National Forest
In central Mississippi.
(601) 469-3811
🛖 🥾 ⛩ ⚓ 🏠

Delta National Forest
In west-central Mississippi.
(662) 873-6256
🚲 🛖 🥾 ⛩ 🏠

De Soto National Forest
In southeastern Mississippi.
(601) 528-6160
🚲 🛖 🥾 ⛩ ⚓ 🏠

🚲 Bicycling Trails   🛖 Camping   🥾 Hiking Trails   ⛩ Picnic Facilities
⚓ Swimming   🏠 Visitor Center   🍴 Food Service

Gulf Islands National Seashore
Along the Gulf of Mexico in southern Mississippi.
(228) 875-9057
[A] [%] [#] [#]

Holly Springs National Forest
In north-central Mississippi.
(662) 236-6550
[A] [%] [#] [±] [#]

Homochitto National Forest
In the southwestern corner of Mississippi.
(601) 384-5876
[&] [A] [%] [#] [±] [#]

Tombigbee National Forest
In east-central Mississippi.
(662) 285-3264
[&] [A] [%] [#] [±] [#]

MISSOURI
Mark Twain National Forest
Southern Missouri.
(573) 364-4621
[&] [A] [%] [#] [±]

Mark Twain National Forest (Big Bay Recreation Area)
1 mi. southeast of Shell Knob on SR 39, then 3 mi. southeast on CR YY.
(573) 364-4621
[A] [#] [±]

Mark Twain National Forest (Crane Lake Recreation Area)
12 mi. south of Ironton off SR 49 and CR E.
(573) 364-4621
[&] [%] [#] [±]

Mark Twain National Forest (Fourche Lake Recreation Area)
18 mi. west of Doniphan on US 160.
(573) 364-4621
[%] [#]

Mark Twain National Forest (Noblett Lake Recreation Area)
8 mi. west of Willow Springs on SR 76, then 1.4 mi. south on SR 181, 3 mi. southeast on CR AP and 1 mi. southwest on CR 857.
(573) 364-4621
[&] [A] [%] [#]

Mark Twain National Forest (Pinewoods Lake Recreation Area)
2 mi. west of Ellsinore on SR 60.
(573) 364-4621
[&] [%] [#] [±]

Mark Twain National Forest (Red Bluff Recreation Area)
1 mi. east of Davisville on CR V, then 1 mi. north on FR 2011.
(573) 364-4621
[A] [%] [#] [±]

Ozarks and Ozark National Scenic Riverways
In southeastern Missouri.
(573) 323-4236
[A] [%] [#] [±] [#] [#]

MONTANA
Beaverhead-Deerlodge National Forest
In southwestern Montana.
(406) 683-3900
[&] [A] [%] [#] [±]

Bighorn Canyon National Recreation Area
In southern Montana and northern Wyoming.
(406) 666-2412
[A] [%] [#] [±] [#] [#]

Bitterroot National Forest
In western Montana.
(406) 363-7100
[&] [A] [%] [#] [±] [#]

Custer National Forest
In southeastern Montana.
(406) 255-1400
[&] [A] [%] [#] [±] [#]

Flathead National Forest
In northwestern Montana.
(406) 758-5204
[&] [A] [%] [#] [±] [#]

Gallatin National Forest
In south-central Montana.
(406) 522-2520
[&] [A] [%] [#] [±] [#] [#]

Glacier National Park
In northwestern Montana.
(406) 888-7800
[A] [%] [#] [±] [#] [#]

Helena National Forest
In west-central Montana.
(406) 449-5201
[A] [%] [#] [±]

Kootenai National Forest
In northwestern Montana.
(406) 293-6211
[&] [A] [%] [#] [±] [#] [#]

Lewis and Clark National Forest
In central Montana.
(406) 791-7700
[A] [%] [#] [±]

NEVADA
Great Basin National Park
In central Nevada, 5 mi. west of Baker near the Nevada-Utah border.
(775) 234-7331
[&] [A] [%] [#] [#] [#]

Humboldt-Toiyabe National Forest
In central, western, northern and southern Nevada and eastern California.
(775) 331-6444
[&] [A] [%] [#]

Lake Mead National Recreation Area
In northwestern Arizona and southeastern Nevada.
(702) 293-8990
[&] [A] [%] [#] [±] [#] [#]

NEW HAMPSHIRE
White Mountains and White Mountain National Forest
In northern New Hampshire.
(603) 528-8721
[icons]

NEW JERSEY
Gateway National Recreation Area (Sandy Hook Unit)
In northeastern New Jersey.
(732) 872-5970
[icons]

NEW MEXICO
Carson National Forest
In north-central New Mexico.
(575) 758-6200
[icons]

Chaco Culture National Historical Park
In northwestern New Mexico.
(505) 786-7014
[icons]

Cibola National Forest
In central New Mexico.
(505) 856-7325
[icons]

El Malpais National Monument and National Conservation Area
23 mi. south of I-40 via SRs 53 and 117.
(505) 783-4774
[icons]

Gila National Forest
In southwestern New Mexico.
(575) 388-8201
[icons]

Lincoln National Forest
In south-central New Mexico.
(575) 434-7200
[icons]

Santa Fe National Forest
In north-central New Mexico between the Jemez Mountains and the Sangre de Cristo Mountains.
(505) 438-5300
[icons]

NEW YORK
Finger Lakes National Forest
In south-central New York on a ridge between Seneca and Cayuga lakes, via I-90, I-81 and SR 17.
(607) 546-4470
[icons]

Gateway National Recreation Area (Jamaica Bay Unit)
In Brooklyn and Queens boroughs in New York City.
(718) 338-3799
[icons]

Gateway National Recreation Area (Staten Island Unit)
On Staten Island borough in New York City.
(718) 354-4500
[icons]

NORTH CAROLINA
Cape Hatteras National Seashore
In eastern North Carolina along the Outer Banks.
(252) 473-2111
[icons]

Croatan National Forest
In southeastern North Carolina.
(252) 638-5628
[icons]

Croatan National Forest (Cedar Point)
1.25 mi. north jct. SRs 24 and 58, 3 mi. southeast of Swansboro.
(252) 638-5628
[icons]

Nantahala National Forest
At North Carolina's southwestern tip.
(828) 257-4200
[icons]

Nantahala National Forest (Hanging Dog)
21 acres 5 mi. northwest of Murphy on SR 1326.
(828) 837-5152
[icons]

Nantahala National Forest (Jackrabbit Mountain)
10 mi. northeast of Hayesville via US 64, SR 175 and SR 1155.
(828) 524-6441
[icons]

Nantahala National Forest (Standing Indian Mountain)
9 mi. west of Franklin on US 64, 2 mi. east on old US 64, then 2 mi. south on FR 67.
(828) 524-6441
[icons]

Pisgah National Forest
In western North Carolina.
(828) 257-4200
[icons]

Pisgah National Forest (Lake Powhatan)
7 mi. southwest of Asheville on SR 191 and FR 3484.
(828) 670-5627
[icons]

Pisgah National Forest (Rocky Bluff)
3 mi. south of Hot Springs on SR 209.
(828) 682-6146
[icons]

Uwharrie National Forest
In central North Carolina.
(910) 576-6391
[icons]

[icon] Bicycling Trails   [icon] Camping   [icon] Hiking Trails   [icon] Picnic Facilities
[icon] Swimming   [icon] Visitor Center   [icon] Food Service

Uwharrie National Forest (Badin Lake)
10 mi. north of Troy on SR 109.
(910) 576-6391
▲ 🚶 🏕 🚤

NORTH DAKOTA
Theodore Roosevelt National Park (North Unit)
In western North Dakota.
(701) 842-2333
▲ 🚶 🏕 🛏

Theodore Roosevelt National Park (South Unit)
In western North Dakota.
(701) 623-4466
▲ 🚶 🏕 🛏

OHIO
Cuyahoga Valley National Park
In northeastern Ohio.
(800) 257-9477
🚴 ▲ 🚶 🏕 🛏 🍴

OKLAHOMA
Black Kettle National Grasslands
Off SR 283 in Cheyenne.
(580) 497-2143
▲ 🚶 🏕 🚤 🍴

Chickasaw National Recreation Area
In south-central Oklahoma.
(580) 622-3161
🚴 ▲ 🚶 🏕 🚤 🛏

OREGON
Crater Lake National Park
On the crest of the Cascade Range off SR 62.
(541) 594-3100
🚴 ▲ 🚶 🏕 🛏 🍴

Deschutes National Forest
In central Oregon 6 mi. south of Bend via US 97.
(541) 383-5300
🚴 ▲ 🚶 🏕 🚤 🛏 🍴

Fremont-Winema National Forests
In south-central Oregon.
(541) 947-2151
🚴 ▲ 🚶 🏕 🚤 🛏 🍴

Hells Canyon National Recreation Area
In northeastern Oregon and western Idaho.
(509) 758-0616
🚴 ▲ 🚶 🏕 🛏

Malheur National Forest
In eastern Oregon.
(541) 575-3000
🚴 ▲ 🚶 🏕 🚤

Mt. Hood and Mt. Hood National Forest
In northwestern Oregon.
(888) 622-4822
🚴 ▲ 🚶 🏕 🚤 🛏 🍴

Ochoco National Forest
In central Oregon off US 26.
(541) 416-6500
🚴 ▲ 🚶 🏕 🚤

Oregon Dunes National Recreation Area
Between North Bend and Florence.
(541) 750-7000
▲ 🚶 🏕 🚤 🛏

Rogue River–Siskiyou National Forest
In southwestern Oregon off I-5 from Medford.
(541) 858-2200
🚴 ▲ 🚶 🏕 🚤 🛏

Siuslaw National Forest
In western Oregon.
(541) 750-7000
🚴 ▲ 🚶 🏕 🚤 🛏

Umatilla National Forest
In northeastern Oregon.
(541) 278-3716
🚴 ▲ 🚶 🏕 🚤 🛏

Umpqua National Forest
In southwestern Oregon 33 mi. east of Roseburg on SR 138.
(541) 672-6601
🚴 ▲ 🚶 🏕 🚤 🛏 🍴

Wallowa-Whitman National Forest
In northeastern Oregon.
(541) 523-6391
▲ 🚶 🏕 🚤

Willamette National Forest
In western Oregon.
(541) 225-6300
🚴 ▲ 🚶 🏕 🚤 🍴

PENNSYLVANIA
Allegheny National Forest
In northwestern Pennsylvania.
(814) 723-5150
🚴 ▲ 🚶 🏕 🚤 🛏 🍴

Delaware Water Gap National Recreation Area
In eastern Pennsylvania and northwestern New Jersey.
(570) 426-2457
▲ 🚶 🏕 🚤 🛏

SOUTH CAROLINA
Congaree National Park
Southeast of Hopkins.
(803) 776-4396
▲ 🚶 🏕 🛏

Francis Marion National Forest
On the Coastal Plain north of Charleston.
(803) 561-4000
🚴 ▲ 🚶 🏕 🛏

Sumter National Forest
In western South Carolina.
(803) 561-4000
🚴 ▲ 🚶 🏕 🚤

SOUTH DAKOTA
Badlands National Park
In southwestern South Dakota.
(605) 433-5361
▲ 🚶 🏕 🛏 🍴

Black Hills National Forest
In southwestern South Dakota.
(605) 673-9200
🚴 🅰 🥾 ⛱ 🏊 👥 🍴

Wind Cave National Park
In southwestern South Dakota.
(605) 745-4600
🚴 🅰 🥾 ⛱ 👥 🍴

TENNESSEE

Big South Fork National River and Recreation Area
In northeastern Tennessee and southeastern Kentucky.
(423) 286-7275
🚴 🅰 🥾 ⛱ 🏊 👥 🍴

Cherokee National Forest
In eastern Tennessee.
(423) 476-9700
🚴 🅰 🥾 ⛱ 🏊 👥

TEXAS

Amistad National Recreation Area
Northwest of Del Rio via US 90.
(830) 775-7491
🅰 🥾 ⛱ 🏊

Angelina National Forest
In east Texas.
(936) 897-1068
🅰 🥾 ⛱ 🏊

Big Bend National Park
In southwest Texas.
(432) 477-2251
🅰 🥾 ⛱ 👥 🍴

Davy Crockett National Forest
In east Texas.
(936) 655-2299
🅰 🥾 ⛱ 🏊

Lake Meredith National Recreation Area
45 mi. northeast of Amarillo and 9 mi. west of Borger via SR 136.
(806) 857-3151
🅰 🥾 ⛱ 🏊

Padre Island National Seashore
On Padre Island near Corpus Christi.
(361) 949-8068
🅰 🥾 ⛱ 🏊 👥 🍴

Sabine National Forest
In east Texas.
(409) 625-1940
🅰 🥾 ⛱ 🏊

Sam Houston National Forest
40 mi. north of Houston in east Texas.
(936) 344-6205
🚴 🅰 🥾 ⛱ 🏊

UTAH

Arches National Park
In eastern Utah.
(435) 719-2100
🅰 🥾 ⛱ 👥

Ashley National Forest
In northeastern Utah.
(435) 789-1181
🚴 🅰 🥾 ⛱ 🏊 👥 🍴

Bryce Canyon National Park
In southwestern Utah.
(435) 834-5322
🅰 🥾 ⛱ 👥 🍴

Canyonlands National Park
In southeastern Utah.
(435) 719-2313
🅰 🥾 ⛱ 👥

Capitol Reef National Park
10 mi. east of Torrey on SR 24.
(435) 425-3791
🚴 🅰 🥾 ⛱ 👥

Dixie National Forest
In southwestern Utah.
(435) 865-3700
🚴 🅰 🥾 ⛱ 🏊 👥 🍴

Fishlake National Forest
In south-central Utah.
(435) 896-9233
🚴 🅰 🥾 ⛱ 👥 🍴

Flaming Gorge National Recreation Area
In northeastern Utah on the Wyoming-Utah border.
(435) 784-3445
🚴 🅰 🥾 ⛱ 🏊 👥 🍴

Manti-La Sal National Forest
In southeastern Utah.
(435) 637-2817
🚴 🅰 🥾 ⛱ 🍴

Uinta National Forest
In north-central, central and northeastern Utah.
(801) 342-5100
🚴 🅰 🥾 ⛱ 🏊 👥

Wasatch-Cache National Forest
In northeastern and north-central Utah.
(801) 342-5100
🚴 🅰 🥾 ⛱ 🏊 👥

Zion National Park
In southwestern Utah.
(435) 772-3256
🚴 🅰 🥾 ⛱ 👥 🍴

VERMONT

Green Mountains and Green Mountain National Forest
In south-central Vermont.
(802) 747-6700
🚴 🅰 🥾 ⛱ 🏊

🚴 Bicycling Trails   🅰 Camping   🥾 Hiking Trails   ⛱ Picnic Facilities
🏊 Swimming   👥 Visitor Center   🍴 Food Service

VIRGINIA

George Washington and Jefferson National Forests
In western Virginia and the eastern edge of West Virginia.
(540) 265-5100

Mount Rogers National Recreation Area
In southwestern Virginia.
(276) 783-5196

Shenandoah National Park
In northwestern Virginia.
(540) 999-3500

WASHINGTON

Colville National Forest
In northeastern Washington.
(509) 684-7000

Gifford Pinchot National Forest
In southwestern Washington.
(360) 891-5000

Gifford Pinchot National Forest (Goose Lake)
13 mi. west of Trout Lake via SR 141, FR 24 and FR 60.
(509) 395-3400

Gifford Pinchot National Forest (Takhlakh Lake)
32 mi. southeast of Randle via SR 131, FR 23 and FR 2329.
(360) 497-1100

Lake Chelan National Recreation Area
In north-central Washington.
(509) 682-1900

Lake Roosevelt National Recreation Area
In northeastern Washington.
(509) 633-9441

Mount Baker-Snoqualmie National Forest
2 mi. east of Glacier on SR 542.
(425) 783-6000

Mount Baker-Snoqualmie National Forest (Douglas Fir)
2 mi. east of Glacier on SR 542.
(425) 783-6000

Mount Baker-Snoqualmie National Forest (Horseshoe Cove)
14 mi. north of Concrete on Baker Lake.
(360) 599-2714

Mount Baker-Snoqualmie National Forest (Shannon Creek)
24 mi. north of Concrete on Baker Lake.
(360) 599-2714

Mount Rainier National Park
In west-central Washington.
(360) 569-2211

Okanogan-Wenatchee National Forest
In north-central Washington.
(509) 826-3275

Okanogan-Wenatchee National Forest (Bonaparte Lake)
7 mi. northwest of Wauconda via SR 20 and CR 4953.
(509) 664-9200

Okanogan-Wenatchee National Forest (Bumping Lake)
3 mi. south of Goose Prairie.
(509) 664-9200

Okanogan-Wenatchee National Forest (Kachess Lake)
15 mi. north of Easton via I-90 and FR 49.
(509) 852-1100

Okanogan-Wenatchee National Forest (Lost Lake)
17 mi. northwest of Wauconda via SR 20, CR 4953, FR 32 and FR 33.
(509) 852-1100

Okanogan-Wenatchee National Forest (Rimrock Lake Area)
At Rimrock off US 12.
(509) 653-1401

Olympic National Forest
In northwestern Washington.
(360) 956-2402

Olympic National Forest (Falls Creek)
3 mi. east of US 101 on Quinault Lake.
(360) 956-2402

Olympic National Forest (Willaby)
2 mi. east of US 101 on Quinault Lake.
(360) 956-2402

Olympic National Forest (Wynoochee Lake-Coho)
1 mi. west of Montesano on US 12, then 37 mi. north on FR 22 (Old Wynoochee Valley Rd.).
(360) 956-2402

Olympic National Park
In the Olympic peninsula in northwestern Washington.
(360) 565-3130

Ross Lake National Recreation Area
Between the north and south sections of North Cascades National Park.
(360) 854-7200

WEST VIRGINIA
Monongahela National Forest
In eastern West Virginia.
(304) 636-1800
[icons]

Monongahela National Forest (Lake Sherwood)
11 mi. northeast of Neola on SR 14.
(304) 636-1800
[icons]

New River Gorge National River
Between Fayetteville and Hinton.
(304) 465-0508
[icons]

Spruce Knob-Seneca Rocks National Recreation Area
In east-central West Virginia.
(304) 257-4488
[icons]

WISCONSIN
Apostle Islands National Lakeshore
Off northern Wisconsin's Bayfield Peninsula in Lake
Superior.
(715) 779-3397
[icons]

Chequamegon-Nicolet National Forest
In north-central and northeastern Wisconsin.
(715) 362-1300
[icons]

St. Croix National Scenic Riverway
Running 252 mi. from Cable to Prescott.
(715) 483-2274
[icons]

WYOMING
Bighorn National Forest
In north-central Wyoming.
(307) 674-2600
[icons]

Devils Tower National Monument
Between Sundance and Hulett.
(307) 467-5283
[icons]

Grand Teton National Park
In northwestern Wyoming.
(307) 739-3300
[icons]

Medicine Bow National Forest
In southeastern Wyoming.
(307) 745-2300
[icons]

Shoshone National Forest
In northwestern Wyoming.
(307) 527-6241
[icons]

Yellowstone National Park
In northwestern Wyoming.
(307) 344-7381
[icons]

Canada

ALBERTA
Banff National Park
In southwestern Alberta, west of Calgary.
(403) 762-1550
[icons]

Elk Island National Park
In central Alberta, east of Edmonton.
(780) 992-2950
[icons]

Jasper National Park
In west-central Alberta along the British Columbia border.
(780) 852-3858
[icons]

Waterton Lakes National Park
In Alberta's southwestern corner.
(403) 859-2224
[icons]

BRITISH COLUMBIA
Glacier National Park
In southeastern British Columbia.
(250) 837-7500
[icons]

Gulf Islands National Park Reserve
Off the southeast coast of Vancouver Island.
(250) 654-4000
[icons]

Kootenay National Park
In southeastern British Columbia.
(250) 343-6783
[icons]

Mount Revelstoke National Park
In southeastern British Columbia.
(250) 837-7500
[icons]

Pacific Rim National Park Reserve
On the southwestern coast of Vancouver Island.
(250) 726-7721
[icons]

Yoho National Park
On the British Columbia-Alberta border.
(250) 343-6783
[icons]

[icon] Bicycling Trails [icon] Camping [icon] Hiking Trails [icon] Picnic Facilities
[icon] Swimming [icon] Visitor Center [icon] Food Service

MANITOBA
Riding Mountain National Park
In southwestern Manitoba.
(204) 848-7275

NEW BRUNSWICK
Fundy National Park
On Hwy. 114, 130 km. southwest of Moncton.
(506) 887-6000

Kouchibouguac National Park
On Hwy. 134, north of Moncton.
(506) 876-2443

NEWFOUNDLAND AND LABRADOR
Gros Morne National Park
On Newfoundland's western coast.
(709) 458-2417

Terra Nova National Park
In eastern Newfoundland.
(709) 533-2801

NORTHWEST TERRITORIES
Wood Buffalo National Park
On the Northwest Territories-Alberta border.
(867) 872-7900

NOVA SCOTIA
Cape Breton Highlands National Park
5 km. northeast of Chéticamp on Cabot Tr.
(902) 224-2306

Kejimkujik National Park and National Historic Site
In southwestern Nova Scotia off Hwy. 8 at Maitland Bridge.
(902) 682-2772

ONTARIO
Bruce Peninsula National Park
In southwestern Ontario.
(519) 596-2233

Fathom Five National Marine Park
Off the northern tip of the Bruce Peninsula in southern Ontario.
(519) 596-2233

Georgian Bay Islands National Park
Along the southeastern portion of Georgian Bay.
(705) 526-9804

Point Pelee National Park
South of Leamington.
(519) 322-2365

Pukaskwa National Park
On the north shore of Lake Superior.
(807) 229-0801

St. Lawrence Islands National Park
In the St. Lawrence River between Kingston and Brockville.
(613) 923-5261

PRINCE EDWARD ISLAND
Prince Edward Island National Park
Along the island's northern shore.
(902) 672-6350

QUEBEC
Forillon National Park
20 km. northeast of Gaspé via Hwy. 132.
(418) 368-5505

La Mauricie National Park
North of Trois-Rivières via Hwy. 55.
(819) 538-3232

SASKATCHEWAN
Grasslands National Park
Between Val Marie and Killdeer in southern Saskatchewan.
(306) 298-2257

Prince Albert National Park
In central Saskatchewan.
(306) 663-4522

EMERGENCY ANIMAL CLINICS

This list of emergency animal clinics in the United States and Canada is provided by the Veterinary Emergency & Critical Care Society (VECCS) as a service to the community for information purposes only. This is not to be construed as a certification or an endorsement of any clinic listed. For further information, contact the society at (210) 698-5575 or online at www.veccs.org. Note: Hours frequently change, and not all clinics are open 24 hours or in the evening. In addition, not all facilities listed here are emergency clinics. In non-emergency situations, it's best to call first.

If you are traveling to an area not covered in this list, be prepared for an emergency by asking your regular veterinarian to recommend a clinic or veterinarian at your destination. The American Animal Hospital Association also can recommend veterinary clinics that meet the association's high standards for veterinary care. For additional information contact the association at (303) 986-2800.

United States

ALABAMA

Auburn University Small Animal Clinic
1010 Wire Rd., Auburn
(334) 844-4690

Animal Medical Center
2864 Acton Rd., Birmingham
(205) 967-7389

Emergency Pet Care
4524 Southlake Pkwy., Suite 28, Birmingham
(205) 988-5988

Southern Regional Veterinary Emergency Services
301 Westgate Pkwy., Dothan
(334) 699-7787

Animal Emergency Clinic of North Alabama
2112 Memorial Pkwy. S.W., Huntsville
(256) 533-7600

Animal Emergency & Referral Center of Mobile, LLC
2573 Government Blvd., Mobile
(251) 706-0890

Emergency Pet Care
7299 Gadsden Hwy., Trussville
(205) 205-2273

ALASKA

Pet Emergency Treatment, Inc.
2320 E. Dowling Rd., Anchorage
(907) 274-5636

After Hours Veterinary Emergency Clinic
8 Bonnie Ave., Fairbanks
(907) 479-2700

Southeast Alaska Animal Medical Center
8231 Glacier Hwy., Juneau
(907) 789-7551

ARIZONA

Emergency Animal Clinic, PLC
13034 W. Rancho Santa Fe Blvd., Avondale
(623) 385-4555

Animal Health Services
37555 N. Cave Creek Rd., Cave Creek
(480) 488-6181

First Regional Animal Hospital
1233 W. Warner Rd., Chandler
(480) 732-0335

Canyon Pet Hospital
1054 E. Old Canyon Ct., Flagstaff
(928) 774-5197

Emergency Animal Clinic, PLC
86 W. Juniper Ave., Gilbert
(480) 497-0222

1st Emergency Pet Care
1423 S. Highley Rd., Suite 102, Mesa
(408) 924-1123

Mesa Veterinary Hospital
858 N. Country Club Dr., Mesa
(480) 833-7330

Emergency Animal Clinic
9875 W. Peoria Ave., Peoria
(623) 974-1520

Emergency Animal Clinic, PLC
2260 W. Glendale Ave., Phoenix
(602) 995-3757

North Valley Animal Emergency Center
3134 W. Carefree Hwy., Suite A-2, Phoenix
(623) 516-8571

Sonora Veterinary Specialists
4015 E. Cactus Rd., Phoenix
(602) 765-3700

Ironwood Animal Hospital
85 W. Combs Rd., Suite 116, San Tan Valley
(480) 888-2299

Emergency Animal Clinic
22595 N. Scottsdale Rd., Suite 110, Scottsdale
(480) 949-8001

Paradise Valley Emergency Animal Clinic
6969 E. Shea Blvd., Suite 225, Scottsdale
(480) 991-1848

Arizona Veterinary Surgery
4131 E. Speedway Blvd., Tucson
(520) 795-9955

Ina Road Animal Hospital
7320 N. La Cholla Blvd., Suite 114, Tucson
(520) 544-7700

Pima Pet Clinic / Animal Emergency Service
4832 E. Speedway Blvd., Tucson
(520) 327-5624

Southern Arizona Veterinary Specialty and Emergency Center
141 E. Fort Lowell Rd., Tucson
(520) 888-3177

Southern Arizona Veterinary Specialty and Emergency Center
7474 E. Broadway Blvd., Tucson
(520) 888-3177

Valley Animal Hospital, P.C.
4984 E. 22nd St., Tucson
(520) 748-0331

Veterinary Specialty Center of Tucson
4909 N. La Canada Dr., Tucson
(520) 795-9955

ARKANSAS
Ft. Smith Animal Emergency Clinic
4301 Regions Park Dr., Suite 3, Fort Smith
(479) 649-3100

Pulaski County Veterinary Emergency Clinic
801 John Barrow Rd., Suite 6, Little Rock
(501) 224-3784

After Hours Animal Hospital
290 Smokey Ln., North Little Rock
(501) 955-0911

Animal Emergency & Specialty Clinic
8735 Sheltie Dr., Suite G, North Little Rock
(501) 224-3784

Animal Emergency Clinic of Northwest Arkansas
1110 Mathias Dr., Suite E, Springdale
(501) 927-0007

CALIFORNIA
East Bay Veterinary Emergency
1312 Sunset Dr., Antioch
(925) 754-5001

Central Coast Pet Emergency Clinic
1558 W. Branch St., Arroyo Grande
(805) 489-6573

Atascadero Pet Hospital and Emergency Center
9575 El Camino Real, Atascadero
(805) 466-3880

Animal Emergency & Urgent Care
4300 Easton Dr., Suite 1, Bakersfield
(661) 322-6019

Pet Emergency Treatment & Specialty (PETS) Referral Center
1048 University Ave., Berkeley
(510) 548-6684

Bolton Veterinary Hospital
222 Boston Tpke., Bolton
(860) 646-6134

United Emergency Animal Clinic
905 Dell Ave., Campbell
(408) 371-6252

Pacific Veterinary Specialists and Emergency Critical Care Center
1980 41st Ave., Capitola
(831) 476-2584

VCA Sacramento Animal Medical Group
4990 Manzanita Ave., Carmichael
(916) 331-7430

North Valley Emergency Veterinary Clinic
2500 Zanella Way, Suite A, Chico
(530) 899-1720

Contra Costa Veterinary Emergency Center
1410 Monument Blvd., Suite 108, Concord
(925) 798-2900

VCA Aacacia Animal Hospital
939 W. 6th St., Corona
(951) 371-1002

UC Davis Veterinary Medical Teaching Hospital - Small Animal Emergency and Critical Care Service
1 Garrod Dr., Davis
(530) 752-1393

Pet Specialists of Monterey
451 Canyon Del Rey Blvd., Del Rey Oaks
(831) 899-7387

SAGE Centers for Veterinary Specialty & Emergency Care
7121 Amador Plaza Rd., Dublin
(925) 891-7839

Vetcare Emergency & Specialty Care Center
7660 Amador Valley Blvd., Dublin
(925) 556-1234

Emergency Pet Clinic of San Gabriel Valley
3254 Santa Anita Ave., El Monte
(626) 579-4550

North Coast Veterinary and Emergency
414 Encinitas Blvd., Encinitas
(760) 632-1072

Animal Urgent Care
2430 S. Escondido Blvd., Escondido
(760) 738-9600

Animal Emergency Center
3954 Jacobs Ave., Eureka
(707) 443-2776

Solano-Napa Pet Emergency Clinic
4437 Central Pl., Fairfield
(707) 864-1444

VCA All-Care Animal Referral Center
18440 Amistad St., Suite E, Fountain Valley
(714) 963-0909

Ohlone Veterinary Emergency Clinic
1618 Washington Blvd., Fremont
(510) 657-6620

Fresno Pet Emergency & Referral Center, Inc.
7375 N. Palm Bluffs Ave., Fresno
(559) 437-3766

Fresno Veterinary Specialty & Emergency Center
6606 N. Blackstone Ave., Fresno
(559) 451-0800

Veterinary Emergency Service, Inc.
1639 N. Fresno St., Fresno
(559) 486-0520

Orange County Emergency Pet Clinic
12750 Garden Grove Blvd., Garden Grove
(714) 537-3032

eMash, Inc. Emergency & Mobile Animal Services Hospital
10825 Watsonville Rd., Gilroy
(408) 847-1122

Pet Medical Center - Chatoak
17659 Chatsworth St., Granada Hills
(818) 363-7444

Animal Emergency Clinic
12022 La Crosse Ave., Grand Terrace
(909) 825-9350

Crossroads Animal Emergency
18364 Beach Blvd., Huntington Beach
(714) 794-6900

Irvine Regional Animal Emergency Hospital
1371 Reynolds Ave., Irvine
(949) 833-9020

North Orange County Emergency Pet Clinic
1474 S. Harbor Blvd., La Habra
(714) 441-2925

Pet Emergency and Specialty Center
5232 Jackson Dr., Suite 105, La Mesa
(619) 462-4800

Animal Emergency Clinic
1055 W. Avenue M, Suite 101, Lancaster
(661) 723-3959

Animal Specialty Group
4641 Colorado Blvd., Los Angeles
(818) 244-7977

Animal Surgical and Emergency Center
1535 S. Sepulveda Blvd., Los Angeles
(310) 473-5906

Eagle Rock Emergency Pet Clinic
4254 Eagle Rock Blvd., Los Angeles
(323) 254-7382

VCA West Los Angeles Animal Hospital
1818 S. Sepulveda Blvd., Los Angeles
(310) 473-2951

Animal Urgent Care
2805 Hillcrest, Mission Viejo
(949) 364-6228

Portola Plaza Veterinary Hospital
27752 Santa Margarita Pkwy., Mission Viejo
(949) 859-2101

Veterinary Emergency Clinic
1800 Prescott Rd., Suite E, Modesto
(209) 527-8844

Monterey Peninsula Veterinary Emergency & Specialty Center
20 Lower Ragsdale Dr., Suite 150, Monterey
(831) 373-7374

All Creatures Emergency Center
22722 Lyons Ave., Suite 5, Newhall
(661) 291-1121

Central Orange County Emergency Animal Clinic
3720 Campus Drive, Suite D, Newport Beach
(949) 261-7979

Crossroads Animal Emergency and Referral Clinic
11057 E. Rosecrans Ave., Norwalk
(562) 863-2522

Orange Veterinary Hospital
1100 W. Chapman Ave., Orange
(714) 997-8200

Extraordinary Veterinary Services
5714 Los Coyotes Dr., Palm Springs
(760) 202-8710

South Peninsula Veterinary Emergency Clinic
3045 Middlefield Rd., Palo Alto
(650) 494-1461

Animal Emergency Clinic of Pasadena
2121 E. Foothill Blvd., Pasadena
(626) 564-0704

Animal Emergency Clinic of San Diego
12775 Poway Rd., Poway
(858) 748-7387

Animal Care Center
6470 Redwood Dr., Rohnert Park
(707) 584-4343

Atlantic Street Veterinary Hospital and Pet Emergency
1100 Atlantic St., Roseville
(916) 783-4655

El Camino Veterinary Hospital
4000 El Camino Ave., Sacramento
(916) 488-6878

Mueller Animal Hospital
6420 Freeport Blvd., Sacramento
(916) 428-9202

Northern California Veterinary Specialists
7425 Greenhaven Dr., Sacramento
(916) 231-0696

VCA Sacramento Veterinary Referral Center
9801 Old Winery Pl., Sacramento
(916) 362-3111

San Carlos Pet Emergency Hospital
718 El Camino Real, San Carlos
(650) 591-5718

Animal ER of San Diego
5610 Kearny Mesa Rd., Suite A, San Diego
(858) 569-0600

VCA Emergency Animal Hospital and Referral Center
2317 Hotel Cir. S., San Diego
(619) 299-2400

Veterinary Specialty Hospital
10435 Sorrento Valley Rd., San Diego
(858) 875-7500

All Animals Emergency Hospital
1333 Ninth Ave., San Francisco
(415) 566-0531

Pets Unlimited
2343 Fillmore St., San Francisco
(415) 563-6700

San Francisco Veterinary Specialists
600 Alabama St., San Francisco
(415) 401-9200

Silicon Valley Veterinary Specialists
7160 Santa Teresa Blvd., San Jose
(408) 649-7070

United Emergency Animal Clinic of South San Jose
5440 Thornwood Dr., Suite E, San Jose
(408) 578-5622

Veterinary Medical and Surgical Group - Orange County
31896 Plaza Dr., Suite C1, San Juan Capistrano
(949) 201-4100

Bay Area Veterinary Emergency Clinic
14790 Washington Ave., San Leandro
(510) 352-6080

California Veterinary Specialists
100 N. Rancho Santa Fe Rd., San Marcos
(760) 734-4433

North Peninsula Veterinary Emergency Clinic, Inc.
227 N. Amphlett Blvd., San Mateo
(650) 348-2575

The Pet Emergency and Specialty Center of Marin
901 E. Francisco Blvd., Suite C, San Rafael
(415) 456-7372

Advanced Veterinary Specialists
414 E. Carrillo St., Santa Barbara
(805) 729-4460

California Animal Referral & Emergency (CARE) Hospital, Inc.
301 E. Haley St., Santa Barbara
(805) 899-2273

Pacific Emergency Pet Hospital, Inc.
2963 State St., Santa Barbara
(805) 682-5120

Santa Cruz Veterinary Hospital
2585 Soquel Dr., Santa Cruz
(831) 475-5400

North Bay Animal Emergency Hospital
1304 Wilshire Blvd., Santa Monica
(310) 451-8962

Emergency Animal Hospital of Santa Rosa
1946 Santa Rosa Ave., Santa Rosa
(707) 544-1647

PetCare Veterinary Hospital
2425 Mendocino Ave., Santa Rosa
(707) 579-3900

PetCare Veterinary Hospital
1370 Fulton Rd., Santa Rosa
(707) 579-5900

Beverly Oaks Animal Hospital and Emergency Animal Clinic
14302 Ventura Blvd., Sherman Oaks
(818) 788-7860

TLC Pet Medical Centers - South Pasadena
1412 Huntington Dr., South Pasadena
(626) 441-8555

Associated Veterinary Emergency Services
3008 E. Hammer Ln., Suite 115, Stockton
(209) 952-8387

Animal Emergency Centre
11730 Ventura Blvd., Studio City
(818) 760-3882

Emergency Pet Clinic of Temecula
27443 Jefferson Ave., Temecula
(951) 695-5044

Conejo Valley Veterinary Hospital
1850 E. Thousand Oaks Blvd., Thousand Oaks
(805) 495-4671

Pet Emergency Clinic
2967 N. Moorepark Rd., Thousand Oaks
(805) 492-2436

Animal Emergency Medical Center
3511 Pacific Coast Hwy., Suite A, Torrance
(310) 325-3000

Emergency Pet Clinic of South Bay
2325 Torrance Blvd., Torrance
(310) 320-8300

Monte Vista Small Animal Hospital
901 E. Monte Vista Ave., Turlock
(209) 634-0023

Advanced Critical Care & Internal Medicine
2965 Edinger Ave., Tustin
(949) 654-8950

Inland Valley Emergency Pet Clinic
10 W. 7th St., Upland
(909) 931-7871

Pet Emergency Clinic
2301 S. Victoria Ave., Ventura
(805) 642-8562

Veterinary Medical and Surgical Group
2199 Sperry Ave., Ventura
(805) 339-2290

Animal Emergency Clinic
15532 Bear Valley Rd., Victorville
(760) 962-1122

Pinnacle Veterinary Service, Inc.
2300 S. Divisadero St., Visalia
(559) 732-8000

Tulare-Kings Veterinary Emergency Service
4240 W. Mineral King, Visalia
(559) 739-7054

Coastal Emergency Animal Hospital
1900 Hacienda Dr., Vista
(760) 630-6343

TLC Pet Medical Centers - West Hollywood
8725 Santa Monica Blvd., West Hollywood
(310) 859-4852

VCA Veterinary Specialists of the Valley
22123 Ventura Blvd., Woodland Hills
(818) 883-8387

COLORADO

Animal Urgent Care, Inc.
7851 Indiana St., Arvada
(303) 420-7387

Aurora Veterinary Emergency Center
18511 E. Hampden Ave., Aurora
(303) 699-1665

Seven Hills Veterinary Hospital
18325 E. Girard Ave., Aurora
(303) 699-1600

Valley Emergency Pet Care
180 Fiou Ln., Suite 101, Basalt
(970) 927-5066

Alpenglow Veterinary Specialty & Emergency Center
3640 Walnut St., Boulder
(303) 443-4569

Animal Emergency & Referral Center
1480 W. Midway Blvd., Boulder
(303) 464-7744

Boulder Emergency Pet Clinic
1658 30th St., Boulder
(303) 440-7722

VCA Douglas County Animal Hospital
531 Jerry St., Castle Rock
(303) 688-2480

Animal Emergency Care Center, Inc.
3775 Airport Rd., Colorado Springs
(719) 578-9300

Animal Emergency Care Centers - North
5520 N. Nevada Ave., Colorado Springs
(719) 260-7141

Animal Emergency Care, Inc.
5752 N. Academy Blvd., Colorado Springs
(719) 260-7141

Alameda East Veterinary Hospital
9770 E. Alameda Ave., Denver
(303) 366-2639

Central Veterinary Emergency Services
3550 S. Jason St., Englewood
(303) 874-7387

Pets of Northern Colorado
3629 23rd Ave., Evans
(970) 339-8700

Fort Collins Veterinary Emergency Hospital
816 S. Lemay Ave., Fort Collins
(970) 484-8080

James L. Voss Veterinary Teaching Hospital - Colorado State University
300 W. Drake Rd., Fort Collins
(970) 221-4535

Grand Valley Veterinary Emergency Center
1660 North Ave., Grand Junction
(970) 255-1911

Animal Hospital Center
5640 County Line Pl., Suite 1, Highlands Ranch
(303) 740-9595

Animal Critical Care & Emergency Services, Inc.
1597 Wadsworth Blvd., Lakewood
(303) 239-1200

Animal E.R.
221 W. County Line Rd., Littleton
(720) 283-9348

Columbine Animal Hospital & Emergency Clinic
5546 W. Canyon Tr., Littleton
(303) 929-4040

Animal Emergency & Critical Care
104 S. Main St., Longmont
(303) 678-8844

Animal Emergency Services of Northern Colorado
201 W. 67th Ct., Loveland
(970) 663-5760

Animal Emergency & Urgent Care
17701 Cottonwood Dr., Parker
(720) 842-5050

Emergency Animal Hospital of Pueblo
472 S. Joe Martinez Blvd., Pueblo
(719) 229-7030

Pueblo Area Pet Emergency Hospital
712 Fortino Blvd., Pueblo
(719) 544-7788

Community Pet Hospital
12311 Washington St., Thornton
(303) 451-1333

Northside Emergency Pet Clinic, P.C.
945 W. 124th Ave., Westminster
(303) 252-7722

Wheat Ridge Animal Hospital / Wheat Ridge Veterinary Specialists
3695 Kipling St., Wheat Ridge
(303) 424-3325

CONNECTICUT

Farmington Valley Veterinary Emergency Hospital
9 Avonwood Rd., Avon
(860) 674-1886

Veterinary Emergency Center
135 Dowd Ave., Canton
(860) 693-6992

Cheshire Veterinary Hospital
1572 S. Main St., Cheshire
(203) 271-1577

New Haven Hospital for Veterinary Medicine, Inc.
843 State St., New Haven
(203) 865-0878

Newtown Veterinary Specialists
52 Church Hill Rd., Newtown
(203) 270-8387

Veterinary Referral & Emergency Center
123 W. Cedar St., Norwalk
(203) 854-9960

V-E-T-S (Veterinary Emergency Treatment Services)
8 Enterprise Ln., Oakdale
(860) 444-8870

Animal Emergency Hospital of Central Connecticut
588 Cromwell Ave., Rocky Hill
(860) 563-4447

Cornell University Veterinary Specialists
880 Canal St., Stamford
(203) 595-2777

Shoreline Animal Emergency Clinic
7365 Main St., Stratford
(203) 375-6500

Connecticut Veterinary Center
470 Oakwood Ave., West Hartford
(860) 233-8564

DELAWARE
VCA Newark Animal Hospital
1360 Marrows Rd., Newark
(302) 737-8100

Veterinary Emergency Center of Delaware
1212 E. Newport Pike, Wilmington
(302) 691-3647

Windcrest Animal Emergency Hospital
3705 Lancaster Pike, Wilmington
(302) 998-2995

DISTRICT OF COLUMBIA
Friendship Hospital for Animals
4105 Brandywine St., Washington
(202) 363-7300

FLORIDA
Calusa Veterinary Center
6900 Congress Ave., Boca Raton
(561) 999-3000

Southwest Florida Veterinary Specialists
28400 Old 41 Rd., Suite 1, Bonita Springs
(239) 992-8387

PetPB Animal Emergency & Advanced Imaging
2246 N. Congress Ave., Boynton Beach
(561) 752-3232

Veterinary Emergency Center
3915 Cortez Rd. W., Bradenton
(941) 896-9420

Animal Emergency Clinic of Brandon
693 W. Lumsden Rd., Brandon
(813) 684-3013

Animal ER of SW Florida
1327 N.E. Pine Island Rd., Suite 110, Cape Coral
(239) 673-7426

Veterinary Emergency Clinic of Central Florida, Inc.
195 Concord Dr., Casselberry
(407) 644-4449

Animal Emergency and Critical Care Services of S. Florida
9410 Stirling Rd., Cooper City
(954) 432-5611

Coral Springs Animal Hospital
2160 N. University Dr., Coral Springs
(954) 753-1800

Doral Centre Animal Hospital
9400 N.W. 58th St., Doral
(305) 598-1234

Florida Veterinary Referral Center & 24 Hour Emergency & Critical Care
9220 Estero Park Commons Blvd., Suite 7, Estero
(239) 992-8878

Animal Emergency Trauma Center
2200 W. Oakland Park Blvd., Fort Lauderdale
(954) 731-4228

Emergency Veterinary Clinic, Inc.
2045 Collier Ave., Fort Myers
(239) 939-5542

Animal Emergency and Referral Center
3984 S. US 1, Fort Pierce
(772) 466-3441

Affiliated Pet Emergency Services
7314 W. University Ave., Gainesville
(352) 373-4444

Hollywood Animal Hospital
2864 Hollywood Blvd., Hollywood
(954) 920-3556

Affiliated Veterinary Emergency Center
3444 Southside Blvd., Suite 101, Jacksonville
(904) 642-5911

Emergency Pet Care, LLC
14185 Beach Blvd., Suite 7, Jacksonville
(904) 223-8000

Emergency Pet Care of Jupiter
300 Central Blvd., Jupiter
(561) 746-0555

Tampa Bay Veterinary Emergency Service
1501 S. Belcher Rd., Suite 1A, Largo
(727) 531-5752

Veterinary Emergency Clinic of Central Florida - Lake County
33040 Professional Dr., Leesburg
(352) 728-4440

Animal Emergency and Critical Care Center of Brevard
2281 W. Eau Gallie Blvd., Melbourne
(321) 725-5365

AEC-Animal Emergency Clinic South
8429 S.W. 132nd St., Miami
(305) 251-2096

Knowles Animal Clinic - Snapper Creek Emergency Clinic
9933 Sunset Dr., Miami
(305) 279-2323

Miami Pet Emergency
11774 N. Kendall Dr., Miami
(305) 273-8100

Miami Veterinary Specialists
8601 Sunset Dr., Miami
(305) 665-2820

The Pet Emergency Room
6394 S. Dixie Hwy., Miami
(305) 666-4142

Animal Specialty Hospital of Florida (ASH)
10130 Market St., Suite 1, Naples
(239) 263-0480

Emergency Pet Hospital of Collier Co.
6530 Dudley Dr., Naples
(941) 263-8010

Ocala Animal Emergency Hospital
1815 N.E. Jacksonville Rd., Ocala
(352) 840-0044

Clay-Duval Pet Emergency Clinic
275 Corporate Way, Suite 200, Orange Park
(904) 264-8281

Veterinary Emergency Clinic of Central Florida - South Facility
2080 Principal Row, Orlando
(407) 438-4449

Pet Emergency and Critical Care Clinic
3816 Northlake Blvd., Palm Beach Gardens
(561) 691-9999

AA Animal ER Center, LLC
36401 US 19N, Palm Harbor
(727) 787-5402

Animal Emergency & Urgent Care
30610 US 19N, Palm Harbor
(727) 786-5755

St. Francis Emergency Animal Hospital
6602 Pines Blvd., Pembroke Pines
(954) 962-0300

Veterinary Emergency Referral Center
4800 N. Davis Hwy., Pensacola
(850) 477-3914

The Veterinary Emergency Clinic
17829 Murdock Cir., Port Charlotte
(941) 255-5222

Animal Specialty and Emergency Hospital
5775 Schenck Ave., Rockledge
(321) 752-7600

Critical Care & Veterinary Specialists of Sarasota
4937 S. Tamiami Tr., Sarasota
(941) 929-1818

Sarasota Veterinary Emergency Hospital
7414 S. Tamiami Tr., Sarasota
(941) 923-7260

Animal Emergency Clinic of St. Petersburg
3165 22nd Ave. N., St. Petersburg
(727) 323-1311

Noah's Animal Hospital and 24 Hour Emergency
2050 62nd Ave. N., St. Petersburg
(727) 522-6640

Pet Emergency & Critical Care Clinic, Inc.
2239 S. Kanner Hwy., Stuart
(772) 781-3302

Allied Veterinary Emergency Hospital
2324 Centerville Rd., Tallahassee
(850) 222-0123

FVS (Florida Veterinary Specialists)
3000 Busch Lake Blvd., Tampa
(813) 933-8944

Tampa Bay Veterinary Emergency Service
238 E. Bearss Ave., Tampa
(813) 265-4043

Animal E.R.
8237 Cooper Creek Blvd., University Park
(941) 355-2884

Animal Emergency Clinic
3425 Forest Hill Blvd., West Palm Beach
(561) 433-2244

Palm Beach Veterinary Specialists
3884 Forest Hill Blvd., West Palm Beach
(561) 434-5700

VCA Cabrera Animal Hospital
6390 S.W. 8th St., West Miami
(305) 261-2374

GEORGIA

All Pets Emergency and Referral Center, P.C.
6460 Hwy. 9N, Alpharetta
(678) 366-2125

University of Georgia Veterinary Teaching Hospital
Carlton St., Athens
(706) 542-3221

Animal Emergency Center of Sandy Springs
228 Sandy Springs Pl. N.E., Atlanta
(404) 252-7881

Georgia Veterinary Specialists & Emergency Care
455 Abernathy Rd. N.E., Atlanta
(404) 459-0963

Brunswick Pet ER
208 Scranton Connector, Suite 122, Brunswick
(912) 275-8246

North Georgia Veterinary Specialists
1328 Buford Hwy., Building 200, Buford
(678) 835-3300

East Metro Animal Emergency Clinic, LLC
6225 Hwy. 278 N.W., Covington
(678) 212-0300

PetFirst 24 Hour Animal Hospital
4075 Pleasant Hill Rd., Duluth
(678) 745-1262

Southern Crescent Animal Emergency
1270 Hwy. 54 E., Fayetteville
(770) 460-8166

An-Emerge
275 Pearl Nix Pkwy., Suite 3, Gainesville
(770) 534-2911

Eastside Animal Medical Center
1835 Grayson Hwy., Grayson
(678) 958-5530

Animal Emergency Center of Gwinnett
1956 Lawrenceville-Suwanee Rd., Lawrenceville
(770) 277-3220

Cobb Emergency Veterinary Clinic
630 Cobb Pkwy. N., Suite C, Marietta
(770) 424-9157

Animal Emergency Center of North Fulton
900 Mansell Rd., Suite 19, Roswell
(770) 594-2266

Savannah Veterinary Emergency Clinic
317 Eisenhower Dr., Savannah
(912) 355-6113

DeKalb-Gwinnett Animal Emergency Clinic
6430 Lawrenceville Hwy., Tucker
(770) 491-0661

Cherokee Emergency Veterinary Clinic
7800 Hwy. 92, Woodstock
(678) 238-0700

HAWAII
Veterinary Emergency & Referral Center of Hawaii
1347 Kapiolani Blvd., Suite 103, Honolulu
(808) 735-7735

IDAHO
Mountain View Animal Hospital / Pet ER
3435 N. Cole Rd., Boise
(208) 375-0251

WestVet Animal Emergency Hospital & Specialty Center
5019 N. Sawyer Ave., Garden City
(208) 375-1600

Idaho Falls Veterinary Emergency Clinic
3151 McNeil Dr., Idaho Falls
(208) 552-0662

All Valley Animal Care Center
2326 E. Cinema Dr., Meridian
(208) 888-0818

WestVet Animal Emergency
3085 E. Magic View Dr., Suite. 110, Meridian
(208) 288-0400

North Idaho Pet Emergency
2700 E. Seltice Way, Suite 12, Post Falls
(208) 777-2707

ILLINOIS
Animal E.R. of Arlington Heights
1195 E. Palatine Rd., Arlington Heights
(847) 394-6049

VCA Aurora Animal Hospital
2600 W. Galena Blvd., Aurora
(630) 896-8541

Animal Emergency Clinic of McLean County
2505 E. Oakland Ave., Bloomington
(309) 665-5020

Veterinary Specialty Center
1515 Busch Pkwy., Buffalo Grove
(847) 459-7535

Animal Emergency Clinic of Champaign County
1713 S. State St., Unit 4, Champaign
(217) 359-1977

Chicago Veterinary Emergency & Specialty Center
3123 N. Clybourne Ave., Chicago
(773) 281-7110

Premier Veterinary Group - Chicago
3927 W. Belmont Ave., Chicago
(773) 516-5800

Animal Emergency Center
2005 Mall St., Collinsville
(618) 346-1898

Countryside Veterinary Center
9823 W. 55th St., Countryside
(708) 469-6050

Emergency Veterinary Care South Assoc.
13715 S. Cicero Ave., Crestwood
(708) 388-3771

Animal Emergency of McHenry County
1095 Pingree Rd., Suite 120, Crystal Lake
(815) 479-9119

Arboretum View Animal Hospital
2551 Warrenville Rd., Downers Grove
(630) 963-0424

Dundee Animal Hospital
199 Penny Ave., Dundee
(847) 428-6114

Elmhurst Animal Care Center
850 S. Riverside Dr., Elmhurst
(630) 530-1900

Midwest Animal Emergency Hospital
7510 W. North Ave., Elmwood Park
(708) 453-4755

VCA Franklin Park Animal Hospital
9846 W. Grand Ave., Franklin Park
(847) 455-4922

Hawthorne Animal Hospital
5 Cougar Dr., Glen Carbon
(618) 288-3971

Wheaton Animal Hospital
266 Roosevelt Rd., Glen Ellyn
(630) 665-1500

Animal Emergency & Treatment Center
1810 E. Belvidere Rd., Grayslake
(847) 548-5300

Emergency Veterinary Services
820 Ogden Ave., Lisle
(630) 960-2900

Animal Emergency of Mokena
19110 S. 88th Ave., Mokena
(708) 326-4800

Naperville Animal Hospital
1023 E. Ogden Ave., Naperville
(630) 355-5300

Springbrook Animal Care Center
2759 Forgue Dr., Naperville
(630) 428-0500

Animal Emergency Clinic of McLeon County
704-B S. Main St., Normal
(309) 454-8802

Animal Emergency & Critical Care Center
1810 Frontage Rd., Northbrook
(847) 564-5775

Tri-County Animal Emergency Clinic
1800 N. Sterling Ave., Peoria
(309) 672-1565

CARE Animal Emergency Services
14411 S. Rte. 59, Plainfield
(877) 859-7387

Animal Emergency Clinic of Rockford
4236 Maray Dr., Rockford
(815) 229-7791

Emergency Veterinary Services of St. Charles
530 Dunham Rd., St. Charles
(630) 584-7447

Animal 911
3735 W. Dempster St., Skokie
(847) 673-9110

Animal Emergency Clinic of Springfield
1333 W. Wabash Ave., Springfield
(617) 698-0870

ASPCA Animal Poison Control Center
1717 S. Philo Rd., Suite 36, Urbana
(217) 337-5030

University of Illinois College of Veterinary Medicine
1008 W. Hazelwood Dr., Urbana
(217) 333-5300

INDIANA
VCA Northwood Animal Hospital
3255 N. SR 9, Anderson
(765) 649-5218

St. Francis Family Pet Health Care
822 W. Plymouth St., Bremen
(574) 546-9005

Circle City Veterinary Specialty & Emergency Hospital
9650 Mayflower Park Dr., Carmel
(317) 872-8387

Northeast Indiana Veterinary Emergency & Specialty Hospital
5818 Maplecrest Rd., Fort Wayne
(260) 426-1062

Airport Animal Emergi-Center, P.C.
5235 W. Washington St., Indianapolis
(317) 248-0832

Animal Emergency Center of Indianapolis
8250 Bash St., Indianapolis
(317) 849-4925

Indianapolis Veterinary Emergency Center
5425 Victory Dr., Indianapolis
(317) 782-4484

Noah's Animal Hospital, P.C.
5510 Millersville Rd., Indianapolis
(317) 253-1327

VCA West 86th St. Animal Hospital
4030 W. 86st St., Indianapolis
(317) 872-0200

Animal Emergency Clinic of Tippecanoe County
1343 Sagamore Pkwy. N., Lafayette
(765) 449-2001

Animal Emergency Clinic
2324 Grape Rd., Mishawaka
(574) 259-8387

Lincolnway Veterinary Clinic, LLC
4043 Lincolnway E., Mishawaka
(574) 256-1871

Calumet Emergency Veterinary Clinic
216 W. Lincoln Hwy., Schererville
(219) 865-0970

IOWA
Iowa State University Veterinary Clinical Sciences Teaching Hospital
1600 S. 16th St., Ames
(515) 294-4900

Animal Emergency Center of the Quad Cities
1510 State St., Bettendorf
(563) 344-9599

Eastern Iowa Veterinary Specialty Center
755 Capital Dr. S.W., Cedar Rapids
(319) 841-5161

Animal Emergency & Referral Center of Central Iowa
6110 Creston Ave., Des Moines
(515) 280-3051

KANSAS
Kansas State University Vet. Med. Teaching Hospital
1800 Denison Ave., Manhattan
(785) 532-4100

VCA Mission Animal Referral & Emergency Center
5914 Johnson Dr., Mission
(913) 722-5566

BluePearl Veterinary Partners - Overland Park
11950 W. 110th St., Overland Park
(913) 642-9563

Central Kansas Veterinary Center
515 W. Blanchard Ave., South Hutchinson
(620) 663-8387

Emergency Animal Clinic of Topeka
839 S.W. Fairlawn Rd., Topeka
(785) 272-2926

Veterinary Emergency & Specialty Hospital of Wichita
727 S. Washington St., Wichita
(316) 262-5321

KENTUCKY
AA Small Animal Emergency Service
150 Dennis Dr., Lexington
(859) 276-2505

Bluegrass Veterinary Specialists & Animal Emergency
1591 Winchester Rd., Suite 106, Lexington
(859) 268-7604

Jefferson Animal Hospital & Regional Emergency Center
4504 Outer Loop, Louisville
(502) 966-4104

Louisville Veterinary Specialty & Emergency Services
13160 Magisterial Dr., Louisville
(502) 244-3036

Greater Cincinnati Veterinary Specialists & Emergency Services
11 Beacon Dr., Wilder
(859) 572-0560

LOUISIANA
Animal Emergency Clinic of Baton Rouge
7353 Jefferson Hwy., Baton Rouge
(225) 927-8800

Baton Rouge Pet Emergency Hospital
1514 Cottondale Dr., Baton Rouge
(225) 925-5566

Sherwood South Animal Emergency & Critical Care Care Center
3803 S. Sherwood Forest Blvd., Baton Rouge
(225) 293-6440

Louisiana Veterinary Referral Center
2611 Florida St., Mandeville
(985) 626-4862

Metairie Small Animal Hospital
101 Metairie Rd., Metairie
(504) 835-4266

Southeast Veterinary Emergency & Critical Care
3409 Division St., Metairie
(504) 219-0444

MAINE
Eastern Maine Emergency Veterinary Clinic
15 Dirigo Dr., Brewer
(207) 989-6267

Animal Emergency Clinic of Mid-Maine
37 Strawberry Ave., Lewiston
(207) 777-1110

Animal Emergency Clinic
739 Warren Ave., Portland
(207) 878-3121

Maine Veterinary Referral Center
1500 Technology Way, Scarborough
(207) 885-1290

MARYLAND
Anne Arundel Veterinary Emergency Clinic
808 Bestgate Rd., Annapolis
(410) 224-0331

Falls Road Animal Hospital
6314 Falls Rd., Baltimore
(410) 825-9100

Animal Emergency Hospital
807B Belair Rd., Bel Air
(410) 420-7297

Harford Emergency Veterinary Services
526 Underwood Ln., Bel Air
(410) 420-8000

Emergency Veterinary Clinic, Inc.
32 Mellor Ave., Catonsville
(410) 788-7042

Emergency Animal Hospital of Ellicott City
10270 Baltimore National Pike (US 40W), Ellicott City
(410) 750-1177

Crossroads Animal Referral and Emergency
1080 W. Patrick St., Frederick
(301) 662-2273

Frederick Emergency Animal Hospital
434 Prospect Blvd., Frederick
(301) 662-6622

VCA Veterinary Referral Associates
500 Perry Pkwy., Gaithersburg
(301) 926-3300, ext. 140

Mountain View Animal Emergency
17747 Virginia Ave., Hagerstown
(301) 733-7339

Rocky Gorge Animal Hospital
7515 Brooklyn Bridge Rd., Laurel
(301) 776-7744

Metropolitan Emergency Animal Clinic
12106 Nebel St., Rockville
(301) 770-5226

Pets ER
329 Tilghman Rd., Suite 100, Salisbury
(410) 543-8400

PET ER
1209 Cromwell Bridge Rd., Towson
(410) 252-8387

Southern Maryland Veterinary Referral Center
3485 Rockefeller Ct., Waldorf
(301) 638-0988

Central Carroll Animal Emergency
1030 Baltimore Blvd., Suite 180, Westminster
(410) 871-9001

Westminster Veterinary Hospital & Emergency / Trauma Center
269 W. Main St., Westminster
(410) 848-3363

MASSACHUSETTS
Animal Emergency Care
164 Great Rd., Acton
(978) 263-1742

Angell Memorial Animal Hospital
350 S. Huntington Ave., Boston
(617) 522-7282

Cape Cod Veterinary Specialists Emergency Service
230 Main St., Buzzards Bay
(508) 759-5125

Wignall Animal Hospital
1837 Bridge St., Dracut
(978) 454-8272

Fall River Animal Hospital, Inc.
33 18th St., Fall River
(508) 675-6374

MetroWest Veterinary Referral Hospital
5 Strathmore Rd., Natick
(508) 319-2117

Essex County Veterinary Emergency Hospital
247 Chickering Rd., North Andover
(978) 725-5544

Tufts University School of Veterinary Medicine
200 Westboro Rd., North Grafton
(508) 839-7826

Animal ER
1634 W. Housatonic St., Pittsfield
(413) 997-3425

Veterinary Emergency & Specialty Hospital
141 Greenfield Rd., South Deerfield
(413) 665-4911

Cape Cod Veterinary Specialists, Inc.
79 Theophilus Smith Rd., South Dennis
(508) 398-7575

VCA South Shore Animal Hospital
595 Columbian St., South Weymouth
(781) 337-6622

Angell Animal Medical Center - Western New England
171 Union St., Springfield
(413) 785-1221

Boston Road Animal Hospital
1235 Boston Rd., Springfield
(413) 783-1203

Mass-RI Veterinary ER
477 Milford Rd., Swansea
(508) 730-1112

BluePearl Veterinary Partners - Waltham
180 Bear Hill Rd., Waltham
(781) 684-8387

New England Animal Medical Center
595 W. Center St., West Bridgewater
(508) 580-2515

Wachusett Animal Hospital
29 Theodore Dr., Westminster
(978) 874-4100

Massachusetts Veterinary Referral Hospital
20 Cabot Rd., Woburn
(781) 932-5802

Woburn Animal Hospital
373 Russell St., Woburn
(718) 933-0170

MICHIGAN
Affiliated Veterinary Emergency Service, P.C.
15220 Southfield Rd., Allen Park
(313) 389-1700

Animal Emergency Clinic
4126 Packard Rd., Ann Arbor
(734) 971-8774

Ann Arbor Animal Hospital
2150 W. Liberty St., Ann Arbor
(734) 662-4474

Emergency Veterinary Hospital
5245 Jackson Rd., Ann Arbor
(734) 369-6446

Michigan Veterinary Specialists
3412 E. Walton Blvd., Auburn Hills
(248) 371-3713

Oakland Veterinary Emergency
1400 Telegraph Rd., Bloomfield Hills
(248) 334-6877

Oakland Veterinary Emergency Group
1948 Telegraph Rd., Bloomfield Hills
(248) 334-1555

Advanced Animal Emergency
43731 Gratiot, Clinton Township
(586) 466-6133

Animal ER Center
1120 Welch Rd., Commerce
(248) 960-7200

Veterinary Emergency Service - West
24400 Ford Rd., Dearborn Heights
(313) 274-3300

Michigan State University Veterinary Teaching Hospital
736 Wilson Rd., East Lansing
(517) 353-5420

Animal Emergency Hospital
1007 S. Ballenger Hwy., Flint
(810) 238-7557

Animal Emergency Hospital
3260 Plainfield Ave. N.E., Grand Rapids
(616) 361-9911

Michigan Veterinary Specialists
1425 Michigan St. N.E., Suite F, Grand Rapids
(616) 284-5300

Southwest Michigan Animal Emergency Hospital
3301 S. Burdick St., Kalamazoo
(616) 381-5228

Lansing Veterinary Urgent Care
3276 E. Jolly Rd., Lansing
(517) 393-9200

Animal Emergency Hospital of Macomb
45245 Romeo Plank Rd., Macomb
(586) 307-3730

Veterinary Emergency Service East
28223 John R Rd., Madison Heights
(248) 547-4677

Veterinary Care Specialists
205 Rowe Rd., Milford
(248) 684-0468

Animal Emergency Center
24360 Novi Rd., Novi
(248) 348-1788

Veterinary Emergency Service West
40850 Ann Arbor Rd., Plymouth
(734) 207-8500

Animal Emergency Center
265 E. 2nd St., Rochester
(248) 651-1788

Great Lakes Pet Emergencies
1221 Tittabawassee Rd., Saginaw
(989) 752-1960

BluePearl - Southfield
29080 Inkster Rd., Southfield
(248) 354-6660

MINNESOTA
South Metro Animal Emergency Care
14690 Pennock Ave., Apple Valley
(952) 953-3737

Affiliated Emergency Veterinary Service
11850 Aberdeen St. N.E., Blaine
(763) 754-5000

Affiliated Emergency Veterinary Hospital
1615 Coon Rapids Blvd., Coon Rapids
(763) 754-9434

Affiliated Emergency Veterinary Service
2314 W. Michigan St., Duluth
(218) 302-8000

Affiliated Emergency Veterinary Service
7717 Flying Cloud Dr., Eden Prairie
(952) 942-8272

Affiliated Emergency Veterinary Service
4708 Hwy. 55, Golden Valley
(763) 529-6560

Animal Emergency Clinic
1163 Helmo Ave. N., Oakdale
(651) 501-3766

Affiliated Emergency Veterinary Service
121 23rd Ave. S.W., Rochester
(507) 424-3976

Affiliated Emergency Veterinary Service
4180 Thielman Ln., Suite 120, St. Cloud
(320) 258-3481

Animal Emergency Clinic
301 University Ave., St. Paul
(651) 293-1800

University of Minnesota College of Veterinary Medicine - Veterinary Medical Center
1365 Gortner Ave., St. Paul
(612) 626-8387

MISSISSIPPI
Gulf Coast Veterinary Emergency Hospital
13095 Hwy. 67, Biloxi
(228) 392-7474

MISSOURI
Animal Emergency Clinic
7095 Metropolitan Blvd., Suite G, Barnhart
(636) 464-2846

Animal Emergency Clinic
12501 Natural Bridge Rd., Bridgeton
(314) 739-1500

University of Missouri - Veterinary Med. Teaching Hospital
900 E. Campus Dr., Columbia
(573) 882-7821

Animal Emergency Center
8141 N. Oak Trfy., Kansas City
(816) 455-5430

Animal Emergency & Referral Hospital
3495 N.E. Ralph Powell Rd., Lee's Summit
(816) 554-4990

VSS Emergency Center
1021 Howard George Dr., Manchester
(636) 227-6100

Animal Emergency Clinic
334 Fort Zumwalt Sq., O'Fallon
(636) 240-5496

Animal Emergency Clinic
9937 Big Bend Blvd., St. Louis
(314) 822-7600

Animal Emergency Center Inc.
3257 E. Outer Rd., Scott City
(573) 334-3400

Emergency Veterinary Clinic of Southwest Missouri
400 S. Glenstone Ave., Springfield
(417) 890-1600

Animal Emergency & Referral Center
16457 Village Plaza View Dr., Wildwood
(636) 458-1777

MONTANA
Pet Emergency Center
1914 S. Reserve St., Missoula
(406) 829-9300

NEBRASKA
United Vet Emergency Treatment Services
3700 S. 9th St., Lincoln
(402) 489-6800

Animal Emergency Clinic
9664 Mockingbird Dr., Omaha
(402) 339-6232

NEVADA
Animal Emergency Center of Las Vegas
3340 E. Patrick Ln., Las Vegas
(702) 457-8050

Las Vegas Animal Emergency Hospital
5231 W. Charleston Blvd., Las Vegas
(702) 822-1045

Veterinary Emergency and Critical Care Center
8650 W. Tropicana Ave., Suite B-104, Las Vegas
(702) 262-7070

Warm Springs Veterinary Emergency Clinic
2500 W. Warm Springs Rd., Las Vegas
(702) 614-5454

Animal Emergency Center of Reno
6425 S. Virginia St., Reno
(775) 851-3600

NEW HAMPSHIRE
Capital Area Veterinary Emergency Service
1 Intervale Rd., Concord
(603) 227-1199

Small Animal Veterinary Emergency Service
63 Evans Dr., Lebanon
(603) 306-0007

Veterinary Emergency Center of Manchester
336 Abby Rd., Manchester
(603) 666-6677

Meredith Place Veterinary Emergency Hospital
8 Maple St., Suite 2, Meredith
(603) 279-1117

Animal Hospital of Nashua
168 Main Dunstable Rd., Nashua
(603) 880-3034

Veterinary Emergency, Critical Care & Referral Center
15 Piscataqua Dr., Newington
(603) 431-3600

Port City Veterinary Referral Hospital
215 Commerce Way, Suite 100, Portsmouth
(603) 433-0056

Rockingham Emergency Veterinary Hospital
3 Cobbetts Pond Rd., Windham
(603) 870-9770

NEW JERSEY
Ocean View Veterinary Hospital
2033 Rt. 9, Cape May Court House
(609) 486-5025

Garden State Veterinary Specialists
643 Rt. 27, Iselin
(732) 283-3535

Jersey Shore Veterinary Emergency Service
1000 Rt. 70, Lakewood
(732) 363-3200

Crown Veterinary Specialists
23 Blossom Hill Rd., Lebanon
(908) 236-4120

Red Bank Veterinary Hospital Linwood
535 Maple Ave., Linwood
(609) 926-5300

North Jersey Veterinary Emergency Services, LLC
724 Ridge Rd., Lyndhurst
(201) 438-7122

Animal Emergency Service of South Jersey
220 Mount Laurel Rd., Mount Laurel
(856) 727-1332

Newton Veterinary Hospital
116 Hampton House Rd., Newton
(973) 383-4321

Oradell Animal Hospital
580 Winters Ave., Paramus
(201) 262-0010

Alliance Emergency Veterinary Clinic
540 Rt. 10 W., Randolph
(973) 328-2844

Animerge
21 Rt. 206 N., Raritan
(908) 707-9077

NorthStar VETS
315 Robbinsville-Allentown Rd., Robbinsville
(609) 259-8300

Garden State Veterinary Specialists
1 Pine St., Tinton Falls
(732) 922-0011

Red Bank Veterinary Hospital
197 Hance Ave., Tinton Falls
(732) 747-3636

Animal Emergency and Referral Center
647 Bloomfield Ave., West Caldwell
(973) 226-3282

NEW MEXICO
Staley's Veterinary Medical Clinic
1407 Indian Wells Rd., Alamogordo
(505) 437-3063

Veterinary Emergency & Specialty Center of New Mexico
4000 Montgomery Blvd. N.E., Albuquerque
(505) 884-3433

ABQ Petcare Hospital
9032 Montgomery Blvd. N.E., Albuquerque
(505) 299-8387

Veterinary Emergency & Specialty Center of Santa Fe
2001 Vivigen Way, Santa Fe
(505) 984-0625

NEW YORK
Greater Buffalo Veterinary Emergency Services
4949 Main St., Amherst
(716) 839-4044

Veterinary Emergency & Critical Care Center
2115 Downer Street Rd., Baldwinsville
(315) 638-3500

Katonah Bedford Veterinary Center
546 N. Bedford Rd., Bedford Hills
(914) 241-7700

Atlantic Coast Veterinary Specialists
3250 Veterans Memorial Hwy., Bohemia
(631) 285-7780

Veterinary Emergency & Referral Group
318 Warren St., Brooklyn
(718) 522-9400

Animal Emergency Service
6230-C Jericho Tpke., Commack
(631) 462-6044

Veterinary Medical Center of Central New York
5841 Bridge St., Suite 200, East Syracuse
(315) 446-7933

New York Veterinary Specialty / Animal Emergency Services
2233 Broadhollow Rd., Farmingdale
(631) 694-3400

Natural Vet For Pets, P.C.
585 Warburton Ave., Hastings-on-Hudson
(914) 478-4100

Animal Emergency Clinic of the Hudson Valley
1112 Morton Blvd., Kingston
(845) 336-0713

Capital District Animal Emergency Clinic
222 Troy Schenectady Rd., Latham
(518) 785-1094

Orange County Animal Emergency Service
517 Rt. 211 E., Middletown
(845) 692-0260

Central Vets Mineola
220 E. Jericho Tpke., Mineola
(516) 294-6680

Flannery Animal Hospital
789 Little Britain Rd., New Windsor
(845) 565-7387

BluePearl - Manhattan
410 W. 55th St., New York
(212) 767-0099

Fifth Avenue Veterinary Specialists
1 W. 15th St., New York
(212) 924-3311

Manhattan Veterinary Group
240 E. 80th St., New York
(212) 988-1000

Orchard Park Veterinary Medical Center
3930 N. Buffalo Rd., Orchard Park
(716) 662-6660

Long Island Veterinary Specialists / Animal Emergency & Critical Care Center
163 S. Service Rd., Plainview
(516) 501-1700

Animal Emergency Clinic of Hudson Valley
84 Patrick Ln., Poughkeepsie
(845) 471-8242

East End Veterinary Emergency Center
67 Commerce Dr., Riverhead
(631) 369-4513

Animal Hospital of Pittsford
2816 Monroe Ave., Rochester
(716) 271-7700

Veterinary Specialists & Emergency Service
825 White Spruce Blvd., Rochester
(585) 424-1277

Animal Hospital of the Rockaways
114-10 Beach Channel Dr., Rockaway Park
(718) 474-0500

Animal Emergency Service
280-L Middle Country Rd., Selden
(631) 698-2225

Valley Cottage Animal Hospital
202 Rt. 303, Valley Cottage
(845) 268-9263

Central Veterinary Associates
73 W. Merrick Rd., Valley Stream
(516) 825-3066

Veterinary Referral & Emergency Center of Westbury
609-5 Cantiague Rock Rd., Westbury
(516) 420-0000

Nassau Animal Emergency Hospital
740 Old Country Rd., Westbury
(516) 333-6262

The Veterinary Emergency Group
193 Tarrytown Rd., White Plains
(914) 949-8779

Animal Specialty Center
9 Odell Plaza, Yonkers
(914) 457-4000

NORTH CAROLINA

Small Animal Emergency Services
1335 N. Sandhills Blvd., Aberdeen
(910) 944-0405

Regional Emergency Animal Care Hospital (REACH)
677 Brevard Rd., Asheville
(828) 665-4399

Animal Emergency Clinic of the High Country, PLLC
1126 Blowing Rock Rd., Suite A, Boone
(828) 268-2833

Animal Emergency Clinic of Cary
220 High House Rd., Cary
(919) 462-8989

Veterinary Specialty Hospital of the Carolinas
6405 Tryon Rd., Cary
(919) 233-4911

Animal Medical Hospital
3832 Monroe Rd., Charlotte
(704) 334-4684

Carolina Veterinary Specialists - Animal Emergency and Trauma Center
2225 Township Rd., Charlotte
(704) 504-9608

Triangle Veterinary Referral Hospital
608 Morreene Rd., Durham
(919) 489-0615

After Hours Veterinary Emergency Clinic
5505 W. Friendly Ave., Greensboro
(336) 851-1990

Carolina Veterinary Specialists - Animal Emergency & Trauma Center
501 Nicholas Rd., Greensboro
(336) 632-0605

Happy Tails Veterinary Emergency Clinic
2936 Battleground Ave., Greensboro
(336) 288-2688

Pet Emergency Clinic of Pitt County
2207-A Evans St., Greenville
(252) 321-1521

Veterinary Referral Hospital of Hickory
126 Hwy. 321 S.W., Hickory
(828) 328-2660

Triangle Veterinary Referral Hospital of Holly Springs
2120 Werrington Dr., Suite 201, Holly Springs
(919) 973-5620

Carolina Veterinary Specialists - Animal Emergency Center
12117 Statesville Rd., Huntersville
(704) 949-1100

Cabarrus Emergency Veterinary Clinic
1317 S. Cannon Blvd., Kannapolis
(704) 932-1182

Charlotte Veterinary Emergency & Trauma Services
2440 Plantation Center Dr., Matthews
(704) 844-6440

Carolina Veterinary Specialists - Matthews
4099 Campus Ridge Rd., Matthews
(704) 815-3939

After Hours Animal Emergency Clinic
409 Vick Ave., Raleigh
(919) 781-5145

North Carolina State University Small Animal Emergency Service
4700 Hillsborough St., Raleigh
(919) 513-6130

Quail Corners Animal Hospital & 24 Hour Emergency Care
1613 E. Millbrook Rd., Raleigh
(919) 876-0739

Thomasville Veterinary Hospital, P.A.
303 National Hwy., Thomasville
(336) 475-9119

Eastern Carolina Veterinary Emergency Treatment Service
4935 Raleigh Rd. Pkwy. W., Wilson
(252) 265-9920

Animal Emergency Services of Forsyth County
7781 North Point Blvd., Winston-Salem
(336) 377-2866

Carolina Veterinary Specialists - Animal Emergency & Trauma Center
1600 Hanes Mall Blvd., Winston-Salem
336-896-0902

NORTH DAKOTA
Red River Animal Emergency Clinic
1401 Oak Manor Ave. S., Suite 2, Fargo
701-478-9299

OHIO
Akron Veterinary Referral & Emergency Center
1321 Centerview Cir., Akron
(330) 665-4996

Animal Emergency Clinic West
2101 N. Cleveland-Massillon Rd., Akron
(216) 362-6001

Metropolitan Veterinary Hospital
1053 S. Cleveland-Massillon Rd., Akron
(330) 666-2976

VCA Great Lakes Veterinary Specialists
4760 Richmond Rd., Bedford Heights
(216) 831-6789

Stark County Veterinary Emergency Clinic, LLC
2705 Fulton Dr. N.W., Canton
(330) 452-5117

CARE Center
6995 E. Kemper Rd., Cincinnati
(513) 530-0911

Capital Veterinary Referral & Emergency Center
5230 Renner Rd., Columbus
(614) 870-0480

Ohio State University Veterinary Medical Center
601 Vernon Tharp St., Columbus
(614) 292-3551

Dayton Care Center
6405 Clyo Rd., Dayton
(937) 428-0911

Dayton Emergency Veterinary Clinic
2714 Springboro W., Dayton
(937) 293-2714

Ohio State University Veterinary Medical Center at Dublin
5020 Bradenton Ave., Dublin
(614) 889-8069

After Hours Animal Emergency Clinic, Inc.
2680 W. Liberty St., Girard
(330) 530-8387

Animal Emergency & Specialty Center
5152 Grove Ave., Lorain
(440) 240-1400

Aaron Animal Clinic and Emergency Hospital
7640 Broadview Rd., Parma
(216) 901-9980

Animal Emergency & Critical Care Center of Toledo, Inc.
2785 W. Central Ave., Toledo
(419) 473-0328

Green Animal Medical Center
1620 Corporate Woods Cir., Uniontown
(330) 896-4040

Cleveland Road Animal Hospital
2752 Cleveland Rd., Wooster
(330) 345-6063

MedVet Associates, Ltd.
300 E. Wilson Bridge Rd., Worthington
(614) 846-5800

OKLAHOMA
Animal Emergency Center
2121 McKown Dr., Norman
(405) 360-7828

Animal Emergency Center
931 S.W. 74th St., Oklahoma City
(405) 631-7828

Neel Veterinary Hospital
2700 N. MacArthur Blvd., Oklahoma City
(405) 947-8387

Veterinary Emergency and Critical Care Hospital
1800 W. Memorial Rd., Oklahoma City
(405) 749-6989

Animal Emergency Center, Inc.
4055 S. 102nd E. Ave., Tulsa
(918) 665-0508

OREGON

Animal Emergency Center of Central Oregon
1245 S.E. 3rd St., Suite C3, Bend
(541) 385-9110

Northwest Veterinary Specialists Emergency Service
16756 S.E. 82nd Dr., Clackamas
(503) 656-3999

Southern Oregon Veterinary Specialty Center
3265 Biddle Rd., Medford
(541) 282-7711

Dove Lewis Emergency Animal Hospital
1945 N.W. Pettygrove St., Portland
(503) 228-7281

VCA Southeast Portland Animal Hospital
13830 S.E. Stark St., Portland
(503) 255-8139

Salem Veterinary Emergency Clinic
3215 Market St. N.E., Salem
(503) 588-8082

Emergency Veterinary Hospital
103 W. Q St., Springfield
(541) 746-0112

Emergency Veterinary Clinic of Tualatin
19314 S.W. Mohave Ct., Tualatin
(503) 691-7922

PENNSYLVANIA

Veterinary Referral and Emergency Center
318 Northern Blvd., Clarks Summit
(570) 587-7777

Northwest Pennsylvania Pet Emergency Center
429 W. 38th St., Erie
(814) 866-5920

Keystone Veterinary Emergency and Referral
1200 W. Chester Pike, Havertown
(484) 454-5412

Center for Animal Referral and Emergency Services
2010 Cabot Blvd. W., Suite D, Langhorne
(215) 750-2774

Gwynedd Veterinary Hospital and Emergency Service
1615 W. Point Pike, Lansdale
(215) 699-9294

Veterinary Specialty & Emergency Center
301 Veterans Hwy., Levittown
(215) 750-7884

Allegheny Veterinary Emergency Trauma & Specialty
4224 Northern Pike, Monroeville
(412) 373-4200

University of Pennsylvania - Ryan Veterinary Hospital
3900 Spruce St., Philadelphia
(215) 746-8911

VCA Castle Shannon Animal Hospital Service
3610 Library Rd., Pittsburgh
(412) 885-2500

Veterinary Emergency Clinic
882 Butler St., Pittsburgh
(412) 492-9855

Hickory Veterinary Hospital
2303 Hickory Rd., Plymouth Meeting
(610) 828-3054

Creature Comforts Veterinary Service
Old Rt. 115, Saylorsburg
(570) 992-0400

Central Pennsylvania Veterinary Emergency Treatment Services
1522 Martin St., State College
(814) 237-4670

Bucks County Veterinary Emergency Trauma Service
978 Easton Rd., Warrington
(215) 918-2200

Animal Emergency Center
395 Susquehanna Tr., Watsontown
(570) 742-7400

Valley Central Emergency Veterinary Hospital
210 Fullerton Ave., Whitehall
(610) 435-5588

Animal Emergency & Referral Center of York
1640 S. Queen St., York
(717) 767-5355

RHODE ISLAND
Ocean State Veterinary Specialists
1480 S. County Tr., East Greenwich
(401) 886-6787

SOUTH CAROLINA
Charleston Veterinary Referral Center
3484 Shelby Ray Ct., Charleston
(843) 614-8387

Palmetto Regional Emergency Hospital for Animals
10298 Two Notch Rd., Columbia
(803) 865-1418

South Carolina Veterinary Emergency Care
3924 Fernandina Rd., Columbia
(803) 798-3837

Animal Emergency Clinic
393 Woods Lake Rd., Greenville
(864) 232-1878

Mt. Pleasant Emergency Veterinary Hospital
930B Pine Hollow Rd., Mt. Pleasant
(843) 216-7554

Animal Emergency Hospital of the Strand
303 Hwy. 15, Suite 1, Myrtle Beach
(843) 445-9797

Veterinary Specialty Care - North Charleston
3163 W. Montague Ave., North Charleston
(843) 744-3372

Care Animal Regional Emergency Clinic of Spartanburg
121 S. Blackstock Rd., Spartanburg
(864) 591-1923

SOUTH DAKOTA
Veterinary Emergency Hospital
3508 S. Minnesota Ave., Suite 104, Sioux Falls
(605) 977-6200

TENNESSEE

Midland Pet Emergency Center, Inc.
235 Calderwood St., Alcoa
(865) 982-1007

Airport Pet Emergency Clinic
2436 Hwy. 75, Blountville
(423) 279-0574

Affiliated Veterinary Specialists
1668 Mallory Ln., Brentwood
(615) 333-1212

Animal Emergency Clinic of Maury County, LLC
1900 Shady Brook St., Suite B, Columbia
(931) 380-1929

PetMed Emergency Center, LLC
830 N. Germantown Pkwy., Suite 105, Cordova
(901) 624-9002

Jackson Pet Emergency Clinic, LLC
2815-D N. Highland, Jackson
(731) 660-4343

Knoxville Pet Emergency Clinic
1819 Ailor Ave., Knoxville
(865) 637-0114

University of Tennessee Veterinary Teaching Hospital
2407 River Dr., Knoxville
(865) 974-8387

Animal Medical Center
234 River Rock Blvd., Murfreesboro
(615) 867-7575

Nashville Pet Emergency Clinic
2000 12th Ave. S., Nashville
(615) 383-2600

Nashville Veterinary Specialists
2971 Sidco Dr., Nashville
(615) 386-0107

TEXAS

I-20 Animal Medical Center
5820 W. I-20, Arlington
(817) 478-9238

AM/PM Animal Hospital
2239 S. Lamar Blvd., Austin
(512) 448-2676

Austin Vet Care - Central
4106 N. Lamar Blvd., Austin
(512) 459-4336

Emergency Animal Hospital of Northwest Austin
12034 Research Blvd., Suite 8, Austin
(512) 331-6121

Emergency Animal Hospital of Northwest Austin - South Branch
4434 Frontier Tr., Austin
(512) 899-0955

White Angel Animal Hospital
1901 RR 620 N., Austin
(512) 266-7838

Southeast Texas Animal Emergency Clinic
3420 W. Cardinal Dr., Beaumont
(409) 842-3239

Burleson Animal Emergency Hospital
805 N.E. Alsbury Blvd., Burleson
(817) 447-9194

North Texas Emergency Pet Clinic
1712 W. Frankford Rd., Suite 108, Carrolton
(972) 323-1310

Texas A&M University Veterinary Teaching Hospital
4475 TAMU, College Station
(979) 845-3541

Heritage Veterinary Hospital
3930 Glade Rd., Suite 120, Colleyville
(817) 358-0404

Emergency Animal Clinic
12101 Greenville Ave., Suite 118, Dallas
(972) 994-9110

The E-Clinic, Inc.
3337 Fitzhugh Ave., Dallas
(214) 520-8388

Veterinary Referral Center of East Dallas
4651 N. Beltline Rd., Dallas
(214) 763-4243

Grayson County Animal Emergency Clinic
3301 Woodlawn Blvd., Denison
(903) 337-0898

Denton County Animal Emergency Room
4145 S. I-35E, Suite 101, Denton
(940) 271-1200

El Paso Animal Emergency Center
1220 Airway Blvd., El Paso
(915) 203-0818

Airport Freeway Animal Emergency Clinic
411 N. Main St., Euless
(817) 571-2088

DFW North Emergency Veterinary Clinic
2311 Cross Timbers, Suite 319, Flower Mound
(469) 464-2964

Metro West Emergency Veterinary Center
3201 Hulen St., Fort Worth
(817) 731-3734

The Animal Emergency Hospital of North Texas
2700 W. Hwy. 114, Grapevine
(817) 410-2273

Animal Emergency Center of West Houston
4823 Hwy. 6N, Houston
(832) 593-8387

Animal Emergency Clinic SH 249
18707 SH 249, Houston
(281) 890-8875

Animal Emergency Clinic Southeast
10331 Gulf Frwy., Houston
(713) 941-8460

Gulf Coast Veterinary Specialists
1111 W. Loop S., Houston
(713) 693-1111

Houston Veterinary Services, Inc.
111 West Loop S., Suite 200, Houston
(713) 693-1100

Veterinary Emergency Referral Group, Inc.
8921 Katy Frwy., Houston
(713) 932-9589

Animal Emergency Clinic North East
10205 Birchridge Dr., Humble
(281) 446-4900

Metroplex Animal Hospital & Pet Lodge
700 W. Airport Frwy., Irving
(972) 438-7113

All Pets Animal Hospital & 24-Hour Emergency Service
24221 Kingsland Blvd., Katy
(281) 392-7387

After Hours Veterinary Services
2501 S. W.S. Young, Suite 413, Killeen
(254) 628-5017

VCA Animal Emergency Hospital Southeast Calder Road
1108 Gulf Frwy. S., Suite 280, League City
(281) 332-1678

Animal Emergency Hospital of Mansfield
301 N. Hwy. 287, Mansfield
(817) 473-7838

Pet Doctor 911 Animal Medical Center
7017 N. 10th St., McAllen
(956) 683-7387

Lake Ray Hubbard Emergency Pet Care Center
4651 N. Belt Line Rd., Mesquite
(972) 226-3377

Pearland 288 Animal Emergency Clinic
10100 Broadway St., Suite 102, Pearland
(713) 482-4592

Emergency Pet Care of Round Rock
301 Chisholm Tr., Round Rock
(512) 961-5200

Angel of Mercy Animal Critical Care, Inc.
8734 Grissom Rd., San Antonio
(210) 684-2105

Animal Emergency Room
4315 Fredericksburg Rd., Suite 2, San Antonio
(210) 737-7380

Emergency Pet Center
8503 Broadway St., Suite 105, San Antonio
(210) 822-2873

Mission Pet Emergency
8202 N. Loop 1604 W., San Antonio
(210) 691-0900

Northeast Emergency Animal Clinic
8365 Perrin Beitel, San Antonio
(210) 650-3141

Veterinary Referral and Emergency Center of South Texas
503 E. Sonterra Blvd., San Antonio
(210) 404-2873

Animal Emergency Clinic - Sugar Land
9920 Hwy. 90A, Suite 100C, Sugar Land
(281) 340-8387

Southwest Freeway Animal Hospital & Emergency Center
15575 Southwest Frwy., Sugar Land
(281) 491-8387

Sugar Land Veterinary Specialists and Emergency Center
1515 Lake Pointe Pkwy., Sugar Land
(281) 491-7800

Texas Animal Medical Center
4900 Steinbeck Bend, Waco
(254) 753-0901

Animal Emergency & Urgent Care Center of the Woodlands
27870 I-45 N., The Woodlands
(281) 367-5444

UTAH
Utah Veterinary Center
308 W. 7200 S., Midvale
(801) 871-0600

Central Emergency Animal Hospital
55 E. Miller Ave., Salt Lake City
(801) 487-1325

Pet E.R. - The Pet Emergency Room
6360 S. Highland Dr., Salt Lake City
(801) 278-3367

Animal Emergency Center
2465 N. Main St., Suite 5, Sunset
(801) 776-8118

VERMONT
Burlington Emergency & Veterinary Specialists
200 Commerce St., Williston
(802) 863-2387

VIRGINIA
Alexandria Veterinary Emergency Service
2660 Duke St., Alexandria
(703) 823-3601

Greenbrier Emergency Animal Hospital
370 Greenbrier Dr., Suite A2, Charlottesville
(434) 202-1616

Veterinary Emergency Treatment Services & Specialty
1540 Airport Rd., Charlottesville
(434) 973-3519

Greenbrier Veterinary Emergency Center
1100 Eden Way N., Suite 101B, Chesapeake
(757) 366-9000

SouthPaws Veterinary Referral Center
8500 Arlington Blvd., Fairfax
(703) 752-9100

Fredericksburg Regional Veterinary Emergency Center, LLC
2301 1/2 Jefferson Davis Hwy., Fredericksburg
(540) 372-3470

Animal Emergency Critical Care Associates
165 Fort Evans Rd. N.E., Leesburg
(703) 777-5755

Animal Emergency & Critical Care of Lynchburg
3432 Odd Fellows Rd., Lynchburg
(434) 846-1504

Veterinary Referral & Critical Care
1596 Hockett Rd., Manakin Sabot
(804) 784-8722

Prince William Emergency Veterinary Clinic
8610 Centreville Rd., Manassas
(703) 361-8287

Animal Emergency Care
12501 Hull Street Rd., Midlothian
(804) 745-4243

Blue Ridge Veterinary Associates
120 E. Cornwell Ln., Purcellville
(540) 338-7387

Dogwood Veterinary Emergency & Specialty Center
5918 W. Broad St., Richmond
(804) 716-4700

Veterinary Emergency Center, Inc.
3312 W. Cary St., Richmond
(804) 353-9000

Emergency Veterinary Services of Roanoke
4902 Frontage Rd. N.W., Roanoke
(540) 563-8575

Regional Veterinary Referral Center
6651 Backlick Rd., Springfield
(703) 451-8900

The Cove - Center of Veterinary Expertise
6550 Hampton Roads Pkwy., Suite 113, Suffolk
(757) 935-9111

The Hope Center for Advanced Veterinary Medicine
140 Park St. S.E., Vienna
(703) 242-4732

Beach Veterinary Emergency Clinic
1124 Lynnhaven Pkwy., Virginia Beach
(757) 468-4900

Tidewater Veterinary Emergency & Critical Care Center
364 S. Independence Blvd., Virginia Beach
(757) 499-5463

Valley Emergency Veterinary Clinic, LLC
164-4 Garber Ln., Winchester
(540) 662-7811

Woodbridge Animal Hospital
2703 Caton Hill Rd., Woodbridge
(703) 897-5665

Animal Emergency Center
5007 Victory Blvd., Yorktown
(757) 234-0461

Peninsula Emergency Veterinary Clinic
1120 George Washington Memorial Hwy., Yorktown
(757) 874-8115

WASHINGTON

After Hours Animal Emergency Clinic
718 Auburn Way N., Auburn
(253) 939-6272

Animal Emergency Care
317 Telegraph Rd., Bellingham
(360) 758-2200

Animal Emergency Clinic of Everett
3625 Rucker Ave., Everett
(425) 258-4466

Alpine Animal Hospital
888 N.W. Sammamish Rd., Issaquah
(425) 392-8888

Animal Emergency & Specialty
636 7th Ave., Kirkland
(425) 827-8727

Seattle Veterinary Specialists
11814 115th Ave. N.E., Suite 102, Kirkland
(425) 823-9111

Agape Pet Emergency Center
16418 7th Pl. W., Lynnwood
(425) 741-2688

Veterinary Specialty Center of Seattle
20115 44th Ave. W., Lynnwood
(425) 697-6106

Pet Emergency Center
14434 Avon Allen Rd., Mount Vernon
(360) 848-5911

Mid-Columbia Pet Emergency Services
8913 Sandifur Pkwy., Pasco
(509) 547-3577

Animal Emergency & Trauma Center
320 Lindvig Way, Poulsbo
(360) 697-7771

VCA Central Kitsap Animal Hospital
10310 Central Valley Rd. N.E., Poulsbo
(360) 692-6162

Washington State University - Veterinary Teaching Hospital
100 Grimes Way, Pullman
(509) 335-0711

Animal Emergency Hospital of Redmond
16421 Cleveland St., Suite H, Redmond
(425) 250-7090

Animal Critical Care & Emergency Services
11536 Lake City Way, N.E., Seattle
(206) 364-1660

Emerald City Emergency Clinic
4102 Stone Way N., Seattle
(206) 634-9000

Five Corners Veterinary Hospital
15707 1st Ave. S., Seattle
(206) 243-2982

Animal Medical Center Of Seattle
14810 15th Ave N.E., Shoreline
(206) 204-3366

PSCVM Small Animal Emergency and Critical Care Center
11308 92nd St. S.E., Snohomish
(360) 563-5300

Pet Emergency Clinic
21 E. Mission Ave., Spokane
(509) 326-6670

The Animal Emergency Clinic - Puget Sound Veterinary Referral Center, PLLC
5608 S. Durango St., Tacoma
(253) 474-0791

Summit Veterinary Referral Center
2505 S. 80th St., Tacoma
(253) 983-1114

Columbia River Veterinary Specialists
6818 N.E. Fourth Plain Blvd., Suite C, Vancouver
(360) 694-3007

St. Francis 24 Hr. Animal Hospital
12010 N.E. 65th St., Vancouver
(360) 253-5446

Yakima Pet Emergency Service
510 W. Chestnut Ave., Yakima
(509) 452-4138

WEST VIRGINIA
Kanawha Valley Animal Emergency Clinic
5304 MacCorkle Ave. S.W., Charleston
(304) 768-2911

Animal Urgent Care, Inc.
4201 Wood St., Wheeling
(304) 233-0002

WISCONSIN
Fox Valley Animal Referral Center
4706 New Horizons Blvd., Appleton
(920) 993-9193

Lakeshore Veterinary Specialists
2100 W. Silver Spring Dr., Glendale
(414) 540-6710

Green Bay Animal Emergency Center
933 Anderson Dr., Suite F, Green Bay
(920) 494-9400

Crawford Animal Hospital
4607 S. 108th St., Greenfield
(414) 543-3499

Emergency Clinic for Animals
229 W. Beltline Hwy., Madison
(608) 274-7772

University of Wisconsin Veterinary Teaching Hospital
2015 Linden Dr., Madison
(608) 263-7600

Veterinary Emergency Service
4902 E. Broadway, Madison
(608) 222-2455

Veterinary Emergency Service
1612 N. High Point Rd., Middleton
(608) 831-1101

Central Wisconsin Animal Emergency Center
1420 Kronenwetter Dr., Mosinee
(715) 693-6934

Lakeshore Veterinary Specialists
207 W. Seven Hills Rd., Port Washington
(262) 268-7800

WVRC - Racine
4333 S. Green Bay Rd., Racine
(262) 553-9223

WVRC - Waukesha
360 Bluemound Rd., Waukesha
(262) 542-3241

Canada

ALBERTA
Calgary Animal Referral and Emergency Centre
7140 12th St. S.E., Calgary
(403) 520-8387

Calgary North Veterinary Hospital and Emergency Service
4204 4th St. N.W., Calgary
(403) 277-0135

McKnight 24 Hour Veterinary Hospital
34-5010 4th St. N.E., Calgary
(403) 457-0911

Western Veterinary Specialist & Emergency Centre
1802 10th Ave. S.W., Calgary
(403) 770-1340

Edmonton South Animal Hospital
3823 99th St. N.W., Edmonton
(780) 989-5595

Edmonton Veterinarians Emergency Clinic
11104 102nd Ave., Edmonton
(780) 433-9505

Guardian Veterinary Centre
5620 99th St. N.W., Edmonton
(780) 436-5880

BRITISH COLUMBIA
Animal Critical Care Group
1410 Boundary Rd., Burnaby
(604) 473-4882

Central Animal Emergency Clinic
812 Roderick Ave., Coquitlam
(604) 931-1911

Animal Emergency Clinic of the Fraser Valley
306-6325 204th St., Langley
(604) 514-1711

Mainland Animal Emergency Clinic
15338 Fraser Hwy., Surrey
(604) 588-4000

Vancouver Animal Emergency Clinic, Ltd.
1590 W. 4th St., Vancouver
(604) 734-5104

Central Victoria Veterinary Hospital
760 Roderick St., Victoria
(250) 475-2495

MANITOBA
Winnipeg Animal Emergency Clinic
400 Pembina Hwy., Winnipeg
(204) 452-9427

NEW BRUNSWICK
The Oaks Veterinary Medical & Emergency Referral Center
565 Mapleton Rd., Moncton
(506) 854-6257

NOVA SCOTIA
Metro Animal Emergency Clinic
201 Brownlow Ave., Unit 32, Dartmouth
(902) 468-0674

ONTARIO
Veterinary Emergency Clinic of York Region
14879 Yonge St., Aurora
(905) 713-2323

Huronia Veterinary Emergency Clinic
115 Bell Farm Rd., Barrie
(705) 722-0377

Pet Hospital of Prince Edward and Hastings Counties
5529 Hwy. 62 S., Belleville
(613) 968-9956

Emergency Veterinary Clinic
1 Wexford Rd., Brampton
(905) 495-9907

North Town Veterinary Hospital
496 Main St. N., Brampton
(905) 451-2000

Burgess Veterinary Emergency Clinic
775 Woodview Rd., Burlington
(905) 637-8111

Alta Vista Animal Health
2616 Bank St., Gloucester
(613) 731-9911

Halton-Wentworth Emergency Vet Clinic
505 King St. W., Hamilton
(905) 529-1004

London Veterinary Emergency Clinic
41 Adelaide St. N., Unit 43, London
(519) 432-7341

Mississauga-Oakville Veterinary Emergency Hospital
2285 Bristol Cir., Oakville
(905) 829-9444

Vaughan-Richmond Hill Veterinary Emergency Clinic
10303 Yonge St., Richmond Hill
(905) 884-1832

Niagara Veterinary Emergency Clinic
2F Tremont Dr., Unit 1, St. Catharines
(905) 641-3185

Veterinary Emergency Clinic
920 Yonge St., Suite 117, Toronto
(416) 920-2002

Veterinary Emergency Hospital of West Toronto
150 Norseman St., Toronto
(416) 239-3453

VETS Toronto
1025 Kingston Rd., Toronto
(416) 690-0625

Animal Emergency Clinic
1910 Dundas St. E., Unit 122, Whitby
(905) 576-3031

QUEBEC
Centre Veterinaire DMV
2300 54e Ave., Montreal
(514) 633-8888

Daubigny Veterinary Centre
3349 Wilfrid-Hamel Blvd., Québec
(418) 872-5355

University of Montreal Veterinary Hospital
3200 Sicotte St., Saint-Hyacinthe
(450) 778-8111

Pet-Friendly Hotels, Restaurants & Campgrounds

How to Use the Listings

U.S. Hotels

Canadian Hotels

Restaurant Listings

Campground Listings

Some 15,000 AAA Approved hotels, restaurants and campgrounds across North America accept traveling pets. This guide provides listings for those lodgings and restaurants in the United States and Canada that roll out the welcome mat for pets as well as the people who love them.

For the purpose of this book, "pets" are domestic cats or dogs. If you are planning to travel with any other kind of animal — particularly such exotic pets as birds or reptiles — check with the property before making definite plans. Expect to keep nontraditional pets crated at all times.

Hotel Listings

Hotels are listed alphabetically under the city or town in which they physically are located — or in some cases — under the nearest recognized city or town. U.S. properties are shown first, followed by Canadian properties. Each hotel listing provides the following information (see sample listing below):

❶ ⓐⓐⓐ or ⓒⓐ logos distinguish establishments that participate in the AAA/CAA logo licensing program.

❷ Diamond Rating

❸ Property name

❹ Hotel classification
(see next page for descriptions)

❺ Special amenities offered. These properties provide an additional benefit to pets, such as treats, toys or gifts, pet sitting and/or walking, a pet menu, food/water dishes, pet sheets or pillows, pet beds or other extras.

❻ Telephone number

❼ Two-person (2P) rate year-round, and cancellation notice validity period (if more than 48 hours). Rates listed are daily. **Note:** Most establishments accept credit cards, but a small number require cash, so please call ahead to verify. "Call for rates" indicates rates were not available at time of printing. Please contact property for current rate information.

❽ Physical address and/or highway location, if available

❾ Exterior or interior corridors

❿ Pet policies. If the phrase "pets accepted" appears, the property does accept pets but specific information was unavailable at press time. Otherwise, pet-specific policies are denoted as follows:

Size. "Very small" denotes pets weighing up to 10 pounds; "small," up to 25 pounds; "medium," up to 50 pounds; and "large," up to 100 pounds. If no size is specified, the property accepts pets of all sizes.

Species. "Other" indicates the property accepts animals other than dogs and cats. Always call ahead and specify the type of pet you plan to bring.

Deposits and fees. Includes the dollar amount, the type of charge (refundable deposit or nonrefundable fee), the frequency of the charge and whether the charge is per pet or per room.

Designated rooms. Guests with pets are placed in certain rooms, often smoking rooms or those on the ground floor.

Housekeeping service. The phrase "service with restrictions" denotes properties that require the pet to be crated, removed or attended by the owner during housekeeping service.

Supervision. The pet is required to be supervised at all times.

Crate. The pet must be crated when the owner is not present.

⓫ Member values, services and facilities:

[SAVE] Discounted standard room rate or lowest public rate available at time of booking for dates of stay

[ECO] Indicates hotels that have been certified by well-established government and/or private eco-certification organizations. For more information about these organizations and their programs, visit AAA.com/eco.

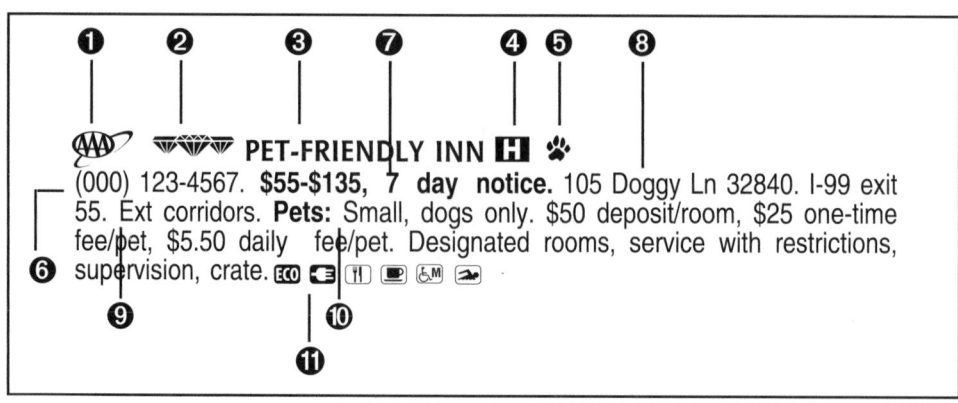

🔌 Electric vehicle charging station on premises. Station locations are provided by Department of Energy.

📶 Free Wireless Internet service on premises

📶 No Wireless Internet service on premises

📶 Wireless Internet service on premises for a fee

☒ Smoke-free premises

&M Accessible features (call property for available services and amenities)

🔲 Refrigerator

▣ Coffee maker

🟊 Restaurant on premises

🏊 Pool

🏊 Recreational activities

🅧 No air conditioning

🕱 No TV

☎ No telephones

Please note: Some in-room amenities represented by the icons in the listings may be available only in selected rooms, and may incur an extra fee. Please inquire when making your reservations.

Always inform the management that you are traveling with an animal; you may be fined if you do not declare your pet. Many properties require guests with pets to sign a waiver or release form and to pay for the room with a credit card. Of course, whether you pay in cash or by credit card, you will be held liable for any damages caused by your pet, even if the property does not charge a deposit or pet fee. It is not a good idea to leave your pet unattended in the room, but if you must, crate him and notify management. When in public areas, keep your pet leashed and do not allow him to disturb other guests.

It is important to remember that animal policies do change; always confirm policies, restrictions and fees with the lodging when making reservations and again 1-2 days before departure.

Listing information is subject to change. All listing information was accurate at press time. However, hotel rates and policies change and the publisher cannot be held liable for changes occurring after publication. AAA cannot guarantee the safety of guests or their pets at any facility.

AAA Hotel Diamond Ratings

Before a property is listed by AAA, it must satisfy a set of minimum standards regarding basic lodging needs as identified by AAA members. If a property meets those requirements (determined during an unannounced evaluation by a AAA inspector), it is assigned a Diamond Rating.

Once an establishment becomes AAA Approved, it is then assigned a rating of one to five Diamonds, indicating the extensiveness of its facilities, amenities and services, from basic to moderate to luxury. The Diamond Ratings guide members in selecting establishments appropriately matched to their needs and expectations.

◈ Budget-oriented, offering basic comfort and hospitality.

◈◈ Affordable, with modestly enhanced facilities, décor and amenities.

◈◈◈ Distinguished, multi-faceted with enhanced physical attributes, amenities and guest comforts.

◈◈◈◈ Refined, stylish with upscale physical attributes, extensive amenities and a high degree of hospitality, service and attention to detail.

◈◈◈◈◈ Ultimate luxury, sophistication and comfort with extraordinary physical attributes, meticulous personalized service, extensive amenities and impeccable standard of excellence.

Hotel Classifications

BB Bed & Breakfast: Typically owner-operated with a high degree of personal touches. Guests are encouraged to interact during evening and breakfast hours. A continental or full, hot breakfast is included in the room rate.

CA Cabin/Cottage: Vacation-oriented, typically small-scale, freestanding units with simple construction, homey design and basic décor. Often located in wooded, rural or waterfront locations. As a rule, essential cleaning supplies, kitchen utensils and complete bed and bath linens are supplied.

CO Condominium: Apartment-style accommodations of varying design or décor, units often contain one or more bedrooms, a living room, full kitchen and an eating area. As a rule, essential cleaning supplies, kitchen utensils and complete bed and bath linens are supplied.

CI Country Inn: Although similar in definition to a bed and breakfast, country inns are usually larger in scale with spacious public areas and offer a dining facility that serves breakfast and dinner.

H Hotel: Typically a multistory property with interior room entrances and a variety of guest unit styles. The magnitude of the public areas is determined by the overall theme, location and service level, but may include a variety of facilities such as a restaurant, shops, a fitness center, a spa, a business center and meeting rooms.

VH House: Freestanding units of varying home-style design. Typically larger scale, often containing two or more bedrooms, a living room, a full kitchen, a dining room and multiple bathrooms. As a rule, essential cleaning supplies, kitchen utensils and complete bed and bath linens are supplied.

M Motel: A one- or two-story roadside property with exterior room entrances and drive up parking. Public areas and facilities are often limited in size and/or availability.

RA Ranch: Typically a working ranch featuring an obvious rustic, Western theme, equestrian-related activities and a variety of guest unit styles.

Restaurant Listings

Restaurants are listed alphabetically under the city or town in which they physically are located — or in some cases — under the nearest recognized city or town. U.S. properties are shown first, followed by Canadian establishments.

Note: Call first before taking your pet to a restaurant, as restaurant policies regarding pets may change. Each listing provides the following information (see sample listing below):

❶ 🐾 or 🐾 logos distinguish establishments that participate in the AAA/CAA logo licensing program.

❷ Diamond Rating

❸ Restaurant name

❹ Telephone number

❺ Cuisine type identifies the predominant food style and classification represents the overall restaurant

❻ Prices represent the minimum and maximum entrée cost per person

❼ Physical address and/or highway location

❽ Restaurant icons:
    🔌 Electric vehicle charging station on premises.

    Ⓑ Breakfast

Ⓛ Lunch

Ⓓ Dinner

㉔ Open 24 hours

LATE Open after 11 p.m.

♿ Accessible features
(call property for available services and amenities)

🌡 No air conditioning

🚭 Designated smoking section

Listing information, including pet policies, is subject to change; always confirm pricing, policies and restrictions with the restaurant before your visit as the publisher cannot be held liable for changes occurring after publication. In addition, AAA cannot guarantee the safety of guests or their pets at any facility.

AAA Restaurant Diamond Ratings

Before a restaurant is listed by AAA, it must satisfy a set of minimum standards regarding basic restaurant needs as identified by AAA members. If an establishment meets those requirements (determined during an unannounced evaluation by a AAA inspector) and is recommended for AAA Approval, it is then assigned a rating of one to five Diamonds.

◆   Simple, familiar specialty food at an economical price. Often self-service, basic surroundings.

◆◆   Familiar, family-oriented experience. Home-style foods and family favorites, often cooked to order, modestly enhanced and reasonable priced. Relaxed service, casual surroundings.

◆◆◆   Fine dining, often adult-oriented. Latest cooking trends and/or traditional cuisine, expanded beverage offerings. Professional service staff and comfortable, well-coordinated ambiance.

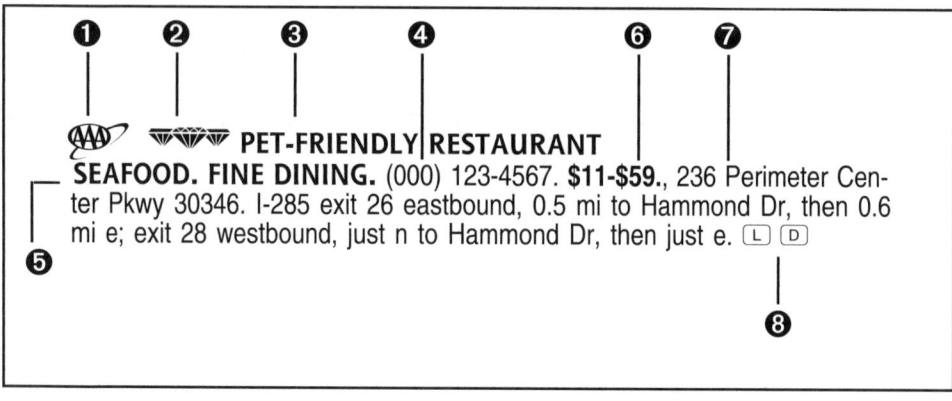

❶   ❷   ❸   ❹   ❻   ❼

🐾 ◆◆◆ **PET-FRIENDLY RESTAURANT**
SEAFOOD. FINE DINING. (000) 123-4567. **$11-$59.**, 236 Perimeter Center Pkwy 30346. I-285 exit 26 eastbound, 0.5 mi to Hammond Dr, then 0.6 mi e; exit 28 westbound, just n to Hammond Dr, then just e. Ⓛ Ⓓ

❺

❽

▼▼ ▼▼ Distinctive fine-dining, typically expensive. Highly creative chefs, imaginative presentations and fresh, top-quality ingredients. Proficient service staff, upscale surroundings. Wine steward may offer menu-specific knowledge.

▼▼ ▼▼ ▼ Luxurious and consistently world-class. Highly acclaimed chefs, artistic and imaginative menu selections using the finest ingredients. Maître d' and unobtrusive, expert service staff.

Campground Listings

Camping information provided by Woodall's®

Geographic listings are used for accuracy and consistency. Campgrounds are listed under the city or town in which they physically are located — or in some cases under the nearest recognized city or town. Not all listings include physical addresses. U.S. campgrounds are listed first, followed by Canadian campgrounds. Listings are alphabetically organized by state or province, city and campground name.

Note: Call first before taking your pet on a camping trip, as campground policies regarding pets may change, including any possible fees that may be assessed.

Each listing provides the following information (see sample listing):

❶ Location

❷ Campground name

❸ Ⓐ or Ⓐ logos distinguish establishments that participate in the AAA/CAA logo licensing program.

❹ Telephone number

❺ Two-person rates are listed as minimum to maximum and include any additional fees that may typically be found at the site such as air conditioning, TV service and heating. Rates and discounts are subject to change. "Call for rates" indicates rates were not available at time of printing. Please contact property for current rate information.

❻ Most campgrounds accept any or all of the major credit cards, including American Express, MasterCard and Visa. If a campground accepts only cash, the phrase "(no credit cards)" appears.

❼ Physical address and/or highway location and mailing address (if available).

❽ Member values, services and facilities:

🚫 No Tents

🏊 Pool

🎯 Recreational activities

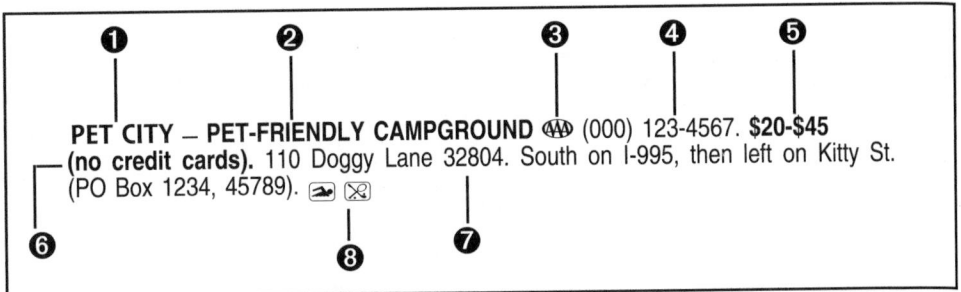

United States Hotels

ALABAMA

ABBEVILLE
◆◆ GuestHouse Inn Abbeville **M**
(334) 585-5060. **Call for rates.** 1237 US Hwy 431 S 36310. Jct SR 27. Ext corridors. **Pets:** Accepted. 🏊 🛜 🍴 🛗 🖥️

ALABASTER
◆◆ Candlewood Suites Alabaster **H**
(205) 620-0188. **Call for rates.** 1004 Balmoral Dr 35007. I-65 exit 238, just e. Int corridors. **Pets:** Accepted. 🛗 🛜 🍴 🛗 🖥️

ALBERTVILLE
◭ ◆◆ Microtel Inn & Suites by Wyndham Albertville **H**
(256) 894-4000. **$69-$89.** 220 Hwy 75 N 35951. Jct US 431 and SR 75, just ne. Int corridors. **Pets:** Small, other species. $10 daily fee/room. Designated rooms, service with restrictions, crate.
SAVE 🏊 🛜 🍴 🖥️

ALEXANDER CITY
◆◆ Baymont Inn & Suites Alexander City **H**
(256) 234-7099. **$49-$89.** 4335 US Hwy 280 35010. US 280, just s of jct SR 22; just nw of jct SR 63. Ext corridors. **Pets:** Accepted.
🏊 🛜 🍴 🖥️

◆◆ Days Inn **M**
(256) 234-6311. **$69-$100.** 3146 US Hwy 280 35010. Jct US 280 and SR 22. Ext corridors. **Pets:** Accepted. 🏊 🛜 🍴 🖥️

ANDALUSIA
◭ ◆◆ Econo Lodge **M**
(334) 222-7511. **$55.** 1421 Dr MLK Jr Expwy 36420. On US 84 Bypass. Ext corridors. **Pets:** Accepted.
SAVE 🍴 🛗 🏊 🛜 🍴 🖥️

ATHENS
◭ ◆◆ BEST WESTERN Athens Inn **H** 🐾
(256) 233-4030. **$95-$120, 3 day notice.** 1329 US 72 35611. I-65 exit 351, just w. Ext corridors. **Pets:** Large, dogs only. $20 one-time fee/pet. Designated rooms, service with restrictions, crate.
SAVE 🏊 🛜 🍴 🖥️

◆◆ Quality Inn Athens **H**
(256) 232-0030. **$63-$80.** 1488 Thrasher Blvd 35611. I-65 exit 351, just e, then just n. Ext corridors. **Pets:** Accepted. 🏊 🛜 🍴 🖥️

◆◆ Sleep Inn Athens **H**
(256) 232-4700. **$67-$82.** 1115 Audubon Ln 35611. I-65 exit 351, just nw. Int corridors. **Pets:** Accepted. 🏊 🛜 🍴 🖥️

ATMORE
◆◆◆ Holiday Inn Express **H**
(251) 368-1585. **Call for rates.** 111 Lakeview Cir 36504. I-65 exit 57, just s. Int corridors. **Pets:** Accepted. 🛗 🏊 🛜 🍴 🖥️

AUBURN
◭ ◆◆◆ Clarion Inn & Suites University Center **H**
(334) 821-7001. **$75-$200.** 1577 S College St 36832. I-85 exit 51, 1.4 mi w on US 29/SR 147. Ext corridors. **Pets:** Accepted.
SAVE 🏊 🛜 🍴 🖥️

◆◆◆◆ The Crenshaw Guest House **BB**
(334) 821-1131. **Call for rates.** 371 N College St 36830. Just w of downtown; in historic district. Ext/int corridors. **Pets:** Accepted.
🛜 🍴 🖥️

◆◆ Quality Inn **M**
(334) 502-5020. **$74-$199.** 1212 Mall Pkwy 36831. Ext corridors. **Pets:** Small. $20 daily fee/pet. Service with restrictions, crate.
🏊 🛜 🍴 🖥️

BESSEMER
◭ ◆◆◆ BEST WESTERN PLUS Bessemer Hotel & Suites **H**
(205) 481-1950. **$90-$100.** 5041 Academy Ln 35022. I-20/59 exit 108, just sw. Int corridors. **Pets:** Medium, other species. $20 daily fee/pet. Supervision. SAVE 🛗 🏊 🛜 ✖️ 🍴 🖥️

◆◆ Sleep Inn **H**
(205) 424-0000. **$70-$150.** 1259 Greenmor Dr 35022. I-459 exit 6, just s, then just w. Int corridors. **Pets:** Accepted. 🏊 🛜 ✖️ 🍴 🖥️

BIRMINGHAM (Restaurants p. 612)
◆◆◆◆ Drury Inn & Suites-Birmingham Southeast **H**
(205) 967-2450. **$110-$189.** 3510 Grandview Pkwy 35243. I-459 exit 19 (US 280 E), just e. Int corridors. **Pets:** $10 daily fee/room. Service with restrictions, supervision. 🏊 🛜 ✖️ 🍴 🖥️

◭ ◆◆◆ Embassy Suites Birmingham **H**
(205) 879-7400. **$129-$209.** 2300 Woodcrest Pl 35209. Just n of jct US 31 and 280 exit 21st Ave southbound, 0.3 mi s. Int corridors.
Pets: Accepted. SAVE 🍴 🛗 🏊 🛜 🍴 🖥️

◆◆◆ The Hotel Highland at Five Points South, an Ascend Collection Hotel Member **H**
(205) 933-9555. **$127-$205.** 1023 20th St S 35205. Jct University Blvd and 20th St S, 0.3 mi s. Int corridors. **Pets:** Accepted.
🛜 ✖️ 🍴 🖥️

◆◆ La Quinta Inn Birmingham / Cahaba Park South **H**
(205) 995-9990. **$65-$214.** 513 Cahaba Park Cir 35242. I-459 exit 19 (US 280), 1.2 mi e. Int corridors. **Pets:** Large, other species. Service with restrictions. 🛜 ✖️ 🍴 🖥️

◆◆◆ Residence Inn by Marriott Birmingham **H**
(205) 991-8686. **$104-$169.** 3 Greenhill Pkwy 35242. I-459 exit 19 (US 280), 2 mi e. Ext corridors. **Pets:** Accepted. 🏊 🛜 ✖️ 🍴 🖥️

◭ ◆◆◆ Residence Inn by Marriott Birmingham Downtown @ UAB **H**
(205) 731-9595. **$103-$179.** 821 20th St S 35205. Jct University Blvd, just s; corner of 8th Ct S. Int corridors. **Pets:** Accepted.
SAVE 🍴 🛗 🏊 🛜 ✖️ 🍴 🖥️

◭ ◆◆◆ Sheraton Birmingham Hotel **H** 🐾
(205) 324-5000. **$129-$299.** 2101 Richard Arrington Jr Blvd N 35203. I-20/59 exit 22nd St. Int corridors. **Pets:** Other species. Designated rooms, service with restrictions, supervision.
SAVE 🍴 ✖️ 🛜 ✖️ 🖥️

◭ ◆◆◆ The Westin Birmingham **H**
(205) 307-3600. **$149-$359.** 2221 Richard Arrington Jr Blvd N 35203. I-20/59 exit 125 westbound; exit 125A eastbound. Int corridors.
Pets: Accepted. SAVE 🍴 🏊 ✖️ 🛜 ✖️ 🍴 🖥️

CALERA
◆◆ Quality Inn **H**
(205) 668-3641. **$86-$96.** 357 Hwy 304 35040. I-65 exit 231, just se. Ext corridors. **Pets:** Accepted. 🏊 🛜 🍴 🖥️

CLANTON

(AAA) ▼▼▼ BEST WESTERN Inn 🅷

(205) 280-1006. **$76-$100, 3 day notice.** 801 Bradberry Ln 35046. I-65 exit 205, 0.5 mi e. Ext corridors. **Pets:** Small, dogs only. $10 daily fee/pet. Designated rooms, service with restrictions, supervision.
🆂🅰🆅🅴 ⮕ 🛜 🍴 💻

CULLMAN *(Restaurants p. 612)*

(AAA) ▼▼▼ BEST WESTERN Fairwinds Inn 🅼

(256) 737-5009. **$77-$135.** 1917 Commerce Ave NW 35055. I-65 exit 310, just e. Ext corridors. **Pets:** Dogs only. $20 daily fee/pet. Designated rooms, service with restrictions. 🆂🅰🆅🅴 ⮕ 🛜 🍴 💻

▼▼ Sleep Inn & Suites 🅷

(256) 734-6166. **$75-$120.** 2050 Old Hwy 157 35057. I-65 exit 310, just ne. Int corridors. **Pets:** Small, dogs only. $20 daily fee/pet. Designated rooms, service with restrictions, supervision. ⮕ 🛜 🍴 💻

DAPHNE

▼▼◈ Hampton Inn Mobile-East Bay Daphne 🅷

(251) 626-2220. **$99-$139.** 29451 US Hwy 98 36526. I-10 exit 35A eastbound; exit 35 westbound, just s. Int corridors. **Pets:** Accepted. ⮕ 🛜 🍴 💻

▼▼◈▼ Homewood Suites by Hilton Mobile East Bay/Daphne 🅷

(251) 621-0100. **$159-$259.** 29474 N Main St 36526. I-10 exit 35A eastbound; exit 35 westbound, just s. Int corridors. **Pets:** Accepted. 🅼⮕ 🛜 🍴 💻

DECATUR *(Restaurants p. 612)*

(AAA) ▼▼▼ BEST WESTERN River City Hotel 🅷 ❀

(256) 301-1388. **$72-$80.** 1305 Front Ave SW 35603. I-65 exit 334, 8 mi n. Int corridors. **Pets:** Small. $20 deposit/pet. Service with restrictions, supervision. 🆂🅰🆅🅴 🅼 ⮕ 🛜 🍴 💻

▼▼ Microtel Inn & Suites by Wyndham 🅷 ❀

(256) 301-9995. **$59-$79, 3 day notice.** 2226 Beltline Rd SW (SR 67) 35601. SR 67, 4 mi w of jct US 31. Int corridors. **Pets:** Small. $20 one-time fee/pet. Service with restrictions, supervision.
🅼 ⮕ 🛜 🍴 💻

▼▼ Quality Inn 🅷

(256) 355-2229. **$67-$79.** 2120 Jameson Pl SW 35603. SR 67, 1.6 mi s of jct US 72A; 3.9 mi n of jct US 31. Ext corridors. **Pets:** $20 daily fee/pet. Service with restrictions, crate. ⮕ 🛜 🍴 💻

DEMOPOLIS

(AAA) ▼▼◈ BEST WESTERN PLUS Two Rivers Hotel & Suites 🅷 ❀

(334) 289-2611. **$110-$120.** 662 US Hwy 80 W 36732. Jct US 43, 0.8 mi w. Int corridors. **Pets:** Large. $100 deposit/room. Service with restrictions, supervision. 🆂🅰🆅🅴 ⮕ 🛜 ✖ 🍴 💻

DOTHAN *(Restaurants p. 612)*

▼▼▼ Comfort Suites 🅷

(334) 792-9000. **$74-$129.** 1650 Westgate Pkwy 36303. 0.7 mi n of jct US 231 and 431, just e. Int corridors. **Pets:** $45 one-time fee/room. Service with restrictions, supervision. 🅼 ⮕ 🛜 ✖ 🍴 💻

▼▼▼ La Quinta Inn & Suites-Dothan 🅷

(334) 793-9090. **$79-$174.** 3593 Ross Clark Cir 36303. Just w of jct US 231; northwest end of town. Int corridors. **Pets:** Large, other species. Service with restrictions. 🅼 ⮕ 🛜 🍴 💻

ENTERPRISE

▼▼ Americas Best Value Inn & Suites 🅼

(334) 348-2378. **$60-$70.** 101 Access Dr 36330. Jct US 84 and SR 167, 0.5 mi w. Ext corridors. **Pets:** Accepted. ⮕ 🛜 🍴 💻

▼▼ Quality Inn 🅼

(334) 393-2304. **$78-$98.** 615 Boll Weevil Cir 36330. On US 84 Bypass. Ext corridors. **Pets:** Accepted. ⮕ 🛜 🍴 💻

EUFAULA *(Restaurants p. 612)*

▼▼▼ Baymont Inn & Suites Eufaula 🅼

(334) 687-7747. **$59-$99.** 136 Towne Center Blvd 36027. On US 431, 1 mi s of US 82 E. Ext corridors. **Pets:** Accepted. ⮕ 🛜 🍴 💻

▼▼▼▼ Eufaula Comfort Suites 🅷

(334) 616-0114. **$105-$140.** 12 Paul Lee Pkwy 36027. 1.7 mi s on US 431 from jct US 82 E, just e. Int corridors. **Pets:** Accepted.
🅼 ⮕ ✖ 🛜 ✖ 🍴 💻

EVERGREEN

▼▼ Econo Lodge Inn & Suites 🅼

(251) 578-2100. **$65-$80.** 215 Hwy 83 36401. I-65 exit 96, just w. Ext corridors. **Pets:** Accepted. 🛜 🍴 💻

▼▼▼ Sleep Inn & Suites 🅷

(251) 578-9590. **$99-$110.** 78 Liberty Hill Pl 36401. I-65 exit 96, just ne. Int corridors. **Pets:** Small. $20 daily fee/pet. Designated rooms, no service, supervision. 🅼 ⮕ 🛜 🍴 💻

FAIRHOPE *(Restaurants p. 612)*

▼▼ Key West Inn 🅼

(251) 990-7373. **$54-$119.** 231 S Greeno Rd 36532. On US 98, 1.9 mi s of jct SR 104. Ext corridors. **Pets:** Accepted. ⮕ 🛜 🍴 💻

FLORENCE

(AAA) ▼▼▼▼ Marriott Shoals Hotel & Spa 🅷

(256) 246-3600. **$159-$245.** 10 Hightower Pl 35630. Jct US 43/72 and SR 133 (Cox Creek Pkwy S), 1.5 mi s; just n of Wilson Dam. Int corridors. **Pets:** Accepted. 🆂🅰🆅🅴 🍴 🅼 ⮕ ✖ 🛜 ✖ 🍴 💻

FOLEY

(AAA) ▼▼▼ Econo Lodge & Suites 🅷

(251) 943-9100. **$55-$109.** 2682 S McKenzie St 36535. On SR 59, 1.9 mi s of jct US 98. Ext corridors. **Pets:** Accepted.
🆂🅰🆅🅴 🅼 ⮕ 🛜 🍴 💻

FORT PAYNE

▼▼▼ Days Inn 🅼

(256) 845-2085. **$66-$76, 3 day notice.** 1416 Glenn Blvd SW 35968. I-59 exit 218, just w. Ext corridors. **Pets:** Accepted. ⮕ 🛜 🍴 💻

FULTONDALE

▼▼▼ Holiday Inn Express & Suites Birmingham-Fultondale 🅷

(205) 439-6300. **$89-$169.** 1733 Fulton Rd 35068. I-65 exit 267, just e. Int corridors. **Pets:** Accepted. ⮕ 🛜 ✖ 🍴 💻

GADSDEN

▼▼▼ Comfort Suites of Gadsden 🅷

(256) 538-5770. **$86-$190.** 96 Walker St 35904. I-59 exit 181, just n. Int corridors. **Pets:** Accepted. 🅼 🛜 ✖ 🍴 💻

GENEVA

▼▼▼ Briarwood Inn of Geneva 🅼

(334) 684-7715. **$79-$108.** 1503 W Magnolia Ave 36340. On SR 52, 0.3 mi w of jct SR 196. Ext corridors. **Pets:** Small, dogs only. $15 daily fee/pet. Designated rooms, service with restrictions, supervision.
⮕ 🛜

GREENVILLE

(AAA) ▼▼▼ BEST WESTERN Inn 🅼

(334) 382-9200. **$60-$90.** 56 Cahaba Rd 36037. I-65 exit 130, just n on SR 185. Ext corridors. **Pets:** Accepted. 🆂🅰🆅🅴 ⮕ 🛜 🍴 💻

△△△ ▽▽▽ **Comfort Inn** H ❀
(334) 383-9595. **$68-$104.** 1029 Fort Dale Rd 36037. I-65 exit 130, just n on SR 185. Int corridors. **Pets:** Medium. $20 daily fee/pet. Service with restrictions, crate. SAVE ⓈM ⌲ ⌘ 🖥

GULF SHORES

▽▽▽ **Staybridge Suites-Gulf Shores** H ❀
(251) 975-1030. **Call for rates.** 3947 Hwy 59 36542. On SR 59, 3.1 mi n of jct SR 180. Int corridors. **Pets:** $75 one-time fee/room. Designated rooms, service with restrictions. ⓈM ⌲ ⌘ 🖥

GUNTERSVILLE

▽▽▽▽ **Wyndham Garden Lake Guntersville** H
(256) 582-2220. **$90-$142.** 2140 Gunter Ave 35976. Jct US 431 (Gunter Ave) and SR 79. Ext corridors. **Pets:** Large. $25 daily fee/pet. Service with restrictions, crate. ⓉⓉ ⓈM ⌲ ⓍⓍ ⌘ ⓍⓍ ⌘ 🖥

HOMEWOOD *(Restaurants p. 612)*

△△△ ▽▽▽ **Aloft Birmingham Soho Square** H
(205) 874-8055. **$129-$199.** 1903 29th Ave S 35209. I-59 exit 126A, 3.5 mi s on US 31, then just w; corner of 19th St S; downtown. Int corridors. **Pets:** Accepted. SAVE ⓉⓉ ⓈM ⌲ ⌘ ⓍⓍ ⌘ 🖥

△△△ ▽▽▽ **BEST WESTERN PLUS Carlton Suites** H
(205) 940-9990. **$119-$169.** 140 State Farm Pkwy 35209. I-65 exit 255, just w to Wildwood Pkwy, then just n. Int corridors. **Pets:** Medium, dogs only. $20 daily fee/pet. Designated rooms, no service, supervision. SAVE ⓈM ⌲ ⌘ ⌘ 🖥

▽▽▽ **Candlewood Suites Birmingham-Homewood** H
(205) 769-9777. **Call for rates.** 400 Commons Dr 35209. I-65 exit 255, 0.7 mi w, then just s. Int corridors. **Pets:** Accepted. ⌘ ⓍⓍ ⌘ 🖥

▽▽▽ **Drury Inn & Suites-Birmingham Southwest** H
(205) 940-9500. **$125-$189.** 160 State Farm Pkwy 35209. I-65 exit 255, 0.5 mi on northwest frontage road. Int corridors. **Pets:** $10 daily fee/room. Service with restrictions, supervision. ⌲ ⌘ ⓍⓍ ⌘ 🖥

▽▽▽ **Residence Inn by Marriott Birmingham Homewood** H
(205) 943-0044. **$109-$179.** 50 State Farm Pkwy 35209. I-65 exit 255, 1 mi nw on northwest frontage road. Int corridors. **Pets:** Other species. $100 one-time fee/pet. Service with restrictions, supervision. ⓈM ⌲ ⌘ ⓍⓍ ⌘ 🖥

▽▽▽ **Super 8** H
(205) 945-9888. **$55-$63, 3 day notice.** 140 Vulcan Rd 35209. I-65 exit 256 northbound; exit 256A southbound, just nw. Int corridors. **Pets:** Small. $10 daily fee/pet. Service with restrictions, crate. ⌘ ⌘ 🖥

▽▽▽ **TownePlace Suites by Marriott Birmingham Homewood** H
(205) 943-0114. **$125-$153.** 500 Wildwood Cir N 35209. I-65 exit 255, 0.6 mi w, then just n. Int corridors. **Pets:** Accepted. ⓔⓒⓞ ⓈM ⌲ ⌘ ⓍⓍ ⌘ 🖥

HOOVER

▽▽ **Days Inn at the Galleria** H
(205) 985-7500. **$69-$109.** 1800 Riverchase Dr 35244. I-459 exit 13, 0.5 mi s on US 31, then 0.4 mi w on SR 150. Ext corridors. **Pets:** Medium. $25 daily fee/pet. Service with restrictions, supervision. ⌲ ⌘ ⌘ 🖥

▽▽▽ **Homewood Suites Birmingham-SW/Riverchase Galleria** H
(205) 637-2900. **$99-$279.** 121 Riverchase Pkwy E 35244. I-65 exit 247, just sw on Valleydale Rd, then just n. Int corridors. **Pets:** Medium. $75 one-time fee/pet. Service with restrictions, supervision. ⓈM ⌲ ⌘ ⌘ 🖥

▽▽▽ **Homewood Suites by Hilton** H
(205) 995-9823. **$109-$169.** 215 Inverness Center Dr 35242. I-459 exit 19 (US 280), 1.8 mi e, then just s. Int corridors. **Pets:** Accepted. ⌲ ⌘ ⌘ 🖥

△△△ ▽▽▽ **Hyatt Place Birmingham/Hoover** H
(205) 988-8444. **$79-$169.** 2980 John Hawkins Pkwy 35244. I-459 exit 13, 0.5 mi s on US 31, then 0.8 mi w on SR 150. Int corridors. **Pets:** Accepted. SAVE ⓈM ⌲ ⌘ ⓍⓍ ⌘ 🖥

△△△ ▽▽▽ **Hyatt Place Birmingham/Inverness** H
(205) 995-9242. **$84-$209.** 4686 Hwy 280 E 35242. I-459 exit 19 (US 280), 1.7 mi e, then just s to Inverness Pkwy. Int corridors. **Pets:** Medium, dogs only. $75 one-time fee/room. Service with restrictions, supervision. SAVE ⓉⓉ ⓈM ⌲ ⌘ ⓍⓍ ⌘ 🖥

△△△ ▽▽▽ **Hyatt Regency Birmingham-The Wynfrey Hotel** H
(205) 705-1234. **$99-$329.** 1000 Riverchase Galleria 35244. I-459 exit 13. Int corridors. **Pets:** Accepted. SAVE ⓉⓉ ⌲ Ⓢ⌘ ⓍⓍ ⌘ 🖥

▽▽ **La Quinta Inn & Suites Birmingham Hoover** H
(205) 403-0096. **$69-$234.** 120 Riverchase Pkwy E 35244. I-65 exit 247, just sw on Valleydale Rd, then just n. Int corridors. **Pets:** Large, other species. Service with restrictions. ⓈM ⌲ ⌘ ⌘ 🖥

▽▽▽ **Residence Inn by Marriott Birmingham/Hoover** H
(205) 733-1655. **$139-$299.** 2725 John Hawkins Pkwy 35244. I-459 exit 13A (Galleria Blvd/SR 150), 0.5 mi se to SR 150, then 1.5 mi s. Int corridors. **Pets:** Other species. $100 one-time fee/room. Service with restrictions, crate. ⓈM ⌲ ⌘ ⓍⓍ ⌘ 🖥

HOPE HULL

▽▽▽ **Hampton Inn Airport** H
(334) 280-9592. **$89-$139.** 60 Wasden Rd 36043. I-65 exit 164, just w. Int corridors. **Pets:** Accepted. ⓈM ⌲ ⌘ ⌘ 🖥

HUNTSVILLE *(Restaurants p. 612)*

△△△ ▽▽▽ **BEST WESTERN PLUS Rocket City Inn & Suites** H
(256) 837-7412. **$70-$85.** 6200 Torok Cir 35806. I-565 exit 14B, 2.6 mi n on SR 255 (Research Park Blvd), then 0.6 mi w on US 72. Int corridors. **Pets:** Accepted. SAVE ⓈM ⌲ ⌘ ⌘ 🖥

▽▽▽ **Country Inn & Suites By Carlson** H
(256) 837-4070. **$95-$135.** 4880 University Dr 35816. I-565 exit 14B, 2.6 mi n on SR 255 (Research Park Blvd), then 1 mi e on US 72. Int corridors. **Pets:** Accepted. ⌲ ⌘ ⓍⓍ ⌘ 🖥

▽▽ **Extended Stay America Huntsville-U.S. Space and Rocket Center** H
(256) 830-9110. **$69-$89.** 4751 Governors House Dr 35805. I-565 exit 17A, just s, then 0.5 mi w. Ext corridors. **Pets:** Other species. $25 daily fee/pet. Service with restrictions, supervision. ⓈM ⌘ ⌘ 🖥

▽▽ **La Quinta Inn & Suites Huntsville Madison Square Mall** H
(256) 830-8999. **$69-$169.** 4890 University Dr NW 35816. I-565 exit 14B, 1.3 mi n on SR 255 (Research Park Blvd) to US 72, then 0.9 mi e. Int corridors. **Pets:** Large, other species. Service with restrictions. ⓈM ⌲ ⌘ ⌘ 🖥

▽▽ **La Quinta Inn Huntsville (Research Park)** H
(256) 830-2070. **$65-$139.** 4870 University Dr NW 35816. I-565 exit 14B, 2.6 mi n on SR 255 (Research Park Blvd), then 1.1 mi e on US 72. Ext/int corridors. **Pets:** Large, other species. Service with restrictions. ⌲ ⌘ ⌘ 🖥

▽▽ **Microtel Inn & Suites by Wyndham Huntsville** H
(256) 859-6655. **$59-$79.** 1820 Chase Creek Row 35811. Jct US 72 and Shields Rd, just n, then just w. Int corridors. **Pets:** Other species. $15 one-time fee/pet. Designated rooms, service with restrictions, supervision. ⓈM ⌲ ⌘ ⌘ 🖥

▼▼▼ **TownePlace Suites by Marriott Huntsville** 🅷
(256) 971-5277. **$89-$299.** 1125 McMurtrie Dr 35806. I-565 exit 14B, 2.6 mi n on SR 255 (Research Park Blvd), 0.8 mi w on US 72, then just s. Int corridors. **Pets:** Medium, other species. $100 one-time fee/room. Service with restrictions, crate. 🖬 ⛖ 🛜 ✕ 🖶 🖵

🅰🅰🅰 ▼▼▼▼ **The Westin Huntsville** 🅷 ❀
(256) 428-2000. **$99-$239.** 6800 Governors West NW 35806. I-565 exit 14A, 0.5 mi n on SR 255 (Research Park Blvd), just w on Madison Pike, then 0.5 mi n. Int corridors. **Pets:** Small, dogs only. $50 one-time fee/room, $15 daily fee/room. Designated rooms, service with restrictions, supervision. 🆂🅰🆅🅴 🍴 🖬 ⛖ ✕ 🦭 ✕ 🖶 🖵

IRONDALE *(Restaurants p. 612)*

▼▼▼▼ **Holiday Inn Express Hotel & Suites Birmingham East** 🅷
(205) 957-0555. **Call for rates.** 811 Old Grants Mill Rd 35210. I-20 exit 133, just sw on Crescent Blvd, then just s. Int corridors. **Pets:** Accepted. ⛖ 🛜 🖶 🖵

JASPER

▼▼ **Quality Inn** 🅼
(205) 387-7710. **$74-$84.** 1100 Hwy 78/118 E 35501. SR 118, 1.8 mi w of jct SR 69. Ext corridors. **Pets:** Accepted. 🖬 ⛖ 🛜 🖶 🖵

LEEDS

▼▼▼▼ **BEST WESTERN PLUS Bass Hotel & Suites** 🅷
(205) 640-5300. **Call for rates.** 1949 Village Dr 35094. I-20 exit 144A westbound; exit 144B eastbound, just ne. Int corridors. **Pets:** Very small. $10 deposit/pet, $10 daily fee/pet. Designated rooms, service with restrictions, supervision. ⛖ 🛜 🖶 🖵

▼▼ **Days Inn of Leeds** 🅼
(205) 699-9833. **$80-$256.** 1838 Ashville Rd 35094. I-20 exit 144A eastbound; exit 144B westbound, just s. Ext corridors. **Pets:** Medium. $10 daily fee/pet. Service with restrictions, supervision. ⛖ 🛜 🖶 🖵

LINCOLN

🅰🅰🅰 ▼▼▼▼ **Comfort Inn** 🅷
(205) 763-9777. **$74-$299.** 850/A Speedway Industrial Dr 35096. I-20 exit 168, just se. Int corridors. **Pets:** Accepted. 🆂🅰🆅🅴 🖬 ⛖ 🛜 🖶 🖵

LUVERNE

▼▼ **GuestHouse Inn & Suites** 🅷
(334) 335-3050. **$65-$75.** 1701 Montgomery Hwy 36049. Jct US 331 and SR 10. Int corridors. **Pets:** Accepted. 🖬 ⛖ 🛜 🖶 🖵

MADISON

▼▼▼ **Country Inn & Suites By Carlson/Huntsville Airport** 🅷
(256) 325-0007. **$75-$200.** 101 Westchester Dr 35758. I-565 exit 9, just n to jct Madison Blvd and SR 20, then just w. Int corridors. **Pets:** Medium. $15 one-time fee/pet. Designated rooms, no service, supervision. 🖬 ⛖ 🛜 ✕ 🖶 🖵

MILLBROOK

▼▼ **Key West Inn** 🅼
(334) 309-2004. **Call for rates.** 2275 Cobbs Ford Rd 36054. I-65 exit 179, just e. Ext corridors. **Pets:** Accepted. ⛖ 🛜 🖶 🖵

MOBILE *(Restaurants p. 612)*

▼▼▼ **Candlewood Suites Downtown** 🅷
(251) 690-7818. **$119-$139.** 121 N Royal St 36602. Corner of St. Louis St; downtown; parking and rear entrance on St. Joseph St. Int corridors. **Pets:** Accepted. ⛖ 🛜 ✕ 🖶 🖵

▼▼▼ **Drury Inn-Mobile** 🅷
(251) 344-7700. **$103-$159.** 824 W I-65 Service Rd S 36609. I-65 exit 3 (Airport Blvd), just w, then just s. Int corridors. **Pets:** $10 daily fee/room. Service with restrictions, supervision. ⛖ 🛜 ✕ 🖶 🖵

🅰🅰🅰 ▼▼▼ **Holiday Inn Mobile West I-10** 🅷
(251) 666-5600. **$109-$139.** 5465 Hwy 90 W 36619. I-10 exit 15B, just e on US 90, then just s on Coca Cola Rd. Int corridors. **Pets:** Service with restrictions, crate. 🆂🅰🆅🅴 🍴 ⛖ 🛜 ✕ 🖶 🖵

▼▼ **La Quinta Inn Mobile** 🅼
(251) 343-4051. **$72-$195.** 816 W I-65 Service Rd S 36609. I-65 exit 3 (Airport Blvd), just w, then just s. Ext/int corridors. **Pets:** Large, other species. Service with restrictions. ⛖ 🛜 🖶 🖵

🅰🅰🅰 ▼▼▼ ▼▼▼ **Renaissance-The Battle House Mobile Hotel & Spa** 🅷 ❀
(251) 338-2000. **$189-$263.** 26 N Royal St 36602. I-10 exit 26B (Water St) eastbound, w on Government St, then just n. Int corridors. **Pets:** Large, other species. $75 one-time fee/room. Service with restrictions. 🆂🅰🆅🅴 🍴 🖬 ⛖ ✕ 🛜 ✕ 🖶 🖵

▼▼▼▼ **Residence Inn by Marriott Mobile** 🅷
(251) 304-0570. **$116-$129.** 950 W I-65 Service Rd S 36609. I-65 exit 3 (Airport Blvd), just w, then 0.4 mi s. Int corridors. **Pets:** Accepted. 🖬 ⛖ 🛜 ✕ 🖶 🖵

▼▼▼▼ **TownePlace Suites by Marriott Mobile** 🅷
(251) 345-9588. **$89-$119.** 1075 Montlimar Dr 36609. I-65 exit 3 (Airport Blvd), 0.5 mi w, then 0.5 mi s. Int corridors. **Pets:** Other species. $83 one-time fee/room. Service with restrictions, crate. ⛖ 🛜 ✕ 🖶 🖵

MONROEVILLE

🅰🅰🅰 ▼▼▼ **BEST WESTERN Inn** 🅼
(251) 575-9999. **$72-$80.** 4419 S Alabama Ave 36460. On SR 21, 0.5 mi n of jct US 84. Ext corridors. **Pets:** Medium. $10 deposit/pet. Supervision. 🆂🅰🆅🅴 ⛖ 🛜 🖶 🖵

▼▼▼ **Country Inn & Suites By Carlson** 🅷
(251) 743-3333. **$77-$139.** 120 Hwy 21 S 36460. On SR 21, just s of jct US 84. Int corridors. **Pets:** Accepted. 🖬 ⛖ 🛜 ✕ 🖶 🖵

▼▼ **Mockingbird Inn & Suites** 🅼
(251) 743-3297. **$75-$140, 3 day notice.** 4389 S Alabama Ave 36460. On SR 21, 0.5 mi n of jct US 84. Ext corridors. **Pets:** Medium. $10 deposit/pet. Supervision. ⛖ 🛜 🖶 🖵

MONTGOMERY *(Restaurants p. 612)*

▼▼ **Baymont Inn & Suites** 🅼
(334) 277-4442. **$49-$69.** 5837 Monticello Dr 36117. I-85 exit 6, just n, then just e. Ext corridors. **Pets:** Small. $10 daily fee/pet. Service with restrictions, supervision. ⛖ 🛜 🖶 🖵

▼▼▼ **Candlewood Suites at EastChase** 🅷
(334) 277-0677. **$90-$109.** 9151 Boyd Cooper Pkwy 36117. I-85 exit 11, just sw. Int corridors. **Pets:** Large. Service $75 one-time fee/room. Service with restrictions, crate. 🖬 ⛖ ✕ 🖶 🖵

▼▼▼ **Drury Inn & Suites-Montgomery** 🅷
(334) 273-1101. **$110-$184.** 1124 Eastern Blvd 36117. I-85 exit 6, just n. Int corridors. **Pets:** $10 daily fee/room. Service with restrictions, supervision. 🖬 ⛖ 🛜 🖶 🖵

▼▼▼ **Embassy Suites Montgomery-Hotel & Conference Center** 🅷 ❀
(334) 269-5055. **$119-$199.** 300 Tallapoosa St 36104. Between Molton and Commerce sts; downtown. Int corridors. **Pets:** Small. $75 one-time fee/pet. Designated rooms, service with restrictions, crate. 🍴 🖬 ⛖ 🦭 🖶 🖵

▼▼▼ **Holiday Inn Express Hotel & Suites** 🅷
(334) 288-8844. **$81.** 4273 Troy Hwy 36116. 1 mi s of jct US 80 and 231 (Troy Hwy). Int corridors. **Pets:** Other species. $50 one-time fee/pet. Service with restrictions, crate. ⛖ 🛜 ✕ 🖶 🖵

▼▼▼ **Homewood Suites by Hilton** 🄷
(334) 272-3010. **$89-$189.** 1800 Interstate Park Dr 36109. I-85 exit 4, just n on Perry Hill Rd, then just e. Int corridors. **Pets:** Accepted.
🐾Ⓜ 🛏 🛜 🖥 💻

▼▼ **La Quinta Inn & Suites Montgomery Carmichael Road** 🄷
(334) 277-6000. **$65-$185.** 5225 Carmichael Rd 36106. I-85 exit 6, just s on Eastern Blvd, then just w. Int corridors. **Pets:** Large, other species. Service with restrictions. 🛏 🛜 🖥 💻

▼▼ **La Quinta Inn Montgomery Eastern Bypass** Ⓜ
(334) 271-1620. **$59-$149.** 1280 Eastern Blvd 36117. I-85 exit 6, just s. Ext corridors. **Pets:** Large, other species. Service with restrictions.
🛏 🛜 🖥 💻

▼▼ **Microtel Inn & Suites by Wyndham Montgomery** 🄷
(334) 649-4465. **$60-$80.** 100 Gibbons Dr 36117. I-85 exit 11, just nw. Int corridors. **Pets:** Accepted. 🐾Ⓜ 🛜 🖥 💻

▼▼ **Motel 6 Montgomery Airport-Hope Hull** Ⓜ
(334) 280-1866. **$46-$60.** 7760 Slade Plaza Blvd 36105. I-65 exit 164, just s. Int corridors. **Pets:** Other species. Service with restrictions, crate.
🐾Ⓜ 🛏 🛜 🖥

ⓐⓐⓐ ▼▼▼ **Quality Inn** 🄷
(334) 280-0306. **$72-$80.** 7731 Slade Plaza Blvd 36105. I-65 exit 164, just s. Int corridors. **Pets:** Accepted. [SAVE] 🛏 🛜 🖥 💻

ⓐⓐⓐ ▼▼▼▼ **Residence Inn by Marriott Montgomery** 🄷
(334) 270-3300. **$89-$139.** 1200 Hilmar Ct 36117. I-85 exit 6, just s on Eastern Blvd, then just e. Ext corridors. **Pets:** Accepted.
[SAVE] 🛏 🛜 ✖ 🖥 💻

▼▼▼▼ **Sleep Inn & Suites** 🄷
(334) 387-1004. **$67-$94.** 5005 Carmichael Rd 36106. I-85 exit 6, just s. Int corridors. **Pets:** $10 daily fee/pet. Service with restrictions.
🛏 🛜 🖥 💻

▼▼▼▼ **Staybridge Suites-EastChase** 🄷
(334) 277-9383. **$119-$149, 3 day notice.** 7800 EastChase Pkwy 36117. I-85 exit 9 (Taylor Rd), just s, then 1 mi e; in The Shoppes of EastChase. Int corridors. **Pets:** Accepted. 🐾Ⓜ 🛏 🛜 🖥 💻

OXFORD
▼▼ **Comfort Inn** Ⓜ
(256) 831-0860. **$60-$250.** 138 Elm St 36203. I-20 exit 185, just s. Ext corridors. **Pets:** Accepted. 🛏 🛜 🖥 💻

ⓐⓐⓐ ▼▼▼▼ **Hampton Inn & Suites** 🄷
(256) 831-8958. **$99-$129.** 210 Colonial Dr 36203. I-20 exit 188, just n, then w. Int corridors. **Pets:** Accepted.
[SAVE] 🐾Ⓜ 🛏 🛜 ✖ 🖥 💻

ⓐⓐⓐ ▼▼▼▼ **Holiday Inn Express & Suites Anniston/Oxford** 🄷
(256) 835-8768. **Call for rates.** 160 Colonial Dr 36203. I-20 exit 188, just n, then w. Int corridors. **Pets:** Medium. $75 daily fee/pet. Service with restrictions, supervision. [SAVE] 🐾Ⓜ 🛏 🛜 ✖ 🖥 💻

ⓐⓐⓐ ▼▼▼▼ **La Quinta Inn & Suites Oxford** 🄷
(256) 241-0950. **$75-$300.** 100 Colonial Dr 36203. I-20 exit 188, just n, then w. Int corridors. **Pets:** Large, other species. Service with restrictions. [SAVE] 🐾Ⓜ 🛏 🛜 🖥 💻

▼▼ **Quality Inn** Ⓜ
(256) 835-2170. **$59-$64.** 161 Colonial Dr 36203. I-20 exit 188, just n, then w. Ext corridors. **Pets:** Medium. $20 daily fee/room. Service with restrictions, crate. 🛏 🛜 🖥 💻

OZARK
▼▼ **Baymont Inn & Suites Ozark** Ⓜ
(334) 774-0233. **$59-$99.** 1360 S US Hwy 231 36360. 0.3 mi s of jct SR 249. Ext corridors. **Pets:** Accepted. 🐾Ⓜ 🛏 🛜 🖥 💻

PELL CITY
▼▼▼▼ **Holiday Inn Express Pell City** 🄷 🐾
(205) 884-0047. **Call for rates.** 240 Vaughan Ln 35125. I-20 exit 158 eastbound; exit 158A westbound, just ne. Int corridors. **Pets:** Small. $50 one-time fee/room. Service with restrictions, supervision.
🐾Ⓜ 🛏 🛜 🖥 💻

PRATTVILLE *(Restaurants p. 613)*
▼▼ **Baymont Inn & Suites Prattville** 🄷
(334) 361-6463. **$59-$79.** 104 Jameson Ct 36067. I-65 exit 179, 1.4 mi w. Ext corridors. **Pets:** Accepted. 🛏 🛜 🖥 💻

▼▼▼▼ **La Quinta Inn & Suites** 🄷
(334) 358-5454. **$81-$184.** 261 Interstate Commercial Park Loop 36066. I-65 exit 181, just w. Int corridors. **Pets:** Large, other species. Service with restrictions. 🐾Ⓜ 🛏 🛜 ✖ 🖥 💻

▼▼ **Quality Inn** 🄷
(334) 365-6003. **$70-$77.** 797 Business Park Dr 36067. I-65 exit 181, just sw, then just n. Int corridors. **Pets:** Small. $10 daily fee/pet. Designated rooms, service with restrictions, supervision.
🐾Ⓜ 🛏 🛜 🖥 💻

PRICEVILLE
▼▼ **Comfort Inn** 🄷
(256) 355-1037. **$79-$99.** 3239 Point Mallard Pkwy 35603. I-65 exit 334, just w. Int corridors. **Pets:** Accepted. 🛏 🛜 ✖ 🖥 💻

RAINSVILLE
ⓐⓐⓐ ▼▼▼ **Super 8 Rainsville** 🄷
(256) 638-1640. **$41-$69.** 46 Roy Sanderson Ave 35986. I-59 exit 218, 5.9 mi nw. Int corridors. **Pets:** Accepted. [SAVE] 🛏 🛜 🖥 💻

SARALAND
▼▼ **Microtel Inn & Suites by Wyndham Saraland/North Mobile** 🄷
(251) 675-5045. **$70-$90.** 1124 Shelton Beach Rd 36571. I-65 exit 13, just e, then just n. Int corridors. **Pets:** Medium, other species. $25 one-time fee/room. Designated rooms, service with restrictions, crate.
🐾Ⓜ 🛜 🖥 💻

SCOTTSBORO
▼▼▼▼ **Comfort Inn & Suites** 🄷
(256) 259-8700. **$89-$119.** 25775 John T Reid Pkwy 35768. Jct US 72 and SR 35/279, 1.2 mi ne, just e on CR 33. Int corridors. **Pets:** Very small. $20 one-time fee/pet. Designated rooms, service with restrictions, crate. 🐾Ⓜ 🛏 🛜 🖥 💻

▼▼ **Quality Inn** 🄷 🐾
(256) 574-6666. **$69-$129.** 208 Micah Way 35769. On US 72, just s of jct SR 35. Ext corridors. **Pets:** Small. $20 daily fee/room. Designated rooms, service with restrictions, crate. 🛏 🛜 🖥 💻

SYLACAUGA
▼▼ **Quality Inn** Ⓜ
(256) 245-4141. **$80-$180.** 89 Gene Stewart Blvd 35151. Jct US 280, just s. Ext corridors. **Pets:** Accepted. 🛏 🛜 🖥 💻

THOMASVILLE
▼▼ **Comfort Inn** 🄷
(334) 636-2000. **$89-$120.** 571 N Park Dr 36784. On US 43, 0.6 mi s of jct SR 5. Int corridors. **Pets:** Accepted. 🐾Ⓜ 🛏 🛜 🖥 💻

TRUSSVILLE

▼▼ Quality Inn 🅷

(205) 661-9323. **$82-$87.** 4730 Norrell Dr 35173. I-59 exit 141, just e on Chalkville Rd, then just n. Ext corridors. **Pets:** Small. $20 daily fee/pet. Designated rooms, service with restrictions, supervision.

🌊 🛜 🖨 💻

TUSCALOOSA *(Restaurants p. 613)*

◈◈◈ ▼▼ BEST WESTERN Park Plaza Motor Inn 🅷

(205) 556-9690. **$80-$239, 7 day notice.** 3801 McFarland Blvd 35405. I-59/20 exit 73, just ne on US 82. Ext corridors. **Pets:** Medium. $10 deposit/pet, $10 daily fee/pet. Designated rooms, service with restrictions, supervision. 🆂🆅🅴 🌊 🛜 🖨 💻

◈◈ Centerstone Inn 🅷

(205) 556-3232. **$70-$300.** 4700 Doris Pate Dr 35405. I-59/20 exit 76, just n. Int corridors. **Pets:** Accepted. 🌊 🛜 ✖ 🖨 💻

▼▼▼ Wingate by Wyndham Tuscaloosa 🅷

(205) 553-5400. **$79-$289.** 4918 Skyland Blvd E 35405. I-59/20 exit 76, just n. Int corridors. **Pets:** Accepted. 🆚Ⓜ 🌊 🛜 ✖ 🖨 💻

TUSCUMBIA

▼▼ Microtel Inn & Suites by Wyndham Tuscumbia/ Muscle Shoals 🅷

(256) 248-0055. **$62-$150.** 1852 Hwy 72 E 35674. Just w of jct US 72 and 43. Int corridors. **Pets:** Small, dogs only. $20 daily fee/pet. Service with restrictions, supervision. 🆚Ⓜ 🌊 🛜 ✖ 🖨 💻

VANCE

▼▼▼ Greystone Inn & Suites 🅷

(205) 556-3606. **$68-$88.** 11170 Will Walker Rd 35490. I-59/20 exit 89 northbound, 0.8 mi n on Mercedes Dr, 0.3 mi w, then just s; exit southbound, just s. Int corridors. **Pets:** Other species. $40 one-time fee/room. Service with restrictions. 🆚Ⓜ 🛜 ✖ 🖨 💻

ALASKA

ANCHORAGE

◈◈◈ ▼▼▼ Clarion Suites Downtown 🅷

(907) 222-5005. **$119-$249, 3 day notice.** 1110 W 8th Ave 99501. Corner of L St and W 8th Ave. Int corridors. **Pets:** Accepted.

🆂🆅🅴 🆚Ⓜ 🌊 🛜 ✖ 🖨 💻

▼▼ Motel 6 - #4216 Midtown Ⓜ

(907) 677-8000. **$59-$189.** 5000 A St 99503. Jct C St, just e on International Airport Rd, just n. Int corridors. **Pets:** Other species. Service with restrictions, crate. 🛜

▼▼▼ Residence Inn by Marriott 🅷

(907) 563-9844. **$129-$299.** 1025 E 35th Ave 99508. Corner of SR 1 (Seward Hwy) and 36th Ave. Int corridors. **Pets:** $100 one-time fee/pet. Service with restrictions, supervision. 🆚Ⓜ 🌊 🛜 ✖ 🖨 💻

◈◈◈ ▼▼▼ Sheraton Anchorage Hotel & Spa 🅷

(907) 276-8700. **$159-$369.** 401 E 6th Ave 99501. Jct 6th Ave and Denali St. Int corridors. **Pets:** Small, dogs only. Designated rooms, service with restrictions, supervision. 🆂🆅🅴 🍽 🆚Ⓜ 🆂 ✖ 🖨 💻

◈◈◈ ▼▼▼ The Voyager Inn 🅷

(907) 277-9501. **Call for rates.** 501 K St 99501. At K St and 5th Ave. Int corridors. **Pets:** Accepted. 🆂🆅🅴 🆚Ⓜ 🛜 ✖ 🖨 💻

CANTWELL

◈◈◈ ▼ Backwoods Lodge Ⓜ 🐾

(907) 987-0960. **$100-$150.** Denali Hwy MP 133.8 99729. SR 3 (Denali Hwy), just e of jct SR 8 (George Parks Hwy). Ext corridors. **Pets:** Dogs only. Supervision. 🆂🆅🅴 🛜 ✖ 🅰🅲 🖨 💻

FAIRBANKS

◈◈◈ ▼▼▼ Pike's Waterfront Lodge 🅷 🐾

(907) 456-4500. **$99-$450, 3 day notice.** 1850 Hoselton Dr 99709. Jct Airport Way and Hoselton Dr. Ext/int corridors. **Pets:** Other species. $25 daily fee/pet. Designated rooms, service with restrictions. 🆂🆅🅴 🍽 🆚Ⓜ ✖ 🛜 ✖ 🖨 💻

HAINES

◈◈◈ ▼ Captain's Choice Motel Ⓜ

(907) 766-3111. **$141-$189.** 108 2nd Ave N 99827. Jct 2nd Ave and Dalton St. Ext corridors. **Pets:** Other species. $25 one-time fee/room. Service with restrictions, supervision. 🆂🆅🅴 🆂 🅰🅲 🖨 💻

HOMER

◈◈◈ ▼▼ BEST WESTERN Bidarka Inn 🅷 🐾

(907) 235-8148. **$90-$210.** 575 Sterling Hwy 99603. Just n of Pioneer Ave on SR 1 (Sterling Hwy). Ext/int corridors. **Pets:** Large, other species. $15 daily fee/pet. Designated rooms, service with restrictions, supervision. 🆂🆅🅴 🍽 🆚Ⓜ 🛜 🅰🅲 🖨 💻

KETCHIKAN

◈◈◈ ▼▼▼ BEST WESTERN PLUS Landing Hotel 🅷 🐾

(907) 225-5166. **$151-$197.** 3434 Tongass Ave 99901. Across from Alaska Marine Hwy ferry terminal. Ext/int corridors. **Pets:** Large, other species. $50 deposit/room, $10 daily fee/pet. Designated rooms, service with restrictions, supervision. 🆂🆅🅴 🍽 🆚Ⓜ 🛜 ✖ 🖨 💻

◈◈◈ ▼▼ Cape Fox Lodge 🅷 🐾

(907) 225-8001. **$99-$245.** 800 Venetia Way 99901. Above Creek St (tramway from Creek St). Ext/int corridors. **Pets:** Other species. $10 daily fee/room. Service with restrictions, crate. 🆂🆅🅴 🍽 🆚Ⓜ 🛜 🅰🅲 🖨 💻

KODIAK

◈◈◈ ▼▼ BEST WESTERN Kodiak Inn & Convention Center 🅷

(907) 486-5712. **$105-$270.** 236 W Rezanof Dr 99615. Just w of ferry terminal; downtown. Ext/int corridors. **Pets:** Medium. $25 one-time fee/pet. Designated rooms, service with restrictions, supervision.

🆂🆅🅴 🍽 🆚Ⓜ 🛜 🅰🅲 🖨 💻

SEWARD

◈◈◈ ▼▼ Hotel Seward 🅷

(907) 224-8001. **$59-$399, 3 day notice.** 221 Fifth Ave 99664. Downtown; just n of Alaska SeaLife Center. Int corridors. **Pets:** Medium, dogs only. $25 daily fee/pet. Designated rooms, service with restrictions, supervision. 🆂🆅🅴 🍽 🆚Ⓜ 🛜 ✖ 🅰🅲 🖨 💻

SITKA

▼▼ Super 8-Sitka 🅷

(907) 747-8804. **$139-$169.** 404 Sawmill Creek Rd 99835. Corner of Lake St and Halibut Point Rd/Sawmill Creek Rd, just e. Int corridors. **Pets:** Accepted. 🆚Ⓜ 🛜 🖨 💻

▼▼ Totem Square Hotel & Marina 🅷

(907) 747-3693. **$149-$259.** 201 Katlian St 99835. In Totem Square Complex near municipal office. Int corridors. **Pets:** Accepted.

🍽 🆚Ⓜ 🛜 ✖ 🅰🅲 🖨 💻

▼▼ Westmark Sitka 🅷

(907) 747-6241. **$159-$230.** 330 Seward St 99835. Center. Int corridors. **Pets:** Accepted. 🍽 🆚Ⓜ 🛜 ✖ 🅰🅲 🖨 💻

SKAGWAY

▼ Westmark Inn Skagway Ⓜ

(907) 983-6000. **$115-$145.** 3rd Ave & Spring St 99840. Jct 3rd Ave and Spring St; downtown. Ext/int corridors. **Pets:** Accepted.

🍽 🆚Ⓜ 🆂 ✖ 🅰🅲 🖨 💻

TOK

Cleft of the Rock Bed & Breakfast BB
(907) 883-4219. **$115-$170, 3 day notice.** 0.5 Sundog Tr 99780. Jct SR 1 and 2 (Alaskan Hwy), 2.5 mi w on SR 2 (Alaskan Hwy) to Sundog Tr, 0.5 mi n. Ext/int corridors. **Pets:** Accepted.

TRAPPER CREEK

Gate Creek Cabins CA
(907) 733-1393. **$120-$150, 10 day notice.** Mile 10.5 Petersville Rd 99683. George Parks Hwy (SR 3), Milepost 114, 10.5 mi w at Petersville Rd. Ext corridors. **Pets:** Dogs only. $25 one-time fee/pet. No service, crate.

Trapper Creek Inn & RV Park M
(907) 733-2302. **Call for rates.** Mile 114.6 Parks Hwy 99683. George Parks Hwy (SR 3), Milepost 114. Ext corridors. **Pets:** Accepted.

VALDEZ

BEST WESTERN Valdez Harbor Inn H
(907) 835-3434. **Call for rates.** 100 N Harbor Dr 99686. Just s at Meals Ave. Int corridors. **Pets:** Small, dogs only. $50 deposit/pet, $10 daily fee/pet. Designated rooms, service with restrictions, supervision.

WASILLA

BEST WESTERN Lake Lucille Inn H
(907) 373-1776. **$89-$199.** 1300 W Lake Lucille Dr 99654. SR 3 (George Parks Hwy), just w on Hallea Ln; center. Int corridors. **Pets:** $20 daily fee/pet. Service with restrictions, crate.

ARIZONA

AJO

La Siesta Motel M
(520) 387-6569. **$60-$65.** 2561 N Ajo-Gila Bend Hwy 85321. On SR 85, 1.8 mi n of town plaza. Ext corridors. **Pets:** Other species. Service with restrictions, supervision.

AMADO

Amado Territory B & B BB
(520) 398-8684. **$129-$139, 7 day notice.** 3001 E Frontage Rd 85645. I-19 exit 48, just e, then just s. Int corridors. **Pets:** Accepted.

ANTHEM

Hampton Inn at Anthem H
(623) 465-7979. **$74-$209.** 42415 N 41st Dr 85086. I-17 exit 229 (Anthem Way), just w. Int corridors. **Pets:** Accepted.

APACHE JUNCTION

Apache Junction Motel M
(480) 982-7702. **$49-$89, 3 day notice.** 1680 W Apache Tr 85120. US 60 exit 195, 2 mi n, then just w. Ext corridors. **Pets:** Very small, dogs only. $20 one-time fee/pet. Designated rooms, service with restrictions, supervision.

BENSON

BEST WESTERN Quail Hollow Inn H ✿
(520) 586-3646. **$79-$199.** 699 N Ocotillo Rd 85602. I-10 exit 304 (Ocotillo Rd), just s. Ext corridors. **Pets:** $10 daily fee/room. Designated rooms, service with restrictions, crate.

BISBEE

Americas Best Value Inn & Suites M
(520) 432-2293. **Call for rates.** 1372 Hwy 92 85603. 0.8 mi w of jct Naco Hwy; southwest of downtown. Ext corridors. **Pets:** Other species. $10 daily fee/pet. Designated rooms, service with restrictions, supervision.

San Jose Lodge M
(520) 432-5761. **Call for rates.** 2102 Naco Hwy 85603. SR 92 W, 1.5 mi s. Ext corridors. **Pets:** Accepted.

BUCKEYE

Days Inn-Buckeye H
(623) 386-5400. **$110-$270.** 25205 W Yuma Rd 85326. I-10 exit 114 (Miller Rd), just sw. Ext corridors. **Pets:** $15 daily fee/pet. Designated rooms, service with restrictions, supervision.

BULLHEAD CITY

BEST WESTERN Bullhead City Inn H
(928) 754-3000. **$70-$149.** 1126 Hwy 95 86429. 1.8 mi s of Laughlin Bridge. Ext corridors. **Pets:** Accepted.

Lake Mohave Resort Motel M
(928) 754-3245. **$95-$170, 3 day notice.** 2690 E Katherine Spur Rd 86429. Jct SR 95, 1.5 mi e on SR 68, 1 mi n, then 5.4 mi e; at Katherine Landing; in Lake Mead National Recreation Area. Ext corridors. **Pets:** Large, other species. $50 deposit/pet, $10 daily fee/pet. Service with restrictions, crate.

CAMERON

Cameron Trading Post Motel, Restaurant & Gift Shop M
(928) 679-2231. **$79-$119.** 466 N Hwy 89 86020. 1 mi from east gate turn off. Ext corridors. **Pets:** $15 daily fee/pet. Service with restrictions, supervision.

CAMP VERDE

Cliff Castle Casino Hotel H
(928) 567-6611. **$69-$199.** 333 Middle Verde Rd 86322. I-17 exit 289, 0.4 mi se. Ext corridors. **Pets:** Medium, dogs only. $20 daily fee/pet. Designated rooms, service with restrictions, crate.

Comfort Inn-Camp Verde H
(928) 567-9000. **Call for rates.** 340 N Goswick Way 86322. I-17 exit 287, just e, then just s. Int corridors. **Pets:** $15 daily fee/pet. Designated rooms, service with restrictions, supervision.

Super 8-Camp Verde H
(928) 567-2622. **$60-$80.** 1550 W Hwy 260 86322. I-17 exit 287, just e. Int corridors. **Pets:** Accepted.

CAREFREE

The Boulders, A Waldorf Astoria Resort H
(480) 488-9009. **$99-$429.** 34631 N Tom Darlington Dr 85377. Jct Scottsdale and Bell rds, 11 mi n. Ext corridors. **Pets:** Accepted.

Carefree Resort & Conference Center H
(480) 488-5300. **$69-$870, 3 day notice.** 37220 Mule Train Rd 85377. SR 101 exit 36 (Pima Rd), 12.2 mi n to Cave Creek Rd, 1 mi w, then 0.4 mi n. Ext/int corridors. **Pets:** Accepted.

CASA GRANDE

(AAA) ✦✦✦✦ Holiday Inn Express & Suites Casa Grande H

(520) 509-6333. **$99-$149.** 805 N Cacheries Ct 85122. I-10 exit 194 (SR 287), 0.6 mi w. Int corridors. **Pets:** Dogs only. $25 daily fee/room. Service with restrictions, supervision.

[SAVE] [&M] [🛏] [📶] [✕] [🎒] [🖥]

(AAA) ✦✦✦✦ Holiday Inn Hotel Casa Grande H

(520) 426-3500. **$79-$159.** 777 N Pinal Ave 85122. I-10 exit 194 (SR 287), 3.9 mi w. Int corridors. **Pets:** Accepted.

[SAVE] [🍴] [🛏] [📶] [🎒] [🖥]

✦✦✦ MainStay Suites Casa Grande H

(520) 426-1177. **$70-$114.** 851 N Henness Rd 85222. I-10 exit 194 (SR 287), 1 mi w, then just n. Int corridors. **Pets:** Medium. $20 daily fee/pet. Service with restrictions, supervision. [📶] [✕] [🎒] [🖥]

(AAA) ✦ Super 8 H

(520) 836-8800. **$59-$79.** 2066 E Florence Blvd 85222. I-10 exit 194 (SR 287), 0.6 mi w. Int corridors. **Pets:** Other species. $10 daily fee/pet. Service with restrictions, supervision. [SAVE] [🛏] [📶] [🎒] [🖥]

CATALINA

✦✦✦ Catalina Inn H

(520) 818-9500. **$78-$120.** 15691 N Oracle Rd 85739. 4.6 mi n of Tangerine Rd. Ext/int corridors. **Pets:** Accepted. [🛏] [📶] [✕] [🎒] [🖥]

CHANDLER *(Restaurants p. 613)*

(AAA) ✦✦✦✦ Comfort Inn Chandler-Phoenix South H

(480) 857-4969. **$79-$199.** 7400 W Boston St 85226. I-10 exit 160 (Chandler Blvd), just e, then just s on Southgate Dr. Int corridors. **Pets:** Medium, dogs only. $20 daily fee/pet. Designated rooms, service with restrictions, supervision. [SAVE] [&M] [🛏] [📶] [✕] [🖥]

✦✦✦✦ Crowne Plaza San Marcos Golf Resort H

(480) 812-0900. **$79-$359, 3 day notice.** 1 N San Marcos Pl 85225. Jct Chandler Blvd, just s on Arizona Ave, then just w on Buffalo St; in historic downtown. Ext corridors. **Pets:** Dogs only. $25 one-time fee/ room. Service with restrictions, crate.

[🍴] [🛏] [✕] [📶] [✕] [🎒] [🖥]

✦✦✦ Hawthorn Suites by Wyndham-Chandler H

(480) 705-8881. **$79-$219.** 5858 W Chandler Blvd 85226. I-10 exit 160 (Chandler Blvd), 1.5 mi e. Int corridors. **Pets:** Accepted.

[🛏] [📶] [🎒] [🖥]

✦✦✦ Hilton Phoenix Chandler H 🐾

(480) 899-7400. **$99-$249.** 2929 W Frye Rd 85224. SR 202 exit 50B (Price Rd), 0.4 mi n, then just w. Int corridors. **Pets:** Other species. $50 one-time fee/room. Service with restrictions, crate.

[🍴] [🛏] [📶] [✕] [🎒] [🖥]

✦✦✦ Homewood Suites by Hilton Phoenix-Chandler H 🐾

(480) 753-6200. **$89-$219.** 7373 W Detroit St 85226. I-10 exit 160 (Chandler Blvd), 0.4 mi e, n on 54th St, then just w. Int corridors. **Pets:** Medium, dogs only. $75 one-time fee/room. Service with restrictions, supervision. [&M] [🛏] [📶] [🎒] [🖥]

✦✦✦ Homewood Suites by Hilton-Phoenix/Chandler Fashion Center H

(480) 963-5700. **$99-$309.** 1221 S Spectrum Blvd 85286. SR 202 exit 50B (Price Rd), just s. Int corridors. **Pets:** Accepted.

[&M] [🛏] [📶] [🎒] [🖥]

(AAA) ✦✦✦ Hyatt Place Phoenix Chandler Fashion Center H

(480) 812-9600. **$79-$225.** 3535 W Chandler Blvd 85226. I-10 exit 160 (Chandler Blvd), 4 mi e. Int corridors. **Pets:** Accepted.

[SAVE] [🛏] [✕] [📶] [✕] [🎒] [🖥]

(AAA) ✦✦✦ Quality Inn H

(480) 705-0922. **$69-$179.** 255 N Kyrene Rd 85226. I-10 exit 160 (Chandler Blvd), 1.5 mi e, then just n. Int corridors. **Pets:** Accepted.

[SAVE] [&M] [🛏] [📶] [✕] [🎒] [🖥]

✦✦✦ Residence Inn by Marriott-Chandler Fashion Center H

(480) 782-1551. **$79-$179.** 200 N Federal St 85226. I-10 exit 160 (Chandler Blvd), 4.2 mi e, just n on N Metro Blvd, then just e. Int corridors. **Pets:** Accepted. [&M] [🛏] [📶] [✕] [🎒] [🖥]

(AAA) ✦✦✦✦ Sheraton Wild Horse Pass Resort & Spa H

(602) 225-0100. **$99-$299, 3 day notice.** 5594 W Wild Horse Pass Blvd 85226. I-10 exit 162, 2.4 mi w. Int corridors. **Pets:** Accepted.

[SAVE] [🍴] [🛏] [✕] [🆘] [✕] [🎒] [🖥]

CHINO VALLEY

✦✦ Days Inn Chino Valley H

(928) 636-0311. **$76-$113.** 688 Fletcher Ct 86323. Center. Int corridors. **Pets:** Accepted. [&M] [📶] [✕] [🎒] [🖥]

COTTONWOOD

✦✦ AZ Pines Motel M

(928) 634-9975. **$65-$135.** 920 S Camino Real 86326. Jct SR 260, just nw on SR 89A, then just s. Ext corridors. **Pets:** Dogs only. $20 one-time fee/room, $5 daily fee/pet. Designated rooms, service with restrictions, supervision. [ECO] [🛏] [📶] [✕] [🎒] [🖥]

(AAA) ✦✦ BEST WESTERN Cottonwood Inn H

(928) 634-5575. **$100-$110.** 993 S Main St 86326. On SR 89A, at SR 260. Ext corridors. **Pets:** Very small, dogs only. $20 daily fee/pet. Designated rooms, service with restrictions, supervision.

[SAVE] [&M] [🛏] [📶] [✕] [🎒] [🖥]

(AAA) ✦✦ Verde Valley Inn M

(928) 634-3678. **$59-$149.** 1089 S SR 260 86326. Just e of jct SR 89A. Ext corridors. **Pets:** Very small, dogs only. $10 daily fee/pet. Designated rooms, service with restrictions, supervision. [SAVE] [📶] [✕] [🎒]

(AAA) ✦ The View Motel M

(928) 634-7581. **$59-$129.** 818 S Main St 86326. On SR 89A, 0.4 mi nw of jct SR 260. Ext corridors. **Pets:** Dogs only. $10 daily fee/pet. Service with restrictions, supervision. [SAVE] [🛏] [📶] [🎒]

EAGAR

(AAA) ✦✦ BEST WESTERN Sunrise Inn M

(928) 333-2540. **$90-$120.** 128 N Main St 85925. Jct SR 260, just n; jct US 60, 1.5 mi s. Ext corridors. **Pets:** Other species. $10 one-time fee/pet. Service with restrictions, crate. [SAVE] [📶] [🎒] [🖥]

EHRENBERG

(AAA) ✦✦ BEST WESTERN Desert Oasis H

(928) 923-9711. **$79-$150.** S Frontage Rd 85334. I-10 exit 1, just s; 0.5 mi e of Colorado River. Int corridors. **Pets:** Accepted.

[SAVE] [🛏] [📶] [🎒] [🖥]

ELOY

✦ Motel 6 #1263 M

(520) 836-3323. **$45-$61.** 4965 S Sunland Gin Rd 85231. I-10 exit 200, just w. Ext corridors. **Pets:** Other species. Service with restrictions, crate. [🛏] [🆘] [🎒]

FLAGSTAFF *(Restaurants p. 613)*

(AAA) ✦✦✦ BEST WESTERN Pony Soldier Inn & Suites H 🐾

(928) 526-2388. **$70-$200.** 3030 E Route 66 86004. I-40 exit 201, just n, then 1 mi w. Int corridors. **Pets:** Large, other species. $20 one-time fee/room. Designated rooms, service with restrictions, supervision.

[SAVE] [&M] [🛏] [📶] [✕] [🎒] [🖥]

▼▼▼ **Comfort Inn I-17/I-40** H
(928) 774-2225. **$90-$190.** 2355 S Beulah Blvd 86001. I-40 exit 195, just n to Forest Meadows St, then 1 blk w. Int corridors.
Pets: Accepted. ⌫ 🛰 🖥 📺

▼▼ **Days Hotel Flagstaff** H
(928) 779-6944. **Call for rates.** 2200 E Butler Ave 86004. I-40 exit 198 (Butler Ave), just n. Int corridors. **Pets:** Accepted.
🍴 ⌫ ✕ 🛰 ✕ 🖥 📺

▲▲▲ ▼▼ **Days Inn & Suites** H
(928) 527-1477. **$63-$150.** 3601 E Lockett Rd 86004. I-40 exit 201, 0.5 mi w on I-40 business loop, then just n on Fanning Dr. Int corridors.
Pets: $25 one-time fee/room, $5 daily fee/room. Designated rooms, service with restrictions, supervision. SAVE ⌫ 🛰 ✕ 🖥 📺

▲▲▲ ▼▼▼ **DoubleTree by Hilton Flagstaff** H
(928) 773-8888. **$109-$189.** 1175 W Route 66 86001. I-40 exit 195, 1.5 mi n on SR 89A (Milton Rd), then 0.5 mi w. Int corridors. **Pets:** Large. $50 one-time fee/room. Designated rooms, service with restrictions.
SAVE 🍴 &M ⌫ ✕ 🛰 ✕ 🖥 📺

▼▼▼ **Drury Inn & Suites-Flagstaff** H
(928) 773-4900. **$155-$224.** 300 S Milton Rd 86001. I-40 exit 195, 1.8 mi n on SR 89A (Milton Rd). Int corridors. **Pets:** $10 daily fee/room. Service with restrictions, supervision.
ECO &M ⌫ 🛰 ✕ 🖥 📺

▲▲▲ ▼▼▼ **Econo Lodge-University** M
(928) 774-7326. **$55-$165.** 914 S Milton Rd 86001. I-40 exit 195, 1.2 mi n on SR 89A (Milton Rd). Ext corridors. **Pets:** Accepted.
SAVE ⌫ 🛰 🖥 📺

▼▼ **Hampton Inn East** H
(928) 526-1885. **$129-$299.** 3501 E Lockett Rd 86004. I-40 exit 201, 0.5 mi w on I-40 business loop, then just n on Fanning Dr. Int corridors.
Pets: Accepted. &M ⌫ 🛰 ✕ 🖥 📺

▼ **Motel 6-Flagstaff West #1000** M
(928) 779-3757. **$49-$105.** 2745 S Woodlands Village Blvd 86001. I-40 exit 195, just n to Forest Meadows St, w to Beulah Blvd, just s, then just w. Ext corridors. **Pets:** Other species. Service with restrictions, crate. &M ⌫ 🛰 🖥 📺

▼ **Quality Inn University** H
(928) 774-8771. **$60-$150.** 2000 S Milton Rd 86001. I-40 exit 195, just n to Forest Meadows St, then right. Int corridors. **Pets:** Accepted.
⌫ 🛰 ✕ 🖥 📺

▼▼ **Ramada West** H
(928) 773-1111. **Call for rates.** 2755 S Woodlands Village Blvd 86001. I-40 exit 195, just n to Forest Meadows St, w to Beulah Blvd, just s, then w. Ext corridors. **Pets:** Accepted. ⌫ 🛰 ✕ 🖥 📺

▲▲▲ ▼▼▼ **Sonesta ES Suites Flagstaff** H
(928) 526-5555. **Call for rates.** 1400 N Country Club Dr 86004. I-40 exit 201, 0.5 mi s. Ext/int corridors. **Pets:** Accepted.
SAVE ⌫ 🛰 ✕ 🖥 📺

▼▼▼ **SpringHill Suites by Marriott** H
(928) 774-8042. **$159-$299.** 2455 S Beulah Blvd 86001. I-40 exit 195, just n to Forest Meadows St, then 1 blk w. Int corridors.
Pets: Accepted. &M ⌫ 🛰 ✕ 🖥 📺

▼▼▼ **Starlight Pines, A Bed & Breakfast** BB
(928) 527-1912. **$159-$179, 14 day notice.** 3380 E Lockett Rd 86004. I-40 exit 201, 0.5 mi w on I-40 business loop, then just n. **Pets:** Very small, dogs only. $10 daily fee/pet. Designated rooms, service with restrictions, supervision. 🛰 ✕ 🌀 🚫

▲▲▲ ▼▼▼ **Super 8-Flagstaff Mall** H
(928) 526-0818. **$50-$102.** 3725 N Kasper Ave 86004. I-40 exit 201, just n, 0.5 mi w on I-40 business loop, then just n. Int corridors.
Pets: Other species. $15 daily fee/pet. Designated rooms, service with restrictions, supervision. SAVE 🛰 🖥 📺

FLORENCE
▼▼▼ **Rancho Sonora Inn** CI
(520) 868-8000. **$89-$225, 3 day notice.** 9198 N Hwy 79 85232. 5 mi s of SR 287. Ext corridors. **Pets:** $10 deposit/pet, $10 daily fee/pet. Designated rooms, service with restrictions, crate.
⌫ 🛰 ✕ 🖥 📺

FOREST LAKES
▲▲▲ ▼ **Forest Lakes Lodge** M
(928) 535-4727. **$67-$89.** 2823 SR 260 85931. Between MM 288 and 289. Ext corridors. **Pets:** Accepted. SAVE 🛰 🐾 🖥

FOUNTAIN HILLS
▼▼▼ **Comfort Inn Fountain Hills** H
(480) 837-5343. **$50-$190.** 17105 E Shea Blvd 85268. 0.5 mi w of SR 87 (Beeline Hwy). Int corridors. **Pets:** Small, other species. $15 daily fee/pet. Designated rooms, service with restrictions, supervision.
⌫ 🛰 🖥 📺

GILA BEND
▲▲▲ ▼▼▼ **BEST WESTERN Space Age Lodge** M
(928) 683-2273. **$109-$169.** 401 E Pima St 85337. Business Loop I-8; center. Ext corridors. **Pets:** Accepted.
SAVE 🍴 ⌫ 🛰 ✕ 🖥 📺

GILBERT
▲▲▲ ▼▼▼ **Hyatt Place Phoenix/Gilbert** H
(480) 899-5900. **$69-$229.** 3275 S Market St 85297. Loop 202 exit 42 (Val Vista Dr), just n, then just e. Int corridors. **Pets:** Medium, dogs only. $75 one-time fee/room. Service with restrictions, supervision.
SAVE 🍴 &M ⌫ 🛰 ✕ 🖥 📺

▼▼▼ **Residence Inn by Marriott Phoenix Gilbert** H
(480) 699-4450. **$119-$359.** 3021 E Banner Gateway Dr 85234. US 60 exit 186 (Higley Rd), just s, then just w. Int corridors. **Pets:** Accepted.
&M ⌫ 🛰 ✕ 🖥 📺

GLENDALE
▼▼▼ **Comfort Suites Glendale University of Phoenix Stadium Area** H ❀
(623) 271-9005. **$99-$999.** 9824 W Camelback Rd 85305. SR 101 exit 5 (Camelback Rd), just w to 99th St, then just n. Int corridors.
Pets: Medium. $25 one-time fee/room. Designated rooms, service with restrictions, crate. &M ⌫ 🛰 ✕ 🖥 📺

▲▲▲ ▼▼▼▼ **Renaissance Glendale Hotel & Spa** H
(623) 937-3700. **$99-$409.** 9495 W Coyotes Blvd 85305. SR 101 exit 7 (Glendale Ave), just e to N 95th Ave, then just n, then just e. Int corridors. **Pets:** Dogs only. $100 one-time fee/pet. Service with restrictions.
SAVE 🍴 &M ⌫ ✕ 🛰 ✕ 🖥 📺

▼▼▼ **Residence Inn by Marriott Phoenix Glendale Sports & Entertainment District** H
(623) 772-8900. **$99-$699.** 7350 W Zanjero Blvd 85305. SR 101 exit 7 (Glendale Ave), then e. Int corridors. **Pets:** Accepted.
&M ⌫ 🛰 ✕ 🖥 📺

▼▼▼ **Staybridge Suites Phoenix/Glendale** H
(623) 842-0000. **Call for rates.** 9340 W Cabela Dr 85305. SR 101 exit 7 (Glendale Ave), 0.6 mi e to N Zanjero Blvd, then just n. Int corridors.
Pets: Accepted. &M ⌫ 🛰 ✕ 🖥 📺

GLOBE
▲▲▲ ▼▼ **BEST WESTERN Copper Hills Inn** H
(928) 425-7575. **$80-$110.** 1565 E South St 85501. On US 60, 1 mi e of town. Ext corridors. **Pets:** Accepted. SAVE ⌫ 🛰 ✕ 🖥 📺

GOODYEAR

AAA ▼▼◆ BEST WESTERN PLUS Phoenix Goodyear Inn H

(623) 932-3210. **$200.** 55 N Litchfield Rd 85338. I-10 exit 128, 0.8 mi s. Ext/int corridors. **Pets:** Accepted.

[SAVE] [❌] [⊷] [�] [✕] [▮] [▭]

▼▼◆◆ Comfort Suites Goodyear H

(623) 266-2884. **Call for rates.** 15575 W Roosevelt St 85338. I-10 exit 126, just s on Estrella Pkwy, then just w. Int corridors. **Pets:** Small. $25 one-time fee/room. Designated rooms, supervision.

[&M] [⊷] [�] [✕] [▮] [▭]

◆◆◆◆ Hampton Inn & Suites Goodyear H

(623) 536-1313. **$99-$219.** 2000 N Litchfield Rd 85395. I-10 exit 128, 0.5 mi n. Int corridors. **Pets:** Accepted. [&M] [⊷] [�] [▮] [▭]

◆◆◆◆ Holiday Inn & Suites Goodyear H

(623) 547-1313. **$139-$229.** 1188 N Dysart Rd 85395. I-10 exit 129 (Dysart Rd), just n. Int corridors. **Pets:** Accepted.

[❌] [⊷] [�] [▮] [▭]

◆◆◆ Holiday Inn Express West Phoenix/Goodyear H

(623) 535-1313. **Call for rates.** 1313 N Litchfield Rd 85395. I-10 exit 128, just n. Int corridors. **Pets:** Accepted.

[&M] [⊷] [�] [✕] [▮] [▭]

◆◆ Quality Inn & Suites Goodyear H

(623) 932-9191. **$70-$170.** 950 N Dysart Rd 85338. I-10 exit 129 (Dysart Rd), just s. Ext corridors. **Pets:** Medium. $15 daily fee/pet. Service with restrictions, supervision. [⊷] [�] [▮] [▭]

◆◆◆◆ Residence Inn by Marriott H

(623) 866-1313. **$89-$189.** 2020 N Litchfield Rd 85395. I-10 exit 128, 0.6 mi n. Int corridors. **Pets:** Accepted. [⊷] [�] [✕] [▮] [▭]

AAA ▼▼◆◆ TownePlace Suites by Marriott Phoenix/Goodyear H

(623) 535-5009. **$69-$599.** 13971 W Celebrate Life Way 85338. I-10 exit 128, just s, then just w. Int corridors. **Pets:** Medium, other species. $100 one-time fee/room. Designated rooms, service with restrictions.

[SAVE] [&M] [⊷] [�] [✕] [▮] [▭]

GRAND CANYON NATIONAL PARK - SOUTH RIM *(Restaurants p. 613)*

AAA ▼▼◆ Canyon Plaza Resort Grand Canyon H 🐾

(928) 638-2673. **$83-$268.** 406 Canyon Plaza Ln 86023. On SR 64; 2 mi s of South Rim entrance. Ext/int corridors. **Pets:** Medium. $50 one-time fee/pet. Designated rooms, service with restrictions, supervision.

[SAVE] [❌] [⊷] [�] [▮] [▭]

AAA ▼▼◆ Red Feather Lodge H

(928) 638-2414. **$75-$350.** 300 SR 64 86023. 2 mi s of South Rim entrance. Ext/int corridors. **Pets:** Other species. $50 deposit/room, $25 one-time fee/pet. Designated rooms, service with restrictions, supervision. [SAVE] [❌] [&M] [⊷] [�] [▮] [▭]

GREEN VALLEY

AAA ▼▼◆◆ BEST WESTERN Green Valley Inn H

(520) 625-2250. **$90-$120.** 111 S La Canada Dr 85614. I-19 exit 65, just w, then just s. Int corridors. **Pets:** $20 daily fee/pet. Designated rooms, supervision. [SAVE] [❌] [⊷] [�] [✕] [▮] [▭]

AAA ▼▼◆ Comfort Inn H

(520) 399-3736. **$85-$150.** 90 W Esperanza Blvd 85614. I-19 exit 65, just w. Int corridors. **Pets:** Accepted. [SAVE] [⊷] [�] [▮] [▭]

◆◆ Holiday Inn Express H

(520) 625-0900. **Call for rates.** 19200 S I-19 Frontage Rd 85614. I-19 exit 69 (Duval Mine Rd), west side of interstate, then just s. Int corridors. **Pets:** $20 daily fee/pet. Service with restrictions, supervision.

[⊷] [�] [▮] [▭]

HEBER

AAA ▼▼◆ BEST WESTERN Sawmill Inn H

(928) 535-5053. **$60-$125.** 1877 Hwy 260 85928. 0.5 mi e of center. Ext corridors. **Pets:** Dogs only. $10 daily fee/pet. Designated rooms, service with restrictions, supervision. [SAVE] [ECO] [�] [▮] [▭]

HOLBROOK

AAA ▼▼◆ BEST WESTERN Arizonian Inn H

(928) 524-2611. **$79-$129.** 2508 Navajo Blvd 86025. I-40 exit 289, 0.5 mi w. Ext corridors. **Pets:** Accepted. [SAVE] [⊷] [�] [✕] [▮] [▭]

AAA ▼▼◆ Days Inn M

(928) 524-6949. **$60-$85.** 2601 Navajo Blvd 86025. I-40 exit 289, 0.3 mi w. Ext corridors. **Pets:** Accepted. [SAVE] [ECO] [⊷] [�] [▮] [▭]

▼▼◆ Howard Johnson H

(928) 524-2566. **$59-$89.** 2608 E Navajo Blvd 86025. I-40 exit 289, just w. Ext corridors. **Pets:** Accepted. [⊷] [�] [▮] [▭]

▼▼◆ Lexington Inn Holbrook H

(928) 524-1466. **$99-$149.** 1308 E Navajo Blvd 86025. I-40 exit 286, just e. Int corridors. **Pets:** Accepted. [⊷] [�] [✕] [▮] [▭]

AAA ▼▼◆ Quality Inn H

(928) 524-6131. **$70-$80.** 2602 Navajo Blvd 86025. I-40 exit 289, just w. Ext corridors. **Pets:** Medium, dogs only. $20 one-time fee/pet. Designated rooms, supervision. [SAVE] [⊷] [�] [✕] [▮] [▭]

JEROME

▼▼ Connor Hotel of Jerome H 🐾

(928) 634-5006. **$95-$165, 3 day notice.** 160 S Main St 86331. Center. Int corridors. **Pets:** Other species. $150 deposit/room. Service with restrictions, supervision. [�] [✕] [▮] [▭]

KAYENTA

▼▼◆◆ Hampton Inn of Kayenta H

(928) 697-3170. **$89-$199.** Hwy 160 86033. Just w of US 163. Int corridors. **Pets:** Accepted. [❌] [&M] [⊷] [�] [✕] [▭]

KINGMAN

AAA ▼▼◆◆ BEST WESTERN PLUS A Wayfarer's Inn & Suites H

(928) 753-6271. **$110-$120.** 2815 E Andy Devine Ave 86401. I-40 exit 53, 0.5 mi w on Route 66. Ext corridors. **Pets:** Accepted.

[SAVE] [⊷] [�] [▮] [▭]

AAA ▼▼◆◆ BEST WESTERN PLUS King's Inn & Suites H

(928) 753-6101. **$105-$115.** 2930 E Andy Devine Ave 86401. I-40 exit 53, just w on Route 66. Ext corridors. **Pets:** $8 one-time fee/room. Designated rooms, service with restrictions, supervision.

[SAVE] [&M] [⊷] [�] [▮] [▭]

▼▼◆ Comfort Inn H

(928) 718-1717. **$90-$120.** 3129 E Andy Devine Ave 86401. I-40 exit 53, just w on Route 66. Int corridors. **Pets:** Medium. $20 one-time fee/room. Designated rooms, service with restrictions, supervision.

[&M] [⊷] [�] [✕] [▮] [▭]

▼▼◆ Days Inn West M

(928) 753-7500. **$54-$99.** 3023 E Andy Devine Ave 86401. I-40 exit 53, just w on Route 66. Ext corridors. **Pets:** Accepted. [⊷] [�] [▮] [▭]

AAA ▼▼◆◆ Holiday Inn Express Hotel & Suites H

(928) 718-4343. **$109-$129.** 3031 E Andy Devine Ave 86401. I-40 exit 53, just w on Route 66. Int corridors. **Pets:** Accepted.

[SAVE] [&M] [⊷] [�] [▮] [▭]

 SpringHill Suites by Marriott H

(928) 753-8766. **$109-$209.** 3101 E Andy Devine Ave 86401. I-40 exit 53, just w on Route 66. Int corridors. **Pets:** Other species. $20 one-time fee/pet. Designated rooms, no service, supervision.

SAVE &M 🏊 🛜 ✕ 🛏 💻

Travelodge Kingman M

(928) 757-1188. **$60-$95.** 3275 E Andy Devine Ave 86401. I-40 exit 53, just e on Route 66. Ext corridors. **Pets:** Medium. $10 one-time fee/room. Service with restrictions, supervision. SAVE 🏊 🛜 🛏 💻

KOHLS RANCH

Kohl's Ranch Lodge CO 🐾

(928) 478-4211. **$89-$149.** 202 S Kohl's Ranch Lodge Rd 85541. SR 87, 16.6 mi e on US 260, between MM 238-239. Ext/int corridors. **Pets:** $20 one-time fee/room. Designated rooms, service with restrictions, supervision. 🍽 🏊 ✕ 🛜 ✕ 🛏 💻

LAKE HAVASU CITY *(Restaurants p. 613)*

Days Inn Lake Havasu M

(928) 855-7841. **$65-$129.** 1700 McCulloch Blvd N 86403. Just ne of Lake Havasu Ave; center. Ext corridors. **Pets:** Accepted.

🏊 🛜 🛏 💻

Hampton Inn Lake Havasu H 🌼

(928) 855-4071. **$107-$206.** 245 London Bridge Rd 86403. 0.5 mi n of London Bridge. Ext/int corridors. **Pets:** Other species. Designated rooms, service with restrictions, supervision.

🏊 ✕ 🛜 ✕ 🛏 💻

Havasu Travelodge M

(928) 680-9202. **$60-$270, 3 day notice.** 480 London Bridge Rd 86403. 1 mi n of London Bridge. Int corridors. **Pets:** Accepted.

🛜 ✕ 🛏 💻

Island Suites H

(928) 855-7333. **$60-$150, 3 day notice.** 236 S Lake Havasu Ave 86403. Just s of jct McCulloch Blvd. Int corridors. **Pets:** Accepted.

🏊 ✕ 🛜 🛏 💻

The Nautical Beachfront Resort H

(928) 855-2141. **$99-$550, 3 day notice.** 1000 McCulloch Blvd N 86403. 1.4 mi w of London Bridge, follow signs. Ext corridors. **Pets:** Other species. $200 deposit/room, $50 one-time fee/room. Designated rooms, service with restrictions, supervision.

🍽 🏊 ✕ 🛜 ✕ 🛏 💻

Quality Inn & Suites H 🌼

(928) 855-1111. **$80-$160.** 271 S Lake Havasu Ave 86403. SR 95, just e on Swanson Ave, then just s. Ext corridors. **Pets:** Other species. $20 one-time fee/room. Service with restrictions. 🍽 🏊 🛜 🛏 💻

LITCHFIELD PARK

The Wigwam H 🐾

(623) 935-3811. **$129-$399, 3 day notice.** 300 Wigwam Blvd 85340. I-10 exit 128 (Litchfield Rd), 2.4 mi n, then 0.4 mi e. Ext corridors. **Pets:** Other species. $15 daily fee/room. Designated rooms, service with restrictions, crate. SAVE 🍽 🏊 ✕ 🍲 ✕ 🛏 💻

MARANA

La Quinta Inn & Suites NW Tucson Marana H

(520) 572-4235. **$70-$314.** 6020 W Hospitality Rd 85743. I-10 exit 246 (Cortaro Rd), just w, then just n. Int corridors. **Pets:** Large, other species. Service with restrictions. &M 🏊 🛜 ✕ 🛏 💻

The Ritz-Carlton, Dove Mountain H

(520) 572-3000. **Call for rates.** 15000 N Secret Springs Dr 85658. I-10 exit 240 (Tangerine Rd), 5 mi e to Dove Mountain Dr, then 4.5 mi n, follow signs. Int corridors. **Pets:** Accepted.

SAVE 🍽 &M 🏊 ✕ 🍲 ✕ 🛏 💻

MARICOPA

Harrah's Ak-Chin Casino Resort H

(480) 802-5000. **Call for rates.** 15406 Maricopa Rd 85239. Jct SR 238, 4.5 mi s on SR 347. Ext/int corridors. **Pets:** Accepted.

🍽 &M 🏊 🛜 🛏 💻

MESA

BEST WESTERN Mezona Inn H

(480) 834-9233. **$78-$150.** 250 W Main St 85201. Just e of Country Club Dr; downtown. Ext corridors. **Pets:** $20 one-time fee/room. Designated rooms, service with restrictions, crate.

SAVE 🍽 🏊 🛜 ✕ 🛏 💻

BEST WESTERN PLUS Mesa H

(480) 926-3600. **Call for rates.** 1563 S Gilbert Rd 85204. US 60 (Superstition Frwy) exit 182 (Gilbert Rd), just n. Int corridors. **Pets:** Medium. $15 daily fee/room. Designated rooms, service with restrictions, supervision. 🏊 🛜 ✕ 🛏 💻

BEST WESTERN Superstition Springs Inn H

(480) 641-1164. **$69-$149.** 1342 S Power Rd 85206. Just n of US 60 (Superstition Frwy) exit 188 (Power Rd); northwest corner of Power Rd and Hampton Ave. Ext corridors. **Pets:** Accepted.

SAVE 🏊 🛜 🛏 💻

Days Hotel Mesa Country Club H

(480) 844-8900. **$66-$160.** 333 W Juanita Ave 85210. US 60 (Superstition Frwy) exit 179 (Country Club Dr), just s, then just e. Int corridors. **Pets:** Other species. $50 daily fee/pet. Service with restrictions, supervision. 🏊 🛜 ✕ 🛏 💻

Days Inn-East Mesa H

(480) 981-8111. **$55-$120.** 5531 E Main St 85205. 0.4 mi e of Higley Rd. Ext corridors. **Pets:** Small, dogs only. $10 daily fee/pet. Designated rooms, service with restrictions. 🏊 🛜 🛏 💻

Hilton Phoenix/Mesa H

(480) 833-5555. **$75-$206.** 1011 W Holmes Ave 85210. US 60 (Superstition Frwy) exit 178 (Alma School Rd), just n, then just e. Int corridors. **Pets:** Accepted. SAVE 🍽 🏊 🍲 🛏 💻

Holiday Inn & Suites Phoenix-Mesa/Chandler H

(480) 964-7000. **$99-$299.** 1600 S Country Club Dr 85210. US 60 (Superstition Frwy) exit 179 (Country Club Dr), just s. Ext/int corridors. **Pets:** Small. $50 one-time fee/pet. Service with restrictions, supervision.

🍽 &M 🏊 🛜 ✕ 🛏 💻

La Quinta Inn & Suites Mesa Superstition Springs H

(480) 654-1970. **$85-$384.** 6530 E Superstition Springs Blvd 85206. US 60 (Superstition Frwy) exit 187 (Superstition Springs Blvd) eastbound, just se; exit 188 (Power Rd) westbound, just sw. Int corridors. **Pets:** Large, other species. Service with restrictions.

&M 🏊 🛜 ✕ 🛏 💻

La Quinta Inn & Suites Phoenix Mesa West H

(480) 844-8747. **$75-$449.** 902 W Grove Ave 85210. US 60 (Superstition Frwy) exit 178 (Alma School Rd), just n, then just e. Int corridors. **Pets:** Large, other species. Service with restrictions.

🏊 🛜 🛏 💻

Quality Inn Mesa - Superstition Springs H

(480) 807-7760. **$54-$229.** 6347 E Southern Ave 85206. US 60 (Superstition Frwy) exit 188 (Power Rd), 0.8 mi n, then 0.4 mi w to mall entrance. Int corridors. **Pets:** Other species. $25 daily fee/pet. Service with restrictions, supervision. 🏊 🛜 🛏 💻

Residence Inn by Marriott Phoenix Mesa H 🐾

(480) 610-0100. **$79-$299.** 941 W Grove Ave 85210. US 60 (Superstition Frwy) exit 178 (Alma School Rd), just n, then just e. Int corridors. **Pets:** $100 one-time fee/room. Designated rooms, service with restrictions, crate. &M 🏊 🛜 ✕ 🛏 💻

NOGALES

▼▼▼▼ Candlewood Suites 🅷

(520) 281-1111. **$99-$159, 3 day notice.** 875 N Frank Reed Rd 85621. I-19 exit 4, just w to Frank Reed Rd, then just nw. Int corridors. **Pets:** Accepted. 🤝 ❌ 🛢 💻

▼▼▼ Holiday Inn Express Hotel Nogales 🅷

(520) 281-0123. **$99-$249, 3 day notice.** 850 W Shell Rd 85621. I-19 exit 4, just w to Frank Reed Rd, then just nw. Int corridors. **Pets:** Other species. $25 one-time fee/room. Designated rooms, service with restrictions, supervision. 🤝 🛰 ❌ 🛢 💻

ORO VALLEY

◈◈◈ ▼▼▼▼ Hilton Tucson El Conquistador Golf & Tennis Resort 🅷 🐾

(520) 544-5000. **$89-$299.** 10000 N Oracle Rd 85704. I-10 exit 248 (Ina Rd); jct Ina Rd, 4.4 mi n. Ext/int corridors. **Pets:** Medium. $50 one-time fee/room. 🆂🅰🆅🅴 🄴🄲🄾 🍽 🛗 🤝 ❌ 📶 ❌ 🛢 💻

PAGE

◈◈◈ ▼▼▼▼ Courtyard by Marriott 🅷

(928) 645-5000. **$119-$329.** 600 Clubhouse Dr 86040. On Loop 89, jct US 89. Int corridors. **Pets:** Accepted.
🆂🅰🆅🅴 🍽 🤝 🛰 ❌ 🛢 💻

▼▼◈ Lake Powell Days Inn & Suites 🅷

(928) 645-2800. **$70-$330.** 961 N Hwy 89 86040. On US 89, just s. Int corridors. **Pets:** Accepted. 🤝 🛰 ❌ 🛢 💻

▼▼◈ Lake Powell Resort and Marina 🅷

(928) 645-2433. **$250-$760.** 100 Lakeshore Dr 86040. 4 mi n of Glen Canyon Dam via US 89. Int corridors. **Pets:** Accepted.
🍽 🤝 ❌ 🛰 ❌ 🛢 💻

PARADISE VALLEY

◈◈◈ ▼▼▼▼ Hermosa Inn 🅷 🐾

(602) 955-8614. **$139-$624, 7 day notice.** 5532 N Palo Cristi Rd 85253. 1 mi s of Lincoln Dr; corner of Stanford Dr. Ext corridors. **Pets:** Medium, dogs only. $75 one-time fee/pet. Service with restrictions, crate. 🆂🅰🆅🅴 🍽 🤝 ❌ 🛰 ❌ 🛢 💻

◈◈◈ ▼▼▼◈ Omni Scottsdale Resort & Spa at Montelucia 🅷 🐾

(480) 627-3200. **$129-$479, 7 day notice.** 4949 E Lincoln Dr 85253. Southeast corner of Lincoln Dr and Tatum Blvd, enter from Lincoln Dr. Ext/int corridors. **Pets:** Small. $100 one-time fee/room. Service with restrictions, supervision. 🆂🅰🆅🅴 🍽 🤝 ❌ 🛰 ❌ 🛢 💻

◈◈◈ ▼▼▼◈ Sanctuary Camelback Mountain 🅷

(480) 948-2100. **$299-$899, 7 day notice.** 5700 E McDonald Dr 85253. SR 101 exit McDonald Dr, 3.9 mi w; 1.8 mi w of jct Scottsdale Rd. Ext corridors. **Pets:** Accepted. 🆂🅰🆅🅴 🍽 🤝 ❌ 📶 ❌ 🛢 💻

PARKER

◈◈◈ ▼▼◈ BEST WESTERN Parker Inn 🅷

(928) 669-6060. **$109-$139.** 1012 Geronimo Ave 85344. Jct SR 95, just e. Int corridors. **Pets:** Very small. $50 one-time fee/room. Designated rooms, service with restrictions, supervision.
🆂🅰🆅🅴 🤝 🛰 ❌ 🛢 💻

◈◈◈ ▼▼▼◈ Blue Water Resort & Casino 🅷

(928) 669-7000. **Call for rates.** 11300 Resort Dr 85344. Jct SR 62, 1.3 mi nw on SR 95. Ext corridors. **Pets:** Accepted.
🆂🅰🆅🅴 🍽 🤝 ❌ 🛰 🛢 💻

PAYSON

▼ Americas Best Value Inn 🅼

(928) 474-2283. **$60-$125.** 811 S Beeline Hwy 85541. SR 87, 0.7 mi s of SR 260. Ext/int corridors. **Pets:** Accepted. 🛰 🛢 💻

▼▼ Quality Inn Payson 🅷 🐾

(928) 474-3241. **$60-$170.** 801 N Beeline Hwy 85541. SR 87, 0.6 mi n of SR 260. Ext corridors. **Pets:** Other species. $20 daily fee/room. Designated rooms, service with restrictions, crate. 🤝 🛰 ❌ 🛢 💻

▼▼ Wooden Nickel Cabins 🅲🅰

(928) 478-4519. **$129-$149, 30 day notice.** 165 S Hunter Creek Dr 85541. SR 87, 22 mi e on SR 260, 0.7 mi n; just w of MM 275, follow signs. Ext corridors. **Pets:** Dogs only. $10 daily fee/pet. Designated rooms, no service, supervision. 🛰 ❌ 🛢 💻

PEACH SPRINGS

◈◈◈ ▼▼▼ Hualapai Lodge 🅷

(928) 769-2230. **$100-$120, 3 day notice.** 900 Route 66 86434. Center. Int corridors. **Pets:** $25 daily fee/room. Designated rooms, service with restrictions, crate. 🆂🅰🆅🅴 🍽 🛗 🤝 🛰 ❌ 🛢 💻

PEORIA

◈◈◈ ▼▼▼◈ Bluegreen Vacation Cibola Vista Resort and Spa, an Ascend Resort Collection Member 🅲🅾

(623) 889-6700. **$89-$449, 3 day notice.** 27501 N Lake Pleasant Pkwy 85383. SR 101 exit 16 (Beardsley Rd), 0.5 mi w, then 6.6 mi nw. Ext/int corridors. **Pets:** $150 one-time fee/room. No service, supervision.
🆂🅰🆅🅴 🍽 ❌ 🛰 ❌ 🛢 💻

▼▼ Comfort Suites by Choice Hotels/Peoria Sports Complex 🅷

(623) 334-3993. **$62-$199.** 8473 W Paradise Ln 85382. SR 101 exit 14 (Bell Rd), just e to 83rd Ave, just s, then just w. Int corridors. **Pets:** Accepted. 🤝 🛰 ❌ 🛢 💻

▼▼ Days Hotel Peoria Glendale Area 🅷

(623) 979-7200. **$53-$113.** 8955 W Grand Ave 85345. SR 101 N exit 11 (Grand Ave), 0.5 mi e. Int corridors. **Pets:** Large. $10 daily fee/pet. Service with restrictions, crate. 🍽 🤝 🛰 ❌ 🛢 💻

▼▼ Extended Stay America Peoria 🅷

(623) 487-0020. **Call for rates.** 7345 W Bell Rd 85382. SR 101 exit 14 (Bell Rd), 1.2 mi e. Int corridors. **Pets:** Other species. $25 daily fee/pet. Service with restrictions, supervision. 🛰 🛢

▼▼ Holiday Inn Express Hotel & Suites Peoria North-Glendale 🅷

(623) 853-1313. **Call for rates.** 16771 N 84th Ave 85382. SR 101 exit 14 (Bell Rd), just w, then just s. Int corridors. **Pets:** Accepted. 🛗 🤝 🛰 ❌ 🛢 💻

▼▼▼ La Quinta Inn & Suites Phoenix West/Peoria 🅷

(623) 487-1900. **$82-$614.** 16321 N 83rd Ave 85382. SR 101 exit 14 (Bell Rd), just e, then just s. Int corridors. **Pets:** Large, other species. Service with restrictions. 🤝 🛰 ❌ 🛢 💻

▼▼▼ Residence Inn by Marriott Glendale/Peoria 🅷

(623) 979-2074. **$120-$340.** 8435 W Paradise Ln 85382. SR 101 exit 14 (Bell Rd), just e to 83rd Ave, just s, then just w. Int corridors. **Pets:** Accepted. 🤝 🛰 ❌ 🛢 💻

PHOENIX *(Restaurants p. 613)*

◈◈◈ ▼▼▼◈ Aloft Phoenix Airport Hotel 🅷

(602) 275-6300. **$99-$399.** 4450 E Washington St 85034. SR 143 exit Washington St, just w. Int corridors. **Pets:** Accepted.
🆂🅰🆅🅴 🛗 🤝 🛰 ❌ 🛢 💻

◈◈◈ ▼▼▼▼ Arizona Biltmore A Waldorf Astoria Resort 🅷

(602) 955-6600. **$109-$499.** 2400 E Missouri Ave 85016. Jct Camelback Rd, 0.5 mi n on 24th St, then 0.4 mi e. Ext/int corridors. **Pets:** Accepted. 🆂🅰🆅🅴 🄴🄲🄾 🍽 🤝 ❌ 📶 ❌ 🛢 💻

BEST WESTERN InnSuites Phoenix Hotel & Suites H

(602) 997-6285. **$69-$149.** 1615 E Northern Ave 85020. SR 51 exit 7, 0.6 mi w. Ext corridors. **Pets:** Accepted. [SAVE] 🍽 🛜 🔌 🖵

BEST WESTERN Phoenix I-17 MetroCenter Inn H

(602) 864-6233. **$49-$240.** 8101 N Black Canyon Hwy 85021. I-17 exit 206 (Northern Ave), just e, then just n; on east side of freeway. Ext corridors. **Pets:** Accepted. [SAVE] 🍽 🛜 🔌 🖵

Candlewood Suites Phoenix H

(602) 861-4900. **Call for rates.** 11411 N Black Canyon Hwy 85029. I-17 exit 208 (Peoria Ave), just e, then 0.4 mi n. Int corridors. **Pets:** Accepted. 🍽 🛜 ✖ 🔌 🖵

Clarion Hotel Phoenix-Chandler H

(480) 893-3900. **$70-$500.** 5121 E La Puenta Ave 85044. I-10 exit 157 (Elliot Rd), just w, just n on 51st St, then just e. Ext corridors. **Pets:** Accepted. 🍽 🛜 🔌 🖵

Comfort Suites Phoenix North H

(602) 861-3900. **$59-$109.** 10210 N 26th Dr 85021. I-17 exit 208 (Peoria Ave), just e, just s on 25th Ave, then 0.3 mi w on W Beryl Ave. Int corridors. **Pets:** $25 one-time fee/room. Service with restrictions. ♿M 🍽 🛜 ✖ 🔌 🖵

Crowne Plaza Phoenix Airport H

(602) 273-7778. **$79-$249.** 4300 E Washington St 85034. SR 202 exit 2 (44th St), 0.7 mi s. Int corridors. **Pets:** Small, dogs only. $50 one-time fee/room. Designated rooms, service with restrictions. [SAVE] 🍴 🍽 🛜 ✖ 🖵

Crowne Plaza Phoenix North H

(602) 943-2341. **$79-$199.** 2532 W Peoria Ave 85029. I-17 exit 208 (Peoria Ave), just e, then just n on 25th Ave. Int corridors. **Pets:** Accepted. 🍴 ♿M 🍽 🛜 ✖ 🔌 🖵

DoubleTree Suites by Hilton Phoenix H 🐾

(602) 225-0500. **$89-$379.** 320 N 44th St 85008. SR 202 exit 2 (44th St), 0.5 mi s. Ext corridors. **Pets:** Large. $75 one-time fee/pet. Service with restrictions, supervision. [SAVE] 🍴 ♿M 🍽 🛜 ✖ 🔌 🖵

Drury Inn & Suites Phoenix Airport H

(602) 437-8400. **$90-$229.** 3333 E University Dr 85034. I-10 exit 151 (University Dr), just e, then just s on Elwood St. Int corridors. **Pets:** $10 daily fee/room. Service with restrictions, supervision. 🍽 🛜 ✖ 🖵

Drury Inn & Suites Phoenix Happy Valley H

(623) 879-8800. **$115-$199.** 2335 W Pinnacle Peak Rd 85027. I-17 exit 217 (Pinnacle Peak Rd), just e. Int corridors. **Pets:** $10 daily fee/room. Service with restrictions, supervision. ♿M 🍽 🛜 ✖ 🔌 🖵

Embassy Suites Phoenix Airport at 24th St H

(602) 957-1910. **$89-$279.** 2333 E Thomas Rd 85016. SR 51 exit 2 (44th St), just e. Ext corridors. **Pets:** Accepted. [SAVE] 🍴 🍽 🛜 🔌 🖵

Embassy Suites Phoenix Biltmore H

(602) 955-3992. **$109-$349.** 2630 E Camelback Rd 85016. Just n of Camelback Rd, on 26th St. Int corridors. **Pets:** Accepted. [SAVE] 🍴 🍽 🛜 ✖ 🔌 🖵

Embassy Suites Phoenix North H

(602) 375-1777. **$109-$259.** 2577 W Greenway Rd 85023. I-17 exit 211, just e. Ext corridors. **Pets:** Accepted. [SAVE] 🍴 🍽 ✖ 🛜 🔌 🖵

Extended Stay America Phoenix-Biltmore H

(602) 265-6800. **Call for rates.** 5235 N 16th St 85016. Jct SR 51, just w on Camelback Rd, then just n. Int corridors. **Pets:** Other species. $25 daily fee/pet. Service with restrictions, supervision. 🍽 🛜 ✖ 🖵

Extended Stay America-Phoenix-Chandler H

(480) 785-0464. **Call for rates.** 14245 S 50th St 85044. I-10 exit 159, just w on Ray Rd, just s, then just e. Int corridors. **Pets:** Other species. $25 daily fee/pet. Service with restrictions, supervision. ♿M 🛜 🔌 🖵

Extended Stay America Phoenix-Chandler-E Chandler Blvd H

(480) 753-6700. **Call for rates.** 5035 E Chandler Blvd 85048. I-10 exit 160 (Chandler Blvd), just w. Ext corridors. **Pets:** Other species. $25 daily fee/pet. Service with restrictions, supervision. 🍽 🛜 🔌 🖵

Extended Stay America Phoenix-Deer Valley H

(623) 879-6609. **Call for rates.** 20827 N 27th Ave 85027. I-17 exit 215A, just w. Int corridors. **Pets:** Other species. $25 daily fee/pet. Service with restrictions, supervision. 🛜 🔌

Extended Stay America Phoenix/Midtown H

(602) 279-9000. **Call for rates.** 217 W Osborn Rd 85013. Just w of Central Ave; between Indian School and Thomas rds. Int corridors. **Pets:** Other species. $25 daily fee/pet. Service with restrictions, supervision. ♿M 🍽 🛜 ✖ 🔌

Hilton Phoenix Suites H

(602) 222-1111. **$79-$269.** 10 E Thomas Rd 85012. Just e of Central Ave; in Phoenix Plaza. Int corridors. **Pets:** Accepted. 🍴 ♿M 🏊 🗞 🔌 🖵

Holiday Inn North Phoenix H

(602) 548-6000. **$59-$450, 14 day notice.** 12027 N 28th Dr 85029. I-17 exit 209 (Cactus Rd), just w, then just s. Int corridors. **Pets:** Accepted. [SAVE] 🍴 🍽 🛜 ✖ 🔌 🖵

Homewood Suites by Hilton Phoenix-Biltmore H

(602) 508-0937. **$99-$279.** 2001 E Highland Ave 85016. Just e of 20th St. Int corridors. **Pets:** Accepted. 🍽 🛜 🔌 🖵

Homewood Suites by Hilton Phoenix Metrocenter H

(602) 674-8900. **$89-$249.** 2536 W Beryl Ave 85021. I-17 exit 208 (Peoria Ave), just e, just s on 25th Ave, then just w. Int corridors. **Pets:** Accepted. ♿M 🍽 🛜 🔌 🖵

Homewood Suites Phoenix North/Happy Valley H

(623) 580-1800. **$119-$359.** 2470 W Charlotte Dr 85085. I-17 exit 217 (Pinnacle Peak Rd), 0.6 mi n on Frontage Rd. Int corridors. **Pets:** Accepted. ♿M 🍽 🛜 🔌 🖵

Hotel Palomar Phoenix-CityScape H

(602) 253-6633. **$119-$439.** 2 E Jefferson St 85004. Northeast corner of Central Ave and Jefferson St. Int corridors. **Pets:** Accepted. 🍴 ♿M 🛜 ✖ 🔌

Hyatt Place Phoenix-North H

(602) 997-8800. **$64-$229.** 10838 N 25th Ave 85029. I-17 exit 208 (Peoria Ave), just e, then 0.3 mi n. Int corridors. **Pets:** $75 one-time fee/pet. Designated rooms, service with restrictions, crate. [SAVE] 🍴 🍽 🛜 ✖ 🔌 🖵

La Quinta Inn & Suites Phoenix Chandler H

(480) 961-7700. **$82-$599.** 15241 S 50th St 85044. I-10 exit 160 (Chandler Blvd), just w, then just n. Int corridors. **Pets:** Large, other species. Service with restrictions. ♿M 🍽 🛜 🔌 🖵

La Quinta Inn & Suites Phoenix I-10 West H

(602) 595-7601. **$59-$1119.** 4929 W McDowell Rd 85035. I-10 exit 139 (51st Ave), just n, then just e. Int corridors. **Pets:** Large, other species. Service with restrictions. 🍽 🛜 ✖ 🔌 🖵

🛦🛦 La Quinta Inn Phoenix-Arcadia 🎖
(602) 956-6500. $54-$514. 4727 E Thomas Rd 85018. Just w of 48th
St. Ext/int corridors. Pets: Large, other species. Service with restrictions. 🅰 🛜 ⊠ 🛏 🖵

🛦🛦 La Quinta Inn Phoenix North 🎖
(602) 993-0800. $49-$559. 2510 W Greenway Rd 85023. I-17 exit 211,
just e. Ext corridors. Pets: Large, other species. Service with restrictions. 🅰 🛜 🛏 🖵

🔷 🛦🛦🛦 Phoenix Residence Inn Desert View at Mayo
Clinic by Marriott 🎖
(480) 563-1500. $99-$329, 3 day notice. 5665 E Mayo Blvd 85054. SR
101 exit 32 (56th St), just s, then just e. Int corridors. Pets: Accepted.
(SAVE) 🅗M 🅰 🛜 ⊠ 🛏 🖵

🔷 🛦🛦🛦🛦 Pointe Hilton Squaw Peak Resort 🎖
(602) 997-2626. $99-$449. 7677 N 16th St 85020. SR 51 exit Glendale
Ave, 0.4 mi w, then 0.6 mi n. Ext corridors. Pets: Accepted.
(SAVE) 🍴 🅰 ⊠ 📶 ⊠ 🛏 🖵

🔷 🛦🛦 Red Roof Inn Phoenix West 🎖
(602) 233-8004. $50-$126. 5215 W Willetta St 85043. I-10 exit 139
(51st Ave), just n, just e on McDowell Rd, then just s. Int corridors.
Pets: Large, other species. Service with restrictions, supervision.
(SAVE) 🅗M 🅰 🛜 ⊠ 🛏 🖵

🛦🛦🛦 Residence Inn by Marriott Phoenix 🎖
(602) 864-1900. $69-$449. 8242 N Black Canyon Hwy 85051. I-17 exit
207 (Dunlap Ave), just w, then 0.8 mi s; on frontage road. Ext/int corridors. Pets: Accepted. 🅰 🛜 ⊠ 🛏 🖵

🛦🛦🛦 Residence Inn by Marriott Phoenix North/Happy
Valley 🎖
(623) 580-8833. $99-$199. 2035 W Whispering Wind Dr 85085. I-17
exit 128 (Happy Valley Rd), 0.4 mi e to 23rd Ave, just s, then just e. Int
corridors. Pets: Accepted. 🅰 🛜 ⊠ 🛏 🖵

🛦🛦🛦🛦 The Ritz-Carlton, Phoenix 🎖
(602) 468-0700. $229-$439, 3 day notice. 2401 E Camelback Rd
85016. Southeast corner of Camelback Rd and 24th St. Int corridors.
Pets: Accepted. 🍴 🅰 ⊠ 📶 ⊠ 🛏 🖵

🔷 🛦🛦🛦🛦 Royal Palms Resort and Spa 🎖
(602) 840-3610. $179-$629, 3 day notice. 5200 E Camelback Rd
85018. Just e of 52nd St. Ext/int corridors. Pets: Accepted.
(SAVE) 🄴🄲🄾 🍴 🅰 ⊠ 📶 ⊠ 🛏 🖵

🔷 🛦🛦🛦🛦 Sheraton Crescent Hotel 🎖 🐾
(602) 943-8200. $89-$349. 2620 W Dunlap Ave 85021. I-17 exit 207
(Dunlap Ave), just e. Int corridors. Pets: Dogs only. Service with restrictions, supervision. (SAVE) 🍴 🅗M 🅰 ⊠ 📶 ⊠ 🛏 🖵

🔷 🛦🛦🛦🛦 Sheraton Phoenix Downtown
Hotel 🎖
(602) 262-2500. Call for rates. 340 N 3rd St 85004. I-10 exit 145A (7th
St), 0.5 mi s to Fillmore St, just w, then just s. Int corridors.
Pets: Accepted. (SAVE) 🄴🄲🄾 🍴 🅗M 🅰 ⊠ 📶 ⊠ 🛏 🖵

🛦🛦 Sleep Inn Airport 🎖
(480) 967-7100. $59-$179. 2621 S 47th Pl 85034. I-10 exit 151 (University Dr), 2 mi n, then just w. Int corridors. Pets: Medium, dogs only.
$25 one-time fee/room. Designated rooms, service with restrictions,
supervision. 🅰 🛜 ⊠ 🛏 🖵

🔷 🛦🛦 Sleep Inn Phoenix North 🎖
(602) 504-1200. $49-$199. 18235 N 27th Ave 85053. I-17 exit 214A
(Union Hills Dr), just w, then just s. Int corridors. Pets: Small, other
species. $15 daily fee/pet. Designated rooms, service with restrictions,
crate. (SAVE) 🅗M 🅰 🛜 ⊠ 🛏 🖵

🔷 🛦🛦🛦 Super 8-Downtown Phoenix/Convention
Center 🎖
(602) 252-6823. $70-$150. 965 E Van Buren St 85006. I-10 exit 145
(7th St), just s, then just e. Ext corridors. Pets: Accepted.
(SAVE) 🅰 🛜 ⊠ 🛏 🖵

🛦🛦 Super 8-Phoenix West 🎖
(602) 415-0888. $55-$80. 1242 N 53rd Ave 85043. I-10 exit 139 (51st
Ave), just s to Latham Rd, then just w. Int corridors. Pets: Accepted.
🅰 🛜 🛏 🖵

🛦🛦🛦 TownePlace Suites by Marriott Phoenix
North 🎖
(602) 943-9510. $59-$189. 9425 N Black Canyon Frwy 85021. I-17 exit
207 (Dunlap Ave), just e, then 0.3 mi n. Int corridors. Pets: Accepted.
🅗M 🅰 🛜 ⊠ 🛏 🖵

🔷 🛦🛦🛦🛦 The Westin Phoenix Downtown 🎖
(602) 429-3500. $159-$329. 333 N Central Ave 85004. Northeast corner
of Central Ave and Van Buren St. Int corridors. Pets: Accepted.
(SAVE) 🍴 🅗M 🅰 📶 ⊠ 🛏 🖵

PINETOP-LAKESIDE (Restaurants p. 613)

🔷 🛦🛦 BEST WESTERN Inn of Pinetop 🅼
(928) 367-6667. $75-$149. 404 E White Mountain Blvd 85935. On SR
260, east end of town. Ext corridors. Pets: Large. $10 daily fee/pet.
Service with restrictions, crate. (SAVE) 🛜 🛏 🖵

🛦🛦 Econo Lodge Inn & Suites 🅼
(928) 367-3636. $71-$290. 458 E White Mountain Blvd 85935. On SR
260; east end of town. Ext corridors. Pets: Accepted. 🛜 🛏 🖵

🛦🛦 Executive Inn & Suites 🅼
(928) 367-4146. $54-$94. 1023 E White Mountain Blvd 85935. On SR
260; east end of town. Ext corridors. Pets: Small, dogs only. $10 daily
fee/room. Designated rooms, service with restrictions, crate.
🛜 ⊠ 🛏 🖵

🔷 🛦🛦🛦 Hon-Dah Resort Casino and Conference
Center 🎖
(928) 369-0299. $129-$199, 3 day notice. 777 Hwy 260 85935. Jct SR
260 and 73; east end of town. Int corridors. Pets: Accepted.
(SAVE) 🍴 🅗M 🅰 ⊠ 🛜 🛏 🖵

🛦🛦 Northwoods Resort 🄲🄰 🐾
(928) 367-2966. Call for rates. 165 E White Mountain Blvd 85935. On
SR 260, MM 352. Ext corridors. Pets: Large, other species. $10 daily
fee/pet. Service with restrictions, supervision. 🛜 🎛 🄖 🛏 🖵

🛦🛦 TimberLodge Inn 🅼
(928) 367-4463. $49-$99, 3 day notice. 1078 E White Mountain Blvd
85935. On SR 260; east end of town. Ext corridors. Pets: Other species. $10 daily fee/pet. Designated rooms, service with restrictions,
crate. 🛜 🎛 🛏 🖵

PRESCOTT (Restaurants p. 613)

🔷 🛦🛦 BEST WESTERN Prescottonian 🅼
(928) 445-3096. $90-$159. 1317 E Gurley St 86301. On SR 89, just s
of jct SR 69. Ext corridors. Pets: Medium, dogs only. $15 daily fee/
room. Service with restrictions, supervision.
(SAVE) 🍴 🅰 🛜 🛏 🖵

🛦🛦🛦 Hassayampa Inn 🎖 🐾
(928) 778-9434. $89-$309. 122 E Gurley St 86301. Jct Marina St;
downtown. Int corridors. Pets: Medium, dogs only. Designated rooms,
service with restrictions, supervision. 🍴 🛜 ⊠ 🛏 🖵

🛦🛦 La Quinta Inn & Suites 🎖
(928) 777-0770. $74-$329. 4499 E SR 69 86301. 3.6 mi e of jct SR 89.
Int corridors. Pets: Large, other species. Service with restrictions.
🍴 🅰 🛜 ⊠ 🛏 🖵

▼▼ **Prescott Cabin Rentals-Lynx Creek Farm** 🆑
(928) 778-9573. **$87-$309, 31 day notice.** 5555 Onyx Dr 86303. Jct SR 89, 5 mi e on SR 69, 0.4 mi s on dirt/gravel road. Ext corridors. **Pets:** Other species. $10 daily fee/pet. No service, crate.
🛜 ✖️ 🈂️ 🛗 🖥️

▼ **Quality Inn** Ⓜ️
(928) 776-1282. **$58-$110.** 1105 E Sheldon St 86301. 0.4 mi e of jct SR 89. Int corridors. **Pets:** Accepted. 🛀 🛜 🛗 🖥️

▼▼▼ **Residence Inn by Marriott** 🅷
(928) 775-2232. **$109-$244.** 3599 Lee Cir 86301. Jct SR 69, just n on Lee Blvd, then just e. Int corridors. **Pets:** Accepted.
👨‍🦽 🛀 🛜 ✖️ 🛗 🖥️

▼▼▼ **SpringHill Suites by Marriott** 🅷
(928) 776-0998. **$99-$209.** 200 E Sheldon St 86301. On SR 89; at Marina St. Int corridors. **Pets:** Dogs only. $50 one-time fee/room. Designated rooms, service with restrictions. 👨‍🦽 🛀 🛜 ✖️ 🛗 🖥️

PRESCOTT VALLEY

🅰🅰🅰 ▼▼ **Americas Best Value Inn** 🅷
(928) 772-2200. **$59-$155.** 8383 E SR 69 86314. Just w of N Navajo Dr. Int corridors. **Pets:** Dogs only. $6 daily fee/pet. Designated rooms, service with restrictions, supervision. 🆂 🛀 🛜 🛗 🖥️

▼▼ **Arizona Inn of Prescott Valley** 🅷
(928) 772-8600. **$69-$125.** 7875 E Hwy 69 86314. Corner of Windsong Rd. Ext corridors. **Pets:** Other species. $50 deposit/room. Service with restrictions. 🛀 🛜 🛗 🖥️

🅰🅰🅰 ▼▼▼ **Comfort Suites Prescott Valley** 🅷 🐾
(928) 771-2100. **$89-$159.** 2601 N Crownpointe Dr 86314. Just w on SR 69, just n on Market St. Int corridors. **Pets:** Medium. $40 one-time fee/room. Designated rooms, service with restrictions, supervision.
🆂 👨‍🦽 🛀 🛜 ✖️ 🛗 🖥️

QUARTZSITE

▼▼ **Super 8-Quartzsite** Ⓜ️
(928) 927-8080. **$70-$140, 3 day notice.** 2050 Dome Rock Rd 85359. I-10 exit 17, just s to Frontage Rd, then 0.6 mi w. Int corridors. **Pets:** Other species. $10 daily fee/pet. Designated rooms, no service, supervision. 🛜 🛗 🖥️

SAFFORD

🅰🅰🅰 ▼▼▼ **BEST WESTERN Desert Inn** Ⓜ️
(928) 428-0521. **$85.** 1391 W Thatcher Blvd 85546. US 191, 1 mi w on US 70. Ext corridors. **Pets:** Accepted. 🆂 🛀 🛜 🛗 🖥️

SCOTTSDALE *(Restaurants p. 613)*

🅰🅰🅰 ▼▼▼ **BEST WESTERN PLUS Scottsdale Thunderbird Suites** 🅷
(480) 951-4000. **$59-$349.** 7515 E Butherus Dr 85260. 0.8 mi n of Thunderbird Rd; 0.5 mi e of Scottsdale Rd. Ext/int corridors.
Pets: Accepted. 🆂 🍴 🛀 🛜 ✖️ 🛗 🖥️

🅰🅰🅰 ▼▼▼ **BEST WESTERN PLUS Sundial** 🅷 🐾
(480) 994-4170. **$130-$300.** 7320 E Camelback Rd 85251. Just e of Scottsdale Rd. Ext corridors. **Pets:** Other species. $25 daily fee/pet. Designated rooms, service with restrictions, supervision.
🆂 👨‍🦽 🛀 🛜 ✖️ 🛗 🖥️

🅰🅰🅰 ▼▼▼▼ **The Canyon Suites at The Phoenician** 🅷
(480) 423-2880. **Call for rates.** 6000 E Camelback Rd 85251. 0.5 mi w of 64th St; in The Phoenician. Int corridors. **Pets:** Accepted.
🆂 🍴 👨‍🦽 🛀 🈳 🛜 ✖️ 🛗 🖥️

🅰🅰🅰 ▼▼▼▼ **Chaparral Suites Scottsdale** 🅷
(480) 949-1414. **$89-$310.** 5001 N Scottsdale Rd 85250. At Chaparral Rd. Ext corridors. **Pets:** Accepted.
🆂 🍴 👨‍🦽 🛀 🈳 🛜 🛗 🖥️

▼▼ **Comfort Suites by Choice Hotels-Old Town** 🅷
(480) 946-1111. **$59-$219.** 3275 N Drinkwater Blvd 85251. N of Thomas Rd; just e of Scottsdale Rd. Int corridors. **Pets:** Accepted.
👨‍🦽 🛀 🛜 ✖️ 🛗 🖥️

▼▼ **Country Inn & Suites By Carlson** 🅷
(480) 314-1200. **$59-$209, 3 day notice.** 10801 N 89th Pl 85260. SR 101 exit 41 (Shea Blvd), just e, then just n. Int corridors. **Pets:** Medium, dogs only. $50 one-time fee/room. Designated rooms, service with restrictions, supervision. 🛀 🛜 ✖️ 🛗 🖥️

🅰🅰🅰 ▼▼▼▼ **Courtyard by Marriott Scottsdale at Mayo Clinic** 🅷
(480) 860-4000. **$99-$409.** 13444 E Shea Blvd 85259. SR 101 exit 41 (Shea Blvd), 5.8 mi e. Int corridors. **Pets:** Accepted.
🆂 🌿 🍴 👨‍🦽 🛀 🛜 ✖️ 🛗 🖥️

▼▼▼▼ **Days Hotel Scottsdale** 🅷
(480) 945-4392. **$59-$260.** 5101 N Scottsdale Rd 85250. Just n of Chaparral Rd. Ext corridors. **Pets:** Accepted.
🍴 👨‍🦽 🈳 🛜 ✖️ 🛗 🖥️

🅰🅰🅰 ▼▼▼ **Days Inn & Suites Scottsdale North** 🅷 🐾
(480) 948-3800. **$89-$389.** 7330 N Pima Rd 85258. 0.4 mi n of Indian Bend Rd; on west side of Pima Rd. Ext/int corridors. **Pets:** Small. $20 daily fee/room. Designated rooms, service with restrictions, crate.
🆂 🛀 🈳 🛜 ✖️ 🛗 🖥️

🅰🅰🅰 ▼▼▼▼ **DoubleTree Resort by Hilton Paradise Valley-Scottsdale** 🅷
(480) 947-5400. **$69-$229.** 5401 N Scottsdale Rd 85250. Just n of Chaparral Rd; on east side of Scottsdale Rd. Ext corridors. **Pets:** Medium, dogs only. $50 one-time fee/room. Service with restrictions, supervision. 🆂 🍴 🛀 🈳 🛜 ✖️ 🛗 🖥️

▼▼ **Extended Stay America Phoenix-Scottsdale** 🅷
(480) 483-1333. **Call for rates.** 10660 N 69th St 85254. Jct Scottsdale Rd, just w on Shea Blvd, then just n. Int corridors. **Pets:** Other species. $25 daily fee/pet. Service with restrictions, supervision. 🛀 🛜 🛗

▼▼ **Extended Stay America-Phoenix-Scottsdale-North** 🅷
(480) 607-3767. **Call for rates.** 15501 N Scottsdale Rd 85254. SR 101 exit 38 (Frank Lloyd Wright Blvd), 2 mi w, 0.5 mi s on Scottsdale Rd, then just e on Tierra Buena Ln. Ext corridors. **Pets:** Other species. $25 daily fee/pet. Service with restrictions, supervision. 🛜 ✖️ 🛗

▼▼ **Extended Stay America-Phoenix-Scottsdale-Old Town** Ⓜ️
(480) 994-0297. **Call for rates.** 3560 N Marshall Way 85251. Just w of Scottsdale Rd on Goldwater Blvd, just s. Ext corridors. **Pets:** Other species. $25 daily fee/pet. Service with restrictions, supervision.
👨‍🦽 🛀 🛜 🛗 🖥️

🅰🅰🅰 ▼▼▼▼ **Fairmont Scottsdale Princess** 🅷
(480) 585-4848. **$159-$2659, 7 day notice.** 7575 E Princess Dr 85255. SR 101 exit 34 (Scottsdale Rd), 0.8 mi s, then just e; 0.6 mi n of Bell Rd. Ext/int corridors. **Pets:** Accepted.
🆂 🌿 🍴 👨‍🦽 🛀 🈳 📶 ✖️ 🛗 🖥️

🅰🅰🅰 ▼▼▼▼ **FireSky Resort & Spa, A Kimpton Hotel** 🅷 🐾
(480) 945-7666. **Call for rates.** 4925 N Scottsdale Rd 85251. Southeast corner of Scottsdale and Chaparral rds. Int corridors. **Pets:** Other species. Designated rooms, service with restrictions, supervision.
🆂 🌿 ⬅️ 🍴 👨‍🦽 🛀 🈳 🛜 ✖️ 🛗 🖥️

🅰🅰🅰 ▼▼▼▼ **Four Seasons Resort Scottsdale at Troon North** 🅷
(480) 515-5700. **$159-$839, 7 day notice.** 10600 E Crescent Moon Dr 85262. SR 101 exit 36 (Pima Rd), 4.7 mi n, 2 mi e on Happy Valley Rd, then 1.5 mi n on Alma School Rd. Ext corridors. **Pets:** Accepted.
🆂 🍴 👨‍🦽 🛀 🈳 📶 ✖️ 🛗 🖥️

Gainey Suites Hotel H
(480) 922-6969. **$129-$279.** 7300 E Gainey Suites Dr 85258. Just e of Scottsdale Rd. Int corridors. **Pets:** Small, dogs only. $100 deposit/pet. Service with restrictions, crate.

Hampton Inn & Suites Scottsdale Riverwalk H
(480) 270-5393. **$69-$249.** 9550 E Indian Bend Rd 85256. SR 101 exit 44 (Indian Bend Rd), just e. Int corridors. **Pets:** Accepted.

Hampton Inn Phoenix-Scottsdale at Shea Blvd H
(480) 443-3233. **$52-$289.** 10101 N Scottsdale Rd 85253. Just s of Shea Blvd. Int corridors. **Pets:** Accepted.

Hilton Scottsdale Resort & Villas H
(480) 948-7750. **$79-$299.** 6333 N Scottsdale Rd 85250. SR 101 exit 45, 2.1 mi w on McDonald Dr, then 0.3 mi n. Int corridors. **Pets:** Large, dogs only. $50 one-time fee/room. Service with restrictions, supervision.

Holiday Inn Express Hotel & Suites-Scottsdale Old Town H
(480) 675-7665. **Call for rates.** 3131 N Scottsdale Rd 85251. Northeast corner of Scottsdale Rd and Earll Dr. Int corridors. **Pets:** Accepted.

Holiday Inn Express Scottsdale North H
(480) 596-6559. **Call for rates.** 7350 E Gold Dust Ave 85258. Just e of Scottsdale Rd; just s of Shea Blvd; on north side of Gold Dust Ave. Int corridors. **Pets:** Accepted.

Homewood Suites by Hilton Phoenix/Scottsdale H
(480) 368-8705. **$69-$259.** 9880 N Scottsdale Rd 85253. 0.5 mi s of Shea Blvd. Int corridors. **Pets:** Medium. $100 one-time fee/room. Designated rooms, service with restrictions, supervision.

Hospitality Suite Resort H
(480) 949-5115. **Call for rates.** 409 N Scottsdale Rd 85257. Just n of McKellips Rd; on east side of Scottsdale Rd. Ext corridors. **Pets:** Medium, dogs only. Service with restrictions.

Hotel Indigo Scottsdale H
(480) 941-9400. **$99-$329, 3 day notice.** 4415 N Civic Center Plaza 85251. Scottsdale Rd, just e on Camelback Rd, just s on 75th St. Ext/int corridors. **Pets:** Accepted.

Hotel Valley Ho H
(480) 248-2000. **$109-$419.** 6850 E Main St 85251. 0.4 mi w of Scottsdale Rd, just s of Indian School Rd; on north side of Main St. Ext/int corridors. **Pets:** Large, other species. Designated rooms, service with restrictions, supervision.

HYATT house Scottsdale/Old Town H
(480) 946-7700. **$79-$329.** 4245 N Drinkwater Blvd 85251. 0.3 mi e of Scottsdale Rd. Ext corridors. **Pets:** Accepted.

Hyatt Place Scottsdale/Old Town H
(480) 423-9944. **$79-$319.** 7300 E 3rd Ave 85251. Just e of Scottsdale Rd. Int corridors. **Pets:** Medium, dogs only. $75 one-time fee/room. Service with restrictions.

Hyatt Regency Scottsdale Resort & Spa at Gainey Ranch H
(480) 444-1234. **$129-$605, 3 day notice.** 7500 E Doubletree Ranch Rd 85258. SR 101 exit 43, 2.6 mi w on Via de Ventura. Ext/int corridors. **Pets:** Medium. $150 one-time fee/room. Designated rooms, service with restrictions, supervision.

JW Marriott Camelback Inn Resort & Spa H
(480) 948-1700. **$119-$559, 3 day notice.** 5402 E Lincoln Dr 85253. 0.5 mi e of Tatum Blvd; on north side of Lincoln Dr. Ext corridors. **Pets:** $75 one-time fee/room. Service with restrictions.

La Quinta Inn & Suites Phoenix Scottsdale H
(480) 614-5300. **$79-$639.** 8888 E Shea Blvd 85260. SR 101 exit 41 (Shea Blvd); northeast corner. Int corridors. **Pets:** Large, other species. Service with restrictions.

The McCormick Scottsdale H
(480) 948-5050. **Call for rates.** 7401 N Scottsdale Rd 85253. 0.8 mi n of Indian Bend Rd. Ext/int corridors. **Pets:** Accepted.

Motel 6 Scottsdale #29 M
(480) 946-2280. **$55-$95, 14 day notice.** 6848 E Camelback Rd 85251. Just w of Scottsdale Rd. Ext corridors. **Pets:** Other species. Service with restrictions, crate.

The Phoenician H
(480) 941-8200. **Call for rates.** 6000 E Camelback Rd 85251. 0.5 mi w of 64th St. Ext/int corridors. **Pets:** Accepted.

Residence Inn by Marriott Scottsdale North H
(480) 563-4120. **$115-$269.** 17011 N Scottsdale Rd 85255. SR 101 exit 34 (Scottsdale Rd), 1.1 mi s; northeast corner of Frank Lloyd Wright Blvd and Scottsdale Rd. Int corridors. **Pets:** Small. $100 one-time fee/room. Service with restrictions, crate.

Residence Inn by Marriott, Scottsdale/Paradise Valley H
(480) 948-8666. **$79-$259.** 6040 N Scottsdale Rd 85253. Just n of McDonald Dr. Ext/int corridors. **Pets:** Other species. $50 one-time fee/room. Service with restrictions.

Scottsdale Marriott at McDowell Mountains H
(480) 502-3836. **$109-$399.** 16770 N Perimeter Dr 85260. SR 101 exit 36 (Princess Dr/Pima Rd), just w to N Perimeter Dr, then 0.6 mi s. Int corridors. **Pets:** Other species. $50 one-time fee/room. Service with restrictions.

Scottsdale Resort & Athletic Club H
(480) 344-0600. **Call for rates.** 8235 E Indian Bend Rd 85250. 1.5 mi e of Scottsdale Rd. Ext corridors. **Pets:** Accepted.

Scottsdale Resort & Conference Center H
(480) 991-9000. **$89-$349, 3 day notice.** 7700 E McCormick Pkwy 85258. Just w of Hayden Rd; 0.7 mi e of Scottsdale Rd. Ext/int corridors. **Pets:** Accepted.

SpringHill Suites by Marriott-Scottsdale North H
(480) 922-8700. **$79-$332.** 17020 N Scottsdale Rd 85255. Just n of Frank Lloyd Wright Blvd. Int corridors. **Pets:** Accepted.

TownePlace Suites by Marriott Scottsdale H
(480) 551-1100. **$69-$299.** 10740 N 90th St 85260. SR 101 exit 41 (Shea Blvd), just e to 90th St, then just n. Int corridors. **Pets:** Accepted.

We-Ko-Pa Resort and Conference Center **H**
(480) 789-5300. **Call for rates.** 10438 N Ft. McDowell Rd 85264. Jct Shea Blvd, 1.6 mi ne on SR 87. Int corridors. **Pets:** Accepted.

The Westin Kierland Resort & Spa **H** ✿
(480) 624-1000. **$149-$709, 7 day notice.** 6902 E Greenway Pkwy 85254. 0.5 mi w of Scottsdale Rd. Int corridors. **Pets:** Other species. Service with restrictions, supervision.

W Scottsdale **H** ✿
(480) 970-2100. **Call for rates.** 7277 E Camelback Rd 85251. Just e of Scottsdale Rd. Int corridors. **Pets:** Small. $100 one-time fee/room, $25 daily fee/room. Service with restrictions, crate.

SEDONA *(Restaurants p. 614)*

Amara Resort & Spa, a Kimpton Hotel **H**
(928) 282-4828. **$169-$499, 3 day notice.** 100 Amara Ln 86336. Jct SR 179, 0.4 mi ne; center. Int corridors. **Pets:** Accepted.

BEST WESTERN PLUS Arroyo Roble Hotel & Creekside Villas **H** ✿
(928) 282-4001. **$175-$499.** 400 N SR 89A 86336. Jct SR 179, 0.5 mi ne. Ext corridors. **Pets:** Medium, dogs only. $20 daily fee/pet. Designated rooms, service with restrictions, supervision.

BEST WESTERN PLUS Inn of Sedona **H** ✿
(928) 282-3072. **$129-$209.** 1200 W SR 89A 86336. Jct SR 179, 1.2 mi w. Ext corridors. **Pets:** Other species. $20 one-time fee/room. Designated rooms, service with restrictions, supervision.

El Portal Sedona Hotel **H**
(928) 203-9405. **$199-$399, 15 day notice.** 95 Portal Ln 86336. Jct SR 89A, just s on SR 179, just w. Ext/int corridors. **Pets:** Accepted.

Hilton Sedona Resort & Spa **H** ✿
(928) 284-4040. **$149-$279.** 90 Ridge Trail Dr 86351. Jct SR 89A, 7.3 mi s on SR 179. Int corridors. **Pets:** Medium, other species. $50 one-time fee/room. Designated rooms, service with restrictions, supervision.

La Quinta Inn Sedona/Village of Oak Creek **H**
(928) 284-0711. **$73-$259.** 6176 SR 179 86351. Jct Bell Rock Blvd, just s. Int corridors. **Pets:** Large, other species. Service with restrictions.

L'Auberge de Sedona Inn and Spa **H** ✿
(928) 282-1661. **$205-$900, 7 day notice.** 301 L'Auberge Ln 86336. Jct SR 179, just n on SR 89A, then ne; down the hill. Ext/int corridors. **Pets:** Dogs only. $50 daily fee/pet. Designated rooms, service with restrictions, supervision.

The Lodge at Sedona **BB**
(928) 204-1942. **$189-$349, 30 day notice.** 125 Kallof Pl 86336. Jct SR 179, 1.8 mi w on SR 89A, then just s. Ext/int corridors. **Pets:** Accepted.

Matterhorn Inn **M** ✿
(928) 282-7176. **$99-$189.** 230 Apple Ave 86336. Jct SR 179, just ne on SR 89A; uptown. Ext corridors. **Pets:** Medium. $15 daily fee/pet. Designated rooms, service with restrictions, crate.

Orchards Inn of Sedona **H**
(928) 282-2405. **Call for rates.** 254 N SR 89A 86336. Jct SR 179, just ne. Ext corridors. **Pets:** Accepted.

Poco Diablo Resort **H** ✿
(928) 282-7333. **$89-$289.** 1752 State Route 179 86336. Jct SR 179, 2 mi s of SR 89A. Ext corridors. **Pets:** Dogs only. $25 daily fee/room. Designated rooms, service with restrictions, supervision.

Sedona Real Inn & Suites **H** ✿
(928) 282-1414. **$99-$240.** 95 Arroyo Pinon Dr 86336. Jct SR 179, 3.4 mi w on SR 89A, just sw. Ext corridors. **Pets:** Large, other species. $30 one-time fee/pet. Designated rooms, service with restrictions, supervision.

Sedona Rouge Hotel & Spa **H** ✿
(928) 203-4111. **$209-$279, 3 day notice.** 2250 W Hwy 89A 86336. Jct SR 179, 2 mi w. Ext/int corridors. **Pets:** Medium, dogs only. $100 deposit/room, $50 one-time fee/pet. Designated rooms, service with restrictions, supervision.

Sedona Super 8 **H**
(928) 282-1533. **$80-$200.** 2545 W Hwy 89A 86336. Jct SR 179, 2.4 mi w. Int corridors. **Pets:** Accepted.

Sky Ranch Lodge **M**
(928) 282-6400. **$120-$299.** 1105 Airport Rd 86336. Jct SR 179, 1 mi w on SR 89A, then 1 mi s. Ext corridors. **Pets:** Large, other species. $10 daily fee/pet. Service with restrictions, supervision.

Southwest Inn at Sedona **H** ✿
(928) 282-3344. **Call for rates.** 3250 W Hwy 89A 86336. Jct SR 179, 3.5 mi w. Ext corridors. **Pets:** $30 one-time fee/room. Designated rooms, service with restrictions, crate.

Village Lodge **M**
(928) 284-3626. **$59-$99, 3 day notice.** 105 Bell Rock Plaza 86351. Jct SR 179, just w. Ext/int corridors. **Pets:** Small, dogs only. $10 deposit/pet. Designated rooms, service with restrictions, supervision.

SELIGMAN *(Restaurants p. 614)*

Canyon Lodge **M**
(928) 422-3255. **$58-$68.** 22340 Old Hwy 66 86337. I-40 exit 121, 1 mi n, then 0.7 mi e. Ext corridors. **Pets:** Medium. $15 daily fee/pet. Designated rooms, service with restrictions, supervision.

Deluxe Inn Motel **M**
(928) 422-3244. **$57-$67.** 22295 Old Hwy 66 86337. I-40 exit 121 eastbound, 1 mi n, then 0.7 mi e; exit 123 westbound, just ne on I-40 business loop, then 2.4 mi w. Ext corridors. **Pets:** Other species. $10 one-time fee/room. Designated rooms, service with restrictions, supervision.

SHOW LOW

BEST WESTERN Paint Pony Lodge **M**
(928) 537-5773. **$81-$200.** 581 W Deuce of Clubs Ave 85901. On US 60 and SR 260. Ext corridors. **Pets:** Medium, other species. $15 daily fee/pet. Service with restrictions, supervision.

Days Inn **M**
(928) 537-4356. **$70-$149, 3 day notice.** 480 W Deuce of Clubs Ave 85901. On US 60 and SR 260. Ext/int corridors. **Pets:** Medium. $10 one-time fee/room. Service with restrictions, supervision.

K C Motel **M**
(928) 537-4433. **$59-$79.** 60 W Deuce of Clubs Ave 85901. On US 60 and SR 260. Ext corridors. **Pets:** Accepted.

Kiva Motel M

(928) 537-4542. **$58-$68, 3 day notice.** 261 E Deuce of Clubs Ave 85901. On US 60 and SR 260; center. Ext corridors. **Pets:** Small, dogs only. $5 deposit/pet, $5 daily fee/pet. Service with restrictions, supervision. [icons]

Super 8 H

(928) 532-7323. **$60-$130.** 1751 W Deuce of Clubs Ave 85901. 2 mi w of jct US 60 and SR 260, south side. Int corridors. **Pets:** Other species. $100 deposit/room. Service with restrictions, supervision.
[icons]

SIERRA VISTA

Candlewood Suites H

(520) 439-8200. **Call for rates.** 1904 S Hwy 92 85635. Jct SR 90 and 92, 1.4 mi s. Int corridors. **Pets:** Other species. $15 daily fee/pet. Service with restrictions, crate. [icons]

Days Inn H

(520) 458-8500. **$69-$73.** 3460 E Fry Blvd 85635. Just w of jct SR 90 and 92. Ext corridors. **Pets:** Accepted. [icons]

Gateway Studio Suites H ❧

(520) 458-5555. **Call for rates.** 203 S Garden Ave 85635. Just s of Fry Blvd; just e of main gate to Fort Huachuca. Int corridors. **Pets:** Large. $10 daily fee/pet. Designated rooms, service with restrictions, crate.
[icons]

Holiday Inn Express H

(520) 439-8800. **$99-$249, 3 day notice.** 1902 S Hwy 92 85635. Jct SR 90 and 92, 1.4 mi s. Int corridors. **Pets:** Accepted.
[icons]

Quality Inn H

(520) 458-7900. **$45-$99.** 1631 S Hwy 92 85635. On SR 92, 1 mi s of jct SR 90. Int corridors. **Pets:** Accepted. [icons]

Sun Canyon Inn H

(520) 459-0610. **$75-$95, 3 day notice.** 260 N Garden Ave 85635. Just n of Fry Blvd; just e of main gate to Fort Huachuca. Int corridors. **Pets:** Other species. $10 daily fee/pet. Service with restrictions, crate.
[icons]

TownePlace Suites by Marriott H

(520) 515-9900. **$99-$209.** 3399 Rodeo Dr 85635. Jct SR 90, 1.5 mi s on SR 92, just w on Avenida Cochise, just s on Oakmont Dr, then just e. Int corridors. **Pets:** $100 one-time fee/room.
[icons]

SURPRISE

Comfort Inn & Suites of Surprise H

(623) 544-6874. **Call for rates.** 13337 W Grand Ave 85374. Jct Bell Rd, 0.4 mi se. Int corridors. **Pets:** Medium. $20 one-time fee/pet. Designated rooms, service with restrictions, crate.
[icons]

Hampton Inn & Suites Surprise H

(623) 537-9122. **$89-$209.** 14783 W Grand Ave 85374. Jct Bell Rd, 2 mi nw. Int corridors. **Pets:** Accepted.
[icons]

Residence Inn by Marriott Phoenix NW Surprise H

(623) 249-6333. **$109-$499.** 16418 N Bullard Ave 85374. Jct US 60 (Grand Ave), 1.4 mi w on Bell Rd, then just s. Int corridors. **Pets:** Accepted. [icons]

Windmill Suites in Surprise H

(623) 583-0133. **$69-$224.** 12545 W Bell Rd 85378. US 60 (Grand Ave), 1 mi e. Int corridors. **Pets:** Accepted.
[icons]

TAYLOR

Rodeway Inn-Silver Creek Inn M

(928) 536-2600. **$54-$70.** 825 N Main St 85939. On SR 77. Ext corridors. **Pets:** Accepted. [icons]

TEMPE *(Restaurants p. 614)*

Aloft Hotel Tempe H

(480) 621-3300. **$99-$209.** 951 E Playa Del Norte Dr 85281. SR 202 (Red Mountain Frwy) exit 7 (Rural Rd), just s on Scottsdale Rd, then just e. Int corridors. **Pets:** Accepted.
[icons]

BEST WESTERN Inn of Tempe H

(480) 784-2233. **$72-$270.** 670 N Scottsdale Rd 85281. SR 202 (Red Mountain Frwy) exit 7 (Rural Rd), just s. Int corridors. **Pets:** Accepted. [icons]

BEST WESTERN PLUS Tempe by the Mall H

(480) 820-7500. **$90-$170.** 5300 S Priest Dr 85283. I-10 exit 155 (Baseline Rd), 0.4 mi e, then just s. Int corridors. **Pets:** Accepted. [icons]

Country Inn & Suites By Carlson, Phoenix Airport at Tempe H ❧

(480) 858-9898. **$69-$229.** 808 N Scottsdale Rd 85281. SR 202 (Red Mountain Frwy) exit 7 (Rural Rd S), just n. Int corridors. **Pets:** Dogs only. $50 one-time fee/room. Designated rooms, service with restrictions. [icons]

Days Inn & Suites H

(480) 345-8585. **$69-$99.** 1660 W Elliot Rd 85284. I-10 exit 157, just e. Ext corridors. **Pets:** Accepted. [icons]

DoubleTree by Hilton Phoenix-Tempe H

(480) 967-1441. **$89-$199.** 2100 S Priest Dr 85282. I-10 exit 153 (Broadway Rd), 0.5 mi e. Ext corridors. **Pets:** Accepted.
[icons]

Extended Stay America-Phoenix/Airport/Tempe H

(480) 557-8880. **Call for rates.** 2165 W 15th St 85281. I-10 exit 153B (Broadway Rd), 0.3 mi ne, just nw on S 52nd St, then just w. Int corridors. **Pets:** Other species. $25 daily fee/pet. Service with restrictions, supervision. [icons]

Four Points by Sheraton Tempe H

(480) 968-3451. **$80-$161.** 1333 S Rural Rd 85281. US 60 (Superstition Frwy) exit 174 (Rural Rd), 2 mi n. Int corridors. **Pets:** Accepted. [icons]

Hawthorn Suites by Wyndham H

(480) 633-2744. **$70-$135.** 2301 E Southern Ave 85282. SR 101 exit 54 (Southern Ave/Baseline Rd); at southeast corner. Int corridors. **Pets:** Accepted. [icons]

Hotel Tempe Phoenix Airport InnSuites Hotel & Suites H

(480) 897-7900. **$59-$199.** 1651 W Baseline Rd 85283. I-10 exit 155 (Baseline Rd), just e. Ext corridors. **Pets:** Accepted.
[icons]

Hyatt Place Tempe/Phoenix Airport H

(480) 804-9544. **$69-$259.** 1413 W Rio Salado Pkwy 85281. Just w of Priest Dr. Int corridors. **Pets:** Large, dogs only. $75 one-time fee/room. Service with restrictions, crate. [icons]

La Quinta Inn Phoenix Sky Harbor Airport South H

(480) 967-4465. **$72-$549.** 911 S 48th St 85281. I-10 exit 153B (Broadway Rd) eastbound; exit 153A (University Dr) westbound, 0.8 mi n; on south side of University Dr; east side of SR 143 (Hohokam Expwy). Ext/int corridors. **Pets:** Large, other species. Service with restrictions. [icons]

▼▼▼▼ **Red Lion Inn & Suites Phoenix/Tempe - ASU** 🅷
(480) 675-9799. **$79-$159.** 1429 N Scottsdale Rd 85281. SR 202 Loop (Red Mountain Frwy) exit 7 (Rural Rd S), 0.5 mi n. Ext corridors. **Pets:** Accepted. 🐾 📶 ✕ 🛅 💻

𝔸𝔸𝔻 ▼▼ **Red Roof Inn Phoenix Airport** 🅷
(480) 449-3205. **$49-$118.** 2135 W 15th St 85281. I-10 exit 153B (Broadway Rd), just nw on S 52nd St, then just w. Int corridors. **Pets:** Large, other species. Service with restrictions, supervision.
SAVE 🐾 📶 ✕ 🛅 💻

▼▼▼ **Residence Inn by Marriott Tempe** 🅷
(480) 756-2122. **$99-$259.** 5075 S Priest Dr 85282. I-10 exit 155 (Baseline Rd), 0.4 mi e, then just n. Ext/int corridors. **Pets:** Accepted.
&M 🐾 📶 ✕ 🛅 💻

𝔸𝔸𝔻 ▼▼▼ **Residence Inn by Marriott Tempe Downtown/University** 🅷
(480) 967-2300. **$64-$599.** 510 S Forest Ave 85281. Jct University Dr, just n on Mill Ave, just e; downtown. Int corridors. **Pets:** Accepted.
SAVE &M 📶 ✕ 🛅 💻

𝔸𝔸𝔻 ▼▼▼ **Sheraton Phoenix Airport Hotel Tempe** 🅷
(480) 967-6600. **$79-$289.** 1600 S 52nd St 85281. I-10 exit 153B (Broadway Rd) westbound; exit 153A (48th St) eastbound, 0.3 mi ne. Int corridors. **Pets:** Accepted. SAVE 🍴 🐾 📶 ✕ 🛅 💻

𝔸𝔸𝔻 ▼▼▼▼ **Tempe Mission Palms Hotel** 🅷
(480) 894-1400. **$109-$329.** 60 E 5th St 85281. Jct University Dr, just n on Mill Ave, just e. Int corridors. **Pets:** Accepted.
SAVE ECO 🍴 🐾 📦 📶 ✕ 🛅 💻

▼▼▼ **TownePlace Suites by Marriott Tempe at Arizona Mills Mall** 🅷
(480) 345-7889. **$59-$249.** 5223 S Priest Dr 85283. I-10 exit 155 (Baseline Rd), southeast corner of Baseline Rd and Priest Dr. Int corridors. **Pets:** Accepted. &M 🐾 📶 ✕ 🛅 💻

THATCHER

▼▼▼ **Comfort Inn & Suites-Thatcher** 🅷
(928) 348-9500. **$96-$135.** 2577 W Hwy 70 85552. 2 mi w of jct US 191. Int corridors. **Pets:** Accepted. 📶 ✕ 🛅 💻

TOLLESON

𝔸𝔸𝔻 ▼▼ **BEST WESTERN Tolleson-Phoenix Hotel** 🅷
(623) 936-6000. **$90-$300.** 8421 W McDowell Rd 85353. I-10 exit 135 (83rd Ave), just n, then just w. Int corridors. **Pets:** Accepted.
SAVE 🐾 📶 ✕ 🛅 💻

▼▼ **Premier Inns** 🅷
(623) 533-4660. **Call for rates.** 8399 W Lynwood St 85353. I-10 exit 135 (83rd Ave), just n, then just w. Ext corridors. **Pets:** Accepted.
🐾 📦 🛅

TOMBSTONE

𝔸𝔸𝔻 ▼▼▼ **Landmark Lookout Lodge** 🅷
(520) 457-2223. **$99-$130.** 781 N Hwy 80 85638. On SR 80, 1 mi n of center. Ext corridors. **Pets:** Accepted. SAVE 🐾 📶 ✕ 🛅 💻

TUBAC

𝔸𝔸𝔻 ▼▼▼▼ **Tubac Golf Resort & Spa** 🅷 🐾
(520) 398-2211. **$109-$339, 3 day notice.** 1 Otero Rd 85646. I-19 exit 40 (Chavez Siding Rd), on east side, then 2 mi s. Ext corridors. **Pets:** $25 daily fee/pet. Designated rooms, service with restrictions, crate. SAVE ECO 🍴 🐾 📦 📶 ✕ 🛅 💻

TUBA CITY

𝔸𝔸𝔻 ▼▼▼ **Quality Inn Navajo Nation** 🅷
(928) 283-4545. **$103-$173.** 10 N Main St 86045. 1 mi n of US 160. Int corridors. **Pets:** Medium. $10 daily fee/pet. Designated rooms, service with restrictions, supervision. SAVE 🍴 📶 🛅 💻

TUCSON *(Restaurants p. 614)*

𝔸𝔸𝔻 ▼▼▼▼ **Aloft Tucson University** 🅷 🐾
(520) 908-6800. **Call for rates.** 1900 E Speedway Blvd 85719. Southeast corner of Speedway Blvd and Campbell Ave. Int corridors. **Pets:** Medium, dogs only. Service with restrictions, crate.
SAVE 🍴 &M 📶 ✕ 🛅 💻

𝔸𝔸𝔻 ▼▼▼ **Americas Best Value Inn-Tucson** 🅷
(520) 884-5800. **$43-$60.** 810 E Benson Hwy 85713. I-10 exit 262, just s. Ext corridors. **Pets:** Medium. $25 deposit/room. Service with restrictions. SAVE &M 🐾 📶 🛅

𝔸𝔸𝔻 ▼▼▼ **Arizona Riverpark Inn** 🅷
(520) 239-2300. **$89-$199, 3 day notice.** 350 S Freeway 85745. I-10 exit 258 (Broadway Blvd/Congress St), just w, then 0.4 mi s. Ext/int corridors. **Pets:** Accepted. SAVE 🍴 🐾 ✕ 🛅 💻

𝔸𝔸𝔻 ▼▼▼ **BEST WESTERN InnSuites Tucson Foothills Hotel & Suites** 🅷 🐾
(520) 297-8111. **$81-$153.** 6201 N Oracle Rd 85704. I-10 exit 250 (Orange Grove Rd), 4 mi e, then just s. Ext corridors. **Pets:** Large, other species. $20 one-time fee/room. Service with restrictions, supervision. SAVE 🐾 ✕ 📶 🛅 💻

𝔸𝔸𝔻 ▼▼▼▼ **BEST WESTERN PLUS Tucson Int'l Airport Hotel & Suites** 🅷
(520) 746-3932. **$69-$299.** 6801 S Tucson Blvd 85756. Just n of Tucson International Airport. Int corridors. **Pets:** Medium. $20 daily fee/room. Service with restrictions, supervision.
SAVE 🍴 🐾 📶 ✕ 🛅 💻

𝔸𝔸𝔻 ▼▼▼ **BEST WESTERN Royal Sun Inn & Suites** 🅷 🐾
(520) 622-8871. **$59-$299.** 1015 N Stone Ave 85705. I-10 exit 257 (Speedway Blvd), 0.8 mi e, then just s. Ext corridors. **Pets:** $20 daily fee/pet. Designated rooms, service with restrictions, supervision.
SAVE ECO 🍴 🐾 📶 ✕ 🛅 💻

𝔸𝔸𝔻 ▼▼▼ **Candlewood Suites Tucson** 🅷 🐾
(520) 373-5799. **Call for rates.** 1995 W River Rd 85704. I-10 exit 250 (Orange Grove Rd), 0.4 mi e to River Rd, then 2.7 mi se. Int corridors. **Pets:** Medium, dogs only. $15 daily fee/pet. Designated rooms, service with restrictions, supervision. SAVE &M 📶 ✕ 🛅 💻

▼▼▼ **Catalina Park Inn Bed and Breakfast** 🅱🅱
(520) 792-4541. **$135-$189, 14 day notice.** 309 E 1st St 85705. I-10 exit 257 (Speedway Blvd), 1 mi e to 5th Ave, just n, then just e; in West University Historic District. Ext/int corridors. **Pets:** Medium, dogs only. Designated rooms, service with restrictions, supervision. 📶 ✕

▼▼▼ **Comfort Suites at Sabino Canyon** 🅷
(520) 298-2300. **$79-$99.** 7007 E Tanque Verde Rd 85715. Jct Grand Rd, 0.4 mi ne. Ext corridors. **Pets:** Medium. $50 daily fee/pet. Designated rooms, service with restrictions, crate. 🐾 📶 ✕ 🛅 💻

▼▼▼ **Comfort Suites at Tucson Mall** 🅷
(520) 888-6676. **$79-$299.** 515 W Auto Mall Dr 85705. I-10 exit 254 (Prince Rd), 1.9 mi e, then 1.2 mi n. Int corridors. **Pets:** Other species. $25 one-time fee/pet. 🐾 📶 ✕ 🛅 💻

𝔸𝔸𝔻 ▼▼▼ **Country Inn & Suites By Carlson-Tucson Airport** 🅷
(520) 741-9000. **$79-$169.** 6681 S Tucson Blvd 85756. 0.4 mi n of Tucson International Airport entrance. Int corridors. **Pets:** $25 one-time fee/room. Designated rooms, service with restrictions, crate.
SAVE &M 🐾 📶 🛅 💻

AAA ▼▼▼ **Country Inn & Suites By Carlson-Tucson City Center** 🅗

(520) 867-6200. **$89-$199.** 705 N Freeway 85745. I-10 exit 257 (Speedway Blvd), just w, then just s. Int corridors. **Pets:** Accepted. SAVE 🏊 🛜 ✖ 🛢 💻

AAA ▼▼▼ **Desert Diamond Casino & Hotel** 🅗

(520) 342-3100. **$99-$209.** 7350 S Nogales Hwy 85756. I-19 exit 95 (Valencia Rd), 1.4 mi e, then 1 mi s. Int corridors. **Pets:** $500 deposit/room. Service with restrictions, crate. SAVE 🍴 ♿ 🏊 🛜 ✖ 🛢 💻

AAA ▼▼▼ **DoubleTree by Hilton Tucson-Reid Park** 🅗

(520) 881-4200. **$119-$349.** 445 S Alvernon Way 85711. I-10 exit 259 (22nd St), 4 mi e, then just n. Ext/int corridors. **Pets:** Accepted. SAVE 🍴 🏊 ✖ 🛜 ✖ 🛢 💻

▼▼▼ **DoubleTree Suites by Hilton Tucson Airport** 🅗 ❄

(520) 225-0800. **$99-$299.** 7051 S Tucson Blvd 85756. At entrance to Tucson International Airport. Ext corridors. **Pets:** Medium, other species. $50 one-time fee/pet. Designated rooms, service with restrictions, supervision. 🍴 ♿ 🏊 🛜 ✖ 🛢 💻

▼ **Econo Lodge University** Ⓜ

(520) 622-6714. **$65.** 1136 N Stone Ave 85705. I-10 exit 257 (Speedway Blvd) eastbound, just e, then just n. Ext corridors. **Pets:** Accepted. 🏊 🛜 🛢

▼▼▼ **Extended Stay America-Tucson Grant Road** 🅗

(520) 795-9510. **Call for rates.** 5050 E Grant Rd 85712. 0.5 mi e of Swan Rd. Ext corridors. **Pets:** Other species. $25 daily fee/pet. Service with restrictions, supervision. 🛜 🛢 💻

▼▼▼ **Hampton Inn Tucson North** 🅗 ❄

(520) 206-0602. **$69-$179.** 1375 W Grant Rd 85745. I-10 exit 256 (Grant Rd), just w. Int corridors. **Pets:** Medium, other species. Designated rooms, service with restrictions, supervision. ♿ 🏊 🛜 ✖ 🛢 💻

AAA ▼▼▼ **Hilton Tucson East** 🅗 ❄

(520) 721-5600. **$72-$220.** 7600 E Broadway Blvd 85710. 0.5 mi e of Kolb Rd. Int corridors. **Pets:** Medium, other species. $50 one-time fee/room. Designated rooms, service with restrictions, crate. SAVE 🍴 ♿ 🏊 🛜 ✖ 🛢 💻

▼▼▼ **Holiday Inn Express Tucson Airport** 🅗

(520) 889-6600. **$104-$199, 14 day notice.** 2548 E Medina Rd 85756. 0.5 mi n of Tucson International Airport entrance. Int corridors. **Pets:** Accepted. ♿ 🏊 🛜 ✖ 🛢 💻

▼▼▼ **Holiday Inn Hotel & Suites-Tucson Airport North** 🅗

(520) 746-1161. **Call for rates.** 4550 S Palo Verde Blvd 85714. I-10 exit 264 westbound; exit 264B eastbound, 0.5 mi n. Ext/int corridors. **Pets:** Accepted. 🍴 ♿ 🏊 🛜 🛢 💻

AAA ▼▼▼ **Hyatt Place Tucson Airport** 🅗

(520) 295-0405. **$69-$199.** 6885 S Tucson Blvd 85756. Just n of Tucson International Airport. Int corridors. **Pets:** Accepted. SAVE 🍴 ♿ 🏊 🛜 ✖ 🛢 💻

▼▼▼ **La Quinta Inn & Suites Tucson Airport** 🅗

(520) 573-3333. **$65-$244.** 7001 S Tucson Blvd 85706. Just n of Tucson International Airport. Int corridors. **Pets:** Large, other species. Service with restrictions. ♿ 🏊 🛜 🛢 💻

AAA ▼▼▼ **The Lodge @ Ventana Canyon** 🅗 ❄

(520) 577-1400. **$89-$599, 21 day notice.** 6200 N Clubhouse Ln 85750. I-10 exit 256 (Grant Rd), 8.6 mi e, 0.6 mi e on Tanque Verde Rd, 2 mi n on Sabino Canyon Rd, then 3.2 mi n on Kolb Rd. Ext/int corridors. **Pets:** Dogs only. $100 one-time fee/room. Designated rooms, service with restrictions. SAVE 🍴 🏊 ✖ 🛜 ✖ 🛢 💻

AAA ▼▼▼ **Lodge on the Desert** 🅗

(520) 320-2000. **$129-$429, 3 day notice.** 306 N Alvernon Way 85711. I-10 exit 258 (Broadway Blvd/Congress St), 4 mi e, then just n. Ext corridors. **Pets:** Medium, dogs only. $25 daily fee/pet. Designated rooms, service with restrictions. SAVE 🍴 🏊 🛜 ✖ 🛢 💻

AAA ▼▼▼ **Loews Ventana Canyon** 🅗 ❄

(520) 299-2020. **$129-$349, 3 day notice.** 7000 N Resort Dr 85750. I-10 exit 256 (Grant Rd), 8.6 mi e, 0.6 mi ne on Tanque Verde Rd, 2 mi n on Sabino Canyon Rd, then 3.5 mi n on Kolb Rd. Ext/int corridors. **Pets:** Large, other species. $50 one-time fee/room. Service with restrictions. SAVE ECO 🍴 ♿ 🏊 🛜 ✖ 🛢 💻

▼ **Motel 6 Tucson North #1127** 🅗

(520) 744-9300. **Call for rates.** 4630 W Ina Rd 85741. I-10 exit 248 (Ina Rd), just e to Camino de Oeste, then just n. Int corridors. **Pets:** Other species. Service with restrictions, crate. 🏊 🛜 🛢

AAA ▼▼▼ **Omni Tucson National Resort** 🅗 ❄

(520) 297-2271. **$109-$459, 3 day notice.** 2727 W Club Dr 85742. I-10 exit 246 (Cortaro Rd), 3.5 mi e, then just n on Shannon Rd. Ext corridors. **Pets:** $100 one-time fee/room. Designated rooms, service with restrictions, supervision. SAVE 🍴 🏊 ✖ 🛜 ✖ 🛢 💻

AAA ▼▼▼ **Quality Inn Tucson Airport** 🅗

(520) 294-2500. **$59-$119.** 2803 E Valencia Rd 85706. 1 mi ne of Tucson International Airport; just e of Tucson Blvd. Ext/int corridors. **Pets:** Accepted. SAVE 🏊 🛜 🛢 💻

AAA ▼▼▼ **Radisson Suites Tucson** 🅗

(520) 721-7100. **$79-$269.** 6555 E Speedway Blvd 85710. Just e of Wilmot Rd. Ext corridors. **Pets:** Accepted. SAVE 🍴 🏊 ✖ 🛜 🛢 💻

AAA ▼▼▼ **Red Lion Inn & Suites Tucson North** 🅗

(520) 575-9255. **$69-$219.** 7411 N Oracle Rd 85704. SR 77 (Oracle Rd), just n of Ina Rd. Ext corridors. **Pets:** Accepted. SAVE ♿ 🏊 🛜 ✖ 🛢 💻

AAA ▼▼▼ **Red Roof Inn-Tucson South** 🅗

(520) 571-1400. **$39-$120.** 3704 E Irvington Rd 85714. I-10 exit 264 westbound; exit 264B eastbound. Ext corridors. **Pets:** Large, other species. Service with restrictions, supervision. SAVE 🏊 🛜 ✖ 🛢 💻

▼▼▼ **Residence Inn by Marriott-Tucson** 🅗

(520) 721-0991. **$69-$129.** 6477 E Speedway Blvd 85710. Just e of Wilmot Rd. Ext corridors. **Pets:** Accepted. 🏊 🛜 ✖ 🛢 💻

▼▼▼ **Residence Inn by Marriott Tucson Airport** 🅗

(520) 294-5522. **$79-$149.** 2660 E Medina Rd 85756. 0.5 mi n of airport entrance on Tucson Blvd, just e. Int corridors. **Pets:** Other species. $50 one-time fee/room. Service with restrictions, crate. 🏊 🛜 ✖ 🛢 💻

▼▼▼ **Residence Inn by Marriott Williams Centre** 🅗

(520) 790-6100. **$99-$249.** 5400 E Williams Cir 85711. Jct Campbell Ave, 3.8 mi e on Broadway Blvd, just s, then just e on Williams Blvd. Int corridors. **Pets:** Other species. $100 one-time fee/room. Service with restrictions. ♿ 🏊 🛜 ✖ 🛢 💻

AAA ▼▼▼ **Sheraton Tucson Hotel & Suites** 🅗

(520) 323-6262. **$69-$229.** 5151 E Grant Rd 85712. Jct Campbell Ave, 3.6 mi e. Ext/int corridors. **Pets:** Accepted. SAVE 🍴 ♿ 🏊 🛜 ✖ 🛢 💻

▼▼▼ **Staybridge Suites Tucson Airport** H

(520) 807-1004. **Call for rates.** 2705 E Executive Dr 85756. 0.7 mi n of Tucson International Airport. Int corridors. **Pets:** Accepted.

&M ⊷ 📶 ✕ 🍴 💻

🔺 ▼ **Stone Inn** M

(520) 622-6446. **$40-$129.** 1248 N Stone Ave 85705. I-10 exit 257 (Speedway Blvd) eastbound, just e, then just n. Ext corridors. **Pets:** Small, dogs only. $10 deposit/pet, $10 daily fee/pet. Designated rooms, service with restrictions, supervision. SAVE ⊷ 📶 🍴

▼▼ **Studio 6 Extended Stay #6002** M

(520) 746-0030. **$53-$93.** 4950 S Outlet Center Dr 85706. I-10 exit 264A eastbound; exit 264B westbound, just s, then just nw on Julian Dr. Ext corridors. **Pets:** Other species. $10 daily fee/room. Service with restrictions, crate. ⊷ 📶 🍴 💻

▼▼▼ **TownePlace Suites by Marriott Tucson Airport** H ❀

(520) 294-6677. **$65-$139.** 6595 S Bay Colony Dr 85756. 0.7 mi n of Tucson International Airport. Int corridors. **Pets:** Other species. $75 one-time fee/room. Service with restrictions, supervision.

&M ⊷ 📶 ✕ 🍴 💻

▼▼▼ **TownePlace Suites by Marriott Tucson Williams Centre** H

(520) 747-0720. **$79-$149.** 384 S Williams Blvd 85711. Jct Campbell Ave, 3.8 mi e on Broadway Blvd, just s. Int corridors. **Pets:** Accepted.

&M ⊷ 📶 ✕ 🍴 💻

🔺 ▼▼▼ **Viscount Suite Hotel** H

(520) 745-6500. **$79-$199, 3 day notice.** 4855 E Broadway Blvd 85711. Just e of Swan Rd. Int corridors. **Pets:** Medium. $75 deposit/pet. Service with restrictions, supervision. SAVE 🍴 ⊷ 📶 ✕ 🍴 💻

🔺 ▼▼▼▼ **The Westin La Paloma Resort & Spa** H ❀

(520) 742-6000. **$109-$329, 3 day notice.** 3800 E Sunrise Dr 85718. SR 77 (Oracle Rd), 4.6 mi e on Ina Rd via Skyline and Sunrise drs, then just s on Via Palomita. Ext corridors. **Pets:** Small, dogs only. Service with restrictions, supervision.

SAVE ECO 🍴 ⊷ 🏊 🛁 ✕ 🍴 💻

🔺 ▼▼▼▼ **Westward Look Wyndham Grand Resort & Spa** H ❀

(520) 297-1151. **$149-$293, 7 day notice.** 245 E Ina Rd 85704. I-10 exit 248 (Ina Rd), 6 mi e, then just n on Westward Look Dr. Ext corridors. **Pets:** Other species. $75 one-time fee/room. Service with restrictions, crate. SAVE ECO 🍴 ⊷ 🏊 🛁 ✕ 🍴 💻

WELLTON

▼▼ **Microtel Inn & Suites by Wyndham Wellton** H

(928) 785-3777. **$67-$95.** 28784 Commerce Way 85356. I-8 exit 30, just s. Int corridors. **Pets:** Accepted. ⊷ 📶 ✕ 🍴 💻

WICKENBURG

🔺 ▼▼▼ **BEST WESTERN Rancho Grande** H ❀

(928) 684-5445. **$72-$114.** 293 E Wickenburg Way 85390. On US 60; center. Ext corridors. **Pets:** Other species. $8 daily fee/room. Service with restrictions, supervision. SAVE ⊷ 📶 ✕ 🍴 💻

▼▼▼ **Quality Inn Wickenburg** H

(928) 684-5461. **$53-$109.** 850 E Wickenburg Way 85390. 1.3 mi se on US 60. Int corridors. **Pets:** Accepted. ⊷ 📶 ✕ 🍴 💻

🔺 ▼▼▼ **Super 8 Wickenburg** M

(928) 684-0808. **$50-$160.** 1021 N Tegner St 85390. 1 mi n of jct US 60 and 93. Ext/int corridors. **Pets:** $10 daily fee/pet. Service with restrictions, crate. SAVE 📶 🍴 💻

WILLCOX

▼▼ **Days Inn** M

(520) 384-4222. **$55-$60.** 724 N Bisbee Ave 85643. I-10 exit 340, just s. Ext corridors. **Pets:** Medium. $7 daily fee/pet. Service with restrictions, supervision. ⊷ 📶 🍴 💻

▼▼▼▼ **Holiday Inn Express & Suites Willcox** H

(520) 384-3333. **$99-$139.** 1251 N Virginia Ave 85643. I-10 exit 340, just n. Int corridors. **Pets:** Medium. $20 daily fee/pet. Designated rooms, service with restrictions, supervision. &M ⊷ 📶 🍴 💻

WILLIAMS *(Restaurants p. 614)*

🔺 ▼▼▼ **BEST WESTERN PLUS Inn of Williams** H

(928) 635-4400. **$80-$190.** 2600 W Route 66 86046. I-40 exit 161, just e. Int corridors. **Pets:** Medium. $25 daily fee/pet. Designated rooms, service with restrictions, supervision.

SAVE 🍴 ⊷ 📶 ✕ 🍴 💻

▼▼ **Days Inn of Williams** M ❀

(928) 635-4051. **$70-$170.** 2488 W Route 66 86046. I-40 exit 161, just e. Int corridors. **Pets:** $20 daily fee/room. Designated rooms, service with restrictions, supervision. ⊷ 📶 ✕ 🍴 💻

🔺 ▼▼ **Mountain Ranch Resort at Beacon Hill** H

(928) 635-2693. **$119-$259.** 6701 E Mountain Ranch Rd 86046. I-40 exit 171 (Deer Farm Rd), just s. Ext corridors. **Pets:** Medium. $50 one-time fee/room. Designated rooms, service with restrictions, supervision.

SAVE 🍴 🏊 📶 ✕ 🍴 💻

▼▼ **Ramada Williams/Grand Canyon Area** H

(928) 635-4114. **$54-$128.** 950 N Grand Canyon Blvd 86046. I-40 exit 163, just s. Int corridors. **Pets:** Accepted.

🍴 &M ⊷ 📶 🍴 💻

🔺 ◆ **Travelodge Williams** M

(928) 635-2651. **$60-$170.** 430 E Route 66 86046. I-40 exit 163, 0.5 mi s, then just e. Ext corridors. **Pets:** Accepted. SAVE ⊷ 📶 🍴 💻

WINDOW ROCK

🔺 ▼▼ **Quality Inn Navajo Nation Capital** H

(928) 871-4108. **$79-$155.** 48 W Hwy 264 86515. Center. Ext corridors. **Pets:** Medium. $50 deposit/pet. Designated rooms, service with restrictions, supervision. SAVE 🍴 📶 🍴 💻

WINSLOW

🔺 ▼▼▼ **BEST WESTERN PLUS Winslow Inn** H

(928) 289-2960. **$99-$159.** 816 Transcon Ln 86047. I-40 exit 255, just n. Int corridors. **Pets:** Medium, dogs only. $10 one-time fee/pet. Supervision. SAVE &M ⊷ 📶 ✕ 🍴 💻

▼▼▼▼ **La Posada Hotel** H

(928) 289-4366. **$119-$169, 7 day notice.** 303 E 2nd St 86047. I-40 exit 253, 1 mi s to Route 66 (2nd St), then just e; in historic downtown. Int corridors. **Pets:** Accepted. 🍴 &M 📶 ✕ 📠

YOUNGTOWN

🔺 ▼▼▼ **BEST WESTERN Inn & Suites of Sun City** H

(623) 933-8211. **$69-$180.** 11201 Grand Ave 85363. On US 60, just se of 113th Ave. Ext/int corridors. **Pets:** Accepted.

SAVE ⊷ 📶 🍴 💻

YUMA

🔺 ▼▼▼ **BEST WESTERN InnSuites Yuma Mall Hotel & Suites** H

(928) 783-8341. **$71-$99.** 1450 Castle Dome Ave 85365. I-8 exit 2 (16th St/US 95), just e to Yuma Palms Pkwy, just n, then just w. Ext corridors. **Pets:** Accepted. SAVE ⊷ ✕ 📶 🍴 💻

▼▼▼ **Candlewood Suites** 🏠
(928) 726-2800. **Call for rates.** 2036 S Ave 3 E 85365. I-8 exit 3, just n, then just w on Frontage Rd. Int corridors. **Pets:** Accepted.
⟨M⟩ 🛰 ✕ 📗 💻

🔷🔷 ▼▼ **Historic Coronado Motor Hotel** 🏠 ❀
(928) 783-4453. **$80-$140.** 233 4th Ave 85364. I-8 exit 172 (4th Ave) eastbound, 0.5 mi s; exit 1 (Harold C. Giss Pkwy) westbound, 1 mi w. Ext corridors. **Pets:** Medium. $130 deposit/room, $10 one-time fee/pet. Designated rooms, service with restrictions, crate.
SAVE 🍴 🛰 📶 ✕ 📗 💻

▼▼▼ **Holiday Inn Express & Suites** 🏠
(928) 317-1400. **Call for rates.** 2044 S Ave 3 E 85365. I-8 exit 3, just n, then just w on Frontage Rd. Int corridors. **Pets:** Other species. $15 daily fee/pet. ⟨M⟩ 🛰 📶 ✕ 📗 💻

▼▼▼ **Homewood Suites by Hilton Yuma** 🏠
(928) 782-4100. **$89-$149.** 1955 E 16th St 85365. I-8 exit 2 (16th St/US 95), 0.4 mi e. Int corridors. **Pets:** Accepted.
⟨M⟩ 🛰 📶 📗 💻

🔷🔷 ▼▼▼ **La Fuente Inn & Suites** 🏠
(928) 329-1814. **$69-$179.** 1513 E 16th St 85365. I-8 exit 2 (16th St/US 95), just e. Ext corridors. **Pets:** Dogs only. $25 one-time fee/room. Service with restrictions, supervision. SAVE 🛰 📶 📗 💻

▼▼ **Quality Inn** 🏠
(928) 782-1200. **$64-$119.** 1691 S Riley Ave 85365. I-8 exit 2 (16th St/US 95), just w. Int corridors. **Pets:** Accepted.
⟨M⟩ 🛰 📶 📗 💻

▼▼▼ **Radisson Hotel Yuma** 🏠
(928) 783-8000. **$99-$180.** 1501 S Redondo Center Dr 85365. I-8 exit 2 (16th St/US 95), just w, then just n. Int corridors. **Pets:** Small, dogs only. $15 daily fee/pet. Designated rooms, service with restrictions, supervision. 🍴 🛰 📶 ✕ 📗 💻

▼▼ **Shilo Inn Hotel & Suites-Yuma** 🏠
(928) 782-9511. **Call for rates.** 1550 S Castle Dome Ave 85365. I-8 exit 2 (16th St/US 95), just e to Yuma Palms Pkwy, just n, then just w. Int corridors. **Pets:** Accepted. ⟨M⟩ 🛰 ✕ 📶 ✕ 📗 💻

▼▼▼ **TownePlace Suites by Marriott** 🏠
(928) 783-6900. **$89-$209.** 1726 S Sunridge Dr 85365. I-8 exit 2 (16th St/US 95), just e to Sunridge Dr, then just s. Int corridors.
Pets: Accepted. ⟨M⟩ 🛰 📶 📗 💻

▼▼ **Yuma Cabana Motel** Ⓜ
(928) 783-8311. **Call for rates.** 2151 S 4th Ave 85364. I-8 exit 2 (16th St/US 95), 1 mi w, then 0.5 mi s. Int corridors. **Pets:** Accepted.
🛰 📶 ✕ 📗 💻

ARKANSAS

ALMA

🔷🔷 ▼▼ **Quality Inn & Suites** 🏠
(479) 632-4141. **$59-$100.** 439 Hwy 71 N 72921. I-40 exit 13, just n. Ext/int corridors. **Pets:** Accepted. SAVE 📶 📗 💻

ARKADELPHIA

🔷🔷 ▼ **BEST WESTERN Continental Inn** Ⓜ
(870) 246-5592. **$70-$110.** 136 Valley St 71923. I-30 exit 78, just e. Ext corridors. **Pets:** Large. $10 daily fee/pet. Service with restrictions, crate.
SAVE 🛰 📶 📗 💻

▼▼▼ **Hampton Inn** 🏠
(870) 403-0800. **$89-$149.** 108 Malvern Rd 71923. I-30 exit 78, just ne. Int corridors. **Pets:** Small. Designated rooms, supervision.
⟨M⟩ 🛰 📶 📗 💻

BATESVILLE

▼ **Super 8-Batesville** Ⓜ
(870) 793-5888. **$55-$59.** 1287 N St. Louis St 72501. 1 mi n on US 167. Int corridors. **Pets:** Accepted. 📶 📗 💻

BENTON

🔷🔷 ▼▼ **BEST WESTERN Benton Inn** Ⓜ ❀
(501) 778-9695. **$75-$80.** 17036 I-30 72019. I-30 exit 117 westbound; exit 118 eastbound; on northwest service road. Ext corridors.
Pets: Large, other species. $10 daily fee/pet. Service with restrictions, supervision. SAVE 🛰 📶 📗 💻

BENTONVILLE

▼▼▼ **21C Museum Hotel** 🏠
(479) 286-6500. **Call for rates.** 200 NE A St 72712. Just n of jct Central Ave; downtown. Int corridors. **Pets:** Accepted.
🔵 🍴 📶 ✕ 📗 💻

▼▼▼ **Comfort Suites Bentonville/Rogers** 🏠
(479) 254-9099. **$69-$169.** 2011 SE Walton Blvd 72712. I-49 exit 85, just w. Int corridors. **Pets:** Accepted. 🛰 📶 ✕ 📗 💻

▼▼▼ **La Quinta Inn & Suites Bentonville** 🏠
(479) 271-7555. **$79-$249.** 1001 SE Walton Blvd 72712. I-49 exit 85, 0.7 mi w. Int corridors. **Pets:** Large, other species. Service with restrictions. ⟨M⟩ 🛰 📶 ✕ 📗 💻

▼▼ **Microtel Inn & Suites by Wyndham Bentonville** 🏠
(479) 271-6699. **$59-$124.** 911 SE Walton Blvd 72712. I-49 exit 85, 0.8 mi w. Int corridors. **Pets:** Accepted. 📶 📗 💻

▼▼ **Simmons Suites Hotel** 🏠 ❀
(479) 254-7800. **$74-$165.** 3001 NE 11th St 72712. I-49 exit 88, just ne. Int corridors. **Pets:** Medium, dogs only. $50 one-time fee/pet, $10 daily fee/pet. Designated rooms, service with restrictions, supervision.
📶 ✕ 📗 💻

▼▼ **Suburban Extended Stay Hotel** 🏠
(479) 268-4400. **$55-$139.** 200 SW Suburban Ln 72712. I-49 exit 85, 1.6 mi w. Int corridors. **Pets:** Accepted. 📶 📗 💻

▼▼ **TownePlace Suites by Marriott Bentonville/Rogers** 🏠 ❀
(479) 621-0202. **$69-$149.** 3100 SE 14th St 72712. I-49 exit 86, just e. Int corridors. **Pets:** Other species. $50 one-time fee/room. Service with restrictions, crate. ⟨M⟩ 🛰 📶 ✕ 📗 💻

🔷🔷 ▼▼▼ **Wingate by Wyndham** 🏠
(479) 418-5400. **$74-$119.** 7400 SW Old Farm Blvd 72712. 7.4 mi w of jct Walton and SW Regional Airport blvds. Int corridors. **Pets:** Other species. $50 one-time fee/room. Designated rooms, service with restrictions, crate. SAVE ⟨M⟩ 🛰 📶 ✕ 📗 💻

BLYTHEVILLE

▼▼▼ **Comfort Inn & Suites** 🏠
(870) 763-0900. **$96-$159.** 1510 E Main St 72315. I-55 exit 67, just w. Int corridors. **Pets:** Medium, dogs only. $15 one-time fee/room. Designated rooms, service with restrictions, crate.
⟨M⟩ 🛰 📶 ✕ 📗 💻

▼▼▼ **Hampton Inn** 🏠
(870) 763-5220. **$104-$124.** 301 N Service Rd 72315. I-55 exit 67, just nw. Int corridors. **Pets:** Accepted. ⟨M⟩ 🛰 📶 ✕ 📗 💻

▼▼ **Quality Inn** H

(870) 763-7081. **$64-$88.** 1520 E Main St 72315. I-55 exit 67, just w. Ext corridors. **Pets:** Accepted. 🍴 ⅃ 🛜 📶 🖥

BRYANT

▼▼ **Americas Best Value Inn** M

(501) 653-7800. **$58-$100.** 407 W Commerce St 72022. I-30 exit 123, just n on SR 183, then just w. Ext corridors. **Pets:** Accepted. 🛜 📶 🖥

▼▼▼ **Comfort Inn & Suites** H ❀

(501) 653-4000. **$80-$130.** 209 W Commerce St 72022. I-30 exit 123, just n on SR 183, then just w. Int corridors. **Pets:** Medium. Designated rooms, service with restrictions, crate. ⅃ 🛜 ✕ 📶 🖥

▼▼▼ **Holiday Inn Express** H

(501) 847-0900. **$89-$119.** 2915 Main St 72022. I-30 exit 123, just n on SR 183, just e on Commerce St, then just n. Int corridors. **Pets:** Accepted. 🔊 ⅃ 🛜 📶 🖥

▼▼ **Hometown Hotel** H

(501) 653-0123. **$64-$89.** 2921 Main St 72022. I-30 exit 123, just n on SR 183, just e on Commerce St, then just n. Ext/int corridors. **Pets:** Accepted. 🔊 🛜 ✕ 📶 🖥

▼▼▼ **La Quinta Inn & Suites Bryant** H

(501) 847-9494. **$89-$215.** 408 W Commerce St 72022. I-30 exit 123, just n on SR 183, then just w. Int corridors. **Pets:** Large, other species. Service with restrictions. ⅃ 🛜 ✕ 📶 🖥

▼▼ **Super 8** M

(501) 847-7888. **$50-$60.** 201 Dell Dr 72022. I-30 exit 123, just s on SR 183, then just e. Ext corridors. **Pets:** Medium, dogs only. $20 deposit/room, $10 one-time fee/pet. Designated rooms, service with restrictions, supervision. 🛜 📶 🖥

CABOT

▼▼ **Days Inn & Suites-Cabot** H

(501) 605-1810. **$80-$145.** 1302 W Locust St 72023. US 67/167 exit 19, just e, then just n. Int corridors. **Pets:** Medium. $10 daily fee/pet. Service with restrictions, supervision. ⅃ 🛜 ✕ 📶 🖥

CLARKSVILLE

Ⓐ ▼▼ **BEST WESTERN Sherwood Inn** H ❀

(479) 754-7900. **$72-$79.** 1207 S Rogers Ave 72830. I-40 exit 58, just n. Ext corridors. **Pets:** $10 one-time fee/room. Crate. SAVE ⅃ 🛜 📶 🖥

▼▼ **Quality Inn & Suites** H

(479) 754-3000. **$60-$150.** 1167 S Rogers Ave 72830. I-40 exit 58, just n. Ext corridors. **Pets:** Medium. $10 one-time fee/room. Designated rooms, service with restrictions, supervision. ⅃ 🛜 📶 🖥

CLINTON

Ⓐ ▼▼ **BEST WESTERN Hillside Inn** M ❀

(501) 745-4700. **$76-$82.** 1025 Hwy 65 B 72031. Jct SR 16, just s on US 65, then just sw. Ext corridors. **Pets:** Large. $8 daily fee/room. Designated rooms, service with restrictions. SAVE ⅃ 🛜 ✕ 📶 🖥

CONWAY

Ⓐ ▼▼ **BEST WESTERN Conway** M

(501) 329-9855. **$78-$86.** 816 E Oak St 72032. I-40 exit 127, just e on US 64. Ext corridors. **Pets:** Accepted. SAVE ⅃ 🛜 📶 🖥

Ⓐ ▼▼▼ **Candlewood Suites** H ❀

(501) 329-8551. **$59-$129.** 2360 Sanders St 72032. I-40 exit 125, just s on US 65 business route, then just e. Int corridors. **Pets:** Medium, other species. $75 one-time fee/room. Service with restrictions, crate. SAVE 🛜 📶 🖥

▼▼ **La Quinta Inn & Suites** H

(501) 328-5100. **$89-$195.** 2350 Sanders St 72032. I-40 exit 125, just s on US 65 business route, then just e. Int corridors. **Pets:** Large, other species. Service with restrictions. 🔊 ⅃ 🛜 ✕ 📶 🖥

▼▼ **Microtel Inn & Suites by Wyndham Conway** H

(501) 327-0898. **$60-$105.** 2475 Sanders St 72032. I-40 exit 125, just s on US 65 business route, then just e. Int corridors. **Pets:** Accepted. 🛜 ✕ 📶 🖥

▼▼ **Quality Inn** M

(501) 329-0300. **$55-$90.** 150 Skyline Dr N 72032. I-40 exit 125, just n. Ext corridors. **Pets:** Accepted. ⅃ 🛜 📶 🖥

▼▼ **Super 8-Conway** H

(501) 505-8880. **$60-$98.** 2430 Sanders St 72032. I-40 exit 125, just s on US 65 business route, then just e. Int corridors. **Pets:** Accepted. ⅃ 🛜 📶 🖥

EL DORADO

▼▼ **La Quinta Inn El Dorado** H

(870) 863-6677. **$70-$167.** 2303 Junction City Rd 71730. Jct US 167, just e on US 82 business route. Int corridors. **Pets:** Large, other species. Service with restrictions. ⅃ 🛜 📶 🖥

EUREKA SPRINGS *(Restaurants p. 614)*

▼▼▼ **1886 Crescent Hotel & Spa** H

(479) 253-9766. **Call for rates.** 75 Prospect Ave 72632. Jct SR 23, 1.3 mi w on US 62B Historic Loop. Int corridors. **Pets:** $25 one-time fee/room. Service with restrictions, crate. 🍴 ⅃ 🛜 ✕ 📶 🖥

▼▼▼ **Arsenic & Old Lace B&B** BB ❀

(479) 253-5454. **$159-$329, 15 day notice.** 60 Hillside Ave 72632. Jct US 62, 1.2 mi n on SR 23, just sw; downtown. Ext/int corridors. **Pets:** Dogs only. $30 one-time fee/room. Designated rooms, service with restrictions, crate. 🛜 ✕ 🗎 📶

▼▼▼ **Basin Park Hotel-A Magnuson Grand Hotel** H

(479) 253-7837. **$95-$195, 12 day notice.** 12 Spring St 72632. Jct US 62, 0.7 mi n on SR 23, then just nw; downtown. Int corridors. **Pets:** Accepted. 🍴 🛜 ✕ 📶 🖥

Ⓐ ▼▼ **BEST WESTERN Eureka Inn** H

(479) 253-9551. **$80-$139.** 101 E Van Buren St 72632. Jct SR 23 and US 62. Ext/int corridors. **Pets:** Medium, dogs only. $15 daily fee/pet. Designated rooms, service with restrictions, crate. SAVE ⅃ ✕ 🛜 ✕ 📶 🖥

Ⓐ ▼▼ **BEST WESTERN Inn of the Ozarks** H ❀

(479) 253-9768. **$90-$130, 3 day notice.** 207 W Van Buren St 72632. Jct SR 23 N, 0.5 mi w on US 62. Ext corridors. **Pets:** Medium, dogs only. $10 one-time fee/pet. Designated rooms, service with restrictions, crate. SAVE 🍴 ⅃ ✕ 🛜 📶 🖥

FAYETTEVILLE

Ⓐ ▼▼ **BEST WESTERN Windsor Suites** H

(479) 587-1400. **$85-$150.** 1122 S Futrall Dr 72701. I-49 exit 62, just se. Ext corridors. **Pets:** Accepted. SAVE ⅃ 🛜 📶 🖥

▼▼ **The Chancellor Hotel** H

(479) 442-5555. **Call for rates.** 70 N East Ave 72701. Center of downtown. Int corridors. **Pets:** Accepted. 🍴 🔊 ⅃ 🛜 📶 🖥

▼▼ **Comfort Inn & Suites** H

(479) 571-5177. **$79-$104.** 1234 Steamboat Dr 72704. I-49 exit 64, just nw. Int corridors. **Pets:** Medium. $25 daily fee/pet. Service with restrictions, crate. ⅃ 🛜 ✕ 📶 🖥

▼▼ **Courtyard by Marriott** H

(479) 571-4900. **$169-$189.** 600 E Van Asche Dr 72703. Just e of jct Mall Ave. Int corridors. **Pets:** Accepted. ECO 🍴 🔊 ⅃ 🛜 ✕ 📶 🖥

▼▼ **Sleep Inn by Choice Hotels** 🚫
(479) 587-8700. **$69-$90.** 728 E Millsap Rd 72703. I-49 exit 67, 1.6 mi e, then just s on US 71B. Int corridors. **Pets:** Other species. $25 one-time fee/room. Service with restrictions, crate. 📶 🔳 💻

▼▼▼ **Staybridge Suites** 🚫 🐾
(479) 695-2400. **$99-$299.** 1577 W 15th St 72701. Just w of jct Razorback Rd. Int corridors. **Pets:** $15 daily fee/room. Service with restrictions, crate. 🅼 📶 💻

FORDYCE
▼▼ **Days Inn** Ⓜ
(870) 352-2400. **$77-$110.** 2500 W 4th St 71742. US 79/167, 1 mi w. Ext/int corridors. **Pets:** Medium. $10 daily fee/pet. Service with restrictions, supervision. 📶 🔳 💻

FORREST CITY
🅐🅐🅐 ▼▼▼ **BEST WESTERN Colony Inn** Ⓜ
(870) 633-0870. **$84.** 2333 N Washington St 72335. I-40 exit 241A, just s. Ext corridors. **Pets:** Accepted. SAVE 📶 🔳 💻

▼▼ **Days Inn Forrest City** 🚫
(870) 633-6300. **$68-$239.** 200 Holiday Dr 72335. I-40 exit 241B, just n. Ext corridors. **Pets:** Accepted. 🍴 📶 🔳 💻

FORT SMITH
▼▼ **Aspen Hotel & Suites** 🚫
(479) 452-9000. **$68.** 2900 S 68th St 72903. I-49 exit 8B (Rogers Ave), just e, then just s. Int corridors. **Pets:** Small. $15 one-time fee/room. Designated rooms, service with restrictions, supervision.
📶 🔳 ✖ 🔳 💻

▼▼▼ **Baymont Inn & Suites Fort Smith** 🚫
(479) 484-5770. **$49-$79.** 2123 Burnham Rd 72903. I-49 exit 8A (Rogers Ave), just w, then just n. Int corridors. **Pets:** Accepted.
📶 🔳 💻

▼▼▼▼ **Beland Manor Bed & Breakfast** 🅱🅱 🐾
(479) 782-3300. **$115-$185, 5 day notice.** 1320 S Albert Pike 72903. I-49 exit 8A (Rogers Ave), 1.3 mi w. Int corridors. **Pets:** Dogs only. Designated rooms, supervision. 📶 ✖

▼▼▼▼ **Courtyard by Marriott Downtown Fort Smith** 🚫
(479) 783-2100. **$139-$155.** 900 Rogers Ave 72901. I-49 exit 8A (Rogers Ave), 3.9 mi w; downtown. Int corridors. **Pets:** Dogs only. $75 one-time fee/room. Service with restrictions, supervision.
🍴 🅼 📶 ✖ 🔳 💻

▼▼▼ **Holiday Inn City Center Fort Smith** 🚫
(479) 783-1000. **$99-$169.** 700 Rogers Ave 72901. I-49 exit 8A (Rogers Ave), 4 mi w; downtown. Int corridors. **Pets:** Accepted.
🍴 🅼 📶 ✖ 📶 🔳 💻

▼▼▼ **Holiday Inn Express** 🚫
(479) 452-7500. **Call for rates.** 6813 Phoenix Ave 72903. I-49 exit 8B (Rogers Ave), 0.6 mi e, then 0.5 mi s on 70th St. Int corridors.
Pets: Accepted. 📶 ✖ 🔳 💻

▼▼ **Quality Inn** 🚫
(479) 484-0227. **Call for rates.** 2120 Burnham Rd 72903. I-49 exit 8A (Rogers Ave), just w, then just n. Int corridors. **Pets:** Accepted.
📶 ✖ 📶 🔳 💻

▼▼▼ **Residence Inn by Marriott** 🚫
(479) 478-8300. **$159-$179.** 3005 S 74th St 72903. I-49 exit 8B (Rogers Ave), 0.8 mi e, then just n. Int corridors. **Pets:** Accepted.
📶 📶 ✖ 🔳 💻

HARDY
🅐🅐🅐 ▼▼▼ **BEST WESTERN Village Inn** Ⓜ
(870) 856-2176. **Call for rates.** 3587 Hwy 62/412 72542. 2 mi sw. Ext corridors. **Pets:** Small, dogs only. $25 daily fee/pet. Designated rooms, service with restrictions, crate. SAVE 📶 📶 🔳 💻

HARRISON
▼▼▼ **Holiday Inn Express Hotel & Suites** 🚫
(870) 741-3636. **$96-$116.** 117 Hwy 43 E 72601. Jct US 62/65/412, just e. Int corridors. **Pets:** Small. $25 deposit/pet. Service with restrictions, supervision. 📶 ✖ 📶 🔳 💻

▼▼ **Quality Inn** 🚫
(870) 741-7676. **$115.** 1210 Hwy 62/65 N 72601. Jct SR 43, 0.4 mi w on US 62/65/412. Ext/int corridors. **Pets:** Accepted. 📶 📶 🔳 💻

HELENA-WEST HELENA
🅐🅐🅐 ▼▼▼ **BEST WESTERN Inn** Ⓜ
(870) 572-2592. **Call for rates.** 1053 Hwy 49 W 72390. US 49, 3 mi w. Ext corridors. **Pets:** Accepted. SAVE 📶 📶 🔳 💻

HOPE
🅐🅐🅐 ▼▼▼ **BEST WESTERN of Hope** 🚫 🐾
(870) 777-9222. **$75-$85.** 1800 Holiday Dr 71801. I-30 exit 30, just nw. Ext corridors. **Pets:** Other species. $10 daily fee/room. Designated rooms, service with restrictions, supervision. SAVE 📶 📶 🔳 💻

HOT SPRINGS
🅐🅐🅐 ▼▼▼ **BEST WESTERN Winners Circle Inn** Ⓜ
(501) 624-2531. **$99-$200, 7 day notice.** 2520 Central Ave 71901. Jct US 70/270, 1.3 mi n on SR 7. Ext corridors. **Pets:** Small, dogs only. $25 one-time fee/room. Service with restrictions, supervision.
SAVE 📶 📶 🔳 💻

🅐🅐🅐 ▼▼▼ **Clarion Resort** 🚫
(501) 525-1391. **$85-$150.** 4813 Central Ave 71913. Jct US 70/270, 2.6 mi s on SR 7. Int corridors. **Pets:** Small, dogs only. $35 daily fee/pet. Designated rooms, supervision.
SAVE 🍴 📶 ✖ 📶 ✖ 🔳 💻

▼▼▼▼ **Embassy Suites Hot Springs-Hotel & Spa** 🚫
(501) 624-9200. **$139-$229.** 400 Convention Blvd 71901. Jct US 70/270 business route, just n on SR 7, then just e. Int corridors.
Pets: Accepted. 🍴 🅼 📶 ✖ 🆘 🔳 💻

▼▼▼▼ **Staybridge Suites** 🚫 🐾
(501) 525-6500. **$99-$199.** 103 Lookout Cir 71913. Jct US 70/270, 3.9 mi s SR 7. Int corridors. **Pets:** Medium, other species. $75 one-time fee/room. Designated rooms, service with restrictions, crate.
🅼 📶 📶 ✖ 🔳 💻

JACKSONVILLE
🅐🅐🅐 ▼▼▼ **BEST WESTERN Jacksonville Inn** Ⓜ
(501) 982-8181. **$70.** 1600 John Harden Dr 72076. US 67/167 exit 11, just s on west service road. Ext corridors. **Pets:** Accepted.
SAVE 📶 📶 🔳 💻

▼▼ **Super 8** Ⓜ
(501) 982-9219. **$65-$100.** 1850 John Harden Dr 72076. US 67/167 exit 11, just s on west service road. Ext corridors. **Pets:** Accepted.
📶 📶 ✖ 🔳 💻

JOHNSON
▼▼▼ **TownePlace Suites by Marriott Fayetteville North/Springdale** 🚫
(479) 966-4400. **$119-$135.** 5437 S 48th St 72741. I-49 exit 69, just se. Int corridors. **Pets:** Accepted. 🅼 📶 📶 ✖ 🔳 💻

LITTLE ROCK
▼▼▼ **Clarion Hotel Medical Center** 🚫
(501) 664-5020. **$89-$129.** 925 S University Ave 72204. I-630 exit 5, just s. Int corridors. **Pets:** Small. $50 one-time fee/pet. Service with restrictions, crate. 🍴 🅼 📶 📶 🔳 💻

🅐🅐🅐 ▼▼▼▼ **Comfort Inn & Suites Little Rock Airport** 🚫
(501) 376-2466. **$86-$91.** 4301 E Roosevelt Rd 72206. I-440 exit 3, just n. Int corridors. **Pets:** Accepted. SAVE 🅼 📶 🔳 💻

Comfort Inn & Suites Presidential H

(501) 687-7700. **$89-$199.** 707 I-30 72202. I-30 exit 140A, just e. Int corridors. **Pets:** Medium, other species. $50 one-time fee/room. Designated rooms, service with restrictions, crate.

SAVE &M ⊇ 🤚 ✕ 🔋 💻

Days Inn & Suites Airport M

(501) 490-2010. **$41-$58.** 3200 Bankhead Dr 72206. I-440 exit 3, just s. Ext corridors. **Pets:** Accepted. ⊇ 🤚 🔋 💻

Embassy Suites Hotel Little Rock H

(501) 312-9000. **$99-$229.** 11301 Financial Centre Pkwy 72211. I-430 exit 5, 1 mi n on Shackleford Rd, then 0.4 mi w. Int corridors. **Pets:** Accepted. 🍽 &M ⊇ ✕ 📶 🔋 💻

Holiday Inn Airport Conference Center H

(501) 490-1000. **$89-$159, 4 day notice.** 3201 Bankhead Dr 72206. I-440 exit 3, just s. Int corridors. **Pets:** Accepted.

🍽 &M ⊇ 🤚 ✕ 💻

Holiday Inn Express Airport H

(501) 490-4000. **Call for rates.** 3121 Bankhead Dr 72206. I-440 exit 3, just s. Ext/int corridors. **Pets:** Accepted. ⊇ 🤚 ✕ 🔋 💻

Holiday Inn-Financial Centre Parkway H

(501) 225-1075. **$119-$159.** 10920 Financial Centre Pkwy 72211. I-430 exit 5, 1 mi n on Shackleford Rd, then just w. Int corridors. **Pets:** Small. $50 one-time fee/room. Service with restrictions, supervision.

🍽 &M ⊇ 🤚 ✕ 🔋 💻

Residence Inn by Marriott H

(501) 312-0200. **$169-$189.** 1401 S Shackleford Rd 72211. I-430 exit 5, just n. Int corridors. **Pets:** Accepted. ⊇ 🤚 ✕ 🔋 💻

Residence Inn by Marriott -Downtown H

(501) 376-7200. **$169-$189.** 219 River Market Ave 72201. I-30 exit 141A, just w on 2nd St, then just s; downtown. Int corridors. **Pets:** Accepted. ⊇ 🤚 ✕ 🔋 💻

TownePlace Suites by Marriott-Little Rock H

(501) 225-6700. **$129-$143.** 12 Crossings Ct 72205. I-430 exit 5, 0.6 mi e on Shackleford Rd, then just w. Int corridors. **Pets:** Accepted.

&M ⊇ 🤚 ✕ 🔋 💻

LONOKE

BEST WESTERN PLUS Lonoke Hotel H

(501) 676-8880. **Call for rates.** 102 Dee Dee Ln 72086. I-40 exit 175, just n. Int corridors. **Pets:** Medium, dogs only. $14 daily fee/pet. Service with restrictions, supervision. SAVE ⊇ 🤚 ✕ 🔋 💻

Days Inn H

(501) 676-5138. **$70-$100.** 105 Dee Dee Ln 72086. I-40 exit 175, just n. Ext corridors. **Pets:** Accepted. SAVE ⊇ 🤚 🔋 💻

Holiday Inn Express Hotel & Suites H

(501) 676-7800. **$114-$129.** 104 Dee Dee Ln 72086. I-40 exit 175, just n. Int corridors. **Pets:** Small, other species. $25 one-time fee/room. Designated rooms, service with restrictions, supervision.

&M ⊇ 🤚 🔋 💻

MAUMELLE

Holiday Inn Express & Suites-Maumelle H 🐾

(501) 851-4422. **$89-$129.** 200 Holiday Dr 72113. I-40 exit 142, just s. Int corridors. **Pets:** Other species. $25 one-time fee/room, $10 daily fee/room. Designated rooms, service with restrictions, supervision.

&M ⊇ 🤚 ✕ 🔋 💻

MCGEHEE

BEST WESTERN McGehee M

(870) 222-3564. **$79, 3 day notice.** 1202 Hwy 65 N 71654. Center. Ext corridors. **Pets:** Accepted. SAVE ⊇ 🤚 🔋 💻

MOUNTAIN HOME

Comfort Inn H 🐾

(870) 424-9000. **$90-$180.** 1031 Highland Cir 72653. Jct US 412/62, 1.8 mi w on US 62 business route. Ext/int corridors. **Pets:** Small, dogs only. $35 one-time fee/room. Service with restrictions, supervision.

SAVE &M ⊇ 🤚 🔋 💻

Teal Point Resort CA

(870) 492-5145. **$105-$425, 60 day notice.** 715 Teal Point Rd 72653. Jct US 62 business route, 3.5 mi e on US 412/62, 0.6 mi n on CR 406. Ext corridors. **Pets:** $10 daily fee/pet. No service.

SAVE ⊇ ✕ 🤚 ✕ 📁 🔋 💻

MOUNTAIN VIEW

BEST WESTERN Fiddlers Inn M

(870) 269-2828. **$70-$90.** 601 Sylamore Ave 72560. Jct Main St, 1 mi n on SR 5/9/14. Ext corridors. **Pets:** Accepted. SAVE ⊇ 🤚 🔋 💻

NORTH LITTLE ROCK

BEST WESTERN PLUS JFK Inn & Suites H

(501) 246-3300. **$96-$146.** 2500 Main St 72114. I-40 exit 153A, just s on JFK Blvd. Int corridors. **Pets:** Medium, other species. $30 one-time fee/pet. Designated rooms, service with restrictions, supervision.

SAVE &M ⊇ 🤚 ✕ 🔋 💻

Clarion Hotel North Little Rock H

(501) 758-1851. **$79.** 120 W Pershing Blvd 72114. I-40 exit 153A, just s on JFK Blvd, then just w. Int corridors. **Pets:** Accepted.

🍽 ⊇ 🤚 🔋 💻

La Quinta Inn & Suites North Little Rock-McCain Mall H

(501) 945-0808. **$75-$199.** 4311 Warden Rd 72116. US 67/167 exit 1 southbound; exit 2 northbound, just s on west service road. Int corridors. **Pets:** Large, other species. Service with restrictions.

⊇ 🤚 🔋 💻

La Quinta Inn Little Rock North Landers Road M

(501) 758-8888. **$69-$179.** 4100 E McCain Blvd 72117. US 67/167 exit 1 southbound; exit 1A northbound, just e on McCain Blvd, then just s. Ext corridors. **Pets:** Large, other species. Service with restrictions.

⊇ 🤚 🔋 💻

Red Roof Inn-North Little Rock H

(501) 945-0080. **$49-$90.** 5711 Pritchard Dr 72117. I-40 exit 157, just s, then just w. Int corridors. **Pets:** Large, other species. Service with restrictions, supervision. SAVE ⊇ 🤚 🔋 💻

Residence Inn by Marriott-North H 🐾

(501) 945-7777. **$119-$164.** 4110 Healthcare Dr 72117. I-40 exit 156, just n, then just w. Int corridors. **Pets:** Other species. $100 one-time fee/room. Service with restrictions. ⊇ 🤚 ✕ 🔋 💻

PINE BLUFF

Comfort Inn H

(870) 535-5300. **$58-$99.** 2809 Pines Mall Dr 71601. I-530 exit 46, just n on Harding Ave. Int corridors. **Pets:** Medium, dogs only. $10 daily fee/room. Service with restrictions, crate. ⊇ 🤚 🔋 💻

POCAHONTAS

Days Inn & Suites H

(870) 892-9500. **$86-$231.** 2805 Hwy 67 S 72455. Jct US 62, 1.7 mi s. Int corridors. **Pets:** Accepted. 🤚 🔋 💻

ROGERS

Candlewood Suites H

(479) 636-2783. **$89-$229, 3 day notice.** 4601 W Rozell St 72757. I-49 exit 85, 0.5 mi n on 46th St. Int corridors. **Pets:** Accepted.

⊇ 🤚 🔋 💻

▼▼▼▼ Country Inn & Suites By Carlson ⊞
(479) 633-0055. $89. 4304 W Walnut St 72756. I-49 exit 85, just e. Int corridors. Pets: Accepted. 🐾 🛜 🛢 🖵

▼▼▼▼ Embassy Suites Northwest Arkansas ⊞
(479) 254-8400. $99-$229. 3303 Pinnacle Hills Pkwy 72758. I-49 exit 83, just w, then 0.6 mi s. Int corridors. Pets: Accepted.
🍴 ⓜ 🐾 ⊠ 🛜 ⊠ 🛢 🖵

(AAA) ▼▼▼▼ Hyatt Place Rogers/Bentonville ⊞
(479) 633-8555. $69-$209. 4610 W Walnut St 72756. I-49 exit 85, just e. Int corridors. Pets: Medium, dogs only. $75 one-time fee/pet. Designated rooms, service with restrictions, supervision.
(SAVE) 🐾 🛜 ⊠ 🛢 🖵

▼▼ Microtel Inn & Suites by Wyndham Rogers ⊞
(479) 636-5551. $50-$79. 909 S 8th St 72756. 0.5 mi s of jct Walnut St. Int corridors. Pets: Accepted. 🛜 🛢 🖵

▼▼▼▼ Residence Inn by Marriott ⊞
(479) 636-5900. $99-$189. 4611 W Locust St 72756. I-49 exit 85, 0.4 mi n on 46th St. Int corridors. Pets: Accepted.
ⓜ 🐾 🛜 ⊠ 🛢 🖵

▼▼▼▼ Staybridge Suites Rogers-Bentonville ⊞
(479) 845-5701. Call for rates. 1801 S 52nd St 72758. I-49 exit 83, just nw. Int corridors. Pets: $75 one-time fee/room. Service with restrictions, crate. ⓜ 🛜 ⊠ 🛢 🖵

RUSSELLVILLE
▼▼▼▼ La Quinta Inn & Suites ⊞
(479) 967-2299. $89-$229. 111 E Harrell Dr 72802. I-40 exit 81, just s, just e, then just n. Int corridors. Pets: Large, other species. Service with restrictions. 🐾 🛜 ⊠ 🛢 🖵

▼▼ Quality Inn Ⓜ
(479) 967-7500. $60-$80. 3019 E Parkway Dr 72802. I-40 exit 84, just s, then just w. Ext corridors. Pets: Accepted. 🐾 🛜 🛢 🖵

(AAA) ▼▼▼ Super 8 Russellville ⊞
(479) 968-8898. $32-$63. 2404 N Arkansas Ave 72802. I-40 exit 81, just s. Int corridors. Pets: Medium, other species. $10 daily fee/pet. Service with restrictions, supervision. (SAVE) 🛜 🛢 🖵

SEARCY
▼▼ Microtel Inn & Suites by Wyndham ⊞
(501) 268-1555. $55-$95. 3668 Ferren Tr 72143. US 67/167 exit 46, just e, then just n. Int corridors. Pets: Accepted. 🛜 🛢 🖵

SPRINGDALE
▼▼▼▼ Hampton Inn & Suites ⊞
(479) 756-3500. $89-$179. 1700 S 48th St 72762. I-49 exit 72, just e. Int corridors. Pets: Accepted. ⓜ 🐾 🛜 🛢 🖵

▼▼▼▼ Holiday Inn Northwest AR Hotel & Convention Center ⊞
(479) 751-8300. $99-$299, 3 day notice. 1500 S 48th St 72762. I-49 exit 72, just e. Int corridors. Pets: Small. $35 one-time fee/room. No service, supervision. 🍴 🐾 🛜 ⊠ 🛢 🖵

▼▼▼▼ Inn at the Mill, an Ascend Hotel Collection Member ⊞
(479) 443-1800. $99-$329. 3906 Johnson Mill Blvd 72762. I-49 exit 69, just e. Int corridors. Pets: Accepted. 🍴 🛜 ⊠ 🛢 🖵

▼▼▼▼ La Quinta Inn & Suites Springdale ⊞
(479) 751-2626. $69-$354. 1300 S 48th St 72764. I-49 exit 72, just e. Int corridors. Pets: Large, other species. Service with restrictions.
ⓜ 🐾 🛜 🛢 🖵

▼▼▼▼ Residence Inn by Marriott ⊞
(479) 872-9100. $99-$299. 1740 S 48th St 72762. I-49 exit 72, just e to 48th St, then just s. Int corridors. Pets: Accepted.
🐾 🛜 ⊠ 🛢 🖵

STAR CITY
▼▼ Star City Inn & Suites ⊞
(870) 628-6883. $62-$125. 1308 N Lincoln Ave 71667. Just n on US 425. Int corridors. Pets: Very small, dogs only. $5 daily fee/pet. Service with restrictions, supervision. 🐾 🛜 🛢 🖵

STUTTGART
(AAA) ▼▼ Super 8 Stuttgart Ⓜ
(870) 673-2611. $37-$245. 701 W Michigan St 72160. On US 79/63. Ext corridors. Pets: Accepted. (SAVE) 🛜 🛢 🖵

VAN BUREN
(AAA) ▼▼ BEST WESTERN Van Buren Inn ⊞ 🐾
(479) 474-8100. $81-$90. 1903 N 6th St 72956. I-40 exit 5, just n, then just e. Ext corridors. Pets: Other species. $20 daily fee/pet. Supervision. (SAVE) 🐾 🛜 ⊠ 🛢 🖵

▼▼▼▼ Sleep Inn & Suites ⊞
(479) 262-6776. $90-$130. 1633 N 12th Ct 72956. I-40 exit 5, just s on Fayetteville Rd, 0.6 mi e on Pointer Tr, then just n. Int corridors. Pets: Accepted. ⓜ 🐾 🛜 ⊠ 🛢 🖵

CALIFORNIA

AGOURA HILLS (Restaurants p. 614)
(AAA) ▼▼▼▼ Sheraton Agoura Hills Hotel ⊞
(818) 707-1220. $119-$199. 30100 Agoura Rd 91301. US 101 exit 38 (Reyes Adobe Rd), just w, then just s. Int corridors. Pets: Accepted.
(SAVE) 🍴 ⓜ 🐾 🛜 ⊠ 🛢 🖵

ALHAMBRA
(AAA) ▼▼▼ Super 8 Los Angeles/Alhambra Ⓜ
(323) 225-2310. $65-$160. 5350 S Huntington Dr 90032. I-10 exit 22 (Fremont Ave), 2.5 mi n, then 0.5 mi w. Ext corridors. Pets: Other species. $20 daily fee/pet. Designated rooms, service with restrictions, supervision. (SAVE) ⓜ 🛜 🛢 🖵

ALPINE
▼▼▼▼ Ayres Lodge Alpine Ⓜ
(619) 445-5800. $109-$169. 1251 Tavern Rd 91901. I-8 exit 30 (Tavern Rd), just s. Ext corridors. Pets: Medium, dogs only. $45 one-time fee/room. Designated rooms, no service, crate. 🐾 🛜 ⊠ 🛢 🖵

ALTURAS
(AAA) ▼▼▼ BEST WESTERN Trailside Inn Ⓜ
(530) 233-4111. $95-$115. 343 N Main St 96101. Just s of jct SR 299/US 395 and Main St; jct W 4th St. Ext corridors. Pets: Small, dogs only. $15 daily fee/pet. Designated rooms, service with restrictions, supervision. (SAVE) ⓜ 🐾 🛜 ⊠ 🛢 🖵

(AAA) ▼▼ Super 8 Ⓜ
(530) 233-3545. $65-$157. 511 N Main St 96101. Jct SR 299 and US 395, 0.4 mi s on US 395; at W 5th St. Ext corridors. Pets: Accepted.
(SAVE) 🛜 🛢 🖵

AMERICAN CANYON
▼▼▼▼ Holiday Inn Express & Suites-Napa Valley American Canyon ⊞
(707) 552-8100. Call for rates. 5001 Main St 94503. I-80 exit 36 (American Canyon Rd), 3.1 mi sw, 1.1 mi n on SR 29 (Broadway St), just e on Eucalyptus Dr, then just s. Int corridors. Pets: Accepted.
ⓜ 🐾 🛜 ⊠ 🛢 🖵

ANAHEIM

▼▼ Anaheim Buena Park Travelodge M
(714) 761-4200. **$60-$150.** 705 S Beach Blvd 92804. I-5 exit 116 (Beach Blvd), 2.9 mi s. Ext corridors. **Pets:** $10 daily fee/pet. Service with restrictions, supervision. 🐾 🛜 📳 💻

▼▼▼ Anaheim Holiday Inn Hotel & Suites H
(714) 535-0300. **$89-$199.** 1240 S Walnut St 92802. I-5 exit 110 (Harbor Blvd/Ball Rd) northbound; exit 110A (Harbor Blvd) southbound, just n, 0.5 mi w on Ball Rd, then just s. Int corridors. **Pets:** Small, dogs only. $25 one-time fee/pet. Designated rooms, service with restrictions, crate. 🍽 ♿M 🐾 🛜 ✖ 📳 💻

▲▲▲ ▼▼ Anaheim Plaza Hotel & Suites H
(714) 772-5900. **Call for rates.** 1700 S Harbor Blvd 92802. I-5 exit 110 (Harbor Blvd/Ball Rd) northbound; exit 110A (Harbor Blvd) southbound, 0.6 mi s. Ext corridors. **Pets:** Accepted.
SAVE 🍽 ♿M 🐾 📶 📳 💻

▲▲▲ ▼▼▼ Anaheim TownePlace Suites by Marriott M 🐾
(714) 939-9700. **$89-$359.** 1730 S State College Blvd 92806. I-5 exit 109 (Katella Ave/Disney Way) northbound; exit 109A (Katella Ave/ Orangewood Ave) southbound, 0.7 mi e, then just n. Int corridors. **Pets:** Medium, other species. $100 one-time fee/room. Service with restrictions. SAVE 🐾 🛜 ✖ 📳 💻

▲▲▲ ▼▼▼ Clarion Hotel Anaheim Resort H
(714) 750-3131. **$89-$299.** 616 Convention Way 92802. I-5 exit 109 (Katella Ave/Disney Way) northbound; exit 109A (Katella Ave/ Orangewood Ave) southbound, 0.8 mi w to Harbor Blvd, just s, then just w. Int corridors. **Pets:** Medium. $25 one-time fee/pet. Designated rooms, service with restrictions, crate.
SAVE 🍽 ♿M 🐾 🛜 ✖ 📳 💻

▼▼ Extended Stay America-Orange County-Anaheim Convention Center M
(714) 502-9988. **Call for rates.** 1742 S Clementine St 92802. I-5 exit 109 (Katella Ave/Disney Way) northbound; exit 109A (Katella Ave/ Orangewood Ave) southbound, just w, then just n. Int corridors. **Pets:** Other species. $25 daily fee/pet. Service with restrictions, supervision. 🐾 🛜 📳

▼▼▼ Hotel Indigo Anaheim M
(714) 772-7755. **$139-$329.** 435 W Katella Ave 92802. I-5 exit 109 (Katella Ave/Disney Way) northbound; exit 109A (Katella Ave/ Orangewood Ave) southbound, 0.6 mi w. Int corridors. **Pets:** Accepted. 🍽 🐾 🛜 ✖ 📳 💻

▼▼▼ Hotel Menage H
(714) 758-0900. **$89-$219, 3 day notice.** 1221 S Harbor Blvd 92805. I-5 exit 110 (Harbor Blvd/Ball Rd) northbound; exit 110A (Harbor Blvd) southbound, just n. Ext corridors. **Pets:** Small. $25 daily fee/room. Designated rooms, service with restrictions, crate.
🍽 🐾 🛜 ✖ 📳 💻

▼▼ Motel 6 Anaheim-Maingate #1066 M
(714) 520-9696. **$65-$101.** 100 W Disney Way 92802. I-5 exit 109 (Katella Ave/Disney Way) northbound; exit 109B (Disney Way/Anaheim Blvd) southbound, just w, just n on Anaheim Blvd, then just w. Ext corridors. **Pets:** Other species. Service with restrictions, crate.
🐾 📶 📳

▼▼▼ Red Lion Hotel Anaheim H
(714) 750-2801. **$109-$259.** 1850 S Harbor Blvd 92802. I-5 exit 109 (Katella Ave/Disney Way) northbound; exit 109A (Katella Ave/ Orangewood Ave) southbound, 0.8 mi w, then just s. Int corridors. **Pets:** Accepted. 🍽 ♿M 🐾 🛜 ✖ 📳 💻

▲▲▲ ▼▼▼ Residence Inn by Marriott Anaheim Maingate H
(714) 533-3555. **$139-$299.** 1700 S Clementine St 92802. I-5 exit 109 (Katella Ave/Disney Way) northbound; exit 109A (Katella Ave/ Orangewood Ave) southbound, just w, then just n. Ext corridors. **Pets:** Large. $100 one-time fee/room. Service with restrictions.
SAVE ♿M 🐾 ✖ 🛜 ✖ 📳 💻

▲▲▲ ▼▼▼ Sheraton Anaheim Hotel H 🐾
(714) 778-1700. **$144-$344.** 900 S Disneyland Dr 92802. I-5 exit 110 (Harbor Blvd/Ball Rd) northbound; exit 110A (Harbor Blvd) southbound, just n, just w on Ball Rd, then just n. Int corridors. **Pets:** Medium. $25 one-time fee/room. Designated rooms, service with restrictions, supervision. SAVE 🍽 ♿M 🐾 ✖ 📶 ✖ 📳 💻

▲▲▲ ▼▼▼ Sheraton Park Hotel at the Anaheim Resort H 🐾
(714) 750-1811. **$109-$450, 3 day notice.** 1855 S Harbor Blvd 92802. I-5 exit 109 (Katella Ave/Disney Way) northbound; exit 109A (Katella Ave/Orangewood Ave) southbound, 0.8 mi w, then just s. Int corridors. **Pets:** Medium, other species. $50 one-time fee/room. Designated rooms, service with restrictions, crate.
SAVE 🍽 🐾 📶 ✖ 📳 💻

▼▼▼ SpringHill Suites by Marriott at Anaheim Resort /Convention Center H
(714) 533-2101. **Call for rates.** 1801 S Harbor Blvd 92802. I-5 exit 109 (Katella Ave/Disney Way) northbound; exit 109A (Katella Ave/ Orangewood Ave) southbound 0.8 mi w, then just s. Int corridors. **Pets:** Accepted. 🛜 ✖ 📳 💻

▼▼▼ Staybridge Suites-Anaheim Resort H
(714) 748-7700. **Call for rates.** 1855 S Manchester Ave 92802. I-5 exit 109 (Katella Ave/Disney Way) northbound; exit 109A (Katella Ave/ Orangewood Ave) southbound, just w, then 0.3 mi s; adjacent to west side of freeway. Int corridors. **Pets:** Accepted. ♿M 🐾 🛜 📳 💻

ANDERSON

▲▲▲ ▼▼▼ BEST WESTERN Anderson Inn H
(530) 365-2753. **$85-$125.** 2688 Gateway Dr 96007. I-5 exit 668 (Central Anderson/Lassen Nat'l Park) northbound, just e on Balls Ferry Rd, then just s; exit southbound, just e, just s on McMurry Dr, just e on Balls Ferry Rd, then just s. Ext corridors. **Pets:** Medium, other species. $20 daily fee/room. Designated rooms, service with restrictions, supervision. SAVE ♿M 🐾 🛜 📳 💻

▲▲▲ ▼▼▼ Gaia Hotel & Spa Redding, an Ascend Hotel Collection Member H 🐾
(530) 365-7077. **$109-$179.** 4125 Riverside Pl 96007. I-5 exit 670 (Riverside Ave), just e, then just n. Ext corridors. **Pets:** Medium, other species. $27 one-time fee/room. Designated rooms, service with restrictions, supervision. SAVE 🌿 🍽 🐾 ✖ 🛜 ✖ 📳 💻

ANGELS CAMP

▲▲▲ ▼▼▼ BEST WESTERN Cedar Inn & Suites H
(209) 736-4000. **$69-$199.** 444 S Main St 95222. On SR 49; center. Ext/int corridors. **Pets:** Small. $15 daily fee/pet. Designated rooms, service with restrictions, supervision. SAVE ♿M 🐾 🛜 ✖ 📳 💻

▲▲▲ ▼▼ Jumping Frog Motel M
(209) 736-2191. **$70-$165, 3 day notice.** 330 Murphys Grade Rd 95222. Just e of jct SR 49; center. Ext corridors. **Pets:** Small, dogs only. $10 daily fee/pet. Designated rooms, no service, supervision. SAVE 🛜 ✖ 📳 💻

▼▼ Travelodge Angels Camp H
(209) 736-4242. **$69-$169.** 600 N Main St 95222. On SR 49; north end of town. Ext corridors. **Pets:** Dogs only. $10 deposit/pet, $10 daily fee/ pet. Service with restrictions, supervision.
♿M 🐾 🛜 ✖ 📳 💻

ANTIOCH

▼▼▼ Comfort Suites Antioch-Oakley H
(925) 755-1222. **$99-$139.** 5549 Bridgehead Rd 94561. In Oakley; SR 4 exit 30 (Rio Vista/SR 160); SR 160 exit Main St, just ne, then just e of SR 160 and 4. Int corridors. **Pets:** Accepted.
♿M 🐾 ✖ 📳 💻

ARCADIA

▼▼ Extended Stay America-Los Angeles-Arcadia H
(626) 446-6422. **Call for rates.** 401 E Santa Clara St 91006. I-210 exit 33 (Huntington Dr), just w to 5th Ave, just n, then just w. Int corridors. **Pets:** Other species. $25 daily fee/pet. Service with restrictions, supervision. ♿M 🛜 📳 💻

▼▼▼▼ Residence Inn by Marriott 🅷
(626) 446-6500. **$149-$249.** 321 E Huntington Dr 91006. I-210 exit 33 (Huntington Dr), 0.5 mi w, then just n on Gateway Dr. Ext corridors. **Pets:** Medium, other species. $100 one-time fee/room. Service with restrictions, crate. 🅴🅲🅾 ⓜ ⤳ 🛜 ✕ 🛗 🖵

ARCATA

◈◈◈◈ ▼▼▼ BEST WESTERN Arcata Inn 🅼 ❀
(707) 826-0313. **$90-$182.** 4827 Valley West Blvd 95521. US 101 exit Giuntoli Ln/Janes Rd, just e, then just s. Ext corridors. **Pets:** Dogs only. $20 one-time fee/room. Designated rooms, service with restrictions, supervision. 🆂🅰🆅🅴 🅼 ⤳ 🛜 🛗 🖵

◈◈◈◈ ▼▼▼ Days Inn & Suites Arcata 🅼
(707) 826-2827. **$90-$140.** 4701 Valley West Blvd 95521. US 101 exit Giuntoli Ln/Janes Rd, just e, then just s. Ext corridors. **Pets:** Dogs only. $15 daily fee/pet. Designated rooms, service with restrictions, supervision. 🆂🅰🆅🅴 🅼 ⤳ 🛜 🛗 🖵

▼▼ Hotel Arcata 🅷
(707) 826-0217. **Call for rates.** 708 9th St 95521. Corner of G St; downtown; in plaza. Int corridors. **Pets:** Accepted. ⓘⓘ 🛜 🐾 🖵

ARNOLD

▼▼ Arnold Meadowmont Lodge 🅼
(209) 795-1394. **$99-$139.** 2011 Hwy 4 95223. On SR 4; south end of town. Ext corridors. **Pets:** Dogs only. $25 daily fee/pet. Designated rooms, service with restrictions, supervision.
🅼 🛜 ✕ 🐾 🛗 🖵

ARROYO GRANDE

◈◈◈◈ ▼▼▼▼ BEST WESTERN Casa Grande Inn 🅼
(805) 481-7398. **$69-$409.** 850 Oak Park Blvd 93420. US 101 exit 188 (Oak Park Blvd), just e. Ext/int corridors. **Pets:** Accepted.
🆂🅰🆅🅴 ⤳ ✕ 🛜 🛗 🖵

◈◈◈◈ ▼▼▼▼ Hampton Inn & Suites Arroyo Grande 🅷
(805) 202-2110. **$109-$239.** 1400 W Branch St 93420. US 101 exit 188 (W Branch St) northbound, just n; exit 188 (Oak Park Blvd) southbound, just e, then 0.6 mi s. Int corridors. **Pets:** Accepted.
🆂🅰🆅🅴 🅼 ⤳ 🛜 ✕ 🛗 🖵

ATASCADERO

▼▼▼▼ Carlton Hotel 🅷
(805) 461-5100. **Call for rates.** 6005 El Camino Real 93422. US 101 exit Traffic Way, just e. Int corridors. **Pets:** Dogs only. $25 daily fee/pet. Designated rooms, crate. 🅼 🆂🅾 ✕ 🛗 🖵

AUBURN

◈◈◈◈ ▼▼▼▼ BEST WESTERN Golden Key 🅷 🐾
(530) 885-8611. **$89-$200.** 13450 Lincoln Way 95603. I-80 exit 121 (Foresthill Rd/Auburn Ravine Rd), just e, then n. Ext corridors. **Pets:** Other species. $15 one-time fee/room. Designated rooms, service with restrictions, supervision. 🆂🅰🆅🅴 🅼 ⤳ 🛜 🛗 🖵

▼▼▼▼ Holiday Inn Auburn 🅷
(530) 887-8787. **$109-$209.** 120 Grass Valley Hwy 95603. I-80 exit 119B (SR 49), just nw. Int corridors. **Pets:** Accepted.
🅴🅲🅾 ⓘⓘ 🅼 ⤳ 🛜 🛗 🖵

BAKERSFIELD

◈◈◈◈ ▼ Americas Best Value Inn 🅼
(661) 366-1630. **$50-$100, 3 day notice.** 8230 E Brundage Ln 93307. SR 99 exit 24 (SR 58 E), 7 mi e, exit 117 (SR 184/Weedpatch Hwy), just n, then just e. Ext/int corridors. **Pets:** Medium, other species. $5 daily fee/pet. Service with restrictions, supervision.
🆂🅰🆅🅴 ⤳ 🛜 🛗 🖵

◈◈◈◈ ▼ BEST WESTERN Heritage Inn 🅼
(661) 764-6268. **$81-$90.** 253 Trask St 93314. I-5 exit 253 (Stockdale Hwy), just e. Ext corridors. **Pets:** Small. $10 daily fee/pet. Designated rooms, service with restrictions, supervision.
🆂🅰🆅🅴 🅼 ⤳ 🛜 🛗 🖵

◈◈◈◈ ▼▼▼▼ BEST WESTERN PLUS Hill House 🅷
(661) 327-4064. **$109-$149.** 700 Truxtun Ave 93301. SR 99 exit 25 (California Ave), 1.2 mi e, 0.4 mi n on Chester Ave, then 0.4 mi e. Int corridors. **Pets:** Medium. $15 daily fee/pet. Designated rooms, service with restrictions, supervision. 🆂🅰🆅🅴 ⓘⓘ ⤳ 🛜 🛗 🖵

▼▼▼ DoubleTree by Hilton Hotel Bakersfield 🅷
(661) 323-7111. **$129-$149.** 3100 Camino Del Rio Ct 93308. SR 99 exit 26 (SR 58 W/Rosedale Hwy), just w, then just s. Int corridors.
Pets: Accepted. 🅴🅲🅾 ⓘⓘ ⤳ 🛜 ✕ 🛗 🖵

▼▼ Extended Stay Deluxe Bakersfield-Chester Lane 🅷
(661) 328-8181. **Call for rates.** 3600 Chester Ln 93309. SR 99 exit 25 (California Ave), just w to Real Rd, just s, then just w. Int corridors.
Pets: Other species. $25 daily fee/pet. Service with restrictions, supervision. 🛜 ✕ 🛗 🖵

◈◈◈◈ ▼▼▼ Garden Suites Inn 🅷
(661) 833-6066. **$59-$99.** 2310 Wible Rd 93304. SR 99 exit 23 (Ming Ave), just e. Int corridors. **Pets:** $10 daily fee/pet. Designated rooms, service with restrictions, supervision. 🆂🅰🆅🅴 ⤳ 🛜 🛗 🖵

▼▼▼ Homewood Suites 🅷
(661) 664-0400. **$139-$189.** 1505 Mill Rock Way 93311. SR 99 exit 23 (Ming Ave), 4 mi w, then just n. Int corridors. **Pets:** Accepted.
⤳ 🛜 🛗 🖵

▼▼▼ La Quinta Inn & Suites Bakersfield North 🅷
(661) 393-7775. **$94-$176.** 8858 Spectrum Park Way 93308. SR 99 exit 30 (SR 65) northbound, just e to Merle Haggard Dr, just n to Spectrum Park Way, then just s; exit 31 (7th Standard Rd) southbound, just e, then just s. Int corridors. **Pets:** Large, other species. Service with restrictions. 🅼 ⤳ 🛜 🛗 🖵

▼▼▼ La Quinta Inn Bakersfield South 🅼
(661) 325-7400. **$69-$169.** 3232 Riverside Dr 93308. SR 99 exit 26A (SR 58 W/Rosedale Hwy) southbound, just e, then just n; exit 26B (Buck Owens Blvd) northbound, just s. Ext corridors. **Pets:** Large, other species. Service with restrictions. 🅼 ⤳ 🛜 🛗 🖵

▼▼▼ The Padre Hotel 🅷
(661) 427-4900. **$109-$159.** 1702 18th St 93301. SR 58 exit 26A (Rosedale Hwy), 1.5 mi e, 0.3 mi s on F St, then 0.3 mi s. Int corridors. **Pets:** $50 one-time fee/pet. Service with restrictions, supervision.
ⓘⓘ 🛜 ✕ 🛗 🖵

◈◈◈◈ ▼▼▼ Palm Garden Inn & Suites 🅷
(661) 327-9651. **$73-$119.** 2620 Buck Owens Blvd 93308. SR 99 exit 26B (Buck Owens Blvd) northbound, just s; exit 26 (SR 58 W/SR 178 E) southbound, just e, then just n. Ext/int corridors. **Pets:** $15 daily fee/pet. Designated rooms, service with restrictions, supervision.
🆂🅰🆅🅴 ⓘⓘ 🅼 ⤳ 🛜 🛗 🖵

◈◈◈◈ ▼▼▼ Residence Inn by Marriott 🅷
(661) 321-9800. **$109-$199.** 4241 Chester Ln 93309. SR 99 exit 25 (California Ave), 0.5 mi w, then just n. Ext corridors. **Pets:** Accepted.
🆂🅰🆅🅴 🅴🅲🅾 ⤳ 🛜 ✕ 🛗 🖵

◈◈◈◈ ▼▼▼ Super 8 🅼
(661) 833-1000. **$50-$72.** 3620 Wible Rd 93309. SR 99 exit 21 (White Ln), just w, then 0.3 mi n. Ext corridors. **Pets:** Small, other species. $5 daily fee/pet. Service with restrictions, supervision.
🆂🅰🆅🅴 ⤳ 🛜 🛗 🖵

◈◈◈◈ ▼▼▼ Super 8 Bakersfield 🅼
(661) 322-1012. **$55-$82.** 901 Real Rd 93309. SR 99 exit 25 (California Ave), just w, then just s. Ext corridors. **Pets:** Accepted.
🆂🅰🆅🅴 ⤳ 🛜 🛗 🖵

◈◈◈◈ ▼▼▼ Travelodge of Bakersfield 🅼
(661) 325-0772. **$50-$100.** 1011 Oak St 93304. SR 99 exit 25 (California Ave), just e, then just s. Ext/int corridors. **Pets:** $15 daily fee/pet. Designated rooms, service with restrictions, supervision.
🆂🅰🆅🅴 ⤳ 🛜 🛗 🖵

BANNING

▼▼▼ Banning Travelodge **M**
(951) 849-1000. **$60-$110.** 1700 W Ramsey St 92220. I-10 exit 99 (22nd St), just n, then 0.4 mi e. Ext corridors. **Pets:** Accepted.

₳₳₳ ▼▼▼ Days Inn **M**
(951) 849-0092. **$70-$134.** 2320 W Ramsey St 92220. I-10 exit 99 (22nd St), just n, then just w. Ext corridors. **Pets:** Very small. $15 daily fee/pet. Service with restrictions, supervision. [SAVE]

▼▼▼▼ Hampton Inn & Suites **H**
(951) 922-1000. **$119-$249.** 6071 Joshua Palmer Way 92220. I-10 exit 96 (Highland Springs Ave), just n, then just e. Int corridors. **Pets:** Medium. $25 daily fee/pet. Service with restrictions, supervision.

▼▼ Super 8 **M**
(951) 849-8888. **$60-$113.** 1690 W Ramsey St 92220. I-10 exit 99 (22nd St), just n, then 0.4 mi e. Int corridors. **Pets:** Accepted.

BARSTOW

▼▼▼▼ Comfort Suites **H** ❖
(760) 253-3600. **$89-$159.** 2571 Fisher Blvd 92311. I-15 exit 178 (Lenwood Rd), just ne; north of Barstow Outlets. Int corridors. **Pets:** Other species. $25 one-time fee/room. Designated rooms, service with restrictions, crate.

▼▼▼▼ Country Inn & Suites By Carlson **H**
(760) 307-3121. **$99-$199.** 2812 Lenwood Rd 92311. I-15 exit 178 (Lenwood Rd), just se, then just s. Int corridors. **Pets:** $20 daily fee/pet. Designated rooms, service with restrictions, crate.

▼▼ Days Inn South at Lenwood **M**
(760) 253-2121. **$80-$90.** 2551 Commerce Pkwy 92311. I-15 exit 178 (Lenwood Rd), just w, then just n; 8 mi s of town. Ext corridors. **Pets:** Accepted.

▼▼▼▼ Hampton Inn & Suites **H**
(760) 253-2600. **$99-$259.** 2710 Lenwood Rd 92311. I-15 exit 178 (Lenwood Rd), just se, then 0.5 mi s. Int corridors. **Pets:** Other species. Service with restrictions, supervision.

₳₳₳ ▼▼▼▼ Holiday Inn Express Hotel & Suites **H**
(760) 253-9200. **$119-$199.** 2700 Lenwood Rd 92311. I-15 exit 178 (Lenwood Rd), just se, then 0.5 mi s. Int corridors. **Pets:** Accepted. [SAVE]

▼▼ Quality Inn **M**
(760) 256-6891. **$79-$199.** 1520 E Main St 92311. I-15 exit 184B (E Main St) northbound; exit 184 (E Main St/I-40 E/Needles) southbound, 0.3 mi w. Ext corridors. **Pets:** Medium. $10 one-time fee/room. Designated rooms, service with restrictions, supervision.

₳₳₳ ▼▼▼ Rodeway Inn **M**
(760) 256-7581. **$55-$83.** 1261 E Main St 92311. I-15 exit 184B (E Main St) northbound; exit 184 (E Main St/I-40 E/Needles) southbound, 0.8 mi w. Ext corridors. **Pets:** Accepted. [SAVE]

▼▼▼ Sleep Inn on Historic Route 66 **M**
(760) 256-1300. **Call for rates.** 1861 W Main St 92311. I-15 exit 181 (L St), 0.5 mi n, then just e. Int corridors. **Pets:** Accepted.

₳₳₳ ▼ Stardust Inn **M**
(760) 256-7116. **$40-$60.** 901 E Main St 92311. I-15 exit 183 (Barstow Rd), 0.8 mi n, then 0.4 mi e. Ext corridors. **Pets:** Small. $8 daily fee/pet. Designated rooms, service with restrictions, supervision. [SAVE]

BASS LAKE

₳₳₳ ▼▼▼ The Pines Resort **CA**
(559) 642-3121. **$99-$339, 3 day notice.** 54432 Rd 432 93604. 6 mi e of SR 41 exit CR 222, e on CR 274, then s on CR 434. Ext/int corridors. **Pets:** Dogs only. $30 one-time fee/room. Designated rooms, service with restrictions, supervision. [SAVE]

BEAUMONT

₳₳₳ ▼▼▼ BEST WESTERN El Rancho Motor Inn **M**
(951) 845-2176. **$75-$250.** 480 E 5th St 92223. I-10 exit 94 (SR 79/Beaumont Ave), just n, then just e. Ext corridors. **Pets:** Accepted. [SAVE]

▼▼ Rodeway Inn **M**
(951) 845-1436. **$60-$100.** 1265 E 6th St 92223. I-10 exit 94 (SR 79/Beaumont Ave), just n, then 0.7 mi e. Ext corridors. **Pets:** Accepted.

BELMONT

₳₳₳ ▼▼▼ HYATT house Belmont/Redwood Shores **H**
(650) 591-8600. **$99-$499.** 400 Concourse Dr 94002. US 101 exit 412 (Ralston Ave), just e, then 0.3 mi n on Island Pkwy. Ext corridors. **Pets:** Accepted. [SAVE]

BENICIA *(Restaurants p. 614)*

₳₳₳ ▼▼▼ BEST WESTERN PLUS Heritage Inn **H**
(707) 746-0401. **$119-$279.** 1955 E 2nd St 94510. I-780 exit Central Benicia/E 2nd St, just ne. Ext/int corridors. **Pets:** Accepted. [SAVE]

BERKELEY *(Restaurants p. 614)*

₳₳₳ ▼ Americas Best Value Golden Bear Inn **M** ❖
(510) 525-6770. **$85-$160.** 1620 San Pablo Ave 94702. I-80 exit 12 (Gilman St), 0.5 mi e, then just s. Ext corridors. **Pets:** Other species. $15 one-time fee/room. Service with restrictions, supervision. [SAVE]

₳₳₳ ▼▼▼ ▼▼▼ Claremont Hotel Club & Spa **H**
(510) 843-3000. **$229-$499.** 41 Tunnel Rd 94705. SR 24 exit SR 13, 0.8 mi n; I-80 exit 11 (University Ave), just e, 1.5 mi s on San Pablo Ave, 2.6 mi e on Ashby Ave, then just e. Int corridors. **Pets:** Accepted. [SAVE]

₳₳₳ ▼▼▼ ▼▼▼ DoubleTree by Hilton Berkeley Marina **H**
(510) 548-7920. **$129-$369.** 200 Marina Blvd 94710. I-80 exit 11 (University Ave), 0.5 mi w; on Berkeley Marina. Int corridors. **Pets:** Large, dogs only. $100 one-time fee/room. Designated rooms, service with restrictions, supervision. [SAVE] [ECO]

▼▼▼ Hotel Durant **H**
(510) 845-8981. **$159-$359, 3 day notice.** 2600 Durant Ave 94704. I-80 exit 11 (University Ave), 2 mi e to Oxford St, 0.3 mi s, then 0.5 mi e; jct Bowditch St. Int corridors. **Pets:** Accepted. [ECO]

BEVERLY HILLS *(Restaurants p. 615)*

▼▼▼▼ Avalon Hotel Beverly Hills **H**
(310) 277-5221. **$189-$399.** 9400 W Olympic Blvd 90212. I-10 exit 6 (Robertson Blvd), 1.7 mi n, then 0.8 mi w. Ext/int corridors. **Pets:** Accepted. [ECO]

₳₳₳ ▼▼▼▼ The Beverly Hills Hotel and Bungalows **H**
(310) 276-2251. **$475-$775.** 9641 Sunset Blvd 90210. I-405 exit 57 (Sunset Blvd), 3.7 mi e. Ext/int corridors. **Pets:** Accepted. [SAVE]

▼▼▼▼ The Beverly Hilton 🅷
(310) 274-7777. **$219-$419.** 9876 Wilshire Blvd 90210. I-405 exit 55 (Wilshire Blvd), 2.2 mi e. Int corridors. **Pets:** Large, other species. $50 one-time fee/room. Service with restrictions, supervision.
[ECO] [🍴] [&M] [➝] [🌊] [✕] [💻]

◇◇◇ ▼▼▼ ▼▼▼ Beverly Wilshire A Four Seasons
Hotel 🅷 ❀
(310) 275-5200. **$455-$875.** 9500 Wilshire Blvd 90212. I-405 exit 55 (Wilshire Blvd), 4.5 mi e. Int corridors. **Pets:** Very small. Supervision.
[SAVE] [🍴] [&M] [➝] [✕] [🛜] [✕] [💻]

◇◇◇ ▼▼▼◇◇ L'Ermitage Beverly Hills 🅷 ❀
(310) 278-3344. **$369-$699.** 9291 Burton Way 90210. I-10 exit 6 (Robertson Blvd), 3.1 mi n, then just w. Int corridors. **Pets:** Medium. $50 daily fee/room. Service with restrictions, supervision.
[SAVE] [🍴] [&M] [➝] [✕] [🛜] [✕] [💻]

▼▼▼◇◇◇ Montage Beverly Hills 🅷
(310) 860-7800. **$525-$1000.** 225 N Canon Dr 90210. I-405 exit 55A (Santa Monica Blvd), 3.4 mi e, then 0.4 mi s. Int corridors.
Pets: Accepted. [ECO] [🍴] [&M] [➝] [✕] [🛜] [✕] [💻] [💻]

◇◇◇ ▼▼▼▼▼ The Peninsula Beverly Hills 🅷 ❀
(310) 551-2888. **$550-$9500.** 9882 S Santa Monica Blvd 90212. I-405 exit 55A (Santa Monica Blvd), 2.2 mi e, at Wilshire Blvd. Ext/int corridors. **Pets:** $35 daily fee/pet.
[SAVE] [🍴] [&M] [➝] [✕] [🛜] [✕] [💻]

BIG BEAR LAKE (Restaurants p. 615)

▼▼▼▼ Bay Meadows Resort 🆑 ❀
(909) 866-4666. **$79-$369, 5 day notice.** 39756 Big Bear Blvd 92315. SR 18, 1 mi w of Village. Ext corridors. **Pets:** Dogs only. $20 one-time fee/pet. Designated rooms, service with restrictions, supervision.
[➝] [🛜] [✕] [🎦] [💻] [💻]

◇◇◇ ▼▼▼▼ BEST WESTERN Big Bear Chateau 🅷
(909) 866-6666. **$98-$279, 3 day notice.** 42200 Moonridge Rd 92315. SR 18, 1.5 mi e of Pine Knot Ave, 0.5 mi s. Int corridors. **Pets:** $30 one-time fee/room. Designated rooms, service with restrictions, crate.
[SAVE] [🍴] [🛜] [✕] [🎦] [💻] [💻]

▼▼ Eagle's Nest Bed & Breakfast 🅱🅱 ❀
(909) 866-6465. **$115-$185, 5 day notice.** 41675 Big Bear Blvd 92315. SR 18, 1 mi e of Pine Knot Ave. Ext/int corridors. **Pets:** Other species. $10 daily fee/pet. Designated rooms, service with restrictions, supervision. [🛜] [✕] [💻] [💻]

▼▼ Golden Bear Cottages 🆑
(909) 866-2010. **$99-$169, 90 day notice.** 39367 Big Bear Blvd 92315. SR 18, 2 mi w of village. Ext corridors. **Pets:** Accepted.
[➝] [✕] [🛜] [✕] [🎦] [💻] [💻]

◇◇◇ ▼▼▼ Grey Squirrel Resort 🆑
(909) 866-4335. **$85-$157, 14 day notice.** 39372 Big Bear Blvd 92315. SR 18, 2 mi w of village. Ext corridors. **Pets:** Other species. $10 daily fee/pet. No service, crate. [SAVE] [➝] [🛜] [✕] [🎦] [💻] [💻]

▼▼ Pine Knot Guest Ranch 🆑
(909) 866-6500. **$99-$199, 7 day notice.** 908 Pine Knot Ave 92315. Just s of SR 18 and downtown area. Ext corridors. **Pets:** Accepted.
[🛜] [💻] [💻]

▼▼ Sleepy Forest Cottages 🆑
(909) 866-7444. **$79-$299, 15 day notice.** 426 Eureka Dr 92315. SR 18, 0.7 mi e of Pine Knot Ave, just n. Ext corridors. **Pets:** Medium, dogs only. $25 one-time fee/pet. Designated rooms, service with restrictions, supervision. [🛜] [✕] [💻] [💻]

BIG PINE

▼▼ Big Pine Motel 🅼
(760) 938-2282. **Call for rates.** 370 S Main St 93513. On US 395 business route. Ext corridors. **Pets:** Accepted. [🛜] [✕] [💻] [💻]

▼▼ ▼▼ Bristlecone Motel 🅼
(760) 938-2067. **$65-$90.** 101 N Main St 93513. On US 395. Ext corridors. **Pets:** Accepted. [🛜] [✕] [💻] [💻]

BISHOP (Restaurants p. 615)

▼▼▼▼ Americas Best Value Inn 🅼
(760) 873-4912. **$69-$199.** 192 Short St 93514. On US 395 to Short St, just e. Ext corridors. **Pets:** Other species. $10 daily fee/pet. Designated rooms, service with restrictions, supervision. [🛜] [💻] [💻]

◇◇◇ ▼▼▼◇◇ BEST WESTERN Bishop Lodge 🅼
(760) 873-3543. **$105-$250.** 1025 N Main St 93514. On US 395. Ext corridors. **Pets:** Accepted. [SAVE] [&M] [➝] [🛜] [💻] [💻]

◇◇◇ ▼▼▼◇◇ Comfort Inn 🅼
(760) 873-4284. **$90-$250.** 805 N Main St 93514. On US 395. Ext corridors. **Pets:** Medium, other species. $15 daily fee/pet. Designated rooms, service with restrictions, supervision.
[SAVE] [&M] [➝] [🛜] [💻] [💻]

◇◇◇ ▼▼▼▼ Holiday Inn Express Hotel & Suites 🅷
(760) 872-2423. **$119-$299.** 636 N Main St 93514. On US 395. Int corridors. **Pets:** Accepted. [SAVE] [&M] [➝] [✕] [🛜] [✕] [💻] [💻]

▼▼▼▼ Joseph House Inn 🅱🅱
(760) 872-3389. **$158-$200, 14 day notice.** 376 W Yaney St 93514. 0.3 mi w of US 395. Int corridors. **Pets:** Dogs only. Designated rooms, service with restrictions, supervision. [🛜] [✕] [🎦]

▼▼ ▼▼ Super 8 🅼
(760) 872-1386. **$60-$89.** 535 S Main St 93514. On US 395; south end of town. Ext corridors. **Pets:** Accepted. [➝] [🛜] [💻] [💻]

▼▼ ▼▼ Travelodge 🅼
(760) 872-1771. **$79-$230.** 155 E Elm St 93514. On US 395, just e. Ext corridors. **Pets:** Accepted. [&M] [➝] [🛜] [💻] [💻]

▼▼ ▼▼ Vagabond Inn 🅼 ❀
(760) 873-6351. **$70-$396.** 1030 N Main St 93514. On US 395. Ext corridors. **Pets:** Medium, dogs only. $15 daily fee/pet. Designated rooms, service with restrictions, supervision. [&M] [➝] [🛜] [💻] [💻]

BLYTHE (Restaurants p. 615)

◇◇◇ ▼▼ ▼▼ BEST WESTERN Sahara 🅼
(760) 922-7105. **$110-$160.** 825 W Hobsonway 92225. I-10 exit 239 (Lovekin Blvd), just n, then just w. Ext corridors. **Pets:** Medium. $10 daily fee/pet. Service with restrictions, supervision.
[SAVE] [&M] [➝] [🛜] [💻] [💻]

◇◇◇ ▼▼ ▼▼ Clarion Inn 🅼
(760) 922-9000. **$79-$139.** 900 W Hobsonway 92225. I-10 exit 239 (Lovekin Blvd), just n, then just w. Ext corridors. **Pets:** Accepted.
[SAVE] [➝] [🛜] [💻] [💻]

BORREGO SPRINGS

▼▼▼▼ La Casa del Zorro Resort 🅷
(760) 767-0100. **$129-$349, 4 day notice.** 3845 Yaqui Pass Rd 92004. 5.5 mi se on CR S-3; jct Yaqui Pass and Borrego Springs rds. Ext corridors. **Pets:** Medium. $50 daily fee/room. Designated rooms, service with restrictions. [🍴] [&M] [➝] [✕] [🛜] [✕] [💻] [💻]

BRAWLEY

◇◇◇ ▼▼▼▼ BEST WESTERN PLUS Main Street
Inn 🅼
(760) 351-9800. **$112-$149.** 1562 E Main St 92227. On SR 78 and 111. Ext/int corridors. **Pets:** $20 deposit/pet, $20 daily fee/pet. Service with restrictions, crate. [SAVE] [➝] [🛜] [✕] [💻] [💻]

AAA ▼▼ **Brawley Inn Hotel & Conference Center** **M**
(760) 344-1199. **$81-$139.** 575 W Main St 92227. On SR 86 and 78.
Ext/int corridors. **Pets:** Medium. $25 daily fee/pet. Designated rooms,
service with restrictions, supervision.
[SAVE] [T1] [&M] [≈] [⬚] [⬚] [⬚]

BREA
▼▼ **Chase Suite Hotels** **M**
(714) 579-3200. **$109-$299.** 3100 E Imperial Hwy 92821. SR 57 exit 9
(SR 90), 1.5 mi e. Ext corridors. **Pets:** Medium. $150 deposit/room, $10
daily fee/pet. Designated rooms, service with restrictions, supervision.
[≈] [⬚] [✕] [⬚] [⬚]

BRIDGEPORT
AAA ▼▼ **Redwood Motel** **M** ✿
(760) 932-7060. **$69-$250.** 425 Main St 93517. On US 395; on north
side of town. Ext corridors. **Pets:** $10 daily fee/pet. Service with restric-
tions, supervision. [SAVE] [≈] [⬚] [⬚]

AAA ▼▼ **Ruby Inn** **M**
(760) 932-7241. **$100-$225.** 333 Main St 93517. On US 395; center.
Ext corridors. **Pets:** Accepted. [SAVE] [≈] [✕] [⬚] [⬚]

AAA ▼▼ **Silver Maple Inn** **M** ✿
(760) 932-7383. **$80-$150, 3 day notice.** 310 Main St 93517. On US
395; center. Ext corridors. **Pets:** Other species. Supervision.
[SAVE] [≈] [✕] [AC] [⬚] [⬚]

AAA ▼▼ **Walker River Lodge** **M** ✿
(760) 932-7021. **$85-$220, 3 day notice.** 100 Main St 93517. On US
395; at south end of town. Ext corridors. **Pets:** Other species. Service
with restrictions, supervision. [SAVE] [≈] [≈] [⬚] [⬚]

BUELLTON
AAA ▼▼ **Quality Inn Santa Ynez Valley** **M**
(805) 688-0022. **$69-$149.** 630 Ave of the Flags 93427. US 101 exit
140B (Ave of the Flags) southbound, just s; exit 140A (SR 246) northbound, just w, then just n. Ext/int corridors. **Pets:** Accepted.
[SAVE] [≈] [✕] [⬚] [⬚]

AAA ▼▼▼ **Santa Ynez Valley Marriott** **H** ✿
(805) 688-1000. **$139-$349, 3 day notice.** 555 McMurray Rd 93427.
US 101 exit 140A (SR 246), just e, then just n. Int corridors.
Pets: Other species. $80 one-time fee/room. Designated rooms, service
with restrictions. [SAVE] [⬚] [T1] [≈] [✕] [≈] [✕] [⬚] [⬚]

BURBANK
AAA ▼▼▼▼ **Hotel Amarano Burbank** **H**
(818) 842-8887. **Call for rates.** 322 N Pass Ave 91505. SR 134 exit 2
(Hollywood Way) westbound, just w on Alameda Ave, then 0.5 mi n;
exit 2 (Pass Ave) eastbound, 0.5 mi n. Ext corridors. **Pets:** Accepted.
[SAVE] [T1] [&M] [≈] [✕] [≈] [✕] [⬚] [⬚]

▼▼▼ **Los Angeles Marriott Burbank Airport Hotel** **H**
(818) 843-6000. **$119-$309.** 2500 N Hollywood Way 91505. I-5 exit 149
(Hollywood Way), 1 mi s. Int corridors. **Pets:** Accepted.
[ECO] [T1] [&M] [≈] [≈] [✕] [⬚] [⬚]

▼▼▼ **Residence Inn by Marriott Burbank**
Downtown **H**
(818) 260-8787. **$152-$299.** 321 S 1st St 91502. I-5 exit 146A (Olive
Ave) northbound, just e on Angeleno Ave, then just s; exit 146A (Verdugo Ave) southbound, just s on Front St, just e on Verdugo Ave, then
just n. Int corridors. **Pets:** Accepted. [≈] [≈] [✕] [⬚] [⬚]

AAA ▼▼ **The Safari Inn** **M**
(818) 845-8586. **$135-$269, 3 day notice.** 1911 W Olive Ave 91506. I-5
exit 146A (Olive Ave), 1.3 mi sw. Ext corridors. **Pets:** Other species.
$200 deposit/room, $25 daily fee/pet. Service with restrictions, supervision. [SAVE] [T1] [≈] [≈] [⬚] [⬚]

BURLINGAME
AAA ▼▼▼ **Crowne Plaza San Francisco Intl**
Airport **H**
(650) 342-9200. **$109-$359.** 1177 Airport Blvd 94010. US 101 exit
Broadway-Burlingame or Old Bayshore Hwy, just e. Int corridors.
Pets: Accepted. [SAVE] [T1] [&M] [≈] [≈] [✕] [⬚] [⬚]

▼▼▼ **DoubleTree by Hilton Hotel San Francisco**
Airport **H**
(650) 344-5500. **$199-$499.** 835 Airport Blvd 94010. US 101 exit
Broadway-Burlingame or Anza Blvd, just e. Int corridors.
Pets: Accepted. [ECO] [T1] [&M] [≈] [✕] [⬚] [⬚]

AAA ▼▼▼ **Embassy Suites San Francisco Airport -**
Waterfront **H**
(650) 342-4600. **$135-$539.** 150 Anza Blvd 94010. US 101 exit
Broadway-Burlingame, just e. Int corridors. **Pets:** Accepted.
[SAVE] [ECO] [T1] [&M] [≈] [≈] [⬚] [⬚]

AAA ▼▼▼ **Hilton San Francisco Airport**
Bayfront **H** ✿
(650) 340-8500. **$109-$479.** 600 Airport Blvd 94010. US 101 exit
Broadway-Burlingame or Anza Blvd, 0.3 mi e. Int corridors. **Pets:** Large.
$75 one-time fee/room. Designated rooms, service with restrictions,
supervision. [SAVE] [T1] [&M] [≈] [≈] [✕] [⬚] [⬚]

AAA ▼▼▼ **Hyatt Regency San Francisco Airport** **H**
(650) 347-1234. **$99-$399.** 1333 Bayshore Hwy 94010. US 101 exit
Broadway-Burlingame, just e. Int corridors. **Pets:** Accepted.
[SAVE] [ECO] [T1] [&M] [≈] [✕] [≈] [✕] [⬚] [⬚]

AAA ▼▼▼ **Red Roof Inn San Francisco Airport** **M**
(650) 342-7772. **$79-$199.** 777 Airport Blvd 94010. US 101 exit
Broadway-Burlingame or Anza Blvd; just s of airport. Ext corridors.
Pets: Large, other species. Service with restrictions, supervision.
[SAVE] [T1] [&M] [≈] [≈] [✕] [⬚] [⬚]

AAA ▼▼▼ **San Francisco Airport Marriott**
Waterfront **H**
(650) 692-9100. **$139-$329.** 1800 Old Bayshore Hwy 94010. US 101
exit Millbrae Ave, just e. Int corridors. **Pets:** Accepted.
[SAVE] [ECO] [T1] [&M] [≈] [✕] [≈] [✕] [⬚] [⬚]

BURNEY
AAA ▼▼ **Charm Motel** **M** ✿
(530) 335-3300. **$65-$215.** 37363 Main St 96013. 0.5 mi ne on SR
299; jct Roff Way. Ext corridors. **Pets:** $10 daily fee/pet. Service with
restrictions, supervision. [SAVE] [&M] [≈] [✕] [⬚] [⬚]

AAA ▼▼ **Green Gables Motel** **M** ✿
(530) 335-3300. **$70-$215.** 37385 Main St 96013. 0.5 mi ne on SR
299; jct Roff Way. Ext corridors. **Pets:** $10 daily fee/pet. Service with
restrictions, supervision. [SAVE] [≈] [✕] [⬚] [⬚]

CALABASAS *(Restaurants p. 615)*
AAA ▼▼▼ **The Anza-A Calabasas Hotel** **H** ✿
(818) 222-5300. **Call for rates.** 23627 Calabasas Rd 91302. US 101
exit 29 (Valley Cir/Mulholland Dr), just w, then 0.6 mi n. Int corridors.
Pets: Medium, dogs only. $25 daily fee/pet. Designated rooms, service
with restrictions, supervision. [SAVE] [≈] [≈] [✕] [⬚] [⬚]

CALEXICO
AAA ▼▼ **BEST WESTERN John Jay Inn** **M** ✿
(760) 768-0442. **$85.** 2421 Scaroni Ave 92231. I-8 exit 118A (SR 111
S), 5.5 mi s, just w on W Cole Rd, then just n. Int corridors.
Pets: Small, dogs only. $20 daily fee/room. Designated rooms, service
with restrictions, crate. [SAVE] [&M] [≈] [≈] [⬚] [⬚]

CALIMESA

Calimesa Inn Motel M

(909) 795-2536. **$60-$120.** 1205 Calimesa Blvd 92320. I-10 exit 88 (Calimesa Blvd), just ne. Ext corridors. **Pets:** Accepted.

CALISTOGA *(Restaurants p. 615)*

Cottage Grove Inn ⓒ

(707) 942-8400. **$295-$450, 10 day notice.** 1711 Lincoln Ave 94515. On SR 29; at Wapoo Ave. Ext corridors. **Pets:** Small, dogs only. $25 daily fee/pet. Designated rooms.

Solage Calistoga H

(707) 226-0800. **$375-$1025, 14 day notice.** 755 Silverado Tr 94515. Jct SR 29, 0.5 mi se. Ext corridors. **Pets:** $100 one-time fee/room. Designated rooms, service with restrictions.

CAMARILLO *(Restaurants p. 615)*

BEST WESTERN Camarillo Inn M

(805) 987-4991. **$90-$140.** 295 E Daily Dr 93010. US 101 exit 55 (Las Posas Rd), just n, then just e. Ext corridors. **Pets:** Accepted.

Camarillo Residence Inn by Marriott H

(805) 388-7997. **$111-$259.** 2912 Petit St 93012. US 101 exit 53A (Flynn Rd) northbound, 0.8 mi n, then just w; exit Dawson Dr southbound, just w. Int corridors. **Pets:** $100 one-time fee/pet. Designated rooms, service with restrictions, supervision.

CAMBRIA *(Restaurants p. 615)*

Bluebird Inn M

(805) 927-4634. **$68-$220.** 1880 Main St 93428. SR 1 exit Main St northbound, 1.9 mi ne; exit Cambria Dr southbound, 0.5 mi se. Ext corridors. **Pets:** Other species. $20 one-time fee/pet. Designated rooms, supervision.

Blue Dolphin Inn H

(805) 927-3300. **$179-$369.** 6470 Moonstone Beach Dr 93428. SR 1 exit Moonstone Beach Dr, just w, then 0.7 mi n. Int corridors. **Pets:** Medium, dogs only. $25 daily fee/room. Designated rooms, service with restrictions, supervision.

Cambria Shores Inn M

(805) 927-8644. **$199-$349, 7 day notice.** 6276 Moonstone Beach Dr 93428. SR 1 exit Moonstone Beach Dr, just w, then 0.8 mi s. Ext corridors. **Pets:** Dogs only. $15 daily fee/pet. Service with restrictions, supervision.

Castle Inn by the Sea M

(805) 927-8605. **$119-$209.** 6620 Moonstone Beach Dr 93428. SR 1 exit Moonstone Beach Dr, just w, then 0.5 mi s. Ext corridors. **Pets:** Medium, dogs only. $25 daily fee/room. Designated rooms, service with restrictions, supervision.

Fireside Inn On Moonstone Beach M

(805) 927-8661. **$129-$499.** 6700 Moonstone Beach Dr 93428. SR 1 exit Moonstone Beach Dr, just w, then 0.5 mi s. Ext/int corridors. **Pets:** Accepted.

Fog Catcher Inn M

(805) 927-1400. **$149-$500, 7 day notice.** 6400 Moonstone Beach Dr 93428. SR 1 exit Moonstone Beach Dr, just w, then 0.7 mi s. Ext corridors. **Pets:** $75 one-time fee/room. Designated rooms, supervision.

Sand Pebbles Inn H

(805) 927-5600. **$129-$319.** 6252 Moonstone Beach Dr 93428. SR 1 exit Moonstone Beach Dr, just w, then 0.9 mi s. Int corridors. **Pets:** Medium, dogs only. $25 daily fee/room. Designated rooms, service with restrictions, supervision.

Sea Otter Inn M

(805) 927-5888. **$119-$239, 3 day notice.** 6656 Moonstone Beach Dr 93428. SR 1 exit Moonstone Beach Dr, just w, then 0.5 mi s. Ext corridors. **Pets:** Accepted.

White Water Inn M

(805) 927-1066. **$149-$339, 7 day notice.** 6790 Moonstone Beach Dr 93428. SR 1 exit Moonstone Beach Dr, just w, then 0.4 mi s. Ext corridors. **Pets:** Medium. $30 one-time fee/room. Designated rooms, service with restrictions, supervision.

CAMPBELL

DoubleTree by Hilton-Campbell PruneYard Plaza H

(408) 559-4300. **$129-$309.** 1995 S Bascom Ave 95008. SR 17 exit Hamilton Ave, 0.3 mi e, then s. Int corridors. **Pets:** Accepted.

Larkspur Landing Campbell H

(408) 364-1514. **$249-$279.** 550 W Hamilton Ave 95008. SR 17 exit Hamilton Ave, 1 mi w. Int corridors. **Pets:** Accepted.

Residence Inn by Marriott-San Jose H

(408) 559-1551. **$189-$369.** 2761 S Bascom Ave 95008. SR 17 exit Camden Ave E, just n. Ext corridors. **Pets:** Accepted.

TownePlace Suites by Marriott-San Jose/Campbell H

(408) 370-4510. **$110-$256.** 700 E Campbell Ave 95008. SR 17 exit Hamilton Ave E, 0.3 mi to Bascom Ave, 0.3 mi s, then 0.3 mi w. Int corridors. **Pets:** Medium, other species. $100 one-time fee/room. Designated rooms, service with restrictions.

CARDIFF-BY-THE-SEA

Holiday Inn Express Encinitas Cardiff Beach H

(760) 944-0427. **Call for rates.** 1661 Villa Cardiff Dr 92007. I-5 exit 40 (Birmingham Dr), just e, then just n. Int corridors. **Pets:** Accepted.

CARLSBAD *(Restaurants p. 615)*

Carlsbad by the Sea Resort H

(760) 438-7880. **$99-$299.** 850 Palomar Airport Rd 92011. I-5 exit 47 (Palomar Airport Rd), just e. Ext corridors. **Pets:** Accepted.

Hilton Carlsbad Oceanfront Resort & Spa H

(760) 602-0800. **$189-$329.** 1 Ponto Rd 92011. I-5 exit 45 (Poinsettia Ln/Aviara Pkwy), just s on Carlsbad Blvd, 0.4 mi w, then just w. Int corridors. **Pets:** Accepted.

HYATT house San Diego/Carlsbad H

(760) 929-8200. **$109-$319.** 5010 Avenida Encinas 92008. I-5 exit 48 (Cannon Rd), just w, then just s. Int corridors. **Pets:** Other species. $75 one-time fee/pet. Service with restrictions, crate.

La Quinta Inn & Suites San Diego Carlsbad M

(760) 438-2828. **$89-$369.** 760 Macadamia Dr 92011. I-5 exit 45 (Poinsettia Ln/Aviara Pkwy), just w to Ave Encinas, just n, then just e. Ext corridors. **Pets:** Large, other species. Service with restrictions.

Park Hyatt Aviara Resort, Golf Club & Spa H

(760) 448-1234. **$195-$579, 7 day notice.** 7100 Aviara Resort Dr 92011. I-5 exit 45 (Poinsettia Ln/Aviara Pkwy), 1 mi e on Poinsettia Ln, 1 mi s on Aviara Pkwy, then just sw. Int corridors. **Pets:** Accepted.

ᵂᵂ Ramada Inn & Suites 🅜

(760) 438-2285. **$69-$299.** 751 Macadamia Dr 92011. I-5 exit 45 (Poinsettia Ln), just w to Ave Encinas, then 0.3 mi n. Ext corridors. **Pets:** Medium, other species. Designated rooms, service with restrictions. 🅛ᴹ 🛌 🛜 ✕ 🆗 ▯

ᵂᵂ West Inn & Suites 🅗

(760) 448-4500. **$159-$399, 3 day notice.** 4970 Avenida Encinas 92008. I-5 exit 48 (Cannon Rd), just w, then just n. Int corridors. **Pets:** Accepted. 🍽 🅛ᴹ 🛌 🛜 ✕ 🆗 ▯

CARMEL-BY-THE-SEA *(Restaurants p. 615)*

ᵂᵂᵂ Adobe Inn 🅗

(831) 624-3933. **Call for rates.** Dolores St & 8th Ave 93921. Just s off Ocean Ave. Ext corridors. **Pets:** Accepted. 🛌 🛜 ✕ 🆔 🆗 ▯

ᴬᴬᴬ ᵂᵂᵂ Briarwood Inn 🅱🅱 🐾

(831) 626-9056. **$115-$490, 3 day notice.** San Carlos St 93921. 3 blks n of Ocean Ave; at 4th Ave. Ext corridors. **Pets:** Small, dogs only. $25 one-time fee/room. Designated rooms, service with restrictions, supervision. 🆂🅰🆅🅴 🛜 ✕ 🆔 🆗 ▯

ᵂᵂ Carmel Country Inn 🅱🅱 🐾

(831) 625-3263. **$225-$425, 7 day notice.** Dolores St & 3rd Ave 93921. 4 blks n of Ocean Ave. Ext corridors. **Pets:** Other species. $20 daily fee/pet. Supervision. 🛜 ✕ 🆔 🆗 ▯

ᴬᴬᴬ ᵂᵂᵂ Carmel Fireplace Inn Bed & Breakfast 🅱🅱

(831) 624-4862. **$99-$365, 3 day notice.** San Carlos St & 4th Ave 93921. 3 blks n of Ocean Ave. Ext corridors. **Pets:** Accepted. 🆂🅰🆅🅴 🛜 ✕ 🆔 🆗 ▯

ᵂᵂ Carmel Garden Inn 🅱🅱

(831) 624-6926. **$159-$249, 3 day notice.** 4th Ave & Torres St 93921. 3 blks n of Ocean Ave. Ext corridors. **Pets:** Accepted. 🛜 ✕ 🆔 🆗 ▯

ᵂᵂ Carmel Lodge 🅗 🐾

(831) 624-1255. **$129-$399, 3 day notice.** San Carlos St & 5th Ave 93921. 2 blks n of Ocean Ave. Ext/int corridors. **Pets:** $35 daily fee/pet. Service with restrictions, supervision. 🛜 ✕ 🆔 🆗 ▯

ᵂᵂ Carmel Mission Inn 🅗

(831) 624-1841. **$99-$529.** 3665 Rio Rd 93923. 1 mi s on SR 1. Ext/int corridors. **Pets:** Large. $35 one-time fee/pet. Designated rooms, service with restrictions, crate. 🍽 🅛ᴹ 🛌 🛜 ✕ 🆗 ▯

ᴬᴬᴬ ᵂᵂᵂ Coachman's Inn 🅗

(831) 624-6421. **$225-$435, 3 day notice.** San Carlos St at 7th Ave 93921. Just s of Ocean Ave on San Carlos St; between 7th and 8th aves. Ext corridors. **Pets:** Dogs only. $20 one-time fee/room. Designated rooms, service with restrictions, supervision. 🆂🅰🆅🅴 🅛ᴹ ✕ 🛜 ✕ 🆔 🆗 ▯

ᵂᵂᵂ Cypress Inn 🅗 🐾

(831) 624-3871. **$245-$595, 7 day notice.** Lincoln & 7th Ave 93921. Just s of Ocean Ave. Ext/int corridors. **Pets:** Other species. $30 daily fee/pet. Supervision. 🍽 🛜 ✕ 🆔 🆗

ᴬᴬᴬ ᵂᵂ Hofsas House 🅗 🐾

(831) 624-2745. **$119-$400, 3 day notice.** San Carlos St 93921. 3 blks n of Ocean Ave; between 3rd and 4th aves. **Pets:** Dogs only. $25 daily fee/pet. Designated rooms, service with restrictions, supervision. 🆂🅰🆅🅴 🛌 🛜 ✕ 🆔 🆗 ▯

ᴬᴬᴬ ᵂᵂᵂ Horizon Inn & Ocean View Lodge 🅗 🐾

(831) 624-5327. **$118-$399, 3 day notice.** 3rd Ave & Junipero Ave 93921. 4 blks n of Ocean Ave. **Pets:** Dogs only. $20 daily fee/pet. Designated rooms, service with restrictions, supervision. 🆂🅰🆅🅴 🅛ᴹ 🛜 ✕ 🆔 🆗 ▯

ᴬᴬᴬ ᵂᵂᵂ Svendsgaard's 🅗 🐾

(831) 624-1511. **$179-$309, 3 day notice.** 4th Ave & San Carlos St 93921. 3 blks n of Ocean Ave. Ext corridors. **Pets:** $25 daily fee/pet. Designated rooms, service with restrictions, supervision. 🆂🅰🆅🅴 🛌 🛜 ✕ 🆔 🆗 ▯

CARMEL VALLEY

ᴬᴬᴬ ᵂᵂᵂᵂ Bernardus Lodge & Spa 🅗 🐾

(831) 658-3400. **$325-$2050, 7 day notice.** 415 W Carmel Valley Rd 93924. 9.5 mi e of SR 1; just e of Los Laureles Grade. Ext corridors. **Pets:** Large, dogs only. $100 one-time fee/pet. Designated rooms, service with restrictions, supervision. 🆂🅰🆅🅴 🍽 🅛ᴹ 🛌 ✕ 🛜 ✕ 🆔 🆗 ▯

ᵂᵂ ᵂᵂ Carmel Valley Ranch 🅗

(831) 625-9500. **$300-$975, 7 day notice.** One Old Ranch Rd 93923. 6.3 mi e of SR 1 via Carmel Valley Rd to Robinson Canyon Rd exit, follow signs. Ext corridors. **Pets:** Accepted. 🍽 🅛ᴹ 🛌 ✕ 🛜 ✕ 🆔 🆗 ▯

CARPINTERIA

ᵂᵂᵂ Holiday Inn Express & Suites 🅗

(805) 566-9499. **$119-$329.** 5606 Carpinteria Ave 93013. US 101 exit 86A (Casitas Pass Rd), just s, then just e. Int corridors. **Pets:** Other species. $15 daily fee/room. Designated rooms, service with restrictions, supervision. 🅛ᴹ 🛌 🛜 ✕ 🆔 🆗 ▯

CARSON

ᵂᵂᵂ DoubleTree by Hilton Hotel Carson 🅗

(310) 830-9200. **$139-$189.** 2 Civic Plaza Dr 90745. I-405 exit 34 (Carson St), just w, then just n. Int corridors. **Pets:** Accepted. 🍽 🛌 🛜 🆔 🆗 ▯

ᵂᵂ Extended Stay America-Los Angeles/Carson 🅗

(310) 323-2080. **Call for rates.** 401 E Albertoni St 90746. SR 91 exit 7B (Avalon Blvd), just s, then just w. Int corridors. **Pets:** Other species. $25 daily fee/pet. Service with restrictions, supervision. 🅛ᴹ 🛜 🆔 🆗 ▯

CASTRO VALLEY

ᵂᵂ Comfort Inn Castro Valley 🅗

(510) 538-9501. **$110-$175.** 2532 Castro Valley Blvd 94546. I-580 exit Castro Valley Blvd, 0.3 mi n. Int corridors. **Pets:** Accepted. 🅛ᴹ 🛌 🛜 🆔 🆗 ▯

CAYUCOS

ᵂᵂ Cayucos Beach Inn 🅜

(805) 995-2828. **$85-$195, 3 day notice.** 333 S Ocean Ave 93430. On SR 1 business route. Ext corridors. **Pets:** Accepted. 🅛ᴹ 🛜 🆔 🆗 ▯

ᴬᴬᴬ ᵂ Cypress Tree Motel 🅜

(805) 995-3917. **$57-$147.** 125 S Ocean Ave 93430. On SR 1 business route. Ext corridors. **Pets:** Accepted. 🆂🅰🆅🅴 🛜 ✕ 🆔 🆗 ▯

ᵂᵂ Pier View Suites 🅗

(805) 995-0014. **$239-$339.** 12 N Ocean Ave 93430. On SR 1 business route. Ext/int corridors. **Pets:** $30 daily fee/pet. Designated rooms, service with restrictions. 🅛ᴹ 🛜 ✕ 🆔 🆗 ▯

ᵂᵂ Shoreline Inn On The Beach 🅜

(805) 995-3681. **$119-$259, 3 day notice.** 1 N Ocean Ave 93430. On SR 1 business route. Ext corridors. **Pets:** Accepted. 🛜 ✕ 🆔 🆗 ▯

CEDARVILLE

ᴬᴬᴬ ᵂ Sunrise Motel 🅜

(530) 279-2161. **$69-$79, 7 day notice.** 62271 Hwy 299 W 96104. Jct SR 299 and CR 1, 0.6 mi w on CR 1. Ext corridors. **Pets:** Medium. $10 daily fee/pet. Designated rooms, service with restrictions, supervision. 🆂🅰🆅🅴 🛜 ✕ 🆔 🆗 ▯

CERRITOS

Sheraton Cerritos Hotel at Towne Center H

(562) 809-1500. **$98-$217.** 12725 Center Court Dr 90703. SR 91 exit 19B (Artesia/Bloomfield Dr), just s to Town Center Dr, just e, then just s. Int corridors. **Pets:** Accepted.

CHATSWORTH

Ramada H

(818) 998-5289. **$76-$200.** 21340 Devonshire St 91311. SR 118 exit 35 (De Soto Ave), 1.5 mi s, then 0.5 mi w. Int corridors. **Pets:** Very small. $20 daily fee/pet. Designated rooms, service with restrictions, supervision.

Staybridge Suites H

(818) 773-0707. **Call for rates.** 21902 Lassen St 91311. SR 118 exit 34 (Topanga Canyon Blvd), 2 mi s, then just e. Ext/int corridors. **Pets:** Accepted.

CHESTER

BEST WESTERN Rose Quartz Inn H

(530) 258-2002. **$111-$186.** 306 Main St 96020. 0.3 mi w of center on SR 36. Int corridors. **Pets:** Accepted.

CHICO

BEST WESTERN Heritage Inn - Chico H

(530) 894-8600. **$90-$130.** 25 Heritage Ln 95926. Just e of SR 99, via Cohasset Rd. Int corridors. **Pets:** Dogs only. $30 one-time fee/room. Designated rooms, service with restrictions, supervision.

Oxford Suites Chico H

(530) 899-9090. **$99-$225.** 2035 Business Ln 95928. SR 99 exit 384 (E 20th St), just e, then just s. Int corridors. **Pets:** Accepted.

Residence Inn by Marriott Chico H

(530) 894-5500. **$118-$159.** 2485 Carmichael Dr 95928. SR 99 exit 383 (Skyway/Park Ave), just w, then just n. Int corridors. **Pets:** Accepted.

Super 8 H

(530) 345-2533. **$57-$90.** 655 Manzanita Ct 95926. SR 99 exit 387A (Mangrove Ave/Cohasset Rd), follow Mangrove Ave, then just se. Int corridors. **Pets:** Medium. $10 deposit/pet, $10 daily fee/pet. Designated rooms, service with restrictions, supervision.

CHOWCHILLA

Days Inn Gateway to Yosemite M

(559) 665-4821. **$59-$74.** 220 E Robertson Blvd 93610. SR 99 exit 170 (Robertson Blvd), just w. Ext corridors. **Pets:** Accepted.

Holiday Inn Express & Suites Gateway to Yosemite H

(559) 665-3300. **$79-$169.** 309 Prosperity Blvd 93610. SR 99 exit 170 (Robertson Blvd), just w, just s on Chowchilla Blvd, then just e. Int corridors. **Pets:** Accepted.

CHULA VISTA

La Quinta Inn San Diego Chula Vista M

(619) 691-1211. **$89-$379.** 150 Bonita Rd 91910. I-805 exit 7C (E St/Bonita Rd), just w. Ext/int corridors. **Pets:** Large, other species. Service with restrictions.

CLAREMONT

Hotel Casa 425 H

(909) 624-2272. **$195-$400, 3 day notice.** 425 W 1st St 91711. I-10 exit 47 (Indian Hill Blvd), 1.2 mi n, then just w. Ext corridors. **Pets:** Dogs only. $65 one-time fee/room. Designated rooms, service with restrictions, supervision.

Hotel Claremont M

(909) 621-4831. **$79-$129, 3 day notice.** 840 S Indian Hill Blvd 91711. I-10 exit 47 (Indian Hill Blvd), just s; enter on Auto Center Dr. Ext corridors. **Pets:** Accepted.

CLEARLAKE

Clear Lake Cottages and Marina CA

(707) 995-5253. **$119-$209, 15 day notice.** 13885 Lakeshore Dr 95422. SR 53 exit Lakeshore Dr, 2.1 mi w. Ext corridors. **Pets:** Other species. $20 daily fee/pet. Designated rooms, service with restrictions, supervision.

CLOVERDALE

Auberge on the Vineyard BB

(707) 894-5556. **$145-$315, 7 day notice.** 29955 River Rd 95425. US 101 exit Citrus Fair Dr, just e, 0.5 mi n on Asti Rd, 0.8 mi e on Crocker Rd, then just s. Ext/int corridors. **Pets:** Accepted.

Old Crocker Inn BB

(707) 894-4000. **$165-$275, 8 day notice.** 1126 Old Crocker Inn Rd 95425. US 101 exit Citrus Fair Dr, just e, 0.5 mi n on Asti Rd, 0.8 mi e on First St, 3.8 mi s on River Rd, 1.1 mi e on Asti Ridge Rd, then just n. Ext corridors. **Pets:** Dogs only. $20 one-time fee/pet. Designated rooms, supervision.

COALINGA

BEST WESTERN Big Country Inn M

(559) 935-0866. **$129-$149.** 25020 W Dorris Ave 93210. I-5 exit SR 198/Hanford-Lemoore, just w. Ext corridors. **Pets:** Medium. $20 daily fee/pet. Designated rooms, service with restrictions, supervision.

The Inn at Harris Ranch H

(559) 935-0717. **$169-$350.** 24505 W Dorris Ave 93210. I-5 exit SR 198/Hanford-Lemoore, just e. Ext/int corridors. **Pets:** Accepted.

COLTON

Holiday Inn Express Colton/Riverside-North H

(951) 788-9900. **$109-$179.** 2830 S Iowa Ave 92324. I-215 exit 37 (La Cadena Dr) northbound; exit 37 (Iowa Ave) southbound, just se. Int corridors. **Pets:** Medium. $250 deposit/room, $25 one-time fee/pet. Designated rooms, service with restrictions, supervision.

COLUMBIA

Columbia Gem Motel M

(209) 532-4508. **$99-$159.** 22131 Parrotts Ferry Rd 95370. SR 49 exit Parrotts Ferry Rd, 1 mi ne; 3 mi n of Sonora; 1 mi from Columbia State Historic Park. Ext corridors. **Pets:** Dogs only. Service with restrictions, crate.

CONCORD

Crowne Plaza Hotel Concord/Walnut Creek H

(925) 825-7700. **$99-$299, 3 day notice.** 45 John Glenn Dr 94520. I-680 exit Concord Ave, just e. Int corridors. **Pets:** Medium, dogs only. $50 one-time fee/pet. Service with restrictions, supervision.

Hilton Concord H

(925) 827-2000. **$129-$229.** 1970 Diamond Blvd 94520. I-680 exit 51 (Willow Pass Rd), just e, then just nw. Int corridors. **Pets:** Large, other species. $50 one-time fee/pet. Service with restrictions, crate.

CORNING

✦✦✦ BEST WESTERN PLUS Corning Inn 🅷 ☸

(530) 824-5200. **$99-$129.** 910 Hwy 99 W 96021. I-5 exit 631 (Central Corning), just e. Int corridors. **Pets:** $100 deposit/pet, $10 daily fee/pet. Designated rooms, service with restrictions, supervision.

[SAVE] 🛍 🛜 🍴 💻

✦✦✦ Econo Lodge Inn & Suites 🅷

(530) 824-2000. **$65-$119.** 3475 Hwy 99 W 96021. I-5 exit 630 (South Ave), just e, then just s. Int corridors. **Pets:** Small. $10 daily fee/pet. No service, supervision. [SAVE] ⌖M 🛍 🛜 🍴 💻

✦✦✦ The Inn at Rolling Hills 🅷

(530) 824-8300. **$104-$119.** 2645 Everett Freeman Way 96021. I-5 exit 628 (Liberal Ave/SR 99), just w, then just s. Int corridors. **Pets:** Accepted. [SAVE] 🛍 🛜 🍴 💻

CORONA (Restaurants p. 615)

✦✦✦ Ayres Suites Corona West 🅷

(951) 738-9113. **$109-$189.** 1900 Frontage Rd 92882. SR 91 exit 48 (Maple St/W 6th St) eastbound; exit Maple St westbound, just sw. Ext/int corridors. **Pets:** Accepted. 🛍 🛜 🍴 💻

✦✦✦ BEST WESTERN Corona 🅼 ☸

(951) 734-4241. **$84-$105.** 1084 Pomona Rd 92882. SR 91 exit 49 (Lincoln Ave), just ne. Ext corridors. **Pets:** Medium, dogs only. $10 daily fee/room. Designated rooms, service with restrictions, supervision.

[SAVE] 🛍 🛜 🍴 💻

✦✦✦ Residence Inn by Marriott Corona 🅷

(951) 371-0107. **$139-$169.** 1015 Montecito Dr 92879. I-15 exit 95 (Magnolia Ave), just e, just n on El Camino, just w on Carly Way, then just n. Int corridors. **Pets:** Accepted. ⌖M 🛍 🛜 ✕ 🍴 💻

CORONADO (Restaurants p. 615)

✦✦ Crown City Inn 🅼 ☸

(619) 435-3116. **$100-$300.** 520 Orange Ave 92118. I-5 exit 14A (Coronado Bridge), 2.4 mi nw, then just sw. Ext corridors. **Pets:** Other species. $25 daily fee/pet. Designated rooms, supervision.

🍴 ⌖M 🛍 🛜 🍴 💻

✦✦✦✦ Hotel del Coronado 🅷 ☸

(619) 435-6611. **$349-$3200, 14 day notice.** 1500 Orange Ave 92118. I-5 exit 14A (Coronado Bridge), 2.4 mi nw, then 1.6 mi sw. Ext/int corridors. **Pets:** Medium, other species. $125 one-time fee/room. Service with restrictions, supervision. [ECO] 🛍 ✕ 🛜 ✕ 🍴 💻

✦✦✦✦ Loews Coronado Bay 🅷

(619) 424-4000. **$199-$409, 3 day notice.** 4000 Loews Coronado Bay Rd 92118. I-5 exit 14A (Coronado Bridge), 2.4 mi nw to Orange Ave, 1 mi sw to Silver Strand Blvd, 4.5 mi s to Coronado Cays, then just e. Int corridors. **Pets:** Accepted. 🍴 ⌖M 🛍 ✕ 🛜 ✕ 🍴 💻

CORTE MADERA

✦✦✦ Marin Suites Hotel 🅷

(415) 924-3608. **$129-$329, 3 day notice.** 45 Tamal Vista Blvd 94925. US 101 exit Lucky Dr southbound, just w on Fifer Ave, 0.4 mi s; exit Tamalpais Rd/Paradise Dr northbound, 0.5 mi n on Madera Blvd (which becomes Tamal Vista Blvd). Ext corridors. **Pets:** $25 daily fee/pet. Designated rooms, supervision. [SAVE] ⌖M 🛍 ✕ 🛜 🎦 🍴 💻

COSTA MESA (Restaurants p. 615)

✦✦✦ Costa Mesa Marriott 🅷

(714) 957-1100. **$99-$259.** 500 Anton Blvd 92626. I-405 exit 9B (Bristol St), just n, then 0.3 mi e. Int corridors. **Pets:** Accepted.

[ECO] 🍴 ⌖M 🛍 🏊 ✕ 🍴 💻

✦✦✦✦ Crowne Plaza Costa Mesa Orange County 🅷

(714) 557-3000. **$109-$299.** 3131 S Bristol St 92626. I-405 exit 9B (Bristol St), just s. Int corridors. **Pets:** Accepted.

[SAVE] 🍴 🛍 🛜 ✕ 💻

✦✦✦ Hilton Orange County/Costa Mesa 🅷

(714) 540-7000. **$119-$299.** 3050 Bristol St 92626. I-405 exit 9B (Bristol St), just s. Int corridors. **Pets:** Accepted.

[ECO] 🍴 ⌖M 🛍 🏊 ✕ 🍴 💻

✦✦ Ramada Inn & Suites 🅷

(949) 645-2221. **$89-$299.** 1680 Superior Ave 92627. SR 55, just w of Newport Blvd at 17th St. Ext corridors. **Pets:** Accepted.

🍴 ⌖M 🛍 🛜 ✕ 💻

✦✦✦ Residence Inn by Marriott 🅷

(714) 241-8800. **$99-$249.** 881 W Baker St 92626. SR 55 exit 5B (Baker St), just w. Ext corridors. **Pets:** Other species. $100 one-time fee/room. Crate. [SAVE] [ECO] 🛍 🛜 ✕ 🍴 💻

✦✦✦ The Westin South Coast Plaza Hotel 🅷

(714) 540-2500. **Call for rates.** 686 Anton Blvd 92626. I-405 exit 9B (Bristol St), just n, then just e. Int corridors. **Pets:** Accepted.

[SAVE] [ECO] 🍴 ⌖M 🛍 🏊 ✕ 🍴 💻

CRESCENT CITY

✦✦✦ Anchor Beach Inn 🅼

(707) 464-2600. **$56-$178.** 880 Hwy US 101 S 95531. At Anchor Way; south end of town. Ext corridors. **Pets:** Accepted. [SAVE] 🛜 🍴 💻

CULVER CITY

✦✦✦ Four Points by Sheraton LA Westside 🅷

(310) 641-7740. **$179-$249.** 5990 Green Valley Cir 90230. I-405 exit 49 (Slauson Ave/Sepulveda Blvd), just ne. Int corridors. **Pets:** Accepted.

[SAVE] 🍴 ⌖M 🛍 🛜 ✕ 💻

CUPERTINO

✦✦✦ Aloft Cupertino 🅷

(408) 766-7000. **Call for rates.** 10165 N De Anza Blvd 95014. I-280 exit Sunnyvale-Saratoga Rd, just s. Int corridors. **Pets:** Accepted.

[SAVE] 🛜 ✕ 🍴 💻

✦✦✦✦ Cypress Hotel 🅷

(408) 253-8900. **Call for rates.** 10050 S De Anza Blvd 95014. I-280 exit De Anza Blvd, 0.7 mi s. Int corridors. **Pets:** Accepted.

[SAVE] [ECO] 🍴 ⌖M 🛍 ✕ 🛜 ✕ 🍴

CYPRESS

✦✦✦ HYATT house Cypress/Anaheim 🅷

(714) 828-4000. **$94-$249.** 5905 Corporate Ave 90630. I-605 exit 1D (Katella Ave) southbound; exit 1B (Katella Ave/Willow St) northbound, 3 mi e, 0.4 mi n on Valley View Ave, then just w. Int corridors. **Pets:** Accepted. [SAVE] 🛍 🛜 ✕ 🍴 💻

DANA POINT

✦✦✦ BEST WESTERN PLUS Marina Shores Hotel 🅷

(949) 248-1000. **$109-$219.** 34280 Pacific Coast Hwy 92629. I-5 exit 79 (Beach Cities Dr) northbound; exit 79 (Pacific Coast Hwy) southbound, 0.6 mi w, then 0.5 mi n. Ext/int corridors. **Pets:** Other species. $20 daily fee/room. Service with restrictions, crate.

[SAVE] ⌖M 🛍 🛜 ✕ 🍴 💻

✦✦✦ Blue Lantern Inn 🅱🅱

(949) 661-1304. **$200-$610, 7 day notice.** 34343 Street of Blue Lantern 92629. I-5 exit 79 (Pacific Coast Hwy) southbound; exit Beach Cities Dr northbound, 1.5 mi n on Pacific Coast Hwy, then just w. Int corridors. **Pets:** Dogs only. $65 one-time fee/room. Designated rooms, service with restrictions, supervision. ⌖M ✕ 🛜 ✕ 🍴 💻

✦✦✦ DoubleTree Suites by Hilton Doheny Beach-Dana Point 🅷

(949) 661-1100. **$139-$229.** 34402 Pacific Coast Hwy 92629. I-5 exit 79 (Beach Cities Dr) northbound; exit 79 (Pacific Coast Hwy) southbound, 0.6 mi w, U-turn at Doheny Park Plaza Dr, then 0.5 mi s. Int corridors. **Pets:** Accepted. [SAVE] [ECO] 🍴 🛍 🏊 ✕ 🍴 💻

AAA ◆◆◆◆ **The Ritz-Carlton, Laguna Niguel** H ❖

(949) 240-2000. **$445-$4000, 3 day notice.** One Ritz-Carlton Dr 92629. I-5 exit 79 (Pacific Coast Hwy) northbound, 3 mi n, then just w; exit 86 (Crown Valley Pkwy) southbound, 3 mi w, 1 mi s on Pacific Coast Hwy, then just w. Int corridors. **Pets:** $150 one-time fee/room, $50 daily fee/room. Designated rooms, service with restrictions.

SAVE ⑪ ♿ 🏊 ✕ 📶 ✕ ⬛ ▭

AAA ◆◆◆◆ **St. Regis Resort, Monarch Beach** H

(949) 234-3200. **$375-$895, 7 day notice.** One Monarch Beach Resort 92629. I-5 exit 79 (Pacific Coast Hwy) northbound, 3 mi n, then 0.5 mi e on Niguel Rd; exit 86 (Crown Valley Pkwy) southbound, 3 mi w, 1 mi s on Pacific Coast Hwy, then 0.5 mi e on Niguel Rd. Int corridors.
Pets: Accepted. SAVE ⑪ ♿ 🏊 ✕ 📶 ✕ ⬛

DANVILLE

AAA ◆◆◆ **BEST WESTERN Danville Sycamore Inn** H ❖

(925) 855-8888. **$95-$175.** 803 Camino Ramon 94526. I-680 exit 38 (Sycamore Valley Rd), just e, then just s. Ext/int corridors.
Pets: Medium. $15 daily fee/pet. Designated rooms, service with restrictions, supervision. SAVE ♿ 🏊 📶 ✕ ⬛ ▭

DAVIS

AAA ◆◆◆ **BEST WESTERN University Lodge** M

(530) 756-7890. **$110-$150.** 123 B St 95616. I-80 exit 72B (Richards Blvd) westbound; exit 72 eastbound, just nw to 1st St, just w to B St, then just n; at 2nd and B sts. Ext corridors. **Pets:** Medium. $15 daily fee/room. Service with restrictions, supervision.

SAVE 📶 ✕ ⬛ ▭

AAA ◆◆◆ **Hyatt Place UC Davis** H

(530) 756-9500. **$99-$239.** 173 Old Davis Rd Ext 95616. I-80 exit 71 (UC Davis), 0.6 mi ne; just n of jct Alumni Ln; follow signs for Mondavi Center. Int corridors. **Pets:** Accepted.

SAVE ⑪ ♿ 🏊 📶 ✕ ⬛ ▭

AAA ◆◆◆ **University Park Inn & Suites** H ❖

(530) 756-0910. **$120-$250.** 1111 Richards Blvd 95616. I-80 exit 72B (Richards Blvd) westbound; exit 72 eastbound, just nw. Ext corridors.
Pets: Medium. $15 daily fee/pet. Service with restrictions, supervision.

SAVE ♿ 🏊 📶 ✕ ⬛ ▭

DEATH VALLEY NATIONAL PARK

◆◆ **Stovepipe Wells Village** M

(760) 786-2387. **Call for rates.** 360 SR 190 92328. 24 mi nw of visitor center. Ext corridors. **Pets:** Accepted.

⑪ ♿ 🏊 📶 ✕ 🈯 ⬛ ▭

DELANO

AAA ◆◆ **BEST WESTERN Liberty Inn** M

(661) 725-0976. **$80-$250.** 14394 County Line Rd 93215. SR 99 exit 58 (County Line Rd), just e, then just n on Girard St. Int corridors.
Pets: Large, dogs only. $20 daily fee/room. Designated rooms, service with restrictions, supervision. SAVE 🏊 📶 ⬛ ▭

AAA ◆◆ **Rodeway Inn** M

(661) 725-1022. **$75-$139.** 2211 Girard St 93215. SR 99 exit 58 (County Line Rd), just e, then just s. Ext corridors. **Pets:** Accepted.

SAVE 🏊 📶 ⬛ ▭

DEL MAR (Restaurants p. 615)

◆◆◆ **Hilton San Diego Del Mar** H

(858) 792-5200. **$89-$369.** 15575 Jimmy Durante Blvd 92014. I-5 exit 36 (Via de la Valle), just w, then just s. Int corridors. **Pets:** Accepted.

⑪ ♿ 🏊 📶 ✕ ⬛ ▭

AAA ◆◆◆ **Hotel Indigo Del Mar** H ❖

(858) 755-1501. **$129-$309, 3 day notice.** 710 Camino Del Mar 92014. I-5 exit 34 (Del Mar Heights Rd), 1 mi w, then just n. Ext corridors.
Pets: Other species. $75 one-time fee/room. Service with restrictions.

SAVE ⑪ ♿ 🏊 ✕ ✕ ⬛ ▭

AAA ◆◆◆◆ **L'Auberge Del Mar** H ❖

(858) 259-1515. **$295-$720, 7 day notice.** 1540 Camino Del Mar 92014. I-5 exit 34 (Del Mar Heights Rd), 1 mi w, then 1 mi n. Int corridors. **Pets:** Small, dogs only. $100 one-time fee/room. Designated rooms, service with restrictions, supervision.

SAVE ECO ⑪ ♿ 🏊 📶 ✕ ⬛ ▭

DIAMOND BAR

◆◆◆ **Ayres Suites Diamond Bar** H

(909) 860-6290. **$99-$169.** 21951 Golden Springs Dr 91765. SR 57/60 exit 24B (Grand Ave), just s, then 0.5 mi w. Int corridors. **Pets:** Other species. $75 one-time fee/room. Service with restrictions, supervision.

🏊 📶 ⬛ ▭

DINUBA

◆◆◆ **Reedley Country Inn Bed & Breakfast** BB

(559) 638-2585. **$95-$105, 3 day notice.** 43137 Rd 52 93618. SR 99 exit 121 (Manning Ave), 10 mi e, then 1 mi s. Ext/int corridors.
Pets: Accepted. 📶

DIXON

AAA ◆◆◆ **BEST WESTERN PLUS Inn Dixon** H

(707) 678-1400. **$99-$200.** 1345 Commercial Way 95620. I-80 exit 64 (Pitt School Rd), just s, then just e on Stratford Ave, then just n. Ext/int corridors. **Pets:** Medium, dogs only. $15 daily fee/room. Designated rooms, service with restrictions, supervision.

SAVE ♿ 🏊 ✕ 📶 ⬛ ▭

◆◆◆ **Country Inn & Suites By Carlson, Dixon, CA-UC Davis Area** H

(707) 676-5000. **$79-$129.** 155 Dorset Dr 95620. I-80 exit 66A (Currey Rd) westbound, follow SR 113 S; exit 66 eastbound, just s on SR 113, then just w. Int corridors. **Pets:** Accepted.

♿ 🏊 📶 ✕ ⬛ ▭

DORRIS

AAA ◆ **Golden Eagle Motel** M

(530) 397-3114. **$39-$99.** 100 W 1st St 96023. US 97; center. Ext corridors. **Pets:** $6 daily fee/pet. Designated rooms, service with restrictions, supervision. SAVE 📶 ⬛

DOUGLAS CITY

AAA ◆◆◆ **Indian Creek Lodge** M

(530) 623-6294. **$72-$99, 3 day notice.** 59741 Hwy 299 W 96024. On SR 299, 1.5 mi e of jct SR 299 and CR 3. Ext corridors.
Pets: Accepted. SAVE 🏊 ✕ 📶 ✕ 🈯 ⬛ ▭

DOWNIEVILLE

◆◆ **Riverside Inn** M

(530) 289-1000. **$90-$185, 3 day notice.** 206 Commercial St (SR 49) 95936. On SR 49; center. Ext corridors. **Pets:** Other species. $15 one-time fee/pet. Service with restrictions, supervision.

📶 🈯 🈯 ⬛ ▭

DUBLIN

◆◆◆ **Holiday Inn Dublin** H

(925) 828-7750. **$99-$169.** 6680 Regional St 94568. I-580 exit San Ramon Rd, just n, just e on Dublin Blvd, then just s; northwest quadrant of I-580 and 680. Int corridors. **Pets:** Accepted.

⑪ ♿ 🏊 ✕ 📶 ✕ ⬛ ▭

AAA ◆◆◆ **Hyatt Place Dublin/Pleasanton** H

(925) 828-9006. **$79-$219.** 4950 Hacienda Dr 94568. I-580 exit Hacienda Dr, then n; in Hacienda Crossing Shopping Center. Int corridors.
Pets: Accepted. SAVE ♿ 🏊 📶 ✕ ⬛ ▭

◆◆◆ **La Quinta Inn & Suites Dublin - Pleasanton** H

(925) 828-9393. **$69-$279.** 6275 Dublin Blvd 94568. I-580 exit Hopyard/Dougherty Rd, just n. Int corridors. **Pets:** Large, other species. Service with restrictions. ♿ 🏊 📶 ⬛ ▭

DUNSMUIR

△△△ ▽▽▽ Oak Tree Inn 🅷
(530) 235-4100. **$65-$150.** 4000 Siskiyou Ave 96025. I-5 exit 732 (Siskiyou Ave), just e. Int corridors. **Pets:** Accepted.
[SAVE] 🍽 🛜 ✕ 🛢 🖵

EAST PALO ALTO

▽▽▽▽ Four Seasons Hotel Silicon Valley at East Palo Alto 🅷 🐾
(650) 566-1200. **$575-$795.** 2050 University Ave 94303. US 101 exit University Ave. Int corridors. **Pets:** Medium, other species. Service with restrictions. 🍽 ㋦ ㋡ ✕ 🛜 ✕ 🖵

EL CAJON

△△△ ▽▽▽ BEST WESTERN Courtesy Inn Ⓜ
(619) 440-7378. **$59-$119.** 1355 E Main St 92021. I-8 exit 19 (2nd St), 0.5 mi s, then just e. Ext corridors. **Pets:** Other species. $20 daily fee/room. Designated rooms, service with restrictions, supervision.
[SAVE] ㋦ 🛜 🛢 🖵

EL CENTRO

▽▽▽▽ TownePlace Suites by Marriott 🅷
(760) 370-3800. **$149-$169.** 3003 S Dogwood Rd 92243. I-8 exit 116 (Dogwood Rd), 0.5 mi s. Int corridors. **Pets:** Accepted.
㋦ ㋦ 🛜 ✕ 🛢 🖵

ELK

▽▽▽▽ Elk Cove Inn & Spa Ⓒ🅸 🐾
(707) 877-3321. **$100-$395, 14 day notice.** 6300 S Hwy 1 95432. On SR 1, 6.3 mi s of jct SR 128; just s of center. Ext/int corridors. **Pets:** Dogs only. Designated rooms, supervision.
🛜 ㋦ 🖉 🛢 🖵

ELK GROVE

▽▽▽▽ Extended Stay America-Sacramento-Elk Grove 🅷
(916) 683-3753. **Call for rates.** 2201 Longport Ct 95758. I-5 exit 508 (Laguna Blvd), 0.5 mi e, just s on Harbour Point Dr, then just w. Int corridors. **Pets:** Other species. $25 daily fee/pet. Service with restrictions, supervision. ㋦ 🛜 🛢 🖵

▽▽▽▽ Fairfield Inn & Suites by Marriott Sacramento Elk Grove 🅷
(916) 681-5400. **$99-$199.** 8058 Orchard Loop Ln 95624. SR 99 exit 289 (Cosumnes River Blvd/Calvine Rd), just e to Calvine Rd, then just s. Int corridors. **Pets:** Medium, other species. $100 one-time fee/room. Service with restrictions, crate. 🄴🄲🄾 ㋦ ㋦ 🛜 ✕ 🛢 🖵

▽▽▽▽ Holiday Inn Express & Suites 🅷
(916) 478-4000. **$99-$140.** 2460 Maritime Dr 95758. I-5 exit 506 (Elk Grove Blvd), just e to Harbour Point Dr, just n, then just w; SR 99 exit Elk Grove Blvd, 5 mi w, just n on Harbour Point Dr, then just w. Int corridors. **Pets:** Medium. $45 one-time fee/pet. Designated rooms, service with restrictions, crate. ㋦ ㋦ 🛜 ✕ 🛢 🖵

△△△ ▽▽▽▽ Holiday Inn Express Hotel & Suites 🅷
(916) 478-9000. **$99-$179.** 9175 W Stockton Blvd 95758. SR 99 exit 287 (Laguna Blvd), just w, then just n; in Laguna Gateway Shopping Center. Int corridors. **Pets:** Accepted.
[SAVE] ㋦ ㋦ 🛜 ✕ 🛢 🖵

EL MONTE

△△△ ▽▽▽ Americas Best Value Inn & Suites Ⓜ
(626) 442-8354. **$90-$110.** 12040 Garvey Ave 91732. I-10 exit 30 (Garvey Ave) westbound, just w; exit 29A (Peck Rd) eastbound, just s to Garvey Ave, then 0.6 mi e. Ext corridors. **Pets:** Small. $20 daily fee/pet. Designated rooms, service with restrictions, supervision.
[SAVE] ㋦ 🛜 ✕ 🛢 🖵

EL PORTAL

△△△ ▽▽▽▽ Yosemite View Lodge 🅷
(209) 379-2681. **$95-$499, 7 day notice.** 11136 Hwy 140 95318. Just w of Yosemite National Park West Gate. Ext corridors. **Pets:** Other species. $11 daily fee/pet. Service with restrictions, supervision.
[SAVE] 🍽 ㋦ ㋦ 🛟 ✕ 🛢 🖵

EL SEGUNDO *(Restaurants p. 615)*

▽▽▽▽ Embassy Suites-LAX South 🅷
(310) 640-3600. **$119-$259.** 1440 E Imperial Ave 90245. I-405 exit 45B (Imperial Hwy), 1.6 mi w. Int corridors. **Pets:** Accepted.
🎛 🍽 ㋦ ㋦ 🛟 🛢 🖵

▽▽▽ Extended Stay America-Los Angeles-LAX Airport-El Segundo Ⓜ
(310) 607-4000. **Call for rates.** 1910 E Mariposa Ave 90245. I-105 exit 1B (Sepulveda Blvd), 1 mi s. Ext corridors. **Pets:** Other species. $25 daily fee/pet. Service with restrictions, supervision. ㋦ 🛜 🛢 🖵

△△△ ▽▽▽▽ HYATT house Los Angeles LAX/El Segundo 🅷
(310) 725-0100. **$109-$299.** 810 S Douglas St 90245. I-405 exit 43 (Rosecrans Ave), 0.5 mi e, then just n. Ext corridors. **Pets:** Accepted.
[SAVE] ㋦ ㋦ 🛜 ✕ 🛢 🖵

△△△ ▽▽▽▽ Hyatt Place Los Angeles/LAX/El Segundo 🅷
(310) 322-2880. **$94-$239.** 750 N Nash St 90245. I-105 exit Nash St, just s. Int corridors. **Pets:** Medium, dogs only. $175 one-time fee/room. Designated rooms, service with restrictions, supervision.
[SAVE] 🍽 ㋦ ㋦ 🛜 ✕ 🛢 🖵

▽▽▽▽ Residence Inn by Marriott-LAX/El Segundo 🅷
(310) 333-0888. **$149-$299.** 2135 E El Segundo Blvd 90245. I-405 exit 44 (El Segundo Blvd), 1.4 mi w. Int corridors. **Pets:** Accepted.
㋦ ㋦ 🛜 ✕ 🛢 🖵

EMERYVILLE

△△△ ▽▽▽▽ HYATT house Emeryville/San Francisco Bay Area 🅷
(510) 601-5880. **$139-$299.** 5800 Shellmound St 94608. I-80 exit Powell St, just e. Int corridors. **Pets:** Accepted.
[SAVE] 🍽 ㋦ ㋦ 🛜 ✕ 🛢 🖵

ENCINITAS

△△△ ▽▽▽▽ BEST WESTERN Encinitas Inn & Suites at Moonlight Beach 🅷
(760) 942-7455. **$109-$249.** 85 Encinitas Blvd 92024. I-5 exit 41B (Encinitas Blvd), just w. Ext corridors. **Pets:** Accepted.
[SAVE] ㋦ 🛜 🛢 🖵

△△△ ▽▽▽ Econo Lodge Moonlight Beach Encinitas Ⓜ
(760) 436-4999. **$75-$299.** 410 N Coast Hwy 101 92024. I-5 exit 41B (Encinitas Blvd), 0.6 mi w, then 0.6 mi n. Ext/int corridors. **Pets:** Small. $25 daily fee/pet. Designated rooms, service with restrictions, supervision. [SAVE] ㋦ 🛜 ✕ 🛢 🖵

△△△ ▽▽▽ Howard Johnson Encinitas near LEGOLAND Ⓜ
(760) 944-3800. **$79-$150.** 607 Leucadia Blvd 92024. I-5 exit 43 (Leucadia Blvd), just e. Ext corridors. **Pets:** Accepted.
[SAVE] ㋦ 🛜 🛢 🖵

ESCONDIDO *(Restaurants p. 615)*

△△△ ▽▽▽▽ BEST WESTERN Escondido Hotel 🅷
(760) 740-1700. **$110-$230.** 1700 Seven Oakes Rd 92026. I-15 exit 33 (El Norte Pkwy), just e, then just n. Int corridors. **Pets:** Small, other species. $25 one-time fee/pet. Service with restrictions, supervision.
[SAVE] ㋦ 🛜 🛢 🖵

▽▽▽ Comfort Inn San Diego/Escondido 🅷
(760) 489-1010. **$95-$139.** 1290 W Valley Pkwy 92029. I-15 exit 31 (Valley Pkwy), just w. Int corridors. **Pets:** $25 daily fee/pet. Designated rooms, service with restrictions, supervision. ㋦ ㋦ 🛜 🛢 🖵

WW Escondido Lodge M
(760) 743-9733. **Call for rates.** 2650 S Escondido Blvd 92025. I-15 exit 29 (Felicita Rd/Citracado Pkwy), 0.8 mi e on Citracado Pkwy, then just s; on frontage road, just past Centre City Pkwy. Ext corridors. **Pets:** Accepted. 🐾 📶 🛗 🖵

EUREKA

AAA WW BEST WESTERN PLUS Bayshore Inn H ❖
(707) 268-8005. **$99-$210.** 3500 Broadway 95503. Jct US 101 and Truesdale St; south end of town. Ext corridors. **Pets:** Large, dogs only. $20 daily fee/room. Designated rooms, supervision.
SAVE 🍴 🐾 ✕ 📶 🛗 🖵

AAA WW Eureka Town House Motel M
(707) 443-4536. **$60-$150.** 933 4th St 95501. On US 101 southbound at K St. Ext corridors. **Pets:** Medium, dogs only. $10 daily fee/pet. Designated rooms, service with restrictions, supervision.
SAVE 📶 ✕ 🛗 🖵

AAA WW Quality Inn Eureka M
(707) 443-1601. **$75-$195.** 1209 4th St 95501. On US 101 southbound; between M and N sts. Ext corridors. **Pets:** Accepted.
SAVE 🐾 ✕ 🛗 🖵

WWW Red Lion Hotel Eureka H
(707) 445-0844. **Call for rates.** 1929 4th St 95501. On US 101 southbound; between T and V sts. Int corridors. **Pets:** Accepted.
🍴 🔊 🐾 📶 ✕ 🛗 🖵

FAIRFIELD

WW Extended Stay America-Fairfield-Napa Valley H
(707) 438-0932. **Call for rates.** 1019 Oliver Rd 94534. I-80 eastbound exit Fairfield/West Texas St, follow signs for Rockville Rd, just w, go under the overpass, then just n; westbound exit 44, West Texas St/Rockville Rd, just s. Int corridors. **Pets:** Other species. $25 daily fee/pet. Service with restrictions, supervision. 🔊 📶 🛗 🖵

WWW Staybridge Suites Fairfield-Napa Valley Area H
(707) 863-0900. **Call for rates.** 4775 Business Center Dr 94534. I-80 exit 41 (Green Valley Rd/Suisun Valley Rd), n on Green Valley Rd, then just e. Int corridors. **Pets:** Accepted. 🔊 🐾 📶 ✕ 🛗 🖵

FALLBROOK *(Restaurants p. 615)*

WWW Quality Inn M
(760) 723-2888. **$45-$299.** 3135 S Old Hwy 395 92028. I-15 exit 46 (SR 76/Pala Rd/Oceanside), just w, then 0.5 mi n. Ext/int corridors. **Pets:** Medium, dogs only. $25 daily fee/room. Designated rooms, service with restrictions, supervision. 🍴 🐾 📶 ✕ 🛗 🖵

FALL RIVER MILLS

AAA WW Hi-Mont Motel M ❖
(530) 336-5541. **$65-$150.** 43021 Bridge St 96028. 0.4 mi sw on SR 299; jct SR 299 E and Bridge St. Ext corridors. **Pets:** Other species. $15 daily fee/pet. Service with restrictions, supervision.
SAVE 🔊 📶 ✕ 🛗 🖵

FERNDALE

WWW Shaw House Inn BB
(707) 786-9958. **Call for rates.** 703 Main St 95536. Center. Ext/int corridors. **Pets:** Accepted. 📶 ✕ 🎾 🐾

FILLMORE

AAA WW BEST WESTERN La Posada Motel M
(805) 524-0440. **$102-$122.** 827 Ventura St 93015. On SR 126. Ext corridors. **Pets:** $20 one-time fee/room. Designated rooms, service with restrictions, crate. SAVE 🐾 📶 🛗 🖵

FIREBAUGH

AAA WW BEST WESTERN Apricot Inn H
(559) 659-1444. **$90-$140.** 46290 W Panoche Rd 93622. I-5 exit W Panoche Rd, just w. Ext corridors. **Pets:** Medium, other species. $20 one-time fee/room. Service with restrictions, supervision.
SAVE 🔊 🐾 📶 🛗 🖵

FISH CAMP

AAA WWW The Cottages at Tenaya Lodge H ❖
(559) 683-6555. **$159-$455, 7 day notice.** 1122 Hwy 41 93623. 2 mi from Yosemite National Park South Gate. Ext corridors. **Pets:** Dogs only. $75 one-time fee/room. Designated rooms, service with restrictions, supervision. SAVE ECO 🔊 🐾 📶 ✕ 🛗 🖵

WW The Narrow Gauge Inn CI ❖
(559) 683-7720. **$79-$369, 4 day notice.** 48571 Hwy 41 93623. 4 mi from Yosemite National Park South Gate. **Pets:** Medium, dogs only. $25 one-time fee/pet. Designated rooms, service with restrictions. 🍴 🐾 📶 ✕ 🖵

AAA WWWW Tenaya Lodge at Yosemite H ❖
(559) 683-6555. **$129-$450, 7 day notice.** 1122 Hwy 41 93623. 2 mi from Yosemite National Park South Gate. Int corridors. **Pets:** Dogs only. $75 one-time fee/room. Designated rooms, service with restrictions, supervision. SAVE ECO 🍴 🔊 🐾 ✕ 📶 ✕ 🛗 🖵

FOLSOM *(Restaurants p. 616)*

AAA WWW Lake Natoma Inn Hotel & Conference Center H ❖
(916) 351-1500. **$89-$169.** 702 Gold Lake Dr 95630. US 50 exit Folsom Blvd, 3 mi n, then 0.5 mi e on Riley St; behind The Lakes Specialty Shopping Center. Int corridors. **Pets:** $45 one-time fee/room, $15 daily fee/pet. Service with restrictions, supervision.
SAVE 🍴 🔊 🐾 ✕ 📶 ✕ 🛗 🖵

AAA WWW Larkspur Landing Folsom H
(916) 355-1616. **Call for rates.** 121 Iron Point Rd 95630. US 50 exit Folsom Blvd, 0.5 mi n to Iron Point Rd, then 0.3 mi e. Int corridors. **Pets:** Accepted. SAVE ECO 🔊 📶 ✕ 🛗 🖵

WWW Residence Inn by Marriott H
(916) 983-7289. **$149-$199.** 2555 Iron Point Rd 95630. US 50 exit E Bidwell St, just n, then just w. Int corridors. **Pets:** Medium, other species. $100 one-time fee/room. Service with restrictions, supervision.
🔊 📶 ✕ 🛗 🖵

FORT BRAGG

AAA WWW Beachcomber Motel M ❖
(707) 964-2402. **$119-$269, 3 day notice.** 1111 N Main St 95437. 1 mi n on SR 1. Ext corridors. **Pets:** Other species. $20 daily fee/room. Designated rooms, service with restrictions, supervision.
SAVE 🐾 ✕ 🎾 🛗 🖵

AAA WWW Beach House Inn M ❖
(707) 961-1700. **$89-$199.** 100 Pudding Creek Rd 95437. 0.7 mi n on SR 1. Int corridors. **Pets:** $10 daily fee/room. Designated rooms, service with restrictions, supervision. SAVE 🔊 ✕ 🎾 🛗 🖵

WW Coast Inn and Spa M
(707) 964-2852. **$80-$390, 3 day notice.** 18661 N Hwy 1 95437. 0.3 mi s of SR 20. Ext corridors. **Pets:** Large, dogs only. $20 daily fee/pet. Designated rooms, service with restrictions, supervision.
🔊 ✕ 🎾 🛗 🖵

AAA WWWW Emerald Dolphin Inn & Mini Golf H ❖
(707) 964-6699. **$74-$205, 7 day notice.** 1211 S Main St 95437. On SR 1; at Harbor View Dr. Ext corridors. **Pets:** Dogs only. $15 daily fee/room. Designated rooms, service with restrictions, supervision.
SAVE 🐾 ✕ 🔊 ✕ 🛗 🖵

AAA WWW Holiday Inn Express H
(707) 964-1100. **Call for rates.** 250 Hwy 20 95437. On SR 20, just e of jct SR 1. Ext/int corridors. **Pets:** Accepted.
SAVE 🐾 🐾 🔊 ✕ 🛗 🖵

▼▼ Super 8 Fort Bragg Ⓜ ❀
(707) 964-4003. **$75-$137.** 888 S Main St 95437. 0.5 mi s on SR 1; north end of Noyo River Bridge. Ext corridors. **Pets:** Other species. $10 daily fee/pet. Designated rooms, service with restrictions, supervision.
ⒺⒸⓄ ⒼⓂ 🛜 ✕ 🖥 💻

ⒶⒶⒶ ▼▼▼▼ Surf & Sand Lodge Ⓜ ❀
(707) 964-9383. **$109-$349, 3 day notice.** 1131 N Main St 95437. 1 mi n on SR 1. Int corridors. **Pets:** $20 daily fee/room. Designated rooms, supervision. 🆂🅰🆅🅴 ⒼⓂ 🛜 ✕ 🅰🅲 🖥 💻

ⒶⒶⒶ ▼▼▼ Surf Motel & Gardens Ⓜ
(707) 964-5361. **$59-$275, 3 day notice.** 1220 S Main St 95437. On SR 1; jct Oceanview Dr. Ext corridors. **Pets:** Other species. $15 daily fee/pet. Designated rooms, supervision. 🆂🅰🆅🅴 🛜 🅰🅲 🖥 💻

▼▼▼ Weller House Inn ⒷⒷ
(707) 964-4415. **Call for rates.** 524 Stewart St 95437. Just w of SR 1 on Pine St, just n. Int corridors. **Pets:** Accepted.
🛜 ✕ 🅰🅲 🆆 🅿 🖥 💻

FORTUNA

ⒶⒶⒶ ▼▼▼ BEST WESTERN Country Inn Ⓜ
(707) 725-6822. **$69-$130.** 2025 Riverwalk Dr 95540. US 101 exit 687 (Kenmar Rd), just w. Ext corridors. **Pets:** Dogs only. $20 one-time fee/ pet. Designated rooms, service with restrictions, supervision.
🆂🅰🆅🅴 ⒼⓂ 🛀 🛜 ✕ 🖥 💻

▼▼ Fortuna Super 8 Ⓜ
(707) 725-2888. **$80-$145.** 1805 Alamar Way 95540. US 101 exit 687 (Kenmar Rd), just w, then just n. Ext corridors. **Pets:** Accepted.
🛜 🖥 💻

▼▼ The Redwood Fortuna Riverwalk Hotel ⒽⒽ
(707) 725-5500. **$89-$169.** 1859 Alamar Way 95540. US 101 exit 687 (Kenmar Rd), just w, then just n. Ext corridors. **Pets:** Medium, other species. $25 one-time fee/room. Designated rooms, service with restrictions, crate. 🛜 ✕ 🖥 💻

FOUNTAIN VALLEY

ⒶⒶⒶ ▼▼▼▼ Residence Inn by Marriott ⒽⒽ
(714) 965-8000. **$149-$329.** 9930 Slater Ave 92708. I-405 exit 14 (Brookhurst St), just n, then just w. Ext corridors. **Pets:** Accepted.
🆂🅰🆅🅴 🛀 🛜 ✕ 🖥 💻

FREMONT *(Restaurants p. 616)*

ⒶⒶⒶ ▼▼▼▼ BEST WESTERN PLUS Garden Court Inn ⒽⒽ
(510) 792-4300. **$109-$239.** 5400 Mowry Ave 94538. I-880 exit Mowry Ave, just e. Int corridors. **Pets:** Accepted.
🆂🅰🆅🅴 ⒼⓂ 🛜 ✕ 🖥 💻

▼▼▼▼ Comfort Inn by Choice Hotels ⒽⒽ
(510) 490-2900. **$105-$150.** 47031 Kato Rd 94538. I-880 exit Warren Ave/Mission Blvd E, just e. Int corridors. **Pets:** Accepted.
ⒼⓂ 🛀 🛜 🖥 💻

ⒶⒶⒶ ▼▼▼▼ Hyatt Place Fremont/Silicon Valley ⒽⒽ ❀
(510) 623-6000. **$79-$269.** 3101 W Warren Ave 94538. I-880 exit Warren Ave, just w. Int corridors. **Pets:** Medium. $175 one-time fee/room. Service with restrictions, supervision.
🆂🅰🆅🅴 ⒼⓂ 🛀 🛜 ✕ 🖥 💻

▼▼▼▼ La Quinta Inn & Suites Fremont ⒽⒽ
(510) 445-0808. **$89-$239.** 46200 Landing Pkwy 94538. I-880 exit Fremont Blvd/Cushing Pkwy, just w. Int corridors. **Pets:** Large, other species. Service with restrictions. ⒼⓂ 🛀 🛜 🖥 💻

▼▼▼▼ Residence Inn by Marriott ⒽⒽ
(510) 794-5900. **$199-$329.** 5400 Farwell Pl 94536. I-880 exit Mowry Ave, just w. Ext corridors. **Pets:** Accepted.
ⒼⓂ 🛀 🛜 ✕ 🖥 💻

FRESNO

ⒶⒶⒶ ▼▼▼▼ BEST WESTERN Village Inn ⒽⒽ
(559) 226-2110. **$79-$229.** 3110 N Blackstone Ave 93703. SR 41 exit 130 (Shields Ave), 0.3 mi w. Int corridors. **Pets:** Other species. $20 daily fee/room. Designated rooms, service with restrictions, crate.
🆂🅰🆅🅴 🛀 🛜 ✕ 🖥 💻

▼▼▼ Extended Stay America Fresno-North ⒽⒽ
(559) 438-7105. **Call for rates.** 7135 N Fresno St 93720. SR 41 exit Herndon Ave, just e, then just n. Ext corridors. **Pets:** Other species. $25 daily fee/pet. Service with restrictions, supervision.
ⒼⓂ 🛜 🖥 💻

ⒶⒶⒶ ▼▼▼▼ La Quinta Inn & Suites Fresno Northwest ⒽⒽ
(559) 275-3700. **$89-$229.** 5077 N Cornelia Ave 93722. SR 99 exit Shaw Ave, just e, then just n. Int corridors. **Pets:** Large, other species. Service with restrictions. 🆂🅰🆅🅴 ⒼⓂ 🛀 🛜 ✕ 🖥 💻

ⒶⒶⒶ ▼▼▼▼ La Quinta Inn & Suites Fresno Riverpark ⒽⒽ
(559) 449-0928. **$99-$304.** 330 E Fir Ave 93720. SR 41 exit Herndon Ave, just e, just n on Fresno St, then just w. Int corridors. **Pets:** Large, other species. Service with restrictions.
🆂🅰🆅🅴 ⒼⓂ 🛀 🛜 ✕ 🖥 💻

▼▼▼▼ La Quinta Inn Fresno Yosemite ⒽⒽ
(559) 442-1110. **$69-$199.** 2926 Tulare St 93721. SR 99 exit Fresno St, 1 mi e to R St, just s, then just e. Ext/int corridors. **Pets:** Large, other species. Service with restrictions. ⒼⓂ 🛀 🛜 🖥 💻

ⒶⒶⒶ ▼▼▼▼ Park Inn by Radisson Fresno ⒽⒽ
(559) 226-2200. **$90-$160.** 3737 N Blackstone Ave 93726. SR 41 exit 130 (Shields Ave), 0.3 mi w, then just n; jct Dakota Ave. Int corridors. **Pets:** Accepted. 🆂🅰🆅🅴 🍽 ⒼⓂ 🛀 🛜 ✕ 🖥 💻

▼▼▼▼ Piccadilly Inn-Shaw ⒽⒽ ❀
(559) 348-5520. **$89-$189.** 2305 W Shaw Ave 93711. SR 99 exit Shaw Ave, 3 mi e; jct Sequoia Dr. Ext/int corridors. **Pets:** Small, dogs only. $100 deposit/room, $15 daily fee/room. Designated rooms, service with restrictions, supervision. 🍽 ⒼⓂ 🛀 🛜 🖥 💻

▼▼▼▼ Residence Inn by Marriott ⒽⒽ
(559) 222-8900. **$98-$170.** 5322 N Diana St 93710. SR 41 exit 132 (Shaw Ave), 0.3 mi w, 0.5 mi n on Blackstone Ave, just e on Barstow Ave, then just s. Int corridors. **Pets:** Accepted.
ⒺⒸⓄ ⒼⓂ 🛀 🛜 ✕ 🖥 💻

ⒶⒶⒶ ▼▼▼ Rodeway Inn ⒽⒽ
(559) 431-3557. **$60-$90.** 6730 N Blackstone Ave 93710. SR 41 exit Herndon Ave, just w, then s. Ext corridors. **Pets:** Accepted.
🆂🅰🆅🅴 🛀 🛜 🖥 💻

▼▼▼▼ TownePlace Suites by Marriott ⒽⒽ ❀
(559) 435-4600. **$99-$179.** 7127 N Fresno St 93720. SR 41 exit Herndon Ave, just e, then just n. Int corridors. **Pets:** Other species. $100 one-time fee/room. Service with restrictions, crate.
ⒼⓂ 🛀 🛜 ✕ 🖥 💻

FULLERTON

ⒶⒶⒶ ▼▼▼▼ Fullerton Marriott Hotel at California State University ⒽⒽ
(714) 738-7800. **$109-$209.** 2701 E Nutwood Ave 92831. SR 57 exit 7 (Nutwood Ave) northbound; exit 7 (Nutwood Ave/Chapman Ave) southbound, just w. Int corridors. **Pets:** Small. $100 one-time fee/room. Service with restrictions.
🆂🅰🆅🅴 ⒺⒸⓄ 🍽 ⒼⓂ 🛀 🗮 🛜 ✕ 🖥 💻

GARBERVILLE *(Restaurants p. 616)*

▼▼▼▼ Benbow Historic Inn ⒽⒽ ❀
(707) 923-2124. **$125-$595, 5 day notice.** 445 Lake Benbow Dr 95542. US 101 exit 636 (Benbow Lake Rd), just w. Ext/int corridors. **Pets:** Medium. $30 deposit/room. Designated rooms, supervision.
🍽 🛀 🗮 🛜 ✕ 🖥 💻

 BEST WESTERN PLUS Humboldt House Inn 🅜 ❀

(707) 923-2771. **$115-$165.** 701 Redwood Dr 95542. US 101 exit Garberville, just e. Ext corridors. **Pets:** Medium, dogs only. $15 one-time fee/pet. Designated rooms, service with restrictions, supervision.

[SAVE] 🐾 🛜 🛗 💻

GARDEN GROVE

Anaheim Marriott Suites 🄷

(714) 750-1000. **$126-$329.** 12015 Harbor Blvd 92840. I-5 exit 107B (Chapman Ave) northbound, 1.5 mi w, then just s; exit 107C (State College/The City Dr) southbound, just s on State College Blvd, 1.5 mi w on Chapman Ave, then just s. Int corridors. **Pets:** Accepted.

🍽 ♿ 🐾 ❎ 📶 ❎ 🛗 💻

Candlewood Suites Garden Grove/Anaheim Area 🄷

(714) 539-4200. **$79-$149.** 12901 Garden Grove Blvd 92843. SR 22 exit 13 (Haster St) westbound; exit 13 (Fairview St) eastbound, just n, then just w. Int corridors. **Pets:** Large, other species. $10 daily fee/room. Designated rooms, service with restrictions, supervision.

♿ 🛜 ❎ 🛗 💻

Hyatt Regency Orange County Near Disneyland Resort 🄷

(714) 750-1234. **$89-$279.** 11999 Harbor Blvd 92840. I-5 exit 107B (Chapman Ave) northbound, 1.5 mi w, then just s; exit 107C (State College Blvd/The City Dr) southbound, just s on State College Blvd, then 1.5 mi w on Chapman Ave. Int corridors. **Pets:** Accepted.

[SAVE] [ECO] 🍽 ♿ 🐾 ❎ 📶 🛗 💻

Residence Inn by Marriott Anaheim Resort Area 🄷

(714) 591-4000. **$129-$199.** 11931 Harbor Blvd 92840. I-5 exit 107B (Chapman Ave) northbound, 1.5 mi w, then just n; exit 107C (State College Blvd/The City Dr) southbound, just s on State College Blvd, 1.5 mi w on Chapman Ave, then just n. Int corridors. **Pets:** Accepted.

♿ 🐾 ❎ 🛜 ❎ 🛗 💻

Sheraton Garden Grove Anaheim South 🄷

(714) 703-8400. **$99-$249.** 12221 Harbor Blvd 92840. I-5 exit 110 (Harbor Blvd/Ball Rd), 2.2 mi s. Int corridors. **Pets:** Accepted.

[SAVE] 🍽 🐾 📶 ❎ 🛗 💻

GEYSERVILLE *(Restaurants p. 616)*

Geyserville Inn 🄷 ❀

(707) 857-4343. **$109-$499, 3 day notice.** 21714 Geyserville Ave 95441. US 101 exit E Canyon Rd, just s. Ext/int corridors. **Pets:** Dogs only. $25 daily fee/room. Designated rooms, service with restrictions, supervision. [SAVE] 🍽 ♿ 🐾 🛜 ❎ 🛗 💻

GILROY

BEST WESTERN PLUS Forest Park Inn 🄷 ❀

(408) 848-5144. **$100-$300.** 375 Leavesley Rd 95020. US 101 exit Leavesley Rd, just w. Int corridors. **Pets:** Medium, dogs only. $20 daily fee/pet. Designated rooms, service with restrictions, supervision.

[SAVE] ♿ 🐾 ❎ 🛜 ❎ 🛗 💻

Quality Inn & Suites 🄷

(408) 847-5500. **$79-$239.** 8430 Murray Ave 95020. US 101 exit Leavesley Rd, just e. Ext corridors. **Pets:** Accepted.

[SAVE] 🐾 🛜 🛗 💻

GLENDALE

Hilton Los Angeles North/Glendale 🄷

(818) 956-5466. **$169-$229.** 100 W Glenoaks Blvd 91202. SR 134 exit 7B (Brand Blvd), just n, then just w. Int corridors. **Pets:** Accepted.

[SAVE] [ECO] 🍽 ♿ 🐾 ❎ 🛜 🛗 💻

GLEN ELLEN

Gaige House, A Four Sisters Inn 🄷

(707) 935-0237. **$275-$595, 7 day notice.** 13540 Arnold Dr 95442. SR 12 exit Arnold Dr, 0.5 mi w. Ext/int corridors. **Pets:** Dogs only. $65 one-time fee/room. Designated rooms, service with restrictions, supervision.

🐾 🛜 ❎ 🛗 💻

GRAEAGLE

Chalet View Lodge 🄷

(530) 832-5528. **$89-$315, 7 day notice.** 72056 Hwy 70 96103. Jct SR 70 and 89, 5.7 mi e on SR 70. Ext corridors. **Pets:** Other species. $25 daily fee/room. Designated rooms, service with restrictions, supervision.

🍽 🐾 ❎ 🛜 ❎ 🛗 💻

GRASS VALLEY

BEST WESTERN Gold Country Inn 🅜

(530) 273-1393. **$99-$179.** 972 Sutton Way 95945. SR 20 and 49 exit 183 (Brunswick Rd), just e, then just n; midway between Grass Valley and Nevada City. Ext corridors. **Pets:** Accepted.

[SAVE] 🐾 🛜 🛗 💻

The Gold Miners Inn Holiday Inn Express & Suites 🄷 ❀

(530) 477-1700. **$109-$249.** 121 Bank St 95945. SR 49 exit 182A (SR 174/Colfax Ave/Central Grass Valley) northbound; exit 182B (E Main St/Grass Valley) southbound, just n on Auburn St, then just e. Int corridors. **Pets:** Other species. $60 one-time fee/room. Service with restrictions, crate. ♿ 🛜 ❎ 🛗 💻

Grass Valley Courtyard Suites Spa & Conference Center 🄷 ❀

(530) 272-7696. **$159-$300, 3 day notice.** 210 N Auburn St 95945. SR 49 exit 182A (SR 174/Colfax Ave/Central Grass Valley) northbound, just w to S Auburn St, then just n; exit 182B (E Main St/Grass Valley) southbound, just n to E Main St, just w to S Auburn St, then just n; just n of jct Richardson St. Ext corridors. **Pets:** Dogs only. $50 one-time fee/pet. Service with restrictions, supervision.

♿ 🐾 ❎ 🛜 ❎ 🛗 💻

Swan Levine House 🄱🄱

(530) 272-1873. **$110-$120, 3 day notice.** 328 S Church St 95945. SR 49 exit 182A (SR 174/Colfax Ave/Central Grass Valley) southbound, just n on S Auburn St, just nw on Neal St, then just sw; exit 182B (E Main St/Grass Valley) southbound, just nw on Neal St, just sw from jct Walsh St. Int corridors. **Pets:** $15 one-time fee/room. Supervision.

🛜 ❎ 🅆 🆉

GUALALA

Gualala Country Inn 🅜

(707) 884-4343. **$83-$190, 3 day notice.** 47975 Center St 95445. Just n of jct Old State Hwy; on SR 1. Ext/int corridors. **Pets:** Other species. $10 one-time fee/pet. Service with restrictions, supervision.

[SAVE] 🛜 ❎ 🄺 🛗 💻

North Coast Country Inn 🄱🄱

(707) 884-4537. **$185-$235, 3 day notice.** 34591 S Hwy 1 95445. On SR 1, 4.5 mi n; jct Fish Rock Rd. Ext corridors. **Pets:** Accepted.

🛜 ❎ 🄺 🅆 🆉 🛗 💻

Surf Motel 🅜

(707) 884-3571. **$99-$299, 3 day notice.** 39170 S Hwy 1 95445. Center. Ext/int corridors. **Pets:** Accepted. [SAVE] 🛜 ❎ 🄺 🛗 💻

GUERNEVILLE

Cottages on River Road 🄲🄰

(707) 869-3848. **Call for rates.** 14880 River Rd 95446. 1.6 mi ne of jct SR 116. Ext corridors. **Pets:** Accepted.

🐾 🛜 ❎ 🄺 🆉 🛗 💻

Ferngrove Cottages 🄲🄰 ❀

(707) 869-8105. **$109-$289, 14 day notice.** 16650 Hwy 116 95446. Just w of downtown. Ext corridors. **Pets:** $25 daily fee/pet. Designated rooms, service with restrictions, supervision.

[SAVE] 🐾 🛜 ❎ 🄺 🆉 🛗 💻

▼▼▼▼ West Sonoma Inn & Spa 🅲🅰
(707) 869-2470. **$149-$299, 30 day notice.** 14100 Brookside Ln 95446. Just n of SR 116; on west end of downtown. Ext corridors. **Pets:** Dogs only. $25 daily fee/pet. Designated rooms, service with restrictions, supervision. 🔁 🛜 ✖ 🅰 🔌 💻

HALF MOON BAY *(Restaurants p. 616)*

◈◈◈ ▼▼▼ Coastside Inn Half Moon Bay 🄷
(650) 726-3400. **$107-$240.** 230 S Cabrillo Hwy 94019. On SR 1, just s of SR 92. Ext corridors. **Pets:** Other species. $35 daily fee/pet. Designated rooms, supervision. 〔SAVE〕 〔ECO〕 🔁 🛜 ✖ 🔌 💻

▼▼▼ Half Moon Bay Lodge 🄷
(650) 726-9000. **Call for rates.** 2400 Cabrillo Hwy S 94019. 2.5 mi s of jct SR 1 and 92, just w. Ext corridors. **Pets:** Accepted.
🔁 🔁 ✖ 🛜 ✖ 🔌 🔌 💻

◈◈◈ ▼▼▼ Harbor View Inn 🅼
(650) 726-2329. **$78-$378.** 51 Ave Alhambra 94018. SR 1 exit Capistrano Ave, just e; 4 mi n of jct SR 92. Ext corridors. **Pets:** Accepted.
〔SAVE〕 🔁 🛜 ✖ 🔌 🔌 💻

▼▼▼▼ Landis Shores Oceanfront Inn 🅱🅱 ❀
(650) 726-6642. **$230-$350, 7 day notice.** 211 Mirada Rd 94019. 3 mi n of jct SR 1 and 92 to Medio Ave, just w, then just n. Int corridors. **Pets:** Medium, dogs only. $30 daily fee/pet. Designated rooms, service with restrictions, supervision. 🔁 🛜 ✖ 🔌 🔌

◈◈◈ ▼▼▼▼ The Ritz-Carlton, Half Moon
Bay 🄷 ❀
(650) 712-7000. **$545-$4500, 3 day notice.** 1 Miramontes Point Rd 94019. 2.5 mi s of jct SR 1 (Cabrillo Hwy S) and 92, 0.8 mi w. Int corridors. **Pets:** Dogs only. $150 one-time fee/room, $50 daily fee/room. Designated rooms, service with restrictions, supervision.
〔SAVE〕 🍴 🔁 🔁 ✖ 🛜 ✖ 🔌 💻

HANFORD

◈◈◈ ▼▼▼ Sequoia Inn 🄷
(559) 582-0338. **$81-$100.** 1655 Mall Dr 93230. SR 198 exit 12th Ave, just n, then just e. Int corridors. **Pets:** Other species. $30 one-time fee/room. Service with restrictions, supervision.
〔SAVE〕 🔁 🛜 ✖ 🔌 💻

HAWTHORNE

▼▼▼▼ Candlewood Suites LAX Hawthorne 🄷 ❀
(310) 973-3331. **$109-$159, 3 day notice.** 14110 Hawthorne Blvd 90250. I-105 exit 3 (Hawthorne Blvd/Prairie Ave), 0.6 mi s. Int corridors. **Pets:** Small. $150 deposit/room, $150 one-time fee/pet. Service with restrictions, supervision. 🔁 🛜 ✖ 🔌 💻

◈◈◈ ▼▼▼ TownePlace Suites by Marriott 🅼
(310) 725-9696. **$139-$269.** 14400 Aviation Blvd 90250. I-405 exit 43 (Rosecrans Ave), 0.4 mi w. Int corridors. **Pets:** Accepted.
〔SAVE〕 〔ECO〕 🔁 🛜 ✖ 🔌 💻

HEALDSBURG *(Restaurants p. 616)*

◈◈◈ ▼▼▼ BEST WESTERN Dry Creek Inn 🄷 ❀
(707) 433-0300. **$99-$329.** 198 Dry Creek Rd 95448. US 101 exit Dry Creek Rd, just se. Ext corridors. **Pets:** Large. $50 daily fee/room. Designated rooms, service with restrictions, supervision.
〔SAVE〕 🔁 🔁 ✖ 🛜 🔌 💻

▼▼▼ Healdsburg Inn on the Plaza 🅱🅱
(707) 433-6991. **$295-$495, 7 day notice.** 112 Matheson St 95448. Just e of Healdsburg Ave; on the Plaza; downtown. Int corridors. **Pets:** Accepted. 🛜 ✖

HEMET *(Restaurants p. 616)*

◈◈◈ ▼▼▼▼ Quality Inn 🅼
(951) 766-1902. **$79-$109.** 1201 W Florida Ave 92543. 1.5 mi w of SR 79 N (San Jacinto St) on SR 74/79. Ext corridors. **Pets:** Small. $20 daily fee/pet. Designated rooms, service with restrictions, supervision.
〔SAVE〕 〔ECO〕 🔁 🛜 🔌 💻

▼▼ ▼▼ Travelodge Inn of Hemet 🅼
(951) 925-6605. **$72-$86.** 2625 W Florida Ave 92545. 2.4 mi w of SR 79 N (San Jacinto St); on SR 74/79. Ext corridors. **Pets:** Accepted.
🔁 🛜 🔌 💻

HERMOSA BEACH

▼▼ ▼▼ Quality Inn & Suites 🄷
(310) 374-2666. **$139-$199.** 901 Aviation Blvd 90254. SR 1 (Pacific Coast Hwy), just e. Ext/int corridors. **Pets:** Accepted.
🛜 ✖ 🔌 💻

HESPERIA *(Restaurants p. 616)*

▼▼ ▼▼ Econo Lodge 🅼
(760) 949-1515. **$59-$119.** 11976 Mariposa Rd 92345. I-15 exit 147 (Bear Valley Rd), just e, then just s. Ext corridors. **Pets:** Accepted.
🛜 🔌 💻

HOLLYWOOD

◈◈◈ ▼▼▼▼ Hollywood Hotel 🄷 ❀
(323) 315-1800. **$99-$349.** 1160 N Vermont Ave 90029. US 101 exit 6A (Vermont Ave), 0.5 mi n. Int corridors. **Pets:** Medium. $35 daily fee/pet. Service with restrictions, supervision.
〔SAVE〕 🎬 🔁 🔁 🛜 ✖ 🔌 💻

▼▼ ▼▼▼▼ Loews Hollywood 🄷 ❀
(323) 856-1200. **$229-$359, 3 day notice.** 1755 N Highland Ave 90028. US 101 exit Highland Ave northbound; exit 9C southbound, 0.6 mi s. Int corridors. **Pets:** Other species. $25 daily fee/pet. Service with restrictions. 〔ECO〕 🍴 🔁 🔁 🛜 ✖ 🔌 💻

▼▼ ▼▼ Motel 6 Los Angeles - Hollywood #4044 🅼
(323) 464-6006. **Call for rates.** 1738 N Whitley Ave 90028. US 101 exit 9C southbound, just s, just w, then just s. Int corridors. **Pets:** Other species. Service with restrictions, crate. 🛜 ✖ 🔌

◈◈◈ ▼▼▼▼ W Hollywood 🄷 ❀
(323) 798-1300. **Call for rates.** 6250 Hollywood Blvd 90028. US 101 exit 8B (Hollywood Blvd), 0.5 mi w. Int corridors. **Pets:** Medium. $100 one-time fee/room, $25 daily fee/room. Service with restrictions, supervision. 〔SAVE〕 〔ECO〕 🍴 🔁 🔁 ✖ 📷 ✖ 🔌 💻

HUNTINGTON BEACH

◈◈◈ ▼▼▼▼ Hyatt Regency Huntington Beach Resort
& Spa 🄷 ❀
(714) 698-1234. **$179-$499, 3 day notice.** 21500 Pacific Coast Hwy 92648. I-405 exit 16 (Beach Blvd), 6.5 mi s, then just w. Ext/int corridors. **Pets:** Medium, dogs only. $150 one-time fee/room. Designated rooms, service with restrictions, supervision.
〔SAVE〕 〔ECO〕 🍴 🔁 🔁 ✖ 📷 ✖ 🔌 💻

◈◈◈ ▼▼▼▼ The Waterfront Beach Resort A Hilton
Hotel 🄷 ❀
(714) 845-8000. **$199-$509.** 21100 Pacific Coast Hwy 92648. I-405 exit 16 (Beach Blvd), 6.5 mi s, then just w. Int corridors. **Pets:** Medium. $50 one-time fee/pet. Designated rooms, service with restrictions, crate.
〔SAVE〕 〔ECO〕 🎬 🍴 🔁 🔁 ✖ 📷 ✖ 🔌 💻

IDYLLWILD *(Restaurants p. 616)*

▼▼ ▼▼ Quiet Creek Inn 🅲🅰
(951) 468-4208. **$125-$245, 14 day notice.** 26345 Delano Dr 92549. SR 243, 0.8 mi sw of town center, 0.4 mi w on Toll Gate Rd, then just n. Ext corridors. **Pets:** Accepted. 🛜 ✖ 🔌 🆉 🔌 💻

▼▼ ▼▼ Woodland Park Manor 🅲🅰
(951) 659-2657. **$99-$205, 10 day notice.** 55350 S Circle Dr 92549. From SR 243 and town center, 1.5 mi ne. Ext corridors. **Pets:** Dogs only. $15 one-time fee/room. Service with restrictions, supervision.
🔁 🛜 ✖ 🆉 🔌 💻

INDIAN WELLS *(Restaurants p. 616)*

AAA ◇◇◇◇ **Hyatt Regency Indian Wells Resort & Spa** H ❀

(760) 341-1000. **$89-$429, 3 day notice.** 44-600 Indian Wells Ln 92210. I-10 exit 134 (Cook St), 4.4 mi s, 1.5 mi e on SR 111, then just n. Ext/int corridors. **Pets:** Large, dogs only. $150 one-time fee/room. Designated rooms, service with restrictions, supervision.

SAVE ECO ❍ & 🅼 ⌖ ✕ 🕾 ✕ 🖥 🖳

AAA ◇◇◇◇ **Miramonte Resort & Spa** H

(760) 341-2200. **$99-$699, 3 day notice.** 45000 Indian Wells Ln 92210. I-10 exit 134 (Cook St), 4.4 mi s, 1.5 mi e on SR 111, then just s. Ext/int corridors. **Pets:** Accepted.

SAVE ECO ❍ ⌖ ✕ 🅢 ✕ 🖥 🖳

INDIO

AAA ◇◇◇ **BEST WESTERN Date Tree Hotel** M ❀

(760) 347-3421. **$80-$400.** 81-909 Indio Blvd 92201. I-10 exit 139 (Jefferson St/Indio Blvd), 2.5 mi se. Int corridors. **Pets:** Other species. $15 daily fee/room. Service with restrictions.

SAVE ➡ ⌖ ✕ 🖥 🖳

AAA ◇◇◇ **Indian Palms Country Club & Resort** H

(760) 775-4444. **$84-$259.** 48-630 Monroe St 92201. I-10 exit 142 (Monroe St), 3 mi s. Ext corridors. **Pets:** Accepted.

SAVE ❍ ⌖ ✕ 🕾 ✕ 🖥 🖳

AAA ◇◇ **Indio Super & Suites** M

(760) 342-0264. **$50-$112.** 81-753 Hwy 111 92201. I-10 exit 142 (Monroe St), 1.5 mi s, then 0.5 mi w. Ext corridors. **Pets:** Accepted.

SAVE & 🅼 ⌖ 🕾 ✕ 🖥 🖳

INDUSTRY *(Restaurants p. 616)*

◇◇◇ **Pacific Palms Resort** H

(626) 810-4455. **Call for rates.** One Industry Hills Pkwy 91744. SR 60 exit 18 (Azusa Ave), 1.3 mi n, then 0.5 mi w. Int corridors. **Pets:** Dogs only. $35 daily fee/pet. Service with restrictions, supervision.

ECO ❍ & 🅼 ⌖ ✕ 🕾 ✕ 🖳

IRVINE *(Restaurants p. 616)*

◇◇◇ **Hilton Irvine/Orange County Airport** H

(949) 833-9999. **$99-$279.** 18800 MacArthur Blvd 92612. I-405 exit 8 (MacArthur Blvd/John Wayne Airport), 0.5 mi n. Int corridors.
Pets: Accepted. ECO ❍ & 🅼 ⌖ ✕ 🅢 ✕ 🖥 🖳

◇◇◇ **Hotel Irvine** H ❀

(949) 230-4452. **Call for rates.** 17900 Jamboree Rd 92614. I-405 exit 7 (Jamboree Rd), just ne. Int corridors. **Pets:** Dogs only. $50 daily fee/room. Service with restrictions, supervision.

ECO ❍ & 🅼 ⌖ ✕ 🅢 🖥 🖳

◇◇◇ **Residence Inn by Marriott Irvine John Wayne Airport** H

(949) 261-2020. **$94-$269.** 2855 Main St 92614. I-405 exit 7 (Jamboree Rd), just n, then just e. Int corridors. **Pets:** Accepted.

& 🅼 ⌖ 🕾 ✕ 🖥 🖳

AAA ◇◇◇ **Residence Inn by Marriott-Irvine Spectrum** H

(949) 380-3000. **$109-$269.** 10 Morgan St 92618. I-5 exit 94 (Alton Pkwy) southbound; exit 94B northbound, 2 mi e, then just se. Ext corridors. **Pets:** Other species. $100 one-time fee/room. Service with restrictions, crate. SAVE ECO & 🅼 ⌖ 🕾 ✕ 🖥 🖳

AAA ◇◇◇ **Wyndham Irvine - Orange County Airport** H

(949) 863-1999. **$139-$236, 3 day notice.** 17941 Von Karman Ave 92614. I-405 exit 7 (Jamboree Rd), 0.3 mi n to Main St, 0.5 mi w, then just sw. Int corridors. **Pets:** Small, dogs only. $55 one-time fee/pet. Service with restrictions, supervision.

SAVE ❍ & 🅼 ⌖ 🕾 ✕ 🖥 🖳

JACKSON

AAA ◇◇◇ **BEST WESTERN Amador Inn** H ❀

(209) 223-0211. **$90-$130.** 200 S Hwy 49 95642. Just se of jct SR 49 and 88. Int corridors. **Pets:** $15 deposit/pet. Service with restrictions, crate. SAVE ⌖ 🕾 🖥 🖳

AAA ◇◇◇ **The Jackson Lodge** M

(209) 223-0486. **$69-$99.** 850 N Hwy 49 95642. On SR 49 and 88, 0.5 mi w. Ext corridors. **Pets:** Medium. $15 one-time fee/pet. Designated rooms, service with restrictions, supervision.

SAVE ⌖ 🕾 ✕ 🖥 🖳

JAMESTOWN

AAA ◇◇◇ **1859 Historic National Hotel, A Country Inn** CI ❀

(209) 984-3446. **$140-$160, 3 day notice.** 18183 Main St 95327. In historic downtown. Int corridors. **Pets:** Medium. $25 daily fee/pet. Designated rooms, service with restrictions, supervision.

SAVE ❍ 🕾 ✕ 🎮 🗲

◇◇ **Country Inn Sonora** M

(209) 984-0315. **$59-$289.** 18730 Hwy 108 95327. SR 108 and 49, 1 mi e of town. Ext corridors. **Pets:** Accepted. ⌖ 🕾 🖥 🖳

AAA ◇◇ **Jamestown Railtown Motel** M

(209) 984-3332. **$50-$80, 3 day notice.** 10301 N Willow St 95327. Center; in historic downtown. Ext corridors. **Pets:** Small, dogs only. $10 daily fee/pet. No service. SAVE ⌖ 🕾 🖥

◇◇◇ **Victorian Gold Bed & Breakfast** BB

(209) 984-3429. **$115-$185, 5 day notice.** 10382 Willow St 95327. Center; in historic downtown. Int corridors. **Pets:** Accepted.

🕾 ✕ 🗲 🖥

JENNER

◇◇◇ **Jenner Inn & Cottages** CI ❀

(707) 865-2377. **$118-$358, 10 day notice.** 10400 Hwy 1 95450. On SR 1, 1 mi n of SR 116. Ext corridors. **Pets:** Dogs only. $35 one-time fee/pet. Designated rooms, service with restrictions, supervision.

❍ 🕾 ✕ 🎮 🖥 🖳

JULIAN *(Restaurants p. 616)*

AAA ◇◇ **Julian Lodge B & B Mountain Inn** M

(760) 765-1420. **$95-$225, 7 day notice.** 2720 C St 92036. Just s of Main St on SR 78 and 79. Ext/int corridors. **Pets:** $30 one-time fee/room. Service with restrictions, supervision.

SAVE & 🕾 ✕ 🗲 🖥 🖳

JUNE LAKE *(Restaurants p. 616)*

AAA ◇◇◇◇ **Double Eagle Resort and Spa** CA

(760) 648-7004. **$169-$649.** 5587 Hwy 158 93529. 3 mi w of village. Ext corridors. **Pets:** Small, dogs only. $50 one-time fee/room. Service with restrictions, crate.

SAVE ❍ & 🅼 ⌖ ✕ 🕾 ✕ 🎮 🖥 🖳

◇◇ **Gull Lake Lodge** M

(760) 648-7516. **$79-$204, 7 day notice.** 132 Leonard Ave 93529. 0.3 mi n on Knoll St, then 0.3 mi e on Bruce St; in village. Ext corridors. **Pets:** Other species. Designated rooms, service with restrictions, supervision. 🕾 ✕ 🎮 🗲 🖥 🖳

◇◇ **June Lake Villager** M

(760) 648-7712. **Call for rates.** 640 Hwy 158 93529. Center of village. Ext corridors. **Pets:** Accepted. 🕾 ✕ 🎮 🗲 🖥 🖳

KERNVILLE *(Restaurants p. 616)*

◇◇ **Barewood Inn & Suites** M

(760) 376-1910. **$87-$220, 3 day notice.** 7013 Wofford Blvd 93285. In Wofford Heights. Ext corridors. **Pets:** Accepted. 🕾 ✕ 🖥 🖳

▼▼ River View Lodge M

(760) 376-6019. **Call for rates.** 2 Sirretta St 93238. On Kernville Rd; at bridge. Ext corridors. **Pets:** Accepted. 🛰 ⊠ 🐾 🖬

KETTLEMAN CITY

◢◣◥◤ ▼▼▼ BEST WESTERN Kettleman City Inn & Suites M

(559) 386-0804. **$99-$132.** 33410 Powers Dr 93239. E of and adjacent to I-5 exit SR 41 N, 0.3 mi to Bernard Dr, then 0.3 mi n. Ext corridors. **Pets:** Accepted. SAVE &M 🛰 🛰 🖬 🖵

KLAMATH

◢◣◥◤ ▼ Motel Trees M

(707) 482-3152. **$75-$150.** 15495 Hwy 101 N 95548. On US 101, 4.5 mi n of Klamath. Ext corridors. **Pets:** $10 daily fee/pet. Designated rooms, service with restrictions, supervision. SAVE 🛰 ⚿ 🖬 🖵

LAGUNA BEACH *(Restaurants p. 616)*

▼▼ Art Hotel-Laguna Beach M

(949) 494-6464. **$109-$199, 3 day notice.** 1404 N Coast Hwy 92651. SR 133 to Coast Hwy, 1.1 mi n on SR 1. Ext corridors. **Pets:** Other species. Designated rooms. 🛰 🛰 ⊠ 🖬 🖵

▼▼▼ Casa Laguna Inn & Spa BB

(949) 494-2996. **$150-$650, 5 day notice.** 2510 S Coast Hwy 92651. SR 133 to Coast Hwy, 1.3 mi s on SR 1. Ext corridors. **Pets:** Accepted. 🛰 🛰 ⊠ 🖬 🖵

▼▼▼ Holiday Inn Laguna Beach H

(949) 494-1001. **$159-$399.** 696 S Coast Hwy 92651. SR 133 to Coast Hwy, 0.5 mi s on SR 1. Ext corridors. **Pets:** Small, dogs only. $75 one-time fee/room. Service with restrictions, supervision.
🍴 🛰 🛰 ⊠ 🖬 🖵

◢◣◥◤ ▼▼▼▼ Montage Laguna Beach H 🐾

(949) 715-6000. **Call for rates.** 30801 S Coast Hwy 92651. SR 133 to Coast Hwy, 3 mi s on SR 1. Ext/int corridors. **Pets:** Medium, dogs only. $150 one-time fee/pet. Designated rooms, service with restrictions, supervision. SAVE ECO 🍴 🛰 ⊠ 🛰 ⊠ 🖬

◢◣◥◤ ▼▼ ▼▼ Surf & Sand Resort H 🐾

(949) 497-4477. **$390-$835, 3 day notice.** 1555 S Coast Hwy 92651. SR 133, 1 mi s. Ext corridors. **Pets:** Small. $150 one-time fee/room. Designated rooms, service with restrictions, supervision.
SAVE 🍴 &M 🛰 ⊠ 🛰 ⊠ 🖬 🖵

▼▼ The Tides Laguna Beach M

(949) 494-2494. **$109-$315, 3 day notice.** 460 N Coast Hwy 92651. SR 133 to Coast Hwy, 0.5 mi n on SR 1. Ext corridors. **Pets:** Accepted. 🛰 🛰 ⊠ 🖬 🖵

LAGUNA HILLS

▼▼▼ The Hills Hotel H

(949) 586-5000. **$119-$389.** 25205 La Paz Rd 92653. I-5 exit 89 (La Paz Rd), just w. Int corridors. **Pets:** Medium. $30 daily fee/pet. Designated rooms, no service, supervision.
🍴 &M 🛰 🛰 ⊠ 🖬 🖵

LA JOLLA *(Restaurants p. 616)*

◢◣◥◤ ▼▼▼ Empress Hotel of La Jolla H 🐾

(858) 454-3001. **$139-$399.** 7766 Fay Ave 92037. I-5 exit 28 (La Jolla Village Dr) southbound, 0.7 mi w to Torrey Pines Rd, 2.5 mi sw to Prospect St, 0.8 mi sw, then just s; exit 26A (La Jolla Pkwy) northbound, 1.5 mi n to Torrey Pines Rd, 1 mi sw to Prospect St, 0.8 mi sw, then just s. Int corridors. **Pets:** Medium. $75 one-time fee/room. Service with restrictions, supervision. SAVE ECO 🍴 🛰 ⊠ 🖬 🖵

◢◣◥◤ ▼▼▼ ▼▼▼ Estancia La Jolla Hotel & Spa H

(858) 550-1000. **$209-$409.** 9700 N Torrey Pines Rd 92037. I-5 exit 28 (La Jolla Village Dr), 0.7 mi w, then 1 mi n. Ext/int corridors.
Pets: Accepted. SAVE 🍴 🛰 ⊠ 🛰 ⊠ 🖬 🖵

◢◣◥◤ ▼▼▼ Holiday Inn Express La Jolla M

(858) 454-7101. **$109-$289.** 6705 La Jolla Blvd 92037. I-5 exit 28 (La Jolla Village Dr) northbound, 0.7 mi w to Torrey Pines Rd, 3 mi sw to Girard Ave, just s to Pearl St, 0.4 mi w, then 0.6 mi s; exit 26A (La Jolla Pkwy) northbound, 1.5 mi n to Torrey Pines Rd, 1.5 mi sw to Girard Ave, just s to Pearl St, 0.4 mi w, then 0.6 mi s. Ext corridors. **Pets:** $75 one-time fee/room. Service with restrictions, supervision.
SAVE 🛰 🛰 ⊠ 🖬 🖵

▼▼▼ Hotel La Jolla H 🐾

(858) 459-0261. **Call for rates.** 7955 La Jolla Shores Dr 92037. I-5 exit 28 (La Jolla Village Dr) southbound, 0.7 mi w to Torrey Pines Rd, 1.7 mi sw, then just n; exit 26A (La Jolla Pkwy) northbound, 1.5 mi n to Torrey Pines Rd, just w, then just n. Ext corridors. **Pets:** Other species. Designated rooms, service with restrictions.
🍴 &M 🛰 ⊠ 🛰 ⊠ 🖬 🖵

◢◣◥◤ ▼▼▼▼ La Valencia Hotel H 🐾

(858) 454-0771. **$279-$795, 3 day notice.** 1132 Prospect St 92037. I-5 exit 26A (La Jolla Pkwy) northbound, 1.5 mi n to Torrey Pines Rd, 1 mi sw to Prospect St, then 0.6 mi sw; exit 28 (La Jolla Village Dr) southbound, 0.7 mi w to Torrey Pines Rd, 2.5 mi sw to Prospect St, then 0.6 mi sw. Ext/int corridors. **Pets:** $30 daily fee/pet. Service with restrictions, supervision. SAVE 🍴 🛰 ⊠ 🛰 ⊠ 🖬

◢◣◥◤ ▼▼▼▼ Residence Inn by Marriott San Diego La Jolla H

(858) 587-1770. **$159-$359.** 8901 Gilman Dr 92037. I-5 exit 27 (Gilman Dr), 1.3 mi nw. Ext corridors. **Pets:** $100 one-time fee/room. Designated rooms, service with restrictions.
SAVE ECO &M 🛰 🛰 ⊠ 🖬 🖵

▼▼▼ San Diego Marriott La Jolla H 🐾

(858) 587-1414. **$99-$359.** 4240 La Jolla Village Dr 92037. I-5 exit 28 (La Jolla Village Dr), 0.8 mi e. Int corridors. **Pets:** Other species. $75 one-time fee/room. Service with restrictions, crate.
🍴 &M 🛰 🛰 ⊠ 🖬 🖵

◢◣◥◤ ▼▼▼ Sheraton La Jolla Hotel H

(858) 453-5500. **$109-$359.** 3299 Holiday Ct 92037. I-5 exit 28 (La Jolla Village Dr), just w to Villa La Jolla Dr, just s, then just e. Ext/int corridors. **Pets:** Accepted.
SAVE ECO 🍴 &M 🛰 🛰 ⊠ 🖬 🖵

LAKE ARROWHEAD

▼▼▼ Arrowhead Saddleback Inn CI

(909) 336-3571. **$137-$648, 7 day notice.** 300 S SR 173 92352. On SR 173; jct SR 189. Ext/int corridors. **Pets:** Other species. $15 daily fee/pet. Designated rooms, service with restrictions, crate.
🍴 🛰 ⊠ 🖬 🖵

▼▼ Arrowhead Tree Top Lodge M

(909) 337-2311. **$109-$189, 7 day notice.** 27992 Rainbow Dr 92352. 0.3 mi s of Lake Arrowhead Village on SR 173. Ext corridors. **Pets:** $18 daily fee/pet. Designated rooms, service with restrictions, supervision.
🛰 🛰 ⊠ 🐾 🖬 🖵

◢◣◥◤ ▼▼▼ ▼▼ Lake Arrowhead Resort and Spa H

(909) 336-1511. **$169-$449.** 27984 Hwy 189 92352. Just w of SR 173; in Lake Arrowhead Village. Int corridors. **Pets:** Accepted.
SAVE 🍴 &M 🛰 ⊠ 🛰 ⊠ 🖬 🖵

LAKE FOREST *(Restaurants p. 617)*

◢◣◥◤ ▼▼▼ BEST WESTERN PLUS Irvine Spectrum Hotel M

(949) 380-9888. **$79-$139, 3 day notice.** 23192 Lake Center Dr 92630. I-5 exit Lake Forest Dr, just e, just s on Rockfield Blvd, just w on Boeing, then just s. Ext corridors. **Pets:** Medium. $20 daily fee/room. Designated rooms, service with restrictions, supervision.
SAVE 🛰 🛰 🖬 🖵

◢◣◥◤ ▼▼▼ The Prominence Hotel and Suites H

(949) 900-1288. **$89-$199.** 20768 Lake Forest Dr 92630. I-5 exit 92A (Lake Forest Dr) northbound; exit 92 (Bake Pkwy/Lake Forest Dr) southbound, 4 mi e. Int corridors. **Pets:** Medium, other species. $20 daily fee/room. Designated rooms, service with restrictions, supervision.
SAVE &M 🛰 🛰 ⊠ 🖬 🖵

Quality Inn & Suites Irvine Spectrum 🅷
(949) 458-1900. **$99-$189.** 23702 Rockfield Blvd 92630. I-5 exit 92A (Lake Forest Dr) northbound; exit 92 (Bake Pkwy/Lake Forest Dr) southbound, 0.5 mi e on Lake Forest Dr, then just s. Int corridors. **Pets:** Medium. $25 daily fee/pet. Designated rooms, service with restrictions, supervision. SAVE 🍴 ➳ 🛜 📶 💻

Staybridge Suites Irvine East/Lake Forest 🅷
(949) 462-9500. **$119-$249.** 2 Orchard Rd 92630. I-5 exit 92B (Bake Pkwy) northbound; exit 92 (Bake Pkwy/Lake Forest Dr) southbound, 4.7 mi e on Bake Pkwy, just n on Rancho Pkwy S, then just w. Int corridors. **Pets:** Accepted. 🅖🄼 ➳ 🛜 📶 💻

LA MIRADA

Residence Inn by Marriott 🅷
(714) 523-2800. **$134-$164.** 14419 Firestone Blvd 90638. I-5 exit 118 (Valley View Ave), just n, then 0.5 mi e. Ext corridors. **Pets:** Accepted. 🅖🄼 ➳ 🛜 ✕ 📶 💻

LANCASTER

Americas Best Value Inn & Suites of Lancaster 🅜
(661) 945-8771. **$75-$85.** 44131 Sierra Hwy 93534. SR 14 exit 42 (Ave K), 2 mi e, then just n. Ext corridors. **Pets:** Accepted.
SAVE 🛜 📶 💻

Comfort Inn & Suites 🅷
(661) 723-2001. **$109-$144.** 1825 W Ave J-12 93534. SR 14 exit 43 (Ave J) northbound; exit 20th St southbound, just s, then just e. Int corridors. **Pets:** Medium, other species. $30 daily fee/pet. Service with restrictions, supervision. 🅖🄼 ➳ ✕ 🛜 📶 💻

Homewood Suites Lancaster 🅷 🐾
(661) 723-8040. **$155-$165.** 2320 W Double Play Way 93536. SR 14 exit 44 (Ave I), just w, s on Valley Central Way, then just e. Int corridors. **Pets:** Large, other species. $200 one-time fee/room. Service with restrictions, supervision. 🅖🄼 ➳ 🛜 📶 💻

Oxford Inn & Suites Lancaster 🅜
(661) 949-3423. **$105-$140, 3 day notice.** 1651 W Ave K 93534. SR 14 exit 42 (Ave K), just w. Int corridors. **Pets:** Accepted.
SAVE 🅖🄼 ➳ 🛜 📶 💻

TownePlace Suites by Marriott 🅷 🐾
(661) 723-6709. **$84-$170.** 2024 W Ave, J-8 93536. SR 14 exit 43 (Ave J), just w. Int corridors. **Pets:** Other species. $100 one-time fee/pet. Service with restrictions, crate. 🅖🄼 🛜 ✕ 📶 💻

LA PALMA

La Quinta Inn & Suites Buena Park 🅷
(714) 670-1400. **$95-$209.** 3 Centerpointe Dr 90623. SR 91 exit 21 (Orangethorpe Ave/Valley View St) eastbound; exit 22 westbound, just n. Int corridors. **Pets:** Large, other species. Service with restrictions.
➳ 🛜 ✕ 📶 💻

LA QUINTA

La Quinta Resort & Club, A Waldorf Astoria Resort 🅷 🐾
(760) 564-4111. **$109-$619.** 49-499 Eisenhower Dr 92253. I-10 exit 137 (Washington St), 4.7 mi s, then 1 mi sw. Ext corridors. **Pets:** Large, dogs only. $100 one-time fee/room. Service with restrictions.
🍴 ➳ ✕ 🛜 ✕ 📶 💻

LATHROP

Comfort Inn 🅷
(209) 983-1177. **Call for rates.** 14730 S Harlan Rd 95330. I-5 exit 463 (Lathrop Rd), just e. Int corridors. **Pets:** Small. $10 daily fee/pet. Designated rooms, service with restrictions, supervision.
🅖🄼 ➳ ✕ 🛜 📶 💻

LEBEC

Holiday Inn Express Frazier Park/Lebec 🅷
(661) 248-1600. **$115-$179, 3 day notice.** 612 Wainright Ct 93243. I-5 exit 205 (Frazer Mountain Rd), just n. Int corridors. **Pets:** Accepted.
➳ 🛜 ✕ 📶 💻

Ramada Limited Grapevine 🅜
(661) 248-1530. **$79-$115.** 9000 Country Side Ct 93243. I-5 exit 215 (Grapevine Rd), just w. Ext corridors. **Pets:** Medium. $10 one-time fee/pet. Designated rooms, service with restrictions, supervision.
SAVE ➳ 🛜 💻

LEE VINING *(Restaurants p. 617)*

Murphey's Motel 🅜
(760) 647-6316. **$50-$153, 3 day notice.** 51493 Hwy 395 93541. Jct Lee Vining Ave and US 395; in town. Ext corridors. **Pets:** $10 daily fee/room. Service with restrictions, supervision.
SAVE 🛜 ✕ 📶 💻

LEGGETT

Redwoods River Resort 🅲🄰
(707) 925-6249. **$75-$300, 7 day notice.** 75000 Hwy 101 95585. 6.5 mi n of jct SR 1. Ext corridors. **Pets:** Accepted.
SAVE ➳ 🛜 ✕ 🐾 🅧 📶 💻

LINCOLN

Holiday Inn Express Hotel & Suites 🅷
(916) 644-3440. **$109-$159.** 155 Ferrari Ranch Rd 95648. SR 65 exit 315 (Ferrari Ranch Rd), just nw; jct Groveland Ln. Int corridors. **Pets:** Accepted. ➳ 🛜 🛜 📶 💻

LITTLE RIVER *(Restaurants p. 617)*

The Inn at Schoolhouse Creek 🅲🅸
(707) 937-5525. **Call for rates.** 7051 N Hwy 1 95456. SR 1, 0.8 mi s of Van Damme State Park entrance. Ext corridors. **Pets:** Accepted.
🍴 ✕ 🛜 ✕ 🐾 📶 💻

Little River Inn 🅲🅸 🐾
(707) 937-5942. **$130-$369, 5 day notice.** 7901 N Hwy 1 95456. On SR 1, just s of Van Damme State Park entrance. Ext/int corridors. **Pets:** $25 daily fee/pet. Designated rooms, service with restrictions, supervision. 🍴 ✕ 🛜 ✕ 🐾 📶 💻

LIVERMORE *(Restaurants p. 617)*

Holiday Inn Express Hotel & Suites-Livermore 🅷
(925) 961-9600. **Call for rates.** 3000 Constitution Dr 94551. I-580 exit 50 (Airway Blvd/Collier Canyon Rd), just n, then just e on N Canyons Pkwy. Int corridors. **Pets:** Accepted. 🅖🄼 ➳ 🛜 ✕ 📶 💻

La Quinta Inn Livermore 🅷
(925) 373-9600. **$84-$199.** 7700 Southfront Rd 94551. I-580 exit Greenville Rd, just s, then just w; jct Mountain Vista Pkwy. Int corridors. **Pets:** Large, other species. Service with restrictions.
🅖🄼 ➳ ✕ 🛜 ✕ 📶 💻

Residence Inn by Marriott 🅷
(925) 373-1800. **$139-$219.** 1000 Airway Blvd 94551. I-580 exit 50 (Airway Blvd/Collier Canyon Rd), just n. Ext corridors. **Pets:** Accepted. 🅖🄼 ➳ 🛜 ✕ 📶 💻

LODI

Holiday Inn Express 🅷
(209) 210-0150. **Call for rates.** 1337 E Kettleman Ln 95240. SR 99 exit Kettleman Ln, 0.4 mi e. Int corridors. **Pets:** Accepted.
🅖🄼 ➳ 🛜 ✕ 📶 💻

Wine & Roses Hotel Spa and Restaurant 🅷
(209) 334-6988. **$235.** 2505 W Turner Rd 95242. I-5 exit Turner Rd, 5 mi e; SR 99 exit Turner Rd, 2.4 mi w. Ext corridors. **Pets:** Small. $45 daily fee/pet. Designated rooms, service with restrictions, crate.
🍴 🅖🄼 ➳ ✕ 🛜 ✕ 📶 💻

LOMA LINDA

▼▼ ▼▼ **Loma Linda Inn** [M]

(909) 583-2500. **$86.** 24532 University Ave 92354. I-10 exit 74 (Tippecanoe Ave), 1 mi s, just w on Stewart St, just s on Campus, then just w. Ext corridors. **Pets:** Accepted. [&M] [⟨] [✕] [🛈] [▣]

LOMPOC

[AAA] ▼▼ ▼▼ **Inn of Lompoc** [M]

(805) 735-7744. **$70-$80.** 1122 N H St 93436. SR 1, 1.2 mi n of Ocean Ave. Ext/int corridors. **Pets:** $25 one-time fee/room. Service with restrictions, supervision. [SAVE] [⟰] [⟨] [🛈] [▣]

LONE PINE

[AAA] ▼▼ ▼▼ **BEST WESTERN PLUS Frontier Motel** [M]

(760) 876-5571. **$82-$160.** 1008 S Main St 93545. On US 395. Ext corridors. **Pets:** Other species. Designated rooms, supervision.
[SAVE] [⟰] [⟨] [✕] [🛈] [▣]

[AAA] ▼▼ ▼▼▼ **Dow Villa Motel** [M]

(760) 876-5521. **$80-$170.** 310 S Main St 93545. On US 395; center. Ext corridors. **Pets:** $50 deposit/room. Designated rooms, service with restrictions, supervision. [SAVE] [⦙⦙] [⟰] [⟨] [✕] [🛈] [▣]

LONG BEACH *(Restaurants p. 617)*

▼▼ ▼▼ **Extended Stay America-Los Angeles-Long Beach Airport** [H]

(562) 989-4601. **Call for rates.** 4105 E Willow St 90815. I-405 exit 27 (Lakewood Blvd), just s, then 0.3 mi w. Int corridors. **Pets:** Other species. $25 daily fee/pet. Service with restrictions, supervision.
[&M] [⟨]

[AAA] ▼▼ ▼▼▼ **Hilton Long Beach & Executive Meeting Center** [H]

(562) 983-3400. **$129-$259.** 701 W Ocean Blvd 90831. I-710 exit Downtown/Broadway, just e to Daisy Ave, just s to Ocean Blvd, then just w. Int corridors. **Pets:** Accepted.
[SAVE] [ECO] [⊂] [⦙⦙] [&M] [⟰] [⟨] [✕] [🛈] [▣]

▼▼ ▼▼▼ **Hotel Current** [M]

(562) 597-1341. **$119-$199.** 5325 E Pacific Coast Hwy 90804. I-405 exit 23 (SR 22/Long Beach) northbound, 2 mi nw; exit 27 (Lakewood Blvd) southbound, 2 mi se on SR 1. Ext corridors. **Pets:** $50 one-time fee/pet. Designated rooms, service with restrictions, crate.
[ECO] [⦙⦙] [&M] [⟰] [⟨] [✕] [🛈] [▣]

▼▼ ▼▼▼ **Hotel Maya - a DoubleTree by Hilton** [H] ❀

(562) 435-7676. **$149-$379.** 700 Queensway Dr 90802. I-710 exit 1A (Harbor Scenic Dr/Queen Mary), 1.3 mi s, then just e. Ext corridors. **Pets:** Medium, dogs only. $50 one-time fee/room.
[ECO] [⦙⦙] [⟰] [✕] [⟨] [✕] [🛈] [▣]

[AAA] ▼▼ ▼▼▼ **Hyatt Regency Long Beach** [H]

(562) 491-1234. **$89-$389.** 200 S Pine Ave 90802. I-710 exit 1C (Shoreline Dr/Downtown), 1 mi s. Int corridors. **Pets:** Accepted.
[SAVE] [ECO] [⊂] [⦙⦙] [&M] [⟰] [🛰] [✕] [🛈] [▣]

[AAA] ▼▼ ▼▼▼ **Renaissance Long Beach Hotel** [H]

(562) 437-5900. **$139-$309.** 111 E Ocean Blvd 90802. I-710 exit Downtown/Broadway, 0.8 mi e to Long Beach Blvd, just s, then just w. Int corridors. **Pets:** $75 one-time fee/room. Service with restrictions, crate. [SAVE] [ECO] [⦙⦙] [&M] [⟰] [🛰] [✕] [🛈] [▣]

[AAA] ▼▼ ▼▼▼ **Residence Inn by Marriott Long Beach** [H]

(562) 595-0909. **$101-$278.** 4111 E Willow St 90815. I-405 exit 27 (Lakewood Blvd), just s, then just w. Ext corridors. **Pets:** Other species. $115 one-time fee/room. Service with restrictions, crate.
[SAVE] [ECO] [&M] [⟰] [⟨] [✕] [🛈] [▣]

[AAA] ▼▼ ▼▼▼ **Residence Inn by Marriott Long Beach Downtown South Waterfront** [H]

(562) 495-0700. **$143-$299.** 600 Queensway Dr 90802. I-710 exit 1A (Harbor Scenic Dr/Queen Mary), 1.3 mi s, then just w. Int corridors. **Pets:** Accepted. [SAVE] [⟰] [⟨] [✕] [🛈] [▣]

LOS ALAMITOS

[AAA] ▼▼ ▼▼ **Residence Inn by Marriott-Cypress/Los Alamitos** [H]

(714) 484-5700. **$134-$199.** 4931 Katella Ave 90720. I-605 exit 1D (Katella Ave) southbound; exit 1B (Katella Ave/Willow St) northbound, 1.9 mi e. Int corridors. **Pets:** Medium, other species. $100 one-time fee/room. Service with restrictions. [SAVE] [ECO] [⟰] [⟨] [✕] [🛈] [▣]

LOS ALTOS

▼▼ ▼▼ **Residence Inn by Marriott-Palo Alto/Los Altos** [H]

(650) 559-7890. **$179-$399.** 4460 El Camino Real 94022. US 101 exit San Antonio Rd, 2 mi w to SR 82, then just n. Int corridors.
Pets: Accepted. [&M] [⟰] [⟨] [✕] [🛈] [▣]

LOS ANGELES *(Restaurants p. 617)*

[AAA] ▼▼ ▼▼ **BEST WESTERN PLUS Dragon Gate Inn** [H]

(213) 617-3077. **$160-$300.** 818 N Hill St 90012. US 101 exit 2C (Broadway/Spring St), 0.6 mi n to Alpine St, just e, then just n. Ext corridors. **Pets:** Accepted. [SAVE] [⟨] [✕] [🛈] [▣]

▼▼ ▼▼▼ **The Concourse Hotel at Los Angeles Airport – A Hyatt Affiliate** [H]

(310) 670-9000. **$159-$399, 3 day notice.** 6225 W Century Blvd at Sepulveda Blvd 90045. I-405 exit 46 (Century Blvd), 1.6 mi w. Int corridors. **Pets:** Accepted. [ECO] [⦙⦙] [⟰] [⟨] [✕] [🛈] [▣]

▼▼ ▼▼ **Extended Stay America-Los Angeles/LAX Airport** [H]

(310) 568-9337. **Call for rates.** 6531 S Sepulveda Blvd 90045. I-405 exit 49 (Howard Hughes Pkwy), 0.9 mi w, then just n. Int corridors. **Pets:** Other species. $25 daily fee/pet. Service with restrictions, supervision. [&M] [⟨] [🛈] [▣]

[AAA] ▼▼ ▼▼ **Four Points by Sheraton LAX** [H]

(310) 645-4600. **$89-$209.** 9750 Airport Blvd 90045. I-405 exit 46 (Century Blvd), 1.5 mi w, then just n. Int corridors. **Pets:** Accepted.
[SAVE] [⦙⦙] [⟰] [⟨] [✕] [🛈] [▣]

▼▼ ▼▼ ▼▼ **Four Seasons Hotel Los Angeles at Beverly Hills** [H] ❀

(310) 273-2222. **$525-$12000.** 300 S Doheny Dr 90048. I-10 exit 6 (Robertson Blvd), 3 mi n to Burton Way, then just w. Int corridors. **Pets:** Small, other species. Service with restrictions.
[⦙⦙] [&M] [⟰] [✕] [⟨] [✕] [🛈] [▣]

[AAA] ▼▼ ▼▼▼ **Hilton Checkers Los Angeles** [H]

(213) 624-0000. **$179-$419.** 535 S Grand Ave 90071. SR 110 exit 23B (4th St), merge to the right up ramp to Hope St, then just s. Int corridors. **Pets:** Accepted. [SAVE] [⦙⦙] [⟰] [🛰] [🛈] [▣]

▼▼ ▼▼ ▼▼ **Hotel Bel-Air** [H] ❀

(310) 472-1211. **$515-$895.** 701 Stone Canyon Rd 90077. I-405 exit 57 (Sunset Blvd), 1.7 mi e, then 0.7 mi n. Ext corridors. **Pets:** Other species. $35 daily fee/pet. Service with restrictions, crate.
[⦙⦙] [⟰] [✕] [⟨] [✕] [🛈] [▣]

[AAA] ▼▼ ▼▼▼ **Hotel Palomar LA Westwood** [H]

(310) 475-8711. **$299-$900.** 10740 Wilshire Blvd 90024. I-405 exit 55B (Wilshire Blvd), 1 mi w; in Westwood. Int corridors. **Pets:** Accepted.
[SAVE] [ECO] [⊂] [⦙⦙] [⟰] [🛰] [✕] [🛈] [▣]

[AAA] ▼▼ ▼▼▼ **The Hotel Wilshire** [H]

(323) 852-6000. **Call for rates.** 6317 Wilshire Blvd 90048. I-10 exit 7B (Washington Blvd) westbound, 3 mi n, then just w. Int corridors.
Pets: Accepted. [SAVE] [ECO] [⦙⦙] [⟰] [⟨] [✕]

[AAA] ▼▼ ▼▼ ▼▼ **Hyatt Regency Century Plaza** [H]

(310) 228-1234. **$195-$499.** 2025 Avenue of the Stars 90067. I-10 exit 6 (Robertson Blvd), 2.7 mi n to Olympic Blvd, 1.9 mi w, then just n. Int corridors. **Pets:** Accepted. [SAVE] [⦙⦙] [&M] [⟰] [🛰] [🛈]

◯◯◯◯ ▽▽▽ ▽▽▽ InterContinental Los Angeles Century City 🅗

(310) 284-6500. **$249-$599.** 2151 Avenue of the Stars 90067. I-10 exit 6 (Robertson Blvd), 2.7 mi n to Olympic Blvd, 1.9 mi w, then just n. Int corridors. **Pets:** Accepted. [SAVE] [❚❙] [➘] [✕] [📶] [✕] [▬]

▽▽▽ ▽▽▽ La Quinta Inn & Suites LAX 🅗

(310) 645-2200. **$89-$249.** 5249 W Century Blvd 90045. I-405 exit 46 (Century Blvd), just w. Int corridors. **Pets:** Large, other species. Service with restrictions. [❚❙] [➘] [🛜] [📱] [▬]

◯◯◯ ▽▽▽ ▽▽▽ Luxe City Center Hotel 🅗

(213) 748-1291. **$189-$559, 3 day notice.** 1020 S Figueroa St 90015. SR 110 exit 22 (9th St), just e to Flower St, just s to 11th St, just w, then just n. Int corridors. **Pets:** Accepted.
[SAVE] [❚❙] [♿] [🛜] [✕] [📱] [▬]

▽▽▽ ▽▽▽ Luxe Sunset Boulevard Hotel 🅗 🐾

(310) 476-6571. **Call for rates.** 11461 Sunset Blvd 90049. I-405 exit 57 (Sunset Blvd), just w. Int corridors. **Pets:** Medium. $250 one-time fee/ room. Designated rooms, service with restrictions, supervision.
[❚❙] [♿] [➘] [🛜] [✕] [📱] [▬]

▽▽▽ ▽▽▽ Omni Los Angeles Hotel at California Plaza 🅗 🐾

(213) 617-3300. **Call for rates.** 251 S Olive St 90012. SR 110 exit 23B (4th St), just n. Int corridors. **Pets:** Small, other species. $50 one-time fee/room. Service with restrictions, supervision.
[❚❙] [➘] [📶] [✕] [📱] [▬]

▽▽▽ ▽▽▽ The Orlando Hotel 🅗 🐾

(323) 658-6600. **$249-$1500.** 8384 W 3rd St 90048. I-10 exit 7A (La Cienega Blvd), 2.3 mi n, then just e. Int corridors. **Pets:** Small. $75 daily fee/pet. Designated rooms, service with restrictions, supervision.
[❚❙] [➘] [🛜] [✕] [▬]

▽▽▽ ▽▽▽ Radisson Hotel Midtown Los Angeles at USC 🅗

(213) 748-4141. **$169-$309.** 3540 S Figueroa St 90007. SR 110 exit 20B (Exposition Blvd), just w, then just n. Int corridors. **Pets:** Accepted.
[❚❙] [♿] [➘] [🛜] [✕] [▬]

▽▽▽ ▽▽▽ Residence Inn by Marriott-Beverly Hills 🅗

(310) 228-4100. **$199-$309.** 1177 S Beverly Dr 90035. I-10 exit 6 (Robertson Blvd), 1.6 mi n to Pico Blvd, then 0.6 mi w. Int corridors.
Pets: Accepted. [♿] [🛜] [✕] [📱] [▬]

◯◯◯ ▽▽▽ ▽▽▽ Residence Inn by Marriott Los Angeles L.A. Live 🅗 🐾

(213) 443-9200. **Call for rates.** 901 W Olympic Blvd 90015. SR 110 exit 22 (9th St), s on Flower St, then just w. Int corridors. **Pets:** $100 one-time fee/room. Service with restrictions, supervision.
[SAVE] [♿] [🛜] [✕] [📱] [▬]

▽▽▽ ▽▽▽ ▽▽▽ The Ritz-Carlton, Los Angeles 🅗

(213) 743-8800. **Call for rates.** 900 W Olympic Blvd 90015. SR 110 exit 9th St, s on Flower St, then just w; adjacent to L.A. Live courtyard area. Int corridors. **Pets:** Accepted.
[❙] [❚❙] [➘] [✕] [📶] [✕] [▬]

◯◯◯ ▽▽▽ ▽▽▽ Sheraton Gateway, Los Angeles 🅗 🐾

(310) 642-1111. **$95-$199.** 6101 W Century Blvd 90045. I-405 exit 46 (Century Blvd), 1.3 mi w. Int corridors. **Pets:** Medium, dogs only. $25 one-time fee/room. Service with restrictions, supervision.
[SAVE] [ECO] [❚❙] [♿] [➘] [📶] [✕] [▬]

◯◯◯ ▽▽▽ ▽▽▽ Sheraton Los Angeles Downtown Hotel 🅗

(213) 488-3500. **$139-$359, 3 day notice.** 711 S Hope St 90017. SR 110 exit 22 (9th St), 0.4 mi s, then just w. Int corridors. **Pets:** Accepted.
[SAVE] [❚❙] [♿] [📶] [✕] [📱] [▬]

▽▽▽ ▽▽▽ Sofitel Los Angeles at Beverly Hills 🅗

(310) 278-5444. **$245-$799, 3 day notice.** 8555 Beverly Blvd 90048. I-10 exit 7A (La Cienega Blvd), 2.5 mi n. Int corridors. **Pets:** Accepted.
[ECO] [◀▬] [❚❙] [➘] [✕] [🛜] [✕]

▽▽▽ ▽▽▽ Travelodge Hotel at Lax 🅗 🐾

(310) 649-4000. **$76-$154.** 5547 W Century Blvd 90045. I-405 exit 46 (Century Blvd), 0.5 mi w. Ext/int corridors. **Pets:** Other species. $20 daily fee/pet. Designated rooms, service with restrictions, crate.
[➘] [🛜] [✕] [▬]

◯◯◯ ▽▽▽ ▽▽▽ The Westin Los Angeles Airport 🅗

(310) 216-5858. **$99-$239.** 5400 W Century Blvd 90045. I-405 exit 46 (Century Blvd), just w. Int corridors. **Pets:** Accepted.
[SAVE] [ECO] [❚❙] [♿] [➘] [📶] [✕] [▬]

◯◯◯ ▽▽▽ ▽▽▽ W Los Angeles-Westwood 🅗

(310) 208-8765. **$339-$699.** 930 Hilgard Ave 90024. I-405 exit 55B (Wilshire Blvd), 0.6 mi to Glendon Ave, just n, then just e. Int corridors. **Pets:** Accepted. [SAVE] [❚❙] [➘] [✕] [📶] [✕] [📱]

LOS BAÑOS

◯◯◯ ▽▽ ▽▽ Americas Best Value Inn Ⓜ

(209) 826-5002. **$68-$82.** 330 W Pacheco Blvd 93635. On SR 152; center. Ext corridors. **Pets:** Small. $12 deposit/pet, $12 daily fee/pet. Designated rooms, service with restrictions, supervision.
[SAVE] [➘] [🛜] [📱] [▬]

◯◯◯ ▽▽ ▽▽ BEST WESTERN Executive Inn 🅗

(209) 827-0954. **$99-$125.** 301 W Pacheco Blvd 93635. On SR 152; center. Int corridors. **Pets:** Medium, dogs only. $20 daily fee/pet. Designated rooms, service with restrictions, supervision.
[SAVE] [♿] [➘] [🛜] [✕] [📱] [▬]

◯◯◯ ▽▽ ▽▽ Vagabond Inn Executive 🅗

(209) 827-4677. **$79-$115.** 20 W Pacheco Blvd 93635. On SR 152; center. Int corridors. **Pets:** Dogs only. $20 one-time fee/pet. Designated rooms, service with restrictions, supervision.
[SAVE] [♿] [➘] [🛜] [✕] [📱] [▬]

LOS OSOS

▽▽ ▽▽ Sea Pines Golf Resort 🅗

(805) 528-5252. **$109-$184.** 1945 Solano St 93402. SR 1 exit Los Osos/Baywood Park, 4 mi s on S Bay Blvd, 1.6 mi w on Los Osos Valley Rd, 0.3 mi n on Pecho Rd, then just w on Skyline Dr. Ext corridors. **Pets:** Dogs only. $25 daily fee/room. Designated rooms, service with restrictions, crate. [❚❙] [🛜] [📱] [▬]

MAMMOTH LAKES *(Restaurants p. 617)*

▽▽▽ ▽▽ Mammoth Mountain Inn 🅗

(760) 934-2581. **$129-$299, 14 day notice.** 1 Minaret Rd 93546. 5 mi w of town on SR 203. Int corridors. **Pets:** Accepted.
[❚❙] [➘] [✕] [🛜] [✕] [AC] [📱] [▬]

▽▽▽ ▽▽ Shilo Inn Suites-Mammoth Lakes 🅗

(760) 934-4500. **Call for rates.** 2963 Main St 93546. On SR 203, just e of Old Mammoth Rd. Int corridors. **Pets:** Accepted.
[➘] [✕] [🛜] [✕] [📱] [▬]

◯◯◯ ▽▽ ▽▽ Sierra Lodge 🅗

(760) 934-8881. **$69-$199.** 3540 Main St 93546. On SR 203, 0.6 mi w of Old Mammoth Rd. Int corridors. **Pets:** Other species. $10 daily fee/ pet. Service with restrictions. [SAVE] [🛜] [✕] [AC] [📱]

▽▽▽ ▽▽ Sierra Nevada Resort & Spa 🅗

(760) 934-2515. **$149-$1099, 14 day notice.** 164 Old Mammoth Rd 93546. Just s of SR 203. Ext/int corridors. **Pets:** Large, dogs only. $25 daily fee/pet. Designated rooms, service with restrictions, supervision.
[❚❙] [➘] [✕] [🛜] [✕] [📱] [▬]

◯◯◯ ▽▽▽ ▽▽▽ The Westin Monache Resort 🅗 🐾

(760) 934-0400. **Call for rates.** 50 Hillside Dr 93546. SR 203, 1 mi w to Minaret Rd, 0.3 mi n to Forest Tr, just w, then just nw. Int corridors. **Pets:** Medium, dogs only. Service with restrictions, supervision.
[SAVE] [❚❙] [♿] [➘] [🛜] [✕] [📱] [▬]

MANHATTAN BEACH

▼▼▼ The Belamar Hotel 🏨

(310) 750-0300. **$179-$499.** 3501 N Sepulveda Blvd 90266. I-405 exit 43 (Rosecrans Ave), 1.5 mi w, then just s. Int corridors. **Pets:** Accepted.

[ECO] 🍴 🔥 🏊 ✕ 🛜 ✕ 🖥 💻

▼▼▼ Manhattan Beach Marriott 🏨

(310) 546-7511. **$169-$309.** 1400 Parkview Ave 90266. I-405 exit 43 (Rosecrans Ave), 1 mi w, then just s. Int corridors. **Pets:** Accepted.

[ECO] 🍴 🏊 ✕ 🛜 ✕ 💻

▼▼▼ Residence Inn by Marriott 🏨

(310) 421-3100. **$139-$299.** 1700 N Sepulveda Blvd 90266. I-405 exit 43B (Rosecrans Ave), 1.5 mi w, then 1 mi s on SR 1. Ext corridors. **Pets:** $100 one-time fee/room. Designated rooms, service with restrictions, crate. 🔥 🏊 🛜 ✕ 🖥 💻

MANTECA

◢◣ ▼▼▼ BEST WESTERN PLUS Executive Inn & Suites 🏨

(209) 825-1415. **$75-$100.** 1415 E Yosemite Ave 95336. Just n of jct SR 99 and 120 exit E Yosemite Ave, just w. Ext corridors. **Pets:** Accepted. [SAVE] 🔥 🏊 🛜 ✕ 🖥 💻

MARINA

▼▼▼ The Sanctuary Beach Resort 🏨 🐾

(831) 883-9478. **$169-$550, 3 day notice.** 3295 Dunes Dr 93933. SR 1 exit Reservation Rd, just w. Ext corridors. **Pets:** Medium, other species. $40 daily fee/pet. Designated rooms, service with restrictions, supervision. 🍴 🔥 🏊 🛜 ✕ 🎦 🖥 💻

MARINA DEL REY *(Restaurants p. 617)*

◢◣ ▼▼▼ HOTEL MDR - A DoubleTree by Hilton 🏨 🐾

(310) 822-8555. **$189-$249.** 13480 Maxella Ave 90292. SR 90 (Marina Frwy), just n on Lincoln Blvd (SR 1). Int corridors. **Pets:** Other species. $75 one-time fee/room. Service with restrictions, crate.

[SAVE] [ECO] 🍴 🔥 🏊 🛜 ✕ 💻

◢◣ ▼▼▼▼ The Ritz-Carlton, Marina del Rey 🏨 🐾

(310) 823-1700. **$299-$899.** 4375 Admiralty Way 90292. SR 90 (Marina Frwy), just s on Lincoln Blvd (SR 1), then just w on Bali Way. Int corridors. **Pets:** Small, other species. $125 one-time fee/room. Service with restrictions, supervision. [SAVE] 🍴 🔥 🏊 🛜 ✕ 💻

MARIPOSA

◢◣ ▼▼▼ BEST WESTERN PLUS Yosemite Way Station Motel Ⓜ

(209) 966-7545. **$69-$219, 3 day notice.** 4999 Hwy 140 95338. SR 140 at SR 49 S. Ext corridors. **Pets:** Small. $20 daily fee/pet. Designated rooms, service with restrictions, supervision.

[SAVE] 🏊 🛜 ✕ 🖥 💻

◢◣ ▼▼▼ The Mariposa Lodge Ⓜ

(209) 966-3607. **$69-$179, 3 day notice.** 5052 Hwy 140 95338. Center. Ext corridors. **Pets:** $25 daily fee/pet. Designated rooms, service with restrictions, supervision. [SAVE] 🏊 🛜 🖥 💻

◢◣ ▼▼▼ Miners Inn Motel Ⓜ

(209) 742-7777. **$69-$249.** 5181 Hwy 49 N 95338. Jct SR 49 and 140; downtown. Ext/int corridors. **Pets:** Small. $20 daily fee/pet. Designated rooms, service with restrictions, supervision.

[SAVE] 🏊 🛜 ✕ 🖥 💻

◢◣ ▼▼▼ The Monarch 🏨

(209) 966-4288. **$59-$199.** 5059 Hwy 140 95338. Center. Int corridors. **Pets:** Small. $20 daily fee/pet. Designated rooms, service with restrictions, supervision. [SAVE] 🏊 🛜 ✕ 🖥 💻

MARTINEZ

◢◣ ▼▼▼ BEST WESTERN PLUS John Muir Inn 🏨

(925) 229-1010. **$125-$159.** 445 Muir Station Rd 94553. Jct I-680 and SR 4, 2.3 mi w on SR 4 exit 10 (Pine St/Center Ave), then just se. Int corridors. **Pets:** Accepted. [SAVE] 🔥 🏊 🛜 🖥 💻

MARYSVILLE *(Restaurants p. 617)*

◢◣ ▼▼▼ Comfort Suites 🏨

(530) 742-9200. **$85-$160.** 1034 N Beale Rd 95901. SR 70 exit 20B (N Beale Rd), just e, then just se. Int corridors. **Pets:** Medium. $10 daily fee/pet. Designated rooms, service with restrictions, supervision.

[SAVE] 🔥 🏊 🛜 ✕ 🖥 💻

MCCLOUD

◢◣ ▼▼▼ McCloud Hotel [BB]

(530) 964-2822. **$128-$199, 10 day notice.** 408 Main St 96057. I-5 exit 736 (SR 89/McCloud), 9 mi e; jct SR 89 and W Minnesota Ave, 0.3 mi ne on W Minnesota Ave to Main St, then just n. Int corridors. **Pets:** Accepted. [SAVE] 🔥 🛜 ✕ [W] 💻

▼▼▼ McCloud Mercantile Hotel [BB]

(530) 964-2330. **Call for rates.** 241 Main St 96057. I-5 exit 736 (SR 89/McCloud), 9 mi e; jct SR 89 and W Minnesota Ave, 0.3 mi ne on W Minnesota Ave to Main St, then just n. Ext/int corridors. **Pets:** Accepted.

🍴 🛜 ✕ 🖥

MENDOCINO *(Restaurants p. 617)*

▼▼▼ Agate Cove Inn [CA] 🐾

(707) 937-0551. **$189-$379, 14 day notice.** 11201 N Lansing St 95460. Just w on Little Lake Rd from jct SR 1, then 0.6 mi n. Ext corridors. **Pets:** Dogs only. $25 deposit/pet, $25 daily fee/pet. Designated rooms, service with restrictions, supervision. 🛜 ✕ 🎦 🖥 💻

▼▼▼ Hill House Inn 🏨

(707) 937-0554. **Call for rates.** 10701 Palette Dr 95460. Jct SR 1, just w on Little Lake Rd, then just n on Lansing St. Ext corridors. **Pets:** Accepted. 🛜 ✕ 🎦 🖥 💻

▼▼▼ Mendocino Hotel & Garden Suites 🏨

(707) 937-0511. **Call for rates.** 45080 Main St 95460. 0.4 mi w on Main St from jct SR 1. Ext/int corridors. **Pets:** Accepted.

🍴 🛜 ✕ 🎦 💻

◢◣ ▼▼▼ Stanford Inn by the Sea Eco-Resort [CI] 🐾

(707) 937-5615. **$250-$475, 7 day notice.** 44850 Comptche-Ukiah Rd 95460. SR 1 exit Comptche-Ukiah Rd, just e. Ext corridors. **Pets:** Other species. $45 one-time fee/room. Supervision.

[SAVE] [ECO] 🔌 🍴 🏊 🛜 ✕ 🎦 🖥 💻

MENLO PARK

▼▼▼ Red Cottage Inn & Suites Ⓜ

(650) 326-9010. **$149-$279.** 1704 El Camino Real 94025. US 101 exit 406 (Marsh Rd), 0.4 mi s on Middlefield Rd, 0.6 mi w on Encinal Ave, then just n. Ext corridors. **Pets:** Accepted.

🔥 🏊 🛜 ✕ 🖥 💻

MERCED

◢◣ ▼▼▼ BEST WESTERN PLUS Inn 🏨

(209) 723-2163. **$86-$96.** 1033 Motel Dr 95340. SR 99 exit SR 140, just e, then just s. Ext corridors. **Pets:** Other species. $15 daily fee/room. Designated rooms, service with restrictions, crate.

[SAVE] 🏊 🛜 🖥 💻

MILLBRAE

◢◣ ▼▼▼ Aloft San Francisco Airport 🏨 🐾

(650) 443-5500. **$119-$420.** 401 E Millbrae Ave 94030. US 101 exit Millbrae Ave, just e. Int corridors. **Pets:** Small, dogs only. Designated rooms, service with restrictions, supervision.

[SAVE] 🍴 🔥 🏊 ✕ 🖥 💻

◈ ▼▼◆ **The Westin San Francisco Airport** 🅗
(650) 692-3500. **$149-$420.** 1 Old Bayshore Hwy 94030. Just e of US 101 exit Millbrae Blvd. Int corridors. **Pets:** Accepted.
[SAVE] [ECO] ⊡ ¶¶ ⌖ᴹ ⇔ 奈 ✕ 🔋 ⫞

MILL VALLEY

▼▼▼ **Acqua Hotel** 🅗
(415) 380-0400. **$159-$299.** 555 Redwood Hwy 94941. US 101 exit Seminary Dr. Ext/int corridors. **Pets:** Accepted. ⌖ᴹ 奈 ✕ 🔋

▼▼▼ **Holiday Inn Express Mill Valley/San Francisco Area** 🅗
(415) 332-5700. **$139-$499.** 160 Shoreline Hwy 94941. US 101 exit Stinson Beach southbound, just nw; exit Mill Valley/SR 1/Stinson Beach northbound, 0.4 mi nw. Int corridors. **Pets:** Medium, other species. $75 one-time fee/room. Designated rooms, service with restrictions, crate.
[ECO] ⌖ᴹ ⇔ ✕ 奈 ✕ 🔋 ⫞

▼▼▼ **Mill Valley Inn** 🅗
(415) 389-6608. **$189-$499, 14 day notice.** 165 Throckmorton Ave 94941. Center. Ext/int corridors. **Pets:** Medium. $80 daily fee/room. Supervision. ⌖ᴹ 奈 ✕ 🔋 ⫞

MILPITAS

◈ ▼▼◆ **BEST WESTERN PLUS Brookside Inn** 🅗
(408) 263-5566. **$189-$209.** 400 Valley Way 95035. I-880 exit Calaveras Blvd (SR 237), just e. Ext/int corridors. **Pets:** Small, dogs only. $40 daily fee/pet. Designated rooms, service with restrictions, supervision. [SAVE] ¶¶ ⌖ᴹ ⇔ 奈 🔋 ⫞

▼▼▼ **Beverly Heritage Hotel** 🅗
(408) 943-9080. **Call for rates.** 1820 Barber Ln 95035. Northwest quadrant of I-880 and Montague Expwy. Int corridors. **Pets:** $75 one-time fee/room. Designated rooms, service with restrictions, supervision.
¶¶ ⌖ᴹ ⇔ 奈 🔋 ⫞

◈ ▼▼▼ **Larkspur Landing Milpitas** 🅗
(408) 719-1212. **$99-$259, 3 day notice.** 40 Ranch Dr 95035. SR 237 exit McCarthy Blvd, just n. Int corridors. **Pets:** Accepted.
[SAVE] [ECO] ⌖ᴹ 奈 ✕ 🔋 ⫞

▼▼▼ **Residence Inn by Marriott** 🅗
(408) 941-9222. **$129-$399.** 1501 California Cir 95035. I-880 exit Dixon Landing Rd E, just s. Int corridors. **Pets:** Accepted.
⌖ᴹ ⇔ 奈 ✕ 🔋 ⫞

◈ ▼▼◆ **Sheraton San Jose Hotel** 🅗
(408) 943-0600. **Call for rates.** 1801 Barber Ln 95035. 4 mi n of San Jose International Airport; 0.3 mi nw of I-880 and Montague Expwy. Ext/int corridors. **Pets:** Accepted.
[SAVE] ¶¶ ⌖ᴹ ⇔ 🅢 ✕ 🔋 ⫞

▼▼▼ **TownePlace Suites by Marriott** 🅗
(408) 719-1959. **$99-$409.** 1428 Falcon Dr 95035. I-680 exit Montague Expwy W, just n. Int corridors. **Pets:** Accepted.
[ECO] ⌖ᴹ ⇔ 奈 🔋 ⫞

MIRANDA

◈ ▼▼▼ **Miranda Gardens Resort** 🅒🅐
(707) 943-3011. **$105-$265, 7 day notice.** 6766 Ave of the Giants 95553. US 101 exit 650, 0.3 mi s on Maple Hills Rd, then 1.5 mi e. Ext corridors. **Pets:** Small. $150 deposit/room, $15 daily fee/pet. Designated rooms, service with restrictions, supervision.
[SAVE] ⇔ 🅢 ✕ 🏂 🐾 🔋 ⫞

MI-WUK VILLAGE

◈ ▼▼◆ **Christmas Tree Inn** 🅗
(209) 586-1005. **$89-$129, 3 day notice.** 24685 Hwy 108 95346. On SR 108, 15 mi e of Sonora. Ext corridors. **Pets:** $25 one-time fee/room. Designated rooms, service with restrictions, supervision.
[SAVE] ⇔ 奈 ✕ 🔋 ⫞

MODESTO

◈ ▼▼▼◆ **BEST WESTERN Palm Court Inn** 🅗
(209) 521-9000. **$95-$110.** 2001 W Orangeburg Ave 95350. SR 99 exit Briggsmore Ave, just ne, then just s. Ext corridors. **Pets:** Medium, other species. $20 daily fee/room. Service with restrictions, supervision.
[SAVE] ⌖ᴹ ⇔ 奈 ✕ 🔋 ⫞

◈ ▼▼▼ **BEST WESTERN Town House Lodge** 🅗
(209) 524-7261. **$85-$100.** 909 16th St 95354. SR 99 exit Central Modesto, 1 mi e; at I St. Ext corridors. **Pets:** Large. $20 daily fee/room. Service with restrictions. [SAVE] ⌖ᴹ ⇔ 奈 🔋 ⫞

◈ ▼▼▼ **Comfort Inn** 🅗
(209) 544-2000. **$74-$144.** 2025 W Orangeburg Ave 95350. SR 99 exit Briggsmore Ave, just e, then just s. Int corridors. **Pets:** Accepted.
[SAVE] ⌖ᴹ ⇔ 奈 ✕ 🔋 ⫞

◈ ▼▼▼◆ **DoubleTree by Hilton Hotel Modesto** 🅗
(209) 526-6000. **$99-$169.** 1150 9th St 95354. SR 99 exit Central Modesto northbound; exit Maze Blvd southbound, 0.7 mi ne; between K and L sts. Int corridors. **Pets:** Accepted.
[SAVE] [ECO] ¶¶ ⌖ᴹ ⇔ 奈 ✕ 🔋 ⫞

◈ ▼▼◆ **Microtel Inn & Suites by Wyndham Modesto Ceres** 🅗
(209) 538-6466. **$65-$89.** 1760 Herndon Rd 95307. SR 99 exit Hatch Rd E, 0.5 mi s; jct Evans Rd. Int corridors. **Pets:** Small. $50 deposit/pet. Service with restrictions, crate. [SAVE] ⌖ᴹ ⇔ 奈 ✕ 🔋 ⫞

▼▼◆ **Super 8 Modesto** 🅜
(209) 543-9000. **$68-$80.** 4100 Salida Blvd 95358. SR 99 exit Pelandale Ave, just w, then just s. Ext corridors. **Pets:** Small. $10 one-time fee/pet. Service with restrictions, supervision. ⇔ 奈 ✕ 🔋 ⫞

MOJAVE

◈ ▼▼◆ **BEST WESTERN Desert Winds** 🅜
(661) 824-3601. **$105-$125.** 16200 Sierra Hwy 93501. On SR 14 and 58; center. Ext corridors. **Pets:** Dogs only. $10 daily fee/pet. Service with restrictions, supervision. [SAVE] ⌖ᴹ ⇔ 奈 🔋 ⫞

◈ ▼▼ **Desert Inn** 🅜
(661) 824-2518. **$49-$69.** 1954 Hwy 58 93501. Just e of SR 14. Ext corridors. **Pets:** Medium, dogs only. Service with restrictions, crate.
[SAVE] 奈 🔋 ⫞

◈ ▼▼◆ **Mariah Country Inn & Suites** 🅗
(661) 824-4980. **$92-$142.** 1385 Hwy 58 93501. SR 14 exit 172 (SR 58), 1.5 mi e. Ext corridors. **Pets:** Medium. $20 one-time fee/room. Service with restrictions, supervision. [SAVE] ¶¶ ⌖ᴹ ⇔ 奈 🔋 ⫞

MONROVIA

▼▼◆ **DoubleTree by Hilton Hotel Monrovia - Pasadena Area** 🅗
(626) 357-1900. **$139-$226.** 924 W Huntington Dr 91016. I-210 exit 33 (Huntington Dr), just s. Int corridors. **Pets:** Accepted.
¶¶ ⌖ᴹ ⇔ 奈 ✕ 🔋 ⫞

MONTECITO

◈ ▼▼▼◆ **Four Seasons Resort The Biltmore Santa Barbara** 🅗 ❀
(805) 969-2261. **$395-$995, 3 day notice.** 1260 Channel Dr 93108. US 101 exit 94A (Olive Mill Rd), 0.3 mi s. Ext/int corridors. **Pets:** Medium. Designated rooms, service with restrictions, supervision.
[SAVE] ¶¶ ⌖ᴹ ⇔ ✕ 🅢 ✕ 🔋 ⫞

MONTEREY *(Restaurants p. 617)*

◈ ▼▼◆ **Bay Park Hotel** 🅗 🐾
(831) 649-1020. **$99-$350.** 1425 Munras Ave 93940. SR 1 exit Soledad Dr/Munras Ave, just w. Int corridors. **Pets:** Medium, dogs only. $30 daily fee/pet. Designated rooms, service with restrictions, supervision.
[SAVE] ¶¶ ⌖ᴹ ⇔ 奈 ✕ 🔋 ⫞

BEST WESTERN PLUS Beach Resort Monterey H ❖
(831) 394-3321. **$119-$389.** 2600 Sand Dunes Dr 93940. SR 1 exit Del Rey Oaks, just w. Ext corridors. **Pets:** Small. $30 daily fee/room. Designated rooms, service with restrictions, supervision.
SAVE ▥ ⓜ ⇌ ⌘ ✕ ▯ ▣

BEST WESTERN PLUS Victorian Inn H ❖
(831) 373-8000. **$109-$559, 3 day notice.** 487 Foam St 93940. SR 1 exit Monterey, 3.4 mi w. Ext/int corridors. **Pets:** $30 deposit/pet. Designated rooms, service with restrictions, crate.
SAVE ECO ⓜ ⌘ ✕ ▧ ▯ ▣

Casa Munras Garden Hotel & Spa H ❖
(831) 375-2411. **$169-$700, 3 day notice.** 700 Munras Ave 93940. SR 1 exit Soledad Dr/Munras Ave, 0.8 mi w. Ext/int corridors. **Pets:** $50 deposit/pet. Designated rooms, service with restrictions, crate.
SAVE ECO ▥ ⓜ ⇌ ⌘ ✕ ▯ ▣

Comfort Inn-Monterey Bay H
(831) 373-3081. **$65-$169.** 2050 N Fremont St 93940. SR 1 exit Fremont St or Casa Verde Way, 0.3 mi e. Ext corridors. **Pets:** Small, other species. $25 daily fee/room. Service with restrictions, supervision. SAVE ⓜ ⌘ ✕ ▯ ▣

Comfort Inn-Monterey by the Sea H
(831) 372-2908. **$69-$189.** 1252 Munras Ave 93940. SR 1 exit Soledad Dr/Munras Ave, just s. Ext corridors. **Pets:** Medium, other species. $25 daily fee/room. Service with restrictions, supervision.
SAVE ECO ⓜ ⇌ ⌘ ✕ ▯ ▣

El Adobe Inn M
(831) 372-5409. **Call for rates.** 936 Munras Ave 93940. SR 1 exit Soledad Dr/Munras Ave, 0.6 mi w. Ext corridors. **Pets:** Accepted.
⌘ ✕ ▧ ▯ ▣

Hotel Pacific H
(831) 373-5700. **$159-$599, 3 day notice.** 300 Pacific St 93940. SR 1 exit Del Monte Ave, 2.2 mi w. Ext/int corridors. **Pets:** Accepted.
SAVE ⓜ ⌘ ✕ ▧ ▯ ▣

Hyatt Regency Monterey Hotel & Spa H ❖
(831) 372-1234. **$119-$499, 3 day notice.** 1 Old Golf Course Rd 93940. SR 1 exit Aguajito Rd northbound; exit Monterey southbound, just e. Int corridors. **Pets:** Medium, dogs only. $100 one-time fee/room. Designated rooms, no service, crate.
SAVE ECO ▥ ⓜ ⇌ ⌘ ▧ ✕ ▯ ▣

InterContinental The Clement Monterey H
(831) 375-4500. **$189-$429, 3 day notice.** 750 Cannery Row 93940. Between Prescott and David aves. Int corridors. **Pets:** Accepted.
SAVE ▥ ⓜ ⇌ ▧ ⌘ ✕ ▣

Mariposa Inn & Suites H
(831) 649-1414. **$109-$409, 3 day notice.** 1386 Munras Ave 93940. SR 1 exit Soledad Dr/Munras Ave, just w. Ext/int corridors. **Pets:** Dogs only. $40 daily fee/pet. Service with restrictions, supervision.
ⓜ ⇌ ⌘ ✕ ▯ ▣

Monterey Bay Lodge H
(831) 372-8057. **$79-$449.** 55 Camino Aguajito 93940. SR 1 exit Aguajito Rd, just w. Ext corridors. **Pets:** Medium, dogs only. $15 daily fee/pet. Designated rooms, service with restrictions, supervision.
SAVE ▥ ⓜ ⌘ ✕ ▯ ▣

Old Monterey Inn BB
(831) 375-8284. **$199-$499, 14 day notice.** 500 Martin St 93940. SR 1 exit Soledad Dr/Munras Ave, 1 mi w; from Fisherman's Wharf, 1 mi s on Pacific St to Martin St, 2 blks w. Ext/int corridors. **Pets:** Accepted.
SAVE ⌘ ✕

Pacific Inn Monterey M
(831) 373-2445. **Call for rates.** 2332 N Fremont St 93940. SR 1 exit Del Rey Oaks or Fremont St, 0.7 mi e. Ext corridors. **Pets:** Medium. $30 daily fee/pet. Designated rooms, service with restrictions, supervision. SAVE ⌘ ✕ ▯ ▣

Portola Hotel & Spa H ❖
(831) 649-4511. **$159-$649.** 2 Portola Plaza 93940. 2 mi w of SR 1 exit Del Monte or Munras aves; near Fisherman's Wharf; downtown. Int corridors. **Pets:** Other species. $50 daily fee/room. Supervision.
SAVE ECO ▥ ⓜ ⇌ ▧ ⌘ ✕ ▯ ▣

MONTE RIO

Rio Villa Beach Resort M ❖
(707) 865-1143. **$130-$250, 7 day notice.** 20292 Hwy 116 95462. Center. Ext corridors. **Pets:** $25 daily fee/pet. Service with restrictions, supervision. ⌘ ✕ ▯ ▣

MORENO VALLEY

BEST WESTERN Moreno Hotel & Suites M ❖
(951) 924-4546. **$72-$99.** 24840 Elder Ave 92557. SR 60 exit 62 (Perris Blvd) westbound, just n, then just w; exit eastbound, just e on Sunnymead Blvd, just n on Perris Blvd, then just w. Ext corridors. **Pets:** Medium, dogs only. $20 daily fee/pet. Designated rooms, service with restrictions, crate. SAVE ⇌ ⌘ ✕ ▯ ▣

La Quinta Inn & Suites H
(951) 486-9000. **$89-$209.** 23090 Sunnymead Blvd 92553. SR 60 exit 60 (Frederick St/Pigeon Pass Rd), just s, then just e. Int corridors. **Pets:** Large, other species. Service with restrictions.
SAVE ⓜ ⌘ ✕ ▯ ▣

MORGAN HILL

Comfort Inn H
(408) 778-3400. **$105-$999.** 16225 Condit Rd 95037. US 101 exit Tennant Ave, just e, then just n. Int corridors. **Pets:** Accepted.
SAVE ⓜ ⇌ ▧ ⌘ ▯ ▣

Residence Inn by Marriott H ❖
(408) 782-8311. **$89-$299.** 18620 Madrone Pkwy 95037. US 101 exit Cochrane W, just n. Int corridors. **Pets:** Other species. $100 one-time fee/pet. Designated rooms, service with restrictions.
ⓜ ⇌ ⌘ ✕ ▯ ▣

MORRO BAY *(Restaurants p. 617)*

Beach Bungalow Inn & Suites M ❖
(805) 772-9700. **$129-$359, 3 day notice.** 1050 Morro Ave 93442. SR 1 exit Morro Bay Blvd, 0.8 mi w, then just n. Ext corridors. **Pets:** Medium, dogs only. $20 daily fee/pet. Designated rooms, service with restrictions, supervision. ⌘ ✕ ▧ ▯ ▣

BEST WESTERN El Rancho M
(805) 772-2212. **$75-$210, 3 day notice.** 2460 Main St 93442. SR 1 exit Morro Bay Blvd, 0.5 mi n. Ext corridors. **Pets:** Accepted.
SAVE ⇌ ⌘ ▧ ▯ ▣

Econo Lodge M
(805) 772-5609. **$65-$376, 3 day notice.** 1100 Main St 93442. SR 1 exit Morro Bay Blvd, 0.7 mi w, then just n. Ext corridors. **Pets:** Accepted. ⌘ ✕ ▯ ▣

Inn at Morro Bay H ❖
(805) 772-5651. **Call for rates.** 60 State Park Rd 93442. SR 1 exit Morro Bay Blvd, 0.7 mi w, then 1 mi s on Main St. Ext corridors. **Pets:** Medium, dogs only. $25 daily fee/room. Service with restrictions, crate. SAVE ▥ ⓜ ⇌ ▧ ⌘ ✕ ▧ ▯ ▣

La Serena Inn H ❖
(805) 772-5665. **$59-$299, 3 day notice.** 990 Morro Ave 93442. SR 1 exit Morro Bay Blvd, 0.7 mi w, then just n. Int corridors. **Pets:** Large, other species. $25 daily fee/pet. Designated rooms, service with restrictions, supervision. SAVE ⌘ ✕ ▯ ▣

Morro Bay Sandpiper Inn M
(805) 772-7503. **$50-$299, 3 day notice.** 540 Main St 93442. SR 1 exit Morro Bay Blvd, 0.7 mi w, then 0.4 mi s. Ext corridors. **Pets:** Medium, other species. $25 daily fee/room. Designated rooms, service with restrictions, supervision.

MOUNTAIN VIEW *(Restaurants p. 618)*

Extended Stay America-San Jose, Mountain View H
(650) 962-1500. **Call for rates.** 190 E El Camino Real 94040. SR 82, just w of SR 85. Ext corridors. **Pets:** Other species. $25 daily fee/pet. Service with restrictions, supervision.

Residence Inn by Marriott-Palo Alto/Mountain View H
(650) 940-1300. **$139-$429, 3 day notice.** 1854 W El Camino Real 94040. US 101 exit 399 (Shoreline Blvd/Mountain View), 2 mi to SR 82, then 0.5 mi n. Ext corridors. **Pets:** Accepted.

MOUNT SHASTA

BEST WESTERN PLUS Tree House H
(530) 926-3101. **$160-$190.** 111 Morgan Way 96067. I-5 exit 738 (Central Mount Shasta), just e. Ext/int corridors. **Pets:** Medium, other species. $20 daily fee/room. Service with restrictions, supervision.

Cold Creek Inn M
(530) 926-9851. **$69-$185.** 724 N Mount Shasta Blvd 96067. I-5 exit 738 (Central Mount Shasta), 0.5 mi ne on W Lake St, then 0.5 mi nw. Ext corridors. **Pets:** Other species. $20 daily fee/pet. Service with restrictions, supervision.

Mount Shasta Resort C
(530) 926-3030. **$109-$339, 14 day notice.** 1000 Siskiyou Lake Blvd 96067. I-5 exit 738 (Central Mount Shasta), 0.4 mi w on Lake St (which becomes Hatchery Ln), just s on S Old Stage Rd; at split follow sign for resort, 1.4 mi s on W A Barr Rd, then just se. Ext corridors. **Pets:** Other species. $20 daily fee/pet. Designated rooms.

MYERS FLAT

Myers Inn BB
(707) 943-3259. **$161-$203, 14 day notice.** 12913 Ave of the Giants 95554. US 101 exit Myers Flat, just w. Int corridors. **Pets:** Accepted.

NAPA

Blackbird Inn BB
(707) 226-2450. **$395, 7 day notice.** 1755 1st St 94559. SR 29 exit 1st St, 0.5 mi e to Jefferson St, then just n. Int corridors. **Pets:** Accepted.

Embassy Suites Napa Valley H
(707) 253-9540. **$159-$399.** 1075 California Blvd 94559. SR 29 exit 1st St, just ne. Ext/int corridors. **Pets:** Medium, other species. $75 one-time fee/room. Designated rooms, service with restrictions, supervision.

The Inn on First BB
(707) 253-1331. **$199-$450, 30 day notice.** 1938 1st St 94559. SR 29 exit 1st St, just e via Clay St. Ext/int corridors. **Pets:** Dogs only. $50 one-time fee/room. Designated rooms, service with restrictions, crate.

The Meritage Resort and Spa H
(707) 251-1900. **$159-$579.** 875 Bordeaux Way 94558. 0.5 mi n of jct SR 29 and 121; SR 121 N, follow Downtown Napa/Lake Berryessa, w on Napa Valley Corporate Way, then just s. Int corridors.
Pets: Accepted.

The Napa Inn BB
(707) 257-1444. **$169-$389, 10 day notice.** 1137 Warren St 94559. SR 29 exit 1st St, 0.5 mi e, then 0.3 mi n. Int corridors. **Pets:** $30 daily fee/room. Designated rooms, service with restrictions, crate.

Napa River Inn H
(707) 251-8500. **$209-$650, 3 day notice.** 500 Main St 94559. Jct 5th St; downtown. Int corridors. **Pets:** Medium. $25 daily fee/room. Supervision.

Napa Valley Hotel & Suites/A 3 Palms Hotel & Resort at the Napa River H
(707) 226-1871. **Call for rates.** 853 Coombs St 94559. At 2nd and Coombs sts; downtown. Ext corridors. **Pets:** Accepted.

Napa Winery Inn, an Ascend Hotel Collection Member H
(707) 257-7220. **$119-$429, 3 day notice.** 1998 Trower Ave 94558. SR 29 exit Trower Ave, just e. Int corridors. **Pets:** Small. $50 one-time fee/room. Designated rooms, service with restrictions, supervision.

The Westin Verasa Napa H
(707) 257-1800. **$179-$749, 3 day notice.** 1314 McKinstry St 94559. Jct Soscol Ave; behind the Napa Valley Wine Train parking area. Int corridors. **Pets:** Medium. Service with restrictions, supervision.

NATIONAL CITY *(Restaurants p. 618)*

BEST WESTERN PLUS Marina Gateway Hotel H
(619) 259-2800. **$100-$335.** 800 Bay Marina Dr 91950. I-5 exit 10 (Bay Marina Dr), just w. Int corridors. **Pets:** Small, other species. $150 deposit/room. Designated rooms, service with restrictions, supervision.

Clarion Hotel National City San Diego South H
(619) 474-2800. **$109-$229.** 700 National City Blvd 91950. I-5 exit 11B (8th St) southbound, just e; exit 11B (Plaza Blvd) northbound, just e, then just n. Ext corridors. **Pets:** Accepted.

NEEDLES *(Restaurants p. 618)*

BEST WESTERN Colorado River Inn M
(760) 326-4552. **$79-$139.** 2371 W Broadway 92363. I-40 exit 141 (W Broadway/River Rd), 0.3 mi se; on Business Loop I-40. Ext corridors. **Pets:** Other species. $15 daily fee/room. Designated rooms, service with restrictions, supervision.

Rio del Sol Inn M
(760) 326-5660. **$62-$99, 3 day notice.** 1111 Pashard St 92363. I-40 exit 141 (W Broadway/River Rd), just sw. Ext corridors. **Pets:** Accepted.

NEWARK

Aloft Silicon Valley H
(510) 494-8800. **Call for rates.** 8200 Gateway Blvd 94560. SR 84 exit Thornton Ave, just s. Int corridors. **Pets:** Medium, dogs only. Service with restrictions, supervision.

Chase Suite Hotel H
(510) 795-1200. **Call for rates.** 39150 Cedar Blvd 94560. I-880 exit Mowry Ave, just w, then 0.3 mi s. Ext corridors. **Pets:** Accepted.

Doubletree by Hilton Newark/Fremont H
(510) 490-8390. **$99-$199.** 39900 Balentine Dr 94560. I-880 exit Stevenson Blvd, just w. Int corridors. **Pets:** $50 deposit/pet. Supervision.

▼▼▼▼ **Homewood Suites by Hilton** H

(510) 791-7700. **$229-$294.** 39270 Cedar Blvd 94560. I-880 exit Mowry Ave, w to Cedar Blvd, then 0.3 mi s. Int corridors. **Pets:** Accepted.

&M ➦ 📶 🔒 💻

▼▼▼▼ **Residence Inn by Marriott Newark/Silicon Valley** H

(510) 739-6000. **$99-$289.** 35466 Dumbarton Ct 94560. SR 84 exit Newark Blvd, just s. Int corridors. **Pets:** Accepted.

ECO &M ➦ 📶 ✕ 🔒 💻

NEWPORT BEACH *(Restaurants p. 618)*

ⓐⓐⓟ ▼▼▼▼ **Balboa Bay Resort** H ❀

(949) 645-5000. **$229-$459, 3 day notice.** 1221 W Coast Hwy 92663. SR 73 exit 15 (Jamboree Rd), 3.5 mi s, then just w. Int corridors. **Pets:** Small, dogs only. $100 one-time fee/room. Designated rooms, service with restrictions. SAVE ¶¶ &M ➦ ✕ 📶 ✕ 🔒 💻

▼▼ **Extended Stay America-Orange County/John Wayne Airport** H

(949) 851-2711. **Call for rates.** 4881 Birch St 92660. I-405 exit 8 (Mac-Arthur Blvd), 0.8 mi s, then just e. Int corridors. **Pets:** Other species. $25 daily fee/pet. Service with restrictions, supervision. &M 📶 🔒

ⓐⓐⓟ ▼▼▼▼ **Fairmont Newport Beach** H ❀

(949) 476-2001. **$119-$299.** 4500 MacArthur Blvd 92660. I-405 exit 8 (MacArthur Blvd), 1 mi s. Int corridors. **Pets:** $25 daily fee/pet. Service with restrictions. SAVE ECO ¶¶ &M ➦ ✕ 📶 🔒 💻

ⓐⓐⓟ ▼▼▼▼ **Hyatt Regency Newport Beach** H

(949) 729-1234. **$99-$319.** 1107 Jamboree Rd 92660. SR 73 exit 15 (Jamboree Rd), 3 mi s. Ext/int corridors. **Pets:** Accepted.

SAVE ECO ¶¶ &M ➦ ✕ 📶 ✕ 🔒 💻

▼▼▼ **Island Hotel Newport Beach** H

(949) 759-0808. **$209-$5000, 3 day notice.** 690 Newport Center Dr 92660. SR 73 exit 14 (MacArthur Blvd) northbound, 3 mi s to San Joaquin Hills Rd, then 0.5 mi w; exit 15 (Jamboree Rd) southbound, 2.5 mi s to San Joaquin Hills Rd, then 0.5 mi e. Int corridors. **Pets:** Accepted.

SAVE ¶¶ &M ➦ ✕ 📶 ✕ 🔒

▼▼▼ **Newport Beach Marriott Bayview Hotel** H

(949) 854-4500. **$159-$359.** 500 Bayview Cir 92660. SR 73 exit 15 (Jamboree Rd), just s, just w on Bayview Pl, then just n. Int corridors. **Pets:** Accepted. ECO ¶¶ &M ➦ 📶 ✕ 🔒 💻

NICE

▼▼ **Featherbed Railroad Co.** BB

(707) 274-8378. **$99-$220, 3 day notice.** 2870 Lakeshore Blvd 95464. 0.5 mi s of SR 20. Ext corridors. **Pets:** Accepted.

➦ ✕ 📶 ✕ 🐾 🔒 💻

NIPOMO

▼▼ **Kaleidoscope Inn & Gardens B&B** BB

(805) 929-5444. **$140-$160, 7 day notice.** 130 E Dana St 93444. US 101 exit 179 (Tefft St), 0.7 mi e, just s on Thompson Rd, then just e. Ext/int corridors. **Pets:** Other species. Designated rooms, no service, supervision. 📶 ✕ 🐾

NORTH HOLLYWOOD

ⓐⓐⓟ ▼▼▼ **Colony Inn** M

(818) 763-2787. **$80-$150.** 4917 Vineland Ave 91601. US 101 exit 12C (Vineland Ave), 1 mi n. Ext corridors. **Pets:** Medium. $35 daily fee/pet. Designated rooms, service with restrictions, supervision. SAVE 📶 🔒

NORTHRIDGE

▼▼ **Extended Stay America-Los Angeles/Northridge** H

(818) 734-1787. **Call for rates.** 19325 Londelius St 91324. SR 118 exit 37 (Tampa Ave), 3 mi s. Int corridors. **Pets:** Other species. $25 daily fee/pet. Service with restrictions, supervision. &M 📶 🔒 💻

NOVATO *(Restaurants p. 618)*

ⓐⓐⓟ ▼▼▼▼ **Inn Marin** M

(415) 883-5952. **$119-$329.** 250 Entrada Dr 94949. US 101 exit Ignacio Blvd, just w, just n on Enfrente Rd, then just e. Ext corridors. **Pets:** Other species. $25 one-time fee/pet. Service with restrictions, supervision. SAVE ECO 📶 ¶¶ &M ➦ 📶 ✕ 🔒 💻

OAKDALE

ⓐⓐⓟ ▼▼▼ **Motel 6** H

(209) 847-8181. **$49-$110.** 825 East F St 95361. 0.8 mi e on SR 108 and 120. Ext corridors. **Pets:** Other species. Service with restrictions, crate. SAVE &M ➦ 📶 🔒

OAKHURST

ⓐⓐⓟ ▼▼▼▼ **BEST WESTERN PLUS Yosemite Gateway Inn** H

(559) 683-2378. **$99-$219.** 40530 Hwy 41 93644. SR 49, 0.8 mi n. Ext corridors. **Pets:** Accepted.

SAVE ¶¶ &M ➦ ✕ 📶 ✕ 🔒 💻

ⓐⓐⓟ ▼▼▼▼▼ **Château du Sureau** CI

(559) 683-6860. **$385-$585, 14 day notice.** 48688 Victoria Ln 93644. Just w of jct SR 41 and 49. Ext/int corridors. **Pets:** Very small. $85 one-time fee/room. Designated rooms, supervision.

SAVE ¶¶ ➦ 📶 ✕ 🐾

ⓐⓐⓟ ▼▼▼ **Comfort Inn Yosemite Area** M

(559) 683-8282. **$60-$200.** 40489 Hwy 41 93644. SR 49, 0.5 mi n. Ext corridors. **Pets:** Large, other species. $25 daily fee/pet. Designated rooms, service with restrictions, supervision.

SAVE ➦ 📶 ✕ 🔒 💻

OAKLAND

▼▼▼ **Hilton Oakland Airport** H

(510) 635-5000. **$179-$299.** 1 Hegenberger Rd 94621. I-880 exit Hegenberger Rd, 1 mi w; 1.3 mi e of Metropolitan Oakland International Airport. Int corridors. **Pets:** Accepted.

ECO 📶 ¶¶ &M ➦ 📶 🔒 💻

▼▼▼ **Homewood Suites by Hilton** H

(510) 663-2700. **$139-$219.** 1103 Embarcadero 94606. I-880 exit 16th Ave/Embarcadero southbound; exit 5th Ave/Embarcadero northbound, just w. Int corridors. **Pets:** Accepted.

ECO &M ➦ 📶 ✕ 🔒 💻

ⓐⓐⓟ ▼▼▼▼ **La Quinta Inn Oakland Airport Coliseum** H

(510) 632-8900. **$79-$205.** 8465 Enterprise Way 94621. I-880 exit Hegenberger Rd, just e. Int corridors. **Pets:** Large, other species. Service with restrictions. SAVE &M ➦ 📶 ✕ 🔒 💻

▼▼ **Quality Inn** H

(510) 562-4888. **$59-$119.** 8471 Enterprise Way 94621. I-880 exit Hegenberger Rd, just e. Ext corridors. **Pets:** Accepted.

&M ➦ 📶 🔒 💻

ⓐⓐⓟ ▼▼▼ **Red Lion Hotel Oakland International Airport** H

(510) 635-5300. **$109-$199, 3 day notice.** 150 Hegenberger Rd 94621. I-880 exit Hegenberger Rd, 0.8 mi w. Int corridors. **Pets:** Accepted.

SAVE ¶¶ &M ➦ 📶 ✕ 🔒 💻

ⓐⓐⓟ ▼▼▼ **Waterfront Hotel, a Joie de Vivre hotel** H

(510) 836-3800. **$105-$279.** 10 Washington St 94607. I-880 exit Broadway, 0.5 mi w. Int corridors. **Pets:** Accepted.

SAVE ECO ¶¶ &M ➦ 📶 ✕ 🔒 💻

OCCIDENTAL

▼▼▼▼ Inn at Occidental BB ❖

(707) 874-1047. **$199-$379, 10 day notice.** 3657 Church St 95465. Just e on 3rd St; town center. Ext/int corridors. **Pets:** Medium, dogs only. $40 daily fee/room. Designated rooms, service with restrictions, supervision. 🛆M 🛜 ⊠

◆▼ Occidental Hotel M

(707) 874-3623. **$95-$180, 3 day notice.** 3610 Bohemian Hwy 95465. In the village. Ext corridors. **Pets:** Medium. $25 deposit/pet, $25 daily fee/pet. Designated rooms, service with restrictions, supervision. 🛆M 🔁 🛜 ⊠ 🖥 🖵

OCEANO *(Restaurants p. 618)*

▼▼ Oceano Inn M

(805) 473-0032. **$69-$249, 3 day notice.** 1252 Pacific Blvd 93445. On SR 1. Ext corridors. **Pets:** Accepted. 🛆M 🛜 ⊠ 🖥 🖵

OCEANSIDE *(Restaurants p. 618)*

▼▼ La Quinta Inn San Diego Oceanside M

(760) 450-0730. **$79-$399.** 937 N Coast Hwy 92054. I-5 exit 54B (Coast Hwy/Oceanside) southbound; exit 54B (Camp Pendleton) northbound, just w. Int corridors. **Pets:** Large, other species. Service with restrictions. 🛜 ⊠ 🖥 🖵

▼▼ Quality Inn I-5 Near Camp Pendleton M

(760) 721-6663. **$65-$249.** 1403 Mission Ave 92058. I-5 exit 53 (Mission Ave), just e. Ext corridors. **Pets:** Other species. $25 daily fee/pet. Service with restrictions. 🔁 🛜 ⊠ 🖥 🖵

◆◆ ▼▼ Super 8 Oceanside M

(760) 757-7700. **$65-$140.** 3240 Mission Ave 92058. I-5 exit 53 (Mission Ave), 2 mi e. Ext/int corridors. **Pets:** Accepted. SAVE 🔁 🛜 🖥 🖵

OJAI *(Restaurants p. 618)*

▼▼▼ Blue Iguana Inn M

(805) 646-5277. **$139-$329, 7 day notice.** 11794 N Ventura Ave 93023. 2.5 mi w of town on SR 33. Ext corridors. **Pets:** Accepted. 🔁 🛜 ⊠ 🗋 🖥 🖵

▼▼▼ Casa Ojai Inn M

(805) 646-8175. **$109-$219.** 1302 E Ojai Ave 93023. 0.8 mi e on SR 150. Ext corridors. **Pets:** Medium, dogs only. $25 daily fee/pet. Designated rooms, service with restrictions, crate. ECO 🔁 🛜 ⊠ 🖥 🖵

◆◆ ▼▼ Oakridge Inn M

(805) 649-4018. **$55-$160, 3 day notice.** 780 N Ventura Ave 93022. 4 mi s on SR 33; 2 mi e of Lake Casitas; in Oak View. Ext corridors. **Pets:** Medium. $15 daily fee/pet. Designated rooms, service with restrictions, supervision. SAVE 🛜 🖥 🖵

◆◆ ▼▼▼▼ Ojai Valley Inn & Spa H ❖

(805) 646-1111. **$309-$409, 3 day notice.** 905 Country Club Rd 93023. 1 mi w on SR 150, just s. Ext/int corridors. **Pets:** Large, other species. $150 one-time fee/room. Designated rooms, service with restrictions, supervision. SAVE 🍴 🛆 🛆M 🔁 ⊠ 🛜 ⊠ 🖥 🖵

OLYMPIC VALLEY

▼▼▼ PlumpJack Squaw Valley Inn H ❖

(530) 583-1576. **$170-$780, 7 day notice.** 1920 Squaw Valley Rd 96146. I-80 exit SR 89, 8.3 mi s, then 2.2 mi sw. Int corridors. **Pets:** Dogs only. $150 one-time fee/pet. Designated rooms, service with restrictions, crate. 🍴 🛆M 🔁 🛜 ⊠ 🖥 🖵

ONTARIO

◆◆ ▼▼▼ BEST WESTERN PLUS InnSuites Ontario Airport E Hotel & Suites H

(909) 466-9600. **$79-$149.** 3400 Shelby St 91764. I-10 exit 56 (Haven Ave), just n to Inland Empire Blvd, just w, then just se. Ext corridors. **Pets:** Accepted. SAVE 🍴 🔁 ⊠ 🛜 🖥 🖵

◆◆ ▼▼▼ Country Inn Ontario M

(909) 923-1887. **$65-$90.** 2359 S Grove Ave 91761. SR 60 exit 36 (Grove Ave), just n. Ext corridors. **Pets:** Medium. $10 daily fee/pet. Service with restrictions, crate. SAVE 🔁 🛜 🖥 🖵

▼▼▼▼ DoubleTree by Hilton Hotel Ontario Airport H

(909) 937-0900. **$89-$174.** 222 N Vineyard Ave 91764. I-10 exit 54 (Vineyard Ave), 0.4 mi s. Int corridors. **Pets:** Accepted. ECO 🍴 🔁 🛜 ⊠ 🖥 🖵

◆◆ ▼▼▼▼ Hyatt Place Ontario/Rancho Cucamonga H

(909) 980-2200. **$89-$249.** 4760 E Mills Cir 91764. I-10 exit 57 (Milliken Ave), just n, 0.5 mi e on Ontario Mills Pkwy, just n on Ontario Mills Dr, then just e. Int corridors. **Pets:** Accepted. SAVE 🍴 🔁 🛜 ⊠ 🖥 🖵

▼▼▼ La Quinta Inn & Suites Ontario Airport H

(909) 476-1112. **$79-$185.** 3555 Inland Empire Blvd 91764. I-10 exit 56 (Haven Ave), just n, then just e. Int corridors. **Pets:** Large, other species. Service with restrictions. 🛆M 🔁 🛜 🖥 🖵

◆◆ ▼▼▼▼ Ontario Airport Hotel & Conference Center H

(909) 980-0400. **$79-$179.** 700 N Haven Ave 91764. I-10 exit 56 (Haven Ave), just n. Int corridors. **Pets:** Accepted. SAVE ECO 🚏 🍴 🔁 🛜 ⊠ 🖥 🖵

▼▼▼ Ontario Grand Inn & Suites H

(909) 948-7000. **$79-$149, 3 day notice.** 3333 Shelby St 91764. I-10 exit 56 (Haven Ave), just n to Inland Empire Blvd, just w, then just s. Int corridors. **Pets:** Medium. $75 one-time fee/room. Designated rooms, service with restrictions, supervision. 🛆M 🔁 🛜 ⊠ 🖥 🖵

▼▼▼ Quality Inn Ontario Airport Convention Center M

(909) 937-2999. **$69-$125.** 514 N Vineyard Ave 91764. I-10 exit 54 (Vineyard Ave), just s. Ext corridors. **Pets:** Medium, dogs only. $20 daily fee/pet. Designated rooms, service with restrictions, supervision. 🔁 🛜 🖥 🖵

▼▼▼ Red Lion Hotel Ontario Airport H

(909) 937-9700. **$89-$169.** 204 N Vineyard Ave 91764. I-10 exit 54 (Vineyard Ave), 0.3 mi s. Int corridors. **Pets:** Accepted. 🔁 🛜 🖥 🖵

▼▼▼▼ Residence Inn by Marriott Ontario-Airport H

(909) 937-6788. **$139-$209.** 2025 Convention Center Way 91764. I-10 exit 54 (Vineyard Ave), just s, then 1 blk e. Ext corridors. **Pets:** Accepted. 🛆M 🔁 ⊠ 🛜 ⊠ 🖥 🖵

◆◆ ▼▼▼▼ Sheraton Ontario Airport Hotel H

(909) 937-8000. **$89-$275, 3 day notice.** 429 N Vineyard Ave 91764. I-10 exit 54 (Vineyard Ave), just s. Int corridors. **Pets:** Accepted. SAVE 🍴 🔁 🛜 ⊠ 🖵

ORANGE

▼▼▼ Ayres Inn Orange H 🐾

(714) 978-9168. **$129-$189.** 3737 W Chapman Ave 92868. I-5 exit 107B (W Chapman Ave) northbound, just w; exit 107C (State College/The City Dr) southbound, just s on State College Blvd, then just w. Int corridors. **Pets:** Medium. $45 one-time fee/room. Designated rooms, no service, supervision. 🍴 🛆M 🔁 🛜 ⊠ 🖥 🖵

▼▼▼▼ DoubleTree by Hilton Hotel Anaheim - Orange County H

(714) 634-4500. **$109-$209.** 100 The City Dr 92868. I-5 exit 107B (W Chapman Ave) northbound, just w; exit 107C (State College Blvd/The City Dr) southbound, just s on State College Blvd, then just w. Int corridors. **Pets:** Accepted. 🍴 🛆M 🔁 ⊠ 📶 ⊠ 🖥 🖵

ORICK

Elk Meadow Cabins
(707) 488-2222. **$200-$300, 30 day notice.** 7 Valley Green Camp Rd 95555. US 101, milepost 124. Ext corridors. **Pets:** Medium, dogs only. $15 daily fee/pet. Designated rooms, no service, supervision.

ORLAND

Orland Inn M
(530) 865-7632. **$59-$89.** 1052 South St 95963. I-5 exit 618 (CR 16/South St), just ne; in Stony Creek Shopping Center. Ext corridors. **Pets:** Medium, other species. $6 daily fee/pet. Service with restrictions, crate.

OROVILLE

Americas Best Value Inn & Suites M
(530) 533-7070. **$65-$95.** 580 Oro Dam Blvd 95965. SR 70 exit 46 (SR 162/Oroville Dam Blvd), 0.3 mi e. Ext corridors. **Pets:** Medium, dogs only. $10 daily fee/pet. Designated rooms, service with restrictions, supervision.

Super 8 Oroville H
(530) 533-9673. **$75-$155.** 1470 Feather River Blvd 95965. SR 70 exit 47 (Montgomery St), just ne, then s. Int corridors. **Pets:** Dogs only. $100 deposit/room, $15 daily fee/pet. Designated rooms, service with restrictions, supervision.

OXNARD

BEST WESTERN Oxnard Inn M
(805) 483-9581. **$109-$299.** 1156 S Oxnard Blvd 93030. US 101 exit 61 (Rose Ave) northbound, 3 mi s, then 1 mi se; exit 62B (Oxnard Blvd) southbound, 3.5 mi s. Ext corridors. **Pets:** Small, dogs only. $40 one-time fee/pet. Designated rooms, service with restrictions, supervision.

GrandStay Residential Suites Hotel H
(805) 983-6808. **$110-$150.** 2211 E Gonzales Rd 93036. US 101 exit Santa Clara Ave to Rice Ave, 0.4 mi w, then just n. Int corridors. **Pets:** Accepted.

Residence Inn by Marriott at River Ridge H
(805) 278-2200. **$129-$299.** 2101 W Vineyard Ave 93036. US 101 exit 62A (Vineyard Ave), 1.8 mi w. Ext corridors. **Pets:** Medium, other species. $100 one-time fee/room. Service with restrictions, crate.

PACIFIC GROVE

Bide-A-Wee Inn & Cottages M
(831) 372-2330. **$79-$399, 3 day notice.** 221 Asilomar Ave 93950. 1 mi n of SR 68. Ext corridors. **Pets:** Medium, dogs only. $25 daily fee/pet. Designated rooms, service with restrictions, supervision.

Centrella Inn BB
(831) 372-3372. **$119-$299.** 612 Central Ave 93950. At 17th St; center. Ext/int corridors. **Pets:** Medium, dogs only. $50 one-time fee/room. Designated rooms, service with restrictions, crate.

Deer Haven Inn M
(831) 373-7784. **Call for rates.** 750 Crocker Ave 93950. Just e of SR 68 via Sinex Ave. Ext corridors. **Pets:** Accepted.

Gosby House Inn BB
(831) 375-1287. **$135-$395, 7 day notice.** 643 Lighthouse Ave 93950. Downtown. Ext/int corridors. **Pets:** Accepted.

Green Gables Inn BB
(831) 375-2095. **$165-$395, 7 day notice.** 301 Ocean View Blvd 93950. At 5th St. Ext/int corridors. **Pets:** Dogs only. $65 one-time fee/room. Designated rooms, service with restrictions, supervision.

Pacific Gardens Inn H
(831) 646-9414. **$99-$203, 7 day notice.** 701 Asilomar Blvd 93950. Just n of SR 68. Ext corridors. **Pets:** Dogs only.

Sea Breeze Inn and Cottages H
(831) 372-7771. **$79-$499, 10 day notice.** 1100 Lighthouse Ave 93950. Just w of Seventeen Mile Dr; jct Lighthouse and Grove Acre aves. Ext/int corridors. **Pets:** $30 one-time fee/pet. Designated rooms, service with restrictions, supervision.

PALMDALE

BEST WESTERN PLUS John Jay Inn & Suites H
(661) 575-9322. **$89-$119.** 600 W Palmdale Blvd 93551. SR 14 exit 35 (Palmdale Blvd), just w. Int corridors. **Pets:** Accepted.

Embassy Suites H
(661) 266-3756. **$119-$199.** 39375 5th St W 93551. SR 14 exit 37 (Rancho Vista Blvd/Ave P), just w, just s to Trade Center Dr, then just e. Int corridors. **Pets:** Accepted.

Holiday Inn Palmdale-Lancaster H
(661) 947-8055. **$99-$149.** 38630 5th St W 93551. SR 14 exit 35 (Palmdale Blvd), 0.5 mi w. Int corridors. **Pets:** Accepted.

Residence Inn by Marriott H
(661) 947-4204. **$89-$179.** 514 W Ave P 93551. SR 14 exit 37 (Rancho Vista Blvd/Ave P), just e. Int corridors. **Pets:** Medium. $100 one-time fee/room. Service with restrictions, supervision.

Staybridge Suites H
(661) 947-9300. **$133-$289.** 420 W Park Dr 93551. SR 14 exit 35 (Palmdale Blvd), 0.5 mi w. Int corridors. **Pets:** Large, other species. $75 one-time fee/room. Designated rooms, service with restrictions, crate.

PALM DESERT *(Restaurants p. 618)*

BEST WESTERN PLUS Palm Desert Resort H
(760) 340-4441. **Call for rates.** 74-695 Hwy 111 92260. I-10 exit 134 (Cook St), 4.4 mi s, then 0.3 mi w. Ext corridors. **Pets:** Accepted.

Comfort Suites H
(760) 360-3337. **$79-$149.** 39585 Washington St 92211. I-10 exit 137 (Washington St), just n. Int corridors. **Pets:** Medium. $20 daily fee/room. Designated rooms, service with restrictions, supervision.

Embassy Suites Hotel H
(760) 340-6600. **$99-$279.** 74-700 Hwy 111 92260. I-10 exit 134 (Cook St), 4.4 mi s, then 0.3 mi w. Ext corridors. **Pets:** Accepted.

Homewood Suites by Hilton-Palm Desert H
(760) 568-1600. **$79-$259.** 36-999 Cook St 92211. I-10 exit 134 (Cook St), 0.5 mi s, in The Village at University Park. Int corridors. **Pets:** Large. $75 one-time fee/room. Supervision.

The Inn at Deep Canyon M
(760) 346-8061. **$59-$219, 3 day notice.** 74470 Abronia Tr 92260. I-10 exit 134 (Cook St), 4.4 mi s to SR 111, 0.5 mi w, then just s on Deep Canyon Rd. Ext corridors. **Pets:** Accepted.

Residence Inn by Marriott H
(760) 776-0050. **$129-$229.** 38-305 Cook St 92211. I-10 exit 134 (Cook St), 0.8 mi s. Ext corridors. **Pets:** Accepted.

PALM SPRINGS (Restaurants p. 618)

▼▼▼ A Place In The Sun Garden Hotel M
(760) 325-0254. **$119-$379, 7 day notice.** 754 E San Lorenzo Rd 92264. Just e of Palm Canyon Dr on Mesquite Ave, just n on Random Rd, then just e. Ext corridors. **Pets:** Accepted.

AAA ▼▼▼ BEST WESTERN Inn At Palm Springs M
(760) 325-9177. **$75-$300.** 1633 S Palm Canyon Dr 92264. 1.3 mi s of Tahquitz Canyon Way. Ext corridors. **Pets:** $10 daily fee/pet. Service with restrictions, supervision.

▼▼▼ Hilton Palm Springs H ✻
(760) 320-6868. **Call for rates.** 400 E Tahquitz Canyon Way 92262. Just e of Indian Canyon Dr. Int corridors. **Pets:** Large. $75 one-time fee/room. Designated rooms, service with restrictions, supervision.

AAA ▼▼▼ Hyatt Palm Springs H
(760) 322-9000. **$109-$399, 3 day notice.** 285 N Palm Canyon Dr 92262. Downtown. Ext/int corridors. **Pets:** Accepted.

▼▼▼ Le Parker Meridien Palm Springs H
(760) 770-5000. **$199-$1500, 7 day notice.** 4200 E Palm Canyon Dr 92264. 4.5 mi se. Ext/int corridors. **Pets:** Accepted.

▼▼▼ Renaissance Palm Springs Hotel H
(760) 322-6000. **$109-$399.** 888 Tahquitz Canyon Way 92262. 0.4 mi e of Indian Canyon Dr. Int corridors. **Pets:** Accepted.

▼▼▼ Villa Royale Inn CI
(760) 327-2314. **Call for rates.** 1620 S Indian Tr 92264. 2 mi se of Tahquitz Canyon Way on Palm Canyon Dr, just n. Ext corridors. **Pets:** Accepted.

PALO ALTO

AAA ▼▼▼ Comfort Inn Palo Alto/Stanford Area M
(650) 493-3141. **$120-$209.** 3945 El Camino Real 94306. US 101 exit Oregon Expwy/Page Mill Rd, 1 mi s on SR 82. Ext corridors. **Pets:** Accepted.

▼▼▼ Crowne Plaza Cabana Hotel H
(650) 857-0787. **$109-$549, 3 day notice.** 4290 El Camino Real 94306. US 101 exit San Antonio Rd, 2 mi s, then 0.4 mi n on SR 82. Ext/int corridors. **Pets:** Accepted.

AAA ▼▼▼ Dinah's Garden Hotel H
(650) 493-1800. **$99-$800.** 4261 El Camino Real 94306. US 101 exit San Antonio Rd, 2 mi s, then 0.4 mi n on SR 82. Ext/int corridors. **Pets:** $25 one-time fee/room. Designated rooms, service with restrictions, crate.

AAA ▼▼▼ Quality Inn Palo Alto/Stanford Area M
(650) 493-2760. **$120-$209.** 3901 El Camino Real 94306. US 101 exit Oregon Expwy/Page Mill Rd, 2 mi w to SR 82, then se to Ventura Ave. Ext corridors. **Pets:** Accepted.

AAA ▼▼▼ Sheraton Palo Alto Hotel H ✻
(650) 328-2800. **Call for rates.** 625 El Camino Real 94301. US 101 exit 402 (Embarcadero Rd/Oregon Expwy), 1.8 mi w, then just n on SR 82. Int corridors. **Pets:** Medium. Service with restrictions, supervision.

AAA ▼▼▼▼ The Westin Palo Alto H ✻
(650) 321-4422. **Call for rates.** 675 El Camino Real 94301. US 101 exit 402 (Embarcadero Rd/Oregon Expwy), 1.8 mi w, then just n on SR 82. Int corridors. **Pets:** Medium, other species. Service with restrictions, supervision.

PARADISE

AAA ▼▼▼ Comfort Inn H
(530) 876-0191. **$85-$115.** 5475 Clark Rd 95969. SR 191 (Skyway Rd), 1.1 mi e on Pearson Rd, 0.3 mi s. Int corridors. **Pets:** Dogs only. $10 daily fee/pet. Designated rooms, service with restrictions, supervision.

AAA ▼ Lantern Inn M
(530) 877-5553. **$66-$91.** 5799 Wildwood Ln 95969. Just n of jct Pearson and Skyway rds, then 1 blk w off Skyway Rd; behind the Cozy Diner. Ext corridors. **Pets:** Dogs only. $10 daily fee/pet. Service with restrictions, supervision.

▼▼ Ponderosa Gardens Motel M ✻
(530) 872-9094. **$129-$199.** 7010 Skyway 95969. 2 blks e; center. Ext corridors. **Pets:** $200 deposit/room, $20 daily fee/pet. Designated rooms, service with restrictions, supervision.

PASADENA (Restaurants p. 618)

▼▼ Hotel Le Rêve Pasadena M
(626) 796-9291. **$109-$399.** 3321 E Colorado Blvd 91107. I-210 exit 29B (Madre St), just s, then 0.3 mi e. Ext corridors. **Pets:** $20 daily fee/pet. Service with restrictions, supervision.

AAA ▼▼ Howard Johnson Pasadena M
(626) 304-9678. **$89-$399.** 1599 E Colorado Blvd 91106. I-210 exit 27B (Allen Ave) westbound; exit 27 (Hill Ave) eastbound, 0.8 mi s. Ext corridors. **Pets:** Accepted.

AAA ▼▼ Saga Motor Hotel M
(626) 795-0431. **$106-$112.** 1633 E Colorado Blvd 91106. I-210 exit 27 (Hill Ave), just s, then just e. Ext/int corridors. **Pets:** Small, dogs only. $35 one-time fee/room. Designated rooms, service with restrictions, crate.

AAA ▼▼▼ Sheraton Pasadena Hotel H
(626) 449-4000. **$149-$399.** 303 E Cordova St 91101. I-210 exit 26B (Lake Ave), 0.7 mi s, then just w. Int corridors. **Pets:** Accepted.

AAA ▼ Super 8 M
(626) 449-3020. **$69-$220.** 2863 E Colorado Blvd 91107. I-210 exit 29A (San Gabriel Blvd), 0.3 mi s, then just e. Ext corridors. **Pets:** Small. $20 daily fee/pet. Designated rooms, service with restrictions, supervision.

AAA ▼▼▼ Vagabond Inn Executive M
(626) 449-3170. **Call for rates.** 1203 E Colorado Blvd 91106. I-210 exit 27A (Hill Ave), just s, then just w. Ext/int corridors. **Pets:** Accepted.

AAA ▼▼▼ The Westin-Pasadena H
(626) 792-2727. **Call for rates.** 191 N Los Robles Ave 91101. I-210 exit Los Robles Ave, just s; in Plaza Las Fuentes. Int corridors. **Pets:** Accepted.

PASO ROBLES

▼▼▼ Holiday Inn Express Hotel & Suites H
(805) 238-6500. **$109-$289, 3 day notice.** 2455 Riverside Ave 93446. US 101 exit 231B (SR 46 E), just w, then just n. Int corridors. **Pets:** Accepted.

▼▼▼ La Quinta Inn & Suites Paso Robles H
(805) 239-3004. **$109-$429.** 2615 Buena Vista Dr 93446. US 101 exit 234 northbound; exit 231B (SR 46 E) southbound, 0.3 mi e, then just n. Int corridors. **Pets:** Large, other species. Service with restrictions.

AAA ▼▼▼ The Oaks Hotel & Suites H
(805) 237-8700. **$109-$329.** 3000 Riverside Ave 93446. US 101 exit 231B (SR 46 E), just w, then 0.4 mi n. Int corridors. **Pets:** Large, dogs only. $150 deposit/pet, $20 one-time fee/pet. Designated rooms, service with restrictions, supervision.

PATTERSON

BEST WESTERN PLUS Villa Del Lago Inn H

(209) 892-5300. **$109-$149.** 2959 Speno Dr 95363. I-5 exit 434 (Sperry Ave), just e. Int corridors. **Pets:** Large. $20 daily fee/room. Designated rooms, service with restrictions, crate.

PEBBLE BEACH

The Lodge at Pebble Beach H

(831) 624-3811. **$765-$2510, 14 day notice.** 1700 Seventeen Mile Dr 93953. Off SR 1, follow signs. Ext/int corridors. **Pets:** Accepted.

PETALUMA *(Restaurants p. 618)*

BEST WESTERN Petaluma Inn H

(707) 763-0994. **$90-$180.** 200 S McDowell Blvd 94954. US 101 exit Washington St, just e. Ext corridors. **Pets:** Accepted.

Quality Inn-Petaluma H

(707) 664-1155. **$99-$254.** 5100 Montero Way 94954. US 101 exit Old Redwood Hwy-Penngrove northbound; exit Petaluma Blvd N-Penngrove southbound (east side), just n on N McDowell Blvd, then just e. Ext/int corridors. **Pets:** Other species. $15 daily fee/room. Service with restrictions, supervision.

Sheraton Sonoma County-Petaluma H

(707) 283-2888. **Call for rates.** 745 Baywood Dr 94954. US 101 exit SR 116 (Lakeville Hwy), just se. Int corridors. **Pets:** Accepted.

PHELAN

BEST WESTERN Cajon Pass M

(760) 249-6777. **$60-$110.** 8317 Hwy 138 92371. I-15 exit 131 (SR 138/Palmdale), just w. Ext corridors. **Pets:** Accepted.

PINOLE

Days Inn-SF/Pinole M

(510) 222-9400. **$48-$80.** 2600 Appian Way 94564. I-80 exit Appian Way, 0.3 mi s. Ext corridors. **Pets:** Accepted.

PISMO BEACH *(Restaurants p. 618)*

BEST WESTERN PLUS Shore Cliff Lodge H 🐾

(805) 773-4671. **$159-$399.** 2555 Price St 93449. US 101 exit 191B (Shell Beach Rd) northbound; exit 191B (Price St) southbound, just w. Ext/int corridors. **Pets:** Dogs only. $20 one-time fee/room. Designated rooms, service with restrictions, supervision.

Cliffs Resort H

(805) 773-5000. **$149-$545, 3 day notice.** 2757 Shell Beach Rd 93449. US 101 exit 193 (Spyglass Dr) northbound; exit 193 (Shell Beach Rd) southbound, just w, then just n. Int corridors. **Pets:** Accepted.

Cottage Inn by the Sea M

(805) 773-4617. **$109-$499, 7 day notice.** 2351 Price St 93449. US 101 exit 191B (Shell Beach Rd) northbound, just w on Mattie Rd, then 0.5 mi s; exit 191B (Price St), just w, then just s. Ext corridors. **Pets:** Accepted.

Dolphin Bay Resort & Spa CO 🐾

(805) 773-4300. **$345-$1270.** 2727 Shell Beach Rd 93449. US 101 exit 193 (Spyglass Dr) northbound; exit 193 (Shell Beach Rd) southbound, just w, then just n; in Shell Beach area. Ext corridors. **Pets:** $65 daily fee/room. Designated rooms, service with restrictions.

Edgewater Inn & Suites M

(805) 773-4811. **$100-$325.** 280 Wadsworth Ave 93449. US 101 exit 191A (Wadsworth Ave) northbound, just w; exit 191B (Price St) southbound, just w, then 0.4 mi s on Dolliver St. Ext corridors. **Pets:** Service with restrictions, supervision.

Inn at the Cove M

(805) 773-3511. **$139-$399, 3 day notice.** 2651 Price St 93449. US 101 exit 191B (Shell Beach Rd) northbound, just w, then 0.3 mi n; exit 191B (Price St) southbound, just w, then 0.4 mi n. Ext corridors. **Pets:** Accepted.

Oxford Suites Pismo Beach H 🐾

(805) 773-3773. **$89-$269.** 651 Five Cities Dr 93449. US 101 exit 189 (4th St), just w, then just s. Ext corridors. **Pets:** Medium. $25 daily fee/pet. Designated rooms, service with restrictions, supervision.

Pismo Lighthouse Suites M 🐾

(805) 773-2411. **Call for rates.** 2411 Price St 93449. US 101 exit 191B (Price St) northbound, just w, then 0.5 mi s; exit southbound, just w, then just s. Ext corridors. **Pets:** Dogs only. $30 one-time fee/room. Designated rooms, service with restrictions, supervision.

SeaCrest OceanFront Hotel M 🐾

(805) 773-4608. **$119-$429, 3 day notice.** 2241 Price St 93449. US 101 exit 191B (Shell Beach Rd) northbound, just w, then 0.5 mi s; exit 191B (Price St) southbound, just w, then just s. Ext/int corridors. **Pets:** Other species. $25 one-time fee/room. Designated rooms, supervision.

Sea Gypsy Motel M 🐾

(805) 773-1801. **$69-$290.** 1020 Cypress St 93449. US 101 exit 191A (Wadsworth Ave) northbound, 0.3 mi w to Cypress St, then just s; exit 191A (SR 1) southbound, just w on Wadsworth Ave, then just s. Ext/int corridors. **Pets:** Other species. $15 daily fee/pet. Service with restrictions, supervision.

Shell Beach Inn M

(805) 773-4373. **$65-$225.** 653 Shell Beach Rd 93449. US 101 exit 191B (Shell Beach Rd) northbound, just w, then 1.2 mi s; exit 191B (Price St) southbound, just w, then 1 mi n; in Shell Beach area. Ext corridors. **Pets:** Dogs only. $20 daily fee/pet. Service with restrictions, supervision.

PLACENTIA

Quality Inn Placentia - Anaheim H

(714) 996-4410. **Call for rates.** 710 W Kimberly Ave 92870. SR 57 exit 6 (Orangethorpe Ave) southbound; exit 6A northbound, just w, just n on Placentia Ave, then just e. Ext/int corridors. **Pets:** Accepted.

Residence Inn by Marriott H

(714) 996-0555. **$159-$229.** 700 W Kimberly Ave 92870. SR 57 exit 6 (Orangethorpe Ave) southbound; exit 6A northbound, just w, just n on Placentia Ave, then just e. Ext corridors. **Pets:** Accepted.

PLACERVILLE

BEST WESTERN PLUS Placerville Inn H

(530) 622-9100. **$90-$300.** 6850 Green Leaf Dr 95667. US 50 exit 44A (Missouri Flat Rd S), just e. Int corridors. **Pets:** Other species. $20 daily fee/pet. Designated rooms, service with restrictions, supervision.

Eden Vale Inn BB

(530) 621-0901. **$179-$419, 10 day notice.** 1780 Springvale Rd 95667. US 50 exit 37 (Ponderosa Rd), just n, 4 mi ne on N Shingle Rd (which becomes Green Valley Rd/Lotus Rd), follow Lotus Rd 1.9 mi, then just nw; from SR 49, 4.7 mi sw on Lotus Rd, then just nw. Int corridors. **Pets:** Accepted.

PLEASANT HILL

▼▼ ▼▼ **Extended Stay America-Pleasant Hill-Buskirk Ave** H

(925) 945-6788. **Call for rates.** 3220 Buskirk Ave 94523. I-680 exit 48 (Treat Blvd/Geary Rd E), just e, then just n. Int corridors. **Pets:** Other species. $25 daily fee/pet. Service with restrictions, supervision.

🛆 📶

🐾 ▼▼▼▼ **HYATT house Pleasant Hill** H

(925) 934-3343. **$89-$269.** 2611 Contra Costa Blvd 94523. I-680 north-bound exit Pleasant Hill/Contra Costa Blvd, just n, then w; southbound exit Monument Blvd, just w, then just s; jct Boyd Rd. Int corridors. **Pets:** Accepted. SAVE 🛆 🔁 📶 ✕ 🛏 💻

▼▼▼▼ **Residence Inn by Marriott-Pleasant Hill** H

(925) 689-1010. **$179-$309.** 700 Ellinwood Way 94523. I-680 exit Willow Pass Rd W to S Contra Costa Blvd, 0.3 mi e on Ellinwood Dr, then n. Ext/int corridors. **Pets:** Accepted.

ECO 🛆 🔁 📶 ✕ 🛏 💻

PLEASANTON

🐾 ▼▼ ▼▼ **BEST WESTERN PLUS Pleasanton Inn** H

(925) 463-1300. **$79-$179.** 5375 Owens Ct 94588. I-580 exit 45 (Hopyard Rd/Dougherty Rd), just s on Hopyard Rd, just e on Owens Dr, then just n. Ext corridors. **Pets:** Small, dogs only. $50 deposit/pet, $35 daily fee/pet. Designated rooms, service with restrictions, supervision.

SAVE 🛆 📶 🛏 💻

▼▼▼ **DoubleTree by Hilton Hotel Pleasanton at the Club** H

(925) 463-8000. **$189-$289.** 7050 Johnson Dr 94588. I-580 exit 45 (Hopyard Rd/Dougherty Rd), just s on Hopyard Rd, just w on Owens Dr, then just n; I-680 exit 29 (Stoneridge Dr), just e, then just n; in southeast quadrant of jct I-580 and 680. Int corridors. **Pets:** Medium. $50 one-time fee/room. Service with restrictions, crate.

🍴 🛆 🔁 🔊 ✕ 🛏 💻

🐾 ▼▼▼▼ **HYATT house Pleasanton** H

(925) 730-0070. **$99-$259.** 4545 Chabot Dr 94588. I-580 exit 45 (Hopyard Rd/Dougherty Rd), 1 mi s on Hopyard Rd, just e on Stoneridge Dr, then just s. Ext corridors. **Pets:** Accepted.

SAVE 🛆 🔁 📶 ✕ 🛏 💻

🐾 ▼▼▼▼ **Larkspur Landing Pleasanton** H

(925) 463-1212. **Call for rates.** 5535 Johnson Dr 94588. I-580 exit 45 (Hopyard Rd/Dougherty Rd), just s on Hopyard Rd, just w on Owens Dr, then just n. Int corridors. **Pets:** Accepted.

SAVE ECO 🛆 📶 ✕ 🛏 💻

🐾 ▼▼▼▼ **Pleasanton Marriott** H

(925) 847-6000. **$99-$189.** 11950 Dublin Canyon Rd 94588. I-580 44A (San Ramon Rd/Foothill Rd); just s, then just w. Int corridors. **Pets:** Accepted. SAVE 🍴 🛆 🔁 📶 ✕ 🛏 💻

▼▼▼▼ **Residence Inn by Marriott** H

(925) 227-0500. **$85-$249.** 11920 Dublin Canyon Rd 94588. I-580 exit 44A (San Ramon Rd/Foothill Rd), just s, then just w. Int corridors. **Pets:** Accepted. 🛆 🔁 📶 ✕ 🛏 💻

🐾 ▼▼▼▼ **Sheraton Pleasanton Hotel** H

(925) 463-3330. **Call for rates.** 5990 Stoneridge Mall Rd 94588. I-680 exit 29 (Stoneridge Dr), just w, then 0.7 mi n; I-580 exit 44A (Foothill Rd/San Ramon Rd), 0.3 mi s, then 0.3 mi e on Canyon Way. Int corridors. **Pets:** Accepted. SAVE 🍴 🛆 🔁 📶 ✕ 🛏 💻

PLYMOUTH

▼▼▼▼ **Shenandoah Inn** H

(209) 245-4491. **$99-$149, 3 day notice.** 17674 Village Dr 95669. On SR 49, south end of town. Ext corridors. **Pets:** Accepted.

🔁 📶 ✕ 🗾 🛏 💻

POINT ARENA

▼▼◆▼ **Wharf Master's Inn** H

(707) 882-3171. **$109-$199, 3 day notice.** 785 Port Rd 95468. 1 mi w on Iversen Ave from jct SR 1; at wharf. Ext corridors. **Pets:** Small, dogs only. $25 one-time fee/room. Designated rooms, service with restrictions, supervision. 📶 ✕ 🍴 🛏 💻

POLLOCK PINES

🐾 ▼▼▼▼ **BEST WESTERN Stagecoach Inn** M

(530) 644-2029. **$129-$169.** 5940 Pony Express Tr 95726. US 50 exit 57 (Pollock Pines) eastbound, just n, then 1 mi e; exit Sly Park Rd westbound, just n, then 1 mi w. Ext corridors. **Pets:** Accepted.

SAVE 🛆 🔁 📶 🛏 💻

POMONA

🐾 ▼▼▼▼ **Sheraton Fairplex** H

(909) 622-2220. **Call for rates.** 601 W McKinley Ave 91768. I-10 exit 45A (White Ave) eastbound, 0.5 mi n, then just w; exit 43 (Fairplex Dr) westbound, 1 mi n, then 0.7 mi e. Int corridors. **Pets:** Accepted.

SAVE 🍴 🛆 🔁 ✕ 🔊 ✕ 🛏 💻

PORTERVILLE

🐾 ▼▼▼▼ **BEST WESTERN Porterville Inn** H

(559) 781-7411. **$95-$105.** 350 W Montgomery Ave 93257. SR 65, 0.8 mi e on SR 190, just s on Jaye St, then just e. Int corridors. **Pets:** Accepted. SAVE 🛆 🔁 📶 ✕ 🛏 💻

PORT HUENEME

▼▼▼▼ **Holiday Inn Express Port Hueneme** H

(805) 986-5353. **$117-$259.** 350 E Port Hueneme Rd 93041. US 101 exit 62A (Vineyard Rd), just s to Oxnard Blvd, 2 mi s to Wooley Rd, 1 mi w to Ventura Rd, then 3 mi s. Int corridors. **Pets:** Accepted.

🔁 📶 💻

PORTOLA

▼▼ **Sleepy Pines Motel** M

(530) 832-4291. **$68-$120.** 74631 Hwy 70 96122. 1 mi w of center on SR 70. Ext corridors. **Pets:** Accepted. 📶 🛏 💻

POWAY

🐾 ▼▼▼▼ **BEST WESTERN Poway San Diego Hotel** M

(858) 748-6320. **$79-$399, 3 day notice.** 13845 Poway Rd 92064. I-15 exit 18 (Poway Rd), 4.5 mi e. Ext corridors. **Pets:** Medium. $15 daily fee/pet. Designated rooms, service with restrictions, supervision.

SAVE ECO 🔁 📶 🛏 💻

RAMONA

🐾 ▼▼▼▼ **Ramona Valley Inn** M

(760) 789-6433. **$68-$125.** 416 Main St 92065. SR 78, 0.5 mi e of jct SR 67. Ext corridors. **Pets:** Accepted. SAVE 🔁 📶 🗾 🛏

RANCHO BERNARDO

🐾 ▼▼▼▼ **Rancho Bernardo Inn** H

(858) 675-8500. **Call for rates.** 17550 Bernardo Oaks Dr 92128. I-15 exit 24 (Rancho Bernardo Rd), 1 mi e, then 1 mi n. Ext/int corridors. **Pets:** Accepted. SAVE 🍴 🛆 🔁 ✕ 📶 ✕ 🛏 💻

RANCHO CORDOVA

🐾 ▼▼ ▼▼ **BEST WESTERN PLUS Rancho Cordova Inn** H

(916) 631-7500. **$69-$119.** 10713 White Rock Rd 95670. US 50 exit 17 (Zinfandel Dr), just s, then just w. Ext/int corridors. **Pets:** Dogs only. $25 one-time fee/pet. Designated rooms, service with restrictions, crate. SAVE 🛆 🔁 📶 ✕ 🛏 💻

▼▼▼ **Extended Stay America-Sacramento-White Rock Rd** H

(916) 635-2363. **Call for rates.** 10721 White Rock Rd 95670. US 50 exit 17 (Zinfandel Dr), just s, then just w. Ext corridors. **Pets:** Other species. $25 daily fee/pet. Service with restrictions, supervision.

🛆 📶 🛏 💻

▼▼▼▼ **Fairfield Inn & Suites by Marriott** H

(916) 858-8680. **$99-$199.** 10745 Gold Center Dr 95670. US 50 exit 17 (Zinfandel Dr), just e. Int corridors. **Pets:** Accepted.

🚹ᴹ 🛏 🤶 ✕ 🛎 🖳

🅐🅐🅐 ▼▼▼▼ **Holiday Inn Rancho Cordova** H

(916) 635-4040. **$89-$149.** 11269 Point East Dr 95742. US 50 exit 18 (Sunrise Blvd), just s, e on Folsom Blvd, then just n. Int corridors. **Pets:** Accepted. SAVE ECO 🍴 🚹ᴹ 🛏 ✕ 🤶 ✕ 🛎 🖳

🅐🅐🅐 ▼▼▼▼ **HYATT house Sacramento/Rancho Cordova** H

(916) 638-4141. **$69-$189.** 11260 Point East Dr 95742. US 50 exit 18 (Sunrise Blvd), just s, e on Folsom Blvd, then just n. Int corridors. **Pets:** Medium, dogs only. $75 one-time fee/room. Designated rooms, service with restrictions, supervision.

SAVE 🍴 🚹ᴹ 🛏 🤶 ✕ 🛎 🖳

🅐🅐🅐 ▼▼▼▼ **Hyatt Place Sacramento/Rancho Cordova** H

(916) 635-4799. **$69-$189.** 10744 Gold Center Dr 95670. U5 50 exit 17 (Zinfandel Dr), just s on Zinfandel Dr, just e on White Rock Rd, just n on Prospect Park Dr, then just w. Int corridors. **Pets:** Other species. $75 one-time fee/room. Designated rooms, service with restrictions, supervision. SAVE 🍴 🚹ᴹ 🛏 🤶 ✕ 🛎 🖳

▼▼▼▼ **Residence Inn by Marriott** H

(916) 851-1550. **$85-$180.** 2779 Prospect Park Dr 95670. US 50 exit 17 (Zinfandel Dr), just e. Int corridors. **Pets:** Accepted.

🚹ᴹ 🛏 🤶 ✕ 🛎 🖳

RANCHO CUCAMONGA
(Restaurants p. 618)

🅐🅐🅐 ▼▼▼▼ **Aloft Ontario-Rancho Cucamonga** H

(909) 484-2018. **Call for rates.** 10480 4th St 91730. I-10 exit 59 (Haven Ave), 0.3 mi n, then just w. Int corridors. **Pets:** Accepted.

SAVE 🚹ᴹ 🛏 🤶 ✕ 🛎 🖳

🅐🅐🅐 ▼▼▼▼ **Four Points by Sheraton Ontario Rancho Cucamonga** H

(909) 204-6100. **$89-$269.** 11960 Foothill Blvd 91739. I-15 exit 112 (Foothill Blvd), 0.8 mi w. Int corridors. **Pets:** $75 one-time fee/room. Service with restrictions. SAVE 🍴 🛏 🤶 ✕ 🛎 🖳

▼▼▼▼ **Homewood Suites by Hilton** H

(909) 481-6480. **$99-$299.** 11433 Mission Vista Dr 91730. I-15 exit 110 (4th St), just w to Richmond Pl, just n, then just w. Int corridors. **Pets:** Medium. $75 one-time fee/room. Service with restrictions, supervision. 🚹ᴹ 🛏 🤶 ✕ 🛎 🖳

▼▼▼ **TownePlace Suites by Marriott** H 🐾

(909) 466-1100. **$98-$188.** 9625 Milliken Ave 91730. I-10 exit 57 (Milliken Ave), 0.6 mi n. Int corridors. **Pets:** $100 one-time fee/room. Service with restrictions, supervision. 🚹ᴹ 🛏 🤶 ✕ 🛎 🖳

RANCHO MIRAGE (Restaurants p. 619)

▼▼▼▼ **The Ritz-Carlton, Rancho Mirage** H

(760) 321-8282. **Call for rates.** 68-900 Frank Sinatra Dr 92270. I-10 exit 130 (Bob Hope Dr), 3.3 mi s on Bob Hope Dr, then 3.2 mi w. Int corridors. **Pets:** Accepted. 🍴 ✕ 🤶 ✕ 🛎 🖳

🅐🅐🅐 ▼▼▼▼ **The Westin Mission Hills Golf Resort & Spa** H

(760) 328-5955. **$119-$469.** 71-333 Dinah Shore Dr 92270. I-10 exit 130 (Ramon Rd/Bob Hope Dr), 1 mi s on Bob Hope Dr, then 0.6 mi w. Ext corridors. **Pets:** Accepted.

SAVE 🍴 🚹ᴹ 🛏 ✕ 🕿 ✕ 🛎 🖳

RANCHO PALOS VERDES

▼▼▼▼ **Terranea Resort** H

(310) 265-2800. **$325-$4750, 7 day notice.** 100 Terranea Way 90275. I-110 exit Gaffey St, 1.5 mi s, 6.5 mi w on 25th St (which becomes Palos Verdes Dr S), then just sw. Ext/int corridors. **Pets:** Accepted.

🛎 🍴 🛏 ✕ 🕿 ✕ 🛎 🖳

RANCHO SANTA FE (Restaurants p. 619)

▼▼▼▼ **The Inn at Rancho Santa Fe** H

(858) 756-1131. **Call for rates.** 5951 Linea del Cielo 92067. I-5 exit 37 (Lomas Santa Fe Dr), 4 mi e on CR S-8. Ext/int corridors. **Pets:** Accepted. 🍴 🛏 ✕ 🤶 ✕ 🛎 🖳

▼▼▼▼ **Morgan Run Resort & Club** H

(858) 756-2471. **$99-$329.** 5690 Cancha de Golf 92091. I-5 exit 36 (Via de la Valle), 3 mi e. Int corridors. **Pets:** Accepted.

🍴 🛏 ✕ 🤶 ✕ 🛎 🖳

🅐🅐🅐 ▼▼▼◆ **Rancho Valencia Resort and Spa** H

(858) 756-1123. **$414-$1089, 7 day notice.** 5921 Valencia Cir 92067. I-5 exit 36 (Via de la Valle), 1.3 mi e, 0.5 mi s on El Camino Real, 2.5 mi e on San Dieguito Rd, just e on Rancho Diegueno Rd, 1 mi ne on Rancho Valencia, then just e at main gate. Ext corridors.

Pets: Accepted. SAVE 🍴 🛏 ✕ 🤶 ✕ 🛎 🖳

RED BLUFF

🅐🅐🅐 ▼▼▼▼ **BEST WESTERN Antelope Inn** H

(530) 527-8882. **$92-$175.** 203 Antelope Blvd 96080. I-5 exit 649 (SR 36), just e. Int corridors. **Pets:** Other species. $14 daily fee/pet. Designated rooms, service with restrictions, crate.

SAVE 🛏 🤶 🛎 🖳

🅐🅐🅐 ▼▼▼▼ **Comfort Inn** H 🐾

(530) 529-7060. **$79-$165.** 90 Sale Ln 96080. I-5 exit 649 (SR 36), 0.3 mi e. Int corridors. **Pets:** $15 daily fee/pet. Designated rooms, service with restrictions, supervision. SAVE 🚹ᴹ 🛏 🤶 🛎 🖳

▼▼▼ **Holiday Inn Express & Suites Red Bluff-South Redding Area** H 🐾

(530) 528-1600. **$95-$130.** 2810 Main St 96080. I-5 exit 650 (Adobe Rd), just w, then just n. Int corridors. **Pets:** Medium. $20 daily fee/room. Designated rooms, service with restrictions, supervision.

🚹ᴹ 🤶 ✕ 🛎 🖳

REDCREST

🅐🅐🅐 ▼▼◆ **Redcrest Resort** CA 🐾

(707) 722-4208. **$100-$300, 14 day notice.** 26459 Ave of the Giants 95569. US 101 exit 667 (Redcrest), just e, then just n. Ext corridors. **Pets:** Large. $10 daily fee/pet. Designated rooms, service with restrictions, supervision. SAVE 🤶 ✕ 🎴 🕿 🛎 🖳

REDDING (Restaurants p. 619)

🅐🅐🅐 ▼▼▼ **Baymont Inn & Suites Redding** H

(530) 722-9100. **$79-$139.** 2600 Larkspur Ln 96002. I-5 exit 677 (Cypress Ave), just e, then just s. Int corridors. **Pets:** Accepted.

SAVE 🚹ᴹ 🛏 🤶 ✕ 🛎 🖳

🅐🅐🅐 ▼▼▼▼ **BEST WESTERN PLUS Hilltop Inn** H 🐾

(530) 221-6100. **$110-$200.** 2300 Hilltop Dr 96002. I-5 exit 677 (Cypress Ave), just e, then just n. Ext corridors. **Pets:** Dogs only. $20 daily fee/room. Designated rooms, service with restrictions, supervision.

SAVE 🍴 🚹ᴹ 🛏 🤶 ✕ 🛎 🖳

🅐🅐🅐 ▼▼▼▼ **BEST WESTERN PLUS Twin View Inn & Suites** H

(530) 241-5500. **$94-$149.** 1080 Twin View Blvd 96003. I-5 exit 681 (Twin View Blvd), just w. Int corridors. **Pets:** $20 one-time fee/pet. Designated rooms, service with restrictions, supervision.

SAVE 🚹ᴹ 🛏 🤶 ✕ 🛎 🖳

🅐🅐🅐 ▼▼▼ **Bridge Bay Resort** M

(530) 275-3021. **$85-$190, 3 day notice.** 10300 Bridge Bay Rd 96003. I-5 exit 690 (Bridge Bay Rd), just w. Ext corridors. **Pets:** Accepted.

SAVE 🍴 🚹ᴹ 🛏 ✕ 🤶 ✕ 🛎 🖳

🅐🅐🅐 ▼▼▼▼ **Comfort Inn** H

(530) 221-4472. **$79-$124.** 850 Mistletoe Ln 96002. I-5 exit 677 (Cypress Ave), 0.8 mi n on Hilltop Dr, then just e. Int corridors. **Pets:** Small. $10 daily fee/pet. Designated rooms, supervision.

SAVE 🛏 🤶 ✕ 🛎 🖳

▼▼▼▼ Fairfield Inn & Suites by Marriott H

(530) 243-3200. **$104-$145.** 5164 Caterpillar Rd 96003. I-5 exit 681 (Twin View Blvd) northbound; exit 681B southbound, just w, then just n. Int corridors. **Pets:** Accepted. 🅰 ➰ 📶 ✕ 🛏 🖥

▼▼ Fawndale Lodge & RV Resort M

(530) 275-8000. **Call for rates.** 15215 Fawndale Rd 96003. I-5 exit 689 (Fawndale Rd), just e, then 0.3 mi s; 10 mi n of town; 1 mi s of Shasta Lake. Ext corridors. **Pets:** Accepted. ➰ 📶 ✕ 🛏 🖥

AAA ▼▼▼▼ Holiday Inn Hotel and Convention Center H

(530) 221-7500. **Call for rates.** 1900 Hilltop Dr 96002. I-5 exit 677 (Cypress Ave), just e, then 0.8 mi n. Int corridors. **Pets:** Accepted. SAVE 🍴 ➰ 📶 🛏 🖥

AAA ▼▼▼▼ Oxford Suites Redding H

(530) 221-0100. **$105-$159, 3 day notice.** 1967 Hilltop Dr 96002. I-5 exit 677 (Cypress Ave), just e, then just n. Ext/int corridors. **Pets:** Accepted. SAVE 🅰 ➰ 📶 ✕ 🛏 🖥

AAA ▼▼▼▼ Redding Travelodge H

(530) 243-5291. **$62-$129.** 540 N Market St 96003. I-5 exit 680 (Lake Blvd) northbound, 0.5 mi w to Market St, then 0.5 mi s; exit Market St southbound, 2 mi s. Ext corridors. **Pets:** Accepted. SAVE 🅰 ➰ 📶 ✕ 🛏 🖥

▼▼▼▼ Red Lion Hotel Redding H

(530) 221-8700. **Call for rates.** 1830 Hilltop Dr 96002. I-5 exit 677 (Cypress Ave), just e, then 0.6 mi n. Int corridors. **Pets:** Accepted. 🍴 🅰 ➰ 📶 ✕ 🛏 🖥

▼▼▼▼ TownePlace Suites by Marriott H 🐾

(530) 223-0690. **$129-$169.** 2180 Larkspur Ln 96002. I-5 exit 677 (Cypress Ave), just e, just n on Hilltop Dr, just e on Industrial St, then just n. Int corridors. **Pets:** Large, other species. $25 daily fee/room. Designated rooms. 🅰 🏊 📶 ✕ 🛏 🖥

REDLANDS

▼▼▼▼ Ayres Hotel Redlands H

(909) 335-9024. **$119-$169.** 1015 W Colton Ave 92374. I-10 exit 77B (Tennessee St) westbound; exit 77C eastbound, just s, then just e. Ext corridors. **Pets:** Accepted. ECO ➰ ✕ 📶 ✕ 🛏 🖥

▼▼▼▼ Country Inn & Suites By Carlson, San Bernardino (Redlands) H

(909) 792-7913. **$89-$199.** 1650 Industrial Park Ave 92374. I-10 E exit 77A (Alabama St), just s, then just w. Int corridors. **Pets:** Accepted. ➰ 📶 ✕ 🛏 🖥

▼▼▼▼ Dynasty Suites-Redlands M

(909) 793-6648. **$79-$149.** 1235 W Colton Ave 92374. I-10 exit 77C (Tennessee St) eastbound; exit 77B westbound, just s, then just e. Ext corridors. **Pets:** Accepted. ECO ➰ 📶 ✕ 🛏 🖥

REDONDO BEACH

▼▼▼▼ Residence Inn by Marriott Los Angeles Redondo Beach H

(310) 725-0108. **$169-$299.** 2420 Marine Ave 90278. I-405 exit 42B (Inglewood Ave), just n, then just w. Int corridors. **Pets:** Accepted. 📶 ✕ 🛏 🖥

REDWOOD CITY

AAA ▼▼▼ ▼▼▼ Sofitel San Francisco Bay H

(650) 598-9000. **$140-$415, 3 day notice.** 223 Twin Dolphin Dr 94065. US 101 exit Ralston Ave E, 0.5 mi s at jct Shoreline Dr. Int corridors. **Pets:** Accepted. SAVE ECO 🍴 🅰 ➰ 📶 ✕ 🛏 🖥

▼▼▼▼ TownePlace Suites by Marriott H

(650) 593-4100. **$149-$299.** 1000 Twin Dolphin Dr 94065. US 101 exit Redwood Shores Pkwy, 0.3 mi e, then just s. Int corridors. **Pets:** Other species. $100 one-time fee/room. Service with restrictions. 🅰 📶 ✕ 🛏 🖥

REEDLEY

AAA ▼▼ ▼▼ Edgewater Inn M

(559) 637-7777. **$75-$79.** 1977 W Manning Ave 93654. 12 mi e of SR 99 via Manning Ave. Ext corridors. **Pets:** Dogs only. $8 daily fee/pet. Designated rooms, service with restrictions, supervision. SAVE ➰ 📶 🛏 🖥

RIDGECREST

AAA ▼▼▼▼ BEST WESTERN PLUS China Lake Inn M

(760) 371-2300. **$85-$115.** 400 S China Lake Blvd 93555. On US 395 business route. Ext corridors. **Pets:** Medium. $25 deposit/pet. Service with restrictions, supervision. SAVE 🅰 ➰ 📶 🛏 🖥

▼▼▼▼ Econo Lodge Inn & Suites M

(760) 446-2551. **Call for rates.** 201 Inyokern Rd 93555. SR 178 and US 395 business route, just w of China Lake Blvd. Ext corridors. **Pets:** Medium, dogs only. $10 one-time fee/pet. Service with restrictions, supervision. ➰ 📶 🛏 🖥

▼▼▼▼ Quality Inn M

(760) 375-9731. **$80-$99.** 507 S China Lake Blvd 93555. On US 395 business route; south end of town. Ext corridors. **Pets:** Medium. $15 daily fee/pet. Designated rooms, no service, supervision. ➰ 📶 ✕ 🛏 🖥

AAA ▼▼▼▼ Ridgecrest Heritage Inn H

(760) 446-6543. **$83-$96.** 1050 N Norma St 93555. On US 395 business route, just w. Int corridors. **Pets:** Accepted. SAVE 🍴 🅰 ➰ 📶 🛏 🖥

RIO DELL

AAA ▼▼ Humboldt Gables Motel M

(707) 764-5609. **$65-$145.** 40 W Davis St 95562. US 101 exit 680 (Davis St), 0.5 mi w. Ext corridors. **Pets:** Small, dogs only. $20 daily fee/room. Service with restrictions, supervision. SAVE 🅰 📶 ✕ 🅰 🛏 🖥

RIPON

AAA ▼▼▼▼ La Quinta Inn & Suites Manteca - Ripon H

(209) 599-8999. **$79-$226.** 1524 Colony Rd 95366. SR 99 exit 237 (Jack Tone Rd), just n, then just e. Int corridors. **Pets:** Large, other species. Service with restrictions. SAVE 🅰 ➰ ✕ 📶 🛏 🖥

RIVERSIDE (Restaurants p. 619)

▼▼▼▼ Comfort Inn University M

(951) 683-6000. **$79-$109.** 1590 University Ave 92507. I-215 and SR 60 exit 32 (University Ave), 0.5 mi w. Ext corridors. **Pets:** Small. $15 daily fee/pet. Designated rooms, service with restrictions, supervision. ➰ 📶 🛏 🖥

▼▼▼▼ Hampton Inn & Suites Riverside/Corona East H

(951) 352-5020. **$89-$169.** 4250 Riverwalk Pkwy 92505. SR 91 exit 54 (Pierce St/Riverwalk Pkwy) eastbound, 0.4 mi n; exit 55A (Magnolia Ave) westbound, just w, then 0.5 mi n on Pierce St/Riverwalk Pkwy. Int corridors. **Pets:** Accepted. 🅰 ➰ 📶 🛏 🖥

AAA ▼▼▼▼ Hyatt Place Riverside Downtown H

(951) 321-3500. **$84-$199.** 3500 Market St 92501. SR 91 exit 64 (University Ave) eastbound; exit 64 (Mission Inn Ave) westbound, 0.5 mi w, then just n; downtown. Int corridors. **Pets:** Medium, dogs only. $75 one-time fee/room. Service with restrictions, supervision. SAVE 🅰 ➰ 📶 ✕ 🛏 🖥

ROCKLIN (Restaurants p. 619)

▼▼▼▼ Staybridge Suites H

(916) 781-7500. **$99-$159.** 6664 Lonetree Blvd 95765. SR 65 exit Blue Oaks Blvd, just e, just n to Redwood Dr, then just w; behind Blue Oaks Town Center; directly behind Petco. Int corridors. **Pets:** Large. $45 one-time fee/pet. Service with restrictions, supervision. 🅰 ➰ 📶 ✕ 🛏 🖥

ROHNERT PARK

BEST WESTERN Inn 🅼 ❀
(707) 584-7435. **$101-$106.** 6500 Redwood Dr 94928. US 101 exit Rohnert Park Expwy, just w. Ext corridors. **Pets:** Medium, dogs only. $20 daily fee/room. Designated rooms, service with restrictions, supervision.

DoubleTree by Hilton Sonoma Wine Country 🄷
(707) 584-5466. **$109-$279.** One Doubletree Dr 94928. US 101 exit Golf Course Dr; 3 mi s of Santa Rosa. Int corridors. **Pets:** Accepted.

ROSEVILLE

BEST WESTERN PLUS Orchid Hotel & Suites 🄷 ❀
(916) 784-2222. **$109-$189.** 130 N Sunrise Ave 95661. I-80 exit 103A (E Douglas Blvd) eastbound; exit 103 westbound, just e, then 0.3 mi n. Ext/int corridors. **Pets:** Other species. $20 daily fee/pet. Designated rooms, service with restrictions, crate.

BEST WESTERN Roseville Inn 🄷
(916) 782-4434. **$76-$90.** 220 Harding Blvd 95678. I-80 exit 103 (Douglas Blvd) westbound; exit 103B eastbound, just e, then just n. Ext corridors. **Pets:** Other species. $10 daily fee/pet. Designated rooms, service with restrictions, supervision.

Extended Stay America-Sacramento-Roseville 🄷
(916) 781-9001. **Call for rates.** 1000 Lead Hill Blvd 95678. I-80 exit 103B (W Douglas Blvd) eastbound; exit 103 westbound, just w, then 0.6 mi n on Harding Blvd, then just e. Int corridors. **Pets:** Other species. $25 daily fee/pet. Service with restrictions, supervision.

Homewood Suites by Hilton 🄷
(916) 783-7455. **$99-$199.** 401 Creekside Ridge Ct 95678. I-80 exit SR 65, 1 mi w to Galleria Blvd, 0.5 mi s to Antelope Creek Rd, just e, then just n. Int corridors. **Pets:** Accepted.

Hyatt Place Sacramento/Roseville 🄷
(916) 781-6400. **$69-$169.** 220 Conference Center Dr 95678. I-80 exit 105A (Atlantic St/Eureka Rd), just e on Eureka Rd, 0.4 mi ne on Taylor Rd, 1.1 mi w on E Roseville Pkwy, just n on Gibson Dr, then just e. Int corridors. **Pets:** Accepted.

Larkspur Landing Roseville 🄷
(916) 773-1717. **$145.** 1931 Taylor Rd 95661. I-80 exit 105A (Atlantic St/Eureka Rd), just e on Eureka Rd, then 0.4 mi n. Int corridors. **Pets:** Accepted.

Residence Inn by Marriott 🄷
(916) 772-5500. **$99-$229.** 1930 Taylor Rd 95661. I-80 exit 105A (Atlantic St/Eureka Rd), just n. Int corridors. **Pets:** Accepted.

TownePlace Suites by Marriott Roseville 🄷
(916) 782-2232. **$109-$154.** 10569 Fairway Dr 95678. SR 65 exit Blue Oaks Blvd, just e. Int corridors. **Pets:** Accepted.

RUTHERFORD

Rancho Caymus 🄷
(707) 963-1777. **Call for rates.** 1140 Rutherford Rd 94573. From SR 29, just e on SR 128 (Rutherford Rd); 4 mi s of St. Helena. Ext corridors. **Pets:** Accepted.

SACRAMENTO *(Restaurants p. 619)*

BEST WESTERN John Jay Inn 🄷
(916) 689-4425. **$83-$93.** 15 Massie Ct 95823. SR 99 exit Stockton Blvd/Mack Rd northbound, 0.8 mi n on Stockton Blvd, then just w; exit 291A (Mack Rd E) southbound, just e, then just n on Stockton Blvd, then just w. Int corridors. **Pets:** Small, dogs only. $20 daily fee/pet. Designated rooms, service with restrictions, supervision.

BEST WESTERN PLUS Sutter House 🄷
(916) 441-1314. **$125-$200.** 1100 H St 95814. 4 blks from state capitol; between 11th and 12th sts. Ext/int corridors. **Pets:** Medium. $25 daily fee/pet. Designated rooms, service with restrictions, crate.

BEST WESTERN Sandman Motel 🄷
(916) 443-6515. **$90-$100.** 236 Jibboom St 95811. I-5 exit Richards Blvd, just sw. Ext corridors. **Pets:** Medium. $15 daily fee/room. Designated rooms, service with restrictions, supervision.

The Citizen, a Joie de Vivre hotel 🄷
(916) 447-2700. **$139-$299, 3 day notice.** 926 J St 95814. I-5 exit J St (Old Sacramento), 0.6 mi e; jct 10th St. Int corridors. **Pets:** Accepted.

Days Inn-Sacramento Downtown 🄷
(916) 443-4811. **$55-$110.** 228 Jibboom St 95814. I-5 exit Richards Blvd, just w. Int corridors. **Pets:** Accepted.

DoubleTree by Hilton Sacramento 🄷
(916) 929-8855. **$99-$239.** 2001 Point West Way 95815. Business Rt I-80 (Capital City Frwy) exit Arden Way, just e. Int corridors. **Pets:** Accepted.

Extended Stay America-Sacramento-Arden Way 🄷
(916) 921-9942. **Call for rates.** 2100 Harvard St 95815. Business Rt I-80 (Capital City Frwy) exit Arden Way, just w, then just n. Ext corridors. **Pets:** Other species. $25 daily fee/pet. Service with restrictions, supervision.

Hawthorn Suites by Wyndham Sacramento Airport 🄷 ·
(916) 441-1200. **$56-$85.** 321 Bercut Dr 95811. I-5 exit Richards Blvd, just e, then just n. Int corridors. **Pets:** Accepted.

Hilton Sacramento Arden West 🄷
(916) 922-4700. **$99-$239.** 2200 Harvard St 95815. Business Rt I-80 (Capital City Frwy) exit Arden Way, just w, then just n. Int corridors. **Pets:** $50 one-time fee/room. Designated rooms, service with restrictions, crate.

Holiday Inn Express Sacramento Convention Center 🄷
(916) 444-4436. **$89-$209, 3 day notice.** 728 16th St 95814. Jct G and 16th sts. Int corridors. **Pets:** Small, dogs only. $50 one-time fee/room. Designated rooms, service with restrictions, supervision.

Hyatt Regency Sacramento 🄷
(916) 443-1234. **$119-$429.** 1209 L St 95814. 1/2 blk from state capitol; jct 12th and L sts. Int corridors. **Pets:** Accepted.

Lions Gate Hotel & Conference Center 🄷 ❀
(916) 643-6222. **$99-$109, 3 day notice.** 3410 Westover St 95652. I-80 exit Watt Ave, 1.3 mi n to Palm St, just w, then just s on Arnold Ave. Ext/int corridors. **Pets:** Other species. $25 daily fee/pet. Service with restrictions, crate.

Quality Inn Sacramento Airport 🄷
(916) 927-7117. **$60-$110.** 3796 Northgate Blvd 95834. I-80 exit Northgate Blvd, just s. Ext corridors. **Pets:** Medium, other species. $25 one-time fee/pet. Designated rooms, service with restrictions, supervision.

▼▼▼ **Red Lion Hotel Woodlake Conference Center Sacramento** H
(916) 922-2020. **$89-$209.** 500 Leisure Ln 95815. Business Rt I-80 exit Cal Expo/Exposition Blvd, 0.4 mi w on Exposition Blvd; SR 160 exit 47B (Royal Oaks Dr) eastbound, just sw; exit 47A (Leisure Ln/Canterbury Rd) westbound, just e. Ext corridors. **Pets:** Accepted.
⊞ 🛌 🛋 ⊠ 🛜 ⊠ 🗎 💻

▼▼ **Red Roof Inn- Sacramento- Elk Grove** M
(916) 688-0248. **$59-$90.** 7780 Stockton Blvd 95823. SR 99 exit Stockton Blvd/Mack Rd northbound, 0.8 mi n on Stockton Blvd; exit 291A (Mack Rd E) southbound, just e; jct Mack Rd. Ext corridors. **Pets:** Large, other species. Service with restrictions, supervision.
🛌 🛜 🗎 💻

🅰🅰🅰 ▼▼▼ **Residence Inn by Marriott-Sacramento Airport Natomas** H
(916) 649-1300. **$98-$179.** 2410 W El Camino Ave 95833. I-5 exit 521B (W El Camino Ave) northbound only, just w, then just s on Gateway Oaks Dr; I-80 exit W El Camino Ave, 1.5 mi e, then just s on Gateway Oaks Dr. Ext corridors. **Pets:** Medium. $75 one-time fee/room. Service with restrictions, supervision. [SAVE] 🛌 🛋 🛜 ⊠ 🗎 💻

▼▼▼ **Residence Inn by Marriott Sacramento Cal Expo** H
(916) 920-9111. **Call for rates.** 1530 Howe Ave 95825. US 50 exit Howe Ave, 2.5 mi n. Ext corridors. **Pets:** Accepted.
[ECO] 🛌 🛋 🛜 ⊠ 🗎 💻

🅰🅰🅰 ▼▼▼▼ **Residence Inn by Marriott- Sacramento Downtown at Capitol Park** H
(916) 443-0500. **$126-$309.** 1121 15th St 95814. Jct 15th and L sts; just e of state capitol. Int corridors. **Pets:** Small, other species. $100 one-time fee/room. Service with restrictions, crate.
[SAVE] 🍴 🛌 🛋 🛜 ⊠ 🗎 💻

🅰🅰🅰 ▼▼▼ ▼▼▼ **Sheraton Grand Sacramento Hotel** H
(916) 447-1700. **$119-$409.** 1230 J St 95814. I-5 exit J St (Old Sacramento), 1 mi e; jct 12th St. Int corridors. **Pets:** Accepted.
[SAVE] [ECO] 🍴 🛌 🛋 🔲 ⊠ 💻

▼▼▼ **Staybridge Suites Sacramento Airport/Natomas** H
(916) 575-7907. **$115-$190, 7 day notice.** 140 Promenade Cir 95834. I-80 exit Truxel Rd, just nw, n on Gateway Park Blvd, e on N Freeway Blvd, then just s. Int corridors. **Pets:** Accepted.
[ECO] 🛌 🛋 🛜 ⊠ 🗎 💻

▼▼▼ **TownePlace Suites by Marriott Sacramento Cal Expo** H
(916) 920-5400. **$123-$169.** 1784 Tribute Rd 95815. Business Rt I-80 exit 9A (Cal Expo) westbound; exit Exposition Blvd eastbound, just w, then just s. Int corridors. **Pets:** Medium, other species. $100 one-time fee/room. Service with restrictions, supervision.
🛋 🛜 ⊠ 🗎 💻

🅰🅰🅰 ▼▼▼ ▼▼▼ **The Westin Sacramento** H ❀
(916) 443-8400. **$180-$219.** 4800 Riverside Blvd 95822. I-5 exit 515 (Fruitridge/Seamas), just w, then 0.7 mi n. Int corridors. **Pets:** Medium, dogs only. Service with restrictions, supervision.
[SAVE] 🍴 🛌 🛋 ⊠ 🔲 ⊠ 💻

ST. HELENA (Restaurants p. 619)

🅰🅰🅰 ▼▼▼ ▼▼▼ **Harvest Inn** H
(707) 963-9463. **$249-$999, 14 day notice.** One Main St 94574. 1 mi s of center on SR 29 at Adams St. Ext corridors. **Pets:** Accepted.
[SAVE] [ECO] 🛌 🛋 ⊠ 🛜 ⊠ 🗎 💻

SALIDA

🅰🅰🅰 ▼▼▼ **La Quinta Inn & Suites Modesto Salida** H
(209) 579-8723. **$84-$249.** 4909 Sisk Rd 95368. SR 99 exit 233 (SR 219), just ne. Int corridors. **Pets:** Large, other species. Service with restrictions. [SAVE] 🛌 🛋 🛜 🗎 💻

SALINAS

🅰🅰🅰 ▼▼▼ **BEST WESTERN Salinas Monterey Hotel** H
(831) 784-0176. **$89-$499.** 175 Kern St 93905. US 101 exit Market St, just e, then just n. Int corridors. **Pets:** Accepted.
[SAVE] 🛋 🛜 🗎 💻

▼▼▼ **Residence Inn by Marriott-Salinas** H
(831) 775-0410. **$189-$229.** 17215 El Rancho Way 93907. US 101 exit Laurel Dr, just w. Int corridors. **Pets:** Medium. $100 one-time fee/room. Service with restrictions, supervision. 🛌 🛋 🛜 ⊠ 🗎 💻

🅰🅰🅰 ▼▼▼ **Travelodge** M
(831) 424-4801. **$149-$269.** 109 John St 93901. US 101 exit John St, 0.7 mi w. Ext corridors. **Pets:** Dogs only. $20 deposit/pet. Service with restrictions, supervision. [SAVE] 🛌 🛜 🗎 💻

SAN ANDREAS

▼▼▼ **The Robins Nest** BB 🐾
(209) 754-1076. **$100-$175, 7 day notice.** 247 W St. Charles St 95249. SR 49 (W St. Charles St), just sw on Russels Rd, then just se on Market St; north end of town. Int corridors. **Pets:** Large, other species. Designated rooms, service with restrictions, crate. 🛜 ⊠ 🗎 💻

SAN BERNARDINO

🅰🅰🅰 ▼▼▼ **BEST WESTERN Hospitality Lane** M
(909) 381-1681. **$85-$100.** 294 E Hospitality Ln 92408. I-10 exit 73 (Waterman Ave) westbound; exit 73B eastbound, just n, then just w. Ext corridors. **Pets:** Accepted. [SAVE] 🛌 🛜 🗎 💻

▼▼▼ **Homewood Suites by Hilton San Bernardino** H
(909) 799-6500. **$89-$199.** 885 E Hospitality Ln 92408. I-10 exit 74 (Tippecanoe Ave) eastbound; exit 74 (Anderson St/Tippecanoe Ave) westbound, just n, then just w. Int corridors. **Pets:** Accepted.
🛌 🛜 ⊠ 🗎 💻

▼▼▼ **The Hotel San Bernardino** H
(909) 889-0133. **Call for rates.** 285 E Hospitality Ln 92408. I-10 exit 73 (Waterman Ave) westbound; exit 73B eastbound, just n, then just w. Int corridors. **Pets:** Accepted. 🍴 🛌 🛋 🛜 ⊠ 💻

▼▼▼ **Residence Inn by Marriott San Bernardino** H
(909) 382-4564. **$119-$209.** 1040 E Harriman Pl 92408. I-10 exit 74 (Tippecanoe Ave) eastbound; exit 74 (Anderson St/Tippecanoe Ave) westbound, just n, then just w. Int corridors. **Pets:** Medium, other species. $100 one-time fee/room. Designated rooms, service with restrictions, supervision. 🛌 🛋 🛜 ⊠ 🗎 💻

SAN BRUNO

🅰🅰🅰 ▼▼▼ ▼▼ **Staybridge Suites** H
(650) 588-0770. **$149-$499.** 1350 Huntington Ave 94066. I-380 exit El Camino Real N, e on Sneath Ln, then just n. Ext corridors. **Pets:** $15 daily fee/room. Service with restrictions. [SAVE] 🛌 🛋 🛜 🗎 💻

SAN CLEMENTE

🅰🅰🅰 ▼▼▼ **BEST WESTERN PLUS Casablanca Inn** H
(949) 361-1644. **$90-$230.** 1601 N El Camino Real 92672. I-5 exit 76 (Avenida Pico), 0.8 mi sw, then just s. Ext/int corridors. **Pets:** Medium. $20 daily fee/pet. Designated rooms, service with restrictions, supervision. [SAVE] 🛋 🛜 ⊠ 🗎 💻

▼▼▼ **Casa Tropicana A Boutique Beach Front Inn** CI
(949) 492-1234. **$225-$745, 10 day notice.** 610 Avenida Victoria 92672. I-5 exit 75 (Avenida Palizada) southbound, just w, just s on El Camino Real, then 1 mi sw on Avenida Del Mar; exit Avenida Presidio northbound, just w, just n on El Camino Real, then 1 mi sw on Avenida Del Mar. Ext corridors. **Pets:** Accepted. 🍴 🛜 ⊠ 🗎

▼▼▼ **Holiday Inn Express** H
(949) 498-8800. **Call for rates.** 35 Via Pico Plaza 92672. I-5 exit 76 (Avenida Pico), just sw, just s. Int corridors. **Pets:** Small, other species. $35 daily fee/room. Designated rooms, service with restrictions, supervision. 🛌 🛋 🛜 ⊠ 🗎 💻

SAN DIEGO *(Restaurants p. 619)*

AAA ▼▼▼▼ Andaz San Diego H
(619) 849-1234. **$149-$679, 3 day notice.** 600 F St 92101. I-5 exit 16B (6th Ave/Downtown) northbound, 1 mi s, then just e; exit 17 (Front St/Civic Center) southbound, 0.9 mi s to Broadway, 0.5 mi e to 8th Ave, just s, then just w. Int corridors. **Pets:** Accepted.

[SAVE] [▯] [➔] [🛜] [🔋] [▭]

AAA ▼▼▼ BEST WESTERN Lamplighter Inn & Suites at SDSU M
(619) 582-3088. **$95-$239.** 6474 El Cajon Blvd 92115. I-8 exit 11 (70th St/Lake Murray Blvd), 0.4 mi s on 70th St, then 0.8 mi w. Ext corridors. **Pets:** Accepted. [SAVE] [➔] [🛜] [🔋] [▭]

AAA ▼▼▼ BEST WESTERN Mission Bay M
(619) 275-5700. **$79-$279.** 2575 Clairemont Dr 92117. I-5 exit 22 (Clairemont Dr/Mission Bay Dr), just e. Ext corridors. **Pets:** Small. $15 daily fee/room. Designated rooms, service with restrictions, crate.

[SAVE] [➔] [🛜] [✕] [🔋] [▭]

AAA ▼▼▼▼ BEST WESTERN PLUS Hacienda Hotel Old Town H
(619) 298-4707. **$169-$279.** 4041 Harney St 92110. I-5 exit 19 (Old Town Ave), just e, 0.3 mi n on San Diego Ave, then just e. Ext corridors. **Pets:** Medium, dogs only. $50 deposit/room.

[SAVE] [▯] [♿M] [➔] [🛜] [✕] [🔋] [▭]

AAA ▼▼▼▼ BEST WESTERN PLUS San Diego/Miramar Hotel M
(858) 578-6600. **$79-$399.** 9310 Kearny Mesa Rd 92126. I-15 exit 14 (Miramar Rd/Pomerado Rd), just w, then just s. Ext corridors. **Pets:** Accepted. [SAVE] [ECO] [➔] [🛜] [🔋] [▭]

AAA ▼▼▼▼ The Bristol H 🐾
(619) 232-6141. **$139-$399.** 1055 1st Ave 92101. I-5 exit 17 (Front St/Civic Center) southbound, 0.5 mi s, just e on C St, then just s; exit 15B (Pershing Dr/Civic Center) northbound, 1 mi w to 1st Ave, then just s. Int corridors. **Pets:** Other species. Service with restrictions, supervision. [SAVE] [ECO] [▯] [🛜] [✕] [🔋] [▭]

▼▼▼ Country Inn & Suites By Carlson San Diego North H
(858) 558-1818. **$99-$289, 3 day notice.** 5975 Lusk Blvd 92121. I-805 exit 27 (Mira Mesa Blvd), 1 mi e, then just n. Int corridors.
Pets: Accepted. [▯] [♿M] [➔] [🛜] [✕] [🔋] [▭]

▼▼▼ Crowne Plaza San Diego H
(619) 297-1101. **$149-$229.** 2270 Hotel Cir N 92108. I-8 exit 3 (Taylor St), just n, then just e. Ext corridors. **Pets:** Accepted.

[ECO] [▯] [♿M] [➔] [✕] [🔊] [✕] [🔋] [▭]

AAA ▼▼▼▼ The Dana On Mission Bay H
(619) 222-6440. **$109-$399.** 1710 W Mission Bay Dr 92109. I-8 exit 1 (Ingraham St/Mission Bay), 0.7 mi n, then just w. Int corridors.
Pets: Accepted. [SAVE] [ECO] [▯] [➔] [✕] [🛜] [🔋] [▭]

▼▼▼ The Declan Suites San Diego H
(619) 696-9800. **Call for rates.** 701 A St 92101. I-5 exit 16 (10th St) southbound, just s to B St, just w, then just n on 7th St; exit 16B (6th Ave/Downtown) northbound, just s, then just e. Int corridors.
Pets: Medium, other species. $75 one-time fee/room. Designated rooms, service with restrictions, supervision.

[▯] [♿M] [➔] [🛜] [✕] [🔋] [▭]

AAA ▼▼▼▼ DoubleTree by Hilton Golf Resort San Diego H
(858) 672-9100. **$99-$269.** 14455 Penasquitos Dr 92129. I-15 exit 21 (Carmel Mountain Rd), just w. Ext corridors. **Pets:** Medium. $75 one-time fee/room. Service with restrictions.

[SAVE] [ECO] [▯] [♿M] [➔] [✕] [🔊] [✕] [🔋] [▭]

▼▼▼ DoubleTree by Hilton Hotel San Diego - Del Mar H
(858) 481-5900. **$129-$259.** 11915 El Camino Real 92130. I-5 exit 33 (Carmel Valley Rd), 0.3 mi e, then just n. Int corridors. **Pets:** Accepted.

[ECO] [▯] [➔] [🛜] [✕] [🔋] [▭]

AAA ▼▼▼▼ The Grand Del Mar H
(858) 314-2000. **$395-$995, 7 day notice.** 5300 Grand Del Mar Ct 92130. I-5 exit 33 (Carmel Valley Rd), 1.5 mi e on SR 56, 0.5 mi s on Carmel Country Rd, 0.5 mi e on Grand Del Mar Way, then just se. Int corridors. **Pets:** Accepted.

[SAVE] [ECO] [▯] [➔] [✕] [🛜] [✕] [🔋] [▭]

▼▼▼ Hampton Inn-Del Mar H
(858) 792-5557. **$94-$269.** 11920 El Camino Real 92130. I-5 exit 33 (Carmel Valley Rd), just ne. Int corridors. **Pets:** Accepted.

[➔] [🛜] [✕] [🔋] [▭]

AAA ▼▼▼ Hilton San Diego Airport/Harbor Island H
(619) 291-6700. **$139-$229.** 1960 Harbor Island Dr 92101. I-5 exit 184 (Laurel St) southbound, 1.5 mi w; exit 17 (Hawthorn St) northbound, 0.5 mi w to Harbor Dr, then 1.5 mi nw. Int corridors. **Pets:** Accepted.

[SAVE] [ECO] [▯] [♿M] [➔] [🛜] [✕] [🔋] [▭]

AAA ▼▼▼▼ Hilton San Diego Bayfront H
(619) 564-3333. **$149-$459.** One Park Blvd 92101. I-5 exit 17 (Front St/Civic Center) southbound, 1.5 mi s, just w to Harbor Dr, then just s; exit 16B (6th Ave/Downtown) northbound, 1.3 mi s, just w on Market, just s on Front St, just w to Harbor Dr, then just s. Int corridors. **Pets:** Large. $50 one-time fee/room. Designated rooms, service with restrictions, crate. [SAVE] [ECO] [▯] [♿M] [➔] [✕] [🔊] [✕] [🔋] [▭]

▼▼▼ Hilton San Diego Gaslamp Quarter H
(619) 231-4040. **$189-$399.** 401 K St 92101. I-5 exit 7B (J St/Marina Pkwy) northbound, 0.8 mi w to 4th Ave, then just s; exit 17 (Front St/Civic Center) southbound, 0.5 mi e to 4th Ave, then 1 mi s; in Historic Gaslamp Quarter. Int corridors. **Pets:** Accepted.

[▯] [♿M] [➔] [✕] [🔊] [✕] [🔋] [▭]

AAA ▼▼▼▼ Hilton San Diego Mission Valley Zoo/SeaWorld Area H
(619) 543-9000. **$99-$299.** 901 Camino del Rio S 92108. I-8 exit 5 (Mission Center Rd), just s, then just w. Int corridors. **Pets:** Accepted.

[SAVE] [ECO] [▯] [♿M] [🔊] [✕] [🔋] [▭]

▼▼▼ Hotel Indigo San Diego Gaslamp Quarter H
(619) 727-4000. **Call for rates.** 509 9th Ave 92101. I-5 exit 17 (Front St/Civic Center) southbound, 0.3 mi s, 0.5 mi e on A St, 0.5 mi s on 6th Ave, then just e on Island Ave; exit 16B (6th Ave/Downtown) northbound, 0.5 mi s, then just e on Island Ave. Int corridors.
Pets: Accepted. [ECO] [▯] [♿M] [🛜] [✕] [🔋] [▭]

AAA ▼▼▼▼ HYATT house San Diego/Sorrento Mesa H
(858) 597-0500. **$109-$319.** 10044 Pacific Mesa Blvd 92121. I-805 exit 27 (Mira Mesa Blvd), 1.5 mi e, just n on Pacific Heights, then just w. Int corridors. **Pets:** Medium, dogs only. $75 one-time fee/room. Designated rooms, service with restrictions, supervision.

[SAVE] [▯] [♿M] [➔] [🛜] [✕] [🔋] [▭]

AAA ▼▼▼▼ Hyatt Regency Mission Bay Spa and Marina H 🐾
(619) 224-1234. **$149-$459.** 1441 Quivira Rd 92109. I-8 exit 1 (Ingraham St/Mission Bay Dr), 0.7 mi n, just w on Mission Bay Dr, then just sw. Ext/int corridors. **Pets:** Medium, dogs only. $100 one-time fee/room. Designated rooms, service with restrictions, supervision.

[SAVE] [ECO] [▯] [♿M] [➔] [✕] [🔊] [🔋] [▭]

▼▼▼ The Keating Hotel by Pininfarina H
(619) 814-5700. **$199-$2500, 3 day notice.** 432 F St 92101. I-5 exit 16B (6th Ave/Downtown) northbound, 1 mi s, then just w; exit 17 (Front St/Civic Center) southbound, 0.9 mi s to Broadway, 0.5 mi e to 8th Ave, just s, then 0.3 mi w. Int corridors. **Pets:** Accepted.

[▯] [🔊] [✕] [🔋] [▭]

▼▼▼ **Kona Kai Resort & Marina** **H**

(619) 221-8000. **Call for rates.** 1551 Shelter Island Dr 92106. I-5 exit 20 (Rosecrans St) southbound, 3 mi sw, then 1.5 mi sw; exit 17 (Hawthorn St) northbound, 3 mi nw on Harbor Dr to Scott Rd, then 1.5 mi sw. Ext/int corridors. **Pets:** Accepted.

❘❙ ⚘M ➜ ✕ 🛜 ✕ 🛢 🖵

▼▼▼ **La Quinta Inn & Suites San Diego SeaWorld Area/Mission Bay** **H**

(858) 483-9800. **$85-$429.** 4610 De Soto St 92109. I-5 exit 23A (Grand Ave/Garnet Ave) northbound, 1 mi n on Mission Bay Dr, then just e on Damon Ave; exit 23B (Balboa Ave/Garnet Ave) southbound, just s, then just e on Damon Ave. Int corridors. **Pets:** Large, other species. Service with restrictions. ⚘M ➜ 🛜 ✕ 🛢 🖵

▼▼ **La Quinta Inn & Suites San Diego SeaWorld/Zoo Area** **M**

(619) 295-6886. **$84-$339.** 641 Camino Del Rio S 92108. I-8 exit 5 (Mission Center Rd), just s, then just w. Ext corridors. **Pets:** Large, other species. Service with restrictions. ⚘M ➜ 🛜 ✕ 🛢 🖵

▼▼▼ **La Quinta Inn San Diego Old Town/Airport** **M**

(619) 291-9100. **$99-$524.** 2380 Moore St 92110. I-5 exit 19 (Old Town Ave), just n via Frontage Rd; on east side of freeway. Ext/int corridors. **Pets:** Large, other species. Service with restrictions.

ECO ⚘M ➜ 🛜 ✕ 🛢 🖵

▲▲▲ ▼▼ ▼▼ **Manchester Grand Hyatt San Diego** **H**

(619) 232-1234. **$109-$459, 7 day notice.** 1 Market Pl 92101. I-5 exit 17 (Front St/Civic Center), 1.3 mi s, then just w. Int corridors. **Pets:** Accepted. SAVE ❘❙ ⚘M ➜ ✕ 🛜 🛢 🖵

▲▲▲ ▼▼▼ **Marina Inn & Suites** **M**

(619) 232-7551. **$49-$289.** 1943 Pacific Hwy 92101. I-5 exit 17 (Front St/Civic Center) southbound, just s to Cedar St, 0.3 mi w, then just n; exit 17A (Hawthorn St/San Diego Airport) northbound, 0.4 mi w, then just s. Ext corridors. **Pets:** Accepted. SAVE 🛜 🛢 🖵

▼▼ **Motel 6 - San Diego Mission Valley East #4917** **M**

(619) 281-2222. **$79-$299, 3 day notice.** 4380 Alvarado Canyon Rd 92120. I-8 exit 7 (Mission Gorge Rd), just ne. Ext corridors. **Pets:** Other species. Service with restrictions, crate. ECO ➜ 🛜 🛢 🖵

▼▼ **Old Town Inn** **M**

(619) 260-8024. **$75-$300.** 4444 Pacific Hwy 92110. I-5 exit 21 (SeaWorld Dr/Tecolote St), just sw, then 1 mi se. Ext corridors. **Pets:** Medium, other species. $15 daily fee/pet. Service with restrictions, supervision. ⚘M ➜ 🛜 ✕ 🛢 🖵

▼▼ ▼▼ **Omni San Diego Hotel** **H**

(619) 231-6664. **Call for rates.** 675 L St 92101. I-5 exit 17 (Front St/Civic Center) southbound, 0.3 mi s, 0.3 mi e on A St, 0.6 mi s on 6th Ave, then just e; exit 16B (6th Ave/Downtown) northbound, just s, then just e; connected via skybridge to Petco Park. Int corridors. **Pets:** Accepted. ❘❙ ⚘M ➜ ✕ 🛜 ✕ 🛢 🖵

▲▲▲ ▼▼▼ **Pacific Inn Hotel & Suites** **M**

(619) 232-6391. **$49-$289.** 1655 Pacific Hwy 92101. I-5 exit 17 (Front St/Civic Center) southbound, just s to Cedar St, 0.5 mi w, then just n; exit 17A (Hawthorn St/San Diego Airport) northbound, 0.6 mi w, then just s. Ext corridors. **Pets:** Accepted. SAVE ➜ 🛜 🛢 🖵

▲▲▲ ▼▼▼ **Pacific Shores Inn** **M**

(858) 483-6300. **$109-$269, 3 day notice.** 4802 Mission Blvd 92109. I-5 exit 23A (Grand Ave/Garnet Ave), via Mission Bay Dr to Garnet Ave, 2.2 mi w, then 0.3 mi n. Ext corridors. **Pets:** Medium, dogs only. $45 one-time fee/room. Service with restrictions, crate.

SAVE ➜ 🛜 ✕ 🛢 🖵

▼▼▼ **Porto Vista Hotel** **H**

(619) 544-0164. **$99-$449.** 1835 Columbia St 92101. I-5 exit 17 (Front St/Civic Center) southbound, just w on Cedar St, then just n on State St; exit 17 (Hawthorn St/San Diego Airport) northbound, just e, then just s. Ext/int corridors. **Pets:** Accepted. ❘❙ 🛜 ✕ 🛢 🖵

▼▼▼ **Quality Inn I-15 Miramar** **M**

(858) 578-4350. **$89-$209.** 9350 Kearny Mesa Rd 92126. I-15 exit 14 (Miramar Rd/Pomerado), just w, then just s. Int corridors. **Pets:** Medium. $10 daily fee/pet. Designated rooms, service with restrictions, crate. ⚘M ➜ 🛜 🛢 🖵

▲▲▲ ▼▼▼ **Red Roof Inn-Pacific Beach/SeaWorld Area, San Diego** **M**

(858) 483-4222. **$59-$349.** 4545 Mission Bay Dr 92109. I-5 exit 23A (Grand Ave/Garnet Ave) northbound, 0.5 mi n; exit 23B (Balboa Ave/Garnet Ave) southbound, 0.3 mi s. Ext corridors. **Pets:** Large, other species. Service with restrictions, supervision.

SAVE ➜ 🛜 ✕ 🛢 🖵

▼▼▼ **Residence Inn by Marriott-San Diego Central** **H** ❀

(858) 278-2100. **$139-$209.** 5400 Kearny Mesa Rd 92111. SR 163 exit 8 (Clairemont Mesa Blvd) just w, then just n. Ext corridors. **Pets:** Other species. $100 one-time fee/room. Service with restrictions, supervision.

⚘M ➜ 🛜 ✕ 🛢 🖵

▼▼▼ **Residence Inn by Marriott San Diego Downtown** **H**

(619) 338-8200. **$139-$539.** 1747 Pacific Hwy 92101. I-5 exit 17 (Front St/Civic Center) southbound, just s to Cedar St, 0.3 mi w, then just n; exit 17A (Hawthorn St/San Diego Airport) northbound, 0.4 mi w, then just s. Int corridors. **Pets:** Accepted. ⚘M ➜ 🛜 ✕ 🛢 🖵

▲▲▲ ▼▼▼ **Residence Inn by Marriott San Diego Downtown Gaslamp Quarter** **H**

(619) 487-1200. **$159-$389.** 356 6th Ave 92101. I-5 exit 17 (Front St/Civic Center) southbound, 0.3 mi s, 0.3 mi e on A St, then 0.6 mi s; exit 16B (6th Ave/Downtown) northbound, 1 mi s. Int corridors. **Pets:** Accepted. SAVE ❘❙ ⚘M ➜ 🛜 ✕ 🛢 🖵

▼▼▼ **Residence Inn by Marriott San Diego/Mission Valley/SeaWorld Area** **H**

(619) 881-3600. **$149-$379.** 1865 Hotel Cir S 92108. I-8 exit 4A (Hotel Cir S). Int corridors. **Pets:** Accepted.

⚘M ➜ ✕ 🛜 ✕ 🛢 🖵

▼▼▼ **Residence Inn by Marriott San Diego Rancho Bernardo/Scripps Poway** **H**

(858) 635-5724. **$139-$259.** 12011 Scripps Highlands Dr 92131. I-805 exit 17 (Mercy Rd/Scripps Poway Pkwy), just e, then just n. Int corridors. **Pets:** Accepted. ⚘M ➜ 🛜 ✕ 🛢 🖵

▲▲▲ ▼▼▼ **Residence Inn by Marriott San Diego-Sorrento Mesa** **H**

(858) 552-9100. **$159-$329.** 5995 Pacific Mesa Ct 92121. I-805 exit 27 (Mira Mesa Blvd), 1.5 mi e, just n on Pacific Heights, then just se. Int corridors. **Pets:** Accepted. SAVE ECO ⚘M ➜ 🛜 ✕ 🛢 🖵

▲▲▲ ▼▼▼ **Residence Inn San Diego/Del Mar** **H**

(858) 481-8800. **$159-$329.** 3525 Valley Centre Dr 92130. I-5 exit 33 (Carmel Valley Rd), just ne. Int corridors. **Pets:** Large, other species. $100 one-time fee/room. Service with restrictions.

SAVE 🛜 ✕ 🛢 🖵

▲▲▲ ▼▼▼ **Residence Inn San Diego Rancho Bernardo/ Carmel Mountain Ranch** **H**

(858) 673-1900. **$84-$279.** 11002 Rancho Carmel Dr 92128. I-15 exit 21 (Carmel Mountain Rd), just e, just s, then just w on Windcrest Ln. Ext/int corridors. **Pets:** Accepted. SAVE ⚘M ➜ 🛜 ✕ 🛢 🖵

▼▼▼ **San Diego Marriott Del Mar** **H**

(858) 523-1700. **$129-$529.** 11966 El Camino Real 92130. I-5 exit 33 (Carmel Valley Rd), just ne. Int corridors. **Pets:** $100 one-time fee/room. Designated rooms, service with restrictions.

ECO ❘❙ ⚘M ➜ 🛜 ✕ 🛢 🖵

Sheraton Mission Valley San Diego Hotel 🏨 🐾

(619) 260-0111. **$109-$329.** 1433 Camino del Rio S 92108. I-8 exit 5 (Mission Center Rd), just s, then just e. Int corridors. **Pets:** Medium. Designated rooms, service with restrictions, supervision.

Sheraton San Diego Hotel & Marina 🏨 🐾

(619) 291-2900. **$159-$549, 3 day notice.** 1380 Harbor Island Dr 92101. I-5 exit 17 (Hawthorn St) northbound, just e to Harbor Dr, 1.5 mi w, then just s; exit 18A (Kettner Blvd/Hancock St) southbound, just s to Laurel St, just w to Harbor Dr, 1.5 mi w, then just s. Ext/int corridors. **Pets:** Small, dogs only. $35 daily fee/pet. Supervision.

The Sofia Hotel 🏨 🐾

(619) 234-9200. **$139-$249.** 150 W Broadway 92101. I-5 exit 17 (Front St/Civic Center) southbound, 0.5 mi s, just w on Broadway; exit 15B (Pershing Dr/Civic Center) northbound, 1 mi w to 3rd Ave, just s to Broadway, then just w. Int corridors. **Pets:** Dogs only. $25 daily fee/pet. Designated rooms, service with restrictions, supervision.

Sommerset Suites Hotel 🏨

(619) 692-5200. **$119-$329.** 606 Washington St 92103. SR 163 exit 2B (Washington St), just w. Ext/int corridors. **Pets:** Medium, other species. $75 one-time fee/pet. Designated rooms, service with restrictions, supervision.

Staybridge Suites San Diego-Rancho Bernardo 🏨

(858) 487-0900. **Call for rates.** 11855 Ave of Industry 92128. I-15 exit 21 (Carmel Mountain Rd), 1 mi ne to second Rancho Carmel Dr, just w to Innovation Dr, just n, then just e. Int corridors. **Pets:** Accepted.

Staybridge Suites-Sorrento Mesa 🏨

(858) 453-5343. **$169-$399, 3 day notice.** 6639 Mira Mesa Blvd 92121. I-805 exit 27 (Mira Mesa Blvd), 2.3 mi e. Int corridors. **Pets:** Accepted.

Town & Country Resort Hotel 🏨

(619) 291-7131. **$159-$269, 3 day notice.** 500 Hotel Cir N 92108. I-8 exit 4A (Hotel Cir N). Ext/int corridors. **Pets:** Accepted.

The US Grant, A Luxury Collection Hotel 🏨

(619) 232-3121. **$199-$699, 3 day notice.** 326 Broadway 92101. I-5 exit 17 (Front St/Civic Center) southbound, 0.9 mi s to Broadway, then just e; exit 16B (6th Ave/Downtown) northbound, 0.6 mi s, then just w. Int corridors. **Pets:** Accepted.

The Westin San Diego 🏨 🐾

(619) 239-4500. **$159-$999.** 400 W Broadway 92101. I-5 exit 17 (Front St/Civic Center) southbound, 0.9 mi s, then just w; exit 16B (6th Ave/Downtown) northbound, 0.6 mi s, then just w. Int corridors. **Pets:** Medium, dogs only. Service with restrictions, supervision.

The Westin San Diego Gaslamp Quarter 🏨 🐾

(619) 239-2200. **$179-$599, 3 day notice.** 910 Broadway Cir 92101. I-5 exit 17 (Front St/Civic Center) southbound, 0.9 mi s to Broadway, just e, then just s; exit 16B (6th Ave/Downtown) northbound, 0.6 mi s, just w, then just s. Int corridors. **Pets:** Medium, dogs only. Designated rooms, service with restrictions, supervision.

W San Diego 🏨 🐾

(619) 398-3100. **$179-$699, 3 day notice.** 421 W B St 92101. I-5 exit 17 (Front St/Civic Center) southbound, 0.6 mi s, then just w; exit 16B (6th Ave/Downtown) northbound, just s, then just w. Int corridors. **Pets:** Medium, other species. $35 one-time fee/room. Service with restrictions, supervision.

Wyndham Garden San Diego near SeaWorld 🏨

(619) 881-6100. **$67-$193.** 3737 Sports Arena Blvd 92110. I-8 exit Sports Arena Blvd, 0.4 mi s. Ext corridors. **Pets:** Medium. $25 daily fee/room. Designated rooms, service with restrictions, crate.

Wyndham San Diego Bayside 🏨

(619) 232-3861. **$139-$284.** 1355 N Harbor Dr 92101. I-5 exit 17 (Hawthorn St/San Diego Airport) northbound, 0.4 mi w, then just s; exit 17 (Front St/Civic Center) southbound, 0.5 mi s to Ash St, then just w. Int corridors. **Pets:** Accepted.

SAN FRANCISCO *(Restaurants p. 619)*

The Argonaut, A Kimpton Hotel 🏨 🐾

(415) 563-0800. **$229-$659, 3 day notice.** 495 Jefferson St 94109. Fisherman's Wharf; adjacent to The Cannery. Int corridors. **Pets:** Other species. Designated rooms, service with restrictions, supervision.

Beresford Hotel 🏨

(415) 673-9900. **Call for rates.** 635 Sutter St 94102. 1 blk nw of Union Square at Mason St. Int corridors. **Pets:** Accepted.

BEST WESTERN PLUS Americania 🏨

(415) 626-0200. **$129-$399.** 121 7th St 94103. Just s of Market St; between Minna and Natoma sts. Ext corridors. **Pets:** Accepted.

BEST WESTERN PLUS The Tuscan 🏨 🐾

(415) 561-1100. **$529.** 425 Northpoint St 94133. Just s of Fisherman's Wharf at Mason St. Int corridors. **Pets:** Other species. Designated rooms, service with restrictions, crate.

The Fairmont San Francisco 🏨 🐾

(415) 772-5000. **$219-$1449.** 950 Mason St (atop Nob Hill) 94108. Atop Nob Hill at California St. Int corridors. **Pets:** Other species. $75 one-time fee/room. Service with restrictions, supervision.

Four Seasons Hotel San Francisco 🏨 🐾

(415) 633-3000. **$445-$5000, 3 day notice.** 757 Market St 94103. Between 3rd and 4th sts. Int corridors. **Pets:** Small, other species. $50 one-time fee/room. Service with restrictions, crate.

Galleria Park Hotel, a Joie de Vivre hotel 🏨

(415) 781-3060. **$209-$609.** 191 Sutter St 94104. 2 blks ne of Union Square; between Kearny and Trinity sts. Int corridors. **Pets:** Accepted.

Good Hotel 🏨

(415) 621-7001. **$109-$349.** 112 7th St 94103. Just s of Market St; at Mission St. Int corridors. **Pets:** Accepted.

Grand Hyatt San Francisco 🏨

(415) 398-1234. **$179-$529.** 345 Stockton St 94108. At Sutter St. Int corridors. **Pets:** Accepted.

The Handlery Union Square Hotel H
(415) 781-7800. **$189-$499.** 351 Geary St 94102. Between Powell and Mason sts; just sw of Union Square. Ext/int corridors. **Pets:** Small, dogs only. $250 deposit/room, $25 daily fee/room. Service with restrictions, crate.

Harbor Court Hotel H
(415) 882-1300. **$189-$479.** 165 Steuart St 94105. On Embarcadero; between Howard and Mission sts. Int corridors. **Pets:** Accepted.

Hilton San Francisco Financial District H
(415) 433-6600. **$175-$389.** 750 Kearny St 94108. Between Clay and Washington sts. Int corridors. **Pets:** Medium. $75 one-time fee/pet. Service with restrictions, supervision.

Hilton San Francisco Union Square H
(415) 771-1400. **$189-$540.** 333 O'Farrell St 94102. Just w of Mason and O'Farrell sts. Int corridors. **Pets:** Accepted.

Holiday Inn Civic Center H
(415) 626-6103. **$99-$529.** 50 8th St 94103. Between Market and Mission sts. Int corridors. **Pets:** Accepted.

Holiday Inn Golden Gateway H
(415) 441-4000. **$169-$499.** 1500 Van Ness Ave 94109. US 101 (Van Ness Ave) at Pine St. Int corridors. **Pets:** Accepted.

Hotel Abri H
(415) 392-8800. **Call for rates.** 127 Ellis St 94102. Just w of Union Square at Mason St. Int corridors. **Pets:** Accepted.

Hotel Adagio, Autograph Collection H
(415) 775-5000. **$139-$369.** 550 Geary St 94102. 2 blks w of Union Square; between Jones and Taylor sts. Int corridors. **Pets:** Large, dogs only. $55 one-time fee/room. Designated rooms, service with restrictions, supervision.

Hotel Bijou H
(415) 771-1200. **$89-$359.** 111 Mason St 94102. Just n of Market St; between Eddy and Ellis sts. Int corridors. **Pets:** Accepted.

The Hotel California H
(415) 441-2700. **Call for rates.** 580 Geary St 94102. 0.3 mi w of Union Square at Jones St. Int corridors. **Pets:** Accepted.

Hotel Carlton, a Joie de Vivre hotel H
(415) 673-0242. **$119-$599, 3 day notice.** 1075 Sutter St 94109. 0.5 mi w of Union Square; between Hyde and Larkin sts. Int corridors. **Pets:** Accepted.

Hotel Cartwright Union Square H
(415) 421-2865. **Call for rates.** 524 Sutter St 94102. Union Square at Powell St. Int corridors. **Pets:** Accepted.

Hotel Del Sol, a Joie de Vivre hotel M
(415) 921-5520. **$159-$389.** 3100 Webster St 94123. Just s of Lombard St at Greenwich St. Ext corridors. **Pets:** Accepted.

Hotel Diva H
(415) 885-0200. **$199-$499, 5 day notice.** 440 Geary St 94102. Between Taylor and Mason sts; on Theater Row. Int corridors. **Pets:** Medium, dogs only. $25 one-time fee/pet. Designated rooms, service with restrictions, supervision.

Hotel Kabuki, a Joie de Vivre hotel H
(415) 922-3200. **$199-$419, 3 day notice.** 1625 Post St 94115. Jct Laguna St; in Japan Center. Int corridors. **Pets:** Accepted.

Hotel Mark Twain H
(415) 673-2332. **$149-$399.** 345 Taylor St 94102. Just w of Union Square. Int corridors. **Pets:** Accepted.

Hotel Monaco, A Kimpton Hotel H
(415) 292-0100. **$189-$549.** 501 Geary St 94102. Just w of Union Square at Taylor St. Int corridors. **Pets:** Accepted.

Hotel Nikko San Francisco H
(415) 394-1111. **$199-$599, 3 day notice.** 222 Mason St 94102. At O'Farrell St. Int corridors. **Pets:** Accepted.

Hotel Palomar H
(415) 348-1111. **Call for rates.** 12 4th St 94103. At Market St. Int corridors. **Pets:** Accepted.

Hotel Rex, a Joie de Vivre hotel H
(415) 433-4434. **$169-$309, 3 day notice.** 562 Sutter St 94102. Just nw of Union Square; between Mason and Powell sts. Int corridors. **Pets:** Accepted.

Hotel Triton H
(415) 394-0500. **$139-$559.** 342 Grant Ave 94108. Near Union Square at Bush St. Int corridors. **Pets:** Other species. No service.

Hotel Union Square H
(415) 397-3000. **$219-$399.** 114 Powell St 94102. At Ellis St; just n of cable car turnaround. Int corridors. **Pets:** Accepted.

Hotel Vitale, a Joie de Vivre hotel H
(415) 278-3700. **Call for rates.** 8 Mission St 94105. At The Embarcadero and Mission St. Int corridors. **Pets:** Dogs only. Designated rooms, service with restrictions, supervision.

Hyatt Fisherman's Wharf H
(415) 563-1234. **$169-$509.** 555 North Point St 94133. Just s of Fisherman's Wharf at Taylor St. Int corridors. **Pets:** Accepted.

Hyatt Regency San Francisco H
(415) 788-1234. **$139-$599.** 5 Embarcadero Center 94111. Foot of California and Market sts; in Financial District. Int corridors. **Pets:** Accepted.

InterContinental Mark Hopkins San Francisco H
(415) 392-3434. **Call for rates.** One Nob Hill 94108. Corner of California and Mason sts. Int corridors. **Pets:** Medium. $50 one-time fee/pet. Designated rooms, service with restrictions, supervision.

InterContinental San Francisco H
(415) 616-6500. **$159-$999.** 888 Howard St 94103. Between 4th and 5th sts; in SoMa District. Int corridors. **Pets:** Other species. $50 one-time fee/pet. Designated rooms, service with restrictions, supervision.

JW Marriott San Francisco H
(415) 771-8600. **$189-$799.** 515 Mason St 94102. Just w of Union Square at Mason St. Int corridors. **Pets:** Accepted.

▼▼▼ **Kensington Park Hotel** H

(415) 788-6400. **$159-$399.** 450 Post St 94102. Just w of Union Square. Int corridors. **Pets:** Accepted.

[ECO] [▮] [&M] [📶] [✕] [AC] [🛎] [💻]

▼▼▼ **Laurel Inn, a Joie de Vivre hotel** H ❖

(415) 567-8467. **$179-$469.** 444 Presidio Ave 94115. 1 mi w of US 101 (Van Ness Ave); 1 mi e of Park Presidio Blvd (SR 1) at California St. Int corridors. **Pets:** Service with restrictions, crate.

[&M] [📶] [✕] [AC] [🛎] [💻]

▼▼▼ **Le Meridien San Francisco** H

(415) 296-2900. **$199-$799.** 333 Battery St 94111. Just s of Clay and Battery sts; in Financial District. Int corridors. **Pets:** Accepted.

[ECO] [▮] [&M] [✕] [🛎]

▼▼▼▼ **Mandarin Oriental San Francisco** H ❖

(415) 276-9888. **$495-$675.** 222 Sansome St 94104. Between Pine and California sts; in Financial District. Int corridors. **Pets:** Small, dogs only. $25 daily fee/pet. Service with restrictions, supervision.

[▮] [&M] [📶] [✕] [🛎]

▼▼ **Marina Motel** M ❖

(415) 921-9406. **Call for rates.** 2576 Lombard St 94123. Between Broderick and Divisadero sts. Ext/int corridors. **Pets:** Dogs only. $15 daily fee/pet. Designated rooms, service with restrictions, crate.

[📶] [✕] [AC] [🛎] [💻]

AAA ▼▼▼▼ **Omni San Francisco Hotel** H

(415) 677-9494. **$229-$759.** 500 California St 94104. At Montgomery St; in Financial District. Int corridors. **Pets:** Accepted.

[SAVE] [▮] [&M] [📶] [✕] [🛎] [💻]

AAA ▼▼▼▼ **Palace Hotel** H

(415) 512-1111. **Call for rates.** 2 New Montgomery St 94105. Just e of Union Square; at Market St. Int corridors. **Pets:** Accepted.

[SAVE] [⬛] [▮] [&M] [🏊] [✕] [📶] [✕] [🛎] [💻]

AAA ▼▼▼▼ **Parc 55 San Francisco-A Hilton Hotel** H

(415) 392-8000. **$158-$429, 3 day notice.** 55 Cyril Magnin St 94102. Corner of Cyril Magnin and Eddy sts; just sw of Union Square. Int corridors. **Pets:** Accepted. [SAVE] [ECO] [⬛] [▮] [&M] [📶] [✕] [🛎] [💻]

AAA ▼▼▼▼ **The Prescott, A Kimpton Hotel** H ❖

(415) 563-0303. **Call for rates.** 545 Post St 94102. Just w of Union Square. Int corridors. **Pets:** Other species. Designated rooms, service with restrictions. [SAVE] [ECO] [▮] [📶] [✕] [🛎] [💻]

▼▼▼ **Radisson Hotel Fisherman's Wharf** H

(415) 392-6700. **Call for rates.** 250 Beach St 94133. At Powell St. Int corridors. **Pets:** Accepted. [▮] [&M] [🏊] [📶] [✕] [🛎] [💻]

AAA ▼▼▼▼ **The Ritz-Carlton, San Francisco** H ❖

(415) 296-7465. **Call for rates.** 600 Stockton St 94108. Just n of Union Square at California st. Int corridors. **Pets:** Small, dogs only. $125 one-time fee/room. Service with restrictions, supervision.

[SAVE] [ECO] [▮] [&M] [✕] [📶] [✕] [🛎] [💻]

AAA ▼▼▼▼ **The St. Regis San Francisco** H

(415) 284-4000. **$425-$825.** 125 3rd St 94103. At Mission St. Int corridors. **Pets:** Accepted. [SAVE] [▮] [&M] [🏊] [✕] [📶] [✕] [🛎]

AAA ▼▼▼ **San Francisco Marriott Fisherman's Wharf** H

(415) 775-7555. **$159-$679.** 1250 Columbus Ave 94133. Just s of Fisherman's Wharf at Bay St. Int corridors. **Pets:** Medium. $100 one-time fee/pet. Designated rooms, service with restrictions, supervision.

[SAVE] [▮] [&M] [📶] [✕] [🛎] [💻]

AAA ▼▼▼ **Serrano Hotel** H

(415) 885-2500. **$259-$899, 3 day notice.** 405 Taylor St 94102. Just w of Union Square at O'Farrell St. Int corridors. **Pets:** Accepted.

[SAVE] [ECO] [▮] [&M] [✕] [📶] [✕] [🛎]

AAA ▼▼▼ **Sheraton Fisherman's Wharf** H

(415) 362-5500. **$159-$699.** 2500 Mason St 94133. Just se of Fisherman's Wharf at Beach St. Int corridors. **Pets:** Accepted.

[SAVE] [ECO] [▮] [&M] [🏊] [📶] [✕] [🛎] [💻]

AAA ▼▼▼ **Sir Francis Drake Hotel** H

(415) 392-7755. **$149-$509.** 450 Powell St 94102. Just n of Union Square at Sutter St. Int corridors. **Pets:** Accepted.

[SAVE] [ECO] [▮] [&M] [✕] [📶] [✕]

AAA ▼▼▼ **Stanford Court Hotel** H

(415) 989-3500. **Call for rates.** 905 California St 94108. Atop Nob Hill; corner of California and Powell sts. Int corridors. **Pets:** Accepted.

[SAVE] [ECO] [▮] [&M] [📶] [✕] [🛎] [💻]

▼▼▼ **Taj Campton Place Hotel San Francisco** H ❖

(415) 781-5555. **Call for rates.** 340 Stockton St 94108. Just n of Union Square; jct Sutter St. Int corridors. **Pets:** Small, dogs only. $100 one-time fee/pet. Service with restrictions.

[ECO] [▮] [&M] [📶] [✕] [🛎] [💻]

▼▼ **Travelodge at the Presidio** M

(415) 931-8581. **$92-$162.** 2755 Lombard St 94123. Between Lyon and Baker sts. Ext corridors. **Pets:** Medium. $20 daily fee/pet. Supervision.

[📶] [✕] [🛎] [💻]

AAA ▼▼▼▼ **The Westin St. Francis San Francisco on Union Square** H

(415) 397-7000. **$239-$799, 3 day notice.** 335 Powell St 94102. Across from Union Square. Int corridors. **Pets:** Accepted.

[SAVE] [▮] [&M] [✕] [📶] [✕] [🛎] [💻]

AAA ▼▼▼ **Westin San Francisco Market Street** H

(415) 974-6400. **$179-$799.** 50 3rd St 94103. Just n of Moscone Convention Center; between Jessie and Stevenson sts. Int corridors. **Pets:** Accepted. [SAVE] [ECO] [▮] [&M] [✕] [✕] [🛎] [💻]

AAA ▼▼▼ **The Wharf Inn** M

(415) 673-7411. **Call for rates.** 2601 Mason St 94133. At Beach St; adjacent to Fisherman's Wharf and San Francisco Bay. Ext corridors. **Pets:** Accepted. [SAVE] [&M] [📶] [✕] [AC]

AAA ▼▼▼▼ **W San Francisco** H ❖

(415) 777-5300. **$199-$729.** 181 3rd St 94103. At Howard St. Int corridors. **Pets:** Other species. $100 one-time fee/room. Designated rooms, service with restrictions.

[SAVE] [ECO] [▮] [&M] [✕] [✕] [📶] [✕] [🛎] [💻]

SAN GABRIEL

AAA ▼▼▼▼ **Hilton Los Angeles/San Gabriel** H

(626) 270-2700. **$169-$349.** 225 W Valley Blvd 91776. I-10 exit 24 (New Ave), 0.6 mi n, then 0.3 mi e. Int corridors. **Pets:** Other species. $50 one-time fee/room. Service with restrictions, supervision.

[SAVE] [▮] [&M] [✕] [✕] [📶] [🛎] [💻]

SANGER

▼▼ **Wonder Valley Ranch Resort & Conference Center** RA

(559) 787-2551. **$149-$278.** 6450 Elwood Rd 93657. Jct SR 180 and N Piedra Rd, 8 mi ne to Elwood Rd, then 5.5 mi e. Ext corridors. **Pets:** Small, dogs only. $25 daily fee/pet. Designated rooms, service with restrictions, crate. [&M] [✕] [✕] [📶] [✕] [🛎] [💻]

SAN JOSE *(Restaurants p. 620)*

AAA ▼▼▼ **DoubleTree by Hilton Hotel San Jose** H ❖

(408) 453-4000. **$199-$359.** 2050 Gateway Pl 95110. 0.3 mi e of Norman Y. Mineta San Jose International Airport via Airport Blvd; w of US 101 exit N 1st St; US 101 exit Brokaw Rd northbound. Int corridors. **Pets:** Large. $50 one-time fee/room. Service with restrictions, crate.

[SAVE] [ECO] [▮] [&M] [✕] [📶] [✕] [🛎] [💻]

▼▼ ▼▼ **Extended Stay America/San Jose Downtown** 🅷
(408) 573-0648. **Call for rates.** 1560 N 1st St 95112. 1 mi e of Norman Y. Mineta San Jose International Airport; US 101 exit N 1st St, then s. Int corridors. **Pets:** Other species. $25 daily fee/pet. Service with restrictions, supervision. 🔧📶📵🔌💻

🅐🅐🅐 ▼▼ ▼▼ **The Fairmont San Jose** 🅷
(408) 998-1900. **$145-$549, 3 day notice.** 170 S Market St 95113. At Fairmont Plaza. Int corridors. **Pets:** Accepted.
🆂🅰🆅🅴 🅴🅲🅾 🍽️ 🔧 ➰ ✖️ 📡 ✖️ 🔌 💻

▼▼▼▼ **Hilton San Jose** 🅷 🐾
(408) 287-2100. **$129-$374.** 300 Almaden Blvd 95110. SR 87 exit Santa Clara St E, 0.4 mi s; at W San Carlos St. Int corridors. **Pets:** $50 one-time fee/room. Service with restrictions, supervision.
🍽️ 🔧 ➰ 📡 ✖️ 🔌 💻

▼▼▼▼ **Homewood Suites by Hilton** 🅷
(408) 428-9900. **$289-$329.** 10 W Trimble Rd 95131. US 101 exit Trimble Rd, 1.3 mi e; 2 mi ne of Norman Y. Mineta San Jose International Airport. Ext/int corridors. **Pets:** Accepted.
📧 🔧 ➰ 📶 🔌 💻

🅐🅐🅐 ▼▼ ▼▼ **Hotel De Anza** 🅷
(408) 286-1000. **$129-$399.** 233 W Santa Clara St 95113. SR 87 exit Santa Clara St, just e. Int corridors. **Pets:** Accepted.
🆂🅰🆅🅴 🍽️ 🔧 📶 ✖️ 🔌 💻

🅐🅐🅐 ▼▼▼▼ **HYATT house San Jose/Silicon Valley** 🅷
(408) 324-1155. **$99-$409.** 75 Headquarters Dr 95134. SR 237 exit N 1st St, just s, then just e. Int corridors. **Pets:** Medium, other species. $75 one-time fee/room. Designated rooms, service with restrictions, crate. 🆂🅰🆅🅴 🔧 ➰ 📶 ✖️ 🔌 💻

🅐🅐🅐 ▼▼▼▼ **Hyatt Place San Jose/Downtown** 🅷
(408) 998-0400. **$124-$319.** 282 Almaden Blvd 95113. I-280 exit Almaden-Vine, 6 blks n. Int corridors. **Pets:** Accepted.
🆂🅰🆅🅴 🍽️ 🔧 ➰ ✖️ 🔌 💻

▼▼▼▼ **La Quinta Inn & Suites San Jose Airport** 🅷
(408) 435-8800. **$102-$979.** 2585 Seaboard Ave 95131. US 101 exit Trimble Rd E; 1 mi ne of Norman Y. Mineta San Jose International Airport. Int corridors. **Pets:** Large, other species. Service with restrictions.
🔧 ➰ 📶 ✖️ 🔌 💻

▼▼▼▼ **Residence Inn by Marriott** 🅷
(408) 226-7676. **$219-$369.** 6111 San Ignacio Ave 95119. US 101 exit Bernal Rd, 0.7 w, then just n. Int corridors. **Pets:** Medium. $100 one-time fee/room. Service with restrictions, supervision.
🔧 ➰ 📶 ✖️ 🔌 💻

🅐🅐🅐 ▼▼▼▼ **San Jose Marriott** 🅷
(408) 280-1300. **$119-$369.** 301 S Market St 95113. SR 87 exit Santa Clara St E, s on Almaden Blvd, then just e on San Carlos St. Int corridors. **Pets:** Accepted. 🆂🅰🆅🅴 🅴🅲🅾 🍽️ 🔧 ➰ 📶 ✖️ 🔌 💻

▼▼▼▼ **Staybridge Suites San Jose** 🅷
(408) 436-1600. **Call for rates.** 1602 Crane Ct 95112. US 101 exit 1st St/Brokaw Rd, 0.4 mi e to Bering Dr, then 0.5 mi s. Ext/int corridors. **Pets:** Accepted. 🔧 ➰ 📶 🔌 💻

▼▼▼▼ **TownePlace Suites by Marriott San Jose/Cupertino** 🅷
(408) 984-5903. **$129-$299.** 440 Saratoga Ave 95129. I-280 exit Saratoga Ave, just n. Int corridors. **Pets:** Accepted.
🔧 ➰ 📶 ✖️ 🔌 💻

SAN JUAN CAPISTRANO
(Restaurants p. 620)

🅐🅐🅐 ▼▼▼▼ **Residence Inn by Marriott Dana Pointe/San Juan Capistrano** 🅷
(949) 443-3600. **$149-$329.** 33711 Camino Capistrano 92675. I-5 exit 81 (Camino Capistrano), 1.3 mi s. Int corridors. **Pets:** Accepted.
🆂🅰🆅🅴 📧 🔧 ➰ 📶 ✖️ 🔌 💻

SAN LUIS OBISPO *(Restaurants p. 620)*

🅐🅐🅐 ▼▼▼▼ **BEST WESTERN PLUS Royal Oak Hotel** 🅷 ❀
(805) 544-4410. **$109-$329.** 214 Madonna Rd 93405. US 101 exit 201 (Madonna Rd), just s. Ext/int corridors. **Pets:** Large. $15 daily fee/pet. Designated rooms, service with restrictions, supervision.
🆂🅰🆅🅴 ➰ 📶 🔌 💻

▼▼▼▼ **Garden Street Inn Bed & Breakfast** 🅱🅱
(805) 545-9802. **$179-$299, 5 day notice.** 1212 Garden St 93401. US 101 exit 202A (Marsh St), 0.5 mi e; downtown. Int corridors. **Pets:** Dogs only. $20 one-time fee/pet. Designated rooms, service with restrictions, crate. 📶 🔌

▼▼▼▼ **Heritage Inn Bed & Breakfast** 🅱🅱
(805) 544-7440. **$105-$200, 7 day notice.** 978 Olive St 93405. US 101 exit 203A (Santa Rosa St) southbound, just ne; exit 203B (SR 1/Morro Bay) northbound, just w on Santa Rosa St, then just s. Int corridors.
Pets: Accepted. 📶 ✖️ 🎵 🎵 ☎️

▼▼▼▼ **Petit Soleil Bed & Breakfast** 🅱🅱 🐾
(805) 549-0321. **$169-$299, 3 day notice.** 1473 Monterey St 93401. US 101 exit 204 (Monterey St), 0.3 mi sw. Ext corridors. **Pets:** Other species. $25 one-time fee/room. Service with restrictions, supervision.
📶 🎵

🅐🅐🅐 ▼▼ ▼▼ **Ramada Inn Olive Tree** 🅼
(805) 544-2800. **$59-$130.** 1000 Olive St 93405. US 101 exit 203A (Santa Rosa St) southbound, just ne; exit 203B (SR 1/Morro Bay) northbound, just w on Santa Rosa St, then just s. Ext corridors.
Pets: Accepted. 🆂🅰🆅🅴 🔧 ➰ 📶 ✖️ 🔌 💻

🅐🅐🅐 ▼▼ ▼▼ **Rose Garden Inn** 🅼
(805) 544-5300. **$69-$269.** 1585 Calle Joaquin 93401. US 101 exit 200 (Los Osos Valley Rd), just w, then just s. Int corridors. **Pets:** Medium, dogs only. $20 daily fee/pet. Service with restrictions, supervision.
🆂🅰🆅🅴 📶 ✖️ 🔌 💻

🅐🅐🅐 ▼▼▼▼ **Sands Inn & Suites** 🅼 🐾
(805) 544-0500. **$79-$299.** 1930 Monterey St 93401. US 101 exit 204 (Monterey St), just sw. Ext corridors. **Pets:** Medium. $25 one-time fee/pet. Designated rooms, service with restrictions, supervision.
🆂🅰🆅🅴 🔧 ➰ ✖️ 🔌 💻

▼▼ ▼▼ **Super 8** 🅼
(805) 544-6888. **$79-$299.** 1951 Monterey St 93401. US 101 exit 204 (Monterey St), just e. Ext corridors. **Pets:** Accepted.
➰ 📶 ✖️ 🔌 💻

SAN MARCOS
▼▼▼▼ **Residence Inn by Marriott San Diego North/San Marcos** 🅷
(760) 591-9828. **$109-$199.** 1245 Los Vallecitos Blvd 92069. SR 78 exit 11B (Las Posas Rd), just ne. Int corridors. **Pets:** Other species. $100 one-time fee/room. Service with restrictions, supervision.
🅴🅲🅾 🔧 ➰ 📶 ✖️ 🔌 💻

SAN MATEO *(Restaurants p. 620)*
▼▼▼▼ **Residence Inn by Marriott** 🅷
(650) 574-4700. **$189-$329, 3 day notice.** 2000 Winward Way 94404. US 101 exit 414B (SR 92/E Hayward/Fashion Island), just e to Mariners Island Blvd, exit 14A, just e. Ext corridors. **Pets:** Accepted.
🔧 ➰ 📶 ✖️ 🔌 💻

SAN RAFAEL
▼▼ ▼▼ **Extended Stay America-San Rafael-Francisco Blvd E** 🅷
(415) 451-1887. **Call for rates.** 1775 Francisco Blvd E 94901. US 101 exit 451 (I-580/Richmond Br/Oakland) northbound; exit 451B (I-580/Richmond/Oakland) southbound, just e on Bellam Blvd, then 1 mi s. Int corridors. **Pets:** Other species. $25 daily fee/pet. Service with restrictions, supervision. 🔧 ➰ 📶 🔌 💻

SAN RAMON

WWWW HYATT house San Ramon ℍ
(925) 743-1882. **$99-$359.** 2323 San Ramon Valley Blvd 94583. I-680 exit 36 (Crow Canyon Rd), just w, then just n. Int corridors. **Pets:** Accepted. [SAVE] [&M] [icons]

WWW Residence Inn by Marriott ℍ
(925) 277-9292. **$139-$329.** 1071 Market Pl 94583. I-680 exit 34 (Bollinger Canyon Rd), 0.5 mi e. Ext corridors. **Pets:** Accepted.
[ECO] [&M] [icons]

WWWW San Ramon Marriott ℍ
(925) 867-9200. **$109-$349.** 2600 Bishop Dr 94583. I-680 exit 34 (Bollinger Canyon Rd), just e, n on Sunset Dr, then just w. Int corridors. **Pets:** Accepted. [ECO] [icons]

SAN SIMEON

WWWW BEST WESTERN PLUS Cavalier Oceanfront Resort ℍ
(805) 927-4688. **$109-$319, 3 day notice.** 9415 Hearst Dr 93452. Just w of SR 1. Ext corridors. **Pets:** Service with restrictions, supervision. [SAVE] [icons]

WM Courtesy Inn Ⓜ
(805) 927-4691. **$50-$250, 7 day notice.** 9450 Castillo Dr 93452. Just e of SR 1. Ext corridors. **Pets:** Dogs only. $25 one-time fee/pet, $25 daily fee/pet. Designated rooms, service with restrictions, supervision. [SAVE] [icons]

WWW The Morgan San Simeon ℍ
(805) 927-3878. **$99-$269.** 9135 Hearst Dr 93452. Just w of SR 1. Int corridors. **Pets:** Accepted. [icons]

WW Sands by the Sea Ⓜ
(805) 927-3243. **$59-$169, 3 day notice.** 9355 Hearst Dr 93452. Just w of SR 1. Ext corridors. **Pets:** Service with restrictions, supervision. [icons]

WWW San Simeon Lodge ℍ
(805) 927-4601. **$49-$299, 3 day notice.** 9520 Castillo Dr 93452. On SR 1. Ext corridors. **Pets:** Small, dogs only. $15 daily fee/pet. Designated rooms, service with restrictions, supervision. [SAVE] [icons]

WWW Silver Surf Motel Ⓜ
(805) 927-4661. **$69-$289.** 9390 Castillo Dr 93452. Just e of SR 1. Ext corridors. **Pets:** Small, dogs only. $15 deposit/pet, $15 daily fee/pet. Designated rooms, service with restrictions, supervision. [SAVE] [icons]

SANTA ANA (Restaurants p. 620)

WWWW La Quinta Inn & Suites Orange County-Santa Ana Ⓜ
(714) 540-1111. **$79-$239.** 2721 Hotel Terrace Dr 92705. SR 55 exit 8 (Dyer Rd) northbound; exit 8B southbound, just w, then just s. Ext corridors. **Pets:** Large, other species. Service with restrictions. [icons]

SANTA BARBARA (Restaurants p. 620)

WWWW BEST WESTERN Beachside Inn Ⓜ
(805) 965-6556. **$179-$400.** 336 W Cabrillo Blvd 93101. US 101 exit 96 (Garden St) northbound, just w; exit 97 (Castillo St/Harbor) southbound, 0.3 mi w to Cabrillo Blvd, then 0.5 mi n; corner of Cabrillo Blvd and Castillo St. Ext corridors. **Pets:** Accepted. [SAVE] [icons]

WWWW BEST WESTERN PLUS Pepper Tree Inn Ⓜ
(805) 687-5511. **$199-$339.** 3850 State St 93105. US 101 exit 101A (La Cumbre/Hope Rd) northbound, just n; exit 101B (State St) southbound, 0.7 mi e. Ext corridors. **Pets:** Accepted. [SAVE] [icons]

WWW Blue Sands Motel Ⓜ
(805) 965-1624. **$105-$285, 3 day notice.** 421 S Milpas St 93103. US 101 exit 96A (Milpas St), 0.3 mi s. Ext corridors. **Pets:** Dogs only. $10 daily fee/pet. Service with restrictions. [icons]

WW Extended Stay America Santa Barbara-Calle Real ℍ
(805) 692-1882. **Call for rates.** 4870 Calle Real 93111. US 101 exit Turnpike Rd, just e, then just n. Int corridors. **Pets:** Other species. $25 daily fee/pet. Service with restrictions, supervision. [&M] [icons]

WWWW The Fess Parker, A DoubleTree by Hilton Resort ℍ 🐾
(805) 564-4333. **$169-$599.** 633 E Cabrillo Blvd 93103. US 101 exit 96A (Milpas St), just s, then just w. Ext/int corridors. **Pets:** Other species. $30 daily fee/pet. Designated rooms, service with restrictions, supervision. [SAVE] [ECO] [icons]

WWW The Goodland Ⓜ
(805) 964-6241. **$159-$359.** 5650 Calle Real 93117. 7 mi nw of town center via US 101 exit 104A (Patterson Ave), just e, then 0.7 mi n. Ext corridors. **Pets:** Accepted. [icons]

WWWW Hyatt Santa Barbara ℍ 🐾
(805) 882-1234. **$139-$549, 3 day notice.** 1111 E Cabrillo Blvd 93103. US 101 exit 96A (Milpas St), 0.3 mi s, then just e. Int corridors. **Pets:** Medium, dogs only. $50 one-time fee/pet. Designated rooms, service with restrictions. [SAVE] [icons]

WWWW La Quinta Inn & Suites Santa Barbara Ⓜ
(805) 966-0807. **$109-$379.** 1601 State St 93101. US 101 exit 99 (Mission St), 0.4 mi e, then 0.3 mi s. Ext corridors. **Pets:** Large, other species. Service with restrictions. [icons]

WWW Marina Beach Motel Ⓜ
(805) 963-9311. **$120-$325.** 21 Bath St 93101. US 101 exit 96B (Garden St), 0.3 mi w to Cabrillo Blvd, 0.4 mi n to Bath St, then just e. Ext corridors. **Pets:** Medium. $15 daily fee/pet. Designated rooms, supervision. [icons]

WWW Pacifica Suites ℍ
(805) 683-6722. **$189-$499.** 5490 Hollister Ave 93111. US 101 exit 104A (Patterson Ave), 0.5 mi w, then 0.5 mi n. Ext/int corridors. **Pets:** Medium, dogs only. $75 one-time fee/room. Designated rooms, service with restrictions, supervision. [icons]

SANTA CLARA (Restaurants p. 620)

WWW Avatar Hotel Great America ℍ
(408) 235-8900. **$89-$329, 3 day notice.** 4200 Great America Pkwy 95054. 0.5 mi e off US 101 exit Great America Pkwy; 0.8 mi s of California's Great America theme park. Ext corridors. **Pets:** Medium, dogs only. $50 one-time fee/room. Designated rooms, service with restrictions, supervision. [SAVE] [ECO] [icons]

WWW Biltmore Hotel & Suites/Silicon Valley ℍ
(408) 988-8411. **$199-$399.** 2151 Laurelwood Rd 95054. US 101 exit Montague Expwy, just e; 1 mi s of Great America Pkwy. Ext/int corridors. **Pets:** Accepted. [SAVE] [icons]

WW Candlewood Suites-Silicon Valley/San Jose ℍ
(408) 241-9305. **Call for rates.** 481 El Camino Real 95050. I-880 exit The Alameda, 1.5 mi w; enter from Railroad Ave. Int corridors. **Pets:** Accepted. [&M] [icons]

WWWW Hilton Santa Clara Hotel ℍ 🐾
(408) 330-0001. **$109-$349.** 4949 Great America Pkwy 95054. US 101 exit Great America Pkwy, 0.5 mi n. Int corridors. **Pets:** Other species. $50 one-time fee/pet. Designated rooms, service with restrictions, crate. [SAVE] [ECO] [icons]

WWW HYATT house Santa Clara ℍ
(408) 486-0800. **$109-$409.** 3915 Rivermark Plaza 95054. US 101 exit Montague Expwy, 1 mi e. Int corridors. **Pets:** Medium, other species. $75 one-time fee/pet. Designated rooms, service with restrictions, crate. [SAVE] [icons]

Hyatt Regency Santa Clara H
(408) 200-1234. **$79-$539.** 5101 Great America Pkwy 95054. US 101 exit Great America Pkwy, 0.8 mi e. Int corridors. **Pets:** Accepted.

Quality Inn & Suites Silicon Valley M
(408) 241-3010. **$85-$150.** 2930 El Camino Real 95051. SR 82, 0.5 mi w of San Tomas Expwy; US 101 exit S Bowers Ave. Ext corridors. **Pets:** Accepted.

SANTA CLARITA

BEST WESTERN Valencia Inn M
(661) 255-0555. **$99-$199.** 27413 Wayne Mills Pl 91355. I-5 exit 170 (Magic Mountain Pkwy), just e. Ext corridors. **Pets:** Accepted.

Embassy Suites Valencia H
(661) 257-3111. **$149-$189.** 28508 Westinghouse Pl 91355. I-5 exit 172 (SR 126/Newhall Ranch Rd), just e on Vanderbilt Way, then just n. Int corridors. **Pets:** Accepted.

Extended Stay America Los Angeles-Valencia H
(661) 255-1044. **Call for rates.** 24940 W Pico Canyon Rd 91381. I-5 exit 167 (Lyons Ave), just w. Int corridors. **Pets:** Other species. $25 daily fee/pet. Service with restrictions, supervision.

Fairfield Inn by Marriott H
(661) 290-2828. **$99-$179.** 25340 The Old Rd 91381. I-5 exit 167 (Lyons Ave), just w, then s. Ext/int corridors. **Pets:** Accepted.

La Quinta Inn & Suites Santa Clarita-Valencia H
(661) 286-1111. **$95-$239.** 25201 The Old Rd 91381. I-5 exit 167 (Lyons Ave), just w to Chiquella Ln, just s, then just sw. Int corridors. **Pets:** Large, other species. Service with restrictions.

Residence Inn by Marriott H
(661) 290-2800. **$99-$499.** 25320 The Old Rd 91381. I-5 exit 167 (Lyons Ave), just w. Int corridors. **Pets:** Accepted.

Super 8-Santa Clarita M
(661) 252-1722. **$65-$109.** 17901 Sierra Hwy 91351. SR 14 exit 6A (Sierra Hwy/Via Princessa), 1.5 mi n. Int corridors. **Pets:** Small, dogs only. $20 daily fee/pet. Service with restrictions, supervision.

SANTA CRUZ

Chaminade Resort & Spa H ❀
(831) 475-5600. **Call for rates.** 1 Chaminade Ln 95065. 1.5 mi e of SR 1 and 17; SR 1 exit Soquel Ave, just w to Paul Sweet Rd, then 0.5 mi n. Int corridors. **Pets:** Medium, dogs only. $75 one-time fee/room. Service with restrictions, supervision.

Continental Inn M ❀
(831) 429-1221. **$59-$399.** 414 Ocean St 95060. 5 blks from beach; between Broadway and Soquel aves. Ext corridors. **Pets:** $30 daily fee/pet. Designated rooms, supervision.

Edgewater Beach Inn & Suites M
(831) 423-0440. **$169-$339, 3 day notice.** 525 Second St 95060. Across from beach and boardwalk. Ext corridors. **Pets:** Accepted.

Hilton Santa Cruz/Scotts Valley H ❀
(831) 440-1000. **$149-$339.** 6001 La Madrona Dr 95060. SR 17 exit Mt Hermon Rd. Int corridors. **Pets:** Dogs only. $50 one-time fee/room. Service with restrictions, supervision.

The Inn at Pasatiempo H
(831) 423-5000. **$75-$305.** 555 Hwy 17 95060. 0.8 mi n of jct SR 1 and 17; SR 17 exit Pasatiempo Dr. Ext corridors. **Pets:** Accepted.

Ocean Pacific Lodge H ❀
(831) 457-1234. **$79-$499.** 301 Pacific Ave 95060. SR 1 and 17 exit w via Ocean St, 1 mi w to Broadway, turn right, left on Front St to Pacific Ave, then just right. Ext corridors. **Pets:** $30 daily fee/pet. Designated rooms, service with restrictions, supervision.

West Cliff Inn BB
(831) 457-2200. **$195-$415, 7 day notice.** 174 W Cliff Dr 95060. Just n of boardwalk and adjacent to Santa Cruz Municipal Wharf. Int corridors. **Pets:** Accepted.

SANTA MARIA *(Restaurants p. 620)*

BEST WESTERN PLUS Big America M ❀
(805) 922-5200. **$112-$223.** 1725 N Broadway 93454. US 101 exit 173 (SR 135/S Broadway), 0.5 mi s. Ext corridors. **Pets:** Large, other species. Service with restrictions, supervision.

Candlewood Suites H
(805) 928-4155. **$79-$199.** 2079 N Roemer Ct 93454. US 101 exit 173 (SR 135/S Broadway), 0.8 mi sw, then just s. Int corridors. **Pets:** Accepted.

Historic Santa Maria Inn H ❀
(805) 928-7777. **$104-$319.** 801 S Broadway 93454. US 101 exit 171 (Main St), 1 mi n, then 0.5 mi s. Int corridors. **Pets:** Large, other species. $50 one-time fee/room. Designated rooms, service with restrictions, supervision.

Holiday Inn & Suites Santa Maria H
(805) 928-6000. **Call for rates.** 2100 N Broadway 93454. US 101 exit 173 (SR 135/S Broadway), just s. Int corridors. **Pets:** Accepted.

Quality Inn & Suites M
(805) 922-5891. **$97-$102.** 210 Nicholson Ave 93454. US 101 exit 171 (Main St), just e, then just s. Int corridors. **Pets:** Accepted.

Radisson Hotel Santa Maria H
(805) 928-8000. **$110-$229, 3 day notice.** 3455 Skyway Dr 93455. US 101 exit 169 (Betteravia Rd), 2.3 mi w, then 1.8 mi s. Ext/int corridors. **Pets:** Medium. $50 one-time fee/room. Designated rooms, service with restrictions, crate.

SANTA MONICA

Channel Road Inn BB
(310) 459-1920. **$195-$425, 7 day notice.** 219 W Channel Rd 90402. SR 1 (Pacific Coast Hwy), just e. Ext/int corridors. **Pets:** Dogs only. $65 one-time fee/room. Designated rooms, service with restrictions, supervision.

The Fairmont Miramar Hotel & Bungalows H
(310) 576-7777. **$339-$4000.** 101 Wilshire Blvd 90401. I-10 exit 1B (Lincoln Blvd), 0.6 mi n, then 0.6 mi w. Ext/int corridors. **Pets:** Accepted.

The Georgian Hotel H
(310) 395-9945. **$274-$374.** 1415 Ocean Ave 90401. I-10 exit 1B (Lincoln Blvd), just n, then 0.5 mi w on Broadway. Int corridors. **Pets:** Accepted.

△△△ ▽▽▽ ▽▽▽ **JW Marriott Santa Monica Le Merigot** H
(310) 395-9700. **$415-$495.** 1740 Ocean Ave 90401. I-10 exit 1B (Lincoln Blvd), 0.3 mi s, 0.6 mi w on Pico Blvd, then just n. Int corridors. **Pets:** Large, other species. $200 deposit/room, $150 one-time fee/room. Service with restrictions, supervision.
SAVE ▯▯ &M ⚊ ⚌ 🕭 ✕ ▱

△△△ ▽▽▽ ▽▽▽ **Le Méridien Delfina Santa Monica** H
(310) 399-9344. **Call for rates.** 530 Pico Blvd 90405. I-10 exit 1B (Lincoln Blvd), just s. Int corridors. **Pets:** Accepted.
SAVE ▯▯ &M ⚊ 🕭 ✕ ▮ ▱

▽▽▽ ▽▽▽ **Loews Santa Monica Beach Hotel** H
(310) 458-6700. **$339-$690.** 1700 Ocean Ave 90401. I-10 exit 1B (Lincoln Blvd), 0.3 mi s, 0.6 mi w on Pico Blvd, then just n. Int corridors. **Pets:** $100 one-time fee/room. Designated rooms, service with restrictions, supervision. ⊟ ▯▯ &M ⚊ ⚌ 🕭 ✕ ▱

△△△ ▽▽▽ ▽▽▽ **Shore Hotel** H 🐾
(310) 458-1515. **$329-$699.** 1515 Ocean Ave 90401. I-10 exit 1B (Lincoln Blvd), 0.3 mi s, 0.6 mi w on Pico Blvd, then just n. Int corridors. **Pets:** Dogs only. $20 daily fee/room. Designated rooms, service with restrictions, supervision. SAVE ⊟ ▯▯ &M ⚊ 🕭 ▮ ▱

△△△ ▽▽ ▽ **Travelodge-Santa Monica/Pico Blvd** M
(310) 450-5766. **$135-$199.** 3102 Pico Blvd 90405. I-10 exit 2 (Centinela Ave), just s, then just w. Ext corridors. **Pets:** Small. Designated rooms, service with restrictions, supervision. SAVE 🕭 ✕ ▮ ▱

▽▽▽ ▽▽ **Viceroy Santa Monica** H
(310) 260-7500. **$380-$3000.** 1819 Ocean Ave 90401. I-10 exit 1B (Lincoln Blvd), 0.3 mi s, 0.6 mi w on Pico Blvd, then just n. Int corridors. **Pets:** Accepted. ▯▯ &M ⚊ 🕭 ✕

△△△ ▽▽▽ **Wyndham Santa Monica At The Pier** H
(310) 451-0676. **$210-$439.** 120 Colorado Ave 90401. I-10 exit 1B (Lincoln Blvd), just n. Int corridors. **Pets:** Accepted.
SAVE ECO ▯▯ ⚊ 🕭 ✕ ▱

SANTA NELLA
△△△ ▽▽ ▽ **BEST WESTERN Andersen's Inn** H
(209) 826-5534. **$95-$120.** 12367 Hwy 33 S 95322. I-5 exit 407 (SR 33), just e. Ext corridors. **Pets:** Dogs only. $20 one-time fee/room. No service, supervision. SAVE &M ⚊ 🕭 ▮ ▱

▽▽▽ **Quality Inn** H
(209) 826-8282. **$79-$139.** 28976 Plaza Dr 95322. I-5 exit 407 (SR 33), just e. Ext corridors. **Pets:** Accepted. &M ⚊ 🕭 ▮ ▱

SANTA PAULA
▽▽ ▽ **Glen Tavern Inn** H
(805) 933-5550. **$89-$119.** 134 N Mill St 93060. SR 126 exit 12 (10th St) northbound, 0.5 mi w, just s on Santa Barbara St, then just e. Int corridors. **Pets:** Accepted. ▯▯ ⚊ 🕭 ✕ ▮ ▱

SANTA ROSA (Restaurants p. 620)
△△△ ▽▽▽ ▽ **BEST WESTERN Garden Inn** H
(707) 546-4031. **$99-$207.** 1500 Santa Rosa Ave 95404. US 101 exit Baker Ave northbound, just n; exit Corby Ave southbound. Ext corridors. **Pets:** Medium, dogs only. $15 daily fee/pet. Designated rooms, service with restrictions, supervision. SAVE ▯▯ &M ⚊ 🕭 ▮ ▱

△△△ ▽▽▽ ▽▽ **BEST WESTERN PLUS Wine Country Inn & Suites** H 🐾
(707) 545-9000. **$139-$259.** 870 Hopper Ave 95403. US 101 northbound exit Mendocino Ave/Old Redwood Hwy, just s to Mendocino Overcross to Cleveland Ave, just n to Hopper Ave, then just w; southbound exit Hopper Ave, then just w. Ext corridors. **Pets:** Dogs only. $20 one-time fee/room. Designated rooms, service with restrictions, supervision. SAVE &M ⚊ 🕭 ▮ ▱

▽▽ ▽▽ **Extended Stay America-Santa Rosa-North** H
(707) 541-0959. **Call for rates.** 100 Fountain Grove Pkwy 95403. US 101 exit Mendocino Ave/Old Redwood Hwy, just e. Int corridors. **Pets:** Other species. $25 daily fee/pet. Service with restrictions, supervision. &M 🕭 ▮ ▱

△△△ ▽▽ ▽ **Extended Stay America-Santa Rosa-South** H
(707) 546-4808. **Call for rates.** 2600 Corby Ave 95407. US 101 exit Hearn Ave/Yolanda Ave northbound; exit Hearn Ave southbound. Ext corridors. **Pets:** Other species. $25 daily fee/pet. Service with restrictions, supervision. SAVE &M 🕭 ▮ ▱

▽▽ ▽▽ **Flamingo Conference Resort and Spa** H
(707) 545-8530. **Call for rates.** 2777 4th St 95405. Off SR 12; at Farmers Ln. Int corridors. **Pets:** Other species. $50 one-time fee/room. Designated rooms, service with restrictions, supervision.
ECO ▯▯ &M ⚊ ⚌ 🕭 ✕ ▮ ▱

▽▽ ▽▽ **Fountaingrove Inn, Hotel & Conference Center** H 🐾
(707) 578-6101. **$99-$499, 3 day notice.** 101 Fountaingrove Pkwy 95403. From US 101 exit Mendocino Ave/Old Redwood Hwy, just e. Int corridors. **Pets:** Medium, dogs only. $25 daily fee/room. Designated rooms, service with restrictions, supervision.
▯▯ &M ⚊ 🕭 ✕ ▮ ▱

△△△ ▽▽ ▽ **Hillside Inn Motel** M
(707) 546-9353. **$84-$99, 3 day notice.** 2901 4th St 95409. US 101, 2.5 mi e on SR 12; at Farmers Ln and 4th St. Ext corridors. **Pets:** Small. Designated rooms, service with restrictions, supervision.
SAVE ▯▯ ⚊ 🕭 ▮ ▱

△△△ ▽▽ ▽ **Hilton Sonoma Wine Country** H 🐾
(707) 523-7555. **$109-$309.** 3555 Round Barn Blvd 95403. US 101 exit Mendocino Ave/Old Redwood Hwy, just e, then just n. Int corridors. **Pets:** Medium, dogs only. $50 one-time fee/pet. Service with restrictions, crate. SAVE ECO ▯▯ &M ⚊ 🕭 ✕ ▮ ▱

▽▽ ▽▽ **Hotel La Rose** H
(707) 579-3200. **$130-$250, 3 day notice.** 308 Wilson St 95401. 2 blks w off US 101 exit downtown Santa Rosa; on Railroad Square. Ext/int corridors. **Pets:** Accepted. &M 🕭 ✕ ▱

△△△ ▽▽▽ ▽▽ **Hyatt Vineyard Creek Hotel and Spa in Sonoma County** H 🐾
(707) 284-1234. **$99-$599.** 170 Railroad St 95401. US 101 exit downtown Santa Rosa, just w; jct 3rd St. Int corridors. **Pets:** Dogs only. $100 one-time fee/room. Service with restrictions, crate.
SAVE ECO ▯▯ &M ⚊ ⚌ 🕭 ✕ ▮ ▱

▽▽ ▽▽ **Quality Inn & Suites Santa Rosa** H
(707) 521-2100. **$100-$400.** 3000 Santa Rosa Ave 95407. US 101 exit Todd Rd, 1.2 mi n. Int corridors. **Pets:** Other species. $20 daily fee/pet. Service with restrictions, supervision. &M 🕭 ✕ ▮ ▱

▽▽ ▽▽ **Sandman Inn** H
(707) 544-8570. **$89-$125, 14 day notice.** 3421 Cleveland Ave 95403. US 101 northbound exit Mendocino Ave/Old Redwood Hwy, then just s to Mendocino Overcross to Cleveland Ave, then just s; southbound exit Hopper Ave, then just e. Ext corridors. **Pets:** Medium, dogs only. $25 one-time fee/pet. Designated rooms, service with restrictions, supervision. SAVE &M ⚊ 🕭 ▮ ▱

SANTEE (Restaurants p. 620)
△△△ ▽▽ ▽ **BEST WESTERN Santee Lodge** M
(619) 449-2626. **$76-$280.** 10726 Woodside Ave 92071. SR 52 exit 14 (Mission Gorge Rd), 2 mi e. Ext corridors. **Pets:** Accepted.
SAVE &M ⚊ 🕭 ✕ ▮ ▱

SAN YSIDRO *(Restaurants p. 621)*

Quality Inn & Suites Near the Border **M**
(619) 690-2633. **$75-$109.** 930 W San Ysidro Blvd 92173. I-5 exit 2 (Dairy Mart Rd), just ne; just n of Tijuana International Border Crossing. Ext corridors. **Pets:** Very small. $25 one-time fee/pet. Designated rooms, service with restrictions, supervision. (SAVE) 🛰 ✕ 🛏 💻

SCOTTS VALLEY

BEST WESTERN PLUS Inn Scotts Valley **H**
(831) 438-6666. **$99-$149.** 6020 Scotts Valley Dr 95066. SR 17 exit Granite Creek, just w. Ext/int corridors. **Pets:** Accepted.
(SAVE) 🛗 🛋 🛰 ✕ 🛏 💻

SEAL BEACH *(Restaurants p. 621)*

The Pacific Inn **H**
(562) 493-7501. **$140-$200, 7 day notice.** 600 Marina Dr 90740. I-405 exit 22 (Seal Beach Blvd/Los Alamitos Blvd), 2.6 mi s, 0.5 mi w on Pacific Coast Hwy, then just sw. Ext/int corridors. **Pets:** Accepted.
(SAVE) 🛗 🛋 ✕ 🛰 ✕ 🛏 💻

SHAVER LAKE

Shaver Lake Village Hotel & Cabins **H**
(559) 841-8289. **Call for rates.** 42135 Tollhouse Rd 93664. Center. Ext/int corridors. **Pets:** Accepted. 🛰 ✕ 🛐 🗲 🛏 💻

SHERMAN OAKS *(Restaurants p. 621)*

BEST WESTERN PLUS Carriage Inn **M**
(818) 787-2300. **$109-$239.** 5525 Sepulveda Blvd 91411. I-405 exit 64 (Burbank Blvd), just e, then just s. Ext/int corridors. **Pets:** Medium. $20 daily fee/pet. Designated rooms, service with restrictions, supervision.
(SAVE) 🌿 🛗 🛋 🛰 ✕ 🛏 💻

SIERRA CITY

Herrington's Sierra Pines Resort **M**
(530) 862-1151. **$79-$140, 10 day notice.** 104 Main St 96125. 0.5 mi w of center on SR 49; 12 mi n of Downieville. Ext corridors. **Pets:** Other species. Supervision. (SAVE) 🍴 🛰 ✕ 🛐 🗲 💻

SIMI VALLEY

Extended Stay America-Los Angeles-Simi Valley **H**
(805) 584-8880. **Call for rates.** 2498 Stearns St 93063. SR 118 exit 28 (Stearns St), just s. Int corridors. **Pets:** Other species. $25 daily fee/pet. Service with restrictions, supervision. 🛰 🛏 💻

SOLEDAD

Valley Harvest Inn **H**
(831) 678-3833. **$89-$149.** 1155 Front St 93960. US 101 exit Soledad, just e. Ext/int corridors. **Pets:** Small. $15 daily fee/pet. Designated rooms, service with restrictions, supervision.
(SAVE) 🍴 🛋 🛰 🛏 💻

SOLVANG *(Restaurants p. 621)*

Hadsten House Inn **M**
(805) 688-3210. **Call for rates.** 1450 Mission Dr 93463. On SR 246. Ext corridors. **Pets:** Accepted.
(SAVE) 🍴 🛗 🛋 🛰 ✕ 🛏 💻

Royal Copenhagen Inn **M**
(805) 688-5561. **$85-$275, 3 day notice.** 1579 Mission Dr 93463. On SR 246; center of town. Ext corridors. **Pets:** Other species. $20 daily fee/pet. Designated rooms, service with restrictions, supervision.
(SAVE) 🛋 🛰 🛏 💻

Viking Motel **M**
(805) 688-1337. **$59-$180, 3 day notice.** 1506 Mission Dr 93463. On SR 246. Ext corridors. **Pets:** Small. $15 daily fee/pet. Designated rooms, service with restrictions, supervision. (SAVE) 🛰 🛏

Wine Valley Inn & Cottages **H**
(805) 688-2111. **$194-$494.** 1564 Copenhagen Dr 93463. SR 246, just s on 5th St. Ext/int corridors. **Pets:** Other species. $25 daily fee/pet. Service with restrictions, supervision. (SAVE) ✕ 🛰 ✕ 🛏 💻

SONOMA *(Restaurants p. 621)*

BEST WESTERN Sonoma Valley Inn & Krug Event Center **H**
(707) 938-9200. **$119-$389, 3 day notice.** 550 2nd St W 95476. 1 blk w of town plaza. Ext corridors. **Pets:** Accepted.
(SAVE) 🛗 🛋 ✕ 🛰 ✕ 🛏 💻

The Fairmont Sonoma Mission Inn & Spa **H**
(707) 938-9000. **$229-$699, 5 day notice.** 100 Boyes Blvd 95476. 2.5 mi n on SR 12. Ext/int corridors. **Pets:** Accepted.
(SAVE) 🌿 🍴 🛗 🛋 ✕ 🔕 ✕ 🛏 💻

Inn at Sonoma **BB**
(707) 939-1340. **$235-$435, 7 day notice.** 630 Broadway 95476. On SR 12, just s of Sonoma Plaza. Int corridors. **Pets:** Dogs only. $65 one-time fee/room. Designated rooms, service with restrictions, supervision. 🛗 🛰 ✕ 🛏 💻

The Lodge at Sonoma, A Renaissance Resort & Spa **H**
(707) 935-6600. **$179-$649, 5 day notice.** 1325 Broadway 95476. On SR 12, 1 mi s of Sonoma Plaza. Ext/int corridors. **Pets:** Accepted.
(SAVE) 🍴 🛗 🛋 ✕ 🛰 ✕ 🛏 💻

Sonoma Creek Inn **M**
(707) 939-9463. **$99-$225, 7 day notice.** 239 Boyes Blvd 95476. SR 12, 0.5 mi w. Ext corridors. **Pets:** Medium, dogs only. $25 one-time fee/pet. Designated rooms, service with restrictions, supervision.
🛗 🛰 ✕ 🛏 💻

SONORA

Aladdin Motor Inn **H**
(209) 533-4971. **Call for rates.** 14260 Mono Way (Hwy 108) 95370. On SR 108, 3.5 mi e. Ext/int corridors. **Pets:** Accepted.
🛋 🛰 🛏 💻

BEST WESTERN PLUS Sonora Oaks Hotel & Conference Center **H** ❀
(209) 533-4400. **$100-$200.** 19551 Hess Ave 95370. SR 108 westbound exit Phoenix Lake Rd, just se to Hess Ave; eastbound exit Hess Ave, just se; jct Mono Way. Ext/int corridors. **Pets:** Large, dogs only. $20 daily fee/room. Designated rooms, service with restrictions, supervision. (SAVE) 🍴 🛗 🛋 🛰 ✕ 🛏 💻

Bradford Place Inn and Gardens **BB** ❀
(209) 536-6075. **$120-$220, 5 day notice.** 56 W Bradford St 95370. Just w of SR 49 (S Washington St); jct Norlin St; downtown. Int corridors. **Pets:** Medium, dogs only. $15 daily fee/room. Designated rooms, supervision. 🛰 ✕ 🗲 🛏 💻

Union Hill Inn **BB**
(209) 533-1494. **$150-$195, 3 day notice.** 21645 Parrotts Ferry Rd 95370. Jct SR 49 and Parrotts Ferry Rd; 3 mi n of downtown. Ext corridors. **Pets:** Accepted. 🛰 ✕ 🗲 🛏 💻

SOUTH LAKE TAHOE *(Restaurants p. 621)*

Alpenrose Inn **M**
(530) 544-2985. **$69-$199, 3 day notice.** 4074 Pine Blvd 96150. Just s of casino area to Stateline Ave, 0.3 mi w to Pine Blvd, then just s. Ext corridors. **Pets:** $50 deposit/pet, $15 daily fee/pet. Designated rooms, service with restrictions, crate. 🛰 ✕ 🛏 💻

Basecamp Hotel **H**
(530) 208-0180. **$99-$199, 3 day notice.** 4143 Cedar Ave 96150. Just s of casino area to Stateline Ave, just w. Ext/int corridors. **Pets:** Other species. $40 one-time fee/room. Designated rooms, service with restrictions, supervision. 🛰 ✕

◆◆ **Beach Retreat & Lodge Lake Tahoe** [H]
(530) 541-6722. **Call for rates.** 3411 Lake Tahoe Blvd 96150. 1.8 mi s of casino area on US 50. Ext corridors. **Pets:** Medium, dogs only. $50 deposit/room, $30 daily fee/pet. Designated rooms, service with restrictions. 🍴 ♿M 🏊 🏋 📶 🚭 ▭

◆ **Econo Lodge** [M]
(530) 544-3959. **$40-$60.** 2659 Lake Tahoe Blvd 96150. 0.8 mi e of jct US 50 and SR 89. Ext corridors. **Pets:** Accepted. 📶 ▮

◆◆◆ **Fireside Lodge - An All Inclusive Premier Bed & Breakfast** [BB] 🐾
(530) 544-5515. **$119-$325, 3 day notice.** 515 Emerald Bay Rd 96150. 1.3 mi n of jct US 50 and SR 89. Ext corridors. **Pets:** Other species. $25 daily fee/pet. 🏋 📶 🚭 AC ▮ ▭

◆◆ **Heavenly Valley Lodge** [M] 🐾
(530) 564-1500. **$145-$295.** 1261 Ski Run Blvd 96150. US 50 exit Ski Run Blvd, 0.5 mi se; jct Pioneer Tr. Ext corridors. **Pets:** Medium, dogs only. $25 daily fee/pet. Designated rooms, service with restrictions, crate. 📶 🚭 AC ☎ ▮ ▭

◆ **Howard Johnson Inn** [M]
(530) 541-4000. **$59-$229.** 3489 Lake Tahoe Blvd 96150. 1.5 mi s of casino area. Ext corridors. **Pets:** Accepted. 🏊 📶 🚭 ▮ ▭

◆◆◆ **Lake Tahoe Vacation Resort - A Diamond Resort** [CO]
(530) 541-6122. **Call for rates.** 901 Ski Run Blvd 96150. 1 mi s of casino area; at US 50 and Ski Run Blvd. Int corridors. **Pets:** Accepted.
ECO 🍴 ♿M 🏊 🏋 📶 🚭 ▮ ▭

◆◆ **Park Tahoe Inn** [M]
(530) 544-6000. **Call for rates.** 4011 Lake Tahoe Blvd 96150. 0.4 mi sw of casino area; at Park Ave and Lake Tahoe Blvd (US 50); across from Heavenly Village. Ext corridors. **Pets:** $25 daily fee/pet. Designated rooms, service with restrictions, supervision. 🏊 📶 🚭 ▮

AAA ◆◆ **Stardust Lodge** [CO]
(530) 544-5211. **$100-$289, 3 day notice.** 4061 Lake Tahoe Blvd 96150. Just sw of casino area; at US 50 and LaSalle Ave. Ext corridors. **Pets:** Accepted. SAVE ♿M 🏊 🏋 📶 🚭 ▮ ▭

AAA ◆◆ **Tahoe Chalet Inn-The Theme Inn and Wedding Chapel** [M]
(530) 544-3311. **$119-$189, 3 day notice.** 3860 Lake Tahoe Blvd 96150. 0.7 mi s of casino area on US 50. Ext corridors. **Pets:** Small. $30 daily fee/pet. Designated rooms, service with restrictions, supervision. SAVE ♿M 🏊 📶 🚭 ▮ ▭

AAA ◆◆◆ **Tahoe Keys Resort** [CO] 🐾
(530) 544-5397. **$112-$1700.** 599 Tahoe Keys Blvd 96150. 0.5 mi e of jct US 50 and SR 89, 1 mi n. Ext corridors. **Pets:** Dogs only. $25 one-time fee/pet. Designated rooms, service with restrictions, crate.
SAVE 🏊 🏋 📶 🚭 AC ▮ ▭

AAA ◆◆ **Tahoe Valley Lodge** [M]
(530) 541-0353. **$125-$495, 7 day notice.** 2241 Lake Tahoe Blvd 96150. 0.5 mi e of jct US 50 and SR 89. Ext corridors. **Pets:** Very small, dogs only. $25 daily fee/pet. Designated rooms, supervision.
SAVE 🏊 📶 🚭 ▮ ▭

SOUTH PASADENA

◆◆◆ **Arroyo Vista Inn** [BB]
(323) 478-7300. **$150-$280, 14 day notice.** 335 Monterey Rd 91030. SR 110 exit 64 (Marmion Way) northbound, 0.8 mi e, then just n; exit 31A (Orange Grove Ave) southbound, 0.3 mi e, 0.6 mi s, then just n. Int corridors. **Pets:** Accepted. 📶 🚭 ☎

SOUTH SAN FRANCISCO

AAA ◆◆◆ **Larkspur Landing South San Francisco** [H]
(650) 827-1515. **Call for rates.** 690 Gateway Blvd 94080. US 101 exit 425A (Grand Ave), 0.4 mi e, then 0.4 mi n. Int corridors.
Pets: Accepted. SAVE ECO ♿M 📶 🚭 ▮ ▭

AAA ◆◆◆ **Residence Inn by Marriott at Oyster Point** [H]
(650) 837-9000. **$299-$409.** 1350 Veterans Blvd 94080. US 101 exit 425B (Oyster Point Blvd), just ne. Int corridors. **Pets:** Large. $100 one-time fee/pet. SAVE ECO 🍴 ♿M 🏊 📶 🚭 ▮ ▭

STOCKTON

AAA ◆◆◆ **BEST WESTERN PLUS Heritage Inn** [H]
(209) 474-3301. **$69-$159.** 111 E March Ln 95207. I-5 exit March Ln, 2.5 mi e; corner of El Dorado St. Int corridors. **Pets:** Accepted.
SAVE 🍴 ♿M 🏊 📶 ▮ ▭

◆◆◆ **Holiday Inn Express Hotel Stockton Southeast** [H]
(209) 946-1234. **$99-$114, 3 day notice.** 5045 S Kingsley Rd 95215. SR 99 exit Arch Rd, just e. Int corridors. **Pets:** Medium. $25 one-time fee/pet. Designated rooms, service with restrictions, supervision.
♿M 🏊 📶 🚭 ▮ ▭

◆◆ **La Quinta Inn Stockton** [H]
(209) 952-7800. **$69-$179.** 2710 W March Ln 95219. I-5 exit March Ln, just w. Ext corridors. **Pets:** Large, other species. Service with restrictions. ♿M 🏊 📶 ▮ ▭

AAA ◆◆◆ **Residence Inn by Marriott** [H]
(209) 472-9800. **$169-$259.** 3240 W March Ln 95219. I-5 exit March Ln, 0.5 mi w; just e of jct Brookside Rd. Int corridors. **Pets:** Accepted.
SAVE ♿M 🏊 📶 🚭 ▮ ▭

AAA ◆◆◆ **University Plaza Waterfront Hotel** [H]
(209) 944-1140. **$109-$149.** 110 W Fremont St 95202. SR 4 exit 66A (Downtown Stockton/El Dorado St), 0.5 mi n on El Dorado St, then just w. Int corridors. **Pets:** $20 daily fee/room. Designated rooms, service with restrictions, supervision.
SAVE ECO 🍴 ♿M 🏊 📶 🚭 ▮ ▭

SUISUN CITY

◆◆◆ **Hampton Inn & Suites Suisun City Waterfront** [H]
(707) 429-0900. **$129-$189.** 2 Harbor Center Dr 94585. I-80 exit 43 (SR 12 E/Rio Vista/Suisun City), 2.6 mi e; exit 58B (Main St/Suisun City), just s. Int corridors. **Pets:** Medium, dogs only. Service with restrictions, crate. ECO ♿M 🏊 📶 🚭 ▮ ▭

SUN CITY

◆◆ **Motel 6 Menifee #4599** [M]
(951) 679-1133. **Call for rates.** 27955 Encanto Dr 92586. I-215 exit 12 (McCall Blvd), just e, then just s. Ext corridors. **Pets:** Other species. Service with restrictions, crate. ♿M 🏊 📶 ▮

SUNNYVALE

AAA ◆◆◆ **Larkspur Landing Sunnyvale** [H]
(408) 733-1212. **Call for rates.** 748 N Mathilda Ave 94085. US 101 exit Mathilda Ave, just s. Int corridors. **Pets:** Accepted.
SAVE ECO ♿M 📶 🚭 ▮ ▭

AAA ◆◆◆ **Maple Tree Inn** [H] 🐾
(408) 720-9700. **$139-$239.** 711 E El Camino Real 94087. US 101 exit 394 (Lawrence Expwy), 2.9 mi w to El Camino Real exit, then 1.8 mi n. Int corridors. **Pets:** Medium, dogs only. $20 daily fee/pet. Service with restrictions, supervision. SAVE ♿M 🏊 📶 🚭 ▮ ▭

◆◆◆ **Quality Inn Santa Clara Convention Center** [H]
(408) 744-1100. **$450-$999.** 1280 Persian Dr 94089. US 101 exit Lawrence Expwy N, 1 mi n to Persian Dr, then 0.3 mi w. Int corridors.
Pets: Accepted. ♿M 🏊 📶 🚭 ▮ ▭

▼▼▼ **Residence Inn by Marriott Silicon Valley I** 🅗
(408) 720-1000. **$159-$499.** 750 Lakeway Dr 94085. US 101 exit Lawrence Expwy S, e on Oakmead Pkwy. Ext corridors. **Pets:** Accepted.
🔙Ⓜ️ 🏊 🛰 ✕ 🛎 💻

▼▼▼ **Residence Inn by Marriott Sunnyvale Silicon Valley II** 🅗
(408) 720-8893. **$159-$499.** 1080 Stewart Dr 94086. US 101 exit Lawrence Expwy S, w on Duane Ave, just s. Ext corridors. **Pets:** Accepted.
🔙Ⓜ️ 🏊 🛰 ✕ 🛎 💻

🅐🅐🅐 ▼▼▼ **Sheraton Sunnyvale** 🅗
(408) 745-6000. **$99-$359.** 1100 N Mathilda Ave 94089. SR 237 exit Mathilda Ave, just n. Int corridors. **Pets:** Accepted.
SAVE 🍴 🔙Ⓜ️ 🏊 🛰 ✕ 🛎 💻

🅐🅐🅐 ▼▼▼ **Staybridge Suites** 🅗
(408) 745-1515. **$300-$370.** 900 Hamlin Ct 94089. SR 237 exit Mathilda Ave S, w on Ross Dr. Ext/int corridors. **Pets:** Other species. $15 one-time fee/room, $10 daily fee/room. Service with restrictions, supervision. SAVE 🔙Ⓜ️ 🏊 🛰 🛎 💻

▼▼▼ **TownePlace Suites by Marriott Sunnyvale/Mountain View** 🅗
(408) 733-4200. **$129-$299.** 606 S Bernardo Ave 94087. SR 85 exit SR 82, 0.5 mi s. Int corridors. **Pets:** Accepted. 🔙Ⓜ️ 🛰 ✕ 🛎 💻

▼▼▼ **Wild Palms Hotel** 🅗
(408) 738-0500. **$99-$209, 3 day notice.** 910 E Fremont Ave 94087. US 101 exit Lawrence Expwy S, 1.5 mi s, 0.9 mi n on E El Camino Real, just w on S Wolfe Rd, then just s. Ext/int corridors.
Pets: Accepted. ECO 🔙Ⓜ️ 🏊 🛰 ✕ 🛎 💻

SUSANVILLE

🅐🅐🅐 ▼▼▼ **BEST WESTERN Trailside Inn** 🅜
(530) 257-4123. **$86-$95.** 2785 Main St 96130. 0.7 mi e on SR 36 from jct SR 139. Ext corridors. **Pets:** Accepted.
SAVE 🍴 🔙Ⓜ️ 🏊 🛰 ✕ 🛎 💻

🅐🅐🅐 ▼▼▼ **Diamond Mountain Casino & Hotel** 🅗
(530) 252-1100. **$86-$189.** 900 Skyline Dr 96130. 1.0 mi ne on SR 139 from jct SR 36, then 1 mi w; follow signs to rancheria. Int corridors. **Pets:** Medium, other species. $15 daily fee/pet. Designated rooms.
SAVE ECO 🍴 🔙Ⓜ️ 🏊 ✕ 🛰 🛎 💻

▼▼▼ **The Roseberry House Bed & Breakfast** 🅑🅑
(530) 257-5675. **$110-$135.** 609 North St 96130. 0.7 mi w on SR 36 from jct SR 139 to N Lassen St, then just n. Int corridors. **Pets:** Other species. $10 daily fee/pet. No service, supervision. 🛰 ✕ 🔁

🅐🅐🅐 ▼▼▼ **Super 8** 🅜
(530) 257-2782. **$72-$82.** 2975 Johnstonville Rd 96130. 1 mi e on SR 36 from jct 139, then just ne. Ext corridors. **Pets:** Accepted.
SAVE 🔙Ⓜ️ 🏊 🛰 🛎 💻

TAHOE CITY (Restaurants p. 621)

▼▼ **Mother Nature's Inn** 🅜 🐾
(530) 581-4278. **$65-$149, 7 day notice.** 551 N Lake Blvd 96145. SR 28 (N Lake Blvd), 0.5 mi e of jct SR 89; behind Mother Nature's Store. Int corridors. **Pets:** $15 daily fee/pet. Service with restrictions.
🛰 ✕ 🛎 💻

▼▼ **River Ranch Lodge** 🅜
(530) 583-4264. **$99-$190, 14 day notice.** 2285 River Rd 96145. I-80 exit SR 89, 11 mi s; 3.5 mi n from City Center. Ext/int corridors.
Pets: Accepted. 🍴 🔙Ⓜ️ 🛰 ✕ 🎦

▼▼▼ **Sunnyside Restaurant & Lodge** 🅗
(530) 583-7200. **$175-$420, 30 day notice.** 1850 W Lake Blvd 96145. SR 89, 2 mi s. Ext/int corridors. **Pets:** $35 one-time fee/room. Designated rooms, service with restrictions, supervision.
🍴 🔙Ⓜ️ 🛰 ✕ 🎦 🛎

TAHOE VISTA

▼▼ **Cedar Glen Lodge** 🅜
(530) 546-4281. **$179-$289, 14 day notice.** 6589 N Lake Blvd 96148. SR 28 (N Lake Blvd), 1.5 mi w of SR 267. Ext corridors.
Pets: Accepted. 🍴 🔙Ⓜ️ 🏊 🛰 ✕ 🛎 💻

▼▼ **Holiday House** 🅜
(530) 546-2369. **Call for rates.** 7276 N Lake Blvd 96148. SR 28 (N Lake Blvd), 1 mi w of SR 267. Ext corridors. **Pets:** Accepted.
🔙Ⓜ️ 🛰 ✕ 🎦 🛎 💻

TARZANA

🅐🅐🅐 ▼▼ **St. George Inn & Suites** 🅜
(818) 345-6911. **Call for rates.** 19454 Ventura Blvd 91356. US 101 exit 24 (Tampa Ave), just s, then just w. Ext corridors. **Pets:** Accepted.
SAVE 🛰 🛰 🛎

TEHACHAPI (Restaurants p. 621)

🅐🅐🅐 ▼▼ **BEST WESTERN Mountain Inn** 🅜
(661) 822-5591. **Call for rates.** 418 W Tehachapi Blvd 93561. SR 58 exit 148 (SR 202), 1 mi s, then e. Ext corridors. **Pets:** Accepted.
SAVE 🛰 🛰 🛎 💻

▼▼▼ **Holiday Inn Express & Suites** 🅗
(661) 822-9837. **$120-$150.** 901 Capital Hills Pkwy 93561. SR 58 exit 149 (Mill St), just n. Int corridors. **Pets:** Accepted.
🔙Ⓜ️ 🛰 🛰 🛎 💻

▼▼ **La Quinta Inn Tehachapi** 🅜
(661) 823-8000. **$99-$259.** 500 E Steuber Rd 93561. SR 58 exit 151 (Monolith St/Tehachapi Blvd), just s. Int corridors. **Pets:** Large, other species. Service with restrictions. 🛰 🛰 ✕ 🛎 💻

TEMECULA (Restaurants p. 621)

▼▼▼ **La Quinta Inn & Suites Temecula** 🅗
(951) 296-1003. **$79-$289.** 27330 Jefferson Ave 92590. I-15 exit 61 (SR 79 N/Winchester Rd), just w, then just n; east side of Rancho Temecula Plaza. Int corridors. **Pets:** Large, other species. Service with restrictions.
🛰 🛰 ✕ 🛎 💻

🅐🅐🅐 ▼▼▼▼ **Ponte Vineyard Inn** 🅗 🐾
(951) 587-6688. **$200-$370, 3 day notice.** 35001 Rancho California Rd 92591. I-15 exit 59 (Rancho California Rd), 6.5 mi e. Ext/int corridors.
Pets: Medium, dogs only. $50 one-time fee/room. Designated rooms, service with restrictions, supervision.
SAVE 🍴 🔙Ⓜ️ 🛰 ✕ 💻

▼▼▼ **Quality Inn Temecula Wine Country** 🅜
(951) 296-3788. **$79-$189.** 27338 Jefferson Ave 92590. I-15 exit 61 (SR 79 N/Winchester Rd), just w, then just n; east side of Rancho Temecula Plaza. Ext corridors. **Pets:** Medium, dogs only. $20 daily fee/room. Designated rooms, service with restrictions, supervision.
🔙Ⓜ️ 🛰 🛰 ✕ 🛎 💻

▼▼▼ **Temecula Creek Inn** 🅗
(951) 694-1000. **$129-$289, 3 day notice.** 44501 Rainbow Canyon Rd 92592. I-15 exit 58 (SR 79 S), 1 mi e to Pechanga Pkwy, just se, then 0.5 mi s. Ext corridors. **Pets:** Medium, dogs only. $50 daily fee/room. Service with restrictions, crate. 🍴 🛰 ✕ 🔊 🛎 💻

THOUSAND OAKS (Restaurants p. 621)

▼▼ **La Quinta Inn & Suites Thousand Oaks Newbury Park** 🅜
(805) 499-5910. **$89-$215.** 1320 Newbury Rd 91320. US 101 exit 46 (Ventu Park Rd), just se. Ext corridors. **Pets:** Large, other species. Service with restrictions. 🔙Ⓜ️ 🛰 🛰 🛎 💻

▼▼▼ **Palm Garden Hotel** 🅗
(805) 716-4200. **$139-$159.** 495 N Ventu Park Rd 91320. US 101 exit 46 (Ventu Park Rd), just n. Ext corridors. **Pets:** Other species. $50 one-time fee/pet. Designated rooms, service with restrictions, crate.
🍴 🔙Ⓜ️ 🛰 🛰 🛎 💻

▽▽▽▽ TownePlace Suites by Marriott 🅷

(805) 499-3111. **$90-$220.** 1712 Newbury Rd 91320. US 101 exit 46 (Ventu Park Rd), just w, then just n. Int corridors. **Pets:** Accepted.

🏊 📶 ✖ 🔋 💻

THREE RIVERS *(Restaurants p. 621)*

🔷🔷🔷 ▽▽ ▽▽ Americas Best Value Inn-Lazy J Ranch Ⓜ

(559) 561-4449. **$155, 3 day notice.** 39625 Sierra Dr 93271. SR 198, 3 mi sw of town center. Ext corridors. **Pets:** Accepted.

SAVE 🏊 📶 ✖ 🔋 💻

▽▽ ▽▽ Buckeye Tree Lodge Ⓜ

(559) 561-5900. **$76-$160, 7 day notice.** 46000 Sierra Dr 93271. SR 198, north end of town; 0.5 mi from entrance to Sequoia National Park. Ext corridors. **Pets:** Other species. $10 daily fee/pet. Service with restrictions, crate. 🏊 📶 ✖ 🔋 💻

🔷🔷🔷 ▽▽▽▽ Comfort Inn & Suites Ⓜ

(559) 561-9000. **$69-$249.** 40820 Sierra Dr 93271. SR 198, 1.5 mi sw of town center. Ext/int corridors. **Pets:** Small. $35 one-time fee/pet. Designated rooms, service with restrictions, crate.

SAVE 🅼 🏊 ✖ 📶 ✖ 🔋 💻

▽▽ ▽▽ Gateway Lodge Ⓜ

(559) 561-4133. **$89-$199, 7 day notice.** 45978 Sierra Dr 93271. SR 198, 6 mi ne of town center; 0.5 mi sw of entrance to Sequoia National Park. Ext corridors. **Pets:** Accepted. 🍽 📶 ✖ 🈂 🔋 💻

▽▽ ▽▽ Sequoia River Dance Bed & Breakfast 🅱🅱

(559) 561-4411. **$105-$145, 14 day notice.** 40534 Cherokee Oaks Dr 93271. SR 198, 2 mi sw of town center, 0.3 mi e. Int corridors. **Pets:** $20 one-time fee/pet. Supervision. 📶 ✖ 🆆 🈂

▽▽ ▽▽ Sequoia Village Inn Ⓜ

(559) 561-3652. **$89-$329, 7 day notice.** 45971 Sierra Dr 93271. SR 198, 6 mi ne of town center; 0.5 mi sw of entrance to Sequoia National Park. Ext corridors. **Pets:** Other species. $10 daily fee/pet. Service with restrictions, crate. 🏊 📶 ✖ 🈂 🔋 💻

TIBURON

▽▽▽▽ The Lodge at Tiburon 🅷 🐾

(415) 435-3133. **$169-$499, 3 day notice.** 1651 Tiburon Blvd 94920. US 101 exit Tiburon-Belvedere, 4 mi e; in village; 1 blk from bay. Ext corridors. **Pets:** Dogs only. $75 one-time fee/pet. Designated rooms, service with restrictions, supervision.

🅴🅲🅾 🍽 🅼 🏊 ✖ 📶 ✖ 🔋 💻

TORRANCE *(Restaurants p. 621)*

🔷🔷🔷 ▽▽▽▽ Holiday Inn Torrance 🅷

(310) 781-9100. **$139-$239.** 19800 S Vermont Ave 90502. I-110 exit 8 (Torrance Blvd/Del Amo Blvd), just n to Del Amo Blvd, just w, then just n. Int corridors. **Pets:** Medium, other species. $50 deposit/room. Service with restrictions, crate.

SAVE 🅴🅲🅾 🍽 🅼 🏊 ✖ 📶 ✖ 🔋 💻

▽▽ ▽▽ Ramada Torrance Ⓜ

(310) 325-0660. **$74-$119.** 2888 Pacific Coast Hwy 90505. I-405 exit 39 (Crenshaw Blvd), 5.2 mi s, then just w. Ext corridors. **Pets:** Small. $30 daily fee/pet. Service with restrictions, supervision. 🏊 📶 🔋 💻

🔷🔷🔷 ▽▽▽▽ Residence Inn by Marriott 🅷

(310) 543-4566. **$149-$289.** 3701 Torrance Blvd 90503. I-405 exit 42A (Hawthorne Blvd), 3.2 mi s, then just e. Ext corridors. **Pets:** Medium, other species. $100 one-time fee/room. Service with restrictions, supervision. SAVE 🅴🅲🅾 🏊 📶 ✖ 🔋 💻

▽▽▽▽ Staybridge Suites Torrance/Redondo Beach 🅷

(310) 371-8525. **$109-$229.** 19901 Prairie Ave 90503. I-405 exit 39 (Crenshaw Blvd), 0.4 mi s to 190th St, 0.9 mi w, then 0.4 mi s. Ext corridors. **Pets:** Accepted. 🅼 🏊 📶 🔋 💻

TRACY

🔷🔷🔷 ▽▽▽▽ BEST WESTERN Luxury Inn 🅷

(209) 832-0271. **$86.** 811 W Clover Rd 95376. I-205 exit 8 (Central Tracy/Tracy Blvd), just s, then just w. Int corridors. **Pets:** Small. $10 daily fee/pet. Service with restrictions, crate.

SAVE 🅼 🏊 📶 🔋 💻

TRINIDAD

▽▽▽▽ Emerald Forest of Trinidad 🅲🅰

(707) 677-3554. **$229-$329, 5 day notice.** 753 Patrick's Point Dr 95570. US 101 exit Trinidad, just w on Main St, then 0.7 mi n. Ext corridors. **Pets:** Accepted. 🅼 📶 ✖ 🅺 🈂 🔋 💻

🔷🔷🔷 ▽▽▽▽ Trinidad Inn Ⓜ 🌼

(707) 677-3349. **$100-$275, 3 day notice.** 1170 Patrick's Point Dr 95570. US 101 exit Trinidad, just w on Main St, then 1.3 mi n. Ext corridors. **Pets:** Dogs only. $10 daily fee/pet. Designated rooms, supervision. SAVE 📶 ✖ 🅺 🔋 💻

TRUCKEE

🔷🔷🔷 ▽▽▽▽ BEST WESTERN PLUS Truckee-Tahoe Hotel 🅷

(530) 587-4525. **Call for rates.** 11331 Brockway Rd 96161. I-80 exit 188 (SR 267) westbound; exit 188B eastbound, 1.5 mi se, then just w. Int corridors. **Pets:** Accepted. SAVE 🅼 🏊 📶 ✖ 🔋 💻

▽▽▽▽ The Cedar House Sport Hotel 🅷 🐾

(530) 582-5655. **$170-$390, 3 day notice.** 10918 Brockway Rd 96161. I-80 exit 188 (SR 267) westbound; exit 188B eastbound, 1.5 mi s, then 0.8 mi nw. Int corridors. **Pets:** Large, dogs only. $50 one-time fee/pet. Designated rooms, service with restrictions, supervision.

🅴 🍽 📶 ✖ 🔋 💻

🔷🔷🔷 ▽▽▽▽▽ The Ritz-Carlton, Lake Tahoe 🅷 🌼

(530) 562-3000. **$249-$899, 7 day notice.** 13031 Ritz-Carlton Highlands Ct 96161. I-80 exit 188 (SR 267) westbound; exit 188B eastbound, 5.6 mi se, then 2.5 mi sw on Highlands View Rd. Int corridors. **Pets:** Other species. $125 one-time fee/room. Designated rooms, service with restrictions, crate. SAVE 🅴🅲🅾 🍽 🅼 🏊 ✖ 📶 ✖ 💻

TULARE

🔷🔷🔷 ▽▽▽▽ BEST WESTERN Town & Country Lodge Ⓜ

(559) 688-7537. **$90-$250.** 1051 N Blackstone St 93274. SR 99 exit 88 (Prosperity Ave/Blackstone St), just w. Int corridors. **Pets:** Medium, dogs only. $20 daily fee/room. Service with restrictions, supervision.

SAVE 🏊 📶 🔋 💻

▽▽▽▽ Charter Inn & Suites 🅷 🌼

(559) 685-9500. **$89-$199.** 1016 E Prosperity Ave 93274. SR 99 exit 88 (Prosperity Ave/Blackstone St), just e. Int corridors. **Pets:** Small. $100 deposit/room, $10 daily fee/pet. Service with restrictions, crate. 🅼 📶 🔋 💻

▽▽▽▽ La Quinta Inn & Suites Tulare 🅷

(559) 685-8900. **$84-$99.** 1500 Cherry Ct 93274. SR 99 exit 88 (Prosperity Ave/Blackstone St), just w. Int corridors. **Pets:** Large, other species. Service with restrictions. 🏊 📶 ✖ 🔋 💻

▽▽▽▽ Quality Inn Ⓜ

(559) 686-3432. **$60-$139.** 1010 E Prosperity Ave 93274. SR 99 exit 88 (Prosperity Ave/Blackstone St), just e. Int corridors. **Pets:** Small, dogs only. $15 daily fee/pet. Designated rooms, no service, supervision. SAVE 🅴🅲🅾 🏊 ✖ 📶 🔋 💻

TURLOCK

🔷🔷🔷 ▽▽▽▽ BEST WESTERN PLUS Orchard Inn 🅷

(209) 667-2827. **$90-$110.** 5025 N Golden State Blvd 95382. SR 99 exit 217 (Taylor Rd), just e, then just n. Ext corridors. **Pets:** Accepted. SAVE 🅼 🏊 📶 🔋 💻

AAA ◆◆◆◆ **Candlewood Suites** H ❀

(209) 250-1501. **$99-$249.** 1000 Powers Ct 95380. SR 99 exit 215 (Monte Vista Ave), just w, then just s on N Tegner Rd, then just e. Int corridors. **Pets:** Large, other species. $150 one-time fee/pet. Service with restrictions, crate. SAVE ⓶M 🛜 ✕ 🛡 ▣

TUSTIN (Restaurants p. 621)

AAA ◆◆◆◆ **Residence Inn by Marriott Tustin Orange County** H

. **$145-$229.** 15181 Newport Ave 92780. SR 55 exit 9 (Edinger Ave), just e. Int corridors. **Pets:** Other species. $100 one-time fee/room. Service with restrictions. SAVE 🛜 ✕ 🛡 ▣

TWAIN HARTE

AAA ◆◆◆◆ **McCaffrey House Bed & Breakfast Inn** BB

(209) 586-0757. **$169-$199, 10 day notice.** 23251 Hwy 108 95383. On SR 108, 0.5 mi e; just beyond 4000' elevation marker. Int corridors. **Pets:** Other species. $25 daily fee/pet. Designated rooms, service with restrictions, supervision. SAVE 🛜 ✕

TWENTYNINE PALMS (Restaurants p. 621)

◆◆◆◆ **Roughley Manor** BB

(760) 367-3238. **$135-$160, 3 day notice.** 74744 Joe Davis Dr 92277. SR 62, 0.7 mi n on Utah Tr, 0.4 mi e. Ext/int corridors. **Pets:** Dogs only. Designated rooms, no service, supervision.

🛎 🛜 ✕ 🅩 🛡 ▣

UKIAH

AAA ◆◆◆◆ **BEST WESTERN Orchard Inn** H

(707) 462-1514. **$89-$189.** 555 S Orchard Ave 95482. US 101 exit Gobbi St, just w, then just n. Int corridors. **Pets:** Accepted.
SAVE ⓶M 🛎 🛜 🛡 ▣

◆◆◆◆ **Comfort Inn & Suites** H

(707) 462-3442. **$89-$199.** 1220 Airport Park Blvd 95482. US 101 exit Talmage Rd, just w, then just s. Int corridors. **Pets:** Dogs only. $20 daily fee/pet. Designated rooms, service with restrictions, supervision.
⓶M 🛎 🛜 🛡 ▣

AAA ◆◆◆ **Days Inn** M

(707) 462-7584. **$59-$149.** 950 N State St 95482. US 101 exit N State St, 0.5 mi s. Ext corridors. **Pets:** Medium. $10 daily fee/pet. Designated rooms, service with restrictions, supervision. SAVE 🛎 🛜 🛡 ▣

AAA ◆◆◆ **Quality Inn** M

(707) 462-2906. **$65-$135.** 1050 S State St 95482. US 101 exit Talmage Rd, 0.4 mi w, then just n. Ext corridors. **Pets:** Accepted.
SAVE ⓶M 🛜 🛡 ▣

◆◆ **Super 8 Ukiah** M

(707) 468-8181. **$55-$85.** 693 S Orchard Ave 95482. US 101 exit Gobbi St W, just w, then just n. Ext corridors. **Pets:** Other species. $10 daily fee/pet. Designated rooms, service with restrictions, supervision.

ECO ⬤ ❒ 🛎 🛜 🛡 ▣

AAA ◆◆◆ **Travelodge Ukiah** H

(707) 462-5745. **$80-$150.** 1720 N State St 95482. US 101 exit N State St, then just n. Int corridors. **Pets:** Accepted.
SAVE ⓶M 🛎 🛜 🛡 ▣

UNIVERSAL CITY

AAA ◆◆◆◆ **Hilton Los Angeles/Universal City** H ❀

(818) 506-2500. **$169-$414.** 555 Universal Hollywood Dr 91608. US 101 exit 12A (Lankershim Blvd), just n, then just e. Int corridors. **Pets:** Medium, other species. $50 one-time fee/pet. Service with restrictions, supervision.

SAVE ECO ⬤ ❒ ⓶M 🛎 🖼 ✕ 🛡 ▣

AAA ◆◆◆◆ **Sheraton Universal Hotel, at Universal Studios** H ❀

(818) 980-1212. **$229-$399, 3 day notice.** 333 Universal Hollywood Dr 91608. US 101 exit 12A (Lankershim Blvd), just n, then just e. Int corridors. **Pets:** Large, other species. Service with restrictions, supervision.

SAVE ❒ 🛎 🛜 ✕ 🛡 ▣

UPPER LAKE (Restaurants p. 621)

AAA ◆◆ **Super 8** M

(707) 275-0888. **$70-$159, 3 day notice.** 450 E Hwy 20 95485. Jct SR 29, 0.5 mi e. Ext corridors. **Pets:** Accepted. SAVE 🛎 🛜 🛡 ▣

VACAVILLE

AAA ◆◆ **BEST WESTERN Heritage Inn** M

(707) 448-8453. **$70-$80.** 1420 E Monte Vista Ave 95688. I-80 exit Monte Vista Ave, just nw of jct Browns Valley Pkwy. Ext corridors. **Pets:** Other species. $20 daily fee/pet. Designated rooms, service with restrictions, supervision. SAVE ⓶M 🛎 🛜 🛡 ▣

◆◆ **Extended Stay America-Sacramento-Vacaville** H

(707) 469-1371. **Call for rates.** 799 Orange Dr 95687. I-80 exit 57 (Leisure Town Rd), just s; just e of I-505 interchange. Int corridors. **Pets:** Other species. $25 daily fee/pet. Service with restrictions, supervision. ⓶M 🛜 🛡 ▣

AAA ◆◆◆ **Hampton Inn & Suites Vacaville/Napa Valley Area** H ❀

(707) 469-6200. **$99-$139.** 800 Mason St 95688. I-80 exit Davis St eastbound, just n, then ne on Porter Way; exit Mason St westbound, just w; jct Porter Way. Int corridors. **Pets:** Other species. Supervision.

SAVE ⓶M 🛎 🛜 🛡 ▣

◆◆ **Quality Inn & Suites Vacaville** M

(707) 446-8888. **$55-$100.** 1050 Orange Dr 95687. I-80 exit 57 (Leisure Town Rd), just s, then just e. Ext corridors. **Pets:** Large, other species. $99 deposit/room. Designated rooms, service with restrictions, crate.
⓶M 🛎 🛜 🛡 ▣

◆◆◆ **Residence Inn by Marriott**

(707) 469-0300. **$89-$159.** 360 Orange Dr 95687. I-80 exit Orange Dr eastbound, 0.5 mi ne; exit Monte Vista Ave westbound to freeway overpass to E Nut Tree Pkwy, then just ne; behind Black Oak Restaurant. Int corridors. **Pets:** Accepted. ⓶M 🛎 🛜 ✕ 🛡 ▣

VALLEJO

◆◆◆ **Courtyard by Marriott Vallejo Napa Valley** H

(707) 644-1200. **$99-$279.** 1000 Fairgrounds Dr 94589. I-80 exit SR 37 (Marine World Pkwy), just w on SR 37, exit 20 (Discovery Kingdom/Fairgrounds Dr), then just se; jct Sage St. Int corridors. **Pets:** Accepted.
⓶M 🛎 🛜 ✕ 🛡 ▣

VALLEY CENTER

AAA ◆◆◆◆ **Harrah's Resort** H

(760) 751-3100. **$130-$500.** 777 Harrah's Rincon Way 92082. I-15 exit 46 (SR 76/Pala/Oceanside), 17 mi e, then 1 mi s on CR 6. Int corridors. **Pets:** Accepted. SAVE ⬤ ❒ ⓶M 🛎 ✕ 🖼 🛡 ▣

VENTURA (Restaurants p. 622)

◆◆◆ **Crowne Plaza Ventura Beach Resort** H

(805) 648-2100. **$119-$219.** 450 E Harbor Blvd 93001. US 101 exit 70A (California St) southbound, just s; exit 71 (Main St) southbound, 0.5 mi e to California St, then just s. Int corridors. **Pets:** Dogs only. $75 one-time fee/room. Designated rooms. ❒ 🛎 ✕ 🖼 ✕ 🛡 ▣

AAA ◆◆◆ **Four Points by Sheraton Ventura Harbor Resort** H

(805) 658-1212. **$125-$185.** 1050 Schooner Dr 93001. US 101 exit 68 (Seaward Ave), just w, then 1.5 mi s on Harbor Blvd; at Ventura Harbor. Ext/int corridors. **Pets:** Other species. $75 one-time fee/room. Service with restrictions, supervision. SAVE ❒ ✕ 🛜 ✕ 🛡 ▣

▼▼▼ **Holiday Inn Express Ventura Harbor** �H
(805) 856-9533. **$139-$278.** 1080 Navigator Dr 93001. US 101 exit 68 (Seaward Ave), just w, then 1.5 mi s; at Ventura Harbor. Ext/int corridors. **Pets:** Other species. $75 one-time fee/room. Service with restrictions, supervision. 🅼 📶 ✕ 🖪 📼

🆔 ▼▼▼▼ **Marriott Ventura Beach Hotel** �H ✤
(805) 643-6000. **$109-$289.** 2055 E Harbor Blvd 93001. US 101 exit 68 (Seaward Ave), just w, then 0.5 mi n. Int corridors. **Pets:** Medium, dogs only. $75 one-time fee/room. Service with restrictions, supervision.
🆂🅰🆅🅴 🅴🅲🅾 🅼 📶 ✕ 📶 ✕ 🖪 📼

▼▼ ▼▼ **Vagabond Inn Ventura** 🅼
(805) 648-5371. **$69-$249.** 756 E Thompson Blvd 93001. US 101 exit 70A (California St) northbound, just n, then just e; exit 70A (Ventura Ave) southbound, 0.6 mi e. Ext corridors. **Pets:** Accepted.
📶 📶 🖪 📼

▼▼ ▼▼ **Wyndham Garden Ventura Pierpont Inn** 🅷
(805) 643-6144. **$73-$162.** 550 Sanjon Rd 93001. US 101 exit 69 (Sanjon Rd) northbound; exit 68 (Seaward Ave) southbound, just w, then 1 mi on Harbor Blvd. Ext/int corridors. **Pets:** Medium, dogs only. $75 deposit/pet. Designated rooms, service with restrictions, supervision.
🍴 📶 📶 ✕ 🖪 📼

VICTORVILLE

🆔 ▼▼▼▼ **Hawthorn Suites by Wyndham** 🅷
(760) 949-4700. **$99-$199.** 11750 Dunia Rd 92392. I-15 exit 147 (Bear Valley Rd), just w, 0.3 mi s on Amargosa Rd, then just w. Int corridors. **Pets:** Small, other species. $15 daily fee/pet. Designated rooms, service with restrictions, supervision. 🆂🅰🆅🅴 🅼 📶 🖪 📼

🆔 ▼▼▼▼ **Hotel Extended Studio** 🅷
(760) 843-3800. **$79-$159.** 14786 Monarch Blvd 92395. I-15 exit 147 (Bear Valley Rd), just e to Mariposa Rd, just n, then just e. Int corridors. **Pets:** Small. $250 one-time fee/pet, $25 daily fee/pet. Designated rooms, service with restrictions, supervision.
🆂🅰🆅🅴 📶 ✕ 📶 🖪 📼

VISALIA *(Restaurants p. 622)*

🆔 ▼▼ ▼▼ **Comfort Inn & Suites** 🅷 ✤
(559) 651-3700. **$78-$96.** 9300 W Airport Dr 93277. SR 198 exit 102 (Plaza Dr), just s, then just w. Int corridors. **Pets:** Small. $50 one-time fee/pet. Designated rooms, service with restrictions, supervision.
🆂🅰🆅🅴 📶 ✕ 📶 ✕ 🖪 📼

▼▼ ▼▼ **Holiday Inn Hotel & Conference Center** 🅷 ✤
(559) 651-5000. **$89-$139.** 9000 W Airport Dr 93277. SR 198 exit 102 (Plaza Dr), just s. Int corridors. **Pets:** Other species. $25 daily fee/pet. Service with restrictions, supervision.
🍴 🅼 📶 📶 ✕ 🖪 📼

🆔 ▼▼ ▼▼ **Lamp Liter Inn** 🅼
(559) 732-4511. **$79-$179.** 3300 W Mineral King Ave 93291. SR 198 exit 105B (SR 63 S/Mooney Blvd) westbound, 0.5 mi w; exit eastbound, just n, then 0.5 mi w. Ext corridors. **Pets:** Accepted.
🆂🅰🆅🅴 🍴 📶 ✕ 🖪 📼

▼▼ ▼▼ ▼▼ **La Quinta Inn & Suites Visalia/Sequoia Gateway** 🅷
(559) 739-9800. **$85-$370.** 5438 W Cypress Ave 93277. SR 198 exit 104 (Akers St), just s, then just w. Int corridors. **Pets:** Large, other species. Service with restrictions. 📶 📶 ✕ 🖪 📼

🆔 ▼▼▼▼ **Marriott Visalia at the Convention Center** 🅷
(559) 636-1111. **$109-$299.** 300 S Court St 93291. SR 198 exit 107A (Central Visalia/SR 63 N), just ne. Int corridors. **Pets:** $75 one-time fee/room. Designated rooms, service with restrictions, supervision.
🆂🅰🆅🅴 🍴 📶 📶 ✕ 🖪 📼

VISTA

🆔 ▼▼▼▼ **Hyatt Place San Diego-Vista/Carlsbad** 🅷
(760) 814-8879. **$89-$359.** 2645 S Melrose Dr 92081. SR 78 exit 6 (Vista Village Dr), just s, just w on Hacienda, then 4 mi se. Int corridors. **Pets:** Accepted. 🆂🅰🆅🅴 🍴 🅼 📶 📶 ✕ 🖪 📼

WALNUT

▼▼ ▼▼ **Quality Inn & Suites** 🅷
(909) 594-9999. **$75-$160.** 1170 Fairway Dr 91789. SR 60 exit 21 (Fairway Dr), 0.3 mi s. Int corridors. **Pets:** Accepted.
🅼 📶 📶 🖪 📼

WALNUT CREEK

🆔 ▼▼▼▼ **Holiday Inn Express Walnut Creek** 🅷
(925) 932-3332. **$89-$199, 3 day notice.** 2730 N Main St 94597. I-680 exit 47 (N Main St), southbound, just n; exit 48 (Geary Rd/Treat Blvd), just w, then just s. Int corridors. **Pets:** Accepted.
🆂🅰🆅🅴 🅼 📶 📶 ✕ 🖪 📼

WATSONVILLE

🆔 ▼▼▼▼ **BEST WESTERN Rose Garden Inn** 🅷
(831) 724-3367. **$90-$250.** 740 Freedom Blvd 95076. On SR 152; jct Main St. Ext corridors. **Pets:** Accepted.
🆂🅰🆅🅴 🅼 📶 📶 ✕ 🖪 📼

WEAVERVILLE

▼▼ ▼▼ **Weaverville Victorian Inn** 🅼
(530) 623-4432. **$79-$169.** 2051 Main St 96093. Jct SR 3 and 299 (Main St), 1.5 mi se. Ext corridors. **Pets:** Accepted.
🅼 📶 📶 🖪 📼

WEST HOLLYWOOD

🆔 ▼▼▼▼ **Andaz West Hollywood** 🅷 ✤
(323) 656-1234. **$189-$545, 3 day notice.** 8401 W Sunset Blvd 90069. I-10 exit 7A (La Cienega Blvd), 4.4 mi n, then just e. Int corridors. **Pets:** Medium. $100 one-time fee/pet. Supervision.
🆂🅰🆅🅴 🅴🅲🅾 🍴 🅼 📶 📶 ✕ 🖪

🆔 ▼▼▼▼ **Chamberlain West Hollywood** 🅷
(310) 657-7400. **$209-$499, 3 day notice.** 1000 Westmount Dr 90069. I-10 exit 7A (La Cienega Blvd), 4 mi n to Santa Monica Blvd, just w, then just n. Int corridors. **Pets:** Accepted.
🆂🅰🆅🅴 🍴 📶 📶 ✕ 🖪 📼

🆔 ▼▼▼▼ **The Grafton on Sunset** 🅷 ✤
(323) 654-4600. **$199-$359, 3 day notice.** 8462 W Sunset Blvd 90069. I-10 exit 7A (La Cienega Blvd), 4.4 mi n, then just e. Int corridors. **Pets:** $100 deposit/pet, $30 daily fee/pet. Designated rooms, service with restrictions, supervision. 🆂🅰🆅🅴 🍴 📶 📶 ✕ 🖪

▼▼▼▼ **Le Montrose Suite Hotel** 🅷
(310) 855-1115. **$219-$599, 3 day notice.** 900 Hammond St 90069. I-10 exit 7A (La Cienega Blvd), 2.6 mi n to San Vicente Blvd, 1.3 mi nw, then just w. Int corridors. **Pets:** Accepted.
🍴 📶 ✕ 📶 ✕ 🖪 📼

▼▼▼▼ **Le Parc Suite Hotel** 🅷 ✤
(310) 855-8888. **$275-$499.** 733 N West Knoll Dr 90069. I-10 exit 7A (La Cienega Blvd), 3.5 mi n, just w on Melrose Ave, then just n. Int corridors. **Pets:** Medium. $100 one-time fee/pet. Designated rooms, service with restrictions, supervision.
🍴 📶 ✕ 📶 ✕ 🖪 📼

▼▼ ▼▼ **The London West Hollywood** 🅷 ✤
(310) 854-1111. **$399-$899, 3 day notice.** 1020 N San Vicente Blvd 90069. I-10 exit 7A (La Cienega Blvd), 2.6 mi n. Int corridors. **Pets:** Small, dogs only. $100 one-time fee/pet, $20 daily fee/pet. Service with restrictions, supervision. 🍴 📶 📶 🖪 📼

🆔 ▼▼▼▼ **Sunset Marquis Hotel & Villas** 🅷
(310) 657-1333. **$305-$950.** 1200 N Alta Loma Rd 90069. I-10 exit 7A (La Cienega Blvd), 4.5 mi n to Holloway Dr, just w, then just n. Int corridors. **Pets:** Very small, dogs only. $200 one-time fee/pet. Service with restrictions, supervision. 🆂🅰🆅🅴 🍴 📶 ✕ 📶 🖪 📼

WESTLAKE VILLAGE *(Restaurants p. 622)*

◇◇◇◇◇◇ Four Seasons Hotel Westlake Village **H**

(818) 575-3000. **$269-$1400, 3 day notice.** Two Dole Dr 91362. US 101 exit 39 (Lindero Canyon Rd), just e, then just n on Via Colinas. Int corridors. **Pets:** Accepted.
[SAVE] [ECO] [¶¶] [&M] [↝] [✕] [≋] [░] [▭]

◇◇◇◇ Hyatt Westlake Plaza Hotel **H**

(805) 557-1234. **$99-$309.** 880 S Westlake Blvd 91361. US 101 exit 40 (Westlake Blvd), just s. Int corridors. **Pets:** Accepted.
[SAVE] [ECO] [¶¶] [&M] [↝] [✕] [≋] [✕] [░] [▭]

◇◇◇◇ Residence Inn by Marriott Westlake Village **H**

(818) 707-4411. **$139-$209.** 30950 Russell Ranch Rd 91362. US 101 exit 39 (Lindero Canyon Rd), just e, then just s. Int corridors. **Pets:** Medium, other species. $100 one-time fee/room. Service with restrictions, crate. [↝] [✕] [≋] [✕] [░] [▭]

◇◇◇◇ ◇◇◇◇ Westlake Village Inn **H**

(818) 889-0230. **$205-$215, 3 day notice.** 31943 Agoura Rd 91361. US 101 exit 40 (Westlake Blvd), 1.3 mi se. Ext corridors. **Pets:** Medium, dogs only. $75 one-time fee/pet. Service with restrictions, supervision.
[SAVE] [¶¶] [&M] [↝] [✕] [≋] [✕] [░] [▭]

WESTLEY

◇◇◇◇ Holiday Inn Express **H**

(209) 894-8940. **$99-$159.** 4525 Howard Rd 95387. I-5 exit 441 (Westley/Howard Rd), just e, then just s. Int corridors. **Pets:** Accepted.
[↝] [≋] [░] [▭]

WESTMORLAND

◇◇◇◇◇ Americas Best Value Inn **M**

(760) 351-7100. **$70-$75.** 351 W Main St 92281. On SR 86/78. Int corridors. **Pets:** Other species. $20 daily fee/pet. Service with restrictions, crate. [SAVE] [↝] [≋] [░] [▭]

WEST SACRAMENTO

◇◇◇◇ Extended Stay America-Sacramento-West Sacramento **H**

(916) 371-1270. **Call for rates.** 795 Stillwater Rd 95605. I-80 exit Reed Ave, just w, then just sw. Int corridors. **Pets:** Other species. $25 daily fee/pet. Service with restrictions, supervision. [≋] [░] [▭]

◇◇◇◇◇ ◇ Rodeway Inn Capitol **M**

(916) 371-6983. **$50-$100.** 817 W Capitol Ave 95691. Business Rt I-80 (Capital City Frwy) exit Jefferson Blvd, 0.3 mi n, then just e. Ext corridors. **Pets:** Accepted. [SAVE] [≋] [░] [▭]

WHITTIER

◇◇◇◇ Radisson Hotel Whittier **H**

(562) 945-8511. **$99-$299, 3 day notice.** 7320 Greenleaf Av 90602. I-605 exit 15 (Whittier Blvd), 2.5 mi e, then 0.6 mi n. Int corridors. **Pets:** Accepted. [ECO] [¶¶] [&M] [↝] [≋] [▭]

◇◇◇◇ Vagabond Inn **M**

(562) 698-9701. **$70-$120.** 14125 E Whittier Blvd 90605. I-605 exit 15 (Whittier Blvd), 3.5 mi e. Ext corridors. **Pets:** Medium. $15 daily fee/pet. Designated rooms, service with restrictions, supervision.
[↝] [≋] [░] [▭]

WILLIAMS

◇◇◇◇◇ ◇◇◇◇ Granzella's Inn **H**

(530) 473-3310. **$99-$117.** 391 6th St 95987. I-5 exit 577 (Williams), 0.5 mi w, then just n. Int corridors. **Pets:** Other species. $10 daily fee/room. Service with restrictions, supervision.
[SAVE] [¶¶] [&M] [↝] [≋] [✕] [░] [▭]

◇◇◇◇◇ ◇◇◇◇ Ramada **H**

(530) 473-5120. **$80-$85.** 374 Ruggieri Way 95987. I-5 exit 577 (Williams), just e. Int corridors. **Pets:** Medium. $10 one-time fee/pet, $10 daily fee/pet. Designated rooms, service with restrictions, supervision.
[SAVE] [&M] [≋] [░] [▭]

◇◇◇◇◇ ◇◇◇◇ Traveler's Inn **M**

(530) 473-5387. **$45-$90.** 215 N 7th St 95987. I-5 exit 577 (Williams), just w on E St (SR 20 business route), then 0.3 mi n. Ext corridors.
Pets: Accepted. [SAVE] [&M] [↝] [≋] [✕] [░] [▭]

WILLITS

◇◇◇◇◇ ◇◇◇◇ Baechtel Creek Inn & Spa, an Ascend Hotel Collection Member **H**

(707) 459-9063. **$109-$250.** 101 Gregory Ln 95490. US 101, just w. Ext corridors. **Pets:** Accepted. [SAVE] [↝] [✕] [≋] [✕] [░] [▭]

WILLOW CREEK

◇◇◇◇ Coho Cottages **CA**

(530) 629-4000. **Call for rates.** 76 Willow Rd 95573. From SR 299, just n. Ext corridors. **Pets:** Dogs only. $25 one-time fee/room. Supervision.
[&M] [≋] [✕] [✕] [░] [▭]

WILLOWS

◇◇◇◇◇ ◇◇ BEST WESTERN Willows Inn **M** 🐾

(530) 934-4444. **$80-$120.** 475 N Humboldt Ave 95988. I-5 exit 603 (SR 162/Willows/Oroville), just e, then just n. Ext corridors. **Pets:** $100 deposit/pet, $10 daily fee/pet. Designated rooms, service with restrictions, supervision. [SAVE] [&M] [↝] [≋] [░] [▭]

◇◇◇◇◇ ◇ Economy Inn **M**

(530) 934-4224. **$70-$100, 3 day notice.** 435 N Tehama St 95988. I-5 exit 603 (SR 162/Willows/Oroville), 1 mi e, then just n. Ext corridors. **Pets:** Medium. $7 daily fee/pet. Designated rooms, service with restrictions, supervision. [SAVE] [≋] [░] [▭]

◇◇◇◇◇ ◇ Holiday Inn Express Willows **H**

(530) 934-8900. **Call for rates.** 545 N Humboldt Ave 95988. I-5 exit 603 (SR 162/Willows/Oroville), just e, then just n. Int corridors.
Pets: Accepted. [SAVE] [&M] [↝] [≋] [✕] [░] [▭]

◇◇◇◇◇ ◇ Motel 6 #4273 **M**

(530) 934-7026. **$49-$149.** 452 N Humboldt Ave 95988. I-5 exit 603 (SR 162/Willows/Oroville), just e, then just n. Ext corridors. **Pets:** Other species. Service with restrictions, crate. [SAVE] [↝] [≋] [░]

WOODLAND

◇◇◇◇◇ ◇◇ Days Inn **H**

(530) 666-3800. **$69-$129.** 1524 E Main St 95776. I-5 exit 537 (Main St) northbound; exit SR 113 (Davis) southbound, just w; behind McDonalds. Int corridors. **Pets:** Medium, dogs only. $15 daily fee/pet. Service with restrictions, supervision. [SAVE] [↝] [≋] [░] [▭]

◇◇◇◇ Econo Lodge **M**

(530) 662-9335. **$49-$89.** 53 W Main St 95695. I-5 exit 537 (Main St) northbound, 2 mi w; exit West St southbound, 1.5 mi s to Main St, then just w. Ext corridors. **Pets:** Accepted. [↝] [≋] [░]

◇◇◇◇◇ ◇◇◇◇ Holiday Inn Express Hotel & Suites **H**

(530) 662-7750. **$109-$179.** 2070 Freeway Dr 95776. I-5 exit 536 (CR 102), just n, just e on E Main St, then just s. Int corridors. **Pets:** Small. $20 daily fee/pet. Designated rooms, service with restrictions, supervision. [SAVE] [&M] [↝] [≋] [✕] [░] [▭]

WOODLAND HILLS *(Restaurants p. 622)*

◇◇◇◇ ◇◇◇◇ Hilton Woodland Hills/Los Angeles **H**

(818) 595-1000. **$99-$269.** 6360 Canoga Ave 91367. US 101 exit 26B (Canoga Ave), 1 mi n. Int corridors. **Pets:** Accepted.
[¶¶] [▨] [✕] [░] [▭]

◇◇◇◇ ◇◇◇◇ Warner Center Marriott Hotel **H**

(818) 887-4800. **$129-$249.** 21850 Oxnard St 91367. US 101 exit 27A (Topanga Canyon Blvd N), 0.6 mi n, then just e. Int corridors.
Pets: Accepted. [¶¶] [&M] [↝] [✕] [▨] [✕] [░] [▭]

YERMO *(Restaurants p. 622)*

▼▼ Oak Tree Inn **M**

(760) 254-1148. **Call for rates.** 35450 Yermo Rd 92398. I-15 exit 191 (Ghost Town Rd), just se. Int corridors. **Pets:** Accepted.

YOSEMITE NATIONAL PARK

▼▼ The Redwoods In Yosemite **VH**

(209) 375-6666. **Call for rates.** 8038 Chilnualna Falls Rd 95389. 6 mi inside southern entrance via SR 41 and Chilnualna Falls Rd. Ext corridors. **Pets:** Accepted.

YOUNTVILLE

▼▼▼ Lavender **BB**

(707) 944-1388. **$295-$595, 7 day notice.** 2020 Webber Ave 94599. From SR 29, just e on Madison St, just s on Washington St, then just e. Ext/int corridors. **Pets:** Dogs only. $65 one-time fee/room. Designated rooms, service with restrictions, supervision.

◆ ▼▼▼▼ Vintage Inn **H** ❀

(707) 944-1112. **$225-$700, 7 day notice.** 6541 Washington St 94599. From SR 29, just e on Madison St, then just s. Ext corridors. **Pets:** Other species. $75 one-time fee/pet. Designated rooms, service with restrictions, crate.

YREKA

▼▼ Baymont Inn & Suites **H**

(530) 841-1300. **$59-$99.** 148 Moonlit Oaks Ave 96097. I-5 exit 773, just w. Int corridors. **Pets:** Other species. $10 one-time fee/room. Designated rooms, service with restrictions, supervision.

◆ ▼▼▼ BEST WESTERN Miner's Inn **M** ❀

(530) 842-4355. **$90-$170.** 122 E Miner St 96097. I-5 exit 775, just w. Ext corridors. **Pets:** $10 daily fee/pet. Designated rooms, service with restrictions, supervision.

▼▼ Comfort Inn **H**

(530) 842-1612. **$90-$150.** 1804-B Fort Jones Rd 96097. I-5 exit 773, just w. Int corridors. **Pets:** Accepted.

◆ ▼▼ Klamath Motor Lodge **M**

(530) 842-2751. **$50-$75.** 1111 S Main St 96097. I-5 exit 775 southbound, just w to Main St, then 0.9 mi s; exit 773 northbound, just w to Main St, then 1.1 mi n; center. Ext corridors. **Pets:** $7 daily fee/pet. Designated rooms, service with restrictions, supervision.

◆ ▼▼ Rodeway Inn **M**

(530) 842-4412. **$56-$85.** 1235 S Main St 96097. I-5 exit 775, just w to Main St, then 0.9 mi s. Ext corridors. **Pets:** Accepted.

◆ ▼▼▼ Super 8 **M**

(530) 842-5781. **$55-$120.** 136 Montague Rd 96097. I-5 exit 776, just w. Ext corridors. **Pets:** $10 daily fee/pet. Designated rooms, service with restrictions, supervision.

YUBA CITY

◆ ▼▼▼ BEST WESTERN Yuba City Inn **M**

(530) 674-1650. **$100-$150.** 894 W Onstott Rd 95991. Just s of jct SR 99 and 20. Ext corridors. **Pets:** Accepted.

▼▼▼ The Harkey House **BB**

(530) 674-1942. **$120-$235, 7 day notice.** 212 C St 95991. At C and 2nd sts; downtown. Int corridors. **Pets:** Small, dogs only. $20 daily fee/room. Designated rooms, service with restrictions, crate.

COLORADO

ALAMOSA

◆ ▼▼▼ BEST WESTERN Alamosa Inn **M** ❀

(719) 589-2567. **$83-$150.** 2005 W Main St 81101. On US 160, 1 mi w of center. Ext corridors. **Pets:** Medium, dogs only. $10 daily fee/pet. Service with restrictions, supervision.

▼▼▼ Comfort Inn & Suites **H**

(719) 587-9000. **$80-$180.** 6301 US 160 S 81101. 2.3 mi w of center. Int corridors. **Pets:** Medium, dogs only. $20 daily fee/pet. Designated rooms, service with restrictions, supervision.

▼▼▼ Holiday Inn Express **H**

(719) 589-4026. **Call for rates.** 3418 Mariposa St 81101. On US 160, 2 mi w of center. Int corridors. **Pets:** Accepted.

◆ ▼▼▼ Super 8 of Alamosa **M**

(719) 589-6447. **$60-$150.** 2505 Main St 81101. On US 160, 1.3 mi w. Int corridors. **Pets:** Accepted.

ASPEN

◆ ▼▼▼▼ Aspen Meadows Resort, A Dolce Resort **H**

(970) 925-4240. **$109-$799, 30 day notice.** 845 Meadows Rd 81611. 0.3 mi n of SR 82 via N 7th Ave, just w. Ext/int corridors. **Pets:** Accepted.

▼▼ Aspen Mountain Lodge **H**

(970) 925-7650. **Call for rates.** 311 W Main St 81611. 0.4 mi w on SR 82; between S 2nd and S 3rd sts. Int corridors. **Pets:** Accepted.

◆ ▼▼▼▼ Hotel Jerome, An Auberge Resort **H**

(970) 920-1000. **Call for rates.** 330 E Main St 81611. Jct E Main and N Mill sts; downtown. Int corridors. **Pets:** Accepted.

◆ ▼▼▼▼ The Limelight Hotel **H** ❀

(970) 925-3025. **$115-$2520, 30 day notice.** 355 S Monarch St 81611. Just s of SR 82; at S Monarch and E Cooper sts; downtown. Int corridors. **Pets:** Other species. $25 daily fee/pet. Designated rooms, service with restrictions, crate.

◆ ▼▼▼▼ The Little Nell **H** ❀

(970) 920-4600. **$280-$1250, 30 day notice.** 675 E Durant Ave 81611. Jct E Durant Ave and S Galena St; downtown. Int corridors. **Pets:** Dogs only. $50 one-time fee/room. Service with restrictions, crate.

▼▼ Mountain House Lodge **M**

(970) 920-2550. **Call for rates.** 905 E Hopkins St 81611. 0.3 mi e on SR 82, just e. Int corridors. **Pets:** Accepted.

▼▼▼▼ The Residence Hotel **H**

(970) 920-6532. **Call for rates.** 305 S Galena St 81611. Jct S Galena St and E Hyman Ave; downtown. **Pets:** Accepted.

AAA ▼▼▼ ▼▼▼ **The St. Regis Aspen Resort** 🅷 ❀
(970) 920-3300. **$249-$2199, 60 day notice.** 315 E Dean St 81611. Jct S Monarch and E Dean sts; downtown. Int corridors. **Pets:** $25 one-time fee/pet, $25 daily fee/pet. Service with restrictions.
[SAVE] 🍽 ⇌ ⊠ 📶 ⊠ 💻

AAA ▼▼▼ **Sky Hotel - A Kimpton Hotel** 🅷 ❀
(970) 925-6760. **$129-$899, 30 day notice.** 709 E Durant Ave 81611. Corner of S Spring St and E Durant Ave; downtown; at base of Aspen Mountain. Ext/int corridors. **Pets:** Other species. Service with restrictions. [SAVE] [ECO] 🍽 ⇌ ⊠ 📶 🅷

AURORA

AAA ▼▼▼ **Aloft Denver International Airport** 🅷
(303) 371-9500. **$99-$209.** 16470 E 40th Cir 80011. I-70 exit 283 (Chambers Rd), just n, 0.7 mi e, then just s. Int corridors. **Pets:** Accepted. [SAVE] 🍽 ⇌ 📶 ⊠ 🅷 💻

AAA ▼▼▼ **BEST WESTERN PLUS Gateway Inn & Suites** 🅷
(720) 748-4800. **$90-$190.** 800 S Abilene St 80012. I-225 exit 7 (Mississippi Ave), just e, then 0.3 mi n. Int corridors. **Pets:** Large. $20 daily fee/room. Service with restrictions, crate.
[SAVE] �& ⇌ 📶 ⊠ 🅷 💻

AAA ▼▼▼ **Hyatt Place Denver Airport** 🅷
(303) 371-0700. **$69-$209.** 16250 E 40th Ave 80011. I-70 exit 283 (Chambers Rd), just n, then 0.5 mi e. Int corridors. **Pets:** Accepted.
[SAVE] 🍽 Ꮖ ⇌ 📶 ⊠ 🅷 💻

▼▼▼ ▼▼▼ **Residence Inn by Marriott** 🅷
(303) 459-8000. **$161-$265.** 16490 E 40th Cir 80011. I-70 exit 283 (Chambers Rd), just n, 0.5 mi e, then just s. Int corridors. **Pets:** Other species. $100 one-time fee/pet. Designated rooms, service with restrictions, crate. Ꮖ ⇌ 📶 ⊠ 🅷 💻

AAA ▼▼▼ ▼▼▼ **Woolley's Classic Suites-Denver Airport** 🅷
(720) 599-3750. **$149-$299.** 16450 E 40th Cir 80011. I-70 exit 283 (Chambers Rd), just n, 0.7 mi e, then just s. Int corridors. **Pets:** $100 one-time fee/pet. Designated rooms, service with restrictions, supervision. [SAVE] 🍽 Ꮖ 📶 ⊠ 🅷 💻

AVON

AAA ▼▼▼ ▼▼▼ **Westin Riverfront Resort & Spa, Avon** 🅒🅞 🐾
(970) 790-6000. **$159-$1199, 30 day notice.** 126 Riverfront Ln 81620. I-70 exit 167, 0.6 mi s on Avon Rd, then just w. Int corridors. **Pets:** Large, dogs only. $25 daily fee/pet. Designated rooms, service with restrictions, supervision.
[SAVE] [ECO] 🍽 ⇌ ⊠ 📶 ⊠ 🅷 💻

BAYFIELD

▼▼▼ **Wilderness Trails Ranch** 🆁🅰
(970) 247-0722. **Call for rates.** 23486 CR 501 81122. 35 mi e of Durango to CR 501, then 24 mi ne. Ext corridors. **Pets:** Accepted.
🍽 ⇌ ⊠ 📶 ⊠ 🄰🄲 🆆 🄯 🅷 💻

BEAVER CREEK

AAA ▼▼▼ ▼▼▼ **Park Hyatt Beaver Creek Resort & Spa** 🅷 ❀
(970) 949-1234. **$129-$949, 3 day notice.** 136 E Thomas Pl 81620. I-70 exit 167, 3 mi s on Avon and Village rds, 0.4 mi e on Offerson Rd, then just s. Int corridors. **Pets:** Large, dogs only. $100 one-time fee/room. Service with restrictions.
[SAVE] [ECO] 🍽 Ꮖ ⇌ ⊠ 📶 🅷 💻

AAA ▼▼▼ ▼▼▼ **The Ritz-Carlton, Bachelor Gulch** 🅷 ❀
(970) 748-6200. **$459-$1299, 45 day notice.** 0130 Daybreak Ridge 81620. I-70 exit 167, just s past the Beaver Creek Village gatehouse to Prater Rd, then just w; follow signs to Bachelor Gulch Village; in The Ritz-Carlton, Bachelor Gulch. Int corridors. **Pets:** Dogs only. $125 one-time fee/room, $25 daily fee/room. Supervision.
[SAVE] 🍽 Ꮖ ᏆᎷ ⇌ ⊠ 📶 ⊠ 🅷 💻

BOULDER *(Restaurants p. 622)*

AAA ▼▼▼ ▼▼▼ **BEST WESTERN PLUS Boulder Inn** 🅷
(303) 449-3800. **$160-$230.** 770 28th St 80303. US 36 (28th St) exit Baseline Rd via Frontage Rd. Int corridors. **Pets:** Medium, other species. $50 deposit/room. Designated rooms, supervision.
[SAVE] [ECO] 🅒🅴 ⇌ ⊠ 📶 ⊠ 🅷 💻

AAA ▼▼▼ **Boulder University Inn** 🅼 ❀
(303) 417-1700. **$79-$179.** 1632 Broadway 80302. US 36 (28th St) exit Baseline Rd, 0.3 mi s, then 3 mi nw. Ext corridors. **Pets:** Medium, other species. $100 deposit/room, $15 daily fee/room. Designated rooms, service with restrictions, supervision.
[SAVE] [ECO] ⇌ 📶 ⊠ 🅷 💻

▼▼▼ **Foot of The Mountain Motel** 🅼 ❀
(303) 442-5688. **$85-$150.** 200 Arapahoe Ave 80302. 1.8 mi w of US 36 (28th St). Ext corridors. **Pets:** Other species. $50 deposit/room, $5 daily fee/pet. Designated rooms, service with restrictions, supervision.
🍽 📶 🄰🄲 🅷 💻

AAA ▼▼▼ ▼▼▼ **Holiday Inn Express** 🅷
(303) 442-6600. **$120-$230.** 4777 N Broadway 80304. 3 mi n of Pearl Street Pedestrian Mall. Int corridors. **Pets:** Accepted.
[SAVE] 🍽 ᏆᎷ ⇌ 📶 ⊠ 🅷 💻

▼▼▼ ▼▼▼ **Homewood Suites by Hilton** 🅷
(303) 499-9922. **$159-$299.** 4950 Baseline Rd 80303. 1.2 mi e of US 36 (28th St); jct SR 157 (Foothills Pkwy), just w; entry off Baseline Rd. Ext/int corridors. **Pets:** Accepted. 🍽 📶 🅷 💻

▼▼▼ ▼▼▼ **Quality Inn & Suites Boulder Creek** 🅷
(303) 449-7550. **$110-$225.** 2020 Arapahoe Ave 80302. US 36 (28th St), 0.5 mi w. Ext/int corridors. **Pets:** Accepted.
⇌ ⊠ 📶 ⊠ 🅷 💻

▼▼▼ ▼▼▼ **Residence Inn by Marriott** 🅷
(303) 449-5545. **$174-$321.** 3030 Center Green Dr 80301. 0.5 mi e of US 36 (28th St); e on Valmont Rd; from Foothills Pkwy, just w on Valmont Rd. Ext corridors. **Pets:** Accepted. [ECO] ⇌ 📶 ⊠ 🅷 💻

BRECKENRIDGE

AAA ▼▼▼ ▼▼▼ **Beaver Run Resort & Conference Center** 🅒🅞
(970) 453-6000. **$120-$690, 3 day notice.** 620 Village Rd 80424. 0.4 mi sw of SR 9 and Village Rd; at base of Peak 9. Int corridors. **Pets:** Medium, dogs only. $40 daily fee/pet. Designated rooms, service with restrictions, supervision.
[SAVE] 🍽 ⇌ ⊠ 📶 ⊠ 🄰🄲 🅷 💻

▼▼▼ ▼▼▼ **DoubleTree by Hilton Breckenridge** 🅷
(970) 547-5550. **$129-$499.** 550 Village Rd 80424. Jct Main St, just w on S Park Ave, just sw. Int corridors. **Pets:** Medium. $50 one-time fee/room. Service with restrictions, crate.
[ECO] 🍽 ⇌ ⊠ 📶 ⊠ 🅷 💻

▼▼▼ ▼▼▼ **The Lodge at Breckenridge** 🅷 ❀
(970) 453-9300. **$129-$340, 30 day notice.** 112 Overlook Dr 80424. 0.3 m s of Main St and Ski Hill Rd to Boreas Pass Rd, then 2.2 mi w (uphill) to Overlook Rd. Ext/int corridors. **Pets:** Dogs only. $30 daily fee/room. Service with restrictions. 🍽 ⊠ 📶 ⊠ 🄰🄲 🅷 💻

BROOMFIELD *(Restaurants p. 622)*

AAA ▼▼▼ **Aloft Broomfield Denver** 🅷
(303) 635-2000. **$79-$299.** 8300 Arista Pl 80021. US 36 (Boulder Tpke) exit US 287/CR 121, 0.6 mi s, then 0.4 mi w on Uptown Ave. Int corridors. **Pets:** Accepted. [SAVE] 🍽 ⇌ 📶 ⊠ 🅷 💻

AAA ▼▼▼ **HYATT house Boulder/Broomfield** Ⓗ

(720) 890-4811. **$99–$239.** 13351 W Midway Blvd 80020. US 36 (Boulder Tpke) exit Storagetek Dr/Interlocken Loop, 0.3 mi n, then just e on Via Varra Rd. Int corridors. **Pets:** Medium, other species. $75 one-time fee/room. Service with restrictions. ⏷ 🍴 🏊 📶 ☒ 🛅 🖥

▼▼ ▼▼ **Omni Interlocken Resort** Ⓗ

(303) 438-6600. **Call for rates.** 500 Interlocken Blvd 80021. US 36 (Boulder Tpke) exit Interlocken Loop, 0.4 mi s, then 0.4 mi e. Int corridors. **Pets:** Accepted. 🍴 ♿ 🏊 ☒ 📶 ☒ 🛅 🖥

▼▼ ▼▼ **TownePlace Suites by Marriott Boulder/Broomfield** Ⓗ

(303) 466-2200. **$111–$206.** 480 Flatiron Blvd 80021. US 36 (Boulder Tpke) exit Interlocken Loop, 0.4 mi s, just w on Interlocken Blvd, then just s. Int corridors. **Pets:** Accepted.
🍴 ♿ 🏊 📶 ☒ 🛅 🖥

BURLINGTON

AAA ▼▼▼ **BEST WESTERN PLUS Carousel Inn & Suites** Ⓗ 🐾

(719) 346-7777. **$110–$175.** 605 S Lincoln St 80807. I-70 exit 437, just s. Int corridors. **Pets:** Medium. $20 daily fee/room. Designated rooms, service with restrictions, supervision.
⏷ 🍴 ♿ 🏊 📶 ☒ 🛅 🖥

▼▼ ▼▼ **Comfort Inn Burlington** Ⓗ

(719) 346-7676. **$85–$159.** 282 S Lincoln St 80807. I-70 exit 437, just n on US 385. Int corridors. **Pets:** Accepted. 🏊 📶 ☒ 🛅 🖥

CAÑON CITY

AAA ▼▼▼ **BEST WESTERN Cañon City** Ⓗ

(719) 275-2400. **$75–$219.** 110 Latigo Ln 81212. From 9th St, 3 mi e on US 50, just n. Int corridors. **Pets:** Medium. $20 daily fee/pet. Designated rooms, no service, supervision.
⏷ 🏊 ☒ 📶 ☒ 🖥

CARBONDALE *(Restaurants p. 622)*

▼▼ ▼▼ **Comfort Inn & Suites** Ⓗ 🐾

(970) 963-8880. **$119–$169.** 920 Cowen Dr 81623. Jct SR 82 and 133, just sw. Int corridors. **Pets:** Medium. $15 daily fee/pet. Designated rooms, no service, supervision. 🍴 🏊 📶 ☒ 🛅 🖥

CASTLE ROCK

AAA ▼▼▼ **BEST WESTERN PLUS Castle Rock** Ⓗ

(303) 814-8800. **Call for rates.** 595 Genoa Way 80109. I-25 exit 184 (Meadows Pkwy), just w to Castleton Way, just s, then e. Int corridors. **Pets:** Accepted. ⏷ 🏊 📶 ☒ 🛅 🖥

CENTENNIAL

▼▼ ▼▼ **Drury Inn & Suites-Denver Near the Tech Center** Ⓗ

(303) 694-3400. **$80–$150.** 9445 E Dry Creek Rd 80112. I-25 exit 196 (Dry Creek Rd), just w; on northwest corner. Int corridors. **Pets:** $10 daily fee/room. Service with restrictions, supervision.
🍴 📶 ☒ 🛅 🖥

▼▼▼ ▼▼▼ **Staybridge Suites Denver Tech Center** Ⓗ

(303) 858-9990. **$99–$169, 5 day notice.** 7150 S Clinton St 80112. I-25 exit 197 (Arapahoe Rd), just e to Clinton St, 0.5 mi s, then just e. Int corridors. **Pets:** Accepted. ♿ 🏊 📶 ☒ 🛅 🖥

▼▼ ▼▼ **TownePlace Suites by Marriott Denver Tech Center** Ⓗ

(720) 875-1113. **$90–$194.** 7877 S Chester St 80112. I-25 exit 196 (Dry Creek Rd), just w to Chester St, then 0.3 mi s. Int corridors. **Pets:** Other species. $25 daily fee/room. Service with restrictions, supervision. 🍴 ♿ 🏊 📶 ☒ 🛅 🖥

CHIPITA PARK

▼▼ ▼▼ **Chipita Lodge B & B** 🅱🅱

(719) 684-8454. **$125–$160, 7 day notice.** 9090 Chipita Park Rd 80809. Jct US 24, just s on Fountain Blvd (Pine Peak Hwy), then 1.5 mi w; right at fork. Ext/int corridors. **Pets:** Dogs only. $25 one-time fee/pet. Designated rooms, no service, supervision.
🍴 📶 ☒ ♿ 🎦 ☒

CLIFTON

AAA ▼▼▼ **BEST WESTERN Grande River Inn & Suites** Ⓗ 🐾

(970) 434-3400. **$109–$159, 3 day notice.** 3228 I-70 Business Loop 81520. I-70 exit 37, 0.8 mi s; east of Grand Junction. Ext corridors. **Pets:** Medium. $10 daily fee/pet. Designated rooms, service with restrictions, supervision. ⏷ 🏊 📶 ☒ 🖥

COLORADO SPRINGS

AAA ▼▼▼▼ **The Broadmoor** Ⓗ 🐾

(719) 634-7711. **$385–$7800, 7 day notice.** 1 Lake Ave 80906. I-25 exit 138, 3 mi w on Circle Dr (which becomes Lake Ave). Ext/int corridors. **Pets:** Other species. $50 daily fee/pet. Designated rooms, service with restrictions, supervision. ⏷ 🍴 ♿ 🏊 ☒ 📶 ☒ 🛅 🖥

AAA ▼▼▼ **Cheyenne Mountain Resort** Ⓗ 🐾

(719) 538-4000. **$109–$399, 7 day notice.** 3225 Broadmoor Valley Rd 80906. I-25 exit 138, 1.4 mi w to SR 115, 0.5 mi s, just w on Cheyenne Mountain Blvd, then just s. Ext/int corridors. **Pets:** Large, dogs only. $35 daily fee/pet. Service with restrictions, crate.
⏷ 🌿 🍴 ♿ 🏊 ☒ 📶 ☒ 🛅 🖥

AAA ▼▼▼ **Comfort Inn North** Ⓗ

(719) 262-9000. **$64–$109.** 6450 Corporate Dr 80919. I-25 exit 149 (Woodmen Rd), just w, then 0.3 mi s. Int corridors. **Pets:** Medium, other species. $15 daily fee/pet. Designated rooms, service with restrictions. ⏷ 🍴 ♿ 🏊 📶 ☒ 🛅 🖥

AAA ▼▼▼ **DoubleTree by Hilton Colorado Springs** Ⓗ

(719) 576-8900. **$99–$139.** 1775 E Cheyenne Mountain Blvd 80906. I-25 exit 138, just w. Int corridors. **Pets:** Accepted.
⏷ 🍴 ♿ 🏊 ☒ 📶 ☒ 🛅 🖥

▼▼ ▼▼ **Drury Inn-Pikes Peak** Ⓗ

(719) 598-2500. **$60–$150.** 8155 N Academy Blvd 80920. I-25 exit 150, just s, then e. Int corridors. **Pets:** $10 daily fee/room. Service with restrictions. 🏊 📶 ☒ 🛅 🖥

AAA ▼▼▼ **Fairfield Inn & Suites by Marriott Colorado Springs North Air Force Academy** Ⓗ

(719) 488-4644. **$104–$183.** 15275 W Struthers Rd 80921. I-25 exit 158, just e on Baptist Rd, then just s. Int corridors. **Pets:** Accepted.
⏷ ♿ 🏊 📶 ☒ 🛅 🖥

▼▼ ▼▼ **Fairfield Inn & Suites by Marriott Colorado Springs/South** Ⓗ 🐾

(719) 576-1717. **$76–$160.** 2725 Geyser Dr 80906. I-25 exit 138, just w to E Cheyenne Mountain Blvd, then just s. Int corridors. **Pets:** Medium. $75 one-time fee/pet. Service with restrictions.
♿ 🏊 📶 ☒ 🛅 🖥

▼▼▼ ▼▼▼ **Hampton Inn & Suites Colorado Springs Air Force Academy/I-25 North @ Interquest** Ⓗ

(719) 598-6911. **$89–$169.** 1307 Republic Dr 80921. I-25 exit 153, 0.5 mi e, then just s. Int corridors. **Pets:** Accepted.
🍴 🏊 📶 ☒ 🛅 🖥

▼▼▼ ▼▼▼ **Homewood Suites by Hilton Colorado Springs-North** Ⓗ

(719) 265-6600. **$92–$219.** 9130 Explorer Dr 80920. I-25 exit 151 (Briargate Pkwy), 0.8 mi e. Int corridors. **Pets:** Accepted.
🍴 ♿ 🏊 📶 🛅 🖥

(AAA) ▼▼◆ Hotel Eleganté Conference & Event Center **H** ❖

(719) 576-5900. **$79-$189.** 2886 S Circle Dr 80906. I-25 exit 138, just e. Int corridors. **Pets:** Medium. $50 one-time fee/room. Designated rooms, service with restrictions, crate.

[SAVE] [¶][➥][✕][📶][✕][🛢][💻]

(AAA) ▼▼▼▼ Hyatt Place Colorado Springs/Garden of the Gods **H**

(719) 265-9385. **$69-$179.** 503 W Garden of the Gods Rd 80907. I-25 exit 146 (Garden of the Gods Rd), just w. Int corridors. **Pets:** Medium, dogs only. $75 one-time fee/pet. No service, supervision.

[SAVE] [¶][➥][📶][✕][🛢][💻]

(AAA) ▼▼▼ ▼▼ The Mining Exchange, a Wyndham Grand Hotel **H** ❖

(719) 323-2000. **$119-$249.** 8 S Nevada Ave 80903. Between Colorado and Pikes Peak aves; downtown. Int corridors. **Pets:** Large, dogs only. $50 one-time fee/room. Service with restrictions, crate.

[SAVE] [¶][↺M][📶][✕][🛢][💻]

(AAA) ▼▼▼ Radisson Hotel Colorado Springs Airport **H** ❖

(719) 597-7000. **$119-$185, 7 day notice.** 1645 N Newport Rd 80916. I-25 exit 139, 4.5 mi e on US 24 Bypass. Int corridors. **Pets:** Medium, dogs only. $100 deposit/room, $25 one-time fee/pet. Designated rooms, service with restrictions, crate.

[SAVE] [¶][↺M][➥][✕][📶][✕][🛢][💻]

▼▼▼ Residence Inn by Marriott Air Force Academy **H**

(719) 388-9300. **$90-$183.** 9805 Federal Dr 80921. I-25 exit 153, just e, then s. Int corridors. **Pets:** Accepted.

[¶][↺M][➥][📶][✕][🛢][💻]

▼▼▼ Residence Inn by Marriott Colorado Springs Central **H** ❖

(719) 574-0370. **$111-$229.** 3880 N Academy Blvd 80917. I-25 exit 146 (Garden of the Gods Rd), 4.5 mi e, then 0.3 mi s. Ext corridors. **Pets:** Other species. $75 one-time fee/room. Service with restrictions, crate. [¶][➥][📶][✕][🛢][💻]

▼▼▼▼ Residence Inn by Marriott-Colorado Springs South **H**

(719) 576-0101. **$90-$183.** 2765 Geyser Dr 80906. I-25 exit 138, just w to E Cheyenne Mountain Blvd, then just s. Int corridors. **Pets:** Accepted. [↺M][➥][📶][✕][🛢][💻]

▼▼▼▼ TownePlace Suites by Marriott Colorado Springs South **H**

(719) 638-0800. **$90-$171.** 1530 N Newport Rd 80916. I-25 exit 139, 5 mi e on US 24 Bypass, then just n. Int corridors. **Pets:** Accepted.

[¶][➥][📶][✕][🛢][💻]

CORTEZ

(AAA) ▼▼▼ BEST WESTERN Turquoise Inn & Suites **M** ❖

(970) 565-3778. **$99-$169.** 535 E Main St 81321. 0.6 mi e of center on US 160. Ext corridors. **Pets:** Small. $20 one-time fee/pet. Designated rooms, service with restrictions, supervision. [SAVE][➥][📶][🛢][💻]

▼▼ Tomahawk Lodge **M**

(970) 565-8521. **$49-$99.** 728 S Broadway 81321. 1 mi w of center on US 160. Ext corridors. **Pets:** Medium. Designated rooms, service with restrictions, supervision. [📶][🛢]

CRAIG

(AAA) ▼▼▼▼ BEST WESTERN PLUS Deer Park Inn & Suites **H** ❖

(970) 824-9282. **$120-$130.** 262 Commerce St 81625. 0.3 mi s of jct US 40 and SR 13. Int corridors. **Pets:** Other species. $10 one-time fee/room. Designated rooms, service with restrictions, supervision.

[SAVE] [¶][➥][📶][✕][🛢][💻]

▼▼◆ Candlewood Suites **H**

(970) 824-8400. **$89-$169.** 92 Commerce St 81625. 0.4 mi s of jct US 40 and SR 13. Int corridors. **Pets:** Medium, dogs only. $150 deposit/room, $150 one-time fee/room. Service with restrictions, crate.

[¶][📶][✕][🛢][💻]

(AAA) ▼▼▼ Hampton Inn & Suites **H**

(970) 826-9900. **$109-$139.** 377 Cedar Ct 81625. 0.4 mi s of jct US 40 and SR 13, just w. Int corridors. **Pets:** Accepted.

[SAVE] [¶][↺M][➥][📶][✕][🛢][💻]

CRESTED BUTTE (Restaurants p. 622)

▼▼▼ Elevation Hotel & Spa **H** ❖

(970) 251-3000. **$119-$399, 3 day notice.** 500 Gothic Rd 81225. 5.9 mi n of Elk Ave. Int corridors. **Pets:** Other species. $35 daily fee/pet. Designated rooms, service with restrictions, supervision.

[¶][➥][✕][📶][✕][🎿][🛢][💻]

▼▼ Elk Mountain Lodge **BB**

(970) 349-7533. **$129-$219, 14 day notice.** 129 Gothic Ave 81224. 0.3 mi w on Elk Ave to 2nd St, just n. Int corridors. **Pets:** Accepted.

[✕][📶][🎿]

(AAA) ▼▼▼ The Grand Lodge **H**

(970) 349-8000. **$99-$269, 3 day notice.** 6 Emmons Loop 81225. 2.3 mi n of center. Int corridors. **Pets:** Accepted.

[SAVE] [¶][➥][✕][📶][✕][🎿][🛢][💻]

▼▼▼ Nordic Inn **BB** ❖

(970) 349-5542. **Call for rates.** 14 Treasury Rd 81225. 2.9 mi n of Elk Ave to Treasury Rd, then just e. Ext corridors. **Pets:** Other species. $25 daily fee/pet. Designated rooms, service with restrictions, supervision.

[📶][✕][🎿][🛢][💻]

▼▼▼ Old Town Inn **H** ❖

(970) 349-6184. **$99-$139.** 708 Sixth St 81224. On SR 135, just s of Elk Ave. Int corridors. **Pets:** Other species. $10 daily fee/room. Designated rooms, service with restrictions. [📶][✕][🛢]

▼▼▼ WestWall Lodge **CO**

(970) 349-1280. **Call for rates.** 14 Hunter Hill Rd 81225. 2.2 mi n, just e; at Mt. Crested Butte. Int corridors. **Pets:** Accepted.

[➥][✕][📶][✕][🎿][🛢][💻]

DENVER (Restaurants p. 622)

(AAA) ▼▼▼ BEST WESTERN PLUS Denver Hotel **H**

(303) 388-6161. **$90-$170.** 3737 Quebec St 80207. I-70 exit 278, just s. Int corridors. **Pets:** Medium. $20 daily fee/room. Designated rooms, no service, supervision. [SAVE][➥][📶][✕][🛢][💻]

(AAA) ▼▼▼ ▼▼ The Brown Palace Hotel and Spa, Autograph Collection **H**

(303) 297-3111. **$209-$344.** 321 17th St 80202. From Broadway and Tremont Pl, just sw. Int corridors. **Pets:** Accepted.

[SAVE] [¶][📶][✕][🛢][💻]

(AAA) ▼▼▼ Courtyard by Marriott Denver Stapleton **H**

(303) 333-3303. **$111-$194.** 7415 E 41st Ave 80216. I-70 exit 278, s on Quebec St, exit Smith Rd, then e to Frontage Rd; I-270 exit 4. Int corridors. **Pets:** Accepted. [SAVE][ECO][¶][➥][📶][✕][🛢][💻]

▼▼◆▼ Crowne Plaza Denver International Airport **H**

(303) 371-9494. **$99-$249.** 15500 E 40th Ave 80239. I-70 exit 283 (Chambers Rd), just n, then just e. Int corridors. **Pets:** Medium, dogs only. $30 one-time fee/room. Service with restrictions, supervision.

[¶][↺M][📶][✕][🛢][💻]

▼▼◆▼ the Curtis - a DoubleTree by Hilton Hotel **H**

(303) 571-0300. **$149-$409.** 1405 Curtis St 80202. Between 14th and 15th sts. Int corridors. **Pets:** Accepted. [¶][↺M][📶][✕][🛢][💻]

▼▼▼ **DoubleTree by Hilton Denver-Stapleton North** 🄷
(303) 321-6666. **$84-$239.** 4040 Quebec St 80216. I-70 exit 278, s on Quebec St to Smith Rd exit, then e to Frontage Rd. Int corridors. **Pets:** Accepted. 🍴 🛏 📶 ✖ 📠 🖥

▼▼▼ **DoubleTree by Hilton Hotel Denver** 🄷
(303) 321-3333. **$89-$249.** 3203 Quebec St 80207. I-70 exit 278, 0.5 mi s; I-270 exit 4. Int corridors. **Pets:** Accepted.
🍴 🛏 ✖ 📶 ✖ 📠 🖥

▼▼▼ **Drury Inn & Suites Denver Stapleton** 🄷
(303) 373-1983. **$129-$199.** 4550 N Central Park Blvd 80238. I-70 exit 279B westbound; exit 279 eastbound, just n. Int corridors.
Pets: Accepted. 🅜 📶 📠 🖥

🄰🄰🄰 ▼▼▼ **Embassy Suites Denver-Stapleton** 🄷
(303) 375-0400. **$119-$179.** 4444 N Havana St 80239. I-70 exit 280, just n. Int corridors. **Pets:** Accepted.
🆂🅰🆅🅴 🍴 🅜 🛏 ✖ 📶 ✖ 📠 🖥

🄰🄰🄰 ▼▼▼▼ **Four Seasons Hotel Denver** 🄷 🐾
(303) 389-3000. **Call for rates.** 1111 14th St 80202. Between Lawrence and Arapahoe sts. Int corridors. **Pets:** Dogs only. Supervision.
🆂🅰🆅🅴 🍴 🛏 ✖ 📶 ✖

🄰🄰🄰 ▼▼▼▼ **Grand Hyatt Denver** 🄷
(303) 295-1234. **$99-$399.** 1750 Welton St 80202. Between 17th and 18th sts. Int corridors. **Pets:** Accepted.
🆂🅰🆅🅴 🄴🄲🄾 🍴 🅜 🛏 ✖ 📶 ✖ 📠 🖥

▼▼▼ **Hampton Inn & Suites Denver Tech Center** 🄷 🐾
(303) 804-9900. **$109-$189.** 5001 S Ulster St 80237. I-25 exit 199, e to Ulster St, then just n. Int corridors. **Pets:** $25 one-time fee/pet. Designated rooms, service with restrictions, supervision.
🅜 🛏 📶 ✖ 📠 🖥

▼▼▼ **Holiday Inn Denver East - Stapleton** 🄷
(303) 321-3500. **Call for rates.** 3333 Quebec St 80207. I-70 exit 278, 0.3 mi s; I-270 exit 4. Int corridors. **Pets:** Accepted.
🍴 🅜 🛏 ✖ 📶 ✖ 📠 🖥

🄰🄰🄰 ▼▼▼ **Holiday Inn Express Denver Downtown** 🄷
(303) 296-0400. **Call for rates.** 401 17th St 80202. From Broadway and Tremont Pl, just sw. Int corridors. **Pets:** Accepted.
🆂🅰🆅🅴 📶 ✖ 📠 🖥

🄰🄰🄰 ▼▼▼▼ **Hotel Monaco Denver** 🄷
(303) 296-1717. **Call for rates.** 1717 Champa St 80202. Between 17th and 18th sts. Int corridors. **Pets:** Accepted.
🆂🅰🆅🅴 🄴🄲🄾 🍴 🅜 ✖ 📶

🄰🄰🄰 ▼▼▼▼ **Hotel Teatro** 🄷
(303) 228-1100. **$179-$699.** 1100 14th St 80202. Between Lawrence and Arapahoe sts. Int corridors. **Pets:** Accepted.
🆂🅰🆅🅴 🍴 ✖ 📶 ✖ 📠 🖥

🄰🄰🄰 ▼▼▼▼ **HYATT house Denver Airport** 🄷
(303) 628-7777. **$79-$209.** 18741 E 71st Ave 80249. I-70 exit 286 (Tower Rd), 4.6 mi n, then just e; from Pena Blvd exit 5 (Tower Rd/SR 32), just s. Int corridors. **Pets:** Accepted.
🆂🅰🆅🅴 🍴 🛏 ✖ 📠 🖥

🄰🄰🄰 ▼▼▼▼ **Hyatt Regency Denver Tech Center** 🄷 🐾
(303) 779-1234. **$99-$429.** 7800 E Tufts Ave 80237. I-225 exit 2 (Tamarac St), just s to Tufts Ave; I-25 exit 199 (Belleview Ave), e to S Ulster St, then 0.5 mi n. Int corridors. **Pets:** Medium, dogs only. $100 one-time fee/room. Designated rooms, service with restrictions, crate.
🆂🅰🆅🅴 🍴 🅜 🛏 ✖ 📶 ✖ 📠 🖥

🄰🄰🄰 ▼▼▼ **The Inn at Cherry Creek** 🄷 🐾
(303) 350-4440. **Call for rates.** 233 Clayton St 80206. Between 2nd and 3rd aves; in Cherry Creek Village. Int corridors. **Pets:** $35 one-time fee/pet. Service with restrictions, supervision.
🆂🅰🆅🅴 🍴 📶 ✖ 📠 🖥

🄰🄰🄰 ▼▼▼▼ **JW Marriott Denver Cherry Creek** 🄷
(303) 316-2700. **$286-$470.** 150 Clayton Ln 80206. I-25 exit 205 (University Blvd), 2.4 mi n to 1st Ave, just e, then just n. Int corridors.
Pets: Accepted. 🆂🅰🆅🅴 🍴 🅜 ✖ 📶 ✖ 📠 🖥

▼▼▼ **La Quinta Inn & Suites Denver Airport DIA** 🄷
(303) 371-0888. **$79-$244.** 6801 Tower Rd 80249. I-70 exit 286 (Tower Rd), 4.2 mi n; 0.8 mi s of Pena Blvd. Int corridors. **Pets:** Large, other species. Service with restrictions. 🅜 🛏 📶 ✖ 📠 🖥

▼▼▼ **La Quinta Inn & Suites Denver Gateway Park** 🄷
(303) 373-2525. **$95-$259.** 4460 Peoria St 80239. I-70 exit 281, just n. Int corridors. **Pets:** Large, other species. Service with restrictions.
🛏 📶 ✖ 📠 🖥

🄰🄰🄰 ▼▼▼ **The Oxford Hotel** 🄷
(303) 628-5400. **Call for rates.** 1600 17th St 80202. Corner of 17th and Wazee sts. Int corridors. **Pets:** Accepted.
🆂🅰🆅🅴 🍴 ✖ 📶 ✖ 📠 🖥

🄰🄰🄰 ▼▼▼ **Renaissance Denver Hotel** 🄷
(303) 399-7500. **$118-$194.** 3801 Quebec St 80207. I-70 exit 278, just s via Smith Rd exit. Int corridors. **Pets:** Accepted.
🆂🅰🆅🅴 🍴 🛏 📶 ✖ 📠 🖥

🄰🄰🄰 ▼▼▼ **Residence Inn by Marriott Denver City Center** 🄷
(303) 296-3444. **$181-$378.** 1725 Champa St 80202. Between 17th and 18th sts. Int corridors. **Pets:** Accepted. 🆂🅰🆅🅴 📶 ✖ 📠 🖥

▼▼▼ **Residence Inn by Marriott Denver Downtown** 🄷
(303) 458-5318. **$132-$240.** 2777 Zuni St 80211. I-25 exit 212B (Speer Blvd) southbound; exit 212A northbound, just w, then just n. Ext corridors. **Pets:** Accepted. 🛏 📶 ✖ 📠 🖥

🄰🄰🄰 ▼▼▼▼ **The Ritz-Carlton, Denver** 🄷 🐾
(303) 312-3800. **$409-$439.** 1881 Curtis St 80202. Between 18th and 19th sts. Int corridors. **Pets:** Other species. $125 one-time fee/room. Service with restrictions, supervision.
🆂🅰🆅🅴 🍴 🅜 🛏 ✖ 📶 ✖ 📠 🖥

▼▼ **Rodeway Inn & Suites** 🄷
(303) 375-1500. **Call for rates.** 4380 Peoria St 80239. I-70 exit 281 eastbound; exit 282 westbound, just n. Int corridors. **Pets:** Accepted.
🛏 📶 📠 🖥

🄰🄰🄰 ▼▼▼ **Sheraton Denver Downtown Hotel** 🄷
(303) 893-3333. **$99-$450.** 1550 Court Pl 80202. Between 15th and 16th sts. Int corridors. **Pets:** Accepted.
🆂🅰🆅🅴 🍴 🅜 🛏 📶 ✖ 📠 🖥

▼▼▼▼ **Staybridge Suites** 🄷
(303) 574-0888. **$99-$220.** 6951 Tower Rd 80249. Just s of jct Pena Blvd. Int corridors. **Pets:** Accepted. 🅜 🛏 📶 ✖ 📠 🖥

🄰🄰🄰 ▼▼▼ **TownePlace Suites by Marriott @ Denver Airport** 🄷
(303) 373-4243. **$125-$206.** 4100 N Kittredge St 80239. I-70 exit 283 (Chambers Rd), just n to 40th Ave, 0.3 mi e, then just n. Int corridors. **Pets:** Other species. $100 one-time fee/room. Designated rooms, service with restrictions, crate. 🆂🅰🆅🅴 🍴 🛏 📶 ✖ 📠 🖥

▼▼ **TownePlace Suites by Marriott-Denver Southeast** 🄷
(303) 759-9393. **$90-$183.** 3699 S Monaco Pkwy 80237. I-25 exit 201, just e to Monaco Pkwy, then s. Int corridors. **Pets:** Accepted.
🛏 📶 ✖ 📠 🖥

TownePlace Suites by Marriott Downtown Denver H

(303) 722-2322. **$153-$252.** 685 Speer Blvd 80204. I-25 exit 209A (6th Ave), 1.4 mi w, then just n on Acoma St. Int corridors. **Pets:** Other species. $100 one-time fee/room. Service with restrictions.

[SAVE] [🍴] [&M] [📶] [✕] [🔒] [💻]

Warwick Denver Hotel H

(303) 861-2000. **Call for rates.** 1776 Grant St 80203. Between 17th and 18th aves. Int corridors. **Pets:** Accepted.

[🍴] [🏊] [🦮] [✕] [🔒] [💻]

The Westin Denver Downtown H ❀

(303) 572-9100. **$159-$509.** 1672 Lawrence St 80202. Between 16th and 17th sts. Int corridors. **Pets:** Dogs only. No service, supervision.

[SAVE] [🍴] [&M] [🏊] [📶] [✕] [🔒] [💻]

DILLON

BEST WESTERN Ptarmigan Lodge M

(970) 468-2341. **$80-$251.** 652 Lake Dillon Dr 80435. I-70 exit 205, 1.3 mi s on US 6 to Lake Dillon Dr stop light, then 0.3 mi s. Ext/int corridors. **Pets:** $10 daily fee/pet. Designated rooms, service with restrictions, supervision. [SAVE] [✕] [📶] [✕] [🎾] [🔒] [💻]

DURANGO (Restaurants p. 622)

Apple Orchard Inn BB

(970) 247-0751. **$90-$250, 21 day notice.** 7758 CR 203 81301. 8.5 mi n on US 550, just w at Trimble Ln, then 1.3 mi n. Ext/int corridors. **Pets:** Accepted. [🍴] [📶] [✕] [🎾] [🔒] [💻]

BEST WESTERN Durango Inn & Suites M ❀

(970) 247-3251. **$79-$179.** 21382 US Hwy 160 W 81303. On US 160, 1 mi w. Ext corridors. **Pets:** $15 daily fee/room. Service with restrictions, supervision. [SAVE] [🍴] [🏊] [📶] [🔒] [💻]

Caboose Motel M

(970) 247-1191. **$58-$190.** 3363 Main Ave 81301. 2.5 mi n on US 550. Ext corridors. **Pets:** Medium, dogs only. $15 daily fee/pet. Service with restrictions, supervision. [📶] [✕] [🚫] [🔒] [💻]

Comfort Inn & Suites H

(970) 259-7900. **$75-$330.** 455 S Camino Del Rio 81303. On US 550 (Frontage Rd), 1.5 mi e of jct US 550. Int corridors. **Pets:** Accepted.

[SAVE] [🍴] [&M] [🏊] [📶] [✕] [🔒] [💻]

DoubleTree by Hilton Hotel Durango H ❀

(970) 259-6580. **Call for rates.** 501 Camino Del Rio 81301. Jct US 160 and 550. Int corridors. **Pets:** Large, other species. $15 daily fee/pet. Service with restrictions, supervision.

[ECO] [🍴] [🏊] [✕] [📶] [✕] [🔒] [💻]

Durango Downtown Inn M

(970) 247-5393. **Call for rates.** 800 Camino Del Rio 81301. On US 550, just n of jct US 160. Ext corridors. **Pets:** Accepted.

[SAVE] [🍴] [🏊] [📶] [🔒] [💻]

Holiday Inn Hotel & Suites Durango Central H

(970) 385-6400. **Call for rates.** 21636 Hwy 160 W 81301. Just w of jct US 160. Int corridors. **Pets:** Other species. $25 one-time fee/pet. Designated rooms, service with restrictions, supervision.

[🍴] [&M] [📶] [✕] [🔒] [💻]

Homewood Suites by Hilton H

(970) 259-2996. **$138-$245.** 15 Girard St 81303. On US 160 (Frontage Rd), 2.2 mi e of jct US 550. Int corridors. **Pets:** Large, dogs only. $75 one-time fee/room. Designated rooms, service with restrictions.

[🍴] [&M] [📶] [✕] [🔒] [💻]

Leland House Bed & Breakfast Suites BB ❀

(970) 385-1920. **$139-$449, 14 day notice.** 721 E 2nd Ave 81301. Just e of Main Ave via 7th St, then just n. Ext/int corridors. **Pets:** Dogs only. $20 daily fee/pet. Designated rooms, service with restrictions, supervision. [📶] [✕] [🔒] [💻]

Quality Inn M ❀

(970) 259-5373. **$65-$129.** 2930 N Main Ave 81301. 2 mi n on US 550. Ext corridors. **Pets:** Dogs only. $15 daily fee/pet. Designated rooms, service with restrictions, crate. [🏊] [📶] [✕] [🔒] [💻]

Residence Inn by Marriott H

(970) 259-6200. **$108-$292.** 21691 Hwy 160 W 81301. On US 160, just w. Int corridors. **Pets:** Accepted. [&M] [🏊] [📶] [✕] [🔒] [💻]

The Rochester Hotel BB ❀

(970) 385-1920. **$139-$449, 14 day notice.** 726 E 2nd Ave 81301. Just e of Main Ave via 7th St, then just n. Int corridors. **Pets:** Dogs only. $20 daily fee/pet. Designated rooms, service with restrictions, supervision. [📶] [✕] [🔒]

Siesta Motel M

(970) 247-0741. **$58-$145.** 3475 N Main Ave 81301. 2.6 mi n on US 550. Ext corridors. **Pets:** Accepted. [📶] [✕] [🔒] [💻]

Strater Hotel H

(970) 247-4431. **$124-$289.** 699 Main 81301. Corner of 7th St and Main Ave; in historic downtown. Int corridors. **Pets:** Accepted.

[SAVE] [ECO] [🍴] [📶] [✕]

EDWARDS

The Lodge & Spa at Cordillera H

(970) 926-2200. **Call for rates.** 2205 Cordillera Way 81632. I-70 exit 163, 0.5 mi s, 2.6 mi w on US 6, then 2 mi nw via Squaw Creek Rd, follow signs; 2.3 mi via paved road from gatehouse. Int corridors. **Pets:** Accepted. [SAVE] [🍴] [🏊] [✕] [📶] [✕] [🔒] [💻]

ENGLEWOOD

Homewood Suites by Hilton - DTC/Inverness H

(303) 706-0102. **$89-$199.** 199 Inverness Dr W 80112. I-25 exit 195 (County Line Rd), 0.3 mi ne to traffic light, then just n. Int corridors. **Pets:** Accepted. [🍴] [🏊] [📶] [🔒] [💻]

Residence Inn by Marriott Denver South / Park Meadows H

(720) 895-0200. **$125-$240.** 8322 S Valley Hwy 80112. I-25 exit 195 (County Line Rd), just e to S Valley Hwy, then just w. Int corridors. **Pets:** Other species. $100 one-time fee/room. Service with restrictions.

[&M] [🏊] [📶] [✕] [🔒] [💻]

ESTES PARK

Castle Mountain Lodge LLC CA

(970) 586-3664. **$80-$575, 30 day notice.** 1520 Fall River Rd 80517. 1 mi w on US 34. Ext corridors. **Pets:** Dogs only. $15 daily fee/pet. Designated rooms, service with restrictions, supervision.

[SAVE] [✕] [📶] [✕] [🎾] [🚫] [🔒] [💻]

Mountain Shadows Resort CA ❀

(970) 577-0397. **Call for rates.** 871 Riverside Dr 80517. Jct Elkhorn and Moraine aves, 1.4 mi sw to Marys Lake Rd, 0.3 mi s, then just e. Ext corridors. **Pets:** Other species. $15 daily fee/pet. No service, crate. [🍴] [📶] [✕] [🚫] [🔒] [💻]

Murphy's River Lodge H

(970) 480-5081. **$119-$219.** 481 W Elkhorn Ave 80517. 0.4 mi w of jct Elkhorn and Moraine aves; west end of downtown. Ext corridors. **Pets:** Accepted. [🍴] [🏊] [📶] [✕] [🚫] [🔒] [💻]

Rocky Mountain Park Inn H

(970) 586-2332. **Call for rates.** 101 S Saint Vrain Ave 80517. 0.4 mi se on US 36 to SR 7, just s. Int corridors. **Pets:** Accepted.

[SAVE] [🍴] [&M] [🏊] [📶] [✕] [🔒] [💻]

EVERGREEN

▼▼▼▼ Comfort Suites Golden West on Evergreen Parkway ℍ ❖

(303) 526-2000. **$115-$170.** 29300 US Hwy 40 80439. I-70 exit 252 (Evergreen Pkwy) westbound; exit 251 eastbound, just s, then just w. Int corridors. **Pets:** Dogs only. $10 daily fee/pet. Designated rooms, service with restrictions, supervision.

FORT COLLINS

ⒶⒶⒶ ▼▼ ▼ BEST WESTERN Kiva Inn ℍ

(970) 484-2444. **Call for rates.** 1638 E Mulberry St 80524. I-25 exit 269B, 1.5 mi w on SR 14. Ext/int corridors. **Pets:** Accepted.

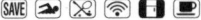

ⒶⒶⒶ ▼▼ ▼ BEST WESTERN University Inn Ⓜ ❖

(970) 484-2984. **$110-$250.** 914 S College Ave 80524. I-25 exit 268, 4 mi w to College Ave, then just n on US 287. Ext/int corridors. **Pets:** $15 daily fee/pet. Designated rooms, supervision.

▼▼▼▼ Cambria Hotel & Suites ℍ

(970) 267-9000. **$119-$239.** 2921 E Harmony Rd 80528. I-25 exit 265 (Harmony Rd), 1.5 mi w, then just s on Ziegler Rd. Int corridors. **Pets:** Accepted. 🍴 🐾 📶 ✕ 🛏 🖥

▼▼▼▼ Courtyard by Marriott ℍ

(970) 282-1700. **$105-$210.** 1200 Oakridge Dr 80525. I-25 exit 265 (Harmony Rd), 3.3 mi w; entry via Lemay Ave. Int corridors. **Pets:** Accepted. 🅴🅲🅾 🍴 ♿ 🐾 📶 ✕ 🛏 🖥

▼▼▼▼ Fort Collins Marriott ℍ

(970) 226-5200. **$118-$217.** 350 E Horsetooth Rd 80525. Jct College Ave and Horsetooth Rd, just e, then just n on John F Kennedy Pkwy. Int corridors. **Pets:** Accepted. 🅴🅲🅾 🍴 ♿ 🐾 📶 ✕ 🛏 🖥

ⒶⒶⒶ ▼▼▼▼ Hilton Ft Collins ℍ

(970) 482-2626. **$92-$199.** 425 W Prospect Rd 80526. I-25 exit 268, 4.3 mi w. Int corridors. **Pets:** Accepted.

🆂🅰🆅🅴 🍴 🐾 📶 ✕ 🛏 🖥

▼▼▼▼ Holiday Inn Express & Suites ℍ

(970) 225-2200. **Call for rates.** 1426 Oakridge Dr 80525. I-25 exit 265 (Harmony Rd), 3 mi w, just s on McMurry Ave, then just w. Int corridors. **Pets:** Accepted. ♿ 🐾 📶 ✕ 🛏 🖥

ⒶⒶⒶ ▼▼▼▼ Homewood Suites by Hilton Fort Collins ℍ

(970) 225-2400. **$109-$279.** 1521 Oakridge Dr 80525. I-25 exit 265 (Harmony Rd), 3 mi w, just s on McMurry Ave, then just w. Int corridors. **Pets:** Accepted. 🆂🅰🆅🅴 🐾 🐾 📶 🛏 🖥

▼▼▼▼ Quality Inn & Suites ℍ ❖

(970) 282-9047. **$79-$179.** 4001 S Mason St 80525. Jct Harmony Rd and College Ave, just w to Mason St, then 0.5 mi n. Int corridors. **Pets:** Other species. $15 daily fee/room. Designated rooms, service with restrictions, supervision. ♿ 🐾 📶 ✕ 🛏 🖥

▼▼▼▼ Residence Inn by Marriott Fort Collins ℍ

(970) 223-5700. **$127-$235.** 1127 Oakridge Dr 80525. I-25 exit 265 (Harmony Rd), 3.3 mi w to Lemay Ave, then s to Oakridge Dr. Int corridors. **Pets:** Accepted. 🅴🅲🅾 🐾 🐾 📶 ✕ 🛏 🖥

▼▼ ▼ Super 8 ℍ

(970) 493-7701. **$55-$135.** 409 Centro Way 80524. I-25 exit 269B, just w. Int corridors. **Pets:** $11 daily fee/pet. Designated rooms, service with restrictions, supervision. 🐾 📶 ✕ 🛏 🖥

FORT MORGAN

ⒶⒶⒶ ▼▼ Central Motel Ⓜ

(970) 867-2401. **$64-$70.** 201 W Platte Ave 80701. I-76 exit 80, 0.6 mi s, then w on US 34. Ext corridors. **Pets:** $10 one-time fee/room. Service with restrictions, supervision. 🆂🅰🆅🅴 📶 🛏 🖥

▼▼ ▼ Rodeway Inn Ⓜ

(970) 867-9481. **Call for rates.** 1409 Barlow Rd 80701. I-76 exit 82 (Barlow Rd), just n. Ext/int corridors. **Pets:** Other species. $15 daily fee/pet. Service with restrictions. 🍴 📶 🛏 🖥

FRISCO

ⒶⒶⒶ ▼▼ ▼ Baymont Inn & Suites Lake Dillon ℍ ❖

(970) 668-5094. **$79-$300.** 1202 N Summit Blvd 80443. I-70 exit 203, just sw. Int corridors. **Pets:** Large. $15 daily fee/room. Designated rooms, service with restrictions. 🆂🅰🆅🅴 🍴 🐾 📶 ✕ 🛏 🖥

▼▼ ▼ Holiday Inn ℍ

(970) 668-5000. **Call for rates.** 1129 N Summit Blvd 80443. I-70 exit 203, just s, then just e. Int corridors. **Pets:** Accepted.

🍴 ♿ 🐾 🐾 📶 ✕ 🛏 🖥

▼▼ ▼ Hotel Frisco ℍ

(970) 668-5009. **Call for rates.** 308 Main St 80443. I-70 exit 201, 0.7 mi e. Int corridors. **Pets:** Large, dogs only. $25 daily fee/room. Service with restrictions, crate. 📶 ✕ 🐾 🛏 🖥

FRUITA

▼▼ ▼ Comfort Inn ℍ

(970) 858-1333. **$69-$139.** 400 Jurassic Ave 81521. I-70 exit 19, 0.3 mi s; just e of Dinosaur Journey Museum. Int corridors. **Pets:** Accepted.

🐾 📶 ✕ 🛏 🖥

GATEWAY

ⒶⒶⒶ ▼▼▼▼ Gateway Canyons Resort & Spa ℍ

(970) 931-2458. **$379-$1899, 3 day notice.** 43200 Hwy 141 81522. 43 mi w of US 50; 49 mi n of CR 90. Ext/int corridors. **Pets:** Accepted.

🆂🅰🆅🅴 🍴 🐾 📶 ✕ 🛏 🖥

GLENDALE

ⒶⒶⒶ ▼▼▼▼ Hyatt Place Denver Cherry Creek ℍ

(303) 782-9300. **$79-$219.** 4150 E Mississippi Ave 80246. I-25 exit 204, 0.8 mi n on Colorado Blvd, then just e. Int corridors. **Pets:** Accepted.

🆂🅰🆅🅴 🍴 ♿ 📶 ✕ 🛏 🖥

▼▼▼▼ Residence Inn by Marriott ℍ

(303) 758-6200. **$125-$240.** 670 S Colorado Blvd 80246. I-25 exit 204, 1.6 mi n. Int corridors. **Pets:** Accepted. 🍴 ♿ 📶 ✕ 🛏 🖥

ⒶⒶⒶ ▼▼▼▼ Staybridge Suites Denver/Cherry Creek ℍ

(303) 321-5757. **Call for rates.** 4220 E Virginia Ave 80246. I-25 exit 204, 1.5 mi n on Colorado Blvd to Virginia Ave, then just e. Int corridors. **Pets:** Accepted. 🆂🅰🆅🅴 🍴 🐾 📶 ✕ 🛏 🖥

GLENWOOD SPRINGS

▼▼ ▼ Caravan Inn Ⓜ

(970) 945-7451. **$59-$159.** 1826 Grand Ave (SR 82) 81601. I-70 exit 116, 0.9 mi s. Ext corridors. **Pets:** Medium, dogs only. $100 deposit/pet, $15 daily fee/pet. Designated rooms, service with restrictions, supervision. 🐾 📶 🖥

▼▼ ▼ Hotel Colorado ℍ

(970) 945-6511. **$79-$431.** 526 Pine St 81601. I-70 exit 116, just ne. Int corridors. **Pets:** Other species. $25 daily fee/pet. Supervision.

🍴 📶 ✕ 🐾 🛏 🖥

▼▼ ▼ The Hotel Denver ℍ

(970) 945-6565. **$159-$239.** 402 7th St 81601. I-70 exit 116; across from historic train station; in town center. Int corridors. **Pets:** Accepted.

🍴 📶 ✕ 🛏 🖥

▼▼ ▼ Quality Inn & Suites ℍ

(970) 945-5995. **$94-$169.** 2650 Gilstrap Ct 81601. I-70 exit 114, just s, then just w. Int corridors. **Pets:** Accepted.

🍴 🐾 📶 ✕ 🛏 🖥

▼▼▼▼ Residence Inn by Marriott ⊞

(970) 928-0900. **$132-$240.** 125 Wulfsohn Rd 81601. I-70 exit 114, 2nd exit at roundabout, 1.5 mi e on Midland Ave, then just s. Int corridors. **Pets:** Accepted. ⊡ 🔌 ⊚ ⊠ 🖥 🖳

GOLDEN

▼▼▼▼ The Golden Hotel, an Ascend Hotel Collection Member ⊞ ❀

(303) 279-0100. **$169-$219.** 800 11th St 80401. At 11th St and Washington Ave; downtown. Int corridors. **Pets:** Other species. $20 daily fee/room. Designated rooms, service with restrictions.

🍴 ⊚ ⊠ 🖥 🖳

▼▼▼▼ Residence Inn by Marriott Denver West/Golden ⊞

(303) 271-0909. **$133-$265.** 14600 W 6th Ave, Frontage Rd 80401. US 6 exit Indiana Ave, just s to Frontage Rd, then just e. Int corridors. **Pets:** Other species. $100 one-time fee/room. Service with restrictions, crate. 🍴 🔌🅼 🔌 ⊚ ⊠ 🖥 🖳

◀◀◀ ▼▼▼ Table Mountain Inn ⊞ ❀

(303) 277-9898. **$184-$269, 3 day notice.** 1310 Washington Ave 80401. US 6 exit 19th St, 0.5 mi n to Washington Ave, 0.5 mi w; downtown, just s of arch. Int corridors. **Pets:** $10 daily fee/pet. Designated rooms, service with restrictions, supervision.

SAVE 🍴 🔌🅼 ⊚ ⊠ 🖥 🖳

GRAND JUNCTION

▼▼ Americas Best Value Inn 🅼

(970) 245-1410. **$60-$120.** 754 Horizon Dr 81506. I-70 exit 31, just n. Ext corridors. **Pets:** Accepted. 🔌 ⊚ 🖥 🖳

▼▼ Candlewood Suites ⊞

(970) 255-8093. **$85-$179.** 654 Market St 81505. I-70 exit 28 (24 Rd), 1.3 mi s to F Rd, just e, then just n. Int corridors. **Pets:** Other species. $15 daily fee/pet. Service with restrictions. ⊚ ⊠ 🖥 🖳

◀◀◀ ▼▼▼ Clarion Inn ⊞ ❀

(970) 243-6790. **$79-$129.** 755 Horizon Dr 81506. I-70 exit 31, just n. Ext/int corridors. **Pets:** Designated rooms, crate.

SAVE 🍴 🔌 ⊠ ⊚ ⊠ 🖥 🖳

▼▼ Comfort Inn ⊞

(970) 245-3335. **$74-$169.** 750 3/4 Horizon Dr 81506. I-70 exit 31, just n. Int corridors. **Pets:** Accepted. 🔌 ⊚ ⊠ 🖥 🖳

◀◀◀ ▼▼▼ Days Inn Grand Junction 🅼 ❀

(970) 243-4150. **$69-$99, 7 day notice.** 708 Horizon Dr 81506. I-70 exit 31, 0.3 mi s. Ext corridors. **Pets:** Other species. $15 daily fee/pet. Designated rooms, service with restrictions, supervision.

SAVE 🔌 ⊚ 🖥 🖳

◀◀◀ ▼▼▼ Econo Lodge ⊞

(970) 257-1140. **$59-$79.** 751 Horizon Dr 81506. I-70 exit 31, just n. Int corridors. **Pets:** Accepted. SAVE ⊚ ⊠ 🖥 🖳

▼▼▼▼ Fairfield Inn & Suites by Marriott Grand Junction Downtown/Historic Main Street ⊞

(970) 242-2525. **$133-$219.** 225 Main St 81501. At 2nd and Main sts. Int corridors. **Pets:** Accepted. 🔌 ⊚ ⊠ 🖥 🖳

▼▼▼▼ Hampton Inn Grand Junction Downtown/Historic Main Street ⊞

(970) 243-3222. **$99-$209.** 205 Main St 81501. At 2nd and Main sts. Int corridors. **Pets:** $25 daily fee/pet. Designated rooms, service with restrictions, crate. 🔌 ⊚ ⊠ 🖥 🖳

▼▼ La Quinta Inn & Suites Grand Junction ⊞

(970) 241-2929. **$79-$269.** 2761 Crossroads Blvd 81506. I-70 exit 31, 0.3 mi n, then 0.3 mi w. Int corridors. **Pets:** Large, other species. Service with restrictions. 🔌 ⊚ ⊠ 🖥 🖳

◀◀◀ ▼▼▼ Quality Inn of Grand Junction ⊞ ❀

(970) 245-7200. **$69-$125.** 733 Horizon Dr 81506. I-70 exit 31, just s. Int corridors. **Pets:** $10 daily fee/pet. Designated rooms, crate.

SAVE 🍴 🔌 ⊚ ⊠ 🖥 🖳

◀◀◀ ▼▼▼ Residence Inn by Marriott ⊞

(970) 263-4004. **$112-$253.** 767 Horizon Dr 81506. I-70 exit 31, 0.3 mi n. Int corridors. **Pets:** Accepted. SAVE 🔌 ⊚ ⊠ 🖥 🖳

▼▼▼▼ SpringHill Suites by Marriott Grand Junction Downtown/Historic Main Street ⊞

(970) 424-5777. **$133-$219.** 236 Main St 81501. At 3rd and Main sts. Int corridors. **Pets:** Other species. $25 daily fee/room. Designated rooms, service with restrictions, supervision.

⊡ 🔌🅼 🔌 ⊚ ⊠ 🖥 🖳

GRAND LAKE

◀◀◀ ▼▼▼ Spirit Lake Lodge 🅼

(970) 627-3344. **$55-$200, 7 day notice.** 829 Grand Ave 80447. 0.3 mi e to Grand Ave, then 0.4 mi e. Ext corridors. **Pets:** Large. $10 daily fee/pet. No service, supervision. SAVE ⊚ ⊠ 🅐 🖥 🖳

GREELEY

◀◀◀ ▼▼▼ Comfort Inn-Greeley ⊞ ❀

(970) 330-6380. **$99-$229.** 2467 W 29th St 80631. US 34 Bypass exit 23rd Ave, just sw. Int corridors. **Pets:** Medium, dogs only. $15 daily fee/pet. Designated rooms, service with restrictions, supervision.

SAVE 🔌 ⊚ ⊠ 🖥 🖳

◀◀◀ ▼▼▼ Country Inn & Suites By Carlson ⊞

(970) 330-3404. **$119-$189.** 2501 W 29th St 80631. US 34 Bypass exit 23rd Ave, just s, then w. Int corridors. **Pets:** Medium. $40 one-time fee/room. Service with restrictions, supervision.

SAVE 🔌🅼 🔌 ⊚ ⊠ 🖥 🖳

GREENWOOD VILLAGE

◀◀◀ ▼▼▼▼ BEST WESTERN PLUS Denver Tech Center Hotel ⊞

(303) 792-9999. **$109-$179.** 9231 E Arapahoe Rd 80112. I-25 exit 197 (Arapahoe Rd), just e. Int corridors. **Pets:** Accepted.

SAVE 🔌🅼 ⊚ ⊠ 🖥 🖳

◀◀◀ ▼▼▼▼ HYATT house Denver Tech Center ⊞

(303) 706-1945. **$69-$209.** 9280 E Costilla Ave 80112. I-25 exit 197 (Arapahoe Rd), e to Clinton St, then just s. Int corridors. **Pets:** Medium. $175 one-time fee/pet. Service with restrictions, supervision.

SAVE 🔌🅼 ⊚ ⊠ 🖥 🖳

◀◀◀ ▼▼▼ Hyatt Place Denver Tech Center ⊞

(303) 804-0700. **$69-$199.** 8300 E Crescent Pkwy 80111. I-25 exit 199, 0.4 mi e to Crescent Pkwy, then just s. Int corridors. **Pets:** Accepted. SAVE 🔌 ⊚ ⊠ 🖥 🖳

▼▼▼ Residence Inn by Marriott-Denver Tech Center ⊞

(303) 740-7177. **$118-$217.** 6565 S Yosemite St 80111. I-25 exit 197 (Arapahoe Rd), just w, then n. Ext corridors. **Pets:** Accepted.

🔌 ⊚ ⊠ 🖥 🖳

◀◀◀ ▼▼▼▼ Sheraton Denver Tech Center ⊞ ❀

(303) 799-6200. **$99-$299.** 7007 S Clinton St 80112. I-25 exit 197 (Arapahoe Rd), just e, then s. Int corridors. **Pets:** Medium, dogs only. Designated rooms, service with restrictions, crate.

SAVE 🍴 🔌🅼 🔌 🔘 ⊠ 🖥 🖳

GUNNISON

▼▼ Alpine Inn ⊞

(970) 641-2804. **$65-$180.** 1011 W Rio Grande Rd 81230. 0.5 mi w of center, 0.5 mi s; at US 50 and Rio Grande Ave. Int corridors. **Pets:** Small. $20 one-time fee/pet. Designated rooms, service with restrictions, supervision. 🍴 🔌 ⊚ 🖥 🖳

▼▼ Econo Lodge Gunnison/Crested Butte ⬛
(970) 641-3068. **$64-$149.** 411 E Tomichi Ave 81230. On US 50, 0.3 mi e of center. Int corridors. **Pets:** Accepted. 🛜 ⬛ ⬛

▼▼▼ The Inn at Tomichi Village Ⓜ ✿
(970) 641-1131. **$109-$159.** 41883 US Hwy 50 E 81230. 2 mi e of center. Ext corridors. **Pets:** Dogs only. $20 daily fee/pet. Designated rooms, service with restrictions, supervision. 🍽 🔌 🛜 ✕ ⬛ ⬛

▼▼ Rodeway Inn Ⓜ
(970) 641-0500. **$75-$119.** 37760 W Hwy 50 81230. 0.5 mi w of center, 2 mi sw. Ext corridors. **Pets:** Accepted. 🛜 ⬛ ⬛

HESPERUS (Restaurants p. 622)

▼▼▼ Blue Lake Ranch 🅱🅱
(970) 385-4537. **Call for rates.** 16919 Hwy 140 81326. Jct US 160 and SR 140, 6.4 mi s. Ext/int corridors. **Pets:** Accepted.
🍽 🛜 ✕ ⬛ ⬛

HIGHLANDS RANCH

ⒶⒶⒶ ▼▼▼ Comfort Suites-Denver South ⬛ ✿
(303) 770-5400. **$79-$219.** 7060 E County Line Rd 80126. SR 470 exit Quebec St, just n to County Line Rd, just w, then just s; at Quebec Highlands Center. Int corridors. **Pets:** Dogs only. $15 daily fee/pet. Designated rooms, service with restrictions, supervision.
🆂🅰🆅🅴 🔌 🛜 ✕ ⬛ ⬛

▼▼ Residence Inn by Marriott Denver Highlands Ranch ⬛
(303) 683-5500. **$140-$230.** 93 W Centennial Blvd 80126. SR 470 exit Broadway, just s, then w. Int corridors. **Pets:** Other species. $100 one-time fee/room. Service with restrictions, supervision.
🔌 🔌 🛜 ✕ ⬛ ⬛

HOT SULPHUR SPRINGS

ⒶⒶⒶ ▼ Canyon Motel Ⓜ
(970) 725-3395. **$59-$139.** 221 Byers Ave 80451. On US 40, center. Ext corridors. **Pets:** Dogs only. $10 one-time fee/room. Service with restrictions, supervision. 🆂🅰🆅🅴 🛜 ✕ 🅐🅒 ⬛ ⬛

IGNACIO

ⒶⒶⒶ ▼▼▼ Sky Ute Casino Resort ⬛
(970) 563-7777. **$81-$135, 3 day notice.** 14324 Hwy 172 N 81137. Jct US 172 and CR 517. Int corridors. **Pets:** Accepted.
🆂🅰🆅🅴 🍽 🔌 🔌 🛜 ⬛ ⬛

KEYSTONE

▼▼ The Inn at Keystone ⬛
(970) 496-4825. **$129-$280, 21 day notice.** 23044 Hwy 6 80435. I-70 exit 205, 6.5 mi e. Int corridors. **Pets:** Dogs only. $40 daily fee/room. Designated rooms, service with restrictions.
🍽 🔌 🛜 ✕ 🅐🅒 ⬛ ⬛

KREMMLING

ⒶⒶⒶ ▼▼ Allington Inn & Suites ⬛
(970) 724-9800. **$97-$149.** 215 W Central Ave 80459. 0.5 mi w of jct US 40 and SR 9, then just n. Int corridors. **Pets:** Accepted.
🆂🅰🆅🅴 🔌 🛜 ✕ ⬛ ⬛

LA JUNTA

▼▼ Holiday Inn Express ⬛
(719) 384-2900. **$99-$119.** 27994 US Hwy 50 Frontage Rd 81050. On US 50 Frontage Rd, 0.8 mi w. Int corridors. **Pets:** $20 deposit/room, $20 daily fee/room. Designated rooms, service with restrictions, supervision. 🔌 🛜 ⬛ ⬛

ⒶⒶⒶ ▼ Stagecoach Motel Ⓜ
(719) 384-5476. **$55-$70.** 905 W 3rd St 81050. Jct US 50 and 350. Ext corridors. **Pets:** Medium. $10 daily fee/pet. Designated rooms, service with restrictions, supervision. 🆂🅰🆅🅴 🔌 🛜 ✕ ⬛ ⬛

LAKE GEORGE

▼▼ M Lazy C Ranch & Mule Creek Outfitters 🆁🅰
(719) 748-3398. **Call for rates.** 801 CR 453 80827. 5 mi w on US 24, then 1 mi n on dirt road. Ext corridors. **Pets:** Accepted.
🍽 ❌ 🛜 ✕ 🅐🅒 🅦 🇿 ⬛ ⬛

LAKEWOOD

ⒶⒶⒶ ▼▼▼ BEST WESTERN Denver Southwest ⬛
(303) 989-5500. **Call for rates.** 3440 S Vance St 80227. Just ne of jct US 285 (Hampden Ave) and S Wadsworth Blvd, e on Girton Dr, then just s. Int corridors. **Pets:** Large, other species. Designated rooms, service with restrictions, supervision. 🆂🅰🆅🅴 🔌 🔌 🛜 ✕ ⬛ ⬛

ⒶⒶⒶ ▼▼▼ Holiday Inn Denver Lakewood ⬛
(303) 980-9200. **$89-$149.** 7390 W Hampden Ave 80227. US 285 (W Hampden Ave) exit S Wadsworth Blvd, just e on Jefferson Ave, then n on Vance St. Int corridors. **Pets:** Accepted.
🆂🅰🆅🅴 🍽 🔌 🛜 ⬛ ⬛

▼▼▼ Home2 Suites by Hilton Denver West/Federal Center ⬛
(303) 985-7100. **$99-$259.** 50 Van Gordon St 80228. US 6 exit Simms St/Union Blvd, 0.6 mi s on Union Blvd to 2nd Pl, just w, then just s. Int corridors. **Pets:** Accepted. 🍽 🔌 🔌 🛜 ✕ ⬛ ⬛

▼▼ Residence Inn by Marriott Denver SW/Lakewood ⬛
(303) 985-7676. **$111-$217.** 7050 W Hampden Ave 80227. Just se of jct US 285 (W Hampden Ave) and Wadsworth Blvd, e on Jefferson Ave, then n on frontage road. Int corridors. **Pets:** Accepted.
🍽 🔌 🔌 🛜 ✕ ⬛ ⬛

ⒶⒶⒶ ▼▼▼ Sheraton-Denver West Hotel ⬛
(303) 987-2000. **$99-$269, 3 day notice.** 360 Union Blvd 80228. US 6 exit Simms St/Union Blvd, just s. Int corridors. **Pets:** Accepted.
🆂🅰🆅🅴 🍽 🔌 🛜 ✕ ⬛ ⬛

LAMAR

▼▼▼ Holiday Inn Express & Suites ⬛
(719) 931-4010. **Call for rates.** 1304 N Main St 81052. 0.8 mi n on US 50 and 287. Int corridors. **Pets:** Accepted.
🔌 🔌 🛜 ✕ ⬛ ⬛

LEADVILLE

ⒶⒶⒶ ▼▼ Alps Motel Ⓜ
(719) 486-1223. **$100, 10 day notice.** 207 Elm St 80461. Just s of center on US 24. Ext corridors. **Pets:** Other species. $18 daily fee/pet. Service with restrictions, supervision. 🆂🅰🆅🅴 🛜 ✕ 🅐🅒 ⬛ ⬛

LIMON

ⒶⒶⒶ ▼ Safari Inn Ⓜ
(719) 775-2363. **$45-$145, 3 day notice.** 637 Main St 80828. I-70 exit 361, 0.8 mi w. Ext corridors. **Pets:** Other species. $10 daily fee/pet. Designated rooms, service with restrictions, supervision.
🆂🅰🆅🅴 🔌 🛜 ⬛ ⬛

LITTLETON

▼▼ Holiday Inn Express Hotel & Suites Denver SW-Littleton ⬛
(720) 981-1000. **$99-$209.** 12683 W Indore Pl 80127. SR 470 exit Ken Caryl Ave, just e to Shaffer Ave, just n, then w. Int corridors. **Pets:** Accepted. 🔌 🔌 🛜 ✕ ⬛ ⬛

▼▼▼ Homewood Suites by Hilton-Denver Littleton ⬛
(720) 981-4763. **$119-$499.** 7630 Shaffer Pkwy 80127. SR 470 exit Ken Caryl Ave, just e, then just s. Int corridors. **Pets:** Medium, other species. $100 one-time fee/room. Designated rooms, service with restrictions, supervision. 🔌 🔌 🛜 ✕ ⬛ ⬛

ⒶⒶⒶ ▼▼▼ TownePlace Suites by Marriott-Denver Southwest/Littleton ⬛
(303) 972-0555. **$90-$183.** 10902 W Toller Dr 80127. SR 470 exit Kipling Pkwy, just s, then 0.4 mi w on Ute St. Int corridors.
Pets: Accepted. 🆂🅰🆅🅴 🍽 🔌 🛜 ✕ ⬛ ⬛

LONE TREE

Element Denver Park Meadows H
(303) 790-2100. **$99-$199.** 9985 Park Meadows Dr 80124. Jct Yosemite St, 0.4 mi e. Int corridors. **Pets:** Accepted.

Hyatt Place Denver - South/Park Meadows H
(303) 662-8500. **$69-$199.** 9030 E Westview Rd 80124. I-25 exit 195 (County Line Rd), 0.5 mi w to Yosemite St, just s to Parkland Rd, then just w; SR 470 exit Yosemite St, 0.5 mi nw, just n on Parkland Rd, then just w. Int corridors. **Pets:** Accepted.

Staybridge Suites Denver South-Lone Tree H
(303) 649-1010. **Call for rates.** 7820 Park Meadows Dr 80124. I-25 exit 195 (County Line Rd), w to Acres Green Dr, s to E Park Meadows Dr, then just w; SR 470 exit Quebec St, just s, then just e. Int corridors. **Pets:** Accepted.

LONGMONT

BEST WESTERN PLUS Plaza Hotel H
(303) 776-2000. **$109-$179.** 1900 Ken Pratt Blvd 80501. Jct US 287, 1.3 mi sw on Ken Pratt Blvd (SR 119). Int corridors. **Pets:** Large. Designated rooms, service with restrictions, supervision.

Holiday Inn Express & Suites H
(303) 684-0404. **$109-$184.** 1355 Dry Creek Dr 80503. Jct Main St and Ken Pratt Blvd (SR 119), 2.2 mi w, just n, then just ne. Int corridors. **Pets:** Other species. $30 one-time fee/room. Service with restrictions, supervision.

Residence Inn by Marriott Boulder/Longmont H
(303) 702-9933. **$146-$275.** 1450 Dry Creek Dr 80503. Jct Main St and Ken Pratt Blvd (SR 119), 2.2 mi w, just n, then just ne; jct Hoover Rd and SR 119. Int corridors. **Pets:** Accepted.

Super 8 Twin Peaks, Longmont H
(303) 772-8106. **$63-$109.** 2446 N Main St 80501. I-25 exit 243, 6.4 mi w on SR 66. Int corridors. **Pets:** Accepted.

LOUISVILLE

BEST WESTERN PLUS Louisville Inn & Suites H
(303) 327-1215. **$79-$199.** 960 W Dillon Rd 80027. US 36 (Boulder Tpke) exit Superior (SR 170), just n on McCaslin Blvd to Dillon Rd, then just e. Int corridors. **Pets:** Accepted.

Residence Inn by Marriott-Boulder/Louisville H
(303) 665-2661. **$132-$252.** 845 Coal Creek Cir 80027. US 36 (Boulder Tpke) exit Superior (SR 170), n on McCaslin Blvd to Dillon Rd, then 0.6 mi e. Int corridors. **Pets:** Accepted.

LOVELAND

BEST WESTERN PLUS Crossroads Inn & Conference Center H
(970) 667-7810. **$130-$300.** 5542 E US Hwy 34 80537. I-25 exit 257B, just w. Ext/int corridors. **Pets:** Accepted.

Candlewood Suites H
(970) 667-5444. **Call for rates.** 6046 E Crossroads Blvd 80538. I-25 exit 259, just e. Int corridors. **Pets:** Medium, dogs only. $50 one-time fee/room. Service with restrictions.

Embassy Suites Loveland H
(970) 593-6200. **$159-$199.** 4705 Clydesdale Pkwy 80538. I-25 exit 259, just e, then just n. Int corridors. **Pets:** Accepted.

MANCOS

Mesa Verde Motel M
(970) 533-7741. **$55-$108, 3 day notice.** 191 W Railroad Ave 81328. On US 160 at SR 184; 7 mi e of Mesa Verde National Park entrance. Ext corridors. **Pets:** Other species. $5 daily fee/pet. Designated rooms, service with restrictions.

MANITOU SPRINGS

Silver Saddle Motel M
(719) 685-5611. **Call for rates.** 215 Manitou Ave 80829. I-25 exit 141, 4 mi w on US 24, then just sw on US 24 business route. Ext corridors. **Pets:** Accepted.

MESA VERDE NATIONAL PARK

Far View Lodge M
(970) 529-4422. **$99-$149, 3 day notice.** 34879 Hwy 160 81328. 14 mi from park gate at MM 15. Ext corridors. **Pets:** Accepted.

MONTE VISTA

BEST WESTERN Movie Manor H
(719) 852-5921. **$80-$150.** 2830 Hwy 160 W 81144. 2 mi w of center. Ext corridors. **Pets:** Accepted.

MONTROSE

Days Inn M
(970) 249-4507. **$55-$230.** 1417 E Main St 81401. 0.8 mi e on US 50. Ext corridors. **Pets:** Accepted.

Hampton Inn H
(970) 252-3300. **$114-$189.** 1980 N Townsend Ave 81401. 1.5 mi n on US 550. Int corridors. **Pets:** Accepted.

Holiday Inn Express & Suites H
(970) 240-1800. **Call for rates.** 1391 S Townsend Ave 81401. 1 mi s on US 550. Int corridors. **Pets:** Accepted.

Super 8 H
(970) 240-8200. **$55-$100.** 1705 E Main St 81401. 1 mi e on US 50. Int corridors. **Pets:** Dogs only. Designated rooms, service with restrictions, supervision.

NEW CASTLE

Econo Lodge Inn & Suites H
(970) 984-2363. **$70-$180.** 781 Burning Mountain Ave 81647. I-70 exit 105, just n, then w. Int corridors. **Pets:** Accepted.

OURAY

Comfort Inn M
(970) 325-7203. **$75-$210.** 191 5th Ave 81427. Just w of US 550 (Main St) via 5th Ave. Ext corridors. **Pets:** Accepted.

Ouray Riverside Inn & Cabins M
(970) 325-4061. **Call for rates.** 1804 N Main St 81427. 1 mi n of center on US 550 (Main St). Ext corridors. **Pets:** Accepted.

Ouray Victorian Inn M
(970) 325-7222. **Call for rates.** 50 3rd Ave 81427. Just w of US 550 (Main St) to 3rd Ave. Ext corridors. **Pets:** Dogs only. $10 daily fee/pet. Designated rooms, service with restrictions, supervision.

PAGOSA SPRINGS

Alpine Inn of Pagosa Springs M
(970) 731-4005. **Call for rates.** 8 Solomon Dr 81147. 2.5 mi w of downtown to Piedra Rd, just n. Ext/int corridors. **Pets:** Accepted.

▼▼ Fireside Inn Cabins 🅲🅰 ❄️
(970) 264-9204. **Call for rates.** 1600 E Hwy 160 81147. 1.3 mi e of downtown. Ext corridors. **Pets:** Dogs only. $12 daily fee/pet. No service, supervision. 🍴 🛜 ✖️ 🕸️ 🛢️ 💻

▼▼ High Country Lodge & Cabins 🄼 ❄️
(970) 264-4181. **$89-$210.** 3821 E Hwy 160 81147. 3 mi e of downtown. Ext corridors. **Pets:** Medium, dogs only. $50 deposit/pet, $20 daily fee/pet. Designated rooms, service with restrictions, supervision.
🖂 🛜 ✖️ 🛢️ 💻

▼▼ Mountain Landing Suites & R.V. Park 🄼 ❄️
(970) 731-5345. **$74-$185, 14 day notice.** 345 Piedra Rd 81147. 2.5 mi w of downtown to Piedra Rd, 0.5 mi n. Ext corridors. **Pets:** Medium, dogs only. $10 daily fee/pet. Designated rooms, no service, supervision.
🍴 🛜 ✖️ 🛢️ 💻

PALISADE
🅐🅐🅐 ▼▼▼ Wine Country Inn 🄷
(970) 464-5777. **$104-$429.** 777 Grande River Dr 81526. I-70 exit 42, 0.3 mi w. Int corridors. **Pets:** Accepted.
🆂🅰🆅🅴 🍴 🛜 🏊 🛜 ✖️ 🛢️ 💻

PARACHUTE
▼▼ Candlewood Suites 🄷
(970) 285-9880. **Call for rates.** 233 Grand Valley Way 81635. I-70 exit 75, just se. Int corridors. **Pets:** Large, other species. $25 one-time fee/room. Service with restrictions. 🛜 🛢️ 💻

▼▼ Comfort Inn & Suites 🄷
(970) 285-1122. **$89-$109.** 228 Railroad Ave 81635. I-70 exit 75, just nw. Int corridors. **Pets:** Accepted. 🏊 🛜 🛢️ 💻

▼▼ Days Inn & Suites 🄷
(970) 285-2330. **Call for rates.** 221 Grand Valley Way 81635. I-70 exit 25, just se. Int corridors. **Pets:** Accepted. 🏊 🛜 🛢️ 💻

PARKER
▼▼▼ Holiday Inn 🄷
(303) 248-2147. **Call for rates.** 19308 Cottonwood Dr 80138. SR 470 (toll road) exit 5 (Parker Rd/SR 83) eastbound, straight at light, follow signs to Cottonwood Dr; exit westbound, just s to Crown Crest Blvd, follow signs to Cottonwood Dr. Int corridors. **Pets:** Accepted.
🍴 🏊 🛜 ✖️ 🛢️ 💻

PUEBLO *(Restaurants p. 622)*
▼▼▼ Holiday Inn Express & Suites 🄷
(719) 542-8888. **Call for rates.** 4530 Dillon Dr 81008. I-25 exit 102, just e, then just s. Int corridors. **Pets:** Accepted.
🍴 🏊 🏊 🛜 ✖️ 🛢️ 💻

▼▼ La Quinta Inn & Suites Pueblo 🄷
(719) 542-3500. **$82-$249.** 4801 N Elizabeth St 81008. I-25 exit 102, just w, then 0.3 mi n. Int corridors. **Pets:** Large, other species. Service with restrictions. 🏊 🛜 🛢️ 💻

▼▼ Microtel Inn & Suites by Wyndham Pueblo 🄷
(719) 242-2020. **$55-$105.** 3343 Gateway Dr 81004. I-25 exit 94, just w, then just s. Int corridors. **Pets:** Accepted. 🍴 🛜 🛢️ 💻

RIFLE
▼▼▼ Comfort Inn & Suites 🄷
(970) 625-9912. **$75-$129.** 301 S 7th St 81650. I-70 exit 90, just s, then just w. Int corridors. **Pets:** Accepted.
🏊 🟑 🛜 ✖️ 🛢️ 💻

▼▼▼ Hampton Inn & Suites 🄷
(970) 625-1500. **$79-$189.** 499 Airport Rd 81650. I-70 exit 90, just s, then just e. Int corridors. **Pets:** Accepted. 🏊 🛜 ✖️ 🛢️ 💻

▼▼ La Quinta Inn & Suites Rifle 🄷
(970) 625-2676. **$74-$223.** 600 Wapiti Ct 81650. I-70 exit 90, just s, then just e. Int corridors. **Pets:** Large, other species. Service with restrictions. 🏊 🛜 ✖️ 🛢️ 💻

SALIDA
▼▼▼ Chalets at Tudor Rose 🅲🅰
(719) 539-2002. **$185-$265, 30 day notice.** 6720 CR 104 81201. East end of US 50, just s on CR 104, then 0.5 mi up the hill. Ext corridors. **Pets:** Accepted. 🍴 🏊 🛜 ✖️ 🛢️ 💻

🅐🅐🅐 ▼▼ Woodland Motel 🄼 ❄️
(719) 539-4980. **$54-$155.** 903 W 1st St 81201. 0.5 mi nw on 1st St (SR 291); nw of historic downtown. Ext corridors. **Pets:** Other species.
🆂🅰🆅🅴 🛜 ✖️ 🛢️ 💻

SILT
▼▼▼ Holiday Inn Express & Suites 🄷
(970) 876-5100. **Call for rates.** 1535 River Frontage Rd 81652. I-70 exit 97, just s, then just e. Int corridors. **Pets:** Accepted.
🍴 🏊 🛜 ✖️ 🛢️ 💻

SILVERTON
🅐🅐🅐 ▼▼ Inn of the Rockies at the Historic Alma House 🅱🅱
(970) 387-5336. **Call for rates.** 220 E 10th St 81433. Just se of 10th and Main sts. Int corridors. **Pets:** Accepted. 🆂🅰🆅🅴 🛜 ✖️ 🕸️ 🈯

▼▼ Villa Dallavalle Bed & Breakfast 🅱🅱
(970) 387-5555. **$109-$125, 3 day notice.** 1257 Blair St 81433. Corner of 13th and Blair sts. Int corridors. **Pets:** Accepted. 🛜 ✖️ 🕸️ 🈯

▼▼ The Wyman Hotel & Inn 🅱🅱
(970) 387-5372. **Call for rates.** 1371 Greene St 81433. Corner of 14th and Main sts. Int corridors. **Pets:** Accepted. 🛜 ✖️ 🕸️ 🛢️ 💻

SNOWMASS VILLAGE
▼▼▼▼ Viceroy Snowmass 🅲🅾
(970) 923-8000. **$225-$875, 45 day notice.** 130 Wood Rd 81615. 6 mi sw of SR 82 via Brush Creek Rd, then 0.3 mi to lower Carriage Way. Int corridors. **Pets:** Accepted. 🍴 🏊 🖂 🛜 ✖️ 🛢️ 💻

🅐🅐🅐 ▼▼▼ The Westin Snowmass Resort 🄷
(970) 923-8200. **$99-$809, 3 day notice.** 100 Elbert Ln 81615. 2.4 mi sw of SR 82 via Brush Creek Rd, 2nd exit at roundabout, then 3 mi to Elbert Ln; Lot 8. Int corridors. **Pets:** Accepted.
🆂🅰🆅🅴 🍴 🏊 🖂 🛜 ✖️ 🛢️ 💻

SOUTH FORK
▼▼ Ute Bluff Lodge & Cabins 🄼
(719) 873-5595. **$57-$77, 3 day notice.** 27680 W Hwy 160 81154. 2.7 mi e of jct US 160 and SR 149. Ext corridors. **Pets:** Accepted.
🍴 🛜 ✖️ 🕸️ 🛢️ 💻

STEAMBOAT SPRINGS
🅐🅐🅐 ▼▼▼ Fairfield Inn & Suites by Marriott 🄷
(970) 870-9000. **$139-$229.** 3200 S Lincoln Ave 80477. On US 40 (Lincoln Ave), 3.1 mi s of downtown; near Steamboat Ski Resort. Int corridors. **Pets:** Dogs only. $20 daily fee/room. Designated rooms, service with restrictions, supervision. 🆂🅰🆅🅴 🏊 🛜 ✖️ 🛢️ 💻

▼▼▼ Hampton Inn & Suites 🄷
(970) 871-8900. **$109-$259.** 725 S Lincoln Ave 80487. 1.1 mi e of center on US 40 (Lincoln Ave). Int corridors. **Pets:** Accepted.
🅼 🏊 🛜 ✖️ 🛢️ 💻

▼▼▼ Holiday Inn Steamboat Springs 🄷 ❄️
(970) 879-2250. **Call for rates.** 3190 S Lincoln Ave 80487. On US 40 (Lincoln Ave), 3 mi s of downtown. Int corridors. **Pets:** Dogs only. $35 daily fee/room. Designated rooms, service with restrictions, supervision.
🍴 🅼 🏊 🖂 🛜 ✖️ 🛢️ 💻

▼▼ ▼▼ **La Quinta Inn & Suites Steamboat Springs** H

(970) 871-1219. **$85-$209.** 3155 Ingles Ln 80487. On US 40 (Lincoln Ave), 3 mi s of downtown; near Steamboat Ski Resort. Int corridors. **Pets:** Large, other species. Service with restrictions.

🛏 📶 ✕ 🅿 💻

▼▼ ▼▼ **Nordic Lodge** M

(970) 879-0531. **Call for rates.** 1036 Lincoln Ave 80477. On US 40 (Lincoln Ave), just w of 10th St; downtown. Ext corridors. **Pets:** Accepted. 🛏 📶 ✕ 🅿

▼▼ ▼▼ **Rabbit Ears Motel** M

(970) 879-1150. **Call for rates.** 201 Lincoln Ave 80477. On US 40 (Lincoln Ave), just se of 3rd St; downtown. Ext corridors. **Pets:** Accepted.

📶 🅿 💻

◆◆◆ ▼▼▼▼ **Sheraton Steamboat Resort** H

(970) 879-2220. **$149-$599, 3 day notice.** 2200 Village Inn Ct 80487. 2.3 mi s from center on US 40 (Lincoln Ave) to Mt. Werner Rd exit, 0.8 mi e, 0.3 mi ne on Mt. Werner Cir, just ne at Ski Time Square, then just s. Int corridors. **Pets:** Accepted.

SAVE 🛏 🏊 ✕ 📶 ✕ 🅿 💻

STERLING

◆◆◆ ▼▼ ▼▼ **BEST WESTERN Sundowner** M ✿

(970) 522-6265. **$99-$148.** 125 Overland Trail St 80751. I-76 exit 125, just w. Ext/int corridors. **Pets:** Other species. $20 daily fee/room. Designated rooms, service with restrictions, supervision.

SAVE ✕ 🛏 🏊 📶 ✕ 🅿 💻

TELLURIDE

▼▼▼▼ **Fairmont Heritage Place, Franz Klammer Lodge** CO ✿

(970) 728-3318. **$350-$2400, 45 day notice.** 567 Mountain Village Blvd 81435. 2.3 mi e; in Mountain Village. Int corridors. **Pets:** Dogs only. $20 daily fee/room. Designated rooms, supervision.

ECO 🛏 🏊 📶 ✕ 🅰 🅿 💻

◆◆◆ ▼▼▼▼ **Hotel Columbia** H ✿

(970) 728-0660. **Call for rates.** 301 W San Juan Ave 81435. At Aspen St and San Juan Ave; opposite gondola. Int corridors. **Pets:** Dogs only. $25 daily fee/pet. Designated rooms, service with restrictions.

SAVE ✕ 📶 ✕ 🅿 💻

◆◆◆ ▼▼▼ ▼▼▼ **Hotel Madeline Telluride** H

(970) 879-0880. **Call for rates.** 568 Mountain Village Blvd 81435. 2.2 mi e; in Mountain Village. Int corridors. **Pets:** Accepted.

SAVE ✕ 🛏 🏊 📶 ✕ 🅿 💻

▼▼▼▼ **The Hotel Telluride** H

(970) 369-1188. **Call for rates.** 199 N Cornet St 81435. Just s of roundabout, then just e. Int corridors. **Pets:** Accepted.

✕ 🅰 🏊 📶 ✕ 🅿 💻

▼▼▼ **Ice House Lodge & Condominiums** H

(970) 728-6300. **Call for rates.** 310 S Fir St 81435. Just s of SR 145 (Colorado Ave); end of Fir St. Int corridors. **Pets:** Accepted.

🛏 🏊 📶 ✕ 🅰 🅿 💻

▼▼▼▼ **The Peaks, A Grand Heritage Resort & Spa** H

(970) 728-6800. **Call for rates.** 136 Country Club Dr 81435. 2.5 mi e; in Mountain Village. Int corridors. **Pets:** Medium, dogs only. $75 one-time fee/pet. Designated rooms, service with restrictions.

✕ 🏊 📶 ✕ 🅰 🅿 💻

THORNTON

▼▼▼ **Holiday Inn Express Hotel & Suites - Denver North/Thornton** H

(303) 452-0800. **$119-$239.** 12030 Grant St 80241. Int corridors. **Pets:** Medium, other species. $150 deposit/room, $25 daily fee/pet. Designated rooms, service with restrictions, supervision.

✕ 🅰 🛏 📶 ✕ 🅿 💻

TRINIDAD

◆◆◆ ▼▼ ▼▼ **Days Inn & Suites Trinidad** M

(719) 846-2215. **$60-$110.** 900 W Adams St 81082. I-25 exit 13A northbound; exit 13B southbound, just e to Santa Fe Tr, then 0.3 mi s. Ext corridors. **Pets:** Medium. $10 daily fee/pet. Designated rooms, service with restrictions, supervision. SAVE ✕ 🛏 📶 🅿 💻

▼▼▼▼ **Holiday Inn & Suites** H

(719) 845-8400. **Call for rates.** 3130 Santa Fe Trail Dr 81082. I-25 exit 11 (Starkville), just e, then just n. Int corridors. **Pets:** Medium, other species. $20 one-time fee/pet. Designated rooms, service with restrictions. ✕ 🅰 🛏 📶 ✕ 🅿 💻

▼▼▼▼ **La Quinta Inn & Suites Trinidad** H

(719) 845-0102. **$89-$241.** 2833 Toupal Dr 81082. I-25 exit 11 (Starkville), just w, then n. Int corridors. **Pets:** Large, other species. Service with restrictions. ✕ 🛏 ✕ 📶 🅿 💻

VAIL *(Restaurants p. 622)*

◆◆◆ ▼▼▼ ▼▼▼ ▼▼▼ **The Arrabelle at Vail Square, A RockResort** H

(970) 754-7750. **Call for rates.** 675 Lionshead Pl 81657. I-70 exit 176, just s to roundabout, 1 mi w on Frontage Rd to W Lionshead Cir, continue just s past No Outlet sign. Int corridors. **Pets:** Accepted.

SAVE ✕ 🛏 ✕ 📶 ✕ 🅿 💻

▼▼▼ ▼▼▼ **Evergreen Lodge at Vail** H

(970) 476-7810. **$99-$570, 30 day notice.** 250 S Frontage Rd W 81657. I-70 exit 176, just s, then just w. Int corridors. **Pets:** Accepted.

✕ 🛏 ✕ 📶 ✕ 🅰 🅿 💻

◆◆◆ ▼▼▼ ▼▼▼ **Four Seasons Resort & Residences Vail** H ✿

(970) 477-8600. **Call for rates.** One Vail Rd 81657. I-70 exit 176, just s, then just w of roundabout. Int corridors. **Pets:** Small, dogs only. Service with restrictions, supervision.

SAVE ✕ 🏊 ✕ 📶 ✕ 🅿 💻

▼▼▼ ▼▼▼ **Holiday Inn Apex Vail** H

(970) 476-2739. **Call for rates.** 2211 N Frontage Rd 81657. I-70 exit 173, just n to roundabout, then 0.3 mi e. Int corridors. **Pets:** Accepted.

✕ 🛏 ✕ 📶 ✕ 🅿 💻

▼▼▼ ▼▼▼ **The Lodge at Vail, A RockResort & Spa** H

(970) 754-7800. **Call for rates.** 174 E Gore Creek Dr 81657. I-70 exit 176, 0.3 mi s on Vail Rd to Gore Creek Dr. Ext/int corridors. **Pets:** Accepted. ✕ 🛏 ✕ 📶 ✕ 🅿 💻

◆◆◆ ▼▼▼ ▼▼▼ **The Sebastian- Vail** H ✿

(970) 315-4214. **$295-$6250, 31 day notice.** 16 Vail Rd 81657. I-70 exit 176, just s, take 2nd exit at roundabout, then just s. Int corridors. **Pets:** Large, dogs only. $150 one-time fee/room. Designated rooms, service with restrictions, supervision.

SAVE ✕ 🅰 🛏 ✕ 📶 ✕ 🅿 💻

▼▼▼ ▼▼▼ **Sonnenalp Hotel** H

(970) 476-5656. **Call for rates.** 20 Vail Rd 81657. I-70 exit 176, just s, take 2nd exit at the roundabout, then just s. Int corridors. **Pets:** Accepted. ECO ✕ 🛏 ✕ 📶

◆◆◆ ▼▼▼ ▼▼▼ **Vail Cascade Resort & Spa** H

(970) 476-7111. **Call for rates.** 1300 Westhaven Dr 81657. I-70 exit 176, 1.3 mi w via S Frontage Rd; 1 mi e of exit 173. Int corridors. **Pets:** Accepted. SAVE ✕ 🅰 🛏 ✕ 📶 ✕ 🅿 💻

WALSENBURG

◆◆◆ ▼▼ ▼▼ **BEST WESTERN Rambler** M ✿

(719) 738-1121. **$72-$106.** 457 US Hwy 85-87 81089. I-25 exit 52, just w. Ext/int corridors. **Pets:** Large, other species. $10 daily fee/pet. Designated rooms, service with restrictions, supervision.

SAVE ✕ 🛏 📶 ✕ 🅿 💻

WESTMINSTER

▼▼▼ Drury Inn & Suites 🅷
(303) 460-1220. **$100-$199.** 10393 Reed St 80021. US 36 (Boulder Tpke) exit Church Ranch Blvd W, just s, then just e. Int corridors. **Pets:** $10 daily fee/room. Service with restrictions, supervision.
🍽 ♿ 📶 ✕ 📦 💻

▼▼▼ Residence Inn by Marriott 🅷
(303) 427-9500. **$108-$189.** 5010 W 88th Pl 80031. US 36 (Boulder Tpke) exit Sheridan Blvd, n to 92nd Ave, e to Yates Dr, then s. Int corridors. **Pets:** Accepted. ♿ 🛋 📶 ✕ 📦 💻

AAA ▼▼▼ The Westin Westminster 🅷
(303) 410-5000. **$99-$389.** 10600 Westminster Blvd 80020. US 36 (Boulder Tpke) exit 104th Ave, just n. Int corridors. **Pets:** Accepted.
🆂 🍽 ♿ 🛋 ✕ 📶 ✕ 📦 💻

WINTER PARK

▼▼ Americas Best Value Inn Sundowner Motel 🅼
(970) 726-9451. **Call for rates.** 78869 US Hwy 40 80482. Downtown. Ext corridors. **Pets:** Accepted. 🛋 📶 ✕ 📦 💻

AAA ▼▼▼ BEST WESTERN Alpenglo Lodge 🅷
(970) 726-8088. **Call for rates.** 78665 US Hwy 40 80482. 0.3 mi n of center. Int corridors. **Pets:** $10 daily fee/pet. Designated rooms.
🆂 ♿ 📶 ✕ 📦 💻

WOODLAND PARK

▼▼▼ Bristlecone Lodge 🅲🅰
(719) 687-9518. **$105-$150, 30 day notice.** 510 N Hwy 67 80863. 0.5 mi n. Ext corridors. **Pets:** Accepted.
🍽 📶 ✕ ♿ 🛋 📦 💻

AAA ▼▼▼ Woodland Country Lodge 🅷
(719) 687-6277. **$99-$189.** 723 US Hwy 24 W 80863. Just w of jct SR 67. Int corridors. **Pets:** $10 daily fee/pet. Designated rooms, service with restrictions, supervision. 🆂 🍽 ♿ 🛋 📶 ✕ 📦 💻

CONNECTICUT

AVON

▼▼ Avon Old Farms Hotel 🅷
(860) 677-1651. **$109-$259.** 279 Avon Mountain Rd 06001. Jct US 44 and SR 10. Ext/int corridors. **Pets:** Other species. $20 daily fee/room. Designated rooms, service with restrictions, crate.
🍽 🛋 📶 ✕ 📦 💻

▼▼▼ Residence Inn by Marriott Hartford-Avon 🅷
(860) 678-1666. **$139-$229.** 55 Simsbury Rd (US 202 & SR 10) 06001. Jct US 44, just n. Int corridors. **Pets:** $100 one-time fee/room. Service with restrictions, crate. 🍽 ♿ 🛋 📶 ✕ 📦 💻

BETHEL

▼▼ Microtel Inn & Suites by Wyndham Bethel 🅷
(203) 748-8318. **$74-$99.** 80 Benedict Rd 06801. I-84 exit 8, 1 mi e on US 6. Int corridors. **Pets:** Medium. $150 deposit/pet, $11 daily fee/pet. Service with restrictions, supervision. ♿ 📶 ✕ 📦 💻

BRIDGEPORT

▼▼▼ Bridgeport Holiday Inn & Convention Center 🅷
(203) 334-1234. **$119-$189.** 1070 Main St 06604. SR 8 exit 2 northbound, 0.7 mi se; exit southbound, just s, then just e. Int corridors. **Pets:** Accepted. 🍽 ♿ 🛋 📶 📦 💻

BROOKFIELD

▼▼ Newbury Inn 🅼
(203) 775-0220. **$89-$129, 3 day notice.** 1030 Federal Rd 06804. Jct SR 25, 0.9 mi nw. Ext/int corridors. **Pets:** Large. $150 deposit/pet, $10 daily fee/pet. Service with restrictions, supervision. 📶 ✕ 📦 💻

CROMWELL

AAA ▼▼▼ Crowne Plaza Hartford-Cromwell 🅷
(860) 635-2000. **$109-$189.** 100 Berlin Rd 06416. I-91 exit 21, just e on SR 372. Int corridors. **Pets:** Accepted.
🆂 🅴🅲🅾 🍽 ♿ 🛋 ✕ 📶 ✕ 📦 💻

DANBURY

▼▼▼ Ethan Allen Hotel 🅷
(203) 744-1776. **$109-$209.** 21 Lake Ave Ext 06811. I-84 exit 4, 0.3 mi w on US 6 and 202. Int corridors. **Pets:** $50 daily fee/pet. Designated rooms, service with restrictions, supervision.
🅴🅲🅾 🍽 🛋 📶 ✕ 📦 💻

▼▼▼ Holiday Inn Express & Suites Danbury - I-84 🅷
(203) 205-0800. **$99-$169.** 89 Mill Plain Rd 06811. I-84 exit 2 eastbound; exit 2B westbound, just n, then just e. Int corridors. **Pets:** Medium, other species. $25 daily fee/pet. Designated rooms, service with restrictions, supervision. ♿ 🛋 📶 ✕ 📦 💻

AAA ▼▼▼ La Quinta Inn & Suites 🅷
(203) 798-1200. **$85-$235.** 116 Newtown Rd 06810. I-84 exit 8 (Newtown Rd), just sw. Int corridors. **Pets:** Large, other species. Service with restrictions. 🆂 🍴 🍽 🛋 📶 ✕ 📦 💻

AAA ▼▼▼ Maron Hotel & Suites 🅷
(203) 791-2200. **$99-$199.** 42 Lake Ave Ext 06811. I-84 exit 4, 0.5 mi w on US 6 and 202. Int corridors. **Pets:** Medium. $25 daily fee/room. Designated rooms, service with restrictions, supervision.
🆂 🍽 ♿ 📶 📦 💻

AAA ▼▼▼ Quality Inn & Suites 🅷
(203) 743-6701. **$81-$119.** 78 Federal Rd 06810. I-84 exit 7 (US 7 N), 0.5 mi n to exit 11 (Federal Rd), 0.8 mi s on White Turkey Rd, then just w. Int corridors. **Pets:** Accepted. 🆂 🛋 📶 📦 💻

▼▼▼ Residence Inn by Marriott Danbury 🅷
(203) 797-1256. **$153-$252.** 22 Segar St 06810. I-84 exit 4 eastbound, just n; exit westbound, just e on Lake Ave Ext, then just s. Int corridors. **Pets:** Accepted. 🅴🅲🅾 🛋 📶 ✕ 📦 💻

DAYVILLE

▼▼▼ Comfort Inn & Suites 🅷 🐾
(860) 779-3200. **$131-$159.** 16 Tracy Rd 06241. I-395 exit 94, just w. Int corridors. **Pets:** Other species. $15 daily fee/pet. Designated rooms, service with restrictions, crate. ♿ 🛋 📶 📦 💻

ENFIELD

▼▼▼ Holiday Inn Springfield-Enfield 🅷
(860) 741-2211. **$109-$159.** 1 Bright Meadow Blvd 06082. I-91 exit 49, just e on service road. Int corridors. **Pets:** Medium, dogs only. $50 one-time fee/room. Designated rooms, service with restrictions, supervision.
🍽 ♿ 🛋 ✕ 📶 📦 💻

FAIRFIELD

AAA ▼▼▼ BEST WESTERN PLUS Black Rock Inn 🅷
(203) 659-2200. **$139-$169.** 100 Kings Hwy Cutoff 06824. I-95 exit 24, just sw. Int corridors. **Pets:** Large, dogs only. $20 daily fee/pet. Designated rooms, supervision. 🆂 ♿ 📶 ✕ 📦 💻

FARMINGTON

▼▼ Extended Stay America Hartford-Farmington 🅷
(860) 676-2790. **Call for rates.** 1 Batterson Park Rd 06032. I-84 exit 37, just ne. Int corridors. **Pets:** Other species. $25 daily fee/pet. Service with restrictions, supervision. 🔊 🛜 🛢 💻

▼▼▼ The Farmington Inn 🅷
(860) 269-3401. **$109-$199.** 827 Farmington Ave 06032. I-84 exit 39, 1.8 mi w on SR 4. Int corridors. **Pets:** Medium. $100 deposit/room, $20 daily fee/pet. Designated rooms, service with restrictions, crate. 🛜 🛢 💻

▼▼▼ Homewood Suites by Hilton
Hartford-Farmington 🅷
(860) 321-0000. **$119-$209.** 2 Farm Glen Blvd 06032. I-84 exit 39, 0.6 mi e on SR 4. Int corridors. **Pets:** Large, other species. $75 one-time fee/room. Service with restrictions. 🍴 🔊 🏊 🛜 🛢 💻

GLASTONBURY

🅰 ▼▼▼ Homewood Suites by Hilton Hartford
South/Glastonbury 🅷
(860) 652-8111. **$99-$229.** 65 Glastonbury Blvd 06033. SR 3 exit Main St, just se. Int corridors. **Pets:** Accepted.
SAVE 🔊 🏊 🛜 🛢 💻

GREENWICH

▼▼▼▼ The Stanton House Inn 🅱🅱
(203) 869-2110. **$189-$259, 7 day notice.** 76 Maple Ave 06830. Just n of US 1; center. Ext/int corridors. **Pets:** Accepted.
🍴 🏊 🛜 ✖ 🛢

GRISWOLD

▼▼ AmericInn Lodge & Suites of Griswold 🅷
(860) 376-3200. **$89-$219.** 375 Voluntown Rd 06351. I-395 exit 85, w on SR 138. Int corridors. **Pets:** Other species. $40 one-time fee/room. Designated rooms, service with restrictions, crate.
🍴 🔊 🏊 🛜 🛢 💻

HAMDEN

▼▼▼ Clarion Hotel & Suites Hamden-New Haven 🅷
(203) 288-3831. **$119-$149.** 2260 Whitney Ave 06518. SR 15 exit 61, just n. Int corridors. **Pets:** Accepted. 🔊 🏊 🛜 ✖ 🛢 💻

HARTFORD *(Restaurants p. 622)*

▼▼▼ The Hilton Hartford Hotel 🅷 ❀
(860) 728-5151. **$129-$339.** 315 Trumbull St 06103. Downtown. Int corridors. **Pets:** Large, other species. $75 one-time fee/room. Designated rooms, service with restrictions, crate.
ECO 🍴 🔊 🏊 ✖ 🛜 🛢 💻

▼▼▼ Homewood Suites by Hilton Hartford
Downtown 🅷
(860) 524-0223. **$169-$339.** 338 Asylum St 06103. Between Ann and High sts; downtown. Int corridors. **Pets:** Accepted. 🔊 🛜 🛢 💻

▼▼▼ Marriott Residence Inn - Downtown
Hartford 🅷 ❀
(860) 524-5550. **$230-$378.** 942 Main St 06103. I-91 exit 29A northbound; exit 31 southbound. Int corridors. **Pets:** $100 one-time fee/pet.
ECO 🛜 ✖ 🛢 💻

▼▼▼ Radisson Hotel Hartford 🅷
(860) 549-2400. **$83-$219.** 50 Morgan St 06120. I-91 exit 32B; I-84 exit 50 eastbound; exit 52 westbound. Int corridors. **Pets:** Accepted.
🍴 🔊 🏊 🛜 ✖ 🛢 💻

IVORYTON

▼▼▼ The Copper Beech Inn 🅲🅸
(860) 767-0330. **Call for rates.** 46 Main St 06442. SR 9 exit 3, 1.7 mi w. Int corridors. **Pets:** Accepted. 🍴 🛜 ✖ 🛢 🛢

LAKEVILLE

▼▼▼ Interlaken Inn Resort and Conference Center 🅷
(860) 435-9878. **$229-$309, 7 day notice.** 74 Interlaken Rd 06039. On SR 112, 0.5 mi w of jct SR 41. Ext/int corridors. **Pets:** Dogs only. $25 daily fee/room. Designated rooms, service with restrictions, supervision.
ECO 🍴 🏊 ✖ 🛜 ✖ 🛢 💻

LEDYARD

▼▼ Almost In Mystic/Mares Inn 🅱🅱
(860) 572-7556. **$125-$225, 14 day notice.** 333 Colonel Ledyard Hwy 06339. I-95 exit 89, 1 mi ne to Gold Star Hwy, 0.6 mi w, then 0.7 mi n. Int corridors. **Pets:** Accepted. 🍴 🛜 ✖ 🛢 🛢 💻

LITCHFIELD

▼▼▼ Litchfield Inn 🅷
(860) 567-4503. **Call for rates.** 432 Bantam Rd 06759. 1.5 mi w on US 202. Int corridors. **Pets:** $25 daily fee/pet. Designated rooms, service with restrictions, supervision. 🍴 🛜 ✖ 🛢 💻

MANCHESTER *(Restaurants p. 622)*

▼▼ Extended Stay America Hartford-Manchester 🅷
(860) 643-5140. **Call for rates.** 340 Tolland Tpke 06040. I-84 exit 63, 0.3 mi se on SR 30, then just sw. Int corridors. **Pets:** Other species. $25 daily fee/pet. Service with restrictions, supervision.
🍴 🔊 🛜 🛢 💻

▼▼▼ Residence Inn by Marriott
Hartford/Manchester 🅷
(860) 432-4242. **$153-$252.** 201 Hale Rd 06042. I-84 exit 63, 0.5 mi nw, then 0.6 mi sw. Int corridors. **Pets:** Accepted.
🔊 🏊 🛜 ✖ 🛢 💻

MASHANTUCKET

▼▼▼ Two Trees Inn at Foxwoods Resort
Casino 🅷 ❀
(860) 312-3000. **Call for rates.** 240 Indiantown Rd 06339. Jct SR 214 and 2. Int corridors. **Pets:** Other species. $40 daily fee/pet. Designated rooms. 🍴 🔊 🏊 ✖ 🛜 🛢 💻

MERIDEN

▼▼ Extended Stay America Hartford-Meriden 🅷
(203) 630-1927. **Call for rates.** 366 Bee St 06450. I-91 exit 17 northbound, just e on E Main St, then 0.7 mi n; exit 19 southbound, 0.5 mi w on Baldwin Ave, then 0.6 mi s. Int corridors. **Pets:** Other species. $25 daily fee/pet. Service with restrictions, supervision.
🍴 🔊 🛢 💻

🅰 ▼▼▼ Four Points by Sheraton Meriden 🅷
(203) 238-2380. **$89-$235.** 275 Research Pkwy 06450. I-91 exit 17 southbound; exit 16 northbound, 0.5 mi e, then 0.5 mi s. Int corridors. **Pets:** Accepted. SAVE 🍴 🔊 🏊 🛜 ✖ 🛢 💻

🅰 ▼▼▼ Hawthorn Suites by Wyndham 🅷
(203) 379-5048. **$94-$99.** 1151 E Main St 06450. I-91 exit 17 southbound; exit 16 northbound, just n. Int corridors. **Pets:** Accepted.
SAVE 🔊 🛜 🛢 💻

MILFORD

🅰 ▼▼▼ Hyatt Place Milford 🅷
(203) 877-9800. **$89-$329.** 190 Old Gate Ln 06460. I-95 exit 40, 0.4 mi s. Int corridors. **Pets:** Accepted. SAVE 🍴 🔊 🛜 ✖ 🛢 💻

🅰 ▼ Red Roof Inn Milford 🅼
(203) 877-6060. **Call for rates.** 10 Rowe Ave 06460. I-95 exit 35, just nw. Ext corridors. **Pets:** Large, other species. Service with restrictions, supervision. SAVE 🍴 🛜 ✖ 🛢 💻

▼▼▼ Residence Inn by Marriott Milford 🅷
(203) 283-2100. **$118-$206.** 62 Rowe Ave 06460. I-95 exit 35, just nw. Int corridors. **Pets:** Accepted. 🍴 🔊 🏊 🛜 ✖ 🛢 💻

MORRIS

◇◇◇ ▼▼▼▼▼▼ Winvian **H** ❀
(860) 567-9600. **Call for rates.** 155 Alain White Rd 06763. Jct SR 109, 1 mi n. Ext/int corridors. **Pets:** Dogs only. $75 daily fee/pet. Designated rooms, service with restrictions. 🏧 🍴 ⊠ 📶 ✕ 🛄 🖥

MYSTIC *(Restaurants p. 622)*

▼▼▼▼▼▼ Hampton Inn & Suites/Mystic **H** ❀
(860) 536-2536. **$109-$239.** 6 Hendel Dr 06355. I-95 exit 90, just s. Int corridors. **Pets:** Other species. Service with restrictions.
🅴🅲🅾 🔥ᴹ ⊇ 📶 🛄 🖥

▼▼▼▼▼▼ Hyatt Place Mystic **H**
(860) 536-9997. **$79-$279.** 224 Greenmanville Ave 06355. I-95 exit 90, just se. Int corridors. **Pets:** Accepted.
🏧 🍴 🔥ᴹ ⊇ 📶 ✕ 🛄 🖥

▼▼▼▼▼▼ Residence Inn by Marriott **H**
(860) 536-5150. **$125-$263.** 40 Whitehall Ave 06355. I-95 exit 90, just n on SR 27. Int corridors. **Pets:** Other species. $100 one-time fee/room. Service with restrictions. 🅴🅲🅾 🍴 ⊇ ⊠ 📶 ✕ 🛄 🖥

NAUGATUCK

▼▼▼▼▼▼ Comfort Inn Naugatuck **H**
(203) 723-9356. **$89-$99.** 716 New Haven Rd 06770. Jct SR 63 and 8, 0.8 mi s. Int corridors. **Pets:** Other species. $25 daily fee/pet. Designated rooms, service with restrictions, supervision.
🔥ᴹ 📶 ✕ 🛄 🖥

NEW BRITAIN

▼▼ ▼▼ La Quinta Inn & Suites New
Britain/Farmington **H**
(860) 348-1463. **$72-$159.** 65 Columbus Blvd 06051. SR 9 exit 26 northbound; exit 27 southbound, just nw. Int corridors. **Pets:** Large, other species. Service with restrictions. 🍴 🔥ᴹ 📶 🛄 🖥

NEW HAVEN *(Restaurants p. 623)*

▼▼▼▼ Omni New Haven Hotel at Yale **H**
(203) 772-6664. **Call for rates.** 155 Temple St 06510. Between Chapel and Crown sts; downtown. Int corridors. **Pets:** Accepted.
🍴 🔥ᴹ 📶 ✕ 🛄 🖥

◇◇◇ ▼▼▼▼ Premiere Hotel & Suites **H**
(203) 777-5337. **$149-$239.** 3 Long Wharf Dr 06511. I-95 exit 46, 0.6 mi nw. Ext corridors. **Pets:** Accepted.
🏧 🅴🅲🅾 🍴 🔥ᴹ 📶 ✕ 🛄 🖥

NEW LONDON

◇◇◇ ▼ Red Roof Inn Mystic New London **M**
(860) 444-0001. **Call for rates.** 707 Colman St 06320. I-95 exit 82A northbound, 0.4 mi e, then just n; exit 83 southbound, 0.6 mi s. Ext corridors. **Pets:** Large, other species. Service with restrictions, supervision. 🏧 🍴 📶 ✕ 🛄 🖥

NEW MILFORD

▼▼ ▼▼ The Homestead Inn **BB**
(860) 354-4080. **$90-$265, 3 day notice.** 5 Elm St 06776. Jct US 202, just w. Ext/int corridors. **Pets:** Other species. Designated rooms, service with restrictions, crate. 📶 ✕ 🛄

NIANTIC

▼ Motel 6 - #1063 **M**
(860) 739-6991. **Call for rates.** 269 Flanders Rd 06357. I-95 exit 74, just s. Ext corridors. **Pets:** Other species. Service with restrictions, crate. 🍴 ⊇ 🍲 🛄

NORTH STONINGTON

▼▼▼▼ The Inn at Lower Farm B & B **BB**
(860) 535-9075. **Call for rates.** 119 Mystic Rd 06359. I-95 exit 90, 1.5 mi n on SR 27, 1.4 mi e on SR 184, then 3.4 mi n on SR 201. Int corridors. **Pets:** Accepted. 🍴 📶 ✕ 🅆 🅩

NORWALK

▼▼ ▼▼ Extended Stay America - Norwalk **H**
(203) 847-6888. **Call for rates.** 400 Main Ave 06851. I-95 exit 15, 3.5 mi n on US 7, just e, then 1 mi s. Int corridors. **Pets:** Other species. $25 daily fee/pet. Service with restrictions, supervision.
🍴 🍲 🛄 🖥

OLD GREENWICH

◇◇◇ ▼▼▼▼▼▼ Hyatt Regency Greenwich **H**
(203) 637-1234. **$89-$399.** 1800 E Putnam Ave 06870. I-95 exit 5, 0.5 mi n on US 1. Int corridors. **Pets:** Medium, dogs only. $100 one-time fee/room. Designated rooms, service with restrictions, crate.
🏧 🍴 🔥ᴹ ⊇ 🛄 🖥

OLD SAYBROOK

▼▼ Liberty Inn **M**
(860) 388-1777. **$58-$130.** 55 Spring Brook Rd 06475. I-95 exit 68 southbound; exit 67 northbound, 0.9 mi n on US 1, then w. Ext corridors. **Pets:** Accepted. 🍴 📶 🛄 🖥

◇◇◇ ▼▼▼ ▼▼▼ Saybrook Point Inn & Spa **H** ❀
(860) 395-2000. **$259-$799, 3 day notice.** 2 Bridge St 06475. On SR 154, 2.2 mi s of jct US 1; at Saybrook Point. Int corridors.
Pets: Medium, dogs only. $50 daily fee/room. Designated rooms, service with restrictions, supervision.
🏧 🅴🅲🅾 🍷 🍴 🔥ᴹ ⊇ ⊠ 📶 ✕ 🛄 🖥

PAWCATUCK

▼▼▼▼ La Quinta Inn & Suites **H**
(860) 599-2400. **$79-$439.** 349 Liberty St 06379. I-95 exit 92, 1 mi s on SR 2. Int corridors. **Pets:** Large, other species. Service with restrictions. 🍴 🔥ᴹ ⊇ 📶 ✕ 🛄 🖥

RIVERTON

▼▼▼▼ Old Riverton Inn **CI**
(860) 379-8678. **Call for rates.** 436 E River Rd (SR 20) 06065. Center. Int corridors. **Pets:** Dogs only. $20 daily fee/room. Designated rooms, service with restrictions, supervision. 📶 ✕ 🛄

ROCKY HILL

▼▼▼▼ Residence Inn by Marriott Hartford-Rocky
Hill **H** ❀
(860) 257-7500. **$146-$240.** 680 Cromwell Ave 06067. I-91 exit 23, 0.4 mi w on West St, then just n. Int corridors. **Pets:** Other species. $100 one-time fee/room. Service with restrictions.
🔥ᴹ ⊇ 📶 ✕ 🛄 🖥

◇◇◇ ▼▼▼▼ Sheraton Hartford South **H**
(860) 257-6000. **$129-$399.** 100 Capital Blvd 06067. I-91 exit 23, just e. Int corridors. **Pets:** Accepted.
🏧 🅴🅲🅾 🍴 🔥ᴹ ⊇ 🍲 ✕ 🛄 🖥

SHELTON

▼▼ ▼▼ Extended Stay America Shelton Connecticut **H**
(203) 926-6868. **Call for rates.** 945 Bridgeport Ave 06484. SR 8 exit 11, 0.5 mi w. Int corridors. **Pets:** Other species. $25 daily fee/pet. Service with restrictions, supervision. 🍴 🔥ᴹ 📶 🛄 🖥

▼▼▼▼ Hampton Inn Shelton **H**
(203) 925-5900. **$109-$169.** 695 Bridgeport Ave 06484. SR 8 exit 12, 0.3 mi w, then just s. Int corridors. **Pets:** Accepted.
🔥ᴹ ⊇ 📶 ✕ 🛄 🖥

◇◇◇ ▼▼▼▼ HYATT house Shelton **H**
(203) 225-0700. **$99-$349.** 830 Bridgeport Ave 06484. SR 8 exit 12, 0.7 mi sw. Int corridors. **Pets:** Accepted.
🏧 🍴 🔥ᴹ ⊇ 📶 ✕ 🛄 🖥

▼▼▼▼ Residence Inn by Marriott Shelton Fairfield
County **H**
(203) 926-9000. **$111-$183.** 1001 Bridgeport Ave 06484. SR 8 exit 11, 0.3 mi w. Ext corridors. **Pets:** Accepted.
🍴 🔥ᴹ ⊇ 📶 ✕ 🛄 🖥

SIMSBURY

◆◆◆ **The Simsbury Inn** [H]
(860) 651-5700. **$169-$329.** 397 Hopmeadow St 06070. On US 202/SR 10, 0.4 mi n of jct SR 185. Int corridors. **Pets:** Accepted.
🍴 ♿ 🏊 🏋 📶 ☒ ▣ ▭

SOUTHBURY

◆◆◆ **Cornucopia at Oldfield Bed and Breakfast** [BB]
(203) 267-6772. **Call for rates.** 782 Main St N 06488. I-84 exit 15, 1.5 mi n. Int corridors. **Pets:** Small, dogs only. $25 one-time fee/pet. Supervision. ECO 🍴 🏊 📶 ☒ ☎

◆◆◆ **Crowne Plaza Southbury** [H]
(203) 598-7600. **Call for rates.** 1284 Strongtown Rd 06488. I-84 exit 16, just n on SR 188. Int corridors. **Pets:** Accepted.
🍴 ♿ 🏊 🏋 📶 ▣ ▭

◆◆◆ **Heritage Hotel, Golf Spa & Conference Center** [H]
(203) 264-8200. **Call for rates.** 522 Heritage Rd 06488. I-84 exit 15, 0.4 mi n on SR 67, then 1 mi w. Int corridors. **Pets:** Accepted.
🍴 ♿ 🏊 🏋 📶 ☒ ▣ ▭

SOUTHINGTON

◆◆ **Days Inn** [H]
(860) 628-0921. **$72-$80.** 30 Laning St 06489. I-84 exit 32, just se. Int corridors. **Pets:** Accepted. 🍴 📶 ▣ ▭

◆◆◆ **Residence Inn by Marriott Southington** [H]
(860) 621-4440. **$129-$212.** 778 West St 06489. I-84 exit 31, just s. Int corridors. **Pets:** Accepted. ECO ♿ 🏊 📶 ☒ ▣ ▭

SOUTHPORT

◆◆◆◆ **Delamar Southport** [H] 🐾
(203) 259-2800. **$355.** 275 Old Post Rd 06890. I-95 exit 19, just e. Int corridors. **Pets:** Medium, dogs only. $50 daily fee/pet. Service with restrictions, supervision. 🍴 🏋 📶 ☒ ▭

STAMFORD *(Restaurants p. 623)*

AAA ◆◆ **Amsterdam Hotel - Greenwich/Stamford** [H]
(203) 327-4300. **$99-$299.** 19 Clarks Hill Ave 06902. I-95 exit 8 northbound, just n on Atlantic St, 0.6 mi ne on Tresser Blvd, then just s; exit southbound, just nw on Elm St, ne on Main St, then just s. Int corridors. **Pets:** $50 deposit/pet, $50 daily fee/pet. Designated rooms, service with restrictions, supervision. SAVE 🍴 ♿ 📶 ▣ ▭

AAA ◆◆◆ **Hilton Stamford Hotel & Executive Meeting Center** [H]
(203) 967-2222. **$119-$329.** 1 First Stamford Pl 06902. I-95 exit 7 northbound, just s on Greenwich Ave, then just w; exit 6 southbound, just s on West Ave, 0.3 mi w on Baxter Ave, just n on Fairfield Ave, then just e. Int corridors. **Pets:** Accepted.
SAVE 🍴 🏊 🏋 📶 ☒ ▣ ▭

AAA ◆◆◆ **Sheraton Stamford Hotel** [H] 🐾
(203) 358-8400. **$99-$349.** 700 E Main St 06901. I-95 exit 8 southbound, just n on Elm St; exit northbound, n on Atlantic St, 0.3 mi e on Tresser Blvd, then just n on Elm St; downtown. Int corridors. **Pets:** Service with restrictions, supervision. SAVE 🍴 🏊 📶 ☒ ▣ ▭

AAA ◆◆◆ **Stamford Marriott Hotel & Spa** [H]
(203) 357-9555. **$230-$424.** 243 Tresser Blvd 06901. I-95 exit 8, just n under viaduct, then n. Int corridors. **Pets:** Accepted.
SAVE 🍴 ♿ 🏊 📶 ☒ ▣ ▭

STONINGTON *(Restaurants p. 623)*

◆◆◆ **Another Second Penny Inn** [BB]
(860) 535-1710. **Call for rates.** 870 Pequot Tr 06378. I-95 exit 91, 0.8 mi s on SR 234. Int corridors. **Pets:** $25 one-time fee/pet. Designated rooms, service with restrictions, crate. 🍴 📶 ☒ ▣

STRATFORD

◆◆◆ **Homewood Suites by Hilton** [H]
(203) 377-3322. **$99-$220.** 6905 Main St 06614. SR 15 exit 53, just n. Int corridors. **Pets:** Accepted. 🍴 ♿ 🏊 📶 ▣ ▭

UNCASVILLE

AAA ◆◆◆ **Hyatt Place Mohegan Sun** [H]
(860) 383-1234. **$109-$429.** 2049 Norwich New London Tpke 06382. I-395 exit 79A, just e on SR 2A, then just s on SR 32. Int corridors. **Pets:** Accepted. SAVE 🍴 ♿ 🏊 📶 ☒ ▣ ▭

WALLINGFORD

◆◆◆ **Homewood Suites by Hilton New Haven/Wallingford** [H]
(203) 284-2600. **$119-$209.** 90 Miles Dr 06492. I-91 exit 15, just nw on SR 68, then just s. Int corridors. **Pets:** Accepted.
🍴 ♿ 🏊 📶 ▣ ▭

WATERFORD

◆ **Rodeway Inn at Crossroad** [M]
(860) 442-7227. **$56-$86.** 211 Parkway N 06385. I-95 exit 81 northbound, just nw; exit southbound, 0.6 mi w. Ext corridors. **Pets:** Accepted. 🍴 🏊 📶 ▣

WESTPORT *(Restaurants p. 623)*

◆◆◆ **The Westport Inn, an Ascend Hotel Collection Member** [H]
(203) 259-5236. **$139-$399.** 1595 Post Rd E 06880. I-95 exit 18 northbound, n to US 1, then 1.5 mi e; exit 19 southbound, 1 mi w. Ext/int corridors. **Pets:** Medium, other species. $50 one-time fee/pet. Designated rooms, service with restrictions, supervision.
🍴 🏊 📶 ☒ ▣ ▭

WETHERSFIELD

AAA ◆◆ **Comfort Inn** [H]
(860) 563-2311. **$79-$99.** 1330 Silas Deane Hwy 06109. I-91 exit 24, 0.4 mi n. Int corridors. **Pets:** Medium. $20 daily fee/pet. Service with restrictions, crate. SAVE ♿ 🏊 📶 ▣ ▭

WINDSOR

AAA ◆◆◆ **HYATT house Hartford North/Windsor** [H]
(860) 298-8000. **$99-$229.** 200 Corporate Dr 06095. I-91 exit 38 northbound; exit 38B southbound. Int corridors. **Pets:** Accepted.
SAVE 🍴 ♿ 🏊 📶 ☒ ▣ ▭

◆◆◆ **Residence Inn by Marriott Hartford-Windsor** [H]
(860) 688-7474. **$111-$183.** 100 Dunfey Ln 06095. I-91 exit 37, just w on SR 305 to Dunfey Ln, then 0.3 mi n. Ext corridors. **Pets:** Accepted.
🍴 ♿ 🏊 📶 ☒ ▣ ▭

WINDSOR LOCKS

◆◆◆ **Candlewood Suites** [H]
(860) 623-2000. **$99-$164.** 149 Ella T Grasso Tpke 06096. I-91 exit 40, 2.5 mi w on SR 20, then 0.6 mi n on SR 75. Int corridors. **Pets:** Accepted. ♿ 🏊 📶 ▣ ▭

◆◆ **La Quinta Inn Hartford Bradley Airport** [H]
(860) 623-3336. **$69-$215.** 64 Ella T Grasso Tpke 06096. I-91 exit 40, 2.5 mi w on SR 20, then just n on SR 75. Int corridors. **Pets:** Large, other species. Service with restrictions. ♿ 📶 ▣ ▭

Sheraton Hartford Hotel At Bradley Airport ✚ ❀

(860) 627-5311. **$99-$299.** 1 Bradley International Airport 06096. Jct SR 75, 0.6 mi w on Schoephoester Rd, 0.5 mi nw on Terminal Rd. Int corridors. **Pets:** Medium. Service with restrictions, supervision.

SAVE ECO ⛔ ♿ ➰ 📶 ✕ 🔋 💻

WOODSTOCK *(Restaurants p. 623)*

Inn at Woodstock Hill 🔵

(860) 928-0528. **$135-$250, 3 day notice.** 94 Plaine Hill Rd 06281. 0.8 mi n on SR 169. Int corridors. **Pets:** $15 daily fee/room. Designated rooms. ECO ⛔ 📶 ✕ 🔋 💻

DELAWARE

BEAR

BEST WESTERN PLUS Newark/Christiana Inn 🟥

(302) 326-2500. **$110-$160.** 875 Pulaski Hwy 19701. I-95 exit 4, 3.3 mi se on SR 1 exit 160, then just e on US 40. Int corridors. **Pets:** Small, dogs only. $20 daily fee/pet. Designated rooms, service with restrictions, crate. SAVE ♿ ➰ 📶 ✕ 🔋 💻

DEWEY BEACH

Hyatt Place Dewey Beach 🟥

(302) 864-9100. **$99-$359.** 1301 Coastal Hwy 19971. On SR 1; center. Int corridors. **Pets:** Medium, dogs only. $75 one-time fee/room. Designated rooms, service with restrictions, supervision.

SAVE ⛔ ♿ ➰ 📶 ✕ 🔋 💻

DOVER

BEST WESTERN Galaxy Inn 🟦

(302) 735-4700. **$70-$95.** 1700 E Lebanon Rd 19901. SR 1 exit 95, just w on SR 10. Int corridors. **Pets:** Other species. $10 daily fee/pet. Service with restrictions, supervision. SAVE ➰ 📶 🔋 💻

Days Inn Dover 🟦

(302) 674-8002. **$62-$275.** 272 N DuPont Hwy 19901. SR 1 exit 104, 2.8 mi s on US 13. Ext corridors. **Pets:** Dogs only. $25 daily fee/room. Service with restrictions, crate. SAVE 📶 🔋 💻

Hampton Inn-Dover 🟥

(302) 736-3500. **$89-$370.** 1568 N DuPont Hwy 19901. SR 1 exit 104, 1 mi s. Int corridors. **Pets:** Accepted. ♿ ➰ 📶 🔋 💻

Holiday Inn Express Hotel & Suites Dover 🟥

(302) 678-0600. **Call for rates.** 1780 N DuPont Hwy 19901. SR 1 exit 104, just s on US 13. Int corridors. **Pets:** Accepted.

♿ ➰ 📶 🔋 💻

MainStay Suites Dover 🟥

(302) 678-8383. **$60-$319.** 201 Stover Blvd 19901. SR 1 exit 95 northbound, just n on Bay Rd; exit 95 southbound, 1.5 mi n on Bay Rd; 0.7 mi s of jct US 13. Int corridors. **Pets:** Accepted.

ECO ⛔ ♿ ➰ 📶 🔋 💻

Residence Inn by Marriott-Dover 🟥

(302) 677-0777. **$97-$189.** 600 Jefferic Blvd 19901. SR 1 exit 104, 2.7 mi s on US 13. Int corridors. **Pets:** Accepted.

♿ ➰ 📶 ✕ 🔋 💻

Sleep Inn & Suites Dover 🟥

(302) 735-7770. **$80-$350.** 1784 N DuPont Hwy 19901. SR 1 exit 104, just s on US 13. Int corridors. **Pets:** Accepted.

♿ ➰ 📶 ✕ 🔋 💻

GEORGETOWN

Comfort Inn & Suites-Georgetown 🟥

(302) 854-9400. **Call for rates.** 20530 DuPont Blvd 19947. On US 113, 0.5 mi n of jct SR 404. Int corridors. **Pets:** Accepted.

⛔ ➰ 📶 🔋 💻

HARRINGTON

Baymont Inn & Suites Harrington 🟥

(302) 398-3900. **$65-$89.** 1259 Corn Crib Rd 19952. On US 13, 0.6 mi s of jct SR 14. Int corridors. **Pets:** Accepted.

⛔ ♿ ➰ 📶 ✕ 🔋 💻

LEWES *(Restaurants p. 623)*

The Inn at Canal Square 🟥

(302) 644-3377. **$105-$310, 7 day notice.** 122 Market St 19958. Just nw of jct Savannah Rd (US 9 business route). Int corridors. **Pets:** Medium, dogs only. Designated rooms, service with restrictions, supervision. SAVE ♿ 📶 ✕ 🔋 💻

Sleep Inn & Suites 🟥

(302) 645-6464. **$70-$380.** 18451 Coastal Hwy 19958. On SR 1, 1.5 mi s. Int corridors. **Pets:** Other species. $25 daily fee/room. Designated rooms, service with restrictions, supervision. ➰ 📶 ✕ 🔋 💻

MIDDLETOWN

Hampton Inn Middletown 🟥

(302) 378-5656. **$109-$299.** 117 Sand Hill Dr 19709. SR 1 exit 136, 2.8 mi w on SR 299, then just n on SR 15. Int corridors. **Pets:** Accepted.

♿ ➰ 📶 🔋 💻

MILLSBORO

Atlantic Inn-Millsboro 🟦

(302) 934-6711. **Call for rates.** 28534 DuPont Blvd 19966. US 113, just s of SR 24. Ext corridors. **Pets:** Accepted. ➰ 📶 ✕ 🔋

NEWARK

Courtyard by Marriott-Newark at the University of Delaware 🟥 ❀

(302) 737-0900. **$132-$229.** 400 David Hollowell Dr 19716. I-95 exit 1B southbound; exit 1 northbound, 3 mi n on SR 896. Int corridors. **Pets:** Medium. $75 one-time fee/room. Designated rooms, service with restrictions, crate. SAVE ECO ⛔ ♿ ➰ 📶 ✕ 🔋 💻

Extended Stay America Newark/Christiana 🟥

(302) 283-0800. **Call for rates.** 333 Continental Dr 19713. I-95 exit 4B, 0.3 mi n on SR 7 exit 166, then 0.4 mi w on SR 58 (Churchmans Rd). Int corridors. **Pets:** Other species. $25 daily fee/pet. Service with restrictions, supervision. ♿ 📶 ✕ 🔋 💻

Hilton Wilmington/Christiana 🟥

(302) 454-1500. **$119-$199.** 100 Continental Dr 19713. I-95 exit 4B, 0.3 mi n on SR 7 exit 166, then 0.4 mi w on SR 58 (Churchmans Rd). Int corridors. **Pets:** $49 one-time fee/room. Designated rooms, service with restrictions. SAVE ECO ⛔ ➰ 📶 🔋 💻

Homewood Suites by Hilton Newark/Wilmington South 🟥

(302) 453-9700. **$109-$179.** 640 S College Ave 19713. I-95 exit 1B southbound; exit 1 northbound, 0.8 mi n on SR 896. Int corridors. **Pets:** Accepted. ♿ ➰ 📶 🔋 💻

Quality Inn Wilmington-Newark/Christiana Mall 🟦

(302) 292-1500. **$89-$299.** 65 Geoffrey Dr 19713. I-95 exit 4B, 0.3 mi n on SR 7 exit 166, then just e on SR 58 (Churchmans Rd). Ext/int corridors. **Pets:** Small. $25 daily fee/pet. Designated rooms, service with restrictions, supervision. SAVE ♿ ➰ 📶 ✕ 🔋 💻

Ramada Newark/Wilmington 🟥

(302) 738-3400. **$79-$129.** 260 Chapman Rd 19702. I-95 exit 3 southbound; exit 3A northbound, 0.3 mi e on SR 273 E, then just s. Int corridors. **Pets:** Medium, other species. $25 daily fee/pet. Service with restrictions, crate. SAVE ⛔ ➰ 📶 ✕ 🔋 💻

Red Roof Plus Wilmington - Newark M
(302) 292-2870. **Call for rates.** 415 Stanton Christiana Rd 19713. I-95 exit 4B, 0.5 mi n on SR 7. Ext corridors. **Pets:** Large, other species. Service with restrictions, supervision.

Residence Inn by Marriott Wilmington/Newark/Christiana H
(302) 453-9200. **$174-$286.** 240 Chapman Rd 19702. I-95 exit 3 southbound; exit 3A northbound, 0.3 mi e on SR 273 E, then 0.5 mi s. Ext corridors. **Pets:** Accepted.

Staybridge Suites-Newark/Wilmington H
(302) 366-8097. **Call for rates.** 270 Chapman Rd 19702. I-95 exit 3 southbound; exit 3A northbound, 0.3 mi e on SR 273 E, then just s. Int corridors. **Pets:** Medium. $150 deposit/pet. Service with restrictions, supervision.

TownePlace Suites by Marriott-Wilmington/Christiana/Newark H
(302) 369-6212. **$122-$200.** 410 Eagle Run Rd 19702. I-95 exit 3 southbound; exit 3A northbound, just e. Int corridors. **Pets:** Accepted.

NEW CASTLE
Clarion Hotel-The Belle H
(302) 428-1000. **$109-$189.** 1612 N DuPont Hwy 19720. Jct I-295, just n on US 13. Int corridors. **Pets:** Medium, other species. $10 daily fee/room. Designated rooms, service with restrictions, supervision.

Sheraton Wilmington South New Castle H
(302) 328-6200. **$99-$239.** 365 Airport Rd 19720. I-95 exit 5A (SR 141 S). Int corridors. **Pets:** Accepted.

REHOBOTH BEACH *(Restaurants p. 623)*
AmericInn Lodge & Suites of Rehoboth Beach H ❀
(302) 226-0700. **$89-$359, 3 day notice.** 36012 Airport Rd 19971. Just w of SR 1; just w on Miller Rd, just s. Int corridors. **Pets:** Large, dogs only. $25 daily fee/pet. Designated rooms, service with restrictions, supervision.

WILMINGTON
BEST WESTERN PLUS Brandywine Valley Inn H
(302) 656-9436. **$139-$169.** 1807 Concord Pike 19803. I-95 exit 8, 1 mi n on US 202. Ext corridors. **Pets:** Accepted.

Hotel du Pont H
(302) 594-3100. **Call for rates.** 11th & Market Streets 19801. I-95 exit 7, 0.5 mi se; at 11th St; downtown. Int corridors. **Pets:** Accepted.

Sheraton Suites Wilmington Downtown H ❀
(302) 654-8300. **$89-$319.** 422 Delaware Ave 19801. I-95 exit 7 northbound; exit 7A southbound, 0.3 mi e; downtown. Int corridors. **Pets:** Medium, dogs only. $25 one-time fee/pet. Designated rooms, service with restrictions, crate.

Westin Wilmington H
(302) 654-2900. **$149-$399.** 818 Shipyard Dr 19801. I-95 exit 6, just w, then 0.5 mi s. Int corridors. **Pets:** Accepted.

DISTRICT OF COLUMBIA

WASHINGTON, D.C. *(Restaurants p. 623)*
Avenue Suites H ❀
(202) 333-8060. **Call for rates.** 2500 Pennsylvania Ave NW 20037. Jct 25th St NW and Pennsylvania Ave. Int corridors. **Pets:** $25 daily fee/pet. Service with restrictions, supervision.

Capella Washington, D.C., Georgetown H
(202) 617-2400. **Call for rates.** 1050 31st St NW 20007. Between M and K sts NW; in Georgetown. Int corridors. **Pets:** Accepted.

Capitol Hill Hotel H
(202) 543-6000. **Call for rates.** 200 C St SE 20003. 2 blks from Capitol grounds; at 2nd and C sts SE. Int corridors. **Pets:** Accepted.

The Churchill Hotel H
(202) 797-2000. **Call for rates.** 1914 Connecticut Ave NW 20009. Just n of Dupont Circle. Int corridors. **Pets:** Accepted.

The Dupont Circle Hotel H
(202) 483-6000. **$169-$609.** 1500 New Hampshire Ave NW 20036. At Dupont Circle, Connecticut and Massachusetts aves NW. Int corridors. **Pets:** Accepted.

Fairmont Washington, D.C., Georgetown H ❀
(202) 429-2400. **$189-$950.** 2401 M St NW 20037. 24th and M sts NW. Int corridors. **Pets:** Service with restrictions, supervision.

Four Seasons Hotel Washington, D.C. H
(202) 342-0444. **$395-$2500.** 2800 Pennsylvania Ave NW 20007. Jct M St NW and Pennsylvania Ave NW. Int corridors. **Pets:** Accepted.

Hamilton Crowne Plaza, Washington DC H
(202) 682-0111. **Call for rates.** 1001 14th St NW 20005. At 14th and K sts NW. Int corridors. **Pets:** Accepted.

The Hay-Adams H
(202) 638-6600. **$399-$1100.** 800 16th St NW 20006. 16th and H sts NW; just n of the White House. Int corridors. **Pets:** Accepted.

Hotel George-A Kimpton Hotel H ❀
(202) 347-4200. **$159-$569.** 15 E St NW 20001. Just n of Capitol grounds. Int corridors. **Pets:** Other species. Service with restrictions, crate.

Hotel Helix-A Kimpton Hotel H ❀
(202) 462-9001. **$119-$409, 3 day notice.** 1430 Rhode Island Ave NW 20005. Just e of Scott Circle. Int corridors. **Pets:** Other species. Service with restrictions.

Hotel Madera-A Kimpton Hotel H
(202) 296-7600. **$149-$449.** 1310 New Hampshire Ave NW 20036. Between 20th and N sts NW. Int corridors. **Pets:** Accepted.

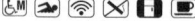

Hotel Monaco DC-A Kimpton Hotel H
(202) 628-7177. **$189-$699.** 700 F St NW 20004. Between 7th and 8th sts NW. Int corridors. **Pets:** Accepted.
SAVE ECO ⊕ ⊠ 🕸 ⊠ 🖥

Hotel Palomar Washington, DC-A Kimpton Hotel H
(202) 448-1800. **Call for rates.** 2121 P St NW 20037. Between 21st and 22nd sts NW; just w of Dupont Circle. Int corridors. **Pets:** Accepted. SAVE ECO ⊕ ⊇ ⊠ 🕸 ⊠ 🖥

Hotel Rouge-A Kimpton Hotel H
(202) 232-8000. **Call for rates.** 1315 16th St NW 20036. Just n of Scott Circle. Int corridors. **Pets:** Accepted.
SAVE ECO ⊕ 🕸 ⊠ 🖥 🖳

Liaison Capitol Hill DC, an Affinia hotel H
(202) 638-1616. **$99-$599.** 415 New Jersey Ave NW 20001. On Capitol Hill, just n of Capitol grounds. Int corridors. **Pets:** Accepted.
SAVE ⊕ 🛆ᴹ ⊇ 🕸 ⊠ 🖥 🖳

The Loews Madison H 🐾
(202) 862-1600. **Call for rates.** 1177 15th St NW 20005. 15th and M sts NW. Int corridors. **Pets:** Other species. $75 one-time fee/room. Service with restrictions. SAVE ⊕ ⊠ 🕸 ⊠ 🖥

Mandarin Oriental, Washington D.C. H
(202) 554-8588. **Call for rates.** 1330 Maryland Ave SW 20024. Jct Independence Ave SW, just s on 12th St SW. Int corridors.
Pets: Accepted. ⊕ 🛆ᴹ ⊇ ⊠ 🕸 ⊠ 🖥

The Mayflower Renaissance Hotel H
(202) 347-3000. **$119-$699.** 1127 Connecticut Ave NW 20036. Just n of K St NW; in business district. Int corridors. **Pets:** Accepted.
SAVE ⊕ 🛆ᴹ 🕸 ⊠ 🖥 🖳

The Melrose Georgetown Hotel H
(202) 955-6400. **$129-$499, 3 day notice.** 2430 Pennsylvania Ave NW 20037. Between 24th and 25th sts NW. Int corridors. **Pets:** Accepted.
SAVE ⊕ 🕸 ⊠ 🖥

The Normandy Hotel H
(202) 483-1350. **Call for rates.** 2118 Wyoming Ave NW 20008. Just w of Connecticut Ave. Int corridors. **Pets:** Accepted. 🕸 ⊠ 🖥 🖳

Omni Shoreham Hotel H
(202) 234-0700. **$149-$599.** 2500 Calvert St NW 20008. Just w of Connecticut Ave. Int corridors. **Pets:** Accepted.
⊕ 🛆ᴹ ⊇ ⊠ 🕸 ⊠ 🖥 🖳

One Washington Circle Hotel H 🐾
(202) 872-1680. **$109-$359.** One Washington Cir NW 20037. Between 23rd St and New Hampshire Ave NW. Int corridors. **Pets:** Designated rooms, service with restrictions, crate.
⊕ 🛆ᴹ ⊇ 🕸 ⊠ 🖥 🖳

Park Hyatt Washington D.C. H
(202) 789-1234. **$179-$999, 3 day notice.** 1201 24th St NW 20037. 24th and M sts NW. Int corridors. **Pets:** Accepted.
SAVE ECO ⊕ 🛆ᴹ ⊇ ⊠ 🕸 ⊠ 🖥 🖳

The Quincy H 🐾
(202) 223-4320. **$122-$209, 3 day notice.** 1823 L St NW 20036. Between 18th and 19th sts NW. Int corridors. **Pets:** Medium. $150 one-time fee/room. Designated rooms, service with restrictions, crate.
⊕ 🕸 ⊠ 🖥 🖳

Residence Inn by Marriott DC/Foggy Bottom H 🐾
(202) 785-2000. **$139-$409.** 801 New Hampshire Ave NW 20037. Just sw at Washington Circle. Int corridors. **Pets:** Other species. $100 one-time fee/room. Designated rooms, service with restrictions.
🛆ᴹ ⊇ 🕸 ⊠ 🖥 🖳

Residence Inn by Marriott-Dupont Circle H
(202) 466-6800. **$151-$395.** 2120 P St NW 20037. Between 21st and 22nd sts NW; just w of Dupont Circle. Int corridors. **Pets:** Accepted.
🛆ᴹ 🕸 ⊠ 🖥 🖳

Residence Inn by Marriott Washington, DC/Capitol H
(202) 484-8280. **$299-$395.** 333 E St SW 20024. Between 3rd and 4th sts SW. Int corridors. **Pets:** $200 one-time fee/room, $10 daily fee/pet. Service with restrictions. SAVE 🛆ᴹ ⊇ 🕸 ⊠ 🖥 🖳

Residence Inn by Marriott-Washington DC-Downtown H
(202) 898-1100. **$89-$599.** 1199 Vermont Ave NW 20005. Jct 14th St and Vermont Ave NW, at Thomas Circle. Int corridors. **Pets:** Accepted.
SAVE ECO 🛆ᴹ 🕸 ⊠ 🖥 🖳

The Ritz-Carlton Georgetown, Washington DC H
(202) 912-4100. **$459-$959.** 3100 South St NW 20007. Just s of jct M St and Wisconsin Ave; in Georgetown. Int corridors. **Pets:** Accepted.
SAVE ⊕ 🛆ᴹ ⊠ 🕸 ⊠ 🖥

The Ritz-Carlton, Washington, D.C. H
(202) 835-0500. **$359-$959.** 1150 22nd St NW 20037. At 22nd and M sts NW. Int corridors. **Pets:** Accepted.
SAVE ⊕ 🛆ᴹ ⊇ ⊠ 🕸 ⊠ 🖥

The River Inn H
(202) 337-7600. **Call for rates.** 924 25th St NW 20037. Between K and I sts NW. Int corridors. **Pets:** Accepted. ⊕ 🕸 ⊠ 🖥 🖳

The St. Regis, Washington, D.C. H
(202) 638-2626. **$295-$975.** 923 16th St NW 20006. 16th and K sts; just n of the White House. Int corridors. **Pets:** Small, dogs only. $150 one-time fee/room. Designated rooms, service with restrictions, supervision. SAVE ⊕ 🕸 ⊠ 🖥

The Savoy Suites Hotel H
(202) 337-9700. **Call for rates.** 2505 Wisconsin Ave NW 20007. 0.3 mi s of Massachusetts Ave NW; in upper Georgetown area. Int corridors.
Pets: Accepted. ⊕ 🛆ᴹ 🕸 ⊠ 🖥 🖳

Topaz Hotel-A Kimpton Hotel H
(202) 393-3000. **Call for rates.** 1733 N St NW 20036. Just e of Connecticut Ave. Int corridors. **Pets:** Accepted.
SAVE ECO ⊕ 🕸 ⊠ 🖥

Twelve & K Hotel H
(202) 289-7600. **$119-$499.** 1201 K St NW 20005. At 12th and K sts NW. Int corridors. **Pets:** Accepted.
SAVE ECO ⊕ ⊇ 🕸 ⊠ 🖥 🖳

The Washington Court Hotel H
(202) 628-2100. **Call for rates.** 525 New Jersey Ave NW 20001. On Capitol Hill, 3 blks n of Capitol grounds. Int corridors. **Pets:** Accepted.
⊕ 🕸 ⊠ 🖥

Washington Hilton H
(202) 483-3000. **$99-$439.** 1919 Connecticut Ave NW 20009. Just n of Dupont Circle at T St NW. Int corridors. **Pets:** Accepted.
SAVE ⊕ ⊇ 🕸 ⊠ 🖥 🖳

Washington Marriott Wardman Park H
(202) 328-2000. **$89-$599.** 2660 Woodley Rd NW 20008. Just w of Connecticut Ave. Int corridors. **Pets:** Accepted.
SAVE ⊕ 🛆ᴹ ⊇ ⊠ 🕸 ⊠ 🖥 🖳

The Westin Georgetown, Washington, D.C. H 🐾
(202) 429-0100. **$149-$549.** 2350 M St NW 20037. At 24th and M sts NW. Int corridors. **Pets:** Small, dogs only. $200 deposit/room.
SAVE ⊕ 🛆ᴹ ⊇ 🕸 ⊠ 🖥 🖳

(AAA) ▼▼▼ The Westin Washington DC City Center Hotel H ✿
(202) 429-1700. **Call for rates.** 1400 M St NW 20005. Just w of Thomas Circle. Int corridors. **Pets:** Medium, dogs only. $200 deposit/room. Service with restrictions, crate. (SAVE) (♦) (🔊) (✕) (🔋) (💻)

(AAA) ▼▼▼ ▼▼▼ The Willard InterContinental H ✿
(202) 628-9100. **$229-$629, 5 day notice.** 1401 Pennsylvania Ave NW 20004. Just e of the White House; jct 14th St NW. Int corridors. **Pets:** Medium. $200 one-time fee/room. Service with restrictions, crate.
(SAVE) (♦) (🅼) (✕) (🔊) (✕) (🔋) (💻)

(AAA) ▼▼▼ W Washington, D.C. H
(202) 661-2400. **$229-$999.** 515 15th St NW 20004. At 15th St and Pennsylvania Ave NW. Int corridors. **Pets:** Accepted.
(SAVE) (♦) (🅼) (✕) (🔊) (✕) (🔋)

FLORIDA

ALTAMONTE SPRINGS

(AAA) ▼▼▼ Embassy Suites Orlando North H
(407) 834-2400. **$129-$249.** 225 Shorecrest Dr 32701. I-4 exit 92 (SR 436), 0.5 mi e, then just n on Cranes Roost Blvd. Int corridors.
Pets: Accepted. (SAVE) (ECO) (♦) (🅼) (✌) (✕) (📶) (✕) (🔋) (💻)

(AAA) ▼▼ ▼▼ Hawthorn Suites by Wyndham Orlando Altamonte Springs H
(407) 767-5757. **$69-$199.** 644 Raymond Ave 32701. I-4 exit 92 (SR 436), just w to Douglas Ave, 0.8 mi n to Central Pkwy, then just e. Int corridors. **Pets:** Accepted. (SAVE) (🅼) (✌) (📶) (🔋) (💻)

▼▼ ▼▼ Quality Inn - Orlando North/Altamonte Springs H
(407) 869-9000. **$59-$89.** 151 N Douglas Ave 32714. I-4 exit 92 (SR 436), just w to Douglas Ave, then just n. Ext corridors. **Pets:** Accepted.
(🅼) (✌) (📶) (🔋) (💻)

▼▼ ▼▼ Ramada Inn Altamonte Springs H
(407) 862-8200. **$59-$119.** 150 Douglas Ave 32714. I-4 exit 92 (SR 436), just w to Douglas Ave, then just n. Ext corridors. **Pets:** Dogs only. $50 deposit/pet, $20 daily fee/pet. Designated rooms, service with restrictions, supervision. (🅼) (✌) (📶) (🔋) (💻)

▼▼▼ ▼▼▼ Residence Inn by Marriott-Orlando Altamonte Springs/Maitland H ✿
(407) 788-7991. **$109-$208.** 270 Douglas Ave 32714. I-4 exit 92 (SR 436), just w to Douglas Ave, then just n. Ext corridors. **Pets:** Medium. $75 one-time fee/room. Service with restrictions, supervision.
(🅼) (✌) (📶) (✕) (🔋) (💻)

APALACHICOLA

▼▼▼ ▼▼▼ Coombs Inn & Suites BB
(850) 653-9199. **Call for rates.** 80 Sixth St 32320. US 98 (Market St) and Ave E. Int corridors. **Pets:** Accepted. (📶) (✕) (🔋) (💻)

▼▼▼ ▼▼▼ Water Street Hotel & Marina CO
(850) 653-3700. **$109-$450.** 329 Water St 32320. Jct Ave I. Ext corridors. **Pets:** Other species. $35 daily fee/pet. Service with restrictions, supervision. (🅼) (✌) (✕) (📶) (✕) (🔋) (💻)

ARCADIA

▼▼▼ ▼▼▼ Holiday Inn Express Hotel & Suites H
(863) 494-5900. **Call for rates.** 2709 SE SR 70 34266. On SR 70, 1.9 mi e of US 17; jct SR 31. Int corridors. **Pets:** Accepted.
(🅼) (✌) (📶) (🔋) (💻)

ATLANTIC BEACH

(AAA) ▼▼ ▼▼ BEST WESTERN Mayport Inn & Suites M ✿
(904) 435-3500. **$99-$129, 3 day notice.** 2389 Mayport Rd 32233. 2 mi n on SR A1A; 1.4 mi s of naval base. Int corridors. **Pets:** Large, dogs only. $15 daily fee/pet. Crate. (SAVE) (✌) (📶) (🔋) (💻)

(AAA) ▼▼▼ ▼▼▼ One Ocean Resort Hotel & Spa H ✿
(904) 249-7402. **$169-$900, 3 day notice.** One Ocean Blvd 32233. Jct SR A1A, just e on Atlantic Blvd. Int corridors. **Pets:** $75 daily fee/pet. Supervision. (SAVE) (ECO) (♦) (🅼) (✌) (✕) (📶) (✕) (🔋)

AVENTURA

(AAA) ▼▼▼ ▼▼▼ Residence Inn by Marriott-Aventura Mall H ✿
(786) 528-1001. **$101-$278.** 19900 W Country Club Dr 33180. I-95 exit 16 (Ives Dairy Rd), 1.1 mi e to US 1 (Biscayne Blvd), 0.5 mi s to 199th St (Aventura Blvd), 0.5 mi e to W Country Club Dr, then just s. Int corridors. **Pets:** Other species. $100 one-time fee/room. Service with restrictions. (SAVE) (ECO) (🅼) (✌) (📶) (✕) (🔋) (💻)

(AAA) ▼▼▼ ▼▼▼ Turnberry Isle Miami, Autograph Collection H
(305) 932-6200. **$179-$699, 7 day notice.** 19999 W Country Club Dr 33180. I-95 exit 16 (Ives Dairy Rd), 1.1 mi e to US 1 (Biscayne Blvd), just s to 199th St (Aventura Blvd), 0.5 mi e to Country Club Dr, then just s. Ext/int corridors. **Pets:** Accepted.
(SAVE) (ECO) (♦) (🅼) (✌) (✕) (🔊) (✕) (🔋) (💻)

BAL HARBOUR

(AAA) ▼▼▼ ▼▼▼ The Ritz-Carlton Bal Harbour, Miami H
(305) 455-5400. **$450-$10000, 3 day notice.** 10295 Collins Ave 33154. On SR A1A (Collins Ave); at Haulover Cswy. Int corridors.
Pets: Accepted. (SAVE) (♦) (✌) (✕) (📶) (✕) (💻)

(AAA) ▼▼▼ ▼▼▼ St. Regis Bal Harbour H
(305) 993-3300. **$509-$1409, 7 day notice.** 9703 Collins Ave 33154. Just n of jct SR A1A (Collins Ave) and 922 (96th St). Int corridors.
Pets: Accepted. (SAVE) (♦) (🅼) (✌) (✕) (📶) (✕) (💻)

BOCA RATON *(Restaurants p. 624)*

(AAA) ▼▼▼ ▼▼▼ Boca Raton Resort & Club, A Waldorf Astoria Resort H
(561) 447-3000. **Call for rates.** 501 E Camino Real 33432. I-95 exit 44 (Palmetto Park Rd), 1.9 mi e to US 1 (Federal Hwy), just s to Camino Real, then 0.5 mi e. Ext/int corridors. **Pets:** Accepted.
(SAVE) (ECO) (♦) (🅼) (✌) (✕) (🔊) (🔋) (💻)

▼▼▼ ▼▼▼ Fairfield Inn & Suites by Marriott-Boca Raton H
(561) 417-8585. **$89-$259.** 3400 Airport Rd 33431. I-95 exit 45 (Glades Rd), just e to Airport Rd, then 1.1 mi n. Int corridors. **Pets:** Accepted.
(ECO) (🅼) (✌) (📶) (✕) (🔋) (💻)

(AAA) ▼▼▼ ▼▼▼ Hilton Boca Raton Suites H
(561) 483-3600. **$89-$229.** 7920 Glades Rd 33434. I-95 exit 45 (Glades Rd), 3.4 mi w; Florida Tpke exit 75 (Glades Rd), just e; in Arvida Parkway Center. Int corridors. **Pets:** Accepted.
(SAVE) (ECO) (✌) (📶) (✕) (🔋) (💻)

AAA ▼▼ Quality Inn-Boca Raton **M**
(561) 395-7172. **$80-$150.** 2899 N Federal Hwy 33431. I-95 exit 48 (Yamato Rd), 1.2 mi e to US 1 (Federal Hwy), then 1.3 mi s. Ext corridors. Pets: Accepted. ⟨SAVE⟩ 🛬 📶 📹 📺

AAA ▼▼▼ Residence Inn by Marriott-Boca Raton **H**
(561) 994-3222. **$79-$269.** 525 NW 77th St 33487. I-95 exit 50 (Congress Ave), merge onto NW 82nd St, just s on Congress Ave to NW 6th Ave, just e, then n; in Boca Commerce Center. Ext corridors. Pets: Accepted. ⟨SAVE⟩ 🛬 📶 ✕ 📹 📺

▼▼▼▼ TownePlace Suites by Marriott-Boca Raton **H**
(561) 994-7232. **$109-$279.** 5110 NW 8th Ave 33487. I-95 exit 48 (Yamato Rd), just w; in Arvida Park of Commerce. Int corridors. Pets: Accepted. ⟨ECO⟩ ⟨&M⟩ 🛬 📶 ✕ 📹 📺

BONITA SPRINGS *(Restaurants p. 624)*
▼▼▼▼ Holiday Inn Express & Suites Bonita Springs **H**
(239) 948-0699. **Call for rates.** 27891 Crown Lake Blvd 34135. I-75 exit 116, 3.4 mi w on Bonita Beach Rd SE (CR 865), then just n. Int corridors. Pets: Accepted. ⟨ECO⟩ ⟨&M⟩ 🛬 📶 ✕ 📹 📺

AAA ▼▼▼▼ Hyatt Regency Coconut Point Resort & Spa **H**
(239) 444-1234. **$139-$569, 3 day notice.** 5001 Coconut Rd 34134. I-75 exit 123, 1.9 mi w on Corkscrew Rd, 2.3 mi s on US 41 (Tamiami Tr), then 1.5 mi w. Int corridors. Pets: Accepted.
⟨SAVE⟩ ⟨ECO⟩ 🛬 ✕ 🔊 ✕ 📹 📺

BOYNTON BEACH *(Restaurants p. 624)*
AAA ▼▼▼ Courtyard by Marriott-Boynton Beach **H**
(561) 737-4600. **$79-$259.** 1601 N Congress Ave 33426. I-95 exit 59 (Gateway Blvd), 1.2 mi w to Congress Ave, then just s. Ext/int corridors. Pets: Accepted. ⟨SAVE⟩ ⟨ECO⟩ 🛬 📶 ✕ 📹 📺

BRADENTON
AAA ▼▼▼ BEST WESTERN PLUS Bradenton Hotel & Suites **H**
(941) 757-5555. **$90-$210.** 648 67th St Cir E 34208. I-75 exit 220 southbound; exit 220B northbound, 0.3 mi w on SR 64, just n on 66th St Ct E. Int corridors. Pets: Accepted.
⟨SAVE⟩ ⟨ECO⟩ ⟨&M⟩ 🛬 📶 ✕ 📹 📺

AAA ▼▼▼ Courtyard by Marriott Bradenton/Sarasota Riverfront **H**
(941) 747-3727. **$89-$269.** 100 Riverfront Dr W 34205. Just w of US 41 and 301; south side of Hernando Desoto Bridge; just n of jct SR 64 (Manatee Ave W) on 3rd St W. Int corridors. Pets: Accepted.
⟨SAVE⟩ ⟨ECO⟩ ⟨&M⟩ 🛬 📶 ✕ 📹 📺

▼▼▼ Hampton Inn & Suites Bradenton-Downtown Historic District **H** ☙
(941) 746-9400. **$119-$199.** 309 10th St W 34205. Just n of jct Manatee Ave W on 9th St W (Business Rt 41); downtown. Int corridors. Pets: Medium, dogs only. $100 one-time fee/pet. Designated rooms, service with restrictions, supervision. ⟨&M⟩ 📶 ✕ 📹 📺

AAA ▼▼ Quality Inn Bradenton **M**
(941) 758-7199. **$59-$189.** 6727 14th St W 34207. On US 41, 2 mi s of jct SR 70. Ext corridors. Pets: Small, dogs only. $10 daily fee/pet. Service with restrictions, supervision. ⟨SAVE⟩ 🛬 📶 📹 📺

AAA ▼▼ Super 8-Bradenton **M**
(941) 756-6656. **$59-$99.** 6516 14th St W 34207. On US 41, 1.5 mi s of jct SR 70. Ext corridors. Pets: Small, dogs only. $10 daily fee/pet. Service with restrictions, supervision. ⟨SAVE⟩ 🛬 📶 📹

BROOKSVILLE
▼▼ Microtel Inn & Suites by Wyndham Brooksville **H**
(352) 796-9025. **$60-$90.** 6298 Nature Coast Blvd 34602. I-75 exit 301, just w on US 98/SR 50 (Cortez Blvd), then just s. Int corridors. Pets: Other species. $25 one-time fee/room. Service with restrictions, supervision. ⟨&M⟩ 🛬 📶 📹 📺

CAPE CANAVERAL
▼▼▼▼ Radisson Resort at the Port **H** ☙
(321) 784-0000. **$80-$175.** 8701 Astronaut Blvd 32920. On SR A1A, 2.7 mi nw of jct SR 520. Ext/int corridors. Pets: Other species. Service with restrictions, supervision. ⟨❸⟩ ⟨&M⟩ 🛬 ✕ 📶 ✕ 📹 📺

▼▼▼ Residence Inn by Marriott Cape Canaveral/Cocoa Beach **H**
(321) 323-1100. **$149-$189.** 8959 Astronaut Blvd 32920. On SR A1A, 0.3 mi s of jct SR 528. Int corridors. Pets: Accepted.
⟨ECO⟩ 🛬 📶 ✕ 📹 📺

CAPE CORAL *(Restaurants p. 624)*
▼▼▼ Hampton Inn & Suites-Cape Coral/Fort Myers Area **H**
(239) 540-1050. **$99-$259.** 619 SE 47th Terr 33904. Just w of jct Coronado Pkwy. Int corridors. Pets: Accepted. ⟨&M⟩ 🛬 📶 📹 📺

▼▼▼ Holiday Inn Express Cape Coral-Fort Myers Area **H**
(239) 542-2121. **$89-$225, 7 day notice.** 1538 Cape Coral Pkwy E 33904. Jct Del Prado Blvd. Int corridors. Pets: Small. $20 daily fee/pet. Designated rooms, service with restrictions, crate.
⟨&M⟩ 🛬 📶 ✕ 📹 📺

AAA ▼▼▼▼ The Westin Cape Coral Resort At Marina Village **H**
(239) 541-5000. **$99-$459.** 5951 Silver King Blvd 33914. 0.9 mi s of jct Cape Coral Pkwy on Pelican Way; 1 mi sw on Rose Garden Rd. Int corridors. Pets: Accepted.
⟨SAVE⟩ ❸ ⟨&M⟩ 🛬 ✕ 🔊 ✕ 📹 📺

CEDAR KEY
AAA ▼▼▼ Park Place Motel & Condominiums **CO**
(352) 543-5737. **$65-$115.** 211 2nd St 32625. Just ne of jct SR 24; at A St. Ext corridors. Pets: Small, other species. $7 daily fee/pet. Designated rooms, service with restrictions, supervision.
⟨SAVE⟩ ⟨ECO⟩ 📶 📹 📺

▼▼▼ Seahorse Landing Waterfront Condominiums **CO**
(352) 543-5860. **$100-$175, 3 day notice.** 4050 G St 32625. Just sw of jct SR 24, on 6th St. Ext corridors. Pets: Large, dogs only. $15 daily fee/room. Designated rooms, service with restrictions, crate.
⟨ECO⟩ 🛬 ✕ 📶 ✕ 📹 📺

CELEBRATION *(Restaurants p. 624)*
AAA ▼▼▼ Bohemian Hotel Celebration, Autograph Collection **H**
(407) 566-6000. **$143-$299, 3 day notice.** 700 Bloom St 34747. I-4 exit 64, 0.5 mi e on US 192 (W Irlo Bronson Hwy); 1.6 mi s on Celebration Ave, then just se on Campus St; downtown. Int corridors. Pets: Accepted. ⟨SAVE⟩ ❸ ⟨&M⟩ 🛬 ✕ 🔊 ✕ 📹 📺

CHAMPIONSGATE
AAA ▼▼▼▼ Omni Orlando Resort at ChampionsGate **H**
(407) 390-6664. **Call for rates.** 1500 Masters Blvd 33896. I-4 exit 58, 0.5 mi w on ChampionsGate Blvd (CR 532) to Masters Blvd, then just n. Int corridors. Pets: Accepted.
⟨SAVE⟩ ⟨ECO⟩ ❸ ⟨&M⟩ 🛬 ✕ 🔊 ✕ 📺

CHIEFLAND

Days Inn Chiefland M
(352) 493-9400. **$64-$80.** 809 NW 21st Ave 32626. Just e of Alt US 27/19/98; 1 mi n of jct US 129. Ext corridors. **Pets:** Accepted.

Quality Inn M
(352) 493-0663. **$71-$95.** 1125 N Young Blvd 32626. On Alternate Rt US 27/19/98, just n of jct US 129. Ext corridors. **Pets:** Accepted.

CLEARWATER (Restaurants p. 624)

Extended Stay America M
(727) 561-9032. **$60-$225.** 3089 Executive Dr 33762. I-275 exit 31 southbound, just w on SR 688 (Ulmerton Rd); exit 30 northbound, 1.4 mi w on SR 686, then 1.6 mi w on SR 688 (Ulmerton Rd). **Pets:** Other species. $25 daily fee/pet. Service with restrictions, supervision.

Holiday Inn Express Clearwater East-Icot Center H
(727) 536-7275. **$79-$129.** 13625 Icot Blvd 33760. 0.5 mi e of jct US 19; just n of SR 688 (Ulmerton Rd); in Icot Center Business Park. Int corridors. **Pets:** Medium. $49 one-time fee/room. Service with restrictions, crate.

Holiday Inn St. Petersburg/Clearwater Airport H
(727) 577-9100. **$109-$199, 3 day notice.** 3535 Ulmerton Rd 33762. I-275 exit 31 southbound, 1.8 mi w on SR 688 (Ulmerton Rd); exit 30 northbound, 1.4 mi w on SR 686, just w on SR 688 (Ulmerton Rd). Int corridors. **Pets:** $50 one-time fee/room. Designated rooms, no service.

Residence Inn by Marriott Clearwater Downtown H
(727) 562-5400. **$79-$395.** 940 Court St 33756. On SR 60, jct S Prospect Ave. Int corridors. **Pets:** Other species. $100 one-time fee/room. Designated rooms, service with restrictions, crate.

Residence Inn by Marriott St. Petersburg/Clearwater H
(727) 573-4444. **$95-$249.** 5050 Ulmerton Rd 33760. I-275 exit 31 southbound, 3.1 mi w on SR 688 (Ulmerton Rd); exit 30 northbound, 1.4 mi w on SR 686, then 1.7 mi w. Ext corridors. **Pets:** Accepted.

TownePlace Suites by Marriott St. Petersburg/Clearwater H
(727) 299-9229. **$109-$219.** 13200 49th St N 33762. I-275 exit 31 southbound, 3.4 mi w on SR 688 (Ulmerton Rd); exit 30 northbound, 1.4 mi w on SR 686, 3 mi w on SR 688 (Ulmerton Rd), then just s; in Turtle Creek. Int corridors. **Pets:** Accepted.

CLERMONT

Days Inn Clermont South H
(863) 424-6099. **$63-$86.** 9240 US Hwy 192 34714. 0.8 mi e of jct US 27. Ext corridors. **Pets:** Accepted.

Fairfield Inn & Suites by Marriott Clermont H
(352) 394-6585. **$99-$169.** 1750 Hunt Trace Blvd 34711. 0.5 mi e of jct US 27 on SR 50, just n on Citrus Tower Blvd. Int corridors. **Pets:** Medium, other species. $75 one-time fee/pet. Designated rooms, service with restrictions, supervision.

COCOA

BEST WESTERN Cocoa Inn M
(321) 632-1065. **$80-$120.** 4225 W King St 32926. I-95 exit 201 (SR 520), just e. Ext corridors. **Pets:** Accepted.

COCOA BEACH

BEST WESTERN Ocean Beach Hotel & Suites H
(321) 783-7621. **$89-$229.** 5600 N Atlantic Ave 32931. SR A1A (Atlantic Ave), 0.8 mi n of jct SR 520. Ext/int corridors. **Pets:** Accepted.

Comfort Inn & Suites Cocoa Beach-Port Canaveral Area H
(321) 783-2221. **$90-$160.** 3901 N Atlantic Ave 32931. On SR A1A (Atlantic Ave), 0.3 mi s of jct SR 520. Ext corridors. **Pets:** Medium, other species. $10 daily fee/room. Designated rooms, service with restrictions, crate.

Days Inn Cocoa Beach M
(321) 784-2550. **$75-$165.** 5500 N Atlantic Ave 32931. SR A1A (Atlantic Ave), 0.8 mi n of SR 520. Ext corridors. **Pets:** Accepted.

Four Points by Sheraton Cocoa Beach H
(321) 783-8717. **$90-$175.** 4001 N Atlantic Ave 32931. SR A1A (Atlantic Ave), just s of SR 520. Int corridors. **Pets:** Accepted.

La Quinta Inn Cocoa Beach-Port Canaveral H
(321) 783-2252. **$72-$204.** 1275 N Atlantic Ave 32931. SR A1A (Atlantic Ave), 1.7 mi s of SR 520. Ext corridors. **Pets:** Large, other species. Service with restrictions.

COCONUT GROVE (Restaurants p. 624)

Mayfair Hotel & Spa H
(305) 441-0000. **Call for rates.** 3000 Florida Ave 33133. At Florida Ave and Virginia St; center. Ext/int corridors. **Pets:** Accepted.

Residence Inn by Marriott Miami Coconut Grove H
(305) 285-9303. **$109-$329.** 2835 Tigertail Ave 33133. S Bayshore Dr, w on SW 27th Ave (Cornelia Dr), then s. Ext corridors. **Pets:** Accepted.

CORAL GABLES (Restaurants p. 624)

The Biltmore Hotel Coral Gables H
(305) 445-1926. **Call for rates.** 1200 Anastasia Ave 33134. US 1, 1.4 mi w on Bird Rd (SW 40th St) to Granada Blvd, 0.5 mi n to Anastasia Ave, then just w. Int corridors. **Pets:** Accepted.

Extended Stay America-Miami-Coral Gables H
(305) 443-7444. **$60-$160.** 3640 Coral Way/SW 22nd St 33145. Just e of Douglas Rd. Int corridors. **Pets:** Other species. $25 daily fee/pet. Service with restrictions, supervision.

CORAL SPRINGS (Restaurants p. 624)

La Quinta Inn & Suites-Coral Springs University Dr H
(954) 753-9000. **$79-$250.** 3701 N University Dr 33065. SR 869 (Sawgrass Expwy) exit 15 (University Dr/SR 817), 1.9 mi s. Int corridors. **Pets:** Large, other species. Service with restrictions.

La Quinta Inn & Suites-Ft. Lauderdale University Drive South H
(954) 344-2200. **$79-$227.** 3100 N University Dr 33065. SR 869 (Sawgrass Expwy) exit 15 (University Dr/SR 817), 2.4 mi s. Int corridors. **Pets:** Large, other species. Service with restrictions.

CRESCENT BEACH

(AAA) ▼▼ Beacher's Lodge Oceanfront Suites **CO**
(904) 471-8849. **Call for rates.** 6970 A1A S 32080. On SR A1A (Atlantic Ave), just s of jct SR 206. Ext corridors. **Pets:** Other species. $50 one-time fee/pet. Service with restrictions.
[SAVE] 🏊 📶 ✕ 📶 💻

CRESTVIEW *(Restaurants p. 624)*

▼▼ Quality Inn **H**
(850) 683-1778. **$71-$89.** 151 Cracker Barrel Dr 32536. I-10 exit 56, just s on SR 85. Int corridors. **Pets:** Small. $20 daily fee/pet. Designated rooms, service with restrictions, supervision. 🏊 📶 📶 💻

CRYSTAL RIVER

(AAA) ▼▼▼ Plantation on Crystal River **H**
(352) 795-4211. **$109-$199, 3 day notice.** 9301 W Fort Island Tr 34429. Just sw of jct US 19. Ext/int corridors. **Pets:** Accepted.
[SAVE] [ECO] 🍴 🏊 ✕ 📶 ✕ 📶 💻

DANIA BEACH

(AAA) ▼▼▼▼ HYATT house Fort Lauderdale Airport & Cruise Port **H**
(954) 922-0271. **$99-$299.** 90 SW 18th Ave 33004. I-95 exit 22 (Stirling Rd), just e to SW 18th Ave, then just n. Int corridors. **Pets:** Accepted.
[SAVE] 🏊 📶 ✕ 📶 💻

(AAA) ▼▼▼▼ Hyatt Place Ft. Lauderdale Airport & Cruise Port **H**
(954) 922-0436. **$89-$279.** 91 SW 18th Ave 33004. I-95 exit 22 (Stirling Rd), just e to SW 18th Ave, then just n. Int corridors. **Pets:** Accepted.
[SAVE] 📶 🏊 📶 ✕ 📶 💻

(AAA) ▼▼▼▼ Sheraton Ft. Lauderdale Airport & Cruise Port Hotel **H**
(954) 920-3500. **$89-$329.** 1825 Griffin Rd 33004. I-95 exit 23 (Griffin Rd), just e. Int corridors. **Pets:** Accepted.
[SAVE] [ECO] 🍴 📶 🏊 ✕ 📶 ✕ 📶 💻

DAYTONA BEACH

(AAA) ▼▼ Comfort Inn & Suites Oceanfront **H**
(386) 255-5491. **$69-$180.** 730 N Atlantic Ave 32118. On SR A1A (Atlantic Ave), 1.1 mi n of jct US 92 (International Speedway Blvd). Ext/int corridors. **Pets:** Accepted. [SAVE] [ECO] 🏊 📶 ✕ 📶 💻

(AAA) ▼▼▼ Hilton Daytona Beach Resort/Ocean Walk Village **H**
(386) 254-8200. **$109-$249.** 100 N Atlantic Ave 32118. I-95 exit 261A, 6.1 mi e to SR A1A (Atlantic Ave), then 0.5 mi n. Int corridors.
Pets: Accepted. [SAVE] [ECO] 🍴 🏊 ✕ 📶 ✕ 📶 💻

▼▼▼ Holiday Inn-Daytona Beach LPGA **H**
(386) 236-0200. **$89-$149.** 137 AutoMall Cir 32124. I-95 exit 265, just sw. Int corridors. **Pets:** Medium. $50 daily fee/room. Designated rooms, service with restrictions, crate. 🍴 📶 🏊 ✕ 📶 💻

▼▼▼ Homewood Suites by Hilton-Daytona Beach Airport/Speedway **H**
(386) 258-2828. **$89-$149.** 165 Bill France Blvd 32114. I-95 exit 261 (US 92), 2.1 mi e to Bill France Blvd, then just n. Int corridors.
Pets: Accepted. 📶 🏊 📶 📶 💻

(AAA) ▼▼▼▼ The Plaza Historic Beach Resort & Spa **H**
(386) 255-4471. **$89-$499, 3 day notice.** 600 N Atlantic Ave 32118. I-95 exit 261 (US 92), 6 mi e to SR A1A (Atlantic Ave), 1 mi n. Int corridors. **Pets:** Accepted. [SAVE] [ECO] 🍴 🏊 ✕ 📶 ✕ 📶 💻

(AAA) ▼▼▼ Residence Inn by Marriott - Daytona Beach **H**
(386) 252-3949. **$116-$179.** 1725 Richard Petty Blvd 32114. I-95 exit 261 (US 92), 2.4 mi e to Midway Ave, just s to Richard Petty Blvd, then just e. Int corridors. **Pets:** Accepted.
[SAVE] [ECO] 📶 🏊 📶 ✕ 📶 💻

DAYTONA BEACH SHORES

(AAA) ▼▼▼ Atlantic Ocean Palm Inn **M**
(386) 761-8450. **$59-$299, 7 day notice.** 3247 S Atlantic Ave 32118. On SR A1A (Atlantic Ave), 5 mi s of jct US 92 (International Speedway Blvd). Ext corridors. **Pets:** Small, dogs only. $25 daily fee/pet. Designated rooms, service with restrictions, supervision.
[SAVE] 🏊 📶 ✕ 📶 💻

(AAA) ▼▼▼ Hyatt Place Daytona Beach Oceanfront **H**
(386) 944-2010. **$89-$599.** 3161 S Atlantic Ave 32118. I-95 exit 256 (SR 421), 5 mi e to SR A1A (Atlantic Ave), then 0.8 mi n. Int corridors. **Pets:** Medium, dogs only. $75 one-time fee/room. Designated rooms, service with restrictions. [SAVE] 📶 🏊 📶 ✕ 📶 💻

(AAA) ▼▼▼ The Shores Resort & Spa **H**
(386) 767-7350. **$119-$659, 3 day notice.** 2637 S Atlantic Ave 32118. On SR A1A (Atlantic Ave), 3.2 mi s of jct US 92 (International Speedway Blvd). Int corridors. **Pets:** Accepted.
[SAVE] [ECO] 🍴 📶 🏊 ✕ 📶 ✕ 💻

DEERFIELD BEACH

(AAA) ▼▼ Comfort Inn Oceanside **H** ❀
(954) 428-0650. **$85-$325, 3 day notice.** 50 S Ocean Dr (SR A1A) 33441. I-95 exit 42 (Hillsboro Blvd), 2.6 mi e; jct Hillsboro Blvd and SR A1A (Ocean Dr). Int corridors. **Pets:** Other species. $50 daily fee/pet. Designated rooms, service with restrictions, supervision.
[SAVE] 🏊 📶 📶 💻

(AAA) ▼▼▼ DoubleTree by Hilton Deerfield Beach-Boca Raton **H**
(954) 427-7700. **$99-$259.** 100 Fairway Dr 33441. I-95 exit 42A (Hillsboro Blvd), just e to Fairway Dr. Int corridors. **Pets:** Accepted.
[SAVE] [ECO] 🍴 🏊 📶 ✕ 📶 💻

▼▼ Extended Stay America - Fort Lauderdale - Deerfield Beach **H**
(954) 428-5997. **$60-$140.** 1200 FAU Research Park Blvd 33441. I-95 exit 41 (SW 10th St), just e to FAU Research Park Rd, then just s. Int corridors. **Pets:** Other species. $25 daily fee/pet. Service with restrictions, supervision. 📶 📶 ✕ 📶 💻

▼▼ La Quinta Inn & Suites-Deerfield Beach I-95 **H**
(954) 428-0661. **$82-$234.** 100 SW 12th Ave 33442. I-95 exit 42B (Hillsboro Blvd), just w to SW 12th Ave, then just s. Int corridors.
Pets: Large, other species. Service with restrictions.
📶 🏊 📶 📶 💻

▼▼ Quality Inn & Suites-Deerfield Beach **H**
(954) 570-8887. **$75-$200.** 1040 E Newport Center Dr 33442. I-95 exit 41 (SW 10th St), just w; in Newport Center Complex. Ext corridors. **Pets:** Small. $25 daily fee/pet. Designated rooms, no service, supervision. 🏊 📶 ✕ 📶 💻

(AAA) ▼▼▼ Wyndham Deerfield Beach Resort **H** ❀
(954) 428-2850. **$159-$479.** 2096 NE 2nd St 33441. I-95 exit 42 (Hillsboro Blvd), 2.6 mi e to SR A1A (Ocean Blvd), then just ne. Int corridors. **Pets:** Small. $35 daily fee/room. Designated rooms, service with restrictions, supervision. [SAVE] 🍴 🏊 ✕ 📶 ✕ 📶 💻

DE FUNIAK SPRINGS

(AAA) ▼▼▼ BEST WESTERN Crossroads Inn **M**
(850) 892-5111. **$90-$100.** 2343 US Hwy 331 S 32435. I-10 exit 85, just s. Ext/int corridors. **Pets:** Accepted. [SAVE] 🍴 🏊 📶 📶 💻

DELRAY BEACH *(Restaurants p. 625)*

∰ ☖☖☖ **Colony Hotel & Cabana Club** 🅷 ❀
(561) 276-4123. **$99-$329, 3 day notice.** 525 E Atlantic Ave 33483.
I-95 exit 52 (Atlantic Ave), 1.4 mi e. Int corridors. **Pets:** Other species.
$25 daily fee/pet. (SAVE) ⓔⓒⓞ ➡ 🛜 ✕

∰ ☖☖ ☖☖ **Delray Beach Marriott** 🅷
(561) 274-3200. **$161-$599.** 10 N Ocean Blvd 33483. I-95 exit 52
(Atlantic Ave), 1.8 mi e, then just n; downtown. Int corridors.
Pets: Small. $125 one-time fee/room. Service with restrictions, supervision. (SAVE) ⓔⓒⓞ ⓣ ➡ 🗴 🛜 ✕ 🔌 🖳

∰ ☖☖ ☖☖ **Hyatt Place Delray Beach** 🅷
(561) 330-3530. **$99-$399.** 104 NE 2nd Ave 33444. I-95 exit 52 (Atlantic Ave), 1.2 mi e to NE 2nd Ave, then just n; in Pineapple Grove district of downtown. Int corridors. **Pets:** Accepted.
(SAVE) ⓖⓜ 🛜 ✕ 🔌 🖳

∰ ☖☖☖ **Residence Inn by Marriott - Delray Beach** 🅷
(561) 276-7441. **$143-$499.** 1111 E Atlantic Ave 33483. I-95 exit 52
(Atlantic Ave), 1.7 mi e; downtown. Int corridors. **Pets:** Accepted.
(SAVE) ⓔⓒⓞ ⓖⓜ ➡ 🛜 ✕ 🔌 🖳

☖☖☖ **Sundy House** 🅷
(561) 272-5678. **Call for rates.** 106 S Swinton Ave 33444. I-95 exit 52
(Atlantic Ave), 1.1 mi e to Swinton Ave, then just s. Ext corridors.
Pets: Accepted. ⓣ ➡ 🛜 ✕ 🔌 🖳

DESTIN *(Restaurants p. 625)*

∰ ☖☖☖ **Residence Inn by Marriott Sandestin at Grand Boulevard** 🅷
(850) 650-7811. **$149-$399.** 300 Grand Blvd 32550. On US 98, jct Baytowne Ln. Int corridors. **Pets:** Accepted.
(SAVE) ⓔⓒⓞ ⓖⓜ ➡ 🗴 🛜 ✕ 🔌 🖳

∰ ☖☖☖ **Sandestin Golf and Beach Resort** 🅷
(850) 267-8000. **$139-$329, 7 day notice.** 9300 Emerald Coast Pkwy
W 32550. On US 98; jct Sandestin Dr, follow signs to The Village. Ext/
int corridors. **Pets:** Dogs only. Designated rooms, service with restrictions, crate. (SAVE) ⓣ ➡ 🗴 🛜 ✕ 🔌 🖳

∰ ☖☖☖ **SummerPlace Inn** 🅷 ❀
(850) 650-8003. **$70-$289, 3 day notice.** 14047 Emerald Coast Pkwy
32541. On US 98, 2.5 mi w at jct SR 293. Int corridors. **Pets:** Large,
other species. $50 one-time fee/pet. Designated rooms, service with
restrictions, crate. (SAVE) ➡ 🛜 ✕ 🔌 🖳

DORAL

☖☖☖ **Aloft Miami Doral** 🅷 ❀
(786) 272-7200. **Call for rates.** 3265 NW 107th Ave 33172. Corner of
NW 33rd St and 107th Ave; 3.7 mi e of Doral. Int corridors.
Pets: Medium, dogs only. Service with restrictions, supervision.
🛜 🗴 Ⓦ 🖳

☖☖☖ **Candlewood Suites-Miami Airport West** 🅷
(305) 591-9099. **Call for rates.** 8855 NW 27th St 33172. Florida Tpke
exit 29 (NW 41st St), 3.2 mi e to NW 87th Ave, 0.7 mi s to NW 27th
St, then just w. Int corridors. **Pets:** Accepted.
ⓖⓜ ➡ 🛜 ✕ 🔌 🖳

☖☖☖ **Extended Stay America-Miami-Doral** 🅷
(305) 716-9005. **$70-$250.** 7750 NW 25th St 33122. SR 826 (Palmetto
Expwy) exit NW 25th St, just w. Int corridors. **Pets:** Other species. $25
daily fee/pet. Service with restrictions, supervision.
ⓖⓜ ➡ 🛜 ✕ 🔌

☖☖☖ **La Quinta Inn & Suites Miami Airport West** 🅷
(305) 436-0830. **$105-$284.** 8730 NW 27th St 33172. Florida Tpke exit
29 (NW 41st St), 3.2 mi e to NW 87th Ave, 0.7 mi s to NW 27th St,
then just w. Int corridors. **Pets:** Large, other species. Service with
restrictions. ⓖⓜ ➡ 🛜 🔌 🖳

∰ ☖☖ ☖☖ **Provident Doral at the Blue Miami** 🅷
(305) 597-8600. **$119-$389.** 5300 NW 87th Ave 33178. Florida Tpke
exit 29 (NW 41st St), 3 mi e to NW 87th Ave, then just n. Ext corridors.
Pets: Accepted. (SAVE) ⓣ ➡ 🗴 🛜 ✕ 🔌 🖳

☖☖ **Residence Inn by Marriott-Miami Airport West/Doral Area** 🅷
(305) 591-2211. **$129-$239.** 1212 NW 82nd Ave 33126. SR 826 (Palmetto Expwy) exit NW 25th St, 0.5 mi w to NW 82nd Ave, then 1 mi s.
Ext corridors. **Pets:** Accepted. ➡ 🛜 ✕ 🔌 🖳

☖☖☖ **Staybridge Suites-Miami Doral** 🅷
(305) 500-9100. **$149-$169, 3 day notice.** 3265 NW 87th Ave 33172.
Florida Tpke exit 29 (NW 41st St), 3.2 mi e to NW 87th Ave, then 0.3
mi s. Int corridors. **Pets:** Other species. $150 one-time fee/pet. Service
with restrictions, crate. ➡ 🛜 🔌 🖳

∰ ☖☖ ☖☖ **TownePlace Suites by Marriott-Miami Airport West/Doral Area** 🅷
(305) 718-4144. **$99-$199.** 5300 NW 36th St 33178. Florida Tpke exit
29 (NW 41st St), 1.2 mi e to 107th Ave, then just s. Int corridors.
Pets: Accepted. (SAVE) ➡ 🛜 ✕ 🔌 🖳

∰ ☖☖ ☖☖ **Trump National Doral® Miami** 🅷
(305) 592-2000. **$133-$425.** 4400 NW 87th Ave 33178. Florida Tpke
exit 29 (NW 41st St), 3 mi e to NW 87th Ave, then just n. Int corridors.
Pets: Accepted. (SAVE) ⓣ ➡ 🗴 🆂 ✕ 🔌 🖳

DUNEDIN

∰ ☖☖☖ **The Blue Moon Inn** Ⓜ
(727) 784-3719. **$159-$189, 30 day notice.** 2920 US Alt 19 N 34698.
0.6 mi n of jct Curlew Rd. Ext corridors. **Pets:** Accepted.
(SAVE) ⓖⓜ ➡ 🗴 🛜 ✕ 🔌 🖳

FERNANDINA BEACH

☖☖ **Amelia Island Hampton Inn** 🅷
(904) 321-1111. **$119-$189.** 2549 Sadler Rd 32034. In Fernandina
Beach; just w of jct SR A1A (Atlantic Ave) and Sadler Rd. Int corridors.
Pets: Accepted. ⓖⓜ ➡ 🛜 🔌 🖳

☖☖ **Days Inn & Suites** Ⓜ
(904) 277-2300. **$70-$400.** 2707 Sadler Rd 32034. In Fernandina
Beach; on east side of island, just w of jct S Fletcher Ave (SR A1A/
105). Ext corridors. **Pets:** Accepted. ➡ 🗴 🛜 ✕

∰ ☖☖☖ **The Hoyt House** 🅱🅱
(904) 277-4300. **$229-$369, 14 day notice.** 804 Atlantic Ave 32034. In
Fernandina Beach; between S 8th and S 9th sts. Int corridors.
Pets: Medium, dogs only. $25 daily fee/pet. Designated rooms, supervision. (SAVE) ➡ 🗴 🛜 ✕

∰ ☖☖ ☖☖ **Omni Amelia Island Plantation Resort** 🅷
(904) 261-6161. **$189-$499, 3 day notice.** 39 Beach Lagoon Rd 32034.
In Fernandina Beach; SR A1A (Atlantic Ave), 6.5 mi s of the bridge. Ext
corridors. **Pets:** Accepted.
(SAVE) ⓔⓒⓞ ⓣ ➡ 🗴 🛜 ✕ 🔌 🖳

∰ ☖☖☖ **Residence Inn by Marriott-Amelia Island** 🅷
(904) 277-2440. **$105-$175.** 2301 Sadler Rd 32034. In Fernandina
Beach; just w of jct S Fletcher Ave (SR A1A/105); on east side of
island. Int corridors. **Pets:** Accepted.
(SAVE) ⓔⓒⓞ ⓖⓜ ➡ 🗴 🛜 ✕ 🔌 🖳

FORT LAUDERDALE *(Restaurants p. 625)*

∰ ☖☖ ☖☖ **The Atlantic Hotel & Spa** 🅷
(954) 567-8020. **$179-$499, 3 day notice.** 601 N Fort Lauderdale
Beach Blvd 33304. I-95 exit 29 (Sunrise Blvd), 4.1 mi e to SR A1A
(Fort Lauderdale Beach Blvd), then 0.5 mi s. Int corridors.
Pets: Accepted. (SAVE) ⓣ ⓖⓜ ➡ 🗴 🛜 ✕ 🔌 🖳

Candlewood Suites Fort Lauderdale Airport/Cruise Port H
(954) 522-8822. **$79-$269.** 1120 W State Rd 84 33315. I-95 exit 25 (SR 84), 0.8 mi e. Int corridors. **Pets:** Accepted.

Embassy Suites Fort Lauderdale-17th Street H
(954) 527-2700. **$119-$319.** 1100 SE 17th St 33316. I-95 exit 25 (SR 84), 2 mi e to US 1 (SE 6th Ave), 0.5 mi n to SE 17th St, then 0.3 mi e. Int corridors. **Pets:** Accepted.

Extended Stay America-Fort Lauderdale-Cypress Creek-NW 6th Way H
(954) 772-3155. **$60-$200.** 6001 NW 6th Way 33309. I-95 exit 33 (Cypress Creek Rd), 0.4 mi w, then just s. Int corridors. **Pets:** Other species. $25 daily fee/pet. Service with restrictions, supervision.

Hampton Inn Ft. Lauderdale Airport North Cruise Port H
(954) 524-9900. **$109-$329.** 2301 SW 12th Ave 33315. I-95 exit 25 (SR 84), 0.7 mi e to SW 12th Ave, then just n. Int corridors.
Pets: Accepted.

Hilton Fort Lauderdale Marina H
(954) 463-4000. **$79-$299.** 1881 SE 17th St 33316. I-95 exit 25 (SR 84), 2 mi e to SE 6th Ave (US 1), 0.5 mi n to SE 17th St, then 1 mi e. Ext/int corridors. **Pets:** Medium. $75 one-time fee/room. Designated rooms, service with restrictions.

Holiday Inn Express & Suites-Ft. Lauderdale Executive Airport H
(954) 772-3032. **Call for rates.** 1500 W Commercial Blvd 33309. I-95 exit 32 (Commercial Blvd), 0.7 mi w. Int corridors. **Pets:** Accepted.

Hyatt Place Fort Lauderdale 17th Street Convention Center H
(954) 763-7670. **$89-$349.** 1851 SE 10th Ave 33316. US 1 (Federal Hwy), just e on SE 17th St to SE 10th Ave, then just s. Int corridors. **Pets:** Accepted.

La Quinta Inn & Suites-Ft Lauderdale Cypress Creek H
(954) 491-7666. **$79-$254.** 999 W Cypress Creek Rd 33309. I-95 exit 33 (Cypress Creek Rd), 0.7 mi w. Int corridors. **Pets:** Large, other species. Service with restrictions.

La Quinta Inn-Ft. Lauderdale Northeast H
(954) 491-2500. **$82-$224.** 5727 N Federal Hwy 33308. I-95 exit 32 (Commercial Blvd), 2.7 mi e to US 1 (Federal Hwy), then 0.7 mi n. Ext/int corridors. **Pets:** Large, other species. Service with restrictions.

The Ritz-Carlton, Fort Lauderdale H ❀
(954) 465-2300. **$219-$2499, 7 day notice.** 1 N Fort Lauderdale Beach Blvd 33304. I-95 exit 29 (Sunrise Blvd), 4.1 mi e to SR A1A (Fort Lauderdale Beach Blvd), then 1.2 mi s. Int corridors. **Pets:** Small, dogs only. $250 one-time fee/room. Service with restrictions.

Riverside Hotel, The International Hotel of Fort Lauderdale H
(954) 467-0671. **$119-$599, 3 day notice.** 620 E Las Olas Blvd 33301. I-95 exit 27 (Broward Blvd), 2.4 mi e to US 1 (Federal Hwy), just s to Las Olas Blvd, then just e. Int corridors. **Pets:** Accepted.

Rodeway Inn & Suites-Fort Lauderdale Airport/Cruise Port H
(954) 792-8181. **Call for rates.** 2440 W SR 84 33312. I-95 exit 25 (SR 84), just w. Ext/int corridors. **Pets:** Accepted.

Sheraton Suites Fort Lauderdale at Cypress Creek H
(954) 772-5400. **$99-$159.** 555 NW 62nd St 33309. I-95 exit 33 (Cypress Creek Rd), just w. Int corridors. **Pets:** Accepted.

TownePlace Suites by Marriott-Fort Lauderdale West H
(954) 484-2214. **$109-$279.** 3100 W Prospect Rd 33309. I-95 exit 33 (Cypress Creek Rd), 2.7 mi w to NW 31st Ave, then 0.5 mi s. Int corridors. **Pets:** Accepted.

The Westin Fort Lauderdale H
(954) 772-1331. **$99-$399.** 400 Corporate Dr 33334. I-95 exit 33 (Cypress Creek Rd), just e; in Radice Corporate Park. Int corridors.
Pets: Accepted.

The Westin Fort Lauderdale Beach Resort H
(954) 467-1111. **$169-$569, 3 day notice.** 321 N Fort Lauderdale Beach Blvd 33304. I-95 exit 29 (Sunrise Blvd), 4.2 mi e to SR A1A (Fort Lauderdale Beach Blvd), then 0.8 mi s. Int corridors. **Pets:** Accepted.

W Fort Lauderdale H
(954) 414-8200. **$159-$699, 3 day notice.** 401 N Fort Lauderdale Beach Blvd 33304. I-95 exit 29 (Sunrise Blvd), 4.2 mi e to SR A1A (Fort Lauderdale Beach Blvd), then 0.7 mi s. Int corridors.
Pets: Accepted.

FORT MYERS *(Restaurants p. 625)*

Baymont Inn & Suites Fort Myers H
(239) 454-0040. **$59-$128.** 9401 Marketplace Rd 33912. I-75 exit 131, just w on CR 879 (Daniels Pkwy), then just n on Danport Blvd. Int corridors. **Pets:** Medium. $15 daily fee/pet. Designated rooms, service with restrictions, supervision.

BEST WESTERN Airport Inn H ❀
(239) 561-7000. **$59-$309.** 8955 Daniels Pkwy 33912. I-75 exit 131, 0.6 mi w on CR 879 (Daniels Pkwy). Int corridors. **Pets:** Large, other species. $20 daily fee/pet. Designated rooms, service with restrictions, supervision.

Candlewood Suites-Fort Myers Sanibel Gateway H
(239) 210-7777. **Call for rates.** 9740 Commerce Center Ct 33908. Just sw of Summerlin Rd on Bass Rd; in Summerlin Park. Int corridors.
Pets: Accepted.

Holiday Inn-Historic Downtown H
(239) 332-3232. **$79-$299.** 2431 Cleveland Ave 33901. On US 41, just s of jct Edison Ave. Int corridors. **Pets:** Accepted.

Homewood Suites by Hilton Fort Myers Airport/FGCU H
(239) 210-7300. **$109-$299.** 16450 Corporate Commerce Way 33913. I-75 exit 128, 0.6 mi e on CR 840 (Alico Rd), just n on Ben Hill Griffin Pkwy, then just w; in Gulfcoast Landings. Int corridors. **Pets:** Accepted.

Homewood Suites by Hilton-Fort Myers at Bell Tower H ❀
(239) 275-6000. **$109-$299.** 5255 Big Pine Way 33907. Just e of jct US 41; just n of jct CR 879 (Daniels Pkwy). Int corridors. **Pets:** Large. $75 one-time fee/room. Service with restrictions, crate.

▼▼▼ **Hotel Indigo-Fort Myers Downtown River District** H

(239) 337-3446. **$119-$289.** 1520 Broadway Ave 33901. Between First and Main sts. Int corridors. **Pets:** Small, dogs only. $75 one-time fee/pet. Designated rooms, crate. ECO ⓘ ⓛM ⌂ ⓦ ⓧ ⓗ ⓟ

AAA ▼▼▼ **Hyatt Place Fort Myers at The Forum** H

(239) 418-1844. **$79-$219.** 2600 Champion Ring Rd 33905. I-75 exit 138, just e on SR 82. Int corridors. **Pets:** Accepted.
SAVE ⓛM ⌂ ⓦ ⓧ ⓗ ⓟ

AAA ▼▼▼ **La Quinta Inn & Suites-Airport** H

(239) 466-0012. **$79-$279.** 9521 Marketplace Rd 33912. I-75 exit 131, 0.4 mi w on CR 879 (Daniels Pkwy), then just n on Danport Blvd. Int corridors. **Pets:** Large, other species. Service with restrictions.
SAVE ECO ⓛM ⌂ ⓦ ⓧ ⓗ ⓟ

▼▼ **Quality Suites Fort Myers Airport** M

(239) 768-0005. **$60-$190.** 13651 Indian Paint Ln 33912. I-75 exit 131, just w on CR 879 (Daniels Pkwy). Int corridors. **Pets:** Accepted.
⌂ ⓦ ⓧ ⓗ ⓟ

▼▼▼ **Residence Inn by Marriott Fort Myers** H

(239) 936-0110. **$89-$249.** 2960 Colonial Blvd 33966. I-75 exit 136, 3.5 mi w on SR 884 (Colonial Blvd); jct Metro Pkwy. Int corridors.
Pets: Accepted. ECO ⓛM ⌂ ⓦ ⓧ ⓗ ⓟ

AAA ▼▼▼ **Residence Inn by Marriott-Fort Myers Sanibel** H

(239) 415-4150. **$99-$299.** 20371 Summerlin Rd 33908. On CR 869, just ne of jct McGregor Blvd. Int corridors. **Pets:** Large, other species. $100 one-time fee/room. Designated rooms, service with restrictions.
SAVE ⓛM ⌂ ⓧ ⓦ ⓧ ⓗ ⓟ

▼▼ **Suburban Extended Stay Hotel** H

(239) 938-0100. **$60-$130.** 10150 Metro Pkwy 33912. I-75 exit 136, 3.4 mi w on SR 884 (Colonial Blvd), then just s on SR 739. Int corridors.
Pets: Accepted. ECO ⓛM ⌂ ⓦ ⓦ ⓟ

FORT MYERS BEACH

AAA ▼▼▼ **BEST WESTERN PLUS Beach Resort** H

(239) 463-6000. **$209-$349, 7 day notice.** 684 Estero Blvd 33931. 0.4 mi n of Matanzas Pass Bridge (SR 865). Ext corridors. **Pets:** Small, dogs only. $20 daily fee/pet. Service with restrictions, supervision.
SAVE ⓛM ⌂ ⓦ ⓧ ⓗ ⓟ

AAA ▼▼▼ **Carousel Inn on the Beach** M

(239) 463-6131. **$199, 7 day notice.** 6230 Estero Blvd 33931. On SR 599, 4 mi se of jct Matanzas Pass Bridge (SR 865). Ext corridors.
Pets: Accepted. SAVE ⌂ ⓦ ⓗ ⓟ

▼▼▼ **Hampton Inn & Suites Ft. Myers Beach-Sanibel Gateway** H ❖

(239) 437-8888. **$79-$259.** 11281 Summerlin Square Rd 33931. Just e of jct Matanzas Pass Bridge (SR 865). Int corridors. **Pets:** Medium, other species. Service with restrictions, supervision.
ECO ⓛM ⌂ ⓦ ⓧ ⓗ ⓟ

AAA ▼▼▼ **Matanzas Inn** M

(239) 463-9258. **$84-$235, 30 day notice.** 414 Crescent St 33931. Just e of Matanzas Pass Bridge (SR 865), then just n. Ext corridors.
Pets: Accepted. SAVE ⓘ ⌂ ⓧ ⓦ ⓗ ⓟ

FORT PIERCE

AAA ▼▼▼ **Fairfield Inn & Suites by Marriott-Fort Pierce** H

(772) 462-2900. **$99-$189.** 6502 Metal Dr 34945. I-95 exit 129 (Okeechobee Rd), 0.6 mi w; Florida Tpke exit 152, 0.3 mi e. Int corridors. **Pets:** Other species. $50 one-time fee/room. Service with restrictions, crate. SAVE ECO ⓛM ⌂ ⓦ ⓧ ⓗ ⓟ

▼▼▼ **Holiday Inn Express & Suites Fort Pierce West** H

(772) 464-5000. **Call for rates.** 7151 Okeechobee Rd 34945. I-95 exit 129 (Okeechobee Rd), 0.7 mi w; Florida Tpke exit 152, just e. Int corridors. **Pets:** Accepted. ⓛM ⌂ ⓦ ⓧ ⓗ ⓟ

AAA ▼▼ **Royal Inn Beach Hotel-South Hutchinson Island** M

(772) 672-8888. **$89-$299.** 222 Hernando St 34949. US 1, 2.5 mi e on Seaway Dr (SR A1A) to Hernando St, then just s. Ext corridors.
Pets: $25 daily fee/room. Service with restrictions, supervision.
SAVE ⓦ ⓧ ⓗ ⓟ

FORT WALTON BEACH

▼▼▼ **La Quinta Inn & Suites Fort Walton Beach** H

(850) 244-1500. **$89-$394.** 3 SW Miracle Strip Pkwy 32548. On US 98; jct SR 189. Int corridors. **Pets:** Large, other species. Service with restrictions. ⌂ ⓦ ⓧ ⓗ ⓟ

▼▼ **Ramada Plaza Beach Resort** H

(850) 243-9161. **$109-$279, 3 day notice.** 1500 Miracle Strip Pkwy SE 32548. On US 98, 1 mi e. Ext/int corridors. **Pets:** Accepted.
ECO ⓘ ⌂ ⓦ ⓧ ⓗ ⓟ

GAINESVILLE

AAA ▼▼▼ **Baymont Inn & Suites Gainesville** H

(352) 332-8292. **$59-$89.** 6901 NW 4th Blvd 32607. I-75 exit 387, just w on SR 26 (W Newberry Rd), then just s on 75th St, then just e. Ext/int corridors. **Pets:** Accepted. SAVE ⌂ ⓦ ⓧ ⓗ ⓟ

AAA ▼▼▼ **BEST WESTERN Gateway Grand** H

(352) 331-3336. **$99-$269, 3 day notice.** 4200 NW 97th Blvd 32606. I-75 exit 390, just w on SR 222, then just n. Int corridors.
Pets: Accepted. SAVE ECO ⓘ ⓛM ⌂ ⓧ ⓦ ⓧ ⓗ ⓟ

AAA ▼▼▼ **Hilton University of Florida Conference Center Gainesville** H

(352) 371-3600. **$109-$249.** 1714 SW 34th St 32607. I-75 exit 384, 0.9 mi e on SR 24 (Archer Rd), then 0.7 mi n on SR 121; in University of Florida. Int corridors. **Pets:** Accepted.
SAVE ECO ⓘ ⓛM ⌂ $ⓦ ⓧ ⓗ ⓟ

AAA ▼▼▼ **Holiday Inn Express** H

(352) 376-0004. **$106-$210, 30 day notice.** 3905 SW 43rd St 32608. I-75 exit 384, just w on SR 24 (Archer Rd), then just n. Int corridors.
Pets: Medium, other species. $25 one-time fee/room, $5 daily fee/room. Designated rooms, service with restrictions, supervision.
SAVE ⓛM ⌂ ⓦ ⓗ ⓟ

AAA ▼▼ **Quality Inn** H

(352) 378-2405. **$70-$221.** 3455 SW Williston Rd 32608. I-75 exit 382, just sw on SR 121. Int corridors. **Pets:** Accepted. ⌂ ⓦ ⓗ ⓟ

AAA ▼▼▼ **Residence Inn by Marriott Gainesville I-75** H

(352) 264-0000. **$116-$170.** 3275 SW 40th Blvd 32608. I-75 exit 384, just e on SR 24 (Archer Rd), then just n. Int corridors. **Pets:** Accepted.
SAVE ECO ⌂ ⓦ ⓧ ⓗ ⓟ

AAA ▼▼▼ **SpringHill Suites by Marriott Gainesville** ❖

(352) 376-8873. **$149-$329.** 4155 SW 40th Blvd 32608. I-75 exit 384, just e, then just s. Int corridors. **Pets:** Other species. $75 one-time fee/room. Designated rooms, service with restrictions, supervision.
SAVE ECO ⌂ ⓦ ⓧ ⓗ ⓟ

AAA ▼▼▼ **Sweetwater Branch Inn Bed & Breakfast** BB ❖

(352) 373-6760. **$139-$289.** 625 E University Ave 32601. On SR 26/20, just w of jct SE 11th St. Int corridors. **Pets:** $50 deposit/room, $50 one-time fee/room. Designated rooms, service with restrictions, crate.
SAVE ⓦ ⓧ ⓗ ⓟ

HILLSBORO BEACH

▼▼ Seabonay Beach Resort 🅷

(954) 427-2525. **Call for rates.** 1159 Hillsboro Mile 33062. I-95 exit 42 (Hillsboro Blvd), 2.6 mi e to SR A1A (Ocean Blvd), then 1.4 mi s. Ext/int corridors. **Pets:** Accepted. 🔲 🆂 ⊠ 🛢 💻

HOLLYWOOD (Restaurants p. 625)

▼▼ Days Inn-Fort Lauderdale/Hollywood Airport South 🅷

(954) 923-7300. **$145-$309.** 2601 N 29th Ave 33020. I-95 exit 21 (Sheridan St), just w. Int corridors. **Pets:** Accepted.
🄴🄲🄾 🔲 📶 🛢 💻

▼▼ La Quinta Inn & Suites-Ft. Lauderdale Airport 🅷

(954) 922-2295. **$115-$294.** 2620 N 26th Ave 33020. I-95 exit 21 (Sheridan St), just e to N 26th Ave, then just n. Int corridors. **Pets:** Large, other species. Service with restrictions.
🔲ᴹ 📶 🛢 💻

◈ ▼◈ Quality Inn & Suites-Fort Lauderdale Airport/Cruise Port South 🅷

(954) 922-1600. **$69-$219.** 2520 Stirling Rd 33020. I-95 exit 22 (Stirling Rd), 0.4 mi e. Ext corridors. **Pets:** Accepted.
🆂🄰🅅🄴 🔲ᴹ 🔲 📶 ⊠ 🛢 💻

◈ ▼◈ ▼◈ Quality Inn & Suites Hollywood Blvd 🅼

(954) 981-1800. **$90-$270.** 4900 Hollywood Blvd 33021. I-95 exit 20 (Hollywood Blvd), 1.6 mi w; Florida Tpke exit 49, 1.3 mi e. Ext corridors. **Pets:** Accepted. 🆂🄰🅅🄴 🔲 📶 ⊠ 🛢 💻

◈ ▼◈ ▼◈ Seminole Hard Rock Hotel & Casino Hollywood 🅷

(954) 327-7625. **Call for rates.** 1 Seminole Way 33314. I-95 exit 22 (Stirling Rd), 2.9 mi w, then just n on SR 7/US 441; Florida Tpke exit 53, 0.5 mi e, then 0.8 mi s. Int corridors. **Pets:** Accepted.
🆂🄰🅅🄴 🄴🄲🄾 🍴 🔲ᴹ 🔲 ⊠ 📶 💻

INDIALANTIC

▼◈◈ Windemere Inn By The Sea 🄱🄱 🐾

(321) 728-9334. **$175-$275, 10 day notice.** 815 S Miramar Ave (A1A) 32903. Jct US 192, 0.3 mi s on SR A1A. Ext/int corridors. **Pets:** Medium. $25 daily fee/pet. Designated rooms, service with restrictions, supervision. 📶 ⊠ 🄯

ISLAMORADA (Restaurants p. 625)

▼▼ Islander Resort, a Guy Harvey Outpost Resort 🅼

(305) 664-2031. **$188-$368, 3 day notice.** 82100 Overseas Hwy 33036. US 1 at MM 82.1. Ext corridors. **Pets:** Accepted.
🍴 🔲 ⊠ 📶 🛢 💻

JACKSONVILLE (Restaurants p. 625)

◈◈ ▼◈◈◈ Aloft Jacksonville Tapestry Park 🅷

(904) 998-4448. **$89-$299.** 4812 Deer Lake Dr W 32246. I-95 exit 340, 4.5 mi n to Southside Blvd, then e. Int corridors. **Pets:** Accepted.
🆂🄰🅅🄴 🔲ᴹ 🔲 📶 ⊠ 🛢 💻

▼▼ Candlewood Suites 🅷

(904) 296-7785. **$70-$90, 3 day notice.** 4990 Belfort Rd 32256. I-95 exit 344 (Butler Blvd/SR 202), ne to Belfort Rd, then just s. Int corridors. **Pets:** Accepted. 🔲ᴹ 📶 ⊠ 🛢 💻

◈◈ ▼◈◈◈ Crowne Plaza Jacksonville Airport/I-95N 🅷

(904) 741-4404. **$89-$179.** 14670 Duval Rd 32218. I-95 exit 363, just w. Int corridors. **Pets:** Medium. $75 one-time fee/room. Designated rooms, service with restrictions. 🆂🄰🅅🄴 🍴 🔲ᴹ 🔲 📶 💻

◈◈ ▼◈◈◈ Days Inn Jacksonville Airport 🅷

(904) 741-4980. **$75-$130.** 1170 Airport Rd 32218. I-95 exit 363B, just w, then just s on Duval Rd. Ext corridors. **Pets:** Medium. $20 daily fee/room. Designated rooms, service with restrictions, supervision.
🆂🄰🅅🄴 🔲ᴹ 🔲 📶 🛢 💻

▼▼▼ Hampton Inn & Suites Jacksonville South-St Johns Town Center Area 🅷

(904) 997-9100. **$89-$149.** 4415 Southside Blvd 32216. I-95 exit 344 (Butler Blvd/SR 202), 2.5 mi e on J Turner Butler Blvd, then 0.9 mi n on SR 115. Int corridors. **Pets:** Service with restrictions, crate.
🔲 📶 ⊠ 🛢 💻

▼▼▼ Holiday Inn Express & Suites Jacksonville Blount Island 🅷

(904) 696-3333. **$83-$209.** 10148 New Berlin Rd 32226. I-95 exit 362A southbound, 4.9 mi s on SR 9A to Heckscher Dr, then just w; exit 358A northbound, 5.8 mi ne on Heckscher Dr; 0.6 mi from Jaxport Cruise Terminal. Int corridors. **Pets:** Accepted. 🔲ᴹ 🔲 📶 ⊠ 🛢 💻

▼▼▼ Holiday Inn Express Hotel & Suites - South 🅷

(904) 332-9500. **$79-$179.** 4675 Salisbury Rd 32256. I-95 exit 344 (Butler Blvd/SR 202), just e to Salisbury Rd, then just s. Int corridors. **Pets:** Other species. $150 deposit/pet. Service with restrictions, supervision. 🔲ᴹ 🔲 📶 ⊠ 🛢 💻

▼▼▼ Holiday Inn Express Jacksonville East 🅷

(904) 997-9190. **$89-$119.** 53 Jefferson Rd 32225. Jct SR 9A and Atlantic Blvd, just ne. Int corridors. **Pets:** Accepted.
🔲 📶 ⊠ 🛢 💻

▼▼▼ Homewood Suites by Hilton Jacksonville South/Town Center St. Johns 🅷

(904) 641-7988. **$109-$400.** 10434 Midtown Pkwy 32246. I-95 exit 344 (SR 202), 3.5 mi e on J Turner Butler Blvd to Gate Pkwy, 0.3 mi n to Town Center Pkwy, 0.5 mi e to Midtown Pkwy, then 0.3 mi s. Int corridors. **Pets:** Accepted. 🔲 📶 🛢 💻

▼▼▼ Homewood Suites Jacksonville Downtown/Southbank 🅷

(904) 396-6888. **$149-$181.** 1201 Kings Ave 32207. I-95 exit 350A (Downtown/Prudential St), 0.3 mi e on Prudential St, then just s. Int corridors. **Pets:** Other species. $75 one-time fee/room. Service with restrictions. 🔲ᴹ 🔲 📶 🛢 💻

▼▼▼ Hotel Indigo Jacksonville Deerwood Park 🅷

(904) 996-7199. **Call for rates.** 9840 Tapestry Park Cir 32246. I-95 exit 340, 4.5 mi n to Southside Blvd, then e. Int corridors. **Pets:** Large, other species. $25 one-time fee/room. Service with restrictions, supervision. 🍴 🔲 📶 ⊠ 🛢 💻

◈◈ ▼◈◈◈ Hyatt Place Jacksonville Airport 🅷

(904) 741-4184. **$79-$199.** 14565 Duval Rd 32218. I-95 exit 363B, just w, then just s. Int corridors. **Pets:** Accepted.
🆂🄰🅅🄴 🍴 🔲ᴹ 🔲 📶 ⊠ 🛢 💻

◈◈ ▼◈◈◈ Hyatt Regency Jacksonville Riverfront 🅷

(904) 588-1234. **$89-$399, 3 day notice.** 225 Coast Line Dr E 32202. Downtown; just e of The Landing. Int corridors. **Pets:** Accepted.
🆂🄰🅅🄴 🄴🄲🄾 🍴 🔲 ⊠ 📶 🛢 💻

▼◈◈◈ Omni Jacksonville Hotel 🅷

(904) 355-6664. **Call for rates.** 245 Water St 32202. Corner of Pearl and Water sts; on north side of St. Johns River; downtown; adjacent to The Landing. Int corridors. **Pets:** Accepted.
🄴🄲🄾 🍴 🔲 📶 ⊠ 💻

▼▼ Residence Inn by Marriott Butler Blvd 🅷

(904) 996-8900. **$85-$139.** 10551 Deerwood Park Blvd 32256. I-95 exit 344 (Butler Blvd/SR 202), 3.3 mi e to Gate Parkway exit, then just s to Deerwood Park Blvd, then just w. Int corridors. **Pets:** $100 one-time fee/pet. Service with restrictions, supervision.
🔲ᴹ 🔲 📶 ⊠ 🛢 💻

◈◈ ▼◈◈◈ Residence Inn by Marriott Jacksonville Baymeadows 🅷

(904) 733-8088. **$74-$124.** 8365 Dix Ellis Tr 32256. I-95 exit 341 (Baymeadows Rd/SR 152), just w to Freedom Commerce Pkwy, then just s. Ext corridors. **Pets:** Accepted. 🆂🄰🅅🄴 🔲 📶 ⊠ 🛢 💻

AAA ▼▼▼▼ Sheraton Jacksonville Hotel 🅷

(904) 564-4772. **$99-$199, 7 day notice.** 10605 Deerwood Park Blvd 32256. I-95 exit 344 (Butler Blvd/SR 202), 3.3 mi e to Gate Parkway exit, just s to Deerwood Park Blvd, then just w. Int corridors. **Pets:** Accepted. [SAVE] [🍴] [&M] [🛏] [🛜] [✕] [📠] [💻]

JACKSONVILLE BEACH *(Restaurants p. 625)*

AAA ▼▼▼▼ Four Points by Sheraton Jacksonville Beachfront 🅷 ❀

(904) 435-3535. **$159-$399.** 11 1st St N 32250. Just n of Beach Blvd (US 90). Int corridors. **Pets:** Medium, dogs only. $35 daily fee/pet. Designated rooms, service with restrictions, supervision.

[SAVE] [ECO] [&M] [🛏] [✕] [🛜] [✕] [📠] [💻]

AAA ▼▼▼▼ Holiday Inn Express Jacksonville Beach-Mayo Clinic 🅷

(904) 435-3000. **$119-$329, 3 day notice.** 1101 Beach Blvd 32250. 0.7 mi w of 3rd St/SR A1A. Int corridors. **Pets:** Accepted.

[SAVE] [ECO] [🛏] [✕] [🛜] [✕] [📠] [💻]

JUNO BEACH *(Restaurants p. 625)*

▼▼▼▼ Holiday Inn Express North Palm Beach-Oceanview 🅷

(561) 622-4366. **Call for rates.** 13950 US Hwy 1 33408. I-95 exit 83 (Donald Ross Rd), 4.5 mi e; jct US 1 and Donald Ross Rd. Ext/int corridors. **Pets:** Accepted. [🛏] [🛜] [✕] [📠] [💻]

JUPITER

▼▼▼▼ Fairfield Inn & Suites by Marriott-Jupiter/West Palm Beach 🅷

(561) 748-5252. **$99-$299.** 6748 W Indiantown Rd 33458. I-95 exit 87A (Indiantown Rd), 0.8 mi e. Int corridors. **Pets:** Small, other species. Designated rooms, service with restrictions, crate.

[ECO] [🛏] [🛜] [✕] [📠] [💻]

AAA ▼▼▼▼ Jupiter Waterfront Inn 🅷

(561) 747-9085. **$99-$279.** 18903 SE Federal Hwy 33469. On US 1 (Federal Hwy), 2.9 mi n of SR 706 (Indiantown Rd). Ext corridors. **Pets:** Small. $25 daily fee/room. Designated rooms, service with restrictions, supervision. [SAVE] [🛏] [🛜] [✕] [📠]

KEY BISCAYNE *(Restaurants p. 625)*

AAA ▼▼▼▼ The Ritz-Carlton Key Biscayne, Miami 🅷

(305) 365-4500. **$229-$699, 7 day notice.** 455 Grand Bay Dr 33149. Jct Crandon Blvd, just e. Int corridors. **Pets:** Accepted.

[SAVE] [ECO] [🍴] [&M] [🛏] [✕] [🛜] [✕] [📠] [💻]

KEY LARGO *(Restaurants p. 625)*

AAA ▼▼▼▼ Courtyard by Marriott Key Largo 🅷

(305) 451-3939. **$129-$429.** 99751 Overseas Hwy 33037. US 1 at MM 100. Int corridors. **Pets:** Accepted.

[SAVE] [ECO] [&M] [🛏] [✕] [🛜] [✕] [📠] [💻]

KEY WEST *(Restaurants p. 625)*

AAA ▼▼▼ BEST WESTERN Key Ambassador Resort Inn 🅼

(305) 296-3500. **$179-$499, 3 day notice.** 3755 S Roosevelt Blvd 33040. On SR A1A, 1 mi s of jct US 1. Ext corridors. **Pets:** Small, dogs only. $20 daily fee/room. Designated rooms, service with restrictions. [SAVE] [🍴] [🛏] [🛜] [✕] [📠] [💻]

AAA ▼▼▼ Casa Marina, A Waldorf Astoria Resort 🅷

(305) 296-3535. **$189-$599.** 1500 Reynolds St 33040. 4 mi s on Flagler Ave (CR 5A) from jct SR A1A. Ext/int corridors. **Pets:** Small, dogs only. $75 daily fee/pet. Service with restrictions, supervision.

[SAVE] [ECO] [🍴] [🛏] [✕] [🛜] [✕] [📠] [💻]

AAA ▼▼▼ Courtney's Place Historic Cottages & Inn 🅱🅱

(305) 294-3480. **$119-$389, 21 day notice.** 720 Whitmarsh Ln 33040. Just e of jct Petronia and Simonton sts; in Old Town. Ext corridors. **Pets:** Other species. $10 daily fee/pet. Service with restrictions.

[SAVE] [🛏] [🛜] [✕] [📠] [💻]

▼▼▼▼ DoubleTree Resort by Hilton Hotel Grand Key-Key West 🅷

(305) 293-1818. **Call for rates.** 3990 S Roosevelt Blvd 33040. From US 1, 0.5 mi s on SR A1A. Int corridors. **Pets:** Accepted.

[ECO] [🍴] [&M] [🛏] [✕] [🛜] [✕] [📠] [💻]

AAA ▼▼▼▼ Hyatt Key West Resort & Spa 🅷 ❀

(305) 809-1234. **$219-$599, 7 day notice.** 601 Front St 33040. Corner of Simonton and Front sts; just n of Mallory Square; in Old Town. Ext corridors. **Pets:** Medium, dogs only. $150 one-time fee/room. Service with restrictions, supervision.

[SAVE] [ECO] [🍴] [🛏] [✕] [🛜] [✕] [📠] [💻]

AAA ▼▼▼▼ The Reach, A Waldorf Astoria Resort 🅷

(305) 296-5000. **$179-$559.** 1435 Simonton St 33040. Just s of jct Truman Ave and Simonton St. Ext corridors. **Pets:** Accepted.

[SAVE] [ECO] [🍴] [🛏] [✕] [🛜] [✕] [📠] [💻]

AAA ▼▼▼▼ Sheraton Suites Key West 🅷

(305) 292-9800. **$134-$368, 3 day notice.** 2001 S Roosevelt Blvd 33040. Jct US 1 and SR A1A, 3 mi s. Ext/int corridors. **Pets:** Accepted.

[SAVE] [ECO] [🍴] [&M] [🛏] [✕] [🛜] [✕] [📠] [💻]

AAA ▼▼▼▼ The Westin Key West Resort & Marina 🅷

(305) 294-4000. **$206-$539, 3 day notice.** 245 Front St 33040. Corner of Front and Greene sts; in Old Town. Ext/int corridors. **Pets:** Accepted.

[SAVE] [ECO] [🍴] [&M] [🛏] [✕] [🛜] [✕] [📠] [💻]

KISSIMMEE

AAA ▼▼▼▼ BEST WESTERN PREMIER Saratoga Resort Villas 🅷 ❀

(407) 997-3300. **$112-$239.** 4787 W Irlo Bronson Memorial Hwy 34746. I-4 exit 64 (US 192), 4.9 mi e. Ext corridors. **Pets:** Medium. $25 daily fee/pet. Designated rooms, service with restrictions, supervision.

[SAVE] [🍴] [&M] [🛏] [✕] [🛜] [✕] [📠] [💻]

AAA ▼▼▼ Champions World Resort 🅼

(407) 396-4500. **Call for rates.** 8660 W Irlo Bronson Memorial Hwy 34747. I-4 exit 64 (US 192), 6.7 mi w. Ext corridors. **Pets:** Accepted.

[SAVE] [🍴] [🛏] [✕] [🛜] [✕] [📠] [💻]

▼▼▼ The Palms Hotel & Villas 🅲🅾

(407) 396-2229. **$79-$199.** 3100 Parkway Blvd 34747. I-4 exit 64 (US 192), 0.3 mi e, then 0.4 mi n. Ext/int corridors. **Pets:** Medium. $25 one-time fee/room. Designated rooms, service with restrictions.

[🛏] [✕] [🛜] [✕] [📠] [💻]

AAA ▼▼▼ Quality Suites Royale Parc Suites 🅷

(407) 396-8040. **$85-$263, 3 day notice.** 5876 W Irlo Bronson Memorial Hwy 34746. I-4 exit 64 (US 192), 3 mi e. Int corridors. **Pets:** Medium, dogs only. $125 one-time fee/pet. Service with restrictions. [SAVE] [🍴] [🛏] [✕] [🛜] [✕] [📠] [💻]

LADY LAKE

AAA ▼▼▼ Comfort Suites at The Villages 🅷

(352) 259-6578. **$85-$129.** 1202 Avenida Central N 32159. Just w of jct US 441/27. Int corridors. **Pets:** Medium. $35 one-time fee/room. Service with restrictions, crate. [SAVE] [🛏] [🛜] [✕] [📠] [💻]

▼▼ ◆◆ **Microtel Inn & Suites by Wyndham Lady Lake/The Villages** H
(352) 259-0184. **$65-$140.** 850 S US 27/441 32159. On US 27/441, 2.9 mi s of The Village Center, just s of jct Rolling Acres Rd. Int corridors. **Pets:** Accepted. 🐾 📶 ❌ 🛢 💻

◆◆◇ ▼▼▼▼ **TownePlace Suites by Marriott The Villages** H
(352) 753-8686. **$109-$219.** 1141 Alonzo Ave 32159. Just w of jct US 27/441 on Main St, just n. Int corridors. **Pets:** Accepted.
SAVE 🔳 🐾 📶 ❌ 🛢 💻

LAKE BUENA VISTA

◆◆◇ ▼▼▼▼ **Clarion Inn Lake Buena Vista** H ❧
(407) 996-7300. **$60-$140.** 8442 Palm Pkwy 32836. I-4 exit 68, 0.6 mi n on SR 535, then 0.5 mi e. Ext corridors. **Pets:** Medium. $15 daily fee/room. Designated rooms, service with restrictions, crate.
SAVE 🔳 🍴 🔳 🐾 📶 ❌ 🛢 💻

◆◆◇ ▼▼▼▼ **Holiday Inn Resort Orlando-Lake Buena Vista** H
(407) 239-4500. **$89-$179, 3 day notice.** 13351 State Road 535 32821. I-4 exit 68, 0.3 mi se. Int corridors. **Pets:** Accepted.
SAVE 🍴 🔳 🐾 ❌ 📶 🛢 💻

◆◆◇ ▼▼▼▼ **Hyatt Regency Grand Cypress** H
(407) 239-1234. **$99-$309, 3 day notice.** 1 Grand Cypress Blvd 32836. I-4 exit 68, 0.8 mi nw on SR 535, just s. Int corridors. **Pets:** Accepted.
SAVE ECO 🔲 🍴 🐾 ❌ 🔳 ❌ 🛢 💻

◆◆◇ ▼▼▼▼ **Residence Inn by Marriott Orlando Lake Buena Vista** H ❧
(407) 465-0075. **$89-$249, 3 day notice.** 11450 Marbella Palms Ct 32836. I-4 exit 68, 0.6 mi n on SR 535, then 1 mi e on Palm Pkwy, just sw. Int corridors. **Pets:** Medium, other species. $100 one-time fee/room. Service with restrictions.
SAVE 🔳 🐾 ❌ 📶 ❌ 🛢 💻

◆◆◇ ▼▼▼▼ **Sheraton Lake Buena Vista Resort** H
(407) 239-0444. **$119-$209, 3 day notice.** 12205 Apopka-Vineland Rd 32836. I-4 exit 68, 0.6 mi n on SR 535. Ext/int corridors.
Pets: Accepted. SAVE ECO 🍴 🔳 🐾 ❌ 🔳 🛢 💻

◆◆◇ ▼▼▼▼ **Westgate Blue Tree Resort at Lake Buena Vista** CO
(407) 597-2200. **$89-$189, 3 day notice.** 12007 Cypress Run Rd 32836. I-4 exit 68, 1 mi n on SR 535 (Apopka-Vineland Rd S), 0.4 mi e on to Vinings Way Blvd. Ext corridors. **Pets:** Accepted.
SAVE 🔳 🐾 ❌ 🔳 ❌ 🛢 💻

◆◆◇ ▼▼▼▼ ▼▼▼▼ **Wyndham Grand Orlando Resort, Bonnet Creek** H
(407) 390-2300. **$259-$479.** 14651 Chelonia Pkwy 32821. I-4 exit 65, 1.3 mi w on W Osceola Pkwy, 1.2 mi n on Victory Way, 0.4 mi ne on Buena Vista Dr, then 0.9 mi s. Int corridors. **Pets:** Accepted.
SAVE 🍴 🔳 🐾 ❌ 🔳 ❌ 🛢 💻

LAKE CITY
▼▼▼▼ **Baymont Inn & Suites Lake City** M
(386) 752-3801. **$64-$75.** 3598 W Hwy 90 32055. I-75 exit 427, just w. Ext corridors. **Pets:** Medium, other species. $15 daily fee/room. Designated rooms, service with restrictions, supervision. 🐾 📶 🛢 💻

▼▼▼▼ **Holiday Inn Hotel & Suites** H
(386) 754-1411. **Call for rates.** 213 SW Commerce Dr 32025. I-75 exit 427, just e on US 90, then just s. Int corridors. **Pets:** Accepted.
ECO 🍴 🔳 🐾 ❌ 📶 ❌ 🛢 💻

LAKELAND
▼▼▼▼ **Baymont Inn & Suites Lakeland** H
(863) 858-9070. **$59-$99.** 4375 Lakeland Park Dr 33809. I-4 exit 33, 0.6 mi s on SR 33, just nw on N Socrum Loop Rd, then just w. Int corridors. **Pets:** Accepted. 🔳 🐾 📶 🛢 💻

▼▼▼▼ **Crestwood Suites Lakeland** H
(863) 904-2050. **$84-$199.** 4360 Lakeland Park Dr 33809. I-4 exit 33, 0.6 mi se on SR 33, 0.4 mi n on Socrum Loop, then just s. Int corridors. **Pets:** Accepted. 🔳 🐾 📶 🛢 💻

◆◆◇ ▼▼▼▼ **Hyatt Place Lakeland Center** H
(863) 413-1122. **$79-$279.** 525 W Orange St 33815. I-4 exit 31, 2.6 mi se on Kathleen Rd, then just w; adjacent to The Lakeland Center. Int corridors. **Pets:** Accepted. SAVE 🔳 🐾 📶 ❌ 🛢 💻

▼▼▼▼ **Residence Inn by Marriott Lakeland** H
(863) 680-2323. **$109-$329.** 3701 Harden Blvd 33803. SR 570 (Polk Pkwy) exit 5, just n on SR 563. Int corridors. **Pets:** Accepted.
🐾 📶 ❌ 🛢 💻

LAKE MARY (Restaurants p. 626)
▼▼ **Candlewood Suites Lake Mary** H
(407) 585-3000. **Call for rates.** 1130 Greenwood Blvd 32746. I-4 exit 98, just e to Lake Emma Rd, 0.7 mi s to Exchange Pl, 0.3 mi w to Greenwood Blvd, then just s. Int corridors. **Pets:** Accepted.
🐾 📶 🛢 💻

▼▼▼ **Extended Stay America-Orlando-Lake Mary** H
(407) 833-0011. **$49-$149.** 1036 Greenwood Blvd 32746. I-4 exit 98, just e to Lake Emma Rd, 0.5 mi s to Greenwood Blvd, then just w. Int corridors. **Pets:** Other species. $25 daily fee/pet. Service with restrictions, supervision. 📶 ❌ 🛢 💻

▼▼▼▼ **Extended Stay America-Orlando-Lake Mary** H
(407) 829-2332. **$54-$139.** 1040 Greenwood Blvd 32746. I-4 exit 98, just e to Lake Emma Rd, 0.5 mi s to Greenwood Blvd, then just w; in Commerce Park. Int corridors. **Pets:** Other species. $25 daily fee/pet. Service with restrictions, supervision. 🔳 🐾 📶 🛢 💻

▼▼▼▼ **Homewood Suites by Hilton Lake Mary** H
(407) 805-9111. **$109-$219.** 755 Currency Cir 32746. I-4 exit 98, just ne via Lake Mary and Primera blvds. Int corridors. **Pets:** Accepted.
🔳 🐾 📶 🛢 💻

◆◆◇ ▼▼▼▼ **Hyatt Place Lake Mary/Orlando-North** H
(407) 995-5555. **$89-$219.** 1255 S International Pkwy 32746. I-4 exit 98, just w. Int corridors. **Pets:** Small, dogs only. $75 one-time fee/room. Service with restrictions, supervision.
SAVE ECO 🐾 📶 ❌ 💻

▼▼▼ **La Quinta Inn & Suites - Orlando Lake Mary** H
(407) 805-9901. **$69-$249.** 1060 Greenwood Blvd 32746. I-4 exit 98, just e to Lake Emma Rd, then 0.5 mi s. Int corridors. **Pets:** Large, other species. Service with restrictions. 🔳 🐾 📶 🛢 💻

▼▼▼▼ **Residence Inn by Marriott-Orlando Lake Mary** H
(407) 995-3400. **$119-$229.** 825 Heathrow Park Ln 32746. I-4 exit 101A, 0.5 mi w to International Pkwy, then just s. Int corridors.
Pets: Accepted. 🔲 🐾 📶 ❌ 🛢 💻

◆◆◇ ▼▼▼▼ **The Westin Lake Mary, Orlando North** H ❧
(407) 531-3555. **$109-$299.** 2974 International Pkwy 32746. I-4 exit 101A, 0.5 mi w. Int corridors. **Pets:** Small, dogs only. Designated rooms, service with restrictions, supervision.
SAVE 🍴 🐾 ❌ 📶 ❌ 🛢 💻

LAKE WORTH (Restaurants p. 626)
◆◆◇ ▼▼▼▼ **Sabal Palm House B & B Inn** BB ❧
(561) 582-1090. **$99-$259, 14 day notice.** 109 N Golfview Rd 33460. Just n of SR 802 (Lake Ave); west side of Intracoastal Bridge. Ext/int corridors. **Pets:** Small, dogs only. $25 daily fee/pet. Designated rooms, service with restrictions. SAVE 📶 ❌ 🛢 💻

LARGO

Hampton Inn & Suites 🄷
(727) 585-3333. **$119-$249.** 100 E Bay Dr 33770. On SR 686, 3.4 mi w of jct US 19; jct Alternate Rt US 19 (Seminole Blvd/Missouri Ave). Int corridors. **Pets:** Accepted. 🆂🄴🄲🄾 ♿M ⛲ 🛜 🍽 🛏 🖥

Holiday Inn Express & Suites Largo Central Park 🄷
(727) 581-3900. **$105-$179, 3 day notice.** 210 Seminole Blvd 33770. On Alternate US 19, just s of jct SR 686 (W Bay Dr/E Bay Dr). Int corridors. **Pets:** Medium. $50 one-time fee/pet. Designated rooms, service with restrictions, supervision. ♿M ⛲ 🛜 🍽 🛏 🖥

LECANTO

Holiday Inn Express Hotel & Suites 🄷
(352) 341-3515. **$80-$180.** 903 E Gulf to Lake Hwy 34461. On SR 44, 4.2 mi e. Int corridors. **Pets:** Other species. $25 daily fee/pet. Designated rooms, service with restrictions.
🄴🄲🄾 ♿M ⛲ 🛜 🍽 🛏 🖥

LEESBURG

BEST WESTERN PLUS Chain of Lakes Inn & Suites 🄷
(352) 460-0118. **$80-$140.** 1321 N 14th St 34748. Jct US 27 and 441. Int corridors. **Pets:** Small, dogs only. $20 daily fee/pet. Designated rooms, service with restrictions, supervision.
🆂🄴 ♿M ⛲ 🛜 🍽 🛏 🖥

Hampton Inn Leesburg/Tavares 🄷
(352) 315-1053. **$89-$149.** 9630 US Hwy 441 34788. Just s of jct College Dr. Int corridors. **Pets:** Accepted. 🄴🄲🄾 ⛲ 🛜 🍽 🛏 🖥

LEHIGH ACRES

Microtel Inn & Suites by Wyndham Lehigh 🄷
(239) 369-2121. **$70-$129, 3 day notice.** 1320 Business Way 33936. Just se of jct Lee Blvd (CR 884) on Homestead Rd N, just s on Beth Stacey Blvd, then just n. Int corridors. **Pets:** Accepted.
🆂🄴 ♿M ⛲ 🛜 🍽 🛏 🖥

LIVE OAK

Quality Inn & Suites 🄼
(386) 362-6000. **$100-$130.** 6819 US 129 N 32060. I-10 exit 283, 0.3 mi s. Ext corridors. **Pets:** Large. $15 daily fee/pet. Designated rooms, service with restrictions, crate. ⛲ 🛜 🛏 🖥

LUTZ

Residence Inn by Marriott Tampa Suncoast Parkway at NorthPointe Village 🄷 🐾
(813) 792-8400. **$129-$219.** 2101 NorthPointe Pkwy 33558. Suncoast Pkwy exit 19, just e on SR 54, then just ne; in NorthPointe at Suncoast Crossings. Int corridors. **Pets:** Other species. $100 one-time fee/room. Service with restrictions, crate. 🄴🄲🄾 ♿M ⛲ 🛜 🍽 🛏 🖥

LYNN HAVEN

Wingate by Wyndham Lynn Haven 🄷
(850) 248-8080. **$95-$136.** 2610 Lynn Haven Pkwy 32444. On SR 77, 1.8 mi n of jct SR 368. Int corridors. **Pets:** Accepted.
🆂🄴 ♿M ⛲ 🛜 🍽 🛏 🖥

MADISON

BEST WESTERN PLUS Madison Inn 🄷
(850) 973-2020. **$99-$169.** 167 SE Bandit St 32340. I-10 exit 258, just n. Int corridors. **Pets:** Accepted. 🆂🄴 ♿M ⛲ 🛜 🛏 🖥

MAITLAND

Homewood Suites by Hilton-Orlando North/Maitland 🄷
(407) 875-8777. **$109-$169.** 290 Southhall Ln 32751. I-4 exit 90B, just w to Lake Destiny Dr, then just s. Int corridors. **Pets:** Accepted.
🆂🄴 ♿M ⛲ 🛜 🛏 🖥

Sheraton Orlando North 🄷
(407) 660-9000. **$89-$249.** 600 N Lake Destiny Dr 32751. I-4 exit 90B, just w. Int corridors. **Pets:** Accepted.
🆂🄴 🄴🄲🄾 🍸 ♿M ⛲ 🗙 🛜 🍽 🛏 🖥

MANALAPAN

Eau Palm Beach Resort & Spa 🄷
(561) 533-6000. **$199-$749, 14 day notice.** 100 S Ocean Blvd 33462. I-95 exit 61 (Lantana Rd), 1.1 mi e to US 1 (Dixie Hwy), just s to Ocean Ave, then 0.8 mi e. Int corridors. **Pets:** Accepted.
🆂🄴 🄴🄲🄾 🍸 ⛲ 🗙 🛜 🍽

MARATHON

Royal Hawaiian Motel/Botel 🄼
(305) 743-7500. **$99-$175, 30 day notice.** 12020 Overseas Hwy 33050. US 1 at MM 53; gulfside. Ext corridors. **Pets:** Small. $25 one-time fee/pet. Service with restrictions, supervision.
⛲ 🗙 🛜 🛏 🖥

MARIANNA

Microtel Inn & Suites by Wyndham Marianna 🄷
(850) 526-5005. **$80-$110.** 4959 Whitetail Dr 32448. I-10 exit 142, just n on SR 71. Int corridors. **Pets:** Accepted. ♿M ⛲ 🛜 🛏 🖥

MELBOURNE *(Restaurants p. 626)*

Candlewood Suites Melbourne/Viera 🄷
(321) 821-9009. **$99-$119.** 2930 Pineda Plaza Way 32940. I-95 exit 191 (CR 509/Wickham Rd), 4.5 mi se to Pineda Plaza Way, then just n. Int corridors. **Pets:** Accepted. 🛜 🗙 🛏 🖥

Extended Stay America Melbourne-Airport 🄷
(321) 733-6050. **$70-$169.** 1701 Evans Rd 32904. I-95 exit 180 (US 192/New Haven Ave), 3.2 mi e to Evans Rd, then 0.4 mi n. Int corridors. **Pets:** Other species. $25 daily fee/pet. Service with restrictions, supervision. ⛲ 🛜 🛏 🖥

Hilton Melbourne Rialto Place 🄷
(321) 768-0200. **$99-$199.** 200 Rialto Pl 32901. I-95 exit 180 (US 192/New Haven Ave), 4.8 mi e to Airport Blvd, then 0.8 mi n to Rialto Pl. Int corridors. **Pets:** Accepted. 🍸 ♿M ⛲ 🗙 🛜 🍽 🛏 🖥

La Quinta Inn & Suites-Melbourne 🄷
(321) 242-9400. **$75-$220.** 7200 George T Edwards Dr 32940. I-95 exit 191 (CR 509/Wickham Rd), just w. Int corridors. **Pets:** Large, other species. Service with restrictions. ⛲ 🛜 🛏 🖥

Residence Inn by Marriott Melbourne 🄷
(321) 723-5740. **$159-$229.** 1430 S Babcock St 32901. I-95 exit 180 (US 192/New Haven Ave), 5.1 mi e to Babcock St, then 0.5 mi n. Int corridors. **Pets:** Other species. $100 one-time fee/room. Service with restrictions, supervision. 🆂🄴 ♿M ⛲ 🛜 🗙 🛏 🖥

MIAMI *(Restaurants p. 626)*

DoubleTree by Hilton Hotel-Miami Airport Convention Center 🄷
(305) 261-3800. **$99-$259.** 711 NW 72nd Ave 33126. SR 836 (Dolphin Expwy) exit NW 57th Ave/Red Rd/SR 959, 0.6 mi s to NW 7th St, 1.5 mi w to NW 72nd Ave/Milam Dairy Rd, then just n. Int corridors. **Pets:** Accepted. 🆂🄴 🍸 ⛲ 🗙 🛜 🗙 🛏 🖥

Element Miami International Airport 🄷
(305) 636-1600. **$89-$699.** 3525 NW 25th St 33142. From LeJeune Rd (NW 42nd Ave), 0.7 mi e. Int corridors. **Pets:** Accepted.
🆂🄴 🍽 🍸 ♿M 🛜 🗙 🛏 🖥

Epic Miami 🄷
(305) 424-5226. **$219-$889, 3 day notice.** 270 Biscayne Blvd Way 33131. Just e of US 1 (SE 2nd Ave). Int corridors. **Pets:** Accepted.
🆂🄴 🄴🄲🄾 🍸 ♿M ⛲ 🗙 📶 🗙

AAA ▼▼▼ Four Seasons Hotel Miami H
(305) 358-3535. **$259-$699, 3 day notice.** 1435 Brickell Ave 33131. Jct 14th Terr on US 1. Int corridors. **Pets:** Accepted.
SAVE ECO ⊞ ⊺⊺ &M ⇆ ⊠ ⑤ ✕ ⌷

AAA ▼▼▼ Hilton Miami Downtown H
(305) 374-0000. **$105-$209.** 1601 Biscayne Blvd 33132. On US 1 (Biscayne Blvd), just n of NE 15th St. Int corridors. **Pets:** Accepted.
SAVE ECO ⊺⊺ &M ⇆ ⑤ ✕ ⌷

AAA ▼▼▼ Hotel Indigo Miami-Dadeland H
(305) 595-6000. **$109-$199.** 7600 N Kendall Dr 33156. SR 826 (Palmetto Expwy) exit SW 88th St (N Kendall Dr), just w. Int corridors.
Pets: Accepted. SAVE ⊺⊺ &M ⇆ ⑤ ✕ ⌷

AAA ▼▼▼ Hotel Urbano at Brickell H
(305) 854-2070. **Call for rates.** 2500 Brickell Ave 33129. Jct SE 25th Rd and Brickell Ave. Int corridors. **Pets:** Accepted.
SAVE ⊺⊺ &M ⇆ ⑤ ✕ ⌷

AAA ▼▼▼ HYATT house Miami Airport H
(305) 269-1922. **$99-$249.** 5710 Blue Lagoon Dr 33126. SR 836 (Dolphin Expwy) exit NW 57th Ave/Red Rd/SR 959, just s. Int corridors.
Pets: Accepted. SAVE &M ⇆ ⑤ ✕ ⊟ ⌷

AAA ▼▼▼ Hyatt Place Miami Airport-West/Doral H
(305) 718-8292. **$99-$229.** 3655 NW 82nd Ave 33166. Florida Tpke exit 29 (NW 41st St), 3.7 mi e to NW 82nd Ave, then just s; just w of SR 826 (Palmetto Expwy). Int corridors. **Pets:** Accepted.
SAVE &M ⇆ ⑤ ✕ ⊟ ⌷

▼▼▼ La Quinta Inn Miami Airport North H
(305) 599-9902. **$95-$264.** 7401 NW 36th St 33166. SR 826 (Palmetto Expwy) exit NW 36th St (SR 948), just e. Ext/int corridors. **Pets:** Large, other species. Service with restrictions. ⇆ ⑤ ⊟ ⌷

AAA ▼▼▼ Mandarin Oriental, Miami H ❀
(305) 913-8288. **Call for rates.** 500 Brickell Key Dr 33131. US 1 (Brickell Ave), just e on SE 8th St (Brickell Key Dr). Int corridors.
Pets: Medium. $100 deposit/room, $100 one-time fee/room. Supervision. SAVE ECO ⊺⊺ &M ⇆ ⊠ ⑤ ✕ ⌷

AAA ▼▼▼ Residence Inn by Marriott Miami Airport H
(305) 642-8570. **$119-$349.** 1201 NW 42nd Ave 33126. SR 836 (Dolphin Expwy) exit LeJeune Rd (NW 42nd Ave), just s. Int corridors.
Pets: Accepted. SAVE &M ⑤ ✕ ⊟ ⌷

AAA ▼▼▼ Sheraton Miami Airport Hotel & Executive Meeting Center H
(305) 871-3800. **$109-$379.** 3900 NW 21st St 33142. SR 112 to LeJeune Rd (NW 42nd Ave), 0.3 mi e. Int corridors. **Pets:** Accepted.
SAVE ECO ⊺⊺ ⇆ ⑤ ✕ ⌷

▼▼▼ Sofitel Miami H
(305) 264-4888. **$95-$500.** 5800 Blue Lagoon Dr 33126. SR 836 (Dolphin Expwy) exit NW 57th Ave/Red Rd/SR 959, just s to Blue Lagoon Dr, then just w. Int corridors. **Pets:** Accepted.
ECO ⊺⊺ ⇆ ⑤ ⊟ ⌷

MIAMI BEACH *(Restaurants p. 626)*

AAA ▼▼▼▼ The Betsy-South Beach H ❀
(305) 531-6100. **$240-$1200, 3 day notice.** 1440 Ocean Dr 33139. Between 14th and 15th sts. Int corridors. **Pets:** Small, dogs only. $250 one-time fee/room. Designated rooms, service with restrictions, supervision. SAVE ⊺⊺ ⇆ ⑤ ✕ ⌷

AAA ▼▼▼▼ Eden Roc Miami Beach H ❀
(305) 531-0000. **Call for rates.** 4525 Collins Ave 33140. SR A1A (Collins Ave), just n of 41st St. Int corridors. **Pets:** Dogs only. Designated rooms, service with restrictions, crate.
SAVE ⊺⊺ ⇆ ⊠ ⑤ ✕ ⊟ ⌷

AAA ▼▼▼ Fontainebleau Miami Beach H
(305) 538-2000. **Call for rates.** 4441 Collins Ave 33140. SR A1A (Collins Ave); just n of Arthur Godfrey Rd. Int corridors. **Pets:** Accepted.
SAVE ECO ⊞ ⊺⊺ ⇆ ⑤ ✕ ⊟ ⌷

▼▼▼ Grand Beach Hotel H
(305) 538-8666. **$189-$999.** 4835 Collins Ave 33140. Between 48th and 49th sts. Int corridors. **Pets:** Accepted.
⊺⊺ &M ⇆ ⊠ ⑤ ⊟ ⌷

AAA ▼▼▼▼ The James Royal Palm Hotel H
(305) 604-5700. **Call for rates.** 1545 Collins Ave 33139. On SR A1A (Collins Ave), just s of 16th Ave. Ext/int corridors. **Pets:** Accepted.
SAVE ⊺⊺ ⇆ ⊠ ⑤ ✕ ⌷

AAA ▼▼▼▼ Loews Miami Beach Hotel H
(305) 604-1601. **$239-$649, 3 day notice.** 1601 Collins Ave 33139. Jct SR A1A (Collins Ave) and 16th Ave. Int corridors. **Pets:** Accepted.
SAVE ⊺⊺ &M ⇆ ⊠ ⑤ ✕ ⌷

AAA ▼▼▼ Marriott Stanton South Beach H
(305) 536-7700. **$233-$576, 3 day notice.** 161 Ocean Dr 33139. Just e of SR A1A (Collins Ave); just s of 2nd St. Int corridors. **Pets:** Accepted.
SAVE ⊺⊺ ⇆ ⊠ ⑤ ✕ ⊟ ⌷

AAA ▼▼▼ The National Hotel H
(305) 532-2311. **$299-$1599, 7 day notice.** 1677 Collins Ave 33139. Jct SR A1A (Collins Ave) and 16th St. Int corridors. **Pets:** Accepted.
SAVE ⊺⊺ ⇆ ⑤ ✕

▼▼▼▼ The Ritz-Carlton, South Beach H
(786) 276-4000. **$299-$949, 7 day notice.** 1 Lincoln Rd 33139. Jct SR A1A (Collins Ave). Int corridors. **Pets:** Accepted.
ECO ⊺⊺ &M ⇆ ⊠ ⑤ ✕ ⌷

AAA ▼▼▼ The Setai, Miami Beach H
(305) 520-6000. **$550-$1650, 14 day notice.** 2001 Collins Ave 33139. SR A1A (Collins Ave); at 20th St. Int corridors. **Pets:** Accepted.
SAVE ECO ⊺⊺ &M ⇆ ⊠ ⑤ ✕ ⊟ ⌷

AAA ▼▼▼ Surfcomber, A Kimpton Hotel H
(305) 532-7715. **$199-$599, 3 day notice.** 1717 Collins Ave 33139. Between 17th and 18th sts. Int corridors. **Pets:** Accepted.
SAVE ECO ⊺⊺ ⇆ ⊠ ⑤ ✕

AAA ▼▼▼ W South Beach H
(305) 938-3000. **$369-$1209, 3 day notice.** 2201 Collins Ave 33139. Jct SR A1A (Collins Ave) and 22nd St. Int corridors. **Pets:** Accepted.
SAVE ⊺⊺ &M ⇆ ⊠ ⑤ ✕ ⊟ ⌷

MIAMI LAKES

▼▼▼ Hotel Indigo Miami Lakes H
(305) 556-0100. **Call for rates.** 7601 Miami Lakes Dr 33014. SR 826 (Palmetto Expwy) exit NW 154th St, just e. Int corridors.
Pets: Accepted. ⊺⊺ &M ⇆ ⑤ ✕ ⌷

▼▼▼ La Quinta Inn & Suites-Miami Lakes H
(305) 821-8274. **$109-$269.** 7925 NW 154th St 33016. Jct SR 826 (Palmetto Expwy) exit NW 154th St, just w. Int corridors. **Pets:** Large, other species. Service with restrictions. ⇆ ⑤ ⊟ ⌷

AAA ▼▼ TownePlace Suites by Marriott-Miami Lakes Miramar Area H
(305) 512-9191. **$99-$199.** 8079 NW 154th St 33016. SR 826 (Palmetto Expwy) exit NW 154th St, 0.4 mi w. Int corridors. **Pets:** Accepted.
SAVE &M ⇆ ⑤ ✕ ⊟ ⌷

MIAMI SPRINGS

▼▼ La Quinta Inn & Suites-Miami Airport East M
(305) 871-1777. **$99-$279.** 3501 NW LeJeune Rd 33142. LeJeune Rd (NW 42nd Ave), just s of SR 112. Int corridors. **Pets:** Large, other species. Service with restrictions. ⇆ ⑤ ⊟ ⌷

AAA ▼▼▼ Red Roof Plus+ Miami Airport H
(305) 871-4221. **$74-$289.** 3401 NW LeJeune Rd (NW 42nd Ave) 33142. Just s of SR 112. Int corridors. **Pets:** Large, other species. Service with restrictions, supervision. SAVE ⌂ ⚟ ✕ ▯ ▣

MIDWAY

AAA ▼▼▼▼ BEST WESTERN PLUS Panhandle Capital Inn & Suites H
(850) 514-2222. **$100-$129.** 85 River Park Dr 32343. I-10 exit 192, just s. Int corridors. **Pets:** Accepted. SAVE ⌂ ⚟ ✕ ▯ ▣

▼▼ Howard Johnson Express Inn M
(850) 574-8888. **$65-$189.** 81 Commerce Blvd 32343. I-10 exit 192, just n. Ext corridors. **Pets:** Medium. $10 daily fee/pet. Service with restrictions, supervision. ⚟ ▯ ▣

MILTON *(Restaurants p. 627)*

AAA ▼▼ Comfort Inn M
(850) 623-1511. **$99-$135.** 8936 Hwy 87 S 32583. I-10 exit 31, just s. Int corridors. **Pets:** Accepted. SAVE ⌂ ⚟ ▯ ▣

AAA ▼▼▼ Red Roof Inn & Suites-Pensacola East Milton H
(850) 995-6100. **$70-$104.** 2672 Avalon Blvd 32583. I-10 exit 22, just s on SR 281. Int corridors. **Pets:** Large, other species. Service with restrictions, supervision. SAVE ⌂ ⚟ ✕ ▯ ▣

MIRAMAR

AAA ▼▼▼ Residence Inn by Marriott-Fort Lauderdale SW/Miramar H
(954) 450-2717. **$99-$299.** 14700 Hotel Rd 33027. I-75 exit 7A (Miramar Pkwy), just e to SW 148th Ave, just n to Hotel Rd, then just e. Int corridors. **Pets:** Accepted. SAVE ECO ⌂ ⚟ ✕ ▯ ▣

MONTICELLO

▼▼ Days Inn M
(850) 997-5988. **$78-$105.** 44 Woodworth Dr 32336. I-10 exit 225, just s on US 19. Ext corridors. **Pets:** Accepted. ⚟ ▯ ▣

NAPLES *(Restaurants p. 627)*

AAA ▼▼ Gulfcoast Inn H
(239) 261-6046. **$90-$200.** 2555 Tamiami Tr N 34103. On US 41 (Tamiami Tr); jct 26th Ave N. Ext corridors. **Pets:** Accepted.
SAVE ⌂ ⚟ ✕ ▯ ▣

AAA ▼▼▼▼ Hawthorn Suites by Wyndham-Naples H ❀
(239) 593-1300. **$99-$300.** 3557 Pine Ridge Rd 34109. I-75 exit 107 (Pine Ridge Rd), 0.8 mi w. Int corridors. **Pets:** Medium. $125 one-time fee/room. Designated rooms, service with restrictions, crate.
SAVE ECO ⌂ ⚟ ✕ ▯ ▣

▼▼ La Quinta Inn & Suites-Naples Downtown H
(239) 793-4646. **$79-$279.** 1555 5th Ave S 34102. Just w of jct SR 84 (Davis Blvd) and US 41 (Tamiami Tr). Int corridors. **Pets:** Large, other species. Service with restrictions. ⌂ ⚟ ▯ ▣

AAA ▼▼▼▼ Naples Bay Resort & Marina H
(239) 530-1199. **$149-$799, 7 day notice.** 1500 5th Ave S 34102. On US 41 (Tamiami Tr), just e of jct Goodlette-Frank Rd. Ext/int corridors. **Pets:** Accepted. SAVE ⌂ ⚟ ✕ ▯ ▣

AAA ▼▼ Red Roof Inn Plus+ Naples H
(239) 774-3117. **$59-$209.** 1925 Davis Blvd 34104. Just e of jct US 41 (Tamiami Tr). Ext corridors. **Pets:** Large, other species. Service with restrictions, supervision. SAVE ⌂ ⚟ ✕ ▯ ▣

▼▼▼ Residence Inn by Marriott Naples H
(239) 659-1300. **$119-$349.** 4075 Tamiami Tr N 34103. I-75 exit 107, 3.8 mi w on Pine Ridge Rd (CR 896) to US 41 (Tamiami Tr), then 1 mi s. Int corridors. **Pets:** Medium. $125 one-time fee/room. Service with restrictions. ⌂ ⚟ ✕ ▯ ▣

AAA ▼▼▼▼▼ The Ritz-Carlton Golf Resort, Naples H ❀
(239) 593-2000. **$219-$1029, 3 day notice.** 2600 Tiburon Dr 34109. I-75 exit 111, 1.8 mi w on Immokalee Rd, 1.3 mi s on CR 31 (Airport-Pulling Rd), then just e. Int corridors. **Pets:** Small. $150 one-time fee/room. Designated rooms, service with restrictions, crate.
SAVE ECO ⌂ ⚟ ✕ ▯ ▣

▼▼▼ Staybridge Suites Naples-Gulf Coast H
(239) 643-8002. **$89-$229.** 4805 Tamiami Tr N 34103. I-75 exit 107, 3.8 mi w on Pine Ridge Rd (CR 896) to US 41 (Tamiami Tr), then 0.9 mi s. Int corridors. **Pets:** Accepted. ⌂ ⚟ ✕ ▯ ▣

NEPTUNE BEACH

▼▼ Days Inn Neptune Beach-Mayo Clinic M
(904) 249-2777. **$60-$110.** 1401 Atlantic Blvd 32266. SR 9A exit SR 10, 6.9 mi e. Int corridors. **Pets:** Accepted. ⚟ ▯ ▣

NEW SMYRNA BEACH *(Restaurants p. 627)*

AAA ▼▼▼▼ Black Dolphin Inn BB ❀
(386) 410-4868. **$139-$319, 5 day notice.** 916 S Riverside Dr 32168. I-95 exit 249 (SR 44), 4.1 mi e to Riverside Dr, then 0.4 mi s. Ext/int corridors. **Pets:** Dogs only. $50 one-time fee/room. Designated rooms. SAVE ⚟ ✕ ▯

AAA ▼▼▼ Longboard Inn BB
(386) 428-3499. **$115-$140, 14 day notice.** 312 Washington St 32168. Just e of US 1 (Dixie Frwy); 0.3 mi w of jct N Riverside Dr. Ext corridors. **Pets:** Accepted. SAVE ⚟ ✕ ▯

▼▼▼ Night Swan Intracoastal Bed & Breakfast BB
(386) 423-4940. **Call for rates.** 512 S Riverside Dr 32168. I-95 exit 249 (SR 44), 4 mi e to Live Oak St, just s to Andrews St, just e to S Riverside Dr, then just s; on west side of Intracoastal Waterway. Ext/int corridors. **Pets:** Accepted. ECO ⚟ ✕ ▯ ▣

NORTH FORT MYERS

AAA ▼▼ BEST WESTERN Ft. Myers Waterfront H ❀
(239) 997-5511. **$90-$170.** 13021 N Cleveland Ave 33903. On US 41, 0.6 mi s of SR 78A (Pondella Rd), jct N Bay Dr; at base of Caloosahatchee Bridge. Ext corridors. **Pets:** Dogs only. $35 one-time fee/room. Designated rooms, service with restrictions, supervision.
SAVE ⌂ ⚟ ✕ ▯ ▣

OCALA

▼▼▼ Hampton Inn & Suites Ocala H
(352) 867-0300. **$119-$189.** 3601 SW 38th Ave 34474. I-75 exit 350, just w on SR 200 (SW College Rd), then just nw. Int corridors. **Pets:** Small. $20 daily fee/pet. Designated rooms, service with restrictions, supervision. ⚟ ✕ ▯ ▣

AAA ▼▼▼ Hilton Ocala H
(352) 854-1400. **$109-$199.** 3600 SW 36th Ave 34474. I-75 exit 350, 0.3 mi e on SR 200 (SW College Rd), just s. Int corridors. **Pets:** Accepted. SAVE ECO ⌂ ⚟ ✕ ▯ ▣

AAA ▼▼▼ Holiday Inn Express Midtown Medical H
(352) 629-7300. **$79-$149.** 1212 S Pine Ave 34474. 0.8 mi s on US 27, 301 and 441; just s of SR 200 (SW College Rd). Int corridors. **Pets:** Small. $25 daily fee/pet. Designated rooms, service with restrictions, supervision. SAVE ⚟ ✕ ▯ ▣

AAA ▼▼▼ Residence Inn by Marriott Ocala H ❀
(352) 547-1600. **$125-$204.** 3610 SW 38th Ave 34474. I-75 exit 350, just w on SR 200 (SW College Rd), then n. Int corridors. **Pets:** Large, other species. $75 one-time fee/room. Service with restrictions, crate.
SAVE ECO ⚟ ✕ ▯ ▣

▼▼▼ **Sleep Inn & Suites** H
(352) 347-8383. **$69-$129.** 13600 SW 17th Ct 34473. I-75 exit 341, just e on CR 484. Int corridors. **Pets:** Medium. $25 daily fee/pet. Designated rooms, service with restrictions, supervision.
🖼 ⊠ 🛜 ⊠ 🔋 💻

OCOEE

▼▼ **Red Roof Inn Orlando West-Ocoee** H
(407) 347-0140. **$55-$83.** 11241 W Colonial Dr 34761. I-4 exit 84 (Ivanhoe Blvd), 10 mi w; SR 429 exit 60, 0.7 mi e. Int corridors. **Pets:** Large, other species. Service with restrictions, supervision.
⊠ 🛜 ⊠ 🔋 💻

OKEECHOBEE

▲▲▲ ▼▼ **BEST WESTERN Lake Okeechobee** M
(863) 357-7100. **$150-$170.** 3975 US Hwy 441 S 34974. US 98/441, 2.5 mi s of jct SR 70; 0.7 mi n of Lake Okeechobee and jct SR 78. Ext corridors. **Pets:** Accepted. 🖼 ⊠ 🛜 🔋 💻

OLDSMAR

▼▼▼ **Residence Inn by Marriott Tampa/Oldsmar** H ❖
(813) 818-9400. **$127-$206.** 4012 Tampa Rd 34677. On SR 580, jct St. Petersburg Dr. Int corridors. **Pets:** Medium, other species. $25 daily fee/room. Service with restrictions. 🖼 ⊠ ⊠ 🛜 ⊠ 🔋 💻

ORANGE CITY

▼▼ **Days Inn Orange City/Deland** M
(386) 775-4522. **$60-$225.** 2501 N Volusia Ave 32763. I-4 exit 114 (SR 472), 2.6 mi w to US 17-92, then 0.3 mi s. Ext corridors.
Pets: Accepted. ⊠ 🛜 🔋 💻

ORLANDO *(Restaurants p. 627)*

▲▲▲ ▼▼ **BEST WESTERN Orlando East Inn & Suites** H
(407) 282-3900. **$89-$109.** 8750 E Colonial Dr 32817. SR 417 exit 34 (Colonial Dr), just w. Ext corridors. **Pets:** Accepted.
🖼 ⊠ 🛜 🔋 💻

▲▲▲ ▼▼▼ **BEST WESTERN Orlando Gateway Hotel** H
(407) 351-5009. **$113-$300.** 7299 Universal Blvd 32819. I-4 exit 74A (Sand Lake Rd), 0.7 mi e to Universal Blvd, then 0.6 mi n; adjacent to Wet 'n Wild. Int corridors. **Pets:** Accepted.
🖼 🍴 🖼 ⊠ ⊠ 🛜 ⊠ 🔋 💻

▲▲▲ ▼▼▼ **BEST WESTERN Orlando West** H
(407) 841-8600. **$69-$139.** 2014 W Colonial Dr 32804. I-4 exit 83A, just n to SR 50 (Colonial Dr), then 1.5 mi w. Int corridors. **Pets:** Accepted.
🖼 🍴 ⊠ 🛜 🔋 💻

▲▲▲ ▼▼▼▼ **Castle Hotel, Autograph Collection** H
(407) 345-1511. **$109-$299.** 8629 International Dr 32819. I-4 exit 74A (Sand Lake Rd), 0.5 mi e to International Dr, then 0.5 mi s. Int corridors. **Pets:** Accepted. 🖼 🍴 🖼 ⊠ ⊠ 🛜 ⊠ 🔋 💻

▼▼▼ **Country Inn & Suites By Carlson-Orlando Airport** H
(407) 856-8896. **$89-$159.** 5440 Forbes Pl 32812. SR 528 (Beachline Expwy) exit 11 (Semoran Blvd), 0.6 mi n to Frontage Rd, then just w. Int corridors. **Pets:** Accepted. ⊠ 🛜 ⊠ 🔋 💻

▲▲▲ ▼▼ **Days Inn Orlando Airport** M
(407) 855-0308. **$58-$130.** 9301 S Orange Blossom Tr 32837. SR 528 (Beachline Expwy) exit 4, then just s on US 17-92/441. Ext corridors. **Pets:** Large, dogs only. $15 daily fee/pet. Service with restrictions.
🖼 🍴 ⊠ 🛜 🔋 💻

▲▲▲ ▼▼▼ **DoubleTree by Hilton Orlando at SeaWorld** H
(407) 352-1100. **$99-$129.** 10100 International Dr 32821. I-4 exit 72, 0.5 mi e on SR 528 (Beachline Expwy) exit 1 (International Dr), just e. Ext/int corridors. **Pets:** Accepted.
🖼 🖼 ⊟ 🍴 🖼 ⊠ ⊠ 🛜 ⊠ 🔋 💻

▼▼▼ **Drury Inn & Suites-Orlando** H
(407) 354-1101. **$145-$224.** 7301 W Sand Lake Rd 32819. I-4 exit 74A (Sand Lake Rd), just w. Int corridors. **Pets:** $10 daily fee/room. Service with restrictions, supervision. 🖼 ⊠ 🛜 ⊠ 🔋 💻

▼▼▼ **Extended Stay America-Orlando-Convention Center-Int'l Drive Area** H
(407) 903-1500. **$60-$189.** 8750 Universal Blvd 32819. I-4 exit 74A (Sand Lake Rd), 0.5 mi e to Universal Blvd, then 0.8 mi s. Int corridors. **Pets:** Other species. $25 daily fee/pet. Service with restrictions, supervision. 🖼 ⊠ 🛜 ⊠ 🔋 💻

▼▼▼ **Extended Stay America-Orlando-Universal Studios** H
(407) 351-1788. **$55-$179.** 5620 Major Blvd 32819. I-4 exit 75B, 1.3 mi n to Vineland Rd, just e to Major Blvd, then just s. Int corridors. **Pets:** Other species. $25 daily fee/pet. Service with restrictions, supervision. 🛜 ⊠ 🔋 💻

▼▼▼ **Extended Stay America-Orlando-Universal Studios-Vineland Rd** H
(407) 370-4428. **$60-$189.** 5610 Vineland Rd 32819. I-4 exit 75B, 1 mi n on SR 435 (Kirkman Rd), then e. Int corridors. **Pets:** Other species. $25 daily fee/pet. Service with restrictions, supervision.
🖼 ⊠ 🛜 ⊠ 🔋 💻

▲▲▲ ▼▼▼ **Floridays Resort Orlando** H 🐾
(407) 238-7700. **$150-$450, 3 day notice.** 12562 International Dr 32821. I-4 exit 72 (SR 528), 1.3 mi e to exit 1 (International Dr), then 3.2 mi s. Ext corridors. **Pets:** Small, dogs only. $200 one-time fee/room. Designated rooms, service with restrictions, crate.
🖼 🖼 🍴 🖼 ⊠ 🖼 ⊠ 🔋 💻

▲▲▲ ▼▼▼ ▼▼▼ **The Grand Bohemian Hotel Orlando, Autograph Collection** H 🐾
(407) 313-9000. **$161-$329.** 325 S Orange Ave 32801. I-4 exit 82B, just e on South St to Orange Ave, then just s; downtown. Int corridors. **Pets:** Small, dogs only. $150 one-time fee/pet. Designated rooms, service with restrictions, supervision.
🖼 🖼 🍴 🖼 ⊠ ⊠ 🛜 ⊠ 💻

▲▲▲ ▼▼▼ ▼▼▼ **Hard Rock Hotel® at Universal Orlando** H 🐾
(407) 503-2000. **$264-$444, 5 day notice.** 5800 Universal Blvd 32819. I-4 exit 74B; exit 75A eastbound, 1.3 mi n to Vineland Rd, just w to Universal Blvd, then just s. Int corridors. **Pets:** Small. $50 daily fee/room. Designated rooms, service with restrictions, crate.
🖼 🖼 🍴 🖼 ⊠ ⊠ 🛜 ⊠ 💻

▲▲▲ ▼▼▼ **Hawthorn Suites by Wyndham Orlando International Drive** H
(407) 345-0117. **$79-$189.** 7975 Canada Ave 32819. I-4 exit 74A (Sand Lake Rd), 0.3 mi e. Ext corridors. **Pets:** Accepted.
🖼 ⊠ 🛜 ⊠ 🔋 💻

▲▲▲ ▼▼▼ ▼▼▼ **Holiday Inn & Suites-Across from Universal Orlando** H
(407) 351-3333. **$89-$169.** 5905 S Kirkman Rd 32819. I-4 exit 75B, 0.9 mi n on SR 435 (Kirkman Rd). Int corridors. **Pets:** Accepted.
🖼 🍴 🖼 ⊠ 🛜 🔋 💻

▼▼▼ **Homewood Suites by Hilton-Orlando Airport at Gateway Village** H
(407) 857-5791. **$109-$219.** 5425 Gateway Village Cir 32812. SR 528 exit 11 (Semoran Blvd/SR 436), just n. Int corridors. **Pets:** Accepted.
🖼 🛜 🔋 💻

ⓐⓐⓐ ▼▼▼▼ Hyatt Place Orlando Airport-Northwest H
(407) 816-7800. **$79-$249.** 5435 Forbes Pl 32812. SR 528 (Beachline Expwy) exit 11, 0.5 mi n on SR 436, then just w. Int corridors. **Pets:** Medium, dogs only. $75 one-time fee/room. Service with restrictions, crate. SAVE ⓛⓜ 🏊 🛜 ✕ 🔌 🖥

ⓐⓐⓐ ▼▼▼▼ Hyatt Place Orlando/Convention Center H
(407) 370-4720. **$79-$249.** 8741 International Dr 32819. I-4 exit 74A (Sand Lake Rd), just e, then 0.7 mi s of SR 482 (Sand Lake Rd). Int corridors. **Pets:** Medium, dogs only. $75 one-time fee/room. Service with restrictions, crate. SAVE ⓛⓜ 🏊 🛜 ✕ 🔌 🖥

ⓐⓐⓐ ▼▼▼▼ Hyatt Place Orlando/Universal H
(407) 351-0627. **$99-$209.** 5895 Caravan Ct 32819. I-4 exit 75B, 0.6 mi n to Major Blvd, just e to Caravan Ct, then just s. Int corridors. **Pets:** Medium. $75 one-time fee/room. Service with restrictions.
SAVE ⓛⓜ 🏊 🛜 ✕ 🔌 🖥

▼▼ ▼▼ International Palms Resort and Conference Center H
(407) 351-3500. **Call for rates.** 6515 International Dr 32819. I-4 exit 74A (Sand Lake Rd), just e to International Dr, then 0.5 mi n. Ext/int corridors. **Pets:** Accepted. 🍴 ⓛⓜ 🏊 ✕ 🔊 🔌 🖥

▼▼▼ La Quinta Inn & Suites-Orlando Convention Center H
(407) 345-1365. **$85-$224.** 8504 Universal Blvd 32819. I-4 exit 74A (Sand Lake Rd), 0.5 mi e to Universal Blvd, then 0.5 mi s. Int corridors. **Pets:** Large, other species. Service with restrictions.
ⓛⓜ 🏊 🛜 🔌 🖥

▼▼▼ La Quinta Inn & Suites-Orlando UCF H
(407) 737-6075. **$75-$244.** 11805 Research Pkwy 32826. SR 408 exit 21 (Alafaya Tr), 2.7 mi n to Research Pkwy, then just e. Int corridors. **Pets:** Large, other species. Service with restrictions.
ⓛⓜ 🏊 🛜 🔌 🖥

ⓐⓐⓐ ▼▼▼ La Quinta Inn-Orlando North International Dr H
(407) 351-4100. **$69-$225.** 5825 International Dr 32819. I-4 exit 75A, 0.6 mi s to International Dr, then just w. Int corridors. **Pets:** Large, other species. Service with restrictions. SAVE 🏊 🛜 ✕ 🔌 🖥

ⓐⓐⓐ ▼▼▼▼ Loews Portofino Bay Hotel at Universal Orlando® H 🐾
(407) 503-1000. **$294-$464, 5 day notice.** 5601 Universal Blvd 32819. I-4 exit 74B westbound; exit 75A eastbound, 1 mi n. Int corridors. **Pets:** $50 daily fee/room. Designated rooms.
SAVE ECO 🍴 ⓛⓜ 🏊 ✕ 🛜 ✕ 🔌 🖥

ⓐⓐⓐ ▼▼▼▼ Loews Royal Pacific Resort at Universal Orlando® H
(407) 503-3000. **$234-$389, 5 day notice.** 6300 Hollywood Way 32819. I-4 exit 74A, just w to Turkey Lake Rd, 1.3 mi n to Hollywood Way, then just e. Int corridors. **Pets:** Accepted.
SAVE ECO 🍴 🏊 ✕ 🛜 ✕ 🔌 🖥

ⓐⓐⓐ ▼▼▼ Red Roof Inn International Dr./Convention Center H
(407) 352-1507. **$50-$130.** 9922 Hawaiian Ct 32819. SR 528 (Beachline Expwy) exit 1 (International Dr), 0.5 mi n to Hawaiian Ct, then just s. Ext corridors. **Pets:** Large, other species. Service with restrictions, supervision. SAVE ⓛⓜ 🏊 🛜 ✕ 🔌 🖥

▼▼ ▼▼ Red Roof Inn Orlando South-Florida Mall M
(407) 240-0570. **$46-$90.** 8296 S Orange Blossom Tr 32809. I-4 exit 80A, 4.7 mi s. Ext corridors. **Pets:** Large, other species. Service with restrictions, supervision. 🏊 🛜 🔌 🖥

ⓐⓐⓐ ▼▼▼ Residence Inn by Marriott-Orlando at SeaWorld H
(407) 313-3600. **$84-$219.** 11000 Westwood Blvd 32821. I-4 exit 71, just e to Westwood Blvd, then just s. Int corridors. **Pets:** Accepted.
SAVE 🍴 ⓛⓜ 🏊 🛜 ✕ 🔌 🖥

ⓐⓐⓐ ▼▼▼ Residence Inn by Marriott-Orlando Convention Center H
(407) 226-0288. **$99-$189.** 8800 Universal Blvd 32819. I-4 exit 74A (Sand Lake Rd), 0.5 mi e on SR 482 (Sand Lake Rd), then 0.8 mi s. Int corridors. **Pets:** Accepted. SAVE ⓛⓜ 🏊 🛜 ✕ 🔌 🖥

▼▼▼ Residence Inn by Marriott-Orlando East/UCF Area H 🐾
(407) 513-9000. **$109-$169.** 11651 University Blvd 32817. SR 417 exit 37A (University Blvd), 1.9 mi e. Int corridors. **Pets:** Small. $100 one-time fee/room. Service with restrictions, crate. 🏊 🛜 ✕ 🔌 🖥

ⓐⓐⓐ ▼▼▼ Residence Inn by Marriott Orlando International Airport H
(407) 856-2444. **$119-$209.** 7024 Augusta National Dr 32822. SR 528 (Beach Line Expwy) exit 11, 0.5 mi n on SR 436, then just e. Int corridors. **Pets:** Accepted. SAVE ⓛⓜ 🏊 🛜 ✕ 🔌 🖥

ⓐⓐⓐ ▼▼ ▼▼ The Ritz-Carlton Orlando, Grande Lakes H
(407) 206-2400. **Call for rates.** 4012 Central Florida Pkwy 32837. I-4 exit 71, 2.8 mi e. Int corridors. **Pets:** Accepted.
SAVE ECO ⬅ 🍴 🏊 ✕ 🛜 ✕ 🖥

▼▼▼ Rosen Centre Hotel H
(407) 996-9840. **Call for rates.** 9840 International Dr 32819. I-4 exit 72 (SR 528), 1 mi e to exit 1 (International Dr), then 0.5 mi n; adjacent to Orange County Convention Center. Int corridors. **Pets:** Accepted.
ECO 🍴 ⓛⓜ 🏊 ✕ 🛜 ✕ 🔌 🖥

ⓐⓐⓐ ▼▼▼ Rosen Inn H
(407) 996-4444. **$60-$150.** 6327 International Dr 32819. I-4 exit 74A, just e to International Dr, then 0.7 mi n. Ext/int corridors. **Pets:** Medium. $50 one-time fee/pet. Designated rooms, service with restrictions, crate.
SAVE ⬅ 🍴 ⓛⓜ 🏊 🛜 ✕ 🔌 🖥

ⓐⓐⓐ ▼▼▼ Rosen Inn at Pointe Orlando H
(407) 996-8585. **$69-$149.** 9000 International Dr 32819. I-4 exit 74A (Sand Lake Rd), just e to International Dr, then 1.1 mi s. Ext corridors.
Pets: Accepted. SAVE 🍴 ⓛⓜ 🏊 🛜 ✕ 🔌 🖥

ⓐⓐⓐ ▼▼▼ Rosen Inn International H
(407) 996-1600. **$55-$109.** 7600 International Dr 32819. I-4 exit 74A (Sand Lake Rd), just e to International Dr, then just n. Ext corridors.
Pets: Accepted. SAVE 🍴 ⓛⓜ 🏊 🛜 ✕ 🔌 🖥

▼▼▼ Rosen Plaza Hotel H
(407) 996-9700. **Call for rates.** 9700 International Dr 32819. I-4 exit 74A (Sand Lake Rd), just e to International Dr, then 1.5 mi s. Int corridors. **Pets:** Accepted. ECO 🍴 ⓛⓜ 🏊 ✕ 🛜 ✕ 🔌 🖥

ⓐⓐⓐ ▼▼ ▼▼ Rosen Shingle Creek H
(407) 996-9939. **Call for rates.** 9939 Universal Blvd 32819. I-4 exit 72 (SR 528), 1.7 mi e to exit 2 (Orangewood Blvd), then 0.5 mi n. Int corridors. **Pets:** Accepted.
SAVE ECO ⬅ 🍴 ⓛⓜ 🏊 ✕ 🛜 ✕ 🔌 🖥

ⓐⓐⓐ ▼▼▼ Sheraton Suites Orlando Airport H
(407) 240-5555. **$79-$209.** 7550 Augusta National Dr 32822. SR 528 exit 11 (Semoran Blvd/SR 436), just n to T.G. Lee Blvd, just e to Augusta National Dr, then just s. Int corridors. **Pets:** Large, dogs only. Service with restrictions, supervision.
SAVE ECO 🍴 ⓛⓜ 🏊 🛜 ✕ 🔌 🖥

▼▼▼ **Staybridge Suites Orlando Airport South** H
(407) 438-2121. **Call for rates.** 7450 Augusta National Dr 32822. SR 528 (Beachline Expwy) exit 11, 0.5 mi n on SR 436, just e, then just s. Int corridors. **Pets:** Medium, other species. $15 daily fee/pet. Service with restrictions, crate. [ECO] [&M] 🏊 🛜 ✕ 🛅 💻

▼▼▼ **TownePlace Suites by Marriott-Orlando East/UCF** H
(407) 243-6100. **$131-$153.** 11801 High Tech Ave 32817. SR 417 exit 37A (University Blvd), 2 mi e to Quadrangle Blvd, just n to High Tech Ave, then just e. Int corridors. **Pets:** Accepted.
🏊 🛜 ✕ 🛅 💻

◇◇◇ ▼▼▼ ▼▼▼ **Villas Of Grand Cypress Golf Resort** H
(407) 239-4700. **$225-$1995, 3 day notice.** 1 N Jacaranda St 32836. I-4 exit 68 (SR 535), 0.8 mi n to Winter Garden Vineland Rd, then 1.6 mi nw. Ext corridors. **Pets:** Accepted.
[SAVE] [ECO] [†1] 🏊 ⊠ 🛜 ✕ 🛅 💻

◇◇◇ ▼▼▼ ▼▼▼ **Westgate Lakes Resort & Spa** H
(407) 345-0000. **$99-$489, 3 day notice.** 10000 Turkey Lake Rd 32819. I-4 exit 74A (Sand Lake Rd), 1.1 mi s to Sand Lake Rd, just w to Turkey Lake Rd, then 2.1 mi s. Ext corridors. **Pets:** Accepted.
[SAVE] ◧ [†1] 🏊 ⊠ 🛜 ✕ 🛅 💻

◇◇◇ ▼▼▼ **Westgate Palace** H
(407) 996-6000. **$125-$206, 3 day notice.** 6145 Carrier Dr 32819. I-4 exit 74A, 0.3 mi n to International Dr, 0.4 mi n to Carrier Dr, then just e. Int corridors. **Pets:** Accepted.
[SAVE] [†1] [&M] 🏊 ⊠ 🛜 ✕ 🛅 💻

◇◇◇ ▼▼▼ **Wyndham Orlando Resort International Drive** H ❖
(407) 351-2420. **$79-$199, 3 day notice.** 8001 International Dr 32819. I-4 exit 74A (Sand Lake Rd), just e. Ext/int corridors. **Pets:** Medium, other species. $50 deposit/pet. Service with restrictions, crate.
[SAVE] [†1] [&M] 🏊 ⊠ 🛜 ✕ 🛅 💻

ORMOND BEACH

▼▼▼▼ **Hampton Inn Daytona/Ormond Beach** H
(386) 677-9999. **$99-$159.** 155 Interchange Blvd 32174. I-95 exit 268 (SR 40/Granada Blvd), just w to Interchange Blvd, then just s. Int corridors. **Pets:** Small, other species. $25 daily fee/pet. Service with restrictions, supervision. [&M] 🏊 🛜 ✕ 🛅 💻

◇◇◇ ▼▼▼ **Howard Johnson Inn & Suites at Destination Daytona** H
(386) 944-1500. **$89-$399, 3 day notice.** 1635 N US Hwy 1 32174. I-95 exit 273 (US 1), just nw. Int corridors. **Pets:** Medium, other species. $25 daily fee/pet. Service with restrictions.
[SAVE] 🏊 🛜 ✕ 🛅 💻

▼▼▼▼ **La Quinta Inn & Suites-Ormond Beach/Daytona Beach** H
(386) 236-2031. **$59-$330.** 1571 N US Hwy 1 32174. I-95 exit 273 (US 1), just se. Int corridors. **Pets:** Large, other species. Service with restrictions. [&M] 🏊 🛜 ✕ 🛅 💻

▼▼▼▼ **Lotus Boutique Inn & Suites** H
(386) 310-7966. **Call for rates.** 505 S Atlantic Ave 32176. I-95 exit 268 (SR 40/Granada Blvd), 5.6 mi e to SR A1A (Atlantic Ave), then 1 mi s. Ext corridors. **Pets:** Medium. $20 daily fee/pet. Service with restrictions, supervision. 🏊 🛜 ✕ 🛅 💻

PALM BAY

◇◇◇ ▼▼▼ **Holiday Inn Express Hotel & Suites-Palm Bay** H
(321) 220-2003. **$99-$169.** 1206 SE Malabar Rd 32907. I-95 exit 173 (SR 514/Malabar Rd), just e; behind Sunoco gas station. Int corridors. **Pets:** Small. $15 daily fee/pet. Designated rooms, service with restrictions, supervision. [SAVE] [&M] 🏊 🛜 🛅 💻

▼▼▼ **Quality Inn Palm Bay** H
(321) 725-2952. **$79-$159.** 890 Palm Bay Rd NE 32905. I-95 exit 176 (Palm Bay Rd NE), 0.5 mi e. Int corridors. **Pets:** Small, dogs only. $20 daily fee/room. Designated rooms, service with restrictions, supervision. [&M] 🏊 🛜 🛅 💻

PALM BEACH *(Restaurants p. 627)*

◇◇◇◇ ▼▼▼ ▼▼▼ **The Brazilian Court Hotel** H
(561) 655-7740. **$249-$2999, 14 day notice.** 301 Australian Ave 33480. From Royal Palm Way, just s on Cocoanut Row, then just e; corner of Hibiscus and Australian aves. Int corridors. **Pets:** Accepted.
[SAVE] 🏊 ⊠ 🛜 ✕ 🛅

◇◇◇◇ ▼▼▼ ▼▼▼ **The Chesterfield Hotel Palm Beach** H ❖
(561) 659-5800. **$175-$1000, 7 day notice.** 363 Cocoanut Row 33480. Jct Australian Ave and Cocoanut Row; 2 blks n of Worth Ave. Int corridors. **Pets:** Medium. $90 one-time fee/pet. Designated rooms, service with restrictions, supervision. [SAVE] [†1] 🏊 🛜 🛅 💻

▼▼▼▼ **The Colony Palm Beach** H
(561) 655-5430. **Call for rates.** 155 Hammon Ave 33480. 1 blk s of Worth Ave; between S County Rd and SR A1A (Ocean Blvd). Int corridors. **Pets:** Small, dogs only. $200 one-time fee/room.
[†1] 🏊 🛜 ✕ 🛅 💻

◇◇◇◇ ▼▼▼ ▼▼▼ **Four Seasons Resort Palm Beach** H
(561) 582-2800. **$249-$5495, 14 day notice.** 2800 S Ocean Blvd 33480. On SR A1A (Ocean Blvd), 0.5 mi n of SR 802 (Lake Ave). Int corridors. **Pets:** Accepted.
[SAVE] [ECO] [†1] [&M] 🏊 ⊠ 🛜 ✕ 💻

◇◇◇◇ ▼▼▼ ▼▼▼ **The Omphoy Ocean Resort & Spa** H
(561) 540-6440. **$199-$839, 14 day notice.** 2842 S Ocean Blvd 33480. On SR A1A (Ocean Blvd), 0.4 mi n of SR 802 (Lake Ave). Int corridors. **Pets:** Accepted. [SAVE] [†1] 🏊 ⊠ 🛜 ✕ 💻

◇◇◇◇ ▼▼▼ **Palm Beach Historic Inn** BB ❖
(561) 832-4009. **Call for rates.** 365 S County Rd 33480. Jct S County Rd and Chilian Ave, just n of Worth Ave. Int corridors. **Pets:** $75 one-time fee/pet. Designated rooms, service with restrictions.
[SAVE] 🛜 [✗] [W] [Z]

PALM BEACH GARDENS *(Restaurants p. 627)*

◇◇◇ ▼▼▼ ▼▼▼ **BEST WESTERN PLUS Windsor Gardens Hotel & Suites & Conference Center** H
(561) 844-8448. **$95-$225.** 11360 US Hwy 1 33408. I-95 exit 79A (PGA Blvd), 2.5 mi e to US 1, then just s; Florida Tpke exit 109, 5 mi e to US 1, then just s. Int corridors. **Pets:** Other species. $20 daily fee/pet. Designated rooms, service with restrictions, supervision.
[SAVE] [ECO] [†1] 🏊 🛜 ✕ 🛅 💻

◇◇◇ ▼▼▼ ▼▼▼ **Homewood Suites by Hilton-Palm Beach Gardens** H ❖
(561) 622-7799. **$129-$279.** 4700 Donald Ross Rd 33418. I-95 exit 83 (Donald Ross Rd), 1.1 mi e; in Donald Ross Village. Int corridors. **Pets:** Small. $75 one-time fee/room. Designated rooms, service with restrictions, supervision. [SAVE] [&M] 🏊 🛜 ✕ 💻

◇◇◇ ▼▼▼ ▼▼▼ **PGA National Resort & Spa** H ❖
(561) 627-2000. **$179-$599, 3 day notice.** 400 Ave of the Champions 33418. I-95 exit 79B (PGA Blvd), 2 mi w; Florida Tpke exit 109, just w. Int corridors. **Pets:** Medium. $150 one-time fee/pet. Designated rooms, supervision. [SAVE] [ECO] ◧ [†1] 🏊 ⊠ 🛜 ✕ 🛅 💻

PALM BEACH SHORES *(Restaurants p. 627)*

◇◇◇ ▼▼▼ **SeaSpray Inn Beach Resort** H
(561) 557-8050. **$100-$250, 14 day notice.** 123 S Ocean Ave 33404. On Singer Island; 0.5 mi s of SR A1A. Int corridors. **Pets:** Small, dogs only. $15 daily fee/pet. Designated rooms, service with restrictions, supervision. [SAVE] [†1] 🏊 🛜 ✕ 🛅 💻

PALM COAST

ΔΔΔ ▼▼▼ BEST WESTERN Palm Coast Ⓜ
(386) 446-4457. **$70-$279.** 5 Kingswood Dr 32137. I-95 exit 289 (Palm Coast Pkwy), just e to Kingswood Dr, then just s; in Kingswood Center. Ext corridors. **Pets:** Other species. $10 daily fee/room. Service with restrictions. SAVE ⇨ ⓦ 🔋 🖥

ΔΔΔ ▼▼▼▼ Days Inn Palm Coast Ⓗ
(386) 627-7734. **$69-$149.** 120 Garden St N 32137. I-95 exit 289 (Palm Coast Pkwy), just w to Boulder Rock Dr, just n to Garden St, then just e. Int corridors. **Pets:** Other species. $25 one-time fee/pet. Designated rooms, service with restrictions. SAVE ⓜ ⇨ ⓦ 🔋 🖥

▼▼▼▼ Fairfield Inn & Suites by Marriott-Palm Coast I-95 Ⓗ
(386) 445-3450. **$75-$125.** 400 Old Kings Rd N 32137. I-95 exit 289 (Palm Coast Pkwy), just e Kingswood Dr, then 0.3 mi s. Int corridors. **Pets:** Accepted. ECO ⓜ ⇨ ⓦ ✖ 🔋 🖥

▼▼▼ Holiday Inn Express Hotel & Suites-Palm Coast Ⓗ
(386) 439-3939. **Call for rates.** 200 Flagler Plaza Dr 32137. I-95 exit 284 (SR 100), just e; behind Hampton Inn & Suites. Int corridors. **Pets:** Accepted. ⓜ ⇨ ⓦ 🔋 🖥

ΔΔΔ ▼▼▼ Red Roof Inn - Palm Coast Ⓗ
(386) 446-8180. **$53-$200.** 10 Kingswood Dr 32137. I-95 exit 289 (Palm Coast Pkwy), just e to Kingswood Dr, then just sw; in Kingswood Center. Int corridors. **Pets:** Large, other species. Service with restrictions, supervision. SAVE ECO ⓜ ⇨ ⓦ ✖ 🔋 🖥

PANAMA CITY

▼▼▼▼ La Quinta Inn & Suites Ⓗ
(850) 914-0022. **$69-$199.** 1030 E 23rd St 32405. On SR 368 (23rd St), jct US 231. Int corridors. **Pets:** Large, other species. Service with restrictions. ⓜ ⇨ ⓦ 🔋 🖥

▼▼▼ Red Roof Inn-Panama City Ⓗ
(850) 215-2727. **$59-$199, 3 day notice.** 217 Hwy 231 32405. On US 231, just ne of jct US 98. Int corridors. **Pets:** Large, other species. Service with restrictions, supervision. ⇨ ⓦ 🔋 🖥

▼▼▼▼ Super 8-Panama City Ⓜ
(850) 784-1988. **$52-$100.** 207 Hwy 231 32405. On US 231, just ne of jct US 98. Ext/int corridors. **Pets:** Medium, dogs only. $15 daily fee/pet. Designated rooms, service with restrictions, crate. ⇨ ⓦ 🔋 🖥

▼▼▼▼ TownePlace Suites by Marriott Panama City Ⓗ
(850) 747-0609. **$99-$199.** 903 E 23rd Pl 32405. Just e of jct SR 77, w of jct US 231 on SR 368 (23rd St), then n on Palo Alto Ave. Int corridors. **Pets:** Accepted. ⓜ ⇨ ⓦ 🔋 🖥

PANAMA CITY BEACH *(Restaurants p. 627)*

▼▼▼▼ Hawthorn Suites by Wyndham Ⓗ
(850) 233-7829. **Call for rates.** 7909 Panama City Beach Pkwy 32407. Jct US 98 and SR 30. Int corridors. **Pets:** Small, dogs only. $20 daily fee/room. Service with restrictions. ⓦ Ⓚ Ⓦ Ⓩ

PENSACOLA *(Restaurants p. 628)*

ΔΔΔ ▼▼▼ Hyatt Place Pensacola Airport Ⓗ
(850) 483-5599. **Call for rates.** 161 Airport Ln 32504. I-110 exit 5, 2.7 mi e on SR 750, just n on 12th Ave, then just e. Int corridors. **Pets:** Accepted. SAVE ⓦ Ⓚ Ⓦ Ⓩ

▼▼▼▼ MainStay Suites Ⓗ
(850) 479-1000. **$79-$159.** 7230 Plantation Rd 32504. I-10 exit 13, just s on SR 291, then 0.3 mi w. Ext corridors. **Pets:** Accepted. ⓜ ⇨ ⓦ ✖ 🔋 🖥

▼▼▼ Red Roof Inn Pensacola West Ⓗ
(850) 941-0908. **$55-$90.** 2591 Wilde Lake Blvd 32526. I-10 exit 7, just s on SR 297, then just w. Int corridors. **Pets:** Large, other species. Service with restrictions, supervision. ⓜ ⇨ ⓦ 🔋 🖥

▼▼▼ TownePlace Suites by Marriott Pensacola Ⓗ 🐾
(850) 484-7022. **$129-$169.** 481 Creighton Rd 32504. I-10 exit 13, 0.3 mi s on SR 291, then just w. Int corridors. **Pets:** Medium, other species. $100 one-time fee/room. Service with restrictions, crate. ECO ⇨ ⓦ ✖ 🔋 🖥

PLANTATION *(Restaurants p. 628)*

▼▼▼ Extended Stay America-Fort Lauderdale-Plantation Ⓗ
(954) 382-8888. **$60-$150.** 7755 SW 6th St 33324. I-595 exit 5 (University Dr), 1.2 mi w to University Dr, 1 mi n to SW 6th St, then just w. Int corridors. **Pets:** Other species. $25 daily fee/pet. Service with restrictions, supervision. ⇨ ⓦ 🔋 🖥

ΔΔΔ ▼▼▼ Hyatt Place Fort Lauderdale/Plantation Ⓗ
(954) 370-2220. **$75-$219.** 8530 W Broward Blvd 33324. I-595 exit 4, 0.4 mi w to Pine Island Rd, 1.4 mi n to Broward Blvd, then just e. Int corridors. **Pets:** Accepted. SAVE ⓜ ⇨ ⓦ ✖ 🔋 🖥

▼▼▼ La Quinta Inn & Suites-Ft. Lauderdale Plantation Ⓗ
(954) 476-6047. **$89-$254.** 8101 Peters Rd 33324. I-595 exit 5 (University Dr), 1.2 mi w to University Dr, 0.4 mi n to Peters Rd, then just w; in Crossroad Office Park. Int corridors. **Pets:** Large, other species. Service with restrictions. ⓜ ⇨ ⓦ 🔋 🖥

▼▼▼ La Quinta Inn & Suites-Plantation at SW 6th St Ⓗ
(954) 473-8257. **$82-$249.** 7901 SW 6th St 33324. I-595 exit 5 (University Dr), 1.2 mi w to University Dr, 1 mi n to SW 6th St, then 0.3 mi w; in Wellesley Corporate Plaza. Int corridors. **Pets:** Large, other species. Service with restrictions. ⇨ ⓦ 🔋 🖥

ΔΔΔ ▼▼▼ Residence Inn by Marriott-Fort Lauderdale Plantation Ⓗ
(954) 723-0300. **$129-$209.** 130 N University Dr 33324. I-95 exit 27 (Broward Blvd), 5.2 mi w to University Dr, then just n. Int corridors. **Pets:** Accepted. SAVE ECO ⓜ ⇨ ⓦ ✖ 🔋 🖥

ΔΔΔ ▼▼▼ Sheraton Suites Plantation Ⓗ
(954) 424-3300. **$89-$219.** 311 N University Dr 33324. I-595 exit 5, 1.2 mi w to University Dr, then 1.8 mi n. Int corridors. **Pets:** Accepted. SAVE ECO 🍴 ⓜ ⇨ ✖ ⓦ ✖ 🔋 🖥

▼▼▼▼ Staybridge Suites-Plantation/Fort Lauderdale Ⓗ
(954) 577-9696. **$99-$169, 3 day notice.** 410 N Pine Island Rd 33324. I-595 exit 4 (Pine Island Rd), 1.7 mi n. Int corridors. **Pets:** Accepted. ⓜ ⇨ ⓦ ✖ 🔋 🖥

PLANT CITY

ΔΔΔ ▼▼▼▼ BEST WESTERN PLUS Plant City Hotel Ⓗ
(813) 707-6000. **$69-$229.** 2003 S Frontage Rd 33566. I-4 exit 22, just s on Park Rd. Int corridors. **Pets:** Accepted. SAVE ⓜ ⇨ ⓦ ✖ 🔋 🖥

POMPANO BEACH

▼▼▼ Extended Stay America-Ft. Lauderdale-Cypress Creek Park North Ⓗ
(954) 783-1050. **$60-$140.** 1401 W McNab Rd 33069. I-95 exit 33B (Cypress Creek Rd), just w to Andrews Ave, 0.7 mi n to McNab Rd, then just w. Int corridors. **Pets:** Other species. $25 daily fee/pet. Service with restrictions, supervision. ⇨ ⓦ 🔋 🖥

▼▼▼ Residence Inn by Marriott-Fort Lauderdale Pompano Beach/Oceanfront Ⓗ
(954) 590-1000. **$143-$399.** 1350 N Ocean Blvd 33062. I-95 exit 36 (Atlantic Blvd), 3.1 mi e to Ocean Blvd (SR A1A), then 1.3 mi n. Ext/int corridors. **Pets:** Accepted. 🍴 ⓜ ⇨ ✖ ⓦ ✖ 🔋 🖥

PONTE VEDRA BEACH

WWWW Sawgrass Marriott Golf Resort & Spa H

(904) 285-7777. **$179-$307, 3 day notice.** 1000 PGA Tour Blvd 32082. SR 202 (Butler Blvd), 4 mi s on SR A1A to PGA Tour Blvd, then just w. Ext/int corridors. **Pets:** Accepted.

SAVE ECO TI 2 X S X H P

PORT CHARLOTTE *(Restaurants p. 628)*

WWW Country Inn & Suites By Carlson H

(941) 235-1035. **Call for rates.** 24244 Corporate Ct 33954. I-75 exit 170, just w on CR 769 (Kings Hwy). Int corridors. **Pets:** Other species. $10 daily fee/room. Service with restrictions.

M 2 X H P

WW Days Inn of Port Charlotte H

(941) 627-8900. **$69-$169.** 1941 Tamiami Tr 33948. On US 41, 2.3 mi s of jct Toledo Blade Blvd (CR 779). Ext corridors. **Pets:** Medium, dogs only. $10 daily fee/pet. Service with restrictions, supervision.

TI 2 X H P

WWWW La Quinta Inn & Suites Port Charlotte H

(941) 979-4200. **$82-$254.** 812 Kings Hwy 33980. I-75 exit 170, just w on CR 769 (Kings Hwy), then just s on Veterans Blvd. Int corridors. **Pets:** Large, other species. Service with restrictions.

SAVE M 2 X H P

PORT ORANGE

WWWW Country Inn & Suites By Carlson-Port Orange/Daytona, FL H

(386) 760-0101. **$99-$599.** 5802 Journey's End Way 32127. I-95 exit 256, just e. Int corridors. **Pets:** Large, other species. $35 one-time fee/room. Designated rooms, service with restrictions, supervision.

SAVE M 2 X H P

WWWW La Quinta Inn & Suites-Port Orange/Daytona H

(386) 756-3440. **$65-$424.** 1791 Dunlawton Ave 32129. I-95 exit 256, just e. Int corridors. **Pets:** Large, other species. Service with restrictions.

M 2 X H P

PORT RICHEY

WWWW Homewood Suites by Hilton Tampa/Port Richey H

(727) 819-1000. **$109-$289.** 11115 US 19 N 34668. 0.9 mi s of SR 52 at jct Hammock/Ranch Rd. Int corridors. **Pets:** Accepted.

M 2 H P

PORT ST. LUCIE

WWW Holiday Inn-Port St Lucie H

(772) 337-2200. **$79-$229.** 10120 S Federal Hwy 34952. On US 1, 0.6 mi n of jct SR 716 (Port St Lucie Blvd). Int corridors. **Pets:** Accepted.

ECO TI 2 X H P

WWWW Homewood Suites by Hilton Port St. Lucie-Tradition H

(772) 345-5300. **$104-$239.** 10301 SW Innovation Way 34987. I-95 exit 118 (Gatlin Blvd), 0.5 mi w to Village Pkwy, then just s. Int corridors. **Pets:** Accepted. M 2 H P

WWWW Residence Inn by Marriott-Port St. Lucie H

(772) 344-7814. **$99-$224.** 1920 SW Fountainview Blvd 34986. I-95 exit 121 (St. Lucie West Blvd), just e to Paramount Dr, just s to SW Fountainview Blvd, just sw. Int corridors. **Pets:** Accepted.

SAVE M 2 X H P

WW Sleep Inn & Mainstay Suites at PGA Village H

(772) 460-8882. **$79-$145.** 8501 Champions Way 34986. I-95 exit 121 (St. Lucie West Blvd), just w. Int corridors. **Pets:** Accepted.

2 X H P

PUNTA GORDA *(Restaurants p. 628)*

WWWW Four Points by Sheraton Punta Gorda Harborside H

(941) 637-6770. **$90-$199.** 33 Tamiami Tr 33950. On US 41; at Peace River Bridge. Int corridors. **Pets:** Medium. $25 one-time fee/room. Designated rooms, service with restrictions, supervision.

SAVE TI M 2 X X H P

QUINCY *(Restaurants p. 628)*

WWW Allison House Inn BB

(850) 875-2511. **$85-$175, 21 day notice.** 215 N Madison St 32351. Just n of town center; in historic district. Int corridors. **Pets:** Small, dogs only. Designated rooms, service with restrictions, crate. X Z

ST. AUGUSTINE

WWWW Bayfront Marin House BB

(904) 824-4301. **$179-$359, 7 day notice.** 142 Avenida Menendez 32084. 1 blk s of Bridge of Lions. Ext corridors. **Pets:** $30 daily fee/pet. Designated rooms, service with restrictions. X

WWWW BEST WESTERN St. Augustine I-95 M

(904) 829-1999. **$70-$180.** 2445 SR 16 32092. I-95 exit 318 (SR 16), just w. Ext corridors. **Pets:** Accepted. SAVE 2 P

WWWW Casablanca Inn on the Bay BB

(904) 829-0928. **$99-$369, 7 day notice.** 24 Avenida Menendez 32084. I-95 exit 318 (SR 16), 5.5 mi e to San Marco Ave, then 1.8 mi s; in historic district. Ext/int corridors. **Pets:** Accepted. SAVE X H

WWWW Casa Monica Hotel, Autograph Collection H

(904) 827-1888. **$152-$409, 3 day notice.** 95 Cordova St 32084. Downtown; across from Lightner Museum and Flagler College. Int corridors. **Pets:** Accepted. SAVE ECO TI 2 X X H P

WWWW Peace and Plenty Inn BB

(904) 829-8209. **$89-$189, 7 day notice.** 87 Cedar St 32084. From King St, just s on Granada St, then just w. Int corridors. **Pets:** Medium, dogs only. $35 one-time fee/pet. Designated rooms, service with restrictions, supervision. X Z H P

ST. AUGUSTINE BEACH

WWWW House of Sea and Sun BB

(904) 461-1716. **$169-$229, 7 day notice.** 2 B St 32080. Jct SR 312 and A1A, 1.9 mi s to B St, then just e. Ext/int corridors. **Pets:** Other species. Service with restrictions. SAVE X Z H

ST. CLOUD

WWWW Budget Inn of St Cloud M

(407) 892-2858. **$35-$90, 3 day notice.** 602 13th St 34769. On US 192/441, 0.5 mi e of the Water Tower, 2 mi w of jct CR 15. Ext corridors. **Pets:** Very small, dogs only. $10 daily fee/pet. Service with restrictions. SAVE H P

ST. PETE BEACH *(Restaurants p. 628)*

WWW Bay Palms Waterfront Resort 2 M

(727) 360-7642. **$79-$249, 14 day notice.** 4237 Gulf Blvd 33706. On SR 699, 0.6 mi n of Pinellas Bayway. Ext corridors. **Pets:** Medium, dogs only. $50 deposit/pet, $25 daily fee/pet. Service with restrictions, crate. SAVE ECO 2 X H

WWW Bayview Plaza Waterfront Resort 1 M

(727) 367-2791. **$79-$249, 14 day notice.** 4321 Gulf Blvd 33706. On SR 699, 0.6 mi n of Pinellas Bayway. Ext/int corridors. **Pets:** Medium, dogs only. $50 deposit/pet, $25 daily fee/pet. Service with restrictions, crate. SAVE ECO 2 X X H P

WWW Island's End Resort CA

(727) 360-5023. **$163-$372, 14 day notice.** 1 Pass-A-Grille Way 33706. 2 mi s of Pinellas Bayway; in historic Pass-A-Grille. Ext corridors. **Pets:** Accepted. SAVE X H P

Loews Don CeSar Hotel H ❧

(727) 360-1881. **$189-$809, 3 day notice.** 3400 Gulf Blvd 33706. On SR 699, jct Pinellas Bayway. Int corridors. **Pets:** $45 daily fee/room. Designated rooms, service with restrictions, crate.

SAVE ECO ⊟ ⊟ &M ⇔ ⋈ 📶 ✕ 🖬 🖵

Sirata Beach Resort & Conference Center H ❧

(727) 363-5100. **$149-$499, 3 day notice.** 5300 Gulf Blvd 33706. On SR 699, 1.2 mi n of Pinellas Bayway. Ext/int corridors. **Pets:** Medium. $100 deposit/room, $30 daily fee/room. Designated rooms, service with restrictions. SAVE ECO ⊟ ⇔ ⋈ 📶 ✕ 🖬 🖵

TradeWinds Island Grand Beach Resort H ❧

(727) 367-6461. **$234-$627.** 5500 Gulf Blvd 33706. On SR 699, 1 mi n of Pinellas Bayway. Ext/int corridors. **Pets:** Large, other species. $100 deposit/room, $30 daily fee/room. Designated rooms, service with restrictions. SAVE ECO ⊟ ⇔ ⋈ 📶 ✕ 🖬 🖵

ST. PETERSBURG (Restaurants p. 628)

Hilton St. Petersburg Bayfront H

(727) 894-5000. **$109-$429.** 333 1st St S 33701. Just s of jct 1st Ave S. Int corridors. **Pets:** Accepted.

SAVE ECO ⊟ &M ⇔ 📶 ✕ 🖬 🖵

Hotel Indigo St. Petersburg Downtown H

(727) 822-4814. **Call for rates.** 234 3rd Ave N 33701. Jct 2nd St N. Int corridors. **Pets:** Medium, other species. $50 one-time fee/room. Service with restrictions, crate. ⊟ &M ⇔ ⋈ 📶 ✕ 🖬 🖵

La Quinta Inn & Suites St. Petersburg Northeast H

(727) 525-1800. **$79-$299.** 6638 4th St N 33702. I-275 exit 26, 1.7 mi e on 54th Ave N (CR 202), then 0.8 mi n. Int corridors. **Pets:** Large, other species. Service with restrictions. &M 📶 ✕ 🖵

Magnuson Hotel Marina Cove M ❧

(727) 867-1151. **$80-$180.** 6800 Sunshine Skyway Ln S 33711. I-275 exit 16, just e on Pinellas Point Dr S, then just s. Ext/int corridors. **Pets:** Medium. $20 daily fee/pet. Designated rooms, service with restrictions, crate. SAVE ⊟ &M ⇔ ⋈ 📶 🖬 🖵

Staybridge Suites Downtown St Petersburg H

(727) 821-0777. **$99-$399.** 940 5th Ave S 33705. I-275 exit 22, 0.4 mi se on US 175, jct Dr Martin Luther King Jr St. Int corridors. **Pets:** Accepted. &M 📶 ✕ 🖬 🖵

SANFORD

BEST WESTERN PLUS Sanford Airport/Lake Mary Hotel H

(407) 320-0845. **$79-$199.** 3401 S Orlando Dr 32773. I-4 exit 98, 4.5 mi e to US 17-92, then 0.7 mi n. Int corridors. **Pets:** Medium, other species. $20 daily fee/pet. Designated rooms, service with restrictions, crate. SAVE &M ⇔ 📶 ✕ 🖬 🖵

SARASOTA (Restaurants p. 628)

Hampton Inn & Suites Sarasota Bradenton Airport H

(941) 355-8140. **$99-$189.** 975 University Pkwy 34234. Just e of jct US 41 (N Tamiami Tr). Int corridors. **Pets:** Accepted.

⊟ &M ⇔ 📶 ✕ 🖬 🖵

Holiday Inn Express & Suites Sarasota East I-75 H

(941) 925-0631. **$89-$279.** 5730 Gantt Rd 34233. I-75 exit 205, 0.3 mi w on SR 72 (Clark Rd), then just n on Hospitality Way. Int corridors. **Pets:** Medium. $25 daily fee/room. Service with restrictions, supervision.

ECO &M ⇔ 📶 ✕ 🖬 🖵

Holiday Inn Lido Beach H

(941) 388-5555. **$199-$599, 7 day notice.** 233 Ben Franklin Dr 34236. On Lido Key at Lido Beach; 0.4 mi s of St. Armands Circle. Int corridors. **Pets:** Accepted. SAVE ECO ⊟ ⇔ 📶 ✕ 🖬 🖵

Holiday Inn Sarasota Bradenton Airport H

(941) 355-9000. **$99-$259.** 8009 15th St E 34243. 1.2 mi nw on W University Pkwy from jct University Pkwy (CR 610). Int corridors. **Pets:** Small, dogs only. $75 one-time fee/room. Designated rooms, service with restrictions, supervision.

SAVE ⊟ &M ⇔ ⋈ 📶 ✕ 🖬 🖵

Hotel Indigo Sarasota H

(941) 487-3800. **$134-$424.** 1223 Boulevard of the Arts 34236. Jct US 41 (N Tamiami Tr). Int corridors. **Pets:** Accepted.

⊟ &M ⋈ 📶 ✕ 🖬 🖵

Hyatt Regency Sarasota H ❧

(941) 953-1234. **$99-$369, 3 day notice.** 1000 Boulevard of the Arts 34236. Just w of jct US 41 (Tamiami Tr). Int corridors. **Pets:** Medium, dogs only. $100 one-time fee/pet. Designated rooms, service with restrictions, crate. SAVE ECO ⊟ &M ⇔ ⋈ 📶 ✕ 🖬 🖵

Lido Beach Resort H

(941) 388-2161. **$179-$359, 3 day notice.** 700 Ben Franklin Dr 34236. On Lido Key at Lido Beach; 0.8 mi s of St. Armands Circle. Ext/int corridors. **Pets:** Small, dogs only. $75 daily fee/pet. Designated rooms, service with restrictions, supervision.

SAVE ECO ⊟ &M ⇔ ⋈ 📶 ✕ 🖬 🖵

Residence Inn by Marriott Sarasota-Bradenton H ❧

(941) 358-1468. **$149-$429.** 1040 University Pkwy 34234. Just e of jct US 41 (Tamiami Tr). Int corridors. **Pets:** Other species. $75 one-time fee/room. Service with restrictions. ECO &M ⇔ 📶 ✕ 🖬 🖵

The Ritz-Carlton, Sarasota H ❧

(941) 309-2000. **$229-$759, 3 day notice.** 1111 Ritz-Carlton Dr 34236. On US 41, jct John Ringling Blvd. Int corridors. **Pets:** Small, dogs only. $250 one-time fee/room. Service with restrictions.

SAVE ECO ⊟ &M ⇔ ⋈ 📶 ✕ 🖬 🖵

SEBASTIAN

BEST WESTERN PLUS Sebastian Hotel & Suites H

(772) 388-9300. **$70-$150.** 1655 US Hwy 1 32958. I-95 exit 156 (Fellsmere Rd/CR 512), 6.5 mi e to US 1, then 1.2 mi n. Int corridors. **Pets:** Accepted. SAVE ⇔ 📶 ✕ 🖬 🖵

SEBRING

Château Élan Hotel & Conference Center H

(863) 655-7200. **$85-$460, 3 day notice.** 150 Midway Dr 33870. Jct US 98, 1.4 mi n on Haywood Taylor Blvd; at entrance to Sebring International Raceway. Int corridors. **Pets:** Accepted.

ECO ⊟ ⇔ 📶 ✕ 🖬 🖵

Inn On The Lakes H ❧

(863) 471-9400. **$110-$300.** 3101 Golfview Rd 33875. On US 27/98, just s of jct Sebring Pkwy. Ext/int corridors. **Pets:** Other species. $40 one-time fee/room. Designated rooms, service with restrictions, supervision. SAVE ⊟ ⇔ 🖬 🖵

La Quinta Inn & Suites Sebring H

(863) 386-1000. **$89-$494.** 4115 US Hwy 27 S 33870. On US 27/98, just n of jct Sebring Pkwy. Int corridors. **Pets:** Large, other species. Service with restrictions. &M ⇔ 📶 ✕ 🖬 🖵

Residence Inn by Marriott - Sebring H

(863) 314-9100. **$109-$189.** 3221 Tubbs Rd 33870. On US 27/98, 4.5 mi n of jct SR 98. Int corridors. **Pets:** Accepted.

SAVE ⇔ 📶 ✕ 🖬 🖵

SEFFNER

AAA **WWW** Country Inn & Suites By Carlson Tampa East/Seffner **H**

(813) 675-8600. **$89-$199.** 11551 Discovery Ln 33584. I-4 exit 10, just n on CR 579. Int corridors. **Pets:** Other species. $25 daily fee/pet. Designated rooms, service with restrictions.

[SAVE] [&M] [≥] [≈] [X] [■] [▣]

WWWW Hampton Inn & Suites Tampa East **H**

(813) 630-4321. **$99-$169.** 11740 Tampa Gateway Blvd 33584. I-4 exit 10, just n on CR 579, just e. Int corridors. **Pets:** Small. Designated rooms, service with restrictions, crate. [&M] [≥] [≈] [■] [▣]

SILVER SPRINGS

WWWW Holiday Inn Express Hotel & Suites **H**

(352) 304-6111. **Call for rates.** 5360 E Silver Springs Blvd 34488. On SR 40, just e of jct NE 25th St. Int corridors. **Pets:** Small. $25 daily fee/pet. Service with restrictions, supervision.

[ECO] [≥] [≈] [X] [■] [▣]

SPRING HILL

WWW Microtel Inn & Suites by Wyndham, Spring Hill **H**

(352) 596-3444. **$60-$100.** 4881 Commercial Way 34606. On US 19, 1 mi s of jct Northcliffe Blvd and Frontage Rd. Int corridors. **Pets:** Dogs only. $25 daily fee/pet. Service with restrictions, supervision.

[&M] [≈] [■] [▣]

STARKE

AAA **WWW** BEST WESTERN Starke **M**

(904) 964-6744. **$89-$135.** 1290 N Temple Ave 32091. 1 mi n on US 301 from jct SR 100 (Reid St). Ext corridors. **Pets:** Large. $10 daily fee/pet. Service with restrictions, supervision. [SAVE] [≥] [≈] [■] [▣]

STUART

AAA **WWWW** BEST WESTERN Downtown Stuart **H**

(772) 287-6200. **$80-$160.** 1209 SE Federal Hwy 34994. On US 1, 0.5 mi s of jct SR 76. Ext corridors. **Pets:** Accepted.

[SAVE] [≥] [≈] [■] [▣]

WWWW Courtyard by Marriott-Stuart **H**

(772) 781-3344. **$89-$259.** 7615 SW Lost River Rd 34997. I-95 exit 101 (SR 76), 0.7 mi e to SW Lost River Rd, then just nw. Int corridors. **Pets:** Accepted. [&M] [≥] [≈] [X] [■] [▣]

WWWW Hampton Inn & Suites Stuart-North **H**

(772) 692-6922. **$109-$199.** 1150 NW Federal Hwy 34994. On US 1, 2.1 mi nw of SR 76 (SW Kanner Hwy). Int corridors. **Pets:** Accepted. [&M] [≥] [≈] [■] [▣]

WWW Monterey Inn & Marina **M**

(772) 283-3500. **Call for rates.** 300 SW Monterey Rd 34994. Jct SR 76 (S Kanner Hwy) and CR 714 (SW Monterey Rd), just w; base of east side of Palm City Bridge. Ext corridors. **Pets:** Accepted. [≈] [■] [▣]

SUNNY ISLES BEACH

AAA **WWWW** Acqualina Resort & Spa on the Beach **H**

(305) 918-8000. **$450-$4200, 30 day notice.** 17875 Collins Ave 33160. I-95 exit 16 (Ives Dairy Rd), 1.2 mi e to US 1 (Biscayne Blvd), 0.6 mi s to William Lehman Cswy, 1.6 mi e to SR A1A (Collins Ave), then 0.8 mi s. Int corridors. **Pets:** Accepted.

[SAVE] [¶] [&M] [≥] [X] [≈] [■] [▣]

SUNRISE

AAA **WWWW** DoubleTree by Hilton Sunrise-Sawgrass Mills **H**

(954) 851-1020. **$109-$209.** 13400 W Sunrise Blvd 33323. Sawgrass Expwy (SR 869) exit 1 (Sunrise Blvd), 1 mi e. Int corridors. **Pets:** Accepted. [SAVE] [¶] [&M] [≥] [≈] [X] [■] [▣]

WWW **WWW** La Quinta Inn & Suites-Ft. Lauderdale Sunrise **H**

(954) 845-9929. **$95-$249.** 13600 NW 2nd St 33325. I-595 exit 1A (SR 84), 0.5 mi w to NW 136th Ave, 0.4 mi n to NW 2nd St, then just w. Int corridors. **Pets:** Large, other species. Service with restrictions.

[≥] [≈] [■] [▣]

WWW **WWW** La Quinta Inn & Suites-Sunrise Sawgrass Mills **H**

(954) 846-1200. **$95-$249.** 13651 NW 2nd St 33325. I-595 exit 1A (SR 84), 0.5 mi w to NW 136th Ave, 0.4 mi n to NW 2nd St, then just w. Int corridors. **Pets:** Large, other species. Service with restrictions.

[≥] [≈] [■] [▣]

TALLAHASSEE *(Restaurants p. 628)*

AAA **WWWW** Aloft Tallahassee Downtown **H**

(850) 513-0313. **$95-$269.** 200 N Monroe St 32301. 0.4 mi n of Capitol. Int corridors. **Pets:** Accepted. [SAVE] [≥] [≈] [X] [■] [▣]

WWW Baymont Inn & Suites Tallahassee Central **H**

(850) 878-5099. **Call for rates.** 2850 Apalachee Pkwy 32301. 3 mi se on US 27. Ext corridors. **Pets:** Accepted. [&M] [≥] [≈] [■] [▣]

AAA **WWWW** BEST WESTERN Pride Inn & Suites **M**

(850) 656-6312. **$70-$400.** 2016 Apalachee Pkwy 32301. 1 mi se on US 27. Ext corridors. **Pets:** $20 daily fee/pet. Service with restrictions, crate. [SAVE] [≥] [≈] [■] [▣]

AAA **WWWW** BEST WESTERN Seminole Inn **M**

(850) 656-2938. **$70-$250.** 6737 Mahan Dr 32308. I-10 exit 209A, just w on US 90. Ext corridors. **Pets:** Medium. $20 daily fee/pet. Designated rooms, service with restrictions, supervision. [SAVE] [≥] [≈] [■] [▣]

WWW Extended Stay America Tallahassee-Killearn **H**

(850) 383-1700. **$60-$225.** 1950 Raymond Diehl Rd 32308. I-10 exit 203, 2.4 mi s, then just n. Int corridors. **Pets:** Other species. $25 daily fee/pet. Service with restrictions, supervision. [&M] [≥] [≈] [■] [▣]

AAA **WWWW** Four Points by Sheraton Tallahassee Downtown **H**

(850) 422-0071. **$99-$549.** 316 W Tennessee St 32301. Just w of US 27; downtown. Int corridors. **Pets:** Medium, dogs only. $25 daily fee/pet. Designated rooms, no service, supervision.

[SAVE] [¶] [≥] [≈] [X] [■] [▣]

WWWW Homewood Suites by Hilton **H**

(850) 402-9400. **$119-$299.** 2987 Apalachee Pkwy 32301. US 27, 3.5 mi s. Int corridors. **Pets:** Accepted. [ECO] [≥] [≈] [■] [▣]

WWW La Quinta Inn Tallahassee (North) **H**

(850) 385-7172. **$59-$309.** 2905 N Monroe St 32303. I-10 exit 199, just s on US 27. Ext corridors. **Pets:** Large, other species. Service with restrictions. [≥] [≈] [■] [▣]

AAA **WWW** Quality Inn & Suites **H**

(850) 877-4437. **$75-$159.** 2020 Apalachee Pkwy 32301. 2.2 mi s on US 27. Int corridors. **Pets:** Accepted.

[SAVE] [ECO] [≥] [≈] [X] [■] [▣]

WWWW Residence Inn by Marriott Tallahassee North I-10 Capital Circle **H**

(850) 422-0093. **$76-$299.** 1880 Raymond Diehl Rd 32308. I-10 exit 203, just s. Int corridors. **Pets:** Accepted.

[ECO] [&M] [≥] [≈] [X] [■] [▣]

AAA **WWWW** Residence Inn by Marriott Tallahassee Universities at the Capitol **H**

(850) 329-9080. **$119-$299.** 600 W Gaines St 32304. 0.5 mi w of S Monroe St; downtown. Int corridors. **Pets:** Accepted.

[SAVE] [ECO] [&M] [≥] [≈] [X] [■] [▣]

▼▼▼▼ Staybridge Suites Tallahassee 🅗

(850) 219-7000. **Call for rates.** 1600 Summit Lake Dr 32317. I-10 exit 209B, just n. Int corridors. **Pets:** Accepted.

ECO 🖬 🛜 ✕ 🛢 🖵

▼▼▼ TownePlace Suites by Marriott Tallahassee Northeast/Capital Circle 🅗

(850) 219-0122. **$85-$375.** 1876 Capital Cir NE 32308. I-10 exit 203, just e to US 319, then 2.1 mi s. Int corridors. **Pets:** Accepted.

ECO 🅑M 🖬 🛜 ✕ 🛢 🖵

▼▼▼ Wyndham Garden Tallahassee Capitol 🅗

(850) 877-3171. **$62-$71.** 1355 Apalachee Pkwy 32301. 1.3 mi se on US 27. Int corridors. **Pets:** Small. $50 one-time fee/room. Service with restrictions, crate. 🍽 🖬 🛜 ✕ 🛢 🖵

TAMARAC

▼▼▼ La Quinta Inn & Suites-Fort Lauderdale/Tamarac 🅗

(954) 484-6909. **$75-$224.** 5070 N SR 7 33319. I-95 exit 32 (Commercial Blvd), 3.2 mi w to SR 7 (US 441), then just n; Florida Tpke exit 62, 0.5 mi e to SR 7 (US 441), then just n. Int corridors. **Pets:** Large, other species. Service with restrictions. 🖬 🛜 🛢 🖵

▼▼▼ La Quinta Inn-Ft. Lauderdale Tamarac East 🅗

(954) 485-7900. **$75-$224.** 3800 W Commercial Blvd 33309. I-95 exit 32 (Commercial Blvd), 3 mi w; Florida Tpke exit 62, 0.7 mi e. Int corridors. **Pets:** Large, other species. Service with restrictions.

🏊 🛜 🛢 🖵

TAMPA *(Restaurants p. 628)*

▼▼▼ Clarion Inn Tampa Conference Center 🅜

(813) 621-5555. **Call for rates.** 9331 Adamo Dr 33619. I-75 exit 257, 1.2 mi w on SR 60. Ext corridors. **Pets:** Accepted.

🍽 🖬 🛜 🛢 🖵

▼▼ Extended Stay America 🅗

(813) 886-5253. **$65-$159.** 4811 Memorial Hwy 33634. SR 589 (Veterans Expwy) exit 3, just sw on CR 576. Int corridors. **Pets:** Other species. $25 daily fee/pet. Service with restrictions, supervision.

🅑M 🖬 🛜 🛢 🖵

▼▼ Extended Stay America-Tampa-Airport-N West Shore Blvd 🅗

(813) 637-8990. **$65-$169.** 1805 N Westshore Blvd 33607. I-275 exit 40A southbound, 0.5 mi nw; exit 39A northbound, 1 mi e on SR 60 (John F Kennedy Blvd), then 1.3 mi nw. Int corridors. **Pets:** Other species. $25 daily fee/pet. Service with restrictions, supervision.

🅑M 🖬 🛜 🛢 🖵

▼▼▼ Fairfield Inn & Suites by Marriott Tampa Fairgrounds/Casino 🅗

(813) 626-3000. **$89-$224.** 6720 Lakeview Center Dr 33619. I-4 exit 5, just e on SR 574 (Dr. Martin Luther King Jr Blvd), just s on Corporex Dr, then just w; in Corporex Park. Int corridors. **Pets:** Accepted.

🅑M 🖬 🛜 ✕ 🛢 🖵

🄰🄰🄰 ▼▼▼ ▼▼▼ Grand Hyatt Tampa Bay 🅗 🐾

(813) 874-1234. **$99-$399.** 2900 Bayport Dr 33607. On SR 60, at east end of Courtney Campbell Cswy. Ext/int corridors. **Pets:** Small, dogs only. $100 one-time fee/pet. Designated rooms, service with restrictions, supervision. SAVE ECO 🍽 🅑M 🖬 ✕ 🖴 ✕ 🛢 🖵

▼▼▼ Hampton Inn Tampa-Veterans Expwy/Airport North 🅗

(813) 901-5900. **$99-$174.** 5628 W Waters Ave 33634. SR 589 (Veterans Expwy) exit 6A, just e on CR 584. Int corridors. **Pets:** Small. $20 deposit/pet, $20 daily fee/pet. Service with restrictions, crate.

🅑M 🖬 🛜 🛢 🖵

🄰🄰🄰 ▼▼▼▼ Holiday Inn Express Hotel & Suites 🅗

(813) 910-7171. **Call for rates.** 8310 Galbraith Rd 33647. I-75 exit 270, 0.3 mi n on CR 581 (Bruce B Downs Blvd), just w on Highwoods Preserve Pkwy, then just n; in Highwoods Preserve. Int corridors. **Pets:** Small, dogs only. $50 one-time fee/room. Designated rooms, service with restrictions, supervision. SAVE ECO 🅑M 🖬 🛜 🛢 🖵

🄰🄰🄰 ▼▼▼▼ Holiday Inn Tampa Westshore Airport 🅗 🐾

(813) 289-8200. **$89-$239, 3 day notice.** 700 N Westshore Blvd 33609. I-275 exit 40A southbound, just nw on CR 587; exit 39A northbound, 1 mi n on SR 60 (Kennedy Blvd), then 0.9 mi nw on CR 587, jct W Cypress St. Int corridors. **Pets:** Medium. $50 one-time fee/room. Service with restrictions, crate. SAVE 🍽 🖬 🛜 ✕ 🛢 🖵

🄰🄰🄰 ▼▼▼▼ Homewood Suites by Hilton Tampa/Brandon 🅗

(813) 685-7099. **$109-$179.** 10240 Palm River Rd 33619. I-75 exit 257, 0.4 mi w on SR 60, just s on S Falkenburg Rd, then 0.3 mi e. Int corridors. **Pets:** Large. $100 one-time fee/room. Service with restrictions, crate. SAVE ECO 🅑M 🖬 🛜 🛢 🖵

▼▼▼▼ Homewood Suites by Hilton Tampa Westshore 🅗

(813) 282-1950. **$149-$229.** 5325 Avion Park Dr 33607. I-275 exit 40A southbound, 0.7 mi n on Westshore Blvd; exit 39A northbound, 1 mi e on Kennedy Blvd (SR 60), 1.2 mi n on Westshore Blvd, just w on Spruce St, then just s on O'Brien St; in Avion Park Westshore. Int corridors. **Pets:** Accepted. ECO 🅑M 🖬 🛜 🛢 🖵

▼▼▼ La Quinta Inn & Suites Tampa Bay Fairgrounds 🅗

(813) 626-0885. **$69-$189.** 4811 US 301 N 33610. I-4 exit 7 westbound; exit 7A eastbound, just se. Int corridors. **Pets:** Large, other species. Service with restrictions. 🖬 🛜 🛢 🖵

▼▼▼ La Quinta Inn & Suites Tampa Brandon West 🅗

(813) 684-4007. **$69-$174.** 602 S Falkenburg Rd 33619. I-75 exit 257, just w on SR 60, then just n. Int corridors. **Pets:** Large, other species. Service with restrictions. 🖬 🛜 🛢 🖵

▼▼▼▼ La Quinta Inn & Suites Tampa North 🅗

(813) 971-7676. **$89-$209.** 17301 Dona Michelle Dr 33647. I-75 exit 270, just n on CR 581 (Bruce B Downs Blvd); in North Palms. Int corridors. **Pets:** Large, other species. Service with restrictions.

ECO 🅑M 🖬 🛜 ✕ 🛢 🖵

▼▼▼▼ La Quinta Inn & Suites USF (near Busch Gardens) 🅗

(813) 910-7500. **$79-$209.** 3701 E Fowler Ave 33612. I-275 exit 51, 2.2 mi e on SR 582. Int corridors. **Pets:** Large, other species. Service with restrictions. 🅑M 🖬 🛜 🛢 🖵

▼▼▼▼ La Quinta Inn Tampa South 🅗

(813) 835-6262. **$95-$239.** 4620 W Gandy Blvd 33611. On US 92, just e of jct S Westshore Blvd. Int corridors. **Pets:** Large, other species. Service with restrictions. 🅑M 🖬 🛜 ✕ 🛢 🖵

🄰🄰🄰 ▼▼▼ Red Roof Inn Tampa Fairgrounds 🅜

(813) 623-5245. **$55-$110.** 5001 N US 301 33610. I-4 exit 7 westbound; exit 7A eastbound, just se. Ext corridors. **Pets:** Large, other species. Service with restrictions, supervision. SAVE 🛜 🛢

▼▼▼ Residence Inn by Marriott Tampa Downtown 🅗

(813) 221-4224. **$95-$199.** 101 E Tyler St 33602. I-275 exit 44, 0.5 mi se on W Ashley Dr/Tampa St; exit 45A southbound, 1.5 mi se on W Ashley Dr. Int corridors. **Pets:** Accepted. 🅑M 🖬 🛜 ✕ 🛢 🖵

▼▼▼ Residence Inn by Marriott Tampa Sabal Park/Brandon 🅗

(813) 627-8855. **$109-$169.** 9719 Princess Palm Ave 33619. I-75 exit 260 southbound; exit 260B northbound, just w on SR 574 (Dr. Martin Luther King Jr Blvd), just s on Falkenburg Rd, then 0.4 mi w; in Sabal Corporate Park. Int corridors. **Pets:** Accepted.

🅑M 🖬 🛜 ✕ 🛢 🖵

▼▼▼ Residence Inn by Marriott Tampa Westshore/Airport 🅗

(813) 877-7988. **$109-$269.** 4312 W Boy Scout Blvd 33607. I-275 exit 40B, 0.8 mi n on Lois Ave. Int corridors. **Pets:** Accepted.

🅑M 🖬 🛜 ✕ 🛢 🖵

Seminole Hard Rock Hotel & Casino Tampa H

(813) 627-7625. **$189-$1009, 3 day notice.** 5223 N Orient Rd 33610. I-4 exit 6, just w. Int corridors. **Pets:** Accepted.

Sheraton Tampa Riverwalk H

(813) 223-2222. **$109-$339.** 200 N Ashley Dr 33602. I-275 exit 44, 0.8 mi s. Int corridors. **Pets:** Accepted.

SpringHill Suites by Marriott Tampa North/Tampa Palms H

(813) 558-0300. **$99-$153.** 5396 Primrose Lake Cir 33647. I-75 exit 270, just s on CR 581 (Bruce B Downs Blvd), then 0.9 mi ne; in The Pointe. Int corridors. **Pets:** Accepted.

Staybridge Suites-Tampa East H 🐾

(813) 227-4000. **$119-$399.** 3624 N Falkenburg Rd 33619. I-75 exit 260 southbound; exit 260B northbound, just w on SR 574 (Dr. Martin Luther King Jr Blvd), then just s. Int corridors. **Pets:** Medium, other species. $75 one-time fee/pet. Service with restrictions, crate.

TownePlace Suites by Marriott Tampa Westshore/Airport H

(813) 282-1081. **$99-$230.** 5302 Avion Park Dr 33607. I-275 exit 40A southbound, 0.7 mi n on Westshore Blvd; exit 39A northbound, 1 mi e on SR 60 (Kennedy Blvd), 1.2 mi n on Westshore Blvd, just w on Spruce St, then just s on O'Brien St; in Avion Park Westshore. Int corridors. **Pets:** Accepted.

The Westin Tampa Bay H

(813) 281-0000. **$109-$369.** 7627 Courtney Campbell Cswy 33607. On SR 60, at east end of causeway. Int corridors. **Pets:** Accepted.

The Westin Tampa Harbour Island H

(813) 229-5000. **$119-$399.** 725 S Harbour Island Blvd 33602. I-275 exit 44, 2.4 mi se on W Ashley Dr/Tampa St; exit 45A southbound, 3.9 mi se; on Harbour Island. Int corridors. **Pets:** Accepted.

TAVARES

BEST WESTERN PLUS Lake County Inn & Suites H

(352) 253-2378. **$109-$229, 3 day notice.** 1380 E Burleigh Blvd 32778-4305. On US 441, 1.5 mi e of SR 19. Int corridors. **Pets:** Dogs only. $50 deposit/pet, $25 daily fee/pet. Designated rooms, service with restrictions, supervision.

TEMPLE TERRACE

Extended Stay America-Tampa North-USF Attractions H

(813) 989-2264. **$65-$130.** 12242 Morris Bridge Rd 33637. I-75 exit 266, just w on Fletcher Ave (CR 582A). Int corridors. **Pets:** Other species. $25 daily fee/pet. Service with restrictions, supervision.

Residence Inn by Marriott Tampa North I-75 Fletcher H

(813) 972-4400. **$107-$179.** 13420 N Telecom Pkwy 33637. I-75 exit 266, 1.1 mi w on Fletcher Ave (CR 582A), then just s; in Telecom Tampa Park. Int corridors. **Pets:** Accepted.

TownePlace Suites by Marriott Tampa North/I-75 Fletcher H

(813) 975-9777. **$79-$119.** 6800 Woodstork Rd 33637. I-75 exit 266, 1.1 mi w on Fletcher Ave (CR 582A), then just s on N Telecom Dr; in Telecom Tampa Park. Int corridors. **Pets:** Accepted.

THE VILLAGES

Hampton Inn & Suites - The Villages H

(352) 259-8246. **$85-$105.** 11727 NE 63rd Dr 32162. 2.6 mi w of jct US 27/441 on CR 466. Int corridors. **Pets:** Accepted.

TITUSVILLE

BEST WESTERN Space Shuttle Inn H

(321) 269-9100. **$69-$200.** 3455 Cheney Hwy 32780. I-95 exit 215 (SR 50), just e. Ext corridors. **Pets:** Other species. $10 daily fee/room. Service with restrictions.

Fairfield Inn & Suites by Marriott - Titusville/ Kennedy Space Center H

(321) 385-1818. **$99-$229.** 4735 Helen Hauser Blvd 32780. I-95 exit 215 (SR 50), just w. Int corridors. **Pets:** Accepted.

Hampton Inn Titusville/I-95 Kennedy Space Center H

(321) 383-9191. **$98-$209.** 4760 Helen Hauser Blvd 32780. I-95 exit 215 (SR 50), just w. Int corridors. **Pets:** Accepted.

Holiday Inn Titusville - Kennedy Space Center H

(321) 383-0200. **Call for rates.** 4715 Helen Hauser Blvd 32780. I-95 exit 215 (SR 50), just w to Helen Hauser Blvd, then just n. Int corridors. **Pets:** Accepted.

Ramada Inn & Suites-Kennedy Space Center H

(321) 269-5510. **$50-$71.** 3500 Cheney Hwy 32780. I-95 exit 215 (SR 50), just e. Int corridors. **Pets:** $10 deposit/pet, $10 daily fee/pet. Designated rooms, service with restrictions, supervision.

TREASURE ISLAND

Residence Inn by Marriott St. Petersburg Treasure Island H

(727) 367-2761. **$179-$330, 3 day notice.** 11908 Gulf Blvd 33706. On SR 699, 0.7 mi n of jct Treasure Island Cswy. Ext/int corridors. **Pets:** Accepted.

VENICE

Holiday Inn Express Hotel & Suites H

(941) 584-6800. **Call for rates.** 380 Commercial Ct 34292. I-75 exit 193, just w on CR 765 (Jacaranda Blvd), then just n. Int corridors. **Pets:** Accepted.

Ramada Venice Resort M

(941) 308-7700. **$72-$135.** 425 US 41 Bypass N 34285. 0.4 mi n of jct Venice Ave (CR 772). Int corridors. **Pets:** Medium. $25 one-time fee/room. Designated rooms, service with restrictions.

VERO BEACH

The Caribbean Court Boutique Hotel H

(772) 231-7211. **$109-$349, 3 day notice.** 1601 S Ocean Dr 32963. US 1, 4.3 mi n on Indian River Blvd (CR 603), 1.3 mi e on 17th St (SR 656) to Ocean Dr, then just s; jct Ocean Dr and Jasmine Ln. Ext corridors. **Pets:** Small. Designated rooms, service with restrictions.

Costa d' Este Beach Resort & Spa H

(772) 562-9919. **$159-$759, 3 day notice.** 3244 Ocean Dr 32963. I-95 exit 147 (SR 60), 8.7 mi e to Indian River Blvd, 1 mi n to Merril P Barber Bridge/SR 60, 1.7 mi e to Ocean Dr, then just s. Int corridors. **Pets:** Accepted.

ⒶⒶⒶ ▼▼▼▼ Country Inn & Suites By Carlson, Vero Beach I-95 🅷

(772) 257-0252. **$69-$159.** 9330 19th Ln 32966. I-95 exit 147 (20th St/SR 60), just w; adjacent to Vero Fashion Outlets Mall. Int corridors. **Pets:** Accepted. ⓈⒶⓋⒺ ⨱ 🛜 ✕ 🛄 ▣

ⒶⒶⒶ ▼▼▼ Holiday Inn Hotel & Suites Vero Beach-Oceanside 🅷

(772) 231-2300. **Call for rates.** 3384 Ocean Dr 32963. E of SR A1A; at end of SR 60. Ext corridors. **Pets:** Accepted.

ⓈⒶⓋⒺ ECO ⓘⓘ ⨱ 🛜 ✕ 🛄 ▣

ⒶⒶⒶ ▼▼▼ ▼▼▼ Vero Beach Hotel & Spa 🅷 ❋

(772) 231-5666. **$229-$559, 7 day notice.** 3500 Ocean Dr 32963. On Ocean Dr, just n of SR 60. Ext/int corridors. **Pets:** Other species. Designated rooms, service with restrictions, supervision.

ⓈⒶⓋⒺ ECO ⓘⓘ ⨱ ✕ 🛰 ✕ 🛄 ▣

ⒶⒶⒶ ▼▼▼ Vero Beach Inn & Suites 🅷 ❋

(772) 567-8321. **$75-$110.** 8797 20th St 32966. I-95 exit 147 (20th St/SR 60), 0.8 mi e. Ext corridors. **Pets:** Small. $25 daily fee/pet. Designated rooms, service with restrictions, crate.

ⓈⒶⓋⒺ ⓘⓘ ⨱ 🛜 ✕ 🛄 ▣

WEEKI WACHEE
▼▼▼ Quality Inn Weeki Wachee 🅼

(352) 596-9000. **$64-$94.** 9373 Cortez Blvd 34613. On SR 50, just e of jct US 19. Ext corridors. **Pets:** Accepted. ⨱ 🛜 🛄 ▣

WEST MELBOURNE
ⒶⒶⒶ ▼▼▼ Fairfield Inn & Suites by Marriott-Melbourne Palm Bay/Viera 🅷

(321) 722-2220. **$89-$169.** 4355 W New Haven Ave 32904. I-95 exit 180 (US 192/New Haven Ave), just e. Int corridors. **Pets:** Accepted.

ⓈⒶⓋⒺ ⓖⓜ ⨱ 🛜 ✕ 🛄 ▣

WESTON
ⒶⒶⒶ ▼▼▼ Comfort Suites Weston-Sawgrass Mills South 🅷

(954) 659-1555. **$99-$189.** 2201 N Commerce Pkwy 33326. I-75 exit 15 (Royal Palm Blvd), just w to Weston Rd, n to Commerce Pkwy, then just e. Int corridors. **Pets:** Medium, other species. $15 daily fee/pet. Designated rooms, service with restrictions.

ⓈⒶⓋⒺ ⓖⓜ ⨱ 🛜 ✕ 🛄 ▣

▼▼▼ Residence Inn by Marriott-Fort Lauderdale Weston 🅷

(954) 659-8585. **$120-$263.** 2605 Weston Rd 33331. I-75 exit 15 (Royal Palm Blvd), 0.3 mi w to Weston Rd, then just s. Int corridors. **Pets:** Accepted. ⓖⓜ ⨱ 🛜 ✕ 🛄 ▣

▼▼ TownePlace Suites by Marriott-Fort Lauderdale Weston 🅷

(954) 659-2234. **$119-$296.** 1545 Three Village Rd 33326. I-75 exit 15 (Royal Palm Blvd), 1.1 mi e to Bonaventure Blvd, 0.4 mi n to Three Village Rd, then just w. Int corridors. **Pets:** Accepted.

ⓖⓜ ⨱ 🛜 ✕ 🛄 ▣

WEST PALM BEACH (Restaurants p. 628)
ⒶⒶⒶ ▼▼ BEST WESTERN Palm Beach Lakes 🅷

(561) 683-8810. **$99-$189.** 1800 Palm Beach Lakes Blvd 33401. I-95 exit 71 (Palm Beach Lakes Blvd), just e. Ext/int corridors. **Pets:** Medium. $100 deposit/pet, $15 daily fee/pet. Designated rooms, service with restrictions, crate. ⓈⒶⓋⒺ ECO ⨱ 🛜 🛄 ▣

▼▼▼ Days Inn-Airport North 🅼

(561) 689-0450. **$66-$120.** 2300 45th St 33407. I-95 exit 74 (45th St), just e. Ext corridors. **Pets:** Medium. $30 daily fee/pet. Designated rooms, service with restrictions, supervision. ⓘⓘ ⨱ 🛜 🛄 ▣

ⒶⒶⒶ ▼▼▼ Hyatt Place West Palm Beach/Downtown 🅷

(561) 655-1454. **$99-$429.** 295 Lakeview Ave 33401. I-95 exit 70 (Okeechobee Blvd), 1.8 mi e to S Olive Ave, then just n. Int corridors. **Pets:** Accepted. ⓈⒶⓋⒺ ⓖⓜ ⨱ 🛜 ✕ 🛄 ▣

▼▼ La Quinta Inn-West Palm Beach City Place 🅼

(561) 697-3388. **$82-$234.** 5981 Okeechobee Blvd 33417. I-95 exit 70B (Okeechobee Blvd), 3.6 mi w; Florida Tpke exit 99 (Okeechobee Blvd), just e. Ext corridors. **Pets:** Large, other species. Service with restrictions. ⨱ 🛜 🛄 ▣

▼▼▼ Residence Inn by Marriott-West Palm Beach 🅷

(561) 687-4747. **$109-$229.** 2461 Metrocentre Blvd E 33407. I-95 exit 74 (45th St), just w to Metrocentre Blvd, then just se; in Metrocentre Corporate Park. Int corridors. **Pets:** Accepted.

ⓖⓜ ⨱ 🛜 ✕ 🛄 ▣

▼▼ Stay Inn West Palm Beach Airport Hotel 🅼

(561) 471-8700. **$80-$180.** 1505 Belvedere Rd 33406. I-95 exit 69 (Belvedere Rd), just w. Ext corridors. **Pets:** Medium. $20 daily fee/pet. Service with restrictions, supervision. ⓈⒶⓋⒺ ⨱ 🛜 🛄 ▣

WILDWOOD
▼▼▼ Sleep Inn & Suites Wildwood- The Villages 🅷

(352) 748-0507. **$69-$129.** 1224 S Main St 34785. Florida Tpke exit 304, just n on US 301. Int corridors. **Pets:** Medium. $25 daily fee/pet. Designated rooms, service with restrictions, supervision.

ECO ⓖⓜ ⨱ 🛜 ✕ 🛄 ▣

WINTER PARK (Restaurants p. 629)
ⒶⒶⒶ ▼▼▼ ▼▼▼ The Alfond Inn 🅷 ❋

(407) 998-8090. **$159-$329, 3 day notice.** 300 E New England Ave 32789. I-4 exit 87 (Fairbanks Ave), 2 mi e to Park Ave, just n to New England Ave, then just e. Int corridors. **Pets:** Dogs only. $75 daily fee/room. Designated rooms, service with restrictions.

ⓈⒶⓋⒺ ⓘⓘ ⓖⓜ 🛜 ✕ 🛄 ▣

YULEE
ⒶⒶⒶ ▼▼▼ BEST WESTERN PLUS First Coast Inn & Suites 🅷

(904) 225-0182. **$69-$119.** 462577 SR 200 32097. I-95 exit 373 (SR 200/A1A), just e. Int corridors. **Pets:** $20 daily fee/room. Designated rooms, service with restrictions, supervision.

ⓈⒶⓋⒺ ⓖⓜ ⨱ 🛜 ✕ 🛄 ▣

▼▼ Comfort Inn 🅷

(904) 225-2600. **$70-$110.** 76043 Sidney Pl 32097. I-95 exit 373 (SR 200/ A1A), just e. Int corridors. **Pets:** Accepted. ⨱ 🛜 🛄 ▣

ZEPHYRHILLS
▼▼ Microtel Inn & Suites by Wyndham Zephyrhills 🅷

(813) 783-2211. **$55-$110.** 7839 Gall Blvd 33541. On US 301, 0.9 mi n of jct Daugherty Rd. Int corridors. **Pets:** Accepted.

ⓖⓜ ⨱ 🛜 🛄 ▣

ACWORTH

BEST WESTERN Acworth Inn M
(770) 974-0116. **$75-$135.** 5155 Cowan Rd 30101. I-75 exit 277, just w. Ext corridors. **Pets:** Medium, other species. $10 daily fee/pet. Designated rooms, service with restrictions, supervision.

Days Inn Acworth M
(770) 975-9000. **$56-$72, 3 day notice.** 164 N Point Way 30102. I-75 exit 277, just e. Ext corridors. **Pets:** Accepted.

La Quinta Inn Acworth H
(770) 975-9920. **$79-$196.** 184 N Point Way 30102. I-75 exit 277, just e. Ext/int corridors. **Pets:** Large, other species. Service with restrictions.

Super 8 M
(770) 966-9700. **$55-$100.** 4970 Cowan Rd 30101. I-75 exit 277, just w. Ext corridors. **Pets:** Medium. $10 daily fee/pet. Service with restrictions, supervision.

ADAIRSVILLE

Hampton Inn & Suites Adairsville-Calhoun H
(770) 773-3100. **$109-$159.** 101 Travelers Path 30103. I-75 exit 306, just w. Int corridors. **Pets:** Accepted.

Quality Inn M
(770) 773-2886. **$70-$149.** 107 Princeton Blvd 30103. I-75 exit 306, just w. Ext corridors. **Pets:** Accepted.

Ramada Limited M
(770) 769-9726. **$60-$100.** 500 Georgia North Cir 30103. I-75 exit 306, 0.3 mi w. Ext corridors. **Pets:** Accepted.

ADEL

Days Inn H
(229) 896-4574. **$50-$90.** 1204 W 4th St 31620. I-75 exit 39, just w. Ext corridors. **Pets:** Large, other species. $10 daily fee/pet. Service with restrictions.

Hampton Inn H 🐾
(229) 896-3099. **$89-$124.** 1500 W 4th St 31620. I-75 exit 39, just w. Int corridors. **Pets:** Other species. Service with restrictions.

ALBANY

Baymont Inn & Suites Albany H
(229) 435-3737. **$59-$79.** 2720 Dawson Rd 31707. 0.5 mi se of jct US 82 and SR 520. Ext corridors. **Pets:** Accepted.

Quality Inn Albany Mall H
(229) 883-3300. **$63-$110.** 806 N Westover Blvd 31707. 7 mi w on Dawson Rd; 0.5 mi se of jct US 82 and SR 520. Ext corridors. **Pets:** Accepted.

ALMA

Days Inn M
(912) 632-7000. **$63-$100.** 930 S Pierce St 31510. Jct SR 32/US 1, 0.4 mi s on US 1. Ext corridors. **Pets:** Accepted.

ALPHARETTA

Holiday Inn Express Alpharetta H
(770) 552-0006. **Call for rates.** 2950 Mansell Rd 30022. SR 400 exit 8, 0.7 mi e. Int corridors. **Pets:** Accepted.

Hyatt Place Alpharetta/North Point Mall H
(770) 594-8788. **$69-$299.** 7500 North Point Pkwy 30022. SR 400 exit 8, just e to North Point Pkwy, then just n. Int corridors. **Pets:** Accepted.

Hyatt Place Atlanta/Alpharetta/Windward Parkway H
(770) 343-9566. **$59-$179.** 5595 Windward Pkwy 30004. SR 400 exit 11, just w. Int corridors. **Pets:** Accepted.

La Quinta Inn & Suites Atlanta Alpharetta H
(770) 754-7800. **$62-$189.** 1350 North Point Dr 30022. SR 400 exit 9, 0.5 mi e. Int corridors. **Pets:** Large, other species. Service with restrictions.

Residence Inn by Marriott Atlanta Alpharetta North Point Mall H
(770) 587-1151. **$79-$299.** 1325 North Point Dr 30022. SR 400 exit 9, just e to North Point Dr, then just s. Int corridors. **Pets:** Accepted.

Residence Inn by Marriott Atlanta Alpharetta/Windward H
(770) 664-0664. **$129-$299.** 5465 Windward Pkwy 30004. SR 400 exit 11, 0.4 mi w. Ext/int corridors. **Pets:** Accepted.

Staybridge Suites H
(770) 569-7200. **$160-$260, 3 day notice.** 3980 North Point Pkwy 30005. SR 400 exit 10, 0.5 mi e. Int corridors. **Pets:** Accepted.

TownePlace Suites by Marriott Alpharetta H
(770) 664-1300. **$69-$219.** 7925 Westside Pkwy 30009. SR 400 exit 9, 0.3 mi w. Int corridors. **Pets:** Accepted.

Wingate by Wyndham Alpharetta H
(770) 649-0955. **$74-$129.** 1005 Kingswood Pl 30004. SR 400 exit 8, 0.7 mi w. Int corridors. **Pets:** Medium. $25 one-time fee/pet. Designated rooms, service with restrictions, crate.

AMERICUS

Quality Inn H
(229) 924-4431. **$76-$100.** 1205 S Martin Luther King Jr Blvd 31709. On US 19 S, 1 mi w of downtown. Ext corridors. **Pets:** Accepted.

ASHBURN

BEST WESTERN Ashburn Inn H
(229) 567-0080. **$70-$85.** 820 Shoney's Dr 31714. I-75 exit 82, just w. Ext corridors. **Pets:** Medium, dogs only. $10 daily fee/pet. Designated rooms, service with restrictions, supervision.

ATHENS *(Restaurants p. 629)*

BEST WESTERN Athens M
(706) 546-7311. **$70-$300.** 170 N Milledge Ave 30601. Jct US 78 business route (Broad St), 0.5 mi w on SR 15. Ext corridors. **Pets:** Medium, dogs only. $10 daily fee/pet. Designated rooms, no service, supervision.

Candlewood Suites H
(706) 548-9663. **Call for rates.** 156 Classic Rd 30606. Jct SR 10 Loop and US 78 business route, 1.1 mi w on US 78 business route to Classic Rd, just s. Int corridors. **Pets:** Large. $75 one-time fee/pet. Designated rooms, service with restrictions, crate.

▼▼ Comfort Inn & Suites H
(706) 227-9700. **$76-$91.** 3980 Atlanta Hwy 30622. SR 10 Loop exit 18 (Atlanta Hwy), 0.7 mi w. Int corridors. **Pets:** Accepted.

◢◣◥◤ ▼▼▼▼ Comfort Suites Downtown Athens H
(706) 995-4000. **$89-$109.** 255 North Ave 30601. SR 10 Loop exit 11B (Dougherty St/North Ave); 1 mi n of downtown. Int corridors. **Pets:** Small. $25 daily fee/pet. Designated rooms, service with restrictions, supervision.

▼▼▼▼ Graduate Athens M
(706) 549-7020. **$109-$299.** 295 E Dougherty St 30601. Jct Thomas and Dougherty sts; downtown. Ext/int corridors. **Pets:** Accepted.

▼▼▼▼ Holiday Inn Express Athens H
(706) 546-8122. **Call for rates.** 513 W Broad St 30601. On US 78 business route (Broad St); center. Int corridors. **Pets:** Accepted.

▼▼▼▼ Hotel Indigo Athens Downtown/Univ. Area H
(706) 546-0430. **Call for rates.** 500 College Ave 30601. Just n of center. Int corridors. **Pets:** Accepted.

◢◣◥◤ ▼▼ ▼ Microtel Inn by Wyndham Athens H
(706) 548-5676. **$50-$175.** 1050 Ultimate Dr 30605. Jct US 78 business route (Broad St) and SR 10 Loop, 1.4 mi e. Int corridors. **Pets:** Accepted.

▼▼▼ Sleep Inn & Suites H
(706) 850-1261. **$65-$109.** 109 Florence Dr 30622. Jct SR 10 Loop and US 78 business route, 1.2 mi w on US 78 to Florence Dr, just s. Int corridors. **Pets:** Small. $20 daily fee/pet. Service with restrictions, supervision.

ATLANTA *(Restaurants p. 629)*

▼▼▼ Artmore Hotel H
(404) 876-6100. **$119-$169, 3 day notice.** 1302 W Peachtree St 30309. I-75/85 exit 250 (14th St), just e, then just n on W Peachtree St to 16th St. Int corridors. **Pets:** Accepted.

◢◣◥◤ ▼▼▼▼ BEST WESTERN PLUS Inn at the Peachtrees M
(404) 577-6970. **$89-$209.** 330 W Peachtree St 30308. I-75/85 exit 248C northbound, 0.4 mi w to Peachtree St, then 0.3 mi n; exit 249C southbound, just s to Peachtree Pl, then just e. Ext/int corridors. **Pets:** Accepted.

◢◣◥◤ ▼▼▼▼ Courtyard by Marriott-Atlanta Vinings H
(770) 432-5555. **$69-$219.** 2857 Paces Ferry Rd SE 30339. I-285 exit 18, 0.6 mi e. Int corridors. **Pets:** Accepted.

◢◣◥◤ ▼▼▼▼ Crowne Plaza: Atlanta-Midtown H
(404) 877-9000. **$109-$350.** 590 W Peachtree St NW 30308. I-75/85 exit 249D southbound; exit 249C northbound, just e. Int corridors. **Pets:** Accepted.

▼▼▼▼ DoubleTree by Hilton Hotel Atlanta-Buckhead H
(404) 231-1234. **$89-$209.** 3342 Peachtree Rd NE 30326. Jct Piedmont and Peachtree rds NE, just n. Int corridors. **Pets:** Accepted.

◢◣◥◤ ▼▼▼▼ Embassy Suites Atlanta-Galleria H
(770) 984-9300. **$149-$209.** 2815 Akers Mill Rd 30339. I-75 exit 258, just w. Int corridors. **Pets:** Accepted.

▼▼ Extended Stay America Atlanta-Clairmont H
(404) 679-4333. **$61-$105.** 3115 Clairmont Rd 30329. I-85 exit 91, 0.6 mi w. Int corridors. **Pets:** Other species. $25 daily fee/pet. Service with restrictions, supervision.

▼▼ Extended Stay America Atlanta-Lenox H
(404) 237-9100. **$75-$110.** 3967 Peachtree Rd NE 30319. I-85 exit 89, 2.8 mi w. Int corridors. **Pets:** Other species. $25 daily fee/pet. Service with restrictions, supervision.

▼▼ Extended Stay America (Atlanta/Marietta/Wildwood Rd) H
(770) 933-8010. **$63-$83.** 2010 Powers Ferry Rd 30339. I-75 exit 260 (Windy Hill Rd), 0.5 mi e, then just s. Int corridors. **Pets:** Other species. $25 daily fee/pet. Service with restrictions, supervision.

▼▼ Extended Stay America (Atlanta/Marietta/Windy Hill/Int N Pkwy) H
(770) 226-0242. **$56-$95.** 2225 Interstate North Pkwy 30339. I-75 exit 260, just e to Interstate North Pkwy, then just s. Int corridors. **Pets:** Other species. $25 daily fee/pet. Service with restrictions, supervision.

▼▼ Extended Stay America Atlanta-Perimeter/Crestline H
(770) 396-5600. **$52-$75.** 905 Crestline Pkwy 30328. SR 400 exit 5A, just e to Peachtree-Dunwoody Rd, then 0.5 mi s. Int corridors. **Pets:** Other species. $25 daily fee/pet. Service with restrictions, supervision.

▼▼ Extended Stay America-Atlanta-Perimeter-Hammond Drive H
(770) 522-0025. **$51-$86.** 1050 Hammond Dr 30328. I-285 exit 26 eastbound, 0.5 mi n to Hammond Dr, then 0.5 mi e; exit 28 westbound, just n to Hammond Dr, then just w. Ext corridors. **Pets:** Other species. $25 daily fee/pet. Service with restrictions, supervision.

▼▼ Extended Stay America Atlanta-Perimeter/Peachtree-Dunwoody H
(770) 379-0111. **$61-$81.** 6330 Peachtree-Dunwoody Rd NE 30328. SR 400 exit 5A, just e to Peachtree-Dunwoody Rd, then 0.5 mi s. Int corridors. **Pets:** Other species. $25 daily fee/pet. Service with restrictions, supervision.

▼▼ Extended Stay America Atlanta-Vinings H
(770) 436-1511. **$58-$109.** 2474 Cumberland Pkwy SE 30339. I-285 exit 18, just e. Int corridors. **Pets:** Other species. $25 daily fee/pet. Service with restrictions, supervision.

◢◣◥◤ ▼▼▼▼▼ Four Seasons Hotel Atlanta H ❀
(404) 881-9898. **$249-$5000.** 75 14th St NE 30309. I-75/85 exit 250 (14th St), 0.3 mi e. Int corridors. **Pets:** Service with restrictions, supervision.

◢◣◥◤ ▼▼▼▼ The Georgian Terrace Hotel H
(404) 897-1991. **$129-$359.** 659 Peachtree St 30308. I-75/85 exit 249D, 0.5 mi e to Peachtree St, then just n. Int corridors. **Pets:** Medium, dogs only. $75 one-time fee/pet. Service with restrictions, crate.

◢◣◥◤ ▼▼▼▼ Grand Hyatt Atlanta H ❀
(404) 237-1234. **$139-$409.** 3300 Peachtree Rd NE 30305. Corner of Peachtree and Piedmont rds. Int corridors. **Pets:** Dogs only. $100 one-time fee/room. Designated rooms, service with restrictions, crate.

◢◣◥◤ ▼▼▼▼ Hilton Atlanta H
(404) 659-2000. **$99-$259.** 255 Courtland St NE 30303. I-75/85 exit 249A southbound; exit 248C northbound, just w to Piedmont Ave, just n to Baker St, then just w. Int corridors. **Pets:** Accepted.

▼▼▼▼ Hilton Atlanta Perimeter Suites H
(770) 668-0808. **$89-$229.** 6120 Peachtree-Dunwoody Rd 30328. I-285 exit 28 westbound, 0.4 mi n; exit 26 eastbound, 0.5 mi n to Hammond Dr, 0.5 mi e to Peachtree-Dunwoody Rd, then just n. Int corridors. **Pets:** Accepted.

Holiday Inn Atlanta Perimeter H
(770) 457-6363. **Call for rates.** 4386 Chamblee-Dunwoody Rd 30341. I-285 exit 30 eastbound, just s; exit westbound, follow access road 1.3 mi to Chamblee-Dunwoody Rd, then just s. Int corridors. **Pets:** Accepted. [SAVE] [Y¹] [&M] [≥] [⌷] [✕] [▮] [▭]

Homewood Suites-Atlanta Buckhead H
(404) 365-0001. **$129-$179.** 3566 Piedmont Rd 30305. SR 400 exit 2, just s to Piedmont Rd, then 1 mi w. Int corridors. **Pets:** Accepted. [&M] [≥] [▮] [▭]

Homewood Suites-Cumberland H
(770) 988-9449. **$132-$259.** 3200 Cobb Pkwy SW 30339. I-285 exit 19 eastbound; exit 20 westbound, 0.7 mi s. Ext/int corridors. **Pets:** Accepted. [&M] [≥] [⌷] [▮] [▭]

Hotel Indigo Atlanta Midtown H 🐾
(404) 874-9200. **$99-$349, 3 day notice.** 683 Peachtree St NE 30308. I-75/85 exit 249D, 0.5 mi s to Peachtree St, then just n. Int corridors. **Pets:** Other species. $25 one-time fee/room. Designated rooms, service with restrictions. [Y¹] [&M] [⌷] [▭]

HYATT house Atlanta/Cobb Galleria H
(770) 541-2960. **$79-$309.** 3595 Cumberland Blvd SE 30339. I-75 exit 258, just e. Int corridors. **Pets:** Accepted. [SAVE] [&M] [⌷] [✕] [▮] [▭]

Hyatt Place Atlanta/Buckhead H
(404) 869-6161. **$89-$219.** 3242 Peachtree Rd NE 30305. Jct Peachtree and Piedmont rds NE, just s. Int corridors. **Pets:** Accepted. [SAVE] [Y¹] [&M] [≥] [⌷] [✕] [▮] [▭]

Hyatt Place, Atlanta/Downtown H
(404) 577-1980. **$99-$299.** 330 Peachtree St NE 30308. I-75/85 exit 249A to Baker St, 0.3 mi w to Peachtree St, then just n. **Pets:** Medium, dogs only. $75 one-time fee/room. Designated rooms, service with restrictions. [SAVE] [&M] [⌷] [✕] [▮] [▭]

Hyatt Place Atlanta/Perimeter Center H
(770) 730-9300. **$69-$199.** 1005 Crestline Pkwy 30328. SR 400 exit 5A (Dunwoody Rd), 0.3 mi e. Int corridors. **Pets:** Accepted. [SAVE] [&M] [≥] [⌷] [✕] [▮] [▭]

InterContinental Buckhead Atlanta H
(404) 946-9000. **$159-$349.** 3315 Peachtree Rd NE 30326. Jct Piedmont and Peachtree rds NE, just e. Int corridors. **Pets:** Accepted. [SAVE] [Y¹] [&M] [≥] [⌷] [🔊] [✕] [▮] [▭]

La Quinta Inn & Suites Atlanta (Paces Ferry/Vinings) H
(770) 801-9002. **$65-$195.** 2415 Paces Ferry Rd SE 30339. I-285 exit 18, just w. Int corridors. **Pets:** Large, other species. Service with restrictions. [&M] [≥] [⌷] [▮] [▭]

La Quinta Inn & Suites Atlanta (Perimeter/Medical Center) H
(770) 350-6177. **$69-$195.** 6260 Peachtree-Dunwoody Rd 30328. I-285 exit 28 westbound, 0.7 mi n; exit 26 eastbound, 0.5 mi n to Hammond Dr, 0.7 mi e, then 0.5 mi n. Int corridors. **Pets:** Large, other species. Service with restrictions. [&M] [≥] [⌷] [▮] [▭]

La Quinta Inn Atlanta Midtown Buckhead H
(404) 321-0999. **$79-$234.** 2535 Chantilly Dr NE 30324. I-85 exit 88 southbound; exit 86 northbound, 2 mi on Buford Hwy to Lenox Rd, then just e under highway. Int corridors. **Pets:** Large, other species. Service with restrictions. [&M] [⌷] [▮] [▭]

Le Méridien Atlanta Perimeter H
(770) 396-6800. **$119-$339.** 111 Perimeter Center W 30346. I-285 exit 29 (Ashford-Dunwoody Rd), 0.5 mi n. Int corridors. **Pets:** Accepted. [SAVE] [Y¹] [&M] [≥] [🔊] [✕] [▮] [▭]

Loews Atlanta Hotel H
(404) 745-5000. **Call for rates.** 1075 Peachtree St NE 30309. I-75/85 exit 251 (10th St), 0.5 mi e to Peachtree St NE, then just n. Int corridors. **Pets:** Accepted. [SAVE] [Y¹] [&M] [⌷] [⌷] [✕] [▮] [▭]

Mandarin Oriental, Atlanta H
(404) 995-7500. **$275-$575, 3 day notice.** 3376 Peachtree Rd NE 30326. Jct Peachtree and Lenox rds, just s. Int corridors. **Pets:** Accepted. [Y¹] [&M] [≥] [⌷] [⌷] [✕] [▭]

Microtel Inn & Suites by Wyndham Atlanta/Buckhead Area H
(404) 325-4446. **$65-$85.** 1840 Corporate Blvd 30329. I-85 exit 89, just w to Buford Hwy, 0.3 mi n to Corporate Blvd, then just e. Int corridors. **Pets:** Small. $25 one-time fee/pet. Service with restrictions, crate. [&M] [⌷] [▮] [▭]

Omni Hotel at CNN Center H
(404) 659-0000. **$159-$399, 3 day notice.** 100 CNN Center 30303. I-75/85 exit 248C northbound, 0.8 mi w; exit 249C southbound to International Blvd, 0.5 mi w. Int corridors. **Pets:** Accepted. [Y¹] [≥] [⌷] [🔊] [✕] [▮] [▭]

Red Roof Plus+ Atlanta-Buckhead M
(404) 321-1653. **$60-$150.** 1960 N Druid Hills Rd 30329. I-85 exit 89, just w. Ext corridors. **Pets:** Large, other species. Service with restrictions, supervision. [SAVE] [⌷] [✕] [▮] [▭]

Renaissance Atlanta Midtown H
(678) 412-2400. **$98-$284.** 866 W Peachtree St NW 30308. I-75/85 exit 249D, just e to W Peachtree St NW, then 0.6 mi n. Int corridors. **Pets:** Accepted. [SAVE] [ECO] [Y¹] [🔊] [✕] [▮] [▭]

Residence Inn by Marriott-Atlanta/Buckhead M
(404) 239-0677. **$123-$225.** 2960 Piedmont Rd NE 30305. Jct Piedmont and Pharr rds, just s. Ext corridors. **Pets:** Accepted. [SAVE] [≥] [⌷] [✕] [▮] [▭]

Residence Inn by Marriott Atlanta Buckhead/Lenox Park H
(404) 467-1660. **$89-$159.** 2220 Lake Blvd 30319. I-85 exit 89, 1.6 mi w on N Druid Hills (which becomes E Roxboro Rd), then just n on Lenox Park Blvd. Int corridors. **Pets:** Accepted. [SAVE] [&M] [≥] [⌷] [✕] [▮] [▭]

Residence Inn by Marriott Atlanta-Downtown H
(404) 522-0950. **$89-$399.** 134 Peachtree St NW 30303. I-75/85 exit 248C northbound, 0.4 mi w, then just s; exit 249A southbound to International Blvd, just w, then just s. Int corridors. **Pets:** Large, other species. $100 one-time fee/room. Service with restrictions, crate. [⌷] [✕] [▮] [▭]

Residence Inn by Marriott Atlanta Midtown at 17th Street H
(404) 745-1000. **$109-$299.** 1365 Peachtree St 30309. I-75/85 exit 250 (17th St) southbound, 0.5 mi n to Peachtree St; exit 251 northbound. Int corridors. **Pets:** Accepted. [&M] [⌷] [✕] [▮] [▭]

Residence Inn by Marriott Atlanta Perimeter Center H
(770) 455-4446. **$99-$219.** 1901 Savoy Dr 30341. I-285 exit 30, just e. Ext corridors. **Pets:** Accepted. [SAVE] [≥] [⌷] [✕] [▮] [▭]

The Ritz-Carlton, Buckhead H
(404) 237-2700. **$249-$559.** 3434 Peachtree Rd NE 30326. I-85 exit 86, 1.8 mi n on Lenox Rd. Int corridors. **Pets:** Accepted. [SAVE] [Y¹] [&M] [≥] [⌷] [🔊] [✕] [▭]

St. Regis Atlanta Hotel & Residences H
(404) 563-7900. **$350-$650.** 88 W Paces Ferry Rd 30305. Jct Peachtree and W Paces Ferry rds, just w. Int corridors. **Pets:** Accepted. [SAVE] [Y¹] [&M] [≥] [⌷] [⌷] [✕]

Sheraton Atlanta Hotel H
(404) 659-6500. **$119-$399, 3 day notice.** 165 Courtland St NE 30303. I-75/85 exit 249A southbound; exit 248C northbound, just w. Int corridors. **Pets:** Accepted. SAVE

Sheraton Suites Galleria H
(770) 955-3900. **$105-$279.** 2844 Cobb Pkwy SE 30339. I-285 exit 20 westbound; exit 19 eastbound, just s. Int corridors. **Pets:** Accepted.

Sonesta ES Suites Atlanta H
(404) 250-0110. **$119-$199.** 760 Mt Vernon Hwy NE 30328. I-285 exit 25, 0.8 mi n on Roswell Rd, then 1 mi e. Ext/int corridors.
Pets: Accepted. SAVE

Staybridge Suites-Atlanta/Buckhead H
(404) 842-0800. **$99-$290.** 540 Pharr Rd 30305. Jct Pharr and Piedmont rds, just w. Int corridors. **Pets:** Accepted.

Staybridge Suites Atlanta Perimeter H
(678) 320-0111. **$99-$219, 3 day notice.** 4601 Ridgeview Rd 30338. I-285 exit 29 (Ashford-Dunwoody Rd), 0.5 mi n, 0.5 mi w on Perimeter Center W to Crowne Pointe Dr, then just n. Int corridors.
Pets: Accepted.

TownePlace Suites by Marriott Atlanta Buckhead H
(404) 949-4820. **$89-$269.** 820 Sidney Marcus Blvd 30324. I-85 exit 86 northbound, 1.9 mi n to Sidney Marcus Blvd, then just w; exit 88 southbound, just w to Sidney Marcus Blvd, then just w. Int corridors.
Pets: Accepted.

TWELVE Atlantic Station H
(404) 961-1212. **$149-$409.** 361 17th St NW 30363. I-75 exit 251 northbound; exit 250 southbound, just w; in Atlantic Station. Int corridors. **Pets:** Accepted. SAVE

TWELVE Centennial Park H
(404) 418-1212. **$149-$409.** 400 W Peachtree St NW 30308. I-75/85 exit 249C, 0.4 mi s; jct W Peachtree St NW. Int corridors.
Pets: Accepted. SAVE

The University Inn at Emory M
(404) 634-7327. **$89-$175.** 1767 N Decatur Rd NE 30307. Adjacent to Emory University. Ext/int corridors. **Pets:** Accepted.

W Atlanta Buckhead H
(678) 500-3100. **$119-$239.** 3377 Peachtree Rd NE 30326. Jct Piedmont and Peachtree rds, 0.3 mi e. Int corridors. **Pets:** Accepted.

W Atlanta Downtown H
(404) 582-5800. **$149-$429.** 45 Ivan Allen Jr Blvd 30308. I-75/85 exit 249C, just s. Int corridors. **Pets:** Accepted.

W Atlanta Midtown H
(404) 892-6000. **Call for rates.** 188 14th St NE 30361. I-75/85 exit 250 (14th St), 0.5 mi e. Int corridors. **Pets:** Accepted.

The Westin Atlanta Perimeter North H ❀
(770) 395-3900. **$89-$329.** 7 Concourse Pkwy 30328. I-285 exit 28 westbound; exit 26 eastbound, 0.5 mi n to Hammond Dr, then 0.4 mi e. Int corridors. **Pets:** Medium, dogs only. Supervision.

The Westin Buckhead Atlanta H ❀
(404) 365-0065. **$109-$459.** 3391 Peachtree Rd NE 30326. Adjacent to Lenox Square Mall. Int corridors. **Pets:** Medium, dogs only. $100 one-time fee/room. Service with restrictions, supervision.

The Westin Peachtree Plaza H ❀
(404) 659-1400. **$129-$459.** 210 Peachtree St NW 30303. I-75/85 exit 248C northbound, 0.4 mi w; exit 249C southbound, 0.5 mi s. Int corridors. **Pets:** Small, dogs only. Designated rooms, service with restrictions, supervision. SAVE ECO

Wyndham Atlanta Galleria H
(770) 955-1700. **$79-$159.** 6345 Powers Ferry Rd NW 30339. I-285 exit 22, just s. Int corridors. **Pets:** Accepted.

AUGUSTA (Restaurants p. 629)

Augusta Marriott At The Convention Center H
(706) 722-8900. **$159-$239.** 2 10th St 30901. I-20 exit 200 (River Watch Pkwy), 5.4 mi se, then just n; downtown. Int corridors. **Pets:** Small. $50 one-time fee/room. Service with restrictions, crate.

Candlewood Suites Augusta H
(706) 733-3300. **$70-$139.** 1080 Claussen Rd 30907. I-20 exit 200 (River Watch Pkwy), just nw, then just sw. Int corridors. **Pets:** Medium, dogs only. $75 one-time fee/pet. Designated rooms, service with restrictions, crate. SAVE

DoubleTree by Hilton Hotel Augusta H
(706) 855-8100. **$109-$159.** 2651 Perimeter Pkwy 30909. I-520 exit 1C (Wheeler Rd), just w to Perimeter Pkwy, then just n. Int corridors.
Pets: Accepted.

Jameson Suites H
(706) 733-4656. **$89-$109.** 1062 Clausen Rd 30907. I-20 exit 200 (River Watch Pkwy), just nw, then just sw. Int corridors. **Pets:** Accepted.

La Quinta Inn Augusta M
(706) 733-2660. **$62-$604.** 3020 Washington Rd 30907. I-20 exit 199 (Washington Rd), just w. Ext/int corridors. **Pets:** Large, other species. Service with restrictions.

The Partridge Inn H
(706) 737-8888. **Call for rates.** 2110 Walton Way 30904. 1.3 mi w off 15th St. Int corridors. **Pets:** Accepted.

Sheraton Augusta Hotel H
(706) 396-1000. **Call for rates.** 1069 Stevens Creek Rd 30907. I-20 exit 199 (Washington Rd), just w, then just ne. Int corridors.
Pets: Accepted. SAVE

AUSTELL

Super 8 Austell/Six Flags M
(770) 944-2110. **$70-$110.** 7377 Six Flags Dr 30168. I-20 exit 46 eastbound; exit 46B westbound, just n. Ext/int corridors. **Pets:** Accepted.

BAINBRIDGE

Quality Inn H
(229) 243-7000. **$75-$80.** 1403 Tallahassee Hwy 39819. Just s of US 84 Bypass on US 27. Ext corridors. **Pets:** Accepted.

BLUE RIDGE

Blue Ridge Hotel M
(706) 632-2100. **$55-$79.** 4970 Appalachian Hwy 30513. On SR 515 and US 76. Ext corridors. **Pets:** Accepted.

The Blue Ridge Lodge by Comfort Inn & Suites H

(706) 946-3333. **$79-$119.** 83 Blue Ridge Overlook 30513. Just off SR 515 and US 76; behind Arby's. Int corridors. **Pets:** $50 one-time fee/room. Service with restrictions, supervision.

BRASELTON

BEST WESTERN Braselton Inn M

(706) 654-3081. **$90-$170, 3 day notice.** 303 Zion Church Rd 30517. I-85 exit 129, just e, then 0.3 mi n. Ext corridors. **Pets:** Medium. $15 daily fee/pet. Designated rooms, service with restrictions, crate.

BRUNSWICK

Quality Inn M

(912) 265-4600. **$59-$199.** 125 Venture Dr 31525. I-95 exit 38 (Golden Isles Pkwy), just nw. Ext/int corridors. **Pets:** Small, other species. $15 daily fee/pet. Designated rooms, service with restrictions, supervision.

Super 8 H

(912) 264-8800. **$50-$56.** 5280 New Jesup Hwy 31523. I-95 exit 36B (New Jesup Hwy/US 25), just nw. Int corridors. **Pets:** $10 daily fee/pet. Service with restrictions, supervision.

BYRON

BEST WESTERN Inn & Suites M 🐾

(478) 956-3056. **$65-$79.** 101 Dunbar Rd 31008. I-75 exit 149 (SR 49), just e. Ext corridors. **Pets:** $15 daily fee/pet. Service with restrictions, supervision.

Super 8 H

(478) 956-3311. **$54-$100.** 305 Hwy 49 N 31008. I-75 exit 149 (SR 49), just e. Ext corridors. **Pets:** Small. $10 daily fee/pet. Service with restrictions, supervision.

CAIRO

BEST WESTERN Executive Inn H

(229) 377-8000. **$73-$140.** 2800 Hwy 84 E 39828. 2 mi e. Ext corridors. **Pets:** Accepted.

CALHOUN

Baymont Inn & Suites M

(706) 629-8133. **$59-$79.** 189 Jameson St 30701. I-75 exit 312, just w. Ext corridors. **Pets:** Accepted.

Days Inn M

(706) 629-9501. **$60-$70.** 915 Hwy 53 SE 30701. I-75 exit 312, just e. Ext corridors. **Pets:** Small, dogs only. $10 daily fee/pet. No service, supervision.

La Quinta Inn H

(706) 629-2559. **$69-$200.** 150 Cracker Barrel Dr 30701. I-75 exit 312, just e. Int corridors. **Pets:** Large, other species. Service with restrictions.

Ramada Calhoun M

(706) 629-9207. **$69-$140.** 1204 Red Bud Rd NE 30701. I-75 exit 315, just w. Ext corridors. **Pets:** Accepted.

Super 8 Calhoun M

(706) 629-0999. **$59-$124.** 115 Hampton Dr SE 30701. I-75 exit 312, just w. Ext corridors. **Pets:** Medium, other species. $15 daily fee/pet. Designated rooms, service with restrictions, supervision.

CANTON *(Restaurants p. 629)*

Econo Lodge Inn & Suites H 🐾

(770) 345-1994. **$59-$79.** 138 Keith Dr 30114. I-575 exit 20, just e. Int corridors. **Pets:** Medium. $25 daily fee/pet. Designated rooms, crate.

Motel 6 - Canton #4839 H

(770) 345-8700. **Call for rates.** 114 River Pointe Pkwy 30114. I-575 exit 20, just e. Int corridors. **Pets:** Other species. Service with restrictions, crate.

CARROLLTON

Quality Inn M

(770) 834-2600. **$80.** 700 S Park St 30117. On US 27, just s of downtown. Ext corridors. **Pets:** Small, other species. $20 daily fee/pet. Designated rooms, service with restrictions, crate.

CARTERSVILLE

BEST WESTERN Garden Inn & Suites M

(770) 386-1569. **$75-$120.** 5663 Hwy 20 NE 30121. I-75 exit 290, 0.3 mi e. Ext corridors. **Pets:** Accepted.

Cartersville North Inn & Suites H

(770) 386-9259. **$60-$74.** 11 Kent Dr 30121. I-75 exit 296, just e. Int corridors. **Pets:** Medium. $15 daily fee/pet. Designated rooms, service with restrictions, supervision.

Country Inn & Suites By Carlson H

(770) 386-5888. **$93-$169, 3 day notice.** 43 SR 20 Spur 30121. I-75 exit 290, 0.3 mi se. Int corridors. **Pets:** Accepted.

Econo Lodge Cartersville H

(770) 382-8881. **Call for rates.** 41 SR 20 Spur SE 30121. I-75 exit 290, 0.3 mi e. Int corridors. **Pets:** Accepted.

Holiday Inn H

(770) 386-0830. **Call for rates.** 2336 Hwy 411 30184. I-75 exit 293, just w. Int corridors. **Pets:** Accepted.

Knights Inn M

(770) 386-7263. **$50-$101.** 420 E Church St 30121. I-75 exit 288, 1.5 mi w. Ext corridors. **Pets:** Medium, dogs only. $10 daily fee/pet. Designated rooms, service with restrictions, supervision.

Microtel Inn & Suites by Wyndham Cartersville H

(678) 605-9331. **$68-$86.** 1348 Joe Frank Harris Pkwy 30120. I-75 exit 290, 1.8 mi w on SR 20 W, just s on Market Pl Blvd, 1.5 mi w on SR 3 N/US 41 N (Joe Frank Harris Pkwy). Int corridors. **Pets:** Accepted.

Motel 6 - #4046 M

(770) 386-1449. **Call for rates.** 5657 Hwy 20 NE 30121. I-75 exit 290, 0.3 mi e. Ext corridors. **Pets:** Other species. Service with restrictions, crate.

Red Roof Inn-Cartersville M

(770) 387-1800. **$52-$80.** 28 SR 20 Spur 30121. I-75 exit 290, 0.3 mi se. Ext corridors. **Pets:** Large, other species. Service with restrictions, supervision.

CEDARTOWN

Country Hearth Inn H

(770) 749-9951. **Call for rates.** 925 N Main St 30125. 1.5 mi n on US 27. Int corridors. **Pets:** Accepted.

CLAYTON

Americas Best Value Inn M

(706) 782-4702. **$50-$90.** 698 Hwy 441 S 30525. 0.8 mi s. Int corridors. **Pets:** Accepted.

COLLEGE PARK

Embassy Suites Hotel at Atlanta Airport H

(404) 767-1988. **$99-$199.** 4700 Southport Rd 30337. I-85 exit 71, 0.3 mi w on Riverdale Rd. Int corridors. **Pets:** Accepted.

▼▼▼▼ Holiday Inn Express-Atlanta Airport H
(404) 761-6500. **Call for rates.** 4601 Best Rd 30337. I-85 exit 71, just
w. Int corridors. **Pets:** Accepted. 🅢Ⓜ 🔁 📶 ✖ 📧 💻

⚜️ ▼▼▼▼ Hyatt Place Atlanta Airport-South H
(770) 994-2997. **$69-$189.** 1899 Sullivan Rd 30337. I-85 exit 71, just e
to Sullivan Rd, then just s; I-285 exit 60 (Riverdale Rd N), 1 mi to Sullivan Rd, then just s. Int corridors. **Pets:** Small, dogs only. $75 one-time
fee/pet. Designated rooms, service with restrictions, supervision.
🅢🅐🆅🅴 🅢Ⓜ 🔁 📶 ✖ 📧 💻

▼▼▼▼ La Quinta Inn & Suites Atlanta Airport H
(770) 996-0000. **$75-$219.** 4820 Massachusetts Blvd 30337. I-85 exit
71, just e to Airport Rd, then just s. Int corridors. **Pets:** Large, other
species. Service with restrictions. 🔁 📶 📧 💻

▼▼▼▼ Quality Hotel & Conference Center-Atlanta
Airport H
(770) 996-4321. **$80-$130.** 1551 Phoenix Blvd 30349. I-285 exit 60
(Riverdale Rd N), just s. Ext/int corridors. **Pets:** Accepted.
🍴 🔁 📶 📧 💻

⚜️ ▼▼▼▼ Sheraton Gateway Hotel, Atlanta
Airport H
(770) 997-1100. **$80-$351.** 1900 Sullivan Rd 30337. I-85 exit 71, just e
to Airport Rd, then just s. Int corridors. **Pets:** $50 one-time fee/room.
Designated rooms, service with restrictions, crate.
🅢🅐🆅🅴 🍴 🅢Ⓜ 🔁 🔁 ✖ 📧 💻

⚜️ ▼▼▼▼ The Westin Hotel-Atlanta
Airport H 🐾
(404) 762-7676. **$99-$379.** 4736 Best Rd 30337. I-85 exit 71, just w, se
on access road to Best Rd, then just s. Int corridors. **Pets:** Small. $100
one-time fee/room. Designated rooms, service with restrictions, supervision. 🅢🅐🆅🅴 🄴🄲🄾 🍴 🅢Ⓜ 🔁 ✖ 📶 ✖ 📧 💻

COLUMBUS (Restaurants p. 629)

▼▼▼ Extended Stay America-Columbus-Bradley
Park H
(706) 653-9938. **$59-$89.** 1721 Rollins Way 31904. I-185 exit 10 (US
80 and SR 22), 1.5 mi w on US 80 exit 3A, just s to Whittlesey Rd, 0.3
mi e to Rollins Way, then just n. Int corridors. **Pets:** Other species. $25
daily fee/pet. Service with restrictions, supervision. 📶 📧 💻

▼▼▼ Holiday Inn Express & Suites H
(706) 507-7080. **$82-$249.** 3901 Victory Dr 31903. I-185 exit 1B, 1 mi
w. Int corridors. **Pets:** Accepted. 🅢Ⓜ 🔁 📶 📧 💻

⚜️ ▼▼▼ Holiday Inn North H
(706) 324-0231. **Call for rates.** 2800 Manchester Expwy 31904. I-185
exit 7, just w. Int corridors. **Pets:** Accepted.
🅢🅐🆅🅴 🍴 🔁 📶 ✖ 📧 💻

⚜️ ▼▼▼▼ Hyatt Place Columbus North H
(706) 507-5000. **$84-$199.** 2974 Northlake Pkwy 31909. US 80 and SR
22 exit Veterans Pkwy, 0.6 mi n. Int corridors.
Pets: Medium. $75 one-time fee/room. Service with restrictions, crate.
🅢🅐🆅🅴 🍴 🅢Ⓜ 🔁 📶 ✖ 📧 💻

▼▼ La Quinta Inn Columbus Midtown M
(706) 568-1740. **$59-$165.** 3201 Macon Rd, Suite 200 31906. I-185 exit
6, just w. Ext/int corridors. **Pets:** Large, other species. Service with
restrictions. 🔁 📶 📧 💻

▼▼ La Quinta Inn Columbus State University H
(706) 323-4344. **$69-$214.** 2919 Warm Springs Rd 31909. I-185 exit 7
southbound; exit 7A northbound, just e. Int corridors. **Pets:** Large, other
species. Service with restrictions. 🅢Ⓜ 🔁 📶 📧 💻

▼▼ Microtel Inn & Suites by Wyndham Columbus/Near
Fort Benning H
(706) 685-2305. **$70-$110.** 3930 St. Mary's Rd 31907. I-185 exit 3, just
e. Int corridors. **Pets:** Accepted. 🔁 📶 📧 💻

▼▼ Microtel Inn & Suites by Wyndham Columbus
North H
(706) 653-7004. **$65-$90.** 1728 Fountain Ct 31904. I-185 exit 12, just
w. Int corridors. **Pets:** Accepted. 🅢Ⓜ 📶 📧 💻

⚜️ ▼▼▼ Staybridge Suites H
(706) 507-7700. **$120-$170.** 1678 Whittlesey Rd 31904. I-185 exit 8,
just w on Whitesville Rd, then just s. Int corridors. **Pets:** Accepted.
🅢🅐🆅🅴 🔁 📶 📧 💻

COMMERCE

⚜️ ▼▼ BEST WESTERN Commerce Inn H
(706) 335-3640. **$50-$300.** 157 Eisenhower Dr 30529. I-85 exit 149,
just ne. Int corridors. **Pets:** Medium. $15 daily fee/pet. Designated
rooms, service with restrictions, supervision.
🅢🅐🆅🅴 🅢Ⓜ 🔁 📶 📧 💻

▼▼▼ Comfort Suites Commerce H
(706) 336-0000. **$89-$219.** 30490 Hwy 441 S 30529. I-85 exit 149, just
w. Int corridors. **Pets:** $25 one-time fee/pet. Designated rooms, service
with restrictions, crate. 🅢Ⓜ 🔁 📶 ✖ 📧 💻

CONYERS

▼▼▼ Country Inn & Suites By Carlson H
(770) 785-2400. **$87-$120, 3 day notice.** 1312 Old Covington Hwy SE
30012. I-20 exit 82, just n. Int corridors. **Pets:** Medium. $50 one-time
fee/room. Designated rooms, service with restrictions, supervision.
🅢Ⓜ 🔁 📶 ✖ 📧 💻

▼▼▼ Hampton Inn H
(770) 483-8838. **$99-$149.** 1340 Dogwood Dr SE 30013. I-20 exit 82,
just n, then just e. Int corridors. **Pets:** Accepted.
🅢Ⓜ 🔁 📶 📧 💻

▼▼▼ La Quinta Inn & Suites Atlanta Conyers H
(770) 918-0092. **$79-$214.** 1184 Dogwood Dr SE 30012. I-20 exit 82,
just n to Dogwood Dr, then just w. Int corridors. **Pets:** Large, other species. Service with restrictions. 🅢Ⓜ 🔁 📶 📧 💻

▼▼ Microtel Inn & Suites by Wyndham Conyers/Atlanta
Area H
(770) 278-0950. **$41-$62.** 1412 Old McDonough Hwy 30094. I-20 exit
82, just s. Int corridors. **Pets:** Accepted. 🅢Ⓜ 📶 📧 💻

▼▼ Quality Inn M
(770) 760-1230. **$69-$84.** 1164 Dogwood Dr SE 30012. I-20 exit 82,
just n to Dogwood Dr, then just w. Ext corridors. **Pets:** Small. $20 daily
fee/pet. Designated rooms, service with restrictions, supervision.
🔁 📶 📧 💻

CORDELE

⚜️ ▼▼▼ Baymont Inn & Suites H
(229) 273-9477. **$70-$119.** 416 S Greer St 31015. I-75 exit 101 (US
280), just w, then just n. Int corridors. **Pets:** Medium, dogs only. $15
daily fee/pet. Service with restrictions, supervision.
🅢🅐🆅🅴 🔁 ✖ 📧 💻

⚜️ ▼▼ BEST WESTERN Colonial Inn H
(229) 273-5420. **$69-$80.** 1706 E 16th Ave (US 280) 31015. I-75 exit
101 (US 280), just w. Ext/int corridors. **Pets:** Medium, other species.
$10 daily fee/pet. Service with restrictions, supervision.
🅢🅐🆅🅴 🔁 📶 📧 💻

▼▼ Hampton Inn H
(229) 273-0737. **$85-$99.** 1603 16th Ave E (US 280) 31015. I-75 exit
101 (US 280), just w. Ext corridors. **Pets:** Accepted.
🔁 📶 📧 💻

⚜️ ▼▼▼▼ Lake Blackshear Resort & Golf Club H
(229) 276-1004. **$99-$199, 7 day notice.** 2459-H US 280 W 31015.
I-75 exit 101 (US 280), 10 mi w. Ext/int corridors. **Pets:** Other species.
Designated rooms, service with restrictions.
🅢🅐🆅🅴 🄴🄲🄾 🍴 🅢Ⓜ 🔁 ✖ 📶 📧 💻

Quality Inn Cordele H

(229) 273-2371. **$59-$109.** 1601 E 16th Ave (US 280) 31015. I-75 exit 101 (US 280), just w. Ext corridors. **Pets:** Accepted.

CORNELIA
Super 8 H

(706) 778-9573. **$50-$100.** 2965 J Warren Rd 30531. Jct SR 365 and US 441 business route, just w. Int corridors. **Pets:** Medium, dogs only. $25 daily fee/pet. Designated rooms, service with restrictions, crate.

COVINGTON
Baymont Inn & Suites M

(770) 787-4900. **$59-$99.** 10111 Alcovy Rd 30014. I-20 exit 92, just n. Ext corridors. **Pets:** Accepted.

DAHLONEGA
Quality Inn Dahlonega M

(706) 864-6191. **$65-$119.** 619 N Grove St 30533. 0.5 mi n on US 19 business route. Ext corridors. **Pets:** Accepted.

DALTON
Baymont Inn & Suites Dalton M

(706) 226-5022. **$49-$79.** 2106 Chattanooga Rd 30720. I-75 exit 336, just w. Ext corridors. **Pets:** Accepted.

Comfort Inn & Suites H

(706) 259-2583. **$90-$119.** 905 Westbridge Rd 30720. I-75 exit 333, just w to Westbridge Rd, then just s. Int corridors. **Pets:** Accepted.

Holiday Inn & Suites Dalton H

(706) 529-6000. **Call for rates.** 879 College Dr 30720. I-75 exit 333, just w. Int corridors. **Pets:** Small. $25 daily fee/pet. Designated rooms, no service, supervision.

Howard Johnson Dalton M

(706) 281-1880. **$69-$99.** 790 College Dr 30720. I-75 exit 333, just w, then 0.3 mi n. Ext corridors. **Pets:** Accepted.

La Quinta Inn & Suites Dalton H

(706) 272-9099. **$79-$229.** 715 College Dr 30720. I-75 exit 333, just w to Holiday Inn Dr, then 0.5 mi n. Int corridors. **Pets:** Large, other species. Service with restrictions.

Quality Inn M

(706) 278-0500. **$70-$115.** 875 College Dr 30720. I-75 exit 333, just w. Ext corridors. **Pets:** Accepted.

DARIEN
Comfort Inn H

(912) 437-4200. **$71-$150.** 12924 GA Hwy 251 Rd 31305. I-95 exit 49 (SR 251), just nw. Int corridors. **Pets:** Accepted.

Days Inn H

(912) 437-2500. **$49-$69.** 12888 GA Hwy 251 31305. I-95 exit 49 (SR 251), just nw. Int corridors. **Pets:** Small. $15 daily fee/pet. Designated rooms, no service, supervision.

DAWSONVILLE
Comfort Inn H

(706) 216-1900. **$76-$100.** 127 Beartooth Pkwy 30534. Jct SR 400/53, 0.5 mi s. Int corridors. **Pets:** Large, other species. $15 daily fee/pet. Designated rooms, service with restrictions.

Dawson Village Inn H

(706) 216-4410. **$70-$73, 4 day notice.** 76 N Georgia Ave 30534. Jct SR 400/53, 0.5 mi s. Int corridors. **Pets:** Small, dogs only. $25 daily fee/pet. Designated rooms, service with restrictions, supervision.

DORAVILLE
Comfort Inn & Conference Center Northeast H

(770) 455-3700. **$69-$132.** 2001 Clearview Ave 30340. I-285 exit 32, just s, just e on Jesse Norman Way, just n on Stewart Rd, then just s. Int corridors. **Pets:** Accepted.

DOUGLAS
Jameson Inn H

(912) 384-9432. **$64-$67.** 1628 S Peterson Ave 31535. Jct US 221/441/SR 31 and SR 206/353, just s. Ext corridors. **Pets:** Accepted.

DOUGLASVILLE
Days Inn M

(770) 949-1499. **$58-$85.** 5489 Westmoreland Plaza 30134. I-20 exit 37, just n. Ext corridors. **Pets:** Medium, other species. $20 daily fee/pet. Service with restrictions, supervision.

Econo Lodge Inn & Suites H

(770) 489-4863. **Call for rates.** 8304 Cherokee Blvd 30134. I-20 exit 37, just n to Cherokee Blvd, then just e. Int corridors. **Pets:** Large. $15 daily fee/pet. Service with restrictions, supervision.

La Quinta Inn & Suites Atlanta Douglasville H

(770) 577-3838. **$79-$174.** 1000 Linnenkohl Dr 30134. I-20 exit 34, just n. Int corridors. **Pets:** Large, other species. Service with restrictions.

DUBLIN
Baymont Inn & Suites Dublin H

(478) 275-3008. **$59-$79.** 100 PM Watson Ln 31021. I-16 exit 51 (US 441), just n. Ext corridors. **Pets:** Accepted.

La Quinta Inn & Suites Dublin H

(478) 272-3110. **$91-$224.** 101 Travel Center Blvd 31021. I-16 exit 51 (US 441), just s. Int corridors. **Pets:** Large, other species. Service with restrictions.

DULUTH *(Restaurants p. 629)*
Candlewood Suites-Atlanta H

(678) 380-0414. **$70-$95.** 3665 Shackleford Rd 30096. I-85 exit 104, just e, then just s. Int corridors. **Pets:** Accepted.

Extended Stay America-Atlanta-Gwinnett Place H

(770) 623-6800. **$64-$90.** 3390 Venture Pkwy NW 30096. I-85 exit 104, just w to Venture Pkwy, then just n. Int corridors. **Pets:** Other species. $25 daily fee/pet. Service with restrictions, supervision.

Holiday Inn Express H

(770) 935-7171. **Call for rates.** 3670 Shackleford Rd 30096. I-85 exit 104, just e to Shackleford Rd, then just s. Int corridors. **Pets:** Accepted.

Holiday Inn-Gwinnett Center H

(770) 476-2022. **Call for rates.** 6310 Sugarloaf Pkwy 30097. I-85 exit 108, just w. Int corridors. **Pets:** Accepted.

Hyatt Place Atlanta/Duluth/Gwinnett Mall H

(770) 623-9699. **$69-$179.** 3530 Venture Pkwy 30096. I-85 exit 104, just w to Venture Pkwy, then just n. Int corridors. **Pets:** Accepted.

▼▼▼ Quality Inn-Gwinnett Mall
(770) 623-9300. **$53-$129.** 3500 Venture Pkwy 30096. I-85 exit 104, just w to Venture Pkwy, then just n. Ext/int corridors. **Pets:** Accepted.

▼▼▼▼ Residence Inn Atlanta NE/Duluth Sugarloaf ⊞
(770) 814-2929. **$109-$259.** 1940 Satellite Blvd 30097. I-85 exit 108, 0.8 mi e. Int corridors. **Pets:** Medium, other species. $100 one-time fee/pet. Designated rooms, service with restrictions, supervision.

▼▼▼▼ Residence Inn by Marriott Atlanta Gwinnett Place ⊞
(770) 921-2202. **$89-$179.** 1760 Pineland Rd 30096. I-85 exit 104, just e to Shackleford Rd, just s to Pineland Rd, then just e. Int corridors. **Pets:** Accepted.

EAST ELLIJAY
▼▼ Stratford Motor Inn M
(706) 276-1080. **Call for rates.** 79 Maddox Cir 30540. Jct Maddox Cir and SR 515. Ext corridors. **Pets:** Accepted.

EAST POINT (Restaurants p. 630)
▼▼▼▼ Crowne Plaza Atlanta Airport ⊞
(404) 768-6660. **$99-$199.** 1325 Virginia Ave 30344. I-85 exit 73 southbound; exit 73B northbound, just w. Int corridors. **Pets:** Accepted.

▼▼▼▼ Drury Inn & Suites-Atlanta Airport ⊞
(404) 761-4900. **$105-$210.** 1270 Virginia Ave 30344. I-85 exit 73 southbound; exit 73A northbound, just e. Int corridors. **Pets:** $10 daily fee/room. Service with restrictions, supervision.

▲▲▲ ▼▼▼▼ Holiday Inn & Suites Atlanta Airport-North ⊞
(404) 305-9990. **$89-$144.** 1380 Virginia Ave 30344. I-85 exit 73 southbound; exit 73B northbound, just w. Int corridors. **Pets:** Accepted.

▲▲▲ ▼▼▼▼ Hyatt Place Atlanta Airport-North ⊞
(404) 768-8484. **$74-$199.** 3415 Norman Berry Dr 30344. I-85 exit 73B northbound; exit 73 southbound, just e to Bobby Brown Pkwy, then just n. Int corridors. **Pets:** Accepted.

FAIRBURN
▼▼▼▼ Country Inn & Suites By Carlson ⊞
(678) 782-4900. **$89-$109.** 7815 Senoia Rd 30213. I-85 exit 61, just e. Int corridors. **Pets:** Accepted.

▼▼▼▼ Sleep Inn & Suites ⊞
(678) 782-4700. **$69-$109.** 1005 Oakley Industrial Blvd 30213. I-85 exit 61, just e. Int corridors. **Pets:** Accepted.

▼▼▼▼ Wingate by Wyndham Atlanta Airport Fairburn ⊞
(770) 892-3006. **$84-$189.** 7882 Senoia Rd 30213. I-85 exit 61, 0.3 mi e. Int corridors. **Pets:** Accepted.

FITZGERALD
▼▼ Quality Inn ⊞
(229) 423-5151. **$55-$100.** 263 Ocilla Hwy 31750. US 319/107, just n. Int corridors. **Pets:** Accepted.

▼▼ Western Motel ⊞
(229) 424-9500. **$60, 3 day notice.** 111 Bull Run Rd 31750. On US 129, just n of US 319/107. Ext corridors. **Pets:** Small. $10 daily fee/pet. Service with restrictions, supervision.

FOREST PARK
▼▼▼ Super 8 M
(404) 363-8811. **$45-$100.** 410 Old Dixie Way 30297. I-75 exit 235, just e. Ext corridors. **Pets:** Accepted.

FORSYTH
▲▲▲ ▼▼▼ Comfort Inn Forsyth ⊞
(478) 994-3400. **$64-$84.** 333 Harold G Clark Pkwy 31029. I-75 exit 185 (SR 18), just w. Ext corridors. **Pets:** Small. $15 daily fee/pet. Designated rooms, service with restrictions, supervision.

▼▼▼▼ Holiday Inn Express ⊞
(478) 994-9697. **$78-$119.** 520 Holiday Cir 31029. I-75 exit 186 (Juliette Rd), just w, then just s on Aaron St. Int corridors. **Pets:** Medium. $20 one-time fee/pet. Designated rooms, service with restrictions, supervision.

▲▲▲ ▼▼▼ Super 8 M
(478) 994-5101. **$57-$101.** 436 Tift College Dr 31029. I-75 exit 186 (Juliette Rd), just w. Ext/int corridors. **Pets:** Medium. $15 daily fee/pet. Designated rooms, service with restrictions, supervision.

FORT OGLETHORPE
▲▲▲ ▼▼▼ BEST WESTERN Battlefield Inn M
(706) 866-0222. **$70-$150.** 2120 Lafayette Rd 30742. Jct US 27 and SR 2, just n. Ext corridors. **Pets:** Small. $15 daily fee/pet. Designated rooms, service with restrictions, supervision.

GAINESVILLE
▲▲▲ ▼▼▼ GuestHouse Inn & Suites M
(770) 535-8100. **$54-$99, 3 day notice.** 520 Queen City Pkwy SW 30501. I-985 exit 20, 1.8 mi nw on SR 60/Queen City Pkwy. Ext corridors. **Pets:** Accepted.

GREENSBORO
▲▲▲ ▼▼▼▼▼ The Ritz-Carlton Lodge, Reynolds Plantation ⊞ 🐾
(706) 467-0600. **$259-$999, 3 day notice.** 1 Lake Oconee Tr 30642. I-20 exit 130, 7.2 mi sw on SR 44 (Old Eatonton Rd), 1.5 mi e on Linger Longer Rd, then 2 mi ne. Ext/int corridors. **Pets:** Dogs only. $150 one-time fee/room. Designated rooms, service with restrictions, supervision.

GROVETOWN
▼▼▼ Hawthorn Suites by Wyndham Augusta ⊞
(706) 228-1990. **$85-$499.** 4049 Jimmie Dyess Pkwy 30909. I-20 exit 194 (SR 383), 0.5 mi s. Int corridors. **Pets:** Accepted.

▼▼▼ Super 8-Augusta ⊞
(706) 396-1600. **$69-$289.** 456 Park West Dr 30813. I-20 exit 194 (SR 383), just s, then w. Int corridors. **Pets:** Accepted.

HAPEVILLE
▲▲▲ ▼▼▼▼ Hilton Atlanta Airport ⊞
(404) 767-9000. **$89-$209.** 1031 Virginia Ave 30354. I-85 exit 73 southbound; exit 73A northbound, just e. Int corridors. **Pets:** Accepted.

▲▲▲ ▼▼▼▼ Residence Inn by Marriott Atlanta Airport North/Virginia Avenue ⊞
(404) 761-0511. **$99-$229.** 3401 International Blvd 30354. I-85 exit 73 southbound; exit 73A northbound, 0.5 mi e to International Blvd, then just n. Ext/int corridors. **Pets:** Accepted.

HARTWELL

 BEST WESTERN Lake Hartwell Inn & Suites H

(706) 376-4700. **$80.** 1357 E Franklin St 30643. I-85 exit 177, 2 mi on US 29 N. Int corridors. **Pets:** Accepted. (SAVE) ⛵ 🛰 ✕ 🛢 🖵

HELEN *(Restaurants p. 630)*

The Helendorf River Inn & Conference Center M

(706) 878-2271. **$54-$209, 10 day notice.** 33 Munich Strasse 30545. SR 17 and 75; center. Ext corridors. **Pets:** Other species. $20 daily fee/pet. Designated rooms, service with restrictions, supervision.
⛵ 🛰 🛢 🖵

Kountry Peddler Tanglewood Resort Cabins CA

(706) 878-3286. **Call for rates.** 3387 Hwy 356 30571. 1 mi n on SR 75, 3 mi ne. Ext corridors. **Pets:** Small, dogs only. $25 one-time fee/pet. No service, crate. 🐾 ✕ 🛢 🖵

Quality Inn M

(706) 878-2268. **$59-$108.** 15 Yonah St 30545. Just w of Mack St. Ext corridors. **Pets:** Accepted. ⛵ 🛰 🛢 🖵

Riverbend Motel & Cabins M

(706) 878-2155. **Call for rates.** 134 River St 30545. Just w off Main St. Ext corridors. **Pets:** Accepted. 🛰 ✕ 🛢 🖵

HIAWASSEE

Enota Mountain Retreat CA

(706) 896-9966. **$80-$165.** 1000 Hwy 180 30546. E on US 76 to SR 75/17, 6 mi s to SR 180, then 2.5 mi s. Ext corridors. **Pets:** Other species. $15 daily fee/pet. No service, supervision.
✕ 🐾 ✕ 🐾 🐾 🛢 🖵

HINESVILLE

Baymont Inn & Suites H

(912) 408-4444. **Call for rates.** 773 Frank Cochran Dr 31313. Jct SR 119/196, 1 mi sw on SR 196, then just nw. Int corridors. **Pets:** Accepted. 🛞M ⛵ 🛰 🛢 🖵

La Quinta Inn & Suites Hinesville/Ft Stewart H

(912) 369-3000. **$79-$199.** 1740 E Oglethorpe Hwy 31313. Jct US 84 and SR 38C, 0.8 mi ne. Int corridors. **Pets:** Large, other species. Service with restrictions. 🛞M ⛵ 🛰 ✕ 🛢 🖵

HIRAM

Country Inn & Suites By Carlson H 🐾

(770) 222-0456. **$85-$140.** 70 Enterprise Path 30134. Jct SR 92/6 and US 278, 0.3 mi w. Int corridors. **Pets:** Small. $15 daily fee/pet. Service with restrictions, supervision. ⛵ 🛰 🛢 🖵

HOGANSVILLE

Woodstream Inn M

(706) 637-9395. **$50-$120.** 1888 E Main St 30230. I-85 exit 28, just w. Ext corridors. **Pets:** Small, dogs only. $20 daily fee/pet. Designated rooms, no service, supervision. ⛵ 🛰 🛢

JASPER

Clairmont Inn M

(706) 253-3297. **$63-$93.** 100 Whitfield Dr 30143. Jct SR 515/53; in Lawsons Crossing. Ext corridors. **Pets:** Accepted.
🛞M ⛵ 🛰 🛢 🖵

Microtel Inn & Suites by Wyndham Jasper H

(706) 299-5500. **$60-$90.** 171 H Mullins Ct 30143. Jct SR 515/53, 0.9 mi n. Int corridors. **Pets:** Accepted. 🛞M 🛰 🛢 🖵

JEKYLL ISLAND *(Restaurants p. 630)*

Hampton Inn & Suites Jekyll Island H

(912) 635-3733. **$129-$249.** 200 S Beachview Dr 31527. Jct Ben Fortson Pkwy (SR 520/Beachview Dr), 2 mi s. Int corridors. **Pets:** Accepted.
(SAVE) 🛞M ⛵ ✕ 🛰 ✕ 🛢 🖵

Villas by the Sea CO

(912) 635-2521. **$119-$399, 7 day notice.** 1175 N Beachview Dr 31527. Jct Ben Fortson Pkwy (SR 520/Beachview Dr), 4 mi n. Ext corridors. **Pets:** Medium, dogs only. $100 one-time fee/room. Designated rooms, service with restrictions. (SAVE) 🍴 🛞M ⛵ ✕ 🛰 ✕ 🛢 🖵

JOHNS CREEK

Hyatt Place Atlanta/Duluth/Johns Creek H

(770) 622-5858. **$59-$259.** 11505 Medlock Bridge Rd 30097. Jct SR 141 and 120, 0.7 mi n. Int corridors. **Pets:** Small, dogs only. $75 one-time fee/pet. Designated rooms, service with restrictions, supervision.
(SAVE) 🛞M ⛵ 🛰 ✕ 🛢 🖵

KENNESAW *(Restaurants p. 630)*

BEST WESTERN Kennesaw Inn M

(770) 424-7666. **$75-$80.** 3375 Busbee Dr 30144. I-75 exit 271, just e. Ext corridors. **Pets:** Medium, other species. $10 daily fee/pet. Designated rooms, service with restrictions, supervision.
(SAVE) ⛵ 🛰 🛢 🖵

Days Inn M

(770) 419-1576. **$50-$85.** 760 Cobb Place Blvd 30144. I-75 exit 269, just w. Ext corridors. **Pets:** Accepted. 🛞M ⛵ 🛰 🛢 🖵

Embassy Suites Atlanta-Kennesaw Town Center H

(770) 420-2505. **$119-$249.** 620 Chastain Rd NW 30144. I-75 exit 271, 0.4 mi w. Int corridors. **Pets:** Small, dogs only. $75 one-time fee/room. Designated rooms, service with restrictions, supervision.
🍴 🛞M ⛵ 🖲 🛢 🖵

Extended Stay America Atlanta Kennesaw H

(770) 422-1403. **$52-$95.** 3000 George Busbee Pkwy 30144. I-75 exit 269, just e to George Busbee Pkwy, then 0.8 mi n. Int corridors. **Pets:** Other species. $25 daily fee/pet. Service with restrictions, supervision. 🛞M 🛰 🛢 🖵

Extended Stay America Atlanta-Kennesaw Chastain Rd H

(770) 425-6101. **$45-$87.** 3316 Busbee Dr 30144. I-75 exit 271, just e to Busbee Dr, then just s. Int corridors. **Pets:** Other species. $25 daily fee/pet. Service with restrictions, supervision. 🛞M ⛵ 🛰 🛢 🖵

La Quinta Inn Kennesaw H

(770) 426-0045. **$80-$200.** 2625 George Busbee Pkwy 30144. I-75 exit 269, just e to George Busbee Pkwy, then just n. Int corridors. **Pets:** Large, other species. Service with restrictions.
🛞M ⛵ 🛰 🛢 🖵

M-Star Kennesaw by Magnuson Hotels M

(770) 529-3370. **$45-$55.** 3027 Cobb Pkwy NW 30152. I-75 exit 271, 2.5 mi w, then 2.2 mi n on US 41. Ext corridors. **Pets:** Accepted.
(SAVE) 🛞M 🛰 🛢 🖵

Quality Inn M

(770) 419-1530. **$65-$85.** 750 Cobb Place Blvd 30144. I-75 exit 269, just w. Ext corridors. **Pets:** Accepted. 🛞M ⛵ 🛰 🛢 🖵

Red Roof Inn Atlanta-Kennesaw M

(770) 429-0323. **$57-$100.** 520 Roberts Ct NW 30144. I-75 exit 269, just e. Ext corridors. **Pets:** Large, other species. Service with restrictions, supervision. 🛞M 🛰 🛢 🖵

Residence Inn by Marriott Atlanta Kennesaw/Town Center H

(770) 218-1018. **$110-$179.** 3443 Busbee Dr 30144. I-75 exit 271, just e. Int corridors. **Pets:** Medium, dogs only. $100 one-time fee/room. Designated rooms, service with restrictions, crate.
(SAVE) 🛞M ⛵ 🛰 ✕ 🛢 🖵

KINGSLAND

▼▼ Baymont Inn & Suites Kingsland H
(912) 729-9600. **$49-$79.** 105 May Creek Dr 31548. I-95 exit 3 (SR 40), just w. Ext corridors. **Pets:** Accepted. 〔M〕 ⌖ 奈 🔒 💻

▼▼▼ La Quinta Inn Kingsland Kings Bay H
(912) 882-8010. **$74-$192.** 104 May Creek Dr 31548. I-95 exit 3 (SR 40), just w. Int corridors. **Pets:** Large, other species. Service with restrictions. 〔M〕 ⌖ 奈 ✕ 🔒 💻

AAA ▼▼ Microtel Inn & Suites by Wyndham Kingsland H
(912) 729-1555. **$49-$79.** 1325 E King Ave 31548. I-95 exit 3 (SR 40), just ne. Int corridors. **Pets:** Other species. $10 daily fee/pet. Designated rooms, service with restrictions, crate. 〔SAVE〕 ⌖ 奈 🔒 💻

▼▼ Quality Inn M 🐾
(912) 576-9400. **$56-$90.** 111 Robert L. Edenfield Dr 31548. I-95 exit 3 (SR 40), just e. Ext corridors. **Pets:** Other species. $10 daily fee/pet. Service with restrictions, supervision. 奈 🔒 💻

▼▼ Sleep Inn & Suites H
(912) 673-7116. **$49-$129.** 1321 Hospitality Ave 31548. I-95 exit 3 (SR 40), just e. Int corridors. **Pets:** Accepted. 〔M〕 ⌖ 奈 🔒 💻

LA FAYETTE

▼▼ Days Inn M
(706) 639-9362. **$60-$95.** 2209 N Main St 30728. 2.5 mi n on US 27. Ext corridors. **Pets:** Accepted. ⌖ 奈 🔒 💻

▼▼ Key West Inn M
(706) 638-8200. **$49-$89.** 2221 N Main St 30728. 2.5 mi n on US 27. Ext corridors. **Pets:** Accepted. 〔M〕 ⌖ 奈 🔒

LAKE PARK

AAA ▼▼ Days Inn H
(229) 559-0229. **$59-$69.** 4913 Timber Dr 31636. I-75 exit 5, just nw. Ext corridors. **Pets:** Accepted. 〔SAVE〕 ⌖ 奈 ✕ 🔒 💻

LAVONIA

▼▼▼▼ Holiday Inn Express & Suites H
(706) 356-2100. **$99-$118.** 110 Owens Dr 30553. I-85 exit 173, just w. Int corridors. **Pets:** Accepted. 〔M〕 ⌖ 奈 🔒 💻

▼▼ Super 8 M
(706) 356-8848. **$40-$58.** 14227 Jones St 30553. I-85 exit 173, just w. Ext corridors. **Pets:** Accepted. 〔M〕 ⌖ 奈 🔒 💻

LAWRENCEVILLE

AAA ▼▼ Days Inn M
(770) 995-7782. **$65-$75.** 731 Duluth Hwy 30046. SR 316 exit SR 120, just e. Ext corridors. **Pets:** Medium. $25 one-time fee/pet. Designated rooms, service with restrictions, supervision. 〔SAVE〕 奈 🔒 💻

LITHONIA

AAA ▼▼▼ Hyatt Place Atlanta-East/Lithonia H
(770) 484-4384. **$69-$189.** 7900 Mall Ring Rd 30038. I-20 exit 75, just s on Turner Hill Rd, then 0.7 mi w. Int corridors. **Pets:** Accepted. 〔SAVE〕 〔M〕 ⌖ 奈 ✕ 🔒 💻

▼▼ Microtel Inn & Suites by Wyndham Lithonia/Stone Mountain H
(678) 287-4400. **$54-$79.** 2980 Evans Mill Rd 30038. I-20 exit 74, just s. Int corridors. **Pets:** Accepted. 〔M〕 奈 🔒 💻

LOCUST GROVE

AAA ▼▼ La Quinta Inn & Suites Locust Grove H
(678) 583-8088. **$81-$230.** 4832 Bill Gardner Pkwy 30248. I-75 exit 212, just e. Int corridors. **Pets:** Large, other species. Service with restrictions. 〔SAVE〕 〔M〕 ⌖ 奈 ✕ 🔒 💻

AAA ▼▼▼ Red Roof Inn-Locust Grove H
(678) 583-0004. **$59-$89.** 4840 Bill Gardner Pkwy 30248. I-75 exit 212, just e. Int corridors. **Pets:** Large, other species. Service with restrictions, supervision. 〔SAVE〕 〔M〕 奈 🔒 💻

AAA ▼▼ Super 8 M
(770) 957-2936. **$54-$96, 3 day notice.** 4605 Bill Gardner Pkwy 30248. I-75 exit 212, just w. Ext corridors. **Pets:** Accepted. 〔SAVE〕 奈 🔒 💻

LAGRANGE

▼▼ Baymont Inn & Suites H
(706) 885-9002. **$69-$89.** 107 Hoffman Dr 30240. I-85 exit 18 (Lafayette Pkwy), just w. Int corridors. **Pets:** Medium. $10 daily fee/pet. Service with restrictions, crate. ⌖ 奈 🔒 💻

▼▼▼▼ Lafayette Garden Inn & Conference Center M
(706) 884-6175. **$59-$74.** 1513 Lafayette Pkwy 30241. I-85 exit 18 (Lafayette Pkwy), just w. Ext corridors. **Pets:** Accepted. 〔¶¶〕 ⌖ 奈 🔒 💻

▼▼▼▼ La Quinta Inn & Suites H
(706) 812-8000. **Call for rates.** 111 Hoffman Dr 30241. I-85 exit 18 (Lafayette Pkwy), just w. Int corridors. **Pets:** Large, other species. Service with restrictions. 〔M〕 ⌖ 奈 ✕ 🔒 💻

AAA ▼▼▼ Quality Inn M
(706) 882-8700. **$60-$69.** 110 Jameson Dr 30240. I-85 exit 18 (Lafayette Pkwy), 0.3 mi w. Ext corridors. **Pets:** Small. $15 daily fee/pet. Designated rooms, service with restrictions, crate. 〔SAVE〕 〔M〕 ⌖ 奈 🔒 💻

▼▼ Red Roof Inn LaGrange M
(706) 882-9540. **$50-$100.** 1601 Lafayette Pkwy 30241. I-85 exit 18 (Lafayette Pkwy), just e. Ext corridors. **Pets:** Large, other species. Service with restrictions, supervision. ⌖ 奈 🔒 💻

MACON *(Restaurants p. 630)*

AAA ▼▼▼▼ 1842 Inn BB
(478) 741-1842. **$189-$255, 7 day notice.** 353 College St 31201. I-75 exit 164 (US 41), 0.5 mi e, then just n. Ext/int corridors. **Pets:** Small. $50 daily fee/pet. Designated rooms, service with restrictions, supervision. 〔SAVE〕 奈 ✕

AAA ▼▼▼ BEST WESTERN Inn & Suites of Macon M 🐾
(478) 781-5300. **$70-$90.** 4681 Chambers Rd 31206. I-475 exit 3 (Eisenhower Pkwy/US 80), just ne, then just se. Ext corridors. **Pets:** Large. $10 daily fee/room. Designated rooms, service with restrictions. 〔SAVE〕 ⌖ 奈 🔒 💻

AAA ▼▼▼ BEST WESTERN Riverside Inn H
(478) 743-6311. **$75-$85, 3 day notice.** 2400 Riverside Dr 31204. I-75 exit 167 (Riverside Dr), just w, then 0.4 mi se. Int corridors. **Pets:** Medium. $15 deposit/pet, $15 daily fee/pet. Designated rooms, supervision. 〔SAVE〕 ⌖ 奈 🔒 💻

▼▼▼ Candlewood Suites H
(478) 254-3530. **Call for rates.** 3957 River Place Dr 31210. I-75 exit 169 (Arkwright Rd), just e, then just s. Int corridors. **Pets:** Accepted. 〔M〕 ⌖ 奈 🔒 💻

AAA ▼▼▼ Days Inn M
(478) 781-4343. **$54-$59.** 4999 Eisenhower Pkwy 31206. I-475 exit 3 (Eisenhower Pkwy/US 80), just w. Ext corridors. **Pets:** Accepted. 〔SAVE〕 ⌖ 奈 🔒 💻

▼▼▼ La Quinta Inn & Suites Macon H
(478) 475-0206. **$79-$165.** 3944 River Place Dr 31210. I-75 exit 169 (Arkwright Rd), just n, then e. Int corridors. **Pets:** Large, other species. Service with restrictions. 〔M〕 ⌖ 奈 🔒 💻

WWW La Quinta Inn & Suites Macon West H
(478) 788-6226. **$82-$194.** 4615 Chambers Rd 31206. I-475 exit 3 (Eisenhower Pkwy/US 80), just e, then 0.5 mi s. Int corridors. **Pets:** Large, other species. Service with restrictions.
⛲ 🛜 ✕ 🛗 🖥

MADISON *(Restaurants p. 630)*

WW Quality Inn M
(706) 342-1839. **Call for rates.** 2001 Eatonton Rd 30650. US 129/441, 0.4 mi w. Ext corridors. **Pets:** Accepted. ᴍ 🛜 🛗 🖥

MARIETTA *(Restaurants p. 630)*

WWW Baymont Inn & Suites Marietta/Atlanta North M
(770) 951-0026. **$69-$104.** 2170 Delk Rd 30067. I-75 exit 261, 0.3 mi w. Ext/int corridors. **Pets:** Accepted. ⛲ 🛜 🛗 🖥

WWWW Drury Inn & Suites-Atlanta Northwest H
(770) 612-0900. **$110-$169.** 1170 Powers Ferry Pl 30067. I-75 exit 261, just e. Int corridors. **Pets:** $10 daily fee/room. Service with restrictions, supervision. ᴍ ⛲ 🛜 ✕ 🛗 🖥

WW Extended Stay America-Atlanta-Marietta-Powers Ferry Rd H
(770) 303-0043. **$45-$86.** 2239 Powers Ferry Rd SE 30067. I-285 exit 22, just n. Int corridors. **Pets:** Other species. $25 daily fee/pet. Service with restrictions, supervision. ᴍ 🛜 🛗 🖥

⚛ WWWW Hilton Atlanta/Marietta Hotel & Conference Center H
(770) 427-2500. **$99-$179.** 500 Powder Springs St 30064. I-75 exit 263, 3.5 mi w to Powder Springs St, then just w. Int corridors. **Pets:** $75 one-time fee/room. Service with restrictions, crate.
SAVE 🍽 ᴍ ⛲ ✕ 📶 ✕ 🛗 🖥

⚛ WWWW Hyatt Regency Suites Atlanta NW H
(770) 956-1234. **$109-$289, 3 day notice.** 2999 Windy Hill Rd 30067. I-75 exit 260, 0.5 mi e. Int corridors. **Pets:** Accepted.
SAVE 🍽 ᴍ ⛲ 📶 ✕ 🛗 🖥

⚛ WWW Quality Inn Atlanta/Marietta H
(770) 955-0004. **$70-$80.** 1255 Franklin Rd SE 30067. I-75 exit 261, 0.3 mi w to Franklin Rd, then just s. Int corridors. **Pets:** Medium, other species. $15 daily fee/pet. Designated rooms, service with restrictions, supervision. SAVE ⛲ 🛜 🛗 🖥

MCDONOUGH

⚛ WWW Country Inn & Suites By Carlson H
(770) 957-0082. **$75-$200.** 115 E Greenwood Rd 30253. I-75 exit 216, just w. Int corridors. **Pets:** Small. $20 one-time fee/room. Service with restrictions, crate. SAVE ᴍ ⛲ 🛜 🛗 🖥

⚛ WWW Econo Lodge M
(770) 957-2651. **$43-$55.** 1279 Hwy 20 W 30253. I-75 exit 218, just w. Ext corridors. **Pets:** Accepted. SAVE 🛜 🛗 🖥

WW Motel 6 McDonough, GA #4847 M
(770) 954-9110. **Call for rates.** 80 Hwy 81 W 30253. I-75 exit 218, just w. Ext corridors. **Pets:** Other species. Service with restrictions, crate.
⛲ 🛜 🛗

⚛ WWW Quality Inn & Suites Conference Center M
(770) 957-5291. **$59-$104.** 930 Hwy 155 S 30253. I-75 exit 216, just w. Ext corridors. **Pets:** $10 daily fee/room. Service with restrictions, supervision. SAVE ᴍ ⛲ 🛜 🛗 🖥

⚛ WWW Sleep Inn H
(770) 898-0804. **$54-$135.** 945 Hwy 155 S 30253. I-75 exit 216, just w. Int corridors. **Pets:** Accepted. SAVE ᴍ ⛲ 🛜 ✕ 🛗 🖥

MILLEDGEVILLE

WWW Antebellum Inn BB
(478) 453-3993. **Call for rates.** 200 N Columbia St 31061. Just s of Business Rt US 441 (Columbia St); between SR 22 and 49; downtown. Int corridors. **Pets:** Accepted. ⛲ 🛜 ✕ 🗑 🖥

WWW Hampton Inn H
(478) 451-0050. **$109-$149.** 2461 N Columbia St 31061. US 441, 2.6 mi n of downtown. Int corridors. **Pets:** Medium, other species. $25 one-time fee/room. Designated rooms, service with restrictions, supervision.
⛲ 🛜 🛗 🖥

WW Super 8 Milledgeville M
(478) 453-9491. **$50-$75.** 2474 N Columbia St 31061. US 441, 2.6 mi n of downtown. Ext corridors. **Pets:** Medium. $10 daily fee/pet. Designated rooms, service with restrictions, supervision. 🛜 🛗 🖥

MORROW

⚛ WWW BEST WESTERN Southlake Inn M
(770) 961-6300. **$66-$110.** 6437 Jonesboro Rd 30260. I-75 exit 233, just e. Ext corridors. **Pets:** Accepted. SAVE ⛲ 🛜 🛗 🖥

WWW Drury Inn & Suites-Atlanta South H
(770) 960-0500. **$115-$174.** 6520 S Lee St 30260. I-75 exit 233, just e. Int corridors. **Pets:** $10 daily fee/room. Service with restrictions, supervision. ᴍ ⛲ 🛜 ✕ 🛗 🖥

WW Extended Stay America-Atlanta-Morrow H
(770) 472-0727. **$55-$85.** 2265 Mt. Zion Pkwy 30260. I-75 exit 231, just w, then just s. Int corridors. **Pets:** Other species. $25 daily fee/pet. Service with restrictions, supervision. 🛜 🛗 🖥

WW Quality Inn & Suites M
(770) 960-1957. **$55-$99.** 6597 Jonesboro Rd 30260. I-75 exit 233, just w. Ext corridors. **Pets:** Accepted. ᴍ ⛲ 🛜 🛗 🖥

WW Red Roof Inn-Atlanta South Morrow M
(770) 968-1483. **$42-$69.** 1348 Southlake Plaza Dr 30260. I-75 exit 233, just e to Southlake Plaza Dr, then just n. Ext corridors.
Pets: Large, other species. Service with restrictions, supervision.
ᴍ 🛜 🛗 🖥

MOULTRIE

WW Econo Lodge H
(229) 890-8652. **$65-$150.** 1300 Veterans Pkwy N 31788. Northern jct US 319 and 319 business route, just e. Int corridors. **Pets:** Accepted.
⛲ 🛜 🛗 🖥

NEWNAN

⚛ WWWW BEST WESTERN Shenandoah Inn M
(770) 304-9700. **$59-$129.** 620 Hwy 34 E 30265. I-85 exit 47, just w. Ext corridors. **Pets:** Medium. $10 daily fee/pet. Service with restrictions, supervision. SAVE ᴍ ⛲ 🛜 🛗 🖥

WW La Quinta Inn & Suites Atlanta South-Newnan H
(770) 502-8430. **$70-$150.** 600 Bullsboro Dr 30265. I-85 exit 47, 0.3 mi w. Int corridors. **Pets:** Large, other species. Service with restrictions.
ᴍ 🛜 🛗 🖥

NORCROSS

WW Comfort Inn & Suites H
(770) 263-8883. **$64-$95.** 5200 Peachtree Industrial Blvd 30071. I-285 exit 31B, 5.5 mi n; I-85 exit 99, 4 mi w to Peachtree Industrial Blvd, then 1.5 mi n. Int corridors. **Pets:** Accepted. ᴍ ⛲ 🛜 🛗 🖥

WW Hilton Atlanta Northeast H
(770) 447-4747. **$79-$249.** 5993 Peachtree Industrial Blvd 30092. I-285 exit 31B, 4.5 mi ne. Int corridors. **Pets:** Accepted.
🍽 ᴍ ⛲ 📶 ✕ 🛗 🖥

▼▼▼ Homewood Suites by Hilton 🅷

(770) 448-4663. **$79-$169.** 450 Technology Pkwy 30092. I-85 exit 99, 4 mi w to Peachtree Industrial Blvd, 0.4 mi n, w on Holcomb Bridge Rd, then 2 blks n on Peachtree Pkwy; I-285 exit 31B, 5 mi n on SR 141. Ext/int corridors. **Pets:** Accepted. 🖪 ⊿ 🖪 🖥

◈ ▼▼▼ Hyatt Place Atlanta/Norcross/Peachtree Parkway 🅷

(770) 416-7655. **$64-$169.** 5600 Peachtree Pkwy 30092. I-285 exit 31B, 4 mi n on SR 141, then 1 mi n. Int corridors. **Pets:** Accepted. 🆂🅰🆅🅴 🍴 🖪 ⊿ 🛜 ✕ 🖪 🖥

▼▼▼ La Quinta Inn Norcross 🅷

(770) 368-9400. **$69-$199.** 5945 Oakbrook Pkwy 30093. I-85 exit 99, 0.3 mi e to Live Oak Pkwy, then 0.8 mi nw. Int corridors. **Pets:** Large, other species. Service with restrictions. ⊿ 🛜 🖪 🖥

▼▼ TownePlace Suites by Marriott Atlanta Norcross/Peachtree Corners 🅷

(770) 447-8446. **$89-$139.** 6640 Bay Cir 30071. I-285 exit 31B, 3 mi n on Peachtree Industrial Blvd to Jones Mill Rd. Int corridors. **Pets:** Accepted. 🅴🅲🅾 🖪 ⊿ 🛜 ✕ 🖪 🖥

OAKWOOD

◈ ▼▼▼ BEST WESTERN PLUS Lake Lanier/Gainesville Hotel & Suites 🅷

(770) 535-8080. **$89-$280.** 4535 Oakwood Rd 30566. I-985 exit 16, just w. Int corridors. **Pets:** Accepted. 🆂🅰🆅🅴 ⊿ 🛜 ✕ 🖪 🖥

▼▼ Jameson Inn 🅼

(770) 533-9400. **Call for rates.** 3530 Thurman Tanner Pkwy 30566. I-985 exit 16, 0.4 mi w. Ext corridors. **Pets:** Accepted. 🖪 ⊿ 🛜 🖪 🖥

PEACHTREE CITY

▼▼ Days Inn & Suites Peachtree City 🅼

(770) 632-9700. **Call for rates.** 976 Crosstown Dr 30269. Jct SR 54 and 74, 2.1 mi s on SR 74. Ext corridors. **Pets:** Accepted. 🖪 ⊿ 🛜 🖪 🖥

◈ ▼▼▼ Wyndham Peachtree Hotel & Conference Center 🅷

(770) 487-2000. **$89-$248.** 2443 Hwy 54 W 30269. Jct SR 74 and 54, 1 mi e. Int corridors. **Pets:** Large. $100 one-time fee/pet. Designated rooms, service with restrictions, supervision. 🆂🅰🆅🅴 🍴 🖪 ⊿ ✕ 🛜 ✕ 🖪 🖥

PERRY

◈ ▼▼ Microtel Inn & Suites by Wyndham Perry 🅷

(478) 987-4004. **$45-$89.** 110 Fairview Dr 31069. I-75 exit 134, just nw. Int corridors. **Pets:** Accepted. 🆂🅰🆅🅴 🖪 ⊿ 🛜 ✕ 🖪 🖥

▼▼ Ramada Inn 🅼

(478) 987-3313. **$66-$110.** 200 Valley Dr 31069. I-75 exit 136 (Sam Nunn Blvd), just w, then s. Ext corridors. **Pets:** Accepted. 🍴 ⊿ 🛜 🖪 🖥

PINE MOUNTAIN

◈ ▼▼▼ Mountain Creek Inn at Callaway Gardens 🅼

(706) 663-2281. **$95-$305, 7 day notice.** 17800 Hwy 27 31822. Jct SR 354, 1.5 mi s on US 27/SR 1; in Callaway Gardens. Ext corridors. **Pets:** Medium, dogs only. $95 one-time fee/pet. Designated rooms, service with restrictions, crate.

🆂🅰🆅🅴 🍴 🖪 ⊿ ✕ 🛜 🖪 🖥

▼ White Columns Motel 🅼

(706) 663-2312. **$59-$80, 3 day notice.** 524 S Main Ave 31822. Jct SR 354, just n on US 27/SR 1. Ext corridors. **Pets:** Medium. $15 daily fee/pet. Designated rooms, service with restrictions, supervision. 🛜 🖪

POOLER

▼▼▼ La Quinta Inn & Suites Savannah Airport-Pooler 🅷

(912) 748-3771. **$85-$239.** 414 Gray St 31322. I-95 exit 102 (US 80), just w. Int corridors. **Pets:** Large, other species. Service with restrictions. ⊿ 🛜 ✕ 🖪 🖥

▼▼ Quality Inn 🅷

(912) 748-0017. **$74-$249.** 125 Bourne Ave 31322. I-95 exit 102 (US 80), just e. Int corridors. **Pets:** $20 one-time fee/pet. Designated rooms, service with restrictions, supervision. ⊿ 🛜 🖪 🖥

PORT WENTWORTH (Restaurants p. 630)

▼▼▼ Comfort Suites Savannah North 🅷

(912) 965-1445. **$74-$200.** 115 Travelers Way 31407. I-95 exit 109 (SR 21), just n. Int corridors. **Pets:** Accepted. 🖪 ⊿ 🛜 ✕ 🖪 🖥

▼▼▼ Hampton Inn Savannah North 🅷

(912) 966-2000. **$99-$149.** 7050 Hwy 21 31407. I-95 exit 109 (SR 21), just s. Int corridors. **Pets:** Accepted. 🖪 ⊿ 🛜 🖪 🖥

▼▼ Sleep Inn I-95 North Savannah 🅷

(912) 966-9800. **$45-$109.** 7206 Hwy 21 N 31407. I-95 exit 109 (SR 21), just n. Int corridors. **Pets:** Accepted. ⊿ 🛜 ✕ 🖪 🖥

RICHMOND HILL

◈ ▼▼▼ BEST WESTERN PLUS Richmond Hill Inn 🅷

(912) 756-7070. **$69-$139.** 4564 Hwy 17 31324. I-95 exit 87 (Ocean Hwy/US 17), just w. Int corridors. **Pets:** Accepted. 🆂🅰🆅🅴 ⊿ ✕ 🛜 🖪 🖥

◈ ▼▼ Econo Lodge-Richmond Hill 🅼

(912) 756-3312. **$52-$75.** 4701 US 17 31324. I-95 exit 87 (Ocean Hwy/US 17), 0.4 mi sw. Ext corridors. **Pets:** Accepted. 🆂🅰🆅🅴 🛜 🖪 🖥

RINGGOLD

◈ ▼▼ Hometown Inn 🅷

(706) 937-7070. **$69-$99.** 22 Gateway Business Park Dr 30736. I-75 exit 350, just e. Int corridors. **Pets:** Accepted. 🆂🅰🆅🅴 🖪 ⊿ 🛜 🖪 🖥

ROME

▼▼▼ La Quinta Inn & Suites 🅷

(706) 291-1034. **$87-$199.** 15 Chateau Dr 30161. 2 mi e on US 411. Int corridors. **Pets:** Large, other species. Service with restrictions. 🖪 ⊿ 🛜 ✕ 🖪 🖥

▼▼ Quality Inn 🅷

(706) 291-7797. **$75-$84.** 40 Grace Dr 30161. 2.2 mi e on US 411. Int corridors. **Pets:** Medium. $20 daily fee/pet. Service with restrictions, crate. 🖪 ⊿ 🛜 🖪 🖥

ST. SIMONS ISLAND (Restaurants p. 630)

◈ ▼▼▼▼ The Lodge at Sea Island 🅷

(912) 634-3992. **$395-$695, 7 day notice.** 100 Retreat Ave 31522. FJ Torras Cswy, 1.6 mi se on Kings Way, just s; on Sea Island Club golf course. Int corridors. **Pets:** Accepted. 🆂🅰🆅🅴 🍴 ✕ 🛜 ✕ 🖪 🖥

SANDERSVILLE

▼▼ Sandersville Inn 🅼

(478) 553-0393. **$69-$129.** 128 Commerce St 31082. On SR 15, jct SR 24/88, just s. Ext corridors. **Pets:** Accepted. 🖪 ⊿ 🛜 🖪 🖥

SAVANNAH (Restaurants p. 630)

◆◆ Baymont Inn & Suites H
(912) 925-9494. $69-$159. 393 Canebrake Rd 31419. I-95 exit 94 (SR 204/Abercorn St), just se. Int corridors. Pets: Medium. $20 daily fee/pet. Designated rooms, service with restrictions, supervision.

⬤M ⤳ 🛜 ✕ 🚹 💻

◆◆◆◆ BEST WESTERN PLUS Savannah Historic District M
(912) 233-1011. $69-$309. 412 W Bay St 31401. Jct Montgomery St. Ext corridors. Pets: Medium, dogs only. $50 deposit/room, $20 daily fee/room. Designated rooms, service with restrictions, crate.

SAVE ⤳ 🛜 ✕ 🚹 💻

◆◆◆ BEST WESTERN Savannah Gateway M
(912) 925-2420. $50-$179. 1 Gateway Blvd E 31419. I-95 exit 94 (SR 204/Abercorn St), just e. Ext corridors. Pets: Accepted.

SAVE �'❙' ⤳ 🛜 🚹 💻

◆◆◆◆ The Bohemian Hotel Savannah Riverfront, Autograph Collection® H
(912) 721-3800. $171-$539, 3 day notice. 102 W Bay St 31401. Between Bull and Whitaker sts. Int corridors. Pets: Accepted.

SAVE ❙❙ ⬤M 🛜 ✕ 💻

◆◆◆◆ Catherine Ward House Inn BB
(912) 234-8564. $179-$289, 3 day notice. 118 E Waldburg St 31401. Between Drayton and Abercorn sts. Ext/int corridors. Pets: Accepted.

🛜 ✕ 📵 🚹

◆◆◆ Comfort Inn & Suites Savannah Airport H
(912) 629-1500. $80-$200. 15 Jay R Turner Dr 31408. I-95 exit 104, 0.4 mi e. Int corridors. Pets: Medium, other species. $25 one-time fee/room. Service with restrictions. ⬤M ⤳ 🛜 ✕ 🚹 💻

◆◆◆ Comfort Suites Historic District H
(912) 629-2001. $99-$259. 630 W Bay St 31401. Between Fahm and W Boundary sts; on west side of historic district. Int corridors. Pets: Small, other species. $50 one-time fee/pet. Service with restrictions, crate. SAVE ⬤M ⤳ 🛜 ✕ 🚹 💻

◆◆◆ East Bay Inn CI
(912) 238-1225. $150-$400, 7 day notice. 225 E Bay St 31401. Between Abercorn and Lincoln sts. Int corridors. Pets: Accepted.

SAVE ❙❙ 🛜 ✕

◆◆ Extended Stay America Savannah-Midtown H
(912) 692-0076. $75-$105. 5511 Abercorn St 31405. Jct SR 21 and 204 (Abercorn St), just s. Int corridors. Pets: Other species. $25 daily fee/pet. Service with restrictions, supervision. 🛜 🚹 💻

◆◆◆◆ Foley House Inn BB 🐾
(912) 232-6622. $159, 3 day notice. 14 W Hull St 31401. Between Bull and Whitaker sts; on Chippewa Square. Ext/int corridors. Pets: Other species. $50 one-time fee/pet. Service with restrictions. SAVE 🛜 ✕

◆◆◆ The Forsyth Park Inn BB
(912) 233-6800. $185-$295, 14 day notice. 102 W Hall St 31401. Between Whitaker and Howard sts; across from Forsyth Park. Int corridors. Pets: Accepted. 🛜 ✕ 🚹

◆◆◆◆ Hamilton-Turner Inn BB
(912) 233-1833. $209-$424, 10 day notice. 330 Abercorn St 31401. Between E Charlton and E Harris sts; overlooking Lafayette Square. Ext/int corridors. Pets: Medium. $50 one-time fee/pet. Designated rooms, service with restrictions, supervision. SAVE 🛜 ✕

◆◆ La Quinta Inn & Suites H
(912) 927-7660. $65-$264. 8484 Abercorn St 31406. 2.4 mi s of jct SR 21 and 204 (Abercorn St). Int corridors. Pets: Large, other species. Service with restrictions. ⤳ 🛜 🚹 💻

◆◆◆◆ Mansion on Forsyth Park, Autograph Collection H
(912) 238-5158. $165-$519. 700 Drayton St 31401. Between E Hall and E Gwinnett sts; on Forsyth Park. Int corridors. Pets: Medium, dogs only. $150 one-time fee/room. Designated rooms, service with restrictions, supervision. SAVE ECO ⬤❙ ❙❙ ⬤M 🛜 ✕ 💻

◆◆◆ Oglethorpe Inn & Suites H 🐾
(912) 354-8560. $79-$250, 3 day notice. 7110 Hodgson Memorial Dr 31406. Jct SR 21 and 204 (Abercorn St), 1.3 mi s, just e on Eisenhower Dr, then just s. Int corridors. Pets: Medium. $35 one-time fee/room. Designated rooms, service with restrictions, supervision.

SAVE ⤳ 🛜 ✕ 🚹 💻

◆◆◆ Olde Harbour Inn BB
(912) 234-4100. $159-$450, 7 day notice. 508 E Factors Walk 31401. Lincoln St ramp off E Bay St. Ext corridors. Pets: Accepted.

SAVE 🛜 ✕ 🚹 💻

◆◆◆ Quality Inn Heart of Savannah M
(912) 236-6321. $109-$299. 300 W Bay St 31401. Between N Montgomery and N Jefferson sts. Ext corridors. Pets: Accepted.

SAVE 🛜 ✕ 🚹 💻

◆◆◆ Residence Inn by Marriott Downtown/Historic District H 🐾
(912) 233-9996. $142-$237. 500 W Charlton St 31401. Jct Martin Luther King Jr Blvd. Int corridors. Pets: Other species. $100 one-time fee/room. Service with restrictions. ⬤M ⤳ 🛜 ✕ 🚹 💻

◆◆◆ Residence Inn by Marriott Savannah Midtown H
(912) 356-3266. $152-$237. 5710 White Bluff Rd 31405. Jct SR 21, 0.5 mi s. Int corridors. Pets: Accepted. ⤳ ✕ 🛜 ✕ 🚹 💻

◆◆◆ Staybridge Suites Savannah Historic District H
(912) 721-9000. $149-$319. 301 E Bay St 31401. Corner of Lincoln St. Int corridors. Pets: Accepted. SAVE ⬤M 🛜 ✕ 🚹 💻

◆◆ Super 8 Gateway H
(912) 925-6996. $60-$135. 387 Canebrake Rd 31419. I-95 exit 94 (SR 204/Abercorn St), just e, then s. Int corridors. Pets: Medium. $10 daily fee/pet. Designated rooms, service with restrictions, supervision.

⬤M 🛜 ✕ 🚹 💻

◆◆◆ TownePlace Suites by Marriott Savannah Airport H
(912) 629-7775. $124-$179. 4 Jay R Turner Dr 31408. I-95 exit 104, just e. Int corridors. Pets: Accepted. ⬤M 🛜 ✕ 🚹 💻

◆◆ TownePlace Suites by Marriott Savannah Midtown H
(912) 920-9080. $95-$190. 11309 Abercorn St 31419. Jct SR 21 and 204 (Abercorn St), 4.6 mi s. Int corridors. Pets: Accepted.

⤳ 🛜 ✕ 🚹 💻

◆◆ Travelodge Savannah Gateway H
(912) 921-1940. $35-$73. 17009 Abercorn St 31419. I-95 exit 94 (SR 204/Abercorn St), just e. Int corridors. Pets: Accepted.

⤳ 🛜 ✕ 🚹 💻

◆◆◆◆ The Westin Savannah Harbor Golf Resort and Spa H
(912) 201-2000. $159-$449, 3 day notice. 1 Resort Dr 31421. On Hutchinson Island; 1 mi se of first exit after Eugene Talmadge Memorial Bridge and US 17. Int corridors. Pets: Accepted.

SAVE ECO ❙❙ ⬤M ⤳ ✕ 🛜 ✕ 🚹 💻

▼▼▼▼ Wingate by Wyndham Savannah Airport **H**
(912) 544-1180. **$69-$259.** 50 Sylvester C Formey Dr 31408. I-95 exit 104, just se to Crossroads Pkwy, sw to Stephen S Green Dr, then just se. Int corridors. **Pets:** Other species. $35 one-time fee/room. Designated rooms, service with restrictions, crate.

SMYRNA
▼▼▼ Baymont Inn & Suites **H**
(404) 794-1600. **$69-$89.** 5130 S Cobb Dr 30082. I-285 exit 15, 0.3 mi w. Int corridors. **Pets:** Medium. $25 deposit/pet, $25 daily fee/pet. Designated rooms, service with restrictions, supervision.

▼▼▼ Extended Stay America-Atlanta-Cumberland Mall **M**
(770) 432-4000. **$48-$89.** 3103 Sports Ave 30080. I-285 exit 20 westbound; exit 19 eastbound, just n to Spring Rd, then 0.3 mi w. Ext corridors. **Pets:** Other species. $25 daily fee/pet. Service with restrictions, supervision.

▲▲▲ **▼▼▼▼** Hyatt Place Atlanta/Cobb Galleria **H**
(770) 384-0060. **$84-$179.** 2876 Spring Hill Pkwy 30080. I-285 exit 20 westbound; exit 19 eastbound, just n to Spring Rd, then just w. Int corridors. **Pets:** Accepted.

▲▲▲ **▼▼▼** Red Roof Inn-Atlanta Smyrna **M**
(770) 952-6966. **$44-$80.** 2200 Corporate Plaza 30080. I-75 exit 260, just w to Corporate Plaza, then just s. Ext corridors. **Pets:** Large, other species. Service with restrictions, supervision.

▲▲▲ **▼▼▼▼** Residence Inn by Marriott-Atlanta Cumberland **H**
(770) 433-8877. **$79-$299.** 2771 Cumberland Blvd 30080. I-285 exit 20 westbound; exit 19 eastbound, just n to Spring Rd, 0.3 mi w to Cumberland Blvd, then just n. Ext corridors. **Pets:** Accepted.

SNELLVILLE
▲▲▲ **▼▼▼** La Quinta Inn & Suites Snellville-Stone Mountain **H**
(770) 736-4723. **$84-$199.** 2971 Main St W 30078. Jct US 78 and SR 124, 0.9 mi w. Int corridors. **Pets:** Large, other species. Service with restrictions.

STOCKBRIDGE
▲▲▲ **▼▼▼▼** La Quinta Inn & Suites Atlanta Stockbridge **H**
(770) 506-9991. **$85-$254.** 3581 Cameron Pkwy 30281. I-75 exit 228, just e; I-675 exit 1, just w. Int corridors. **Pets:** Large, other species. Service with restrictions.

▼▼▼▼ Microtel Inn & Suites by Wyndham Stockbridge/Atlanta South/At Eagles Landing **H**
(678) 782-6100. **$70-$110, 3 day notice.** 195 Country Club Dr 30281. I-75 exit 224, just e, then just s. Int corridors. **Pets:** Accepted.

▼▼▼▼ Red Roof Inn Atlanta/Southeast **H**
(678) 782-4100. **$57-$127.** 637 Hwy 138 30281. I-75 exit 228, just e; I-675 exit 1, just w. Int corridors. **Pets:** Large, other species. Service with restrictions, supervision.

▼▼ Sleep Inn & Suites **H**
(770) 474-3870. **$59-$79.** 7423 Davidson Cir W 30281. I-675 exit 1, just e, then just s; I-75 exit 228, 1 mi e, then just s. Int corridors. **Pets:** Accepted.

STONE MOUNTAIN
▲▲▲ **▼▼▼** Quality Inn Stone Mountain **M**
(770) 465-1022. **Call for rates.** 1595 E Park Place Blvd 30087. US 78 exit 9, 0.7 mi n. Ext corridors. **Pets:** Accepted.

SUWANEE
▲▲▲ **▼▼▼** Quality Inn **M**
(770) 945-1608. **$60-$80.** 2945 Lawrenceville Suwanee Rd 30024. I-85 exit 111, just e. Ext corridors. **Pets:** Accepted.

THOMASTON
▼▼ Quality Inn **M**
(706) 648-2232. **$69-$74.** 1010 Hwy 19 N 30286. Jct SR 74, 2.3 mi n. Ext corridors. **Pets:** Accepted.

THOMASVILLE *(Restaurants p. 631)*
▼▼ Quality Inn & Suites Conference Center **M**
(229) 225-2134. **$60-$120.** 15138 US Hwy 19 S 31757. On US 319, 0.3 mi s. Ext corridors. **Pets:** Medium. $10 daily fee/room. Designated rooms, service with restrictions, supervision.

THOMSON
▼▼ White Columns Inn **M**
(706) 595-8000. **$62-$68.** 1890 Washington Rd 30824. I-20 exit 172 (US 78), just s. Ext corridors. **Pets:** $10 daily fee/pet. Designated rooms, no service, crate.

TIFTON *(Restaurants p. 631)*
▼▼▼ Country Inn & Suites By Carlson **H**
(229) 382-8100. **Call for rates.** 310 S Virginia Ave 31794. I-75 exit 62, just e on US 82 and 319. Int corridors. **Pets:** Accepted.

▼▼ Days Inn & Suites **H**
(229) 382-8505. **$57-$173.** 1199 Hwy 82 W 31793. I-75 exit 62, just w. Int corridors. **Pets:** Accepted.

▼▼ Microtel Inn & Suites by Wyndham Tifton **H**
(229) 387-0112. **$51-$139.** 196 S Virginia Ave 31794. I-75 exit 62, just n. Int corridors. **Pets:** Accepted.

TUCKER
▲▲▲ **▼▼▼▼** DoubleTree by Hilton Hotel Atlanta-Northlake **H**
(770) 938-1026. **$99-$129.** 4156 Lavista Rd 30084. I-285 exit 37, just w. Int corridors. **Pets:** Accepted.

▲▲▲ **▼▼** Quality Inn Atlanta/Northlake **M**
(770) 491-7444. **$68-$84.** 2155 Ranchwood Dr 30345. I-285 exit 37, 0.4 mi w, then just n. Ext/int corridors. **Pets:** Accepted.

▼▼ TownePlace Suites by Marriott Atlanta Northlake **H**
(770) 938-0408. **$89-$139.** 3300 Northlake Pkwy 30345. I-285 exit 36 southbound, just w; exit 37 northbound, just w to Parklake Dr, 0.5 mi n, then just w. Int corridors. **Pets:** Other species. $100 one-time fee/room. Service with restrictions, crate.

UNION CITY
▼▼ Magnuson Hotel Atlanta South **M**
(770) 306-6067. **$50-$125.** 6840 Shannon Pkwy S 30291. I-85 exit 64, 0.3 mi w to Shannon Pkwy, then just s. Ext corridors. **Pets:** Accepted.

VALDOSTA *(Restaurants p. 631)*
▲▲▲ **▼▼▼▼** BEST WESTERN PLUS Valdosta Hotel & Suites **H** 🐾
(229) 241-9221. **$90-$150.** 4025 Northlake Dr 31602. I-75 exit 22, just e on N Valdosta Rd, then just n. Int corridors. **Pets:** $20 daily fee/room. Designated rooms, service with restrictions, crate.

WV WV **Clarion Inn Conference Center** H

(229) 242-1212. **$70-$102.** 2101 W Hill Ave 31601. I-75 exit 16, just w. Ext/int corridors. **Pets:** Accepted. 🍴 🐾 📶 🛗 💻

AAA WV WV **Econo Lodge** H

(229) 671-1511. **$50-$90.** 3022 James Rd 31602. I-75 exit 18, just w. Int corridors. **Pets:** Medium, other species. $15 daily fee/pet. Designated rooms, service with restrictions, crate.

SAVE 👤M 🐾 📶 🛗 💻

WV WV **Howard Johnson Valdosta** H

(229) 244-4460. **$50-$60.** 4598 N Valdosta Rd 31602. I-75 exit 22, just w. Ext corridors. **Pets:** Accepted. 🐾 📶 🛗 💻

WV WV **Quality Inn South** H

(229) 244-4520. **$59-$75.** 1902 W Hill Ave 31601. I-75 exit 16, just e on US 84. Ext corridors. **Pets:** Accepted. 🍴 🐾 📶 🛗 💻

VILLA RICA

WV WV **Days Inn** H

(770) 459-8888. **$53-$100.** 195 Hwy 61 Connector 30180. I-20 exit 24, just n. Int corridors. **Pets:** Medium. $10 daily fee/pet. Designated rooms, service with restrictions, supervision. 👤M 🐾 📶 🛗 💻

WV WV **Econo Lodge-Villa Rica Inn** M

(770) 459-6669. **$57-$120.** 124 Hwy 61 Connector 30180. I-20 exit 24, just n. Ext corridors. **Pets:** Accepted. 👤M 🐾 📶 🛗 💻

WV WV **Super 8** M

(770) 459-8000. **$55-$99, 3 day notice.** 128 Hwy 61 Connector 30180. I-20 exit 24, just n. Ext corridors. **Pets:** Accepted. 🐾 📶 🛗 💻

WARNER ROBINS

WV WV **Baymont Inn & Suites Warner Robins** H

(478) 953-5522. **$59-$79.** 2731 Watson Blvd 31093. I-75 exit 146 (SR 247C), 4.1 mi e. Ext corridors. **Pets:** Accepted. 🐾 📶 🛗 💻

AAA WV WV **BEST WESTERN Peach Inn** H

(478) 953-3800. **$59-$69.** 2739 Watson Blvd 31093. I-75 exit 146 (SR 247C), 4.1 mi e. Ext corridors. **Pets:** Other species. $10 daily fee/pet. Designated rooms, service with restrictions. SAVE 🐾 📶 🛗 💻

WV WV **Comfort Inn & Suites** H

(478) 922-7555. **$85-$99.** 95 Georgia Hwy 247 S 31088. Jct SR 247C and US 129/SR 247, 1.6 mi s on US 129/SR 247. Ext/int corridors. **Pets:** Medium. $15 daily fee/room. Service with restrictions, crate.

🐾 📶 ✖ 🛗 💻

WAYCROSS

WV WV **Baymont Inn & Suites Waycross** M

(912) 283-3800. **$59-$79.** 950 S City Blvd 31501. Between US 1 and 82; e of city. Ext corridors. **Pets:** Accepted. 👤M 🐾 📶 🛗 💻

WV WV WV **Comfort Suites** H

(912) 548-0555. **$79-$109.** 1922 Memorial Dr 31501. Between US 1 and 82. Int corridors. **Pets:** Accepted. 🐾 📶 ✖ 🛗 💻

WV WV WV **Holiday Inn Express & Suites** H

(912) 548-0720. **$95-$118.** 1761 Memorial Dr 31501. Between US 1 and 82. Int corridors. **Pets:** Accepted. 🐾 ✖ 📶 ✖ 🛗 💻

WV WV **Motel 6** M

(912) 283-3300. **Call for rates.** 1903 Memorial Dr 31501. Between US 1 and 82; at S City Blvd. Ext corridors. **Pets:** Other species. Service with restrictions, crate. 🐾 📶 🛗 💻

WAYNESBORO

WV WV **Quality Inn** M

(706) 437-0500. **$90-$100.** 1436 N Liberty St 30830. 0.9 mi n of downtown center on US 25. Ext corridors. **Pets:** Accepted.

🐾 📶 🛗 💻

WINDER

AAA WV WV **BEST WESTERN Winder Hotel** H

(770) 868-5303. **$85-$150.** 177 W Athens St 30680. Jct Broad St, 0.8 mi n; downtown. Int corridors. **Pets:** Accepted.

SAVE 🐾 📶 🛗 💻

YOUNG HARRIS

WV WV WV **Brasstown Valley Resort** H

(706) 379-9900. **$129-$299, 7 day notice.** 6321 US Hwy 76 30582. US 76 and US 76/SR 515. Int corridors. **Pets:** Accepted.

ECO 🍴 🐾 ✖ 📶 ✖ 🛗 💻

HAWAII

HONOLULU

AAA WV WV **Airport Honolulu Hotel** H 🐾

(808) 836-0661. **$109-$189, 3 day notice.** 3401 N Nimitz Hwy 96819. Jct Rodgers Blvd. Int corridors. **Pets:** Dogs only. $30 daily fee/room. Designated rooms, service with restrictions, crate.

SAVE 🍴 👤M 🐾 📶 ✖ 🛗 💻

AAA WV WV **Aqua Waikiki Wave Hotel** H 🐾

(808) 922-1262. **$99-$299, 3 day notice.** 2299 Kuhio Ave 96815. Just s of Seaside Ave. Int corridors. **Pets:** Medium. $35 daily fee/room. Designated rooms, service with restrictions, crate.

SAVE 🍴 👤M 📶 ✖ 🛗 💻

AAA WV WV **BEST WESTERN The Plaza Hotel** H 🐾

(808) 836-3636. **$169-$209.** 3253 N Nimitz Hwy 96819. Just e of jct Paiea St. Ext/int corridors. **Pets:** Other species. $30 daily fee/room. Designated rooms, service with restrictions, crate.

SAVE ECO 🍴 👤M 🐾 📶 ✖ 🛗 💻

AAA WV WV WV **Courtyard by Marriott Waikiki Beach** H

(808) 954-4000. **$119-$399, 3 day notice.** 400 Royal Hawaiian Ave 96815. Jct Kuhio Ave. Ext/int corridors. **Pets:** Accepted.

SAVE 🍴 👤M 🐾 ✖ 📶 ✖ 🛗 💻

AAA WV WV WV **Hotel Renew by Aston** H

(808) 687-7700. **$229-$359, 3 day notice.** 129 Paoakalani Ave 96815. Between Kalakaua Ave and Lemon Rd. Int corridors. **Pets:** Accepted.

SAVE 👤M 📶 ✖ 🛗 💻

AAA WV WV WV **Hyatt Place Waikiki Beach** H

(808) 922-3861. **$139-$449.** 175 Paoakalani Ave 96815. Jct Kuhio Ave. Int corridors. **Pets:** Medium. $75 one-time fee/room. Service with restrictions, crate. SAVE 🍴 👤M 🐾 📶 ✖ 🛗 💻

AAA WV WV WV **Hyatt Regency Waikiki Beach Resort & Spa** H

(808) 923-1234. **$180-$510, 3 day notice.** 2424 Kalakaua Ave 96815. Between Kaiulani Ave and Uluniu St; entrance on Uluniu St. Int corridors. **Pets:** Accepted.

SAVE ECO 🍴 👤M 🐾 ✖ 🛁 ✖ 🛗 💻

AAA WV WV WV WV **The Kahala Hotel & Resort** H 🐾

(808) 739-8888. **$395-$595, 3 day notice.** 5000 Kahala Ave 96816. E of Diamond Head at end of Kahala Ave. Int corridors. **Pets:** Medium, dogs only. $150 one-time fee/room. Service with restrictions, supervision. SAVE ECO 🍴 👤M 🐾 ✖ 📶 🛗 💻

WV WV WV **Lotus Honolulu** H

(808) 922-1700. **$319-$409, 3 day notice.** 2885 Kalakaua Ave 96815. East end of Kapiolani Park. Ext corridors. **Pets:** Accepted.

🍴 👤M 📶 ✖ 🛗 💻

⚫ ▼▼ ▼▼ The Modern Honolulu 🅷 ✿
(808) 943-5800. **$299-$899, 3 day notice.** 1775 Ala Moana Blvd 96815. Jct Hobron Ln. Int corridors. **Pets:** Small, dogs only. $50 daily fee/room. Service with restrictions, supervision.

[SAVE] 🍴 ⚙M ⤵ 🛜 ✕ 📶

▼▼ ▼▼ Trump International Hotel Waikiki Beach Walk ▼
(808) 683-7777. **$489-$775, 3 day notice.** 223 Saratoga Rd 96815. Just sw on Kalakaua Ave via Saratoga Rd. Int corridors.
Pets: Accepted. 🍴 ⚙M ⤵ ✕ 🛜 📶 🖥

KĀ'ANAPALI

⚫ ▼▼ ▼▼ Hyatt Regency Maui Resort & Spa 🅷
(808) 661-1234. **$259-$599, 3 day notice.** 200 Nohea Kai Dr 96761. SR 30 exit Kaanapali Pkwy, just w, then just s; in Kaanapali Beach resort area. Ext/int corridors. **Pets:** Accepted.

[SAVE] [ECO] 📶 🍴 ⚙M ⤵ ✕ 🛜 ✕ 📶 🖥

⚫ ▼▼ ▼▼ Sheraton Maui Resort & Spa 🅷
(808) 661-0031. **$279-$639, 3 day notice.** 2605 Kaanapali Pkwy 96761. SR 30 exit Kaanapali Pkwy, just nw; in Kaanapali Beach resort area. Ext/int corridors. **Pets:** Accepted.

[SAVE] 📶 🍴 ⚙M ⤵ ✕ 🛜 ✕ 📶 🖥

KAHUKU

▼▼▼ Turtle Bay Resort 🅷
(808) 293-6000. **$279-$1499, 14 day notice.** 57-091 Kamehameha Hwy 96731. 3 mi nw off SR 83. Ext/int corridors. **Pets:** Small, dogs only. $300 deposit/room. Designated rooms, service with restrictions, crate.

[ECO] 📶 🍴 ⚙M ⤵ ✕ 🛜 ✕ 📶 🖥

KAPALUA

⚫ ▼▼▼▼ The Ritz-Carlton, Kapalua 🅷
(808) 669-6200. **$559-$919, 21 day notice.** One Ritz-Carlton Dr 96761. SR 30 exit Office Rd; in Kapalua resort area; on northwest shore. Int corridors. **Pets:** Accepted.

[SAVE] [ECO] 📶 🍴 ⚙M ⤵ ✕ 🛜 ✕ 📶 🖥

KAUPULEHU

⚫ ▼▼▼▼ Four Seasons Resort Hualalai at Historic Ka'upulehu 🅷 ✿
(808) 325-8000. **$695-$1645, 21 day notice.** 72-100 Ka'upulehu Dr 96740. 6 mi n of Kona International Airport on SR 19, 1.3 mi sw. Ext corridors. **Pets:** Other species.

[SAVE] 📶 🍴 ⚙M ⤵ ✕ 🛜 ✕ 📶 🖥

KEAUHOU

⚫ ▼▼ Sheraton Kona Resort & Spa at Keauhou Bay 🅷
(808) 930-4900. **$135-$379, 3 day notice.** 78-128 Ehukai St 96740. SR 11, 1.4 mi sw (toward ocean) on Kamehameha III Rd, 0.7 mi s on Alii Dr, then just w on Kaleiopapa St, watch for Keauhou Bay sign. Ext/int corridors. **Pets:** Accepted. [SAVE] 🍴 ⚙M ✕ 🛜 ✕ 📶 🖥

KOHALA COAST

⚫ ▼▼ ▼▼ The Fairmont Orchid, Hawaii 🅷
(808) 885-2000. **$400-$3900, 14 day notice.** One N Kaniku Dr 96743. 19 mi n of Kona International Airport on SR 19, 1 mi w on Mauna Lani Dr, then 1 mi n; in Mauna Lani resort area. Int corridors.
Pets: Accepted.

[SAVE] [ECO] 📶 🍴 ⚙M ⤵ ✕ 🛜 ✕ 📶 🖥

LĀNA'I CITY

⚫ ▼▼ ▼▼ Four Seasons Resort Lana'i at Manele Bay 🅷
(808) 565-2000. **$750-$5500, 21 day notice.** 1 Manele Bay Rd 96763. From airport, 4 mi e on Kaumalapau Hwy to Lana'i City, 7 mi s on SR 440. Ext corridors. **Pets:** Accepted.

[SAVE] 🍴 ⚙M ⤵ ✕ 🛜 ✕ 📶 🖥

PO'IPŪ

⚫ ▼▼▼ Sheraton Kauai Resort 🅷
(808) 742-1661. **$199-$509, 3 day notice.** 2440 Hoonani Rd 96756. 1.8 mi se of Koloa on Poipu Rd, just se; in Poipu Beach area. Ext corridors. **Pets:** Accepted.

[SAVE] [ECO] 📶 🍴 ⤵ ✕ 🛜 ✕ 📶 🖥

WAILEA

⚫ ▼▼ ▼▼ The Fairmont Kea Lani, Maui 🅷
(808) 875-4100. **$549-$6000, 21 day notice.** 4100 Wailea Alanui Dr 96753. From end of SR 31, 0.7 mi s. Ext corridors. **Pets:** Small, dogs only. $25 daily fee/room. Service with restrictions, supervision.

[SAVE] [ECO] 🍴 ⚙M ⤵ ✕ 🛜 ✕ 📶 🖥

⚫ ▼▼ ▼▼ Four Seasons Resort Maui at Wailea 🅷 ✿
(808) 874-8000. **$489-$899, 21 day notice.** 3900 Wailea Alanui Dr 96753. From end of SR 31, 0.5 mi s. Int corridors. **Pets:** Very small, other species. Service with restrictions.

[SAVE] 📶 🍴 ⚙M ⤵ ✕ 🛜 📶 🖥

IDAHO

AHSAHKA

⚫ ▼▼▼ High Country Inn Orofino/Ahsahka 🅱🅱
(208) 476-7570. **$99-$450, 7 day notice.** 70 High Country Ln 83520. 0.5 mi w to Dworshak Visitors Center Rd, 2 mi n, then 1 mi w, follow signs. Ext/int corridors. **Pets:** $25 one-time fee/pet. Service with restrictions, crate. [SAVE] 🔗 ✕ 🆆 🅉 📶 🖥

ATHOL

⚫ ▼▼▼ Log Spirit Bed & Breakfast 🅱🅱
(208) 683-4722. **$140-$200, 14 day notice.** 31328 N Tiara Ln 83801. US 95, just e on SR 54 to Howard Rd, 1.8 mi n, then 0.5 mi e. Int corridors. **Pets:** $25 daily fee/pet. Supervision.

[SAVE] ⚙M 🛜 ✕ 🅇 🆆 🅉 📶

BLACKFOOT

⚫ ▼▼ BEST WESTERN Blackfoot Inn 🅷 ✿
(208) 785-4144. **$80-$130.** 750 Jensen Grove Dr 83221. I-15 exit 93, 0.3 mi e to Parkway Dr, then 0.4 mi n. Int corridors. **Pets:** Dogs only. Designated rooms, service with restrictions, supervision.

[SAVE] ⤵ 🛜 📶 🖥

▼ Super 8 🅷
(208) 785-9333. **$51-$79.** 1279 Parkway Dr 83221. I-15 exit 93, just se, then just w. Int corridors. **Pets:** Accepted. 🛜 📶 🖥

BOISE

⚫ ▼▼ BEST WESTERN Airport Inn Ⓜ
(208) 384-5000. **$80-$150.** 2660 Airport Way 83705. I-84 exit 53 (Vista Ave), just se. Ext corridors. **Pets:** Medium, dogs only. $10 daily fee/pet. Service with restrictions, supervision. [SAVE] ⤵ 🛜 📶 🖥

⚫ ▼▼ BEST WESTERN Northwest Lodge 🅷
(208) 287-2300. **$82-$150.** 6989 Federal Way 83716. I-84 exit 57 (Gowen Rd/Idaho City), just e, then just s. Int corridors. **Pets:** $20 daily fee/room. Service with restrictions, supervision.

[SAVE] ⚙M ⤵ 🛜 ✕ 📶 🖥

⚫ ▼▼ ▼▼ BEST WESTERN Vista Inn at the Airport 🅷
(208) 336-8100. **$89-$109, 3 day notice.** 2645 Airport Way 83705. I-84 exit 53 (Vista Ave), just s. Ext/int corridors. **Pets:** Medium, dogs only. $20 daily fee/room. Designated rooms, service with restrictions, crate.

[SAVE] ⚙M ⤵ 🛜 📶 🖥

▼▼▼ **Candlewood Suites-Boise Towne Square** ⛫

(208) 322-4300. **Call for rates.** 700 N Cole Rd 83704. I-84 exit 50A westbound; exit 50B eastbound, 2 mi n on Cole Rd, then just w. Int corridors. **Pets:** Accepted. 〔&M〕 〔🛜〕 〔✕〕 〔📋〕 〔💻〕

▼▼ **Fairfield Inn by Marriott - Airport** ⛫

(208) 331-5656. **$70-$179.** 3300 S Shoshone St 83705. I-84 exit 53 (Vista Ave), just n to Elder St, then just w. Int corridors. **Pets:** Accepted. 〔&M〕 〔≈〕 〔🛜〕 〔✕〕 〔📋〕 〔💻〕

▼▼▼ **Hampton Inn - Airport** ⛫

(208) 331-5600. **$99-$159.** 3270 S Shoshone St 83705. I-84 exit 53 (Vista Ave), just n to Elder St, then just w. Int corridors. **Pets:** Accepted. 〔&M〕 〔≈〕 〔🛜〕 〔📋〕 〔💻〕

▼▼▼ **Holiday Inn Boise - Airport** ⛫

(208) 344-7444. **Call for rates.** 2970 W Elder St 83705. I-84 exit 53 (Vista Ave), just n to Elder St, then just w. Int corridors. **Pets:** Accepted. 〔�11〕 〔&M〕 〔≈〕 〔🛜〕 〔✕〕 〔📋〕 〔💻〕

▼▼▼ **Holiday Inn Express - Downtown/Parkcenter** ⛫

(208) 345-2002. **Call for rates.** 475 W Parkcenter Blvd 83706. I-84 exit 54 (Broadway Ave), 2.3 mi n to Beacon St, then 0.3 mi e. Int corridors. **Pets:** Accepted. 〔&M〕 〔≈〕 〔✕〕 〔🛜〕 〔✕〕 〔📋〕 〔💻〕

⬥⬥⬥ ▼▼▼▼ **Hyatt Place-Boise Towne Square** ⛫

(208) 375-1200. **$79-$219.** 925 N Milwaukee St 83704. I-84 exit 49 (Franklin St), just w, then 0.5 mi n. Int corridors. **Pets:** Accepted. 〔SAVE〕 〔�11〕 〔&M〕 〔≈〕 〔🛜〕 〔✕〕 〔📋〕 〔💻〕

⬥⬥⬥ ▼▼ **Inn America - Airport** ⛫

(208) 389-9800. **$49-$76.** 2275 Airport Way 83705. I-84 exit 53 (Vista Ave), 0.3 mi se. Int corridors. **Pets:** Dogs only. $20 daily fee/room. Designated rooms, service with restrictions. 〔SAVE〕 〔≈〕 〔🛜〕 〔📋〕 〔💻〕

▼▼ **La Quinta Inn & Suites Boise Airport** ⛫

(208) 388-0800. **$79-$249.** 2613 S Vista Ave 83705. I-84 exit 53 (Vista Ave), 0.6 mi n. Int corridors. **Pets:** Large, other species. Service with restrictions. 〔&M〕 〔≈〕 〔🛜〕 〔✕〕 〔📋〕 〔💻〕

▼▼▼ **La Quinta Inn & Suites Boise Towne Square** ⛫

(208) 378-7000. **$85-$219.** 7965 W Emerald St 83704. I-84 exit 49 (Franklin St), just w, 0.5 mi n on Milwaukee St to Emerald St, then just e. Int corridors. **Pets:** Large, other species. Service with restrictions. 〔&M〕 〔≈〕 〔🛜〕 〔✕〕 〔📋〕 〔💻〕

▼▼ **Modern Hotel & Bar** Ⓜ

(208) 424-8244. **$104-$114.** 1314 W Grove St 83702. At 13th and W Grove sts; downtown. Ext/int corridors. **Pets:** Accepted. 〔�11〕 〔🛜〕 〔✕〕 〔📋〕 〔💻〕

⬥⬥⬥ ▼▼▼▼ **Oxford Suites Boise** ⛫

(208) 322-8000. **$105-$189, 3 day notice.** 1426 S Entertainment Ave 83709. I-84 exit 50A, just s to Spectrum Way, just w, then just n. Int corridors. **Pets:** Accepted. 〔SAVE〕 〔≈〕 〔✕〕 〔🛜〕 〔✕〕 〔📋〕 〔💻〕

▼▼▼ **Red Lion Hotel Boise Downtowner** ⛫

(208) 344-7691. **$79-$259.** 1800 Fairview Ave 83702. I-184 exit 3 (Fairview Ave), 1 mi n. Int corridors. **Pets:** Accepted. 〔�11〕 〔&M〕 〔≈〕 〔✕〕 〔🛜〕 〔✕〕 〔📋〕 〔💻〕

▼▼▼ **Residence Inn by Marriott Boise Downtown** ⛫

(208) 344-1200. **$139-$159.** 1401 S Lusk Ave 83706. I-84 exit 53 (Vista Ave), 2.4 mi n, just w on Ann Morrison Park Dr, then just s on Lois Ave. Ext corridors. **Pets:** Accepted. 〔≈〕 〔🛜〕 〔✕〕 〔📋〕 〔💻〕

▼▼▼ **Residence Inn by Marriott Boise West** ⛫

(208) 385-9000. **$169-$189.** 7303 W Denton St 83704. I-84 exit 50A westbound; exit 50B eastbound, 2 mi n on Cole Rd, then just w. Int corridors. **Pets:** Accepted. 〔&M〕 〔≈〕 〔🛜〕 〔✕〕 〔📋〕 〔💻〕

▼▼▼ **The Riverside Hotel** ⛫ 🐾

(208) 343-1871. **$119-$159.** 2900 W Chinden Blvd 83714. I-84 exit 49 (Franklin Rd), 2.7 mi ne on I-184 exit 3 (Fairview Ave), just n, then just w. Int corridors. **Pets:** Medium. $25 one-time fee/room. Designated rooms, service with restrictions, supervision.

〔ECO〕 〔�11〕 〔&M〕 〔≈〕 〔✕〕 〔🛜〕 〔📋〕 〔💻〕

▼▼ **Safari Inn Downtown** ⛫

(208) 344-6556. **$79-$119, 3 day notice.** 1070 Grove St 83702. Corner of 11th and Grove sts. Int corridors. **Pets:** $10 one-time fee/room. Designated rooms, service with restrictions, supervision.

〔&M〕 〔≈〕 〔✕〕 〔🛜〕 〔✕〕 〔📋〕 〔💻〕

▼▼▼ **SpringHill Suites by Marriott - Boise/Eagle** ⛫

(208) 939-8266. **$139-$159.** 6325 N Cloverdale Rd 83713. I-84 exit 46 (Eagle Rd), 4.5 mi n to Chinden Blvd, 1 mi e, then just s. Int corridors. **Pets:** Accepted. 〔&M〕 〔≈〕 〔🛜〕 〔✕〕 〔📋〕 〔💻〕

▼▼▼ **SpringHill Suites by Marriott - Boise/Parkcenter** ⛫

(208) 342-1044. **$89-$179.** 424 E Parkcenter Blvd 83706. I-84 exit 54 (Broadway Ave), 2.3 mi n to Beacon St, 0.3 mi e, then 0.7 mi se. Int corridors. **Pets:** Accepted. 〔&M〕 〔≈〕 〔🛜〕 〔✕〕 〔📋〕 〔💻〕

⬥⬥⬥ ▼▼▼ **TownePlace Suites by Marriott - Downtown** ⛫

(208) 429-8881. **$89-$199.** 1455 S Capitol Blvd 83706. I-84 exit 53 (Vista Ave), 2.4 mi n. Int corridors. **Pets:** Accepted. 〔SAVE〕 〔&M〕 〔≈〕 〔🛜〕 〔✕〕 〔📋〕 〔💻〕

BONNERS FERRY

⬥⬥⬥ ▼▼▼▼ **BEST WESTERN PLUS Kootenai River Inn Casino & Spa** ⛫

(208) 267-8511. **$109-$184.** 7169 Plaza St 83805. On US 95; City Center. Int corridors. **Pets:** Medium. $20 daily fee/pet. Service with restrictions, supervision. 〔SAVE〕 〔�11〕 〔≈〕 〔✕〕 〔🛜〕 〔✕〕 〔📋〕 〔💻〕

BURLEY

⬥⬥⬥ ▼▼▼▼ **BEST WESTERN PLUS Burley Inn & Convention Center** ⛫

(208) 678-3501. **$85-$98.** 800 N Overland Ave 83318. I-84 exit 208, just s. Ext/int corridors. **Pets:** Accepted. 〔SAVE〕 〔�11〕 〔&M〕 〔≈〕 〔🛜〕 〔📋〕 〔💻〕

⬥⬥⬥ ▼▼ **Super 8 Burley** ⛫

(208) 678-7000. **$75-$116.** 336 S 600 W 83318. I-84 exit 208, just n. Int corridors. **Pets:** Accepted. 〔SAVE〕 〔≈〕 〔🛜〕 〔📋〕 〔💻〕

CALDWELL

⬥⬥⬥ ▼▼▼ **BEST WESTERN PLUS Caldwell Inn & Suites** ⛫

(208) 454-7225. **$74-$104.** 908 Specht Ave 83605. I-84 exit 29, just s. Int corridors. **Pets:** Accepted. 〔SAVE〕 〔≈〕 〔🛜〕 〔✕〕 〔📋〕 〔💻〕

▼▼ **La Quinta Inn Caldwell** ⛫

(208) 454-2222. **$74-$249.** 901 Specht Ave 83605. I-84 exit 29, just s. Int corridors. **Pets:** Large, other species. Service with restrictions. 〔≈〕 〔🛜〕 〔✕〕 〔📋〕 〔💻〕

COEUR D'ALENE

⬥⬥⬥ ▼▼▼ **BEST WESTERN PLUS Coeur d'Alene Inn** ⛫

(208) 765-3200. **$129-$219.** 506 W Appleway Ave 83814. I-90 exit 12, just nw. Int corridors. **Pets:** Other species. $20 daily fee/room. Designated rooms, service with restrictions, supervision. 〔SAVE〕 〔�11〕 〔≈〕 〔🛜〕 〔✕〕 〔📋〕 〔💻〕

▼▼▼ ▼▼▼ **The Coeur d'Alene Resort** ⛫

(208) 209-5026. **$129-$549, 3 day notice.** 115 S 2nd St 83814. I-90 exit 11 (Northwest Blvd), 2 mi s. Ext/int corridors. **Pets:** Accepted. 〔�11〕 〔≈〕 〔✕〕 〔🛜〕 〔✕〕 〔📋〕 〔💻〕

▼▼ **Comfort Inn Coeur d'Alene** H
(208) 664-1649. **$63-$287.** 2303 N 4th St 83814. I-90 exit 13 (4th St), just n. Int corridors. **Pets:** Accepted. 🐾 🖥 ✕ 🛏 ☕

▼▼ **Days Inn-Coeur d'Alene** H
(208) 667-8668. **$65-$200.** 2200 Northwest Blvd 83814. I-90 exit 11 (Northwest Blvd), just se. Int corridors. **Pets:** Accepted.
🖥 ✕ 🛏 ☕

▼▼▼ **Holiday Inn Express Hotel & Suites Coeur d'Alene** H ❀
(208) 667-3100. **$99-$400.** 2300 W Seltice Way 83814. I-90 exit 11 (Northwest Blvd), just s. Ext/int corridors. **Pets:** Dogs only. Designated rooms, service with restrictions, supervision.
🐾M 🐾 🖥 ✕ 🛏 ☕

▼▼▼ **La Quinta Inn & Suites Coeur d'Alene** H
(208) 665-9000. **$79-$394.** 333 Ironwood Dr 83814. I-90 exit 12, just s. Int corridors. **Pets:** Accepted. 🐾M 🐾 🖥 🛏 ☕

▼▼ **La Quinta Inn & Suites Coeur d'Alene East** H
(208) 667-6777. **$65-$259.** 2209 E Sherman Ave 83814. I-90 exit 15 (Sherman Ave), just s. Int corridors. **Pets:** Large, other species. Service with restrictions. 🐾M 🐾 🖥 ✕ 🛏 ☕

▼▼▼ **Quality Inn & Suites Coeur d'Alene** H
(208) 765-5500. **Call for rates.** 280 W Appleway Ave 83814. I-90 exit 12, just ne. Int corridors. **Pets:** Other species. Designated rooms, service with restrictions, crate. 🐾M 🐾 🖥 ✕ 🛏 ☕

▼▼▼ **The Roosevelt Inn and Spa** BB
(208) 765-5200. **Call for rates.** 105 E Wallace Ave 83814. I-90 exit 13 (4th St), 2 mi s, then just w; downtown. Int corridors. **Pets:** Accepted.
🍴 ✕ 🖥 ✕ 🕎 ✉

▼▼ **Shilo Inn Suites - Coeur d'Alene** H
(208) 664-2300. **Call for rates.** 702 W Appleway Ave 83814. I-90 exit 12, just n, then just w. Int corridors. **Pets:** Accepted.
🐾M 🐾 ✕ 🖥 ✕ 🛏 ☕

DRIGGS
▼ **Teton Valley Cabins** CA
(208) 354-8153. **$69-$99, 7 day notice.** 388 Ski Hill Rd 83422. Jct SR 33 E, 0.8 mi e on Little Ave/Ski Hill Rd. Ext corridors. **Pets:** Accepted.
🖥 ✕ 🕎 ✉ 🛏 ☕

GRANGEVILLE
AAA ▼▼ **Gateway Inn** M
(208) 983-2500. **$55-$99.** 700 W Main St 83530. Jct US 95 and SR 13. Ext corridors. **Pets:** $10 one-time fee/room, $10 daily fee/room. Designated rooms, service with restrictions, supervision.
SAVE 🐾 🖥 ✕ 🛏 ☕

HAGERMAN
AAA ▼ **Hagerman Valley Inn** M
(208) 837-6196. **$68-$108.** 661 Frog's Landing 83332. South end of town on US 30. Ext corridors. **Pets:** $8 one-time fee/room. Designated rooms, supervision. SAVE 🍴 🖥 ✕ 🛏 ☕

HAILEY
▼ **Airport Inn** M
(208) 788-2477. **$85-$120, 3 day notice.** 820 S 4th Ave 83333. 1 mi s of center to 4th Ave via Main St (SR 75); south end of town. Ext corridors. **Pets:** Accepted. 🖥 🛏 ☕

▼▼▼ **AmericInn Lodge & Suites Hailey/Sun Valley** H
(208) 788-7950. **Call for rates.** 51 Cobblestone Ln 83333. 0.5 mi n of center. Int corridors. **Pets:** Dogs only. $25 one-time fee/room. Designated rooms, service with restrictions, supervision.
🐾M 🐾 ✕ 🖥 ✕ 🛏 ☕

▼▼▼ **Wood River Inn** H
(208) 578-0600. **$99-$159.** 601 N Main St 83333. 0.3 mi n of center. Int corridors. **Pets:** Accepted. 🐾M 🐾 ✕ 🖥 ✕ 🛏 ☕

HAYDEN
▼▼ **Holiday Inn Express Hotel & Suites** H
(208) 772-7900. **$90-$399.** 151 W Orchard Ave 83835. I-90 exit 12, 4 mi n. Int corridors. **Pets:** Other species. $10 daily fee/pet. Supervision.
🐾M ✕ 🖥 ✕ 🛏 ☕

IDAHO FALLS
AAA ▼▼ **BEST WESTERN PLUS CottonTree Inn** H
(208) 523-6000. **$100-$180.** 900 Lindsay Blvd 83402. I-15 exit 119, just e. Int corridors. **Pets:** $15 daily fee/pet. Service with restrictions, supervision. SAVE ECO 🐾 🖥 ✕ 🛏 ☕

AAA ▼▼▼ **BEST WESTERN PLUS Driftwood Inn** M ❀
(208) 523-2242. **$79-$159.** 575 River Pkwy 83402. I-15 exit 118 (Broadway), 0.5 mi e, then 0.3 mi n. Ext corridors. **Pets:** Other species. $10 daily fee/room. Service with restrictions, supervision.
SAVE 🐾M 🐾 ✕ 🖥 ✕ 🛏 ☕

▼▼ **Candlewood Suites** H
(208) 525-9800. **Call for rates.** 665 Pancheri Dr 83402. I-15 exit 118 (Broadway), 1 mi e (cross bridge), then 0.5 mi s on S Capital Ave. Int corridors. **Pets:** Accepted. 🐾M 🖥 🛏 ☕

▼▼▼ **La Quinta Inn & Suites Idaho Falls** H
(208) 552-2500. **$92-$269.** 2501 S 25th St E 83406. I-15 exit 118 (Broadway), 1 mi e, 0.5 mi s on Yellowstone Hwy, 3.8 mi e on 17th St to Hitt Rd, then just s. Int corridors. **Pets:** Large, other species. Service with restrictions. 🐾M 🐾 🖥 ✕ 🛏 ☕

▼▼ **Le Ritz Hotel & Suites** H
(208) 528-0880. **$69-$149, 3 day notice.** 720 Lindsay Blvd 83402. I-15 exit 118 (Broadway), 0.5 mi e, then 0.4 mi n. Int corridors. **Pets:** Accepted. 🐾M 🐾 🖥 🛏 ☕

▼▼▼ **Residence Inn by Marriott** H
(208) 542-0000. **$159-$209.** 635 W Broadway 83402. I-15 exit 118 (Broadway), 0.4 mi e. Int corridors. **Pets:** Small. $100 one-time fee/room. Designated rooms, service with restrictions, crate.
🐾 🖥 ✕ 🛏 ☕

AAA ▼▼▼ **Sleep Inn & Suites** H ❀
(208) 821-3647. **$99-$169.** 3200 Outlet Blvd 83405. I-15 exit 116, just w. Int corridors. **Pets:** Other species. $25 one-time fee/room. Designated rooms, service with restrictions, supervision.
SAVE 🐾M 🐾 🖥 ✕ 🛏 ☕

JEROME
AAA ▼▼▼ **BEST WESTERN Sawtooth Inn & Suites** H ❀
(208) 324-9200. **$89-$139.** 2653 S Lincoln Ave 83338. I-84 exit 168, just n. Int corridors. **Pets:** Other species. $100 deposit/room. Designated rooms, service with restrictions, crate.
SAVE 🐾M 🐾 🖥 ✕ 🛏 ☕

▼▼▼ **Comfort Inn & Suites** H
(208) 644-1200. **$99-$129.** 379 Crossroads Point Blvd 83338. I-84 exit 173 (US 93), 0.7 mi n. Int corridors. **Pets:** Small. $15 one-time fee/pet. Designated rooms, service with restrictions, crate.
🐾M 🐾 🖥 ✕ 🛏 ☕

KAMIAH
▼▼ **Clearwater 12 Motel** M
(208) 935-2671. **Call for rates.** 108 E 3rd St (Hwy 12) 83536. On US 12, just e of center. Ext corridors. **Pets:** Accepted. 🖥 🛏 ☕

AAA ▼▼▼ **Hearthstone Elegant Lodge on the River** BB
(208) 935-1492. **$125-$235, 3 day notice.** 3250 Hwy 12 at Milepost 64 83536. 2.2 mi w of center. Ext corridors. **Pets:** Medium, dogs only. $20 daily fee/pet. Designated rooms, service with restrictions, supervision.
SAVE 🖥 ✕ 🛏 ☕

KELLOGG

▼▼ GuestHouse Inn & Suites 🅷 ❀
(208) 783-1234. **$99-$289.** 601 Bunker Ave 83837. I-90 exit 49, 0.5 mi se. Int corridors. **Pets:** $15 daily fee/room. Service with restrictions, supervision. 🅛🄼 🔁 🛜 🎁 💻

▼▼▼ Morning Star Lodge 🄲🄾
(208) 783-0202. **$101-$720, 3 day notice.** 602 Bunker Ave 83837. I-90 exit 49, 0.5 mi se. Int corridors. **Pets:** Accepted.
🍴 ⊠ 🛜 ⊠ 🎁 💻

▼ Silverhorn Motor Inn 🅷 ❀
(208) 783-1151. **$69-$130.** 699 W Cameron Ave 83837. I-90 exit 49, just ne. Int corridors. **Pets:** Other species. Supervision. 🍴 🛜 🎁

KETCHUM

ⒶⒶⒶ ▼▼ BEST WESTERN Tyrolean Lodge 🅷
(208) 726-5336. **Call for rates.** 260 Cottonwood St 83340. Just s of center to Rivers St, w to 2nd Ave, s to Cottowood St, then just w. Int corridors. **Pets:** Accepted. 🅂🄰🅅🄴 🔁 ⊠ 🛜 ⊠ 🎁 💻

▼▼ Tamarack Lodge 🄼
(208) 726-3344. **$101-$179.** 291 Walnut Ave N 83340. 0.3 mi e on Sun Valley Rd. Ext corridors. **Pets:** Accepted. 🔁 🛜 ⊠ 🎁 💻

KOOSKIA

▼▼ River Dance Lodge 🄲🄰
(208) 926-4300. **$109-$419, 45 day notice.** 7743 Hwy 12 83539. On US 12, 16 mi e of Kooskia at MM 89. Ext corridors. **Pets:** Accepted.
🍴 ⊠ 🛜 🄺 🅆 🅩 🎁 💻

LEWISTON

ⒶⒶⒶ ▼▼▼ Holiday Inn Express 🅷
(208) 750-1600. **Call for rates.** 2425 Nez Perce Dr 83501. 1.2 mi s on US 12 from jct US 95, 1.2 mi s on 21st St, just e. Int corridors. **Pets:** Other species. $25 daily fee/pet. Service with restrictions, supervision. 🅂🄰🅅🄴 🅛🄼 🔁 🛜 ⊠ 🎁 💻

▼▼ Inn America 🅷
(208) 746-4600. **Call for rates.** 702 21st St 83501. 1.2 mi s on US 12 from jct US 95, just s. Int corridors. **Pets:** Accepted.
🅛🄼 🔁 🛜 🎁 💻

MCCALL *(Restaurants p. 631)*

ⒶⒶⒶ ▼▼▼ BEST WESTERN PLUS McCall Lodge & Suites 🅷
(208) 634-2230. **$83-$163.** 211 S 3rd St 83638. 1 mi s of center on SR 55. Int corridors. **Pets:** Dogs only. $20 daily fee/room. Designated rooms, service with restrictions, supervision.
🅂🄰🅅🄴 🅛🄼 🔁 ⊠ 🛜 ⊠ 🎁 💻

ⒶⒶⒶ ▼▼▼ Shore Lodge 🅷 ❀
(208) 634-2244. **$509, 14 day notice.** 501 W Lake St 83638. 1 mi w of center on SR 55. Int corridors. **Pets:** Dogs only. $25 daily fee/pet. Designated rooms, service with restrictions, supervision.
🅂🄰🅅🄴 🍴 🅛🄼 🔁 ⊠ 🛜 ⊠ 🎁 💻

MERIDIAN

ⒶⒶⒶ ▼▼▼ BEST WESTERN PLUS Rama Inn 🅷
(208) 887-7888. **$90-$130.** 1019 S Progress Ave 83642. I-84 exit 44 (Meridian/Kuna), just ne. Int corridors. **Pets:** Accepted.
🅂🄰🅅🄴 🅛🄼 🔁 🛜 ⊠ 🎁 💻

▼▼▼ Candlewood Suites-Boise/Meridian 🅷
(208) 888-5121. **Call for rates.** 1855 S Silverstone Way 83642. I-84 exit 46 (Eagle Rd), 0.6 mi s, just e on Overland Rd, then just s. Int corridors. **Pets:** Accepted. 🅛🄼 🛜 ⊠ 🎁 💻

ⒶⒶⒶ ▼▼▼ Country Inn & Suites By Carlson Boise West 🅷
(208) 639-3300. **Call for rates.** 3355 E Pine Ave 83642. I-84 exit 46 (Eagle Rd), 0.8 mi n, then just e. Int corridors. **Pets:** Accepted.
🅂🄰🅅🄴 🅛🄼 🔁 🛜 ⊠ 🎁 💻

ⒶⒶⒶ ▼▼▼ Holiday Inn Express & Suites-Boise West/Meridian 🅷
(208) 288-2060. **$109-$179.** 2610 E Freeway Dr 83642. I-84 exit 46 (Eagle Rd), just n, then 0.3 mi w. Int corridors. **Pets:** Dogs only. $30 daily fee/pet. Designated rooms, service with restrictions, crate.
🅂🄰🅅🄴 🅛🄼 🔁 🛜 ⊠ 🎁 💻

▼▼▼ La Quinta Inn & Suites Meridian Boise 🅷
(208) 288-2100. **$82-$264.** 800 S Allen St 83642. I-84 exit 46 (Eagle Rd), just nw. Int corridors. **Pets:** Large, other species. Service with restrictions. 🅛🄼 🔁 🛜 ⊠ 🎁 💻

ⒶⒶⒶ ▼▼▼ TownePlace Suites by Marriott-Boise/Meridian 🅷 ❀
(208) 884-8550. **$110-$153.** 1415 S Eagle Rd 83642. I-84 exit 46 (Eagle Rd), just sw. Int corridors. **Pets:** Other species. $50 one-time fee/room. Service with restrictions, supervision.
🅂🄰🅅🄴 🅛🄼 🔁 🛜 ⊠ 🎁 💻

MONTPELIER

ⒶⒶⒶ ▼▼▼ Clover Creek Inn 🄼
(208) 847-1782. **$75-$125.** 243 N 4th St 83254. On US 30, just n of jct US 89. Ext corridors. **Pets:** Dogs only. $10 one-time fee/room. Designated rooms, service with restrictions, supervision. 🅂🄰🅅🄴 🛜 🎁 💻

MOSCOW

ⒶⒶⒶ ▼▼▼ BEST WESTERN PLUS University Inn 🅷
(208) 882-0550. **$99-$229.** 1516 W Pullman Rd 83843. Jct US 95, 1 mi w on SR 8. Int corridors. **Pets:** Accepted.
🅂🄰🅅🄴 🍴 🅛🄼 🔁 ⊠ 🛜 ⊠ 🎁 💻

▼▼▼ Fairfield Inn & Suites by Marriott Moscow 🅷
(208) 882-4600. **$95-$135.** 1000 W Pullman Rd 83843. Jct US 95, 1 mi w on SR 8. Int corridors. **Pets:** Accepted. 🅛🄼 🛜 ⊠ 🎁 💻

▼▼▼ La Quinta Inn & Suites Moscow Pullman 🅷
(208) 882-5365. **$95-$349.** 185 Warbonnet Dr 83843. 1.6 mi w on SR 8 from jct US 95, just n. Int corridors. **Pets:** Large, other species. Service with restrictions. 🅛🄼 🔁 🛜 ⊠ 🎁 💻

MOUNTAIN HOME

ⒶⒶⒶ ▼▼▼ BEST WESTERN Foothills Inn 🄼 ❀
(208) 587-8477. **$89-$149.** 1080 Hwy 20 83647. I-84 exit 95, just n. Ext corridors. **Pets:** Dogs only. $15 daily fee/room. Designated rooms, service with restrictions, supervision. 🅂🄰🅅🄴 🔁 🛜 🎁 💻

▼▼ Mountain Home Inn 🅷
(208) 587-9743. **$84-$99.** 1180 Hwy 20 83647. I-84 exit 95, just n. Int corridors. **Pets:** Accepted. 🛜 🎁 💻

NAMPA

▼▼▼ Holiday Inn Express & Suites 🅷
(208) 466-4045. **Call for rates.** 4104 E Flamingo Ave 83687. I-84 exit 38, just s, then just w. Int corridors. **Pets:** Dogs only. $25 one-time fee/pet. Designated rooms, service with restrictions, supervision.
🅛🄼 🛜 ⊠ 🎁 💻

▼▼ Sleep Inn 🅷
(208) 463-6300. **$68-$100.** 1315 Industrial Rd 83687. I-84 exit 36 (Franklin Blvd), just s. Int corridors. **Pets:** Medium, dogs only. $25 one-time fee/pet. Designated rooms, service with restrictions, supervision.
🔁 🛜 🎁 💻

OROFINO

AAA ▼▼/▼▼ BEST WESTERN PLUS Lodge at River's Edge ℍ ✿

(208) 476-9999. **Call for rates.** 615 Main St 83544. US 12, 0.3 mi e to Main St, 0.3 mi s. Int corridors. **Pets:** Medium, dogs only. $20 daily fee/pet. Designated rooms, service with restrictions, supervision.

SAVE 🚹ᴹ ☎ 🏋 🛜 🏊 📶 🛏 💻

▼▼ ▼▼ Helgeson Hotel Suites ℍ

(208) 476-5729. **$63-$90.** 125 Johnson Ave 83544. US 12, 0.3 mi e; downtown. Int corridors. **Pets:** Accepted. 🚹ᴹ 🛜 🏊 🛏 💻

▼▼ ▼▼ Konkolville Motel Ⓜ

(208) 476-5584. **$57-$87, 3 day notice.** 2600 Michigan Ave 83544. US 12, 3 mi e. Ext corridors. **Pets:** $15 daily fee/pet. Designated rooms, service with restrictions, supervision. 🚹ᴹ ☎ 🛜 🛏 💻

POCATELLO

▼▼ ▼▼ AmeriTel Inn ℍ

(208) 234-7500. **Call for rates.** 1440 Bench Rd 83201. I-15 exit 71, just e. Int corridors. **Pets:** Accepted. 🚹ᴹ ☎ 🛜 🛏 💻

AAA ▼▼ ▼▼ BEST WESTERN Pocatello Inn ℍ

(208) 237-7650. **$99-$119.** 1415 Bench Rd 83201. I-15 exit 71, just e. Int corridors. **Pets:** Accepted. SAVE ☎ 🛜 🏊 🛏 💻

AAA ▼▼ ▼▼ Clarion Inn ℍ

(208) 237-1400. **$79-$109.** 1399 Bench Rd 83201. I-15 exit 71, just e. Ext/int corridors. **Pets:** $10 daily fee/room. Designated rooms, service with restrictions, crate. SAVE 🍴 🚹ᴹ ☎ 🏋 🛜 🛏 💻

AAA ▼▼ ▼▼ Comfort Inn ℍ ✿

(208) 237-8155. **$85-$100.** 1333 Bench Rd 83201. I-15 exit 71, just e. Int corridors. **Pets:** Other species. $10 daily fee/pet. Service with restrictions, supervision. SAVE 🚹ᴹ ☎ 🛜 🏊 🏋 🛏 💻

▼▼ ▼▼ Red Lion Hotel ℍ

(208) 233-2200. **Call for rates.** 1555 Pocatello Creek Rd 83201. I-15 exit 71, just e. Int corridors. **Pets:** Accepted. ☎ 🛜 🏋 🛏 💻

AAA ▼▼ ▼▼ Super 8 ℍ

(208) 234-0888. **$60-$90.** 1330 Bench Rd 83201. I-15 exit 71, just e. Int corridors. **Pets:** $15 one-time fee/room. Designated rooms, service with restrictions, crate. SAVE 🛜 🏋 🛏 💻

▼▼▼▼ TownePlace Suites by Marriott ℍ

(208) 478-7000. **$159-$186.** 2376 Via Caporatti Dr 83201. I-15 exit 69 (Clark St), 0.3 mi e. Int corridors. **Pets:** Accepted.

🚹ᴹ ☎ 🛜 🏋 🛏 💻

PONDERAY

▼▼ ▼▼ GuestHouse Lodge-Sandpoint ℍ

(208) 263-2210. **$52-$159, 3 day notice.** 476841 Hwy 95 N 83852. 0.7 mi n on US 95 from jct SR 200. Int corridors. **Pets:** Small, dogs only. $10 daily fee/room. Designated rooms, service with restrictions, supervision. 🚹ᴹ 🛜 🏋 🛏 💻

▼▼ ▼▼ Holiday Inn Express & Suites ℍ

(208) 255-4500. **Call for rates.** 477326 Hwy 95 N 83852. 0.7 mi n on US 95 from jct SR 200. Int corridors. **Pets:** Accepted.

🚹ᴹ ☎ 🛜 🏋 🛏 💻

▼▼ ▼▼ Hotel Ruby Ponderay ℍ ✿

(208) 263-5383. **$80-$200.** 477255 Hwy 95 N 83852. 1.2 mi n on US 95 from jct SR 200. Int corridors. **Pets:** Large, other species. $10 daily fee/room. Service with restrictions, supervision. 🚹ᴹ 🛜 🛏 💻

POST FALLS

▼▼▼▼ Red Lion Templin's Hotel on the River - Post Falls ℍ

(208) 773-1611. **$109-$229.** 414 E 1st Ave 83854. I-90 exit 5 eastbound, just s to 1st Ave; exit 6 westbound, 0.7 mi w on Seltice Way to Spokane St, 0.5 mi s, then just e. Ext/int corridors. **Pets:** Accepted.

🍴 🚹ᴹ ☎ 🏋 🛜 🏋 🛏 💻

▼▼ ▼▼ Sleep Inn ℍ

(208) 777-9394. **$45-$259.** 157 S Pleasant View Rd 83854. I-90 exit 2, just s. Int corridors. **Pets:** Dogs only. $25 one-time fee/room. Service with restrictions, supervision. 🚹ᴹ ☎ 🛜 🏋 🛏 💻

PRIEST RIVER

▼▼ Eagle's Nest Motel Ⓜ

(208) 448-2000. **$59-$125, 3 day notice.** 5678 Hwy 2 83856. US 2, 0.5 mi w. Ext corridors. **Pets:** $10 daily fee/pet. Designated rooms, service with restrictions, supervision. 🚹ᴹ 🛜 🛏

REXBURG

▼▼ ▼▼ AmericInn Lodge & Suites of Rexburg ℍ

(208) 356-5333. **Call for rates.** 1098 Golden Beauty Dr 83440. US 20 exit 332 (S Rexburg). Int corridors. **Pets:** Accepted.

🚹ᴹ ☎ 🛜 🏋 🛏 💻

AAA ▼▼ ▼▼ Quality Inn ℍ

(208) 359-1311. **$89-$149.** 885 W Main St 83440. US 20 exit 333 (Salmon), just e. Int corridors. **Pets:** Accepted.

SAVE ☎ 🛜 🏋 🛏 💻

RIGGINS

▼▼ ▼▼ Pinehurst Resort Cabins & RV 🅲🅰

(208) 628-3323. **$65-$95.** 5604 Hwy 95 83654. 12 mi s of Riggins; MM 182. Ext corridors. **Pets:** $15 daily fee/pet. Designated rooms, no service, supervision. 🛜 🏋 🎾 📶 🛏 💻

▼▼▼▼ Salmon Rapids Lodge ℍ

(208) 628-2743. **$110-$201.** 1010 S Main St 83549. 0.3 mi s of center. Int corridors. **Pets:** Accepted. ☎ 🛜 🏋 🛏 💻

SAGLE

AAA ▼▼▼▼ The Lodge at Sandpoint ℍ

(208) 263-2211. **$129-$479, 14 day notice.** 41 Lakeshore Dr 83860. 1 mi s of Sandpoint on US 95; just s of Long Bridge. Int corridors. **Pets:** Small, dogs only. $20 daily fee/pet. Designated rooms, service with restrictions, supervision. SAVE 🍴 🏋 🛜 🏋 🛏 💻

SALMON

▼▼ ▼▼ Stagecoach Inn Ⓜ

(208) 756-2919. **$79-$109.** 201 Riverfront Dr (US 93 N) 83467. Just n on US 93 from jct SR 28. Int corridors. **Pets:** Accepted.

☎ 🛜 🛏 💻

SANDPOINT

AAA ▼▼▼▼ BEST WESTERN Edgewater Resort ℍ

(208) 263-3194. **$99-$359.** 56 Bridge St 83864. Just e of US 95; downtown. Int corridors. **Pets:** Accepted.

SAVE 🍴 ☎ 🏋 🛜 🏋 🛏 💻

▼▼ ▼▼ La Quinta Inn Sandpoint ℍ

(208) 263-9581. **$64-$309.** 415 Cedar St 83864. Jct US 2 and 95; downtown. Ext/int corridors. **Pets:** Large, other species. Service with restrictions. 🍴 🚹ᴹ ☎ 🛜 🏋 🛏 💻

▼▼ ▼▼ Quality Inn Sandpoint ℍ

(208) 263-2111. **$59-$199.** 807 N 5th Ave 83864. US 2 and 95, just s of jct SR 200. Int corridors. **Pets:** Accepted. 🍴 ☎ 🛜 🛏 💻

TWIN FALLS

BEST WESTERN PLUS Twin Falls Hotel H

(208) 736-8000. **$89-$129.** 1377 Blue Lakes Blvd N 83301. I-84 exit 173, 4 mi s on US 93. Int corridors. **Pets:** Medium, dogs only. $20 daily fee/room. Designated rooms, service with restrictions, supervision.

La Quinta Inn & Suites H

(208) 736-9600. **$94-$280.** 539 Pole Line Rd 83301. I-84 exit 173, 3 mi s to Pole Line Rd, then 0.3 mi w. Int corridors. **Pets:** Large, other species. Service with restrictions.

Quality Inn & Suites H

(208) 734-7494. **$89-$159.** 1910 Fillmore St N 83301. I-84 exit 173, 3.3 mi s. Int corridors. **Pets:** Medium, other species. $20 daily fee/pet. Service with restrictions, supervision.

Red Lion Hotel Canyon Springs H

(208) 734-5000. **Call for rates.** 1357 Blue Lakes Blvd N 83301. I-84 exit 173, 4 mi s on US 93. Int corridors. **Pets:** Accepted.

WALLACE *(Restaurants p. 631)*

The Wallace Inn H

(208) 752-1252. **$72-$175, 3 day notice.** 100 Front St 83873. I-90 exit 61 (Business Rt 90), just se. Int corridors. **Pets:** Other species. $20 daily fee/room. Service with restrictions, supervision.

WHITE BIRD

Hells Canyon Jet Boat Trips & Lodging M

(208) 839-2255. **$80-$90, 7 day notice.** 3252 Waterfront Dr 83554. US 95 exit White Bird, 1.5 mi s of center. Ext corridors. **Pets:** $15 daily fee/pet. Service with restrictions, crate.

WORLEY

Coeur d'Alene Casino Resort Hotel H

(208) 769-2600. **$100-$190.** 37914 S Nukwalqw Rd 83876. On US 95, 3 mi n. Int corridors. **Pets:** Accepted.

ILLINOIS

ALSIP

Baymont Inn & Suites Chicago/Alsip H

(708) 597-3900. **$79-$159.** 12801 S Cicero Ave 60803. I-294 exit SR 50 (S Cicero Ave). Int corridors. **Pets:** Accepted.

ALTON

BEST WESTERN PLUS Parkway Hotel H

(618) 433-9900. **$84-$114.** 1900 Homer M Adams Pkwy 62002. On SR 111, 1.8 mi e of jct US 67. Int corridors. **Pets:** Other species. $10 daily fee/pet. Service with restrictions, crate.

Comfort Inn H

(618) 465-9999. **$89-$104.** 11 Crossroads Ct 62002. Jct SR 3, just w on SR 140. Int corridors. **Pets:** Other species. $10 daily fee/room. Service with restrictions, supervision.

ANNAWAN

BEST WESTERN Annawan Inn H

(309) 935-6565. **$80-$165.** 315 N Canal St 61234. I-80 exit 33, just s. Int corridors. **Pets:** $20 deposit/pet. Designated rooms, no service, supervision.

ARCOLA

BEST WESTERN PLUS Green Mill Village Hotel & Suites H

(217) 268-5000. **$81-$170.** 917 Green Mill Rd 61910. I-57 exit 203 (SR 133), just e. Int corridors. **Pets:** Large, other species. $50 deposit/room, $10 daily fee/pet. Designated rooms, service with restrictions, supervision.

Comfort Inn H

(217) 268-4000. **$75-$130.** 610 E Springfield Rd 61910. I-57 exit 203 (SR 133), just w. Int corridors. **Pets:** Accepted.

ARLINGTON HEIGHTS

DoubleTree by Hilton Chicago-Arlington Heights H

(847) 364-7600. **$99-$229.** 75 W Algonquin Rd 60005. I-90 exit Arlington Heights Rd, just n to Algonquin Rd, then just w. Int corridors. **Pets:** Accepted.

Holiday Inn Express H

(847) 593-9400. **Call for rates.** 2120 S Arlington Heights Rd 60005. I-90 exit Arlington Heights Rd, 0.6 mi n. Int corridors. **Pets:** Accepted.

La Quinta Inn Chicago Arlington Heights H

(847) 253-8777. **$65-$183.** 1415 W Dundee Rd 60004. SR 53 exit Dundee Rd, just e. Int corridors. **Pets:** Large, other species. Service with restrictions.

Red Roof Inn Chicago – O'Hare Airport / Arlington Heights M

(847) 228-6650. **$45-$90.** 22 W Algonquin Rd 60005. I-90 exit Arlington Heights Rd, 0.5 mi n, then just w. Ext corridors. **Pets:** Large, other species. Service with restrictions, supervision.

AURORA

Candlewood Suites Chicago-Aurora H

(630) 907-9977. **Call for rates.** 2625 W Sullivan Rd 60506. I-88 exit Orchard Rd, just sw. Int corridors. **Pets:** Accepted.

Staybridge Suites Aurora/Naperville H

(630) 978-2222. **Call for rates.** 4320 Meridian Pkwy 60504. I-88 exit SR 59, 2 mi s to Meridian Pkwy, then just w. Int corridors. **Pets:** Accepted.

BANNOCKBURN

La Quinta Inn & Suites Chicago Bannockburn/Deerfield H

(847) 317-7300. **$79-$279.** 2000 S Lakeside Dr 60015. I-94 exit Half Day Rd (SR 22), just e to Lakeside Dr, then just s. Int corridors. **Pets:** Large, other species. Service with restrictions.

BEDFORD PARK

Extended Stay America Chicago-Midway H

(708) 496-8211. **$104-$159.** 7524 State Rd 60638. Jct SR 50, just w. Int corridors. **Pets:** Other species. $25 daily fee/pet. Service with restrictions, supervision.

Residence Inn by Marriott Chicago Midway Airport H

(708) 458-7790. **$139-$298.** 6638 S Cicero Ave 60638. Jct 65th St. Int corridors. **Pets:** Accepted.

Sleep Inn-Chicago/Midway Airport H

(708) 594-0001. **$130-$180.** 6650 S Cicero Ave 60638. Jct 65th St. Int corridors. **Pets:** Accepted.

BLOOMINGDALE

▼▼▼ Courtyard by Marriott Chicago Bloomingdale 🏠
(630) 529-9200. **$97-$171.** 275 Knollwood Dr 60108. I-355 exit Army Trail Rd, 4 mi w, then just n. Int corridors. **Pets:** Accepted.
🍽 🔥M 🏊 📶 ✕ 🔌 💻

◈ ▼▼▼▼ Hilton Chicago Indian Lakes Resort 🏠 ❀
(630) 529-0200. **$89-$249.** 250 W Schick Rd 60108. I-355 exit Lake St (US 20), 2.5 mi w, just s on Bloomingdale Rd, then 0.6 mi w. Int corridors. **Pets:** Large, other species. $50 one-time fee/room. Designated rooms, service with restrictions. 🆂🅰🆅🅴 🍽 🏊 ✕ 📶

▼▼▼ Residence Inn by Marriott Chicago Bloomingdale 🏠
(630) 893-9200. **$104-$183.** 295 Knollwood Dr 60108. I-355 exit Army Trail Rd, 4 mi w, then just n. Int corridors. **Pets:** Accepted.
🔥M 🏊 📶 ✕ 🔌 💻

BLOOMINGTON

◈ ▼▼ Baymont Inn & Suites 🏠
(309) 662-2800. **$69-$99.** 604 1/2 IAA Dr 61701. I-55 exit 167 southbound, follow I-55 business route (Veterans Pkwy), 2.8 mi s to jct SR 9, just e, then just n via service road; exit 157B (Veterans Pkwy) northbound, 4 mi n to SR 9. Int corridors. **Pets:** Accepted.
🆂🅰🆅🅴 🏊 📶 🔌 💻

▼▼▼ The Chateau Hotel and Conference Center 🏠
(309) 662-2020. **$79-$119.** 1601 Jumer Dr 61704. I-55 exit 167, follow I-55 business route (Veterans Pkwy), just e; 1.3 mi n of jct SR 9; 1 mi s of jct I-55. Int corridors. **Pets:** Accepted.
🍽 🏊 ✕ 📶 ✕ 🔌 💻

▼▼ Country Inn & Suites By Carlson Bloomington/ Normal West 🏠 ❀
(309) 828-7177. **$85-$159.** 923 Maple Hill Rd 61704. I-55/74 exit 160 (SR 9), 0.3 mi w to Wylie Dr, just n, then just e. Int corridors. **Pets:** $25 daily fee/room. Service with restrictions, crate.
🔥M 🏊 📶 ✕ 🔌 💻

▼▼▼ DoubleTree by Hilton Bloomington 🏠
(309) 664-6446. **$99-$139.** 10 Brickyard Dr 61701. I-55 business route (Veterans Pkwy), just n of US 150. Int corridors. **Pets:** Accepted.
🍽 🏊 📠 ✕ 🔌 💻

▼▼▼ Eastland Suites Hotel & Conference Center 🏠
(309) 662-0000. **Call for rates.** 1801 Eastland Dr 61704. Jct I-55 business route (Veterans Pkwy) and SR 9, just s to Eastland Dr, then just e. Ext/int corridors. **Pets:** Accepted. 🏊 📶 🔌 💻

▼▼▼ Holiday Inn Express Bloomington West 🏠
(309) 820-9990. **$104-$169, 3 day notice.** 1031 Wylie Dr 61705. I-55/74 exit 160 (SR 9), just w, then just n. Int corridors. **Pets:** Medium. $15 daily fee/pet. Service with restrictions, crate.
🏊 📶 ✕ 🔌 💻

▼▼▼ Holiday Inn Hotel & Suites 🏠 ❀
(309) 662-4700. **$99-$219.** 3202 E Empire St 61704. Jct I-55 business route (Veterans Pkwy) and SR 9, 2.3 mi e on SR 9. Int corridors. **Pets:** Dogs only. $20 daily fee/pet. Designated rooms, service with restrictions, supervision. 🍽 🔥M 🏊 ✕ 📶 ✕ 🔌 💻

▼▼ La Quinta Inn Bloomington - Normal 🏠
(309) 828-6000. **$60-$250.** 505 Brock Dr 61701. I-55/74 exit 160 (SR 9), just e. Int corridors. **Pets:** Large, other species. Service with restrictions. 📶 🔌 💻

▼▼▼ Residence Inn by Marriott Bloomington/Normal 🏠 ❀
(309) 661-9822. **$104-$171.** 2160 Ireland Grove Rd 61704. Jct I-55 business route (Veterans Pkwy) and Ireland Grove Rd, 3 mi e. Int corridors. **Pets:** $100 one-time fee/room. Service with restrictions.
🔥M 📶 ✕ 🔌 💻

BOLINGBROOK

◈ ▼▼▼▼ Aloft Bolingbrook 🏠
(630) 410-6367. **Call for rates.** 500 Janes Ave 60440. I-355 exit Boughton Rd, just sw. Int corridors. **Pets:** Accepted.
🆂🅰🆅🅴 🔥M 🏊 📶 ✕ 🔌 💻

◈ ▼▼▼ Quality Inn by Choice Hotels 🏠
(630) 378-5300. **$85-$120.** 175 W Remington Blvd 60440. I-55 exit 267, just n on SR 53. Int corridors. **Pets:** Accepted.
🆂🅰🆅🅴 🔥M 🏊 📶 🔌 💻

BRIDGEVIEW

▼ Motel 6 Bridgeview 🏠
(708) 430-1818. **$74-$85.** 9625 S 76th Ave 60455. I-294 exit 95th St, just sw. Int corridors. **Pets:** Other species. Service with restrictions, crate. 📶 🔌 💻

BUFFALO GROVE

▼▼ Extended Stay America-Chicago-Buffalo Grove-Deerfield 🏠
(847) 215-0641. **$74-$109.** 1525 Busch Pkwy 60089. I-94 exit W Lake Cook Rd, 2 mi w to Milwaukee Ave (US 45/SR 21), then 1.3 mi n. Int corridors. **Pets:** Other species. $25 daily fee/pet. Service with restrictions, supervision. 📶 🔌 💻

BURR RIDGE

▼▼ Extended Stay America Chicago-Burr Ridge 🏠
(630) 323-6630. **$74-$119.** 15 W 122nd S Frontage Rd 60527. I-55 exit 276A (County Line Rd), just sw. Int corridors. **Pets:** Other species. $25 daily fee/pet. Service with restrictions, supervision. 📶 🔌

CARBONDALE

◈ ▼▼▼ BEST WESTERN Saluki Inn 🏠
(618) 351-6611. **$84-$149.** 801 N Giant City Rd 62901. I-57 exit 54B, 14 mi w on SR 13, just s. Int corridors. **Pets:** Accepted.
🆂🅰🆅🅴 📶 🔌 💻

▼▼▼ Holiday Inn Hotel and Conference Center 🏠
(618) 549-2600. **Call for rates.** 2300 Reed Station Pkwy 62901. I-57 exit 54B, 12 mi w on SR 13. Int corridors. **Pets:** Accepted.
🍽 🏊 📶 🔌 💻

▼ Super 8 🏠
(618) 457-8822. **$45-$110.** 1180 E Main St 62901. I-57 exit 54B, 13.9 mi w on SR 13. Int corridors. **Pets:** $10 daily fee/pet. Service with restrictions, crate. 📶 ✕ 🔌 💻

CHAMPAIGN

▼▼ Baymont Inn & Suites 🏠
(217) 356-8900. **$69-$199.** 302 W Anthony Dr 61822. I-74 exit 182 (Neil St), just nw. Int corridors. **Pets:** Other species. $15 daily fee/pet. Designated rooms, service with restrictions, crate. 📶 🔌 💻

▼▼▼ Drury Inn & Suites-Champaign 🏠
(217) 398-0030. **$100-$169.** 905 W Anthony Dr 61821. I-74 exit 181 (Prospect Ave), just n. Int corridors. **Pets:** $10 daily fee/room. Service with restrictions, supervision. 🔥M 🏊 📶 ✕ 🔌 💻

▼▼ Extended Stay America-Champaign-Urbana 🏠
(217) 351-8899. **Call for rates.** 610 W Marketview Dr 61822. I-74 exit 181 (Prospect Ave), just n, then just e. Int corridors. **Pets:** Other species. $25 daily fee/pet. Service with restrictions, supervision.
📶 🔌 💻

◈ ▼▼▼▼ Hawthorn Suites by Wyndham Champaign 🏠
(217) 398-3400. **$95-$310.** 101 Trade Centre Dr 61820. I-74 exit 182 (Neil St), 2.7 mi s. Int corridors. **Pets:** $25 one-time fee/room. Service with restrictions, crate. 🆂🅰🆅🅴 🔥M 🏊 📶 ✕ 🔌 💻

◈ ▼▼▼▼ Hyatt Place Champaign Urbana 🏠
(217) 531-2800. **$79-$349.** 217 N Neil St 61820. Jct W Church St. Int corridors. **Pets:** Accepted. 🆂🅰🆅🅴 🔥M 📶 ✕ 🔌 💻

▼▼ La Quinta Inn Champaign 🅷
(217) 356-4000. **$69-$269.** 1900 Center Dr 61820. I-74 exit 182 (Neil St), just n. Int corridors. **Pets:** Large, other species. Service with restrictions. 🅢🅜 🕿 🛜 🅗 🖵

▼▼ Quality Inn & Suites 🅷
(217) 352-4055. **$65-$175.** 305 Marketview Dr 61821. I-74 exit 182 (Neil St), just n to Marketview Dr, then just w. Int corridors. **Pets:** Accepted. 🕿 🛜 🅗 🖵

▼▼▼ Residence Inn by Marriott Champaign 🅷
(217) 398-0000. **$90-$183.** 502 W Marketview Dr 61822. I-74 exit 181, 1 mi ne. Int corridors. **Pets:** Accepted. 🛜 ⊠ 🅗 🖵

▼▼▼ Wingate by Wyndham 🅷
(217) 355-5566. **$79-$109.** 516 W Marketview Dr 61822. I-74 exit 181, 1 mi ne. Int corridors. **Pets:** $30 one-time fee/pet. Designated rooms, service with restrictions, crate. 🛜 ⊠ 🅗 🖵

CHESTER

AAA ▼▼ BEST WESTERN Reid's Inn 🅷
(618) 826-3034. **$85.** 2150 State St 62233. SR 150, 1 mi e of SR 3. Int corridors. **Pets:** Accepted. 🅢 🅜 🕿 🛜 🅗 🖵

CHICAGO

AAA ▼▼▼ Allegro Chicago, A Kimpton Hotel 🅷
(312) 236-0123. **$129-$409.** 171 W Randolph St 60601. Jct LaSalle St. Int corridors. **Pets:** Accepted. 🅢 ☘ ⑪ 🕿 ⊠ 🅗 🖵

AAA ▼ Aloft Chicago City Center 🅷 🐾
(312) 661-1000. **$89-$499.** 515 N Clark St 60654. Jct W Grand Ave. Int corridors. **Pets:** Medium, dogs only. Service with restrictions, supervision. 🅢 ⑪ 🅜 🛜 ⊠ 🅗 🖵

AAA ▼▼▼ BEST WESTERN PLUS Hawthorne Terrace Hotel 🅷
(773) 244-3434. **$119-$299.** 3434 N Broadway St 60657. Between Belmont Ave and Addison St. Int corridors. **Pets:** Accepted.
🅢 ⊠ 🛜 🅗 🖵

AAA ▼▼ Carlton Inn Midway 🅼
(773) 582-0900. **$99-$189.** 4944 S Archer Ave 60632. I-55 exit 287 (Pulaski Rd), 1.8 mi s to Archer Ave, then just e. Ext corridors. **Pets:** Accepted. 🅢 🛜 🅗 🖵

AAA ▼▼▼ Conrad Chicago 🅷
(312) 645-1500. **$175-$325.** 521 N Rush St 60611. Jct Grand Ave. Int corridors. **Pets:** Accepted. 🅢 ⑪ 🅜 🛜 ⊠ 🅗 🖵

AAA ▼▼▼ Crowne Plaza Chicago Metro 🅷
(312) 829-5000. **Call for rates.** 733 W Madison St 60661. I-90/94 exit 51D (Madison St); jct Halsted St. Int corridors. **Pets:** Small, other species. $50 one-time fee/pet. Supervision. 🅢 ⑪ 🛜 ⊠ 🖵

AAA ▼▼▼ The Drake 🅷
(312) 787-2200. **$89-$499.** 140 E Walton Pl 60611. Jct N Michigan Ave and Lake Shore Dr. Int corridors. **Pets:** Dogs only. $75 one-time fee/pet. Designated rooms, service with restrictions, supervision.
🅢 ⑪ 🕿 ⊠ 🅗 🖵

AAA ▼▼▼▼ Fairmont Chicago, Millennium Park 🅷
(312) 565-8000. **$159-$389.** 200 N Columbus Dr 60601. Jct Michigan Ave and Wacker Dr, just e. Int corridors. **Pets:** Accepted.
🅢 ☘ ⑪ 🅜 🕿 ⊠ 🖵

▼▼▼▼ Four Seasons Hotel Chicago 🅷 🐾
(312) 280-8800. **Call for rates.** 120 E Delaware Pl 60611. Jct Michigan Ave; just nw of John Hancock Building. Int corridors. **Pets:** Small. $40 daily fee/room. Designated rooms, supervision.
☘ ⑪ 🅜 🕿 ⊠ 🛜 ⊠ 🅗 🖵

▼▼▼ Hampton Inn Chicago Downtown/Magnificent Mile 🅷
(312) 706-0888. **$89-$239.** 160 E Huron St 60611. Just e of N Michigan Ave. Int corridors. **Pets:** Accepted. ⑪ 🕿 🛜 ⊠ 🅗 🖵

AAA ▼▼▼ Hard Rock Hotel Chicago 🅷
(312) 345-1000. **Call for rates.** 230 N Michigan Ave 60601. Between Lake St and Wacker Dr. Int corridors. **Pets:** Accepted.
🅢 ⑪ 🅜 🛜 ⊠ 🖵

AAA ▼▼▼ Hilton Chicago 🅷
(312) 922-4400. **$85-$525.** 720 S Michigan Ave 60605. I-290 (Congress Pkwy) exit Michigan Ave, just s. Int corridors. **Pets:** Other species. Service with restrictions, crate. 🅢 ☘ ⑪ 🕿 ⊠ 🛜 ⊠ 🖵

AAA ▼▼▼ Hilton Chicago O'Hare Airport 🅷
(773) 686-8000. **$99-$429.** O'Hare Int'l Airport 60666. Opposite and connected to terminal buildings at Chicago O'Hare International Airport, accessed via I-190. Int corridors. **Pets:** Accepted.
🅢 ⑪ 🕿 ⊠ 🛜 ⊠ 🖵

AAA ▼▼▼ Hilton Suites Chicago/Magnificent Mile 🅷
(312) 664-1100. **$99-$329.** 198 E Delaware Pl 60611. Just e of Michigan Ave. Int corridors. **Pets:** Accepted.
🅢 ⑪ 🅜 🕿 🛜 🅗 🖵

▼▼▼ Holiday Inn Chicago O'Hare 🅷
(773) 693-5800. **Call for rates.** 5615 N Cumberland Ave 60631. I-90 exit 79B (N Cumberland Ave), just s. Int corridors. **Pets:** Small. $50 deposit/pet. Designated rooms, service with restrictions, supervision.
⑪ 🅜 🕿 🅗 🖵

AAA ▼▼▼ Homewood Suites by Hilton Chicago Downtown 🅷
(312) 644-2222. **$119-$349.** 40 E Grand Ave 60611. Jct Wabash Ave, just w of Michigan Ave. Int corridors. **Pets:** Medium. $150 one-time fee/room. Designated rooms, service with restrictions.
🅢 🅜 🕿 🛜 🅗 🖵

▼▼▼ Homewood Suites Chicago Downtown/Magnificent Mile 🅷
(312) 585-9333. **$99-$259.** 152 E Huron St 60611. Just e of N Michigan Ave. Int corridors. **Pets:** Accepted. ⑪ 🅜 🛜 ⊠ 🅗 🖵

AAA ▼▼▼ Hotel Blake, an Ascend Hotel Collection Member 🅷
(312) 986-1234. **Call for rates.** 500 S Dearborn St 60605. Jct I-290 (Congress Pkwy). Int corridors. **Pets:** Accepted.
🅢 ⑪ 🛜 ⊠ 🅗 🖵

AAA ▼▼▼ Hotel Burnham Chicago 🅷 🐾
(312) 782-1111. **Call for rates.** One W Washington St 60602. Jct State St. Int corridors. **Pets:** Other species. Service with restrictions, crate.
🅢 ☘ ⑪ ⊠ 🛜 ⊠

▼▼▼ Hotel Indigo Chicago Downtown Gold Coast 🅷 🐾
(312) 787-4980. **Call for rates.** 1244 N Dearborn Pkwy 60610. Just n of Division St. Int corridors. **Pets:** $75 one-time fee/room. Service with restrictions, crate. ⑪ 🛜 ⊠ 🖵

AAA ▼▼▼▼ Hotel Monaco Chicago 🅷 🐾
(312) 960-8500. **$199-$509.** 225 N Wabash Ave 60601. Jct Wacker Dr. Int corridors. **Pets:** Other species. Designated rooms, service with restrictions. 🅢 ☘ ⑪ 🛜 ⊠ 🖵

▼▼▼▼ Hotel Palomar Chicago 🅷 🐾
(312) 755-9703. **$209-$799.** 505 N State St 60654. Between Grand and Illinois sts. Int corridors. **Pets:** Other species. Service with restrictions, crate. ⑪ 🅜 🕿 🛜 ⊠

AAA ▼▼▼▼ **Hyatt Place Chicago-South/University Medical Center** ⊞
(773) 752-5300. **$109-$339.** 5225 S Harper Dr 60615. Lake Shore Dr exit 53rd St, 0.4 mi e to S Harper Dr, then just n. Int corridors. **Pets:** Medium, dogs only. $75 one-time fee/pet. Service with restrictions, crate. [SAVE] [&M] [📶] [✕] [🛡] [💻]

AAA ▼▼▼▼ **InterContinental Chicago Magnificent Mile** ⊞
(312) 944-4100. **Call for rates.** 505 N Michigan Ave 60611. Just n of Chicago River; between E Grand Ave and E Illinois St. Int corridors. **Pets:** Accepted. [SAVE] [ECO] [◁] [†1] [⇌] [✕] [so] [✕] [💻]

▼▼▼▼ **The James Chicago** ⊞
(312) 337-1000. **Call for rates.** 55 E Ontario St 60611. Just w of N Michigan Ave. Int corridors. **Pets:** Accepted.
[†1] [&M] [✕] [📶] [🛡] [💻]

AAA ▼▼▼▼ **Kinzie Hotel** ⊞
(312) 395-9000. **$139-$649.** 20 W Kinzie St 60654. Between State and Dearborn sts. Int corridors. **Pets:** Accepted.
[SAVE] [&M] [📶] [✕] [🛡] [💻]

AAA ▼▼▼▼ **The Langham, Chicago** ⊞
(312) 923-9988. **$319-$770.** 330 N Wabash Ave 60611. Jct Kinzie St, just s; at Chicago River. Int corridors. **Pets:** Accepted.
[SAVE] [†1] [&M] [📶] [✕] [🛡] [💻]

▼▼▼▼ **La Quinta Inn & Suites Chicago Downtown** ⊞
(312) 558-1020. **$89-$504.** 1 S Franklin St 60606. Jct Madison Ave. Int corridors. **Pets:** Large, other species. Service with restrictions.
[†1] [&M] [⇌] [📶] [🛡] [💻]

▼▼▼▼ **MileNorth, A Chicago Hotel** ⊞
(312) 787-6000. **$169-$499.** 166 E Superior St 60611. Just e of Michigan Ave. Int corridors. **Pets:** Accepted. [📶] [✕] [🛡] [💻]

AAA ▼▼▼▼ **Omni Chicago Hotel** ⊞
(312) 944-6664. **Call for rates.** 676 N Michigan Ave 60611. Jct Huron St. Int corridors. **Pets:** Accepted.
[SAVE] [†1] [&M] [⇌] [✕] [so] [✕] [🛡] [💻]

AAA ▼▼▼▼ **Palmer House - A Hilton Hotel** ⊞ ✿
(312) 726-7500. **$89-$529.** 17 E Monroe St 60603. Between State St and Wabash Ave. Int corridors. **Pets:** Other species. $50 one-time fee/room. Service with restrictions, supervision.
[SAVE] [ECO] [†1] [⇌] [✕] [so] [✕] [🛡]

AAA ▼▼▼▼ **Park Hyatt Chicago** ⊞
(312) 335-1234. **$265-$845, 3 day notice.** 800 N Michigan Ave 60611. Jct Chicago Ave at Water Tower Square. Int corridors. **Pets:** Accepted.
[SAVE] [ECO] [†1] [&M] [⇌] [✕] [📶] [✕] [💻]

AAA ▼▼▼▼ **The Peninsula Chicago** ⊞
(312) 337-2888. **Call for rates.** 108 E Superior St 60611. Jct Michigan Ave. Int corridors. **Pets:** Accepted.
[SAVE] [ECO] [†1] [&M] [⇌] [✕] [📶] [🛡]

AAA ▼▼▼▼ **Radisson Blu Aqua Hotel** ⊞
(312) 565-5258. **$199-$459.** 221 N Columbus Dr 60601. Jct E Water St, just s of the Chicago River. Int corridors. **Pets:** Accepted.
[SAVE] [†1] [&M] [⇌] [✕] [✕] [🛡] [💻]

▼▼▼▼ **Renaissance Blackstone Chicago Hotel** ⊞
(312) 447-0955. **$160-$459.** 636 S Michigan Ave 60605. Jct Congress Pkwy, just s. Int corridors. **Pets:** Accepted.
[SAVE] [†1] [so] [✕] [🛡] [💻]

AAA ▼▼▼▼ **Residence Inn by Marriott Chicago Downtown/Magnificent Mile** ⊞
(312) 943-9800. **$167-$321.** 201 E Walton Pl 60611. Just e of Michigan Ave at Mies van der Rohe Way. Int corridors. **Pets:** Accepted.
[SAVE] [&M] [📶] [✕] [🛡] [💻]

▼▼▼▼ **Residence Inn by Marriott Chicago Downtown River North** ⊞
(312) 494-9301. **$174-$551.** 410 N Dearborn St 60654. Between W Kinzie and W Hubbard sts. Int corridors. **Pets:** Accepted.
[&M] [⇌] [📶] [✕] [🛡] [💻]

▼▼▼▼ **The Ritz-Carlton Chicago (A Four Seasons Hotel)** ⊞
(312) 266-1000. **Call for rates.** 160 E Pearson St 60611. Jct N Michigan Ave. Int corridors. **Pets:** Accepted.
[ECO] [†1] [&M] [⇌] [✕] [📶] [✕] [🛡] [💻]

AAA ▼▼▼▼ **Sheraton Chicago Hotel & Towers** ⊞
(312) 464-1000. **$199-$579.** 301 E North Water St 60611. Columbus Dr at Chicago River; just e of Michigan Ave. Int corridors. **Pets:** Accepted.
[SAVE] [ECO] [†1] [⇌] [✕] [✕] [🛡] [💻]

AAA ▼▼▼▼ **Sofitel Chicago Water Tower** ⊞
(312) 324-4000. **$140-$595, 3 day notice.** 20 E Chestnut St 60611. Jct Wabash Ave and Chestnut St, 1/2 blk w of Rush St. Int corridors. **Pets:** Accepted. [SAVE] [ECO] [†1] [&M] [📶] [✕] [🛡] [💻]

AAA ▼▼▼▼ **Thompson Chicago** ⊞
(312) 266-2100. **$159-$699, 3 day notice.** 21 E Bellevue Pl 60611. Jct Rush St. Int corridors. **Pets:** Accepted. [SAVE] [†1] [📶] [✕] [🛡]

AAA ▼▼▼▼ **Trump International Hotel & Tower** ⊞
(312) 588-8000. **Call for rates.** 401 N Wabash Ave 60611. Between Hubbard and Kinzie sts; just s of Kinzie St. Int corridors. **Pets:** Accepted. [SAVE] [†1] [&M] [⇌] [✕] [📶] [✕] [🛡] [💻]

AAA ▼▼▼▼ **Waldorf Astoria Chicago** ⊞ ✿
(312) 646-1300. **$285-$1100.** 11 E Walton St 60611. Between State and Rush sts. Int corridors. **Pets:** Medium, dogs only. $40 one-time fee/room. Supervision. [SAVE] [†1] [&M] [⇌] [✕] [📶] [✕] [🛡] [💻]

AAA ▼▼▼▼ **W Chicago-City Center** ⊞
(312) 332-1200. **Call for rates.** 172 W Adams St 60603. Between LaSalle and Wells sts. Int corridors. **Pets:** Accepted.
[SAVE] [†1] [so] [✕] [🛡]

AAA ▼▼▼▼ **W Chicago Lakeshore** ⊞
(312) 943-9200. **Call for rates.** 644 N Lake Shore Dr 60611. Jct Ontario St. Int corridors. **Pets:** Accepted.
[SAVE] [†1] [⇌] [so] [✕] [🛡]

AAA ▼▼▼▼ **The Westin Chicago River North** ⊞
(312) 744-1900. **$119-$629.** 320 N Dearborn St 60654. Just n of Chicago River; between Dearborn and Clark sts. Int corridors.
Pets: Accepted. [SAVE] [†1] [✕] [so] [✕] [🛡] [💻]

AAA ▼▼▼▼ **The Westin Michigan Avenue Chicago** ⊞ ✿
(312) 943-7200. **Call for rates.** 909 N Michigan Ave 60611. Across from John Hancock Center. Int corridors. **Pets:** Medium, dogs only. Designated rooms, service with restrictions, supervision.
[SAVE] [ECO] [†1] [&M] [so] [✕] [💻]

AAA ▼▼▼▼ **Wyndham Grand Chicago Riverfront** ⊞ ✿
(312) 346-7100. **$99-$499.** 71 E Wacker Dr 60601. Jct N Michigan Ave, just w. Int corridors. **Pets:** Medium, dogs only. $100 one-time fee/room. Designated rooms, service with restrictions, crate.
[SAVE] [†1] [&M] [📶] [✕] [🛡] [💻]

COLLINSVILLE

▼▼▼▼ **Drury Inn Collinsville-St. Louis** Ⓗ

(618) 345-7700. **$110-$184.** 602 N Bluff Rd 62234. I-55/70 exit 11 (SR 157), just n. Int corridors. **Pets:** $10 daily fee/room. Service with restrictions, supervision. 🅼 �'🍃 ⛟ 🖥

▼▼ **Super 8-Collinsville** Ⓗ

(618) 345-8008. **$59-$85.** 2 Gateway Dr 62234. I-55/70 exit 11 (SR 157), just n. Int corridors. **Pets:** Other species. $15 one-time fee/room. Supervision. 🍃 ⛟ 🖥

COLUMBIA

▼▼▼▼ **Hampton Inn** Ⓗ

(618) 281-9000. **$99-$149.** 165 Admiral Trost Dr 62236. I-255 exit 6 (SR 3), 1.5 mi s, then just e. Int corridors. **Pets:** Accepted.
🅼 �'🍃 ✕ ⛟ 🖥

CRYSTAL LAKE

▼▼ **Comfort Inn by Choice Hotels** Ⓗ

(815) 444-0040. **$79-$109.** 595 Tracy Tr 60014. Jct US 14 and SR 31, 0.4 mi w, just n on Pingree Rd, then just n. Int corridors. **Pets:** Medium. $15 daily fee/pet. Designated rooms, service with restrictions, supervision. �'🍃 ✕ ⛟ 🖥

▼▼▼▼ **Holiday Inn Chicago-Crystal Lake** Ⓗ

(815) 477-7000. **$89-$209.** 800 S SR 31 60014. At Three Oaks Rd, 0.3 mi s of jct US 14. Int corridors. **Pets:** Small. $25 daily fee/pet. Designated rooms, service with restrictions, crate. 🍴 �'🍃 ⛟ 🖥

▼ **Super 8** Ⓗ

(815) 788-8888. **$60-$89.** 577 Crystal Point Dr 60014. On US 14, 1 mi w of jct SR 31. Int corridors. **Pets:** Small. $20 daily fee/pet. Designated rooms, supervision. 🍃 ⛟ 🖥

DANVILLE

🄰🄰🄰 ▼▼ **BEST WESTERN Regency Inn** Ⓗ

(217) 446-2111. **$83-$150.** 360 Eastgate Dr 61834. I-74 exit 220 (Lynch Dr), just n. Ext/int corridors. **Pets:** $20 daily fee/pet. Designated rooms, service with restrictions, supervision. SAVE �'🍃 ⛟ 🖥

▼▼ **Sleep Inn & Suites** Ⓗ

(217) 442-6600. **$110-$160.** 361 Lynch Dr 61834. I-74 exit 220 (Lynch Dr), just n. Int corridors. **Pets:** Other species. $15 daily fee/pet. Service with restrictions, supervision. �'🍃 ✕ ⛟ 🖥

▼▼ **Super 8** Ⓗ

(217) 443-4499. **$55-$97.** 377 Lynch Dr 61834. I-74 exit 220 (Lynch Dr), just n. Int corridors. **Pets:** Accepted. 🍃 ⛟ 🖥

DARIEN

▼▼ **Extended Stay America Chicago-Darien** Ⓗ

(630) 985-4708. **$79-$99.** 2345 Sokol Ct 60561. I-55 exit 271A, 0.5 mi s to Westgate Rd, then 0.5 mi ne via frontage road. Int corridors. **Pets:** Other species. $25 daily fee/pet. Service with restrictions, supervision. 🍃 ⛟ 🖥

DECATUR

▼▼▼▼ **Decatur Conference Center & Hotel** Ⓗ

(217) 422-8800. **Call for rates.** 4191 W Hwy 36 62522. I-72 exit 133A (US 36), 1 mi e. Int corridors. **Pets:** Accepted.
🍴 🅼 �'✕ 🍃 ⛟ 🖥

▼▼▼▼ **Sleep Inn** Ⓗ

(217) 872-7700. **$79-$159.** 3920 E Hospitality Ln 62521. I-72 exit 144 (SR 48), just s to Brush College Rd, then just e. Int corridors. **Pets:** Accepted. �'🍃 ⛟ 🖥

DEERFIELD

🄰🄰🄰 ▼▼▼▼ **Chicago Marriott Suites Deerfield** Ⓗ

(847) 405-9666. **$202-$332.** 2 Parkway North 60015. I-94 exit Deerfield Rd northbound, just w; exit Lake Cook Rd southbound, 0.3 mi e to Saunders Rd, then 0.5 mi n. Int corridors. **Pets:** Small, other species. $75 one-time fee/pet. Designated rooms, service with restrictions, crate.
SAVE 🍴 �'🍃 ✕ ⛟ 🖥

▼ **Red Roof Inn Chicago - Northbrook/Deerfield** Ⓜ

(847) 205-1755. **$54-$99.** 340 S Waukegan Rd 60015. I-94 exit SR 43 (Waukegan Rd). Ext corridors. **Pets:** Large, other species. Service with restrictions, supervision. 🍃 ⛟ 🖥

▼▼▼▼ **Residence Inn by Marriott Chicago/Deerfield** Ⓗ

(847) 940-4644. **$132-$252.** 530 Lake Cook Rd 60015. I-94 exit Lake Cook Rd, 1.8 mi e, then 3 blks n on Corporate 500 Dr access road. Ext corridors. **Pets:** Accepted. �'🍃 ✕ ⛟ 🖥

DEKALB

🄰🄰🄰 ▼▼ **Red Roof Inn & Suites DeKalb** Ⓗ

(815) 758-8661. **$89-$149.** 1212 W Lincoln Hwy 60115. I-88 exit Annie Glidden Rd, 2 mi n to W Lincoln Hwy (SR 38), then just w. Ext/int corridors. **Pets:** Large, other species. Service with restrictions, supervision. SAVE 🚑'🍃 ✕ ⛟ 🖥

DES PLAINES

🄰🄰🄰 ▼▼▼ **Comfort Inn O'Hare** Ⓗ

(847) 635-1300. **$89-$149.** 2175 E Touhy Ave 60018. I-294 exit Touhy Ave westbound, just w; exit Golf Rd (SR 58) eastbound, 0.3 mi w to River Rd, then 5.5 mi s. Int corridors. **Pets:** Accepted.
SAVE 🍃 ✕ ⛟ 🖥

▼▼ **Extended Stay America-Chicago O'Hare** Ⓗ

(847) 294-9693. **$79-$109.** 1201 E Touhy Ave 60018. SR 72 (Higgins Rd), 0.6 mi w of US 12/45 (Mannheim Rd). Int corridors. **Pets:** Other species. $25 daily fee/pet. Service with restrictions, supervision.
🅼 🍃 ⛟ 🖥

▼▼ **Extended Stay America-Chicago O'Hare South** Ⓗ

(847) 768-0395. **$84-$120.** 1207 E Touhy Ave 60018. SR 72 (Higgins Rd), 0.6 mi w of US 12/45 (Mannheim Rd). Int corridors. **Pets:** Other species. $25 daily fee/pet. Service with restrictions, supervision.
🅼 🍃 ✕ ⛟ 🖥

DIXON

🄰🄰🄰 ▼▼▼ **Comfort Inn by Choice Hotels** Ⓗ

(815) 284-0500. **$100-$155.** 136 Plaza Dr 61021. I-88 exit SR 26, just n, then just e. Int corridors. **Pets:** Medium, other species. $15 daily fee/pet. Service with restrictions, crate. SAVE 🚑'🍃 ⛟ 🖥

DOWNERS GROVE

▼▼ **Holiday Inn Express** Ⓗ

(630) 810-9500. **Call for rates.** 3031 Finley Rd 60515. I-355 exit Butterfield Rd (SR 56), just e. Int corridors. **Pets:** Accepted. 🍃 ⛟ 🖥

🄰🄰🄰 ▼▼ **Red Roof Inn Chicago - Downers Grove** Ⓜ

(630) 963-4205. **$49-$129.** 1113 Butterfield Rd 60515. I-355 exit Butterfield Rd (SR 56), on frontage road; I-88 exit Highland Ave N, just w. Ext corridors. **Pets:** Large, other species. Service with restrictions, supervision. SAVE 🍃 ✕ ⛟

EAST MOLINE

▼▼▼ **Comfort Inn & Suites** Ⓗ

(309) 792-4660. **$85-$180.** 2209 John Deere Rd 61244. I-74 exit 4B (John Deere Rd), 5 mi e on SR 5. Int corridors. **Pets:** Accepted.
🅼 🚑'🍃 ✕ ⛟ 🖥

EAST PEORIA

▼▼▼▼ **Embassy Suites East Peoria-Hotel and Conference Center** Ⓗ

(309) 694-0200. **$129-$389.** 100 Conference Center Dr 61611. I-74 exit 94 (Riverfront Dr), 0.4 mi sw, follow signs. Int corridors. **Pets:** Accepted.
🍴 🅼 🚑'🍃 ✕ ⛟ 🖥

▼▼◆ **Stoney Creek Hotel & Conference Center** Ⓗ

(309) 694-1300. **Call for rates.** 101 Mariners Way 61611. I-74 exit 95 (Main St) westbound; exit 95A eastbound, just n. Int corridors. **Pets:** Accepted. 🅼 🚑'✕ 🍃 ✕ ⛟ 🖥

▼▼ **Super 8 Peoria East** Ⓗ

(309) 698-8889. **$60-$75.** 725 Taylor St 61611. I-74 exit 96, just e. Int corridors. **Pets:** Accepted. 🍃 ✕ ⛟ 🖥

EFFINGHAM

BEST WESTERN Raintree Inn
(217) 342-4121. **$70-$80.** 1811 W Fayette Ave 62401. I-57/70 exit 159, just n. Ext/int corridors. **Pets:** Medium, other species. $10 one-time fee/room. Service with restrictions, supervision.

Delta Inn
(217) 342-4499. **$89-$93, 7 day notice.** 1509 Hampton Dr 62401. I-57/70 exit 160 (SR 32/33), just s. Int corridors. **Pets:** Other species. $25 one-time fee/room. Designated rooms, service with restrictions, crate.

Fairfield Inn & Suites by Marriott Effingham
(217) 540-5454. **$70-$115.** 1111 N Henrietta St 62401. I-57/70 exit 160 (SR 32/33), just se. Int corridors. **Pets:** Other species. $20 one-time fee/room. Service with restrictions, supervision.

Quality Inn
(217) 347-5050. **$69-$79.** 1304 W Evergreen Ave 62401. I-57/70 exit 160 (SR 32/33), just e, then just n. Int corridors. **Pets:** Large, other species. $10 one-time fee/pet. Designated rooms, service with restrictions, supervision.

Super 8-Effingham
(217) 342-6888. **$50-$62.** 1400 Thelma Keller Ave 62401. I-57/70 exit 160 (SR 32/33), 0.5 mi n. Int corridors. **Pets:** Accepted.

ELGIN

Candlewood Suites
(847) 888-0600. **$100-$120.** 1780 Capital St 60124. I-90 exit N Randall Rd, just s to Westfield Dr, then 0.3 mi w. Int corridors. **Pets:** Medium. $25 daily fee/pet. Designated rooms, service with restrictions.

Quality Inn by Choice Hotels-Elgin
(847) 608-7300. **$65-$89.** 500 Tollgate Rd 60123. I-90 exit SR 31 N, just n. Int corridors. **Pets:** Medium. $10 daily fee/pet. Designated rooms, service with restrictions, supervision.

ELK GROVE VILLAGE

La Quinta Inn Chicago O'Hare Airport
(847) 439-6767. **$75-$254.** 1900 E Oakton St 60007. Jct SR 72 (Higgins Rd) and 83 (Busse Rd). Int corridors. **Pets:** Large, other species. Service with restrictions.

Motel 6 O'Hare
(847) 803-9400. **$59-$109.** 2881 Touhy Ave 60007. Jct SR 72 (Higgins Rd) and 83 (Busse Rd), 1.5 mi e on SR 72 (Higgins Rd). Int corridors. **Pets:** Other species. Service with restrictions, crate.

Motel 6 Schaumburg/Elk Grove
(847) 895-2085. **$59-$109.** 1000 W Devon Ave 60007. I-290 exit Thorndale Ave, 0.5 mi w to Rohlwing Rd, 0.3 mi n to Devon Ave, then 0.3 mi e. Int corridors. **Pets:** Other species. Service with restrictions, crate.

Sheraton Suites Chicago Elk Grove
(847) 290-1600. **$79-$179.** 121 Northwest Point Blvd 60007. I-90 exit Arlington Heights Rd, just s; in Northwest Point Corporate Park. Int corridors. **Pets:** Accepted.

Super 8 O'Hare
(847) 827-3133. **$63-$128.** 2951 Touhy Ave 60007. Jct SR 72 (Higgins Rd) and 83 (Busse Rd); 1.5 mi e on SR 72 (Higgins Rd). Int corridors. **Pets:** Accepted.

ELMHURST

Clarion Inn Elmhurst-Oakbrook
(630) 279-0700. **Call for rates.** 933 S Riverside Dr 60126. 2.4 mi s of SR 64 (North Ave), just off SR 83. Int corridors. **Pets:** Accepted.

Extended Stay America Chicago-Elmhurst-O'Hare
(630) 530-4353. **$75-$109.** 550 W Grand Ave 60126. Jct US 20 (Lake St), 0.4 mi ne; adjacent to I-290 overpass. Int corridors. **Pets:** Other species. $25 daily fee/pet. Service with restrictions, supervision.

EVANSTON

Hilton Orrington/Evanston
(847) 866-8700. **$129-$399.** 1710 Orrington Ave 60201. Jct Church St. Int corridors. **Pets:** Medium, dogs only. $50 one-time fee/room. Designated rooms, service with restrictions.

FAIRVIEW HEIGHTS

Americas Best Value Inn
(618) 624-3636. **$50-$90.** 305 Salem Pl 62208. I-64 exit 12 (SR 159), just n. Int corridors. **Pets:** Medium. $10 daily fee/pet. Designated rooms, crate.

Comfort Suites
(618) 394-0202. **$84-$155.** 137 Ludwig Dr 62208. I-64 exit 12 (SR 159), just n, then 0.4 mi w. Int corridors. **Pets:** Accepted.

Drury Inn & Suites-Fairview Heights
(618) 398-8530. **$115-$189.** 12 Ludwig Dr 62208. I-64 exit 12 (SR 159), just n. Int corridors. **Pets:** $10 daily fee/room. Service with restrictions, supervision.

Fairfield Inn by Marriott
(618) 398-7124. **$129-$149.** 140 Ludwig Dr 62208. I-64 exit 12 (SR 159), just n, then 0.5 mi w. Int corridors. **Pets:** Medium, other species. $25 daily fee/room. Designated rooms, service with restrictions, supervision.

FLORA

BEST WESTERN Lorson Inn
(618) 662-3054. **$76-$90.** 201 Hagen Dr 62839. Jct US 45 and 50. Int corridors. **Pets:** Accepted.

FORSYTH

Hampton Inn Decatur-Forsyth
(217) 877-5577. **$99-$199.** 1429 Hickory Point Dr 62535. I-72 exit 141B (US 51), 0.5 mi n. Int corridors. **Pets:** Medium, other species. $50 deposit/room. Service with restrictions, crate.

Quality Inn Forsyth
(217) 875-1166. **$85-$216.** 134 Barnett Ave 62535. I-72 exit 141B (US 51), 0.5 mi n. Int corridors. **Pets:** Small. $10 daily fee/pet. Service with restrictions, supervision.

FREEPORT

Baymont Inn & Suites-Freeport
(815) 599-8510. **$89-$119.** 1060 Riverside Dr 61032. Jct US 20 Bypass and SR 26, just s. Int corridors. **Pets:** Large, other species. $35 one-time fee/room. Designated rooms, service with restrictions, crate.

GALENA

BEST WESTERN Designer Inn & Suites
(815) 777-2577. **$99-$260.** 9923 US Rt 20 W 61036. On US 20, 1 mi e. Ext/int corridors. **Pets:** Small, dogs only. $15 daily fee/pet. Designated rooms, service with restrictions, crate.

Eagle Ridge Resort & Spa
(815) 777-5000. **$139-$319, 7 day notice.** 444 Eagle Ridge Dr 61036. US 20, 6 mi e to E Glen Hollow Rd, 4.5 mi n. Ext/int corridors. **Pets:** Small, dogs only. $75 one-time fee/pet. Designated rooms, service with restrictions, crate.

▼▼ Stoney Creek Inn **H**

(815) 777-2223. **Call for rates.** 940 Galena Square Dr 61036. On US 20, 1.8 mi w. Int corridors. **Pets:** Accepted.

🔁 ✕ 🛜 ✕ 🔋 🖳

GALESBURG

🌀 ▼▼ BEST WESTERN Prairie Inn & Conference Center **H**

(309) 343-7151. **$94-$159, 3 day notice.** 300 S Soangetaha Rd 61401. I-74 exit 48 (Main St), just e, then just s. Int corridors. **Pets:** Medium. $20 daily fee/pet. Designated rooms, service with restrictions, supervision. **SAVE** 🍴 🔁 🛜 ✕ 🔋 🖳

▼▼ Holiday Inn Express **H**

(309) 343-7100. **$109-$149.** 2285 Washington St 61401. I-74 exit 48A (US 150), just w to Michigan Ave, just s to Washington St, then just e. Int corridors. **Pets:** Other species. $25 one-time fee/room. Service with restrictions, supervision. **M** 🔁 🛜 ✕ 🔋 🖳

GENESEO

🌀 ▼▼ BEST WESTERN Geneseo Inn **H**

(309) 945-9345. **Call for rates.** 1375 S Oakwood Ave 61254. I-80 exit 19 (US 6/SR 82), just n. Int corridors. **Pets:** Accepted.

SAVE 🛜 ✕ 🔋 🖳

GENEVA

🌀 ▼▼▼▼ The Herrington Inn & Spa **CI** 🐾

(630) 208-7433. **$179-$550.** 15 S River Ln 60134. Just off SR 38, 0.5 mi w of jct SR 25. **Pets:** Dogs only. $100 one-time fee/room, $25 daily fee/room. Designated rooms, service with restrictions, crate. **SAVE** 🍴 🛜 ✕ 🖳

GILMAN

🌀 ▼ Super 8 **H**

(815) 265-7000. **$58-$102.** 1301 S Crescent St 60938. I-57 exit 283, 0.3 mi e. Int corridors. **Pets:** Medium, dogs only. $25 deposit/pet, $10 daily fee/pet. Service with restrictions, crate. **SAVE** 🛜 🔋 🖳

GLEN ELLYN

▼▼▼ Crowne Plaza Lombard Downers Grove **H**

(630) 629-6000. **Call for rates.** 1250 Roosevelt Rd 60137. I-355 exit Roosevelt Rd, 0.8 mi e on SR 38. Int corridors. **Pets:** Accepted.

🍴 **M** 🔁 🛜 ✕ 🔋 🖳

GLENVIEW

▼▼▼ Staybridge Suites Glenview **H**

(847) 657-0002. **Call for rates.** 2600 Lehigh Ave 60026. I-294 exit Willow Rd, 2.4 mi e. Int corridors. **Pets:** Medium, other species. $13 daily fee/pet. Service with restrictions, crate. **M** 🔁 🛜 ✕ 🔋 🖳

GRAYSLAKE

▼▼▼ Comfort Suites by Choice Hotels **H**

(847) 223-5050. **$89-$199.** 1775 E Belvidere Rd 60030. Just w of jct US 45. Int corridors. **Pets:** $35 one-time fee/room. Supervision.

🔁 🛜 ✕ 🔋 🖳

GRAYVILLE

▼▼ Super 8 **H**

(618) 375-7288. **$55-$105.** 2060 CR 2450 N 62844. I-64 exit 130 (SR 1), just n. Int corridors. **Pets:** Medium, other species. $15 one-time fee/room. Service with restrictions, supervision. **M** 🛜 ✕ 🔋 🖳

GREENVILLE

▼▼ Econo Lodge Inn & Suites **M**

(618) 664-3030. **$53-$120.** 1731 S SR 127 62246. I-70 exit 45, just n. Ext/int corridors. **Pets:** $10 daily fee/pet. Designated rooms, service with restrictions, supervision. 🔁 🛜 🔋 🖳

▼▼ Super 8-Greenville **H**

(618) 664-0800. **$50-$96.** 1700 SR 127 S 62246. I-70 exit 45, just n. Int corridors. **Pets:** Accepted. 🛜 🔋 🖳

GURNEE

🌀 ▼▼ BEST WESTERN Gurnee Hotel & Suites **H**

(847) 782-0890. **$79-$119, 3 day notice.** 5430 Grand Ave 60031. I-94 exit Grand Ave (SR 132 E), 0.5 mi e. Int corridors. **Pets:** Accepted.

SAVE **M** 🔁 🛜 ✕ 🔋 🖳

▼▼ Comfort Inn by Choice Hotels **H**

(847) 855-8866. **$80-$139.** 6080 Gurnee Mills Cir E 60031. I-94 exit Grand Ave (SR 132 W), just nw. Int corridors. **Pets:** Accepted.

🔁 🛜 🔋 🖳

▼▼ Country Inn & Suites By Carlson **H**

(847) 625-9700. **Call for rates.** 5420 Grand Ave 60031. I-94 exit Grand Ave (SR 132 E), 0.5 mi e. Int corridors. **Pets:** Accepted.

M 🔁 🛜 ✕ 🔋 🖳

▼▼ La Quinta Inn & Suites Chicago Gurnee **H**

(847) 662-7600. **$65-$200.** 5688 Northridge Dr 60031. I-94 exit Grand Ave (SR 132 E), just e via service road. Int corridors. **Pets:** Large, other species. Service with restrictions. **M** 🔁 🛜 🔋 🖳

HANOVER PARK

▼▼ Extended Stay America-Chicago-Hanover Park **H**

(630) 893-4823. **$79-$109.** 1075 Lake St 60133. On US 20; between Gary Ave and Elgin-O'Hare Expwy. Int corridors. **Pets:** Other species. $25 daily fee/pet. Service with restrictions, supervision. 🛜 🔋 🖳

HILLSIDE

🌀 ▼▼▼ BEST WESTERN PLUS Chicago Hillside **H**

(708) 544-9300. **$79-$159.** 4400 Frontage Rd 60162. I-290 exit 14B eastbound; exit 17 westbound to US 12/45 (Mannheim Rd), just nw via frontage road. Int corridors. **Pets:** Medium. $50 one-time fee/room. Service with restrictions, crate. **SAVE** 🍴 🔁 🛜 🔋 🖳

HOFFMAN ESTATES

🌀 ▼▼ Hawthorn Suites by Wyndham **H**

(847) 490-1686. **$79-$114.** 2875 Greenspoint Pkwy 60169. I-90 exit Barrington Rd westbound, just s to SR 72 (Higgins Rd), then just w; exit SR 59 eastbound, 0.5 mi n to SR 72 (Higgins Rd), then 2 mi e. Int corridors. **Pets:** Accepted. **SAVE** 🛜 ✕ 🔋 🖳

🌀 ▼▼▼ Hyatt Place Chicago/Hoffman Estates **H**

(847) 839-1800. **$75-$199.** 2750 Greenspoint Pkwy 60169. I-90 exit Barrington Rd westbound, 0.3 mi s; exit SR 59 eastbound, 0.5 mi n to SR 72 (Higgins Rd), 2 mi e to Barrington Rd, then just n. Int corridors. **Pets:** Accepted. **SAVE** **M** 🔁 🛜 ✕ 🔋 🖳

▼▼ La Quinta Inn Chicago Hoffman Estates **H**

(847) 882-3312. **$62-$195.** 2280 Barrington Rd 60169. I-90 exit Barrington Rd westbound, 0.3 mi s; exit SR 59 eastbound, 0.5 mi n to SR 72 (Higgins Rd), 2 mi e to Barrington Rd, then just n. Int corridors. **Pets:** Large, other species. Service with restrictions. 🔁 🛜 🔋 🖳

ITASCA

▼▼ Extended Stay America-Chicago-Itasca **H**

(630) 250-1111. **$64-$99.** 1181 Rohlwing Rd 60143. I-290 exit Thorndale Ave, 0.5 mi w. Int corridors. **Pets:** Other species. $25 daily fee/pet. Service with restrictions, supervision. **M** 🛜 🔋 🖳

🌀 ▼▼▼ Hyatt Place Chicago/Itasca **H**

(630) 875-1400. **$69-$509.** 1150 Arlington Heights Rd 60143. I-290 exit Thorndale Ave, 0.6 mi e, then 0.5 mi n. Int corridors. **Pets:** Accepted.

SAVE 🍴 **M** 🔁 🛜 ✕ 🔋 🖳

🌀 ▼▼▼▼ The Westin Chicago Northwest **H** 🐾

(630) 773-4000. **$79-$299.** 400 Park Blvd 60143. I-290 exit Thorndale Ave, just e. Int corridors. **Pets:** Medium. Service with restrictions, crate.

SAVE 🍴 🔁 ✕ 🛜 ✕ 🔋 🖳

JACKSONVILLE

BEST WESTERN Jacksonville Inn M

(217) 245-4500. **Call for rates.** 1709 W Morton Ave 62650. I-72 exit 64, 2.3 mi n on SR 267 (Main St) to SR 104 (Morton Ave), then 1.5 mi w. Int corridors. **Pets:** $10 daily fee/pet. Service with restrictions, crate.

Starlite Motel M

(217) 245-7184. **$40-$85.** 1910 W Morton Ave 62650. I-72 exit 64, 2.3 mi n on SR 267 (Main St) to SR 104 (Morton Ave), then 1.8 mi w. Ext corridors. **Pets:** Small. $5 daily fee/pet. Service with restrictions.

Super 8 H

(217) 479-0303. **$58-$105.** 1003 W Morton Ave 62650. I-72 exit 64, 2.3 mi n on SR 267 (Main St) to SR 104 (Morton Ave), then 0.8 mi w. Int corridors. **Pets:** $10 daily fee/pet. Service with restrictions, crate.

JOLIET

Comfort Inn by Choice Hotels Joliet North H

(815) 436-5141. **$80-$219.** 3235 Norman Ave 60435. I-55 exit 257, just e. Int corridors. **Pets:** Medium. $34 one-time fee/pet. Service with restrictions, supervision.

Fairfield Inn by Marriott Joliet South H

(815) 741-3499. **$83-$171.** 1501 Riverboat Center Dr 60436. I-80 exit 127, just n. Int corridors. **Pets:** Accepted.

Quality Inn & Suites South H

(815) 744-1770. **$79-$180.** 135 S Larkin Ave 60436. I-80 exit 130B, 0.5 mi n. Int corridors. **Pets:** Medium. $35 one-time fee/pet. Service with restrictions, supervision.

Red Roof Inn Chicago - Joliet M

(815) 741-2304. **$49-$189.** 1750 McDonough St 60436. I-80 exit 130B, just off Larkin Ave. Ext corridors. **Pets:** Large, other species. Service with restrictions, supervision.

TownePlace Suites by Marriott Joliet South H ✿

(815) 741-2400. **$97-$183.** 1515 Riverboat Center Dr 60431. I-80 exit 127, just n. Int corridors. **Pets:** Large, other species. $25 one-time fee/room. Service with restrictions, crate.

KEWANEE

AmericInn Lodge & Suites of Kewanee H

(309) 856-7200. **Call for rates.** 925 Tenney St 61443. On SR 78, 1.9 mi s of jct US 34. Int corridors. **Pets:** Accepted.

LAKE ZURICH

Holiday Inn Express & Suites Lake Zurich-Barrington H

(847) 726-7500. **Call for rates.** 197 S Rand Rd 60047. On US 12, 0.3 mi nw of SR 22. Int corridors. **Pets:** Accepted.

LANSING

Extended Stay America-Chicago-Lansing H

(708) 895-6402. **$79-$109.** 2520 173rd St 60438. I-80/94 exit 161 (Torrence Ave), just n to 173rd St, then just e. Int corridors. **Pets:** Other species. $25 daily fee/pet. Service with restrictions, supervision.

LEROY

Days Inn Le Roy - Bloomington SE M

(309) 962-4700. **$54-$63.** 1 Demma Dr 61752. I-74 exit 149, just sw. Int corridors. **Pets:** Accepted.

Holiday Inn Express H

(309) 962-4439. **Call for rates.** 705 S Persimmons Ct 61752. I-74 exit 149, just ne. Int corridors. **Pets:** Accepted.

LIBERTYVILLE

Candlewood Suites Chicago-Libertyville H

(847) 247-9900. **Call for rates.** 1100 N US 45 60048. I-94 exit SR 137 (Buckley Rd), 5.6 mi w to US 45, then 1.4 mi s. Int corridors. **Pets:** Accepted.

Holiday Inn Express & Suites H

(847) 549-7878. **$99-$299.** 77 Buckley Rd 60048. I-94 exit SR 137 (Buckley Rd), 2.3 mi w. Int corridors. **Pets:** Accepted.

LINCOLN

BEST WESTERN PLUS Lincoln Inn H

(217) 732-9641. **$75-$90.** 1750 5th St 62656. I-55 exit 126 (US 121), 1.6 mi e to Lincoln Pkwy, then 0.5 mi s. Int corridors. **Pets:** Accepted.

Hampton Inn - Lincoln H

(217) 732-6729. **$94-$119.** 1019 N Heitman Dr 62656. I-55 exit 126 (US 121), just e. Int corridors. **Pets:** Medium, other species. Service with restrictions, supervision.

Holiday Inn Express H

(217) 735-5800. **$89-$129, 3 day notice.** 130 Olson Dr 62656. I-55 exit 126 (US 121), just e. Int corridors. **Pets:** Accepted.

LINCOLNSHIRE

Homewood Suites by Hilton Chicago-Lincolnshire H

(847) 945-9300. **$89-$219.** 10 Westminster Way 60069. I-94 exit Half Day Rd, just w. Int corridors. **Pets:** Accepted.

Staybridge Suites Lincolnshire H

(847) 821-0002. **Call for rates.** 100 Barclay Blvd 60069. I-94 exit Half Day Rd, 2.2 mi w to Barclay Blvd, then just s; just w of jct US 45 and SR 21; in Lincolnshire Corporate Center. Int corridors. **Pets:** Accepted.

LISLE

Extended Stay America-Chicago-Lisle H

(630) 434-7710. **$69-$99.** 445 Warrenville Rd 60532. I-355 exit Ogden Ave, just nw. Int corridors. **Pets:** Other species. $25 daily fee/pet. Service with restrictions, supervision.

Hyatt Lisle H

(630) 852-1234. **$49-$239.** 1400 Corporetum Dr 60532. I-88 exit SR 53 westbound, 0.3 mi s; exit Naperville Rd eastbound to Warrenville Rd, 2 mi e to jct SR 53. Int corridors. **Pets:** Accepted.

Sheraton Lisle Hotel H ✿

(630) 505-1000. **Call for rates.** 3000 Warrenville Rd 60532. I-88 exit Naperville Rd, just n, then 0.3 mi e. Int corridors. **Pets:** Small. $200 deposit/room. Designated rooms, service with restrictions, supervision.

LITCHFIELD

Hampton Inn H

(217) 324-4441. **$74-$154.** 11 Thunderbird Cir 62056. I-55 exit 52 (SR 16), on Corvette Dr, then just e. Int corridors. **Pets:** Large. $100 deposit/room. Service with restrictions, crate.

Holiday Inn Express H

(217) 324-4556. **$109-$169.** 1405 W Hudson Dr 62056. I-55 exit 52 (SR 16), just e to Ohren Ln, just s to W Hudson Dr, then just w. Int corridors. **Pets:** Other species. Service with restrictions, supervision.

 Quality Inn Litchfield 🅷

(217) 324-9260. **$77-$120.** 1010 E Columbian Blvd N 62056. I-55 exit 52 (SR 16), just e to Ohren Ln, just s to W Hudson Dr, then just w. Int corridors. **Pets:** Small. $10 daily fee/pet. Crate.

LOMBARD

 Embassy Suites Chicago-Lombard/Oak Brook 🅷

(630) 969-7500. **$109-$219.** 707 E Butterfield Rd 60148. I-88 exit Highland Ave, just n to Butterfield Rd (SR 56), then 0.5 mi e. Int corridors. **Pets:** Other species. $50 one-time fee/room. Designated rooms, service with restrictions, crate.

Extended Stay America-Chicago-Lombard-Oak Brook 🅷

(630) 928-0202. **$69-$99.** 2701 Technology Dr 60148. I-88 exit Highland Ave, just n, 0.6 mi e on Butterfield Rd (SR 56), then just s. Int corridors. **Pets:** Other species. $25 daily fee/pet. Service with restrictions, supervision.

Extended Stay America-Chicago-Yorktown-Oak Brook 🅷

(630) 424-1000. **$74-$99.** 260 E 22nd St 60148. I-88 exit Highland Ave, 0.8 mi n to 22nd St, then just e. Int corridors. **Pets:** Other species. $25 daily fee/pet. Service with restrictions, supervision.

Residence Inn by Marriott Chicago-Lombard 🅷

(630) 629-7800. **$104-$171.** 2001 S Highland Ave 60148. I-88 exit Highland Ave, 0.8 mi n. Ext corridors. **Pets:** Accepted.

TownePlace Suites by Marriott Chicago Lombard 🅷

(630) 932-4400. **$90-$160.** 455 E 22nd St 60148. I-88 exit Highland Ave, 0.8 mi n, then 0.3 mi e. Int corridors. **Pets:** Accepted.

The Westin Lombard Yorktown Center 🅷 ❀

(630) 719-8000. **$129-$359.** 70 Yorktown Center 60148. I-88 exit Highland Ave, just n to Butterfield Rd (SR 56), then just w; in The Shops on Butterfield. Int corridors. **Pets:** Medium, dogs only. Service with restrictions, supervision.

LOVES PARK

Holiday Inn Express Hotel & Suites Rockford North 🅷

(815) 654-4100. **$100-$150.** 7552 Park Pl 61111. I-39/90 exit E Riverside Blvd, just nw. Int corridors. **Pets:** Accepted.

Quality Inn & Suites Rockford/Loves Park 🅷

(815) 282-9300. **$75-$150.** 4313 N Bell School Rd 61111. I-39/90 exit E Riverside Blvd, just nw. Int corridors. **Pets:** Accepted.

MARION

Country Inn & Suites By Carlson 🅷

(618) 997-2444. **Call for rates.** 1306 Halfway Rd 62959. I-57 exit 54, 2.8 mi w on SR 13, 1 mi n on DeYoung St, then just e. Int corridors. **Pets:** Accepted.

Drury Inn-Marion 🅷

(618) 997-9600. **$95-$149.** 2706 W DeYoung St 62959. I-57 exit 54B (SR 13), 0.5 mi w. Int corridors. **Pets:** $10 daily fee/room. Service with restrictions, supervision.

Quality Inn & Suites 🅷

(618) 993-6221. **$64-$139.** 2600 W Main St 62959. I-57 exit 53 (Main St), just w. Int corridors. **Pets:** Small. $15 daily fee/pet. Designated rooms, service with restrictions, supervision.

Super 8 🅷

(618) 993-5577. **$61-$85.** 2601 W Vernell Rd 62959. I-57 exit 54B (SR 13), just w. Int corridors. **Pets:** Small. $10 daily fee/pet. Service with restrictions, supervision.

MATTOON

Baymont Inn & Suites 🅷 ❀

(217) 234-2420. **$69-$99.** 206 McFall Rd 61938. I-57 exit 190B, just w. Int corridors. **Pets:** Other species. $20 daily fee/pet. Designated rooms, service with restrictions, supervision.

Holiday Inn Express Hotel & Suites 🅷

(217) 235-2060. **$90-$139.** 121 Swords Dr 61938. I-57 exit 190B, just w. Int corridors. **Pets:** $10 daily fee/pet. Service with restrictions, supervision.

Quality Inn & Suites Conference Center 🅷

(217) 235-0222. **Call for rates.** 4922 Paradise Rd 61938. I-57 exit 184, just w. Int corridors. **Pets:** Accepted.

Super 8 🅼

(217) 235-8888. **$69-$114.** 205 McFall Rd 61938. I-57 exit 190B, just w. Int corridors. **Pets:** Small. $15 one-time fee/pet. Designated rooms, service with restrictions, supervision.

METROPOLIS

Harrah's Metropolis Casino & Hotel 🅷

(618) 524-2628. **Call for rates.** 100 E Front St 62960. I-24 exit 37 (US 45), 3.5 mi w, then just s on Ferry St; between Metropolis and Ferry sts. Int corridors. **Pets:** Accepted.

METTAWA

Residence Inn by Marriott Chicago Lake Forest/Mettawa 🅷

(847) 615-2701. **$182-$299.** 26325 N Riverwoods Blvd 60045. I-94 exit SR 60 (Townline Rd), just nw. Int corridors. **Pets:** Accepted.

MOLINE

Comfort Inn by Choice Hotels 🅷 ❀

(309) 762-7000. **$95-$150.** 2600 52nd Ave 61265. I-280/74 exit 18A eastbound; exit 5B westbound, just s on US 6 and 150, then 0.5 mi nw on 27th St. Int corridors. **Pets:** $10 daily fee/pet. Designated rooms, service with restrictions.

Fairfield Inn by Marriott 🅷

(309) 762-9083. **$90-$160.** 2705 48th Ave 61265. I-280/74 exit 5B westbound; exit 18A eastbound, just s on US 6 to traffic light, then 1 mi nw on 27th St. Int corridors. **Pets:** $75 one-time fee/room. Service with restrictions, crate.

La Quinta Inn Moline Airport 🅷

(309) 762-9008. **$59-$199.** 5450 27th St 61265. I-280/74 exit 18A eastbound; exit 5B westbound, just s on US 6 and 150 to traffic light, then just nw. Int corridors. **Pets:** Large, other species. Service with restrictions.

Stoney Creek Inn & Conference Center 🅷

(309) 743-0101. **$104-$199.** 101 18th St 61265. Jct 18th St and 2nd Ave. Int corridors. **Pets:** Accepted.

MONMOUTH

AmericInn Lodge & Suites of Monmouth 🅷

(309) 734-9958. **$99, 3 day notice.** 1 AmericInn Way 61462. Jct US 34 and N Main St, just s; 18 mi w of jct I-74 and US 34. Int corridors. **Pets:** Small, dogs only. $75 one-time fee/room. Service with restrictions, supervision.

MONTICELLO

BEST WESTERN Monticello Gateway Inn H

(217) 762-9436. **$75-$180.** 805 Iron Horse Pl 61856. I-72 exit 166, just s. Ext/int corridors. **Pets:** Other species. $10 daily fee/pet. Service with restrictions, crate. SAVE ⊇ ⊚ ✕ ☐ ▣

MORRIS

Holiday Inn Express & Suites H

(815) 941-8700. **Call for rates.** 222 Gore Rd 60450. I-80 exit 112 (SR 47), just nw. Int corridors. **Pets:** Accepted. ⓂⒶ ⊇ ⊚ ☐ ▣

Quality Inn by Choice Hotels H

(815) 942-6600. **$85-$125.** 200 Gore Rd 60450. I-80 exit 112 (SR 47), 0.3 mi nw. Int corridors. **Pets:** Accepted. ❚❙ ⊇ ☐ ▣

MORTON

Baymont Inn & Suites H

(309) 266-8888. **$75-$105.** 210 E Ashland St 61550. I-74 exit 102, 0.4 mi ne. Int corridors. **Pets:** Accepted. SAVE ⊇ ⊚ ☐ ▣

BEST WESTERN Ashland House & Conference Center H

(309) 263-5116. **$86-$120.** 201 E Ashland St 61550. I-74 exit 102, 0.3 mi ne. Int corridors. **Pets:** Small, dogs only. $10 daily fee/pet. Designated rooms, service with restrictions, supervision.

SAVE ❚❙ ⊇ ⊚ ☐ ▣

Holiday Inn Express Hotel & Suites Morton-Peoria H

(309) 263-4400. **Call for rates.** 140 E Ashland St 61550. I-74 exit 102, 0.3 mi ne. Int corridors. **Pets:** Accepted. Ⓜ ⊚ ✕ ☐ ▣

Quality Inn by Choice Hotels H

(309) 266-8310. **$65-$80.** 115 E Ashland Ave 61550. I-74 exit 102B, just w. Ext/int corridors. **Pets:** Dogs only. $25 daily fee/pet. Designated rooms, service with restrictions, supervision. ⊚ ☐ ▣

MORTON GROVE

BEST WESTERN Morton Grove Inn M

(847) 965-6400. **Call for rates.** 9424 Waukegan Rd 60053. SR 43, just s of Golf Rd (SR 58). Ext corridors. **Pets:** Accepted.

SAVE ⊚ ☐ ▣

MOUNT VERNON

Comfort Suites H

(618) 244-2700. **$104-$160.** 404 S 44th St 62864. I-57/64 exit 95 (SR 15), just e. Int corridors. **Pets:** Accepted. ⊇ ⊚ ✕ ☐ ▣

Holiday Inn H

(618) 244-7100. **Call for rates.** 222 Potomac Blvd 62864. I-57/64 exit 95 (SR 15), just w to Potomac Blvd, then just n. Int corridors. **Pets:** Accepted. ❚❙ Ⓜ ⊇ ⊚ ☐ ▣

MUNDELEIN

DoubleTree by Hilton Libertyville - Mundelein H ❀

(847) 949-5100. **$79-$199.** 510 E Illinois (Rt 83) 60060. Jct US 45. Int corridors. **Pets:** Other species. $50 one-time fee/room. Service with restrictions, crate. ❚❙ ⊇ ⊚ ✕ ☐ ▣

NAPERVILLE

BEST WESTERN Naperville Inn H ❀

(630) 505-0200. **$79-$150.** 1617 N Naperville Wheaton Rd 60563. I-88 exit Naperville Rd, just e on Diehl Rd to Naperville Rd, then just s. Ext/int corridors. **Pets:** Medium, dogs only. $10 daily fee/pet. Designated rooms, service with restrictions, supervision. SAVE ⊚ ☐ ▣

Country Inn & Suites By Carlson H

(630) 505-3353. **$69-$219, 3 day notice.** 1837 Centre Point Cir 60563. I-88 exit Naperville Rd, 0.3 mi s to Diehl Rd, 0.7 mi w, then just n. Int corridors. **Pets:** Accepted. SAVE ECO ⊇ ⊚ ✕ ☐ ▣

Extended Stay America Chicago-Naperville-East H

(630) 577-0200. **$64-$99.** 1827 Centre Point Cir 60563. I-88 exit Naperville Rd, just s to Diehl Rd, 0.8 mi w, then just n. Int corridors. **Pets:** Other species. $25 daily fee/pet. Service with restrictions, supervision. Ⓜ ⊚ ☐

Hotel Arista at CityGate Centre H

(630) 579-4100. **Call for rates.** 2139 CityGate Ln 60563. I-88 exit SR 59, just n. Int corridors. **Pets:** Accepted.

SAVE ECO ❚❙ Ⓜ ⊚ ✕ ☐ ▣

Red Roof Plus+ Chicago - Naperville M

(630) 369-2500. **$59-$90.** 1698 W Diehl Rd 60563. I-88 exit SR 59, just s. Ext corridors. **Pets:** Large, other species. Service with restrictions, supervision. SAVE ⊚ ✕ ☐

TownePlace Suites by Marriott Naperville H

(630) 548-0881. **$91-$171.** 1843 W Diehl Rd 60563. I-88 exit SR 59, just s to Diehl Rd, then just w. Int corridors. **Pets:** Accepted.

⊇ ⊚ ✕ ☐ ▣

NASHVILLE

BEST WESTERN U. S. Inn H

(618) 478-5341. **$69-$76.** 11640 SR 127 62263. I-64 exit 50 (SR 127), 0.3 mi s. Int corridors. **Pets:** Small. $10 daily fee/pet. Service with restrictions, supervision. SAVE Ⓜ ⊇ ⊚ ☐ ▣

NORMAL

Comfort Suites by Choice Hotels Bloomington/Normal H

(309) 452-8588. **$79-$139.** 310 B Greenbriar Dr 61761. I-55 exit 167, follow I-55 business route (Veterans Pkwy), 1.3 mi s; jct Fort Jesse Rd. Int corridors. **Pets:** Accepted. Ⓜ ⊇ ⊚ ✕ ☐ ▣

NORTHBROOK

Hilton Chicago/Northbrook H

(847) 480-7500. **$94-$236.** 2855 N Milwaukee Ave 60062. On SR 21, s of jct US 45 and Willow Rd. Int corridors. **Pets:** Accepted.

SAVE ❚❙ ⊇ ✕ ⊚ ✕ ☐ ▣

Renaissance Chicago North Shore H

(847) 498-6500. **$174-$286.** 933 Skokie Blvd 60062. I-94 exit Dundee Rd W northbound; exit SR 43 (Waukegan Rd) southbound, 0.5 mi s to SR 68, then 1.5 mi e. Int corridors. **Pets:** Other species. $75 one-time fee/room. Designated rooms, service with restrictions, crate.

SAVE ❚❙ ⊇ ⊚ ✕ ☐ ▣

Sheraton Chicago Northbrook Hotel H ❀

(847) 480-1900. **$84-$199.** 1110 Willow Rd 60062. 2 mi w of jct I-94; 3.2 mi e of jct I-294. Int corridors. **Pets:** Other species. Service with restrictions, crate. SAVE ❚❙ Ⓜ ⊇ ⊚ ✕ ☐ ▣

OAK BROOK

Hilton Chicago/Oak Brook Hills Resort & Conference Center H ❀

(630) 850-5555. **$119-$209.** 3500 Midwest Rd 60523. I-88 exit SR 83 westbound, 0.5 mi s to 31st St, 1 mi w to Midwest Rd, then 0.6 mi s; exit Midwest Rd eastbound, 1.3 mi s. Int corridors. **Pets:** Medium, dogs only. $50 one-time fee/room. Designated rooms, service with restrictions, supervision. SAVE ❚❙ Ⓜ ⊇ ✕ ⊚ ✕ ☐ ▣

Le Meridien Chicago - Oakbrook Center H

(630) 368-9900. **$129-$409.** 2100 Spring Rd 60523. Just e of SR 83, just n of 22nd St (Cermak Rd). Int corridors. **Pets:** Accepted.

SAVE ❚❙ Ⓜ ⊇ ⊚ ✕ ☐ ▣

▼▼▼▼ Residence Inn by Marriott Chicago/Oak Brook **H**

(630) 571-1200. **$133-$240.** 790 Jorie Blvd 60523. I-88 exit Midwest Rd eastbound, just n to 22nd St (Cermak Rd), 1.7 mi e to Jorie Blvd, then just sw; exit 22nd St (Cermak Rd) westbound, 0.4 mi e to Jorie Blvd. Int corridors. **Pets:** Accepted. ⓜ ⌫ 🛜 ✕ ❚ 💻

OAKBROOK TERRACE

ⒶⒶⒶ ▼▼▼▼ Holiday Inn Chicago-Oak Brook **H**

(630) 833-3600. **Call for rates.** 17 W 350 22nd St 60181. I-88 exit Midwest Rd eastbound, 0.4 mi n to 22nd St (Cermak Rd), then just e; exit 22nd St (Cermak Rd) westbound, then 0.9 mi w. Int corridors. **Pets:** Accepted. ⓢⒶⓥⒺ ¶¶ ⌫ 🛜 ❚ 💻

ⒶⒶⒶ ▼▼◆ La Quinta Inn Chicago Oakbrook Terrace **H**

(630) 495-4600. **$69-$234.** 1 S 666 Midwest Rd 60181. I-88 exit Midwest Rd eastbound, 0.4 mi n, then just n of 22nd St (Cermak Rd); exit 22nd St (Cermak Rd) westbound, 1.1 mi w to Midwest Rd, then just n. Int corridors. **Pets:** Large, other species. Service with restrictions. ⓢⒶⓥⒺ ⌫ 🛜 ❚ 💻

ⒶⒶⒶ ▼▼▼▼ Staybridge Suites Chicago-Oakbrook Terrace **H**

(630) 953-9393. **$79-$219.** 200 Royce Blvd 60181. I-88 exit Midwest Rd eastbound to 22nd St (Cermak Rd), 0.4 mi w to Butterfield Rd (SR 56), just n, then just n on Renaissance Blvd; exit 22nd St (Cermak Rd) westbound, 2.5 mi w on 22nd St to SR 56, just n, then just n on Renaissance Blvd. Int corridors. **Pets:** Accepted. ⓢⒶⓥⒺ ⓜ 🛜 ❚ 💻

O'FALLON

▼▼▼▼ Candlewood Suites **H**

(618) 622-9555. **Call for rates.** 1332 Park Plaza Dr 62269. I-64 exit 14 (US 50), just s on Lincoln Hwy, 0.5 mi e on Hartman Ln, then just n on 2nd entrance to Park Plaza Dr. Int corridors. **Pets:** Accepted. ⓜ 🛜 ❚ 💻

▼▼▼▼ Drury Inn & Suites-O'Fallon **H**

(618) 624-2211. **$120-$209.** 1118 Central Park Dr 62269. I-64 exit 16, just s. Int corridors. **Pets:** $10 daily fee/room. Service with restrictions, supervision. ⓜ ⌫ 🛜 ❚ 💻

▼▼ Extended Stay America-St. Louis-O'Fallon **H**

(618) 624-1757. **Call for rates.** 154 Regency Park Dr 62269. I-64 exit 14 (US 50), just w to Regency Park Dr, then 0.4 mi s. Int corridors. **Pets:** Other species. $25 daily fee/pet. Service with restrictions, supervision. ⓜ 🛜 ❚ 💻

ⒶⒶⒶ ▼▼ Super 8 O'Fallon **H**

(618) 624-6060. **$55-$150.** 1100 Eastgate Dr 62269. I-64 exit 19B (SR 158), 0.5 mi n, then just sw. Int corridors. **Pets:** Small. $10 daily fee/pet. Designated rooms, service with restrictions, supervision. ⓢⒶⓥⒺ ⌫ 🛜 ✕ ❚ 💻

OGLESBY

ⒶⒶⒶ ▼▼▼ BEST WESTERN Oglesby Inn **H**

(815) 883-3535. **$80-$110.** 900 Holiday St 61348. I-39 exit 54, just e. Int corridors. **Pets:** Accepted. ⓢⒶⓥⒺ ⌫ 🛜 ❚ 💻

▼▼ Days Inn Oglesby/Starved Rock **H**

(815) 883-9600. **$100-$120.** 120 N Lewis Ave 61348. I-39 exit 54, just e. Int corridors. **Pets:** Other species. $15 one-time fee/pet. Designated rooms, service with restrictions. ⓜ ⌫ 🛜 ✕ ❚ 💻

OTTAWA

▼▼▼▼ Fairfield Inn & Suites by Marriott Ottawa/Starved Rock Area **H**

(815) 431-8955. **$101-$166.** 3000 Fairfield Ln 61350. I-80 exit 90 (SR 23), just s to Etna Rd, then just e. Int corridors. **Pets:** Accepted. ⓜ ⌫ 🛜 ✕ ❚ 💻

▼▼▼▼ Hampton Inn-Starved Rock Area **H**

(815) 434-6040. **$94-$179.** 4115 Holiday Ln 61350. I-80 exit 90 (SR 23), just n. Int corridors. **Pets:** Accepted. ⓜ ⌫ 🛜 ❚ 💻

▼▼ Holiday Inn Express **H**

(815) 433-0029. **$100-$130.** 120 W Stevenson Rd 61350. I-80 exit 90 (SR 23), just n. Int corridors. **Pets:** Accepted. ⌫ 🛜 ❚ 💻

PALATINE

▼▼▼▼ Holiday Inn Express Palatine/Arlington Heights **H**

(847) 934-4900. **Call for rates.** 1550 E Dundee Rd 60074. SR 53 exit Dundee Rd (SR 68), just w. Int corridors. **Pets:** Accepted. ⓜ ⌫ ✕ 🛜 ❚ 💻

PEORIA

▼▼ Candlewood Suites Peoria at Grand Prairie **H**

(309) 691-1690. **Call for rates.** 5300 W Landens Way 61615. SR 6 exit 2 (US 150/War Memorial Dr), follow US 150 NW to Summershade Cir, then just w. Int corridors. **Pets:** Accepted. ⓜ 🛜 ❚ 💻

▼▼ Comfort Suites by Choice Hotels **H** 🐾

(309) 688-3800. **$119-$139.** 1812 W War Memorial Dr 61614. I-74 exit 89 (US 150/War Memorial Dr), just e, then just s. Int corridors. **Pets:** Other species. $25 one-time fee/room. Designated rooms, service with restrictions, crate. ⌫ 🛜 ✕ ❚ 💻

▼▼▼▼ Country Inn & Suites By Carlson Peoria-North **H**

(309) 589-0044. **Call for rates.** 5309 W Landens Way 61615. SR 6 exit 2 (US 150/War Memorial Dr), just n. Int corridors. **Pets:** Accepted. ⓜ ⌫ 🛜 ✕ ❚ 💻

▼▼▼▼ Hampton Inn & Suites Peoria at Grand Prairie **H**

(309) 589-0001. **$149-$169.** 7806 N Rt 91 61615. SR 6 exit 2 (US 150/War Memorial Dr), just w, then 0.3 mi n. Int corridors. **Pets:** Accepted. ⓜ ⌫ 🛜 ✕ ❚ 💻

ⒶⒶⒶ ▼▼▼▼ Quality Inn & Suites **H**

(309) 685-2556. **$100-$200.** 4112 N Brandywine Dr 61614. I-74 exit 89 (US 150/War Memorial Dr), just e. Int corridors. **Pets:** $20 daily fee/room. Service with restrictions, crate. ⓢⒶⓥⒺ ⌫ 🛜 ❚ 💻

▼▼▼▼ Residence Inn by Marriott **H**

(309) 681-9000. **$133-$219.** 2000 W War Memorial Dr 61614. I-74 exit 89 (US 150/War Memorial Dr), just w; entrance through Northwoods Mall. Int corridors. **Pets:** Accepted. ⌫ 🛜 ✕ ❚ 💻

▼▼▼▼ Staybridge Suites Peoria Downtown **H**

(309) 673-7829. **$139-$219.** 300 W Romeo B Garrett Ave 61605. I-74 exit 92, 0.5 mi w on Glendale Ave (which becomes William Kumpf St), then just w on Fourth Ave. Int corridors. **Pets:** Accepted. ⌫ 🛜 ✕ ❚ 💻

▼▼▼▼ Super 8 **H**

(309) 688-8074. **$59-$105.** 1816 W War Memorial Dr 61614. I-74 exit 89 (US 150/War Memorial Dr), just e. Int corridors. **Pets:** Accepted. 🛜 ❚ 💻

▼▼▼▼ Wingate by Wyndham Peoria **H** 🐾

(309) 589-0033. **$109-$189.** 7708 N Rt 91 61615. SR 6 exit 2 (US 150/War Memorial Dr), just w, then 0.3 mi n. Int corridors. **Pets:** Other species. $75 one-time fee/room. Service with restrictions, crate. ⓜ ⌫ 🛜 ✕ ❚ 💻

PERU

▼▼▼▼ Holiday Inn Express & Suites Peru **H**

(815) 224-2500. **$96-$138.** 5253 Trompeter Rd 61354. I-80 exit 75 (SR 251), just n. Int corridors. **Pets:** Other species. $35 one-time fee/room. Service with restrictions, supervision. ⓜ 🛜 ✕ ❚ 💻

▼▼▼▼ La Quinta Inn & Suites Peru **H**

(815) 224-9000. **$78-$205.** 4389 Venture Dr 61354. I-80 exit 75 (SR 251), 0.4 mi s to 38th St, just w to Venture Dr, then 0.4 mi nw. Int corridors. **Pets:** Large, other species. Service with restrictions. ⌫ 🛜 ❚ 💻

PONTIAC

BEST WESTERN Pontiac Inn H

(815) 842-2777. **$90-$105.** 1821 W Reynolds St 61764. I-55 exit 197 (SR 116), just e. Int corridors. **Pets:** Accepted.

PONTOON BEACH

Super 8 H

(618) 931-8808. **$24-$64.** 4141 Timber Lake Dr 62040. I-270 exit 6A (SR 11), just s. Int corridors. **Pets:** Small, dogs only. $20 daily fee/pet. Designated rooms, service with restrictions, crate.

PROSPECT HEIGHTS

Country Inn & Suites By Carlson, Prospect Heights H

(847) 419-3600. **$104-$149.** 600 N Milwaukee Ave 60070. Jct SR 21 and US 45. Int corridors. **Pets:** Accepted.

QUINCY

Comfort Inn by Choice Hotels H

(217) 228-2700. **Call for rates.** 4122 Broadway St 62305. I-172 exit 14 (SR 104), 1.3 mi w. Int corridors. **Pets:** Other species. $20 one-time fee/pet. Service with restrictions.

Microtel Inn & Suites by Wyndham Quincy H

(217) 222-5620. **$69-$159.** 200 S 3rd St 62301. Jct US 24 and SR 57, just sw. Int corridors. **Pets:** Small. $15 daily fee/pet. Service with restrictions, crate.

Quincy Inn & Suites H

(217) 228-8808. **$69-$79, 7 day notice.** 224 N 36th St 62301. I-172 exit 14 (SR 104), 1.8 mi w, then just s. Int corridors. **Pets:** Accepted.

Stoney Creek Hotel & Conference Center H

(217) 223-2255. **Call for rates.** 3809 E Broadway St 62305. I-172 exit 14 (SR 104), 1 mi w. Int corridors. **Pets:** Accepted.

RANTOUL

Magnuson Hotel Heritage Inn M

(217) 892-9292. **$65-$70.** 420 S Murray Rd 61866. I-57 exit 250 (US 136), 0.5 mi e, then just s. Ext corridors. **Pets:** Medium. $10 daily fee/pet. Service with restrictions, supervision.

Super 8 H

(217) 893-8888. **$60-$145.** 207 S Murray Rd 61866. I-57 exit 250 (US 136), just e. Int corridors. **Pets:** Small, dogs only. $10 daily fee/pet. Designated rooms, service with restrictions, supervision.

RICHMOND

Super 8 Richmond/Geneva Lakes H

(815) 678-4711. **$65-$165.** 11200 N US Hwy 12 60071. 0.5 mi n of jct SR 173. Int corridors. **Pets:** Accepted.

ROBINSON

BEST WESTERN Robinson Inn H

(618) 544-8448. **$82-$94.** 1500 W Main St 62454. 1.2 mi w on SR 33. Int corridors. **Pets:** Other species. $5 daily fee/room. Service with restrictions, crate.

ROCHELLE

Comfort Inn & Suites by Choice Hotels H

(815) 562-5551. **$80-$170.** 1133 N 7th St 61068. I-39 exit 99 (SR 38), 2.5 mi w; jct SR 38 and 251; downtown. Int corridors. **Pets:** Accepted.

Holiday Inn Express H

(815) 562-9994. **$129-$149.** 1240 Dement Rd 61068. I-39 exit 99 (SR 38), just nw. Int corridors. **Pets:** Medium. $25 one-time fee/pet. Designated rooms, service with restrictions, supervision.

ROCKFORD

Baymont Inn & Suites Rockford H

(815) 229-8200. **$74-$134.** 662 N Lyford Rd 61107. I-90 exit US 20 business route, just e, then just n. Int corridors. **Pets:** Other species. $10 daily fee/pet. Designated rooms, service with restrictions, supervision.

Candlewood Suites H

(815) 229-9300. **$99-$139.** 7555 Walton St 61108. I-90 exit US 20 business route, 0.3 mi e to Bell School Rd, just s to Walton St, then just e. Int corridors. **Pets:** Large, other species. $75 one-time fee/pet. Designated rooms, service with restrictions, crate.

Comfort Inn by Choice Hotels H

(815) 398-7061. **$72-$89.** 7392 Argus Dr 61107. I-90 exit US 20 business route, just w to Bell School Rd, then just n. Int corridors. **Pets:** Medium. $25 one-time fee/room. Service with restrictions, supervision.

Days Inn Rockford H

(815) 332-4915. **$54-$109.** 220 S Lyford Rd 61108. I-90 exit US 20 business route, just e, then just s. Int corridors. **Pets:** Other species. $10 daily fee/room. Service with restrictions, crate.

Extended Stay America - Rockford East H

(815) 397-8316. **$69-$119.** 747 N Bell School Rd 61107. I-90 exit US 20 business route, just w to Bell School Rd, then 0.3 mi n. Int corridors. **Pets:** Other species. $25 daily fee/pet. Service with restrictions, supervision.

Extended Stay America - Rockford - I-90 H

(815) 226-8969. **$64-$114.** 653 Clark Dr 61107. I-90 exit US 20 business route, just w. Int corridors. **Pets:** Other species. $25 daily fee/pet. Service with restrictions, supervision.

Holiday Inn H

(815) 398-2200. **Call for rates.** 7550 E State St 61108. I-90 exit US 20 business route, 0.3 mi w to Bell School Rd. Int corridors. **Pets:** Accepted.

Red Roof Inn Rockford M

(815) 398-9750. **$49-$119.** 7434 E State St 61108. I-90 exit US 20 business route, just w. Ext corridors. **Pets:** Large, other species. Service with restrictions, supervision.

Residence Inn by Marriott H 🐾

(815) 227-0013. **$119-$196.** 7542 Colosseum Dr 61107. I-90 exit US 20 business route, 0.3 mi w to Bell School Rd, then just n. Int corridors. **Pets:** Other species. $100 one-time fee/room. Service with restrictions, crate.

Sleep Inn-Rockford H

(815) 398-8900. **$65-$94.** 725 Clark Dr 61107. I-90 exit US 20 business route, just w to Bell School Rd, just n to Clark Dr, then 0.4 mi ne. Int corridors. **Pets:** Accepted.

Staybridge Suites H

(815) 397-0200. **$139-$249, 3 day notice.** 633 N Bell School Rd 61107. I-90 exit US 20 business route, 0.3 mi w to Bell School Rd, then just n. Int corridors. **Pets:** Accepted.

ROMEOVILLE

Comfort Inn by Choice Hotels Romeoville/Bolingbrook H

(630) 226-1900. **$82-$140.** 1235 Lakeview Dr 60446. I-55 exit 263, just n. Int corridors. **Pets:** Small. $20 one-time fee/room. Designated rooms, service with restrictions, crate.

⚑ ▼▼ ◈ Country Inn & Suites By Carlson, Romeoville (Chicago) H
(630) 378-1052. **$88-$116.** 1265 Lakeview Dr 60446. I-55 exit 263, just n. Int corridors. **Pets:** Medium. $25 daily fee/pet. Designated rooms, service with restrictions, supervision. SAVE ⌂ ⌂ 🖥 🖥 🖥

▼▼ Extended Stay America Chicago-Romeoville H
(630) 226-8966. **$74-$99.** 1225 Lakeview Dr 60446. I-55 exit 263, just n. Int corridors. **Pets:** Other species. $25 daily fee/pet. Service with restrictions, supervision. ⌂ 🖥

ROSEMONT

⚑ ▼▼▼ Aloft Chicago O'Hare H
(847) 671-4444. **$129-$299.** 9700 Balmoral Ave 60018. I-190 exit 1B, just s. Int corridors. **Pets:** Accepted.
SAVE ⌂M ⌂ ⌂ ✕ 🖥 🖥

⚑ ▼▼▼ Crowne Plaza Chicago O'Hare Hotel & Conference Center H
(847) 671-6350. **$79-$199, 3 day notice.** 5440 N River Rd 60018. I-190 exit 1B (River Rd), just s. Int corridors. **Pets:** Small. $50 one-time fee/pet. Designated rooms, service with restrictions, supervision.
SAVE ⌂ ⌂M ⌂ ⌂ 🖥 🖥

⚑ ▼▼▼ ▼▼▼ DoubleTree by Hilton Chicago O'Hare Airport-Rosemont H
(847) 292-9100. **$109-$299.** 5460 N River Rd 60018. I-190 exit 1B (River Rd), just s. Int corridors. **Pets:** Accepted.
SAVE ⌂ ⌂M ⌂ ⌂ ✕ 🖥 🖥

⚑ ▼▼▼ Embassy Suites Hotel O'Hare Rosemont H
(847) 678-4000. **$129-$299.** 5500 N River Rd 60018. I-190 exit 1B (River Rd), just s. Int corridors. **Pets:** Accepted.
SAVE ⌂ ⌂ ⌂ ✕ 🖥

⚑ ▼▼▼ Hilton Rosemont Chicago O'Hare H
(847) 678-4488. **$109-$359.** 5550 N River Rd 60018. I-190 exit 1B (River Rd), just s. Int corridors. **Pets:** Accepted.
SAVE ⌂ ⌂M ⌂ ⌂ ✕ 🖥

▼▼▼ Loews Chicago O'Hare Hotel H ❀
(847) 544-5300. **$149-$329, 3 day notice.** 5300 N River Rd 60018. I-190 exit 1B (River Rd), 0.4 mi s. Int corridors. **Pets:** Medium, other species. $120 one-time fee/room. Service with restrictions, crate.
⌂ ⌂M ⌂ ✕ 🖥 🖥

▼▼▼ Residence Inn by Marriott Chicago-O'Hare H
(847) 375-9000. **$97-$217.** 7101 Chestnut St 60018. Jct US 12, 45 and Touhy Ave. Int corridors. **Pets:** Accepted. ⌂ ⌂ ✕ 🖥 🖥

⚑ ▼▼▼▼ Sheraton Chicago O'Hare H
(847) 699-6300. **$99-$369.** 6501 N Mannheim Rd 60018. On US 12 and 45, at SR 72 (Higgins Rd). Int corridors. **Pets:** Accepted.
SAVE ⌂ ⌂ ✕ 🖥 🖥

⚑ ▼▼▼ ▼▼▼ The Westin O'Hare H
(847) 698-6000. **$99-$459.** 6100 N River Rd 60018. I-190 exit 1B (River Rd), just n. Int corridors. **Pets:** Accepted.
SAVE ⌂ ⌂M ⌂ ✕ ⌂ ✕ 🖥 🖥

ST. CHARLES

▼▼ Country Inn & Suites By Carlson H
(630) 587-6564. **$79-$299.** 155 38th Ave 60174. On SR 64, 3.1 mi w of SR 59. Int corridors. **Pets:** Medium, dogs only. $150 deposit/room, $10 daily fee/pet. Designated rooms, service with restrictions, crate.
⌂M ⌂ ⌂ 🖥 🖥

▼▼▼ Courtyard by Marriott Chicago-St Charles H
(630) 377-6370. **$90-$160.** 700 Courtyard Dr 60174. Jct SR 59 and 64, 3.4 mi w on SR 64, just n on Kirk Rd, then just w on Foxfield. Int corridors. **Pets:** Accepted. ECO ⌂ ⌂M ⌂ ⌂ ✕ 🖥 🖥

▼▼ Geneva Motel Inn H
(630) 513-6500. **$65-$120, 3 day notice.** 100 S Tyler Rd 60174. Jct SR 64, just s. Int corridors. **Pets:** Accepted. ⌂ ⌂ 🖥 🖥

⚑ ▼▼▼▼ Pheasant Run Resort H
(630) 584-6300. **Call for rates.** 4051 E Main St 60174. On SR 64, 2.4 mi w of SR 59. Int corridors. **Pets:** Accepted.
SAVE ⌂ ⌂ ✕ ⌂ ✕ 🖥 🖥

⚑ ▼▼▼ Quality Inn & Suites Saint Charles H
(630) 584-5300. **Call for rates.** 1600 E Main St 60174. On SR 64, 0.5 mi e of SR 25. Int corridors. **Pets:** Accepted. SAVE ⌂ ⌂ 🖥 🖥

SALEM

▼ Super 8 H
(618) 548-5882. **$64-$95.** 118 Woods Ln 62881. I-57 exit 116 (US 50), just w. Ext/int corridors. **Pets:** Medium. Service with restrictions, supervision. ⌂M ⌂ 🖥 🖥

SAVOY

⚑ ▼▼▼ BEST WESTERN Paradise Inn H ❀
(217) 356-1824. **Call for rates.** 709 N Dunlap Ave 61874. I-57 exit 229, 2.5 mi e to US 45, then 2.5 mi n. Ext corridors. **Pets:** Small, dogs only. $25 deposit/pet, $10 daily fee/pet. Designated rooms, service with restrictions, crate. SAVE ⌂ ⌂ 🖥 🖥

SCHAUMBURG

⚑ ▼▼▼ AmericInn Hotel & Suites Schaumburg H
(847) 619-1000. **$89-$159, 7 day notice.** 1300 E Higgins Rd 60173. I-290 exit SR 72 (Higgins Rd), 0.5 mi w. Int corridors. **Pets:** Medium. $30 one-time fee/room. Service with restrictions, crate.
SAVE ⌂M ⌂ 🖥 🖥

▼▼ Extended Stay America Chicago-Schaumburg Convention Center H
(847) 882-6900. **$69-$99.** 51 E State Pkwy 60173. I-90 exit Roselle Rd, 0.8 mi s, then just e. Int corridors. **Pets:** Other species. $25 daily fee/pet. Service with restrictions, supervision. ⌂M ⌂ 🖥 🖥

▼▼ Extended Stay America Chicago-Schaumburg I-90 H
(847) 882-7011. **$69-$99.** 2000 N Roselle Rd 60195. I-90 exit Roselle Rd, just sw. Int corridors. **Pets:** Other species. $25 daily fee/pet. Service with restrictions, supervision. ⌂ ✕ 🖥 🖥

▼▼ Extended Stay America-Chicago-Woodfield H
(847) 517-7255. **$79-$119.** 1200 American Ln 60173. I-290 exit SR 72 (Higgins Rd), 0.5 mi w to Meacham Rd, 0.5 mi n to American Ln, then just w. Int corridors. **Pets:** Other species. $25 daily fee/pet. Service with restrictions, supervision. ⌂ 🖥 🖥

⚑ ▼▼ Hawthorn Suites by Wyndham Chicago-Schaumburg H ❀
(847) 517-7644. **$80-$150.** 1200 E Bank Dr 60173. I-290 exit SR 72 (Higgins Rd), 0.8 mi w to National Pkwy, then just n. Int corridors. **Pets:** Other species. $15 daily fee/room. Service with restrictions.
SAVE ⌂ ✕ 🖥 🖥

⚑ ▼▼▼ Homewood Suites by Hilton-Schaumburg H
(847) 605-0400. **Call for rates.** 815 E American Ln 60173. I-290 exit SR 72 (Higgins Rd), 1.5 mi w, then 0.4 mi n on Plum Grove Rd. Ext/int corridors. **Pets:** Accepted. SAVE ⌂M ⌂ ⌂ 🖥 🖥

⚑ ▼▼▼ HYATT house Chicago/Schaumburg H
(847) 706-9007. **$69-$209.** 1251 E American Ln 60173. I-290 exit SR 72 (Higgins Rd), 0.5 mi w to Meacham Rd, 0.5 mi n to American Ln, then just w. Int corridors. **Pets:** Medium. $75 one-time fee/room. Service with restrictions, crate. SAVE ⌂M ⌂ ✕ ⌂ ✕ 🖥 🖥

▼▼▼▼ Hyatt Place Chicago/Schaumburg 🅗
(847) 330-1060. **$64-$399.** 1851 McConnor Pkwy 60173. I-290 exit 1A (Woodfield Rd/Golf Rd) northbound, just n to Golf Rd, just w to McConnor Pkwy, then just n; exit 1B (Woodfield Rd/Golf Rd) southbound. Int corridors. **Pets:** Accepted. [SAVE] [ⓜ] [🏊] [🛜] [✕] [🔋] [💻]

▼▼ La Quinta Inn (Schaumburg) 🅗
(847) 517-8484. **$62-$175.** 1730 E Higgins Rd 60173. I-290 exit SR 72 (Higgins Rd), just w. Int corridors. **Pets:** Large, other species. Service with restrictions. [🛜] [🔋] [💻]

▼▼▼ Residence Inn by
Marriott-Chicago/Schaumburg 🅗
(847) 517-9200. **$154-$253.** 1610 McConnor Pkwy 60173. I-290 exit 1A (Woodfield Rd/Golf Rd) northbound, follow signs just n to Golf Rd, just w to McConnor Pkwy, then 0.8 mi n; exit 1B (Woodfield Rd/Golf Rd) southbound. Int corridors. **Pets:** Accepted.
[ⓜ] [🏊] [🛜] [✕] [🔋] [💻]

▼▼▼ Sonesta ES Suites
Chicago/Schaumburg 🅗 🐾
(847) 619-6677. **Call for rates.** 901 E Woodfield Office Ct 60173. I-290 exit SR 72 (Higgins Rd), 1.5 mi w, then 0.3 mi n on Plum Grove Rd. Ext/int corridors. **Pets:** Medium, other species. $75 daily fee/room. Designated rooms, service with restrictions, crate.
[SAVE] [🏊] [🛜] [✕] [🔋] [💻]

SCHILLER PARK

▼▼ Comfort Suites O'Hare Airport 🅗 🐾
(847) 233-9000. **$95-$199.** 4200 N River Rd 60176. Jct SR 19 (Irving Park Rd) and Des Plaines St/River Rd, just n. Int corridors. **Pets:** Medium, dogs only. $50 daily fee/room. Designated rooms, service with restrictions, crate. [🍽] [ⓜ] [🛜] [✕] [🔋] [💻]

▼▼▼▼ Four Points by Sheraton Chicago O'Hare
Airport 🅗
(847) 671-6000. **$89-$299.** 10249 W Irving Park Rd 60176. Jct US 12, 45 and SR 19 (Irving Park Rd). Int corridors. **Pets:** Medium. $100 deposit/room. Designated rooms, service with restrictions, crate.
[SAVE] [🍽] [ⓜ] [🏊] [✕] [🛜] [✕] [🔋] [💻]

▼▼▼ Hampton Inn Chicago O'Hare Airport 🅗
(847) 671-1700. **$99-$259.** 3939 N Mannheim Rd 60176. Jct US 12 and 45, 0.5 mi s of SR 19 (Irving Park Rd). Int corridors.
Pets: Accepted. [🏊] [🛜] [🔋] [💻]

SKOKIE

▼▼▼ Extended Stay America-Chicago-Skokie 🅗
(847) 663-9031. **$84-$134.** 5211 Old Orchard Rd 60077. I-94 exit 35 (Old Orchard Rd). Int corridors. **Pets:** Other species. $25 daily fee/pet. Service with restrictions, supervision. [🛜] [🔋] [💻]

▼▼▼ Holiday Inn Chicago North Shore 🅗
(847) 679-8900. **Call for rates.** 5300 W Touhy Ave 60077. I-94 exit 39A, 0.5 mi w. Int corridors. **Pets:** Accepted. [🍽] [🏊] [🛜] [🔋] [💻]

SOUTH BELOIT

▼▼▼ BEST WESTERN Legacy Inn & Suites
Beloit/South Beloit 🅗
(815) 389-4211. **$89-$119.** 5910 Technology Dr 61080. I-90/39 exit 1, just sw. Int corridors. **Pets:** Accepted.
[SAVE] [ⓜ] [🏊] [🛜] [✕] [🔋] [💻]

SOUTH JACKSONVILLE

▼▼▼ Holiday Inn Express & Suites Jacksonville 🅗
(217) 245-6500. **Call for rates.** 2501 Holliday Ln 62650. I-72 exit 64, just n. Int corridors. **Pets:** Accepted. [ⓜ] [🏊] [🛜] [✕] [🔋] [💻]

SPRINGFIELD

▼▼ Baymont Inn & Suites Springfield 🅗 🐾
(217) 529-6655. **$69-$159.** 5871 S 6th St 62703. I-55 exit 90 (Toronto Rd), just e to 6th St, then just n. Int corridors. **Pets:** Medium. $10 daily fee/pet. Designated rooms, service with restrictions, supervision.
[ⓜ] [🏊] [🛜] [✕] [🔋] [💻]

▼▼▼ BEST WESTERN Clearlake Plaza 🅗
(217) 525-7420. **$89-$110.** 3440 E Clear Lake Ave 62702. I-55 exit 98B, just w. Int corridors. **Pets:** $20 daily fee/room. Service with restrictions, supervision. [SAVE] [ⓜ] [🏊] [✕] [🔋] [💻]

▼▼▼ Candlewood Suites 🅗
(217) 522-5100. **Call for rates.** 2501 Sunrise Dr 62703. I-55 exit 94 (Stevenson Dr), just w to Dirksen Pkwy, then 0.4 mi n. Int corridors. **Pets:** Other species. $75 one-time fee/room. Service with restrictions, crate. [ⓜ] [🛜] [✕] [🔋] [💻]

▼▼▼ Drury Inn & Suites-Springfield 🅗
(217) 529-3900. **$100-$169.** 3180 S Dirksen Pkwy 62703. I-55 exit 94 (Stevenson Dr), just w to Dirksen Pkwy, then just n. Int corridors. **Pets:** $10 daily fee/room. Service with restrictions, supervision.
[ⓜ] [🏊] [🛜] [✕] [🔋] [💻]

▼▼▼▼ Holiday Inn Express Hotel & Suites 🅗
(217) 529-7771. **$89-$115.** 3050 S Dirksen Pkwy 62703. I-55 exit 94 (Stevenson Dr), just w to S Dirksen Pkwy, then 0.4 mi n. Int corridors. **Pets:** Other species. $40 deposit/room. Service with restrictions, crate. [SAVE] [ⓜ] [🛜] [✕] [🔋] [💻]

▼▼ Microtel Inn & Suites by Wyndham Springfield 🅗
(217) 753-2636. **$74-$99.** 2636 Sunrise Dr 62703. I-55 exit 94 (Stevenson Dr), just w to Dirksen Pkwy, then 0.4 mi n. Int corridors.
Pets: Accepted. [ⓜ] [🏊] [🛜] [✕] [🔋] [💻]

▼▼▼ Quality Inn & Suites Springfield 🅗
(217) 787-2250. **$90-$190.** 3442 Freedom Dr 62704. I-72 exit 93 (Veterans Pkwy), 0.7 mi n to Lindbergh Blvd, just w to Freedom Dr, then just s. Int corridors. **Pets:** Accepted. [🏊] [🛜] [🔋] [💻]

▼▼ Sleep Inn by Choice Hotels 🅗
(217) 787-6200. **$69-$100.** 3470 Freedom Dr 62704. I-72 exit 93 (Veterans Pkwy), 0.7 mi n to Lindbergh Blvd, just w to Freedom Dr, then just s. Int corridors. **Pets:** Accepted. [🏊] [🛜] [🔋] [💻]

▼▼▼ Staybridge Suites Springfield South 🅗
(217) 793-6700. **Call for rates.** 4231 Schooner Dr 62711. I-72 exit 93 (Veterans Pkwy), 0.4 mi se. Int corridors. **Pets:** Accepted.
[ⓜ] [🏊] [🛜] [🔋] [💻]

STAUNTON

▼▼ Super 8 Staunton 🅗
(618) 635-5353. **$50-$70.** 1527 Herman Rd 62088. I-55 exit 41, 0.6 mi w. Int corridors. **Pets:** Medium. $10 one-time fee/room. Service with restrictions, supervision. [🛜] [🔋] [💻]

STOCKTON

▼▼▼ Country Inn & Suites By Carlson 🅗
(815) 947-6060. **$95-$145.** 200 Dillon Ave 61085. On US 20, just e of SR 78. Int corridors. **Pets:** Accepted. [ⓜ] [🏊] [🛜] [✕] [🔋] [💻]

TINLEY PARK

▼▼ La Quinta Inn & Suites Chicago-Tinley Park 🅗
(708) 633-1200. **$92-$249.** 7255 W 183rd St 60477. I-80 exit 148B, 0.5 mi n to 183rd St, then just w to North Creek Business Center. Int corridors. **Pets:** Large, other species. Service with restrictions.
[ⓜ] [🏊] [🛜] [🔋] [💻]

TUSCOLA

▼▼ Baymont Inn & Suites 🅗
(217) 253-3500. **$69-$109.** 1006 Southline Rd 61953. I-57 exit 212 (US 36), 0.3 mi w. Int corridors. **Pets:** Small, dogs only. $10 daily fee/pet. Designated rooms, service with restrictions, supervision.
[ⓜ] [🏊] [🛜] [🔋] [💻]

▼▼▼▼ Holiday Inn Express ⊞
(217) 253-6363. **$98-$130, 3 day notice.** 1201 Tuscola Blvd 61953. I-57 exit 212 (US 36), 0.3 mi w to Progress Blvd, just s to Tuscola Blvd, then 0.4 mi se. Int corridors. **Pets:** Small. Service with restrictions, supervision. 🐾 🛜 🛗 💻

URBANA
▼▼▼▼ Comfort Suites by Choice Hotels
Urbana/Champaign ⊞ 🐾
(217) 328-3500. **$99-$139.** 2001 N Lincoln Ave 61801. I-74 exit 183 (Lincoln Ave), 0.5 mi s. Int corridors. **Pets:** Other species. $20 daily fee/room. Designated rooms, service with restrictions, crate.
⟨M 🐾 🛜 ✕ 🛗 💻

🐾🐾🐾 ▼▼▼ Ramada-Urbana/Champaign ⊞
(217) 328-4400. **$79-$100.** 902 W Killarney St 61801. I-74 exit 183 (Lincoln Ave), just s to Killarney St, then just w. Int corridors. **Pets:** Medium. $25 deposit/pet, $10 daily fee/pet. Service with restrictions, supervision. SAVE 🐾 🛜 ✕ 🛗 💻

VANDALIA
▼▼▼▼ Holiday Inn Express Hotel & Suites ⊞
(618) 283-0010. **Call for rates.** 21 Mattes Ave 62471. I-70 exit 61, just s. Int corridors. **Pets:** Accepted. ⟨M 🐾 🛜 ✕ 🛗 💻

🐾🐾🐾 ▼ Jay's Inn M
(618) 283-1200. **$56-$65.** 720 Gochenour St 62471. I-70 exit 63 (US 51), just s. Ext corridors. **Pets:** Other species. Service with restrictions, crate. SAVE 🛜 🛗 💻

▼▼▼▼ Ramada Inn Vandalia ⊞
(618) 283-1400. **$59-$89.** 2707 Veterans Ave 62471. I-70 exit 61, just s. Int corridors. **Pets:** Medium. $10 daily fee/pet. Service with restrictions, crate. 🐾 🛜 🛗 💻

VERNON HILLS
▼▼ Extended Stay America-Chicago-Vernon Hills-Lake Forest ⊞
(847) 821-7101. **$89-$114.** 215 N Milwaukee Ave 60061. I-94 exit SR 60 (Townline Rd), 2.1 mi w to SR 21 (Milwaukee Ave), then 0.3 mi s. Int corridors. **Pets:** Other species. $25 daily fee/pet. Service with restrictions, supervision. ⟨M 🛜 🛗 💻

▼▼ Extended Stay America Chicago/Vernon Hills-Lincolnshire ⊞
(847) 955-1111. **$89-$114.** 675 Woodlands Pkwy 60061. I-94 exit SR 60 (Townline Rd), 2.1 mi w to SR 21 (Milwaukee Ave), 1.9 mi s to Woodlands Pkwy, then just w. Int corridors. **Pets:** Other species. $25 daily fee/pet. Service with restrictions, supervision. 🛜 ✕ 🛗 💻

▼▼▼▼ Holiday Inn Express/Vernon Hills ⊞
(847) 367-8031. **Call for rates.** 975 Lakeview Pkwy 60061. Jct SR 21 (Milwaukee Ave), 0.7 mi w on SR 60 (Townline Rd) to Lakeview Pkwy, then just n. Int corridors. **Pets:** Accepted.
⟨M 🐾 🛜 ✕ 🛗 💻

▼▼▼▼ Hotel Indigo Chicago/Vernon Hills ⊞
(847) 918-1400. **Call for rates.** 450 N Milwaukee Ave 60061. I-94 exit SR 60 (Townline Rd), 2.1 mi w to SR 21 (Milwaukee Ave), then 0.3 mi s. Int corridors. **Pets:** Accepted. 🍴 ⟨M 🐾 🛜 ✕ 🛗 💻

WARRENVILLE
🐾🐾🐾 ▼▼▼▼ HYATT house
Chicago/Naperville/Warrenville ⊞
(630) 836-2960. **$79-$229.** 27554 Maecliff Dr 60555. I-88 exit Winfield Rd, just n to Ferry Rd, then just e. Int corridors. **Pets:** Accepted.
SAVE ⟨M 🐾 🛜 ✕ 🛗 💻

▼▼▼▼ Residence Inn by Marriott Chicago
Naperville/Warrenville ⊞
(630) 393-3444. **$119-$230.** 28500 Bella Vista Pkwy 60555. I-88 exit Winfield Rd, just n to Ferry Rd, then just e. Int corridors.
Pets: Accepted. ⟨M 🐾 🛜 ✕ 🛗 💻

WASHINGTON
▼▼▼ Super 8 ⊞
(309) 444-8881. **$56-$63.** 1884 Washington Rd 61571. On Business Rt US 24, 1.5 mi w. Int corridors. **Pets:** Accepted. 🛜 🛗 💻

WATSEKA
🐾🐾🐾 ▼▼▼ Super 8 ⊞
(815) 432-6000. **$58-$87.** 710 W Walnut St 60970. On US 24; center of downtown. Int corridors. **Pets:** Medium. $10 daily fee/pet. Service with restrictions, supervision. SAVE 🛜 ✕ 🛗 💻

WAUKEGAN
▼▼▼ Candlewood Suites Chicago/Waukegan ⊞
(847) 578-5250. **Call for rates.** 1151 S Waukegan Rd 60085. I-94 exit SR 137 (Buckley Rd), 0.5 mi e to SR 43 (Waukegan Rd), then 1.9 mi n. Int corridors. **Pets:** Accepted. 🛜 🛗 💻

▼▼▼▼ Residence Inn by Marriott
Chicago-Waukegan/Gurnee ⊞
(847) 689-9240. **$97-$206.** 1440 S White Oak Dr 60085. I-94 exit SR 137 (Buckley Rd), 0.5 mi e to SR 43 (Waukegan Rd), 1.5 mi n to Lakeside Dr, then just e. Int corridors. **Pets:** Accepted.
ECO ⟨M 🐾 ✕ 🛜 ✕ 🛗 💻

WENONA
▼▼▼ Super 8 M
(815) 853-4371. **$50-$65.** 5 Cavalry Dr 61377. I-39 exit 35, just e. Int corridors. **Pets:** Accepted. 🛜 🛗 💻

WEST DUNDEE
▼▼ TownePlace Suites by Marriott Chicago West
Dundee/Elgin ⊞
(847) 608-6320. **$90-$148.** 2185 Marriott Dr 60118. I-90 exit SR 31, 0.4 mi n to Marriott Dr, then just e. Int corridors. **Pets:** Accepted.
ECO 🐾 🛜 ✕ 🛗 💻

WESTMONT
🐾🐾🐾 ▼▼▼ ClubHouse Inn & Suites ⊞
(630) 920-2200. **Call for rates.** 630 Pasquinelli Dr 60559. Just off US 34 (Ogden Ave); 0.3 mi nw of jct SR 83. Int corridors. **Pets:** Accepted.
SAVE 🐾 🛜 ✕ 🛗 💻

▼▼▼ Extended Stay America - Chicago - Westmont - Oak
Brook ⊞
(630) 323-9292. **$79-$99.** 855 Pasquinelli Dr 60559. SR 83 exit US 34 (Ogden Ave), just w to Pasquinelli Dr, then 0.5 mi n. Int corridors.
Pets: Other species. $25 daily fee/pet. Service with restrictions, supervision. ⟨M 🛜 🛗 💻

WHEELING
▼▼▼ Hawthorn Suites by Wyndham -
Northbrook/Wheeling ⊞
(847) 520-1684. **$75-$130.** 8000 Capitol Dr 60090. Jct S Wolf and E Palatine rds. Int corridors. **Pets:** Accepted. ⟨M 🛜 ✕ 🛗 💻

🐾🐾🐾 ▼▼▼▼ The Westin Chicago North Shore ⊞
(847) 777-6500. **$109-$299.** 601 N Milwaukee Ave 60090. Jct Lake Cook Rd, just s. Int corridors. **Pets:** Accepted.
SAVE ECO 🍴 ⟨M 🐾 ✕ 🐾 ✕ 🛗 💻

WILLOWBROOK
▼▼▼ La Quinta Inn Chicago-Willowbrook ⊞
(630) 654-0077. **$79-$225.** 855 79th St 60527. I-55 exit 274, just n. Int corridors. **Pets:** Large, other species. Service with restrictions.
🛜 🛗 💻

🐾🐾🐾 ▼ Red Roof Inn Chicago - Willowbrook M
(630) 323-8811. **$48-$99.** 7535 Kingery Hwy Rt 83 60527. I-55 exit 274, 0.5 mi n on SR 83. Ext corridors. **Pets:** Large, other species. Service with restrictions, supervision. SAVE 🛜 🛗 💻

WILMETTE

▼▼▼▼ **Residence Inn by Marriott Chicago Wilmette** 🅷
(847) 251-6600. **$139-$229.** 3205 Old Glenview Rd 60091. I-94 exit 35 (Old Orchard Rd), just w to Old Glenview Rd, then just n. Int corridors. **Pets:** Accepted. 🔊Ⓜ 📶 ✖ 🚽 💻

WOODSTOCK

🔺 ▼▼▼ **BEST WESTERN Woodstock Inn** 🅷
(815) 337-0065. **$80-$135.** 990 Lake Ave 60098. On SR 47, 0.5 mi n of jct US 14. Int corridors. **Pets:** Medium, dogs only. $20 deposit/pet, $20 daily fee/pet. Designated rooms, service with restrictions, supervision.
SAVE 📶 ✖ 🚽 💻

▼▼▼ **Super 8** 🅷
(815) 337-8808. **$65-$120.** 1220 Davis Rd 60098. On SR 47, s of jct US 14. Int corridors. **Pets:** Accepted. 📶 🚽 💻

INDIANA

ANDERSON

🔺 ▼▼▼▼ **BEST WESTERN PLUS Anderson** 🅷
(765) 649-2500. **$79-$159.** 2114 E 59th St 46013. I-69 exit 226, just nw. Int corridors. **Pets:** Accepted. SAVE Ⓜ 📶 ✖ 🚽 💻

▼▼▼ **Motel 6 Indianapolis Anderson #4898** 🅷
(765) 644-4422. **Call for rates.** 2205 E 59th St 46013. I-69 exit 226, just nw. Int corridors. **Pets:** Accepted. 📶 ✖ 🚽

ANGOLA

▼▼▼ **Ramada Angola Hotel** 🅷
(260) 665-9471. **$85-$119.** 3855 N SR 127 46703. I-69 exit 354, just e, then 0.4 mi s. Int corridors. **Pets:** Other species. $25 daily fee/room. Service with restrictions, crate. 🍴 📶 ✖ 💻

AUBURN

▼▼▼▼ **Holiday Inn Express Auburn** 🅷
(260) 925-1900. **$86-$110.** 404 Touring Dr 46706. I-69 exit 329 (SR 8), just e, then just s. Int corridors. **Pets:** Other species. Service with restrictions, supervision. Ⓜ 📶 ✖ 🚽

▼▼ **La Quinta Inn & Conference Center** 🅷
(260) 920-1900. **$80-$429.** 306 Touring Dr 46706. I-69 exit 329 (SR 8), 0.5 mi e. Int corridors. **Pets:** Large, other species. Service with restrictions. 📶 ✖ 🚽 💻

BATESVILLE

▼▼▼▼ **Hampton Inn Batesville** 🅷
(812) 934-6262. **$99-$135.** 1030 SR 229 N 47006. I-74 exit 149, just n. Int corridors. **Pets:** Medium. Service with restrictions, crate.
Ⓜ 📶 ✖ 🚽 💻

BEDFORD

🔺 ▼▼▼▼ **Holiday Inn Express & Suites** 🅷
(812) 279-1206. **$125-$175, 3 day notice.** 2800 Express Ln 47421. On US 50/SR 37, 1.4 mi s of jct SR 450. Int corridors. **Pets:** Accepted.
SAVE 📶 ✖ 🚽 💻

🔺 ▼▼◆ **Quality Inn & Suites Bedford** 🅷
(812) 279-8111. **$69-$99.** 911 Constitution Ave 47421. Jct SR 37 and 58, just s on SR 37. Int corridors. **Pets:** Small. $25 one-time fee/pet. Designated rooms, supervision. SAVE Ⓜ 📶 ✖ 🚽 💻

▼▼ **Super 8 Bedford** 🅷
(812) 275-8881. **$89-$125.** 501 Bell Back Rd 47421. Jct SR 37 and 58, just e on SR 58. Int corridors. **Pets:** Accepted.
📶 ✖ 🚽 💻

BERNE

▼▼ **Clock Tower Inn** 🅷
(260) 589-8955. **$70-$79.** 1335 US 27 N 46711. On US 27, 1 mi n. Int corridors. **Pets:** Medium. $10 daily fee/room. Designated rooms, service with restrictions, crate. 📶 ✖ 🚽 💻

BLOOMINGTON

▼▼ **Comfort Inn Bloomington** 🅷 🐾
(812) 650-0010. **$99-$299.** 1700 N Kinser Pike 47404. On SR 45 and 45 Bypass, 1 mi e of jct SR 37. Int corridors. **Pets:** Medium, other species. $25 one-time fee/room. Designated rooms, service with restrictions, crate. 📶 ✖ 🚽 💻

▼▼▼▼ **Fairfield Inn by Marriott** 🅷
(812) 331-1122. **$83-$137.** 120 Fairfield Dr 47404. Just e from SR 37 at 3rd St. Int corridors. **Pets:** Accepted. Ⓜ 📶 ✖ 🚽 💻

▼▼▼▼ **Hampton Inn Bloomington** 🅷
(812) 334-2100. **$129-$159.** 2100 N Walnut St 47404. 1 mi e of jct SR 37 on SR 45 and 46 Bypass, then just s on College Ave/Walnut St. Int corridors. **Pets:** Accepted. 📶 ✖ 🚽 💻

▼▼▼▼ **Holiday Inn Bloomington** 🅷
(812) 334-3252. **$89-$289, 3 day notice.** 1710 N Kinser Pike 47404. On SR 45 and 46 Bypass, 1 mi e of jct SR 37. Int corridors. **Pets:** Accepted. 🍴 Ⓜ 📶 ✖ 🚽 💻

🔺 ▼▼▼▼ **Hyatt Place Bloomington** 🅷
(812) 339-5950. **$89-$659.** 217 W Kirkwood Ave 47404. Jct S Gentry St. Int corridors. **Pets:** Accepted. SAVE 🍴 Ⓜ 📶 ✖ 🚽 💻

▼▼▼▼ **TownePlace Suites by Marriott** 🅷
(812) 334-1234. **$83-$137.** 105 S Franklin Rd 47404. Just e from SR 37 at 3rd St, then 0.3 mi n. Int corridors. **Pets:** Accepted.
📶 ✖ 🚽 💻

BLUFFTON

▼▼ **Bluffton Inn & Suites** 🅷
(260) 824-5553. **$69-$89.** 100 Charles Deam Ct 46714. Jct SR 1 and 124 (E Division Rd), just n. Int corridors. **Pets:** Accepted.
📶 ✖ 🚽 💻

BREMEN

▼▼▼ **Scottish Bed and Breakfast** 🅱🅱
(574) 220-6672. **$109-$169, 14 day notice.** 2180 Miami Tr 46506. Jct SR 331, 2 mi w on SR 106, just s. Int corridors. **Pets:** Small, dogs only. $25 one-time fee/room. Designated rooms, service with restrictions, crate. 📶 ✖ 🌀 🚽

BROWNSBURG

▼▼ **Quality Inn & Suites Brownsburg** 🅷
(317) 852-5353. **Call for rates.** 31 Maplehurst Dr 46112. I-74 exit 66, just n on SR 267. Int corridors. **Pets:** Accepted.
Ⓜ 📶 ✖ 🚽 💻

CARMEL (Restaurants p. 631)

▼▼▼ **Comfort Inn Carmel** 🅷
(317) 816-1616. **$85-$209.** 10201 N Meridian St 46290. I-465 exit 31, 0.3 mi n on US 31. Int corridors. **Pets:** Accepted.
Ⓜ 📶 ✖ 🚽 💻

▼▼▼▼ **Residence Inn by Marriott Indianapolis/Carmel** 🅷
(317) 846-2000. **$112-$207.** 11895 N Meridian St 46032. I-465 exit 31, 2 mi n on US 31, just e on 116th St, then just n on N Pennsylvania St. Int corridors. **Pets:** Medium. $100 one-time fee/room. Service with restrictions, supervision. 🅜 ⊠ 🛜 ✖ 🔋 💻

▼▼▼▼ **Staybridge Suites Indianapolis-Carmel** 🅷
(317) 582-1500. **Call for rates.** 10675 N Pennsylvania St 46280. I-465 exit 31, 0.7 mi n to 106th St, just e, then just n. Int corridors.
Pets: Accepted. 🅜 ⊠ 🛜 ✖ 🔋 💻

CHESTERTON
▼▼▼▼ **Gray Goose Inn** 🆑 🐾
(219) 926-5781. **$110-$195, 10 day notice.** 350 Indian Boundary Rd 46304. I-94 exit 26A, 0.6 mi s, then just w. Int corridors. **Pets:** Medium. $25 one-time fee/pet. Designated rooms, service with restrictions, supervision. 🛜 ✖

CLARKSVILLE
🆂 ▼▼▼ **BEST WESTERN Green Tree Inn** 🅼
(812) 288-9281. **$80-$275, 30 day notice.** 1425 Broadway St 47129. I-65 exit 4, just w. Ext corridors. **Pets:** Medium, dogs only. $15 daily fee/pet. Designated rooms, service with restrictions, crate.
🆂🅰🆅🅴 ⊠ 🛜 🔋 💻

🆂 ▼▼▼▼ **Candlewood Suites Louisville North** 🅷
(812) 284-6113. **$124, 3 day notice.** 1419 Bales Ln 47129. I-65 exit 4, just w, then just n on Broadway St. Int corridors. **Pets:** Accepted.
🆂🅰🆅🅴 🅜 ⊠ 🛜 ✖ 🔋 💻

CLOVERDALE
▼▼ **Super 8 Cloverdale/Greencastle** 🅷
(765) 795-7373. **$57-$219.** 1020 N Main St 46120. I-70 exit 41, just s on US 231. Int corridors. **Pets:** Dogs only. $10 daily fee/room. Service with restrictions, crate. ⊠ 🛜 ✖ 🔋 💻

COLUMBIA CITY
▼▼ **Quality Inn** 🅷
(260) 248-4551. **$65-$150.** 701 W Connexion Way 46725. 1 mi w of SR 9, just off US 30. Int corridors. **Pets:** Small, other species. $15 one-time fee/room. Service with restrictions, supervision.
🅜 ⊠ 🛜 ✖ 🔋 💻

COLUMBUS
▼▼▼ **Hotel Indigo** 🅷
(812) 375-9100. **$119-$229.** 400 Brown St 47201. Jct 4th St. Int corridors. **Pets:** Accepted. 🍽 🅜 ⊠ 🛜 ✖ 🔋 💻

▼▼▼ **La Quinta Inn & Suites** 🅷
(812) 379-4657. **$89-$229.** 101 Carrie Ln 47201. I-65 exit 68, just w on SR 46. Int corridors. **Pets:** Large, other species. Service with restrictions. 🅜 ⊠ 🛜 ✖ 🔋 💻

▼▼▼ **Residence Inn by Marriott** 🅷
(812) 342-2400. **$104-$240.** 4525 W SR 46 47201. I-65 exit 68, 0.8 mi w on SR 46. Int corridors. **Pets:** Accepted.
🅜 ⊠ ✖ 🛜 ✖ 🔋 💻

CORYDON
▼▼▼▼ **Comfort Inn Corydon** 🅷
(812) 738-3900. **$69-$109.** 115 Skypark Dr 47112. I-64 exit 105, just n. Int corridors. **Pets:** Other species. $10 daily fee/pet. Designated rooms, service with restrictions, supervision. ⊠ 🛜 ✖ 🔋 💻

▼▼▼ **Holiday Inn Express** 🅷
(812) 738-1623. **$94-$129.** 249 Federal Dr 47112. I-64 exit 105, 0.6 mi s, then just w. Int corridors. **Pets:** Accepted. ⊠ 🛜 ✖ 🔋 💻

CRAWFORDSVILLE
▼▼ **Comfort Inn** 🅷
(765) 361-0665. **$97-$154.** 2991 Gandhi Dr 47933. I-74 exit 34, just s on US 231. Int corridors. **Pets:** Accepted. ⊠ 🛜 ✖ 🔋 💻

▼▼▼ **Hampton Inn & Suites** 🅷
(765) 362-8884. **$99-$189.** 2895 Gandhi Dr 47933. I-74 exit 34, just s on US 231. Int corridors. **Pets:** Dogs only. $25 daily fee/pet. Designated rooms, service with restrictions, supervision.
🅜 ⊠ 🛜 ✖ 🔋 💻

▼▼▼ **Holiday Inn Express Hotel & Suites** 🅷
(765) 323-4575. **$98-$195.** 2506 N Lafayette Rd 47933. I-74 exit 34, 0.3 mi s on US 231. Int corridors. **Pets:** Accepted.
🅜 ⊠ 🛜 ✖ 🔋 💻

DALE
🆂 ▼▼▼ **Baymont Inn & Suites Dale** 🅷
(812) 937-7000. **$72-$180.** 1339 N Washington St 47523. I-64 exit 57A, just s. Int corridors. **Pets:** Accepted.
🆂🅰🆅🅴 🅜 ⊠ 🛜 ✖ 🔋 💻

EDINBURGH
🆂 ▼▼▼ **BEST WESTERN Horizon Inn** 🅷
(812) 526-9883. **$80-$300.** 11780 N US 31 46124. I-65 exit 76B, just n. Int corridors. **Pets:** Accepted. 🆂🅰🆅🅴 ⊠ 🛜 ✖ 🔋 💻

ELKHART
▼▼▼▼ **Baymont Inn & Suites Elkhart** 🅷
(574) 264-7222. **$49-$99.** 3010 Brittany Ct 46514. I-80/90 exit 92, 0.3 mi s on SR 19. Int corridors. **Pets:** $20 one-time fee/pet. Service with restrictions, supervision. 🅜 ⊠ 🛜 ✖ 🔋 💻

▼▼▼▼ **Candlewood Suites** 🅷
(574) 262-8600. **$90-$299.** 300 Northpointe Blvd 46514. I-80/90 exit 92, just n on SR 19, then just w. Int corridors. **Pets:** Large, other species. $25 daily fee/pet. Service with restrictions, crate.
🅜 🛜 ✖ 🔋 💻

🆂 ▼▼▼▼ **Staybridge Suites Elkhart North** 🅷
(574) 970-8488. **Call for rates.** 3252 Cassopolis St 46514. I-80/90 exit 92, just n on SR 19. Int corridors. **Pets:** Accepted.
🆂🅰🆅🅴 ⊠ 🛜 ✖ 🔋 💻

EVANSVILLE
▼▼▼ **Baymont Inn & Suites Evansville East** 🅷
(812) 477-2677. **$74-$114.** 8005 E Division St 47715. I-164 exit 7B (SR 66/Lloyd Expwy), 0.5 mi w to Cross Pointe Blvd, just n to Division St, then 0.5 mi e. Int corridors. **Pets:** Accepted.
🅜 ⊠ 🛜 ✖ 🔋 💻

▼▼ **Comfort Inn East** 🅷
(812) 476-3600. **$79-$99.** 8331 E Walnut St 47715. I-164 exit 7B (SR 66/Lloyd Expwy), 0.5 mi w to Eagle Crest Blvd, 0.3 mi se to Fuquay St, just s to Walnut St, then 0.4 mi e. Int corridors. **Pets:** Small. $10 one-time fee/room. Designated rooms, service with restrictions, supervision. 🅜 ⊠ 🛜 ✖ 🔋 💻

▼▼▼ **Comfort Inn Evansville North** 🅷
(812) 867-1600. **$80-$300.** 19622 Elpers Rd 47725. I-64 exit 25A (US 41), 0.5 mi s, then just w. Int corridors. **Pets:** Accepted.
⊠ 🛜 ✖ 🔋 💻

▼▼▼ **Drury Inn & Suites-Evansville East** 🅷
(812) 471-3400. **$95-$169.** 100 Cross Pointe Blvd 47715. I-164 exit 7B (SR 66/Lloyd Expwy), 0.5 mi w. Int corridors. **Pets:** $10 daily fee/room. Service with restrictions, supervision. 🅜 ⊠ 🛜 ✖ 🔋 💻

▼▼ **Extended Stay America Evansville East** 🅷
(812) 479-0103. **Call for rates.** 301 Eagle Crest Dr 47715. I-164 exit 7B (SR 66/Lloyd Expwy), 0.5 mi w to Eagle Crest Blvd, 0.5 mi s, then just e. Int corridors. **Pets:** Other species. $25 daily fee/pet. Service with restrictions, supervision. ⊠ 🛜 ✖ 🔋 💻

▼▼▼ **Gateway Inn & Suites** 🅷
(812) 868-8000. **Call for rates.** 324 Rusher Creek Rd 47725. I-64 exit 25A (US 41), 0.5 mi s, then just w. Int corridors. **Pets:** Accepted.
🅜 ⊠ 🛜 ✖ 🔋 💻

▼▼▼ Holiday Inn Express - Evansville West 🅷
(812) 421-9773. **$120-$200.** 5737 Pearl Dr 47712. Jct US 41 and SR 62 (Lloyd Expwy), 5.7 mi w on SR 62 (Lloyd Expwy), then just s on Boehne Camp Rd. Int corridors. **Pets:** Medium. $15 daily fee/pet. Service with restrictions, supervision. 🅂🅼 🖾 🛜 ✕ 🔋 💻

▼▼▼ Howard Johnson Evansville East 🅷
(812) 476-9626. **$59-$139.** 1101 N Green River Rd 47715. I-164 exit 9 (SR 62 E/Morgan Ave), 1.3 mi w on SR 62, then just s. Int corridors. **Pets:** Medium, other species. $20 one-time fee/pet. Service with restrictions, crate. 🅂🅼 🖾 🛜 ✕ 🔋 💻

▼▼▼ La Quinta Inn & Suites Evansville 🅷
(812) 471-3414. **$79-$199.** 8015 E Division St 47715. I-164 exit 7B (SR 66/Lloyd Expwy), 0.5 mi w to Cross Pointe Blvd, just n, then 0.5 mi e. Int corridors. **Pets:** Large, other species. Service with restrictions.
🖾 🛜 ✕ 🔋 💻

▼▼▼ Residence Inn by Marriott Evansville East 🅷
(812) 471-7191. **$118-$194.** 8283 E Walnut St 47715. I-164 exit 7B (SR 66/Lloyd Expwy), 0.5 mi w to Eagle Crest Blvd, 0.3 mi se to Fuquay St, then 0.3 mi e. Int corridors. **Pets:** $100 one-time fee/room. Designated rooms, service with restrictions, crate. 🅂🅼 🖾 🛜 ✕ 🔋 💻

ⒶⒶⒶ ▼▼▼ Tropicana Evansville 🅷
(812) 433-4000. **$99-$299.** 421 NW Riverside Dr 47708. SR 62 (Lloyd Expwy), just s on Fulton. Int corridors. **Pets:** Medium. $100 deposit/room. Designated rooms, service with restrictions.
🆂🅰🆅🅴 🍴 🅂🅼 🛜 🔋 💻

FISHERS

ⒶⒶⒶ ▼▼▼ AmericInn Hotel & Suites Indianapolis - Northeast 🅷
(317) 578-9000. **Call for rates.** 9780 North by Northeast Blvd 46037. I-69 exit 203, just ne. Int corridors. **Pets:** Accepted.
🆂🅰🆅🅴 🅂🅼 🖾 🛜 ✕ 🔋 💻

ⒶⒶⒶ ▼▼▼ Baymont Inn and Suites Fishers / Indianapolis Area 🅷
(317) 578-2000. **$79-$159.** 9790 North by Northeast Blvd 46038. I-69 exit 203, just ne. Int corridors. **Pets:** Accepted.
🆂🅰🆅🅴 🅂🅼 🖾 🛜 ✕ 🔋 💻

▼▼ Comfort Suites 🅷
(317) 578-1200. **$99-$159.** 9760 Crosspoint Blvd 46256. I-69 exit 203, just w on 96th St, then just n. Int corridors. **Pets:** Medium. $25 daily fee/pet. Service with restrictions. 🖾 🛜 ✕ 🔋 💻

▼▼▼ Residence Inn by Marriott Indianapolis/Fishers 🅷
(317) 842-1111. **$112-$207.** 9765 Crosspoint Blvd 46256. I-69 exit 203, just nw. Int corridors. **Pets:** Medium. $100 one-time fee/room. Service with restrictions, supervision. 🅂🅼 🖾 🛜 ✕ 🔋 💻

▼▼▼ Staybridge Suites Indianapolis-Fishers 🅷
(317) 577-9500. **$139-$179.** 9780 Crosspoint Blvd 46256. I-69 exit 203, just nw. Int corridors. **Pets:** Medium, other species. $125 one-time fee/room. Service with restrictions, crate.
🅂🅼 🖾 🖾 🛜 ✕ 🔋 💻

FORT WAYNE

▼▼ Avenir Inn 🅷
(260) 489-2220. **Call for rates.** 1005 W Washington Center Rd 46825. I-69 exit 311B, just n on SR 3, then 0.4 mi e. Int corridors. **Pets:** Accepted. 🛜 ✕ 🔋 💻

ⒶⒶⒶ ▼▼▼ BEST WESTERN Luxbury Inn Fort Wayne 🅷 🐾
(260) 436-0242. **$90-$120.** 5501 Coventry Ln 46804. I-69 exit 302, just w. Int corridors. **Pets:** Medium. $20 daily fee/room. Designated rooms, service with restrictions, supervision. 🆂🅰🆅🅴 🖾 🛜 ✕ 🔋 💻

ⒶⒶⒶ ▼▼▼ BEST WESTERN PLUS Fort Wayne Inn & Suites-North 🅷
(260) 490-6060. **$99-$120.** 5926 Cross Creek Blvd 46818. I-69 exit 311B, just n. Int corridors. **Pets:** Accepted.
🆂🅰🆅🅴 🖾 🛜 ✕ 🔋 💻

▼▼▼ Candlewood Suites 🅷
(260) 484-1400. **$89-$99.** 5250 Distribution Dr 46825. I-69 exit 311A, just e. Int corridors. **Pets:** Accepted.
🍴 🅂🅼 🖾 🛜 ✕ 🔋 💻

▼▼▼ Comfort Suites Southwest 🅷 🐾
(260) 436-4300. **$89-$119.** 5775 Coventry Ln 46804. I-69 exit 302, just w. Int corridors. **Pets:** $25 daily fee/pet. Designated rooms, service with restrictions, crate. 🅂🅼 🖾 🛜 ✕ 🔋 💻

▼▼ Don Hall's Guesthouse 🅷
(260) 489-2524. **$99-$109.** 1313 W Washington Center Rd 46825. I-69 exit 311B, just n on SR 3, then 0.3 mi e. Ext/int corridors. **Pets:** Accepted. 🍴 🖾 🖾 🛜 ✕ 🔋 💻

▼▼ Extended Stay America-Fort Wayne-South 🅷
(260) 432-1916. **Call for rates.** 8309 W Jefferson Blvd 46804. I-69 exit 302, 0.4 mi e on US 24, then 0.6 mi s. Int corridors. **Pets:** Other species. $25 daily fee/pet. Service with restrictions, supervision.
🍴 🛜 ✕ 🔋 💻

▼▼ Hawthorn Suites by Wyndham Fort Wayne 🅷
(260) 484-4700. **$109-$142.** 4919 Lima Rd 46808. I-69 exit 311A, 0.4 mi s on US 27. Ext corridors. **Pets:** Other species. $50 one-time fee/room. Designated rooms, service with restrictions, crate.
🖾 🛜 ✕ 🔋 💻

ⒶⒶⒶ ▼▼▼ Hilton Fort Wayne at the Grand Wayne Convention Center 🅷 🐾
(260) 420-1100. **$109-$229.** 1020 S Calhoun St 46802. Jct Jefferson Blvd; center. Int corridors. **Pets:** $50 one-time fee/pet. Service with restrictions, supervision. 🆂🅰🆅🅴 🍴 🅂🅼 🖾 🛜 ✕ 🔋 💻

▼▼▼ Homewood Suites by Hilton Fort Wayne 🅷
(260) 432-5100. **$109-$184.** 8621 US 24 W 46804. I-69 exit 302, just w. Int corridors. **Pets:** Accepted. 🅂🅼 🛜 ✕ 🔋 💻

▼▼ Hotel Fort Wayne 🅷 🐾
(260) 484-0411. **$89-$169.** 305 E Washington Center Rd 46825. I-69 exit 312A, just s. Int corridors. **Pets:** $50 one-time fee/room. Designated rooms, service with restrictions, supervision.
🍴 🖾 🛜 ✕ 🔋 💻

ⒶⒶⒶ ▼▼▼ Hyatt Place Fort Wayne 🅷
(260) 471-8522. **$79-$189.** 111 W Washington Center Rd 46825. I-69 exit 312A, just s on Coldwater Rd, then just w. Int corridors. **Pets:** Accepted. 🆂🅰🆅🅴 🍴 🅂🅼 🖾 🛜 ✕ 🔋 💻

ⒶⒶⒶ ▼▼▼ Quality Inn 🅷
(260) 489-5554. **$75-$100.** 1734 W Washington Center Rd 46818. I-69 exit 311B, just n on SR 3. Int corridors. **Pets:** Medium. $15 daily fee/pet. Designated rooms, service with restrictions, supervision.
🆂🅰🆅🅴 🖾 🛜 ✕ 💻

▼▼▼ Residence Inn by Marriott Southwest 🅷
(260) 432-8000. **$97-$160.** 7811 W Jefferson Blvd 46804. I-69 exit 302, 0.5 mi e. Int corridors. **Pets:** Accepted. 🍴 🖾 🛜 ✕ 🔋 💻

▼▼▼ Staybridge Suites - Fort Wayne 🅷
(260) 432-2427. **Call for rates.** 5925 Ellison Rd 46804. I-69 exit 302, just w. Int corridors. **Pets:** Accepted. 🅂🅼 🖾 🛜 ✕ 🔋 💻

▼▼▼ TownePlace Suites by Marriott Fort Wayne North 🅷
(260) 483-1160. **$83-$154.** 3949 Ice Way 46805. I-69 exit 311A, 1.2 mi se on Lima Rd. Int corridors. **Pets:** Accepted.
🍴 🅂🅼 🖾 🛜 ✕ 🔋 💻

FREMONT

▼▼ Holiday Inn Express Fremont (Angola Area) H
(260) 833-6464. **Call for rates.** 6245 N Old 27, Suite 400 46737. I-80/90 exit 144, just s; I-69 exit 357, just w, then 1 mi s. Int corridors. **Pets:** Accepted. 🛅M 🛏 📶 ✕ 📧 💻

FRENCH LICK

▼▼▼ Comfort Suites H
(812) 936-5300. **$108-$141.** 9530 W SR 56 47432. Jct SR 145, 1.2 mi sw. Int corridors. **Pets:** Medium. $35 one-time fee/pet. Designated rooms, service with restrictions, crate. 🛅M 🛏 📶 ✕ 📧 💻

◈◈◈ ▼▼▼▼ French Lick Springs Hotel H
(812) 936-9300. **Call for rates.** 8670 W SR 56 47432. Jct SR 145. Int corridors. **Pets:** Accepted.
[SAVE] 🍴 🛅M 🛏 📶 ✕ 📧 💻

GAS CITY

◈◈◈ ▼▼▼▼ BEST WESTERN PLUS Gas City H
(765) 998-2331. **$100-$185.** 4936 Kaybee Dr 46143. I-69 exit 259, just e. Int corridors. **Pets:** Other species. $20 one-time fee/pet. Designated rooms, service with restrictions, supervision.
[SAVE] 🛅M 🛏 📶 ✕ 📧 💻

GOSHEN

◈◈◈ ▼▼▼ BEST WESTERN Inn M ❀
(574) 533-0408. **$99.** 900 Lincolnway E 46526. 1 mi se on US 33. Ext corridors. **Pets:** Crate. [SAVE] 📶 ✕ 📧 💻

GREENFIELD

◈◈◈ ▼▼▼ Comfort Inn-Greenfield H
(317) 467-9999. **$90-$126.** 178 E Martindale Dr 46140. I-70 exit 104, 0.4 mi s on State St. Int corridors. **Pets:** Accepted.
[SAVE] 🛏 📶 ✕ 📧 💻

▼▼▼ Quality Inn & Suites Greenfield H ❀
(317) 462-7112. **$89-$99.** 2270 N State St 46140. I-70 exit 104, just s. Int corridors. **Pets:** Other species. $10 daily fee/pet.
🛏 📶 ✕ 📧 💻

GREENSBURG

▼▼▼▼ Hampton Inn & Suites H
(812) 663-5000. **$99-$169.** 2075 N Michigan Ave 47240. I-74 exit 132, 1.5 mi s on SR 3, then 0.6 mi w. Int corridors. **Pets:** Accepted.
🛅M 🛏 📶 ✕ 📧 💻

▼▼▼ Holiday Inn Express H
(812) 663-5500. **$89-$119.** 915 Ann Blvd 47240. I-74 exit 134A, 1.4 mi s on SR 3. Int corridors. **Pets:** Other species. $15 daily fee/pet. Service with restrictions, supervision. 🛅M 🛏 📶 ✕ 📧 💻

GREENWOOD

▼▼▼▼ Candlewood Suites Indy-South H
(317) 882-4300. **$89-$130.** 1190 N Graham Rd 46143. I-65 exit 101, just e. Int corridors. **Pets:** Other species. $25 one-time fee/room. Service with restrictions, crate. 🛅M 📶 ✕ 📧 💻

HAMMOND

◈◈◈ ▼▼▼ BEST WESTERN Northwest Indiana Inn H
(219) 844-2140. **$100-$150.** 3830 179th St 46323. I-80/94 exit 5, 0.6 mi s on Cline Ave (SR 912), then 0.6 mi n on frontage road (179th St). Int corridors. **Pets:** Small, other species. $50 deposit/pet, $20 daily fee/pet. Designated rooms, service with restrictions, crate.
[SAVE] 🍴 🛏 📶 ✕ 📧 💻

▼▼▼▼ Residence Inn by Marriott Chicago Southeast H
(219) 844-8440. **$125-$217.** 7740 Corinne Dr 46323. I-80/94 exit 3 (Kennedy Ave S), just s. Int corridors. **Pets:** Accepted.
🛅M 🛏 📶 ✕ 📧 💻

HOWE

▼▼▼ Holiday Inn Express-Howe/Sturgis H
(260) 562-3660. **Call for rates.** 45 W 750 N 46746. I-80/90 exit 121 (US 66). Int corridors. **Pets:** Accepted. 🛅M 🛏 📶 ✕ 📧 💻

HUNTINGTON

▼▼ Super 8 H
(260) 358-8888. **$65-$90.** 2801 Guilford St 46750. US 24, just n. Int corridors. **Pets:** Accepted. 🛏 📶 ✕ 📧 💻

INDIANAPOLIS *(Restaurants p. 631)*

▼▼▼▼ The Alexander - A Dolce Hotel H ❀
(317) 624-8200. **$189-$339, 3 day notice.** 333 S Delaware St 46204. Jct Delaware and South sts. Int corridors. **Pets:** Medium, dogs only. $25 one-time fee/pet. Service with restrictions, supervision.
🍴 🛅M 📶 ✕ 📧 💻

▼▼▼ Baymont Inn & Suites H
(317) 322-2000. **$89-$159, 3 day notice.** 1540 Brookville Crossing Way 46239. I-465 exit 47, 0.3 mi e. Int corridors. **Pets:** Other species. $15 daily fee/room. Designated rooms, service with restrictions, crate.
🛅M 🛏 📶 ✕ 📧 💻

▼▼▼ Baymont Inn & Suites Indianapolis South H
(317) 784-7006. **$59-$99.** 4402 E Creekview Dr 46237. I-65 exit 103, just w. Int corridors. **Pets:** Medium. $20 daily fee/pet. Designated rooms, service with restrictions, supervision. 🛏 📶 ✕ 📧 💻

▼▼▼ Baymont Inn & Suites Indianapolis West H
(317) 299-6165. **$85-$105.** 3850 Eagle View Dr 46254. I-465 exit 17, just w on 38th St, then just n. Int corridors. **Pets:** Medium. $20 daily fee/room. Service with restrictions, supervision.
🛏 📶 ✕ 📧 💻

◈◈◈ ▼▼▼ BEST WESTERN Airport Suites H
(317) 246-1505. **Call for rates.** 55 S High School Rd 46241. I-465 exit 13B, just w. Int corridors. **Pets:** Accepted. [SAVE] 📶 ✕ 📧 💻

◈◈◈ ▼▼▼ BEST WESTERN Country Suites H
(317) 879-1700. **$59-$120.** 3871 W 92nd St 46268. I-465 exit 27, just s on Michigan Rd. Int corridors. **Pets:** Accepted.
[SAVE] 🛅M 📶 ✕ 📧 💻

◈◈◈ ▼▼▼ BEST WESTERN Crossroads H
(317) 353-6966. **$79-$199.** 7610 Old Trails Rd 46219. I-465 exit 46, just sw. Int corridors. **Pets:** Accepted. [SAVE] 🛏 📶 ✕ 📧 💻

▼▼▼ Candlewood Suites Indianapolis NE H
(317) 595-9292. **$99-$119.** 8111 Bash St 46250. I-69 exit 201, just w. Int corridors. **Pets:** Accepted. 🛏 📶 ✕ 📧 💻

▼▼▼ Candlewood Suites Indianapolis NW H
(317) 298-8000. **Call for rates.** 7455 Woodland Dr 46278. I-465 exit 21 (73rd St), just n. Int corridors. **Pets:** Accepted.
🛅M 🛏 📶 ✕ 📧 💻

◈◈◈ ▼▼▼ Comfort Inn-East H
(317) 359-9999. **$75-$110.** 2295 N Shadeland Ave 46219. I-70 exit 89, 0.5 mi w of jct I-465. Int corridors. **Pets:** $25 one-time fee/pet. Designated rooms, service with restrictions, supervision.
[SAVE] 🛏 📶 ✕ 📧 💻

▼▼▼ Conrad Indianapolis H ❀
(317) 713-5000. **$139-$399.** 50 W Washington St 46204. Jct Illinois St. Int corridors. **Pets:** Medium, other species. $100 deposit/room, $150 one-time fee/room. Service with restrictions, crate.
🍴 🛅M 🛏 📶 ✕ 📧 💻

▼▼▼ Drury Inn & Suites Indianapolis Northeast H
(317) 849-8900. **$100-$179.** 8180 N Shadeland Ave 46250. I-69 exit 201, just e. Int corridors. **Pets:** $10 daily fee/room. Service with restrictions, supervision. 🛅M 🛏 📶 ✕ 📧 💻

▼▼▼▼ **Drury Inn-Indianapolis** 🏠
(317) 876-9777. **$95-$169.** 9320 N Michigan Rd 46268. I-465 exit 27, just s. Int corridors. **Pets:** $10 daily fee/room. Service with restrictions, supervision. 🛁 📶 ✕ 🖥 💻

▼▼ **Extended Stay America - 86th Street/Northwest** 🏠
(317) 334-7829. **Call for rates.** 8520 Northwest Blvd 46278. I-465 exit 23, just e. Int corridors. **Pets:** Other species. $25 daily fee/pet. Service with restrictions, supervision. 👤 🛁 📶 ✕ 🖥 💻

▼▼ **Extended Stay America Indianapolis - North - Carmel** 🏠
(317) 843-1181. **Call for rates.** 9750 Lakeshore Dr 46280. I-465 exit 33, 0.4 mi n on Keystone Ave, 0.6 mi e on 96th St, then just n on Bauer Dr. Int corridors. **Pets:** Other species. $25 daily fee/pet. Service with restrictions, supervision. 🛁 📶 ✕ 🖥 💻

▼▼▼▼ **GuestHouse Inn Indianapolis Airport** 🏠
(317) 247-4100. **Call for rates.** 5845 Rockville Rd 46224. I-465 exit 13A, just e. Int corridors. **Pets:** Accepted. 📶 ✕ 🖥 💻

🅐🅐🅐 ▼▼▼▼ **Hilton Indianapolis Hotel & Suites** 🏠
(317) 972-0600. **$89-$399.** 120 W Market St 46204. Jct Illinois St. Int corridors. **Pets:** Accepted.
SAVE 🍴 👤 🛁 ✕ 📶 ✕ 🖥 💻

🅐🅐🅐 ▼▼▼▼ **Holiday Inn Express South** 🏠
(317) 783-5151. **$92-$144.** 5151 S East St 46227. I-465 exit 2B, 0.3 mi s. Int corridors. **Pets:** Other species. $55 one-time fee/room. Designated rooms, service with restrictions, crate. SAVE 🛁 📶 ✕ 🖥 💻

🅐🅐🅐 ▼▼▼▼ **Hyatt Place Indianapolis Airport** 🏠
(317) 227-0950. **$69-$179.** 5500 W Bradbury Ave 46241. I-465 exit 11A, 0.3 mi e on Sam Jones Expwy to Executive Dr. Int corridors.
Pets: Accepted. SAVE 🍴 👤 🛁 📶 ✕ 🖥 💻

🅐🅐🅐 ▼▼▼▼ **Hyatt Place Indianapolis/Keystone** 🏠
(317) 843-0064. **$89-$189.** 9104 Keystone Crossing 46240. I-465 exit 33, 0.5 mi s on SR 431, just e on 86th St, then 0.5 mi n. Int corridors.
Pets: Accepted. SAVE 🍴 👤 🛁 📶 ✕ 🖥 💻

▼▼▼▼ **Indianapolis Marriott East** 🏠
(317) 352-1231. **$132-$217.** 7202 E 21st St 46219. I-70 exit 89, 0.3 mi se; 0.5 mi w of jct I-465. Int corridors. **Pets:** Accepted.
🍴 👤 🛁 📶 ✕ 🖥 💻

▼▼▼ **La Quinta Inn Indianapolis Airport Executive Drive** 🏠
(317) 244-8100. **$65-$294.** 2650 Executive Dr 46241. I-465 exit 11 southbound; exit 11B northbound, 0.3 mi e. Int corridors. **Pets:** Large, other species. Service with restrictions. 👤 📶 ✕ 🖥 💻

▼▼▼ **La Quinta Inn Indianapolis Airport Lynhurst** 🏠
(317) 247-4281. **$62-$274.** 5316 W Southern Ave 46241. I-465 exit 11A, 0.5 mi e on Sam Jones Expwy to Lynhurst Dr. Int corridors.
Pets: Large, other species. Service with restrictions.
🛁 📶 ✕ 🖥 💻

▼▼▼ **La Quinta Inn Indianapolis East** 🏠
(317) 359-1021. **$69-$494.** 7304 E 21st St 46219. I-70 exit 89, just s, then just e; 0.5 mi w of jct I-465. Int corridors. **Pets:** Large, other species. Service with restrictions. 🛁 📶 ✕ 🖥 💻

▼▼▼▼ **Omni Severin Hotel** 🏠
(317) 634-6664. **$159-$369, 14 day notice.** 40 W Jackson Pl 46225. Corner of Illinois and Georgia sts. Int corridors. **Pets:** Accepted.
🍴 🛁 ✕ 🖥 💻

▼▼▼ **Quality Inn Indy Castleton** 🏠
(317) 849-8555. **$72-$125.** 8380 Kelly Ln 46250. I-465 exit 35 (Allison-ville Rd), just s. Int corridors. **Pets:** Accepted.
🍴 👤 🛁 📶 ✕ 🖥 💻

▼▼▼▼ **Radisson Hotel Indianapolis Airport** 🏠
(317) 244-3361. **$99-$309.** 2500 S High School Rd 46241. I-465 exit 11 southbound; exit 11B northbound, just w. Int corridors. **Pets:** Large. $50 one-time fee/pet. Service with restrictions, supervision.
🍴 📶 🖥 💻

▼▼▼ **Ramada Limited** Ⓜ
(317) 297-1848. **$72-$105, 3 day notice.** 3851 Shore Dr 46254. I-465 exit 17, just w on 38th St, then just n. Ext corridors. **Pets:** Accepted.
🛁 📶 ✕ 🖥 💻

🅐🅐🅐 ▼▼▼ **Red Roof Inn Indianapolis North-College Park** 🏠
(317) 872-3030. **$45-$99.** 9520 Valparaiso Ct 46268. I-465 exit 27, just n. Ext corridors. **Pets:** Large, other species. Service with restrictions, supervision. SAVE 👤 📶 ✕ 🖥 💻

▼▼▼▼ **Residence Inn by Marriott Indianapolis Airport** 🏠
(317) 244-1500. **$119-$196.** 5224 W Southern Ave 46241. I-465 exit 11A, 0.5 mi e on Sam Jones Expwy to Lynhurst Dr. Int corridors.
Pets: Accepted. 👤 🛁 📶 ✕ 🖥 💻

▼▼▼▼ **Residence Inn by Marriott Indianapolis Downtown on the Canal** 🏠
(317) 822-0840. **$132-$217.** 350 W New York St 46202. Jct Senate Ave. Int corridors. **Pets:** Accepted. 👤 🛁 ✕ 📶 ✕ 🖥 💻

▼▼▼▼ **Residence Inn by Marriott Northwest-Indianapolis** 🏠
(317) 275-6000. **$125-$206.** 6220 Digital Way 46278. I-465 exit 21, just w. Int corridors. **Pets:** Accepted. 👤 🛁 📶 ✕ 🖥 💻

🅐🅐🅐 ▼▼▼▼ **Sheraton Indianapolis at Keystone Crossing** 🏠
(317) 846-2700. **$119-$399.** 8787 Keystone Crossing 46240. I-465 exit 33, 0.5 mi s on SR 431, just e on 86th St, then just n. Int corridors.
Pets: Accepted. SAVE ECO 🍴 👤 🛁 ✕ 💻

🅐🅐🅐 ▼▼▼▼ **Sheraton Indianapolis City Centre** 🏠
(317) 635-2000. **$179-$299.** 31 W Ohio St 46204. Jct Meridian St; just n of Monument Cir. Int corridors. **Pets:** Accepted.
SAVE 🍴 👤 🛁 📶 ✕ 🖥 💻

▼▼▼▼ **Staybridge Suites City Centre** 🏠
(317) 536-7500. **Call for rates.** 535 S West St 46225. Just s of South St. Int corridors. **Pets:** Accepted. 👤 🛁 📶 ✕ 🖥 💻

▼▼▼ **Suburban Extended Stay Hotel** 🏠
(317) 598-1914. **$39-$89.** 8055 Bash St 46250. I-69 exit 201, just w. Int corridors. **Pets:** Other species. $25 one-time fee/room. Service with restrictions, crate. 👤 📶 ✕ 🖥 💻

▼▼▼ **TownePlace Suites by Marriott Keystone** 🏠
(317) 255-3700. **$83-$160.** 8468 Union Chapel Rd 46240. I-465 exit 33, 0.5 mi s on SR 431, just e on 86th St, then just s. Int corridors.
Pets: Accepted. 🛁 📶 ✕ 🖥 💻

▼▼▼ **TownePlace Suites by Marriott Park 100** 🏠
(317) 290-8900. **$90-$160.** 5802 W 71st St 46278. I-465 exit 21, 0.3 mi e. Int corridors. **Pets:** Accepted. 🛁 📶 ✕ 🖥 💻

🅐🅐🅐 ▼▼▼▼ **The Westin Indianapolis** 🏠
(317) 262-8100. **$135-$349.** 50 S Capitol Ave 46204. Jct Washington and Maryland sts. Int corridors. **Pets:** Accepted.
SAVE 🍴 👤 🛁 ✕ 🛁 ✕ 🖥 💻

▼▼▼▼ **Wingate By Wyndham Indianapolis Airport-Rockville Rd** 🏠
(317) 243-8310. **$99-$200.** 5797 Rockville Rd 46224. I-465 exit 13A, just e. Int corridors. **Pets:** Accepted. 👤 🛁 📶 ✕ 🖥 💻

◇◇◇ **Wyndham Indianapolis West** ⓗ
(317) 248-2481. **$99-$189.** 2544 Executive Dr 46241. I-465 exit 11A southbound; exit 11B northbound, just e on Sam Jones Expwy to Executive Dr. Int corridors. **Pets:** Accepted.
⊞ 🍽 🛥 🛜 ✕ 🔋 🖥

JEFFERSONVILLE

AAA ◇◇◇◇ **Sheraton Louisville Riverside Hotel** ⓗ
(812) 284-6711. **Call for rates.** 700 W Riverside Dr 47130. I-65 exit 0, just w. Int corridors. **Pets:** Accepted.
SAVE 🍽 🛥 🛜 ✕ 🔋 🖥

◇◇ **TownePlace Suites by Marriott** ⓗ
(812) 280-8200. **$90-$171.** 703 N Shore Dr 47130. I-65 exit 0, just w. Int corridors. **Pets:** Accepted. 🛥 🛜 ✕ 🔋 🖥

KENDALLVILLE

AAA ◇◇ **BEST WESTERN Kendallville Inn** ⓗ 🐾
(260) 347-5263. **$86-$129.** 621 Professional Way 46755. 1 mi e on US 6. Int corridors. **Pets:** Medium. $15 daily fee/room. Designated rooms, service with restrictions, crate. SAVE 🛥 🛜 ✕ 🖥

◇◇◇ **Holiday Inn Express Kendallville** ⓗ
(260) 343-0000. **Call for rates.** 1917 Dowling St 46755. I-69 exit 334, 9.3 mi e on US 6. Int corridors. **Pets:** Accepted.
🦽 🛥 🛜 ✕ 🔋 🖥

KOKOMO

◇◇ **Comfort Inn by Choice Hotels** ⓗ
(765) 452-5050. **$75-$109.** 522 Essex Dr 46901. Jct US 35, 0.3 mi n on US 31. Int corridors. **Pets:** Accepted. 🛥 🛜 ✕ 🔋 🖥

◇◇◇ **Hampton Inn & Suites** ⓗ
(765) 455-2900. **$124-$159.** 2920 S Reed Rd (US Hwy 31) 46902. US 31, 2 mi s of jct US 35. Int corridors. **Pets:** Designated rooms, service with restrictions, crate. 🦽 🛥 🛜 🔋 🖥

LAFAYETTE

◇◇ **Baymont Inn & Suites** ⓗ
(765) 449-4808. **$69-$299.** 201 Frontage Rd 47905. I-65 exit 172, just e on SR 26, then just n. Int corridors. **Pets:** Accepted.
🛜 ✕ 🔋 🖥 .

AAA ◇◇◇ **BEST WESTERN Lafayette Executive Plaza & Conference Center** ⓗ
(765) 447-0575. **$109-$243.** 4343 South St 47905. I-65 exit 172, just w. Int corridors. **Pets:** Medium. $20 daily fee/pet. Designated rooms, service with restrictions, supervision.
SAVE 🍽 🦽 🛥 ✕ 🛜 ✕ 🔋 🖥

◇◇◇ **Candlewood Suites** ⓗ
(765) 807-5735. **$95-$280.** 240 Meijer Dr 47905. I-65 exit 172, just e on SR 26. Int corridors. **Pets:** $100 one-time fee/pet. Service with restrictions, crate. 🦽 🛥 🛜 ✕ 🔋 🖥

◇◇ **Comfort Inn** ⓗ
(765) 447-3434. **$80-$120.** 4701 Meijer Ct 47905. I-65 exit 172, just e on SR 26. Int corridors. **Pets:** Small, other species. $15 one-time fee/ pet. Designated rooms, service with restrictions, supervision.
🛥 🛜 ✕ 🔋 🖥

◇◇ **Days Inn & Suites** ⓗ
(765) 446-8558. **$60-$229.** 151 Frontage Rd 47905. I-65 exit 172, just e. Int corridors. **Pets:** Accepted. 🛜 ✕ 🔋 🖥

◇◇◇ **Homewood Suites by Hilton** ⓗ
(765) 448-9700. **$149-$279.** 3939 South St 47905. I-65 exit 172, 0.8 mi w. Ext/int corridors. **Pets:** Other species. $250 deposit/pet, $10 daily fee/pet. Service with restrictions, crate. 🛥 🛜 ✕ 🔋 🖥

◇◇◇ **Lafayette Comfort Suites** ⓗ
(765) 447-0016. **$85-$144.** 31 Frontage Rd 47905. I-65 exit 172, just e. Int corridors. **Pets:** Other species. $10 daily fee/pet. Designated rooms, service with restrictions, supervision.
🦽 🛥 ✕ 🛜 ✕ 🔋 🖥

◇ **Motel 6 #4291** Ⓜ
(765) 447-7566. **$50-$119.** 139 Frontage Rd 47905. I-65 exit 172, just e on SR 26, then just n. Ext corridors. **Pets:** Other species. Service with restrictions, crate. 🛜 ✕ 🔋

AAA ◇◇◇ **TownePlace Suites by Marriott** ⓗ
(765) 446-8668. **$111-$183.** 163 Frontage Rd 47905. I-65 exit 172, just e. Int corridors. **Pets:** Accepted. SAVE 🛥 🛜 ✕ 🔋 🖥

LAWRENCEBURG

◇◇ **Comfort Inn & Suites** ⓗ
(812) 539-3600. **$89-$119.** 1610 Flossie Dr 47025. I-275 exit 16, 0.3 mi e. Int corridors. **Pets:** Accepted. 🦽 🛥 🛜 ✕ 🔋 🖥

LEBANON

◇◇◇ **Holiday Inn Express** ⓗ
(765) 483-4100. **$99-$149.** 335 N Mt Zion Rd 46052. I-65 exit 140, just w. Int corridors. **Pets:** Accepted. 🍽 🦽 🛥 🛜 ✕ 🔋 🖥

LA PORTE

AAA ◇◇◇ **BEST WESTERN PLUS LaPorte Hotel & Conference Center** ⓗ
(219) 362-4585. **$100-$250.** 444 Pine Lake Ave 46350. 1.5 mi n on US 35. Int corridors. **Pets:** Other species. $25 one-time fee/pet. Designated rooms, service with restrictions, supervision.
SAVE 🍽 🛥 ✕ 🛜 ✕ 🔋 🖥

◇◇◇ **Holiday Inn Express-LaPorte @ Pine Lake** ⓗ
(219) 326-7900. **Call for rates.** 100 Eastshore Ct 46350. I-80/90 exit 49, 2.5 mi s on SR 39/US 35. Int corridors. **Pets:** Accepted.
🦽 🛥 🛜 ✕ 🔋 🖥

MARION

◇◇◇ **Comfort Suites Marion** ⓗ
(765) 651-1006. **$120-$170.** 1345 N Baldwin Ave 46952. On SR 9, 1.5 mi n of SR 18. Int corridors. **Pets:** $10 one-time fee/pet. Designated rooms, service with restrictions, crate. 🛥 🛜 ✕ 🔋 🖥

MARTINSVILLE

AAA ◇◇◇ **Holiday Inn Express Bloomington N/Martinsville** ⓗ
(765) 813-3999. **Call for rates.** 2233 Burton Ln 46151. SR 37 to Burton Ln, just e. Int corridors. **Pets:** Accepted. SAVE 🛜 ✕ 🔋 🖥

MERRILLVILLE

◇◇ **Candlewood Suites** ⓗ
(219) 791-9100. **$99-$129.** 8339 Ohio St 46410. I-65 exit 253, 0.3 mi e, just s on Mississippi St, 0.4 mi w on 83rd Ave, then just s. Int corridors. **Pets:** Medium, dogs only. $75 one-time fee/pet. Designated rooms, service with restrictions, supervision. 🛜 ✕ 🔋 🖥

◇◇◇ **Clarion Inn Merrillville** ⓗ
(219) 756-1600. **$105-$178.** 7850 Rhode Island Ave 46410. I-65 exit 253, just nw. Int corridors. **Pets:** Accepted.
ECO 🦽 🛥 🛜 ✕ 🔋 🖥

AAA ◇◇◇ **Country Inn & Suites By Carlson** ⓗ
(219) 736-1300. **$90-$130.** 8311 Ohio St 46410. I-65 exit 253, 0.3 mi e, just s on Mississippi St, 0.4 mi w on 83rd Ave, then just s. Int corridors. **Pets:** Accepted. SAVE 🛥 🛜 ✕ 🔋 🖥

◇◇ **Extended Stay America-Merrillville-US Rte 30** ⓗ
(219) 769-4740. **$69-$99.** 1355 E 83rd Ave 46410. I-65 exit 253, 0.3 mi e on US 30, just s on Mississippi St, then 0.4 mi w. Int corridors. **Pets:** Other species. $25 daily fee/pet. Service with restrictions, supervision. 🛜 ✕ 🔋 🖥

AAA **♦♦♦** **Red Roof Inn Merrillville** **H**
(219) 738-2430. **$55-$110.** 8290 Georgia St 46410. I-65 exit 253B (US 30), 0.3 mi sw. Ext corridors. **Pets:** Large, other species. Service with restrictions, supervision. (SAVE) 📶 ✖ 🛏 🖥

♦♦♦♦ **Residence Inn by Marriott Merrillville** **H**
(219) 791-9000. **$126-$213.** 8018 Delaware Pl 46410. I-65 exit 253, just nw. Int corridors. **Pets:** Large. $100 one-time fee/room. Service with restrictions, crate. 🅑M 🛄 📶 ✖ 🛏 🖥

MISHAWAKA
AAA **♦♦♦♦** **BEST WESTERN PLUS Mishawaka Inn** **H**
(574) 273-2309. **$89-$149.** 445 W University Dr 46545. I-80/90 exit 83, just n on SR 23, 1.6 mi sw to Main St, just s to University Dr, then just w. Int corridors. **Pets:** Accepted.
(SAVE) 🅑M 🛄 📶 ✖ 🛏 🖥

♦♦♦ **Country Inn & Suites By Carlson** **H**
(574) 271-1700. **Call for rates.** 120 W University Dr 46545. I-80/90 exit 83, just n on SR 331 to SR 23, 0.6 mi sw on SR 23, then just s on Main St. Int corridors. **Pets:** Accepted. 🅑M 🛄 📶 ✖ 🛏 🖥

♦♦ **Holiday Inn Express Mishawaka** **H**
(574) 277-2520. **Call for rates.** 420 W University Dr 46545. I-80/90 exit 83, just n on SR 331 to 23, 1.6 mi sw to Main St, just s to University Dr, then just w. Int corridors. **Pets:** Accepted.
🅑M 🛄 📶 ✖ 🛏 🖥

AAA **♦♦♦♦** **Hyatt Place South Bend/Mishawaka** **H**
(574) 258-7777. **$79-$499.** 215 W Day Rd 46545. I-80/90 exit 83, just n on SR 331 to SR 23, 1.6 mi sw, then 1.3 mi s on Main St. Int corridors. **Pets:** Medium, dogs only. $75 one-time fee/room. Designated rooms, service with restrictions.
(SAVE) 🍴 🅑M 🛄 📶 ✖ 🛏 🖥

♦♦♦♦ **Residence Inn by Marriott South Bend/Mishawaka** **H**
(574) 271-9283. **$105-$184.** 231 Park Pl 46545. I-80/90 exit 83, just n on SR 331 to SR 23, 1.6 mi sw, then 1.3 mi s on Main St. Int corridors. **Pets:** Accepted. 🅑M 🛄 📶 ✖ 🛏 🖥

MOUNT VERNON
♦♦ **Four Seasons Motel** **M**
(812) 838-4821. **$82-$104.** 70 Hwy 62 W 47620. 1.8 mi w. Ext corridors. **Pets:** Small, other species. $25 one-time fee/pet. Service with restrictions, supervision. 🛄 📶 ✖ 🛏 🖥

MUNCIE
♦♦ **Super 8** **H**
(765) 286-4333. **$57-$61, 3 day notice.** 3601 W Fox Ridge Ln 47304. I-69 exit 241, 6.3 mi e on SR 332. Int corridors. **Pets:** Medium, dogs only. $10 daily fee/pet. Service with restrictions, supervision. 📶 ✖ 🛏 🖥

NEW HARMONY
AAA **♦♦♦♦** **New Harmony Inn** **H**
(812) 682-4431. **$120-$135, 3 day notice.** 504 North St 47631. Jct Brewery St. Int corridors. **Pets:** Small. $250 deposit/room, $25 daily fee/room. Designated rooms, service with restrictions, crate.
(SAVE) 🍴 🅑M 🛄 ✖ 📶 ✖ 🛏 🖥

NOBLESVILLE
♦♦ **Quality Inn & Suites** **H**
(317) 770-6772. **$105-$190.** 16025 Prosperity Dr 46060. I-69 exit 205, 4 mi n on SR 37. Int corridors. **Pets:** Accepted. 🛄 📶 ✖ 🛏 🖥

♦♦ **Super 8 Noblesville** **H**
(317) 776-7088. **$59-$174.** 17070 Dragonfly Dr 46060. Jct SR 37 and 38, 0.5 mi s on SR 37. Int corridors. **Pets:** Accepted.
🛄 📶 ✖ 🛏 🖥

NORTH VERNON
♦♦♦ **Comfort Inn** **H**
(812) 352-9999. **$85-$105.** 150 FDR Dr 47265. Jct US 50, 0.6 mi n on SR 7. Int corridors. **Pets:** Small. $15 daily fee/pet. Service with restrictions, supervision. 🛄 📶 ✖ 🛏 🖥

PERU
AAA **♦♦♦** **BEST WESTERN Circus City Inn** **H** 🐾
(765) 473-8800. **$100-$110.** 2642 Business Rt US 31 S 46970. Just e of jct US 31. Int corridors. **Pets:** Other species. $10 daily fee/pet. Designated rooms, service with restrictions, crate.
(SAVE) 🛄 📶 ✖ 🛏 🖥

PLAINFIELD
♦♦♦ **Holiday Inn Express-Indianapolis Airport** **H**
(317) 839-9000. **Call for rates.** 6296 Cambridge Way 46168. I-70 exit 66, 0.4 mi n on SR 267, just e on Hadley Rd, then just s. Int corridors. **Pets:** Accepted. 🅑M 🛄 📶 ✖ 🛏 🖥

AAA **♦♦♦♦** **La Quinta Inn & Suites Indianapolis Airport-Plainfield** **H**
(317) 279-2650. **$94-$234.** 2251 Manchester Dr 46168. I-70 exit 66, 0.4 mi n on SR 267, just e on Perry Rd. Int corridors. **Pets:** Large, other species. Service with restrictions. (SAVE) 🅑M 🛄 📶 ✖ 🛏 🖥

♦♦♦ **Staybridge Suites Indianapolis Airport** **H**
(317) 839-2700. **Call for rates.** 6295 Cambridge Way 46168. I-70 exit 66, 0.4 mi n on SR 267, just e on Hadley Rd, then just s. Int corridors. **Pets:** Accepted. 🅑M 🛄 📶 ✖ 🛏 🖥

PORTAGE
♦♦ **Comfort Inn** **H**
(219) 763-7177. **$75-$180.** 2300 Willowcreek Rd 46368. I-80/90 exit 23; I-94 exit 19, 1.5 mi s on CR 249. Int corridors. **Pets:** Accepted.
📶 ✖ 🛏 🖥

♦♦ **Holiday Inn Express-Portage** **H**
(219) 762-7777. **Call for rates.** 2323 Willowcreek Rd 46368. I-80/90 exit 23; I-94 exit 19, 1.5 mi s. Int corridors. **Pets:** Accepted.
🅑M 🛄 📶 ✖ 🛏 🖥

PRINCETON
♦♦♦ **Fairfield Inn by Marriott** **H**
(812) 385-4300. **$83-$137.** 2828 Dixon St 47670. Jct US 41 and SR 64, 0.3 mi w. Int corridors. **Pets:** Accepted.
🅑M 🛄 📶 ✖ 🛏 🖥

REMINGTON
♦♦ **Super 8-Remington** **H**
(219) 261-2883. **$73-$150.** 4278 W US 24 47977. I-65 exit 201, 0.5 mi w. Int corridors. **Pets:** Accepted. 📶 ✖ 🛏 🖥

RICHMOND
AAA **♦♦♦♦** **BEST WESTERN Classic Inn** **H** 🐾
(765) 939-9500. **$89-$109.** 533 W Eaton Pike 47374. I-70 exit 156A, just s. Int corridors. **Pets:** $10 one-time fee/pet. Service with restrictions, crate. (SAVE) 🛄 📶 ✖ 🛏 🖥

RUSHVILLE
♦♦ **Comfort Inn** **H**
(765) 932-2999. **$88-$119.** 320 Conrad Harcourt Way 46173. Just e of SR 3. Int corridors. **Pets:** Accepted. 📶 ✖ 🛏 🖥

SCHERERVILLE
♦♦♦♦ **Staybridge Suites - Schererville** **H**
(219) 227-5125. **Call for rates.** 1758 Fountain Park Dr 46375. I-65 exit 253, 7.3 mi w on US 30. Int corridors. **Pets:** Accepted.
🅑M 📶 🛏 🖥

SCOTTSBURG

▼▼▼▼ Hampton Inn & Suites 🅷
(812) 752-1999. **$94-$229.** 1535 W McClain Ave 47170. I-65 exit 29, just w. Int corridors. **Pets:** Accepted. 🐾 📶 ✖ 🛗 💻

SELLERSBURG

▼▼ Ramada 🅷
(812) 246-3131. **$79-$105.** 360 Triangle Dr 47172. I-65 exit 9, just e. Int corridors. **Pets:** Medium, other species. $25 one-time fee/room. Service with restrictions, supervision. 🐾 📶 ✖ 🛗 💻

SHELBYVILLE

AAA ▼▼ Comfort Inn 🅷
(317) 398-8044. **$65-$99.** 36 W Rampart Dr 46176. I-74 exit 113, just s. Int corridors. **Pets:** Small. $30 daily fee/pet. Designated rooms, service with restrictions, supervision. SAVE 🐾 📶 ✖ 🛗 💻

SOUTH BEND

▼▼▼▼ Comfort Suites University Area 🅷 🐾
(574) 272-1500. **$84-$419.** 52939 US 933 N 46637. I-80/90 exit 77, just e to Business Rt US 31/SR 933, then 1 mi n. Int corridors. **Pets:** Large. $20 daily fee/pet. Designated rooms, service with restrictions, supervision. 🐾 ✖ 📶 ✖ 🛗 💻

▼▼▼▼ Cushing Manor Inn 🅱🅱
(574) 288-1990. **Call for rates.** 508 W Washington St 46601. 0.4 mi w of jct SR 933 and Business Rt US 31. Int corridors. **Pets:** Accepted. 📶 ✖

▼▼▼▼ The Oliver Inn Bed & Breakfast 🅱🅱
(574) 232-4545. **$140-$339, 14 day notice.** 630 W Washington St 46601. 0.3 mi w of SR 933 and Business Rt US 31. Int corridors. **Pets:** Accepted. 📶 ✖ 🛗 💻

AAA ▼▼ Sleep Inn 🅷
(574) 232-3200. **$75-$110.** 4134 Lincolnway W 46628. I-80/90 exit 72, 1.5 mi s on US 31 to South Bend Regional Airport exit, then 2 mi e. Int corridors. **Pets:** Medium. $10 daily fee/pet. Designated rooms, service with restrictions, crate. SAVE 🐾 📶 ✖ 🛗 💻

▼▼▼ Staybridge Suites South Bend-University Area 🅷
(574) 968-7440. **Call for rates.** 52860 SR 933 N 46637. I-80/90 exit 77, 1 mi n. Int corridors. **Pets:** Accepted. 🅼 🐾 📶 ✖ 🛗 💻

▼▼ Suburban Extended Stay Hotel 🅷
(574) 968-4737. **$69-$159.** 52825 SR 933 N 46637. I-80/90 exit 77, 1 mi n. Int corridors. **Pets:** Accepted. 🅼 🐾 📶 ✖ 🛗 💻

AAA ▼▼▼ Super 8 - South Bend 🅷
(574) 243-0200. **$70-$130, 3 day notice.** 4124 Ameritech Dr 46628. I-80/90 exit 72, 0.7 mi n on US 31, just e on Cleveland Rd, then just s. Int corridors. **Pets:** Medium. $10 daily fee/pet. Service with restrictions, supervision. SAVE 🐾 📶 ✖ 🛗 💻

▼▼▼▼ Waterford Estates Lodge 🅷
(574) 272-5220. **$109-$119.** 52890 SR 933 N 46637. I-80/90 exit 77, 1 mi n. Int corridors. **Pets:** Accepted. 🍽 🅼 🐾 📶 ✖ 🛗 💻

TAYLORSVILLE

▼▼ Red Roof Inn Columbus – Taylorsville 🅼
(812) 526-9747. **$69-$100.** 10330 US 31 47280. I-65 exit 76A, just s. Ext corridors. **Pets:** Large, other species. Service with restrictions, supervision. 🐾 📶 ✖ 🛗 💻

TELL CITY

▼▼▼ Holiday Inn Express 🅷
(812) 547-0800. **Call for rates.** 310 Orchard Hill Dr 47586. Just off SR 66, 1.7 mi se of jct SR 37. Int corridors. **Pets:** $25 daily fee/pet. Designated rooms, service with restrictions, supervision. 🅼 🐾 📶 ✖ 🛗 💻

▼▼ Ramada Limited 🅷
(812) 547-3234. **$79-$119.** 235 Orchard Hill Dr 47586. Just off SR 66, 1.7 mi se of jct SR 37. Int corridors. **Pets:** Other species. $50 deposit/room, $15 daily fee/room. Supervision. 🐾 📶 ✖ 🛗 💻

TERRE HAUTE

▼▼▼ Candlewood Suites 🅷
(812) 234-3400. **$89-$99.** 721 Wabash Ave 47807. I-70 exit 7 (US 41/150), 2.2 mi n, 0.4 mi e, then just s. Int corridors. **Pets:** Accepted. 🅼 📶 ✖ 🛗 💻

▼▼▼▼ Drury Inn-Terre Haute 🅷
(812) 238-1206. **$80-$149.** 3040 Hwy 41 S 47802. I-70 exit 7 (US 41/150), just n. Int corridors. **Pets:** $10 daily fee/room. Service with restrictions, supervision. 🅼 🐾 📶 ✖ 🛗 💻

▼▼ Holiday Inn 🅷
(812) 232-6081. **$99-$169.** 3300 Hwy 41 S 47802. I-70 exit 7 (US 41/150), just s. Int corridors. **Pets:** Accepted. 🍽 🐾 ✖ 📶 ✖ 🛗 💻

▼▼▼ Holiday Inn Express & Suites 🅷
(812) 234-3200. **Call for rates.** 2645 S Joe Fox St 47803. I-70 exit 11, just n. Int corridors. **Pets:** Accepted. 🅼 🐾 📶 ✖ 🛗 💻

▼▼ Pear Tree Inn by Drury-Terre Haute 🅷
(812) 234-4268. **$55-$109.** 3050 Hwy 41 S 47802. I-70 exit 7 (US 41/150), just n. Int corridors. **Pets:** $10 daily fee/room. Service with restrictions, supervision. 📶 ✖ 🛗 💻

VALPARAISO

AAA ▼▼▼▼ The Inn at Aberdeen 🅱🅱
(219) 465-3753. **$108-$205.** 3158 S SR 2 46385. Jct US 30 and SR 2, 2.7 mi s. Int corridors. **Pets:** Other species. $25 daily fee/pet. Designated rooms, service with restrictions, supervision. SAVE 📶 ✖ 🛗 💻

VINCENNES

▼▼▼ TownePlace Suites by Marriott Vincennes 🅷
(812) 255-1500. **$97-$160.** 1320 Willow St 47591. Jct US 41 Bypass and Willow St, 1.2 mi nw. Int corridors. **Pets:** Accepted. 🅼 🐾 📶 ✖ 🛗 💻

WARSAW

▼▼▼ Holiday Inn Express Hotel & Suites-Warsaw 🅷
(574) 268-1600. **Call for rates.** 3825 Lake City Hwy 46580. Jct US 30 and SR 15, 4 mi e on US 30. Int corridors. **Pets:** Accepted. 🐾 📶 ✖ 🛗 💻

▼▼▼▼ Wyndham Garden of Warsaw 🅷
(574) 269-2323. **$119-$159.** 2519 E Center St 46580. 2.8 mi e of SR 15 on US 30, just s. Int corridors. **Pets:** Accepted. 🍽 🐾 ✖ 📶 ✖ 🛗 💻

WASHINGTON

▼▼ Baymont Inn & Suites Washington 🅷
(812) 254-7000. **$75-$135.** 7 Cumberland Dr 47501. Just ne of jct US 50 and SR 257. Int corridors. **Pets:** Accepted. 🐾 ✖ 📶 ✖ 🛗 💻

▼▼▼ Holiday Inn Express 🅷
(812) 254-6666. **Call for rates.** 1808 E National Hwy 47501. On US 50 business route, 0.4 mi e of SR 257. Int corridors. **Pets:** Accepted. 🐾 📶 ✖ 🛗 💻

WEST BADEN SPRINGS

West Baden Springs Hotel 🅷
(812) 936-5501. **$180-$325, 3 day notice.** 8538 W Baden Ave 47469.
On SR 56. Int corridors. **Pets:** Accepted.
⟨SAVE⟩ ⟨⟩ ⟨⟩ ⟨⟩ ⟨⟩ ⟨⟩ ⟨⟩ ⟨⟩ ⟨⟩

WEST LAFAYETTE

Four Points by Sheraton West Lafayette 🅷
(765) 463-5511. **Call for rates.** 1600 Cumberland Ave 47906. I-65 exit
175, 1.5 mi sw on Schuyler Ave, then 3.8 mi nw on US 52. Int corridors. **Pets:** Accepted. ⟨SAVE⟩ ⟨⟩ ⟨⟩ ⟨⟩ ⟨⟩ ⟨⟩ ⟨⟩

IOWA

ALGONA

Americinn Lodge & Suites of Algona 🅷
(515) 295-3333. **Call for rates.** 600 Hwy 18 W 50511. Just w of jct US
169/18. Int corridors. **Pets:** Accepted.
⟨⟩ ⟨⟩ ⟨⟩ ⟨⟩ ⟨⟩ ⟨⟩ ⟨⟩

ALTOONA

Settle Inn & Suites-Altoona 🅷
(515) 967-7888. **Call for rates.** 2101 Adventureland Dr 50009. I-80 exit
142A, just se. Int corridors. **Pets:** Accepted. ⟨⟩ ⟨⟩ ⟨⟩ ⟨⟩

AMES

Americinn of Ames 🅷
(515) 233-1005. **$89-$249.** 2507 SE 16th St 50010. US 30 exit 150,
just ne. Int corridors. **Pets:** Accepted.
⟨SAVE⟩ ⟨⟩ ⟨⟩ ⟨⟩ ⟨⟩ ⟨⟩ ⟨⟩

Baymont Inn & Suites 🅷
(515) 232-0689. **$95-$150.** 1605 S Dayton Pl 50010. US 30 exit 150,
just ne. Int corridors. **Pets:** Accepted. ⟨⟩ ⟨⟩ ⟨⟩ ⟨⟩

BEST WESTERN PLUS University Park Inn & Suites 🅷
(515) 296-2500. **$99-$209.** 2500 University Blvd 50010. US 30 exit 146,
just s. Int corridors. **Pets:** Large. $10 one-time fee/room. Service with
restrictions, supervision. ⟨SAVE⟩ ⟨⟩ ⟨⟩ ⟨⟩ ⟨⟩ ⟨⟩

Country Inn & Suites By Carlson 🅷
(515) 233-3935. **$99-$200.** 2605 SE 16th St 50010. US 30 exit 150,
just ne. Int corridors. **Pets:** Medium, other species. $30 one-time fee/
room. Designated rooms, service with restrictions, supervision.
⟨⟩ ⟨⟩ ⟨⟩ ⟨⟩ ⟨⟩ ⟨⟩

Econo Lodge 🅷
(515) 233-6060. **$60-$175.** 2600 SE 16th St 50010. US 30 exit 150,
just ne. Int corridors. **Pets:** Accepted. ⟨⟩ ⟨⟩ ⟨⟩ ⟨⟩

Gateway Hotel & Conference Center 🅷
(515) 292-8600. **Call for rates.** 2100 Green Hills Dr 50014. US 30 exit
146, just sw. Int corridors. **Pets:** Accepted.
⟨⟩ ⟨⟩ ⟨⟩ ⟨⟩ ⟨⟩ ⟨⟩ ⟨⟩

GrandStay Residential Suites Hotel 🅷
(515) 232-8363. **$90-$260.** 1606 S Kellogg Ave 50010. US 30 exit 148,
just n. Int corridors. **Pets:** $15 daily fee/pet. Service with restrictions,
crate. ⟨SAVE⟩ ⟨⟩ ⟨⟩ ⟨⟩ ⟨⟩ ⟨⟩ ⟨⟩

Holiday Inn Ames Conference Center at ISU 🅷
(515) 268-8808. **$79-$499, 3 day notice.** 2609 University Blvd 50010.
US 30 exit 146, just s. Int corridors. **Pets:** Accepted.
⟨⟩ ⟨⟩ ⟨⟩ ⟨⟩ ⟨⟩

Quality Inn & Suites Starlite Village Conference Center 🅷 ❖
(515) 232-9260. **$129-$289, 3 day notice.** 2601 E 13th St 50010. I-35
exit 113 (13th St), 0.5 mi w. Int corridors. **Pets:** Medium, other species.
$10 one-time fee/pet. Service with restrictions, crate.
⟨⟩ ⟨⟩ ⟨⟩ ⟨⟩ ⟨⟩ ⟨⟩ ⟨⟩

ANAMOSA

Americinn Lodge & Suites 🅷
(319) 462-4119. **Call for rates.** 101 Harley Ave 52205. US 151, exit 54,
1 mi n. Int corridors. **Pets:** Small, dogs only. $50 deposit/pet. Designated rooms, service with restrictions, crate.
⟨⟩ ⟨⟩ ⟨⟩ ⟨⟩ ⟨⟩ ⟨⟩

ANKENY

Comfort Inn 🅷
(515) 963-1100. **$90-$140.** 2602 SE Creekview Dr 50021. I-35 exit 90,
just ne. Int corridors. **Pets:** Small. $35 one-time fee/pet. Designated
rooms, service with restrictions, supervision.
⟨SAVE⟩ ⟨⟩ ⟨⟩ ⟨⟩ ⟨⟩ ⟨⟩

ARNOLDS PARK

Fillenwarth Beach Ⓜ
(712) 332-5646. **$82-$1838, 60 day notice.** 87 Lake Shore Dr 51331.
Just w of US 71. Ext corridors. **Pets:** Other species. Service with
restrictions, crate. ⟨⟩ ⟨⟩ ⟨⟩ ⟨⟩ ⟨⟩ ⟨⟩

ATLANTIC

Super 8 🅷
(712) 243-4723. **$80-$110.** 1902 E 7th St 50022. I-80 exit 60 (US 71),
6 mi s, then 2 mi w; east side of town. Int corridors. **Pets:** Other species. $5 one-time fee/room. Designated rooms, service with restrictions,
supervision. ⟨⟩ ⟨⟩ ⟨⟩ ⟨⟩ ⟨⟩ ⟨⟩

BETTENDORF

Econo Lodge Inn & Suites 🅷
(563) 355-6336. **$65-$149.** 815 Golden Valley Dr 52722. I-74 exit 2,
just e, then just n on Utica Ridge Rd. Int corridors. **Pets:** Accepted.
⟨⟩ ⟨⟩ ⟨⟩ ⟨⟩ ⟨⟩

Isle Casino Hotel Bettendorf 🅷
(563) 441-7000. **$70-$300, 3 day notice.** 1777 Isle Pkwy 52722. I-74
exit 4 (US 67/State St), just e on State St, then just s, follow signs. Int
corridors. **Pets:** Accepted. ⟨⟩ ⟨⟩ ⟨⟩ ⟨⟩ ⟨⟩ ⟨⟩

Ramada Bettendorf/Davenport 🅷
(563) 355-7575. **$86-$176.** 3020 Utica Ridge Rd 52722. I-74 exit 2, just
e. Int corridors. **Pets:** Accepted. ⟨⟩ ⟨⟩ ⟨⟩ ⟨⟩ ⟨⟩ ⟨⟩

BURLINGTON

Comfort Suites Hotel & Conference Center 🅷
(319) 753-1300. **$97-$190.** 1780 Stonegate Center Dr 52601. On US
61, 2 mi s of US 34. Int corridors. **Pets:** Accepted.
⟨⟩ ⟨⟩ ⟨⟩ ⟨⟩ ⟨⟩ ⟨⟩ ⟨⟩

CARTER LAKE

Holiday Inn Express & Suites-Omaha Airport 🅷
(402) 505-4900. **Call for rates.** 2510 Abbott Plaza 51510. I-480 W exit
4 to 10th St, 2 mi n, follow Eppley Airfield signs. Int corridors.
Pets: Accepted. ⟨⟩ ⟨⟩ ⟨⟩ ⟨⟩ ⟨⟩ ⟨⟩ ⟨⟩

La Quinta Inn & Suites Omaha Airport-Carter Lake 🅷
(712) 347-6595. **$89-$314.** 1201 Ave H 51510. I-480 W exit 4 to 10th
St, 2 mi n, follow Eppley Airfield signs. Int corridors. **Pets:** Large, other
species. Service with restrictions. ⟨SAVE⟩ ⟨⟩ ⟨⟩ ⟨⟩ ⟨⟩ ⟨⟩

▼▼ **Super 8** 🏨
(712) 347-5588. **$66-$176.** 3000 Airport Dr 51510. I-480 W exit 4 to 10th St, 2.3 mi n, follow Eppley Airfield signs. Int corridors.
Pets: Accepted. 🐾 🛜 🖥 🖵

CEDAR FALLS

▼▼ **AmericInn Lodge & Suites of Cedar Falls** 🏨
(319) 277-6166. **Call for rates.** 5818 Nordic Dr 50613. US 20 exit 225, 1.4 mi n on SR 58. Int corridors. **Pets:** Accepted. 🐾 🛜 🖥 🖵

▼▼▼ **Comfort Suites** 🏨
(319) 273-9999. **$95-$180.** 7402 Nordic Dr 50613. US 20 exit 225, just nw. Int corridors. **Pets:** Medium, dogs only. $15 daily fee/room. Designated rooms, service with restrictions, crate.
🍴 👤M 🐾 🛜 ✕ 🖥 🖵

▼▼▼ **Suburban Extended Stay Hotel** 🏨
(319) 268-2222. **$89-$179.** 300 Viking Rd 50613. US 20 exit 225, 1.4 mi n on SR 58, then just w. Int corridors. **Pets:** Small, dogs only. $75 one-time fee/room. Designated rooms, service with restrictions, crate.
👤M 🐾 🛜 ✕ 🖥 🖵

CEDAR RAPIDS

▼▼ **AmericInn Lodge & Suites of Cedar Rapids** 🏨
(319) 632-1800. **$100-$196.** 8910 6th St SW 52404. I-380 exit 13, just nw. Int corridors. **Pets:** $25 daily fee/pet. Designated rooms, service with restrictions, supervision. 🍴 👤M 🐾 🛜 ✕ 🖥 🖵

▼▼ **Baymont Inn & Suites** 🏨
(319) 378-8000. **$59-$119.** 1220 Park Pl NE 52402. I-380 exit 24A (SR 100/Collins Rd), 0.9 mi e, then just n. Int corridors. **Pets:** Accepted.
👤M 🐾 🛜 ✕ 🖥 🖵

ⒶⒶⒶ ▼▼▼ **BEST WESTERN Cooper's Mill Hotel** 🏨
(319) 366-5323. **$90-$150.** 100 F Ave NW 52405. I-380 exit 19C northbound, at south end of exit make immediate U-turn under I-380; exit 20A southbound, cross river, then just n on 1st St NW. Int corridors. **Pets:** Large. $10 daily fee/pet. Service with restrictions, supervision.
SAVE 🍴 👤M 🐾 🛜 ✕ 🖥 🖵

ⒶⒶⒶ ▼▼▼ **BEST WESTERN PLUS Longbranch Hotel & Convention Center** 🏨
(319) 377-6386. **$120-$140.** 90 Twixt Town Rd NE 52402. I-380 exit 24A (SR 100/Collins Rd), 2.5 mi e, then just n. Int corridors. **Pets:** Medium, other species. $10 daily fee/room. Designated rooms, service with restrictions. SAVE 🍴 👤M 🐾 ✕ 🛜 ✕ 🖥 🖵

▼▼ **Clarion Hotel & Convention Center** 🏨
(319) 366-8671. **$68-$129.** 525 33rd Ave SW 52404. I-380 exit 17 (33rd Ave SW), just w. Int corridors. **Pets:** $15 daily fee/room. Service with restrictions. 🍴 🐾 🛜 ✕ 🖥 🖵

▼▼ **Country Inn & Suites By Carlson, Cedar Rapids Airport** 🏨
(319) 363-3789. **$99-$199.** 9100 Atlantic Dr SW 52405. I-380 exit 13, just w. Int corridors. **Pets:** Accepted. 👤M 🐾 🛜 ✕ 🖥 🖵

▼▼ **Hometown Inn & Suites** 🏨
(319) 362-9012. **Call for rates.** 3315 Southgate Ct SW 52404. I-380 exit 17 (33rd Ave SW), just sw. Int corridors. **Pets:** Accepted.
🐾 🛜 🖥 🖵

▼▼▼ **Homewood Suites** 🏨
(319) 378-1140. **$99-$149.** 1140 Park Pl NE 52402. I-380 exit 24A (SR 100/Collins Rd) to Collins Rd, n on Council St, then just e. Int corridors. **Pets:** Medium. $75 one-time fee/room. Service with restrictions, crate.
👤M 🐾 🛜 🖥 🖵

▼▼ **MainStay Suites** 🏨
(319) 363-7829. **$89-$169.** 5145 Rockwell Dr NE 52402. I-380 exit 24A (SR 100/Collins Rd), 1 mi e, then just n. Int corridors. **Pets:** Accepted.
👤M 🐾 🛜 🖥 🖵

▼▼ **Quality Inn at Collins Road** 🏨
(319) 393-8247. **$60-$120.** 5055 Rockwell Dr NE 52402. I-380 exit 24A (SR 100/Collins Rd), 1 mi e. Int corridors. **Pets:** Small, other species. $15 daily fee/pet. Designated rooms, service with restrictions, supervision. 🛜 🖥 🖵

▼▼ **Quality Inn South by Choice Hotels** 🏨
(319) 363-7934. **$60-$82.** 390 33rd Ave SW 52404. I-380 exit 17 (33rd Ave SW), just w. Int corridors. **Pets:** Small, dogs only. $20 daily fee/room. Designated rooms, service with restrictions, crate. 🛜 🖥 🖵

▼▼ **Red Roof Inn Cedar Rapids** 🏨
(319) 364-2000. **$54-$89.** 3243 S Ridge Dr SW 52404. I-380 exit 17 (33rd Ave SW), just nw. Ext/int corridors. **Pets:** Large, other species. Service with restrictions. 🐾 🛜 🖥 🖵

▼▼▼ **Residence Inn by Marriott** 🏨 🐾
(319) 395-0111. **$125-$229.** 1900 Dodge Rd NE 52402. I-380 exit 24A (SR 100/Collins Rd), just e. Int corridors. **Pets:** Other species. $100 one-time fee/room. Service with restrictions, crate.
👤M 🐾 🛜 ✕ 🖥 🖵

▼▼ **Super 8** 🏨
(319) 362-6002. **$56-$110, 3 day notice.** 720 33rd Ave SW 52404. I-380 exit 17 (33rd Ave SW), 0.4 mi w. Int corridors. **Pets:** Accepted.
🛜 🖥 🖵

CHARLES CITY

▼▼▼ **Sleep Inn & Suites** 🏨
(641) 257-6700. **$85-$150.** 1416 S Grand Ave 50616. US 218/18 exit 218, 0.7 mi n on US 218 business route; south side of town. Int corridors. **Pets:** Accepted. 👤M 🐾 🛜 🖥 🖵

▼▼ **Super 8-Charles City** 🏨
(641) 228-2888. **$62-$100.** 1411 S Grand Ave 50616. US 218/18 exit 218, 0.8 mi n on US 218 business route; south side of town. Int corridors. **Pets:** Small. $10 daily fee/pet. Designated rooms, service with restrictions, supervision. 🍴 👤M 🛜 🖥 🖵

CHEROKEE

ⒶⒶⒶ ▼▼ **BEST WESTERN La Grande Hacienda** 🏨
(712) 225-5701. **$79-$200.** 1401 N 2nd St 51012. Just s of jct SR 3 and US 59 (N 2nd St). Int corridors. **Pets:** Accepted.
SAVE 🍴 👤M 🐾 🛜 ✕ 🖥 🖵

CLARINDA

▼▼ **Clarinda Super 8** 🏨
(712) 542-6333. **$66-$124.** 1203 S 12th St 51632. Jct US 71 and SR 2, just e. Int corridors. **Pets:** Accepted.
🍴 👤M 🐾 🛜 ✕ 🖥 🖵

CLEAR LAKE

▼▼ **AmericInn Lodge & Suites of Clear Lake** 🏨
(641) 357-8954. **$91-$111.** 1406 N 25th St 50428. I-35 exit 194 (US 18), just nw. Int corridors. **Pets:** Accepted. 🐾 🛜 ✕ 🖥 🖵

ⒶⒶⒶ ▼▼▼ **BEST WESTERN Holiday Lodge** 🏨
(641) 357-5253. **$89-$149.** 2023 7th Ave N 50428. I-35 exit 194 (US 18), 0.3 mi w. Ext/int corridors. **Pets:** Accepted.
SAVE 🍴 👤M 🐾 🛜 🖥 🖵

▼▼ **Microtel Inn by Wyndham Clear Lake** 🏨
(641) 357-0966. **$70-$103.** 1305 N 25th St 50428. I-35 exit 194 (US 18), just nw. Int corridors. **Pets:** Other species. Service with restrictions, supervision. 👤M 🛜 ✕ 🖥 🖵

CLINTON

ⒶⒶⒶ ▼▼▼ **Country Inn & Suites By Carlson** 🏨
(563) 244-9922. **$89-$149.** 2224 Lincoln Way 52732. On US 30, just e of jct US 30 and 67. Int corridors. **Pets:** $10 daily fee/pet. Service with restrictions, supervision. SAVE 👤M 🐾 🛜 🖥 🖵

Oak Tree Inn H
(563) 243-1000. **Call for rates.** 2300 Valley W Ct 52732. Just n of jct US 30 and 67; west side of town. Int corridors. **Pets:** Accepted.
🆘 ♿ 📶 ✖ 🍴 💻

CLIVE

BEST WESTERN PLUS Des Moines West Inn & Suites H
(515) 221-2345. **$100-$140.** 1450 NW 118th St 50325. I-80/35 exit 124 (University Ave), just nw. Int corridors. **Pets:** Dogs only. $20 daily fee/pet. Supervision. 🆘 ♿ 🏊 📶 ✖ 🍴 💻

Country Inn & Suites By Carlson, Des Moines-West H
(515) 223-9254. **$99-$169.** 1350 NW 118th St 50325. I-80/35 exit 124 (University Ave), just nw. Int corridors. **Pets:** Medium, dogs only. $25 daily fee/room. Designated rooms, service with restrictions, supervision.
🆘 ♿ 🏊 📶 ✖ 🍴 💻

Wildwood Lodge H 🐾
(515) 222-9876. **$89-$179.** 11431 Forest Ave 50325. I-80/35 exit 124 (University Ave), just e. Int corridors. **Pets:** Large. $20 daily fee/pet. Designated rooms, service with restrictions, crate.
🏊 ✖ 📶 🍴 💻

COLFAX

Microtel Inn & Suites by Wyndham Colfax/Newton H
(515) 674-0600. **$60-$149.** 11000 Federal Ave 50054. I-80 exit 155 (SR 117), just nw. Int corridors. **Pets:** Other species. $15 daily fee/room. Service with restrictions. 🆘 🍴 ♿ 📶 ✖ 🍴 💻

CORALVILLE

Baymont Inn & Suites H
(319) 337-9797. **$59-$199.** 200 6th St 52241. I-80 exit 242, just s on 1st Ave, then just w. Int corridors. **Pets:** Other species. $25 daily fee/pet. Service with restrictions, crate. 🏊 📶 🍴 💻

BEST WESTERN Cantebury Inn & Suites H
(319) 351-0400. **Call for rates.** 704 1st Ave 52241. I-80 exit 242, just s. Int corridors. **Pets:** Accepted. 🆘 🏊 📶 🍴 💻

Comfort Inn & Suites H
(319) 337-8382. **$85-$120.** 214 W 9th St 52241. I-80 exit 242, just s. Int corridors. **Pets:** Medium. $20 daily fee/pet. Service with restrictions, crate. ♿ 🏊 📶 ✖ 🍴 💻

Country Inn & Suites By Carlson H
(319) 545-8464. **$109-$239.** 2571 Heartland Pl 52241. I-80 exit 240, just n. Int corridors. **Pets:** Small. $30 one-time fee/room. Designated rooms, supervision. ♿ 🏊 📶 ✖ 🍴 💻

Holiday Inn H
(319) 351-5049. **Call for rates.** 1220 1st Ave 52241. I-80 exit 242, just n. Int corridors. **Pets:** Accepted. 🍴 ♿ 🏊 📶 🍴 💻

Quality Inn H
(319) 351-8144. **$65-$110.** 209 W 9th St 52241. I-80 exit 242, just s. Int corridors. **Pets:** Medium. $15 daily fee/pet. Service with restrictions, crate. ♿ 🏊 📶 🍴 💻

Residence Inn by Marriott H
(319) 338-6000. **$97-$183.** 2681 James St 52241. I-80 exit 240, just s. Int corridors. **Pets:** Accepted. ♿ 🏊 📶 ✖ 🍴 💻

Super 8 H
(319) 337-8388. **$70-$180.** 611 1st Ave 52241. I-80 exit 242, 0.4 mi s. Int corridors. **Pets:** Other species. $10 one-time fee/room. Service with restrictions, supervision. ♿ 📶 🍴 💻

COUNCIL BLUFFS

BEST WESTERN Crossroads of the Bluffs H
(712) 322-3150. **Call for rates.** 2216 27th Ave 51501. I-29/80 exit 1B (24th St), just ne. Int corridors. **Pets:** Accepted.
🆘 🍴 🏊 📶 🍴 💻

Comfort Suites H
(712) 323-9760. **$79-$129.** 1801 S 35th St 51503. I-29 exit 52, just e. Int corridors. **Pets:** Very small. $20 daily fee/room. Service with restrictions, supervision. 🆘 🍴 ♿ 🏊 📶 ✖ 🍴 💻

Days Inn H
(712) 366-9699. **$56-$271.** 3208 S 7th St 51501. I-29/80 exit 3 (US 92), just sw. Int corridors. **Pets:** Accepted. 📶 🍴 💻

Days Inn H
(712) 323-2200. **$55-$140.** 3619 9th Ave 51501. I-29 exit 53A (9th Ave), just s. Int corridors. **Pets:** Accepted. 📶 🍴 💻

Harrah's Casino & Hotel H 🐾
(712) 329-6000. **Call for rates.** 1 Harrahs Blvd 51501. I-29 exit 53A (9th Ave), just w. Int corridors. **Pets:** Dogs only. $40 daily fee/room. Designated rooms, service with restrictions, crate.
🍴 ♿ 📶 🍴 💻

Microtel Inn & Suites by Wyndham Council Bluffs H
(712) 256-2900. **$75-$200.** 2141 S 35th St 51501. I-29/80 exit 1B (24th St), 0.4 mi n, then 0.8 mi w on 23rd Ave. Int corridors. **Pets:** Large. $25 one-time fee/room. Service with restrictions, crate.
🆘 ♿ 🏊 📶 ✖ 🍴 💻

Super 8 H
(712) 322-2888. **$66-$78.** 2712 S 24th St 51501. I-29/80 exit 1B (24th St), just nw. Int corridors. **Pets:** Accepted. 📶 🍴 💻

Western Inn H
(712) 322-4499. **$59-$145.** 1842 Madison Ave 51503. I-80 exit 5 (Madison Ave), just s. Int corridors. **Pets:** Small. $10 daily fee/pet. Service with restrictions, crate. 🏊 📶 ✖

CRESCO

Cresco Motel M
(563) 547-2240. **$53-$81.** 620 2nd Ave SE (Hwy 9) 52136. East side of town. Ext corridors. **Pets:** Dogs only. Designated rooms, service with restrictions, supervision. 🆘 🍴 ♿ 📶 🍴 💻

CRESTON

Super 8-Creston H
(641) 782-6541. **$65-$80.** 804 W Taylor St 50801. Jct US 34 and SR 25, on US 34. Int corridors. **Pets:** Accepted. 📶 🍴 💻

DAVENPORT

BEST WESTERN PLUS SteepleGate Inn H
(563) 386-6900. **$119-$199.** 100 W 76th St 52806. I-80 exit 295A (US 61), 0.5 mi s to 65th St and west frontage road entrance, then just nw. Int corridors. **Pets:** Accepted. 🆘 🍴 ♿ 🏊 📶 🍴 💻

Clarion Hotel & Conference Center H
(563) 391-1230. **$70-$140.** 5202 Brady St 52806. I-80 exit 295A (US 61), 1.6 mi s. Int corridors. **Pets:** Large, other species. $10 daily fee/pet. Designated rooms, crate. 🆘 🍴 ♿ 🏊 ✖ 📶 💻

Country Inn & Suites By Carlson H
(563) 388-6444. **Call for rates.** 140 E 55th St 52806. I-80 exit 295A (US 61), 1.4 mi s. Int corridors. **Pets:** Medium, other species. $25 one-time fee/room. Service with restrictions, supervision.
♿ 🏊 📶 ✖ 🍴 💻

▼▼ ▼▼ **Days Inn Davenport** 🅷
(563) 391-8222. **$60-$110.** 7222 Northwest Blvd 52806. I-80 exit 292 (Northwest Blvd), 0.3 mi s. Ext corridors. **Pets:** Accepted.
🔊 🛜 🛏 💻

▼▼ ▼▼ **Fairfield Inn by Marriott** 🅷
(563) 355-2264. **$97-$160.** 3206 E Kimberly Rd 52807. I-74 exit 2, just w. Int corridors. **Pets:** Large, other species. $35 one-time fee/room. Service with restrictions. 🔊 🛜 🛜 ✖ 🛏 💻

▲▲ ▼▼ ▼▼ **Hotel Blackhawk, Autograph**
Collection 🅷
(563) 322-5000. **$209-$499.** 200 E 3rd St 52801. Between Brady St (US 61 N) and Pershing Ave; downtown. Int corridors. **Pets:** Accepted.
🆂 🍽 🔊 🛜 ✖ 🛜 ✖ 🛏 💻

▼▼ ▼▼ **Residence Inn by Marriott** 🅷
(563) 391-8877. **$104-$206.** 120 E 55th St 52806. I-80 exit 295A (US 61), 1.4 mi s. Int corridors. **Pets:** Accepted.
🍽 🔊 🛜 🛜 ✖ 🛏 💻

▼▼ ▼▼ **Staybridge Suites** 🅷
(563) 359-7829. **$110-$300.** 4729 Progress Dr 52807. I-74 exit 1 (53rd St), 0.5 mi e, then 0.4 mi s on CR 216 (Utica Ridge Rd). Int corridors. **Pets:** Large, other species. $13 daily fee/pet. Service with restrictions, crate. 🔊 🛜 🛜 ✖ 🛏 💻

▼▼ ▼▼ **Super 8 of Davenport** 🅷
(563) 386-5000. **$80-$190, 7 day notice.** 301 Jason Way Ct 52806. I-80 exit 295A (US 61), just s to 65th St, then 0.4 mi ne on frontage road. Int corridors. **Pets:** Small. $20 daily fee/pet. Designated rooms, service with restrictions, supervision. 🔊 🛜 🛜 ✖ 🛏 💻

DECORAH
▼▼ ▼▼ **Quality Inn & Suites** 🅷
(563) 382-2269. **$99-$185.** 705 Commerce Dr 52101. Jct US 52, 1.5 mi e on SR 9. Int corridors. **Pets:** Accepted.
🍽 🔊 🛜 ✖ 🛏 💻

DES MOINES
▲▲ ▼▼ ▼▼ **Des Moines Marriott Downtown** 🅷
(515) 245-5500. **$153-$298.** 700 Grand Ave 50309. Downtown. Int corridors. **Pets:** Accepted. 🆂 🍽 🔊 🛜 🛜 ✖ 🛏 💻

▼▼ ▼▼ **Holiday Inn Airport & Conference Center** 🅷
(515) 287-2400. **$135-$265.** 6111 Fleur Dr 50321. SR 5 exit 97, 1 mi n; opposite the airport. Int corridors. **Pets:** Dogs only. $25 one-time fee/room. Designated rooms, service with restrictions, crate.
🍽 🔊 🛜 ✖ 🛜 ✖ 🛏 💻

▼▼ ▼▼ **Quality Inn & Suites** 🅷
(515) 287-3434. **$99-$199.** 5231 Fleur Dr 50321. Opposite the airport. Int corridors. **Pets:** Accepted. 🔊 🛜 🛜 ✖ 🛏 💻

▼▼ ▼▼ **Residence Inn by Marriott Des Moines**
Downtown 🅷
(515) 288-4500. **$125-$240.** 100 SW Water St 50309. Jct Court Ave, just s; downtown. Int corridors. **Pets:** Large, other species. $100 one-time fee/room. Service with restrictions. 🔊 🛜 ✖ 🛏 💻

DE WITT
▼▼ ▼▼ **De Witt Super 8** 🅷
(563) 659-8888. **$55-$95.** 918 Westwood Dr 52742. On US 30, just e of jct US 30 and 61. Int corridors. **Pets:** Accepted.
🍽 🔊 🛜 🛏 💻

DUBUQUE
▲▲ ▼▼ ▼▼ **BEST WESTERN PLUS Dubuque Hotel &**
Conference Center 🅷
(563) 557-8000. **$90-$180.** 3100 Dodge St 52003. US 20, 2.3 mi w of jct US 52/61/151 and Mississippi Bridge. Int corridors. **Pets:** Accepted.
🆂 🍽 🔊 🛜 ✖ 🛜 🛏 💻

▲▲ ▼▼ ▼▼ **Days Inn** 🅷
(563) 583-3297. **$60-$130.** 1111 Dodge St 52003. US 20, 0.8 mi w of jct US 52/61/151 and Mississippi Bridge exit Hill/Bryant sts. Ext corridors. **Pets:** Other species. $15 one-time fee/pet. Service with restrictions, crate. 🆂 🍽 🔊 🛜 🛏 💻

▼▼ ▼▼ ▼▼ **Holiday Inn Dubuque/Galena** 🅷
(563) 556-2000. **$85-$145, 3 day notice.** 450 Main St 52001. At Main and 4th sts; downtown. Int corridors. **Pets:** Other species. $35 one-time fee/room. Service with restrictions.
🍽 🔊 🛜 ✖ 🛜 ✖ 🛏 💻

▼▼ ▼▼ ▼▼ **Holiday Inn Express & Suites** 🅷
(563) 556-4600. **$79-$179.** 2080 Holiday Dr 52002. Jct US 20 and SR 32, 1.5 mi n. Int corridors. **Pets:** Medium, other species. $50 deposit/pet, $10 daily fee/pet. Designated rooms, service with restrictions, supervision. 🔊 🛜 ✖ 🛏 💻

▼▼ ▼▼ **MainStay Suites** 🅷
(563) 557-7829. **$80-$171.** 1275 Associates Dr 52002. Just n of jct US 20 and NW Arterial Rd; west side of town. Int corridors. **Pets:** Other species. $20 daily fee/room. Service with restrictions, crate.
🔊 🛜 🛏 💻

▼▼ ▼▼ **Quality Inn** 🅷
(563) 556-3006. **$80-$100.** 4055 McDonald Dr 52002. US 20, 3.8 mi w of jct US 52/61/151 and Mississippi Bridge. Int corridors.
Pets: Accepted. 🍽 🔊 🛜 🛏 💻

DYERSVILLE
▼▼ ▼▼ **Comfort Inn** 🅷
(563) 875-7700. **$90-$160.** 527 16th Ave SE 52040. US 20 exit 294 (SR 136), just nw. Int corridors. **Pets:** Small. $20 daily fee/room. Designated rooms, service with restrictions, supervision.
🔊 🛜 ✖ 🛏 💻

EMMETSBURG
▼▼ ▼▼ **Super 8** 🅷
(712) 852-2667. **$60-$112.** 3501 Main St 50536. Jct US 18 and SR 4, 0.8 mi w. Int corridors. **Pets:** $10 daily fee/pet. Service with restrictions, supervision. 🛜 ✖ 🛏 💻

ESTHERVILLE
▼▼ ▼▼ **Estherville Hotel & Suites** 🅷
(712) 362-5522. **$124.** 2008 Central Ave 51334. Jct SR 4 and 9, 1 mi e. Int corridors. **Pets:** Other species. $20 one-time fee/room. Service with restrictions. 🔊 🛜 ✖ 🛏 💻

▼▼ ▼▼ **Super 8** 🅷
(712) 362-2400. **$56-$85.** 1919 Central Ave 51334. Jct SR 4 and 9, 1 mi e. Int corridors. **Pets:** Small, dogs only. $5 daily fee/pet. Designated rooms, service with restrictions, supervision. 🛜 🛏 💻

EVANSDALE
▼▼ ▼▼ **Days Inn** 🅷
(319) 235-1111. **$79-$145.** 450 Evansdale Dr 50707. I-380/US 20 exit 68, just n. Int corridors. **Pets:** Accepted. 🔊 🛜 🛜 🛏 💻

FAIRFIELD
▲▲ ▼▼ ▼▼ **BEST WESTERN Fairfield Inn** 🅷
(641) 472-2200. **$81-$121.** 2200 W Burlington Ave 52556. On US 34, 1 mi w of jct SR 1. Int corridors. **Pets:** Medium. $10 daily fee/room. Service with restrictions, supervision. 🆂 🍽 🛜 🛜 🛏 💻

▲▲ ▼▼ ▼▼ **Super 8** 🅷
(641) 469-2000. **$65-$121.** 3001 W Burlington Ave 52556. On US 34, 1.5 mi w of jct SR 1. Int corridors. **Pets:** Medium. $100 deposit/room, $25 daily fee/pet. Designated rooms, service with restrictions, crate.
🆂 🛜 🛜 🛏 💻

FORT DODGE

▼▼ AmericInn Lodge & Suites of Fort Dodge 🅷
(515) 576-2100. **$99-$225.** 100 Kenyon Rd 50501. 3 mi n of jct US 20 and 169. Int corridors. **Pets:** Medium, dogs only. $15 daily fee/room. Designated rooms, service with restrictions, supervision.
🛦 ➠ 🤝 ✕ 🖪 🖵

(A) **▼▼◆ BEST WESTERN Starlite Village** 🅷
(515) 573-7177. **$94-$134.** 1518 3rd Ave NW 50501. Jct US 169 and SR 7. Ext/int corridors. **Pets:** Dogs only. $10 daily fee/pet. Service with restrictions, crate. SAVE 🍴 ➠ ✕ 🤝 🖪 🖵

▼▼ Comfort Inn 🅷
(515) 573-5000. **$99-$149.** 2938 5th Ave S 50501. US 20 exit 124 (Coalville), 3.5 mi n on CR P59, 1.3 mi w on 5th Ave and Business Rt US 20. Int corridors. **Pets:** Accepted.
🛦 ➠ 🤝 ✕ 🖪 🖵

GRINNELL

(A) **▼▼▼ BEST WESTERN PLUS Pioneer Inn & Suites** 🅷
(641) 236-6116. **Call for rates.** 2210 West St S 50112. I-80 exit 182, just n. Int corridors. **Pets:** Accepted. SAVE 🛦 ➠ 🤝 🖪 🖵

▼▼◆ Comfort Inn & Suites 🅷
(641) 236-5236. **$89-$180.** 1630 West St S 50112. I-80 exit 182, 0.7 mi n. Int corridors. **Pets:** $15 daily fee/room. Designated rooms, service with restrictions, supervision. 🍴 🛦 ➠ 🤝 ✕ 🖪 🖵

▼▼◆ Country Inn & Suites By Carlson 🅷
(641) 236-9600. **$75-$189.** 1710 West St S 50112. I-80 exit 182, 0.7 mi n. Int corridors. **Pets:** Accepted. 🍴 🛦 ➠ 🤝 ✕ 🖪 🖵

GRUNDY CENTER

▼▼ AmericInn Motel & Suites of Grundy Center 🅷
(319) 824-5272. **$78-$105.** 2101 Commerce Dr 50638. Jct SR 175 and 14, 1.2 mi w; west side of town. Int corridors. **Pets:** $25 one-time fee/pet. Service with restrictions, supervision.
🛦 ➠ 🤝 ✕ 🖪 🖵

HAMPTON

▼▼ AmericInn Lodge & Suites of Hampton 🅷
(641) 456-5559. **Call for rates.** 702 Central Ave W 50441. On SR 3 (Central Ave W), 0.7 mi w of jct US 65 and SR 3. Int corridors. **Pets:** Other species. $15 daily fee/pet. Designated rooms, service with restrictions, supervision. 🛦 ➠ ✕ 🖪 🖵

IDA GROVE

▼▼ Super 8 🅷
(712) 364-3988. **$66-$103.** 90 E Hwy 175 51445. Just n of SR 175/US 59. Int corridors. **Pets:** Other species. $10 one-time fee/room. Designated rooms, service with restrictions. 🛦 🤝 🖪 🖵

INDEPENDENCE

▼▼ Super 8 🅷
(319) 334-7041. **$70-$111.** 2000 1st St W 50644. US 20 exit 252, 1.4 mi n. Int corridors. **Pets:** Medium. Designated rooms, service with restrictions, crate. 🛦 🤝 🖪 🖵

IOWA CITY

(A) **▼▼▼ hotelVetro conference center** 🅷
(319) 337-4961. **$139-$399.** 201 S Linn St 52240. I-80 exit 244, s on Dubuque St, e on Washington St, then just s. Int corridors. **Pets:** Accepted. SAVE 🛦 ➠ 🤝 ✕ 🖪 🖵

(A) **▼▼▼ Sheraton Iowa City Hotel** 🅷
(319) 337-4058. **$109-$399.** 210 S Dubuque St 52240. Jct Dubuque and Burlington sts (SR 1); downtown. Int corridors. **Pets:** Accepted.
SAVE 🍴 🛦 ➠ 🤝 ✕ 🖪 🖵

IOWA FALLS

▼▼ Iowa Falls Super 8 🅷
(641) 648-4618. **$64-$135.** 839 S Oak St 50126. Jct US 65 and Washington Ave, 1 mi s; US 20 exit 168, 3.8 mi n. Int corridors. **Pets:** $15 deposit/pet. Service with restrictions, crate. ➠ 🤝 🖪 🖵

KEOKUK

▼▼ Baymont Inn & Suites 🅷
(319) 524-8000. **$59-$99.** 325 Main St 52632. Jct 4th and Main sts; downtown. Int corridors. **Pets:** Large, other species. $15 daily fee/pet. Service with restrictions, crate. 🛦 ➠ ✕ 🤝 ✕ 🖪 🖵

LE CLAIRE

▼▼ Comfort Inn & Suites-Riverview 🅷 🐾
(563) 289-4747. **$114-$174.** 902 Mississippi View Ct 52753. I-80 exit 306 (US 67), 0.5 mi n to Eagle Ridge Rd, then just sw. Int corridors. **Pets:** Medium. $10 daily fee/pet. Service with restrictions, crate.
🛦 ➠ 🤝 🖪 🖵

▼▼▼ Holiday Inn Express 🅷
(563) 289-9978. **$140-$280.** 1201 Canal Shore Dr SW 52753. I-80 exit 306 (US 67), just n. Int corridors. **Pets:** Medium. $35 one-time fee/room. Service with restrictions, supervision.
🛦 ➠ 🤝 ✕ 🖪 🖵

▼▼ Super 8 of Le Claire 🅷 🐾
(563) 289-5888. **$73-$106.** 1552 Welcome Center Dr 52753. I-80 exit 306 (US 67), 0.5 mi n to Eagle Ridge Rd, then just sw to Mississippi View Ct. Int corridors. **Pets:** Medium. $10 daily fee/pet. Service with restrictions, crate. 🛦 🤝 ✕ 🖪 🖵

MARQUETTE

▼ The Frontier Motel Ⓜ
(563) 873-3497. **$60-$110.** 101 S 1st St 52158. Just s of jct US 18 and SR 76; between Mississippi River Bridge and casino. Ext corridors. **Pets:** $10 daily fee/room. Designated rooms, service with restrictions, crate. 🍴 ➠ 🤝 🖪 🖵

MARSHALLTOWN

(A) **▼▼▼ BEST WESTERN Regency Inn** 🅷
(641) 752-6321. **$70-$200.** 3303 S Center St 50158. Jct US 30 and SR 14. Int corridors. **Pets:** Accepted. SAVE 🍴 🛦 ➠ 🤝 🖪 🖵

▼▼ Comfort Inn 🅷
(641) 752-6000. **$80-$120.** 2613 S Center St 50158. 0.5 mi n of jct US 30 and SR 14. Int corridors. **Pets:** Dogs only. $10 daily fee/pet. Service with restrictions, crate. ➠ 🤝 ✕ 🖪 🖵

▼▼ Super 8 🅷
(641) 753-3333. **$65-$95.** 3315 S Center St 50158. Just n of jct US 30 and SR 14. Int corridors. **Pets:** Accepted. 🤝 🖪 🖵

MASON CITY

▼▼ Mason City Super 8 🅷
(641) 423-8855. **$70-$141.** 3010 4th St SW 50401. I-35 exit 194 (SR 122), 5.3 mi e. Int corridors. **Pets:** Other species. $10 daily fee/pet. Service with restrictions, supervision. 🛦 ➠ 🤝 🖪 🖵

▼▼ Quality Inn & Suites 🅷
(641) 423-4444. **$95-$177.** 410 5th St SW 50401. Jct US 65 and SR 122, 0.3 mi w. Int corridors. **Pets:** Accepted.
🛦 ➠ 🤝 ✕ 🖪 🖵

MISSOURI VALLEY

▼▼ Oak Tree Inn 🅷
(712) 642-3000. **Call for rates.** 128 S Willow Rd 51555. I-29 exit 75, 0.4 mi ne. Int corridors. **Pets:** Accepted. 🛦 🤝 ✕ 🖪 🖵

MORAVIA

▼▼▼▼ **Honey Creek Resort State Park on Rathbun Lake** H

(641) 724-9100. **$109-$199, 14 day notice.** 12633 Resort Dr 52571. Jct SR 5 and CR J18, 5.4 mi w on CR J18, 1.3 mi s. Ext/int corridors. **Pets:** Accepted. ECO ⟦⟧ ⟦M ⟦∼ ⟦⟧ ⟦≋ ⟦×⟧ ⟦⟧ ⟦⟧

MOUNT PLEASANT

AAA ▼▼▼ **BEST WESTERN Mt. Pleasant Inn** H

(319) 385-2102. **Call for rates.** 810 N Grand Ave 52641. US 218 exit 45, 0.6 mi s. Int corridors. **Pets:** Accepted.
SAVE ⟦∼ ⟦×⟧ ⟦≋ ⟦×⟧ ⟦⟧ ⟦⟧

▼▼ **Super 8** H

(319) 385-8888. **$57-$77.** 1000 N Grand Ave 52641. US 218 exit 45, 0.6 mi s. Int corridors. **Pets:** Accepted. ⟦M ⟦≋ ⟦⟧ ⟦⟧

MOUNT VERNON

▼▼▼ **Sleep Inn & Suites** H

(319) 895-0055. **$85-$145.** 310 Virgil Ave 52314. Jct US 30 and SR 1, just se. Int corridors. **Pets:** Medium, dogs only. $25 daily fee/pet. Designated rooms, service with restrictions, supervision.

⟦M ⟦∼ ⟦≋ ⟦×⟧ ⟦⟧ ⟦⟧

MUSCATINE

▼▼ **AmericInn Lodge & Suites of Muscatine** H

(563) 263-0880. **Call for rates.** 3115 Hwy 61 N 52761. Jct US 61 and SR 38, just n. Int corridors. **Pets:** Accepted.

⟦M ⟦∼ ⟦≋ ⟦×⟧ ⟦⟧ ⟦⟧

▼▼ **The Hotel Muscatine** H

(563) 264-5550. **$100.** 2915 N Hwy 61 52761. Jct US 61 and SR 38, just n. Int corridors. **Pets:** Accepted. ⟦∼ ⟦×⟧ ⟦≋ ⟦×⟧ ⟦⟧ ⟦⟧

▼▼ **Pearl City Inn** H

(563) 264-5566. **$69-$114.** 305 Cleveland St 52761. Jct US 61 and SR 38. Int corridors. **Pets:** Accepted. ⟦M ⟦∼ ⟦≋ ⟦×⟧ ⟦⟧ ⟦⟧

NEW HAMPTON

▼▼ **Southgate Inn** M

(641) 394-4145. **Call for rates.** 2199 S Linn Ave 50659. US 63 exit 201, 0.9 mi ne on US 63 business route. Ext corridors. **Pets:** Accepted.
⟦M ⟦≋ ⟦⟧ ⟦⟧

▼▼ **Super 8-New Hampton** H

(641) 394-3838. **$65-$117.** 825 S Linn Ave 50659. US 63 exit 201, 1.5 mi ne on US 63 business route. Int corridors. **Pets:** Dogs only. $15 daily fee/room. Designated rooms, service with restrictions, crate.
⟦⟧ ⟦M ⟦∼ ⟦≋ ⟦×⟧ ⟦⟧ ⟦⟧

NEWTON

AAA ▼▼▼ **AmericInn Lodge & Suites of Newton** H

(641) 791-1160. **$120-$220.** 4401 S 22nd Ave E 50208. I-80 exit 168, just sw. Int corridors. **Pets:** Medium. $40 daily fee/pet. Designated rooms, service with restrictions, supervision.
SAVE ⟦⟧ ⟦M ⟦∼ ⟦≋ ⟦×⟧ ⟦⟧ ⟦⟧

NORTH LIBERTY

▼▼ **Sleep Inn & Suites** H

(319) 665-2700. **$85-$145.** 485 Madison Ave N 52317. I-380 exit 4, just se. Int corridors. **Pets:** Accepted. ⟦⟧ ⟦M ⟦∼ ⟦≋ ⟦×⟧ ⟦⟧ ⟦⟧

NORTHWOOD

▼▼▼▼ **Country Inn & Suites By Carlson** H

(641) 323-7000. **$109-$130, 14 day notice.** 711 Diamond Jo Ln 50459. I-35 exit 214, just nw. Int corridors. **Pets:** Medium, other species. $25 one-time fee/room. Service with restrictions, supervision.

⟦M ⟦∼ ⟦≋ ⟦⟧ ⟦⟧

AAA ▼▼▼ **Holiday Inn Express & Suites** H

(641) 323-7500. **Call for rates.** 4712 Wheelerwood Rd 50459. I-35 exit 214, just nw. Int corridors. **Pets:** Other species. $25 daily fee/room. Service with restrictions, crate. SAVE ⟦M ⟦∼ ⟦≋ ⟦×⟧ ⟦⟧ ⟦⟧

OELWEIN

▼▼ **Super 8-Oelwein** M

(319) 283-2888. **$70-$146.** 210 10th St SE 50662. Jct SR 3 and 150, 1 mi s on SR 150; south end of downtown. Int corridors. **Pets:** Accepted.
⟦⟧ ⟦M ⟦≋ ⟦⟧ ⟦⟧

OKOBOJI

▼▼ **AmericInn Lodge & Suites of Okoboji** H

(712) 332-9000. **$94-$319, 7 day notice.** 1005 Brooks Park Dr 51355. Jct US 71 and SR 9, 2.5 mi s. Int corridors. **Pets:** Accepted.
⟦M ⟦∼ ⟦≋ ⟦×⟧ ⟦⟧ ⟦⟧

▼▼▼ **Arrowwood Resort & Conference Center** H

(712) 332-2161. **Call for rates.** 1405 Hwy 71 N 51355. Jct US 71 and SR 9, 3 mi s. Ext/int corridors. **Pets:** Accepted.
⟦⟧ ⟦M ⟦∼ ⟦×⟧ ⟦≋ ⟦×⟧ ⟦⟧ ⟦⟧

▼▼ **The Inn at Okoboji Resort & Conference Center** H

(712) 332-2113. **$99-$355, 15 day notice.** 3301 Lakeshore Dr 51355. Jct US 71 and Sanborn Ave, 1 mi w. Ext corridors. **Pets:** Accepted.
⟦⟧ ⟦∼ ⟦×⟧ ⟦≋ ⟦×⟧ ⟦⟧ ⟦⟧

OSCEOLA

AAA ▼▼ **Americas Best Value Inn** M

(641) 342-2123. **$68-$96.** 1520 Jeffreys Dr 50213. I-35 exit 33 (Osceola/US 34), just e. Int corridors. **Pets:** Accepted. SAVE ⟦≋ ⟦⟧

▼▼ **AmericInn Lodge & Suites of Osceola** H

(641) 342-9400. **$100-$250.** 111 Ariel Cir 50213. I-35 exit 33 (Osceola/US 34), just w. Int corridors. **Pets:** Accepted.
⟦M ⟦∼ ⟦≋ ⟦×⟧ ⟦⟧ ⟦⟧

AAA ▼▼▼ **Lakeside Hotel Casino** H

(641) 342-9511. **$81.** 777 Casino Dr 50213. I-35 exit 34, 0.5 mi w. Int corridors. **Pets:** Accepted. SAVE ⟦⟧ ⟦M ⟦×⟧ ⟦≋ ⟦⟧

▼▼ **Super 8 Osceola** H

(641) 342-6594. **$50-$70.** 720 Warren Ave 50213. I-35 exit 33 (Osceola/US 34), just e. Int corridors. **Pets:** Accepted. ⟦≋ ⟦⟧ ⟦⟧

OTTUMWA

▼▼ **AmericInn of Ottumwa** H

(641) 684-8222. **Call for rates.** 222 W 2nd St 52501. Just se of US 63 and 4th St W; downtown. Int corridors. **Pets:** Accepted.
⟦M ⟦∼ ⟦≋ ⟦×⟧ ⟦⟧ ⟦⟧

▼▼ **Quality Inn & Suites** H

(641) 682-8526. **$70-$129.** 125 W Joseph Ave 52501. Jct US 34, 2 mi n on US 63. Int corridors. **Pets:** Accepted. ⟦∼ ⟦≋ ⟦×⟧ ⟦⟧ ⟦⟧

PELLA

▼▼ **Super 8** H

(641) 628-8181. **$70-$80.** 105 E Oskaloosa St 50219. SR 163 exit 42, 1 mi n, then 0.5 mi e. Int corridors. **Pets:** Dogs only. $15 daily fee/pet. Designated rooms, service with restrictions, supervision.
⟦M ⟦≋ ⟦⟧ ⟦⟧

PEOSTA

▼▼ **Quality Inn & Suites** H

(563) 557-8878. **$65-$190.** 100 Peosta St 52068. US 20 exit 308, just n. Int corridors. **Pets:** Accepted. ⟦M ⟦∼ ⟦≋ ⟦×⟧ ⟦⟧ ⟦⟧

PERCIVAL

AAA ▼▼ **Americas Best Value Inn & Suites-Percival/Nebraska City** H

(712) 382-2100. **Call for rates.** 2113 Sapp Bros Dr 51648. I-29 exit 10 (SR 2), just w. Int corridors. **Pets:** Accepted.
SAVE ⟦⟧ ⟦≋ ⟦×⟧ ⟦⟧ ⟦⟧

 **Super 8-Percival/Nebraska City** H
(712) 382-2828. **$62-$82.** 2103 249th St 51648. I-29 exit 10 (SR 2), just w. Int corridors. **Pets:** Dogs only. $10 one-time fee/room. Service with restrictions, supervision. SAVE ⊟ ⛺ ⟲ ✕ 🛎 ▯

PLEASANT HILL
Sleep Inn & Suites H
(515) 299-9922. **Call for rates.** 5850 Morning Star Ct 50327. US 65 exit 79 (SR 163/E University Ave), just e. Int corridors. **Pets:** Accepted.
⊟ ⛺ ⟲ 🛎 ▯

RIVERSIDE
Riverside Casino & Golf Resort H
(319) 648-1234. **$80-$250.** 3184 Hwy 22 52327. I-218 exit 80, 1.5 mi ne. Int corridors. **Pets:** Accepted. ⊟ ⛺ ⟲ ✕ S 🛎 ▯

SHELDON
Holiday Inn Express & Suites Sheldon H
(712) 324-3000. **Call for rates.** 201 34th Ave 51201. SR 60 exit 34, just sw. Int corridors. **Pets:** Accepted.
⊟ ⛺ ⟲ ⟲ ✕ 🛎 ▯

Super 8 M
(712) 324-8400. **$82-$130.** 210 N 2nd Ave 51201. SR 60 exit 34, 2 mi w on US 18, then just n on Business Rt SR 60. Int corridors.
Pets: Accepted. ⊟ ⛺ ⟲ ⟲ 🛎 ▯

SIGOURNEY
Belva Deer Inn H
(641) 622-3200. **$74-$99, 3 day notice.** 21638 Hwy 92 52591. Jct SR 149 and 92, 1.1 mi e. Int corridors. **Pets:** $25 one-time fee/room. Service with restrictions, crate. ⛺ ⟲ ✕ 🛎 ▯

SIOUX CENTER
Econo Lodge M
(712) 722-4000. **$75-$125.** 86 9th St Cir NE 51250. On US 75, 1 mi n of jct SR 840; north side of town. Ext/int corridors. **Pets:** Other species. $10 daily fee/pet. Designated rooms, service with restrictions, supervision. ⛺ ⟲ ✕ 🛎 ▯

SIOUX CITY
AmericInn Lodge & Suites of Sioux City H
(712) 255-1800. **Call for rates.** 4230 S Lewis Blvd 51106. I-29 exit 143, just e. Int corridors. **Pets:** Accepted. ⛺ ⟲ ⟲ 🛎 ▯

Days Inn Sioux City M
(712) 258-8000. **$33-$148.** 3000 Singing Hills Blvd 51106. I-29 exit 143, just se. Ext/int corridors. **Pets:** Medium, dogs only. $15 daily fee/pet. Designated rooms, service with restrictions, supervision.
⛺ ⟲ ⟲ 🛎 ▯

Fairfield Inn by Marriott H
(712) 276-5600. **$90-$160.** 4716 Southern Hills Dr 51106. I-29 exit 144A, 1 mi e on US 20, then just s. Int corridors. **Pets:** Accepted.
⟲ ⟲ ✕ 🛎 ▯

Hilton Garden Inn-Sioux City Riverfront H
(712) 255-4200. **Call for rates.** 1132 Larsen Park Rd 51103. I-29 exit 149, just sw. Int corridors. **Pets:** Medium. $30 one-time fee/pet. Designated rooms, service with restrictions, crate.
⊟ ⛺ ⟲ ✕ ⟲ ✕ 🛎 ▯

Quality Inn & Suites H
(712) 274-1400. **$65-$100.** 4230 S Lakeport St 51106. I-29 exit 144A, 1 mi e on US 20, then just s. Int corridors. **Pets:** Accepted.
⛺ ⟲ 🛎 ▯

Super 8 H
(712) 274-1520. **$61-$116.** 4307 Stone Ave 51106. I-29 exit 144A north-bound; US 75 exit 4B, 1.5 mi w on Gordon Dr; exit 147B southbound to Gordon Dr, 3 mi e. Int corridors. **Pets:** Accepted. ⟲ 🛎 ▯

Super 8 Singing Hills M
(712) 255-8888. **$25-$63.** 2530 Singing Hills Blvd 51111. I-29 exit 143, just w. Int corridors. **Pets:** Other species. $10 daily fee/pet. Designated rooms, service with restrictions, supervision. ⛺ ⟲ 🛎 ▯

SPENCER
AmericInn Hotel & Suites of Spencer H
(712) 262-7525. **$89-$169.** 1005 13th St SW 51301. On US 71, 1 mi w of southern jct US 18 and 71. Int corridors. **Pets:** Medium. $10 daily fee/room. Service with restrictions, supervision.
⊟ ⛺ ⟲ ⟲ ✕ 🛎 ▯

SPIRIT LAKE
Spirit Lake Super 8 H 🐾
(712) 336-4901. **$80-$175.** 2203 Circle Dr W 51360. Jct US 71 and SR 9. Int corridors. **Pets:** Other species. $10 one-time fee/room. Service with restrictions, crate. ⛺ ⟲ 🛎 ▯

STORM LAKE
King's Pointe Waterpark Resort H
(712) 213-4500. **$99-$409, 3 day notice.** 1520 E Lakeshore Dr 50588. Jct Business Rt US 71 and SR 7, just n. Int corridors. **Pets:** Accepted.
⊟ ⛺ ⟲ ✕ ⟲ ✕ 🛎 ▯

STORY CITY
Comfort Inn H
(515) 733-6363. **$90-$139.** 425 Timberland Dr 50248. I-35 exit 124, just sw. Int corridors. **Pets:** Accepted. ⛺ ⟲ ⟲ 🛎 ▯

STUART
Americas Best Value Inn & Suites H
(515) 523-2888. **$62-$97.** 203 SE 7th St 50250. I-80 exit 93, just ne. Int corridors. **Pets:** Accepted. ⊟ ⛺ ⟲ ⟲ 🛎 ▯

URBANDALE
Holiday Inn Hotel & Suites Northwest H
(515) 278-4755. **Call for rates.** 4800 Merle Hay Rd 50322. I-35/80 exit 131 (Merle Hay Rd), just s. Int corridors. **Pets:** Accepted.
⊟ ⛺ ⟲ ⟲ ✕ 🛎 ▯

Microtel Inn & Suites by Wyndham Urbandale/Des Moines H
(515) 727-5424. **$59-$150.** 8711 Plum Dr 50322. I-35/80 exit 129 (86th St). Int corridors. **Pets:** $10 daily fee/pet. Service with restrictions, supervision. ⛺ ⟲ 🛎 ▯

Ramada Tropics Resort/Conference Center Des Moines H
(515) 278-0271. **$101-$189.** 5000 Merle Hay Rd 50322. I-35/80 exit 131 (Merle Hay Rd), just s. Int corridors. **Pets:** Other species. $10 daily fee/pet. Designated rooms, service with restrictions, crate.
⊟ ⟲ ✕ ⟲ ✕ 🛎 ▯

Sleep Inn H
(515) 270-2424. **$94-$150.** 11211 Hickman Rd 50322. I-35/80 exit 125 (Hickman Rd), just ne. Int corridors. **Pets:** Accepted.
⛺ ⟲ ⟲ 🛎 ▯

TownePlace Suites by Marriott Des Moines/Urbandale H
(515) 727-4066. **$91-$150.** 8800 Northpark Dr 50131. I-35/80 exit 129 (86th St), just nw. Int corridors. **Pets:** Medium. $100 one-time fee/room. Designated rooms, service with restrictions, crate.
⟲ ⟲ ✕ 🛎 ▯

VINTON
Cobblestone Inn & Suites H
(319) 472-2220. **$90-$110.** 1202 W 11th St 52349. Jct US 218, just sw. Int corridors. **Pets:** Accepted. ⛺ ⟲ ✕ 🛎 ▯

WALCOTT

AAA ▼▼ ◆◆ **Davenport/Walcott Comfort Inn** H

(563) 284-9000. **$95-$199.** 501 W Walker St 52773. I-80 exit 284, just nw. Int corridors. **Pets:** Small. $15 daily fee/pet. Designated rooms, service with restrictions, supervision.

WALNUT

◆◆ ◆ **Super 8** H

(712) 784-2221. **$70-$100.** 2109 Antique City Dr 51577. I-80 exit 46, just n. Int corridors. **Pets:** Accepted.

WATERLOO

▼▼ ▼▼ **Baymont Inn & Suites Waterloo** H

(319) 234-7411. **$65-$78.** 1945 LaPorte Rd 50702. I-380 exit 72 (E San Marnan Dr), just sw. Int corridors. **Pets:** Accepted.

▼▼ ▼▼ **Days Inn & Suites** H

(319) 235-4461. **$79-$156.** 1809 LaPorte Rd 50702. I-380 exit 72 (E San Marnan Dr), just nw. Int corridors. **Pets:** Accepted.

▼▼ ▼▼ **Howard Johnson** H

(319) 232-7467. **$79-$129.** 3052 Marnie Ave 50701. 1 mi n of jct US 20 and 63 exit 227. Int corridors. **Pets:** Dogs only. $10 daily fee/pet. Designated rooms, service with restrictions, supervision.

AAA ▼▼ ▼▼ **Ramada Hotel & Convention Center** H

(319) 233-7560. **$89-$102.** 205 W 4th St 50701. At 4th and Commercial sts; downtown. Int corridors. **Pets:** Accepted.

WAUKON

◆◆ ◆ **Stoney Creek Inn** H

(563) 568-2220. **$69-$142.** 407 Rossville Rd 52172. Jct SR 9 and 76, 1.7 mi n. Int corridors. **Pets:** Accepted.

WAVERLY

▼▼ ▼▼ **Comfort Inn** H

(319) 352-0399. **$89-$179.** 404 29th Ave SW 50677. US 218 exit 198, 0.7 mi n. Int corridors. **Pets:** Accepted.

▼▼ ▼▼ **Super 8 Waverly** H

(319) 352-0888. **$66-$138.** 301 13th Ave SW 50677. US 218 exit 198, 1.4 mi n. Int corridors. **Pets:** Accepted.

WEBSTER CITY

▼▼ ▼▼ **AmericInn Motel & Suites of Webster City** H 🐾

(515) 832-3999. **$75-$125.** 411 Closz Dr 50595. Just s of jct US 20 and SR 17. Int corridors. **Pets:** Other species. $25 one-time fee/room. Service with restrictions, crate.

WEST DES MOINES

▼▼ ▼▼ **Candlewood Suites-West Des Moines** H

(515) 221-0001. **Call for rates.** 7625 Office Plaza Dr N 50266. I-80 exit 121 (Jordan Creek Pkwy), just sw. Int corridors. **Pets:** Accepted.

▼▼ ▼▼ **Drury Inn & Suites** H

(515) 457-9500. **$115-$220.** 5505 Mills Civic Pkwy 50266. I-35 exit 70 (Mills Civic Pkwy), just w. Int corridors. **Pets:** $10 daily fee/room. Service with restrictions, supervision.

▼▼ ▼▼ **Residence Inn by Marriott-Des Moines West** H

(515) 267-0338. **$132-$217.** 160 S Jordan Creek Pkwy 50266. I-35 exit 70 (Mills Civic Pkwy), 1.2 mi w to 68th St, then just nw. Int corridors. **Pets:** Other species. $100 one-time fee/room. Service with restrictions.

AAA ◆◆◆◆ **Sheraton West Des Moines** H

(515) 223-1800. **$109-$199.** 1800 50th St 50266. I-35/80 exit 124 (University Ave), just e. Int corridors. **Pets:** Accepted.

▼▼ ▼▼ **Staybridge Suites** H

(515) 223-0000. **$129-$229.** 6905 Lake Dr 50266. I-80 exit 121 (Jordan Creek Pkwy), just ne. Int corridors. **Pets:** Medium, other species. $35 one-time fee/room. Service with restrictions, crate.

▼▼ ▼▼ **West Des Moines Marriott** H

(515) 267-1500. **$157-$258.** 1250 Jordan Creek Pkwy 50266. I-80 exit 121 (Jordan Creek Pkwy), just sw. Int corridors. **Pets:** Accepted.

WILLIAMS

AAA ▼▼ ▼▼ **BEST WESTERN Norseman Inn** M

(515) 854-2281. **$76-$95.** 3086 220th St 50271. I-35 exit 144, just e. Int corridors. **Pets:** Medium, dogs only. $10 daily fee/pet. Designated rooms, service with restrictions, supervision.

WILLIAMSBURG

▼▼ ▼▼ **Best Inn Cozy House & Suites** H

(319) 668-9777. **$90-$150.** 1708 N Highland St 52361. I-80 exit 220, 0.8 mi n. Int corridors. **Pets:** Large, other species. $20 daily fee/pet. Designated rooms, service with restrictions, supervision.

AAA ▼▼ ▼▼ **Crest Country Inn** M

(319) 668-1522. **$70-$90.** 340 W Evans St 52361. I-80 exit 220, just nw. Ext corridors. **Pets:** Accepted.

AAA ▼▼▼▼ **Ramada Williamsburg and Wasserbahn Waterpark** H

(319) 668-1175. **$81-$108.** 2211 U Ave 52361. I-80 exit 225 (US 151), just sw. Int corridors. **Pets:** Accepted.

KANSAS

ABILENE

▼▼▼▼ **Holiday Inn Express Hotel & Suites** H

(785) 263-4049. **$115-$125.** 110 E Lafayette Ave 67410. I-70 exit 275, just n. Int corridors. **Pets:** $20 daily fee/pet. Designated rooms, service with restrictions, supervision.

ANDOVER

AAA ▼▼ ▼▼ **Days Inn Andover** M

(316) 733-8881. **$65-$85.** 222 W US Hwy 54 67002. 2.2 mi e of jct SR 96. Ext corridors. **Pets:** Dogs only. $10 daily fee/pet. Service with restrictions, crate.

▼▼▼▼ **Holiday Inn Express & Suites** H

(316) 733-8833. **$109.** 600 S Allen St 67002. 2.2 mi e of jct SR 96 and US 54. Int corridors. **Pets:** Accepted.

ARKANSAS CITY

AAA ▼▼▼▼ **BEST WESTERN PLUS Patterson Park Inn** H

(620) 307-6767. **Call for rates.** 6100 Patterson Pkwy 67005. Just w of jct US 77. Int corridors. **Pets:** Accepted.

BELOIT

▼▼ ▼▼ Super 8 **H**
(785) 738-4300. **$58-$89, 3 day notice.** 3018 W US Hwy 24 67420. Just e of jct SR 14. Ext/int corridors. **Pets:** Accepted.
&M 🛜 ✕ 🛢 ▣

BONNER SPRINGS

▼▼▼ Holiday Inn Express **H**
(913) 721-5300. **Call for rates.** 13031 Ridge Dr 66012. I-70 exit 224. Int corridors. **Pets:** Accepted. &M 🛜 ✕ 🛢 ▣

BURLINGTON

▼▼ Country Haven Inn **H**
(620) 364-8260. **$69-$75.** 207 Cross St 66839. Just e of US 75; 1 mi n of center. Int corridors. **Pets:** Very small, dogs only. $50 deposit/pet. Designated rooms, service with restrictions, supervision.
&M 🛜 ✕ 🛢 ▣

CLAY CENTER

▼▼ Cedar Court Motel **M**
(785) 632-2148. **$58-$85.** 905 Crawford St 67432. On US 24, just e of jct SR 15. Ext corridors. **Pets:** Small, dogs only. $15 daily fee/pet. Designated rooms, service with restrictions, supervision.
&M 🛜 🛢 ▣

COFFEYVILLE

AAA ▼▼▼ BEST WESTERN Bricktown Lodge **H**
(620) 251-3700. **$96.** 605 Northeast St 67337. 1 mi e of center. Int corridors. **Pets:** $20 daily fee/pet. Service with restrictions, crate.
SAVE 🛜 ✕ 🛢 ▣

COLBY

▼▼ Comfort Inn **H**
(785) 462-3833. **$95-$150.** 2225 S Range Ave 67701. I-70 exit 53 (SR 25), just s. Int corridors. **Pets:** Accepted.
🍴 &M 🛜 🛢 ▣

AAA ▼▼▼ Days Inn **H**
(785) 462-8691. **$77-$100.** 1925 S Range Ave 67701. I-70 exit 53 (SR 25), 0.3 mi n. Int corridors. **Pets:** Small, dogs only. $15 daily fee/pet. Designated rooms, service with restrictions, supervision.
SAVE 🛜 🛢 ▣

▼▼▼ Holiday Inn Express Hotel & Suites **H**
(785) 462-8787. **$115-$145.** 645 W Willow St 67701. I-70 exit 53 (SR 25), just ne. Int corridors. **Pets:** Medium. $25 one-time fee/room. Designated rooms, service with restrictions, supervision.
&M 🛜 ✕ 🛢 ▣

▼▼▼ Sleep Inn & Suites **H**
(785) 460-0310. **$90-$120.** 2075 Sewell Ave 67701. I-70 exit 53 (SR 25), just ne. Int corridors. **Pets:** Accepted. 🛜 ✕ 🛢 ▣

AAA ▼▼▼ Super 8 **H**
(785) 462-8248. **$65-$85.** 1040 Zelfer Ave 67701. I-70 exit 53 (SR 25), 0.3 mi n, then just w. Int corridors. **Pets:** Accepted.
SAVE 🛜 🛢 ▣

COTTONWOOD FALLS *(Restaurants p. 631)*

AAA ▼▼▼ Grand Central Hotel **CI**
(620) 273-6763. **$160-$190, 3 day notice.** 215 Broadway 66845. US 177, just w on Main St, then just s; center of downtown. Int corridors. **Pets:** Service with restrictions, supervision. SAVE 🍴 🛜 ✕ ▣

DERBY

▼▼▼ Hampton Inn Derby **H**
(316) 425-7900. **$109-$169.** 1701 Cambridge St 67037. Just sw of jct Rock Rd. Int corridors. **Pets:** Accepted. &M 🛜 🛜 ✕ 🛢 ▣

DODGE CITY

AAA ▼▼▼ BEST WESTERN PLUS Country Inn & Suites **H**
(620) 225-7378. **$104-$179.** 506 N 14th Ave 67801. Just n of jct US 50 business route. Ext/int corridors. **Pets:** Accepted.
SAVE &M 🛜 🛜 ✕ 🛢 ▣

▼▼▼ Holiday Inn Express **H**
(620) 227-5000. **$114-$135.** 2320 W Wyatt Earp Blvd 67801. 1.4 mi w on US 50 business route. Int corridors. **Pets:** $30 one-time fee/room. Service with restrictions, crate. 🛜 🛜 ✕ 🛢 ▣

▼▼ Super 8 **H**
(620) 225-3924. **$75-$116.** 1708 W Wyatt Earp Blvd 67801. 1.2 mi w on US 50 business route. Int corridors. **Pets:** Accepted.
🛜 🛜 🛢 ▣

EL DORADO

AAA ▼▼▼ BEST WESTERN Red Coach Inn **H**
(316) 321-6900. **$69-$119.** 2525 W Central Ave 67042. I-35 exit 71, 0.5 mi e. Ext corridors. **Pets:** Very small, dogs only. $15 daily fee/pet. Designated rooms, no service, supervision. SAVE 🛜 🛜 🛢 ▣

▼ Super 8-El Dorado **M**
(316) 321-4888. **$69-$74.** 2530 W Central Ave 67042. I-35 exit 71, 0.5 mi e. Int corridors. **Pets:** Accepted. 🛜 🛢 ▣

ELLIS

▼▼▼ Days Inn **H**
(785) 726-2511. **$75-$90.** 205 N Washington St 67637. I-70 exit 145, just s. Int corridors. **Pets:** Other species. $5 daily fee/pet. Designated rooms, supervision. &M 🛜 🛜 ✕ 🛢 ▣

EMPORIA

▼▼ Candlewood Suites **H**
(620) 343-7756. **Call for rates.** 2602 Candlewood Dr 66801. I-35 exit 128 (Industrial St), just n, then just e. Int corridors. **Pets:** Accepted.
🛜 ✕ 🛢 ▣

▼▼ Flint Hills Inn & Suites **H**
(620) 341-9393. **Call for rates.** 2921 W 18th Ave 66801. I-35 exit 128 (Industrial St), just nw. Int corridors. **Pets:** Accepted.
🛜 🛜 ✕ 🛢 ▣

AAA ▼▼ Super 8 **H**
(620) 342-7567. **$55-$75.** 2913 W US Hwy 50 66801. I-35 exit 127A, just s to US 50, follow roundabout directions, then 0.7 mi e. Int corridors. **Pets:** Small. $10 daily fee/pet. Designated rooms, service with restrictions, supervision. SAVE 🛜 ✕ 🛢 ▣

FORT SCOTT

▼▼▼ Lyons' Twin Mansions B & B Hotel **CI**
(620) 223-3644. **$109-$225, 14 day notice.** 742 S National Ave 66701. Jct US 69 and 54 E, 0.3 mi w on Wall St, 0.6 mi s. Ext/int corridors. **Pets:** Dogs only. Designated rooms, service with restrictions, supervision. 🍴 🛜 ✕ 🎦 🛢 ▣

GARDEN CITY

▼▼▼ AmericInn Lodge & Suites of Garden City **H** 🐾
(620) 272-9860. **$89-$165.** 3020 E Kansas Ave 67846. Jct US 50, 83 and SR 156. Int corridors. **Pets:** Small, other species. $20 one-time fee/room. Designated rooms, service with restrictions, supervision.
🛜 🛜 ✕ 🛢 ▣

AAA ▼▼▼ Clarion Inn & Conference Center **H**
(620) 275-7471. **$110-$150.** 1911 E Kansas Ave 67846. 0.5 mi w of US 50 and 83 Bypass, on SR 156. Int corridors. **Pets:** Medium, dogs only. $45 one-time fee/pet. Designated rooms, service with restrictions, crate.
SAVE 🍴 🛜 🛜 ✕ 🛢 ▣

▼▼ Comfort Inn **H**
(620) 275-5800. **$95-$120.** 2608 E Kansas Ave 67846. Jct US 50, 83 and SR 156. Int corridors. **Pets:** Accepted.
🛜 ✕ 🛜 ✕ 🛢 ▣

▼▼▼ Holiday Inn Express Hotel & Suites 🅷

(620) 275-5900. **Call for rates.** 2502 E Kansas Ave 67846. Jct US 50, 83 and SR 156. Int corridors. **Pets:** Accepted.

🙾 🛜 ✕ 🛏 💻

▼▼ Magnuson Hotel Red Baron 🅷

(620) 275-4164. **$79-$119, 5 day notice.** 2205 E Fulton St 67846. 2.3 mi e on US 50 business route, at US 83 Bypass. Ext corridors.
Pets: Accepted. 🙾 🛜 ✕ 🛏 💻

GARDNER
▼▼ Super 8 🅷

(913) 856-8887. **$64-$114.** 2001 E Santa Fe 66030. I-35 exit 210, just w. Int corridors. **Pets:** Other species. $10 daily fee/pet. Service with restrictions, supervision. 🅼 🙾 🛜 🛏 💻

GOODLAND
🆬 ▼▼▼ Holiday Inn Express Hotel & Suites 🅷

(785) 890-9060. **Call for rates.** 2631 Enterprise Rd 67735. I-70 exit 17 (SR 27), just s. Int corridors. **Pets:** Medium. $25 daily fee/room. Designated rooms, service with restrictions, supervision.

SAVE 🔌 🅼 🙾 🛜 ✕ 🛏 💻

GREAT BEND
🆬 ▼▼ BEST WESTERN Angus Inn 🅷 🐾

(620) 792-3541. **$85-$95.** 2920 10th St 67530. 0.8 mi w on US 56 and SR 96/156. Ext/int corridors. **Pets:** Other species. $10 daily fee/pet. Service with restrictions, crate. SAVE 🍽 🏊 ✕ 🛜 🛏 💻

GREENSBURG
🆬 ▼▼▼ BEST WESTERN PLUS Night Watchman Inn & Suites 🅷 🐾

(620) 723-2244. **$109-$126.** 515 W Kansas Ave 67054. Just e of jct US 54 and 183. Int corridors. **Pets:** Other species. $50 deposit/pet. Designated rooms, service with restrictions, crate.

SAVE 🙾 🛜 ✕ 🛏 💻

HAYSVILLE
▼▼▼ Sleep Inn & Suites 🅷

(316) 425-6077. **Call for rates.** 651 E 71 St S 67060. I-35 exit 39, just w. Int corridors. **Pets:** Medium. $10 one-time fee/pet. Service with restrictions, crate. 🅼 🛜 ✕ 🛏 💻

HERINGTON
▼▼▼ Herington Inn & Suites 🅷

(785) 258-3300. **$72-$92.** 565 Hwy 77 67449. US 77, just w. Int corridors. **Pets:** Very small, dogs only. $25 one-time fee/pet. Supervision.
🅼 🛜 ✕ 🛏 💻

HESSTON
🆬 ▼▼ AmericInn Lodge & Suites of Hesston 🅷

(620) 327-2053. **Call for rates.** 2 Leonard Ct 67062. I-135 exit 40, just e. Int corridors. **Pets:** Other species. $15 one-time fee/room. Designated rooms, service with restrictions, crate. SAVE 🙾 🛜 🛏 💻

HIAWATHA
🆬 ▼▼▼ BEST WESTERN PLUS Hiawatha Hotel 🅷

(785) 740-7000. **Call for rates.** 119 E Lodge Rd 66434. Jct US 73 and 36, just ne. Int corridors. **Pets:** $25 daily fee/pet. Service with restrictions, crate. SAVE 🅼 🛜 ✕ 🛏 💻

HILLSBORO
▼▼ Country Haven Inn 🅷

(620) 947-2929. **$73-$85.** 804 Western Heights Cir 67063. On US 56; center. Int corridors. **Pets:** Accepted. 🛜 ✕ 🛏 💻

HUTCHINSON
▼▼ Comfort Inn & Suites 🅷

(620) 669-5200. **$85-$170.** 1601 Super Plaza 67501. Just w of jct SR 61 and N 17th Ave. Int corridors. **Pets:** Small, other species. $25 one-time fee/pet. Designated rooms, service with restrictions, supervision.
🅼 🏊 🛜 🛏 💻

INDEPENDENCE
▼▼ Appletree Inn 🅷

(620) 331-5500. **Call for rates.** 201 N 8th St 67301. At 8th and Laurel sts. Ext/int corridors. **Pets:** Accepted. 🙾 🛜 🛏 💻

IOLA
▼▼ Super 8 Iola 🅷

(620) 365-3030. **$68-$101.** 200 Bills Way 66749. Jct US 54 and 169. Int corridors. **Pets:** Accepted. 🅼 🙾 🛜 ✕ 🛏 💻

JUNCTION CITY
🆬 ▼▼ BEST WESTERN J.C. Inn 🅷

(785) 210-1212. **$72-$159.** 604 E Chestnut St 66441. I-70 exit 298, just w. Int corridors. **Pets:** Accepted. SAVE 🅼 🙾 🛜 🛏 💻

▼▼ Candlewood Suites 🅷

(785) 238-1454. **$83-$93.** 100 S Hammons Dr 66441. I-70 exit 298, just w. Int corridors. **Pets:** Accepted. 🅼 🛜 ✕ 🛏 💻

▼▼▼ Courtyard by Marriott Junction City 🅷

(785) 210-1500. **$81-$117.** 310 Hammons Dr 66441. I-70 exit 298, just w. Int corridors. **Pets:** Accepted. 🅼 🙾 🛜 ✕ 🛏 💻

▼▼▼ Holiday Inn Express 🅷

(785) 762-4200. **Call for rates.** 120 N East St 66441. I-70 exit 298, just nw. Int corridors. **Pets:** Accepted. 🅼 🙾 🛜 🛏 💻

KANSAS CITY
▼▼▼ Candlewood Suites 🅷

(913) 788-9929. **$119-$149.** 10920 Parallel Pkwy 66109. I-435 exit 14B, just w. Int corridors. **Pets:** Medium. $10 daily fee/pet. Designated rooms, service with restrictions, crate. 🅼 🛜 ✕ 🛏 💻

▼▼▼ Comfort Suites Speedway 🅷

(913) 299-4466. **Call for rates.** 3000 N 103rd Terr 66109. I-435 exit 15A, just e. Int corridors. **Pets:** Small. $40 daily fee/room. Designated rooms, service with restrictions, supervision. 🛜 ✕ 🛏 💻

▼▼▼ Oak Tree Inn 🅷

(913) 677-3060. **$80-$110, 3 day notice.** 501 Southwest Blvd 66103. I-35 exit 234 (7th St), 0.4 mi s to Southwest Blvd, then just w. Int corridors. **Pets:** Accepted. 🙾 🛜 🛏 💻

LANSING
▼▼ Econo Lodge Lansing/Leavenworth 🅷

(913) 727-2777. **$54-$85.** 504 N Main 66043. I-70 exit 224 (Leavenworth), 10 mi n on US 73 and SR 7. Int corridors. **Pets:** Accepted.
🛜 🛏 💻

LAWRENCE
🆬 ▼▼▼ Baymont Inn & Suites 🅷

(785) 838-4242. **$69-$159.** 740 Iowa St 66044. I-70 exit 202, 1 mi s on US 59. Int corridors. **Pets:** Medium. $15 deposit/pet, $15 daily fee/pet. Designated rooms, service with restrictions, supervision.
SAVE 🅼 🙾 🛜 🛏 💻

🆬 ▼▼▼ BEST WESTERN Lawrence 🅷

(785) 843-9100. **$90-$170.** 2309 Iowa St 66046. On US 59; jct SR 10. Ext/int corridors. **Pets:** Accepted. SAVE 🅼 🙾 🛜 🛏 💻

🆬 ▼▼▼ Holiday Inn Express Hotel & Suites 🅷

(785) 749-7555. **Call for rates.** 3411 SW Iowa St 66046. I-70 exit 197 (SR 10), 8.4 mi e to US 59, then just n. Int corridors. **Pets:** Small. $20 daily fee/room. Designated rooms, service with restrictions, supervision.
SAVE 🅼 🙾 ✕ 🛜 ✕ 🛏 💻

 Holiday Inn Hotel & Convention Center 🅷
(785) 841-7077. **$89-$199.** 200 McDonald Dr 66044. I-70 exit 202, 0.5
mi s on US 59. Int corridors. **Pets:** Other species. $25 one-time fee/
room. Designated rooms, service with restrictions.
🍴 🏊 ⊠ 🛜 ✕ 🛅 💻

LEAWOOD

◈ 🔷🔷🔷 Aloft Leawood-Overland Park 🅷 🐾
(913) 345-9430. **$109-$199.** 11620 Ash St 66211. I-435 exit 77B (Nall
Ave), 1.1 mi s, then just e. Int corridors. **Pets:** Small, dogs only. Designated rooms, service with restrictions, supervision.
SAVE ♿ 🏊 🛜 ✕ 🛅 💻

LENEXA

🔷🔷 La Quinta Inn Kansas City Lenexa 🅷
(913) 492-5500. **$65-$209.** 9461 Lenexa Dr 66215. I-35 exit 224 (95th
St), just ne; entrance left on Monrovia Rd off 95th St. Int corridors.
Pets: Large, other species. Service with restrictions.
🏊 🛜 ✕ 🛅 💻

LIBERAL

◈ 🔷 Americas Best Value Inn Ⓜ
(620) 624-6203. **$62-$72.** 564 E Pancake Blvd 67901. 0.8 mi w of jct
US 54 and 83. Ext corridors. **Pets:** Small. $10 daily fee/pet. Designated
rooms, service with restrictions, supervision. SAVE 🛜 🛅 💻

LYONS

🔷🔷 Celebration Centre Inn & Suites 🅷
(620) 680-6022. **$68-$100.** 1108 E Hwy 56 67554. 2 mi e of jct SR 14
and US 56. Int corridors. **Pets:** $20 one-time fee/room. Designated
rooms, service with restrictions, crate. 🛜 🛅 💻

MANHATTAN

◈ 🔷🔷 BEST WESTERN Manhattan Inn 🅷
(785) 537-8300. **$95-$105.** 601 E Poyntz Ave 66502. SR 177, 0.5 mi e
on US 24 (Frontage Rd). Int corridors. **Pets:** Accepted.
SAVE ♿ 🏊 🛜 ✕ 🛅 💻

🔷🔷🔷 Candlewood Suites 🅷
(785) 320-7995. **Call for rates.** 210 Blue Earth Pl 66502. Just w of jct
SR 177 and 18 (Ft. Riley Blvd). Int corridors. **Pets:** Accepted.
🛜 ✕ 🛅 💻

🔷🔷🔷 Holiday Inn at the Campus 🅷
(785) 539-7531. **$99-$199.** 1641 Anderson Ave 66502. 1 mi n of SR 18
(Ft. Riley Blvd). Int corridors. **Pets:** Accepted.
🍴 🏊 🛜 ✕ 🛅 💻

◈ 🔷🔷🔷 Parkwood Inn & Suites 🅷
(785) 320-5440. **$90-$190.** 505 S 17th St 66502. 1.5 mi w of jct SR
177 and 18 (Ft. Riley Blvd), just n. Int corridors. **Pets:** $10 daily fee/
pet. Service with restrictions, crate. SAVE 🛜 ✕ 🛅 💻

MARYSVILLE

🔷🔷🔷 Heritage Inn Express 🅷
(785) 562-5588. **$56-$95.** 1155 Pony Express Hwy 66508. 2 mi e on
US 36 (Pony Express Hwy). Int corridors. **Pets:** Accepted.
🛜 🛅 💻

🔷🔷 Marysville Surf Motel Ⓜ
(785) 562-2354. **Call for rates.** 2105 Center St 66508. 1 mi e on US
36 (Pony Express Hwy). Ext/int corridors. **Pets:** Accepted.
🛜 🛅 💻

◈ 🔷🔷 Oak Tree Inn 🅷
(785) 562-1234. **$69-$79.** 1127 Pony Express Hwy 66508. 1.6 mi e on
US 36 (Pony Express Hwy). Ext/int corridors. **Pets:** Other species. Designated rooms, service with restrictions, supervision.
SAVE 🛜 ✕ 🛅 💻

MCPHERSON

◈ 🔷🔷 BEST WESTERN Holiday Manor 🅷 🐾
(620) 241-5343. **$75-$119.** 2211 E Kansas Ave 67460. I-135 exit 60,
just w. Ext/int corridors. **Pets:** Other species. $10 daily fee/pet. Service
with restrictions, supervision. SAVE 🍴 🏊 🛜 🛅 💻

MERRIAM

🔷🔷🔷 Drury Inn-Merriam/Shawnee Mission Parkway 🅷
(913) 236-9200. **$115-$169.** 9009 W Shawnee Mission Pkwy 66202.
I-35 exit 228B (Shawnee Mission Pkwy), just se. Int corridors.
Pets: $10 daily fee/room. Service with restrictions, supervision.
♿ 🏊 🛜 🛅 💻

MULVANE

🔷🔷🔷 Hampton Inn & Suites 🅷 🐾
(316) 524-3777. **$79-$229.** 785 Kansas Star Dr 67110. I-35 exit 33, just
w. Int corridors. **Pets:** Small, other species. Service with restrictions,
supervision. 🍴 ♿ 🛜 🛅 💻

NEWTON

◈ 🔷🔷🔷 Comfort Inn & Suites 🅷
(316) 804-4866. **$90-$160.** 1205 E 1st St 67114. I-135 exit 31, just w;
exit southbound, just w at 2nd roundabout. Int corridors.
Pets: Accepted. SAVE 🏊 🛜 ✕ 🛅 💻

OLATHE

◈ 🔷🔷🔷 BEST WESTERN PLUS Olathe Hotel &
Suites 🅷
(913) 440-9762. **$115-$179.** 1580 S Hamilton Cir 66061. I-35 exit 215
(151st St), just nw. Int corridors. **Pets:** Medium. $10 daily fee/pet. Des-
ignated rooms, service with restrictions, supervision.
SAVE 🏊 🛜 ✕ 🛅 💻

🔷🔷 Candlewood Suites Olathe 🅷
(913) 768-8888. **$80-$150.** 15490 S Rogers Rd 66062. I-35 exit 215
(151st St), just sw. Int corridors. **Pets:** Accepted. ♿ 🛜 🛅 💻

🔷🔷🔷 Days Inn Olathe Medical Center 🅷
(913) 390-9500. **$58-$87.** 20662 W 151st St 66061. I-35 exit 215
(151st St), 0.4 mi sw, follow signs. Int corridors. **Pets:** Accepted.
♿ 🏊 🛜 🛅 💻

🔷🔷🔷 Residence Inn by Marriott 🅷
(913) 829-6700. **$169-$186.** 12215 S Strang Line Rd 66062. I-35 exit
220 (119th St), just e to Strang Line Rd, then 0.8 mi s. Int corridors.
Pets: Accepted. ♿ 🏊 🛜 ✕ 🛅 💻

OTTAWA

◈ 🔷🔷 BEST WESTERN Ottawa Inn 🅷
(785) 242-2224. **$72-$100.** 212 E 23rd St 66067. I-35 exit 183 (US 59),
just w. Ext/int corridors. **Pets:** $18 daily fee/pet. Service with restric-
tions, supervision. SAVE ♿ 🏊 🛜 🛅 💻

OVERLAND PARK

🔷🔷 Candlewood Suites 🅷
(913) 469-5557. **Call for rates.** 11001 Oakmont St 66210. I-435 exit 82
(Quivira Rd), 0.5 mi s, 0.3 mi w on College Blvd, then just n. Int corridors. **Pets:** Accepted. ♿ 🛜 ✕ 🛅 💻

🔷🔷 Chase Suite Hotels-Overland Park 🅷
(913) 491-3333. **$99-$229.** 6300 W 110th St 66211. I-435 exit 79 (Metcalf Ave/US 169), 0.3 mi s on US 169, 0.5 mi e on College Blvd to
Lamar Ave, then just n. Ext corridors. **Pets:** Accepted.
🏊 🛜 ✕ 🛅 💻

🔷🔷 Days Inn Overland Park-Convention Center Ⓜ
(913) 341-0100. **$50-$55.** 6800 W 108th St 66211. I-435 exit 79 (Metcalf Ave/US 169), just ne. Ext corridors. **Pets:** Accepted.
♿ 🛜 ✕ 🛅 💻

▼▼▼▼ Drury Inn & Suites-Overland Park H

(913) 345-1500. **$95-$224.** 10963 Metcalf Ave 66210. I-435 exit 79 (Metcalf Ave/US 169), just se. Int corridors. **Pets:** $10 daily fee/room. Service with restrictions, supervision. 🅼 ➰ 🤜 ✕ 🗄 🖵

▼▼ Econo Lodge Inn & Suites H

(913) 262-9600. **$60-$120.** 7508 Shawnee Mission Pkwy 66202. I-35 exit 228B, 0.5 mi e. Ext corridors. **Pets:** Accepted.
➰ 🤜 ✕ 🗄 🖵

ⓐⓐⓐ ▼▼▼▼ Hyatt Place Kansas City/Overland Park/ Convention Center H

(913) 491-9002. **$79-$189.** 5001 W 110th St 66211. I-435 exit 77B (Nall Ave), just se. Int corridors. **Pets:** Accepted.
SAVE 🅼 ➰ 🤜 ✕ 🗄 🖵

ⓐⓐⓐ ▼▼▼▼ Hyatt Place Kansas City/Overland Park/Metcalf H

(913) 451-2553. **$69-$189.** 6801 W 112th St 66211. I-435 exit 79 (Metcalf Ave/US 169), 0.6 mi s. Int corridors. **Pets:** Accepted.
SAVE 🅼 ➰ 🤜 ✕ 🗄 🖵

▼▼ Pear Tree Inn by Drury-Overland Park H

(913) 451-0200. **$80-$149.** 10951 Metcalf Ave 66210. I-435 exit 79 (Metcalf Ave/US 169), just se. Int corridors. **Pets:** $10 daily fee/room. Service with restrictions, supervision. 🅼 ➰ 🤜 ✕ 🗄 🖵

▼▼▼▼ Residence Inn by Marriott H

(913) 491-4444. **$179-$209.** 12010 Blue Valley Pkwy 66213. I-435 exit 79 (Metcalf Ave/US 169), 1.3 mi s. Int corridors. **Pets:** Accepted.
🅼 ➰ 🤜 ✕ 🗄 🖵

ⓐⓐⓐ ▼▼▼▼ Sheraton Overland Park Hotel at the Convention Center H

(913) 234-2100. **$99-$279.** 6100 College Blvd 66211. I-435 exit 79 (Metcalf Ave/US 169), just s to College Blvd, then 0.6 mi e. Int corridors. **Pets:** Small, dogs only. $40 one-time fee/pet. Service with restrictions, supervision. SAVE ECO 🍽 🅼 ➰ 🤜 ✕ 🖵

PARK CITY

ⓐⓐⓐ ▼▼▼ BEST WESTERN Wichita North Hotel & Suites H

(316) 832-9387. **$89-$108.** 915 E 53rd St N 67219. I-135 exit 13, just w. Ext/int corridors. **Pets:** Accepted.
SAVE 🍽 ➰ 🤜 🤜 🗄 🖵

ⓐⓐⓐ ▼▼▼ Quality Inn & Suites H

(316) 927-3900. **$65-$95.** 792 Beaumont St 67219. I-135 exit 14, just sw. Int corridors. **Pets:** Accepted. SAVE ➰ 🤜 🗄 🖵

▼▼ Super 8-Wichita North/Park City M

(316) 744-2071. **$60-$85.** 6075 N Air Cap Dr 67219. I-135 exit 14, just sw. Int corridors. **Pets:** Accepted. 🤜 🗄 🖵

PARSONS

ⓐⓐⓐ ▼▼▼ BEST WESTERN Parsons Inn H

(620) 423-0303. **$95-$105.** 101 E Main St 67357. 1.5 mi e; center. Int corridors. **Pets:** Small. $20 daily fee/pet. Service with restrictions, supervision. SAVE ➰ 🤜 ✕ 🗄 🖵

ⓐⓐⓐ ▼▼▼ Sleep Inn & Suites H

(620) 421-6126. **$80-$110.** 1807 Harding Dr 67357. Just sw of jct US 59 and 400. Int corridors. **Pets:** Accepted.
SAVE 🅼 ➰ 🤜 ✕ 🗄 🖵

PHILLIPSBURG

▼▼ Cottonwood Inn M

(785) 543-2125. **$80-$199, 7 day notice.** 1200 State St 67661. 1 mi e on US 36/183. Ext corridors. **Pets:** Other species. Service with restrictions, supervision. ➰ 🤜 ✕ 🗄

PITTSBURG

ⓐⓐⓐ ▼▼▼ Lamplighter Inn & Suites H

(620) 231-8700. **$69-$109.** 4020 Parkview Dr 66762. 2.3 mi n on US 69 from jct SR 126. Ext/int corridors. **Pets:** Accepted.
SAVE 🅼 ➰ 🤜 ✕ 🗄 🖵

PRATT

ⓐⓐⓐ ▼▼▼▼ BEST WESTERN PLUS Pratt H

(620) 508-6466. **$110-$120.** 112 NE SR Hwy 61 67124. Just n of jct US 54 and SR 61. Int corridors. **Pets:** Accepted.
SAVE 🅼 🤜 ✕ 🗄 🖵

ⓐⓐⓐ ▼▼▼▼ Comfort Suites H

(620) 672-9999. **$110-$130.** 704 Allison Ln 67124. Just n of jct US 54 and SR 61. Int corridors. **Pets:** Accepted.
SAVE 🅼 ➰ 🤜 ✕ 🗄 🖵

▼▼ Evergreen Inn & RV Park M

(620) 672-6431. **$59-$100.** 20001 W US Hwy 54 67124. 3 mi w. Ext corridors. **Pets:** Accepted. ➰ 🤜 🗄

▼▼▼▼ Holiday Inn Express H

(620) 508-6350. **Call for rates.** 1903 Pauline Pl 67124. Jct US 54 and SR 61, just n. Int corridors. **Pets:** Accepted.
🅼 ➰ 🤜 ✕ 🗄 🖵

SALINA

ⓐⓐⓐ ▼▼▼ BEST WESTERN PLUS Midwest Inn & Suites H

(785) 493-9800. **Call for rates.** 745 W Schilling Rd 67401. I-135 exit 89 (Schilling Rd), just w. Int corridors. **Pets:** $20 daily fee/room. Designated rooms, service with restrictions, crate.
SAVE ➰ 🤜 ✕ 🗄 🖵

▼▼ Candlewood Suites H

(785) 823-6939. **Call for rates.** 2650 Planet Ave 67401. I-135 exit 89 (Schilling Rd), just e to S 9th St, 0.5 mi n to Belmont Blvd, then just w. Int corridors. **Pets:** Accepted. 🅼 🤜 ✕ 🗄 🖵

▼▼▼▼ La Quinta Inn & Suites H

(785) 827-9000. **$89-$249.** 201 E Diamond Dr 67401. I-70 exit 252, just ne. Int corridors. **Pets:** Large, other species. Service with restrictions.
🅼 ➰ 🤜 ✕ 🗄 🖵

ⓐⓐⓐ ▼▼▼ Super 8 I-70 H

(785) 823-8808. **$72-$78.** 120 E Diamond Dr 67401. I-70 exit 252, just ne. Int corridors. **Pets:** Medium. $15 one-time fee/room. Service with restrictions, crate. SAVE 🅼 ➰ 🤜 ✕ 🗄 🖵

SHARON SPRINGS

▼▼ Oak Tree Inn H

(785) 852-4664. **Call for rates.** 801 N Hwy 27 67758. Jct US 40 and SR 27. Ext/int corridors. **Pets:** Accepted.
🍽 🅼 🤜 ✕ 🗄 🖵

TOPEKA

ⓐⓐⓐ ▼▼▼ BEST WESTERN Topeka Inn & Suites H

(785) 228-2223. **Call for rates.** 700 SW Fairlawn Rd 66606. I-70 exit 357A, just ne. Int corridors. **Pets:** $25 one-time fee/pet, $10 daily fee/ pet. Designated rooms, service with restrictions, supervision.
SAVE ➰ 🤜 ✕ 🗄 🖵

ⓐⓐⓐ ▼▼▼▼ ClubHouse Inn & Suites H

(785) 273-8888. **$79-$159.** 924 SW Henderson Rd 66615. I-70 exit 356 (Wanamaker Rd), just sw. Int corridors. **Pets:** Accepted.
SAVE 🅼 ➰ 🤜 ✕ 🗄 🖵

▼▼▼▼ Comfort Suites H

(785) 246-6777. **$95-$139.** 6213 SW 10th Ave 66615. I-70 exit 356 (Wanamaker Rd), just s. Int corridors. **Pets:** $40 one-time fee/room. Service with restrictions, crate. 🅼 🤜 ✕ 🗄 🖵

AAA ◆◆◆◆ **Hyatt Place Topeka** H
(785) 273-0066. **$69-$189.** 6021 SW 6th Ave 66615. I-70 exit 356 (Wanamaker Rd), just n. Int corridors. **Pets:** Accepted.
SAVE &M 🛏 🛜 ✕ 🛗 📺

◆◆ **Sleep Inn & Suites** H 🐾
(785) 228-2500. **$90-$100.** 1024 SW Wanamaker Rd 66604. I-70 exit 356 (Wanamaker Rd), just s. Int corridors. **Pets:** Medium, other species. $10 daily fee/pet. Service with restrictions, supervision.
&M 🛏 🛜 🛗 📺

AAA ◆◆◆ **Super 8 at Forbes Landing** H
(785) 862-2222. **$73-$90.** 5922 SW Topeka Blvd 66619. I-470 exit 6, 2.2 mi s. Int corridors. **Pets:** $20 one-time fee/room. Crate.
SAVE &M 🛏 🛜 🛗 📺

ULYSSES
◆◆ **Single Tree Inn** H
(620) 356-1500. **$73-$77.** 2033 W Oklahoma Ave 67880. 1.5 mi w on US 160. Int corridors. **Pets:** Accepted. 🛜 ✕ 🛗 📺

WAKEENEY
AAA ◆◆◆ **BEST WESTERN PLUS Wakeeney Inn & Suites** H 🐾
(785) 743-2700. **$81-$90.** 525 S 1st St 67672. I-70 exit 127, just n. Int corridors. **Pets:** Other species. $10 daily fee/pet. Designated rooms, service with restrictions, supervision.
SAVE &M 🛏 🛜 ✕ 🛗 📺

◆◆ **Super 8** H
(785) 743-6442. **$68-$78.** 709 S 13th St 67672. I-70 exit 128, just n. Int corridors. **Pets:** Small, other species. $10 one-time fee/pet. Designated rooms, service with restrictions, supervision. SAVE 🛜 🛗 📺

WICHITA
AAA ◆◆◆ ◆◆◆ **Ambassador Hotel Wichita, Autograph Collection** H
(316) 239-7100. **$189-$1500.** 104 S Broadway 67202. Jct Douglass Ave; downtown. Int corridors. **Pets:** Small, dogs only. $50 one-time fee/pet. Designated rooms, service with restrictions, supervision.
SAVE 🍴 &M 🛜 ✕ 🛗 📺

AAA ◆◆ ◆◆ **BEST WESTERN Airport Inn & Conference Center** H
(316) 942-5600. **$89-$125.** 6815 W Kellogg St 67209. I-235 exit 7, 0.6 mi w on US 54 (S Frontage Rd). Int corridors. **Pets:** Small. Service with restrictions, supervision. SAVE 🍴 🛏 🖾 🛜 ✕ 🛗 📺

AAA ◆◆ ◆◆ **BEST WESTERN Governors Inn & Suites** H
(316) 522-0775. **$80-$99.** 4742 S Emporia St 67216. I-135 exit 1A/B (47th St S), just sw. Int corridors. **Pets:** Accepted.
SAVE 🛏 🛜 🛗 📺

◆◆◆ **Candlewood Suites** H
(316) 942-0400. **$69-$129.** 570 S Julia St 67209. I-235 exit 7, 0.3 mi w to Dugan St, just n to Taft St, just e, then just s. Int corridors. **Pets:** Accepted. 🛜 🛗 📺

◆◆ **Candlewood Suites-Wichita Northeast** H
(316) 634-6070. **$72-$79, 14 day notice.** 3141 N Webb Rd 67226. SR 96 exit Webb Rd, just nw. Int corridors. **Pets:** Accepted.
&M 🛜 🛗 📺

◆◆ **Comfort Inn by Choice Hotels** H
(316) 686-2844. **$90-$130.** 9525 E Corporate Hills Dr 67207. I-35 exit 50, just ne. Int corridors. **Pets:** Medium. $15 one-time fee/room. Designated rooms, service with restrictions, crate. 🛏 🛜 ✕ 🛗 📺

AAA ◆◆ ◆◆ **Country Inn & Suites By Carlson Wichita Northeast** H
(316) 634-3900. **$99-$159.** 7824 E 32nd St N 67226. SR 96 E exit Rock Rd, just sw. Int corridors. **Pets:** Accepted.
SAVE 🛏 🛜 🛗 📺

◆◆◆ **Drury Plaza Hotel Broadview-Wichita** H
(316) 262-5000. **$110-$199.** 400 W Douglas Ave 67202. Jct Waco St; downtown. Int corridors. **Pets:** $10 daily fee/room. Service with restrictions, supervision. 🍴 🛏 🛜 ✕ 🛗 📺

◆◆◆ **Hampton Inn by Hilton** H
(316) 686-3576. **$99-$149.** 9449 E Corporate Hills Dr 67207. I-35 exit 50, just ne. Int corridors. **Pets:** Accepted. &M 🛏 🛜 🛗 📺

◆◆◆ **Homewood Suites by Hilton at The Waterfront** H 🐾
(316) 260-8844. **$139-$209.** 1550 N Waterfront Pkwy 67206. Just e of jct 13th St and Webb Rd, then just n. Int corridors. **Pets:** Large. $100 deposit/room, $50 one-time fee/room, $50 daily fee/room. Designated rooms, service with restrictions, supervision.
&M 🛏 🛜 ✕ 🛗 📺

◆◆ **La Quinta Inn & Suites Wichita Airport** H
(316) 943-2181. **$69-$219.** 5500 W Kellogg Dr 67209. I-235 exit 7, just nw. Int corridors. **Pets:** Large, other species. Service with restrictions.
🍴 🛏 🛜 ✕ 🛗 📺

◆◆◆ **Residence Inn by Marriott at Plazzio** H
(316) 682-7300. **$179-$209.** 1212 N Greenwich Rd 67206. SR 96 exit 13th St, 0.5 mi sw. Int corridors. **Pets:** Medium, other species. $75 one-time fee/room. Service with restrictions. &M 🛏 🛜 ✕ 🛗 📺

◆◆◆ **Staybridge Suites** H
(316) 927-3888. **$99-$309.** 2250 N Greenwich Rd 67226. Just e of jct 21st St and Greenwich Rd. Int corridors. **Pets:** Medium. $75 one-time fee/room. Service with restrictions, crate. &M 🛏 🛜 🛗 📺

◆◆ **TownePlace Suites by Marriott** H
(316) 631-3773. **$124-$137.** 9444 E 29th St N 67226. SR 96 exit Webb Rd, just sw. Int corridors. **Pets:** Accepted. &M 🛜 ✕ 🛗 📺

◆◆ **Wesley Inn** H
(316) 858-3343. **$91.** 3343 E Central Ave 67208. Just e of jct Hillside St. Int corridors. **Pets:** Accepted. 🛜 ✕ 🛗 📺

WINFIELD
◆◆ **Comfort Inn** H
(620) 221-7529. **$110-$140.** 3800 S Pike Rd 67156. On US 77, 1 mi s. Ext/int corridors. **Pets:** Small. $25 daily fee/pet. Designated rooms, service with restrictions, crate. 🛏 🛜 🛗 📺

KENTUCKY

ASHLAND
AAA ◆◆◆◆ **BEST WESTERN River Cities** H
(606) 326-0357. **$114-$124.** 31 Russell Plaza Dr 41101. I-64 exit 185, 6 mi nw on US 60, then 3 mi n on US 23. Int corridors. **Pets:** Accepted.
SAVE &M 🛏 🛜 🛗 📺

◆◆ **Quality Inn** H
(606) 325-8989. **$71-$77.** 4708 Winchester Ave 41101. I-64 exit 191, 4.8 mi n on US 23. Ext corridors. **Pets:** Accepted.
&M 🛏 🛜 🛗 📺

BARDSTOWN

General Nelson Inn M

(502) 348-3977. **Call for rates.** 411 W Stephen Foster Ave 40004. 0.5 mi w on US 62. Ext corridors. **Pets:** Medium. $15 one-time fee/room. Service with restrictions, crate.

Hampton Inn H

(502) 349-0100. **$104-$199.** 985 Chambers Blvd 40004. Just s of SR 245. Int corridors. **Pets:** Accepted.

BENTON

Comfort Inn & Suites H

(270) 527-5300. **$80-$120.** 173 Carroll Rd 42025. Purchase Pkwy (SR 9003) exit 47, just e. Int corridors. **Pets:** Other species. $15 daily fee/pet. Supervision.

BEREA

Boone Tavern Hotel & Restaurant of Berea College H

(859) 985-3700. **$99-$159.** 100 Main St 40404. I-75 exit 76, 1.5 mi ne on SR 21. Int corridors. **Pets:** Medium. $50 one-time fee/room. Service with restrictions, crate.

Comfort Inn & Suites H

(859) 985-5500. **$89-$129.** 219 Paint Lick Rd 40403. I-75 exit 76, just w. Int corridors. **Pets:** Accepted.

Red Roof Inn & Suites Berea H

(859) 228-0340. **$75-$109.** 330 Walnut Creek Dr 40403. I-75 exit 77, just w. Int corridors. **Pets:** Large, other species. Service with restrictions, supervision.

BOWLING GREEN *(Restaurants p. 631)*

Candlewood Suites H

(270) 843-5505. **$99-$189, 3 day notice.** 540 Wall St 42103. I-65 exit 22 (Scottsville Rd), just n. Int corridors. **Pets:** Accepted.

Country Inn & Suites By Carlson H

(270) 781-7200. **$89-$199.** 535 Wall St 42104. I-65 exit 22 (Scottsville Rd), just w. Int corridors. **Pets:** Accepted.

Drury Inn-Bowling Green H

(270) 842-7100. **$100-$159.** 3250 Scottsville Rd 42104. I-65 exit 22 (Scottsville Rd), just w. Int corridors. **Pets:** $10 daily fee/room. Service with restrictions, supervision.

Econo Lodge Bowling Green M

(270) 781-3460. **Call for rates.** 3160 Scottsville Rd 42104. I-65 exit 22 (Scottsville Rd), just w. Ext corridors. **Pets:** Accepted.

Hampton Inn H

(270) 842-4100. **$109-$149.** 233 Three Springs Rd 42104. I-65 exit 22 (Scottsville Rd), 0.3 mi w. Int corridors. **Pets:** Accepted.

Holiday Inn Express H

(270) 843-3200. **Call for rates.** 165 Three Springs Rd 42104. I-65 exit 22 (Scottsville Rd), 0.3 mi w. Int corridors. **Pets:** Accepted.

Holiday Inn University Plaza H

(270) 745-0088. **Call for rates.** 1021 Wilkinson Trace 42103. I-65 exit 22 (Scottsville Rd), 2.5 mi w, then just n. Int corridors. **Pets:** Accepted.

La Quinta Inn & Suites H

(270) 783-0083. **$89-$269.** 1953 Mel Browning St 42104. I-65 exit 22 (Scottsville Rd), just e. Int corridors. **Pets:** Large, other species. Service with restrictions.

Ramada Bowling Green H

(270) 781-3000. **$49-$67.** 4767 Scottsville Rd 42104. I-65 exit 22 (Scottsville Rd), 0.3 mi e. Int corridors. **Pets:** Medium. $10 daily fee/pet. Designated rooms, service with restrictions, supervision.

Red Roof Inn Bowling Green M

(270) 781-6550. **$50-$150.** 3140 Scottsville Rd 42104. I-65 exit 22 (Scottsville Rd), 0.3 mi w. Ext corridors. **Pets:** Large, other species. Service with restrictions, supervision.

Staybridge Suites Bowling Green H

(270) 904-0480. **Call for rates.** 680 Campbell Ln 42101. I-65 exit 20B (Natcher Pkwy), 3.7 mi w to exit 6 (SR 31 W), then 1.7 mi n. Int corridors. **Pets:** Other species. $13 daily fee/room. Service with restrictions, crate.

TownePlace Suites by Marriott H

(270) 782-4714. **$97-$160.** 1818 Cave Mill Rd 42104. I-65 exit 22, w to traffic light 9, then just s. Int corridors. **Pets:** Accepted.

CALVERT CITY

Super 8 Calvert City/KY Lake Area H

(270) 395-5566. **$54-$74.** 86 Campbell Dr 42029. I-24/69 exit 27, just e. Int corridors. **Pets:** Small, dogs only. $10 one-time fee/pet. Service with restrictions.

CARROLLTON

BEST WESTERN Executive Inn H

(502) 732-7027. **$84-$99.** 10 Slumber Ln 41008. I-71 exit 44, just nw. Int corridors. **Pets:** Accepted.

Holiday Inn Express H

(502) 732-6770. **Call for rates.** 147 Hospitality Way 41008. I-71 exit 44, just nw. Int corridors. **Pets:** Accepted.

Super 8 Carrollton H

(502) 732-0252. **$60-$199.** 130 Slumber Ln 41008. I-71 exit 44, just nw. Int corridors. **Pets:** Accepted.

CATLETTSBURG

Ramada Limited Hotel H

(606) 739-5700. **$89-$110.** 6000 Crider Dr 41129. I-64 exit 191, 0.5 mi n on US 23. Int corridors. **Pets:** Accepted.

CAVE CITY *(Restaurants p. 631)*

Super 8 M

(270) 773-2500. **$60-$80.** 799 Mammoth Cave St 42127. I-65 exit 53, just ne. Ext corridors. **Pets:** Small, dogs only. $15 daily fee/pet. Designated rooms, service with restrictions, supervision.

CENTRAL CITY

Super 8 H

(270) 757-1700. **$74-$94.** 635 S 2nd St 42330. Western Kentucky Pkwy exit 58, just n. Int corridors. **Pets:** Small, dogs only. $20 daily fee/pet. Designated rooms, service with restrictions, supervision.

COLUMBIA

BEST WESTERN Columbia M

(270) 384-9744. **$90-$140.** 710 Bomar Heights 42728. Cumberland Pkwy exit 49, just n on SR 55, then just w. Ext corridors. **Pets:** Accepted.

CORBIN

BEST WESTERN Corbin Inn M

(606) 528-2100. **$79-$169.** 2630 Cumberland Falls Hwy 40701. I-75 exit 25, just w. Ext corridors. **Pets:** $15 daily fee/pet. Service with restrictions, supervision.

COVINGTON

Embassy Suites Cincinnati RiverCenter H

(859) 261-8400. **$179-$259.** 10 E RiverCenter Blvd 41011. I-71/75 exit 192, 0.8 mi e on 5th St, then 0.3 mi n on Madison Ave. Int corridors. **Pets:** Very small, dogs only. $50 one-time fee/room.

DANVILLE

Comfort Suites H

(859) 936-9300. **Call for rates.** 864 Ben Ali Dr 40422. Jct US 127 Bypass, just w on US 150 (Perryville Rd). Int corridors. **Pets:** Accepted.

Quality Inn H ✿

(859) 236-8600. **$94-$104.** 96 Daniel Dr 40422. Jct US 127, just e on US 150. Int corridors. **Pets:** Medium. $10 daily fee/pet. Designated rooms, service with restrictions, supervision.

DRY RIDGE

Comfort Inn H

(859) 824-7121. **$79-$99.** 1050 Fashion Ridge Rd 41035. I-75 exit 159, just nw. Int corridors. **Pets:** Medium. $15 daily fee/pet. Designated rooms, service with restrictions, supervision.

EDDYVILLE

Eddy Creek Marina Resort M

(270) 388-2271. **Call for rates.** 7612 SR 93 S 42038. I-24 exit 45, just w to SR 93, then 4 mi s. Ext corridors. **Pets:** Accepted.

Holiday Hills Resort Townhouses CO

(270) 388-7236. **$80-$210, 30 day notice.** 1 Holiday Hills Rd 42038. I-24 exit 45, just w to SR 93, then 2 mi s. Ext corridors. **Pets:** $15 daily fee/pet. Designated rooms, no service, crate.

ELIZABETHTOWN

Holiday Inn Express H

(270) 769-1334. **Call for rates.** 107 Buffalo Creek Dr 42701. I-65 exit 94, just w. Int corridors. **Pets:** Small. $50 daily fee/pet. Service with restrictions, crate.

La Quinta Inn & Suites Elizabethtown H

(270) 765-4747. **$85-$249.** 210 Commerce Dr 42701. I-65 exit 94, just nw. Int corridors. **Pets:** Large, other species. Service with restrictions.

Quality Inn & Suites H

(270) 765-4166. **$55-$139.** 2009 N Mulberry St 42701. I-65 exit 94, just sw. Int corridors. **Pets:** Large, other species. $10 one-time fee/room. Supervision.

Wingfield Inn & Suites H

(270) 769-3030. **Call for rates.** 1043 Executive Dr 42701. I-65 exit 94, just nw. Int corridors. **Pets:** Accepted.

ERLANGER

Residence Inn by Marriott, Cincinnati Airport H

(859) 282-7400. **$111-$183.** 2811 Circleport Dr 41018. I-275 exit 2, just s. Int corridors. **Pets:** Accepted.

FLORENCE

Ashley Quarters Hotel H

(859) 525-9997. **$100-$175.** 4880 Houston Rd 41042. I-71/75 exit 182, 0.6 mi w on Turfway and Houston rds. Int corridors. **Pets:** Accepted.

BEST WESTERN Inn Florence H

(859) 525-0090. **Call for rates.** 7821 Commerce Rd 41042. I-71/75 exit 181, just ne. Int corridors. **Pets:** Accepted.

Comfort Inn Greater Cincinnati Airport on Turfway Rd H

(859) 647-2700. **Call for rates.** 7454 Turfway Rd 41042. I-71/75 exit 182, 0.8 mi sw. Int corridors. **Pets:** $10 daily fee/room. Service with restrictions, supervision.

Hilton Cincinnati Airport H

(859) 371-4400. **$90-$179.** 7373 Turfway Rd 41042. I-71/75 exit 182, 0.4 mi sw. Int corridors. **Pets:** Large, dogs only. $75 one-time fee/room. Service with restrictions, crate.

Hyatt Place Cincinnati Airport/Florence H

(859) 647-1170. **$79-$219.** 300 Meijer Dr 41042. I-71/75 exit 182, 0.4 mi sw. Int corridors. **Pets:** Accepted.

La Quinta Inn & Suites Cincinnati Airport Florence H

(859) 282-8212. **$99-$299.** 350 Meijer Dr 41042. I-71/75 exit 182, 0.4 mi sw. Int corridors. **Pets:** Large, other species. Service with restrictions.

Microtel Inn & Suites by Wyndham Florence/ Cincinnati Airport H

(859) 746-8100. **$70-$160.** 7490 Woodspoint Dr 41042. I-71/75 exit 181, just w. Int corridors. **Pets:** Very small, dogs only. $20 daily fee/pet. Service with restrictions, supervision.

FRANKFORT

BEST WESTERN Parkside Inn H

(502) 695-6111. **$89-$139.** 80 Chenault Rd 40601. I-64 exit 58, just e. Ext/int corridors. **Pets:** Large, other species. $20 daily fee/pet. Designated rooms, service with restrictions, crate.

Capital Plaza Hotel H

(502) 227-5100. **$77-$94.** 405 Wilkinson Blvd 40601. I-64 exit 53B, 4 mi n on US 127. Int corridors. **Pets:** Medium, other species. $25 one-time fee/pet. Designated rooms, service with restrictions, crate.

FRANKLIN

Holiday Inn Express & Suites-Franklin H

(270) 586-7626. **Call for rates.** 85 Neha Dr 42134. I-65 exit 2, just nw. Int corridors. **Pets:** Accepted.

GEORGETOWN

BEST WESTERN PLUS Georgetown Corporate Center Hotel H

(502) 868-0055. **$75-$172.** 132 Darby Dr 40324. I-75 exit 126, just nw. Int corridors. **Pets:** Accepted.

Comfort Suites H

(502) 868-9500. **$81-$105.** 121 Darby Dr 40324. I-75 exit 126, just nw. Int corridors. **Pets:** Medium. $20 daily fee/pet. Service with restrictions, supervision.

Country Inn & Suites By Carlson H

(502) 868-6800. **Call for rates.** 131 Darby Dr 40324. I-75 exit 126, just nw. Int corridors. **Pets:** Accepted.

Fairfield Inn & Suites by Marriott Lexington Georgetown/College Inn H

(502) 868-9955. **$76-$148.** 200 Tiger Way 40324. I-75 exit 126, just nw. Int corridors. **Pets:** Accepted.

Holiday Inn Express Lexington North-Georgetown H

(502) 570-0220. **Call for rates.** 140 Osbourne Way 40324. I-75 exit 126, 0.3 mi e on Cherry Blossom Way, then just n. Int corridors. **Pets:** Accepted.

GLASGOW

 Comfort Inn **M**

(270) 651-9099. **Call for rates.** 210 Cavalry Dr 42141. Cumberland Pkwy exit 11, just n, just w. Ext corridors. **Pets:** Small. $10 daily fee/pet. Service with restrictions, crate.

GRAND RIVERS *(Restaurants p. 631)*

Green Turtle Bay Resort **CO**

(270) 362-8364. **$125-$500, 7 day notice.** 263 Green Turtle Bay Dr 42045. I-24 exit 31 (SR 453), 3 mi s to W Commerce Ave, just e to JH O'Bryan Ave, just n to Barkley Dr, then 0.7 mi w. Ext corridors. **Pets:** $45 one-time fee/pet. Designated rooms, no service, crate.

Patti's Inn and Suites **H**

(270) 928-2740. **$66-$85.** 1017 Dover Rd 42045. I-24 exit 31 (SR 453), just n. Int corridors. **Pets:** Small, dogs only. $15 one-time fee/pet. Designated rooms, service with restrictions, supervision.

GRAYSON

Quality Inn-Grayson, KY **M**

(606) 474-7854. **$59-$99.** 205 SR 1947 41143. I-64 exit 172, just n. Ext corridors. **Pets:** Accepted.

Super 8 **H**

(606) 474-8811. **$50-$70.** 125 Super 8 Ln 41143. I-64 exit 172, just s. Int corridors. **Pets:** Small. $10 daily fee/pet. Designated rooms, service with restrictions, supervision.

HARLAN

Comfort Inn **H**

(606) 573-3385. **Call for rates.** 2608 S Hwy 421 40831. On US 421, 2.8 mi s. Int corridors. **Pets:** Accepted.

HARRODSBURG

Baymont Inn & Suites Harrodsburg **H**

(859) 734-2400. **$65-$149, 7 day notice.** 105 Commercial Dr 40330. Jct US 68, 1 mi n on US 127, just e. Int corridors. **Pets:** Small. $20 one-time fee/pet. Service with restrictions, supervision.

Shaker Village of Pleasant Hill **CI**

(859) 734-5411. **Call for rates.** 3501 Lexington Rd 40330. On US 68, 7 mi ne; jct SR 33. Ext/int corridors. **Pets:** Accepted.

HEBRON

DoubleTree by Hilton Hotel Cincinnati Airport **H**

(859) 371-6166. **$105-$149.** 2826 Terminal Dr 41048. I-275 exit 4B, 1.2 mi w. Int corridors. **Pets:** Medium. Service with restrictions, crate.

HENDERSON

Sleep Inn **H**

(270) 830-6500. **$75-$90.** 2224 US Hwy 41 N 42420. On US 41, 1.4 mi n. Int corridors. **Pets:** Small, dogs only. $10 daily fee/pet. Designated rooms, service with restrictions, supervision.

HOPKINSVILLE

BEST WESTERN Hopkinsville **H**

(270) 886-9000. **Call for rates.** 4101 Ft Campbell Blvd 42240. Pennyrile Pkwy exit 7, just s. Int corridors. **Pets:** Accepted.

Holiday Inn **H**

(270) 886-4413. **$99-$159.** 2910 Ft Campbell Blvd 42240. Pennyrile Pkwy exit 7, 0.6 mi n on US 41A. Int corridors. **Pets:** Other species. $25 one-time fee/room, $13 daily fee/room. Service with restrictions.

HURSTBOURNE

Drury Inn & Suites-Louisville **H**

(502) 326-4170. **$100-$189.** 9501 Blairwood Rd 40222. I-64 exit 15, just n. Int corridors. **Pets:** $10 daily fee/room. Service with restrictions, supervision.

Red Roof Inn Louisville East - Hurstbourne **M**

(502) 426-7621. **$44-$250.** 9330 Blairwood Rd 40222. I-64 exit 15, 0.3 mi nw of Hurstbourne Pkwy. Ext corridors. **Pets:** Large, other species. Service with restrictions, supervision.

JEFFERSONTOWN

BEST WESTERN Louisville East **H**

(502) 499-0000. **$59-$199, 3 day notice.** 9802 Bunsen Way 40299. I-64 exit 15, 0.4 mi s, then 0.5 mi e. Int corridors. **Pets:** Small. $10 daily fee/pet. Designated rooms, service with restrictions, supervision.

Hyatt Place Louisville-East **H**

(502) 426-0119. **$79-$219.** 701 S Hurstbourne Pkwy 40222. I-64 exit 15, 1 mi n. Int corridors. **Pets:** Accepted.

La Quinta Inn & Suites Louisville **H**

(502) 267-8889. **$80-$425.** 1501 Alliant Ave 40299. I-64 exit 17, just s. Int corridors. **Pets:** Large, other species. Service with restrictions.

Microtel Inn by Wyndham Louisville East **H**

(502) 266-6590. **$53-$200.** 1221 Kentucky Mills Dr 40299. I-64 exit 17, just s. Int corridors. **Pets:** Accepted.

KUTTAWA

Days Inn **M**

(270) 388-4060. **$65-$90.** 139 Days Inn Dr 42055. I-24 exit 40 (US 62), just s. Ext corridors. **Pets:** Accepted.

Relax Inn **M** ❖

(270) 388-2285. **$55-$90, 7 day notice.** 224 New Circle Dr 42055. I-24 exit 40 (US 62), just e. Ext corridors. **Pets:** Large, other species. $10 daily fee/pet. Designated rooms, service with restrictions, crate.

LA GRANGE

Comfort Inn & Suites La Grange **H**

(502) 222-5678. **Call for rates.** 1001 Paige Pl 40031. I-71 exit 22, just se. Int corridors. **Pets:** Other species. $25 daily fee/pet. Designated rooms, service with restrictions, supervision.

LEBANON

Hampton Inn Lebanon **H**

(270) 699-4000. **$99-$120.** 1125 Loretto Rd 40033. Jct SR 49/52 (Loretto Rd) and 2154 (Veterans Memorial Hwy). Int corridors. **Pets:** Medium. $45 one-time fee/room. Service with restrictions, crate.

LEITCHFIELD

Hatfield Inn **H**

(270) 259-0464. **$87-$135.** 769 White St 42754. Western Kentucky Pkwy exit 107, just nw. Int corridors. **Pets:** Medium. $20 daily fee/pet. Service with restrictions, crate.

LEXINGTON

Candlewood Suites **H**

(859) 967-1940. **$129.** 603 Adcolor Dr 40511. Jct SR 4 (New Circle Rd) exit 9A, and Newtown Pike, just s. Int corridors. **Pets:** Large. $25 daily fee/pet. Service with restrictions, supervision.

▼▼ Clarion Hotel Lexington Conference Center 🅷 ❀

(859) 263-5241. **$100-$149.** 5532 Athens-Boonesboro Rd 40509. I-75 exit 104, just e. Int corridors. **Pets:** Medium, other species. $20 daily fee/pet. Service with restrictions, crate. 🐾 🛜 ⛌ 🛏 🖥

▼▼ Comfort Suites by Choice Hotels 🅷 ❀

(859) 296-4446. **$89-$189.** 3060 Fieldstone Way 40513. Jct SR 4 (New Circle Rd) and US 68 (Harrodsburg Rd), just sw. Int corridors. **Pets:** Large, other species. $40 one-time fee/pet. Service with restrictions, supervision. 🅂🄼 🐾 🛜 ⛌ 🛏 🖥

▼▼ Days Inn-South 🄼

(859) 263-3100. **$55-$64.** 5575 Athens-Boonesboro Rd 40509. I-75 exit 104, just e. Ext corridors. **Pets:** Accepted. 🛜 🛏 🖥

▼▼ DoubleTree Suites by Hilton Hotel Lexington 🅷

(859) 268-0060. **Call for rates.** 2601 Richmond Rd 40509. SR 4 (New Circle Rd) exit 15, just s; in French Quarter Square. Int corridors. **Pets:** Accepted. 🍽 🅂🄼 🐾 🛜 ⛌ 🛏 🖥

⊛ ▼▼ Fairfield Inn & Suites by Marriott-Lexington North 🅷

(859) 977-5870. **$87-$143.** 2100 Hackney Pl 40511. I-75/64 exit 115, just n, then 0.3 mi e on Stanton Way. Int corridors. **Pets:** $75 one-time fee/room. Service with restrictions. 🅂🄰🅅🄴 🅂🄼 🐾 🛜 ⛌ 🛏 🖥

⊛ ▼▼ Four Points by Sheraton Hotel 🅷

(859) 259-1311. **$96-$139.** 1938 Stanton Way 40511. I-75/64 exit 115, just n on SR 922, then just e. Int corridors. **Pets:** Accepted. 🅂🄰🅅🄴 🍽 🅂🄼 🐾 🛜 ⛌ 🛏 🖥

⊛ ▼▼ Hampton Inn I-75 🅷

(859) 299-2613. **$99-$169.** 2251 Elkhorn Rd 40505. I-75 exit 110, just nw, just off US 60. Int corridors. **Pets:** Medium. Designated rooms, service with restrictions, supervision. 🅂🄰🅅🄴 🅂🄼 🐾 🛜 🛏 🖥

▼▼ Hilton Suites of Lexington Green 🅷

(859) 271-4000. **$129-$279.** 245 Lexington Green Cir 40503. SR 4 (New Circle Rd) exit 19, just s on US 27 (Nicholasville Rd), then just w. Int corridors. **Pets:** Accepted. 🍽 🅂🄼 🐾 🛰 ⛌ 🛏 🖥

▼▼ Holiday Inn Express Hotel & Suites-Lexington Downtown at the University 🅷

(859) 389-6800. **Call for rates.** 1000 Export St 40504. I-75/64 exit 113, 4.5 mi s, then just e on Virginia Ave. Int corridors. **Pets:** Accepted. 🅂🄼 🐾 🛜 ⛌ 🛏 🖥

⊛ ▼▼ Hyatt Place Lexington 🅷

(859) 296-0091. **$94-$209.** 2001 Bryant Rd 40509. I-75 exit 108, 0.3 mi w on Man O' War Blvd, just s on Pleasant Ridge Dr, 0.3 mi e on Justice Dr, then just s. Int corridors. **Pets:** Accepted. 🅂🄰🅅🄴 🍽 🅂🄼 🐾 🛜 ⛌ 🛏 🖥

▼▼ La Quinta Inn 🅷

(859) 231-7551. **$69-$235.** 1920 Stanton 40511. I-75/64 exit 115, just ne off SR 922. Int corridors. **Pets:** Large, other species. Service with restrictions. 🐾 🛜 🛏 🖥

▼▼ La Quinta Inn & Suites Lexington South/Hamburg 🅷

(859) 543-1877. **$79-$214.** 100 Canebrake Dr 40509. I-75 exit 104, just e. Int corridors. **Pets:** Large, other species. Service with restrictions. 🅂🄼 🐾 🛜 ⛌ 🛏 🖥

▼▼ Marriott Griffin Gate Resort & Spa 🅷

(859) 231-5100. **$146-$275.** 1800 Newtown Pike 40511. I-75/64 exit 115, 0.5 mi s on SR 922. Int corridors. **Pets:** Accepted. 🍽 🅂🄼 🐾 ⛌ 🛰 ⛌ 🛏 🖥

⊛ ▼▼ Microtel Inn by Wyndham Lexington 🅷

(859) 299-9600. **$50-$90, 14 day notice.** 2240 Buena Vista Rd 40505. I-75 exit 110, just w. Int corridors. **Pets:** Small. $20 one-time fee/pet. Designated rooms, service with restrictions, supervision. 🅂🄰🅅🄴 🅂🄼 🛜 ⛌ 🛏

⊛ ▼▼ Red Roof Inn Lexington South 🅷

(859) 277-9400. **$55-$99.** 2651 Wilhite Dr 40503. Jct US 27 and SR 4 (New Circle Rd). Ext corridors. **Pets:** Large, other species. Service with restrictions, supervision. 🅂🄰🅅🄴 🅂🄼 🛜 ⛌ 🛏 🖥

▼▼ Residence Inn by Marriott Lexington Keeneland/Airport 🅷

(859) 296-0460. **$105-$207.** 3110 Wall St 40513. Jct SR 4 (New Circle Rd) and US 68 (Harrodsburg Rd). Int corridors. **Pets:** Accepted. 🅂🄼 🐾 🛜 ⛌ 🛏 🖥

▼▼ Residence Inn by Marriott Lexington North 🅷

(859) 231-6191. **$90-$183.** 1080 Newtown Pike 40511. I-75/64 exit 115, 1 mi s on SR 922. Ext corridors. **Pets:** Other species. $75 one-time fee/room. Service with restrictions, supervision. 🐾 🛜 ⛌ 🛏 🖥

▼▼ Residence Inn by Marriott Lexington South/ Hamburg Place 🅷

(859) 263-9979. **$118-$194.** 2688 Pink Pigeon Pkwy 40509. I-75 exit 108, 0.6 mi w, then 0.3 mi n. Int corridors. **Pets:** Accepted. 🅂🄼 🐾 🛜 ⛌ 🛏 🖥

LONDON

▼▼ Country Inn & Suites By Carlson 🅷

(606) 878-9900. **Call for rates.** 2035 W Hwy 192 40741. I-75 exit 38, just e. Int corridors. **Pets:** Medium. $25 one-time fee/pet. Designated rooms, service with restrictions, supervision. 🅂🄼 🐾 🛜 ⛌ 🛏 🖥

▼▼ Red Roof Inn London I-75 🅷

(606) 862-8844. **$59-$114.** 110 Melcon Ln 40741. I-75 exit 41, southwest corner. Int corridors. **Pets:** Large, other species. Service with restrictions, supervision. 🅂🄼 🐾 🛜 🛏 🖥

LOUISA

▼▼ Super 8-Louisa 🅷

(606) 638-7888. **$63-$85.** 191 Falls Creek Dr 41230. Jct US 23 and SR 3. Int corridors. **Pets:** Accepted. 🅂🄼 🛜 🛏 🖥

LOUISVILLE

▼▼ 21c Museum Hotel 🅷

(502) 217-6300. **Call for rates.** 700 W Main St 40202. Jct 7th and Main sts. Int corridors. **Pets:** Accepted. 🍽 🅂🄼 ⛌ 🛜 ⛌ 🖥

⊛ ▼▼ BEST WESTERN Airport East/Expo Center 🅷

(502) 456-4411. **Call for rates.** 1921 Bishop Ln 40218. I-264 exit 15 eastbound; 15B westbound, 0.3 mi s. Int corridors. **Pets:** $25 one-time fee/room. Designated rooms, service with restrictions, crate. 🅂🄰🅅🄴 🅂🄼 🐾 🛜 🖥

▼▼ Candlewood Suites Louisville Airport 🅷

(502) 357-3577. **Call for rates.** 1367 Gardiner Ln 40213. I-264 exit 14, just s on Poplar Level Rd, then 0.4 mi e. Int corridors. **Pets:** Accepted. 🛜 ⛌ 🛏 🖥

▼▼ Crowne Plaza Louisville 🅷

(502) 367-2251. **Call for rates.** 830 Phillips Ln 40209. I-264 exit 11 (Fairgrounds/Expo Center Main Gate). Int corridors. **Pets:** Other species. $150 one-time fee/room. Service with restrictions, supervision. 🍽 🅂🄼 🐾 🛜 ⛌ 🛏 🖥

▼▼ Hawthorn Suites by Wyndham Louisville/Jeffersontown 🅷

(502) 261-0085. **$77-$88.** 11762 Commonwealth Dr 40299. I-64 exit 17, 0.5 mi s on Blankenbaker Pkwy. Int corridors. **Pets:** Accepted. 🅂🄼 🛜 ⛌ 🛏 🖥

▼▼▼ **Homewood Suites Louisville East** H
(502) 429-9070. **$119-$899.** 9401 Hurstbourne Trace 40222. I-64 exit 15, 2.5 mi n. Int corridors. **Pets:** Other species. $100 one-time fee/room. Service with restrictions, crate. 🚹M 🛏 🛜 ✖ 🛗 💻

◈◈◈ ▼▼▼ **La Quinta Inn & Suites Louisville Airport Expo** H
(502) 368-0007. **$92-$659.** 4125 Preston Hwy 40213. I-65 exit 130, 1 mi n. Int corridors. **Pets:** Large, other species. Service with restrictions. SAVE 🚹M 🛏 🛜 ✖ 🛗 💻

▼▼ **Ramada Limited Airport & Fair/Expo Center** H
(502) 637-6336. **$69-$159.** 2912 Crittenden Dr 40209. I-264 exit 11 (Fairgrounds/Expo Center Main Gate), 0.6 mi n. Int corridors. **Pets:** Medium. $25 one-time fee/pet. Service with restrictions, crate. 🛏 🛜 ✖ 🛗 💻

◈◈◈ ▼▼ **Red Roof Inn Louisville Expo Airport** H
(502) 968-0151. **$54-$250.** 4704 Preston Hwy 40213. I-65 exit 130, just e. Ext corridors. **Pets:** Large, other species. Service with restrictions, supervision. SAVE 🛜 ✖ 🛗 💻

◈◈◈ ▼▼ **Red Roof Inn Louisville Fair And Expo** H
(502) 456-2993. **$55-$250.** 3322 Red Roof Inn Pl 40218. I-264 exit 15 eastbound; exit 15B westbound, 0.3 mi s. Ext corridors. **Pets:** Large, other species. Service with restrictions, supervision. SAVE 🛜 ✖ 🛗 💻

▼▼▼ **Residence Inn by Marriott-Louisville Airport** H
(502) 363-8800. **$111-$183.** 700 Phillips Ln 40209. I-264 exit 11 (Fairgrounds/Expo Center Main Gate), 0.4 mi w. Int corridors. **Pets:** Accepted. 🚹M 🛏 🛜 ✖ 🛗 💻

▼▼▼ **Residence Inn by Marriott Louisville Downtown** H
(502) 589-8998. **$139-$229.** 333 E Market St 40202. Corner of Preston and E Market sts. Int corridors. **Pets:** Accepted. 🚹M 🛏 🛜 ✖ 🛗 💻

▼▼▼ **Residence Inn by Marriott Louisville East** H
(502) 425-1821. **$90-$194.** 120 N Hurstbourne Pkwy 40222. I-64 exit 15, 1.8 mi n. Ext corridors. **Pets:** Accepted. 🛏 🛜 ✖ 🛗 💻

▼▼▼ **Residence Inn by Marriott-Louisville NE** H
(502) 412-1311. **$125-$206.** 3500 Springhurst Commons Dr 40241. I-265 exit 32, 0.5 mi w on Westport Rd, then just n. Int corridors. **Pets:** Accepted. 🚹M 🛏 🛜 ✖ 🛗 💻

◈◈◈ ▼▼▼ **The Seelbach Hilton Louisville** H
(502) 585-3200. **$149-$299.** 500 4th St 40202. I-65 exit 136C (Muhammad Ali Blvd), 0.3 mi w, then just s. Int corridors. **Pets:** Accepted. SAVE 🍴 🛏 ✖ 🛗 💻

▼▼▼ **Staybridge Suites Louisville East** H
(502) 244-9511. **Call for rates.** 11711 Gateworth Way 40299. I-64 exit 17, just n. Int corridors. **Pets:** Accepted. 🚹M 🛏 🛜 🛗 💻

MADISONVILLE

◈◈◈ ▼▼▼▼ **BEST WESTERN PLUS Madisonville Inn** H
(270) 821-2121. **$90-$100.** 1891 Lantaff Blvd 42431. Pennyrile Pkwy exit 44. Int corridors. **Pets:** Medium, dogs only. $10 daily fee/pet. Service with restrictions. SAVE 🚹M 🛏 🛜 🛗 💻

MAYSVILLE

▼▼▼▼ **French Quarter Inn** H
(606) 564-8000. **$89-$175.** 25 E McDonald Pkwy 41056. Corner of Limestone St and McDonald Pkwy; near Ohio River Bridge; downtown. Int corridors. **Pets:** Small, other species. Designated rooms, service with restrictions. 🚹M 🛏 🛜 🛗 💻

▼▼ **Quality Inn** M
(606) 759-5696. **Call for rates.** 1428A US 68 41056. Jct US 68 and SR 9 (AA Hwy). Ext corridors. **Pets:** Accepted. 🚹M 🛏 🛜 🛗 💻

MOREHEAD

◈◈◈ ▼▼▼▼ **Comfort Inn & Suites** H
(606) 780-7378. **$69-$109.** 2650 Kentucky 801 N 40351. I-64 exit 133, just s. Int corridors. **Pets:** $10 daily fee/pet. Service with restrictions, crate. SAVE 🚹M 🛏 🛜 🛗 💻

▼▼▼ **Holiday Inn Express of Morehead** H
(606) 784-5796. **Call for rates.** 110 Toms Dr 40351. I-64 exit 137 (SR 32), just sw. Int corridors. **Pets:** Accepted. 🚹M 🛏 🛜 🛗 💻

MOUNT VERNON

▼▼ **Days Inn-Renfro Valley/Mt. Vernon** H
(606) 256-3300. **$55-$100.** 1630 Richmond St 40456. I-75 exit 62, just w. Ext corridors. **Pets:** Small. $20 one-time fee/pet. Service with restrictions, supervision. 🛜 🛗 💻

MURRAY

◈◈◈ ▼▼▼ **BEST WESTERN University Inn** H
(270) 753-5353. **Call for rates.** 1503 N 12th St 42071. 1.9 mi n on US 641. Ext corridors. **Pets:** Accepted. SAVE 🛏 🛗 💻

OAK GROVE

◈◈◈ ▼▼▼ **Quality Inn @ Ft. Campbell** H
(270) 439-3311. **$60-$89.** 201 Auburn St 42262. I-24 exit 86, just s. Ext corridors. **Pets:** Medium, other species. $20 daily fee/pet. Service with restrictions, crate. SAVE 🚹M 🛏 🛜 🛗 💻

◈◈◈ ▼▼▼▼ **Sleep Inn & Suites** H
(270) 640-7170. **Call for rates.** 220 Auburn St 42262. I-24 exit 86, just e. Ext corridors. **Pets:** Other species. $25 daily fee/pet. No service, supervision. SAVE 🚹M 🛜 ✖ 🛗 💻

PADUCAH *(Restaurants p. 632)*

▼▼ **Candlewood Suites** H
(270) 442-3969. **Call for rates.** 3940 Coleman Crossing Cir 42001. I-24 exit 4, just nw. Int corridors. **Pets:** Accepted. 🚹M 🛜 🛗 💻

◈◈◈ ▼▼▼▼ **Courtyard by Marriott** H
(270) 442-3600. **$97-$160.** 3835 Technology Dr 42001. I-24 exit 4, just ne. Int corridors. **Pets:** Large, dogs only. $75 one-time fee/pet. Service with restrictions, supervision. SAVE 🍴 🚹M 🛏 🛜 ✖ 🛗 💻

▼▼▼ **Days Inn** H
(270) 442-7500. **$55-$65.** 3901 Hinkleville Rd 42001. I-24 exit 4, just ne. Ext corridors. **Pets:** Accepted. 🛏 🛜 🛗 💻

▼▼▼ **Drury Inn** H
(270) 443-3313. **$90-$149.** 3975 Hinkleville Rd 42001. I-24 exit 4, just e. Int corridors. **Pets:** $10 daily fee/room. Service with restrictions, supervision. 🚹M 🛏 🛜 ✖ 🛗 💻

▼▼▼ **Drury Suites** H
(270) 441-0024. **$100-$149.** 2930 James Sanders Blvd 42001. I-24 exit 4, just s. Int corridors. **Pets:** $10 daily fee/room. Service with restrictions, supervision. 🚹M 🛏 🛜 ✖ 🛗 💻

▼▼ **Pear Tree Inn by Drury** H
(270) 444-7200. **$70-$129.** 5006 Hinkleville Rd 42001. I-24 exit 4, just s. Int corridors. **Pets:** $10 daily fee/room. Service with restrictions, supervision. 🛏 🛜 🛗 💻

▼▼▼ **Residence Inn by Marriott** H
(270) 444-3966. **$108-$177.** 3900 Coleman Crossing Cir 42001. I-24 exit 4, just nw. Int corridors. **Pets:** $50 one-time fee/room. Service with restrictions. 🚹M 🛏 🛜 ✖ 🛗 💻

RICHMOND

▼▼▼ **Holiday Inn Express Hotel & Suites** H
(859) 624-4055. **$109-$149.** 1990 Colby Taylor Dr 40745. I-75 exit 87, just w. Int corridors. **Pets:** $25 daily fee/pet. Designated rooms, service with restrictions, supervision. 🚹M 🛏 🛜 ✖ 🛗 💻

RUSSELLVILLE

▼▼▼ Econo Lodge **H**

(270) 726-2488. **$80-$100.** 1450 Bowling Green Rd 42276. 1.4 mi e on SR 80 and US 68. Ext corridors. **Pets:** Accepted. 🐾 🛜 🍴 💻

SHELBYVILLE

AAA ▼▼▼ BEST WESTERN Shelbyville Lodge **H**

(502) 633-4400. **Call for rates.** 115 Isaac Shelby Dr 40065. I-64 exit 32, 0.5 mi n on SR 55. Int corridors. **Pets:** Accepted.

SAVE 🐾 🛜 🍴 💻

AAA ▼▼▼ Country Hearth Inn **H**

(502) 633-5771. **$55-$145.** 100 Howard Dr 40065. I-64 exit 32, 0.5 mi n on SR 55. Int corridors. **Pets:** Accepted. SAVE 🛜 🍴 💻

▼▼▼ Ramada **H**

(502) 633-9933. **$84-$149, 3 day notice.** 251 Breighton Cir 40065. I-64 exit 32, just s. Int corridors. **Pets:** Accepted.

🅼 🐾 🛜 ✖ 🍴 💻

SHEPHERDSVILLE

AAA ▼▼▼ BEST WESTERN PLUS South **H**

(502) 543-7097. **$76-$220.** 211 S Lakeview Dr 40165. I-65 exit 117 (SR 44 W), just se. Int corridors. **Pets:** Designated rooms, service with restrictions, supervision. SAVE 🐾 🛜 ✖ 🍴 💻

▼▼▼ Comfort Inn Louisville South **H** ❀

(502) 955-5566. **$74-$119.** 191 Brenton Way 40165. I-65 exit 121, just ne. Int corridors. **Pets:** Large, other species. $25 one-time fee/pet. Designated rooms, service with restrictions. 🐾 🛜 ✖ 🍴 💻

▼▼▼ Fairfield Inn by Marriott Louisville South **H**

(502) 955-5533. **$80-$131.** 362 Brenton Way 40165. I-65 exit 121, just ne. Int corridors. **Pets:** Accepted. 🅼 🐾 🛜 ✖ 🍴 💻

▼▼▼ Sleep Inn & Suites-Louisville South **H**

(502) 921-1001. **$69-$299.** 130 Spring Pointe Dr 40165. I-65 exit 117 (SR 44 W), just e. Int corridors. **Pets:** Accepted.

🅼 🐾 🛜 ✖ 🍴 💻

▼▼▼ Super 8 **H**

(502) 543-8870. **$59-$79.** 275 Keystone Crossroads 40165. I-65 exit 117 (SR 44 W), just w. Int corridors. **Pets:** Accepted.

🐾 🛜 🍴 💻

SHIVELY

▼▼▼ Holiday Inn Southwest Fair Expo **H**

(502) 448-2020. **Call for rates.** 4110 Dixie Hwy 40216. I-264 exit 8B, just n on US 31 W and 60. Int corridors. **Pets:** Accepted.

🍴 🅼 🐾 🛜 🍴 💻

SMITHS GROVE

▼▼▼ Bryce Inn **M**

(270) 563-5141. **$59-$77.** 592 S Main St 42171. I-65 exit 38, 0.3 mi n. Ext corridors. **Pets:** Accepted. 🐾 🛜 🍴 💻

SOMERSET

▼▼▼ Quality Inn & Suites **H**

(606) 678-2023. **$69-$79.** 240 N Hwy 27 42503. Jct SR 80, just n; at traffic light 2. Int corridors. **Pets:** Accepted. 🅼 🐾 🛜 🍴 💻

SPARTA

▼▼▼ Ramada at the Kentucky Speedway **H**

(859) 567-7223. **$69-$144, 3 day notice.** 525 Dale Dr 41086. I-71 exit 57, just w. Int corridors. **Pets:** Medium. $25 one-time fee/room. Service with restrictions. 🅼 🐾 🛜 🍴 💻

WEST LIBERTY

▼▼▼ Days Inn **H**

(606) 743-4206. **$70-$90.** 1613 W Main St 41472. Jct SR 519 and 460, just w. Int corridors. **Pets:** Accepted. 🅼 🛜 🍴 💻

WILLIAMSBURG

▼▼▼ Cumberland Inn **H**

(606) 539-4100. **Call for rates.** 649 S 10th St 40769. I-75 exit 11, just e on SR 92, then just n on SR 2386. Int corridors. **Pets:** Accepted.

🍴 🅼 🐾 🛜 ✖ 🍴 💻

WINCHESTER

AAA ▼▼▼ BEST WESTERN Country Squire **M**

(859) 744-7210. **$79-$169.** 1307 W Lexington Ave 40391. I-64 exit 94 (US 60), 0.9 mi se. Ext corridors. **Pets:** Very small. $20 daily fee/pet. Designated rooms, service with restrictions, supervision.

SAVE 🐾 🛜 🍴 💻

LOUISIANA

ALEXANDRIA

AAA ▼▼▼ BEST WESTERN of Alexandria Inn & Suites & Conf. Ctr. **H**

(318) 445-5530. **$89-$129.** 2720 N MacArthur Dr 71303. I-49 exit 86 (MacArthur Dr), 1.3 mi sw. Ext/int corridors. **Pets:** Medium. $10 daily fee/pet. Designated rooms, service with restrictions, supervision.

SAVE 🐾 🛜 🍴 💻

▼▼▼ Candlewood Suites **H**

(318) 427-9020. **$119-$149.** 2344 N MacArthur Dr 71303. I-49 exit 86 (MacArthur Dr), just s. Int corridors. **Pets:** Large, other species. $150 one-time fee/room. Service with restrictions, supervision.

🅼 🛜 🍴 💻

▼▼▼ La Quinta Inn & Suites Alexandria Airport **H**

(318) 442-3700. **$89-$230.** 6116 W Calhoun Dr 71303. I-49 exit 90 (Air Base Rd), just w. Int corridors. **Pets:** Large, other species. Service with restrictions. 🅼 🐾 🛜 🍴 💻

BATON ROUGE (Restaurants p. 632)

AAA ▼▼▼ BEST WESTERN Chateau Louisianne Suite Hotel **H**

(225) 927-6700. **$58-$180.** 710 N Lobdell Blvd 70806. 4.6 mi e on Florida Blvd, 0.3 mi n. Int corridors. **Pets:** Accepted.

SAVE 🐾 ✖ 🛜 🍴 💻

AAA ▼▼▼▼ BEST WESTERN PLUS Richmond Inn & Suites - Baton Rouge **H** ❀

(225) 924-6500. **$119-$189.** 2683 Energy Dr 70808. I-10 exit 158 (College Dr), just n, just e on Corporate Dr, then just s. Int corridors. **Pets:** Other species. $20 daily fee/room. Service with restrictions, crate.

SAVE 🐾 🛜 ✖ 🍴 💻

▼▼▼ Chase Suites by Woodfin **H** ❀

(225) 927-5630. **$119-$159.** 5522 Corporate Blvd 70808. I-10 exit 158 (College Dr), just n, then just e. Ext corridors. **Pets:** Medium, other species. $150 deposit/room, $250 one-time fee/room, $10 daily fee/pet. Service with restrictions, crate. 🐾 🛜 ✖ 🍴 💻

▼▼▼ **Drury Inn & Suites Baton Rouge** 🏨

(225) 766-2022. **$110-$239.** 7939 Essen Park Ave 70809. I-10 exit 160 (Essen Ln), just s. Int corridors. **Pets:** $10 daily fee/room. Service with restrictions, supervision. 🅼 🛗 🛜 🛗 🖥

▼▼▼ **Holiday Inn-South Baton Rouge** 🏨

(225) 924-7021. **$99-$119, 3 day notice.** 9940 Airline Hwy 70816. I-12 exit 2B, just n. Ext/int corridors. **Pets:** Accepted.
🍽 🛗 🛜 🛗 🖥

▼▼▼ **Hotel Indigo Baton Rouge Downtown Riverfront** 🏨

(225) 343-1515. **$189-$389, 3 day notice.** 200 Convention St 70801. Corner of Lafayette St; downtown. Int corridors. **Pets:** Accepted.
🍽 🅼 🛜 ✖ 🛗 🖥

🔺 ▼▼▼ **Hyatt Place Baton Rouge/I-10** 🏨

(225) 769-4400. **$89-$219.** 6080 Bluebonnet Blvd 70809. I-10 exit 162 (Bluebonnet Blvd), just s. Int corridors. **Pets:** Accepted.
🆂🅰🆅 🅼 🛗 🛜 ✖ 🛗 🖥

▼▼ **La Quinta Inn Baton Rouge University Area** Ⓜ

(225) 924-9600. **$72-$279.** 2333 S Acadian Thruway 70808. I-10 exit 157B, just n. Ext corridors. **Pets:** Large, other species. Service with restrictions. 🛗 🛜 🛗 🖥

▼▼ **Microtel Inn & Suites by Wyndham Baton Rouge Airport** 🏨

(225) 356-9191. **$60-$109.** 3444 Harding Blvd 70807. I-110 exit 6, just e. Int corridors. **Pets:** Small, other species. $35 daily fee/pet. Service with restrictions, crate. 🅼 🛗 🛜 ✖ 🛗 🖥

▼▼▼ **Quality Suites** 🏨

(225) 615-8890. **$76-$99.** 1755 O'Neal Ln 70816. I-12 exit 7, just n. Int corridors. **Pets:** Large. $10 daily fee/pet. Designated rooms, service with restrictions, supervision. 🅼 🛗 🛜 ✖ 🛗 🖥

▼▼▼ **Radisson Hotel Baton Rouge** 🏨

(225) 236-4000. **Call for rates.** 2445 S Acadian Thruway 70808. I-10 exit 157B, just n. Int corridors. **Pets:** Accepted.
🍽 🛗 ✖ 🛜 ✖ 🛗 🖥

🔺 ▼▼ **Red Roof Inn Baton Rouge** 🏨

(225) 275-6600. **Call for rates.** 11314 Boardwalk Dr 70816. I-12 exit 4, just n. Ext corridors. **Pets:** Large, other species. Service with restrictions, supervision. 🆂🅰🆅 🛜 🅺 🐾 🆉

🔺 ▼▼▼ **Residence Inn by Marriott-Baton Rouge-Siegen Lane** 🏨

(225) 293-8700. **$142-$219.** 10333 N Mall Dr 70809. I-10 exit 163 (Siegen Ln), just s; in Siegen Marketplace. Int corridors. **Pets:** Medium, other species. $109 one-time fee/room. Service with restrictions, crate.
🆂🅰🆅 🅼 🛗 🛜 ✖ 🛗 🖥

▼▼ **TownePlace Suites by Marriott Baton Rouge South** 🏨

(225) 819-2112. **$109-$179.** 8735 Summa Ave 70809. I-10 exit 162 (Bluebonnet Blvd), just s to Picardy Ave, just w to Summa Ave, then 0.5 mi nw. Int corridors. **Pets:** Accepted. 🅼 🛗 🛜 ✖ 🛗 🖥

BELLE CHASSE

▼▼ **Microtel Inn & Suites by Wyndham, Belle Chasse** 🏨

(504) 684-8540. **$80-$150.** 14740 Hwy 23 70037. Jct SR 428 and 23, 14.4 mi s. Int corridors. **Pets:** Accepted. 🛜 ✖ 🛗 🖥

BOSSIER CITY

▼▼▼ **Hampton Inn** 🏨

(318) 752-1112. **$94-$139.** 1005 Gould Dr 71111. I-20 exit 21 (Old Minden Rd), just e, then 0.5 mi n. Int corridors. **Pets:** Accepted.
🅼 🛗 🛜 🛗 🖥

🔺 ▼▼▼ **Homewood Suites Shreveport/Bossier City** 🏨

(318) 759-1940. **Call for rates.** 2015 Old Minden Rd 71111. I-20 exit 21 (Old Minden Rd), just e. Int corridors. **Pets:** Dogs only. $20 daily fee/room. Service with restrictions. 🆂🅰🆅 🛜 🅺 🐾 🆉

▼▼ **Microtel Inn & Suites by Wyndham Bossier City** 🏨

(318) 742-7882. **$60-$100.** 2713 Village Ln 71112. I-20 exit 22 (Airline Dr), just s, then just w. Int corridors. **Pets:** Small. $25 one-time fee/pet. Designated rooms, service with restrictions, supervision.
🅼 🛜 🛗 🖥

▼▼ **TownePlace Suites by Marriott** 🏨 🐾

(318) 741-9090. **$99-$149.** 1009 Gould Dr 71111. I-20 exit 21 (Old Minden Rd), just e, then 0.5 mi n. Int corridors. **Pets:** Medium, other species. Service with restrictions, crate. 🛜 ✖ 🛗 🖥

BREAUX BRIDGE

▼▼▼ **Holiday Inn Express of Breaux Bridge** 🏨

(337) 667-8913. **$100-$160.** 2942 H Grand Point Hwy 70517. I-10 exit 115, just n. Int corridors. **Pets:** Other species. $25 one-time fee/room. Service with restrictions. 🅼 🛗 🛜 🛗 🖥

▼▼ **Microtel Inn & Suites by Wyndham Breaux Bridge** 🏨

(337) 332-0432. **Call for rates.** 2280 Rees St Ext 70517. I-10 exit 109 (Breaux Bridge), just e. Int corridors. **Pets:** Small. $25 one-time fee/room. Service with restrictions, crate. 🛜 🅺 🐾 🆉

BROUSSARD

▼▼▼ **La Quinta Inn & Suites Broussard - Lafayette Area** 🏨

(337) 330-8081. **$89-$249.** 104 Sweetland Dr 70518. US 90, just w on Albertson Pkwy, just n. Int corridors. **Pets:** Large, other species. Service with restrictions. 🅼 🛗 🛜 ✖ 🛗 🖥

COVINGTON *(Restaurants p. 632)*

🔺 ▼▼ **BEST WESTERN Northpark Inn** 🏨 🐾

(985) 892-2681. **$89-$199.** 625 N Hwy 190 70433. I-12 exit 63B, just n. Ext/int corridors. **Pets:** Large, other species. $20 daily fee/room. Designated rooms, service with restrictions, crate. 🆂🅰🆅 🛗 🛜 🛗 🖥

🔺 ▼▼▼ **Residence Inn New Orleans Covington/ North Shore** 🏨

. **$116-$199.** 101 Park Pl Blvd 70433. I-12 exit 63B, 0.5 mi n, then just w. Int corridors. **Pets:** Other species. $100 one-time fee/pet. Service with restrictions, crate. 🆂🅰🆅 🛗 🛜 ✖ 🛗 🖥

▼▼▼ **Staybridge Suites Covington-Northpark** 🏨

(985) 892-0003. **$94-$999.** 140 Holiday Blvd 70433. I-12 exit 63B, just n, then just w. Int corridors. **Pets:** Accepted. 🛗 🛜 🛗 🖥

DELHI

🔺 ▼▼ **BEST WESTERN Delhi Inn** Ⓜ

(318) 878-5126. **$85.** 135 Snider Rd 71232. I-20 exit 153, just s. Ext corridors. **Pets:** Accepted. 🆂🅰🆅 🛗 🛜 🛗 🖥

GONZALES

▼▼ **TownePlace Suites by Marriott Baton Rouge Gonzales** 🏨

(225) 450-3400. **Call for rates.** 2823 S Outfitters Dr 70737. I-10 exit 177, just w, then just s. Int corridors. **Pets:** Small, other species. $100 one-time fee/room. Service with restrictions, supervision.
🛜 🅺 🐾 🆉

GRETNA

▼▼ **La Quinta Inn New Orleans West Bank/Gretna** 🏨

(504) 368-5600. **$79-$379.** 50 Terry Pkwy 70056. US 90 business route exit 9A (Terry Pkwy) southbound; US 90 (Westbank Expwy) exit 9 (Terry Pkwy/General DeGaulle) northbound. Ext corridors. **Pets:** Large, other species. Service with restrictions. 🛗 🛜 🛗 🖥

HAMMOND (Restaurants p. 632)

AAA◇ ▼▼▼ Historic Michabelle Inn **CI**
(985) 419-0550. **$90-$150, 3 day notice.** 1106 S Holly St 70403. I-12 exit 40 (US 51), 0.8 mi n, just e on Old Covington Hwy, then n, follow signs. Ext/int corridors. **Pets:** Accepted.
[SAVE] [符] [≥] [?] [✕] [✈] [🛗] [▣]

▼▼ Lexington Inn **H**
(985) 345-0003. **Call for rates.** 46053 N Puma Dr 70401. I-55 exit 32 (Wardline/University), just e. Ext corridors. **Pets:** Accepted.
[≥] [?] [🛗] [▣]

HOUMA

▼▼▼ La Quinta Inn & Suites Houma **H**
(985) 879-1646. **$89-$194.** 189 Synergy Center Blvd 70364. US 90 exit 202, 3.4 mi s on Main St to Martin Luther King Blvd, then just w. Int corridors. **Pets:** Large, other species. Service with restrictions.
[&M] [≥] [?] [✕] [🛗] [▣]

IOWA

▼▼▼ La Quinta Inn & Suites Iowa **H**
(337) 582-2261. **$89-$285.** 204 W Frontage Rd 70647. I-10 exit 43, just n. Int corridors. **Pets:** Large, other species. Service with restrictions.
[≥] [?] [✕] [🛗] [▣]

KENNER

▼▼ Days Inn New Orleans Airport **H**
(504) 464-1644. **$89-$199.** 1021 Airline Dr 70062. US 61, 0.6 mi w from jct SR 49. Ext corridors. **Pets:** Accepted.
[符] [≥] [?] [🛗] [▣]

AAA◇ ▼▼▼ Hilton New Orleans Airport **H**
(504) 469-5000. **$109-$219.** 901 Airline Dr 70062. I-10 exit 223A (Williams Blvd), 2 mi s, then 0.8 mi w. Int corridors. **Pets:** Accepted.
[SAVE] [符] [≥] [🕹] [🛗] [▣]

▼▼▼ La Quinta Inn New Orleans (Airport) **H**
(504) 466-1401. **$89-$369.** 2610 Williams Blvd 70062. I-10 exit 223A (Williams Blvd), 0.3 mi s. Int corridors. **Pets:** Large, other species. Service with restrictions.
[符] [&M] [≥] [?] [🛗] [▣]

LAFAYETTE (Restaurants p. 632)

▼▼ Baymont Inn & Suites Lafayette Airport **H**
(337) 291-2916. **$69-$89.** 2200 NE Evangeline Thruway 70501. I-10 exit 103A, just s. Int corridors. **Pets:** Accepted.
[≥] [?] [🛗] [▣]

AAA◇ ▼▼▼ BEST WESTERN Lafayette Inn **H**
(337) 769-2900. **$110-$150.** 2207 NW Evangeline Thruway 70501. I-10 exit 103A, just s. Int corridors. **Pets:** Medium, other species. $20 daily fee/pet. Service with restrictions, crate.
[SAVE] [≥] [?] [🛗] [▣]

▼▼▼▼ Candlewood Suites **H**
(337) 984-6900. **Call for rates.** 2105 Kaliste Saloom Rd 70508. I-10 exit 103A, 3.9 mi s on US 90/Evangeline Thruway to Kaliste Saloom Rd, then 3.6 mi w. Int corridors. **Pets:** Accepted.
[&M] [?] [✕] [🛗] [▣]

▼▼▼▼ Drury Inn & Suites-Lafayette **H**
(337) 262-0202. **$110-$174.** 120 Alcide Dominique 70506. I-10 exit 101, just s on University Ave, then just w. Int corridors. **Pets:** $10 daily fee/room. Service with restrictions, supervision.
[&M] [≥] [?] [🛗] [▣]

▼▼▼▼ Fairfield Inn & Suites by Marriott I-10
(337) 235-9898. **$89-$149.** 2225 NW Evangeline Thruway 70501. I-10 exit 103A, just sw. Int corridors. **Pets:** Medium. $35 one-time fee/room. Designated rooms, service with restrictions, supervision.
[&M] [≥] [?] [✕] [🛗] [▣]

▼▼▼▼ La Quinta Inn & Suites Lafayette Oil Center **H**
(337) 291-1088. **$94-$255.** 1015 W Pinhook Rd 70503. I-10 exit 103A, 2.9 mi s on US 90/Evangeline Thruway, then 1 mi w. Int corridors. **Pets:** Large, other species. Service with restrictions.
[≥] [?] [✕] [🛗] [▣]

▼▼ Pear Tree Inn By Drury **H**
(337) 289-9907. **$80-$144.** 126 Alcide Dominique 70506. I-10 exit 101, just s on University Ave, then just w. Int corridors. **Pets:** $10 daily fee/ room. Service with restrictions, supervision.
[&M] [≥] [?] [🛗] [▣]

▼▼▼ Residence Inn by Marriott, Lafayette Airport **H**
(337) 232-3341. **$98-$161.** 128 James Comeaux Rd 70508. I-10 exit 103A, 3.9 mi s on US 90/Evangeline Thruway to Kaliste Saloom Rd, then 1 mi w. Int corridors. **Pets:** Accepted.
[&M] [≥] [?] [✕] [🛗] [▣]

▼▼▼ Staybridge Suites Lafayette Airport **H**
(337) 267-4666. **$89-$219.** 129 E Kaliste Saloom Rd 70508. I-10 exit 103A, 3.9 mi s on US 90/Evangeline Thruway to Kaliste Saloom Rd, then 0.7 mi w. Int corridors. **Pets:** Small. $15 daily fee/room. Designated rooms, service with restrictions, supervision.
[&M] [≥] [?] [✕] [🛗] [▣]

LAKE CHARLES

▼▼▼ Comfort Suites **H**
(337) 436-6400. **$99-$140.** 1016 N Martin Luther King Hwy 70601. I-10 exit 33, 0.3 mi n on US 171 (Martin Luther King Hwy). Int corridors. **Pets:** Accepted. [&M] [≥] [?] [✕] [🛗] [▣]

AAA◇ ▼▼▼ La Quinta Inn & Suites-Prien **H**
(337) 478-9889. **$125-$254.** 1201 W Prien Lake Rd 70601. I-210 exit 4 (Nelson Rd), just n, then 0.5 mi e. Int corridors. **Pets:** Large, other species. Service with restrictions. [SAVE] [≥] [?] [✕] [🛗] [▣]

▼▼ Super 8-Lake Charles **H**
(337) 477-1606. **$75-$95, 3 day notice.** 1350 E Prien Lake Rd 70601. I-210 exit 6B (Enterprise Blvd), 0.3 mi e, then just n. Int corridors. **Pets:** Accepted. [&M] [≥] [?] [🛗] [▣]

LA PLACE

AAA◇ ▼▼▼ BEST WESTERN La Place Inn **M**
(985) 651-4000. **$90-$200.** 4289 Main St 70068. I-10 exit 209, just s. Ext corridors. **Pets:** Accepted. [SAVE] [≥] [?] [🛗] [▣]

METAIRIE

▼▼▼ La Quinta Inn New Orleans Causeway **M**
(504) 835-8511. **$85-$349.** 3100 S I-10 Service Rd E 70001. I-10 exit 228 (Causeway Blvd), just s. Ext corridors. **Pets:** Large, other species. Service with restrictions. [&M] [≥] [?] [🛗] [▣]

AAA◇ ▼▼▼ Residence Inn by Marriott New Orleans Metairie **H** 🐾
(504) 832-0888. **$194-$244.** 3 Galleria Blvd 70001. I-10 exit 228 (Causeway Blvd), just se to 36th St, then just e. Int corridors. **Pets:** Medium, other species. $100 one-time fee/room. Service with restrictions, crate. [SAVE] [≥] [?] [✕] [🛗] [▣]

AAA◇ ▼▼▼ Sheraton Metairie New Orleans **H** 🐾
(504) 837-6707. **$109-$399.** 4 Galleria Blvd 70001. I-10 exit 228 (Causeway Blvd), just s to 36th St, just e, then just n. Int corridors. **Pets:** Other species. Supervision. [SAVE] [符] [&M] [≥] [🕹] [✕] [▣]

MINDEN

AAA◇ ▼▼▼ BEST WESTERN Minden Inn **H**
(318) 377-1001. **$91.** 1411 Sibley Rd 71055. I-20 exit 47, just n. Ext corridors. **Pets:** Medium. $15 daily fee/pet. Service with restrictions, supervision. [SAVE] [≥] [?] [🛗] [▣]

MONROE

▼▼▼ Residence Inn by Marriott **H**
(318) 387-0210. **$128-$144.** 4960 Millhaven Rd 71203. I-20 exit 120, just n of Pecanland Mall. Int corridors. **Pets:** Accepted.
[&M] [≥] [?] [✕] [🛗] [▣]

AAA◇ ▼▼▼ TownePlace Suites by Marriott **H**
(318) 387-7277. **$109-$175.** 4919 Pecanland Mall Dr 71203. I-20 exit 120, just w of Pecanland Mall. Int corridors. **Pets:** Medium. $75 one-time fee/room. Service with restrictions, crate.
[SAVE] [&M] [≥] [?] [✕] [🛗] [▣]

MORGAN CITY

◆◆ **Holiday Inn-Morgan City** H
(985) 385-2200. **$110-$260.** 520 Roderick St 70380. 1.5 mi s of jct US 90 and SR 70. Ext corridors. **Pets:** Medium. $50 one-time fee/room. Service with restrictions, supervision. ⊞ ⌂M ⇌ 🛜 🛢 🖵

◆◆ **La Quinta Inn & Suites Morgan City** H
(985) 300-0200. **$80-$200.** 2018 Allison St 70380. US 90 exit Dr Martin Luther King Jr Blvd, just s. Int corridors. **Pets:** Large, other species. Service with restrictions. ⌂M ⇌ 🛜 ✕ 🛢 🖵

NATCHITOCHES

◆◆◆ **BEST WESTERN Natchitoches Inn** H
(318) 352-6655. **$95-$189.** 5131 University Pkwy 71457. I-49 exit 138, just e. Int corridors. **Pets:** Accepted. SAVE ⇌ 🛜 🛢 🖵

NEW IBERIA

◆◆◆ **La Quinta Inn & Suites** H
(337) 321-6000. **$89-$204.** 611A Queen City Dr 70560. US 90 exit SR 14, just e. Int corridors. **Pets:** Large, other species. Service with restrictions. SAVE ⇌ 🛜 ✕ 🛢 🖵

NEW ORLEANS *(Restaurants p. 632)*

◆◆◆ **BEST WESTERN PLUS St. Charles Inn** H 🐾
(504) 899-8888. **$140-$325.** 3636 St. Charles Ave 70115. US 90 business route exit St. Charles Ave, 1.8 mi s. Int corridors. **Pets:** $50 one-time fee/room, $20 daily fee/room. Service with restrictions.
SAVE 🛜 ✕ 🛢 🖵

◆◆◆ **BEST WESTERN PLUS St. Christopher Hotel** H
(504) 648-0444. **$79-$600, 30 day notice.** 114 Magazine St 70130. Between Canal and Common sts. Int corridors. **Pets:** Large. $50 deposit/room. Designated rooms, service with restrictions, supervision.
SAVE 🛜 🛢 🖵

◆◆◆ **The Bienville House Hotel** H 🐾
(504) 529-2345. **$89-$369, 3 day notice.** 320 Decatur St 70130. Between Conti and Bienville sts. Ext/int corridors. **Pets:** $100 one-time fee/pet, $25 daily fee/pet. Service with restrictions, supervision.
SAVE ⊞ ⇌ 🛜 ✕ 🛢 🖵

◆◆◆◆ **Clarion Inn & Suites** H
(504) 299-9900. **$90-$1000, 3 day notice.** 1300 Canal St 70112. Jct Saratoga St. Int corridors. **Pets:** Accepted. 🛜 ✕ 🛢 🖵

◆◆◆◆ **Drury Inn & Suites-New Orleans** H
(504) 529-7800. **$175-$259.** 820 Poydras St 70112. Between Baronne and Carondelet sts. Int corridors. **Pets:** $10 daily fee/room. Service with restrictions, supervision. ⌂M ⇌ 🛜 🛢 🖵

◆◆◆ **Hilton New Orleans St. Charles Avenue** H 🐾
(504) 524-8890. **$119-$299.** 333 St. Charles Ave 70130. Jct Perdido St. Int corridors. **Pets:** Small, dogs only. $75 one-time fee/room. Service with restrictions, crate. SAVE ⊞ ⌂M ⇌ 🛜 🛢 🖵

◆◆◆ **Historic Streetcar Inn** H
(504) 521-8000. **$79-$279, 7 day notice.** 1509 St. Charles Ave 70130. US 90 business route, exit St. Charles Ave, just sw. Ext/int corridors. **Pets:** Small, other species. $10 daily fee/pet. Service with restrictions, crate. SAVE 🛜 ✕ 🛢 🖵

◆◆◆◆ **Hotel Indigo New Orleans Garden District** H
(504) 522-3650. **$149-$299.** 2203 St. Charles Ave 70130. 1 mi w of US 90; corner of Jackson Ave. Int corridors. **Pets:** Accepted.
⊞ ⌂M 🛜 ✕ 🛢 🖵

◆◆ **The Hotel Modern New Orleans** H
(504) 962-0900. **$99-$299.** 2 Lee Cir 70130. Just e of US 90 business route exit St. Charles Ave; on southeast block of circle. Int corridors. **Pets:** Other species. $55 one-time fee/room. Service with restrictions, crate. SAVE ⊞ 🛜 ✕ 🛢 🖵

◆◆◆◆ **Hotel Monteleone** H 🐾
(504) 523-3341. **$159-$399, 3 day notice.** 214 Royal St 70130. Between Iberville and Bienville sts. Int corridors. **Pets:** $100 one-time fee/room, $25 daily fee/room. Service with restrictions, supervision.
SAVE ECO ⊞ ⇌ 🛜 ✕ 🛢 🖵

◆◆◆ **Hyatt Place New Orleans Convention Center** H
(504) 524-1881. **$99-$349.** 881 Convention Center Blvd 70130. Between N Diamond and St. Joseph sts. Int corridors. **Pets:** Accepted. SAVE 🛜 ✕ 🛢 🖵

◆◆◆◆ **InterContinental New Orleans** H
(504) 525-5566. **$109-$699, 3 day notice.** 444 St. Charles Ave 70130. Between Perdido and Poydras sts. Int corridors. **Pets:** Accepted.
SAVE ⊞ ⌂M ⇌ 🛜 🛢 🖵

◆◆◆ **La Quinta Inn & Suites New Orleans French Quarter** H
(504) 598-9977. **$89-$589.** 301 Camp St 70130. Corner of Gravier and Camp sts. Int corridors. **Pets:** Large, other species. Service with restrictions. ⌂M ⇌ 🛜 🛢 🖵

◆◆◆ **Le Méridien New Orleans** H 🐾
(504) 525-9444. **$109-$409, 3 day notice.** 333 Poydras St 70130. Jct Poydras and S Peters sts; close to Riverfront area/convention center. Int corridors. **Pets:** Small. $100 one-time fee/room, $25 daily fee/room. Designated rooms, service with restrictions, supervision.
SAVE ⊞ ⌂M ⇌ 🛜 ✕ 🖵

◆◆◆ **Loews New Orleans Hotel** H 🐾
(504) 595-3300. **Call for rates.** 300 Poydras St 70130. Corner of S Peters St. Int corridors. **Pets:** Medium, other species. $100 one-time fee/room, $25 daily fee/pet. Designated rooms, service with restrictions, supervision. SAVE ⊞ ⇌ ✕ 🛢 🖵

◆◆◆ **Maison St. Charles Quality Inn & Suites** H 🐾
(504) 522-0187. **$79-$999.** 1319 St. Charles Ave 70130. Just s of US 90 business route (Pontchartrain Expwy). Ext corridors. **Pets:** $50 one-time fee/pet. No service, crate. SAVE ⇌ 🛜 ✕ 🛢 🖵

◆◆◆ **Omni Royal Crescent Hotel** H
(504) 527-0006. **$109-$349, 3 day notice.** 535 Gravier St 70130. 0.3 mi w of Canal St. Int corridors. **Pets:** Accepted.
⊞ ✕ 🛜 ✕ 🖵

◆◆◆ **Omni Royal Orleans Hotel** H
(504) 529-5333. **$139-$459, 3 day notice.** 621 St. Louis St 70140. At Royal and St. Louis sts. Int corridors. **Pets:** Accepted.
⊞ ⇌ 🛜 ✕ 🛢 🖵

◆◆◆ **Residence Inn by Marriott Downtown New Orleans** H 🐾
(504) 522-1300. **$74-$313, 3 day notice.** 345 St. Joseph St 70130. At Tchoupitoulas St. Int corridors. **Pets:** Large. $100 one-time fee/room. Service with restrictions, crate. SAVE ⌂M ⇌ 🛜 ✕ 🛢 🖵

◆◆◆ **The Ritz-Carlton, New Orleans** H
(504) 524-1331. **$159-$499, 3 day notice.** 921 Canal St 70112. Between Burgundy and Dauphine sts. Int corridors. **Pets:** Accepted.
SAVE ⊞ ⌂M ✕ 🛜 ✕ 🛢 🖵

◆◆◆ **The Roosevelt New Orleans, A Waldorf Astoria Hotel** H
(504) 648-1200. **$199-$599.** 130 Roosevelt Way 70112. Just s of Canal St. Int corridors. **Pets:** Accepted.
SAVE ⊞ ⌂M ⇌ ✕ 🛜 ✕ 🛢

△△△ ▽▽▽ ▽▽▽ **Royal Sonesta Hotel New Orleans** H
(504) 586-0300. **$179-$499, 3 day notice.** 300 Bourbon St 70130. Garage entrance on Conti or Bienville sts. Int corridors. **Pets:** Accepted.
SAVE ⊞ 🏊M 🛁 🛜 🖥 📺

△△△ ▽▽▽ ▽▽▽ **Sheraton New Orleans Hotel** H ❀
(504) 525-2500. **$99-$489, 3 day notice.** 500 Canal St 70130. Between Camp and Magazine sts. Int corridors. **Pets:** Medium, dogs only. Service with restrictions, crate. SAVE ⊞ 🏊M 🛁 🛜 ✕ 📺

△△△ ▽▽▽ ▽▽▽ **Staybridge Suites Hotel** H
(504) 571-1818. **$99-$500.** 501 Tchoupitoulas St 70130. Corner of Poydras St. Int corridors. **Pets:** Accepted. SAVE 🏊M 🛁 🛜 🖥 📺

△△△ ▽▽▽ ▽▽▽ **The Westin New Orleans Canal Place** H
(504) 566-7006. **$139-$439, 3 day notice.** 100 Iberville St 70130. At Canal Place, near Mississippi River. Int corridors. **Pets:** Accepted.
SAVE ⊞ 🛁 🛜 ✕ 🖥 📺

△△△ ▽▽▽ ▽▽▽ **W French Quarter** H
(504) 581-1200. **$179-$809, 3 day notice.** 316 Chartres St 70130. Between Conti and Bienville sts. Int corridors. **Pets:** Accepted.
SAVE ⊞ 🏊M 🛁 🛜 ✕ 🖥 📺

△△△ ▽▽▽ ▽▽▽ **Windsor Court Hotel** H
(504) 523-6000. **Call for rates.** 300 Gravier St 70130. Between Magazine and Tchoupitoulas sts. Int corridors. **Pets:** Accepted.
SAVE ⊞ 🛁 ✕ 🛜 ✕ 📺

△△△ ▽▽▽ ▽▽▽ **Wyndham New Orleans - French Quarter** H
(504) 529-7211. **$159-$279.** 124 Royal St 70130. Between Iberville and Canal sts. Int corridors. **Pets:** Accepted.
SAVE ⊞ 🏊M 🛁 🛜 ✕ 🖥 📺

OPELOUSAS

▽▽▽ ▽▽▽ **Comfort Inn Opelousas** H
(337) 942-4900. **$90-$146.** 5454 I-49 N Service Rd 70570. I-49 exit 18, just s. Int corridors. **Pets:** Accepted. 🏊M 🛁 🛜 🖥 📺

▽▽▽ ▽▽▽ **Evangeline Downs Hotel, an Ascend Hotel Collection Member** H
(337) 407-2121. **$92-$190.** 2235 Creswell Ln Lot B 70570. I-49 exit 18, 0.6 mi e on SR 31, then 0.7 mi n on entry driveway. Int corridors. **Pets:** $25 one-time fee/room. Service with restrictions, crate.
⊞ 🏊M 🛁 🛜 🖥 📺

PONCHATOULA

▽▽▽ ▽▽▽ **Microtel Inn & Suites by Wyndham** H ❀
(985) 386-8866. **$40-$82.** 727 W Pine St 70454. I-55 exit 26, 0.5 mi e on SR 22. Int corridors. **Pets:** Other species. $10 daily fee/room. Service with restrictions, crate. 🏊M 🛁 🛜 🖥 📺

RUSTON

△△△ ▽▽▽ ▽▽▽ **Holiday Inn Express Hotel & Suites** H
(318) 513-9777. **$104-$159.** 1825 Roberta Ave 71270. I-20 exit 86, just se. Int corridors. **Pets:** Medium. $50 one-time fee/room. Designated rooms, service with restrictions, supervision.
SAVE 🏊M 🛁 🛜 🖥 📺

ST. FRANCISVILLE

▽▽▽ ▽▽▽ **Lake Rosemound Inn Bed & Breakfast** BB
(225) 635-3176. **$90-$145, 3 day notice.** 10473 Lindsey Ln 70775. 13 mi n on SR 61, then 3 mi w using Rosemound Loop, Sligo Rd, Lake Rosemound Rd and Lindsey Ln, follow signs. Ext/int corridors.
Pets: Accepted. ✕ 🛜 ✕

ST. ROSE

▽▽▽ ▽▽▽ ▽▽▽ **Holiday Inn Express & Suites New Orleans Airport South** H
(504) 466-1355. **Call for rates.** 110 James Dr E 70087. I-310 exit 2, 1.5 mi e on SR 61. Int corridors. **Pets:** Accepted.
⊞ 🏊M 🛁 🛜 ✕ 🖥 📺

SCOTT

▽▽▽ ▽▽▽ **Comfort Inn & Suites** H
(337) 706-8128. **$79-$125.** 1636 Saint Mary St 70583. I-10 exit 97, just s. Int corridors. **Pets:** Small. $25 one-time fee/pet. Designated rooms, service with restrictions, supervision. 🏊M 🛜 ✕ 🖥 📺

SHREVEPORT

△△△ ▽▽▽ ▽▽▽ ▽▽▽ **Eldorado Resort Casino Shreveport** H
(318) 220-0711. **$89-$299, 3 day notice.** 451 Clyde Fant Pkwy 71101. I-20 exit 19A (Spring St), 0.8 mi n to Crockett St, just e, then just n. Int corridors. **Pets:** Accepted. SAVE ⊞ 🛜 🖥 📺

▽▽▽ ▽▽▽ **Homewood Suites - Shreveport** H
(318) 549-2000. **$109-$229.** 5485 Financial Plaza 71129. I-20 exit 10 (Pines Rd), just s, then 1.2 mi e. Int corridors. **Pets:** Other species. $20 daily fee/room. Service with restrictions, supervision.
🏊M 🛁 🛜 🖥 📺

▽▽▽ ▽▽▽ **La Quinta Inn & Suites Shreveport Airport** H
(318) 671-1100. **$85-$205.** 6700 Financial Cir 71129. I-20 exit 10 (Pines Rd), just s, then 0.5 mi e. Int corridors. **Pets:** Large, other species. Service with restrictions. 🏊M 🛁 🛜 🖥 📺

△△△ ▽▽▽ ▽▽▽ **Residence Inn by Marriott Shreveport - Airport** H
(318) 635-8000. **$99-$159.** 4910 W Monkhouse Dr 71109. I-20 exit 13, just nw. Int corridors. **Pets:** Accepted.
SAVE 🏊M 🛁 🛜 ✕ 🖥 📺

SLIDELL

▽▽▽ ▽▽▽ **Candlewood Suites - Slidell/Northshore** H
(985) 326-0120. **Call for rates.** 100 Holiday Blvd 70460. I-10 exit 80, just sw. Int corridors. **Pets:** Accepted. 🏊M 🛜 ✕ 🖥 📺

▽▽▽ ▽▽▽ **La Quinta Inn New Orleans/Slidell** H
(985) 643-9770. **$69-$204.** 794 E I-10 Service Rd 70461. I-10 exit 266 (Gause Blvd), just se. Ext corridors. **Pets:** Large, other species. Service with restrictions. 🛁 🛜 🖥 📺

VILLE PLATTE

△△△ ▽▽▽ ▽▽▽ **BEST WESTERN Ville Platte** H
(337) 360-9961. **$96.** 1919 E Main St (Hwy 167) 70586. I-49 exit 23, 14 mi nw. Int corridors. **Pets:** Accepted. SAVE 🛁 🛜 🖥 📺

WALKER

▽▽▽ ▽▽▽ **La Quinta Inn & Suites Walker** H
(225) 667-1966. **$89-$219.** 13450 Vera McGowan 70785. I-12 exit 15, just n. Int corridors. **Pets:** Large, other species. Service with restrictions. 🛁 🛜 ✕ 🖥 📺

WESTLAKE

▽▽▽ ▽▽▽ **Isle of Capri Casino & Hotel** H
(337) 430-2400. **$99-$249, 3 day notice.** 100 Westlake Ave 70669. I-10 exit 27, just s. Int corridors. **Pets:** Accepted.
⊞ 🏊M 🛁 ✕ 🛜 🖥 📺

WEST MONROE

▽▽▽ ▽▽▽ **Quality Inn & Suites-West Monroe** H
(318) 387-2711. **$74-$130.** 503 Constitution Dr 71292. I-20 exit 114 (Thomas Rd), just s to Constitution Dr, then 0.6 mi w. Int corridors.
Pets: Accepted. 🏊M 🛁 🛜 🖥 📺

WINNFIELD

(AAA) ▼▼▼ BEST WESTERN of Winnfield M
(318) 628-3993. **$66-$100.** 700 W Court St 71483. Jct US 84 and 167, just e. Ext corridors. **Pets:** Accepted. [SAVE] [⊤] [⊅] [⊚] [⊟] [⊑]

ZACHARY

(AAA) ▼▼▼ BEST WESTERN Zachary Inn H
(225) 658-2550. **$96-$120.** 4030 Hwy 19 70791. Just s of jct SR 64. Int corridors. **Pets:** Other species. $20 daily fee/room. Service with restrictions, supervision. [SAVE] [⊅] [⊚] [⊟] [⊑]

MAINE

AUBURN

▼▼ Fireside Inn & Suites M
(207) 777-1777. **Call for rates.** 1777 Washington St 04210. I-95 exit 75, 0.5 mi s on US 202, SR 4 and 100. Ext/int corridors.
Pets: Accepted. [⊤] [⊅] [⊚] [⊟] [⊑]

(AAA) ▼▼▼▼ Residence Inn by Marriott Auburn H
(207) 777-3400. **$111-$263.** 670 Turner St 04210. I-95 exit 80 southbound; exit 75 northbound; from SR 100, just w. Int corridors.
Pets: Accepted. [SAVE] [⌂M] [⊅] [⊚] [⊠] [⊟] [⊑]

AUGUSTA

**(AAA) ▼▼▼ BEST WESTERN PLUS Civic Center
Inn H ✿**
(207) 622-4751. **$99-$199.** 110 Community Dr 04330. I-95 exit 112A northbound; exit 112 southbound, just s on SR 8, 11 and 27. Int corridors. **Pets:** Other species. $10 daily fee/pet. Service with restrictions, supervision. [SAVE] [⊤] [⌂M] [⊅] [⊚] [⊟] [⊑]

(AAA) ▼▼▼▼ Senator Inn & Spa H ✿
(207) 622-5804. **$80-$229.** 284 Western Ave 04330. I-95 exit 109 northbound; exit 109A southbound, on US 202, SR 11 and 100. Ext/int corridors. **Pets:** $12 daily fee/room. Designated rooms, no service, supervision. [SAVE] [ECO] [⊤] [⊅] [⊠] [⊚] [⊠] [⊟] [⊑]

BANGOR

**(AAA) ▼▼▼▼ Bangor TownePlace Suites by
Marriott H**
(207) 262-4000. **$104-$206.** 240 Sylvan Rd 04401. I-95 exit 187 (Hogan Rd), just se, then 0.5 mi sw; in Sylvan Business Park. Int corridors. **Pets:** Accepted. [SAVE] [⊤] [⌂M] [⊚] [⊠] [⊟] [⊑]

**(AAA) ▼▼▼▼ BEST WESTERN White House
Inn H ✿**
(207) 862-3737. **$145-$300.** 155 Littlefield Ave 04401. I-95 exit 180 (Coldbrook Rd), 5.5 mi s of downtown. Ext/int corridors. **Pets:** Other species. $10 daily fee/pet. Designated rooms, service with restrictions, supervision. [SAVE] [⊅] [⊚] [⊟] [⊑]

▼▼ Econo Lodge Inn & Suites M
(207) 945-0111. **$90-$150.** 327 Odlin Rd 04401. I-95 exit 182B, just e on US 2 and SR 100. Int corridors. **Pets:** Dogs only. $10 one-time fee/room. Designated rooms, service with restrictions, supervision.
[⌂M] [⊅] [⊚] [⊠] [⊟] [⊑]

(AAA) ▼▼▼▼ Fairfield Inn by Marriott Bangor H
(207) 990-0001. **$90-$183.** 300 Odlin Rd 04401. I-95 exit 182B, just e on US 2 and SR 100. Int corridors. **Pets:** Accepted.
[SAVE] [ECO] [⌂M] [⊅] [⊠] [⊚] [⊠] [⊟] [⊑]

▼▼ Fireside Inn & Suites H ✿
(207) 942-1234. **$89-$199.** 570 Main St 04401. I-395 exit 3B. Int corridors. **Pets:** Medium, dogs only. $10 daily fee/pet. Service with restrictions, supervision. [ECO] [⊤] [⊚] [⊠] [⊟] [⊑]

**(AAA) ▼▼▼▼ Four Points by Sheraton Bangor
Airport H**
(207) 947-6721. **$135-$250.** 308 Godfrey Blvd 04401. At Bangor International Airport. Int corridors. **Pets:** Accepted.
[SAVE] [⊤] [⌂M] [⊅] [⊚] [⊠] [⊟] [⊑]

▼▼▼ Holiday Inn-Bangor H
(207) 947-0101. **Call for rates.** 404 Odlin Rd 04401. I-95 exit 182B; jct Odlin Rd and I-395. Int corridors. **Pets:** Accepted.
[⊤] [⌂M] [⊅] [⊚] [⊠] [⊟] [⊑]

▼▼▼ Howard Johnson Inn H
(207) 942-5251. **$59-$120.** 336 Odlin Rd 04401. I-95 exit 182B; jct Odlin Rd and I-395. Int corridors. **Pets:** Medium, dogs only. $10 daily fee/pet. Designated rooms, service with restrictions, supervision.
[⊤] [⊅] [⊚] [⊟] [⊑]

▼▼▼ Quality Inn Bangor H
(207) 942-7899. **$80-$145.** 750 Hogan Rd 04401. I-95 exit 187 (Hogan Rd), 0.5 mi nw. Int corridors. **Pets:** Accepted. [⊚] [⊠] [⊟] [⊑]

▼▼ Ramada H
(207) 947-6961. **$89-$149.** 357 Odlin Rd 04401. I-95 exit 182B; jct Odlin Rd and I-395. Int corridors. **Pets:** Accepted.
[⊤] [⊅] [⊚] [⊟] [⊑]

BAR HARBOR *(Restaurants p. 632)*

(AAA) ▼▼▼ Atlantic Eyrie Lodge H
(207) 288-9786. **Call for rates.** 6 Norman Rd 04609. 1 mi w on SR 3 to Highbrook Rd. Ext corridors. **Pets:** Other species. $35 one-time fee/room. Designated rooms, service with restrictions, supervision.
[SAVE] [⌂M] [⊅] [⊚] [⊠] [⊟] [⊑]

▼▼▼ A Wonder View Inn H
(207) 288-3358. **$99-$279, 3 day notice.** 50 Eden St 04609. 0.5 mi w on SR 3. Ext corridors. **Pets:** Accepted. [⊤] [⊅] [⊚] [⊠] [⊟] [⊑]

(AAA) ▼▼▼▼ Balance Rock Inn 1903 BB
(207) 288-2610. **Call for rates.** 21 Albert Meadow 04609. Just s of Main St; center. Ext/int corridors. **Pets:** Accepted.
[SAVE] [⊤] [⊅] [⊚] [⊠] [⊟] [⊑]

(AAA) ▼▼▼ Bar Harbor Quality Inn H ✿
(207) 288-5403. **$189, 3 day notice.** 40 Kebo St 04609. Jct SR 3 and 233; center. Ext corridors. **Pets:** Dogs only. $25 daily fee/pet. Designated rooms, service with restrictions, supervision.
[SAVE] [⊤] [⊅] [⊚] [⊠] [⊟] [⊑]

(AAA) ▼▼▼▼ Bar Harbor Regency Holiday Inn H
(207) 288-9723. **Call for rates.** 123 Eden St 04609. 1 mi w on SR 3. Int corridors. **Pets:** Accepted. [SAVE] [⊤] [⊅] [⊠] [⊚] [⊠] [⊟] [⊑]

▼▼ Hutchins Mountain View Cottages CA
(207) 288-4833. **$80-$98, 14 day notice.** 286 State Hwy 3 04609. On SR 3, 4 mi w. Ext corridors. **Pets:** Other species. Service with restrictions. [ECO] [⊤] [⊅] [⊚] [⊠] [AC] [☿] [⊟] [⊑]

(AAA) ▼▼▼▼ West Street Hotel H
(207) 288-0825. **Call for rates.** 50 West St 04609. Jct Main St. Int corridors. **Pets:** Accepted. [SAVE] [⊤] [⌂M] [⊅] [⊚] [⊠] [⊟]

BELFAST

▼▼ Belfast Harbor Inn H
(207) 338-2740. **$89-$209, 3 day notice.** 91 Searsport Ave (Rt 1) 04915. On US 1, 2 mi n from jct SR 3. Ext/int corridors. **Pets:** Dogs only. $20 daily fee/pet. Designated rooms, service with restrictions, supervision. [⊅] [⊚] [⊠] [⊟] [⊑]

◆◆ Fireside Inn & Suites, Ocean's Edge 🄷

(207) 338-2090. **Call for rates.** 159 Searsport Ave 04915. On US 1, 2.6 mi n from jct SR 3. Int corridors. **Pets:** Accepted.

◆ Gull Motel 🅼

(207) 338-4030. **$69-$159.** 196 Searsport Ave 04915. On US 1, 3 mi n from jct SR 3. Ext corridors. **Pets:** Medium, dogs only. $25 daily fee/pet. Designated rooms, service with restrictions, supervision.

◆ Yankee Clipper Motel 🅼

(207) 338-2353. **$79-$139, 3 day notice.** 50 Searsport Ave 04915. On US 1, 1.6 mi n from jct SR 3. Ext corridors. **Pets:** Dogs only. $20 daily fee/pet. Designated rooms, service with restrictions, supervision.

BETHEL

◆◆ The Inn At the Rostay 🅼

(207) 824-3111. **$79-$160, 14 day notice.** 186 Mayville Rd (US 2) 04217. On US 2, 2 mi e. Ext corridors. **Pets:** Other species. $20 daily fee/pet. Designated rooms, service with restrictions, supervision.

BOOTHBAY HARBOR

◆◆ Beach Cove Waterfront Inn 🅼

(207) 633-0353. **Call for rates.** 48 Lakeview Rd 04538. Off SR 27. Ext corridors. **Pets:** Accepted.

◆◆ Boothbay Harbor Inn 🄷 🐾

(207) 633-6302. **$89-$249, 3 day notice.** 31 Atlantic Ave 04538. 0.3 mi e of SR 27; on east side of Boothbay Harbor. Ext/int corridors. **Pets:** $20 daily fee/pet. Designated rooms, service with restrictions, supervision.

◆◆ Cap'n Fish's Waterfront Inn 🄷

(207) 633-6605. **$75-$175, 7 day notice.** 65 Atlantic Ave 04538. 0.3 mi se of SR 27; on east side of Boothbay Harbor. Ext corridors. **Pets:** Accepted.

◆ ◆◆ Flagship Inn & Suites 🅼 🐾

(207) 633-5094. **$74-$144, 3 day notice.** 200 Townsend Ave 04538. On SR 27, just n of jct SR 96. Ext corridors. **Pets:** Designated rooms, service with restrictions, supervision.

◆◆ Tugboat Inn 🄷 🐾

(207) 633-4434. **$99-$249, 3 day notice.** 80 Commercial St 04538. Center. Ext corridors. **Pets:** $20 daily fee/pet. Designated rooms, service with restrictions, supervision.

BRUNSWICK

◆ ◆◆ BEST WESTERN PLUS Brunswick Bath 🄷

(207) 725-5251. **Call for rates.** 71 Gurnet Rd 04011. On SR 24, 1 mi s of US 1. Int corridors. **Pets:** Accepted.

◆ ◆◆◆ The Brunswick Hotel & Tavern 🄷

(207) 837-6565. **Call for rates.** 4 Noble St 04011. Center. Int corridors. **Pets:** $50 one-time fee/room. Service with restrictions, supervision.

BRYANT POND

◆ Mollyockett Motel & Swim Spa 🅼

(207) 674-2345. **Call for rates.** 1132 S Main St 04219. 1.3 mi n on SR 26 from jct SR 219. Ext/int corridors. **Pets:** Accepted.

BUCKSPORT

◆ Bucksport Motor Inn 🅼

(207) 469-3111. **$69-$109.** 70 US Route 1 04416. Just e of downtown. Ext corridors. **Pets:** Dogs only. $15 one-time fee/room. Designated rooms, supervision.

CAMDEN

◆ ◆◆ ◆◆ Grand Harbor Inn 🄷 🐾

(207) 230-7177. **$169-$639, 4 day notice.** 14 Bay View Landing 04843. Just e of Main St; center. Int corridors. **Pets:** Dogs only. $35 daily fee/pet. Designated rooms, service with restrictions, supervision.

◆ ◆◆ ◆◆ Hartstone Inn & Restaurant 🄲🄸

(207) 236-4259. **Call for rates.** 41 Elm St 04843. On US 1, just s of Washington St; center. Ext/int corridors. **Pets:** Accepted.

◆ ◆◆ ◆◆ Lord Camden Inn 🄷 🐾

(207) 236-4325. **$99-$399.** 24 Main St 04843. Just n of Washington St; center. Int corridors. **Pets:** Dogs only. $35 daily fee/pet. Designated rooms, service with restrictions, supervision.

CAPE ELIZABETH *(Restaurants p. 632)*

◆ ◆◆ ◆◆ Inn by the Sea 🄷

(207) 799-3134. **$199-$2199, 14 day notice.** 40 Bowery Beach Rd (SR 77) 04107. On SR 77, 7 mi s. Ext/int corridors. **Pets:** Accepted.

CASTINE

◆◆ Pentagoet Inn 🄲🄸

(207) 326-8616. **Call for rates.** 26 Main St 04421. Center. Int corridors. **Pets:** Accepted.

EAGLE LAKE

◆◆ Overlook Motel & Lakeside Cabins 🅼

(207) 444-4535. **Call for rates.** 3232 Aroostook Rd 04739. On SR 11; center. Ext/int corridors. **Pets:** Other species. $10 daily fee/pet. Service with restrictions, supervision.

ELLSWORTH

◆ ◆◆ Comfort Inn 🄷 🐾

(207) 667-1345. **$109-$179.** 130 High St 04605. On US 1 and SR 3; center. Int corridors. **Pets:** $25 daily fee/room. Designated rooms, supervision.

◆◆ The Eagle's Lodge 🅼 🐾

(207) 667-3311. **$75-$130.** 278 High St 04605. Jct US 1 and 1A, 1.3 mi se on SR 3. Int corridors. **Pets:** Dogs only. $10 daily fee/room. Designated rooms, service with restrictions, supervision.

◆ ◆◆◆ Ellsworth Ramada 🄷

(207) 667-9341. **$119-$189.** 215 High St 04605. Jct US 1, 1A and SR 3. Int corridors. **Pets:** Accepted.

◆ ◆ Knights Inn 🅼

(207) 667-3621. **$79-$159.** 19 Thorsen Rd 04605. US 1, 1.5 mi n of SR 3. Ext corridors. **Pets:** Accepted.

◆ ◆ Sunset Motel 🄲🄰

(207) 667-8390. **Call for rates.** 210 Twin Hill Rd 04605. 6 mi s on US 1 and SR 3. Ext corridors. **Pets:** Small, dogs only. $15 daily fee/pet. Service with restrictions, supervision.

◆◆ Twilite Motel 🅼

(207) 667-8165. **$59-$126.** 147 Bucksport Rd 04605. Jct US 1A, 1.5 mi w on US 1 and SR 3. Ext corridors. **Pets:** Small, dogs only. $15 daily fee/room. Designated rooms, service with restrictions, supervision.

FALMOUTH

◆ ◆ Falmouth Inn 🅼

(207) 781-2120. **$69-$156.** 209 US 1 04105. I-295 exit 10, just e on Buckman Rd, then just s. Ext corridors. **Pets:** Dogs only. $10 daily fee/pet. Designated rooms, no service, supervision.

FREEPORT

◈◈◈ BEST WESTERN Freeport Inn 🅷
(207) 865-3106. **$70-$220.** 31 US 1 04032. I-295 exit 17, 1 mi n. Ext/int corridors. **Pets:** Accepted. 🆂 ⬛ ⬛ ⬛ ⬛ ⬛

◈◈◈ Candlebay Inn 🅱🅱
(207) 865-1868. **$105-$235, 5 day notice.** 8 Maple Ave 04032. Just w. of downtown, just w. Int corridors. **Pets:** Dogs only. $15 one-time fee/room. Supervision. ⬛ ⬛ ⬛

◈◈ Econo Lodge 🅼
(207) 865-3777. **$60-$180.** 537 US Rt 1 04032. I-295 exit 20, 0.3 mi s. Ext corridors. **Pets:** Medium, other species. $10 daily fee/room. Designated rooms, supervision. ⬛ ⬛ ⬛ ⬛

◈◈◈◈ Harraseeket Inn 🅲🅸
(207) 865-9377. **$140-$350, 3 day notice.** 162 Main St 04032. I-295 exit 22, 0.5 mi e. Int corridors. **Pets:** Accepted.
🆂 🅴🅲🅾 ⬛ ⬛ ⬛ ⬛ ⬛ ⬛

GREENVILLE

◈◈ Chalet Moosehead Lakefront Motel 🅼
(207) 695-2950. **Call for rates.** 12 N Birch St 04442. 1.5 mi w on SR 15. Ext corridors. **Pets:** Dogs only. $20 daily fee/pet. Designated rooms, service with restrictions, supervision. ⬛ ⬛ ⬛ ⬛

◈◈ Kineo View Motor Lodge 🅼
(207) 695-4470. **Call for rates.** 50 Overlook Dr 04441. 2.5 mi s on SR 15; gravel access road from highway. Ext corridors. **Pets:** Dogs only. $10 daily fee/room. Designated rooms, service with restrictions, supervision. ⬛ ⬛ ⬛ ⬛ ⬛

◈◈◈◈ The Lodge at Moosehead Lake 🅲🅸
(207) 695-4400. **$259-$695, 2 day notice.** 368 Lily Bay Rd 04441. 2.5 mi n. Int corridors. **Pets:** Accepted. 🆂 ⬛ ⬛ ⬛ ⬛ ⬛ ⬛

JACKMAN

◈◈ Bishop's Country Inn Motel 🅼
(207) 668-3231. **$65-$100.** 461 Main St 04945. On US 201; center. Ext corridors. **Pets:** $100 daily fee/pet. Service with restrictions, crate. ⬛ ⬛ ⬛ ⬛ ⬛

KENNEBUNK

◈◈◈ Port Inn Kennebunk, an Ascend Hotel Collection Member 🅼
(207) 985-6100. **$89-$309.** 55 York St (US 1) 04043. Jct SR 35 (US 1), 0.7 mi s. Ext corridors. **Pets:** Accepted. 🆂 ⬛ ⬛ ⬛ ⬛ ⬛

◈◈ Turnpike Motel 🅼
(207) 985-4404. **Call for rates.** 77 Old Alewive Rd 04043. I-95 exit 25, just e on SR 35, then just n. Ext/int corridors. **Pets:** Accepted.
🆂 ⬛ ⬛ ⬛

KENNEBUNKPORT *(Restaurants p. 632)*

◈◈◈ The Captain Jefferds Inn 🅱🅱 🐾
(207) 967-2311. **$159-$429, 7 day notice.** 5 Pearl St 04046. From Dock Square, 0.3 mi s on Ocean Ave, just ne; corner of Pearl and Pleasant sts. Ext/int corridors. **Pets:** Other species. $30 daily fee/pet. Designated rooms, supervision. ⬛ ⬛ ⬛ ⬛

◈◈◈ The Colony Hotel 🅷 🐾
(207) 967-3331. **Call for rates.** 140 Ocean Ave 04046. From Dock Square, 1 mi s. Int corridors. **Pets:** Other species. $30 daily fee/pet. Service with restrictions, crate. 🅴🅲🅾 ⬛ ⬛ ⬛ ⬛ ⬛

◈◈◈ Lodge At Turbat's Creek 🅼
(207) 967-8700. **Call for rates.** 7 Turbats Creek Rd 04046. From Dock Square, 0.5 mi se on Maine St, 0.6 mi ne on Wildes District Rd, then just se. Ext corridors. **Pets:** Accepted. ⬛ ⬛ ⬛ ⬛ ⬛ ⬛

◈◈◈ The Yachtsman Lodge & Marina 🅼 🐾
(207) 967-2511. **Call for rates.** 57 Ocean Ave 04046. From Dock Square, just s. Ext corridors. **Pets:** Other species. $35 daily fee/pet. Designated rooms, service with restrictions, crate.
⬛ ⬛ ⬛ ⬛ ⬛

KITTERY

◈◈◈ The Coachman Inn 🅼
(207) 439-4434. **$69-$209.** 380 US Rt 1 03904. I-95 exit 2, 1.5 mi n. Ext/int corridors. **Pets:** Other species. $10 daily fee/pet. Designated rooms, service with restrictions, supervision.
🆂 ⬛ ⬛ ⬛ ⬛ ⬛ ⬛

LEWISTON

◈◈◈ Hampton Inn Lewiston-Auburn 🅷
(207) 344-1000. **$99-$349.** 15 Lincoln St 04243. On SR 196, just s of SR 11 and 202. Int corridors. **Pets:** Accepted.
🆂 ⬛ ⬛ ⬛ ⬛ ⬛

◈◈ Ramada Conference Center 🅷
(207) 784-2331. **$90-$170.** 490 Pleasant St 04240. I-95 exit 80, right turn on Foch St, follow signs. Int corridors. **Pets:** Accepted.
⬛ ⬛ ⬛ ⬛ ⬛ ⬛ ⬛ ⬛

LINCOLNVILLE

◈◈◈ Victorian By The Sea 🅱🅱
(207) 236-3785. **Call for rates.** 33 Sea View Dr 04849. On US 1, 1.2 mi s of jct SR 173. Int corridors. **Pets:** Accepted.
⬛ ⬛ ⬛ ⬛ ⬛ ⬛

LUBEC

◈◈ The Eastland Motel 🅼
(207) 733-5501. **Call for rates.** 385 County Rd 04652. Jct US 1 and SR 189, 8.4 mi e on SR 189. Ext/int corridors. **Pets:** Accepted.
⬛ ⬛ ⬛ ⬛ ⬛

MACHIAS

◈◈◈ Machias Motor Inn 🅼
(207) 255-4861. **$83-$139.** 103 Main St 04654. 0.5 mi e on US 1. Ext corridors. **Pets:** Dogs only. $10 daily fee/pet. Designated rooms, service with restrictions, supervision. 🆂 ⬛ ⬛ ⬛

MILFORD

◈◈ Milford Motel On The River 🅼
(207) 827-3200. **Call for rates.** 174 Main Rd 04461. 0.5 mi n on US 2. Ext corridors. **Pets:** Small, dogs only. Service with restrictions, supervision. 🆂 ⬛ ⬛ ⬛ ⬛

MILLINOCKET

◈◈ Baxter Park Inn 🅷
(207) 723-9777. **$90-$120.** 935 Central St 04462. 0.8 mi e on SR 11 and 157. Int corridors. **Pets:** Accepted. ⬛ ⬛ ⬛ ⬛ ⬛

NAPLES

◈◈ Augustus Bove House 🅱🅱
(207) 693-6365. **Call for rates.** 11 Sebago Rd 04055. Corner of US 302 and SR 114. Int corridors. **Pets:** Accepted.
⬛ ⬛ ⬛ ⬛ ⬛

NEWCASTLE

◈◈◈ Newcastle Inn 🅱🅱 🐾
(207) 563-5685. **$155-$275, 14 day notice.** 60 River Rd 04553. Jct US 1, 0.5 mi ne via Snead Spur. Ext/int corridors. **Pets:** Medium, dogs only. $35 daily fee/pet. Designated rooms, service with restrictions, crate. ⬛ ⬛ ⬛ ⬛

NORTHEAST HARBOR

◈◈ Asticou Inn 🅷
(207) 276-3344. **Call for rates.** 15 Peabody Dr 04662. Jct SR 3 and Peabody Dr; center. Int corridors. **Pets:** Accepted.
⬛ ⬛ ⬛ ⬛ ⬛ ⬛

NORTHPORT

Point Lookout Resort & Conference Center [CA]

(207) 789-2000. **$119-$449, 3 day notice.** 67 Atlantic Hwy 04849. 4 mi s on US 1; at Lincolnville town line. Ext corridors. **Pets:** Accepted.

OGUNQUIT

Studio East Motor Inn [M]

(207) 646-7297. **Call for rates.** 267 Main St 03907. On US 1, just n. Ext corridors. **Pets:** Accepted.

OLD ORCHARD BEACH

Sea View Inn [M]

(207) 934-4180. **Call for rates.** 65 W Grand Ave (SR 9) 04064. 0.5 mi w on SR 9 (W Grand Ave). Ext corridors. **Pets:** Accepted.

ORONO

Black Bear Inn Conference Center & Suites [H]

(207) 866-7120. **Call for rates.** 4 Godfrey Dr 04473. I-95 exit 193 (Stillwater Ave), just se. Int corridors. **Pets:** Accepted.

University Inn Academic Suites [H]

(207) 866-4921. **$92-$199, 3 day notice.** 5 College Ave (US 2) 04473. I-95 exit 191, 1 mi e on Kelley, then 1.5 mi n on US 2; 8 mi n of Bangor. Int corridors. **Pets:** Accepted.

POLAND SPRING

Wolf Cove Inn [BB]

(207) 998-4976. **Call for rates.** 5 Jordan Shore Dr 04274. Just w of SR 11. Int corridors. **Pets:** Large, other species. $30 daily fee/room. Designated rooms, service with restrictions, supervision.

PORTLAND

Clarion Portland [H]

(207) 774-5611. **$79-$219.** 1230 Congress St 04102. I-295 exit 5, w on SR 22. Int corridors. **Pets:** Medium. Designated rooms, no service, supervision.

Embassy Suites Hotel [H]

(207) 775-2200. **$119-$329.** 1050 Westbrook St 04102. At Portland International Jetport. Int corridors. **Pets:** Accepted.

Fireside Inn & Suites [H]

(207) 774-5601. **$100-$220.** 81 Riverside St 04103. I-95 exit 48, just s. Int corridors. **Pets:** Accepted.

Hilton Garden Inn Portland Airport [H]

(207) 828-1117. **$125-$429.** 145 Jetport Blvd 04102. At Portland International Jetport. Int corridors. **Pets:** Accepted.

Hilton Garden Inn Portland Downtown Waterfront [H]

(207) 780-0780. **$179-$409.** 65 Commercial St 04101. In the Old Port; across from Casco Bay ferry terminal. Int corridors. **Pets:** Accepted.

Hyatt Place Portland Old Port [H]

(207) 775-1000. **$99-$699.** 433 Fore St 04101. At Union St; in Old Port. Int corridors. **Pets:** Accepted.

La Quinta Inn & Suites Portland [H]

(207) 871-0611. **$82-$295.** 340 Park Ave 04102. I-295 exit 5A southbound; exit 5 northbound, e on SR 22. Int corridors. **Pets:** Large, other species. Service with restrictions.

Portland Harbor Hotel [H]

(207) 775-9090. **$189-$650.** 468 Fore St 04101. In the Old Port. Int corridors. **Pets:** Accepted.

Portland Regency Hotel & Spa [H]

(207) 774-4200. **$149-$339.** 20 Milk St 04101. In the Old Port; between Market and Silver sts; downtown. Int corridors. **Pets:** Accepted.

Residence Inn by Marriott Portland Downtown/Waterfront [H]

(207) 761-1660. **$118-$344.** 145 Fore St 04101. In the Old Port; across from Casco Bay ferry terminal. Int corridors. **Pets:** Accepted.

The Westin Portland Harborview [H]

(207) 775-5411. **$149-$529.** 157 High St 04101. At Congress St. Int corridors. **Pets:** Medium, dogs only. Service with restrictions, supervision.

RANGELEY

Rangeley Saddleback Inn [H]

(207) 864-3434. **Call for rates.** 2303 Main St 04970. On SR 4, just s of village. Ext corridors. **Pets:** Accepted.

ROCKLAND

Navigator Inn [H]

(207) 594-2131. **Call for rates.** 520 Main St 04841. On US 1; between Talbot and Summer sts. Ext/int corridors. **Pets:** Accepted.

Trade Winds Inn [H]

(207) 596-6661. **$84-$234.** 2 Park Dr 04841. On US 1; center. Int corridors. **Pets:** Dogs only. $10 daily fee/pet. Designated rooms, service with restrictions, supervision.

ROCKPORT

The Country Inn At Camden/Rockport [H]

(207) 236-2725. **$119-$249.** 8 Country Inn Way 04856. Jct SR 90, 0.9 mi n on US 1. Ext/int corridors. **Pets:** $10 daily fee/pet. Designated rooms, service with restrictions, supervision.

Samoset Resort On The Ocean [H]

(207) 594-2511. **Call for rates.** 220 Warrenton St 04856. Jct SR 90, 4.8 mi s on US 1, 0.5 mi e. Int corridors. **Pets:** Small, dogs only. $75 one-time fee/pet. Designated rooms, service with restrictions, supervision.

Schooner Bay Motor Inn [M]

(207) 236-2205. **Call for rates.** 337 Commercial St 04856. Jct SR 90, 0.5 mi s on US 1. Ext corridors. **Pets:** $10 daily fee/pet. Designated rooms, service with restrictions, supervision.

SACO

Hampton Inn [H]

(207) 282-7222. **$99-$329.** 48 Industrial Park Rd 04072. I-95 exit 36 (I-195) to exit 1 (Industrial Park Rd), just ne. Int corridors. **Pets:** Other species. $200 deposit/room. Designated rooms, service with restrictions, supervision.

Ramada Saco Old Orchard Beach Area [H]

(207) 286-9600. **$80-$230.** 352 North St (SR 112) 04072. I-95 exit 36 (I-195) to exit 1 (Industrial Park Rd), 0.6 mi sw to SR 112, then 0.4 mi nw. Int corridors. **Pets:** Other species. $25 one-time fee/room. Supervision.

▼▼ Wagon Wheel Motel **M** ✿

(207) 283-3258. **Call for rates.** 726 Portland Rd (US 1) 04072. I-95 exit 36 (I-195), 1.5 mi se to US 1, then 0.7 mi ne. Ext corridors. **Pets:** Dogs only. $25 one-time fee/pet. Designated rooms, service with restrictions, crate. 🍴 🛏 ⛱ 🛜 ✕ 🄯 📱 📺

SANFORD

▼▼ Super 8 **H**

(207) 324-8823. **$52-$97.** 1892 Main St (Rt 109) 04073. I-95 exit 19, 7 mi nw. Int corridors. **Pets:** Accepted. 🍴 🛜 📱 📺

SCARBOROUGH

△△△ ▼▼▼ Homewood Suites Portland **H** ✿

(207) 775-2700. **$119-$369.** 200 Southborough Dr 04074. I-95 exit 45, just s. Int corridors. **Pets:** Other species. $75 one-time fee/room. Service with restrictions, supervision. 📳 ♿ ⛱ 🛜 📱 📺

▼ Pride Motel & Cottages **CA**

(207) 883-4816. **Call for rates.** 677 US Rt 1 04074. I-95 exit 36, 0.5 mi e to US 1, then 4.5 mi n. Ext corridors. **Pets:** Accepted. ♻ 🍴 ⛱ 🛜 ✕ 🄯 📱 📺

▼▼ Residence Inn by Marriott **H**

(207) 883-0400. **$92-$281.** 800 Roundwood Dr 04074. I-95 exit 42, 1.5 mi n on Payne Rd. Int corridors. **Pets:** Medium. $75 one-time fee/room. Service with restrictions, supervision. 🍴 ♿ ⛱ 🛜 ✕ 📱 📺

▼▼ TownePlace Suites by Marriott **H**

(207) 883-6800. **$118-$344.** 700 Roundwood Dr 04074. I-95 exit 42, 1.5 mi n on Payne Rd. Int corridors. **Pets:** Accepted. 🍴 ♿ ⛱ 🛜 ✕ 📱 📺

SKOWHEGAN

△△△ ▼▼ Belmont Motel **M**

(207) 474-8315. **$77-$107.** 273 Madison Ave 04976. 1 mi n on US 201. Ext corridors. **Pets:** Accepted. 📳 ♿ ⛱ 🛜 ✕ 📱 📺

SOUTHPORT

△△△ ▼▼▼ Ocean Gate Resort **H**

(207) 633-3321. **$119-$384, 7 day notice.** 70 Ocean Gate Rd 04576. SR 27, 2.5 mi s of Boothbay Harbor, 0.5 mi s of bridge to Southport Island. Ext corridors. **Pets:** Medium. $25 one-time fee/room. Designated rooms, service with restrictions, crate. 📳 🍴 ⛱ 🄯 🛜 ✕ 📱 📺

SOUTH PORTLAND

△△△ ▼▼▼ BEST WESTERN Merry Manor Inn **H** ✿

(207) 774-6151. **Call for rates.** 700 Main St 04106. I-95 exit 45, 1.3 mi e to US 1. Ext/int corridors. **Pets:** Dogs only. $20 one-time fee/pet. Designated rooms, service with restrictions, supervision. 📳 🍴 ♿ ⛱ 🛜 ✕ 📱 📺

△△△ ▼▼ Comfort Inn Airport **H**

(207) 775-0409. **$79-$199.** 90 Maine Mall Rd 04106. I-95 exit 45, 1 mi n. Int corridors. **Pets:** Other species. Designated rooms, service with restrictions, supervision. 📳 ♻ 🍴 ♿ 🛜 ✕ 📱 📺

△△△ ▼▼▼ Days Inn Airport/Maine Mall **H**

(207) 772-3450. **$53-$220.** 461 Maine Mall Rd 04106. I-95 exit 45. Int corridors. **Pets:** Medium. $10 deposit/pet, $10 daily fee/pet. Designated rooms, service with restrictions, supervision. 📳 ⛱ 🛜 ✕ 📱 📺

▼▼▼ Hampton Inn Portland Airport **H**

(207) 773-4400. **$99-$269.** 171 Philbrook Ave 04106. I-95 exit 45, just ne. Int corridors. **Pets:** Accepted. ♿ ⛱ 🛜 ✕ 📱 📺

△△△ ▼▼▼ Holiday Inn Express & Suites **H**

(207) 775-3900. **Call for rates.** 303 Sable Oaks Dr 04106. I-95 exit 45, just n on Maine Mall Rd, then just w on Running Hill Rd. Int corridors. **Pets:** Accepted. 📳 ♻ 🍴 ⛱ 🛜 ✕ 📱 📺

△△△ ▼▼▼ Portland Marriott at Sable Oaks **H**

(207) 871-8000. **$125-$286.** 200 Sable Oaks Dr 04106. I-95 exit 45, just n on Maine Mall Rd, then just w on Running Hill Rd. Int corridors. **Pets:** Small. $75 one-time fee/room. Designated rooms, supervision. 📳 ♻ 🍴 ♿ ⛱ 🄯 🛜 ✕ 📱 📺

SPRUCE HEAD

▼▼ The Craignair Inn & Restaurant **CI**

(207) 594-7644. **Call for rates.** 5 Third St 04859. 2.5 mi w on SR 73, 1.5 mi s on Clark Island Rd; 10 mi s of Rockland. Ext/int corridors. **Pets:** Accepted. ♻ 🍴 🛜 ✕ 🄯

STANDISH

▼▼ Sebago Lake Lodge and Cottages **BB**

(207) 892-2698. **$62-$275, 30 day notice.** 661 White's Bridge Rd 04084. 1 mi w on US 302. Ext/int corridors. **Pets:** Accepted. 🍴 🄯 🛜 ✕ 🎿 📱 📺

WATERVILLE

△△△ ▼▼▼ BEST WESTERN PLUS Waterville Grand Hotel **H**

(207) 873-0111. **$99-$249.** 375 Main St 04901. I-95 exit 130 (Main St), on SR 104. Int corridors. **Pets:** Other species. Service with restrictions. 📳 ♻ 🍴 ⛱ 🛜 📱 📺

▼▼ Fireside Inn & Suites **H** ✿

(207) 873-3335. **Call for rates.** 376 Main St 04901. I-95 exit 130 (Main St). Int corridors. **Pets:** $20 one-time fee/room. Designated rooms, service with restrictions, crate. ♻ 🍴 ♿ ⛱ 🛜 ✕ 📱 📺

WELLS

▼▼ Wells-Moody Motel **M**

(207) 646-5601. **Call for rates.** 119 Post Rd 04054. I-95 exit 19, jct SR 109 and US 1, 3.4 mi s. Ext corridors. **Pets:** Accepted. ⛱ 🛜 ✕ 📱 📺

WESTBROOK

△△△ ▼ Super 8 **H**

(207) 854-1881. **$99-$114.** 208 Larrabee Rd 04092. I-95 exit 48, jut w. Int corridors. **Pets:** Accepted. 📳 🍴 ⛱ 🛜 📱 📺

WEST FORKS

▼▼ Inn by the River **CI**

(207) 663-2181. **Call for rates.** 2777 US Rt 201 04985. Center. Int corridors. **Pets:** Other species. Service with restrictions, crate. 🍴 🛜 ✕ 🎿 🄯 📺

WESTPORT

▼▼▼ The Squire Tarbox Inn **CI**

(207) 882-7693. **Call for rates.** 1181 Main Rd 04578. Jct US 1, 8.5 mi s on SR 144, follow signs. Ext/int corridors. **Pets:** Accepted. 🍴 🛜 ✕ 🎿 🄯

WILTON

▼▼▼ Farmington/Wilton Comfort Inn & Suites **H** ✿

(207) 645-5155. **$99-$189.** 1026 US Rt 2 E 04294. On US 2, just w of jct SR 133. Int corridors. **Pets:** Medium. $35 one-time fee/room. Designated rooms, service with restrictions, crate. 🍴 ♿ ⛱ 🛜 ✕ 📱 📺

YORK HARBOR

▼▼◆ York Harbor Inn **CI** ✿

(207) 363-5119. **$109-$349, 14 day notice.** 480 York St 03911. On US 1A; center. Ext/int corridors. **Pets:** Dogs only. Designated rooms, service with restrictions, supervision. ♻ 🍴 🛜 ✕

MARYLAND

ABERDEEN

Home2 Suites by Hilton Baltimore - Aberdeen 🅷
(410) 272-0203. **$109-$189.** 20 Newton Rd 21001. I-95 exit 85, 2 mi e on SR 22, then 2 mi w on US 40; jct US 40 and SR 715. Int corridors. **Pets:** Accepted. 🛗 📶 📡 🍴 💻

La Quinta Inn Aberdeen 🅷
(410) 272-6000. **$79-$214.** 793 W Bel Air Ave 21001. I-95 exit 85, just e. Int corridors. **Pets:** Large, other species. Service with restrictions. 🛗 📶 🍴 💻

Red Roof Inn Aberdeen 🅷
(410) 273-7800. **$60-$99.** 988 Hospitality Way 21001. I-95 exit 85, just e on SR 22. Ext corridors. **Pets:** Large, other species. Service with restrictions, supervision. SAVE 🛗 📶 ✖ 🍴 💻

Residence Inn by Marriott Aberdeen at Ripken Stadium 🅷
(410) 272-0444. **$99-$245.** 830 Long Dr 21001. I-95 exit 85, 0.5 mi w on SR 22, then 0.5 mi n. Int corridors. **Pets:** Accepted.
🛗 📶 📡 ✖ 🍴 💻

ANNAPOLIS (Restaurants p. 632)

BEST WESTERN Annapolis Ⓜ
(410) 224-2800. **$110-$180, 30 day notice.** 2520 Riva Rd 21401. 2.3 mi sw on US 50 and 301 exit 22, just e; in Parole area. Ext/int corridors. **Pets:** Accepted. SAVE 📶 📡 🍴 💻

Country Inn & Suites By Carlson 🅷
(410) 571-6700. **$79-$299.** 2600 Housley Rd 21401. US 50 and 301 exit 23 eastbound; exit 23B westbound, 1 mi w on SR 450. Int corridors. **Pets:** Accepted. 🛗 📶 📡 ✖ 🍴 💻

DoubleTree by Hilton Hotel Annapolis 🅷
(410) 224-3150. **$99-$204.** 210 Holiday Ct 21401. 2.3 mi sw on US 50 and 301 exit 22 to Riva Rd, 0.3 mi n. Int corridors. **Pets:** Accepted.
SAVE 🍴 📶 📡 ✖ 🍴 💻

Extended Stay America-Annapolis-Admiral Cochrane Dr 🅷
(410) 571-6600. **Call for rates.** 120 Admiral Cochrane Dr 21401. 2.3 mi sw on US 50 and 301 exit 22, just s, then just e. Int corridors. **Pets:** Other species. $25 daily fee/pet. Service with restrictions, supervision. 🛗 📶 ✖ 🍴

Hampton Inn & Suites-Annapolis 🅷 🐾
(410) 571-0200. **$99-$219.** 124 Womack Dr 21401. 2.3 mi sw on US 50 and 301 exit 22, just s, then just e on Admiral Cochrane Dr; n on Spruill Rd, then just w; in Parole area. Int corridors. **Pets:** Large. $50 deposit/room. Service with restrictions, crate. 🛗 📶 📡 ✖ 🍴 💻

Loews Annapolis Hotel 🅷
(410) 263-7777. **$119-$309, 3 day notice.** 126 West St 21401. US 50 and 301 exit 24 eastbound; exit 24A westbound, 1.4 mi s on SR 70, just sw on Calvert St, then just w. Int corridors. **Pets:** Accepted.
SAVE ECO 🍴 📶 ✖ 🍴 💻

Residence Inn by Marriott 🅷
(410) 573-0300. **$132-$217.** 170 Admiral Cochrane Dr 21401. 2.3 mi sw on US 50 and 301, exit 22 to Riva Rd, just s, then just e; in Parole area. Ext corridors. **Pets:** Accepted.
SAVE 🛗 📶 📡 ✖ 🍴 💻

Sheraton Annapolis Hotel 🅷
(410) 266-3131. **$109-$249.** 173 Jennifer Rd 21401. North side of US 50 and 301 exit 23B westbound; exit 23 eastbound. Int corridors. **Pets:** Accepted. SAVE 🍴 🛗 📶 📡 ✖ 🍴 💻

The Westin Annapolis 🅷
(410) 972-4300. **Call for rates.** 100 Westgate Cir 21401. US 50 and 301 exit 24 eastbound; exit 24A westbound, 0.7 mi s on SR 70, then 0.8 mi e on SR 435; 0.5 mi n of Church Circle. Int corridors. **Pets:** Accepted. SAVE ECO 🍴 🛗 📡 ✖ 📡 ✖ 💻

BALTIMORE (Restaurants p. 632)

Admiral Fell Inn, an Ascend Hotel Collection Member 🅷 🐾
(410) 522-7377. **$149-$319.** 888 S Broadway St 21231. Corner of Broadway and Thames sts; facing waterfront. Int corridors. **Pets:** Large. Designated rooms, service with restrictions.
SAVE 🍴 📡 ✖ 🍴 💻

Baltimore Harbor Hotel 🅷
(410) 752-1100. **$89-$399, 3 day notice.** 101 W Fayette St 21201. Between Charles and Liberty sts. Int corridors. **Pets:** Accepted.
📡 📶 ✖ 🍴 💻

Brookshire Suites 🅷
(410) 625-1300. **$119-$299.** 120 E Lombard St 21202. Corner of Calvert and Lombard sts. Int corridors. **Pets:** Medium. $35 one-time fee/room, $10 daily fee/pet. Designated rooms, service with restrictions.
📶 ✖ 🍴 💻

Celie's Waterfront Inn 🅱🅱
(410) 522-2323. **$99-$249, 14 day notice.** 1714 Thames St 21231. In historic Fell's Point area. **Pets:** Dogs only. Designated rooms. 📶 ✖ 📡 🍴 💻

Days Inn Inner Harbor Baltimore 🅷
(410) 576-1000. **$139-$189.** 100 Hopkins Pl 21201. Opposite First Mariner Arena; 1 blk from Baltimore Convention Center. Int corridors. **Pets:** Small, dogs only. $100 deposit/room. Service with restrictions, supervision. SAVE 🍴 📶 📡 ✖ 🍴 💻

Embassy Suites Baltimore-Inner Harbor 🅷
(410) 727-2222. **$129-$399.** 222 St. Paul Pl 21202. At St. Paul Pl and Saratoga St. Int corridors. **Pets:** Accepted.
SAVE 🍴 📡 📡 ✖ 🍴 💻

Four Seasons Hotel Baltimore 🅷 🐾
(410) 576-5800. **$359-$579, 3 day notice.** 200 International Dr 21202. In Harbor East. Int corridors. **Pets:** Small. Service with restrictions, supervision. 🍴 🛗 📡 📶 ✖ 🍴 💻

Hilton Baltimore 🅷
(443) 573-8700. **$107-$359.** 401 W Pratt St 21201. I-95 exit 53, just w of Camden Yards. Int corridors. **Pets:** Accepted.
SAVE 🍴 🛗 📡 ✖ 📡 ✖ 🍴 💻

Holiday Inn Express Baltimore/Downtown 🅷
(410) 400-8045. **$109-$189.** 221 N Gay St 21202. Jct N Gay St and Fallsway. Int corridors. **Pets:** Small. $50 one-time fee/pet. Service with restrictions, crate. 🛗 📶 ✖ 🍴 💻

Holiday Inn-Inner Harbor 🅷
(410) 685-3500. **Call for rates.** 301 W Lombard St 21201. Just w of Camden Yards; between S Howard and Eutaw sts. Int corridors. **Pets:** Accepted. 🍴 📡 📶 ✖ 🍴 💻

Home2 Suites by Hilton-Downtown Baltimore 🅷
(410) 576-1200. **$129-$209.** 8 E Pleasant St 21202. Just e of Charles St. Int corridors. **Pets:** Accepted. 🛗 📶 🍴 💻

Homewood Suites by Hilton Baltimore Inner Harbor 🅷
(410) 234-0999. **$169-$329.** 625 S President St 21202. In Harbor East, at President St traffic circle. Int corridors. **Pets:** Accepted.
🛗 📶 🍴 💻

◆◆ ◆◆ **Hotel Brexton** 🅷

(443) 478-2100. **Call for rates.** 868 Park Ave 21201. Between Tyson and Brexton sts; 1 blk e of Martin Luther King Jr Blvd. Int corridors. **Pets:** Accepted. 🕭 ⊠ ▤ 🖵

◆◆◆ ◆◆ ◆◆ **Hotel Monaco Baltimore** 🅷

(443) 692-6170. **$149-$399.** 2 N Charles St 21201. Jct Baltimore and N Charles sts. Int corridors. **Pets:** Accepted.

[SAVE] [ECO] 🍽 🕭 ⊠ 🖵

◆◆ ◆◆ **Inn at The Colonnade Baltimore - A DoubleTree by Hilton Hotel** 🅷

(410) 235-5400. **Call for rates.** 4 W University Pkwy 21218. I-83 exit 9A, 0.5 mi e on Cold Springs Ln to Roland Ave/University Pkwy, then 1 mi s. Int corridors. **Pets:** Accepted. [ECO] 🍽 ⌚ ⊠ ▤ 🖵

◆◆ ◆◆ **Pier 5, an Ascend Hotel Collection Member** 🅷 🐾

(410) 539-2000. **$159-$339.** 711 Eastern Ave 21202. On the Inner Harbor, at Pier 5. Int corridors. **Pets:** Large. Designated rooms, service with restrictions. 🍽 🕭 ⊠ ▤ 🖵

◆◆ ◆◆ **Radisson Hotel at Cross Keys** 🅷 🐾

(410) 532-6900. **$119-$189.** 5100 Falls Rd 21210. I-83 exit 10A (Northern Pkwy), just e, then 0.4 mi s on Falls Rd; in Village of Cross Keys. Int corridors. **Pets:** $50 one-time fee/pet. Service with restrictions, supervision. 🍽 ⌚ ⌚ ⌚ ⊠ ▤ 🖵

◆◆ ◆◆ **Residence Inn by Marriott-Baltimore Downtown/Inner Harbor** 🅷

(410) 962-1220. **$179-$285.** 17 Light St 21202. Jct Redwood and Light sts. Int corridors. **Pets:** Medium, dogs only. $100 one-time fee/room. Designated rooms, service with restrictions, crate.

🍽 ⌚ ⌚ ⊠ ▤ 🖵

◆◆◆ ◆◆ ◆◆ **Sheraton Inner Harbor Hotel** 🅷

(410) 962-8300. **$109-$499.** 300 S Charles St 21201. At Conway St; 1 blk from the Inner Harbor. Int corridors. **Pets:** Accepted.

[SAVE] 🍽 ⌚ 🕭 ⊠ ▤ 🖵

◆◆◆ ◆◆ **Sleep Inn & Suites Downtown/Inner Harbor** 🅷 🐾

(410) 779-6166. **$89-$359.** 301 Fallsway 21202. Between E Lexington and Gay sts. Int corridors. **Pets:** Medium, other species. $35 daily fee/room. Designated rooms, service with restrictions, crate.

[SAVE] ⌚ ⌚ ⊠ ▤ 🖵

◆◆ ◆◆ ◆◆ **Wyndham Baltimore Peabody Court** 🅷

(410) 727-7101. **$129-$223.** 612 Cathedral St 21201. Cathedral St and Mt. Vernon Square. Int corridors. **Pets:** Accepted.

🍽 ⌚ ▤ 🖵

BELCAMP

◆◆ ◆◆ **Candlewood Suites Aberdeen** 🅷

(410) 914-3060. **Call for rates.** 4216 Philadelphia Rd 21015. I-95 exit 80 (SR 543), just s to SR 7 (Philadelphia Rd N), then just w. Int corridors. **Pets:** Accepted. ⌚ ⌚ ▤ 🖵

◆◆ ◆◆ **Extended Stay America-Baltimore-Bel Air-Aberdeen** 🅷

(410) 273-0194. **Call for rates.** 1361 James Way 21015. I-95 exit 80 (SR 543), just ne. Int corridors. **Pets:** Other species. $25 daily fee/pet. Service with restrictions, supervision. ⌚ ⌚ ▤

◆◆ ◆◆ ◆◆ **Homewood Suites by Hilton Aberdeen/Bel Air** 🅷

(410) 297-8585. **Call for rates.** 4170 Philadelphia Rd 21015. I-95 exit 80 (SR 543), just s to SR 7 (Philadelphia Rd N), then just w. Int corridors. **Pets:** $75 one-time fee/room. Service with restrictions, crate.

⌚ ⌚ ⌚ ▤ 🖵

BELTSVILLE

◆◆ ◆◆ **Comfort Inn Capital Beltway/I-95 North** 🅷

(301) 572-7100. **$79-$129.** 4050 Powder Mill Rd 20705. I-95 exit 29B, just w on SR 212. Int corridors. **Pets:** Medium. $25 one-time fee/pet. Service with restrictions, supervision. ⌚ ⌚ ⌚ ⊠ ▤ 🖵

◆◆◆ ◆◆ ◆◆ **Sheraton College Park North Hotel** 🅷

(301) 937-4422. **$89-$299.** 4095 Powder Mill Rd 20705. I-95 exit 29B, just w on SR 212; 2 mi n of I-495. Int corridors. **Pets:** Accepted.

[SAVE] [ECO] 🍽 ⌚ ⌚ 🕭 ⊠ ▤ 🖵

BETHESDA *(Restaurants p. 633)*

◆◆◆ ◆◆ ◆◆ **Hyatt Regency Bethesda near Washington, D.C.** 🅷

(301) 657-1234. **$99-$499.** One Bethesda Metro Center 20814. I-495 exit 34, 2.5 mi s on SR 355; jct Wisconsin Ave and Old Georgetown Rd; downtown. Int corridors. **Pets:** Accepted.

[SAVE] 🍽 ⌚ ⌚ 🕭 ▤ 🖵

◆◆◆ ◆◆ ◆◆ **Residence Inn by Marriott-Bethesda Downtown** 🅷

(301) 718-0200. **$209-$340.** 7335 Wisconsin Ave 20814. I-495 exit 34, 2.5 mi s on SR 355; entrance on Waverly St. Int corridors. **Pets:** Accepted. [SAVE] ⌚ ⌚ ⊠ ▤ 🖵

BOWIE

◆◆◆ ◆◆ ◆◆ **Comfort Inn Conference Center-Bowie** 🅷 🐾

(301) 464-0089. **$89-$195.** 4500 NW Crain Hwy 20716. US 50 exit 13A, jct US 50/301 and SR 3. Int corridors. **Pets:** Medium, other species. $15 daily fee/pet. Designated rooms, service with restrictions, crate. [SAVE] 🍽 ⌚ ⌚ ⌚ ▤ 🖵

CALIFORNIA

◆◆ ◆◆ **La Quinta Inn & Suites Lexington Park - Patuxent** 🅷

(301) 862-4100. **$89-$190.** 22769 Three Notch Rd 20619. On SR 235, 1.4 mi s of jct SR 4. Int corridors. **Pets:** Large, other species. Service with restrictions. ⌚ ⌚ ⊠ ▤ 🖵

CAMBRIDGE

◆◆ ◆◆ ◆◆ **Comfort Inn & Suites Cambridge** 🅷

(410) 901-0926. **$65-$169.** 2936 Ocean Gateway 21613. On US 50, 0.8 mi e of jct SR 16. Int corridors. **Pets:** Large. $25 daily fee/pet. Service with restrictions, supervision. ⌚ ⌚ ⌚ ⊠ ▤ 🖵

◆◆◆ ◆◆ ◆◆ ◆◆ **Hyatt Regency Chesapeake Bay Golf Resort, Spa and Marina** 🅷 🐾

(410) 901-1234. **$159-$469, 3 day notice.** 100 Heron Blvd 21613. US 50, 1.2 mi e of Frederick C Malkus Jr Bridge. Int corridors. **Pets:** Medium, dogs only. $150 one-time fee/pet. Designated rooms, service with restrictions, crate.

[SAVE] [ECO] 🍽 ⌚ ⌚ ⊠ ⌚ ▤ 🖵

CAMP SPRINGS

◆◆ ◆◆ **Country Inn & Suites By Carlson Andrews Air Force Base/DC Area** 🅷

(240) 492-1070. **$99-$200.** 4950 Mercedes Blvd 20746. I-95/495 exit 7B, just e to Auth Rd, then just n. Int corridors. **Pets:** Accepted. ⌚ ⌚ ▤ 🖵

CHESTERTOWN

◆◆ ◆◆ ◆◆ **Holiday Inn Express Hotel & Suites Chestertown** 🅷

(410) 778-0778. **$99-$239, 3 day notice.** 150 Scheeler Rd 21620. 0.4 mi ne of jct SR 213 and 291. Int corridors. **Pets:** Accepted.

⌚ ⌚ ⌚ ⊠ ▤ 🖵

CHEVERLY

▼▼ Howard Johnson Washington, DC North/BW Pkwy 🄷 ❀

(301) 779-7700. **$89-$139.** 5811 Annapolis Rd 20784. Jct Baltimore-Washington Pkwy and SR 202, then just n on SR 202. Int corridors. **Pets:** Other species. $35 one-time fee/room. Service with restrictions, supervision. 🍴 ⇌ 🛜 🛜 📟

CLEAR SPRING

◈ ▼▼▼ Sleep Inn & Suites 🄷

(301) 842-0290. **$89-$115.** 12426 Houck Ave 21722. I-70 exit 18, just n. Int corridors. **Pets:** Accepted. [SAVE] ⇌ 🛜 ⊠ 📞 📟

CLINTON

◈ ▼▼▼ TownePlace Suites by Marriott at Joint Base Andrews 🄷

(301) 856-2266. **$119-$169.** 7800 Ferry Ave 20735. I-95/495 exit 7A, 2.9 mi s on SR 5 exit Coventry Way E, follow signs to Andrews AFB, then 0.5 mi ne on Old Alexandria Ferry Rd. Int corridors. **Pets:** Accepted. [SAVE] [&M] ⇌ 🛜 ⊠ 📞 📟

COLLEGE PARK

▼▼ Clarion Inn & Fundome 🄷

(301) 474-2800. **$84-$129.** 8601 Baltimore Ave 20740. I-95/495 exit 25 northbound; exit 25B southbound, 1.5 mi s on US 1. Ext/int corridors. **Pets:** Small. $20 daily fee/room. Designated rooms, service with restrictions, crate. 🍴 ⇌ 🛜 📞 📟

▼▼ Comfort Inn & Suites College Park 🄷

(301) 441-8110. **$85-$179.** 9020 Baltimore Ave 20740. I-95/495 exit 25 northbound; exit 25B southbound, 1.3 mi s on US 1. Int corridors. **Pets:** Accepted. ⇌ 🛜 ⊠ 📞 📟

COLUMBIA *(Restaurants p. 633)*

▼▼▼ Homewood Suites by Hilton Columbia 🄷

(410) 872-9200. **$109-$209.** 8320 Benson Dr 21045. I-95 exit 41B, 0.5 mi w on SR 175 (Little Patuxent Pkwy), just nw on SR 108, then just w on Lark Brown Rd. Int corridors. **Pets:** Other species. $15 daily fee/pet. Service with restrictions, crate. [&M] ⇌ 🛜 📞 📟

◈ ▼◈◈◈ Sheraton Columbia Town Center Hotel 🄷

(410) 730-3900. **$89-$249.** 10207 Wincopin Cir 21044. 1.2 mi w on SR 175 (Little Patuxent Pkwy) from jct US 29, then just s; center. Int corridors. **Pets:** Accepted. [SAVE] [ECO] 🍴 ⇌ 🛜 ⊠ 📞 📟

◈ ▼◈◈◈ Sonesta ES Suites Columbia 🄷

(410) 964-9494. **Call for rates.** 8844 Columbia 100 Pkwy 21045. I-95 exit 43B, 4 mi w on SR 100 exit 1B, then just e. Int corridors. **Pets:** Accepted. [SAVE] [&M] ⇌ 🛜 📞 📟

CUMBERLAND

▼▼▼ Ramada Cumberland Downtown 🄷

(301) 724-8800. **$81-$183.** 100 S George St 21502. I-68 exit 43C, just n; downtown. Int corridors. **Pets:** Medium. $25 one-time fee/room. Designated rooms, service with restrictions, supervision. 🍴 ⇌ 🛜 ⊠ 📞 📟

EASTON

▼▼ Comfort Inn Easton Ⓜ

(410) 820-8333. **$85-$149.** 8523 Ocean Gateway 21601. US 50, 0.7 mi n of jct SR 331. Ext corridors. **Pets:** Medium. $25 daily fee/room. Designated rooms, service with restrictions, crate. ⇌ 🛜 📞 📟

◈ ▼▼▼ Inn at 202 Dover 🄲

(410) 819-8007. **$299-$550, 7 day notice.** 202 E Dover St 21601. 0.7 mi w on SR 331 from jct US 50. Int corridors. **Pets:** Dogs only. $50 one-time fee/room. Designated rooms, service with restrictions, crate. [SAVE] 🍴 🛜 ⊠

▼▼ Tidewater Inn 🄷

(410) 822-1300. **Call for rates.** 101 E Dover St 21601. On SR 231, 0.8 mi w of US 50; center. Int corridors. **Pets:** Accepted. 🍴 🛜 ⊠ 📞 📟

EDGEWOOD

▼▼ La Quinta Inn & Suites 🄷

(410) 676-6969. **$84-$179.** 2112B Emmorton Park Rd 21040. I-95 exit 77A, just e on SR 24. Int corridors. **Pets:** Large, other species. Service with restrictions. [&M] 🛜 ⊠ 📞 📟

▼▼ Ramada Edgewood Hotel and Conference Center 🄷

(410) 679-0770. **$74-$119.** 1700 Van Bibber Rd 21040. I-95 exit 77A, just e on SR 24. Ext corridors. **Pets:** Accepted. ⇌ 🛜 📞 📟

ELKTON

▼▼▼ Elk Forge Bed & Breakfast Inn Retreat and Day Spa 🄱🄱

(410) 392-9007. **Call for rates.** 807 Elk Mills Rd 21921. I-95 exit 109B, 1 mi w on SR 279 to Fletchwood Rd (SR 277), then 2 mi s. Ext/int corridors. **Pets:** Accepted. ⊠ 🛜 ⊠ 📞

ELLICOTT CITY

▼▼▼ Residence Inn by Marriott Columbia 🄷

(410) 997-7200. **$189-$209.** 4950 Beaver Run Way 21043. I-95 exit 43B, 4 mi w on SR 100 exit 1B. Int corridors. **Pets:** Accepted. [ECO] [&M] ⇌ 🛜 ⊠ 📞 📟

◈ ▼▼▼ Turf Valley 🄷

(410) 465-1500. **$125-$245.** 2700 Turf Valley Rd 21042. I-70 exit 82 eastbound, 1.5 mi e on US 40; exit 83 westbound, 0.6 mi s on Marriottsville Rd, then 0.8 mi e on US 40. Int corridors. **Pets:** Accepted. [SAVE] [ECO] 🍴 ⇌ ⊠ 🛜 ⊠ 📞 📟

EMMITSBURG

▼▼ Sleep Inn & Suites in Emmitsburg 🄷

(301) 447-0044. **$74-$129.** 501 Silo Hill Pkwy 21727. US 15 exit SR 140, just w, then just n. Int corridors. **Pets:** Accepted. ⇌ 🛜 ⊠ 📞 📟

FREDERICK *(Restaurants p. 633)*

◈ ▼◈◈ Country Inn & Suites By Carlson, Frederick, MD 🄷

(301) 695-2881. **$89-$179.** 5579 Spectrum Dr 21703. I-270 exit 31A, just e on SR 85. Int corridors. **Pets:** Small. $20 daily fee/room. Designated rooms, service with restrictions, supervision. [SAVE] 🛜 ⊠ 📞 📟

◈ ▼▼ Days Inn Ⓜ ❀

(301) 694-6600. **$79-$122.** 5646 Buckeystown Pike 21704. I-270 exit 31A, 0.5 mi e on SR 85; I-70 exit 54, 0.5 mi w. Ext corridors. **Pets:** Small. $20 daily fee/pet. Designated rooms, service with restrictions, crate. [SAVE] ⇌ 🛜 📞 📟

▼▼ Extended Stay America-Frederick-Westview Dr Ⓜ

(301) 668-0808. **Call for rates.** 5240 Westview Dr 21703. I-270 exit 31B, 0.5 mi sw on SR 85, then 0.4 mi n. Int corridors. **Pets:** Other species. $25 daily fee/pet. Service with restrictions, supervision. [&M] 🛜 📞 📟

▼▼▼ Hampton Inn Frederick 🄷

(301) 698-2500. **$99-$179.** 5311 Buckeystown Pike 21704. I-270 exit 31B, 0.6 mi w. Int corridors. **Pets:** Accepted. ⇌ 🛜 ⊠ 📞 📟

▼▼▼ Holiday Inn & Conference Center 🄷

(301) 694-7500. **Call for rates.** 5400 Holiday Dr 21703. I-270 exit 31A, just se of SR 85. Int corridors. **Pets:** Accepted. 🍴 ⇌ ⊠ 🛜 📞 📟

ΔΔΔ ▽▼▽ MainStay Suites Frederick H ❀
(301) 668-4600. **$89-$149.** 7310 Executive Way 21704. I-270 exit 31B, 0.7 mi sw on SR 85. Int corridors. **Pets:** Large, other species. $10 daily fee/pet. Service with restrictions, crate. (SAVE) 🏊 🛜 🍴 📺

▽▼▽▼ Residence Inn by Marriott Frederick H
(301) 360-0010. **$99-$199.** 5230 Westview Dr 21703. I-270 exit 31B, 0.5 mi sw on SR 85, then 0.3 mi n on Crestwood Blvd. Int corridors. **Pets:** Accepted. (&M) 🏊 🛜 ✕ 🍴 📺

▽▼▽▼ TownePlace Suites by Marriott Frederick H
(301) 624-0050. **$99-$199.** 5050 Westview Dr 21703. I-270 exit 31B, 0.9 mi sw on SR 85. Int corridors. **Pets:** Large. $100 one-time fee/ room. Service with restrictions. (&M) 🏊 🛜 ✕ 🍴 📺

ΔΔΔ ▽▼▽ Travelodge Frederick H
(301) 663-0500. **$60-$156.** 20 Monocacy Blvd 21704. I-70 exit 54, just n. Int corridors. **Pets:** Accepted. (SAVE) 🛜 🍴 📺

FROSTBURG

▽▼▽ Days Inn & Suites M
(301) 689-2050. **$80-$200.** 11100 New Georges Creek Rd 21532. I-68 exit 34, 1 mi n on SR 36. Int corridors. **Pets:** Accepted.
✕ 🛜 🍴 📺

GAITHERSBURG

▽▼▽▼ Comfort Inn Shady Grove H
(301) 330-0023. **$89-$159.** 16216 Frederick Rd 20877. I-270 exit 8, 1 mi e on Shady Grove Rd at SR 355. Int corridors. **Pets:** Medium. $15 daily fee/pet. Designated rooms, service with restrictions, crate.
🍴 🏊 🛜 ✕ 🍴 📺

ΔΔΔ ▽▼▽▼ Hilton Washington DC North/Gaithersburg H
(301) 977-8900. **$89-$219.** 620 Perry Pkwy 20877. I-270 exit 11, then e. Int corridors. **Pets:** Medium. $50 one-time fee/pet. Designated rooms, service with restrictions, crate. (SAVE) 🍴 🏊 🛜 ✕ 🍴 📺

ΔΔΔ ▽▼▽▼ HYATT house Gaithersburg H
(301) 527-6000. **$89-$269.** 200 Skidmore Blvd 20877. I-370 exit SR 355, just n to Westland Rd. Ext corridors. **Pets:** Accepted.
(SAVE) (&M) 🏊 🛜 ✕ 🍴 📺

▽▼▽▼ Residence Inn by Marriott-Gaithersburg H
(301) 590-3003. **$179-$219.** 9721 Washingtonian Blvd 20878. I-270 exit 9B (I-370/Sam Eig Hwy), just w to Fields Rd, 0.8 mi se, then just ne. Int corridors. **Pets:** Accepted. (&M) 🏊 🛜 ✕ 🍴 📺

▽▼▽▼ TownePlace Suites by Marriott-Gaithersburg H
(301) 590-2300. **$99-$249.** 212 Perry Pkwy 20877. I-270 exit 10 north-bound, just ne; exit 11 southbound, just e on SR 124 to SR 355, 0.3 mi s, then 0.5 mi sw. Int corridors. **Pets:** Accepted.
(&M) 🛜 ✕ 🍴 📺

GLEN BURNIE *(Restaurants p. 633)*

▽▼▽ Extended Stay America Baltimore-Glen Burnie H
(410) 761-2708. **Call for rates.** 104 Chesapeake Centre Ct 21061. I-695 exit 3B eastbound; exit 2 westbound, 0.9 mi s on SR 2, just e on E Ordnance Rd, then just s. Int corridors. **Pets:** Other species. $25 daily fee/pet. Service with restrictions, supervision. (&M) 🛜 🍴 📺

ΔΔΔ ▽▼▽ La Quinta Inn & Suites Baltimore South Glen Burnie H
(410) 636-4300. **$82-$205.** 6323 Ritchie Hwy 21061. I-695 exit 3A east-bound; exit 2 westbound, jct SR 2. Int corridors. **Pets:** Large, other species. Service with restrictions. (SAVE) (&M) 🏊 🛜 🍴 📺

GRANTSVILLE

ΔΔΔ ▽▼▽▼ Comfort Inn H
(301) 895-5993. **$84-$107.** 2541 Chestnut Ridge Rd 21536. I-68 exit 22, just s on US 219. Int corridors. **Pets:** Accepted.
(SAVE) 🏊 🛜 ✕ 🍴 📺

GRASONVILLE

ΔΔΔ ▽▼▽ BEST WESTERN Kent Narrows Inn M
(410) 827-6767. **$149-$255.** 3101 Main St 21638. US 50 and 301 exit 42; at Kent Narrows Bridge. Ext corridors. **Pets:** Accepted.
(SAVE) 🏊 🛜 📺

GREENBELT

ΔΔΔ ▽▼▽▼ Residence Inn by Marriott-Greenbelt H
(301) 982-1600. **$99-$229.** 6320 Golden Triangle Dr 20770. I-95/495 exit 23, 0.5 mi sw of jct SR 201, off SR 193 (Greenbelt Rd), then just n on Walker Dr. Int corridors. **Pets:** Accepted.
(SAVE) (&M) 🏊 🛜 ✕ 🍴 📺

HAGERSTOWN

ΔΔΔ ▽▼▽ BEST WESTERN Grand Venice Hotel Wedding & Conference Center H
(301) 733-0830. **$79-$94.** 431 Dual Hwy 21740. I-70 exit 32B, 2.7 mi w on US 40. Int corridors. **Pets:** Accepted.
(SAVE) (ECO) (🍴) 🏊 🛜 ✕ 🍴 📺

ΔΔΔ ▽▼▽▼ Clarion Hotel & Conference Center H
(301) 733-5100. **$49-$275.** 901 Dual Hwy 21740. I-70 exit 32B, 1.1 mi n on US 40. Int corridors. **Pets:** Accepted.
(SAVE) 🏊 🛜 ✕ 🍴 📺

ΔΔΔ ▽▼▽▼ Comfort Suites H
(301) 791-8100. **$70-$129.** 1801 Dual Hwy 21740. I-70 exit 32B, 0.8 mi w on US 40. Int corridors. **Pets:** Small, dogs only. Designated rooms, service with restrictions, crate. (SAVE) 🏊 🛜 ✕ 🍴 📺

▽▼▽ Days Inn Hagerstown M
(301) 733-2700. **$60-$140.** 1101 Dual Hwy 21740. I-70 exit 32B, 2.2 mi w on US 40. Int corridors. **Pets:** Accepted. 🛜 🍴 📺

▽▼▽ Halfway Hagerstown Super 8 M
(301) 582-1992. **$63-$130.** 16805 Blake Rd 21740. I-81 exit 5B, just w. Int corridors. **Pets:** Medium. $20 deposit/pet, $15 daily fee/pet. Service with restrictions, supervision. 🛜 🍴 📺

▽▼▽▼ Holiday Inn Express Hotel & Suites H
(301) 745-5644. **$119-$139.** 241 Railway Ln 21740. I-81 exit 5A, just e. Int corridors. **Pets:** Accepted. (&M) 🏊 ✕ 🛜 ✕ 🍴 📺

▽▼▽▼ Homewood Suites by Hilton H
(301) 665-3816. **$129-$169.** 1650 Pullman Ln 21740. I-81 exit 5, 0.3 mi e; 0.5 mi n of jct I-70 and 81. Int corridors. **Pets:** Accepted.
🏊 🛜 🍴 📺

▽▼▽ Sleep Inn & Suites H ❀
(301) 766-9449. **$89-$139.** 18216 Col Henry K Douglas Dr 21740. I-70 exit 29, just s. Int corridors. **Pets:** Large. $10 daily fee/pet. Designated rooms, service with restrictions, supervision. 🏊 🛜 🍴 📺

HANOVER *(Restaurants p. 633)*

ΔΔΔ ▽▼▽▼ Aloft Arundel Mills H
(443) 577-0077. **$129-$199.** 7520 Teague Rd 21076. I-95 exit 43A, 3.6 mi e on SR 100 exit 10A (Arundel Mills Blvd), then 0.4 mi s to SR 713. Int corridors. **Pets:** Accepted. (SAVE) (ECO) (&M) 🏊 🛜 ✕ 🍴 📺

ΔΔΔ ▽▼▽▼ Element Arundel Mills H
(443) 577-0050. **$139-$209.** 7522 Teague Rd 21076. I-95 exit 43A, 3.6 mi e on SR 100 exit 10A (Arundel Mills Blvd), then 0.4 mi s to SR 713. Int corridors. **Pets:** Accepted.
(SAVE) (ECO) (🍴) (&M) 🏊 🛜 ✕ 🍴 📺

▽▼▽▼ Homewood Suites by Hilton Baltimore/Arundel Mills H
(410) 878-7201. **$149-$209.** 7491-B New Ridge Rd 21076. SR 100 exit 10B, 0.3 mi n on SR 713. Int corridors. **Pets:** Accepted.
(&M) 🏊 🛜 ✕ 🍴 📺

AAA **♦♦♦** Red Roof Plus+ Baltimore- Washington DC/BW Parkway **M**

(410) 712-4070. **$60-$130.** 7306 Parkway Dr S 21076. I-95 exit 43A, 2 mi e on SR 100 exit 8 (Coca Cola Dr), then 0.5 mi se. Ext corridors. **Pets:** Large, other species. Service with restrictions, supervision.

[SAVE] [♿M] [📶] [✕] [🛎] [🖥]

♦♦♦ Residence Inn by Marriott-Arundel Mills/BWI **H**

(410) 799-7332. **$169-$189.** 7035 Arundel Mills Cir 21076. I-95 exit 43A, 3.6 mi e on SR 100 exit 10A (Arundel Mills Blvd). Int corridors. **Pets:** Accepted. [♿M] [🏊] [📶] [✕] [🛎] [🖥]

♦♦♦ TownePlace Suites by Marriott Arundel Mills/BWI **H** 🐾

(410) 379-9000. **$159-$209.** 7021 Arundel Mills Cir 21076. I-95 exit 43A, 3.6 mi e on SR 100 exit 10A (Arundel Mills Blvd). Int corridors. **Pets:** Small. $100 one-time fee/room. Designated rooms, service with restrictions, crate. [♿M] [🏊] [📶] [✕] [🛎] [🖥]

HUNT VALLEY

♦♦♦♦ Hunt Valley Inn, A Wyndham Grand Hotel **H**

(410) 785-7000. **$88-$221.** 245 Shawan Rd 21031. I-83 exit 20A (Shawan Rd), just e. Int corridors. **Pets:** Accepted.

[🍽] [♿M] [🏊] [✕] [📶] [✕] [🖥]

♦♦♦ Residence Inn by Marriott Baltimore Hunt Valley **H**

(410) 527-2333. **$179-$209.** 45 Schilling Rd 21031. I-83 exit 20A (Shawan Rd), just e, just s on McCormick Rd, then just e. Int corridors. **Pets:** Other species. $75 one-time fee/room. Service with restrictions.

[♿M] [🏊] [📶] [✕] [🛎] [🖥]

JESSUP

♦♦♦ Extended Stay America-Columbia-Laurel-Ft. Meade **H**

(301) 725-3877. **Call for rates.** 8550 Washington Blvd 20794. I-95 exit 38A, 1.4 mi e on SR 32, then 0.5 mi n on US 1. Int corridors. **Pets:** Other species. $25 daily fee/pet. Service with restrictions, supervision. [♿M] [📶] [🛎]

♦♦♦ La Quinta Inn & Suites Columbia Jessup **H**

(410) 799-1500. **$72-$219.** 7300 Crestmount Rd 20794. I-95 exit 41A, just e on SR 175, then just s on US 1. Int corridors. **Pets:** Large, other species. Service with restrictions. [♿M] [📶] [🛎] [🖥]

AAA **♦♦♦** Red Roof Inn Washington DC- Columbia/Fort Meade **M**

(410) 796-0380. **$60-$130.** 8000 Washington Blvd 20794. I-95 exit 41A, 0.3 mi s of jct US 1 and SR 175. Ext corridors. **Pets:** Large, other species. Service with restrictions, supervision.

[SAVE] [♿M] [📶] [✕] [🛎] [🖥]

LARGO

♦♦♦ Radisson Hotel Largo/Washington, D.C. **H**

(301) 773-0700. **$99-$259.** 9100 Basil Ct 20774. I-95/495 exit 17A (SR 202), just se. Int corridors. **Pets:** Accepted.

[🍽] [♿M] [🏊] [📶] [✕] [🛎] [🖥]

♦♦♦ Residence Inn Largo Capital Beltway **H**

(301) 925-7806. **$109-$299.** 1330 Caraway Ct 20774. I-95/495 exit 16, 0.4 mi e on Arena Dr, 0.3 mi n on Lottsford Rd, then just w on McCormick Dr. Int corridors. **Pets:** Accepted. [♿M] [📶] [✕] [🛎] [🖥]

LAUREL

AAA **♦♦♦** Holiday Inn Express & Suites Laurel Lakes **H**

(301) 206-2600. **Call for rates.** 14402 Laurel Pl 20707. On US 1, 0.9 mi s of jct SR 198. Int corridors. **Pets:** Accepted.

[SAVE] [♿M] [🏊] [📶] [✕] [🛎] [🖥]

♦♦♦ Holiday Inn Laurel-West **H** 🐾

(301) 776-5300. **Call for rates.** 15101 Sweitzer Ln 20707. I-95 exit 33B, just w on SR 198. Ext/int corridors. **Pets:** Large. $75 one-time fee/pet. Designated rooms, service with restrictions, crate.

[🍽] [♿M] [📶] [✕] [🛎] [🖥]

LA VALE

AAA **♦♦♦** BEST WESTERN Braddock Motor Inn **H**

(301) 729-3300. **$68-$130.** 1268 National Hwy 21502. On US 40, jct SR 53. Int corridors. **Pets:** Accepted.

[SAVE] [🍽] [🏊] [✕] [📶] [🛎] [🖥]

♦ Super 8 LaVale **M**

(301) 729-6265. **$41-$71.** 1301 National Hwy 21502. I-68 exit 40 eastbound, 0.5 mi s; exit 39 westbound, 0.4 mi n. Int corridors. **Pets:** Accepted. [📶] [🛎] [🖥]

LEXINGTON PARK

AAA **♦♦♦** Hampton Inn Lexington Park **H**

(301) 863-3200. **$99-$159.** 22211 Three Notch Rd 20653. On SR 235, 0.9 mi n of jct SR 246. Int corridors. **Pets:** Dogs only. Designated rooms, service with restrictions, supervision.

[SAVE] [♿M] [🏊] [📶] [✕] [🛎] [🖥]

♦♦♦ Home2 Suites by Hilton Lexington Park/Pax River NAS **H**

(301) 866-1416. **$119-$169.** 46058 Valley Dr 20653. On SR 235, 0.9 mi n of jct SR 246. Int corridors. **Pets:** Accepted.

[ECO] [♿M] [🏊] [📶] [✕] [🛎] [🖥]

♦♦♦ TownePlace Suites by Marriott Patuxent River Naval Air Station **H**

(301) 863-1111. **$159-$179.** 22520 Three Notch Rd 20653. On SR 235, 1 mi n of Gate 1 at Naval Air Station Patuxent River. Int corridors. **Pets:** Accepted. [♿M] [🏊] [📶] [✕] [🛎] [🖥]

LINTHICUM HEIGHTS

AAA **♦♦♦** Aloft Baltimore Washington Intl Airport **H**

(410) 691-6969. **$89-$249.** 1741 W Nursery Rd 21090. I-695 exit 7A, 1 mi s on SR 295, then 1.2 mi e. Int corridors. **Pets:** Accepted.

[SAVE] [♿M] [🏊] [📶] [🛎] [🖥]

♦♦ BEST WESTERN PLUS BWI Airport North Inn & Suites **H**

(410) 789-7223. **Call for rates.** 6055 Belle Grove Rd 21225. I-695 exit 6A eastbound; exit 5 westbound, 0.4 mi n to jct SR 170/648, just n on SR 170. Int corridors. **Pets:** Accepted. [♿M] [📶] [🛎] [🖥]

♦♦♦ Candlewood Suites-BWI **H**

(410) 850-9214. **Call for rates.** 1247 Winterson Rd 21090. I-695 exit 7A, 1 mi s on SR 295, 1.3 mi w on W Nursery Rd, then 0.3 mi w. Int corridors. **Pets:** Accepted. [📶] [✕] [🛎] [🖥]

♦♦♦ DoubleTree by Hilton Baltimore - BWI Airport **H**

(410) 859-8400. **$109-$209.** 890 Elkridge Landing Rd 21090. I-695 exit 7A, 1 mi s on SR 295, 1.3 mi w on W Nursery Rd, then 0.5 mi w. Int corridors. **Pets:** Accepted. [🍽] [♿M] [🏊] [📶] [✕] [🛎] [🖥]

♦♦♦ Hampton Inn BWI Airport **H**

(410) 850-0600. **$119-$299.** 829 Elkridge Landing Rd 21090. I-695 exit 7A, 1 mi s on SR 295, 1.3 mi e on W Nursery Rd, then just w. Int corridors. **Pets:** Accepted. [♿M] [📶] [✕] [🛎] [🖥]

AAA **♦♦♦** Holiday Inn BWI **H**

(410) 691-1000. **Call for rates.** 815 Elkridge Landing Rd 21090. I-695 exit 7A, 1 mi s on SR 295, then 1.3 mi e on W Nursery Rd. Int corridors. **Pets:** Accepted. [SAVE] [🍽] [♿M] [📶] [✕] [🛎] [🖥]

AAA **♦♦♦** Hyatt Place Baltimore/BWI Airport **H**

(410) 859-3366. **$79-$229.** 940 International Dr 21090. I-695 exit 7A, 1 mi s on SR 295, then just e on W Nursery Rd. Int corridors. **Pets:** Accepted. [SAVE] [♿M] [🏊] [📶] [✕] [🛎] [🖥]

La Quinta Inn & Suites BWI Airport 🏨
(410) 859-2333. **$79-$204.** 1734 W Nursery Rd 21090. I-695 exit 7A, 1 mi s on SR 295, then 1.3 mi e. Int corridors. **Pets:** Large, other species. Service with restrictions.

Red Roof Plus+ Baltimore-Washington DC/BWI Airport 🅼
(410) 850-7600. **$60-$130.** 827 Elkridge Landing Rd 21090. I-695 exit 7A, 1 mi s on SR 295, 1.3 mi e on W Nursery Rd, then just w. Ext corridors. **Pets:** Large, other species. Service with restrictions, supervision.

Residence Inn by Marriott-BWI Airport 🏨
(410) 691-0255. **$89-$241.** 1160 Winterson Rd 21090. I-695 exit 7A, 1 mi s on SR 295, 0.7 mi e on W Nursery Rd, then just n. Int corridors. **Pets:** Accepted.

Staybridge Suites BWI 🏨
(410) 850-5666. **Call for rates.** 1301 Winterson Rd 21090. I-695 exit 7A, 1 mi s on SR 295, 1.3 mi e on Nursery Rd, then 0.4 mi w. Int corridors. **Pets:** Accepted.

TownePlace Suites by Marriott Baltimore/ BWI Airport 🏨
(410) 694-0060. **$69-$199.** 1171 Winterson Rd 21090. I-695 exit 7A, 1 mi s on SR 295, 0.7 mi e on W Nursery Rd, then just n. Int corridors. **Pets:** Other species. $100 one-time fee/room. Service with restrictions, crate.

The Westin-Baltimore Washington Airport 🏨
(443) 577-2300. **Call for rates.** 1110 Old Elkridge Landing Rd 21090. I-695 exit 7A, 1 mi s on SR 295, 1.3 mi e on W Nursery Rd, then 0.4 mi w on Winterson Rd. Int corridors. **Pets:** Accepted.

MCHENRY

Wisp Resort Hotel & Conference Center 🏨
(301) 387-5581. **$79-$369, 7 day notice.** 290 Marsh Hill Rd 21541. 1 mi s on US 219 from jct SR 42, just on Sang Run Rd, then 0.3 mi s. Int corridors. **Pets:** Medium, dogs only. $50 one-time fee/room. Designated rooms, service with restrictions, crate.

NATIONAL HARBOR (Restaurants p. 633)

Aloft Washington National Harbor 🏨
(301) 749-9000. **$99-$449.** 156 Waterfront St 20745. I-95/495 exit 2A, 0.5 mi e. Int corridors. **Pets:** Accepted.

Residence Inn by Marriott National Harbor 🏨
(301) 749-4755. **$129-$389.** 192 Waterfront St 20745. I-95/495 exit 2A, 0.5 mi e. Int corridors. **Pets:** Accepted.

The Westin Washington National Harbor 🏨 🐾
(301) 567-3999. **Call for rates.** 171 Waterfront St 20745. I-95/495 exit 2A, 0.5 mi e. Int corridors. **Pets:** Medium. Designated rooms, service with restrictions, crate.

NORTH EAST (Restaurants p. 633)

BEST WESTERN North East Inn 🏨
(410) 287-5450. **$90-$120.** 39 Elwoods Rd 21901. I-95 exit 100 southbound; exit 100B northbound, 0.5 mi n on SR 272, then just w on Joseph Biggs Hwy to Old Bayview Rd. Int corridors. **Pets:** $10 daily fee/pet. Designated rooms, service with restrictions, crate.

Comfort Inn & Suites North East 🏨
(410) 287-7100. **$90-$140.** 1 Center Dr 21901. I-95 exit 100 southbound; exit 100A northbound, just s on SR 272. Int corridors. **Pets:** Small, dogs only. $15 daily fee/pet. Designated rooms, service with restrictions, supervision.

OCEAN CITY (Restaurants p. 633)

Clarion Resort Fontainebleau Hotel 🏨
(410) 524-3535. **Call for rates.** 10100 Coastal Hwy 21842. At 101st St. Int corridors. **Pets:** Other species. $39 daily fee/pet. Designated rooms, service with restrictions.

Comfort Suites Ocean City 🏨 🐾
(410) 213-7171. **$89-$129, 3 day notice.** 12718 Ocean Gateway 21842. US 50; 0.7 mi w of Ocean City Bridge. Int corridors. **Pets:** Medium. $35 daily fee/pet. Designated rooms, service with restrictions, crate.

Paradise Plaza Inn 🏨
(410) 289-6381. **$65-$465, 3 day notice.** 3 9th St 21842. 9th St and The Boardwalk. Int corridors. **Pets:** Accepted.

OWINGS MILLS

Hyatt Place Baltimore/Owings Mills 🏨
(410) 998-3630. **$89-$189.** 4730 Painters Mill Rd 21117. I-795 exit 4 (Owings Mills Blvd), 0.5 mi s, then 0.7 mi e on Red Run Blvd. Int corridors. **Pets:** Medium, dogs only. $75 one-time fee/pet. Designated rooms, service with restrictions, supervision.

PERRYVILLE

Days Inn Perryville 🅼
(410) 642-2866. **$69-$84.** 61 Heather Ln 21903. I-95 exit 93, just e. Ext corridors. **Pets:** Accepted.

ROCK HALL

Inn at Huntingfield Creek 🅱🅱
(410) 639-7779. **$185-$325, 14 day notice.** 4928 Eastern Neck Rd 21661. 1.8 mi s on SR 445 from jct SR 20. Ext/int corridors. **Pets:** $25 daily fee/pet. Designated rooms, crate.

Mariners Motel 🅼
(410) 639-2291. **$80-$95.** 5681 S Hawthorne Ave 21661. 0.3 mi e of SR 20. Ext corridors. **Pets:** Accepted.

ROCKVILLE (Restaurants p. 633)

BEST WESTERN PLUS Rockville Hotel & Suites 🏨
(301) 424-4940. **$89-$159.** 1251 W Montgomery Ave 20850. I-270 exit 6B, just w on SR 28. Int corridors. **Pets:** Accepted.

Crowne Plaza Washington DC-Rockville 🏨
(301) 840-0200. **$79-$199.** 3 Research Ct 20850. I-270 exit 8 (Shady Grove Rd), just sw. Int corridors. **Pets:** Medium, other species. $20 daily fee/pet.

EVEN Hotels-Rockville/Washington, DC Area 🏨
(301) 881-3836. **Call for rates.** 1775 Rockville Pike 20852. SR 355, 2 mi s of jct SR 28. Int corridors. **Pets:** Accepted.

Extended Stay America-Washington DC-Rockville 🏨
(301) 987-9100. **Call for rates.** 2621 Research Blvd 20850. I-270 exit 8 (Shady Grove Rd), just w, then just n. Int corridors. **Pets:** Other species. $25 daily fee/pet. Service with restrictions, supervision.

Hilton Rockville Hotel & Executive Meeting Center H
(301) 468-1100. **$99-$309.** 1750 Rockville Pike 20852. SR 355, 2 mi s of jct SR 28. Int corridors. **Pets:** Accepted.

Quality Suites Rockville H
(301) 590-9880. **Call for rates.** 1380 Piccard Dr 20850. I-270 exit 8 (Shady Grove Rd) northbound to Redland Blvd, just n; exit 8 (Shady Grove Rd) southbound, 0.3 mi e to Choke Cherry Rd, just s to Piccard Dr, then 0.6 sw; 1 mi w of SR 355 via Redland Blvd. Ext corridors. **Pets:** Accepted.

Red Roof Plus+ Washington DC-Rockville M
(301) 987-0965. **$79-$150.** 16001 Shady Grove Rd 20850. I-270 exit 8 (Shady Grove Rd), 0.5 mi e. Ext corridors. **Pets:** Large, other species. Service with restrictions, supervision.

Sheraton Rockville H ✿
(240) 912-8200. **Call for rates.** 920 King Farm Blvd 20850. I-270 exit 8 (Shady Grove Rd), 0.3 mi e to Choke Cherry Rd, just s to Piccard Dr, then just sw; 1 mi w of SR 355 via Redland Blvd. Int corridors. **Pets:** Medium, dogs only. Designated rooms, service with restrictions, supervision.

Sleep Inn-Rockville H ✿
(301) 948-8000. **$69-$99.** 2 Research Ct 20850. I-270 exit 8 (Shady Grove Rd), just sw. Int corridors. **Pets:** Large, other species. $25 daily fee/pet. Designated rooms, service with restrictions.

ROSEDALE

La Quinta Inn & Suites Baltimore North H
(410) 574-8100. **$82-$214.** 4 Philadelphia Ct 21237. I-695 exit 34, just n. Int corridors. **Pets:** Large, other species. Service with restrictions.

ST. MICHAELS

BEST WESTERN St. Michaels Motor Inn M
(410) 745-3333. **$110-$205.** 1228 S Talbot St 21663. 1 mi e on SR 33. Ext/int corridors. **Pets:** Accepted.

St. Michaels Harbour Inn, Marina & Spa H
(410) 745-9001. **Call for rates.** 101 N Harbor Rd 21663. 0.3 mi e on SR 33, just n on Seymour Ave, just w. Int corridors. **Pets:** Dogs only. $50 one-time fee/pet. Service with restrictions, supervision.

SALISBURY

BEST WESTERN Salisbury Plaza M ✿
(410) 546-1300. **$49-$130.** 1735 N Salisbury Blvd 21801. US 13 business route, 0.5 mi s of US 50 Bypass. Ext corridors. **Pets:** $10 daily fee/room. Service with restrictions, crate.

Hampton Inn-Salisbury H ✿
(410) 334-3080. **$77-$139.** 121 E Naylor Mill Rd 21804. US 13, 0.5 mi n of jct US 50 Bypass. Int corridors. **Pets:** Large, other species. Service with restrictions.

Residence Inn by Marriott Salisbury H
(410) 543-0033. **$139-$230.** 140 Centre Rd 21801. Just off US 13 business route at US 50. Int corridors. **Pets:** Other species. $100 one-time fee/room. Service with restrictions.

SILVER SPRING

Residence Inn by Marriott Silver Spring H
(301) 572-2322. **$89-$239.** 12000 Plum Orchard Dr 20904. I-95 exit 29B, 1.2 mi w on SR 212, then 1 mi n on Cherry Hill Rd. Int corridors. **Pets:** Accepted.

Sheraton Silver Spring H
(301) 589-0800. **Call for rates.** 8777 Georgia Ave 20910. I-495 exit 31B, 1 mi s. Int corridors. **Pets:** Accepted.

SNOW HILL

River House Inn BB
(410) 632-2722. **$99-$350, 7 day notice.** 201 E Market St 21863. 1 mi w on SR 394 from jct SR 113. Ext/int corridors. **Pets:** Dogs only. $15 daily fee/pet. Designated rooms, service with restrictions.

SYKESVILLE *(Restaurants p. 633)*

Inn at Norwood BB
(410) 549-7868. **$135-$225, 7 day notice.** 7514 Norwood Ave 21784. I-70 exit 80 (SR 32), 3.6 mi n, 0.6 mi w on W Friendship Rd (which becomes Main St), then just s on Church St. Ext/int corridors. **Pets:** Dogs only. $20 daily fee/pet. Designated rooms, service with restrictions.

THURMONT

Super 8-Thurmont M
(301) 271-7888. **$59-$140.** 300 Tippin Dr 21788. US 15, just w on SR 806. Int corridors. **Pets:** Accepted.

TILGHMAN ISLAND

Knapp's Narrows Marina & Inn M
(410) 886-2720. **$90-$260, 7 day notice.** 6176 Tilghman Island Rd 21671. On SR 33, east side of the bridge. Ext corridors. **Pets:** Other species. $25 daily fee/room. Designated rooms, service with restrictions, crate.

TIMONIUM

Red Roof Plus+ Baltimore North-Timonium M
(410) 666-0380. **$65-$110.** 111 W Timonium Rd 21093. I-83 exit 16A northbound; exit 16 southbound, just e. Ext corridors. **Pets:** Large, other species. Service with restrictions, supervision.

TOWSON

Sheraton Baltimore North Hotel H
(410) 321-7400. **Call for rates.** 903 Dulaney Valley Rd 21204. I-695 exit 27A (Dulaney Valley Rd), 0.3 mi s. Int corridors. **Pets:** Accepted.

UPPER MARLBORO

Executive Inn & Suites M
(301) 627-3969. **$80-$130.** 2901 Crain Hwy 20774. On US 301, 2.5 mi n of jct SR 4; 7 mi s of jct US 50. Ext corridors. **Pets:** Medium. $10 daily fee/pet. Service with restrictions, supervision.

WALDORF

Holiday Inn Express Waldorf H
(301) 932-9200. **$70-$120, 45 day notice.** 11370 Days Ct 20603. 0.5 mi s on US 301 from jct SR 228. Int corridors. **Pets:** Accepted.

La Quinta Inn Waldorf H
(301) 645-0022. **$80-$224.** 11770 Business Park Dr 20601. 1 mi n on US 301 from jct SR 228. Int corridors. **Pets:** Large, other species. Service with restrictions.

Residence Inn by Marriott Waldorf H
(301) 632-2111. **$132-$152.** 3020 Technology Pl 20601. SR 228, just w of jct US 301. Int corridors. **Pets:** Accepted.

WESTMINSTER *(Restaurants p. 633)*

◇◇◇ ▼▼◆ BEST WESTERN Westminster Catering & Conference Center 🅷 ❖

(410) 857-1900. **$99-$179.** 451 WMC Dr 21158. 1.7 mi w on SR 140 from jct SR 27. Int corridors. **Pets:** Large, dogs only. $15 daily fee/pet. Service with restrictions, crate. 🆂🅰🆅🅴 🛀 🛜 ⌧ 🛏 🖵

▼▼ The Boston Inn 🅼

(410) 848-9095. **$47-$75.** 533 Baltimore Blvd 21157. 0.9 mi se on SR 140 and 97 from jct SR 27. Ext corridors. **Pets:** Dogs only. Service with restrictions, crate. 🛀 🛜 🛏 🖵

WHITE MARSH *(Restaurants p. 633)*

▼▼◆ Home2 Suites by Hilton Baltimore White Marsh 🅷

(410) 933-1010. **$99-$299.** 10465 Philadelphia Rd 21162. I-95 exit 67, 0.5 mi e on SR 43, then just s on CR 7. Int corridors. **Pets:** Accepted. 🅼 🛀 🛜 ⌧ 🛏 🖵

▼▼◆ Residence Inn by Marriott Baltimore/White Marsh 🅷

(410) 933-9554. **$169-$230.** 4980 Mercantile Rd 21236. I-95 exit 67, 0.5 mi w on SR 43 (White Marsh Blvd), just s on Honeygo Blvd, then just e. Int corridors. **Pets:** Accepted. 🅼 🛀 🛜 ⌧ 🛏 🖵

WILLIAMSPORT

◇◇◇ ▼▼◆ Red Roof Inn- Hagerstown-Williamsport 🅼

(301) 582-3500. **$60-$175.** 310 E Potomac St 21795. I-81 exit 2, 0.3 mi sw on US 11. Ext corridors. **Pets:** Large, other species. Service with restrictions, supervision. 🆂🅰🆅🅴 🛜 🛏

MASSACHUSETTS

ANDOVER

▼▼◆ Homewood Suites by Hilton Boston/Andover 🅷

(978) 475-6000. **$139-$189.** 4 Riverside Dr 01810. I-93 exit 45, 0.5 mi e. Int corridors. **Pets:** Accepted. 🍽 🅼 🛀 🛜 🛏 🖵

▼▼◆ Residence Inn by Marriott Boston-Andover 🅷 ❖

(978) 683-0382. **$125-$229.** 500 Minuteman Rd 01810. I-93 exit 45, 0.3 mi w, then 0.5 mi n. Int corridors. **Pets:** Large. $100 one-time fee/room. Designated rooms, service with restrictions.

🍽 🅼 🛀 🛜 ⌧ 🛏 🖵

◇◇◇ ▼▼◆ Sonesta ES Suites 🅷

(978) 686-2000. **$139-$209.** 4 Tech Dr 01810. I-93 exit 45, just sw to Shattuck Rd. Int corridors. **Pets:** Accepted.
🆂🅰🆅🅴 🍽 🅼 🛀 🛜 🛏 🖵

◇◇◇ ▼▼◆ Wyndham Boston/Andover Hotel 🅷

(978) 975-3600. **$119-$192.** 123 Old River Rd 01810. I-93 exit 45, just e on River Rd. Int corridors. **Pets:** Accepted.
🆂🅰🆅🅴 🍽 🛀 🛜 ⌧ 🛏 🖵

AUBURN

▼▼ La Quinta Inn Auburn Worcester 🅷

(508) 832-7000. **$82-$239.** 446 Southbridge St 01501. I-90 exit 10, 1.2 mi n on SR 12. Int corridors. **Pets:** Large, other species. Service with restrictions. 🛜 🛏 🖵

BARRE

▼▼◆ Jenkins Inn 🅶

(978) 355-6444. **Call for rates.** 7 West St 01005. On SR 122 and 32. Int corridors. **Pets:** Dogs only. $10 daily fee/pet. Service with restrictions, supervision. 🍽 🛜 ⌧ 🛏 🖵

BEDFORD

▼▼◆ Homewood Suites by Hilton 🅷

(978) 670-7111. **$98-$206.** 35 Middlesex Tpke 01730. I-95 exit 32B, 2.5 mi n. Int corridors. **Pets:** Accepted. 🅼 🛀 🛜 🛏 🖵

BOSTON *(Restaurants p. 633)*

▼▼ ▼▼◆ Ames Hotel 🅷

(617) 979-8100. **$229-$450.** 1 Court St 02108. At Washington St; across from Old State House. Int corridors. **Pets:** Accepted.
🍽 🅼 🛜 ⌧

◇◇◇ ▼▼◆▼ Battery Wharf Hotel, Boston Waterfront 🅷

(617) 994-9000. **$229-$2399, 3 day notice.** Three Battery Wharf 02109. At Battery Wharf; east of North End. Int corridors. **Pets:** Accepted.
🆂🅰🆅🅴 🄴🄲🄾 🍽 🅼 ⌧ 🍲 ⌧ 🖵

◇◇◇ ▼▼◆ BEST WESTERN PLUS Roundhouse Suites 🅷

(617) 989-1000. **$180-$310.** 891 Massachusetts Ave 02118. I-93 exit 18, just sw; just n of Newmarket Square; in South Boston. Int corridors. **Pets:** Accepted. 🆂🅰🆅🅴 🅼 🛜 ⌧ 🛏 🖵

◇◇◇ ▼▼◆▼ Boston Harbor Hotel 🅷

(617) 439-7000. **$320-$745.** 70 Rowes Wharf 02110. At Atlantic Ave. Int corridors. **Pets:** Accepted. 🆂🅰🆅🅴 🍽 🛀 ⌧ 🛜 ⌧

◇◇◇ ▼▼◆ Boston Park Plaza 🅷

(617) 426-2000. **Call for rates.** 50 Park Plaza 02116. At Park Plaza and Arlington St, just s of Boston Common and Public Gardens. Int corridors. **Pets:** Accepted. 🆂🅰🆅🅴 🍽 🍲 ⌧ 🖵

◇◇◇ ▼▼◆ The Boxer 🅷

(617) 624-0202. **Call for rates.** 107 Merrimac St 02114. At Merrimac and Causeway sts. Int corridors. **Pets:** Accepted.
🆂🅰🆅🅴 🍽 🛜 ⌧ 🛏 🖵

◇◇◇ ▼▼◆▼ The Colonnade Hotel Boston 🅷

(617) 424-7000. **Call for rates.** 120 Huntington Ave 02116. Just s of Copley Square. Int corridors. **Pets:** Accepted.
🆂🅰🆅🅴 🍽 🛀 🍲 ⌧ 🛏 🖵

▼▼ ◆ Comfort Inn Boston 🅷

(617) 287-9200. **$109-$309.** 900 William T Morrissey Blvd 02122. I-93 exit 13 northbound, 0.5 mi sw; exit 12 southbound, follow signs. Int corridors. **Pets:** Accepted. 🍲 ⌧ 🛏 🖵

◇◇◇ ▼▼◆▼ Copley Square Hotel 🅷

(617) 536-9000. **Call for rates.** 47 Huntington Ave 02116. I-90 exit 22, just n. Int corridors. **Pets:** Accepted. 🆂🅰🆅🅴 🍽 🅼 🛜 ⌧

◇◇◇ ▼▼◆▼ The Eliot Hotel 🅷 ❖

(617) 267-1607. **$285-$545.** 370 Commonwealth Ave 02215. Corner of Massachusetts Ave; in historic Back Bay. Int corridors. **Pets:** Other species. Service with restrictions, crate. 🆂🅰🆅🅴 🍽 🅼 🛜 ⌧ 🖵

enVision Hotel Boston, an Ascend Hotel Collection Member H

(617) 383-5229. **$139-$239.** 81 S Huntington Ave 02130. Jct Huntington Ave (SR 9). Int corridors. **Pets:** Medium. $25 daily fee/pet. Service with restrictions, supervision.

The Fairmont Copley Plaza Boston H ❧

(617) 267-5300. **$299-$579.** 138 St. James Ave 02116. At Copley Square. Int corridors. **Pets:** $25 daily fee/pet. Service with restrictions, supervision.

Four Seasons Hotel Boston H

(617) 338-4400. **$395-$1300.** 200 Boylston St 02116. Between Arlington and Charles sts. Int corridors. **Pets:** Accepted.

Hilton Boston Downtown/Faneuil Hall H ❧

(617) 556-0006. **$249-$599.** 89 Broad St 02110. Corner of Broad and Franklin sts. Int corridors. **Pets:** Large, dogs only. $75 one-time fee/pet. Service with restrictions, supervision.

Hilton Boston Logan Airport H

(617) 568-6700. **$139-$409.** 1 Hotel Dr 02128. At Boston Logan International Airport. Int corridors. **Pets:** Accepted.

Hotel Commonwealth H ❧

(617) 933-5000. **Call for rates.** 500 Commonwealth Ave 02215. On SR 2; at Beacon St and Brookline Ave. Int corridors. **Pets:** Dogs only. $150 deposit/room. Service with restrictions, supervision.

Hyatt Boston Harbor H

(617) 568-1234. **$129-$599.** 101 Harborside Dr 02128. I-90 exit 20, follow Hotel Dr to Harborside Dr. Int corridors. **Pets:** Accepted.

Hyatt Regency Boston H

(617) 912-1234. **$159-$599.** One Avenue de Lafayette 02111. Just e of Boston Common. Int corridors. **Pets:** Accepted.

InterContinental Boston H

(617) 747-1000. **Call for rates.** 510 Atlantic Ave 02210. I-93 exit 23 southbound; exit 20 northbound; at Pearl St. Int corridors. **Pets:** Accepted.

The Lenox Hotel H ❧

(617) 536-5300. **Call for rates.** 61 Exeter St 02116. I-90 exit 22, just n at Boylston St. Int corridors. **Pets:** Medium, dogs only. $125 one-time fee/pet. Service with restrictions, supervision.

The Liberty, A Luxury Collection Hotel H

(617) 224-4000. **$299-$699.** 215 Charles St 02114. I-93 exit 26 (Storrow Dr), just n. Int corridors. **Pets:** Accepted.

Loews Boston Hotel H

(617) 266-7200. **Call for rates.** 154 Berkeley St 02116. At Berkeley St. Int corridors. **Pets:** Accepted.

Mandarin Oriental Boston H ❧

(617) 535-8888. **Call for rates.** 776 Boylston St 02199. At Prudential Center. Int corridors. **Pets:** Small, dogs only. Service with restrictions, supervision.

The Midtown Hotel H ❧

(617) 262-1000. **$99-$309.** 220 Huntington Ave 02115. 3 blks sw of Copley Pl; just n of Symphony Hall and Massachusetts Ave. Int corridors. **Pets:** Other species. $30 one-time fee/room. Service with restrictions, crate.

Nine Zero Hotel H ❧

(617) 772-5800. **Call for rates.** 90 Tremont St 02108. Just ne of Boston Common; motor entrance on Bosworth St. Int corridors. **Pets:** Other species. Designated rooms, service with restrictions, crate.

Omni Parker House H

(617) 227-8600. **Call for rates.** 60 School St 02108. Corner of Tremont St; northeast corner of Boston Common. Int corridors. **Pets:** Accepted.

Onyx Hotel H

(617) 557-9955. **$159-$499.** 155 Portland St 02114. Corner of Merrimac and Traverse sts, just n; 3 blks s of TD Bank North Garden. Int corridors. **Pets:** Accepted.

Ramada Boston H

(617) 287-9100. **$99-$269.** 800 William T Morrissey Blvd 02122. I-93 exit 13 northbound, 0.5 mi sw; exit 12 southbound, follow signs. Int corridors. **Pets:** Accepted.

Residence Inn by Marriott Boston Back Bay - Fenway H

(617) 236-8787. **$279-$689.** 125 Brookline Ave 02215. Just sw of Kenmore Square; at Burlington Ave. Int corridors. **Pets:** Accepted.

Residence Inn by Marriott Boston Downtown/Seaport Hotel H

(617) 478-0840. **$223-$689.** 370 Congress St 02210. At Congress and Stilings sts; in Seaport District. Int corridors. **Pets:** Accepted.

Residence Inn by Marriott Boston Harbor on Tudor Wharf H

(617) 242-9000. **$279-$689.** 34-44 Charles River Ave 02129. Just se of SR 99 at Charlestown Bridge. Int corridors. **Pets:** $100 one-time fee/room. Service with restrictions.

Revere Hotel/Boston Common H

(617) 482-1800. **$179-$699.** 200 Stuart St 02116. At Park Square and Charles St; in Back Bay. Int corridors. **Pets:** Accepted.

The Ritz-Carlton, Boston Common H

(617) 574-7100. **Call for rates.** 10 Avery St 02111. At Washington and Avery sts; 1 blk e of Boston Common. Int corridors. **Pets:** Accepted.

Seaport Hotel & Seaport World Trade Center H

(617) 385-4000. **$149-$699.** 1 Seaport Ln 02210. At Seaport World Trade Center. Int corridors. **Pets:** Accepted.

Sheraton Boston H

(617) 236-2000. **$139-$669.** 39 Dalton St 02199. I-90 exit 22, At Belvedere St. Int corridors. **Pets:** Accepted.

Taj Boston H ❧

(617) 536-5700. **$249-$5000.** 15 Arlington St 02117. At Arlington and Newbury sts; overlooks the Public Gardens. Int corridors. **Pets:** Medium, dogs only. Service with restrictions, supervision.

◢◣ ▼▼ The Verb Hotel **M**
(617) 566-4500. **Call for rates.** 1271 Boylston St 02215. Between Ipswich St and Yawkey Way. Int corridors. **Pets:** Accepted.
[SAVE] [&M] [📶] [✕] [🛏] [💻]

◢◣ ▼▼▼ W Boston Hotel &
Residences **H** ❀
(617) 261-8700. **$189-$599.** 100 Stuart St 02116. At Tremont St. Int corridors. **Pets:** Medium, other species. $50 one-time fee/room. Service with restrictions. [SAVE] [¶] [&M] [📶] [✕]

◢◣ ▼▼▼ Westin Boston Waterfront **H**
(617) 532-4600. **$179-$599.** 425 Summer St 02210. I-93 exit 23, 1 mi se on Purchase St to Summer St. Int corridors. **Pets:** Accepted.
[SAVE] [¶] [&M] [📶] [📶] [✕] [💻]

◢◣ ▼▼▼ The Westin Copley Place
Boston **H** ❀
(617) 262-9600. **$279-$389.** 10 Huntington Ave 02116. I-90 exit 22; at Copley Square. Int corridors. **Pets:** Medium, dogs only. Service with restrictions, supervision. [SAVE] [ECO] [¶] [&M] [📶] [📶] [✕] [💻]

◢◣ ▼▼▼ XV Beacon **H** ❀
(617) 670-1500. **$335-$2650, 3 day notice.** 15 Beacon St 02108. Between Bowdoin and Somerset sts. Int corridors. **Pets:** Dogs only. Designated rooms, service with restrictions, supervision.
[SAVE] [¶] [📶] [✕]

BOXBOROUGH

▼▼▼ Holiday Inn Boxborough **H**
(978) 263-8701. **Call for rates.** 242 Adams Pl 01719. I-495 exit 28, just e on SR 111. Int corridors. **Pets:** Accepted.
[¶] [📶] [📶] [✕] [🛏] [💻]

BRAINTREE

▼▼▼ Candlewood Suites Boston - Braintree **H**
(781) 849-7450. **Call for rates.** 235 Wood Rd 02184. I-93 exit 6, just n on SR 37, then 0.5 mi w. Int corridors. **Pets:** Accepted. [📶] [🛏] [💻]

▼▼▼ Hampton Inn Braintree **H**
(781) 380-3300. **$159-$239.** 215 Wood Rd 02184. I-93 exit 6, just n on SR 37, then 0.5 mi w. Int corridors. **Pets:** Accepted.
[&M] [📶] [📶] [✕] [🛏] [💻]

◢◣ ▼▼▼ Hyatt Place Boston Braintree **H**
(781) 848-0600. **$89-$299.** 50 Forbes Rd 02184. I-93 exit 6, just se. Int corridors. **Pets:** Medium, dogs only. $75 one-time fee/room. Supervision. [SAVE] [&M] [📶] [✕] [📶] [✕] [🛏] [💻]

BROCKTON

▼▼▼ Residence Inn by Marriott Boston Brockton **H**
(508) 583-3600. **$108-$189.** 124 Liberty St 02301. SR 24 exit 17B, just w, just s on Pearl St, then 0.3 mi se to Mill St connector. Int corridors. **Pets:** Other species. $100 one-time fee/room. Service with restrictions, crate. [&M] [📶] [📶] [✕] [🛏] [💻]

BROOKLINE

▼▼▼ Holiday Inn Boston Brookline **H**
(617) 277-1200. **$179-$399.** 1200 Beacon St 02446. On SR 2; 1 mi sw of Kenmore Square. Int corridors. **Pets:** Medium, dogs only. $25 daily fee/pet. Designated rooms, service with restrictions, supervision.
[¶] [&M] [📶] [📶] [✕] [🛏] [💻]

BURLINGTON

▼▼▼ Candlewood Suites Boston-Burlington **H**
(781) 229-4300. **Call for rates.** 130 Middlesex Tpke 01803. I-95 exit 32B, just n. Int corridors. **Pets:** Other species. $75 one-time fee/room. Service with restrictions, supervision. [¶] [&M] [📶] [🛏] [💻]

◢◣ ▼▼ HYATT house Boston/Burlington **H**
(781) 270-0800. **$89-$399.** 2 Van de Graaff Dr 01803. I-95 exit 33A, just s on US 3, then 0.5 mi w on Wayside Rd. Int corridors.
Pets: Accepted. [SAVE] [¶] [&M] [📶] [📶] [✕] [🛏] [💻]

◢◣ ▼▼▼ Sonesta ES Suites **H**
(781) 221-2233. **Call for rates.** 11 Old Concord Rd 01803. I-95 exit 32B, just s on Middlesex Tpke. Int corridors. **Pets:** Accepted.
[SAVE] [¶] [&M] [📶] [📶] [🛏] [💻]

BUZZARDS BAY

◢◣ ▼▼ Bay Motor Inn **M**
(508) 759-3989. **Call for rates.** 223 Main St 02532. SR 25 exit 3, 0.5 mi w of Bourne rotary. Ext corridors. **Pets:** Other species. $15 daily fee/room. Service with restrictions, supervision.
[SAVE] [📶] [📶] [✕] [🛏] [💻]

CAMBRIDGE *(Restaurants p. 633)*

◢◣ ▼▼▼ BEST WESTERN PLUS Hotel
Tria **H** ❀
(617) 491-8000. **$139-$399.** 220 Alewife Brook Pkwy 02138. Jct SR 2, 16 and US 3; I-90 (Massachusetts Tpke) exit Cambridge/Allston to SR 2 W (Fresh Pond Pkwy). Int corridors. **Pets:** Medium, other species. $20 daily fee/room. Designated rooms, service with restrictions, crate.
[SAVE] [¶] [&M] [📶] [✕] [🛏] [💻]

◢◣ ▼▼▼ The Charles Hotel, Harvard
Square **H**
(617) 864-1200. **Call for rates.** 1 Bennett St 02138. Just s of Harvard Square; at Eliot St. Int corridors. **Pets:** Accepted.
[SAVE] [📶] [¶] [&M] [📶] [✕] [📶] [✕]

◢◣ ▼▼▼ Hotel Marlowe **H**
(617) 868-8000. **Call for rates.** 25 Edwin H Land Blvd 02141. Just sw of jct SR 28. Int corridors. **Pets:** Accepted.
[SAVE] [ECO] [¶] [&M] [📶] [✕]

◢◣ ▼▼▼ Hyatt Regency Cambridge **H** ❀
(617) 492-1234. **$119-$459.** 575 Memorial Dr 02139. On US 3 and SR 2. Int corridors. **Pets:** Medium. $100 one-time fee/room. Designated rooms, service with restrictions, supervision.
[SAVE] [¶] [&M] [📶] [✕] [📶] [🛏] [💻]

◢◣ ▼▼▼ Le Meridien Cambridge **H**
(617) 577-0200. **$205-$650.** 20 Sidney St 02139. On SR 2A, 1 mi n of river. Int corridors. **Pets:** Medium. $150 deposit/room. Service with restrictions, crate. [SAVE] [¶] [&M] [📶] [✕] [💻]

▼▼▼ Residence Inn by Marriott Boston Cambridge
Center **H**
(617) 349-0700. **$244-$804.** 6 Cambridge Center 02142. Corner of Ames St and Broadway. Int corridors. **Pets:** Other species. $150 one-time fee/room. [&M] [📶] [📶] [✕] [🛏] [💻]

◢◣ ▼▼▼ Sheraton Commander Hotel **H**
(617) 547-4800. **$99-$519.** 16 Garden St 02138. Just n of Harvard Square. Int corridors. **Pets:** Accepted. [SAVE] [¶] [&M] [📶] [✕] [💻]

CHELSEA

▼▼▼ Residence Inn by Marriott Boston Logan
Airport/Chelsea **H**
(617) 889-9990. **$251-$574.** 200 Maple St 02150. 0.3 mi se of SR 16. Int corridors. **Pets:** Accepted. [¶] [&M] [📶] [📶] [✕] [🛏] [💻]

CHICOPEE

▼▼▼ Residence Inn by Marriott -
Springfield/Chicopee **H**
(413) 331-4440. **$139-$229.** 500 Memorial Dr 01020. I-90 exit 5, just s. Int corridors. **Pets:** Medium, dogs only. $100 one-time fee/pet. Designated rooms, service with restrictions, crate. [&M] [📶] [✕] [🛏] [💻]

CONCORD

◢◣ ▼▼▼ BEST WESTERN at Historic
Concord **H** ❀
(978) 369-6100. **$149-$209.** 740 Elm St 01742. 1.8 mi w, just off SR 2 and 2A. Int corridors. **Pets:** Medium. $15 daily fee/room. Designated rooms, service with restrictions. [SAVE] [📶] [📶] [✕] [🛏] [💻]

▼▼▼ The Hawthorne Inn **BB**
(978) 369-5610. **$169-$359, 14 day notice.** 462 Lexington Rd 01742. 0.8 mi e of town square. Int corridors. **Pets:** Small. $100 deposit/room. Designated rooms, supervision. 🍽 📶 ✕ 🎦

DANVERS

AAA ▼▼▼ Comfort Inn North Shore **H**
(978) 777-1700. **$80-$170.** 50 Dayton St 01923. Just w of US 1, 0.8 mi n of jct SR 114 exit Center St northbound; w under US 1 exit Dayton St southbound. Int corridors. **Pets:** Medium. $35 one-time fee/pet. Service with restrictions, supervision. SAVE 🍽 ᰳM ᰢ 📶 🔋 💻

AAA ▼▼▼▼ DoubleTree by Hilton Boston North Shore **H**
(978) 777-2500. **$99-$259.** 50 Ferncroft Rd 01923. I-95 exit 50, follow signs for US 1 S to Ferncroft Village. Int corridors. **Pets:** Accepted. SAVE 🍽 ᰳM ᰢ ✕ 📶 🔋 💻

▼▼▼▼ Residence Inn by Marriott Boston-North Shore/Danvers **H**
(978) 777-7171. **$104-$217.** 51 Newbury St 01923. US 1 N, just s of jct SR 114. Ext corridors. **Pets:** Accepted. ᰢ 📶 ✕ 🔋 💻

▼▼▼ TownePlace Suites by Marriott Boston-North Shore/Danvers **H**
(978) 777-6222. **$83-$183.** 238 Andover St 01923. SR 114 eastbound, enter just w of US 1 (no westbound entrance); US 1 southbound, enter through shopping center; southwest corner of jct US 1 and SR 114. Int corridors. **Pets:** Accepted. ECO 🍽 ᰳM ᰢ 📶 ✕ 🔋 💻

DEDHAM

▼▼▼▼ Residence Inn by Marriott **H**
(781) 407-0999. **$195-$355.** 259 Elm St 02026. I-95 exit 15A, just n, then 0.4 mi e. Int corridors. **Pets:** Accepted. ᰢ 📶 ✕ 🔋 💻

DEERFIELD

▼▼▼ Deerfield Inn **CI**
(413) 774-5587. **$170-$280, 7 day notice.** 81 Old Main St 01342. Center. Int corridors. **Pets:** Accepted. 🍽 📶 ✕

EAST FALMOUTH

▼▼ Capewind Waterfront Motel **M**
(508) 548-3400. **Call for rates.** 34 Maravista Ext 02536. 2.2 mi e to SR 28, just s, follow signs. Ext corridors. **Pets:** Accepted. 🍽 ᰢ 📶 ✕ 🔋 💻

EASTHAM

▼ Ocean Park Inn **M**
(508) 255-1132. **Call for rates.** 3900 State Hwy 02642. On US 6; 1 mi n of National Seashore Visitor's Center. Ext corridors. **Pets:** Other species. $25 daily fee/room. Designated rooms, service with restrictions, supervision. 🍽 ᰢ 📶 ✕ 🔋

EAST WAREHAM

AAA ▼ Atlantic Motel **M**
(508) 295-0210. **Call for rates.** 7 Depot St 02538. Jct SR 25 exit 1; between eastbound and westbound lanes of US 6/SR 28. Ext corridors. **Pets:** Medium, dogs only. $20 daily fee/pet. Designated rooms, service with restrictions, supervision. SAVE 🍽 ᰢ 📶 🔋 💻

EDGARTOWN

AAA ▼▼▼▼ Clarion Inn Martha's Vineyard **H**
(508) 627-5161. **$99-$381, 3 day notice.** 227 Upper Main St 02539. 0.8 mi nw; center. Int corridors. **Pets:** Accepted. SAVE 🍽 📶 ✕ 🔋 💻

AAA ▼▼▼▼ Harbor View Hotel **H**
(508) 627-7000. **Call for rates.** 131 N Water St 02539. 0.3 mi n; center. Ext/int corridors. **Pets:** Accepted. SAVE 🍽 ᰢ ✕ 📶 ✕ 🔋 💻

AAA ▼▼▼▼ The Kelley House Hotel **H**
(508) 627-7900. **Call for rates.** 23 Kelley St 02539. At N Water St; center. Ext/int corridors. **Pets:** Accepted. SAVE 🍽 ᰢ 📶 ✕ 🔋 💻

▼▼▼ Vineyard Square Hotel & Suites **CI**
(508) 627-4711. **Call for rates.** 38 N Water St 02539. Just n from Main St. Int corridors. **Pets:** Accepted. 🍽 ✕ 📶 ✕ 🔋 💻

FAIRHAVEN

▼▼ Seaport Inn Conference Center & Marina **H**
(508) 997-1281. **$89-$239.** 110 Middle St 02719. I-195 exit 15, 1 mi s, then just off US 6. Int corridors. **Pets:** Other species. $25 deposit/pet. Service with restrictions, supervision. 🍽 📶 ✕ 🔋 💻

FALMOUTH

AAA ▼▼ Seaside Inn **M**
(508) 540-4120. **$62-$345, 14 day notice.** 263 Grand Ave 02540. Jct SR 28, 1.3 mi s from Falmouth Heights Rd. Ext/int corridors. **Pets:** Medium. $15 daily fee/pet. Designated rooms, service with restrictions, supervision. SAVE 🍽 📶 ✕ 🔋 💻

FOXBORO

▼▼▼ Residence Inn by Marriott Foxborough **H**
(508) 698-2800. **$209-$401.** 250 Foxborough Blvd 02035. I-95 exit 7A, 0.6 mi s on SR 140, 0.7 mi e, then just n. Int corridors. **Pets:** Accepted. ᰳM ᰢ 📶 ✕ 🔋 💻

FRAMINGHAM

AAA ▼▼ BEST WESTERN Framingham **H**
(508) 872-8811. **$127.** 130 Worcester Rd 01702. I-90 exit 13, 0.5 mi s to SR 9; 1 mi w of Speen St; just w of Shopper's World Mall. Int corridors. **Pets:** Designated rooms, service with restrictions, supervision. SAVE 🍽 ᰢ 📶 ✕ 🔋 💻

AAA ▼▼▼ Red Roof Inn Boston Framingham **M**
(508) 872-4499. **Call for rates.** 650 Cochituate Rd 01701. I-90 exit 13, 0.6 mi ne on SR 30. Ext corridors. **Pets:** Large, other species. Service with restrictions, supervision. SAVE 📶 🔋 💻

AAA ▼▼▼ Residence Inn by Marriott Boston/Framingham **H**
(508) 370-0001. **$146-$252.** 400 Staples Dr 01702. SR 9 W to Crossing Blvd, then s. Int corridors. **Pets:** Accepted. SAVE 🍽 ᰳM ᰢ 📶 ✕ 🔋 💻

AAA ▼▼▼ Sheraton Framingham Hotel & Conference Center **H**
(508) 879-7200. **$99-$299.** 1657 Worcester Rd 01701. I-90 exit 12, follow signs to SR 9 W. Int corridors. **Pets:** Accepted. SAVE 🍽 ᰢ ✕ 📶 ✕ 💻

FRANKLIN

AAA ▼▼▼ Hawthorn Suites by Wyndham Franklin **H**
(508) 553-3500. **$99-$179.** 835 Upper Union St 02038. I-495 exit 16, just s, then 0.3 mi e. Int corridors. **Pets:** Accepted. SAVE 🍽 ᰳM ᰢ 📶 ✕ 🔋 💻

▼▼▼ Residence Inn by Marriott-Boston/Franklin **H**
(508) 541-8188. **$153-$309.** 4 Forge Pkwy 02038. I-495 exit 17, 0.7 mi nw off SR 140 N. Int corridors. **Pets:** Medium, other species. $100 one-time fee/room. Service with restrictions. 🍽 ᰳM ᰢ 📶 ✕ 🔋 💻

GARDNER

▼▼▼ Colonial Hotel **H**
(978) 630-2500. **Call for rates.** 625 Betty Spring Rd 01440. SR 2 exit 24 eastbound; exit 24B westbound, 0.9 mi n on SR 140, then 0.5 mi w. Int corridors. **Pets:** Accepted. 🍽 ᰢ ✕ 📶 🔋 💻

GLOUCESTER

▽ Castle Manor Inn CI

(978) 515-7386. **Call for rates.** 141 Essex Ave 01930. On SR 133, 2.3 mi e of exit 14 (SR 128). Ext/int corridors. **Pets:** Accepted.
▥ ⊚ ⊠

GREENFIELD

▽▽▽▽ The Brandt House B&B BB

(413) 774-3329. **Call for rates.** 29 Highland Ave 01301. I-91 exit 26, 1.8 mi e on SR 2A, then se on Crescent St. Int corridors. **Pets:** Accepted. ▥ ⊚ ⊠

HADLEY

▽ ▽ Comfort Inn H

(413) 584-9816. **$89-$169.** 237 Russell St 01035. I-91 exit 19 northbound; exit 20 southbound, 3 mi e on SR 9. Int corridors. **Pets:** Small. $35 daily fee/room. Designated rooms, service with restrictions, crate.
⊇ ⊚ ⊟ ⊑

▽ ▽ Howard Johnson Inn Hadley H

(413) 586-0114. **$72-$180.** 401 Russell St 01035. I-91 exit 19 northbound, 4.3 mi e on SR 9; exit 24 southbound, 10 mi s on SR 116, then just w on SR 9. Int corridors. **Pets:** Accepted. ⊾M ⊇ ⊚ ⊟ ⊑

HAVERHILL

△△△ ▽▽▽▽ BEST WESTERN PLUS Merrimack Valley H

(978) 373-1511. **$89-$209.** 401 Lowell Ave 01832. I-495 exit 49 (SR 110). Int corridors. **Pets:** Accepted. SAVE ⊇ ⊚ ⊠ ⊟ ⊑

▽▽▽ Hampton Inn H

(978) 374-7755. **$99-$179.** 106 Bank Rd 01832. I-495 exit 49 (SR 110), 0.5 mi s. Int corridors. **Pets:** Designated rooms, service with restrictions, supervision. ▥ ⊾M ⊚ ⊠ ⊟ ⊑

HOLLAND

▽▽▽ The Inn at Restful Paws BB ☙

(413) 245-7792. **Call for rates.** 70 Allen Hill Rd 01521. SR 20, 2.1 mi s on E Brimfield Rd, 0.4 mi on Alexander Rd, then 0.7 mi n. Int corridors. **Pets:** No service, supervision. ▥ ⊚ ⊠ ▥ ⊠ ⊑

HOLYOKE

▽▽▽▽ Homewood Suites by Hilton Holyoke-Springfield North H

(413) 532-3100. **$109-$209.** 375 Whitney Ave 01040. I-91 exit 15, just w on Lower Westfield Rd, then 0.4 mi s. Int corridors. **Pets:** Accepted.
▥ ⊾M ⊇ ⊚ ⊟ ⊑

HYANNIS *(Restaurants p. 634)*

▽ Cape Cod Harbor House Inn M

(508) 771-1880. **Call for rates.** 119 Ocean St 02601. Opposite ferry docks. Ext corridors. **Pets:** Small, dogs only. $27 daily fee/pet. Designated rooms, service with restrictions, supervision. ⊚ ⊠ ⊟ ⊑

▽ ▽ Comfort Inn Cape Cod H

(508) 771-4804. **$169-$229.** 1470 Iyannough Rd 02601. US 6 exit 6, 1.3 mi se on SR 132. Ext/int corridors. **Pets:** Accepted.
▥ ⊇ ⊠ ⊚ ⊠ ⊟ ⊑

LAWRENCE

△△△ ▽ ▽ Holiday Inn Express H

(978) 975-4050. **$79-$159.** 224 Winthrop Ave 01843. I-495 exit 42A, just s on SR 114. Int corridors. **Pets:** Accepted.
SAVE ⊾M ⊚ ⊠ ⊑

LENOX

▽▽▽ ▽▽▽▽ Wheatleigh CI ☙

(413) 637-0610. **Call for rates.** 11 Hawthorne Rd 01240. 1.8 mi s on SR 183, 1 mi e. Int corridors. **Pets:** Medium, dogs only. $200 one-time fee/room. Designated rooms, service with restrictions, supervision.
▥ ⊇ ⊠ ⊚ ⊠

LEXINGTON

△△△ ▽▽▽▽ Aloft Lexington H ☙

(781) 761-1700. **$89-$369.** 727 Marrett Rd - A 02421. I-95 exit 30B, just w. Int corridors. **Pets:** Designated rooms, service with restrictions, crate. SAVE ⊟ ▥ ⊇ ⊚ ⊠ ⊟ ⊑

△△△ ▽▽▽▽ Element Lexington H ☙

(781) 761-1750. **$99-$389.** 727 Marrett Rd - B 02421. I-95 exit 30B, just w. Int corridors. **Pets:** Designated rooms, service with restrictions, supervision. SAVE ECO ⊟ ▥ ⊾M ⊇ ⊚ ⊠ ⊟ ⊑

MANSFIELD

▽▽▽ Holiday Inn Mansfield/Foxboro H

(508) 339-2200. **$109-$329.** 31 Hampshire St 02048. I-95 exit 7A, 0.5 mi s on SR 140, then 1 mi w on Forbes Rd; I-495 exit 12, 2 mi n on SR 140, then w on Forbes Rd. Int corridors. **Pets:** Accepted.
▥ ⊾M ⊇ ⊠ ⊚ ⊟ ⊑

△△△ ▽▽▽ Red Roof Inn Boston - Mansfield/Foxboro H

(508) 339-2323. **Call for rates.** 60 Forbes Blvd 02048. I-95 exit 7A, 1.3 mi n; I-495 exit 12, just off SR 140. Int corridors. **Pets:** Large, other species. Service with restrictions, supervision.
SAVE ▥ ⊇ ⊚ ⊠ ⊟ ⊑

MARLBOROUGH

△△△ ▽▽▽ BEST WESTERN Royal Plaza Hotel & Trade Ctr. H

(508) 460-0700. **$119-$369.** 181 Boston Post Rd W 01752. I-495 exit 24B, 1 mi w on US 20. Int corridors. **Pets:** Accepted.
SAVE ▥ ⊇ ⊚ ⊟ ⊑

▽▽▽ Courtyard by Marriott Boston Marlborough H

(508) 480-0015. **$160-$263.** 75 Felton St 01752. I-495 exit 24B, just w; just off US 20. Int corridors. **Pets:** Medium, other species. $75 one-time fee/room. Designated rooms, no service, crate.
▥ ⊾M ⊇ ⊚ ⊠ ⊟ ⊑

▽▽▽ Embassy Suites Hotel-Boston Marlborough H ☙

(508) 485-5900. **$130-$230.** 123 Boston Post Rd W 01752. I-495 exit 24B, 0.5 mi w; just off US 20. Int corridors. **Pets:** Dogs only. $25 daily fee/room. Designated rooms, service with restrictions.
▥ ⊾M ⊇ ⊠ ⊚ ⊟ ⊑

▽▽▽ Residence Inn by Marriott Boston Marlborough H

(508) 481-1500. **$160-$263.** 112 Donald Lynch Blvd 01752. I-290 exit 25B, 3 mi ne. Int corridors. **Pets:** Accepted.
▥ ⊾M ⊇ ⊚ ⊠ ⊟ ⊑

MEDFORD

△△△ ▽▽▽▽ Hyatt Place Boston/Medford H

(781) 395-8500. **$109-$369.** 116 Riverside Ave NE 02155. I-93 exit 32, just sw to SR 60 and River St. Int corridors. **Pets:** Accepted.
SAVE ⊾M ⊇ ⊚ ⊠ ⊟ ⊑

MILFORD

▽▽▽ Holiday Inn Express H ☙

(508) 634-1054. **$109-$169.** 50 Fortune Blvd 01757. I-495 exit 20, just sw on SR 85, then just se. Int corridors. **Pets:** Dogs only. $35 one-time fee/pet. Designated rooms, service with restrictions, supervision.
⊾M ⊇ ⊚ ⊠ ⊟ ⊑

NATICK

△△△ ▽▽▽▽ The Verve Crowne Plaza H

(508) 653-8800. **Call for rates.** 1360 Worcester St 01760. I-90 exit 12, 5 mi e; SR 9, 4 mi e of Framingham Center. Int corridors.
Pets: Accepted. SAVE ▥ ⊾M ⊚ ⊠ ⊟ ⊑

NEEDHAM

AAA ▼▼▼▼ Sheraton Needham Hotel **H**

(781) 444-1110. **$99-$349.** 100 Cabot St 02494. I-95 exit 19A, just e. Int corridors. **Pets:** Accepted. [SAVE] [icons]

NEWBURYPORT

▼▼▼ Garrison Inn **H**

(978) 499-8500. **Call for rates.** 11 Brown Square 01950. I-95 exit 57, 2.6 mi e on SR 1A, just n on Green St, just w on Pleasant St, then just s. Int corridors. **Pets:** Other species. $30 daily fee/pet. Service with restrictions, supervision. [icons]

NEWTON

AAA ▼▼▼▼ Hotel Indigo Boston-Newton Riverside **H**

(617) 969-5300. **Call for rates.** 399 Grove St 02462. I-95 exit 22, just e. Int corridors. **Pets:** Medium. $50 one-time fee/pet. Designated rooms, service with restrictions, crate.

 [icons]

NORTHAMPTON

▼▼▼ Clarion Hotel & Conference Center **H**

(413) 586-1211. **$109-$299.** 1 Atwood Dr 01060. I-91 exit 18, just s on US 5. Int corridors. **Pets:** $20 daily fee/room. Designated rooms, service with restrictions, supervision. [icons]

NORTH DARTMOUTH

AAA ▼▼▼▼ Residence Inn by Marriott New Bedford/Dartmouth **H**

(508) 984-5858. **$118-$229.** 181 Faunce Corner Rd 02747. I-195 exit 12A westbound; exit 12 eastbound, just s. Int corridors. **Pets:** Other species. $100 one-time fee/room. Service with restrictions.

[SAVE] [icons]

NORWOOD

▼▼▼ Hampton Inn Boston - Norwood **H**

(781) 769-7000. **$100-$299.** 434 Providence Hwy 02062. I-95 exit 9 northbound, 5.9 mi ne on US 1; exit 11B southbound, 1.3 mi nw on Neponset St, then 0.4 mi n on US 1. Int corridors. **Pets:** Accepted.

 [icons]

AAA ▼▼▼▼ Residence Inn by Marriott Boston-Norwood-Canton **H**

(781) 278-9595. **$139-$240.** 275 Norwood Park S 02062. I-95 exit 9 northbound, 3.7 mi n on US 1; exit 11B southbound, 0.5 mi nw on Neponset St, 0.6 mi w on Dean St, then 0.8 mi s on US 1. Int corridors. **Pets:** Accepted. [SAVE] [icons]

ORLEANS

▼▼ Orleans Inn **CI**

(508) 255-2222. **$250-$450.** 3 Old County Rd 02653. On SR 28 and 6A exit rotary, just w. Int corridors. **Pets:** Accepted. [icons]

AAA ▼▼▼ Skaket Beach Motel **M**

(508) 255-1020. **$67-$175, 10 day notice.** 203 Cranberry Hwy (Rt 6A) 02653. US 6 exit 12, just e. Ext corridors. **Pets:** Dogs only. $15 daily fee/pet. Designated rooms, service with restrictions, supervision.

[SAVE] [icons]

PITTSFIELD

▼▼▼▼ Crowne Plaza Hotel-Berkshires **H** ❀

(413) 499-2000. **$99-$349, 3 day notice.** 1 West St 01201. Center. Int corridors. **Pets:** Medium. $50 one-time fee/room. Designated rooms, service with restrictions, supervision.

[icons]

PLYMOUTH

▼▼▼▼ Hampton Inn & Suites-Plymouth Kingston **H**

(508) 747-5000. **$119-$259.** 10 Plaza Way 02360. SR 3 exit 7. Int corridors. **Pets:** Other species. $35 daily fee/pet. Designated rooms.

[icons]

PROVINCETOWN

▼▼▼ Bayshore & Chandler **CO**

(508) 487-9133. **Call for rates.** 493 Commercial St 02657. 0.8 mi e of Town Hall. Ext corridors. **Pets:** $25 daily fee/room. Service with restrictions. [icons]

AAA ▼▼▼▼ Crowne Pointe Historic Inn & Spa **CI**

(508) 487-6767. **$109-$659, 21 day notice.** 82 Bradford St 02657. On SR 6A, just w of Town Hall. Ext/int corridors. **Pets:** Accepted.

[SAVE] [icons]

▼▼▼▼ White Wind Inn **BB**

(508) 487-1526. **Call for rates.** 174 Commercial St 02657. Just w of Town Hall. Int corridors. **Pets:** Dogs only. $15 daily fee/pet. Designated rooms, service with restrictions. [icons]

RAYNHAM

AAA ▼▼▼ Quality Inn of Raynham-Taunton **M**

(508) 824-8647. **$90-$135.** 164 New State Hwy 02767. SR 24 exit 13B, 0.8 mi w on US 44. Ext/int corridors. **Pets:** Medium. $20 daily fee/pet. Designated rooms, service with restrictions, supervision.

[SAVE] [icons]

REHOBOTH

▼▼▼ Five Bridge Inn Bed & Breakfast **BB**

(508) 252-3190. **Call for rates.** 152 Pine St 02769. 1.6 mi n of US 44; 3.3 mi w of jct SR 118; US 44, n on Blanding Rd, e on Broad St, n on Salisbury St, then w. Int corridors. **Pets:** Accepted.

[icons]

REVERE

▼▼▼ Comfort Inn & Suites Boston Logan International Airport **H** ❀

(781) 485-3600. **$149-$339.** 85 American Legion Hwy 02151. Jct SR 1A and 60; 3 mi n of Boston Logan International Airport. Int corridors. **Pets:** Other species. $50 one-time fee/pet. Designated rooms, service with restrictions, supervision. [ECO] [icons]

▼▼▼ Hampton Inn Boston Logan Airport **H**

(781) 286-5665. **$159-$339.** 230 Lee Burbank Hwy 02151. On SR 1A, 0.6 mi s of terminus SR 60; 1.9 mi n of Boston Logan International Airport. Int corridors. **Pets:** Accepted.

[icons]

RICHMOND

▼▼▼ The Inn at Richmond **BB**

(413) 698-2566. **Call for rates.** 802 State Rd (SR 41) 01254. 2.5 mi s of jct US 20. Ext/int corridors. **Pets:** Accepted.

[icons]

ROCKPORT

AAA ▼▼▼▼ Rockport Inn & Suites **M** ❀

(978) 546-3300. **$109-$279, 3 day notice.** 183 Main St 01966. On SR 127. Ext corridors. **Pets:** Large, other species. $30 daily fee/pet. Service with restrictions. [SAVE] [icons]

SALEM

AAA ▼▼▼▼ Hawthorne Hotel **H** ❀

(978) 744-4080. **$119-$365, 3 day notice.** 18 Washington Square W 01970. On SR 1A. Int corridors. **Pets:** Other species. $100 deposit/room, $15 daily fee/pet. Designated rooms, service with restrictions.

[SAVE] [icons]

▼▼▼ The Salem Inn **BB**

(978) 741-0680. **$139-$390, 7 day notice.** 7 Summer St 01970. On SR 114 at Essex St; SR 128 exit 25A, 3 mi e. Int corridors. **Pets:** Other species. $20 daily fee/pet. Designated rooms, service with restrictions.

[icons]

SAUGUS

Red Roof Inn - Boston Logan 🅷
(781) 941-1400. **Call for rates.** 920 Broadway 01906. I-95 exit 44 northbound, 3.2 mi s on US 1 exit Main St/Saugus; exit southbound to U-turn. Int corridors. **Pets:** Large, other species. Service with restrictions, supervision. SAVE &M 🛜 ✕ 🛏 🖵

SEEKONK

Clarion Providence-Seekonk 🅷 🐾
(508) 336-7300. **$89-$189.** 940 Fall River Ave 02771. I-195 exit 1, just s. Int corridors. **Pets:** Medium, dogs only. $75 one-time fee/room. Designated rooms, service with restrictions, supervision.
🍽 &M 🛜 🛜 ✕ 🛏 🖵

Comfort Inn Providence/Seekonk 🅷
(508) 336-7900. **$79-$210.** 341 Highland Ave 02771. I-195 exit 1, just s on US 6. Int corridors. **Pets:** Medium. $10 daily fee/pet. Designated rooms, service with restrictions, crate. SAVE 🛜 🛜 🛏 🖵

Motel 6 - #1289 Ⓜ
(508) 336-7800. **Call for rates.** 821 Fall River Ave 02771. I-195 exit 1, just n on SR 114A. Int corridors. **Pets:** Other species. Service with restrictions, crate. &M 🛜

SOMERVILLE

La Quinta Inn & Suites Boston Somerville 🅷
(617) 625-5300. **$105-$385.** 23 Cummings St 02143. I-93 exit 29 northbound, just ne on SR 28, then just s on Middlesex Ave; exit southbound 1 mi e on SR 16, then 0.5 mi s on SR 28 to Middlesex Ave. Int corridors. **Pets:** Large, other species. Service with restrictions.
&M 🛜 🛏 🖵

SOUTHBOROUGH

Red Roof Inn Boston-Southborough/Worcester Ⓜ
(508) 481-3904. **Call for rates.** 367 Turnpike Rd 01772. I-495 exit 23A, just e on SR 9. Ext corridors. **Pets:** Large, other species. Service with restrictions, supervision. SAVE 🍽 🛜 ✕ 🛏 🖵

SOUTH YARMOUTH

Red Jacket Beach Resort 🅷
(508) 398-6941. **Call for rates.** 1 S Shore Dr 02664. 2 mi s off SR 28. Ext/int corridors. **Pets:** Accepted.
SAVE 🍽 🛜 ✕ 🛜 ✕ 🛏 🖵

Red Jacket Blue Rock Resort Ⓜ
(508) 398-6962. **$89-$219, 10 day notice.** 39 Todd Rd 02664. SR 28, 1 mi ne via N Main St and High Bank Rd, then 0.5 mi nw on Country Club Dr, follow signs. Ext corridors. **Pets:** Accepted.
SAVE 🍽 🛜 🛜 ✕ 🛏 🖵

Red Jacket Blue Water Resort on the Ocean 🅷 🐾
(508) 398-2288. **$100-$395, 30 day notice.** 291 S Shore Dr 02664. 1 mi s off SR 28. Ext/int corridors. **Pets:** Medium, dogs only. $35 deposit/pet. Designated rooms, service with restrictions, supervision.
SAVE 🍽 🛜 🛜 ✕ 🛏 🖵

SPRINGFIELD

La Quinta Inn & Suites 🅷
(413) 781-0900. **$95-$234.** 100 Congress St 01104. I-291 exit 2A, just s of Chestnut St. Int corridors. **Pets:** Large, other species. Service with restrictions. 🍽 🛜 ✕ 🛏 🖵

Sheraton Springfield Monarch Place Hotel 🅷
(413) 781-1010. **$109-$239.** One Monarch Pl 01144. I-91 exit 6 northbound; exit 7 southbound, just n; downtown. Int corridors.
Pets: Accepted. SAVE 🍽 &M 🛜 ✕ 🛜 ✕ 🛏 🖵

STURBRIDGE

Publick House Historic Inn & Country Lodge Ⓒ🅸
(508) 347-3313. **Call for rates.** 277 Main St 01566. I-84 exit 3B, 0.5 mi s of jct US 20. Ext/int corridors. **Pets:** Accepted.
🍽 🛜 🛜 🛏 🖵

Sturbridge Host Hotel & Conference Center on Cedar Lake 🅷
(508) 347-7393. **$115-$199.** 366 Main St 01566. I-90 exit 9, just w on US 20; I-84 exit 3B. Int corridors. **Pets:** Other species. $25 daily fee/room. Designated rooms, service with restrictions, supervision.
SAVE 🍽 🛜 ✕ 🛜 🛏 🖵

Super 8 Sturbridge Ⓜ
(508) 347-9000. **$69-$315.** 358 Main St 01566. I-84 exit 3B; on US 20. Ext corridors. **Pets:** Accepted. 🛜 🛜 🛏 🖵

TAUNTON

Holiday Inn Taunton/Foxboro 🅷 🐾
(508) 823-0430. **$119-$229.** 700 Myles Standish Blvd 02780. I-495 exit 9, just sw. Int corridors. **Pets:** Small. $26 daily fee/room. Designated rooms, service with restrictions, supervision.
SAVE 🍽 &M 🛜 ✕ 🛜 🛏 🖵

TEWKSBURY

Holiday Inn Tewksbury-Andover 🅷
(978) 640-9000. **Call for rates.** 4 Highwood Dr 01876. I-495 exit 39, just w on SR 133. Int corridors. **Pets:** Accepted.
SAVE 🍽 🛜 ✕ 🛜 ✕ 🛏 🖵

Residence Inn by Marriott Boston-Tewksbury-Andover 🅷
(978) 640-1003. **$118-$229.** 1775 Andover St 01876. I-495 exit 39, 0.3 mi w on SR 133. Ext corridors. **Pets:** Accepted.
&M 🛜 🛜 ✕ 🛏 🖵

TownePlace Suites by Marriott Boston Tewksbury 🅷
(978) 863-9800. **$90-$148.** 20 International Pl 01876. I-495 exit 39, 0.3 mi nw. Int corridors. **Pets:** Accepted.
ECO &M 🛜 🛜 ✕ 🛏 🖵

VINEYARD HAVEN

The Doctor's House Bed & Breakfast 🅱🅱
(508) 696-0859. **Call for rates.** 60 Mt. Aldworth Rd 02568. 0.4 mi sw to road to Edgartown, 1 blk e. Int corridors. **Pets:** Dogs only. $25 daily fee/pet. Supervision. 🍽 🛜 ✕ 🛜

Mansion House Inn, Health Club & Spa 🅷
(508) 693-2200. **$99-$509, 14 day notice.** 9 Main St 02568. West of ferry dock; corner of Beach Rd. Int corridors. **Pets:** Accepted.
🛜 ✕ 🛜 ✕ 🛏 🖵

WAKEFIELD

Sheraton Colonial Hotel Boston North & Conference Center 🅷
(781) 245-9300. **$99-$399.** 1 Audubon Rd 01880. I-95 exit 42, just n. Int corridors. **Pets:** Accepted.
SAVE 🍽 &M 🛜 ✕ 🛜 🛏 🖵

WALTHAM

Courtyard by Marriott Boston-Waltham 🅷
(781) 419-0900. **$167-$367.** 387 Winter St 02451. I-95 exit 27B northbound; exit 27A southbound; on northeast corner. Int corridors.
Pets: Accepted. 🍽 &M 🛜 🛜 ✕ 🛏 🖵

Holiday Inn Express Boston/Waltham 🅷
(781) 890-2800. **$89-$329.** 385 Winter St 02451. I-95 exit 27B northbound; exit 27A southbound, just ne. Int corridors. **Pets:** Accepted.
&M 🛜 ✕ 🛏 🖵

▼▼ ▼▼▼▼ The Westin Waltham-Boston ⊞

(781) 290-5600. **$109-$399.** 70 3rd Ave 02451. I-95 exit 27A, just se. Int corridors. **Pets:** Accepted. (SAVE) (ECO) ⊞ ⓜ ⌂ 🐾 ✕ 💻

WESTBOROUGH

▼▼ ▼▼ Extended Stay America-Boston-Westborough ⊞

(508) 616-9213. **Call for rates.** 180 E Main St 01581. I-495 exit 23B, 1.4 mi w, then just sw on SR 30. Int corridors. **Pets:** Other species. $25 daily fee/pet. Service with restrictions, supervision.

⊞ ⓜ 🛜 ✕ 🔋 💻

▲▲▲ ▼▼▼▼ Residence Inn by Marriott Boston
Westborough ⊞

(508) 366-7700. **$160-$263.** 25 Connector Rd 01581. I-495 exit 23B, just w on SR 9 exit Computer and Research drs, then 0.3 mi s. Ext/int corridors. **Pets:** Accepted.

(SAVE) (ECO) ⊞ ⓜ ⌂ 🛜 ✕ 🔋 💻

WEST DENNIS

▼▼ ▼▼ Inn at Swan River ⓜ

(508) 394-5415. **Call for rates.** 829 Main St 02670. On SR 28, just w of SR 134. Ext corridors. **Pets:** Accepted.

⊞ ⌂ 🛜 ✕ 🔋 💻

WESTFORD

▼▼▼▼ Residence Inn by Marriott Boston Westford ⊞

(978) 392-1407. **$139-$229.** 7 Lan Dr 01886. I-495 exit 32, just s, then 0.5 w on SR 110. Int corridors. **Pets:** Accepted.

ⓜ ⌂ 🛜 ✕ 🔋 💻

WESTPORT

▼▼▼ Hampton Inn-Fall River-Westport ⊞

(508) 675-8500. **$99-$219.** 53 Old Bedford Rd 02790. I-195 exit 9 eastbound; exit 10 westbound, just s to US 6, then 1.3 mi w. Int corridors. **Pets:** Medium. $35 daily fee/pet. Designated rooms, supervision.

⌂ ✕ 🛜 ✕ 🔋 💻

WEST SPRINGFIELD

▼▼ ▼▼ Candlewood Suites ⊞

(413) 739-1122. **Call for rates.** 572 Riverdale St 01089. I-91 exit 13B, 1.3 mi s. Int corridors. **Pets:** Accepted. ⊞ ⓜ ⌂ 🛜 🔋 💻

▼▼▼▼ Hampton Inn ⊞

(413) 732-1300. **$129-$179.** 1011 Riverdale St (US 5) 01089. I-91 exit 13B, 0.3 mi s. Int corridors. **Pets:** Accepted.

ⓜ ⌂ 🛜 ✕ 🔋 💻

▼▼▼▼ Residence Inn by Marriott West Springfield ⊞

(413) 732-9543. **$104-$194.** 64 Border Way 01089. I-91 exit 13A, on US 5. Int corridors. **Pets:** Medium. $75 one-time fee/room. Service with restrictions, crate. ⊞ ⓜ ⌂ 🛜 ✕ 🔋 💻

WEST YARMOUTH

▼▼ ▼▼ The Yarmouth Resort ⓜ 🐾

(508) 775-5155. **$69-$239.** 343 Main St 02673. On SR 28, 2 mi e of jct SR 132. Ext/int corridors. **Pets:** Medium, dogs only. $20 daily fee/pet. Designated rooms, service with restrictions, supervision.

⌂ ✕ 🛜 🔋 💻

WILLIAMSTOWN

▼▼ ▼▼ The 1896 House Country Motels ⓜ

(413) 458-1896. **$84-$232, 7 day notice.** 910 Cold Spring Rd (Rt 7) 01267. 1.8 mi s on US 7 and SR 2. Ext corridors. **Pets:** Accepted.

⊞ ⌂ 🛜 ✕ 🔋 💻

▼▼ ▼▼ Maple Terrace Motel ⓜ

(413) 458-9677. **Call for rates.** 555 Main St 01267. On SR 2, 1 mi e of jct US 7. Ext corridors. **Pets:** Dogs only. $19 one-time fee/pet. Designated rooms, service with restrictions, supervision.

⊞ ⌂ 🛜 ✕ 🔋 💻

WOBURN

▲▲▲ ▼▼▼▼ BEST WESTERN PLUS New Englander ⊞

(781) 935-8160. **$129-$189.** 1 Rainin Rd 01801. I-93 exit 36, just e. Int corridors. **Pets:** Medium, dogs only. $20 daily fee/room. Designated rooms, service with restrictions, supervision.

(SAVE) ⊞ ⓜ ⌂ 🛜 ✕ 🔋 💻

▼▼ ▼▼ Extended Stay America Boston-Woburn ⊞

(781) 938-3737. **Call for rates.** 831 Main St 01801. I-95 exit 35, just n on SR 38. Int corridors. **Pets:** Other species. $25 daily fee/pet. Service with restrictions, supervision. ⓜ ⌂ 🛜 🔋 💻

▼▼▼▼ Hilton Boston/Woburn ⊞

(781) 932-0999. **$109-$269.** 2 Forbes Rd 01801. I-95 exit 36, 0.5 mi s via Washington St, then just e at Lukoil; jct Cedar St. Int corridors. **Pets:** Accepted. ⊞ ⌂ 🛜 ✕ 🔋 💻

▲▲▲ ▼▼▼▼ Residence Inn by
Marriott-Boston/Woburn ⊞ 🐾

(781) 376-4000. **$153-$344.** 300 Presidential Way 01801. I-93 exit 37C, just nw. Int corridors. **Pets:** Other species. $100 one-time fee/room. Service with restrictions. (SAVE) ⊞ ⓜ ⌂ 🛜 ✕ 🔋 💻

WORCESTER

▲▲▲ ▼▼▼ ▼▼▼ Beechwood Hotel ⊞

(508) 754-5789. **$169-$399.** 363 Plantation St 01605. I-290 exit 22 westbound, 0.5 mi w on Lincoln St, then 1.5 mi s; exit 21 eastbound, 1.3 mi s. Int corridors. **Pets:** Accepted.

(SAVE) ⊞ ⓜ 🛜 ✕ 🔋 💻

▼▼▼ ▼▼▼ Residence Inn by Marriott Worcester ⊞

(508) 753-6300. **$209-$355.** 503 Plantation St 01605. I-290 exit 21, 0.5 mi sw. Int corridors. **Pets:** Accepted.

⊞ ⓜ ⌂ 🛜 ✕ 🔋 💻

MICHIGAN

ACME

▼▼ ▼▼ Sleep Inn & Suites ⊞⊞

(231) 938-7000. **$50-$350.** 5520 US 31 N 49610. Jct US 31 and SR 72, 0.5 mi sw. Int corridors. **Pets:** Accepted.

ⓜ ⌂ 🛜 ✕ 🔋 💻

ADRIAN

▼▼ ▼▼ Carlton Lodge ⊞

(517) 263-7000. **$100-$240.** 1629 W Maumee St 49221. Jct SR 52, 3 mi w on US 223. Int corridors. **Pets:** Accepted.

⊞ ⌂ 🛜 ✕ 🔋 💻

▼▼ ▼▼ Holiday Inn Express ⊞

(517) 265-5700. **Call for rates.** 1077 W US 223 49221. Jct SR 52, just w. Int corridors. **Pets:** Accepted. ⌂ 🛜 ✕ 🔋 💻

▼▼ ▼▼ Super 8 ⊞

(517) 265-8888. **$76-$291.** 1091 W US 223 49221. Jct SR 52, just w. Int corridors. **Pets:** $25 one-time fee/room. Service with restrictions, supervision. 🛜 ✕ 🔋 💻

ALLEN PARK

▲▲▲ ▼▼▼ ▼▼▼ BEST WESTERN Greenfield Inn ⊞

(313) 271-1600. **$115-$155.** 3000 Enterprise Dr 48101. I-94 exit 206 (Oakwood Blvd), just s, then just w. Int corridors. **Pets:** Dogs only. $10 daily fee/room. Service with restrictions.

(SAVE) ⊞ ⌂ ✕ ✕ 🔋 💻

ALMA

Triangle Motel M

(989) 463-2296. **$70-$85.** 131 W Lincoln Rd 48801. US 127 exit 123 (Lincoln Rd) northbound; exit 124 (State Rd) southbound, just w on US 127 business route. Ext corridors. **Pets:** Dogs only. Designated rooms, supervision.

ALPENA

BEST WESTERN of Alpena H

(989) 356-9087. **Call for rates.** 1285 Hwy M-32 W 49707. 2.3 mi w of jct US 23. Ext/int corridors. **Pets:** Dogs only. $5 daily fee/pet. Service with restrictions, supervision.

Days Inn H

(989) 356-6118. **$80-$122.** 1496 Hwy M-32 W 49707. 2.5 mi w of jct US 23. Int corridors. **Pets:** Dogs only. $10 daily fee/room. Designated rooms, service with restrictions, supervision.

The Sanctuary Inn and Conference Center H

(989) 356-2151. **$99-$150, 3 day notice.** 1000 Hwy 23 N 49707. On US 23, 1 mi n. Int corridors. **Pets:** Accepted.

ANN ARBOR *(Restaurants p. 634)*

Candlewood Suites H

(734) 663-2818. **Call for rates.** 701 Waymarket Dr 48103. I-94 exit 175 (Ann Arbor/Saline Rd), just n, just e on Eisenhower Rd, then just s. Int corridors. **Pets:** Large, other species. $15 daily fee/pet. Service with restrictions, crate.

Extended Stay America University South H

(734) 997-7623. **$105-$110.** 3265 Boardwalk Dr 48108. I-94 exit 177 (State St), just n, just e on Victors Way, then just n. Int corridors. **Pets:** Other species. $25 daily fee/pet. Service with restrictions, supervision.

Hampton Inn-North H

(734) 996-4444. **$119-$399.** 2300 Green Rd 48105. US 23 exit 41 (Plymouth Rd), just nw. Int corridors. **Pets:** Medium. $50 one-time fee/room. Designated rooms, service with restrictions, crate.

Holiday Inn Near the University of Michigan H

(734) 769-9800. **Call for rates.** 3600 Plymouth Rd 48105. US 23 exit 41 (Plymouth Rd), just sw. Int corridors. **Pets:** Accepted.

Red Roof Plus+ Ann Arbor – University of Michigan North M

(734) 996-5800. **$60-$190.** 3621 Plymouth Rd 48105. US 23 exit 41 (Plymouth Rd), just nw. Ext corridors. **Pets:** Large, other species. Service with restrictions, supervision.

Residence Inn by Marriott H

(734) 996-5666. **$125-$206.** 800 Victors Way 48108. I-94 exit 177 (State St), just n, then just e. Ext/int corridors. **Pets:** Accepted.

Residence Inn by Marriott H

(734) 327-0011. **$109-$299.** 3535 Green Ct 48105. US 23 exit 41 (Plymouth Rd), just sw. Int corridors. **Pets:** Accepted.

Sheraton Ann Arbor Hotel H

(734) 996-0600. **Call for rates.** 3200 Boardwalk Dr 48108. I-94 exit 177 (State St), just n, just e on Victors Way, then just n. Int corridors. **Pets:** Accepted.

AUBURN HILLS

Extended Stay America Detroit-Auburn Hills-Featherstone Road H

(248) 335-5200. **$100-$105.** 2100 Featherstone Rd 48326. I-75 exit 79, 0.5 mi w on University Dr, then 0.8 mi s on Opdyke Rd. Int corridors. **Pets:** Other species. $25 daily fee/pet. Service with restrictions, supervision.

Extended Stay America Detroit-Auburn Hills-University Drive H

(248) 340-8888. **$100-$110.** 3315 University Dr 48326. I-75 exit 79, 0.9 mi e. Int corridors. **Pets:** Other species. $25 daily fee/pet. Service with restrictions, supervision.

Hawthorn Suites by Wyndham Detroit Auburn Hills H

(248) 373-3342. **$68-$145.** 1650 N Opdyke Rd 48326. I-75 exit 79, just w on University Dr, then 0.4 mi n. Int corridors. **Pets:** Accepted.

Hilton Suites Auburn Hills H

(248) 334-2222. **$109-$220.** 2300 Featherstone Rd 48326. I-75 exit 79, just w on University Dr, 0.5 mi s on Opdyke Rd, then just e. Int corridors. **Pets:** Accepted.

Hyatt Place Detroit/Auburn Hills H

(248) 475-9393. **$84-$199.** 1545 N Opdyke Rd 48326. I-75 exit 79, 0.5 mi w on University Dr, then just n. Int corridors. **Pets:** Accepted.

Sonesta ES Suites H

(248) 322-4600. **Call for rates.** 2050 Featherstone Rd 48326. I-75 exit 79, just w on University Dr, 0.5 mi s on Opdyke Rd, then just e. Int corridors. **Pets:** Accepted.

BAD AXE

Ameriway Inn & Suites H

(989) 269-3200. **$70-$116.** 898 N Van Dyke Rd 48413. 0.4 mi s of jct SR 142 and 53 (Van Dyke Rd). Int corridors. **Pets:** Small. $10 daily fee/pet. Designated rooms, service with restrictions, supervision.

BATTLE CREEK

Baymont Inn & Suites-Battle Creek H

(269) 979-5400. **$99-$239.** 4725 Beckley Rd 49015. I-94 exit 97 (Capital Ave), just sw. Int corridors. **Pets:** Accepted.

BAY CITY *(Restaurants p. 634)*

AmericInn Bay City H

(989) 671-0071. **$89-$159, 7 day notice.** 3915 Three Mile Rd 48706. I-75 exit 164 (Wilder Rd), just n. Int corridors. **Pets:** Large, dogs only. $35 one-time fee/pet, $10 daily fee/pet. Service with restrictions, supervision.

Fairfield Inn by Marriott H

(989) 667-7050. **$90-$160.** 4105 E Wilder Rd 48706. 1 mi e of SR 13. Int corridors. **Pets:** Other species. $50 one-time fee/room. Service with restrictions, supervision.

Holiday Inn Express & Suites H

(989) 667-3800. **$99-$169.** 3959 Traxler Ct 48706. I-75 exit 164 (Wilder Rd), 0.3 mi e. Int corridors. **Pets:** Accepted.

BELLAIRE

▼▼▼ **Shanty Creek Resorts Lakeview Hotel** 🅷
(231) 533-8621. **$149-$268, 5 day notice.** 5780 Shanty Creek Rd 49615. Jct SR 88/US 131, 4 mi nw to Shanty Creek Rd, then 1.5 mi e; in Summit Village. Int corridors. **Pets:** Accepted.

🍴 🕹 🏊 🏋 🛜 ✕ 🔋 💻

BELLEVILLE

▼▼▼ **Holiday Inn Express Hotel & Suites-Belleville (Airport Area)** 🅷
(734) 857-6200. **$99-$199.** 46194 N I-94 Service Dr 48111. I-94 exit 190 (Belleville Rd), just n, then just w. Int corridors. **Pets:** Medium, dogs only. $50 one-time fee/pet. Service with restrictions.

🕹 🏊 🏋 🛜 ✕ 🔋 💻

BENTON HARBOR

▼▼▼ **Holiday Inn Express & Suites** 🅷
(269) 927-4599. **$75-$175, 3 day notice.** 2276 Pipestone Rd 49022. I-94 exit 29 (Pipestone Rd), just se. Int corridors. Designated rooms, service with restrictions, supervision. 🏊 🛜 ✕ 🔋 💻

BEULAH

🔺🔺🔺 ▼▼▼ **BEST WESTERN Scenic Hill Resort** 🅷
(231) 882-7754. **$105-$200.** 1400 US Hwy 31 49617. On US 31, 0.8 mi e. Int corridors. **Pets:** Accepted.

[SAVE] 🍴 🏊 🏋 🛜 ✕ 🔋 💻

BIG RAPIDS

▼▼ ▼ **Country Inn & Suites By Carlson** 🅷
(231) 527-9000. **Call for rates.** 15344 Waldron Way 49307. US 131 exit 139, just e. Int corridors. **Pets:** Accepted.

🍴 🕹 🏊 🛜 ✕ 🔋 💻

BIRCH RUN

▼▼▼ **Americas Best Value Inn & Suites** 🅷
(989) 624-4440. **$50-$155.** 9235 E Birch Run Rd 48415. I-75 exit 136 (Birch Run Rd), just e. Int corridors. **Pets:** Service with restrictions, supervision. 🛜 ✕ 🔋 💻

🔺🔺🔺 ▼▼ ▼ **BEST WESTERN of Birch Run/Frankenmuth** 🅷
(989) 624-9395. **$75-$190.** 9087 Birch Run Rd 48415. I-75 exit 136 (Birch Run Rd), just e. Ext/int corridors. **Pets:** Accepted.

[SAVE] 🍴 🕹 🏊 🏋 🛜 ✕ 🔋 💻

▼▼▼ **Holiday Inn Express** 🅷
(989) 624-9300. **Call for rates.** 12150 Dixie Hwy 48415. I-75 exit 136 (Birch Run Rd), just e. Int corridors. **Pets:** Accepted.

🏊 🏋 🛜 ✕ 🔋 💻

BIRMINGHAM

🔺🔺🔺 ▼▼▼▼ **The Townsend Hotel** 🅷 🐾
(248) 642-7900. **$340-$550.** 100 Townsend St 48009. Center. Int corridors. **Pets:** Dogs only. $150 one-time fee/room, $5 daily fee/room. Service with restrictions, supervision.

[SAVE] [ECO] 🍴 🕹 🎙 ✕ 🔋 💻

BRIDGEPORT

▼▼ ▼ **Baymont Inn & Suites-Frankenmuth/Bridgeport** 🅷
(989) 777-3000. **$55-$159.** 6460 Dixie Hwy 48722. I-75 exit 144A. Int corridors. **Pets:** Accepted. 🕹 🏊 🛜 ✕ 🔋 💻

BRIGHTON

🔺🔺🔺 ▼▼ ▼ **Courtyard by Marriott** 🅷
(810) 225-9200. **$108-$177.** 7799 Conference Center Dr 48114. I-96 exit 145 (Grand River Ave S), just n, then 0.4 mi w. Int corridors. **Pets:** Accepted. [SAVE] 🕹 🏊 🛜 ✕ 🔋 💻

BROOKLYN

▼▼ ▼ **Super 8-Brooklyn** 🅷
(517) 592-0888. **$76-$138.** 419 S Main/M-50 49230. Jct SR 50 (Main St) and 124; downtown. Int corridors. **Pets:** $5 daily fee/pet. Designated rooms, service with restrictions, supervision. 🕹 🛜 ✕ 🔋 💻

BYRON CENTER

▼▼▼ **Comfort Suites-Grand Rapids South** 🅷
(616) 301-2255. **$90-$135.** 7644 Caterpillar Ct SW 49548. US 131 exit 75, just se. Int corridors. **Pets:** Accepted.

🕹 🏊 🏋 🛜 ✕ 🔋 💻

CADILLAC

▼▼▼ **McGuire's Resort** 🅷
(231) 775-9947. **$99-$169, 7 day notice.** 7880 Mackinaw Tr 49601. US 131 exit 177, 0.7 mi n, then 0.5 mi w. Int corridors. **Pets:** Accepted.

🍴 🏊 🏋 🛜 ✕ 🔋 💻

CALUMET

▼▼ ▼ **AmericInn Lodge & Suites of Calumet** 🅷 🐾
(906) 337-6463. **$107-$147.** 56925 S 6th St 49913. On US 41; just w of Visitors Center. Int corridors. **Pets:** Dogs only. $20 one-time fee/room. Designated rooms, service with restrictions.

🏊 🏋 🛜 ✕ 🔋 💻

CANTON

▼▼ ▼ **La Quinta Inn Detroit Canton** 🅷
(734) 981-1808. **$72-$169.** 41211 Ford Rd 48187. I-275 exit 25 (Ford Rd), just w on SR 153. Int corridors. **Pets:** Large, other species. Service with restrictions. 🛜 ✕ 🔋 💻

CASCADE

🔺🔺🔺 ▼▼ ▼ **BEST WESTERN Hospitality Hotel & Suites** 🅷
(616) 949-8400. **$90-$199.** 5500 28th St SE 49512. I-96 exit 43B, just e on SR 11. Int corridors. **Pets:** Accepted.

[SAVE] 🏊 🏋 🛜 ✕ 🔋 💻

▼▼ ▼ **Clarion Inn & Suites Grand Rapids Airport** 🅷
(616) 956-9304. **$109-$149.** 4981 28th St SE 49512. I-96 exit 43A, 0.4 mi w on SR 11. Int corridors. **Pets:** Accepted. 🏊 🛜 ✕ 🔋 💻

▼▼▼▼ **Crowne Plaza Grand Rapids** 🅷
(616) 957-1770. **$82-$199.** 5700 28th St SE 49546. I-96 exit 43B, 0.3 mi e on SR 11. Int corridors. **Pets:** Accepted.

🍴 🕹 🏊 🏋 🛜 ✕ 🔋 💻

▼▼▼ **Holiday Inn Express & Suites Grand Rapids Airport** 🅷
(616) 940-8100. **$99-$169.** 5401 28th St Ct SE 49546. I-96 exit 43B, just e on SR 11. Int corridors. **Pets:** Accepted.

🍴 🕹 🏊 🛜 ✕ 🔋 💻

CHARLEVOIX

▼▼ ▼ **AmericInn Lodge & Suites of Charlevoix** 🅷
(231) 237-0988. **Call for rates.** 11800 US 31 N 49720. On US 31, 2.4 mi n. Int corridors. **Pets:** Accepted. 🍴 🕹 🏊 🛜 ✕ 🔋 💻

▼▼ ▼ **Charlevoix Inn & Suites** 🅷 🐾
(231) 547-0300. **$69-$259.** 800 Petoskey Ave 49720. 1 mi n on US 31. Int corridors. **Pets:** Other species. $10 daily fee/pet. Designated rooms, service with restrictions, crate. 🏊 🛜 ✕ 🔋 💻

CHEBOYGAN

🔺🔺🔺 ▼▼ ▼ **BEST WESTERN River Terrace** 🅷
(231) 627-5688. **$79-$229.** 847 S Main St 49721. 1 mi s on SR 27. Ext/int corridors. **Pets:** Medium, dogs only. $10 daily fee/pet. Designated rooms, service with restrictions, supervision.

[SAVE] 🏊 🏋 🛜 ✕ 🔋 💻

▼ **Birch Haus Motel** **M**

(231) 627-5862. **$40-$85.** 1301 Mackinaw Ave 49721. On US 23, 0.8 mi nw. Ext corridors. **Pets:** Small, dogs only. $10 daily fee/pet. Designated rooms, service with restrictions, supervision. ⬚ ⬚ ⬚ ⬚

▼▼ **Continental Inn** **M**

(231) 627-7164. **$45-$130, 3 day notice.** 613 N Main St 49721. Jct US 23 and SR 27. Ext corridors. **Pets:** Small, dogs only. $10 daily fee/room. Designated rooms, service with restrictions, supervision. ⬚ ⬚ ⬚ ⬚ ⬚

CHELSEA

▼▼ **Chelsea Comfort Inn & Village Conference Center** **H**

(734) 433-8000. **$99-$129.** 1645 Commerce Park Dr 48118. I-94 exit 159 (SR 52/Main St), just n. Int corridors. **Pets:** Other species. $20 daily fee/room. Service with restrictions. ⬚ ⬚ ⬚ ⬚ ⬚ ⬚

▼▼ **Holiday Inn Express** **H**

(734) 433-1600. **Call for rates.** 1540 Commerce Park Dr 48118. I-94 exit 159 (SR 52/Main St), just n, then just w. Int corridors. **Pets:** Medium, other species. $40 one-time fee/pet. Service with restrictions, crate. ⬚ ⬚ ⬚ ⬚ ⬚ ⬚

CLARE

▼▼ **Days Inn of Clare** **H**

(989) 386-1111. **$80-$180.** 10318 S Clare Ave 48617. On Business Rt US 10 and 127; just w of jct US 127 and Old US 27. Int corridors. **Pets:** Other species. $10 daily fee/pet. Service with restrictions, supervision. ⬚ ⬚ ⬚ ⬚ ⬚

COLDWATER

▲▲▲ ▼▼▼ **BEST WESTERN PLUS Coldwater Hotel** **H**

(517) 279-0900. **$99-$139.** 630 E Chicago St 49036. I-69 exit 13 (US 12), just sw. Int corridors. **Pets:** Medium. $50 deposit/room, $10 daily fee/room. Designated rooms, service with restrictions, crate. ⬚ ⬚ ⬚ ⬚ ⬚ ⬚ ⬚

COMSTOCK PARK

▼▼▼ **Comfort Suites Grand Rapids North** **H**

(616) 785-7899. **$109-$169.** 350 Dodge St 49321. US 131 exit 91, just ne. Int corridors. **Pets:** Accepted. ⬚ ⬚ ⬚ ⬚ ⬚ ⬚ ⬚

COPPER HARBOR

▼ **Lake Fanny Hooe Resort** **M**

(906) 289-4451. **$100-$135, 7 day notice.** 505 2nd St 49918. Just s on Manganese Rd. Ext corridors. **Pets:** Other species. $10 daily fee/pet. Service with restrictions, crate. ⬚ ⬚ ⬚ ⬚ ⬚ ⬚ ⬚

DAVISON

▲▲▲ ▼▼▼▼ **BEST WESTERN Davison Inn** **H**

(810) 658-2700. **$90-$110.** 10082 Lapeer Rd 48423. I-69 exit 145 (SR 15), just n, then e. Int corridors. **Pets:** Medium. Designated rooms, service with restrictions, crate. ⬚ ⬚ ⬚ ⬚ ⬚ ⬚

DEARBORN

▲▲▲ ▼▼▼▼ **adoba hotel Dearborn/Detroit** **H**

(313) 592-3622. **Call for rates.** 600 Town Center Dr 48126. SR 39 (Southfield Frwy), 0.3 mi w on Michigan Ave, 0.3 mi n on Evergreen Rd, then e on Fairlane Rd. Int corridors. **Pets:** Accepted. ⬚ ⬚ ⬚ ⬚ ⬚ ⬚ ⬚ ⬚ ⬚

▼▼ **Extended Stay America Detroit Dearborn** **H**

(313) 336-0021. **$115-$120.** 260 Towne Center Dr 48126. SR 39 (Southfield Frwy); between Ford Rd and Michigan Ave exits; just w of jct Service and Hubbard drs. Int corridors. **Pets:** Other species. $25 daily fee/pet. Service with restrictions, supervision. ⬚ ⬚ ⬚ ⬚ ⬚

▲▲▲ ▼▼▼ ▼▼▼ **The Henry, Autograph Collection** **H**

(313) 441-2000. **$181-$298.** 300 Town Center Dr 48126. SR 39 (Southfield Frwy); between Ford Rd and Michigan Ave exits, on Service Dr. Int corridors. **Pets:** Accepted. ⬚ ⬚ ⬚ ⬚ ⬚ ⬚ ⬚ ⬚ ⬚

▲▲▲ ▼▼▼ **Red Roof Inn-Dearborn** **M**

(313) 278-9732. **$61-$106.** 24130 Michigan Ave 48124. Jct US 24 (Telegraph Rd) and 12 (Michigan Ave). Ext corridors. **Pets:** Large, other species. Service with restrictions, supervision. ⬚ ⬚ ⬚ ⬚ ⬚ ⬚

▼▼ ▼▼ **TownePlace Suites by Marriott-Detroit Dearborn** **H**

(313) 271-0200. **$136-$229.** 6141 Mercury Dr 48126. SR 39 (Southfield Frwy) exit 7 (Ford Rd), just e, then 0.8 mi n. Int corridors. **Pets:** Accepted. ⬚ ⬚ ⬚ ⬚ ⬚

DETROIT

▼▼▼▼ **Crowne Plaza Detroit Convention Center** **H**

(313) 965-0200. **Call for rates.** 2 Washington Blvd 48226. Jct W Jefferson Ave. Int corridors. **Pets:** Accepted. ⬚ ⬚ ⬚ ⬚ ⬚ ⬚ ⬚ ⬚

▼▼▼▼ **DoubleTree Suites by Hilton Detroit Downtown-Fort Shelby** **H**

(313) 963-5600. **$119-$229.** 525 W Lafayette Blvd 48226. Jct First Ave. Int corridors. **Pets:** Accepted. ⬚ ⬚ ⬚ ⬚ ⬚

▼▼ ▼▼ **Holiday Inn Express & Suites-Detroit** **H**

(313) 887-7000. **$99-$299.** 1020 Washington Blvd 48226. Corner of Washington Blvd and Michigan Ave. Int corridors. **Pets:** Other species. $25 one-time fee/room. Service with restrictions, supervision. ⬚ ⬚ ⬚ ⬚ ⬚ ⬚ ⬚

▲▲▲ ▼▼▼ ▼▼▼ **MotorCity Casino Hotel** **H**

(313) 237-7711. **$149-$499, 3 day notice.** 2901 Grand River Ave 48201. I-75 exit 50 (Grand River Ave), just n. Int corridors. **Pets:** Small, dogs only. $125 one-time fee/pet. Service with restrictions, supervision. ⬚ ⬚ ⬚ ⬚ ⬚ ⬚ ⬚

▲▲▲ ▼▼▼ ▼▼▼ **The Westin Book Cadillac Detroit** **H**

(313) 442-1600. **$109-$329.** 1114 Washington Blvd 48226. Corner of Washington Blvd and Michigan Ave. Int corridors. **Pets:** Accepted. ⬚ ⬚ ⬚ ⬚ ⬚ ⬚ ⬚ ⬚

DEWITT

▲▲▲ ▼▼▼ **Sleep Inn** **H**

(517) 669-8823. **$80-$160.** 1101 Commerce Park Dr 48820. I-69 exit 87 (Old US 27), 0.8 mi n. Int corridors. **Pets:** Accepted. ⬚ ⬚ ⬚ ⬚ ⬚

EAST LANSING

▼▼▼ **Hampton Inn East Lansing** **H**

(517) 324-2072. **$139-$209.** 2500 Coolidge Rd 48823. US 127 exit 79 (Lake Lansing Rd), just e. Int corridors. **Pets:** Other species. Service with restrictions. ⬚ ⬚ ⬚ ⬚ ⬚ ⬚

EAST TAWAS

▲▲▲ ▼▼▼ **Tawas Bay Beach Resort** **H**

(989) 362-8600. **$70-$210, 3 day notice.** 300 E Bay St 48730. On US 23; jct Main St. Int corridors. **Pets:** Accepted. ⬚ ⬚ ⬚ ⬚ ⬚ ⬚ ⬚

ESCANABA

▼▼ **Bay View Motel** **M**

(906) 786-2843. **$45-$80.** 7110 US Hwy 2 & 41 & M-35 49837. 4.5 mi n on US 2/41 and SR 35. Ext/int corridors. **Pets:** Other species. $5 one-time fee/pet. Supervision. ⬚ ⬚ ⬚ ⬚ ⬚

Econo Lodge H
(906) 789-1066. **$61-$89.** 921 N Lincoln Rd 49829. 0.5 mi n on US 2/41 and SR 35. Int corridors. **Pets:** Accepted.
SAVE 🛰 ✕ 🛏 💻

FARMINGTON HILLS
Extended Stay America Detroit-Farmington Hills H
(248) 473-4000. **$95-$100.** 27775 Stansbury Blvd 48334. I-696 exit 5 (Orchard Lake Rd), just n, just e on 12 Mile Rd, then just s. Int corridors. **Pets:** Other species. $25 daily fee/pet. Service with restrictions, supervision. 🅼 🛰 ✕ 🛏 💻

Hawthorn Suites by Wyndham Detroit Farmington Hills H
(248) 324-0540. **$73-$150.** 37555 Hills Tech Dr 48331. I-696 exit I-96 E/I-275 S/SR 5, just s to SR 5 N, 2 mi n to 12 Mile Rd, 1.3 mi e, then 0.3 mi s on Halsted Rd. Int corridors. **Pets:** Medium, other species. $15 daily fee/room. Service with restrictions. 🅼 🛰 ✕ 🛏 💻

Holiday Inn & Suites H
(248) 477-7800. **Call for rates.** 37529 Grand River Ave 48335. I-275 exit 165 (SR 5/Grand River Ave), 1 mi e. Int corridors. **Pets:** Accepted.
🍴 🅼 🛰 🛰 ✕ 🛏 💻

Radisson Hotel Detroit-Farmington Hills H
(248) 553-0000. **Call for rates.** 31525 W 12 Mile Rd 48334. I-696 exit 5 (Orchard Lake Rd), just w. Int corridors. **Pets:** Accepted.
🍴 🛰 🛰 ✕ 🛏 💻

Red Roof Inn Detroit - Farmington Hills M
(248) 478-8640. **$45-$99.** 24300 Sinacola Ct 48335. I-96/275 and SR 5 exit 165 (Grand River Ave), just w. Ext corridors. **Pets:** Large, other species. Service with restrictions, supervision.
SAVE 🅼 🛰 ✕ 🛏 💻

FENTON
Comfort Inn & Suites H
(810) 714-7171. **Call for rates.** 17800 Silver Pkwy 48430. US 23 exit 78 (Owen Rd), just w, then 0.4 mi n. Int corridors. **Pets:** Accepted.
🅼 🛰 🛰 ✕ 🛏 💻

FLINT
Americas Best Value Inn & Suites H
(810) 233-9000. **$79-$139.** 6075 Hill 23 Dr 48507. US 23 exit 90 (Hill Rd), just w. Int corridors. **Pets:** Large, other species. $25 one-time fee/room. Service with restrictions. 🍴 🅼 🛰 🛰 ✕ 🛏 💻

Baymont Inn & Suites-Flint/Flushing H
(810) 732-2300. **$59-$129.** 4160 Pier North Blvd 48504. I-75 exit 122 (Pierson Rd), just w. Int corridors. **Pets:** Medium, other species. $25 one-time fee/pet. Designated rooms, service with restrictions, crate.
🛰 🛰 ✕ 🛏 💻

Courtyard by Marriott H
(810) 232-3500. **$97-$171.** 5205 Gateway Center 48507. US 23 exit 90 (Hill Rd), just e to Gateway Center, then just n. Int corridors.
Pets: Accepted. 🍴 🅼 🛰 🛰 ✕ 🛏 💻

Holiday Inn Express Flint Campus Area H
(810) 238-7744. **Call for rates.** 1150 Robert T Longway Blvd 48503. I-475 exit 8A (Robert T Longway Blvd), just w. Int corridors.
Pets: Accepted. 🅼 🛰 ✕ 🛏 💻

Residence Inn by Marriott H
(810) 424-7000. **$104-$183.** 2202 W Hill Rd 48507. US 23 exit 90 (Hill Rd), just e. Int corridors. **Pets:** Other species. $100 one-time fee/room. Service with restrictions, crate. 🍴 🅼 🛰 🛰 ✕ 🛏 💻

FRANKENMUTH
Drury Inn & Suites H
(989) 652-2800. **$90-$160.** 260 S Main St 48734. On SR 83; downtown. Int corridors. **Pets:** $10 daily fee/room. Service with restrictions, supervision. 🅼 🛰 🛰 ✕ 🛏 💻

Frankenmuth Motel M
(989) 652-6171. **$49-$115.** 1218 Weiss St 48734. Just e of SR 83. Ext corridors. **Pets:** Other species. $10 daily fee/pet. Service with restrictions, crate. SAVE 🍴 🛰 ✕ 🛏 💻

GAYLORD
Downtown Motel M
(989) 732-5010. **Call for rates.** 208 S Otsego Ave 49735. I-75 exit 282, 0.5 mi e, then 0.3 mi s on I-75 business loop. Ext corridors.
Pets: Accepted. 🛰 ✕ 🛏 💻

GLEN ARBOR
The Homestead H
(231) 334-5000. **$83-$265, 28 day notice.** 4800 Wood Ridge Rd 49636. In Homestead Resort. Ext/int corridors. **Pets:** $10 daily fee/pet. Designated rooms, service with restrictions, supervision.
🍴 🅼 🛰 🛰 🛰 ✕ 🛏 💻

GRAND BLANC
Comfort Inn H
(810) 694-0000. **$70-$140.** 9040 Holly Rd 48439. I-75 exit 108 (Holly Rd), just e. Int corridors. **Pets:** Accepted.
🍴 🅼 🛰 🛰 ✕ 🛏 💻

GRAND RAPIDS *(Restaurants p. 634)*
Holiday Inn Grand Rapids Downtown H
(616) 235-7611. **$169-$249.** 310 Pearl St NW 49504. US 131 exit 85B (Pearl St), just se. Int corridors. **Pets:** Other species. $25 daily fee/room. Service with restrictions, crate.
SAVE ECO 🍴 🅼 🛰 🛰 ✕ 🛏 💻

Homewood Suites by Hilton H
(616) 285-7100. **$113-$189.** 3920 Stahl Dr SE 49546. I-96 exit 43A, 1.6 mi w on SR 11, just n on E Paris Ave, then just w. Int corridors.
Pets: Accepted. 🍴 🅼 🛰 🛰 ✕ 🛏 💻

GRANDVILLE
Days Inn & Suites H
(616) 531-5263. **$70-$150.** 3825 28th St SW 49418. I-196 exit 70/70A, 0.3 mi e. Int corridors. **Pets:** Small. $50 deposit/room, $10 daily fee/pet. Designated rooms, service with restrictions, supervision.
🍴 🛰 ✕ 🛏 💻

Grandvillage Inn H
(616) 532-3222. **Call for rates.** 3425 Fairlanes Ave 49418. I-196 exit 69A, just e on Chicago Dr, then just s. Int corridors. **Pets:** Accepted.
🛰 ✕ 🛰 ✕ 🛏 💻

Residence Inn by Marriott Grand Rapids West H
(616) 538-1100. **$111-$206.** 3451 Rivertown Point Ct SW 49418. I-196 exit 67, 1.5 mi e. Int corridors. **Pets:** Accepted.
ECO 🅼 🛰 🛰 ✕ 🛏 💻

GRAYLING
Ramada Hotel & Conference Center H
(989) 348-7611. **$80-$120.** 2650 S I-75 Business Loop 49738. I-75 exit 254 northbound, 1 mi nw; exit 256 southbound, 1 mi sw. Ext/int corridors. **Pets:** $10 daily fee/pet. Designated rooms, service with restrictions, crate. 🍴 🛰 🛰 🛰 ✕ 🛏 💻

Super 8 H
(989) 348-8888. **$62-$100.** 5828 Nelson A Miles Pkwy 49738. I-75 exit 251, just w. Int corridors. **Pets:** $8 daily fee/room. Designated rooms, supervision. 🍴 🛰 🛰 ✕ 🛏 💻

GREENVILLE
AmericInn Lodge & Suites of Greenville H
(616) 754-4500. **$90-$120.** 2525 W Washington St 48838. Jct SR 91, 1.9 mi w on SR 57. Int corridors. **Pets:** Accepted.
🍴 🅼 🛰 🛰 ✕ 🛏 💻

HANCOCK

▼▼▼ **Magnuson Hotel Copper Crown** 🅗
(906) 482-6111. **$70-$74.** 235 Hancock St 49930. On US 41 S; downtown. Ext/int corridors. **Pets:** Small, dogs only. $10 daily fee/room. Designated rooms, service with restrictions, supervision.

🍴 🛆 🛜 ✖ 🛎 💻

HARRISON

▼▼ **Lakeside Motel & Cottages** Ⓜ
(989) 539-0706. **$62-$99.** 515 E Park St, US 127 Business Rt 48625. US 127 exit US 127 business route/SR 61, 2.2 mi w. Ext corridors. **Pets:** Other species. Service with restrictions, supervision.

🍴 🛜 ✖ 🛎 💻

HARTLAND

🅐🅐🅐 ▼▼▼ **BEST WESTERN of Hartland** Ⓜ
(810) 632-7177. **$79-$115.** 10087 M-59 48353. US 23 exit 67 (SR 59), just w. Ext corridors. **Pets:** Accepted.

🆂🅰🆅🅴 🍴 🛆ᴹ 🛆 🛜 ✖ 🛎 💻

HASTINGS

▼▼▼▼ **Holiday Inn Express Hastings** 🅗
(269) 945-0000. **Call for rates.** 1099 W SR 43 Hwy 49058. 1.3 mi w on SR 43; center of town. Int corridors. **Pets:** Accepted.

🛆ᴹ 🛜 ✖ 🛎 💻

HOLLAND

🅐🅐🅐 ▼▼▼▼ **BEST WESTERN PLUS Holland Inn & Suites** 🅗
(616) 994-0400. **$90-$400, 3 day notice.** 2888 W Shore Dr 49424. US 31 exit Felch St E, just ne. Ext/int corridors. **Pets:** Medium, dogs only. $25 daily fee/pet. Designated rooms, service with restrictions.

🆂🅰🆅🅴 🛆ᴹ 🛆 🛜 🛎 💻

▼▼▼ **Residence Inn by Marriott** 🅗
(616) 393-6900. **$97-$160.** 631 Southpoint Ridge Rd 49423. I-196 exit 49, 0.7 mi n on SR 40. Int corridors. **Pets:** Large. $75 one-time fee/room. Service with restrictions, crate.

🔌 🍴 🛆ᴹ 🛆 🛜 ✖ 🛎 💻

HOUGHTON

▼▼▼▼ **Country Inn & Suites By Carlson** 🅗 🐾
(906) 487-6700. **Call for rates.** 919 Razorback Dr 49931. 1.3 mi w on SR 26. Int corridors. **Pets:** Dogs only. $10 one-time fee/room. Designated rooms, service with restrictions, supervision.

🛆ᴹ 🛆 🛜 ✖ 🛎 💻

▼▼▼▼ **Holiday Inn Express Houghton** 🅗 🐾
(906) 482-1066. **$109-$209.** 1110 Century Way 49931. 1 mi w on SR 26. Int corridors. **Pets:** Dogs only. $20 one-time fee/room. Service with restrictions, supervision. 🍴 🛆 🗙 🛜 ✖ 🛎 💻

▼▼▼ **Magnuson Hotel-Franklin Square Inn** 🅗
(906) 487-1700. **$90-$120.** 820 Shelden Ave 49931. On US 41; downtown. Int corridors. **Pets:** $20 daily fee/room. Designated rooms, service with restrictions, supervision. 🍴 🛆 🗙 🛜 ✖ 🛎 💻

HOUGHTON LAKE

▼▼ **Super 8** 🅗
(989) 422-3119. **$65-$85.** 9580 W Lake City Rd 48629. Jct US 127 and SR 55. Int corridors. **Pets:** Accepted. 🛆 🗙 🛜 ✖ 💻

HOWELL

▼▼▼ **Baymont Inn & Suites-Howell** 🅗
(517) 546-0712. **$69-$139.** 4120 Lambert Dr 48855. I-96 exit 133 (US 59/Grand River Ave), just n, then 0.5 mi e. Int corridors. **Pets:** Dogs only. $50 deposit/room, $10 daily fee/pet. Designated rooms, service with restrictions. 🍴 🛆ᴹ 🛆 🛜 ✖ 🛎 💻

🅐🅐🅐 ▼▼▼ **BEST WESTERN of Howell** Ⓜ
(517) 548-2900. **$99-$195, 3 day notice.** 1500 Pinckney Rd 48843. I-96 exit 137 (Pinckney Rd), just s on CR D19 (Michigan Ave). Ext corridors. **Pets:** Accepted. 🆂🅰🆅🅴 🍴 🛆 🛜 ✖ 🛎 💻

IMLAY CITY

▼▼▼ **Super 8-Imlay City** 🅗
(810) 724-8700. **$60-$100.** 6951 Newark Rd 48444. I-69 exit 168 (SR 53/Van Dyke Rd), just n, then just e. Int corridors. **Pets:** Accepted.

🗙 🛜 ✖ 🛎 💻

IRON MOUNTAIN

🅐🅐🅐 ▼▼▼ **Comfort Inn by Choice Hotels** 🅗 🐾
(906) 774-5505. **$99-$109.** 1565 N Stephenson Ave 49801. On US 2, 1.3 mi nw. Int corridors. **Pets:** Medium, dogs only. $15 daily fee/pet. Designated rooms, service with restrictions, supervision.

🆂🅰🆅🅴 🛜 ✖ 🛎 💻

▼▼▼▼ **Country Inn & Suites By Carlson** 🅗
(906) 774-1900. **$80-$160.** 2005 S Stephenson Ave 49801. Jct SR 141, 0.8 mi w on US 2. Int corridors. **Pets:** Accepted.

🍴 🛆ᴹ 🛆 🛜 ✖ 🛎 💻

IRON RIVER

▼▼▼ **AmericInn Lodge & Suites of Iron River** 🅗
(906) 265-9100. **$100-$137.** 40 E Adams St 49935. On US 2; downtown. Int corridors. **Pets:** Accepted. 🛆 🗙 🛜 ✖ 🛎 💻

IRONWOOD

▼▼ **Americas Best Value Inn** 🅗
(906) 932-3395. **$70-$90.** 160 E Cloverland Dr 49938. Jct US 2 and 2 business route. Int corridors. **Pets:** $15 daily fee/pet. Supervision.

🛜 ✖ 🛎 💻

▼▼▼ **AmericInn of Ironwood** 🅗 🐾
(906) 932-7200. **Call for rates.** 1117 E Cloverland Dr 49938. 0.8 mi e on US 2. Int corridors. **Pets:** Other species. $20 daily fee/room. Service with restrictions, supervision. 🛆ᴹ 🛆 🗙 🛜 ✖ 🛎 💻

ISHPEMING

🅐🅐🅐 ▼▼▼ **BEST WESTERN Country Inn** 🅗
(906) 485-6345. **$100-$117, 3 day notice.** 850 US 41 W 49849. US 41, just w of town. Int corridors. **Pets:** Designated rooms, service with restrictions, crate. 🆂🅰🆅🅴 🍴 🛆 🛜 ✖ 💻

JACKSON

▼▼▼ **Baymont Inn-Jackson** 🅗
(517) 789-6000. **$69-$189.** 2035 Bondsteel Dr 49202. I-94 exit 138 (US 127), just nw. Int corridors. **Pets:** Medium. $10 daily fee/pet. Service with restrictions, crate. 🛜 ✖ 🛎 💻

▼▼▼ **Hampton Inn by Hilton** 🅗
(517) 789-5151. **$129-$189.** 2225 Shirley Dr 49202. I-94 exit 138 (US 127), just n to Springport Rd, then just e. Int corridors. **Pets:** Medium. Designated rooms, service with restrictions, supervision.

🛆ᴹ 🛆 🛜 ✖ 🛎 💻

KALAMAZOO

▼▼▼ **AmericInn Hotel & Suites** 🅗
(269) 344-7774. **Call for rates.** 1550 E Kilgore Rd 49001. I-94 exit 78 (Portage Rd), just n, then just w. Int corridors. **Pets:** Accepted.

🍴 🛆ᴹ 🛆 🛜 ✖ 🛎 💻

▼▼▼ **Baymont Inn & Suites Kalamazoo** 🅗
(269) 372-7999. **$69-$139.** 2203 S 11th St 49009. US 131 exit 36B (Stadium Dr), just nw. Int corridors. **Pets:** Accepted.

🛜 ✖ 🛎 💻

🅐🅐🅐 ▼▼▼▼ **BEST WESTERN PLUS Kalamazoo Suites** 🅗
(269) 350-5522. **$90-$160.** 2575 S 11th St 49009. US 131 exit 36B (Stadium Dr), just sw. Int corridors. **Pets:** Medium. $25 one-time fee/room. Service with restrictions, supervision.

🆂🅰🆅🅴 🛆ᴹ 🛆 🛜 ✖ 🛎 💻

▼▼▼ Candlewood Suites H

(269) 270-3203. **$114.** 3443 Retail Place Dr 49048. I-94 exit 80 (Sprinkle Rd), just s. Int corridors. **Pets:** Medium. $25 daily fee/room. Service with restrictions, crate. ⊞ 🍴 ⟨M⟩ 🛜 ✕ 🛏 🖵

▼▼▼ Clarion Inn Kalamazoo H

(269) 381-1900. **Call for rates.** 3640 E Cork St 49001. I-94 exit 80 (Sprinkle Rd), just nw. Int corridors. **Pets:** Other species. $25 daily fee/ pet. Designated rooms, service with restrictions, crate.
🔁 🛜 🛏 🖵

AAA ▼▼▼▼ Four Points by Sheraton Kalamazoo H ❀

(269) 385-3922. **Call for rates.** 3600 E Cork St Ct 49001. I-94 exit 80 (Sprinkle Rd), 0.3 mi n, then 0.4 mi w. Int corridors. **Pets:** Medium, dogs only. $25 one-time fee/pet. Designated rooms, service with restrictions, supervision. SAVE 🍴 🔁 🛜 ✕ 🛏 🖵

▼▼▼▼ Henderson Castle Bed & Breakfast, Restaurant and Spa C

(269) 344-1827. **$99-$299, 8 day notice.** 100 Monroe St 49006. US 131 exit 38A, 2.9 mi e. Int corridors. **Pets:** Other species. $25 daily fee/pet. Service with restrictions, supervision.
🍴 ⟨M⟩ ✕ 🛜 ✕ ✍

AAA ▼▼▼ Holiday Inn Kalamazoo H

(269) 375-6000. **$109-$159.** 2747 S 11th St 49009. US 131 exit 36B (Stadium Dr), just sw. Int corridors. **Pets:** Accepted.
SAVE ECO 🍴 ⟨M⟩ 🔁 ✕ 🛜 ✕ 🛏 🖵

AAA ▼▼▼ Quality Inn H

(269) 381-7000. **$70-$130.** 3820 S Sprinkle Rd 49001. I-94 exit 80 (Sprinkle Rd), 0.3 mi s. Int corridors. **Pets:** Accepted.
SAVE 🔁 🛜 🛏 🖵

AAA ▼▼▼ Red Roof Inn Kalamazoo West-Western Michigan Univ. H

(269) 375-7400. **$49-$110.** 5425 W Michigan Ave 49009. US 131 exit 36B (Stadium Dr), just nw. Ext corridors. **Pets:** Large, other species. Service with restrictions, supervision. SAVE ⟨M⟩ 🛜 ✕ 🛏 🖵

▼▼▼ Residence Inn by Marriott H

(269) 349-0855. **$115-$189.** 1500 E Kilgore Rd 49001. I-94 exit 78 (Portage Rd), just n, then just w. Int corridors. **Pets:** Accepted.
ECO 🍴 ⟨M⟩ 🔁 🛜 ✕ 🛏 🖵

▼▼▼ Staybridge Suites-Kalamazoo H

(269) 372-8000. **Call for rates.** 2001 Seneca Ln 49008. US 131 exit 36A (Stadium Dr), 0.3 mi e. Int corridors. **Pets:** Accepted.
⟨M⟩ 🔁 🛜 ✕ 🛏 🖵

▼▼▼ TownePlace Suites by Marriott Kalamazoo H

(269) 353-1500. **$104-$183.** 5683 S 9th St 49009. I-94 exit 72 (9th St), just s. Int corridors. **Pets:** Accepted. ⟨M⟩ 🔁 🛜 ✕ 🛏 🖵

KALKASKA

▼▼▼ All Seasons Resort H

(231) 258-0000. **Call for rates.** 760 S Cedar St 49646. On US 131 and SR 72, 0.8 mi n. Int corridors. **Pets:** Accepted.
🔁 ✕ 🛜 ✕ 🛏

KENTWOOD

▼▼▼ Residence Inn by Marriott Grand Rapids Airport H

(616) 285-1280. **$111-$183.** 4443 28th St 49512. I-96 exit 43A, 1 mi w on SR 11. Int corridors. **Pets:** Accepted. 🛜 ✕ 🛏 🖵

▼▼▼ Staybridge Suites - Grand Rapids H

(616) 464-3200. **Call for rates.** 3000 Lake Eastbrook Blvd SE 49512. I-96 exit 43A, 2 mi w on SR 11, then just s. Int corridors.
Pets: Accepted. 🍴 ⟨M⟩ 🔁 🛜 ✕ 🛏 🖵

LANSING

AAA ▼▼▼▼ Candlewood Suites H ❀

(517) 351-8181. **Call for rates.** 3545 Forest Rd 48910. I-496 exit 11 (Jolly Rd), 0.3 mi e to Collins Rd, 0.7 mi n, then just w. Int corridors. **Pets:** Other species. $150 one-time fee/pet. Designated rooms.
SAVE 🍴 ⟨M⟩ 🛜 ✕ 🛏 🖵

AAA ▼▼▼▼ Causeway Bay Lansing Hotel & Convention Center H

(517) 694-8123. **Call for rates.** 6820 S Cedar St 48911. I-96 exit 104. Int corridors. **Pets:** Accepted.
SAVE 🍴 ⟨M⟩ 🔁 ✕ 🛜 ✕ 🛏 🖵

▼▼▼ Comfort Inn H ❀

(517) 627-8381. **$79-$114.** 525 N Canal Rd 48917. I-96 exit 93B (SR 43/Saginaw Hwy), just e. Int corridors. **Pets:** Other species. Designated rooms, service with restrictions. 🔁 🛜 ✕ 🛏 🖵

AAA ▼▼▼▼ Courtyard by Marriott H

(517) 482-0500. **$132-$217.** 2710 Lake Lansing Rd 48912. US 127 exit 79 (Lake Lansing Rd), just w. Int corridors. **Pets:** Accepted.
SAVE 🍴 ⟨M⟩ 🔁 🛜 ✕ 🛏 🖵

AAA ▼▼▼▼ Crowne Plaza Lansing West H

(517) 323-7100. **$159-$375.** 925 S Creyts Rd 48917. I-496 exit 1 (Creyts Rd), just n. Int corridors. **Pets:** Accepted.
SAVE 🍴 🔁 🛜 ✕ 🛏 🖵

AAA ▼▼▼▼ Quality Suites Hotel H ❀

(517) 886-0600. **$85-$119.** 901 Delta Commerce Dr 48917. I-96 exit 93B (SR 43/Saginaw Hwy), 0.3 mi e, then just n. Int corridors.
Pets: Other species. $25 one-time fee/room. Service with restrictions.
SAVE ECO 🛜 ✕ 🛏 🖵

▼▼▼▼ Residence Inn by Marriott West H

(517) 886-5030. **$126-$207.** 922 Delta Commerce Dr 48917. I-96 exit 93B (SR 43/Saginaw Hwy), 0.4 mi e. Int corridors. **Pets:** Accepted.
⟨M⟩ 🔁 🛜 ✕ 🛏 🖵

LIVONIA

▼▼▼ Comfort Inn Livonia H

(734) 458-7111. **$74-$110.** 29235 Buckingham Dr 48154. I-96 exit 176 (Middlebelt Rd), just n. Int corridors. **Pets:** Medium, dogs only. Designated rooms, service with restrictions, crate. 🛜 ✕ 🛏 🖵

▼▼▼▼ Embassy Suites Hotel H

(734) 462-6000. **$119-$219.** 19525 Victor Pkwy 48152. I-96/275 exit 169 (7 Mile Rd), just e, then 0.5 mi n. Int corridors. **Pets:** Accepted.
🍴 🔁 🍲 ✕ 🛏 🖵

AAA ▼▼▼▼ Hyatt Place Detroit/Livonia H

(734) 953-9224. **$74-$199.** 19300 Haggerty Rd 48152. I-96/275 exit 169 (7 Mile Rd), just w, then just n. Int corridors. **Pets:** Accepted.
SAVE ⟨M⟩ 🔁 🛜 ✕ 🛏 🖵

▼▼▼▼ Livonia Marriott H

(734) 462-3100. **$109-$178.** 17100 Laurel Park Dr N 48152. I-96/275 exit 170 (6 Mile Rd), just e, then just n. Int corridors. **Pets:** Small. $75 one-time fee/room. Service with restrictions, crate.
ECO 🍴 🔁 🍲 ✕ 🛏 🖵

▼▼▼ Residence Inn by Marriott Detroit-Livonia H

(734) 462-4201. **$111-$183.** 17250 Fox Dr 48152. I-96/275 exit 170 (6 Mile Rd), just w, then just n. Int corridors. **Pets:** Accepted.
⟨M⟩ 🔁 🛜 ✕ 🛏 🖵

▼▼▼ TownePlace Suites by Marriott H ❀

(734) 542-7400. **$97-$171.** 17450 Fox Dr 48152. I-96/275 exit 170 (6 Mile Rd), just w, then just n. Int corridors. **Pets:** Other species. $100 one-time fee/room. Designated rooms. ⟨M⟩ 🔁 🛜 ✕ 🛏 🖵

LUDINGTON

AAA ▼▼▼ BEST WESTERN Lakewinds H ❀
(231) 843-2140. **$80-$250.** 5005 W US 10 49431. US 31 exit 170B, 0.9 mi w. Int corridors. **Pets:** Dogs only. $10 daily fee/pet. Designated rooms, service with restrictions, crate.
SAVE ⊺⊦ 🛌 ⊠ 🛜 ✕ 🛢 💻

▼▼▼ Holiday Inn Express H
(231) 845-7004. **$89-$249.** 5323 W US 10 49431. US 31 exit 170B, 1.3 mi w. Int corridors. **Pets:** Accepted.
ECO ⊺⊦ 🛌 ⊠ 🛜 ✕ 🛢 💻

MACKINAW CITY

▼▼ Baymont Inn & Suites H
(231) 436-7737. **$59-$148.** 109 S Nicolet St 49701. I-75 exit 338 southbound, just n. Int corridors. **Pets:** Accepted. 🛌 🛜 ✕ 🛢 💻

▼▼ The Beach House CA
(231) 436-5353. **$49-$218, 14 day notice.** 11490 W US 23 49701. 1.3 mi s. Ext corridors. **Pets:** Accepted. ⊺⊦ 🛌 🛜 ✕ 🐾 🛢

▼▼ Days Inn & Suites "Bridgeview Lodge" M
(231) 436-8961. **$75-$200.** 206 N Nicolet St 49701. I-75 exit 339; at bridge. Ext/int corridors. **Pets:** Medium, dogs only. $50 deposit/room. Designated rooms, service with restrictions, supervision.
🛌 🛜 ✕ 🛢 💻

AAA ▼▼ Days Inn Lakeview M
(231) 436-5557. **$39-$299, 3 day notice.** 825 S Huron Ave 49701. I-75 exit 337 northbound, 0.5 mi n to US 23, then 0.3 mi e; exit 338 southbound, 0.8 mi se on US 23. Ext corridors. **Pets:** Accepted.
SAVE 🛌 ⊠ 🛜 ✕ 🛢 💻

AAA ▼▼ Econo Lodge Bayview M
(231) 436-5777. **$39-$299, 3 day notice.** 712 S Huron Ave 49701. I-75 exit 337 northbound, 0.5 mi n to US 23, 0.3 mi e, then just n; exit 338 southbound, 0.8 mi se on US 23, then just n. Ext corridors.
Pets: Accepted. SAVE 🛌 ⊠ 🛜 ✕ 🛢 💻

AAA ▼▼ Fairview Beachfront Inn M
(231) 436-8831. **$38-$198, 3 day notice.** 907 S Huron Ave 49701. 0.8 mi se on US 23. Ext corridors. **Pets:** Accepted.
SAVE 🛌 🛜 ✕ 🛢 💻

▼▼ Holiday Inn Express at the Bridge H
(231) 436-7100. **$69-$299.** 364 Louvigny St 49701. I-75 exit 339. Int corridors. **Pets:** Medium, dogs only. $50 deposit/room. Designated rooms, service with restrictions, supervision.
🛜M 🛌 ⊠ 🛜 ✕ 🛢 💻

▼▼ Knights Inn Mackinaw City M
(231) 436-5026. **$60-$100.** 412 N Nicolet St 49701. I-75 exit 339, just ne. Ext corridors. **Pets:** Accepted. 🛜 ✕ 🛢 💻

▼▼ Lamplighter Motel M
(231) 436-5350. **$29-$102.** 303 Jamet St 49701. I-75 exit 339, just n of town. Ext corridors. **Pets:** Other species. $5 daily fee/pet. Crate.
⊺⊦ 🛜 ✕ 🛢 💻

AAA ▼ Mackinaw Waterfront Inn M
(231) 436-5527. **$38-$288, 3 day notice.** 1009 S Huron Ave 49701. 1.2 mi se on US 23. Ext corridors. **Pets:** Accepted.
SAVE ⊺⊦ 🛌 🛜 ✕ 🛢

AAA ▼▼▼ Quality Inn & Suites Lakefront M
(231) 436-5051. **$39-$249, 3 day notice.** 917 S Huron Ave 49701. 1 mi se on US 23. Ext corridors. **Pets:** Accepted.
SAVE 🛌 🛜 ✕ 🛢 💻

AAA ▼▼ Super 8 Beachfront M
(231) 436-7111. **$39-$299, 3 day notice.** 519 S Huron Ave 49701. I-75 exit 337 northbound, 0.5 mi n to US 23, 0.3 mi e, then just n; exit 338 southbound, 0.8 mi se on US 23, then just n. Ext corridors.
Pets: Accepted. SAVE 🛌 🛜 ✕ 🛢 💻

AAA ▼▼ Super 8 Bridgeview H
(231) 436-5252. **$39-$299, 3 day notice.** 601 N Huron Ave 49701. I-75 exit 339 northbound, just n, then just e. Ext/int corridors.
Pets: Accepted. SAVE 🛌 🛜 ✕ 🛢 💻

MADISON HEIGHTS

▼▼ Red Roof Inn Detroit - Royal Oak/Madison Heights M
(248) 583-4700. **$40-$99.** 32511 Concord Dr 48071. I-75 exit 65A, just e on 14 Mile Rd, then just s. Ext corridors. **Pets:** Large, other species. Service with restrictions, supervision. 🛜M 🛜 ✕ 🛢 💻

▼▼▼ Residence Inn by Marriott-Detroit Troy/Madison Heights H
(248) 583-4322. **$109-$178.** 32650 Stephenson Hwy 48071. I-75 exit 65B, just w on W 14 Mile Rd, then just s. Ext corridors.
Pets: Accepted. 🛌 🛜 ✕ 🛢 💻

MANISTIQUE

▼▼ Comfort Inn by Choice Hotels H
(906) 341-6981. **$80-$160.** 617 E Lakeshore Dr 49854. 0.5 mi e on US 2. Int corridors. **Pets:** $25 one-time fee/room. Service with restrictions, supervision. 🛜 ✕ 🛢 💻

▼▼ Quality Inn & Suites Manistique H
(906) 341-3777. **Call for rates.** 955 E Lakeshore Dr 49854. 1.4 mi e on US 2. Int corridors. **Pets:** Accepted. 🛜 ✕ 🛢 💻

MARQUETTE

AAA ▼ Birchmont Motel M
(906) 228-7538. **$67-$87.** 2090 US 41 S 49855. On US 41, 1.8 mi n of jct SR 28; 2.8 mi s of downtown. Ext corridors. **Pets:** Other species. $10 daily fee/pet. Designated rooms, service with restrictions, supervision. SAVE ⊺⊦ 🛌 🛜 ✕ 🛢

AAA ▼ Cedar Motor Inn M
(906) 228-2280. **$49-$99, 3 day notice.** 2523 US Hwy 41 W 49855. On US 41 and SR 28, 2.8 mi w. Ext/int corridors. **Pets:** Dogs only. $10 daily fee/pet. Designated rooms, service with restrictions, crate.
SAVE ⊺⊦ 🛌 🛜 ✕ 🛢 💻

▼▼ Days Inn H
(906) 225-1393. **$89-$159, 3 day notice.** 2403 US 41 W 49855. On US 41 and SR 28, 2.3 mi w. Int corridors. **Pets:** Accepted.
🛌 ⊠ 🛜 ✕ 🛢 💻

▼▼ Econo Lodge Lakeside M
(906) 225-1305. **$64-$169.** 2050 US 41 S 49855. On US 41, 2 mi n of SR 28; 2.6 mi s of downtown. Ext/int corridors. **Pets:** Accepted.
⊺⊦ 🛜 ✕ 🛢 💻

▼▼ Holiday Inn H
(906) 225-1351. **$129-$199.** 1951 US 41 W 49855. On US 41 and SR 28, 1.8 mi w. Int corridors. **Pets:** Dogs only. $25 daily fee/pet. Designated rooms, service with restrictions, supervision.
⊺⊦ 🛜M 🛌 ⊠ 🛜 ✕ 🛢 💻

▼▼ Ramada Marquette H
(906) 228-6000. **$100-$190.** 412 W Washington St 49855. 0.4 mi w on US 42 business route. Int corridors. **Pets:** Accepted.
⊺⊦ 🛌 ⊠ 🛜 ✕ 🛢 💻

▼▼ Settle Inn H
(906) 228-8100. **$87-$94.** 1275 US 41 W 49855. On US 41 and SR 28, 1 mi w. Int corridors. **Pets:** Dogs only. $20 one-time fee/room. Designated rooms, supervision. 🛌 🛜 ✕ 🛢 💻

MARSHALL

AAA ▼▼▼ Arbor Inn of Historic Marshall M
(269) 781-7772. **$45-$79.** 15435 W Michigan Ave 49068. I-69 exit 36 (Michigan Ave), just w. Ext corridors. **Pets:** $5 daily fee/pet. Service with restrictions, crate. SAVE ⊺⊦ 🛌 🛜 ✕ 🛢

▼▼ Comfort Inn 🅷
(269) 789-7890. **$90-$150.** 204 Winston Dr 49068. I-69 exit 36 (Michigan Ave), just se. Int corridors. **Pets:** Accepted.

▼▼ Hampton Inn Marshall 🅷
(269) 789-0131. **$139-$189.** 325 Sam Hill Dr 49068. I-94 exit 110 (SR 227), just s. Int corridors. **Pets:** Small, other species. $25 daily fee/pet. Service with restrictions, crate.

▼▼ Holiday Inn Express-Marshall 🅷
(269) 789-9301. **$119-$179.** 329 Sam Hill Dr 49068. I-94 exit 110 (SR 227), just s. Int corridors. **Pets:** Accepted.

MENOMINEE

▼▼ AmericInn Menominee on the Bay 🅷
(906) 863-8699. **$89-$135.** 2330 10th St 49858. 0.8 mi n on US 41. Int corridors. **Pets:** Accepted.

▼▼ Econo Lodge On The Bay 🅷
(906) 863-4431. **$61-$130.** 2516 10th St 49858. 1 mi n on US 41. Int corridors. **Pets:** Small. $20 daily fee/pet. Supervision.

MIDLAND

▼▼ Baymont Inn & Suites Midland 🅷
(989) 631-0070. **Call for rates.** 2200 W Wackerly St 48640. US 10 exit 122 (Eastman Ave), just s, then just w. Int corridors. **Pets:** Accepted.

ⓐⓐⓐ ▼▼ BEST WESTERN Valley Plaza Inn 🅷
(989) 496-2700. **$81-$100.** 5221 Bay City Rd 48642. US 10 exit 129 (Bay City Rd). Int corridors. **Pets:** Accepted.

▼▼▼ Residence Inn by Marriott 🅷
(989) 837-9990. **$122-$200.** 850 Joe Mann Blvd 48642. US 10 exit 122 (Eastman Ave), 1 mi e. Int corridors. **Pets:** Accepted.

▼▼ Sleep Inn of Midland 🅷
(989) 837-1010. **$90-$130.** 2100 W Wackerly St 48640. US 10 exit 122 (Eastman Ave), just s, then just w. Int corridors. **Pets:** Dogs only. $10 daily fee/room. Service with restrictions, supervision.

MOUNT PLEASANT

▼▼▼ Comfort Inn & Suites Hotel and Conference Center 🅷 🌸
(989) 772-4000. **$139-$159.** 2424 S Mission St 48858. 2 mi s on US 127 business route. Int corridors. **Pets:** $20 daily fee/room. Service with restrictions.

▼▼ Fairfield Inn & Suites by Marriott 🅷
(989) 775-5000. **$111-$183.** 2525 S University Park Dr 48858. 2.5 mi s on US 127 business route. Int corridors. **Pets:** Accepted.

MUNISING

▼ Alger Falls Motel 🅼
(906) 387-3536. **$55-$185.** E9427 Hwy M-28 49862. 2 mi e on SR 28 and 94. Ext corridors. **Pets:** Small, dogs only. $5 one-time fee/pet. Service with restrictions, supervision.

▼ AmericInn Lodge & Suites of Munising 🅷
(906) 387-2000. **Call for rates.** E9926 Hwy M-28 49854. On SR 28, 2.7 mi e. Int corridors. **Pets:** Accepted.

▼▼▼ Holiday Inn Express Lakeview 🅷
(906) 387-4800. **$80-$240.** E8890 M-28 49862. On SR 28, 2 mi w of town. Int corridors. **Pets:** $15 daily fee/room. Designated rooms, service with restrictions.

ⓐⓐⓐ ▼▼ Terrace Motel 🅼
(906) 387-2735. **$50-$150.** 420 Prospect St 49862. 0.5 mi e, just off SR 28. Ext corridors. **Pets:** Small, dogs only. $10 daily fee/room. Service with restrictions, crate.

NEWBERRY

▼▼ Comfort Inn Tahquamenon Falls 🅷
(906) 293-3218. **$100-$145.** 13954 Hwy M-28 49868. Jct SR 28 and 123. Int corridors. **Pets:** Accepted.

NILES

▼▼ Comfort Inn & Suites 🅷
(269) 684-3900. **$90-$150.** 1265 S 11th St (M-51) 49120. Jct US 12, 0.8 mi n on SR 51. Int corridors. **Pets:** Large. $25 daily fee/pet. Service with restrictions, crate.

NORWAY

ⓐⓐⓐ ▼▼ Norway Inn Lodge & Suites 🅷 🌸
(906) 563-7500. **$81-$88.** W6002 US Hwy 2 49870. 0.7 mi w. Int corridors. **Pets:** Other species. $20 one-time fee/room. Designated rooms, service with restrictions, crate.

NOVI

▼▼ Extended Stay America-Detroit-Novi 🅷
(248) 305-9955. **$95-$100.** 21555 Haggerty Rd 48375. I-96/275 exit 167 (8 Mile Rd), just w, then 0.5 mi n. Int corridors. **Pets:** Other species. $25 daily fee/pet. Service with restrictions, supervision.

▼▼▼ Residence Inn by Marriott-Detroit/Novi 🅷
(248) 735-7400. **$154-$253.** 27477 Cabaret Dr 48377. I-96 exit 162 (Novi Rd), just n, just w on 12 Mile Rd, then just s. Int corridors. **Pets:** Accepted.

ⓐⓐⓐ ▼▼▼▼ Sheraton-Detroit-Novi 🅷
(248) 349-4000. **Call for rates.** 21111 Haggerty Rd 48375. I-96/275 exit 167 (8 Mile Rd), just w, then just n. Int corridors. **Pets:** Accepted.

▼▼▼ Staybridge Suites 🅷
(248) 349-4600. **$99-$399, 7 day notice.** 27000 Providence Pkwy 48374. I-96 exit 160 (Beck Rd), just s, 0.6 mi w on Grand River Ave, then just s. Int corridors. **Pets:** $100 one-time fee/room. Designated rooms, service with restrictions, crate.

▼▼ TownePlace Suites by Marriott 🅷
(248) 305-5533. **$101-$166.** 42600 11 Mile Rd 48375. I-96 exit 162 (Novi Rd), 0.4 mi s, just e on Grand River Ave, just n on Town Center Dr, then just e. Int corridors. **Pets:** Accepted.

OKEMOS

▼▼ Comfort Inn-E Lansing/Okemos 🅷
(517) 347-6690. **$105-$200.** 2187 University Park Dr 48864. I-96 exit 110 (Okemos Rd), just n, then just e. Int corridors. **Pets:** Dogs only. $25 one-time fee/pet. Service with restrictions, crate.

▼▼▼ Holiday Inn Express & Suites 🅷
(517) 349-8700. **$126-$136.** 2209 University Park Dr 48864. I-96 exit 110 (Okemos Rd), just n, then just e. Int corridors. **Pets:** Large, dogs only. $25 deposit/pet. Designated rooms, service with restrictions, supervision.

▼▼▼ Staybridge Suites-Lansing/Okemos 🅷
(517) 347-3044. **Call for rates.** 3553 Meridian Crossing Dr 48864. I-96 exit 110 (Okemos Rd), just n. Int corridors. **Pets:** Other species. $75 one-time fee/room. Designated rooms, service with restrictions, supervision.

PAW PAW

▼▼▼ **Comfort Inn & Suites** 🏨
(269) 655-0303. **$79-$139.** 153 Ampey Rd 49079. I-94 exit 60 (SR 40), just nw. Int corridors. **Pets:** Large, other species. $50 deposit/room. Service with restrictions, supervision. 🅜 ⊠ 📶 ✕ 🔌 💻

PETOSKEY *(Restaurants p. 634)*

🔷 ▼▼▼ **@ Michigan Inn & Lodge** Ⓜ
(231) 348-3900. **$64-$149.** 1420 S US 131 49770. US 131, 1.3 mi s. Ext corridors. **Pets:** $12 daily fee/pet. Service with restrictions, supervision. 🅢 🍴 📶 ✕ 🔌 💻

▼▼▼ **Holiday Inn Express Hotel & Suites** 🏨
(231) 487-0991. **$89-$399.** 1751 US 131 S 49770. US 131, 1.5 mi s. Int corridors. **Pets:** Accepted. 🍴 ⊠ ✕ 📶 🔌 💻

PLAINWELL

🔷 ▼▼▼ **Comfort Inn** 🏨
(269) 685-9891. **$89-$169.** 622 Allegan St 49080. US 131 exit 49A, just e. Int corridors. **Pets:** Large. $15 daily fee/pet. Designated rooms, service with restrictions, supervision. 🅢 ⊠ 📶 ✕ 🔌 💻

PLYMOUTH

▼▼ **Red Roof Inn Detroit - Plymouth/Canton** Ⓜ
(734) 459-3300. **$45-$110.** 39700 Ann Arbor Rd 48170. I-275 exit 28 (Ann Arbor Rd), just e, then just n. Ext corridors. **Pets:** Large, other species. Service with restrictions, supervision. 📶 ✕ 🔌 💻

PONTIAC

▼▼ **Residence Inn by Marriott Detroit Pontiac/Auburn Hills** 🏨
(248) 858-8664. **$112-$184.** 3333 Centerpoint Pkwy 48341. I-75 exit 75, 1 mi w on Square Lake Rd, then just n on Opdyke Rd. Int corridors. **Pets:** Medium. $100 one-time fee/room. Service with restrictions.
⊠ ⊠ 📶 ✕ 🔌 💻

PORT HURON

🔷 ▼▼▼ **Baymont Inn & Suites** 🏨
(810) 364-8000. **$69-$129.** 1611 Range Rd 48074. I-94 exit 269 (Range Rd), just w. Int corridors. **Pets:** Medium. $15 daily fee/pet. Designated rooms, service with restrictions, crate. 🅢 ⊠ 📶 ✕ 🔌 💻

▼▼🔷 **Comfort Inn** 🏨 🐾
(810) 982-5500. **$83-$149.** 1700 Yeager St 48060. I-94 exit 274B (Water St), just s, then just w. Int corridors. **Pets:** Large, dogs only. $30 daily fee/pet. Designated rooms, service with restrictions, supervision.
⊠ 📶 ✕ 🔌 💻

ROMULUS

▼▼ **Days Inn-Detroit Metro Airport** 🏨
(734) 946-4300. **$70-$150.** 9501 Middlebelt Rd 48174. I-94 exit 199 (Middlebelt Rd), 0.4 mi s. Int corridors. **Pets:** Small, other species. $25 daily fee/room. Designated rooms, service with restrictions.
🍴 📶 ✕ 🔌 💻

▼▼ **Extended Stay America-Detroit-Metropolitan Airport** 🏨
(734) 722-7780. **$80-$85.** 30325 Flynn Dr 48174. I-94 exit 198 (Merriman Rd), just n, then 0.4 mi e. Int corridors. **Pets:** Other species. $25 daily fee/pet. Service with restrictions, supervision. 📶 ✕ 🔌 💻

▼▼▼ **Holiday Inn Express-Detroit Metro Airport** 🏨
(734) 641-9006. **$99-$159.** 7680 Merriman Rd 48174. I-94 exit 198 (Merriman Rd), 0.4 mi n. Int corridors. **Pets:** Accepted.
📶 ✕ 🔌 💻

▼▼▼ **La Quinta Inn & Suites-Detroit Metro Airport** 🏨
(734) 721-1100. **$79-$194.** 30847 Flynn Dr 48174. I-94 exit 198 (Merriman Rd), just n, then just e. Int corridors. **Pets:** Large, other species. Service with restrictions. ⊠ 📶 ✕ 🔌 💻

▼▼ **Romulus Quality Inn & Suites** 🏨
(734) 946-1400. **$69-$110.** 9555 Middlebelt Rd 48174. I-94 exit 199 (Middlebelt Rd), 0.4 mi s. Int corridors. **Pets:** Accepted.
📶 ✕ 🔌 💻

🔷 ▼▼▼ **Sheraton Detroit Metro Airport** 🏨
(734) 729-2600. **$129-$329.** 8000 Merriman Rd 48174. I-94 exit 198 (Merriman Rd), 0.4 mi n. Int corridors. **Pets:** Accepted.
🅢 🍴 ⊠ 📶 ✕ 💻

🔷 ▼▼▼ ▼▼▼ **The Westin Detroit Metropolitan Airport** 🏨
(734) 942-6500. **Call for rates.** 2501 Worldgateway Pl 48242. I-94 exit 198 (Merriman Rd). Int corridors. **Pets:** Accepted.
🅢 🍴 🅜 ⊠ ⊠ 📶 ✕ 💻

ROSEVILLE

▼▼ **Days Inn & Suites – Roseville** Ⓜ
(586) 294-0400. **$54-$94.** 31327 Gratiot Ave 48066. I-94 exit 232 (Little Mack Ave), just s, 0.5 mi e on 13 Mile Rd, then just n on SR 3. Ext corridors. **Pets:** Accepted. 🍴 ⊠ 📶 ✕ 🔌 💻

🔷 ▼▼▼ **Red Roof Inn Detroit - St Clair Shores** Ⓜ
(586) 296-0310. **$45-$89.** 31800 Little Mack Ave 48066. I-94 exit 232 (Little Mack Ave), just n. Ext corridors. **Pets:** Large, other species. Service with restrictions, supervision. 🅢 🅜 📶 ✕ 🔌 💻

SAGINAW

▼▼▼ **Comfort Suites by Choice Hotels** 🏨
(989) 797-8000. **$95-$135.** 5180 Fashion Square Blvd 48603. I-675 exit 6, 0.6 mi w on Tittabawassee Rd. Int corridors. **Pets:** Medium. $50 one-time fee/room. Designated rooms, service with restrictions, supervision. 🅜 ⊠ 📶 ✕ 🔌 💻

▼▼▼ **Country Inn & Suites By Carlson Saginaw** 🏨
(989) 792-7666. **Call for rates.** 2222 Tittabawassee Rd 48604. I-675 exit 6, just w. Int corridors. **Pets:** Accepted. ⊠ 📶 ✕ 🔌 💻

▼▼▼ **Residence Inn by Marriott** 🏨
(989) 799-9000. **$118-$194.** 5230 Fashion Square Blvd 48604. I-675 exit 6, 0.8 mi w, then just n. Int corridors. **Pets:** Accepted.
⊠ 📶 ✕ 🔌 💻

▼▼▼ **TownePlace Suites by Marriott Saginaw** 🏨
(989) 792-2200. **$108-$177.** 5368 Fashion Square Blvd 48604. I-675 exit 6, 0.8 mi w, then just n. Int corridors. **Pets:** Accepted.
🅜 📶 ✕ 🔌 💻

ST. IGNACE

🔷 ▼▼▼ **Budget Host Inn & Suites** 🏨
(906) 643-9666. **$73-$254.** 700 N State St 49781. 1.8 mi n of bridge tollgate on I-75 business route. Ext/int corridors. **Pets:** Other species. $10 one-time fee/pet. Service with restrictions, supervision.
🅢 ⊠ ⊠ 📶 🔌 💻

ST. JOSEPH

▼▼ **Silver Beach Hotel** 🏨
(269) 983-7341. **$94-$400.** 100 Main St 49085. I-94 exit 23, 6 mi nw on Business Rt I-94. Int corridors. **Pets:** Medium. $35 one-time fee/room. Designated rooms, service with restrictions, supervision.
⊠ ⊠ 📶 ✕ 🔌 💻

SANDUSKY

▼▼ **DeMott's West Park Inn** 🏨
(810) 648-4300. **Call for rates.** 440 W Sanilac Rd 48471. 0.7 mi w on SR 46. Ext/int corridors. **Pets:** Accepted. 🍴 📶 ✕ 🔌 💻

SAULT STE. MARIE

▼▼ **Americas Best Value Inn** 🏨
(906) 632-8882. **Call for rates.** 3826 I-75 Business Loop 49783. I-75 exit 392, 0.5 mi ne. Int corridors. **Pets:** Accepted. 📶 ✕ 🔌 💻

▼ **Budget Host Crestview Inn** Ⓜ

(906) 635-5213. **$59-$119, 3 day notice.** 1200 Ashmun St 49783. I-75 exit 392, 2.8 mi ne on I-75 business loop. Ext corridors. **Pets:** Other species. $5 daily fee/pet. Designated rooms, service with restrictions, supervision. 🍴 📶 ✕ 🛗

◈◈◈ Days Inn Ⓗ

(906) 635-5200. **$72-$129.** 3651 I-75 Business Spur 49783. I-75 exit 392, 0.8 mi ne on I-75 business loop. Int corridors. **Pets:** $5 deposit/pet. Designated rooms, service with restrictions.

[SAVE] ➳ ✕ 📶 ✕ 🛗 🖥

▼▼ **Super 8 Sault Ste. Marie** Ⓗ

(906) 632-6000. **$53-$68.** 3525 I-75 Business Spur 49783. I-75 exit 392, 0.8 mi ne. Int corridors. **Pets:** Accepted.

🚹 ➳ ✕ 📶 ✕ 🛗 🖥

SILVER CITY

▼ **AmericInn Lodge & Suites** Ⓗ

(906) 885-5311. **Call for rates.** 120 Lincoln Ave 49953. SR 107, 0.3 mi w of SR 64. Int corridors. **Pets:** Accepted.

🍴 ➳ ✕ 📶 ✕ 🛗 🖥

SOUTHFIELD

◈◈◈◈ **The Westin Southfield Detroit** Ⓗ

(248) 827-4000. **$109-$369.** 1500 Town Center 48075. SR 10 (Northwestern Hwy) exit 10 (10 Mile Rd/Evergreen Rd), 0.3 mi n. Int corridors. **Pets:** Accepted. [SAVE] 🍴 🚹 ➳ ✕ 📶 ✕ 🖥

SOUTHGATE

◈◈ **La Quinta Inn-Detroit Southgate** Ⓗ

(734) 374-3000. **$69-$189.** 12888 Reeck Rd 48195. I-75 exit 37 (Northline Rd), just w. Int corridors. **Pets:** Large, other species. Service with restrictions. 📶 ✕ 🛗 🖥

SOUTH HAVEN

◈◈◈ **Comfort Suites** Ⓗ

(269) 639-2014. **$80-$230.** 1755 Phoenix St 49090. I-196 exit 20, 0.5 mi e. Int corridors. **Pets:** Accepted. [SAVE] 🚹 ➳ 📶 ✕ 🛗 🖥

SPRING LAKE

◈◈◈ **Grand Haven/Spring Lake Waterfront Holiday Inn** Ⓗ ❀

(616) 846-1000. **$89-$299, 3 day notice.** 940 W Savidge St 49456. On SR 104, just e of US 31. Int corridors. **Pets:** Dogs only. $26 daily fee/pet. Designated rooms, service with restrictions, supervision.

🍴 📶 ✕ 🛗 🖥

STERLING HEIGHTS

◈◈◈ **The Sterling Inn Banquet & Conference Center** Ⓗ

(586) 979-1400. **$125-$189.** 34911 Van Dyke Ave 48312. On SR 53 (Van Dyke Ave); jct 15 Mile Rd. Ext/int corridors. **Pets:** Small, other species. $50 deposit/room, $20 one-time fee/room. Service with restrictions. 🍴 🚹 ➳ ✕ 📶 ✕ 🛗 🖥

◈◈ **TownePlace Suites by Marriott Detroit Sterling Heights** Ⓗ

(586) 566-0900. **$90-$194.** 14800 Lakeside Cir 48313. 1 mi e of jct SR 53 (Van Dyke Ave) on SR 59 (Hall Rd), then just s. Int corridors. **Pets:** Accepted. 🚹 ➳ 📶 ✕ 🛗 🖥

SUTTONS BAY *(Restaurants p. 634)*

▼ **Red Lion Motor Lodge** Ⓜ

(231) 271-6694. **$79-$195.** 4290 S West Bayshore Dr 49682. 5 mi s on SR 22. Ext corridors. **Pets:** Medium. $10 daily fee/pet. Designated rooms, no service, supervision. 🍴 📶 ✕ 🅿 🛗 🖥

TAWAS CITY

◈◈◈ **Bay Inn Tawas** Ⓗ

(989) 362-0088. **$63-$135, 3 day notice.** 1020 W Lake St 48763. 1.5 mi s on US 23. Int corridors. **Pets:** Accepted.

[SAVE] 🍴 ➳ ✕ 📶 ✕ 🛗 🖥

TAYLOR

◈◈ ◈◈◈ **Red Roof Inn Detroit Southwest - Taylor** Ⓜ

(734) 374-1150. **$44-$89.** 21230 Eureka Rd 48180. I-75 exit 36 (Eureka Rd), just w. Ext corridors. **Pets:** Large, other species. Service with restrictions, supervision. [SAVE] 📶 ✕ 🛗 🖥

THOMPSONVILLE

◈◈ ◈◈◈ **Crystal Mountain** Ⓗ ❀

(231) 378-2000. **$159-$429, 14 day notice.** 12500 Crystal Mountain Dr 49683. On SR 115, 2 mi w. Ext/int corridors. **Pets:** $50 one-time fee/room. Designated rooms, service with restrictions, supervision.

[SAVE] [ECO] 🔌 🍴 ➳ ✕ 📶 ✕ 🛗 🖥

TRAVERSE CITY

◈◈ ◈◈ **BEST WESTERN Four Seasons** Ⓗ

(231) 946-8424. **$59-$350.** 305 Munson Ave 49686. 2 mi e on US 31/SR72. Int corridors. **Pets:** Accepted. [SAVE] ➳ 📶 ✕ 🛗 🖥

◈◈◈ **Country Inn & Suites by Carlson - Traverse City** Ⓗ

(231) 941-0208. **$110-$266.** 420 Munson Ave 49686. 2 mi e on US 31. Ext/int corridors. **Pets:** $25 daily fee/pet. Designated rooms, service with restrictions, supervision. 🍴 🚹 ➳ ✕ 📶 ✕ 🛗 🖥

◈◈◈ **Park Place Hotel** Ⓗ

(231) 946-5000. **Call for rates.** 300 E State St 49684. Corner of E State and Park sts; downtown. Int corridors. **Pets:** Accepted.

[ECO] 🍴 ➳ ✕ 📶 ✕ 🛗 🖥

◈◈ ◈◈ **Quality Inn** Ⓗ ❀

(231) 929-4423. **$59-$279.** 1492 US 31 N 49686. On US 31, 3.3 mi e. Ext/int corridors. **Pets:** Other species. $10 daily fee/room.

[SAVE] ➳ 📶 ✕ 🛗 🖥

◈◈ ◈◈◈ **West Bay Beach, a Holiday Inn Resort** Ⓗ

(231) 947-3700. **$90-$350, 3 day notice.** 615 E Front St 49686. 0.5 mi e on US 31. Int corridors. **Pets:** Accepted.

[SAVE] 🍴 🚹 ➳ ✕ 📶 ✕ 🛗 🖥

TROY

◈◈◈ **Drury Inn & Suites-Troy** Ⓗ

(248) 528-3330. **$95-$165.** 575 W Big Beaver Rd 48084. I-75 exit 69A, just e. Int corridors. **Pets:** $10 daily fee/room. Service with restrictions, supervision. 🍴 🚹 ➳ ✕ 📶 ✕ 🛗 🖥

◈◈ ◈◈◈ **Hawthorn Suites by Wyndham Troy** Ⓗ

(248) 689-6856. **$99-$129.** 2600 Livernois Rd 48083. I-75 exit 69A, 0.5 mi e on E Big Beaver Rd, then 0.5 mi s. Ext corridors. **Pets:** Small. $15 daily fee/pet. Designated rooms, service with restrictions, supervision. [SAVE] ➳ 📶 ✕ 🛗 🖥

◈◈ **The MET Hotel Troy Detroit** Ⓗ

(248) 879-2100. **Call for rates.** 5500 Crooks Rd 48098. I-75 exit 72 (Crooks Rd), just n. Int corridors. **Pets:** Accepted.

🚹 ➳ 📶 ✕ 🛗

◈◈ **Quality Inn Detroit-Troy** Ⓗ

(248) 689-7500. **$84-$120.** 2537 Rochester Ct 48083. I-75 exit 67 (Stephenson Hwy), 0.3 mi sw on Rochester Rd, then just w. Int corridors. **Pets:** Accepted. [ECO] 🍴 ➳ 📶 🛗 🖥

◈◈ **Red Roof Inn Detroit - Troy** Ⓜ

(248) 689-4391. **$40-$99.** 2350 Rochester Ct 48083. I-75 exit 67 (Stephenson Hwy), 0.3 mi sw. Ext corridors. **Pets:** Large, other species. Service with restrictions, supervision. 📶 ✕ 🛗 🖥

UTICA

◈◈ ◈◈◈ **Comfort Inn** Ⓗ

(586) 739-7111. **$97-$170.** 11401 Hall Rd 48317. Van Dyke Ave (SR 53) exit 17, just w on Hall Rd (SR 59). Int corridors. **Pets:** Medium, dogs only. Crate. [SAVE] 🍴 📶 ✕ 🛗 🖥

AAA ◆◆◆◆ Hyatt Place Detroit/Utica H
(586) 803-0100. **$79-$199.** 45400 Park Ave 48315. Van Dyke Ave (SR 53) exit 17A, just e on Hall Rd (SR 59), then just n. Int corridors.
Pets: Accepted. [SAVE] [&M] [≈] [⊚] [✕] [🛊] [▣]

◆◆ La Quinta Inn & Suites Detroit Utica H
(586) 731-4700. **$85-$204.** 45311 Park Ave 48315. Van Dyke Ave (SR 53) exit 17A, just 2 on Hall Rd (SR 59), then just n. Int corridors.
Pets: Large, other species. Service with restrictions.
[≈] [⊚] [✕] [🛊] [▣]

◆◆◆ Staybridge Suites-Utica H
(586) 323-0101. **$129-$145.** 46155 Utica Park Blvd 48315. Van Dyke Ave (SR 53) exit 17A, just e on Hall Rd (SR 59), then just n. Int corridors. **Pets:** Accepted. [¶] [&M] [≈] [⊚] [✕] [🛊] [▣]

WALKER

◆◆◆ Hampton Inn-Grand Rapids North H
(616) 647-1000. **$109-$199.** 500 Center Dr NW 49544. I-96 exit 30, just n on Alpine Rd, then 0.3 mi e. Int corridors. **Pets:** $25 one-time fee/pet. Service with restrictions, supervision.
[¶] [&M] [≈] [⊚] [✕] [🛊] [▣]

WARREN

◆◆◆ Candlewood Suites-Detroit Warren H
(586) 978-1261. **$89-$99.** 7010 Convention Blvd 48092. I-696 exit 23, 2.8 mi on Van Dyke Ave (SR 53). Int corridors. **Pets:** Accepted.
[&M] [⊚] [✕] [🛊] [▣]

◆◆◆ Extended Stay America Detroit-Warren H
(586) 558-5554. **$80-$85.** 30125 N Civic Center Blvd 48093. I-696 exit 23, 1.5 mi n on Van Dyke Ave (SR 53), then just e. Int corridors. **Pets:** Other species. $25 daily fee/pet. Service with restrictions, supervision. [&M] [🔊] [✕] [🛊] [▣]

◆◆◆ Hawthorn Suites by Wyndham Warren H
(586) 558-7870. **$79-$119, 3 day notice.** 30180 N Civic Center Blvd 48093. I-696 exit 23, 1.8 mi on Van Dyke Ave (SR 53), then just e. Ext/int corridors. **Pets:** $10 daily fee/pet. Designated rooms, service with restrictions, supervision. [&M] [≈] [⊚] [✕] [🛊] [▣]

AAA ◆◆◆ Red Roof Inn Detroit - Warren M
(586) 573-4300. **$56-$89.** 26300 Dequindre Rd 48091. I-696 exit 20, just ne. Ext corridors. **Pets:** Large, other species. Service with restrictions, supervision. [SAVE] [¶] [&M] [⊚] [✕] [🛊] [▣]

AAA ◆◆◆◆ TownePlace Suites by Marriott-Warren H
(586) 264-8800. **$104-$171.** 7601 Chicago Rd 48092. I-696 exit 23, 2.4 mi n on Van Dyke Ave (SR 53), then just w. Int corridors. **Pets:** Small. $100 one-time fee/pet. Designated rooms, service with restrictions, supervision. [SAVE] [&M] [≈] [⊚] [✕] [🛊] [▣]

WATERSMEET

◆◆◆ Dancing Eagles Resort Lac Vieux Desert Casino H
(906) 358-4949. **Call for rates.** N5384 US Hwy 45 49969. 1.8 mi n of US 2. Int corridors. **Pets:** Accepted. [¶] [≈] [✕] [⊚] [🛊] [▣]

WHITEHALL

◆◆◆ Comfort Inn H
(231) 893-4833. **$69-$250.** 2822 N Durham Rd 49461. US 31 exit 128, just ne. Int corridors. **Pets:** Accepted. [¶] [≈] [⊚] [✕] [🛊] [▣]

WHITMORE LAKE

AAA ◆◆◆ BEST WESTERN of Whitmore Lake M
(734) 449-2058. **$90-$100.** 9897 Main St 48189. US 23 exit 53, just e. Ext corridors. **Pets:** Other species. $20 daily fee/pet. Designated rooms, service with restrictions, crate. [SAVE] [≈] [⊚] [✕] [🛊] [▣]

WOODHAVEN

AAA ◆◆◆ BEST WESTERN Woodhaven Inn H
(734) 676-8000. **$80-$89.** 21700 West Rd 48183. I-75 exit 32 (West Rd), just w. Int corridors. **Pets:** Accepted.
[SAVE] [¶] [≈] [⊠] [⊚] [✕] [🛊] [▣]

WYOMING

AAA ◆◆◆◆ Hyatt Place Grand Rapids-South H
(616) 724-1234. **$89-$189.** 2150 Metro Ln 49519. SR 6 exit 5 (Byron Center Ave), just ne. Int corridors. **Pets:** Accepted.
[SAVE] [ECO] [¶] [&M] [≈] [⊚] [✕] [🛊] [▣]

MINNESOTA

AITKIN

◆◆◆ Ripple River Motel & RV Park M
(218) 927-3734. **$57-$97.** 701 Minnesota Ave S 56431. US 169, 0.8 mi s of jct SR 210. Ext corridors. **Pets:** Accepted.
[¶] [≈] [✕] [🛊] [▣]

ALBERT LEA

◆◆◆ AmericInn Lodge & Suites of Albert Lea H
(507) 373-4324. **Call for rates.** 811 E Plaza St 56007. I-90 exit 157 (CR 22), just se. Int corridors. **Pets:** Accepted.
[⊟] [&M] [≈] [⊚] [✕] [🛊] [▣]

AAA ◆◆◆◆ BEST WESTERN PLUS Albert Lea I-90/I-35 Hotel H ❀
(507) 373-4000. **Call for rates.** 821 E Plaza St 56007. I-90 exit 157 (CR 22), just se. Int corridors. **Pets:** Medium, dogs only. $20 daily fee/room. Designated rooms, service with restrictions, crate.
[SAVE] [&M] [≈] [⊚] [✕] [🛊] [▣]

◆◆◆ Comfort Inn H
(507) 377-1100. **$99-$159.** 810 Happy Trails Ln 56007. I-35 exit 11, just se. Int corridors. **Pets:** Other species. $25 one-time fee/room. Service with restrictions, supervision. [&M] [≈] [⊚] [✕] [🛊] [▣]

◆◆◆◆ Country Inn & Suites By Carlson H
(507) 373-5513. **Call for rates.** 2214 E Main St 56007. I-35 exit 12 southbound; exit 11 northbound, 1 mi w. Int corridors. **Pets:** Accepted.
[&M] [≈] [⊚] [✕] [🛊] [▣]

ALEXANDRIA

◆◆◆ AmericInn Lodge & Suites of Alexandria H
(320) 763-6808. **Call for rates.** 4520 Hwy 29 S 56308. I-94 exit 103, 0.3 mi n. Int corridors. **Pets:** Accepted. [&M] [≈] [⊚] [✕] [🛊] [▣]

AAA ◆◆◆ BEST WESTERN Alexandria Inn H
(320) 762-5161. **$99-$129.** 508 Twin Blvd 56308. I-94 exit 103, just n, then just e on 50th St. Int corridors. **Pets:** Accepted.
[SAVE] [¶] [≈] [⊚] [✕] [🛊] [▣]

◆◆◆ Holiday Inn Alexandria H
(320) 763-6577. **$130-$180.** 5637 Hwy 29 S 56308. I-94 exit 103, just s. Int corridors. **Pets:** Medium, other species. Designated rooms, service with restrictions. [¶] [&M] [≈] [⊠] [⊚] [✕] [🛊] [▣]

◆◆◆ Super 8 H
(320) 763-6552. **$64-$98, 3 day notice.** 4620 Hwy 29 S 56308. I-94 exit 103, 0.3 mi nw. Int corridors. **Pets:** Medium, dogs only. $15 one-time fee/pet. Designated rooms, service with restrictions, crate.
[≈] [✕] [🛊] [▣]

ANNANDALE

◆◆◆ Annandale Lodge & Suites H
(320) 274-3006. **Call for rates.** 620 Elm St E 55302. On SR 55. Int corridors. **Pets:** Accepted. [&M] [≈] [⊚] [🛊] [▣]

AUSTIN

▼▼▼ AmericInn Lodge & Suites of Austin 🅗
(507) 437-7337. **$99-$177.** 1700 8th St NW 55912. I-90 exit 178A (4th St NW), just nw. Int corridors. **Pets:** Accepted.
🅂🅼 🛤 🗶 🛜 🗙 🔋 💻

▼▼▼ Days Inn 🅗
(507) 433-8600. **$59-$88.** 700 16th Ave NW 55912. I-90 exit 178A (4th St NW), just nw. Int corridors. **Pets:** Accepted. 🅂🅼 🛜 🔋 💻

▼▼▼ Holiday Inn & Austin Conference Center 🅗
(507) 433-1000. **Call for rates.** 1701 4th St NW 55912. I-90 exit 178A (4th St NW), just nw. Int corridors. **Pets:** Accepted.
🍴 🅂🅼 🛤 🛜 🗙 🔋 💻

BABBITT

▼▼▼ Timber Bay Lodge & Houseboats 🅒🅐
(218) 827-3682. **$165-$798, 60 day notice.** 8347 Timber Bay Rd 55706. 2.8 mi e of jct CR 21 via CR 70. Ext corridors. **Pets:** Accepted.
🍴 🗶 🛜 🗙 🔋 💻

BAUDETTE

▼▼▼ AmericInn Lodge & Suites of Baudette 🅗
(218) 634-3200. **Call for rates.** 1179 Main St W 56623. 0.5 mi w on SR 11. Int corridors. **Pets:** Dogs only. $25 one-time fee/pet. Designated rooms, service with restrictions, supervision.
🅂🅼 🛤 🗶 🛜 🗙 🔋 💻

BAXTER

▼▼▼ Baymont Inn & Suites 🅗
(218) 822-1133. **$58-$106.** 7208 Fairview Rd 56425. Just nw of jct SR 371 on SR 210. Int corridors. **Pets:** Accepted.
🍴 🅂🅼 🛤 🗶 🛜 🗙 🔋 💻

▼▼ Country Inn & Suites By Carlson 🅗
(218) 828-2161. **$99-$179.** 15058 Dellwood Dr N 56425. Jct SR 371 and 210, 1 mi n on SR 371. Int corridors. **Pets:** Small. $30 one-time fee/room. Designated rooms, service with restrictions, supervision.
🍴 🛤 🛜 🗙 🔋 💻

▼▼▼ Holiday Inn Express, Three Bear Waterpark 🅗
(218) 824-3232. **Call for rates.** 15739 Audubon Way 56425. Just se of jct SR 371 and CR 77. Int corridors. **Pets:** Medium, dogs only. $150 deposit/room, $40 daily fee/pet. Designated rooms, service with restrictions, supervision. 🍴 🅂🅼 🗶 🛜 🗙 🔋 💻

🄰🄰🄰 ▼▼▼ Super 8 🅜 🐾
(218) 828-4288. **$75-$95.** 14341 Edgewood Dr 56425. 0.5 mi n of jct SR 371 on SR 210. Int corridors. **Pets:** Other species. Designated rooms, service with restrictions, supervision.
🆂🅰🆅🅴 🍴 🛜 🗙 🔋 💻

BEMIDJI

🄰🄰🄰 ▼▼▼ AmericInn Lodge & Suites of Bemidji 🅗 🐾
(218) 751-3000. **$80-$160.** 1200 Paul Bunyan Dr NW 56601. 0.5 mi e of northwest jct US 2, 71 and SR 197. Int corridors. **Pets:** $15 daily fee/room. Designated rooms, service with restrictions, supervision.
🆂🅰🆅🅴 🛤 🗶 🛜 🗙 🔋 💻

🄰🄰🄰 ▼▼▼ BEST WESTERN Bemidji Inn 🅗
(218) 751-0390. **$79-$119.** 2420 Paul Bunyan Dr 56601. Jct US 71 N and SR 197. Int corridors. **Pets:** Other species. $15 daily fee/room. Designated rooms, service with restrictions, crate.
🆂🅰🆅🅴 🍴 🛤 🛜 🗙 🔋 💻

▼▼▼ Country Inn & Suites by Carlson 🅗
(218) 441-4800. **$129-$209.** 927 Lake Shore Dr NE 56601. Jct SR 197 and CR 12 (1st St SE), just ne. Int corridors. **Pets:** Accepted.
🍴 🅂🅼 🛜 🔋 💻

🄰🄰🄰 ▼▼▼ Quality Inn 🅗
(218) 444-7700. **$109-$149.** 3500 Moberg Dr NW 56601. On US 2, just w of jct US 71 N and SR 197. Int corridors. **Pets:** Medium, other species. $15 daily fee/pet. Designated rooms, service with restrictions, supervision. 🆂🅰🆅🅴 🍴 🛤 🗶 🛜 🗙 🔋 💻

▼▼▼ Ruttger's Birchmont Lodge 🅒🅐
(218) 444-3463. **$76-$460, 30 day notice.** 7598 Bemidji Rd NE 56601. On CR 21 (Bemidji Ave N), 3.6 mi n of jct SR 197. Ext/int corridors. **Pets:** Accepted. 🍴 🛤 🗶 🛜 🗙 🔋 💻

BLAINE

🄰🄰🄰 ▼▼▼ Centerstone Suites 🅗
(763) 792-0750. **Call for rates.** 10580 Baltimore St NE 55449. US 10 exit SR 65, 2 mi n on Central Ave, just e on 107th Ave NE, then just s. Int corridors. **Pets:** Accepted. 🆂🅰🆅🅴 🅂🅼 🛤 🗶 🛜 🗙 🔋 💻

▼▼ Super 8 🅗
(763) 786-8888. **$80-$140.** 9410 Baltimore St NE 55449. Just n of jct US 10 and SR 65 to 93rd Ln, just e to Baltimore St NE, then just n. Int corridors. **Pets:** Small, dogs only. $15 daily fee/pet. Designated rooms, service with restrictions, supervision.
🍴 🅂🅼 🛤 🛜 🗙 💻

BLOOMINGTON

▼▼▼ Days Inn-Bloomington West 🅗
(952) 835-7400. **$63-$92.** 7851 Normandale Blvd 55435. I-494 exit 7A (SR 100), just ne. Int corridors. **Pets:** Accepted.
🅂🅼 🛤 🛜 🗙 🔋 💻

🄰🄰🄰 ▼▼▼▼ DoubleTree by Hilton Bloomington-Minneapolis South 🅗
(952) 835-7800. **Call for rates.** 7800 Normandale Blvd 55439. Just nw of jct I-494 and SR 100, access via SR 100 and Industrial Blvd. Int corridors. **Pets:** Large, dogs only. $50 one-time fee/pet. Designated rooms, service with restrictions, crate.
🆂🅰🆅🅴 🍴 🛤 🛜 🗙 🔋 💻

▼▼ Extended Stay America Minneapolis-Bloomington 🅗
(952) 884-1400. **Call for rates.** 7956 Lyndale Ave 55420. I-494 exit 4B (Lyndale Ave), just sw. Int corridors. **Pets:** Other species. $25 daily fee/pet. Service with restrictions, supervision. 🛜 🗙 🔋 💻

🄰🄰🄰 ▼▼▼ Hilton Minneapolis/Bloomington 🅗
(952) 893-9500. **$99-$239.** 3900 American Blvd W 55437. I-494 exit 6B (France Ave), just sw. Int corridors. **Pets:** Accepted.
🆂🅰🆅🅴 ⬅ 🍴 🛤 🛜 🔋 💻

🄰🄰🄰 ▼▼▼▼ Hilton Minneapolis/St. Paul Airport Mall of America 🅗 🐾
(952) 854-2100. **$109-$229.** 3800 American Blvd E 55425. I-494 exit 1B (34th Ave), just se. Int corridors. **Pets:** $50 one-time fee/pet. Service with restrictions, crate. 🆂🅰🆅🅴 🍴 🅂🅼 🛤 📶 🗙 🔋 💻

▼▼▼ La Quinta Inn & Suites Minneapolis Bloomington West 🅗
(952) 830-1300. **$72-$205.** 5151 American Blvd W 55437. I-494 exit 6B (France Ave), just se of SR 100, 1 mi w on frontage road. Int corridors. **Pets:** Large, other species. Service with restrictions.
🍴 🅂🅼 🛤 🗶 🛜 🔋 💻

▼▼▼ La Quinta Inn Minneapolis Airport Bloomington 🅗
(952) 881-7311. **$65-$164.** 7815 Nicollet Ave S 55420. I-494 exit 4A (Nicollet Ave), just s. Int corridors. **Pets:** Large, other species. Service with restrictions. 🛜 🔋 💻

▼▼▼ Park Plaza Hotel Bloomington 🅗
(952) 831-3131. **Call for rates.** 4460 W 78th Street Cir 55435. I-494 exit 6B (France Ave), 0.5 mi nw. Int corridors. **Pets:** Accepted.
🄴🄲🄾 🍴 🛤 🛜 🗙 🔋 💻

Radisson Blu Mall of America [H]
(952) 881-5258. **Call for rates.** 2100 Killebrew Dr 55425. SR 77, 0.3 mi e. Int corridors. **Pets:** Accepted.
SAVE [icons]

Residence Inn by Marriott [H] 🐾
(952) 876-0900. **$139-$252.** 7850 Bloomington Ave S 55425. I-494 exit 3 (Portland Ave/12th Ave), on south frontage road; behind Courtyard by Marriott Minneapolis/Bloomington. Int corridors. **Pets:** Large. $75 one-time fee/room. Service with restrictions. [icons]

Sheraton Bloomington Hotel [H] 🐾
(952) 835-1900. **$109-$349.** 5601 W 78th St 55439. Just nw of jct I-494 and SR 100, access via SR 100 and Industrial Blvd. Int corridors. **Pets:** Designated rooms, service with restrictions, crate.
SAVE ECO [icons]

Staybridge Suites [H]
(952) 831-7900. **$89-$299.** 5150 American Blvd W 55437. I-494 exit 6B (France Ave), 1 mi w on frontage road. Int corridors. **Pets:** Accepted.
[icons]

Super 8 [H]
(952) 888-8800. **$64-$129.** 7800 2nd Ave S 55420. I-494 exit 4A (Nicollet Ave), just se. Int corridors. **Pets:** Medium. $10 daily fee/pet. Service with restrictions, supervision. SAVE [icons]

BROOKLYN CENTER

BEST WESTERN PLUS Minneapolis-Northwest [H]
(763) 566-7500. **$99-$109.** 2050 Freeway Blvd 55430. I-94/694 exit 34 (Shingle Creek Pkwy), just nw. Int corridors. **Pets:** Dogs only. $10 daily fee/pet. Designated rooms, service with restrictions, supervision.
SAVE [icons]

Country Inn & Suites By Carlson [H]
(763) 561-0900. **$81-$159.** 2550 Freeway Blvd 55430. I-94/694 exit 34 (Shingle Creek Pkwy), just nw. Int corridors. **Pets:** Accepted.
[icons]

Extended Stay America-Minneapolis-Brooklyn Center [H]
(763) 549-5571. **Call for rates.** 2701 Freeway Blvd 55430. I-94/694 exit 34 (Shingle Creek Pkwy), 0.5 mi nw. Int corridors. **Pets:** Other species. $25 daily fee/pet. Service with restrictions, supervision.
[icons]

Quality Inn [H]
(763) 560-7464. **$89-$129.** 1600 James Cir N 55430. I-94/694 exit 34 (Shingle Creek Pkwy), just ne. Int corridors. **Pets:** Small. $15 one-time fee/pet. Designated rooms, service with restrictions, supervision.
[icons]

BROOKLYN PARK

La Quinta Inn & Suites Minneapolis Northwest [H]
(763) 971-8000. **$64-$199.** 7011 Northland Cir 55428. I-94/694 exit 30 (Boone Ave), just ne. Int corridors. **Pets:** Large, other species. Service with restrictions. [icons]

BURNSVILLE

BEST WESTERN PREMIER Nicollet Inn [H]
(952) 435-2100. **$149-$200.** 14201 Nicollet Ave 55337. Just n of jct I-35W and CR 42. Int corridors. **Pets:** Large, dogs only. $20 one-time fee/room. Designated rooms, service with restrictions, supervision.
SAVE [icons]

CANBY

Canby Inn & Suites [M]
(507) 223-6868. **$90-$175.** 127 1st St W 56220. Just w of US 75; center. Int corridors. **Pets:** Other species. $20 one-time fee/room. Designated rooms, service with restrictions, supervision.
[icons]

CANNON FALLS

Saratoga Inn & Suites [H]
(507) 263-7272. **Call for rates.** 31591 64th Ave 55009. Jct SR 19, 1 mi sw on US 52. Int corridors. **Pets:** Accepted. [icons]

CHANHASSEN

AmericInn of Chanhassen [H]
(952) 934-3888. **Call for rates.** 570 Pond Promenade 55317. Just se of jct SR 5 and 101 S. Int corridors. **Pets:** Accepted.
SAVE [icons]

CLOQUET

AmericInn Lodge & Suites of Cloquet [H]
(218) 879-1231. **Call for rates.** 111 Big Lake Rd 55720. I-35 exit 237 (SR 33), 2 mi nw. Int corridors. **Pets:** Dogs only. $15 daily fee/room. Designated rooms, supervision. [icons]

Super 8 [H]
(218) 879-1250. **$70-$100.** 121 Big Lake Rd 55720. I-35 exit 237 (SR 33), 2 mi nw. Int corridors. **Pets:** Accepted. [icons]

COOK

Ludlow's Island Resort [CA]
(218) 666-5407. **$265-$700, 90 day notice.** 8166 Ludlow Dr 55723. US 53, 3.5 mi ne on CR 24, 5.1 mi e on CR 78 and 540. Ext corridors. **Pets:** Accepted. [icons]

COON RAPIDS

Fairfield Inn by Marriott [H]
(763) 785-8922. **$90-$160.** 8965 Springbrook Dr 55433. US 10 exit Foley Blvd, 0.8 mi s to Coon Rapids Blvd, 0.5 mi e to Springbrook Dr, then 0.4 mi s. Int corridors. **Pets:** Accepted.
[icons]

CROSSLAKE

Pine Peaks Lodge and Suites [H]
(218) 692-7829. **$80-$170, 3 day notice.** 14047 Swann Dr 56442. Jct CR 66 and Swann Dr. Int corridors. **Pets:** Accepted.
[icons]

DEER RIVER

White Oak Inn & Suites [H]
(218) 246-9400. **$67-$160.** 201 4th Ave NW 56636. On US 2. Int corridors. **Pets:** $15 one-time fee/pet. Designated rooms, service with restrictions, supervision. SAVE [icons]

DEERWOOD

Country Inn of Deerwood [H]
(218) 534-3101. **$79-$159.** 23885 Front St 56444. On SR 6 and 210, e of jct CR 12. Int corridors. **Pets:** Accepted.
SAVE [icons]

DETROIT LAKES

AmericInn Lodge & Suites of Detroit Lakes [H]
(218) 847-8795. **$85-$200.** 777 Hwy 10 E 56501. 1.4 mi se. Int corridors. **Pets:** Accepted. SAVE [icons]

BEST WESTERN PLUS Holland House [H] 🐾
(218) 847-4483. **$89-$199, 3 day notice.** 615 Hwy 10 E 56501. 1.3 mi se. Ext/int corridors. **Pets:** Medium. $15 daily fee/pet. Designated rooms, service with restrictions, supervision.
SAVE [icons]

Holiday Inn on the Lake [H]
(218) 847-2121. **$79-$349, 3 day notice.** 1155 US 10 E 56501. 2 mi se. Int corridors. **Pets:** Accepted.
[icons]

DULUTH

AAA ♦♦♦ **AmericInn Hotel & Suites of Duluth South** [H]
(218) 624-1026. **$85-$300.** 185 US 2 55810. Jct I-35 and US 2, 0.8 mi n. Int corridors. **Pets:** $25 one-time fee/room. Designated rooms, service with restrictions, supervision. [SAVE] [YI] ⌦ ⌂ ⌧ ▮ ▯

♦♦♦ **Country Inn & Suites By Carlson Duluth North** [H] ❀
(218) 740-4500. **$139-$249.** 4257 Haines Rd 55811. Just n of US 53. Int corridors. **Pets:** Other species. $30 one-time fee/room. Service with restrictions, crate. ⌦ ⌂ ⌧ ▯

♦♦ **Days Inn-Duluth** [H]
(218) 727-3110. **$85-$399.** 909 Cottonwood Ave 55811. SR 194, just n of jct US 53. Int corridors. **Pets:** Other species. $5 daily fee/room. Service with restrictions, supervision. ⌂ ▮ ▯

AAA ♦♦♦ **Days Inn Lakewalk** [M]
(218) 728-5141. **$77-$144.** 2211 London Rd 55812. I-35 exit 258 (21st Ave E), just nw. Int corridors. **Pets:** Accepted.
[SAVE] ⌂ ⌧ ▮ ▯

AAA ♦♦♦ **Downtown Duluth Motel** [M]
(218) 727-6851. **$72-$179.** 131 W 2nd St 55802. 2nd St at 2nd Ave W; center. Ext/int corridors. **Pets:** Accepted. [SAVE] ⌂ ⌧ ▮ ▯

♦♦ **Econo Lodge Airport** [H]
(218) 722-5522. **$79-$209.** 4197 Haines Rd 55811. Just s of US 53. Int corridors. **Pets:** Medium. $10 daily fee/pet. Designated rooms, no service, supervision. ⌦ ⌧ ⌂ ▮ ▯

AAA ♦♦♦♦ **Edgewater Hotel & Waterpark** [H] ❀
(218) 728-3601. **Call for rates.** 2400 London Rd 55812. I-35 exit 258 (21st Ave E), just nw. Ext/int corridors. **Pets:** $20 daily fee/pet. Service with restrictions, supervision.
[SAVE] [YI] ⌕M ⌦ ⌧ ⌂ ⌧ ▮ ▯

AAA ♦♦♦ **Fairfield Inn by Marriott** [H]
(218) 723-8607. **$101-$213.** 901 Joshua Ave 55811. Jct US 53 and SR 194. Int corridors. **Pets:** Accepted.
[SAVE] [ECO] [YI] ⌕M ⌦ ⌂ ⌧ ▮ ▯

AAA ♦♦♦ **Fitger's Inn** [H]
(218) 722-8826. **$145-$375.** 600 E Superior St 55802. I-35 exit 256B (Lake Ave), just ne. Int corridors. **Pets:** Other species. Designated rooms, service with restrictions, supervision.
[SAVE] [YI] ⌂ ⌧ ▮ ▯

♦♦♦♦ **Residence Inn by Marriott** [H] ❀
(218) 279-2885. **$90-$206.** 517 W Central Entrance 55811. Just e on SR 194 from jct US 53. Int corridors. **Pets:** $75 one-time fee/room. Service with restrictions, crate. [YI] ⌕M ⌦ ⌂ ⌧ ▮ ▯

AAA ♦♦♦♦ **Sheraton Duluth Hotel** [H]
(218) 733-5660. **Call for rates.** 301 E Superior St 55802. I-35W exit 256B (Lake Ave), just nw. Int corridors. **Pets:** Accepted.
[SAVE] [YI] ⌦ ⌂ ⌧ ▮ ▯

♦♦♦♦ **The Suites Hotel at Waterfront Plaza** [H]
(218) 727-4663. **$96-$549.** 325 Lake Ave S 55802. In Canal Park area. Int corridors. **Pets:** Large. $50 deposit/room, $15 daily fee/pet. Supervision. [YI] ⌕M ⌦ ⌧ ⌂ ▮ ▯

♦♦ **Super 8** [H]
(218) 628-2241. **$67-$160.** 4100 W Superior St 55807. I-35 exit 253B (40th Ave W), just sw. Int corridors. **Pets:** Dogs only. $50 deposit/room, $12 daily fee/room. Designated rooms, service with restrictions, supervision. ⌂ ▮ ▯

♦♦ **Voyageur Lakewalk Inn** [M]
(218) 722-3911. **Call for rates.** 333 E Superior St 55802. I-35 exit 256 (Superior St), just n. Ext corridors. **Pets:** Accepted. ⌂ ▮ ▯

EAGAN

AAA ♦♦♦♦ **BEST WESTERN PLUS Dakota Ridge** [H]
(651) 452-0100. **$109-$159.** 3450 Washington Dr 55122. I-35E exit 97B (Yankee Doodle Rd), just sw. Int corridors. **Pets:** Accepted.
[SAVE] ⌂ ⌧ ▮ ▯

♦♦ **Days Inn** [H]
(651) 681-1770. **$83-$97.** 4510 Erin Dr 55122. Just ne of jct SR 77 and Cliff Rd. Int corridors. **Pets:** Accepted.
[YI] ⌕M ⌦ ⌧ ⌂ ▮ ▯

♦♦ **Microtel Inn & Suites by Wyndham Eagan/St Paul** [H]
(651) 405-0988. **$55-$110, 3 day notice.** 3000 Denmark Ave 55121. I-35E exit 98 (Lone Oak Rd), just se. Int corridors. **Pets:** Accepted.
[YI] ⌂ ▮ ▯

♦♦♦ **Residence Inn by Marriott Minneapolis-St. Paul Airport/Eagan** [H]
(651) 688-0363. **$111-$194.** 3040 Eagandale Pl 55121. I-35E exit 98 (Lone Oak Rd), just sw. Ext corridors. **Pets:** Other species. $50 one-time fee/room. Service with restrictions. ⌦ ⌂ ⌧ ▮ ▯

♦♦ **Staybridge Suites** [H]
(651) 994-7810. **$89-$249.** 4675 Rahncliff Rd 55122. I-35E exit 93 (Cliff Rd), just w, then just s. Int corridors. **Pets:** Other species. $15 daily fee/room. Service with restrictions, supervision. ⌦ ⌂ ▮ ▯

♦♦ **TownePlace Suites by Marriott Minneapolis St. Paul Airport/Eagan** [H]
(651) 994-4600. **$115-$206.** 3615 Crestridge Dr 55122. I-35E exit 97A (Pilot Knob Rd), just se. Int corridors. **Pets:** Accepted.
⌕M ⌦ ⌂ ⌧ ▮ ▯

EDEN PRAIRIE

AAA ♦♦♦ **BEST WESTERN Eden Prairie Inn** [H]
(952) 829-0888. **$91-$150.** 11500 W 78th St 55344. I-494 exit 11A (Prairie Center Dr), just sw. Int corridors. **Pets:** Other species. $20 daily fee/pet. Service with restrictions, crate. [SAVE] ⌦ ⌂ ▮ ▯

♦♦ **Extended Stay America Minneapolis-Eden Prairie** [H]
(952) 941-1113. **Call for rates.** 7550 Office Ridge Cir 55344. I-494 exit 12, just se. Int corridors. **Pets:** Other species. $25 daily fee/pet. Service with restrictions, supervision. ⌂ ▮ ▯

♦♦ **Extended Stay America-Minneapolis-Eden Prairie** [H]
(952) 942-6818. **Call for rates.** 11905 Technology Dr 55344. Just sw of jct I-494 and US 212 (Flying Cloud Dr). Int corridors. **Pets:** Other species. $25 daily fee/pet. Service with restrictions, supervision.
⌕M ⌂ ▮ ▯

AAA ♦♦♦ **Hyatt Place Minneapolis/Eden Prairie** [H]
(952) 944-9700. **$79-$219.** 11369 Viking Dr 55344. I-494 exit 11A (Prairie Center Dr), just w. Int corridors. **Pets:** Accepted.
[SAVE] ⌕M ⌦ ⌧ ▮ ▯

♦♦♦ **Residence Inn by Marriott-Minneapolis SW** [H]
(952) 829-0033. **$116-$229.** 7780 Flying Cloud Dr 55344. I-494 exit 11A (Prairie Center Dr); on US 169 S and 212. Int corridors.
Pets: Accepted. ⌦ ⌂ ⌧ ▮ ▯

EDINA

AAA ♦♦♦ **Residence Inn by Marriott Minneapolis-Edina** [H]
(952) 893-9300. **$132-$309.** 3400 Edinborough Way 55435. I-494 exit 6B (France Ave), 0.3 mi n to Minnesota Dr, then just e. Int corridors.
Pets: Accepted. [SAVE] ⌂ ⌧ ▮ ▯

The Westin Edina Galleria H ❖
(952) 567-5000. **$119-$439.** 3201 Galleria 55435. I-494 exit 6B (France Ave), 1.5 mi n, then just e; at the Galleria. Int corridors. **Pets:** Medium. Designated rooms, service with restrictions, supervision.
SAVE ❌ ⊷ 🕳 ✕ 🛑 🖵

ELY

Grand Ely Lodge Resort and Conference Center H
(218) 365-6565. **$109-$329, 14 day notice.** 400 N Pioneer Rd 55731. SR 169 to Central Ave, just n to Pioneer Rd, then 1 mi n. Ext/int corridors. **Pets:** $15 daily fee/pet. Designated rooms, service with restrictions, crate. SAVE ❌ ⊷ ✕ 🕳 🛑 🖵

Motel Ely M
(218) 365-3237. **$50-$130.** 1047 E Sheridan St 55731. SR 1 and 169. Ext corridors. **Pets:** Dogs only. $15 one-time fee/pet. Designated rooms, service with restrictions, crate. SAVE ❌ 🕳 ✕ 🛑 🖵

EVELETH

Super 8 H
(218) 744-1661. **$80-$160.** 1080 Industrial Park Dr 55734. On US 53, 0.5 mi n of jct SR 37. Int corridors. **Pets:** Accepted.
❌ 🚹 ⊷ ✕ 🕳 🛑 🖵

FAIRMONT

Comfort Inn H ❖
(507) 238-5444. **$110-$170.** 2225 N State St 56031. I-90 exit 102 (SR 15), just s. Int corridors. **Pets:** Other species. $25 one-time fee/room. Designated rooms, service with restrictions, supervision.
SAVE ⊷ 🕳 ✕ 🛑 🖵

Hampton Inn Fairmont H ❖
(507) 235-2626. **$139-$179.** 100 Hampton Dr 56031. I-90 exit 102 (SR 15), just sw. Int corridors. **Pets:** Other species. $25 one-time fee/room. Service with restrictions, supervision.
SAVE 🚹 ⊷ 🕳 ✕ 🛑 🖵

Holiday Inn H ❖
(507) 238-4771. **Call for rates.** 1201 Torgerson Dr 56031. I-90 exit 102 (SR 15), just s. Int corridors. **Pets:** $25 one-time fee/room. Supervision.
❌ 🚹 ⊷ ✕ 🕳 ✕ 🛑 🖵

Super 8 H ❖
(507) 238-9444. **$75-$90.** 1200 Torgerson Dr 56031. I-90 exit 102 (SR 15), just s. Int corridors. **Pets:** Other species. $25 one-time fee/room. Service with restrictions, supervision. 🕳 🛑 🖵

FARIBAULT

Boarders Inn & Suites H
(507) 334-9464. **$85-$140.** 1801 Lavender Dr 55021. I-35 exit 59 (SR 21), just e. Int corridors. **Pets:** Accepted.
⊷ ✕ 🕳 ✕ 🛑 🖵

Days Inn & Suites H
(507) 334-6835. **$67-$96.** 1920 Cardinal Ln 55021. I-35 exit 59 (SR 21), just ne. Int corridors. **Pets:** Accepted.
🚹 ❌ ⊷ 🕳 🛑 🖵

FERGUS FALLS

AmericInn Lodge & Suites of Fergus Falls H
(218) 739-3900. **$90-$170.** 526 Western Ave N 56537. I-94 exit 54 (SR 210), just se. Int corridors. **Pets:** Other species. $10 one-time fee/room. Designated rooms, service with restrictions, supervision.
❌ ⊷ ✕ 🕳 ✕ 🛑 🖵

FINLAYSON

Americas Best Value Inn M
(320) 245-5284. **Call for rates.** 60671 State Hwy 23 55735. I-35 exit 195 (SR 23), just ne. Int corridors. **Pets:** Accepted. 🕳 🛑

FOREST LAKE

AmericInn Motel of Forest Lake H
(651) 464-1930. **Call for rates.** 1291 W Broadway Ave 55025. I-35 exit 131 (CR 2), just ne. Int corridors. **Pets:** Accepted. ⊷ 🕳 🛑 🖵

FOSSTON

Super 8 H
(218) 435-1088. **$58-$128.** 108 S Amber Ave 56542. US 2, 0.5 mi e. Int corridors. **Pets:** Accepted. 🚹 🕳 ✕ 🛑 🖵

GARRISON

Garrison Inn & Suites H
(320) 692-4050. **$79-$169, 7 day notice.** 9243 Hwy 169 56540. SR 169, just s of jct SR 18. Int corridors. **Pets:** Accepted.
⊷ 🕳 🛑 🖵

GRAND MARAIS

BEST WESTERN PLUS Superior Inn & Suites H ❖
(218) 387-2240. **$99-$199, 3 day notice.** 104 1st Ave E 55604. SR 61, just ne of center. Int corridors. **Pets:** $15 daily fee/pet. Designated rooms, service with restrictions, supervision. SAVE 🕳 ✕ 🛑 🖵

Gunflint Lodge VH ❖
(218) 388-2294. **$99-$499, 31 day notice.** 143 S Gunflint Lake Rd 55604. 43 mi nw on CR 12 (Gunflint Tr) from jct SR 61; 0.8 mi e on CR 50. Ext corridors. **Pets:** Other species. $20 daily fee/pet. Service with restrictions, crate. 🚹 ❌ ✕ 🕳 ✕ 🏌 Ⓩ 🛑 🖵

Nor'Wester Lodge and Outfitter CA
(218) 388-2252. **$119-$289, 60 day notice.** 7778 Gunflint Tr 55604. 30 mi nw on CR 12 (Gunflint Tr) from jct SR 61. Ext corridors. **Pets:** $15 daily fee/pet. Designated rooms, service with restrictions, crate.
🚹 ✕ 🕳 ✕ 🏌 ♺ Ⓩ 🛑 🖵

Outpost Motel M
(218) 387-1833. **$49-$95.** 2935 SR 61 E 55604. On SR 61, 9 mi ne. Ext corridors. **Pets:** Other species. $10 daily fee/pet. Supervision.
🚹 🕳 ✕ 🏌 🛑 🖵

GRAND RAPIDS

AmericInn of Grand Rapids H
(218) 326-8999. **$89-$154, 14 day notice.** 1812 S Pokegama Ave 55744. US 2, 1.8 mi s on US 169. Int corridors. **Pets:** Accepted.
🚹 ❌ ⊷ 🕳 ✕ 🛑 🖵

Country Inn & Suites By Carlson H ❖
(218) 327-4960. **$92-$150.** 2601 S Hwy 169 55744. US 2, 2 mi s. Int corridors. **Pets:** Medium, dogs only. Supervision.
SAVE ❌ ⊷ 🕳 🛑 🖵

Sawmill Inn H
(218) 326-8501. **$69-$109.** 2301 S Pokegama Ave 55744. US 2, 2 mi s. Ext/int corridors. **Pets:** Other species. Service with restrictions, supervision. SAVE 🚹 ⊷ ✕ 🕳 🛑 🖵

Super 8 H ❖
(218) 327-1108. **$90-$100.** 1702 S Pokegama Ave 55744. 1.5 mi s on US 169. Int corridors. **Pets:** Other species. Service with restrictions, supervision. SAVE 🚹 ❌ 🕳 🛑 🖵

GRANITE FALLS

Granite Falls Super Motel M
(320) 564-4075. **$59-$149.** 845 W SR 212 56241. Jct SR 23, 0.5 mi w. Int corridors. **Pets:** Small. $15 daily fee/pet. Designated rooms, service with restrictions, supervision. ❌ ⊷ 🕳 🛑

HAM LAKE

AmericInn Lodge & Suites of Ham Lake H
(763) 755-2100. **$90-$110.** 13440 Hwy 65 55304. 1 mi n of jct SR 65 and CR 242. Int corridors. **Pets:** Accepted.
🚹 ❌ ⊷ 🕳 🛑 🖵

Hoyt Lakes 🏨 🐾
...y notice. 99 Kennedy Memorial Dr
...s. **Pets:** Large, other species. $25 daily
...oms, service with restrictions, supervision.

HUTCHINSON
▼▼▼ **AmericInn of Hutchinson** 🏨 🐾
(320) 587-5515. **$79-$150.** 1115 Hwy 7 E 55350. 1 mi e of jct SR 15. Int corridors. **Pets:** Dogs only. $15 daily fee/room. Designated rooms, service with restrictions, supervision.

▼▼▼ **Days Inn Hutchinson** 🏨
(320) 587-6030. **$59-$88.** 1000 Hwy 7 W 55350. SR 15, 1 mi w. Int corridors. **Pets:** Accepted.

INTERNATIONAL FALLS
▼▼ **AmericInn of International Falls** 🏨
(218) 283-8000. **Call for rates.** 1500 US 71 W 56649. 1.5 mi w on US 71 and SR 11 W. Int corridors. **Pets:** Accepted.

⊛ **Hilltop Motel** Ⓜ
(218) 283-2505. **$59-$89.** 2002 2nd Ave W 56649. US 53, 1 mi s of jct US 53 and SR 11. Ext corridors. **Pets:** Service with restrictions.

JACKSON
⊛ ▼▼▼ **AmericInn Lodge & Suites of Jackson** 🏨
(507) 847-2444. **$117-$189.** 110 Belmont Ln 56143. I-90 exit 73 (US 71), just sw. Int corridors. **Pets:** Small, dogs only. $50 deposit/room, $25 daily fee/pet. Designated rooms, service with restrictions, supervision.

KASSON
▼▼ **AmericInn Motel & Suites of Kasson** 🏨
(507) 634-3444. **$79-$159.** 301 8th St SE 55944. Just se of jct US 14 and SR 57. Int corridors. **Pets:** Accepted.

LAKE ELMO
▼▼▼ **Holiday Inn & Suites St. Paul NE-Lake Elmo** 🏨
(651) 714-8068. **Call for rates.** 8511 Hudson Blvd 55042. I-94 exit 250 (Inwood Ave/Radio Dr), just ne. Int corridors. **Pets:** Accepted.

LAKEVILLE
▼▼▼ **Holiday Inn & Suites** 🏨
(952) 469-1134. **Call for rates.** 20800 Kenrick Ave 55044. I-35 exit 81 (CR 70), just ne. Int corridors. **Pets:** Accepted.

LE CENTER
⊛ **Guardian Inn Motel** Ⓜ
(507) 357-2239. **Call for rates.** 550 Commerce Dr 56057. 1 mi e on SR 99. Ext/int corridors. **Pets:** Accepted.

LITCHFIELD
▼▼▼ **Knights Inn** Ⓜ
(320) 693-2496. **$52-$120.** 1017 E Frontage Rd 55355. 1 mi se on US 12. Int corridors. **Pets:** Accepted.

LUTSEN
▼▼ **Solbakken Resort on Superior** Ⓜ
(218) 663-7566. **$61-$93, 14 day notice.** 4874 W SR 61 55612. SR 61, 1.3 mi n of jct CR 4 (Caribou Trl). Ext corridors. **Pets:** Other species. $10 daily fee/pet. Designated rooms, service with restrictions, crate.

LUVERNE
⊛ ▼▼▼ **GrandStay Hotel & Suites of Luverne** 🏨
(507) 449-4949. **$80-$129.** 908 S Kniss Ave 56156. I-90 exit 12 (US 75), just n. Int corridors. **Pets:** $20 one-time fee/room. Designated rooms, service with restrictions, crate.

MANHATTAN BEACH
▼▼▼ **Manhattan Beach Lodge** 🏨
(218) 692-3381. **$99-$259, 14 day notice.** 39051 CR 66 56442. On CR 66. Int corridors. **Pets:** Accepted.

MANKATO
⊛ ▼▼▼ **BEST WESTERN Hotel & Restaurant** 🏨 🐾
(507) 625-9333. **$90-$145.** 1111 Range St 56003. 0.6 mi s of jct US 169 and 14. Int corridors. **Pets:** $10 daily fee/room. Designated rooms, service with restrictions, supervision.

▼▼ **Days Inn** 🏨
(507) 387-3332. **$85-$120.** 1285 Range St 56001. 0.3 mi s of jct US 169 and 14. Int corridors. **Pets:** Accepted.

▼▼▼ **Holiday Inn Express & Suites** 🏨
(507) 388-1880. **$99-$159.** 2051 Adams St 56001. Jct US 14 and SR 22, 0.4 mi s, just e. Int corridors. **Pets:** Accepted.

⊛ ▼▼▼ **Mankato City Center Hotel** 🏨
(507) 345-1234. **$90-$120.** 101 E Main St 56001. Main St at Riverfront Dr; downtown. Int corridors. **Pets:** Other species. $35 one-time fee/room. Service with restrictions, crate.

⊛ ▼▼▼ **Mankato Quality Inn** 🏨
(507) 388-5107. **$69-$119.** 131 Apache Pl 56001. Just s of jct US 14 and SR 22. Int corridors. **Pets:** Accepted.

⊛ ▼▼▼ **Microtel Inn & Suites by Wyndham Mankato** 🏨 🐾
(507) 388-2818. **$66-$92.** 200 St. Andrews Dr 56001. US 14 exit CR 3, 0.4 mi n. Int corridors. **Pets:** Other species. $15 one-time fee/room. Service with restrictions, crate.

MAPLE GROVE
▼▼▼▼ **Staybridge Suites Minneapolis-Maple Grove** 🏨
(763) 494-8856. **Call for rates.** 7821 Elm Creek Blvd 55369. Just ne of jct I-94/494/694. Int corridors. **Pets:** Accepted.

MARSHALL
▼▼ **AmericInn Lodge & Suites of Marshall** 🏨
(507) 537-9424. **$94-$171.** 1406 E Lyon St 56258. Just se on US 59 from jct SR 23. Int corridors. **Pets:** Accepted.

▼▼ **Comfort Inn** 🏨
(507) 532-3070. **$85-$200.** 1511 E College Dr 56258. SR 19, w of jct SR 23. Int corridors. **Pets:** Accepted.

▼▼ **Ramada Marshall** 🏨
(507) 532-3221. **$99-$199.** 1500 E College Dr 56258. SR 19, just w of jct SR 23. Int corridors. **Pets:** Accepted.

▼▼ **Super 8** Ⓜ
(507) 537-1461. **$68-$98.** 1106 E Main St 56258. 0.3 mi se on US 59 from jct SR 23. Int corridors. **Pets:** Accepted.

MINNEAPOLIS *(Restaurants p. 634)*

Aloft Minneapolis H ❀
(612) 455-8400. **$99-$299.** 900 Washington Ave S 55415. Jct 9th Ave. Int corridors. **Pets:** Medium, dogs only. Designated rooms.
[SAVE] [♦] [&M] [≈] [🖻] [✕] [🗎] [💻]

BEST WESTERN PLUS The Normandy Inn & Suites H
(612) 370-1400. **$99-$209.** 405 S 8th St 55404. Corner of S 8th St and S 4th Ave. Int corridors. **Pets:** Dogs only. $10 daily fee/room. Designated rooms, service with restrictions, crate.
[SAVE] [♦] [≈] [✕] [🖻] [✕] [🗎] [💻]

Courtyard by Marriott H
(612) 333-4646. **$125-$298.** 1500 Washington Ave S 55454. Jct Washington and S 15th aves. Int corridors. **Pets:** Accepted.
[SAVE] [&M] [≈] [🖻] [✕] [🗎] [💻]

Days Hotel on University H
(612) 623-3999. **$75-$300.** 2407 University Ave SE 55414. I-35W exit University Ave, 1 mi se. Int corridors. **Pets:** $20 one-time fee/pet. Designated rooms, service with restrictions, supervision.
[SAVE] [🖻] [✕] [🗎] [💻]

The Depot Renaissance Minneapolis Hotel H
(612) 375-1700. **$146-$378.** 225 3rd Ave S 55401. Jct 3rd and Washington aves. Int corridors. **Pets:** Accepted.
[🗐] [♦] [≈] [🖂] [🖻] [✕] [🗎]

The Grand Hotel Minneapolis-A Kimpton Hotel H ❀
(612) 288-8888. **$199-$599.** 615 2nd Ave S 55402. Corner of 2nd Ave S and S 7th St. Int corridors. **Pets:** Other species. Designated rooms, service with restrictions, crate. [SAVE] [♦] [≈] [🖂] [🖻] [✕] [🗎]

Hilton Minneapolis H
(612) 376-1000. **$89-$299.** 1001 Marquette Ave S 55403. Between S 10th and S 11th sts. Int corridors. **Pets:** Accepted.
[SAVE] [♦] [&M] [≈] [🖂] [🖻] [🗎] [💻]

Hotel Ivy, a Luxury Collection Hotel, Minneapolis H
(612) 746-4600. **$189-$699.** 201 S 11th St 55403. Jct 2nd Ave and S 11th St. Int corridors. **Pets:** Accepted. [SAVE] [♦] [🖻] [✕]

The Hotel Minneapolis, Autograph Collection H
(612) 340-2000. **$99-$459.** 215 4th St S 55401. On 2nd Ave. Int corridors. **Pets:** Accepted. [♦] [🖻] [✕] [🗎] [💻]

Hyatt Regency Minneapolis H
(612) 370-1234. **$89-$399.** 1300 Nicollet Mall 55403. Jct Grant St. Int corridors. **Pets:** Accepted.
[SAVE] [ECO] [♦] [&M] [≈] [🖻] [✕] [🗎] [💻]

Loews Minneapolis Hotel H
(612) 677-1100. **$164-$289.** 601 1st Ave N 55403. Between 6th and 7th sts. Int corridors. **Pets:** Accepted. [SAVE] [♦] [🖻] [✕]

The Marquette Hotel H
(612) 333-4545. **$89-$399.** 710 Marquette Ave 55402. Jct Marquette Ave and S 7th St. Int corridors. **Pets:** Accepted. [SAVE] [♦] [🖻] [💻]

Minneapolis Marriott City Center H
(612) 349-4000. **$178-$384.** 30 S 7th St 55402. Between Hennepin and Nicollet aves; in City Center Shopping Complex. Int corridors.
Pets: Accepted. [♦] [&M] [🖂] [🖻] [✕] [🗎] [💻]

Radisson Blu Minneapolis Downtown H
(612) 339-4900. **$99-$499.** 35 S 7th St 55402. Between Nicollet and Hennepin aves. Int corridors. **Pets:** Accepted.
[SAVE] [ECO] [♦] [&M] [🖻] [✕] [🗎] [💻]

Ramada Plaza Minneapolis H
(612) 331-1900. **$109-$295.** 1330 Industrial Blvd NE 55413. I-35W exit 22, 3 mi n of downtown. Int corridors. **Pets:** Accepted.
[SAVE] [♦] [&M] [≈] [🖻] [✕] [🗎] [💻]

Residence Inn by Marriott Minneapolis Downtown City Center H
(612) 677-1000. **$129-$413.** 45 S 8th St 55402. At 8th St and LaSalle Ave. Int corridors. **Pets:** Accepted. [SAVE] [🖻] [✕] [🗎] [💻]

The Residence Inn Minneapolis Downtown at The Depot H
(612) 340-1300. **$146-$355.** 425 S 2nd St 55401. Jct S 2nd St and 5th Ave S. Int corridors. **Pets:** Accepted. [SAVE] [🖻] [✕] [🗎] [💻]

Sheraton Minneapolis Midtown Hotel H
(612) 821-7600. **$109-$349.** 2901 Chicago Ave S 55407. At Lake St. Int corridors. **Pets:** Accepted. [SAVE] [♦] [&M] [≈] [🖻] [✕] [🗎] [💻]

TownePlace Suites by Marriott Minneapolis Downtown H
(612) 340-1000. **$169-$209.** 525 N 2nd St 55401. Jct N 5th Ave. Int corridors. **Pets:** Accepted. [SAVE] [🖻] [✕] [🗎] [💻]

The Westin Minneapolis H ❀
(612) 333-4006. **$129-$679.** 88 S 6th St 55402. At Marquette Ave. Int corridors. **Pets:** Medium, dogs only. Service with restrictions, supervision. [SAVE] [♦] [≈] [🖂] [🖻] [✕] [🗎] [💻]

W Minneapolis-The Foshay H 🐾
(612) 215-3700. **$139-$799.** 821 Marquette Ave 55402. Between 9th and 8th sts. Int corridors. **Pets:** Medium. $100 one-time fee/room, $25 daily fee/pet. Service with restrictions. [SAVE] [♦] [🖂] [✕] [🗎]

MINNETONKA *(Restaurants p. 634)*

La Quinta Inn & Suites H
(952) 541-1094. **$89-$474.** 10420 Wayzata Blvd 55305. I-394 exit 2 (Hopkins Crossroad), just n, then 0.3 mi e on north frontage road. Int corridors. **Pets:** Large, other species. Service with restrictions.
[&M] [🖻] [✕]

Minneapolis Marriott-Southwest H
(952) 935-5500. **$150-$281.** 5801 Opus Pkwy 55343. Jct US 169 and SR 62, exit Bren Rd, just nw. Int corridors. **Pets:** Accepted.
[SAVE] [♦] [≈] [🖂] [🖻] [✕] [🗎] [💻]

Sheraton Minneapolis West Hotel H
(952) 593-0000. **$99-$279.** 12201 Ridgedale Dr 55305. I-394 exit 1C (Ridgedale Dr), 0.3 mi s. Int corridors. **Pets:** Accepted.
[SAVE] [♦] [≈] [🖻] [✕] [🗎] [💻]

MONTEVIDEO

Crossings by GrandStay Inn & Suites H
(320) 269-8000. **$95-$189.** 1805 E SR 7 56265. On SR 7; east of downtown. Int corridors. **Pets:** Other species. $200 deposit/room, $10 daily fee/pet. Designated rooms, service with restrictions, supervision.
[♦] [≈] [🖻] [🗎] [💻]

MONTICELLO

BEST WESTERN Chelsea Inn & Suites H
(763) 271-8880. **$99-$139.** 89 Chelsea Rd 55362. I-94 exit 193, 0.3 mi se. Int corridors. **Pets:** Accepted. [SAVE] [≈] [🖻] [✕] [🗎] [💻]

Days Inn H
(763) 295-1111. **$69-$109.** 200 E Oakwood Dr 55362. I-94 exit 193, 0.3 mi se. Int corridors. **Pets:** Large. $12 daily fee/pet. Designated rooms, service with restrictions, supervision. [SAVE] [♦] [🖻] [✕] [🗎] [💻]

△△△ ▼▼▼ Super 8 H
(763) 295-5900. **$70-$130.** 1114 Cedar St 55362. I-94 exit 193, 0.3 mi se. Int corridors. **Pets:** $10 daily fee/room. Designated rooms, service with restrictions, supervision. [SAVE] ⬤ ⬤ ⬤ ⬤ ⬤ ⬤

MOORHEAD
▼▼ Travelodge & Suites H
(218) 233-5333. **$50-$115.** 3027 S Frontage Rd 56560. Just s of US 10 E; east of downtown. Int corridors. **Pets:** Accepted.
⬤ ⬤ ⬤ ⬤ ⬤

MOOSE LAKE
▼▼ AmericInn Lodge & Suites of Moose Lake H
(218) 485-8885. **Call for rates.** 400 Park Place Dr 55767. I-35 exit 214 (SR 73), just sw. Int corridors. **Pets:** Accepted.
⬤ ⬤ ⬤ ⬤ ⬤ ⬤

MOUNTAIN IRON
▼▼ AmericInn Lodge & Suites of Virginia H ❀
(218) 741-7839. **Call for rates.** 5480 Mountain Iron Dr 55792. US 53, just s of jct US 169. Int corridors. **Pets:** Medium, dogs only. $15 daily fee/pet. Designated rooms, supervision. ⬤ ⬤ ⬤ ⬤ ⬤

▼▼▼ Holiday Inn Express & Suites H ❀
(218) 741-7411. **Call for rates.** 8570 Rock Ridge Dr 55768. On US 169, just w of jct US 53. Int corridors. **Pets:** Other species. $20 daily fee/pet. Service with restrictions. ⬤ ⬤ ⬤ ⬤ ⬤

MCGREGOR
▼▼ Country Meadows Inn & Suites H
(218) 768-7378. **$69-$149.** 403 Meadow Dr 55760. Jct SR 65 and 210. Int corridors. **Pets:** Accepted. ⬤ ⬤ ⬤ ⬤

NEW BRIGHTON
▼▼▼ Homewood Suites New Brighton H
(651) 631-8002. **$99-$199.** 1815 Old Hwy 8 NW 55112. I-35W exit 28A (CR 96). Int corridors. **Pets:** Medium. $150 one-time fee/room. Service with restrictions, crate. ⬤ ⬤ ⬤ ⬤ ⬤

NEW ULM
▼▼▼ Holiday Inn H
(507) 359-2941. **Call for rates.** 2101 S Broadway 56073. SR 15/68, 1.8 mi se. Int corridors. **Pets:** Accepted. ⬤ ⬤ ⬤ ⬤ ⬤ ⬤

NISSWA
▼▼ Nisswa Motel M
(218) 963-7611. **$59-$115, 5 day notice.** 5370 Merrill Ave 56468. Just sw of Main St; center. Ext corridors. **Pets:** Dogs only. $10 daily fee/pet. Designated rooms, service with restrictions, supervision. ⬤ ⬤ ⬤

NORTH BRANCH
▼▼ AmericInn Lodge & Suites of North Branch H
(651) 674-8627. **$99-$190.** 38675 14th Ave 55056. I-35 exit 147 (SR 95), just e, just s on Oakview Ave, then w on Oak St. Int corridors. **Pets:** Other species. $30 one-time fee/room. Service with restrictions, supervision. ⬤ ⬤ ⬤ ⬤ ⬤ ⬤

NORTHFIELD
▼▼ AmericInn Lodge & Suites of Northfield M
(507) 645-7761. **$109-$199.** 1320 Bollenbacher Dr 55057. Jct SR 3 and 19, 1 mi s. Int corridors. **Pets:** Accepted. ⬤ ⬤ ⬤ ⬤ ⬤

OAKDALE
△△△ ▼▼▼ BEST WESTERN Regency Plaza Hotel H
(651) 578-8466. **$99-$159.** 970 Helena Ave N 55128. I-694 exit 57, just se. Int corridors. **Pets:** Accepted. [SAVE] ⬤ ⬤ ⬤ ⬤ ⬤

OAK PARK HEIGHTS
▼▼ AmericInn Lodge & Suites of Oak Park Heights M
(651) 275-0980. **Call for rates.** 13025 60th St N 55082. SR 36 at Stillwater Blvd, just se. Int corridors. **Pets:** Other species. $25 daily fee/room. Service with restrictions, crate. ⬤ ⬤ ⬤ ⬤ ⬤ ⬤

ORR
▼▼ North Country Inn H
(218) 757-3778. **Call for rates.** 4483 Hwy 53 55771. 0.3 mi s. Int corridors. **Pets:** Accepted. ⬤ ⬤ ⬤ ⬤ ⬤

OTTERTAIL
△△△ ▼▼▼▼ Thumper Pond Resort H
(218) 367-2000. **Call for rates.** 300 Thumper Lodge Rd 56571. Jct SR 108 and 78. Int corridors. **Pets:** Accepted.
[SAVE] ⬤ ⬤ ⬤ ⬤ ⬤ ⬤

OWATONNA
▼▼ AmericInn of Owatonna H ❀
(507) 455-1142. **$90-$130.** 245 Florence Ave 55060. I-35 exit 41 (Bridge St), 0.3 mi ne. Int corridors. **Pets:** Other species. $10 daily fee/pet. Designated rooms, service with restrictions, crate.
⬤ ⬤ ⬤ ⬤ ⬤

▼▼▼ Comfort Inn H
(507) 444-0818. **$105-$150.** 2345 43rd St NW 55060. I-35 exit 45 (Clinton Falls), just sw. Int corridors. **Pets:** Other species. $10 daily fee/pet. Designated rooms, service with restrictions, supervision.
⬤ ⬤ ⬤ ⬤ ⬤ ⬤

▼▼ Oakdale Motel M
(507) 451-5480. **$45-$75.** 1418 S Oak Ave 55060. I-35 exit 40, 1 mi e on US 14 and 218, then 0.5 mi n on CR 45. Ext corridors.
Pets: Accepted. ⬤ ⬤ ⬤

PARKERS PRAIRIE
△△△ ▼▼▼ Crossings by GrandStay Inn & Suites of Parkers Prairie H
(218) 338-3380. **$62-$119.** 211 W Main St 56361. Just w of jct SR 29 and 235 (Main St). Int corridors. **Pets:** Medium. $25 daily fee/room. Service with restrictions, crate. [SAVE] ⬤ ⬤ ⬤ ⬤ ⬤ ⬤

PARK RAPIDS
▼▼ C'mon Inn H
(218) 732-1471. **$90-$174.** 1009 1st St E 56470. SR 34, 0.8 mi e of jct US 71. Int corridors. **Pets:** Accepted.
⬤ ⬤ ⬤ ⬤ ⬤ ⬤

PAYNESVILLE
▼▼ Paynesville Inn & Suites H
(320) 243-4146. **$90-$99.** 700 Diekmann Dr 56362. Jct SR 55, 0.3 mi s. Int corridors. **Pets:** Accepted. ⬤ ⬤ ⬤ ⬤ ⬤

PEQUOT LAKES
▼▼ AmericInn Lodge & Suites of Pequot Lakes H
(218) 568-8400. **Call for rates.** 32912 Paul Bunyan Trail Dr (SR 371/CR 16) 56472. SR 371, 2 mi n of downtown. Int corridors.
Pets: Accepted. ⬤ ⬤ ⬤ ⬤ ⬤ ⬤ ⬤

PERHAM
▼▼ Super 8-Perham H
(218) 346-7888. **$60-$95.** 106 Jake St SE 56573. SR 78, just nw of jct US 10. Int corridors. **Pets:** Accepted. ⬤ ⬤ ⬤ ⬤

PLYMOUTH
△△△ ▼▼▼▼ BEST WESTERN Kelly Inn H
(763) 553-1600. **$100-$229.** 2705 N Annapolis Ln 55441. I-494 exit 22 (SR 55), just e. Int corridors. **Pets:** Accepted.
[SAVE] ⬤ ⬤ ⬤ ⬤ ⬤

◆◆ **Comfort Inn** Ⓗ
(763) 559-1222. **$95-$150.** 3000 Harbor Ln 55447. I-494 exit 22 (SR 55), 0.3 mi nw. Int corridors. **Pets:** Accepted.
🍴 🏊 🏋 📶 🚭 ▣ ☕

AAA ◆◆◆ **Crowne Plaza Minneapolis West** Ⓗ
(763) 559-6600. **Call for rates.** 3131 Campus Dr 55441. I-494 exit 22 (SR 55), just e to CR 61 (Northwest Blvd), then 0.8 mi nw. Int corridors. **Pets:** Accepted. SAVE 🍴 🏊 🏋 📶 ☕

◆◆◆ **Residence Inn by Marriott** Ⓗ
(763) 577-1600. **$132-$223.** 2750 Annapolis Cir 55441. I-494 exit 22 (SR 55), just e to CR 61, just nw. Int corridors. **Pets:** Accepted.
🏊 📶 🚭 ▣ ☕

RED WING

◆◆◆ **St. James Hotel** Ⓗ
(651) 388-2846. **Call for rates.** 406 Main St 55066. On US 61; downtown. Int corridors. **Pets:** Accepted. 🍴 ♿ 📶 🚭 ▣

RICHFIELD

◆◆◆ **Candlewood Suites** Ⓗ
(612) 869-7704. **$105-$150.** 351 W 77th St 55423. I-494 exit 4B (Lyndale Ave), just ne. Int corridors. **Pets:** Accepted.
🍴 ♿ 📶 🚭 ▣ ☕

AAA ◆◆◆ **Four Points by Sheraton Minneapolis Airport** Ⓗ
(612) 861-1000. **$99-$149.** 7745 Lyndale Ave S 55423. I-494 exit 4B (Lyndale Ave), just ne. Int corridors. **Pets:** Accepted.
SAVE 🍴 🏊 📶 🚭 ▣ ☕

ROCHESTER

◆◆◆ **Aspen Suites** Ⓗ
(507) 289-6600. **Call for rates.** 1211 2nd St SW 55902. US 52/14 exit 55B (2nd St SW), just e. Int corridors. **Pets:** Medium. $75 one-time fee/room. Designated rooms, service with restrictions, crate.
♿ 🏊 🏋 📶 🚭 ▣ ☕

◆◆ **Centerstone Plaza Hotel Soldiers Field** Ⓗ
(507) 288-2677. **$107-$130.** 401 6th St SW 55902. 4th Ave SW at 6th St; just s of Mayo Clinic. Ext/int corridors. **Pets:** Accepted.
🍴 🏊 🏋 📶 ▣ ☕

◆◆◆ **Clarion Inn** Ⓗ
(507) 288-1844. **$70-$200.** 1630 S Broadway 55904. 0.5 mi s of jct US 14 and 63 (Broadway). Ext/int corridors. **Pets:** Accepted.
🍴 🏊 🏋 📶 ▣ ☕

◆◆ **Comfort Inn** Ⓗ
(507) 289-3344. **$86-$95.** 5708 Bandel Rd NW 55901. US 52 exit 59 (55th St), just n on E Frontage Rd. Int corridors. **Pets:** Medium, dogs only. $35 one-time fee/room. Designated rooms, no service, supervision.
🍴 ♿ 🏊 🏋 📶 🚭 ▣ ☕

◆◆ **Extended Stay America-Rochester North** Ⓗ
(507) 289-7444. **Call for rates.** 2814 43rd St NW 55901. Just nw from jct US 52. Int corridors. **Pets:** Other species. $25 daily fee/pet. Service with restrictions, supervision. 📶 ▣ ☕

◆◆ **Extended Stay America-Rochester-South** Ⓗ
(507) 536-7444. **Call for rates.** 55 Woodlake Dr SE 55904. US 63 (Broadway) exit 49th St S, 0.7 mi ne. Int corridors. **Pets:** Other species. $25 daily fee/pet. Service with restrictions, supervision. 📶 ▣ ☕

AAA ◆◆ **GuestHouse International Inn & Suites** Ⓗ
(507) 288-9090. **$70-$76.** 435 16th Ave NW 55901. US 52 exit 56A (Civic Center Dr), just se jct US 14. Int corridors. **Pets:** Accepted.
SAVE 🍴 ♿ 🏊 🏋 📶 🚭 ▣ ☕

◆◆◆ **Holiday Inn Express & Suites** Ⓗ
(507) 226-8700. **$133-$162.** 155 16th Ave SW 55902. Jct US 52. Int corridors. **Pets:** Accepted. ♿ 📶 🚭 ▣ ☕

◆◆◆ **Holiday Inn Rochester Downtown** Ⓗ
(507) 252-8200. **$129-$149.** 220 S Broadway 55904. On US 63 (Broadway); downtown. Int corridors. **Pets:** Small. $75 one-time fee/room. Designated rooms, service with restrictions, supervision.
🍴 ♿ 🏊 📶 🚭 ▣ ☕

AAA ◆◆◆ **The Kahler Grand Hotel** Ⓗ
(507) 280-6200. **Call for rates.** 20 SW 2nd Ave 55902. Opposite Mayo Clinic and Methodist Hospital. Int corridors. **Pets:** Accepted.
SAVE 🍴 🏊 🏋 📶 🚭 ▣ ☕

AAA ◆◆ **Kahler Inn & Suites** Ⓗ
(507) 285-9200. **Call for rates.** 9 NW 3rd Ave 55901. Just n of Mayo Clinic. Int corridors. **Pets:** Accepted.
SAVE 🍴 🏊 🏋 📶 🚭 ▣ ☕

◆◆◆ **Marriott Hotel** Ⓗ
(507) 280-6000. **$202-$332.** 101 1st Ave SW 55902. Just e of Mayo Clinic; downtown. Int corridors. **Pets:** Accepted.
🍴 🏊 ● 🚭 ▣ ☕

◆◆ **Quality Inn & Suites** Ⓗ
(507) 282-8091. **$90-$215.** 1620 1st Ave SE 55904. 0.5 mi s from jct US 14 and 63, just e on 16th St, then just s. Ext/int corridors. **Pets:** Accepted. 📶 🚭 ▣ ☕

◆◆◆ **Residence Inn by Marriott** Ⓗ
(507) 292-1400. **$146-$240.** 441 W Center St 55902. Just n of Mayo Clinic; downtown. Int corridors. **Pets:** Accepted.
♿ 📶 🚭 ▣ ☕

AAA ◆◆◆◆ **The Towers at Kahler Grand** Ⓗ
(507) 328-8000. **$399-$579.** 20 SW 2nd Ave 55902. Opposite Mayo Clinic and Methodist Hospital; 10th and 11th Floor of The Kahler Grand Hotel. Int corridors. **Pets:** $300 one-time fee/room. Service with restrictions, crate. SAVE 🍴 🏊 🏋 📶 🚭 ▣

◆◆◆ **TownePlace Suites by Marriott** Ⓗ
(507) 281-1200. **$108-$177.** 2829 NW 43rd St 55901. US 52 exit 41st St NW, just w, just n on W Frontage Rd, then just w. Int corridors. **Pets:** $100 one-time fee/room. Service with restrictions, supervision.
♿ 🏊 📶 🚭 ▣ ☕

ROGERS

◆◆ **AmericInn Lodge & Suites of Rogers** Ⓗ 🐾
(763) 428-4346. **$79-$149.** 21800 Industrial Blvd 55374. I-94 exit 207 (SR 101), just sw. Int corridors. **Pets:** $10 daily fee/pet. Designated rooms, service with restrictions, supervision. 🏊 📶 🚭 ▣ ☕

AAA ◆◆◆ **Hampton Inn & Suites** Ⓗ 🐾
(763) 425-0044. **$109-$149.** 13550 Commerce Blvd 55374. I-94 exit 207 (SR 101), 0.4 mi ne. Int corridors. **Pets:** Medium. Designated rooms, service with restrictions, supervision.
SAVE 🍴 ♿ 🏊 📶 🚭 ▣ ☕

ROSEAU

AAA ◆◆ **AmericInn Lodge & Suites of Roseau** Ⓗ
(218) 463-1045. **$86-$135.** 1110 3rd St NW 56751. 1 mi w on SR 11. Int corridors. **Pets:** $25 one-time fee/room. Service with restrictions.
SAVE ♿ 🏊 🏋 📶 🚭 ▣ ☕

◆◆ **North Country Inn** Ⓗ
(218) 463-9444. **$79-$129.** 902 3rd St NW 56751. 0.8 mi w on SR 11. Int corridors. **Pets:** Medium. $7 daily fee/pet. Designated rooms, service with restrictions, supervision. 🏊 📶 🚭 ▣ ☕

ROSEVILLE

◆◆◆ **Residence Inn by Marriott** Ⓗ
(651) 636-0680. **$125-$240.** 2985 Centre Pointe Dr 55113. I-35W exit 25A (CR D), just se. Int corridors. **Pets:** Accepted.
🍴 ♿ 🏊 📶 🚭 ▣ ☕

ST. CLOUD

AmericInn Lodge & Suites of St. Cloud 🏨 ❀

(320) 253-6337. **Call for rates.** 4385 Clearwater Rd 56301. I-94 exit 171 (CR 75), just ne. Int corridors. **Pets:** $50 deposit/room, $10 daily fee/pet. Service with restrictions, supervision.

SAVE ⓜ 🛏 🤶 🛁 💻

BEST WESTERN PLUS Kelly Inn 🏨

(320) 253-0606. **$114-$145.** 100 4th Ave S 56301. SR 23 at 4th Ave S; center. Int corridors. **Pets:** $100 deposit/room. Service with restrictions, supervision. SAVE 🍴 ⓜ 🛏 🤶 ❌ 🛁 💻

Country Inn & Suites By Carlson-St. Cloud West 🏨

(320) 259-8999. **Call for rates.** 235 S Park Ave 56301. Jct SR 15 and 23 W, just w. Int corridors. **Pets:** Small, dogs only. $15 one-time fee/pet. Designated rooms, service with restrictions, supervision.

SAVE 🍴 ⓜ 🛏 🤶 🛁 💻

GrandStay Residential Suites Hotel 🏨

(320) 251-5400. **$83-$200.** 213 6th Ave S 56301. SR 23 at 6th Ave S; center. Int corridors. **Pets:** Accepted. 🛏 🤶 🛁 💻

Holiday Inn Express & Suites 🏨 ❀

(320) 240-8000. **$90-$180.** 4322 Clearwater Rd 56301. I-94 exit 171 (CR 75), just ne. Int corridors. **Pets:** Designated rooms, service with restrictions, supervision. ⓜ 🛏 🤶 🛁 💻

Holiday Inn Hotel & Suites 🏨

(320) 253-9000. **$100-$160, 3 day notice.** 75 S 37th Ave 56301. Jct SR 15 and 23. Int corridors. **Pets:** Service with restrictions, supervision. 🍴 🛏 🤶 🛁 💻

Le St-Germain Suite Hotel 🏨

(320) 654-1661. **$89-$159, 3 day notice.** 404 W St. Germain St 56301. Just n of SR 23; center. Int corridors. **Pets:** Accepted.

🍴 ⓜ 🛏 🤶 🛁 💻

Quality Inn 🏨

(320) 251-1500. **$89-$119.** 4040 2nd St S 56301. Jct SR 15 and 23 W, just w. Int corridors. **Pets:** Small, dogs only. $20 one-time fee/pet. Designated rooms, service with restrictions, supervision.

🍴 ⓜ 🛏 🤶 ❌ 🛁 💻

ST. JAMES

Super 8 St. James 🏨

(507) 375-4708. **$73-$106.** 1210 Heckman Ct 56081. SR 60 exit 30/730th Ave, just n, then just e. Int corridors. **Pets:** Other species. $10 daily fee/pet. Service with restrictions, crate. ⓜ 🛏 🤶 🛁 💻

ST. LOUIS PARK

DoubleTree by Hilton Hotel Minneapolis-Park Place 🏨

(952) 542-8600. **$89-$249.** 1500 Park Place Blvd 55416. I-394 exit 5 (Park Place Blvd), just sw. Int corridors. **Pets:** Medium, dogs only. $50 one-time fee/room. Service with restrictions, crate.

🍴 🛏 🤶 ❌ 🛁 💻

Homewood Suites St. Louis Park/Minneapolis West 🏨

(952) 544-0495. **$99-$229.** 5305 Wayzata Blvd 55416. I-394 exit 5 (Park Place Blvd), just se. Int corridors. **Pets:** Small. $75 one-time fee/room. Service with restrictions, crate.

🍴 ⓜ 🛏 🤶 ❌ 🛁 💻

TownePlace Suites by Marriott Minneapolis West St. Louis Park 🏨

(952) 847-6900. **$118-$229.** 1400 Zarthan Ave S 55416. I-394 exit 5 (Park Place Blvd), 0.3 mi w on 16th, then just n. Int corridors. **Pets:** Accepted. 🛏 🤶 ❌ 🛁 💻

ST. PAUL

BEST WESTERN Plus Bandana Square 🏨

(651) 647-1637. **Call for rates.** 1010 Bandana Blvd W 55108. I-94 exit 239B (Lexington Pkwy), 1.3 mi n, then 0.3 mi w on Energy Park Dr. Int corridors. **Pets:** Accepted. SAVE ⓜ 🛏 🤶 🤶 ❌ 🛁 💻

BEST WESTERN PLUS Capitol Ridge 🏨

(651) 227-8711. **Call for rates.** 161 St. Anthony Ave 55103. Jct I-35E and 94. Int corridors. **Pets:** Accepted.

SAVE 🍴 🛏 🤶 🤶 🛁 💻

SAUK CENTRE

AmericInn Lodge & Suites of Sauk Centre 🏨 ❀

(320) 352-2800. **$84-$149.** 1230 Timberlane Dr 56378. I-94 exit 127, just ne. Int corridors. **Pets:** Medium, dogs only. $10 daily fee/pet. Designated rooms, service with restrictions, crate.

🍴 🛏 🤶 🤶 ❌ 🛁 💻

GuestHouse International Hotel 🏨

(320) 351-7256. **$72-$89.** 322 12th St S 56378. I-94 exit 127, just ne. Int corridors. **Pets:** Dogs only. $10 daily fee/pet. Designated rooms, service with restrictions, supervision. 🍴 🛏 🤶 🛁 💻

SHAKOPEE

Americas Best Value Inn & Suites 🏨

(952) 445-3644. **$72-$162.** 1244 Canterbury Rd 55379. Just nw of US 169. Int corridors. **Pets:** Medium. $10 daily fee/pet. Service with restrictions, supervision. 🍴 🛏 🤶 ❌ 🛁 💻

BEST WESTERN PLUS Shakopee Inn 🏨

(952) 445-9779. **$100-$140.** 511 S Marshall Rd 55379. On CR 17, 0.5 mi s of CR 101. Int corridors. **Pets:** Accepted.

SAVE ECO 🛏 🤶 🤶 ❌ 🛁 💻

Country Inn & Suites By Carlson 🏨

(952) 445-0200. **Call for rates.** 1204 Ramsey St 55379. Just ne of US 169. Int corridors. **Pets:** Medium, other species. $50 one-time fee/pet, $15 daily fee/pet. Designated rooms, service with restrictions, supervision. SAVE 🍴 ⓜ 🛏 🤶 ❌ 🛁 💻

Sandalwood Studios & Suites 🏨

(952) 277-0100. **$49-$129.** 3910 12th Ave E 55379. Just nw of US 169. Int corridors. **Pets:** Accepted. 🍴 🤶 🛁

SILVER BAY

AmericInn Lodge & Suites of Silver Bay 🏨 ❀

(218) 226-4300. **$110-$175, 3 day notice.** 150 Mensing Dr 55614. On SR 61, 0.5 mi ne of jct Outer Dr. Int corridors. **Pets:** Dogs only. $20 daily fee/pet. Service with restrictions, supervision.

🍴 ⓜ 🛏 🤶 🤶 ❌ 🛁 💻

Mariner Motel Ⓜ

(218) 226-4488. **$55-$75, 3 day notice.** 46 Outer Dr 55614. On SR 61; at traffic signal. Ext corridors. **Pets:** Dogs only. $10 daily fee/pet. Service with restrictions, supervision. SAVE 🍴 🤶 Ⓚ 🛁 💻

SOUTH ST. PAUL

Clarion South Saint Paul Hotel & Conference Center 🏨

(651) 455-3600. **$89-$169.** 701 Concord St S 55075. I-494 exit 64B (SR 56/Concord St), just n. Int corridors. **Pets:** Large, other species. $10 daily fee/pet. Service with restrictions, crate.

🍴 ⓜ 🛏 🤶 ❌ 🛁 💻

SPRINGFIELD

Microtel Inn & Suites by Wyndham Springfield 🏨

(507) 723-8200. **$65-$95.** 502 E Rock St 56087. On US 14. Int corridors. **Pets:** Accepted. ⓜ 🛏 🤶 ❌ 🛁 💻

STILLWATER

◆◆ Americas Best Value Inn H
(651) 430-1300. Call for rates. 1750 W Frontage Rd 55082. SR 36 at Washington Ave, just ne. Int corridors. Pets: Accepted.

◆◆ Crossings by GrandStay Inn & Suites H
(651) 430-2699. Call for rates. 2200 W Frontage Rd 55082. SR 36 at Washington Ave, just nw. Int corridors. Pets: Accepted.

◆◆ Lexington Inn & Suites H ❀
(651) 275-1401. Call for rates. 2000 Washington Ave S 55082. SR 36 at Washington Ave, just n. Int corridors. Pets: Medium. $25 one-time fee/pet. Service with restrictions, crate.

◆◆ Super 8 H
(651) 430-3990. $49-$79. 2190 W Frontage Rd 55082. SR 36 at Washington Ave, just nw. Int corridors. Pets: Accepted.

THIEF RIVER FALLS

◆◆ C'mon Inn H
(218) 681-3000. Call for rates. 1586 US 59 SE 56701. 1 mi se. Int corridors. Pets: Accepted.

TOFTE

◆◆◆ ◆◆ AmericInn Lodge & Suites of Tofte H
(218) 663-7899. $70-$165. 7231 W SR 61 55615. On SR 61. Int corridors. Pets: $15 daily fee/pet. Designated rooms, service with restrictions, crate.

◆◆◆ ◆◆◆ Bluefin Bay on Lake Superior CO
(218) 663-7296. $75-$595, 7 day notice. 7192 W Hwy 61 55615. On SR 61. Ext corridors. Pets: Other species. $20 daily fee/room. Designated rooms, service with restrictions, supervision.

◆◆◆ Surfside on Lake Superior CO
(218) 663-6870. $169-$549, 7 day notice. 10 Surfside (Hwy 61) Dr 55615. On SR 61. Ext corridors. Pets: Accepted.

TWO HARBORS

◆◆◆ ◆◆ AmericInn Lodge & Suites of Two Harbors H ❀
(218) 834-3000. Call for rates. 1088 SR 61 N 55616. On SR 61, 0.7 mi s. Int corridors. Pets: Medium, dogs only. $15 daily fee/room. Designated rooms, service with restrictions, crate.

◆◆◆ Superior Shores Resort & Conference Center CO ❀
(218) 834-5671. $79-$529, 14 day notice. 1521 Superior Shores Dr 55616. On SR 61, 1.5 mi n of center. Ext/int corridors. Pets: Dogs only. $15 daily fee/room. Designated rooms, service with restrictions, supervision.

VIRGINIA

◆◆ Lakeshor Motor Inn M
(218) 741-3360. $55-$104. 404 6th Ave N 55792. Just n of Chestnut St; center. Ext corridors. Pets: Accepted.

◆◆◆ ◆◆ Pine View Inn M
(218) 741-8918. $60-$109. 903 N 17th St 55792. 0.5 mi n on US 53 from jct US 169, 0.7 mi e on 9th St N, then 0.5 mi n. Ext corridors. Pets: $10 daily fee/room. Designated rooms, service with restrictions, supervision.

WABASHA

◆◆ ◆◆ AmericInn Lodge & Suites of Wabasha H
(651) 565-5366. $90-$180. 150 Commerce Dr 55981. Just ne of jct US 61 and SR 60. Int corridors. Pets: Accepted.

WACONIA

◆◆◆◆ AmericInn Lodge & Suites of Waconia H ❀
(952) 442-8787. $90-$120. 550 Cherry Dr 55387. Just nw of jct SR 5. Int corridors. Pets: Small, dogs only. $10 daily fee/pet. Designated rooms, service with restrictions, supervision.

WALKER

◆◆◆ Country Inn Walker H
(218) 547-1400. $89-$235. 442 Walker Bay Blvd 56484. 1 mi s on SR 371. Int corridors. Pets: Accepted.

WARROAD

◆◆ The Patch Motel H
(218) 386-2723. Call for rates. 801 State St N 56763. 0.6 mi w on SR 11. Int corridors. Pets: Accepted.

WASECA

◆◆◆ Crossings by GrandStay Inn & Suites H ❀
(507) 835-0022. $95-$126, 3 day notice. 2201 N State St 56093. Jct US 14, 1.4 mi n on SR 13. Int corridors. Pets: Other species. $10 daily fee/pet. Designated rooms, service with restrictions, crate.

WHITE BEAR LAKE

◆◆ AmericInn Lodge & Suites of White Bear Lake H
(651) 429-7131. $109-$119. 4675 White Bear Pkwy 55110. I-35E exit 117, just ne of jct SR 96. Int corridors. Pets: Medium, dogs only. $10 daily fee/pet. Designated rooms, service with restrictions, supervision.

◆◆◆ ◆◆◆ BEST WESTERN PLUS White Bear Country Inn H
(651) 429-5393. $90-$150. 4940 N Hwy 61 55110. Jct SR 96, 1 mi n. Int corridors. Pets: Medium, dogs only. $10 daily fee/room. Service with restrictions, supervision.

WILLMAR

◆◆ AmericInn Motel of Willmar H
(320) 231-1962. Call for rates. 2404 E US 12 56201. 2 mi e. Int corridors. Pets: Medium, dogs only. $15 daily fee/pet. Designated rooms, service with restrictions, supervision.

◆◆◆ ◆◆◆ BEST WESTERN PLUS Willmar H
(320) 235-6060. Call for rates. 2100 US 12 E 56201. 1.8 mi e. Int corridors. Pets: $10 daily fee/pet. Service with restrictions, supervision.

◆◆ Days Inn Willmar H
(320) 231-1275. $70-$96. 225 28th St SE 56201. 2.3 mi e on US 12. Int corridors. Pets: Other species. $10 daily fee/pet. Service with restrictions, supervision.

WINDOM

◆◆ Guardian Inn Motel M
(507) 831-1809. Call for rates. 1955 1st Ave 56101. Just ne on SR 60 from jct US 71. Ext/int corridors. Pets: Accepted.

WINONA

◆◆◆ Holiday Inn Express & Suites H
(507) 474-1700. $140-$170. 1128 Homer Rd 55987. Jct SR 43, just sw. Int corridors. Pets: Accepted.

◆◆◆ The Plaza Hotel & Suites H
(507) 453-0303. Call for rates. 1025 Hwy 61 E 55987. Jct SR 43, just sw. Int corridors. Pets: Accepted.

WOODBURY

▼▼▼ **Extended Stay America-Minneapolis-Woodbury** 🅷
(651) 501-1085. **Call for rates.** 10020 Hudson Rd 55125. I-94 exit 251, just se. Int corridors. **Pets:** Other species. $25 daily fee/pet. Service with restrictions, supervision. 🔳📶🔌🖥

▼▼▼ **Holiday Inn Express Hotel & Suites** 🅷
(651) 702-0200. **$109-$208.** 9840 Norma Ln 55125. I-94 exit 251, sw. Int corridors. **Pets:** Medium. $25 daily fee/room. Designated rooms, service with restrictions, supervision. 🌊📶🗙🔌🖥

🆎 ▼▼◆ **Sheraton St. Paul Woodbury Hotel** 🅷 🐾
(651) 209-3280. **Call for rates.** 676 Bielenberg Dr 55125. I-494 exit 59C (Tamarack Rd), just ne. Int corridors. **Pets:** Dogs only. Designated rooms, supervision. 🆂🍽🔳🌊📶🗙🔌🖥

WORTHINGTON

🆎 ▼▼◆ **AmericInn Lodge & Suites of Worthington** 🅷
(507) 376-4500. **$117-$165.** 1475 Darling Dr 56187. I-90 exit 43 (US 59), just se. Int corridors. **Pets:** Accepted.
🆂🔳🌊📶🗙🔌🖥

▼▼◆ **Comfort Suites & Conference Center** 🅷 🐾
(507) 295-9185. **$109-$169.** 1447 Prairie Dr 56187. I-90 exit 43, just n. Int corridors. **Pets:** Dogs only. $20 daily fee/room. Designated rooms, service with restrictions, supervision. 🍽🔳📶🗙🔌🖥

MISSISSIPPI

BILOXI

▼▼ **Edgewater Inn** 🅷
(228) 388-1100. **Call for rates.** 1936 Beach Blvd 39531. I-110 exit 1B, 3.4 mi w on US 90. Ext corridors. **Pets:** Accepted. 🌊📶🔌🖥

🆎 ▼▼◆ ▼▼◆ **Hard Rock Hotel & Casino Biloxi** 🅷
(228) 374-7625. **$109-$499.** 777 Beach Blvd 39530. I-110 exit 1A (US 90), just e. Int corridors. **Pets:** Accepted.
🆂🍽🔳🌊🗙📶🔌🖥

▼▼◆ **La Quinta Inn & Suites** 🅷
(228) 392-5978. **$93-$239.** 957 Cedar Lake Rd 39532. I-10 exit 44, just s. Int corridors. **Pets:** Large, other species. Service with restrictions.
🔳🌊📶🗙🔌🖥

BRANDON

▼◆ **Microtel Inn & Suites by Wyndham** 🅷
(601) 591-5858. **$47-$64.** 1130 Oak St 39042. I-20 exit 56, just n. Int corridors. **Pets:** Medium, other species. $25 one-time fee/pet. Service with restrictions, supervision. 🔳📶🔌🖥

CANTON

🆎 ▼▼◆ **BEST WESTERN Canton Inn** 🅷
(601) 859-8600. **$70-$150.** 137 Soldier Colony Rd 39046. I-55 exit 119, just se. Int corridors. **Pets:** Accepted. 🆂🌊📶🔌🖥

CLARKSDALE

▼▼ **Comfort Inn of Clarksdale** 🅷
(662) 627-5122. **$85-$120.** 818 S State St 38614. 1.2 mi s of jct US 49 and SR 161. Int corridors. **Pets:** Accepted. 🌊📶🔌🖥

CLEVELAND

▼▼◆ **Holiday Inn Express** 🅷
(662) 843-9300. **Call for rates.** 808 N Davis Ave 38732. 1 mi n of jct US 61 and SR 8. Int corridors. **Pets:** Accepted.
🔳📶🗙🔌🖥

CLINTON

🆎 ▼▼◆ **BEST WESTERN Ridgeland Inn** 🅷
(601) 926-4323. **$68-$79.** 102 Clinton Loop Dr 39056. I-20 exit 36, just s, then just w on Clinton Center Dr. Int corridors. **Pets:** Medium. $15 daily fee/pet. Designated rooms, service with restrictions, supervision.
🆂🌊📶🔌🖥

COLUMBUS *(Restaurants p. 634)*

▼▼ **Quality Inn** 🅷
(662) 329-2422. **$80-$85.** 1210 US 45 N 39705. Jct US 82 Bypass and 45 N. Ext corridors. **Pets:** Accepted. 📶🔌🖥

D'IBERVILLE

▼▼▼ **Home2 Suites by Hilton Biloxi North/D'Iberville** 🅷
(228) 392-6265. **Call for rates.** 3810 Promenade Pkwy 39540. I-10 exit 46B, just nw; in The Promenade. Int corridors. **Pets:** Accepted.
📶🐾🔳🆎

▼▼ **Suburban Extended Stay Hotel** 🅷
(228) 396-5780. **$54-$130.** 10221 Rodriguez St 39540. I-110 exit 2, just sw. Ext corridors. **Pets:** Accepted. 📶🔌🖥

▼▼▼ **Wingate by Wyndham** 🅷
(228) 396-0036. **$84-$159.** 12009 Indian River Rd 39540. I-10 exit 46B, just ne. Int corridors. **Pets:** Accepted. 🌊📶🗙🔌🖥

GRENADA

▼▼▼ **Comfort Inn & Suites** 🅷
(662) 227-8444. **$99-$125.** 255 SW Frontage Rd 38901. I-55 exit 206, just sw. Int corridors. **Pets:** Medium. $25 one-time fee/room. Service with restrictions, crate. 🌊📶🔌🖥

GULFPORT

🆎 ▼▼◆ **BEST WESTERN PLUS Seaway Inn** 🅷 🐾
(228) 864-0050. **$100-$150.** 9475 Hwy 49 39503. I-10 exit 34A, just sw. Ext corridors. **Pets:** Other species. $15 daily fee/pet. Designated rooms, service with restrictions, supervision. 🆂🌊📶🔌🖥

🆎 ▼▼◆ **Clarion Inn Gulfport/Airport** 🅷
(228) 868-3300. **$72-$149.** 9445 Hwy 49 39503. I-10 exit 34A, just sw. Ext corridors. **Pets:** Accepted. 🆂🌊📶🔌🖥

▼▼ **Quality Inn Gulfport** 🅷
(228) 864-7222. **$60-$130.** 9435 Hwy 49 39503. I-10 exit 34A, 0.6 mi s. Ext corridors. **Pets:** Small. $20 daily fee/pet. Service with restrictions, supervision. 📶🔌🖥

▼▼◆ **Residence Inn by Marriott Gulfport-Biloxi Airport** 🅷
(228) 867-1722. **$144-$495.** 14100 Airport Rd 39503. I-10 exit 34A, 0.8 mi s on US 49, then 1.2 mi e. Int corridors. **Pets:** $100 one-time fee/room. Service with restrictions. 🔳🌊📶🗙🔌🖥

HATTIESBURG

▼▼▼ **Candlewood Suites** 🅷
(601) 264-9666. **Call for rates.** 9 Gateway Dr 39402. I-59 exit 67B, just nw to Classic Dr, then just sw. Int corridors. **Pets:** Accepted.
🔳📶🔌🖥

▼▼▼ **Hampton Inn of Hattiesburg** H
(601) 264-8080. **$89-$99.** 4301 Hardy St 39402. I-59 exit 65, just nw. Ext/int corridors. **Pets:** Accepted.

▼▼▼ **Residence Inn by Marriott Hattiesburg** H
(601) 264-9202. **$149-$175.** 116 Grand Dr 39401. I-59 exit 65, jct N 40th St, then just w. Int corridors. **Pets:** Accepted.

HOLLY SPRINGS
▼▼ **Econo Lodge** H
(662) 252-5444. **$80-$100.** 100 Brooks Rd 38635. US 78 exit 30, just sw. Int corridors. **Pets:** Accepted.

HORN LAKE
 ▼▼▼▼ **BEST WESTERN PLUS Goodman Inn & Suites** H
(662) 510-6999. **$100-$300.** 6910 Windchase Dr 38637. I-55 exit 289, just w, then just s. Int corridors. **Pets:** Accepted.

▼▼▼ **Comfort Inn** H
(662) 349-3493. **$84-$114.** 801 Desoto Cove 38637. I-55 exit 289, just w, then just n. Int corridors. **Pets:** Small, dogs only. $10 daily fee/pet. Service with restrictions, supervision.

▼▼▼ **Drury Inn & Suites-Memphis South** H
(662) 349-6622. **$130-$199.** 735 Goodman Rd W 38637. I-55 exit 289, just w, then just s. Int corridors. **Pets:** $10 daily fee/room. Service with restrictions, supervision.

▼▼▼ **La Quinta Inn & Suites Horn Lake Southaven** H
(662) 510-6500. **$89-$229.** 721 Southwest Dr 38637. I-55 exit 289, just sw. Int corridors. **Pets:** Large, other species. Service with restrictions.

JACKSON
▲▲▲ ▼▼▼▼ **Fairview Inn** BB ❀
(601) 948-3429. **$179-$449, 3 day notice.** 734 Fairview St 39202. I-55 exit 98A (Woodrow Wilson Ave), 0.8 mi w to State St, 0.4 mi s, then just e. Int corridors. **Pets:** Small, dogs only. $35 daily fee/pet. Designated rooms, service with restrictions, crate.

▲▲▲ ▼▼▼▼ **Hilton Jackson** H ❀
(601) 957-2800. **$99-$179.** 1001 E County Line Rd 39211. I-55 exit 103 (County Line Rd), just e. Int corridors. **Pets:** Large, other species. $75 one-time fee/room. Service with restrictions, supervision.

▼▼ **Quality Inn & Suites Southwest** H
(601) 922-5600. **$65-$110.** 2800 Greenway Dr 39204. I-20 exit 40 eastbound; exit 40A westbound, just se. Ext corridors. **Pets:** Small, dogs only. $15 daily fee/pet. Designated rooms, service with restrictions, supervision.

KOSCIUSKO
▼▼ **Econo Lodge** M
(662) 289-6252. **$59-$64.** 1052 Veterans Memorial Dr 39090. Just sw of jct SR 35 and Natchez Trace Pkwy. Ext corridors. **Pets:** $5 daily fee/pet. Service with restrictions, crate.

LUCEDALE
▼▼▼ **Holiday Inn Express & Suites** H
(601) 947-2099. **Call for rates.** 1287 Beaver Dam Rd 39452. Jct US 98 and SR 63, 1.5 mi se. Int corridors. **Pets:** Accepted.

MCCOMB
▼▼ **Ramada Inn** H
(601) 684-8655. **$90-$120.** 2001 Veterans Blvd 39648. I-55 exit 18, just w. Int corridors. **Pets:** Accepted.

MERIDIAN
▼▼▼ **Baymont Inn & Suites Meridian** H
(601) 483-3315. **$59-$79.** 524 Bonita Lakes Dr 39301. I-20/59 exit 154 southbound; exit 154A northbound, just s. Ext corridors. **Pets:** Accepted.

▼▼▼ **Drury Inn & Suites** H
(601) 483-5570. **$130-$209.** 112 Hwy 11 & 80 N 39301. I-20/59 exit 154, jct US 11/80 N. Int corridors. **Pets:** $10 daily fee/room. Service with restrictions, supervision.

▼▼▼ **Hamilton Inn** H
(601) 693-3210. **$79.** 2219 S Frontage Rd 39301. I-20/59 exit 153, just sw. Ext/int corridors. **Pets:** Accepted.

▼▼ **La Quinta Inn & Suites - Meridian** H
(601) 693-2300. **$79-$189.** 1400 Roebuck Dr 39301. I-20/59 exit 153, just s. Int corridors. **Pets:** Large, other species. Service with restrictions.

▲▲▲ ▼▼▼ **Super 8** M
(601) 482-8088. **$67-$79.** 124 Hwy 11 & 80 E 39301. I-20/59 exit 154 westbound; exit 154B eastbound, on northeast frontage road. Ext corridors. **Pets:** Accepted.

MOSS POINT
▲▲▲ ▼▼▼ **BEST WESTERN Flagship Inn** H
(228) 475-5000. **$70-$100.** 4830 Amoco Dr 39563. I-10 exit 69, just s. Ext corridors. **Pets:** Accepted.

▼▼▼ **Quality Inn** H ❀
(228) 475-2477. **$60-$90.** 6800 Hwy 63 N 39563. I-10 exit 69, just s. Ext corridors. **Pets:** Medium, other species. $15 one-time fee/room. Designated rooms, service with restrictions, crate.

NATCHEZ
▼▼▼ **Hampton Inn & Suites** H
(601) 446-6770. **$129-$249.** 627 S Canal St 39120. US 84/65 exit just before Mississippi River. Int corridors. **Pets:** Medium. $50 one-time fee/room. Service with restrictions, supervision.

OLIVE BRANCH
▼▼ **Candlewood Suites** H
(662) 890-7491. **$89-$149.** 7448 Craft Goodman Rd 38654. US 78 exit 1 westbound, 0.5 mi se; exit 2 (SR 302) eastbound, 1.4 mi ne. Int corridors. **Pets:** $15 daily fee/pet. Designated rooms, service with restrictions, supervision.

▼▼ **Magnolia Inn & Suites** H
(662) 895-4545. **Call for rates.** 6935 W Hamilton Cir 38654. US 78 exit 2 (SR 302), 0.5 mi w. Int corridors. **Pets:** Small, dogs only. $20 daily fee/pet. Designated rooms, service with restrictions, crate.

▼▼ **Whispering Woods Hotel and Conference Center** H
(662) 895-2941. **$79-$109, 3 day notice.** 11200 E Goodman Rd 38654. US 78 exit 2 (SR 302), 3.6 mi e. Int corridors. **Pets:** Accepted.

PASCAGOULA
▼▼ **Super 8** M
(228) 762-9414. **$90-$120, 3 day notice.** 4919 Denny Ave 39581. I-10 exit 69, 3.5 mi s on SR 63, then just w on US 90. Int corridors. **Pets:** Small. $50 deposit/room, $15 one-time fee/pet. Designated rooms, service with restrictions, supervision.

PEARL
▼▼▼ **Candlewood Suites** H
(601) 936-3442. **$89-$99.** 632 S Pearson Rd 39208. I-20 exit 48, just s. Int corridors. **Pets:** Medium. $25 one-time fee/room. Service with restrictions, crate.

▼▼▼ **La Quinta Inn & Suites Jackson Airport** H
(601) 664-0065. **$85-$185.** 501 S Pearson Rd 39208. I-20 exit 48, just s. Int corridors. **Pets:** Large, other species. Service with restrictions.

▼▼ **Ramada Jackson Airport** H
(601) 933-1122. **$60-$80.** 341 Airport Rd 39208. I-20 exit 52, just nw. Int corridors. **Pets:** Medium. $25 one-time fee/room. Service with restrictions, crate.

PHILADELPHIA
▼▼▼ **Dancing Rabbit Inn** H
(601) 389-6600. **Call for rates.** 13240 Hwy 16 W 39350. Jct SR 15, 2 mi w. Int corridors. **Pets:** Accepted.

▼▼▼ **Golden Moon Hotel & Casino** H
(601) 650-1234. **$89-$499, 3 day notice.** 13541 Hwy 16 W 39350. Jct SR 15, 2 mi w. Int corridors. **Pets:** Accepted.

▼▼▼ **Silver Star Hotel & Casino** H
(601) 650-1234. **$89-$499, 3 day notice.** 13540 Hwy 16 W 39350. Jct SR 15, 2 mi w. Int corridors. **Pets:** Accepted.

PICAYUNE
▼▼ **Days Inn** H
(601) 799-1339. **$80-$130.** 450 S Lofton Ave 39466. I-59 exit 4, just nw. Ext corridors. **Pets:** Accepted.

RIDGELAND
▼▼▼ **Drury Inn & Suites Ridgeland-Jackson** H
(601) 956-6100. **$118-$199.** 610 E County Line Rd 39157. I-55 exit 103 (County Line Rd), just w. Int corridors. **Pets:** $10 daily fee/room. Service with restrictions, supervision.

▼▼▼ **Homewood Suites by Hilton** H
(601) 899-8611. **$129-$159.** 853 Centre St 39157. I-55 exit 103 (County Line Rd), just e to Ridgewood Rd, 0.4 mi ne, then just e. Int corridors. **Pets:** Accepted.

AAA ▼▼▼ **Hyatt Place Jackson/Ridgeland** H
(601) 898-8815. **$89-$189.** 1016 Highland Colony Pkwy 39157. I-55 exit 105, just w. Int corridors. **Pets:** Accepted.

▼▼▼ **Residence Inn by Marriott Jackson Ridgeland** H
(601) 206-7755. **$109-$197.** 855 Centre St 39157. I-55 exit 103 (County Line Rd), just e to Ridgewood Rd, then just e. Int corridors. **Pets:** Medium, other species. $75 one-time fee/room. Service with restrictions, supervision.

▼▼▼ **TownePlace Suites by Marriott Jackson Ridgeland/ The Township at Colony Park** H
(601) 898-9880. **Call for rates.** 310 Southlake Ave 39157. I-55 exit 105C (Old Agency Rd), just w, 0.8 mi n on Highland Colony Pkwy, just w on Steed Rd, then just n. Int corridors. **Pets:** Other species. $100 one-time fee/room. Service with restrictions, crate.

RIPLEY
AAA ▼▼▼ **BEST WESTERN Ripley** M
(662) 837-0002. **$75-$83, 3 day notice.** 922 City Ave S 38663. Jct US 4 and 15, 0.5 mi s. Ext corridors. **Pets:** Medium, dogs only. $10 daily fee/pet. Service with restrictions, supervision.

SOUTHAVEN
▼▼ **Magnolia Inn & Suites** H
(662) 280-5555. **$50-$95.** 5069 Pepper Chase Dr 38671. I-55 exit 287, just w. Int corridors. **Pets:** Accepted.

▼▼▼ **Residence Inn by Marriott Memphis Southaven** H
(662) 996-1500. **$114-$186.** 7165 Sleepy Hollow Dr 38671. I-55 exit 289, just e, just n on Southcrest Pkwy, then w on Market Plaza. Int corridors. **Pets:** Accepted.

STARKVILLE
▼▼▼ **Comfort Suites Starkville** H
(662) 324-9595. **$89-$249.** 801 Russell St 39759. 0.5 mi s of jct US 82 and SR 12. Int corridors. **Pets:** Accepted.

▼▼▼ **Hampton Inn** H
(662) 324-1333. **$99-$149.** 700 Hwy 12 E 39759. 1.1 mi sw of jct SR 182. Int corridors. **Pets:** Accepted.

TUNICA
▼ **Key West Inn Tunica** M
(662) 363-0021. **$35-$199.** 11635 Hwy 61 N 38664. US 61, 0.3 mi n of SR 304. Ext corridors. **Pets:** Small. $10 daily fee/pet. Designated rooms, service with restrictions, supervision.

TUPELO *(Restaurants p. 634)*
▼▼▼ **Candlewood Suites Tupelo North** H 🐾
(662) 553-4649. **Call for rates.** 979 N Gloster St 38804. US 45 exit McCullough Blvd, just w, then just s. Int corridors. **Pets:** $50 one-time fee/pet. Service with restrictions, crate.

▼▼ **La Quinta Inn & Suites** H
(662) 847-8000. **$92-$230.** 1013 N Gloster St 38804. On SR 145, just n of McCullough Blvd. Int corridors. **Pets:** Large, other species. Service with restrictions.

▼▼ **Quality Inn Tupelo** M
(662) 842-5100. **$75-$90.** 1190 N Gloster St 38804. Jct McCullough Blvd and SR 145, 1.3 mi s to McCullough Blvd, w to N Gloster St, then 0.3 mi n. Ext corridors. **Pets:** Small, other species. $25 one-time fee/pet. Service with restrictions, crate.

VICKSBURG
▼▼▼ **Anchuca** CI
(601) 661-0111. **$135-$210, 3 day notice.** 1010 1st East St 39183. I-20 exit 4B, 2.2 mi w on Clay St, then 0.4 mi n on Cherry St; in historic downtown. Ext/int corridors. **Pets:** Accepted.

▼▼▼ **Baymont Inn & Suites Vicksburg** H
(601) 619-7799. **$59-$79.** 3975 S Frontage Rd 39180. I-20 exit 4A, on southeast frontage road. Ext corridors. **Pets:** Accepted.

AAA ▼▼▼ **BEST WESTERN Vicksburg** H
(601) 636-5800. **$79-$139.** 2445 N Frontage Rd 39180. I-20 exit 3, just w on NW Frontage Rd. Ext corridors. **Pets:** Medium. $15 daily fee/pet. Service with restrictions, supervision.

▼▼▼ **Candlewood Suites** H
(601) 638-6900. **$89-$139.** 1296 S Frontage Rd 39180. I-20 exit 1C, just s, then just e. Int corridors. **Pets:** Accepted.

AAA ▼▼▼ **Cedar Grove Mansion Inn & Restaurant** CI
(601) 636-1000. **$100-$215, 3 day notice.** 2200 Oak St 39180. I-20 exit 1A, 2.3 mi n on Washington St, then w on Klein St; to gated entrance. Ext/int corridors. **Pets:** Accepted.

▼▼▼ **Corners Mansion Inn, a Bed & Breakfast** BB
(601) 636-7421. **$125-$210, 3 day notice.** 601 Klein St 39180. I-20 exit 1A, 2.3 mi n on Washington St, then just w. Ext/int corridors. **Pets:** Accepted.

WWWW La Quinta Inn & Suites **H**
(601) 802-0525. **$89-$214.** 4160 S Frontage Rd 39180. I-20 exit 4A eastbound; exit 5B westbound, just s. Int corridors. **Pets:** Large, other species. Service with restrictions. 🛗M 🏊 🛜 ✖ 🛎 💻

WW WW Travel Inn **M**
(601) 630-0100. **$45-$100.** 1675 N Frontage Rd 39180. I-20 exit 1C, just ne. Ext corridors. **Pets:** Accepted. 🛜 🛎

WIGGINS
WWWW Hampton Inn & Suites **H**
(601) 528-5255. **$89-$108.** 1121 E Frontage Rd 39577. Jct US 49 and SR 26, 1.2 mi s. Int corridors. **Pets:** Small. Designated rooms, service with restrictions, supervision. 🛗M 🏊 🛜 ✖ 🛎 💻

WINONA
AAA WWWW Holiday Inn Express Inn & Suites Winona North Mississippi **H**
(662) 283-9992. **Call for rates.** 413 SE Frontage Rd 38967. I-55 exit 185, just e, then just s. Int corridors. **Pets:** Accepted.
SAVE 🛗M 🏊 🛜 🛎 💻

MISSOURI

ARNOLD
WWWW Drury Inn & Suites Arnold **H**
(636) 287-3111. **$110-$189.** 3800 SR 141 63010. I-55 exit 191 (SR 141), just e. Int corridors. **Pets:** $10 daily fee/room. Service with restrictions, supervision. 🛗M 🏊 🛜 ✖ 🛎 💻

WW WW Pear Tree Inn Arnold **H**
(636) 296-9600. **$95-$144.** 1201 Drury Ln 63010. I-55 exit 191 (SR 141), just e. Int corridors. **Pets:** $10 daily fee/room. Service with restrictions, supervision. 🏊 🛜 🛎 💻

AVA
WW WW Ava Super 8 **H**
(417) 683-1343. **$75-$135.** 1711 S Jefferson St 65608. 1.8 mi s of jct SR 5, 14 and 76. Int corridors. **Pets:** Accepted. 🛗M 🛜 🛎 💻

BLUE SPRINGS
WWWW Hampton Inn Blue Springs **H**
(816) 220-3844. **$99-$189.** 900 NW South Outer Rd 64015. I-70 exit 20, just s on SR 7, then just w. Int corridors. **Pets:** Other species. Service with restrictions. 🏊 🛜 🛎 💻

BOONVILLE
AAA WW WW Boonville Comfort Inn **H**
(660) 882-5317. **$69-$109.** 2427 Mid America Industrial Dr 65233. I-70 exit 101, just sw. Int corridors. **Pets:** Small. $10 daily fee/pet. Designated rooms, service with restrictions, supervision.
SAVE 🏊 🛜 ✖ 🛎 💻

BRANSON
AAA WW WW Baymont Inn & Suites **H**
(417) 334-1985. **$59-$119.** 1000 W Main St 65616. Just sw of jct US 65 and SR 76 (Country Blvd). Int corridors. **Pets:** Accepted.
SAVE 🏊 🛜 ✖ 🛎 💻

AAA WWWWW BEST WESTERN PLUS Landing View Inn & Suites **H**
(417) 334-6464. **$89-$199.** 403 W Main (Hwy 76) 65616. 0.3 mi e of jct SR 76 (Country Blvd) and US 65. Ext corridors. **Pets:** Accepted.
SAVE 🏊 🛜 🛎 💻

WW WW Branson Plantation Inn **H**
(417) 336-3300. **Call for rates.** 3470 Keeter St 65616. Just sw of jct SR 76 (Country Blvd). Ext corridors. **Pets:** Accepted.
🛗M 🏊 🛜 🛎 💻

AAA WWWWWW Chateau on the Lake Resort & Spa **H**
(417) 334-1161. **$129-$329, 3 day notice.** 415 N State Hwy 265 65616. Just n of jct SR 165. Int corridors. **Pets:** Small, dogs only. $50 one-time fee/room. Designated rooms, service with restrictions, crate.
SAVE 🍴 🛗M 🏊 ✖ 🛜 ✖ 🛎 💻

AAA WW WW Econo Lodge **M**
(417) 336-4849. **$59-$99.** 230 S Wildwood Dr 65616. Just s of jct SR 76 (Country Blvd). Ext corridors. **Pets:** Accepted.
SAVE 🛗M 🏊 🛜 🛎 💻

WW WW Fall Creek Inn & Suites **H** ✿
(417) 348-1683. **$49-$99.** 995 Hwy 165 65616. Jct SR 76 (Country Blvd), 1.5 mi s on SR 165. Ext corridors. **Pets:** Medium, other species. $50 deposit/pet, $15 daily fee/pet. Designated rooms, service with restrictions. SAVE 🏊 🛜 🛎 💻

WWWW Hampton Inn Branson Hills **H**
(417) 243-7800. **$99-$149.** 200 Payne Stewart Dr 65616. 1.5 mi nw of jct US 65 and Branson Hills Pkwy. Int corridors. **Pets:** Accepted.
🛗M 🏊 🛜 ✖ 🛎 💻

AAA WWWWWW Hilton Branson Convention Center Hotel **H** ✿
(417) 336-5400. **$109-$249.** 200 E Main St 65616. Center. Int corridors. **Pets:** Medium, dogs only. $50 daily fee/room. Service with restrictions, supervision. SAVE 🍴 🏊 🍽 🛎 💻

AAA WWWWW Hilton Promenade at Branson Landing **H** ✿
(417) 336-5500. **$99-$229.** 3 Branson Landing 65616. Jct Main St, just e; in Branson Landing Shopping District. Int corridors. **Pets:** Medium, dogs only. $50 daily fee/room. Service with restrictions, supervision. SAVE 🍴 🛗M 🏊 🍽 🛎 💻

AAA WW WW HomeStay Inn Branson **H**
(417) 336-2666. **$49-$89.** 3221 Shepherd of the Hills Expwy 65616. 0.3 mi e of jct SR 76 (Country Blvd). Ext corridors. **Pets:** Accepted.
SAVE 🏊 🛜 ✖ 🛎 💻

AAA WW WW Hotel Grand Victorian **H**
(417) 336-2935. **$70-$229.** 2325 W Hwy 76 (Country Blvd) 65616. 2.3 mi w of jct US 65. Int corridors. **Pets:** Accepted.
SAVE 🏊 ✖ 🛜 ✖ 🛎 💻

WW WW La Quinta Inn **H**
(417) 336-1600. **$50-$250.** 1835 W Hwy 76 65616. 1.6 mi w of jct US 65. Ext/int corridors. **Pets:** Large, other species. Service with restrictions. 🏊 ✖ 🛜 ✖ 🛎 💻

WW WW Lazy Valley Resort **M**
(417) 334-2397. **$69-$250, 49 day notice.** 285 River Ln 65616. Jct SR 76 (Country Blvd), 2.5 mi s on Fall Creek Rd to River Valley Rd. Ext corridors. **Pets:** Small, dogs only. $10 daily fee/pet. Supervision.
🛗M 🏊 ✖ 🦮 🛎 💻

AAA WW WW Ozark Regal Hotel **H**
(417) 336-2200. **$80-$85, 3 day notice.** 3010 Green Mountain Dr 65616. From jct US 65, 2 mi w on SR 76 (Country Blvd), just s. Int corridors. **Pets:** Small, dogs only. $20 one-time fee/pet, $5 daily fee/pet. Designated rooms, service with restrictions, crate. SAVE 🛜 ✖ 🛎

◆◆ **Quality Inn on the Strip** 🄷
(417) 334-1194. **$70-$170.** 2834 W Hwy 76 65616. 2.5 mi w of jct US 65. Ext corridors. **Pets:** Accepted. 🐾 🛜 🛗 🖵

◆◆◆ ◆◆◆◆ **Radisson Hotel Branson** 🄷
(417) 335-5767. **$89-$239.** 120 S Wildwood Dr 65616. Just s of jct SR 76 (Country Blvd). Int corridors. **Pets:** Accepted.
[SAVE] 🍴 ♿ 🐾 ✕ 🛜 ✕ 🛗 🖵

◆◆◆ **Residence Inn by Marriott** 🄷
(417) 336-4077. **$99-$199.** 280 Wildwood Dr S 65616. Just s of jct Green Mountain Dr. Int corridors. **Pets:** Other species. $100 one-time fee/room. Service with restrictions, crate. 🐾 🛜 ✕ 🛗 🖵

◆◆◆ **Thousand Hills Golf Resort** 🄲🄾
(417) 336-5873. **Call for rates.** 245 S Wildwood Dr 65616. 0.5 mi s of jct SR 76 (Country Blvd). Ext corridors. **Pets:** Accepted.
♿ 🐾 ✕ 🛜 ✕ 🛗 🖵

◆◆◆ ◆◆◆◆ **The Village At Indian Point** 🄲🄾
(417) 338-8800. **$140-$300, 31 day notice.** 24 Village Tr 65616. 2.5 mi s of jct SR 76 (Country Blvd) on Indian Point Rd. Ext corridors. **Pets:** Large, dogs only. $15 daily fee/room. Designated rooms, no service, crate. [SAVE] 🐾 ✕ 🛜 ✕ 🛗 🖵

BROOKFIELD

◆◆◆ ◆◆◆ **BEST WESTERN Brookfield** 🄷
(660) 258-4900. **$103-$123.** 28622 Hwy 11 64628. US 36 exit Business Rt 36, just se. Int corridors. **Pets:** Medium, dogs only. $10 daily fee/room. Designated rooms, service with restrictions, crate.
[SAVE] ♿ 🐾 🛜 🛗 🖵

CANTON

◆ **Centerstone Inn Canton** 🄷
(573) 288-8800. **$70-$104, 3 day notice.** 1701 Oak St 63435. US 61 exit US 61 business route/CR P, just e. Int corridors. **Pets:** Accepted.
🐾 ✕ 🛜 🛗 🖵

CAPE GIRARDEAU

◆◆ **Auburn Place Hotel & Suites** 🄷
(573) 651-4486. **Call for rates.** 3265 William St 63701. I-55 exit 96 (William St), just e. Ext/int corridors. **Pets:** Accepted.
♿ 🐾 ✕ 🛜 🛗 🖵

◆◆◆ **Drury Lodge-Cape Girardeau** 🄷
(573) 334-7151. **$90-$144.** 104 S Vantage Dr 63701. I-55 exit 96 (William St), just e. Ext/int corridors. **Pets:** $10 daily fee/room. Service with restrictions, supervision. 🐾 🛜 🛗 🖵

◆◆◆ **Drury Suites-Cape Girardeau** 🄷
(573) 339-9500. **$130-$154.** 3303 Campster Dr 63701. I-55 exit 96 (William St), just w. Int corridors. **Pets:** $10 daily fee/room. Service with restrictions, supervision. ♿ 🐾 🛜 ✕ 🛗 🖵

◆◆◆ **Hampton Inn-Cape Girardeau** 🄷
(573) 651-3000. **$109-$144.** 103 Cape W Pkwy 63701. I-55 exit 96 (William St), 0.3 mi sw. Int corridors. **Pets:** Accepted.
♿ 🛜 ✕ 🛗 🖵

◆ **Pear Tree Inn by Drury-Cape Girardeau** 🄷
(573) 334-3000. **$74-$124.** 3248 William St 63701. I-55 exit 96 (William St), just e. Int corridors. **Pets:** $10 daily fee/room. Service with restrictions, supervision. 🐾 🛜 🖵

CARTHAGE

◆◆◆ ◆◆◆ **BEST WESTERN Precious Moments Hotel** 🄷
(417) 359-5900. **$69-$89.** 2701 Hazel St 64836. Just e of jct US 71 and SR HH. Int corridors. **Pets:** Medium, dogs only. $10 daily fee/pet. Designated rooms, service with restrictions, crate.
[SAVE] 🐾 🛜 ✕ 🛗 🖵

◆◆ **Econo Lodge** 🄷
(417) 358-3900. **$60-$250.** 1441 W Central Ave 64836. I-49 exit 53, just ne. Ext/int corridors. **Pets:** Accepted. 🐾 🛜 🛗

CHESTERFIELD

◆◆◆ **Drury Plaza Hotel-Chesterfield** 🄷
(636) 532-3300. **$115-$239.** 355 Chesterfield Center E 63017. I-64/US 40 exit 19B (Clarkson Rd/Olive Blvd), just s on Clarkson Rd, then just w. Int corridors. **Pets:** $10 daily fee/room. Service with restrictions, supervision. 🍴 ♿ 🐾 🛜 ✕ 🛗 🖵

◆◆◆ **Hampton Inn-Chesterfield** 🄷
(636) 537-2500. **$99-$159.** 16201 Swingley Ridge Rd 63017. I-64/US 40 exit 19B (Clarkson Rd/Olive Blvd), just n on Olive Blvd, then just w. Int corridors. **Pets:** Accepted. 🐾 🛜 ✕ 🛗 🖵

◆◆◆ **Homewood Suites by Hilton** 🄷
(636) 530-0305. **$99-$189.** 840 Chesterfield Pkwy W 63017. I-64/US 40 exit 19B (Clarkson Rd/Olive Blvd), 0.5 mi n on Olive Blvd, then just w. Int corridors. **Pets:** Accepted. 🐾 🛜 🛗 🖵

◆◆◆ ◆◆◆ **Hyatt Place St. Louis/Chesterfield** 🄷
(636) 536-6262. **$79-$259.** 333 Chesterfield Center E 63017. I-64/US 40 exit 19B (Clarkson Rd/Olive Blvd), just s on Clarkson Rd, then just w. Int corridors. **Pets:** Accepted. [SAVE] 🍴 ♿ 🛜 ✕ 🛗 🖵

CLAYTON

◆◆◆ **Crowne Plaza St. Louis-Clayton** 🄷
(314) 726-5400. **$99-$210.** 7750 Carondelet Ave 63105. I-64/US 40 exit 31B (Brentwood/Hanley Rd), 1.3 mi n on Hanley Rd, then just w. Int corridors. **Pets:** Accepted. 🍴 🐾 ✕ 🛜 ✕ 🛗 🖵

◆◆◆ ◆◆◆◆ **The Ritz-Carlton, St. Louis** 🄷
(314) 863-6300. **$239-$499.** 100 Carondelet Plaza 63105. I-64/US 40 exit 31B (Brentwood/Hanley Rd), 1.2 mi n on Hanley Rd, then just e. Int corridors. **Pets:** Accepted. [SAVE] 🍴 🐾 🛜 ✕ 🛗 🖵

◆◆◆ ◆◆◆ **Sheraton Clayton Plaza Hotel** 🄷
(314) 863-0400. **$99-$329.** 7730 Bonhomme Ave 63105. I-64/US 40 exit 31B (Brentwood/Hanley Rd), 1.2 mi n on Hanley Rd, then just w. Int corridors. **Pets:** Accepted. [SAVE] 🍴 🐾 🛜 ✕ 🛗 🖵

COLUMBIA

◆◆◆ **Drury Inn-Columbia** 🄷
(573) 445-1800. **$120-$199.** 1000 Knipp St 65203. I-70 exit 124 (Stadium Blvd), just s. Int corridors. **Pets:** $10 daily fee/room. Service with restrictions, supervision. 🐾 🛜 ✕ 🛗 🖵

◆◆◆ **Holiday Inn Executive Center** 🄷 🐾
(573) 445-8531. **$112-$300.** 2200 I-70 Dr SW 65203. I-70 exit 124 (Stadium Blvd), just w. Int corridors. **Pets:** $30 one-time fee/room. Designated rooms, service with restrictions, supervision.
🍴 ♿ 🐾 🛜 🛗 🖵

◆◆ **Ramada** 🄷
(573) 443-4141. **$59-$129.** 901 Conley Rd 65201. I-70 exit 128A (US 63), just sw. Int corridors. **Pets:** Medium. $15 deposit/pet, $15 one-time fee/pet. Designated rooms, no service, supervision.
♿ 🐾 🛜 ✕ 🛗 🖵

◆◆◆ ◆◆◆ **Residence Inn by Marriott** 🄷
(573) 442-5601. **$149-$164.** 1100 Woodland Springs Ct 65202. I-70 exit 128A (US 63), just n, then 0.4 mi e. Int corridors. **Pets:** Accepted.
[SAVE] ♿ 🐾 🛜 ✕ 🛗 🖵

◆◆◆ ◆◆◆ **Staybridge Suites** 🄷
(573) 442-8600. **$99-$189.** 805 N Keene St 65201. I-70 exit 128A (US 63), just w to N Keene St, then just s. Int corridors. **Pets:** Other species. $50 one-time fee/pet. Service with restrictions, crate.
[SAVE] ♿ 🐾 🛜 🛗 🖵

▼▼▼▼ **Stoney Creek Hotel & Conference Center** 🅷
(573) 442-6400. **$109-$179, 3 day notice.** 2601 S Providence Rd 65203. I-70 exit 126 (Providence Rd), 3 mi s; on west outer road. Int corridors. **Pets:** Accepted. 🔁 ⊠ 📶 ✕ 🛗 💻

▼▼ **Super 8 Columbia Clark Lane** Ⓜ
(573) 474-8488. **$63-$180.** 3216 Clark Ln 65202. I-70 exit 128A (US 63); northeast corner. Int corridors. **Pets:** Accepted. 📶 🛗 💻

CREVE COEUR
▼▼▼▼ **Drury Inn & Suites-Creve Coeur** 🅷
(314) 989-1100. **$90-$179.** 11980 Olive Blvd 63141. I-270 exit 14 (Olive Blvd), just e. Int corridors. **Pets:** $10 daily fee/room. Service with restrictions, supervision. 🅼 🔁 📶 ✕ 🛗 💻

CUBA
🅰🅰🅰 ▼▼▼ **BEST WESTERN Cuba Inn** Ⓜ
(573) 885-7707. **Call for rates.** 246 Hwy P 65453. I-44 exit 208 (SR 19), just n, then just e. Ext corridors. **Pets:** Accepted.
SAVE 🔁 📶 🛗 💻

▼▼ ▼▼ **Super 8** 🅷
(573) 885-2087. **$67-$122.** 28 Hwy P 65453. I-44 exit 208 (SR 19), just n, then just w. Ext/int corridors. **Pets:** $15 one-time fee/pet. Designated rooms, service with restrictions, supervision. 📶 🛗 💻

EARTH CITY
▼▼ ▼▼ **Candlewood Suites St. Louis** 🅷
(314) 770-2744. **$70-$200.** 3250 Rider Tr S 63045. I-70 exit 231B (Earth City Expwy), just n, then just e. Int corridors. **Pets:** Accepted.
📶 🛗 💻

▼▼▼▼ **Residence Inn by Marriott St. Louis Airport/Earth City** 🅷
(314) 209-0995. **$94-$159.** 3290 Rider Tr S 63045. I-70 exit 231B (Earth City Expwy), just n, then just e. Int corridors. **Pets:** Accepted.
🅼 🔁 📶 ✕ 🛗 💻

EDMUNDSON
▼▼▼ **Drury Inn-St. Louis Airport** 🅷
(314) 423-7700. **$90-$179.** 10490 Natural Bridge Rd 63134. I-70 exit 236 (Lambert Airport), just s, then just e. Int corridors. **Pets:** $10 daily fee/room. Service with restrictions, supervision.
🅼 🔁 📶 ✕ 🛗 💻

🅰🅰🅰 ▼▼▼▼ **Marriott-St. Louis Airport** 🅷
(314) 423-9700. **$79-$409.** 10700 Pear Tree Ln 63134. I-70 exit 236 (Lambert Airport), just s. Int corridors. **Pets:** Accepted.
SAVE 🍽 🔁 🐾 ✕ 🛗 💻

EUREKA
▼▼▼ **Holiday Inn at Six Flags** 🅷 🐾
(636) 938-6661. **$99-$184, 3 day notice.** 4901 Six Flags Rd 63025. I-44 exit 261 (Allenton Rd), just e. Ext/int corridors. **Pets:** Other species. $25 daily fee/room. Service with restrictions, crate.
🍽 🔁 ⊠ 📶 🛗 💻

EXCELSIOR SPRINGS
🅰🅰🅰 ▼▼▼▼ **The Elms Hotel & Spa** 🅷
(816) 630-5500. **$149-$189, 3 day notice.** 401 Regent St 64024. Off SR 10; at Elms Blvd. Int corridors. **Pets:** Accepted.
SAVE 🍽 ⊠ 📶 🛗 💻

FENTON
▼▼▼▼ **Drury Inn & Suites-Fenton** 🅷
(636) 343-1842. **$115-$184.** 1088 S Highway Dr 63026. I-44 exit 274A eastbound, just e; exit 274 westbound, just s on Bowles Ave, then just e. Int corridors. **Pets:** $10 daily fee/room. Service with restrictions, supervision. 🔁 📶 ✕ 🛗 💻

▼▼ ▼▼ **Pear Tree Inn by Drury-Fenton** 🅷
(636) 343-8820. **$82-$144.** 1100 S Highway Dr 63026. I-44 exit 274A eastbound, just e; exit 274 westbound, just s on Bowles Ave, then just e. Int corridors. **Pets:** $10 daily fee/room. Service with restrictions, supervision. 🔁 📶 🛗 💻

▼▼ ▼▼ **TownePlace Suites by Marriott** 🅷
(636) 305-7000. **$99-$139.** 1662 Fenton Business Park Ct 63026. I-44 exit 275 westbound, 0.5 mi ne on Soccer Park Rd, 0.7 mi nw on Rudder Rd, then just s; exit 274B eastbound, 1 mi e on S Highway Dr, just sw on Rudder Rd, then just s. Int corridors. **Pets:** Accepted.
🅼 🔁 📶 ✕ 🛗 💻

FESTUS
▼▼ ▼▼ **Drury Inn-Festus** 🅷
(636) 933-2400. **$105-$159.** 1001 Veterans Blvd 63028. I-55 exit 175, just e on Route A. Int corridors. **Pets:** $10 daily fee/room. Service with restrictions, supervision. 🔁 📶 🛗 💻

FULTON
▼▼▼▼ **Loganberry Inn Bed & Breakfast** 🅱🅱 🐾
(573) 642-9229. **$109-$199, 14 day notice.** 310 W 7th St 65251. Jct US 54 exit CR F, 1 mi e, just n to Westminster Ave, then just e. Int corridors. **Pets:** Medium, dogs only. $15 one-time fee/room. Designated rooms, service with restrictions. 📶 ✕ 🐾 🛗 💻

HANNIBAL
🅰🅰🅰 ▼▼▼▼ **Quality Inn & Suites** 🅷
(573) 221-4001. **$99-$139.** 120 Lindsey Dr 63401. 2 mi w on US 36 exit Shinn Ln to south service road, then 0.6 mi e. Int corridors. **Pets:** Medium. $20 daily fee/pet. Designated rooms, service with restrictions, supervision. SAVE 🔁 ⊠ 📶 🛗 💻

▼▼▼ **Super 8** Ⓜ
(573) 221-5863. **$56-$95.** 120 Huckleberry Heights Dr 63401. Jct US 36, 1.5 mi s on US 61. Int corridors. **Pets:** $15 daily fee/pet. Designated rooms, no service, crate. 🔁 📶 🛗 💻

HAYTI
▼▼▼ **Drury Inn & Suites Hayti/Caruthersville** 🅷
(573) 359-2702. **$105-$159.** 1317 Hwy 84 63851. I-55 exit 19 (US 412/SR 84), just w. Int corridors. **Pets:** $10 daily fee/room. Service with restrictions, supervision. 🔁 📶 🛗 💻

HERMANN
▼▼▼ **Hermann Hill** 🅱🅱 🐾
(573) 486-4455. **$204-$582, 10 day notice.** 711 Wein St 65041. SR 19 (Market St), just w on W 6th St, just s on Washington St, then 0.3 mi w on W 10th St. Ext/int corridors. **Pets:** Medium, dogs only. $50 one-time fee/room. Designated rooms, supervision. 📶 ✕ 🛗 💻

HOLLISTER
🅰🅰🅰 ▼▼▼▼ **Westgate Branson Lakes at Emerald Pointe** 🅲🅾
(417) 334-4944. **Call for rates.** 750 Emerald Pointe Dr 65672. Jct US 65 and SR 265, 1 mi w to Hill Haven Rd, then 2 mi s. Ext corridors. **Pets:** Medium. $100 deposit/room, $170 one-time fee/room. Designated rooms, service with restrictions, supervision.
SAVE 🅼 🔁 ⊠ 📶 ✕ 🛗 💻

INDEPENDENCE
🅰🅰🅰 ▼▼▼ **BEST WESTERN Truman Inn** 🅷
(816) 254-0100. **$70-$150.** 4048 S Lynn Court Dr 64055. I-70 exit 12, just n on Noland Rd, then just w. Ext corridors. **Pets:** Medium. $50 deposit/room, $10 daily fee/pet. Service with restrictions, crate.
SAVE 🔁 📶 🛗 💻

▼▼▼ **Comfort Suites-Independence** 🅷 🐾
(816) 373-9880. **$104-$144.** 19751 E Valley View Pkwy 64057. I-70 exit 17 (Little Blue Pkwy), just s, then just w. Int corridors. **Pets:** $25 one-time fee/pet. Designated rooms, no service.
🅼 🔁 📶 ✕ 🛗 💻

▼▼▼▼ Drury Inn & Suites Kansas City-Independence 🅷

(816) 795-9393. **$100-$200.** 20300 E 42nd St S 64015. I-70 exit 17 (Little Blue Pkwy), just s. Int corridors. **Pets:** $10 daily fee/room. Service with restrictions, supervision. 🅔🅜 ➤ 🛜 ✕ 🛏 🖵

⨁⨁ ▼▼▼▼ Holiday Inn Express & Suites-Independence/ Kansas City 🅷 🐾

(816) 795-8889. **Call for rates.** 19901 E Valley View Pkwy 64057. I-70 exit 17 (Little Blue Pkwy), just s, then just w. Int corridors. **Pets:** Other species. $25 one-time fee/room. Service with restrictions, supervision.

🆂🅰🆅🅴 🅔🅜 ➤ 🛜 ✕ 🛏 🖵

JACKSON

▼▼▼▼ Drury Inn & Suites-Jackson, MO 🅷

(573) 243-9200. **$100-$174.** 225 Drury Ln 63755. I-55 exit 105 (SR 61), just w. Int corridors. **Pets:** $10 daily fee/room. Service with restrictions, supervision. 🅔🅜 ➤ 🛜 🛏 🖵

JANE

▼▼ Booneslick Lodge 🅷

(417) 226-1888. **$56-$70.** 21140 US Hwy 71 64856. Just s on US 71. Int corridors. **Pets:** Accepted. ➤ 🛜 🛏 🖵

JEFFERSON CITY

▼▼▼▼ Capitol Plaza Hotel & Convention Center 🅷

(573) 635-1234. **$83-$169.** 415 W McCarty St 65101. On US 50 and 63 S, just e of jct US 54. Int corridors. **Pets:** Medium, dogs only. $25 one-time fee/pet. Service with restrictions, crate.

🍴 🅔🅜 ➤ 🛜 ✕ 🛏 🖵

▼▼▼ Oak Tree Inn Jefferson City 🅷

(573) 636-5456. **Call for rates.** 1710 Jefferson St 65110. US 54 exit Ellis Blvd, 0.3 mi nw on frontage road. Int corridors. **Pets:** Service with restrictions, supervision. 🛜 ✕ 🛏 🖵

JOPLIN

⨁⨁ ▼▼▼ BEST WESTERN Oasis Inn & Suites 🅷

(417) 781-6776. **$69-$129.** 3508 S Range Line Rd 64804. I-44 exit 8, just nw. Ext corridors. **Pets:** Accepted. 🆂🅰🆅🅴 ➤ 🛜 🛏 🖵

⨁⨁ ▼▼▼▼ Candlewood Suites 🅷

(417) 623-9595. **$89-$139.** 3512 S Range Line Rd 64804. I-44 exit 8, just nw. Int corridors. **Pets:** $75 one-time fee/room. Designated rooms, service with restrictions, supervision. 🆂🅰🆅🅴 🅔🅜 ➤ 🛜 🛏 🖵

▼▼▼▼ Drury Inn & Suites-Joplin 🅷

(417) 781-8000. **$120-$199.** 3601 S Range Line Rd 64804. I-44 exit 8, just ne. Int corridors. **Pets:** $10 daily fee/room. Service with restrictions, supervision. 🅔🅜 ➤ 🛜 🛏 🖵

▼▼▼▼ Holiday Inn and Convention Center Joplin 🅷

(417) 782-1000. **Call for rates.** 3615 S Range Line Rd 64804. I-44 exit 8B, just ne. Int corridors. **Pets:** Accepted. 🍴 ➤ 🛜 ✕ 🛏 🖵

▼▼▼▼ Homewood Suites by Hilton 🅷

(417) 623-1900. **Call for rates.** 2642 E 32nd St 64804. I-44 exit 8B, just w of US 71 business route (Range Line Rd). Int corridors. **Pets:** Accepted. 🅔🅜 🛜 🛏 🖵

▼▼▼▼ La Quinta Inn & Suites Joplin 🅷

(417) 781-0500. **$79-$289.** 3320 S Range Line Rd 64804. I-44 exit 8B, just n. Int corridors. **Pets:** Large, other species. Service with restrictions. 🍴 ➤ 🛜 ✕ 🛏 🖵

▼▼▼▼ Residence Inn by Marriott-Joplin 🅷 🐾

(417) 782-0908. **$149-$169.** 3128 E Hammons Blvd 64804. I-44 exit 8, just ne. Int corridors. **Pets:** Medium, other species. $75 one-time fee/room. Service with restrictions. 🅔🅜 ➤ 🛜 ✕ 🛏 🖵

▼▼ Sleep Inn 🅷

(417) 782-1212. **$95.** 4100 Hwy 43 S 64803. I-44 exit 4, just s. Int corridors. **Pets:** Accepted. 🛜 🖵

⨁⨁ ▼▼▼▼ TownePlace Suites by Marriott Joplin 🅷

(417) 659-8111. **$124-$136.** 4026 Arizona Ave 64804. I-44 exit 8, just sw. Int corridors. **Pets:** Large, other species. $25 one-time fee/pet. Service with restrictions. 🆂🅰🆅🅴 🅔🅜 ➤ 🛜 ✕ 🛏 🖵

KANSAS CITY *(Restaurants p. 634)* .

⨁⨁ ▼▼▼ ▼▼▼ The Ambassador Kansas City, Autograph Collection 🅷 🐾

(816) 298-7700. **$189-$229.** 1111 Grand Blvd 64106. Jct 11th St, southeast corner. Int corridors. **Pets:** Small, dogs only. $50 one-time fee/pet. Designated rooms, service with restrictions, supervision.

🆂🅰🆅🅴 🍴 🅔🅜 🛜 ✕ 🛏 🖵

⨁⨁ ▼▼▼ BEST WESTERN Country Inn-North Ⓜ

(816) 459-7222. **$56-$190.** 2633 NE 43rd St 64117. I-35 exit 8C (Antioch Rd), just s on SR 1, then just e. Ext corridors. **Pets:** Accepted. 🆂🅰🆅🅴 🍴 ➤ 🛜 🛏 🖵

⨁⨁ ▼▼▼ BEST WESTERN PLUS Seville Plaza Hotel 🅷 🐾

(816) 561-9600. **$95-$125, 3 day notice.** 4309 Main St 64111. Jct 43rd St, just s. Int corridors. **Pets:** Medium, dogs only. $15 daily fee/pet. Designated rooms, service with restrictions, supervision. 🆂🅰🆅🅴 🅔🅜 🛜 ✕ 🛏 🖵

▼▼▼▼ Candlewood Suites Kansas City Airport 🅷

(816) 886-9700. **$89-$139.** 11110 NW Ambassador Dr 64153. I-29 exit 12, just se. Int corridors. **Pets:** Medium. $20 daily fee/pet. Service with restrictions, crate. 🅔🅜 🛜 🛏 🖵

▼▼▼▼ Candlewood Suites Kansas City Northeast 🅷

(816) 886-9311. **Call for rates.** 4450 N Randolph Rd 64117. I-435 exit 54, just s. Int corridors. **Pets:** Accepted. ➤ 🛜 🛏 🖵

▼▼▼▼ Chase Suite Hotel 🅷

(816) 891-9009. **Call for rates.** 9900 NW Prairie View Rd 64153. I-29 exit 10, just w, then just n. Ext corridors. **Pets:** Accepted.

➤ 🛜 ✕ 🛏 🖵

▼▼▼▼ Drury Inn & Suites-Kansas City Airport 🅷

(816) 880-9700. **$105-$209.** 7900 NW Tiffany Springs Pkwy 64153. I-29 exit 10, just w. Int corridors. **Pets:** $10 daily fee/room. Service with restrictions, supervision. 🅔🅜 ➤ 🛜 🛏 🖵

▼▼▼▼ Drury Inn & Suites-Kansas City Stadium 🅷

(816) 923-3000. **$130-$194.** 3830 Blue Ridge Cutoff 64133. I-70 exit 9 (Blue Ridge Cutoff), just nw. Int corridors. **Pets:** $10 daily fee/room. Service with restrictions, supervision. 🅔🅜 ➤ 🛜 ✕ 🛏 🖵

▼▼▼▼ Embassy Suites Kansas City-International Airport 🅷

(816) 891-7788. **$109-$239.** 7640 NW Tiffany Springs Pkwy 64153. I-29 exit 10, just e. Int corridors. **Pets:** Large. $75 one-time fee/room. Service with restrictions, crate. 🍴 🅔🅜 ➤ 🍽 🛏 🖵

▼▼ Fairfield Inn & Suites by Marriott Kansas City North Near Worlds of Fun 🅷

(816) 452-6212. **$79-$159.** 4231 N Corrington Ave 64117. I-435 exit 54 northbound, just w on Parvin Rd; exit southbound, 1 mi s on service road, just w on Parvin Rd, then just n. Int corridors. **Pets:** Accepted.

🅔🅜 ➤ 🛜 ✕ 🛏 🖵

⨁⨁ ▼▼▼▼ Holiday Inn Country Club Plaza 🅷

(816) 753-7400. **$99-$209.** 1 E 45th St 64111. Jct Main St; in Country Club Plaza. Int corridors. **Pets:** Other species. $25 one-time fee/pet. Designated rooms, service with restrictions, supervision.

🆂🅰🆅🅴 🍴 🅔🅜 ➤ 🛜 ✕ 🛏 🖵

◬ ▽▽▽▽ Holiday Inn Kansas City Northeast 🅷
(816) 455-1060. **Call for rates.** 7333 NE Parvin Rd 64117. I-435 exit 54, just w. Int corridors. **Pets:** Accepted.
[SAVE] [🍴][🔥M][🏊][✕][📶][✕][🛄][💻]

◬ ▽▽▽▽ Holiday Inn KCI Airport & KCI Expo Center 🅷
(816) 801-8400. **$79-$169.** 11728 NW Ambassador Dr 64153. I-29 exit 13, just e on CR D, then just s. Int corridors. **Pets:** Small, other species. $25 deposit/room. Designated rooms, service with restrictions, supervision. [SAVE] [🍴][🔥M][🏊][📶][✕][🛄][💻]

▽▽▽ Homewood Suites by Hilton Kansas City Airport 🅷
(816) 880-9880. **$99-$229.** 7312 NW Polo Rd 64153. I-29 exit 10, just e. Int corridors. **Pets:** Other species. $75 one-time fee/room. Service with restrictions. [🏊][📶][🛄][💻]

▽▽▽▽ Hotel Phillips 🅷 🐾
(816) 221-7000. **$109-$299, 3 day notice.** 106 W 12th St 64105. Jct Wyandotte St, just e. Int corridors. **Pets:** Small. $50 one-time fee/room. Designated rooms, service with restrictions, crate. [🍴][📶][✕][💻]

◬ ▽▽▽▽ Hyatt Place Kansas City/Airport 🅷
(816) 891-0871. **$74-$199.** 7600 NW 97th Terr 64153. I-29 exit 10, just sw. Int corridors. **Pets:** Accepted. [SAVE][🏊][📶][✕][🛄][💻]

◬ ▽▽▽▽ The InterContinental Kansas City at the Plaza 🅷
(816) 756-1500. **Call for rates.** 401 Ward Pkwy 64112. Jct Wornall Rd; in Country Club Plaza. Int corridors. **Pets:** Accepted.
[SAVE][🍴][🏊][✕][📶][✕][🛄][💻]

▽▽▽▽ Residence Inn by Marriott Downtown/Union Hill 🅷
(816) 561-3000. **$123-$199.** 2975 Main St 64108. Jct 31st St, just n. Ext corridors. **Pets:** Accepted. [ECO][🏊][📶][✕][🛄][💻]

▽▽▽▽ Residence Inn by Marriott, Kansas City Airport 🅷
(816) 741-2300. **$179-$199.** 10300 N Ambassador Dr 64153. I-29 exit 10, 1.5 mi ne. Int corridors. **Pets:** Other species. $100 one-time fee/room. Service with restrictions, crate.
[🍴][🔥M][🏊][📶][✕][🛄][💻]

▽▽▽▽ Residence Inn by Marriott Kansas City Country Club Plaza 🅷
(816) 753-0033. **$125-$265.** 4601 Broadway Blvd 64112. Jct J.C. Nichols Pkwy, just w on 46th Terr; in Country Club Plaza. Int corridors. **Pets:** Medium. $100 one-time fee/room. Designated rooms, service with restrictions, supervision. [🏊][📶][✕][🛄][💻]

◬ ▽▽▽▽ The Sheraton Kansas City Hotel at Crown Center 🅷
(816) 841-1000. **$119-$329.** 2345 McGee St 64108. In Crown Center area. Int corridors. **Pets:** Accepted.
[SAVE][ECO][🍴][🔥M][🏊][📶][✕][🛄][💻]

◬ ▽▽▽▽ Sheraton Suites Country Club Plaza 🅷
(816) 931-4400. **$149-$329.** 770 W 47th St 64112. Jct Summit St; in Country Club Plaza. Int corridors. **Pets:** Accepted.
[SAVE][🍴][🔥M][🏊][📶][✕][🛄][💻]

◬ ▽▽▽▽ The Westin Kansas City at Crown Center 🅷 🐾
(816) 474-4400. **$129-$339.** 1 E Pershing Rd 64108. 0.5 mi s. Int corridors. **Pets:** Large. $25 one-time fee/pet. Service with restrictions, supervision. [SAVE][🍴][🔥M][🏊][✕][📶][✕][🛄][💻]

KEARNEY

▽▽▽▽ Kearney Super 8 🅷
(816) 628-6800. **$63-$113.** 210 Platte Clay Way 64060. I-35 exit 26, just e on SR 92, then just n. Int corridors. **Pets:** Accepted.
[🍴][🏊][📶][🛄][💻]

KIRKSVILLE

▽ Super 8-Kirksville 🅷
(660) 665-8826. **$56-$95.** 1101 Country Club Dr 63501. On US 63 and SR 6. Int corridors. **Pets:** Other species. $10 daily fee/pet. Service with restrictions, crate. [📶][🛄][💻]

KIRKWOOD

◬ ▽▽▽ BEST WESTERN Kirkwood Inn 🅷 🐾
(314) 821-3950. **$109-$139.** 1200 S Kirkwood Rd 63122. I-44 exit 277B (Lindbergh Blvd), just n. Int corridors. **Pets:** $10 daily fee/pet. Designated rooms, service with restrictions, crate.
[SAVE][🍴][🏊][📶][✕][🛄][💻]

LAMAR

▽▽ Super 8-Lamar 🅷
(417) 682-6888. **$60-$100.** 45 SE 1st Ln 64759. I-49 exit 77, just ne. Ext/int corridors. **Pets:** Accepted. [🏊][📶][🛄][💻]

LEBANON

▽▽▽ Super 8 🅷
(417) 588-2574. **$70-$85.** 1831 W Elm St 65536. I-44 exit 127, just n. Int corridors. **Pets:** Accepted. [🏊][📶][🛄][💻]

LICKING

▽ Scenic Rivers Inn 🅼
(573) 674-4809. **$65-$75.** 209 S Hwy 63 65542. On US 63. Ext corridors. **Pets:** Small, dogs only. $10 daily fee/pet. Service with restrictions, supervision. [🏊][📶][🛄][💻]

MACON

▽▽ Super 8 🅷
(660) 385-5788. **$65-$100.** 203 E Briggs Dr 63552. Jct US 36 and 63. Int corridors. **Pets:** Accepted. [📶][✕][🛄][💻]

MARSHFIELD

▽▽▽ Holiday Inn Express 🅷
(417) 859-6000. **$85-$105.** 1301 Banning St 65706. I-44 exit 100 (SR 38), just se. Int corridors. **Pets:** Other species. $25 one-time fee/room. Designated rooms, service with restrictions, supervision.
[🔥M][🏊][📶][🛄][💻]

MARYLAND HEIGHTS

◬ ▽▽▽▽ Comfort Inn Westport 🅷
(314) 878-1400. **$85-$150.** 12031 Lackland Rd 63146. I-270 exit 16A (Page Ave), just e to Lackland Rd, then just w. Int corridors. **Pets:** Medium. $10 daily fee/pet. Designated rooms, service with restrictions, crate. [SAVE][🍴][🔥M][🏊][📶][✕][🛄][💻]

◬ ▽▽▽▽ DoubleTree by Hilton Hotel St. Louis-Westport 🅷
(314) 434-0100. **$99-$329.** 1973 Craigshire Rd 63146. I-270 exit 16A (Page Ave), just e, then 0.4 mi s on Concourse Dr, just w on Lackland Rd, then just w. Int corridors. **Pets:** Accepted.
[SAVE][ECO][🍴][🔥M][🏊][📶][✕][🛄][💻]

▽▽▽▽ Drury Inn & Suites-St. Louis-Westport 🅷
(314) 576-9966. **$105-$189.** 12220 Dorsett Rd 63043. I-270 exit 17 (Dorsett Rd), just e. Int corridors. **Pets:** $10 daily fee/room. Service with restrictions, supervision. [🏊][📶][🛄][💻]

◬ ▽▽▽▽ Hollywood Casino & Hotel 🅷
(314) 770-8100. **$89-$559.** 777 Casino Center Dr 63043. I-70 exit 231A (Earth City Expwy S), 1 mi s, then 1.2 mi nw. Int corridors.
Pets: Accepted. [SAVE][🍴][🔥M][📶][🛄][💻]

WWW **Residence Inn by Marriott-Westport** H

(314) 469-0060. **$124-$159.** 1881 Craigshire Rd 63146. I-270 exit 16A (Page Ave), just e, just s on Concourse Dr, just s on Craig Rd, then just w. Ext corridors. **Pets:** Accepted.

WWW **Sheraton Westport Lakeside Chalet** H

(314) 878-1500. **Call for rates.** 191 Westport Plaza Dr 63146. I-270 exit 16A (Page Ave), just e, just s on Concourse Dr, just w on Lackland Rd, then 0.4 mi n. Int corridors. **Pets:** Accepted.

WWW **Sheraton Westport Plaza Tower** H

(314) 878-1500. **Call for rates.** 900 Westport Plaza 63146. I-270 exit 16A (Page Ave), just e, just s on Concourse Dr, just w on Lackland Rd, then 0.4 mi n. Int corridors. **Pets:** Accepted.

WWW **Sonesta ES Suites St. Louis** H

(314) 878-1555. **Call for rates.** 1855 Craigshire Rd 63146. I-270 exit 16A (Page Ave), just e, just s on Concourse Dr, just s on Craig Rd, then just w. Ext/int corridors. **Pets:** Accepted.

MARYVILLE

WW **Americas Best Value Inn** H

(660) 582-8088. **$52-$62.** 222 E Summit Dr 64468. On Business Rt US 71; just n of US 71 Bypass. Int corridors. **Pets:** Service with restrictions, supervision.

WW **Comfort Inn** H

(660) 562-2002. **$85-$100.** 2817 S Main St 64468. On Business Rt US 71; just n of US 71 Bypass. Int corridors. **Pets:** Small, dogs only. Designated rooms, service with restrictions, supervision.

MEHLVILLE

WWW **BEST WESTERN St. Louis Inn** H

(314) 416-7639. **$75-$89, 3 day notice.** 6224 Heimos Industrial Park Dr 63129. I-55 exit 193, just e on Meramec Bottom Rd, then just n. Int corridors. **Pets:** Medium. $12 daily fee/pet. Designated rooms, service with restrictions, crate.

MINER

WWW **Drury Inn & Suites-Sikeston** H

(573) 472-2299. **$120-$179.** 2608 E Malone Ave 63801. I-55 exit 67, just nw. Int corridors. **Pets:** $10 daily fee/room. Service with restrictions, supervision.

WW **Pear Tree Inn by Drury** H

(573) 471-4100. **$92-$149.** 2602 E Malone Ave 63801. I-55 exit 67, just nw. Int corridors. **Pets:** $10 daily fee/room. Service with restrictions, supervision.

O'FALLON

WWW **Staybridge Suites O'Fallon** H

(636) 300-0999. **Call for rates.** 1155 Technology Dr 63368. US 40/61 exit 9 (CR K), just nw. Int corridors. **Pets:** Accepted.

OSAGE BEACH

W **Scottish Inns** M

(573) 348-3123. **$50-$95, 3 day notice.** 5404 Osage Beach Pkwy 65065. US 54 exit Case Rd, just s. Ext/int corridors. **Pets:** Small. $10 daily fee/pet. Designated rooms, service with restrictions, crate.

PACIFIC

WW **Quality Inn Near Six Flags** H

(636) 257-8400. **$69-$109.** 1400 W Osage St 63069. I-44 exit 257, just se. Ext/int corridors. **Pets:** Accepted.

PERRYVILLE

WW **Days Inn** M

(573) 547-1091. **$72-$99.** 1500 Liberty St 63775. I-55 exit 129 (SR 51). Int corridors. **Pets:** Small, dogs only. $10 daily fee/pet. Designated rooms, service with restrictions, supervision.

PLATTE CITY

WWW **BEST WESTERN Airport Inn & Suites/KCI North** H

(816) 858-0200. **$56-$129.** 2512 NW Prairie View Rd 64079. I-29 exit 18, just e, then just s. Int corridors. **Pets:** Accepted.

WWW **Quality Inn & Suites Kansas City Airport North** H

(816) 858-5430. **$70-$120.** 1201 Branch St 64079. I-29 exit 18, 1 mi w. Int corridors. **Pets:** Medium, other species. $15 daily fee/pet. Designated rooms, supervision.

POPLAR BLUFF

WW **Comfort Inn** H

(573) 686-5200. **$78-$115.** 2582 N Westwood Blvd 63901. 1.3 mi se of jct US 60 and 67. Int corridors. **Pets:** Accepted.

WW **Drury Inn-Poplar Bluff** H

(573) 686-2451. **$105-$154.** 2220 N Westwood Blvd 63901. 1.4 mi se of jct US 60 and 67. Int corridors. **Pets:** $10 daily fee/room. Service with restrictions, supervision.

POTOSI

W **Potosi Super 8** H

(573) 438-8888. **$62-$98.** 820 E High St 63664. Jct SR 8 and 21. Ext/int corridors. **Pets:** Accepted.

REPUBLIC

WW **AmericInn Lodge & Suites of Republic** H ✿

(417) 732-5335. **$85-$140.** 950 N Austin Ln 65738. I-44 exit 67, 4.4 mi s to SR 174, then 0.7 mi e. Int corridors. **Pets:** Medium. $10 daily fee/pet. Designated rooms, service with restrictions, supervision.

RICHMOND HEIGHTS

WWW **Residence Inn by Marriott-St. Louis Galleria** H

(314) 862-1900. **$161-$199.** 8011 Galleria Pkwy 63117. I-64/US 40 exit 31B (Brentwood/Hanley Rd), 0.4 mi n on Brentwood Blvd, then 0.5 mi e. Ext corridors. **Pets:** Accepted.

ROLLA

WWW **BEST WESTERN Coachlight** M

(573) 341-2511. **$75-$130, 7 day notice.** 1403 Martin Springs Dr 65401. Jct I-44 and Business Rt 44 S exit 184. Ext corridors. **Pets:** Accepted.

WW **Drury Inn-Rolla** H

(573) 364-4000. **$102-$139.** 2006 N Bishop Ave 65401. I-44 exit 186 (US 63), just ne. Int corridors. **Pets:** $10 daily fee/room. Service with restrictions, supervision.

ST. ANN

WWW **Hampton Inn-St. Louis Airport** H

(314) 429-2000. **$89-$179.** 10820 Pear Tree Ln 63074. I-70 exit 236 (Airport Dr), just s, then just w. Int corridors. **Pets:** Accepted.

WW **Pear Tree Inn by Drury-St. Louis Airport** H

(314) 427-3400. **$95-$159.** 10810 Pear Tree Ln 63074. I-70 exit 236 (Airport Dr), just s, then just w. Int corridors. **Pets:** $10 daily fee/room. Service with restrictions, supervision.

ST. CHARLES

BEST WESTERN PLUS The Charles Hotel H ❖

(636) 946-6936. **$89-$169.** 1425 S 5th St 63301. I-70 exit 229B (5th St N), just n, then w. Int corridors. **Pets:** Medium. $10 daily fee/room. Service with restrictions, supervision. SAVE ☐ ☐ ☐ ☐ ☐

Comfort Suites-St. Charles H

(636) 949-0694. **$99-$199.** 1400 S 5th St 63301. I-70 exit 229 and 229B, just n on 5th St, just e on Ameristar Blvd, then just s. Int corridors. **Pets:** Other species. $10 daily fee/pet. Supervision. ☐ ☐ ☐ ☐ ☐ ☐

TownePlace Suites by Marriott H

(636) 949-6800. **$89-$139.** 1800 Zumbehl Rd 63303. I-70 exit 227 (Zumbehl Rd), 0.6 mi s, then just se. Int corridors. **Pets:** Accepted. ☐ ☐ ☐ ☐ ☐

ST. CLAIR

Budget Lodging M ❖

(636) 629-1000. **$74-$89.** 866 S Outer Rd 63077. I-44 exit 240, just w. Ext corridors. **Pets:** Dogs only. $10 daily fee/room. Designated rooms, service with restrictions, supervision. ☐ ☐ ☐ ☐

ST. JOSEPH

Candlewood Suites H

(816) 232-2600. **$80-$135, 14 day notice.** 3505 N Village Dr 64506. I-29 exit 50, just sw, then 0.3 mi n. Int corridors. **Pets:** Accepted. ☐ ☐ ☐ ☐

Drury Inn & Suites-St. Joseph H

(816) 364-4700. **$115-$184.** 4213 Frederick Blvd 64506. I-29 exit 47, just e. Int corridors. **Pets:** $10 daily fee/room. Service with restrictions, supervision. ☐ ☐ ☐ ☐ ☐

St. Joseph Holiday Inn-Riverfront H

(816) 279-8000. **Call for rates.** 102 S Third St 64501. I-229 exit Edmond St northbound; exit Felix St southbound; downtown. Int corridors. **Pets:** Accepted. ☐ ☐ ☐ ☐ ☐ ☐ ☐

Stoney Creek Hotel & Conference Center H

(816) 901-9600. **Call for rates.** 1201 N Woodbine Rd 64506. I-29 exit 47, just w to Woodbine Rd. Int corridors. **Pets:** Accepted. ☐ ☐ ☐ ☐ ☐

ST. LOUIS (Restaurants p. 634)

The Cheshire H

(314) 647-7300. **$149-$499.** 6300 Clayton Rd 63117. I-64/US 40 exit 33C (McCausland Ave/Skinker Blvd), just n on Skinker Blvd, then just w. Int corridors. **Pets:** Accepted. SAVE ☐ ☐ ☐ ☐ ☐ ☐ ☐

Drury Inn & Suites Near Forest Park H

(314) 646-0770. **$100-$199.** 2111 Sulphur Ave 63139. I-44 exit 286, just s. Int corridors. **Pets:** $10 daily fee/room. Service with restrictions, supervision. ☐ ☐ ☐ ☐ ☐ ☐

Drury Inn & Suites-St. Louis-Convention Center H

(314) 231-8100. **$100-$190.** 711 N Broadway 63102. Between Convention Plaza and Lucas Ave. Int corridors. **Pets:** $10 daily fee/room. Service with restrictions, supervision. ☐ ☐ ☐ ☐ ☐

Drury Inn-St. Louis/Union Station H

(314) 231-3900. **$90-$180.** 201 S 20th St 63103. I-64/US 40 exit 39 westbound (Market St at 21st St), just n, just e on Market St, then just s; exit 38A eastbound, just n on Jefferson Ave, 0.5 mi e on Market St, then just s. Int corridors. **Pets:** $10 daily fee/room. Service with restrictions, supervision. ☐ ☐ ☐ ☐ ☐

Drury Plaza Hotel-St. Louis at the Arch H

(314) 231-3003. **$115-$234.** 2 S 4th St 63102. Between Walnut and Market sts. Int corridors. **Pets:** $10 daily fee/room. Service with restrictions, supervision. ☐ ☐ ☐ ☐ ☐ ☐

Four Seasons Hotel St. Louis H ❖

(314) 881-5800. **$219-$699.** 999 N 2nd St 63102. Jct Washington Ave, just n on 4th St, just e on Cole St, just e on Carr St, just s. Int corridors. **Pets:** Medium. Service with restrictions, supervision. SAVE ☐ ☐ ☐ ☐ ☐ ☐

Hilton St. Louis at the Ballpark H

(314) 421-1776. **$109-$599.** 1 S Broadway 63102. Between Walnut and Market sts. Int corridors. **Pets:** Accepted. ☐ ☐ ☐ ☐ ☐ ☐ ☐

Hilton-St. Louis Downtown H ❖

(314) 436-0002. **$119-$259.** 400 Olive St 63102. Jct 4th St. Int corridors. **Pets:** Large. $50 one-time fee/room. Service with restrictions, crate. ☐ ☐ ☐ ☐ ☐ ☐

Holiday Inn Forest Park H

(314) 645-0700. **$99-$229.** 5915 Wilson Ave 63110. I-44 exit 286, just s on Hampton Ave. Int corridors. **Pets:** Large, dogs only. $75 deposit/room, $25 one-time fee/room. Designated rooms, service with restrictions, supervision. SAVE ☐ ☐ ☐ ☐ ☐ ☐

Hotel Ignacio H

(314) 977-4411. **$220.** 3411 Olive St 63103. I-64/US 40 exit 38A westbound, just w on Forest Park Ave, just n on Grand Blvd, then just e on Lindell Blvd; exit 37B eastbound, 0.4 mi n on Grand Blvd, then just e on Lindell Blvd. Int corridors. **Pets:** Dogs only. $75 one-time fee/pet. Designated rooms, service with restrictions, crate. SAVE ☐ ☐ ☐ ☐ ☐ ☐

Hyatt Regency St. Louis at The Arch H

(314) 655-1234. **$79-$399.** 315 Chestnut St 63102. Jct 4th St. Int corridors. **Pets:** Accepted. SAVE ☐ ☐ ☐ ☐ ☐

Moonrise Hotel H ❖

(314) 721-1111. **$139-$319.** 6177 Delmar Blvd 63112. I-64/US 40 exit 33C (McCausland Ave/Skinker Blvd), 1.7 mi n on Skinker Blvd, then just e; in The Loop. Int corridors. **Pets:** $40 one-time fee/room. Designated rooms, service with restrictions. SAVE ☐ ☐ ☐ ☐ ☐ ☐

Omni Majestic Hotel H

(314) 436-2355. **$159-$329.** 1019 Pine St 63101. Jct N Broadway, just w; at 10th St. Int corridors. **Pets:** Accepted. ☐ ☐ ☐ ☐ ☐

The Parkway Hotel H

(314) 256-7777. **$129-$279.** 4550 Forest Park Ave 63108. I-64/US 40 exit 36A (Kingshighway Blvd), 0.6 mi n, then just e. Int corridors. **Pets:** Medium. $20 daily fee/pet. Designated rooms, service with restrictions, crate. SAVE ☐ ☐ ☐ ☐ ☐

Pear Tree Inn Union Station H

(314) 241-3200. **$90-$170.** 2211 Market St 63103. I-64/US 40 exit 39 westbound (Market St at 21st St), just n, then just w; exit 38A eastbound just n on Jefferson Ave, then just e. Int corridors. **Pets:** $10 daily fee/room. Service with restrictions, supervision. ☐ ☐ ☐ ☐ ☐ ☐

Red Roof Plus+ St. Louis-Forest Park/Hampton Ave. H

(314) 645-0101. **$79-$129.** 5823 Wilson Ave 63110. I-44 exit 286, 0.3 mi se. Ext corridors. **Pets:** Large, other species. Service with restrictions, supervision. ☐ ☐ ☐ ☐ ☐

Residence Inn by Marriott St. Louis Downtown H

(314) 289-7500. **$109-$299.** 525 S Jefferson Ave 63103. I-64/US 40 exit 38A eastbound, just s; 39 westbound (Market St at 21st St), just n, just w on Market St, then just s. Int corridors. **Pets:** Other species. $75 one-time fee/room. Service with restrictions, supervision. SAVE ☐ ☐ ☐ ☐ ☐ ☐

St. Louis Union Station Hotel A DoubleTree by Hilton Hotel H

(314) 231-1234. **$109-$599.** 1820 Market St 63103. I-64/US 40 exit 39 westbound (Market St at 21st St), just n, then just e; exit 38A eastbound, just n on Jefferson Ave, then 0.5 mi e. Int corridors. **Pets:** Accepted.

The Westin St. Louis H

(314) 621-2000. **Call for rates.** 811 Spruce St 63102. I-64/US 40 exit 39C eastbound, just n on 11th St, then just e; exit 40A westbound, just n, just e on Clark Ave, just s on 8th St, then just w. Int corridors. **Pets:** Dogs only. Service with restrictions, supervision.

ST. PETERS

Drury Inn St. Peters H

(636) 397-9700. **$100-$169.** 170 Mid Rivers Mall Cir 63376. I-70 exit 222 (Mid Rivers Mall Dr), just s, then just e. Int corridors. **Pets:** $10 daily fee/room. Service with restrictions, supervision.

ST. ROBERT

BEST WESTERN Montis Inn H

(573) 336-4299. **$75-$80.** 14086 Hwy Z 65584. I-44 exit 163, just s. Ext corridors. **Pets:** Dogs only. $10 daily fee/pet. Service with restrictions, supervision.

MainStay Suites H

(573) 451-2700. **$99-$159.** 227 St. Robert Blvd 65584. I-44 exit 159, 0.8 mi nw. Ext/int corridors. **Pets:** Other species. $15 daily fee/room. Service with restrictions.

Quality Inn H

(573) 451-2535. **$74-$89.** 114 Vickie Lynn Ln 65584. I-44 exit 161, just s, then 0.3 mi e on frontage road. Int corridors. **Pets:** Small. $20 one-time fee/pet. Designated rooms, service with restrictions, supervision.

STE. GENEVIEVE

Microtel Inn & Suites by Wyndham Sainte Genevieve H

(573) 883-8884. **$80-$132.** 21958 Hwy 32 63670. I-55 exit 150 (SR 32), 3.9 mi e. Int corridors. **Pets:** $10 daily fee/pet. Service with restrictions.

SEDALIA

BEST WESTERN State Fair Inn H

(660) 826-6100. **$80-$150.** 3120 S Limit Ave 65301. Jct US 50, 1.5 mi s on US 65. Ext/int corridors. **Pets:** Medium. Designated rooms, service with restrictions, crate.

SEYMOUR

Americas Best Value Inn H

(417) 935-9888. **$68-$73.** 1000 E Clinton Rd 65746. Just s of jct US 60. Int corridors. **Pets:** Accepted.

SIKESTON

Comfort Inn & Suites H

(573) 472-0197. **$96-$180.** 109 Matthews Ln 63801. I-55 exit 67, just sw. Int corridors. **Pets:** Accepted.

SPRINGFIELD

Baymont Inn & Suites H

(417) 889-8188. **$69-$149.** 3776 S Glenstone Ave 65804. On US 60 (James River Frwy). Int corridors. **Pets:** Accepted.

BEST WESTERN PLUS Coach House H

(417) 862-0701. **$79-$129.** 2535 N Glenstone Ave 65803. I-44 exit 80, just s. Ext corridors. **Pets:** Large. $10 daily fee/pet. Designated rooms, service with restrictions, crate.

BEST WESTERN PLUS Springfield Airport Inn H

(417) 799-2200. **$90-$100.** 4445 W Chestnut Expwy 65802. I-44 exit 72, 0.8 mi s. Int corridors. **Pets:** Large, other species. $10 daily fee/pet. Service with restrictions, supervision.

BEST WESTERN Route 66 Rail Haven M

(417) 866-1963. **$69-$199.** 203 S Glenstone Ave 65802. I-44 exit 80, 3 mi s. Ext corridors. **Pets:** Medium. $10 daily fee/pet. Designated rooms, service with restrictions, supervision.

Candlewood Suites South H

(417) 881-8500. **$89-$139.** 1035 E Republic Rd 65807. US 60 (James River Frwy) exit National Ave, just s. Int corridors. **Pets:** Medium. $150 one-time fee/pet. Service with restrictions.

Candlewood Suites Springfield I-44 H

(417) 866-4242. **$89-$139.** 1920 E Kerr St 65803. I-44 exit 80, just e to Evergreen St. Int corridors. **Pets:** Accepted.

Courtyard by Marriott Airport H

(417) 869-6700. **$79-$154.** 3527 W Kearney St 65803. I-44 exit 75 (US 160 W Bypass), just se to SR 744, then just w. Int corridors. **Pets:** $75 one-time fee/room. Service with restrictions.

DoubleTree by Hilton Hotel Springfield H

(417) 831-3131. **$109-$179.** 2431 N Glenstone Ave 65803. I-44 exit 80, just s. Int corridors. **Pets:** Large. $25 one-time fee/room. Designated rooms.

Drury Inn & Suites-Springfield H

(417) 863-8400. **$110-$209.** 2715 N Glenstone Ave 65803. I-44 exit 80, just s. Int corridors. **Pets:** $10 daily fee/room. Service with restrictions, supervision.

Greenstay Hotel & Suites H

(417) 863-1440. **$69-$109.** 222 N Ingram Mill Rd 65802. US 65 exit Chestnut Expwy, just sw. Int corridors. **Pets:** Accepted.

Hilton Garden Inn Springfield H

(417) 875-8800. **$124-$179.** 4155 S Nature Center Way 65804. US 60 (James River Frwy) exit Glenstone Ave (US 65 business route), just s. Int corridors. **Pets:** Small, other species. $75 one-time fee/room. Designated rooms, service with restrictions, crate.

La Quinta Inn & Suites Springfield Airport Plaza H

(417) 447-4466. **$83-$230.** 2445 N Airport Plaza Ave 65803. I-44 exit 75 (US 160 W Bypass), just se. Int corridors. **Pets:** Large, other species. Service with restrictions.

La Quinta Inn & Suites Springfield South H

(417) 890-6060. **$82-$197.** 2535 S Campbell Ave 65807. Jct Battlefield Rd and Campbell Ave, 0.5 mi n. Int corridors. **Pets:** Large, other species. Service with restrictions.

University Plaza Hotel and Convention Center H

(417) 864-7333. **$102-$157.** 333 John Q Hammons Pkwy 65806. 0.5 mi e on St. Louis St. Int corridors. **Pets:** $25 one-time fee/room. Designated rooms, service with restrictions, crate.

SULLIVAN

Baymont Inn & Suites H

(573) 860-3333. **$79-$114.** 275 N Service Rd W 63080. I-44 exit 225, just e, then 0.4 mi n. Int corridors. **Pets:** $10 daily fee/pet. Designated rooms, service with restrictions, supervision.

Comfort Inn 🅷
(573) 468-7800. **$89-$109.** 736 S Service Rd W 63080. I-44 exit 225, just sw. Int corridors. **Pets:** Accepted. [SAVE] ⊡ 🛜 ⊠ 🛗 🖵

SUNSET HILLS

Holiday Inn St. Louis SW-Route 66 🅷 ❄
(314) 821-6600. **$109-$229.** 10709 Watson Rd 63127. I-44 exit 277B (Lindbergh Blvd), just s on US 61/67. Int corridors. **Pets:** $35 daily fee/ pet. Service with restrictions, crate. [SAVE] 🍽 ⊡ 🛜 🛗 🖵

SWEET SPRINGS

Night Inn 🅼
(660) 335-4162. **$55-$65.** 1001 N Locust St 65351. I-70 exit 66, just se. Ext corridors. **Pets:** $10 daily fee/pet. Designated rooms, service with restrictions, supervision. 🛜 🛗

TRENTON

Country Home Inn 🅷
(660) 359-2988. **Call for rates.** 1845A E 28th St 64683. US 65, 1 mi n of jct SR 6 and US 65. Int corridors. **Pets:** $50 one-time fee/room. Service with restrictions, supervision. 🛜 🛗

UNION

Super 8 🅷
(636) 583-8808. **$80-$93.** 1015 E Main St 63084. I-44 exit 247 (US 50), 4.7 mi w; just w of jct SR 47. Int corridors. **Pets:** Medium, dogs only. $35 deposit/pet, $10 daily fee/pet. Designated rooms, service with restrictions, supervision. ⌨M ⊡ 🛜 🛗 🖵

VALLEY PARK

Drury Inn & Suites-St. Louis Southwest 🅷
(636) 861-8300. **$120-$174.** 5 Lambert Drury Dr 63088. I-44 exit 272 (SR 141), just sw. Int corridors. **Pets:** $10 daily fee/room. Service with restrictions, supervision. ⊡ 🛜 ⊠ 🛗 🖵

Hampton Inn-St. Louis Southwest near Six Flags 🅷 ❄
(636) 529-9020. **$119-$134.** 9 Lambert Drury Dr 63088. I-44 exit 272 (SR 141), just sw. Int corridors. **Pets:** Medium. Service with restrictions, crate. ⊡ 🛜 🛗 🖵

WASHINGTON

Super 8 Washington 🅷
(636) 390-0088. **$80-$97.** 2081 Eckelkamp Ct 63090. I-44 exit 251, 10 mi w on SR 100; just s of SR 100 and 47. Int corridors. **Pets:** Small, dogs only. $35 deposit/room, $10 daily fee/pet. Service with restrictions, crate. 🛜 🛗 🖵

WEST PLAINS

Econo Lodge 🅷
(417) 257-2711. **Call for rates.** 220 Jan Howard Expwy 65775. 0.5 mi nw of jct US 63 and 160. Int corridors. **Pets:** Accepted. ⊡ 🛜 🛗 🖵

WILLOW SPRINGS

Comfort Inn of Willow Springs 🅷
(417) 469-0410. **$84-$169.** 1204 E Main St 65793. Just n of US 60/63. Int corridors. **Pets:** Accepted. 🛜 🛗 🖵

WOODSON TERRACE

Hilton St. Louis Airport 🅷
(314) 426-5500. **$89-$239.** 10330 Natural Bridge Rd 63134. I-70 exit 236 (Lambert Airport), 0.5 mi se. Int corridors. **Pets:** Accepted.
[SAVE] 🍽 ⊡ 🛋 ⊠ 🛗 🖵

MONTANA

BELGRADE

Gallatin River Lodge 🅲🅸
(406) 388-0148. **$170-$500, 7 day notice.** 9105 Thorpe Rd 59718. I-90 exit 298, 2.7 mi s on SR 85, 1 mi w on Valley Center Rd (gravel), then 0.5 mi s, follow signs. Ext/int corridors. **Pets:** Dogs only. $30 daily fee/ room. Designated rooms, supervision. 🍽 🛜 ⊠ 🖵

Holiday Inn Express & Suites Belgrade 🅷 ❄
(406) 388-7100. **$109-$189.** 309 W Madison Ave 59714. I-90 exit 298, just n on SR 85. Int corridors. **Pets:** Dogs only. $20 daily fee/pet. Service with restrictions, supervision. [SAVE] ⌨M 🛜 ⊠ 🛗 🖵

La Quinta Inn & Suites Belgrade / Bozeman 🅷
(406) 388-2222. **$69-$259.** 6445 Jackrabbit Ln 59714. I-90 exit 298, just s on SR 85. Int corridors. **Pets:** Large, other species. Service with restrictions. ⊡ ⊠ 🛜 🛗 🖵

Quality Inn 🅷
(406) 388-0800. **$59-$139.** 6261 Jackrabbit Ln 59714. I-90 exit 298, just s on SR 85. Int corridors. **Pets:** Accepted.
[SAVE] ⌨M 🛜 ⊠ 🛗 🖵

Super 8-Belgrade/Bozeman Airport 🅷
(406) 388-1493. **$70-$99.** 6450 Jackrabbit Ln 59714. I-90 exit 298, just s on SR 85. Int corridors. **Pets:** Accepted. ⊡ 🛜 🛗 🖵

BIGFORK

Mountain Lake Lodge 🅷 ❄
(406) 837-3800. **$239-$285, 7 day notice.** 14735 Sylvan Dr 59911. On SR 35, 5 mi s. Ext corridors. **Pets:** Dogs only. $15 daily fee/room. Designated rooms, service with restrictions, supervision.
[SAVE] 🍽 ⌨M ⊡ 🛜 🛗 🖵

Timbers Motel 🅼
(406) 837-6200. **Call for rates.** 8540 Hwy 35 59911. Just n on SR 35 from jct SR 209. Ext corridors. **Pets:** Accepted. ⊡ 🛜 🛗 🖵

BIG SKY

Buck's T-4 Lodge 🅷
(406) 995-4111. **Call for rates.** 46625 Gallatin Rd 59716. US 191, 1 mi s of Big Sky entrance. Ext/int corridors. **Pets:** Other species. $10 daily fee/pet. Supervision. 🍽 ⊠ 🛜 ⊠ 🛗 🖵

Rainbow Ranch Lodge 🅷
(406) 995-4132. **Call for rates.** 42950 Gallatin Rd 59730. 5 mi s on US 191. Ext corridors. **Pets:** Other species. $40 one-time fee/pet. Designated rooms, service with restrictions, supervision.
🍽 ⊠ 🛜 ⊠ 🐾 🛗 🖵

BIG TIMBER

Big Timber Super 8 🅷
(406) 932-8888. **$84-$109.** 20A Big Timber Loop Rd 59011. I-90 exit 367. Int corridors. **Pets:** Accepted. ⌨M 🛜 🛗 🖵

River Valley Inn 🅷
(406) 932-4943. **$68-$100.** 600 W 2nd St 59011. I-90 exit 367, just n, then 0.6 mi e. Int corridors. **Pets:** Small, other species. $10 one-time fee/room. Service with restrictions, supervision. 🛜 🛗

BILLINGS

◬◬ ♦♦♦♦ BEST WESTERN PLUS Clocktower Inn 🄷 ❀

(406) 259-5511. **$89-$159.** 2511 1st Ave N 59101. On I-90 business loop; downtown. Ext/int corridors. **Pets:** Other species. $20 daily fee/pet. Designated rooms, service with restrictions.

[SAVE] 🍴 🏊 📶 ✕ 🛁 🖥

◬◬ ♦♦♦♦ BEST WESTERN PLUS Kelly Inn & Suites 🄷 ❀

(406) 256-9400. **$120-$180.** 4915 Southgate Dr 59101. I-90 exit 447, just w. Ext/int corridors. **Pets:** Small. Designated rooms, service with restrictions, supervision. [SAVE] 🛗 🏊 📶 ✕ 🛁 🖥

♦♦♦ Billings Inn by Riversage 🄷

(406) 252-6800. **$85-$95.** 880 N 29th St 59101. I-90 exit 450, 2 mi n on 27th St, then just w on 9th Ave. Int corridors. **Pets:** Other species. $8 daily fee/pet. Designated rooms, service with restrictions, supervision. [SAVE] 📶 ✕ 🛁 🖥

♦♦ Billings Super 8 🄷

(406) 248-8842. **$79-$94.** 5400 Southgate Dr 59102. I-90 exit 447, just n on S Billings Blvd, 0.8 mi w on King Ave, then just s on Parkway Ln. Int corridors. **Pets:** Accepted. 🛗 📶 🛁 🖥

♦♦ Comfort Inn by Choice Hotels 🄷

(406) 652-5200. **$110-$140.** 2030 Overland Ave 59102. I-90 exit 446, 0.5 mi n, then just s. Int corridors. **Pets:** Accepted.

🛗 🏊 📶 ✕ 🛁 🖥

♦♦ Days Inn 🄷

(406) 252-4007. **$73-$125.** 843 Parkway Ln 59101. I-90 exit 447, just n on S Billings Blvd, 0.8 mi w on King Ave, then just s. Int corridors. **Pets:** Accepted. 📶 ✕ 🛁 🖥

♦♦ Econo Lodge 🄷

(406) 252-2700. **$65-$90.** 5425 Midland Rd 59101. I-90 exit 446, just se. Ext/int corridors. **Pets:** Accepted. 🏊 📶 🛁 🖥

♦♦ Extended Stay America-Billings-West End 🄷

(406) 245-3980. **Call for rates.** 4950 Southgate Dr 59101. I-90 exit 447, just w. Int corridors. **Pets:** Other species. $25 daily fee/pet. Service with restrictions, supervision. 🛗 📶 🛁 🖥

◬◬ ♦♦♦ Hilltop Inn by Riversage 🄷

(406) 245-5000. **$85-$95.** 1116 N 28th St 59101. I-90 exit 450, 2 mi n on 27th St, just w on 11th Ave, then just n. Int corridors. **Pets:** Other species. $8 daily fee/pet. Designated rooms, service with restrictions, supervision. [SAVE] 🛗 📶 ✕ 🛁 🖥

◬◬ ♦♦♦♦ Holiday Inn Grand Montana Billings 🄷

(406) 248-7701. **$119-$149.** 5500 Midland Rd 59101. I-90 exit 446. Int corridors. **Pets:** Accepted. [SAVE] 🍴 🛗 🏊 📶 ✕ 🛁 🖥

♦♦ Kelly Inn 🄷

(406) 248-9800. **Call for rates.** 5610 S Frontage Rd 59101. I-90 exit 446, just s. Ext/int corridors. **Pets:** Accepted.

🛗 🏊 📶 ✕ 🛁 🖥

♦♦♦ La Quinta Inn and Suites 🄷

(406) 252-1188. **Call for rates.** 5720 S Frontage Rd 59101. I-90 exit 446, just s. Int corridors. **Pets:** Accepted. 🛗 📶 ✕ 🛁 🖥

♦♦ My Place Hotel 🄷

(406) 259-9970. **Call for rates.** 4770 King Ave E 59101. I-90 exit 447, just e. Int corridors. **Pets:** Accepted. 📶 ✕ 🛁 🖥

♦♦ Quality Inn Homestead 🄷

(406) 652-1320. **$129.** 2036 Overland Ave 59102. I-90 exit 446, 0.5 mi n, then just s. Int corridors. **Pets:** Accepted. 🏊 ✕ 📶 🛁 🖥

♦♦♦ Residence Inn by Marriott 🄷

(406) 656-3900. **$189-$209.** 956 S 25th St W 59102. I-90 exit 446, 1.5 mi w, just s on S 24th St, then just s. Int corridors. **Pets:** Accepted.

🛗 🏊 📶 ✕ 🛁 🖥

◬◬ ♦♦♦ Western Executive Inn 🄷

(406) 294-8888. **$80-$210.** 3121 King Ave W 59102. I-90 exit 446, 2.5 mi w. Int corridors. **Pets:** Medium. $10 daily fee/pet. Service with restrictions, supervision. [SAVE] 🛗 📶 🛁 🖥

◬◬ ♦ Westwood's Rimview Inn Ⓜ

(406) 248-2622. **Call for rates.** 1025 N 27th St 59101. I-90 exit 450, 2 mi n. Ext/int corridors. **Pets:** Accepted. [SAVE] 📶 🛁 🖥

BOZEMAN *(Restaurants p. 634)*

◬◬ ♦♦♦♦ BEST WESTERN PLUS GranTree Inn 🄷

(406) 587-5261. **$99-$209, 3 day notice.** 1325 N 7th Ave 59715. I-90 exit 306, just s. Int corridors. **Pets:** $10 daily fee/room. Designated rooms, service with restrictions, supervision.

[SAVE] 🍴 🏊 📶 ✕ 🛁 🖥

♦♦ Bozeman Days Inn & Suites 🄷 ❀

(406) 587-5251. **$65-$135.** 1321 N 7th Ave 59715. I-90 exit 306, just s. Int corridors. **Pets:** $5 one-time fee/pet. Service with restrictions, supervision. 🏊 ✕ 📶 ✕ 🛁 🖥

♦ Bozeman Inn Ⓜ

(406) 587-3176. **Call for rates.** 1235 N 7th Ave 59715. I-90 exit 306, just s. Ext corridors. **Pets:** Accepted. 🏊 📶 🛁 🖥

♦♦ Bozeman's Western Heritage Inn 🄷 ❀

(406) 586-8534. **$73-$189.** 1200 E Main St 59715. I-90 exit 309, 0.5 mi w. Int corridors. **Pets:** Dogs only. $10 daily fee/pet. Supervision.

📶 ✕ 🛁 🖥

♦♦ Comfort Inn of Bozeman 🄷

(406) 587-2322. **$94-$209.** 1370 N 7th Ave 59715. I-90 exit 306, just s. Int corridors. **Pets:** $10 daily fee/pet. Designated rooms, service with restrictions, supervision. 🏊 📶 ✕ 🛁 🖥

♦♦♦ Holiday Inn Bozeman 🄷

(406) 587-4561. **Call for rates.** 5 E Baxter Ln 59715. I-90 exit 306, just s. Int corridors. **Pets:** Accepted. 🍴 🏊 📶 🛁 🖥

♦♦♦ Holiday Inn Express & Suites 🄷

(406) 582-4995. **Call for rates.** 2305 Catron St 59718. I-90 exit 305, just s on CR 41 (19th St), then just w on E Valley Center Rd. Int corridors. **Pets:** Accepted. [ECO] 🛗 🏊 📶 ✕ 🛁 🖥

♦♦♦ La Quinta Inn & Suites 🄷

(406) 585-9300. **$79-$299.** 620 Nikles Dr 59715. I-90 exit 306, just ne. Int corridors. **Pets:** Large, other species. Service with restrictions.

🛗 🏊 📶 ✕ 🛁 🖥

♦♦ Microtel Inn & Suites by Wyndham Bozeman 🄷

(406) 586-3797. **$60-$140.** 612 Nikles Dr 59715. I-90 exit 306, just ne. Int corridors. **Pets:** Accepted. 🏊 📶 ✕ 🛁 🖥

♦♦ Motel 6 Bozeman #4818 🄷

(406) 585-7888. **Call for rates.** 817 Wheat Dr 59718. I-90 exit 306, just n. Int corridors. **Pets:** Other species. Service with restrictions, crate.

🛗 🏊 📶 ✕ 🛁 🖥

♦♦ MountainView Lodge & Suites 🄷

(406) 522-8686. **$89-$179.** 1121 Reeves Rd W 59718. I-90 exit 305, just n. Int corridors. **Pets:** Dogs only. $10 daily fee/pet. Designated rooms, service with restrictions, supervision.

🛗 🏊 ✕ 📶 🛁 🖥

♦♦ My Place Hotel 🄷

(406) 586-8228. **$85.** 5889 E Valley Center Rd 59718. I-90 exit 305, just s on CR 41 (19th St), then just w. Int corridors. **Pets:** Dogs only. $10 daily fee/room. Service with restrictions, crate.

🛗 📶 ✕ 🛁 🖥

△△△ ▽ Rainbow Motel M
(406) 587-4201. **$75-$95.** 510 N 7th Ave 59715. I-90 exit 306, 0.8 mi s. Ext corridors. **Pets:** Accepted. [SAVE] 🏊 🛜 📶 💻

▽▽ Ramada Limited H
(406) 585-2626. **$60-$140, 3 day notice.** 2020 Wheat Dr 59715. I-90 exit 306, just n, then just w. Ext/int corridors. **Pets:** Accepted.
🏊 🛜 ✕ 📶 💻

△△△ ▽ Royal '7' Budget Inn M
(406) 587-3103. **$60-$89, 3 day notice.** 310 N 7th Ave 59715. I-90 exit 306, 0.8 mi s. Ext corridors. **Pets:** $5 daily fee/pet. Designated rooms, service with restrictions, supervision. [SAVE] 🛜 ✕ 📶 💻

▽▽ Super 8 H
(406) 586-1521. **$59-$159.** 800 Wheat Dr 59715. I-90 exit 306, just n, then just w. Int corridors. **Pets:** Accepted. 🛜 ✕ 📶 💻

BROWNING

△△△ ▽ Going to the Sun Inn & Suites M
(406) 338-7572. **$88-$174, 4 day notice.** 121 Central Ave E 59417. On US 2; center. Ext corridors. **Pets:** Medium, other species. $10 daily fee/pet. Supervision. [SAVE] 🛜 ✕ 📶

BUTTE

△△△ ▽ Americas Best Value Inn M
(406) 723-5464. **$55-$70.** 122001 W Brown's Gulch Rd 59701. I-90/15 exit 122 (Rocker Rd). Int corridors. **Pets:** Medium. $10 daily fee/room. Designated rooms, service with restrictions, supervision. [SAVE] 🛜 📶

△△△ ▽▽▽ BEST WESTERN PLUS Butte Plaza Inn H 🐾
(406) 494-3500. **$107-$147.** 2900 Harrison Ave 59701. I-90/15 exit 127 (Harrison Ave). Int corridors. **Pets:** Designated rooms, service with restrictions, supervision. [SAVE] 🍽 🏊 ✕ 🛜 ✕ 📶 💻

△△△ ▽▽ Comfort Inn of Butte H 🐾
(406) 494-8850. **$95-$135.** 2777 Harrison Ave 59701. I-90/15 exit 127 (Harrison Ave), just s. Int corridors. **Pets:** Other species. $20 daily fee/room. Designated rooms, service with restrictions, supervision. [SAVE] [ECO] [&M] 🏊 ✕ 📶 💻

▽▽ Finlen Hotel H
(406) 723-5461. **$76-$110.** 100 E Broadway 59701. Jct Wyoming St; in Historic Uptown. Ext/int corridors. **Pets:** Designated rooms, service with restrictions, supervision. 🛜 ✕ 📶

▽▽▽ La Quinta Inn & Suites H
(406) 494-6999. **$85-$244.** 1 Holiday Park Dr 59701. I-90/15 exit 127 (Harrison Ave), just n to Cornell St, then just e, follow signs. Int corridors. **Pets:** Large, other species. Service with restrictions.
[&M] 🛜 ✕ 📶 💻

▽▽ Quality Inn & Suites Butte H
(406) 494-7800. **$80-$150.** 2100 Cornell Ave 59701. I-90/15 exit 127B (Harrison Ave), just n, then just e. Int corridors. **Pets:** Accepted.
🏊 🛜 📶 💻

△△△ ▽▽ Super 8 of Butte H
(406) 494-6000. **$72-$115.** 2929 Harrison Ave 59701. I-90/15 exit 127 (Harrison Ave), just s. Int corridors. **Pets:** Medium. $15 one-time fee/pet. Service with restrictions, supervision. [SAVE] 🛜 ✕ 📶 💻

COLUMBUS

▽▽ Super 8 of Columbus H 🐾
(406) 322-4101. **$73-$120.** 602 8th Ave N 59019. I-90 exit 408, just s on SR 78. Int corridors. **Pets:** Large, dogs only. $25 daily fee/pet. Service with restrictions, supervision. [&M] 🛜 📶 💻

CONRAD

▽▽ Super 8 H 🐾
(406) 278-7676. **$86-$103.** 215 N Main St 59425. I-15 exit 339, just w. Int corridors. **Pets:** Other species. $10 daily fee/pet. Service with restrictions, supervision. 🛜 ✕ 📶 💻

DARBY

▽▽ Rye Creek Lodge CA
(406) 821-3366. **$250-$750, 60 day notice.** 458 Rye Creek Rd 59829. US 93, 4.5 mi s, 1.5 mi e. Ext corridors. **Pets:** Accepted.
✕ 🛜 ✕ 📶 💻

DEER LODGE

△△△ ▽ Travelodge M
(406) 846-2370. **$80-$200.** 1150 N Main St 59722. I-90 exit 184, 0.3 mi s. Int corridors. **Pets:** Accepted. [SAVE] 🛜 ✕ 📶 💻

▽ Western Big Sky Inn M
(406) 846-2590. **Call for rates.** 210 N Main St 59722. I-90 exit 184, 1 mi w. Ext corridors. **Pets:** Accepted. 🛜 ✕ 📶 💻

DILLON

△△△ ▽▽ BEST WESTERN Paradise Inn H
(406) 683-4214. **Call for rates.** 650 N Montana St 59725. I-15 exit 63, 0.3 mi s on SR 41. Ext corridors. **Pets:** Accepted.
[SAVE] 🏊 🛜 ✕ 📶 💻

△△△ ▽▽▽ Comfort Inn of Dillon H 🐾
(406) 683-6831. **$118-$139.** 450 N Interchange 59725. I-15 exit 63. Int corridors. **Pets:** Other species. $15 daily fee/pet. Designated rooms, service with restrictions, supervision. [SAVE] 🏊 🛜 ✕ 📶 💻

▽▽ GuestHouse International Inn & Suites H
(406) 683-3636. **$69-$249.** 580 Sinclair St 59725. I-15 exit 63, just e. Int corridors. **Pets:** Other species. $15 daily fee/pet. Designated rooms, service with restrictions, supervision. [&M] 🏊 🛜 ✕ 📶 💻

EAST GLACIER PARK

△△△ ▽ Dancing Bears Inn & Suites M
(406) 226-4402. **$88-$174, 4 day notice.** 40 Montana Ave 59434. Just off US 2, follow signs; center. Ext/int corridors. **Pets:** Medium, other species. $10 daily fee/pet. Supervision. [SAVE] 🛜 ✕ 📶 💻

EMIGRANT

△△△ ▽▽▽ Paradise Gateway Bed & Breakfast & Guest Cabin BB
(406) 333-4063. **$85-$450, 14 day notice.** 2644 Hwy 89 S 59027. I-90 exit 333 (US 89), 4.5 mi s of town; between MM 26 and 27, 0.3 mi e on gravel road. Ext/int corridors. **Pets:** Accepted.
[SAVE] 🛜 ✕ 📶 💻

FORSYTH

△△△ ▽▽▽ Magnuson Hotels Sundowner Inn M
(406) 346-2115. **$95-$130.** 1018 Front St 59327. I-94 exit 95, 0.5 mi nw. Ext corridors. **Pets:** Dogs only. $15 daily fee/pet. Service with restrictions, supervision. [SAVE] 🛜 📶 💻

△△△ ▽ Rails Inn Motel H
(406) 346-2242. **$69-$92, 3 day notice.** 290 Front St 59327. I-94 exit 93, just n, then 0.5 mi e. Int corridors. **Pets:** Other species. $6 daily fee/pet. Designated rooms, service with restrictions, supervision.
[SAVE] 🛜 ✕ 📶 💻

△△△ ▽ Restwel Motel M
(406) 346-2771. **$72-$90.** 810 Front St 59327. I-94 exit 95, 0.8 mi nw. Ext corridors. **Pets:** Accepted. [SAVE] 🛜 📶

△△△ ▽ Westwind Motor Inn M
(406) 346-2038. **$69-$92, 3 day notice.** 225 Westwind Ln 59327. I-94 exit 93, 0.3 mi n. Int corridors. **Pets:** Other species. $6 daily fee/pet. Designated rooms, service with restrictions, supervision.
[SAVE] 🛜 ✕ 📶 💻

GARDINER

⬙ ⬙⬙ BEST WESTERN PLUS By Mammoth Hot Springs Ⓜ

(406) 848-7311. **$89-$219.** 905 Scott St W 59030. 0.5 mi n. Ext/int corridors. **Pets:** Accepted. 🆂🅰🆅🅴 🍽 🔛 🗙 🛜 🗙 🔋 🖥

⬙ ⬙ Yellowstone River Motel Ⓜ

(406) 848-7303. **$65-$121.** 14 E Park St 59030. Just e of US 89. Ext corridors. **Pets:** Accepted. 🆂🅰🆅🅴 🅼 🛜 🗙 🔋 🖥

⬙ ⬙ Yellowstone Super 8-Gardiner 🅷

(406) 848-7401. **$50-$210.** Hwy 89 S 59030. 0.4 mi n. Int corridors. **Pets:** Other species. $10 daily fee/pet. Designated rooms, supervision. 🔛 🛜 🗙 🔋 🖥

GLASGOW

⬙ ⬙ Cottonwood Inn 🅷

(406) 228-8213. **$88-$112.** 45 1st Ave NE 59230. 0.5 mi e on US 2. Int corridors. **Pets:** $5 daily fee/room. Designated rooms, service with restrictions, supervision. 🍽 🔛 🛜 🔋 🖥

GREAT FALLS

⬙ ⬙⬙⬙ BEST WESTERN PLUS Heritage Inn 🅷

(406) 761-1900. **$120-$160.** 1700 Fox Farm Rd 59404. I-15 exit 278, 0.8 mi e on 10th Ave S, US 87/89 and SR 3/200. Int corridors. **Pets:** Small, other species. $15 one-time fee/room. Designated rooms, service with restrictions, crate.

🆂🅰🆅🅴 🍽 🔛 🗙 🛜 🗙 🔋 🖥

⬙ ⬙⬙ Comfort Inn by Choice Hotels 🅷

(406) 454-2727. **$77-$165.** 1120 9th St S 59405. I-15 exit 278, 3 mi e on 10th Ave S, US 87/89 and SR 3/200, then just s. Int corridors. **Pets:** Other species. $20 daily fee/pet. Service with restrictions, supervision. 🆂🅰🆅🅴 🅼 🔛 🛜 🔋 🖥

⬙ ⬙ Days Inn of Great Falls 🅷

(406) 727-6565. **$78-$93.** 101 14th Ave NW 59404. I-15 exit 280 (Central Ave), 1.3 mi e on Central Ave/Business Rt I-15, 0.8 mi n on 3rd St NW, then just w. Int corridors. **Pets:** Dogs only. $5 daily fee/room. Designated rooms, service with restrictions, supervision.

🛜 🗙 🔋 🖥

⬙ ⬙ Extended Stay America-Great Falls-Missouri River 🅷

(406) 761-7524. **Call for rates.** 800 River Dr S 59405. I-15 exit 278, 1.7 mi e on 10th Ave S, then 0.7 mi n. Int corridors. **Pets:** Other species. $25 daily fee/pet. Service with restrictions, supervision.

🅼 🛜 🔋 🖥

⬙ ⬙⬙ The Great Falls Inn by Riversage 🅷 🐾

(406) 453-6000. **$85-$95.** 1400 28th St S 59405. I-15 exit 278, 5.3 mi e on 10th Ave S, 0.3 mi s on 26th St S, then just e on 15th Ave S. Int corridors. **Pets:** Other species. $7 daily fee/pet. Designated rooms, service with restrictions, supervision. 🆂🅰🆅🅴 🅼 🛜 🗙 🔋 🖥

⬙⬙⬙ Hampton Inn 🅷

(406) 453-2675. **$109-$149.** 2301 14th St SW 59404. I-15 exit 278, just sw. Int corridors. **Pets:** Accepted. 🅼 🔛 🛜 🔋 🖥

⬙⬙⬙ Holiday Inn 🅷

(406) 727-7200. **$89-$169.** 1100 5th St S 59405. I-15 exit 278, 2 mi e on 10th Ave S, then just s. Int corridors. **Pets:** Dogs only. $20 one-time fee/room. Designated rooms, service with restrictions, supervision.

🍽 🅼 🔛 🛜 🗙 🔋 🖥

⬙⬙⬙ La Quinta Inn & Suites Great Falls 🅷

(406) 761-2600. **$84-$314.** 600 River Dr S 59405. I-15 exit 278, 1.7 mi e on 10th Ave S, then 0.8 mi n. Int corridors. **Pets:** Large, other species. Service with restrictions. 🅼 🔛 🗙 🛜 🔋 🖥

⬙ ⬙ Motel 6 #4238 Ⓜ

(406) 453-1602. **$67-$95.** 2 Treasure State Dr 59404. I-15 exit 278, 0.8 mi e on 10th Ave S and US 87/89 and SR 3/200. Int corridors. **Pets:** Other species. Service with restrictions, crate.

🆂🅰🆅🅴 🛜 🗙 🔋

⬙ O'Haire Motor Inn Ⓜ

(406) 454-2141. **Call for rates.** 17 7th St S 59403. Center of downtown. Ext/int corridors. **Pets:** Accepted. 🍽 🔛 🛜 🔋 🖥

⬙⬙⬙ Quality Inn 🅷

(406) 761-3410. **$69-$109.** 220 Central Ave 59401. Downtown. Ext/int corridors. **Pets:** Accepted. 🆂🅰🆅🅴 🍽 🔛 🛜 🔋 🖥

⬙⬙⬙ Staybridge Suites 🅷

(406) 761-4903. **$99-$199.** 201 3rd St NW (US 87) 59404. I-15 exit 280 (Central Ave), 1 mi w, then just n. Int corridors. **Pets:** Accepted.

🅼 🔛 🛜 🗙 🔋 🖥

⬙ ⬙⬙ TownHouse Inn of Great Falls Ⓜ 🐾

(406) 761-4600. **Call for rates.** 1411 10th Ave S 59405. I-15 exit 278, 2.6 mi e on 10th Ave S, US 87/89 and SR 3/200. Int corridors. **Pets:** Other species. $10 daily fee/pet. Service with restrictions, supervision. 🆂🅰🆅🅴 🅴🅲🅾 🔛 🗙 🛜 🗙 🔋 🖥

HAMILTON

⬙ ⬙ Bitterroot River Inn & Conference Center 🅷

(406) 375-2525. **$79-$159.** 139 Bitterroot Plaza Dr 59840. US 93, 1 mi n, then just w. Ext/int corridors. **Pets:** Large. Designated rooms, service with restrictions, supervision. 🅼 🔛 🗙 🛜 🗙 🔋 🖥

⬙ ⬙ ⬙ Town House Inns 🅷 🐾

(406) 363-6600. **$65-$100.** 1113 N 1st St 59840. On US 93, n of City Center. Int corridors. **Pets:** Other species. $10 daily fee/pet. Designated rooms, service with restrictions, supervision. 🆂🅰🆅🅴 🅼 🛜 🔋 🖥

HARLOWTON

⬙ Countryside Inn Ⓜ

(406) 632-4119. **$55-$65.** 309 3rd St NE 59036. US 12 E. Ext corridors. **Pets:** Accepted. 🛜 🔋

HAVRE

⬙ ⬙ ⬙ TownHouse Inn of Havre 🅷

(406) 265-6711. **Call for rates.** 601 1st St W 59501. Just w of town center on US 2. Int corridors. **Pets:** Accepted.

🆂🅰🆅🅴 🔛 🛜 🔋 🖥

HELENA

⬙⬙⬙ Barrister Bed & Breakfast 🅱🅱 🐾

(406) 443-7330. **Call for rates.** 416 N Ewing St 59601. I-15 exit 192 (Prospect Ave), 1.5 mi sw via Prospect and Montana aves to 9th Ave, 0.8 mi w, then just s. Int corridors. **Pets:** Dogs only. 🛜 🗙 🖥

⬙ ⬙⬙⬙ BEST WESTERN PREMIER Helena Great Northern Hotel 🅷

(406) 457-5500. **$171-$195.** 835 Great Northern Blvd 59601. I-15 exit 193 (Cedar St), 2 mi w, just w on Lyndale Ave, then just s on Getchell St; downtown. Int corridors. **Pets:** Accepted.

🆂🅰🆅🅴 🍽 🅼 🔛 🛜 🗙 🔋 🖥

⬙ ⬙⬙⬙ Comfort Suites 🅷 🐾

(406) 495-0505. **$120-$140.** 3180 N Washington St 59602. I-15 exit 194 (Custer Ave), just e. Int corridors. **Pets:** Other species. $20 daily fee/room. Designated rooms, supervision.

🆂🅰🆅🅴 🅼 🔛 🛜 🗙 🔋 🖥

⬙ ⬙ Days Inn Helena 🅷

(406) 442-3280. **$80-$250.** 2001 Prospect Ave 59601. I-15 exit 192 (Prospect Ave), just w. Int corridors. **Pets:** Accepted.

🅼 🛜 🔋 🖥

⬙ Helena Super 8 🅷

(406) 443-2450. **$65-$75.** 2200 11th Ave 59601. I-15 exit 192 (Prospect Ave) northbound; exit west business district southbound on US 12. Int corridors. **Pets:** Accepted. 🛜 🔋 🖥

▼▼▼ **Holiday Inn Conference Center Downtown** H
(406) 443-2200. **$119-$159, 3 day notice.** 22 N Last Chance Gulch 59601. Jct Park Ave and Broadway St. Int corridors. **Pets:** $10 daily fee/pet. Designated rooms, service with restrictions, supervision.
🍽 ⊠ 🛜 ✕ 🛗 ▭

▼▼ **Jorgenson's Inn & Suites** H 🐾
(406) 442-1770. **$80-$129.** 1714 11th Ave 59601. I-15 exit 192 (Prospect Ave), just w of I-15 and US 287/12. Ext/int corridors. **Pets:** Other species. $20 one-time fee/room. Service with restrictions, crate.
🍽 ᴍ ⊠ 🛜 🛗 ▭

▼▼ **La Quinta Inn & Suites Helena** H
(406) 449-4000. **$85-$211.** 701 Washington St 59601. I-15 exit 192 (Prospect Ave), just w. Int corridors. **Pets:** Large, other species. Service with restrictions. ᴍ 🛜 ✕ 🛗 ▭

▼▼▼ **Red Lion Colonial Hotel** H
(406) 443-2100. **Call for rates.** 2301 Colonial Dr 59601. I-15 exit 192 (Prospect Ave) southbound; exit 192B northbound. Int corridors.
Pets: Accepted. 🍽 ᴍ ⊠ 🛜 ✕ 🛗 ▭

▼▼▼ **Residence Inn by Marriott** H
(406) 443-8010. **$159-$175.** 2500 E Custer Ave 59602. I-15 exit 194 (Custer Ave), just e. Int corridors. **Pets:** Large, other species. $100 one-time fee/room. Service with restrictions. ᴍ ⊠ 🛜 ✕ 🛗 ▭

ⓐⓐⓐ ▼▼▼ **Wingate by Wyndham** H
(406) 449-3000. **$99-$225.** 2007 N Oakes St 59601. I-15 exit 193 (Cedar St), just sw. Int corridors. **Pets:** Accepted.
SAVE ᴍ ⊠ 🛜 ✕ 🛗 ▭

HUNGRY HORSE

ⓐⓐⓐ ▼ **Mini Golden Inns Motel** M
(406) 387-4313. **$86-$160, 30 day notice.** 8955 US 2 E 59919. East end of town. Ext corridors. **Pets:** Small. $6 one-time fee/pet. Designated rooms, no service, supervision. SAVE ᴍ 🛜 🛗 ▭

KALISPELL

ⓐⓐⓐ ▼ **Aero Inn** H 🐾
(406) 755-3798. **$49-$104.** 1830 US 93 S 59901. 1.3 mi s on US 93 from jct US 2. Int corridors. **Pets:** $20 deposit/room. Designated rooms, service with restrictions, supervision. SAVE ⊠ 🛜 🛗

▼▼ **Americas Best Value Inn** H
(406) 756-3222. **$65-$140.** 1550 Hwy 93 N 59901. 1.3 mi n on US 93 from jct US 2. Int corridors. **Pets:** Accepted. 🛜 ✕ 🛗 ▭

ⓐⓐⓐ ▼▼▼ **BEST WESTERN PLUS Flathead Lake Inn & Suites** H
(406) 857-2400. **$95-$250.** 4824 Hwy 93 S 59901. 7 mi s; jct SR 82. Int corridors. **Pets:** Medium, dogs only. $20 daily fee/room. Designated rooms, service with restrictions, supervision.
SAVE ᴍ ⊠ 🛜 ✕ 🛗 ▭

▼▼ **Comfort Inn** H
(406) 755-6700. **Call for rates.** 1330 Hwy 2 W 59901. 1 mi w on US 2 from jct US 93. Int corridors. **Pets:** $20 one-time fee/room. Designated rooms, service with restrictions, supervision. ⊠ 🛜 ✕ 🛗 ▭

▼▼▼ **Holiday Inn Express & Suites** H
(406) 755-7405. **Call for rates.** 275 Treeline Rd 59901. 3 mi n on US 93 from jct US 2, just w. Int corridors. **Pets:** Accepted.
ᴍ ⊠ 🛜 ✕ 🛗 ▭

▼▼▼ **Homewood Suites by Hilton** H
(406) 755-8080. **$129-$349.** 195 Hutton Ranch Rd 59901. US 93 N, just e. Int corridors. **Pets:** Accepted. ᴍ ⊠ 🛜 ✕ 🛗 ▭

▼▼ **Kalispell/Glacier Int'l Airport area Super 8** H 🐾
(406) 755-1888. **$53-$120.** 1341 1st Ave E 59901. 1.2 mi s on US 93 from jct US 2. Int corridors. **Pets:** Other species. $15 daily fee/pet. Designated rooms, service with restrictions, supervision.
ᴍ 🛜 ✕ 🛗 ▭

▼▼ **Kalispell Grand Hotel** H 🐾
(406) 755-8100. **$88-$162.** 100 Main St 59901. On US 93; jct 1st St; downtown. Int corridors. **Pets:** Other species. Crate. 🛜 ✕

▼▼▼ **La Quinta Inn & Suites Kalispell** H
(406) 257-5255. **$86-$339.** 255 Montclair Dr 59901. Jct US 93 and 2, 1 mi e. Int corridors. **Pets:** Large, other species. Service with restrictions.
ᴍ ⊠ 🛜 ✕ 🛗 ▭

▼▼ **Red Lion Hotel Kalispell** H
(406) 751-5050. **Call for rates.** 20 N Main St 59901. Just s on US 93 from jct US 2; connected to Kalispell Center Mall. Int corridors.
Pets: Accepted. ᴍ ⊠ ✕ 🛜 ✕ 🛗 ▭

LAUREL

ⓐⓐⓐ ▼▼ **BEST WESTERN Yellowstone Crossing** H
(406) 628-6888. **$89-$99.** 205 SE 4th St 59044. I-90 exit 434, just n, then just e. Int corridors. **Pets:** Medium. $15 daily fee/pet. Designated rooms, service with restrictions, supervision.
SAVE ᴍ ⊠ 🛜 🛗 ▭

LEWISTOWN

▼ **B & B Motel** M
(406) 535-5496. **Call for rates.** 520 E Main St 59457. Downtown. Ext corridors. **Pets:** Small, dogs only. $10 daily fee/pet. Designated rooms, service with restrictions, supervision. 🛜 🛗 ▭

▼▼ **Lewistown Super 8** H
(406) 538-2581. **$72-$125.** 102 Wendell Ave 59457. West side of town, on US 87; near airport. Int corridors. **Pets:** $10 one-time fee/pet. Designated rooms, service with restrictions, supervision. 🛜 ✕ 🛗 ▭

LIBBY

▼ **Sandman Motel** M 🐾
(406) 293-8831. **$55-$85.** 31901 US 2 59923. Just w on US 2 from jct SR 37. Ext corridors. **Pets:** Medium, other species. $8 daily fee/pet. Designated rooms, service with restrictions, supervision. 🛜 🛗

▼▼▼ **Venture Motor Inn** H
(406) 293-7711. **$75-$112.** 1015 W 9th St (US 2) 59923. Just w on US 2 from jct SR 37. Int corridors. **Pets:** Dogs only. $10 daily fee/pet. Designated rooms, service with restrictions, supervision.
SAVE 🍽 ⊠ 🛜 ✕ 🛗 ▭

LIVINGSTON

ⓐⓐⓐ ▼▼▼ **BEST WESTERN Yellowstone Inn** H
(406) 222-6110. **Call for rates.** 1515 W Park St 59047. I-90 exit 333, just n. Int corridors. **Pets:** Accepted. SAVE 🍽 ⊠ 🛜 🛗 ▭

▼▼ **Livingston Rodeway Inn** M
(406) 222-6320. **$66-$155.** 102 Rogers Ln 59047. I-90 exit 333, just n on US 89, then just w. Ext/int corridors. **Pets:** Accepted.
🍽 ⊠ 🛜 🛗 ▭

LOLO

▼▼ **Days Inn** H
(406) 273-2121. **$80-$110, 3 day notice.** 11225 US 93 S 59847. North edge of town. Ext/int corridors. **Pets:** Accepted.
ᴍ 🛜 ✕ 🛗 ▭

MALTA

ⓐⓐⓐ ▼ **Maltana Motel** M
(406) 654-2610. **$74-$87.** 138 S 1st Ave W 59538. Just s of US 2 via US 191, just w; downtown. Ext corridors. **Pets:** Accepted.
SAVE 🛜 ✕ 🛗 ▭

MILES CITY

ⓐⓐⓐ ▼▼▼ **BEST WESTERN War Bonnet Inn** M
(406) 234-4560. **$110-$200.** 1015 S Haynes Ave 59301. I-94 exit 138 (Broadus), 0.3 mi n. Ext corridors. **Pets:** Other species. $20 daily fee/room. Designated rooms, service with restrictions, crate.
SAVE ⊠ ✕ 🛜 ✕ 🛗 ▭

▼▼ Comfort Inn Miles City H
(406) 234-3141. **$100-$145.** 1615 S Haynes Ave 59301. I-94 exit 138 (Broadus), just s. Int corridors. **Pets:** Medium. $15 daily fee/pet. Designated rooms, service with restrictions, supervision.

♿ ≋ 📶 ✖ 🛄 📺

▲▲ ▼▼▼▼ Sleep Inn & Suites Miles City H
(406) 232-3000. **$109-$209.** 1006 S Haynes Ave 59301. I-94 exit 138 (Broadus), 0.3 mi n. Int corridors. **Pets:** Accepted.

SAVE ♿ 📶 ✖ 🛄 📺

MISSOULA

▲▲ ▼▼▼▼ BEST WESTERN PLUS Grant Creek Inn H 🐾
(406) 543-0700. **$109-$179.** 5280 Grant Creek Rd 59808. I-90 exit 101 (Reserve St), just n. Int corridors. **Pets:** Large. $10 daily fee/room. Designated rooms, service with restrictions, supervision.

SAVE ♿ ≋ ✖ 📶 ✖ 🛄 📺

▼▼ Broadway Inn Conference Center H 🐾
(406) 532-3300. **$70-$200.** 1609 W Broadway 59808. I-90 exit 104 (Orange St), 0.5 mi s, then 1 mi w. Int corridors. **Pets:** Dogs only. $10 daily fee/pet. Designated rooms, service with restrictions, supervision.

🍴 ≋ 📶 🛄 📺

▼▼ Campus Inn M
(406) 549-5134. **Call for rates.** 744 E Broadway 59802. I-90 exit 105 (Van Buren St), just s to Broadway, then just w. Ext/int corridors. **Pets:** Accepted. ≋ 📶 ✖ 🛄 📺

▼▼▼▼ Comfort Inn - University H 🐾
(406) 549-7600. **$99-$199.** 1021 E Broadway 59802. I-90 exit 105 (Van Buren St), just s, then just e. Int corridors. **Pets:** $25 daily fee/room. Designated rooms, service with restrictions, crate.

♿ 📶 ✖ 🛄 📺

▲▲ ▼▼▼▼ Courtyard by Marriott H
(406) 549-5260. **$79-$259.** 4559 N Reserve St 59808. I-90 exit 101 (Reserve St), just s, then just w. Int corridors. **Pets:** Accepted.

SAVE 🍴 ♿ ≋ 📶 ✖ 🛄 📺

▼▼ Days Inn/Missoula Airport H
(406) 721-9776. **$64-$104.** 8600 Truck Stop Rd 59808. I-90 exit 96, just n. Int corridors. **Pets:** Accepted. 📶 🛄 📺

▼▼ Days Inn University H
(406) 543-7221. **$80-$100.** 201 E Main St 59802. I-90 exit 104 (Orange St), 0.5 mi s to Broadway, 0.5 mi e to Washington St, just s to Main St, then just w. Ext corridors. **Pets:** Dogs only. $15 daily fee/pet. Service with restrictions, supervision. ≋ 📶 🛄 📺

▲▲ ▼▼▼▼ DoubleTree by Hilton Hotel Missoula - Edgewater H
(406) 728-3100. **$109-$250.** 100 Madison St 59802. I-90 exit 105 (Van Buren St), just s, then just w on Front St. Int corridors. **Pets:** Accepted.

SAVE 🍴 ♿ ≋ 📶 🛄 📺

▼▼ Econo Lodge H
(406) 542-7550. **$65-$95.** 4953 N Reserve St 59808. I-90 exit 101 (Reserve St), just s. Int corridors. **Pets:** Accepted. ♿ 📶 🛄 📺

▼▼ GuestHouse Inn & Suites - Missoula H
(406) 251-2665. **$69-$109.** 3803 Brooks St 59804. I-90 exit 101 (Reserve St), 5 mi s to Brooks St, then just w. Int corridors. **Pets:** Accepted. ♿ 📶 ✖ 🛄 📺

▲▲ ▼▼▼▼ Hampton Inn H
(406) 549-1800. **$99-$169.** 4805 N Reserve St 59808. I-90 exit 101 (Reserve St), just s. Int corridors. **Pets:** Accepted.

SAVE ♿ ≋ 📶 🛄 📺

▲▲ ▼▼▼▼ Holiday Inn Missoula-Downtown at the Park H
(406) 721-8550. **$99-$209.** 200 S Pattee St 59802. I-90 exit 104 (Orange St), 0.5 mi s to Broadway, just e to Pattee St, then just s. Int corridors. **Pets:** Accepted.

SAVE 🍴 ♿ ≋ ✖ 📶 ✖ 🛄 📺

▼▼ La Quinta Inn Missoula H
(406) 549-9000. **$74-$279.** 5059 N Reserve St 59808. I-90 exit 101 (Reserve St), just s. Int corridors. **Pets:** Large, other species. Service with restrictions. ♿ 📶 ✖ 🛄 📺

▼▼ Quality Inn & Suites-Missoula H
(406) 542-0888. **$99-$165.** 4545 N Reserve St 59808. I-90 exit 101 (Reserve St), 0.7 mi s. Int corridors. **Pets:** Small, dogs only. $20 daily fee/room. Designated rooms, service with restrictions, crate.

♿ ≋ 📶 🛄 📺

▼▼ Red Lion Inn M
(406) 728-3300. **$89-$149.** 700 W Broadway 59802. I-90 exit 104 (Orange St), just s, then just w. Ext corridors. **Pets:** Accepted.

≋ 📶 ✖ 🛄 📺

▲▲ ▼▼▼▼ Ruby's Inn & Convention Center H
(406) 721-0990. **$79-$125, 7 day notice.** 4825 N Reserve St 59808. I-90 exit 101 (Reserve St), just s. Ext/int corridors. **Pets:** $10 daily fee/room. Service with restrictions, supervision.

SAVE ♿ ≋ ✖ 📶 🛄 📺

▼▼ Sleep Inn by Choice Hotels H
(406) 543-5883. **$69-$139.** 3425 Dore Ln 59801. I-90 exit 101 (Reserve St), 5 mi s, then just e on Brooks St. Int corridors. **Pets:** Accepted.

♿ ≋ 📶 🛄 📺

▼▼▼▼ Staybridge Suites H 🐾
(406) 830-3900. **$99-$299.** 120 Expressway Blvd 59808. I-90 exit 101 (Reserve St), just s. Int corridors. **Pets:** Medium. $50 one-time fee/room. Designated rooms, service with restrictions, supervision.

♿ ≋ 📶 ✖ 🛄 📺

▼▼ Super 8-Brooks St H
(406) 251-2255. **$78-$87.** 3901 Brooks St 59804. I-90 exit 101 (Reserve St), 5 mi s to Brooks St, then just w. Int corridors. **Pets:** Accepted. 📶 ✖ 🛄 📺

▲▲ ▼▼▼▼ Thunderbird Motel M
(406) 543-7251. **$75-$95.** 1009 E Broadway 59802. I-90 exit 105 (Van Buren St), just s to Broadway, then just e. Ext/int corridors. **Pets:** Accepted. SAVE ≋ 📶 🛄 📺

▼▼▼▼ Wingate by Wyndham H
(406) 541-8000. **$99-$195.** 5252 Airway Blvd 59808. I-90 exit 99 (Airway Blvd), just s to E Harrier Dr. Int corridors. **Pets:** Dogs only. $15 one-time fee/room. Designated rooms, service with restrictions.

♿ ≋ 📶 ✖ 🛄 📺

MONTANA CITY

▼▼ Elkhorn Mountain Inn H
(406) 442-6625. **$70-$90.** 1 Jackson Creek Rd 59634. I-15 exit 187 (Montana City), just w. Int corridors. **Pets:** $10 one-time fee/room. Designated rooms, service with restrictions, supervision.

♿ 📶 ✖ 🛄 📺

POLSON

▼▼ Americas Best Value Port Polson Inn M
(406) 883-5385. **$69-$160.** 49825 US Hwy 93 E 59860. Just s of downtown. Ext/int corridors. **Pets:** Small, dogs only. $20 daily fee/pet. Designated rooms, service with restrictions, supervision. 📶 🛄 📺

▲▲ ▼▼▼▼ BEST WESTERN PLUS KwaTaqNuk Resort H
(406) 883-3636. **$95-$250, 3 day notice.** 49708 US Hwy 93 E 59860. Just s of downtown. Int corridors. **Pets:** Accepted.

SAVE 🍴 ♿ ≋ ✖ 📶 ✖ 🛄 📺

RED LODGE

▼▼ Comfort Inn of Red Lodge H

(406) 446-4469. **$99-$210.** 612 N Broadway Ave 59068. Jct US 212 and SR 78, north entrance. Int corridors. **Pets:** Other species. $15 daily fee/room. Designated rooms, supervision.

🅜 ⊇ 🤝 ✕ 🔒 💻

⚡ ▼▼ Rock Creek Resort H 🐾

(406) 446-1111. **$130-$390, 15 day notice.** 6380 US Hwy 212 S 59068. 5.8 mi s. Ext/int corridors. **Pets:** Dogs only. $20 one-time fee/pet. Designated rooms, supervision.

SAVE 🍴 ⊇ ✕ 🤝 ✕ 🐾 🔒 💻

▼ Yodeler Motel M

(406) 446-1435. **$60-$140.** 601 S Broadway Ave 59068. Just s on US 212. Ext corridors. **Pets:** Other species. $5 daily fee/pet. Designated rooms, service with restrictions, supervision. 🤝 ✕ 🔒 💻

RONAN

▼ Starlite Motel M

(406) 676-7000. **$63-$100, 3 day notice.** 18 Main St SW 59864. Just w of jct US 93 and Main St. Ext corridors. **Pets:** Dogs only. $10 daily fee/pet. Designated rooms. 🤝 🔒 💻

ST. IGNATIUS

▼ Sunset Motel M

(406) 745-3900. **$60-$80.** 333 Mountain View 59865. Just s of downtown, exit US 93. Ext corridors. **Pets:** Dogs only. $5 daily fee/pet. Service with restrictions, supervision. 🤝 ✕ 🔒

ST. REGIS

⚡ ▼ Little River Motel M

(406) 649-2713. **$45-$85.** 424 Little River Ln 59866. I-90 exit 33, just n to flashing light, just w, then just sw. Ext corridors. **Pets:** $10 one-time fee/pet. Service with restrictions, supervision.

SAVE 🤝 ✕ 🐾 🆔 🔒 💻

⚡ ▼▼ Super 8-St. Regis H

(406) 649-2422. **$59-$93.** 9 Old Hwy 10 E 59866. I-90 exit 33, just n. Ext/int corridors. **Pets:** $10 daily fee/pet. Service with restrictions.

SAVE 🤝 🔒 💻

SHELBY

⚡ ▼▼▼ BEST WESTERN Shelby Inn & Suites H

(406) 424-4560. **$89-$160.** 1948 Roosevelt Hwy 59474. I-15 exit 363, just w. Int corridors. **Pets:** Other species. $15 one-time fee/pet. Designated rooms, service with restrictions, supervision.

SAVE 🅜 🤝 ✕ 🔒 💻

⚡ ▼▼ Comfort Inn of Shelby H 🐾

(406) 434-2212. **$95-$160.** 455 McKinley Ave 59474. I-15 exit 363, just e, then just s. Int corridors. **Pets:** Other species. $15 one-time fee/room. Service with restrictions, supervision.

SAVE ✕ 🤝 ✕ 🔒 💻

SIDNEY

⚡ ▼▼▼ BEST WESTERN Golden Prairie Inn & Suites H

(406) 433-4560. **$125-$170.** 820 S Central Ave 59270. 1.8 mi n of jct SR 16 and 200. Int corridors. **Pets:** Accepted.

SAVE ⊇ 🤝 ✕ 🔒 💻

▼▼ Microtel Inn & Suites by Wyndham Sidney H

(406) 482-9011. **$116-$179.** 1500 S Central Ave 59270. 1.3 mi n of jct SR 16 and 200. Int corridors. **Pets:** Other species. $20 daily fee/pet. Service with restrictions, supervision. 🅜 🤝 ✕ 🔒 💻

⚡ ▼▼ Richland Inn & Suites M

(406) 433-6400. **$110-$150.** 1200 S Central Ave 59270. 1.5 mi n of jct SR 16 and 200. Int corridors. **Pets:** Dogs only. $10 daily fee/pet. Designated rooms, crate. SAVE 🤝 🔒 💻

SUPERIOR

▼ Big Sky Motel M

(406) 822-4831. **$86-$96.** 103 4th Ave E 59872. I-90 exit 47, just n. Ext corridors. **Pets:** $10 one-time fee/pet. Designated rooms, supervision.

🤝 ✕ 🔒

THREE FORKS

⚡ ▼ Broken Spur Motel M

(406) 285-3237. **$69-$130.** 124 W Elm (Hwy 2) 59752. I-90 exit 278 westbound, 1.3 mi sw; exit 274 eastbound, 1 mi s on SR 287 to jct SR 2, then 3 mi se. Ext corridors. **Pets:** $10 one-time fee/pet. Designated rooms, service with restrictions, supervision. SAVE 🤝 🔒

▼ Fort Three Forks Motel & RV Park M

(406) 285-3233. **$68-$116, 3 day notice.** 10776 Hwy 287 59752. I-90 exit 274, just n. Ext corridors. **Pets:** Accepted. 🤝 🔒 💻

WEST YELLOWSTONE

⚡ ▼▼▼ BEST WESTERN Desert Inn H 🐾

(406) 646-7376. **$85-$270.** 133 Canyon St 59758. Jct US 191 (Canyon St) and Firehole Ave; 0.3 mi n of park entrance. Int corridors. **Pets:** Dogs only. Designated rooms, service with restrictions, supervision. SAVE 🅜 ⊇ 🤝 ✕ 🔒 💻

⚡ ▼▼▼ BEST WESTERN Weston Inn M

(406) 646-7373. **$62-$250.** 103 Gibbon Ave 59758. Jct US 191 (Canyon St) and Gibbon Ave; 0.5 mi n of park entrance. Ext/int corridors. **Pets:** Accepted. SAVE ⊇ 🤝 ✕ 🔒 💻

⚡ ▼▼ Brandin' Iron Inn M

(406) 646-9411. **$79-$199, 3 day notice.** 201 Canyon St 59758. Jct US 20 (Firehole Ave) and US 191 (Canyon St); 0.3 mi n of park entrance. Ext corridors. **Pets:** Accepted. SAVE 🅜 🤝 ✕ 🔒 💻

⚡ ▼ City Center Motel M

(406) 646-7337. **$69-$139, 3 day notice.** 214 Madison Ave 59758. Jct Madison Ave and Dunraven St; 0.4 mi nw of park entrance. Ext corridors. **Pets:** Accepted. SAVE 🤝 ✕ 🐾 💻

▼▼▼ ClubHouse Inn H

(406) 646-4892. **$100-$270.** 105 S Electric St 59758. Just sw of jct US 20/191/287; 0.4 mi w of park entrance. Int corridors. **Pets:** Other species. Designated rooms, service with restrictions, supervision.

🅜 ⊇ 🤝 ✕ 🔒 💻

▼▼▼ Crosswinds Inn M 🐾

(406) 646-9557. **$70-$230.** 201 Firehole Ave 59758. Just w of US 191 (Canyon St); at US 20 (Firehole Ave) and Dunraven St; 0.5 mi nw of park entrance. Ext corridors. **Pets:** Dogs only. $20 one-time fee/room. Designated rooms, service with restrictions, supervision.

⊇ 🤝 ✕ 🔒 💻

⚡ ▼▼▼ Explorer Cabins at Yellowstone CA

(406) 646-7075. **Call for rates.** 201 Grizzly Ave 59758. 0.4 mi w of park entrance. Ext corridors. **Pets:** Accepted. SAVE 🤝 ✕ 🔒 💻

⚡ ▼▼ Gray Wolf Inn and Suites H

(406) 646-0000. **$89-$259, 3 day notice.** 250 S Canyon St 59758. Just e of park entrance, just s. Int corridors. **Pets:** Accepted.

SAVE 🅜 ⊇ 🤝 ✕ 🔒 💻

⚡ ▼▼▼ Holiday Inn West Yellowstone Conference Hotel H

(406) 646-7365. **$119-$319, 5 day notice.** 315 Yellowstone Ave 59758. 0.4 mi w of park entrance. Int corridors. **Pets:** $50 one-time fee/room. Designated rooms, service with restrictions, supervision.

SAVE 🍴 🅜 ⊇ ✕ 🤝 ✕ 🔒 💻

⚡ ▼▼▼ Stage Coach Inn H

(406) 646-7381. **$49-$279, 3 day notice.** 209 Madison Ave 59758. Corner of Dunraven St and Madison Ave; 0.4 mi nw of park entrance. Int corridors. **Pets:** Accepted. SAVE 🅜 ✕ 🤝 ✕ 🔒 💻

Three Bear Lodge H
(406) 646-7353. **$69-$239.** 217 Yellowstone Ave 59758. Just w of park entrance. Ext/int corridors. **Pets:** Accepted.
[SAVE] [†] [≈] [⊠] [≋] [✕] [☎] [▭]

Yellowstone Lodge H
(406) 646-0020. **$79-$239.** 251 S Electric St 59758. Just s of Yellowstone Ave and Electric St; 0.6 mi from park entrance. Int corridors.
Pets: Accepted. [≈] [≋] [⊠] [☎] [▭]

Yellowstone Westgate Hotel H
(406) 646-4212. **Call for rates.** 638 Madison Ave 59758. At Iris St and Madison Ave; 1 mi nw of park entrance. Int corridors. **Pets:** Designated rooms, service with restrictions. [≈] [≋] [✕] [☎] [▭]

WHITEFISH
Bay Point on the Lake CO
(406) 862-2331. **Call for rates.** 300 Bay Point Dr 59937. Jct US 93 and SR 487, 0.6 mi n on SR 487 to Skyles Pl, 0.3 mi w to Dakota Ave, 0.3 mi n, then just w. Ext corridors. **Pets:** Accepted.
[≈] [⊠] [≋] [☎] [▭]

BEST WESTERN Rocky Mountain Lodge H ❀
(406) 862-2569. **Call for rates.** 6510 Hwy 93 S 59937. 1.3 mi s on US 93 from jct SR 487. Ext/int corridors. **Pets:** Medium. $20 daily fee/room. Designated rooms, service with restrictions, supervision.
[SAVE] [&M] [≈] [≋] [✕] [☎] [▭]

Grouse Mountain Lodge H
(406) 862-3000. **$114-$219, 3 day notice.** 2 Fairway Dr 59937. 1 mi w on US 93 from jct SR 487. Int corridors. **Pets:** Dogs only. $25 one-time fee/pet. Designated rooms, service with restrictions, supervision.
[SAVE] [†] [≈] [⊠] [≋] [✕] [☎] [▭]

North Forty Resort CA
(406) 862-7740. **$119-$289, 14 day notice.** 3765 Hwy 40 W 59912. 2.5 mi e on SR 40 from jct US 93. Ext corridors. **Pets:** Other species. $10 daily fee/pet. Designated rooms, service with restrictions, crate.
[≈] [✕] [⅀] [☎] [▭]

Pine Lodge H
(406) 862-7600. **$82-$170.** 920 Spokane Ave 59937. 1 mi s on US 93 from jct SR 487. Int corridors. **Pets:** Dogs only. $25 one-time fee/pet. Service with restrictions, supervision.
[SAVE] [&M] [≈] [≋] [✕] [☎] [▭]

NEBRASKA

BELLEVUE
BEST WESTERN White House Inn H
(402) 293-1600. **$94-$190.** 305 Fort Crook Rd N 68005. US 75, 1.8 mi n of jct SR 370 and Fort Crook Rd N. Int corridors. **Pets:** Accepted.
[SAVE] [&M] [≋] [✕] [☎] [▭]

Hampton Inn H
(402) 292-1607. **$109-$259.** 3404 Samson Way 68123. US 75, 1 mi n on SR 370, just w on Golden Blvd, 0.3 mi n. Int corridors.
Pets: Accepted. [SAVE] [&M] [≈] [≋] [✕] [☎] [▭]

Microtel Inn & Suites by Wyndham Bellevue H
(402) 292-0191. **$65-$170.** 3008 Samson Way 68123. Jct US 75, 1 mi w on SR 370, just n on Golden Blvd, just w. Int corridors.
Pets: Accepted. [SAVE] [&M] [≋] [✕] [☎] [▭]

CHADRON
BEST WESTERN West Hills Inn H ❀
(308) 432-3305. **$87-$157.** 1100 W 10th St 69337. Just s of jct US 385 and 20. Ext/int corridors. **Pets:** $12 daily fee/room. Designated rooms, service with restrictions, crate. [SAVE] [≈] [≋] [✕] [☎] [▭]

Grand Westerner Motel M
(308) 432-5595. **Call for rates.** 1050 W Hwy 20 69337. On US 20, 0.8 mi w; just e of jct US 385. Ext corridors. **Pets:** Accepted.
[≋] [✕] [☎]

Westerner Motel M
(308) 432-5577. **$55-$65.** 300 Oak St 69337. On US 20; 0.5 mi e of jct US 385 and SR 87. Ext corridors. **Pets:** Dogs only. $10 one-time fee/room. Designated rooms, service with restrictions, supervision.
[SAVE] [≋] [☎]

COLUMBUS
Sleep Inn & Suites Hotel H
(402) 562-5200. **$74-$89.** 303 23rd St 68601. On US 30, 2 mi e of jct US 30 and 81; east side of town. Int corridors. **Pets:** Medium. $25 daily fee/room. No service, crate. [&M] [≋] [✕] [☎] [▭]

COZAD
Rodeway Inn H
(308) 784-4900. **$55-$85.** 809 S Meridian Ave 69130. I-80 exit 222, just n. Int corridors. **Pets:** Accepted. [†] [&M] [≋] [✕] [☎] [▭]

FREMONT
Oak Tree Inn H
(402) 721-3700. **Call for rates.** 2700 N Diers Pkwy 68025. US 30, just n. Int corridors. **Pets:** Accepted. [&M] [≋] [✕] [☎] [▭]

GERING
Monument Inn & Suites H
(308) 436-1950. **$75-$105.** 1130 M St 69341. 1 mi e of SR 71, just w of M (SR 92) and 10th sts. Int corridors. **Pets:** Medium, dogs only. $15 one-time fee/room. Designated rooms, service with restrictions, crate.
[≋] [☎] [▭]

GOTHENBURG
Comfort Suites H
(308) 537-7378. **$99-$119.** 315 Platte River Dr 69138. I-80 exit 211 (SR 47), just n, then just w. Int corridors. **Pets:** Other species. $15 daily fee/pet. Designated rooms, supervision. [&M] [≈] [≋] [✕] [☎] [▭]

GRAND ISLAND
Days Inn-Grand Island I-80 H
(308) 384-5006. **$69-$120.** 7800 S US Hwy 281 68803. I-80 exit 312 (US 281), just s. Int corridors. **Pets:** Other species. $15 daily fee/room. Service with restrictions, crate. [&M] [≋] [✕] [☎] [▭]

Quality Inn and Conference Center H
(308) 384-7770. **$85-$180.** 7838 S US Hwy 281 68803. I-80 exit 312 (US 281), just s. Int corridors. **Pets:** Medium. $15 daily fee/room. Designated rooms, service with restrictions, supervision.
[†] [&M] [≈] [⊠] [≋] [☎] [▭]

Rodeway Inn H
(308) 384-1333. **$65-$75.** 3205 S Locust St 68801. I-80 exit 314, 4 mi n. Int corridors. **Pets:** Accepted. [≋] [☎] [▭]

Super 8 H
(308) 384-4380. **$74-$115.** 2603 S Locust St 68801. I-80 exit 314, 4.7 mi n. Int corridors. **Pets:** Accepted. [SAVE] [&M] [≈] [≋] [☎] [▭]

KEARNEY
AmericInn Lodge & Suites of Kearney H
(308) 234-7800. **Call for rates.** 215 W Talmadge Rd 68845. I-80 exit 272 (SR 44), just n. Int corridors. **Pets:** Medium, dogs only. $10 daily fee/room. Designated rooms, service with restrictions, supervision.
[SAVE] [&M] [≈] [≋] [✕] [☎] [▭]

▼▼ **Econo Lodge** 🅗
(308) 237-2671. **$62-$120.** 709 2nd Ave 68847. I-80 exit 272 (SR 44), 1 mi n. Int corridors. **Pets:** Accepted. 🛜 ✖ 🔋 🖵

🆔 ▼▼ **Microtel Inn & Suites by Wyndham Kearney** 🅗 🐾
(308) 698-3003. **$64-$95.** 104 Talmadge Rd 68847. I-80 exit 272 (SR 44), just se. Int corridors. **Pets:** Medium, other species. $10 daily fee/room. Designated rooms, service with restrictions, supervision.
[SAVE] 🛜 ✖ 🔋 🖵

▼▼ **New Victorian Inn & Suites** 🅗
(308) 237-5858. **Call for rates.** 903 2nd Ave 68847. I-80 exit 272 (SR 44), 1 mi n. Int corridors. **Pets:** Accepted. 🛜 🔋

▼▼ **Quality Inn by Choice Hotels** 🅗
(308) 237-0838. **$74-$169.** 121 3rd Ave 68845. I-80 exit 272 (SR 44), 0.3 mi n. Int corridors. **Pets:** Accepted. 🏊 🛜 ✖ 🔋 🖵

▼▼ **Rodeway Inn & Suites** 🅗
(308) 698-2810. **$70-$141.** 411 2nd Ave 68847. I-80 exit 272 (SR 44), 0.8 mi n. Int corridors. **Pets:** Accepted. 🛜 ✖ 🔋 🖵

LEXINGTON
▼▼ **Days Inn** 🅗
(308) 324-6440. **$80-$130.** 2506 Plum Creek Pkwy 68850. I-80 exit 237 (US 283), 0.6 mi n. Int corridors. **Pets:** Dogs only. $15 daily fee/pet. Designated rooms, no service, supervision. 🍴 🛜 🔋 🖵

▼▼▼ **Holiday Inn Express & Suites** 🅗
(308) 324-9900. **Call for rates.** 2605 Plum Creek Pkwy 68850. I-80 exit 237 (US 283), 0.5 mi n. Int corridors. **Pets:** Other species. $25 daily fee/room. Designated rooms, service with restrictions, supervision.
🍴 🏊 🛜 ✖ 🔋 🖵

▼▼ **Lexington Comfort Inn** 🅗
(308) 324-3747. **$80-$130.** 2810 Plum Creek Pkwy 68850. I-80 exit 237 (US 283), 0.3 mi n. Ext/int corridors. **Pets:** Small. $15 one-time fee/pet. Designated rooms, service with restrictions, supervision.
🍴 🏊 🛜 🔋 🖵

LINCOLN
🆔 ▼▼ **AmericInn Lodge & Suites of Lincoln North** 🅗
(402) 435-1600. **$80-$200, 3 day notice.** 6555 N 27th St 68521. I-80 exit 403 (27th St), 0.3 mi s, just w on Whitehead Dr, then just s. Int corridors. **Pets:** Accepted. [SAVE] 🏊 🛜 🔋 🖵

▼▼ **AmericInn Lodge & Suites of Lincoln South** 🅗
(402) 420-0027. **Call for rates.** 8701 Amber Hill Ct 68526. 5.8 mi se on SR 2 (Nebraska Hwy), just w at 87th St. Int corridors. **Pets:** Accepted.
🏊 🛜 ✖ 🔋 🖵

▼▼▼ **Comfort Suites** 🅗
(402) 476-8080. **$80-$120, 3 day notice.** 4231 Industrial Ave 68504. I-80 exit 403 (27th St), 2.3 mi s. Int corridors. **Pets:** Medium. $10 daily fee/pet. Service with restrictions, supervision.
🏊 🛜 ✖ 🔋 🖵

▼▼▼ **Comfort Suites East** 🅗
(402) 325-8800. **$80-$119.** 331 N Cotner Blvd 68505. I-180 exit 9th St, 3.3 mi e on US 34 (O St), then 0.3 mi n. Int corridors. **Pets:** Accepted.
🏊 🛜 ✖ 🔋 🖵

🆔 ▼▼ **Country Inn & Suites By Carlson-Lincoln Airport** 🅗 🐾
(402) 474-2080. **$69-$199.** 1301 W Bond Cir 68521. I-80 exit 399 (Airport), just nw. Int corridors. **Pets:** $10 deposit/pet, $10 daily fee/pet. Service with restrictions. [SAVE] 🏊 🛜 ✖ 🔋 🖵

🆔 ▼▼ **Country Inn & Suites By Carlson Lincoln North** 🅗
(402) 476-5353. **$89-$299.** 5353 N 27th St 68521. I-80 exit 403 (27th St), 1.5 mi s. Int corridors. **Pets:** Accepted.
[SAVE] 🍴 🏊 🛜 ✖ 🔋 🖵

▼▼▼ **Holiday Inn Express & Suites Lincoln Airport** 🅗
(402) 464-0588. **$99-$289.** 1101 W Commerce Way 68521. I-80 exit 399, just n, then just e. Int corridors. **Pets:** Accepted.
🏊 🛜 ✖ 🔋 🖵

▼▼▼ **Hyatt Place Lincoln/Downtown-Haymarket** 🅗 🐾
(402) 742-6007. **$99-$399.** 600 Q St 68508. Jct Q and 6th sts; in Historic Haymarket District. Int corridors. **Pets:** Medium, dogs only. $75 one-time fee/room. Designated rooms, service with restrictions, crate.
[SAVE] 🛜 ✖ 🔋 🖵

🆔 ▼▼▼ **La Quinta Inn Lincoln** 🅗
(402) 476-2222. **$74-$209.** 4433 N 27th St 68521. I-80 exit 403 (27th St), 2.3 mi s. Int corridors. **Pets:** Large, other species. Service with restrictions. [SAVE] 🏊 🛜 ✖ 🔋 🖵

▼▼ **New Victorian Suites** 🅗
(402) 464-4400. **$64-$189.** 225 N 50th St 68504. 2.5 mi e on US 6 and 34; just ne of jct O St; entrance off 48th St. Int corridors. **Pets:** Medium, dogs only. $15 daily fee/pet. Service with restrictions, supervision. 🏊 🛜 ✖ 🔋

▼▼▼ **Residence Inn by Marriott-Lincoln South** 🅗
(402) 423-1555. **$104-$171.** 5865 Boboli Ln 68516. 1 mi s of SR 2 (Nebraska Hwy) via 56th St, just e on Pine Lake Rd. Int corridors. **Pets:** Accepted. 🍴 🏊 🛜 ✖ 🔋 🖵

▼▼▼ **Staybridge Suites Lincoln-I-80** 🅗
(402) 438-7829. **$99-$326.** 2701 Fletcher Ave 68504. I-80 exit 403 (27th St), 0.4 mi s, then just e. Int corridors. **Pets:** Other species. $75 one-time fee/room. Designated rooms, service with restrictions, crate.
🏊 🛜 🔋 🖵

▼▼ **Super 8-Lincoln/West 'O' Street** 🅗
(402) 476-8887. **$53-$129.** 2635 West O St 68528. I-80 exit 396 eastbound, 0.5 mi e; exit 397 westbound, 0.5 mi w. Int corridors. **Pets:** Small. $10 daily fee/pet. Designated rooms, service with restrictions, supervision. 🍴 🛜 🔋 🖵

MORRILL
▼▼ **Oak Tree Inn** Ⓜ
(308) 247-2111. **Call for rates.** 707 E Webster St 69358. 0.4 mi e of center on US 26. Ext/int corridors. **Pets:** Accepted.
🍴 🛜 ✖ 🔋 🖵

NORTH PLATTE
▼ **Americas Best Value Travelers Inn** Ⓜ
(308) 534-4020. **$40-$70.** 602 E 4th St 69101. I-80 exit 177 (US 83), 1.5 mi n, then 0.3 mi e. Ext corridors. **Pets:** Small, other species. Service with restrictions, supervision. 🍴 🏊 🛜 ✖ 🔋 🖵

▼▼ **Comfort Inn** 🅗 🐾
(308) 532-6144. **$89-$139.** 2901 S Jeffers St 69101. I-80 exit 177 (US 83), just s. Int corridors. **Pets:** Medium, other species. $15 daily fee/pet. Designated rooms, service with restrictions, crate.
🏊 🛜 🔋 🖵

▼▼ **Holiday Inn Express Hotel & Suites** 🅗
(308) 532-9500. **$119-$229.** 300 Holiday Frontage Rd 69101. I-80 exit 177 (US 83), just s. Int corridors. **Pets:** Accepted.
🏊 🛜 ✖ 🔋 🖵

🆔 ▼▼▼ **La Quinta Inn & Suites North Platte** 🅗
(308) 534-0700. **$95-$227.** 2600 Eagles Wings Pl 69101. I-80 exit 179, just n, then just w. Int corridors. **Pets:** Large, other species. Service with restrictions. [SAVE] 🍴 🏊 🛜 ✖ 🔋 🖵

OGALLALA

Days Inn M

(308) 284-6365. **$80-$90.** 601 Stagecoach Tr 69153. I-80 exit 126 (US 26/SR 61), just n, then e on frontage road. Int corridors. **Pets:** $10 deposit/room, $10 one-time fee/room. Service with restrictions, supervision. (SAVE) Ⓜ 🛈 🍽️ 💻

OMAHA (Restaurants p. 634)

BEST WESTERN PLUS Kelly Inn H ✿

(402) 339-7400. **$99-$229.** 4706 S 108th St 68137. I-80 exit 445 (L St E), 0.3 mi e, then just s. Int corridors. **Pets:** Other species. Service with restrictions, crate. (SAVE) 🍴 Ⓜ 🏊 🛈 🍽️ ☒ 🔌 ☕ 💻

Comfort Inn at the Zoo H

(402) 342-8000. **$79-$129.** 2920 S 13th Ct 68108. I-80 exit 454 (13th St) westbound; exit 454 (13th St N) eastbound, just w. Int corridors. **Pets:** Very small. $20 daily fee/room. Service with restrictions, crate. (SAVE) Ⓜ 🏊 🛈 ☒ 🔌 ☕ 💻

DoubleTree by Hilton Hotel Omaha Downtown H

(402) 346-7600. **$99-$189.** 1616 Dodge St 68102. Downtown. Int corridors. **Pets:** Accepted. (SAVE) 🍴 Ⓜ 🏊 🛈 ☒ 🔌 ☕ 💻

DoubleTree Suites by Hilton Hotel Omaha H ✿

(402) 397-5141. **$89-$159.** 7270 Cedar St 68124. I-80 exit 449 (72nd St), 1.3 mi n. Int corridors. **Pets:** Medium. $50 one-time fee/room. Designated rooms, service with restrictions, crate.

🍴 Ⓜ 🏊 ☒ 🛈 ☒ 🔌 ☕ 💻

Element Omaha Midtown Crossing H ✿

(402) 614-8080. **$99-$189.** 3253 Dodge St 68131. I-480 exit 2B westbound; exit 2A northbound, just w; in Midtown Crossing. Int corridors. **Pets:** Other species. Service with restrictions, crate.

(SAVE) 🛈 ☒ 🔌 ☕ 💻

Hawthorn Suites by Wyndham Omaha H

(402) 758-2848. **$79-$149.** 360 S 108th Ave 68154. I-680 exit 3 (W Dodge Rd), 0.7 mi to 108th Ave, then 0.8 mi s. Int corridors. **Pets:** Medium, other species. $50 one-time fee/pet. Service with restrictions, crate. (SAVE) 🍴 Ⓜ 🛈 🔌 ☕ 💻

Hilton Omaha H

(402) 998-3400. **$89-$399.** 1001 Cass St 68102. Jct Cass and 10th sts; downtown. Int corridors. **Pets:** Accepted.

(SAVE) 🍴 Ⓜ 🏊 ☒ 📶 ☒ 🔌 ☕ 💻

Holiday Inn Express Hotel & Suites-Omaha West H

(402) 333-5566. **Call for rates.** 17677 Wright St 68130. I-80 exit 445 (L St W), 5.5 mi w, then just s. Int corridors. **Pets:** Accepted.

Ⓜ 🏊 🛈 ☒ 🔌 ☕ 💻

Home2 Suites by Hilton Omaha West H

(402) 289-9886. **$129-$149.** 17889 Chicago St 68118. I-680 exit 6 (W Dodge Rd), 6 mi w on US 6 (180th St), just s, then e. Int corridors. **Pets:** Accepted. 🍴 Ⓜ 🛈 ☒ 🔌 ☕ 💻

Hotel Deco XV H

(402) 991-4981. **Call for rates.** 1504 Harney St 68102. Jct Harney and 15th sts; downtown. Int corridors. **Pets:** Accepted.

(SAVE) 🍴 🛈 ☒ 🔌

Magnolia Hotel H

(402) 341-2500. **$129-$199.** 1615 Howard St 68102. Jct 16th St. Int corridors. **Pets:** Accepted. (SAVE) 🍴 Ⓜ 🛈 ☒ 🔌 ☕ 💻

Residence Inn by Marriott Omaha-Central H

(402) 553-8898. **$123-$229.** 6990 Dodge St 68132. I-680 exit 3 (Dodge St E), 3 mi e. Ext corridors. **Pets:** Accepted.

Ⓜ 🏊 🛈 ☒ 🔌 ☕ 💻

Sheraton Omaha Hotel H

(402) 496-0850. **$79-$179.** 655 N 108th Ave 68154. I-680 exit 3 (W Dodge Rd), 0.7 mi to 108th St to 108th Ave and N Old Mill Rd exits, then just n. Int corridors. **Pets:** Accepted.

(SAVE) 🍴 Ⓜ 🏊 🛈 ☒ 🔌 ☕ 💻

Sleep Inn & Suites H

(402) 342-2525. **$69-$89.** 2525 Abbott Dr 68110. I-480 E exit 14th St (Cuming St), 2 mi n, follow signs. Int corridors. **Pets:** Accepted.

Ⓜ 🛈 ☒ 🔌 ☕ 💻

Staybridge Suites Omaha H

(402) 933-8901. **Call for rates.** 7825 Davenport St 68114. I-680 exit 3 (Dodge St E), 2.2 mi e, then just n. Int corridors. **Pets:** Accepted.

🏊 🛈 ☒ 🔌 ☕ 💻

TownePlace Suites by Marriott Omaha West H

(402) 590-2800. **$104-$206.** 10865 W Dodge Rd 68154. I-680 exit 3 (W Dodge Rd), 0.7 mi to 108th St to 108th Ave and N Old Mill Rd exits, then just s. Int corridors. **Pets:** Accepted.

Ⓜ 🏊 🛈 ☒ 🔌 ☕ 💻

SCOTTSBLUFF

Scottsbluff Super 8 H

(308) 635-1600. **$59-$99.** 2202 Delta Dr 69361. 1.8 mi e on US 26. Int corridors. **Pets:** Accepted. 🏊 🛈 🔌 ☕ 💻

SIDNEY

BEST WESTERN PLUS Sidney Lodge H

(308) 254-0100. **$110-$150.** 645 Cabela Dr 69162. I-80 exit 59, just nw. Int corridors. **Pets:** Accepted. (SAVE) Ⓜ 🏊 🛈 ☒ 🔌 ☕ 💻

Country Inn & Suites By Carlson H

(308) 254-2000. **Call for rates.** 664 Chase Blvd 69162. I-80 exit 59, just s. Int corridors. **Pets:** Accepted. 🍴 Ⓜ 🏊 🛈 🔌 ☕ 💻

Sidney Comfort Inn H

(308) 254-5011. **$109-$189.** 730 E Jennifer Ln 69162. I-80 exit 59, just n. Int corridors. **Pets:** Accepted. (SAVE) Ⓜ 🏊 🛈 🔌 ☕ 💻

SOUTH SIOUX CITY

Marina Inn Conference Center H

(402) 494-4000. **Call for rates.** 385 E 4th St 68776. I-29 exit 149 southbound; exit 148 northbound, e at traffic light by Nebraska side of bridge; on banks of Missouri River. Int corridors. **Pets:** Accepted.

🍴 Ⓜ 🏊 🛈 ☒ 🔌 ☕ 💻

VALENTINE

Econo Lodge Inn & Suites M

(402) 376-3131. **$90-$170.** 340 E Hwys 20 & 83 69201. Jct US 20/83, 0.3 mi e. Ext corridors. **Pets:** Accepted. 🛈 🔌 ☕ 💻

Trade Winds Motel M

(402) 376-1600. **$75-$115.** 1009 E Hwy 20 69201. Jct US 20/83, 1 mi se. Ext corridors. **Pets:** Other species. $10 daily fee/pet. Designated rooms, service with restrictions, supervision. 🛈 🔌 ☕ 💻

YORK

Americas Best Value Inn-Palmer Inn M

(402) 362-5585. **$45-$95.** 2426 S Lincoln Ave 68467. I-80 exit 353 (US 81), 1 mi n. Ext corridors. **Pets:** Accepted.

(SAVE) 🍴 Ⓜ 🏊 🛈 🔌 ☕ 💻

BEST WESTERN PLUS York Hotel & Conference Center H ✿

(402) 362-6661. **$89-$120.** 4619 S Lincoln Ave 68467. I-80 exit 353 (US 81), just s. Int corridors. **Pets:** Other species. $25 one-time fee/room. Designated rooms, service with restrictions.

(SAVE) 🍴 Ⓜ 🏊 🛈 ☒ 🔌 ☕ 💻

NEVADA

BEATTY *(Restaurants p. 635)*

▼▼ Death Valley Inn & RV Park 🄷
(775) 553-9400. **$70-$125.** 651 Hwy 95 S 89003. Just s. Ext corridors.
Pets: Other species. $10 deposit/room, $5 one-time fee/room. Service
with restrictions, supervision. ➴ 🛜 ✕ 🛄 🖭

⟨ⒶⒶⒶ⟩ ▼▼ Stagecoach Hotel Casino 🄷
(775) 553-2419. **$68-$78.** 900 E Hwy 95 N 89003. North end of town;
west side of US 95. Ext/int corridors. **Pets:** Other species. $10 deposit/
room, $5 one-time fee/room. Designated rooms, service with restric-
tions, crate. (SAVE) 🍽 🅼 ➴ 🛜 🛄 🖭

CARSON CITY *(Restaurants p. 635)*

▼▼▼ Holiday Inn Express & Suites 🄷
(775) 283-4055. **$100-$209.** 4055 N Carson St 89701. US 395 exit 43,
0.7 mi se. Int corridors. **Pets:** Medium. $20 one-time fee/pet. Service
with restrictions, supervision. 🅼 ➴ 🛜 🛄 🖭

**▼▼ Wyndham Garden Carson Station Casino
Hotel** 🄷
(775) 883-0900. **$69-$94.** 900 S Carson St 89701. US 395, 0.3 mi s of
Capitol building. Int corridors. **Pets:** Other species. $50 deposit/room,
$25 daily fee/pet. Service with restrictions, crate. 🍽 🛜 🛄 🖭

ELKO

**⟨ⒶⒶⒶ⟩ ▼▼ Americas Best Value Gold Country Inn &
Casino** 🄼 🐾
(775) 738-8421. **$79-$169, 14 day notice.** 2050 Idaho St 89801. I-80
exit 303, just s. Ext corridors. **Pets:** Other species. $15 one-time fee/
room. Designated rooms, service with restrictions, crate.
(SAVE) 🍽 🅼 ➴ 🛜 🛄 🖭

⟨ⒶⒶⒶ⟩ ▼ BEST WESTERN Elko Inn 🄷
(775) 738-8787. **$110-$290.** 1930 Idaho St 89801. I-80 exit 303, 0.3 mi
sw. Int corridors. **Pets:** Accepted. (SAVE) ➴ 🛜 ✕ 🛄 🖭

⟨ⒶⒶⒶ⟩ ▼ Oak Tree Inn 🄷
(775) 777-2222. **$89-$119.** 95 Spruce Rd 89801. I-80 exit 301, just n.
Int corridors. **Pets:** Accepted. (SAVE) 🛜 ✕ 🛄 🖭

⟨ⒶⒶⒶ⟩ ▼▼▼ Red Lion Hotel & Casino 🄷
(775) 738-2111. **$89-$289.** 2065 Idaho St 89801. I-80 exit 303, just s.
Int corridors. **Pets:** Accepted. (SAVE) 🍽 ➴ ✕ 🛜 🛄 🖭

⟨ⒶⒶⒶ⟩ ▼▼ Rodeway Inn 🄼
(775) 738-7152. **$130-$150.** 736 Idaho St 89801. I-80 exit 303, just sw
of 8th and Idaho sts. Ext corridors. **Pets:** Accepted.
(SAVE) 🛜 ✕ 🛄 🖭

⟨ⒶⒶⒶ⟩ ▼▼ Thunderbird Motel 🄼
(775) 738-7115. **$79-$107.** 345 Idaho St 89801. Just sw of 4th and
Idaho sts. Ext corridors. **Pets:** $15 daily fee/room. Designated rooms,
supervision. (SAVE) ➴ 🛜 🛄

▼▼▼ TownePlace Suites by Marriott 🄷 🐾
(775) 738-9900. **$79-$189.** 2625 E Jennings Way 89801. I-80 exit 303,
0.3 mi nw. Int corridors. **Pets:** Other species. $100 one-time fee/room.
Service with restrictions. ➴ 🛜 ✕ 🛄 🖭

▼ Travelodge 🄷
(775) 753-7747. **$24-$63.** 1785 Idaho St 89801. I-80 exit 303, 0.5 mi
sw. Int corridors. **Pets:** Accepted. 🛜 🛄 🖭

ELY

⟨ⒶⒶⒶ⟩ ▼ Four Sevens Motel 🄼
(775) 289-4747. **$35-$48.** 500 High St 89301. Just n of 5th St; downtown. Ext corridors. **Pets:** Medium, other species. $15 daily fee/room.
Designated rooms, service with restrictions, supervision.
(SAVE) 🛜 🛄 🖭

⟨ⒶⒶⒶ⟩ ▼▼ Historic Hotel Nevada & Gambling Hall 🄷
(775) 289-6665. **Call for rates.** 501 Aultman St 89301. 1.1 mi w of jct
US 50 and 93. Int corridors. **Pets:** Medium, other species. $15 daily
fee/pet. Designated rooms, service with restrictions, supervision.
(SAVE) 🍽 🛜 🛄 🖭

▼▼▼ La Quinta Inn & Suites-Ely 🄷
(775) 289-8833. **$89-$254.** 1591 Great Basin Blvd 89301. 0.4 mi s of
jct US 6, 50 and 93. Int corridors. **Pets:** Large, other species. Service
with restrictions. ➴ 🛜 ✕ 🛄 🖭

▼▼ Park Vue Motel 🄼
(775) 289-4497. **Call for rates.** 930 Aultman St 89301. 0.8 mi w of jct
US 50 and 93. Ext corridors. **Pets:** Accepted. 🛜 ✕ 🛄 🖭

⟨ⒶⒶⒶ⟩ ▼▼ Prospector Hotel Gambling Hall 🄷 🐾
(775) 289-8900. **$79.** 1501 E Aultman St 89301. 0.8 mi e of jct US 50
and 93. Int corridors. **Pets:** Other species. $10 daily fee/pet. Designated
rooms, service with restrictions, supervision.
(SAVE) 🍽 🅼 ➴ 🛜 ✕ 🛄 🖭

EUREKA

▼▼ Eureka Gold Country Inn 🄷
(775) 237-5247. **$102-$107.** 251 N Main St 89316. On east side of
Main St; center. Int corridors. **Pets:** $15 daily fee/pet. Designated
rooms, service with restrictions. 🅼 🛜 🛄 🖭

FALLON

⟨ⒶⒶⒶ⟩ ▼▼ BEST WESTERN Fallon Inn & Suites 🄷
(775) 423-6005. **$95-$130.** 1035 W Williams Ave 89406. 0.4 mi w of jct
US 50 and 95. Ext corridors. **Pets:** Accepted.
(SAVE) 🅼 ➴ 🛜 🛄 🖭

⟨ⒶⒶⒶ⟩ ▼ Econo Lodge Fallon Naval Air Station 🄼
(775) 423-2194. **$45-$120.** 70 E Williams Ave 89406. Just e of jct US
50 and 95. Ext corridors. **Pets:** Medium, dogs only. $10 daily fee/pet.
Designated rooms, service with restrictions, supervision.
(SAVE) ➴ 🛜 🛄 🖭

▼▼▼ Holiday Inn Express 🄷
(775) 428-2588. **$119-$139.** 55 Commercial Way 89406. At Williams
Ave, 0.8 mi w of US 95. Int corridors. **Pets:** $30 one-time fee/room.
Designated rooms, service with restrictions, crate.
🅼 ➴ 🛜 ✕ 🛄 🖭

⟨ⒶⒶⒶ⟩ ▼ Motel 6 #4140 🄼
(775) 423-2277. **$51-$95.** 1705 S Taylor St 89406. 0.8 mi s of jct US
50. Ext corridors. **Pets:** Other species. Service with restrictions, crate.
(SAVE) ➴ 🛜 🛄

⟨ⒶⒶⒶ⟩ ▼ Super 8 🄷
(775) 423-6031. **$60-$70.** 855 W Williams Ave 89406. 0.4 mi w of jct
US 50 and 95. Ext/int corridors. **Pets:** $20 one-time fee/room. Desig-
nated rooms, service with restrictions, supervision.
(SAVE) 🍽 🛜 🛄 🖭

FERNLEY

⟨ⒶⒶⒶ⟩ ▼▼ BEST WESTERN Fernley Inn 🄼 🐾
(775) 575-6776. **$87-$117.** 1405 E Newlands Dr 89408. I-80 exit 48
(Craig Rd), just s. Ext corridors. **Pets:** Other species. $10 daily fee/pet.
Designated rooms, service with restrictions, crate.
(SAVE) ➴ 🛜 🛄 🖭

GARDNERVILLE

⟨ⒶⒶⒶ⟩ ▼▼ BEST WESTERN Topaz Lake Inn 🄷
(775) 266-4661. **$70-$175.** 3410 Sandy Bowers Ave 89410. US 395 S
at Topaz Lake, 20 mi s. Ext/int corridors. **Pets:** Accepted.
(SAVE) 🅼 🛜 ✕ 🛄 🖭

ⓐⓐⓐ ▼▼ **Westerner Motel** **M**
(775) 782-3602. **$45-$89.** 1353 US Hwy 395 S 89410. US 395, south end of town. Ext corridors. **Pets:** Dogs only. $5 daily fee/pet. Designated rooms, service with restrictions, supervision.
SAVE 🖼 🛜 🛢 💻

GENOA
▼▼▼ **1862 David Walley's Resort** **CO**
(775) 782-8155. **Call for rates.** 2001 Foothill Rd (SR 206) 89411. US 395 exit Genoa Ln, 3.5 mi w, then 1.6 mi s. Ext/int corridors.
Pets: Accepted. 🍴 🖼 ✖ 🛜 🛢 💻

GOLD HILL
▼ **Gold Hill Hotel** **H**
(775) 847-0111. **$45-$225.** 1540 S Main St 89440. 1 mi s on SR 342. Ext/int corridors. **Pets:** Accepted. 🍴 🛜 ✖ 🛢 💻

HAWTHORNE
ⓐⓐⓐ ▼▼ **America's Best Inn & Suites** **M**
(775) 945-2660. **$100-$120.** 1402 E 5th St 89415. US 95, 0.5 mi e. Ext corridors. **Pets:** Other species. $10 daily fee/pet. Designated rooms, service with restrictions, supervision. **SAVE** 🖼 🛜 🛢 💻

HENDERSON *(Restaurants p. 635)*
ⓐⓐⓐ ▼▼▼ **BEST WESTERN PLUS Henderson Hotel** **H**
(702) 564-9200. **$75-$149.** 1553 N Boulder Hwy 89011. Jct Sunset Rd, 0.5 mi s. Int corridors. **Pets:** Medium. $20 daily fee/pet. Designated rooms, service with restrictions. **SAVE** 🖼 🖼 🛜 ✖ 🛢 💻

▼▼▼ **BEST WESTERN PLUS St. Rose Pkwy/Las Vegas South Hotel** **H**
(702) 568-0027. **$79-$289.** 3041 St. Rose Pkwy 89052. I-215 exit 6 (St. Rose Pkwy), 2 mi s. Int corridors. **Pets:** Accepted.
🖼 🖼 🛜 ✖ 🛢 💻

ⓐⓐⓐ ▼▼ **Fiesta-Henderson** **H**
(702) 558-7000. **$30-$299, 3 day notice.** 777 W Lake Mead Pkwy 89015. I-515 exit 61A southbound; exit 61 (Lake Mead Pkwy) northbound, just e. Int corridors. **Pets:** Medium, dogs only. $50 one-time fee/room. Designated rooms, service with restrictions, supervision.
SAVE 🍴 🖼 🖼 🛜

▼▼▼ **Hampton Inn & Suites** **H**
(702) 992-9292. **$99-$199.** 421 Astaire Dr 89014. I-215 exit 3A (Stephanie St) eastbound; exit 3 westbound, 1.8 mi n, just e on Warm Springs Rd, then just n. Int corridors. **Pets:** Accepted. 🖼 🖼 🛜 🛢 💻

▼▼▼ **Hampton Inn & Suites** **H**
(702) 385-2200. **$99-$169.** 3245 St. Rose Pkwy 89052. I-215 exit 6 (St. Rose Pkwy), 2.1 mi s. Int corridors. **Pets:** Accepted.
🖼 🛜 ✖ 🛢 💻

▼▼ **Hawthorn Suites by Wyndham** **H**
(702) 568-7800. **$66-$222.** 910 S Boulder Hwy 89015. Jct Lake Mead Pkwy, 1.4 mi s. Int corridors. **Pets:** Accepted. 🖼 🛜 ✖ 🛢 💻

ⓐⓐⓐ ▼▼▼ **Hilton Lake Las Vegas Resort & Spa** **H**
(702) 567-4700. **$119-$299.** 1610 Lake Las Vegas Pkwy 89011. I-515 exit 61A southbound; exit 61 northbound (Lake Mead Pkwy), 6.3 mi ne, then 2.8 mi n, follow signs. Int corridors. **Pets:** Accepted.
SAVE 🍴 🖼 🖼 🖼 🛜 ✖ 🛢 💻

ⓐⓐⓐ ▼▼▼ **Residence Inn by Marriott Las Vegas/ Henderson/Green Valley** **H** ❀
(702) 434-2700. **$107-$199.** 2190 Olympic Ave 89014. I-215 exit 5 (Green Valley Pkwy), 3 mi n at Sunset Rd. Int corridors. **Pets:** Medium, other species. $100 one-time fee/pet. Designated rooms, service with restrictions, crate. **SAVE** **ECO** 🖼 🖼 🛜 ✖ 🛢 💻

▼▼▼ **TownePlace Suites by Marriott Las Vegas Henderson** **H**
(702) 896-2900. **$80-$149.** 1471 Paseo Verde Pkwy 89012. I-215 exit 3A (Stephanie St) eastbound; exit 3 westbound, just s. Int corridors.
Pets: Accepted. 🖼 🖼 🛜 ✖ 🛢 💻

ⓐⓐⓐ ▼▼▼ ▼▼▼ **The Westin Lake Las Vegas Resort & Spa** **H** ❀
(702) 567-6000. **$129-$369, 3 day notice.** 101 Montelago Blvd 89011. I-515 exit 61A southbound; exit 61 northbound (Lake Mead Pkwy), 6.3 mi ne, then 4 mi n, follow signs. Int corridors. **Pets:** Other species. $35 one-time fee/room. Designated rooms, supervision.
SAVE 🍴 🖼 🖼 ✖ 🛜 ✖ 🛢 💻

INCLINE VILLAGE
ⓐⓐⓐ ▼▼▼ ▼▼▼ **Hyatt Regency Lake Tahoe Resort, Spa and Casino** **H**
(775) 832-1234. **$119-$529, 3 day notice.** 111 Country Club Dr at Lakeshore 89450. 0.4 mi w of SR 28, toward lake via Country Club Dr; 2 mi s of Mt. Rose Hwy. Int corridors. **Pets:** Accepted.
SAVE **ECO** 🍴 🖼 🖼 ✖ 🛜 ✖ 🛢 💻

JACKPOT
▼▼ **Horseshu Hotel & Casino** **H**
(775) 755-2321. **$49-$109.** 1385 Hwy 93 89825. Center. Int corridors. **Pets:** Other species. $10 one-time fee/room. Designated rooms, service with restrictions, supervision. 🍴 🖼 🛜 💻

LAS VEGAS *(Restaurants p. 635)*
▼▼▼ **Alexis Park All Suite Resort** **H**
(702) 796-3300. **Call for rates.** 375 E Harmon Ave 89169. Jct Las Vegas Blvd, just e. Ext corridors. **Pets:** Accepted.
🍴 🖼 🖼 ✖ 🛜 ✖ 🛢 💻

ⓐⓐⓐ ▼▼ **Americas Best Value Inn Downtown Las Vegas** **M**
(702) 382-3455. **$50-$180.** 1000 N Main St 89101. I-15 exit 43E northbound; exit 44E southbound. Ext corridors. **Pets:** Other species. $15 daily fee/room. Designated rooms, service with restrictions, supervision.
SAVE 🍴 🖼 🛜 🛢 💻

▼▼ **Artisan Hotel** **H**
(702) 214-4000. **Call for rates.** 1501 W Sahara Ave 89102. I-15 exit 40 (Sahara Ave), just s. Int corridors. **Pets:** Accepted.
🍴 🖼 🔊 ✖ 🛢

ⓐⓐⓐ ▼▼ **Baymont Inn & Suites Las Vegas South Strip** **H**
(702) 273-2500. **$69-$199.** 55 E Robindale Rd 89123. I-15 exit 33 (Blue Diamond Rd), just e, then just n. Int corridors. **Pets:** Accepted.
SAVE 🖼 🛜 ✖ 🛢 💻

ⓐⓐⓐ ▼▼▼ **BEST WESTERN PLUS Las Vegas West** **H**
(702) 256-3766. **$95-$165.** 8669 W Sahara Ave 89117. Jct Durango Dr. Int corridors. **Pets:** Accepted. **SAVE** 🖼 🛜 ✖ 🛢 💻

▼▼▼ **Caesars Palace** **H**
(702) 731-7110. **Call for rates.** 3570 Las Vegas Blvd S 89109. I-15 exit 38 (Flamingo Rd), just e to the Strip. Int corridors. **Pets:** Accepted.
🍴 🖼 🖼 ✖ 🛜 🛢 💻

▼▼▼ **Candlewood Suites** **H**
(702) 836-3660. **Call for rates.** 4034 S Paradise Rd 89169. I-15 exit 38 (Flamingo Rd) to Paradise Rd, just ne. Int corridors. **Pets:** Accepted.
🖼 🖼 🛜 🛢 💻

ⓐⓐⓐ ▼▼▼ ▼▼▼ **The Cosmopolitan of Las Vegas** **H**
(702) 698-7000. **$200-$660, 3 day notice.** 3708 Las Vegas Blvd S 89109. Between Flamingo Rd and Tropicana Ave; on the Strip. Int corridors. **Pets:** Accepted. **SAVE** 🍴 🖼 🖼 ✖ 🛜 ✖ 🛢

▼▼▼ ▼▼▼ **Delano Las Vegas** 🄷 ❀
(702) 632-7777. **Call for rates.** 3940 Las Vegas Blvd S 89119. I-15 exit 36 (Russell Rd), e to the Strip, then just n. Int corridors. **Pets:** Medium, dogs only. $50 daily fee/pet. Designated rooms, service with restrictions, crate. 🍴 🕭ᴹ 🛏 ⊠ 🛜 🛢

🄰🄰🄰 ▼▼▼ **Element by Westin Las Vegas Summerlin** 🄷 ❀
(702) 589-2000. **Call for rates.** 10555 Discovery Dr 89135. I-215 exit 23 (Town Center), just n. Int corridors. **Pets:** Dogs only. $50 one-time fee/room. Designated rooms, service with restrictions, crate.
🆂🅰🆅🅴 🄴 🕭ᴹ 🛏 🛜 ⊠ 🛢 💻

▼▼ **Extended Stay America-Las Vegas/Midtown** 🄷
(702) 369-1414. **Call for rates.** 3045 S Maryland Pkwy 89109. I-15 exit 40 (Sahara Ave), 1.7 mi e, then 0.6 mi s. Int corridors. **Pets:** Other species. $25 daily fee/pet. Service with restrictions, supervision.
🕭ᴹ 🛜 🛢 💻

▼▼ **Flamingo Las Vegas** 🄷
(702) 733-3111. **Call for rates.** 3555 Las Vegas Blvd S 89109. I-15 exit 38 (Flamingo Rd), just n on the Strip. Int corridors. **Pets:** Accepted.
🍴 🕭ᴹ 🛏 ⊠ 🛜 🛢 💻

🄰🄰🄰 ▼▼▼ ▼▼▼ **Four Seasons Hotel Las Vegas** 🄷 ❀
(702) 632-5000. **$239-$3500.** 3960 Las Vegas Blvd S 89119. I-15 exit 37 (Tropicana Ave), just s on the Strip. Int corridors. **Pets:** Small, other species. $100 one-time fee/pet. Designated rooms, service with restrictions, supervision. 🆂🅰🆅🅴 🍴 🕭ᴹ 🛏 ⊠ 🛜 ⊠ 🛢 💻

▼▼▼ **Harrah's-Las Vegas** 🄷
(702) 369-5000. **Call for rates.** 3475 Las Vegas Blvd S 89109. I-15 exit 38 (Flamingo Rd), just n on the Strip. Int corridors. **Pets:** Accepted.
🍴 🕭ᴹ 🛏 🛜 🛢 💻

🄰🄰🄰 ▼▼▼▼ **Holiday Inn Express-Nellis** 🄷
(702) 644-5700. **$79-$350.** 4035 N Nellis Blvd 89115. I-15 exit 48 (Craig Rd), 2.3 mi e, then just s. Int corridors. **Pets:** Other species. $20 daily fee/pet. Service with restrictions, crate.
🆂🅰🆅🅴 🕭ᴹ 🛏 🛜 ⊠ 🛢 💻

🄰🄰🄰 ▼▼▼▼ **Hyatt Place Las Vegas** 🄷
(702) 369-3366. **$99-$309.** 4520 Paradise Rd 89169. Jct Harmon Ave, just s. Int corridors. **Pets:** Accepted.
🆂🅰🆅🅴 🕭ᴹ 🛏 🛜 ⊠ 🛢 💻

▼▼▼ **La Quinta Inn & Suites Airport South** 🄷
(702) 492-8900. **$74-$289.** 6560 Surrey St 89119. Jct Eastern Ave and Sunset Rd, just w, just s. Int corridors. **Pets:** Large, other species. Service with restrictions. 🕭ᴹ 🛏 🛜 ⊠ 🛢 💻

▼▼▼ **La Quinta Inn & Suites Las Vegas Redrock/Summerlin** 🄷
(702) 243-0356. **$89-$244.** 9570 W Sahara Ave 89117. Jct Fort Apache Rd, just w. Int corridors. **Pets:** Large, other species. Service with restrictions. 🕭ᴹ 🛏 🛜 ⊠ 🛢 💻

▼▼▼ **La Quinta Inn & Suites Tropicana** 🄷
(702) 798-7736. **$79-$239.** 4975 S Valley View Blvd 89118. I-15 exit 37 (Tropicana Ave), 0.6 mi w. Int corridors. **Pets:** Large, other species. Service with restrictions. 🛏 🛜 ⊠ 🛢 💻

▼▼ **La Quinta Inn Las Vegas Nellis** 🄷
(702) 632-0229. **$79-$284.** 4288 N Nellis Blvd 89115. Jct Las Vegas Blvd, just n. Int corridors. **Pets:** Large, other species. Service with restrictions. 🕭ᴹ 🛏 🛜 🛢 💻

🄰🄰🄰 ▼▼▼ **The Mardi Gras Hotel & Casino** 🄷
(702) 731-2020. **$49-$149, 3 day notice.** 3500 Paradise Rd 89169. 0.5 mi s of Las Vegas Convention Center. Ext corridors. **Pets:** Accepted.
🆂🅰🆅🅴 🍴 🛏 🛜 🛢 💻

▼▼▼ ▼▼▼ **Platinum Hotel & Spa** 🄷
(702) 365-5000. **$132-$302, 3 day notice.** 211 E Flamingo Rd 89169. I-15 exit 38 (Flamingo Rd), 1.2 mi e. Int corridors. **Pets:** Accepted.
🍴 🕭ᴹ 🛏 ⊠ 🛜 ⊠ 🛢 💻

🄰🄰🄰 ▼▼▼▼ **Residence Inn by Marriott-Hughes Center** 🄷
(702) 650-0040. **$107-$219.** 370 Hughes Center Dr 89169. Jct Flamingo and Paradise rds, just n. Int corridors. **Pets:** Accepted.
🆂🅰🆅🅴 🄴🄲🄾 🕭ᴹ 🛏 🛜 ⊠ 🛢 💻

🄰🄰🄰 ▼▼▼ **Residence Inn by Marriott Las Vegas Convention Center** 🄷
(702) 796-9300. **$98-$249.** 3225 Paradise Rd 89109. Opposite Las Vegas Convention Center. Ext corridors. **Pets:** Medium, other species. $100 one-time fee/room. Service with restrictions.
🆂🅰🆅🅴 🄴🄲🄾 🕭ᴹ 🛏 ⊠ 🛢 💻

▼▼▼ ▼▼▼ **Residence Inn by Marriott Las Vegas South** 🄷
(702) 795-7378. **$89-$169.** 5875 Dean Martin Rd 89118. I-15 exit 36 (Russell Rd), just sw. Int corridors. **Pets:** Accepted.
🕭ᴹ 🛏 🛜 ⊠ 🛢 💻

🄰🄰🄰 ▼▼▼ ▼▼▼ **Trump International Hotel Las Vegas** 🄷 ❀
(702) 982-0000. **$129-$499, 3 day notice.** 2000 Fashion Show Dr 89109. Jct Las Vegas Blvd, just w. Int corridors. **Pets:** Small, dogs only. $200 one-time fee/room. Service with restrictions.
🆂🅰🆅🅴 🍴 🛏 ⊠ 🛜 ⊠ 🛢 💻

🄰🄰🄰 ▼▼▼ ▼▼▼ **Vdara Hotel & Spa** 🄷
(702) 590-2767. **$99-$775.** 2600 W Harmon Ave 89158. Between Flamingo Rd and Tropicana Ave; on the Strip. Int corridors.
Pets: Accepted. 🆂🅰🆅🅴 🄴🄲🄾 🍴 🛏 ⊠ 🛜 ⊠ 🛢 💻

🄰🄰🄰 ▼▼▼▼ **The Westin Las Vegas Hotel, Casino and Spa** 🄷
(702) 836-5900. **$89-$299.** 160 E Flamingo Rd 89109. I-15 exit 38 (Flamingo Rd), 1.1 mi e. Int corridors. **Pets:** Accepted.
🆂🅰🆅🅴 🍴 🕭ᴹ 🛏 ⊠ 🛰 ⊠ 🛢 💻

LAUGHLIN
▼▼▼ **Don Laughlin's Riverside Resort Hotel & Casino** 🄷
(702) 298-2535. **Call for rates.** 1650 S Casino Dr 89029. 2 mi s of Davis Dam. Int corridors. **Pets:** Accepted.
🍴 🕭ᴹ 🛏 ⊠ 🛜 🛢 💻

▼▼▼ **Harrah's Casino Hotel** 🄷
(702) 298-4600. **Call for rates.** 2900 S Casino Dr 89029. 5 mi s of Davis Dam. Int corridors. **Pets:** Accepted.
🍴 🕭ᴹ 🛏 ⊠ 🛜 🛢 💻

MESQUITE
🄰🄰🄰 ▼▼▼ **BEST WESTERN Mesquite Inn** 🄼
(702) 346-7444. **$79-$129.** 390 N Sandhill Blvd 89027. I-15 exit 122. Ext corridors. **Pets:** Medium. $20 daily fee/room. Designated rooms, service with restrictions, supervision. 🆂🅰🆅🅴 🛏 🛜 🛢 💻

🄰🄰🄰 ▼▼▼ **Holiday Inn Express & Suites** 🄷
(702) 346-2200. **$80-$300.** 1030 W Pioneer Blvd 89027. I-15 exit 120, just w. Int corridors. **Pets:** Large, other species. $20 daily fee/room. Designated rooms, service with restrictions, supervision.
🆂🅰🆅🅴 🛏 ⊠ 🛜 ⊠ 🛢 💻

▼▼▼ **Virgin River Hotel Casino Bingo** 🄼
(702) 346-7777. **Call for rates.** 100 Pioneer Blvd 89027. I-15 exit 122, just w. Ext corridors. **Pets:** Accepted. 🍴 🕭ᴹ 🛏 🛜 🛢

MINDEN

▼▼▼▼ **Holiday Inn Express & Suites Minden** 🏨
(775) 782-7500. **$109-$259.** 1659 SR 88 89423. Jct US 395 N. Int corridors. **Pets:** Other species. $20 one-time fee/pet. Designated rooms, service with restrictions, supervision. 🛒 🛜 ✖ 🔌 🖥

NORTH LAS VEGAS

♨ ▼▼▼▼ **Aliante Casino + Hotel + Spa** 🏨
(702) 692-7777. **$75, 3 day notice.** 7300 Aliante Pkwy 89084. I-215 exit 43 (Aliante Pkwy), just n. Int corridors. **Pets:** Accepted.
🆂🅰🆅🅴 🍴 🛒 ✖ 🛜 🔌 🖥

♨ ▼▼▼▼ **BEST WESTERN PLUS North Las Vegas Inn & Suites** 🏨
(702) 649-3000. **$99-$299.** 4540 Donovan Way 89081. I-15 exit 48 (Craig Rd), just w to Donovan Way. Int corridors. **Pets:** Accepted.
🆂🅰🆅🅴 🛒 🛜 ✖ 🔌 🖥

OVERTON

▼▼ **North Shore Inn at Lake Mead** 🏨
(702) 397-6000. **$77-$125, 3 day notice.** 520 N Moapa Valley Blvd 89040. I-15 exit 93, 10 mi ne on SR 169. Int corridors. **Pets:** Accepted.
🛒 🛜 ✖ 🔌 🖥

PAHRUMP

♨ ▼▼▼ **BEST WESTERN Pahrump Station** Ⓜ ✿
(775) 727-5100. **$85-$136.** 1101 S Hwy 160 89048. Downtown. Ext/int corridors. **Pets:** Dogs only. $12 daily fee/pet. Designated rooms, service with restrictions, supervision. 🆂🅰🆅🅴 🍴 ♿ 🛒 🛜 🔌 🖥

RENO *(Restaurants p. 635)*

♨ ▼▼▼ **BEST WESTERN Airport Plaza Hotel** 🏨
(775) 348-6370. **$80-$90, 3 day notice.** 1981 Terminal Way 89502. I-580/US 395 exit 65A southbound (E Plumb Ln/Villanova Dr), just e on Villanova Dr; exit 65 northbound, just e on E Plumb Ln. Int corridors.
Pets: Accepted. 🆂🅰🆅🅴 🍴 ♿ 🛒 ✖ 🛜 🔌 🖥

▼▼▼ **Extended Stay America-Reno-South Meadows** 🏨
(775) 852-5611. **Call for rates.** 9795 Gateway Dr 89521. I-580/US 395 exit 60 (S Meadows Pkwy), just e, then n. Int corridors. **Pets:** Other species. $25 daily fee/pet. Service with restrictions, supervision.
🛜 🔌 🖥

♨ ▼▼▼▼ **Grand Sierra Resort & Casino** 🏨
(775) 789-2000. **$59-$409, 3 day notice.** 2500 E 2nd St 89595. Jct I-80 and I-580/US 395, 0.5 mi s; I-580/US 395 exit 66 (Mill St). Int corridors. **Pets:** Accepted. 🆂🅰🆅🅴 🍴 ♿ 🛒 ✖ 🛜 🔌 🖥

♨ ▼▼▼▼ **Harrah's Reno** 🏨 🐾
(775) 786-3232. **Call for rates.** 219 N Center St 89501. I-80 exit 13 (Virginia St), 0.6 mi s; jct 2nd st; downtown. Int corridors.
Pets: Medium, dogs only. Designated rooms, service with restrictions, crate. 🆂🅰🆅🅴 🎫 🍴 ♿ 🛒 ✖ 🛜 🔌 🖥

▼▼▼▼ **Holiday Inn Express & Suites Reno Airport** 🏨
(775) 229-7070. **$99-$189.** 2375 Market St 89502. I-580/US 395 exit 66, just n. Int corridors. **Pets:** Medium. $100 deposit/pet, $30 one-time fee/pet, $30 daily fee/pet. Designated rooms, service with restrictions, supervision. ♿ 🛒 🛜 ✖ 🔌 🖥

♨ ▼▼▼▼ **Homewood Suites by Hilton Reno** 🏨 ✿
(775) 853-7100. **$109-$209.** 5450 Kietzke Ln 89511. I-580/US 395 exit 62 (Neil Rd), just sw. Int corridors. **Pets:** Other species. $75 one-time fee/room. Service with restrictions, crate. 🆂🅰🆅🅴 🛒 🛜 🔌 🖥

♨ ▼▼▼▼ **Hyatt Place Reno-Tahoe Airport** 🏨
(775) 826-2500. **$79-$209.** 1790 E Plumb Ln 89502. I-580/US 395 exit 65A southbound (E Plumb Ln/Villanova Dr); exit 65 northbound, just se. Int corridors. **Pets:** Medium, dogs only. $75 one-time fee/room. Service with restrictions, supervision. 🆂🅰🆅🅴 🍴 ♿ 🛒 ✖ 🛜 🔌 🖥

▼▼▼ **La Quinta Inn Reno** Ⓜ
(775) 348-6100. **$65-$209.** 4001 Market St 89502. I-580/US 395 exit 65A southbound (E Plumb Ln/Villanova Dr), just w on Villanova Dr; exit 65 northbound, just n, then just w on Villanova Dr. Ext corridors. **Pets:** Large, other species. Service with restrictions.
♿ 🛒 🛜 🔌 🖥

♨ ▼▼▼▼ **Ramada Reno Hotel & Casino** 🏨
(775) 786-5151. **$44-$140.** 1000 E 6th St 89512. I-80 exit 14 (Wells Ave), just s, then just e. Int corridors. **Pets:** Large, other species. $10 daily fee/pet. Designated rooms, service with restrictions, supervision.
🆂🅰🆅🅴 🍴 🛒 🛜 🔌 🖥

♨ ▼▼▼▼ **Residence Inn by Marriott** 🏨
(775) 853-8800. **$116-$233.** 9845 Gateway Dr 89521. I-580/US 395 exit 60 (S Meadows Pkwy), just e. Int corridors. **Pets:** Other species. $100 one-time fee/room. Service with restrictions, crate.
🆂🅰🆅🅴 🅴🅲🅾 ♿ 🛒 🛜 ✖ 🔌 🖥

▼▼ **Sands Regency Casino Hotel** 🏨
(775) 348-2200. **Call for rates.** 345 N Arlington Ave 89501. At 3rd St. Int corridors. **Pets:** Medium, dogs only. $75 deposit/room, $15 daily fee/pet. Designated rooms, service with restrictions, crate.
🍴 🛒 ✖ 🛜 🔌

▼▼▼▼ **Siena Hotel Spa Casino** 🏨 ✿
(775) 682-3900. **$49-$389, 3 day notice.** 1 S Lake St 89501. I-80 exit 13 (Virginia St), 0.8 mi s; at Mill St. Int corridors. **Pets:** Small. $50 deposit/room, $50 one-time fee/pet. Designated rooms, service with restrictions, crate. 🍴 ♿ 🛒 ✖ 🛜 🔌 🖥

▼▼▼ **Staybridge Suites Reno** 🏨
(775) 657-8999. **$89-$299.** 10559 Professional Cir 89511. I-580/US 395 exit 59 (Damonte Ranch Pkwy), just e, just n on Double R Blvd, then just w. Int corridors. **Pets:** Accepted. ♿ 🛒 🛜 ✖ 🔌 🖥

▼▼▼ **Whitney Peak Hotel** 🏨
(775) 398-5400. **Call for rates.** 255 N Virginia St 89501. I-80 exit 13 (Virginia St), 0.6 mi s; jct W Commercial Row; downtown. Int corridors.
Pets: Accepted. 🍴 🛜 ✖ 🔌 🖥

SPARKS

♨ ▼▼▼▼ **Holiday Inn-Reno/Sparks** 🏨
(775) 358-6900. **$89-$169.** 55 E Nugget Ave 89431. I-80 exit 19 (McCarran Blvd), just se. Int corridors. **Pets:** Accepted.
🆂🅰🆅🅴 🍴 ♿ 🛒 🛜 🔌 🖥

♨ ▼▼▼ **Super 8-Sparks/Reno** 🏨
(775) 358-8884. **$72-$152.** 1900 E Greg St 89431. I-80 exit 20, 0.6 mi s, then just e. Int corridors. **Pets:** $10 daily fee/pet. Service with restrictions, supervision. 🆂🅰🆅🅴 🛒 🛜 🔌 🖥

TONOPAH

♨ ▼▼▼ **BEST WESTERN Hi-Desert Inn** 🏨 ✿
(775) 482-3511. **$110-$120.** 320 Main St 89049. On US 6 and 95. Int corridors. **Pets:** Other species. Designated rooms, supervision.
🆂🅰🆅🅴 ♿ 🛜 🔌 🖥

▼▼ **Mizpah Hotel** 🏨 🐾
(775) 482-3030. **$89-$159.** 100 N Main St 89049. Center. Int corridors. **Pets:** Large, dogs only. $10 daily fee/pet. Designated rooms, service with restrictions, supervision. 🍴 🛜 ✖ 🔌

♨ ▼▼▼ **Tonopah Station** 🏨
(775) 482-9777. **$69-$79.** 1137 S Main St 89049. On US 6 and 95. Int corridors. **Pets:** Other species. $10 one-time fee/room. Service with restrictions, supervision. 🆂🅰🆅🅴 🍴 ♿ 🛜 ✖ 🔌 🖥

WINNEMUCCA

BEST WESTERN PLUS Gold Country Inn H ❀
(775) 623-6999. **$119-$135.** 921 W Winnemucca Blvd 89445. 0.6 mi sw of center. Int corridors. **Pets:** Other species. $10 one-time fee/room. Designated rooms, service with restrictions, supervision.
SAVE ⊇ 🛜 🛅 💻

Candlewood Suites H
(775) 623-2700. **$100-$200.** 460 E Winnemucca Blvd 89445. I-80 exit 178, just s. Int corridors. **Pets:** Accepted. 🛜 ✕ 🛅 💻

Holiday Inn Express H
(775) 625-3100. **$129-$224.** 1987 W Winnemucca Blvd 89445. I-80 exit 176, just s. Int corridors. **Pets:** Accepted.
🍴 ㋖ 🏊 🛜 ✕ 🛅 💻

Town House Motel M
(775) 623-3620. **$85-$95.** 375 Monroe St 89445. 0.4 mi sw of center to Monroe St, just se. Ext corridors. **Pets:** Small, dogs only. $10 deposit/pet. Designated rooms, service with restrictions, supervision.
SAVE ⊇ 🛜 ✕ 🛅 💻

Winnemucca Holiday Motel M
(775) 623-3684. **$79-$149.** 670 W Winnemucca Blvd 89445. 0.4 mi sw of center. Ext corridors. **Pets:** Other species. $75 deposit/room. Designated rooms, service with restrictions, supervision.
SAVE ⊇ 🛜 🛅 💻

The Winnemucca Inn H
(775) 623-2565. **Call for rates.** 741 W Winnemucca Blvd 89445. I-80 exit 176, 1.1 mi nw. Ext/int corridors. **Pets:** Accepted.
SAVE 🍴 ⊇ ✕ 🛜 🛅 💻

ZEPHYR COVE

Zephyr Cove Resort CA
(775) 589-4980. **Call for rates.** 760 Hwy 50 89448. 4 mi n of Stateline, NV. Ext/int corridors. **Pets:** Dogs only. Designated rooms.
SAVE 🍴 ✕ 🛜 ✕ 🛅 💻

NEW HAMPSHIRE

ASHLAND

Comfort Inn H
(603) 968-7668. **$80-$250.** 53 West St 03217. I-93 exit 24 (SR 25 and US 3), just e. Int corridors. **Pets:** Dogs only. $15 daily fee/pet. Designated rooms, service with restrictions. 🍴 ⊇ 🛜 🛅 💻

Glynn House Inn BB
(603) 968-3775. **Call for rates.** 59 Highland St 03217. I-93 exit 24 (SR 25 and US 3), 0.8 mi e to flag pole in center of town (Highland St), then 0.3 mi nw. Ext/int corridors. **Pets:** Accepted.
ECO 🍴 🛜 ✕ ㋖

BARTLETT

The Bartlett Inn BB ❀
(603) 374-2353. **Call for rates.** 1477 US Rt 302 03812. On US 302, 7 mi w of jct SR 16. Ext/int corridors. **Pets:** Dogs only. $25 one-time fee/pet. Designated rooms, service with restrictions, supervision.
🍴 ⊇ ✕ 🛜 ㋖ 🛅 💻

BEDFORD

Country Inn & Suites By Carlson, Manchester Airport H
(603) 666-4600. **Call for rates.** 250 S River Rd 03110. I-293 exit US 3 (Kilton Rd/S River Rd), 0.7 mi s. Int corridors. **Pets:** Accepted.
🍴 ㋖ ⊇ ✕ 🛜 ✕ 🛅 💻

BRETTON WOODS

The Lodge at Bretton Woods M
(603) 278-4000. **$99-$249, 7 day notice.** 2653 US 302 03575. Center. Ext corridors. **Pets:** Accepted. ⊇ ✕ 🛜 ✕ 🛅

Omni Bretton Arms Inn CI
(603) 278-3000. **$139-$449, 7 day notice.** 173 Mount Washington Hotel Rd (US 302) 03575. Center. Int corridors. **Pets:** Accepted.
🍴 ㋖ ✕ 🛜 ✕ 🛅 💻

CHESTERFIELD

Chesterfield Inn CI
(603) 256-3211. **$149-$345, 5 day notice.** 20 Cross Rd 03466. I-91 exit 3, 2 mi e on SR 9. Ext/int corridors. **Pets:** Large, other species. Designated rooms, service with restrictions, crate.
ECO 🍴 🛜 ✕ 🛅 💻

COLEBROOK

Northern Comfort Motel M
(603) 237-4440. **Call for rates.** 1 Trooper Scott Phillips Hwy 03576. 1.5 mi s on US 3. Ext corridors. **Pets:** Accepted.
SAVE 🍴 ⊇ 🛜 ✕ 🛅

CONCORD

BEST WESTERN Concord Inn & Suites H
(603) 228-4300. **$99-$299.** 97 Hall St 03301. I-93 exit 13, just n on Main St, then 0.5 mi w. Int corridors. **Pets:** Other species. $50 deposit/room, $15 daily fee/pet. Designated rooms, service with restrictions, crate. SAVE 🍴 ⊇ 🛜 🛅 💻

Concord Comfort Inn H
(603) 226-4100. **$99-$289.** 71 Hall St 03301. I-93 exit 13, just n on Main St, then 0.3 mi w. Int corridors. **Pets:** Accepted.
🍴 ㋖ ⊇ ✕ 🛜 🛅 💻

Residence Inn by Marriott Concord H
(603) 226-0012. **$111-$200.** 91 Hall St 03301. I-93 exit 13, just n on Main St, then 0.5 mi w. Int corridors. **Pets:** Accepted.
🦮 🍴 ㋖ ⊇ 🛜 ✕ 🛅 💻

DOVER

Comfort Inn & Suites H
(603) 750-7507. **$99-$199.** 10 Hotel Dr 03820. SR 16 exit 9, 0.4 mi ne. Int corridors. **Pets:** Accepted. ㋖ ⊇ 🛜 🛅 💻

Homewood Suites Dover H
(603) 516-0929. **$129-$259.** 21 Members Way 03820. SR 16 exit 9, 0.4 mi w. Int corridors. **Pets:** Accepted. ㋖ ⊇ 🛜 🛅 💻

DURHAM

Holiday Inn Express Durham-UNH H ❀
(603) 868-1234. **$99-$359.** 2 Main St 03824. On SR 108; center. Int corridors. **Pets:** Large, other species. $50 one-time fee/room. Designated rooms, service with restrictions, supervision. 🛜 ✕ 🛅 💻

Three Chimneys Inn CI
(603) 868-7800. **Call for rates.** 17 Newmarket Rd 03824. On SR 108; center. Ext/int corridors. **Pets:** Accepted. 🍴 🛜 ✕ 💻

EXETER

▼◆▼ Hampton Inn & Suites **H**

(603) 658-5555. **$109-$189.** 59 Portsmouth Ave 03833. SR 101 exit 11, just s. Int corridors. **Pets:** Designated rooms, service with restrictions, supervision.

FRANCONIA

ⒶⒶⒶ ▼◆▼ BEST WESTERN White Mountain Inn **H**

(603) 823-7422. **$88-$220, 3 day notice.** 87 Wallace Hill Rd 03580. I-93 exit 38, just e. Int corridors. **Pets:** Medium, other species. $20 daily fee/pet. Designated rooms, service with restrictions, supervision.

🆂🅰🆅🅴 🍽 ➳ 🛜 ✕ 🔋 🖥

▼ Gale River Motel **M** ❀

(603) 823-5655. **Call for rates.** 1 Main St 03580. I-93 exit 38, 0.8 mi n on SR 18. Ext corridors. **Pets:** Dogs only. $10 daily fee/pet. Designated rooms, service with restrictions, supervision.

🄴🄲🄾 🍽 🛗 ➳ 🛜 ✕ 🔋 🖥

▼◆▼ Lovetts Inn by Lafayette Brook **CI**

(603) 823-7761. **Call for rates.** 1474 Profile Rd 03580. I-93 exit 38, just w on Wallace Hill Rd, then 2.1 mi s on SR 18. Ext/int corridors.

Pets: Accepted. 🍽 ➳ 🛜 ✕ 🐾 🖥

GILFORD

▼◆▼ Fireside Inn & Suites **H** ❀

(603) 293-7526. **$79-$299.** 17 Harris Shore Rd 03249. Jct SR 11 and 11B, 2.5 mi e of jct US 3 N. Int corridors. **Pets:** Medium. $25 daily fee/pet. Designated rooms, service with restrictions, supervision.

🛗 ➳ ✕ 🛜 ✕ 🔋 🖥

▼◆▼ TownePlace Suites by Marriott Gilford **H** ❀

(603) 524-5533. **$111-$367.** 14 Sawmill Rd 03249. Just e of jct SR 3 and 11A. Int corridors. **Pets:** Other species. $100 one-time fee/room. Designated rooms. 🍽 🛗 ➳ 🛜 ✕ 🔋 🖥

GORHAM

▼ Moose Brook Motel **M**

(603) 466-5400. **Call for rates.** 65 Lancaster Rd 03581. Jct SR 16, 0.5 mi w on US 2. Ext corridors. **Pets:** $5 one-time fee/pet. Service with restrictions, crate. ➳ 🛜 ✕ 🔋 🖥

▼◆▼ Royalty Inn **H**

(603) 466-3312. **$84-$169.** 130 Main St 03581. On US 2 and SR 16; center. Ext/int corridors. **Pets:** Accepted.

🄴🄲🄾 🛗 ➳ ✕ 🛜 🔋 🖥

ⒶⒶⒶ ▼◆▼ Top Notch Inn **M** ❀

(603) 466-5496. **Call for rates.** 265 Main St 03581. On US 2 and SR 16; center. Ext/int corridors. **Pets:** Medium, dogs only. Designated rooms, service with restrictions, supervision.

🆂🅰🆅🅴 🗑 ➳ 🛜 ✕ 🔋 🖥

▼◆▼ Town & Country Inn & Resort **H**

(603) 466-3315. **Call for rates.** 20 SR 2 03581. 0.5 mi e of jct SR 16. Ext/int corridors. **Pets:** Accepted. 🍽 ➳ ✕ 🛜 🔋 🖥

HAMPTON

ⒶⒶⒶ ▼◆▼ Lamie's Inn and The Old Salt Restaurant **CI**

(603) 926-0330. **$99-$180, 3 day notice.** 490 Lafayette Rd 03842. Jct SR 27 on US 1. Int corridors. **Pets:** Accepted.

🆂🅰🆅🅴 🍽 🛜 ✕ 🔋

HANCOCK (Restaurants p. 635)

▼◆▼ The Hancock Inn **CI**

(603) 525-3318. **Call for rates.** 33 Main St 03449. Jct SR 123 and 137; center. Int corridors. **Pets:** Accepted. 🍽 🛜 ✕

HANOVER

ⒶⒶⒶ ▼◆▼ ▼◆▼ The Hanover Inn Dartmouth **H**

(603) 643-4300. **$199-$579, 3 day notice.** 2 E Wheelock St 03755. Center. Int corridors. **Pets:** Accepted. 🆂🅰🆅🅴 🍽 🛜 ✕ 🖥

▼◆▼ Six South Street Hotel Hanover **H**

(603) 643-0600. **Call for rates.** 6 South St 03755. I-89 exit 18, n on SR 120 to Lebanon St, left on Sanborn Rd (which becomes South St). Int corridors. **Pets:** Accepted. 🍽 🛜 ✕ 🔋 🖥

HARTS LOCATION

▼◆▼ Notchland Inn **CI**

(603) 374-6131. **Call for rates.** 2 Morey Rd 03812. On US 302, 6.4 mi w of town. Ext/int corridors. **Pets:** $20 daily fee/pet. Designated rooms, service with restrictions, crate. 🄴🄲🄾 🍽 🛜 ✕ 🅿 🔋 🖥

HEBRON

▼◆▼ Coppertoppe Inn & Retreat Center **BB** ❀

(603) 744-3636. **$159-$295, 14 day notice.** 8 Range Rd 03241. I-93 exit 23, 6 mi w on SR 104, 8.7 mi n on SR 3A, then 0.6 mi w on N Shore Rd. Int corridors. **Pets:** Other species. $15 deposit/pet, $15 daily fee/pet. Service with restrictions.

🄴🄲🄾 🍽 ✕ 🛜 ✕ 🅉 🔋 🖥

HENNIKER

▼◆▼ Henniker Motel **M**

(603) 428-3536. **Call for rates.** 61 Craney Pond Rd 03242. I-89 exit 5, 6.5 mi w on US 202 and SR 9 to jct SR 114, 3 mi s to Flanders Rd, then 0.5 mi w, follow signs; adjacent to Pat's Peak. Ext/int corridors. **Pets:** Other species. Designated rooms, service with restrictions, crate.

🍽 🛜 ✕ 🔋 🖥

INTERVALE

▼◆▼ The New England Inn & Lodge **CI**

(603) 356-5541. **$139-$249, 15 day notice.** 336 SR 16A 03845. Jct US 302/SR 16, follow SR 16A Intervale Resort Loop. Ext/int corridors. **Pets:** Dogs only. $25 one-time fee/pet. Designated rooms, no service, crate. 🍽 ➳ 🛜 ✕ 🔋 🖥

JACKSON

▼◆▼ The Eagle Mountain House & Golf Club **H**

(603) 383-9111. **Call for rates.** 179 Carter Notch Rd 03846. Jct SR 16B, from village center follow SR 16B across the Jackson Covered Bridge to immediate right turn, 0.7 mi n. Int corridors. **Pets:** Accepted.

🄴🄲🄾 🍽 ➳ 🛜 ✕

▼◆▼ Nordic Village Resort **CO**

(603) 383-9101. **$129-$869, 7 day notice.** Rt 16 03846. 1 mi n of jct US 302. Ext/int corridors. **Pets:** Other species. $25 deposit/pet. Designated rooms, no service, supervision.

🍽 ➳ ✕ 🛜 ✕ 🔋 🖥

▼◆▼ Snowflake Inn **BB** ❀

(603) 383-8259. **$179-$375, 14 day notice.** 95 Main St (SR 16A) 03846. On SR 16A; center. Int corridors. **Pets:** Dogs only. $30 daily fee/pet. Designated rooms. ➳ 🛜 ✕

JEFFERSON

ⒶⒶⒶ ▼◆▼ Jefferson Inn **BB**

(603) 586-7998. **Call for rates.** 6 Renaissance Ln 03583. US 2, just e of SR 116. Int corridors. **Pets:** Accepted.

🆂🅰🆅🅴 🍽 ✕ 🛜 ✕ 🅉 🔋

KEENE

ⒶⒶⒶ ▼◆▼ BEST WESTERN PLUS Sovereign Hotel **H**

(603) 357-3038. **Call for rates.** 401 Winchester St 03431. SR 10, just s of jct SR 12 and 101. Int corridors. **Pets:** $20 daily fee/pet. Designated rooms, supervision. 🆂🅰🆅🅴 🍽 ➳ 🛜 ✕

▼◆▼ Courtyard by Marriott Keene Downtown **H**

(603) 354-7900. **$118-$252.** 75 Railroad St 03431. Just off Main St; downtown. Int corridors. **Pets:** Accepted.

🄴🄲🄾 🍽 🛗 🏊 🛜 ✕ 🔋 🖥

∰ ⚟⚟ Days Inn of Keene H
(603) 352-9780. **$75-$260.** 3 Ash Brook Rd 03431. Jct SR 9 and 12, just w. Int corridors. **Pets:** $20 one-time fee/room. Service with restrictions, supervision. SAVE ⟰M ⟲ ⬛ ⬜

⚟⚟⚟ Fairfield Inn & Suites by Marriott Keene Downtown H
(603) 357-7070. **Call for rates.** 30 Main St 03431. Between Church and Roxbury sts; downtown. Int corridors. **Pets:** Accepted.
⟦⟧ ⟰M ⟲ ⟲ ⬛ ⬜

⚟⚟⚟ Holiday Inn Express H
(603) 352-7616. **Call for rates.** 175 Key Rd 03431. SR 101, just n, via Winchester St, then 0.3 mi w. Int corridors. **Pets:** Medium, dogs only. $250 deposit/room, $25 daily fee/pet. Designated rooms, service with restrictions, crate. ⟰M ⟲ ⟲ ⬛ ⬜

LANCASTER

∰ ⚟⚟ The Cabot Inn & Suites H
(603) 788-3346. **$79-$159.** 200 Portland St 03584. On US 2, 1.2 mi e of jct US 3. Int corridors. **Pets:** $10 one-time fee/pet. Designated rooms, no service, crate.
SAVE ⟦⟧ ⟰M ⟲ ⟲ ⟲ ⬛ ⬜

∰ ⚟⚟ Coos Motor Inn H
(603) 788-3079. **$49-$110.** 209 Main St 03584. On US 2 and 3; center. Int corridors. **Pets:** Accepted. SAVE ⟦⟧ ⟰M ⟲ ⟲

LEBANON

∰ ⚟⚟⚟ Residence Inn by Marriott Hanover Lebanon H
(603) 643-4511. **$146-$263.** 32 Centerra Pkwy 03766. I-89 exit 18, 2.5 mi n on SR 120. Int corridors. **Pets:** Accepted.
SAVE ⟰M ⟲ ⟲ ⟲ ⬛ ⬜

LINCOLN

∰ ⚟⚟ Econo Lodge Inn & Suites M
(603) 745-3661. **$70-$205.** 381 US Rt 3 03251. I-93 exit 33 (US 3), 0.3 mi ne. Ext/int corridors. **Pets:** Accepted. SAVE ⟲ ⟲ ⟲ ⟲ ⬛

∰ ⚟⚟ Woodward's Resort M
(603) 745-8141. **Call for rates.** 527 US 3 03251. I-93 exit 33 (US 3), 1.4 mi ne. Ext/int corridors. **Pets:** Accepted.
SAVE ⟦⟧ ⟲ ⟲ ⟲ ⬛ ⬜

LITTLETON

⚟⚟⚟ The Beal House Inn CI
(603) 444-2661. **Call for rates.** 2 W Main St 03561. I-93 exit 42, 0.8 mi e on US 302 and SR 10. Int corridors. **Pets:** Accepted.
⟦⟧ ⟲ ⟲ ⟲ ⬛

∰ ⚟⚟ Eastgate Motor Inn M
(603) 444-3971. **$70-$140, 3 day notice.** 335 Cottage St 03561. I-93 exit 41, just e. Ext/int corridors. **Pets:** Small, dogs only. $20 one-time fee/pet, $20 daily fee/pet. Designated rooms, service with restrictions, supervision. SAVE ⟦⟧ ⟲ ⬛ ⬜

MANCHESTER *(Restaurants p. 635)*

∰ ⚟⚟⚟ BEST WESTERN PLUS Executive Court Inn & Conf. Ctr. H
(603) 627-2525. **$105-$200.** 13500 S Willow St 03103. I-293 exit 1, 0.5 mi s on SR 28, then 1 mi e. Int corridors. **Pets:** Accepted.
SAVE ⟦⟧ ⟲ ⟲ ⟲ ⟲ ⬛ ⬜

⚟⚟ Comfort Inn H
(603) 668-2600. **$89-$149.** 298 Queen City Ave 03102. I-293 exit 4, just w. Int corridors. **Pets:** Large. $25 one-time fee/room. Designated rooms, service with restrictions, supervision.
⟦⟧ ⟲ ⟲ ⟲ ⬛ ⬜

⚟⚟⚟ Holiday Inn Express Hotel & Suites-Manchester Airport H
(603) 669-6800. **Call for rates.** 1298 S Porter St 03103. I-293 exit 1. Int corridors. **Pets:** Accepted. ⟦⟧ ⟰M ⟲ ⟲ ⟲ ⬛ ⬜

⚟⚟⚟ Homewood Suites by Hilton H
(603) 668-2200. **$104-$229.** 1000 Perimeter Rd 03103. I-293 exit 2, follow signs to Manchester-Boston Regional Airport. Int corridors. **Pets:** Accepted. ⟦⟧ ⟰M ⟲ ⟲ ⟲ ⬛ ⬜

⚟⚟⚟ La Quinta Inn & Suites Manchester H
(603) 669-5400. **$95-$239.** 21 Front St 03102. I-293 exit 6, just se. Int corridors. **Pets:** Large, other species. Service with restrictions.
⟦⟧ ⟰M ⟲ ⟲ ⟲ ⬛ ⬜

∰ ⚟⚟⚟ Quality Inn Manchester Airport H
(603) 668-6110. **$79-$250.** 55 John E Devine Dr 03103. I-293 exit 1, just nw on SR 28. Int corridors. **Pets:** Accepted.
SAVE ⟦⟧ ⟰M ⟲ ⟲ ⟲ ⬛ ⬜

∰ ⚟⚟⚟ Radisson Hotel Manchester Downtown H
(603) 625-1000. **$119-$219.** 700 Elm St 03101. Jct Granite St; downtown. Int corridors. **Pets:** Accepted.
SAVE ECO ⟦⟧ ⟰M ⟲ ⟲ ⟲ ⟲ ⬛ ⬜

⚟⚟ TownePlace Suites by Marriott Manchester-Boston Regional Airport H
(603) 641-2288. **$111-$183.** 686 Huse Rd 03103. I-293 exit 1, 0.5 mi se on SR 28. Int corridors. **Pets:** Accepted.
⟰M ⟲ ⟲ ⟲ ⬛ ⬜

MEREDITH

⚟⚟⚟ Church Landing at Mill Falls H ✿
(603) 279-7006. **$250-$525, 3 day notice.** 281 Daniel Webster Hwy 03253. Jct US 3 and SR 104, 0.6 mi n. Ext/int corridors. **Pets:** Other species. $350 deposit/room, $25 daily fee/pet. Designated rooms, service with restrictions. ⟲ ⟦⟧ ⟰M ⟲ ⟲ ⟲ ⟲ ⬛ ⬜

MERRIMACK

∰ ⚟⚟ Hawthorn Suites by Wyndham H
(603) 424-8100. **$79-$179.** 246 Daniel Webster Hwy 03054. Everett Tpke exit 11, just e, then 0.6 mi s on US 3. Ext/int corridors.
Pets: Other species. $10 daily fee/room. Service with restrictions, crate.
SAVE ECO ⟦⟧ ⟰M ⟲ ⟲ ⟲ ⬛ ⬜

NASHUA

⚟⚟⚟ Hampton Inn Nashua H
(603) 883-5333. **$89-$179.** 407 Amherst St 03063. US 3 (Everett Tpke) exit 8; on SR 101A. Int corridors. **Pets:** Accepted.
ECO ⟰M ⟲ ⟲ ⟲ ⬛ ⬜

∰ ⚟⚟⚟ Holiday Inn & Suites Nashua H
(603) 888-1551. **$109-$189.** 9 Northeastern Blvd 03062. US 3 (Everett Tpke) exit 4, just w, then 0.3 mi n. Int corridors. **Pets:** Accepted.
SAVE ⟦⟧ ⟰M ⟲ ⟲ ⟲ ⬛ ⬜

⚟⚟⚟ Radisson Hotel Nashua H
(603) 888-9970. **$89-$229.** 11 Tara Blvd 03062. US 3 (Everett Tpke) exit 1, just w. Int corridors. **Pets:** Accepted.
ECO ⟦⟧ ⟰M ⟲ ⟲ ⟲ ⟲ ⬛ ⬜

⚟⚟⚟ Residence Inn by Marriott Nashua H
(603) 882-8300. **$143-$186.** 25 Trafalgar Sq 03063. US 3 (Everett Tpke) exit 8, just w. Int corridors. **Pets:** Accepted.
⟦⟧ ⟰M ⟲ ⟲ ⟲ ⬛ ⬜

NEWBURY

⚟⚟ Sunapee Lake Lodge H
(603) 763-2010. **Call for rates.** 1403 SR 103 03255. Jct SR 103B, just e. Int corridors. **Pets:** Accepted. ⟦⟧ ⟰M ⟲ ⟲ ⟲ ⬛ ⬜

NEW CASTLE

Wentworth By The Sea Marriott Hotel & Spa H
(603) 422-7322. **$153-$459, 3 day notice.** 588 Wentworth Rd 03854. On SR 1B, 2 mi e of SR 1A. Ext/int corridors. **Pets:** Accepted.

NEW LONDON

New London Inn CI
(603) 526-2791. **Call for rates.** 353 Main St 03257. Center. Int corridors. **Pets:** Other species. $25 one-time fee/room. Designated rooms, service with restrictions.

NORTH CONWAY

North Conway Hampton Inn & Suites H
(603) 356-7736. **$89-$249.** 1788 White Mountain Hwy 03860. Jct US 302/SR 16, 1 mi n. Int corridors. **Pets:** Other species. Designated rooms, service with restrictions, crate.

North Conway Mountain Inn M
(603) 356-2803. **$79-$199.** 2114 White Mountain Hwy 03860. 1 mi s on US 302/SR 16. Ext corridors. **Pets:** Accepted.

Red Jacket Mountain View Resort and Indoor Water Park H
(603) 356-5411. **Call for rates.** 2251 White Mountain Hwy 03860. 1 mi s on US 302/SR 16. Ext/int corridors. **Pets:** Accepted.

Residence Inn by Marriott, North Conway H
(603) 356-3024. **$146-$286.** 1801 White Mountain Hwy 03860. Jct US 302/SR 16, 1 mi n. Int corridors. **Pets:** Accepted.

PLYMOUTH

Red Carpet Inn & Suites M
(603) 536-2155. **Call for rates.** 166 Highland St 03264. 1 mi w of center. Ext corridors. **Pets:** Other species. $10 one-time fee/pet, $10 daily fee/pet. Designated rooms, service with restrictions, supervision.

PORTSMOUTH

Anchorage Inn & Suites H
(603) 431-8111. **Call for rates.** 417 Woodbury Ave 03801. I-95 exit 6 at Portsmouth Traffic Circle, follow Woodbury Ave exit, then just n. Int corridors. **Pets:** Medium, dogs only. $20 daily fee/pet. Designated rooms, service with restrictions, supervision.

BEST WESTERN PLUS Wynwood Hotel & Suites H
(603) 436-7600. **$99-$199.** 580 US 1 Bypass 03801. I-95 exit 5, jct US 1 Bypass and Portsmouth Traffic Circle. Ext/int corridors. **Pets:** Accepted.

Hampton Inn-Portsmouth H
(603) 431-6111. **$119-$249.** 99 Durgin Ln 03801. I-95 exit 7, 1 mi w via Market St and Woodbury Ave to Durgin Ln, then 0.3 mi s. Int corridors. **Pets:** Accepted.

Homewood Suites by Hilton H
(603) 427-5400. **$109-$409.** 100 Portsmouth Blvd 03801. I-95 exit 7, 0.5 mi w, then 0.3 mi n. Int corridors. **Pets:** Accepted.

Port Inn Portsmouth, An Ascend Collection Member M
(603) 436-4378. **$99-$399.** 505 US 1 Bypass 03801. I-95 exit 5, jct US 1 Bypass and Portsmouth Traffic Circle. Ext corridors. **Pets:** Accepted.

Residence Inn by Marriott H
(603) 436-8880. **$125-$367.** 1 International Dr 03801. SR 4/16 exit 1, just s. Int corridors. **Pets:** Accepted.

Residence Inn by Marriott Downtown/Waterfront H
(603) 422-9200. **$132-$390.** 100 Deer St 03801. Downtown. Int corridors. **Pets:** Accepted.

Sheraton Portsmouth Harborside Hotel H
(603) 431-2300. **$119-$369.** 250 Market St 03801. Downtown. Int corridors. **Pets:** Designated rooms, supervision.

ROCHESTER

Anchorage Inn M
(603) 332-3350. **$79-$179.** 13 Wadleigh Rd 03867. Jct Spaulding Tpke (SR 16), exit 12, just n on SR 125. Ext corridors. **Pets:** Accepted.

Holiday Inn Express Hotel & Suites Rochester H
(603) 994-1175. **$89-$209.** 77 Farmington Rd 03867. I-16 exit 15, 1 mi w on SR 11. Int corridors. **Pets:** Other species. $50 one-time fee/room. Designated rooms, service with restrictions, supervision.

SALEM

Red Roof Inn Salem M
(603) 898-6422. **Call for rates.** 15 Red Roof Ln 03079. I-93 exit 2, just se. Ext corridors. **Pets:** Large, other species. Service with restrictions, supervision.

SUGAR HILL

The Hilltop Inn BB
(603) 823-5695. **Call for rates.** 9 Norton Ln 03586. I-93 exit 38, 0.5 mi n on SR 18, then 2.8 mi w on SR 117. Int corridors. **Pets:** Dogs only. $10 daily fee/room.

SUNAPEE

Dexter's Inn CI
(603) 763-5571. **$110-$185, 7 day notice.** 258 Stagecoach Rd 03782. Jct SR 103B and 11, 0.4 mi e on SR 11, then 1.8 mi s on Winn Hill Rd. Ext/int corridors. **Pets:** Other species. $10 daily fee/pet. Designated rooms, service with restrictions.

THORNTON

Shamrock Motel M
(603) 726-3534. **Call for rates.** 2913 US 3 03285. I-93 exit 29, 2.3 mi n. Ext corridors. **Pets:** Other species. $5 one-time fee/room. Designated rooms, no service, supervision.

TILTON

Black Swan Inn BB
(603) 286-4524. **Call for rates.** 354 W Main St 03276. I-93 exit 20 southbound, 1.5 mi w on SR 3 and 11. Int corridors. **Pets:** Other species. Designated rooms, service with restrictions.

TROY

The Inn at East Hill Farm CI
(603) 242-6495. **Call for rates.** 460 Monadnock St 03465. Jct SR 12 and Monadnock St, 2 mi e. Ext/int corridors. **Pets:** $20 daily fee/pet. Designated rooms, service with restrictions, crate.

WEST LEBANON

A Fireside Inn and Suites 🅷 🐾

(603) 298-5900. **$120-$280.** 25 Airport Rd 03784. I-89 exit 20 (SR 12A), just s. Int corridors. **Pets:** Dogs only. $20 daily fee/pet. Supervision. 🍴 🛎 🛜 ✕ 🛗 💻

Baymont Inn 🅼

(603) 298-8888. **$79-$129.** 45 Airport Rd 03784. I-89 exit 20 (SR 12A), just s, then just e. Int corridors. **Pets:** Accepted.
🍴 🅼 🛎 🛜 🛗 💻

WOODSVILLE

All Seasons Motel 🅼

(603) 747-2157. **$60-$125, 3 day notice.** 36 Smith St 03785. I-91 exit 17, 4.1 mi e on US 302, then just s. Ext corridors. **Pets:** $5 daily fee/pet. Designated rooms, service with restrictions, supervision.
(SAVE) 🛎 🛜 ✕ 🛗 💻

Nootka Lodge 🅼

(603) 747-2418. **$70-$250, 3 day notice.** 4982 Dartmouth College Hwy 03785. I-91 exit 17, 4.5 mi e on US 302. Ext corridors. **Pets:** $5 daily fee/pet. Designated rooms, service with restrictions, supervision.
(SAVE) 🛎 ✕ 🛜 ✕ 🛗

NEW JERSEY

ABSECON

Quality Inn & Suites Atlantic City Marina District 🅷

(609) 652-3300. **$45-$260.** 328 E White Horse Pike (US 30) 08205. Garden State Pkwy exit 40 southbound; exit northbound, U-turn through Atlantic City Service Plaza, s to exit 40, then just e. Ext corridors.
Pets: Accepted. 🛎 🛜 🛗 💻

Red Roof Inn & Suites Atlantic City 🅷

(609) 646-5000. **Call for rates.** 405 E Absecon Blvd 08201. Garden State Pkwy exit 40 southbound; exit northbound, U-turn through Atlantic City Service Plaza, s to exit 40, then 3.3 mi e. Int corridors.
Pets: Large, other species. Service with restrictions, supervision.
🍴 🛎 🛜 ✕ 🛗 💻

ATLANTIC CITY

Harrah's Resort Atlantic City 🅷

(609) 441-5000. **Call for rates.** 777 Harrah's Blvd 08401. 0.9 mi n of US 30 on Brigantine Blvd. Int corridors. **Pets:** Accepted.
🍴 🅼 🛎 ✕ 🛜 🛗 💻

Sheraton Atlantic City Convention Center Hotel 🅷

(609) 344-3535. **$79-$299.** 2 Convention Blvd 08401. Garden State Pkwy exit 38 to Atlantic City Expwy to Arctic Ave, just e to Michigan Ave, then just n. Int corridors. **Pets:** Accepted.
(SAVE) 🍴 🛎 🛜 ✕ 🛗 💻

BASKING RIDGE

Dolce Basking Ridge 🅷

(908) 953-3000. **Call for rates.** 300 N Maple Ave 07920. I-287 exit 30A, 0.3 mi e. Int corridors. **Pets:** Accepted.
🍴 🅼 🛎 ✕ 🛜 ✕ 🛗 💻

Hotel Indigo Basking Ridge 🅷

(908) 580-1300. **Call for rates.** 80 Allen Rd 07920. I-78 exit 33, 0.3 mi n on CR 525, then 0.3 mi w. Int corridors. **Pets:** Accepted.
🍴 🛜 ✕ 🛗 💻

BAY HEAD

The Grenville Hotel 🅷

(732) 892-3100. **Call for rates.** 345 Main Ave (SR 35) 08742. SR 35 S; at Bridge Ave. Int corridors. **Pets:** Medium, dogs only. $50 one-time fee/pet. Designated rooms, no service, supervision.
🍴 🛜 ✕ 🅕 🛗

BORDENTOWN

BEST WESTERN Bordentown Inn 🅼

(609) 298-8000. **$80-$120.** 1068 US Hwy 206 S 08505. New Jersey Tpke exit 7, 0.8 mi n. Ext corridors. **Pets:** Accepted.
(SAVE) 🛎 ✕ 🛜 🛗 💻

Days Inn-Bordentown 🅼

(609) 298-6100. **$70-$99.** 1073 US Hwy 206 N 08505. New Jersey Tpke exit 7, 0.8 mi n. Ext corridors. **Pets:** Accepted.
(SAVE) 🛎 🛜 🛗 💻

BRANCHBURG

HYATT house Branchburg 🅷

(908) 704-2191. **$89-$329.** 3141 Rt 22 E 08876. I-287 exit 14B northbound, 6.7 mi w; exit 17 southbound, 3.7 mi w. Int corridors.
Pets: Accepted. (SAVE) 🍴 🛎 🛜 ✕ 🛗 💻

BRIDGEPORT

Hampton Inn-Bridgeport 🅷 🐾

(856) 467-6200. **$139-$159.** 2 Pureland Dr 08085. I-295 exit 10, just se. Int corridors. **Pets:** Other species. Designated rooms, service with restrictions, supervision. 🅼 🛎 🛜 ✕ 🛗 💻

BRIDGEWATER

HYATT house Bridgewater 🅷

(908) 725-0800. **$89-$299.** 530 US 22 E 08807. I-287 exit 14B northbound, 4.7 mi w; exit 17 southbound, 1.8 mi w. Ext corridors.
Pets: Accepted. (SAVE) 🍴 🅼 🛎 🛜 ✕ 🛗 💻

CAPE MAY

Madison Avenue Beach Club Motel 🅼

(609) 884-8266. **Call for rates.** 605 Madison Ave 08204. Jct Columbia Ave. Ext corridors. **Pets:** Designated rooms, service with restrictions.
🍴 🛎 🛜 ✕ 🛗 💻

Marquis de Lafayette Hotel 🅷

(609) 884-3500. **Call for rates.** 501 Beach Ave 08204. Between Decatur and Ocean sts. Ext/int corridors. **Pets:** Other species. $100 deposit/room, $25 daily fee/pet. Designated rooms, service with restrictions.
(SAVE) 🍴 🅼 🛎 🛜 ✕ 🛗 💻

Palace Hotel of Cape May 🅷 🐾

(609) 898-8100. **$89-$339, 7 day notice.** 1101 Beach Ave 08204. Jct Beach and Philadelphia aves. Int corridors. **Pets:** Dogs only. $25 daily fee/pet. Designated rooms, service with restrictions, supervision.
(SAVE) 🅼 🛜 ✕ 🛗 💻

Victorian Lace Inn 🅱🅱

(609) 884-1772. **$135-$395, 14 day notice.** 901 Stockton Ave 08204. At Jefferson St; just w of Beach Ave. Ext/int corridors. **Pets:** Accepted.
🍴 🛜 ✕ 🅩 🛗 💻

CAPE MAY COURT HOUSE

The Doctors Inn 🅱🅱

(609) 463-9330. **$99-$250, 14 day notice.** 2 N Main St 08210. At Main (US 9) and Mechanic sts; just s of Garden State Pkwy. Int corridors.
Pets: Medium, dogs only. $25 daily fee/pet. Designated rooms, service with restrictions, supervision. 🍴 🛜 ✕ 🅩 🛗

CARNEYS POINT

Comfort Inn & Suites 🅷

(856) 299-8282. **$99-$150.** 634 Sodders Rd 08069. I-295 exit 2B, just e on Pennsville-Auburn Rd, then 0.3 mi s. Int corridors. **Pets:** $10 daily fee/pet. Designated rooms, service with restrictions, crate.
🅼 🛜 🛗 💻

◆◆◆ ▽▽◆◆◆ Holiday Inn Express Hotel & Suites �H

(856) 351-9222. **$110-$140.** 506 S Pennsville-Auburn Rd 08069. I-295 exit 2B, just e. Int corridors. **Pets:** Other species. $10 daily fee/pet. Service with restrictions, supervision. 🆂🅰🆅🅴 🛜 ✖ 🛎 🖥

CARTERET

▽▽◆◆ Hotel Executive Suites �H

(732) 541-2005. **$99-$299.** 30 Minue St 07008. I-95 (New Jersey Tpke) exit 12, 0.3 mi e on Roosevelt Ave, just s. Int corridors. **Pets:** Accepted.
🍽 🅰🅼 🛜 🛎 🖥

CHERRY HILL

▽▽ ▽▽ Extended Stay America-Philadelphia/Cherry Hill �H

(856) 616-1200. **Call for rates.** 1653 E SR 70 (Marlton Pike) 08034. I-295 exit 34A, just e. Int corridors. **Pets:** Other species. $25 daily fee/pet. Service with restrictions, supervision. 🍽 🛜 🛎 🖥

◆◆◆ ▽▽◆◆ Holiday Inn Philadelphia-Cherry Hill �H 🐾

(856) 663-5300. **Call for rates.** 2175 W Marlton Pike 08002. I-295 exit 34B, 2.5 mi w. Int corridors. **Pets:** Other species. $75 deposit/room. Designated rooms, service with restrictions, crate.

🆂🅰🆅🅴 🍽 🅰🅼 🛟 🛜 ✖ 🛎 🖥

CLINTON

▽▽◆▽▽ Holiday Inn-Clinton �H

(908) 735-5111. **$99-$199.** 111 Rt 173 08809. I-78 exit 15, just nw. Int corridors. **Pets:** Accepted. 🍽 🛟 🛜 ✖ 🛎 🖥

COOKSTOWN

▽▽ ▽▽ Quality Inn McGuire AFB �H

(609) 723-6500. **$80-$159.** 21 Wrightstown/Cookstown Rd 08511. 0.3 mi n of main entrance to McGuire Air Force Base. Int corridors. **Pets:** Other species. $100 deposit/room. Designated rooms, service with restrictions. 🅰🅼 🛟 🛜 🛎 🖥

CRANBURY

◆◆◆ ▽▽◆▽▽ Courtyard by Marriott Cranbury/South Brunswick �H

(609) 655-9950. **$125-$206.** 420 Forsgate Dr 08512. New Jersey Tpke exit 8A to SR 32 W toward town, just s. Int corridors. **Pets:** Accepted.
🆂🅰🆅🅴 🍽 🅰🅼 🛟 🛜 ✖ 🛎 🖥

◆◆◆ ▽▽◆▽▽ Residence Inn by Marriott/Cranbury-South Brunswick �H

(609) 395-9447. **$111-$229.** 2662 US 130 08512. New Jersey Tpke exit 8A to SR 32 W toward town, 2 mi s on River Rd. Int corridors. **Pets:** Medium. $100 one-time fee/room. Designated rooms, service with restrictions. 🆂🅰🆅🅴 🅰🅼 🛟 🛜 ✖ 🛎 🖥

▽▽◆▽▽ Staybridge Suites/Cranbury �H

(609) 409-7181. **$130-$150.** 1272 S River Rd 08512. New Jersey Tpke exit 8A to SR 32 W toward town, 2 mi s. Int corridors. **Pets:** Large. $75 daily fee/room. Service with restrictions. 🛟 🛜 ✖ 🛎 🖥

DEPTFORD

▽▽◆▽▽ Residence Inn by Marriott Deptford �H

(856) 686-9188. **$125-$229.** 1154 Hurffville Rd 08096. SR 42 exit Deptford, Runnemede, Woodbury to CR 544, just e to SR 41 S. Int corridors. **Pets:** Accepted. 🛟 🛜 ✖ 🛎 🖥

DOVER

▽▽◆▽▽ Homewood Suites by Hilton Dover-Rockaway �H

(973) 989-8899. **$135-$175.** 2 Commerce Center Dr 07801. 1.2 mi n on Mt Hope Ave, just w on Mt Pleasant Ave. Int corridors. **Pets:** Accepted.
🍽 🅰🅼 🛟 🛜 🛎 🖥

EAST BRUNSWICK

◆◆◆ ▽▽◆▽▽ BEST WESTERN East Brunswick Inn �H

(732) 238-4900. **$90-$300.** 764 SR 18 N 08816. Between Rue Ln and Racetrack Rd; New Jersey Tpke exit 9 (SR 18 N), 4 mi s. Ext/int corridors. **Pets:** Accepted. 🆂🅰🆅🅴 🅰🅼 🛜 🛎 🖥

▽▽ Motel 6 East Brunswick #1083 Ⓜ

(732) 390-4545. **Call for rates.** 244 SR 18 N 08816. New Jersey Tpke exit 9 (SR 18), 1 mi s, U-turn at Edgeboro Rd, then just e. Ext/int corridors. **Pets:** Other species. Service with restrictions, crate.
🍽 🅰🅼 🛟 🛎

▽▽ ▽▽ Studio 6 East Brunswick #6020 �H

(732) 238-3330. **Call for rates.** 246 Rt 18 at Edgeboro Rd 08816. New Jersey Tpke exit 9 (SR 18), 1 mi s, U-turn at Edgeboro Rd, then just e. Int corridors. **Pets:** Other species. $10 daily fee/room. Service with restrictions, crate. 🍽 🅰🅼 🛟 🛎 🖥

EAST RUTHERFORD

▽▽◆▽▽ Residence Inn by Marriott East Rutherford Meadowlands �H

(201) 939-0020. **$195-$321.** 10 Murray Hill Pkwy 07073. New Jersey Tpke exit 16W (from western spur) to SR 3 W to SR 17 N, 1.5 mi n to Paterson Plank Rd (SR 120), then just e. Int corridors. **Pets:** Accepted.
🍽 🅰🅼 🛟 🛜 ✖ 🛎 🖥

EAST WINDSOR

▽▽ ▽▽ Days Inn East Windsor �H

(609) 448-3200. **$69-$149.** 460 Rt 33 E 08520. New Jersey Tpke exit 8, just e. Int corridors. **Pets:** Medium. $50 one-time fee/room. Designated rooms, service with restrictions, crate. 🍽 🛟 🛜 🛎 🖥

◆◆◆ ▽▽ ▽▽ Quality Inn East Windsor �H 🐾

(609) 448-7399. **$70-$199.** 351 Franklin St 08520. New Jersey Tpke exit 8, just w. Ext/int corridors. **Pets:** Medium. $20 daily fee/pet. Designated rooms, service with restrictions, crate.
🆂🅰🆅🅴 🍽 🅰🅼 🛎 🖥

EATONTOWN

◆◆◆ ▽▽◆▽▽ Staybridge Suites Hotel Eatontown-Tinton Falls �H

(732) 380-9300. **$89-$259.** 4 Industrial Way E 07724. Garden State Pkwy exit 105, 0.7 mi e on SR 36, then 1 mi s on SR 35. Int corridors. **Pets:** Large. $75 one-time fee/pet. Designated rooms, service with restrictions, crate. 🆂🅰🆅🅴 🍽 🅰🅼 🛟 🛜 ✖ 🛎 🖥

EDISON

▽▽ ▽▽ Quality Inn Edison �H

(732) 548-7000. **$80-$95.** 21 Cortlandt St 08837. I-287 exit 1B, just s to Prince St. Int corridors. **Pets:** Accepted. 🅰🅼 🛜 🛎 🖥

▽▽ Red Roof Inn Edison Ⓜ

(732) 248-9300. **Call for rates.** 860 New Durham Rd 08817. I-287 exit 2A northbound, 0.3 mi w via Bridge St, then left; exit 3 southbound, just w. Ext corridors. **Pets:** Large, other species. Service with restrictions, supervision. 🅰🅼 🛜 🛎 🖥

◆◆◆ ▽▽◆▽▽ Sheraton Edison Hotel Raritan Center �H

(732) 225-8300. **Call for rates.** 125 Raritan Center Pkwy 08837. New Jersey Tpke exit 10, 0.5 mi se on CR 514, keep right after tolls. Int corridors. **Pets:** Accepted.
🆂🅰🆅🅴 🍽 🅰🅼 ✖ 🛟 ✖ 🛎 🖥

ELIZABETH

◆◆◆ ▽▽◆▽▽ Residence Inn by Marriott Newark Elizabeth/Liberty International Airport �H

(908) 352-4300. **$174-$286.** 83 Glimcher Realty Way 07201. New Jersey Tpke exit 13A, 1 mi se on Jersey Garden Blvd, just n on Kapkowski Rd, then just w. Int corridors. **Pets:** Accepted.
🆂🅰🆅🅴 🅰🅼 🛟 🛜 ✖ 🛎 🖥

EWING

 Element by Westin Ewing Princeton **H** ✿

(609) 671-0050. **$109-$199.** 1000 Sam Weinroth Rd E 08628. I-95 exit 3A, just e. Int corridors. **Pets:** Small. Service with restrictions, crate.

SAVE ⊟ ⊺⊺ ⅙ᴹ ⇶ ⊠ 📶 ⊠ 🔒 💻

FAIRFIELD

La Quinta Inn & Suites Fairfield **H**

(973) 575-1742. **$85-$225.** 38 Two Bridges Rd 07004. I-80 exit 52 westbound; exit 47B (Caldwells) eastbound, 7 mi e on US 46 exit Passaic Ave. Int corridors. **Pets:** Large, other species. Service with restrictions. ⇶ 📶 🔒 💻

FAIR LAWN

 Hyatt Place Fair Lawn/Paramus **H**

(201) 475-3888. **$74-$209.** 41-01 Broadway (Rt 4 W) 07410. Garden State Pkwy exit 161 northbound, 0.7 mi w; exit 163 southbound; entrance from SR 4 W. Int corridors. **Pets:** Accepted.

SAVE ⅙ᴹ ⇶ 📶 ⊠ 🔒 💻

FLORHAM PARK

Wyndham Hamilton Park Hotel & Conference Center **H**

(973) 377-2424. **$135-$289.** 175 Park Ave 07932. SR 24 exit 2A, 0.4 mi w on CR 510, then 1 mi s on CR 623. Int corridors. **Pets:** Accepted.

SAVE ⊺⊺ ⇶ ⊠ 📶 ⊠ 🔒 💻

FORT LEE

BEST WESTERN Fort Lee **M**

(201) 461-7000. **$100-$250, 3 day notice.** 2300 Rt 4 W 07024. 0.5 mi w of George Washington Bridge (SR 4 W). Int corridors.

Pets: Accepted. SAVE ⊺⊺ ⅙ᴹ 📶 🔒 💻

GALLOWAY

Stockton Seaview Hotel & Golf Club-A Dolce Resort **H**

(609) 652-1800. **$99-$379.** 401 S New York Rd 08205. US 9, 2.5 mi ne of White Horse Pike (US 30). Int corridors. **Pets:** Accepted.

⊺⊺ ⇶ ⊠ 📶 ⊠ 🔒 💻

HADDONFIELD

Haddonfield Inn **BB** ✿

(856) 428-2195. **Call for rates.** 44 W End Ave 08033. I-295 exit 28, 0.7 mi n on SR 168, 2.6 mi e on Kings Hwy, then just n. Int corridors. **Pets:** Dogs only. $25 daily fee/pet. Designated rooms, supervision.

⅙ᴹ 📶 ⊠ 🔒

HARRISON

Element Harrison-Newark **H**

(973) 484-1500. **$139-$299.** 399 Somerset St 07029. I-95 exit 15W; I-280 exit 16 (Essex St), just s on Frank E Rodgers Blvd S. Int corridors. **Pets:** Accepted. SAVE ⊺⊺ ⅙ᴹ 📶 ⊠ 🔒 💻

HAZLET

Holiday Inn/Hazlet **H**

(732) 888-2000. **Call for rates.** 2870 SR 35 07730. Garden State Pkwy exit 117 to SR 35 S, 2.5 mi s. Int corridors. **Pets:** Accepted.

⊺⊺ ⇶ 📶 🔒 💻

HOBOKEN *(Restaurants p. 635)*

W Hoboken **H**

(201) 253-2400. **$209-$619.** 225 River St 07030. Between 1st and 2nd sts. Int corridors. **Pets:** Accepted. SAVE ⊺⊺ ⅙ᴹ 📶 ⊠ 🔒 💻

JERSEY CITY

The Westin Jersey City Newport **H** ✿

(201) 626-2900. **$199-$569.** 479 Washington Blvd 07310. At The Waterfront, just n of 6th St. Int corridors. **Pets:** Medium, dogs only. Designated rooms, service with restrictions, supervision.

SAVE ⊺⊺ ⅙ᴹ ⇶ ⊠ 📶 ⊠ 🔒 💻

LAWRENCEVILLE

Red Roof Inn Princeton **M**

(609) 896-3388. **Call for rates.** 3203 Brunswick Pike (US 1) 08648. I-295 exit 67A, just n. Ext corridors. **Pets:** Large, other species. Service with restrictions, supervision. SAVE 📶 ⊠ 🔒 💻

LONG BRANCH

Ocean Place Resort & Spa **H**

(732) 571-4000. **Call for rates.** 1 Ocean Blvd 07740. Jct SR 71, 3 mi e on SR 36, then 0.5 mi s. Int corridors. **Pets:** Medium. $150 one-time fee/room. Designated rooms, no service.

SAVE ⊺⊺ ⇶ ⊠ 📶 ⊠ 🔒 💻

MAHWAH

Homewood Suites by Hilton **H**

(201) 760-9994. **$113-$179.** 375 Corporate Dr 07430. I-287 exit 66, 1.7 mi on SR 17 S to MacArthur Blvd, then 0.4 mi w. Int corridors.

Pets: Accepted. ⊺⊺ ⇶ 📶 🔒 💻

Sheraton Mahwah Hotel **H**

(201) 529-1660. **$129-$309.** 1 International Blvd (Rt 17) 07495. I-287 exit 66, at SR 17 N. Int corridors. **Pets:** Accepted.

SAVE ⊺⊺ ⇶ ⊠ 📶 ⊠ 🔒 💻

Super 8 Mahwah **H**

(201) 512-0800. **$80-$120.** 160 Rt 17 S 07430. I-287 exit 66, 0.7 mi s. Int corridors. **Pets:** Other species. $15 daily fee/pet. Designated rooms, service with restrictions, crate. 📶 🔒 💻

MANCHESTER

Comfort Inn Toms River / Manchester **H**

(732) 657-7100. **$75-$999.** 2016 Rt 37 W 08759. Garden State Pkwy exit 82A, 5 mi w. Int corridors. **Pets:** Medium, dogs only. $25 daily fee/pet. Service with restrictions, supervision. ⊺⊺ 📶 🔒 💻

MIDDLETOWN

Comfort Inn Middletown-Red Bank **H**

(732) 671-3400. **$89-$250.** 750 State Rt 35 S 07748. Garden State Pkwy exit 114, 2 mi e on Red Hill Rd, 1 mi s on Kings Hwy to SR 35, then 0.3 mi s. Int corridors. **Pets:** Large. $30 daily fee/room. Service with restrictions, supervision. SAVE ⊺⊺ ⇶ 📶 🔒 💻

MONMOUTH JUNCTION

Residence Inn by Marriott Princeton-South Brunswick **H**

(732) 329-9600. **$104-$207.** 4225 US 1 S 08543. 0.5 mi s of Raymond Rd. Int corridors. **Pets:** Accepted. ⊺⊺ ⅙ᴹ ⇶ 📶 ⊠ 🔒 💻

MORRIS PLAINS

Candlewood Suites Parsippany-Morris Plains **H**

(973) 984-9960. **Call for rates.** 100 Candlewood Dr 07950. I-287 exit 39 northbound; exit 39B southbound, 2 mi w on SR 10. Int corridors. **Pets:** Accepted. ⅙ᴹ 📶 ⊠ 🔒 💻

MORRISTOWN

HYATT house Morristown **H**

(973) 971-0008. **$99-$359.** 194 Park Ave 07960. SR 24 exit 2A (Morristown), just w. Int corridors. **Pets:** Accepted.

SAVE ⊺⊺ ⅙ᴹ ⇶ 📶 ⊠ 🔒 💻

◇◇◇◇◇ The Westin Governor Morris ⓗ ❀

(973) 539-7300. **$139-$499.** 2 Whippany Rd 07960. I-287 exit 36 southbound, left lane to light, left to stop sign, then 1 mi e; exit 36A northbound to Morris Ave, 0.8 mi e, follow signs. Int corridors.
Pets: Medium, dogs only. $50 one-time fee/pet. Service with restrictions, supervision. 🅢🅐🅥🅔 ⓘⓘ ⓖ🄼 ⌁ 🛜 ⌧ 🛏 ▣

MOUNT LAUREL

◇◇ Candlewood Suites Mt. Laurel ⓗ

(856) 642-7567. **Call for rates.** 4000 Crawford Pl 08054. New Jersey Tpke exit 4, 1 mi s on SR 73 S. Int corridors. **Pets:** Accepted.
🛜 ⌧ 🛏 ▣

◇◇ Extended Stay America Pacilli Place Philadelphia/Mt. Laurel ⓗ

(856) 608-9820. **Call for rates.** 500 Diemer Dr 08054. New Jersey Tpke exit 4, 1 mi se on SR 73, just n on Crawford Pl, then just e. Int corridors. **Pets:** Other species. $25 daily fee/pet. Service with restrictions, supervision. 🛜 ⌧ 🛏 ▣

◇◇◇ ◇◇◇◇ Hyatt house Mt. Laurel ⓗ

(856) 222-1313. **$99-$189.** 3000 Crawford Pl 08054. I-295 exit 36A, 1.5 mi s on SR 73. Ext corridors. **Pets:** Accepted.
🅢🅐🅥🅔 ⓖ🄼 ⌁ 🛜 ⌧ 🛏 ▣

◇◇◇ ◇◇◇◇ Hyatt Place Mt. Laurel ⓗ

(856) 840-0770. **$99-$199.** 8000 Crawford Pl 08054. New Jersey Tpke exit 4, 1 mi se on SR 73; I-295 exit 36A, 1.7 mi se on SR 73. Int corridors. **Pets:** Accepted. 🅢🅐🅥🅔 ⓖ🄼 ⌁ 🛜 ⌧ 🛏 ▣

◇◇◇ ◇◇◇◇ La Quinta Mt. Laurel-Philadelphia ⓗ

(856) 235-7500. **$79-$249.** 5000 Clover Rd 08054. New Jersey Tpke exit 4, just se; I-295 exit 36A, 0.8 mi se. Int corridors. **Pets:** Accepted.
🅢🅐🅥🅔 ⓖ🄼 🛜 ⌧ 🛏 ▣

◇◇◇◇ Philadelphia/Mount Laurel Homewood Suites by Hilton ⓗ

(856) 222-9001. **$109-$199.** 1422 Nixon Dr 08054. I-295 exit 36B, follow ramp to end, then just n. Int corridors. **Pets:** Medium. $100 one-time fee/room. Service with restrictions, crate.
ⓖ🄼 ⌁ 🛜 ⌧ 🛏 ▣

◇◇◇ ◇◇◇ Red Roof Inn #7066 Ⓜ

(856) 234-5589. **Call for rates.** 603 Fellowship Rd 08054. I-295 exit 36A, just se on SR 73 to Fellowship Rd, then just s. Ext corridors. **Pets:** Large, other species. Service with restrictions, supervision.
🅢🅐🅥🅔 🛜 🛏 ▣

◇◇◇◇ Residence Inn by Marriott Mount Laurel at Bishop's Gate ⓗ

(856) 234-1025. **$118-$194.** 1000 Bishops Gate Blvd 08054. I-295 exit 40A, just e. Int corridors. **Pets:** Accepted.
ⓖ🄼 ⌁ 🛜 ⌧ 🛏 ▣

◇◇◇ ◇◇◇◇ Staybridge Suites ⓗ

(856) 722-1900. **$149-$359.** 4115 Church Rd 08054. New Jersey Tpke exit 4, 0.5 mi s on SR 73, then 0.5 mi w. Int corridors. **Pets:** Medium, other species. $50 one-time fee/pet. Designated rooms, service with restrictions, crate. 🅢🅐🅥🅔 ⌁ 🛜 ⌧ 🛏 ▣

◇◇◇ ◇◇◇◇ The Westin Mount Laurel ⓗ

(856) 778-7300. **$99-$399.** 555 Fellowship Rd 08054. I-295 exit 36A, just se on SR 73 to Fellowship Rd, then just n. Int corridors.
Pets: Accepted. 🅢🅐🅥🅔 ⓘⓘ ⓖ🄼 ⌁ ⌧ 🛜 ⌧ 🛏 ▣

◇◇◇ ◇◇◇◇ Wyndham Philadelphia-Mount Laurel ⓗ

(856) 234-7000. **$109-$189.** 1111 SR 73 08054. New Jersey Tpke exit 4; I-295 exit 36A, 0.5 mi se. Int corridors. **Pets:** Accepted.
🅢🅐🅥🅔 🄴🄲🄾 ⓘⓘ ⓖ🄼 ⌁ 🛜 ⌧ 🛏 ▣

MOUNT OLIVE

◇◇◇◇ Residence Inn by Marriott Mt. Olive at The International Trade Center ⓗ

(973) 691-1720. **$140-$230.** 271 Continental Dr 07828. I-80 exit 25, just n, follow signs for International Trade Center. Int corridors.
Pets: Accepted. ⓘⓘ ⓖ🄼 ⌁ 🛜 ⌧ 🛏 ▣

NEPTUNE

◇◇◇◇ Residence Inn by Marriott Neptune at Gateway Centre ⓗ ❀

(732) 643-9350. **$118-$206.** 230 Jumping Brook Rd 07753. Garden State Pkwy exit 100B, 0.5 mi e on SR 33, then 0.5 mi n. Int corridors.
Pets: Other species. $100 one-time fee/room. Service with restrictions.
ⓘⓘ ⓖ🄼 ⌁ 🛜 ⌧ 🛏 ▣

NEWARK

◇◇◇◇ Fairfield Inn & Suites by Marriott Newark Liberty International Airport ⓗ

(973) 242-2600. **$108-$177.** 618-50 Rt 1 & 9 S 07114. I-95 (New Jersey Tpke) exit 14, 1 mi sw via US 1 and 9 S. Int corridors.
Pets: Accepted. ⓘⓘ ⓖ🄼 ⌁ 🛜 ⌧ 🛏 ▣

◇◇◇◇ Hilton Newark Penn Station ⓗ

(973) 622-5000. **$169-$399.** Gateway Center - 1048 Raymond Blvd 07102. I-95 (New Jersey Tpke) exit 15E, 3 mi w via Raymond Blvd. Int corridors. **Pets:** Accepted. ⓘⓘ 🄯 ⌧ 🛏 ▣

NORTH BERGEN *(Restaurants p. 635)*

◇◇ Meadowlands View Hotel ⓗ

(201) 348-3600. **$99-$152.** 2750 Tonnelle Ave 07047. Jct SR 3, 0.4 mi s. Int corridors. **Pets:** $100 deposit/pet. Designated rooms, service with restrictions, crate. ⓘⓘ 🛜 🛏 ▣

PARSIPPANY

◇◇◇◇ Embassy Suites Parsippany ⓗ

(973) 334-1440. **$101-$256.** 909 Parsippany Blvd 07054. I-80 exit 42 to US 202 N; just ne of jct US 202 and 46 W. Int corridors.
Pets: Accepted. ⓘⓘ ⌁ 🄯 🛏 ▣

◇◇◇ ◇◇◇◇ HYATT house Parsippany-East ⓗ

(973) 428-8875. **$109-$299.** 299 Smith Rd 07054. I-287 exit 41A northbound; exit 42 southbound to US 46 E, 0.5 mi s. Int corridors.
Pets: Accepted. 🅢🅐🅥🅔 ⓘⓘ ⓖ🄼 ⌁ 🛜 ⌧ 🛏 ▣

◇◇◇ ◇◇◇ Red Roof Inn Parsippany Ⓜ

(973) 334-3737. **Call for rates.** 855 US Hwy 46 E 07054. I-80 exit 47 westbound; exit 45 eastbound, 0.5 mi e. Ext corridors. **Pets:** Large, other species. Service with restrictions, supervision.
🅢🅐🅥🅔 🛜 🛏 ▣

◇◇◇ ◇◇◇◇ Residence Inn by Marriott Parsippany ⓗ

(973) 984-3313. **$188-$309.** 3 Gatehall Dr 07054. I-287 exit 39 northbound; exit 39B southbound, 2 mi w on SR 10. Ext/int corridors.
Pets: Accepted. 🅢🅐🅥🅔 ⓘⓘ ⓖ🄼 ⌁ ⌧ 🛜 ⌧ 🛏 ▣

◇◇◇ ◇◇◇◇ Sheraton Parsippany Hotel ⓗ

(973) 515-2000. **$75-$369.** 199 Smith Rd 07054. I-287 exit 41A northbound; exit 42 to US 46 E, 0.4 mi s. Int corridors. **Pets:** Accepted.
🅢🅐🅥🅔 🄴🄲🄾 ⓘⓘ ⓖ🄼 ⌁ ⌧ 🄯 ⌧ 🛏 ▣

◇◇◇ ◇◇◇◇ Sonesta ES Suites Parsippany ⓗ

(973) 334-2907. **Call for rates.** 61 Interpace Pkwy 07054. I-80 exit 42, 0.3 mi s on Cherry Hill Rd, then just w. Int corridors. **Pets:** Accepted.
🅢🅐🅥🅔 ⓘⓘ ⓖ🄼 ⌁ 🛜 ⌧ 🛏 ▣

PISCATAWAY *(Restaurants p. 635)*

◇◇◇ Embassy Suites Hotel Piscataway-Somerset ⓗ

(732) 980-0500. **$119-$209.** 121 Centennial Ave 08854. I-287 exit 9 (Highland Park), just s to Centennial Ave. Int corridors. **Pets:** Accepted.
ⓘⓘ ⌁ 🛜 🛏 ▣

◆◆ **Extended Stay America Piscataway-Rutgers University** H
(732) 235-1000. **Call for rates.** 410 S Randolphville Rd 08854. I-287 exit 7, 0.4 mi s. Int corridors. **Pets:** Other species. $25 daily fee/pet. Service with restrictions, supervision. 🍴 ➿ 🛜 🖥 🖨

◆ **Motel 6 Piscataway #1084** H
(732) 981-9200. **Call for rates.** 1012 Stelton Rd 08854. I-287 exit 5, just e. Ext/int corridors. **Pets:** Other species. Service with restrictions, crate. 🛞 🖥

PRINCETON

◆◆◆ ◆◆◆ **Chauncey Hotel and Conference Center** H
(609) 921-3600. **Call for rates.** 660 Rosedale Rd 08541. 0.5 mi w on Stockton Rd, 0.5 mi n on Elm Rd, 1.8 mi w. Int corridors.
Pets: Accepted. SAVE 🍴 ♿M ➿ 🛜 ✖ 🖥 🖨

◆◆◆ ◆◆◆ **Clarion Hotel Palmer Inn** H
(609) 452-2500. **$80-$263.** 3499 US 1 S 08540. 2 mi s of jct CR 526 and 571. Ext/int corridors. **Pets:** Accepted.
SAVE 🍴 ➿ 🛜 🖥 🖨

◆◆◆ **Courtyard by Marriott Princeton** H
(609) 716-9100. **$167-$275.** 3815 US 1 S 08540. 0.4 mi s of Scudders Mill Rd at Mapleton Rd. Int corridors. **Pets:** Accepted.
🍴 ♿M ➿ 🛜 ✖ 🖥 🖨

◆◆◆ **Hampton Inn Princeton** H
(609) 951-0066. **$99-$179.** 4385 US 1 S 08540. Just past Ridge Rd. Int corridors. **Pets:** Accepted. 🍴 ♿M ➿ 🛜 ✖ 🖥 🖨

◆◆◆ **Holiday Inn Princeton** H
(609) 520-1200. **Call for rates.** 100 Independence Way 08540. I-295 exit 67A (SR 1) northbound; exit 67 (SR 1) southbound, 7 mi n. Int corridors. **Pets:** Accepted. 🍴 ♿M ➿ 🛜 ✖ 🖥 🖨

◆◆◆ ◆◆◆ **Hyatt Place Princeton** H
(609) 720-0200. **$89-$379.** 3565 US 1 S 08540. 1.5 mi s of jct CR 526 and 571. Int corridors. **Pets:** Accepted.
SAVE ♿M ➿ 🛜 ✖ 🖥 🖨

◆◆◆ ◆◆◆ **Nassau Inn** H 🐾
(609) 921-7500. **$199-$305.** 10 Palmer Square E 08542. Center. Int corridors. **Pets:** Large. $75 one-time fee/room. Designated rooms, service with restrictions, crate. SAVE 🍴 🛞 ✖ 🖥 🖨

◆◆◆ **Residence Inn by Marriott-Princeton at Carnegie Center** H
(609) 799-0550. **$174-$286.** 3563 US 1 S 08540. 1.5 mi s of jct CR 527 and 571. Int corridors. **Pets:** Accepted.
♿M ➿ 🛜 ✖ 🖥 🖨

◆◆◆ ◆◆ **Sonesta ES Suites Princeton** H
(609) 951-0009. **Call for rates.** 4375 US 1 S 08543. Just past Ridge Rd. Ext corridors. **Pets:** Accepted. SAVE ➿ 🛜 🖥 🖨

◆◆◆ ◆◆◆ **Westin Princeton at Forrestal Village** H
(609) 452-7900. **$139-$299.** 201 Village Blvd 08540. On US 1 southbound, 1.5 mi n of CR 571. Int corridors. **Pets:** Accepted.
SAVE 🍴 ♿M ➿ 🛞 ✖ 🖥 🖨

RAMSEY

◆◆◆ ◆◆◆ **BEST WESTERN The Inn at Ramsey** H
(201) 327-6700. **$89-$129.** 1315 Rt 17 S 07446. Jct I-287 and SR 17 S, 3 mi s. Int corridors. **Pets:** Accepted. SAVE 🍴 ♿M 🛜 🖥 🖨

ROBBINSVILLE

◆◆◆ **Hampton Inn & Suites** H
(609) 259-0300. **$119-$159.** 153 W Manor Way 08691. I-195 exit 7, just n. Int corridors. **Pets:** Accepted. 🍴 ♿M 🛜 ✖ 🖥 🖨

RUNNEMEDE

◆◆◆ ◆◆◆ **La Quinta Inn & Suites Runnemede** H
(856) 312-8521. **$89-$239.** 109 E 9th Ave 08078. New Jersey Tpke exit 3, 0.3 mi se, then just e; I-295 exit 28, 1.2 mi se. Int corridors.
Pets: Accepted. SAVE 🍴 ➿ 🛜 ✖ 🖥 🖨

RUTHERFORD

◆◆ **Extended Stay America-Meadowlands-Rutherford** H
(201) 635-0266. **Call for rates.** 750 Edwin L Ward Sr Memorial Hwy 07070. I-95 exit 16W, 1.5 mi w on SR 3 to SR 17 N service road exit, then 0.5 mi e. Int corridors. **Pets:** Other species. $25 daily fee/pet. Service with restrictions, supervision. 🍴 🛜 🖥 🖨

SECAUCUS

◆◆◆ ◆◆◆ **Hyatt Place Secaucus/Meadowlands** H
(201) 422-9480. **$109-$349.** 575 Park Plaza Dr 07094. New Jersey Tpke exits 16E, 17 or 16W via SR 3 to Harmon Meadow Blvd, then just w. Int corridors. **Pets:** Accepted. SAVE ♿M 🛜 ✖ 🖥 🖨

◆◆ **La Quinta Inn & Suites Secaucus Meadowlands** H
(201) 863-8700. **$125-$434.** 350 Lighting Way 07094. Between eastern and western spurs of New Jersey Tpke exits 16E, 17 or 16W via SR 3 W and Harmon Meadow Blvd; in Mill Creek Mall. Int corridors.
Pets: Large, other species. Service with restrictions.
➿ 🛜 🖥 🖨

SOMERSET

◆◆ **Candlewood Suites** H
(732) 748-1400. **Call for rates.** 41 Worlds Fair Dr 08873. I-287 exit 10 (CR 527), left on ramp (CR 527 S/Easton Ave), 0.3 mi, then 0.5 mi w. Int corridors. **Pets:** Accepted. 🍴 ♿M 🛜 🖥 🖨

◆◆◆ ◆◆◆ **Holiday Inn-Somerset** H
(732) 356-1700. **Call for rates.** 195 Davidson Ave 08873. I-287 exit 10 (CR 527), just n toward Bound Brook, then 0.5 mi sw. Int corridors.
Pets: Accepted. SAVE 🍴 ♿M ➿ 🛜 🖥 🖨

◆◆◆ **Homewood Suites by Hilton-Somerset** H
(732) 868-9155. **$109-$179.** 101 Pierce St 08873. I-287 exit 10 (CR 527), left on ramp (CR 527 S/Easton Ave), 0.3 mi, 0.7 mi w on Worlds Fair Dr, then just s. Int corridors. **Pets:** Accepted.
🍴 ♿M ➿ 🛜 ✖ 🖥 🖨

◆◆◆ **La Quinta Inn & Suites Somerset** H
(732) 560-9880. **$74-$224.** 60 Cottontail Ln 08873. I-287 exit 12, just sw via Weston Canal Rd. Int corridors. **Pets:** Large, other species. Service with restrictions. 🍴 ➿ 🛜 🖥 🖨

◆◆◆ ◆◆◆ **Residence Inn by Marriott-Somerset** H
(732) 627-0881. **$167-$275.** 37 Worlds Fair Dr 08873. I-287 exit 10 (CR 527), 0.3 mi left on ramp (CR 527 S/Easton Ave), then 0.5 mi w. Int corridors. **Pets:** Accepted. SAVE 🍴 ♿M ➿ 🛜 ✖ 🖥 🖨

◆◆◆ ◆◆◆ **Sonesta ES Suites Somerset** H
(732) 356-8000. **$125-$225, 3 day notice.** 260 Davidson Ave 08873. I-287 exit 10 (CR 527), just n toward Bound Brook to Davidson Ave, then 0.8 mi sw. Ext corridors. **Pets:** Medium, dogs only. $150 one-time fee/room. Designated rooms, service with restrictions.
SAVE ➿ 🛜 🖥 🖨

SOMERS POINT

◆◆◆ **Residence Inn by Marriott Atlantic City Somers Point** H
(609) 927-6400. **$139-$344.** 900 Mays Landing Rd 08244. Garden State Pkwy exit 30 southbound; exit 29 northbound, 1 mi e. Ext corridors. **Pets:** Accepted. ➿ 🛜 ✖ 🖥 🖨

SOUTH PLAINFIELD

BEST WESTERN The Garden Executive Hotel H
(908) 561-4488. **$94-$124.** 101 New World Way 07080. I-287 exit 5, just s. Int corridors. **Pets:** $50 deposit/room. Designated rooms, service with restrictions, crate. SAVE

STOCKTON

Woolverton Inn BB
(609) 397-0802. **$150-$435, 10 day notice.** 6 Woolverton Rd 08559. Jct CR 523 N and SR 29 N, just n to Woolverton Rd, then just w. Int corridors. **Pets:** Accepted.

SWEDESBORO

Holiday Inn H
(856) 467-3322. **Call for rates.** 1 Pureland Dr 08085. I-295 exit 10, 0.4 mi e. Int corridors. **Pets:** Accepted.

THOROFARE

BEST WESTERN West Deptford Inn H
(856) 848-4111. **$110.** 98 Friars Blvd 08086. I-295 exit 20, just e on Mid Atlantic Pkwy, then 0.4 mi n. Int corridors. **Pets:** Medium, dogs only. $25 one-time fee/pet. Designated rooms, service with restrictions, supervision. SAVE

TINTON FALLS

Red Roof Inn Tinton Falls Jersey Shore M
(732) 389-4646. **Call for rates.** 11 Centre Plaza 07724. Garden State Pkwy exit 105, just right at 1st light after toll. Ext corridors. **Pets:** Large, other species. Service with restrictions, supervision.

Residence Inn by Marriott Tinton Falls H
(732) 389-8100. **$111-$206.** 90 Park Rd 07724. Garden State Pkwy exit 105, 1st jughandle after toll, then just n. Ext corridors. **Pets:** Accepted.

TOMS RIVER

Howard Johnson Hotel-Toms River H
(732) 244-1000. **$99-$399.** 955 Hooper Ave 08753. Garden State Pkwy exit 82, 1 mi e on SR 37. Int corridors. **Pets:** Other species. $50 daily fee/pet. Designated rooms, service with restrictions, supervision. SAVE

VERNON

Appalachian Motel M
(973) 764-6070. **$55-$125, 3 day notice.** 367 Rt 94 N 07462. 1 mi n. Ext corridors. **Pets:** Other species. $20 daily fee/pet. Designated rooms, service with restrictions, supervision. SAVE

VINELAND

Comfort Inn H
(856) 692-8070. **$68-$170.** 29 W Landis Ave 08360. SR 55 exit 32A, 2 mi e. Int corridors. **Pets:** Medium. $15 daily fee/pet. Designated rooms, service with restrictions, supervision.

Wingate by Wyndham H
(856) 690-9900. **$79-$159.** 2196 W Landis Ave 08360. SR 55 exit 32A, just e. Int corridors. **Pets:** Accepted. SAVE

WANTAGE

High Point Country Inn M
(973) 702-1860. **Call for rates.** 1328 SR 23 N 07461. 1 mi n of Colesville Village Center. Ext corridors. **Pets:** Accepted.

WAYNE

La Quinta Inn & Suites H
(973) 696-8050. **$72-$185.** 1850 SR 23 07470. I-80 exit 53 (Butler-Verona) westbound to SR 23 N, 3 mi to Ratzer Rd (service road), then just n; exit 54 eastbound to Minnisink Rd, U-turn for US 80 W exit 53. Int corridors. **Pets:** Large, other species. Service with restrictions.

Ramada Wayne Fairfield Area H
(973) 256-7000. **$90-$150.** 334 Rt 46 E/Service Rd 07470. I-80 exit 53 (Butler-Verona) westbound to SR 23 S, service road off US 46 eastbound Caldwells; exit 47B eastbound, 7 mi e on US 46 to service road. Ext corridors. **Pets:** Accepted.

Residence Inn by Marriott Wayne H
(973) 872-7100. **$146-$240.** 30 Nevins Rd 07470. Jct CR 640 (Riverview Dr) and 681 (Valley Rd), 3.5 mi n, just w on Barbour Pond Dr, then just n. Int corridors. **Pets:** Accepted.

WEEHAWKEN

Sheraton Lincoln Harbor Hotel H
(201) 617-5600. **$189-$449.** 500 Harbor Blvd 07086. Just se of Lincoln Tunnel entrance, at 19th St. Int corridors. **Pets:** Accepted.

WESTAMPTON

BEST WESTERN Burlington Inn H
(609) 261-3800. **$99-$139.** 2020 Burlington Mt Holly Rd 08060. New Jersey Tpke exit 5, just n. Int corridors. **Pets:** Small. $10 daily fee/pet. Designated rooms, service with restrictions, supervision. SAVE

WEST LONG BRANCH

La Quinta Inn H
(732) 403-8700. **$85-$294.** 109 Rt 36 07764. 1.9 mi w of jct SR 35. Int corridors. **Pets:** Large, other species. Service with restrictions.

WEST ORANGE

Residence Inn by Marriott-West Orange H ❖
(973) 669-4700. **$139-$286.** 107 Prospect Ave 07052. I-280 exit 8B, 1 mi n on CR 577 (Prospect Ave). Int corridors. **Pets:** Other species. $100 one-time fee/room. Service with restrictions.

The Wilshire Grand Hotel H ❖
(973) 731-7007. **$199-$449, 3 day notice.** 350 Pleasant Valley Way 07052. I-280 exit 8B, just n to Eagle Rock Ave, 0.9 mi w, then just n. Int corridors. **Pets:** Other species. $35 one-time fee/room. Designated rooms, supervision. SAVE

WHIPPANY

HYATT house Parsippany/Whippany H
(973) 605-1001. **$99-$299.** 1 Ridgedale Ave N 07981. I-287 exit 39, just nw. Int corridors. **Pets:** Accepted. SAVE

WILLIAMSTOWN

BEST WESTERN Monroe Inn & Suites H ❖
(856) 340-7900. **$99-$199.** 1151 N Black Horse Pike 08094. New Jersey Tpke exit 3, 3.2 mi s on SR 168, then 9 mi s on SR 42; 2 mi s of jct CR 689. Int corridors. **Pets:** Medium, dogs only. $20 daily fee/pet. Service with restrictions, supervision. SAVE

WOODBRIDGE

Extended Stay America Woodbridge-Newark H
(732) 442-8333. **Call for rates.** 1 Hoover Way 07095. I-95 (New Jersey Tpke) exit 11, 1.4 mi to US 9 N, then just w on King Georges Post Rd. Int corridors. **Pets:** Other species. $25 daily fee/pet. Service with restrictions, supervision.

▼▼▼ **Residence Inn by Marriott-Woodbridge Edison/ Raritan Center** �H

(732) 510-7100. **$160-$263.** 2 Regency Pl 07095. I-95 (New Jersey Tpke) exit 11, just e on SR 184 (Pond Rd), then 1.2 mi n on US 9. Int corridors. **Pets:** Small. $100 one-time fee/room. Service with restrictions, supervision. 🍴 🛴 🌊 🛜 ✕ 🛗 🖵

WOODCLIFF LAKE

▼▼▼▼ **Hilton Woodcliff Lake** �H

(201) 391-3600. **$159-$289.** 200 Tice Blvd 07677. Garden State Pkwy exit 171 northbound, left on Glen Rd from exit ramp, right on Chestnut Ridge Rd, 0.5 mi to Tice Blvd, then just left. Int corridors. **Pets:** Small. $75 one-time fee/pet. Designated rooms, service with restrictions, supervision. 🍴 🛴 🛎 ✕ 📶 🛗 🖵

NEW MEXICO

ALAMOGORDO (Restaurants p. 635)

🏵 ▼▼ **Magnuson Hotel and Suites Alamogordo** Ⓜ

(575) 437-2110. **Call for rates.** 1021 S White Sands Blvd 88310. 1.6 mi s of jct US 82/70 and 54. Ext corridors. **Pets:** Dogs only. $10 daily fee/pet. Designated rooms, service with restrictions, supervision. 🆂🅰🆅🅴 🛴 🛎 🛜 🛗 🖵

🏵 ▼▼ **Super 8-Alamogordo** �H

(575) 434-4205. **$59-$80.** 3204 N White Sands Blvd 88310. Just s of jct US 54/70 and 82. Int corridors. **Pets:** Other species. $10 deposit/pet, $10 daily fee/pet. Service with restrictions, crate. 🆂🅰🆅🅴 🛜 ✕ 🛗 🖵

ALBUQUERQUE (Restaurants p. 635)

🏵 ▼▼▼▼ **Albuquerque Sheraton Uptown Hotel** �H 🐾

(505) 881-0000. **Call for rates.** 2600 Louisiana Blvd NE 87110. I-40 exit 162, 0.8 mi n; in Northeast Heights. Int corridors. **Pets:** Medium, dogs only. $25 one-time fee/pet. Service with restrictions, supervision. 🆂🅰🆅🅴 🍴 🛴 📶 ✕ 🛗 🖵

🏵 ▼▼▼ **BEST WESTERN Airport Albuquerque InnSuites Hotel & Suites** �H

(505) 242-7022. **$69-$199.** 2400 Yale Blvd SE 87106. I-25 exit 222 (Gibson Blvd) northbound; exit 222A southbound, 1 mi e, then just s. Int corridors. **Pets:** Other species. $20 one-time fee/room. Designated rooms, service with restrictions, crate. 🆂🅰🆅🅴 🛴 🛜 🛗 🖵

🏵 ▼▼▼ **BEST WESTERN PLUS Rio Grande Inn** �H

(505) 843-9500. **$89-$159.** 1015 Rio Grande Blvd NW 87104. I-40 exit 157A (Rio Grande Blvd), just s. Int corridors. **Pets:** Accepted. 🆂🅰🆅🅴 🍴 🛴 🛜 ✕ 🛗 🖵

▼▼▼▼ **Bottger Mansion Bed and Breakfast** 🅱🅱

(505) 243-3639. **$115-$179, 7 day notice.** 110 San Felipe St NW 87104. I-40 exit 157A (Rio Grande Blvd), 1.5 mi s, then just e; off Central Ave. Int corridors. **Pets:** Accepted. 🛜 ✕

▼▼▼▼ **Candlewood Suites** �H

(505) 888-3424. **$90-$190.** 3025 Menaul Blvd NE 87107. I-40 exit 160, just n to Menaul Blvd, then 0.5 mi w. Int corridors. **Pets:** Large, other species. $15 daily fee/room. Service with restrictions, crate. 🛴 🛜 🛗 🖵

🏵 ▼▼▼ **ClubHouse Inn & Suites** �H

(505) 345-0010. **$89-$139.** 1315 Menaul Blvd NE 87107. I-25 exit 227A southbound, 1.5 mi s to Menaul Blvd, then just w; exit 225 northbound, 1.8 mi n, then just w. Int corridors. **Pets:** Other species. $15 daily fee/pet. Service with restrictions, crate. 🆂🅰🆅🅴 🍴 🛴 🛜 ✕ 🛗 🖵

🏵 ▼▼▼ **Comfort Inn Airport** �H

(505) 242-0036. **$69-$135.** 1801 Yale Blvd SE 87106. I-25 exit 222 (Gibson Blvd) northbound; exit 222A southbound, 1 mi e on Gibson Blvd, then just n. Int corridors. **Pets:** Small. $15 one-time fee/pet. Designated rooms, service with restrictions, supervision. 🆂🅰🆅🅴 🛴 🛜 🛗 🖵

▼▼ **Comfort Inn & Suites by Choice Hotels** �H

(505) 822-1090. **$62-$92.** 5811 Signal Ave NE 87113. I-25 exit 233 (Alameda Blvd), just e. Int corridors. **Pets:** Accepted. 🛴 🛜 🛗 🖵

▼▼ **Country Inn & Suites By Carlson Albuquerque Airport** �H

(505) 246-9600. **Call for rates.** 2601 Mulberry St SE 87106. I-25 exit 222 (Gibson Blvd), just e. Int corridors. **Pets:** Small. $25 one-time fee/room. Service with restrictions, supervision. 🛴 🛜 ✕ 🛗 🖵

🏵 ▼▼▼▼ **Courtyard by Marriott Journal Center** �H

(505) 823-1919. **$89-$169.** 5151 Journal Center Blvd NE 87109. I-25 exit 232, just s on Pan American Frwy NE. Int corridors. **Pets:** Accepted. 🆂🅰🆅🅴 🍴 🛴 🛜 ✕ 🛗 🖵

▼▼▼ **Drury Inn & Suites-Albuquerque** �H

(505) 341-3600. **$125-$189.** 4310 The 25 Way NE 87109. I-25 exit 229 (Jefferson St); northwest quadrant of exchange. Int corridors. **Pets:** $10 daily fee/room. Service with restrictions, supervision. 🛴 🛜 ✕ 🛗 🖵

▼▼ **Econo Lodge Midtown** �H

(505) 880-0080. **$55-$120.** 2412 Carlisle Blvd NE 87110. I-40 exit 160, just n. Ext corridors. **Pets:** Accepted. 🛜 🛗

▼▼ **Econo Lodge Old Town Albuquerque** �H

(505) 243-8475. **$73-$110.** 2321 Central Ave NW 87104. I-40 exit 157A, 0.6 mi s on Rio Grande Blvd, then 0.4 mi w. Ext corridors. **Pets:** Accepted. 🛴 🛜 🛗 🖵

🏵 ▼▼▼▼ **Fairfield Inn by Marriott Albuquerque-University Area** �H

(505) 889-4000. **$131-$179.** 1760 Menaul Blvd NE 87102. I-40 exit 160, just n to Menaul Blvd, then 1 mi w. Int corridors. **Pets:** Accepted. 🆂🅰🆅🅴 🛴 ✕ 🛜 ✕ 🛗 🖵

▼▼▼ **Holiday Inn Express Hotel & Suites Albuquerque Historic Old Town** �H

(505) 842-5000. **Call for rates.** 2300 12th St NW 87104. I-40 exit 157B eastbound; exit 158 westbound; just s of Menaul Blvd. Int corridors. **Pets:** Accepted. 🛴 🛜 ✕ 🛗 🖵

🏵 ▼▼▼▼ **Hotel Andaluz** �H

(505) 242-9090. **$139-$269, 3 day notice.** 125 2nd St NW 87102. I-25 exit 224A northbound; exit 224B southbound, jct Copper Ave and 2nd St. Int corridors. **Pets:** Accepted. 🆂🅰🆅🅴 🍴 ✕ 🛗 🖵

🏵 ▼▼▼▼ **Hotel Parq Central** �H

(505) 242-0040. **$140-$420.** 806 Central Ave SE 87102. I-25 exit 224A northbound; exit 224B southbound, just w. Int corridors. **Pets:** Accepted. 🆂🅰🆅🅴 🍴 🛴 ✕ 🛜 ✕ 🛗 🖵

🏵 ▼▼▼▼ **Hyatt Place Albuquerque Uptown** �H

(505) 872-9000. **$79-$209.** 6901 Arvada Ave NE 87110. I-40 exit 162, 0.7 mi n. Int corridors. **Pets:** Medium, dogs only. $75 one-time fee/pet. Designated rooms, service with restrictions, supervision. 🆂🅰🆅🅴 🍴 🛴 🛜 ✕ 🛗 🖵

Hyatt Regency Albuquerque H
(505) 842-1234. **$99-$299.** 330 Tijeras Ave NW 87102. I-25 exit 224B (Central Ave), 0.5 mi w. Int corridors. **Pets:** Accepted.
SAVE ECO 🍴 ⓜ 🏊 🗙 📶 🗙 🛢 💻

La Quinta Inn Albuquerque Airport H
(505) 243-5500. **$65-$244.** 2116 Yale Blvd SE 87106. I-25 exit 222 (Gibson Blvd) northbound; exit 222A southbound, 1 mi e. Ext corridors. **Pets:** Large, other species. Service with restrictions.
ⓜ 🏊 📶 🛢 💻

La Quinta Inn & Suites Albuquerque Midtown H
(505) 761-5600. **$97-$269.** 2011 Menaul Blvd 87107. Jct University and Menaul blvds, just e. Int corridors. **Pets:** Large, other species. Service with restrictions. ⓜ 🏊 📶 🗙 🛢 💻

La Quinta Inn & Suites Albuquerque West H
(505) 839-1744. **$59-$230.** 6101 Iliff Rd NW 87121. I-40 exit 155, just sw. Int corridors. **Pets:** Large, other species. Service with restrictions.
ⓜ 🏊 📶 🛢 💻

Mauger Bed & Breakfast Inn BB 🐾
(505) 242-8755. **$99-$204, 10 day notice.** 701 Roma Ave NW 87102. I-25 exit 225, 1 mi w, then just s on 7th Ave. Int corridors. **Pets:** Dogs only. $20 one-time fee/room. Designated rooms, service with restrictions. 📶 🗙 🛢 💻

MCM Elegante Hotel H
(505) 884-2511. **$84-$200.** 2020 Menaul Blvd NE 87107. I-40 exit 160, 0.3 mi n to Menaul Blvd, then 1 mi w. Int corridors. **Pets:** Accepted.
🍴 ⓜ 🏊 📶 🗙 🛢 💻

Nativo Lodge H
(505) 798-4300. **$89-$199.** 6000 Pan American Frwy NE 87109. I-25 exit 230, just e. Int corridors. **Pets:** Medium, dogs only. $25 one-time fee/pet. Service with restrictions, supervision.
🍴 🏊 📶 🗙 🛢 💻

Residence Inn by Marriott Albuquerque Airport H
(505) 242-2844. **$83-$207.** 2301 International Dr SE 87106. I-25 exit 222 (Gibson Blvd) northbound; exit 222A southbound, 1 mi e, just n of jct Yale Blvd. Int corridors. **Pets:** $100 one-time fee/room. Service with restrictions, crate. ⓜ 🏊 📶 🗙 🛢 💻

Residence Inn by Marriott North H 🐾
(505) 761-0200. **$76-$208.** 4331 The Lane at 25 NE 87109. I-25 exit 229 (Jefferson St), just w, just n to The Lane at 25 NE, then just e. Int corridors. **Pets:** Medium. $100 one-time fee/pet. Designated rooms, service with restrictions, supervision. ⓜ 🏊 📶 🗙 🛢 💻

Sheraton Albuquerque Airport Hotel H
(505) 843-7000. **$89-$179.** 2910 Yale Blvd SE 87106. I-25 exit 222 (Gibson Blvd) northbound; exit 222A southbound, 1 mi e, then 0.5 mi s. Int corridors. **Pets:** Accepted. SAVE 🍴 ⓜ 🏊 📶 🗙 🛢 💻

Staybridge Suites Albuquerque Airport H
(505) 338-3900. **Call for rates.** 1350 Sunport Pl SE 87106. I-25 exit 221, 0.3 mi e to University Blvd exit, then just n to Woodward Rd. Int corridors. **Pets:** Accepted. ⓜ 🏊 📶 🗙 🛢 💻

Staybridge Suites Albuquerque North H 🐾
(505) 266-7829. **$90-$220.** 5817 Signal Ave NE 87113. I-25 exit 233 (Alameda Blvd), just e; jct Alameda Blvd and Signal Ave. Int corridors. **Pets:** Other species. $10 daily fee/pet. Service with restrictions, supervision. SAVE 🏊 📶 🗙 🛢 💻

TownePlace Suites by Marriott H
(505) 232-5800. **$55-$159.** 2400 Centre Ave SE 87106. I-25 exit 222 (Gibson Blvd) northbound; exit 222A southbound, 1 mi e to Yale Blvd, at northeast jct of Gibson and Yale blvds, then just e. Int corridors. **Pets:** Accepted. ⓜ 🏊 📶 🗙 🛢 💻

ALGODONES

Hacienda Vargas Bed and Breakfast Inn BB 🐾
(505) 867-9115. **Call for rates.** 1431 SR 313 (El Camino Real) 87001. I-25 exit 248, 0.3 mi w, then 0.3 mi s. Int corridors. **Pets:** Other species. $10 daily fee/room. Service with restrictions, supervision.
📶 🗙 🗙 🛢

ARROYO SECO

Adobe and Stars B & B BB 🐾
(575) 776-2776. **Call for rates.** 584 State Hwy 150 87571. 1.1 mi ne of Arroyo Seco village, at Valdez Rd. Ext/int corridors. **Pets:** Medium. $50 deposit/pet. Designated rooms, service with restrictions, crate.
📶 🗙 🗙 🛢

ARTESIA

Artesia Inn M
(575) 746-9801. **Call for rates.** 1820 S 1st St 88210. 1.5 mi s on US 285. Ext corridors. **Pets:** Accepted. 🏊 📶 🛢 💻

BEST WESTERN Pecos Inn H
(575) 748-3324. **$150-$260.** 2209 W Main St 88210. 1.5 mi w on US 82. Int corridors. **Pets:** Accepted. SAVE 🍴 🏊 📶 🛢 💻

Hotel Artesia H
(575) 746-2066. **$129.** 203 N 2nd St 88210. Jct US 285 and Main St, just n. Int corridors. **Pets:** Small, dogs only. $39 one-time fee/pet. Designated rooms, service with restrictions, supervision.
📶 🗙 🛢 💻

AZTEC

Microtel Inn & Suites by Wyndham H 🐾
(505) 334-4014. **$53-$89.** 623 Phoenix Ct 87410. Jct SR 516 and US 550, 3 mi s. Int corridors. **Pets:** Dogs only. $25 daily fee/pet. Designated rooms, service with restrictions, supervision. 📶 🗙 🛢 💻

BERNALILLO *(Restaurants p. 635)*

Days Inn Bernalillo H
(505) 771-7000. **$65-$95.** 107 N Camino del Pueblo 87004. I-25 exit 242, just w. Int corridors. **Pets:** Accepted.
SAVE 🏊 📶 🗙 🛢 💻

Hyatt Regency Tamaya Resort and Spa H 🐾
(505) 867-1234. **$119-$309, 3 day notice.** 1300 Tuyuna Tr 87004. I-25 exit 242, 1 mi w on US 550 to Tamaya Blvd, then 1 mi n, follow signs. Int corridors. **Pets:** Medium, dogs only. $150 one-time fee/pet. Designated rooms, service with restrictions.
SAVE ECO 🍴 ⓜ 🏊 🗙 📶 🛢 💻

BLOOMFIELD

Super 8 M
(505) 632-8886. **$79-$94, 3 day notice.** 525 W Broadway Blvd 87413. Jct of US 64 and 550. Int corridors. **Pets:** Medium, other species. $15 one-time fee/room. Service with restrictions, supervision. 📶 🛢 💻

CHIMAYÓ *(Restaurants p. 636)*

Casa Escondida Bed & Breakfast BB 🐾
(505) 351-4805. **$119-$179, 14 day notice.** 64 CR 100 87522. Jct SR 76 and 98, just w on SR 76, then 0.5 mi ne, follow signs; 7.5 mi e of Espanola on SR 76. Ext/int corridors. **Pets:** Other species. $15 daily fee/pet. Designated rooms, service with restrictions, supervision.
📶 🗙 🗙 🛢 💻

CIMARRON

Cimarron Inn & RV Park M 🐾
(575) 376-2268. **$49-$75.** 212 10th St 87714. On US 64. Ext corridors. **Pets:** Other species. $10 one-time fee/room. Designated rooms, service with restrictions. SAVE 📶 🗙 🛢 💻

CLAYTON

BEST WESTERN Kokopelli Lodge H ❀
(575) 374-2589. **$105-$175.** 702 S 1st St 88415. US 87, 0.5 mi se of jct US 56 and 64. Ext corridors. **Pets:** Other species. $10 daily fee/pet. Service with restrictions, supervision. (SAVE) 🌊 🛜 ✕ 🛏 🖭

Days Inn & Suites H
(575) 374-0133. **$105-$145.** 1120 S 1st St 88415. US 87, 1 mi s of jct US 56 and 64. Int corridors. **Pets:** Accepted. 🌊 🛜 ✕ 🛏 🖭

CLOUDCROFT *(Restaurants p. 636)*

The Lodge Resort H
(575) 682-2566. **$115-$335, 14 day notice.** 601 Corona Pl 88317. US 82, 0.3 mi s on Curlew Pl/Corona Pl. Int corridors. **Pets:** Accepted.
(SAVE) 🍴 ♿ 🌊 ✕ 🛜 ✕ 🛏 🖭

CLOVIS

Clovis Inn & Suites H
(575) 762-5600. **Call for rates.** 2912 Mabry Dr 88101. 1.8 mi e on US 60/70/84. Ext corridors. **Pets:** Accepted. 🌊 🛜 🛏 🖭

Comfort Inn & Suites H
(575) 762-4536. **$119.** 201 Schepps Blvd 88101. Jct US 60/70/84, just n. Int corridors. **Pets:** Accepted. 🌊 🛜 🛏 🖭

La Quinta Inn & Suites Clovis H
(575) 763-8777. **$89-$205.** 4521 N Prince St 88101. Jct US 60/84, 3 mi n. Int corridors. **Pets:** Large, other species. Service with restrictions.
🌊 🛜 ✕ 🛏 🖭

DEMING *(Restaurants p. 636)*

BEST WESTERN Mimbres Valley Inn H ❀
(575) 546-4544. **$80-$149.** 1500 W Pine St 88030. I-10 exit 81, just e. Ext corridors. **Pets:** Other species. $15 daily fee/pet. Designated rooms, service with restrictions, supervision. (SAVE) 🌊 🛜 🛏 🖭

Days Inn M
(575) 546-8813. **$57-$72.** 1601 E Pine St 88030. I-10 exit 85 westbound, 2 mi w on business loop; exit 81 eastbound, 1 mi e on business loop. Ext corridors. **Pets:** Accepted. 🍴 🌊 🛜 🛏 🖭

Grand Motor Inn H
(575) 546-2632. **$46-$69.** 1721 E Pine St 88030. I-10 exit 85 westbound, 2 mi w on business loop; exit 82 eastbound, 1 mi e on business loop. Ext/int corridors. **Pets:** Medium. $5 daily fee/pet. Service with restrictions, supervision. (SAVE) 🍴 🌊 🛜 🛏

Hampton Inn H
(575) 546-2022. **$99-$129.** 3751 E Cedar St 88030. I-10 exit 85, just s to Cedar St, then just w. Int corridors. **Pets:** Accepted.
♿ 🌊 🛜 ✕ 🛏 🖭

La Quinta Inn & Suites Deming H
(575) 546-0600. **$79-$189.** 4300 E Pine St 88030. I-10 exit 85, just w. Int corridors. **Pets:** Large, other species. Service with restrictions.
(SAVE) ♿ 🌊 🛜 ✕ 🛏 🖭

ELEPHANT BUTTE

Elephant Butte Inn & Spa H ❀
(575) 744-5431. **$79-$139.** 401 Hwy 195 87935. I-25 exit 83, 4 mi e. Ext corridors. **Pets:** Other species. $20 one-time fee/pet. Designated rooms, service with restrictions, supervision.
(SAVE) 🍴 ♿ 🌊 🛜 ✕ 🛏 🖭

ESPAÑOLA *(Restaurants p. 636)*

Inn at the Delta BB
(505) 753-9466. **Call for rates.** 243 Paseo de Onate 87532. US 84 and 285, 1 mi n of jct SR 68; 0.3 mi n of jct SR 30. Ext corridors.
Pets: Accepted. 🛜 ✕ 🛏 🖭

Rodeway Inn H
(505) 753-2419. **$45-$66.** 604-B S Riverside Dr 87532. US 84 and 285, just s of jct SR 68. Int corridors. **Pets:** Accepted. 🌊 🛜 🛏 🖭

Santa Claran Hotel Casino H
(505) 367-4900. **Call for rates.** 464 N Riverside Dr 87532. SR 68; center. Int corridors. **Pets:** Accepted. 🍴 ♿ 🛜 🛏 🖭

FARMINGTON

Comfort Inn H
(505) 325-2626. **$83-$104.** 555 Scott Ave 87401. 1 mi e on SR 516 (Main St), just s. Int corridors. **Pets:** Accepted.
(SAVE) 🌊 🛜 ✕ 🛏 🖭

Holiday Inn Express H
(505) 325-2545. **Call for rates.** 2110 Bloomfield Blvd 87401. 1.6 mi e on US 64 (Bloomfield Blvd), just past jct Broadway; on Frontage Rd. Int corridors. **Pets:** Medium, other species. $25 one-time fee/room. Service with restrictions, crate. 🌊 🛜 ✕ 🛏 🖭

TownePlace Suites by Marriott H
(505) 327-2442. **$107-$152.** 4200 Sierra Vista Dr 87402. 5 mi e on SR 516 (E Main St), just s. Int corridors. **Pets:** Medium. $100 one-time fee/room. Service with restrictions, crate.
📧 🌊 🛜 ✕ 🛏 🖭

GALLUP

Americas Best Value Inn & Suites M
(505) 722-0757. **$49-$79.** 2003 Hwy 66 W 87301. I-40 exit 20, 1 mi w. Ext/int corridors. **Pets:** Accepted. (SAVE) 🛜 🛏 🖭

Comfort Suites H
(505) 863-3445. **$110-$125.** 3940 E Hwy 66 87301. I-40 exit 26, just e. Int corridors. **Pets:** Accepted. (SAVE) 🌊 🛜 ✕ 🛏 🖭

Holiday Inn Express & Suites H
(505) 722-7500. **$120-$190.** 3850 E Hwy 66 87301. I-40 exit 26, just e. Int corridors. **Pets:** Accepted. ♿ 🛜 ✕ 🛏 🖭

La Quinta Inn & Suites Gallup H
(505) 722-2233. **$94-$215.** 3880 E Hwy 66 87301. I-40 exit 26, just e. Int corridors. **Pets:** Large, other species. Service with restrictions.
🌊 ✕ 🛜 ✕ 🛏 🖭

Quality Inn & Suites M
(505) 726-1000. **$80-$140.** 1500 W Maloney Ave 87301. I-40 exit 20, just n on Muñoz Dr, then just w. Ext/int corridors. **Pets:** Small, dogs only. $15 one-time fee/pet. Designated rooms, service with restrictions, supervision. (SAVE) 🌊 🛜 🛏 🖭

Red Roof Inn - Gallup M
(505) 722-7765. **$40-$80.** 3304 W Hwy 66 87301. I-40 exit 16, just se. Ext corridors. **Pets:** Large, other species. Service with restrictions, supervision. (SAVE) 🌊 🛜 🛏 🖭

GRANTS

Red Lion Hotel Grants H
(505) 287-7901. **$60-$100.** 1501 E Santa Fe Ave 87020. I-40 exit 85, just w. Int corridors. **Pets:** Accepted. 🍴 🌊 🛜 🛏 🖭

HOBBS

BEST WESTERN Executive Inn H
(575) 397-7171. **$99-$120.** 309 N Marland Blvd 88240. US 62, 180 and Snyder St. Ext corridors. **Pets:** Dogs only. $10 daily fee/pet. Designated rooms, service with restrictions, supervision. (SAVE) 🌊 🛜 🛏 🖭

La Quinta Inn & Suites Hobbs H
(575) 397-8777. **$109-$239.** 3312 N Lovington Hwy 88240. SR 18 N (Lovington Hwy), just s of jct Joe Harvey Blvd. Int corridors.
Pets: Large, other species. Service with restrictions.
♿ 🌊 🛜 ✕ 🛏 🖭

Sleep Inn & Suites 🄷
(575) 393-3355. **$199.** 4630 N Lovington Hwy 88240. Jct SR 18 N (Lovington Hwy) and W Millen Dr, 0.8 mi s. Int corridors.
Pets: Accepted. 🖥️🏊‍♀️🛜✕🔋🖥️

LAS CRUCES (Restaurants p. 636)

BEST WESTERN Mission Inn 🄷 🐾
(575) 524-8591. **$80-$140.** 1765 S Main St 88005. I-10 exit 142 (University Ave), 1 mi n. Ext corridors. **Pets:** Other species. $10 daily fee/pet. Designated rooms, service with restrictions, crate.
SAVE 🏊‍♀️🛜🔋🖥️

Comfort Inn & Suites de Mesilla 🄷 🐾
(575) 527-1050. **$80-$100.** 1300 Avenida de Mesilla 88005. I-10 exit 140, just s. Int corridors. **Pets:** Other species. $10 daily fee/pet. Service with restrictions, supervision. 🖥️🏊‍♀️🛜🔋🖥️

Comfort Suites by Choice Hotels 🄷 🐾
(575) 522-1300. **$79-$149.** 2101 S Triviz Dr 88001. I-25 exit 1 (University Ave), just w, then just n. Int corridors. **Pets:** Medium, other species. $25 one-time fee/room. Designated rooms, service with restrictions, supervision. 🖥️🏊‍♀️🛜✕🔋🖥️

Days Inn Las Cruces 🄷
(575) 526-8311. **$46-$70.** 755 Avenida de Mesilla 88005. I-10 exit 140, just e. Ext corridors. **Pets:** Accepted. SAVE 🏊‍♀️🛜🔋🖥️

Drury Inn & Suites Las Cruces 🄷
(575) 523-4100. **$110-$169.** 1631 Hickory Loop 88005. I-10 exit 140, just e. Int corridors. **Pets:** $10 daily fee/room. Service with restrictions, supervision. 🖥️🏊‍♀️🛜🔋🖥️

Holiday Inn Express & Suites 🄷
(575) 522-0700. **$124-$164.** 2142 Telshor Ct 88011. I-25 exit 6 (US 70), just s. Int corridors. **Pets:** Medium, dogs only. $15 daily fee/pet. Designated rooms, service with restrictions, supervision.
🖥️🏊‍♀️🛜✕🔋🖥️

Hotel Encanto de Las Cruces 🄷
(575) 522-4300. **$127-$179.** 705 S Telshor Blvd 88011. I-25 exit 3 (Lohman Ave), just e, then just s. Int corridors. **Pets:** Accepted.
🍴🏊‍♀️🛜✕🔋🖥️

La Quinta Inn & Suites Las Cruces Organ Mountain 🄷
(575) 523-0100. **$69-$184.** 1500 Hickory Dr 88005. I-10 exit 140, just se of jct I-25 and Avenida de Mesilla. Int corridors. **Pets:** Large, other species. Service with restrictions. 🖥️🏊‍♀️🛜🔋🖥️

Lundeen's Inn of the Arts 🄱🄱
(575) 526-3326. **$79-$125, 3 day notice.** 618 S Alameda Blvd 88005. Jct Lohman Ave, just s; center. Int corridors. **Pets:** Medium. $15 daily fee/room. Service with restrictions, supervision. 🛜✕🔋🖥️

Ramada Palms de Las Cruces 🄷
(575) 526-4411. **$79-$199.** 201 E University Ave 88005. I-10 exit 142 (University Ave), just n. Int corridors. **Pets:** Accepted.
🍴🖥️🏊‍♀️🛜✕🔋🖥️

Staybridge Suites 🄷
(575) 521-7999. **Call for rates.** 2651 Northrise Dr 88011. I-25 exit 6 (US 70), just e. Int corridors. **Pets:** Other species. $75 one-time fee/room. Service with restrictions, supervision.
🖥️🏊‍♀️🛜✕🔋🖥️

TownePlace Suites by Marriott Las Cruces 🄷 🐾
(575) 532-6500. **$116-$162.** 2143 Telshor Ct 88011. I-25 exit 6 (US 70), just s. Int corridors. **Pets:** Other species. $75 one-time fee/room, $10 daily fee/pet. Service with restrictions, supervision.
🖥️🏊‍♀️🛜✕🔋🖥️

LAS VEGAS

BEST WESTERN PLUS Montezuma Inn & Suites 🄷 🐾
(505) 426-8000. **$90-$140.** 2020 N Grand Ave 87701. I-25 exit 347, just sw. Int corridors. **Pets:** Other species. $20 daily fee/room. Designated rooms, service with restrictions, supervision.
SAVE 🖥️🏊‍♀️✕🛜✕🔋🖥️

Holiday Inn Express Hotel & Suites 🄷
(505) 426-8182. **$95-$125.** 816 S Grand Ave 87701. I-25 exit 343, just n. Int corridors. **Pets:** Other species. $20 daily fee/room. Designated rooms, service with restrictions, crate. 🖥️🏊‍♀️🛜🔋🖥️

LORDSBURG

Comfort Inn & Suites 🄷
(575) 542-3355. **$89-$114.** 400 W Wabash St 88045. I-10 exit 22, just n, then w. Int corridors. **Pets:** Accepted. 🖥️🏊‍♀️✕🛜🔋🖥️

Hampton Inn 🄷
(575) 542-8900. **$89-$119.** 412 W Wabash St 88045. I-10 exit 22, just w. Int corridors. **Pets:** Medium, other species. Designated rooms, service with restrictions, supervision. 🖥️🏊‍♀️🛜✕🔋🖥️

LOS ALAMOS (Restaurants p. 636)

Holiday Inn Express & Suites 🄷
(505) 661-2646. **Call for rates.** 60 Entrada Dr 87544. Jct Airport Basin Dr and SR 502. Int corridors. **Pets:** Accepted.
🖥️🏊‍♀️🛜✕🔋🖥️

LOS LUNAS

Western Skies Inn & Suites 🄷
(505) 865-0001. **$65-$95, 3 day notice.** 2258 Sun Ranch Village Loop 87031. I-25 exit 203, just w. Int corridors. **Pets:** Other species. $10 daily fee/pet. Service with restrictions, supervision.
SAVE 🖥️🏊‍♀️🛜🔋🖥️

MORIARTY

Americas Best Value Inn 🄷
(505) 832-4457. **$52-$85.** 1316 Route 66 W 87035. I-40 exit 194, 0.5 mi se on US 66 and I-40 business loop. Int corridors. **Pets:** Medium, other species. $10 daily fee/pet. Designated rooms, service with restrictions, supervision. SAVE 🛜🔋🖥️

BEST WESTERN Moriarty Heritage Inn 🄷
(505) 832-5000. **$100.** 111 Anaya Blvd 87035. I-40 exit 194, 0.4 mi e. Int corridors. **Pets:** Other species. $15 one-time fee/room. Designated rooms, service with restrictions, supervision.
SAVE 🖥️🏊‍♀️🛜✕🔋🖥️

Comfort Inn 🄷 🐾
(505) 832-6666. **Call for rates.** 119 Route 66 E 87035. I-40 exit 196, just s, then just e. Int corridors. **Pets:** Large, other species. $20 one-time fee/room. Designated rooms, service with restrictions, crate.
🖥️🏊‍♀️🛜🔋🖥️

Super 8 🄷
(505) 832-6730. **$62-$108.** 1611 W Old Route 66 87035. I-40 exit 194, 0.5 mi e on Central Ave. Int corridors. **Pets:** Medium, other species. $10 daily fee/pet. Designated rooms, service with restrictions, supervision. 🛜🔋🖥️

PINOS ALTOS

Bear Creek Motel & Cabins 🄲🄰
(575) 388-4501. **$99-$269, 5 day notice.** 88 Main St 88053. 1 mi n of town on SR 15. Ext corridors. **Pets:** Accepted. 🛜🐾🔋🖥️

RATON

BEST WESTERN PLUS Raton Hotel 🄷
(575) 445-8501. **$110-$180.** 473 Clayton Rd 87740. I-25 exit 451, just w. Ext/int corridors. **Pets:** Accepted.
SAVE 🍴🖥️🏊‍♀️🛜✕🔋🖥️

▼▼ ▼▼ **Holiday Inn Express Hotel & Suites** 🅷 ❄️
(575) 445-1500. **$140-$190.** 101 Card Ave 87740. I-25 exit 450, just w.
Int corridors. **Pets:** Dogs only. $250 deposit/room, $20 daily fee/pet.
Designated rooms, service with restrictions. 🛏 🛜 ✕ 🔋 🖵

RED RIVER

◈◈◈ ▼▼▼▼ **BEST WESTERN Rivers Edge** 🅷
(575) 754-1766. **$80-$230, 7 day notice.** 301 W River St 87558. 1 blk
s of W Main St (SR 38); center. Ext corridors. **Pets:** Large, dogs only.
$10 daily fee/room. Service with restrictions, supervision.
SAVE 🗗 🛜 ✕ 🔋 🖵

RIO RANCHO

▼▼ ▼▼ **Extended Stay America Albuquerque-Rio
Rancho** 🅼
(505) 792-1338. **Call for rates.** 2608 The American Rd NW 87124.
Corner of SR 528 and Cottonwood Dr, just n, just w. Int corridors.
Pets: Other species. $25 daily fee/pet. Service with restrictions, supervision. 🛜 🔋 🖵

ROSWELL

◈◈◈ ▼▼▼▼ **BEST WESTERN El Rancho Palacio** 🅷
(575) 622-2721. **$70-$110.** 2205 N Main St 88201. Jct US 70 and 285,
1.8 mi n. Ext corridors. **Pets:** Large. Service with restrictions, supervision. SAVE 🗗 🛜 🔋 🖵

◈◈◈ ▼▼▼▼ **BEST WESTERN Sally Port Inn &
Suites** 🅷
(575) 622-6430. **$99-$119, 3 day notice.** 2000 N Main St 88201. Jct
US 70 and 285, 1.5 mi n. Int corridors. **Pets:** Medium. $10 daily fee/
pet. Service with restrictions, supervision.
SAVE 🍴 🗗 🗙 🛜 ✕ 🔋 🖵

▼▼▼▼ **Candlewood Suites Roswell** 🅷
(575) 623-4300. **$109-$159.** 4 Military Heights Dr 88201. Jct US 70 and
285, just n of US 385. Int corridors. **Pets:** Accepted.
🗗ᴹ 🗗 🗙 🔋 🖵

◈◈◈ ▼▼▼▼ **Comfort Inn** 🅷
(575) 623-4567. **$89-$104.** 3595 N Main St 88201. Jct US 70 and 285,
3 mi n. Int corridors. **Pets:** Small, other species. Service with restrictions, supervision. SAVE 🗗ᴹ 🗗 🛜 🔋 🖵

◈◈◈ ▼▼ ▼▼ **Days Inn** 🅷
(575) 623-4021. **$70-$110.** 1310 N Main St 88201. Jct US 70 and 285,
0.8 mi n. Ext corridors. **Pets:** Large. Service with restrictions, supervision. SAVE 🗗 🛜 🔋 🖵

▼▼▼▼ **Holiday Inn** 🅷
(575) 623-3216. **Call for rates.** 3620 N Main St 88201. Jct US 70 and
285 N, 1 mi s. Int corridors. **Pets:** Medium. $25 daily fee/pet. Designated rooms, service with restrictions, supervision.
🍴 🗗ᴹ 🗙 🛜 ✕ 🔋 🖵

◈◈◈ ▼▼▼▼ **Holiday Inn Express & Suites** 🅷
(575) 627-9900. **$110-$139.** 2300 N Main St 88201. Jct US 70 and
285, 1.8 mi n. Int corridors. **Pets:** Medium. $10 daily fee/pet. Service
with restrictions, supervision. SAVE 🗗ᴹ 🗗 🗙 🛜 ✕ 🔋 🖵

▼▼▼▼ **TownePlace Suites by Marriott** 🅷
(575) 622-5460. **$89-$199.** 180 E 19th St 88201. Jct Main St, just e. Int
corridors. **Pets:** Other species. $100 one-time fee/room. Service with
restrictions, crate. 🗗ᴹ 🛜 🗙 🔋 🖵

RUIDOSO *(Restaurants p. 636)*

▼▼▼▼ **The Lodge at Sierra Blanca** 🅷
(575) 258-5500. **$119-$239, 3 day notice.** 107 Sierra Blanca Dr 88345.
Jct Sudderth Dr. Int corridors. **Pets:** Accepted.
🗗 🗙 🛜 ✕ 🔋 🖵

▼▼ ▼▼ **Ruidoso Mountain Inn** 🅷
(575) 257-3736. **Call for rates.** 400 W Hwy 70 88345. US 70, just w of
jct Sudderth Dr. Int corridors. **Pets:** Small. $20 deposit/pet. Designated
rooms, no service, supervision. 🗗ᴹ 🗗 🛜 🔋 🖵

▼▼ ▼▼ **Whispering Pine Cabins** 🅲🅰
(575) 257-4311. **Call for rates.** 422 Main Rd 88345. 0.9 mi w of jct SR
48 and Sudderth Dr. Ext corridors. **Pets:** Accepted.
🛜 🗙 🗗 🔋 🖵

RUIDOSO DOWNS

◈◈◈ ▼▼ ▼▼ **BEST WESTERN Pine Springs Inn** 🅷 ❄️
(575) 378-8100. **$70-$200.** 111 Pine Springs Dr 88346. Just e of jct US
70 and SR 48. Ext corridors. **Pets:** Large, other species. $50 deposit/
room, $10 daily fee/room. Service with restrictions, supervision.
SAVE 🗗 🛜 🔋 🖵

SANTA FE *(Restaurants p. 636)*

◈◈◈ ▼▼▼▼ **BEST WESTERN PLUS Inn of Santa
Fe** 🅷
(505) 438-3822. **$90-$150.** 3650 Cerrillos Rd 87507. I-25 exit 278, 2.8
mi n. Int corridors. **Pets:** Accepted. SAVE 🗗 🛜 🗙 🔋 🖵

◈◈◈ ▼▼▼▼ **Bishop's Lodge Ranch Resort & Spa** 🅷
(505) 983-6377. **Call for rates.** 1297 N Bishop's Lodge Rd 87501. 3.5
mi n of jct Paseo de Peralta. Ext/int corridors. **Pets:** Accepted.
SAVE 🍴 🗗 🗙 🛜 ✕ 🔋 🖵

◈◈◈ ▼▼▼▼ **Courtyard by Marriott-Santa Fe** 🅷
(505) 473-2800. **$89-$199.** 3347 Cerrillos Rd 87507. I-25 exit 278, 3.2
mi n. Ext/int corridors. **Pets:** Accepted.
SAVE 🗗ᴹ 🗗 🛜 🗙 🔋 🖵

◈◈◈ ▼▼▼ ▼▼ **Eldorado Hotel & Spa** 🅷
(505) 988-4455. **$149-$419, 3 day notice.** 309 W San Francisco St
87501. Just w of The Plaza; at Sandoval St. Int corridors.
Pets: Accepted. SAVE 🍴 🗗ᴹ 🗗 🗙 🛜 ✕ 🔋 🖵

◈◈◈ ▼▼▼▼ **El Paradero Bed & Breakfast** 🅱🅱
(505) 988-1177. **$100-$200, 14 day notice.** 220 W Manhattan Ave
87501. 0.3 mi s on Cerrillos Rd, 1/2 blk e. Ext/int corridors. **Pets:** Dogs
only. $20 daily fee/pet. Designated rooms, service with restrictions,
crate. SAVE 🛜 🗙 🔋 🖵

◈◈◈ ▼▼▼ ▼▼ **Four Seasons Resort Rancho Encantado
Santa Fe** 🅷 ❄️
(505) 946-5700. **$209-$909, 3 day notice.** 198 State Road 592 87506.
US 285/84 N exit 172 (CR 73/Tesuque), 0.5 mi se to SR 592, then 2
mi ne. Ext corridors. **Pets:** Other species. $100 one-time fee/room. Service with restrictions, supervision.
SAVE 🍴 🗗 🗙 🛜 ✕ 🔋 🖵

◈◈◈ ▼▼▼▼ **Hampton Inn Santa Fe** 🅷 ❄️
(505) 474-3900. **$99-$129.** 3625 Cerrillos Rd 87505. I-25 exit 278, 2.5
mi n. Int corridors. **Pets:** Other species. Designated rooms, service with
restrictions, supervision. SAVE 🗗ᴹ 🗗 🛜 🔋 🖵

◈◈◈ ▼▼▼ ▼▼ **Hilton Santa Fe Buffalo Thunder** 🅷
(505) 455-5555. **$99-$399.** 20 Buffalo Thunder Tr 87506. N on US 285
exit Buffalo Thunder Rd, just e. Int corridors. **Pets:** Accepted.
SAVE 🍴 🗗ᴹ 🗗 🔇 🗙 🔋 🖵

◈◈◈ ▼▼▼▼ **Hilton Santa Fe Historic Plaza** 🅷 🐾
(505) 988-2811. **$129-$399.** 100 Sandoval St 87501. Just sw of The
Plaza; between San Francisco and W Alameda sts. Ext/int corridors.
Pets: $50 one-time fee/room. Service with restrictions, supervision.
SAVE 🍴 🗗 🔇 🗙 🔋 🖵

▼▼▼▼ **Holiday Inn Express-Santa Fe** 🅷
(505) 474-7570. **$79-$199.** 3450 Cerrillos Rd 87507. I-25 exit 278, 3 mi
n. Int corridors. **Pets:** Medium. $15 daily fee/pet. Designated rooms,
service with restrictions, supervision. 🗗ᴹ 🗗 🛜 🗙 🔋 🖵

◈◈◈ ▼▼ ▼▼ **Homewood Suites By Hilton-Santa Fe
North** 🅷
(505) 455-9100. **$109-$209.** 10 Buffalo Thunder Tr 87506. US 84/285
exit 177, just e. Ext/int corridors. **Pets:** Medium, dogs only. $75 one-
time fee/room. Service with restrictions. SAVE 🗗ᴹ 🗗 🛜 🔋 🖵

◈◈◈◈◈ ◈◈◈◈◈ Hotel Chimayó de Santa Fe H
(505) 988-4900. **$159-$299, 3 day notice.** 125 Washington Ave 87501. Just ne of The Plaza; center. Ext/int corridors. **Pets:** Accepted.
[SAVE] [≈] [✕] [⊟] [▣]

◈◈◈ Hotel Santa Fe, The Hacienda & Spa H ❖
(505) 982-1200. **$119-$600, 3 day notice.** 1501 Paseo de Peralta 87501. At Cerrillos Rd, 0.6 mi s of The Plaza. Int corridors. **Pets:** Dogs only. $20 daily fee/pet. Service with restrictions, supervision.
[⊺⊺] [≈] [✕] [≈] [✕] [⊟] [▣]

◈◈◈◈ ◈◈◈◈ Hyatt Place Santa Fe H
(505) 474-7777. **$79-$249.** 4320 Cerrillos Rd 87507. I-25 exit 278, 2 mi e. Int corridors. **Pets:** Medium, dogs only. $75 one-time fee/pet. Designated rooms, service with restrictions, supervision.
[SAVE] [⊺⊺] [♿M] [≈] [≈] [✕] [⊟] [▣]

◈◈◈◈ ◈◈◈ ◈◈◈ The Inn & Spa at Loretto H
(505) 988-5531. **$189-$599, 3 day notice.** 211 Old Santa Fe Tr 87501. Just s of The Plaza. Int corridors. **Pets:** Accepted.
[SAVE] [⊺⊺] [♿M] [≈] [≈] [✕] [⊟] [▣]

◈◈◈◈ ◈◈◈ Inn at Santa Fe H
(505) 474-9500. **$79-$249.** 8376 Cerrillos Rd 87507. I-25 exit 278, 0.3 mi n. Int corridors. **Pets:** Accepted.
[SAVE] [⊟] [⊺⊺] [♿M] [≈] [✕] [≈] [✕] [⊟] [▣]

◈◈◈◈◈ ◈◈◈◈◈ The Inn of The Five Graces CI ❖
(505) 992-0957. **$425-$2500, 7 day notice.** 150 E DeVargas St 87501. Jct Old Pecos Trail. Ext/int corridors. **Pets:** Medium, dogs only. $500 deposit/pet, $75 daily fee/pet. Designated rooms, service with restrictions, crate. [≈] [✕] [⊟] [▣]

◈◈◈◈◈ Inn On The Alameda H ❖
(505) 984-2121. **$159-$599, 3 day notice.** 303 E Alameda St 87501. Just e of The Plaza; jct Paseo de Peralta. Ext/int corridors. **Pets:** Dogs only. $50 daily fee/pet. Designated rooms, service with restrictions.
[⊺⊺] [✕] [≈] [✕] [⊟] [▣]

◈◈◈ Inn on the Paseo BB
(505) 982-8200. **Call for rates.** 630 Paseo de Peralta 87501. I-25 exit 282, 2 mi e; jct St. Francis Dr. Ext/int corridors. **Pets:** Accepted.
[≈] [✕]

◈◈◈◈ ◈◈◈◈ La Fonda On the Plaza H
(505) 982-5511. **$159-$599.** 100 E San Francisco St 87501. On The Plaza. Int corridors. **Pets:** Accepted.
[⊺⊺] [♿M] [≈] [✕] [≈] [✕] [⊟] [▣]

◈◈◈ ◈◈◈◈ ◈◈◈◈ La Posada de Santa Fe Resort & Spa H ❖
(505) 986-0000. **$149-$599, 3 day notice.** 330 E Palace Ave 87501. Jct Paseo de Peralta and E Palace Ave. Ext corridors. **Pets:** Medium. $75 one-time fee/room. Service with restrictions, crate.
[SAVE] [⊺⊺] [≈] [✕] [≈] [⊟] [▣]

◈◈◈ La Quinta Inn Santa Fe H
(505) 471-1142. **$62-$235.** 4298 Cerrillos Rd 87507. I-25 exit 278, 1.8 mi n. Ext/int corridors. **Pets:** Large, other species. Service with restrictions. [≈] [≈] [⊟] [▣]

◈◈◈◈ Las Palomas H ❖
(505) 982-5560. **$99-$600.** 460 W San Francisco St 87501. Just w of jct Guadalupe St. Ext corridors. **Pets:** Dogs only. $20 daily fee/pet. Service with restrictions, supervision. [≈] [✕] [⊟] [▣]

◈◈◈◈ ◈◈◈ The Lodge at Santa Fe H
(505) 992-5800. **$99-$159, 3 day notice.** 750 N St. Francis Dr 87501. Jct of Cerrillos Rd and St. Francis Dr (US 84/285), 1.1 mi nw to Alamo Dr, just w, then just n. Ext/int corridors. **Pets:** Accepted.
[SAVE] [⊺⊺] [≈] [≈] [✕] [⊟] [▣]

◈◈◈ Motel 6-150 M
(505) 473-1380. **$45-$75.** 3007 Cerrillos Rd 87507. I-25 exit 278, 3.8 mi n. Ext corridors. **Pets:** Other species. Service with restrictions, crate.
[≈] [📶] [⊟]

◈◈◈◈ ◈◈◈◈ The Old Santa Fe Inn M
(505) 995-0800. **$99-$390, 3 day notice.** 320 Galisteo St 87501. Just sw of The Plaza; center. Ext/int corridors. **Pets:** Medium. $20 daily fee/pet. Designated rooms, service with restrictions, supervision.
[SAVE] [≈] [✕] [⊟] [▣]

◈◈◈◈ ◈◈◈ Pecos Trail Inn M ❖
(505) 982-1943. **$89-$155.** 2239 Old Pecos Tr 87505. I-25 exit 284, 0.8 mi n on CR 466 (Old Pecos Tr). Ext corridors. **Pets:** $25 one-time fee/room. Designated rooms, service with restrictions, crate.
[SAVE] [⊺⊺] [≈] [≈] [✕] [⊟] [▣]

◈◈◈◈ ◈◈◈◈ Rosewood Inn of the Anasazi H
(505) 988-3030. **Call for rates.** 113 Washington Ave 87501. Just ne of The Plaza. Int corridors. **Pets:** Accepted. [⊺⊺] [≈] [✕] [⊟] [▣]

◈◈◈ ◈◈◈ Santa Fe Motel & Inn M
(505) 982-1039. **$99-$249, 3 day notice.** 510 Cerrillos Rd 87501. 4 blks sw of The Plaza. Ext corridors. **Pets:** Other species. $20 daily fee/pet. Designated rooms, service with restrictions, supervision.
[≈] [⊟] [▣]

◈◈◈◈ ◈◈◈◈ Santa Fe Sage Inn H
(505) 982-5952. **$59-$169, 7 day notice.** 725 Cerrillos Rd 87505. 0.4 mi ne of St. Francis Dr (US 84). Ext corridors. **Pets:** Accepted.
[SAVE] [≈] [≈] [⊟] [▣]

SANTA ROSA

◈◈◈◈ ◈◈◈ BEST WESTERN Santa Rosa Inn M
(575) 472-5877. **$80-$140.** 2491 Historic Route 66 88435. I-40 exit 277, 0.5 mi w. Ext corridors. **Pets:** Medium. $15 daily fee/pet. Service with restrictions, supervision. [SAVE] [≈] [≈] [⊟] [▣]

◈◈◈◈ ◈◈◈ Days Inn & Suites H
(575) 472-3446. **Call for rates.** 2255 Historic Route 66 88435. I-40 exit 275. Ext corridors. **Pets:** Medium. $10 one-time fee/room. Service with restrictions, supervision. [SAVE] [≈] [≈] [⊟] [▣]

◈◈◈ ◈◈◈◈ Holiday Inn Express H
(575) 472-5411. **$80-$199, 3 day notice.** 2516 Historic Route 66 88435. I-40 exit 277, 0.4 mi w. Int corridors. **Pets:** Other species. $25 one-time fee/room. Designated rooms, service with restrictions, supervision.
[♿M] [≈] [✕] [≈] [✕] [⊟] [▣]

◈◈◈ ◈◈◈◈ La Quinta Inn Santa Rosa H
(575) 472-4800. **$85-$189.** 2277 Historic Route 66 88435. I-40 exit 275, just e. Int corridors. **Pets:** Large, other species. Service with restrictions. [≈] [≈] [⊟] [▣]

◈◈◈ Quality Inn H
(575) 472-5570. **$65-$95.** 2533 E Historic Route 66 88435. I-40 exit 277, 0.3 mi w. Ext corridors. **Pets:** Accepted. [≈] [≈] [⊟] [▣]

◈◈◈ Super 8-Santa Rosa M
(575) 472-5388. **$53-$96.** 2075 Historic Route 66 88435. I-40 exit 275, just w. Int corridors. **Pets:** Accepted. [♿M] [≈] [⊟] [▣]

SILVER CITY

◈◈◈ ◈◈◈ Comfort Inn H
(575) 534-1883. **$80-$300.** 1060 E Hwy 180 88061. Just e of jct SR 15. Int corridors. **Pets:** Dogs only. $7 daily fee/pet. Designated rooms, crate. [SAVE] [≈] [≈] [✕] [⊟] [▣]

◈◈◈ ◈◈◈ Econo Lodge Silver City H
(575) 534-1111. **$79-$159.** 1120 Hwy 180 E 88061. 1.5 mi ne on US 180 and SR 90. Int corridors. **Pets:** Medium. $30 deposit/pet. Designated rooms, service with restrictions, supervision.
[♿M] [≈] [≈] [⊟] [▣]

▼▼ Holiday Inn Express ⊞
(575) 538-2525. **$115-$143.** 1103 Superior St 88061. 3 mi ne on US 180 and SR 90. Int corridors. **Pets:** Other species. Designated rooms, service with restrictions, supervision. 🛜 ⊠ 🛢 💻

SOCORRO

◈ ▼▼▼ BEST WESTERN Socorro Hotel & Suites ⊞
(575) 838-0556. **$105.** 1100 California Ave NE 87801. I-25 exit 150, just s. Ext/int corridors. **Pets:** Medium. $10 deposit/pet. Designated rooms, service with restrictions, supervision.
[SAVE] ⟨M⟩ ⥤ ⊠ 🛜 ⊠ 🛢 💻

▼▼▼ Comfort Inn & Suites ⊞
(575) 838-4400. **$83-$134.** 1259 Frontage Rd NW 87801. I-25 exit 150, just nw. Int corridors. **Pets:** Accepted. ⟨M⟩ ⥤ 🛜 🛢 💻

◈ ▼▼ Econo Lodge M
(575) 835-1500. **$55-$105.** 713 California St NW 87801. I-25 exit 150, 1 mi s. Ext corridors. **Pets:** Medium. $10 daily fee/pet. Service with restrictions, supervision. [SAVE] ⥤ ⊠ 🛜 ⊠ 🛢 💻

TAOS *(Restaurants p. 636)*

◈ ▼▼▼ American Artists Gallery House Bed & Breakfast ⓑⓑ
(575) 758-4446. **$119-$250, 14 day notice.** 132 Frontier Ln 87571. 1 mi s of jct US 64 and Taos Plaza, 0.3 mi e. Ext/int corridors. **Pets:** Dogs only. $25 daily fee/pet. Designated rooms, service with restrictions, supervision. [SAVE] 🛜 ⊠ ⟨K⟩ 🛢 💻

▼▼▼ An Inn On The Rio ⓑⓑ
(575) 758-7199. **$125-$225, 14 day notice.** 910 Kit Carson Rd 87571. US 64, 1.5 mi e of jct SR 68 and Taos Plaza. Ext corridors. **Pets:** Accepted. ⥤ 🛜 ⊠ ⟨K⟩ 💻

◈ ▼▼▼▼ El Monte Sagrado, Autograph Collection ⊞
(575) 758-3502. **$127-$339, 3 day notice.** 317 Kit Carson Rd 87571. 0.5 mi e of jct US 64 and SR 68. Ext/int corridors. **Pets:** Accepted.
[SAVE] ⟨Y⟩ ⥤ ⊠ 🛰 ⊠ 🛢 💻

◈ ▼▼▼▼ La Posada de Taos ⓑⓑ
(575) 758-8164. **$149-$250, 14 day notice.** 309 Juanita Ln 87571. From Taos Plaza, just w on Don Fernando St, just s on Manzanares St, then just w. Ext/int corridors. **Pets:** Accepted. [SAVE] 🛜 ⊠ ⟨Z⟩ 💻

TRUTH OR CONSEQUENCES
(Restaurants p. 636)

▼▼▼ Holiday Inn Express & Suites ⊞
(575) 894-3900. **$90-$99.** 2201 FG Amin St 87901. I-25 exit 79, just e. Int corridors. **Pets:** Other species. $25 one-time fee/room. Designated rooms, service with restrictions. ⟨M⟩ ⥤ 🛜 ⊠ 🛢 💻

▼▼▼ Sierra Grande Lodge & Spa ⊞
(575) 894-6976. **$99-$395.** 501 McAdoo St 87901. Just w of Foch St; center. Ext/int corridors. **Pets:** Accepted. ⊠ 🛜 ⊠

TUCUMCARI

◈ ▼▼▼ BEST WESTERN Discovery Inn ⊞
(575) 461-4884. **Call for rates.** 200 E Estrella Ave 88401. I-40 exit 332, just n. Ext corridors. **Pets:** Accepted. [SAVE] ⥤ 🛜 ⊠ 🛢 💻

▼▼ Days Inn ⊞
(575) 461-3158. **$60-$102.** 2623 S 1st St 88401. I-40 exit 332, just n. Ext/int corridors. **Pets:** Accepted. 🛜 🛢 💻

NEW YORK

ALBANY *(Restaurants p. 636)*

◈ ▼▼▼ BEST WESTERN Sovereign Hotel-Albany ⊞
(518) 489-2981. **$99-$169.** 1228 Western Ave 12203. I-90 exit 1S, 1 mi e on US 20 (Western Ave). Int corridors. **Pets:** $25 daily fee/pet. Designated rooms, service with restrictions, crate.
[SAVE] ⟨Y⟩ ⥤ 🛜 ⊠ 🛢 💻

▼▼▼▼ CrestHill Suites ⊞
(518) 454-0007. **Call for rates.** 1415 Washington Ave 12206. I-90 exit 2 westbound, just s on Fuller Rd, then just e; exit eastbound, just e. Int corridors. **Pets:** Accepted. ⟨Y⟩ ⟨M⟩ ⥤ 🛜 🛢 💻

▼▼ Days Inn-Albany/SUNY ⊞
(518) 489-4423. **$79-$99.** 1230 Western Ave 12203. I-90 exit 1S, 0.7 mi e on US 20 (Western Ave). Int corridors. **Pets:** Accepted.
⟨M⟩ 🛜 🛢 💻

▼▼ Extended Stay America Albany-SUNY ⊞
(518) 446-0680. **Call for rates.** 1395 Washington Ave 12206. I-90 exit 2 westbound, just s on Fuller Rd, then 0.5 mi e; exit eastbound, just e. Int corridors. **Pets:** Other species. $25 daily fee/pet. Service with restrictions, supervision. 🛜 🛢 💻

▼▼▼▼ TownePlace Suites by Marriott Albany Downtown/ Medical Center ⊞ ☙
(518) 860-1500. **$104-$183.** 22 Holland Ave 12209. I-90 exit 5 (Everett Rd), 2.6 mi on SR 5, then just e. Int corridors. **Pets:** Small, other species. $100 one-time fee/room. Designated rooms, crate.
⥤ 🛜 ⊠ 🛢 💻

▼▼▼ TownePlace Suites by Marriott Albany University Area ⊞
(518) 435-1900. **$111-$217.** 1379 Washington Ave 12206. I-90 exit 2 westbound, just s on Fuller Rd, then 0.6 mi e; exit eastbound, just e. Int corridors. **Pets:** Accepted. ⟨Y⟩ ⟨M⟩ ⥤ 🛜 ⊠ 🛢 💻

ALLEGANY

▼▼ Microtel Inn & Suites by Wyndham Olean/Allegany ⊞
(716) 373-5333. **$79-$149.** 3234 NYS Rt 417 14760. I-86 exit 24, 2.1 mi e on SR 417 (State St). Int corridors. **Pets:** Other species. $15 daily fee/room. Service with restrictions, supervision.
⟨M⟩ 🛜 ⊠ 🛢 💻

▼▼ The New Lantern Motel M
(716) 373-1672. **Call for rates.** 4004 NYS Rt 417 14706. I-86 exit 24, 0.4 mi w on SR 417 (State St). Ext corridors. **Pets:** Large. $20 one-time fee/room. Service with restrictions, supervision.
⟨Y⟩ 🛜 ⊠ 🛢

AMHERST

▼▼▼ Candlewood Suites ⊞
(716) 688-2100. **Call for rates.** 20 Flint Rd 14226. I-290 exit 5B, just n on SR 263 (Millersport Hwy). Int corridors. **Pets:** $25 one-time fee/pet. Service with restrictions, supervision. ⟨M⟩ 🛜 ⊠ 🛢 💻

▼▼▼ Comfort Inn University ⊞ ☙
(716) 688-0811. **$70-$180.** 1 Flint Rd 14226. I-290 exit 5B, just n on SR 263 (Millersport Hwy), then just w. Int corridors. **Pets:** Large, other species. $20 one-time fee/pet. Designated rooms, service with restrictions, crate. ⥤ 🛜 ⊠ 🛢 💻

▼▼▼ DoubleTree by Hilton Buffalo-Amherst 🅷
(716) 689-4414. **$149-$189.** 10 Flint Rd 14226. I-290 exit 5B, just n on SR 263 (Millersport Hwy). Int corridors. **Pets:** Accepted.
🍽 ᕫᴹ ➣ 🛜 ✕ 📳 📼

▼▼▼ Homewood Suites Buffalo/Amherst 🅷
(716) 833-2277. **$129-$234.** 1138 Millersport Hwy 14226. I-290 exit 5A, just w. Int corridors. **Pets:** Accepted. 🍽 ᕫᴹ ➣ 🛜 📳 📼

◈◈ ▼▼▼ Red Roof Inn University at Buffalo Amherst Ⓜ
(716) 689-7474. **Call for rates.** 42 Flint Rd 14226. I-290 exit 5B, just n on SR 263 (Millersport Hwy), then just w. Ext corridors. **Pets:** Large, other species. Service with restrictions, supervision.
🆂🅰🆅🅴 ᕫᴹ 🛜 ✕ 📳 📼

AMSTERDAM
▼▼ Super 8 🅷
(518) 843-5888. **$60-$99.** 5502 Rt 30 S 12010. I-90 exit 27 (SR 30), just sw. Int corridors. **Pets:** Accepted. 🍽 🛜 📳 📼

APALACHIN
▼▼ Quality Inn 🅷
(607) 625-4441. **Call for rates.** 7666 SR 434 13732. SR 17 exit 66, just e. Int corridors. **Pets:** Accepted. 🛜 📳 📼

ARMONK
▼▼ La Quinta Inn & Suites Armonk 🅷
(914) 273-9090. **$92-$219.** 94 Business Park Dr 10504. I-684 exit 3S northbound; exit 3 southbound, 0.3 mi s on SR 22. Int corridors. **Pets:** Large, other species. Service with restrictions.
🍽 ᕫᴹ 🛜 ✕ 📳 📼

AUBURN
▼▼▼ Days Inn Auburn/Finger Lakes Region 🅷
(315) 252-7567. **$60-$134.** 37 William St 13021. Just s on SR 34, just w. Ext/int corridors. **Pets:** Accepted. 🍽 🛜 📳 📼

▼▼ Inn at the Finger Lakes 🅷
(315) 253-5000. **$99-$189, 3 day notice.** 12 Seminary Ave 13021. Jct SR 34/38, just e on US 20/SR 5; center. Int corridors. **Pets:** $15 one-time fee/pet. Designated rooms, service with restrictions, supervision.
ᕫᴹ 🛜 ✕ 📳 📼

BALDWINSVILLE
◈◈ ▼▼▼ Microtel Inn & Suites by Wyndham Baldwinsville/Syracuse 🅷
(315) 635-9556. **$70-$125.** 131 Downer St 13027. SR 690 exit SR 31 W, 0.4 mi e. Int corridors. **Pets:** Other species. $10 daily fee/pet. Service with restrictions, crate. 🆂🅰🆅🅴 ᕫᴹ 🛜 📳 📼

▼▼▼▼ The Red Mill Inn 🅷
(315) 635-4871. **Call for rates.** 4 Syracuse St 13027. Just w of jct SR 31 on SR 48; center. Int corridors. **Pets:** Accepted. 🛜 ✕ 📳 📼

BATAVIA
◈◈ ▼ Budget Inn Ⓜ
(585) 343-7921. **$49-$129.** 301 Oak St 14020. I-90 exit 48, just n on SR 98. Int corridors. **Pets:** Medium. $8 daily fee/pet. Designated rooms, service with restrictions, supervision. 🆂🅰🆅🅴 🛜 📳

◈◈ ▼▼▼ Clarion Hotel Palm Island Indoor Water Park 🅷
(585) 344-2100. **$89-$139.** 8250 Park Rd 14020. I-90 exit 48, just w. Int corridors. **Pets:** Accepted. 🆂🅰🆅🅴 🍽 🛜 📳 📼

◈◈ ▼▼▼ Comfort Inn 🅷
(585) 344-9999. **$68-$280.** 4371 Federal Dr 14020. I-90 exit 48, just n on SR 98. Int corridors. **Pets:** Accepted.
🆂🅰🆅🅴 🍽 ᕫᴹ ➣ 🛜 📳 📼

◈◈ ▼▼▼ Quality Inn & Suites 🅷
(585) 344-7000. **$79-$189.** 8200 Park Rd 14020. I-90 exit 48, just w. Int corridors. **Pets:** Accepted. 🆂🅰🆅🅴 ᕫᴹ ➣ 🛜 📳 📼

▼▼ Super 8 🅷
(585) 345-0800. **$55-$88.** 202 Oak St 14020. I-90 exit 48, just s. Int corridors. **Pets:** Large. $10 deposit/pet. Designated rooms, service with restrictions, supervision. 🅴🅲🅾 🛜 📳 📼

BATH
▼▼ Bath Super 8 🅷
(607) 776-2187. **$50-$75, 3 day notice.** 333 W Morris St 14810. I-86 exit 38, just n. Int corridors. **Pets:** Accepted. 🛜 📳 📼

▼▼ Microtel Inn & Suites by Wyndham Bath 🅷
(607) 776-5333. **$70-$115.** 370 W Morris St 14810. I-86 exit 38, just n. Int corridors. **Pets:** Accepted. ᕫᴹ 🛜 ✕ 📳 📼

BINGHAMTON
◈◈ ▼▼▼ Comfort Inn of Binghamton 🅷
(607) 724-3297. **$110-$180.** 1000 Upper Front St 13905. I-81 exit 6 southbound, 2 mi s on US 11 (Front St); exit 5 northbound, 1 mi n on US 11 (Front St). Int corridors. **Pets:** Accepted.
🆂🅰🆅🅴 ᕫᴹ 🛜 📳 📼

▼▼▼ DoubleTree by Hilton-Binghamton 🅷
(607) 722-7575. **$119-$209.** 225 Water St 13901. SR 17 exit 72 to US 11 (Front St), 1 mi s, just e on E Clinton St, then just s; downtown. Int corridors. **Pets:** Other species. $25 one-time fee/room. Designated rooms, service with restrictions. 🍽 ➣ ✕ 🛜 ✕ 📳 📼

◈◈ ▼▼▼ Holiday Inn Binghamton 🅷 🐾
(607) 722-1212. **$99-$169.** 2-8 Hawley St 13901. Downtown. Int corridors. **Pets:** Other species. $35 one-time fee/room. Designated rooms, service with restrictions, supervision. 🆂🅰🆅🅴 🍽 ➣ 🛜 📳 📼

BLASDELL
◈◈ ▼▼ Econo Lodge South Ⓜ
(716) 825-7530. **$62-$120.** 4344 Milestrip Rd 14219. I-90 exit 56, just e on SR 179. Ext corridors. **Pets:** Medium. $10 daily fee/room. Designated rooms, service with restrictions, supervision. 🆂🅰🆅🅴 🛜 📳 📼

BOHEMIA
▼▼▼ La Quinta Inn & Suites Islip Macarthur Airport 🅷
(631) 881-7700. **$95-$265.** 10 Aero Rd 11716. I-495 exit 57, 5.1 mi se on SR 454, just s on Johnson Ave, then just e. Int corridors. **Pets:** Large, other species. Service with restrictions.
🍽 ᕫᴹ 🛜 📳 📼

BOWMANSVILLE
▼▼ La Quinta Inn Buffalo Airport 🅷
(716) 633-1011. **$79-$279.** 6619 Transit Rd 14026. I-90 exit 49, just n. Int corridors. **Pets:** Large, other species. Service with restrictions.
🛜 ✕ 📳 📼

◈◈ ▼▼▼ Red Roof Inn Buffalo Niagara Airport Ⓜ
(716) 633-1100. **Call for rates.** 146 Maple Dr 14026. Just e of SR 78; just n of entrance to I-90 (New York State Thruway) exit 49. Ext corridors. **Pets:** Large, other species. Service with restrictions, supervision.
🆂🅰🆅🅴 🛜 ✕ 📳 📼

BREWERTON
▼▼ Days Inn Brewerton/Syracuse 🅷
(315) 676-3222. **$61-$121.** 5552 Bartell Rd 13029. I-81 exit 31 (Bartell Rd), just w. Int corridors. **Pets:** Medium. $25 one-time fee/pet. Designated rooms, service with restrictions, supervision.
🍽 ᕫᴹ 🛜 ✕ 📳 📼

BRIGHTON

La Quinta Inn & Suites Rochester South H
(585) 272-7800. **$99-$239.** 717 E Henrietta Rd 14623. I-390 exit 16B (Henrietta Rd) southbound; exit 16 northbound, just w. Int corridors. **Pets:** Large, other species. Service with restrictions.

BROCKPORT

Dollinger's Inn and Suites H
(585) 395-1000. **$75-$150.** 4908 Lake Rd S 14420. On SR 19 S, just s of jct SR 31. Int corridors. **Pets:** Other species. $25 one-time fee/room. Service with restrictions.

BROOKLYN

Aloft New York Brooklyn H
(718) 256-3833. **$139-$349.** 216 Duffield St 11201. Between Willoughby St and Fulton Mall. Int corridors. **Pets:** Accepted.

Comfort Inn Downtown Brooklyn H
(718) 855-9600. **$89-$299.** 279 Butler St 11217. In Park Slope; between 3rd Ave and Nevins St. Int corridors. **Pets:** Medium, other species. $50 one-time fee/room. Service with restrictions, crate.

Fairfield Inn & Suites by Marriott New York-Brooklyn H
(718) 522-4000. **$167-$413.** 181 3rd Ave 11217. In Park Slope; jct Butler St. Int corridors. **Pets:** Accepted.

Holiday Inn Express Brooklyn H
(718) 797-1133. **$119-$369.** 625 Union St 11215. Between 3rd and 4th aves. Int corridors. **Pets:** Accepted.

Hotel Indigo Brooklyn H
(718) 254-7800. **Call for rates.** 229 Duffield St 11201. Between Willoughby St and Fulton Mall. Int corridors. **Pets:** Accepted.

McCarren Hotel & Pool H
(718) 218-7500. **Call for rates.** 160 N 12th St 11211. In Williamsburg; between Bedford Ave and Berry St. Int corridors. **Pets:** Accepted.

NU Hotel Brooklyn H
(718) 852-8585. **Call for rates.** 85 Smith St 11201. Between Atlantic and State sts. Int corridors. **Pets:** Accepted.

Sheraton Brooklyn New York Hotel H
(718) 855-1900. **$139-$739.** 228 Duffield St 11201. Between Willoughby St and Fulton Mall. Int corridors. **Pets:** Accepted.

Wythe Hotel H
(718) 460-8000. **Call for rates.** 80 Wythe Ave 11249. In Williamsburg; between 11th and 12th sts. Int corridors. **Pets:** Accepted.

BUFFALO

BEST WESTERN On The Avenue H
(716) 886-8333. **$129-$229.** 510 Delaware Ave 14202. Between Virginia and Allen sts; downtown. Int corridors. **Pets:** Medium, dogs only. $50 deposit/room. Designated rooms, service with restrictions, supervision.

Hyatt Regency Buffalo/Hotel and Conference Center H
(716) 856-1234. **$89-$249.** 2 Fountain Plaza 14202. On Pearl St at W Huron St; downtown. Int corridors. **Pets:** Accepted.

CALCIUM

Microtel Inn by Wyndham Calcium/Near Fort Drum H
(315) 629-5000. **$55-$149.** 8000 Virginia Smith Dr 13616. Jct SR 342 and US 11, just s. Int corridors. **Pets:** Accepted.

CANANDAIGUA

The Inn On The Lake H
(585) 394-7800. **$111-$345.** 770 S Main St 14424. I-90 exit 44 (SR 332), just s of jct US 20 and SR 5. **Pets:** Dogs only. $25 daily fee/pet. Designated rooms, service with restrictions, supervision.

Morgan-Samuels Inn/BB & Spa BB
(585) 394-9232. **Call for rates.** 2920 Smith Rd 14424. I-90 exit 43, 4.1 mi s on SR 21, just e on SR 488 to East Ave/Smith Rd, then 2 mi s. Ext/int corridors. **Pets:** Accepted.

Super 8 H
(585) 396-7224. **$60-$120.** 4450 Eastern Blvd 14424. Jct SR 332, 5 and US 20, 0.5 mi e. Int corridors. **Pets:** Other species. $10 daily fee/pet. Designated rooms, service with restrictions, supervision.

CARLE PLACE *(Restaurants p. 636)*

Homewood Suites by Hilton Carle Place-Garden City H
(516) 747-0230. **Call for rates.** 40 Westbury Ave 11514. Jct SR 25, 0.5 mi s on Glen Cove Rd, just w. Int corridors. **Pets:** Accepted.

CARTHAGE

Pleasant Night Inn H
(315) 493-2500. **$71-$99.** 30 N Broad St 13619. Just se on SR 126. Int corridors. **Pets:** Accepted.

CAZENOVIA

Brae Loch Inn CI
(315) 655-3431. **Call for rates.** 5 Albany St 13035. On US 20. Int corridors. **Pets:** Accepted.

CHEEKTOWAGA

Comfort Inn-Cheektowaga H 🐾
(716) 896-2800. **$80-$199.** 475 Dingens St 14206. Just n of I-90 exit 53 (I-190); I-190 exit 1 (S Ogden St), just w. Int corridors. **Pets:** Large. $20 daily fee/pet. Designated rooms, service with restrictions, crate.

Comfort Suites-Buffalo Airport H 🐾
(716) 633-6000. **$96-$160.** 901 Dick Rd 14225. SR 33 exit Dick Rd, just sw. Int corridors. **Pets:** Other species. $15 one-time fee/room. Crate.

Holiday Inn-Buffalo Airport H
(716) 634-6969. **Call for rates.** 4600 Genesee St 14225. I-90 exit 51, 1 mi e on SR 33. Int corridors. **Pets:** Accepted.

Holiday Inn Express Hotel & Suites-Buffalo Airport H
(716) 631-8700. **Call for rates.** 131 Buell Ave 14225. I-90 exit 51, just e on Genesee St (SR 33), then just s. Int corridors. **Pets:** Accepted.

Homewood Suites by Hilton H 🐾
(716) 685-0700. **$159-$219.** 760 Dick Rd 14225. SR 33 exit Dick Rd, 0.3 mi sw. Int corridors. **Pets:** $75 one-time fee/room. Service with restrictions, crate.

Oak Tree Inn H
(716) 681-2600. **Call for rates.** 3475 Union Rd 14225. I-90 exit 52, 0.3 mi e on Walden Ave, then just n on SR 277 (Union Rd). Int corridors. **Pets:** Accepted.

▼▼▼ Residence Inn by Marriott Buffalo-Cheektowaga

(716) 892-5410. **$123-$263.** 107 Anderson Rd 14225. I-90 exit 52 westbound, stay to left off exit ramp. Int corridors. **Pets:** Other species. $100 one-time fee/room. Service with restrictions, crate.

🛗 🛆ᴹ 🛆 🛜 🗙 🔋 🖵

▼▼ TownePlace Suites by Marriott-Buffalo Airport 🖪

(716) 839-1880. **$90-$148.** 4265 Genesee St 14225. I-90 exit 51, 1.4 mi e on SR 33. Int corridors. **Pets:** Accepted.

🔌 🍴 🛆ᴹ 🛜 🗙 🔋 🖵

CHESTER

🔺 ▼▼▼ Holiday Inn Express Hotel & Suites Chester/Monroe/Goshen 🖪

(845) 469-3000. **Call for rates.** 2 Bryle Pl 10918. SR 17 exit 126, just n on SR 94, then just w on SR 17M (Brookside Ave). Int corridors. **Pets:** $30 one-time fee/room. Designated rooms, service with restrictions, supervision. 🆂🅰🆅🅴 🛆ᴹ 🛆 🛜 🗙 🔋 🖵

CHESTERTOWN

▼▼▼ Friends Lake Inn 🇨🇮

(518) 494-4751. **Call for rates.** 963 Friends Lake Rd 12817. I-87 exit 25, 3.3 mi sw on SR 8, then 2.2 mi s. Int corridors. **Pets:** Accepted.

🍴 🛆 🗙 🛜 🗙 🔋 🖵

CICERO

🔺 ▼ Budget Inn Ⓜ

(315) 458-3510. **$55-$225, 7 day notice.** 901 South Bay Rd 13039. I-481 exit 10, just n. Ext corridors. **Pets:** Medium, dogs only. $10 daily fee/pet. Designated rooms, service with restrictions, supervision.

🆂🅰🆅🅴 🍴 🛜 🔋 🖵

🔺 ▼▼▼ Comfort Suites Cicero Syracuse North 🖪

(315) 752-0150. **$99-$159.** 5875 Carmenica Dr 13039. I-80 exit 31, just e. Int corridors. **Pets:** Medium. $25 one-time fee/pet. Designated rooms, service with restrictions, supervision.

🆂🅰🆅🅴 🛆ᴹ 🛆 🛜 🗙 🔋 🖵

CLARENCE

🔺 ▼▼▼ Asa Ransom House 🇨🇮

(716) 759-2315. **Call for rates.** 10529 Main St 14031. Jct SR 78 (Transit Rd), 5.3 mi e on SR 5 (Main St). Int corridors. **Pets:** Dogs only. Designated rooms, service with restrictions, crate.

🆂🅰🆅🅴 🅴🅲🅾 🍴 🛆ᴹ 🛜 🗙 🔋

▼▼▼ Staybridge Suites-Buffalo Airport 🖪 🐾

(716) 810-7829. **$169-$249, 3 day notice.** 8005 Sheridan Dr 14221. I-90 exit 49, 3 mi n on SR 78 (Transit Rd); jct SR 324; next to Eastern Hills Mall. Int corridors. **Pets:** $75 one-time fee/room. Service with restrictions, crate. 🛆ᴹ 🛆 🛜 🔋 🖵

CLAY

▼▼▼ Hampton Inn-Syracuse/Clay 🖪

(315) 622-3443. **$149-$169.** 3948 SR 31 13090. SR 481 exit 12, just w. Int corridors. **Pets:** Medium, dogs only. $100 deposit/room. Designated rooms, service with restrictions, supervision. 🛆ᴹ 🛆 🛜 🔋 🖵

CLAYTON

▼ Fair Wind Lodge Ⓜ

(315) 686-5251. **Call for rates.** 38201 NYS Rt 12E 13624. 2.3 mi sw. Ext corridors. **Pets:** Accepted. 🍴 🛆 🛜 🗙 🆩 🔋 🖵

CLIFTON PARK

▼▼▼ Comfort Suites of Clifton Park 🖪

(518) 373-2255. **$99-$279.** 7 Northside Dr 12065. I-87 exit 9, just w on SR 146, then just n. Int corridors. **Pets:** Accepted.

🛆 🛜 🗙 🔋 🖵

CLINTON

▼▼▼ Amidst the Hedges 🅱🅱

(315) 723-2035. **Call for rates.** 180 Sanford Ave 13323. SR 412 (College St), 0.3 mi n on Elm St. Int corridors. **Pets:** Dogs only. Designated rooms, no service, supervision. 🗙 🛜 🗙 🔋 🖵

COBLESKILL

🔺 ▼▼▼ BEST WESTERN Inn of Cobleskill 🖪

(518) 234-4321. **$90-$210.** 121 Burgin Dr 12043. I-88 exit 21 eastbound on SR 7, 0.8 mi e of jct SR 10; exit 22 westbound, 2.9 mi w on SR 7. Int corridors. **Pets:** Accepted.

🆂🅰🆅🅴 🍴 🛆ᴹ 🛆 🛜 🗙 🔋 🖵

▼▼▼ Super 8 🖪

(518) 234-4888. **$85-$125.** 955 E Main St 12043. I-88 exit 22 westbound, 2.4 mi w on SR 7; exit 21 eastbound, 3.1 mi e on SR 7. Int corridors. **Pets:** Medium, dogs only. $10 daily fee/pet. Service with restrictions, supervision. 🛆ᴹ 🛜 🔋 🖵

COLONIE

🔺 ▼▼▼ BEST WESTERN Albany Airport Inn 🖪

(518) 458-1000. **$79-$169.** 200 Wolf Rd 12205. I-87 exit 4, just se to Wolf Rd, then just sw. Int corridors. **Pets:** Other species. $20 daily fee/pet. Service with restrictions, crate. 🆂🅰🆅🅴 🍴 🛆 🛜 🗙 🔋 🖵

🔺 ▼▼ Cocca's Inn & Suites, Wolf Rd Ⓜ

(518) 459-2240. **$59-$149.** 2 Wolf Rd 12205. I-87 exit 2E, just e. Ext/int corridors. **Pets:** $10 daily fee/pet. Service with restrictions, supervision. 🆂🅰🆅🅴 🛜 🔋 🖵

▼▼▼ Holiday Inn Albany on Wolf Road 🖪

(518) 458-7250. **$99-$199.** 205 Wolf Rd 12205. I-87 exit 4, 0.3 mi se. Int corridors. **Pets:** $100 one-time fee/room, $35 daily fee/room. Designated rooms, service with restrictions.

🍴 🛆ᴹ 🛆 🗙 🛜 🔋 🖵

🔺 ▼▼ Travelodge Inn & Suites, Albany Airport 🖪

(518) 459-5670. **$60-$169.** 42 Wolf Rd 12205. I-87 exit 2E, just e, then just n. Int corridors. **Pets:** Medium. $10 daily fee/pet. Service with restrictions, supervision. 🆂🅰🆅🅴 🛜 🔋 🖵

CORNING

▼▼▼ Radisson Hotel Corning 🖪

(607) 962-5000. **$109-$399.** 125 Denison Pkwy E 14830. Downtown. Int corridors. **Pets:** Accepted. 🅴🅲🅾 🍴 🛆 🛜 🔋 🖵

▼▼▼ Staybridge Suites 🖪

(607) 936-7800. **Call for rates.** 201 Townley Ave 14830. I-86/SR 17 exit 46, just s. Int corridors. **Pets:** Accepted.

🍴 🛆ᴹ 🛆 🛜 🗙 🔋 🖵

CORNWALL

▼▼▼ Cromwell Manor Inn 🅱🅱 🐾

(845) 534-7136. **Call for rates.** 174 Angola Rd 12518. Jct US 9W and SR 94, 5.5 mi s on US 9W, 0.5 mi w. Ext/int corridors. **Pets:** Large, dogs only. $25 one-time fee/pet. Designated rooms, service with restrictions, supervision. 🍴 🛆ᴹ 🛆 🗙 🆩

CROTON-ON-HUDSON

▼▼▼ Alexander Hamilton House 🅱🅱

(914) 271-6737. **Call for rates.** 49 Van Wyck St 10520. US 9 exit SR 129, just e on Municipal Place, just n on Riverside Ave, just e on Grand St, then just n on Hamilton Ave. Int corridors. **Pets:** Accepted.

🍴 🛆 🛜 🗙 🆩 🔋

CUBA

▼▼ Cuba Econo Lodge Ⓜ

(585) 968-1992. **$90-$120.** 1 N Branch Rd 14727. I-86 exit 28, just n to N Branch Rd, then just e. Int corridors. **Pets:** Accepted. 🍴 🛜 🔋

DEWITT

AAA ▼▼ Econo Lodge **M**
(315) 446-3300. **$89-$175.** 3400 Erie Blvd E 13214. I-481 exit 3, 1.2 mi w on SR 5; I-690 exit 17 S (Bridge St), just e on Erie Blvd (SR 5). Ext corridors. **Pets:** Accepted. [SAVE] 🛜 📶

DUNKIRK

AAA ▼▼▼ BEST WESTERN PLUS Dunkirk & Fredonia Inn **H**
(716) 366-7100. **$90-$200.** 3912 Vineyard Dr 14048. I-90 exit 59, just w. Int corridors. **Pets:** Medium, other species. $10 daily fee/pet. Service with restrictions, supervision. [SAVE] 🛁 🛜 ✕ 📶

AAA ▼▼▼ Comfort Inn **H**
(716) 672-4450. **$130-$200.** 3925 Vineyard Dr 14048. I-90 exit 59, just se on SR 75 (Camp Rd), then just w. Int corridors. **Pets:** Accepted.
[SAVE] 🛜 📶

EAST GREENBUSH

▼▼▼ Residence Inn by Marriott Albany East Greenbush/ Tech Valley **H** 🐾
(518) 720-3600. **$125-$240.** 3 Tech Valley Dr 12061. I-90 exit 9, just e. Int corridors. **Pets:** Other species. $75 one-time fee/room. Service with restrictions. 🍽 🛜 🛁 🛜 ✕ 📶

EAST SYRACUSE

AAA ▼▼▼ BEST WESTERN PLUS Carrier Circle Syracuse **H** 🐾
(315) 437-2761. **$89-$189.** 6555 Old Collamer Rd S 13057. I-90 exit 35 (Carrier Cir) to SR 298 E, just n. Int corridors. **Pets:** Large, other species. $20 daily fee/pet. Service with restrictions.
[SAVE] 🍽 🛁 ✕ 🛜 ✕ 📶

▼▼▼ CrestHill Suites **H**
(315) 432-5595. **$109-$249.** 6410 New Venture Gear Dr 13057. I-90 exit 35 (Carrier Cir) to SR 298 E, 0.7 mi s, then just e. Int corridors. **Pets:** $15 daily fee/room. Service with restrictions, crate.
🍽 🛁 🛜 📶

▼▼ Quality Inn Syracuse **H**
(315) 432-9333. **$60-$90.** 6611 Old Collamer Rd 13057. I-90 exit 35 (Carrier Cir) to SR 298 E, just n. Ext/int corridors. **Pets:** Large. $15 daily fee/pet. Designated rooms, service with restrictions, supervision.
🛜 🛁 🛜 📶

▼▼▼ Residence Inn by Marriott Syracuse **H**
(315) 432-4488. **$139-$229.** 6420 Yorktown Cir 13057. I-90 exit 35 (Carrier Cir) to SR 298 E, just n. Ext/int corridors. **Pets:** Accepted.
📶 🛜 🛁 🛜 ✕ 📶

ELLICOTTVILLE

▼▼▼ The Jefferson Inn of Ellicottville **BB** 🐾
(716) 699-5869. **Call for rates.** 3 Jefferson St 14731. Just n of jct US 219 and SR 242. Ext/int corridors. **Pets:** Other species. $15 daily fee/pet. Designated rooms, service with restrictions. 🛜 ✕ 📶

▼▼▼ Sugar Pine Lodge **BB**
(716) 699-4855. **Call for rates.** 6158 Jefferson St (Rt 219 S) 14731. Jct US 219 and SR 242, 0.5 mi s on US 219. Ext/int corridors.
Pets: Accepted. 🍽 🛁 🛜 ✕ 📶

ELMIRA

AAA ▼▼ Coachman Motor Lodge **M**
(607) 733-5526. **$90-$120.** 908 Pennsylvania Ave 14904. I-86/SR 17 exit 56, 0.7 mi w on SR 352 (Church St), 0.5 mi s on Madison Ave (which becomes Pennsylvania Ave), then 1.4 mi s. Ext corridors.
Pets: Accepted. [SAVE] 🍽 🛜 📶

▼▼▼ Holiday Inn-Elmira Riverview **H**
(607) 734-4211. **$99-$300.** 760 E Water St 14901. I-86/SR 17 exit 56, 0.5 mi s. Int corridors. **Pets:** $250 one-time fee/room. Designated rooms, service with restrictions, supervision.
🍽 🛁 🛜 ✕ 📶

ELMSFORD

▼▼ Extended Stay America-White Plains-Elmsford **H**
(914) 347-8073. **Call for rates.** 118 W Main St 10523. I-87 exit 8, just w. Int corridors. **Pets:** Other species. $25 daily fee/pet. Service with restrictions, supervision. 🍽 🛜 🛜 📶

EVANS MILLS

▼▼▼ Candlewood Suites Watertown/Fort Drum **H**
(315) 629-6990. **$89-$160.** 26513 Herrick Dr 13637. Jct US 11, just n. Int corridors. **Pets:** Large, other species. $150 one-time fee/pet. Service with restrictions, crate. 🛜 🛜 ✕ 📶

FARMINGTON

AAA ▼ Budget Inn **M**
(585) 924-5020. **$54-$129, 3 day notice.** 6001 Rt 96 14425. I-90 exit 44, 1 mi s on SR 332, then just e. Ext corridors. **Pets:** Small, dogs only. $15 daily fee/pet. Designated rooms, service with restrictions, supervision. [SAVE] 🛜 📶

FAYETTEVILLE

▼▼ Craftsman Inn and Conference Center **H**
(315) 637-8000. **Call for rates.** 7300 E Genesee St (SR 5) 13066. Across from Fayetteville Towne Center. Int corridors. **Pets:** Accepted.
🍽 🛜 🛜 ✕ 📶

FISHKILL

▼▼ Extended Stay America-Fishkill-Poughkeepsie **H**
(845) 896-0592. **Call for rates.** 55 W Merritt Blvd 12524. I-84 exit 13, just n. Int corridors. **Pets:** Other species. $25 daily fee/pet. Service with restrictions, supervision. 🛜 🛜 📶

▼▼ Extended Stay America Fishkill Route 9 **H**
(845) 897-2800. **Call for rates.** 25 Merritt Blvd 12524. I-84 exit 13, just n. Int corridors. **Pets:** Other species. $25 daily fee/pet. Service with restrictions, supervision. 🛜 📶

AAA ▼▼▼ HYATT house Fishkill/Poughkeepsie **H**
(845) 897-5757. **$79-$269.** 100 Westage Business Center Dr 12524. I-84 exit 13, just n on US 9, just w on Merritt Blvd, then just s. Int corridors. **Pets:** Medium, dogs only. $75 one-time fee/room. Designated rooms, service with restrictions, crate.
[SAVE] 🛜 🛁 🛜 ✕ 📶

FLORAL PARK

▼▼ Quality Inn Floral Park **H**
(718) 343-9600. **$89-$229.** 256-15 Jericho Tpke 11001. At Keene Ave. Int corridors. **Pets:** Accepted. 🍽 🛜 ✕ 📶

FLUSHING

▼▼ Extended Stay America-NY City-LaGuardia Airport **H**
(718) 357-3661. **Call for rates.** 18-30 Whitestone Expwy 11357. In Whitestone; I-678 (Van Wyck Expwy) exit 15, just w. Int corridors.
Pets: Other species. $25 daily fee/pet. Service with restrictions, supervision. 🍽 🛜 🛜 📶

▼▼▼ The Parc Hotel **H**
(718) 358-8897. **Call for rates.** 39-16 College Point Blvd 11354. In Flushing; Whitestone Expwy exit 14, just s on Linden Pl, just w on 28th ave. Int corridors. **Pets:** Accepted. 🛜 ✕ 📶

AAA ▼▼▼ Sheraton LaGuardia East Hotel **H** 🐾
(718) 460-6666. **$189-$489.** 135-20 39th Ave 11354. In Flushing; Grand Central Pkwy to Northern Blvd, 1 mi e to Main St, 0.3 mi s to 39th Ave, then just w. Int corridors. **Pets:** Medium. Service with restrictions, crate.
[SAVE] 🍽 🛜 ✕ 📶

GARDEN CITY

▼▼▼ La Quinta Inn & Suites Garden City **H**
(516) 705-9000. **$135-$369.** 821 Stewart Ave 11530. Meadowbrook Pkwy exit 3, 0.5 mi w. Int corridors. **Pets:** Large, other species. Service with restrictions. 🍽 🛜 🛜 📶

GATES

▼▼▼ **Holiday Inn-Rochester Airport** 🆗
(585) 328-6000. **Call for rates.** 911 Brooks Ave 14624. I-390 exit 18A (SR 204), just e. Int corridors. **Pets:** Accepted.
🍴 🔁 ⊠ 🛜 🔌 🖵

▼◆ **Quality Inn-Rochester** 🆗
(585) 464-8800. **$95-$145.** 1273 Chili Ave 14624. I-390 exit 19, just w on SR 33. Int corridors. **Pets:** Accepted. 🍴 🔁 🛜 🔌 🖵

GENESEO

▼▼ **Quality Inn Geneseo** 🆗
(585) 243-0500. **$109-$299.** 4242 Lakeville Rd 14454. I-390 exit 8, 3.4 mi w on US 20A. Int corridors. **Pets:** Accepted.
🔁 🛜 ⊠ 🔌 🖵

GENEVA

🅰🅰🅰 ▼▼▼ **Cobtree Vacation Rentals Resort** 🆅🅷
(315) 789-1144. **$130-$660, 90 day notice.** 440-458 Armstrong Rd 14456. 3 mi n on SR 14. Ext corridors. **Pets:** Accepted.
🆂🅰🆅🅴 🍴 🛜 ⊠ 🔌 🖵

▼▼ **Microtel Inn & Suites by Wyndham Geneva** 🆗
(315) 789-7890. **$59-$125.** 550 Hamilton St 14456. Jct SR 14, 2 mi w on US 20/SR 5. Int corridors. **Pets:** Accepted.
🅼 ⊠ 🔌 🖵

GLENS FALLS

🅰🅰🅰 ▼▼ **Queensbury Hotel** 🆗
(518) 792-1121. **$79-$199.** 88 Ridge St 12801. Corner of Maple St. Int corridors. **Pets:** Accepted. 🆂🅰🆅🅴 🍴 🔁 ⊠ 🛜 ⊠ 🔌 🖵

GREAT NECK

▼▼▼ **The Andrew Hotel** 🆗 🐾
(516) 482-2900. **$179-$269.** 75 N Station Plaza 11021. Jct SR 25A, 0.8 mi n on Middle Neck Rd, just e. Int corridors. **Pets:** Small. $150 one-time fee/pet. Service with restrictions, supervision.
🍴 🔁 ⊠ 🔌 🖵

GREECE

▼▼ **Comfort Inn West** 🆗
(585) 621-5700. **$84-$145.** 1501 W Ridge Rd 14615. Jct I-390 and SR 104 (Ridge Rd), 0.5 mi e. Int corridors. **Pets:** Other species. $15 daily fee/room. Service with restrictions, crate. 🛜 🔌 🖵

▼▼▼ **Hampton Inn-Rochester North** 🆗 🐾
(585) 663-6070. **$119-$199.** 500 Center Place Dr 14615. I-390 exit 24A, just e on SR 104 (Ridge Rd), then just n on Buckman Rd. Int corridors. **Pets:** Other species. Service with restrictions, crate.
🅼 🔁 🛜 ⊠ 🔌 🖵

▼▼▼ **Residence Inn by Marriott Rochester West/Greece** 🆗
(585) 865-2090. **$118-$194.** 500 Paddy Creek Cir 14615. I-390 exit 24A, just e on SR 104 (Ridge Rd), just s on Hoover Dr, then just w. Int corridors. **Pets:** Accepted. 🔁 🛜 ⊠ 🔌 🖵

HAMBURG

▼▼ **Comfort Inn & Suites** 🆗
(716) 648-2922. **$70-$165.** 3615 Commerce Pl 14075. I-90 exit 57, just w. Int corridors. **Pets:** Accepted. 🅼 🔁 🛜 🔌 🖵

🅰🅰🅰 ▼▼▼ **Quality Inn Hamburg** 🆗
(716) 649-0500. **$69-$209.** 5440 Camp Rd 14075. I-90 exit 57, 0.3 mi se on SR 75. Int corridors. **Pets:** Accepted.
🆂🅰🆅🅴 🍴 🔁 🛜 🔌 🖵

🅰🅰🅰 ▼▼ **Red Roof Inn Buffalo Hamburg** Ⓜ
(716) 648-7222. **Call for rates.** 5370 Camp Rd 14075. I-90 exit 57, just se on SR 75. Ext corridors. **Pets:** Large, other species. Service with restrictions, supervision. 🆂🅰🆅🅴 🛜 🔌 🖵

HANCOCK

▼▼ **Smith's Colonial Motel** Ⓜ
(607) 637-2989. **Call for rates.** 23085 State Hwy 97 13783. SR 17 exit 87, 2.7 mi s. Ext corridors. **Pets:** Dogs only. $15 daily fee/pet. Service with restrictions, supervision. 🍴 🛜 ⊠ 🔌 🖵

HAUPPAUGE

🅰🅰🅰 ▼▼▼ **Residence Inn by Marriott Long Island-Hauppauge/Islandia** 🆗
(631) 724-4188. **$118-$229.** 850 Veterans Memorial Hwy 11788. I-495 exit 57, 1.2 mi nw. Int corridors. **Pets:** Accepted.
🆂🅰🆅🅴 🔌 🍴 🅼 🔁 🛜 ⊠ 🔌 🖵

HENRIETTA

▼▼▼ **Homewood Suites by Hilton-Rochester** 🆗 🐾
(585) 334-9150. **$139-$229.** 2095 Hylan Dr 14623. I-390 exit 13, just e. Int corridors. **Pets:** Medium, other species. $75 one-time fee/room. Service with restrictions, crate. 🅼 🔁 🛜 🔌 🖵

▼▼ **Microtel Inn by Wyndham Henrietta/Rochester** 🆗
(585) 334-3400. **$60-$119.** 905 Lehigh Station Rd 14467. I-390 exit 12 northbound; exit 12A southbound, just w on SR 253. Int corridors. **Pets:** Accepted. 🛜 🔌

▼▼▼ **Radisson Rochester Airport** 🆗
(585) 475-1910. **$109-$239.** 175 Jefferson Rd 14623. I-390 exit 14A southbound; exit 14 northbound, 3 mi w on SR 252 (Jefferson Rd). Int corridors. **Pets:** $25 one-time fee/room. Designated rooms, service with restrictions, crate. 🍴 🅼 🔁 🛜 ⊠ 🔌 🖵

🅰🅰🅰 ▼▼ **Red Roof Inn Rochester Henrietta** Ⓜ
(585) 359-1100. **Call for rates.** 4820 W Henrietta Rd 14467. I-390 exit 12 northbound; exit 12A southbound, 0.5 mi w on SR 253, then just s on SR 15 (Henrietta Rd). Ext corridors. **Pets:** Large, other species. Service with restrictions, supervision. 🆂🅰🆅🅴 🛜 🔌 🖵

▼▼◆ **Residence Inn by Marriott Rochester** 🆗
(585) 272-8850. **$118-$194.** 1300 Jefferson Rd 14623. I-390 exit 14A southbound, 0.5 mi e on SR 252 (Jefferson Rd); exit 14 northbound, just n on SR 15A, then 0.5 mi e on SR 252 (Jefferson Rd). Ext/int corridors. **Pets:** Accepted. 🔁 🛜 ⊠ 🔌 🖵

▼▼▼ **R I T Inn & Conference Center** 🆗
(585) 359-1800. **Call for rates.** 5257 W Henrietta Rd 14467. I-390 exit 12 northbound; exit 12A southbound, 0.5 mi w on SR 253, then 0.7 mi s. Int corridors. **Pets:** Accepted.
🅴🅲🅾 🍴 🔁 ⊠ 🛜 ⊠ 🔌 🖵

HERKIMER

🅰🅰🅰 ▼▼◆ **Red Roof Inn & Suites-Herkimer** Ⓜ
(315) 866-0490. **$78-$150, 3 day notice.** 100 Marginal Rd 13350. I-90 exit 30, just n on SR 28. Ext/int corridors. **Pets:** Accepted.
🆂🅰🆅🅴 🔁 🛜 ⊠ 🔌 🖵

HIGHLAND

▼▼ **Super 8** Ⓜ
(845) 691-6888. **$47-$96.** 3423 Rt 9W 12528. Just s of jct SR 299 and US 9W. Int corridors. **Pets:** Accepted. 🍴 🅼 🛜 🔌 🖵

HOGANSBURG

🅰🅰🅰 ▼▼▼ **Comfort Inn & Suites Hogansburg** 🆗
(518) 358-1000. **$99-$209.** 865 State Route 37 13655. Jct SR 95, 0.3 mi w. Int corridors. **Pets:** Medium. $10 daily fee/pet. Designated rooms, service with restrictions, supervision. 🆂🅰🆅🅴 🔁 🛜 ⊠ 🔌 🖵

HORSEHEADS

▼▼▼ **Candlewood Suites** 🆗
(607) 873-7676. **$79-$299.** 198 Colonial Dr 14845. I-86/SR 17 exit 51B westbound; exit 51A eastbound, just e. Int corridors. **Pets:** Accepted.
🛜 ⊠ 🔌 🖵

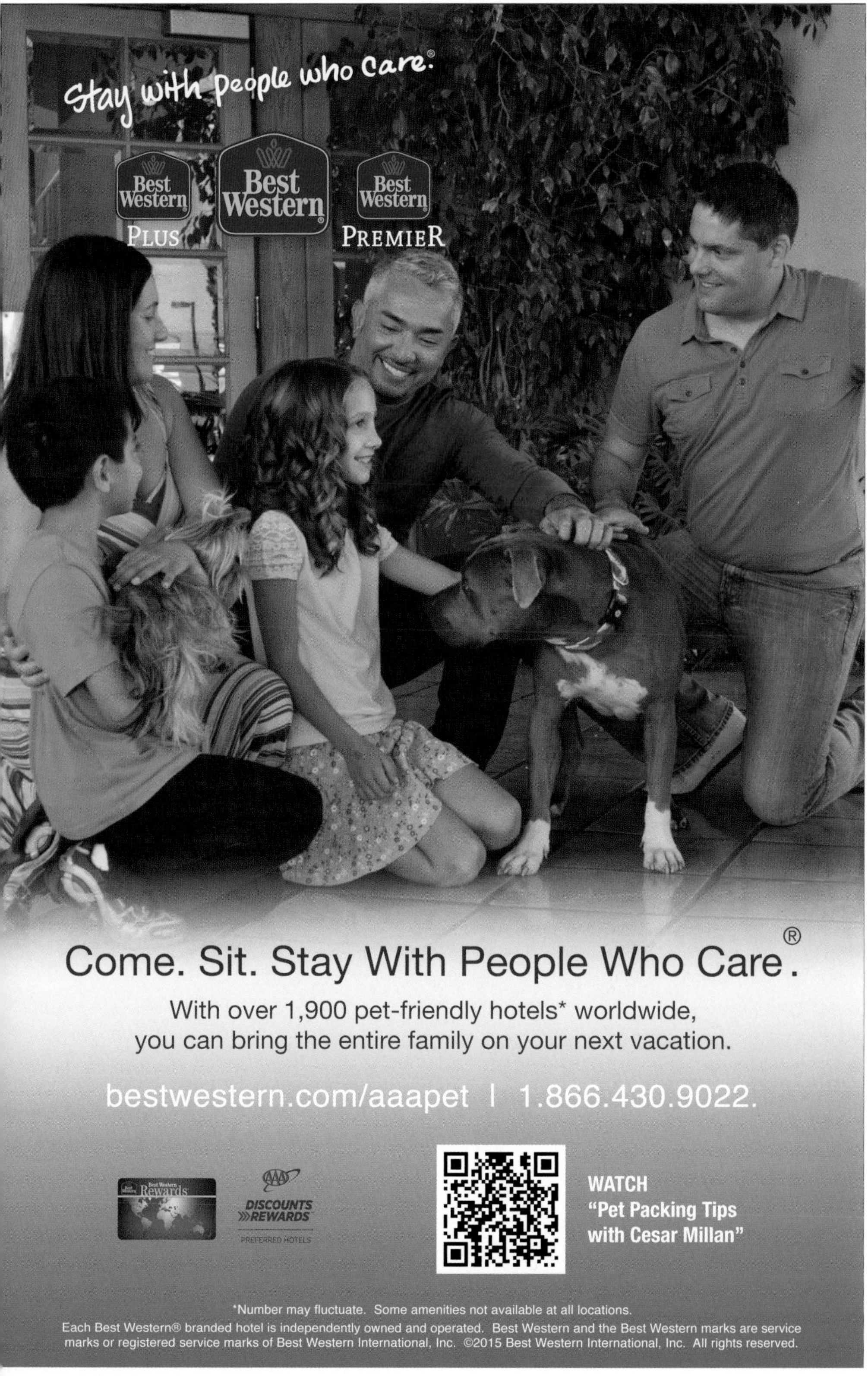
Stay with People who Care.®
Best Western PLUS
Best Western
Best Western PREMIER
Come. Sit. Stay With People Who Care®.
With over 1,900 pet-friendly hotels* worldwide, you can bring the entire family on your next vacation.
bestwestern.com/aaapet | 1.866.430.9022.
Best Western Rewards
AAA DISCOUNTS REWARDS PREFERRED HOTELS
WATCH "Pet Packing Tips with Cesar Millan"
*Number may fluctuate. Some amenities not available at all locations.
Each Best Western® branded hotel is independently owned and operated. Best Western and the Best Western marks are service marks or registered service marks of Best Western International, Inc. ©2015 Best Western International, Inc. All rights reserved.

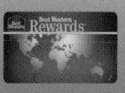

AAA/CAA Members Save Up to 20% Every Day plus 10% Bonus Points with Best Western Rewards®

BEST WESTERN®   **BEST WESTERN PLUS®**   **BEST WESTERN PREMIER®**

With three types of hotels, there's always a Best Western that's perfect for your stay. At every **BEST WESTERN®**, **BEST WESTERN PLUS®** and **BEST WESTERN PREMIER®**, you'll find convenient amenities and extras like breakfast and FREE high-speed internet*. Join our FREE AAA/CAA Preferred Best Western Rewards program and start earning free nights.

AAA/CAA members save up to 20% off room rates and earn 10% more Best Western Rewards® points.
Book now! 1-866-430-9022 bestwestern.com/AAA
(US) bestwestern.com/CAA (Canada)

AAA PetBook® Photo Contest Entries

Each year, the winning entry in AAA's PetBook Photo Contest, sponsored by Best Western®appears on a cover of *Traveling With Your Pet: The AAA PetBook®* and also receives other great prizes. You have already met the contest winners, but here are more great entries that we just had to make room for!

Check out AAA.com/PetBook for pictures, contest rules and an entry form for next year's contest. And keep traveling with your pet!

Brunsen at Coyote Hills Regional Park in Fremont, Calif.
Owner: Jeralyn Terry from Fremont, Calif.

Jackson on Main Street in Chatham, Mass.
Owner: Brooke Conti from Melrose, Mass.

Scarlett at Carmel Country Inn in
Carmel-by-the-Sea, Calif.
Owner: Ted Rose from Pasadena, Calif.

Rukas enjoying Hoboken, N.J.
Owner: Athina Glindmeyer from Long Branch, N.J.

Mimi at Balboa Park in San Diego, Calif.
Owner: Hideo Honjo from San Diego, Calif.

Pippin at Hidden Arch in Monument Valley, Utah
Owners: Charles & Norma Roberts from Costa Mesa, Calif.

Dillon on a scenic overlook near Mount of the
Holy Cross, Colo.
Owner: Mary Jodziewicz from Los Angeles, Calif.

Bowie at the shore in Cannon Beach, Ore.
Owner: Ellis Brasch from Bend, Ore.

Ellie in Bangor, Maine
Owner: Melissa Franco from
Acushnet, Mass.

Lola & Liam enjoying Sanibel, Fla.
Owner: Nancy Kirby from Leesburg, Fla.

Loba on the Alpine Loop in Silverton, Colo.
Owner: Susan Deleon from San Jacinto, Calif.

Buster Moe enjoying the beach in Pacific Grove, Calif.
Owner: Dr. Tran Hong from Tustin, Calif.

Bella Mae at Lake Superior in Munising, Mich.
Owner: Sharon Matulewicz from Marquette, Mich.

Aiden at Truckee River in Nev.
Owners: Mark & Rosa Overstreet from Los
Angeles, Calif.

Miss Marlee & Rusty at Salisbury Beach State Reservation in Salisbury, Mass.
Owners: Lou & Kathy Diamontopoulos from Haverhill, Mass.

Nina relaxing on the beach in Dennis Port, Mass.
Owner: Robin Hodder from Natick, Mass.

Koa & Makana at Copalis Beach, Wash.
Owner: Lisa Wakida from Kirkland, Wash.

Buddha at the park in Vancouver, Wash.
Owner: Pam Link from Vancouver, Wash.

Bierstadt at Fisher Towers near Moab, Utah
Owner: Bret Edge from Moab, Utah

Candy & Frodo romping at Crissy Field Beach in San Francisco, Calif.
Owner: Ramesh Subramonian from Portola Valley, Calif.

Nico & Jill at Glacier National Park, West Glacier, Mont.
Owner: Robert Mastrandrea from Essex, Mont.

Diego at Point Cabrillo Light Station in Mendocino, Calif.
Owners: Andrew Nance & Jim Maloney from
San Francisco, Calif.

Finn at Eastshore State Park, San Francisco
Bay in Albany, Calif.
Owner: Jane Stutfield from Berkeley, Calif.

Chara visiting Peggy's Cove in Nova Scotia, Canada
Owners: Arthur & Linda Everly from Blackstone, Mass.

Biscuit in Kennebunk, Maine
Owners: Dave & Carol Santora from Lyman, Maine

Gunner enjoying Paulina Lake near La Pine, Ore.
Owner: Ramona Welle from Beavercreek, Ore.

Hampton viewing Crater Lake National Park in Ore.
Owner: Ken Koenig from San Francisco, Calif.

Amber at Bridal Veil State Park in Corbett, Ore.
Owner: Patty Runner from Gresham, Ore.

Mini outside Galaxy Diner in Hatch, Utah
Owner: Michael McCollum from Patterson, Calif.

Buddy visiting White Pines Lake in Arnold, Calif.
Owner: Tim Dowling from Murphys, Calif.

Lilly at Mendocino Coast Botanical Gardens in Fort Bragg, Calif.
Owner: Tina Chandler from Clovis, Calif.

Ruby exploring the Sierra Nevada Mountains in Calif.
Owner: Kathleen Mocharski from Placerville, Calif.

Roxi on the Corona Arch Trail in Moab, Utah
Owner: Kathy Farnsworth from Corvallis, Ore.

Zoe enjoying the coastline in Lincoln City, Ore.
Owner: Gibson Holub from Ashland, Ore.

Joey at the Land O' Lakes overlook in Grand Mesa, Colo.
Owners: Art Trevena & Joyce Tanihara from Cedaredge, Colo.

Vinny at Fish Creek Marina in Saratoga Springs, N.Y.
Owner: Joann Verderosa from Clifton Park, N.Y.

A few more tail-wagging travelers

1) BB on the bay in Boothbay Harbor, Maine, Owner: Paula Kane from Avon, Maine 2) Huck at Mt. Hood National Forest in Sandy, Ore., Owner: Jim Arnold from Beavercreek, Ore. 3) Foxy at San Bernardino National Forest in San Bernardino, Calif., Owners: Chuck & Michelle Mayfield from Forest Falls, Calif. 4) Bosley in Bar Harbor, Maine, Owner: Carolyn Corrente from Abington, Mass. 5) Mr. Chubs at the dog beach in Huntington Beach, Calif., Owner: Stacy Zar from Rancho Santa Margarita, Calif. 6) Banjo playing on Crissy Field in San Francisco, Calif., Owner: Kristen Dutro from Ukiah, Calif. 7) Ollie at Graveyard Lakes in the John Muir Wilderness in Lakeshore, Calif., Owner: Bridget Keimel from Petaluma, Calif. 8) Faith at Lake Tahoe, Calif., Owner: Stacey Pownell from Santa Rosa, Calif.

HUNTINGTON

Oheka Castle Hotel & Estate [CI]
(631) 659-1400. **$395-$1095, 3 day notice.** 135 West Gate Dr 11743. Jct SR 25, 0.5 mi ne. Int corridors. **Pets:** Accepted.

INLET

Marina Motel [M]
(315) 357-3883. **$79-$189, 14 day notice.** 6 S Shore Rd 13360. Center. Ext corridors. **Pets:** Accepted.

IRONDEQUOIT

Holiday Inn Express [H]
(585) 342-0430. **Call for rates.** 2200 Goodman St N 14609. SR 104 exit Goodman St, just n. Int corridors. **Pets:** Accepted.

ITHACA *(Restaurants p. 636)*

BEST WESTERN University Inn [M]
(607) 272-6100. **$129-$249.** 1020 Ellis Hollow Rd 14850. SR 79 E, 1 mi ne on Pine Tree Rd, just n; in East Hill Plaza. Int corridors. **Pets:** Small, other species. $20 daily fee/pet. Designated rooms, service with restrictions, supervision.

Country Inn & Suites By Carlson [H] ❖
(607) 256-1100. **$109-$359.** 1100 Danby Rd (SR 96B) 14850. 0.5 mi past entrance to Ithaca College and jct SR 96B. Int corridors. **Pets:** Other species. $25 daily fee/pet. Designated rooms, service with restrictions, supervision.

Hampton Inn [H]
(607) 277-5500. **$139-$249.** 337 Elmira Rd 14850. On SR 13. Int corridors. **Pets:** Dogs only. Service with restrictions, supervision.

La Tourelle Resort and Spa [CI]
(607) 273-2734. **Call for rates.** 1150 Danby Rd 14850. 2.7 mi s on SR 96B. Int corridors. **Pets:** Dogs only. Designated rooms, service with restrictions, crate.

JAMAICA

Sheraton JFK Airport Hotel [H] ❖
(718) 322-7190. **Call for rates.** 132-26 S Conduit Ave 11430. In Jamaica; between S Conduit and 149th aves; off Nassau Expwy. Int corridors. **Pets:** Medium, dogs only. Designated rooms, service with restrictions, supervision.

JAMESTOWN

Comfort Inn [H] ❖
(716) 664-5920. **$99-$159.** 2800 N Main St 14701. I-86/SR 17 exit 12, just s on SR 60 (Main St). Int corridors. **Pets:** Other species. $25 one-time fee/pet. Designated rooms, service with restrictions, supervision.

JOHNSON CITY

BEST WESTERN PLUS of Johnson City [H]
(607) 729-9194. **$104-$139.** 569 Harry L Dr 13790. SR 17 exit 70N, 0.3 mi n. Int corridors. **Pets:** Accepted.

La Quinta Inn Binghamton - Johnson City [H]
(607) 770-9333. **$94-$269.** 581 Harry L Dr 13790. SR 17 exit 70N, 0.3 mi n. Int corridors. **Pets:** Large, other species. Service with restrictions.

Red Roof Inn Binghamton [M]
(607) 729-8940. **Call for rates.** 590 Fairview St 13790. SR 17 exit 70N, 0.3 mi n, then just n on Reynolds Rd. Ext corridors. **Pets:** Large, other species. Service with restrictions, supervision.

JOHNSTOWN

Holiday Inn [H]
(518) 762-4686. **$100-$175.** 308 N Comrie Ave 12095. Jct SR 30A and 29 E, 1.3 mi n. Int corridors. **Pets:** Accepted.

Microtel Inn & Suites by Wyndham Johnstown [H]
(518) 762-5425. **$76-$99.** 136 N Comrie Ave 12095. I-90 exit 28 (SR 30A), 4 mi n. Int corridors. **Pets:** Accepted.

Super 8 [H]
(518) 736-1800. **$70-$100.** 301 N Comrie Ave 12095. Jct SR 30A and 29 E, 1.2 mi n. Int corridors. **Pets:** Accepted.

KENMORE

Super 8-Buffalo/Niagara Falls [H]
(716) 876-4020. **$48-$82.** 1288 Sheridan Dr 14217. I-190 exit 15, 1.5 mi e on SR 324 (Sheridan Dr). Int corridors. **Pets:** Medium, dogs only. Service with restrictions, supervision.

KINGSTON

BEST WESTERN PLUS Kingston Hotel & Conference Center [H]
(845) 338-0400. **$139-$229, 3 day notice.** 503 Washington Ave 12401. I-87 exit 19, just e of traffic circle. Int corridors. **Pets:** Accepted.

LAKE GEORGE

Green Haven Resort [M]
(518) 668-2489. **Call for rates.** 3136 Lake Shore Dr 12845. I-87 exit 22, 0.8 mi n on SR 9N. Ext corridors. **Pets:** Dogs only. $25 one-time fee/room. Service with restrictions, crate.

Lake George Inn [M]
(518) 668-2673. **Call for rates.** 444 Canada St 12845. I-87 exit 22, 0.3 mi s on US 9. Ext corridors. **Pets:** Other species. $15 daily fee/pet. Designated rooms, service with restrictions.

Lake Haven Motel [M]
(518) 668-2260. **Call for rates.** 442 Canada St 12845. I-87 exit 22, 0.4 mi s on US 9. Ext corridors. **Pets:** Medium, dogs only. $20 daily fee/pet. Designated rooms, service with restrictions.

Roaring Brook Ranch & Tennis Resort [H]
(518) 668-5767. **$170-$246, 10 day notice.** 2206 State Rt 9N S 12845. I-87 exit 21, 1 mi s. Ext/int corridors. **Pets:** $10 daily fee/room. Service with restrictions, crate.

Travelodge Lake George [M]
(518) 668-5421. **$69-$169.** 2011 US 9 12845. I-87 exit 21, just s. Ext/int corridors. **Pets:** Dogs only. $20 daily fee/room. Service with restrictions, supervision.

LAKE LUZERNE

Luzerne Court [M]
(518) 696-2734. **Call for rates.** 508 Lake Ave 12846. I-87 exit 21, 8.7 mi s on SR 9N. Ext corridors. **Pets:** Accepted.

LAKE PLACID

Art Devlin's Olympic Motor Inn, Inc. [M]
(518) 523-3700. **$78-$498, 14 day notice.** 2764 Main St 12946. 0.5 mi e on SR 86. Ext corridors. **Pets:** Dogs only. $6 daily fee/pet. Service with restrictions, crate.

Crowne Plaza Resort & Golf Club Lake Placid [H]
(518) 523-2556. **$119-$259, 7 day notice.** 101 Olympic Dr 12946. Downtown. Ext/int corridors. **Pets:** Dogs only. $10 daily fee/pet. Service with restrictions, supervision.

▼▼▼▼ **Golden Arrow Lakeside Resort** �H🏠

(518) 523-3353. **Call for rates.** 2559 Main St 12946. On SR 86; center. Int corridors. **Pets:** Accepted. 🌱 🍴 🏊 ✕ 🛰 ✕ 📱 💻

▼▼▼ **High Peaks Resort** 🏠

(518) 523-4411. **$129-$349, 7 day notice.** 2384 Saranac Ave 12946. 0.3 mi w on SR 86. Int corridors. **Pets:** Accepted.
🍴 ⚙ 🏊 ✕ 🛰 ✕ 📱 💻

▼▼ **The Lake House at High Peaks Resort** 🏠 🐾

(518) 523-4422. **Call for rates.** 1 Mirror Lake Dr 12946. 0.3 mi w on SR 86. Int corridors. **Pets:** Dogs only. $50 one-time fee/pet. Designated rooms, service with restrictions, supervision.
⚙ 🏊 🛰 ✕ 📱 💻

🅰🅰 ▼▼▼ **Quality Inn on Lake Placid** 🏠

(518) 523-9555. **$80-$330.** 2125 Saranac Ave 12946. 0.5 mi w on SR 86. Ext/int corridors. **Pets:** Accepted.
🆂🅰🆅🅴 🍴 🏊 ✕ 🛰 ✕ 📱 💻

LANSING

▼▼▼ **Courtyard by Marriott Ithaca** 🏠

(607) 330-1000. **$132-$217.** 29 Thornwood Dr 14850. Jct SR 13 N and Warren Rd, just w to Brown Rd, just e. Int corridors. **Pets:** Other species. $75 one-time fee/room. Designated rooms, service with restrictions, crate. 🍴 ⚙ 🏊 ✕ 🛰 ✕ 📱 💻

▼▼▼▼ **Homewood Suites by Hilton** 🏠

(607) 266-0000. **$159-$249.** 36 Cinema Dr 14850. SR 13 exit Triphammer Rd, just e, then just n on Sheraton Dr (which becomes Cinema Dr). Int corridors. **Pets:** Accepted. ⚙ 🏊 🛰 📱 💻

LATHAM

🅰🅰 ▼▼▼▼ **The Century House, an Ascend Hotel Collection Member** 🏠 🐾

(518) 785-0931. **$99-$229.** 997 New Loudon Rd 12110. I-87 exit 7 (SR 7), just e, then 0.5 mi n on US 9. Int corridors. **Pets:** $25 daily fee/pet. Designated rooms, service with restrictions, crate.

🆂🅰🆅🅴 🍴 🏊 🛰 ✕ 📱 💻

▼▼▼ **Days Inn Airport & Conference Center** 🏠

(518) 783-1900. **$75-$125.** 20 Airport Park Blvd 12110. I-87 exit 4, 2.2 mi nw on Albany Shaker Rd. Int corridors. **Pets:** Accepted.
🍴 🛰 📱 💻

▼▼▼▼ **Hotel Indigo** 🏠

(518) 869-9100. **Call for rates.** 254 Old Wolf Rd 12110. I-87 exit 4, just w on Albany Shaker Rd. Int corridors. **Pets:** Accepted.
🍴 ⚙ 🛰 ✕ 📱 💻

🅰🅰 ▼▼▼▼ **La Quinta Inn & Suites Latham Albany Airport** 🏠

(518) 640-2200. **$92-$240.** 833 New Loudon Rd 12110. I-87 exit 7 (SR 7), just s on US 9 to Latham Cir, then just n on US 9. Int corridors. **Pets:** Large, other species. Service with restrictions.
🆂🅰🆅🅴 ⚙ 🏊 🛰 ✕ 📱 💻

▼▼▼▼ **Microtel Inn by Wyndham Albany Airport** 🏠

(518) 782-9161. **$65-$120.** 7 Rensselaer Ave 12110. I-87 exit 6, just w. Int corridors. **Pets:** Accepted. ⚙ 🛰 📱

▼▼▼▼ **Residence Inn by Marriott Albany Airport** 🏠

(518) 783-0600. **$125-$240.** 1 Residence Inn Dr 12110. I-87 exit 6, 2 mi w on SR 7. Ext corridors. **Pets:** Accepted. 🏊 🛰 ✕ 📱 💻

LITTLE FALLS

🅰🅰 ▼▼▼ **Travelodge Inn & Suites Little Falls** 🏠

(315) 823-4954. **$70-$110, 3 day notice.** 20 Albany St 13365. On SR 5 and 167. Int corridors. **Pets:** Other species. $10 one-time fee/pet. Designated rooms, service with restrictions, crate.

🆂🅰🆅🅴 🍴 🛰 ✕ 📱 💻

LIVERPOOL

🅰🅰 ▼▼▼ **BEST WESTERN PLUS Liverpool Grace Inn & Suites** 🏠

(315) 701-4400. **$99-$229.** 136 Transistor Pkwy 13088. I-90 exit 37 (Electronics Pkwy), just n. Int corridors. **Pets:** Large. $25 daily fee/pet. Designated rooms, service with restrictions, supervision.

🆂🅰🆅🅴 🍴 🏊 🛰 ✕ 📱 💻

▼▼▼ **Homewood Suites by Hilton** 🏠

(315) 451-3800. **Call for rates.** 275 Elwood Davis Rd 13088. I-81 exit 25 (7th North St), 1 mi w; I-90 exit 36. Int corridors. **Pets:** Other species. $100 one-time fee/room. Designated rooms, service with restrictions. 🍴 ⚙ 🛰 📱 💻

🅰🅰 ▼▼▼ **Knights Inn** Ⓜ

(315) 453-6330. **$59-$169.** 430 Electronics Pkwy 13088. I-90 exit 37 (Electronics Pkwy), just w; I-81 exit 25 (7th North St), 1.3 mi nw, then just w. Ext corridors. **Pets:** Accepted. 🆂🅰🆅🅴 🛰 📱

🅰🅰 ▼▼▼ **Super 8 Route 57** 🏠

(315) 451-8550. **$69-$99, 3 day notice.** 7360 Oswego Rd 13090. I-90 exit 38, 1 mi n on CR 57. Int corridors. **Pets:** Small, dogs only. $25 daily fee/pet. Service with restrictions, supervision. 🆂🅰🆅🅴 🛰 📱 💻

LOCKPORT

🅰🅰 ▼▼▼ **Comfort Inn** 🏠

(716) 434-4411. **$70-$160.** 551 S Transit St 14094. 1 mi s on SR 78. Int corridors. **Pets:** Small. $10 daily fee/pet. Designated rooms, service with restrictions, supervision. 🆂🅰🆅🅴 ⚙ 🛰 ✕ 📱 💻

LONG ISLAND CITY

▼▼ **Wyndham Garden Long Island City Manhattan View** 🏠

(718) 906-1900. **$179-$599.** 44-29 9th St 11101. At 44th Ave and Vernon Blvd. Int corridors. **Pets:** Accepted. 🛰 ✕ 📱 💻

MALONE

🅰🅰 ▼▼▼ **Four Seasons Motel** Ⓜ

(518) 483-3490. **$55-$99.** 206 W Main St 12953. 1 mi w on US 11. Ext corridors. **Pets:** Accepted. 🆂🅰🆅🅴 🏊 🛰 📱

▼▼ **Red Roof Inn Malone** 🏠

(518) 483-8123. **Call for rates.** 42 Finney Blvd 12953. On SR 30, just s of jct US 11. Int corridors. **Pets:** Large, other species. Service with restrictions, supervision. 🍴 ⚙ 🛰 ✕ 📱 💻

MALTA

🅰🅰 ▼▼▼ **Hyatt Place Saratoga/Malta** 🏠

(518) 885-1109. **$110-$400.** 20 State Farm Pl 12020. I-87 exit 12, just w. Int corridors. **Pets:** Accepted.
🆂🅰🆅🅴 🌱 🍴 ⚙ 🏊 🛰 ✕ 📱 💻

MANCHESTER

▼ **Manchester Inn** Ⓜ

(585) 289-3811. **$55-$165.** 4078 Rt 96 14504. I-90 exit 43, just s, then just w. Ext/int corridors. **Pets:** Medium. $15 daily fee/pet. Designated rooms, no service, supervision. 🍴 🛰 📱

MARGARETVILLE

▼▼ **Hanah Mountain Resort and Country Club** 🏠

(845) 586-4849. **Call for rates.** 576 W Hubbell Hill Rd 12455. 2.5 mi n on SR 30. Ext corridors. **Pets:** Accepted.
🍴 🏊 🛰 ✕ 📱 💻

MASSENA

▼▼ **Econo Lodge-Meadow View Motel** 🏠

(315) 764-0246. **$65-$100.** 15054 State Hwy 37 13662. On SR 37, 2.7 mi sw. Int corridors. **Pets:** Medium. $10 daily fee/pet. Designated rooms, service with restrictions, crate. 🍴 🛰 📱 💻

MCGRAW

Cortland Days Inn 🅗
(607) 753-7594. **$54-$144.** 3775 US Rt 11 13101. I-81 exit 10 (McGraw/Cortland), just n. Int corridors. **Pets:** Accepted. 📶 🏢 💻

MELVILLE

Extended Stay America-Long Island-Melville 🅗
(631) 777-3999. **Call for rates.** 100 Spagnoli Rd 11747. I-495 exit 49S eastbound, 0.5 mi e on south service road, then 1.1 mi s on SR 110; exit westbound, 1.5 mi s on SR 110. Int corridors. **Pets:** Other species. $25 daily fee/pet. Service with restrictions, supervision.
🍴 ♿ 📶 ❎ 🏢 💻

Hilton Long Island/Huntington 🅗
(631) 845-1000. **$149-$269.** 598 Broad Hollow Rd (SR 110) 11747. I-495 exit 49, 1 mi s on SR 110. Int corridors. **Pets:** Accepted.
🍴 ♿ ❎ 🐾 ❎ 🏢 💻

MIDDLETOWN *(Restaurants p. 636)*

Hampton Inn Middletown 🅗
(845) 344-3400. **$134-$219.** 20 Crystal Run Crossing 10941. SR 17 exit 122, just ne. Int corridors. **Pets:** Accepted. ♿ ♿ 📶 🏢 💻

Microtel Inn & Suites by Wyndham Middletown 🅗
(845) 692-0098. **$99-$139.** 19 Crystal Run Crossing 10941. SR 17 exit 122, just nw. Int corridors. **Pets:** Accepted. ♿ 📶 ❎ 🏢 💻

MOUNT KISCO *(Restaurants p. 636)*

Holiday Inn 🅗
(914) 241-2600. **Call for rates.** 1 Holiday Inn Dr 10549. Saw Mill River Pkwy exit 37, just e. Int corridors. **Pets:** Accepted.
🍴 ♿ ♿ 📶 ❎ 🏢 💻

MOUNT MORRIS

Country Inn & Suites By Carlson 🅗 🐾
(585) 658-4080. **$120-$289.** 130 N Main St 14510. On SR 36; center. Int corridors. **Pets:** Other species. $25 daily fee/room. Designated rooms, service with restrictions, crate. ♿ 📶 ❎ 🏢 💻

NANUET

Candlewood Suites 🅗
(845) 371-4445. **Call for rates.** 20 Overlook Blvd 10954. I-287/87 (New York State Thruway) exit 14 (SR 59 W) to New Clarkstown Rd. Int corridors. **Pets:** Accepted. ♿ 📶 🏢 💻

DoubleTree by Hilton Hotel Nanuet 🅗
(845) 642-6000. **$129-$229.** 425 E Rt 59 10954. Palisades Interstate Pkwy exit 8W, just w. Int corridors. **Pets:** Medium, other species. $50 one-time fee/pet. Designated rooms, service with restrictions.
🍴 ♿ 📶 ❎ 🏢 💻

NEWARK

Quality Inn Finger Lakes Region 🅗
(315) 331-9500. **$89-$209.** 125 N Main St 14513. Jct SR 31, just n on SR 88. Int corridors. **Pets:** Accepted.
🅂🅰🅅🅴 🍴 ♿ 📶 ❎ 🏢 💻

NEWBURGH

Super 8 Ⓜ
(845) 564-5700. **$55-$392.** 1287 Rt 300 12550. I-87 exit 17, just w; I-84 exit 6, 2 mi e. Int corridors. **Pets:** Accepted. 🍴 ❎ 📶 🏢 💻

NEWFANE

Lake Ontario Motel Ⓜ
(716) 778-5004. **$69-$105, 5 day notice.** 3330 Lockport-Olcott Rd 14108. 2.5 mi n of jct SR 104 on SR 78. Int corridors. **Pets:** Other species. $5 daily fee/pet. Service with restrictions, supervision.
📶 ❎ 🏢

NEW HARTFORD

Holiday Inn Utica 🅗
(315) 797-2131. **Call for rates.** 1777 Burrstone Rd 13413. I-90 (New York State Thruway) exit 31, 4.5 mi w on SR 5 W and 12 S exit Burrstone Rd, then 1 mi nw. Int corridors. **Pets:** Accepted.
ⒺⒸⓄ 🍴 ♿ ♿ 📶 ❎ 🏢 💻

NEW ROCHELLE

Radisson Hotel New Rochelle 🅗
(914) 576-3700. **Call for rates.** 1 Radisson Plaza 10801. I-95 exit 16, via Cedar St. Int corridors. **Pets:** Accepted.
🅂🅰🅅🅴 🍴 ♿ 📶 ❎ 🏢 💻

NEW YORK *(Restaurants p. 637)*

70 Park Avenue Hotel 🅗
(212) 973-2400. **Call for rates.** 70 Park Ave 10016. At 38th St. Int corridors. **Pets:** Accepted. 🅂🅰🅅🅴 ⒺⒸⓄ 🍴 ♿ 📶 ❎ 💻

Algonquin Hotel Autograph Collection 🅗 🐾
(212) 840-6800. **$293-$769.** 59 W 44th St 10036. Between 5th and 6th (Ave of the Americas) aves. Int corridors. **Pets:** Other species. Service with restrictions, supervision. 🅂🅰🅅🅴 ⒺⒸⓄ 🍴 ♿ 📶 ❎ 🏢 💻

Aloft Harlem Hotel 🅗
(212) 749-4000. **$189-$429.** 2296 Frederick Douglass Blvd 10027. At W 124th St. Int corridors. **Pets:** Accepted. 🅂🅰🅅🅴 ♿ 📶 ❎ 🏢 💻

Andaz 5th Avenue 🅗
(212) 601-1234. **$200-$925.** 485 5th Ave 10017. At 41st St. Int corridors. **Pets:** Accepted. 🅂🅰🅅🅴 🍴 ♿ 📶 ❎ 🏢 💻

Andaz Wall Street 🅗 🐾
(212) 590-1234. **$170-$625.** 75 Wall St 10005. Between Pearl and Water sts. Int corridors. **Pets:** Large. Designated rooms, service with restrictions. 🅂🅰🅅🅴 🍴 ♿ 📶 ❎ 🏢 💻

Archer New York 🅗
(212) 719-4100. **Call for rates.** 45 W 38th St 10018. Between 5th and 6th (Ave of the Americas) aves. Int corridors. **Pets:** Accepted.
🍴 ♿ 📶 ❎ 🏢 💻

The Benjamin Hotel 🅗
(212) 715-2500. **$249-$799.** 125 E 50th St 10022. Between Lexington and 3rd aves. Int corridors. **Pets:** Accepted.
🅂🅰🅅🅴 🍴 ❎ 🐾 ❎ 🏢 💻

Bentley Hotel 🅗
(212) 644-6000. **Call for rates.** 500 E 62nd St 10021. At York Ave. Int corridors. **Pets:** Accepted. 🍴 🐾 ❎ 🏢 💻

BEST WESTERN PLUS Seaport Inn Downtown 🅗
(212) 766-6600. **$229-$699.** 33 Peck Slip on Front St 10038. North end of South St Seaport. Int corridors. **Pets:** Accepted.
🅂🅰🅅🅴 ♿ 📶 ❎ 🏢 💻

The Bowery Hotel 🅗
(212) 505-9100. **Call for rates.** 335 Bowery 10003. Between E 2nd and 3rd sts. Int corridors. **Pets:** Accepted. 🍴 🐾 📶 💻

Candlewood Suites Times Square 🅗
(212) 967-2254. **$129-$699, 3 day notice.** 339 39th St 10018. Between 8th and 9th aves. Int corridors. **Pets:** Accepted.
🅂🅰🅅🅴 🍴 ♿ 📶 ❎ 🏢 💻

The Carlton Hotel Autograph Collection 🅗 🐾
(212) 532-4100. **$258-$562.** 88 Madison Ave 10016. Between 28th and 29th sts. Int corridors. **Pets:** $50 one-time fee/room. Service with restrictions. 🅂🅰🅅🅴 🍴 📶 ❎ 🏢 💻

The Carlyle, A Rosewood Hotel H
(212) 744-1600. **Call for rates.** 35 E 76th St 10021. At Madison Ave.
Int corridors. **Pets:** Accepted.

Chambers Hotel H
(212) 974-5656. **Call for rates.** 15 W 56th St 10019. Between 5th and
6th (Ave of the Americas) aves. Int corridors. **Pets:** Accepted.

The Chatwal, A Luxury Collection Hotel H
(212) 764-6200. **Call for rates.** 130 W 44th St 10036. Between 6th
(Ave of the Americas) and 7th aves. Int corridors. **Pets:** Accepted.

Comfort Inn Manhattan Bridge H
(212) 925-1212. **$119-$399.** 61-63 Chrystie St 10002. At Hester and
Canal sts. Int corridors. **Pets:** Small. $50 daily fee/room. Designated
rooms, service with restrictions, supervision.

Conrad New York H
(212) 945-0100. **$189-$509.** 102 North End Ave 10282. In Battery Park
City; between Vesey and Murray sts. Int corridors. **Pets:** Accepted.

Courtyard by Marriott Central Park H
(212) 324-3773. **$265-$815.** 1717 Broadway 10019. Between 54th and
55th sts; entrance on 54th St. Int corridors. **Pets:** Accepted.

Courtyard by Marriott/Manhattan-Times Square H
(212) 391-0088. **$258-$804.** 114 W 40th St 10018. Between Broadway
and 6th Ave (Ave of the Americas). Int corridors. **Pets:** Accepted.

Crowne Plaza Times Square Manhattan H
(212) 977-4000. **Call for rates.** 1605 Broadway 10019. Between 48th
and 49th sts. Int corridors. **Pets:** $75 deposit/room, $75 daily fee/room.
Designated rooms, service with restrictions.

DoubleTree by Hilton Metropolitan Hotel-New York City H
(212) 752-7000. **$139-$599.** 569 Lexington Ave 10022. At E 51st St. Int
corridors. **Pets:** Accepted.

DoubleTree by Hilton New York City-Chelsea H
(212) 564-0994. **$199-$999.** 128 W 29th St 10001. Between 6th (Ave of
the Americas) and 7th aves. Int corridors. **Pets:** Accepted.

DoubleTree by Hilton Times Square South H
(212) 542-8990. **$129-$559.** 341 W 36th St 10018. Between 8th and
9th aves. Int corridors. **Pets:** Accepted.

DoubleTree Suites by Hilton New York City - Times Square H
(212) 719-1600. **$169-$599.** 1568 Broadway 10036. Jct 47th St and 7th
Ave. Int corridors. **Pets:** Accepted.

Dream Downtown H
(212) 229-2559. **$292-$2500.** 355 W 16th St 10011. Between 8th and
9th aves. Int corridors. **Pets:** Accepted.

Duane Street Hotel H
(212) 964-4600. **Call for rates.** 130 Duane St 10013. Between Church
St and W Broadway. Int corridors. **Pets:** Accepted.

Dumont NYC, an Affinia hotel H 🐾
(212) 481-7600. **Call for rates.** 150 E 34th St 10016. Between Lexington and 3rd aves. Int corridors. **Pets:** Other species. $100 one-time
fee/room. Service with restrictions.

Element by Westin Times Square West H
(212) 643-0770. **$199-$629.** 311 W 39th St 10018. Between 8th and
9th aves. Int corridors. **Pets:** Accepted.

Eventi-A Kimpton Hotel H
(212) 564-4567. **Call for rates.** 851 6th Ave (Ave of the Americas)
10001. At 30th St. Int corridors. **Pets:** Accepted.

Fifty NYC, an Affinia hotel H 🐾
(212) 751-5710. **Call for rates.** 155 E 50th St 10022. Between 3rd and
Lexington aves. Int corridors. **Pets:** Other species. $50 one-time fee/pet.
Service with restrictions, supervision.

Four Seasons Hotel New York H
(212) 758-5700. **Call for rates.** 57 E 57th St 10022. Between Park and
Madison aves. Int corridors. **Pets:** Accepted.

The Franklin Hotel H
(212) 369-1000. **Call for rates.** 164 E 87th St 10128. Between 3rd and
Lexington aves. Int corridors. **Pets:** Accepted.

Gansevoort Meatpacking NYC H
(212) 660-6700. **Call for rates.** 18 9th Ave 10014. At 13th St. Int corridors. **Pets:** Accepted.

Gardens NYC, an Affinia hotel H
(212) 355-1230. **Call for rates.** 215 E 64th St 10065. Between 2nd and
3rd aves. Int corridors. **Pets:** Accepted.

Gild Hall A Thompson Hotel H 🐾
(212) 232-7700. **$209-$629, 3 day notice.** 15 Gold St 10038. At Platt
St. Int corridors. **Pets:** Other species. Service with restrictions.

Gracie Inn Hotel/B & B BB
(212) 628-1700. **$149-$399, 3 day notice.** 502 E 81st St 10028.
Between York and East End aves. Int corridors. **Pets:** Other species.
$100 deposit/room, $25 daily fee/pet. Crate.

Hampton Inn Empire State Building H
(212) 564-3688. **$199-$419.** 59 W 35th St 10001. Between 5th and 6th
(Ave of the Americas) aves. Int corridors. **Pets:** Accepted.

Hampton Inn-Manhattan/Chelsea H
(212) 414-1000. **$199-$699.** 108 W 24th St 10011. Between 6th (Ave of
the Americas) and 7th aves. Int corridors. **Pets:** Accepted.

Hampton Inn Manhattan/Downtown- Financial District H
(212) 480-3500. **$199-$509.** 32 Pearl St 10004. Between Broad and
Whitehall sts. Int corridors. **Pets:** Accepted.

Hampton Inn Manhattan/Madison Square Garden Area H
(212) 947-9700. **$199-$699.** 116 W 31st St 10001. Between 6th (Ave of
the Americas) and 7th aves. Int corridors. **Pets:** Accepted.

Hampton Inn-Manhattan/Seaport/Financial District H
(212) 571-4400. **$189-$509.** 320 Pearl St 10038. Between Peck Slip and Dover St. Int corridors. **Pets:** Medium. Service with restrictions.

Hampton Inn Manhattan/Times Square South H
(212) 967-2344. **$159-$559.** 337 W 39th St 10018. Between 8th and 9th aves. Int corridors. **Pets:** Accepted.

Hilton Club New York H
(646) 459-6500. **$309-$899.** 1335 Ave of the Americas, 37th Floor 10019. Between 53rd and 54th sts. Int corridors. **Pets:** Small. $75 one-time fee/pet. Service with restrictions, supervision.

Hilton Garden Inn New York/Midtown Park Avenue H
(212) 755-1108. **$109-$599.** 45 E 33rd St 10016. Between Park and Madison aves. Int corridors. **Pets:** Accepted.

Hilton Times Square H ❀
(212) 840-8222. **$169-$699.** 234 W 42nd St 10036. Between 7th and 8th aves. Int corridors. **Pets:** Large, other species. $75 one-time fee/room. Service with restrictions, crate.

Holiday Inn Express Fifth Ave H
(212) 302-9088. **$159-$599.** 15 W 45th St 10036. Between 5th and 6th (Ave of the Americas) aves. Int corridors. **Pets:** Accepted.

Holiday Inn Express Manhattan Times Square South H
(212) 897-3388. **Call for rates.** 60 W 36th St 10018. Between 5th and 6th (Ave of the Americas) aves. Int corridors. **Pets:** Accepted.

Holiday Inn Express NYC/Madison Square Garden H
(212) 695-7200. **Call for rates.** 232 W 29th St 10001. Between 7th and 8th aves. Int corridors. **Pets:** Accepted.

Holiday Inn Manhattan 6th Ave Chelsea H
(212) 430-8500. **Call for rates.** 125 W 26th St 10001. Between 6th (Ave of the Americas) and 7th aves. Int corridors. **Pets:** Accepted.

Hotel 373 Fifth Avenue H
(212) 213-3388. **Call for rates.** 373 Fifth Ave 10016. Jct 35th St. Int corridors. **Pets:** Accepted.

Hotel Indigo New York City-Chelsea H
(212) 973-9000. **Call for rates.** 127 W 28th St 10001. Between 6th (Ave of the Americas) and 7th aves. Int corridors. **Pets:** Accepted.

Hotel Mela H
(212) 710-7000. **Call for rates.** 120 W 44th St 10036. Between Broadway and 6th Ave (Ave of the Americas). Int corridors. **Pets:** Accepted.

Hotel Plaza Athénée H
(212) 734-9100. **$695.** 37 E 64th St 10065. Between Madison and Park aves. Int corridors. **Pets:** Accepted.

Hotel Wales H
(212) 876-6000. **Call for rates.** 1295 Madison Ave 10128. Between 92nd and 93rd sts E. Int corridors. **Pets:** Accepted.

Hyatt 48Lex H
(212) 838-1234. **$219-$699.** 517 Lexington Ave 10017. At 48th St. Int corridors. **Pets:** Accepted.

Hyatt Place New York/Midtown-South H
(212) 239-9100. **$149-$1299.** 52 W 36th St 10018. Between 5th and 6th (Ave of the Americas) aves. Int corridors. **Pets:** Accepted.

Hyatt Union Square New York H
(212) 253-1234. **$199-$699.** 134 Fourth Ave 10003. At 13th St. Int corridors. **Pets:** Accepted.

Ink 48 New York City, A Kimpton Hotel H
(212) 757-0088. **$199-$589.** 653 11th Ave 10036. Between 47th and 48th sts. Int corridors. **Pets:** Accepted.

InterContinental New York Times Square H
(212) 803-4500. **$229-$780.** 300 W 44th St 10036. Between 8th and 9th aves. Int corridors. **Pets:** Accepted.

The James Hotel New York Soho H
(212) 465-2000. **Call for rates.** 27 Grand St 10013. Between 6th Ave (Ave of the Americas) and Thompson St. Int corridors. **Pets:** Accepted.

JW Marriott Essex House New York H
(212) 247-0300. **$349-$919.** 160 Central Park S 10019. Between 6th (Ave of the Americas) and 7th aves. Int corridors. **Pets:** Accepted.

Langham Place, Fifth Avenue H
(212) 695-4005. **$495-$1095, 3 day notice.** 400 Fifth Ave 10018. Between 36th and 37th sts. Int corridors. **Pets:** Accepted.

Le Parker Meridien New York H ❀
(212) 245-5000. **$299-$1213.** 119 W 56th St 10019. Between 6th (Ave of the Americas) and 7th aves. Int corridors. **Pets:** Other species. $50 daily fee/pet. Service with restrictions, crate.

The Lexington New York City, Autograph Collection H ❀
(212) 755-4400. **$149-$804.** 511 Lexington Ave 10017. At E 48th St. Int corridors. **Pets:** Medium, dogs only. $150 one-time fee/room. Service with restrictions, supervision.

Loews Regency Hotel H
(212) 759-4100. **Call for rates.** 540 Park Ave 10021. At 61st St. Int corridors. **Pets:** Accepted.

The London NYC H
(212) 307-5000. **Call for rates.** 151 W 54th St 10019. Between 6th (Ave of the Americas) and 7th aves. Int corridors. **Pets:** Accepted.

The Lowell Hotel H
(212) 838-1400. **Call for rates.** 28 E 63rd St 10021. Between Park and Madison aves. Int corridors. **Pets:** Accepted.

Mandarin Oriental, New York H ❀
(212) 805-8800. **$1095-$1495.** 80 Columbus Cir at 60th St 10023. Entrance on 60th St. Int corridors. **Pets:** Small, dogs only. Service with restrictions, supervision.

The Manhattan at Times Square Hotel H
(212) 581-3300. **Call for rates.** 790 7th Ave 10019. Between 51st and 52nd sts. Int corridors. **Pets:** Accepted. SAVE 📶 📶 ⊠ 🔋 💻

Manhattan NYC, an Affinia hotel H
(212) 563-1800. **$199-$599.** 371 7th Ave 10001. At 31st St. Int corridors. **Pets:** Accepted. SAVE 🍴 📶 ⊠ 🔋 💻

The Mansfield Hotel H
(212) 277-8700. **Call for rates.** 12 W 44th St 10036. Between 5th and 6th (Ave of the Americas) aves. Int corridors. **Pets:** Accepted.
SAVE 🍴 📶 ⊠

Millennium Broadway Hotel-Times Square-New York H
(212) 768-4400. **Call for rates.** 145 W 44th St 10036. Between 6th Ave (Ave of the Americas) and Broadway; in Times Square. Int corridors. **Pets:** Accepted. 🍴 📶 📶 ⊠ 🔋 💻

Mondrian SoHo H
(212) 389-1000. **Call for rates.** 9 Crosby St 10013. Just s of Grand St. Int corridors. **Pets:** Accepted. 🍴 📶 ⊠ 💻

The Muse New York, A Kimpton Hotel H
(212) 485-2400. **Call for rates.** 130 W 46th St 10036. Between 6th (Ave of the Americas) and 7th aves. Int corridors. **Pets:** Accepted.
SAVE ECO 🍴 📶 ⊠ 🔋 💻

The New York Hilton Midtown H
(212) 586-7000. **$179-$699.** 1335 Ave of the Americas 10019. Between 53rd and 54th sts. Int corridors. **Pets:** Accepted.
SAVE 🍴 📶 📶 ⊠ 🔋

The New York Palace H
(212) 888-7000. **Call for rates.** 455 Madison Ave 10022. Between 50th and 51st sts. Int corridors. **Pets:** Accepted.
🍴 📶 ⊠ 📶 ⊠ 🔋 💻

The New York Renaissance Home and Guesthouse BB
(212) 470-3696. **Call for rates.** 464 W 141 St 10031. Between Amsterdam and Convent aves. Int corridors. **Pets:** Accepted.
🍴 📶 🔋 💻

The NoMad Hotel H
(212) 796-1500. **Call for rates.** 1170 Broadway 10001. At 28th St. Int corridors. **Pets:** Accepted. 🍴 📶 ⊠ 🔋

Novotel New York Times Square H
(212) 315-0100. **Call for rates.** 226 W 52nd St 10019. At Broadway. Int corridors. **Pets:** Accepted. 🍴 📶 📶 ⊠ 🔋 💻

NYLO New York City H
(212) 362-1100. **Call for rates.** 2178 Broadway 10024. At 77th St. Int corridors. **Pets:** Accepted. SAVE 🍴 📶 ⊠ 🔋 💻

Omni Berkshire Place H
(212) 753-5800. **Call for rates.** 21 E 52nd St 10022. Between Madison and 5th aves. Int corridors. **Pets:** Accepted.
SAVE 🍴 📶 📶 ⊠ 🔋 💻

The Paramount Hotel New York H
(212) 764-5500. **Call for rates.** 235 W 46th St 10036. Between Broadway and 8th Ave. Int corridors. **Pets:** Small, dogs only. $250 one-time fee/pet. Supervision. SAVE 🍴 📶 ⊠ 🔋

Park Hyatt New York H
(646) 774-1234. **Call for rates.** 153 W 57th St 10019. Between 6th (Ave of the Americas) and 7th aves. Int corridors. **Pets:** Accepted.
🍴 📶 ⊠ 📶 ⊠ 🔋 💻

The Peninsula New York H
(212) 956-2888. **Call for rates.** 700 5th Ave 10019. At 55th St. Int corridors. **Pets:** Accepted. SAVE 🍴 📶 ⊠ 📶 🔋 💻

The Pierre New York-A Taj Hotel H 🐾
(212) 838-8000. **$495-$1500.** 2 E 61st St 10065. At 5th Ave and E 61st St. Int corridors. **Pets:** Very small, dogs only. Supervision.
SAVE ECO 🍴 📶 📶 💻

The Plaza Hotel H
(212) 759-3000. **Call for rates.** 5th Ave at Central Park S 10019. Corner of 5th Ave and Central Park S. Int corridors. **Pets:** Accepted.
SAVE 🍴 📶 ⊠ 📶 ⊠ 🔋 💻

Radisson Martinique on Broadway H
(212) 736-3800. **Call for rates.** 49 W 32nd St 10001. Between Broadway and 5th Ave. Int corridors. **Pets:** Small, dogs only. $100 deposit/pet, $25 one-time fee/pet, $25 daily fee/pet. Service with restrictions, crate. SAVE 🍴 📶 📶 ⊠ 🔋 💻

Refinery Hotel New York H 🐾
(646) 664-0310. **Call for rates.** 63 W 38th St 10018. Between 5th and 6th (Ave of the Americas) aves. Int corridors. **Pets:** Large. $500 deposit/room. Service with restrictions, crate.
🍴 📶 📶 ⊠ 🔋 💻

Renaissance New York Hotel 57 H
(212) 753-8841. **$300-$769.** 130 E 57th St 10022. At Lexington Ave. Int corridors. **Pets:** Accepted. SAVE 🍴 📶 📶 ⊠ 🔋 💻

Renaissance New York Hotel Times Square H
(212) 765-7676. **$314-$804.** 2 Times Square, 7th Ave at W 48th St 10036. At Broadway and 7th Ave; motor access from 7th Ave, s of W 48th St. Int corridors. **Pets:** Accepted.
SAVE 🍴 📶 ⊠ 📶 ⊠ 🔋 💻

Residence Inn by Marriott Central Park H
(212) 324-3774. **$279-$838.** 1717 Broadway 10019. Between 54th and 55th sts; entrance on 54th St. Int corridors. **Pets:** Accepted.
SAVE 🍴 📶 📶 ⊠ 🔋 💻

Residence Inn by Marriott Manhattan/Midtown East H
(212) 980-1003. **$356-$746.** 148 E 48th St 10017. Between 3rd and Lexington aves. Int corridors. **Pets:** Accepted. 📶 📶 ⊠ 🔋 💻

The Ritz-Carlton New York, Battery Park H
(212) 344-0800. **$295-$895.** Two West St 10004. Jct Battery Pl. Int corridors. **Pets:** Accepted. SAVE 🍴 📶 ⊠ 📶 ⊠ 🔋 💻

The Ritz-Carlton New York, Central Park H
(212) 308-9100. **Call for rates.** 50 Central Park S 10019. Jct 59th St (Central Park S) and 6th Ave (Ave of the Americas). Int corridors.
Pets: Accepted. SAVE 🍴 📶 ⊠ 📶 ⊠ 🔋 💻

Royalton Hotel H
(212) 869-4400. **Call for rates.** 44 W 44th St 10036. Between 5th and 6th (Ave of the Americas) aves. Int corridors. **Pets:** Accepted.
🍴 📶 ⊠

The St. Regis New York H
(212) 753-4500. **$595-$1495.** 2 E 55th St 10022. Between Madison and 5th aves. Int corridors. **Pets:** Accepted.
SAVE 🍴 📶 📶 ⊠ 🔋 💻

Shelburne NYC, an Affinia hotel H
(212) 689-5200. **Call for rates.** 303 Lexington Ave 10016. Between 37th and 38th sts. Int corridors. **Pets:** Accepted.

Sheraton New York Times Square Hotel H ❖
(212) 581-1000. **$199-$699.** 811 7th Ave 10019. At 52nd St. Int corridors. **Pets:** Medium, dogs only. Service with restrictions, crate.

Sheraton Tribeca New York Hotel H
(212) 966-3400. **$299-$699.** 370 Canal St 10013. Just e of Broadway. Int corridors. **Pets:** Accepted.

The Shoreham Hotel H
(212) 247-6700. **Call for rates.** 33 W 55th St 10019. Between 5th and 6th (Ave of the Americas) aves. Int corridors. **Pets:** Accepted.

Skyline Hotel H ❖
(212) 586-3400. **Call for rates.** 725 10th Ave 10019. At 49th and 50th sts. Int corridors. **Pets:** Dogs only. $200 deposit/room. Service with restrictions, crate.

Smyth, a Thompson Hotel H
(212) 587-7000. **$365-$709, 3 day notice.** 85 W Broadway 10007. Between Chambers and Warren sts. Int corridors. **Pets:** Accepted.

Sofitel New York H
(212) 354-8844. **$199-$1200.** 45 W 44th St 10036. Between 5th and 6th (Ave of the Americas) aves. Int corridors. **Pets:** Accepted.

Staybridge Suites Times Square H
(212) 757-9000. **$169-$899, 3 day notice.** 340 W 40th St 10018. Between 8th and 9th aves. Int corridors. **Pets:** Accepted.

St Giles The Court-A Premier Hotel H
(212) 685-1100. **Call for rates.** 130 E 39th St 10016. Between Park and Lexington aves. Int corridors. **Pets:** Accepted.

The Surrey H
(212) 288-3700. **Call for rates.** 20 E 76th St 10021. Jct E 76th St and Madison Ave. Int corridors. **Pets:** Accepted.

Trump International Hotel & Tower H ❖
(212) 299-1000. **$795-$3700, 3 day notice.** 1 Central Park W 10023. Jct Central Park S; at Columbus Cir. Int corridors. **Pets:** Small, dogs only. $250 one-time fee/room. Service with restrictions.

Trump SoHo® New York H ❖
(212) 842-5500. **Call for rates.** 246 Spring St 10013. Between Varick St and 6th Ave (Ave of the Americas). Int corridors. **Pets:** Small. $250 one-time fee/room. Service with restrictions, supervision.

TRYP Times Square South H
(212) 600-2440. **$179-$499.** 345 W 35th St 10001. Between 8th and 9th aves. Int corridors. **Pets:** Medium. $30 daily fee/room. Service with restrictions, crate.

Viceroy New York H
(212) 830-8000. **Call for rates.** 120 W 57th St 10019. Between 6th (Ave of the Americas) and 7th aves. Int corridors. **Pets:** Accepted.

Waldorf Astoria New York H ❖
(212) 355-3000. **$217-$665.** 301 Park Ave 10022. Between E 49th and 50th sts. Int corridors. **Pets:** Small. $50 one-time fee/pet. Service with restrictions, supervision.

Warwick New York Hotel H
(212) 247-2700. **Call for rates.** 65 W 54th St 10019. At 6th Ave (Ave of the Americas). Int corridors. **Pets:** Medium, dogs only. $50 one-time fee/pet. Designated rooms, service with restrictions, supervision.

The Westin New York at Times Square H
(212) 201-2700. **$199-$549.** 270 W 43rd St 10036. Corner of 8th Ave. Int corridors. **Pets:** Accepted.

The Westin New York Grand Central H
(212) 490-8900. **$199-$599.** 212 E 42nd St 10017. Between 2nd and 3rd aves. Int corridors. **Pets:** Accepted.

W New York H
(212) 755-1200. **$179-$799.** 541 Lexington Ave 10022. At 49th St. Int corridors. **Pets:** Accepted.

W New York Downtown H
(646) 826-8600. **$249-$789.** 123 Washington St 10006. At Albany St. Int corridors. **Pets:** Accepted.

W New York Times Square H
(212) 930-7400. **$299-$1499.** 1567 Broadway at 47th St 10036. Corner of 47th St. Int corridors. **Pets:** Accepted.

W New York-Union Square H ❖
(212) 253-9119. **$299-$5000.** 201 Park Ave S 10003. At 17th St. Int corridors. **Pets:** Medium, other species. $100 one-time fee/room, $25 daily fee/room. Designated rooms, service with restrictions, supervision.

Wyndham Garden Chinatown H
(646) 329-3400. **$149-$549.** 93 Bowery 10002. At Hester St. Int corridors. **Pets:** Accepted.

Wyndham Midtown 45 H
(212) 867-5100. **$199-$499.** 205 E 45th St 10017. At 3rd Ave. Int corridors. **Pets:** Accepted.

NIAGARA FALLS

Four Points by Sheraton Niagara Falls H
(716) 299-0344. **$145-$295.** 7001 Buffalo Ave 14304. I-190 exit 21 (Robert Moses Pkwy), just e. Int corridors. **Pets:** Accepted.

Motel 6 H
(716) 297-9902. **Call for rates.** 9100 Niagara Falls Blvd 14304. I-190 exit 22, 1.8 mi e. Int corridors. **Pets:** Other species. Service with restrictions, crate.

Quality Hotel & Suites "At the Falls" H
(716) 282-1212. **$80-$210.** 240 First St 14303. I-190 exit 21 (Robert Moses Pkwy) eastbound to City Traffic exit, just w; downtown. Int corridors. **Pets:** $30 one-time fee/pet. Service with restrictions, crate.

Sheraton At The Falls H
(716) 285-3361. **$99-$299.** 300 3rd St 14303. I-190 exit 21 (Robert Moses Pkwy) to City Traffic exit, just w on Rainbow Blvd, just n. Int corridors. **Pets:** Accepted.

NORHT SYRACUSE

△△△ **▽▽▽▽** **BEST WESTERN Syracuse Airport Inn** **H**
(315) 455-7362. **$90-$200.** 900 Col. Eileen Collins Blvd 13212. I-81 exit 27 (Syracuse Hancock International Airport). Int corridors.
Pets: Accepted. [SAVE] [⊓] [≥] [☞] [✕] [⊟] [▣]

▽▽▽▽ **Candlewood Suites Syracuse Airport** **H** ❀
(315) 454-8999. **$89-$249.** 5414 South Bay Rd 13212. I-90 exit 36; I-81 exit 26 (Mattydale Rd), follow South Bay Rd signs, just n. Int corridors.
Pets: $10 daily fee/pet. Service with restrictions, crate. [☞] [⊟] [▣]

▽▽▽▽ **Comfort Inn & Suites/Syracuse Airport** **H**
(315) 457-4000. **$86-$146.** 6701 Buckley Rd 13212. I-81 exit 25 (7th North St), just w. Int corridors. **Pets:** Large, other species. $25 one-time fee/pet. Designated rooms, service with restrictions, crate.
[⊓] [≥] [☞] [✕] [⊟] [▣]

NORWICH

▽▽▽ **Super 8 of Norwich** **H**
(607) 336-8880. **$55-$110.** 6067 State Hwy 12 13815. On SR 12, 0.9 mi n. Int corridors. **Pets:** $11 daily fee/pet. Service with restrictions, supervision. [☞] [⊟] [▣]

OGDENSBURG

△△△ **▽▽▽▽** **Quality Inn Gran-View** **M**
(315) 393-4550. **$115-$365.** 6765 SR 37 13669. On SR 37, 3 mi sw. Ext/int corridors. **Pets:** $10 daily fee/pet. Designated rooms, service with restrictions, crate. [SAVE] [⊓] [≥] [✕] [☞] [✕] [⊟] [▣]

△△△ **▽▽▽** **Windjammer Lodge** **M**
(315) 393-6300. **Call for rates.** 5843 SR 37 13669. On SR 37, 5 mi sw. Ext corridors. **Pets:** Other species. $10 daily fee/pet. Designated rooms, service with restrictions, crate. [SAVE] [⊓] [≥] [☞] [⊟] [▣]

OLD FORGE

▽▽▽ **Adirondack Lodge Old Forge** **M**
(315) 369-6836. **$69-$229.** 2752 SR 28 13420. 0.3 mi s. Ext/int corridors. **Pets:** Dogs only. $25 one-time fee/room. Designated rooms, service with restrictions, supervision. [⊓] [≥] [✕] [☞] [⊟] [▣]

ONEIDA

▽▽ **Super 8-Oneida** **H**
(315) 363-5168. **$60-$190.** 215 Genesee St 13421. I-90 exit 33, 4 mi s on SR 365 to SR 5, then 0.5 mi w. Int corridors. **Pets:** Accepted.
[☞] [⊟] [▣]

ONEONTA

▽▽▽▽ **Holiday Inn Oneonta/Cooperstown Area** **H**
(607) 433-2250. **Call for rates.** 5206 State Hwy 23 13820. I-88 exit 15 (SR 23 and 28), 1.5 mi e. Int corridors. **Pets:** Accepted.
[⊓] [♿M] [≥] [☞] [✕] [⊟] [▣]

OSWEGO

▽▽▽ **Quality Inn & Suites - Riverfront** **H**
(315) 343-1600. **$135-$184.** 70 E 1st St 13126. Just n on SR 481. Int corridors. **Pets:** Accepted. [⊓] [☞] [✕] [⊟] [▣]

PAINTED POST

△△△ **▽** **Americas Best Value Inn Lodge on the Green** **M** ❀
(607) 962-2456. **$76-$160.** 196 S Hamilton St 14870. I-86/SR 17 exit 44B, 0.5 mi sw on SR 417 W; US 15 exit 3, 0.8 mi ne on SR 417 E, then just w on Canada Rd. Ext corridors. **Pets:** Dogs only. $10 one-time fee/room. Service with restrictions, supervision.
[SAVE] [⊓] [≥] [☞] [⊟] [▣]

PEMBROKE

▽▽▽▽ **Darien Lakes Econo Lodge** **H**
(585) 599-4681. **$59-$199.** 8493 Alleghany Rd 14036. I-90 exit 48A, just s. Int corridors. **Pets:** Other species. $20 deposit/room. Designated rooms, service with restrictions, supervision. [☞] [⊟] [▣]

PENN YAN

△△△ **▽▽▽▽** **BEST WESTERN PLUS Vineyard Inn & Suites** **H**
(315) 536-8473. **$120-$185.** 142 Lake St 14527. I-90 exit 43, just e on SR 54, then just s; corner of SR 54 and 14A. Int corridors.
Pets: Accepted. [SAVE] [≥] [☞] [✕] [⊟] [▣]

PINE VALLEY

▽▽ **Rodeway Inn Marshall Manor** **M**
(607) 739-3891. **$86-$186.** 3527 Watkins Rd 14845. I-86 exit 52B, 5 mi n on SR 14. Ext corridors. **Pets:** Accepted. [≥] [☞] [⊟] [▣]

PLAINVIEW

▽▽▽ **Homewood Suites Long Island Melville** **H**
(516) 293-4663. **$209-$259.** 1585 Round Swamp Rd 11803. I-495 exit 48, just s. Int corridors. **Pets:** Accepted.
[⊏] [⊓] [♿M] [≥] [☞] [⊟] [▣]

▽▽▽▽ **Residence Inn by Marriott Plainview Long Island** **H**
(516) 433-6200. **$172-$282.** 9 Gerhard Rd 11803. I-495 exit 44, 1.6 mi s on SR 135 exit 10, then just e on Old Country Rd. Int corridors.
Pets: Accepted. [⊓] [♿M] [≥] [✕] [☞] [✕] [⊟] [▣]

PLATTSBURGH

△△△ **▽▽▽▽** **BEST WESTERN PLUS The Inn at Smithfield** **H**
(518) 561-7750. **$110-$140.** 446 Rt 3 12901. I-87 exit 37, just e. Int corridors. **Pets:** Accepted. [SAVE] [⊓] [♿M] [≥] [☞] [✕] [⊟] [▣]

▽▽▽ **Comfort Inn & Suites Plattsburgh New York** **H**
(518) 562-2730. **$129-$259.** 411 Rt 3 12901. I-87 exit 37, 0.5 mi e. Int corridors. **Pets:** Accepted. [⊓] [♿M] [≥] [✕] [☞] [✕] [⊟] [▣]

▽▽▽ **La Quinta Inn & Suites Plattsburgh** **H**
(518) 562-4000. **$72-$329.** 16 Plaza Blvd 12901. I-87 exit 37, just w. Int corridors. **Pets:** Large, other species. Service with restrictions.
[♿M] [≥] [☞] [⊟] [▣]

▽▽ **Microtel Inn & Suites by Wyndham Plattsburgh** **H**
(518) 324-3800. **$69-$154.** 554 SR 3 12901. I-87 exit 37, just w. Int corridors. **Pets:** Medium. $10 daily fee/room. Service with restrictions, supervision. [♿M] [☞] [✕] [⊟] [▣]

POUGHKEEPSIE

△△△ **▽▽▽** **BEST WESTERN PLUS The Inn & Suites at the Falls** **H**
(845) 462-5770. **$99-$350.** 50 Red Oaks Mill Rd (CR 44) 12603. Jct SR 376 and CR 113, just se. Int corridors. **Pets:** Medium, dogs only. $25 daily fee/pet. Designated rooms, service with restrictions, supervision. [SAVE] [⊓] [♿M] [☞] [✕] [⊟] [▣]

△△△ **▽▽▽** **Days Inn** **M**
(845) 454-1010. **$100-$160.** 536 Haight Ave 12603. 2 mi e of Mid-Hudson Bridge on US 44 and SR 55. Ext/int corridors. **Pets:** Dogs only. $30 one-time fee/pet. Designated rooms, service with restrictions, crate.
[SAVE] [≥] [☞] [⊟] [▣]

QUEENSBURY

▽▽ **Quality Inn of Glens Falls** **H**
(518) 793-3800. **$85-$229.** 547 Aviation Rd 12804. I-87 exit 19, just e. Int corridors. **Pets:** Accepted. [♿M] [≥] [☞] [✕] [⊟] [▣]

RHINEBECK

▽▽▽▽ **Beekman Arms & Delamater Inn and Conference Center** **CI**
(845) 876-7077. **Call for rates.** 6387 Mill St (Rt 9) 12572. Jct US 9 and SR 308; center of village. Ext/int corridors. **Pets:** Accepted.
[⊓] [☞] [⊟] [▣]

RIVERHEAD

▼▼▼ Holiday Inn Express East End 🄷
(631) 548-1000. **$126-$400.** 1707 Old Country Rd (SR 58) 11901. I-495 exit 73, 0.5 mi e. Int corridors. **Pets:** Accepted.
�

▼▼▼ Hotel Indigo East End 🄷
(631) 369-2200. **Call for rates.** 1830 SR 25 11901. I-495 exit 72 (SR 25 E). Int corridors. **Pets:** Accepted. 🍽 ⤳ 📶 ✕ 🛏 🖥

🔺 ▼▼▼ Hyatt Place Long Island/East End 🄷
(631) 208-0002. **$119-$419.** 451 E Main St 11901. On SR 25. Int corridors. **Pets:** Accepted. 〔SAVE〕 🍽 📶 ⤳ 📶 ✕ 🛏 🖥

ROCHESTER

▼▼ La Quinta Inn Rochester North 🄷
(585) 254-1000. **$72-$205.** 1956 Lyell Ave 14606. I-390 exit 21 (SR 31), just e. Int corridors. **Pets:** Large, other species. Service with restrictions. 🍽 📶 🛏 🖥

▼▼▼ Radisson Hotel Rochester Riverside 🄷
(585) 546-6400. **Call for rates.** 120 E Main St 14604. Downtown. Int corridors. **Pets:** Accepted. 🍽 📶 📶 ✕ 🛏 🖥

🔺 ▼▼▼ Rochester Plaza Hotel & Conference Center
(585) 546-3450. **$99-$269.** 70 State St 14614. Jct Main St; downtown. Int corridors. **Pets:** Small. $25 one-time fee/pet. Designated rooms, service with restrictions, supervision.
〔SAVE〕 🍽 ⤳ 📶 ✕ 🛏 🖥

ROME

🔺 ▼▼▼ Inn at the Beeches 🄼
(315) 336-1775. **$95-$295.** 7900 Turin Rd 13440. Jct SR 46, 2 mi n on SR 26 (Turin Rd). Ext corridors. **Pets:** Accepted.
〔SAVE〕 🍽 ⤳ 📶 🛏 🖥

RYE BROOK

🔺 ▼▼▼ Hilton Westchester 🄷 🐾
(914) 939-6300. **$149-$269.** 699 Westchester Ave 10573. I-287 (Cross Westchester Expwy) exit 10 eastbound, 0.6 mi ne on SR 120A; exit westbound, 0.3 mi n on Webb Ave, then 0.4 mi ne on SR 120A. Int corridors. **Pets:** Large, dogs only. $75 one-time fee/room. Service with restrictions, supervision. 〔SAVE〕 🍽 📶 ⤳ ✕ 📶 ✕ 🛏 🖥

SACKETS HARBOR

▼▼ Ontario Place Hotel 🄷 🐾
(315) 646-8000. **Call for rates.** 103 General Smith Dr 13685. Corner of W Main St; center. Int corridors. **Pets:** Other species. $25 one-time fee/room. Designated rooms, service with restrictions.
📶 ✕ 🛏 🖥

SALAMANCA

▼▼▼ Holiday Inn Express & Suites 🄷
(716) 945-7600. **$140-$190.** 779 Broad St 14779. I-86 exit 20, just n. Int corridors. **Pets:** Other species. $50 deposit/room, $25 one-time fee/room. Designated rooms, service with restrictions, supervision.
📶 ⤳ 📶 ✕ 🛏 🖥

SARANAC LAKE

▼ Adirondack Motel 🄼
(518) 891-2116. **$79-$285.** 248 Lake Flower Ave 12983. 0.5 mi e on SR 86. Ext corridors. **Pets:** Dogs only. $15 daily fee/pet. Service with restrictions, supervision. 🍽 📶 ✕ 🛏 🖥

🔺 ▼▼▼ BEST WESTERN Mountain Lake Inn 🄷
(518) 891-1970. **$92-$299.** 487 Lake Flower Ave 12983. 1.1 mi e on SR 86. Int corridors. **Pets:** Other species. $20 one-time fee/room. Designated rooms, service with restrictions, supervision.
〔SAVE〕 🍽 ⤳ 📶 ✕ 🛏 🖥

▼ Lake Flower Inn 🄼
(518) 891-2310. **Call for rates.** 234 Lake Flower Ave 12983. 0.5 mi e on SR 86. Ext corridors. **Pets:** Accepted. 🍽 ⤳ 📶 ✕ 🛏

▼ Lake Side Motel 🄼
(518) 891-4333. **Call for rates.** 256 Lake Flower Ave 12983. 0.6 mi e on SR 86. Ext corridors. **Pets:** Accepted. 🍽 ⤳ 📶 ✕ 🛏

SARATOGA SPRINGS

🔺 ▼▼▼ BEST WESTERN PLUS Park Inn 🄷
(518) 584-2350. **$99-$400, 3 day notice.** 3291 S Broadway 12866. I-87 exit 13N, 1.1 mi n on US 9. Int corridors. **Pets:** $20 daily fee/pet. Service with restrictions. 〔SAVE〕 🍽 📶 ⤳ 📶 ✕ 🛏 🖥

▼▼▼ Holiday Inn 🄷 🐾
(518) 584-4550. **$149-$499.** 232 Broadway 12866. Jct SR 50, on US 9. Int corridors. **Pets:** Other species. Service with restrictions.
🍽 ⤳ 📶 ✕ 🛏 🖥

▼▼▼ Residence Inn by Marriott-Saratoga Springs 🄷
(518) 584-9600. **$118-$401.** 295 Excelsior Ave 12866. I-87 exit 15, just n, just s, then just e. Int corridors. **Pets:** Accepted.
🍽 📶 ⤳ 📶 ✕ 🛏 🖥

🔺 ▼▼▼ Saratoga Downtowner Motel 🄼
(518) 584-6160. **$79-$309, 7 day notice.** 413 Broadway 12866. On US 9; corner of Division St. Ext/int corridors. **Pets:** Accepted.
〔SAVE〕 ⤳ 📶 ✕ 🛏

▼▼▼ The Saratoga Hilton 🄷
(518) 584-4000. **$109-$529.** 534 Broadway 12866. I-87 exit 15, on SR 50. Int corridors. **Pets:** Accepted. 🍽 📶 ⤳ 📶 🛏 🖥

▼▼▼ Union Gables Inn and Suites 🄱🄱
(518) 584-1558. **Call for rates.** 55 Union Ave 12866. I-87 exit 14, 1.5 mi w. Int corridors. **Pets:** Accepted. 📶 ✕ 🗾 🛏 🖥

SENECA FALLS

🔺 ▼▼▼ Microtel Inn & Suites by Wyndham Seneca Falls 🄷
(315) 539-8438. **$60-$130.** 1966 Rt 5 & 20 13148. I-90 (New York State Thruway) exit 41, 4 mi s on SR 414, then just e. Int corridors. **Pets:** Other species. $15 daily fee/room. Service with restrictions, supervision. 〔SAVE〕 📶 📶 🛏 🖥

SKANEATELES

🔺 ▼▼▼ Finger Lakes Lodging 🄼
(315) 217-0222. **$69-$285, 7 day notice.** 834 W Genesee St 13152. On US 20, just w. Ext/int corridors. **Pets:** Accepted.
〔SAVE〕 📶 ✕ 🛏

▼▼▼ Skaneateles Suites 🄼
(315) 685-7568. **$99-$175.** 4114 W Genesee St 13152. On US 20, 2 mi w. Ext corridors. **Pets:** Other species. $35 one-time fee/pet. Service with restrictions. 🍽 📶 ✕ 🛏 🖥

SOLVAY

▼▼ Clarion Inn & Suites 🄷
(315) 457-8700. **$70-$129.** 100 Farrell Rd 13209. I-690 exit 3 (Farrell Rd) westbound; exit 4 (John Glenn Blvd) eastbound, just n to Farrell Rd. Int corridors. **Pets:** Medium, other species. $25 one-time fee/pet. Service with restrictions, crate. 🍽 ⤳ 📶 ✕ 🛏 🖥

SOUTHAMPTON

🔺 ▼▼▼ Southampton Inn 🄷 🐾
(631) 283-6500. **$159-$499, 30 day notice.** 91 Hill St 11968. 0.3 mi n from corner of Main St and Jobs Ln. Int corridors. **Pets:** Other species. $49 daily fee/pet. Designated rooms, service with restrictions, supervision. 〔SAVE〕 🍽 📶 ⤳ 📶 📶 ✕ 🛏

SPRINGVILLE

▼▼ Microtel Inn & Suites by Wyndham Springville ⛊
(716) 592-3141. **$70-$119.** 270 S Cascade Dr 14141. Just s off SR 39 E. Int corridors. **Pets:** Accepted. ⛊Ⓜ 🛜 ✕ ⛊ 🖥

STATEN ISLAND

◈◈◈ ▼▼▼ Hilton Garden Inn Staten Island ⛊
(718) 477-2400. **$189-$219.** 1100 South Ave 10314. I-278 exit 6 (South Ave) westbound, just s; exit 5 eastbound to SR 440 S to South Ave exit, just s, then 1 mi n to Lois Ln. Int corridors. **Pets:** Accepted.
⟨SAVE⟩ 🍽 ⛊Ⓜ 🏊 ✕ 🛜 ✕ ⛊ 🖥

STONY BROOK

▼▼▼ Holiday Inn Express Stony Brook ⛊
(631) 471-8000. **$139-$199.** 3131 Nesconset Hwy 11720. I-495 exit 62 (CR 97/Nicolls Rd N), 8 mi n, then 0.6 mi e on SR 347. Int corridors. **Pets:** Accepted. 🍽 ⛊Ⓜ 🏊 🛜 ✕ ⛊ 🖥

SUFFERN

◈◈◈ ▼▼▼ Crowne Plaza Suffern-Mahwah Hotel and Conference Center ⛊
(845) 357-4800. **$129-$189.** 3 Executive Blvd 10901. I-87 (New York State Thruway) exit 14B, just n. Int corridors. **Pets:** Medium, dogs only. $50 one-time fee/room. Designated rooms, service with restrictions, supervision. ⟨SAVE⟩ 🍽 🛜 ✕ ⛊ 🖥

SYRACUSE *(Restaurants p. 637)*

▼▼ Comfort Inn-Carrier Circle ⛊
(315) 437-0222. **$78-$139.** 6491 Thompson Rd S 13206. I-90 exit 35 (Carrier Cir), just s. Ext/int corridors. **Pets:** Accepted.
🍽 🛜 ⛊ 🖥

◈◈◈ ▼▼▼▼ Crowne Plaza Syracuse-Hotel & Conference Center ⛊ 🐾
(315) 479-7000. **Call for rates.** 701 E Genesee St 13210. Jct Almond St; downtown. Int corridors. **Pets:** Other species. $50 one-time fee/pet. Designated rooms, service with restrictions, crate.
⟨SAVE⟩ 🍽 ⛊Ⓜ 🛜 ✕ ⛊ 🖥

▼▼▼ Genesee Grande Hotel ⛊
(315) 476-4212. **Call for rates.** 1060 E Genesee St 13210. I-81 exit 18, 0.7 mi e on SR 92 (Genesee St). Int corridors. **Pets:** Accepted.
🍽 🛜 ✕ ⛊ 🖥

◈◈◈ ▼▼▼▼ Red Roof Inn Syracuse Ⓜ
(315) 437-3309. **Call for rates.** 6614 N Thompson Rd 13206. I-90 exit 35 (Carrier Cir), just n. Ext corridors. **Pets:** Large, other species. Service with restrictions, supervision. ⟨SAVE⟩ 🛜 ✕ ⛊ 🖥

◈◈◈ ▼▼▼▼ Sheraton Syracuse University Hotel & Conference Center ⛊ 🐾
(315) 475-3000. **$150-$350.** 801 University Ave 13210. I-81 exit 18, just e. Int corridors. **Pets:** Medium, dogs only. Service with restrictions, supervision. ⟨SAVE⟩ ⓔⓒⓞ 🍽 🏊 🛜 ⛊ 🖥

TARRYTOWN

▼▼▼▼ DoubleTree by Hilton Hotel Tarrytown ⛊
(914) 631-5700. **$169-$259.** 455 S Broadway 10591. I-87 (New York State Thruway) exit 9, just s on US 9. Int corridors. **Pets:** Accepted.
🍽 ⛊Ⓜ 🏊 ✕ 🔊 ✕ ⛊ 🖥

◈◈◈ ▼▼▼▼ Sheraton Tarrytown Hotel ⛊
(914) 332-7900. **$139-$249.** 600 White Plains Rd 10591. I-87 exit 9 northbound, 0.8 mi e on SR 119; exit southbound, just n on US 9, then 1 mi e on SR 119. Int corridors. **Pets:** Accepted.
⟨SAVE⟩ 🍽 ⛊Ⓜ 🏊 🛜 ✕ ⛊ 🖥

▼▼▼ Westchester Marriott Hotel ⛊
(914) 631-2200. **$187-$307.** 670 White Plains Rd 10591. I-87 (New York State Thruway) exit 9 northbound, 0.8 mi e on SR 119; exit southbound, just n on US 9, then 1 mi e on SR 119. Int corridors.
Pets: Accepted. ⓔⓒⓞ 🍽 🏊 ✕ 🛜 ✕ ⛊ 🖥

TICONDEROGA

▼▼ Super 8-Ticonderoga ⛊
(518) 585-2617. **$70-$75.** 1144 Wicker St 12883. Jct SR 9N and 74/22. Int corridors. **Pets:** Accepted. 🛜 ✕ ⛊ 🖥

TONAWANDA

▼▼ Econo Lodge Ⓜ
(716) 694-6696. **$230.** 2000 Niagara Falls Blvd 14150. I-290 exit 3 (Niagara Falls Blvd), 0.5 mi n on US 62. Ext/int corridors.
Pets: Accepted. 🍽 🛜 ⛊

TROY

◈◈◈ ▼▼▼▼ BEST WESTERN PLUS Franklin Square Inn Troy/Albany ⛊ 🐾
(518) 274-8800. **$102-$180.** One 4th St 12180. I-787 exit 8, just e on 23rd to Federal St, just e to 4th St, then just s; downtown. Int corridors. **Pets:** Other species. $25 one-time fee/room. Service with restrictions, supervision. ⟨SAVE⟩ ⛊Ⓜ 🛜 ✕ ⛊ 🖥

TULLY

◈◈◈ ▼▼▼ BEST WESTERN Tully Inn ⛊
(315) 696-6061. **$80-$299.** 5779 SR 80 13159. I-81 exit 14, just e. Int corridors. **Pets:** Accepted. ⟨SAVE⟩ 🍽 🛜 🖥

UTICA

◈◈◈ ▼▼▼ BEST WESTERN Gateway Adirondack Inn ⛊
(315) 732-4121. **$89-$179.** 175 N Genesee St 13502. I-90 (New York State Thruway) exit 31, 0.5 mi s. Int corridors. **Pets:** Accepted.
⟨SAVE⟩ 🛜 ✕ ⛊ 🖥

▼▼▼▼ Hotel Utica, an Ascend Hotel Collection Member ⛊
(315) 724-7829. **$119-$169.** 102 Lafayette St 13502. I-90 (New York State Thruway) exit 31, 1.1 mi s on Genesee St; center. Int corridors.
Pets: Accepted. 🍽 🛜 ✕ ⛊ 🖥

◈◈◈ ▼▼▼ Red Roof Inn Utica Ⓜ
(315) 724-7128. **Call for rates.** 20 Weaver St 13502. I-90 (New York State Thruway) exit 31. Ext corridors. **Pets:** Large, other species. Service with restrictions, supervision. ⟨SAVE⟩ 🛜 ✕ ⛊ 🖥

▼▼▼ Rosemont Inn Bed & Breakfast ⒷⒷ
(315) 797-9033. **Call for rates.** 1423 Genesee St 13501. I-90 (New York State Thruway) exit 31, 2.5 mi s. Int corridors. **Pets:** Accepted.
🍽 🛜 ✕ ⓩ

VERONA

▼▼▼ La Quinta Inn & Suites Verona ⛊
(315) 231-5080. **$129-$364.** 5394 Willow Pl 13478. I-90 exit 33, just s on SR 365, then 0.5 mi n. Int corridors. **Pets:** Large, other species. Service with restrictions. 🍽 ⛊Ⓜ 🏊 🛜 ⛊ 🖥

▼▼ Microtel Inn & Suites by Wyndham Verona ⛊ 🐾
(315) 363-1850. **$81-$135.** 5118 NY S Rt 365 13478. I-90 (New York State Thruway) exit 33, 0.5 mi s. Int corridors. **Pets:** Large. $20 one-time fee/pet. Service with restrictions, crate. 🍽 🛜 ✕ ⛊ 🖥

VICTOR

◈◈◈ ▼▼▼▼ BEST WESTERN PLUS Victor Inn & Suites ⛊
(585) 924-3933. **$100-$130.** 7449 SR 96 14564. I-90 (New York State Thruway) exit 45, 0.5 mi s. Int corridors. **Pets:** Small, dogs only. $35 daily fee/room. Designated rooms, service with restrictions, supervision.
⟨SAVE⟩ ⛊Ⓜ 🏊 🛜 ⛊ 🖥

 **Hampton Inn & Suites-Rochester/Victor** H ❖

(585) 924-4400. **$119-$219.** 7637 Pittsford-Victor Rd/SR 96 14564. I-90 (New York State Thruway) exit 45, just n. Int corridors. **Pets:** Large, other species. Designated rooms, service with restrictions, supervision.

SAVE 🏊 📶 ⊗ 🔌 📺

Homewood Suites by Hilton H

(585) 869-7500. **$129-$199.** 575 Fishers Station Dr 14564. I-90 (New York State Thruway) exit 45, just s on SR 96, then just w. Int corridors. **Pets:** Accepted. 📶 🏊 📶 ⊗ 🔌 📺

Microtel Inn by Wyndham Victor/Rochester H

(585) 924-9240. **$55-$119.** 7498 Main St Fishers 14564. I-90 (New York State Thruway) exit 45, just s on SR 96, then just e. Int corridors. **Pets:** $15 daily fee/room. Service with restrictions, supervision.

📶 ⊗ 🔌 📺

WARNERS

Holiday Inn Express Syracuse/Fairgrounds H

(315) 701-5000. **$109-$239, 3 day notice.** 6946 Winchell Rd 13164. I-690 exit 5 eastbound, just n on State Fair Blvd; exit westbound, just s on State Fair Blvd, 1 mi w on Walters Rd, then just n. Int corridors. **Pets:** Medium, dogs only. $50 one-time fee/room. Service with restrictions, crate. 📶 🏊 📶 ⊗ 🔌 📺

WARRENSBURG

Warrensburg Super 8 M ❖

(518) 623-2811. **$85-$95.** 3619 SR 9 12845. I-87 exit 23, just w. Int corridors. **Pets:** Other species. $15 one-time fee/room. Designated rooms, service with restrictions, crate. 🍴 📶 ⊗ 🔌 📺

WATERLOO

Holiday Inn Waterloo-Seneca Falls H

(315) 539-5011. **$89-$249.** 2468 SR 414 13165. I-90 (New York State Thruway) exit 41, 4 mi s; just n of jct SR 414/5 and US 20. Int corridors. **Pets:** Large. $15 daily fee/room. Service with restrictions, supervision. 🍴 📶 🏊 ⊗ 📶 ⊗ 🔌 📺

WATERTOWN

BEST WESTERN Watertown Fort Drum H ❖

(315) 782-8000. **$90-$170.** 300 Washington St 13601. Center. Int corridors. **Pets:** Medium, other species. $15 daily fee/room. Designated rooms, service with restrictions, crate.

SAVE ECO 🍴 🏊 📶 ⊗ 🔌 📺

Comfort Inn & Suites H ❖

(315) 782-2700. **$89-$149.** 110 Commerce Park Dr 13601. I-81 exit 45, 0.4 mi e on Arsenal St, then just n. Int corridors. **Pets:** Other species. $25 one-time fee/pet. Service with restrictions, crate.

🏊 📶 🔌 📺

WATKINS GLEN

Anchor Inn and Marina M ❖

(607) 535-4159. **$69-$189, 15 day notice.** 3425 Salt Point Rd 14891. Just n on SR 14, 0.8 mi n. Ext corridors. **Pets:** Medium, dogs only. $25 deposit/pet. Service with restrictions, supervision. 🍴 📶 ⊗

WELLSVILLE

Microtel Inn & Suites by Wyndham Wellsville H

(585) 593-3449. **$70-$119.** 30 W Dyke St 14895. Just n off SR 19 and 417. Int corridors. **Pets:** Medium, other species. $15 daily fee/pet. Service with restrictions, supervision. 📶 🔌 📺

WESTBURY

Viana Hotel & Spa H

(516) 338-7777. **Call for rates.** 3998 Brush Hollow Rd 11590. Northern Pkwy exit 34, just ne. Int corridors. **Pets:** Accepted.

🍴 🏊 ⊗ 📶 ⊗ 🔌 📺

WEST COXSACKIE

BEST WESTERN New Baltimore Inn H

(518) 731-8100. **$100-$140.** 12600 Rt 9W 12192. I-87 (New York State Thruway) exit 21B, 0.5 mi s. Int corridors. **Pets:** Medium. $20 daily fee/room. Designated rooms, service with restrictions, supervision.

SAVE 🍴 🏊 ⊗ 📶 ⊗ 🔌 📺

WEST SENECA

Staybridge Suites Buffalo-South H

(716) 939-3100. **$139-$429.** 164 Slade Ave 14224. I-90 exit 55 (Ridge Rd E), just n. Int corridors. **Pets:** Accepted. 📶 🏊 📶 🔌 📺

WHITE PLAINS

HYATT house White Plains H

(914) 251-9700. **$119-$339.** 101 Corporate Park Dr 10604. I-287 (Cross Westchester Expwy) exit 9A eastbound, 0.6 mi e on Westchester Ave, then 0.3 mi n; exit 9N-S westbound, 0.9 mi w on Westchester Ave. Int corridors. **Pets:** Medium. $200 one-time fee/room. Designated rooms, service with restrictions, crate.

SAVE 🍴 📶 🏊 📶 ⊗ 🔌 📺

Residence Inn by Marriott White Plains H

(914) 761-7700. **$195-$321.** 5 Barker Ave 10601. I-287 exit 6 westbound, w on service road to SR 22 (Broadway), 0.8 mi s to Barker Ave, then 0.5 mi w; exit eastbound, s on Broadway. Int corridors. **Pets:** Accepted. 🍴 📶 ⊗ 🔌 📺

WILLIAMSVILLE

Residence Inn by Marriott Buffalo/Amherst H

(716) 632-6622. **$111-$217.** 100 Maple Rd 14221. I-290 exit 5B, just n on Millersport Hwy exit Maple Rd, then just e. Ext corridors. **Pets:** Other species. $50 one-time fee/room. Service with restrictions.

🍴 📶 🏊 📶 ⊗ 🔌 📺

WILMINGTON

Hungry Trout Resort M

(518) 946-2217. **Call for rates.** 5239 Rt 86 12997. On SR 86, 2 mi w. Ext corridors. **Pets:** Accepted. 🍴 🏊 ⊗ 📶 ⊗ 🔌 📺

Ledge Rock at Whiteface M

(518) 946-2379. **Call for rates.** 5078 NYS Rt 86 12997. On SR 86, 3 mi w. Ext corridors. **Pets:** $25 daily fee/pet. Service with restrictions.

🍴 🏊 📶 ⊗ 🔌 📺

Willkommen Hof Bed & Breakfast BB ❖

(518) 946-7669. **$79-$259, 21 day notice.** 5367 SR 86 12997. On SR 86, 1.5 mi sw of jct CR 431. Int corridors. **Pets:** Large, other species. $50 deposit/room, $10 daily fee/pet. Designated rooms, service with restrictions, crate. SAVE 🍴 ⊗ 📶 ⊗ 🎦 🔌 📺

WOODBURY

BEST WESTERN Woodbury Inn M

(516) 921-6900. **$109-$189.** 7940 Jericho Tpke (SR 25) 11797. Jct SR 25 and 135, 0.9 mi e. Ext/int corridors. **Pets:** Accepted.

SAVE 🍴 🏊 📶 ⊗ 🔌 📺

The Inn at Fox Hollow H

(516) 224-8100. **Call for rates.** 7755 Jericho Tpke 11797. Jct SR 25 and 135, 0.4 mi e. Int corridors. **Pets:** Accepted.

SAVE 📶 ⊗ 🔌 📺

YONKERS

Hampton Inn & Suites H ❖

(914) 377-1144. **$189-$269.** 160 Corporate Blvd 10701. Sawmill Pkwy exit 9, 0.8 mi w. Int corridors. **Pets:** $250 deposit/room. Designated rooms, service with restrictions, crate. 🍴 🏊 📶 🔌 📺

ABERDEEN

Hampton Inn & Suites H
(910) 693-4330. **$89-$189.** 200 Columbus Dr 28315. Jct US 1, just n on US 15/501, then just s. Int corridors. **Pets:** Accepted.

ALBEMARLE

Quality Inn M
(704) 983-6990. **$76-$85.** 735 NC 24/27 Bypass E 28001. Jct US 52 S, 1.4 mi e. Ext corridors. **Pets:** Accepted.

APEX

Candlewood Suites-Apex/Raleigh H
(919) 387-8595. **Call for rates.** 1005 Marco Dr 27502. US 1 exit 95, just w on SR 55. Int corridors. **Pets:** Accepted.

ARCHDALE

Comfort Inn - High Point H
(336) 434-4797. **$69-$84.** 10123 N Main St 27263. I-85 exit 111, just n on US 311 business route. Int corridors. **Pets:** Accepted.

Hampton Inn-High Point H
(336) 434-5200. **$99-$109.** 10066 N Main St 27263. I-85 exit 111, just n on US 311 business route. Int corridors. **Pets:** Accepted.

Holiday Inn Express Hotel & Suites H
(336) 861-3310. **$69-$199.** 10050 N Main St 27263. I-85 exit 111, just n on US 311 business route. Int corridors. **Pets:** Other species. $50 one-time fee/room. Designated rooms, no service, supervision.

Quality Inn-High Point H
(336) 861-3000. **$59-$109.** 1202 Liberty Rd 27263. I-85 exit 113A, just s on SR 62. Int corridors. **Pets:** Accepted.

ASHEBORO

Holiday Inn Express Hotel & Suites H
(336) 636-5222. **Call for rates.** 1113 E Dixie Dr 27203. Jct SR 42, 0.5 mi w on US 64. Int corridors. **Pets:** Accepted.

ASHEVILLE *(Restaurants p. 637)*

1889 WhiteGate Inn & Cottage BB ✿
(828) 253-2553. **$169-$379, 14 day notice.** 173 E Chestnut St 28801. I-240 exit 5B (Charlotte St), just n, then just w; in historic district. Ext/int corridors. **Pets:** Dogs only. $50 one-time fee/room. Designated rooms, service with restrictions, supervision.

1900 Inn on Montford BB ✿
(828) 254-9569. **$155-$625, 14 day notice.** 296 Montford Ave 28801. I-240 exit 4C (Montford Ave/Haywood St), 0.7 mi n; in historic district. Ext/int corridors. **Pets:** Other species. Designated rooms, service with restrictions.

Abbington Green Bed & Breakfast Inn BB
(828) 251-2454. **$175-$450, 30 day notice.** 46 Cumberland Cir 28801. I-240 exit 4C (Montford Ave/Haywood St), just n on Montford Ave, just e on W Chestnut St, just n on Cumberland Avenue, then just ne; in Montford Historic District. Ext/int corridors. **Pets:** Accepted.

Aloft Asheville Downtown H ✿
(828) 232-2838. **$149-$449.** 51 Biltmore Ave 28801. On US 25. Int corridors. **Pets:** Dogs only. Service with restrictions, supervision.

Applewood Manor Inn Bed & Breakfast BB
(828) 254-2244. **$160-$250, 7 day notice.** 62 Cumberland Cir 28801. I-240 exit 4C (Montford Ave/Haywood St), just n on Montford Ave, just e on W Chestnut St, just n on Cumberland Ave, then just ne. Ext/int corridors. **Pets:** Dogs only. Designated rooms, service with restrictions, crate.

BEST WESTERN of Asheville Biltmore East M ✿
(828) 298-5562. **$89-$159.** 501 Tunnel Rd 28805. I-240 exit 7, 0.5 mi e on US 70 (Tunnel Rd). Ext corridors. **Pets:** Small, dogs only. $10 daily fee/pet. Designated rooms, service with restrictions, supervision.

Biltmore Village Inn BB ✿
(828) 274-8707. **$199-$345, 30 day notice.** 119 Dodge St 28803. I-40 exit 50/50B (US 25 N), 0.5 mi n, just e on Lula St, just n on Reed St, just e on Warren Ave, then just s. Ext/int corridors. **Pets:** Dogs only. $45 daily fee/pet. Designated rooms, service with restrictions, crate.

Biltmore Village Lodge H ✿
(828) 277-1800. **$59-$249, 3 day notice.** 117 Hendersonville Rd 28803. I-40 exit 50 eastbound; exit 50B westbound, just n on US 25. Int corridors. **Pets:** Large, other species. $50 one-time fee/room. Designated rooms, service with restrictions, crate.

Cedar Crest Inn BB
(828) 252-1389. **Call for rates.** 674 Biltmore Ave 28803. I-40 exit 50, 1.1 mi n. Ext/int corridors. **Pets:** Accepted.

Comfort Inn-West H
(828) 665-6500. **$80-$220.** 15 Crowell Rd 28806. I-40 exit 44, just n on US 19 and 23, just w on Old Haywood Rd, then just s. Int corridors. **Pets:** Medium, other species. $25 daily fee/pet. Designated rooms, no service, supervision.

Comfort Suites Biltmore H ✿
(828) 665-4000. **$69-$229.** 890 Brevard Rd 28806. I-26 exit 33, 0.3 mi w. Int corridors. **Pets:** Other species. $25 daily fee/room. Designated rooms, service with restrictions, crate.

Crowne Plaza Tennis & Golf Resort H ✿
(828) 254-3211. **$99-$229, 3 day notice.** One Resort Dr 28806. I-240 exit 3B (Resort Dr), just w. Int corridors. **Pets:** Medium. $25 daily fee/pet. Designated rooms, service with restrictions, supervision.

Days Inn-Biltmore East H ✿
(828) 298-4000. **$65-$160.** 1435 Tunnel Rd 28805. I-40 exit 55, just n. Int corridors. **Pets:** Small, dogs only. $10 daily fee/pet. Designated rooms, service with restrictions, supervision.

DoubleTree by Hilton Hotel Asheville-Biltmore H ✿
(828) 274-1800. **$129-$299.** 115 Hendersonville Rd 28803. I-40 exit 50 eastbound; exit 50B westbound, just n on US 25. Int corridors. **Pets:** Large, other species. $50 one-time fee/room. Designated rooms, service with restrictions, crate.

Extended Stay America Asheville-Tunnel Rd H
(828) 253-3483. **$79-$199.** 6 Kenilworth Knoll 28805. I-240 exit 6, 0.7 mi e on US 70 (Tunnel Rd), then just n. Int corridors. **Pets:** Other species. $25 daily fee/pet. Service with restrictions, supervision.

Four Points by Sheraton Asheville Downtown H
(828) 253-1851. **$129-$189.** 22 Woodfin St 28801. I-240 exit 5A (Merrimon Ave), just s, then just w. Int corridors. **Pets:** Medium. $50 one-time fee/pet. Designated rooms, service with restrictions.

Grand Bohemian Hotel Asheville, Autograph Collection H
(828) 505-2949. **$152-$509, 3 day notice.** 11 Boston Way 28803. I-40 exit 50/50B, just se of US 25; at Biltmore Village. Int corridors.
Pets: Accepted.

Haywood Park Hotel & Atrium H ✿
(828) 252-2522. **$195-$450, 3 day notice.** One Battery Park Ave 28801. I-240 exit 4C (Montford Ave/Haywood St), just s, 0.6 mi se on Haywood St, then just w. Int corridors. **Pets:** Medium, dogs only. $50 one-time fee/pet. Designated rooms, service with restrictions, crate.

Hilton Asheville Biltmore Park H
(828) 209-2700. **$119-$279.** 43 Town Square Blvd 28803. I-26 exit 37, just e on Long Shoals Rd, then w; in Biltmore Park Town Square. Int corridors. **Pets:** $50 one-time fee/room. Designated rooms, service with restrictions.

Holiday Inn-Biltmore East at the Blue Ridge Parkway H ✿
(828) 298-5611. **Call for rates.** 1450 Tunnel Rd 28805. I-40 exit 55, just n. Int corridors. **Pets:** $25 daily fee/room. Designated rooms, service with restrictions, supervision.

Hotel Indigo H ✿
(828) 239-0239. **$159-$539, 7 day notice.** 151 Haywood St 28801. I-240 exit 4C (Montford Ave/Haywood St), just s, then just w. Int corridors. **Pets:** Large. $50 one-time fee/room. Designated rooms, service with restrictions, supervision.

The Omni Grove Park Inn H
(828) 252-2711. **$199-$329, 7 day notice.** 290 Macon Ave 28804. I-240 exit 5B (Charlotte St), 2 mi n on Macon Ave via Charlotte St, follow signs. Int corridors. **Pets:** Large, dogs only. $130 one-time fee/room. Designated rooms, service with restrictions, supervision.

Quality Inn & Suites M ✿
(828) 298-5519. **$70-$180.** 1430 Tunnel Rd 28805. I-40 exit 55, just n. Ext corridors. **Pets:** Other species. $15 daily fee/room. Designated rooms, service with restrictions, crate.

Ramada H
(828) 298-9141. **$79-$129, 3 day notice.** 800 Fairview Rd 28803. I-240 exit 8, jct I-40 and US 74. Int corridors. **Pets:** Medium. $15 one-time fee/pet, $10 daily fee/pet. Designated rooms, service with restrictions, supervision.

Red Roof Inn-Asheville West M
(828) 667-9803. **$50-$159.** 16 Crowell Rd 28806. I-40 exit 44, just n on US 19 and 23, just w on Old Haywood Rd, then just s. Ext corridors. **Pets:** Large, other species. Service with restrictions, supervision.

Renaissance Asheville Hotel H
(828) 252-8211. **$109-$329.** 31 Woodfin St 28801. I-240 exit 5A (Merrimon Ave), Jct US 25 (Broadway St), just e. Int corridors.
Pets: Accepted.

Rodeway Inn & Suites Biltmore Square H
(828) 670-8800. **$49-$149.** 9 Wedgefield Dr 28806. I-26 exit 33, just nw. Int corridors. **Pets:** Medium. $15 daily fee/pet. Service with restrictions, supervision.

Sleep Inn Biltmore West H
(828) 670-7600. **$69-$139.** 1918 Old Haywood Rd 28806. I-40 exit 44, just n on US 19 and 23, then just w. Int corridors. **Pets:** Accepted.

ATLANTIC BEACH
Doubletree by Hilton Hotel Atlantic Beach Oceanfront H
(252) 240-1155. **Call for rates.** 2717 W Ft Macon Rd 28512. 2.3 mi n on SR 58 N, at MP 4.5. Int corridors. **Pets:** Accepted.

BANNER ELK
BEST WESTERN Mountain Lodge at Banner Elk H ✿
(828) 898-4571. **$70-$170.** 1615 Tynecastle Hwy 28604. Jct SR 194, 1.3 mi s on SR 184. Ext corridors. **Pets:** Other species. $10 daily fee/room. Designated rooms, service with restrictions, supervision.

BLACK MOUNTAIN
Quality Inn Black Mountain M
(828) 669-9950. **$70-$140.** 585 NC Hwy 9 28711. I-40 exit 64, just s. Ext corridors. **Pets:** $15 daily fee/pet. Service with restrictions.

BLOWING ROCK (Restaurants p. 637)
Alpine Village Inn M
(828) 295-7206. **Call for rates.** 297 Sunset Dr 28605. Jct US 321, just w. Ext corridors. **Pets:** Dogs only. $10 daily fee/pet. Designated rooms, service with restrictions, supervision.

Hillwinds Inn M
(828) 295-7660. **$69-$229, 3 day notice.** 315 Sunset Dr 28605. Jct US 321 bypass, just w. Ext/int corridors. **Pets:** Large. $25 daily fee/room. Designated rooms, service with restrictions.

Homestead Inn M
(828) 295-9559. **$49-$99, 4 day notice.** 153 Morris St 28605. Jct US 321 business route (Main St), just e. Ext corridors. **Pets:** Accepted.

BOONE
Baymont Inn & Suites Boone South H
(828) 264-0077. **$70-$125.** 1075 Hwy 105 28607. Jct US 321, just sw. Int corridors. **Pets:** Accepted.

La Quinta Inn & Suites Boone H
(828) 262-1234. **$75-$310.** 165 Hwy 105 N Ext 28607. Jct US 421, just s. Int corridors. **Pets:** Large, other species. Service with restrictions.

BREVARD
Hampton Inn-Brevard H
(828) 883-4800. **$99-$179.** 275 Forest Gate Dr 28768. Jct US 64, just e on SR 280, then just n. Int corridors. **Pets:** Medium, other species. $50 one-time fee/pet. Service with restrictions.

Holiday Inn Express & Suites Brevard H
(828) 862-8900. **Call for rates.** 2228 Asheville Hwy 28712. Jct SR 280, just w on US 64. Int corridors. **Pets:** Accepted.

The Inn at Brevard BB
(828) 884-2105. **$150-$235, 14 day notice.** 315 E Main St 28712. Jct US 64 (Broad St), just e; center. Ext/int corridors. **Pets:** Accepted.

BRYSON CITY

 Settlers Mountain 🆅🅷 ✿

(828) 488-8622. **$90-$200, 30 day notice.** 340 E Alarka Rd 28713. US 74 exit 64, 1.5 mi s on Alarka Rd, then 0.4 mi e. Ext corridors. **Pets:** Large, dogs only. $50 one-time fee/room. No service.
🛜 ✖ 🅗 💻

BUXTON

🆅🆅 Lighthouse View Oceanfront Lodging 🅗

(252) 995-5680. **$74-$169, 7 day notice.** 46677 NC Hwy 12 27920. 0.5 mi n of Cape Hatteras Lighthouse. Ext corridors. **Pets:** $10 daily fee/ pet. Designated rooms, no service. 🏊 🛜 🅗 💻

CANDLER

🅰🅰🅰 🆅🆅 Days Inn Asheville West 🅼

(828) 667-9321. **$50-$80.** 2551 Smokey Park Hwy 28715. I-40 exit 37, just s, then w. Ext corridors. **Pets:** $10 daily fee/room. Service with restrictions, supervision. 🆂🅰🆅🅴 🏊 🛜 🅗 💻

CANTON

🅰🅰🅰 🆅🆅 Americas Best Value Inn Canton 🅼

(828) 648-0300. **Call for rates.** 1963 Champion Dr 28716. I-40 exit 31, just n. Ext corridors. **Pets:** Accepted. 🆂🅰🆅🅴 🏊 🛜 🅗 💻

CARY

🅰🅰🅰 🆅🆅 BEST WESTERN PLUS Cary Inn - NC State 🅗

(919) 481-1200. **$74-$89.** 1722 Walnut St 27511. I-40 exit 293A, just s on US 1 exit 101A, then just e. Ext/int corridors. **Pets:** Medium, dogs only. $20 daily fee/pet. Designated rooms, service with restrictions, supervision. 🆂🅰🆅🅴 🏊 🛜 ✖ 🅗 💻

🆅🆅🆅 Comfort Suites Hotel 🅗

(919) 852-4318. **$74-$129.** 350 Ashville Ave 27518. US 1 exit 98A, 0.8 mi e on Tryon Rd, then just n. Int corridors. **Pets:** Accepted.
🆱🅼 🏊 🛜 ✖ 🅗 💻

🆅🆅🆅 Extended Stay America-Raleigh-Cary-Harrison Ave 🅗

(919) 677-9910. **$74-$104.** 600 Weston Pkwy 27513. I-40 exit 287, 0.5 mi s on Harrison Ave, then just w. Int corridors. **Pets:** Other species. $25 daily fee/pet. Service with restrictions, supervision.
🏊 🛜 🅗 💻

🆅🆅🆅 Hampton Inn & Suites 🅗

(919) 233-1798. **$89-$189.** 111 Hampton Woods Ln 27607. I-40 exit 290, just w on SR 54, then just s. Int corridors. **Pets:** Accepted.
🆱🅼 🛜 ✖ 🅗 💻

🅰🅰🅰 🆅🆅🆅 Hawthorn Suites by Wyndham Raleigh 🅗

(919) 468-4222. **$79-$120.** 1020 Buck Jones Rd 27606. I-40 exit 293A, just s on US 1 exit 101B, 0.5 mi nw; in Buck Jones Village. Int corridors. **Pets:** Other species. $15 daily fee/room. Service with restrictions. 🆂🅰🆅🅴 🆱🅼 ✖ 🅗 💻

🆅🆅🆅 La Quinta Inn & Suites Raleigh (Cary) 🅗

(919) 851-2850. **$75-$189.** 191 Crescent Commons Dr 27511. US 1 exit 98A, 0.5 mi e on Tryon Rd, then just n. Int corridors. **Pets:** Large, other species. Service with restrictions. 🆱🅼 🏊 🛜 🅗 💻

🅰🅰🅰 🆅🆅 Red Roof Inn Raleigh NCSU-Cary 🅗

(919) 469-3400. **$49-$99.** 1800 Walnut St 27518. I-40 exit 293A, just s on US 1 exit 101A, just e. Int corridors. **Pets:** Large, other species. Service with restrictions, supervision. 🆂🅰🆅🅴 🛜 ✖ 🅗 💻

🆅🆅🆅 Residence Inn by Marriott Raleigh Cary 🅗

(919) 467-4080. **$79-$289.** 2900 Regency Pkwy 27518. US 1 exit 98A, 0.5 mi e on Tryon Rd, then just s. Int corridors. **Pets:** Accepted.
🅴🅲🅾 🆱🅼 🏊 🛜 ✖ 🅗 💻

🅰🅰🅰 🆅🆅🆅 TownePlace Suites by Marriott-Raleigh/Cary/ Weston Parkway 🅗

(919) 678-0005. **$84-$179.** 120 Sage Commons Way 27513. I-40 exit 287, 0.5 mi s on Harrison Ave, 2.3 w on Weston Pkwy, then just n. Int corridors. **Pets:** Accepted. 🆂🅰🆅🅴 🆱🅼 🏊 🛜 ✖ 🅗 💻

🅰🅰🅰 🆅🆅🆅🆅 The Umstead Hotel & Spa 🅗 ✿

(919) 447-4000. **$279-$639.** 100 Woodland Pond Dr 27513. I-40 exit 287, just s on Harrison Ave, just e on SAS Campus Dr, then just n. Int corridors. **Pets:** Dogs only. $200 one-time fee/room.
🆂🅰🆅🅴 🆔 🆈🅻 🆱🅼 🏊 ✖ 🛜 ✖ 🅗 💻

CASHIERS *(Restaurants p. 637)*

🅰🅰🅰 🆅🆅🆅🆅 High Hampton Inn & Country Club 🅗 ✿

(828) 743-2411. **$280-$390, 21 day notice.** 1525 Hwy 107 S 28717. Jct US 64, 1.5 mi s. Ext/int corridors. **Pets:** Dogs only. $50 one-time fee/ room. Designated rooms, service with restrictions.
🆂🅰🆅🅴 🆈🅻 ✖ 🛜 ✖ 🆇 🆆 🗳

CHAPEL HILL

🅰🅰🅰 🆅🆅🆅 Aloft - Chapel Hill 🅗 ✿

(919) 932-7772. **$109-$319.** 1001 S Hamilton Rd 27517. I-40 exit 273/ 273A, 2.6 mi w on SR 54, then just s. Int corridors. **Pets:** Medium, dogs only. Designated rooms, service with restrictions, supervision.
🆂🅰🆅🅴 🆱🅼 🏊 🛜 ✖ 🅗 💻

🅰🅰🅰 🆅🆅 Chapel Hill University Inn 🅼

(919) 929-2171. **$65-$115.** 1301 Fordham Blvd 27514. I-40 exit 270, 2 mi s on US 15/501. Ext corridors. **Pets:** Accepted.
🆂🅰🆅🅴 🆈🅻 🏊 🛜 🅗 💻

🅰🅰🅰 🆅🆅 Quality Inn 🅗

(919) 968-3000. **$59-$119.** 1740 Fordham Blvd 27514. I-40 exit 270, 1 mi s on US 15/501, just e on Europa Dr, then just s on service road. Ext corridors. **Pets:** Small. $25 one-time fee/pet. Designated rooms, service with restrictions, supervision. 🆂🅰🆅🅴 🆱🅼 🏊 🛜 🅗 💻

🅰🅰🅰 🆅🆅🆅 Residence Inn by Marriott-Chapel Hill 🅗

(919) 933-4848. **$149-$299.** 101 Erwin Rd 27514. I-40 exit 270, 1.2 mi s on US 15/501, then just w. Int corridors. **Pets:** Accepted.
🆂🅰🆅🅴 🆱🅼 🏊 🛜 ✖ 🅗 💻

🅰🅰🅰 🆅🆅🆅 Sheraton Chapel Hill 🅗

(919) 968-4900. **$109-$199.** 1 Europa Dr 27517. I-40 exit 270, 1 mi s, then just e. Int corridors. **Pets:** Accepted.
🆂🅰🆅🅴 🆈🅻 🏊 🛜 ✖ 🅗 💻

🅰🅰🅰 🆅🆅🆅🆅 The Siena Hotel, Autograph Collection 🅗 ✿

(919) 929-4000. **$139-$395.** 1505 E Franklin St 27514. I-40 exit 270, 2 mi s on US 15/501, then 0.5 mi w. Int corridors. **Pets:** Dogs only. $75 one-time fee/room. Designated rooms, supervision.
🆂🅰🆅🅴 🆈🅻 🆱🅼 ✖ 🅗 💻

CHARLOTTE

🅰🅰🅰 🆅🆅🆅 Aloft Charlotte-Ballantyne 🅗 ✿

(704) 247-2222. **$99-$299.** 13139 Ballantyne Corporate Pl 28277. I-485 exit 61 or 61B, 0.5 mi s on US 521 (Johnston Rd), just e on Ballantyne Commons Pkwy, then just n. Int corridors. **Pets:** $100 one-time fee/pet. Designated rooms, service with restrictions, supervision.
🆂🅰🆅🅴 🅴🅲🅾 🆱🅼 🏊 🛜 ✖ 🅗 💻

🅰🅰🅰 🆅🆅🆅 Aloft Charlotte Uptown @ the EpiCentre 🅗

(704) 333-1999. **$109-$199.** 210 E Trade St 28202. I-77 exit 10 or 10B, 0.9 mi e, then just n; jct College St. Int corridors. **Pets:** Accepted.
🆂🅰🆅🅴 🆱🅼 🏊 🛜 ✖ 🅗 💻

🆅🆅🆅 Candlewood Suites-Charlotte University 🅗

(704) 598-9863. **Call for rates.** 8812 University East Dr 28213. I-85 exit 45A (W.T. Harris Blvd), 2.5 mi e on SR 24, then just s; in University East Business Park. Int corridors. **Pets:** Accepted. 🛜 ✖ 🅗 💻

⚠️ ▼▼▼ Comfort Suites-Airport H
(704) 971-4400. **$89-$299.** 3425 Mulberry Church Rd 28208. I-85 exit 33, just e, then just n. Int corridors. **Pets:** Accepted.
SAVE &M 🐾 ✕ 📶 📺

▼▼ Country Inn & Suites By Carlson-Charlotte University H
(704) 549-8770. **Call for rates.** 131 E McCullough Dr 28262. I-85 exit 45A (W.T. Harris Blvd), 0.5 mi e on SR 24, 0.4 mi s on US 29 (N Tryon St), then just e. Int corridors. **Pets:** Accepted.
&M 🐾 🛜 ✕ 📶 📺

⚠️ ▼▼▼ DoubleTree Suites by Hilton Hotel Charlotte-SouthPark H
(704) 364-2400. **$119-$289.** 6300 Morrison Blvd 28211. I-77 exit 5 (Tyvola Rd), 3.3 mi e on Tyvola/Fairview rds, just n on Barclay Downs, then just e. Int corridors. **Pets:** Accepted.
SAVE ❌ 🐾 🐾 ✕ 📶 📺

▼▼▼ Drury Inn & Suites-Charlotte Northlake H
(704) 599-8882. **$115-$214.** 6920 Northlake Mall Dr 28216. I-77 exit 18 (W.T. Harris Blvd), just w on SR 24. Int corridors. **Pets:** $10 daily fee/room. Service with restrictions, supervision. &M 🐾 🛜 📶 📺

▼▼▼ Drury Inn & Suites-Charlotte University Place H
(704) 593-0700. **$115-$214.** 415 W W.T. Harris Blvd 28262. I-85 exit 45A (W.T. Harris Blvd), just e on SR 24. Int corridors. **Pets:** $10 daily fee/room. Service with restrictions, supervision.
&M 🐾 🛜 ✕ 📶 📺

▼▼ Extended Stay America-Charlotte/Airport M
(704) 676-0083. **$65-$225.** 710 Yorkmont Rd 28217. I-77 exit 6B northbound; exit southbound, just s on S Tryon St, then just w. Ext corridors. **Pets:** Other species. $25 daily fee/pet. Service with restrictions, supervision. 🛜 📶 📺

▼▼ Extended Stay America-Charlotte-Pineville-Park Rd H
(704) 341-0929. **$65-$225.** 10930 Park Rd 28226. I-485 exit 64A, just n on SR 51, then just e; behind Terraces at Park Place Shopping Center. Int corridors. **Pets:** Other species. $25 daily fee/pet. Service with restrictions, supervision. &M 🛜 📶 📺

▼▼ Extended Stay America-Charlotte-Pineville-Pineville Matthews Rd H
(704) 542-9521. **$79-$299.** 8405 Pineville-Matthews Rd 28226. I-485 exit 64A, 0.7 mi n on SR 51. Int corridors. **Pets:** Other species. $25 daily fee/pet. Service with restrictions, supervision. 🐾 🛜 📶 📺

▼▼ Extended Stay America-Charlotte-Tyvola Rd-Executive Park H
(704) 527-1960. **$65-$225.** 5830 Westpark Dr 28217. I-77 exit 5 (Tyvola Rd), just e, then 0.4 mi s. Int corridors. **Pets:** Other species. $25 daily fee/pet. Service with restrictions, supervision. 🐾 🛜 ✕ 📶 📺

⚠️ ▼▼▼ Extended Stay America-Charlotte-University Place H
(704) 510-1636. **$65-$109.** 8211 University Executive Park Dr 28262. I-85 exit 45A (W.T. Harris Blvd), 0.5 mi w on SR 24, then 0.5 mi s on US 29 (N Tryon St). Int corridors. **Pets:** Other species. $25 daily fee/pet. Service with restrictions, supervision. SAVE 🛜 📶 📺

⚠️ ▼▼▼ Fairfield Inn & Suites Charlotte Uptown H
(704) 372-7550. **$99-$309.** 201 S McDowell St 28204. I-277 exit 2A, just w on 4th St, then just s. Int corridors. **Pets:** Accepted.
SAVE ❌ 🐾 🛜 ✕ 📶 📺

⚠️ ▼▼▼ Four Points by Sheraton-Charlotte H
(704) 522-0852. **Call for rates.** 315 E Woodlawn Rd 28217. I-77 exit 6A, 0.5 mi e. Int corridors. **Pets:** Accepted.
SAVE ❌ 🐾 🛜 ✕ 📶 📺

⚠️ ▼▼▼ Hawthorn Suites by Wyndham Charlotte Executive Park H
(704) 529-7500. **$69-$299.** 5840 Westpark Dr 28217. I-77 exit 5 (Tyvola Rd), just e, then 0.5 mi s. Int corridors. **Pets:** Accepted.
SAVE &M 🛜 ✕ 📶 📺

▼▼▼ Home2 Suites by Hilton Charlotte/I-77 South H 🐾
(704) 405-4000. **$109-$169.** 6025 Tyvola Glen Cir 28217. I-77 exit 5 (Tyvola Rd), just n. Int corridors. **Pets:** Medium, other species. $50 one-time fee/pet. Service with restrictions, supervision.
&M 🛜 📶 📺

▼▼▼ Homewood Suites by Hilton Airport H
(704) 357-0500. **$119-$299.** 2770 Yorkmont Rd 28208. I-77 exit 6B, 2 mi nw on Billy Graham Pkwy exit Coliseum/Tyvola Rd, just se on Tyvola Rd, then just w. Int corridors. **Pets:** Accepted.
&M 🐾 🛜 ✕ 📶 📺

▼▼▼ Homewood Suites by Hilton-University Research Park H
(704) 549-8800. **$139-$179.** 8340 N Tryon St 28262. I-85 exit 45A (W.T. Harris Blvd), 0.5 mi e on SR 24, then just s on US 29 (N Tryon St). Ext/int corridors. **Pets:** Accepted. &M 🐾 🛜 📶 📺

⚠️ ▼▼▼ HYATT house Charlotte Airport H
(704) 525-2600. **$69-$199.** 4920 S Tryon St 28217. I-77 exit 6B northbound, just w, then just s; exit southbound, just s. Int corridors. **Pets:** Dogs only. $75 one-time fee/room. Service with restrictions, supervision. SAVE &M 🐾 🛜 ✕ 📶 📺

⚠️ ▼▼▼ Hyatt Place Charlotte/Airport/Lake Pointe H
(704) 357-8555. **$69-$209.** 4119 South Stream Blvd 28217. I-77 exit 6B, 2 mi nw on Billy Graham Pkwy exit Coliseum/Tyvola Rd, then 0.8 mi se on Tyvola Rd, then just s. Int corridors. **Pets:** Medium, dogs only. $50 one-time fee/pet. Service with restrictions.
SAVE 🐾 🛜 ✕ 📶 📺

⚠️ ▼▼▼ Hyatt Place Charlotte Airport/Tyvola Road-Yorkmont H
(704) 423-9931. **$69-$209.** 2950 Oak Lake Blvd 28208. I-77 exit 6B, 2 mi nw on Billy Graham Pkwy exit Coliseum/Tyvola Rd, just se on Tyvola Rd, just w on Yorkmont Rd, then just n. Int corridors. **Pets:** Medium, dogs only. $75 one-time fee/room. Service with restrictions, supervision. SAVE 🐾 🛜 ✕ 📶 📺

⚠️ ▼▼▼ Hyatt Place Charlotte/Arrowood H
(704) 522-8400. **$89-$209.** 7900 Forest Point Blvd 28273. I-77 exit 3 southbound; exit 2 northbound, just e. Int corridors. **Pets:** Accepted.
SAVE &M 🐾 🛜 ✕ 📶 📺

▼▼ La Quinta Inn & Suites Charlotte Airport North H
(704) 392-1600. **$72-$279.** 3127 Sloan Rd 28208. I-85 exit 33, just w, then just s. Int corridors. **Pets:** Large, other species. Service with restrictions. &M 🛜 📶 📺

▼▼▼ La Quinta Inn & Suites Charlotte Airport South H
(704) 523-5599. **$69-$279.** 4900 S Tryon St 28217. I-77 exit 6B northbound, just w, then just s; exit southbound, just s. Int corridors. **Pets:** Large, other species. Service with restrictions.
&M 🐾 🛜 📶 📺

▼▼ MainStay Suites H
(704) 521-3232. **$109-$149.** 7926 Forest Pine Dr 28273. I-77 exit 3 southbound; exit 2 northbound, just e, then just s. Int corridors. **Pets:** Medium, other species. $35 daily fee/pet. Service with restrictions, crate. &M 🐾 🛜 📶 📺

Microtel Inn & Suites by Wyndham Charlotte/Northlake H

(704) 227-3377. **$59-$140.** 6309 Banner Elk Dr 28216. I-77 exit 16B, just w on Sunset Rd, then just s. Int corridors. **Pets:** Small. $20 one-time fee/pet. Service with restrictions, supervision.

Morehead Inn BB

(704) 376-3357. **$149-$289.** 1122 E Morehead St 28204. I-277 exit Kenilworth Ave, 0.9 mi s, then just w; corner of Berkeley Ave. Ext/int corridors. **Pets:** Accepted.

Omni Charlotte Hotel H ❀

(704) 377-0400. **$149-$549, 3 day notice.** 132 E Trade St 28202. I-77 exit 10 or 10B, 0.8 mi e; jct Tryon St. Int corridors. **Pets:** Small. $50 one-time fee/room. Service with restrictions, crate.

Residence Inn by Marriott Charlotte South at I-77/Tyvola Rd H

(704) 527-8110. **$85-$143.** 5816 Westpark Dr 28217. I-77 exit 5 (Tyvola Rd), just e, then 0.4 mi s. Ext/int corridors. **Pets:** Accepted.

Residence Inn by Marriott Charlotte SouthPark H

(704) 554-7001. **$179-$199.** 6030 Piedmont Row Dr S 28210. I-77 exit 5 (Tyvola Rd), 3.2 mi e on Tyvola/Fairview rds, then just s. Int corridors. **Pets:** Accepted.

Residence Inn by Marriott-Charlotte University Research Park H

(704) 547-1122. **$104-$189.** 8503 N Tryon St 28262. I-85 exit 45A (W.T. Harris Blvd), 0.5 mi w on SR 24, then just s on US 29 (N Tryon St). Ext corridors. **Pets:** Accepted.

Residence Inn by Marriott-Charlotte Uptown H

(704) 340-4000. **$119-$299.** 404 S Mint St 28202. I-77 exit 10 or 10B, 0.6 mi e on Trade St, then just s. Int corridors. **Pets:** Other species. $100 one-time fee/room. Designated rooms, service with restrictions, crate.

Residence Inn by Marriott-Piper Glen H

(704) 319-3900. **$89-$299.** 5115 Piper Station Dr 28277. I-485 exit 59, just s on Rea Rd, then just e. Int corridors. **Pets:** Accepted.

Sheraton Charlotte Airport Hotel H

(704) 392-1200. **$89-$279.** 3315 Scott Futrell Dr 28208. I-85 exit 33, just e, then just s. Int corridors. **Pets:** Accepted.

Sleep Inn-Billy Graham Parkway H

(704) 525-5005. **$70-$170.** 701 Yorkmont Rd 28217. I-77 exit 6B northbound, just w, just s on S Tryon St, then just w; exit southbound, just s on S Tryon St, then just w. Int corridors. **Pets:** Other species. $25 daily fee/pet. Designated rooms, service with restrictions, supervision.

Sleep Inn Northlake H

(704) 399-7778. **$59-$79.** 6300 Banner Elk Dr 28216. I-77 exit 16B, just w on Sunset Rd, then just s. Int corridors. **Pets:** Medium. $20 one-time fee/room. Designated rooms, service with restrictions, supervision.

Sleep Inn University Place H

(704) 549-4544. **$77-$169.** 8525 N Tryon St 28262. I-85 exit 45A (W.T. Harris Blvd), 0.5 mi e on SR 24, just s on US 29 (N Tryon St). Int corridors. **Pets:** Accepted.

Sonesta ES Suites Charlotte H

(704) 527-6767. **Call for rates.** 7925 Forest Pine Dr 28273. I-77 exit 3 southbound; exit 2 northbound, just e, then just s. Int corridors. **Pets:** Accepted.

Staybridge Suites Charlotte-Ballantyne H

(704) 248-5000. **$109-$160, 3 day notice.** 15735 Brixham Hill Ave 28277. I-485 exit 61 or 61B, just s, then just w. Int corridors. **Pets:** Accepted.

TownePlace Suites by Marriott Charlotte Arrowood H

(704) 227-2000. **$89-$189.** 7805 Forest Point Blvd 28217. I-77 exit 3 southbound; exit 2 northbound, just e. Int corridors. **Pets:** Other species. $75 one-time fee/room. Service with restrictions.

TownePlace Suites by Marriott-University H

(704) 548-0388. **$79-$159.** 8710 Research Dr 28262. I-85 exit 45B (W.T. Harris Blvd), just w on SR 24, then just n. Int corridors. **Pets:** Accepted.

The Westin Charlotte H

(704) 375-2600. **$99-$389.** 601 S College St 28202. I-277 exit College St, just n; jct E Stonewall St. Int corridors. **Pets:** Accepted.

CHEROKEE

Magnuson's Great Smokies Inn M

(828) 497-2020. **$59-$149.** 1636 Acquoni Rd 28719. Jct US 19, 1.7 mi n. Ext corridors. **Pets:** Accepted.

Microtel Inn & Suites by Wyndham Cherokee H ❀

(828) 497-7800. **$65-$150.** 674 Casino Tr 28719. Jct US 441, just n on US 441 business route. Int corridors. **Pets:** Small, other species. $25 deposit/pet, $25 daily fee/pet. Designated rooms, service with restrictions, crate.

CHOCOWINITY

Baymont Inn & Suites Chocowinity/Washington M

(252) 946-8001. **$69-$89.** 3635 US Hwy 17 S 27817. On US 17 business route. Ext corridors. **Pets:** Small. $10 daily fee/pet. Designated rooms, service with restrictions, supervision.

CLEMMONS

Holiday Inn Express H

(336) 778-1500. **$81-$130.** 6320 Amp Dr 27012. I-40 exit 184, just n, then just e. Int corridors. **Pets:** Accepted.

Super 8 Clemmons H

(336) 778-0931. **$59-$109.** 6204 Ramada Dr 27012. I-40 exit 184, just s, then just e. Int corridors. **Pets:** Accepted.

COLUMBUS

Days Inn M

(828) 894-3303. **$95-$110.** 626 W Mills St 28722. I-26 exit 67, just w on SR 108. Ext corridors. **Pets:** Accepted.

CONCORD

Americas Best Value Inn M

(704) 788-8550. **$60-$145, 7 day notice.** 2451 Kannapolis Hwy 28025. I-85 exit 58, just s on US 29, then just w. Ext corridors. **Pets:** Accepted.

Comfort Suites-Concord Mills H

(704) 979-3800. **$89-$249.** 7800 Gateway Ln NW 28027. I-85 exit 49, just e, just n on Weddington Rd, then just w. Int corridors. **Pets:** Accepted.

Embassy Suites Charlotte-Concord Golf Resort & Spa H

(704) 455-8200. **$109-$269.** 5400 John Q Hammons Dr 28027. I-85 exit 49, 1 mi e on Bruton Smith Blvd, then just n. Int corridors. **Pets:** Accepted.

Residence Inn by Marriott Charlotte Concord H
(704) 454-7862. **$79-$299.** 7601 Scott Padgett Pkwy 28027. I-85 exit 49, 1 mi e, then just n. Int corridors. **Pets:** Accepted.

Sleep Inn-Concord H
(704) 788-2150. **$69-$159.** 1120 Copperfield Blvd 28025. I-85 exit 60, just e. Int corridors. **Pets:** Accepted.

CONOVER
La Quinta Inn & Suites Hickory/Conover H
(828) 465-1100. **$98-$198.** 1607 Fairgrove Church Rd 28613. I-40 exit 128, just s. Int corridors. **Pets:** Large, other species. Service with restrictions.

CORNELIUS
Comfort Inn & Suites H
(704) 896-7622. **Call for rates.** 19521 Liverpool Pkwy 28031. I-77 exit 28, just w, then just s. Int corridors. **Pets:** Accepted.

Hampton Inn Lake Norman H
(704) 892-9900. **$89-$149.** 19501 Statesville Rd 28031. I-77 exit 28, just e, then just s. Int corridors. **Pets:** Accepted.

DUNN
Baymont Inn & Suites Dunn M
(910) 891-5758. **$49-$79.** 901 Jackson Rd 28334. I-95 exit 73, just w, then just s. Ext corridors. **Pets:** Medium. $20 daily fee/pet. Service with restrictions, crate.

DURHAM
Candlewood Suites H
(919) 484-9922. **$70-$109.** 1818 E NC Hwy 54 27713. I-40 exit 278, just s, then just w. Int corridors. **Pets:** Accepted.

Extended Stay America-Durham-RTP-Miami Blvd-North H
(919) 941-2878. **$79-$109.** 4610 S Miami Blvd 27703. I-40 exit 281, just n. Int corridors. **Pets:** Other species. $25 daily fee/pet. Service with restrictions, supervision.

Extended Stay America-Durham-RTP-Miami Blvd-South H
(919) 998-0400. **$84-$114.** 4919 S Miami Blvd 27703. I-40 exit 281, just s. Int corridors. **Pets:** Other species. $25 daily fee/pet. Service with restrictions, supervision.

Hilton Durham near Duke University H 🐾
(919) 564-2900. **$99-$299.** 3800 Hillsborough Rd 27705. I-85 exit 173, just e on Cole Mill Rd, then 0.5 mi w on US 70 business route. Int corridors. **Pets:** Large, dogs only. $50 one-time fee/pet. Service with restrictions.

Holiday Inn Express H
(919) 313-3244. **Call for rates.** 2516 Guess Rd 27705. I-85 exit 175, just e. Int corridors. **Pets:** Accepted.

Holiday Inn Express Hotel & Suites-RTP H 🐾
(919) 474-9800. **$79-$139.** 4912 S Miami Blvd 27703. I-40 exit 281, just s. Int corridors. **Pets:** Medium. $50 one-time fee/room. Designated rooms, service with restrictions, supervision.

Hotel Indigo RDU at RTP H
(919) 474-3000. **$89-$279, 3 day notice.** 151 Tatum Dr 27703. I-40 exit 281, just s on Miami Blvd, then just e. Int corridors. **Pets:** $75 one-time fee/room. Designated rooms, service with restrictions, crate.

La Quinta Inn & Suites Raleigh (Durham-Chapel Hill) H
(919) 401-9660. **$75-$289.** 4414 Durham Chapel Hill Blvd 27707. I-40 exit 270, 1.7 mi n on US 15/501. Int corridors. **Pets:** Large, other species. Service with restrictions.

La Quinta Inn & Suites Raleigh (Research Triangle Park) H
(919) 484-1422. **$72-$245.** 1910 W Westpark Dr 27713. I-40 exit 278, just n on SR 55, then just e. Int corridors. **Pets:** Large, other species. Service with restrictions.

Quality Inn & Suites H
(919) 382-3388. **$55-$95.** 3710 Hillsborough Rd 27705. I-85 exit 173, just e on Cole Mill Rd, then just w on US 70 business route. Ext/int corridors. **Pets:** Accepted.

Red Roof Inn Chapel Hill-UNC M
(919) 489-9421. **$45-$85.** 5623 Durham-Chapel Hill Blvd 27707. I-40 exit 270, just s on US 15/501, then just ne on E Lakeview Dr. Ext corridors. **Pets:** Large, other species. Service with restrictions, supervision.

Red Roof Inn Durham Triangle Park M
(919) 361-1950. **$45-$105.** 4405 Hwy 55 E 27713. I-40 exit 278, just n. Ext corridors. **Pets:** Large, other species. Service with restrictions, supervision.

Residence Inn by Marriott Durham/Research Triangle Park H
(919) 361-1266. **$88-$169.** 201 Residence Inn Blvd 27713. I-40 exit 278, just s on SR 55, then just w. Ext/int corridors. **Pets:** Medium, other species. $75 one-time fee/room. Service with restrictions.

Staybridge Suites of Durham H
(919) 401-9800. **Call for rates.** 3704 Mt. Moriah Rd 27707. I-40 exit 270, just n on US 15/501, then just e. Int corridors. **Pets:** Accepted.

Washington Duke Inn & Golf Club H
(919) 490-0999. **$209-$389.** 3001 Cameron Blvd 27705. US 15/501 Bypass exit 107, 0.8 mi s on SR 751. Int corridors. **Pets:** Accepted.

EDEN
Baymont Inn & Suites Eden M
(336) 627-0472. **$49-$82.** 716 Linden Dr 27288. Jct SR 700/770, 1.4 mi s on SR 87/14, just e. Ext corridors. **Pets:** Accepted.

Econo Lodge M
(336) 627-5131. **$59-$225.** 110 E Arbor Ln 27288. Jct SR 700/770, 1.4 mi s on SR 87/14, just e. Ext corridors. **Pets:** Accepted.

FAYETTEVILLE
Ambassador Inn M
(910) 485-8135. **$63-$70.** 2035 Eastern Blvd 28306. Jct SR 87, 1.2 mi s on I-95 business route/US 301; jct Owen Dr. Ext corridors. **Pets:** $10 daily fee/room. Designated rooms, service with restrictions, crate.

Candlewood Suites-Fayetteville/Ft. Bragg H
(910) 868-0873. **$109-$159.** 4108 Legend Ave 28303. US 401 Bypass, just e on McPherson Church Rd, just n on Sycamore Dairy Rd, then just w. Int corridors. **Pets:** Large, other species. $75 one-time fee/room. Service with restrictions.

Comfort Inn near Fort Bragg H
(910) 867-1777. **$80-$95.** 1922 Skibo Rd 28314. All American Frwy exit US 401 Bypass, 0.8 mi s. Int corridors. **Pets:** Medium, other species. $50 one-time fee/room. Designated rooms, service with restrictions, supervision.

◆◆ Days Inn & Suites - Cross Creek M

(910) 867-7659. $50-$100. 1720 Skibo Rd 28303. All American Frwy exit US 401 Bypass, just s; enter through Cross Creek Plaza entrance. Ext/int corridors. Pets: Accepted.

◆◆◆ ◆◆ Econo Lodge I-95 M

(910) 433-2100. $60-$80. 1952 Cedar Creek Rd 28312. I-95 exit 49, just w. Ext corridors. Pets: Accepted.

◆◆ Extended Stay America Fayetteville-Cross Creek Mall H

(910) 868-5662. $114-$140. 4105 Sycamore Dairy Rd 28303. All American Frwy exit Morganton Rd, just e, then just n. Int corridors. Pets: Other species. $25 daily fee/pet. Service with restrictions, supervision.

◆◆ Extended Stay America Fayetteville-Owen Dr. M

(910) 485-2747. $94-$120. 408 Owen Dr 28304. Jct All American Frwy. Ext corridors. Pets: Other species. $25 daily fee/pet. Service with restrictions, supervision.

◆◆◆ Home2 Suites by Hilton H

(910) 223-1170. Call for rates. 4035 Sycamore Dairy Rd 28303. US 401 Bypass, just e on McPherson Church Rd, then just s. Int corridors. Pets: Accepted.

◆◆◆ ◆◆ Red Roof Inn M

(910) 438-0748. $60-$90. 1902 Cedar Creek Rd 28312. I-95 exit 49, just w. Ext corridors. Pets: Large, other species. Service with restrictions, supervision.

◆◆◆ Residence Inn by Marriott Fayetteville Cross Creek H ◢

(910) 868-9005. $90-$144. 1468 Skibo Rd 28303. Jct SR 24/87, just s on US 401 Bypass. Int corridors. Pets: Other species. $100 one-time fee/room. Service with restrictions, supervision.

◆◆◆ ◆◆ Sleep Inn H

(910) 433-9090. $79-$119. 1915 Cedar Creek Rd 28312. I-95 exit 49, just w. Int corridors. Pets: Accepted.

◆◆◆ ◆◆◆ TownePlace Suites by Marriott Fayetteville Cross Creek H

(910) 764-1100. $99-$149. 1464 Skibo Rd 28303. Jct SR 24/87, just s on US 401 Bypass. Int corridors. Pets: Accepted.

FEARRINGTON VILLAGE

◆◆◆ ◆◆◆◆ The Fearrington House Inn CI ◢

(919) 542-2121. $325-$695, 3 day notice. 2000 Fearrington Village Center 27312. US 64 exit 383, 6 mi n on US 15/501. Ext/int corridors. Pets: Dogs only. $50 daily fee/pet. Designated rooms, service with restrictions, crate.

FLAT ROCK

◆◆ Highland Lake Inn H

(828) 693-6812. $99-$359, 7 day notice. 86 Lily Pad Ln 28731. I-26 exit 53, 1.1 mi w on Upward Rd, 0.5 mi w on N Highland Lake Rd, then just s on Highland Lake Dr. Ext/int corridors. Pets: Accepted.

FLETCHER

◆◆ Comfort Inn Asheville Airport H

(828) 687-9199. $80-$199. 15 Rockwood Rd 28732. I-26 exit 40, just e on SR 280, then just s. Int corridors. Pets: Accepted.

FOREST CITY

◆◆ Baymont Inn & Suites Forest City M

(828) 287-8788. $59-$99. 164 Jameson Inn Dr 28043. US 74 Bypass exit 181, 1.8 mi nw on US 74A. Ext corridors. Pets: Accepted.

FRANKLIN

◆◆◆ ◆◆◆ Microtel Inn by Wyndham Franklin H

(828) 349-9000. $70-$100. 81 Allman Dr 28734. Jct US 441 Bypass, 0.4 mi s on US 441/23. Int corridors. Pets: Accepted.

FUQUAY-VARINA

◆◆◆ Comfort Inn H

(919) 557-9000. $80-$110. 7616 Purfoy Rd 27526. Jct SR 55, 1 mi n on US 401/SR 55, then just e. Int corridors. Pets: Other species. $10 daily fee/pet. Designated rooms, service with restrictions, supervision.

GARNER

◆◆ Super 8 M

(919) 661-1991. $62-$79. 101 Leone Ct 27529. I-40 exit 312, just e on SR 42, then just s. Ext corridors. Pets: Medium. $10 daily fee/pet. Service with restrictions, supervision.

GARYSBURG

◆◆◆ Super 8 Roanoke Rapids M

(252) 537-1011. $54-$77. 6785 NC 46 Hwy 27831. I-95 exit 176, just w. Ext corridors. Pets: Medium, other species. Designated rooms, service with restrictions, crate.

GASTONIA

◆◆◆ ◆◆ BEST WESTERN Gastonia H

(704) 868-2000. $80-$200. 360 Best Western Ct 28054. I-85 exit 20, just nw on SR 279, then just e. Ext/int corridors. Pets: Accepted.

◆◆◆ ◆◆ Days Inn M

(704) 864-9981. $50-$58. 1700 N Chester St 28052. I-85 exit 17, just s on US 321. Ext/int corridors. Pets: Other species. $10 daily fee/pet. Service with restrictions, supervision.

◆◆◆ Hampton Inn H

(704) 866-9090. $99-$169. 1859 Remount Rd 28054. I-85 exit 20, just nw on SR 279, then just e. Int corridors. Pets: Accepted.

GOLDSBORO

◆◆◆ ◆◆◆◆ BEST WESTERN PLUS Goldsboro H

(919) 751-1999. $59-$109. 909 N Spence Ave 27534. US 70 E Bypass exit Spence Ave, just s. Int corridors. Pets: Accepted.

◆◆◆ ◆◆ Days Inn Goldsboro M

(919) 735-7911. $59-$90. 801 US 70 E Bypass 27534. US 70 E Bypass exit Wayne Memorial Dr eastbound, just n, just w on 11th St, then 0.5 mi sw on Lincoln Mercury Dr; exit westbound, straight on 11th St, then 0.5 mi sw on Lincoln Mercury Dr. Ext corridors. Pets: Medium, dogs only. $10 daily fee/pet. Designated rooms, service with restrictions, supervision.

◆◆◆ Hampton Inn H

(919) 778-1800. $92-$169. 905 N Spence Ave 27534. US 70 E Bypass exit Spence Ave, just s. Int corridors. Pets: Accepted.

GREENSBORO (Restaurants p. 637)

◆◆◆ ◆◆ BEST WESTERN PLUS Greensboro Airport Hotel H

(336) 454-0333. $74-$165, 3 day notice. 7800 National Service Rd 27409. I-40 exit 210 (SR 68), just s, just w on Thorndike Rd, then just n. Int corridors. Pets: Accepted.

◆◆◆ ◆◆◆ BEST WESTERN PLUS Windsor Suites H ◢

(336) 294-9100. $89-$209. 2006 Veasley St 27407. I-40 exit 217, just s on High Point Rd, then just w. Int corridors. Pets: Medium. $20 daily fee/pet. Designated rooms, service with restrictions, supervision.

W W Comfort Inn Greensboro H
(336) 297-1055. **$85-$230.** 1103 Lanada Rd 27407. I-40 exit 214 or 214A, just sw on Wendover Ave, then just e on Stanley Rd. Int corridors. **Pets:** Medium. $25 daily fee/room. Designated rooms.

WWW Comfort Suites Airport H
(336) 882-6666. **$74-$139.** 7619 Thorndike Rd 27409. I-40 exit 210 (SR 68), just s. Int corridors. **Pets:** Accepted.

WWW Drury Inn & Suites-Greensboro H
(336) 856-9696. **$105-$184.** 3220 High Point Rd 27407. I-40 exit 217, just s. Int corridors. **Pets:** $10 daily fee/room. Service with restrictions, supervision.

WW Extended Stay America-Greensboro-Airport H
(336) 454-0080. **$225.** 7617 Thorndike Rd 27409. I-40 exit 210 (SR 68), just s. Int corridors. **Pets:** Other species. $25 daily fee/pet. Service with restrictions, supervision.

WW WW Fairfield Inn by Marriott Greensboro Airport H
(336) 841-0140. **$85-$220.** 7615 Thorndike Rd 27409. I-40 exit 210 (SR 68), just s, then just w. Int corridors. **Pets:** Accepted.

WW WW Grandover Resort & Conference Center Golf & Spa H
(336) 294-1800. **$169-$250.** 1000 Club Rd 27407. I-85 exit 118, 0.7 mi s on I-85 business route exit Guilford College Rd, 0.4 mi w, then 1.3 mi n on Grandover Pkwy. Int corridors. **Pets:** Accepted.

AAA WWW Hawthorn Suites by Wyndham Greensboro H
(336) 454-0078. **$69-$199.** 7623 Thorndike Rd 27409. I-40 exit 210 (SR 68), just s, then just w. Int corridors. **Pets:** Other species. $15 daily fee/room. Service with restrictions.

WWWW Holiday Inn Express & Suites-Airport H
(336) 882-0004. **$99-$119.** 645 S Regional Rd 27409. I-40 exit 210 (SR 68), just s, then just e. Int corridors. **Pets:** Accepted.

WWWW Holiday Inn Express-I-40 at Wendover H
(336) 854-0090. **Call for rates.** 4305 Big Tree Way 27409. I-40 exit 214 or 214B, just ne on Wendover Ave, then just w. Int corridors. **Pets:** Accepted.

WWWW Holiday Inn Greensboro Airport H
(336) 668-0421. **$79-$225, 14 day notice.** 6426 Burnt Poplar Rd 27409. I-40 exit 211, just n on Gallimore Dairy Rd, then just w. Int corridors. **Pets:** Small. $10 daily fee/pet. Designated rooms, service with restrictions, crate.

AAA WWW Hyatt Place Greensboro H
(336) 852-1200. **$99-$229.** 1619 Stanley Rd 27407. I-40 exit 214 or 214A, just sw on Wendover Ave, then just e. Int corridors. **Pets:** Medium, dogs only. $75 one-time fee/room. Service with restrictions, crate.

WWWW La Quinta Inn & Suites H
(336) 316-0100. **$79-$259.** 1201 Lanada Rd 27407. I-40 exit 214 or 214A, just sw on Wendover Ave, just e on Stanley Rd, then just se. Int corridors. **Pets:** Large, other species. Service with restrictions.

WWWW Quality Inn & Suites-Airpark East H
(336) 668-3638. **$70-$160.** 7067 Albert Pick Rd 27409. I-40 exit 210 (SR 68) westbound, just s, then just e; exit eastbound, just e. Int corridors. **Pets:** Medium. $25 one-time fee/pet. Designated rooms, service with restrictions, supervision.

AAA WWW Red Roof Inn Greensboro Coliseum M
(336) 852-6560. **$51-$120.** 2101 W Meadowview Rd 27403. I-40 exit 217, just n on High Point Rd, then just e. Ext corridors. **Pets:** Large, other species. Service with restrictions, supervision.

WWW Residence Inn by Marriott-Greensboro Airport H
(336) 632-4666. **$109-$180.** 7616 Thorndike Rd 27409. I-40 exit 210 (SR 68), just s, then just w. Int corridors. **Pets:** Accepted.

WW Sleep Inn-Airport H
(336) 931-1272. **$49-$79.** 7 Sharps Airpark Ct 27409. I-40 exit 210 (SR 68) westbound, follow Regional Rd sign, then just n; exit eastbound, straight on Albert Pick Rd, then just n on Regional Rd. Int corridors. **Pets:** Medium. $20 daily fee/pet. Service with restrictions, crate.

GREENVILLE
WWWW Candlewood Suites H
(252) 317-3000. **Call for rates.** 1055 Waterford Commons Dr 27834. Just e of US 264; jct Stantonsburg and B's Barbeque rds; just w of Pitt County Memorial Hospital. Int corridors. **Pets:** Accepted.

WWWW City Hotel & Bistro H
(252) 355-8300. **Call for rates.** 203 W Greenville Blvd 27834. Jct SR 11/903, 1 mi e on US 264A. Int corridors. **Pets:** Medium, dogs only. $75 one-time fee/pet. Service with restrictions, crate.

WW Econo Lodge M
(252) 752-7382. **$59-$140.** 920 Crosswinds St 27834. Jct US 264 alternate route, just s on US 13/SR 11, just w; behind Waffle House. Ext corridors. **Pets:** Accepted.

WWW Hilton Greenville H
(252) 355-5000. **$109-$359.** 207 SW Greenville Blvd 27834. Jct SR 11/903, 1 mi e on US 264 alternate route. Int corridors. **Pets:** Accepted.

WW Home-Towne Suites H
(252) 752-3411. **Call for rates.** 2111 W Arlington Blvd 27834. Jct US 13/SR 11, 0.4 mi w on Stantonsburg Rd, then just s. Int corridors. **Pets:** Accepted.

WWW Residence Inn by Marriott Greenville H
(252) 364-8999. **$149-$169.** 1820 W 5th St 27834. Jct 5th St (SR 43); across from north entrance, Pitt County Memorial Hospital. Int corridors. **Pets:** Accepted.

GROVER
WW The Inn of the Patriots BB
(704) 937-2940. **$149-$309, 30 day notice.** 301 Cleveland Ave 28073. On SR 226. Int corridors. **Pets:** Medium, other species. $30 one-time fee/pet. Service with restrictions, supervision.

HAVELOCK
WWWW Holiday Inn Express & Suites H
(252) 447-9000. **Call for rates.** 103 Branchside Dr 28532. Jct SR 101, 1 mi w on US 70. Int corridors. **Pets:** Medium, dogs only. $35 one-time fee/room. Designated rooms, service with restrictions, supervision.

HENDERSON
WW Budget Host Inn M
(252) 492-2013. **$49-$69.** 1727 N Garnett St 27536. I-85 exit 215, just e, then just w on US 158. Ext corridors. **Pets:** Accepted.

WW Red Roof Inn Henderson H
(252) 438-6300. **$89-$119.** 200 Simmons Dr 27536. I-85 exit 212, just w on Ruin Creek Rd, 0.5 mi n on N Cooper Dr, then just e. Int corridors. **Pets:** Accepted.

Sleep Inn 🅷
(252) 433-9449. **$70-$90.** 18 Market St 27537. I-85 exit 212, just w on Ruin Creek Rd, then just se on Zeb Robinson Rd. Int corridors.
Pets: Accepted. (SAVE) 📶 🛄 🖵

HENDERSONVILLE
BEST WESTERN Hendersonville Inn 🅼
(828) 692-0521. **$69-$159.** 105 Sugarloaf Rd 28792. I-26 exit 49A, just e on US 64. Ext corridors. **Pets:** Large, other species. $10 daily fee/pet. Designated rooms, service with restrictions, crate.
(SAVE) 🍽 🚹 🏊 📶 🛄 🖵

Econo Lodge 🅼
(828) 693-8800. **$60-$120.** 206 Mitchelle Dr 28792. I-26 exit 49B, just w on US 64, just s on Orr Camp Dr, then just e. Ext corridors.
Pets: Accepted. 🏊 📶 🛄 🖵

Mountain Inn & Suites 🅷
(828) 692-7772. **$69-$169.** 755 Upward Rd 28731. I-26 exit 53, just e. Int corridors. **Pets:** Accepted. 🚹 📶 🛄 🖵

Mountain Lodge 🅷
(828) 693-9910. **$99-$159.** 755 Upward Rd 28731. I-26 exit 53, just e. Int corridors. **Pets:** Accepted. 🚹 🏊 📶 ✖ 🛄 🖵

Ramada 🅷
(828) 697-0006. **$55-$90.** 150 Sugarloaf Rd 28792. I-26 exit 49A, just e on US 64, then just s. Int corridors. **Pets:** Medium, dogs only. $15 daily fee/pet. Service with restrictions, supervision. 🚹 📶 ✖ 🛄 🖵

HICKORY
Baymont Inn & Suites Hickory 🅼
(828) 304-0410. **$49-$79.** 1120 13th Ave Dr SE 28602. I-40 exit 125, just s on Lenoir Rhyne Blvd, then 0.4 mi w. Ext corridors.
Pets: Accepted. 🚹 🏊 📶 🛄 🖵

BEST WESTERN Hickory 🅷 🐾
(828) 323-1150. **$90-$95.** 1520 13th Ave Dr SE 28602. I-40 exit 125, just s on Lenoir Rhyne Blvd, then just e. Ext/int corridors. **Pets:** Large, other species. $20 one-time fee/pet. Designated rooms, service with restrictions. (SAVE) 🏊 📶 🛄 🖵

Crowne Plaza 🅷
(828) 323-1000. **$109-$119, 10 day notice.** 1385 Lenoir Rhyne Blvd SE 28602. I-40 exit 125, just s. Ext/int corridors. **Pets:** Accepted.
🍽 🏊 📶 🛄 🖵

Red Roof Inn Hickory 🅼
(828) 323-1500. **$39-$79.** 1184 Lenoir Rhyne Blvd 28602. I-40 exit 125, just n. Ext corridors. **Pets:** Large, other species. Service with restrictions, supervision. (SAVE) 🚹 📶 ✖ 🛄 🖵

HIGHLANDS
Highlands Inn Lodge 🅷
(828) 526-5899. **Call for rates.** 96 Log Cabin Ln 28741. Jct US 64, just s on SR 106 (Dillard Rd), just w. Ext/int corridors. **Pets:** Accepted.
🚹 📶 ✖ 🛄 🖵

The Park on Main 🅷
(828) 526-4502. **Call for rates.** 205 Main St 28741. Just w on US 64; downtown. Ext/int corridors. **Pets:** Accepted. 🚹 📶 ✖ 🛄 🖵

HILLSBOROUGH
Holiday Inn Express 🅷
(919) 644-7997. **Call for rates.** 202 Cardinal Dr 27278. I-85 exit 164, just se, then just s; I-40 exit 261, 1.2 mi n, then just w. Int corridors.
Pets: Accepted. 🚹 🏊 📶 🛄 🖵

HUNTERSVILLE
BEST WESTERN PLUS Huntersville Inn & Suites Near Lake Norman 🅷
(704) 875-7880. **$76.** 13830 Statesville Rd 28078. I-77 exit 23, just e, then s on US 21. Int corridors. **Pets:** Large, other species. $20 daily fee/pet. Designated rooms, service with restrictions, supervision.
(SAVE) 🏊 📶 🛄 🖵

Candlewood Suites 🅷
(704) 895-3434. **$83-$103.** 16530 Northcross Dr 28078. I-77 exit 25, just w on SR 73, then just s. Int corridors. **Pets:** Medium. $25 daily fee/pet. Designated rooms, service with restrictions, crate.
📶 🛄 🖵

Hampton Inn & Suites-Huntersville 🅷
(704) 947-5510. **$119-$179.** 10305 Wilmington St 28078. I-77 exit 23, just e, then just n on US 21. Int corridors. **Pets:** Medium, other species. Designated rooms, service with restrictions, supervision.
🚹 🏊 📶 🛄 🖵

Quality Inn 🅷
(704) 892-6597. **$62-$99.** 16825 Caldwell Creek Dr 28078. I-77 exit 25, just e on SR 73, just n on US 21, then just w. Ext/int corridors.
Pets: Medium. $25 daily fee/pet. Service with restrictions, supervision.
(SAVE) 🚹 📶 🛄 🖵

Residence Inn by Marriott-Lake Norman 🅷
(704) 584-0000. **$89-$199.** 16830 Kenton Dr 28078. I-77 exit 25, 1 mi w on SR 73, then just n. Int corridors. **Pets:** Accepted.
🚹 🏊 📶 ✖ 🛄 🖵

Sleep Inn & Suites 🅷
(704) 766-2500. **$90-$285.** 16508 Northcross Dr 28078. I-77 exit 25, just w on SR 73, then just s. Int corridors. **Pets:** Accepted.
📶 🛄 🖵

JACKSONVILLE
Baymont Inn & Suites Jacksonville 🅷
(910) 347-6500. **$89-$149, 3 day notice.** 474 Western Blvd 28546. Jct US 17, just n. Ext corridors. **Pets:** Medium, other species. $15 daily fee/pet. Service with restrictions, crate.
🏊 📶 🛄 🖵

Candlewood Suites 🅷
(910) 333-0494. **$92-$129.** 119 Penny Ln 28546. Jct Western Blvd, just n on US 17 business route, just w. Int corridors. **Pets:** Accepted.
🚹 📶 ✖ 🛄 🖵

Home2 Suites by Hilton 🅷
(910) 355-3500. **$109-$154.** 139 Circuit Ln 28546. Jct US 17, 0.4 mi w on Western Blvd, just s. Int corridors. **Pets:** Accepted.
🚹 📶 🛄 🖵

Suburban Extended Stay Hotel-Camp Lejeune 🅷
(910) 346-7759. **$84-$119.** 1323 Lejeune Blvd 28540. On SR 24 business route, just e of US 17. Int corridors. **Pets:** Small. $25 daily fee/room. Designated rooms, service with restrictions, crate.
🚹 📶 🛄 🖵

TownePlace Suites by Marriott Jacksonville 🅷 🐾
(910) 478-9795. **$89-$139.** 400 Northwest Cir 28546. Jct US 17, 2 mi w on Western Blvd, just s. Int corridors. **Pets:** Other species. $100 one-time fee/room. Service with restrictions, supervision.
🚹 🏊 📶 ✖ 🛄 🖵

JONESVILLE
BEST WESTERN Yadkin Valley Inn & Suites 🅷 🐾
(336) 835-6000. **$89-$109.** 1713 NC Hwy 67 28642. I-77 exit 82, just e. Int corridors. **Pets:** Medium. $15 daily fee/pet. Designated rooms, service with restrictions, supervision. (SAVE) 🚹 🏊 📶 🛄 🖵

◆◆ ▼▼▼ Comfort Inn M ❀
(336) 835-9400. **$74-$109.** 1633 Winston Rd 28642. I-77 exit 82, just w on SR 67. Ext corridors. **Pets:** Other species. $15 one-time fee/room. Service with restrictions, crate. SAVE ⛄M 🏊 🛜 🍴 📶 💻

KANNAPOLIS
▼▼▼ Comfort Inn & Suites H ❀
(704) 795-4888. **Call for rates.** 3033 Cloverleaf Pkwy 28083. I-85 exit 58, just n on US 29, just e on Cloverleaf Plaza, then just s. Int corridors. **Pets:** Other species. $25 daily fee/room. Designated rooms, service with restrictions, crate. ⛄M 🏊 🛜 🍴 📶 💻

KENLY
▼▼▼ Motel 6 # 4918 M
(919) 284-3800. **$50-$135.** 843 Johnston Pkwy 27542. I-95 exit 106, just w. Ext corridors. **Pets:** Other species. Service with restrictions, crate. 🛜 📶

KILL DEVIL HILLS
◆◆ ▼▼▼ Comfort Inn North Oceanfront H
(252) 441-6333. **$69-$229.** 1601 S Virginia Dare Tr 27948. SR 12, at MM 9.5. Int corridors. **Pets:** Medium. $25 daily fee/room. Designated rooms, service with restrictions, supervision.
SAVE 🍴 🏊 🛜 🍴 📶 ☕

▼▼▼ First Flight Retreat Condominiums CO
(252) 489-4747. **$145-$399.** 815 S Virginia Dare Tr 27948. SR 12, at MM 8.5. Int corridors. **Pets:** Dogs only. $125 one-time fee/pet. Designated rooms, no service. 🏊 ✂ 🛜 🍴 📶 💻

▼▼ John Yancey Oceanfront Inn M
(252) 441-7141. **$50-$259, 3 day notice.** 2009 S Virginia Dare Tr 27948. SR 12, at MM 10.3. Ext/int corridors. **Pets:** Dogs only. $20 daily fee/pet. Designated rooms, service with restrictions, supervision.
🏊 🛜 📶 💻

◆◆ ▼▼▼ Ramada Plaza Nags Head Oceanfront H
(252) 441-2151. **$89-$219, 3 day notice.** 1701 S Virginia Dare Tr 27948. SR 12, at MM 9.5. Int corridors. **Pets:** $25 daily fee/pet. Designated rooms, service with restrictions, supervision.
SAVE 🍴 ⛄M 🏊 🛜 ✂ 📶 💻

▼▼ Travelodge-Nags Head Beach Hotel H
(252) 441-0411. **$70-$240, 3 day notice.** 804 N Virginia Dare Tr 27948. SR 12, at MM 8.1. Ext/int corridors. **Pets:** Large, other species. Designated rooms, service with restrictions. ⛄M 🏊 🛜 📶 💻

LAKE TOXAWAY
▼▼▼ Cabins at Seven Foxes CA ❀
(828) 877-6333. **$180-$295, 30 day notice.** Seven Foxes Ln 28747. Jct US 64, 1.4 mi n on SR 281, 1.4 mi w on Slick Fisher Rd, then just s. Ext corridors. **Pets:** Dogs only. $75 one-time fee/pet. No service, supervision. 📷 ✂ 📶 💻

LAURINBURG
▼▼ Quality Inn M
(910) 277-0080. **$70-$100.** 14 Jameson Inn Ct 28352. US 74 Bypass exit 183, just n on US 15/401 Bypass, then just e. Ext corridors. **Pets:** Large. $20 daily fee/pet. Service with restrictions, crate.
🏊 🛜 📶 💻

LELAND
◆◆ ▼▼▼ BEST WESTERN PLUS Westgate Inn & Suites H ❀
(910) 371-2858. **$70-$190.** 1120 Towne Lake Dr 28451. Jct US 74/76, 2 mi s on US 17. Int corridors. **Pets:** Medium, dogs only. $20 daily fee/room. Designated rooms, service with restrictions, supervision.
SAVE ⛄M 🏊 🛜 ✂ 📶 💻

▼▼▼ Holiday Inn Express Leland - Wilmington Area H
(910) 383-3300. **Call for rates.** 1020 Grandiflora Dr 28451. Jct US 74/76, 2 mi s on US 17, just w. Int corridors. **Pets:** Accepted.
⛄M 🏊 🛜 ✂ 📶 💻

LEXINGTON
◆◆ ▼▼▼ Days Inn & Suites H
(336) 357-2333. **$80-$99.** 1620 Cotton Grove Rd 27292. I-85 exit 91, just s on SR 8, then just ne. Ext/int corridors. **Pets:** Other species. $10 daily fee/pet. Designated rooms, service with restrictions, crate.
SAVE ⛄M 🏊 🛜 📶 💻

LILLINGTON
▼▼ Microtel Inn & Suites by Wyndham Lillington H
(910) 893-2626. **$70-$90.** 300 E Cornelius Harnett Blvd 27546. Jct US 401/SR 210, just ne on US 421/SR 27. Int corridors. **Pets:** Accepted.
⛄M 🏊 🛜 📶 💻

LUMBERTON
◆◆ ▼▼ BEST WESTERN Lumberton M
(910) 618-9799. **$90-$169.** 201 Jackson Ct 28358. I-95 exit 22, just e, then just s. Ext corridors. **Pets:** Other species. $10 daily fee/pet. Service with restrictions, supervision. SAVE 🏊 🛜 📶 💻

MAGGIE VALLEY
▼▼ Microtel Inn & Suites by Wyndham Maggie Valley H
(828) 926-8554. **$55-$170.** 3777 Soco Rd 28751. Jct US 276, 4 mi w on US 19. Int corridors. **Pets:** Accepted. ⛄M 🏊 🛜 ✂ 📶 💻

MARION
▼▼ Comfort Inn H
(828) 652-4888. **$90-$190.** 178 Hwy 70 W 28752. I-40 exit 85, 5 mi n; jct US 221 N Bypass and 70. Int corridors. **Pets:** Accepted.
♿ 🏊 🛜 📶 💻

MARS HILL
▼▼ Comfort Inn H
(828) 689-9000. **$80-$120.** 167 J F Robinson Ln 28754. US 19/23 exit 11. Int corridors. **Pets:** Accepted. ⛄M 🏊 🛜 ✂ 📶 💻

MATTHEWS
▼▼▼ Quality Inn & Suites H
(704) 821-9800. **$69-$199.** 13470 E Independence Blvd 28105. I-485 exit 51B, 1 mi e on US 74. Ext/int corridors. **Pets:** Accepted.
🏊 🛜 ✂ 📶 💻

MILLS RIVER
▼▼▼ Barkwells CA
(828) 891-8288. **$235-$380, 30 day notice.** 234-333 Barkwells Ln 28759. I-26 exit 40, 0.8 mi n on US 25 (Boylston Hwy), 2.4 mi w on Old Fanning Bridge Rd, then 0.3 mi s, follow signs to gated entrance. Ext corridors. **Pets:** Accepted. 🛜 ✂ 📶 💻

MOCKSVILLE
▼▼ Quality Inn M
(336) 751-7310. **$70-$100.** 1500 Yadkinville Rd 27028. I-40 exit 170, just s on US 601. Ext corridors. **Pets:** Accepted. 🏊 🛜 📶 💻

MOORESVILLE
▼▼▼ Candlewood Suites Mooresville/Lake Norman H
(704) 360-4899. **Call for rates.** 3247 Charlotte Hwy 28117. I-77 exit 33, 0.4 mi ne on US 21. Int corridors. **Pets:** Medium. $15 one-time fee/pet, $10 daily fee/pet. Designated rooms, service with restrictions, crate.
⛄M 🛜 ✂ 📶 💻

▼▼▼ Holiday Inn Express Hotel & Suites H
(704) 662-6900. **$94-$139.** 130 Norman Station Blvd 28117. I-77 exit 36, just e on SR 150, then just s. Int corridors. **Pets:** Medium, other species. $50 one-time fee/room. Designated rooms, service with restrictions. ⛄M 🏊 🛜 ✂ 📶 ☕

▼▼▼ TownePlace Suites by Marriott Charlotte Mooresville H
(704) 659-8600. **$75-$132.** 139 Gateway Blvd 28117. I-77 exit 33, just ne on US 21, then just w. Int corridors. **Pets:** Accepted.
⛄M 🏊 🛜 ✂ 📶 💻

MOREHEAD CITY

Econo Lodge Crystal Coast M
(252) 247-2940. **$60-$90.** 3410 Bridges St 28557. Jct US 70, just n on 35th St. Ext corridors. **Pets:** Accepted. SAVE

Holiday Inn Express Hotel & Suites H
(252) 247-5001. **$79-$229.** 5063 Executive Dr 28557. Jct US 70 and SR 24. Int corridors. **Pets:** Accepted.

Quality Inn M
(252) 247-3434. **$60-$159.** 3100 Arendell St 28557. 2 mi w on US 70. Ext corridors. **Pets:** Accepted.

MORGANTON

Comfort Inn & Suites H
(828) 430-4000. **$95-$140.** 1273 Burkemont Ave 28655. I-40 exit 103, just s. Int corridors. **Pets:** Accepted. SAVE

Quality Inn H
(828) 437-0171. **$75-$130.** 2400 S Sterling St 28655. I-40 exit 105 (SR 18), just s. Ext corridors. **Pets:** Accepted.

Sleep Inn H
(828) 433-9000. **$70-$80.** 2400A S Sterling St 28655. I-40 exit 105 (SR 18), just s. Int corridors. **Pets:** Accepted.

MORRISVILLE

Holiday Inn Express H
(919) 653-2260. **Call for rates.** 1014 Airport Blvd 27560. I-40 exit 284 or 284A, just s. Int corridors. **Pets:** Accepted.

Holiday Inn-Raleigh-Durham Airport H
(919) 465-1910. **$79-$179.** 930 Airport Blvd 27560. I-40 exit 284 or 284A, 0.5 mi s. Int corridors. **Pets:** Accepted.

HYATT house Raleigh Durham Airport H
(919) 388-5355. **$79-$239.** 10962 Chapel Hill Rd 27560. I-40 exit 283A, 1 mi s on SR 540 exit 69, then just e on SR 54. Int corridors.
Pets: Accepted. SAVE

Hyatt Place Raleigh-Durham Airport H
(919) 405-2400. **$69-$219.** 200 Airgate Dr 27560. I-40 exit 284 or 284B, just n, just w on Pleasant Grove Church Rd, then just s. Int corridors. **Pets:** Medium, dogs only. $75 one-time fee/room. Service with restrictions, crate. SAVE

La Quinta Inn & Suites Raleigh Durham Airport South H
(919) 481-3600. **$72-$205.** 1001 Aerial Center Pkwy 27560. I-40 exit 284 or 284A, just s, then just e; in Aerial Center Park. Int corridors. **Pets:** Large, other species. Service with restrictions.

La Quinta Inn & Suites (Raleigh-Durham Int'l Airport) H
(919) 461-1771. **$69-$239.** 1001 Hospitality Ct 27560. I-40 exit 284 or 284A, just s, just e on Aerial Center Pkwy, then just ne; in Aerial Center Park. Int corridors. **Pets:** Large, other species. Service with restrictions.

Residence Inn by Marriott Raleigh-Durham Airport H ❀
(919) 467-8689. **$85-$170.** 2020 Hospitality Ct 27560. I-40 exit 284 or 284A, just s on Airport Blvd, just e on Aerial Center Pkwy, then just ne. Int corridors. **Pets:** Other species. $100 one-time fee/room. Designated rooms, service with restrictions, crate. SAVE ECO

Staybridge Suites Raleigh Durham Airport H
(919) 468-0180. **Call for rates.** 1012 Airport Blvd 27560. I-40 exit 284 or 284A, just s; enter between Hampton Inn-RDU and Holiday Inn Express. Int corridors. **Pets:** Accepted.

MOUNT AIRY

Holiday Inn Express & Suites H
(336) 719-1731. **$100-$140.** 1320 EMS Dr 27030. Jct US 52, 0.5 mi s on US 601, then just w. Int corridors. **Pets:** Small, other species. $25 daily fee/pet. Designated rooms, service with restrictions, supervision.

Quality Inn M
(336) 789-2000. **$80-$130.** 2136 Rockford St 27030. Jct US 52, 0.6 mi s on US 601. Ext corridors. **Pets:** Medium. $25 one-time fee/pet. Designated rooms, service with restrictions, supervision.

MOUNT OLIVE

Sleep Inn & Suites Mount Olive H
(919) 658-1002. **$90-$160.** 203 NC Hwy 55 W 28365. Jct US 117, just w. Int corridors. **Pets:** Small. $20 daily fee/pet. Designated rooms, service with restrictions, supervision.

MURPHY

BEST WESTERN of Murphy M
(828) 837-3060. **$64-$110.** 1522 Andrews Rd 28906. US 74, 19 and 129 exit Andrews Rd. Ext corridors. **Pets:** Medium, other species. $10 daily fee/room. Designated rooms, service with restrictions. SAVE

NAGS HEAD

Comfort Inn Oceanfront South H 🐾
(252) 441-6315. **$59-$239.** 8031 Old Oregon Inlet Rd 27959. SR 12, at MM 17. Int corridors. **Pets:** Other species. $25 daily fee/room. Designated rooms, service with restrictions, crate. SAVE

Dolphin Oceanfront Motel M
(252) 441-7488. **$49-$399, 30 day notice.** 8017 S Old Oregon Inlet Rd 27959. SR 12, at MM 16.5. Ext corridors. **Pets:** Accepted.

Sea Foam Motel M
(252) 441-7320. **$71-$170, 14 day notice.** 7111 S Virginia Dare Tr 27959. SR 12, at MM 16.5. Ext corridors. **Pets:** Other species. $10 daily fee/pet. Designated rooms, service with restrictions, supervision. SAVE

NEW BERN

Bridge Pointe Hotel & Marina H
(252) 636-3637. **$80-$135.** 101 Howell Rd 28562. US 70 Bypass exit 417, just w on US 70 business route, then just s. Int corridors.
Pets: Accepted.

DoubleTree by Hilton New Bern Riverfront H
(252) 638-3585. **$109-$249.** 100 Middle St 28560. Downtown; on waterfront. Int corridors. **Pets:** Accepted.

OCEAN ISLE BEACH

The Islander Inn H
(910) 575-7000. **$69-$209, 3 day notice.** 57 W First St 28469. SR 904, just s. Int corridors. **Pets:** Accepted. SAVE

The Winds Resort Beach Club H
(910) 579-6275. **$75-$387, 30 day notice.** 310 E First St 28469. SR 904, 1.6 mi n. Ext/int corridors. **Pets:** Small. $25 daily fee/pet. Designated rooms, service with restrictions, crate. SAVE

OCRACOKE

The Anchorage Inn M
(252) 928-1101. **Call for rates.** 205 Irvin Garrish Hwy (SR 12) 27960. From Cedar Island Ferry, just n. Ext corridors. **Pets:** Accepted.

OLD FORT

▼▼◆▼ **Inn On Mill Creek** **BB** ❀
(828) 668-1115. **$159-$199, 14 day notice.** 3895 Mill Creek Rd 28762.
I-40 exit 66, just n, 0.9 mi e on Ridgecrest Rd, 0.9 mi n on Yates Ave,
then 1.5 mi n. Ext/int corridors. **Pets:** $10 daily fee/pet. Designated
rooms, service with restrictions. 🤝 ✕ 🗐

ORIENTAL

▼▼ **Oriental Marina & Inn** **CO**
(252) 249-1818. **$104-$234, 3 day notice.** 103 Wall St 28571. Jct SR
55 (Broad St), just ne on Hodges St. Ext corridors. **Pets:** Accepted.
🍴 🏊 🛜 ✕ 🛏 🖵

OXFORD

▼▼ **Comfort Inn & Suites** **H**
(919) 692-1000. **$89-$129.** 1000 Linden Ave 27565. I-85 exit 204, just
e. Int corridors. **Pets:** Medium. $15 daily fee/pet. Designated rooms,
service with restrictions, crate. 🏊 🛜 ✕ 🛏 🖵

PEMBROKE

▼▼◆▼ **Holiday Inn Express** **H**
(910) 521-1311. **Call for rates.** 605 Redmond Rd 28372. Jct SR 710,
just se on SR 711, then just s. Int corridors. **Pets:** Accepted.
&M 🏊 🛜 🛏 🖵

PINEHURST

⬙ ▼▼◆▼ **Homewood Suites by Hilton-Olmsted Village
near Pinehurst** **H**
(910) 255-0300. **$99-$239.** 250 Central Park Ave 28374. Jct SR 5 and
211, just n; in Olmsted Village. Int corridors. **Pets:** Accepted.
SAVE &M 🏊 🛜 ✕ 🛏 🖵

PLYMOUTH

▼▼◆▼ **Holiday Inn Express** **H**
(252) 793-4700. **Call for rates.** 840 US Hwy 64 W 27962. Jct SR 32 S,
1 mi w. Ext/int corridors. **Pets:** Accepted.
&M 🏊 🛜 ✕ 🛏 🖵

RALEIGH

▼▼ **Candlewood Suites-Crabtree** **H** ❀
(919) 789-4840. **Call for rates.** 4433 Lead Mine Rd 27612. I-440 exit 7
or 7B, just w, then just n. Int corridors. **Pets:** Large. $25 daily fee/room.
Service with restrictions, crate. &M 🛜 ✕ 🛏 🖵

▼▼◆▼ **Comfort Inn & Suites Crabtree** **H**
(919) 782-1112. **$79-$95.** 6209 Glenwood Ave 27612. I-440 exit 7 or
7B, 2.5 mi w on US 70. Int corridors. **Pets:** Medium. $25 daily fee/
room. Designated rooms, service with restrictions, crate.
&M 🏊 🛜 🛏 🖵

▼▼ **Days Inn** **M**
(919) 878-9310. **$55-$63.** 3201 Wake Forest Rd 27609. I-440 exit 10
(Wake Forest Rd), just n, then just w. Ext corridors. **Pets:** Accepted.
🏊 🛜 🛏 🖵

▼▼ **Extended Stay America West - Raleigh/North
Raleigh** **H**
(919) 829-7271. **$64-$94.** 911 Wake Towne Dr 27609. I-440 exit 10
(Wake Forest Rd), just s, then w. Int corridors. **Pets:** Other species.
$25 daily fee/pet. Service with restrictions, supervision. 🛜 🛏 🖵

⬙ ▼▼◆▼ **Fairfield Inn & Suites by Marriott Raleigh
Crabtree Valley** **H**
(919) 881-9800. **$94-$149.** 2201 Summit Park Ln 27612. I-440 exit 7 or
7B, just w on US 70, just s on Blue Ridge Rd, then just e. Int corridors.
Pets: Accepted. SAVE &M 🏊 🛜 ✕ 🛏 🖵

▼▼◆▼ **Hilton North Raleigh Midtown** **H**
(919) 872-2323. **$99-$229.** 3415 Wake Forest Rd 27609. I-440 exit 10
(Wake Forest Rd), 0.4 mi n. Int corridors. **Pets:** Accepted.
🍴 &M 🏊 🛜 ✕ 🛏 🖵

▼▼◆▼ **Holiday Inn Crabtree Valley** **H**
(919) 782-8600. **$89-$299, 3 day notice.** 4100 Glenwood Ave 27612.
I-440 exit 7 or 7B, just w on US 70. Int corridors. **Pets:** Accepted.
🍴 &M 🏊 🛜 🛏 🖵

▼▼◆▼ **Holiday Inn Express & Suites near NC
State/Southwest** **H**
(919) 854-0001. **$89-$139, 3 day notice.** 3741 Thistledown Dr 27606.
I-40 exit 295, just n on Gorman St, then just e. Int corridors.
Pets: Accepted. &M 🏊 🛜 ✕ 🛏 🖵

▼▼◆▼ **Holiday Inn Express Hotel & Suites** **H**
(919) 570-5550. **$90-$130.** 11400 Common Oaks Dr 27614. Jct SR 98,
1.2 mi s on US 1, then just w. Int corridors. **Pets:** Small. $25 daily fee/
room. Designated rooms, service with restrictions, crate.
&M 🏊 🛜 ✕ 🛏 🖵

⬙⬙⬙ ▼▼◆▼ **HYATT house Raleigh North Hills** **H**
(919) 363-0771. **$99-$259.** 160 Park at North Hills St 27609. I-440 exit
8B, just n on Six Forks Rd, then just ne. Int corridors. **Pets:** Accepted.
SAVE &M 🛜 ✕ 🛏 🖵

⬙⬙⬙ ▼▼◆▼ **Hyatt Place North Raleigh - Midtown** **H**
(919) 877-9997. **$69-$179.** 1105 Navaho Dr 27609. I-440 exit 10 (Wake
Forest Rd), just n, then just w. Int corridors. **Pets:** Medium, dogs only.
$75 one-time fee/room. Service with restrictions, crate.
SAVE &M 🏊 🛜 ✕ 🛏 🖵

⬙⬙⬙ ▼▼◆▼ **Hyatt Place Raleigh West** **H** ❀
(919) 233-2205. **$69-$189.** 710 Corporate Center Dr 27607. I-40 exit
290, just e on SR 54 (Chapel Hill Rd). Int corridors. **Pets:** Large, dogs
only. $75 one-time fee/room. Designated rooms, service with restric-
tions, crate. SAVE &M 🏊 🛜 ✕ 🛏 🖵

▼▼◆▼ **La Quinta Inn & Suites Raleigh (Crabtree)** **H**
(919) 785-0071. **$72-$224.** 2211 Summit Park Ln 27612. I-440 exit 7 or
7B, just w on US 70, just s on Blue Ridge Rd, then just e. Int corridors.
Pets: Large, other species. Service with restrictions.
&M 🏊 🛜 🛏 🖵

⬙⬙⬙ ▼▼◆▼ **Ramada-Blue Ridge** **H**
(919) 832-4100. **$79-$159.** 1520 Blue Ridge Rd 27607. I-40 exit 289, 2
mi e on Wade Ave exit Blue Ridge Rd, then just s; I-440 exit 4 or 4B,
just w on Wade Ave exit Blue Ridge Rd, then just s. Int corridors.
Pets: Other species. $25 one-time fee/pet. Designated rooms, service
with restrictions, supervision. SAVE 🍴 &M 🏊 🛜 ✕ 🛏 🖵

⬙⬙⬙ ▼▼ **Red Roof Plus+ Raleigh NCSU- Convention
Center** **H**
(919) 833-6005. **$54-$120.** 1813 S Saunders St 27603. I-40 exit 298B,
just n. Int corridors. **Pets:** Large, other species. Service with restrictions, supervision. SAVE &M 🛜 ✕ 🛏 🖵

⬙⬙⬙ ▼▼◆▼ **Residence Inn by Marriott Raleigh Crabtree
Valley** **H**
(919) 279-3000. **$109-$209.** 2200 Summit Park Ln 27612. I-440 exit 7
or 7B, just w on US 70, just s on Blue Ridge Rd, then just e. Int corridors. **Pets:** Accepted. SAVE &M 🏊 🛜 ✕ 🛏 🖵

⬙⬙⬙ ▼▼◆▼ **Residence Inn by Marriott-Raleigh
Midtown** **H**
(919) 878-6100. **$89-$199.** 1000 Navaho Dr 27609. I-440 exit 10 (Wake
Forest Rd), just n, then w. Ext corridors. **Pets:** Accepted.
SAVE &M 🏊 🛜 ✕ 🛏 🖵

REIDSVILLE

⬙⬙⬙ ▼▼ **Days Inn of Reidsville** **M**
(336) 342-2800. **$64-$79.** 2205 Barnes St 27320. US 29 exit 150
(Barnes St), just e. Ext corridors. **Pets:** Accepted. SAVE 🛜 🛏 🖵

⬙⬙⬙ ▼▼ **Quality Inn** **M**
(336) 634-1275. **$65-$119.** 2203 Barnes St 27320. US 29 exit 150
(Barnes St), just e. Ext corridors. **Pets:** Accepted.
SAVE &M 🏊 🛜 🛏 🖵

ROANOKE RAPIDS

▼▼▼ Baymont Inn & Suites Roanoke Rapids M
(252) 533-0022. **$49-$79.** 101 S Old Farm Rd 27870. I-95 exit 173, 0.5 mi w on US 158, then just s. Ext corridors. **Pets:** Accepted.
🏊 📶 🛗 💻

AAA ▼▼▼▼ Hilton Garden Inn-Roanoke Rapids H
(252) 519-2333. **$89-$123.** 111 Carolina Crossroads Pkwy 27870. I-95 exit 171, just s on SR 125, then just n. Int corridors. **Pets:** Accepted.
SAVE ¶ 🛗 🏊 📶 🛗 💻

▼▼▼ Quality Inn M
(252) 537-9927. **$94-$104.** 1914 Julian R Allsbrook Hwy 27870. I-95 exit 173, just w. Ext corridors. **Pets:** Accepted. 🏊 📶 🛗 💻

ROBBINSVILLE

▼▼ Microtel Inn & Suites by Wyndham Robbinsville H
(828) 479-6772. **$65-$85.** 111 Rodney Orr Bypass (US 129) 28771. Center of downtown. Int corridors. **Pets:** Other species. $50 one-time fee/room. Service with restrictions, supervision. 📶 ✕ 🛗 💻

ROCKY MOUNT

AAA ▼▼▼ BEST WESTERN Inn I-95/Goldrock M
(252) 985-1450. **$70-$89.** 7095 NC 4 27809. I-95 exit 145, just e. Ext corridors. **Pets:** Other species. $20 one-time fee/room. Service with restrictions, supervision. SAVE 🏊 📶 🛗 💻

▼▼▼▼ Candlewood Suites H ❀
(252) 467-2550. **$90-$200.** 688 English Rd 27804. I-95 exit 138, 1 mi e on US 64 exit 466, just n on Winstead Ave, then just w. Int corridors. **Pets:** Large, other species. $25 one-time fee/room. Service with restrictions, crate. 🛗 🏊 📶 🛗 💻

AAA ▼▼▼ Comfort Inn H
(252) 937-7765. **$74-$124.** 200 Gateway Blvd 27804. I-95 exit 138, 1 mi e on US 64 exit 466, just s on Winstead Ave, just e on Curtis Ellis Dr, then just ne. Int corridors. **Pets:** Accepted.
SAVE 🏊 📶 🛗 💻

▼▼▼▼ Country Inn & Suites By Carlson H
(252) 442-0500. **$89-$129, 14 day notice.** 672 English Rd 27804. I-95 exit 138, 1 mi e on US 64 exit 466, just n on Winstead Ave, then just w. Int corridors. **Pets:** $20 one-time fee/room. Designated rooms, service with restrictions, supervision. 🛗 🏊 📶 ✕ 🛗 💻

▼▼▼ Residence Inn by Marriott Rocky Mount H
(252) 451-5600. **$119-$164.** 230 Gateway Blvd 27804. I-95 exit 138, 1 mi e on US 64 exit 466, just s on Winstead Ave, just e on Curtis Ellis Dr, then just ne. Int corridors. **Pets:** Accepted.
🛗 🏊 📶 ✕ 🛗 💻

AAA ▼▼▼ Rocky Mount Inn M
(252) 442-8101. **$50-$90.** 1921 N Wesleyan Blvd 27804. US 64 exit 468A, 2.2 mi n on US 301 Bypass. Ext corridors. **Pets:** $20 one-time fee/room. Service with restrictions, supervision.
SAVE 🏊 📶 🛗 💻

ROXBORO

▼▼▼ Hampton Inn H
(336) 599-8800. **$114-$139.** 920 Durham Rd 27573. Jct US 158, just n on US 501. Int corridors. **Pets:** Accepted. 🏊 📶 🛗 💻

▼▼ Innkeeper M
(336) 599-3800. **Call for rates.** 906 Durham Rd 27573. Jct US 158, just n on US 501. Ext/int corridors. **Pets:** Medium. $50 one-time fee/room. Designated rooms, service with restrictions, supervision.
🏊 📶 🛗

SALISBURY

▼▼▼▼ Hampton Inn H
(704) 637-8000. **$99-$199.** 1001 Klumac Rd 28144. I-85 exit 75, just n on US 601, then just sw. Int corridors. **Pets:** Other species. Designated rooms, service with restrictions, supervision. 🏊 📶 🛗 💻

▼▼▼ Hotel Salisbury & Conference Center H
(704) 637-3100. **$79-$139.** 530 Jake Alexander Blvd S 28147. I-85 exit 75, 0.5 mi n on US 601. Ext/int corridors. **Pets:** Accepted.
¶ 🛗 🏊 ✕ 📶 ✕ 🛗 💻

SALUDA

▼▼▼ The Oaks Bed & Breakfast BB ❀
(828) 749-2000. **$165-$199, 14 day notice.** 339 Greenville St 28773. I-26 exit 59, 1.1 mi sw, 0.5 mi w on US 176, then cross railway tracks. Ext/int corridors. **Pets:** Large, other species. $50 one-time fee/room. Designated rooms, service with restrictions, crate.
📶 ✕ 🖂 🛗 💻

SANFORD

▼▼▼ Baymont Inn & Suites Sanford M
(919) 708-7400. **$49-$79.** 2614 S Horner Blvd 27330. US 1 exit 69A, 4.1 mi s on US 421 and SR 87. Ext corridors. **Pets:** Accepted.
🛗 🏊 📶 🛗 💻

SCOTLAND NECK

▼▼ Scotland Neck Inn M
(252) 826-5141. **$60-$90, 3 day notice.** 308 S Main St 27874. Jct SR 125 S, just s on US 258. Int corridors. **Pets:** Medium, other species. $10 daily fee/pet. Designated rooms, service with restrictions, supervision. 🏊 📶 🛗 💻

SELMA

▼▼▼ Days Inn H
(919) 965-4000. **$65-$95.** 115 US 70A 27576. I-95 exit 97, just e, then just n. Int corridors. **Pets:** Medium, other species. $10 one-time fee/pet. Service with restrictions, supervision. 🛗 🏊 📶 🛗 💻

▼▼ Quality Inn M
(919) 965-5200. **$61-$114.** 1705 Industrial Park Dr 27576. I-95 exit 97, just w, then just s. Ext corridors. **Pets:** Accepted. 🏊 📶 🛗 💻

SHALLOTTE

▼▼ Days Inn Shallotte H
(910) 754-3300. **$55-$105.** 3670 Express Dr 28470. Jct SR 130, 0.9 mi n on US 17, just w on N Mulberry Dr, then just s. Int corridors.
Pets: Accepted. 🏊 📶 ✕ 🛗 💻

SMITHFIELD

▼▼ Baymont Inn & Suites Smithfield M
(919) 989-5901. **$49-$79.** 125 S Equity Dr 27577. I-95 exit 95, just w on US 70 business route, just n on Industrial Park Dr, then just w. Ext corridors. **Pets:** Accepted. 🛗 🏊 📶 🛗 💻

AAA ▼▼▼ Super 8 H ❀
(919) 989-8988. **$59-$129.** 735 Industrial Park Dr 27577. I-95 exit 95, just w on US 70 business route, then just n. Ext corridors. **Pets:** Other species. $15 daily fee/room. Service with restrictions, supervision.
SAVE 🛗 🏊 📶 🛗 💻

SOUTHERN PINES

AAA ▼▼▼ BEST WESTERN Pinehurst Inn H
(910) 692-0640. **$80-$110.** 1675 US Hwy 1 S 28387. Jct US 15/501, 0.5 mi n. Ext corridors. **Pets:** Dogs only. $10 daily fee/pet. Service with restrictions. SAVE 🏊 📶 🛗 💻

▼▼ Econo Lodge Inn & Suites H
(910) 692-2063. **$65-$95.** 408 W Morganton Rd 28387. US 1 exit Morganton Rd, just w. Int corridors. **Pets:** Accepted. 📶 🛗 💻

▼▼▼ Residence Inn by Marriott-Pinehurst/Southern Pines H
(910) 693-3400. **$109-$199.** 105 Brucewood Rd 28387. Jct US 1, 1.2 mi n on US 15/501, then just e. Int corridors. **Pets:** Accepted.
🏊 📶 ✕ 🛗 💻

SOUTHPORT

AAA ▼▼▼▼ Comfort Suites 🄷
(910) 454-7444. **$89-$159.** 4963 Southport Supply Rd (SR 211) 28461. Jct SR 87, 1.8 mi n. Int corridors. **Pets:** Accepted.
SAVE 🄼 ⤴ 📶 ✕ 🄱 🖵

STATESVILLE

AAA ▼▼▼ BEST WESTERN Statesville Inn 🄼 🐾
(704) 881-0111. **$79-$129.** 1121 Morland Dr 28677. I-77 exit 49A, just e on US 70. Ext corridors. **Pets:** Small. $20 daily fee/room. Designated rooms, service with restrictions, supervision.
SAVE 🄼 ⤴ 📶 🄱 🖵

AAA ▼▼▼ Comfort Inn & Suites 🄷
(704) 873-2044. **$79-$119.** 1214 Greenland Dr 28677. I-77 exit 49A, just e on US 70, then just s. Int corridors. **Pets:** Medium. $20 one-time fee/room. Designated rooms, service with restrictions, supervision.
SAVE 🄼 ⤴ 📶 ✕ 🄱 🖵

AAA ▼▼▼ Courtyard by Marriott Statesville Mooresville/Lake Norman 🄷
(704) 768-2400. **$126-$190.** 1530 Cinema Dr 28625. I-77 exit 49B, just e on Salisbury Rd, 0.6 mi n on Folger Dr, then just e. Int corridors.
Pets: Accepted. SAVE 🄼 ⤴ 📶 ✕ 🄱 🖵

▼▼ Quality Inn & Suites 🄼
(704) 878-2721. **$67-$129.** 715 Sullivan Rd 28677. I-40 exit 151, just s on US 21. Ext corridors. **Pets:** Accepted. ⤴ 📶 🄱 🖵

AAA ▼▼▼ Ramada 🄷
(704) 878-9691. **Call for rates.** 1215 E Garner Bagnal Blvd 28677. I-77 exit 49A, just e on US 70. Int corridors. **Pets:** Medium. $20 daily fee/pet. Designated rooms, service with restrictions, supervision.
SAVE 🍴 ⤴ 📶 🄱 🖵

AAA ▼▼▼ Red Roof Plus+ Statesville 🄼
(704) 878-2051. **$56-$100.** 1508 E Broad St 28625. I-77 exit 50, just e, then just s on Middleton St. Ext corridors. **Pets:** Large, other species. Service with restrictions, supervision. SAVE 🄼 📶 ✕ 🄱 🖵

THOMASVILLE

AAA ▼▼▼▼ Comfort Inn-Thomasville 🄷
(336) 472-6600. **$80-$140.** 895 Lake Rd 27360. I-85 exit 102, just w, then just s. Int corridors. **Pets:** Accepted. SAVE ⤴ 📶 🄱 🖵

▼▼ Microtel Inn & Suites by Wyndham Thomasville/High Point/Lexington 🄷
(336) 474-4515. **$55-$130.** 959 Lake Rd 27360. I-85 exit 102, just w, then just s. Int corridors. **Pets:** Small, dogs only. $20 daily fee/pet. Designated rooms, service with restrictions, supervision.
🄼 📶 🄱 🖵

WAKE FOREST

▼▼▼▼ Candlewood Suites 🄷 🐾
(919) 554-6901. **$110-$120.** 12050 Retail Dr 27587. US 1 exit 125, just w on SR 98 (Durham Rd), then just s. Int corridors. **Pets:** Other species. $75 one-time fee/room. Service with restrictions, supervision.
🄼 📶 🄱 🖵

▼▼▼ Hampton Inn 🄷
(919) 554-0222. **$89-$149.** 12318 Wake Union Church Rd 27587. Jct SR 98 (Durham Rd), 0.5 mi n on US 1, 0.5 mi w. Int corridors.
Pets: Accepted. ⤴ 📶 ✕ 🄱 🖵

WASHINGTON

▼▼ Comfort Inn 🄷
(252) 946-4444. **$70-$99.** 1636 Carolina Ave 27889. Jct US 264, 1 mi n on US 17 Business. Int corridors. **Pets:** Accepted. 🏊 📶 🄱 🖵

WAYNESVILLE *(Restaurants p. 637)*

▼▼ Super 8 🄼
(828) 454-9667. **$59-$129.** 79 Liner Cove Rd 28786. I-40 exit 27, to US 23/74, 3 mi; exit 104 (Liner Cove Rd). Ext corridors. **Pets:** Accepted.
🄼 ⤴ 📶 🄱 🖵

AAA ▼▼◆ The Waynesville Inn Golf Resort & Spa 🄷
(828) 456-3551. **$88-$198.** 176 Country Club Dr 28786. US 23 S/74 W exit 100, 0.6 mi s on Hazelwood Ave, then 0.3 mi e on Virginia Ave. Ext/int corridors. **Pets:** Dogs only. $25 daily fee/room. Designated rooms, service with restrictions, supervision.
SAVE 🍴 🄼 ⤴ ✕ 📶 ✕ 🄱 🖵

▼▼▼▼ The Yellow House on Plott Creek Road 🄱🄱
(828) 452-0991. **Call for rates.** 89 Oakview Dr 28786. US 23/74 exit 100 eastbound, 1.3 mi nw on Plott Creek Rd; exit 100 westbound, just se, just w on Sulphur Springs Rd, then 1.4 mi nw on Plott Creek Rd. Ext/int corridors. **Pets:** Accepted. 📶 ✕ 🄱 🖵

WEST JEFFERSON

▼▼ Nation's Inn 🄼
(336) 246-2080. **Call for rates.** 107 Beaver Creek School Rd 28694. Jct US 221, just n on SR 194, just w. Ext corridors. **Pets:** Accepted.
🄼 📶 🄱 🖵

WILLIAMSTON

▼▼▼ Holiday Inn Express 🄷
(252) 799-0100. **$96-$116.** 1071 Cantle Ct 27892. US 64 exit 512. Int corridors. **Pets:** Accepted. 🄼 ⤴ 📶 🄱 🖵

WILMINGTON

▼▼ Baymont Inn 🄼
(910) 392-6767. **$59-$109, 3 day notice.** 306 S College Rd 28403. Jct US 17 business route, just s on SR 132. Ext/int corridors. **Pets:** $10 daily fee/pet. Designated rooms, service with restrictions, supervision.
🄼 ⤴ 📶 🄱 🖵

AAA ▼▼▼▼ BEST WESTERN PLUS Coastline Inn 🄷 🐾
(910) 763-2800. **$109-$191.** 503 Nutt St 28401. Jct Market St, just w on Front St, just s on Red Cross St, then just w. Ext corridors. **Pets:** Large, dogs only. $50 deposit/room, $20 daily fee/room. Designated rooms, service with restrictions, crate. SAVE 📶 ✕ 🄱 🖵

AAA ▼▼▼▼ BEST WESTERN PLUS University Inn 🄷
(910) 799-4292. **$79-$169.** 5345 Market St 28405. Jct SR 132, just s on US 17 business route. Int corridors. **Pets:** Accepted.
SAVE ⤴ 📶 🄱 🖵

▼▼ Days Inn 🄼
(910) 799-6300. **$53-$100.** 5040 Market St 28405. Jct SR 132, 0.6 mi s on US 17 business route. Ext corridors. **Pets:** Other species. $15 daily fee/room. Service with restrictions, crate. 🍴 ⤴ 📶 🄱 🖵

▼▼ Jameson Inn 🄷
(910) 452-5660. **Call for rates.** 5102 Dunlea Ct 28405. Jct SR 132, 0.5 mi s on US 17 business route, just w on New Centre Dr. Int corridors.
Pets: Accepted. ⤴ 📶 🄱 🖵

▼▼ MainStay Suites 🄷
(910) 392-1741. **Call for rates.** 5229 Market St 28405. Jct SR 132, just s on US 17 business route. Int corridors. **Pets:** Small, other species. $50 one-time fee/pet. Designated rooms, service with restrictions, supervision. 🄼 📶 🄱 🖵

▼▼ Quality Inn 🄼
(910) 791-8850. **$60-$140.** 4926 Market St 28405. Jct SR 132, 0.9 mi s on US 17 business route. Ext corridors. **Pets:** Accepted.
⤴ 📶 🄱 🖵

Residence Inn by Marriott Wilmington Landfall H
(910) 256-0098. **$99-$229.** 1200 Culbreth Dr 28405. Jct US 17 business route, 2.4 mi e on US 74, 0.4 mi n on Military Cutoff Rd, then just e. Int corridors. **Pets:** Accepted. [SAVE] [&M] [≥] [≈] [✕] [⊟] [⬚]

Staybridge Suites Wilmington East H
(910) 202-8500. **$89-$239.** 5010 New Centre Dr 28403. Jct SR 132, 0.5 mi s on US 17 business route, just e. Int corridors. **Pets:** $75 one-time fee/room. Service with restrictions, crate. [&M] [≥] [≈] [⊟] [⬚]

TownePlace Suites by Marriott Wilmington/ Wrightsville Beach H
(910) 332-3326. **$89-$209.** 305 Eastwood Rd 28403. Jct US 17 business route, just e on US 74. Int corridors. **Pets:** Accepted.
[SAVE] [&M] [≥] [≈] [✕] [⊟] [⬚]

WILSON

Country Inn & Suites By Carlson H
(252) 281-5501. **$75-$150.** 4910 Hayes Pl 27893. I-95 exit 121, just w, then just s. Int corridors. **Pets:** Other species. $20 daily fee/room. Service with restrictions, crate. [SAVE] [&M] [≥] [≈] [✕] [⊟] [⬚]

Days Inn M
(252) 291-2323. **$85-$95.** 1801 S Tarboro St 27893. US 264 exit 40, 3.3 mi e on SR 42. Ext corridors. **Pets:** Medium. $15 deposit/pet, $15 daily fee/pet. Supervision. [SAVE] [≥] [≈] [⊟] [⬚]

Microtel Inn by Wyndham Wilson H
(252) 234-0444. **$44-$62.** 5013 Hayes Pl 27896. I-95 exit 121, just w, then just n. Int corridors. **Pets:** Accepted. [≈] [⊟]

Sleep Inn H
(252) 234-2900. **$80-$120.** 5011 Hayes Pl 27896. I-95 exit 121, just w. Int corridors. **Pets:** Accepted. [≥] [≈] [⊟] [⬚]

WINDSOR

The Inn at Grays Landing CI
(252) 794-2255. **$70-$140.** 401 S King St 27983. US 17, just w on SR 308. Int corridors. **Pets:** $25 one-time fee/pet. Designated rooms, service with restrictions. [۞] [≈] [✕] [z]

WINSTON-SALEM

Embassy Suites-Winston-Salem H
(336) 724-2300. **$119-$279.** 460 N Cherry St 27101. I-40 business route exit 5C (Cherry St), just n. Int corridors. **Pets:** Accepted.
[۞] [&M] [≥] [≈] [⊟] [⬚]

Fairfield Inn & Suites by Marriott Winston-Salem Hanes Mall H 🐾
(336) 714-3000. **$99-$209.** 1680 Westbrook Plaza Dr 27103. I-40 exit 189 (Stratford Rd), 0.5 mi n, just w, then just s. Int corridors. **Pets:** Medium. $50 one-time fee/room. Designated rooms, service with restrictions, supervision. [&M] [≥] [≈] [✕] [⊟] [⬚]

The Hawthorne Inn & Conference Center H
(336) 777-3000. **$81-$142.** 420 High St 27101. I-40 business route exit 5C (Cherry St) eastbound, just e; exit westbound, just w on 1st St, then just s on Marshall St. Int corridors. **Pets:** Accepted.
[SAVE] [۞] [&M] [≥] [≈] [✕] [⊟] [⬚]

La Quinta Inns & Suites Winston-Salem H
(336) 765-8777. **$75-$224.** 2020 Griffith Rd 27103. I-40 exit 189 (Stratford Rd), just s, just e on Hanes Mall Blvd, then just s. Int corridors. **Pets:** Large, other species. Service with restrictions.
[&M] [≥] [≈] [⊟] [⬚]

Quality Inn & Suites-Hanes Mall H
(336) 765-6670. **$60-$140.** 2008 S Hawthorne Rd 27103. I-40 business route exit 2A, 0.5 mi s on Silas Creek Pkwy, then just e. Ext corridors. **Pets:** Accepted. [SAVE] [۞] [&M] [≥] [≈] [⊟] [⬚]

Quality Inn-Coliseum H
(336) 767-8240. **$60-$120.** 531 Akron Dr 27105. US 52 exit 112, just e. Int corridors. **Pets:** Large, other species. $15 daily fee/pet. Designated rooms, service with restrictions, crate. [≥] [≈] [⊟] [⬚]

Ramada Plaza Hotel & Spa Winston-Salem North H
(336) 723-2911. **$90-$160.** 3050 University Pkwy 27105. I-40 business route exit 5C (Cherry St), 3 mi n. Int corridors. **Pets:** Accepted.
[۞] [≥] [≈] [⊟] [⬚]

Residence Inn by Marriott Winston-Salem H
(336) 759-0777. **$154-$269.** 7835 North Point Blvd 27106. US 52 exit 115B, 2 mi s on University Pkwy, then just e. Ext corridors. **Pets:** Large. $75 one-time fee/room. Service with restrictions, crate.
[≥] [≈] [✕] [⊟] [⬚]

Sleep Inn-Hanes Mall H
(336) 774-8020. **$65-$130.** 1985 Hampton Inn Ct 27103. I-40 exit 189 (Stratford Rd), just s, just e on Hanes Mall Blvd, then just n. Int corridors. **Pets:** Accepted. [&M] [≈] [⊟] [⬚]

WRIGHTSVILLE BEACH

Summer Sands Motel M
(910) 256-4175. **Call for rates.** 104 S Lumina Ave 28480. US 76, just e of causeway. Ext corridors. **Pets:** Dogs only. $100 deposit/room, $15 daily fee/room. Designated rooms, service with restrictions, crate.
[≥] [≈] [✕] [⊟] [⬚]

NORTH DAKOTA

BEULAH

AmericInn Lodge & Suites of Beulah H
(701) 873-2220. **$119-$186.** 2100 2nd Ave NW 58523. Jct SR 49/200, 1.2 mi s. Int corridors. **Pets:** Dogs only. $25 one-time fee/pet. Service with restrictions, supervision. [۞] [&M] [≥] [≈] [✕] [⊟] [⬚]

BISMARCK

Americas Best Value Inn & Suites M
(701) 223-8060. **$79-$135, 3 day notice.** 1505 Interchange Ave 58501. I-94 exit 159 (US 83), just se. Int corridors. **Pets:** Other species. $10 daily fee/pet. Designated rooms, service with restrictions, crate.
[SAVE] [&M] [≈] [✕] [⊟] [⬚]

BEST WESTERN PLUS Ramkota Hotel H
(701) 258-7700. **$109-$129.** 800 S 3rd St 58504. Just s of jct I-94 business loop (Bismarck Expwy) and S 3rd St. Int corridors.
Pets: Accepted. [SAVE] [۞] [&M] [≥] [✕] [≈] [✕] [⊟] [⬚]

Candlewood Suites H
(701) 751-8900. **$96-$143, 3 day notice.** 4400 Skyline Crossings 58503. I-94 exit 159 (US 83), 1.7 mi n, then just e. Int corridors.
Pets: Accepted. [۞] [&M] [≥] [≈] [✕] [⊟] [⬚]

Comfort Inn H
(701) 223-1911. **$77-$82.** 1030 E Interstate Ave 58503. I-94 exit 159 (US 83), 0.3 mi nw. Int corridors. **Pets:** Service with restrictions, crate.
[&M] [≥] [✕] [≈] [✕] [⊟] [⬚]

Comfort Suites H
(701) 223-4009. **$80-$94.** 929 Gateway Ave 58503. I-94 exit 159 (US 83), 0.3 mi nw. Int corridors. **Pets:** $10 daily fee/pet. Service with restrictions, crate. 🅼 ➔ 📶 ✕ 🛏 💻

Days Inn-Bismarck H
(701) 223-9151. **$89-$160.** 1300 E Capitol Ave 58501. I-94 exit 159 (US 83), just s. Int corridors. **Pets:** Accepted.
🅼 ➔ ✕ 📶 ✕ 🛏 💻

Kelly Inn M
(701) 223-8001. **$100-$189.** 1800 N 12th St 58501. I-94 exit 159 (US 83), 0.3 mi s. Int corridors. **Pets:** Medium, other species. Service with restrictions, supervision. 🍴 🅼 ➔ ✕ 📶 ✕ 🛏 💻

La Quinta Inn & Suites Bismarck H
(701) 751-3313. **$119-$309.** 2240 N 12th St 58501. I-94 exit 159 (US 83), just s. Int corridors. **Pets:** Large, other species. Service with restrictions. 🅼 ➔ 📶 ✕ 🛏 💻

Radisson Hotel Bismarck H
(701) 255-6000. **$116-$144.** 605 E Broadway Ave 58501. Jct 6th St; center. Int corridors. **Pets:** Accepted.
🍴 🅼 ➔ ✕ 📶 ✕ 🛏 💻

Ramada Bismarck Hotel & Conference Center H
(701) 258-7000. **$81-$249.** 1400 E Interchange Ave 58501. I-94 exit 159 (US 83), just s. Int corridors. **Pets:** Medium, dogs only. $50 deposit/pet, $10 daily fee/pet. Designated rooms, no service, supervision. SAVE 🍴 🅼 ➔ ✕ 📶 ✕ 🛏 💻

Ramada Limited Bismarck H
(701) 221-3030. **$99-$249.** 3808 E Divide Ave 58501. I-94 exit 161, just s on E Bismarck Expwy. Int corridors. **Pets:** Other species. $15 deposit/pet, $15 daily fee/pet. Designated rooms, service with restrictions, crate. SAVE 🅼 ➔ 📶 🛏 💻

Residence Inn by Marriott Bismarck H
(701) 258-6088. **$102-$191.** 3421 N 14th St 58503. I-94 exit 159 (US 83), just n. Int corridors. **Pets:** Accepted.
🅼 ➔ 📶 ✕ 🛏 💻

Super 8 M
(701) 255-1314. **$55-$160, 3 day notice.** 1124 E Capitol Ave 58501. I-94 exit 159 (US 83), just s. Int corridors. **Pets:** Very small, dogs only. $10 daily fee/pet. Designated rooms, supervision. SAVE 📶 🛏 💻

BOTTINEAU
Super 8 of Bottineau H
(701) 228-2125. **$43-$78.** 1007 11th St E 58318. 0.5 mi e on SR 5. Int corridors. **Pets:** Accepted. SAVE 🅼 📶 ✕ 🛏 💻

CARRINGTON
Carrington Inn & Suites M
(701) 652-3982. **$64-$105.** 101 4th Ave S 58421. Jct US 52 and 281, 0.5 mi s on US 52; just s of jct SR 200. Int corridors. **Pets:** $15 daily fee/pet. Designated rooms, service with restrictions, supervision.
📶 ✕ 🛏

CASSELTON
Days Inn & Governors Conference Center H
(701) 347-4524. **$73-$190.** 2050 Governors Dr 58012. I-94 exit 331, just n on SR 18. Int corridors. **Pets:** Accepted.
🍴 🅼 ➔ ✕ 📶 ✕ 🛏 💻

DICKINSON
Comfort Inn H
(701) 264-7300. **$139-$169.** 493 Elks Dr 58601. I-94 exit 61 (SR 22), just n, then w. Int corridors. **Pets:** Accepted.
🅼 ➔ 📶 ✕ 🛏 💻

Holiday Inn Express Hotel & Suites H
(701) 456-8000. **$160-$300.** 103 14th St W 58601. I-94 exit 61 (SR 22), just n, then just e. Int corridors. **Pets:** $50 one-time fee/room. Designated rooms, service with restrictions, supervision.
🅼 ➔ 📶 🛏 💻

La Quinta Inn & Suites H
(701) 456-2500. **$99-$249.** 552 12th St W 58601. I-94 exit 61 (SR 22), just s, then just w. Int corridors. **Pets:** Large, other species. Service with restrictions. 🅼 ➔ 📶 ✕ 🛏 💻

Microtel Inn & Suites by Wyndham Dickinson H
(701) 456-2000. **$130-$190.** 1597 6th Ave W 58601. I-94 exit 61 (SR 22), just n, then w. Int corridors. **Pets:** Accepted.
🅼 ➔ 📶 ✕ 🛏 💻

Quality Inn & Suites-Dickinson H
(701) 225-9510. **$109-$149.** 71 Museum Dr 58601. I-94 exit 61 (SR 22), just s, then just e. Int corridors. **Pets:** Accepted.
SAVE 🅼 ➔ 📶 🛏 💻

Ramada Grand Dakota Hotel H
(701) 483-5600. **$139-$179.** 532 15th St W 58601. I-94 exit 61 (SR 22), just n, then w. Int corridors. **Pets:** Accepted.
🍴 🅼 ➔ 📶 ✕ 🛏 💻

FARGO
AmericInn Hotel & Suites Fargo South-45th Street H ✿
(701) 235-4699. **Call for rates.** 4325 23rd Ave S 58104. I-94 exit 348 (45th St SW), just se. Int corridors. **Pets:** Medium, other species. $20 daily fee/pet. Designated rooms, service with restrictions, crate.
🍴 🅼 ➔ 📶 ✕ 🛏 💻

AmericInn Lodge & Suites Fargo West Acres H
(701) 234-9946. **Call for rates.** 1423 35th St SW 58103. I-29 exit 64 (13th Ave S), just e, just s on 34th St SW, then just w. Int corridors. **Pets:** Other species. $10 daily fee/pet. Designated rooms, service with restrictions, supervision. SAVE 🅼 ➔ ✕ 📶 ✕ 🛏 💻

Baymont Inn and Suites by Wyndham H
(701) 235-3333. **$95-$149, 3 day notice.** 3333 13th Ave S 58103. I-29 exit 64 (13th Ave S), 0.3 mi e. Int corridors. **Pets:** Medium, dogs only. $15 one-time fee/pet. Service with restrictions, supervision.
SAVE 🍴 🅼 ➔ ✕ 📶 ✕ 🛏 💻

BEST WESTERN PLUS Kelly Inn & Suites H ✿
(701) 282-2143. **$122-$250.** 1767 44th St S 58103. I-94 exit 348 (45th St SW), just n, then just e on 18th Ave. Ext/int corridors. **Pets:** Medium. Service with restrictions, supervision.
SAVE 🅼 ➔ ✕ 📶 ✕ 🛏 💻

Biltmore Hotel and Suites H
(701) 281-9700. **$84-$150, 3 day notice.** 3800 Main Ave (US 10) 58103. I-29 exit 65, just sw. Ext/int corridors. **Pets:** Accepted.
🍴 🅼 ➔ ✕ 📶 ✕ 🛏 💻

Candlewood Suites H
(701) 235-8200. **$92-$170.** 1831 NDSU Research Park Dr 58102. I-29 exit 67 (19th Ave), 1.6 mi e. Int corridors. **Pets:** Accepted.
SAVE 🅼 📶 🛏 💻

Country Inn & Suites By Carlson H
(701) 234-0565. **Call for rates.** 3316 13th Ave S 58103. I-29 exit 64 (13th Ave S), 0.3 mi e. Int corridors. **Pets:** Accepted.
➔ 📶 ✕ 🛏 💻

Days Inn Fargo H
(701) 235-5566. **$80-$170.** 3431 14th Ave S 58103. I-29 exit 64 (13th Ave S), just e, just s on 34th St S, then just w. Int corridors. **Pets:** Accepted. 🅼 ➔ 📶 ✕ 🛏 💻

▼▼ ▼▼ **Econo Lodge East** 🅜

(701) 232-3412. **$59-$115.** 1401 35th St SW 58103. I-29 exit 64 (13th Ave S), just e, just s on 34th St SW, then just w. Int corridors. **Pets:** Accepted. 🖼

▼▼ ▼▼ **Econo Lodge West** 🅗

(701) 282-9596. **$59-$129.** 3825 9th Ave SW 58103. I-29 exit 64 (13th Ave S), just n on west frontage road (38th St SW), then just w. Int corridors. **Pets:** Accepted. 🖼

🆔 ▼▼ **Fargo Inn & Suites** 🅗

(701) 282-6300. **$65-$85.** 1025 38th St SW 58103. I-29 exit 64 (13th Ave S), just n on west frontage road (38th St SW). Int corridors. **Pets:** Medium. $10 daily fee/pet. Designated rooms, service with restrictions, supervision. 🖼

▼▼ ▼▼ **Kelly Inn 13th Avenue** 🅗

(701) 277-8821. **$88-$150, 5 day notice.** 4207 13th Ave SW 58103. I-29 exit 64 (13th Ave S), 0.4 mi w. Ext/int corridors. **Pets:** Medium, dogs only. Service with restrictions, supervision. 🖼

▼▼▼▼ **La Quinta Inn & Suites Fargo** 🅗

(701) 499-2000. **$99-$269.** 2355 46th St S 58104. I-94 exit 348 (45th St SW), just s, then just w. Int corridors. **Pets:** Large, other species. Service with restrictions. 🖼

▼▼▼▼ **MainStay Suites** 🅗

(701) 277-4627. **$95-$108.** 1901 44th St SW 58103. I-94 exit 348 (45th St SW), just n, then just e. Int corridors. **Pets:** Medium. $75 one-time fee/room. Designated rooms, service with restrictions, supervision. 🖼

▼▼▼▼ **Quality Suites** 🅗

(701) 237-5911. **$79-$149.** 1415 35th St SW 58103. I-29 exit 64 (13th Ave S), just e, just s on 34th St SW, then just w. Int corridors. **Pets:** Accepted. 🖼

▼▼ ▼▼ **Red Roof Inn of Fargo** 🅗

(701) 281-8240. **$59-$117.** 1921 44th St SW 58103. I-94 exit 348 (45th St SW), just n, just e on 19th Ave S, then just s. Int corridors. **Pets:** Large, other species. Service with restrictions, supervision. 🖼

▼▼▼▼ **Residence Inn by Marriott Fargo** 🅗

(701) 282-2240. **$83-$148.** 4335 23rd St S 58104. I-94 exit 63B, just s. Int corridors. **Pets:** Other species. $100 one-time fee/room. Service with restrictions. 🖼

🆔 ▼▼▼▼ **Staybridge Suites** 🅗

(701) 281-4900. **$99-$199, 3 day notice.** 4300 20th Ave S 58103. I-94 exit 348 (45th St SW), just n, just e on 19th Ave, just s on 44th St S, then just e. Int corridors. **Pets:** Accepted. 🖼

▼▼ **Super 8 Fargo/I-29/West Acres Mall** 🅗

(701) 232-9202. **$60-$146.** 3518 Interstate Blvd 58103. I-29 exit 64 (13th Ave S), just n on east frontage road via 35th St. Int corridors. **Pets:** Accepted. 🖼

GRAND FORKS

🆔 ▼▼ **Americas Best Value Inn of Grand Forks** 🅜

(701) 775-0555. **$50-$110.** 1000 N 42nd St 58203. I-29 exit 141, just e on US 2 (Gateway Dr), then just s. Int corridors. **Pets:** Other species. $15 daily fee/pet. Designated rooms, service with restrictions, crate. 🖼

🆔 ▼▼ **Days Inn - Columbia Mall** 🅗

(701) 775-0060. **$75-$130.** 3101 S 34th St 58201. I-29 exit 138, 0.4 mi e on 32nd Ave S, then just n. Int corridors. **Pets:** Small. $10 daily fee/pet. Designated rooms, service with restrictions, supervision. 🖼

▼▼ ▼▼ **GuestHouse International Town House** 🅗

(701) 746-5411. **$73-$150.** 710 1st Ave N 58203. I-29 exit 140, 2.8 mi e on DeMers Ave, then just n; downtown. Int corridors. **Pets:** Other species. Designated rooms, service with restrictions, supervision. 🖼

🆔 ▼▼ ▼▼ **Ramada Inn** 🅗

(701) 775-3951. **$79-$129.** 1205 N 43rd St 58203. I-29 exit 141, just e on US 2 (Gateway Dr), then just s. Int corridors. **Pets:** Medium. $10 daily fee/pet. Designated rooms, service with restrictions, supervision. 🖼

🆔 ▼▼▼▼ **Staybridge Suites** 🅗

(701) 772-9000. **$129-$209.** 1175 42nd St S 58201. I-29 exit 140, just e on DeMers Ave, then 0.3 mi s. Int corridors. **Pets:** Large, other species. $50 one-time fee/room. Designated rooms, service with restrictions, crate. 🖼

JAMESTOWN

▼▼ ▼▼ **Quality Inn & Suites** 🅗

(701) 252-3611. **$89-$119.** 507 25th St SW 58401. I-94 exit 258 (US 281), just se. Int corridors. **Pets:** Accepted. 🖼

🆔 ▼▼ ▼▼ **Super 8** 🅗

(701) 252-4715. **$70-$110.** 2623 Hwy 281 S 58401. I-94 exit 258 (US 281), just s. Int corridors. **Pets:** Accepted. 🖼

MANDAN

🆔 ▼▼ ▼▼ **BEST WESTERN Seven Seas Hotel & Waterpark** 🅗

(701) 663-7401. **$90-$149.** 2611 Old Red Tr 58554. I-94 exit 152, just n on Sunset Dr, then just w. Int corridors. **Pets:** Accepted. 🖼

MINOT

▼▼ ▼▼ ▼▼ **Baymont Inn & Suites** 🅗

(701) 837-1700. **$67-$112.** 1609 35th Ave SW 58701. US 83 (S Broadway) exit 37th Ave SW, 0.8 mi w to 16th St SW, then just n. Int corridors. **Pets:** Accepted. 🖼

🆔 ▼▼ ▼▼ **BEST WESTERN Kelly Inn** 🅗 ❀

(701) 852-4300. **$95-$250.** 1510 26th Ave SW 58701. US 2 and 52 Bypass, at 16th St SW. Ext/int corridors. **Pets:** Service with restrictions, supervision. 🖼

▼▼▼▼ **Candlewood Suites** 🅗

(701) 858-7700. **Call for rates.** 900 37th Ave SW 58701. US 83, 0.6 mi s of US 2 and 52 Bypass, then just w. Int corridors. **Pets:** Accepted. 🖼

▼▼ ▼▼ **Comfort Inn** 🅗

(701) 852-2201. **$84-$170.** 1515 22nd Ave SW 58701. US 2 and 52 Bypass, at 16th St SW. Int corridors. **Pets:** Medium. $10 daily fee/room. Designated rooms, service with restrictions, supervision. 🖼

▼▼ ▼▼ **Comfort Suites** 🅗

(701) 852-9700. **Call for rates.** 601 22th Ave SW 58701. Just w of S Broadway (US 83). Int corridors. **Pets:** Accepted. 🖼

▼▼ **Days Inn Minot** 🅗

(701) 852-3646. **$80-$150.** 2100 4th St SW 58701. Jct US 2 and 52 Bypass, just n. Int corridors. **Pets:** Accepted. 🖼

🆔 ▼▼▼▼ **HYATT house Minot** 🅗

(701) 838-7300. **$89-$249.** 2301 Landmark Dr NW 58703. 0.4 mi ne of jct US 83 Bypass and 21st Ave NW. Int corridors. **Pets:** Medium, dogs only. $75 one-time fee/room. Designated rooms, service with restrictions, crate. 🖼

▼▼▼▼ **La Quinta Inn & Suites** 🅷
(701) 837-7900. **$94-$279.** 1605 35th St SW 58701. US 83 (S Broadway) exit 37th Ave SW, 0.8 mi w to 16th St SW, then just n. Int corridors. **Pets:** Large, other species. Service with restrictions.
🔟 📶 ⊠ 🔋 🖥

▼▼▼ **Microtel Inn & Suites by Wyndham Minot** 🅷
(701) 839-2200. **$99-$153.** 414 37th Ave SW 58701. 1.5 mi n on US 83, just w. Int corridors. **Pets:** Accepted. 🍴 ♿ 📶 ⊠ 🔋 🖥

▼▼▼▼ **Sleep Inn & Suites** 🅷
(701) 837-3100. **$105-$189.** 2400 10th St SW 58701. US 2 and 52 Bypass, 0.4 mi s on 16th St SW, 0.4 mi e. Int corridors. **Pets:** Very small, dogs only. $25 one-time fee/room. Service with restrictions, supervision. 🍴 ♿ ≋ ⊠ 📶 ⊠ 🔋 🖥

▼▼▼▼ **Souris Valley Suites** 🅷
(701) 858-7300. **$109-$199.** 800 37th Ave SW 58701. 0.4 mi w of S Broadway (US 83). Int corridors. **Pets:** Other species. $25 one-time fee/pet. Service with restrictions, supervision.
🔟 ♿ 📶 ⊠ 🔋 🖥

▲▲▲⁀ ▼▼▼ **Staybridge Suites** 🅷
(701) 852-0852. **$140-$210, 6 day notice.** 3009 S Broadway 58701. US 83, just s of US 2 and 52 Bypass. Int corridors. **Pets:** Other species. $25 daily fee/room. Service with restrictions, crate.
🆂🅰🆅🅴 🔟 ♿ 📶 ⊠ 🔋 🖥

STANLEY
▼▼ **Microtel Inn & Suites by Wyndham Stanley** 🅷
(701) 628-4090. **$144-$155.** 901 Jarard St 58784. US 2 exit SR 8, just nw. Int corridors. **Pets:** Accepted. 🍴 ♿ 📶 ⊠ 🔋 🖥

VALLEY CITY
▼▼ **AmericInn Lodge & Suites of Valley City** 🅷
(701) 845-5551. **$90-$140.** 280 Winter Show Rd SW 58072. I-94 exit 292, just ne. Int corridors. **Pets:** Accepted.
♿ ≋ ⊠ 📶 ⊠ 🔋 🖥

WAHPETON
▼▼ **Baymont Inn & Suites** 🅷
(701) 642-5000. **$75-$155.** 1800 Two Ten Dr 58075. 1 mi n on SR 210 Bypass. Int corridors. **Pets:** Accepted.
🔟 ♿ ≋ ⊠ 📶 🔋 🖥

WATFORD CITY
▲▲▲ ▼▼▼ **Roosevelt Inn & Suites** 🅷
(701) 842-3686. **$125-$215.** 600 2nd Ave SW 58854. US 85, 0.3 mi w. Int corridors. **Pets:** Other species. $25 daily fee/pet. Designated rooms, service with restrictions, supervision.
🆂🅰🆅🅴 ≋ ⊠ 📶 ⊠ 🔋 🖥

WILLISTON
▼▼▼▼ **Candlewood Suites** 🅷 ❧
(701) 572-3716. **$140-$300.** 3716 6th Ave W 58801. 1.3 mi n on US 2 and 85 Bypass, just w. Int corridors. **Pets:** $5 daily fee/pet. Service with restrictions, crate. ♿ 📶 ⊠ 🔋 🖥

▲▲▲ ▼▼▼ **El Rancho Motor Hotel** 🅷
(701) 572-6321. **Call for rates.** 1623 2nd Ave W 58801. 1 mi n on US 2 and 85 Bypass. Ext/int corridors. **Pets:** Accepted.
🆂🅰🆅🅴 🔟 ♿ 📶 🔋 🖥

▼▼▼▼ **HomStay Suites** 🅷
(701) 577-3701. **$200-$210.** 3701 4th Ave W 58801. 1.3 mi n on US 2 and 85 Bypass, just w. Int corridors. **Pets:** Accepted.
🔟 📶 ⊠ 🔋 🖥

▼▼▼▼ **MainStay Suites of Williston** 🅷
(701) 572-5793. **$139-$279.** 200 26th St E 58801. Just w of 2nd Ave W. Int corridors. **Pets:** Accepted. 🔟 ♿ 📶 ⊠ 🔋 🖥

▲▲▲ ▼▼▼ **Marquis Plaza & Suites** 🅷
(701) 774-3250. **$125-$147.** 1525 9th Ave NW 58801. US 2 and 85 Bypass, 4 mi e of jct US 85 Bypass. Int corridors. **Pets:** Small, dogs only. $15 daily fee/pet. Designated rooms, service with restrictions, supervision. 🆂🅰🆅🅴 ♿ ≋ 📶 ⊠ 🔋 🖥

▼▼ **Microtel Inn & Suites by Wyndham Williston** 🅷
(701) 577-4900. **$139-$239, 3 day notice.** 3820 4th Ave W 58801. 1.3 mi n on US 2 and 85 Bypass, just w. Int corridors. **Pets:** Accepted.
♿ ≋ 📶 ⊠ 🔋 🖥

OHIO

AKRON
▲▲▲⁀ ▼▼▼ **Red Roof Inn Akron** 🅼
(330) 644-7748. **$54-$119.** 2939 S Arlington Rd 44312. I-77 exit 120, just n. Ext corridors. **Pets:** Large, other species. Service with restrictions, supervision. 🆂🅰🆅🅴 📶 ⊠ 🔋 🖥

▼▼▼▼ **Residence Inn by Marriott Akron South Green** 🅷
(330) 644-2111. **$132-$217.** 897 Arlington Ridge E 44312. I-77 exit 120, just s. Int corridors. **Pets:** Accepted. ♿ 📶 ⊠ 🔋 🖥

ALLIANCE
▼▼ **Americas Best Value Inn Alliance** 🅼
(330) 821-5688. **$58-$92.** 2330 W State St 44601. 2 mi w on US 62. Ext corridors. **Pets:** $5 daily fee/pet. Service with restrictions, crate.
≋ 📶 🔋 🖥

▼▼▼ **Holiday Inn Express Hotel & Suites** 🅷
(330) 821-6700. **$100-$200.** 2341 W State St 44601. 2 mi w on US 62. Int corridors. **Pets:** Large, other species. $20 daily fee/pet. Designated rooms, service with restrictions, supervision. ♿ ≋ 📶 🔋 🖥

AMHERST
▼▼ **Days Inn** 🅼
(440) 985-1428. **$65-$150.** 934 N Leavitt Rd 44001. I-80/90 exit 140, 2.7 mi n on SR 58. Ext/int corridors. **Pets:** Accepted.
≋ 📶 🔋 🖥

ASHTABULA
▼▼ **Cedars Motel** 🅼
(440) 992-5406. **$50-$140, 3 day notice.** 2015 W Prospect Rd 44004. Jct SR 11, 3 mi w on US 20. Ext corridors. **Pets:** Accepted. 📶 🔋

ATHENS
▼▼▼▼ **The Ohio University Inn & Conference Center** 🅷
(740) 593-6661. **Call for rates.** 331 Richland Ave 45701. 1 mi w on US 33 and 50. Int corridors. **Pets:** Accepted.
🔟 ♿ ≋ 📶 ⊠ 🔋 🖥

AUSTINBURG
▲▲▲⁀ ▼▼▼ **Hampton Inn** 🅷
(440) 275-2000. **$105-$159.** 2900 GH Dr 44010. I-90 exit 223, just s. Int corridors. **Pets:** Accepted. 🆂🅰🆅🅴 📶 🔋 🖥

▼▼▼ **Sleep Inn & Suites** 🄷 🐾
(440) 275-6800. **$109-$179.** 9350 Center Rd 44010. I-90 exit 223, just n. Int corridors. **Pets:** Medium, other species. $25 daily fee/pet. Designated rooms, service with restrictions, supervision.
🄼 ⟲ 🛇 🗡 🔋 🖵

AUSTINTOWN

🅐🅐🅐 ▼▼▼ **Austintown Super 8** 🄼
(330) 793-7788. **$60-$72.** 5280 76 Dr 44515. I-80 exit 223, just s on SR 46. Int corridors. **Pets:** $10 daily fee/pet. Designated rooms, service with restrictions, supervision. 🆂🅰🆅🅴 ⟲ 🔋 🖵

🅐🅐🅐 ▼▼▼ **BEST WESTERN Meander Inn** 🄷
(330) 544-2378. **$76-$85.** 870 N Canfield-Niles Rd 44515. I-80 exit 223, 0.3 mi s on SR 46. Int corridors. **Pets:** Large, other species. $10 daily fee/pet. Service with restrictions, crate. 🆂🅰🆅🅴 🍴 ⟲ ⟲ 🔋 🖵

▼▼▼ **Comfort Inn** 🄼
(330) 792-9740. **$90-$170.** 5425 Clarkins Dr 44515. I-80 exit 223B, just n. Ext corridors. **Pets:** Accepted. ⟲ ⟲ 🔋 🖵

▼▼▼ **Holiday Inn Express & Suites** 🄷
(330) 505-5700. **$119-$169.** 5555 Cerni Pl 44515. I-80 exit 223B, just n. Int corridors. **Pets:** Accepted. 🄼 🅂⟲ 🗡 🔋 🖵

🅐🅐🅐 ▼▼▼ **Sleep Inn** 🄷
(330) 544-5555. **$79-$139.** 5555 Interstate Blvd 44515. I-80 exit 223, just s on SR 46. Int corridors. **Pets:** Accepted.
🆂🅰🆅🅴 ⟲ ⟲ 🔋 🖵

BATAVIA

▼▼▼ **Ameristay Inn & Suites** 🄷
(513) 735-4678. **$76-$139.** 2188 Winemiller Ln 45103. I-275 exit 63B (SR 32), 7.3 mi e. Int corridors. **Pets:** Accepted. ⟲ ⟲ 🔋 🖵

▼▼ **Hampton Inn-Cincinnati Eastgate** 🄷
(513) 752-8584. **$99-$159.** 858 Eastgate North Dr 45245. I-275 exit 63B (SR 32), just e, just n on Glen Este Withamsville Rd, then just w. Int corridors. **Pets:** Accepted. ⟲ ⟲ 🔋 🖵

▼▼▼ **Holiday Inn & Suites Cincinnati Eastgate** 🄷
(513) 752-4400. **$119-$179.** 4501 Eastgate Blvd 45245. I-275 exit 63B (SR 32), 0.4 mi e to Eastgate Mall exit, then just n. Int corridors. **Pets:** Accepted. 🍴 ⟲ ⟲ 🔋 🖵

BEACHWOOD

▼▼▼ **DoubleTree by Hilton Hotel Cleveland East Beachwood** 🄷
(216) 464-5950. **$109-$199.** 3663 Park East Dr 44122. I-271 exit 29, just w on Chagrin Blvd, then just n. Int corridors. **Pets:** Accepted.
🍴 ⟲ 🛇 ⟲ 🗡 🔋 🖵

🅐🅐🅐 ▼▼▼ **Embassy Suites** 🄷
(216) 765-8066. **$116-$206.** 3775 Park East Dr 44122. I-271 exit 29, just w on Chagrin Blvd. Int corridors. **Pets:** Accepted.
🆂🅰🆅🅴 🍴 ⟲ ⟲ 🔋 🖵

▼▼ **Extended Stay America-Cleveland/Beachwood-North** 🄷
(216) 896-5555. **Call for rates.** 3625 Orange Pl 44122. I-271 exit 29, just e on Chagrin Blvd, then just s. Int corridors. **Pets:** Other species. $25 daily fee/pet. Service with restrictions, supervision. ⟲ 🔋 🖵

▼▼ **Extended Stay America-Cleveland-Beachwood -South** 🄷
(216) 595-9551. **Call for rates.** 3820 Orange Pl 44122. I-271 exit 29, 0.3 mi w on Chagrin Blvd, then 0.4 mi s. Int corridors. **Pets:** Other species. $25 daily fee/pet. Service with restrictions, supervision.
⟲ 🔋 🖵

▼▼▼ **Homewood Suites by Hilton** 🄷 🐾
(216) 464-9600. **$129-$209.** 25725 Central Pkwy 44122. I-271 exit 29, just w on Chagrin Blvd, then just n on Enterprise Pkwy. Int corridors. **Pets:** Medium, dogs only. $50 one-time fee/room, $10 daily fee/room. Service with restrictions, crate. 🄼 ⟲ ⟲ 🔋 🖵

▼▼▼ **Residence Inn by Marriott Cleveland-Beachwood** 🄷
(216) 831-3030. **$146-$275.** 3628 Park East Dr 44122. I-271 exit 29, just w on Chagrin Blvd. Int corridors. **Pets:** Accepted.
🄼 ⟲ 🛇 ⟲ 🗡 🔋 🖵

BEAVERCREEK

▼▼▼ **Residence Inn by Marriott Beavercreek** 🄷
(937) 427-3914. **$116-$201.** 2779 Fairfield Commons Blvd 45431. I-675 exit 17, just s on N Fairfield Rd, just w on Pentagon Rd, then just s. Int corridors. **Pets:** Accepted. 🄼 ⟲ ⟲ 🗡 🔋 🖵

BELLVILLE

▼▼▼ **Comfort Inn Splash Harbor** 🄷
(419) 886-4000. **$63-$135.** 855 Comfort Plaza Dr 44813. I-71 exit 165, 0.3 mi e on SR 97. Int corridors. **Pets:** Medium, dogs only. $15 daily fee/pet. Designated rooms, service with restrictions, crate.
⟲ 🛇 ⟲ 🗡 🔋 🖵

▼▼▼ **Quality Inn & Suites-Conference Center** 🄷
(419) 886-7000. **$65-$140.** 1000 Comfort Plaza Dr 44813. I-71 exit 165, 0.3 mi e on SR 97. Int corridors. **Pets:** Medium, dogs only. Designated rooms, service with restrictions, crate. ⟲ 🛇 ⟲ 🔋 🖵

BERLIN

🅐🅐🅐 ▼▼▼ **Berlin Grande Hotel** 🄷
(330) 403-3050. **$109-$279.** 4787 Township Rd 366 44610. SR 39, just n on US 62. Int corridors. **Pets:** Large. $25 daily fee/pet. Designated rooms, service with restrictions, crate.
🆂🅰🆅🅴 🄼 ⟲ ⟲ 🗡 🔋 🖵

BLUE ASH

▼▼▼ **Embassy Suites Hotel-Cincinnati Northeast** 🄷
(513) 733-8900. **$119-$239.** 4554 Lake Forest Dr 45242. I-275 exit 47, 2.3 mi s; I-71 exit 15, 1 mi w on Pfeiffer Rd. Int corridors.
Pets: Accepted. 🍴 🄼 ⟲ 🛇 ⟲ 🗡 🔋 🖵

▼▼ **Extended Stay America-Cincinnati-Blue Ash-Kenwood Road** 🄷
(513) 469-8900. **Call for rates.** 11145 Kenwood Rd 45242. I-71 exit 15, 0.5 mi w on Pfeiffer Rd, then 1.3 mi n. Int corridors. **Pets:** Other species. $25 daily fee/pet. Service with restrictions, supervision.
⟲ 🔋 🖵

▼▼ **Extended Stay America-Cincinnati-Blue Ash-Reagan Highway** 🄷
(513) 793-6750. **Call for rates.** 4260 Hunt Rd 45242. I-71 exit 14, 1.3 mi w on Ronald Reagan Hwy exit Hunt Rd, then just e. Int corridors. **Pets:** Other species. $25 daily fee/pet. Service with restrictions, supervision. ⟲ ⟲ 🔋 🖵

▼▼ **Hawthorn Suites by Wyndham** 🄷
(513) 733-0100. **$82-$97.** 10665 Techwood Cir 45242. I-275 exit 47, 1.9 mi s, just e on Creek Rd, then just s. Int corridors. **Pets:** Medium. $15 daily fee/room. Designated rooms, service with restrictions, crate.
⟲ 🔋 🖵

🅐🅐🅐 ▼▼▼ **Hyatt Place Cincinnati/Blue Ash** 🄷
(513) 489-3666. **$79-$179.** 11435 Reed Hartman Hwy 45241. I-275 exit 47, 0.8 mi s. Int corridors. **Pets:** Accepted.
🆂🅰🆅🅴 🍴 🄼 ⟲ ⟲ 🗡 🔋 🖵

▼▼▼ **Residence Inn by Marriott-Blue Ash** 🄷
(513) 530-5060. **$118-$194.** 11401 Reed Hartman Hwy 45241. I-275 exit 47, 0.8 mi s. Ext/int corridors. **Pets:** Other species. $100 one-time fee/room. Service with restrictions. 🄼 ⟲ ⟲ 🗡 🔋 🖵

AAA ◈◈ **TownePlace Suites by Marriott Blue Ash** H

(513) 469-8222. **$115-$212.** 4650 Cornell Rd 45241. I-275 exit 47, 0.9 mi s on Reed Hartman Hwy, then just w. Int corridors. **Pets:** Accepted.

[SAVE] [≈] [🛜] [✖] [🛏] [💻]

BOARDMAN

◈◈ **Americas Best Value Inn & Suites** M

(330) 549-0157. **$59-$121, 3 day notice.** 9988 Market St 44452. 0.5 mi n on SR 7. Int corridors. **Pets:** Medium. $10 daily fee/pet. Service with restrictions, supervision. [&M] [🛜] [🛏] [💻]

BOWLING GREEN

◈◈◈ **Holiday Inn Express and Suites** H

(419) 353-5500. **Call for rates.** 2150 E Wooster St 43402. I-75 exit 181, just e. Int corridors. **Pets:** Accepted.

[&M] [≈] [🛜] [✖] [🛏] [💻]

BROOKLYN

◈◈ **Extended Stay America Cleveland-Brooklyn** H

(216) 485-0101. **Call for rates.** 10300 Cascade Crossing 44144. I-480 exit 13, just s. Int corridors. **Pets:** Other species. $25 daily fee/pet. Service with restrictions, supervision. [🛜] [🛏] [💻]

BROOK PARK

AAA ◈◈◈ **BEST WESTERN Airport Inn & Suites Cleveland** H

(216) 267-9364. **$80-$100.** 16501 Snow Rd 44142. I-71 exit 237, just e. Int corridors. **Pets:** Accepted. [SAVE] [&M] [≈] [🛜] [🛏] [💻]

BROOKVILLE

◈◈◈ **Holiday Inn Express Hotel & Suites Dayton West - Brookville** H

(937) 833-9998. **Call for rates.** 95 N Parkview Dr 45309. I-70 exit 21, just s. Int corridors. **Pets:** Accepted. [&M] [≈] [🛜] [🛏] [💻]

BRUNSWICK

◈◈ **Quality Inn** H

(330) 273-1112. **$73-$150.** 1435 S Carpenter Rd 44212. I-71 exit 226, 0.3 mi w on SR 303, then just s. Int corridors. **Pets:** Accepted.

[≈] [🛜] [🛏] [💻]

BRYAN

◈ **Plaza Motel** M

(419) 636-3159. **$69-$93.** 1604 S Main St 43506. 1.3 mi s on US 127 and SR 15. Ext corridors. **Pets:** Designated rooms, service with restrictions, supervision. [🛜] [✖] [🛏] [💻]

BUCYRUS

◈◈◈ **Hideaway Country Inn** CI 🐾

(419) 562-3013. **$129-$375, 14 day notice.** 1601 SR 4 44820. 4.5 mi s. Ext/int corridors. **Pets:** Medium, dogs only. $50 daily fee/pet. Designated rooms, service with restrictions, supervision.

[🍴] [🛜] [✖] [🛏] [💻]

CAMBRIDGE

◈◈ **Baymont Inn & Suites** M

(740) 439-1505. **$69-$129.** 61595 Southgate Pkwy 43725. I-70 exit 178, just s on SR 209. Int corridors. **Pets:** Accepted.

[&M] [≈] [🛜] [🛏] [💻]

AAA ◈◈ **Comfort Inn** H 🐾

(740) 435-3200. **$120-$140.** 2327 Southgate Pkwy 43725. I-70 exit 178, just w on SR 209. Int corridors. **Pets:** $25 daily fee/pet. Service with restrictions, crate. [SAVE] [≈] [🛜] [✖] [🛏] [💻]

◈◈ **Days Inn-Cambridge** M

(740) 432-5691. **$90-$100, 3 day notice.** 2328 Southgate Pkwy 43725. I-70 exit 178, just n on SR 209. Int corridors. **Pets:** $20 daily fee/pet. Service with restrictions, crate. [≈] [🛜] [🛏] [💻]

◈◈ **Salt Fork Lodge & Conference Center** H

(740) 435-9050. **$120-$340, 3 day notice.** US Rt 22 E 43725. I-77 exit 47 (US 22/Cambridge), 11.5 mi e. Ext/int corridors. **Pets:** Large. $15 daily fee/pet. Designated rooms, service with restrictions, crate.

[🍴] [≈] [✖] [🛜] [🛏] [💻]

CANTON

AAA ◈◈ **Comfort Inn-Hall of Fame** H

(330) 492-1331. **$99-$279.** 5345 Broadmoor Cir NW 44709. I-77 exit 109, 0.5 mi e on Everhard Rd. Int corridors. **Pets:** Small, other species. $25 daily fee/pet. Service with restrictions. [SAVE] [≈] [🛜] [🛏] [💻]

◈◈◈ **La Quinta Inn & Suites Canton** H

(330) 492-0151. **$84-$124.** 5335 Broadmoor Cir NW 44709. I-77 exit 109, 0.5 mi e on Everhard Rd. Int corridors. **Pets:** Large, other species. Service with restrictions. [&M] [≈] [🛜] [🛏] [💻]

AAA ◈◈ **Red Roof Inn Canton** M

(330) 499-1970. **$59-$120.** 5353 Inn Circle Ct NW 44720. I-77 exit 109, just w on Everhard Rd. Ext corridors. **Pets:** Large, other species. Service with restrictions, supervision. [SAVE] [🛜] [✖] [🛏] [💻]

◈◈◈ **Residence Inn by Marriott** H

(330) 493-0004. **$130-$213.** 5280 Broadmoor Cir NW 44709. I-77 exit 109, 0.5 mi e on Everhard Rd. Int corridors. **Pets:** Accepted.

[&M] [≈] [🛜] [✖] [🛏] [💻]

CARROLLTON

◈◈ **Carrollton Days Inn** H

(330) 627-9314. **$94-$149, 3 day notice.** 1111 Canton Rd 44615. On SR 43, 0.5 mi n of SR 39. Int corridors. **Pets:** Accepted.

[≈] [🛜] [✖] [🛏] [💻]

CEDARVILLE

◈◈ **Hearthstone Inn & Suites** H

(937) 766-3000. **$119-$169, 7 day notice.** 10 S Main St 45314. I-70 exit 54, 11 mi s. Int corridors. **Pets:** Dogs only. $15 daily fee/pet. Service with restrictions, supervision. [🛜] [✖] [🛏] [💻]

CHERRY GROVE

AAA ◈◈◈ **BEST WESTERN Clermont** M

(513) 528-7702. **$90-$200.** 4004 Williams Dr 45255. I-275 exit 65, just w, then just s. Ext corridors. **Pets:** Medium. $20 daily fee/room. Service with restrictions, supervision. [SAVE] [≈] [🛜] [🛏] [💻]

CHILLICOTHE

◈◈ **Christopher Inn & Suites** H

(740) 774-6835. **Call for rates.** 30 N Plaza Blvd 45601. US 35 exit Bridge St, just n on US 23. Int corridors. **Pets:** Accepted.

[≈] [🛜] [🛏] [💻]

CINCINNATI

◈◈◈ **21c Museum Hotel Cincinnati** H

(513) 578-6600. **Call for rates.** 609 Walnut St 45202. Between 6th and 7th sts. Int corridors. **Pets:** Accepted. [🍴] [&M] [🛜] [✖] [💻]

AAA ◈◈◈◈ **The Cincinnatian Hotel** H

(513) 381-3000. **$129-$349.** 601 Vine St 45202. Corner of 6th and Vine sts; entrance on 6th St. Int corridors. **Pets:** Accepted.

[SAVE] [🍴] [&M] [✖] [🛜] [✖] [🛏]

◈◈◈ **Holiday Inn Express Cincinnati West** H

(513) 574-6000. **$104-$299.** 5505 Rybolt Rd 45248. I-74 exit 11, just s. Int corridors. **Pets:** Medium. $25 one-time fee/room. Designated rooms, service with restrictions, supervision. [&M] [≈] [🛜] [🛏] [💻]

AAA ◈◈◈ **Hyatt Regency Cincinnati** H

(513) 579-1234. **$99-$359.** 151 W 5th St 45202. At Hyatt-Saks Fifth Avenue Center. Int corridors. **Pets:** Accepted.

[SAVE] [ECO] [🍴] [&M] [≈] [☕] [✖] [🛏] [💻]

Residence Inn by Marriott Cincinnati Downtown H
(513) 651-1234. **$189-$311.** 506 E Fourth St 45202. Center. Int corridors. **Pets:** Accepted.

The Westin Cincinnati H ❖
(513) 621-7700. **$309-$399.** 21 E 5th St 45202. Between Vine and Walnut sts. Int corridors. **Pets:** Small. Service with restrictions, supervision.

CIRCLEVILLE

Holiday Inn Express Hotel & Suites H
(740) 420-7711. **Call for rates.** 23911 US 23 S 43113. Jct US 22, 1.2 mi s. Int corridors. **Pets:** Accepted.

CLEVELAND

Comfort Inn Downtown Cleveland H
(216) 861-0001. **$99-$299.** 1800 Euclid Ave 44115. Corner of Euclid Ave and E 18th St. Int corridors. **Pets:** Accepted.

Hyatt Regency Cleveland at The Arcade H
(216) 575-1234. **$89-$329.** 420 Superior Ave E 44114. Just e of Public Square. Int corridors. **Pets:** Accepted.

La Quinta Inn Cleveland Airport North H
(216) 251-8500. **$79-$214.** 4222 W 150th St 44135. I-71 exit 240, just n. Int corridors. **Pets:** Large, other species. Service with restrictions.

Radisson Hotel Cleveland-Gateway H
(216) 377-9000. **Call for rates.** 651 Huron Rd E 44115. North side of Progressive Field. Int corridors. **Pets:** Accepted.

Residence Inn by Marriott H
(216) 443-9043. **$244-$401.** 527 Prospect Ave E 44115. Between E 9th and Ontario sts. Int corridors. **Pets:** Accepted.

The Ritz-Carlton, Cleveland H ❖
(216) 623-1300. **$199-$419.** 1515 W 3rd St 44113. In Tower City Center (3rd St side). Int corridors. **Pets:** Medium. $125 one-time fee/pet. Designated rooms, service with restrictions, crate.

Sheraton Cleveland Airport Hotel H ❖
(216) 267-1500. **$99-$260.** 5300 Riverside Dr 44135. I-71 exit 237, just s of I-480 on SR 237, follow signs. Int corridors. **Pets:** Other species. $50 deposit/room. Designated rooms, service with restrictions, supervision.

CLYDE

Red Roof Inn Clyde H
(419) 547-6660. **$74-$140.** 1363 W McPherson Hwy 43410. 1 mi w on SR 20. Int corridors. **Pets:** Large, other species. Service with restrictions, supervision.

COLUMBUS

Baymont Inn & Suites Columbus at Rickenbacker H
(614) 491-4400. **$69-$119.** 2323 Rickenbacker Pkwy W 43217. I-270 exit 49, 3.6 mi s, then just w. Int corridors. **Pets:** Accepted.

BEST WESTERN PLUS Columbus North H
(614) 888-8230. **$63-$90.** 888 E Dublin Granville Rd 43229. I-71 exit 117, 0.5 mi w on SR 161. Int corridors. **Pets:** Medium, other species. $25 one-time fee/room. No service, crate.

BEST WESTERN Port Columbus H
(614) 337-8400. **Call for rates.** 1450 Airpointe Dr 43219. I-670 exit 9 (Johnstown Rd) eastbound; exit 9 (Cassady Ave) westbound. Int corridors. **Pets:** Accepted.

Candlewood Suites Polaris H ❖
(614) 436-6600. **$90-$119.** 8515 Lyra Dr 43240. I-71 exit 121, just w on Polaris Pkwy. Int corridors. **Pets:** Other species. $15 daily fee/room. Service with restrictions, crate.

DoubleTree by Hilton Hotel Columbus-Worthington H
(614) 885-3334. **Call for rates.** 175 Hutchinson Ave 43235. I-270 exit 23, just n on US 23, just e on Dimension Dr, then just s on High Cross Blvd. Int corridors. **Pets:** Accepted.

Drury Inn & Suites-Columbus Convention Center H
(614) 221-7008. **$100-$219.** 88 E Nationwide Blvd 43215. 0.3 mi n on US 23. Int corridors. **Pets:** $10 daily fee/room. Service with restrictions, supervision.

Extended Stay America-Columbus-Easton H
(614) 428-6022. **Call for rates.** 4200 Stelzer Rd 43230. I-270 exit 32, just w on Morse Rd, then just n. Int corridors. **Pets:** Other species. $25 daily fee/pet. Service with restrictions, supervision.

Extended Stay America Columbus/Polaris H
(614) 431-5522. **Call for rates.** 8555 Lyra Dr 43240. I-71 exit 121, just w on Polaris Pkwy. Int corridors. **Pets:** Other species. $25 daily fee/pet. Service with restrictions, supervision.

German Village Guest House BB
(614) 437-9712. **$180-$290.** 748 Jaeger St 43206. I-70 exit 100B, just s on S 3rd St, 0.4 mi e on E Sycamore St, then just s. Int corridors. **Pets:** Accepted.

Hilton Columbus at Easton H ❖
(614) 414-5000. **$189-$309.** 3900 Chagrin Dr 43219. I-270 exit 33, 0.5 mi w. Int corridors. **Pets:** Medium, dogs only. $50 one-time fee/room. Service with restrictions, supervision.

Hilton Columbus Downtown H ❖
(614) 384-8600. **$159-$299.** 401 N High St 43215. Jct Nationwide Blvd, just n. Int corridors. **Pets:** $50 one-time fee/room. Service with restrictions, crate.

Holiday Inn Columbus Downtown Capitol Square H
(614) 221-3281. **Call for rates.** 175 E Town St 43215. I-70 exit 100B, 0.3 mi n on 4th St. Int corridors. **Pets:** Accepted.

Hyatt Place Columbus/Worthington H
(614) 846-4355. **$79-$189.** 7490 Vantage Dr 43235. I-270 exit 23, 0.4 mi n on US 23, just e on Dimension Dr, then just s. Int corridors. **Pets:** Medium. $75 one-time fee/pet. Service with restrictions.

Hyatt Regency Columbus H
(614) 463-1234. **$99-$349.** 350 N High St 43215. 0.3 mi n on US 23. Int corridors. **Pets:** Accepted.

La Quinta Inn & Suites Columbus West-Hilliard H
(614) 878-8844. **$89-$214.** 5510 Trabue Rd 43228. I-70 exit 91 eastbound; exit 91B westbound, just n on Renner Rd, then just e. Int corridors. **Pets:** Large, other species. Service with restrictions.

AAA ▼▼▼ Red Roof Plus+ Columbus#121, The Ohio State University **M**

(614) 267-9941. **$69-$249.** 441 Ackerman Rd 43202. SR 315 exit Ackerman Rd, 0.6 mi e. Ext corridors. **Pets:** Large, other species. Service with restrictions, supervision. 〔SAVE〕 ⟨&M⟩ 🛜 ∎ ⊡

AAA ▼▼▼ Red Roof Plus+ Columbus Downtown-Convention Center **H**

(614) 224-6539. **$81-$180.** 111 E Nationwide Blvd 43215. Jct 3rd St. Int corridors. **Pets:** Large, other species. Service with restrictions, supervision. 〔SAVE〕 ⟨&M⟩ 🛜 ✕ ∎ ⊡

▼▼▼ Residence Inn by Marriott **H**

(614) 885-0799. **$118-$194.** 7300 Huntington Park Dr 43235. I-270 exit 23, 0.4 mi n on US 23, 0.3 mi e on E Campus View Blvd, then 0.5 mi s. Int corridors. **Pets:** Accepted. ⟨&M⟩ ⤳ 🛜 ✕ ∎ ⊡

▼▼▼ Residence Inn by Marriott **H**

(614) 436-3955. **$90-$171.** 8865 Lyra Dr 43240. I-71 exit 121, 0.3 mi w on Polaris Pkwy, then just n. Int corridors. **Pets:** Medium. $100 one-time fee/room. Designated rooms, service with restrictions, crate. ⟨&M⟩ 🛜 ✕ ∎ ⊡

▼▼▼ Residence Inn by Marriott **H**

(614) 222-2610. **$153-$252.** 36 E Gay St 43215. Between High and S 3rd sts. Int corridors. **Pets:** Other species. $100 one-time fee/room. Service with restrictions. ⟨&M⟩ 🛜 ✕ ∎ ⊡

▼▼▼ Residence Inn by Marriott Easton **H**

(614) 414-1000. **$146-$240.** 3999 Easton Loop W 43219. I-270 exit 33, 1 mi w, then just n. Int corridors. **Pets:** Small. $100 one-time fee/room. Service with restrictions, crate. ⤳ 🛜 ✕ ∎ ⊡

AAA ▼▼▼ Sheraton Columbus at Capitol Square **H** 🐾

(614) 365-4500. **$119-$399.** 75 E State St 43215. Corner of State and 3rd sts. Int corridors. **Pets:** Medium, dogs only. Service with restrictions, crate. 〔SAVE〕 〔ECO〕 ⟨¶⟩ 🍴 📶 ✕ ∎ ⊡

AAA ▼▼▼ Sheraton Suites Columbus **H** 🐾

(614) 436-0004. **$101-$189.** 201 Hutchinson Ave 43235. I-270 exit 23, 0.3 mi n on US 23, just e on Dimension Dr, then 0.4 mi se on Vantage Dr. Int corridors. **Pets:** Large. Service with restrictions, crate. 〔SAVE〕 🍴 ⟨&M⟩ ⤳ 📶 ✕ ∎ ⊡

AAA ▼▼ TownePlace Suites by Marriott **H**

(614) 885-1557. **$97-$160.** 7272 Huntington Park Dr 43235. I-270 exit 23, 0.4 mi n, 0.3 mi e on E Campus View Blvd, then 0.3 mi s. Int corridors. **Pets:** Accepted. 〔SAVE〕 〔ECO〕 ⤳ 🛜 ✕ ∎ ⊡

AAA ▼▼ Varsity Inn North **M**

(614) 267-4646. **Call for rates.** 3246 Olentangy River Rd 43202. SR 315 exit N Broadway, 0.3 mi s. Ext corridors. **Pets:** Accepted. 〔SAVE〕 ⤳ 🛜 ∎ ⊡

AAA ▼▼ The Varsity Inn South **M**

(614) 291-2983. **Call for rates.** 1445 Olentangy River Rd 43212. SR 315 exit King Ave southbound; exit Lane Ave northbound, 1 mi s. Ext corridors. **Pets:** Accepted. 〔SAVE〕 ⤳ 🛜 ∎ ⊡

AAA ▼▼▼ The Westin Columbus **H**

(614) 228-3800. **$149-$349.** 310 S High St 43215. Corner of Main and High sts. Int corridors. **Pets:** Accepted. 〔SAVE〕 🍴 📶 ✕ ∎ ⊡

CONNEAUT

▼▼ Days Inn of Conneaut **H**

(440) 593-6000. **$70-$129.** 600 Days Blvd 44030. I-90 exit 241, 0.3 mi n. Int corridors. **Pets:** Accepted. 🍴 ⤳ 🛜 ∎ ⊡

CUYAHOGA FALLS

AAA ▼▼▼ Sheraton Suites Akron-Cuyahoga Falls **H** 🐾

(330) 929-3000. **$129-$369, 3 day notice.** 1989 Front St 44221. SR 8 exit Broad Blvd, just w. Int corridors. **Pets:** Large, other species. Service with restrictions, crate. 〔SAVE〕 🍴 ⟨&M⟩ ⤳ ✕ 🛜 ✕ ∎ ⊡

DANVILLE

▼▼▼ The White Oak Inn **BB**

(740) 599-6107. **$155-$275, 14 day notice.** 29683 Walhonding Rd (SR 715) 43014. 3.6 mi w on US 62, 1.3 mi se on US 36, then 2.7 mi e on SR 715. Ext/int corridors. **Pets:** Accepted. 🛜 ✕ 🗹 ∎ ⊡

DAYTON

▼▼▼ Comfort Suites-Wright Patterson **H**

(937) 425-6498. **Call for rates.** 5220 Huberville Ave 45431. Jct Woodman Dr, just e. Int corridors. **Pets:** Accepted. 🛜 ✕ ∎ ⊡

AAA ▼▼▼ Crowne Plaza Dayton **H**

(937) 224-0800. **$99-$209.** 33 E 5th St 45402. 5th and Jefferson sts; downtown. Int corridors. **Pets:** Accepted. 〔SAVE〕 🍴 ⟨&M⟩ ⤳ 🛜 ✕ ∎ ⊡

▼▼▼ Dayton Marriott Hotel **H**

(937) 223-1000. **$167-$275.** 1414 S Patterson Blvd 45409. I-75 exit 51, 0.6 mi e on Edwin C Moses Blvd, just s on Stewart St, then just w. Int corridors. **Pets:** Accepted. 🍴 ⟨&M⟩ ⤳ ✕ 🛜 ✕ ∎ ⊡

▼▼▼ Drury Inn & Suites-Dayton North **H**

(937) 454-5200. **$95-$199.** 6616 Miller Ln 45414. I-75 exit 59 (Wyse Rd/Benchwood Rd), just w on Benchwood Rd, then just n. Int corridors. **Pets:** $10 daily fee/room. Service with restrictions, supervision. ⟨&M⟩ ⤳ 🛜 ∎ ⊡

▼▼ Fairfield Inn by Marriott Dayton North **H** 🐾

(937) 898-1120. **$59-$108.** 6960 Miller Ln 45414. I-75 exit 59 (Wyse Rd/Benchwood Rd), just w on Benchwood Rd, then 0.5 mi n. Ext/int corridors. **Pets:** $35 one-time fee/room. Designated rooms, service with restrictions. ⟨&M⟩ ⤳ 🛜 ✕ ∎ ⊡

AAA ▼▼ Red Roof Inn Dayton North Airport **M**

(937) 898-1054. **$39-$159.** 7370 Miller Ln 45414. I-75 exit 59 (Wyse Rd/Benchwood Rd), just w on Benchwood Rd, then 0.8 mi n. Ext corridors. **Pets:** Large, other species. Service with restrictions, supervision. 〔SAVE〕 🛜 ✕ ∎ ⊡

▼▼▼ Residence Inn by Marriott Dayton North **H**

(937) 890-2244. **$104-$194.** 7227 York Center Dr 45414. I-75 exit 59 (Wyse Rd/Benchwood Rd), just w on Benchwood Rd, 0.6 mi n on Miller Ln, then just w. Int corridors. **Pets:** Accepted. ⟨&M⟩ ⤳ 🛜 ✕ ∎ ⊡

▼▼▼ TownePlace Suites by Marriott Dayton North **H**

(937) 898-5700. **$76-$125.** 3642 Maxton Rd 45414. I-75 exit 59 (Wyse Rd/Benchwood Rd), just w on Wyse Rd, then 0.5 mi n on Miller Ln. Int corridors. **Pets:** Accepted. ⟨&M⟩ 🛜 ✕ ∎ ⊡

DELAWARE

AAA ▼▼▼ BEST WESTERN PLUS Delaware Inn **H**

(740) 363-3510. **$79-$159.** 1720 Columbus Pike 43015. I-270 exit 23, 11 mi n on US 23. Int corridors. **Pets:** Large, dogs only. $20 daily fee/pet. Designated rooms, service with restrictions, crate. 〔SAVE〕 ⟨&M⟩ ⤳ ✕ 🛜 ✕ ∎ ⊡

▼▼ Pacer Inn & Suites Motel **M**

(740) 362-0050. **$60-$200, 3 day notice.** 259 S Sandusky St 43015. Jct US 23, 0.7 mi w. Ext/int corridors. **Pets:** Medium, dogs only. $25 daily fee/pet. Designated rooms, service with restrictions, supervision. 🛜 ✕ ∎ ⊡

DELPHOS

▼▼ Microtel Inn & Suites by Wyndham Delphos **H**
(567) 765-1500. **$69-$89.** 480 Moxie Ln 45833. US 30 exit 5th St, 0.5 mi s. Int corridors. **Pets:** Accepted. (ᴹ) 🛜 ✕ 🛈 🖵

DUBLIN

▼▼ Chase Suite Hotel **H**
(614) 766-7762. **Call for rates.** 4130 Tuller Rd 43017. I-270 exit 20, 0.3 mi s on Sawmill Rd via Village Pkwy and Dublin Center Dr. Ext corridors. **Pets:** Accepted. 🌊 🛜 ✕ 🛈 🖵

▼▼▼ Drury Inn & Suites-Columbus Northwest **H**
(614) 798-8802. **$100-$199.** 6170 Parkcenter Cir 43017. I-270 exit 15 (Tuttle Crossing Blvd), 0.3 mi e, then just n on Blazer Pkwy. Int corridors. **Pets:** $10 daily fee/room. Service with restrictions, supervision. (ᴹ) 🌊 🛜 🛈 🖵

▼▼◆ Dublin Homewood Suites by Hilton **H**
(614) 791-8675. **$99-$179.** 5300 Parkcenter Ave 43017. I-270 exit 15 (Tuttle Crossing Blvd), just e, just n on Blazer Pkwy, then just e. Int corridors. **Pets:** Accepted. (ᴹ) 🌊 🛜 🛈 🖵

▼▼ Extended Stay America-Columbus-Dublin **H**
(614) 760-0053. **Call for rates.** 450 Metro Pl N 43017. I-270 exit 17A, just e on SR 161, just s on Frantz Rd, then just w. Int corridors. **Pets:** Other species. $25 daily fee/pet. Service with restrictions, supervision. 🛜 🛈 🖵

▼▼ Extended Stay America (Columbus/Tuttle) **H**
(614) 760-0245. **Call for rates.** 5530 Tuttle Crossing Blvd 43016. I-270 exit 15 (Tuttle Crossing Blvd), 0.3 mi w. Int corridors. **Pets:** Other species. $25 daily fee/pet. Service with restrictions, supervision. 🛜 🛈 🖵

▼◆◆◆ Holiday Inn Express **H**
(614) 793-5500. **Call for rates.** 5500 Tuttle Crossing Blvd 43016. I-270 exit 15 (Tuttle Crossing Blvd), just w. Int corridors. **Pets:** Accepted. (ᴹ) 🌊 🛜 ✕ 🛈 🖵

(AAA) ▼▼◆ Hyatt Place Columbus/Dublin **H**
(614) 799-1913. **$69-$179.** 6161 Parkcenter Cir 43017. I-270 exit 15 (Tuttle Crossing Blvd), just e, then just n on Blazer Pkwy. Int corridors. **Pets:** Medium, dogs only. $75 one-time fee/room. Service with restrictions, supervision. [SAVE] (🍴) (ᴹ) 🌊 🛜 ✕ 🛈 🖵

▼▼ La Quinta Inn Columbus Dublin **H**
(614) 792-8300. **$72-$229.** 6145 Parkcenter Cir 43017. I-270 exit 15 (Tuttle Crossing Blvd), just e, then just n on Blazer Pkwy. Int corridors. **Pets:** Large, other species. Service with restrictions. (ᴹ) 🛜 🛈 🖵

(AAA) ▼▼◆ Red Roof Plus+ Columbus/Dublin **M**
(614) 764-3993. **$59-$169.** 5125 Post Rd 43017. I-270 exit 17A, just ne. Ext corridors. **Pets:** Large, other species. Service with restrictions, supervision. [SAVE] (ᴹ) 🛜 ✕ 🛈 🖵

(AAA) ▼▼◆ Sonesta ES Suites Dublin **H**
(614) 791-0403. **$89-$199.** 435 Metro Pl S 43017. I-270 exit 17A, 0.5 mi e on SR 161, 0.5 mi s on Frantz Rd, then just w. Ext/int corridors. **Pets:** Medium. $75 one-time fee/room. Designated rooms, service with restrictions. [SAVE] (ᴹ) 🌊 🛜 ✕ 🛈 🖵

EASTLAKE

▼▼ Radisson Hotel & Suites Cleveland-Eastlake **H**
(440) 953-8000. **Call for rates.** 35000 Curtis Blvd 44095. Jct SR 2 and 91. Int corridors. **Pets:** Accepted. (🍴) 🌊 🛜 ✕ 🛈 🖵

ELYRIA

▼▼ Red Roof Inn & Suites Cleveland – Elyria **H**
(440) 324-4444. **$74-$130.** 621 Midway Blvd 44035. I-80 exit 145, just n on SR 57 exit Midway Blvd. Int corridors. **Pets:** Large, other species. Service with restrictions, supervision. (ᴹ) 🌊 🛜 🛈 🖵

ENGLEWOOD

▼▼ Comfort Inn & Suites-Dayton **H**
(937) 836-9400. **$60-$100.** 9305 N Main St 45415. I-70 exit 29, just s. Int corridors. **Pets:** Medium, other species. $15 one-time fee/room. Service with restrictions. 🌊 🛜 🛈 🖵

FAIRBORN

▼▼ Extended Stay America **H**
(937) 429-0140. **Call for rates.** 3131 Presidential Dr 45324. I-675 exit 15 (Colonel Glenn Hwy), 1.2 mi e, then just s. Int corridors. **Pets:** Other species. $25 daily fee/pet. Service with restrictions, supervision. 🌊 🛜 🛈 🖵

(AAA) ▼▼▼ Holiday Inn Dayton/Fairborn **H**
(937) 426-7800. **Call for rates.** 2800 Presidential Dr 45324. I-675 exit 17 (N Fairfield Rd), just w. Int corridors. **Pets:** Accepted. [SAVE] (🍴) (ᴹ) 🌊 🛜 🛈 🖵

▼▼◆ Homewood Suites by Hilton Dayton-Fairborn **H**
(937) 429-0600. **$89-$299.** 2750 Presidential Dr 45324. I-675 exit 17 (N Fairfield Rd), just w, then just s on Colonel Glenn Hwy. Ext/int corridors. **Pets:** Accepted. 🌊 🛜 🛈 🖵

(AAA) ▼▼ Red Roof Inn Dayton-Fairborn/Nutter Center **M**
(937) 426-6116. **$50-$180.** 2580 Colonel Glenn Hwy 45324. I-675 exit 17 (N Fairfield Rd), just n. Ext corridors. **Pets:** Large, other species. Service with restrictions, supervision. [SAVE] 🛜 ✕ 🛈 🖵

FAIRLAWN

▼▼ Extended Stay America Akron-Copley **H**
(330) 668-9818. **Call for rates.** 185 Montrose West Ave 44321. I-77 exit 137B, just w on SR 18, then 0.6 mi s. Int corridors. **Pets:** Other species. $25 daily fee/pet. Service with restrictions, supervision. 🛜 🛈 🖵

▼▼ Extended Stay America-Akron-Copley **H**
(330) 666-3177. **Call for rates.** 170 Montrose West Ave 44321. I-77 exit 137B, 0.3 mi w on SR 18, then 0.5 mi s. Int corridors. **Pets:** Other species. $25 daily fee/pet. Service with restrictions, supervision. 🌊 🛜 🛈 🖵

FINDLAY

▼▼▼ Country Inn & Suites By Carlson **H**
(419) 422-4200. **Call for rates.** 903 Interstate Dr 45840. I-75 exit 159, just w. Int corridors. **Pets:** Accepted. (ᴹ) 🌊 🛜 🛈 🖵

▼▼▼ Drury Inn & Suites **H**
(419) 422-9700. **$105-$169.** 820 Trenton Ave 45840. I-75 exit 159, just e. Int corridors. **Pets:** $10 daily fee/room. Service with restrictions, supervision. (ᴹ) 🌊 🛜 🛈 🖵

▼▼ Extended Stay America Findlay-Tiffin Ave **H**
(419) 425-9696. **Call for rates.** 2355 Tiffin Ave 45840. 3 mi e on US 224. Int corridors. **Pets:** Other species. $25 daily fee/pet. Service with restrictions, supervision. 🌊 🛜 🛈 🖵

▼▼▼ Holiday Inn Express Hotel & Suites **H** 🐾
(419) 420-1776. **$109-$129.** 941 Interstate Dr 45840. I-75 exit 159, just w. Int corridors. **Pets:** Medium, dogs only. $25 one-time fee/pet. Service with restrictions, supervision. (ᴹ) 🌊 🛜 🛈 🖵

▼▼ Quality Inn **M**
(419) 423-4303. **$70-$85.** 1020 Interstate Ct 45840. I-75 exit 159, just w. Ext corridors. **Pets:** Accepted. 🌊 🛜 🛈 🖵

(AAA) ▼▼▼ TownePlace Suites by Marriott Findlay **H**
(419) 425-9545. **$118-$194.** 2501 Tiffin Ave 45840. 3 mi e on US 224. Int corridors. **Pets:** Accepted. [SAVE] 🌊 🛜 ✕ 🛈 🖵

FOSTORIA

◉ ▼▼ BEST WESTERN Fostoria Inn & Suites **H**
(419) 436-3600. **$83-$130.** 1690 N County Line Rd 44830. SR 12, 2 mi n on SR 23. Int corridors. **Pets:** Medium. $100 deposit/room, $10 daily fee/pet. Designated rooms, service with restrictions, crate.
[SAVE] [&M] [▲] [◉] [📶] [■] [💻]

FREDERICKTOWN

▼▼▼ Heartland Country Resort **CA**
(216) 577-2090. **Call for rates.** 3020 Township Rd 190 43019. I-71 exit 151, 2 mi e on SR 95, 0.5 mi s on SR 314, then 1.3 mi e. Ext corridors. **Pets:** Accepted. [📶] [✕] [■] [💻]

FREMONT

▼▼ Days Inn **H**
(419) 334-9551. **$77-$155.** 3701 SR 53 N 43420. I-80/90 exit 91, just n. Int corridors. **Pets:** Small, dogs only. Service with restrictions, supervision. [🍴] [▲] [📶] [■] [💻]

GAHANNA

▼▼ Candlewood Suites Columbus Airport **H**
(614) 863-4033. **Call for rates.** 590 Taylor Rd 43230. I-270 exit 37, 0.4 mi e, 0.6 mi s on Morrison Rd, then just e. Int corridors. **Pets:** Accepted. [📶] [✕] [■] [💻]

◉ ▼▼ TownePlace Suites by Marriott Columbus Airport **H**
(614) 861-1400. **$97-$183.** 695 Taylor Rd 43230. I-270 exit 37, just e, 0.6 mi s on Morrison Rd, then just e. Int corridors. **Pets:** Large. $100 one-time fee/room. Designated rooms, service with restrictions, crate.
[SAVE] [ECO] [▲] [📶] [✕] [■] [💻]

GALLIPOLIS

◉ ▼▼ Super 8 **M**
(740) 446-8080. **$74-$165, 3 day notice.** 321 Upper River Rd 45631. On SR 7, jct US 35. Int corridors. **Pets:** Accepted.
[SAVE] [&M] [▲] [📶] [■] [💻]

GENEVA

▼ Motel 6 #4476 **H**
(440) 466-1168. **Call for rates.** 1715 SR 534 S 44041. I-90 exit 218, just n. Ext/int corridors. **Pets:** Other species. Service with restrictions, crate. [▲] [📶] [■]

GENEVA-ON-THE-LAKE

◉ ▼▼▼ The Lodge & Conference Center at Geneva-on-the-Lake **H** ❀
(440) 466-7100. **$89-$219, 3 day notice.** 4888 N Broadway (SR 534) 44041. I-90 exit 218, 6.1 mi n. Int corridors. **Pets:** Other species. $50 one-time fee/room. Designated rooms, service with restrictions, supervision. [SAVE] [🍴] [&M] [▲] [✕] [📶] [✕] [■] [💻]

GRANDVIEW HEIGHTS

◉ ▼▼▼ Hyatt Place Columbus/OSU **H**
(614) 280-1234. **$79-$229.** 795 Yard St 43212. US 315 exit Goodale Blvd, just w. Int corridors. **Pets:** Accepted.
[SAVE] [🍴] [&M] [▲] [📶] [✕] [■] [💻]

GREEN

▼▼ Super 8 Akron-Canton Airport **H**
(330) 899-9888. **$150-$170.** 1605 Corporate Woods Pkwy 44685. I-77 exit 118, just w. Int corridors. **Pets:** Accepted. [▲] [📶] [■] [💻]

GROVE CITY

◉ ▼▼ BEST WESTERN Executive Inn **M**
(614) 875-7770. **$77-$110.** 4026 Jackpot Rd 43123. I-71 exit 100, just e. Ext corridors. **Pets:** Small, dogs only. $12 daily fee/pet. Designated rooms, service with restrictions, supervision. [SAVE] [▲] [📶] [■] [💻]

▼▼▼ Drury Inn & Suites-Columbus South **H**
(614) 875-7000. **$100-$199.** 4109 Parkway Centre Dr 43123. I-71 exit 100, just e. Int corridors. **Pets:** $10 daily fee/room. Service with restrictions, supervision. [&M] [▲] [📶] [■] [💻]

▼▼▼ La Quinta Inn Grove City **H**
(614) 539-6200. **$89-$279.** 3962 Jackpot Rd 43123. I-71 exit 100, just e. Int corridors. **Pets:** Large, other species. Service with restrictions.
[▲] [✕] [📶] [✕] [■] [💻]

▼▼ Microtel Inn by Wyndham Grove City/Columbus **H**
(614) 277-0705. **$56-$100.** 1800 Stringtown Rd 43123. I-71 exit 100, just e. Int corridors. **Pets:** Accepted. [📶] [■]

HILLIARD

▼▼▼ Comfort Suites by Choice Hotels-Columbus **H**
(614) 529-8118. **$90-$130.** 3831 Park Mill Run Dr 43026. I-270 exit 13 southbound; exit 13A northbound, 0.4 mi e on Fishinger Blvd. Int corridors. **Pets:** Medium. $10 daily fee/room. Designated rooms, service with restrictions, supervision. [&M] [▲] [📶] [✕] [■] [💻]

▼▼▼ Homewood Suites by Hilton-Columbus **H**
(614) 529-4100. **$109-$199.** 3841 Park Mill Run Dr 43026. I-270 exit 13 southbound; exit 13A northbound, 0.4 mi e on Fishinger Blvd. Int corridors. **Pets:** Accepted. [&M] [▲] [📶] [■] [💻]

HILLSBORO

▼▼ Days Inn Hillsboro **H**
(937) 393-0299. **$75-$115.** 103 Harry Sauner Rd 45133. 1.9 mi ne on US 62. Int corridors. **Pets:** Accepted. [▲] [📶] [■] [💻]

HOLIDAY CITY

▼▼▼ Holiday Inn Express Hotel & Suites Bryan/Montpelier **H**
(419) 485-0008. **$93-$220.** 13399 SR 15 43543. I-80/90 exit 13, just s. Int corridors. **Pets:** Other species. $10 daily fee/pet. Service with restrictions. [▲] [📶] [■] [💻]

HOLLAND

▼ Extended Stay America Toledo-Holland **H**
(419) 861-1133. **Call for rates.** 6155 W Trust Dr 43528. I-475 exit 8, 0.5 mi e to Holland-Sylvania Rd, then just n. Int corridors. **Pets:** Other species. $25 daily fee/pet. Service with restrictions, supervision.
[📶] [■] [💻]

HUBBARD

▼▼ Travelodge Hubbard **H**
(330) 534-8191. **$28-$68.** 6985 Truck World Blvd 44425. I-80 exit 234, just n. Int corridors. **Pets:** Accepted. [&M] [📶] [✕] [💻]

HUBER HEIGHTS

◉ ▼▼▼ Holiday Inn Express Hotel & Suites **H**
(937) 235-2000. **Call for rates.** 5612 Merily Way 45424. I-70 exit 36, just se on SR 202. Int corridors. **Pets:** Accepted.
[SAVE] [&M] [▲] [📶] [■] [💻]

HUDSON

◉ ▼▼ Baymont Inn & Suites Hudson/Boston Heights **H** ❀
(330) 650-2040. **$59-$149.** 6731 Industrial Pkwy 44236. SR 8 exit 15 southbound. Int corridors. **Pets:** Medium, other species. $10 daily fee/pet. Designated rooms, service with restrictions.
[SAVE] [&M] [▲] [📶] [✕] [■] [💻]

◉ ▼▼ Clarion Inn and Conference Center **H**
(330) 653-9191. **$69-$129.** 6625 Dean Memorial Pkwy 44236. SR 8 exit 15 southbound; exit 14A northbound. Int corridors. **Pets:** Medium, other species. $10 daily fee/room. Service with restrictions, supervision.
[SAVE] [🍴] [&M] [▲] [✕] [📶] [■] [■] [💻]

HURON

▼▼▼▼ Motel 6 Huron 🄷
(419) 433-7829. **$39-$169, 3 day notice.** 601 Rye Beach Rd 44839. SR 2 exit Rye Beach, 2.5 mi w on US 6. Int corridors. **Pets:** Other species. Service with restrictions, crate. 🄼 ⊶ 🕸 ✕ 📧 💻

Ⓐ ▼▼▼▼ Sawmill Creek Resort 🄷
(419) 433-3800. **$129-$219, 3 day notice.** 400 Sawmill Creek W 44839. SR 2 exit Rye Beach, 0.5 mi w on US 6. Int corridors. **Pets:** Medium, dogs only. $25 daily fee/pet. Service with restrictions, crate. 🆂🅰🆅🅴 🍴 ⊶ ✕ 🕸 ✕ 📧 💻

INDEPENDENCE

Ⓐ ▼▼▼▼ Hyatt Place Cleveland/Independence 🄷
(216) 328-1060. **$74-$179.** 6025 Jefferson Dr 44131. I-77 exit 155 (Rockside Rd), just w, then just n. Int corridors. **Pets:** Medium, dogs only. $75 one-time fee/room. Service with restrictions, supervision. 🆂🅰🆅🅴 🍴 🄼 ⊶ 🕸 ✕ 📧 💻

▼▼ La Quinta Inn Cleveland Independence 🄷
(216) 447-1133. **$72-$194.** 6161 Quarry Ln 44131. I-77 exit 155 (Rockside Rd), just e, then just s. Int corridors. **Pets:** Large, other species. Service with restrictions. 🕸 📧 💻

Ⓐ ▼▼ Red Roof Inn Cleveland -
Independence 🄼
(216) 447-0030. **$59-$110.** 6020 Quarry Ln 44131. I-77 exit 155 (Rockside Rd), just e, then just s. Ext corridors. **Pets:** Large, other species. Service with restrictions, supervision. 🆂🅰🆅🅴 🄼 🕸 📧 💻

▼▼▼▼ Residence Inn by Marriott 🄷
(216) 520-1450. **$160-$263.** 5101 W Creek Rd 44131. I-77 exit 155 (Rockside Rd), just w, then just n. Ext/int corridors. **Pets:** Accepted. 🄼 ⊶ 🕸 ✕ 📧 💻

JACKSON

▼▼ Days Inn 🄷
(740) 286-3464. **$78-$90.** 972 E Main St 45640. Just s of SR 93. Int corridors. **Pets:** Accepted. 🕸 📧 💻

▼▼ Red Roof Inn Jackson, OH 🄼
(740) 288-1200. **$72-$107.** 1000 Acy Ave 45640. US 35 exit McCarty Ln, just nw. Int corridors. **Pets:** Large, other species. Service with restrictions, supervision. 🕸 📧

KENT

▼▼ Days Inn-Akron Kent 🄼
(330) 677-9400. **$55-$149.** 4422 Edson Rd 44240. I-76 exit 33, just n. Ext corridors. **Pets:** Accepted. ⊶ 🕸 📧 💻

▼▼▼▼ Kent State University Hotel & Conference
Center 🄷
(330) 346-0100. **Call for rates.** 215 S Depeyster St 44240. Jct Erie St. Int corridors. **Pets:** Accepted. 🍴 🕸 ✕ 📧 💻

KENWOOD

Ⓐ ▼▼▼▼ BEST WESTERN PLUS Hannaford Inn &
Suites 🄷
(513) 936-0525. **$119-$150.** 5900 E Galbraith Rd 45236. I-71 exit 12, 0.5 mi e, then 0.3 mi n. Int corridors. **Pets:** Small, other species. $150 one-time fee/room. Supervision. 🆂🅰🆅🅴 ⊶ 🕸 ✕ 📧 💻

KINSMAN

▼▼▼▼ Dream Horse Guesthouse 🅱🅱
(330) 876-0428. **$85-$150, 14 day notice.** 9532 SR 7 44428. 0.5 mi n on SR 7. Int corridors. **Pets:** Other species. $20 daily fee/pet. Service with restrictions, supervision. 🕸 ✕ 📧 💻

LIMA

▼▼▼▼ Country Inn & Suites By Carlson 🄷
(419) 999-9992. **$99-$139.** 804 S Leonard Ave 45804. I-75 exit 125A southbound; exit 125 northbound, just w. Int corridors. **Pets:** Accepted. ⊶ 🕸 📧 💻

Ⓐ ▼▼▼▼ Howard Johnson Lima 🄷
(419) 222-0004. **$79-$129.** 1920 Roschman Ave 45804. I-75 exit 125A southbound; exit 125 northbound. Int corridors. **Pets:** Dogs only. $25 daily fee/pet. Service with restrictions, supervision. 🆂🅰🆅🅴 🍴 🄼 ⊶ ✕ 🕸 📧 💻

LOGAN

▼▼▼▼ Holiday Inn Express Hocking Hills 🄷
(740) 385-7700. **$109-$279.** 12916 Grey St 43138. SR 664, just w to Lake Logan Rd, then just n. Int corridors. **Pets:** Other species. Service with restrictions, supervision. 🄼 ⊶ 🕸 📧 💻

▼▼▼▼ The Inn & Spa At Cedar Falls 🄲 🐾
(740) 380-7489. **$135-$339, 30 day notice.** 21190 SR 374 43138. 9.5 mi s on SR 664, 1 mi e. Int corridors. **Pets:** Large, dogs only. $45 one-time fee/room. Designated rooms, service with restrictions, crate. 🍴 🕸 ✕ ✕ 📧 💻

MANSFIELD

Ⓐ ▼▼ BEST WESTERN Richland
Inn-Mansfield 🄷 🐾
(419) 756-6670. **$72-$189.** 180 E Hanley Rd 44903. I-71 exit 169, jct SR 13. Int corridors. **Pets:** Large. $15 daily fee/room. Service with restrictions, crate. 🆂🅰🆅🅴 ⊶ 🕸 📧 💻

▼▼ La Quinta Inn & Suites Mansfield 🄷
(419) 774-0005. **$79-$369.** 120 Stander Ave 44903. I-71 exit 169, just e. Int corridors. **Pets:** Large, other species. Service with restrictions. 🄼 ⊶ 🕸 📧 💻

▼▼▼▼ Quality Inn & Suites 🄷
(419) 529-1000. **$84-$500.** 500 N Trimble Rd 44906. Jct US 30, just s. Int corridors. **Pets:** Accepted. ⊶ 🕸 📧 💻

Ⓐ ▼▼▼ Super 8 🄷
(419) 756-8875. **$50-$189.** 2425 Interstate Cir 44903. I-71 exit 169, just w. Int corridors. **Pets:** Medium. $15 daily fee/pet. Designated rooms, service with restrictions, supervision. 🆂🅰🆅🅴 🕸 📧 💻

MARIETTA

▼▼▼▼ The Lafayette Hotel 🄷
(740) 373-5522. **$80-$210.** 101 Front St 45750. I-77 exit 1; downtown. Int corridors. **Pets:** Accepted. 🍴 🕸 📧 💻

▼▼ Magnuson Hotel By The River 🄼
(740) 374-7211. **$66-$99.** 279 Muskingum Dr 45750. I-77 exit 6, 3.5 mi sw on SR 821, then 1 mi s on SR 60. Ext corridors. **Pets:** Accepted. 🕸 📧 💻

Ⓐ ▼▼▼▼ Quality Inn Marietta 🄷
(740) 374-8190. **$85-$100.** 700 Pike St 45750. I-77 exit 1, just e. Int corridors. **Pets:** Other species. $10 daily fee/pet. 🆂🅰🆅🅴 🍴 🄼 ⊶ 🕸 📧 💻

MARYSVILLE

▼▼▼▼ Comfort Inn 🄷
(937) 644-0400. **$90-$95.** 16420 Allenby Dr 43040. Jct US 33 and 36. Int corridors. **Pets:** $15 daily fee/pet. Service with restrictions. ⊶ 🕸 📧 💻

MASON

Ⓐ ▼▼▼▼ Hyatt Place Cincinnati-Northeast 🄷
(513) 754-0003. **$79-$199.** 5070 Natorp Blvd 45040. I-71 exit 19, 0.5 mi w. Int corridors. **Pets:** Accepted. 🆂🅰🆅🅴 🍴 🄼 ⊶ 🕸 ✕ 📧 💻

▼▼▼ **Red Roof Inn & Suites-Cincinnati North-Mason** ⓗ
(513) 683-3086. **$60-$99.** 8870 Governor's Hill Dr 45249. I-71 exit 19, just se. Int corridors. **Pets:** Large, other species. Service with restrictions, supervision. 🐾 🛜 🛟 📺

⟨AAA⟩ ▼▼▼ **TownePlace Suites by Marriott** ⓗ
(513) 774-0610. **$118-$217.** 9369 Waterstone Blvd 45249. I-71 exit 19, just e on Mason-Montgomery Rd, then 0.9 mi n on Fields-Ertel and Union Cemetery rds. Int corridors. **Pets:** Accepted.
【SAVE】【ECO】【&M】🐾 🛜 ✕ 🛟 📺

MAUMEE

▼▼ **Extended Stay America-Toledo-Maumee** ⓗ
(419) 891-1211. **$80-$85.** 542 W Dussel Dr 43537. I-475 exit 6, just e. Int corridors. **Pets:** Other species. $25 daily fee/pet. Service with restrictions, supervision. 🐾 🛜 🛟 📺

▼▼▼ **Homewood Suites by Hilton Toledo/Maumee** ⓗ
(419) 897-0980. **$89-$189.** 1410 Arrowhead Rd 43537. I-475 exit 6, just e. Int corridors. **Pets:** Accepted. 【&M】🏊 🐾 🛜 🛟 📺

⟨AAA⟩ ▼▼ **Red Roof Inn Toledo - Maumee** Ⓜ
(419) 893-0292. **$45-$100.** 1570 Reynolds Rd 43537. I-80/90 exit 59, just s. Ext/int corridors. **Pets:** Large, other species. Service with restrictions, supervision. 【SAVE】🛜 🛟 📺

▼▼▼ **Residence Inn by Marriott Maumee** ⓗ
(419) 891-2233. **$132-$229.** 1370 Arrowhead Dr 43537. I-475 exit 6, just e. Int corridors. **Pets:** Accepted. 🐾 ✕ 🛜 ✕ 🛟 📺

MAYFIELD HEIGHTS

▼▼ **Staybridge Suites Cleveland East** ⓗ
(440) 442-9200. **$109-$169.** 6103 Landerhaven Dr 44124. I-271 exit 32, just e on Cedar Rd, 0.7 mi n on Lander Rd, then just e. Int corridors. **Pets:** Accepted. 【&M】🐾 🛜 ✕ 🛟 📺

MEDINA

▼▼ **Quality Inn & Suites** ⓗ
(330) 723-4994. **$75-$170.** 2850 Medina Rd 44256. I-71 exit 218, just e. Int corridors. **Pets:** Medium. $10 daily fee/pet. Service with restrictions, supervision. 🐾 🛜 🛟 📺

▼▼ **Red Roof Inn Cleveland-Medina** Ⓜ
(330) 725-1395. **$55-$130.** 5021 Eastpointe Dr 44256. I-71 exit 218, just w. Ext corridors. **Pets:** Large, other species. Service with restrictions, supervision. 🐾 🛜 🛟

MENTOR

⟨AAA⟩ ▼▼▼ **BEST WESTERN PLUS Lawnfield Inn & Suites** ⓗ 🐾
(440) 205-7378. **Call for rates.** 8434 Mentor Ave 44060. I-90 exit 195, 1.5 mi n to US 20 (Mentor Ave), then just e. Int corridors. **Pets:** $20 daily fee/room. Designated rooms, service with restrictions, supervision.
【SAVE】【🍴】【&M】🏊 🐾 🛜 ✕ 🛟 📺

▼▼▼ **Residence Inn by Marriott** ⓗ
(440) 392-0800. **$167-$275.** 5660 Emerald Ct 44060. Jct SR 2 and Heisley Rd, just s. Int corridors. **Pets:** Accepted.
🐾 🛜 ✕ 🛟 📺

▼▼ **Super 8** ⓗ
(440) 951-8558. **$47-$99.** 7325 Palisades Pkwy 44060. On SR 306, just s of SR 2. Int corridors. **Pets:** Accepted. 🛜 🛟 📺

MIAMISBURG

▼▼▼ **DoubleTree Suites by Hilton Dayton-Miamisburg** ⓗ 🐾
(937) 436-2400. **$89-$189.** 300 Prestige Pl 45342. I-75 exit 44, just e on SR 725, just s on Prestige Plaza Dr, then just se. Int corridors. **Pets:** Large. $25 daily fee/room. Service with restrictions, supervision.
【🍴】【&M】🐾 🛜 🛟 📺

▼▼▼ **Homewood Suites by Hilton-Dayton South** ⓗ 🐾
(937) 432-0000. **$109-$179.** 3100 Contemporary Ln 45342. I-75 exit 44, just e on SR 725, just se on Prestige Plaza Dr, then just s. Int corridors. **Pets:** Other species. $200 deposit/room, $30 daily fee/pet. Service with restrictions, crate. 【&M】🐾 🛜 🛟 📺

MIDDLEBURG HEIGHTS

▼▼ **Comfort Inn-Cleveland Airport** ⓗ
(440) 234-3131. **$72-$129, 3 day notice.** 17550 Rosbough Dr 44130. I-71 exit 235, 0.3 mi w to Engle Rd, then 0.3 mi n. Int corridors. **Pets:** $50 one-time fee/pet. Service with restrictions, crate.
【&M】🐾 🛜 ✕ 🛟 📺

⟨AAA⟩ ▼▼▼ **Days Inn Cleveland Airport South** Ⓜ
(440) 243-2277. **$59-$69.** 7233 Engle Rd 44130. I-71 exit 235, just w. Ext corridors. **Pets:** $10 daily fee/pet. Designated rooms, service with restrictions, supervision. 【SAVE】🐾 🛜 🛟 📺

▼▼ **Extended Stay America Cleveland-Middleburg Heights** ⓗ
(440) 243-7024. **Call for rates.** 17552 Rosbough Dr 44130. I-71 exit 235, 0.3 mi w to Engle Rd, then 0.3 mi n. **Pets:** Other species. $25 daily fee/pet. Service with restrictions, supervision.
🛜 🛟 📺

⟨AAA⟩ ▼▼▼ **Red Roof Inn Cleveland - Middleburg Heights** ⓗ
(440) 243-2441. **$49-$120.** 17555 Bagley Rd 44130. I-71 exit 235, just w, then just s. Ext/int corridors. **Pets:** Large, other species. Service with restrictions, supervision. 【SAVE】🛜 ✕ 🛟 📺

▼▼▼ **Residence Inn by Marriott** ⓗ
(440) 234-6688. **$139-$229.** 17525 Rosbough Dr 44130. I-71 exit 235, just w on Bagley Rd, then just n on Engle Rd. Ext/int corridors. **Pets:** Accepted. 🐾 🛜 ✕ 🛟 📺

⟨AAA⟩ ▼▼▼ **TownePlace Suites by Marriott Cleveland Airport** ⓗ
(440) 816-9300. **$125-$240.** 7325 S Engle Rd 44130. I-71 exit 235, just w on Bagley Rd, then just s. Int corridors. **Pets:** Accepted.
【SAVE】【ECO】🐾 🛜 ✕ 🛟 📺

MIDDLETOWN

▼▼▼ **Drury Inn & Suites Middletown** ⓗ
(513) 425-6650. **$90-$139.** 3320 Village Dr 45005. I-75 exit 32, just w on SR 122. Int corridors. **Pets:** $10 daily fee/room. Service with restrictions, supervision. 【&M】🏊 🛜 🛟 📺

MILAN

▼▼ **Motel 6 - 4016** ⓗ
(419) 499-8001. **$39-$169, 3 day notice.** 11406 US 250 Milan Rd 44846. I-80/90 exit 118, 1.5 mi n. Int corridors. **Pets:** Other species. Service with restrictions, crate. 【ECO】🐾 🛜

▼▼ **Red Roof Inn Sandusky-Milan** ⓗ
(419) 499-4347. **$54-$175.** 11303 US 250 Milan Rd 44846. I-80/90 exit 118, 0.5 mi n. Int corridors. **Pets:** Large, other species. Service with restrictions, supervision. 🐾 🛜 🛟

▼▼ **Super 8** ⓗ
(419) 499-4671. **$49-$278.** 11313 US 250 Milan Rd 44846. I-80/90 exit 118, 0.5 mi n. Ext/int corridors. **Pets:** Small, dogs only. Service with restrictions, supervision. 🐾 🛜 📺

MILFORD

▼▼▼ **Homewood Suites by Hilton** ⓗ
(513) 248-4663. **$109-$189.** 600 Chamber Dr 45150. I-275 exit 59 southbound; exit 59A northbound, 0.5 mi w on Milford Pkwy, then 0.5 mi s. Int corridors. **Pets:** Accepted. 【&M】🐾 🛜 🛟 📺

MILLERSBURG

▼▼▼▼ Comfort Inn Millersburg [H]

(330) 674-7400. **$90-$200.** 1102 Glen Dr 44654. SR 39, 0.5 mi s on S Clay. Int corridors. **Pets:** Dogs only. $20 daily fee/pet. Designated rooms, service with restrictions, supervision. 🔁 🛰 ✖ 🔋 🖵

▼▼ ▼▼ Hotel Millersburg [H]

(330) 674-1457. **$69-$219, 3 day notice.** 35 W Jackson St 44654. Just w of jct SR 83; downtown. Int corridors. **Pets:** Cats only. $15 daily fee/room. Designated rooms, service with restrictions, crate.

🍴 🛰 ✖ 🔋 🖵

▲▲▲ ▼▼▼▼ The Inn at Honey Run [CI]

(330) 674-0011. **$139-$259.** 6920 CR 203 44654. SR 241 N/Massillon Rd, 1.7 mi n, just e. Int corridors. **Pets:** Accepted.

[SAVE] 🍴 🛰 ✖ 🔋 🖵

MONROE

▲▲▲ ▼▼ ▼▼ BEST WESTERN Monroe Inn [H]

(513) 539-4400. **$99-$109.** 40 New Garver Rd 45050. I-75 exit 29, just w. Int corridors. **Pets:** Accepted. [SAVE] 🔁 🔁 🛰 🔋 🖵

MOUNT ORAB

▲▲▲ ▼▼ ▼▼ BEST WESTERN Mount Orab Inn [H]

(937) 444-6666. **Call for rates.** 100 Leininger St 45154. Jct US 68 and SR 32, just n on US 68. Int corridors. **Pets:** $15 daily fee/pet. Designated rooms, service with restrictions, crate.

[SAVE] 🔁 🛰 🔋 🖵

MOUNT VERNON

▼▼▼▼ Comfort Inn [H]

(740) 392-6886. **$100-$200.** 150 Howard St 43050. Jct SR 13; s of downtown. Int corridors. **Pets:** Other species. $10 daily fee/pet. Service with restrictions, supervision. 🔁 🛰 🔋 🖵

▼▼▼▼ Holiday Inn Express [H]

(740) 392-1900. **$120-$180.** 11555 Upper Gilchrist Rd 43050. 2.6 mi e on US 36, then just s. Int corridors. **Pets:** Small, other species. Designated rooms, service with restrictions, supervision.

🔁 🔁 🛰 ✖ 🔋 🖵

NAPOLEON

▲▲▲ ▼▼ ▼▼ BEST WESTERN Napoleon Inn & Suites [H]

(419) 599-0850. **$85-$130.** 1290 Independence Dr 43545. US 6 and 24, exit 41, just se. Int corridors. **Pets:** Accepted. [SAVE] 🔁 🛰 🔋 🖵

▼▼ ▼▼ Holiday Inn Express Hotel & Suites [H]

(419) 592-5599. **Call for rates.** 590 Bonaparte Dr 43545. Jct US 6 and 24, exit 40, just n on SR 108. Int corridors. **Pets:** $50 one-time fee/pet. Designated rooms, no service. 🔁 🔁 🛰 🔋 🖵

NEWARK

▼▼▼▼ Cherry Valley Lodge [H]

(740) 788-1200. **$99-$239.** 2299 Cherry Valley Rd 43055. 4.2 mi w on SR 16, 0.3 mi s. Int corridors. **Pets:** $25 daily fee/pet. Designated rooms, service with restrictions, crate.

🍴 🔁 🔁 ✖ 🛰 ✖ 🔋 🖵

NEWCOMERSTOWN

▼▼▼ Hampton Inn [H]

(740) 498-9800. **$99-$179.** 200 Morris Crossing 43832. I-77 exit 65, 0.8 mi w. Int corridors. **Pets:** Accepted. 🔁 🔁 🛰 🔋 🖵

NEW PHILADELPHIA

▲▲▲ ▼▼▼▼ BEST WESTERN Dutch Valley Inn [H] 🐾

(330) 339-6500. **$100-$150.** 161 Bluebell Dr SW 44663. I-77 exit 81, 0.7 mi e. Int corridors. **Pets:** Large. $15 daily fee/room. Designated rooms, service with restrictions, supervision.

[SAVE] 🔁 🔁 🛰 🔋 🖵

NEWTON FALLS

▼▼ Econo Lodge [M]

(330) 872-0988. **$58-$65.** 4248 SR 5 44444. I-80 exit 209, just w. Ext corridors. **Pets:** Accepted. 🛰 🔋 🖵

NILES

▼▼▼▼ Residence Inn by Marriott Youngstown/Warren-Niles [H]

(330) 505-3655. **$125-$206.** 5555 Youngstown-Warren Rd 44446. I-80 exit 227, 2.6 mi w on US 422. Int corridors. **Pets:** Accepted.

🔁 🛰 ✖ 🔋 🖵

NORTH OLMSTED

▼▼▼▼ Candlewood Suites Cleveland/North Olmsted [H]

(440) 716-0584. **Call for rates.** 24741 Country Club Blvd 44070. I-480 exit 6B westbound; exit 6 eastbound, just n on SR 252. Int corridors. **Pets:** Accepted. 🔁 🛰 🔋 🖵

▼▼ ▼▼ Extended Stay America Cleveland/Airport-N Olmsted [H]

(440) 716-2412. **Call for rates.** 25801 Country Club Blvd 44070. I-480 exit 6B westbound; exit 6 eastbound, just n on SR 252, then 0.3 mi w. Int corridors. **Pets:** Other species. $25 daily fee/pet. Service with restrictions, supervision. 🔁 🛰 🔋 🖵

▼▼ ▼▼ Extended Stay America-North Olmsted [H]

(440) 777-8585. **Call for rates.** 24851 Country Club Blvd 44070. I-480 exit 6B westbound; exit 6 eastbound, just n on SR 252. Int corridors. **Pets:** Other species. $25 daily fee/pet. Service with restrictions, supervision. 🔁 🛰 🔋 🖵

▼▼▼▼ La Quinta Inn & Suites Cleveland Airport West [H]

(440) 734-4477. **$84-$285.** 25105 Country Club Blvd 44070. I-480 exit 6B westbound; exit 6 eastbound, just n on SR 252. **Pets:** Large, other species. Service with restrictions.

🔁 🔁 🛰 ✖ 🔋 🖵

NORWALK

▲▲▲ ▼▼ ▼▼ All American Inn & Suites [H]

(419) 663-1922. **$79-$257.** 415 Milan Ave 44857. 4 mi n on US 250; 5 mi s of I-80/90 (Ohio Tpke). Int corridors. **Pets:** Medium. $25 one-time fee/pet. Service with restrictions, supervision. [SAVE] 🔁 🛰 🔋 🖵

▼▼ Econo Lodge [M]

(419) 668-5656. **$149-$225.** 342 Milan Ave 44857. 3 mi n on US 250; 6 mi s of I-80/90 (Ohio Tpke). Ext corridors. **Pets:** Accepted.

🔁 🛰 🔋

OBERLIN

▼▼ Oberlin Inn [H]

(440) 775-1111. **$109-$219, 3 day notice.** 7 N Main St 44074. On SR 58; jct College and Main sts; center. Int corridors. **Pets:** Accepted.

🍴 🛰 🔋 🖵

OBETZ

▼▼▼▼ Comfort Inn Obetz Rickenbacker [H]

(614) 492-9000. **$65-$135.** 4870 Old Rathmell Ct 43207. I-270 exit 49, just e. Int corridors. **Pets:** Accepted. 🛰 🔁 🛰 ✖ 🔋 🖵

OREGON

▲▲▲ ▼▼ ▼▼ Comfort Inn East [H]

(419) 691-8911. **$80-$100.** 2930 Navarre Ave 43616. I-280 exit 7, 0.3 mi n on access road, then 0.6 mi e on SR 2 (Navarre Ave). Int corridors. **Pets:** Accepted. [SAVE] 🔁 🛰 🔋 🖵

▲▲▲ ▼▼ ▼▼ Sleep Inn & Suites [H]

(419) 697-7800. **$86-$126.** 1761 Meijer Cir 43616. I-280 exit 6 (Curtice Rd), just w. Int corridors. **Pets:** Accepted. [SAVE] 🔁 🛰 🔋 🖵

PAINESVILLE

▼▼▼ Quail Hollow Resort ⊞
(440) 497-1100. $99-$129. 11080 Concord-Hambden Rd 44077. I-90 exit 200, 0.3 mi s on SR 44, then just e on Auburn Rd. Int corridors. Pets: Small, dogs only. $150 deposit/room, $50 one-time fee/room. Designated rooms, service with restrictions, crate.

⊙ ⌨ ⇌ ⊠ 🔊 ✕ 🔋 🖥

PERRYSBURG

▼▼ Candlewood Suites ⊞
(419) 872-6161. Call for rates. 27350 Lake Vue Dr 43551. I-75 exit 193, just e. Int corridors. Pets: Accepted. ⌨ 🔊 🔋 🖥

▼▼ La Quinta Inn Toledo Perrysburg ⊞
(419) 872-0000. $69-$219. 1154 Professional Dr 43551. I-75 exit 193, just w. Int corridors. Pets: Large, other species. Service with restrictions. 🔊 🔋 🖥

PERRYSVILLE

▼▼ Mohican Resort & Conference Center ⊞
(419) 938-5411. Call for rates. 4700 Goon Rd 44864. I-71 exit 165, 2 mi e on SR 95. Ext/int corridors. Pets: $15 daily fee/pet. Designated rooms, service with restrictions. ⊙ ⊠ 🔊 ✕ 🔋 🖥

PIQUA

▼▼ Comfort Inn, Piqua, at Miami Valley Centre Mall ⊞
(937) 778-8100. $79-$179. 987 E Ash St 45356. I-75 exit 82, just w. Int corridors. Pets: Other species. $20 daily fee/room. Supervision.

⇌ 🔊 🔋 🖥

POLAND

ⒶⒶⒶ ▼▼▼ Red Roof Inn Boardman ⊞
(330) 758-1999. $50-$200. 1051 Tiffany S 44514. I-680 exit 11, just w. Int corridors. Pets: Large, other species. Service with restrictions, supervision. 🆂🅰🆅🅴 🔊 ✕ 🔋 🖥

▼▼▼ Residence Inn by Marriott-Youngstown ⊞
(330) 726-1747. $126-$207. 7396 Tiffany S 44514. I-680 exit 11, just w. Int corridors. Pets: Accepted. ⇌ 🔊 ✕ 🔋 🖥

PORT CLINTON

ⒶⒶⒶ ▼▼ BEST WESTERN Port Clinton ⊞
(419) 734-2274. $59-$199. 1734 E Perry St 43452. 1.7 mi e on SR 163, w of jct SR 2. Ext/int corridors. Pets: Medium, dogs only. Designated rooms, service with restrictions, supervision.

🆂🅰🆅🅴 ⇌ 🔊 🔋 🖥

▼▼ Commodore Perry Inn & Business Center ⊞
(419) 732-2645. Call for rates. 255 W Lakeshore Dr 43452. SR 2 exit 121A, 2.4 mi e on SR 163. Int corridors. Pets: Accepted.
⊙ ⇌ 🔊 ✕ 🔋 🖥

▼▼ Quality Inn ⊞
(419) 732-2929. $60-$230. 1723 E Perry St 43452. 1.5 mi e on SR 163, w of jct SR 2. Ext corridors. Pets: Accepted. ⇌ 🔊 🔋 🖥

▼▼ Super 8 ⊞
(419) 734-4446. $49-$189. 1704 E Perry St 43452. 1.7 mi e on SR 163, w of jct SR 2. Int corridors. Pets: Medium, dogs only. Designated rooms, service with restrictions, supervision. 🔊 🖥

▼▼ Travelodge Port Clinton Ⓜ
(419) 734-0769. $69-$179. 1811 E Perry St 43452. SR 163, 1.8 mi e to jct SR 2, then w. Ext/int corridors. Pets: $50 deposit/room. Service with restrictions, supervision. ⇌ 🔊 🔋 🖥

PORTSMOUTH

▼▼ Comfort Inn Ⓜ
(740) 353-3232. $80-$150. 5100 Old Scioto Tr 45662. 3.8 mi n of downtown. Int corridors. Pets: Small, dogs only. $25 one-time fee/pet. Service with restrictions, supervision. ⌨ ⇌ 🔊 🔋 🖥

REYNOLDSBURG

▼▼▼ The Fairfield Inn & Suites by Marriott Columbus East ⊞
(614) 864-4555. $87-$160. 2826 Taylor Rd Ext 43068. I-70 exit 112B eastbound; exit 112 westbound, just n, then just e. Int corridors. Pets: Accepted. ⌨ ⇌ 🔊 ✕ 🔋 🖥

RICHFIELD

▼▼ Days Inn & Suites Richfield ⊞
(330) 659-6151. $79-$300. 4742 Brecksville Rd 44286. I-80 exit 173, just s; I-77 exit 145, 0.5 mi n. Int corridors. Pets: $25 one-time fee/room. Designated rooms, service with restrictions, supervision.

⊙ ⇌ ⊠ 🔊 🔋 🖥

ROSSFORD

ⒶⒶⒶ ▼▼▼ Country Inn & Suites By Carlson, Toledo South ⊞
(419) 872-9900. $69-$169. 9790 Clark Dr 43460. I-75 exit 195, just e. Int corridors. Pets: Medium. $25 daily fee/pet. Designated rooms, service with restrictions, crate. 🆂🅰🆅🅴 ⌨ ⇌ 🔊 ✕ 🔋 🖥

ST. CLAIRSVILLE

ⒶⒶⒶ ▼ Americas Best Value Inn St. Clairsville/Wheeling Ⓜ
(740) 695-5038. $79-$169. 51260 National Rd 43950. I-70 exit 218, 0.5 mi ne on US 40. Ext corridors. Pets: Other species. $10 one-time fee/room. Designated rooms, service with restrictions.

🆂🅰🆅🅴 ⇌ 🔊 🔋 🖥

ⒶⒶⒶ ▼▼ Red Roof Inn St Clairsville-Wheeling West Ⓜ
(740) 695-4057. $59-$99. 68301 Red Roof Ln 43950. I-70 exit 218, just n. Ext corridors. Pets: Large, other species. Service with restrictions, supervision. 🆂🅰🆅🅴 🔊 🔋

SANDUSKY

▼▼ Knights Inn Sandusky Ⓜ
(419) 621-9000. $45-$105. 2405 Cleveland Rd 44870. US 6, 2 mi e of Cedar Point Cswy. Ext/int corridors. Pets: Accepted.
⇌ 🔊 🔋 🖥

▼▼ La Quinta Inn Sandusky-Cedar Point Ⓜ
(419) 626-6766. $69-$414. 3304 Milan Rd 44870. US 250, 2 mi n of SR 2. Int corridors. Pets: Large, other species. Service with restrictions.
⇌ 🔊 🔋 🖥

▼▼ South Shore Inn Ⓜ
(419) 626-4436. Call for rates. 2047 Cleveland Rd 44870. US 6, just e of Cedar Point Cswy. Ext/int corridors. Pets: Accepted.
⊙ ⇌ ⊠ 🔊 🔋 🖥

SEAMAN

▼▼ Comfort Inn Ⓜ
(937) 386-2511. $85-$125. 55 Stern Dr 45679. Jct SR 32 and 247. Int corridors. Pets: Accepted. ⇌ 🔊 ✕ 🔋 🖥

SEVILLE

▼▼ Comfort Inn ⊞
(330) 769-4949. $85-$200. 4949 Park Ave W 44273. I-76/US 224 exit 2, just n. Int corridors. Pets: Accepted. ⇌ 🔊 🔋 🖥

▼▼▼ Hawthorn Suites by Wyndham ⊞
(330) 769-5025. $99-$109, 3 day notice. 5025 Park Ave W 44273. I-76/US 224 exit 2, just n. Int corridors. Pets: Accepted.
⇌ 🔊 🔋 🖥

▼▼ Super 8-Seville ⊞
(330) 769-8880. $60-$95. 6116 Speedway Dr 44273. Jct US 224 and Lake Rd, just s. Int corridors. Pets: Medium. $25 one-time fee/pet. Designated rooms, service with restrictions, supervision.
⌨ 🔊 🔋 🖥

SHARONVILLE

▼▼▼ **Drury Inn & Suites-Cincinnati North** �H
(513) 771-5601. **$95-$169.** 2265 E Sharon Rd 45241. I-75 exit 15, just e. Int corridors. **Pets:** $10 daily fee/room. Service with restrictions, supervision. ⌖Ⓜ 🔁 📶 🖥 🖵

▼▼ **Hawthorn Suites by Wyndham** �H
(513) 354-1000. **$63-$150.** 11180 Dowlin Dr 45241. I-75 exit 15, just e on Sharon Rd, then just n. Int corridors. **Pets:** Medium, dogs only. $15 daily fee/pet. Designated rooms, service with restrictions, crate.
🔁 📶 ✕ 🖥 🖵

▼▼▼ **Homewood Suites by Hilton-Cincinnati North/Sharonville** �H
(513) 772-8888. **$109-$169.** 2670 E Kemper Rd 45241. I-275 exit 44, jct Mosteller Rd. Int corridors. **Pets:** Other species. $20 daily fee/room. Service with restrictions. 🔁 📶 🖥 🖵

▼▼ **La Quinta Inn & Suites Cincinnati Sharonville** �H
(513) 771-0300. **$79-$259.** 11029 Dowlin Dr 45241. I-75 exit 15, just e. Int corridors. **Pets:** Large, other species. Service with restrictions.
⌖Ⓜ 🔁 📶 🖥 🖵

▼▼▼ **Residence Inn by Marriott** �H
(513) 771-2525. **$111-$183.** 11689 Chester Rd 45246. I-75 exit 15, just w on Sharon Rd, then 1 mi n. Ext corridors. **Pets:** Accepted.
⌖Ⓜ 🔁 📶 ✕ 🖥 🖵

SPRINGFIELD

🅰🅰🅰 ▼▼▼ **Courtyard by Marriott Springfield Downtown** �H
(937) 322-3600. **$97-$160.** 100 S Fountain Ave 45502. I-70 exit 54, 2 mi n on SR 72 (Limestone St), just w on Main St, then just s; downtown. Int corridors. **Pets:** Accepted.
 🅢🅐🅥🅔 🍴 🔁 📶 ✕ 🖥 🖵

🅰🅰🅰 ▼▼▼ **Red Roof Inn Springfield, OH** �H
(937) 325-5356. **$59-$129.** 155 W Leffel Ln 45506. I-70 exit 54, just n, then w. Int corridors. **Pets:** Large, other species. Service with restrictions, supervision. 🅢🅐🅥🅔 🔁 📶 🖥 🖵

STRASBURG

🅰🅰🅰 ▼▼▼ **Ramada Limited Dover/Strasburg** �H
(330) 878-1400. **$79-$149.** 509 S Wooster Ave 44680. I-77 exit 87, 0.4 mi n on US 250 and SR 21. Int corridors. **Pets:** Medium, dogs only. $15 daily fee/room. Service with restrictions, supervision.
🅢🅐🅥🅔 ⌖Ⓜ 🔁 📶 🖥 🖵

STREETSBORO

▼▼ **TownePlace Suites by Marriott** �H
(330) 422-1855. **$83-$171.** 795 Mondial Pkwy 44241. I-80 exit 187, 0.8 mi s. Int corridors. **Pets:** Other species. $75 one-time fee/room. Designated rooms, service with restrictions, crate. 🔁 📶 ✕ 🖥 🖵

SWANTON

▼▼ **Days Inn** �H
(419) 865-2002. **$55-$65.** 10753 Airport Hwy 43558. I-80/90 exit 52, just s, then 0.5 mi e. Int corridors. **Pets:** Accepted. 🔁 📶 🖥 🖵

TIFFIN

▼▼▼ **Holiday Inn Express** �H
(419) 443-5100. **$99-$159, 7 day notice.** 78 Shaffer Park Dr 44883. US 224, just n on Market St, then just w. Int corridors. **Pets:** Medium, other species. $25 daily fee/room. Designated rooms, service with restrictions, supervision. 🔁 📶 🖥 🖵

TIPP CITY

🅰🅰🅰 ▼▼ **La Quinta Inn & Suites Dayton North-Tipp City** �H
(937) 667-1574. **$64-$237.** 19 Weller Dr 45371. I-75 exit 68, just w. Int corridors. **Pets:** Large, other species. Service with restrictions.
 🅢🅐🅥🅔 ⌖Ⓜ 🔁 📶 🖥 🖵

TOLEDO

▼▼▼ **Holiday Inn Express/Toledo North** �H
(419) 574-0292. **Call for rates.** 5855 Hagman Rd 43612. I-75 exit 210, 0.8 mi w on SR 184, then just n. Int corridors. **Pets:** Accepted.
⌖Ⓜ 📶 ✕ 🖥 🖵

▼▼ **Park Inn Hotel Toledo** �H
(419) 241-3000. **Call for rates.** 101 N Summit St 43604. Between Jefferson and Monroe sts; downtown. Int corridors. **Pets:** Accepted.
🍴 📶 ✕ 🖥 🖵

TROY

▼▼▼ **Holiday Inn Express Hotel & Suites** �H
(937) 332-1700. **Call for rates.** 60 Troy Town Dr 45373. I-75 exit 74, just w. Int corridors. **Pets:** Accepted. ⌖Ⓜ 🔁 📶 🖥 🖵

▼▼ **Residence Inn by Marriott** �H
(937) 440-9303. **$101-$183.** 87 Troy Town Dr 45373. I-75 exit 74, just w. Int corridors. **Pets:** Accepted. 🔁 📶 ✕ 🖥 🖵

TWINSBURG

🅰🅰🅰 ▼▼▼ **Comfort Suites-Twinsburg** �H
(330) 963-5909. **$110-$180.** 2716 Creekside Dr 44087. I-480 exit 37, just n. Int corridors. **Pets:** Dogs only. $25 daily fee/room. Designated rooms, service with restrictions, supervision.
🅢🅐🅥🅔 ⌖Ⓜ 🔁 📶 ✕ 🖥 🖵

UHRICHSVILLE

🅰🅰🅰 ▼▼ **BEST WESTERN Country Inn** Ⓜ
(740) 922-0774. **Call for rates.** 111 W McCauley Dr 44683. US 250 exit McCauley Dr. Ext corridors. **Pets:** $10 daily fee/pet. Service with restrictions, crate. 🅢🅐🅥🅔 📶 🖥 🖵

UPPER ARLINGTON

▼▼▼ **Homewood Suites by Hilton Columbus/OSU** �H
(614) 488-1500. **$139-$309.** 1576 W Lane Ave 43221. US 315, 1.2 mi w. Int corridors. **Pets:** Accepted. ⌖Ⓜ 📶 🖥 🖵

VAN WERT

▼▼ **Comfort Inn** �H
(419) 232-6040. **$85-$135.** 840 N Washington St 45891. US 127, s of jct US 30 and 224. Int corridors. **Pets:** Accepted. 🔁 📶 🖥 🖵

VERMILION

▼▼▼ **Holiday Inn Express** �H
(440) 967-8770. **$109-$209.** 2417 SR 60 44089. Jct SR 2 and 60. Int corridors. **Pets:** Medium, other species. $35 one-time fee/pet. Service with restrictions, crate. 🔁 📶 🖥 🖵

WAPAKONETA

🅰🅰🅰 ▼▼▼ **BEST WESTERN Wapakoneta Inn** �H
(419) 738-2050. **$90-$149.** 1008 Lunar Dr 45895. I-75 exit 111, just w. Int corridors. **Pets:** Medium. $20 daily fee/pet. Designated rooms, service with restrictions, supervision. 🅢🅐🅥🅔 ⌖Ⓜ 🔁 📶 ✕ 🖥 🖵

WASHINGTON COURT HOUSE

▼▼▼ **Holiday Inn Express Washington Court House Jeffersonville South** �H
(740) 335-9310. **Call for rates.** 101 Courthouse Pkwy 43160. Jct US 35, 0.4 mi sw on US 62. Int corridors. **Pets:** Accepted.
⌖Ⓜ 🔁 📶 🖥 🖵

WAUSEON

🅰🅰🅰 ▼▼▼ **BEST WESTERN Del Mar** �H
(419) 335-1565. **$76-$136.** 8319 SR 108 43567. I-80/90 exit 34, just s. Ext corridors. **Pets:** Accepted. 🅢🅐🅥🅔 🔁 📶 🖥 🖵

WEST CHESTER

◆◆◆◆ Residence Inn by Marriott Cincinnati North/West Chester ◻H◻

(513) 341-4040. **$139-$229.** 6240 Muhlhauser Rd 45069. I-75 exit 19, just w on Union Centre Blvd, then just n. Int corridors. **Pets:** Accepted.
(icons)

◆◆◆◆ Staybridge Suites Cincinnati North ◻H◻ ❖

(513) 874-1900. **$99-$250.** 8955 Lakota Dr W 45069. I-75 exit 19, just w on Union Centre Blvd, then 0.5 mi n. Int corridors. **Pets:** Other species. $75 one-time fee/room. Service with restrictions.
(icons)

WESTERVILLE

◆◆◆ ◆◆ Red Roof Inn Columbus Northeast-Westerville ◻M◻

(614) 890-1244. **$69-$149.** 909 S State St 43081. I-270 exit 29, 0.4 mi n on SR 3, then just s. Ext corridors. **Pets:** Large, other species. Service with restrictions, supervision.
(icons)

WESTLAKE

◆◆ ◆◆ Extended Stay America Cleveland-Westlake ◻H◻

(440) 899-4160. **Call for rates.** 30360 Clemens Rd 44145. I-90 exit 156, just n. Int corridors. **Pets:** Other species. $25 daily fee/pet. Service with restrictions, supervision. (icons)

◆◆◆◆ Holiday Inn Cleveland Westlake ◻H◻

(440) 871-6000. **Call for rates.** 1100 Crocker Rd 44145. I-90 exit 156, just n. Int corridors. **Pets:** Accepted.
(icons)

◆◆◆ ◆◆ Red Roof Inn Cleveland - Westlake ◻M◻

(440) 892-7920. **$40-$99.** 29595 Clemens Rd 44145. I-90 exit 156, just n. Ext corridors. **Pets:** Large, other species. Service with restrictions, supervision. (icons)

◆◆◆◆ Residence Inn by Marriott Cleveland/Westlake ◻H◻

(440) 892-2254. **$146-$240.** 30100 Clemens Rd 44145. I-90 exit 156, just n. Ext corridors. **Pets:** Accepted. (icons)

◆◆◆ ◆◆◆◆ TownePlace Suites by Marriott Cleveland Westlake ◻H◻

(440) 892-4275. **$122-$200.** 25052 Sperry Dr 44145. I-90 exit 159, just n. Int corridors. **Pets:** Accepted. (icons)

WICKLIFFE

◆◆◆◆ Quality Inn-Wickliffe ◻H◻

(440) 944-4030. **$70-$175.** 28611 Euclid Ave 44092. I-90 exit 186, just n on US 20. Int corridors. **Pets:** $10 daily fee/pet. Designated rooms, service with restrictions, supervision. (icons)

WILLOUGHBY

◆◆◆ ◆◆◆◆ Red Roof Inn Cleveland East - Willoughby ◻M◻

(440) 946-9872. **$50-$90.** 4166 SR 306 44094. I-90 exit 193, just s. Ext corridors. **Pets:** Large, other species. Service with restrictions, supervision. (icons)

WILMINGTON

◆◆◆◆ Hampton Inn & Suites Wilmington ◻H◻

(937) 382-4400. **$99-$139.** 201 Holiday Dr 45177. 1.5 mi e on US 22. Int corridors. **Pets:** Medium. Service with restrictions, crate.
(icons)

◆◆◆◆ Holiday Inn Wilmington & Roberts Conference Centre ◻H◻

(937) 283-3200. **$129, 7 day notice.** 123 Gano Rd 45177. I-71 exit 50, just w. Int corridors. **Pets:** Accepted.
(icons)

WOOSTER

◆◆◆ ◆◆◆◆ Econo Lodge ◻M◻

(330) 264-8883. **$60-$99.** 2137 E Lincoln Way 44691. US 30, 3 mi e. Ext corridors. **Pets:** Accepted. (icons)

ZANESVILLE

◆◆◆ ◆◆◆◆ BEST WESTERN B. R. Guest ◻H◻

(740) 453-6300. **$90-$130.** 4929 East Pike 43701. I-70 exit 160, just s. Int corridors. **Pets:** Other species. $10 daily fee/pet. Designated rooms, service with restrictions, supervision. (icons)

◆◆◆ ◆◆◆◆ Comfort Inn ◻H◻

(740) 454-4144. **Call for rates.** 500 Monroe St 43701. I-70 exit 155 westbound; exit 7th St eastbound, e on Elberon Ave to light, just n on Underwood St. Int corridors. **Pets:** Medium. $20 daily fee/pet. Designated rooms, service with restrictions, supervision.
(icons)

◆◆ Super 8-Zanesville ◻M◻

(740) 455-3124. **$64-$100.** 2440 National Rd 43701. I-70 exit 152, just n. Int corridors. **Pets:** Accepted. (icons)

OKLAHOMA

ADA

◆◆◆ ◆◆ Raintree Inn ◻H◻

(580) 332-6262. **$75-$79.** 1100 N Mississippi Ave 74820. Just e of jct J A Richardson Rd. Ext corridors. **Pets:** Medium, dogs only. $25 one-time fee/pet. Service with restrictions, crate. (icons)

ALTUS

◆◆◆◆ Days Inn Altus ◻H◻

(580) 482-9300. **$59-$149.** 2804 N Main St 73521. 2 mi n on US 283. Ext corridors. **Pets:** Accepted. (icons)

◆◆◆◆ Hampton Inn & Suites Altus ◻H◻

(580) 482-1273. **$109-$139.** 3601 N Main St 73521. 2.2 mi n on US 283. Int corridors. **Pets:** Accepted. (icons)

ARDMORE

◆◆◆ La Quinta Inn Ardmore North ◻H◻

(580) 223-7976. **$85-$170.** 2432 Veterans Blvd 73401. I-35 exit 33, just e. Ext corridors. **Pets:** Large, other species. Service with restrictions.
(icons)

◆◆◆ Lexington Inn ◻H◻

(580) 223-7525. **$99-$149.** 136 Holiday Dr 73401. I-35 exit 31A, just ne. Int corridors. **Pets:** Accepted. (icons)

◆◆◆ Quality Hotel ◻H◻

(580) 223-7130. **$70-$160.** 2705 W Broadway 73401. I-35 exit 31A, just e. Ext corridors. **Pets:** Accepted. (icons)

ATOKA

◆◆◆ ◆◆◆◆ BEST WESTERN Atoka Inn ◻H◻

(580) 889-7381. **Call for rates.** 2101 S Mississippi Ave 74525. 1 mi s. Ext corridors. **Pets:** Accepted. (icons)

◆◆◆ ◆◆◆◆ Comfort Inn & Suites ◻H◻

(580) 889-8999. **$82-$125.** 1502 S Mississippi Ave 74525. Just s of center. Int corridors. **Pets:** Accepted. (icons)

BARTLESVILLE

▼▼ Candlewood Suites H

(918) 766-0044. **$65-$86.** 3812 SE Washington Pl 74006. Just s of jct US 60. Int corridors. **Pets:** Accepted. ♿ 🛏 📶 ✕ 🍴 📶 💻

▼▼ Motel 6 Bartlesville #4870 H

(918) 333-2100. **Call for rates.** 2696 SE Washington Blvd 74006. 1.4 mi s of jct US 60. Int corridors. **Pets:** Other species. Service with restrictions, crate. ♿ 📶 📶 💻

BIG CABIN

▼▼ Super 8-Big Cabin M

(918) 783-5888. **$60-$70.** 30954 S Hwy 69 74301. I-44 exit 283, just ne. Ext/int corridors. **Pets:** Accepted. ♿ 📶 🍴 💻

BLACKWELL

ⒶⒶⒶ ▼▼▼▼ BEST WESTERN Blackwell Inn H 🐾

(580) 363-1300. **$110-$120.** 4545 W White Ave 74631. I-35 exit 222, just ne. Int corridors. **Pets:** Medium. $10 daily fee/pet. Designated rooms, service with restrictions, crate. SAVE ♿ 📶 ✕ 🍴 💻

ⒶⒶⒶ ▼▼▼ Econo Lodge Blackwell H

(580) 363-7000. **$98.** 1201 N 44th St 74631. I-35 exit 222, just ne. Int corridors. **Pets:** Accepted. SAVE ♿ 📶 ✕ 🍴 💻

BROKEN ARROW

▼▼ Clarion Hotel H

(918) 258-7085. **$70-$199.** 2600 N Aspen Ave 74012. Just s of jct SR 51. Int corridors. **Pets:** Medium. $25 one-time fee/room. Service with restrictions, supervision. ♿ 📶 🍴 💻

▼▼▼ Homewood Suites by Hilton Tulsa South H

(918) 392-7700. **$104-$124.** 4900 W Madison Pl 74012. Just ne of jct 71st St and Garnett Ave. Int corridors. **Pets:** Accepted.

♿ ♿ 📶 🍴 💻

▼▼ Quality Inn H

(918) 258-8585. **$64-$74.** 2301 W Concord St 74012. Just sw of jct SR 51 and Aspen Ave (145th St). Ext/int corridors. **Pets:** Small. $8 daily fee/pet. No service, supervision. ♿ 📶 🍴 💻

▼▼▼ TownePlace Suites by Marriott H

(918) 355-9600. **$129-$149.** 2251 N Stonewood Cir 74012. Just ne of jct SR 51 and Elm Pl. Int corridors. **Pets:** Accepted.

♿ ♿ 📶 ✕ 🍴 💻

BROKEN BOW

▼▼ HiWay Inn Express Hotel & Suites H

(580) 584-7400. **Call for rates.** 1699 S Park Dr 74728. On US 70/259, 1 mi s of SR 3. Int corridors. **Pets:** Accepted. ♿ 📶 🍴 💻

CATOOSA

▼▼▼ Hampton Inn & Suites-Catoosa H

(918) 739-3939. **$99-$139.** 100 McNabb Field Rd 74015. I-44 exit 240A, just ne. Int corridors. **Pets:** Accepted.

♿ ♿ 📶 ✕ 🍴 💻

ⒶⒶⒶ ▼▼▼ La Quinta Inn & Suites H

(918) 739-4600. **$94-$249.** 2009 S Cherokee St 74015. I-44 exit 240A, just n. Int corridors. **Pets:** Large, other species. Service with restrictions. SAVE ♿ 📶 ✕ 🍴 💻

CHICKASHA

ⒶⒶⒶ ▼▼▼ BEST WESTERN Chickasha H

(405) 224-4890. **Call for rates.** 2101 S 4th St 73018. I-44 exit 80, just nw. Ext/int corridors. **Pets:** Other species. $25 one-time fee/room. Designated rooms, service with restrictions, crate. SAVE ♿ 📶 🍴 💻

▼▼▼ Hampton Inn H

(405) 320-5955. **$124-$154.** 3004 S 4th St 73018. I-44 exit 80, 0.4 mi e. Int corridors. **Pets:** Accepted. ♿ 📶 ✕ 🍴 💻

CLAREMORE

▼▼ Claremore Motor Inn M

(918) 342-4545. **Call for rates.** 1709 N Lynn Riggs Blvd 74017. 1.2 mi n on SR 66. Ext/int corridors. **Pets:** Accepted. 📶 🍴 💻

▼▼ Comfort Inn Claremore H

(918) 343-3297. **$92-$135.** 1720 S Lynn Riggs Blvd 74017. 1.6 mi s on SR 66. Int corridors. **Pets:** Accepted. ♿ 📶 ✕ 🍴 💻

▼▼ Microtel Inn & Suites by Wyndham Claremore H

(918) 343-2868. **$75-$95.** 10600 E Mallard Lake Rd 74017. 2.6 mi s on SR 66. Int corridors. **Pets:** Accepted. ♿ 📶 ✕ 🍴 💻

ⒶⒶⒶ ▼▼▼ Super 8 H

(918) 341-2323. **$65-$105.** 1100 E Will Rogers Blvd 74017. I-44 exit 255, just w. Ext/int corridors. **Pets:** Medium. $10 daily fee/pet. Designated rooms, service with restrictions, crate. SAVE 📶 ✕ 🍴 💻

CLINTON

▼▼▼▼ Holiday Inn Express H

(580) 323-1950. **$107-$135.** 2000 Boulevard of Champions 73601. I-40 exit 65A, 0.5 mi nw. Int corridors. **Pets:** Accepted.

♿ 📶 ✕ 🍴 💻

DURANT

▼▼ Comfort Inn & Suites H

(580) 924-8881. **$79-$89.** 2112 W Main St 74701. Just e of jct US 69/75 and 70. Int corridors. **Pets:** Accepted. ♿ 📶 🍴 💻

EDMOND

ⒶⒶⒶ ▼▼▼ BEST WESTERN Edmond Inn & Suites H

(405) 216-0300. **Call for rates.** 2700 E 2nd St 73034. I-35 exit 141, 1.1 mi w. Int corridors. **Pets:** Accepted. SAVE ♿ 📶 ✕ 🍴 💻

▼▼▼▼ La Quinta Inn & Suites Edmond H

(405) 513-5353. **$105-$219.** 200 Meline Dr 73034. I-35 exit 141, just w. Int corridors. **Pets:** Accepted. ♿ ♿ 📶 ✕ 🍴 💻

▼▼▼ Sleep Inn & Suites H

(405) 844-3000. **$69-$135.** 3608 S Broadway Extension 73013. John Kilpatrick Tpke, 1.5 mi n on US 77. Int corridors. **Pets:** Accepted.

♿ ♿ 📶 ✕ 🍴 💻

ELK CITY

ⒶⒶⒶ ▼▼▼ Holiday Inn Express & Suites H

(580) 303-4556. **$131-$161, 7 day notice.** 2101 E 3rd St 73644. I-40 exit 40, just n. Int corridors. **Pets:** Accepted.

SAVE ♿ 📶 ✕ 🍴 💻

EL RENO

ⒶⒶⒶ ▼▼▼ BEST WESTERN Hensley's H

(405) 262-6490. **$90-$95, 3 day notice.** 2701 S Country Club Rd 73036. I-40 exit 123, just s. Ext corridors. **Pets:** Medium. $25 deposit/room, $5 daily fee/pet. Service with restrictions, supervision.

SAVE 📶 🍴 💻

ⒶⒶⒶ ▼▼▼ Motel 6 El Reno #4267 H

(405) 262-6060. **$63-$75.** 1506 Domino Dr 73036. I-40 exit 123, just ne. Int corridors. **Pets:** Other species. Service with restrictions, crate.

SAVE ♿ 📶 🍴

ENID

▼▼ Baymont Inn & Suites-Enid H

(580) 234-6800. **$79-$129.** 3614 W Owen K Garriott Rd 73703. 2 mi w of jct US 81. Int corridors. **Pets:** Dogs only. $100 deposit/room, $12 daily fee/pet. Designated rooms, service with restrictions, supervision.

♿ 📶 🍴 💻

▼▼ Days Inn H

(580) 242-7110. **$109.** 2818 S Van Buren St 73703. 1.6 mi s of jct US 412. Ext corridors. **Pets:** Accepted. 🍴 📶 🍴 💻

GLENPOOL

🛆 ▼▼ BEST WESTERN Glenpool/Tulsa 🏠 🐾
(918) 322-5201. **$80-$90.** 14831 S Casper St 74033. I-44 exit 224, 9.5
mi s on US 75. Ext corridors. **Pets:** $10 daily fee/pet. Designated
rooms, service with restrictions, supervision. [SAVE] 🌊 🛜 📶 🖵

▼▼▼ Comfort Inn & Suites Glenpool 🏠
(918) 995-2225. **$90-$150.** 12119 N Casper St 74033. Just se of jct US
75 and 121st St. Int corridors. **Pets:** Other species. $8 daily fee/pet.
Service with restrictions. 🛃M 🛜 ✕ 📶 🖵

GROVE

🛆 ▼▼ BEST WESTERN TimberRidge Inn 🏠
(918) 786-6900. **$96-$136.** 120 W 18th St 74344. Just w of jct US 59.
Ext/int corridors. **Pets:** Dogs only. $20 daily fee/pet. Designated rooms,
service with restrictions, supervision. [SAVE] 🌊 🛜 ✕ 📶 🖵

GUYMON

🛆 ▼▼▼ BEST WESTERN PLUS Guymon Hotel &
Suites 🏠
(580) 338-0800. **$101-$141.** 1102 NE 6th St 73942. Just s of jct US 64.
Ext/int corridors. **Pets:** Accepted.
[SAVE] 🍴 🛃M 🌊 ✕ 🛜 📶 🖵

▼▼ Comfort Inn & Suites 🏠
(580) 338-0831. **$80-$135.** 501 Hwy 54 E 73942. Just s of jct US 64.
Int corridors. **Pets:** Accepted. 🌊 🛜 📶 🖵

▼▼▼ Holiday Inn Express Hotel & Suites Guymon 🏠
(580) 338-4208. **$100-$150, 3 day notice.** 701 SE Hwy 3 73942. Jct
US 54/412, just e. Int corridors. **Pets:** Medium. $35 daily fee/pet. Ser-
vice with restrictions, supervision. 🛃M 🌊 🛜 ✕ 📶 🖵

HENRYETTA

🛆 ▼▼ Green Country Inn 🅼
(918) 652-9988. **$48-$62.** 2004 Old Hwy 75 W 74437. I-40 exit 237,
just ne. Ext corridors. **Pets:** Medium. $10 daily fee/pet. Designated
rooms, service with restrictions, supervision. [SAVE] 🌊 🛜 📶

IDABEL

▼▼ Comfort Suites 🏠
(580) 286-9393. **$95-$115.** 400 SE Lincoln Rd 74745. Just s of jct US
70 and 259. Int corridors. **Pets:** Small, other species. $5 daily fee/pet.
Service with restrictions, supervision. 🌊 🛜 ✕ 📶 🖵

▼▼ Super 8 🏠
(580) 286-2888. **$66-$110.** 401 NE Lincoln Rd 74745. Just s of jct US
70 and 259. Ext corridors. **Pets:** Accepted. 🌊 🛜 📶 🖵

LAWTON

🛆 ▼▼▼ BEST WESTERN PLUS Lawton Hotel &
Convention Center 🏠
(580) 353-0200. **$79-$109.** 1125 E Gore Blvd 73501. I-44 exit 37, just
e. Ext/int corridors. **Pets:** Accepted. [SAVE] 🍴 🌊 🛜 📶 🖵

▼▼▼ Homewood Suites 🏠
(580) 357-9800. **$99-$159.** 415 SE Interstate Dr 73501. I-44 exit 37,
just sw. Int corridors. **Pets:** Accepted. 🛃M 🛜 📶 🖵

🛆 ▼▼▼ Sleep Inn & Suites 🏠 🐾
(580) 353-5555. **$91-$117.** 421 SE Interstate Dr 73501. I-44 exit 37,
just sw. Int corridors. **Pets:** Large, dogs only. $25 one-time fee/room.
Designated rooms, service with restrictions, supervision.
[SAVE] 🛃M 🌊 🛜 ✕ 📶 🖵

LOCUST GROVE

🛆 ▼▼ BEST WESTERN Locust Grove Inn &
Suites 🏠
(918) 479-8082. **$79-$249.** 106 Holiday Ln 74352. Just nw of jct US
412 and SR 82. Int corridors. **Pets:** Small. $25 one-time fee/pet. Ser-
vice with restrictions, crate. [SAVE] 🌊 🛜 📶 🖵

MADILL

🛆 ▼▼▼ BEST WESTERN PLUS Sand Bass Inn &
Suites 🏠
(580) 677-9890. **$100-$140.** 827 S 1st St 73446. Just s on US 70 from
jct US 377. Int corridors. **Pets:** Accepted.
[SAVE] 🛃M 🛜 ✕ 📶 🖵

MCALESTER

🛆 ▼▼▼ BEST WESTERN Inn of McAlester 🏠
(918) 426-0115. **$69-$89.** 1215 George Nigh Expwy 74502. 3 mi s on
US 69. Ext corridors. **Pets:** Accepted. [SAVE] 🌊 🛜 📶 🖵

▼▼ Candlewood Suites 🏠
(918) 426-4171. **Call for rates.** 425 S George Nigh Expwy 74501. 2 mi
e on US 69. Int corridors. **Pets:** Accepted. 🛃M 🛜 ✕ 📶 🖵

▼▼ Comfort Suites 🏠
(918) 302-0001. **$70-$89.** 650 S George Nigh Expwy 74501. 1.2 mi s
on US 69. Int corridors. **Pets:** Small. $10 daily fee/pet. Service with
restrictions, crate. 🌊 🛜 ✕ 📶 🖵

▼▼ Econo Lodge 🅼
(918) 426-4420. **$49-$65.** 731 S George Nigh Expwy 74501. 1.5 mi s
on US 69. Ext corridors. **Pets:** Accepted. 🛜 📶 🖵

▼▼ Happy Days Hotel 🏠
(918) 429-0910. **Call for rates.** 1400 S George Nigh Expwy 74501. 3.3
mi s on US 69. Int corridors. **Pets:** Accepted. 🌊 🛜 ✕ 📶 🖵

▼▼ Oak Tree Inn 🏠
(918) 420-5002. **$62-$71.** 530 S George Nigh Expwy 74501. Just e of
jct US 69. Int corridors. **Pets:** Accepted. 🛃M 🛜 ✕ 📶 🖵

MIDWEST CITY

🛆 ▼▼ Hawthorn Suites by Wyndham 🏠
(405) 737-7777. **$95-$110, 3 day notice.** 5701 Tinker Diagonal 73110.
I-40 exit 156A (Sooner Rd), just n. Int corridors. **Pets:** Accepted.
[SAVE] 🛃M 🌊 🛜 📶 🖵

🛆 ▼▼▼ Sheraton Midwest City Hotel at the Reed
Conference Center 🏠
(405) 455-1800. **$129-$149.** 5750 Will Rogers Rd 73110. I-40 exit 156A
(Sooner Rd), just ne. Int corridors. **Pets:** Accepted.
[SAVE] 🍴 🌊 🛜 ✕ 📶 🖵

MOORE *(Restaurants p. 637)*

🛆 ▼▼▼ BEST WESTERN PLUS Greentree Inn &
Suites 🏠
(405) 912-8882. **$95-$119.** 1811 N Moore Ave 73160. I-35 exit 118, just
n on west frontage road. Int corridors. **Pets:** Small, dogs only. $10 daily
fee/pet. Service with restrictions, supervision. [SAVE] 🌊 🛜 📶 🖵

MUSKOGEE

▼▼ Comfort Inn 🏠
(918) 682-3724. **$85-$95.** 3133 Azalea Park Dr 74401. Just sw of jct
US 62 and 69. Int corridors. **Pets:** Accepted. 🌊 🛜 📶 🖵

▼▼▼ Quality Inn & Suites 🏠
(918) 687-9000. **$84-$129.** 3031 Military Blvd 74401. Just se of jct US
62 and 69. Int corridors. **Pets:** Accepted. 🌊 🛜 ✕ 📶 🖵

NORMAN

▼▼ Econo Lodge 🅼
(405) 364-5554. **$52-$93.** 100 SW 26th Dr 73069. I-35 exit 109 (Main
St), just se. Ext corridors. **Pets:** Accepted. 🛜 📶 🖵

▼▼▼ Embassy Suites Norman-Hotel & Conference
Center 🏠
(405) 364-8040. **$109-$299.** 2501 Conference Dr 73069. Jct 24th Ave
NW and Robinson St, 0.7 mi n on 24th Ave NW. Int corridors.
Pets: Accepted. [ECO] 🍴 🛃M 🌊 🛜 📶 🖵

▼▼▼▼ **La Quinta Inn & Suites Norman** 🅗
(405) 579-4000. **$65-$322.** 930 Ed Noble Dr 73072. I-35 exit 108B (Lindsey St), just nw. Int corridors. **Pets:** Large, other species. Service with restrictions. 🚭🛌📶📴📺

▼▼▼ **Quality Inn & Suites** 🅗
(405) 701-4011. **$80-$91.** 2841 S Classen Blvd 73071. Just n of jct SR 9. Int corridors. **Pets:** Accepted. 🚭🛌📶✖️📴📺

OKLAHOMA CITY
▼▼▼▼ **The Ambassador Oklahoma City, Autograph Collection** 🅗 ❀
(405) 600-6200. **$189-$249.** 1200 N Walker Ave 73103. Jct 12th St. Int corridors. **Pets:** Medium, dogs only. $50 one-time fee/room. Service with restrictions, supervision. 🍴🚭📶✖️📺

▼ **Americas Best Value Inn Bricktown** Ⓜ
(405) 677-1000. **Call for rates.** 3030 S Prospect 73129. I-35 exit 124B northbound; exit 125A southbound, just n on service road. Ext corridors. **Pets:** Medium. $10 daily fee/pet. Service with restrictions, supervision.
📶📺

▼▼▼ **Americas Best Value Inn-Oklahoma City/I-35 North** 🅗
(405) 478-0400. **Call for rates.** 12001 N I-35 Service Rd 73131. I-35 exit 137 (122nd St), just sw. Ext corridors. **Pets:** Small, dogs only. $10 one-time fee/pet. Designated rooms, service with restrictions, supervision. 🛌📶📴📺

⬨⬨⬨ ▼▼▼ **Baymont Inn & Suites** 🅗
(405) 943-4400. **$59-$79.** 4240 W I-40 Service Rd 73108. I-40 exit 145 (Meridian Ave), just e on south frontage road. Ext/int corridors. **Pets:** Accepted. [SAVE]🛌📶✖️📴📺

⬨⬨⬨ ▼▼▼ **BEST WESTERN PLUS Broadway Inn & Suites** 🅗
(405) 848-1919. **$67-$119.** 6101 N Santa Fe 73118. I-44 exit 127, just e on 63rd St, then just s. Int corridors. **Pets:** Large. $20 daily fee/room. Designated rooms, service with restrictions, crate. [SAVE]🍴🚭📶✖️📴📺

⬨⬨⬨ ▼▼▼ **BEST WESTERN PLUS Memorial Inn & Suites** 🅗
(405) 286-5199. **$92-$250.** 1301 W Memorial Rd 73114. John Kilpatrick Tpke exit Western Ave, just nw. Int corridors. **Pets:** Accepted. [SAVE]🚭🛌📶📴📺

⬨⬨⬨ ▼▼▼▼ **BEST WESTERN PLUS Saddleback Inn & Conference Center** 🅗
(405) 947-7000. **$99-$160.** 4300 SW 3rd St 73108. I-40 exit 145 (Meridian Ave), just ne. Ext/int corridors. **Pets:** Small. $15 daily fee/room. Designated rooms, service with restrictions, crate. [SAVE]🍴🚭🛌✖️📶✖️📴📺

▼▼ **Candlewood Suites Hotel** 🅗
(405) 680-8770. **$99-$119.** 4400 W River Park Dr 73108. I-40 exit 145 (Meridian Ave), 1.1 mi s. Int corridors. **Pets:** Accepted. 🚭📶📴📺

▼▼▼ **Colcord Hotel** 🅗
(405) 601-4300. **$159-$209.** 15 N Robinson Ave 73102. Jct Sheridan and Robinson aves. Int corridors. **Pets:** Large, dogs only. $50 daily fee/room. Service with restrictions, crate. [ECO]🍴📶✖️📴

▼▼▼ **Comfort Inn North** 🅗
(405) 478-7282. **$80-$100.** 4625 NE 120th St 73131. I-35 exit 137 (122nd St), just sw. Int corridors. **Pets:** Accepted. 🛌📶📴📺

▼▼▼▼ **Country Inn & Suites By Carlson** 🅗
(405) 286-3555. **$84-$109.** 13501 Memorial Park Dr 73120. Just sw of jct Memorial Rd and Memorial Park Ln. Int corridors. **Pets:** Accepted. 🚭🛌📶✖️📴📺

⬨⬨⬨ ▼▼▼ **Courtyard by Marriott-NW** 🅗
(405) 848-0808. **$99-$179.** 1515 Northwest Expwy 73118. I-44 exit 125C westbound; exit 125B eastbound, just e. Int corridors.
Pets: Accepted. [SAVE][ECO]🚭🛌📶✖️📴📺

⬨⬨⬨ ▼▼▼ **Courtyard by Marriott Oklahoma City Downtown** 🅗
(405) 232-2290. **$129-$379.** 2 W Reno Ave 73102. Jct Gaylord Blvd and Reno Ave. Int corridors. **Pets:** Accepted.
[SAVE]🍴🚭🛌📶✖️📴📺

⬨⬨⬨ ▼▼▼ **Embassy Suites** 🅗
(405) 682-6000. **$119-$189.** 1815 S Meridian Ave 73108. I-40 exit 145 (Meridian Ave), 1 mi s. Int corridors. **Pets:** Medium. $50 one-time fee/room. Service with restrictions, crate. [SAVE]🍴🛌📶📴📺

▼▼▼▼ **Homewood Suites Oklahoma City-West** 🅗
(405) 789-3600. **$169-$219.** 6920 W Reno Ave 73127. Just e of jct Rockwell Ave. Int corridors. **Pets:** Accepted. 🚭🛌📶📴📺

⬨⬨⬨ ▼▼▼ **Hyatt Place Oklahoma City Airport** 🅗
(405) 682-3900. **$69-$189.** 1818 S Meridian Ave 73108. I-40 exit 145 (Meridian Ave), 1 mi s. Int corridors. **Pets:** Medium, dogs only. $75 one-time fee/room. Service with restrictions, supervision.
[SAVE]🍴🛌📶✖️📴📺

▼▼▼ **La Quinta Inn & Suites OKC North-Quail Springs** 🅗
(405) 755-7000. **$89-$269.** 3003 W Memorial Rd 73134. John Kilpatrick Tpke exit May Ave, just nw. Int corridors. **Pets:** Large, other species. Service with restrictions. 🚭🛌📶✖️📴📺

▼▼▼ **Quality Inn** 🅗
(405) 632-6666. **$60-$75.** 7800 CA Henderson Blvd 73139. I-240 exit 2A, just s. Ext corridors. **Pets:** Accepted. 🛌📶📴📺

⬨⬨⬨ ▼▼▼▼ **Renaissance Oklahoma City Convention Center, Hotel & Spa** 🅗
(405) 228-8000. **$129-$399.** 10 N Broadway Ave 73102. Jct Sheridan and Broadway aves. Int corridors. **Pets:** Accepted.
[SAVE]🍴🚭🛌✖️📶✖️📴📺

▼▼▼ **Residence Inn by Marriott** 🅗
(405) 601-1700. **$149-$449.** 400 E Reno Ave 73104. Just se of jct Joe Carter Ave; in Bricktown. Int corridors. **Pets:** Other species. $100 one-time fee/room. Service with restrictions, crate.
🚭🛌📶✖️📴📺

▼▼▼ **Residence Inn by Marriott Oklahoma City South-Crossroads Mall** 🅗
(405) 634-9696. **$89-$199.** 1111 E I-240 Service Rd 73149. I-240 exit 4C eastbound, 0.4 mi nw; exit 5 westbound, 0.8 mi nw. Int corridors.
Pets: Accepted. 🛌📶✖️📴📺

▼▼▼ **Residence Inn by Marriott-Oklahoma City West** 🅗
(405) 942-4500. **$95-$135.** 4361 W Reno Ave 73107. I-40 exit 145 (Meridian Ave), 0.3 mi n, then just e. Ext corridors. **Pets:** Accepted.
🛌📶✖️📴📺

⬨⬨⬨ ▼▼▼▼ **Sheraton Oklahoma City** 🅗 🐾
(405) 235-2780. **$139-$359.** 1 N Broadway Ave 73102. Jct Sheridan and Broadway aves. Int corridors. **Pets:** Medium, dogs only. Service with restrictions, supervision. [SAVE]🍴🛌📶✖️📴📺

⬨⬨⬨ ▼▼▼▼ **Skirvin Hilton** 🅗 ❀
(405) 272-3040. **$149-$329.** 1 Park Ave 73102. Corner of N Broadway and Park aves. Int corridors. **Pets:** Medium, dogs only. $250 one-time fee/pet. Service with restrictions, supervision.
[SAVE]🍴🚭🛌📶✖️📴📺

▼▼▼▼ **SpringHill Suites by Marriott** 🅗
(405) 604-0200. **$79-$199.** 510 S MacArthur Blvd 73128. I-40 exit 144, just ne. Int corridors. **Pets:** Accepted. 🚭🛌📶✖️📴📺

▼▼▼ **SpringHill Suites by Marriott** H
(405) 749-1595. **$130-$165.** 3201 W Memorial Rd 73134. John Kilpatrick Tpke exit May Ave, 0.4 mi w on north service road. Int corridors.
Pets: Accepted. ⬚ 🛇 ⊗ 🗒 💻

▼▼▼ **Staybridge Suites** H
(405) 429-4400. **$99, 5 day notice.** 4411 SW 15th St 73108. I-40 exit 145 (Meridian Ave), 1 mi se. Int corridors. **Pets:** Accepted.
🅼 ⬚ 🛇 🗒 💻

▼▼▼ **Wyndham Garden Hotel Oklahoma City Airport** H
(405) 685-4000. **$89-$139.** 2101 S Meridian Ave 73108. I-40 exit 145 (Meridian Ave), 1.3 mi s. Int corridors. **Pets:** Small. $75 one-time fee/room. Service with restrictions, crate. 🍴 ⬚ 🛇 ⊗ 🗒 💻

OKMULGEE

AAA ▼▼ **BEST WESTERN Okmulgee** H
(918) 756-9200. **$84-$87.** 3499 N Wood Dr 74447. Just n of jct US 75 and SR 56. Int corridors. **Pets:** Other species. $10 daily fee/room. Service with restrictions. SAVE ⬚ 🛇 🗒 💻

OWASSO

AAA ▼ ▼ **BEST WESTERN Owasso Inn & Suites** H
(918) 272-2000. **$85-$95.** 7653 N Owasso Expwy 74055. Just ne of jct US 169 and 76th St. Ext/int corridors. **Pets:** Large. $20 daily fee/pet. Service with restrictions, supervision. SAVE ⬚ 🛇 ⊗ 🗒 💻

▼ ▼ **Candlewood Suites** H
(918) 272-4334. **$76-$96.** 11699 E 96th St N 74055. 0.4 mi nw of jct US 169. Int corridors. **Pets:** $150 one-time fee/room. Service with restrictions, crate. 🅼 🛇 🗒 💻

▼▼▼ **TownePlace Suites by Marriott Tulsa North/Owasso** H
(918) 376-4400. **$99-$129.** 9355 N Owasso Expwy 74055. Just se of jct US 169 and 96th St. Int corridors. **Pets:** Accepted.
🅼 ⬚ 🛇 ⊗ 🗒 💻

PAULS VALLEY

▼▼▼ **Comfort Inn & Suites** H
(405) 207-9730. **$111-$136.** 103 S Humphrey Blvd 73075. I-35 exit 72, just e. Int corridors. **Pets:** Small. $20 daily fee/room. Designated rooms, service with restrictions, supervision. 🅼 ⬚ 🛇 🗒 💻

PERRY

AAA ▼▼▼ **Comfort Inn & Suites** H
(580) 336-3800. **$110-$170.** 3112 W Fir St 73077. I-35 exit 186, just w. Int corridors. **Pets:** Accepted. SAVE 🅼 ⬚ 🛇 ⊗ 🗒 💻

▼▼▼ **Holiday Inn Express** H
(580) 336-5050. **Call for rates.** 3002 W Fir St 73077. I-35 exit 186, just w. Int corridors. **Pets:** Accepted. 🅼 ⬚ 🛇 ⊗ 🗒 💻

PONCA CITY

AAA ▼ ▼ **Comfort Inn & Suites** H 🐾
(580) 765-2322. **$105-$149.** 3101 N 14th St 74604. I-35 exit 214, 3 mi n on US 77. Int corridors. **Pets:** Small. $10 daily fee/pet. Service with restrictions, crate. SAVE 🅼 ⬚ 🛇 ⊗ 🗒 💻

POTEAU

▼▼▼ **Holiday Inn Express & Suites-Poteau** H
(918) 649-0123. **Call for rates.** 201 Hillview Pkwy 74953. Just ne of jct US 59/271 and SR 112. Int corridors. **Pets:** Accepted.
🅼 ⬚ 🛇 ⊗ 🗒 💻

PRYOR

AAA ▼ ▼ **Comfort Inn & Suites** H
(918) 476-6660. **$80-$200.** 307 Mid America Dr 74361. 5 mi s on US 69. Int corridors. **Pets:** Accepted. SAVE ⬚ 🛇 🗒 💻

▼▼▼ **Holiday Inn Express & Suites** H
(918) 476-5400. **$109-$159.** 271 Mid America Dr 74361. 5 mi s on US 69. Int corridors. **Pets:** Accepted. 🅼 ⬚ 🛇 🗒 💻

SHAWNEE

AAA ▼▼▼ **La Quinta Inn & Suites Shawnee** H
(405) 275-7930. **$80-$210.** 5401 Enterprise Ct 74804. I-40 exit 186, just ne. Int corridors. **Pets:** Large, other species. Service with restrictions.
SAVE 🅼 ⬚ 🛇 🗒 💻

STILLWATER

AAA ▼▼▼ **BEST WESTERN PLUS Cimarron Hotel & Suites** H
(405) 372-2878. **$119-$265.** 315 N Husband St 74074. Just w of jct Hall of Fame Blvd and Main St. Int corridors. **Pets:** Other species. $20 daily fee/room. Service with restrictions.
SAVE 🅼 ⬚ 🛇 ⊗ 🗒 💻

▼▼▼ **Residence Inn by Marriott** H 🐾
(405) 707-0588. **$129-$154.** 800 S Murphy St 74074. Just s of jct SR 51. Int corridors. **Pets:** Dogs only. $75 one-time fee/room. Designated rooms, service with restrictions, supervision.
🅼 ⬚ 🛇 ⊗ 🗒 💻

▼▼▼ **Wyndham Garden Stillwater** H
(405) 377-7010. **$81-$115.** 600 E McElroy Rd 74075. 1 mi n on US 177 (Perkins Rd). Int corridors. **Pets:** Other species. $25 daily fee/pet. Service with restrictions, crate. 🍴 ⬚ ⊗ 🛇 ⊗ 🗒 💻

THACKERVILLE

▼▼ **The Inn at WinStar** H
(580) 276-4487. **Call for rates.** 21943 Red River Rd 73459. I-35 exit 1, 1.2 mi n on E Service Rd. Int corridors. **Pets:** Small. $10 one-time fee/pet. Designated rooms, service with restrictions, crate.
⬚ 🛇 🗒 💻

TULSA *(Restaurants p. 637)*

AAA ▼▼▼ **Aloft Tulsa** H
(918) 949-9000. **Call for rates.** 6716 S 104th E Ave 74133. Just nw of jct US 169 and 71st St. Int corridors. **Pets:** Accepted.
SAVE 🅼 ⬚ ⊗ 🛇 🗒 💻

AAA ▼▼▼ **Aloft-Tulsa Downtown** H
(918) 947-8200. **Call for rates.** 200 Civic Center 74103. Just w of jct Denver and 4th St. Int corridors. **Pets:** Accepted.
SAVE 🅼 🛇 ⊗ 🗒 💻

AAA ▼▼▼ **Ambassador Hotel Tulsa** H 🐾
(918) 587-8200. **$189-$309, 3 day notice.** 1324 S Main St 74119. Jct 14th St. Int corridors. **Pets:** Small, dogs only. $50 one-time fee/room. Service with restrictions, crate. SAVE 🍴 🛇 ⊗ 🗒 💻

▼▼ **Baymont Inn & Suites Tulsa** H
(918) 488-8777. **$49-$79.** 4530 E Skelly Dr 74135. I-44 exit 229 (Yale Ave), just sw. Int corridors. **Pets:** Small, dogs only. $15 daily fee/pet. Designated rooms, service with restrictions, supervision.
⬚ 🛇 ⊗ 🗒 💻

AAA ▼▼ **BEST WESTERN-Airport** H
(918) 438-0780. **$72-$90.** 222 N Garnett Rd 74116. I-244 exit 14 (Garnett Rd), just s. Ext corridors. **Pets:** Medium. $20 one-time fee/pet. Service with restrictions, supervision. SAVE ⬚ 🛇 🗒 💻

▼▼ **Candlewood Suites** H
(918) 294-9000. **Call for rates.** 10008 E 73rd St S 74133. Just sw of jct 71st St and 101st E Ave. Int corridors. **Pets:** Accepted.
🅼 🛇 ⊗ 🗒 💻

▼▼ **Comfort Suites East** H
(918) 628-0900. **$60-$75.** 1737 S 101st E Ave 74128. I-44 exit 233 eastbound; exit 233B westbound, follow signs. Int corridors.
Pets: Accepted. ⬚ 🛇 ⊗ 🗒 💻

(AAA) ▼▼▼▼ Country Inn & Suites Tulsa Central H
(918) 663-1000. **Call for rates.** 3209 S 79th E Ave 74145. I-44 exit 231 (31st St) eastbound; exit 232 (Memorial Dr) westbound, just sw. Int corridors. **Pets:** Accepted. [SAVE] [≈] [⌂] [✕] [🔌] [💻]

▼▼▼▼ Crowne Plaza Tulsa-Southern Hills H
(918) 492-5000. **Call for rates.** 7902 S Lewis Ave 74136. I-44 exit 227 (Lewis Ave), 3 mi s. Int corridors. **Pets:** Small. $50 one-time fee/room. Designated rooms, service with restrictions, supervision.
[⑪] [≈] [⌂] [✕] [🔌] [💻]

▼▼▼▼ DoubleTree by Hilton Hotel Tulsa Downtown H
(918) 587-8000. **$92-$209.** 616 W 7th St 74127. Jct 7th St and Houston Ave. Int corridors. **Pets:** Other species. $50 one-time fee/room. Service with restrictions, crate. [⑪] [≈] [⌂] [✕] [🔌] [💻]

▼▼▼▼ DoubleTree by Hilton Hotel Tulsa-Warren Place H 🐾
(918) 495-1000. **$129-$189.** 6110 S Yale Ave 74136. I-44 exit 229 (Yale Ave), 1.3 mi s. Int corridors. **Pets:** Very small, dogs only. $50 one-time fee/pet. Supervision. [⑪] [🖥M] [≈] [✕] [⌂] [🔌] [💻]

▼▼▼▼ Embassy Suites Hotel H
(918) 622-4000. **$109-$149.** 3332 S 79th E Ave 74145. I-44 exit 231 (31st St) eastbound; exit 232 (Memorial Dr) westbound, just sw. Int corridors. **Pets:** Accepted. [⑪] [≈] [⌂] [✕] [🔌] [💻]

▼▼▼▼ Holiday Inn & Suites H
(918) 994-5000. **Call for rates.** 10020 E 81st St 74133. Just w of jct US 169. Int corridors. **Pets:** Accepted.
[⑪] [🖥M] [≈] [⌂] [✕] [🔌] [💻]

(AAA) ▼▼▼▼ Holiday Inn Tulsa City Center H
(918) 585-5898. **$84-$159.** 17 W 7th St 74119. Jct Boulder Ave. Int corridors. **Pets:** Large. $35 one-time fee/room. Designated rooms, service with restrictions, supervision.
[SAVE] [⑪] [🖥M] [≈] [⌂] [✕] [🔌] [💻]

(AAA) ▼◆▼▼ Hyatt Place Tulsa/South Medical District H
(918) 491-4010. **$64-$199.** 7037 S Zurich Ave 74136. I-44 exit 229 (Yale Ave), 3 mi s to 71st St, then just e. Int corridors. **Pets:** Medium, dogs only. $75 one-time fee/pet. Service with restrictions, supervision.
[SAVE] [🖥M] [≈] [⌂] [✕] [🔌] [💻]

(AAA) ▼◆▼▼ Hyatt Regency Tulsa H
(918) 234-1234. **$69-$279.** 100 E 2nd St 74103. Jct 2nd St and Boston Ave; downtown. Int corridors. **Pets:** Accepted.
[SAVE] [⑪] [🖥M] [≈] [✕] [🔌] [💻]

▼▼▼▼ La Quinta Inn & Suites Tulsa Airport/Expo Square H
(918) 949-3600. **$82-$199.** 23 N 67th E Ave 74115. I-244 exit 11 (Sheridan Rd), just se. Int corridors. **Pets:** Large, other species. Service with restrictions. [🖥M] [≈] [⌂] [✕] [🔌] [💻]

▼▼▼ La Quinta Inn & Suites Tulsa Central H
(918) 665-2630. **$94-$214.** 6030 E Skelly Dr 74135. I-44 exit 230, just s. Int corridors. **Pets:** Large, other species. Service with restrictions.
[≈] [⌂] [✕] [🔌] [💻]

▼▼▼▼ Ramada H
(918) 828-9128. **$80-$110, 3 day notice.** 8175 E Skelly Dr 74129. I-44 exit 231 (31st St) eastbound; exit 232 (Memorial Dr) westbound, just ne. Int corridors. **Pets:** Accepted. [≈] [⌂] [✕] [🔌] [💻]

▼▼▼ Red Roof Inn-Tulsa M
(918) 622-6776. **$50-$149.** 4717 S Yale Ave 74135. I-44 exit 229 (Yale Ave), just s. Ext corridors. **Pets:** Large, other species. Service with restrictions, supervision. [≈] [⌂] [🔌]

(AAA) ▼▼▼▼ Renaissance Tulsa Hotel & Convention Center H
(918) 307-2600. **$89-$229.** 6808 S 107th E Ave 74133. Just ne of jct US 169 and 71st St. Int corridors. **Pets:** Accepted.
[SAVE] [⑪] [🖥M] [≈] [✕] [⌂] [✕] [🔌] [💻]

▼▼▼▼ Residence Inn by Marriott H
(918) 250-4850. **$139-$175.** 11025 E 73rd St 74133. Just se of jct US 169 and 71st St. Int corridors. **Pets:** Accepted.
[≈] [⌂] [✕] [🔌] [💻]

▼▼▼ Sleep Inn & Suites Tulsa Central H
(918) 663-2777. **$62-$120.** 8021 E 33rd St S 74145. I-44 exit 231 (31st St) eastbound; exit 232 (Memorial Dr) westbound, just sw. Int corridors. **Pets:** Accepted. [≈] [✕] [⌂] [✕] [🔌] [💻]

▼▼▼▼ Staybridge Suites H
(918) 461-2100. **$99-$155.** 11111 E 73rd St 74133. Just se of jct US 169 and 71st St. Int corridors. **Pets:** Accepted.
[🖥M] [≈] [⌂] [✕] [🔌] [💻]

▼▼▼▼ Wyndham Tulsa H
(918) 627-5000. **$109-$139.** 10918 E 41st St 74146. Just e of US 169. Int corridors. **Pets:** Small, dogs only. $75 one-time fee/pet. Designated rooms, service with restrictions, crate. [⑪] [≈] [⌂] [✕] [🔌] [💻]

WAGONER
▼▼▼▼ The Canebrake H
(918) 485-1810. **Call for rates.** 33241 E 732nd Rd 74467. 1.7 mi n of jct SR 51 and S 330th Rd. Ext corridors. **Pets:** Accepted.
[ECO] [⑪] [🖥M] [≈] [✕] [🔌] [💻]

WEATHERFORD
(AAA) ▼▼◆▼ BEST WESTERN PLUS Mark Motor Hotel H
(580) 772-3325. **$90-$170.** 525 E Main St 73096. I-40 exit 82, 0.5 mi n. Ext corridors. **Pets:** Medium, dogs only. $20 daily fee/pet. Designated rooms, service with restrictions, supervision. [SAVE] [≈] [⌂] [🔌] [💻]

WOODWARD
(AAA) ▼▼▼▼ Northwest Inn H
(580) 256-7600. **$99-$119.** Hwy 270 S & 1st St 73802. 1.4 mi s of jct US 183, 270 and 412. Ext/int corridors. **Pets:** Designated rooms, service with restrictions, crate. [SAVE] [⑪] [≈] [⌂] [✕] [🔌] [💻]

YUKON
(AAA) ▼▼◆▼ BEST WESTERN PLUS Yukon H
(405) 265-2995. **$122.** 11440 W I-40 Service Rd 73099. I-40 exit 138, just sw. Ext/int corridors. **Pets:** Medium. $25 deposit/room, $6 daily fee/pet. Designated rooms, service with restrictions, supervision.
[SAVE] [≈] [⌂] [🔌] [💻]

▼▼▼▼ Comfort Suites H
(405) 577-6500. **$109-$179.** 11424 NW 4th St 73099. I-40 exit 138, just nw. Int corridors. **Pets:** $20 deposit/room, $20 daily fee/pet. Designated rooms, service with restrictions, supervision. [≈] [⌂] [✕] [🔌] [💻]

▼▼▼ La Quinta Inn & Suites Oklahoma City-Yukon H
(405) 494-7600. **$89-$195.** 11500 W I-40 73099. I-40 exit 138, just s. Int corridors. **Pets:** Large, other species. Service with restrictions.
[🖥M] [≈] [⌂] [🔌] [💻]

OREGON

ALBANY

BEST WESTERN PLUS Prairie Inn H ❀

(541) 928-5050. **$95-$180.** 1100 Price Rd SE 97322. I-5 exit 233, just e on Santiam Hwy (US 20), then just n. Int corridors. **Pets:** Dogs only. $20 daily fee/pet. Designated rooms, service with restrictions, supervision. SAVE ⌂M ⤳ 🛜 ✕ 🛏 ☕

Comfort Suites-Linn County Fairgrounds and Expo H

(541) 928-2053. **$99-$219.** 100 Opal Ct NE 97322. I-5 exit 234A southbound; exit 234 northbound, just se. Int corridors. **Pets:** Accepted. SAVE ⌂M ⤳ 🗙 🛜 ✕ 🛏 ☕

Econo Lodge M

(541) 926-0170. **$59-$79.** 1212 SE Price Rd 97322. I-5 exit 233, just e on Santiam Hwy (US 20), then just n. Ext corridors. **Pets:** Accepted. 🛜 🛏

Holiday Inn Express Hotel & Suites H ❀

(541) 928-8820. **$109-$249.** 105 Opal Ct NE 97322. I-5 exit 234A southbound; exit 234 northbound, just se. Int corridors. **Pets:** Medium. $20 daily fee/room. Service with restrictions, crate. SAVE ⌂M ⤳ 🗙 🛜 ✕ 🛏 ☕

Motel 6-#4124 M

(541) 926-4233. **Call for rates.** 2735 E Pacific Blvd 97321. I-5 exit 234B southbound; exit 234 northbound, 0.5 mi w. Ext corridors. **Pets:** Other species. Service with restrictions, crate. 🛜 🛏

Phoenix Inn Suites-Albany H

(541) 926-5696. **Call for rates.** 3410 Spicer Rd SE 97322. I-5 exit 233, just se. Int corridors. **Pets:** Accepted. ⤳ 🛜 🛏 ☕

ASHLAND

Ashland Chanticleer Inn BB

(541) 482-1919. **$130-$205, 31 day notice.** 120 Gresham St 97520. Just se of downtown on SR 99 (E Main St), just s; jct Pearl St. Int corridors. **Pets:** Dogs only. $20 daily fee/pet. Designated rooms, service with restrictions, crate. 🛜 ✕ 🐾

Ashland Hills Hotel & Suites H

(541) 482-8310. **$89-$159, 3 day notice.** 2525 Ashland St 97520. I-5 exit 14, just e on SR 66 (Ashland St). Int corridors. **Pets:** Accepted. 🗙 🛜 ✕ 🛏 ☕

Ashland Springs Hotel H

(541) 488-1700. **$89-$299, 3 day notice.** 212 E Main St 97520. Corner of 1st St; center. Int corridors. **Pets:** Medium. $30 one-time fee/pet. Designated rooms, service with restrictions, crate. 🍴 🛜 ✕ 🛏 ☕

BEST WESTERN Bard's Inn H

(541) 482-0049. **$120-$280.** 132 N Main St 97520. From Downtown Plaza, just nw on SR 99 (N Main St). Ext/int corridors. **Pets:** Accepted. SAVE ⤳ 🛜 ✕ 🛏 ☕

BEST WESTERN Windsor Inn H

(541) 488-2330. **$90-$190.** 2520 Ashland St 97520. I-5 exit 14, just e on SR 66 (Ashland St). Ext corridors. **Pets:** Accepted. SAVE ⤳ 🛜 ✕ 🛏 ☕

Callahan's Lodge CI

(541) 482-1299. **Call for rates.** 7100 Old Hwy 99 S 97520. I-5 exit 6 (Mt. Ashland), just e; 8 mi s of town. Int corridors. **Pets:** Accepted. 🍴 🛜 ✕ 🛏 ☕

Flagship Inn of Ashland M

(541) 482-2641. **Call for rates.** 1193 Siskiyou Blvd 97520. I-5 exit 14, 1.3 mi w on SR 66 (Ashland St), then just n. Ext corridors. **Pets:** Accepted. SAVE ⤳ 🛜 ✕ 🛏 ☕

Holiday Inn Express Hotel & Suites H

(541) 201-0202. **$116-$189.** 565 Clover Ln 97520. I-5 exit 14, just e on SR 66 (Ashland St), then just s. Int corridors. **Pets:** Accepted. SAVE ⌂M ⤳ 🛜 ✕ 🛏 ☕

La Quinta Inn & Suites Ashland H

(541) 482-6932. **$89-$234.** 434 S Valley View Rd 97520. I-5 exit 19, just sw. Int corridors. **Pets:** Large, other species. Service with restrictions. ⤳ 🛜 ✕ 🛏 ☕

Plaza Inn & Suites At Ashland Creek H ❀

(541) 488-8900. **$89-$309.** 98 Central Ave 97520. From Downtown Plaza, just nw on SR 99 (N Main St), just ne on Helman St, then just e. Int corridors. **Pets:** Other species. $25 daily fee/room. Designated rooms, service with restrictions, supervision. SAVE 🛜 ✕ 🛏 ☕

Timbers Motel of Ashland M

(541) 482-4242. **$52-$135, 3 day notice.** 1450 Ashland St 97520. I-5 exit 14, 1.2 mi w on SR 66 (Ashland St). Ext corridors. **Pets:** Dogs only. Designated rooms, service with restrictions, crate. SAVE ⤳ 🛜 ✕ 🛏 ☕

ASTORIA *(Restaurants p. 637)*

Astoria Crest Motel M

(503) 325-3141. **Call for rates.** 5366 Leif Erickson Dr 97103. 4 mi e of Astoria Bridge on US 30. Ext corridors. **Pets:** Accepted. 🛜 🐾 🛏 ☕

Astoria Dunes Motel M

(503) 325-7111. **$75-$195.** 288 W Marine Dr 97103. Just e of Astoria Bridge on US 30. Ext corridors. **Pets:** Medium, dogs only. $10 daily fee/pet. Service with restrictions, supervision. SAVE ⤳ 🛜 🛏 ☕

Astoria Holiday Inn Express Hotel & Suites H

(503) 325-6222. **$119-$389.** 204 W Marine Dr 97103. On US 30; west side of town. Int corridors. **Pets:** Accepted. ⌂M ⤳ 🗙 🛜 ✕ 🛏 ☕

BEST WESTERN Lincoln Inn H

(503) 325-2205. **$90-$400.** 555 Hamburg Ave 97103. On US 101/30; at east end of Youngs Bay Bridge. Int corridors. **Pets:** Medium, dogs only. $15 daily fee/pet. Designated rooms, service with restrictions, supervision. SAVE ⤳ 🗙 🛜 ✕ 🛏 ☕

Clementine's Bed & Breakfast BB

(503) 325-2005. **$98-$165, 7 day notice.** 847 Exchange St 97103. At 8th and Exchange sts; in historic downtown. Int corridors. **Pets:** Other species. $15 one-time fee/room. Designated rooms, no service, supervision. 🛜 ✕ 🐾 🛏 ☕

Comfort Suites Columbia River H

(503) 325-2000. **$99-$289.** 3420 Leif Erickson Dr 97103. 2.5 mi e of Astoria Bridge on US 30. Int corridors. **Pets:** Dogs only. $10 daily fee/pet. Designated rooms, service with restrictions, supervision. ⤳ 🗙 🛜 ✕ 🛏 ☕

BAKER CITY

BEST WESTERN Sunridge Inn H ❀

(541) 523-6444. **$79-$237.** 1 Sunridge Ln 97814. I-84 exit 304, just w. Int corridors. **Pets:** Other species. $15 daily fee/room. Designated rooms, service with restrictions, crate. SAVE 🍴 ⤳ 🛜 🛏 ☕

▼▼▼▼ **Geiser Grand Hotel** 🅷 ❀

(541) 523-1889. **$99-$279, 7 day notice.** 1996 Main St 97814. I-84 exit 304, 0.9 mi w on Campbell St, then 0.3 mi s; downtown. Int corridors. **Pets:** Other species. $15 daily fee/pet. Service with restrictions, crate.

🍽️ 👤ᴹ 🛜 ✕ 🔲

BANDON

▼▼ ▼▼ **Bandon Beach Vacation Rentals** 🆅🅷

(541) 347-4801. **$100-$200, 30 day notice.** 54515 Beach Loop Rd 97411. 1 mi s on US 101, 0.8 mi w on Seabird Rd, then 1 mi s; registration in house behind property. Ext corridors. **Pets:** Dogs only. $20 one-time fee/pet. No service, supervision. 🛜 ✕ 🅰️ 🔲

🅐🅐🅐 ▼▼ ▼▼ **Bandon Inn** 🅼 ❀

(541) 347-4417. **$84-$185, 3 day notice.** 355 US 101 97411. Center. Ext corridors. **Pets:** Medium. $15 daily fee/pet. Designated rooms, service with restrictions, supervision. 🆂🅰🆅🅴 🛜 ✕ 🅰️ 🔲

🅐🅐🅐 ▼▼▼▼ **BEST WESTERN Inn at Face Rock** 🅷

(541) 347-9441. **$125-$335.** 3225 Beach Loop Dr 97411. 1 mi s on US 101, 0.8 mi w on Seabird Rd, just s. Ext corridors. **Pets:** Accepted.

🆂🅰🆅🅴 🌊 ✕ 🛜 🅰️ 🔲

BEAVERTON

▼▼ ▼▼ **Comfort Inn & Suites** 🅷

(503) 643-9100. **$84-$149.** 13455 SW Tualatin Valley Hwy 97005. SR 217 exit 2A (Canyon Rd/SR 8), 1 mi w. Int corridors. **Pets:** Small, dogs only. $10 daily fee/pet. Service with restrictions, supervision.

🌊 ✕ 🅰️ 🔲

🅐🅐🅐 ▼▼ ▼▼ **DoubleTree by Hilton-Portland/Beaverton** 🅷

(503) 614-8100. **$99-$229.** 15402 NW Cornell Rd 97006. US 26 exit 65, just ne. Int corridors. **Pets:** Accepted.

🆂🅰🆅🅴 🍽️ 👤ᴹ 🌊 🛜 ✕ 🅰️ 🔲

▼▼▼▼ **Homewood Suites by Hilton** 🅷

(503) 614-0900. **$109-$229.** 15525 NW Gateway Ct 97006. US 26 exit 65, just sw on NW Cornell Rd, just s on NW 158th Ave, just se on NW Waterhouse Ave, then just e. Int corridors. **Pets:** Accepted.

👤ᴹ 🌊 🛜 🅰️ 🔲

BEND *(Restaurants p. 637)*

▼▼ ▼▼ **Bend Riverside Inn & Suites** 🅼

(541) 389-2363. **$85-$159, 3 day notice.** 1565 NW Wall St 97701. US 97 exit 137 (Revere Ave), just s. Ext corridors. **Pets:** Accepted.

🌊 🛜 ✕ 🔲

▼▼ ▼▼ **Bend Three Sisters Inn & Suites** 🅼

(541) 382-1515. **$89-$180.** 721 NE 3rd St 97701. Jct US 20 and Business Rt US 97 (NE 3rd St), just s. Ext corridors. **Pets:** Other species. $10 daily fee/pet. Designated rooms, service with restrictions, supervision. 🌊 🛜 ✕ 🅰️ 🔲

▼▼ ▼▼ **Holiday Inn Express Hotel & Suites** 🅷

(541) 317-8500. **Call for rates.** 20615 Grandview Dr 97701. On US 97; north end of town. Int corridors. **Pets:** Accepted.

👤ᴹ 🌊 🛜 ✕ 🅰️ 🔲

▼▼ ▼▼ **La Quinta Inn Bend** 🅷

(541) 388-2227. **$95-$299.** 61200 SE 3rd St (Business Rt US 97) 97702. From south end of jct US 97 and Business Rt 97 (NE 3rd St), 0.5 mi n. Int corridors. **Pets:** Large, other species. Service with restrictions. 🌊 🛜 ✕ 🅰️ 🔲

🅐🅐🅐 ▼▼▼▼ ▼▼▼▼ **The Oxford Hotel** 🅷 ❀

(541) 382-8436. **$209-$539, 10 day notice.** 10 NW Minnesota Ave 97701. Jct NW Minnesota Ave and NW Lava Rd; downtown. Int corridors. **Pets:** Other species. $55 one-time fee/pet. Designated rooms, supervision. 🆂🅰🆅🅴 🍽️ 👤ᴹ ✕ 🛜 ✕ 🅰️ 🔲

▼▼▼▼ **Pine Ridge Inn Hotel & Suites** 🅷 ❀

(541) 389-6137. **$179-$299, 3 day notice.** 1200 SW Mt Bachelor Dr 97702. US 97 exit 138 (Downtown/Mt Bachelor Dr), 1.6 mi sw on Colorado Ave, just s on Century Dr, then just w. Int corridors. **Pets:** Dogs only. $55 one-time fee/room. Designated rooms, service with restrictions, supervision. 👤ᴹ 🛜 ✕ 🅰️ 🔲

🅐🅐🅐 ▼▼▼▼ **The Riverhouse Hotel & Convention Center** 🅷

(541) 389-3111. **$119-$175, 3 day notice.** 3075 N US 97 Business 97701. US 97 exit 137 (Revere Ave) northbound, just n on NE Division St, then just n; exit 136 (Butler Market Rd) southbound, just w. Ext/int corridors. **Pets:** Accepted. 🆂🅰🆅🅴 🍽️ 🌊 ✕ 🛜 ✕ 🅰️ 🔲

▼▼▼▼ **Tetherow Lodges** 🅷 ❀

(541) 388-2582. **Call for rates.** 61240 Skyline Ranch Rd 97702. US 97 exit 139 (Reed Market Rd), 4 mi sw; at Tetherow Golf Club. Int corridors. **Pets:** Large, dogs only. $50 one-time fee/pet. Designated rooms, service with restrictions, crate. 🍽️ 🛜 ✕ 🅰️ 🔲

▼▼ ▼▼ **TownePlace Suites by Marriott** 🅷

(541) 382-5006. **$89-$229.** 755 SW 13th Pl 97702. US 97 exit 138 (Downtown/Mt Bachelor Dr), 1.6 mi sw on NW Colorado Ave. Int corridors. **Pets:** Accepted. 👤ᴹ 🌊 🛜 ✕ 🅰️ 🔲

BROOKINGS

🅐🅐🅐 ▼▼▼▼ **BEST WESTERN PLUS Beachfront Inn** 🅷

(541) 469-7779. **$129-$275.** 16008 Boat Basin Rd 97415. US 101 exit Benham Ln, 0.6 mi w; 1.2 mi s of Chetco River Bridge. Ext corridors. **Pets:** Large. $10 daily fee/pet. Designated rooms, service with restrictions, supervision. 🆂🅰🆅🅴 👤ᴹ 🌊 🛜 ✕ 🅰️ 🔲

🅐🅐🅐 ▼▼ ▼▼ **Spindrift Motel** 🅼

(541) 469-5345. **$89-$99.** 1215 Chetco Ave (US 101) 97415. On US 101; north end of town. Ext corridors. **Pets:** Accepted.

🆂🅰🆅🅴 🛜 ✕ 🅰️ 🔲

🅐🅐🅐 ▼▼ ▼▼ **Westward Inn** 🅼

(541) 469-7471. **$69-$150, 3 day notice.** 1026 Chetco Ave (US 101) 97415. On US 101; just n of downtown. Ext corridors. **Pets:** Medium, dogs only. $12 daily fee/pet. Designated rooms, service with restrictions, supervision. 🆂🅰🆅🅴 🛜 ✕ 🅰️ 🔲

▼▼ ▼▼ **Wild Rivers Motorlodge** 🅼 ❀

(541) 469-5361. **$59-$119.** 437 Chetco Ave (US 101) 97415. On US 101; just n of Chetco River Bridge. Ext corridors. **Pets:** $10 daily fee/pet. Designated rooms, service with restrictions, supervision.

🛜 🅰️ 🔲

BURNS

🅐🅐🅐 ▼▼ ▼▼ **America's Best Inn** 🅼

(541) 573-1700. **$66-$82.** 999 Oregon Ave (US 395/20) 97720. 1 mi w on US 395/20 from jct SR 78. Ext/int corridors. **Pets:** Small, dogs only. $50 deposit/room, $5 daily fee/pet. Designated rooms, service with restrictions, supervision. 🆂🅰🆅🅴 🌊 🛜 ✕ 🅰️ 🔲

🅐🅐🅐 ▼▼ **Silver Spur Motel** 🅼

(541) 573-2077. **$43-$56.** 789 N Broadway Ave 97720. US 395; corner of W "D" St. Ext corridors. **Pets:** Other species. $5 daily fee/room. Designated rooms, service with restrictions, supervision.

🆂🅰🆅🅴 🛜 🅰️ 🔲

CANNON BEACH

▼▼ ▼▼ **Ecola Creek Lodge** 🅼

(503) 436-2776. **$79-$244, 3 day notice.** 208 E 5th St 97110. US 101 exit Ecola State Park northbound, just w; north end of downtown. Ext corridors. **Pets:** Accepted. 👤ᴹ 🛜 ✕ 🅰️ 🔲

▼▼▼▼ **Inn at Cannon Beach** 🅷 ❀

(503) 436-9085. **$125-$299, 7 day notice.** 3215 S Hemlock St 97110. US 101 exit Tolovana Park, just w on Warren Way, then just n. Ext corridors. **Pets:** Dogs only. $15 daily fee/pet. Designated rooms, service with restrictions, supervision. 🛜 ✕ 🅰️ 🔲

▼▼▼ The Ocean Lodge ℍ
(503) 436-2241. **$199-$429, 7 day notice.** 2864 S Pacific St 97110. US 101 exit Tolovana Park, just w on Warren Way, just n on S Hemlock St, just w on W Chisana St, then just n. Ext/int corridors. **Pets:** Accepted.
🛜 ✕ 🛏 💻

ⒶⒶⒶ ▼▼▼ Surfsand Resort ℍ 🐾
(503) 436-2274. **$119-$469, 3 day notice.** 148 W Gower St 97110. US 101 exit Cannon Beach (2nd exit); downtown. Ext corridors. **Pets:** Other species. $15 daily fee/pet. Designated rooms, supervision.
🆂🅰🆅🅴 🍽 🏊 ✕ 🛜 ✕ 🛏 💻

ⒶⒶⒶ ▼▼▼ Tolovana Inn 🆖 🐾
(503) 436-2211. **$72-$474, 7 day notice.** 3400 S Hemlock St 97145. US 101 exit Tolovana Park, just w on Warren Way, then just s. Ext corridors. **Pets:** Large, other species. $20 daily fee/pet. Designated rooms, service with restrictions, supervision.
🆂🅰🆅🅴 🏊 ✕ 🛜 ✕ 🆇 🛏 💻

CANYONVILLE
▼▼▼ Holiday Inn Express & Suites Canyonville ℍ
(541) 839-4200. **$109-$209.** 200 Creekside Dr 97417. I-5 exit 99, just w. Int corridors. **Pets:** Small. $10 daily fee/pet. Designated rooms, service with restrictions, supervision. 🅼 🏊 🛜 ✕ 🛏 💻

CASCADE LOCKS
ⒶⒶⒶ ▼▼▼ BEST WESTERN PLUS Columbia River Inn ℍ
(541) 374-8777. **$115-$180.** 735 WaNaPa St (US 30) 97014. I-84 exit 44 eastbound, 0.4 mi ne; exit westbound, 1.4 mi nw. Int corridors. **Pets:** Medium. $10 daily fee/pet. Designated rooms, service with restrictions, supervision. 🆂🅰🆅🅴 🅼 🏊 🛜 ✕ 🛏 💻

CENTRAL POINT
▼▼▼ Holiday Inn Express Hotel & Suites ℍ
(541) 423-1010. **$89-$169.** 285 Peninger St 97502. I-5 exit 33, just se. Int corridors. **Pets:** Small. $25 daily fee/room. Designated rooms, service with restrictions, supervision. 🅼 🏊 🛜 🛏 💻

▼▼▼ Medford Inn & Suites ℍ
(541) 665-4141. **Call for rates.** 1777 Larue Dr 97502. I-5 exit 33, just se. Int corridors. **Pets:** Accepted. 🅼 🏊 🛜 ✕ 🛏 💻

▼▼ Super 8 Inn & Suites ℍ
(541) 664-5888. **$80-$103.** 4999 Biddle Rd 97502. I-5 exit 33, 0.5 mi e. Int corridors. **Pets:** Large. $15 one-time fee/room. Service with restrictions, crate. 🅼 🏊 🛜 🛏 💻

CLACKAMAS
▼▼ Comfort Suites ℍ
(503) 723-3450. **$77-$110.** 15929 SE McKinley Ave 97015. I-205 exit 12 northbound; exit 12B southbound, just w. Int corridors.
Pets: Accepted. 🏊 ✕ 🛜 ✕ 🛏 💻

CLATSKANIE
ⒶⒶⒶ ▼▼ Clatskanie River Inn ℍ
(503) 728-9000. **$89-$159.** 600 E Columbia River Hwy (US 30) 97016. On US 30, just e. Int corridors. **Pets:** Other species. $20 daily fee/room. Designated rooms, service with restrictions, supervision.
🆂🅰🆅🅴 🏊 🛜 ✕ 🛏 💻

COOS BAY
ⒶⒶⒶ ▼▼▼ BEST WESTERN PLUS Holiday Hotel ℍ
(541) 269-5111. **$110-$180.** 411 N Bayshore Dr 97420. On US 101; just n of downtown. Ext corridors. **Pets:** Medium, dogs only. $15 daily fee/pet. Service with restrictions. 🆂🅰🆅🅴 🏊 🛜 ✕ 🛏 💻

ⒶⒶⒶ ▼▼▼ Red Lion Hotel Coos Bay ℍ
(541) 267-4141. **$89-$156.** 1313 N Bayshore Dr 97420. On US 101; 0.5 mi n of downtown. Ext corridors. **Pets:** Accepted.
🆂🅰🆅🅴 🍽 🅼 🏊 🛜 ✕ 🛏 💻

▼▼ Super 8 Coos Bay 🅼
(541) 808-0700. **$70-$125.** 1001 N Bayshore Dr 97420. On US 101; just n of downtown. Ext corridors. **Pets:** Accepted.
🛜 ✕ 🆇 🛏 💻

COQUILLE
▼▼ Myrtle Lane Motel 🅼
(541) 396-2102. **$60-$85.** 787 N Central Blvd 97423. SR 42, 0.4 mi n. Ext corridors. **Pets:** Small. $10 daily fee/pet. Designated rooms, service with restrictions, supervision. 🛜 🆇 🛏 💻

CORVALLIS
ⒶⒶⒶ ▼▼▼ BEST WESTERN Grand Manor Inn & Suites ℍ
(541) 758-8571. **$99-$249.** 925 NW Garfield Ave 97330. Jct SR 34 and US 20, 0.3 mi w on NW Harrison Blvd, 1 mi n on NW 9th St, then just w. Int corridors. **Pets:** Large. $100 deposit/room, $10 daily fee/pet. Designated rooms, service with restrictions, supervision.
🆂🅰🆅🅴 🅼 🏊 🛜 ✕ 🛏 💻

ⒶⒶⒶ ▼▼▼ Comfort Suites Corvallis ℍ
(541) 753-4320. **$110-$160.** 1730 NW 9th St 97330. Jct SR 34 and US 20, 0.3 mi w on NW Harrison Blvd, 1.1 mi n. Int corridors.
Pets: Accepted. 🆂🅰🆅🅴 🏊 🛜 ✕ 🛏 💻

ⒶⒶⒶ ▼▼ Days Inn ℍ
(541) 754-7474. **$65-$360.** 1113 NW 9th St 97330. Jct SR 34 and US 20, 0.3 mi w on NW Harrison Blvd, 0.5 mi n. Int corridors.
Pets: Accepted. 🆂🅰🆅🅴 🏊 🛜 ✕ 🛏 💻

▼▼ Econo Lodge Corvallis ℍ
(541) 758-9125. **Call for rates.** 935 NW Garfield Ave 97330. Jct SR 34 and US 20, 0.3 mi w on NW Harrison Blvd, 1 mi n on NW 9th St, then just w. Int corridors. **Pets:** Very small. $20 one-time fee/pet. Designated rooms, service with restrictions, supervision. 🅼 🛜 🛏 💻

ⒶⒶⒶ ▼▼▼ Holiday Inn Express On The River ℍ
(541) 752-0800. **$99-$309, 3 day notice.** 781 NE 2nd St 97330. Jct SR 34 and US 20, 0.4 mi n. Int corridors. **Pets:** Other species. $25 daily fee/room. Service with restrictions. 🆂🅰🆅🅴 🅼 🏊 🛜 ✕ 🛏 💻

▼▼ Rodeway Inn Willamette River 🅼
(541) 752-9601. **$58-$190.** 345 NW 2nd St 97330. Between NW Harrison Blvd and NW Van Buren St; downtown. Ext/int corridors.
Pets: Accepted. 🛜 🛏 💻

▼▼ Super 8 ℍ
(541) 758-8088. **$55-$166.** 407 NW 2nd St 97330. Jct SR 34 and US 20, just n; downtown. Int corridors. **Pets:** Accepted.
🅼 🏊 🛜 🛏 💻

COTTAGE GROVE
ⒶⒶⒶ ▼▼ BEST WESTERN Cottage Grove Inn ℍ
(541) 942-1000. **Call for rates.** 1601 Gateway Blvd 97424. I-5 exit 174, just sw. Int corridors. **Pets:** Accepted.
🆂🅰🆅🅴 🅼 🏊 🛜 ✕ 🛏 💻

CRESWELL
▼▼▼ Comfort Inn & Suites ℍ 🐾
(541) 895-4025. **$79-$209.** 247 Melton Rd 97426. I-5 exit 182, just ne. Int corridors. **Pets:** Other species. $20 one-time fee/room. Service with restrictions, supervision. 🏊 🛜 ✕ 🛏 💻

DALLAS
ⒶⒶⒶ ▼▼▼ BEST WESTERN Dallas Inn & Suites ℍ
(503) 623-6000. **$99-$150.** 250 Orchard Dr 97338. SR 223, just n. Int corridors. **Pets:** Accepted. 🆂🅰🆅🅴 🅼 🛜 🛏 💻

ENTERPRISE *(Restaurants p. 637)*

▼▼▼ Eagle's View Inn & Suites 🅷

(541) 426-2700. **$83-$125, 7 day notice.** 1200 Highland Ave 97828. On SR 82, 1 mi e of downtown. Int corridors. **Pets:** Dogs only. $15 one-time fee/pet. Designated rooms, service with restrictions, supervision.

▼▼ Ponderosa Motel Ⓜ

(541) 426-3186. **$65-$79.** 102 E Greenwood St 97828. At S River (SR 82) and Greenwood sts. Ext corridors. **Pets:** Medium, dogs only. $10 daily fee/pet. Service with restrictions, supervision. 🔗🅘🖱

▼ Wilderness Inn Ⓜ

(541) 426-4535. **$59-$79.** 301 W North St 97828. Just w of downtown; on SR 82. Ext corridors. **Pets:** Medium, dogs only. $10 daily fee/pet. Service with restrictions, supervision. 🔗🅘🖱

EUGENE *(Restaurants p. 637)*

🆎 ▼ Americas Best Value Inn Ⓜ

(541) 343-0730. **$49-$149.** 1140 W 6th Ave 97402. I-5 exit 194B, 3.5 mi w on I-105, then 0.3 mi w on SR 99 N (6th Ave). Ext corridors. **Pets:** Accepted. [SAVE] 🔗

🆎 ▼▼▼ BEST WESTERN Greentree Inn 🅷 🐾

(541) 485-2727. **$110-$193.** 1759 Franklin Blvd 97403. I-5 exit 194B southbound to I-105 exit University of Oregon, 0.9 mi e; exit 192 northbound, 1.2 mi w. Ext/int corridors. **Pets:** Large, other species. $20 daily fee/room. Designated rooms, service with restrictions, supervision.

[SAVE] 🔗🅘🖱

🆎 ▼▼▼ BEST WESTERN New Oregon 🅷 🐾

(541) 683-3669. **$111-$170.** 1655 Franklin Blvd 97403. I-5 exit 194B southbound to I-105 exit University of Oregon, 0.9 mi e; exit 192 northbound, 1.2 mi w. Ext corridors. **Pets:** Large, other species. $20 daily fee/room. Designated rooms, service with restrictions, supervision.

[SAVE] 🔗🅘🖱

🆎 ▼▼▼ Campus Inn & Suites Ⓜ

(541) 343-3376. **$81-$168.** 390 E Broadway 97401. I-5 exit 192 north-bound, 2.2 mi w; exit 194B southbound, 1.3 mi w on I-105 exit 2 (Coburg Rd), 1.5 mi s, follow signs to University of Oregon. Ext corri-dors. **Pets:** Medium. $50 deposit/pet, $10 daily fee/pet. Designated rooms, service with restrictions, supervision. [SAVE] 🔗🅘🖱

▼▼▼ Excelsior Inn & Ristorante Italiano 🅲🅸

(541) 342-6963. **$135-$300.** 754 E 13th Ave 97401. I-5 exit 194B southbound, 1.3 mi w on I-105 exit 2 (Coburg Rd), 1.5 mi s, follow signs to University of Oregon, just e on Broadway/Franklin Blvd, just s on Patterson St, then just e; exit 192 northbound, 1.5 mi w, then just s on Alder St. Int corridors. **Pets:** Small, dogs only. $200 deposit/room, $25 one-time fee/pet. Designated rooms, service with restrictions, crate. 🅘🔗🅧

🆎 ▼▼▼ Hilton Eugene 🅷

(541) 342-2000. **$104-$159.** 66 E 6th Ave 97401. At 6th Ave and Oak St; center. Int corridors. **Pets:** Accepted.

[SAVE] 🅲🅘🔗🅢🅧🅘🖱

🆎 ▼▼▼ Inn at the 5th 🅷 🐾

(541) 743-4099. **$199-$399, 3 day notice.** 205 E 6th Ave 97401. Jct Pearl St; downtown. Int corridors. **Pets:** $55 one-time fee/pet. Service with restrictions. [SAVE] 🅶🅼🅧🔗🅧🅘🖱

▼▼▼ La Quinta Inn & Suites Eugene 🅷

(541) 344-8335. **$94-$374.** 155 Day Island Rd 97401. I-5 exit 194B, 1.3 mi w on I-105 exit 2 (Coburg Rd), straight through jct Coburg Rd to Southwood Ln, just w, then 0.5 mi se on Country Club Rd, follow signs for Autzen Stadium. Int corridors. **Pets:** Large. Service with restrictions. 🔗🅧🅘🖱

▼▼▼ Residence Inn by Marriott Eugene Springfield 🅷

(541) 342-7171. **$134-$319.** 25 Club Rd 97401. I-5 exit 194B, 1.3 mi w on I-105 exit 2 (Coburg Rd), straight through jct Coburg Rd to South-wood Ln, just w, then se on Country Club Rd, follow signs for Autzen Stadium. Int corridors. **Pets:** Accepted. 🅶🅼🔗🅧🅘🖱

🆎 ▼▼▼ Valley River Inn 🅷

(541) 743-1000. **$109-$239.** 1000 Valley River Way 97401. I-5 exit 194B, 2.5 mi w on I-105 exit 1, follow signs for Valley River Center. Int corridors. **Pets:** $40 one-time fee/room. Designated rooms, service with restrictions, supervision. [SAVE] 🅘🔗🅧🔗🅧🅘🖱

FLORENCE

🆎 ▼▼▼ BEST WESTERN Pier Point Inn 🅷 🐾

(541) 997-7191. **$140-$230.** 85625 US 101 S 97439. Jct SR 126, 1.1 mi s. Ext/int corridors. **Pets:** $20 daily fee/room. Designated rooms, service with restrictions, supervision.

[SAVE] 🅘🔗🅧🔗🅧🅘🖱

🆎 ▼ Le Chateau Inn Ⓜ

(541) 997-3481. **Call for rates.** 1084 US 101 N 97439. Jct SR 126, just n. Ext corridors. **Pets:** Accepted. [SAVE] 🔗🅧🔗🅧🅘

🆎 ▼ Ocean Breeze Motel Ⓜ 🐾

(541) 997-2642. **$69-$130.** 85165 US 101 S 97439. Jct SR 126, 2 mi s. Ext corridors. **Pets:** Dogs only. $10 daily fee/pet. Designated rooms, supervision. [SAVE] 🔗🅧🅐🅘🖱

🆎 ▼ Park Motel Ⓜ

(541) 997-2634. **$55-$150, 3 day notice.** 85034 US 101 S 97439. Jct SR 126, 2.2 mi s. Ext corridors. **Pets:** Other species. $15 daily fee/room. Designated rooms, service with restrictions, supervision.

[SAVE] 🔗🅧🅐🅘🖱

FOREST GROVE

🆎 ▼▼ BEST WESTERN University Inn & Suites 🅷

(503) 992-8888. **$90-$220.** 3933 Pacific Ave 97116. East end of town on SR 8. Int corridors. **Pets:** Accepted.

[SAVE] 🅶🅼🔗🅧🔗🅧🅘🖱

GEARHART *(Restaurants p. 637)*

▼▼▼ Gearhart By The Sea 🅲🅞

(503) 738-8331. **$126-$300, 3 day notice.** 1157 N Marion Ave 97138. US 101 exit City Center, 1 mi w. Ext corridors. **Pets:** Accepted.

🅘🔗🅧🔗🅐🅘🖱

GLADSTONE

▼▼▼ Holiday Inn Express Portland SE-Clackamas Area 🅷

(503) 722-7777. **Call for rates.** 75 82nd Dr 97027. I-205 exit 11, 0.3 mi sw. Int corridors. **Pets:** Accepted. 🔗🅧🔗🅧🅘🖱

GOLD BEACH

🆎 ▼▼▼ Gold Beach Inn Ⓜ

(541) 247-7091. **Call for rates.** 29346 Ellensburg Ave (US 101) 97444. On US 101; center. Ext corridors. **Pets:** Accepted.

[SAVE] 🔗🅧🅐🅘🖱

🆎 ▼▼▼ Gold Beach Resort 🅷 🐾

(541) 247-7066. **$80-$180.** 29232 Ellensburg Ave 97444. On US 101; south end of town. Ext corridors. **Pets:** Large, dogs only. $15 daily fee/pet. Designated rooms, service with restrictions, supervision.

[SAVE] 🔗🔗🅧🅘🖱

GOVERNMENT CAMP

🆎 ▼▼▼ BEST WESTERN Mt. Hood Inn 🅷 🐾

(503) 272-3205. **$120-$200.** 87450 E Government Camp Loop 97028. 0.5 mi w of center. Int corridors. **Pets:** Medium, other species. $15 daily fee/pet. Designated rooms, service with restrictions, supervision.

[SAVE] 🔗🅧🅐🅘🖱

GRANTS PASS *(Restaurants p. 638)*

🆎 ▼ Bestway Inn Ⓜ

(541) 479-2952. **$65-$80.** 1253 NE 6th St 97526. I-5 exit 58, 0.9 mi s on SR 99. Ext corridors. **Pets:** Small, dogs only. $10 daily fee/pet. Service with restrictions, supervision. [SAVE] 🔗🅘🖱

BEST WESTERN Grants Pass Inn H
(541) 476-1117. **$110-$150.** 111 NE Agness Ave 97526. I-5 exit 55, just nw. Ext corridors. **Pets:** Accepted. [SAVE] [&M] [≈] [⌂] [▤] [▦]

BEST WESTERN Inn at the Rogue H
(541) 582-2200. **$99-$159.** 8959 Rogue River Hwy 97527. I-5 exit 48, just nw. Int corridors. **Pets:** Accepted.
[SAVE] [&M] [≈] [⌂] [✕] [▤] [▦]

Holiday Inn Express Grants Pass H
(541) 471-6144. **$119-$169.** 105 NE Agness Ave 97526. I-5 exit 55, just nw. Int corridors. **Pets:** Accepted. [≈] [✕] [▤] [▦]

Knights Inn Motel M
(541) 479-5595. **$65-$89.** 104 SE 7th St 97526. I-5 exit 58, 1.7 mi s on SR 99, just e on G St, then just n. Ext corridors. **Pets:** Small, dogs only. $10 one-time fee/pet, $10 daily fee/pet. Service with restrictions, supervision. [SAVE] [≈] [▤]

La Quinta Inn & Suites Grants Pass H
(541) 472-1808. **$89-$264.** 243 NE Morgan Ln 97526. I-5 exit 58, 0.4 mi s on SR 99, just e on Hillcrest Dr to SR 99 N, then just n. Int corridors. **Pets:** Large, other species. Service with restrictions.
[&M] [≈] [≋] [⌂] [▤] [▦]

Motel 6-#253 M
(541) 474-1331. **$51-$75.** 1800 NE 7th St 97526. I-5 exit 58, just s on SR 99. Ext corridors. **Pets:** Other species. Service with restrictions, crate. [&M] [≈] [$≋] [▤]

Redwood Hyperion Suites H ✿
(541) 476-0878. **$82-$418.** 815 NE 6th St 97526. I-5 exit 58, 1.2 mi s on SR 99. Ext corridors. **Pets:** Designated rooms, service with restrictions, supervision. [SAVE] [&M] [≈] [✕] [≈] [✕] [▤] [▦]

Riverside Inn H
(541) 476-6873. **$135-$155, 3 day notice.** 986 SW 6th St 97526. I-5 exit 58, 2.5 mi s on SR 99. Ext corridors. **Pets:** Accepted.
[SAVE] [&M] [≈] [≈] [✕] [▤] [▦]

Shilo Inn-Grants Pass H
(541) 479-8391. **Call for rates.** 1880 NW 6th St 97526. I-5 exit 58, 0.3 mi s on SR 99. Int corridors. **Pets:** Accepted.
[&M] [≈] [≈] [✕] [▤] [▦]

Super 8-Grants Pass H
(541) 474-0888. **$57-$247.** 1949 NE 7th St 97526. I-5 exit 58, 0.4 mi s on SR 99, just e on Hillcrest Dr to SR 99 N, then just n. Int corridors. **Pets:** Accepted. [&M] [≈] [≈] [✕] [▤] [▦]

Travelodge M ✿
(541) 479-6611. **$70-$105.** 1950 NW Vine St 97526. I-5 exit 58, just s on SR 99. Ext corridors. **Pets:** Medium. $10 daily fee/pet. Designated rooms, service with restrictions, supervision. [SAVE] [≈] [≈] [▤] [▦]

GRESHAM

Days Inn & Suites H
(503) 465-1515. **$62-$120.** 24124 SE Stark St 97030. I-84 exit 16, 1.5 mi s on NE 238th and NE 242nd drs, then just w. Int corridors. **Pets:** Dogs only. $10 daily fee/pet. Designated rooms, service with restrictions, supervision. [SAVE] [≈] [≈] [▤] [▦]

Days Inn-Portland/Gresham H
(503) 618-8400. **$55-$85.** 2261 NE 181st Ave 97230. I-84 exit 13, just sw. Int corridors. **Pets:** Accepted. [&M] [≈] [≈] [✕] [▤] [▦]

Extended Stay America Portland/Gresham H
(503) 661-0226. **Call for rates.** 17777 NE Sacramento St 97230. I-84 exit 13, 0.3 mi s on NE 181st Ave, just w on NE San Rafael St, then just n on NE 178th Ave. Int corridors. **Pets:** Other species. $25 daily fee/pet. Service with restrictions, supervision. [&M] [≈] [▦]

Holiday Inn Portland/Gresham H
(503) 907-1777. **$89-$299.** 2752 NE Hogan Dr 97030. I-84 exit 16, 1.8 mi s on NE 238th, NE 242nd and NE Hogan drs. Int corridors. **Pets:** Small, dogs only. $35 daily fee/pet. Designated rooms, service with restrictions, supervision. [¶¶] [&M] [≈] [✕] [▤] [▦]

Super 8 H
(503) 661-5100. **$50-$65.** 121 NE 181st Ave 97230. I-84 exit 13, 1.3 mi s. Int corridors. **Pets:** Medium, dogs only. $10 daily fee/pet. Service with restrictions, supervision. [SAVE] [≈] [▤] [▦]

HALSEY

Pioneer Villa Travelodge M
(541) 369-2804. **$53-$85.** 33180 SR 228 97348. I-5 exit 216, just se. Ext corridors. **Pets:** Other species. $10 daily fee/room. Service with restrictions. [¶¶] [≈] [≈] [▤] [▦]

HERMISTON

Comfort Inn & Suites H
(541) 564-5911. **$104-$190.** 77514 SR 207 97838. I-84 exit 182, just n. Int corridors. **Pets:** Other species. $20 daily fee/pet. Service with restrictions, supervision. [&M] [≈] [≈] [▤] [▦]

Oak Tree Inn H
(541) 567-2330. **$72-$87.** 1110 SE 4th St 97838. 0.4 mi s on US 395, just w. Int corridors. **Pets:** Accepted. [≈] [✕] [▤] [▦]

Oxford Suites Hermiston H ✿
(541) 564-8000. **$109-$209, 3 day notice.** 1050 N 1st St 97838. I-84 exit 188 (US 395), 7.8 mi nw. Int corridors. **Pets:** Small, dogs only. $25 one-time fee/pet. Designated rooms, service with restrictions, supervision. [SAVE] [&M] [≈] [≈] [✕] [▤] [▦]

HILLSBORO

Extended Stay America-Portland-Beaverton H
(503) 439-1515. **Call for rates.** 18665 NW Eider Ct 97006. US 26 exit 64, 0.7 mi s on NW 185th Ave, then just w. Int corridors. **Pets:** Other species. $25 daily fee/pet. Service with restrictions, supervision.
[≈] [✕] [▤] [▦]

Larkspur Landing Hillsboro H
(503) 681-2121. **Call for rates.** 3133 NE Shute Rd 97124. US 26 exit 61, 1.1 mi s. Int corridors. **Pets:** Accepted. [SAVE] [≈] [✕] [▤] [▦]

Residence Inn by Marriott-Portland West/Hillsboro H
(503) 531-3200. **$119-$299.** 18855 NW Tanasbourne Dr 97124. US 26 exit 64, just s on NW 185th Ave, then just w. Ext/int corridors. **Pets:** Accepted. [&M] [≈] [≈] [✕] [▤] [▦]

TownePlace Suites by Marriott-Portland Hillsboro H
(503) 268-6000. **$89-$259.** 6550 NE Brighton St 97124. US 26 exit 62A westbound; exit 62 eastbound, 1 mi s on Cornelius Pass Rd, 0.7 mi w on NE Cornell Rd, just n on NW 229th Ave, then just w. Ext corridors. **Pets:** Accepted. [≈] [≈] [✕] [▤] [▦]

HINES

BEST WESTERN Rory & Ryan Inns H
(541) 573-5050. **$95-$135.** 534 US 20 N 97738. On US 20 (Central Oregon Hwy). Int corridors. **Pets:** Medium, dogs only. $15 daily fee/pet. Designated rooms, service with restrictions, supervision.
[SAVE] [≈] [≈] [✕] [▤] [▦]

Rory & Ryan Inns H
(541) 573-3370. **$55-$125.** 504 US 20 N 97738. On US 20 (Central Oregon Hwy). Int corridors. **Pets:** Medium, dogs only. $10 daily fee/pet. Designated rooms, service with restrictions, supervision.
[≈] [≈] [✕] [▤] [▦]

HOOD RIVER

BEST WESTERN PLUS Hood River Inn 🅷 ❀

(541) 386-2200. **$180-$500.** 1108 E Marina Way 97031. I-84 exit 64, just ne. Int corridors. **Pets:** Dogs only. $12 daily fee/pet. Designated rooms, service with restrictions, supervision.

SAVE 🍽 🖘 ❌ 🖨 🖵

Columbia Gorge Hotel & Spa 🆑

(541) 386-5566. **$159-$299.** 4000 Westcliff Dr 97031. I-84 exit 62, just nw of overpass. Int corridors. **Pets:** Medium. $20 daily fee/room. Designated rooms, service with restrictions, supervision. 🍽 🖘 ❌ 🖨

Riverview Lodge 🅼

(541) 386-8719. **$79-$189, 7 day notice.** 1505 Oak St 97031. I-84 exit 62, 1 mi e on Cascade Ave. Ext/int corridors. **Pets:** Medium, dogs only. $50 deposit/room, $15 daily fee/pet. Designated rooms, service with restrictions, supervision. SAVE 🖘 🖨 🖵

Sunset Motel 🅼

(541) 386-6322. **$79-$129, 3 day notice.** 2300 Cascade Ave 97031. I-84 exit 62, 0.7 mi se. Ext corridors. **Pets:** Medium, dogs only. $15 daily fee/pet. Designated rooms, service with restrictions, supervision.

SAVE 🅼 🖘 ❌ 🖨 🖵

Vagabond Lodge 🅼 ❀

(541) 386-2992. **$55-$155.** 4070 Westcliff Dr 97031. I-84 exit 62, 0.3 mi nw. Ext corridors. **Pets:** Other species. $10 daily fee/pet. Designated rooms, service with restrictions, supervision. 🖘 🖨 🖵

JACKSONVILLE

Country House Inns Jacksonville 🆑 ❀

(541) 899-2050. **$99-$325, 3 day notice.** 830 N 5th St 97530. 0.5 mi ne of downtown; in historic district. Ext/int corridors. **Pets:** Other species. $25 daily fee/room. Designated rooms, service with restrictions, supervision. SAVE 🅼 🖘 ❌ 🖬 🖨 🖵

Jacksonville Inn 🆑 ❀

(541) 899-1900. **$159-$465, 3 day notice.** 175 E California St 97530. Between 3rd and 4th sts; in historic district; center. Ext/int corridors. **Pets:** Medium, dogs only. $15 daily fee/pet. Designated rooms, service with restrictions, supervision. SAVE 🍽 🖘 ❌ 🖨 🖵

Jacksonville's Magnolia Inn 🅱🅱 ❀

(541) 899-0255. **$114-$174, 7 day notice.** 245 N 5th St 97530. At 5th (SR 238) and D sts; in historic district. Int corridors. **Pets:** Dogs only. $25 one-time fee/room. Designated rooms, service with restrictions, supervision. 🅼 🖘 ❌

JOHN DAY

BEST WESTERN John Day Inn 🅼

(541) 575-1700. **$105-$130.** 315 W Main St 97845. Just w of jct US 26 and 395. Ext corridors. **Pets:** Other species. $15 one-time fee/room. Designated rooms, service with restrictions, supervision.

SAVE 🖘 ❌ 🖨 🖵

Dreamers Lodge 🅼

(541) 575-0526. **$49-$99.** 144 N Canyon Blvd 97845. Just n of jct US 26 and 395. Ext corridors. **Pets:** Medium, dogs only. $5 deposit/pet, $5 daily fee/pet. Service with restrictions, supervision.

SAVE 🖘 ❌ 🖨 🖵

JOSEPH

Mountain View Motel & RV Park 🅼

(541) 432-2982. **$55-$75.** 83450 Joseph Hwy 97846. 1.8 mi n of downtown; on SR 82. Ext corridors. **Pets:** Large. $10 daily fee/pet. Service with restrictions, crate. SAVE 🖘 ❌ 🖬 🖨 🖵

KING CITY

BEST WESTERN PLUS Northwind Inn & Suites 🅷 ❀

(503) 431-2100. **$110-$210.** 16105 SW Pacific Hwy 97224. I-5 exit 292, just nw on SR 217 exit 6 (SR 99 W), then 2.5 mi s. Int corridors. **Pets:** Very small, dogs only. $15 daily fee/pet. Designated rooms, supervision. SAVE 🅼 🖘 🖨 🖵

KLAMATH FALLS

Cimarron Inn Klamath Falls 🅼 ❀

(541) 882-4601. **$59-$99, 3 day notice.** 3060 S 6th St 97603. 0.4 mi w on 6th St (SR 140); jct SR 140 E/39 S and SR 39 N/US 97 business route. Ext corridors. **Pets:** Medium. $25 one-time fee/pet. Designated rooms, service with restrictions, supervision.

SAVE 🖘 🖘 ❌ 🖨 🖵

Golden West Motel 🅼 ❀

(541) 882-1758. **$42-$68.** 6402 S 6th St 97603. On S 6th St (SR 140); at eastern edge of town. Ext corridors. **Pets:** Dogs only. $10 one-time fee/room. Supervision. SAVE 🖘 ❌ 🖨

The Lodge At Running Y Ranch-A Holiday Inn Resort 🅷

(541) 850-5500. **Call for rates.** 5500 Running Y Rd 97601. Jct US 97, 7.5 mi nw on SR 140. Int corridors. **Pets:** Accepted.

SAVE 🍽 🅼 🖘 ❌ 🖘 ❌ 🖨 🖵

Majestic Inn & Suites 🅼

(541) 883-7771. **$35-$99.** 5543 S 6th St 97603. 1 mi e on 6th St (SR 140) from jct SR 140 E/39 S and SR 39 N/US 97 business route. Ext corridors. **Pets:** Small, dogs only. $10 daily fee/pet. Designated rooms, service with restrictions, supervision. SAVE 🖘 🖨

Maverick Motel 🅼

(541) 882-6688. **$39-$99.** 1220 Main St 97601. US 97 exit City Center Dr, 0.9 mi e on S Klamath Ave, just n on S 12th St, then just e. Ext corridors. **Pets:** Medium. $6 daily fee/pet. Designated rooms, service with restrictions, supervision. SAVE 🖘 🖨 🖵

Microtel Inn & Suites by Wyndham Klamath Falls 🅷

(541) 273-0206. **$79-$99.** 2716 Dakota Ct 97603. US 97 exit 277, 2.7 mi e on SR 140 exit 3, 1 mi n on Washburn Way, just e on Laverne Ave, then just s on Brooke Dr. Int corridors. **Pets:** Medium, other species. $35 one-time fee/room. Designated rooms, service with restrictions, supervision. SAVE 🅼 🖘 🖘 ❌ 🖨 🖵

Motel 6-#226 🅼

(541) 884-2110. **$51-$65.** 5136 S 6th St 97603. 0.5 mi e on 6th St (SR 140) from jct SR 140 E/39 S and SR 39 N/US 97 business route. Ext corridors. **Pets:** Other species. Service with restrictions, crate.

🖘 🖘 🖨

Shilo Inn Suites Hotel-Klamath Falls 🅷

(541) 885-7980. **Call for rates.** 2500 Almond St 97601. On US 97; 1.5 mi n of downtown. Int corridors. **Pets:** Accepted.

🍽 🅼 🖘 ❌ 🖘 ❌ 🖨 🖵

Super 8 🅷 ❀

(541) 884-8880. **$61-$96.** 3805 US 97 97601. 2 mi n of downtown. Int corridors. **Pets:** Other species. $10 daily fee/room. Service with restrictions, supervision. 🅼 🖘 🖨 🖵

LA GRANDE

Americas Best Value Sandman Inn 🅷

(541) 963-3707. **$89-$149.** 2410 E 'R' Ave 97850. I-84 exit 261, just s on Island Ave, just e on N Albany St, then just n. Int corridors. **Pets:** Dogs only. $25 one-time fee/pet. Designated rooms, service with restrictions, supervision. 🖘 🖘 🖨 🖵

LAKE OSWEGO

▼▼▼ Crowne Plaza Hotel H ❀

(503) 624-8400. **Call for rates.** 14811 Kruse Oaks Dr 97035. I-5 exit 292B northbound; exit 292 southbound, just e on Kruse Way, then just s. Int corridors. **Pets:** Dogs only. $25 daily fee/pet. Designated rooms, service with restrictions, supervision.

🍴 ♿ 🛬 🛜 ✕ 🛄 💻

▼▼ Lakeshore Inn H ❀

(503) 636-9679. **$89-$199, 3 day notice.** 210 N State St 97034. Jct N State St and Foothills Rd; downtown. Ext corridors. **Pets:** Dogs only. $15 daily fee/pet. Designated rooms, service with restrictions, crate.

♿ 🛬 🛜 ✕ 🛄 💻

▼▼▼ Phoenix Inn Suites-Lake Oswego H

(503) 624-7400. **Call for rates.** 14905 SW Bangy Rd 97035. I-5 exit 292B northbound; exit 292 southbound, just s. Int corridors. **Pets:** Accepted. ♿ 🛬 🛜 ✕ 🛄 💻

▼▼▼ Residence Inn by Marriott-Portland South H

(503) 684-2603. **$80-$214.** 15200 SW Bangy Rd 97035. I-5 exit 292B northbound; exit 292 southbound, just e, then 0.3 mi s. Ext corridors. **Pets:** Accepted. ♿ 🛬 🛜 ✕ 🛄 💻

LAKEVIEW

ⓐⓐⓐ ▼▼▼ BEST WESTERN Skyline Motor Lodge M ❀

(541) 947-2194. **$101-$131.** 414 N G St 97630. Jct US 395 and SR 140. Ext corridors. **Pets:** Medium, dogs only. $10 daily fee/pet. Designated rooms, service with restrictions, supervision.

SAVE 🛬 🛜 ✕ 🛄 💻

ⓐⓐⓐ ▼ Interstate 8 Motel M

(541) 947-3341. **$60-$72.** 354 N K St 97630. On SR 140, 0.3 mi w of jct US 395. Ext corridors. **Pets:** Small, dogs only. $50 deposit/room, $5 daily fee/pet. Designated rooms, service with restrictions, supervision.

SAVE 🛜 🛄 💻

LA PINE

ⓐⓐⓐ ▼▼ BEST WESTERN Newberry Station H

(541) 536-5130. **$100-$150.** 16515 Reed Rd 97739. Just off US 97; north end of town. Int corridors. **Pets:** Dogs only. $15 daily fee/room. Designated rooms, supervision. SAVE 🛬 🛜 ✕ 🛄 💻

LINCOLN CITY

ⓐⓐⓐ ▼▼▼▼ The Coho Oceanfront Lodge H ❀

(541) 994-3684. **$99-$299.** 1635 NW Harbor Ave 97367. US 101 exit N 17th St, just w. Ext corridors. **Pets:** Small, dogs only. $20 daily fee/pet. Designated rooms, service with restrictions, supervision.

SAVE 🛬 🛝 🛜 ✕ 🛝 💻

ⓐⓐⓐ ▼▼▼ Comfort Inn & Suites H

(541) 994-8155. **$69-$229.** 136 NE US 101 97367. Just n of D River. Int corridors. **Pets:** Medium, dogs only. $20 daily fee/pet. Designated rooms, service with restrictions, supervision.

SAVE 🛬 🛜 ✕ 💻

ⓐⓐⓐ ▼▼▼ Inn at Wecoma H 🐾

(541) 994-2984. **$59-$219.** 2945 NW US 101 97367. Just s of NW 30th St; north of downtown. Int corridors. **Pets:** Small, dogs only. $15 daily fee/pet. Designated rooms, service with restrictions, supervision.

SAVE 🛬 🛝 🛜 ✕ 🛝 🛄 💻

▼▼ Looking Glass Inn H ❀

(541) 996-3996. **$79-$269, 3 day notice.** 861 SW 51st St 97367. US 101, just w on 51st St; south end of town. Ext corridors. **Pets:** Dogs only. $15 daily fee/pet. Designated rooms, service with restrictions, crate. 🛜 ✕ 🛝 🛄 💻

▼ Motel 6-#4172 H

(541) 996-9900. **$46-$114.** 3517 NW US 101 97367. North end of downtown. Int corridors. **Pets:** Other species. Service with restrictions, crate. ♿ 🛜 🛄

ⓐⓐⓐ ▼▼▼ Palace Inn & Suites H

(541) 996-9466. **$59-$249.** 550 SE Hwy 101 97367. Center. Int corridors. **Pets:** Dogs only. $25 daily fee/room. Designated rooms, service with restrictions, supervision. SAVE 🛝 🛜 ✕ 🛄 💻

▼▼▼ Shearwater Inn H

(541) 994-4121. **Call for rates.** 120 NW Inlet Ct 97367. From US 101, just w on NW 2nd Dr, just s. Int corridors. **Pets:** Accepted.

🛜 ✕ 🛝 🛄 💻

MADRAS

ⓐⓐⓐ ▼▼▼ BEST WESTERN Madras Inn M

(541) 475-6141. **$100-$140.** 12 SW 4th St 97741. On US 97/26 S; at B and 4th sts; downtown. Ext corridors. **Pets:** Accepted.

SAVE ♿ 🛬 🛜 🛄 💻

ⓐⓐⓐ ▼▼▼ Inn at Cross Keys Station H

(541) 475-5800. **Call for rates.** 66 NW Cedar St 97741. On US 26; north end of town. Int corridors. **Pets:** Medium, dogs only. $30 daily fee/pet. Designated rooms, service with restrictions, supervision.

SAVE ♿ 🛬 🛜 ✕ 🛄 💻

▼ Sonny's Motel M

(541) 475-7217. **$58-$150.** 1539 SW US 97 97741. South end of town. Ext corridors. **Pets:** Other species. $10 daily fee/room. Designated rooms, service with restrictions, supervision. 🛬 🛜 🛄

MEDFORD (Restaurants p. 638)

ⓐⓐⓐ ▼▼▼ BEST WESTERN Horizon Inn H

(541) 779-5085. **Call for rates.** 1154 E Barnett Rd 97504. I-5 exit 27 (Barnett Rd), just e. Ext corridors. **Pets:** Other species. $12 daily fee/pet. Designated rooms, service with restrictions, supervision.

SAVE 🛬 🛜 🛄 💻

ⓐⓐⓐ ▼▼▼ Candlewood Suites Medford Airport H

(541) 772-2800. **$85-$145, 3 day notice.** 3548 Heathrow Way 97504. I-5 exit 33, 1.5 mi se via E Pine St and Biddle Rd, just w on O'Hare Pkwy, then just n. Int corridors. **Pets:** Other species. $10 daily fee/room. Designated rooms, service with restrictions, crate.

SAVE ♿ 🛜 🛄 💻

ⓐⓐⓐ ▼▼▼ Comfort Inn North Medford H

(541) 772-9500. **$79-$159.** 2280 Biddle Rd 97504. I-5 exit 30 southbound, just ne on Crater Lake Hwy, follow signs to Biddle Rd/Airport, then just n; exit northbound, follow signs to Biddle Rd/Airport, just ne. Int corridors. **Pets:** Small, dogs only. $10 daily fee/pet. Designated rooms, service with restrictions. SAVE 🛬 🛜 ✕ 🛄 💻

ⓐⓐⓐ ▼◆▼ Comfort Inn South H

(541) 772-8000. **$79-$159.** 60 E Stewart Ave 97501. I-5 exit 27 (Barnett Rd), just w on Garfield St, 0.4 mi n on S Pacific Hwy, then just e. Int corridors. **Pets:** Small, dogs only. $10 daily fee/pet. Designated rooms, service with restrictions. SAVE 🛜 🛄 💻

ⓐⓐⓐ ▼▼▼▼ Homewood Suites by Hilton H ❀

(541) 779-9800. **$119-$189.** 2010 Hospitality Way 97504. I-5 exit 27 (Barnett Rd), 0.4 mi, just s on Ellendale Dr, then just w. Int corridors. **Pets:** Large, other species. $75 one-time fee/room. Service with restrictions, supervision. SAVE ♿ 🛬 🛜 🛄 💻

▼▼ Inn at the Commons H

(541) 779-5811. **Call for rates.** 200 N Riverside Ave 97501. I-5 exit 27 (Barnett Rd), 0.4 mi w on Garfield St, then 1.7 mi n on S Pacific Hwy. Ext corridors. **Pets:** Accepted. 🍴 ♿ 🛬 🛜 ✕ 🛄 💻

▼ Motel 6-Medford North-#739 M

(541) 779-0550. **$51-$65.** 2400 Biddle Rd 97504. I-5 exit 30 southbound, just ne on Crater Lake Hwy, follow signs to Biddle Rd/Airport, then just n; exit northbound, follow signs to Biddle Rd/Airport, just n. Ext corridors. **Pets:** Other species. Service with restrictions, crate. ♿ 🛬 🛜 🛄

(AAA) ▼▼▼ Quality Inn & Suites 🅷

(541) 779-0050. **$75-$95.** 1950 Biddle Rd 97504. I-5 exit 30 southbound, just ne on Crater Lake Hwy, follow signs to Biddle Rd/Airport, then just s; exit northbound, follow signs to Biddle Rd/Airport, then just s. Int corridors. **Pets:** Accepted.

[SAVE] [&M] [⇆] [⊠] [⌧] [✕] [♦] [▣]

(AAA) ▼▼▼ Ramada Medford and Convention Center 🅷

(541) 779-3141. **$70-$90.** 2250 Biddle Rd 97504. I-5 exit 30 southbound, just ne on Crater Lake Hwy, follow signs to Biddle Rd/Airport, then just s; exit northbound, follow signs to Biddle Rd/Airport, just s. Int corridors. **Pets:** Accepted. [SAVE] [⇆] [⊠] [♦] [▣]

▼▼▼ Rogue Regency Inn & Suites 🅷

(541) 770-1234. **$113-$128.** 2300 Biddle Rd 97504. I-5 exit 30 southbound, just ne on Crater Lake Hwy, follow signs to Biddle Rd/Airport, then just n; exit northbound, follow signs to Biddle Rd/Airport, then just n. Int corridors. **Pets:** Dogs only. Designated rooms, service with restrictions, supervision. [❦] [&M] [⇆] [⊠] [⌧] [♦] [▣]

▼▼ Shilo Inn-Medford 🅷

(541) 770-5151. **Call for rates.** 2111 Biddle Rd 97504. I-5 exit 30 southbound, just ne on Crater Lake Hwy, follow signs to Biddle Rd/Airport, then just s; exit northbound, follow signs to Biddle Rd/Airport, then just s. Int corridors. **Pets:** Accepted.

[⌧] [✕] [♦] [▣]

MERLIN

▼▼ Morrison's Rogue River Lodge 🅲🅰

(541) 476-3825. **Call for rates.** 8500 Galice Rd 97532. I-5 exit 61, 12 mi w on Merlin-Galice Rd. Ext/int corridors. **Pets:** Accepted.

[❦] [⇆] [⊠] [⌧] [✕] [♦] [▣]

MCMINNVILLE (Restaurants p. 638)

▼▼▼ Comfort Inn & Suites 🅷

(503) 472-1700. **$95-$185.** 2520 SE Stratus Ave 97128. Jct SR 99 W; 2.3 mi ne on SR 18; across from Willamette Valley Medical Center. Int corridors. **Pets:** Accepted. [&M] [⇆] [⌧] [✕] [♦] [▣]

(AAA) ▼▼▼ GuestHouse Vineyard Inn 🅷

(503) 472-4900. **$95-$131.** 2035 S SR 99 W 97128. Jct SR 99 W and 18. Int corridors. **Pets:** Accepted. [SAVE] [⇆] [⌧] [✕] [♦] [▣]

(AAA) ▼▼▼ McMinnville Inn 🅼

(503) 472-5187. **$69-$89, 3 day notice.** 381 NE SR 99 W 97128. North end of SR 99 W. Ext corridors. **Pets:** Medium, dogs only. $10 daily fee/pet. Designated rooms, service with restrictions, supervision.

[SAVE] [⌧] [♦] [▣]

(AAA) ▼▼▼ Red Lion Inn & Suites McMinnville 🅷

(503) 472-1500. **$95-$136.** 2535 NE Cumulus Ave 97128. Jct SR 99 W; 2.3 mi ne on SR 18. Int corridors. **Pets:** Accepted.

[SAVE] [&M] [⇆] [⌧] [✕] [♦] [▣]

MYRTLE POINT

(AAA) ▼ Myrtle Trees Motel 🅼

(541) 572-5811. **$76-$90.** 1010 8th St (SR 42) 97458. On SR 42, just s of center. Ext corridors. **Pets:** Accepted. [SAVE] [⌧] [✕] [✕] [♦]

NEWBERG

▼▼ The Allison Inn & Spa 🅷 ❖

(503) 554-2525. **$370-$1220, 3 day notice.** 2525 Allison Ln 97132. Jct Portland Rd (SR 99), 1 mi n on Springbrook Rd; north of center. Int corridors. **Pets:** Dogs only. $50 one-time fee/pet. Designated rooms, service with restrictions, supervision.

[ECO] [❦] [⇆] [⊠] [⌧] [✕] [♦]

(AAA) ▼▼▼ BEST WESTERN Newberg Inn 🅷

(503) 537-3000. **$85-$140.** 2211 Portland Rd 97132. Ne of center. Int corridors. **Pets:** Medium. $20 daily fee/pet. Designated rooms, service with restrictions, supervision. [SAVE] [⇆] [⊠] [⌧] [♦] [▣]

NEWPORT (Restaurants p. 638)

(AAA) ▼▼▼ BEST WESTERN Agate Beach Inn 🅷

(541) 265-9411. **$99-$175, 3 day notice.** 3019 N Coast Hwy (US 101) 97365. Jct US 20, 1.5 mi n on US 101. Int corridors. **Pets:** Accepted.

[SAVE] [❦] [⇆] [⌧] [✕] [✕] [♦] [▣]

▼▼▼ Elizabeth Street Inn 🅷 ❖

(541) 265-9400. **$170-$310.** 232 SW Elizabeth St 97365. Jct US 20, 0.5 mi s on US 101, just w on SW Falls St, just n. Int corridors. **Pets:** Large, dogs only. $25 one-time fee/room. Designated rooms, service with restrictions, supervision. [&M] [⇆] [⊠] [⌧] [✕] [♦] [▣]

▼▼▼ Hallmark Resort Newport 🅷

(541) 265-2600. **$89-$339.** 744 SW Elizabeth St 97365. Jct US 20, 0.7 mi s on US 101, just w on SW Bay St. Ext corridors. **Pets:** Accepted.

[❦] [&M] [⇆] [⊠] [⌧] [✕] [✕] [♦] [▣]

(AAA) ▼▼▼ The Landing at Newport 🅲🅾 ❖

(541) 574-6777. **$99-$388.** 890 SE Bay Blvd 97365. Jct US 101, 0.5 mi e on US 20, 0.3 mi s on Moore Dr. Ext corridors. **Pets:** $75 deposit/room, $25 one-time fee/room, $10 daily fee/room. Designated rooms, service with restrictions, supervision.

[SAVE] [&M] [⌧] [✕] [✕] [♦] [▣]

▼▼ La Quinta Inn & Suites Newport 🅷

(541) 867-7727. **$69-$259.** 45 SE 32nd St 97365. US 101, just s of Yaquina Bay Bridge, just e. Int corridors. **Pets:** Large, other species. Service with restrictions. [&M] [⇆] [⌧] [✕] [♦] [▣]

▼▼ Newport Belle Riverboat Bed & Breakfast 🅱🅱 ❖

(541) 867-6290. **$150-$165, 7 day notice.** 2126 SE Marine Science Dr, Dock H 97365. South end of Yaquina Bay Bridge, follow signs to Marine Science Center, around traffic circle exit at boat ramp, then just w; moored at Dock H. Ext corridors. **Pets:** Small, dogs only. $25 one-time fee/room. Designated rooms, service with restrictions.

[⌧] [✕] [✕] [☂] [☇] [♦] [▣]

▼▼ Shilo Inn Suites Oceanfront Hotel-Newport 🅷

(541) 265-7701. **Call for rates.** 536 SW Elizabeth St 97365. Jct US 20, 0.5 mi s on US 101, just w on SW Falls St. Ext/int corridors. **Pets:** Accepted. [❦] [⇆] [⌧] [✕] [✕] [♦] [▣]

(AAA) ▼▼▼ The Whaler Motel 🅼

(541) 265-9261. **$117-$197, 3 day notice.** 155 SW Elizabeth St 97365. Jct US 20, just s on US 101, 0.4 mi w on SW 2nd St. Ext corridors. **Pets:** Dogs only. $10 daily fee/pet. Designated rooms, service with restrictions, supervision. [SAVE] [&M] [⇆] [⌧] [✕] [✕] [♦] [▣]

NORTH BEND

▼▼▼ The Mill Casino & Hotel 🅷 ❖

(541) 756-8800. **$110-$175.** 3201 Tremont Ave (US 101) 97459. 0.7 mi n of Coos Bay on US 101; on bayfront. Int corridors. **Pets:** Large, dogs only. $25 one-time fee/pet. Designated rooms, service with restrictions, supervision. [◁] [❦] [&M] [⇆] [⊠] [♦] [▣]

▼▼▼ Quality Inn & Suites at Coos Bay 🅷

(541) 756-3191. **$100-$199.** 1503 Virginia Ave 97459. 0.5 mi w of US 101. Ext/int corridors. **Pets:** Small, dogs only. $25 daily fee/pet. Designated rooms, supervision. [&M] [⌧] [✕] [♦] [▣]

OAKLAND

▼▼ Motel 6-Rice Hill 🅷

(541) 849-3335. **$59-$75.** 621 John Long Rd 97462. I-5 exit 148, just e. Ext corridors. **Pets:** Other species. Service with restrictions, crate.

[◁] [⇆] [⌧] [♦]

OAKRIDGE

(AAA) ▼▼▼ BEST WESTERN Oakridge Inn 🅷

(541) 782-2212. **$104-$116.** 47433 SR 58 97463. West end of town. Ext corridors. **Pets:** Medium. $15 one-time fee/pet. Designated rooms, supervision. [SAVE] [⇆] [⌧] [♦] [▣]

AAA ♦ Cascade Motel **M** ❀

(541) 782-2489. **$53-$80.** 47487 SR 58 97463. West end of town. Ext corridors. **Pets:** Medium, dogs only. $10 one-time fee/room. Service with restrictions, supervision. [SAVE] 🛈 ⊠ 🖥

ONTARIO

AAA ♦♦ Clarion Inn **H** ❀

(541) 889-8621. **$124-$134.** 1249 Tapadera Ave 97914. I-84 exit 376B, just nw. Int corridors. **Pets:** Other species. $10 one-time fee/room. Designated rooms, service with restrictions, crate.

[SAVE] 🍴 ⊷ 🛈 🖥 🖳

OREGON CITY

AAA ♦♦ BEST WESTERN PLUS Rivershore Hotel **H**

(503) 655-7141. **$89-$299.** 1900 Clackamette Dr 97045. I-205 exit 9, just n. Int corridors. **Pets:** Accepted.

[SAVE] 🍴 ⊷ 🛈 ⊠ 🖥 🖳

PACIFIC CITY

♦♦♦ Inn at Cape Kiwanda **H** ❀

(503) 965-7001. **Call for rates.** 33105 Cape Kiwanda Dr 97135. Just w on Pacific Ave, 1 mi n. Ext corridors. **Pets:** Dogs only. $20 daily fee/ pet. Service with restrictions, supervision.

🍴 ⊷ 🛈 ⊠ 🖥 🖳

AAA ♦ Pacific City Inn **M**

(503) 965-6464. **$105, 7 day notice.** 35280 Brooten Rd 97135. Center. Ext corridors. **Pets:** Dogs only. $18 daily fee/pet. Designated rooms, service with restrictions, supervision.

[SAVE] 🍴 🛈 ⊠ 🖥 🖳

PENDLETON

♦♦ Americas Best Value Inn **M**

(541) 276-1400. **$79-$99.** 201 SW Court Ave 97801. I-84 exit 210 (SR 11), 0.7 mi ne on SE 3rd Dr, then 0.6 mi w. Ext corridors.

Pets: Accepted. ⊷ 🛈 ⊠ 🖥

AAA ♦♦♦ BEST WESTERN Pendleton Inn **H** ❀

(541) 276-2135. **$109-$139.** 400 SE Nye Ave 97801. I-84 exit 210 (SR 11), just se. Int corridors. **Pets:** Small. $20 one-time fee/pet. Designated rooms, service with restrictions, supervision.

[SAVE] 🛈 ⊷ 🛈 ⊠ 🖥 🖳

♦♦♦ Holiday Inn Express **H**

(541) 966-6520. **$119-$159.** 600 SE Nye Ave 97801. I-84 exit 210 (SR 11), just se. Int corridors. **Pets:** Other species. $20 daily fee/room. Designated rooms, service with restrictions, supervision.

🛈 ⊷ 🛈 ⊠ 🖥 🖳

♦ Motel 6 - #349 **M**

(541) 276-3160. **$49-$115.** 325 SE Nye Ave 97801. I-84 exit 210 (SR 11), just se. Ext corridors. **Pets:** Other species. Service with restrictions, crate. ⊷ 📶 🖥

AAA ♦♦♦ Oxford Suites Pendleton **H**

(541) 276-6000. **$99-$499.** 2400 SW Court Pl 97801. I-84 exit 209, just n on SW Emigrant Ave, just nw on SW 20th St, then just sw to SW Court Pl. Int corridors. **Pets:** Accepted.

[SAVE] 🛈 ⊷ 🛈 ⊠ 🖥 🖳

♦♦♦ Red Lion Hotel Pendleton **H**

(541) 276-6111. **$99-$249.** 304 SE Nye Ave 97801. I-84 exit 210 (SR 11), just sw. Int corridors. **Pets:** Accepted.

🍴 ⊷ 🛈 ⊠ 🖥 🖳

AAA ♦♦♦ Travelodge **M**

(541) 276-7531. **$59-$138.** 411 SW Dorion Ave 97801. I-84 exit 209, 0.9 mi ne on SW Frazer Ave, then just nw on SW 4th St. Ext corridors. **Pets:** Accepted. [SAVE] 🛈 ⊠ 🖥 🖳

PORTLAND *(Restaurants p. 638)*

AAA ♦♦♦ Aloft Portland Airport at Cascade Station **H**

(503) 200-5678. **$109-$209.** 9920 NE Cascades Pkwy 97220. I-205 exit 24A northbound; exit 24 southbound, 0.5 mi w on Airport Way, 0.5 mi s on NE Mt Hood Ave, then just e. Int corridors. **Pets:** Accepted.

[SAVE] [ECO] 🛈 ⊷ 🛈 ⊠ 🖥 🖳

AAA ♦♦♦ The Benson Hotel, a Coast Hotel **H**

(503) 228-2000. **$169-$399.** 309 SW Broadway 97205. At SW Broadway and Oak St. Int corridors. **Pets:** Accepted.

[SAVE] 🍴 🛈 🛈 ⊠ 🖥 🖳

AAA ♦♦♦ BEST WESTERN Inn at the Meadows **H** ❀

(503) 286-9600. **$88-$228.** 1215 N Hayden Meadows Dr 97217. I-5 exit 306B, just e. Int corridors. **Pets:** Medium, dogs only. $30 daily fee/ room. Designated rooms, service with restrictions, supervision.

[SAVE] 🛈 ⊠ 🖥 🖳

AAA ♦♦♦ BEST WESTERN Pony Soldier Inn-Airport **H**

(503) 256-1504. **$90-$142.** 9901 NE Sandy Blvd 97220. I-205 exit 23A, just e. Int corridors. **Pets:** $10 daily fee/room. Service with restrictions, crate. [SAVE] 🛈 ⊷ ⊠ 🛈 🖥 🖳

AAA ♦♦♦ Candlewood Suites-Portland Airport **H** ❀

(503) 255-4003. **$89-$199.** 11250 NE Holman St 97220. I-205 exit 24B northbound; exit 24 southbound, 0.4 mi e on Airport Way, then just sw. Int corridors. **Pets:** Small, dogs only. $75 one-time fee/pet. Designated rooms, service with restrictions, supervision.

[SAVE] 🛈 🛈 ⊠ 🖥 🖳

♦♦♦ Courtyard by Marriott Portland City Center **H** ❀

(503) 505-5000. **$139-$299.** 550 SW Oak St 97204. At SW Oak St and SW 6th Ave. Int corridors. **Pets:** Other species. $50 one-time fee/room. Designated rooms, service with restrictions, crate.

[ECO] 🍴 🛈 🛈 ⊠ 🖥 🖳

♦♦ Days Inn-Portland **H**

(503) 289-1800. **$85-$105.** 9930 N Whitaker Rd 97217. I-5 exit 306B, just e. Int corridors. **Pets:** Other species. $10 daily fee/pet. Service with restrictions, supervision. 🛈 🖥 🖳

AAA ♦♦♦ DoubleTree by Hilton Portland **H**

(503) 281-6111. **$110-$275.** 1000 NE Multnomah St 97232. I-5 exit 302A, just e, just s on 9th Ave, then just e; I-84 exit Lloyd Center westbound. Int corridors. **Pets:** Accepted.

[SAVE] [ECO] ▣ 🍴 🛈 ⊷ 🛈 ⊠ 🖥 🖳

♦♦♦ Embassy Suites at Portland Airport **H**

(503) 460-3000. **$107-$209.** 7900 NE 82nd Ave 97220. I-205 exit 24A northbound; exit 24 southbound, 1.3 mi w. Int corridors. **Pets:** Accepted.

🍴 🛈 ⊷ 📶 ⊠ 🖥 🖳

AAA ♦♦♦ The Heathman Hotel **H** ❀

(503) 241-4100. **$249-$2500, 7 day notice.** 1001 SW Broadway 97205. At SW Broadway and Salmon St. Int corridors. **Pets:** Dogs only. $35 daily fee/pet. Service with restrictions, supervision.

[SAVE] [ECO] 🍴 🛈 🛈 ⊠ 🖳

AAA ♦♦♦ Hilton Portland & Executive Tower **H**

(503) 226-1611. **$139-$329.** 921 SW 6th Ave 97204. I-405 exit 1B (6th Ave); at 6th Ave and Taylor St. Int corridors. **Pets:** Large. $25 one-time fee/room. Service with restrictions, supervision.

[SAVE] [ECO] 🍴 ⊷ 🛈 📶 ⊠ 🖥 🖳

AAA ♦♦♦ Holiday Inn Express Hotel & Suites at Jantzen Beach **H**

(503) 283-8000. **$84-$204.** 2300 N Hayden Island Dr 97217. I-5 exit 308, 0.6 mi w. Int corridors. **Pets:** $25 daily fee/room. Service with restrictions, supervision. [SAVE] 🛈 ⊷ 🛈 📶 ⊠ 🖥 🖳

▼▼▼ Holiday Inn Portland Airport Hotel & Convention Center H

(503) 256-5000. **$99-$179.** 8439 NE Columbia Blvd 97220. I-205 exit 23B, 0.5 mi w. Int corridors. **Pets:** Medium, dogs only. $25 daily fee/pet. Designated rooms, service with restrictions, supervision.

▼▼ Hospitality Inn H

(503) 244-6684. **$85-$135, 3 day notice.** 10155 SW Capitol Hwy 97219. I-5 exit 295 southbound, just e; exit 294 northbound, 1 mi n on SW Barbur Blvd, then just e. Int corridors. **Pets:** Medium, dogs only. $15 daily fee/pet. Designated rooms, service with restrictions, supervision.

▼▼▼ Hotel deLuxe H

(503) 219-2094. **$149-$599.** 729 SW 15th Ave 97205. I-5 to I-405 exit Salmon St northbound, just n on 14th Ave, w on Morrison St, then s; exit Couch St/Burnside St southbound; at SW 15th Ave and Yamhill St. Int corridors. **Pets:** Accepted.

▼▼▼ Hotel Lucia H

(503) 225-1717. **$169-$449, 3 day notice.** 400 SW Broadway 97205. At SW Broadway and Stark St. Int corridors. **Pets:** Accepted.

▼▼▼ Hotel Modera H

(503) 484-1084. **$139-$599, 3 day notice.** 515 SW Clay St 97201. Between 5th and 6th sts. Int corridors. **Pets:** Accepted.

▼▼▼▼ Hotel Monaco Portland-A Kimpton Hotel H 🐾

(503) 222-0001. **$159-$459.** 506 SW Washington St 97204. At SW 5th Ave and SW Washington St. Int corridors. **Pets:** Other species. Designated rooms, service with restrictions, supervision.

▼▼▼▼ Hotel Vintage Portland-A Kimpton Hotel H

(503) 228-1212. **$159-$429.** 422 SW Broadway 97205. At Broadway and Washington St. Int corridors. **Pets:** Accepted.

▼▼▼ Hyatt Place Portland Airport/Cascade Station H

(503) 288-2808. **$84-$189.** 9750 NE Cascades Pkwy 97220. I-205 exit 24A northbound; exit 24 southbound, 0.5 mi w on Airport Way, 0.5 mi s on NE Mt Hood Ave, then just e. Int corridors. **Pets:** Medium, dogs only. $75 one-time fee/room. Service with restrictions, crate.

▼▼ La Quinta Inn & Suites Portland Airport H

(503) 382-3820. **$74-$234.** 11207 NE Holman St 97220. I-205 exit 24B northbound; exit 24 southbound, 0.4 mi e on Airport Way, then just sw. Int corridors. **Pets:** Large, other species. Service with restrictions.

▼▼▼ The Mark Spencer Hotel H 🐾

(503) 224-3293. **$159-$299.** 409 SW 11th Ave 97205. At SW Stark St and SW 11th Ave. Int corridors. **Pets:** Other species. $25 daily fee/pet. Designated rooms, service with restrictions.

◆ Motel 6 North Portland - #4198 H

(503) 247-3700. **$49-$80.** 1125 N Schmeer Rd 97217. I-5 exit 306B, 0.4 mi s on N Whitaker Rd, then just e. Int corridors. **Pets:** Other species. Service with restrictions, crate.

▼▼▼▼ The Nines H

(503) 222-9996. **$169-$599.** 525 SW Morrison St 97204. At SW Morrison St and SW 5th Ave. Int corridors. **Pets:** Accepted.

▼▼▼ Oxford Suites Portland-Jantzen Beach H 🐾

(503) 283-3030. **$95-$199.** 12226 N Jantzen Dr 97217. I-5 exit 308, just e on Hayden Island Dr. Int corridors. **Pets:** $25 one-time fee/pet. Service with restrictions, supervision.

▼▼ The Portlander Inn H

(503) 345-0300. **$80-$120.** 10350 N Vancouver Way 97217. I-5 exit 307, follow signs for Marine Dr E, just ne, then 0.7 mi se. Int corridors. **Pets:** Accepted.

▼▼▼ Ramada Portland South I-205 H

(503) 252-7400. **$79-$99.** 9707 SE Stark St 97216. I-205 exit 21A southbound; exit 20 northbound, just e on Washington St, just n on SE 99th Ave, then just w. Int corridors. **Pets:** Accepted.

▼▼▼ Red Lion Hotel on the River Jantzen Beach-Portland H

(503) 283-4466. **$99-$189.** 909 N Hayden Island Dr 97217. I-5 exit 308, just ne. Int corridors. **Pets:** Accepted.

▼▼▼ Red Lion Hotel Portland Airport H

(503) 255-6722. **Call for rates.** 7101 NE 82nd Ave 97220. I-205 exit 24A northbound; exit 24 southbound, 1.3 mi w on NE Airport Way, then 0.5 mi s. Ext/int corridors. **Pets:** Accepted.

▼▼▼ Residence Inn by Marriott Portland Airport at Cascade Station H

(503) 284-1800. **$119-$279.** 9301 NE Cascades Pkwy 97220. I-205 exit 24A northbound; exit 24 southbound, 0.5 mi w on Airport Way, 0.5 mi s on NE Mt Hood Ave, then just w. Int corridors. **Pets:** Accepted.

▼▼▼ Residence Inn by Marriott Portland Downtown at RiverPlace H

(503) 552-9500. **$129-$299.** 2115 SW River Pkwy 97201. At SW Moody Ave and SW River Pkwy; on Willamette River Waterfront. Int corridors. **Pets:** Accepted.

▼▼▼ Residence Inn by Marriott Portland Downtown/ Lloyd Center H

(503) 288-1400. **$129-$289.** 1710 NE Multnomah St 97232. I-5 exit 302A, 0.8 mi e on Weidler St, then just s on 15th Ave; I-84 exit 1 (Lloyd Center) westbound, just n on 13th St, then just e. Ext corridors. **Pets:** Accepted.

▼▼▼ Residence Inn by Marriott Portland Downtown/Pearl District H 🐾

(503) 220-1339. **$239-$296.** 1150 NW 9th Ave 97209. Between NW Marshall and NW Northrup sts. Int corridors. **Pets:** Other species. $100 one-time fee/room. Service with restrictions, crate.

▼▼▼ Residence Inn by Marriott-Portland North Harbour H

(503) 285-9888. **$149-$269.** 1250 N Anchor Way 97217. I-5 exit 307, follow signs to Marine Dr E, then just n. Int corridors. **Pets:** Accepted.

▼▼▼▼ RiverPlace Hotel-A Kimpton Hotel H 🐾

(503) 228-3233. **$189-$950.** 1510 SW Harbor Way 97201. At Naito Pkwy (formerly Front Ave) and SW Harbor Way. Int corridors. **Pets:** Other species. Crate.

▼▼▼ River's Edge Hotel & Spa H

(503) 802-5800. **$189-$499.** 0455 SW Hamilton Ct 97239. I-5 exit 298 northbound, just s on SW Corbett Ave, e on SW Richardson Ct, 0.3 mi n on Macadam Ave (SR 43), then just e; exit 299A southbound, follow signs for Johns Landing/Lake Oswego, 0.8 mi s, then just e. Int corridors. **Pets:** Accepted.

△△△▽ ▽▽▽▽ Sentinel H ❖
(503) 224-3400. **$169-$499, 3 day notice.** 614 SW 11th Ave 97205. At 11th Ave and Alder St. Int corridors. **Pets:** $45 one-time fee/room. Service with restrictions, supervision. [SAVE] [❶] [👋M] [📶] [✕] [❶] [💻]

△△△▽ ▽▽▽▽ Sheraton Portland Airport Hotel H
(503) 281-2500. **$109-$309.** 8235 NE Airport Way 97220. I-205 exit 24A northbound; exit 24 southbound, 1.5 mi w. Int corridors. **Pets:** Dogs only. Service with restrictions, supervision.
[SAVE] [❶] [👋M] [👋] [✕] [📶] [✕] [💻]

▽▽ ▽▽ Shilo Inn-Portland/Rose Garden H
(503) 736-6300. **Call for rates.** 1506 NE 2nd Ave 97232. I-5 exit 302A, just e on NE Weidler St, then just s. Int corridors. **Pets:** Accepted.
[📶] [✕] [❶] [💻]

▽▽ ▽▽ Shilo Inn Suites Hotel-Portland Airport H
(503) 252-7500. **Call for rates.** 11707 NE Airport Way 97220. I-205 exit 24B northbound; exit 24 southbound, 0.5 mi e. Int corridors.
Pets: Accepted. [❶] [👋M] [👋] [✕] [📶] [✕] [❶] [💻]

▽▽▽▽ Staybridge Suites Portland-Airport H
(503) 262-8888. **Call for rates.** 11936 NE Glenn Widing Dr 97220. I-205 exit 24B northbound; exit 24 southbound, 0.7 mi e, then just nw. Int corridors. **Pets:** Accepted. [👋M] [👋] [📶] [✕] [❶] [💻]

▽▽ ▽▽ University Place Hotel & Conference Center H
(503) 221-0140. **Call for rates.** 310 SW Lincoln St 97201. I-5 to I-405 exit 4th Ave, just n, then just e. Ext/int corridors. **Pets:** Dogs only. $15 daily fee/pet. Designated rooms, service with restrictions, supervision.
[❶] [👋] [✕] [❶] [💻]

△△△▽ ▽▽▽▽ ▽▽▽▽ The Westin Portland H
(503) 294-9000. **$179-$329.** 750 SW Alder St 97205. At Park Ave and SW Alder St. Int corridors. **Pets:** Accepted.
[SAVE] [❶] [👋M] [📶] [✕] [💻]

PRINEVILLE
▽▽ Econo Lodge M
(541) 447-6231. **$59-$89.** 123 NE 3rd St 97754. On US 26; downtown. Int corridors. **Pets:** Medium, dogs only. $10 daily fee/pet. Supervision.
[📶] [❶] [💻]

PROSPECT
▽▽ Prospect Historic Hotel, Motel & Dinner House M ❖
(541) 560-3664. **$75-$210.** 391 Mill Creek Dr 97536. Jct SR 62, 0.7 mi e of MM 43, 0.3 mi s on 1st St, then just w. Ext/int corridors.
Pets: Other species. $20 one-time fee/pet. Designated rooms, service with restrictions, supervision. [❶] [📶] [✕] [❶] [💻]

REDMOND
▽▽▽▽ Comfort Suites Airport H
(541) 504-8900. **$99-$199.** 2243 SW Yew Ave 97756. US 97 exit 124 (Yew Ave/Airport Way/Redmond Airport), just nw; 2 mi s of jct SR 126. Int corridors. **Pets:** $25 one-time fee/room. Service with restrictions, supervision. [👋] [📶] [✕] [❶] [💻]

△△△▽ ▽▽▽▽ The Lodge At Eagle Crest, A Holiday Inn Resort H
(541) 923-2453. **$109-$229, 3 day notice.** 1522 Cline Falls Rd 97756. 4.5 mi w of center on SR 126, 1 mi s. Int corridors. **Pets:** Other species. $25 one-time fee/room. Designated rooms, service with restrictions, crate. [SAVE] [❶] [👋M] [👋] [📶] [✕] [❶] [💻]

△△△▽ ▽▽▽▽ Redmond Inn Motel M
(541) 548-1091. **$45-$125.** 1545 S US 97 97756. Jct SR 126, 0.7 mi s. Ext corridors. **Pets:** Medium. $5 deposit/pet, $5 daily fee/pet. Service with restrictions, supervision. [SAVE] [👋] [📶] [❶] [💻]

△△△▽ ▽▽▽▽ Sleep Inn & Suites Redmond H ❖
(541) 504-1500. **$99-$199.** 1847 NW US 97 97756. US 97 exit 119, 0.6 mi s on Business Rt US 97; 1 mi n of downtown. Int corridors.
Pets: Medium, other species. $10 one-time fee/pet. Designated rooms, supervision. [SAVE] [👋M] [👋] [📶] [✕] [❶] [💻]

REEDSPORT (Restaurants p. 638)
△△△▽ ▽▽▽ BEST WESTERN Salbasgeon Inn & Suites of Reedsport H
(541) 271-4831. **$110-$386.** 1400 US 101 S 97467. Jct SR 38, 0.4 mi s. Ext corridors. **Pets:** Medium, dogs only. $20 daily fee/pet. Designated rooms, service with restrictions, supervision.
[SAVE] [👋] [📶] [✕] [❶] [💻]

ROCKAWAY BEACH
△△△▽ ▽▽▽ Silver Sands Oceanfront Motel H
(503) 355-2206. **$88-$166.** 215 S Pacific St 97136. US 101, just w on SW 2nd Ave. Ext corridors. **Pets:** Accepted.
[SAVE] [👋] [✕] [📶] [✕] [✕] [❶] [💻]

ROSEBURG (Restaurants p. 638)
△△△▽ ▽▽▽ BEST WESTERN Garden Villa Inn M ❖
(541) 672-1601. **$80-$170.** 760 NW Garden Valley Blvd 97470. I-5 exit 125, just nw. Ext corridors. **Pets:** $15 daily fee/pet. Service with restrictions, supervision. [SAVE] [👋] [📶] [✕] [❶] [💻]

▽▽▽ Holiday Inn Express H
(541) 673-7517. **Call for rates.** 375 W Harvard Blvd 97470. I-5 exit 124, just se. Ext/int corridors. **Pets:** $15 daily fee/room. Designated rooms, service with restrictions, supervision.
[👋M] [👋] [📶] [✕] [❶] [💻]

▽▽ Motel 6-#4108 H
(541) 464-8000. **$55-$120.** 3100 NW Aviation Dr 97470. I-5 exit 127, just se. Int corridors. **Pets:** Other species. Service with restrictions, crate. [👋M] [📶] [❶]

△△△▽ ▽▽▽ Quality Inn M
(541) 673-5561. **$99-$119.** 427 NW Garden Valley Blvd 97470. I-5 exit 125, just se. Ext corridors. **Pets:** Dogs only. $10 one-time fee/room. Designated rooms, service with restrictions, supervision.
[SAVE] [👋] [📶] [❶] [💻]

△△△▽ ▽▽▽ Roseburg Travelodge M
(541) 672-4836. **$95-$115.** 315 W Harvard Ave 97470. I-5 exit 124, just se. Ext corridors. **Pets:** Medium. $10 deposit/pet, $10 daily fee/pet. Designated rooms, service with restrictions, supervision.
[SAVE] [👋] [📶] [❶] [💻]

△△△▽ ▽▽ Shady Oaks Motel M
(541) 672-2608. **$45-$79.** 2954 Old Hwy 99 S 97471. I-5 exit 120, 0.5 mi n. Ext corridors. **Pets:** Dogs only. $10 daily fee/pet. Designated rooms, service with restrictions, supervision. [SAVE] [📶] [❶]

▽▽ ▽▽ Sleep Inn & Suites H
(541) 464-8338. **$95-$160.** 2855 NW Edenbower Blvd 97471. I-5 exit 127, just sw. Int corridors. **Pets:** Accepted.
[👋M] [👋] [📶] [✕] [❶] [💻]

▽▽ ▽▽ Super 8 H
(541) 672-8880. **$69-$83.** 3200 NW Aviation Dr 97470. I-5 exit 127, just ne. Int corridors. **Pets:** $10 daily fee/pet. Service with restrictions, supervision. [👋M] [👋] [📶] [✕] [❶] [💻]

△△△▽ ▽▽▽ Windmill Inn of Roseburg H ❖
(541) 673-0901. **Call for rates.** 1450 NW Mulholland Dr 97470. I-5 exit 125, just e, then just n. Int corridors. **Pets:** Dogs only. $10 one-time fee/room. Designated rooms, service with restrictions, supervision.
[SAVE] [👋] [📶] [✕] [❶] [💻]

ST. HELENS

BEST WESTERN Oak Meadows Inn H ❖

(503) 397-3000. **$121-$180.** 585 S Columbia River Hwy (US 30) 97051. South end of town. Int corridors. **Pets:** Other species. $20 one-time fee/pet. SAVE

SALEM *(Restaurants p. 638)*

BEST WESTERN Pacific Highway Inn H ❖

(503) 390-3200. **$85-$120.** 4646 Portland Rd NE 97305. I-5 exit 258, 0.3 mi e. Ext corridors. **Pets:** Dogs only. $20 daily fee/room. Designated rooms, service with restrictions, supervision.

BEST WESTERN PLUS Mill Creek Inn H

(503) 585-3332. **$127-$162.** 3125 Ryan Dr SE 97301. I-5 exit 253, just w on Mission St (SR 22), just n on Hawthorne Ave SE, then just w. Int corridors. **Pets:** Dogs only. $20 daily fee/room. Service with restrictions, supervision. SAVE

Comfort Suites Airport H ❖

(503) 585-9705. **$129-$275.** 630 Hawthorne Ave SE 97301. I-5 exit 253, just w on Mission St (SR 22), 0.3 mi n on Hawthorne Ave SE, then just e; on Creekside Corporate Center (private drive). Int corridors. **Pets:** Medium. $25 daily fee/pet. Designated rooms, service with restrictions, supervision.

Days Inn Black Bear H

(503) 581-1559. **$60-$110.** 1600 Motor Ct NE 97301. I-5 exit 256, just e on Market St NE, then just s. Ext corridors. **Pets:** Medium. $11 daily fee/room. Designated rooms, service with restrictions, supervision. SAVE

DoubleTree by Hilton Salem-Oregon H

(503) 581-7004. **$129-$179.** 1590 Weston Ct NE 97301. I-5 exit 256, just w on Market St, then just s. Int corridors. **Pets:** $15 daily fee/pet. Designated rooms, service with restrictions, supervision. SAVE

Howard Johnson Inn H

(503) 375-7710. **$55-$100.** 2250 Mission St SE 97302. I-5 exit 253, 1.4 mi w. Int corridors. **Pets:** Small, dogs only. $15 daily fee/pet. Designated rooms, service with restrictions, supervision. SAVE

La Quinta Inn & Suites Salem H

(503) 391-7000. **$79-$229.** 890 Hawthorne Ave SE 97301. I-5 exit 253, just w on Mission St (SR 22), then just n. Int corridors. **Pets:** Large, other species. Service with restrictions. SAVE

Phoenix Inn Suites-South Salem H

(503) 588-9220. **Call for rates.** 4370 Commercial St SE 97302. I-5 exit 252, 1.5 mi w on Kuebler Blvd, then 0.7 mi n. Int corridors. **Pets:** Accepted.

Residence Inn by Marriott H

(503) 585-6500. **$169-$189.** 640 Hawthorne Ave SE 97301. I-5 exit 253, just w on Mission St (SR 22), 0.3 mi n on Hawthorne Ave SE, then just e; on Creekside Corporate Center (private drive). Int corridors. **Pets:** Medium. $100 one-time fee/room. Designated rooms, service with restrictions, crate.

Shilo Inn Suites-Salem H

(503) 581-4001. **Call for rates.** 3304 Market St NE 97301. I-5 exit 256, just w. Int corridors. **Pets:** Accepted.

Super 8 Salem H

(503) 370-8888. **$55-$115.** 1288 Hawthorne Ave NE 97301. I-5 exit 256, just w on Market St, then just s. Int corridors. **Pets:** Small. $10 daily fee/pet. Designated rooms, supervision.

SANDY

BEST WESTERN Sandy Inn H

(503) 668-7100. **$106-$146.** 37465 US 26 97055. West side of town. Int corridors. **Pets:** Accepted. SAVE

SEASIDE

BEST WESTERN Ocean View Resort H

(503) 738-3334. **$79-$229, 7 day notice.** 414 N Prom 97138. US 101 exit 1st Ave, just w, just n on Necanicum Dr, then just w on 4th Ave. Ext/int corridors. **Pets:** Accepted. SAVE

Comfort Inn & Suites by Seaside Convention Center/Boardwalk H ❖

(503) 738-3011. **$89-$499.** 545 Broadway St 97138. US 101, just w on Ave A; downtown. Int corridors. **Pets:** Medium, dogs only. $25 daily fee/pet. Designated rooms, service with restrictions, supervision. SAVE

Ebb-Tide Resort H

(503) 738-8371. **Call for rates.** 300 N Prom 97138. US 101 exit 1st Ave, 0.4 mi w, just n on Columbia St, then just w on 2nd Ave. Ext/int corridors. **Pets:** Accepted. SAVE

GuestHouse Inn & Suites Seaside H

(503) 738-8971. **Call for rates.** 2455 S Roosevelt Dr (US 101) 97138. Just s of downtown on US 101. Int corridors. **Pets:** Accepted.

Hi-Tide Resort M

(503) 738-8414. **$100-$160, 3 day notice.** 30 Ave G 97138. US 101 exit Ave G, 0.6 mi w. Ext corridors. **Pets:** Accepted. SAVE

Holiday Inn Express Hotel & Suites-Seaside Convention Center H

(503) 717-8000. **$89-$499.** 34 N Holladay Dr 97138. US 101 exit Broadway St, just w, then just n. Int corridors. **Pets:** Medium, dogs only. $25 daily fee/pet. Designated rooms, service with restrictions, supervision. SAVE

Inn at Seaside H

(503) 738-9581. **$79-$299, 3 day notice.** 441 2nd Ave 97138. US 101 exit 1st Ave, just w. Ext/int corridors. **Pets:** Accepted. SAVE

Inn At The Shore M

(503) 738-3113. **Call for rates.** 2275 S Prom 97138. US 101 exit Ave U, just w. Ext corridors. **Pets:** Accepted.

River Inn at Seaside H ❖

(503) 717-5744. **Call for rates.** 531 Ave A 97138. US 101, just w; downtown. Int corridors. **Pets:** $20 daily fee/pet. Service with restrictions.

Rivertide Suites Hotel H

(503) 717-1100. **$79-$449.** 102 N Holladay Dr 97138. US 101, just w on Broadway St, just n. Int corridors. **Pets:** Accepted. SAVE

Seashore Inn...on the Beach H

(503) 738-6368. **$75-$289.** 60 N Prom 97138. US 101 exit 1st Ave, 0.4 mi w. Ext/int corridors. **Pets:** Small. $20 daily fee/pet. Designated rooms, service with restrictions, supervision. SAVE

The Seaside Oceanfront Inn & Restaurant H

(503) 738-6403. **$99-$319, 5 day notice.** 581 S Prom 97138. US 101 exit Ave G, 0.6 mi w, then just n. Int corridors. **Pets:** Dogs only. $25 daily fee/pet. Designated rooms, supervision.

▼▼▼ **Shilo Inn Suites Oceanfront Hotel-Seaside** 🅷

(503) 738-9571. **Call for rates.** 30 N Prom 97138. US 101 exit Broadway St, 0.4 mi w. Ext corridors. **Pets:** Accepted.

🍴 🐕 ⊠ 📶 ✕ 🎿 📧 🖵

SISTERS

🆎 ▼▼▼ **BEST WESTERN Ponderosa Lodge** Ⓜ ❀

(541) 549-1234. **$110-$180.** 500 US 20 W 97759. Jct SR 242, 1.3 mi w on US 20; at Barclay Dr. Ext corridors. **Pets:** Large, dogs only. $15 daily fee/room. Designated rooms, service with restrictions, supervision.

[SAVE] 🐕 📶 ✕ 📧 🖵

🆎 ▼▼▼▼ **FivePine Lodge & Spa** 🅲🅰 ❀

(541) 549-5900. **$149-$329, 7 day notice.** 1021 Desperado Tr 97759. Jct SR 126 and US 20, just e on US 20; east end of town. Int corridors. **Pets:** $25 daily fee/room. Designated rooms, service with restrictions, crate. [SAVE] 🍴 🐕 ⊠ 📶 ✕ 📧 🖵

SPRINGFIELD

🆎 ▼▼ **BEST WESTERN Grand Manor Inn** 🅷

(541) 726-4769. **Call for rates.** 971 Kruse Way 97477. I-5 exit 195A, just se. Int corridors. **Pets:** Accepted.

[SAVE] 🛗 🐕 📶 ✕ 📧 🖵

▼▼▼ **Comfort Suites Springfield** 🅷 🐾

(541) 746-5359. **$99-$189.** 969 Kruse Way 97477. I-5 exit 195, just se. Int corridors. **Pets:** Other species. $25 one-time fee/room. Designated rooms, service with restrictions, supervision. 🐕 📶 ✕ 📧 🖵

▼▼▼ **Holiday Inn Eugene-Springfield** 🅷

(541) 284-0707. **$119-$169.** 919 Kruse Way 97477. I-5 exit 195A, just se. Int corridors. **Pets:** Accepted.

🎴 🍴 🛗 🐕 📶 ✕ 📧 🖵

▼▼▼ **Holiday Inn Express Hotel & Suites** 🅷

(541) 746-8471. **$109-$189.** 3480 Hutton St 97477. I-5 exit 195A, just se. Int corridors. **Pets:** Accepted. 🐕 📶 ✕ 📧 🖵

▼ **Motel 6-#418** Ⓜ

(541) 741-1105. **$55-$101.** 3752 International Ct 97477. I-5 exit 195A, just e on Beltline Rd, just nw on Gateway St, then just n. Ext corridors. **Pets:** Other species. Service with restrictions, crate.

🛗 🐕 🛋 📧

▼▼ **Quality Inn & Suites** 🅷

(541) 726-9266. **$99-$179.** 3550 Gateway St 97477. I-5 exit 195A, just e on Beltline Rd, then just nw. Int corridors. **Pets:** Other species. $5 daily fee/pet. Designated rooms, service with restrictions, supervision.

🛗 🐕 📶 📧 🖵

🆎 ▼▼▼ **Super 8** 🅷

(541) 746-1314. **$65-$91.** 3315 Gateway St 97477. I-5 exit 195A, just e on Beltline Rd, then just s. Int corridors. **Pets:** Accepted.

[SAVE] 📶 📧 🖵

▼▼ **Village Inn** Ⓜ

(541) 747-4546. **$69-$129.** 1875 Mohawk Blvd 97477. I-5 exit 194A, 2.5 mi e on SR 126 exit Mohawk Blvd, then just n. Ext corridors. **Pets:** Other species. $10 daily fee/pet. Service with restrictions.

🐕 ⊠ 📶 📧 🖵

SUNRIVER

🆎 ▼▼▼▼ **Sunriver Resort** 🅷 🐾

(541) 593-1000. **$119-$359, 21 day notice.** 17600 Center Dr 97707. US 97 exit 153 (S Century Dr), 1.5 mi w to Abbott Dr, then 0.6 mi w. Ext corridors. **Pets:** Other species. $75 one-time fee/room. Designated rooms, service with restrictions, supervision.

[SAVE] 🍴 🐕 ⊠ 📶 ✕ 📧 🖵

SUTHERLIN

🆎 ▼▼▼ **BEST WESTERN PLUS Hartford Lodge** 🅷 ❀

(541) 459-1424. **$100-$160.** 150 Myrtle St 97479. I-5 exit 136, just ne. Ext corridors. **Pets:** $20 daily fee/pet. Designated rooms, service with restrictions, supervision. [SAVE] 🐕 📶 ✕ 📧 🖵

▼▼ **GuestHouse Inn & Suites Sutherlin** 🅷 ❀

(541) 459-6800. **Call for rates.** 1400 Hospitality Way 97479. I-5 exit 136, just se. Int corridors. **Pets:** Other species. $10 daily fee/room. Designated rooms, service with restrictions, supervision.

🛗 📶 ✕ 📧 🖵

SWEET HOME

🆎 ▼▼▼ **Sweet Home Inn** Ⓜ

(541) 367-5137. **$69-$155.** 805 Long St 97386. Just se of jct US 20 and SR 228, just s on 10th Ave, just w; jct Terrace Ln. Ext corridors. **Pets:** Medium, dogs only. $10 daily fee/pet. Service with restrictions, supervision. [SAVE] 📶 📧 🖵

THE DALLES

▼▼ **Celilo Inn** Ⓜ

(541) 769-0001. **$99-$300.** 3550 E 2nd St 97058. I-84 exit 87, just s on US 197, just w on US 30, then 0.8 mi ne on SE Frontage Rd. Ext corridors. **Pets:** Accepted. 🐕 📶 ✕ 📧 🖵

▼▼ **Comfort Inn Columbia Gorge** 🅷

(541) 298-2800. **$79-$299.** 351 Lone Pine Dr 97058. I-84 exit 87, just nw. Int corridors. **Pets:** Other species. $15 daily fee/pet. Designated rooms, service with restrictions, supervision.

🐕 ⊠ 📶 ✕ 📧 🖵

▼▼ **Cousins' Country Inn** Ⓜ

(541) 298-5161. **$69-$155.** 2114 W 6th St 97058. I-84 exit 83 eastbound, just nw; exit 84 westbound, just nw on W 2nd St, just sw on Webber St, then just n. Ext corridors. **Pets:** Accepted.

🎴 🍴 🛗 🐕 📶 📧 🖵

▼▼ **The Dalles Inn** 🅷 ❀

(541) 296-9107. **$79-$199.** 112 W 2nd St 97058. I-84 exit 84 eastbound, 0.6 mi se; exit 85 westbound, 0.8 mi nw; at Liberty and W 2nd sts; downtown. Ext/int corridors. **Pets:** Dogs only. $12 daily fee/pet. Designated rooms, service with restrictions, crate.

🛗 🐕 📶 📧 🖵

▼▼▼ **Fairfield Inn & Suites by Marriott-The Dalles** 🅷

(541) 769-0753. **$129-$155.** 2014 W 7th St 97058. I-84 exit 83 eastbound, just nw on W 6th St, then just sw on Walnut St; exit 84 westbound, 0.3 mi nw on W 2nd St, just sw on Webber St, 0.3 mi nw on W 6th St, then just sw on Walnut St. Int corridors. **Pets:** Accepted.

🛗 📶 ✕ 📧 🖵

▼ **Motel 6-#4268** 🅷

(541) 296-1191. **Call for rates.** 2500 W 6th St 97058. I-84 exit 83 eastbound, just nw; exit 84 westbound, just nw on W 2nd St, just sw on Webber St, then just n. Int corridors. **Pets:** Other species. Service with restrictions, crate. 🛗 🐕 📶 📧

▼▼ **Shilo Inn Suites Hotel-The Dalles** 🅷

(541) 298-5502. **Call for rates.** 3223 Bret Clodfelter Way 97058. I-84 exit 87, just ne. Int corridors. **Pets:** Accepted.

🍴 🐕 📶 ✕ 📧 🖵

▼▼ **Super 8** 🅷

(541) 296-6888. **$80-$135.** 609 Cherry Heights Rd 97058. I-84 exit 84 eastbound, just se on W 2nd St, then just sw; exit westbound, just nw on W 2nd St, just sw on Webber St, then just se on W 8th St. Int corridors. **Pets:** Accepted. 🐕 📶 ✕ 📧 🖵

TIGARD

🆎 ▼▼▼ **DoubleTree by Hilton Hotel Portland – Tigard** 🅷

(503) 624-9000. **Call for rates.** 9575 SW Locust St 97223. SR 217 exit 5 (Greenburg Rd), just ne on SW Greenburg Rd, then just e. Int corridors. **Pets:** Accepted. [SAVE] 🛗 🐕 📶 📧 🖵

TILLAMOOK

▽▽▽ **Ashley Inn of Tillamook** [H]
(503) 842-7599. **$107-$300.** 1722 N Makinster Rd 97141. 1 mi n on US 101. Int corridors. **Pets:** Accepted. 🌿 ➹ ⊠ 🛰 ✕ 🔋 💻

▽▽ **Shilo Inn Suites Hotel-Tillamook** [H]
(503) 842-7971. **Call for rates.** 2515 N Main Ave 97141. 1 mi n on US 101. Int corridors. **Pets:** Accepted. 🍴 ➹ ⊠ 🛰 ✕ 🔋 💻

TROUTDALE

▽▽▽ **Comfort Inn Columbia Gorge-Gateway** [H]
(503) 492-2900. **Call for rates.** 1000 NW Graham Rd 97060. I-84 exit 17 eastbound, e on Frontage Rd, then just n; exit westbound, just n. Int corridors. **Pets:** Accepted. 🛰 ✕ 🔋 💻

▽ **Motel 6-Portland Troutdale-#407** [M]
(503) 665-2254. **$51-$71.** 1610 NW Frontage Rd 97060. I-84 exit 17 eastbound, just sw; exit westbound, just w on Frontage Rd, then just sw. Ext corridors. **Pets:** Other species. Service with restrictions, crate. 🕭 ➹ 🎶

TUALATIN

(AAA) ▽▽▽ **Comfort Inn & Suites** [H]
(503) 612-9952. **$90-$220.** 7640 SW Warm Springs St 97062. I-5 exit 289, just w on Nyberg St, just s on Martinazzi Ave, then just e; just behind Fred Meyer. Int corridors. **Pets:** Small, dogs only. $20 daily fee/pet. Designated rooms, service with restrictions, supervision. (SAVE) 🕭 ➹ 🛰 ✕ 🔋 💻

WARRENTON

▽▽ **Shilo Inn Suites Hotel-Warrenton/Astoria** [H]
(503) 861-2181. **Call for rates.** 1609 E Harbor Dr 97146. On US 26/101; near west end of Youngs Bay Bridge. Int corridors. **Pets:** Accepted. 🍴 ➹ ⊠ 🛰 ✕ 🔋 💻

WELCHES

(AAA) ▽▽▽▽ **The Resort at The Mountain** [H] ❀
(503) 622-3101. **$109-$499, 5 day notice.** 68010 E Fairway Ave 97067. 0.6 mi s of US 26 on E Welches Rd. Ext corridors. **Pets:** Medium. $25 daily fee/room. Designated rooms, service with restrictions, supervision. (SAVE) 🍴 ➹ ⊠ 🛰 ✕ 🔋 💻

WHITE CITY

▽▽▽▽ **Brookside Inn & Suites** [H]
(541) 826-0800. **$90-$144.** 2020 Leigh Way 97503. I-5 exit 30, 5.6 mi ne on Crater Lake Hwy (SR 62), then just w. Int corridors. **Pets:** Accepted. 🕭 ➹ 🛰 ✕ 🔋 💻

WILSONVILLE (Restaurants p. 638)

▽▽ **GuestHouse Inn & Suites** [H]
(503) 682-9000. **Call for rates.** 8855 SW Citizens Dr 97070. I-5 exit 283, just e on Wilsonville Rd, just n on Town Center Loop W, then just w. Int corridors. **Pets:** Accepted. 🕭 ➹ 🛰 🔋 💻

▽▽▽▽ **Holiday Inn-Wilsonville** [H]
(503) 682-2211. **Call for rates.** 25425 SW 95th Ave 97070. I-5 exit 286, just w on Boones Ferry Rd, then just se. Int corridors. **Pets:** Accepted. 🍴 ➹ 🛰 ✕ 🔋 💻

(AAA) ▽▽▽ **La Quinta Inn Wilsonville** [H]
(503) 682-3184. **$92-$229.** 8815 SW Sun Pl 97070. I-5 exit 286, just e on Elligsen Rd, just n on Parkway Ave, then just w. Int corridors. **Pets:** Large, other species. Service with restrictions. (SAVE) 🕭 ➹ 🛰 ✕ 🔋 💻

▽▽▽ **Quality Inn Wilsonville** [H]
(503) 682-2288. **$75-$118.** 30800 SW Parkway Ave 97070. I-5 exit 283, just e on Wilsonville Rd, just s on Town Center Loop W, just w on Main St, then 0.4 mi s. Int corridors. **Pets:** Accepted. ➹ 🛰 ✕ 🔋 💻

▽▽ **Super 8 - Wilsonville** [H]
(503) 682-2088. **$57-$75.** 25438 SW Parkway Ave 97070. I-5 exit 286, just e on Elligsen Rd, then just n. Int corridors. **Pets:** Medium, dogs only. $10 one-time fee/pet. Designated rooms, service with restrictions, supervision. 🛰 🔋 💻

WOODBURN

(AAA) ▽▽▽ **BEST WESTERN Woodburn** [H] ❀
(503) 982-6515. **$90-$130.** 2887 Newberg Hwy 97071. I-5 exit 271, just ne. Int corridors. **Pets:** Medium, dogs only. $10 daily fee/pet. Designated rooms, service with restrictions, supervision. (SAVE) 🕭 ➹ 🛰 🔋 💻

▽▽ **La Quinta Inn & Suites Woodburn** [H]
(503) 982-1727. **$74-$219.** 120 Arney Rd NE 97071. I-5 exit 271, just nw. Int corridors. **Pets:** Large, other species. Service with restrictions. ➹ 🛰 ✕ 🔋 💻

▽▽ **Super 8-Woodburn** [H]
(503) 981-8881. **$55-$88.** 821 Evergreen Rd 97071. I-5 exit 271, just se. Int corridors. **Pets:** Medium. $10 daily fee/pet. Designated rooms, service with restrictions, supervision. ➹ 🛰 🔋 💻

YACHATS

(AAA) ▽▽▽ **The Adobe Resort** [H]
(541) 547-3141. **$75-$405.** 1555 US 101 N 97498. 0.5 mi n; just w of US 101. Int corridors. **Pets:** Accepted. (SAVE) 🍴 ➹ ⊠ 🛰 ✕ 〔A〕 🔋 💻

(AAA) ▽ **The Dublin House** [M]
(541) 547-3703. **$59-$135, 3 day notice.** 251 W 7th St 97498. US 101 at 7th St; center. Ext corridors. **Pets:** Dogs only. $10 daily fee/pet. Designated rooms, service with restrictions, supervision. (SAVE) ➹ 🛰 〔A〕 🔋 💻

▽▽ **Fireside Motel** [M] ❀
(541) 547-3636. **$70-$165.** 1881 US 101 N 97498. 0.6 mi n; just w of US 101. Ext corridors. **Pets:** $12 daily fee/pet. Service with restrictions, supervision. 🛰 ✕ 〔A〕 🔋 💻

PENNSYLVANIA

ABBOTTSTOWN

▽▽▽▽ **The Altland House Inn and Suites** [CI]
(717) 259-9535. **Call for rates.** 1 Center Square 17301. Jct SR 194 and US 30; on circle. Int corridors. **Pets:** Accepted. 🍴 🛰 ✕ 🔋 💻

ADAMSTOWN

▽▽▽▽ **Adamstown Inns & Cottages** [BB]
(717) 484-0800. **$109-$270, 14 day notice.** 144 W Main St 19501. Center. Ext/int corridors. **Pets:** Dogs only. $50 one-time fee/pet. Designated rooms, no service, supervision. 🛰 ✕ 🎛 🔋 💻

AKRON

▽▽▽ **Boxwood Inn** [BB]
(717) 859-3466. **Call for rates.** 1320 Diamond St 17501. SR 272, 0.4 mi se on Main St to Diamond St, 0.3 mi s. Ext/int corridors. **Pets:** Accepted. 🍴 🛰 ✕ 🎛 🔋 💻

ALLENTOWN

▽▽▽ **Allentown Comfort Suites** [H]
(610) 437-9100. **$99-$189.** 3712 Hamilton Blvd 18103. I-78 exit 54 (Hamilton Blvd), just n. Int corridors. **Pets:** $50 one-time fee/room. Designated rooms, service with restrictions. 🍴 🛰 ✕ 🔋 💻

AAA ♦♦♦ **Allentown Howard Johnson Inn & Suites Dorney Park** H

(610) 439-4000. **$49-$159.** 3220 Hamilton Blvd 18103. I-78 exit 54 (Hamilton Blvd), 0.8 mi n. Int corridors. **Pets:** $25 daily fee/room. Designated rooms, service with restrictions, supervision.

SAVE 🚹 ⊛ 🛜 🖥 🖵

♦♦ **Comfort Inn Lehigh Valley-West** H 🐾

(610) 391-0344. **Call for rates.** 7625 Imperial Way 18106. I-78 exit 49B (SR 100), just n. Int corridors. **Pets:** Other species. $20 daily fee/room. Designated rooms, service with restrictions. 🍴 🛜 🖥 🖵

♦♦♦ **Staybridge Suites Allentown Bethlehem Airport** H

(610) 443-5000. **Call for rates.** 1787-A Airport Rd 18109. US 22 exit Airport Rd S, 0.3 mi s. Int corridors. **Pets:** Accepted.

🚹 ⊛ 🛜 ✖ 🖥 🖵

ALTOONA

♦♦♦ **Holiday Inn Express Altoona** H 🐾

(814) 944-9661. **$139-$299, 3 day notice.** 3306 Pleasant Valley Blvd 16602. I-99/US 220 exit 32, 0.5 mi w, then just n. Int corridors. **Pets:** Medium. $75 one-time fee/room. Designated rooms, service with restrictions, crate. 🚹 🛜 ✖ 🖥 🖵

♦ **Motel 6 #1415** M

(814) 946-7601. **Call for rates.** 1500 Sterling St 16602. I-99/US 220 exit 31 (Plank Rd), just w. Ext corridors. **Pets:** Other species. Service with restrictions, crate. 🚹 ⊛ 🛜

♦♦ **Super 8 Altoona** M

(814) 942-5350. **$68-$91.** 3535 Fairway Dr 16602. I-99/US 220 exit 32, just w. Int corridors. **Pets:** Small, dogs only. $15 daily fee/pet. Designated rooms, service with restrictions, supervision.

🍴 🚹 🛜 🖥 🖵

AUDUBON

AAA ♦♦♦ **Homewood Suites by Hilton** H

(610) 539-7300. **$109-$199.** 681 Shannondell Blvd 19403. US 422 exit S Trooper Rd, 1.2 mi n. Int corridors. **Pets:** Accepted.

SAVE 🚹 ⊛ 🛜 🖥 🖵

BARKEYVILLE

AAA ♦♦ **Quality Inn-Barkeyville** M

(814) 786-7901. **$60-$130.** 137 Gibb Rd 16038. I-80 exit 29, just n on SR 8. Ext corridors. **Pets:** Accepted. SAVE 🛜 🖥 🖵

BARNESVILLE

♦♦ **MainStay Suites Barnesville/Frackville** H 🐾

(570) 773-5252. **$85-$135.** 1252 Morea Rd 18214. I-81 exit 131A southbound; exit 131B northbound, just s. Int corridors. **Pets:** Other species. $10 daily fee/room. Service with restrictions, crate.

🍴 🚹 🛜 🖥 🖵

BARTONSVILLE

AAA ♦♦ **Baymont Inn & Suites** H

(570) 476-1500. **$90-$150.** 116 Turtlewalk Ln 18321. I-80 exit 302B, 0.4 mi n. Int corridors. **Pets:** Accepted. SAVE 🍴 ⊛ ✖ 🛜 🖥 🖵

BEAVER FALLS

♦♦♦ **Park Inn by Radisson Beaver Falls** H

(724) 846-3700. **Call for rates.** 7195 Eastwood Rd 15010. I-76 (Pennsylvania Tpke) exit 13, just n. Int corridors. **Pets:** $35 one-time fee/room. Service with restrictions, supervision.

🍴 ⊛ ✖ 🛜 🖥 🖵

BEDFORD

AAA ♦♦♦♦ **Omni Bedford Springs Resort & Spa** H 🐾

(814) 623-8100. **Call for rates.** 2138 Business Rt 220 15522. I-70/76 (Pennsylvania Tpke) exit 146, 3.9 mi s. Int corridors. **Pets:** $150 one-time fee/room. Designated rooms, service with restrictions, supervision.

SAVE 🍴 ⊛ ✖ 🛜 ✖ 🖥 🖵

AAA ♦♦ **Quality Inn Bedford** H

(814) 623-5188. **$79-$165.** 4407 Business Rt 220 N 15522. I-70/76 (Pennsylvania Tpke) exit 146, just n. Ext/int corridors. **Pets:** Medium, other species. $15 one-time fee/room. Designated rooms, service with restrictions, crate. SAVE 🍴 ⊛ 🛜 🖥 🖵

♦♦ **Travelodge Bedford** H

(814) 623-9006. **$50-$82.** 4517 Business Rt 220 15522. I-70/76 (Pennsylvania Tpke) exit 146, 0.3 mi n. Ext/int corridors. **Pets:** $50 deposit/room, $15 daily fee/room. Service with restrictions, supervision.

🍴 ⊛ ✖ 🛜 🖥 🖵

BENSALEM

AAA ♦♦♦ **BEST WESTERN PLUS Philadelphia Bensalem** H

(215) 638-1500. **$99-$139.** 3499 Street Rd 19020. I-276 (Pennsylvania Tpke) exit 351, just s on US 1, then 0.3 mi e on SR 132. Ext/int corridors. **Pets:** Small. $50 one-time fee/pet. Designated rooms, service with restrictions, crate. SAVE 🍴 ⊛ 🛜 🖥 🖵

♦♦ **Extended Stay America-Philadelphia/Bensalem** H

(215) 633-6900. **Call for rates.** 3216 Tillman Dr 19020. I-95 exit 37 (SR 132), 2.5 mi w, then just s; I-276 (Pennsylvania Tpke) exit 351, 0.9 mi on US 1, 1.4 mi e, then just s. Int corridors. **Pets:** Other species. $25 daily fee/pet. Service with restrictions, supervision. 🚹 🛜 🖥 🖵

♦♦ **Sleep Inn & Suites-Bensalem** H

(215) 244-2300. **$90-$120.** 3427 Street Rd 19020. I-276 (Pennsylvania Tpke) exit 351, just s on US 1, then 0.3 mi e on SR 132. Int corridors. **Pets:** Accepted. 🚹 🛜 ✖ 🖥 🖵

BENTLEYVILLE

AAA ♦♦♦ **BEST WESTERN Garden Inn** H

(724) 239-4321. **$130.** 101 Gosai Dr 15314. I-70 exit 32B, just s. Int corridors. **Pets:** Medium, other species. $20 one-time fee/room. Designated rooms, service with restrictions, supervision.

SAVE ⊛ 🛜 🖥 🖵

BERWYN

♦♦♦ **Residence Inn by Marriott Philadelphia-Valley Forge** H

(610) 640-9494. **$146-$240.** 600 W Swedesford Rd 19312. US 202 exit Paoli/SR 252, 1 mi n. Ext corridors. **Pets:** Accepted.

ECO 🚹 ⊛ 🛜 ✖ 🖥 🖵

BETHEL

AAA ♦♦♦ **Comfort Inn-Bethel/Midway** H

(717) 933-8888. **$85-$129.** 41 Diner Dr 19507. I-78 exit 16, just w. Int corridors. **Pets:** Other species. $10 daily fee/pet. Designated rooms, service with restrictions, crate. SAVE 🚹 ⊛ 🛜 🖥 🖵

BETHEL PARK

♦♦♦ **Crowne Plaza Pittsburgh South** H

(412) 833-5300. **$119-$219.** 164 Ft Couch Rd 15241. 1 mi n on US 19. Int corridors. **Pets:** Medium. $45 one-time fee/room. Designated rooms, service with restrictions, supervision.

🍴 🚹 ⊛ 🛜 ✖ 🖥 🖵

BETHLEHEM

AAA ♦♦♦ **BEST WESTERN Lehigh Valley Hotel & Conference Center** H

(610) 866-5800. **$79-$119, 3 day notice.** 300 Gateway Dr 18017. US 22 exit Center St and SR 512. Ext/int corridors. **Pets:** Accepted.

SAVE 🍴 🚹 ⊛ 🛜 ✖ 🖥 🖵

♦♦ **Comfort Suites University** H

(610) 882-9700. **$95-$240.** 120 W 3rd St 18015. SR 378 exit 3rd St; jct W 3rd and Brodhead sts; center. Int corridors. **Pets:** Large, other species. $20 daily fee/pet. Designated rooms, service with restrictions.

🍴 🛜 ✖ 🖥 🖵

▽▽▽ **Historic Hotel Bethlehem** H

(610) 625-5000. **$165-$235, 7 day notice.** 437 Main St 18018. SR 378 S exit 3 (City Center), just n on 3rd Ave, 0.3 mi e on Union, then 0.3 mi s. Int corridors. **Pets:** Accepted. 🍴 ♿M 🛜 ✕ 🔋 💻

▽▽▽ **Homewood Suites - Allentown/Bethlehem Airport** H

(610) 264-7500. **$129-$199.** 2031 Avenue C 18017. US 22 exit SR 378/Schoenersville Rd, follow signs for Schoenersville Rd, then 0.7 mi n. Int corridors. **Pets:** Accepted. ♿M 🛗 ✕ 🛜 🔋 💻

⚐ ▽▽▽ **Hyatt Place Bethlehem** H

(610) 625-0500. **$139-$249.** 45 W North St 18018. SR 378 exit 2 (Eighth Ave), just s, 0.7 mi w on Broad St, just n on Main St, then just w. Int corridors. **Pets:** Accepted.

SAVE 🍴 ♿M 🛗 🛜 ✕ 🔋 💻

⚐ ▽▽▽ **Residence Inn by Marriott Allentown Bethlehem/Lehigh Valley Airport** H

(610) 317-2662. **$118-$194.** 2180 Motel Dr 18018. US 22 exit Airport Rd S, 0.8 mi se on Catasauqua Rd. Int corridors. **Pets:** Other species. $100 one-time fee/room. Service with restrictions, crate.

SAVE 🛗 🛜 ✕ 🔋 💻

⚐ ▽▽▽ **The View Inn & Suites** H

(610) 865-6300. **$69-$109.** 3191 Highfield Dr 18020. US 22 exit SR 191, just s. Ext/int corridors. **Pets:** Accepted. SAVE 🛜 🔋 💻

▽▽▽▽ **Wydnor Hall Inn** BB

(610) 867-6851. **Call for rates.** 3612 Old Philadelphia Pike 18015. I-78 exit 60, 0.3 mi s to Center Valley Pkwy, 2.3 mi e to SR 378, 1.5 mi n to Black River Rd, just w to Old Philadelphia Pike, then 0.3 mi s. Int corridors. **Pets:** Accepted. 🛜 ✕ ☎ 🔋 💻

BIRD-IN-HAND

▽▽ **Amish Country Motel** M

(717) 768-8396. **$84-$120.** 3013 Old Philadelphia Pike (Rt 340) 17505. On SR 340, 1 mi e. Ext corridors. **Pets:** Small, other species. $100 deposit/room, $50 one-time fee/pet. Designated rooms, service with restrictions, crate. 🍴 🛗 🛜 ✕ 🔋 💻

BLAKESLEE

⚐ ▽▽ **BEST WESTERN Inn at Blakeslee-Pocono** H

(570) 646-6000. **$77-$250.** 107 Parkside Ave 18610. I-80 exit 284, just n. Int corridors. **Pets:** Accepted.

SAVE 🍴 ♿M 🛗 🛜 ✕ 🔋 💻

BLOOMSBURG

⚐ ▽▽▽ **Econo Lodge** H ❀

(570) 387-0490. **$55-$150.** 189 Columbia Mall Dr 17815. I-80 exit 232 (SR 42), just n. Int corridors. **Pets:** Medium, dogs only. $15 daily fee/pet. Service with restrictions, crate. SAVE 🛜 🔋 💻

▽▽▽ **The Inn at Turkey Hill** CI

(570) 387-1500. **$140-$250.** 991 Central Rd 17815. I-80 exit 236 eastbound; exit 236A westbound, just s. Ext/int corridors. **Pets:** $20 daily fee/room. Designated rooms, service with restrictions, crate.

🍴 🛜 ✕ 🔋 💻

BLUE MOUNTAIN

⚐ ▽▽ **Kenmar Motel** M

(717) 423-5915. **$65-$90, 3 day notice.** 17788 Cumberland Hwy 17240. I-76 (Pennsylvania Tpke) exit 201, just e on SR 997 N. Ext corridors. **Pets:** Small, dogs only. $10 one-time fee/pet. Designated rooms, service with restrictions, supervision. SAVE 🛜 🔋

BRADFORD

⚐ ▽▽▽ **BEST WESTERN PLUS Bradford Inn** H

(814) 362-4501. **$105-$145.** 100 Davis St S 16701. US 219 exit Forman St southbound, just w to Davis St, then 0.3 mi s; exit Elm St northbound, just w. Ext/int corridors. **Pets:** $10 daily fee/pet. Designated rooms, service with restrictions, crate.

SAVE 🍴 ♿M 🛗 🛜 🔋 💻

▽▽▽▽ **Comfort Inn-Bradford** H

(814) 368-6772. **$79-$150.** 76 Elm St 16701. US 219 exit Forman St southbound, just w to Davis St, then 0.3 mi s; exit Elm St northbound, just w. Int corridors. **Pets:** Accepted. 🛗 🛜 🔋 💻

⚐ ▽▽▽▽ **Glendorn** CI 🐾

(814) 362-6511. **$450-$2275, 30 day notice.** 1000 Glendorn Dr 16701. US 219 exit Forman St, just s on Mechanic St, then 4.3 mi w on W Corydon St. Ext/int corridors. **Pets:** Dogs only. $75 daily fee/pet. Designated rooms, service with restrictions, crate.

SAVE 🍴 🛗 ✕ 🛜 ✕ 🔋 💻

BREEZEWOOD

⚐ ▽▽ **BEST WESTERN Plaza Inn** M

(814) 735-4352. **$80-$100.** 16407 Lincoln Hwy 15533. I-76 (Pennsylvania Tpke) exit 161, just w on US 30; I-70 exit 147. Ext corridors.
Pets: Accepted. SAVE 🛗 🛜 ✕ 🔋 💻

▽▽ **Wiltshire Motel** M

(814) 735-4361. **Call for rates.** 140 S Breezewood Rd 15533. I-76 (Pennsylvania Tpke) exit 161, just w on US 30; I-70 exit 147. Ext corridors. **Pets:** Other species. No service, supervision. 🛜 💻

BURNHAM

⚐ ▽▽▽ **Quality Inn & Suites of Lewistown** M

(717) 248-4961. **$89-$269.** 13015 Ferguson Valley Rd 17009. US 322 exit Burnham, just w. Ext corridors. **Pets:** Medium, other species. $25 one-time fee/pet. Designated rooms, service with restrictions, supervision. SAVE 🍴 🛗 🛜 🔋 💻

BUTLER

▽▽▽ **Butler Days Inn Conference Center** H

(724) 287-6761. **$89-$399.** 139 Pittsburgh Rd 16001. 2 mi s. Int corridors. **Pets:** Accepted. 🍴 🛗 🛜 🔋 💻

▽▽▽ **Locust Brook Lodge** BB

(724) 283-8453. **$90, 3 day notice.** 179 Eagle Mill Rd 16001. 5 mi w on US 422 to jct Eagle Mill Rd, 0.8 mi s; I-79 exit 99, 10 mi e on US 422 to jct Eagle Mill Rd, then 0.8 mi s. Ext/int corridors.
Pets: Accepted. 🍴 🛜 🔋 💻

▽▽▽ **Super 8** M

(724) 287-8888. **$51-$72.** 138 Pittsburgh Rd 16001. 2 mi s. Int corridors. **Pets:** Accepted. 🛜 🔋 💻

CAMP HILL

▽▽▽ **Radisson Hotel Harrisburg** H

(717) 763-7117. **$95-$189.** 1150 Camp Hill Bypass 17011. Jct US 11, 15 and Erford Rd. Ext/int corridors. **Pets:** Accepted.
🍴 ♿M 🛗 🛜 ✕ 🔋 💻

CARLISLE

⚐ ▽▽▽ **BEST WESTERN Carlisle** H

(717) 243-6200. **$79-$199.** 1155 Harrisburg Pike 17013. I-76 (Pennsylvania Tpke) exit 226, just s. Int corridors. **Pets:** Accepted.
SAVE 🛗 🛜 🔋 💻

▽▽▽ **Comfort Suites Hotel** H ❀

(717) 960-1000. **$89-$169.** 10 S Hanover St 17013. I-81 exit 47, 0.8 mi n on SR 34, just s of square; downtown. Int corridors. **Pets:** Large, other species. $20 daily fee/pet. Designated rooms, service with restrictions, crate. 🍴 ♿M 🛜 ✕ 🔋 💻

⚐ ▽▽▽ **Country Inn & Suites By Carlson - Carlisle, PA** H

(717) 241-4900. **$99-$249.** 1529 Commerce Ave 17015. I-81 exit 44 (Plainfield Rd), s on SR 465 (Allen Rd), then left. Int corridors.
Pets: Accepted. SAVE ♿M 🛗 🛜 ✕ 🔋 💻

⚐ ▽▽▽▽ **Days Inn Carlisle-South** H

(717) 258-4147. **$79-$175.** 101 Alexander Spring Rd 17015. I-81 exit 45, just sw. Int corridors. **Pets:** Accepted.
SAVE ♿M 🛗 🛜 ✕ 🔋 💻

WWW Fairfield Inn & Suites by Marriott Carlisle H
(717) 243-2080. **$94-$154.** 1528 E Commerce Ave 17015. I-81 exit 44
(Plainfield Rd), just s, then just e. Int corridors. **Pets:** Accepted.

WWW Hampton Inn Carlisle H
(717) 240-0200. **$129-$209.** 1164 Harrisburg Pike 17013. I-76 (Pennsylvania Tpke) exit 226, just n; I-81 exit 52 (US 11) southbound; exit 52B
northbound, 0.8 mi s. Int corridors. **Pets:** Medium. Designated rooms,
service with restrictions, supervision.

WWW Pheasant Field Bed & Breakfast BB
(717) 258-0717. **$135-$255, 7 day notice.** 150 Hickorytown Rd 17015.
I-76 (Pennsylvania Tpke) exit 226, 0.4 mi n on US 11, 2.3 mi right on S
Middlesex Rd, 0.4 mi left on Ridge Dr, then right. Ext/int corridors.
Pets: Medium, other species. $25 daily fee/pet. Designated rooms, ser-
vice with restrictions, supervision.

WWW Residence Inn by Marriott Harrisburg
Carlisle H
(717) 610-9050. **$111-$183.** 1 Hampton Ct 17013. I-76 (Pennsylvania
Tpke) exit 226, just n; I-81 exit 52 (US 11) southbound; exit 52B northbound, 0.8 mi s. Int corridors. **Pets:** $100 one-time fee/room. Service
with restrictions.

WW Sleep Inn Carlisle H
(717) 249-8863. **$90-$189.** 5 E Garland Dr 17013. I-81 exit 47 northbound; exit 47A southbound, just ne. Int corridors. **Pets:** Large. $15
daily fee/pet. Designated rooms, service with restrictions, crate.

WWW Super 8/Carlisle South M
(717) 245-9898. **$49-$160.** 100 Alexander Spring Rd 17015. I-81 exit
45, just se. Int corridors. **Pets:** Medium, other species. $10 daily fee/
pet. Service with restrictions, crate.

CHADDS FORD
WW Brandywine River Hotel H
(610) 388-1200. **$129-$159.** 1609 Baltimore Pike, Bldg 300 19317. Jct
US 1 (Baltimore Pike) and SR 100, 2 mi w of US 202 (Wilmington
Pike). Int corridors. **Pets:** Dogs only. $45 daily fee/pet. Designated
rooms, service with restrictions, crate.

CHALK HILL
WWW The Lodge at Chalk Hill M
(724) 438-8880. **$70-$150.** 2920 National Pike Rd 15421. I-40 exit 14B,
just w. Ext corridors. **Pets:** Small, dogs only. $10 daily fee/pet. Desig-
nated rooms, service with restrictions, crate.

CHAMBERSBURG *(Restaurants p. 638)*
WWW BEST WESTERN Chambersburg H
(717) 262-4994. **$70-$300.** 211 Walker Rd 17201. I-81 exit 16, just w
on US 30, then just n. Int corridors. **Pets:** Accepted.

WWW Candlewood Suites H
(717) 263-2800. **Call for rates.** 231 Walker Rd 17201. I-81 exit 16, just
w on US 30, then just n. Int corridors. **Pets:** Accepted.

WWW Country Inn & Suites By Carlson H
(717) 261-0900. **Call for rates.** 399 Bedington Blvd 17201. I-81 exit 17
(Walker Rd), 0.6 mi s, then just w. Int corridors. **Pets:** $15 one-time
fee/pet. Designated rooms, service with restrictions, crate.

WWW La Quinta Inn & Suites Chambersburg H
(717) 446-0770. **$89-$254.** 199 Walker Rd 17201. I-81 exit 16, just w
on US 30, then just n. Int corridors. **Pets:** Large, other species. Service
with restrictions.

WWW Sleep Inn & Suites H
(717) 263-0596. **$74-$130.** 1435 Doron Dr 17202. I-81 exit 20, just w.
Int corridors. **Pets:** Accepted.

CHESTER
WWW BEST WESTERN PLUS Philadelphia Airport
South at Widener University H
(610) 872-8100. **$120-$150.** 1450 Providence Ave (SR 320) 19013. I-95
exit 6, just e to SR 320, follow signs. Int corridors. **Pets:** Accepted.

CLARION
WW Comfort Inn-Clarion H
(814) 226-5230. **$70-$135.** 129 Dolby St 16214. I-80 exit 62, 0.6 mi n
on SR 68. Int corridors. **Pets:** Accepted.

WW Park Inn By Radisson Clarion H
(814) 226-8850. **$109-$149.** 45 Holiday Inn Rd 16214. I-80 exit 62, 0.5
mi n on SR 68. Int corridors. **Pets:** $10 daily fee/room. Service with
restrictions, crate.

CLEARFIELD
WWW BEST WESTERN PLUS Clearfield H
(814) 768-1049. **$87-$135.** 14424 Clearfield Shawville Hwy (Rt 879)
16830. I-80 exit 120, just s. Int corridors. **Pets:** Other species. $20 daily
fee/room. Designated rooms, service with restrictions, supervision.

WW Super 8-Clearfield M
(814) 768-7580. **$68-$103.** 14597 Clearfield Shawville Hwy (Rt 879)
16830. I-80 exit 120, just s. Int corridors. **Pets:** Other species. $5 daily
fee/room. Service with restrictions, supervision.

CONSHOHOCKEN
WWWW Residence Inn by Marriott
Philadelphia/Conshohocken H
(610) 828-8800. **$174-$286.** 191 Washington St 19428. I-76 (Schuylkill
Expwy) exit 332 (SR 23), 0.3 mi over Fayette Bridge to Elm St, then
just se along river. Int corridors. **Pets:** Accepted.

CORAOPOLIS
WWWW Embassy Suites-Pittsburgh International
Airport H
(412) 269-9070. **$139-$279.** 550 Cherrington Pkwy 15108. Business
I-376 Loop exit Thorn Run Rd. Int corridors. **Pets:** Medium, dogs only.
$75 one-time fee/room. Designated rooms, service with restrictions,
supervision.

WWWW Hampton Inn Pittsburgh Airport H
(412) 264-0020. **$149-$179.** 8514 University Blvd 15108. Jct Business
I-376 Loop, 0.5 mi n. Int corridors. **Pets:** Accepted.

WWWW Hyatt Regency Pittsburgh International
Airport H
(724) 899-1234. **$99-$359.** 1111 Airport Blvd 15231. I-376 exit 53 (Airport Blvd). Int corridors. **Pets:** Small. $100 one-time fee/room. Desig-
nated rooms, service with restrictions, supervision.

WWWW La Quinta Inn Pittsburgh Airport H
(412) 269-0400. **$92-$194.** 8507 University Blvd 15108. Jct Business
I-376 Loop, 1 mi n. Int corridors. **Pets:** Large, other species. Service
with restrictions.

WWWW Pittsburgh Airport Super 8 M
(412) 264-7888. **$60-$70.** 8991 University Blvd 15108. Jct Business
I-376 Loop, 1 mi n. Int corridors. **Pets:** Accepted.

WWWW Sheraton Pittsburgh Airport Hotel H
(412) 262-2400. **$99-$289.** 1160 Thorn Run Rd 15108. Business I-376
Loop exit Thorn Run Rd. Int corridors. **Pets:** Accepted.

COUDERSPORT

▼▼▼ Westgate Inn 🏨

(814) 274-0400. **$82-$99.** 307 Rt 6 W 16915. On US 6, 1 mi w. Int corridors. **Pets:** Small, dogs only. $15 deposit/pet, $15 daily fee/pet. Designated rooms, service with restrictions, crate. 📶 🛗 🖥

CRANBERRY TOWNSHIP

▼▼▼ Candlewood Suites 🏨

(724) 591-8666. **$149-$189.** 20036 Rt 19 16066. I-76 (Pennsylvania Tpke) exit 28; I-79 exit 76 northbound; exit 78 southbound. Int corridors. **Pets:** Accepted. 🔥M 🛍 ⊠ 📶 🛗 🖥

▼▼▼ Hampton Inn Cranberry 🏨

(724) 776-1000. **$99-$189.** 210 Executive Dr 16066. I-79 (Pennsylvania Tpke) exit 76, 0.5 mi n on US 19, then 0.3 mi w on Freedom Rd; exit 78 southbound, 0.5 mi w on Freedom Rd. Int corridors. **Pets:** Accepted. 🔥M 🛍 ⊠ 📶 🛗 🖥

▼▼▼ Holiday Inn Express Cranberry Township 🏨

(724) 772-1000. **Call for rates.** 20003 Rt 19 16066. I-76 (Pennsylvania Tpke) exit 28; I-79 exit 76 northbound; exit 78 southbound, just s. Int corridors. **Pets:** Accepted. 🔥M 📶 🛗 🖥

🅰🅰🅰 ▼▼▼ Hyatt Place Pittsburgh/Cranberry 🏨

(724) 779-7900. **$84-$199.** 136 Emeryville Dr 16066. I-76 (Pennsylvania Tpke) exit 28; I-79 exit 76 northbound; exit 78 southbound, 0.3 mi s on US 19. Int corridors. **Pets:** Accepted.
🆂🅰🆅🅴 🍴 🔥M 🛍 📶 ⊠ 🛗 🖥

🅰🅰🅰 ▼▼ Red Roof Inn Pittsburgh North Cranberry Township Ⓜ

(724) 776-5670. **Call for rates.** 20009 Rt 19 16066. I-76 (Pennsylvania Tpke) exit 28; I-79 exit 76 northbound; exit 78 southbound. Ext corridors. **Pets:** Large, other species. Service with restrictions, supervision.
🆂🅰🆅🅴 📶 ⊠ 🛗 🖥

▼▼▼ Residence Inn by Marriott Pittsburgh Cranberry Township 🏨

(724) 779-1000. **$167-$275.** 1308 Freedom Rd 16066. I-76 (Pennsylvania Tpke) exit 76, 0.5 mi n on US 19, then 0.3 mi w; I-79 exit 78 southbound, 0.5 mi w. Int corridors. **Pets:** Accepted.
🎫 🛗 🔥M 🛍 ⊠ 📶 ⊠ 🛗 🖥

DANVILLE

🅰🅰🅰 ▼▼▼ BEST WESTERN PLUS Danville Inn 🏨

(570) 275-5750. **$119-$139.** 79 Old Valley School Rd 17821. I-80 exit 224, just s. Int corridors. **Pets:** Other species. $15 one-time fee/room. Service with restrictions, supervision. 🆂🅰🆅🅴 🔥M 🛍 📶 🛗 🖥

🅰🅰🅰 ▼▼▼ Danville Super 8 Ⓜ

(570) 275-4640. **$130-$230, 3 day notice.** 35 Sheraton Rd 17821. I-80 exit 224, just sw on SR 54. Ext corridors. **Pets:** Accepted.
🆂🅰🆅🅴 📶 🛗 🖥

DELMONT

▼▼ Super 8 🏨

(724) 468-4888. **$70-$110.** 180 Sheffield Dr 15626. SR 66, just s of US 22. Int corridors. **Pets:** $15 daily fee/pet. Supervision.
🔥M 📶 🛗 🖥

DENVER

▼▼▼ Comfort Inn Lancaster County North 🏨

(717) 336-7541. **$95-$135.** 1 Denver Rd 17517. I-76 (Pennsylvania Tpke) exit 286, 1 mi w to SR 272, then just s. Int corridors.
Pets: Accepted. 🍴 🔥M 🛍 📶 🛗 🖥

▼▼▼ Red Roof Inn Denver 🏨

(717) 336-4649. **Call for rates.** 2017 N Reading Rd 17517. I-76 (Pennsylvania Tpke) exit 286, 1 mi w to SR 272, then just s. Int corridors. **Pets:** Large, other species. Service with restrictions, supervision.
🍴 📶 🛗 🖥

DICKSON CITY

▼▼▼ Residence Inn by Marriott-Scranton 🏨

(570) 343-5121. **$111-$206.** 947 Viewmont Dr 18519. I-81 exit 190, just e, follow signs to Viewmont Dr. Int corridors. **Pets:** Accepted.
🛍 📶 ⊠ 🛗 🖥

DONEGAL

▼▼▼ Days Inn at Donegal 🏨

(724) 593-7536. **$84-$94.** 3620 Rt 31 15628. I-70/76 (Pennsylvania Tpke) exit 91, just e. Ext/int corridors. **Pets:** Small, dogs only. $35 one-time fee/room. Service with restrictions, crate. 🛍 📶 ⊠ 🛗 🖥

DU BOIS

🅰🅰🅰 ▼▼▼ BEST WESTERN PLUS Inn & Conference Center 🏨

(814) 371-6200. **$109-$149.** 82 N Park Pl 15801. I-80 exit 97 eastbound, 2.5 mi e on DuBois Ave (US 219/SR 255), then just s; exit 101 westbound, 2.7 mi w on DuBois Ave (US 219/SR 255), then just s on US 219. Int corridors. **Pets:** Other species. $12 daily fee/pet. Service with restrictions, crate. 🆂🅰🆅🅴 📶 🛗 🖥

DUNMORE

🅰🅰🅰 ▼▼▼ BEST WESTERN PLUS Scranton East Hotel & Convention Center 🏨

(570) 343-4771. **Call for rates.** 200 Tigue St 18512. I-84/380 exit 1 (Tigue St), 0.3 mi e of jct I-81. Int corridors. **Pets:** Other species. $15 daily fee/room. Designated rooms, service with restrictions, supervision.
🆂🅰🆅🅴 🍴 🛍 ⊠ 📶 🛗 🖥

🅰🅰🅰 ▼▼ Quality Inn Scranton 🏨

(570) 348-6101. **$79-$299.** 1226 Oneill Hwy 18512. I-81 exit 188 (Throop), just e at SR 347 N (Oneill Hwy). Int corridors. **Pets:** Large. $15 daily fee/pet. Service with restrictions, supervision.
🆂🅰🆅🅴 📶 🛗 🖥

▼▼ Sleep Inn & Suites 🏨

(570) 961-1116. **$80-$107.** 102 Monahan Ave 18512. I-81 exit 188 (Throop), just e at SR 347 N (Oneill Hwy), then just s. Int corridors. **Pets:** Large. $15 daily fee/pet. Designated rooms, service with restrictions, crate. 🔥M 🛍 📶 🛗 🖥

EAGLES MERE

▼▼ Crestmont Inn Ⓒ🄸

(570) 525-3519. **$120-$250, 7 day notice.** 180 Crestmont Dr 17731. Just n on SR 42 (Eagles Mere Ave), just w on Lakewood Ave. Int corridors. **Pets:** Accepted. 🍴 📶 ⊠ 🛗

EAST NORRITON

🅰🅰🅰 ▼▼▼ HYATT house Philadelphia/Plymouth Meeting 🏨

(610) 313-9990. **$94-$299.** 501 E Germantown Pike 19401. I-476 exit 20, 2.5 mi w. Int corridors. **Pets:** Medium. $75 one-time fee/room. Service with restrictions, crate. 🆂🅰🆅🅴 🍴 🛍 📶 ⊠ 🛗 🖥

EASTON

▼▼▼ Grand Eastonian Suites Hotel 🏨

(610) 258-6350. **$109-$239.** 140 N Northampton St 18042. US 22 exit 4th St (SR 611), just e to 3rd St, just s to downtown square, then just e towards river. Int corridors. **Pets:** Medium. $25 daily fee/room. Designated rooms, service with restrictions, crate.
🍴 🔥M 🛍 📶 ⊠ 🛗 🖥

▼▼▼ The Lafayette Inn 🅱🅱 🐾

(610) 253-4500. **Call for rates.** 525 W Monroe St 18042. US 22 exit 4th St (SR 611), just n on 3rd St, 0.3 mi ne on College Ave, then 0.3 mi n on Cattell St to jct Monroe St. Ext/int corridors. **Pets:** $200 deposit/room, $20 daily fee/room. Designated rooms, service with restrictions, supervision. 📶 ⊠ 🛗 🖥

TownePlace Suites by Marriott - Bethlehem/Easton H

(610) 829-2000. **$118-$194.** 3800 Easton-Nazareth Hwy 18045. SR 33 exit SR 248 (Easton-Nazareth Hwy), 0.6 mi w. Int corridors. **Pets:** Large, other species. $100 one-time fee/room. Service with restrictions, crate.

EAST STROUDSBURG

Budget Inn & Suites H

(570) 424-5451. **$70-$116.** 320 Greentree Dr 18301. I-80 exit 308, just se. Ext/int corridors. **Pets:** $10 daily fee/room. Designated rooms, service with restrictions, supervision.

Super 8 East Stroudsburg M

(570) 424-7411. **$55-$149.** 340 Greentree Dr 18301. I-80 exit 308, just se. Int corridors. **Pets:** Accepted.

EBENSBURG

Comfort Inn H

(814) 472-6100. **Call for rates.** 111 Cook Rd 15931. Jct US 219, just e on US 22. Int corridors. **Pets:** Accepted.

ELIZABETHTOWN

Holiday Inn Express Elizabethtown (Hershey Area) H

(717) 367-4000. **$131-$175.** 147 Merts Dr 17022. SR 283 exit Elizabethtown/Rheems. Int corridors. **Pets:** Accepted.

ERIE

Baymont Inn Erie PA H

(814) 866-8808. **$72-$189.** 8170 Perry Hwy 16509. I-90 exit 27, just s. Int corridors. **Pets:** Accepted.

Fairfield Inn by Marriott Erie H

(814) 868-0985. **$69-$148.** 2082 Interchange Rd 16565. I-79 exit 180, just e; in Pavilion Marketplace. Int corridors. **Pets:** Accepted.

Homewood Suites by Hilton H

(814) 866-8292. **Call for rates.** 2084 Interchange Rd 16565. I-79 exit 180, just e; in Pavilion Marketplace. Int corridors. **Pets:** Accepted.

La Quinta Inn & Suites H

(814) 864-1812. **$65-$244.** 7820 Perry Hwy 16509. I-90 exit 27, just n. Int corridors. **Pets:** Large, other species. Service with restrictions.

Microtel Inn by Wyndham Erie M

(814) 864-1010. **$59-$119.** 8100 Peach St 16509. I-90 exit 24, just s. Int corridors. **Pets:** Large. $10 daily fee/pet. Service with restrictions.

Red Roof Inn Erie M

(814) 868-5246. **Call for rates.** 7865 Perry Hwy 16509. I-90 exit 27, just n on SR 97. Ext/int corridors. **Pets:** Large, other species. Service with restrictions, supervision.

Sheraton Erie Bayfront Hotel H

(814) 454-2005. **$109-$399.** 55 West Bay Dr 16507. I-90 exit 22B to Bayfront Connector; I-79 to Bayfront Pkwy. Int corridors. **Pets:** Large, dogs only. $50 one-time fee/room. Service with restrictions, supervision.

TownePlace Suites by Marriott Erie H

(814) 866-7100. **$83-$171.** 2090 Interchange Rd 16565. I-79 exit 180, just e; in Pavilion Marketplace. Int corridors. **Pets:** Accepted.

Wingate by Wyndham H

(814) 860-3050. **$109-$179.** 8060 Old Oliver Rd 16509. I-90 exit 24, just s on Peach St, just w, just n, then just e. Int corridors. **Pets:** Accepted.

ESSINGTON

Red Roof Inn Philadelphia Airport M

(610) 521-5090. **Call for rates.** 49 Industrial Hwy 19029. I-95 exit 9A, 0.3 mi sw on SR 291. Ext corridors. **Pets:** Large, other species. Service with restrictions, supervision.

FARMINGTON

Historic Summit Inn H

(724) 438-8594. **Call for rates.** 101 Skyline Dr 15437. On US 40; center. Int corridors. **Pets:** Dogs only. $20 daily fee/pet. Service with restrictions, supervision.

Nemacolin Woodlands Resort H

(724) 329-8555. **$209-$969, 14 day notice.** 1001 Lafayette Dr 15437. 1 mi e on US 40. Ext/int corridors. **Pets:** Accepted.

FOGELSVILLE

Glasbern C

(610) 285-4723. **Call for rates.** 2141 Packhouse Rd 18051. I-78 exit 49B (SR 100), 0.3 mi n to 1st traffic light, 0.3 mi w on Main St, 0.6 mi n on Church St, then 0.8 mi ne. Ext/int corridors. **Pets:** Dogs only. $25 daily fee/pet. Designated rooms, service with restrictions.

Holiday Inn Conference Center H

(610) 391-1000. **Call for rates.** 7736 Adrienne Dr 18031. I-78 exit 49A, 0.3 mi s on SR 100. Int corridors. **Pets:** Accepted.

Sleep Inn H

(610) 395-6603. **$69-$129.** 327 Star Rd 18106. I-78 exit 49A, 0.3 mi s on SR 100, e at traffic light, then n on service road. Int corridors. **Pets:** Accepted.

Staybridge Suites-Allentown West H

(610) 841-5100. **Call for rates.** 327 Star Rd 18106. I-78 exit 49A, 0.3 mi s on SR 100, e at traffic light, then n on service road. Int corridors. **Pets:** Accepted.

FORT WASHINGTON

BEST WESTERN Fort Washington Inn H

(215) 542-7930. **$95-$141.** 285 Commerce Dr 19034. I-276 (Pennsylvania Tpke) exit 339 (SR 309 S), just w on Pennsylvania Ave, just n to Commerce Dr, then 0.3 mi e. Int corridors. **Pets:** Large. $15 deposit/pet, $15 daily fee/pet. Designated rooms, service with restrictions, supervision.

Hilton Garden Inn Philadelphia/Fort Washington H

(215) 646-4637. **$119-$229.** 530 W Pennsylvania Ave 19034. I-276 (Pennsylvania Tpke) exit 339 (SR 309 S), just w. Int corridors. **Pets:** Accepted.

FRANKLIN (VENANGO COUNTY)

Franklin Super 8 H

(814) 432-2101. **$64-$125.** 847 Allegheny Blvd 16323. 2 mi n on SR 8. Int corridors. **Pets:** Accepted.

GETTYSBURG

1863 Inn of Gettysburg H

(717) 334-6211. **$105-$345, 7 day notice.** 516 Baltimore St 17325. Jct US 15 business route and SR 97. Ext/int corridors. **Pets:** Other species. $20 daily fee/room. Designated rooms, service with restrictions, supervision.

▼▼ **Americas Best Value Inn** **M**
(717) 334-1188. **$57-$156.** 301 Steinwehr Ave 17325. 1 mi s on US 15 business route, just s of jct SR 134. Ext/int corridors. **Pets:** Other species. Designated rooms, service with restrictions. 🛇 🛜 ✕ 🖬

▼▼ **Battlefield Bed & Breakfast Inn** **BB**
(717) 334-8804. **Call for rates.** 2264 Emmitsburg Rd 17325. 3.8 mi s on Steinwehr Ave/Emmitsburg Rd from jct Baltimore St. Int corridors. **Pets:** Accepted. 🍴 🛜 ✕ 🗷 🖬

◈◈◈ ▼▼ **Country Inn & Suites By Carlson** **H**
(717) 337-9518. **$89-$189.** 1857 Gettysburg Village Dr 17325. US 15 exit SR 97, just e. Int corridors. **Pets:** Other species. $20 daily fee/room. Service with restrictions. [SAVE] 🛇 🛜 ✕ 🖬 🖳

▼▼ **Gettysburg Travelodge** **M**
(717) 334-9281. **$76-$130.** 613 Baltimore St 17325. On SR 97; at US 15 business route. Ext/int corridors. **Pets:** Accepted.
🛜 ✕ 🖬 🖳

▼▼ **Quality Inn & Suites** **H**
(717) 337-2400. **$45-$119.** 871 York Rd 17325. 1 mi e on US 30. Int corridors. **Pets:** Accepted. 🛇 🛜 ✕ 🖬 🖳

◈◈◈ ▼▼ **Super 8** **M**
(717) 337-1400. **$49-$210.** 869 York Rd 17325. 1 mi e on US 30. Int corridors. **Pets:** Other species. $10 daily fee/pet. Service with restrictions, crate. [SAVE] 🛦M 🛇 🛜 🖬 🖳

◈◈◈ ▼▼ **Wyndham Gettysburg** **H**
(717) 339-0020. **$119-$349.** 95 Presidential Cir 17325. US 15 exit York St, just e on US 30. Int corridors. **Pets:** Accepted.
[SAVE] 🍴 🛦M 🛇 🛜 ✕ 🖳

GIBSONIA
▼▼ **Quality Inn & Suites Pittsburgh-Gibsonia** **M**
(724) 444-8700. **$90-$200.** 5137 William Flynn Hwy 15044. I-76 (Pennsylvania Tpke) exit 39, just n. Ext corridors. **Pets:** Large, other species. $15 daily fee/pet. Service with restrictions, crate. 🛜 🖬 🖳

GLEN MILLS
▼▼ **Sweetwater Farm Bed & Breakfast** **BB** ❀
(610) 459-4711. **$150-$435, 14 day notice.** 50 Sweetwater Rd 19342. US 1, 2 mi w on Valley Rd, 0.6 mi s. Ext/int corridors. **Pets:** Other species. $50 one-time fee/pet. Designated rooms, service with restrictions, supervision. 🍴 🛇 🛜 ✕ 🖬 🖳

GORDONVILLE
◈◈◈ ▼▼ **Motel 6-Lancaster #4174** **M**
(717) 687-3880. **Call for rates.** 2959 Lincoln Hwy E 17529. On US 30 (Lincoln Hwy); center. Int corridors. **Pets:** Other species. Service with restrictions, crate. [SAVE] 🛦M 🛜 ✕ 🖬

GRANTVILLE
▼▼ **Days Inn Grantville-Hershey** **M**
(717) 469-0631. **$90-$110.** 252 Bow Creek Rd 17028. I-81 exit 80, 0.3 mi s. Ext corridors. **Pets:** Accepted. 🛜 🖬 🖳

◈◈◈ ▼▼ **Holiday Inn Harrisburg-Hershey Area, I-81** **H**
(717) 469-0661. **$99-$229.** 604 Station Rd 17028. I-81 exit 80. Int corridors. **Pets:** Dogs only. $25 one-time fee/room. Designated rooms, service with restrictions, supervision.
[SAVE] 🍴 🛦M 🛇 🛜 ✕ 🖬 🖳

GREENCASTLE
◈◈◈ ▼▼ **Comfort Inn** **H**
(717) 597-8164. **$70-$120.** 50 Pine Dr 17225. I-81 exit 3, just s on US 11. Int corridors. **Pets:** Other species. $10 daily fee/pet. Designated rooms, service with restrictions, supervision.
[SAVE] 🍴 🛜 ✕ 🖬 🖳

GREENSBURG
▼▼▼ **Ramada Hotel and Conference Greensburg** **H**
(724) 836-6060. **$85-$140.** 100 Ramada Inn Dr 15601. I-76 (Pennsylvania Tpke) exit 75, 5.6 mi on US 119 N, 3 mi e on US 30, then just n. Int corridors. **Pets:** Accepted. 🍴 🛦M 🛇 🛜 ✕ 🖬 🖳

GREEN TREE
◈◈◈ ▼▼▼ **DoubleTree by Hilton Pittsburgh-Green Tree** **H**
(412) 922-8400. **$189-$289.** 500 Mansfield Ave 15205. I-376 exit 67, 1.1 mi nw to Mansfield Ave. Int corridors. **Pets:** $50 one-time fee/room. Designated rooms, service with restrictions, crate.
[SAVE] 🍴 🛦M 🛇 🛜 ✕ 🖬 🖳

▼▼▼ **Hampton Inn Pittsburgh Green Tree** **H**
(412) 922-0100. **$109-$199.** 555 Trumbull Dr 15205. I-376 exit 67; jct US 22 and 30, 1 mi nw via Mansfield Ave. Int corridors.
Pets: Accepted. 🍴 🛇 🛜 🖬 🖳

HAMBURG
▼▼ **Microtel Inn & Suites by Wyndham Hamburg** **H**
(610) 562-4234. **$77-$118.** 50 Industrial Dr 19526. I-78 exit 29B, 0.3 mi n on SR 61, then just e. Int corridors. **Pets:** Other species. $10 daily fee/pet. Service with restrictions, supervision. 🍴 🛦M 🛜 🖬 🖳

HAMLIN
▼▼ **Comfort Inn-Pocono Lakes Region** **H**
(570) 689-4148. **$80-$160.** 117 Twin Rocks Rd 18427. I-84 exit 17, just n on SR 191. Int corridors. **Pets:** $15 daily fee/pet. Designated rooms, service with restrictions, supervision. 🛦M 🛜 🖬 🖳

HARRISBURG *(Restaurants p. 638)*
◈◈◈ ▼▼▼ **BEST WESTERN PREMIER The Central Hotel & Conference Center** **H**
(717) 561-2800. **$100-$200.** 800 E Park Dr 17111. I-83 exit 48, just e on Union Deposit Rd, then 0.5 mi s. Int corridors. **Pets:** Accepted.
[SAVE] 🍴 🛇 🛜 ✕ 🖬 🖳

▼▼▼ **Candlewood Suites Harrisburg** **H**
(717) 652-7800. **$110-$200.** 504 N Mountain Rd 17112. I-81 exit 72B, 0.4 mi n. Int corridors. **Pets:** Accepted. 🛇 🛜 🖬 🖳

▼▼▼ **Candlewood Suites Harrisburg-Hershey** **H**
(717) 561-9400. **$80-$240, 3 day notice.** 117 Twin Rocks Dr 17111. I-83 exit 45, 0.7 mi on Paxton St, then 0.4 mi s. Int corridors.
Pets: Accepted. 🍴 🛦M 🛜 ✕ 🖬 🖳

◈◈◈ ▼▼ **Comfort Inn Harrisburg/Hershey** **H**
(717) 657-2200. **$75-$175.** 5680 Allentown Blvd 17112. I-81 exit 72, just s on N Mountain Rd, then just w on US 22. Int corridors. **Pets:** Other species. $25 daily fee/room. Service with restrictions, supervision.
[SAVE] 🛦M 🛇 🛜 🖬 🖳

▼▼▼ **Comfort Inn Riverfront** **H**
(717) 233-1611. **$79-$189.** 525 S Front St 17104. I-83 exit 43, 0.5 mi n. Int corridors. **Pets:** Small. $25 one-time fee/pet. Service with restrictions. 🍴 🛇 🛜 ✕ 🖬 🖳

◈◈◈ ▼▼▼ **Hilton Harrisburg** **H**
(717) 233-6000. **$159-$219.** One N 2nd St 17101. Jct Market St; downtown. Int corridors. **Pets:** Medium. $50 one-time fee/room. Service with restrictions, supervision. [SAVE] 🍴 🛦M 🛇 🛜 🖬 🖳

▼▼▼ **Holiday Inn Express East** **H** 🐾
(717) 561-8100. **$99-$199.** 4021 Union Deposit Rd 17109. I-83 exit 48, just w. Int corridors. **Pets:** Medium, other species. $25 daily fee/room. Crate. 🛇 🛜 ✕ 🖬 🖳

◈◈◈ ▼▼▼ **Holiday Inn Harrisburg East-Airport** **H**
(717) 939-7841. **$99-$179.** 4751 Lindle Rd 17111. I-283 exit 2, just e. Int corridors. **Pets:** Accepted.
[SAVE] 🍴 🛦M 🛇 ✕ 🛜 ✕ 🖬 🖳

▼▼▼▼ **La Quinta Inn & Suites Harrisburg Hershey** 🄷
(717) 566-7666. **$79-$274.** 265 N Hershey Rd 17112. I-81 exit 77, just s. Int corridors. **Pets:** Large, other species. Service with restrictions.
🅂🄼 📶 ✕ 🛢 🖥

🅰🅰🅰 ▼▼▼ **Ramada Harrisburg** 🄷
(717) 652-7180. **$75-$165.** 300 N Mountain Rd 17112. I-81 exit 72 southbound; exit 72B northbound, just s. Int corridors. **Pets:** Medium, other species. $10 daily fee/pet. Designated rooms, service with restrictions, crate. 🅂🄰🅅🄴 🍽 🛁 📶 🖥

🅰🅰🅰 ▼▼▼ **Red Roof Inn Harrisburg - Hershey** 🄼
(717) 939-1331. **Call for rates.** 950 Eisenhower Blvd 17111. I-283 exit 2, just e. Ext/int corridors. **Pets:** Large, other species. Service with restrictions, supervision. 🅂🄰🅅🄴 📶 ✕ 🛢 🖥

🅰🅰🅰 ▼▼▼ **Red Roof Inn Harrisburg North** 🄼
(717) 657-1445. **Call for rates.** 400 Corporate Cir 17110. I-81 exit 69 (Progress Ave), just n. Ext/int corridors. **Pets:** Large, other species. Service with restrictions, supervision. 🅂🄰🅅🄴 🍽 📶 ✕ 🛢 🖥

▼▼▼ **Residence Inn by Marriott Harrisburg-Hershey** 🄷
(717) 561-1900. **$118-$217.** 4480 Lewis Rd 17111. US 322 exit Penhar Dr, just e. Ext/int corridors. **Pets:** $100 one-time fee/room. Designated rooms, service with restrictions. 🍽 🛁 📶 ✕ 🛢 🖥

🅰🅰🅰 ▼▼▼▼ **Sheraton Harrisburg Hershey** 🄷 🐾
(717) 564-5511. **$161-$329, 3 day notice.** 4650 Lindle Rd 17111. I-283 exit 2, just e. Int corridors. **Pets:** Medium, dogs only. Designated rooms, service with restrictions, crate.
🅂🄰🅅🄴 🍽 🅂🄼 🛁 📶 ✕ 🛢 🖥

🅰🅰🅰 ▼▼▼ **Staybridge Suites Harrisburg** 🄷
(717) 233-3304. **Call for rates.** 920 Wildwood Park Dr 17110. I-81 exit 67A/B, just w. Int corridors. **Pets:** Medium, other species. $75 one-time fee/room. Service with restrictions, supervision.
🅂🄰🅅🄴 🍽 🛁 📶 ✕ 🛢 🖥

🅰🅰🅰 ▼▼▼ **TownePlace Suites by Marriott Harrisburg Hershey** 🄷 🐾
(717) 558-0200. **$139-$229.** 450 Friendship Rd 17111. I-83 exit 45, 0.7 mi on Paxton St, then 0.3 mi s. Int corridors. **Pets:** Other species. $100 one-time fee/room. Service with restrictions, crate.
🅂🄰🅅🄴 🛁 📶 ✕ 🛢 🖥

HAWLEY
▼▼▼ **The Settlers Inn at Bingham Park** 🄲🄸
(570) 226-2993. **Call for rates.** 4 Main Ave 18428. On Main Ave (US 6), 0.3 mi w. Int corridors. **Pets:** Accepted. 🍽 📶 ✕ 🛢

HAZLETON
🅰🅰🅰 ▼▼▼ **BEST WESTERN Genetti Inn & Suites** 🄷 🐾
(570) 454-2494. **$91-$101, 3 day notice.** 1341 N Church St 18202. I-80 exit 262, 6 mi s on SR 309. Ext/int corridors. **Pets:** $10 daily fee/pet. Designated rooms, service with restrictions, crate.
🅂🄰🅅🄴 🛁 📶 🛢 🖥

▼▼▼ **Ramada Inn Hazleton** 🄷
(570) 455-2061. **$70-$140.** 1221 N Church St 18202. I-80 exit 262, 6 mi s on SR 309. Ext/int corridors. **Pets:** Accepted.
🍽 🛁 📶 🛢 🖥

▼▼▼ **Residence Inn by Marriott-Hazleton** 🄷
(570) 455-9555. **$90-$148.** 1 Station Circle Dr 18202. I-81 exit 143, just s on SR 924 S; at Humboldt Station, just e on Commerce Dr. Int corridors. **Pets:** Accepted. 🍽 🅂🄼 🛁 📶 ✕ 🛢 🖥

HERSHEY
🅰🅰🅰 ▼▼▼ **BEST WESTERN Inn Hershey** 🄼
(717) 533-5665. **$79-$329, 3 day notice.** US 422 & Sipe Ave 17033. Jct US 322, just e. Ext/int corridors. **Pets:** Accepted.
🅂🄰🅅🄴 🍽 🛁 📶 📶 ✕ 🛢 🖥

🅰🅰🅰 ▼▼▼ **Days Inn Hershey** 🄷 🐾
(717) 534-2162. **$110-$300.** 350 W Chocolate Ave 17033. On US 422; center. Int corridors. **Pets:** Medium, dogs only. $15 daily fee/pet. Designated rooms, service with restrictions, crate.
🅂🄰🅅🄴 🅂🄼 🛁 📶 📶 ✕ 🛢 🖥

🅰🅰🅰 ▼▼▼ **Hampton Inn & Suites Hershey** 🄷
(717) 533-8400. **$99-$239.** 749 E Chocolate Ave 17033. 0.9 mi e on US 422. Int corridors. **Pets:** Accepted.
🅂🄰🅅🄴 🅂🄼 🛁 📶 📶 ✕ 🛢 🖥

🅰🅰🅰 ▼▼▼ **Holiday Inn Express - Hershey/Hummelstown** 🄷
(717) 583-0500. **$99-$259.** 610 Walton Ave 17036. Just nw of jct US 322, 422 and SR 39 (Hersheypark Dr); just off Hersheypark Dr. Int corridors. **Pets:** Large. Service with restrictions, supervision.
🅂🄰🅅🄴 🍽 🅂🄼 🛁 📶 ✕ 🛢 🖥

HORSHAM
🅰🅰🅰 ▼▼▼ **Days Inn-Horsham/Philadelphia** 🄷
(215) 674-2500. **$59-$130.** 245 Easton Rd 19044. I-276 (Pennsylvania Tpke) exit 343 (SR 611), 1 mi n. Int corridors. **Pets:** Other species. $10 daily fee/pet. Designated rooms, service with restrictions, crate.
🅂🄰🅅🄴 📶 🛢 🖥

▼▼▼ **Extended Stay America-Philadelphia/Horsham** 🄷
(215) 784-9045. **Call for rates.** 114 Welsh Rd 19044. I-276 (Pennsylvania Tpke) exit 343 (SR 611), s toward Jenkintown, 0.6 mi w on Maryland Rd, 0.5 mi sw on Computer Ave, then just n. Int corridors. **Pets:** Other species. $25 daily fee/pet. Service with restrictions, supervision. 🅂🄼 📶 🛢 🖥

▼▼▼ **Residence Inn by Marriott-Willow Grove** 🄷
(215) 443-7330. **$139-$229.** 3 Walnut Grove Dr 19044. I-276 (Pennsylvania Tpke) exit 343, 1 mi n on Easton Rd, then 1.3 mi w on Dresher Rd. Ext corridors. **Pets:** Medium, other species. $150 one-time fee/room, $5 daily fee/room. Service with restrictions, supervision.
🍽 🅂🄼 🛁 📶 ✕ 🛢 🖥

HUNTINGDON
🅰🅰🅰 ▼▼▼ **Comfort Inn** 🄷
(814) 643-1600. **$63-$159.** 100 S 4th St 16652. I-99 exit 48, 8.8 mi on SR 453, then 9.8 mi on US 22 and S 4th St; just off US 22. Int corridors. **Pets:** Medium, other species. $15 daily fee/room. Designated rooms, service with restrictions, supervision.
🅂🄰🅅🄴 🅂🄼 🛁 📶 🛢 🖥

▼▼▼ **Huntingdon Motor Inn** 🄼
(814) 643-1133. **Call for rates.** 6920 Motor Inn Dr 16652. On US 22 (William Penn Hwy) at SR 26. Ext corridors. **Pets:** Small. $10 daily fee/pet. Designated rooms, service with restrictions, supervision.
📶 🛢 🖥

▼▼▼ **The Mill Stone Manor** 🄼
(814) 643-0108. **$49-$100, 3 day notice.** 11979 William Penn Hwy 16652. On US 22 (William Penn Hwy); 3 mi n of downtown. Ext/int corridors. **Pets:** Accepted. 🍽 📶 ✕ 🛢 🖥

INDIANA (INDIANA COUNTY)
▼▼▼ **Park Inn by Radisson** 🄷 🐾
(724) 463-3561. **$109-$159.** 1395 Wayne Ave 15701. US 422 exit Wayne Ave, 1 mi n. Ext/int corridors. **Pets:** Other species. $30 one-time fee/pet. Designated rooms, service with restrictions.
🍽 🅂🄼 🛁 📶 🛢 🖥

JOHNSTOWN

▼▼▼ Comfort Inn & Suites 🅷
(814) 266-3678. **$99-$112.** 455 Theatre Dr 15904. US 219 exit Elton (SR 756), just e. Int corridors. **Pets:** Accepted.
🅰🕭 🏊 🛜 ✕ 📶 🅿

▼▼ Econo Lodge Ⓜ
(814) 536-1114. **$80-$190.** 430 Napoleon Pl 15901. Jct SR 271 and 403; downtown. Int corridors. **Pets:** Accepted. 🅰🕭 🛜 📶

▼▼ Holiday Inn Downtown 🅷
(814) 535-7777. **Call for rates.** 250 Market St 15901. Corner of Market and Vine sts; downtown. Int corridors. **Pets:** Accepted.
🍴 🅰🕭 🏊 ✕ 🛜 ✕ 📶 🅿

▼▼ Holiday Inn Express Johnstown Ⓜ
(814) 266-8789. **Call for rates.** 1440 Scalp Ave 15904. US 219 exit Windber (SR 56 E), just e. Int corridors. **Pets:** Accepted.
🅰🕭 🛜 📶 🅿

▼▼ Sleep Inn 🅷
(814) 262-9292. **$81-$89.** 453 Theatre Dr 15904. US 219 exit Elton (SR 756), just e. Int corridors. **Pets:** Accepted. 🅰🕭 🛜 ✕ 📶 🅿

♨ ▼▼▽ Super 8 Johnstown 🅷
(814) 535-5600. **$60-$150.** 627 Solomon Run Rd 15904. US 219 exit Galleria Dr, just w. Int corridors. **Pets:** $10 daily fee/pet. Service with restrictions, supervision. 🆂🅰🆅🅴 🍴 🛜 ✕ 📶 🅿

JONES MILLS

▼▼ Log Cabin Lodge & Suites Ⓜ
(724) 593-8200. **Call for rates.** 288 Rt 711 15646. I-76 (Pennsylvania Tpke) exit 91, 2 mi on SR 31 E, then just s. Ext corridors.
Pets: Accepted. 🅰🕭 🛜 📶 🅿

JONESTOWN

♨ ▼▼▽ BEST WESTERN Lebanon Valley Inn & Suites 🅷
(717) 865-4234. **$79-$119.** 4 Fisher Ave 17038. I-81 exit 90, just e. Int corridors. **Pets:** Accepted. 🆂🅰🆅🅴 🏊 🛜 ✕ 📶 🅿

▼▼▽ Comfort Inn Lebanon Valley-Ft. Indiantown Gap Ⓜ
(717) 865-8080. **$79-$169.** 16 Marsanna Ln 17038. I-81 exit 90, just w. Int corridors. **Pets:** Medium. $25 daily fee/pet. Service with restrictions, supervision. 🆂🅰🆅🅴 🏊 🛜 ✕ 📶 🅿

▼▼ Days Inn Lebanon/Fort Indiantown Gap 🅷
(717) 865-4064. **$89-$219.** 3 Everest Ln 17038. I-81 exit 90. Int corridors. **Pets:** Other species. $10 daily fee/pet. Service with restrictions, supervision. 🍴 🛜 📶 🅿

KING OF PRUSSIA

♨ ▼▼▽ DoubleTree by Hilton Philadelphia Valley Forge 🅷
(610) 337-1200. **$104-$199.** 301 W Dekalb Pike 19406. I-76 (Pennsylvania Tpke) exit 326 (Valley Forge Rd), 1.4 mi ne on US 202 N. Int corridors. **Pets:** Accepted. 🆂🅰🆅🅴 🍴 🏊 🛜 ✕ 📶 🅿

♨ ▼▼▽ HYATT house Philadelphia/King of Prussia 🅷
(610) 265-0300. **$109-$349.** 240 Mall Blvd 19406. I-76 (Pennsylvania Tpke) exit 326 (Valley Forge Rd), 1 mi n of jct US 202 on Gulph Rd. Int corridors. **Pets:** Accepted. 🆂🅰🆅🅴 🅰🕭 🏊 🛜 ✕ 📶 🅿

♨ ▼▼▽ Hyatt Place Philadelphia/King of Prussia 🅷
(484) 690-3000. **$99-$249.** 440 American Ave 19406. I-76 (Pennsylvania Tpke) exit 326 (Valley Forge Rd); Schuylkill Expwy exit 328A (Mall Blvd), 1.3 mi n on N Gulph Rd, 1 mi ne on 1st Ave, then just e. Int corridors. **Pets:** Medium, dogs only. $75 one-time fee/pet. Service with restrictions, supervision. 🆂🅰🆅🅴 🍴 🏊 🛜 ✕ 📶 🅿

♨ ▼▼▽ Sheraton Valley Forge 🅷 🐾
(484) 238-1800. **$99-$349.** 480 N Gulph Rd 19406. I-76 (Pennsylvania Tpke) exit 326 (Valley Forge Rd), 0.5 mi w. Int corridors. **Pets:** Small, dogs only. Designated rooms, service with restrictions, supervision.
🆂🅰🆅🅴 🍴 🅰🕭 🏊 🛜 ✕ 📶 🅿

KITTANNING

▼▼ Quality Inn Royle 🅷
(724) 543-1159. **$85-$140.** 405 Butler Rd 16201. SR 28 exit US 422 W. Ext/int corridors. **Pets:** Accepted. 🛜 ✕ 📶 🅿

KULPSVILLE

▼▼▽ Holiday Inn Lansdale 🅷
(215) 368-3800. **Call for rates.** 1750 Sumneytown Pike 19443. I-476 (Pennsylvania Tpke NE Ext) exit 31, just e. Int corridors. **Pets:** Other species. $20 daily fee/pet. Service with restrictions, supervision.
🍴 🅰🕭 🏊 🛜 📶 🅿

LAMAR

▼▼ Comfort Inn of Lamar 🅷
(570) 726-4901. **$85-$210.** 31 Hospitality Ln 17751. I-80 exit 173, just n on SR 64. Int corridors. **Pets:** Accepted. 🏊 🛜 📶 🅿

LANCASTER

♨ ▼▼▽▽ BEST WESTERN PREMIER Eden Resort & Suites 🅷
(717) 569-6444. **$105-$180.** 222 Eden Rd 17601. Jct US 30 (Lincoln Hwy) and SR 272 (Oregon Pike). Ext/int corridors. **Pets:** Large, other species. $20 deposit/pet. Designated rooms, service with restrictions, supervision. 🆂🅰🆅🅴 🍴 🅰🕭 🏊 🛜 ✕ 📶 🅿

♨ ▼▼▽ Hawthorn Suites by Wyndham 🅷
(717) 290-7100. **$89-$170.** 2045 Lincoln Hwy 17602. Jct US 30 (Lincoln Hwy). Int corridors. **Pets:** Medium, dogs only. $50 one-time fee/pet. Designated rooms, service with restrictions, crate.
🆂🅰🆅🅴 🛜 ✕ 📶 🅿

♨ ▼▼▽ Red Roof Inn Lancaster Ⓜ
(717) 299-9700. **Call for rates.** 2307 Lincoln Hwy E 17602. On US 30 (Lincoln Hwy), 5 mi e. Ext/int corridors. **Pets:** Large, other species. Service with restrictions, supervision.
🆂🅰🆅🅴 🅰🕭 🏊 🛜 ✕ 📶 🅿

LANGHORNE

♨ ▼▼▽ Red Roof Inn Philadelphia Oxford Valley Ⓜ
(215) 750-6200. **Call for rates.** 3100 Cabot Blvd W 19047. I-95 exit 46A (Oxford Valley Rd), just e off US 1 N; 0.5 mi n of Sesame Place. Ext corridors. **Pets:** Large, other species. Service with restrictions, supervision. 🆂🅰🆅🅴 🍴 🛜 ✕ 📶 🅿

▼▼▽ Residence Inn by Marriott Philadelphia Langhorne 🅷
(215) 946-6500. **$153-$367.** 15 E Cabot Blvd 19047. I-95 exit 46A (Oxford Valley Rd), just e off US 1 N; 0.5 mi n of Sesame Place. Int corridors. **Pets:** Accepted. 🅰🕭 🏊 🛜 ✕ 📶 🅿

♨ ▼▼▽▽ Sheraton Bucks County Hotel 🅷
(215) 547-4100. **$89-$289.** 400 Oxford Valley Rd 19047. I-95 exit 46A (Oxford Valley Rd), 0.8 mi e to exit off US 1 N. Int corridors.
Pets: Accepted. 🆂🅰🆅🅴 🍴 🅰🕭 🏊 🛜 ✕ 📶 🅿

LEBANON (LEBANON COUNTY)

▼▼▽ Berry Patch Bed and Breakfast 🅱🅱
(717) 865-7219. **$135-$239, 14 day notice.** 115 Moore Rd 17046. I-81 exit 90, 2.8 mi s on SR 72, 1 mi e on New Bunker Hill St, 0.8 mi s on S Lancaster St, then just e, follow signs. Ext/int corridors.
Pets: Accepted. 🍴 🛜 ✕ 🆉 📶

LEHIGHTON

Country Inn & Suites By Carlson H
(610) 379-5066. **$92-$300.** 1619 Interchange Rd 18235. I-476 (Pennsylvania Tpke NE Ext) exit 74 (US 209), just w. Int corridors. Pets: $25 daily fee/room. Designated rooms, service with restrictions.

LINCOLN FALLS

Morgan Century Farm BB
(570) 924-4909. **Call for rates.** 7043 Rt 154 18616. Just w on SR 87, 0.6 mi s; in village. Ext/int corridors. Pets: Medium. $15 one-time fee/pet. Designated rooms, service with restrictions, supervision.

LIONVILLE

Comfort Suites Exton H
(610) 594-4770. **$119-$200.** 700 W Uwchlan Ave 19341. I-76 (Pennsylvania Tpke) exit 312, 1 mi s on SR 100. Int corridors. Pets: Accepted.

Extended Stay America-Philadelphia/Exton H
(610) 524-7185. **Call for rates.** 877 N Pottstown Pike (Rt 100) 19353. I-76 (Pennsylvania Tpke) exit 312, 1.8 mi s. Int corridors. Pets: Other species. $25 daily fee/pet. Service with restrictions, supervision.

Hampton Inn Exton/Downingtown H
(610) 363-5555. **$119-$159.** 4 N Pottstown Pike 19341. I-76 (Pennsylvania Tpke) exit 312, 0.5 mi s; jct SR 113 and 100. Int corridors. Pets: Other species. Service with restrictions, supervision.

Residence Inn by Marriott Philadelphia Great Valley/Exton H
(610) 594-9705. **$132-$217.** 10 N Pottstown Pike 19341. I-76 (Pennsylvania Tpke) exit 312, 1 mi s on SR 100. Int corridors. Pets: Other species. $100 one-time fee/room. Service with restrictions.

LITITZ

Holiday Inn Express & Suites H
(717) 625-2366. **$121-$308.** 101 Crosswinds Dr 17543. 1.4 mi s on SR 501 (Lititz Pike), just w on Trolley Run Rd. Int corridors. Pets: Accepted.

LOCK HAVEN

BEST WESTERN Lock Haven H
(570) 748-3297. **$99-$199, 30 day notice.** 101 E Walnut St 17745. US 220 exit 111 (SR 120 W), just w. Int corridors. Pets: Other species. $12 daily fee/pet. Service with restrictions.

MALVERN

The Desmond Hotel and Conference Center Malvern H
(610) 296-9800. **$169-$299.** 1 Liberty Blvd 19355. US 202 exit SR 29 N, 0.5 mi w. Int corridors. Pets: Accepted.

Extended Stay America Malvern H
(610) 695-9200. **Call for rates.** 8 E Swedesford Rd 19355. Just w of US 202 and SR 29 N. Int corridors. Pets: Other species. $25 daily fee/pet. Service with restrictions, supervision.

Extended Stay America-Philadelphia Great Valley H
(610) 240-0455. **Call for rates.** 300 Morehall Rd (SR 29) 19355. US 202 exit SR 29 N. Int corridors. Pets: Other species. $25 daily fee/pet. Service with restrictions, supervision.

Homewood Suites by Hilton H
(610) 296-3500. **$129-$249.** 12 E Swedesford Rd 19355. US 202 exit SR 29, follow signs. Int corridors. Pets: Large, dogs only. $50 one-time fee/pet. Service with restrictions.

Sheraton Great Valley Hotel H
(610) 524-5500. **$109-$229.** 707 Lancaster Pike 19355. Jct US 202 and 30 E. Int corridors. Pets: Accepted.

Sonesta ES Suites Malvern H
(610) 296-4343. **Call for rates.** 20 Morehall Rd 19355. Jct US 30 and SR 29, just nw. Ext/int corridors. Pets: Accepted.

MANSFIELD

Comfort Inn H
(570) 662-3000. **$109-$179.** 300 Gateway Dr 16933. Jct US 6 and 15. Int corridors. Pets: Accepted.

MARIENVILLE

The Forest Lodge & Campground M
(814) 927-8790. **Call for rates.** 44078 Rt 66 16239. 6 mi n of town. Ext/int corridors. Pets: Dogs only. $10 daily fee/pet. Designated rooms, service with restrictions, supervision.

MARS

Comfort Inn Cranberry Township H
(724) 772-2700. **$99-$159.** 924 Sheraton Dr 16046. I-76 (Pennsylvania Tpke) exit 28; I-79 exit 76 (US 19) northbound; exit 78 southbound, 0.5 mi s on US 19. Int corridors. Pets: Medium, other species. $20 one-time fee/room. Designated rooms, service with restrictions, crate.

Super 8-Cranberry H
(724) 776-9700. **$90-$175.** 929 Sheraton Dr 16046. I-76 (Pennsylvania Tpke) exit 28; I-79 exit 76 (US 19 N) northbound; exit 78 southbound, 0.5 mi s on US 19. Int corridors. Pets: Accepted.

MATAMORAS

BEST WESTERN Inn at Hunt's Landing H
(570) 491-2400. **$109-$199.** 120 Rt 6 & 209 18336. I-84 exit 53, just s. Int corridors. Pets: Accepted.

MEADVILLE

Quality Inn Meadville M
(814) 333-8883. **Call for rates.** 17259 Conneaut Lake Rd 16335. I-79 exit 147B, just w on US 322. Ext/int corridors. Pets: Accepted.

MECHANICSBURG

Comfort Inn Capital City H
(717) 766-3700. **$79-$189.** 1012 Wesley Dr 17055. I-76 (Pennsylvania Tpke) exit 236, 1 mi n to Wesley Dr exit, then just w. Int corridors. Pets: Accepted.

Hampton Inn-Harrisburg West H
(717) 691-1300. **$109-$189.** 4950 Ritter Rd 17055. I-76 (Pennsylvania Tpke) exit 236, 1 mi n to Rossmoyne Rd exit. Int corridors. Pets: Accepted.

Holiday Inn Express Harrisburg SW-Mechanicsburg H
(717) 790-0924. **$119-$209.** 6325 Carlisle Pike 17050. Jct Carlisle Pike and US 11, 1 mi w on US 11. Int corridors. Pets: Medium. $25 daily fee/room. Service with restrictions, crate.

Homewood Suites by Hilton-Harrisburg West H
(717) 697-4900. **$119-$199.** 5001 Ritter Rd 17055. I-76 (Pennsylvania Tpke) exit 236, 1 mi n to Rossmoyne Rd exit. Int corridors. Pets: Accepted.

Motel 6 M
(717) 766-0238. **$60-$120.** 381 Cumberland Pkwy 17055. I-76 (Pennsylvania Tpke) exit 236, just s, then exit Cumberland Pkwy. Ext corridors. Pets: Other species. Service with restrictions, crate.

▽▽▽ Park Inn by Radisson Harrisburg West 🅷

(717) 697-0321. **$99-$179.** 5401 Carlisle Pike 17050. Jct Carlisle Pike and US 11, just w. Ext/int corridors. **Pets:** Accepted.

🍽 ⊠ 🗙 🛜 🗙 🛢 ▣

▽▽▽ Wingate by Wyndham Mechanicsburg/Harrisburg West 🅷

(717) 766-2710. **$109-$269.** 385 Cumberland Pkwy 17055. I-76 (Pennsylvania Tpke) exit 236, just s. Int corridors. **Pets:** Accepted.

🅼 ⊠ 🛜 🗙 🛢 ▣

MERCER

▽▽▽ Comfort Inn Mercer 🅷

(724) 748-3030. **$90-$120.** 835 Perry Hwy 16137. I-80 exit 15, just n on US 19. Int corridors. **Pets:** Accepted. 🍽 🅼 ⊠ 🛜 🛢 ▣

MIFFLINVILLE

▽▽▽ Super 8 - Mifflinville 🅼

(570) 759-6778. **$65-$110.** 450 W 3rd St 18631. I-80 exit 242 (SR 339), just n. Ext corridors. **Pets:** Accepted. 🛜 🛢 ▣

MILFORD

▽▽▽ Hotel Fauchère 🅷 ❀

(570) 409-1212. **$189-$594, 14 day notice.** 401 Broad St 18337. In historic downtown. Int corridors. **Pets:** Medium, dogs only. $25 daily fee/pet. Designated rooms, service with restrictions, supervision.

🍽 🛜 🗙 🛢 ▣

◈◈◈ ▽▽▽ Scottish Inns 🅼

(570) 491-4414. **$50-$110, 3 day notice.** 274 Rt 6 & 209 18337. I-84 exit 53, 1 mi s. Ext corridors. **Pets:** Accepted. SAVE 🛜 🛢 ▣

MILROY

◈◈◈ ▽▽▽ BEST WESTERN Nittany Inn Milroy 🅷

(717) 667-9595. **$80-$100.** 5 Commerce Dr 17063. US 322 exit Milroy, just e. Int corridors. **Pets:** Small, dogs only. $20 daily fee/pet. Service with restrictions, supervision. SAVE 🍽 ⊠ 🛜 🗙 🛢 ▣

MONACA

▽▽▽ Hampton Inn Beaver Valley/Pittsburgh 🅷

(724) 774-5580. **$134-$164.** 202 Fairview Dr 15061. I-376 exit 39, just n. Int corridors. **Pets:** Medium, other species. Service with restrictions, supervision. 🅼 ⊠ 🛜 🛢 ▣

▽▽▽ Holiday Inn Express Hotel & Suites-Center Township 🅷

(724) 728-5121. **Call for rates.** 105 Stone Quarry Rd 15061. I-376 exit 39 (SR 18 N/Frankfort Rd), just n. Int corridors. **Pets:** Accepted.

🅼 ⊠ 🗙 🛢 ▣

▽▽ The Inn 🅷

(724) 728-9270. **Call for rates.** 1525 Old Brodhead Rd 15061. I-376 exit 39, 1 mi e. Int corridors. **Pets:** Accepted. 🛜 🛢 ▣

MONROEVILLE

◈◈◈ ▽▽▽ DoubleTree by Hilton Hotel Pittsburgh - Monroeville Convention Center 🅷

(412) 373-7300. **$99-$169.** 101 Mall Blvd 15146. I-76 (Pennsylvania Tpke) exit 57, 2 mi w on US 22. Int corridors. **Pets:** Small, other species. $50 one-time fee/room. Service with restrictions.

SAVE 🍽 ⊠ 🛜 🗙 ▣

▽▽▽ Extended Stay America-Pittsburgh-Monroeville 🅷

(412) 856-8400. **Call for rates.** 3851 Northern Pike 15146. I-76 (Pennsylvania Tpke) exit 57, 1.2 mi w on Business Rt US 22. Int corridors. **Pets:** Other species. $25 daily fee/pet. Service with restrictions, supervision. 🛜 ▣

▽▽▽ Hampton Inn Monroeville/Pittsburgh 🅷

(412) 380-4000. **$109-$159.** 3000 Mosside Blvd 15146. I-76 (Pennsylvania Tpke) exit 57; I-376 exit 84A, 0.3 mi s on SR 48. Int corridors. **Pets:** Accepted. 🅼 ⊠ 🛜 🗙 🛢 ▣

◈◈◈ ▽▽▽ Red Roof Inn Pittsburgh East - Monroeville 🅼

(412) 856-4738. **Call for rates.** 2729 Mosside Blvd 15146. I-76 (Pennsylvania Tpke) exit 57; I-376 exit 84A, 0.8 mi s on SR 48. Ext corridors. **Pets:** Large, other species. Service with restrictions, supervision.

SAVE 🛜 🛢 ▣

▽▽▽ Super 8 Pittsburgh/Monroeville 🅼

(724) 733-8008. **$80-$175.** 1807 Golden Mile Hwy (Rt 286) 15239. I-76 (Pennsylvania Tpke) exit 57; I-376 exit 84A, 2 mi e on US 22 E, then 2 mi e. Int corridors. **Pets:** Accepted. 🛜 🗙 🛢 ▣

MONTGOMERYVILLE

▽▽▽ Comfort Inn 🅷

(215) 361-3600. **$89-$179.** 678 Bethlehem Pike 18936. Jct SR 463 and US 202, 0.3 mi n on SR 309. Int corridors. **Pets:** Large, other species. $25 daily fee/pet. Service with restrictions, supervision.

🅼 🛜 🛢 ▣

▽▽▽ Residence Inn by Marriott Philadelphia/Montgomeryville 🅷

(267) 468-0111. **$132-$217.** 1110 Bethlehem Pike 19454. I-276 (Pennsylvania Tpke) exit 339, 6.5 mi n on SR 309. Int corridors.

Pets: Accepted. ⊠ 🛜 🗙 🛢 ▣

MOON RUN

▽▽▽ Extended Stay America Pittsburgh Airport 🅷

(412) 490-0979. **Call for rates.** 200 Chauvet Dr 15275. I-376 exit 59 (Robinson Town Center Blvd), left on Summit Park Dr, then just s. Int corridors. **Pets:** Other species. $25 daily fee/pet. Service with restrictions, supervision. 🅼 🛜 🗙 🛢 ▣

▽▽▽ MainStay Suites Pittsburgh Airport 🅷

(412) 490-7343. **$90-$120.** 1000 Park Lane Dr 15275. I-376 exit 58 (Montour Run Rd), just w on Cliff Mine Rd, then just s. Int corridors.

Pets: Accepted. 🅼 🛜 🛢 ▣

▽▽▽ Pittsburgh Airport Marriott 🅷

(412) 788-8800. **$188-$309.** 777 Aten Rd 15108. I-376 exit 58 (Montour Run Rd). Int corridors. **Pets:** Accepted. 🍽 ⊠ 🛜 🗙 🛢 ▣

◈◈◈ ▽▽▽ Red Roof Inn Plus Pittsburgh South - Airport 🅼

(412) 787-7870. **Call for rates.** 6404 Steubenville Pike 15205. I-79 exit 60A, 3.2 mi w on SR 60 (Steubenville Pike). Ext/int corridors. **Pets:** Large, other species. Service with restrictions, supervision.

SAVE 🅼 🛜 🗙 🛢 ▣

▽▽▽ Residence Inn by Marriott Pittsburgh Airport Coraopolis 🅷

(412) 787-3300. **$133-$219.** 1500 Park Lane Dr 15275. I-376 exit 58 (Montour Run Rd), just w on Cliff Mine Dr to Summit Park Dr, just s to Park Lane Dr, then just e. Int corridors. **Pets:** Accepted.

🅼 ⊠ 🗙 🛜 🗙 🛢 ▣

MOON TOWNSHIP

▽▽▽ Homewood Suites 🅷

(412) 490-0440. **$129-$219.** 2000 GSK Dr 15108. I-376 exit 59 (Montour Run Rd), 0.9 mi w, then just w to Fedex Dr; jct Montour Run Rd and Fedex Dr. Int corridors. **Pets:** Accepted. 🍽 🛜 🗙 🛢 ▣

MORGANTOWN

▽▽▽ Holiday Inn 🅷

(610) 286-3000. **Call for rates.** 6170 Morgantown Rd 19543. I-76 (Pennsylvania Tpke) exit 298, just s on SR 10. Int corridors.

Pets: Accepted. 🍽 ⊠ 🛜 🗙 🛢 ▣

MORRISVILLE

◈◈◈ ▽▽▽ Comfort Inn NJ State Capital Area 🅷

(215) 428-2600. **$89-$190.** 7 S Pennsylvania Ave 19067. US 1 exit Pennsylvania Ave, just n. Int corridors. **Pets:** Medium, dogs only. $15 daily fee/room. Designated rooms, service with restrictions, crate.

SAVE 🅼 🛜 🗙 🛢 ▣

MOUNTVILLE

◎◎◎ ▽▽ MainStay Suites 🄷

(717) 285-2500. **$90-$160.** 314 Primrose Ln 17554. US 30 (Lincoln Hwy) exit Mountville, just n on Stoney Battery Rd, just w on Highland Dr, then just s. Int corridors. **Pets:** Accepted.

[SAVE] [†¶] [🕭ᴹ] [🏊] [📶] [🔋] [🖵]

NEW CASTLE

▽▽ Comfort Inn-New Castle 🄷 🐾

(724) 658-7700. **$79-$139.** 1740 New Butler Rd (US Business 422) 16101. Jct SR 65, 1 mi e on US 422, 1 mi w on US 422 business route. Int corridors. **Pets:** Medium, other species. $25 one-time fee/pet. Designated rooms, service with restrictions, supervision.

[†¶] [📶] [🔋] [🖵]

NEW COLUMBIA

◎◎◎ ▽▽▽ Holiday Inn Express 🄷

(570) 568-1100. **$99-$229.** 160 Commerce Park Dr 17856. I-80 exit 210A (US 15/New Columbia), just s. Int corridors. **Pets:** Medium, other species. $20 daily fee/pet. Designated rooms, service with restrictions, crate. [SAVE] [🕭ᴹ] [🏊] [📶] [✕] [🔋] [🖵]

NEW CUMBERLAND

◎◎◎ ▽▽▽▽ BEST WESTERN PLUS New Cumberland Inn & Suites 🄷

(717) 774-4440. **$95-$170.** 702 Limekiln Rd 17070. I-83 exit 40A, just w. Int corridors. **Pets:** Medium. $15 daily fee/pet. Service with restrictions, crate. [SAVE] [🏊] [📶] [🔋] [🖵]

◎◎◎ ▽▽▽▽ Clarion Hotel & Conference Center Harrisburg 🄷

(717) 774-2721. **Call for rates.** 148 Sheraton Dr 17070. I-83 exit 40A, just se. Int corridors. **Pets:** Accepted.

[SAVE] [†¶] [🏊] [📶] [✕] [🔋] [🖵]

▽▽ Days Inn Harrisburg South 🄷

(717) 774-4156. **$65-$110.** 353 Lewisberry Rd 17070. I-83 exit 39A, just ne. Int corridors. **Pets:** Accepted. [†¶] [🏊] [📶] [🔋] [🖵]

NEW HOPE

▽▽▽ 1870 Wedgwood Inn of New Hope ⒷⒷ

(215) 862-2570. **Call for rates.** 111 W Bridge St (SR 179) 18938. 0.5 mi w of SR 32; downtown. Int corridors. **Pets:** Medium, dogs only. $20 daily fee/pet. Designated rooms, service with restrictions, supervision.

[📶] [✕] [🔋] [🖵]

▽▽▽ Aaron Burr House Inn & Conference Center ⒷⒷ

(215) 862-3937. **Call for rates.** 80 W Bridge St (SR 179) 18938. 0.5 mi w of SR 32; at W Bridge and Chestnut sts. Int corridors. **Pets:** Medium, dogs only. $20 daily fee/pet. Service with restrictions, supervision.

[📶] [✕] [🄯] [🔋]

NEW STANTON

▽▽▽ Super 8-New Stanton Ⓜ

(724) 925-8915. **$69-$84.** 103 Bair Blvd 15672. I-76 (Pennsylvania Tpke) exit 75, 0.5 mi se; I-70 exit 57B westbound; exit 57 eastbound. Int corridors. **Pets:** Accepted. [🕭ᴹ] [📶] [🔋] [🖵]

OAKDALE

▽▽▽ Quality Inn Pittsburgh Airport 🄷

(412) 787-2600. **$95-$199.** 7011 Old Steubenville Pike 15071. I-376 exit 60A; jct US 22 and 30. Ext/int corridors. **Pets:** Accepted.

[🕭ᴹ] [📶] [🔋] [🖵]

PHILADELPHIA *(Restaurants p. 638)*

◎◎◎ ▽▽▽▽ Aloft Philadelphia 🄷 🐾

(267) 298-1700. **$129.** 4301 Island Ave 19153. Jct I-95 and SR 291 exit 13 northbound; exit 15 southbound. Int corridors. **Pets:** Medium, dogs only. $75 deposit/pet. Service with restrictions, supervision.

[SAVE] [†¶] [🕭ᴹ] [🏊] [📶] [✕] [🔋] [🖵]

◎◎◎ ▽▽▽▽ Four Points by Sheraton Philadelphia Airport 🄷 🐾

(215) 492-0400. **$99.** 4101 Island Ave 19153. Jct I-95 and SR 291 exit 13 northbound; exit 15 southbound. Int corridors. **Pets:** Medium, dogs only. $75 deposit/pet. Service with restrictions, supervision.

[SAVE] [†¶] [🏊] [📶] [✕] [🔋] [🖵]

▽▽▽▽ Four Seasons Hotel Philadelphia 🄷

(215) 963-1500. **Call for rates.** 1 Logan Square 19103. Corner of 18th St and Benjamin Franklin Pkwy. Int corridors. **Pets:** Accepted.

[†¶] [🕭ᴹ] [🏊] [📶] [✕] [🔋] [🖵]

◎◎◎ ▽▽▽ Hawthorn Suites by Wyndham Philadelphia Airport 🄷

(215) 492-1611. **$111-$179.** 4630 Island Ave 19153. I-95 exit 13 northbound; exit 15 southbound, 0.5 mi e; just e of SR 291. Ext corridors. **Pets:** Accepted. [SAVE] [🕭ᴹ] [🏊] [📶] [✕] [🔋] [🖵]

◎◎◎ ▽▽▽▽ Hilton Philadelphia at Penn's Landing 🄷 🐾

(215) 928-1234. **$99-$499.** 201 S Columbus Blvd 19106. Jct S Columbus Blvd and Dock St. Int corridors. **Pets:** Medium, dogs only. $100 one-time fee/room. Designated rooms, service with restrictions, supervision. [SAVE] [†¶] [🕭ᴹ] [🏊] [📶] [✕] [🔋] [🖵]

▽▽▽ Home2 Suites by Hilton Philadelphia Convention Center 🄷

(215) 627-1850. **$149-$399.** 1200 Arch St 19107. Between Market and Arch sts. Int corridors. **Pets:** Accepted. [🕭ᴹ] [📶] [✕] [🔋] [🖵]

◎◎◎ ▽▽▽▽ Hotel Monaco Philadelphia, A Kimpton Hotel 🄷 🐾

(215) 925-2111. **Call for rates.** 433 Chestnut St 19106. Jct 5th and Chestnut sts. Int corridors. **Pets:** Other species. Designated rooms, service with restrictions. [SAVE] [†¶] [🕭ᴹ] [📶] [✕] [🔋] [🖵]

◎◎◎ ▽▽▽▽ Hotel Palomar-Philadelphia 🄷

(215) 563-5006. **Call for rates.** 117 S 17th St 19103. Corner of 17th and Samson sts. Int corridors. **Pets:** Accepted.

[SAVE] [ECO] [†¶] [🕭ᴹ] [📶] [✕] [🔋] [🖵]

◎◎◎ ▽▽▽▽ Hyatt at The Bellevue 🄷 🐾

(215) 893-1234. **$119-$449, 3 day notice.** 200 S Broad St 19102. Between Walnut and Locust sts. Int corridors. **Pets:** Small, dogs only. $100 one-time fee/pet. Designated rooms, service with restrictions, crate. [SAVE] [†¶] [🕭ᴹ] [📶] [✕] [🔋] [🖵]

◎◎◎ ▽▽▽ The Latham Hotel 🄷

(215) 563-7474. **$129-$549.** 135 S 17th St 19103. Jct 17th and Walnut sts. Int corridors. **Pets:** Small, dogs only. $75 one-time fee/room. Designated rooms, service with restrictions, crate.

[SAVE] [†¶] [📶] [✕] [🔋] [🖵]

◎◎◎ ▽▽▽▽ Le Meridien Philadelphia 🄷

(215) 422-8200. **$139-$999.** 1421 Arch St 19102. Between Broad and 15th sts. Int corridors. **Pets:** Accepted.

[SAVE] [†¶] [🕭ᴹ] [📶] [✕] [🔋] [🖵]

◎◎◎ ▽▽▽▽ Loews Philadelphia Hotel 🄷

(215) 627-1200. **$149-$489.** 1200 Market St 19107. Corner of 12th and Market sts. Int corridors. **Pets:** Accepted.

[SAVE] [†¶] [🕭ᴹ] [🏊] [📶] [✕] [📶] [🔋] [🖵]

◎◎◎ ▽▽▽▽ Omni Hotel at Independence Park 🄷

(215) 925-0000. **Call for rates.** 401 Chestnut St 19106. Jct 4th St. Int corridors. **Pets:** Accepted.

[SAVE] [†¶] [🕭ᴹ] [🏊] [📶] [✕] [🔋] [🖵]

▽▽▽▽ Residence Inn by Marriott Center City Philadelphia 🄷

(215) 557-0005. **$174-$286.** 1 E Penn Square 19107. Jct Market and Juniper sts. Int corridors. **Pets:** Accepted. [📶] [✕] [🔋] [🖵]

◇◇◇◇ The Rittenhouse ⊞ ❀
(215) 546-9000. **Call for rates.** 210 W Rittenhouse Square 19103. Jct
W Rittenhouse Square and Walnut St. Int corridors. **Pets:** $150 one-
time fee/pet. Service with restrictions, supervision.
[SAVE] [🍴] [&M] [⊇] [✕] [📶] [✕] [📋] [💻]

◇◇◇◇ The Ritz-Carlton Philadelphia ⊞
(215) 523-8000. **Call for rates.** Ten Avenue of the Arts 19102. On
Broad St; between Market and Chestnut sts. Int corridors.
Pets: Accepted. [🍴] [✕] [📶] [✕] [📋]

◇◇◇◇ Sheraton Philadelphia Downtown ⊞ ❀
(215) 448-2000. **$129-$499.** 201 N 17th St 19103. Jct 17th and Race
sts. Int corridors. **Pets:** Medium, dogs only. $50 one-time fee/room.
Designated rooms, service with restrictions, supervision.
[SAVE] [🍴] [⊇] [📶] [✕] [📋] [💻]

◇◇◇◇ Sheraton Philadelphia Society Hill ⊞
(215) 238-6000. **$159.** One Dock St 19106. Just s of jct 2nd and Wal-
nut sts. Int corridors. **Pets:** Accepted.
[SAVE] [🍴] [⊇] [📶] [✕] [📋] [💻]

◇◇◇◇ Sheraton Philadelphia University City
Hotel ⊞ ❀
(215) 387-8000. **$119-$399.** 3549 Chestnut St 19104. I-76 (Schuylkill
Expwy) exit 345, 0.5 mi w; jct 36th St; at University of Pennsylvania. Int
corridors. **Pets:** Large, dogs only. Service with restrictions, supervision.
[SAVE] [ECO] [🍴] [&M] [⊇] [📶] [✕] [📋] [💻]

◇◇◇◇ Sheraton Suites Philadelphia
Airport ⊞ ❀
(215) 365-6600. **$129.** 4101 Island Ave 19153. Jct I-95 and SR 291 exit
13 northbound; exit 15 southbound. Int corridors. **Pets:** Medium, dogs
only. $75 deposit/pet. Service with restrictions, supervision.
[SAVE] [🍴] [⊇] [📶] [✕] [📋] [💻]

◇◇◇◇ Sofitel Philadelphia ⊞ ❀
(215) 569-8300. **Call for rates.** 120 S 17th St 19103. Jct Sansom and
17th sts. Int corridors. **Pets:** Medium. $300 deposit/room. Service with
restrictions, crate. [SAVE] [ECO] [🍴] [&M] [📶] [✕] [📋]

◇◇◇◇ The Westin Philadelphia ⊞
(215) 563-1600. **Call for rates.** 99 S 17th St at Liberty Pl 19103.
Between Market and Chestnut sts. Int corridors. **Pets:** Accepted.
[SAVE] [🍴] [✕] [📶] [✕] [📋] [💻]

PINE GROVE
◇◇ Comfort Inn ⊞
(570) 345-8031. **$70-$170.** 433 Suedberg Rd 17963. I-81 exit 100, just
e. Int corridors. **Pets:** Other species. $10 daily fee/pet. Crate.
[&M] [⊇] [📶] [📋] [💻]

◇◇◇ Hampton Inn Pine Grove ⊞
(570) 345-4505. **$109-$159.** 481 Suedberg Rd 17963. I-81 exit 100, just
w. Int corridors. **Pets:** Accepted. [&M] [⊇] [📶] [📋] [💻]

PITTSBURGH
◇◇◇ Comfort Inn ⊞
(412) 415-3867. **$103-$125.** 4607 McKnight Rd 15237. I-279 exit 4, 4
mi n on US 19. Int corridors. **Pets:** Accepted.
[🍴] [&M] [📶] [✕] [📋] [💻]

◇◇◇◇ DoubleTree by Hilton Hotel & Suites Pittsburgh
Downtown ⊞
(412) 281-5800. **$189-$309.** One Bigelow Square 15219. Jct Bigelow
Square and 6th St; just n of Grant St. Int corridors. **Pets:** Accepted.
[ECO] [🍴] [⊇] [📶] [✕] [📋] [💻]

◇◇◇◇ Fairmont Pittsburgh ⊞ ❀
(412) 773-8800. **Call for rates.** 510 Market St 15222. Between Market
St and 5th Ave; in cultural district. Int corridors. **Pets:** Other species.
$25 daily fee/pet. Service with restrictions, supervision.
[SAVE] [ECO] [🍴] [&M] [✕] [📶] [✕] [📋] [💻]

◇◇◇ Hampton Inn University Center/Pittsburgh ⊞
(412) 681-1000. **$149-$179.** 3315 Hamlet St 15213. I-376 exit 72A, 0.6
mi e, then e. Int corridors. **Pets:** Accepted. [🍴] [&M] [📶] [📋] [💻]

◇◇◇ Home2 Suites by Hilton
Pittsburgh/McCandless ⊞
(412) 630-8400. **$129-$169.** 8630 Duncan Ave 15237. I-279 exit 4, 7 mi
n on US 19 Truck Babcock, then left to Duncan Ave. Int corridors.
Pets: Accepted. [&M] [📶] [📋] [💻]

◇◇◇◇ Hyatt Place Pittsburgh-North Shore ⊞
(412) 321-3000. **$129-$499.** 260 N Shore Dr 15212. I-279/376 exit 70B
(Fort Duquesne Blvd), exit 6C, stay right, n on 6th St/Roberto Clemente
Bridge (which becomes Federal St), w on W General Robinson St, s on
Mazeroski Way, then just w. Int corridors. **Pets:** Accepted.
[SAVE] [🍴] [&M] [⊇] [📶] [✕] [📋] [💻]

◇◇◇◇ Omni William Penn Hotel ⊞ ❀
(412) 281-7100. **Call for rates.** 530 William Penn Pl 15219. Jct 6th St
and William Penn Pl. Int corridors. **Pets:** Small. $50 one-time fee/room.
Service with restrictions, crate. [SAVE] [🍴] [&M] [📶] [📋] [💻]

◇◇◇ The Parador Inn ⒷⒷ
(412) 231-4800. **Call for rates.** 939 Western Ave 15233. At North
Shore. Int corridors. **Pets:** Medium. Designated rooms, service with
restrictions, supervision. [🍴] [📶] [✕] [📋] [💻]

◇◇◇◇ Residence Inn by Marriott Pittsburgh North
Shore ⊞
(412) 321-2099. **$160-$275.** 574 W General Robinson St 15212. I-279
exit 70B (Fort Duquesne Blvd), left on 6th St, corner of Federal and
General Robinson sts; across from PNC Park. Int corridors.
Pets: Accepted. [SAVE] [&M] [📶] [✕] [📋] [💻]

◇◇◇◇ Residence Inn by Marriott Pittsburgh
University/Medical Center ⊞ ❀
(412) 621-2200. **$153-$263.** 3896 Bigelow Blvd 15213. On SR 380. Int
corridors. **Pets:** Other species. $100 one-time fee/room. Designated
rooms, service with restrictions, crate. [SAVE] [⊇] [📶] [✕] [📋] [💻]

◇◇◇ Residence Inn by
Marriott-Wilkins ⊞ ❀
(412) 816-1300. **$104-$171.** 3455 William Penn Hwy 15235. I-76 (Pennsylvania Tpke) exit 57, 3.5 mi n. Int corridors. **Pets:** Other species.
$100 one-time fee/room. Designated rooms, service with restrictions,
supervision. [SAVE] [&M] [⊇] [📶] [✕] [📋] [💻]

◇◇◇◇ Sheraton Pittsburgh Station Square
Hotel ⊞
(412) 261-2000. **$159-$425.** 300 W Station Square Dr 15219. I-376 exit
Grant St, south end of Smithfield St Bridge. Int corridors.
Pets: Accepted. [SAVE] [🍴] [⊇] [✕] [📶] [✕] [📋] [💻]

◇◇◇ The Westin Convention Center
Pittsburgh ⊞ ❀
(412) 281-3700. **$149-$299.** 1000 Penn Ave 15222. Jct 10th St; at Liberty Center. Int corridors. **Pets:** Medium, dogs only. Service with restrictions, supervision. [SAVE] [🔌] [🍴] [&M] [⊇] [✕] [📶] [✕] [📋] [💻]

◇◇◇ Wyndham Grand Pittsburgh
Downtown ⊞ ❀
(412) 391-4600. **$199-$369.** 600 Commonwealth Pl 15222. Jct I-279/
376/SR 885; in Gateway Center. Int corridors. **Pets:** Medium. $50 one-
time fee/room. Service with restrictions, supervision.
[SAVE] [🍴] [&M] [📶] [✕] [📋] [💻]

PITTSTON
◇◇◇ Comfort Inn Pittston ⊞ ❀
(570) 655-1234. **$39-$179.** 400 Hwy 315 18640. I-81 exit 175 northbound, 1 mi n; exit 175B southbound, just w; in Pittston Crossings
Plaza. Int corridors. **Pets:** Other species. Service with restrictions.
[📶] [✕] [📋] [💻]

POCONO MANOR

△△△◬ ▼▼▼▼ **The Inn at Pocono Manor** Ⓗ

(570) 839-7111. **$119-$249, 3 day notice.** 1 Manor Dr 18349. I-380 exit 3, just e on SR 314, follow signs for 1.3 mi. Int corridors.
Pets: Accepted. [SAVE] ⓘ ⌕ ⤬ ⌕ ⤬ ⓘ

POTTSTOWN

▼▼▼▼ **Comfort Inn & Suites** Ⓗ

(610) 326-5000. **$99-$179.** 99 Robinson St 19464. SR 100, 1 mi n of jct US 422. Int corridors. **Pets:** Accepted.
Ⓜ ⌕ ⌕ ⤬ ⓘ ⓘ

QUAKERTOWN

▼▼▼▼ **Hampton Inn-Quakertown** Ⓗ

(215) 536-7779. **$119-$149.** 1915 John Fries Hwy (SR 663) 18951. I-476 (Pennsylvania Tpke) exit 44, just e. Int corridors. **Pets:** Accepted.
Ⓜ ⌕ ⌕ ⓘ ⓘ

▼▼▼ **Quality Inn & Suites** Ⓗ 🐾

(215) 538-3000. **$79-$159.** 1905 John Fries Hwy (SR 663) 18951. I-476 (Pennsylvania Tpke) exit 44, just e. Ext corridors. **Pets:** Other species. $10 daily fee/room. Service with restrictions, crate. ⌕ ⓘ ⓘ

RONKS

△△△◬ ▼▼▼▼ **La Quinta Inn & Suites** Ⓗ

(717) 392-8100. **$82-$189.** 25 Eastbrook Rd 17572. Jct US 30 (Lincoln Hwy), just n on SR 896. Int corridors. **Pets:** Large, other species. Service with restrictions. [SAVE] ⓘ Ⓜ ⌕ ⌕ ⤬ ⓘ ⓘ

ROYERSFORD

▼▼▼▼ **Staybridge Suites Royersford/Valley Forge** Ⓗ

(610) 792-9300. **Call for rates.** 88 Anchor Pkwy 19468. I-422 exit Royersford, just n. Int corridors. **Pets:** Large, other species. $75 one-time fee/room. Service with restrictions, crate.
Ⓜ ⌕ ⌕ ⤬ ⓘ ⓘ

SAYRE

△△△◬ ▼▼▼▼ **BEST WESTERN Grand Victorian Inn** Ⓗ 🐾

(570) 888-7711. **$139-$199.** 255 Spring St 18840. SR 17 exit 61, just s. Int corridors. **Pets:** Other species. $10 daily fee/pet. Service with restrictions, supervision. [SAVE] ⓘ ⌕ ⤬ ⌕ ⤬ ⓘ ⓘ

SCRANTON

▼▼▼▼ **Hilton Scranton & Conference Center** Ⓗ

(570) 343-3000. **Call for rates.** 100 Adams Ave 18503. I-81 exit 185, just w of jct Lackawanna Ave, Jefferson Ave and Spruce St; downtown. Int corridors. **Pets:** Accepted. [ECO] ⓘ Ⓜ ⌕ ⌕ ⤬ ⓘ ⓘ

▼▼▼▼ **Radisson Lackawanna Station Hotel Scranton** Ⓗ 🐾

(570) 342-8300. **$119-$239.** 700 Lackawanna Ave 18503. I-81 exit 185, jct Lackawanna Ave, Jefferson Ave and Spruce St; downtown. Int corridors. **Pets:** Large, dogs only. $75 one-time fee/room. Service with restrictions, crate. ⓘ ⌕ ⤬ ⓘ ⓘ

▼▼▼▼ **TownePlace Suites by Marriott Scranton Wilkes-Barre** Ⓗ

(570) 207-8500. **$97-$160.** 26 Radcliffe Dr 18507. I-81 exit 182 northbound; exit 182A southbound, 0.5 mi se on Montage Mountain Rd, then just se to Glenmaura Blvd. Int corridors. **Pets:** Accepted.
Ⓜ ⌕ ⌕ ⤬ ⓘ ⓘ

SELINSGROVE

▼▼ **Comfort Inn** Ⓗ

(570) 374-8880. **Call for rates.** 613 N Susquehanna Tr 17870. US 11 and 15, just n of US 522. Int corridors. **Pets:** Accepted.
ⓘ ⌕ ⌕ ⓘ ⓘ

SHAMOKIN DAM

▼▼▼ **Econo Lodge Inn & Suites** Ⓗ 🐾

(570) 743-1111. **$79-$139.** 3249 N Susquehanna Tr 17876. US 11 and 15, just n of jct SR 61. Ext corridors. **Pets:** Medium, other species. $15 daily fee/room. Service with restrictions, crate.
ⓘ ⌕ ⌕ ⓘ ⓘ

▼▼ **Phillips Motel** Ⓜ

(570) 743-3100. **Call for rates.** 2943 N Susquehanna Tr 17876. 3 mi n of Selinsgrove. Ext corridors. **Pets:** Accepted. ⌕ ⓘ ⓘ

SHILLINGTON

△△△◬ ▼▼▼▼ **BEST WESTERN PLUS Reading Inn & Suites** Ⓗ

(610) 777-7888. **$129-$329.** 2299 Lancaster Pike 19607. I-76 (Pennsylvania Tpke) exit 286, 9 mi n on US 222. Int corridors. **Pets:** Accepted.
[SAVE] ⌕ ⌕ ⓘ ⓘ

SHIPPENSBURG

△△△◬ ▼▼▼ **BEST WESTERN Shippensburg Hotel** Ⓗ

(717) 532-5200. **$70-$150.** 125 Walnut Bottom Rd 17257. I-81 exit 29, 0.5 mi w on SR 174. Int corridors. **Pets:** Medium, other species. $10 daily fee/pet. Designated rooms, service with restrictions, supervision.
[SAVE] ⓘ ⌕ ⤬ ⌕ ⓘ ⓘ

SMOKETOWN

▼▼▼ **Mill Stream Country Inn** Ⓗ

(717) 299-0931. **Call for rates.** 170 Eastbrook Rd 17576. Jct SR 340, 0.3 mi s on SR 896. Ext corridors. **Pets:** Accepted.
ⓘ ⌕ ⌕ ⤬ ⓘ

SOMERSET

▼▼ **Budget Host Inn** Ⓜ

(814) 445-7988. **$45-$95, 3 day notice.** 799 N Center Ave 15501. I-70/76 (Pennsylvania Tpke) exit 110, 0.3 mi s. Ext corridors. **Pets:** Very small. $10 daily fee/pet. Designated rooms, no service, supervision.
⌕ ⓘ

△△△◬ ▼▼▼▼ **Comfort Inn** Ⓗ

(814) 445-9611. **$105-$150.** 202 Harmon St 15501. I-70/76 (Pennsylvania Tpke) exit 110, just s. Int corridors. **Pets:** Medium. $35 one-time fee/room. Designated rooms, service with restrictions, supervision.
[SAVE] Ⓜ ⌕ ⌕ ⓘ ⓘ

▼ **Dollar Inn** Ⓜ

(814) 445-2977. **Call for rates.** 1146 N Center Ave 15501. I-70/76 (Pennsylvania Tpke) exit 110, 0.3 mi s, then just n on SR 601/N Central Ave; at top of hill. Ext corridors. **Pets:** Medium. $7 daily fee/pet. Designated rooms, service with restrictions. ⌕ ⓘ

▼▼ **Glades Pike Inn** ⒷⒷ

(814) 443-4978. **Call for rates.** 2684 Glades Pike Rd 15501. I-70/76 (Pennsylvania Tpke) exit 110, 6 mi w on SR 31; exit 91, 13 mi e on SR 31. Int corridors. **Pets:** Dogs only. Service with restrictions, supervision.
ⓘ ⤬ ⌕ ⤬ ⌕

STARLIGHT

▼▼▼ **The Inn at Starlight Lake** Ⓒ

(570) 798-2519. **Call for rates.** 289 Starlight Lake Rd 18461. Off SR 370, 1 mi n, follow signs. Ext/int corridors. **Pets:** Accepted.
ⓘ ⤬ ⌕ ⤬ Ⓚ Ⓦ ⌕

STATE COLLEGE

▼▼▼ **Comfort Suites** Ⓗ 🐾

(814) 235-1900. **$89-$149.** 132 Village Dr 16803. SR 26, 1.1 mi on US 322 W (Atherton St), just ne; center. Int corridors. **Pets:** Large, other species. $25 one-time fee/room. Designated rooms, crate.
ⓘ ⌕ ⤬ ⓘ ⓘ

▼▼▼ **Days Inn Penn State** Ⓗ 🐾

(814) 238-8454. **$104-$250.** 240 S Pugh St 16801. Just e of SR 26 northbound; 0.4 mi n of jct US 322 business route; downtown. Int corridors. **Pets:** $10 daily fee/pet. Service with restrictions.
ⓘ ⌕ ⌕ ⓘ ⓘ

Nittany Budget Motel M
(814) 238-0015. **$49-$225.** 2070 Cato Ave 16801. SR 26, 2.6 mi s of jct US 322 business route. Ext corridors. **Pets:** Dogs only. $5 daily fee/pet. Service with restrictions. (SAVE) 📶 🔒 📺

Quality Inn Penn State M
(814) 234-1600. **$59-$329.** 1274 N Atherton St 16803. US 322 business route, 1 mi w of jct SR 26. Int corridors. **Pets:** Accepted.
&M 📶 ✕ 🔒 📺

Residence Inn by Marriott State College H
(814) 235-6960. **$132-$217.** 1555 University Dr 16801. US 322 business route, 1.5 mi e of jct SR 26. Int corridors. **Pets:** Accepted.
🛆 📶 🔒 📺

TANNERSVILLE
The Chateau Resort & Conference Center H
(570) 629-5900. **$89-$324.** 475 Camelback Rd 18372. I-80 exit 299, 1 mi w on Sullivan Tr, then 1.7 mi, follow signs to Camelback Ski area or Camelback Beach Water Park. Int corridors. **Pets:** Accepted.
(SAVE) 🍴 🛆 ✕ 📶 ✕ 🔒 📺

TREVOSE
Comfort Inn Trevose H
(215) 638-4554. **$85-$105.** 2779 Lincoln Hwy N 19053. I-276 (Pennsylvania Tpke) exit 351, 0.5 mi s. Int corridors. **Pets:** Medium. $15 daily fee/pet. Designated rooms, service with restrictions, supervision.
🛆 📶 🔒 📺

Red Roof Inn Philadelphia Trevose M
(215) 244-9422. **Call for rates.** 3100 Lincoln Hwy 19053. I-276 (Pennsylvania Tpke) exit 351, 0.5 mi s on US 1 at US 132. Ext corridors. **Pets:** Large, other species. Service with restrictions, supervision.
(SAVE) 🍴 &M 📶 ✕ 🔒 📺

TUNKHANNOCK
Comfort Inn & Suites Tunkhannock H
(570) 836-4100. **$149-$179.** 5 N Eaton Rd 18657. 0.4 mi s; just across bridge. Int corridors. **Pets:** Medium, other species. $25 daily fee/pet. Designated rooms, service with restrictions.
🍴 &M 📶 ✕ 🔒 📺

UPPER BLACK EDDY
The Bridgeton House on the Delaware BB 🐾
(610) 982-5856. **Call for rates.** 1525 River Rd 18972. On SR 32; center. Int corridors. **Pets:** Small, dogs only. $100 deposit/room, $25 daily fee/pet. Designated rooms, service with restrictions.
🍴 📶 ✕ 🔒 📺

WARREN
Allegheny Inn & Suites H
(814) 723-8881. **$74-$106.** 204 Struthers St 16365. 1.5 mi w on US 6 exit Ludlow St, w on Allegheny, then s. Ext/int corridors.
Pets: Accepted. 📶 ✕ 🔒 📺

Holiday Inn of Warren H
(814) 726-3000. **$119-$129.** 210 Ludlow St 16365. Jct US 6, just n on US 62 N (Ludlow St). Int corridors. **Pets:** Accepted.
(SAVE) 🍴 &M 🛆 📶 ✕ 📺

WARRINGTON
Homewood Suites Warrington H
(215) 343-1300. **$149-$259.** 2650 Kelly Rd 18976. 2.4 mi s of jct US 202 and SR 611. Int corridors. **Pets:** Small, other species. $20 daily fee/pet. Service with restrictions, crate. (SAVE) &M 📶 🔒 📺

WASHINGTON
Microtel Inn & Suites by Wyndham H
(724) 705-7676. **$95-$130.** 501 Racetrack Rd 15301. I-79 exit 41, just e. Int corridors. **Pets:** Accepted. 🍴 📶 ✕ 🔒 📺

Ramada H
(724) 225-9750. **$82-$130.** 1170 W Chestnut St 15301. I-70 exit 15, 0.5 mi e on US 40. Ext/int corridors. **Pets:** Small. $40 daily fee/room. Designated rooms, service with restrictions, supervision.
(SAVE) 🍴 &M 🛆 📶 🔒 📺

Red Roof Inn Washington, PA M
(724) 228-5750. **Call for rates.** 1399 W Chestnut St 15301. I-70 exit 15, just e on US 40. Ext/int corridors. **Pets:** Large, other species. Service with restrictions, supervision. (SAVE) 📶 🔒 📺

WAYNESBURG
Comfort Inn H
(724) 627-3700. **$95-$130.** 100 Comfort Ln 15370. I-79 exit 14, just e. Int corridors. **Pets:** Small, other species. $25 one-time fee/room. Service with restrictions, supervision. 📶 🔒 📺

WEST HAZLETON
Candlewood Suites H
(570) 459-1600. **$78-$95.** 9 Bowman's Mill Rd 18202. I-81 exit 145 southbound; exit SR 93 S northbound to Tom Hicken Rd. Int corridors. **Pets:** Large. $10 daily fee/pet. Designated rooms, service with restrictions, crate. 🍴 &M 📶 🔒 📺

WEST MIFFLIN
Extended Stay America-Pittsburgh-West Mifflin H
(412) 650-9096. **Call for rates.** 1303 Lebanon Church Rd 15122. 0.5 mi e of jct SR 51. Int corridors. **Pets:** Other species. $25 daily fee/pet. Service with restrictions, supervision. &M 📶 ✕ 🔒 📺

Holiday Inn Express Hotel & Suites H
(412) 469-1900. **Call for rates.** 3122 Lebanon Church Rd 15122. 1.5 mi e of jct SR 51. Int corridors. **Pets:** Accepted. &M 📶 🔒 📺

WEST READING
Candlewood Suites H 🐾
(610) 898-1910. **Call for rates.** 55 S 3rd Ave 19611. Jct Penn Ave. Int corridors. **Pets:** Medium. $75 one-time fee/room. Service with restrictions, crate. &M 📶 🔒 📺

WHITE HAVEN
Comfort Inn-Pocono Mountain H
(570) 443-8461. **$69-$259.** Rt 940 at I-80 & 476 18661. I-476 exit 95, just e; I-80 exit 277 (Lake Harmony). Int corridors. **Pets:** Accepted.
🍴 🛆 ✕ 📶 🔒 📺

WILKES-BARRE
BEST WESTERN Genetti Hotel & Conference Center H 🐾
(570) 823-6152. **$99-$169.** 77 E Market St 18701. Jct Washington St; downtown. Int corridors. **Pets:** Large, other species. $15 daily fee/pet. Designated rooms, service with restrictions.
(SAVE) 🍴 &M 🛆 📶 ✕ 🔒 📺

Days Inn H
(570) 826-0111. **$65-$250.** 760 Kidder St 18702. I-81 exit 170B to exit 1 (SR 309 S business route), just w; I-76 (Pennsylvania Tpke) exit 105 to exit 1 (SR 115 N). Int corridors. **Pets:** Accepted. (SAVE) 📶 🔒 📺

Econo Lodge Arena H 🐾
(570) 823-0600. **$69-$99.** 1075 Wilkes-Barre Township Blvd 18702. I-81 exit 165 southbound; exit 165B northbound, on SR 309 business route. Int corridors. **Pets:** Large, other species. $15 daily fee/pet. Designated rooms, service with restrictions, crate. (SAVE) 📶 🔒 📺

Extended Stay America Wilkes-Barre Hwy 315 H
(570) 970-2500. **Call for rates.** 1067 Hwy 315 18702. I-81 exit 170B to exit 1 (SR 309 S business route), 0.3 mi n. Int corridors. **Pets:** Other species. $25 daily fee/pet. Service with restrictions, supervision.
🍴 &M 📶 ✕ 🔒 📺

△△△ ▽▽▽ Host Inn All Suites 🏠 ❀

(570) 270-4678. **$109-$199.** 860 Kidder St 18702. I-81 exit 170B to exit 1 (SR 309 S business route), 0.5 mi w. Int corridors. **Pets:** Other species. $20 one-time fee/pet. Service with restrictions, crate.

[SAVE] [&M] [🛏] [🛜] [🛎] [💻]

△△△ ▽▽▽ Quality Inn & Suites Conference Center 🏠 ❀

(570) 824-8901. **$79-$129.** 880 Kidder St 18702. I-81 exit 170B to exit 1 (SR 309 S business route) off expressway, 0.5 mi w. Ext corridors. **Pets:** Medium. $15 daily fee/pet. Designated rooms, service with restrictions, crate. [SAVE] [🍴] [🛜] [🛎] [💻]

△△△ ▽▽▽ Red Roof Inn Wilkes-Barre Arena Ⓜ

(570) 829-6422. **Call for rates.** 1035 Hwy 315 18702. I-81 exit 170B to exit 1 (SR 309 S business route) to SR 315, just n. Ext corridors. **Pets:** Large, other species. Service with restrictions, supervision.

[SAVE] [🍴] [🛜] [✖] [🛎] [💻]

▽▽▽▽ The Woodlands Inn, an Ascend Hotel Collection Member 🏠 ❀

(570) 824-9831. **$99-$219.** 1073 Hwy 315 18702. I-81 exit 170B to exit 1 (SR 309 S business route), 0.3 mi n. Int corridors. **Pets:** Medium, dogs only. $30 one-time fee/room. Designated rooms, service with restrictions, crate. [🍴] [🛏] [✖] [🛜] [✖] [🛎] [💻]

WILLIAMSPORT

△△△ ▽▽▽▽ BEST WESTERN Williamsport Inn 🏠

(570) 326-1981. **$80-$190.** 1840 E 3rd St 17701. I-180 exit 25 (Faxon St), 0.5 mi e. Ext corridors. **Pets:** Other species. $15 daily fee/room. Designated rooms, service with restrictions, crate.

[SAVE] [🍴] [&M] [🛏] [🛜] [✖] [🛎] [💻]

▽▽▽▽ Candlewood Suites 🏠

(570) 601-9100. **Call for rates.** 1836 E 3rd St 17701. I-180 exit 25 (Faxon St), 0.5 mi e. Int corridors. **Pets:** Accepted.

[&M] [🛏] [🛜] [✖] [🛎] [💻]

△△△ ▽▽▽ Comfort Inn 🏠

(570) 601-9300. **$110-$140.** 1959 E 3rd St 17701. I-180 exit 23A westbound; exit 23 eastbound, just w. Int corridors. **Pets:** Accepted.

[SAVE] [&M] [🛜] [✖] [🛎] [💻]

△△△ ▽▽ Genetti Hotel & Suites 🏠

(570) 326-6600. **$129-$229.** 200 W 4th St 17701. Jct William St; downtown. Ext/int corridors. **Pets:** Dogs only. $15 daily fee/pet. Designated rooms, service with restrictions, crate. [SAVE] [🍴] [🛏] [🛜] [🛎] [💻]

▽▽▽▽ Residence Inn by Marriott Williamsport 🏠

(570) 505-3140. **$108-$177.** 150 W Church St 17701. I-180 exit 27B eastbound; exit 26 westbound; just w of Market St; downtown. Int corridors. **Pets:** Large. $45 one-time fee/pet. Designated rooms, service with restrictions, supervision. [&M] [🛜] [✖] [🛎] [💻]

▽▽▽▽ TownePlace Suites by Marriott Williamsport 🏠 ❀

(570) 567-7467. **$97-$160.** 10 W Church St 17701. I-180 exit 27B eastbound; exit 26 westbound; at Market St; downtown. Int corridors. **Pets:** Other species. $45 one-time fee/pet. Designated rooms, service with restrictions, supervision. [&M] [🛜] [✖] [🛎] [💻]

WIND GAP

▽▽▽ Red Carpet Inn Ⓜ

(610) 863-7782. **$70-$125.** 1395 Jacobsburg Rd 18091. SR 33 exit Wind Gap/Bath (SR 512 S), just s, follow signs. Ext/int corridors. **Pets:** Accepted. [🛜] [🛎]

WYOMISSING

▽▽▽▽ Crowne Plaza Reading Hotel 🏠

(610) 376-3811. **$149-$249, 3 day notice.** 1741 W Papermill Rd 19610. US 422 exit Papermill Rd. Int corridors. **Pets:** Accepted.

[🍴] [&M] [🛏] [🛜] [✖] [🛎] [💻]

▽▽▽▽ Homewood Suites-Reading/Wyomissing 🏠

(610) 736-3100. **$129-$214.** 2801 Papermill Rd 19610. US 422 exit Papermill Rd, 1.8 mi nw; US 222 exit Spring Ridge Rd. Int corridors. **Pets:** Accepted. [&M] [🛏] [🛜] [✖] [🛎] [💻]

▽▽▽ The Inn at Reading Hotel & Conference Center 🏠 ❀

(610) 372-7811. **$89-$199.** 1040 N Park Rd 19610. US 222 exit N Wyomissing Blvd, just n, then 0.3 mi e. Int corridors. **Pets:** Small. $10 daily fee/pet. Designated rooms, service with restrictions, crate.

[🍴] [&M] [🛏] [🛜] [✖] [🛎] [💻]

WYSOX

▽▽ Comfort Inn 🏠

(570) 265-5691. **$150-$170.** 898 Golden Mile Rd 18854. On US 6 E. Int corridors. **Pets:** Other species. $25 one-time fee/room. Designated rooms, service with restrictions, supervision. [🛏] [🛜] [✖] [🛎] [💻]

YORK

▽▽ Comfort Inn & Suites 🏠

(717) 699-1919. **$95-$169.** 2250 N George St 17402. I-83 exit 22, just n. Int corridors. **Pets:** Medium, other species. $50 one-time fee/pet. Service with restrictions, crate. [&M] [🛜] [🛎] [💻]

△△△ ▽▽ Country Inn & Suites By Carlson York 🏠

(717) 747-5833. **$129-$189.** 245 St. Charles Way 17402. I-83 exit 16A, 0.3 mi se. Int corridors. **Pets:** Accepted. [SAVE] [🛏] [🛜] [✖] [🛎] [💻]

▽▽▽ Holiday Inn Express & Suites 🏠

(717) 741-1000. **Call for rates.** 140 Leader Heights Rd 17403. I-83 exit 14, just w on SR 182. Int corridors. **Pets:** Accepted.

[🍴] [🛜] [✖] [🛎] [💻]

▽▽ Wyndham Garden York 🏠

(717) 846-9500. **$109-$169, 7 day notice.** 2000 Loucks Rd 17408. I-83 exit 21B, 2.5 mi w on US 30, then just n; exit 22 southbound, 0.5 mi s on SR 181, 2.2 mi w on US 30, then just n. Int corridors. **Pets:** Accepted. [🍴] [🛏] [🛜] [🛎] [💻]

△△△ ▽▽▽▽ The Yorktowne Hotel 🏠

(717) 848-1111. **Call for rates.** 48 E Market St 17401. SR 462 eastbound and I-83 business route, just e of square, follow signs. Int corridors. **Pets:** Accepted. [SAVE] [🍴] [✖] [🛜] [🛎] [💻]

RHODE ISLAND

COVENTRY

▽▽▽ La Quinta Inn & Suites Coventry 🏠

(401) 821-3322. **$79-$274.** 4 Universal Blvd 02816. I-95 exit 7, just ne. Int corridors. **Pets:** Large, other species. Service with restrictions.

[🍴] [&M] [🛏] [🛜] [✖] [🛎] [💻]

EAST PROVIDENCE

▽▽ Extended Stay America East Providence 🏠

(401) 272-1661. **Call for rates.** 1000 Warren Ave 02914. I-195 exit 8 eastbound, just e; exit 6 westbound, 1.1 mi e. Int corridors. **Pets:** Other species. $25 daily fee/pet. Service with restrictions, supervision.

[🍴] [&M] [🛜] [✖] [🛎] [💻]

MIDDLETOWN

◆◆◆ Homewood Suites by Hilton
Newport/Middletown 🅷

(401) 848-2700. **$89-$339.** 348 W Main Rd 02842. On SR 114, 0.3 mi
s of jct SR 138. Int corridors. **Pets:** Accepted.
♿Ⓜ 🏊 🛜 ✕ 🛄 💻

◆◆◆ ◆◆◆ Howard Johnson Inn-Newport 🅷

(401) 849-2000. **$69-$500.** 351 W Main Rd 02842. On SR 114, 0.3 mi
s of jct SR 138. Int corridors. **Pets:** Other species. $10 daily fee/pet.
Designated rooms, service with restrictions, supervision.
SAVE 🍽 ♿Ⓜ 🏊 ✕ 🛜 🛄 💻

◆◆◆ ◆◆◆ Residence Inn by
Marriott-Newport/Middletown 🅷 🐾

(401) 845-2005. **$97-$332, 3 day notice.** 325 W Main Rd 02842. On
SR 114, 0.3 mi s of jct SR 138. Int corridors. **Pets:** Other species. $75
one-time fee/room. Designated rooms, service with restrictions.
SAVE 🍽 ♿Ⓜ 🏊 🛜 ✕ 🛄 💻

NEWPORT (Restaurants p. 638)

◆◆◆ ◆◆◆ Beech Tree Inn 🅱🅱 🐾

(401) 847-9794. **$119-$359, 14 day notice.** 34 Rhode Island Ave
02840. Just e of SR 114; 0.8 mi s of jct SR 138. Int corridors.
Pets: Other species. $25 daily fee/pet. Designated rooms, no service.
SAVE 🍽 🛜 ✕ 🛄

◆◆◆ ◆◆◆ Cliffside Inn 🅱🅱 🐾

(401) 847-1811. **$190-$509.** 2 Seaview Ave 02840. Just s of Memorial
Blvd via Cliff Ave. Ext/int corridors. **Pets:** Small, dogs only. $50 one-
time fee/room. Designated rooms, service with restrictions, crate.
SAVE 🍽 🛜 ✕ 🛄

◆◆◆ The Francis Malbone House Inn 🅱🅱

(401) 846-0392. **Call for rates.** 392 Thames St 02840. Just s of Memorial Blvd; downtown. Int corridors. **Pets:** Accepted. 🛜 ✕ 🛄

◆◆◆ ◆◆◆ Hyatt Regency Newport Hotel & Spa 🅷

(401) 851-1234. **$109-$499, 3 day notice.** 1 Goat Island 02840. 0.8 mi
w of America's Cup Ave, follow signs to Goat Island. Int corridors.
Pets: Accepted. SAVE ECO 🍽 ♿Ⓜ 🏊 ✕ 🛜 🛄 💻

◆◆ ◆◆ Mainstay Hotel & Conference Center 🅷

(401) 849-9880. **$59-$300, 3 day notice.** 151 Admiral Kalbfus Rd
02840. SR 138; from Newport Bridge, 2nd exit. Int corridors.
Pets: Accepted. 🍽 🏊 🛜 🛄 💻

◆◆◆ ◆◆◆ Mill Street Inn 🅷 🐾

(401) 849-9500. **Call for rates.** 75 Mill St 02840. Just e of Thames St;
between Spring and Corne sts; downtown. Int corridors. **Pets:** Medium,
dogs only. $50 one-time fee/pet. Designated rooms, service with restric-
tions. SAVE 🛜 ✕ 🛄

◆◆◆ Pelham Court Hotel 🅲🅾

(401) 619-4950. **$99-$529, 7 day notice.** 14 Pelham St 02840. Just n
of Memorial Blvd (SR 138A) via Spring St, then just w. Int corridors.
Pets: Accepted. 🛜 ✕ 🛄 💻

◆◆◆ ◆◆◆ ◆◆◆ The Vanderbilt Grace 🅷

(401) 846-6200. **Call for rates.** 41 Mary St 02840. Just n of Thames
St; downtown. Int corridors. **Pets:** Accepted.
SAVE 🍽 ♿Ⓜ 🏊 ✕ 🛜 ✕ 💻

NORTH KINGSTOWN

◆◆ Hamilton Village Inn 🅼

(401) 295-0700. **$79-$139, 7 day notice.** 642 Boston Neck Rd 02852.
SR 1A, 1.3 mi s of jct SR 102. Ext corridors. **Pets:** Other species. Designated rooms, service with restrictions, supervision.
🍽 🛜 🛄 💻

◆◆◆ TownePlace Suites by Marriott Providence/North
Kingstown 🅷

(401) 667-7500. **$167-$355.** 55 Gate Rd 02852. Jct SR 403, just n on
US 1, then just e. Int corridors. **Pets:** Other species. $100 one-time
fee/room. Designated rooms, service with restrictions, supervision.
🍽 🏊 🛜 ✕ 🛄 💻

PROVIDENCE (Restaurants p. 638)

◆◆◆ ◆◆◆ ◆◆◆ Hotel Providence 🅷 🐾

(401) 861-8000. **$169-$299.** 139 Mathewson St 02903. Corner of Westminster St. Int corridors. **Pets:** Medium. $75 one-time fee/room. Super-
vision. SAVE ECO 🍽 🛜 ✕ 🛄 💻

◆◆◆ ◆◆◆ Omni Providence Hotel 🅷

(401) 598-8000. **Call for rates.** One W Exchange St 02903. I-95 exit
22A. Int corridors. **Pets:** Accepted.
ECO 🍽 ♿Ⓜ 🏊 ✕ 🛰 ✕ 🛄 💻

◆◆◆ ◆◆◆ Providence Marriott Downtown 🅷

(401) 272-2400. **$153-$309.** 1 Orms St 02904. I-95 exit 23 to state
offices. Int corridors. **Pets:** Accepted.
SAVE ECO 🍽 ♿Ⓜ 🏊 ✕ 🛜 ✕ 🛄 💻

SMITHFIELD

◆◆◆ ◆◆◆ All Seasons Inn & Suites 🅷

(401) 232-2400. **$100-$220, 7 day notice.** 355 George Washington Hwy
02917. I-295 exit 8B, 0.3 mi n on SR 7, then 0.6 mi e on SR 116. Int
corridors. **Pets:** Accepted. SAVE 🍽 ♿Ⓜ 🏊 🛜 🛄 💻

◆◆◆ ◆◆◆ Hampton Inn & Suites
Providence/Smithfield 🅷 🐾

(401) 232-9200. **$129-$229.** 945 Douglas Pike 02917. I-295 exit 8B, 0.6
mi nw on SR 7. Int corridors. **Pets:** Other species. Service with restrictions, supervision. SAVE 🍽 ♿Ⓜ 🏊 🛜 ✕ 🛄 💻

WAKEFIELD

◆◆◆ The Kings' Rose Inn 🅱🅱

(401) 783-5222. **Call for rates.** 1747 Mooresfield Rd (SR 138) 02879.
I-95 exit 3A, 11 mi e on SR 138; 3.3 mi w of US 1. Int corridors.
Pets: Service with restrictions, crate. 🍽 🛜 ✕ 🛝

WARWICK (Restaurants p. 639)

◆◆◆ ◆◆ BEST WESTERN Airport Inn 🅷

(401) 737-7400. **$68-$135.** 2138 Post Rd 02886. I-95 exit 13, e to US
1, then just ne. Int corridors. **Pets:** Small. $20 daily fee/room. Desig-
nated rooms, service with restrictions, supervision. SAVE 🛜 🛄 💻

◆◆◆ ◆◆ Comfort Inn-Airport 🅷

(401) 732-0470. **$69-$169.** 1940 Post Rd 02886. I-95 exit 13, e to US
1, then 0.5 mi n. Int corridors. **Pets:** Medium, other species. $50
deposit/pet. Service with restrictions, supervision.
SAVE 🛜 ✕ 🛄 💻

◆◆◆ ◆◆◆ Crowne Plaza Hotel at the Crossings 🅷

(401) 732-6000. **$129-$259.** 801 Greenwich Ave 02886. I-95 exit 12A
southbound; exit 12 northbound, 0.3 mi se on SR 5. Int corridors.
Pets: Accepted. ECO 🍽 ♿Ⓜ 🏊 🛜 🛄 💻

◆◆◆ ◆◆◆ Extended Stay America-Providence-Airport 🅷

(401) 732-6667. **Call for rates.** 268 Metro Center Blvd 02886. I-95 exit
12A, 0.4 mi e on SR 113, 0.4 mi n on SR 5, then 0.4 mi e. Int corridors. **Pets:** Other species. $25 daily fee/pet. Service with restrictions,
supervision. 🍽 ♿Ⓜ 🛜 🛄 💻

◆◆◆ ◆◆◆ Extended Stay America Providence-Warwick 🅷

(401) 732-2547. **Call for rates.** 245 W Natick Rd 02886. I-295 exit 2
northbound, just sw; exit 3A southbound, 1.1 mi e on SR 37, 2 mi s on
SR 2, then just sw. Int corridors. **Pets:** Other species. $25 daily fee/pet.
Service with restrictions, supervision. 🍽 ♿Ⓜ 🛜 🛄 💻

(AAA) ▼▼▼ Hampton Inn & Suites Providence-Warwick Airport H

(401) 739-8888. **$99-$199.** 2100 Post Rd 02886. I-95 exit 13, e to US 1, then just n. Int corridors. **Pets:** Accepted.
[SAVE] 🛌M 🛏 🛜 📶 💻

▼▼▼▼ Holiday Inn Express Hotel & Suites H ❀

(401) 736-5000. **$89-$299.** 901 Jefferson Blvd 02886. I-95 exit 13, 0.4 mi on Airport Connector Rd exit Jefferson Blvd. Int corridors. **Pets:** Medium, dogs only. $25 one-time fee/pet. Designated rooms, service with restrictions, supervision.
[ECO] 🍴 🛌M 🛏 🛜 ✕ 📶 💻

▼▼▼ Homewood Suites by Hilton Providence/Warwick H

(401) 738-0008. **$119-$169.** 33 International Way 02886. I-95 exit 13, 0.4 mi n on Jefferson Blvd, 0.5 mi nw on Kilvert St, then 0.4 mi sw on Metro Center Blvd. Int corridors. **Pets:** Medium, other species. $75 one-time fee/room. Service with restrictions. 🍴 🛌M 🛏 🛜 📶 💻

▼▼▼ NYLO Providence/Warwick H

(401) 734-4460. **$89-$269.** 400 Knight St 02886. Jct SR 5, just ne. Int corridors. **Pets:** Accepted. [ECO] 🍴 🛌M ✕ 🛜 ✕ 📶

▼▼▼ Residence Inn by Marriott H

(401) 737-7100. **$132-$217.** 500 Kilvert St 02886. I-95 exit 13 to Jefferson Blvd, 0.4 mi n, then 0.6 mi w. Ext corridors. **Pets:** Accepted.
🍴 🛌M 🛏 🛜 ✕ 📶 💻

(AAA) ▼▼▼ Sheraton Providence Airport Hotel H ❀

(401) 738-4000. **$89-$279.** 1850 Post Rd 02886. I-95 exit 13, 0.6 mi n on US 1. Int corridors. **Pets:** $50 one-time fee/pet. Designated rooms, service with restrictions, supervision.
[SAVE] 🍴 🛌M 🛏 🛜 ✕ 📶 💻

WATCH HILL

(AAA) ▼▼▼▼ Ocean House H

(401) 584-7000. **$193-$2970, 3 day notice.** 1 Bluff Ave 02891. Jct SR 1A, 0.4 mi sw via Westerly Rd. Int corridors. **Pets:** Accepted.
[SAVE] 🍴 🛌M 🛏 ✕ 🛜 ✕ 📶 💻

WESTERLY

▼▼▼ Shelter Harbor Inn [CI]

(401) 322-8883. **Call for rates.** 10 Wagner Rd 02891. 4 mi ne of jct SR 78 on US 1. Ext/int corridors. **Pets:** Other species. Designated rooms, supervision. 🍴 ✕ 🛜 ✕

(AAA) ▼▼▼ ▼▼ The Weekapaug Inn H

(401) 637-7600. **Call for rates.** 25 Spray Rock Rd 02891. SR 1A, 1 mi s on Noyes Neck Rd, just e on Shawmut Ave, then just s. Int corridors. **Pets:** Accepted. [SAVE] 🍴 ✕ 🛜 ✕ 🐾

WEST GREENWICH

▼▼▼ Residence Inn by Marriott Providence/Coventry H

(401) 828-1170. **$97-$194.** 725 Center of New England Blvd 02817. I-95 exit 7, just ne. Int corridors. **Pets:** Medium, other species. $100 one-time fee/room. Service with restrictions, crate.
🛌M 🛏 🛜 ✕ 📶 💻

WEST WARWICK

▼▼ Extended Stay America Providence-Airport-West Warwick H

(401) 885-3161. **Call for rates.** 1235 Division Rd 02893. I-95 exit 8A northbound, just s on SR 2, then just w; exit 8 southbound, just s on SR 2, then just w. Int corridors. **Pets:** Other species. $25 daily fee/pet. Service with restrictions, supervision. 🛌M 🛜 📶 💻

▼▼▼ SpringHill Suites by Marriott Providence West Warwick H

(401) 822-1244. **$83-$206.** 14 James P Murphy Industrial Hwy 02893. I-95 exit 8 southbound, just nw; exit 8B northbound, just n on Old Quaker Ln, then 0.5 mi nw. Int corridors. **Pets:** Accepted.
🍴 🛌M 🛏 🛜 ✕ 📶 💻

WYOMING

(AAA) ▼▼▼ Stagecoach House Inn [BB] ❀

(401) 539-9600. **$100-$199.** 1136 Main St (SR 138) 02898. I-95 exit 3B northbound, 0.7 mi nw; exit southbound, 0.4 mi nw. Ext/int corridors. **Pets:** Dogs only. $25 daily fee/room. Designated rooms, service with restrictions, supervision. [SAVE] 🛜 ✕ 📶 💻

SOUTH CAROLINA

AIKEN

▼▼ Clarion Inn [M]

(803) 648-0999. **Call for rates.** 155 Colony Pkwy/Whiskey Rd 29803. Jct US 1/78 and SR 19 (Whiskey Rd), 1.8 mi s on SR 19 (Whiskey Rd). Ext corridors. **Pets:** Accepted. 🛏 🛜 📶 💻

▼▼ Quality Inn & Suites [M]

(803) 641-1100. **$59-$89.** 3608 Richland Ave W 29801. Jct US 1/78 and SR 19 (Whiskey Rd), 2.9 mi w on US 1/78. Ext corridors. **Pets:** Large. $20 daily fee/pet. Service with restrictions.
🛏 🛜 📶 💻

▼▼▼ TownePlace Suites by Marriott Aiken H ❀

(803) 641-7373. **$119-$169.** 1008 Monterey Dr 29803. Jct US 1/78 and SR 19 (Whiskey Rd), 3 mi s on SR 19 (Whiskey Rd). Int corridors. **Pets:** Medium. $100 one-time fee/room. Designated rooms, service with restrictions, supervision. 🛌M 🛜 ✕ 📶 💻

ANDERSON

▼▼ Baymont Inn & Suites Anderson/Clemson [M]

(864) 375-9800. **$59-$109.** 128 Interstate Blvd 29621. I-85 exit 19B, just n, then just se. Ext corridors. **Pets:** Small, other species. $20 daily fee/pet. Designated rooms, service with restrictions, crate.
🛌M 🛏 🛜 📶 💻

▼▼▼ Country Inn & Suites By Carlson H

(864) 622-2200. **$80-$200.** 116 Interstate Blvd 29621. I-85 exit 19B, just n, then just se. Int corridors. **Pets:** Accepted. 🛌M 🛏 🛜 📶 💻

▼▼ Days Inn [M]

(864) 375-0375. **$69-$194.** 1007 Smith Mill Rd 29625. I-85 exit 19A, just se. Ext corridors. **Pets:** Dogs only. $25 one-time fee/room, $5 daily fee/pet. Service with restrictions, supervision. 🛌M 🛏 🛜 📶 💻

▼▼ Holiday Inn Express H

(864) 231-0231. **Call for rates.** 410 Alliance Pkwy 29621. I-85 exit 27, just s on SR 81. Int corridors. **Pets:** Accepted.
🛌M 🛏 🛜 ✕ 📶 💻

▼▼ Home-Towne Suites H

(864) 226-1112. **Call for rates.** 151 Civic Center Blvd 29625. I-85 exit 19A, 2.2 mi se on US 76, then 0.6 mi s. Int corridors. **Pets:** $15 daily fee/pet. Service with restrictions, supervision. 🛏 🛜 ✕ 📶 💻

▼▼ Howard Johnson Anderson [M]

(864) 225-3721. **$49-$209.** 3430 Clemson Blvd 29621. I-85 exit 19A northbound, 2.9 mi se on US 76/SR 28 (Clemson Blvd); exit 21 southbound, 2.6 mi s on US 178. Ext corridors. **Pets:** Accepted.
🛏 🛜 📶 💻

▼▼ Microtel Inn & Suites by Wyndham Anderson/Clemson H

(864) 224-9707. **$70-$100.** 102 Electric City Blvd 29621. I-85 exit 19B, just n, then just e. Int corridors. **Pets:** $20 one-time fee/room. Service with restrictions, supervision. 🛌M 🛏 🛜 📶 💻

▼▼ Super 8 H

(864) 225-8384. **$59-$99.** 3302 Cinema Ave 29621. I-85 exit 19A north-bound, 2.8 mi se on US 76/SR 28 (Clemson Blvd); exit 21 southbound, 2.5 mi s on US 178. Int corridors. **Pets:** Dogs only. $15 daily fee/pet. Designated rooms, service with restrictions, supervision. 📶 🛗 💻

BEAUFORT

▼▼▼ City Loft Hotel M

(843) 379-5638. **Call for rates.** 311 Carteret St 29902. Jct Port Republic St. Ext corridors. **Pets:** Accepted. 📶 ✕ 🛗 💻

▼▼ Quality Inn at Town Center M

(843) 524-2144. **$69-$99.** 2001 Boundary St 29902. Jct US 21/SR 170, 1 mi e. Ext corridors. **Pets:** Medium, other species. $10 daily fee/pet. Designated rooms, service with restrictions, crate. 🐾 📶 🛗 💻

BENNETTSVILLE

▼▼ Quality Inn M

(843) 479-1700. **$85-$130.** 213 US Hwy 15 & 401 Bypass E 29512. Jct SR 38/Broad St, just ne on US 15/401/SR 9. Ext corridors.
Pets: Accepted. 🐾 📶 🛗 💻

BLUFFTON *(Restaurants p. 639)*

ⒶⒶ▽ ▼▼▼▼ Candlewood Suites H

(843) 705-9600. **$79-$149.** 5 Young Clyde Ct 29909. I-95 exit 8 (US 278), 7.2 mi e to Okatie Center Blvd S, then just s. Int corridors. **Pets:** Other species. $75 one-time fee/room. Designated rooms, service with restrictions, crate. 📶 🐾 📶 🛗 💻

ⒶⒶ▽ ▼▼▼▼ Holiday Inn Express Hotel & Suites H ✤

(843) 757-2002. **$89-$169.** 35 Bluffton Rd 29910. Jct US 278 (William Hilton Pkwy)/SR 46 (Bluffton Rd), just se; in Kittie's Crossing Shopping Center. Int corridors. **Pets:** Large. $50 one-time fee/room. Service with restrictions, crate. 📶 🐾 📶 ✕ 🛗 💻

ⒶⒶ▽ ▼▼▼▼ The Inn at Palmetto Bluff, A Montage Resort CA ✤

(843) 706-6500. **$395-$2500, 7 day notice.** 476 Mount Pelia Rd 29910. Jct US 278/SR 170, 4.4 mi sw on SR 170, 2.2 mi e on SR 46 (Bluffton Rd) to Palmetto Bluff Rd; check-in at gatehouse. Ext corridors. **Pets:** $25 daily fee/room. Designated rooms, service with restrictions. 📶 🍽 🐾 ✕ 📶 ✕ 🛗 💻

CAMDEN

▼▼▼ Comfort Inn & Suites H

(803) 425-1010. **$95-$199.** 220 Wall St 29020. I-20 exit 98, just n on US 521. Int corridors. **Pets:** Accepted. 🐾 📶 ✕ 🛗 💻

CHARLESTON *(Restaurants p. 639)*

ⒶⒶ▽ ▼▼▼ BEST WESTERN Sweetgrass Inn M

(843) 571-6100. **$69-$269.** 1540 Savannah Hwy 29407. US 17, 3.6 mi w of Ashley River Bridge; jct I-526 W terminus and US 17, 1.7 mi e. Ext corridors. **Pets:** Large, other species. $20 daily fee/room. Designated rooms, service with restrictions, crate. 📶 🐾 📶 🛗 💻

ⒶⒶ▽ ▼▼▼ Days Inn Historic District M

(843) 722-8411. **$109-$249.** 155 Meeting St 29401. Between Cumberland and S Market sts. Ext corridors. **Pets:** Medium. $10 daily fee/pet. Designated rooms, service with restrictions.
📶 🍽 🐾 📶 🛗 💻

▼▼ Hawthorn Suites by Wyndham H

(843) 225-4411. **$99-$279, 3 day notice.** 2455 Savannah Hwy 29414. I-526 exit US 17 (terminus), 1.3 mi w on US 17. Int corridors.
Pets: Accepted. 📶 🐾 📶 ✕ 🛗 💻

ⒶⒶ▽ ▼▼▼▼ Holiday Inn Express Charleston Downtown Ashley River H

(843) 722-4000. **$89-$359.** 250 Spring St 29403. I-26 exit 221A (US 17), 1.2 mi sw; just e of Ashley River. Int corridors. **Pets:** Accepted.
📶 🐾 📶 ✕ 🛗 💻

ⒶⒶ▽ ▼▼▼ Indigo Inn H

(843) 577-5900. **$139-$269, 3 day notice.** 1 Maiden Ln 29401. Corner of Meeting and Pinckney sts. Ext corridors. **Pets:** Medium. $40 daily fee/pet. Designated rooms, service with restrictions.
📶 📶 ✕ 🛗

ⒶⒶ▽ ▼▼▼▼ The Inn at Middleton Place CI ✤

(843) 556-0500. **$149-$749, 3 day notice.** 4290 Ashley River Rd 29414. I-526 exit 11B (Ashley River Rd/SR 61), 2.8 mi nw on Paul Cantrell Blvd/Glenn McConnell Pkwy to Bees Ferry Rd, 1.8 mi ne to Ashley River Rd/SR 61, then 9.2 mi nw, follow signs to historic plantations; adjacent to Middleton Place, National Historic Landmark. Ext corridors. **Pets:** Medium, other species. $75 one-time fee/room. Designated rooms, service with restrictions, crate.
📶 🍽 🐾 📶 🛗 💻

ⒶⒶ▽ ▼▼▼▼ John Rutledge House Inn BB ✤

(843) 723-7999. **$239-$385, 3 day notice.** 116 Broad St 29401. Corner of King St. Int corridors. **Pets:** Medium, dogs only. $25 daily fee/room. Designated rooms, service with restrictions. 📶 📶 ✕ 🛗

ⒶⒶ▽ ▼▼▼▼ Kings Courtyard Inn H

(843) 723-7000. **$189-$310, 3 day notice.** 198 King St 29401. Between Market St and Horlbeck Alley. Ext/int corridors. **Pets:** Accepted.
📶 📶 ✕ 🛗

▼▼▼▼ Residence Inn by Marriott Charleston Downtown/Riverview H

(843) 571-7979. **$149-$399.** 90 Ripley Point Dr 29407. US 17, just over Ashley River Bridge to Albermarle Rd, just s. Int corridors.
Pets: Accepted. 📶 🐾 📶 ✕ 🛗 💻

ⒶⒶ▽ ▼▼▼▼ Town & Country Inn & Suites H

(843) 571-1000. **$99-$359, 3 day notice.** 2008 Savannah Hwy 29407. US 17, 3.5 mi nw of Ashley River Bridge; I-526 exit US 17 (terminus), just se. Ext/int corridors. **Pets:** Accepted.
📶 🍽 🐾 📶 🛗 💻

CHERAW

▼▼ Quality Inn M

(843) 537-5625. **$85-$140.** 885 Chesterfield Hwy 29520. Jct US 1/52/SR 9, 1.6 mi w on SR 9. Ext corridors. **Pets:** Very small. $20 daily fee/pet. Service with restrictions, crate. 🐾 📶 🛗 💻

CLEMSON

▼▼ Comfort Inn-Clemson H

(864) 653-3600. **$89-$109.** 1305 Tiger Blvd 29631. Jct SR 133 (College Ave) and US 76/123, 0.5 mi e. Int corridors. **Pets:** Accepted.
🐾 📶 🛗 💻

▼▼ Days Inn-Clemson M

(864) 653-4411. **$69-$306.** 1387 Tiger Blvd 29631. Jct SR 133 (College Ave) and US 76/123, 0.9 mi e. Ext corridors. **Pets:** Accepted.
📶 🛗 💻

CLINTON

ⒶⒶ▽ ▼▼ Quality Inn M

(864) 833-5558. **$65-$118.** 105 Trade St 29325. I-26 exit 52, just n. Ext corridors. **Pets:** Accepted. 📶 🐾 📶 🛗 💻

COLUMBIA *(Restaurants p. 639)*

ⒶⒶ▽ ▼▼▼▼ Candlewood Suites Columbia-Fort Jackson H

(803) 727-1299. **Call for rates.** 921 Atlas Rd 29209. I-77 exit 9A (Garners Ferry Rd), 0.9 mi se to Atlas Rd, then just sw. Int corridors.
Pets: Accepted. 📶 📶 🐾 📶 🛗 💻

▼▼▼ Chesnut Cottage Bed & Breakfast BB

(803) 256-1718. **$159-$229, 14 day notice.** 1718 Hampton St 29201. SR 12 (Taylor St), just s; between Henderson and Barnwell sts; downtown. Int corridors. **Pets:** Other species. 📶 ✕ 🔲 🛗 💻

▼▼▼ Comfort Inn Columbia H

(803) 798-5101. **$90-$150.** 911 Bush River Rd 29210. I-26 exit 108A, just e. Int corridors. **Pets:** Small, other species. $15 daily fee/pet. Designated rooms, service with restrictions, crate. [SAVE] ⊇ 🛜 🛢 🖃

▼▼▼▼ DoubleTree by Hilton Columbia H ❀

(803) 731-0300. **$109-$189.** 2100 Bush River Rd 29210. I-20 exit 63 (Bush River Rd), just e; I-26 exit 108 (Bush River Rd), 0.7 mi w. Int corridors. **Pets:** Medium, other species. $40 one-time fee/room. Designated rooms, service with restrictions, crate.
[🍴] ⊇ 🛜 ✕ 🛢 🖃

▼▼▼▼ Fairfield Inn & Suites by Marriott Columbia Northeast H

(803) 760-1700. **$99-$139.** 120 Blarney Dr 29223. I-77 exit 17 (Two Notch Rd), just s on US 1, just w on Daulton Dr, then just n; I-20 exit 74 (Two Notch Rd), 0.5 mi n on US 1, just w on Daulton Dr, then just n. Int corridors. **Pets:** Accepted. [SAVE] [ᏹM] ⊇ 🛜 ✕ 🛢 🖃

▼▼▼▼ Hampton Inn Harbison H

(803) 749-6999. **$99-$179.** 101 Woodcross Dr 29212. I-26 exit 103 (Harbison Blvd), just ne, then se. Int corridors. **Pets:** Accepted.
[ᏹM] ⊇ 🛜 ✕ 🛢 🖃

▼▼▼▼ Hilton Columbia Center H ❀

(803) 744-7800. **Call for rates.** 924 Senate St 29201. Jct US 1/SR 48, just s; downtown. Int corridors. **Pets:** Large, other species. $50 one-time fee/room. Designated rooms, service with restrictions, crate.
[SAVE] [🍴] [ᏹM] ⊇ 🛜 ✕ 🛢 🖃

▼▼ Home-Towne Suites of Columbia H

(803) 781-9391. **Call for rates.** 350 Columbiana Dr 29212. I-26 exit 103 (Harbison Blvd), just sw, then 0.7 mi nw. Int corridors.
Pets: Accepted. [ᏹM] ⊇ 🛜 ✕ 🛢 🖃

▼▼ La Quinta Inn & Suites Columbia NE/Ft. Jackson Area H

(803) 736-6400. **$69-$209.** 1538 Horseshoe Dr 29223. I-20 exit 74 (Two Notch Rd), just n on US 1, then just w; I-77 exit 17 (Two Notch Rd), 0.6 mi s on US 1, then just w. Int corridors. **Pets:** Large, other species. Service with restrictions. ⊇ 🛜 🛢 🖃

▼▼ La Quinta Inn-Maingate Ft. Jackson H

(803) 783-5410. **$79-$180.** 7333 Garners Ferry Rd 29209. I-77 exit 9A (Garners Ferry Rd), just se. Int corridors. **Pets:** Large, other species. Service with restrictions. ⊇ 🛜 ✕ 🛢 🖃

▼▼ Red Roof Inn Columbia East Ft. Jackson M

(803) 736-0850. **$36-$74.** 7580 Two Notch Rd 29223. I-20 exit 74 (Two Notch Rd), just n on US 1, then just e; I-77 exit 17 (Two Notch Rd), 0.5 mi s on US 1, then just e. Ext corridors. **Pets:** Large, other species. Service with restrictions, supervision. [SAVE] 🛜 ✕ 🛢 🖃

▼▼▼ Residence Inn by Marriott Columbia Northeast H

(803) 788-8850. **$119-$229.** 2320 Legrand Rd 29223. I-77 exit 19, just ne on Farrow Rd (SR 555), just e on Rabon Rd, then just s. Int corridors. **Pets:** Accepted. ⊇ 🛜 ✕ 🛢 🖃

▼▼▼ Sheraton Columbia Downtown Hotel H

(803) 988-1400. **$99-$499.** 1400 Main St 29201. Jct Washington St; center of downtown. Int corridors. **Pets:** Accepted.
[SAVE] [🍴] 🛜 ✕ 🖃

▼▼▼ Staybridge Suites Columbia H

(803) 451-5000. **Call for rates.** 1913 Huger St 29201. I-126 exit 3B (US 21/Huger St), just s. Int corridors. **Pets:** Accepted.
[ᏹM] ⊇ 🛜 ✕ 🛢 🖃

▼▼▼ Suburban Extended Stay Hotel H

(803) 779-7000. **$80-$90.** 150 Stoneridge Dr 29210. I-126 exit Greystone Blvd, just n, then just e. Ext corridors. **Pets:** Accepted.
⊇ 🛜 ✕ 🛢 🖃

CONWAY

▼▼▼ Comfort Suites at the University H

(843) 347-9292. **$70-$190.** 2480 Hwy 501 E 29526. Jct US 501/501 business route, 1.6 mi se. Int corridors. **Pets:** Accepted.
⊇ 🛜 ✕ 🛢 🖃

DILLON

▼▼▼ Quality Inn M

(843) 774-0222. **$79-$170.** 817 Radford Blvd 29536. I-95 exit 193, just se on SR 9. Ext corridors. **Pets:** Accepted. ⊇ 🛜 🛢 🖃

DUNCAN

▼▼ Baymont Inn & Suites Duncan/Spartanburg M

(864) 433-8405. **$49-$79.** 1546 E Main St 29334. I-85 exit 63, 0.4 mi se on SR 290. Ext corridors. **Pets:** Accepted. ⊇ 🛜 🛢 🖃

▼▼▼▼ Holiday Inn Express & Suites H

(864) 486-9191. **$109-$129.** 275 Frontage Rd 29334. I-85 exit 63, just nw on SR 290, just ne on S Main St, then just se. Int corridors.
Pets: $50 daily fee/pet. Designated rooms, service with restrictions, supervision. [SAVE] [ᏹM] ⊇ 🛜 ✕ 🛢 🖃

EASLEY

▼▼ Baymont Inn & Suites Easley/Greenville M

(864) 306-9000. **$59-$79.** 211 Dayton School Rd 29642. Jct US 123/SR 93, 0.6 mi e on US 123; jct US 123/SR 153, 1.4 mi w. Ext corridors.
Pets: Accepted. ⊇ 🛜 🛢 🖃

▼▼ Quality Inn M

(864) 859-7520. **$70-$199.** 5539 Calhoun Memorial Hwy 29640. Jct US 123/SR 93, just e on US 123. Ext corridors. **Pets:** Accepted.
⊇ 🛜 🛢 🖃

FLORENCE

▼▼▼ Baymont Inn & Suites M

(843) 468-9994. **$69-$169, 3 day notice.** 1826 W Lucas St 29501. I-95 exit 164, just e on US 52. Ext corridors. **Pets:** Accepted.
[SAVE] ⊇ 🛜 🛢 🖃

▼▼▼ BEST WESTERN Inn M

(843) 678-9292. **$103-$119.** 1808 W Lucas St 29501. I-95 exit 164, just se. Ext corridors. **Pets:** Other species. $15 deposit/pet, $15 one-time fee/room. Designated rooms, service with restrictions, supervision.
[SAVE] ⊇ 🛜 🛢 🖃

▼▼▼ Florence Inn & Suites M

(843) 664-9494. **$59-$89.** 3821 Bancroft Rd 29501. I-95 exit 157, just ne on US 76. Ext corridors. **Pets:** Accepted. [SAVE] ⊇ 🛜 🛢 🖃

▼▼▼▼ La Quinta Inn & Suites Florence H

(843) 629-1111. **$105-$349.** 2123 W Lucas St 29501. I-95 exit 164, 0.4 mi nw. Int corridors. **Pets:** Large, other species. Service with restrictions. [ᏹM] ⊇ 🛜 ✕ 🛢 🖃

▼▼▼ Quality Inn & Suites M

(843) 664-2400. **Call for rates.** 150 Dunbarton Dr 29501. I-95 exit 160A, just e, then just n. Ext corridors. **Pets:** Accepted.
[SAVE] ⊇ 🛜 🛢 🖃

▼▼▼ Red Roof Inn-Florence Civic Center M

(843) 678-9000. **$45-$180.** 2690 David McLeod Blvd 29501. I-95 exit 160A, just e on service road. Ext corridors. **Pets:** Large, other species. Service with restrictions, supervision. [SAVE] [ᏹM] 🛜 ✕ 🛢

▼▼▼▼ Residence Inn by Marriott Florence H

(843) 468-2800. **$139-$219.** 2660 Hospitality Blvd 29501. I-95 exit 160A, just e, then s. Int corridors. **Pets:** Accepted.
⊇ 🛜 ✕ 🛢 🖃

▼▼▼ Super 8 M

(843) 661-7267. **$59-$179.** 1832 1/2 W Lucas St 29501. I-95 exit 164, just se. Ext corridors. **Pets:** Small, other species. $10 daily fee/pet. Service with restrictions, supervision. [SAVE] ⊇ 🛜 🛢 🖃

FOLLY BEACH *(Restaurants p. 639)*

▼▼▼ Tides Folly Beach **H**

(843) 588-6464. **Call for rates.** 1 Center St 29439. Terminus of SR 171; center. Ext corridors. **Pets:** Accepted.

🍴 � 🤶 ✕ 🛏 💻

GAFFNEY

▼▼ Baymont Inn & Suites Gaffney **M**

(864) 489-0240. **$69-$99.** 101 Stuard St 29341. I-85 exit 92, 0.5 mi se on SR 11/W Floyd Baker Blvd. Ext corridors. **Pets:** Small, other species. $20 one-time fee/room. Designated rooms, service with restrictions, supervision. 🌀 🤶 🛏 💻

🌐 ▼▼▼ Super 8 **M**

(864) 489-1699. **$59-$89.** 100 Ellis Ferry Ave 29341. I-85 exit 92, 0.7 mi se on SR 11/W Floyd Baker Blvd. Ext corridors. **Pets:** Very small. $10 one-time fee/pet. Designated rooms, no service, supervision.

SAVE 🌀 🤶 🛏 💻

GEORGETOWN *(Restaurants p. 639)*

▼▼ Baymont Inn & Suites Georgetown/Near Georgetown Marina **M**

(843) 546-6090. **$59-$109.** 120 Church St 29440. Jct US 17/17 alternate route/701, 1.2 mi se on US 17; just w of ICW Bridge at Georgetown Landing. Ext corridors. **Pets:** Small. $20 daily fee/room. Designated rooms, service with restrictions, crate. 🌀 🤶 🛏 💻

GREENVILLE *(Restaurants p. 639)*

🌐 ▼▼ BEST WESTERN Greenville Airport Inn **M**

(864) 297-5353. **$70-$100.** 5009 Pelham Rd 29615. I-85 exit 54 (Pelham Rd), just se. Ext corridors. **Pets:** Accepted.

SAVE 🌀 🤶 🛏 💻

🌐 ▼▼▼ Clarion Inn & Suites **M**

(864) 254-6383. **$65-$105.** 50 Orchard Park Dr 29615. I-385 exit 39 (Haywood Rd), just n, just e on Orchard Park Dr, then just s. Ext corridors. **Pets:** Medium, other species. $15 daily fee/room. Service with restrictions, crate. SAVE 🌀 🤶 🛏 💻

▼▼▼ Drury Inn & Suites-Greenville **H**

(864) 288-4401. **$115-$229.** 10 Carolina Point Pkwy 29607. I-85 exit 51A (Woodruff Rd), just se; I-385 exit 35 (Woodruff Rd), 0.6 mi nw. Int corridors. **Pets:** $10 daily fee/room. Service with restrictions, supervision. 🌀 🤶 🛏 💻

▼▼▼ Extended Stay America-Greenville Airport **H**

(864) 213-9698. **$59-$99.** 3715 Pelham Rd 29615. I-85 exit 54 (Pelham Rd), 0.5 mi w. Int corridors. **Pets:** Other species. $25 daily fee/pet. Service with restrictions, supervision. 🤶 🛏 💻

🌐 ▼▼▼▼ Hyatt Place Greenville/Haywood **H**

(864) 232-3000. **$64-$159.** 40 W Orchard Park Dr 29615. I-385 exit 39 (Haywood Rd), just n, then w. Int corridors. **Pets:** Accepted.

SAVE 🍴 🌀 🤶 ✕ 🛏 💻

🌐 ▼▼▼▼ Hyatt Regency Greenville **H**

(864) 235-1234. **$149-$329.** 220 N Main St 29601. Just n of center. Int corridors. **Pets:** Accepted. SAVE ECO 🍴 🌀 🤶 ✕ 🛏 💻

▼▼▼ La Quinta Inn & Suites Greenville Haywood **H**

(864) 233-8018. **$85-$206.** 65 W Orchard Park Dr 29615. I-385 exit 39 (Haywood Rd), just n, then w. Int corridors. **Pets:** Large, other species. Service with restrictions. 🌀 🤶 🛏 💻

▼▼ La Quinta Inn Greenville (Woodruff Rd) **M**

(864) 297-3500. **$59-$175.** 31 Old Country Rd 29607. I-85 exit 51A (Woodruff Rd), just nw on SR 146; I-385 exit 37, just sw on Roper Mountain Rd, then 0.9 mi se. Ext/int corridors. **Pets:** Large, other species. Service with restrictions. 🌀 🤶 🛏 💻

▼▼ The Phoenix Greenville's Inn **M**

(864) 233-4651. **Call for rates.** 246 N Pleasantburg Dr 29607. I-385 exit 40B, 0.6 mi s on SR 291. Ext corridors. **Pets:** Accepted.

🍴 🌀 🤶 🛏 💻

▼▼▼ Red Roof Inn-Greenville **M**

(864) 297-4458. **$49-$79.** 2801 Laurens Rd 29607. I-85 exit 48A, just se to Millennium Blvd, then just nw on Vision Ct. Ext corridors. **Pets:** Large, other species. Service with restrictions, supervision.

SAVE 🌀 🤶 🛏

▼▼▼ Residence Inn by Marriott Greenville-Spartanburg Airport **H**

(864) 627-0001. **$109-$259.** 120 Milestone Way 29615. I-85 exit 54 (Pelham Rd), 0.6 mi w to Milestone Way, then just n. Int corridors.

Pets: Accepted. 🌀 🌀 🤶 ✕ 🛏 💻

▼▼▼ Staybridge Suites Greenville/Spartanburg **H**

(864) 288-4448. **$109-$229.** 31 Market Point Dr 29607. I-85 exit 51A (Woodruff Rd), 0.5 mi se to Miller Rd, 0.5 mi s to S Oak Forest Dr, then just nw; I-385 exit 35 (Woodruff Rd), nw to Miller Rd, 0.5 mi s to S Oak Forest Dr, then just nw. Int corridors. **Pets:** Accepted.

🌀 🤶 ✕ 🛏 💻

▼▼ TownePlace Suites by Marriott Greenville Haywood Mall **H**

(864) 675-1670. **$101-$143.** 75 Mall Connector Rd 29607. I-385 exit 39 (Haywood Rd), just s to Woods Crossing Rd, just se to Mall Connector Rd, then just s. Int corridors. **Pets:** Accepted.

🌀 🌀 🤶 ✕ 🛏 💻

🌐 ▼▼▼▼ The Westin Poinsett **H** 🐾

(864) 421-9700. **$139-$399.** 120 S Main St 29601. Just s of center. Int corridors. **Pets:** Medium, dogs only. $75 one-time fee/pet. Designated rooms, service with restrictions, supervision.

SAVE ECO 🍴 🌀 ✕ 🛏 💻

GREENWOOD

▼▼ Quality Inn **M**

(864) 229-5329. **$67-$99.** 719 Bypass Hwy 25 NE 29646. Jct US 25 Bypass NE/221, just se. Ext corridors. **Pets:** Accepted.

🌀 🤶 🛏 💻

GREER

▼▼▼ Holiday Inn Express Hotel & Suites Greenville Airport **H**

(864) 213-9331. **$109-$149, 3 day notice.** 2681 Dry Pocket Rd 29650. I-85 exit 54 (Pelham Rd), just w to The Parkway, just n to Parkway E, then just se. Int corridors. **Pets:** Accepted. 🌀 🤶 ✕ 🛏 💻

▼▼ MainStay Suites-Greenville **H**

(864) 987-5566. **$54-$99.** 2671 Dry Pocket Rd 29650. I-85 exit 54 (Pelham Rd), just w to The Parkway, just n to Parkway E, then just se. Int corridors. **Pets:** Accepted. 🌀 🤶 🛏 💻

HARDEEVILLE

▼▼▼ Holiday Inn Express & Suites **H**

(843) 784-2800. **$79-$159.** 145 Independence Blvd 29927. I-95 exit 8, just w. Int corridors. **Pets:** Medium. $35 one-time fee/room. Service with restrictions, crate. 🌀 🌀 🤶 🛏 💻

HILTON HEAD ISLAND *(Restaurants p. 639)*

🌐 ▼▼▼ Comfort Inn South Forest Beach **H**

(843) 842-6662. **$69-$199.** 2 Tanglewood Dr 29928. Sea Pines Cir, 1.1 mi se on Pope Ave, just sw on Coligny Plaza. Int corridors. **Pets:** Medium, other species. $25 daily fee/room. Designated rooms, service with restrictions, crate. SAVE 🌀 🤶 🛏 💻

🌐 ▼▼▼ Omni Hilton Head Oceanfront Resort **H** 🐾

(843) 842-8000. **$99-$469.** 23 Ocean Ln 29928. Jct US 278 business route/Queens Folly Rd, 0.9 mi se to Ocean Ln, just sw; in Palmetto Dunes Plantation. Ext/int corridors. **Pets:** Medium. $150 one-time fee/room. Designated rooms, service with restrictions, supervision.

SAVE 🍴 🌀 🌀 ✕ 🤶 ✕ 🛏 💻

Red Roof Inn-Hilton Head Ⓜ

(843) 686-6808. **$49-$149.** 5 Regency Pkwy 29928. 9 mi e of J Wilton Graves Bridge on US 278 business route; between Shipyard Plantation and Palmetto Dunes. Ext corridors. **Pets:** Large, other species. Service with restrictions, supervision. (SAVE) 🛬 🛜 🖥

Sonesta Resort Hilton Head Island Ⓗ 🐾

(843) 842-2400. **$119-$399, 3 day notice.** 130 Shipyard Dr 29928. Jct US 278 business route/Shipyard Dr, 1.3 mi se; in Shipyard Plantation. Int corridors. **Pets:** Small, dogs only. $150 one-time fee/room. Designated rooms, service with restrictions, crate. (SAVE) (ECO) 🍴 🛬 ⊠ 🛜 ✕ 🖥

The Westin Hilton Head Island Resort & Spa Ⓗ

(843) 681-4000. **$119-$599, 5 day notice.** Two Grasslawn Ave 29928. 5.6 mi e of J Wilton Graves Bridge on US 278 business route to Coggins Point Rd, just e, follow signs; in Port Royal Plantation. Int corridors. **Pets:** Accepted. (SAVE) 🍴 🛬 ⊠ 🛜 ✕ 🖥

IRMO

Hyatt Place Columbia/Harbison Ⓗ

(803) 407-1560. **$79-$199.** 1130 Kinley Rd 29063. I-26 exit 102B, just e on SR 60, then just n. Int corridors. **Pets:** Accepted.
(SAVE) (&M) 🛬 🛜 ✕ 🖥

Residence Inn by Marriott Columbia Northwest/Harbison Ⓗ

(803) 749-7575. **$119-$299.** 944 Lake Murray Blvd 29063. I-26 exit 102A, just w on SR 60. Int corridors. **Pets:** Accepted.
(&M) 🛜 ✕ 🖥

KIAWAH ISLAND

Kiawah Island Golf Resort-Courtside Villas Ⓒⓞ

(843) 768-2121. **Call for rates.** 1401 Shipwatch Rd 29455. Just e of main gate to Kiawah Beach Dr, just s; in West Beach Village area. Ext corridors. **Pets:** Accepted. 🛬 ⊠ 🛜 ✕ 🖥

Kiawah Island Golf Resort-Fairway Oaks Villas Ⓒⓞ

(843) 768-2121. **Call for rates.** 1301 Kiawah Beach Dr 29455. Just e of main gate, just s; in West Beach Village area. Ext corridors. **Pets:** Accepted. 🛬 ⊠ 🛜 ✕ 🖥

Kiawah Island Golf Resort-Mariners Watch Villas Ⓒⓞ

(843) 768-2121. **Call for rates.** 4200 Sea Forest Dr 29455. 1.6 mi e of main gate, just s; in East Beach Village area. Ext corridors. **Pets:** Accepted. 🛬 ⊠ 🛜 ✕ 🖥

Kiawah Island Golf Resort-Parkside Villas Ⓒⓞ

(843) 768-2121. **Call for rates.** 4501 Park Lake Dr 29455. 2 mi e of main gate, just s; in East Beach Village area. Ext corridors. **Pets:** Accepted. 🛬 ⊠ 🛜 ✕ 🖥

Kiawah Island Golf Resort-Seascape Villas Ⓒⓞ

(843) 768-2121. **Call for rates.** 3510 Shipwatch Rd 29455. Just e of main gate, just s; in West Beach Village area. Ext corridors. **Pets:** Accepted. 🛬 ⊠ 🛜 ✕ 🖥

Kiawah Island Golf Resort-Tennis Club Villas Ⓒⓞ

(843) 768-2121. **Call for rates.** 4659 Tennis Club Ln 29455. 2.2 mi e of main gate, just s; at Roy Barth Tennis Center. Ext corridors. **Pets:** Accepted. 🛬 ⊠ 🛜 ✕ 🖥

Kiawah Island Golf Resort-Turtle Cove Villas Ⓒⓞ

(843) 768-2121. **Call for rates.** 5501 Green Dolphin Way 29455. 2.4 mi e of main gate, just se; at Roy Barth Tennis Center. Ext corridors. **Pets:** Accepted. 🛬 ⊠ 🛜 ✕ 🖥

Kiawah Island Golf Resort-Turtle Point Villas Ⓒⓞ

(843) 768-2121. **Call for rates.** 4901 Green Dolphin Way 29455. 2.4 mi e of main gate, just se; at Roy Barth Tennis Center and Turtle Point Golf Club. Ext corridors. **Pets:** Accepted.
🛬 ⊠ 🛜 ✕ 🖥

Kiawah Island Golf Resort-Windswept Villas Ⓒⓞ

(843) 768-2121. **Call for rates.** 4300 Sea Forest Dr 29455. 1.6 mi e of main gate, just s; in East Beach Village area. Ext corridors. **Pets:** Accepted. 🛬 ⊠ 🛜 ✕ 🖥

LADSON

BEST WESTERN Magnolia Inn & Suites Ⓗ

(843) 553-8888. **$99-$179.** 747 Treeland Dr 29456. I-26 exit 203 (College Park Rd), just ne. Int corridors. **Pets:** Small. $20 daily fee/pet. Service with restrictions. (SAVE) (&M) 🛬 🛜 🖥

LANCASTER

Quality Inn Ⓜ

(803) 283-1188. **$80-$100.** 114 Commerce Blvd 29720. Jct US 521, 1.3 mi w on SR 9 Bypass, just n. Ext corridors. **Pets:** Medium. $20 daily fee/pet. Service with restrictions, crate. (&M) 🛬 🛜 🖥

LANDRUM

The Red Horse Inn Cottages ⒸⒶ 🐾

(864) 909-1575. **$210-$320, 30 day notice.** 45 Winstons Chase Ct 29356. Jct SR 14/414, 1.5 mi w on SR 414 to Campbell Rd, 0.7 mi n. Ext corridors. **Pets:** $25 one-time fee/pet. Designated rooms, no service, crate. 🛜 ✕ Ⓩ 🖥

LATTA

BEST WESTERN Executive Inn Ⓗ

(843) 752-5060. **$81-$99.** 1534 Hwy 38 W 29565. I-95 exit 181B, just nw. Int corridors. **Pets:** Accepted. (SAVE) 🛬 🛜 🖥

LEXINGTON

Quality Inn & Suites Ⓜ

(803) 359-3099. **Call for rates.** 328 W Main St 29072. I-20 exit 58 (US 1), 3.5 mi w. Ext corridors. **Pets:** Medium. $20 daily fee/pet. Service with restrictions, supervision. 🛬 🛜 🖥

LITTLE RIVER

Holiday Inn Express Hotel & Suites-North Myrtle Beach Ⓗ

(843) 281-9400. **$79-$299, 3 day notice.** 722 Hwy 17 N 29566. Jct SR 9/US 17, 1 mi e; at Coquina Harbor. Int corridors. **Pets:** Accepted.
(SAVE) (&M) 🛬 🛜 ✕ 🖥

MANNING

Baymont Inn & Suites Ⓜ

(803) 473-5334. **$59-$109.** 2284 Raccoon Rd 29102. I-95 exit 119 (SR 261), just se, then s. Ext corridors. **Pets:** Accepted.
(SAVE) 🛬 🛜 🖥

MOUNT PLEASANT *(Restaurants p. 639)*

Days Inn Patriots Point Ⓜ

(843) 881-1800. **$79-$179, 3 day notice.** 261 Johnnie Dodds Blvd 29464. Just e of base of Arthur Ravenel Jr Bridge on US 17 (Johnnie Dodds Blvd). Ext corridors. **Pets:** Small, dogs only. $10 daily fee/pet. Designated rooms, service with restrictions, supervision.
(SAVE) 🛬 🛜 🖥

Hampton Inn-Patriots Point Ⓗ

(843) 881-3300. **$119-$259.** 255 Sessions Way 29464. Just ne of base of Arthur Ravenel Jr Bridge to McGrath Darby Blvd, just s. Int corridors. **Pets:** Accepted. (&M) 🛬 🛜 🖥

Homewood Suites by Hilton Ⓗ

(843) 881-6950. **$149-$359.** 1998 Riviera Dr 29464. I-526 exit 32 (Georgetown/US 17 N), 1.4 mi ne on US 17, 1 mi se on SR 517 (Isle of Palms Connector), then just sw. Int corridors. **Pets:** Accepted.
(&M) 🛬 🛜 🖥

◆◆◆ MainStay Suites Mount Pleasant 🄷
(843) 881-1722. **$69-$189.** 400 McGrath Darby Blvd 29464. Base of Arthur Ravenel Jr Bridge, just ne on US 17 (Johnnie Dodds Blvd), just n. Int corridors. **Pets:** Accepted. 🛧🅼 🛜 🯄 🖵

◆◆◆ Red Roof Plus+ Mt. Pleasant Patriot Point 🄼
(843) 884-1411. **$59-$150.** 301 Johnnie Dodds Blvd 29464. Just e of base of Arthur Ravenel Jr Bridge on US 17 (Johnnie Dodds Blvd), just s on McGrath Darby Blvd. Ext corridors. **Pets:** Large, other species. Service with restrictions, supervision. (SAVE) ⌘ 🛜 🗙 🯄

◆◆◆ Residence Inn by Marriott Charleston Mt. Pleasant 🄷
(843) 881-1599. **$170-$260.** 1116 Isle of Palms Connector 29464. I-526 exit 30 (Georgetown/US 17 N), 1.4 mi ne on US 17 to SR 517 (Isle of Palms Connector), then just se. Int corridors. **Pets:** Accepted.
🛧🅼 ⌘ 🛜 🗙 🯄 🖵

◆◆ Sleep Inn Mt. Pleasant 🄷
(843) 856-5000. **$79-$169.** 299 Wingo Way 29464. Just ne of base of Arthur Ravenel Jr Bridge to McGrath Darby Blvd, just n. Int corridors. **Pets:** Large. $40 one-time fee/room. Designated rooms, service with restrictions, crate. 🛧🅼 ⌘ 🛜 🯄 🖵

MURRELLS INLET

◆◆◆ Holiday Inn Express Hotel & Suites 🄷
(843) 357-0100. **$72-$189.** 1303-A Tadlock Dr 29576. Jct US 17 Bypass and 17 S business route. Int corridors. **Pets:** Other species. $50 one-time fee/room. Service with restrictions. ⌘ 🛜 🗙 🯄 🖵

MYRTLE BEACH *(Restaurants p. 640)*

◆◆◆ BEST WESTERN PLUS Myrtle Beach Hotel 🄷 ❀
(843) 213-1440. **$59-$219.** 9551 Hwy 17 N 29572. Jct SR 22, 1.4 mi sw. Int corridors. **Pets:** Dogs only. $10 daily fee/pet. Designated rooms, service with restrictions. (SAVE) 🛧🅼 ⌘ 🛜 🗙 🯄 🖵

◆◆◆ Clarion Hotel 🄷
(843) 236-1000. **$70-$300.** 101 Fantasy Harbour Blvd 29579. Jct US 17 Bypass, 0.7 mi n on US 501 exit River Oaks Rd/George Bishop Pkwy, just w on River Oaks Rd, then 0.7 mi s. Int corridors. **Pets:** Accepted.
(SAVE) 🍴 ⌘ 🗙 🛜 🗙 🯄 🖵

◆◆◆ Comfort Suites 🄷 ❀
(843) 448-4884. **$70-$270.** 710 Frontage Rd E 29577. Jct US 17 Bypass, just se on US 501, just ne. Int corridors. **Pets:** Medium, other species. $20 daily fee/pet. Designated rooms, service with restrictions. ⌘ 🛜 🗙 🯄 🖵

◆◆ La Quinta Inn & Suites Myrtle Beach At 48th Avenue 🄷
(843) 449-5231. **$55-$334.** 4709 N Kings Hwy 29577. Jct 48th Ave N and US 17 business route. Int corridors. **Pets:** Large, other species. Service with restrictions. ⌘ 🛜 🯄 🖵

◆◆ La Quinta Inn & Suites Myrtle Beach Broadway Area 🄷
(843) 916-8801. **$55-$399.** 1561 21st Ave N 29577. Jct US 17 Bypass, just se. Int corridors. **Pets:** Large, other species. Service with restrictions. 🛧🅼 ⌘ 🛜 🯄 🖵

◆◆◆ Ocean Park Resort 🄷
(843) 448-1915. **$44-$199.** 1905 S Ocean Blvd 29577. Jct 20th Ave S. Int corridors. **Pets:** Accepted. (SAVE) ⌘ 🗙 🛜 🗙 🯄 🖵

◆◆◆ Patricia Grand Resort Hotel 🄷
(843) 448-8453. **$49-$214.** 2710 N Ocean Blvd 29577. Jct 27th Ave N. Ext corridors. **Pets:** Accepted.
(SAVE) 🍴 ⌘ 🗙 🛜 🗙 🯄 🖵

◆◆◆ Red Roof Inn & Suites Myrtle Beach 🄷
(843) 626-4444. **$39-$235.** 2801 S Kings Hwy 29577. Between 27th Ave S and 29th Ave S on US 17 business route. Int corridors. **Pets:** Large, other species. Service with restrictions, supervision.
(SAVE) ⌘ 🛜 🯄 🖵

◆◆◆ Springmaid Beach Resort & Conference Center 🄷
(843) 315-7100. **$59-$359.** 3200 S Ocean Blvd 29577. Jct 30th Ave S, 0.4 mi s. Ext corridors. **Pets:** Accepted.
(SAVE) 🍴 ⌘ 🗙 🛜 🗙 🯄 🖵

◆◆◆ Staybridge Suites 🄷 ❀
(843) 903-4000. **$65-$199.** 303 Fantasy Harbour Blvd 29579. Jct US 17 Bypass, 0.7 mi n on US 501 exit River Oaks Rd/George Bishop Pkwy, just w on River Oaks Rd, then 0.4 mi s. Int corridors. **Pets:** Large. $20 daily fee/room. Designated rooms, service with restrictions.
(SAVE) ⌘ 🛜 🯄 🖵

◆◆◆ Westgate Myrtle Beach Oceanfront Resort 🄷
(843) 448-4481. **$59-$299, 3 day notice.** 415 S Ocean Blvd 29577. Jct 6th Ave S, just ne. Int corridors. **Pets:** Accepted.
(SAVE) 🍴 ⌘ 🗙 🛜 🗙 🯄 🖵

NORTH CHARLESTON *(Restaurants p. 640)*

◆◆◆ Aloft Charleston Airport & Convention Center 🄷
(843) 566-7300. **Call for rates.** 4875 Tanger Outlet Blvd 29418. I-26 exit 213 westbound; exit 213A eastbound, follow signs to Tanger Outlet Mall. Int corridors. **Pets:** Accepted. (SAVE) ⌘ 🗙 🯄 🖵

◆◆ Candlewood Suites 🄷
(843) 797-3535. **Call for rates.** 2177 Northwoods Blvd 29406. I-26 exit 209A eastbound; exit 209B (Ashley Phosphate Rd) westbound, just e, then just n. Int corridors. **Pets:** Accepted. 🛜 🯄 🖵

◆◆ Charleston Plaza Hotel 🄷
(843) 747-1900. **Call for rates.** 4770 Goer Dr 29406. I-26 exit 213 westbound; exit 213B eastbound, just n. Int corridors. **Pets:** Accepted.
🍴 ⌘ 🛜 🗙 🯄 🖵

◆◆ Embassy Suites Hotel Airport-Convention Center North Charleston 🄷
(843) 747-1882. **$159-$249.** 5055 International Blvd 29418. I-26 exit 213 westbound; exit 213A eastbound, just s, then w; I-526 exit 10 (International Blvd), 0.4 mi e. Int corridors. **Pets:** Medium. $25 one-time fee/pet. Service with restrictions, crate.
🍴 🛧🅼 ⌘ 🗙 🛜 🯄 🖵

◆◆ Fairfield Inn & Suites by Marriott Charleston North/Ashley Phosphate 🄷
(843) 725-5400. **$89-$209.** 2520 N Forest Dr 29420. I-26 exit 209A eastbound; exit 209B (Ashley Phosphate Rd) westbound, just w of Northside Dr. Int corridors. **Pets:** $50 one-time fee/room. Designated rooms, service with restrictions, supervision.
🛧🅼 ⌘ 🛜 🗙 🯄 🖵

◆◆ Hawthorn Suites by Wyndham-North Charleston 🄷
(843) 572-5757. **$89-$172.** 7645 Northwoods Blvd 29406. I-26 exit 209A eastbound; exit 209B (Ashley Phosphate Rd) westbound, just e, then n. Ext corridors. **Pets:** Accepted. ⌘ 🛜 🯄 🖵

◆◆ Home2 Suites by Hilton Charleston Airport/Convention Center 🄷
(843) 744-4202. **$119-$189.** 3401 W Montague Ave 29418. I-26 exit 213 westbound; exit 213A eastbound, 0.9 mi sw; I-526 exit 16. Int corridors. **Pets:** Accepted. 🛧🅼 ⌘ 🛜 🯄 🖵

◆◆ La Quinta Inn Charleston North 🄼
(843) 797-8181. **$65-$284.** 2499 La Quinta Ln 29420. I-26 exit 209A eastbound; exit 209B (Ashley Phosphate Rd) westbound, just w. Ext/int corridors. **Pets:** Large, other species. Service with restrictions.
⌘ 🛜 🯄 🖵

Red Roof Inn-North Charleston Coliseum M

(843) 572-9100. **$50-$100.** 7480 Northwoods Blvd 29406. I-26 exit 209A eastbound; exit 209B (Ashley Phosphate Rd) westbound, just e, just n. Ext corridors. **Pets:** Large, other species. Service with restrictions, supervision. [SAVE] 🛰 ☒ 🖬

Residence Inn by Marriott Charleston Airport H

(843) 266-3434. **$139-$249.** 5035 International Blvd 29418. I-26 exit 213 westbound; exit 213A eastbound, just s; I-526 exit 16 (International Blvd), 0.7 mi e. Int corridors. **Pets:** Large, other species. $100 one-time fee/room. Service with restrictions. 🛰 🛰 🖬 ☒ 🖬 🖳

Staybridge Suites North Charleston H

(843) 377-4600. **$139-$199, 3 day notice.** 7329 Mazyck Rd 29406. I-26 exit 209A eastbound; exit 209B (Ashley Phosphate Rd) westbound, just sw, then just s. Int corridors. **Pets:** Accepted. 🛰 🛰 🖬 🖳

RICHBURG

Motel 6 H

(803) 789-7770. **Call for rates.** 2912 Parkway Blvd 29729. I-77 exit 65, just w on SR 9. Int corridors. **Pets:** Other species. Service with restrictions, crate. 🛰 🖬

RIDGELAND *(Restaurants p. 640)*

Quality Inn & Suites M

(843) 726-2121. **$66-$96.** Hwy 336 & I-95 29936. I-95 exit 21 (US 336), just nw. Ext/int corridors. **Pets:** Accepted. [SAVE] 🛰 🛰 🖬 🖳

ROCK HILL

Comfort Suites H

(803) 326-3300. **$99-$139.** 1323 Old Springdale Rd 29730. I-77 exit 79, just e on Dave Lyle Blvd, just s on Galleria Blvd, then just e. Int corridors. **Pets:** Accepted. 🛰 🛰 ☒ 🖬 🖳

Hampton Inn Rock Hill H

(803) 325-1100. **$119-$189.** 2111 Tabor Dr 29730. I-77 exit 79, just e on Dave Lyle Blvd, just n on Galleria Blvd, then just w. Int corridors. **Pets:** Accepted. 🛰 🛰 ☒ 🖬 🖳

TownePlace Suites by Marriott Rock Hill H

(803) 327-0700. **$109-$139.** 2135 Tabor Dr 29730. I-77 exit 79, just e on Dave Lyle Blvd, just n on Galleria Blvd, then just w. Int corridors. **Pets:** Accepted. 🛰 🛰 🛰 ☒ 🖬 🖳

Wingate By Wyndham H

(803) 324-9000. **$79-$165.** 760 Galleria Blvd 29730. I-77 exit 79, just e on Dave Lyle Blvd, then just s. Int corridors. **Pets:** Accepted.

🛰 🛰 🛰 ☒ 🖬 🖳

SANTEE

Econo Lodge Santee M

(803) 854-3870. **$55-$60.** 9112 Old Hwy 6 29142. I-95 exit 98 (SR 6), 0.4 mi se. Ext corridors. **Pets:** Accepted. [SAVE] 🛰 🛰 🖬 🖳

Holiday Inn Santee H

(803) 854-9800. **Call for rates.** 139 Bradford Blvd 29142. I-95 exit 98 (SR 6), just nw, then just sw. Int corridors. **Pets:** Small, other species. $20 daily fee/pet. Designated rooms, service with restrictions, supervision. 🍴 🛰 🛰 🛰 🖬 🖳

Super 8 M

(803) 854-3456. **$51-$89.** 9125 Old Hwy 6 29142. I-95 exit 98 (SR 6), 0.4 mi se. Ext corridors. **Pets:** $10 daily fee/pet. Service with restrictions. [SAVE] 🛰 🛰 🖬 🖳

SENECA

Quality Inn M

(864) 888-8300. **$81-$149.** 226 Hi-Tech Rd 29678. Jct SR 28 and US 76/123, 0.9 mi w on US 76/123, just se. Ext corridors. **Pets:** Small, other species. $20 daily fee/pet. Designated rooms, service with restrictions, supervision. 🛰 🛰 🛰 🖬 🖳

SIMPSONVILLE *(Restaurants p. 640)*

Comfort Suites H

(864) 757-1552. **$109-$124.** 3971 Grandview Dr 29680. I-385 exit 26, just s on Fairview Rd, then 0.5 mi se along Service Rd. Int corridors. **Pets:** Medium, other species. $25 daily fee/room. Designated rooms, service with restrictions, supervision. 🛰 🛰 🛰 ☒ 🖬 🖳

Days Inn M

(864) 963-7701. **$70-$80.** 45 Ray E Talley Ct 29680. I-385 exit 27, just s, then just se. Ext corridors. **Pets:** Accepted. 🛰 🛰 🖬 🖳

Quality Inn M

(864) 963-2777. **$59-$89.** 3755 Grandview Dr 29680. I-385 exit 27, just s. Ext corridors. **Pets:** Accepted. [SAVE] 🛰 🛰 🖬 🖳

SPARTANBURG

Holiday Inn Express Hotel & Suites H

(864) 699-7777. **Call for rates.** 895 Spartan Blvd 29301. I-26 exit 21B (US 29), just e to W Blackstock Rd, then 0.7 mi n. Int corridors. **Pets:** Accepted. [SAVE] 🛰 🛰 🛰 🖬 🖳

Quality Inn & Suites H

(864) 542-0333. **$69-$94.** 160 Simuel Rd 29303. I-85 business route exit 4 (SR 56), just sw. Int corridors. **Pets:** Accepted.

🛰 🛰 ☒ 🖬 🖳

SUMMERVILLE *(Restaurants p. 640)*

Holiday Inn Express-Charleston/Summerville H

(843) 875-3300. **$109-$149.** 120 Holiday Dr 29483. I-26 exit 199A, just w on US 17 alternate route to Holiday Dr, then just n. Int corridors. **Pets:** Accepted. 🛰 🛰 🛰 🖬 🖳

SUMTER

Candlewood Suites H

(803) 469-4000. **Call for rates.** 2541 Broad St 29150. 1.1 mi w of jct US 76/378/521. Int corridors. **Pets:** Accepted. 🛰 🛰 ☒ 🖬 🖳

Travelers Inn & Suites M

(803) 469-9210. **Call for rates.** 1210 Camden Rd 29151. Jct US 521/76. Ext corridors. **Pets:** Medium. $10 daily fee/pet. Service with restrictions, supervision. 🛰 🛰 🖬 🖳

SURFSIDE BEACH

Holiday Inn Oceanfront at Surfside Beach H

(843) 238-5601. **$49-$229.** 1601 N Ocean Blvd 29575. Jct 16th Ave N and N Ocean Blvd. Int corridors. **Pets:** Accepted.

[SAVE] 🍴 🛰 🛰 ☒ 🛰 ☒ 🖬 🖳

WALTERBORO

BEST WESTERN of Walterboro M

(843) 538-3600. **$90-$100.** 1428 Sniders Hwy 29488. I-95 exit 53 (SR 63), just e. Ext corridors. **Pets:** Medium. $15 daily fee/room. Designated rooms, service with restrictions, supervision. [SAVE] 🛰 🛰 🖬 🖳

Super 8 M

(843) 538-5383. **$62-$77.** 1972 Bells Hwy 29488. I-95 exit 57 (SR 64), just nw. Ext corridors. **Pets:** Accepted. [SAVE] 🛰 🛰 🖬 🖳

WEST COLUMBIA

Quality Inn M

(803) 791-5160. **$60-$70.** 2516 Augusta Rd 29169. I-26 exit 111B (US 1 N), just e. Ext/int corridors. **Pets:** Accepted. 🛰 🛰 🖬 🖳

WINNSBORO

▼▼▼ **Americas Best Value Inn Winnsboro** Ⓜ
(803) 635-1447. **$56-$99.** 1894 US Hwy 321 Bypass 29180. I-77 exit 34 (SR 34), 6.5 mi w; jct US 321/SR 34/213. Ext corridors. **Pets:** Small. $15 daily fee/pet. Designated rooms, service with restrictions, supervision. 🐾 🛜 🔋 🖥

YEMASSEE

◆◆◆ ▼▼▼ **BEST WESTERN Point South** Ⓜ ❧
(843) 726-8101. **$84-$94.** 3536 Point South Dr 29945. I-95 exit 33 (US 17), just ne. Ext corridors. **Pets:** $12 one-time fee/room. Designated rooms, service with restrictions, supervision. 🆂🅰🆅🅴 🐾 🛜 🔋 🖥

SOUTH DAKOTA

ABERDEEN

▼▼▼ **Aberdeen East Super 8** 🅷 ❧
(605) 229-5005. **$70-$115.** 2405 6th Ave SE 57401. 1.8 mi e on US 12. Int corridors. **Pets:** $10 deposit/room, $10 one-time fee/room. Service with restrictions, supervision. 🅼 🐾 ✕ 🛜 🔋 🖥

▼▼▼ **Aberdeen North Super 8** Ⓜ
(605) 226-2288. **$60-$100.** 1023 8th Ave NW 57401. 1.5 mi nw on US 281. Int corridors. **Pets:** Accepted. 🅼 🛜 🔋 🖥

◆◆◆ ▼▼▼ **AmericInn Lodge & Suites of Aberdeen** 🅷
(605) 225-4565. **$105.** 301 Centennial St 57401. 2.2 mi e on US 12, just n. Int corridors. **Pets:** Accepted.
🆂🅰🆅🅴 🅼 🐾 ✕ 🛜 ✕ 🔋 🖥

◆◆◆ ▼▼▼ **BEST WESTERN Ramkota Hotel** 🅷
(605) 229-4040. **$90-$130.** 1400 8th Ave NW 57401. 1.5 mi nw on US 281. Ext/int corridors. **Pets:** Service with restrictions, crate.
🆂🅰🆅🅴 🍽 🅼 🐾 🛜 ✕ 🔋 🖥

▼▼▼▼ **Holiday Inn Express Hotel & Suites** 🅷
(605) 725-4000. **Call for rates.** 3310 7th Ave SE 57401. 2.1 mi e on US 12. Int corridors. **Pets:** Accepted. 🅼 🐾 🛜 ✕ 🔋 🖥

◆◆◆ ▼▼▼ **TownePlace Suites by Marriott** 🅷 ❧
(605) 725-3500. **$104-$171.** 402 Norwood St S 57401. Between 3rd and 6th aves SE. Int corridors. **Pets:** Other species. $20 daily fee/room. Service with restrictions. 🆂🅰🆅🅴 🍽 🐾 🛜 ✕ 🔋 🖥

BRANDON

▼▼▼▼ **Holiday Inn Express & Suites** 🅷 ❧
(605) 582-2901. **$109-$169.** 1103 N Splitrock Blvd 57005. I-90 exit 406, just s. Int corridors. **Pets:** $15 daily fee/pet. Service with restrictions, crate. 🅼 🐾 🛜 ✕ 🔋 🖥

BROOKINGS

▼▼ **Brookings Super 8** 🅷
(605) 692-6920. **$71-$155.** 3034 Lefevre Dr 57006. I-29 exit 132, just e. Int corridors. **Pets:** $10 daily fee/pet. Service with restrictions, crate. 🅼 🐾 🛜 ✕ 🔋 🖥

▼▼▼▼ **Holiday Inn Express Hotel & Suites** 🅷
(605) 692-9060. **$120-$180.** 3020 Lefevre Dr 57006. I-29 exit 132, just se. Int corridors. **Pets:** Accepted. 🅼 🐾 🛜 ✕ 🔋 🖥

BUFFALO

▼▼ **Tipperary Motel and Lodge** Ⓜ
(605) 375-3721. **$56.** 604 1st St W 57720. 0.5 mi n on US 85, turn at sign. Int corridors. **Pets:** Accepted. 🍽 🛜 ✕ 🔋

CHAMBERLAIN

◆◆◆ ▼▼▼ **BEST WESTERN Lee's Motor Inn** Ⓜ
(605) 734-5575. **$50-$120.** 220 W King Ave 57325. US 16 and I-90 business loop; downtown. Ext/int corridors. **Pets:** Small. $10 deposit/pet. Service with restrictions, supervision. 🆂🅰🆅🅴 🅼 🐾 🛜 ✕ 🖥

CUSTER CITY

◆◆◆ ▼▼▼ **Bavarian Inn** Ⓜ ❧
(605) 673-2802. **$59-$149.** 855 N 5th St 57730. 1 mi n on US 16 and 385. Ext/int corridors. **Pets:** $25 one-time fee/room. Service with restrictions. 🆂🅰🆅🅴 🍽 🅼 🐾 🛜 ✕ 🔋 🖥

▼▼ **Rock Crest Lodge and Cabins** 🅒🅐
(605) 673-4323. **Call for rates.** 15 W Mt. Rushmore Rd 57730. US 16, 0.5 mi w. Ext/int corridors. **Pets:** Accepted. 🐾 🛜 ✕ 🔋 🖥

◆◆◆ ▼ **Rocket Motel** Ⓜ
(605) 673-4401. **$59-$124, 3 day notice.** 211 Mt. Rushmore Rd 57730. On US 16; center. Ext corridors. **Pets:** Dogs only. $10 daily fee/pet. Designated rooms, service with restrictions, crate. 🆂🅰🆅🅴 🛜 ✕ 🔋

◆◆◆ ▼▼ **Super 8-Custer** 🅷
(605) 673-2200. **$80-$180.** 535 W Mt. Rushmore Rd 57730. US 16, 0.8 mi w. Int corridors. **Pets:** Accepted.
🆂🅰🆅🅴 🅼 🐾 🛜 ✕ 🔋 🖥

DEADWOOD

◆◆◆ ▼▼▼ **Cadillac Jack's Gaming Resort** 🅷
(605) 578-1500. **$44-$879.** 360 Main St 57732. 0.6 mi n on US 85. Int corridors. **Pets:** Accepted. 🆂🅰🆅🅴 🍽 🅼 🛜 🔋 🖥

◆◆◆ ▼▼▼ **Deadwood Gulch Gaming Resort** 🅷 ❧
(605) 578-1294. **$49-$169.** 304 Cliff St 57732. 0.7 mi s on US 85 S. Ext/int corridors. **Pets:** Dogs only. $500 deposit/room, $20 one-time fee/pet. Designated rooms, service with restrictions.
🆂🅰🆅🅴 🍽 🅼 🛜 ✕ 🔋 🖥

◆◆◆ ▼▼▼ **First Gold Hotel & Gaming** 🅷
(605) 578-9777. **$79-$349, 45 day notice.** 270 Main St 57732. 0.7 mi n on US 85. Ext/int corridors. **Pets:** $25 one-time fee/room. Designated rooms, service with restrictions.
🆂🅰🆅🅴 🍽 🅼 🛜 🔋 🖥

▼▼▼▼ **Holiday Inn Express Hotel & Suites** 🅷
(605) 578-3330. **Call for rates.** 22 Lee St 57732. Jct Main St; center. Int corridors. **Pets:** Medium, dogs only. $35 one-time fee/room. Designated rooms, service with restrictions, supervision.
🅼 🐾 🛜 ✕ 🔋 🖥

▼▼▼▼ **Holiday Inn Resort Deadwood Mountain Grand** 🅷
(605) 559-0386. **Call for rates.** 1906 Deadwood Mountain Dr 57732. Jct US 14 and Pine St; downtown. Int corridors. **Pets:** Accepted.
🍽 🅼 🐾 🛜 ✕ 🔋 🖥

▼▼▼▼ **The Lodge at Deadwood** 🅷 ❧
(605) 584-4800. **$89-$799, 3 day notice.** 100 Pine Crest Ln 57732. Jct US 14, 1 mi n on US 85. Ext/int corridors. **Pets:** Other species. Service with restrictions, crate. 🍽 🐾 🛜 ✕ 🔋 🖥

FAITH

▼▼ **Prairie Vista Inn** Ⓜ
(605) 967-2343. **$80-$130.** 204 E 1st St 57626. On US 212; east end of town. Int corridors. **Pets:** $15 one-time fee/room. Designated rooms, service with restrictions, supervision. 🅼 🛜 🔋 🖥

FAULKTON

▼▼ **Faulkton Inn** Ⓜ
(605) 598-4567. **Call for rates.** 700 Main St 57438. On US 212; center. Int corridors. **Pets:** Accepted. 🛜 🔋 🖥

FORT PIERRE

 **AmericInn Lodge & Suites of Pierre/Fort Pierre** 🏠 🐾

(605) 223-2358. **$106-$199.** 312 Island Dr 57532. Jct US 14 and SR 34, just w of Missouri River Bridge, just s. Int corridors. **Pets:** $20 one-time fee/pet. Service with restrictions, supervision.

🌊 🛜 ✕ 📵 🖵

FREEMAN

Freeman Country Inn 🅼

(605) 925-4888. **$75-$123.** 1019 S Hwy 81 57029. On US 81, just s. Int corridors. **Pets:** Other species. $20 daily fee/pet. Designated rooms, service with restrictions, supervision. 🅼 🛜 ✕ 📵

HILL CITY

BEST WESTERN Golden Spike Inn & Suites 🏠 🐾

(605) 574-2577. **Call for rates.** 601 E Main St 57745. Just n on US 16 and 385. Ext/int corridors. **Pets:** $15 daily fee/pet. Designated rooms, service with restrictions, supervision.

[SAVE] 🍴 🅼 🌊 🛜 ✕ 📵 🖵

Lantern Inn 🅼

(605) 574-2582. **Call for rates.** 580 E Main St 57745. On US 16 and 385; north side of town. Ext corridors. **Pets:** Accepted.

🌊 🛜 ✕ 📵

The Lodge at Palmer Gulch 🏠

(605) 574-2525. **$70-$750, 10 day notice.** 12620 SR 244 57745. On SR 244, 5 mi w of Mt. Rushmore. Int corridors. **Pets:** Accepted.

[SAVE] 🍴 🅼 🌊 ✕ 🛜 ✕ 📵 🖵

HOT SPRINGS

BEST WESTERN Sundowner Inn 🏠

(605) 745-7378. **$69-$200.** 737 S 6th St 57747. 0.5 mi se off US 18 and 385. Int corridors. **Pets:** Accepted.

[SAVE] 🅼 🌊 🛜 ✕ 📵 🖵

Dollar Inn Hot Springs 🅼

(605) 745-3182. **$50-$300.** 402 Battle Mountain Ave 57747. 1 mi n on US 385. Ext corridors. **Pets:** Accepted. [SAVE] 🛜 ✕ 📵 🖵

Hills Inn 🅼

(605) 745-3130. **$50-$250.** 640 S 6th St 57747. 0.5 mi se off US 18 and 385. Ext corridors. **Pets:** Accepted. [SAVE] 🌊 🛜 📵 🖵

Motel 6 🏠

(605) 745-6666. **$45-$156.** 541 Indianapolis Ave 57747. US 18 and 385, just w; jct S 6th St. Int corridors. **Pets:** Other species. Service with restrictions, crate. 🍴 🅼 🌊 🛜 📵

Stay USA Hotel and Suites 🏠

(605) 745-4411. **$58-$280.** 1401 Hwy 18 Bypass 57747. Jct US 18 and 385, 0.7 mi w on US 18 Bypass. Int corridors. **Pets:** Accepted.

[SAVE] 🅼 🛜 ✕ 📵 🖵

Super 8-Hot Springs 🏠

(605) 745-3888. **$44-$109.** 800 Mammoth St 57747. Jct US 18 and 385, 1 mi w on US 18 Bypass. Int corridors. **Pets:** Accepted.

🅼 🛜 📵 🖵

HURON

BEST WESTERN Of Huron 🏠 🐾

(605) 352-2000. **$91-$99.** 2000 Dakota Ave 57350. 1.3 mi s on SR 37. Ext/int corridors. **Pets:** Medium. $10 one-time fee/room. Service with restrictions, supervision. [SAVE] 🅼 🛜 📵 🖵

KEYSTONE

Econo Lodge of Mt. Rushmore 🏠

(605) 666-4417. **$60-$500.** 908 Madill St 57751. SR 40, 1 mi e of jct US 16A. Int corridors. **Pets:** Accepted. [SAVE] 🍴 🌊 🛜 📵 🖵

Holy Smoke Resort 🆑

(605) 666-4616. **$60-$225, 14 day notice.** 24105 Hwy 16A 57751. On US 16A, 2 mi n. Ext corridors. **Pets:** Accepted.

🍴 🛜 ✕ 🅩 📵 🖵

Mt. Rushmore's Washington Inn & Suites 🏠

(605) 666-5070. **$49-$99, 3 day notice.** 231 Winter St 57751. On US 16A; downtown. Ext/int corridors. **Pets:** Accepted.

🍴 🅼 🌊 🛜 📵

Mt. Rushmore's White House Resort 🏠

(605) 666-4917. **$49-$99, 3 day notice.** 115 Swanzey St 57751. Just e of jct US 16A and SR 40. Ext/int corridors. **Pets:** Accepted.

🍴 🅼 🌊 🛜 ✕ 📵

Powder House Lodge 🆑

(605) 666-4646. **$80-$500, 3 day notice.** 24125 Hwy 16A 57751. On US 16A, 1.5 mi n. Ext corridors. **Pets:** Accepted.

[SAVE] 🍴 🅼 🌊 🛜 ✕ 📵 🖵

MADISON

AmericInn Lodge & Suites Madison 🏠

(605) 256-3076. **Call for rates.** 504 10th St SE 57042. SR 34, 0.5 mi se; south side of town. Int corridors. **Pets:** Accepted.

🍴 🅼 🌊 🛜 ✕ 📵

MITCHELL

AmericInn Lodge & Suites 🏠

(605) 996-9700. **$90-$160.** 1421 S Burr St 57301. I-90 exit 332, just n. Int corridors. **Pets:** Accepted. 🌊 🛜 ✕ 📵 🖵

Days Inn of Mitchell 🏠

(605) 996-6208. **$74-$104.** 1506 S Burr St 57301. I-90 exit 332, just n. Int corridors. **Pets:** Dogs only. $10 daily fee/pet. Designated rooms, service with restrictions, supervision. [SAVE] 🅼 🌊 🛜 📵 🖵

Kelly Inn & Suites 🏠

(605) 995-0500. **Call for rates.** 1010 Cabela Dr 57301. I-90 exit 332, just sw. Ext/int corridors. **Pets:** Accepted.

🅼 🌊 🛜 ✕ 📵 🖵

MOBRIDGE

Wrangler Inn 🏠

(605) 845-3641. **$82-$159.** 820 W Grand Crossing 57601. 0.5 mi w on US 12. Ext/int corridors. **Pets:** Accepted.

🍴 🌊 ✕ 🛜 ✕ 📵 🖵

MURDO

BEST WESTERN Graham's 🅼

(605) 669-2441. **Call for rates.** 301 W 5th St 57559. On I-90 business loop, 0.5 mi w of jct US 83; I-90 exit 191 or 192. Ext corridors. **Pets:** Large, other species. $20 one-time fee/room. Designated rooms, service with restrictions, supervision.

[SAVE] 🅼 🌊 🛜 ✕ 📵 🖵

Range Country 🏠

(605) 669-2425. **$65-$159.** 302 W 5th St 57559. I-90 business loop, 0.5 mi w of jct US 83 exit 192 or 191. Ext/int corridors. **Pets:** Accepted.

[SAVE] 🍴 🅼 🌊 🛜 📵 🖵

OACOMA

Oasis Inn 🏠

(605) 734-6061. **$80-$141.** 1100 E Hwy 16 57365. I-90 exit 260, 0.4 mi e on US 16 and I-90 business loop. Ext/int corridors. **Pets:** Other species. Designated rooms, service with restrictions, supervision.

🅼 🌊 🛜 ✕ 📵 🖵

Quality Inn 🏠

(605) 734-5593. **Call for rates.** 100 W Hwy 16 57365. I-90 exit 260, just n. Int corridors. **Pets:** Accepted.

🍴 🅼 🌊 🛜 ✕ 📵 🖵

PIERRE

AAA ▼▼▼ **BEST WESTERN Ramkota Hotel** H ❖
(605) 224-6877. **$109-$125, 3 day notice.** 920 W Sioux Ave 57501. 1 mi w on US 14/83. Ext/int corridors. **Pets:** Other species. Service with restrictions, supervision. SAVE ▢ ▢ ▢ ▢ ▢ ▢ ▢

AAA ▼▼▼ **ClubHouse Hotel & Suites** H
(605) 494-2582. **$109-$209.** 808 W Sioux Ave 57501. I-90 exit 212. Ext/int corridors. **Pets:** Designated rooms, service with restrictions, supervision. SAVE ▢ ▢ ▢ ▢ ▢ ▢ ▢

▼▼ **Governor's Inn** H
(605) 224-4200. **$75-$140.** 700 W Sioux Ave 57501. 0.8 mi w on 14/83 and SR 34. Ext/int corridors. **Pets:** Accepted.
▢ ▢ ▢ ▢ ▢ ▢

AAA ▼▼ **River Lodge** M
(605) 224-4140. **Call for rates.** 713 W Sioux Ave 57501. 0.8 mi w on US 14/83 and SR 34. Int corridors. **Pets:** Accepted.
SAVE ▢ ▢ ▢ ▢

▼ **Super 8** M
(605) 224-1617. **$55-$72.** 320 W Sioux Ave 57501. 0.3 mi w on US 14/83 and SR 34. Int corridors. **Pets:** Accepted. ▢ ▢ ▢

PINE RIDGE

AAA ▼▼ **Prairie Wind Casino & Hotel** H
(605) 867-6300. **$40-$76.** HC 49 Box 10 57770. On US 18, 13 mi w of Oglala; 29 mi w of Pine Ridge; on Pine Ridge Indian Reservation. Int corridors. **Pets:** Accepted. SAVE ▢ ▢ ▢ ▢ ▢ ▢

RAPID CITY

▼▼▼ **Adoba Hotel Rapid City/Mt. Rushmore** H
(605) 348-8300. **$79-$289.** 445 Mt. Rushmore Rd 57701. On I-90 business loop; jct Main St; center. Int corridors. **Pets:** Small. $15 daily fee/room. Designated rooms, service with restrictions, supervision.
▢ ▢ ▢ ▢ ▢ ▢

▼▼▼ **Americas Best Value Inn** H
(605) 343-5434. **$59-$280, 7 day notice.** 620 Howard St 57701. I-90 exit 58 (Haines Ave), just nw. Int corridors. **Pets:** $10 daily fee/room. Service with restrictions, supervision. ▢ ▢ ▢ ▢ ▢

AAA ▼▼▼ **AmericInn Lodge & Suites Rapid City** H
(605) 343-8424. **$39-$299, 3 day notice.** 1632 Rapp St 57701. I-90 exit 59 (LaCrosse St), just s, then just w on Eglin St. Int corridors. **Pets:** Accepted. SAVE ▢ ▢ ▢ ▢ ▢ ▢

▼▼▼ **Baymont Inn & Suites** H
(605) 791-5151. **$54-$133.** 4040 Cheyenne Blvd 57703. I-90 exit 61 (Elk Vale Rd), just s. Int corridors. **Pets:** Medium. $10 daily fee/pet. Designated rooms, service with restrictions, supervision.
▢ ▢ ▢ ▢

AAA ▼▼▼ **BEST WESTERN Ramkota Hotel** H ❖
(605) 343-8550. **$100-$170, 30 day notice.** 2111 N LaCrosse St 57701. I-90 exit 59 (LaCrosse St), just n. Ext/int corridors. **Pets:** Medium, other species. Designated rooms, no service, supervision.
SAVE ▢ ▢ ▢ ▢ ▢ ▢ ▢

AAA ▼▼▼ **Country Inn & Suites By Carlson** H
(605) 394-0017. **Call for rates.** 2321 N LaCrosse St 57701. I-90 exit 59 (LaCrosse St), just n. Int corridors. **Pets:** Accepted.
SAVE ▢ ▢ ▢ ▢ ▢ ▢ ▢

▼▼▼ **Days Inn I-90** H
(605) 348-8410. **$55-$290.** 1570 N LaCrosse St 57701. I-90 exit 59 (LaCrosse St), just s. Int corridors. **Pets:** Accepted.
▢ ▢ ▢ ▢ ▢ ▢

AAA ▼▼▼ **Grand Gateway Hotel** H
(605) 342-1300. **Call for rates.** 1721 N LaCrosse St 57701. I-90 exit 59 (LaCrosse St), just n. Int corridors. **Pets:** Accepted.
SAVE ▢ ▢ ▢ ▢ ▢ ▢ ▢

AAA ▼▼▼ **GrandStay Residential Suites Hotel** H
(605) 341-5100. **$89-$299.** 660 Disk Dr 57701. I-90 exit 58 (Haines Ave), just n, then just w. Int corridors. **Pets:** Accepted.
▢ ▢ ▢ ▢ ▢ ▢ ▢

AAA ▼▼▼ **Holiday Inn-Rushmore Plaza** H
(605) 348-4000. **$119-$189.** 505 N 5th St 57701. I-90 exit 58 (Haines Ave), 1.3 mi s. Int corridors. **Pets:** Accepted.
SAVE ▢ ▢ ▢ ▢ ▢ ▢ ▢ ▢

AAA ▼▼▼ **The Hotel Alex Johnson** H ❖
(605) 342-1210. **$59-$250.** 523 6th St 57701. I-90 exit 57 (I-190/US 16 W/Mt. Rushmore), 1.8 mi s, just e on SR 44 (Omaha St), then just s; jct St Joseph St. Int corridors. **Pets:** Other species. $25 daily fee/pet. Designated rooms, service with restrictions, supervision.
SAVE ▢ ▢ ▢ ▢

AAA ▼▼▼ **Howard Johnson Inn & Suites** H
(605) 737-4656. **$79-$450.** 950 North St 57701. I-90 exit 57 (I-190 S/US-16 W Mt. Rushmore); exit 1C, then just e. Int corridors.
Pets: Accepted. SAVE ▢ ▢ ▢ ▢ ▢ ▢

AAA ▼▼▼ **La Quinta Inn & Suites** H
(605) 718-7000. **$49-$509.** 1416 N Elk Vale Rd 57701. I-90 exit 61 (Elk Vale Rd), just s. Int corridors. **Pets:** Large, other species. Service with restrictions. SAVE ▢ ▢ ▢ ▢ ▢

▼ **Lazy U Motel** M
(605) 343-4242. **Call for rates.** 2215 Mt. Rushmore Rd 57701. 1 mi s on US 16. Ext corridors. **Pets:** Accepted. ▢ ▢ ▢

AAA ▼▼▼ **MainStay Suites** H
(605) 719-5151. **$79-$279.** 3321 Outfitter Rd 57701. I-90 exit 61, just n on Elk Vale Rd, w on E Mall Dr, then just s. Int corridors. **Pets:** Large. $25 one-time fee/pet. Designated rooms, service with restrictions, supervision. SAVE ▢ ▢ ▢ ▢ ▢

AAA ▼▼ **Microtel Inn & Suites by Wyndham Rapid City** H
(605) 348-2523. **$53-$239.** 1740 Rapp St 57701. I-90 exit 59 (LaCrosse St), just se. Int corridors. **Pets:** Other species. $10 daily fee/room. Designated rooms, service with restrictions, crate.
SAVE ▢ ▢ ▢ ▢ ▢ ▢

▼▼ **Rapid City Ramada** H
(605) 342-3322. **$48-$170.** 1902 N LaCrosse St 57701. I-90 exit 59 (LaCrosse St), just s. Ext/int corridors. **Pets:** Accepted.
▢ ▢ ▢ ▢ ▢ ▢ ▢

▼▼ **Sleep Inn & Suites** H
(605) 791-5678. **$69-$229.** 4031 Cheyenne Blvd 57703. I-90 exit 61 (Elk Vale Rd), just s. Int corridors. **Pets:** Accepted.
▢ ▢ ▢ ▢ ▢ ▢

AAA ▼▼ **Super 8 LaCrosse St** M
(605) 348-8070. **$44-$130.** 2124 LaCrosse St 57701. I-90 exit 59 (LaCrosse St), just n. Int corridors. **Pets:** Medium, other species. $10 daily fee/pet. Service with restrictions, supervision.
SAVE ▢ ▢ ▢ ▢ ▢

▼▼ **Travelodge-Rapid City** H
(605) 343-5383. **$49-$350.** 2505 Mt. Rushmore Rd 57701. 1.3 mi s on US 16. Ext corridors. **Pets:** Accepted. ▢ ▢ ▢ ▢ ▢ ▢

SIOUX FALLS

AAA ▼▼▼ **BEST WESTERN Empire Towers** H
(605) 361-3118. **$75-$175.** 4100 W Shirley Pl 57106. I-29 exit 77 (41st St), just ne. Int corridors. **Pets:** $25 daily fee/room. Designated rooms, service with restrictions, supervision.
SAVE ▢ ▢ ▢ ▢ ▢ ▢

AAA ▼▼▼ BEST WESTERN PLUS Ramkota Hotel 🄷 🐾

(605) 336-0650. **$100-$140.** 3200 W Maple St 57107. I-29 exit 81 (Airport/Russell St), just e. Ext/int corridors. **Pets:** Other species. Service with restrictions, supervision.

[SAVE] 🍽 🕭M 🛋 🗙 📶 ⨉ 🔋 🔲

▼▼ Center Inn 🄼

(605) 334-9002. **$67-$115.** 900 E 20th St 57105. I-90 exit 399 (Cliff Ave), 5 mi s, then just w. Int corridors. **Pets:** Accepted.

🕭M 📶 🗙 🔋

AAA ▼▼▼ ClubHouse Hotel & Suites 🄷

(605) 361-8700. **$129-$179.** 2320 S Louise Ave 57106. I-29 exit 78 (26th St), just e. Ext/int corridors. **Pets:** Accepted.

[SAVE] 🍽 🕭M 🛋 🗙 📶 ⨉ 🔋 🔲

▼▼ Comfort Suites by Choice Hotels 🄷

(605) 362-9711. **$80-$160.** 3208 S Carolyn Ave 57106. I-29 exit 77 (41st St), just e, then n. Int corridors. **Pets:** Accepted.

🕭M 🛋 📶 🗙 🔋 🔲

▼▼ Dakotah Lodge 🄼

(605) 332-2000. **$69-$150.** 3200 W Russell St 57107. I-29 exit 81 (Airport/Russell St), just e. Int corridors. **Pets:** Other species. $10 daily fee/pet. Service with restrictions, supervision. 🍽 🛋 📶 🔋 🔲

▼▼▼ Homewood Suites by Hilton 🄷

(605) 338-8585. **$69-$249.** 3620 W Avera Dr 57108. I-229 exit 1C (Louise Ave), just s. Int corridors. **Pets:** Accepted. 🕭M 🛋 📶 🔋 🔲

▼▼ Microtel Inn & Suites by Wyndham Sioux Falls 🄼

(605) 361-7484. **$55-$85.** 2901 S Carolyn Ave 57106. I-29 exit 77 (41st St), just e, then n. Int corridors. **Pets:** Accepted. 🕭M 📶 🔋 🔲

▼▼▼ Quality Inn & Suites 🄷 🐾

(605) 336-1900. **$90-$145.** 5410 N Granite Ln 57107. I-29 exit 83 (SR 38), just e, then 0.3 mi n. Int corridors. **Pets:** Other species. $20 daily fee/pet. Designated rooms, service with restrictions, supervision.

🕭M 🛋 📶 🗙 🔋 🔲

▼▼ Quality Inn & Suites South 🄷

(605) 361-2822. **$70-$150.** 3216 S Carolyn Ave 57106. I-29 exit 77 (41st St), just e, then n. Int corridors. **Pets:** Accepted.

🕭M 🛋 📶 🔋 🔲

▼▼▼ Red Roof Inn Sioux Falls 🄼

(605) 361-1864. **$55-$86.** 3500 S Gateway Blvd 57106. I-29 exit 77 (41st St), just w, then s. Int corridors. **Pets:** Large, other species. Service with restrictions, supervision. 📶 🔋 🔲

▼▼▼ Residence Inn by Marriott 🄷

(605) 361-2202. **$97-$189.** 4509 W Empire Pl 57106. I-29 exit 77 (41st St), 0.5 mi se. Int corridors. **Pets:** Medium. $75 one-time fee/pet. Service with restrictions, crate. 🕭M 🛋 📶 🗙 🔋 🔲

AAA ▼▼▼ Sheraton Sioux Falls 🄷 🐾

(605) 331-0100. **$109-$229.** 1211 N West Ave 57104. I-29 exit 81 (Airport/Russell St), 1.3 mi e. Int corridors. **Pets:** Medium, dogs only. Designated rooms, service with restrictions, supervision.

[SAVE] 🍽 🕭M 🛋 🗙 🔋 🔲

▼▼▼ Staybridge Suites 🄷 🐾

(605) 361-2298. **Call for rates.** 2505 S Carolyn Ave 57106. I-29 exit 78 (26th St), just se. Int corridors. **Pets:** Medium. $50 daily fee/pet. Designated rooms, service with restrictions, supervision.

🕭M 🛋 📶 🗙 🔋 🔲

▼▼▼ TownePlace Suites by Marriott 🄷

(605) 361-2626. **$111-$183.** 4545 W Homefield Dr 57106. I-29 exit 78 (26th St), just w. Int corridors. **Pets:** Accepted.

🍽 🕭M 🛋 📶 🗙 🔋 🔲

SPEARFISH

▼▼ Bell's Motor Lodge Motel 🄼

(605) 642-3812. **$40-$78.** 230 N Main St 57783. 0.5 mi s of center. Ext corridors. **Pets:** Small, dogs only. $2 daily fee/pet. Designated rooms, supervision. 🛋 📶 🔋 🔲

AAA ▼▼ BEST WESTERN Black Hills Lodge 🄷

(605) 642-7795. **$69-$179.** 540 E Jackson Blvd 57783. I-90 exit 12, just s. Ext/int corridors. **Pets:** Accepted.

[SAVE] 🍽 🕭M 🛋 📶 🗙 🔋 🔲

▼▼ Days Inn 🄷

(605) 642-7101. **$54-$350.** 240 Ryan Rd 57783. I-90 exit 10, 1.2 mi s. Ext/int corridors. **Pets:** Other species. $10 daily fee/pet. Designated rooms, service with restrictions, crate. 🕭M 📶 🗙 🔋 🔲

AAA ▼▼▼ Holiday Inn Hotel & Convention Center 🄷 🐾

(605) 642-4683. **$99-$199, 3 day notice.** 305 N 27th St 57783. I-90 exit 14 (Spearfish Canyon), just n. Ext/int corridors. **Pets:** Other species. $25 one-time fee/pet. Designated rooms, service with restrictions, supervision. [SAVE] 🍽 🕭M 🛋 🗙 📶 🔋 🔲

AAA ▼▼▼ Quality Inn 🄷

(605) 642-2337. **$69-$149.** 2725 1st Ave 57783. I-90 exit 14 (Spearfish Canyon), just n. Int corridors. **Pets:** $10 daily fee/pet. Service with restrictions, supervision. [SAVE] 🕭M 🛋 📶 🗙 🔋 🔲

▼▼▼ Spearfish Canyon Lodge 🄷 🐾

(605) 584-3435. **$89-$275, 5 day notice.** 10619 Roughlock Falls Rd 57754. I-90 exit 14 (Spearfish Canyon), 13 mi s. Int corridors. **Pets:** Other species. $25 daily fee/pet. Service with restrictions, supervision. 🍽 🕭M 🗙 📶 🗙 🔋 🔲

▼▼ Super 8-Spearfish 🄷

(605) 642-4721. **$55-$315.** 440 Heritage Dr 57783. I-90 exit 14 (Spearfish Canyon), just e, then just s. Int corridors. **Pets:** Other species. $10 daily fee/pet. Designated rooms, service with restrictions, supervision. 🛋 📶 🔋 🔲

STURGIS

AAA ▼▼▼ BEST WESTERN Sturgis Inn 🄷

(605) 347-3604. **$69-$149.** 2431 Junction Ave 57785. I-90 exit 32, just n. Ext/int corridors. **Pets:** Other species. $10 daily fee/room. Designated rooms, service with restrictions, crate.

[SAVE] 🍽 🕭M 🛋 📶 🔋 🔲

▼▼▼ Holiday Inn Express & Suites-Sturgis 🄷

(605) 347-4140. **Call for rates.** 2721 Lazelle St 57785. I-90 exit 30 (US 14A), just s. Int corridors. **Pets:** Accepted.

🕭M 🛋 🗙 📶 🗙 🔋 🔲

SUMMERSET

AAA ▼▼ Ramada 🄷

(605) 787-4844. **$59-$159.** 7900 Stagestop Rd 57718. I-90 exit 48, just s. Int corridors. **Pets:** Small, other species. $10 daily fee/pet. Designated rooms, service with restrictions, supervision.

[SAVE] 🕭M 🛋 📶 🗙 🔋 🔲

VERMILLION

AAA ▼▼ BEST WESTERN Vermillion Inn 🄷

(605) 624-8333. **$109-$129.** 701 W Cherry St 57069. I-29 exit 26 (SR 50), 7.5 mi w on Business Rt SR 50. Int corridors. **Pets:** $20 daily fee/pet. Designated rooms, service with restrictions, supervision.

[SAVE] 🍽 🕭M 🛋 🗙 📶 🗙 🔋 🔲

▼▼ Prairie Inn 🄷

(605) 624-2824. **Call for rates.** 916 N Dakota St 57069. I-29 exit 26 (SR 50), 7 mi w, then 0.3 mi n. Int corridors. **Pets:** Accepted.

🍽 📶 🗙 🔋 🔲

WALL

BEST WESTERN Plains Motel 🅷 ❀
(605) 279-2145. **$72-$162.** 712 Glenn St 57790. I-90 exit 110, just n.
Ext corridors. **Pets:** Other species. $20 daily fee/pet. Designated rooms,
service with restrictions, supervision.
SAVE ⬛ ➰ ✖ 📶 🍴 💲

Econo Lodge 🅼
(605) 279-2121. **$159.** 804 Glenn St 57790. I-90 exit 110, just n. Ext
corridors. **Pets:** Accepted. SAVE ⬛ ➰ 📶 🍴 💲

Sunshine Inn 🅼
(605) 279-2178. **$59-$79.** 608 Main St 57790. Downtown. Ext corridors.
Pets: Accepted. SAVE 📶

WATERTOWN

BEST WESTERN Ramkota Hotel 🅷 ❀
(605) 886-8011. **$89-$129.** 1901 9th Ave SW 57201. I-29 exit 177 (US
212), 4 mi w. Int corridors. **Pets:** Dogs only. Designated rooms, service
with restrictions, crate. SAVE 🍴 ⬛ ➰ ✖ 📶 ✖ 🍴 💲

Country Inn & Suites By Carlson 🅷
(605) 886-8900. **Call for rates.** 3400 8th Ave SE 57201. I-29 exit 177
(US 212), just w. Int corridors. **Pets:** Accepted.
⬛ ➰ 📶 ✖ 🍴 💲

Days Inn 🅷
(605) 886-3500. **$70-$120.** 2900 9th Ave SE 57201. I-29 exit 177 (US
212), 0.5 mi w. Ext/int corridors. **Pets:** $15 one-time fee/room. Service
with restrictions, supervision. ⬛ ➰ 📶 ✖ 🍴 💲

Econo Lodge 🅼
(605) 882-2243. **$59-$80.** 920 14th St SE 57201. I-29 exit 177 (US
212), 1.5 mi w, then just s. Int corridors. **Pets:** Accepted.
📶 🍴 💲

Holiday Inn Express Hotel & Suites 🅷 ❀
(605) 882-3636. **$115-$134.** 3901 9th Ave SE 57201. I-29 exit 177 (US
212), just e. Int corridors. **Pets:** Large, dogs only. $15 daily fee/pet.
Service with restrictions, supervision. ⬛ ➰ 📶 🍴 💲

Quality Inn & Suites 🅷
(605) 886-3010. **$84-$94.** 800 35th St Cir 57201. I-29 exit 177 (US
212), just w. Ext/int corridors. **Pets:** $20 one-time fee/room. Designated
rooms, service with restrictions, crate. ⬛ ➰ 📶 🍴 💲

Super 8-Watertown 🅼
(605) 882-1900. **$74-$88.** 503 14th Ave SE 57201. On US 81, 0.3 mi s
of jct US 212. Int corridors. **Pets:** Accepted.
🍴 ⬛ ➰ 📶 🍴 💲

WINNER

Holiday Inn Express Hotel & Suites Winner 🅷
(605) 842-2255. **$115-$125.** 1360 E Hwy 44 57580. Just ne of jct US
18 and 183. Int corridors. **Pets:** Very small. $25 one-time fee/room.
Service with restrictions, supervision. ⬛ ➰ 📶 ✖ 🍴 💲

YANKTON

BEST WESTERN Kelly Inn 🅷 ❀
(605) 665-2906. **$99-$119.** 1607 Hwy 50 E 57078. On US 50, 1.8 mi e.
Ext/int corridors. **Pets:** Other species. Service with restrictions, supervision. SAVE 🍴 ⬛ ➰ ✖ 📶 ✖ 🍴 💲

Days Inn-Yankton 🅼
(605) 665-8717. **$78-$135.** 2410 Broadway St 57078. US 81, 1.7 mi n.
Int corridors. **Pets:** Small, dogs only. $10 one-time fee/pet. Service with
restrictions, crate. SAVE ⬛ ➰ 📶 🍴 💲

Lewis & Clark Resort 🅼
(605) 665-2680. **$75-$145, 30 day notice.** 43496 Shore Dr 57078. 4 mi
w on SR 52; in Lewis and Clark State Park, just w of marina. Ext corridors. **Pets:** Accepted. 🍴 ⬛ ➰ ✖ 📶 ✖ ✖ 🍴 💲

TENNESSEE

ALCOA

Candlewood Suites Knoxville Airport/Alcoa 🅷
(865) 233-4411. **$74-$79.** 176 Cusick Rd 37701. US 129, just e. Int
corridors. **Pets:** Accepted. ⬛ ➰ 📶 🍴 💲

La Quinta Inn & Suites Knoxville Airport 🅷
(865) 984-9350. **$75-$200.** 126 Cusick Rd 37701. US 129, just e. Int
corridors. **Pets:** Large, other species. Service with restrictions.
⬛ ➰ 📶 ✖ 🍴 💲

MainStay Suites 🅷
(865) 379-7799. **$70-$110.** 361 Fountain View Cir 37701. US 129, just
n on SR 35, just se on Associates Blvd, then just w. Int corridors.
Pets: Medium, other species. $25 one-time fee/room. Service with
restrictions, crate. 🔌 ⬛ ➰ 📶 🍴 💲

Quality Inn 🅷
(865) 984-6800. **$70-$130.** 206 Corporate Pl 37701. US 129, just s. Int
corridors. **Pets:** Small, other species. $20 daily fee/pet. Service with
restrictions, crate. ⬛ ➰ 📶 🍴 💲

ANTIOCH

Rodeway Inn & Suites 🅼 ❀
(615) 641-7721. **$89-$199, 3 day notice.** 13010 Old Hickory Blvd
37013. I-24 exit 62, just n. Ext corridors. **Pets:** Medium. $20 daily fee/
room. Designated rooms, service with restrictions, supervision.
SAVE ⬛ ➰ 📶 🍴 💲

ATOKA

Comfort Inn & Suites 🅷
(901) 837-7729. **$65-$100.** 10772 Hwy 51 S 38004. SR 206, 0.5 mi n.
Int corridors. **Pets:** Accepted. SAVE ⬛ ➰ 📶 ✖ 🍴 💲

BRENTWOOD (Restaurants p. 640)

Candlewood Suites 🅷
(615) 309-0600. **Call for rates.** 5129 Virginia Way 37027. I-65 exit 74B
(SR 254 W), 0.3 mi s on Franklin Rd (US 31), 1.2 mi w on Maryland
Way, just s on Ward Circle, then just s. Int corridors. **Pets:** Accepted.
📶 ✖ 🍴 💲

Hyatt Place Nashville/Brentwood 🅷
(615) 661-9477. **$94-$209.** 202 Summit View Dr 37027. I-65 exit 74A,
just e. Int corridors. **Pets:** Accepted.
SAVE 🍴 ⬛ ➰ 📶 ✖ 🍴 💲

Residence Inn by Marriott Nashville-Brentwood 🅷
(615) 371-0100. **$109-$269.** 206 Ward Cir 37027. I-65 exit 74B, 0.3 mi
s on Franklin Rd (US 31), then 0.5 mi w on Maryland Way. Ext/int corridors. **Pets:** Accepted. SAVE ➰ 📶 ✖ 🍴 💲

Sleep Inn 🅷
(615) 376-2122. **$85-$110.** 1611 Galleria Blvd 37027. I-65 exit 69 (SR
441), just w, then just n. Int corridors. **Pets:** Accepted.
⬛ ➰ 📶 ✖ 🍴 💲

BULLS GAP

Quality Inn 🅷
(423) 235-9111. **$73-$100.** 50 Speedway Ln 37711. I-81 exit 23, just w.
Int corridors. **Pets:** Accepted. ⬛ ➰ 📶 🍴 💲

BUTLER

▼▼▼▼ Iron Mountain Inn B & B and Creekside Chalet 🅱🅱

(423) 768-2446. **$150-$400, 14 day notice.** 268 Moreland Dr 37640. 1.6 mi w on Pine Orchard Rd from SR 67 at Stout Store, follow signs; 13 mi w on SR 67 from US 421 in Mountain City, follow sign at Stout Store area; 15.1 mi from Shell station in Hampton to Pine Orchard Rd, 1.6 mi to Moreland Dr. Ext/int corridors. **Pets:** Dogs only. $50 one-time fee/pet. Designated rooms, no service, supervision. 🤖 ✕ 🛑 🖥

CHATTANOOGA *(Restaurants p. 640)*

⟨AAA⟩ ▼▼▼ BEST WESTERN Heritage Inn Ⓜ

(423) 899-3311. **$60-$80.** 7641 Lee Hwy 37421. I-75 exit 7B northbound; exit 7 southbound, just w. Ext corridors. **Pets:** Small, dogs only. $15 daily fee/pet. Service with restrictions, crate.

🆂🆅 🍴 🕸 🤖 ✕ 🛑 🖥

⟨AAA⟩ ▼▼▼ BEST WESTERN Royal Inn Ⓜ

(423) 821-6840. **$82-$120.** 3644 Cummings Hwy 37419. I-24 exit 174, 0.4 mi s. Ext corridors. **Pets:** Accepted. 🆂🆅 🤖 🤖 🛑 🖥

⟨AAA⟩ ▼▼▼ Chattanooga Choo-Choo Ⓗ

(423) 266-5000. **$119-$229.** 1400 Market St 37402. I-24 exit 178 (Broad St) eastbound; exit Market St westbound, 0.5 mi n. Ext/int corridors. **Pets:** Accepted. 🆂🆅 🆓 🍴 🆖🅼 🤖 ✕ 🤖 ✕ 🛑 🖥

▼▼▼ Comfort Inn Downtown-Lookout Mountain Ⓗ

(423) 265-0077. **$69-$115.** 2420 Williams St 37408. I-24 exit 178 (Market St), just s. Int corridors. **Pets:** Medium, dogs only. $35 daily fee/room. Service with restrictions, supervision. 🆖🅼 🤖 🤖 🛑 🖥

⟨AAA⟩ ▼▼▼ Country Inn & Suites By Carlson, Chattanooga I-24 West Ⓗ

(423) 825-6100. **Call for rates.** 3725 Modern Industries Blvd 37419. I-24 exit 174, just s. Int corridors. **Pets:** Accepted.

🆂🆅 🆖🅼 🤖 🤖 🖥

⟨AAA⟩ ▼▼▼ Days Inn-Lookout Mountain/Tiftonia Ⓜ

(423) 821-6044. **$59-$85.** 3801 Cummings Hwy 37419. I-24 exit 174, just n. Ext corridors. **Pets:** $10 daily fee/pet. Service with restrictions, crate. 🆂🆅 🆖🅼 🤖 🤖 ✕ 🛑 🖥

⟨AAA⟩ ▼▼▼ Econo Lodge-Hamilton Mall Area Ⓜ

(423) 499-9550. **$55.** 7421 Bonny Oaks Dr 37421. I-75 exit 7B northbound; exit 7 southbound, just w. Ext corridors. **Pets:** Accepted.

🆂🆅 🤖 🤖 🛑 🖥

▼ Extended Stay America-Chattanooga-Airport Ⓗ

(423) 892-1315. **$49-$69.** 6240 Airpark Dr 37421. SR 153 exit 1 (Lee Hwy), 0.3 mi s to Vance Rd, then just w to cul-de-sac. Ext corridors. **Pets:** Other species. $25 daily fee/pet. Service with restrictions, supervision. 🆖🅼 🤖 🛑 🖥

▼▼▼▼ Homewood Suites by Hilton Ⓗ

(423) 510-8020. **$99-$199.** 2250 Center St 37421. I-75 exit 5 (Shallowford Rd), 0.5 mi w. Int corridors. **Pets:** Other species. $35 one-time fee/room. Service with restrictions, supervision. 🤖 🤖 🛑 🖥

▼▼ La Quinta Inn Chattanooga Ⓗ

(423) 265-3151. **$69-$199.** 100 W 21st St 37408. I-24 exit 178 (Broad St) eastbound; exit Market St westbound, US 11 to Lookout Mountain, w to 20th St, w to Williams St, then w. Int corridors. **Pets:** Large, other species. Service with restrictions. 🆖🅼 🤖 🤖 ✕ 🛑 🖥

▼▼ La Quinta Inn Chattanooga/Hamilton Place Ⓜ

(423) 855-0011. **$59-$165.** 7015 Shallowford Rd 37421. I-75 exit 5 (Shallowford Rd), just w. Ext corridors. **Pets:** Large, other species. Service with restrictions. 🆖🅼 🤖 🤖 🛑 🖥

▼▼ MainStay Suites-Chattanooga Ⓗ

(423) 485-9424. **$89-$119.** 7030 Amin Dr 37421. I-75 exit 5 (Shallowford Rd), just w, then s. Int corridors. **Pets:** Accepted.

🆖🅼 🤖 🛑 🖥

⟨AAA⟩ ▼▼▼ Quality Inn Ⓜ

(423) 821-1499. **$60-$150.** 3109 Parker Ln 37419. I-24 exit 175, just s. Ext corridors. **Pets:** Accepted. 🆂🆅 🤖 🤖 🛑 🖥

⟨AAA⟩ ▼▼▼ Quality Suites Ⓜ

(423) 892-1500. **$89-$119.** 7324 Shallowford Rd 37421. I-75 exit 5 (Shallowford Rd), just e. Ext corridors. **Pets:** Accepted.

🆂🆅 🤖 🤖 🖥

⟨AAA⟩ ▼▼▼ Ramada Limited-Lookout Mountain I-24 West Ⓜ

(423) 821-7162. **$56-$120.** 30 Birmingham Hwy 37419. I-24 exit 174, just s. Ext/int corridors. **Pets:** Small, dogs only. $15 daily fee/pet. Designated rooms, service with restrictions, supervision.

🆂🆅 🤖 🛑 🖥

⟨AAA⟩ ▼▼▼ The Read House Historic Inn & Suites Ⓗ

(423) 266-4121. **$109-$189.** 827 Broad St 37402. US 27 exit 1A, just e. Int corridors. **Pets:** Accepted. 🆂🆅 🍴 🆖🅼 🤖 🤖 ✕ 🛑 🖥

⟨AAA⟩ ▼▼▼ Red Roof Inn Chattanooga Airport Ⓜ

(423) 899-0143. **$39-$99.** 7014 Shallowford Rd 37421. I-75 exit 5 (Shallowford Rd), just w. Ext corridors. **Pets:** Large, other species. Service with restrictions, supervision. 🆂🆅 🆖🅼 🤖 🛑 🖥

▼▼▼ Residence Inn by Marriott Chattanooga near Hamilton Place Ⓗ

(423) 468-7700. **$119-$249.** 2340 Center St 37421. I-75 exit 5 (Shallowford Rd), 0.5 mi w to Lee Hwy, then just n. Int corridors. **Pets:** Other species. $75 one-time fee/room. Service with restrictions, crate.

🆖 🆖🅼 🤖 🤖 ✕ 🛑 🖥

▼▼▼ Staybridge Suites Ⓗ

(423) 267-0900. **$129-$199.** 1300 Carter St 37402. US 27 N exit 1A (Dr Martin Luther King Blvd), just e to Carter St, then 0.3 mi s. Int corridors. **Pets:** Other species. $50 one-time fee/room. Service with restrictions. 🆓 🆖 🆖🅼 🤖 🤖 ✕ 🛑 🖥

▼▼▼ Staybridge Suites-Hamilton Place Ⓗ

(423) 826-2700. **$130-$260.** 7015 Shallowford Rd 37421. I-75 exit 5 (Shallowford Rd), just w. Int corridors. **Pets:** Accepted.

🆖🅼 🤖 🤖 ✕ 🛑 🖥

▼▼ Super 8 Ⓗ

(423) 490-8560. **$55-$65.** 7024 McCutcheon Rd 37421. I-75 exit 5 (Shallowford Rd), just w, then 0.3 mi n on Shallowford Village Dr. Int corridors. **Pets:** Accepted. 🤖 🤖 🛑 🖥

▼▼▼ TownePlace Suites by Marriott Chattanooga near Hamilton Place Ⓗ

(423) 834-9444. **$79-$109.** 7010 McCutcheon Rd 37421. I-75 exit 5 (Shallowford Rd), 0.5 mi w to Lee Hwy, then just n. Int corridors. **Pets:** Accepted. 🆖🅼 🤖 🤖 ✕ 🛑 🖥

CLARKSVILLE

▼▼▼ Candlewood Suites Ⓗ

(931) 906-0900. **$108-$135.** 3050 Clay Lewis Rd 37040. I-24 exit 4, just s. Int corridors. **Pets:** Accepted. 🆖🅼 🤖 🛑 🖥

▼▼▼ La Quinta Inn & Suites Clarksville Ⓗ

(931) 906-0606. **$95-$225.** 251 Holiday Dr 37040. I-24 exit 4, just se. Int corridors. **Pets:** Large, other species. Service with restrictions.

🆖🅼 🤖 🤖 ✕ 🛑 🖥

▼▼▼ MainStay Suites Ⓗ

(931) 648-3400. **$70-$149.** 115 Fairbrook Pl 37043. I-24 exit 4, just sw. Int corridors. **Pets:** Accepted. 🆖🅼 🤖 🤖 ✕ 🛑 🖥

⟨AAA⟩ ▼▼▼ Quality Inn-Exit 4 Ⓗ

(931) 648-4848. **$89-$99.** 3095 Wilma Rudolph Blvd 37040. I-24 exit 4, just se. Ext corridors. **Pets:** Medium. $25 daily fee/room. Designated rooms, service with restrictions, crate.

🆂🆅 🍴 🤖 ✕ 🤖 🛑 🖥

▼▼▼ **Red Roof Inn Clarksville** Ⓜ
(931) 905-1555. **$41-$119.** 197 Holiday Dr 37040. I-24 exit 4, just s.
Ext corridors. **Pets:** Large, other species. Service with restrictions,
supervision. 🐾 📶 🛏 💻

CLEVELAND

▼▼▼ **Baymont Inn & Suites Cleveland** 🅷
(423) 614-5583. **$69-$99.** 360 Paul Huff Pkwy 37312. I-75 exit 27, 0.8
mi e. Ext corridors. **Pets:** Accepted. 🅼 🐾 📶 🛏 💻

◈◈ ▼▼▼ **Douglas Inn & Suites** 🅷
(423) 559-5579. **$55-$115.** 2600 Westside Dr NW 37312. I-75 exit 25,
just e, then just n. Ext/int corridors. **Pets:** Small. $15 daily fee/pet. Ser-
vice with restrictions, supervision. 🆂 🅼 📶 ❌ 🛏 💻

▼▼ **Quality Inn** 🅷
(423) 478-5265. **$70-$110.** 153 James Asbury Dr 37312. I-75 exit 27,
just w, then just s. Ext/int corridors. **Pets:** Accepted.
🐾 📶 🛏 💻

▼ **Super 8** Ⓜ
(423) 476-5555. **$57-$141.** 163 Bernham Dr 37312. I-75 exit 27, just w,
then just s. Ext/int corridors. **Pets:** Accepted. 🐾 📶 🛏 💻

CLINTON

▼▼▼ **Holiday Inn Express Hotel & Suites** 🅷
(865) 457-2233. **$99-$159.** 111 Hillvale Rd 37716. I-75 exit 122, just w.
Int corridors. **Pets:** Accepted. 🔌 🅼 🐾 📶 ❌ 🛏 💻

▼▼ **Red Roof Inn & Suites-Clinton** 🅷
(865) 457-9070. **$45-$99.** 141 Buffalo Rd 37716. I-75 exit 122, just w.
Ext corridors. **Pets:** Large, other species. Service with restrictions,
supervision. 🅼 🐾 📶 🛏 💻

COLLIERVILLE

▼▼ **Hampton Inn Collierville** 🅷
(901) 854-9400. **$99-$144.** 1280 W Poplar Ave 38017. 0.9 mi w of jct
CR 175 on US 72. Int corridors. **Pets:** Medium, dogs only. $10 daily
fee/pet. Service with restrictions, supervision.
🅼 🐾 📶 ❌ 🛏 💻

COLUMBIA *(Restaurants p. 640)*

◈◈ ▼▼▼ **Baymont Inn & Suites Columbia/Maury** 🅷
(931) 388-3326. **$61-$99.** 715 S James M Campbell Blvd 38401. Jct
SR 50 and US 31, 0.9 mi w. Int corridors. **Pets:** Accepted.
🆂 🅼 🐾 📶 🛏 💻

▼▼ **Super 8 Columbia** 🅷
(931) 380-1227. **$75-$110.** 1554 Bear Creek Pike 38401. I-65 exit 46,
just w. Ext corridors. **Pets:** Accepted. 🅼 🐾 📶 🛏 💻

COOKEVILLE

◈◈ ▼▼▼ **BEST WESTERN Thunderbird
Motel** 🅷 ❀
(931) 526-7115. **$65-$121.** 900 S Jefferson Ave 38501. I-40 exit 287,
just n. Ext corridors. **Pets:** $15 daily fee/room. Designated rooms, ser-
vice with restrictions. 🆂 🍽 🅼 🐾 📶 🛏 💻

▼▼ **Country Inn & Suites By Carlson Cookeville** 🅷
(931) 525-6668. **Call for rates.** 1151 S Jefferson Ave 38506. I-40 exit
287, just s. Int corridors. **Pets:** Medium, other species. $15 daily fee/
pet. Designated rooms, no service, crate.
🅼 🐾 📶 ❌ 🛏 💻

▼▼▼▼ **La Quinta Inn & Suites** 🅷
(931) 520-3800. **$90-$240.** 1131 S Jefferson Ave 38506. I-40 exit 287,
just s. Int corridors. **Pets:** Large, other species. Service with restrictions.
🅼 🐾 📶 ❌ 🛏 💻

◈◈ ▼▼▼ **Red Roof Inn Cookeville-Tennessee
Tech.** Ⓜ
(931) 528-2020. **$50-$125.** 1292 S Walnut Ave 38501. I-40 exit 287,
just n. Ext corridors. **Pets:** Large, other species. Service with restrictions, supervision. 🆂 🐾 📶 🛏 💻

CORDOVA

◈◈ ▼▼▼ **Microtel Inn & Suites by Wyndham** 🅷
(901) 213-4141. **$60-$130.** 2423 N Germantown Pkwy 38018. I-40 exit
16 or 16A, just s, then just w on Rock Creek Cove. Int corridors.
Pets: $50 deposit/pet, $35 daily fee/pet. Designated rooms, service with
restrictions, supervision. 🆂 📶 🛏 💻

COUNCE *(Restaurants p. 640)*

▼▼ **Pickwick Landing State Resort Park Inn** 🅷
(731) 689-3135. **$74-$88, 3 day notice.** 120 Playground Loop 38326.
Jct SR 128, just se on SR 57, then just e; in state park. Int corridors.
Pets: Accepted. 🍽 🅼 🐾 ❌ 📶 ❌ 🛏 💻

CROSSVILLE

◈◈ ▼▼ **Quality Inn Crossville** 🅷
(931) 484-1551. **$79-$249.** 4035 Hwy 127 N 38571. I-40 exit 317 (US
127), just n. Int corridors. **Pets:** Small. $15 daily fee/pet. Designated
rooms, service with restrictions. 🆂 🐾 📶 🛏 💻

DANDRIDGE

▼▼ **Jefferson Inn** 🅷
(865) 940-5042. **$50-$110.** 127 Sharon Dr 37725. I-40 exit 417, just s.
Int corridors. **Pets:** Small, dogs only. $15 daily fee/pet. Designated
rooms, service with restrictions, supervision. 🅼 🐾 📶 🛏 💻

▼▼ **Super 8** 🅷
(865) 397-1200. **$60-$70.** 125 Sharon Dr 37725. I-40 exit 417, just s.
Int corridors. **Pets:** Accepted. 🐾 📶 🛏 💻

DAYTON

◈◈ ▼▼ **BEST WESTERN Dayton** Ⓜ
(423) 775-6560. **$85-$125.** 7835 Rhea County Hwy 37321. 1 mi n on
US 27. Ext corridors. **Pets:** Accepted. 🆂 🐾 📶 🛏 💻

DECHERD

▼▼ **Quality Inn** Ⓜ
(931) 962-0130. **$80-$85.** 1838 Decherd Blvd 37324. Jct Main St and
SR 41A, just s. Ext corridors. **Pets:** Small. $20 daily fee/pet. Service
with restrictions, crate. 🐾 📶 🛏 💻

DICKSON

◈◈ ▼▼ **BEST WESTERN Executive Inn** 🅷
(615) 446-0541. **$65-$99.** 2338 Hwy 46 S 37055. I-40 exit 172, just n.
Ext corridors. **Pets:** Dogs only. $10 one-time fee/pet. Supervision.
🆂 🐾 📶 🛏 💻

◈◈ ▼▼ **Comfort Inn** 🅷
(615) 740-1000. **$75-$110.** 1085 E Christi Dr 37055. I-40 exit 172, just
ne. Int corridors. **Pets:** Accepted. 🆂 🅼 🐾 📶 🛏 💻

◈◈ ▼▼▼ **Holiday Inn Express & Suites** 🅷
(615) 446-2781. **$90-$150.** 100 Barzani Blvd 37055. I-40 exit 172, just
se. Int corridors. **Pets:** Small. $25 daily fee/pet. Supervision.
🆂 🅼 🐾 📶 ❌ 🛏 💻

▼▼ **Super 8** 🅷
(615) 446-1923. **$50-$100, 3 day notice.** 150 Suzanne Dr 37055. I-40
exit 172, just ne. Int corridors. **Pets:** Accepted. 🐾 📶 🛏 💻

DYERSBURG

▼▼ **Days Inn** 🅷
(731) 287-0888. **$61-$68.** 2600 Lake Rd 38024. I-155 exit 13, just s on
SR 78. Int corridors. **Pets:** Accepted. 🅼 📶 🛏 💻

▼▼ Executive Inn & Suites **M**
(731) 287-0044. **$45-$60.** 2331 Lake Rd 38024. I-155 exit 13, 0.5 mi s on SR 78. Ext corridors. **Pets:** Other species. $10 daily fee/pet. Designated rooms, service with restrictions, supervision. 🛜 🛜

▼▼▼ Hampton Inn **H**
(731) 285-4778. **$69-$119.** 2750 Mall Loop Rd 38024. I-155 exit 13, just s on SR 78, then just e. Int corridors. **Pets:** Medium. Service with restrictions, crate. 🛜 🛜 🛜 🛜

▼▼▼ Holiday Inn Express & Suites **H**
(731) 286-1021. **Call for rates.** 822 Reelfoot Dr 38024. I-155 exit 13, just s on SR 78, then just w. Int corridors. **Pets:** Very small. $10 daily fee/pet. Service with restrictions, supervision.
🛜🛜 🛜 🛜 🛜 🛜

▼▼▼ Sleep Inn & Suites **H**
(731) 287-0248. **$70-$90.** 824 Reelfoot Dr 38024. I-155 exit 13, just s on SR 78, then just w. Int corridors. **Pets:** Accepted.
🛜🛜 🛜 🛜 🛜 🛜

FARRAGUT

▼▼ Americas Best Value Inn & Suites-West Knoxville/
Turkey Creek **M**
(865) 288-3641. **Call for rates.** 11717 Campbell Lakes Dr 37934. I-40/75 exit 373 (Campbell Station Rd), just s. Ext corridors.
Pets: Accepted. 🛜🛜 🛜 🛜 🛜 🛜

▼▼▼ Country Inn & Suites By Carlson, Knoxville West **H**
(865) 675-9800. **$79-$159.** 805 N Campbell Station Rd 37934. I-40/75 exit 373 (Campbell Station Rd), just n. Int corridors. **Pets:** Accepted.
🛜🛜 🛜 🛜 🛜

FAYETTEVILLE

▲▲▲ ▼▼ BEST WESTERN Fayetteville Inn **H**
(931) 433-0100. **$95-$100.** 3021 Thornton Taylor Pkwy 37334. 0.7 mi e of US 431, on US 64 and 231 Bypass. Ext corridors. **Pets:** Accepted.
🛜🛜 🛜 🛜 🛜

FRANKLIN *(Restaurants p. 640)*

▲▲▲ ▼▼▼ Aloft Nashville-Cool Springs **H** 🐾
(615) 435-8700. **$89-$209.** 7109 S Springs Dr 37067. I-65 exit 68B, 0.4 mi w, 0.3 mi n on Mallory Ln, then just e. Int corridors. **Pets:** Medium, dogs only. Designated rooms, service with restrictions, crate.
🛜🛜 🛜 🛜 🛜 🛜 🛜

▼▼▼ Baymont Inn & Suites **H**
(615) 591-6660. **$63-$101, 3 day notice.** 4202 Franklin Commons Ct 37067. I-65 exit 65, just e. Int corridors. **Pets:** Medium, dogs only. $30 daily fee/pet. Designated rooms, service with restrictions, supervision.
🛜🛜 🛜 🛜 🛜 🛜

▲▲▲ ▼▼▼ BEST WESTERN Franklin Inn **H** 🐾
(615) 790-0570. **$70-$140.** 1308 Murfreesboro Rd 37064. I-65 exit 65, just w. Ext corridors. **Pets:** Medium. $20 daily fee/room. Service with restrictions, supervision. 🛜🛜 🛜 🛜 🛜 🛜

▼▼ Comfort Inn **M**
(615) 791-6675. **$78-$170.** 4206 Franklin Commons Ct 37067. I-65 exit 65, just e. Ext corridors. **Pets:** Accepted. 🛜 🛜 🛜 🛜 🛜

▼▼▼ Drury Plaza Hotel Franklin **H**
(615) 771-6778. **$145-$264.** 1874 W McEwen Dr 37067. I-65 exit 67, just w. Int corridors. **Pets:** $10 daily fee/room. Service with restrictions, supervision. 🛜 🛜 🛜 🛜 🛜 🛜

▼▼▼ Embassy Suites Nashville South/Cool Springs **H**
(615) 515-5151. **$189-$249.** 820 Crescent Centre Dr 37067. I-65 exit 68A to Carothers Rd. Int corridors. **Pets:** Accepted.
🛜🛜 🛜 🛜 🛜 🛜 🛜

▲▲▲ ▼▼▼ Hyatt Place Nashville/Franklin/Cool Springs **H**
(615) 771-8900. **$99-$209.** 650 Bakers Bridge Ave 37067. I-65 exit 69 (SR 441), 0.3 mi e to Carothers Pkwy, 0.5 mi s, then 0.3 mi w. Int corridors. **Pets:** Accepted. 🛜🛜 🛜 🛜 🛜 🛜 🛜 🛜 🛜

▼▼▼ Residence Inn by Marriott Franklin Cool Springs **H**
(615) 778-0002. **$129-$299.** 2009 Meridian Blvd 37067. I-65 exit 68A, just e on Cool Springs Blvd, then just n on Carothers Pkwy. Int corridors. **Pets:** Accepted. 🛜🛜 🛜 🛜 🛜 🛜 🛜

GALLATIN

▼▼▼ Quality Inn of Gallatin **H**
(615) 451-4494. **$85-$90.** 1001 Village Green Crossing 37066. 2 mi s on US 31 E. Ext corridors. **Pets:** Accepted. 🛜 🛜 🛜 🛜

GATLINBURG

▼▼▼ Cobbly Nob Rentals **CA**
(865) 436-5298. **$100-$185, 30 day notice.** 3722 E Parkway 37738. Jct US 441, 10.3 mi n on US 321. Ext corridors. **Pets:** Accepted.
🛜🛜 🛜 🛜 🛜 🛜 🛜

▼▼ Motel 6 Gatlinburg Smoky Mountains #4767 **M**
(865) 436-7813. **Call for rates.** 309 Ownby St 37738. Traffic light 10 (Ski Mountain Rd), 0.4 mi n. Ext corridors. **Pets:** Other species. Service with restrictions, crate. 🛜 🛜 🛜 🛜

▼▼▼ Outback Resort Rentals & Sales **VH**
(865) 430-9385. **$120-$799, 30 day notice.** 902 Street of Dreams Way 37738. Jct US 441 on north end of town at Great Smoky Mountains Welcome Center, 1 mi sw on Wiley Oakley Dr, then 0.5 mi w on N Woodland Dr. Ext corridors. **Pets:** Medium. $150 deposit/pet. No service. 🛜 🛜 🛜 🛜 🛜

▲▲▲ ▼▼▼ Westgate Smoky Mountain Resort & Spa **CO**
(865) 430-4800. **$79-$339, 3 day notice.** 915 Westgate Resort Rd 37738. Jct US 441, just on Little Smoky Rd, then just s. Ext corridors. **Pets:** Medium, dogs only. $100 deposit/room, $170 one-time fee/room. Designated rooms, service with restrictions, crate.
🛜🛜 🛜 🛜 🛜 🛜 🛜 🛜

GERMANTOWN

▼▼▼ Comfort Inn & Suites-Germantown **H**
(901) 757-7800. **$79-$129.** 7787 Wolf River Blvd 38138. I-40 exit 16A, 5.7 mi s on Germantown Pkwy, then just w. Int corridors.
Pets: Accepted. 🛜🛜 🛜 🛜 🛜 🛜 🛜

▼▼▼ Homewood Suites by Hilton-Germantown **H**
(901) 751-2500. **$109-$169.** 7855 Wolf River Blvd 38138. I-40 exit 16, 5.7 mi s on Germantown Pkwy, then just e. Int corridors.
Pets: Accepted. 🛜 🛜 🛜 🛜

▲▲▲ ▼▼▼ Hyatt Place Memphis/Germantown **H**
(901) 759-1174. **$89-$209.** 9161 Winchester Rd 38138. SR 177 (Germantown Pkwy), 3 mi e on US 72 (Poplar Ave), just s on Forest Hill Irene Rd, then just e. Int corridors. **Pets:** Accepted.
🛜🛜 🛜 🛜 🛜 🛜 🛜 🛜

▼▼▼ Residence Inn by Marriott Memphis/Germantown **H**
(901) 752-0900. **$104-$179.** 9314 Poplar Pike 38138. SR 177 (Germantown Pkwy), 3 mi e on US 72 (Poplar Ave), just s on Forest Hill Irene Rd, then just e. Int corridors. **Pets:** Accepted.
🛜🛜 🛜 🛜 🛜 🛜 🛜

GOODLETTSVILLE

▲▲▲ ▼▼▼ BEST WESTERN Fairwinds Inn **H**
(615) 851-1067. **$63-$200.** 100 Northcreek Blvd 37072. I-65 exit 97 (Long Hollow Pike), just e, then just s. Ext corridors. **Pets:** Large. $15 daily fee/pet. Designated rooms, service with restrictions, supervision.
🛜🛜 🛜 🛜 🛜

▼▼▼ Country Inn & Suites By Carlson 🅗

(615) 851-4444. **$90-$149, 5 day notice.** 641 Wade Cir 37072. I-65 exit 96, just ne. Int corridors. **Pets:** Medium, dogs only. $15 deposit/pet. Service with restrictions, crate. 🔄 🛎️ 📶 ❌ 🔌 💻

GREENEVILLE

▼▼ Quality Inn 🅗

(423) 638-7511. **$90-$123.** 3160 E Andrew Johnson Hwy 37745. US 11 E Bypass, 3.6 mi ne. Int corridors. **Pets:** Accepted.

🔄 🛎️ 📶 🔌 💻

HARRIMAN

▼▼ Days Inn Harriman Ⓜ

(865) 882-6200. **$59-$70.** 120 Childs Rd 37748. I-40 exit 347, just n on US 27. Ext corridors. **Pets:** Accepted. 🔄 📶 🔌 💻

HENDERSONVILLE

🆎 ▼▼▼ Hyatt Place Nashville - Northeast 🅗

(615) 826-4301. **$79-$189.** 330 E Main St 37075. US 31 E, 1 mi n. Int corridors. **Pets:** Medium, dogs only. $100 one-time fee/room. Service with restrictions, crate. 🅢 🍴 🔄 🛎️ 📶 ❌ 🔌 💻

HERMITAGE

🆎 ▼▼ Super 8 🅗

(615) 871-4545. **$70-$100.** 1414 Princeton Pl 37076. I-40 exit 221 westbound; exit 221B eastbound, just n. Ext corridors. **Pets:** Small. $15 daily fee/pet. Service with restrictions. 🅢 🛎️ 📶 🔌 💻

HUNTINGDON

▼▼ Heritage Inn Ⓜ

(731) 986-2281. **$78-$83.** 11790 Lexington St 38344. Jct US 70, just n on SR 22 business route. Ext corridors. **Pets:** Small, dogs only. $10 daily fee/pet. Designated rooms, service with restrictions.

🛎️ 📶 🔌 💻

HURRICANE MILLS

🆎 ▼▼ BEST WESTERN of Hurricane Mills 🅗

(931) 296-4251. **$120-$140.** 15542 Hwy 13 S 37078. I-40 exit 143, just n. Ext corridors. **Pets:** Other species. $15 daily fee/pet. Designated rooms, service with restrictions. 🅢 🛎️ 📶 🔌 💻

JACKSON *(Restaurants p. 640)*

🆎 ▼▼ BEST WESTERN Carriage House Inn & Suites Ⓜ

(731) 664-3030. **$85-$100.** 1936 Hwy 45 Bypass 38305. I-40 exit 80A, just s. Ext corridors. **Pets:** Accepted. 🅢 🛎️ 📶 🔌 💻

▼▼▼ Courtyard by Marriott 🅗

(731) 256-7073. **$129-$209.** 200 Campbell Oaks Dr 38305. I-40 exit 83, just s on Campbell St, then just w. Int corridors. **Pets:** Accepted.

🍴 🔄 🛎️ 📶 ❌ 🔌 💻

▼▼▼ Hampton Inn & Suites 🅗

(731) 427-6100. **$119-$129.** 150 Campbell Oaks Dr 38305. I-40 exit 83, just s on Campbell St, then just w. Int corridors. **Pets:** Accepted.

🔄 🏊 📶 🔌 💻

▼▼ Howard Johnson - Jackson 🅗

(731) 660-8651. **$89-$109.** 1292 Vann Dr 38305. I-40 exit 80B, just n on US 45 Bypass, then 0.6 mi w. Int corridors. **Pets:** Accepted.

🛎️ 📶 🔌 💻

▼▼ Quality Inn 🅗

(731) 668-1400. **$69-$81.** 535 Wiley Parker Rd 38305. I-40 exit 80A, just s, then just e on Carriage House Dr. Ext/int corridors. **Pets:** Accepted. 🛎️ 📶 🔌 💻

▼▼▼ Residence Inn by Marriott Jackson 🅗

(731) 935-4100. **$149-$179.** 126 Old Medina Crossing 38305. I-40 exit 83, just ne. Int corridors. **Pets:** Accepted. 🛎️ 📶 ❌ 🔌 💻

JOHNSON CITY *(Restaurants p. 640)*

🆎 ▼▼ BEST WESTERN Johnson City Hotel & Conference Center 🅗

(423) 282-2161. **$80-$170.** 2406 N Roan St 37601. I-26 exit 20A westbound; exit 20 eastbound, just n. Ext/int corridors. **Pets:** Accepted.

🅢 🍴 🔄 🛎️ 📶 🔌 💻

🆎 ▼▼▼▼ Carnegie Hotel 🅗

(423) 979-6400. **$126-$136.** 1216 W State of Franklin Rd 37604. I-26 exit 24, 2.2 mi se on US 321 S. Int corridors. **Pets:** Medium, dogs only. $30 daily fee/pet. Designated rooms, service with restrictions, supervision. 🅢 🍴 🛎️ 📶 ❌ 🔌 💻

▼▼▼ Comfort Suites 🅗

(423) 610-0010. **$89-$112.** 3118 Browns Mill Rd 37604. I-26 exit 19, just e, then just n. Int corridors. **Pets:** Large, other species. $15 daily fee/pet. Designated rooms, service with restrictions.

🔄 🛎️ 📶 ❌ 🔌 💻

▼▼▼ DoubleTree by Hilton Hotel Johnson City 🅗

(423) 929-2000. **$99-$389.** 211 Mockingbird Ln 37604. I-26 exit 20A westbound; exit 20 eastbound, just w on N Roan St. Int corridors. **Pets:** $25 one-time fee/room. Designated rooms, service with restrictions. 🅔 🍴 🔄 🛎️ 📶 ❌ 🔌 💻

▼▼▼ Holiday Inn-Johnson City 🅗

(423) 282-4611. **Call for rates.** 101 W Springbrook Dr 37604. I-26 exit 20A westbound; exit 20 eastbound, just e on N Roan St, then just n. Int corridors. **Pets:** Small. $25 one-time fee/pet. Designated rooms, service with restrictions, supervision. 🍴 🔄 🛎️ 📶 🔌 💻

▼▼ Quality Inn Ⓜ

(423) 282-0488. **$69-$210.** 119 Pinnacle Dr 37615. I-26 exit 17, just w on CR 354, then just s. Ext corridors. **Pets:** Small, other species. $20 daily fee/pet. Service with restrictions, supervision.

🔄 🛎️ 📶 🔌 💻

🆎 ▼▼ Red Roof Inn-Johnson City Ⓜ

(423) 282-3040. **$50-$100.** 210 Broyles Dr 37601. I-26 exit 20A westbound; exit 20 eastbound, just w on N Roan St. Ext corridors. **Pets:** Large, other species. Service with restrictions, supervision.

🅢 🔄 📶 ❌ 🔌

▼▼ Sleep Inn & Suites 🅗

(423) 915-0081. **$89-$126.** 2020 Franklin Terrace Ct 37604. I-26 exit 19, just w, then just n, follow signs; entrance on Oakland Ave at light. Int corridors. **Pets:** Accepted. 🔄 📶 🔌 💻

KIMBALL

🆎 ▼▼ Comfort Inn 🅗

(423) 837-2478. **$55-$150.** 205 Kimball Crossing 37347. I-24 exit 152B, 0.3 mi n. Int corridors. **Pets:** Medium. $15 daily fee/pet. Designated rooms, supervision. 🅢 🛎️ 📶 ❌ 🔌 💻

🆎 ▼▼ Super 8 - Kimball 🅗

(423) 837-7185. **$63-$102.** 395 Main St 37347. I-24 exit 152, 0.5 mi n. Ext corridors. **Pets:** Medium, other species. $10 one-time fee/pet. Designated rooms, service with restrictions, supervision.

🅢 🛎️ 📶 🔌 💻

KINGSPORT

▼▼ Colonial Inn Ⓜ

(423) 239-3400. **Call for rates.** 4234 Fort Henry Dr 37663. I-81 exit 59, 0.7 mi n on SR 36. Ext corridors. **Pets:** Accepted. 🔄 📶 🔌 💻

▼▼▼ La Quinta Inn & Suites Kingsport Tri-Cities Airport 🅗

(423) 323-0500. **$69-$321.** 10150 Airport Pkwy 37663. I-81 exit 63, just e. Int corridors. **Pets:** Large, other species. Service with restrictions.

🔄 🛎️ 📶 🔌 💻

▼▼ Quality Inn 🅗

(423) 230-0534. **$79-$300.** 3004 Bay Meadow Pl 37664. I-26 exit 4, just n. Int corridors. **Pets:** Small. $20 daily fee/pet. Crate.

🔄 🛎️ 📶 🔌 💻

◆◆ Sleep Inn **H**
(423) 279-1811. **$75-$450.** 200 Hospitality Pl 37663. I-81 exit 63, just s. Int corridors. **Pets:** Medium, other species. $10 daily fee/room. Designated rooms, service with restrictions, crate. 🛜 🖥 💻

KINGSTON
◆◆ Motel 6 #4403 **M**
(865) 376-2069. **$43-$90.** 495 Gallaher Rd 37763. I-40 exit 356, just n. Ext corridors. **Pets:** Other species. Service with restrictions, crate. 🛜 🖥

KINGSTON SPRINGS
AAA ◆◆ BEST WESTERN Harpeth Inn **H**
(615) 952-3961. **$55-$100.** 116 Luyben Hills Rd 37082. I-40 exit 188, just n. Ext corridors. **Pets:** Accepted. [SAVE] 🛌 🛜 🖥 💻

KNOXVILLE *(Restaurants p. 640)*
◆◆ Candlewood Suites-Knoxville **H** 🐾
(865) 777-0400. **$95-$125.** 10206 Parkside Dr 37922. I-40/75 exit 374 (Lovell Rd), 0.5 mi s, then 1 mi e. Int corridors. **Pets:** $15 daily fee/room. Service with restrictions, crate. 🔱ᴹ 🛜 ✖ 🖥 💻

◆◆ The Clarion Inn **H** 🐾
(865) 687-8989. **$55-$99.** 5634 Merchants Center Blvd 37912. I-75 exit 108 (Merchants Dr), just w, then just n. Int corridors. **Pets:** Small, other species. $20 daily fee/pet. Service with restrictions, crate.
🔱ᴹ 🛌 🛜 ✖ 🖥 💻

◆◆◆ Country Inn & Suites By Carlson, West Knoxville/Cedar Bluff **H**
(865) 693-4500. **$99-$249.** 9137 Cross Park Dr 37923. I-40/75 exit 378 (Cedar Bluff Rd), just e. Int corridors. **Pets:** Accepted.
🔱ᴹ 🛌 🛜 ✖ 🖥 💻

AAA ◆◆◆◆ Crowne Plaza Knoxville **H** 🐾
(865) 522-2600. **$99-$350.** 401 W Summit Hill Dr 37902. Corner of Walnut St; downtown. Int corridors. **Pets:** Other species. $35 one-time fee/room. Service with restrictions.
[SAVE] 🍴 🔱ᴹ 🛌 🛜 ✖ 🖥 💻

◆◆ Econo Lodge Inn & Suites-East Knoxville **M**
(865) 932-1217. **$55-$85.** 7424 Strawberry Plains Pike 37924. I-40 exit 398 (Strawberry Plains Pike), just n. Ext corridors. **Pets:** $15 daily fee/pet. Service with restrictions, crate. 🛌 🛜 💻

◆◆ Econo Lodge-North **M**
(865) 687-5680. **$49-$90.** 5505 Merchants Center Blvd 37912. I-75 exit 108 (Merchants Dr), just w, then just n. Ext corridors. **Pets:** Accepted. 🛜 🖥

◆◆ Extended Stay America Knoxville-Cedar Bluff **M**
(865) 769-0822. **$49-$99.** 214 Langley Pl 37922. I-40/75 exit 378 (Cedar Bluff Rd), just s, then 1 mi w on N Peters Rd. Ext corridors. **Pets:** Other species. $25 daily fee/pet. Service with restrictions, supervision. 🔱ᴹ 🛜 🖥 💻

◆◆ Extended Stay America Knoxville-West Hills **H**
(865) 694-4178. **$49-$99.** 1700 Winston Rd 37919. I-40/75 exit 380 (West Hills), just w on Kingston Pike, then just s. Int corridors. **Pets:** Other species. $25 daily fee/pet. Service with restrictions, supervision. 🛌 🛜 🖥 💻

◆◆◆ Hilton Knoxville Downtown **H**
(865) 523-2300. **$99-$179.** 501 W Church Ave 37902. Between Locust and Walnut sts; downtown. Int corridors. **Pets:** Accepted.
🍴 🔱ᴹ 🛌 🛜 ✖ 🖥 💻

◆◆◆ Holiday Inn Cedar Bluff **H**
(865) 693-1011. **$109-$169.** 9134 Executive Park Dr 37923. I-40/75 exit 378 (Cedar Bluff Rd) eastbound; exit 378B westbound, just n to Executive Park Dr. Int corridors. **Pets:** $35 one-time fee/room. Designated rooms, service with restrictions, supervision.
🍴 🔱ᴹ 🛌 ✖ 🛜 ✖ 🖥 💻

◆◆◆ Holiday Inn Express Knoxville-East **H** 🐾
(865) 525-5100. **$109-$119.** 730 Rufus Graham Rd 37924. I-40 exit 398 (Strawberry Plains Pike), just n. Int corridors. **Pets:** Large. $30 daily fee/pet. Service with restrictions, crate. 🔳 🔱ᴹ 🛌 🛜 🖥 💻

◆◆◆ Holiday Inn World's Fair Park **H** 🐾
(865) 522-2800. **$99-$359.** 525 Henley St 37902. Corner of Clinch Ave; downtown. Int corridors. **Pets:** Small. $35 one-time fee/room. Service with restrictions, crate. [ECO] 🍴 🔱ᴹ 🛌 🛜 ✖ 🖥 💻

◆◆◆ Homewood Suites by Hilton **H**
(865) 777-0375. **$139-$189.** 10935 Turkey Dr 37922. I-40/75 exit 374 (Lovell Rd), just s to Parkside Dr, then 0.5 mi n on Snow Goose Dr. Int corridors. **Pets:** Accepted. 🔱ᴹ 🛌 🛜 ✖ 🖥 💻

◆◆◆ La Quinta Inn & Suites Knoxville Strawberry Plains **H**
(865) 633-5100. **$79-$199.** 7210 Saddlerack St 37914. I-40 exit 398 (Strawberry Plains Pike), just s, just e on Region Ln, then just se on Shumard Ave. Int corridors. **Pets:** Large, other species. Service with restrictions. 🔱ᴹ 🛌 🛜 🖥 💻

AAA ◆◆◆◆ MainStay Suites Knoxville **H** 🐾
(865) 247-0222. **$59-$129.** 144 Merchants Dr 37912. I-75 exit 108 (Merchants Dr), just n. Int corridors. **Pets:** Medium, other species. $25 one-time fee/room. Designated rooms, service with restrictions, crate. [SAVE] 🔱ᴹ 🛜 🖥 💻

◆◆ Quality Inn Merchants Dr **M**
(865) 342-3701. **$65-$80.** 117 Cedar Ln 37912. I-75 exit 108 (Merchants Dr), just e. Ext corridors. **Pets:** Medium. $10 daily fee/pet. Designated rooms, service with restrictions, supervision.
🔱ᴹ 🛌 🛜 🖥 💻

◆◆ Red Roof Inn & Suites Knoxville - East **H**
(865) 546-5700. **$49-$119.** 7525 Crosswood Blvd 37924. I-40 exit 398 (Strawberry Plains Pike), just n, then w. Int corridors. **Pets:** Large, other species. Service with restrictions, supervision. 🔱ᴹ 🛌 🛜 🖥 💻

AAA ◆◆◆ Red Roof Inn Knoxville - University of Tennessee **M**
(865) 691-1664. **$50-$120.** 209 Advantage Pl 37922. I-40/75 exit 378 (Cedar Bluff Rd), just s to N Peters Rd, then w. Ext corridors. **Pets:** Large, other species. Service with restrictions, supervision.
[SAVE] 🔱ᴹ 🛜 🖥 💻

◆◆◆ Residence Inn by Marriott Knoxville Cedar Bluff **H**
(865) 539-5339. **$124-$209.** 215 Langley Pl 37922. I-40/75 exit 378 (Cedar Bluff Rd), just s, then 1 mi w on N Peters Rd. Int corridors. **Pets:** Other species. $100 one-time fee/room. Service with restrictions, crate. 🔱ᴹ 🛌 🛜 ✖ 🖥 💻

◆◆ Rodeway Inn **M**
(865) 246-3600. **$39-$79.** 814 Brakebill Rd 37914. I-40 exit 398 (Strawberry Plains Pike), just n, then w. Ext corridors. **Pets:** Medium. $10 daily fee/pet. Service with restrictions, crate. 🛌 🛜 🖥 💻

LA VERGNE
◆◆ Quality Inn & Suites **H**
(615) 793-9999. **$79-$169.** 110 Enterprise Blvd 37086. I-24 exit 64, just e. Int corridors. **Pets:** Large. $25 daily fee/room. Service with restrictions, supervision. 🔱ᴹ 🛌 🛜 🖥 💻

LAWRENCEBURG
◆◆ Americas Best Value Inn **M**
(931) 762-4467. **$70-$80.** 1940 N Locust Ave 38464. Jct US 43 and 64, 1.6 mi n. Ext corridors. **Pets:** Very small. $15 deposit/pet, $15 daily fee/pet. Designated rooms, service with restrictions, crate.
🔱ᴹ 🛌 🛜 🖥 💻

LEBANON

▼▼ Econo Lodge Ⓜ
(615) 444-1001. **$55-$70.** 829 S Cumberland St 37087. I-40 exit 238, just n. Ext corridors. **Pets:** Medium. $10 daily fee/room. Designated rooms, supervision. 🛌 🛜 🔌 💻

ⒶⒶⒶ ▼▼▼ La Quinta Inn & Suites 🄷
(615) 470-1001. **$85-$215.** 140 Dixie Ave 37090. I-40 exit 238, just s. Int corridors. **Pets:** Large, other species. Service with restrictions.
🅂🄰🅅🄴 ⬛ 🅂🄼 🛌 🛜 ✖ 🔌 💻

▼▼ Quality Inn Ⓜ
(615) 444-7020. **$70-$110.** 641 S Cumberland St 37087. I-40 exit 238, 0.5 mi n. Ext corridors. **Pets:** Accepted. 🅂🄼 🛌 🛜 🔌 💻

▼▼ Sleep Inn & Suites-Lebanon/Nashville 🄷
(615) 449-7005. **$69-$159.** 150 S Eastgate Ct 37090. I-40 exit 232, just n. Int corridors. **Pets:** Accepted. 🅂🄼 🛌 🛜 ✖ 🔌 💻

LENOIR CITY

▼▼ Days Inn 🄷
(865) 986-2011. **$50-$90.** 1110 Hwy 321 N 37771. I-75 exit 81, just e. Ext corridors. **Pets:** Accepted. 🍴 🛌 🛜 🔌 💻

ⒶⒶⒶ ▼▼▼ Econo Lodge 🄷
(865) 986-0295. **$69-$74.** 1211 Hwy 321 N 37771. I-75 exit 81, just w. Ext corridors. **Pets:** Accepted. 🅂🄰🅅🄴 🛌 🛜 🔌

MANCHESTER

▼▼ Microtel Inn & Suites by Wyndham Manchester 🄷
(937) 723-7001. **$67-$250.** 201 Expressway Dr 37355. I-24 exit 114, 0.5 mi nw on SR 41, then just n. Int corridors. **Pets:** Accepted.
🅂🄼 🛌 🛜 ✖ 🔌 💻

ⒶⒶⒶ ▼▼▼ Sleep Inn & Suites 🄷
(931) 954-0580. **$70-$350.** 84 Relco Dr 37355. I-24 exit 114, just e. Int corridors. **Pets:** Accepted. 🅂🄰🅅🄴 🅂🄼 🛌 🛜 ✖ 🔌 💻

MARYVILLE

▼ LuxBury Inn & Suites Ⓜ
(865) 983-9839. **$55-$159.** 805 Foothills Mall Dr 37801. Jct US 321 (Lamar Alexander Pkwy). Ext corridors. **Pets:** Small, dogs only. $25 one-time fee/pet. Designated rooms, service with restrictions, supervision. 🅂🄼 🛜 🔌 💻

MCKENZIE

ⒶⒶⒶ ▼▼▼ BEST WESTERN McKenzie Ⓜ
(731) 352-1083. **$73-$75.** 16180 N Highland Ave 38201. Jct SR 22, 1 mi s on US 79. Ext corridors. **Pets:** Small. $10 daily fee/pet. Designated rooms, service with restrictions, supervision.
🅂🄰🅅🄴 🛌 🛜 🔌 💻

MEMPHIS *(Restaurants p. 641)*

▼▼ Baymont Inn & Suites Memphis East 🄷
(901) 377-2233. **$59-$79.** 6020 Shelby Oaks Dr 38134. I-40 exit 12, just n, then just e. Int corridors. **Pets:** Medium. $15 one-time fee/pet. Designated rooms, service with restrictions, supervision.
🛌 🛜 🔌 💻

▼▼ Econo Lodge Inn & Suites 🄷
(901) 385-1999. **$64-$94.** 6045 Macon Cove Rd 38134. I-40 exit 12, just s on Sycamore View Rd, then just w. Ext corridors. **Pets:** Accepted.
🅂🄼 🛌 🛜 🔌 💻

▼▼▼ Hampton Inn Memphis-Walnut Grove/Baptist Hospital East 🄷
(901) 747-3700. **$99-$169.** 33 Humphreys Center Dr 38120. I-240 exit 13 (Walnut Grove E), just e. Int corridors. **Pets:** Accepted.
🅂🄼 🛌 🛜 🔌 💻

▼▼▼ Hilton Memphis 🄷
(901) 684-6664. **$99-$239.** 939 Ridge Lake Blvd 38120. I-240 exit 15 (Poplar Ave), just e, then n under overpass. Int corridors.
Pets: Accepted. 🍴 🅂🄼 🛌 🍽 ✖ 🔌 💻

▼▼▼ Homewood Suites by Hilton Memphis-Poplar 🄷
(901) 763-0500. **$119-$189.** 5811 Poplar Ave 38119. I-240 exit 15 (Poplar Ave), just e. Ext/int corridors. **Pets:** Accepted.
🛌 🛜 ✖ 🔌 💻

▼▼▼ Homewood Suites by Hilton Southwind-Hacks Cross 🄷
(901) 758-5018. **$119-$179.** 3583 Hacks Cross Rd 38125. I-240 exit 16, 4 mi e on SR 385, then 1 mi n. Int corridors. **Pets:** Accepted.
🅂🄼 🛌 🛜 🔌 💻

ⒶⒶⒶ ▼▼▼ Hyatt Place-Memphis/Primacy Parkway 🄷
(901) 680-9700. **$79-$179.** 1220 Primacy Pkwy 38119. I-240 exit 15 (Poplar Ave), 0.5 mi e, s on Ridgeway Rd, just w. Int corridors. **Pets:** Medium, dogs only. $75 one-time fee/pet. Designated rooms, service with restrictions, supervision.
🅂🄰🅅🄴 🅂🄼 🛌 🛜 ✖ 🔌 💻

ⒶⒶⒶ ▼▼▼ Hyatt Place Memphis/Wolfchase Galleria 🄷
(901) 371-0010. **$84-$189.** 7905 Giacosa Pl 38133. I-40 exit 16 or 16B, just n on Germantown Rd, then just w. Int corridors. **Pets:** Medium, dogs only. $75 one-time fee/pet. Service with restrictions, crate.
🅂🄰🅅🄴 🅂🄼 🛌 🛜 ✖ 🔌 💻

▼▼ The Inn at Thousand Oaks 🄷
(901) 367-1234. **Call for rates.** 2700 Perkins Rd S 38118. I-240 exit 18, just se. Int corridors. **Pets:** Accepted. 🅂🄼 🛌 🛜 🔌 💻

▼▼▼ La Quinta Inn & Suites Memphis East-Sycamore View 🄷
(901) 381-0044. **$79-$259.** 6069 Macon Cove Rd 38134. I-40 exit 12, just s, then just w. Int corridors. **Pets:** Large, other species. Service with restrictions. 🅂🄰🅅🄴 🅂🄼 🛌 🛜 ✖ 🔌 💻

▼▼▼ La Quinta Inn & Suites-Memphis Primacy Parkway 🄷
(901) 374-0330. **$75-$210.** 1236 Primacy Pkwy 38119. I-240 exit 15 (Poplar Ave), 0.5 mi e, just s on Ridgeway Rd, just w on Park Ave, then just s. Int corridors. **Pets:** Large, other species. Service with restrictions. 🅂🄼 🛌 🛜 🔌 💻

ⒶⒶⒶ ▼▼▼▼ Madison Hotel 🄷
(901) 333-1200. **$187-$374, 3 day notice.** 79 Madison Ave 38103. Jct Main St, just w. Int corridors. **Pets:** Accepted.
🅂🄰🅅🄴 🍴 🅂🄼 🛜 ✖ 💻

ⒶⒶⒶ ▼▼▼ Peabody Memphis 🄷 🐾
(901) 529-4000. **$325-$570, 3 day notice.** 149 Union Ave 38103. Jct 2nd St. Int corridors. **Pets:** Medium. $75 one-time fee/room. Designated rooms, service with restrictions, supervision.
🅂🄰🅅🄴 ⬛ 🍴 🛌 ✖ 🍽 ✖ 🔌 💻

▼▼▼ Residence Inn by Marriott Memphis Downtown 🄷
(901) 578-3700. **$167-$312.** 110 Monroe Ave 38103. Jct Main St. Int corridors. **Pets:** Accepted. 🅂🄼 🛜 ✖ 🔌 💻

ⒶⒶⒶ ▼▼▼ Residence Inn by Marriott Memphis East 🄷
(901) 685-9595. **$99-$186.** 6141 Poplar Pike 38119. I-240 exit 15 (Poplar Ave), 0.5 mi e. Int corridors. **Pets:** Small. $100 one-time fee/pet. Service with restrictions, supervision.
🅂🄰🅅🄴 🅂🄼 🛌 🛜 ✖ 🔌 💻

Sheraton Memphis Downtown Hotel H 🐾

(901) 527-7300. **$109-$299.** 250 N Main St 38103. I-40 exit 1A westbound; exit 1 eastbound, just s. Int corridors. **Pets:** Medium, dogs only. Supervision. [SAVE] [🍴] [🏊] [📶] [✕] [🛗] [📺]

Sleep Inn H

(901) 312-7777. **$75-$89.** 2855 Old Austin Peay Hwy 38128. I-40 exit 8 or 8A, 0.8 mi ne. Int corridors. **Pets:** Accepted.
[♿M] [🏊] [📶] [🛗] [📺]

Staybridge Suites Memphis-Poplar Ave East H

(901) 682-1722. **Call for rates.** 1070 Ridge Lake Blvd 38120. I-240 exit 15 (Poplar Ave), just e, then n under overpass. Int corridors.
Pets: Accepted. [♿M] [🏊] [📶] [✕] [🛗] [📺]

Travelers Inn and Suites M

(901) 363-8430. **Call for rates.** 5024 Lamar Ave (US Hwy 78) 38118. I-240 exit 21 (US 78), 5 mi s. Ext corridors. **Pets:** Accepted.
[🍴] [🏊] [📶] [🛗] [📺]

The Westin Memphis Beale Street H

(901) 334-5900. **$179-$329.** 170 Lt. George W. Lee Ave 38103. Jct S 3rd St. Int corridors. **Pets:** Accepted. [SAVE] [🍴] [♿M] [📶] [✕] [📺]

MILLINGTON

Plantation Oaks Suites & Inn M

(901) 872-8000. **Call for rates.** 6656 Hwy 51 N 38053. SR 385, 2.4 mi s. Ext/int corridors. **Pets:** Accepted. [🏊] [📶] [🛗] [📺]

MONTEAGLE

BEST WESTERN Smoke House Lodge H

(931) 924-2091. **$72-$140.** 844 W Main St 37356. I-24 exit 134, just s. Ext corridors. **Pets:** Accepted.

[SAVE] [🔌] [🍴] [🏊] [✕] [📶] [🛗] [📺]

Edgeworth Inn CI

(931) 924-4000. **$139-$225, 7 day notice.** 19 Wilkins Ave 37356. I-24 exit 134, 0.4 mi e on SR 41A. Ext/int corridors. **Pets:** Medium. $45 deposit/pet. Service with restrictions, crate.

[🍴] [🏊] [📶] [✕] [🎬] [🛗] [📺]

Monteagle Inn & Retreat Center BB

(931) 924-3869. **$165-$275, 15 day notice.** 204 W Main St 37356. I-24 exit 134, 0.4 mi e on US 41A. Ext/int corridors. **Pets:** Accepted.
[🍴] [♿M] [📶] [✕]

MORRISTOWN

BEST WESTERN PLUS Morristown Conference Center Hotel H 🐾

(423) 587-2400. **$115-$195.** 130 Cracker Rd 37813. I-81 exit 8, just w. Int corridors. **Pets:** Large, other species. $20 daily fee/room. Service with restrictions, supervision. [SAVE] [♿M] [🏊] [📶] [🛗] [📺]

Days Inn M

(423) 587-2200. **$55-$145, 3 day notice.** 2512 E Andrew Johnson Hwy 37814. I-81 exit 8, 6 mi n on US 25 E to exit 2B (Greeneville-Morristown), then just w. Ext corridors. **Pets:** Accepted.
[♿M] [🏊] [📶] [🛗] [📺]

Super 8 M

(423) 318-8888. **$50-$102.** 5400 S Davy Crockett Pkwy 37813. I-81 exit 8, just n. Int corridors. **Pets:** Dogs only. $9 daily fee/pet. Service with restrictions, supervision. [♿M] [📶] [🛗] [📺]

MOUNT JULIET

Quality Inn & Suites H

(615) 773-3600. **$60-$130.** 1000 Hershel Dr 37122. I-40 exit 226A eastbound; exit 226 westbound, just s. Int corridors. **Pets:** Accepted.
[🏊] [📶] [🛗] [📺]

MCMINNVILLE

BEST WESTERN Tree City Inn H

(931) 473-2159. **$70-$127.** 809 Sparta St 37110. Jct US 70 S Bypass and Red Rd, 1 mi s, follow signs. Ext corridors. **Pets:** Dogs only. $10 daily fee/pet. Service with restrictions, supervision.
[SAVE] [🏊] [📶] [🛗] [📺]

MURFREESBORO

Baymont Inn & Suites M

(615) 896-1172. **$69-$109.** 2230 Armory Dr 37129. I-24 exit 78B, just n. Ext corridors. **Pets:** Accepted. [🏊] [📶] [🛗] [📺]

BEST WESTERN Chaffin Inn M

(615) 895-3818. **$60-$160.** 168 Chaffin Pl 37129. I-24 exit 78B, just s. Ext corridors. **Pets:** Medium. $15 daily fee/room. Designated rooms, service with restrictions, supervision. [SAVE] [🏊] [📶] [🛗] [📺]

DoubleTree by Hilton Hotel Murfreesboro H

(615) 895-5555. **$109-$189.** 1850 Old Fort Pkwy 37129. I-24 exit 78B, 0.6 mi ne. Int corridors. **Pets:** Medium. Service with restrictions, crate.
[SAVE] [ECO] [🔌] [🍴] [♿M] [🏊] [📶] [✕] [🛗] [📺]

Hampton Inn & Suites H 🐾

(615) 890-2424. **$109-$300.** 325 N Thompson Ln 37129. I-24 exit 78B, just n. Int corridors. **Pets:** Medium. $25 daily fee/room. Designated rooms, service with restrictions, supervision.
[♿M] [🏊] [📶] [✕] [🛗] [📺]

Quality Inn Murfreesboro H

(615) 890-1006. **$65-$175.** 2135 S Church St 37130. I-24 exit 81 westbound; exit 81B eastbound. Int corridors. **Pets:** Large, other species. $10 one-time fee/room. Service with restrictions, supervision.
[SAVE] [♿M] [🏊] [📶] [🛗] [📺]

NASHVILLE *(Restaurants p. 641)*

Aloft Nashville West End H

(615) 329-4200. **$209-$399.** 1719 West End Ave 37203. I-40 exit 209B (Broadway), 0.4 mi w. Int corridors. **Pets:** Accepted.
[SAVE] [🍴] [🏊] [✕] [🛗] [📺]

Comfort Inn Downtown H

(615) 255-9977. **$100-$400.** 1501 Demonbreun St 37203. I-40 exit 209B, just w. Ext corridors. **Pets:** Accepted.
[♿M] [🏊] [📶] [✕] [🛗] [📺]

Days Inn North M

(615) 228-3421. **$65-$150.** 3312 Dickerson Pike 37207. I-65 exit 90A (Dickerson Pike), just s. Ext corridors. **Pets:** $10 daily fee/pet. Designated rooms, service with restrictions, crate. [SAVE] [🏊] [📶] [🛗] [📺]

Days Inn Opryland H

(615) 889-0090. **$65-$107.** 2460 Music Valley Dr 37214. I-40 exit 215B (SR 155 N/Briley Pkwy), 5.3 mi n to exit 12 (McGavock Pike), just w, then 0.3 mi n. Int corridors. **Pets:** Accepted. [🏊] [📶] [🛗] [📺]

Drury Inn & Suites-Nashville Airport H

(615) 902-0400. **$135-$209.** 555 Donelson Pike 37214. I-40 exit 216 (Donelson Pike), just n. Int corridors. **Pets:** $10 daily fee/room. Service with restrictions, supervision. [♿M] [🏊] [📶] [✕] [🛗] [📺]

The Hermitage Hotel H

(615) 244-3121. **$289-$489.** 231 6th Ave N 37219. Corner of Union St. Int corridors. **Pets:** Accepted. [SAVE] [🍴] [♿M] [📶] [✕] [🛗] [📺]

Hilton Garden Inn Nashville-Vanderbilt H

(615) 369-5900. **$139-$399.** 1715 Broadway 37203. Corner of 17th Ave S and Broadway; in West End. Int corridors. **Pets:** Medium. $75 one-time fee/room. Designated rooms, service with restrictions, supervision.
[🍴] [♿M] [🏊] [📶] [✕] [🛗] [📺]

AAA ◆◆◆ **Hilton Nashville Downtown** 🏨 🐾
(615) 620-1000. **$227-$389.** 121 4th Ave S 37201. Center. Int corridors.
Pets: Large, other species. $50 one-time fee/room. Service with restrictions, supervision. SAVE ⊟ 🔲

AAA ◆◆◆ **Holiday Inn Express-Airport/Opryland**
Area 🏨
(615) 883-1366. **$99-$171.** 1111 Airport Center Dr 37214. I-40 exit 216C
(Donelson Pike N), 1 mi n, then 0.5 mi e. Int corridors. **Pets:** Accepted.
SAVE 🔲

◆◆◆ **Home2 Suites by Hilton-Nashville/Vanderbilt** 🏨
(615) 254-2170. **$139-$239.** 1800 Division St 37203. I-40 exit 209
(Demonbreun St), 0.5 mi sw. Int corridors. **Pets:** Accepted.

◆◆◆ **Homewood Suites by Hilton Nashville Vanderbilt/**
West End 🏨
(615) 340-8000. **Call for rates.** 2400 West End Ave 37203. I-40 exit
209A (Broadway), 0.7 mi w. Int corridors. **Pets:** Accepted.

◆◆◆ **Homewood Suites Nashville Downtown** 🏨
(615) 742-5550. **$179-$239.** 706 Church St 37203. Jct 7th Ave N and
Church St. Int corridors. **Pets:** Accepted.

AAA ◆◆◆ **Hotel Indigo-Nashville Downtown** 🏨
(615) 891-6000. **$199-$469, 3 day notice.** 301 Union St 37201. I-40
exit 209A (Church St), 0.8 mi e on Charlotte Ave, then just s. Int corridors. **Pets:** Accepted. SAVE

◆◆◆ **Hotel Preston** 🏨 🐾
(615) 361-5900. **$129-$299, 3 day notice.** 733 Briley Pkwy 37217. I-40
exit 215 (SR 155 N/Briley Pkwy), just s. Int corridors. **Pets:** Small. $45
one-time fee/room. Designated rooms, service with restrictions, supervision.

AAA ◆◆◆ **Hutton Hotel** 🏨
(615) 340-9333. **$259-$399.** 1808 West End Ave 37203. I-40 W exit
209B (Broadway), 1 mi w. Int corridors. **Pets:** Accepted.
SAVE ECO

AAA ◆◆◆ **Hyatt Place Nashville Airport** 🏨
(615) 493-5200. **$79-$209.** 721 Royal Pkwy 37214. I-40 exit 216C
(Donelson Pike), just n, then just e. Int corridors. **Pets:** Accepted.
SAVE

AAA ◆◆◆ **Hyatt Place Nashville Downtown** 🏨
(615) 687-9995. **Call for rates.** 301 3rd Ave S 37201. I-40 exit 210C,
0.6 mi n on 2nd Ave S, then w at Korean Veterans Blvd. Int corridors.
Pets: Accepted. SAVE

AAA ◆◆◆ **Hyatt Place Nashville/Opryland** 🏨
(615) 872-0422. **$89-$209.** 220 Rudy Cir 37214. I-40 exit 215B (SR
155 N/Briley Pkwy), 5.3 mi n to exit 12 (McGavock Pike), just w, then
0.3 mi n on Music Valley Dr. Int corridors. **Pets:** Accepted.
SAVE

◆ **La Quinta Inn & Suites Nashville-Airport** 🏨
(615) 885-3100. **$72-$239.** 531 Donelson Pike 37214. I-40 exit 216C
(Donelson Pike), 0.3 mi n. Int corridors. **Pets:** Large, other species.
Service with restrictions.

AAA ◆◆ **Loews Vanderbilt Hotel Nashville** 🏨
(615) 320-1700. **$199-$549, 3 day notice.** 2100 West End Ave 37203.
I-40 exit 209B (Broadway), 1.3 mi w. Int corridors. **Pets:** Accepted.
SAVE ECO

AAA ◆◆ **Red Roof Inn Airport** 🅼
(615) 872-0735. **$50-$130.** 510 Claridge Dr 37214. I-40 exit 216C
(Donelson Pike), 0.3 mi n. Ext corridors. **Pets:** Large, other species.
Service with restrictions, supervision. SAVE

AAA ◆◆◆ **Residence Inn by Marriott Nashville**
Airport 🏨
(615) 889-8600. **$109-$269.** 2300 Elm Hill Pike 37214. I-40 exit 215B
(SR 155 N/Briley Pkwy), 1.5 mi n. Ext corridors. **Pets:** Accepted.
SAVE ECO

AAA ◆◆◆ **Sheraton Music City Hotel** 🏨
(615) 885-2200. **$129-$355.** 777 McGavock Pike 37214. I-40 exit 215B
(SR 155 N/Briley Pkwy), 1 mi n to exit 7 (Elm Hill Pike), 0.5 mi e, then
s. Int corridors. **Pets:** Accepted.
SAVE

AAA ◆◆ **Super 8-West** 🅼
(615) 356-6005. **$50-$100.** 6924 Charlotte Pike 37209. I-40 exit 201B,
just n. Ext corridors. **Pets:** Medium. $15 daily fee/pet. Service with
restrictions, supervision. SAVE

◆◆◆ **TownePlace Suites by Marriott Nashville**
Airport 🏨
(615) 232-3830. **$159-$299.** 2700 Elm Hill Pike 37214. I-40 exit 215
(SR 155 N/Briley Pkwy), 1 mi n to exit 7 (Elm Hill Pike), then just e. Int
corridors. **Pets:** Accepted.

NEWPORT

AAA ◆◆ **BEST WESTERN Newport Inn** 🅼
(423) 623-8713. **$70-$170.** 1015 Cosby Hwy 37821. I-40 exit 435, just
w. Ext corridors. **Pets:** Medium, other species. $10 daily fee/pet. Designated rooms, no service, supervision.
SAVE

AAA ◆◆ **Comfort Inn** 🏨
(423) 623-5355. **$49-$89.** 1149 Smokey Mountain Ln 37821. I-40 exit
432B, just n. Int corridors. **Pets:** Large. $20 daily fee/room. Designated
rooms, service with restrictions, supervision.
SAVE

◆◆ **Motel 6 #4090** 🅼
(423) 623-1850. **$40-$50.** 255 Heritage Blvd 37822. I-40 exit 435, just
n. Int corridors. **Pets:** Other species. Service with restrictions, crate.

OAK RIDGE

◆◆◆ **DoubleTree by Hilton Hotel Oak Ridge** 🏨
(865) 481-2468. **$89-$159.** 215 S Illinois Ave 37830. 0.3 mi se of SR
95 on SR 62 (Oak Ridge Hwy). Int corridors. **Pets:** Accepted.
ECO

◆◆ **Quality Inn** 🏨
(865) 483-6809. **$79-$94.** 216 S Rutgers Ave 37830. Jct SR 95 and 62,
0.9 mi se on SR 62 (Oak Ridge Hwy) to Rutgers Ave, 0.7 mi n. Int
corridors. **Pets:** Small, other species. $20 daily fee/room. Service with
restrictions, crate.

◆◆ **Staybridge Suites** 🏨
(865) 298-0050. **$109-$129, 3 day notice.** 420 S Illinois Ave 37830. Jct
Lafayette St and SR 62 (Oak Ridge Hwy). Int corridors. **Pets:** Accepted.

OOLTEWAH

◆◆ **Super 8** 🅼
(423) 238-5951. **$50-$56.** 8934 Lee Hwy 37363. I-75 exit 11, just w. Ext
corridors. **Pets:** Accepted.

PARIS

◆◆ **Quality Inn Paris** 🏨
(731) 642-2838. **$75-$140.** 1510 E Wood St 38242. Jct US 641, 2 mi n
on US 79. Ext corridors. **Pets:** Other species. Service with restrictions,
crate.

◆◆ **Super 8** 🏨
(731) 644-7008. **$58-$72.** 1309 E Wood St 38242. Jct US 641, 1.5 mi
n on US 79. Ext/int corridors. **Pets:** Accepted.

PIGEON FORGE *(Restaurants p. 641)*

▼▼ Bear Creek Crossing by Eden Crest Vacation Rentals CA

(865) 774-0059. **$100-$390, 90 day notice.** 652 Wears Valley Rd 37863. Jct US 441, 1 mi s on US 321 at traffic light 3. Ext corridors. **Pets:** Small, dogs only. $50 one-time fee/pet. No service, crate.

🐾 📷 ✕ 🛏 💻

▼▼▼ Black Bear Ridge by Eden Crest Vacation Rentals CA

(865) 774-0059. **$100-$1300.** 652 Wears Valley Rd 37863. Jct US 441, 1 mi s on US 321 at traffic light 3. Int corridors. **Pets:** Small, dogs only. $50 one-time fee/pet. No service, crate. 📷 ✕ 🛏 💻

▼▼▼ Hampton Inn & Suites H

(865) 428-1600. **$99-$189.** 2025 Parkway 37863. On US 441, at traffic light 0. Int corridors. **Pets:** Accepted. 🚶M 🐾 📶 🛏 💻

▼▼ Microtel Inn & Suites by Wyndham H

(865) 453-1116. **$45-$120.** 2045 Parkway 37863. On US 441, just s of traffic light 0. Int corridors. **Pets:** Medium, dogs only. $25 daily fee/pet. Designated rooms, no service. 🚶M 🐾 📶 ✕ 🛏 💻

AAA ▼▼▼▼ RiverStone Resort & Spa CO

(865) 908-0660. **$110-$479, 7 day notice.** 212 Dollywood Ln 37863. Jct US 441, just e at traffic light 8. Ext corridors. **Pets:** Very small, dogs only. $25 daily fee/pet. Designated rooms, no service.

SAVE 🐾 ✕ 📶 ✕ 🛏 💻

▼▼▼▼ Smoky Cove by Eden Crest Vacation Rentals CA

(865) 774-0059. **$100-$1000.** 652 Wears Valley Rd 37863. Jct US 441, 1 mi s on US 321 at traffic light 3. Ext corridors. **Pets:** Small, dogs only. $50 one-time fee/pet. No service, crate. 🐾 📷 ✕ 🛏 💻

▼▼ Timbers Lodge M

(865) 428-5216. **Call for rates.** 134 Wears Valley Rd E 37863. Jct US 441, just e at traffic light 3. Ext corridors. **Pets:** Accepted.

🐾 📶 ✕ 🛏 💻

POWELL

▼▼▼▼ Comfort Inn H

(865) 938-5500. **$85-$150.** 7585 Barnett Way 37849. I-75 exit 112, 0.4 mi e on Emory Rd, then just w. Int corridors. **Pets:** Medium. $10 daily fee/pet. Service with restrictions, crate. 🚶M 🐾 📶 ✕ 🛏 💻

▼▼▼ Country Inn & Suites By Carlson H

(865) 947-7500. **$75-$155.** 7534 Conner Rd 37849. I-75 exit 112, just e. Int corridors. **Pets:** $25 daily fee/pet. Designated rooms, service with restrictions, crate. 🚶M 🐾 📶 🛏 💻

▼▼▼ Super 8 of Powell M

(865) 938-5501. **$60-$80.** 323 E Emory Rd 37849. I-75 exit 112. Ext corridors. **Pets:** Accepted. 🐾 📶 🛏 💻

ROGERSVILLE

▼▼▼▼ Comfort Inn & Suites H

(423) 272-8700. **$85-$200.** 128 James Richardson Ln 37857. US 11 W/SR 1/70, 1.6 mi w, just n. Int corridors. **Pets:** $25 daily fee/pet. Designated rooms. 🚶M 🐾 📶 🛏 💻

SELMER

▼▼ America's Best Inn M

(731) 645-8880. **Call for rates.** 644 Mulberry Ave 38375. Jct US 64, just s on US 45. Ext corridors. **Pets:** Accepted. 🐾 📶 🛏 💻

SEVIERVILLE

AAA ▼▼▼ BEST WESTERN Greenbrier Inn M

(865) 428-1000. **$50-$120.** 711 Parkway 37862. Jct US 411, 0.7 mi s. Ext corridors. **Pets:** Accepted. SAVE 🐾 📶 🛏 💻

▼▼ Econo Lodge M

(865) 429-7797. **$40-$90.** 680 Winfield Dunn Pkwy 37864. Jct US 411, 0.7 mi n on SR 66. Int corridors. **Pets:** Small, dogs only. $15 daily fee/pet. Designated rooms, no service, supervision.

🚶M 🐾 📶 🛏 💻

▼▼ La Quinta Inn & Suites Sevierville/Kodak H

(865) 933-3339. **$65-$199.** 2428 Winfield Dunn Pkwy 37764. I-40 exit 407, 3.2 mi s on SR 66. Int corridors. **Pets:** Large, other species. Service with restrictions. 🚶M 🐾 📶 ✕ 🛏 💻

AAA ▼▼▼ Quality Inn & Suites River Suites M

(865) 428-5519. **$60-$130.** 860 Winfield Dunn Pkwy 37876. Jct US 411, 1.2 mi n on SR 66. Ext corridors. **Pets:** Accepted.

SAVE 🐾 📶 ✕ 🛏 💻

▼▼ Sleep Inn H

(865) 429-0484. **$80-$130.** 1020 Parkway 37862. On US 441, 1.2 mi s of jct US 411. Int corridors. **Pets:** Accepted. 🚶M 🐾 📶 🛏 💻

SHELBYVILLE

AAA ▼▼▼▼ BEST WESTERN Celebration Inn & Suites H

(931) 684-2378. **$59-$169.** 724 Madison St 37160. Jct US 231 and 41. Ext corridors. **Pets:** Accepted. SAVE 🐾 📶 ✕ 🛏 💻

▼▼ Microtel Inn & Suites by Wyndham H

(931) 684-8343. **$49-$85.** 1207 N Main St 37160. Jct US 231 and 41, 0.9 mi n. Int corridors. **Pets:** Accepted. 🚶M 📶 ✕ 🛏 💻

SMYRNA

▼▼▼ La Quinta Inn & Suites H

(615) 220-8845. **$89-$239.** 2537 Highwood Blvd 37167. I-24 exit 66A, just w. Int corridors. **Pets:** Large, other species. Service with restrictions. 🔲 🚶M 🐾 📶 ✕ 🛏 💻

SWEETWATER *(Restaurants p. 641)*

▼▼ Quality Inn & Suites H

(423) 337-4900. **Call for rates.** 1116 New Hwy 68 37874. I-75 exit 60, just w. Int corridors. **Pets:** Accepted. 🚶M 🐾 📷 🛏 💻

▼▼ Quality Inn West H

(423) 337-3353. **$70-$110.** 249 New Hwy 68 37874. I-75 exit 60, just e. Ext/int corridors. **Pets:** Small. $10 daily fee/pet. Designated rooms, service with restrictions, supervision. 🐾 📶 ✕ 🛏 💻

TOWNSEND

AAA ▼▼▼ BEST WESTERN Cades Cove Inn M

(865) 448-9000. **$80-$249.** 7824 E Lamar Alexander Pkwy 37882. Jct SR 73, 0.7 mi s on US 321. Ext corridors. **Pets:** Small, dogs only. $20 daily fee/pet. Designated rooms, service with restrictions, supervision.

SAVE 🚶M 🐾 📶 ✕ 🛏 💻

TULLAHOMA

▼▼ Baymont Inn Tullahoma M

(931) 455-7891. **$49-$99.** 2113 N Jackson St 37388. 3 mi n on SR 41A (N Jackson St). Ext corridors. **Pets:** Accepted. 🐾 📶 🛏 💻

WHITE HOUSE

▼▼▼ BEST WESTERN PLUS White House H 🐾

(615) 672-3993. **Call for rates.** 404 Hester Dr 37188. I-65 exit 108, just e, then just s. Int corridors. **Pets:** Medium, other species. $20 daily fee/room. Service with restrictions, supervision.

🚶M 🐾 📶 ✕ 🛏 💻

(AAA) ▼▼▼ **Holiday Inn Express** H
(615) 672-7200. **$90-$200.** 206 Knight Cir 37188. I-65 exit 108, just e. Int corridors. **Pets:** Medium. $25 daily fee/pet. Designated rooms, service with restrictions, supervision. [SAVE] [&M] [🛏] [🤶] [✕] [🛢] [🖵]

WINCHESTER

(AAA) ▼▼▼ **BEST WESTERN Winchester Inn** M
(931) 967-9444. **$84-$94.** 1602 Dinah Shore Blvd 37398. Jct US 41A and 41 Bypass, just w. Ext corridors. **Pets:** Accepted.
[SAVE] [&M] [🛏] [🤶] [🛢] [🖵]

TEXAS

ABILENE

(AAA) ▼▼▼ **BEST WESTERN Whitten South** H
(325) 695-1262. **$89-$129.** 3950 Ridgemont Dr 79606. US 83/84 exit Buffalo Gap Rd to Ridgemont Dr, just w. Ext corridors. **Pets:** Accepted.
[SAVE] [🛏] [🤶] [🛢] [🖵]

▼▼▼ **Comfort Inn & Suites** H
(325) 232-8801. **$84-$159.** 6350 Directors Pkwy 79606. US 83/84 S exit Antilley Rd, just w. Int corridors. **Pets:** Dogs only. $25 one-time fee/pet. Designated rooms, service with restrictions, crate.
[&M] [🛏] [🤶] [✕] [🛢] [🖵]

▼▼▼ **MCM Elegante Suites** H
(325) 698-1234. **$129-$349.** 4250 Ridgemont Dr 79606. US 83/84 exit Buffalo Gap Rd, 1 mi s of W Frontage Rd to Ridgemont Dr, then 0.5 mi w. Ext/int corridors. **Pets:** Accepted. [🍴] [🛏] [🤶] [🛢] [🖵]

▼▼▼ **Residence Inn by Marriott** H
(325) 677-8700. **$79-$149.** 1641 Musgrave Blvd 79601. I-20 exit 288; on N Frontage Rd. Int corridors. **Pets:** Accepted.
[&M] [🛏] [🤶] [✕] [🛢] [🖵]

▼▼▼ **Sleep Inn & Suites** H
(325) 437-1525. **$79-$165.** 3225 S Danville Dr 79605. US 83/84/277S exit Buffalo Gap Rd; on E Frontage Rd. Int corridors. **Pets:** Accepted.
[&M] [🛏] [🤶] [🛢] [🖵]

(AAA) ▼▼▼ **Super 8** H
(325) 701-4779. **$79-$109.** 4397 Sayles Blvd 79605. US 83/84 exit Buffalo Gap Rd northbound, just e; exit southbound, just e to Industrial Blvd, 0.5 mi e to Sayles Blvd, then just s. Int corridors. **Pets:** Medium. $20 daily fee/pet. Designated rooms, service with restrictions, supervision. [SAVE] [🛏] [🤶] [🛢] [🖵]

ADDISON *(Restaurants p. 641)*

▼▼▼ **Comfort Suites by Choice Hotels** H
(972) 503-6500. **$79-$149.** 4555 Belt Line Rd 75001. Just w of Addison Rd; behind Macaroni Grill. Int corridors. **Pets:** Medium. $20 daily fee/pet. Designated rooms, service with restrictions, crate.
[🛏] [🤶] [✕] [🛢] [🖵]

▼▼▼ **Homewood Suites by Hilton** H
(972) 788-1342. **$99-$259.** 4451 Belt Line Rd 75001. Just e of jct Belt Line and Midway rds. Ext/int corridors. **Pets:** Accepted.
[&M] [🛏] [🤶] [🛢] [🖵]

(AAA) ▼▼▼ **HYATT house Dallas/Addison** H
(972) 661-3113. **$64-$169.** 4900 Edwin Lewis Dr 75001. Just n of jct Belt Line Rd and Quorum Dr to Edwin Lewis Dr, just w. Ext corridors.
Pets: Accepted. [SAVE] [&M] [🤶] [✕] [🛢] [🖵]

▼▼▼ **La Quinta Inn & Suites Dallas Addison Galleria** H
(972) 404-0004. **$59-$214.** 14925 Landmark Blvd 75254. Jct Belt Line Rd and Landmark Blvd, just s. Int corridors. **Pets:** Large, other species. Service with restrictions. [&M] [🛏] [🤶] [🛢] [🖵]

▼▼▼ **Residence Inn by Marriott-Addison** H
(972) 866-9933. **$179-$199.** 14975 Quorum Dr 75254. Just s of jct Belt Line Rd and Quorum Dr. Int corridors. **Pets:** Accepted.
[🛏] [🤶] [✕] [🛢] [🖵]

ALAMO

▼▼▼ **La Quinta Inn & Suites Alamo At East McAllen** H
(956) 783-6955. **$79-$244.** 909 E Frontage Rd 78516. US 83 exit Alamo Rd. Int corridors. **Pets:** Large, other species. Service with restrictions. [&M] [🛏] [🤶] [✕] [🛢] [🖵]

ALICE

(AAA) ▼▼▼ **BEST WESTERN Executive Inn** M
(361) 664-2133. **$120-$180.** 1350 S US 281 Business Rt 78332. Just s of Cecilia St. Ext corridors. **Pets:** Accepted.
[SAVE] [🛏] [🤶] [✕] [🛢] [🖵]

ALPINE

(AAA) ▼▼▼ **BEST WESTERN Alpine Classic Inn** H
(432) 837-1530. **$95-$116.** 2401 E Hwy 90 79830. Jct SR 118 and US 67/90, 1.5 mi e. Int corridors. **Pets:** Accepted.
[SAVE] [&M] [🛏] [🤶] [✕] [🛢] [🖵]

▼▼▼ **The Holland Hotel** H
(432) 837-2800. **$115-$225, 3 day notice.** 209 W Holland Ave 79830. On US 90 eastbound and 6th St. Int corridors. **Pets:** Accepted.
[🍴] [🤶] [✕] [🎽] [🛢] [🖵]

▼▼ **The Maverick Inn** H ❀
(432) 837-0628. **Call for rates.** 1200 E Holland Ave 79830. Just e of downtown. Ext corridors. **Pets:** $15 one-time fee/room. Designated rooms, service with restrictions, crate. [🤶] [✕] [🎽] [🛢] [🖵]

▼▼ **Oak Tree Inn** H
(432) 837-5711. **Call for rates.** 2407 E Holland Ave (Hwy 90/67) 79830. On US 90, 2 mi e. Int corridors. **Pets:** Accepted.
[🍴] [&M] [🤶] [✕] [🛢] [🖵]

ALVARADO

▼▼ **Super 8** H
(817) 790-7378. **$50-$120.** 5445 S I-35W 76009. I-35W exit 27A (US 67), just e to 1st traffic light, then 0.4 mi n on access road. Int corridors. **Pets:** Accepted. [&M] [🛏] [🤶] [🛢] [🖵]

ALVIN

▼▼ **Americas Best Value Inn & Suites** M
(281) 331-0335. **Call for rates.** 1588 S Hwy 35 Loop 77511. SR 35 Bypass, 0.5 mi sw of SR 6. Ext corridors. **Pets:** Medium. $15 daily fee/pet. Service with restrictions, supervision. [🛏] [🤶] [🛢] [🖵]

AMARILLO

▼▼ **Baymont Inn & Suites** H
(806) 372-1425. **$59-$89.** 1700 I-40 E 79103. I-40 exit 71 (Ross-Osage), just e on south frontage road. Int corridors. **Pets:** Accepted.
[🛏] [🤶] [🛢] [🖵]

(AAA) ▼▼▼ **BEST WESTERN Santa Fe** H ❀
(806) 372-1885. **$90-$110.** 4600 I-40 E 79103. I-40 exit 73 (Eastern St) eastbound; exit Bolton St westbound, U-turn on south frontage road. Int corridors. **Pets:** $20 one-time fee/room. Designated rooms, supervision.
[SAVE] [🛏] [🤶] [🛢] [🖵]

(AAA) ▼▼▼ **Big Texan Inn** M
(806) 372-5000. **Call for rates.** 7701 I-40 E 79118. I-40 exit 75 (Lakeside Dr), just w; on north frontage road. Ext corridors. **Pets:** Accepted.
[SAVE] [🍴] [🛏] [🤶] [🛢] [🖵]

▼▼▼ **Country Inn & Suites By Carlson, I-40 West** H
(806) 356-9977. **$79-$229.** 2000 Soncy Rd 79121. I-40 exit 64 (Soncy Rd), just n. Int corridors. **Pets:** Accepted. 🐾 🛜 🍴 💻

🔵 ▼▼ **Days Inn** H
(806) 359-9393. **$60-$130.** 2102 S Coulter St 79106. I-40 exit 65 (Coulter St), just n. Ext corridors. **Pets:** Accepted.
SAVE 🐾 🛜 🍴 💻

▼▼▼ **Drury Inn & Suites-Amarillo** H
(806) 351-1111. **$120-$199.** 8540 W I-40 79106. I-40 exit 65 (Coulter St), 0.8 mi w; on north service road. Int corridors. **Pets:** $10 daily fee/room. Service with restrictions, supervision. 🅼 🐾 🛜 🍴 💻

▼▼▼ **Holiday Inn Express & Suites** H
(806) 335-2500. **Call for rates.** 9401 I-40 E 79118. I-40 exit 76 (Airport Blvd), just w on north frontage road. Int corridors. **Pets:** Accepted.
🅼 🐾 ✕ 🍴 💻

🔵 ▼▼ **Microtel Inn & Suites by Wyndham Amarillo** H
(806) 372-8373. **$70-$100.** 1501 S Ross St 79102. I-40 exit 71 (Ross-Osage), just n. Int corridors. **Pets:** Dogs only. $25 one-time fee/pet. Designated rooms, service with restrictions, supervision.
SAVE 🅼 🐾 🛜 🍴 💻

🔵 ▼▼ **Quality Inn & Suites Medical Center** H
(806) 358-7861. **$90-$300.** 1610 Coulter St 79106. I-40 exit 65 (Coulter St), 0.6 mi n. Ext/int corridors. **Pets:** Medium. $20 deposit/pet. Designated rooms, service with restrictions, supervision.
SAVE 🐾 🛜 ✕ 🍴 💻

▼▼▼ **Residence Inn by Marriott** H
(806) 354-2978. **$130-$250.** 6700 I-40 W 79106. I-40 exit 66 (Bell St), 0.5 mi w on north frontage road. Int corridors. **Pets:** Large. $50 one-time fee/room. Designated rooms, service with restrictions, supervision.
🅼 🐾 🛜 ✕ 🍴 💻

ANGLETON

🔵 ▼▼ **BEST WESTERN Angleton Inn** H
(979) 849-5822. **Call for rates.** 1809 N Velasco St 77515. Jct SR 35 and Business Rt SR 288, 1 mi n. Ext corridors. **Pets:** $20 one-time fee/room. Service with restrictions, crate. SAVE 🐾 🛜 🍴 💻

▼▼▼ **La Quinta Inn & Suites Angelton** H
(979) 864-3383. **$92-$259.** 2400 W Mulberry St 77515. Jct SR 35 and 288; on northwest corner. Int corridors. **Pets:** Large, other species. Service with restrictions. 🅼 🐾 🛜 ✕ 🍴 💻

ARLINGTON

🔵 ▼▼▼ **Comfort Suites Six Flags in Arlington** H
(817) 460-8700. **$81-$152.** 411 W Road To Six Flags St 76011. I-30 exit 27 (Cooper St) eastbound; exit 28 (Collins St) westbound, just s, then just e. Int corridors. **Pets:** Accepted.
SAVE 🅼 🐾 🛜 ✕ 🍴 💻

▼▼▼ **Hawthorn Suites by Wyndham** H
(817) 640-1188. **$89-$269.** 2401 Brookhollow Plaza Dr 76006. I-30 exit 30 (SR 360), just n to Lamar Blvd, just w to Brookhollow Plaza Dr, then just n. Ext corridors. **Pets:** Large, dogs only. $50 one-time fee/pet. Service with restrictions, crate. 🐾 🛜 🍴 💻

▼▼▼ **Holiday Inn Express Hotel & Suites Arlington Six Flags Area** H
(817) 640-5454. **$89-$199.** 2451 E Randol Mill Rd 76011. I-30 exit 30 (SR 360), 0.4 mi s, then just w. Int corridors. **Pets:** Accepted.
🐾 🛜 ✕ 🍴 💻

▼▼▼ **Homewood Suites by Hilton** H
(817) 633-1594. **$109-$299.** 2401 Road to Six Flags St E 76011. I-30 exit 30 (SR 360), 0.5 mi s on southbound frontage road, then just w. Int corridors. **Pets:** Accepted. 🅼 🐾 🛜 🍴 💻

🔵 ▼▼▼ **Hyatt Place Dallas/Arlington** H
(817) 649-7676. **$79-$299.** 2380 Road to Six Flags St E 76011. I-30 exit 30 (SR 360), 0.5 mi s on southbound frontage road, then just w. Int corridors. **Pets:** Accepted. SAVE 🐾 🛜 ✕ 🍴 💻

▼▼▼ **La Quinta Inn & Suites Dallas/Arlington 6 Flags Dr** H
(817) 640-4142. **$99-$379.** 825 N Watson Rd 76011. SR 360 exit Six Flags Dr northbound; exit Ave H/Lamar Blvd southbound; on southbound frontage road. Int corridors. **Pets:** Large, other species. Service with restrictions. 🐾 🛜 🍴 💻

🔵 ▼▼▼ **Sheraton Arlington Hotel** H
(817) 261-8200. **$99-$399.** 1500 Convention Center Dr 76011. I-30 exit 29 (Ballpark Way), 0.4 mi e on Copeland Rd to Convention Center Dr, then just s. Int corridors. **Pets:** Accepted.
SAVE 🍴 🅼 🐾 🛜 ✕ 🍴 💻

AUSTIN *(Restaurants p. 641)*

🔵 ▼▼▼ **Aloft Austin at the Domain** H
(512) 491-0777. **$139-$299.** 11601 Domain Dr 78758. Loop 1 (Mo-Pac Expwy) exit Burnett Rd/Duval Rd, just e; in The Domain. Int corridors. **Pets:** Accepted. SAVE 🅼 🐾 🛜 ✕ 🍴 💻

🔵 ▼▼▼ **BEST WESTERN Atrium North** H
(512) 339-7311. **$80-$249.** 7928 Gessner Dr 78753. I-35 exit 240A, 0.4 mi w on US 183. Int corridors. **Pets:** Accepted.
SAVE 🐾 🛜 🍴 💻

🔵 ▼▼▼ **BEST WESTERN PLUS Austin Airport Inn & Suites** H
(512) 386-5455. **$99-$159.** 1805 Airport Commerce Dr 78741. Jct SR 71 (E Ben White Blvd) and Riverside Dr, just n; in Airport Commerce Park. Int corridors. **Pets:** Accepted.
SAVE 🅼 🐾 🛜 ✕ 🍴 💻

🔵 ▼▼▼ **BEST WESTERN PLUS Austin City Hotel** H
(512) 444-0561. **$120-$430.** 2200 S I-35 78704. I-35 exit 232A (Oltorf Blvd); on west side access road. Ext/int corridors. **Pets:** Accepted.
SAVE 🍴 🐾 🛜 ✕ 🍴 💻

▼▼ **Candlewood Suites Austin Northwest** H
(512) 338-1611. **Call for rates.** 9701 Stonelake Blvd 78759. Jct Capital of Texas Hwy (SR 360) and Stonelake Blvd, just s. Int corridors. **Pets:** Accepted. 🅼 🛜 🍴 💻

▼▼▼ **Candlewood Suites-South** H
(512) 444-8882. **Call for rates.** 4320 S I-35 78745. I-35 exit 230 (Ben White Blvd/SR 71) northbound; exit 231 (Woodward Rd) southbound; on southbound frontage road. Int corridors. **Pets:** Small. $15 daily fee/room. Service with restrictions, crate. 🅼 🛜 🍴 💻

▼▼▼ **DoubleTree Suites by Hilton Hotel Austin** H
(512) 478-7000. **$184-$609.** 303 W 15th St 78701. Just nw of state capitol building. Int corridors. **Pets:** Accepted.
🍴 🐾 🔊 ✕ 🍴 💻

🔵 ▼▼▼ ▼▼ **The Driskill** H
(512) 474-5911. **$179-$649.** 604 Brazos St 78701. Jct 6th St. Int corridors. **Pets:** Accepted. SAVE ECO 🍴 ✕ 🛜 ✕ 🍴

▼▼▼ **Drury Inn & Suites-Austin North** H
(512) 467-9500. **$120-$194.** 6711 N I-35 78752. I-35 exit 238A; on east frontage road. Int corridors. **Pets:** $10 daily fee/room. Service with restrictions, supervision. 🐾 🛜 🍴 💻

▼▼ **Econo Lodge** H
(512) 835-7070. **$70-$280.** 9102 Burnet Rd 78758. US 183 and Burnet Rd; on northeast corner. Ext corridors. **Pets:** Accepted. 🛜 🍴 💻

▼▼▼ **Embassy Suites Austin Central** H
(512) 454-8004. **$109-$199.** 5901 N I-35 78723. I-35 exit 238A; on east frontage road. Int corridors. **Pets:** Accepted. 🍴 🐾 🛜 🍴 💻

▼▼▼ Extended Stay America Austin Arboretum 🄷

(512) 231-1520. **Call for rates.** 10100 N Capital of Texas Hwy 78759. Jct Loop 1 (Mo-Pac Expwy) and Capital of Texas Hwy (SR 360), just w. Int corridors. **Pets:** Other species. $25 daily fee/pet. Service with restrictions, supervision. 🄼 📶 🛇 🔲 💻

▼▼ Extended Stay America Austin-Arboretum-North 🄷

(512) 833-0898. **Call for rates.** 2700 Gracy Farms Ln 78758. 2 mi n of US 183 on Loop 1 (Mo-Pac Expwy) exit Burnet Rd. Int corridors. **Pets:** Other species. $25 daily fee/pet. Service with restrictions, supervision. 🔼 📶 🔲 💻

▼▼ Extended Stay America Austin Arboretum South 🄷

(512) 837-6677. **Call for rates.** 9100 Waterford Centre Blvd 78758. US 183 exit Burnet Rd; on westbound frontage road. Ext corridors. **Pets:** Other species. $25 daily fee/pet. Service with restrictions, supervision. 📶 🔲 💻

▼▼▼ Extended Stay America-Austin/Downtown/Town Lake 🄷

(512) 476-1818. **Call for rates.** 507 S 1st St 78704. I-35 exit 234B southbound; exit 234A northbound, 1.8 mi w on Cesar Chavez St/E 1st St, then 0.5 mi s. Int corridors. **Pets:** Other species. $25 daily fee/pet. Service with restrictions, supervision. 📶 🔲 💻

▼▼ Extended Stay America Austin-North Central 🄷

(512) 339-6005. **Call for rates.** 8221 N I-35 78753. I-35 exit 241; on east frontage road. Int corridors. **Pets:** Other species. $25 daily fee/pet. Service with restrictions, supervision. 🔼 📶 🔲 💻

▼▼ Extended Stay America Austin Northwest Lakeline Mall 🄷

(512) 258-3365. **Call for rates.** 13858 US Hwy 183 N 78750. Jct US 183 and SR 620; on southwest corner. Int corridors. **Pets:** Other species. $25 daily fee/pet. Service with restrictions, supervision. 🄼 📶 🔲 💻

▼▼ Extended Stay America (Austin/Northwest/Research Park) 🄷

(512) 219-6500. **Call for rates.** 12424 Research Blvd 78759. US 183 exit Oak Knoll Dr; on eastbound frontage road. Int corridors. **Pets:** Other species. $25 daily fee/pet. Service with restrictions, supervision. 🄼 📶 🛇 🔲 💻

▼▼ Extended Stay America Austin Southwest 🄷

(512) 892-4272. **Call for rates.** 5100 US Hwy 290 W 78735. I-35 exit 230; US 290 W exit Brodie Ln, 1 mi w. Int corridors. **Pets:** Other species. $25 daily fee/pet. Service with restrictions, supervision. 🄼 📶 🔲 💻

ⒶⒶⒶ ▼▼▼ Four Seasons Hotel 🄷 ❖

(512) 478-4500. **Call for rates.** 98 San Jacinto Blvd 78701. Jct Congress Ave and Cesar Chavez St; 2 blks e on Lady Bird Lake Tr. Int corridors. **Pets:** $100 one-time fee/room. Designated rooms, service with restrictions, supervision. SAVE 🍽 🔼 🛇 📶 🛇 🔲 💻

▼▼▼ Hampton Inn Northwest 🄷 🐾

(512) 349-9898. $99-$209. 3908 W Braker Ln 78759. 1 mi n of US 183 on Loop 1 (Mo-Pac Expwy) exit W Braker Ln. Int corridors. **Pets:** Designated rooms, service with restrictions, supervision. 🄼 🔼 📶 🛇 🔲 💻

ⒶⒶⒶ ▼▼▼ Hilton Austin 🄷

(512) 482-8000. $129-$389. 500 E 4th St 78701. Jct 4th and Neches sts. Int corridors. **Pets:** Large. $50 one-time fee/pet. Service with restrictions. SAVE 🍽 🄼 🔼 🛇 🔊 🛇 🔲 💻

ⒶⒶⒶ ▼▼ Hilton Austin Airport 🄷

(512) 385-6767. $99-$199. 9515 Hotel Dr 78719. SR 71; service road exit at airport. Int corridors. **Pets:** Accepted. SAVE ECO 🍽 🄼 🔼 🛇 📶 🛇 🔲 💻

▼▼▼ Holiday Inn Express & Suites Austin Airport 🄷

(512) 386-7600. $90-$499. 7601 E Ben White Blvd 78741. I-35 exit 230B (Ben White Blvd/SR 71), 3.2 mi e. Int corridors. **Pets:** Small, dogs only. $50 one-time fee/pet. Designated rooms, service with restrictions, crate. 🄼 🔼 📶 🛇 🔲 💻

▼▼ Holiday Inn Express Hotel & Suites 🄷

(512) 251-9110. **Call for rates.** 14620 N I-35 78728. I-35 exit 247; on west frontage road. Int corridors. **Pets:** Accepted. 🄼 🔼 📶 🛇 🔲 💻

ⒶⒶⒶ ▼▼▼ Homewood Suites-Austin South/Airport 🄷

(512) 445-5050. $129-$199. 4143 Governor's Row 78744. I-35 exit 231 (Ben White Blvd/SR 71) southbound; exit 229 northbound; at Ben White Blvd. Int corridors. **Pets:** Small. $75 one-time fee/pet. Designated rooms, service with restrictions, crate. SAVE 🄼 🔼 📶 🔲 💻

▼▼▼ Homewood Suites by Hilton Arboretum NW 🄷

(512) 349-9966. $109-$229. 10925 Stonelake Blvd 78759. US 183 N to Loop 1 (Mo-Pac Expwy), 1.5 mi n to Braker Ln; on northwest corner. Int corridors. **Pets:** Accepted. 🄼 🔼 📶 🔲 💻

ⒶⒶⒶ ▼▼▼ ▼▼ Hotel Ella 🄷

(512) 495-1800. $269-$849, 3 day notice. 1900 Rio Grande St 78705. Jct Rio Grande St and Martin Luther King Jr Blvd. Int corridors. **Pets:** Accepted. SAVE 🍽 📶 🛇 💻

ⒶⒶⒶ ▼▼▼ HYATT house Austin/Arboretum 🄷

(512) 342-8080. $79-$425. 10001 N Capital of Texas Hwy 78759. US 183, N Capital of Texas Hwy (SR 360), just e. Int corridors. **Pets:** Accepted. SAVE 🔼 📶 🛇 🔲 💻

ⒶⒶⒶ ▼▼▼ Hyatt Place Austin-North Central 🄷

(512) 323-2121. $79-$219. 7522 N I-35 78752. I-35 exit 240A; on west frontage road. Int corridors. **Pets:** Accepted. SAVE 🄼 🔼 📶 🛇 🔲 💻

ⒶⒶⒶ ▼▼▼ ▼▼ Hyatt Regency Austin 🄷

(512) 477-1234. $129-$399. 208 Barton Springs Rd 78704. At south end of Congress Avenue Bridge; on south bank of Town Lake. Int corridors. **Pets:** Accepted. SAVE ECO ➕ 🍽 🄼 🔼 🛇 📶 🛇 🔲 💻

ⒶⒶⒶ ▼▼▼ ▼▼ Hyatt Regency Lost Pines Resort and Spa 🄷

(512) 308-1234. $129-$519, 3 day notice. 575 Hyatt Lost Pines Rd 78612. SR 71, 13 mi e of Austin-Bergstrom International Airport; 9 mi w of Bastrop. Int corridors. **Pets:** Accepted. SAVE ECO 🍽 🄼 🔼 🛇 📶 🛇 🔲 💻

▼▼▼ La Quinta Inn & Suites Austin Airport 🄷

(512) 386-6800. $102-$479. 7625 E Ben White Blvd 78741. I-35 exit 230B (Ben White Blvd/SR 71), 8.8 mi e. Int corridors. **Pets:** Large, other species. Service with restrictions. 🄼 🔼 📶 🔲 💻

ⒶⒶⒶ ▼▼▼ La Quinta Inn & Suites-Austin/Cedar Park-Lakeline 🄷

(512) 568-3538. $79-$469. 10701 Lakeline Mall Dr 78717. Jct US 183 and Lakeline Dr, 0.5 mi e, then just s on Lake Creek Dr. Int corridors. **Pets:** Large, other species. Service with restrictions. SAVE 🄼 🔼 📶 🛇 🔲 💻

▼▼▼ La Quinta Inn & Suites Austin Mopac North 🄷

(512) 832-2121. $89-$384. 11901 N Mo-Pac Expwy 78759. US 183, 2 mi n on Loop 1 (Mo-Pac Expwy) exit Duval Rd. Int corridors. **Pets:** Large, other species. Service with restrictions. 🄼 🔼 📶 🔲 💻

▼▼▼ La Quinta Inn & Suites Austin Southwest at Mopac 🄷

(512) 899-3000. $112-$489. 4525 S Gaines Ranch Loop 78735. Jct Loop 1 (Mo-Pac Expwy), US 290 and SR 71 E; on southbound frontage road. Int corridors. **Pets:** Large, other species. Service with restrictions. 🄼 🔼 📶 🔲 💻

▼▼▼▼ **La Quinta Inn & Suites Round Rock South** H
(512) 246-2800. **$82-$284.** 150 Parker Dr 78728. I-35 exit 250; on west frontage road. Int corridors. **Pets:** Large, other species. Service with restrictions. 🛅M 🛏 🛜 🖥 📱 📺

▼▼▼ **La Quinta Inn Austin Capitol** H
(512) 476-1166. **$112-$709.** 300 E 11th St 78701. Just e of state capitol building. Ext/int corridors. **Pets:** Large, other species. Service with restrictions. 🛏 🛜 🖥 📱 📺

🆎 ▼▼▼▼ **Omni Austin Hotel Downtown** H 🐾
(512) 476-3700. **Call for rates.** 700 San Jacinto Blvd 78701. At 8th St and San Jacinto Blvd. Int corridors. **Pets:** Small. $50 one-time fee/room. Service with restrictions, crate.
[SAVE] 🍽 🛅M 🛏 🖲 ✕ 🖥 📱 📺

🆎 ▼▼▼▼ **Omni Austin Hotel Southpark** H 🐾
(512) 448-2222. **$109-$799.** 4140 Governor's Row 78744. I-35 exit 230B (Ben White Blvd/SR 71) southbound; exit 230 northbound; on east frontage road. Int corridors. **Pets:** Small, other species. $50 one-time fee/room. Service with restrictions, crate.
[SAVE] 🍽 🛅M 🛏 ✕ 🖲 ✕ 🖥 📱 📺

▼▼▼ **Quality Inn & Suites Airport** H
(512) 385-1000. **$80-$130.** 2751 Hwy 71 E 78617. On SR 71, 0.5 mi e of airport. Int corridors. **Pets:** Accepted.
🍽 🛅M 🛏 🛜 ✕ 🖥 📱 📺

🆎 ▼▼▼ **Red Roof Inn Austin South** H
(512) 448-0091. **$69-$260.** 4701 S I-35 78744. I-35 exit 230B (Ben White Blvd/SR 71) southbound; exit 229 (Stassney Rd) northbound; on northbound frontage road. Int corridors. **Pets:** Large, other species. Service with restrictions, supervision. [SAVE] 🛅M 🛏 🛜 ✕ 🖥

🆎 ▼▼▼▼ **Renaissance Austin Hotel** H
(512) 343-2626. **$119-$499.** 9721 Arboretum Blvd 78759. Jct US 183 and N Capital of Texas Hwy (SR 360); southwest corner. Int corridors. **Pets:** Other species. $75 one-time fee/room. Service with restrictions, crate. [SAVE] 🍽 🛅M 🛏 ✕ 🖲 ✕ 🖥 📱 📺

🆎 ▼▼▼ **Residence Inn by Marriott Austin Airport/South** H
(512) 912-1100. **$100-$500.** 4537 S I-35 78744. I-35 exit 229 (Stassney Rd) southbound; exit 230 (Ben White Blvd/SR 71) northbound; on northbound frontage road. Int corridors. **Pets:** Accepted.
[SAVE] 🛏 🛜 ✕ 🖥 📱 📺

🆎 ▼▼▼ **Residence Inn by Marriott Austin/Downtown/ Convention Center** H
(512) 472-5553. **$169-$369.** 300 E 4th St 78701. Between Trinity St and San Jacinto Blvd. Int corridors. **Pets:** Accepted.
[SAVE] 🍽 🛏 🛜 ✕ 🖥 📱 📺

🆎 ▼▼▼ **Residence Inn by Marriott-Austin North/ Parmer Lane** H
(512) 977-0544. **$135-$171.** 12401 N Lamar Blvd 78753. I-35 exit 245, just w. Int corridors. **Pets:** Accepted.
[SAVE] 🛅M 🛏 🛜 ✕ 🖥 📱 📺

▼▼▼ **Staybridge Suites Austin Airport** H
(512) 386-7800. **$130-$150.** 1611 Airport Commerce Dr 78741. Jct SR 71 (E Ben White Blvd) and Riverside Dr, just n. Int corridors. **Pets:** Accepted. 🛅M 🛏 🛜 🖥 📱 📺

▼▼▼ **Staybridge Suites Austin Arboretum** H
(512) 349-0888. **Call for rates.** 10201 Stonelake Blvd 78759. Jct N Capital of Texas Hwy (SR 360) and Stonelake Blvd, 1 blk n. Int corridors. **Pets:** Accepted. 🛅M 🛏 🛜 ✕ 🖥 📱 📺

▼▼▼ **Staybridge Suites Austin Northwest** H
(512) 336-7829. **Call for rates.** 13087 Hwy 183 N, Lot 3 78750. US 183 N exit Anderson Mill Rd, just n of exit on east frontage road; south of Anderson Mill Rd. Int corridors. **Pets:** Accepted.
🛅M 🛏 🛜 ✕ 🖥 📱 📺

▼▼▼ **Studio 6-Northwest #6032** M
(512) 258-3556. **$68-$87.** 11901 Pavilion Blvd 78759. US 183 exit Oak Knoll Dr westbound; exit Duval Rd/Balcones Woods Dr eastbound; on eastbound frontage road. Ext corridors. **Pets:** Other species. $10 daily fee/room. Service with restrictions, crate. 🛜 ✕ 🖥 📱 📺

▼▼▼ **Super 8 Austin North** H
(512) 339-1300. **$64-$209.** 8128 N I-35 78753. I-35 exit 241; on west frontage road. Int corridors. **Pets:** Other species. $25 one-time fee/room. Service with restrictions, supervision. 🛏 🛜 🖥 📱 📺

🆎 ▼▼▼▼ **W Austin** H 🐾
(512) 542-3600. **$299-$699.** 200 Lavaca St 78701. At Lavaca and 2nd sts. Int corridors. **Pets:** Medium. $100 deposit/room, $25 daily fee/room. Service with restrictions. [SAVE] 🍽 🛅M 🛏 ✕ 🖲 ✕ 🖥 📱 📺

🆎 ▼▼▼▼ **Westin Austin at the Domain** H
(512) 832-4197. **$199-$699.** 11301 Domain Dr 78758. Jct Braker Ln and Burnet Rd; on northwest corner; in The Domain. Int corridors. **Pets:** Accepted. [SAVE] 🍽 🛅M 🛏 🛜 ✕ 🖥 📱 📺

▼▼▼ **Wyndham Garden Hotel** H 🐾
(512) 448-2444. **$89-$169.** 3401 I-35 S 78741. I-35 exit 231 (Woodward St) southbound; exit 230 (Ben White Blvd/SR 71) northbound; on northbound frontage road. Ext/int corridors. **Pets:** $50 one-time fee/room. Designated rooms, service with restrictions.
🍽 🛅M 🛏 🛜 ✕ 🖥 📱 📺

BASTROP
▼▼▼ **Comfort Suites** H
(512) 321-3377. **$79-$279.** 505 Agnes St 78602. SR 71 exit Hasler Blvd; on south frontage road. Int corridors. **Pets:** Medium. $35 one-time fee/pet. Designated rooms, no service, supervision.
🛅M 🛏 🛜 ✕ 🖥 📱 📺

▼▼▼ **Quality Inn** H
(512) 321-3303. **$69-$295.** 106 Hasler Blvd 78602. Jct SR 71. Int corridors. **Pets:** Accepted. 🛅M 🛏 🛜 🖥 📱 📺

BAY CITY
▼▼▼ **Comfort Suites** H
(979) 245-9300. **$110-$140.** 5100 7th St 77414. On SR 35 (7th St), 2.2 mi e. Int corridors. **Pets:** Accepted. 🛏 🛜 ✕ 🖥 📱 📺

▼▼▼▼ **La Quinta Inn & Suites Bay City** H
(979) 323-9095. **$89-$199.** 5300 7th St 77414. On SR 35 (7th St), 3 mi e of downtown. Int corridors. **Pets:** Large, other species. Service with restrictions. 🛅M 🛏 🛜 ✕ 🖥 📱 📺

BAYTOWN
▼▼▼ **Baymont Inn & Suites by Wyndham** H
(281) 839-1400. **$79-$159.** 7212 E Point Blvd 77521. I-10 exit 792 (Garth Rd), just n. Int corridors. **Pets:** Accepted. 🛏 🛜 🖥 📱 📺

▼▼▼ **Comfort Suites** H
(281) 421-9764. **$90-$180.** 7209 Garth Rd 77521. I-10 exit 792 (Garth Rd), just n. Int corridors. **Pets:** Very small, other species. $25 daily fee/pet. Designated rooms, service with restrictions, supervision.
🛅M 🛏 🛜 ✕ 🖥 📱 📺

▼▼ **La Quinta Inn & Suites Baytown East** H
(281) 421-5566. **$75-$249.** 5215 I-10 E 77521. I-10 exit 792 (Garth Rd), just ne. Int corridors. **Pets:** Large, other species. Service with restrictions. 🛅M 🛏 🛜 🖥 📱 📺

BEAUMONT
▼▼▼ **Holiday Inn Express Inn & Suites** H
(409) 892-3600. **$119.** 7140 Eastex Frwy 77708. US 69 exit 105; on northbound service road. Int corridors. **Pets:** Medium, dogs only. $50 one-time fee/room. Service with restrictions, crate.
🛅M 🛏 🛜 ✕ 🖥 📱

🔺🔺 ▽▽▽ Holiday Inn Hotel & Suites Beaumont Plaza 🅷

(409) 842-5995. **$109-$149.** 3950 I-10 S 77705. I-10 exit 848 (Walden Rd), just n. Int corridors. **Pets:** Accepted.
SAVE ❕🍴 ➡️ 🛜 ✖️ 🔋 💻

▽▽▽▽ Homewood Suites by Hilton 🅷

(409) 842-9990. **$119-$279.** 3745 IH-10 S 77705. I-10 exit 848 (Walden Rd); on eastbound frontage road. Int corridors. **Pets:** Other species. Service with restrictions, supervision. ⚙️M ➡️ 🛜 🔋 💻

BEEVILLE

🔺🔺 ▽▽▽ BEST WESTERN Texan Inn 🅷

(361) 358-9999. **$110.** 2001 Hwy 59 78102. US 181 at US 59, just e. Ext/int corridors. **Pets:** Large, other species. $10 daily fee/pet. Service with restrictions, crate. SAVE ➡️ 🛜 🔋 💻

BELTON

🔺🔺 ▽▽▽ Budget Host Inn 🅷

(254) 939-0744. **$49-$75, 3 day notice.** 1520 S I-35 76513. I-35 exit 292 southbound; exit 293A northbound; on east frontage road. Ext corridors. **Pets:** $7 daily fee/pet. Service with restrictions, supervision.
SAVE ➡️ 🛜 🔋 💻

BENBROOK

🔺🔺 ▽▽▽ Comfort Suites 🅷

(817) 249-8008. **$90-$170.** 8004 Winbrook Dr 76126. I-20 exit 429B, just n. Int corridors. **Pets:** Accepted. SAVE ➡️ 🛜 ✖️ 🔋 💻

🔺🔺 ▽▽▽ Days Inn 🅷

(817) 249-0076. **$70-$150.** 590 Winscott Rd 76126. I-20 exit 429B, just n. Int corridors. **Pets:** Accepted. SAVE ➡️ 🛜 🔋 💻

▽ Motel 6-#4051 🅷

(817) 249-8885. **$71-$77, 3 day notice.** 8601 Benbrook Blvd (Hwy 377 S) 76126. I-20 exit 429A, 0.7 mi s. Int corridors. **Pets:** Other species. Service with restrictions, crate. ⚙️M ➡️ 🛜 🔋

BIG SPRING

▽▽▽ Holiday Inn Express 🅷

(432) 263-5400. **Call for rates.** 1109 N Aylesford St 79720. I-20 exit 177, just s. Int corridors. **Pets:** Accepted. ⚙️M ➡️ 🛜 🔋 💻

▽▽▽ La Quinta Inn & Suites Big Spring 🅷

(432) 264-0222. **$119-$299.** 1102 I-20 W 79720. I-20 exit 177, just nw. Int corridors. **Pets:** Large, other species. Service with restrictions.
⚙️M ➡️ 🛜 ✖️ 🔋 💻

BOERNE

▽▽▽ Comfort Inn & Suites 🅷

(830) 249-6800. **$79-$179.** 35000 I-10 W 78006. I-10 exit 540 (SR 46), just e. to Norris Ln, then just s. Int corridors. **Pets:** Accepted.
➡️ 🛜 🔋 💻

▽▽▽ Fairfield Inn & Suites by Marriott San Antonio Boerne 🅷

(830) 368-4167. **$93-$229.** 6 Cascade Caverns Rd 78006. I-10 exit 543 (Cascade Caverns Rd), just off westbound access road. Int corridors. **Pets:** Accepted. ➡️ 🛜 ✖️ 🔋 💻

▽▽▽▽ La Quinta Inn & Suites Boerne 🅷

(830) 249-1212. **$75-$239.** 36756 IH-10 W 78006. I-10 exit 539 (Johns Rd) westbound; exit 540 (Bandera Rd) eastbound, U-turn; on westbound frontage road. Int corridors. **Pets:** Large, other species. Service with restrictions. ⚙️M ➡️ 🛜 ✖️ 🔋 💻

BORGER

🔺🔺 ▽▽▽ BEST WESTERN Borger Inn 🅷 🐾

(806) 274-7050. **$89-$159.** 206 S Cedar St 79007. Jct SR 136 and 207, just n. Int corridors. **Pets:** Other species. $20 daily fee/pet. Designated rooms, service with restrictions, crate. SAVE ➡️ 🛜 🔋 💻

▽▽▽ Borger Ambassador Inn 🅷

(806) 273-6000. **$99-$155.** 900 E 3rd St 79007. Corner of SR 152 and Florida St. Int corridors. **Pets:** Medium, dogs only. $250 deposit/room. Designated rooms, service with restrictions, supervision.
⚙️M ➡️ ✖️ 🛜 ✖️ 🔋 💻

BOWIE

🔺🔺 ▽▽▽▽ BEST WESTERN Bowie Inn & Suites 🅷

(940) 872-9595. **$90-$120.** 900 W US Hwy 287 S 76230. Just s of jct SR 59. Int corridors. **Pets:** Small. $15 daily fee/pet. Designated rooms, service with restrictions, supervision. SAVE ➡️ 🛜 ✖️ 🔋 💻

🔺🔺 ▽ Park's Inn Ⓜ

(940) 872-1111. **$60-$70.** 708 W Wise St 76230. 0.5 mi n of jct SR 59; downtown. Ext corridors. **Pets:** Small. $10 daily fee/pet. Designated rooms, service with restrictions, supervision. SAVE 🛜 🔋 💻

BRADY

🔺🔺 ▽▽▽ BEST WESTERN Brady Inn 🅷

(325) 597-3997. **$73-$99.** 2200 S Bridge St 76825. 1.1 mi s on US 87/377. Ext corridors. **Pets:** Small. $10 daily fee/pet. Designated rooms, service with restrictions, crate. SAVE ➡️ 🛜 ✖️ 🔋 💻

BRENHAM

🔺🔺 ▽▽▽▽ BEST WESTERN Inn of Brenham 🅷

(979) 251-7791. **$105-$120.** 1503 Hwy 290 E 77833. Jct SR 36 and US 290, 1.3 mi e. Ext corridors. **Pets:** Medium. $20 daily fee/room. Designated rooms, service with restrictions, crate.
SAVE ❕🍴 ➡️ 🛜 🔋 💻

▽▽▽ Comfort Suites 🅷

(979) 421-8100. **$74-$180.** 2350 S Day St 77833. US 290 exit SR 36 S, just n on Business Rt SR 36. Int corridors. **Pets:** Accepted.
⚙️M ➡️ 🛜 ✖️ 🔋 💻

BROOKSHIRE

▽▽▽ La Quinta Inn & Suites Brookshire 🅷

(281) 375-8888. **$106-$237.** 721 FM 1489 77423. I-10 exit 731; on south frontage road. Int corridors. **Pets:** Large, other species. Service with restrictions. ⚙️M ➡️ 🛜 ✖️ 🔋 💻

BROWNFIELD

🔺🔺 ▽▽▽ BEST WESTERN Caprock Inn 🅷

(806) 637-9471. **$110-$180.** 321 Lubbock Rd 79316. Jct US 385 and 82, just n. Ext corridors. **Pets:** Large, other species. $10 daily fee/pet. Service with restrictions, crate. SAVE ➡️ 🛜 🔋 💻

BROWNSVILLE

🔺🔺 ▽▽▽ Holiday Inn 🅷

(956) 547-1500. **$77-$85.** 3777 North Expwy 78520. US 77 and 83 exit Ruben Torres Sr Blvd (FM 802); on southbound frontage road. Int corridors. **Pets:** Small. $50 one-time fee/pet. Service with restrictions, supervision. SAVE ❕🍴 ➡️ 🛜 🔋 💻

🔺🔺 ▽▽▽ Homewood Suites by Hilton 🅷

(956) 574-6900. **$99-$189.** 3759 North Expwy 78520. US 77 and 83 exit Ruben Torres Sr Blvd (FM 802); on southbound frontage road. Int corridors. **Pets:** Accepted. SAVE ➡️ 🛜 🔋 💻

🔺🔺 ▽▽▽ La Quinta Inn & Suites Brownsville North 🅷

(956) 350-2118. **$79-$189.** 5051 North Expwy (US 77) 78520. US 77 exit Alton Gloor Rd southbound; exit Stillman Rd northbound U-turn; on southbound frontage road. Int corridors. **Pets:** Large, other species. Service with restrictions. SAVE ➡️ 🛜 ✖️ 🔋 💻

▽▽▽ Residence Inn by Marriott Brownsville 🅷

(956) 350-8100. **$149-$159.** 3975 N Expwy 83 78520. US 77 and 83 exit Ruben Torres Sr Blvd (FM 802). Int corridors. **Pets:** Accepted.
⚙️M ➡️ 🛜 ✖️ 🔋 💻

WWWW **Staybridge Suites** H
(956) 504-9500. **$103-$148.** 2900 Pablo Kisel Blvd 78526. US 77 and 83 exit Ruben Torres Sr Blvd (FM 802), 0.8 mi n on frontage road to Pablo Kisel Blvd, then 0.5 mi e. Int corridors. **Pets:** Accepted.

BROWNWOOD
WWWW **La Quinta Inn & Suites** H
(325) 641-1731. **$99-$209.** 103 Market Place Blvd 76801. US 183, just e. Int corridors. **Pets:** Large, other species. Service with restrictions.

BRYAN
AAA WWWW **BEST WESTERN PREMIER Old Town Center** H
(979) 731-5300. **$130-$360.** 1920 Austins Colony Pkwy 77803. SR 6 exit Briarcrest Dr; just n on east frontage road. Int corridors. **Pets:** Accepted. SAVE

WWWW **LaSalle Hotel** H ✿
(979) 822-2000. **$139-$169, 30 day notice.** 120 S Main St 77803. SR 6 exit W William Joel Bryan Pkwy, 2.2 mi w to Main St, then 2 blks s. Int corridors. **Pets:** Medium. $25 daily fee/pet. Designated rooms, service with restrictions, crate.

BUDA
WWWW **Comfort Suites - Buda** H
(512) 295-8600. **Call for rates.** 15295 IH-35 78610. I-35 exit 221; on east frontage road. Int corridors. **Pets:** Accepted.

BURKBURNETT
WWWW **Red River Inn** H
(940) 569-8109. **Call for rates.** 1008 Sheppard Rd 76354. I-44 exit 12, just e. Int corridors. **Pets:** Accepted.

BURLESON
AAA WWWW **BEST WESTERN PLUS Burleson Inn & Suites** H
(817) 744-7747. **Call for rates.** 516 Memorial Plaza 76028. I-35W exit 36 northbound; exit 35 southbound; on northbound access road. Int corridors. **Pets:** Small. $15 daily fee/pet. Designated rooms, service with restrictions, supervision. SAVE

WWWW **La Quinta Inn & Suites** H
(817) 447-6565. **$84-$239.** 225 E Alsbury Blvd 76028. I-35W exit 38 (E Alsbury Blvd), just e. Int corridors. **Pets:** Large, other species. Service with restrictions.

BURNET
AAA WWWW **BEST WESTERN Post Oak Inn** M
(512) 756-4747. **$70-$130.** 908 Buchanan Dr 78611. Jct US 281 and FM 29, 1 mi w. Ext corridors. **Pets:** Accepted.
SAVE

WWWW **Comfort Inn & Suites** H
(512) 756-1789. **$70-$200.** 810 S Water St (US 281) 78611. Jct US 281 and FM 29, 0.5 mi s. Int corridors. **Pets:** Small, dogs only. $10 daily fee/pet. Designated rooms, service with restrictions, supervision.

CAMERON
AAA WWW **Budget Host Inn & Suites** H
(254) 605-0610. **$89-$200.** 102 Lafferty Ave 76520. US 77/190, 0.5 mi s. Int corridors. **Pets:** Medium. $50 daily fee/pet. Designated rooms, service with restrictions, supervision. SAVE

CANTON
AAA WW WW **BEST WESTERN Canton Inn** H
(903) 567-6591. **$89-$189, 3 day notice.** 2251 N Trade Days Blvd 75103. Jct I-20 and SR 19 exit 527. Ext corridors. **Pets:** Accepted.
SAVE

CANYON
AAA WWWW **BEST WESTERN Palo Duro Canyon Inn & Suites** H
(806) 655-1818. **$93-$111.** 2801 4th Ave 79015. I-27 exit 106, 1.6 mi w. Int corridors. **Pets:** Accepted. SAVE

AAA WWWW **Holiday Inn Express Hotel & Suites** H
(806) 655-4445. **Call for rates.** 2901 4th Ave 79015. I-27 exit 106, 1.5 mi w. Int corridors. **Pets:** Accepted.
SAVE

CEDAR PARK
WWW **Candlewood Suites** H
(512) 986-4825. **$89-$159.** 1100 Cottonwood Creek Tr 78613. Jct SR 183A and CR 1431, 1 mi e. Int corridors. **Pets:** Accepted.

WW WW **Comfort Inn** H
(512) 259-1810. **$75-$140.** 300 E Whitestone Blvd 78613. Jct US 183 and CR 1431, just e. Int corridors. **Pets:** Accepted.

WWWW **La Quinta Inn & Suites Austin-Cedar Park** H
(512) 528-9300. **$89-$389.** 1010 E Whitestone Blvd 78613. Jct SR 183A and CR 1431; on southwest corner. Int corridors. **Pets:** Large, other species. Service with restrictions.

CENTER
WWW **Americas Best Value Inn** H
(936) 598-3384. **Call for rates.** 1005 Hurst St 75935. On US 96; jct SR 87. Ext corridors. **Pets:** Accepted.

AAA WWWW **BEST WESTERN PLUS Classic Inn & Suites** H
(936) 591-0002. **$60-$80.** 210 Moffett Dr 75935. Jct US 96 and SR 87, just n. Int corridors. **Pets:** Very small. $10 daily fee/pet. Service with restrictions, crate. SAVE

CHANNELVIEW
WW WW **Days Inn & Suites of Channelview** M
(281) 457-0140. **$70-$110.** 15765 I-10 E Frwy 77530. I-10 exit 783 (Sheldon Rd); on westbound frontage road. Ext corridors. **Pets:** Medium, dogs only. $20 daily fee/pet. Designated rooms, service with restrictions, supervision.

CHILDRESS
AAA WW W **BEST WESTERN Childress** H
(940) 937-6353. **$85.** 1801 Ave F NW (Hwy 287) 79201. Jct US 62/83, just s. Ext corridors. **Pets:** Accepted. SAVE

AAA WWWW **Super 8 Childress** M
(940) 937-8825. **$62-$122.** 411 Ave F NE (Hwy 287 S) 79201. Jct US 83/287, 1.5 mi e. Ext corridors. **Pets:** $13 daily fee/pet. Designated rooms, service with restrictions, crate. SAVE

CLARENDON
AAA WWWW **BEST WESTERN PLUS Red River Inn** H
(806) 874-0160. **$99-$119.** 902 W 2nd St 79226. Jct US 287 and SR 70. Int corridors. **Pets:** Large. $20 daily fee/room. Designated rooms, service with restrictions, crate. SAVE

CLEAR LAKE CITY
WW WW **Candlewood Suites-Houston-Clear Lake** H
(281) 461-3060. **Call for rates.** 2737 Bay Area Blvd 77058. I-45 exit 26 (Bay Area Blvd), 3.7 mi e. Int corridors. **Pets:** Accepted.

WWWW **Residence Inn by Marriott Houston Clear Lake** H
(281) 486-2424. **$98-$159.** 525 Bay Area Blvd 77058. I-45 exit 26 (Bay Area Blvd), 1.2 mi e. Ext/int corridors. **Pets:** Accepted.

CLEBURNE

BEST WESTERN Smithfield Inn M
(817) 556-3330. **$50-$60.** 1707 W Henderson St 76033. 2.5 mi s of jct
SR 4/171/174 and US 67 business route (Courthouse Square); on US
67 business route. Ext corridors. **Pets:** Accepted.

Comfort Inn H
(817) 641-4702. **$80-$118.** 2117 N Main St 76033. On SR 174, just s
of jct US 67. Int corridors. **Pets:** Other species. $10 daily fee/pet. Des-
ignated rooms, service with restrictions, crate.

CLEVELAND

**BEST WESTERN Cleveland Inn &
Suites** H
(281) 659-2700. **$75-$140.** 708 US Hwy 59 S 77328. US 59 exit SR
105; northwest corner. Int corridors. **Pets:** Accepted.

Holiday Inn Express & Suites H
(281) 592-7500. **$70-$110.** 600 Hwy 59 S 77327. US 59 exit Cleveland/
Conroe northbound; exit Cleveland southbound; on northbound frontage
road. Int corridors. **Pets:** Medium. $10 daily fee/pet. Designated rooms,
service with restrictions, supervision.

La Quinta Inn & Suites H
(281) 806-3007. **$79-$199.** 1004 Hwy 59 S 77327. US 59 exit Washington Ave; on northbound frontage road. Int corridors. **Pets:** Large, other
species. Service with restrictions.

CLIFTON

BEST WESTERN Velkommen H
(254) 675-8999. **$95-$105.** 1215 N Ave G 76634. SR 6, 1.5 mi n. Int
corridors. **Pets:** Accepted.

CLUTE

TownePlace Suites by Marriott H
(979) 388-9300. **$149-$169.** 1003 W Hwy 332 77531. On SR 288/332,
just w of jct Business Rt SR 288. Int corridors. **Pets:** Small. $100 one-
time fee/pet. Service with restrictions, supervision.

COLLEGE STATION

Hawthorn Suites by Wyndham H
(979) 695-9500. **$109-$269.** 1010 University Dr E 77840. SR 6 exit
University Dr, 0.5 mi w. Int corridors. **Pets:** Accepted.

Hilton College Station & Conference Center H
(979) 693-7500. **$139-$199.** 801 University Dr E 77840. SR 6 exit University Dr, 1.1 mi w. Int corridors. **Pets:** Accepted.

Homewood Suites-College Station H
(979) 846-0400. **$109-$209.** 950 University Dr E 77840. Jct SR 6 and
60, 1.5 mi e. Int corridors. **Pets:** Small. $100 one-time fee/room. Ser-
vice with restrictions, crate.

Hyatt Place College Station H
(979) 846-9800. **$99-$409.** 1100 University Dr E 77840. Jct University
Dr and Texas Ave, 1 mi e. Int corridors. **Pets:** Accepted.

La Quinta Inn College Station H
(979) 696-7777. **$69-$289.** 607 Texas Ave 77840. Just s on jct SR 60
and 6 business route to Live Oak St, just e. Ext corridors. **Pets:** Large,
other species. Service with restrictions.

Manor Inn College Station H
(979) 764-9540. **$69-$189, 14 day notice.** 2504 Texas Ave S 77840.
2.4 mi s of jct SR 60 (University Dr). Ext corridors. **Pets:** Accepted.

Quality Suites H
(979) 695-9400. **$100-$225.** 3610 Hwy 6 S 77845. Jct SR 6 business
route; just s on west access road. Int corridors. **Pets:** Accepted.

**Residence Inn by Marriott College
Station** H
(979) 268-2200. **$119-$229.** 720 University Dr E 77840. Jct Texas Ave,
0.5 mi e. Int corridors. **Pets:** Accepted.

TownePlace Suites by Marriott H
(979) 260-8500. **$149-$209.** 1300 University Dr E 77840. SR 6 exit
University Dr, 1 mi w. Ext corridors. **Pets:** Accepted.

COLUMBUS *(Restaurants p. 641)*

Americas Best Value Inn H
(979) 732-6293. **Call for rates.** 2436 Hwy 71 S 78934. I-10 exit 696
(SR 71). Ext corridors. **Pets:** Accepted.

Holiday Inn Express Hotel & Suites H
(979) 733-9300. **$114-$123.** 4321 I-10 78934. I-10 exit 696 (SR 71),
just w on westbound service road. Int corridors. **Pets:** Medium. $25
one-time fee/pet. Service with restrictions, supervision.

CONROE

Baymont Inn & Suites-Conroe/Woodlands H
(936) 539-5100. **$69-$99.** 1506 Interstate 45 S 77304. I-45 exit 85
(Gladstell St) northbound; exit 84 (Frazier St) southbound. Int corridors.
Pets: Dogs only. $10 daily fee/pet. Service with restrictions.

La Quinta Inn & Suites Conroe H
(936) 228-0790. **$94-$234.** 4006 Sprayberry Ln 77303. I-45 exit 91
(League Line Rd), just e. Int corridors. **Pets:** Large, other species. Service with restrictions.

COPPERAS COVE

Comfort Suites H
(254) 518-8840. **Call for rates.** 1816 Martin Luther King Jr Dr 76522.
Jct US 190 and Constitution Dr, just s. Int corridors. **Pets:** Accepted.

CORPUS CHRISTI

BEST WESTERN Marina Grand Hotel H
(361) 883-5111. **$99-$299.** 300 N Shoreline Blvd 78401. Center of
downtown. Int corridors. **Pets:** Medium. $20 daily fee/pet. Designated
rooms, service with restrictions, supervision.

BEST WESTERN on the Island M
(361) 949-2300. **$70-$300.** 14050 S Padre Island Dr 78418. On Park
Rd 22. Ext corridors. **Pets:** Accepted.

Budget Inn & Suites M
(361) 884-2485. **$60-$200.** 801 S Shoreline Blvd 78401. I-37 exit
Shoreline Blvd; between Park and Fuman aves. Ext corridors.
Pets: $25 daily fee/pet. Designated rooms, service with restrictions,
supervision.

Econo Lodge Inn & Suites M
(361) 883-7400. **$60-$160.** 722 N Port Ave 78408. I-37 exit 1D (Port
Ave); on southbound frontage road. Ext corridors. **Pets:** Accepted.

Emerald Beach Hotel H
(361) 883-5731. **$139-$199.** 1102 S Shoreline Blvd 78401. 1.5 mi s on
bay from downtown marina. Ext/int corridors. **Pets:** Medium. $35 one-
time fee/room. Service with restrictions, crate.

▼▼▼ **Homewood Suites by Hilton** 🄷

(361) 854-1331. **$109-$249.** 5201 Crosstown Expwy (SR 286) 78417. I-37 exit SR 358 E (Greenwood Dr), 0.6 mi e; on eastbound access road. Int corridors. **Pets:** Large, other species. $75 one-time fee/room. Service with restrictions, supervision. 🈁 🛜 🛏 💻

▼▼▼ **La Quinta Inn & Suites Corpus Christi Airport** 🄷

(361) 299-2600. **$105-$259.** 546 S Padre Island Dr 78405. SR 358 exit Old Brownsville Rd; on frontage road. Int corridors. **Pets:** Large, other species. Service with restrictions. 🅼 🈁 🛜 ✖ 🛏 💻

▼▼▼ **La Quinta Inn & Suites Northwest** 🄷

(361) 241-4245. **$95-$229.** 10446 I-37 78410. I-37 exit 11A (McKinzie Rd); on northbound frontage road. Int corridors. **Pets:** Large, other species. Service with restrictions. 🛜 ✖ 🛏 💻

▼▼ **La Quinta Inn Corpus Christi South** 🄷

(361) 991-5730. **$69-$254.** 6225 S Padre Island Dr 78412. SR 358 exit Airline Rd. Ext corridors. **Pets:** Large, other species. Service with restrictions. 🈁 🛜 🛏 💻

🄰🄰🄰 ▼▼▼▼ **Omni Corpus Christi Hotel** 🄷 ❀

(361) 887-1600. **$149-$289.** 900 N Shoreline Blvd 78401. Downtown. Int corridors. **Pets:** Small, dogs only. $50 one-time fee/room. Service with restrictions, supervision. (SAVE) 🍽 🈁 ✖ 🛰 ✖ 🛏 💻

▼▼▼ **Residence Inn by Marriott** 🄷

(361) 985-1113. **$150-$220.** 5229 Blanche Moore Dr 78411. SR 358 E exit Everhart Rd, 0.3 mi e. Int corridors. **Pets:** Accepted. 🈁 🛜 ✖ 🛏 💻

▼▼▼ **Staybridge Suites** 🄷

(361) 857-7766. **$150-$250.** 5201 Oakhurst Dr 78411. SR 358 exit Weber St. Int corridors. **Pets:** Large. $75 one-time fee/room. Service with restrictions, supervision. 🛜 ✖ 🛏 💻

🄰🄰🄰 ▼▼▼ **Surfside Condominiums** 🄲🄾

(361) 949-8128. **$140-$265, 3 day notice.** 15005 Windward Dr 78418. Park Rd 22 on N Padre Island Dr, jct Whitecap Blvd, 0.6 mi n to Windward Dr, then 0.8 mi w. Ext corridors. **Pets:** Small. $20 daily fee/pet. Service with restrictions. (SAVE) 🈁 🛜 ✖ 🛏 💻

CORSICANA

🄰🄰🄰 ▼▼▼ **BEST WESTERN PLUS Executive Inn** 🄷 ❀

(903) 872-0020. **$76-$169.** 2100 E Hwy 31 75109. I-45 exit 231, just e. Int corridors. **Pets:** Other species. $10 daily fee/pet. Designated rooms, service with restrictions, supervision. (SAVE) 🅼 🈁 🛜 🛏 💻

COTULLA

🄰🄰🄰 ▼▼▼ **BEST WESTERN Cowboy Inn** 🄷

(830) 879-3100. **$146-$230.** 145 W FM 468 78014. I-35 exit 57 (FM 468), just w. Ext/int corridors. **Pets:** Medium. $10 daily fee/pet. Service with restrictions, supervision. (SAVE) 🈁 🛜 ✖ 🛏 💻

CRESSON

🄰🄰🄰 ▼▼▼ **Scottish Inn** 🄷

(817) 396-4480. **$90-$150.** 9120 E Hwy 377 76035. 0.4 mi s of jct US 377 and SR 171. Int corridors. **Pets:** Accepted. (SAVE) 🈁 🛜 💻

DALHART

🄰🄰🄰 ▼▼▼ **BEST WESTERN Nursanickel Motel** 🄷

(806) 244-5637. **$100-$150.** 102 Scott Ave (Hwy 87 S) 79022. Just s of jct US 54 and 87. Ext corridors. **Pets:** Medium. $10 daily fee/pet. Designated rooms, service with restrictions, supervision. (SAVE) 🈁 🛜 🛏 💻

🄰🄰🄰 ▼▼▼ **Super 8 Dalhart** 🄼

(806) 249-8526. **$60-$85.** 403 Tanglewood Rd (Hwy 54 E) 79022. Jct US 87 and 54, 0.5 mi e. Int corridors. **Pets:** Medium. $25 deposit/pet. Designated rooms, supervision. (SAVE) 🛜 🛏 💻

DALLAS *(Restaurants p. 641)*

🄰🄰🄰 ▼▼▼ **Aloft Downtown Dallas** 🄷

(214) 761-0000. **$199-$399.** 1033 Young St 75202. Northeast corner of Griffin and Young sts. Int corridors. **Pets:** Accepted. (SAVE) 📶 🅼 🈁 🛜 ✖ 🛏 💻

🄰🄰🄰 ▼▼▼ **Baymont Inn & Suites Dallas Love Field** 🄷

(214) 350-5577. **$79-$129.** 2370 W Northwest Hwy 75220. I-35E exit 436 (Northwest Hwy/Loop 12), 0.8 mi e. Int corridors. **Pets:** Very small. $100 deposit/room, $10 daily fee/pet. Designated rooms, service with restrictions, crate. (SAVE) 🈁 🛜 ✖ 🛏 💻

🄰🄰🄰 ▼▼▼ **BEST WESTERN Cityplace Inn** 🄷

(214) 827-6080. **$99-$179.** 4150 N Central Expwy 75204. US 75 exit 1B (Fitzhugh Ave) southbound; exit 2 (Fitzhugh Ave) northbound. Ext corridors. **Pets:** Accepted. (SAVE) 🍽 🈁 🛜 🛏 💻

▼▼ **Candlewood Suites-Dallas by the Galleria** 🄷

(972) 233-6888. **$85-$135.** 13939 Noel Rd 75240. Jct Dallas Pkwy and Spring Valley, just e to Noel Rd, just s. Int corridors. **Pets:** Accepted. 🅼 🛜 🛏 💻

🄰🄰🄰 ▼▼ **Candlewood Suites Dallas Market Center** 🄷

(214) 631-3333. **$89-$119, 3 day notice.** 7930 N Stemmons Frwy 75247. I-35 exit 433B (Mockingbird Ln); on northbound frontage road. Int corridors. **Pets:** Accepted. (SAVE) 🈁 🛜 ✖ 🛏 💻

▼▼ **Candlewood Suites Dallas North/Richardson** 🄷

(972) 669-9606. **Call for rates.** 12525 Greenville Ave 75243. I-635 exit 18A (Greenville Ave), just n, then just w on Amberton Pkwy. Int corridors. **Pets:** Accepted. 🅼 🛏 💻

🄰🄰🄰 ▼▼ **Comfort Inn & Suites Market Center** 🄷

(214) 461-2677. **$80-$109.** 7138 N Stemmons Frwy 75247. I-35E exit 433B (Mockingbird Ln) northbound; exit 432B (Commonwealth Dr) southbound, turn under freeway, 0.7 mi on north access road. Int corridors. **Pets:** Large, other species. $25 one-time fee/pet. Service with restrictions, crate. (SAVE) 🛜 ✖ 🛏 💻

▼▼▼ **Country Inn & Suites Dallas Love Field/Medical Center** 🄷

(214) 352-7676. **Call for rates.** 2383 Stemmons Tr 75220. I-35E exit 436 (Northwest Hwy/Loop 12), just e, then just s. Int corridors. **Pets:** Accepted. 🄴🄲🄾 🈁 🛜 ✖ 🛏 💻

▼▼▼ **Dallas Marriott Suites Medical/Market Center** 🄷

(214) 905-0050. **$89-$269.** 2493 N Stemmons Frwy 75207. I-35E exit 431 (Medical District Dr); on southbound frontage road. Int corridors. **Pets:** Accepted. 🄴🄲🄾 🍽 🅼 🈁 🛰 ✖ 🛏 💻

🄰🄰🄰 ▼▼▼ **Embassy Suites Hotel-Dallas/Love Field** 🄷

(214) 357-4500. **$99-$259.** 3880 W Northwest Hwy 75220. Just se of jct Northwest Hwy (Loop 12) and Marsh Ln. Int corridors. **Pets:** Accepted. (SAVE) 🍽 🅼 🈁 🛜 🛏 💻

🄰🄰🄰 ▼▼▼ **The Fairmont Dallas** 🄷

(214) 720-2020. **$149-$649, 3 day notice.** 1717 N Akard St 75201. Corner of Ross Ave and N Akard St. Int corridors. **Pets:** Accepted. (SAVE) 🄴🄲🄾 🍽 🅼 🈁 🛰 ✖ 💻

🄰🄰🄰 ▼▼▼ **Hawthorn Suites by Wyndham Dallas Park Central** 🄷

(972) 391-0000. **$85-$120.** 7880 Alpha Rd 75240. I-635 exit 19B (Coit Rd), 0.3 mi n, then just w. Int corridors. **Pets:** Accepted. (SAVE) 🈁 🛜 ✖ 🛏 💻

The Highland Dallas, Curio Collection by Hilton 🅷
(214) 520-7969. **Call for rates.** 5300 E Mockingbird Ln 75206. US 75 exit 3 (Mockingbird Ln); on southeast corner. Int corridors.
Pets: Accepted.

Hilton Dallas Lincoln Centre 🅷 ☙
(972) 934-8400. **$131-$183.** 5410 LBJ Frwy 75240. Jct I-635 and Dallas North Tollway/Dallas Pkwy; I-635 exit 22D (Dallas Pkwy) eastbound; exit 22B (Dallas Pkwy/Inwood Rd) westbound, just e on frontage road. Int corridors. **Pets:** Large. $50 one-time fee/room. Service with restrictions.

Holiday Inn Dallas Market Center 🅷
(214) 219-3333. **Call for rates.** 4500 Harry Hines Blvd 75219. I-35E exit 430B (Market Center Blvd), just e. Int corridors. **Pets:** Accepted.

Holiday Inn Dallas Park Cities 🅷
(214) 750-6060. **$99-$199.** 6070 N Central Expwy 75206. US 75 exit 3 (Mockingbird Ln); on northbound frontage road. Int corridors.
Pets: Accepted.

Homewood Suites by Hilton - I-635 Greenville 🅷
(972) 437-6966. **$99-$179.** 9169 Markville Dr 75243. I-635 exit 18A (Greenville Ave S), just s, then just e. Int corridors. **Pets:** Accepted.

Homewood Suites Dallas Market Center 🅷
(214) 819-9700. **$129-$259.** 2747 N Stemmons Frwy 75207. I-35E exit 432A (Inwood Rd), just s. Int corridors. **Pets:** Accepted.

Hotel Indigo Dallas Downtown 🅷
(214) 741-7700. **$89-$149, 3 day notice.** 1933 Main St 75201. Jct Main and Harwood sts; on northwest corner. Int corridors. **Pets:** Accepted.

Hotel St. Germain 🅲🅸
(214) 871-2516. **$305-$700, 7 day notice.** 2516 Maple Ave 75201. I-35 exit 430A (Oak Lawn Ave), 0.5 mi e, then 1 mi s. Int corridors.
Pets: Accepted.

Hotel ZaZa 🅷
(214) 468-8399. **$295.** 2332 Leonard St 75201. Jct Maple Ave/Routh St and McKinney Ave; southeast corner. Int corridors. **Pets:** Accepted.

HYATT house Dallas/Lincoln Park 🅷
(214) 696-1555. **$89-$299.** 8221 N Central Expwy 75225. US 75 exit 5A southbound; exit 4B northbound, just w on Caruth Haven to Lincoln Pl, then just n. Int corridors. **Pets:** Accepted.

HYATT house Dallas/Uptown 🅷
(214) 965-9990. **$89-$299.** 2914 Harry Hines Blvd 75201. I-35 exit 430A (Oak Lawn Ave), just n to Harry Hines Blvd, then 0.6 mi s. Int corridors. **Pets:** Accepted.

Hyatt Place Dallas-North/by the Galleria 🅷
(972) 716-2001. **$74-$189.** 5229 Spring Valley Rd 75254. Jct Dallas North Tollway, just e. Int corridors. **Pets:** Accepted.

Hyatt Place Dallas/Park Central 🅷
(972) 458-1224. **$69-$199.** 12411 N Central Expwy 75243. US 75 exit 8B (Coit Rd) northbound; exit 8 (Coit Rd) southbound; on southbound access road. Int corridors. **Pets:** Accepted.

Hyatt Regency Dallas at Reunion 🅷 ☙
(214) 651-1234. **$99-$499.** 300 Reunion Blvd 75207. I-35E and US 77 exit Reunion Blvd, just e; I-30 exit Commerce St eastbound, just n. Int corridors. **Pets:** Medium, dogs only. $100 one-time fee/pet. Designated rooms, service with restrictions, supervision.

The Joule 🅷
(214) 748-1300. **Call for rates.** 1530 Main St 75201. Center. Int corridors. **Pets:** Accepted.

La Quinta Inn & Suites Dallas North Central 🅷
(214) 361-8200. **$79-$384.** 10001 N Central Expwy 75231. US 75 exit 6 (Walnut Hill Ln/Meadow Rd) northbound, 0.5 mi n to Meadow Rd, then U-turn under highway; exit 7 (Royal St/Meadow Rd) southbound, 1 mi s on feeder. Int corridors. **Pets:** Large, other species. Service with restrictions.

Le Meridien Dallas by the Galleria 🅷
(972) 503-8700. **Call for rates.** 13402 Noel Rd 75240. Dallas Pkwy exit Alpha Rd, just e to Noel Rd, just s. Int corridors. **Pets:** Accepted.

Le Méridien Dallas, The Stoneleigh 🅷
(214) 871-7111. **Call for rates.** 2927 Maple Ave 75201. I-35E exit 430A (Oak Lawn Ave), 0.5 mi n, then 1.2 mi s. Int corridors. **Pets:** Accepted.

Magnolia Hotel Dallas 🅷
(214) 915-6500. **$129-$259.** 1401 Commerce St 75201. Corner of Commerce and Akard sts. Int corridors. **Pets:** Accepted.

MCM Elegante Hotel & Suites 🅷
(214) 351-4477. **$89-$139, 7 day notice.** 2330 W Northwest Hwy 75220. I-35E exit 436, just e. Ext/int corridors. **Pets:** Small. $50 one-time fee/pet. Service with restrictions, supervision.

Residence Inn by Marriott Dallas Central Expressway 🅷
(214) 750-8220. **$79-$151.** 10333 N Central Expwy 75231. US 75 exit 6 (Walnut Hill Ln/Meadow Rd) northbound, 0.5 mi n to Meadow Rd, U-turn under highway; exit 7 (Royal St/Meadow Rd) southbound, 1 mi s on access road. Ext/int corridors. **Pets:** Accepted.

Residence Inn by Marriott-Dallas Market Center 🅷
(214) 631-2472. **$79-$199.** 6950 N Stemmons Frwy 75247. I-35E exit 432B (Commonwealth Ln), 0.6 mi n on northbound frontage road. Ext/int corridors. **Pets:** Accepted.

The Ritz-Carlton, Dallas 🅷
(214) 922-0200. **$399-$799.** 2121 McKinney Ave 75201. SR 366 (Woodall Rodgers Frwy) exit Pearl St, just sw to Olive St, then just nw. Int corridors. **Pets:** Accepted.

Rosewood Crescent Hotel 🅷
(214) 871-3200. **$300-$3000.** 400 Crescent Ct 75201. Corner of Crescent Ct and McKinney Ave; uptown. Int corridors. **Pets:** Accepted.

Rosewood Mansion on Turtle Creek 🅷 ☙
(214) 559-2100. **$270-$5000.** 2821 Turtle Creek Blvd 75219. 2 mi nw, entrance on Gillespie St, just e of jct Gillespie St and Oak Lawn Ave. Int corridors. **Pets:** $100 one-time fee/pet. Service with restrictions, supervision.

Sheraton Dallas Hotel 🅷
(214) 922-8000. **$99-$369.** 400 N Olive St 75201. At Live Oak and Olive sts, just w off Central Expwy. Int corridors. **Pets:** Accepted.

▼▼▼ **Staybridge Suites North Dallas** 🅷

(972) 726-9990. **$89-$249.** 16060 N Dallas Pkwy 75248. Dallas North Tollway exit Keller Springs, just e to Knoll Tr, then just s. Int corridors. **Pets:** Small, dogs only. $75 one-time fee/pet. Designated rooms, service with restrictions, supervision. 🆓ᴹ 🛄 ⊠ 🛜 ✕ 🗎 📺

ⒶⒶⒶ ▼▼▼▼ **Warwick Melrose Hotel**
Dallas 🅷 🐾

(214) 521-5151. **$149-$599.** 3015 Oak Lawn Ave 75219. I-35E exit 430 (Oak Lawn Ave), 0.8 mi n; entrance off Cedar Springs, just n. Int corridors. **Pets:** Medium, dogs only. $50 daily fee/pet. Designated rooms, service with restrictions, crate. 🆓 🍽 🆂⊚ ✕ 🗎 📺

ⒶⒶⒶ ▼▼▼▼ **W Dallas Victory Hotel &**
Residences 🅷

(214) 397-4100. **$299-$399.** 2440 Victory Park Ln 75219. Southwest corner of Olive and N Houston sts; uptown Dallas; across from American Airlines Center. Int corridors. **Pets:** Accepted.

🆓 🍽 🛄 🆂⊚ ✕

ⒶⒶⒶ ▼▼▼▼ **The Westin Dallas Park Central** 🅷

(972) 385-3000. **Call for rates.** 12720 Merit Dr 75251. I-635 exit 19C (Coit Rd) eastbound; exit 19B (US 75/Coit Rd) westbound; 0.3 mi w of jct US 75. Int corridors. **Pets:** Accepted.

🆓 🍽 🛄 🛜 ✕ 🗎 📺

ⒶⒶⒶ ▼▼▼▼ **The Westin Galleria, Dallas** 🅷

(972) 934-9494. **Call for rates.** 13340 Dallas Pkwy 75240. Just n of jct I-635 and N Dallas Pkwy. Int corridors. **Pets:** Accepted.

🆓 🍽 🆓ᴹ 🛄 🆂⊚ ✕ 📺

ⒶⒶⒶ ▼▼▼▼ **Wyndham Dallas Suites Park Central** 🅷

(972) 233-7600. **$79-$149.** 7800 Alpha Rd 75240. I-635 exit 19C (Coit Rd) eastbound; exit 19B (Coit Rd) westbound, just n, then just w. Int corridors. **Pets:** Accepted. 🆓 🍽 🛄 🛜 ✕ 🗎 📺

DECATUR

ⒶⒶⒶ ▼▼▼ **Baymont Inn & Suites** 🅷

(940) 627-3338. **$46-$88.** 600 W Hale Ave 76234. Just s of jct Business Rt US 380 and 287. Int corridors. **Pets:** Medium. $18 daily fee/pet. Designated rooms, service with restrictions, supervision.

🆓 🛜 ✕ 🗎 📺

ⒶⒶⒶ ▼▼▼ **BEST WESTERN Decatur Inn** Ⓜ

(940) 627-5982. **$72-$80.** 1801 S Hwy 287 76234. 0.6 mi s of jct Business Rt US 380. Ext corridors. **Pets:** Accepted.

🆓 🛄 🛜 🗎 📺

▼▼ **Econo Lodge Decatur** 🅷

(940) 627-6919. **$55-$65.** 1709 US 287 76234. 0.6 mi s of jct Business Rt US 380. Ext corridors. **Pets:** $10 daily fee/pet. Service with restrictions, supervision. 🛄 🛜 🗎 📺

ⒶⒶⒶ ▼▼▼ **Holiday Inn Express Hotel & Suites** 🅷

(940) 627-0776. **Call for rates.** 1051 N Hwy 287 76234. Just n of jct US 380 and 287. Int corridors. **Pets:** Accepted.

🆓 🛄 🛜 🗎 📺

DEL RIO

ⒶⒶⒶ ▼▼▼ **BEST WESTERN Inn of Del Rio** Ⓜ

(830) 775-7511. **$80-$85.** 810 Veterans Blvd 78840. Between E 6th and E 7th sts. Ext corridors. **Pets:** Accepted. 🆓 🛄 🛜 🗎 📺

ⒶⒶⒶ ▼▼▼▼ **Ramada** 🅷

(830) 775-1511. **$89-$169.** 2101 Veterans Blvd 78840. 1.8 mi nw on US 90, 277 and 377. Ext/int corridors. **Pets:** Accepted.

🆓 🍽 🛄 ⊠ 🛜 🗎 📺

DENISON

ⒶⒶⒶ ▼▼▼▼ **BEST WESTERN PLUS Texoma Hotel &**
Suites 🅷

(903) 327-8883. **$100-$160.** 810 N US Hwy 75 75020. US 75 exit 69 (Morton Rd); on northbound frontage road. Int corridors. **Pets:** Accepted. 🆓 🆓ᴹ 🛄 🛜 ✕ 🗎 📺

DENTON

▼▼ **Days Inn Denton** 🅷

(940) 383-1471. **$46-$70.** 4211 I-35N 76207. I-35 exit 469 (University Dr), just w, then just n. Int corridors. **Pets:** Accepted.

🛄 🛜 🗎 📺

▼▼▼ **Homewood Suites by Hilton-Denton** 🅷

(940) 382-0420. **$139-$189.** 2907 Shoreline Dr 76210. I-35E exit 462 (State School Rd), just w to Unicorn Lake, 0.4 mi n, then just w. Int corridors. **Pets:** Accepted. 🛄 🛜 🗎 📺

DESOTO

▼▼▼ **TownePlace Suites by Marriott Dallas**
DeSoto 🅷

(972) 780-9300. **$109-$239.** 2700 Travis St 75115. US 67 exit Cockrell Hill; on northbound service road. Int corridors. **Pets:** Accepted.

🆓ᴹ 🛄 🛜 ✕ 🗎 📺

DONNA

▼▼ **Victoria Palms Inn & Suites** 🅷

(956) 464-7801. **$55-$145, 3 day notice.** 602 N Victoria Rd 78537. US 83 exit Victoria Rd. Ext corridors. **Pets:** Small. $75 one-time fee/room, $20 daily fee/room. Designated rooms, service with restrictions, crate.

🍽 🛄 ⊠ 🛜 ✕ 🗎 📺

DRIPPING SPRINGS

▼▼▼ **Sleep Inn & Suites** 🅷

(512) 858-2400. **$50-$75.** 2720 E US Hwy 290 78620. On US 290, 2.5 mi e. Int corridors. **Pets:** Accepted. 🆓ᴹ 🛄 🛜 ✕ 🗎 📺

DUMAS

ⒶⒶⒶ ▼▼▼ **BEST WESTERN Windsor Inn** 🅷

(806) 935-9644. **$90-$110.** 1701 S Dumas Ave 79029. US 287, 2 mi s of US 87 and SR 152. Ext corridors. **Pets:** Accepted.

🆓 🛄 ⊠ 🛜 🗎 📺

ⒶⒶⒶ ▼▼▼ **Days Inn & Suites** 🅷

(806) 935-2222. **$75-$108.** 1610 S Dumas Ave 79029. Just s on US 287. Int corridors. **Pets:** Dogs only. $25 one-time fee/pet. Service with restrictions, supervision. 🆓 🆓ᴹ 🛄 ⊠ 🛜 ✕ 🗎 📺

EAGLE PASS

▼▼▼ **TownePlace Suites by Marriott Eagle Pass** 🅷

(830) 757-0077. **$99-$189.** 2033 N Veterans Blvd 78852. 1.5 mi n on Loop 431 (US 277). Int corridors. **Pets:** Accepted. 🛜 ✕ 🗎 📺

EASTLAND

▼▼▼ **La Quinta Inn & Suites Eastland** 🅷

(254) 629-1414. **$89-$199.** 10150 IH-20 76448. I-20 exit 343; on north service road. Int corridors. **Pets:** Large, other species. Service with restrictions. 🆓ᴹ 🛄 🛜 ✕ 🗎 📺

▼▼ **Super 8 & RV Park** Ⓜ

(254) 629-3336. **$50-$80.** 3900 I-20 E 76448. I-20 exit 343; on north service road. Ext corridors. **Pets:** Accepted. 🛄 🛜 🗎 📺

EDINBURG

ⒶⒶⒶ ▼▼▼ **BEST WESTERN PLUS Edinburg Inn &**
Suites 🅷

(956) 318-0442. **$90-$200.** 2708 S Bus Hwy 281 78539. US 281 exit Canton Ave, 1 mi w to Business Rt US 281. Ext corridors. **Pets:** Very small. $15 daily fee/pet. Designated rooms, service with restrictions, supervision. 🆓 🆓ᴹ 🛜 🗎 📺

EL PASO

AAA ▼▼▼ BEST WESTERN Sunland Park Inn M
(915) 587-4900. **$69-$89.** 1045 Sunland Park Dr 79922. I-10 exit 13 (Sunland Park Dr), just s. Ext corridors. **Pets:** Accepted.
[SAVE] [≈] [≋] [🛏] [🖵]

▼▼▼ Candlewood Suites H
(915) 755-9000. **$99-$119.** 4631 Cohen Ave 79924. US 54 exit 28 (Diana Dr) northbound, 1 mi n, then just e; exit southbound, 1 mi s, U-turn under freeway, 1 mi n, then just e. Int corridors. **Pets:** Accepted.
[&M] [≋] [✕] [🛏] [🖵]

▼▼ Chase Suites Hotel H
(915) 772-8000. **Call for rates.** 6791 Montana Ave 79925. I-10 exit 25 (Airway Blvd), 1 mi n, then just e. Ext corridors. **Pets:** Accepted.
[≈] [≋] [✕] [🛏] [🖵]

▼▼ Comfort Suites by Choice Hotels H
(915) 587-5300. **$79-$124.** 949 Sunland Park Dr 79922. I-10 exit 13 (Sunland Park Dr), just s. Int corridors. **Pets:** Accepted.
[≈] [≋] [✕] [🛏] [🖵]

AAA ▼▼▼ Country Inn & Suites El Paso Sunland H
(915) 833-2900. **$99-$149.** 900 Sunland Park Dr 79922. I-10 exit 13 (Sunland Park Dr), just s. Ext corridors. **Pets:** $50 one-time fee/room. Designated rooms, service with restrictions, crate.
[SAVE] [¶] [≈] [≋] [🛏] [🖵]

▼▼▼ GuestHouse International Suites H
(915) 772-0395. **$79-$104.** 1940 Airway Blvd 79925. I-10 exit 25 (Airway Blvd), 1.2 mi n. Int corridors. **Pets:** Small. $75 deposit/room, $10 daily fee/pet. Service with restrictions, supervision.
[&M] [≈] [≋] [✕] [🛏] [🖵]

AAA ▼▼▼ Holiday Inn Express El Paso-Central H ✿
(915) 544-3333. **$79-$139.** 409 E Missouri St 79901. I-10 exit 19B westbound (downtown); exit 19 eastbound, just e. Int corridors.
Pets: $25 one-time fee/room. Crate. [SAVE] [≈] [≋] [✕] [🛏] [🖵]

AAA ▼▼▼ Hyatt Place El Paso Airport H
(915) 771-0022. **$89-$205.** 6030 Gateway Blvd E 79905. I-10 exit 24B (Geronimo Dr) eastbound; exit 24 westbound, 0.6 mi to Trowbridge Dr, U-turn under interstate; on eastbound service road. Int corridors.
Pets: Accepted. [SAVE] [¶] [&M] [≈] [≋] [✕] [🛏] [🖵]

▼▼ La Quinta Inn & Suites El Paso East H
(915) 591-3300. **$49-$200.** 7944 Gateway Blvd E 79915. I-10 exit 28B. Int corridors. **Pets:** Large, other species. Service with restrictions.
[&M] [≈] [≋] [🛏] [🖵]

▼▼ La Quinta Inn El Paso Lomaland H
(915) 591-2244. **$62-$160.** 11033 Gateway Blvd W 79935. I-10 exit 29 eastbound; exit 30 westbound, 1 mi w. Ext corridors. **Pets:** Large, other species. Service with restrictions. [&M] [≈] [≋] [🖵]

▼▼ La Quinta Inn El Paso West M
(915) 833-2522. **$62-$184.** 7550 Remcon Cir 79912. I-10 exit 11 (Mesa St). Ext corridors. **Pets:** Large, other species. Service with restrictions.
[≈] [≋] [🛏] [🖵]

▼▼ Microtel Inn & Suites by Wyndham El Paso Airport H
(915) 772-3650. **$50-$89.** 2001 Airway Blvd 79925. I-10 exit 25 (Airway Blvd), 1.3 mi n. Int corridors. **Pets:** Small, other species. $100 deposit/ pet, $5 daily fee/pet. Service with restrictions, supervision.
[&M] [≋] [✕] [🛏] [🖵]

▼▼ Red Roof Inn El Paso West H
(915) 587-9977. **$43-$69.** 7530 Remcon Cir 79912. I-10 exit 11 (Mesa St), just se. Ext/int corridors. **Pets:** Large, other species. Service with restrictions, supervision. [&M] [≈] [≋] [✕] [🛏] [🖵]

▼▼▼ Residence Inn by Marriott El Paso H
(915) 771-0504. **$79-$199.** 6355 Gateway Blvd W 79925. I-10 exit 24B (Geronimo Dr) eastbound, n to Edgemere, then just e; exit 25 (Airway Blvd) westbound; on westbound frontage road. Int corridors.
Pets: Accepted. [≈] [≋] [✕] [🛏] [🖵]

▼▼▼ Sleep Inn by Choice Hotels H
(915) 585-7577. **$58-$89.** 953 Sunland Park Dr 79922. I-10 exit 13 (Sunland Park Dr), just w. Int corridors. **Pets:** Accepted.
[≈] [≋] [🛏] [🖵]

▼▼▼ Staybridge Suites Airport H ✿
(915) 775-1212. **Call for rates.** 6680 Gateway Blvd E 79915. I-10 exit 25 (Airway Blvd) eastbound, just e; exit westbound, 0.5 mi w to Airway Blvd, then just sw. Int corridors. **Pets:** $150 one-time fee/room. Service with restrictions, supervision. [&M] [≈] [≋] [✕] [🛏] [🖵]

▼▼▼ Wyndham El Paso Airport H
(915) 778-4241. **$90-$179, 3 day notice.** 2027 Airway Blvd 79925. I-10 exit 25 (Airway Blvd), 1.3 mi n. Int corridors. **Pets:** $25 one-time fee/ room. Service with restrictions, supervision.
[¶] [≈] [≋] [≋] [✕] [🛏] [🖵]

EMORY

AAA ▼▼▼ BEST WESTERN PLUS Emory at Lake Fork Inn & Suites H
(903) 473-2022. **$100-$110.** 1026 E Lennon Dr 75440. On US 69, just s of jct SR 515. Int corridors. **Pets:** Accepted.
[SAVE] [≋] [✕] [🛏] [🖵]

FARMERS BRANCH

▼▼ Fairfield Inn & Suites by Marriott Dallas North by the Galleria H
(972) 661-9800. **$69-$140.** 13900 Parkside Center Blvd 75244. I-635 exit 23 (Midway Rd), 0.9 mi n to Spring Valley Rd, just w, then just s. Int corridors. **Pets:** Accepted. [≈] [≋] [✕] [🛏] [🖵]

▼▼▼ Omni Dallas Hotel Park West H
(972) 869-4300. **$99-$219.** 1590 LBJ Frwy 75234. I-635 exit 29 (Luna Rd), just s. Int corridors. **Pets:** Accepted.
[¶] [≈] [✕] [≋] [✕] [🖵]

AAA ▼▼▼ Sheraton Dallas Hotel by the Galleria H
(972) 661-3600. **Call for rates.** 4801 LBJ Frwy 75244. I-635 exit 22D (Dallas Pkwy) eastbound; exit 22B (Dallas Pkwy) westbound; on west-bound frontage road. Int corridors. **Pets:** Very small. $75 one-time fee/ room. Service with restrictions, supervision.
[SAVE] [¶] [&M] [≈] [≋] [✕] [🖵]

FLORESVILLE

AAA ▼▼▼ BEST WESTERN Floresville Inn M
(830) 393-0443. **$99-$129.** 1720 S 10th St 78114. US 181, just s of downtown. Ext corridors. **Pets:** Accepted. [SAVE] [≈] [≋] [🛏] [🖵]

FOREST HILL

AAA ▼▼▼ BEST WESTERN PLUS Forest Hill Inn & Suites H
(817) 293-1667. **$80-$160.** 3230 Forest Hill Cir 76140. I-20/SE Loop 820 exit 440A (Wichita St), just s, then just e. Int corridors.
Pets: Medium. $50 deposit/pet, $15 daily fee/pet. Designated rooms, service with restrictions, supervision. [SAVE] [≋] [✕] [🛏] [🖵]

▼▼ La Quinta Inn & Suites H
(817) 293-5800. **$79-$230.** 3346 Forest Hill Cir 76140. I-20 exit 440B (Forest Hill Cir), just s, then just w. Int corridors. **Pets:** Large, other species. Service with restrictions. [≈] [≋] [✕] [🛏] [🖵]

FORNEY

AAA ▼▼▼ BEST WESTERN PLUS Christopher Inn & Suites H ✿
(972) 552-1412. **$89-$119.** 752 Pinson Rd 75126. US 80 exit FM 740 (Pinson Rd), just ne. Int corridors. **Pets:** Medium. $10 daily fee/pet. Service with restrictions, crate. [SAVE] [&M] [≈] [≋] [✕] [🛏] [🖵]

FORT DAVIS

▼▼▼ ◆ **Historical Prude Guest Ranch** RA
(432) 426-3202. **$61-$180, 3 day notice.** 6 mi n Hwy 118 79734. 4.5 mi n of jct SR 118 and 17. Ext corridors. **Pets:** Accepted.
🛏 📷 ✖ 🕸 🔋 🔌 💻

FORT STOCKTON

▼▼▼ ◆ **Candlewood Suites** H
(432) 336-7700. **$149-$159, 3 day notice.** 2469 I-10 W 79735. I-20 exit 257, just s. Int corridors. **Pets:** Accepted. 🛏 📶 ✖ 🔌 💻

AAA ▼▼ **Days Inn** H
(432) 336-7500. **$69-$189.** 1408 N US Hwy 285 79735. I-10 exit 257, just s. Ext corridors. **Pets:** Medium. $12 daily fee/pet. Designated rooms, service with restrictions, supervision. SAVE 🛏 📶 🔌 💻

▼▼ **La Quinta Inn Fort Stockton** H
(432) 336-9781. **$69-$189.** 1537 N US Hwy 285 79735. I-10 exit 257, just sw. Ext corridors. **Pets:** Large, other species. Service with restrictions. 🛏 📶 🔌 💻

AAA ▼▼▼ **Sleep Inn & Suites** H
(432) 336-8338. **$95-$139.** 3401 W Dickinson Blvd 79735. I-10 exit 256, just e. Int corridors. **Pets:** Accepted.
SAVE 🔋M 🛏 📶 🔌 💻

FORT WORTH

▼▼▼ **Candlewood Suites** H
(817) 838-8229. **$89-$109.** 5201 Endicott Ave 76137. I-820 exit 17B (Beach St), just s, then w. Int corridors. **Pets:** Accepted. 📶 🔌 💻

AAA ▼▼▼ **Candlewood Suites DFW Airport South** M
(817) 868-1900. **Call for rates.** 4200 Reggis Ct 76155. SR 360 exit Trinity Blvd, just e, then just n. Int corridors. **Pets:** Accepted.
SAVE 📶 🔌 💻

▼▼▼ **Courtyard by Marriott Fort Worth Downtown/Blackstone** H
(817) 885-8700. **Call for rates.** 601 Main St 76102. Center. Int corridors. **Pets:** Accepted. 📶 ✖ 🔌 💻

▼▼▼ **Dallas Fort Worth Marriott Hotel & Golf Club at Champions Circle** H
(817) 961-0800. **$86-$204.** 3300 Championship Pkwy 76177. I-35W exit 70, 1.2 mi w on SR 114 to Championship Pkwy, then 0.4 mi s. Int corridors. **Pets:** Accepted. 🍽 🔋M 🛏 ✖ 📡 ✖ 🔋 🔌 💻

▼▼▼ **Historic Hilton Fort Worth** H
(817) 870-2100. **$149-$269.** 815 Main St 76102. Northeast corner of Main and 8th sts; center. Int corridors. **Pets:** Accepted.
🍽 🔋M 📶 ✖ 🔋 🔌 💻

▼▼▼ **Holiday Inn Express Hotel & Suites** H 🐾
(817) 744-7755. **$99-$125.** 3541 NW Loop 820 76106. I-820 exit 10A (Azle Ave) eastbound; exit 10B westbound. Int corridors. **Pets:** Small. $20 daily fee/pet. Service with restrictions. 🔋M 🛏 📶 🔋 🔌 💻

AAA ▼▼▼ **Holiday Inn Express Hotel & Suites Fort Worth Downtown** H
(817) 698-9595. **$99-$249.** 1111 W Lancaster Ave 76102. I-30 exit 13B (Henderson St), just n. Int corridors. **Pets:** Accepted.
SAVE 🔋M 🛏 📶 ✖ 🔋 💻

▼▼ **Holiday Inn Express Hotel & Suites-Fort Worth West** H
(817) 560-4200. **Call for rates.** 2730 S Cherry Ln 76116. I-30 exit 7A (Cherry Ln), just s. Int corridors. **Pets:** Accepted. 🛏 📶 🔋 🔌 💻

▼▼▼ **Homewood Suites by Hilton** H
(817) 834-7400. **$129-$229.** 3701 Tanacross Dr 76137. I-820 exit 17B (Beach St), just s, then just w. Int corridors. **Pets:** Accepted.
🔋M 🛏 📶 🔋 🔌 💻

▼▼▼ **Homewood Suites Fort Worth Medical Center** H
(817) 921-0202. **$139-$209.** 2200 Charlie Ln 76104. I-30 exit 12B (Forest Park Blvd), just s. Int corridors. **Pets:** Accepted.
📶 ✖ 🔋 🔌 💻

AAA ▼▼▼ **Hyatt Place Ft. Worth/Cityview** H
(817) 361-9797. **$64-$219.** 5900 Cityview Blvd 76132. I-20 exit 431 (Bryant Irvin Rd), just e on frontage road, then just s. Int corridors.
Pets: Accepted. SAVE 🔋M 🛏 📶 ✖ 🔋 🔌 💻

AAA ▼▼▼ **Hyatt Place Fort Worth/Historic Stockyards** H
(817) 626-6000. **$109-$309.** 132 E Exchange Ave 76164. In Historic Fort Worth Stockyards. Int corridors. **Pets:** Accepted.
SAVE 🛏 📶 ✖ 🔋 🔌 💻

▼▼ **La Quinta Inn & Suites Fort Worth North** H
(817) 222-2888. **$89-$254.** 4700 North Frwy 76137. I-35W exit 56A (Meacham Blvd), on northbound frontage road. Int corridors.
Pets: Large, other species. Service with restrictions.
🛏 📶 🔋 🔌 💻

▼▼▼ **La Quinta Inn & Suites Lake Worth** H
(817) 237-9300. **$89-$229.** 5800 Quebec St 76135. I-820 exit 9 (Quebec St), just sw. Int corridors. **Pets:** Large, other species. Service with restrictions. 🛏 📶 ✖ 🔋 🔌 💻

▼▼▼ **Omni Hotel** H
(817) 535-6664. **Call for rates.** 1300 Houston St 76102. Between 12th and 14th sts. Int corridors. **Pets:** Accepted.
🍽 🛏 ✖ 📡 ✖ 💻

▼▼▼ **Radisson Hotel Fort Worth North Fossil Creek** H
(817) 625-9911. **$89-$169.** 2540 Meacham Blvd 76106. I-35W exit 56A (Meacham Blvd), just w. Int corridors. **Pets:** Medium, dogs only. $35 one-time fee/room. Service with restrictions, supervision.
🍽 🛏 📶 ✖ 🔋 🔌 💻

▼▼▼ **Residence Inn by Marriott Fort Worth Alliance Airport** H
(817) 750-7000. **$93-$127.** 13400 North Frwy 76177. I-35W exit 66. Int corridors. **Pets:** Accepted. 🛏 📶 ✖ 🔋 🔌 💻

AAA ▼▼▼ **Residence Inn by Marriott-Fossil Creek** H
(817) 439-1300. **$189-$219.** 5801 Sandshell Dr 76137. I-35W exit 58 (Western Center Blvd) northbound, 0.7 mi s; exit southbound, first road to right through strip center, just s to Sandshell Dr, then 0.7 mi s. Int corridors. **Pets:** Accepted. SAVE ECO 🔋M 🛏 📶 ✖ 🔋 🔌 💻

▼▼▼ **Staybridge Suites West Fort Worth** H
(817) 935-6500. **$92-$219.** 229 Clifford Center Dr 76108. I-820 N exit 5A (Clifford Center Dr), just w. Int corridors. **Pets:** Accepted.
🛏 📶 ✖ 🔋 🔌 💻

▼▼ **Super 8 Fort Worth/Downtown Area** H
(817) 551-6700. **$65-$95.** 6500 South Frwy 76134. I-35 exit 44; on southbound frontage road. Int corridors. **Pets:** Accepted.
🔋M 🛏 📶 🔋 🔌 💻

▼▼▼ **The Worthington Renaissance Fort Worth Hotel** H
(817) 870-1000. **$129-$319.** 200 Main St 76102. Northwest corner of 2nd and Main sts. Int corridors. **Pets:** Accepted.
🍽 🛏 ✖ 📡 ✖ 🔋 🔌 💻

FREDERICKSBURG

BEST WESTERN PLUS Fredericksburg H

(830) 992-2929. **$110-$180.** 314 E Highway St 78624. Jct US 87 (Washington St) and US 290, 0.7 mi s to E Highway St, then just e. Int corridors. **Pets:** Large. $20 daily fee/pet. Designated rooms, service with restrictions, supervision.

Days Inn Suites H

(830) 997-1086. **$64-$240.** 808 S Adams St 78624. 0.6 mi sw of jct US 290 and SR 16. Ext corridors. **Pets:** Accepted.

Dietzel Motel M

(830) 997-3330. **Call for rates.** 1141 W US 290 78624. On US 290, 1 mi w; at US 87. Ext corridors. **Pets:** Accepted.

Fredericksburg Econo Lodge M

(830) 997-3437. **$60-$120.** 810 S Adams St 78624. Jct US 290 and SR 16 S, 1 mi s. Ext corridors. **Pets:** Accepted.

Fredericksburg Inn & Suites H

(830) 997-0202. **$79-$229.** 201 S Washington St 78624. US 290 and 87 (Washington St), 3 blks s. Ext corridors. **Pets:** Small, dogs only. $35 one-time fee/room. Designated rooms, service with restrictions, crate.

La Quinta Inn & Suites Fredericksburg H

(830) 990-2899. **$92-$259.** 1465 E Main St 78624. 1 mi e of downtown. Int corridors. **Pets:** Large, other species. Service with restrictions.

Quality Inn H

(830) 997-9811. **$70-$90.** 908 S Adams St 78624. 0.8 mi sw on SR 16; 0.8 mi sw of jct US 87 and 290. Ext corridors. **Pets:** Accepted.

FRISCO *(Restaurants p. 641)*

Aloft Frisco H

(972) 668-6011. **$84-$259.** 3202 Parkwood Blvd 75034. Dallas North Tollway exit Warren Pkwy, 0.5 mi e to Parkwood Blvd, then just s. Int corridors. **Pets:** Accepted.

Embassy Suites Dallas-Frisco Hotel, Convention Center & Spa H

(972) 712-7200. **$129-$249.** 7600 John Q Hammons Dr 75034. SR 121 exit Parkwood, just n. Int corridors. **Pets:** Accepted.

Sheraton Stonebriar Dallas-Frisco H

(972) 668-8700. **$89-$419.** 5444 State Hwy 121 75034. SR 121 exit Legacy Dr; northwest corner. Int corridors. **Pets:** Accepted.

The Westin Stonebriar Hotel and Golf Club H

(972) 668-8000. **$109-$539.** 1549 Legacy Dr 75034. 0.3 mi n of jct SR 121. Int corridors. **Pets:** Accepted.

GAINESVILLE

La Quinta Inn & Suites Gainesville H

(940) 665-5700. **$85-$214.** 4201 N I-35 76240. I-35 exit 501, just w on FM 1202, then just s on access road. Int corridors. **Pets:** Large, other species. Service with restrictions.

GALVESTON

Hotel Galvez and Spa-A Wyndham Grand Hotel H

(409) 765-7721. **$135-$398, 3 day notice.** 2024 Seawall Blvd 77550. Jct 21st St. Int corridors. **Pets:** Accepted.

La Quinta Inn & Suites Galveston Seawall West H

(409) 740-9100. **$79-$429.** 8710 Seawall Blvd 77554. Between 85th and 89th sts. Int corridors. **Pets:** Large, other species. Service with restrictions.

TownePlace Suites by Marriott Galveston Island Gulf Front H

(409) 497-2840. **$99-$266.** 9540 Seawall Blvd 77554. 5 mi w. Int corridors. **Pets:** Accepted.

The Tremont House-A Wyndham Grand Hotel H

(409) 763-0300. **$124-$350, 3 day notice.** 2300 Ship's Mechanic Row 77550. Broadway Ave, 0.4 mi n on 23rd St; just w to entrance; downtown. Int corridors. **Pets:** Small. $75 one-time fee/pet. Service with restrictions, supervision.

GARLAND

Hyatt Place Dallas/Garland/Richardson at Firewheel Convention Center H

(972) 414-3500. **$64-$219.** 5101 N President George Bush Hwy 75040. Jct N Garland Ave, just e on frontage road. Int corridors. **Pets:** Accepted.

Quality Inn & Suites H

(972) 303-1601. **$70-$85.** 1635 E I-30 at Bass Pro Rd 75043. I-30 exit 62 (Bass Pro Rd) eastbound, just s on Chaha Rd, over bridge to north frontage road. Ext corridors. **Pets:** Accepted.

GATESVILLE

BEST WESTERN Chateau Ville Motor Inn H

(254) 865-2281. **$82.** 2501 E Main St 76528. Jct US 84 and SR 36, 0.5 mi w. Ext corridors. **Pets:** $25 one-time fee/room. Service with restrictions, supervision.

GEORGETOWN *(Restaurants p. 641)*

BEST WESTERN PLUS Georgetown Inn & Suites H

(512) 868-8555. **$89-$109.** 600 San Gabriel Village Blvd 78626. I-35 exit 261A, 0.5 mi n on east frontage road, then just e. Int corridors. **Pets:** Accepted.

GEORGE WEST

BEST WESTERN George West Executive Inn M

(361) 449-3300. **$110-$130.** 208 N Nueces St 78022. Just n of US 59 on US 281. Ext corridors. **Pets:** Medium, dogs only. $20 one-time fee/room. Service with restrictions, crate.

GLEN ROSE

BEST WESTERN Dinosaur Valley Inn & Suites H

(254) 897-4818. **$78-$164.** 1311 NE Big Bend Tr 76043. On US 67. Int corridors. **Pets:** Small. $25 one-time fee/pet. Service with restrictions, crate.

GRANBURY

BEST WESTERN Granbury Inn & Suites H

(817) 573-4239. **Call for rates.** 1517 N Plaza Dr 76048. On US 377 Bypass; 2.2 mi n of jct SR 144 and US 377 Bypass. Int corridors. **Pets:** Accepted.

Comfort Suites H

(817) 579-5559. **Call for rates.** 903 Harbor Lakes Dr 76048. Jct SR 144 and US 377 Bypass, 1.9 mi n on US 377 Bypass. Int corridors. **Pets:** Small, dogs only. $10 daily fee/pet. Designated rooms, service with restrictions, supervision.

GRAND PRAIRIE

▼▼▼ Comfort Suites **H**
(214) 412-1022. **$89-$239.** 2504 I-20 W 75052. I-20 exit 454 (Great Southwest Pkwy), just n, then just e. Int corridors. **Pets:** Accepted.

🛥 🛜 ✕ 📶 🖵

AAA ▼▼▼▼ Hyatt Place Dallas/North Arlington/Grand Prairie **H**
(972) 988-6800. **$79-$279.** 1542 N Hwy 360 75050. SR 360 exit K/J aves southbound, U-turn at Ave J; exit Lamar Dr northbound, just n on frontage road. Int corridors. **Pets:** Accepted.
[SAVE] 🗹M 🛥 🛜 ✕ 📶 🖵

▼▼▼ Super 8 **H**
(972) 606-2800. **$59-$99.** 4020 Great Southwest Pkwy 75052. I-20 exit 454 (Great Southwest Pkwy), just s. Ext corridors. **Pets:** Accepted.
🛥 🛜 📶 🖵

GRAPEVINE *(Restaurants p. 641)*

▼▼▼▼ Embassy Suites Outdoor World **H**
(972) 724-2600. **$139-$289.** 2401 Bass Pro Dr 76051. SR 121 exit Bass Pro Dr, just w. Int corridors. **Pets:** Accepted.
[¶] 🗹M 🛥 🛜 🌀 ✕ 📶 🖵

▼▼▼▼ Homewood Suites by Hilton **H**
(972) 691-2427. **$140-$150.** 2214 Grapevine Mills Cir W 76051. SR 121 N exit Bass Pro Dr. Int corridors. **Pets:** Medium. $75 one-time fee/room. Service with restrictions, crate. 🗹M 🛥 🛜 📶 🖵

AAA ▼▼▼▼ Hyatt Place Dallas/Grapevine **H**
(972) 691-1199. **$69-$219.** 2220 Grapevine Mills Cir W 76051. SR 121 exit Bass Pro Dr, just w, then just e on SR 26. Int corridors.
Pets: Accepted. [SAVE] 🗹M 🛥 🛜 ✕ 📶 🖵

AAA ▼▼▼▼ Hyatt Regency DFW **H**
(972) 453-1234. **$89-$379.** 2334 N International Pkwy 75261. In Dallas-Fort Worth International Airport Terminal C area. Int corridors.
Pets: Accepted. [SAVE] [ECO] [¶] 🗹M 🛥 🌀 ✕ 📶 🖵

▼▼▼ Super 8-Grapevine **H**
(817) 329-7222. **$79-$109.** 250 E Hwy 114 76051. SR 114 exit Main St. Int corridors. **Pets:** Other species. $10 daily fee/pet. Service with restrictions, crate. 🗹M 🛥 🛜 📶 🖵

GREENVILLE

AAA ▼▼▼▼ BEST WESTERN PLUS Monica Royale Inn & Suites **H**
(903) 454-3700. **$100-$110.** 3001 Mustang Crossing 75402. I-30 exit 93. Int corridors. **Pets:** Accepted. [SAVE] 🗹M 🛥 🛜 ✕ 📶 🖵

GROOM

AAA ▼▼▼ Chalet Inn **M**
(806) 248-7524. **Call for rates.** I-40 FM 2300 79039. I-40 exit 113, just s. Ext corridors. **Pets:** Medium. $5 daily fee/pet. Service with restrictions, supervision. [SAVE] 🛜 📶

HALLETTSVILLE

AAA ▼▼▼▼ Hotel Texas **H**
(361) 798-5900. **Call for rates.** 1632 N Texana St 77964. Just s of CR 200. Int corridors. **Pets:** Accepted. [SAVE] 🛥 🛜 ✕ 📶 🖵

HARLINGEN

▼▼▼ La Quinta Inn Harlingen **H**
(956) 428-6888. **$65-$169.** 1002 S Expwy 83 78552. US 83 and 77 exit M St. Ext corridors. **Pets:** Large, other species. Service with restrictions. 🗹M 🛥 🛜 📶 🖵

HEBBRONVILLE

AAA ▼▼▼ BEST WESTERN Hebbronville Inn **H**
(361) 527-3600. **$106-$120.** 37 E Hwy 359 78361. On CR 359, just e of SR 16. Int corridors. **Pets:** Accepted. [SAVE] 🛥 🛜 📶 🖵

HENDERSON

▼▼▼▼ Baymont Inn & Suites Henderson **H**
(903) 657-7900. **$79-$119.** 410 Hwy 79 S 75654. Just n of jct US 259. Int corridors. **Pets:** Small. $50 deposit/pet, $10 daily fee/pet. Service with restrictions, supervision. [¶] 🛥 🛜 📶 🖵

AAA ▼▼▼ BEST WESTERN Inn of Henderson **H**
(903) 657-9561. **$80-$90.** 1500 Hwy 259 S 75654. 2 mi s, 0.7 mi s of jct US 79 and 259 S. Ext/int corridors. **Pets:** Accepted.
[SAVE] 🛥 🛜 📶 🖵

HEREFORD

AAA ▼▼▼ BEST WESTERN Red Carpet Inn **H**
(806) 364-0540. **$80-$90.** 830 W 1st St 79045. Just w of jct US 385 and 60. Ext corridors. **Pets:** Medium. Service with restrictions, crate.
[SAVE] 🛥 🛜 📶 🖵

AAA ▼▼▼▼ Holiday Inn Express **H**
(806) 364-3322. **$130-$169.** 1400 W 1st St 79045. Just w of jct US 385 and 60. Int corridors. **Pets:** Accepted. [SAVE] 🗹M 🛥 🛜 📶 🖵

HEWITT

▼▼▼▼ Sleep Inn & Suites **H**
(254) 420-3200. **$73-$300.** 209 Enterprise Blvd 76643. I-35 exit 328; on northwest corner. Int corridors. **Pets:** Medium, other species. $25 one-time fee/room. Service with restrictions, supervision.
🗹M 🛥 🛜 📶 🖵

HILLSBORO

AAA ▼▼▼▼ La Quinta Inn & Suites Hillsboro I-35 **H**
(254) 580-1300. **$89-$184.** 1513 Old Brandon Rd 76645. I-35 exit 368A northbound; exit 368B southbound, just w. Int corridors. **Pets:** Large, other species. Service with restrictions. [SAVE] 🛥 🛜 ✕ 📶 🖵

▼▼▼ Super 8 **H**
(254) 580-0404. **$70-$150.** 1512 Hillview Dr 76645. I-35 exit 368A northbound; exit 368 southbound, just e. Int corridors. **Pets:** Accepted.
🛥 🛜 📶 🖵

HONDO

AAA ▼▼▼▼ BEST WESTERN Hondo Inn **H**
(830) 426-4466. **$94-$134.** 301 Hwy 90 E 78861. Just e of downtown. Int corridors. **Pets:** Accepted. [SAVE] 🗹M 🛥 🛜 ✕ 📶 🖵

HORSESHOE BAY

AAA ▼▼▼▼ Horseshoe Bay Resort **H**
(830) 598-8600. **$179-$339, 3 day notice.** 200 Hi Cir N 78657. Jct US 281 and SR 2147, 6.6 mi w. Ext/int corridors. **Pets:** Accepted.
[SAVE] [¶] 🗹M 🛥 🗙 🛜 ✕ 📶 🖵

HOUSTON *(Restaurants p. 641)*

AAA ▼▼▼▼ Aloft Houston by the Galleria **H** 🐾
(713) 622-7010. **Call for rates.** 5415 Westheimer Rd 77056. I-610 exit 8C (Westheimer Rd) northbound; exit 9A (San Felipe Rd/Westheimer Rd) southbound, 0.8 mi w. Int corridors. **Pets:** Medium. Service with restrictions, supervision. [SAVE] 🗹M 🛥 🛜 ✕ 📶 🖵

AAA ▼▼▼▼ BEST WESTERN PLUS Westchase Mini-Suites **H**
(713) 782-1515. **$99-$249.** 2950 W Sam Houston Pkwy S 77042. Just w of Sam Houston Pkwy (Beltway 8) and Westheimer Rd; on southbound frontage road. Int corridors. **Pets:** Accepted.
[SAVE] 🗹M 🛥 🛜 ✕ 📶 🖵

▼▼▼ Candlewood Suites at CITYCENTRE - Energy Corridor **H**
(713) 464-2677. **$99-$192, 3 day notice.** 10503 Town & Country Way 77024. I-10 exit 755 eastbound, 1.2 mi on frontage road to Attingham Dr, just s to Town and Country Way, then just w; exit 756A westbound, U-turn under I-10, just e to Attingham Dr, just s to Town and Country Way, then just w. Int corridors. **Pets:** Accepted. 🗹M 🛜 📶 🖵

▼▼ Candlewood Suites Houston by the Galleria 🅷
(713) 839-9411. **$156.** 4900 Loop Central Dr 77081. I-610 exit 7 (Furnace Rd) southbound; exit 7 (Westpark Dr) northbound; on northbound frontage road. Int corridors. **Pets:** Accepted. 📶 🛄 💻

▼▼ Candlewood Suites-Westchase 🅷
(713) 780-7881. **Call for rates.** 4033 W Sam Houston Pkwy S 77042. Sam Houston Pkwy (Beltway 8) exit Westpark Dr; southeast corner of Westpark Dr and Sam Houston Pkwy (Beltway 8); on northbound frontage road. Int corridors. **Pets:** Accepted. 🅼 📶 🛄 💻

▼▼ Candlewood Suites Willowbrook 🅷
(832) 237-7300. **Call for rates.** 8719 FM 1960 W 77070. Corner of Mills Rd and FM 1960 W; just w of Tomball Pkwy. Int corridors. **Pets:** Accepted. 🅼 🔁 📶 🛄 💻

ⒶⒶⒶ ▼▼▼ Crowne Plaza Northwest Hotel 🅷
(713) 462-9977. **$59-$179.** 12801 Northwest Frwy 77040. Northwest on US 290 exit Hollister Rd, 0.7 mi e; on south service road. Ext/int corridors. **Pets:** Medium, other species. $25 one-time fee/room. Designated rooms, service with restrictions, crate.
SAVE 🍴 🔁 📶 ✕ 🛄 💻

▼▼▼ Crowne Plaza Suites Houston-Near Sugar Land 🅷 ❀
(713) 995-0123. **$79-$159.** 9090 Southwest Frwy 77074. US 59 (Southwest Frwy) exit Beechnut St/Gessner Rd; on southbound frontage road. Int corridors. **Pets:** Medium. $40 one-time fee/room. Designated rooms, service with restrictions, crate. 🍴 🅼 🔁 📶 ✕ 🛄 💻

▼▼▼ DoubleTree by Hilton Hotel Houston Downtown 🅷
(713) 759-0202. **$189-$299.** 400 Dallas St 77002. At Dallas and Bagby sts. Int corridors. **Pets:** Large. $25 one-time fee/room. Service with restrictions, supervision. 🍴 🔁 ✕ 🛄 💻

ⒶⒶⒶ ▼▼▼ DoubleTree Suites by Hilton Hotel Houston by the Galleria 🅷
(713) 961-9000. **$129-$499.** 5353 Westheimer Rd 77056. I-610 8C (Westheimer Rd) northbound; exit 9A (San Felipe Rd/Westheimer Rd) southbound, 0.8 mi w. Int corridors. **Pets:** Accepted.
SAVE 🍴 🔁 📶 ✕ 🛄 💻

▼▼▼ Drury Inn & Suites-Houston Hobby 🅷
(713) 941-4300. **$100-$179.** 7902 Mosley Rd 77061. I-45 exit 36 (Airport Blvd/College St) northbound, just w on Airport Blvd, then just n; exit southbound, follow frontage road to Mosley Rd. Int corridors. **Pets:** $10 daily fee/room. Service with restrictions, supervision.
🅼 🔁 📶 ✕ 🛄 💻

▼▼▼ Drury Inn & Suites-Houston Near the Galleria 🅷
(713) 963-0700. **$115-$264.** 1615 West Loop S 77027. I-610 exit 9 (San Felipe Rd) northbound; exit 9A (San Felipe Rd/Westheimer Rd) southbound; on east frontage road. Int corridors. **Pets:** $10 daily fee/room. Service with restrictions, supervision.
🅼 🔁 📶 ✕ 🛄 💻

▼▼▼ Drury Inn & Suites-Houston West 🅷
(281) 558-7007. **$100-$179.** 1000 N Hwy 6 77079. I-10 exit 751 (Addicks Rd/SR 6), just n. Int corridors. **Pets:** $10 daily fee/room. Service with restrictions, supervision. 🅼 🔁 📶 ✕ 🛄 💻

ⒶⒶⒶ ▼▼▼ Element by Westin Houston Vintage Park 🅷
(281) 379-7300. **$95-$309.** 14555 Vintage Preserve Pkwy 77070. SR 249 exit Louetta Rd, just e to Chasewood Park, then just s. Int corridors. **Pets:** Accepted. SAVE ECO ⊞ 🔁 📶 ✕ 🛄 💻

▼▼▼ Embassy Suites Houston Downtown 🅷
(713) 739-9100. **$179-$499.** 1515 Dallas St 77010. Between Crawford and La Branch sts. Int corridors. **Pets:** Accepted.
🍴 🅼 🔁 📶 ✕ 🛄 💻

ⒶⒶⒶ ▼▼▼ Four Points by Sheraton Houston Hobby Airport 🅷 ❀
(713) 948-0800. **$99-$219.** 8720 Gulf Frwy 77017. I-45 exit 38 (Monroe Rd); on south frontage road. Int corridors. **Pets:** Medium. $30 one-time fee/pet. Service with restrictions, supervision.
SAVE 🍴 🔁 📶 ✕ 🛄 💻

ⒶⒶⒶ ▼▼▼ Four Points by Sheraton Houston West 🅷
(281) 501-4600. **$178-$198.** 10655 Katy Frwy 77024. I-10 exit 756A westbound; exit 755 eastbound; southeast corner of I-10 and Sam Houston Pkwy (Beltway 8). Ext/int corridors. **Pets:** Accepted.
SAVE 🍴 🔁 📶 ✕ 🛄 💻

ⒶⒶⒶ ▼▼▼▼ Four Seasons Hotel Houston 🅷
(713) 650-1300. **$229-$750, 3 day notice.** 1300 Lamar St 77010. Jct Lamar and Austin sts. Int corridors. **Pets:** Accepted.
SAVE 🍴 🔁 📶 ✕ 🛄 💻

▼▼▼ Hilton Houston North 🅷
(281) 875-2222. **$69-$249.** 12400 Greenspoint Dr 77060. I-45 exit 61 (Greens Rd), 0.5 mi e. Int corridors. **Pets:** Large. $75 one-time fee/room. Service with restrictions. 🍴 🅼 🔁 📶 💻

ⒶⒶⒶ ▼▼▼ Hilton Houston Post Oak 🅷 🐾
(713) 961-9300. **$99-$329.** 2001 Post Oak Blvd 77056. I-610 exit 8C (Westheimer Rd) northbound; exit 9A (San Felipe Rd/Westheimer Rd) southbound; between San Felipe and Westheimer rds. Ext/int corridors. **Pets:** $75 one-time fee/room. Service with restrictions, crate. SAVE 🍴 🔁 📶 ✕ 💻

▼▼▼ Hilton Houston Westchase 🅷
(713) 974-1000. **$109-$259.** 9999 Westheimer Rd 77042. Sam Houston Pkwy (Beltway 8) exit Westheimer Rd/Briar Forest Dr northbound; exit Westheimer Rd/Richmond Ave southbound, 0.5 mi e. Int corridors. **Pets:** Accepted. 🍴 🅼 🔁 📶 ✕ 💻

▼▼▼ Holiday Inn Express Hotel & Suites Memorial Area 🅷
(713) 688-2800. **Call for rates.** 7625 Katy Frwy 77024. I-10 exit 762 (Silber Rd); on eastbound frontage road. Int corridors. **Pets:** Accepted.
🔁 📶 ✕ 🛄 💻

▼▼▼ Holiday Inn Express Northwest 🅷
(832) 237-4300. **$89-$299.** 12915 FM 1960 W 77065. US 290 exit FM 1960, just e. Int corridors. **Pets:** Accepted.
🅼 🔁 📶 ✕ 🛄 💻

ⒶⒶⒶ ▼▼▼ Holiday Inn Houston Hobby Airport 🅷
(713) 946-8900. **$89-$329.** 8611 Airport Blvd 77061. I-45 exit 36 (Airport Blvd/College St), 1.3 mi w. Int corridors. **Pets:** Small. $75 one-time fee/room, $25 daily fee/pet. Designated rooms, service with restrictions, supervision. SAVE 🍴 🅼 🔁 📶 ✕ 🛄 💻

ⒶⒶⒶ ▼▼▼ Holiday Inn Houston Intercontinental Airport 🅷
(281) 449-2311. **Call for rates.** 15222 John F Kennedy Blvd 77032. Jct N Sam Houston Pkwy (Beltway 8) E and John F Kennedy Blvd. Int corridors. **Pets:** Medium, other species. $100 deposit/pet, $125 one-time fee/room. Service with restrictions, supervision.
SAVE 🍴 🔁 📶 ✕ 🛄 💻

ⒶⒶⒶ ▼▼▼ Holiday Inn Houston-NRG/Medical Center Area 🅷
(713) 790-1900. **Call for rates.** 8111 Kirby Dr 77054. I-610 exit 1C, 0.9 mi n. Int corridors. **Pets:** Accepted. SAVE 🍴 🔁 📶 🛄 💻

ⒶⒶⒶ ▼▼▼ Homewood Suites by Hilton Intercontinental Airport 🅷
(281) 219-9100. **Call for rates.** 1340 N Sam Houston Pkwy E 77032. Sam Houston Pkwy (Beltway 8) exit Aldine Westfield Rd eastbound, 0.8 mi e on frontage road; exit Hardy Toll Rd westbound, U-turn, 1 mi e on frontage road. Int corridors. **Pets:** Accepted.
SAVE 🅼 🔁 📶 🛄 💻

▼▼▼ **Homewood Suites by Hilton Near the Galleria** H

(713) 439-1305. **$129-$389.** 2950 Sage Rd 77056. I-610 exit 8C (Westheimer Rd), just w to Sage Rd, then just s. Int corridors. **Pets:** Accepted. 🔣M 🔣 🛜 🔲 🔲

▼▼▼ **Homewood Suites by Hilton-Westchase** H

(713) 334-2424. **$99-$279.** 2424 Rogerdale Rd 77042. Sam Houston Pkwy (Beltway 8) exit Westheimer Rd, just w to Rogerdale Rd, then just n. Int corridors. **Pets:** Accepted. 🔣M 🔲 🛜 ✕ 🔲 🔲

▼▼▼ **Hotel Derek** H

(713) 961-3000. **$139-$269, 3 day notice.** 2525 West Loop S 77027. I-610 exit 9A (San Felipe Rd/Westheimer Rd) southbound; exit 8C (Westheimer Rd) northbound. Int corridors. **Pets:** Accepted. 🔲 🔲 🛜 ✕ 🔲 🔲

▼▼▼ **Hotel Icon, Autograph Collection** H

(713) 224-4266. **$129-$699.** 220 Main St 77002. Between Travis and Main sts; entrance on Congress St. Int corridors. **Pets:** Accepted. 🔲 🛜 ✕ 🔲

▼▼▼ **Hotel Indigo Houston at the Galleria** H

(713) 621-8988. **$119-$259.** 5160 Hidalgo St 77056. I-610 exit 9A (San Felipe Rd/Westheimer Rd) southbound; exit 8C (Westheimer Rd) northbound, s to Post Oak, just e to Hidalgo St, then just s. Int corridors. **Pets:** Accepted. 🔲 🔣M 🛜 ✕ 🔲 🔲

🅐🅐🅐 ▼▼▼▼ **Hotel ZaZa Houston Museum District** H

(713) 526-1991. **$295.** 5701 Main St 77005. US 59 (Southwest Frwy) exit Main St northbound, 0.5 mi s; exit Fannin St southbound, 0.5 mi s to Ewing St, then just w. Int corridors. **Pets:** Accepted. 🆂🅰🆅🅴 🔲 🔣M 🔲 ✕ 🛜 ✕ 🔲

▼▼▼ **Houston Marriott South at Hobby Airport** H

(713) 943-7979. **$79-$249.** 9100 Gulf Frwy 77017. I-45 exit 36 (Airport Blvd/College St) southbound; exit 38 (Monroe Rd) northbound; on southbound frontage road. Int corridors. **Pets:** Accepted. 🔲 🔲 🛜 ✕ 🔲 🔲

🅐🅐🅐 ▼▼▼ **HYATT house Houston/Galleria** H

(713) 629-9711. **$89-$449.** 3440 Sage Rd 77056. I-610 exit 9A (San Felipe Rd/Westheimer Rd) southbound; exit 8C (Westheimer Rd) northbound, just w to Sage Rd, then 0.8 mi s. Int corridors. **Pets:** Accepted. 🆂🅰🆅🅴 🔲 🛜 ✕ 🔲 🔲

🅐🅐🅐 ▼▼▼ **HYATT house Houston-West/Energy Corridor** H

(281) 646-9990. **$59-$229.** 15405 Katy Frwy (I-10) 77094. I-10 exit 751 (SR 6), just s to Grisby Rd, then just w. Int corridors. **Pets:** $75 one-time fee/room. Service with restrictions, supervision. 🆂🅰🆅🅴 🔲 🛜 ✕ 🔲 🔲

🅐🅐🅐 ▼▼▼ **Hyatt North Houston** H

(281) 249-1234. **$79-$249.** 425 N Sam Houston Pkwy E 77060. Sam Houston Pkwy (Beltway 8) exit Imperial Valley Dr westbound; exit Hardy Toll Rd eastbound; on westbound frontage road. Int corridors. **Pets:** Accepted. 🆂🅰🆅🅴 🔲 🔣M 🔲 🛜 ✕ 🔲

🅐🅐🅐 ▼▼▼ **Hyatt Place Bush Houston Intercontinental Airport** H

(281) 820-6060. **$69-$209.** 300 Ronan Park Pl 77060. Sam Houston Pkwy (Beltway 8) exit Imperial Valley Dr westbound, 0.8 mi w on frontage road; exit Hardy Toll Rd eastbound, turn under parkway, 1.2 mi w; on west frontage road. Int corridors. **Pets:** Accepted. 🆂🅰🆅🅴 🔲 🛜 ✕ 🔲 🔲

▼▼▼ **La Quinta Inn & Suites Energy Corridor** H

(281) 668-1068. **$89-$694.** 2451 Shadow View Ln 77077. 2.5 mi w of Sam Houston Pkwy (Beltway 8) on Westheimer Rd, just n. Int corridors. **Pets:** Large, other species. Service with restrictions. 🔣M 🔲 🛜 ✕ 🔲 🔲

▼▼▼ **La Quinta Inn & Suites Houston Bush Intercontinental Airport South** H

(281) 219-2000. **$85-$299.** 15510 John F Kennedy Blvd 77032. Sam Houston Pkwy (Beltway 8) exit John F Kennedy Blvd/Vickery Dr, just n. Int corridors. **Pets:** Large, other species. Service with restrictions. 🔣M 🔲 🛜 🔲 🔲

🅐🅐🅐 ▼▼▼ **La Quinta Inn & Suites Houston Channelview** H

(281) 452-4402. **$89-$254.** 5520 E Sam Houston Pkwy N 77015. Sam Houston Pkwy exit Woodforest Blvd. Int corridors. **Pets:** Large, other species. Service with restrictions. 🆂🅰🆅🅴 🔣M 🔲 🛜 ✕ 🔲 🔲

▼▼▼ **La Quinta Inn & Suites-Houston Clay Road** H

(713) 939-1400. **$89-$269.** 4424 Westway Park Blvd 77041. Sam Houston Pkwy (Beltway 8) exit Clay Rd, just e. Int corridors. **Pets:** Large, other species. Service with restrictions. 🔣M 🔲 🛜 ✕ 🔲 🔲

▼▼▼ **La Quinta Inn & Suites Houston Galleria Area** H

(713) 355-3440. **$89-$479.** 1625 West Loop S 77027. I-610 exit 9 (San Felipe Rd) northbound; exit 9A (San Felipe Rd/Westheimer Rd) southbound; on northbound frontage road. Int corridors. **Pets:** Large, other species. Service with restrictions. 🔣M 🔲 🛜 🔲 🔲

▼▼▼ **La Quinta Inn & Suites Houston Hobby Airport** H

(713) 490-1008. **$84-$374.** 8776 Airport Blvd 77061. I-45 exit 36 (Airport Blvd/College St), 1.3 mi w. Int corridors. **Pets:** Large, other species. Service with restrictions. 🔣M 🔲 🛜 ✕ 🔲 🔲

🅐🅐🅐 ▼▼▼ **La Quinta Inn & Suites Houston I-45/1960** H

(281) 784-1112. **$99-$334.** 415 FM 1960 Rd E 77073. I-45 exit 66 (FM 1960), just e. Int corridors. **Pets:** Large, other species. Service with restrictions. 🆂🅰🆅🅴 🔲 🛜 🔲 🔲

▼▼▼ **La Quinta Inn & Suites Houston-Normandy** H

(713) 451-0009. **$94-$354.** 930 Normandy St 77015. I-10 exit 778B, just n. Int corridors. **Pets:** Large, other species. Service with restrictions. 🔲 🛜 ✕ 🔲 🔲

▼▼▼ **La Quinta Inn & Suites Houston-Westchase** H

(281) 495-7700. **$89-$479.** 10850 Harwin Dr 77072. Sam Houston Pkwy (Beltway 8) exit Bellaire Blvd/Harwin Dr northbound; exit Westpark Dr/Harwin Dr southbound. Int corridors. **Pets:** Large, other species. Service with restrictions. 🔲 🛜 ✕ 🔲 🔲

▼▼▼ **La Quinta Inn & Suites Houston West Park 10** H

(281) 646-9200. **$89-$359.** 15225 Katy Frwy 77094. I-10 exit 748 (Barker Cypress Rd) eastbound, 2.6 mi on eastbound service road; exit 751 (SR 6) westbound, just s to Grisby Rd, then 0.5 mi w. Int corridors. **Pets:** Large, other species. Service with restrictions. 🔲 🛜 🔲 🔲

▼▼▼ **Omni Houston Hotel** H

(713) 871-8181. **$199-$599, 3 day notice.** Four Riverway 77056. I-610 exit 10 (Woodway Dr), 0.3 mi w. Int corridors. **Pets:** Accepted. 🔲 🔲 ✕ 🔲 ✕ 🔲

🅐🅐🅐 ▼▼▼▼ **Omni Houston Hotel Westside** H 🐾

(281) 558-8338. **$109-$379, 3 day notice.** 13210 Katy Frwy 77079. I-10 exit 753A (Eldridge St), just n. Int corridors. **Pets:** Small, other species. $50 one-time fee/pet. Service with restrictions. 🆂🅰🆅🅴 🔲 🔲 🔲 ✕ 🔲 🔲

🅐🅐🅐 ▼▼▼ **Residence Inn by Marriott Houston by the Galleria** H

(713) 840-9757. **$109-$309.** 2500 McCue Rd 77056. I-610 exit 8C (Westheimer Rd) northbound; exit 9A (San Felipe Rd/Westheimer Rd) southbound, just w to McCue Rd, then just n. Ext/int corridors. **Pets:** Accepted. 🆂🅰🆅🅴 🔲 🛜 ✕ 🔲 🔲

▼▼▼ **Residence Inn by Marriott Houston Downtown/ Convention Center** H

(832) 366-1000. **$99-$319.** 904 Dallas St 77002. At Main St. Int corridors. **Pets:** Accepted. 🏋M 🛋 🛜 ✕ 🛎 🖳

▼▼▼ **Residence Inn by Marriott-Medical Center/NRG Park** H

(713) 660-7993. **$109-$199.** 7710 S Main St 77030. I-610 exit 2 (S Main St/Buffalo Speedway), 1.5 mi n. Ext corridors. **Pets:** Accepted. 🏋M 🛋 🛜 ✕ 🛎 🖳

▼▼▼ **Residence Inn by Marriott-West University** H

(713) 661-4660. **$109-$319.** 2939 Westpark Dr 77005. US 59 (Southwest Frwy) exit Kirby Dr, just s, then just w. Int corridors. **Pets:** Accepted. 🏋M 🏊 🛋 🛜 ✕ 🛎 🖳

▼▼▼ **Residence Inn by Marriott Willowbrook** H

(832) 237-2002. **$129-$269.** 7311 W Greens Rd 77064. SR 249 exit Greens Rd, just e. Int corridors. **Pets:** Accepted. 🛋 🛜 ✕ 🛎 🖳

🅰🅰🅰 ▼▼▼ **Royal Sonesta Hotel Houston** H

(713) 627-7600. **Call for rates.** 2222 West Loop S 77027. I-610 exit 9 (San Felipe Rd) northbound; exit 9A (San Felipe Rd/Westheimer Rd) southbound. Int corridors. **Pets:** Accepted. SAVE 🍴 🛋 🐶 ✕ 🛎 🖳

🅰🅰🅰 ▼▼▼ **The St. Regis Houston** H

(713) 840-7600. **$229-$1200.** 1919 Briar Oaks Ln 77027. I-610 exit 9A (San Felipe Rd/Westheimer Rd), 0.3 mi e. Int corridors. **Pets:** Accepted. SAVE 🍴 🛋 🐾 🐶 ✕ 🛎 🖳

🅰🅰🅰 ▼▼▼ **Sheraton Houston Brookhollow** H 🐾

(713) 688-0100. **$79-$309.** 3000 North Loop W 77092. I-610 exit 13C (T C Jester Blvd); on southbound frontage road. Int corridors. **Pets:** Small, dogs only. Service with restrictions, supervision. SAVE 🍴 🏋M 🛋 🛜 ✕ 🖳

🅰🅰🅰 ▼▼▼ **Sheraton Houston West Hotel** H 🐾

(281) 501-4200. **$99-$329.** 11191 Clay Rd 77041. Sam Houston Pkwy (Beltway 8) exit Clay Rd, just e. Int corridors. **Pets:** Small, dogs only. Designated rooms, service with restrictions, crate. SAVE 🍴 🏋M 🛋 🛜 ✕ 🖳

🅰🅰🅰 ▼▼▼ **Sheraton North Houston Hotel** H

(281) 442-5100. **$99-$299.** 15700 John F Kennedy Blvd 77032. Sam Houston Pkwy (Beltway 8) exit John F Kennedy Blvd, just n. Int corridors. **Pets:** Accepted. SAVE 🍴 🛋 🛜 ✕ 🛎 🖳

🅰🅰🅰 ▼▼▼ **Sheraton Suites Houston Near The Galleria** H 🐾

(713) 586-2444. **$109-$639.** 2400 West Loop S 77027. I-610 exit 9 (San Felipe Rd) northbound; exit 9A (San Felipe Rd/Westheimer Rd) southbound. Int corridors. **Pets:** Medium, dogs only. Service with restrictions, supervision. SAVE 🍴 🛋 🛜 ✕ 🛎 🖳

🅰🅰🅰 ▼▼▼ **Sonesta ES Suites Houston** H

(713) 355-8888. **Call for rates.** 5190 Hidalgo St 77056. I-610 exit 9A (San Felipe Rd/Westheimer Rd) southbound; exit 8C (Westheimer Rd) northbound, 0.4 mi w to Sage Rd, then just s. Int corridors. **Pets:** Accepted. SAVE 🏋M 🛋 🛜 ✕ 🛎 🖳

▼▼▼ **Staybridge Suites Houston West Energy Corridor** H

(281) 759-7829. **Call for rates.** 1225 Eldridge Pkwy 77077. I-10 exit 753A (Eldridge Pkwy), 1.8 mi s. Int corridors. **Pets:** Accepted. 🛋 🛜 ✕ 🛎 🖳

▼▼ **TownePlace Suites by Marriott Houston I-10 West/Energy Corridor** H

(281) 646-0058. **$122-$140.** 15155 Katy Frwy 77094. I-10 exit 751, just s on SR 6 to Grisby Rd, then w. Int corridors. **Pets:** Accepted. 🛋 🛜 ✕ 🛎 🖳

▼▼▼ **TownePlace Suites by Marriott-Northwest Central** H

(713) 690-4035. **$150-$179.** 12820 Northwest Frwy (US 290) 77040. US 290 exit Bingle Rd/43rd St eastbound; exit Bingle Rd/Pinemont Dr/43rd St westbound; on westbound frontage road. Int corridors. **Pets:** Accepted. 🏋M 🛜 ✕ 🛎 🖳

🅰🅰🅰 ▼▼▼ **The Westin Galleria, Houston** H

(713) 960-8100. **$89-$449.** 5060 W Alabama St 77056. I-610 exit 8C (Westheimer Rd) northbound; exit 9A (San Felipe Rd/Westheimer Rd) southbound, 0.5 mi w on Westheimer Rd to Sage Rd, just s, then just e. Int corridors. **Pets:** Accepted. SAVE 🍴 🏋M 🛋 🐶 ✕ 🛎 🖳

🅰🅰🅰 ▼▼▼▼ **Westin Houston Memorial City** H

(281) 501-4300. **$149-$469.** 945 Gessner Rd 77024. I-10 exit 757 (Gessner Rd), just s. Int corridors. **Pets:** Accepted. SAVE 🍴 🏋M 🛋 ✕ 🛜 ✕ 🛎 🖳

🅰🅰🅰 ▼▼▼▼ **Westin Oaks Houston at the Galleria** H

(713) 960-8100. **$89-$449.** 5011 Westheimer Rd 77056. I-610 exit 8C (Westheimer Rd) northbound; exit 9A (San Felipe Rd/Westheimer Rd) southbound. Int corridors. **Pets:** Accepted. SAVE 🍴 🏋M 🛋 🛜 ✕ 🛎 🖳

🅰🅰🅰 ▼▼▼ **Wingate by Wyndham Houston Bush Intercontinental Airport IAH** H

(281) 372-1000. **$89-$180.** 1330 N Sam Houston Pkwy E 77032. Off Sam Houston Pkwy (Beltway 8) exit Aldine Westfield Rd eastbound, 0.8 mi e on service road; exit Hardy Toll Rd westbound, U-turn, then 1 mi e on service road. Int corridors. **Pets:** Small, other species. $50 one-time fee/pet. Service with restrictions, supervision. SAVE 🛋 🛜 ✕ 🛎 🖳

🅰🅰🅰 ▼▼▼ **Wyndham Houston West Energy Corridor** H

(281) 558-5580. **$99-$249.** 14703 Park Row Blvd 77079. I-10 exit 751 (Addicks Rd/SR 6), just n. Int corridors. **Pets:** Small, dogs only. $75 one-time fee/pet. Service with restrictions, crate. SAVE 🍴 🏋M 🛋 🛜 ✕ 🛎 🖳

HUMBLE

🅰🅰🅰 ▼▼▼ **BEST WESTERN PLUS Atascocita Inn & Suites** H

(281) 852-5665. **$90-$800.** 7730 FM 1960 Rd E 77346. Jct US 59 and FM 1960, 6.8 mi e. Int corridors. **Pets:** $10 daily fee/pet. Designated rooms, service with restrictions, supervision. SAVE 🏋M 🛋 🛜 ✕ 🛎 🖳

HUNTSVILLE

🅰🅰🅰 ▼▼▼ **BEST WESTERN Huntsville Inn & Suites** H

(936) 295-9000. **$109-$189.** 201 W Hill Park Cir 77320. I-45 exit 116, just w on US 190. Ext corridors. **Pets:** Accepted. SAVE 🏋M 🛋 🛜 🛎 🖳

HURST

🅰🅰🅰 ▼▼▼ **Hyatt Place Ft. Worth/Hurst** H

(817) 577-3003. **$69-$209.** 1601 Hurst Town Center Dr 76054. SR 183 exit Precinct Line Rd, just n to Thousand Oaks Dr, then just w. Int corridors. **Pets:** Medium, dogs only. $75 one-time fee/pet. Service with restrictions, crate. SAVE 🏋M 🛋 🛜 ✕ 🛎 🖳

INGLESIDE

🅰🅰🅰 ▼▼▼ **BEST WESTERN Naval Station Inn** M

(361) 776-2767. **$100-$155.** 2025 State Hwy 361 78362. Jct SR 1069, 1 mi e. Ext corridors. **Pets:** Dogs only. $15 daily fee/pet. Service with restrictions, supervision. SAVE 🛋 🛜 🛎 🖳

IRVING

▼▼ **Candlewood Suites Dallas/Las Colinas** H

(972) 714-9990. **$81-$109, 3 day notice.** 5300 Green Park Dr 75038. SR 114 exit Walnut Hill Ln, just s. Int corridors. **Pets:** Accepted. 🏋M 🛜 🛎 🖳

▼▼▼ Courtyard by Marriott-DFW Airport North H
(972) 929-4004. **$85-$190.** 4949 Regent Blvd 75063. I-635 exit 34 (Freeport Pkwy), 0.5 mi s, then 0.5 mi w. Int corridors. **Pets:** $75 one-time fee/pet. Service with restrictions, supervision.
🔵ᴹ 🔵 🔵 🔵 🔵 🔵

▲▲▲ ▼▼▼ DoubleTree by Hilton Hotel DFW Airport-North H
(972) 929-8181. **$99-$209.** 4441 W John Carpenter Frwy 75063. North off SR 114 exit Esters Blvd. Int corridors. **Pets:** Accepted.
🔵 🔵 🔵 🔵 🔵 🔵 🔵

▲▲▲ ▼▼▼ Element Dallas Fort Worth Airport North H
(972) 929-9800. **$89-$161.** 3550 IH 635 75063. I-635 exit 33 (Belt Line Rd), just s. Int corridors. **Pets:** Accepted.
🔵 🔵 🔵 🔵 🔵 🔵 🔵

▲▲▲ ▼▼▼ ▼▼▼ Four Seasons Resort and Club H
(972) 717-0700. **Call for rates.** 4150 N MacArthur Blvd 75038. SR 114 exit MacArthur Blvd, 1.5 mi s. Int corridors. **Pets:** Accepted.
🔵 🔵 🔵 🔵 🔵 🔵 🔵 🔵

▼▼▼ Hotel Las Colinas H
(972) 650-1600. **Call for rates.** 110 W John Carpenter Frwy 75039. Sw off SR 114 exit O'Connor Rd. Int corridors. **Pets:** Accepted.
🔵 🔵 🔵 🔵 🔵 🔵

▲▲▲ ▼▼▼ HYATT house Dallas/Las Colinas H
(972) 831-0909. **$83-$189.** 5901 N MacArthur Blvd 75039. SR 114 exit MacArthur Blvd; northwest corner. Ext corridors. **Pets:** Accepted.
🔵 🔵ᴹ 🔵 🔵 🔵 🔵 🔵

▲▲▲ ▼▼▼ Hyatt Place Dallas/Las Colinas H
(972) 550-7400. **$74-$199.** 5455 Green Park Dr 75038. SR 114 exit Walnut Hill Ln, just se. Int corridors. **Pets:** Medium, dogs only. $75 one-time fee/room. Service with restrictions, supervision.
🔵 🔵ᴹ 🔵 🔵 🔵 🔵 🔵

▼▼ La Quinta Inn & Suites Dallas DFW Airport North H
(972) 915-4022. **$69-$449.** 4850 W John Carpenter Frwy 75063. SR 114 exit Freeport Pkwy; on eastbound frontage road. Int corridors. **Pets:** Large, other species. Service with restrictions.
🔵ᴹ 🔵 🔵 🔵 🔵

▼▼ La Quinta Inn & Suites Dallas DFW Airport South/Irving H
(972) 252-6546. **$79-$339.** 4105 W Airport Frwy 75062-5997. SR 183 exit Esters Rd westbound; exit N Belt Line Rd eastbound; on westbound frontage road. Int corridors. **Pets:** Large, other species. Service with restrictions.
🔵 🔵 🔵 🔵

▼▼▼ La Quinta Inn & Suites Dallas-Las Colinas H
(972) 261-4900. **$75-$239.** 4225 N MacArthur Blvd 75038. Se off SR 114 exit MacArthur Blvd, 1.4 mi s. Int corridors. **Pets:** Large, other species. Service with restrictions. 🔵 🔵 🔵 🔵 🔵

▼▼ Motel 6 - #4728 DFW North M
(972) 915-3993. **Call for rates.** 7800 Heathrow Dr 75063. SR 114 exit Freeport Pkwy, just se. Int corridors. **Pets:** Other species. Service with restrictions, crate. 🔵 🔵

▲▲▲ ▼▼▼▼ NYLO Irving/Las Colinas H 🐾
(972) 373-8900. **$89-$499.** 1001 W Royal Ln 75039. SR 114 exit MacArthur Blvd, just n, then just w. Int corridors. **Pets:** Medium. $50 one-time fee/room. Service with restrictions. 🔵 🔵 🔵 🔵 🔵

▼▼▼▼ Omni Mandalay Dallas at Las Colinas H 🐾
(972) 556-0800. **$99-$379.** 221 E Las Colinas Blvd 75039. SR 114 exit O'Connor Rd, just n, then just e. Int corridors. **Pets:** Small. $50 one-time fee/room. Service with restrictions, supervision.
🔵 🔵 🔵 🔵 🔵 🔵 🔵

▲▲▲ ▼▼▼ Residence Inn by Marriott at Las Colinas H
(972) 580-7773. **$79-$209.** 950 W Walnut Hill Ln 75038. SR 114 exit MacArthur Blvd, 0.5 mi s, then just e. Ext corridors. **Pets:** $100 one-time fee/pet. Service with restrictions.
🔵 🔵 🔵ᴹ 🔵 🔵 🔵 🔵 🔵

▼▼▼ Residence Inn by Marriott-DFW North H
(972) 871-1331. **$89-$209.** 8600 Esters Blvd 75063. SR 114 exit Esters Blvd, 0.9 mi n. Int corridors. **Pets:** Accepted.
🔵ᴹ 🔵 🔵 🔵 🔵 🔵

▼▼▼ Sheraton DFW Airport Hotel H
(972) 929-8400. **$129-$259, 3 day notice.** 4440 W John Carpenter Frwy 75063. SR 114 exit Esters Blvd, just s. Int corridors.
Pets: Accepted. 🔵 🔵 🔵 🔵 🔵 🔵 🔵

▼▼▼ Staybridge Suites Dallas-Las Colinas H
(972) 465-9400. **$99-$229, 7 day notice.** 1201 Executive Cir 75038. SR 114 exit MacArthur Blvd, just s to W Walnut Hill Ln, just w. Int corridors. **Pets:** Medium. $10 daily fee/pet. Service with restrictions.
🔵 🔵 🔵 🔵

▼▼ Super 8 DFW South Irving H
(972) 257-1810. **$55-$85.** 4245 W Airport Frwy 75062. SR 183 exit Esters Rd; on westbound frontage road. Int corridors. **Pets:** Accepted.
🔵 🔵 🔵

▲▲▲ ▼▼▼ The Westin Dallas Fort Worth Airport H 🐾
(972) 929-4500. **$109-$459.** 4545 W John Carpenter Frwy 75063. SR 114 exit Esters Blvd, just n. Int corridors. **Pets:** Dogs only. Service with restrictions, supervision. 🔵 🔵 🔵 🔵 🔵 🔵 🔵

JOHNSON CITY

▲▲▲ ▼▼▼ BEST WESTERN Johnson City Inn H
(830) 868-4044. **$90-$150.** 107 S Hwy 290/281 78636. Jct US 281 and 290 N. Ext corridors. **Pets:** Accepted. 🔵 🔵 🔵 🔵 🔵

JUNCTION

▼▼▼ Rodeway Inn H
(325) 446-4588. **$68-$85.** 184 Dos Rios Dr 76849. I-10 exit 456, just s on US 377. Ext corridors. **Pets:** Accepted. 🔵 🔵 🔵 🔵

KATY

▼▼▼▼ Residence Inn by Marriott Houston Katy Mills H
(281) 391-7501. **$204-$244.** 25401 Katy Mills Pkwy 77494. I-10 exit 740 (Pin Oak Rd) westbound; exit 741 (Pin Oak Rd) eastbound, just s; on south side of Kay Mills Mall. Int corridors. **Pets:** Accepted.
🔵 🔵 🔵 🔵 🔵

KAUFMAN

▲▲▲ ▼▼▼ BEST WESTERN La Hacienda Inn M
(972) 962-6272. **$80-$130, 3 day notice.** 200 E Hwy 175 75142. Just e of jct US 175 and SR 34. Ext corridors. **Pets:** Accepted.
🔵 🔵 🔵 🔵 🔵

KERRVILLE

▲▲▲ ▼▼▼ BEST WESTERN Sunday House Inn H
(830) 896-1313. **$74-$114.** 2124 Sidney Baker St 78028. I-10 exit 508 (SR 16), just s. Ext corridors. **Pets:** Small, dogs only. $10 daily fee/pet. Designated rooms, service with restrictions, supervision.
🔵 🔵 🔵 🔵 🔵 🔵

▼▼▼ Days Inn of Kerrville M
(830) 896-1000. **$49-$99.** 2000 Sidney Baker St 78028. I-10 exit 508 (SR 16), 0.5 mi s. Ext/int corridors. **Pets:** Small, other species. $15 daily fee/pet. Designated rooms, no service, supervision.
🔵 🔵 🔵 🔵

▼▼ **La Quinta Inn Kerrville** H

(830) 896-9200. **$75-$229.** 1940 Sidney Baker St 78028. I-10 exit 508 (SR 16), 0.4 mi s. Int corridors. **Pets:** Large, other species. Service with restrictions. 🛏️ 🛜 ✖️ 🛢️ 💻

▼▼ **Quality Inn of Kerrville** H

(830) 792-7700. **$79-$149.** 2001 Sidney Baker St 78028. I-10 exit 508 (SR 16), 0.4 mi s. Int corridors. **Pets:** Accepted. 🛏️ 🛜 🛢️ 💻

👓 ▼▼▼ **Y. O. Ranch Hotel & Conference Center** H

(830) 257-4440. **$79-$129, 3 day notice.** 2033 Sidney Baker St 78028. I-10 exit 508 (SR 16), 0.3 mi s. Ext/int corridors. **Pets:** Accepted.

SAVE 🍴 🛏️ ✖️ 🛜 ✖️ 🛢️ 💻

KILGORE

👓 ▼▼▼ **BEST WESTERN Inn of Kilgore** H

(903) 986-1195. **$85-$150.** 1411 N Hwy 259 75662. I-20 exit 589, 3.9 mi s. Ext corridors. **Pets:** Accepted. SAVE 🛏️ 🛜 🛢️ 💻

KILLEEN

▼▼▼ **Candlewood Suites-Ft. Hood/Killeen** H 🐾

(254) 501-3990. **$77-$139.** 2300 Florence Rd 76542. US 90 exit Jasper Rd, just s. Int corridors. **Pets:** Medium, other species. $75 one-time fee/room. Service with restrictions, crate. 🛜 🛢️ 💻

👓 ▼▼▼ **Days Inn Killeen Mall** M

(254) 554-2727. **$69-$99.** 1602 E Central Texas Expwy 76541. US 190 exit Trimmier Rd. Ext corridors. **Pets:** Small, other species. $25 one-time fee/pet. Service with restrictions, crate. SAVE 🛜 🛢️ 💻

👓 ▼▼▼ **Hawthorn Suites by Wyndham** H

(254) 634-7795. **$89-$125.** 1502 E Central Texas Expwy 76541. US 190 exit Trimmier Rd; on south frontage road. Int corridors. **Pets:** Small, other species. $25 one-time fee/pet. Service with restrictions, crate.

SAVE 🛜 🛢️ 💻

▼▼▼ **Residence Inn by Marriott** H

(254) 634-1020. **$89-$129.** 400 E Central Texas Expwy 76541. US 190 exit Fort Hood St/Jasper Rd (SR 195); on south frontage road. Int corridors. **Pets:** Accepted. 🛏️ ✖️ 🛜 ✖️ 🛢️ 💻

▼▼▼ **Shilo Inn Suites Hotel - Killeen** H

(254) 699-0999. **Call for rates.** 3701 S W S Young Dr 76542. US 190 exit W S Young Dr, 1 mi s. Int corridors. **Pets:** Accepted.

🍴 🛏️ ✖️ 🛜 ✖️ 🛢️ 💻

▼▼▼ **TownePlace Suites by Marriott** H

(254) 554-8899. **$79-$99.** 2401 Florence Rd 76542. US 190 exit Trimmier Rd to Jasper Rd, on south frontage road, 1 blk e to Florence Rd, then just s. Int corridors. **Pets:** Accepted.

🛏️ 🛜 ✖️ 🛢️ 💻

KINGSLAND

▼▼▼ **Rio Vista Resort** CO

(325) 388-6331. **$90-$950, 30 day notice.** 234 Rio Vista Dr 78639. Colorado River Bridge, 0.5 mi nw on FM 1431, 0.5 mi s on Reynolds St. Ext corridors. **Pets:** Accepted. 🛏️ ✖️ 🛜 ✖️ 🛢️ 💻

KINGSVILLE

👓 ▼▼▼ **BEST WESTERN Kingsville Inn** M

(361) 595-5656. **$90-$120.** 2402 E King Ave 78363. 1.5 mi e on US 77 Bypass; opposite jct SR 141. Ext corridors. **Pets:** Small. $30 daily fee/pet. Service with restrictions. SAVE 🛏️ 🛜 🛢️ 💻

👓 ▼▼▼ **Quality Inn** H

(361) 592-5251. **$70-$160.** 221 S Hwy 77 Bypass 78363. On US 77, just s of jct SR 141. Ext corridors. **Pets:** Accepted.

SAVE 🛏️ 🛜 🛢️ 💻

KINGWOOD

👓 ▼▼▼ **Comfort Suites K-Humble Houston North** H 🐾

(281) 359-4448. **$90-$300.** 22223 Hwy 59 N 77339. US 59 exit Kingwood Dr northbound; exit McClellan southbound. Int corridors. **Pets:** Small. $25 daily fee/pet. Service with restrictions, supervision.

SAVE 🛏️ 🛜 ✖️ 🛢️ 💻

KYLE

▼▼▼ **La Quinta Inn & Suites Kyle** H

(512) 295-5599. **$95-$279.** 18869 IH-35 N 78640. I-35 exit 217; on east frontage road. Int corridors. **Pets:** Large, other species. Service with restrictions. 🛏️ 🛜 ✖️ 🛢️ 💻

LA GRANGE *(Restaurants p. 642)*

👓 ▼▼▼ **BEST WESTERN PLUS La Grange Inn & Suites** H

(979) 968-6800. **$106-$129.** 600 E State Hwy 71 Bypass 78945. Jct US 77 and SR 71, just e on N Frontage Rd. Int corridors. **Pets:** Accepted.

SAVE 🛏️ 🛜 ✖️ 🛢️ 💻

LAJITAS

▼▼▼ **Lajitas Golf Resort and Spa** H

(432) 424-5000. **Call for rates.** 1 Main St 79852. Center. Ext/int corridors. **Pets:** Accepted. 🍴 🛏️ ✖️ 🛜 ✖️ 🛢️ 💻

LAKE DALLAS

👓 ▼▼▼ **BEST WESTERN PLUS Lake Dallas Inn & Suites** H

(940) 497-1007. **$80-$200.** 305 Swisher Rd 75065. I-35E exit 458 (Swisher Rd), 0.6 mi on N Frontage Rd. Int corridors. **Pets:** Medium. $25 one-time fee/room. Designated rooms, service with restrictions, supervision. SAVE 🛏️ 🛜 ✖️ 🛢️ 💻

LAKE JACKSON *(Restaurants p. 642)*

▼▼▼ **Candlewood Suites-Lake Jackson-Clute** H

(979) 297-0011. **$110-$149.** 506 Hwy 332 77566. Jct SR 288/332 and Plantation Dr, just n. Int corridors. **Pets:** Medium. $150 one-time fee/room. Designated rooms, service with restrictions, supervision.

🛏️ 🛜 🛢️ 💻

LAKEWAY *(Restaurants p. 642)*

👓 ▼▼▼▼ **Lakeway Resort & Spa** H

(512) 261-6600. **$119-$1300, 3 day notice.** 101 Lakeway Dr 78734. Jct FM 620 and Lakeway Blvd W, 1.5 mi to Lakeway Dr, 2.1 mi n. Int corridors. **Pets:** Medium, dogs only. $75 one-time fee/pet. Designated rooms, service with restrictions, supervision.

SAVE 🍴 🛏️ ✖️ 🛜 ✖️ 🛢️ 💻

LAREDO

▼▼ **Days Inn & Suites** H

(956) 724-8221. **$90-$170.** 7060 N San Bernardo Ave 78041. I-35 exit 4 (San Bernardo Ave), just s; on southbound access road. Ext/int corridors. **Pets:** Small. $10 daily fee/pet. Designated rooms, service with restrictions, supervision. 🍴 🛏️ 🛜 🛢️ 💻

▼▼▼ **La Posada Hotel & Suites** H

(956) 722-1701. **Call for rates.** 1000 Zaragoza St 78040. I-35 exit downtown; just e of International Bridge 1. Ext/int corridors. **Pets:** Accepted. 🍴 🛏️ 🛜 🛢️ 💻

▼▼▼ **La Quinta Inn & Suites Laredo Airport** H

(956) 724-7222. **$112-$234.** 7220 Bob Bullock Loop 78041. I-35 exit 8 (Bob Bullock Loop E), 5.8 mi e. Int corridors. **Pets:** Large, other species. Service with restrictions. 🛏️ 🛜 🛢️ 💻

▼▼ **La Quinta Inn Laredo I-35** M

(956) 722-0511. **$79-$204.** 3610 Santa Ursula Ave 78041. I-35 exit 2 (Jefferson St); on southbound frontage road. Ext corridors. **Pets:** Large, other species. Service with restrictions. 🛏️ 🛜 🛢️ 💻

◆◆◆ **Residence Inn by Marriott Laredo** H

(956) 753-9700. **$98-$153.** 310 Lost Oaks Blvd 78041. I-35 exit 3B (Mann Rd), just n; on northbound frontage road. Int corridors.
Pets: Accepted. 🅜 ≫ 🛜 ✕ 🛢 🔲

◆◆◆ **Staybridge Suites-Laredo** H

(956) 722-0444. **Call for rates.** 7010 Bob Bullock Loop 78041. US 83 exit on Loop 20 (Bob Bullock Loop); on west side. Int corridors.
Pets: Accepted. ≫ 🛜 🛢 🔲

LEVELLAND
◆◆◆ **Holiday Inn Express Hotel & Suites** H

(806) 894-8555. **Call for rates.** 703 E SR 114 79336. 0.5 mi e of jct US 385. Int corridors. **Pets:** Accepted. ≫ 🛜 🛢 🔲

LEWISVILLE
◆◆◆ **Country Inn & Suites By Carlson** H

(972) 315-6565. **Call for rates.** 755 E Vista Ridge Mall Dr 75067. I-35E exit 447B northbound, just w on SR 121 Bypass; exit 448A (Round Grove Rd) southbound, 0.5 mi s on service road to Vista Ridge Mall Dr, then just w. Int corridors. **Pets:** Accepted. ≫ 🛜 🛢 🔲

◆ **Motel 6-#1288** H

(972) 436-5008. **$49-$70.** 1705 Lakepointe Dr 75057. I-35E exit 449 (Corporate Dr), just n on service road. Int corridors. **Pets:** Other species. Service with restrictions, crate. ≫ 📶 🛢

◆◆◆ **Residence Inn by Marriott Dallas/Lewisville** H

(972) 315-3777. **$119-$179.** 755 E Vista Ridge Mall Dr 75067. I-35E exit 448A (Round Grove Rd) southbound, 0.5 mi s on frontage road, then just w; exit 447B northbound, just w to Lake Vista, then just n. Int corridors. **Pets:** Small. $100 one-time fee/pet. Service with restrictions, supervision. 🅜 ≫ 🛜 ✕ 🛢 🔲

◆◆◆ **TownePlace Suites by Marriott Dallas Lewisville** H

(972) 459-1275. **$120-$150.** 731 E Vista Ridge Mall Dr 75067. I-35 exit 447B northbound (SR 121); exit 448A southbound (SR 121), just w to Lake Vista Dr, then just n. Int corridors. **Pets:** Accepted.
≫ 🛜 ✕ 🛢 🔲

LITTLEFIELD
◆◆◆ **BEST WESTERN Littlefield Inn & Suites** H

(806) 385-3400. **$112-$149.** 2600 Hall Ave 79339. Just s of jct US 84 and 385. Int corridors. **Pets:** Accepted.
🆂🅰🆅🅴 🅜 ≫ 🛜 ✕ 🛢 🔲

LIVE OAK
◆◆ **La Quinta Inn San Antonio I-35 North at Toepperwein** H

(210) 657-5500. **$65-$229.** 12822 I-35 N 78233. I-35 exit 170B (Toepperwein Rd); on northbound access road. Ext/int corridors. **Pets:** Large, other species. Service with restrictions. ≫ 🛜 🛢 🔲

LIVINGSTON
◆◆◆ **BEST WESTERN PLUS Livingston Inn & Suites** H

(936) 327-8500. **$109-$189.** 335 Hwy 59 Loop S 77351. Just s of jct US 59 and 190; on southbound frontage road. Int corridors. **Pets:** Small. $100 deposit/room. Designated rooms, service with restrictions, crate. 🆂🅰🆅🅴 ≫ 🛜 🛢 🔲

LLANO
◆◆◆ **BEST WESTERN Llano** H

(325) 247-4101. **$70-$110.** 901 W Young St 78643. 1 mi w on SR 71 and 29. Ext corridors. **Pets:** $10 daily fee/pet. Service with restrictions, crate. 🆂🅰🆅🅴 ≫ 🛜 🛢 🔲

LONGVIEW
◆◆◆ ◆◆◆ **BEST WESTERN Regency Inn & Suites** H

(903) 212-3333. **$89-$94.** 707 N Access Rd 75602. I-20 exit 596 (Eastman Rd), just w; on north frontage road. Int corridors. **Pets:** Accepted.
🆂🅰🆅🅴 ≫ 🛜 🛢 🔲

◆◆◆ **Holiday Inn Express Hotel & Suites Longview South** H

(903) 247-3000. **Call for rates.** 900 S Access Rd 75602. I-20 exit 596. Int corridors. **Pets:** Other species. $25 one-time fee/pet. Service with restrictions, supervision. ≫ 🛜 🛢 🔲

◆◆◆ **La Quinta Inn & Suites Longview North** H

(903) 663-6611. **$90-$205.** 908 E Hawkins Pkwy 75605. Just w of jct US 259. Int corridors. **Pets:** Large, other species. Service with restrictions. 🅜 ≫ 🛜 ✕ 🛢 🔲

◆◆◆ **Staybridge Suites** H

(903) 212-3800. **Call for rates.** 3409 N Fourth St 75605. Just n of jct SR 281/Loop 281. Int corridors. **Pets:** Accepted. 🛜 ✕ 🛢 🔲

LUBBOCK
◆◆◆ ◆◆◆ **Arbor Inn & Suites** H

(806) 722-2726. **$89-$249.** 5310 Englewood Ave 79424. Loop 289 exit 50th St, just w. Int corridors. **Pets:** Accepted.
🆂🅰🆅🅴 🅜 ≫ 🛜 🛢 🔲

◆◆◆ **Baymont Inn & Suites Lubbock** H

(806) 792-5181. **$69-$198.** 3901 19th St 79410. Jct US 62/82 W and 19th St. Int corridors. **Pets:** Accepted. 🅜 ≫ 🛜 ✕ 🛢 🔲

◆◆◆ ◆◆◆ **BEST WESTERN PLUS Lubbock Windsor Inn** H

(806) 762-8400. **$80-$200.** 5410 I-27 79404. I-27 1B southbound; 1A (50th St) northbound. Int corridors. **Pets:** Large. $20 daily fee/pet. Service with restrictions, supervision. 🆂🅰🆅🅴 ≫ 🛜 🛢 🔲

◆◆◆ ◆◆◆ **La Quinta Inn & Suites Lubbock North** H

(806) 749-1600. **$92-$289.** 5006 Auburn St 79416. 1 mi sw of jct Loop 289 N and Quaker Ave; on N Service Rd. Int corridors. **Pets:** Large, other species. Service with restrictions. 🆂🅰🆅🅴 ≫ 🛜 ✕ 🛢 🔲

◆◆◆ **La Quinta Inn & Suites Lubbock West Medical Center** H

(806) 792-0065. **$79-$330.** 4115 Marsha Sharp Frwy 79407. Jct US 62/82 and Quaker Ave, just se. Ext/int corridors. **Pets:** Large, other species. Service with restrictions. ≫ 🛜 ✕ 🛢 🔲

◆◆◆ **La Quinta Inn Lubbock Civic Center** H

(806) 763-9441. **$65-$307.** 601 Ave Q 79401. 0.8 mi nw on US 84. Ext corridors. **Pets:** Large, other species. Service with restrictions.
≫ 🛜 🛢 🔲

◆◆◆ **Residence Inn by Marriott** H 🐾

(806) 745-1963. **$99-$350.** 2551 S Loop 289 79423. Just w of jct University Ave; on south frontage road. Ext corridors. **Pets:** Other species. $100 one-time fee/room. Service with restrictions, crate.
≫ 🛜 ✕ 🛢 🔲

◆◆◆ **Staybridge Suites** H

(806) 765-8900. **Call for rates.** 2515 19th St 79410. Just sw of jct University Ave. Int corridors. **Pets:** Accepted.
🅜 ≫ 🛜 ✕ 🛢 🔲

◆◆◆ **TownePlace Suites by Marriott** H

(806) 799-6226. **$79-$299.** 5310 W Loop 289 79424. 0.5 mi s of jct US 62/82. Int corridors. **Pets:** Accepted. 🅜 ≫ 🛜 ✕ 🛢 🔲

LUFKIN

AAA BEST WESTERN PLUS Crown Colony Inn & Suites ⓗ

(936) 634-3481. **$115-$149.** 3211 S 1st St 75901. 2 mi s of jct US 59 and Loop 287. Int corridors. **Pets:** Medium. $20 one-time fee/room. Service with restrictions, crate. ⟨SAVE⟩ ⟨≈⟩ ⟨✕⟩ ⟨🖫⟩ ⟨💻⟩

LULING

AAA BEST WESTERN PLUS Longhorn Inn & Suites ⓗ

(830) 875-5442. **$130-$160.** 4120 E Pierce St 78648. I-10 exit 632; on northwest corner. Int corridors. **Pets:** Accepted.
⟨SAVE⟩ ⟨≈⟩ ⟨✕⟩ ⟨🖫⟩ ⟨💻⟩

MADISONVILLE

AAA BEST WESTERN Executive Inn & Suites ⓗ

(936) 349-1700. **$110-$120.** 3307 E Main St 77864. I-45 exit 142, just e. Int corridors. **Pets:** Accepted. ⟨SAVE⟩ ⟨♿⟩ ⟨≈⟩ ⟨≈⟩ ⟨🖫⟩ ⟨💻⟩

Woodbine Hotel and Restaurant ⓒ

(936) 348-3333. **$85-$165, 7 day notice.** 209 N Madison St 77864. I-45 exit 142, 2.2 mi w to town square, then 2 blks n. Ext/int corridors. **Pets:** Small. Service with restrictions, supervision.
⟨🍴⟩ ⟨≈⟩ ⟨✕⟩ ⟨🛁⟩ ⟨🖫⟩

MANSFIELD

AAA BEST WESTERN PLUS Mansfield Inn & Suites ⓗ

(817) 539-0707. **$89-$94.** 775 N Hwy 287 76063. US 287 exit Walnut Creek Rd; on southbound frontage road. Int corridors. **Pets:** Medium. $20 daily fee/pet. Service with restrictions, supervision.
⟨SAVE⟩ ⟨♿⟩ ⟨≈⟩ ⟨≈⟩ ⟨🖫⟩ ⟨💻⟩

Holiday Inn Express Hotel & Suites ⓗ

(817) 453-8722. **Call for rates.** 201 Hwy 287 N 76063. US 287 exit Walnut Creek Rd, just s on frontage road. Int corridors. **Pets:** Accepted.
⟨♿⟩ ⟨≈⟩ ⟨≈⟩ ⟨✕⟩ ⟨🖫⟩ ⟨💻⟩

La Quinta Inn & Suites Mansfield ⓗ

(817) 453-5040. **$87-$210.** 1503 Breckenridge Rd 76063. US 287 exit Walnut Creek Rd/Debbie Ln, 1.2 mi n to Debbie Ln, then just e. Int corridors. **Pets:** Large, other species. Service with restrictions.
⟨♿⟩ ⟨≈⟩ ⟨≈⟩ ⟨✕⟩ ⟨🖫⟩ ⟨💻⟩

MANVEL

AAA BEST WESTERN PLUS Manvel Inn & Suites ⓗ

(281) 489-2266. **$86-$239.** 19301 Hwy 6 77578. 1.3 mi e of jct SR 288. Int corridors. **Pets:** Accepted. ⟨SAVE⟩ ⟨≈⟩ ⟨≈⟩ ⟨✕⟩ ⟨🖫⟩ ⟨💻⟩

MARBLE FALLS

AAA BEST WESTERN Marble Falls Inn ⓗ 🐾

(830) 693-5122. **$89-$139.** 1403 US Hwy 281 78654. 0.4 mi n of jct US 281 and FM 1431. Ext/int corridors. **Pets:** $10 daily fee/room. Designated rooms, service with restrictions. ⟨SAVE⟩ ⟨♿⟩ ⟨≈⟩ ⟨≈⟩ ⟨🖫⟩ ⟨💻⟩

Quality Inn-Marble Falls ⓗ

(830) 693-7531. **$100-$130.** 1206 Hwy 281 N 78654. 0.3 mi n of jct US 281 and FM 1431. Ext corridors. **Pets:** Accepted. ⟨≈⟩ ⟨≈⟩ ⟨🖫⟩ ⟨💻⟩

MARFA

Hotel Paisano ⓗ

(432) 729-3669. **$99-$289, 5 day notice.** 207 N Highland Ave 79843. Jct US 90 and SR 17, 3 blks n. Int corridors. **Pets:** Accepted.
⟨🍴⟩ ⟨≈⟩ ⟨≈⟩ ⟨✕⟩ ⟨🛁⟩ ⟨🖫⟩ ⟨💻⟩

MARSHALL

AAA BEST WESTERN Executive Inn ⓗ

(903) 935-0707. **$69-$79.** 5201 E End Blvd S 75672. I-20 exit 617, 0.4 mi n on US 59. Ext corridors. **Pets:** Accepted.
⟨SAVE⟩ ⟨≈⟩ ⟨≈⟩ ⟨🖫⟩ ⟨💻⟩

La Quinta Inn & Suites ⓗ

(903) 934-3080. **$92-$194.** 6015 E End Blvd S 75672. I-20 exit 617, just s. Int corridors. **Pets:** Large, other species. Service with restrictions.
⟨♿⟩ ⟨≈⟩ ⟨✕⟩ ⟨🖫⟩ ⟨💻⟩

Motel 6 Marshall-#422 Ⓜ

(903) 934-3104. **$45-$60.** 300 I-20 E 75670. I-20 exit 617, just s, then just e. Ext corridors. **Pets:** Other species. Service with restrictions, crate. ⟨≈⟩ ⟨≈⟩

MESQUITE

Hampton Inn & Suites at Rodeo Center ⓗ

(972) 329-3100. **$109-$125.** 1700 Rodeo Dr 75149. I-635 exit 4 (Military Pkwy), 0.5 mi s on Hickory Tree Rd. Int corridors. **Pets:** Large. Service with restrictions, crate. ⟨♿⟩ ⟨≈⟩ ⟨≈⟩ ⟨✕⟩ ⟨🖫⟩ ⟨💻⟩

MEXIA

AAA BEST WESTERN Limestone Inn & Suites ⓗ

(254) 562-0200. **Call for rates.** 1314 E Milam St 76667. Just e of CR 1365 on US 84; east side of town. Int corridors. **Pets:** Accepted.
⟨SAVE⟩ ⟨≈⟩ ⟨≈⟩ ⟨🖫⟩ ⟨💻⟩

MIDLAND

La Quinta Inn & Suites Midland North ⓗ

(432) 694-1200. **$139-$369.** 2606 N Loop 250 W 79707. 0.5 mi n of jct SR 158/191; on east frontage road. Int corridors. **Pets:** Large, other species. Service with restrictions. ⟨♿⟩ ⟨≈⟩ ⟨≈⟩ ⟨✕⟩ ⟨🖫⟩ ⟨💻⟩

Residence Inn by Marriott Midland ⓗ

(432) 689-3511. **$149-$329.** 5509 Deauville Blvd 79706. Just w of jct Loop 250; on south frontage road. Int corridors. **Pets:** Accepted.
⟨♿⟩ ⟨≈⟩ ⟨≈⟩ ⟨✕⟩ ⟨🖫⟩ ⟨💻⟩

MINERAL WELLS

AAA BEST WESTERN Club House Inn & Suites ⓗ 🐾

(940) 325-2270. **$70-$130.** 4410 Hwy 180 E 76067. Jct US 180 and CR 1195; in East Mineral Wells. Int corridors. **Pets:** Other species. $10 daily fee/pet. Service with restrictions, supervision.
⟨SAVE⟩ ⟨♿⟩ ⟨≈⟩ ⟨≈⟩ ⟨🖫⟩ ⟨💻⟩

MISSION

El Rocio Retreat Ⓑ Ⓑ

(956) 584-7432. **$75-$315, 3 day notice.** 2519 S Inspiration Rd 78572. Jct US 83 at Inspiration Rd, 2 mi s. Ext/int corridors. **Pets:** Accepted.
⟨≈⟩ ⟨✕⟩ ⟨🖫⟩

La Quinta Inn & Suites ⓗ

(956) 581-7772. **$85-$249.** 805 Travis St 78572. US 83 exit Bryan Rd; on eastbound access road. Int corridors. **Pets:** Large, other species. Service with restrictions. ⟨≈⟩ ⟨≈⟩ ⟨✕⟩ ⟨🖫⟩ ⟨💻⟩

MONAHANS

AAA BEST WESTERN PLUS Monahans Inn & Suites ⓗ

(432) 943-3360. **$190.** 2101 S Betty St 79756. I-20 exit 80, just se. Int corridors. **Pets:** Small. $20 daily fee/pet. Service with restrictions, supervision. ⟨SAVE⟩ ⟨≈⟩ ⟨≈⟩ ⟨🖫⟩ ⟨💻⟩

MONTGOMERY

AAA BEST WESTERN Lake Conroe Inn ⓗ

(936) 588-3030. **$105-$125.** 14643 Hwy 105 W 77356. Just w of McCaleb Rd. Ext corridors. **Pets:** Accepted. ⟨SAVE⟩ ⟨≈⟩ ⟨≈⟩ ⟨🖫⟩ ⟨💻⟩

AAA ▼▼ ▼▼ **La Torretta Lake Resort & Spa** H
(936) 448-4400. **Call for rates.** 600 La Torretta Blvd 77356. SR 105, 2.5 mi n on Walden Rd to La Torretta Blvd. Ext/int corridors. **Pets:** Small, dogs only. $250 deposit/room, $50 one-time fee/room. Designated rooms, service with restrictions, crate.
SAVE ▯ ▭ ▭ ▭ ▭ ▭

MOUNT PLEASANT

AAA ▼▼ ▼▼ **BEST WESTERN Mt. Pleasant Inn** M
(903) 577-7377. **$61.** 102 E Burton Rd 75455. I-30 exit 162, just e. Ext corridors. **Pets:** Accepted. SAVE ▭ ▭ ▭ ▭

AAA ▼▼ ▼▼ **Quality Inn** H
(903) 577-7553. **$55-$90.** 2515 W Ferguson Rd 75455. I-30 exit 160, just s. Ext corridors. **Pets:** Accepted. SAVE ▭ ▭ ▭ ▭

▼▼ ▼▼ **Super 8** M
(903) 572-9808. **$50-$155.** 204 Lakewood Dr 75455. I-30 exit 162 east-bound; exit 162A westbound, then just n, then just w. Ext corridors. **Pets:** Accepted. ▭ ▭ ▭ ▭

MCALLEN

▼▼ ▼▼ **Drury Inn-McAllen** H
(956) 687-5100. **$100-$159.** 612 W Expwy 83 78501. US 83 exit 2nd St; on northwest frontage road. Int corridors. **Pets:** $10 daily fee/room. Service with restrictions, supervision. ▭ ▭ ▭ ▭

▼▼ ▼▼ **Drury Suites-McAllen** H
(956) 682-3222. **$125-$239.** 228 W Expwy 83 78501. At US 83 and 6th St. Int corridors. **Pets:** $10 daily fee/room. Service with restrictions, supervision. ▭ ▭ ▭ ▭ ▭

▼▼ **Motel 6 McAllen-#212** M
(956) 687-3700. **$51-$70.** 700 W Expwy 83 78501. US 83 exit 2nd St; on northwest frontage road. Ext corridors. **Pets:** Other species. Service with restrictions, crate. ▭ ▭

▼▼ **Pear Tree Inn by Drury** H
(956) 682-4900. **$90-$134.** 300 W Expwy 83 78501. US 83 exit 2nd St; on northwest frontage road. Int corridors. **Pets:** $10 daily fee/room. Service with restrictions, supervision. ▭ ▭ ▭ ▭

▼▼ **Posada Ana Inn** H
(956) 631-6700. **$77-$99.** 620 W Expwy 83 78501. US 83 exit 2nd St; on northwest frontage road. Int corridors. **Pets:** $10 daily fee/room. Service with restrictions, supervision. ▭ ▭

▼▼ ▼▼ **Residence Inn by Marriott** H
(956) 994-8626. **$119-$199.** 220 W Expwy 83 78501. US 83 exit 2nd St, just w, then just n on 2nd St. Int corridors. **Pets:** Accepted.
▭ ▭ ▭ ▭ ▭ ▭

▼▼ ▼▼ **Staybridge Suites McAllen-Airport** H
(956) 213-7829. **Call for rates.** 620 Wichita Ave 78503. 0.4 mi s of US 83, just e of S 10th St. Int corridors. **Pets:** Accepted.
▭ ▭ ▭ ▭ ▭ ▭

MCKINNEY

AAA ▼▼▼▼ **La Quinta Inn & Suites at The Ballfields at Craig Ranch** H
(972) 908-2370. **$79-$196.** 6501 Henneman Way 75070. SR 121 exit Stacy Rd, just n, then just w. Int corridors. **Pets:** Large, other species. Service with restrictions. SAVE ▭ ▭ ▭ ▭ ▭

▼▼ ▼▼ **Quality Inn** H
(972) 542-9471. **$65-$110.** 1300 N Central Expwy 75070. US 75 exit 40B (Bob White Ave); on northbound frontage road. Ext corridors. **Pets:** Accepted. ▭ ▭ ▭ ▭

▼▼ ▼▼ **Super 8-McKinney** H
(972) 548-8880. **$59-$99.** 910 N Central Expwy 75070. US 75 exit 40A (Virginia St/Louisiana St), 0.5 mi n on northbound frontage road. Int corridors. **Pets:** Accepted. ▭ ▭ ▭ ▭ ▭

NACOGDOCHES

AAA ▼▼ ▼▼ **BEST WESTERN Northpark Inn** H
(936) 560-1906. **$65-$150.** 4809 US 59 N 75964. Jct US 59 N and Loop 224 exit Westward Dr. Ext corridors. **Pets:** Accepted.
SAVE ▭ ▭ ▭ ▭

▼▼▼▼ **Holiday Inn Express Nacogdoches** H
(936) 564-0100. **$105-$145.** 200 Holiday Ln 75964. US 59, just s of jct Loop 224 and US 59 business route. Int corridors. **Pets:** Accepted.
▭M ▭ ▭ ▭

▼▼ ▼▼ **Super 8 Nacogdoches** H
(936) 560-2888. **$59-$129.** 3909 South St 75964. On US 59, just s of jct Loop 224. Int corridors. **Pets:** Accepted. ▭ ▭ ▭ ▭

NASSAU BAY

▼▼▼▼ **Hilton Houston NASA Clear Lake** H
(281) 333-9300. **$109-$209.** 3000 NASA Pkwy 77058. 2 mi e of NASA Bypass road. Int corridors. **Pets:** Accepted.
▯ ▭ ▭ ▭ ▭ ▭

NAVASOTA

AAA ▼▼ ▼▼ **BEST WESTERN Inn of Navasota** H
(936) 870-4100. **Call for rates.** 8965 Hwy 6 N 77868. Jct SR 6 and 90; on southeast corner. Ext corridors. **Pets:** Dogs only. $50 deposit/room, $20 one-time fee/pet, $20 daily fee/pet. Service with restrictions, crate.
SAVE ▭ ▭ ▭ ▭

▼▼ ▼▼ **Comfort Inn & Suites** H
(936) 825-9464. **$96-$240.** 9345 State Hwy 6 Loop S 77868. SR 6 exit SR 105 and 90, 0.5 mi n on E Frontage Rd. Int corridors.
Pets: Accepted. ▭ ▭ ▭ ▭ ▭

NEW BRAUNFELS

▼▼ ▼▼ **Executive Inn & Suites** M
(830) 625-3932. **$49-$199.** 808 Hwy 46 S 78130. I-35 exit 189 (SR 46), 0.4 mi e. Ext corridors. **Pets:** Very small, dogs only. $25 daily fee/pet. Designated rooms, service with restrictions, crate.
▭M ▭ ▭ ▭

▼▼▼▼ **La Quinta Inn & Suites New Braunfels** H
(830) 627-3333. **$84-$269.** 365 Hwy 46 S 78130. I-35 exit 189 (SR 46), just e. Int corridors. **Pets:** Large, other species. Service with restrictions. ▭M ▭ ▭ ▭ ▭ ▭

▼▼ ▼▼ **Quality Inn & Suites** H
(830) 643-9300. **$59-$359.** 1533 IH-35 N 78130. I-35 exit 190; on southbound frontage road. Int corridors. **Pets:** Accepted.
▭ ▭ ▭ ▭

▼▼ ▼▼ **Ramada New Braunfels** H
(830) 625-8017. **$80-$200.** 1051 I-35 E 78130. I-35 exit 189 (SR 46); on southbound frontage road. Ext corridors. **Pets:** Small, other species. $25 one-time fee/pet. Service with restrictions, supervision.
▭M ▭ ▭ ▭

▼▼ ▼▼ **Super 8-New Braunfels** M
(830) 629-1155. **$60-$220.** 510 Hwy 46 S 78130. I-35 exit 189 (SR 46), just e. Ext corridors. **Pets:** Accepted. ▭ ▭ ▭ ▭

▼▼▼▼ **Wingate by Wyndham** H
(830) 515-4701. **$84-$149.** 245 FM 306 N 78130. I-35 exit 191 (FM 306), just w. Int corridors. **Pets:** Medium, dogs only. Service with restrictions, supervision. ▭M ▭ ▭ ▭ ▭ ▭

NEW CANEY

AAA ▼▼▼▼ **BEST WESTERN PLUS New Caney Inn & Suites** H
(281) 354-7222. **$85-$120.** 22033 N Hwy 59 77357. US 59 exit north-bound Community Dr, just e; exit southbound FM 1314, make U-turn. Int corridors. **Pets:** Accepted. SAVE ▭M ▭ ▭ ▭ ▭ ▭

La Quinta Inn & Suites-New Caney H
(281) 354-1904. **$79-$219**. 22025 US Hwy 59 77357. US 59 exit north-bound Community Dr, just e; exit southbound FM 1314, U-turn 1 mi n. Int corridors. **Pets:** Large, other species. Service with restrictions.

NORTH RICHLAND HILLS

BEST WESTERN N.E. Mall Inn & Suites H
(817) 656-8881. **$80-$90**. 8709 Airport Frwy 76180. SR 121/183 exit Precinct Line Rd eastbound; exit Bedford Euless Rd westbound; on westbound frontage road. Ext corridors. **Pets:** Accepted.

ODESSA

BEST WESTERN Garden Oasis H
(432) 337-3006. Call for rates. 110 W I-20 79761. I-20 exit 116, just w. Ext/int corridors. **Pets:** Medium. $25 one-time fee/room. Service with restrictions, supervision.

Comfort Suites H
(432) 362-1500. **$205-$233**. 4801 E 50th St 79762. Jct JBS Pkwy and 52nd St, just s. Int corridors. **Pets:** Accepted.

TownePlace Suites by Marriott H
(432) 362-1077. **$119-$309**. 4412 Tanglewood Ln 79762. Just nw of jct JBS Pkwy and 42nd St. Int corridors. **Pets:** Accepted.

ORANGE

Holiday Inn Express & Suites Orange H
(409) 882-9222. **$99-$139**. 2655 I-10 E 77630. I-10 exit 877 eastbound; exit 876 westbound; on eastbound frontage road. Int corridors. **Pets:** Medium. $10 daily fee/pet. Service with restrictions, supervision.

La Quinta Inn & Suites Orange H
(409) 883-0011. **$89-$244**. 2220 Hwy 62 S 77630. I-10 exit 873, just s. Int corridors. **Pets:** Large, other species. Service with restrictions.

OZONA

Hillcrest Inn & Suites M
(325) 392-5515. **$70-$90**. 1204 Sheffield Rd/Loop 466 W 76943. I-10 exit 365, 2 blks n to Loop 466, then 1 mi w. Ext corridors. **Pets:** Medium. $20 daily fee/pet. Service with restrictions, supervision.

Travelodge Ozona M
(325) 392-2656. **$99-$130**. 8 11th St 76943. I-10 exit 368 westbound, 2 mi w; exit 365 eastbound to Loop 466, 1 mi e. Ext corridors. **Pets:** Accepted.

PALESTINE

BEST WESTERN Palestine Inn H
(903) 723-4655. **$79-$115**. 1601 W Palestine Ave 75801. Jct US 287/SR 19, 0.7 mi sw on US 79. Ext corridors. **Pets:** Small. $10 daily fee/pet. Designated rooms, service with restrictions, supervision.

Holiday Inn Express H
(903) 723-4884. Call for rates. 1030 E Palestine Ave 75801. Jct US 79 and Loop 256, 0.3 mi s on US 79. Int corridors. **Pets:** Accepted.

La Quinta Inn & Suites Palestine H
(903) 723-1387. **$89-$204**. 3000 S Loop 256 75801. 1.8 mi e of jct US 79 and Loop 256. Int corridors. **Pets:** Large, other species. Service with restrictions.

PAMPA

AmericInn Lodge & Suites of Pampa H
(806) 665-4404. **$105-$125**. 1101 N Hobart St 79065. Just n of jct SR 70 and 152. Int corridors. **Pets:** $15 daily fee/room. Designated rooms, service with restrictions, crate.

BEST WESTERN Northgate Inn H
(806) 665-0926. **$90-$105**. 2831 Perryton Pkwy 79065. 2.1 mi n of jct SR 70 and 152. Ext corridors. **Pets:** Accepted.

PARIS

Americas Best Value Inn Paris H
(903) 785-5566. **$59-$79**. 3755 NE Loop 286 75460. Jct US 82 and E Loop 286, just n. Ext corridors. **Pets:** Medium, other species. $15 daily fee/pet. Designated rooms, service with restrictions, crate.

PEARLAND

BEST WESTERN Pearland Inn H 🐾
(281) 997-2000. **$90-$111**. 1855 N Main St 77581. Jct Loop 8 S and SR 35, 1.5 mi s. Ext corridors. **Pets:** Other species. $20 daily fee/pet. Service with restrictions, supervision.

La Quinta Inn & Suites Pearland H
(281) 412-5454. **$95-$289**. 9002 Broadway St 77584. Jct SR 288 and 518, 1.6 mi e. Int corridors. **Pets:** Large, other species. Service with restrictions.

PEARSALL

Baymont Inn & Suites Pearsall H
(830) 334-4900. **$110-$130**. 1808 W Comal St 78061. I-35 exit 101, just e. Ext/int corridors. **Pets:** Accepted.

La Quinta Inn & Suites H
(830) 872-3277. **$99-$279**. 170 Medical Dr 78061. I-35 exit 101, just w; on southbound frontage road. Int corridors. **Pets:** Large, other species. Service with restrictions.

PECOS

BEST WESTERN Swiss Clock Inn H 🐾
(432) 447-2215. **$137-$142**. 133 S Frontage Rd, I-20 79772. I-20 exit 40, just s. Ext corridors. **Pets:** Dogs only. $15 daily fee/pet. Designated rooms, service with restrictions, supervision.

Knights Inn Laura Lodge Motel & Suites M
(432) 445-4924. **$100-$144**. 1000 E 3rd St 79772. I-20 exit 42, 1 mi nw to Business Rt I-20, then 0.5 mi e. Ext corridors. **Pets:** Small. $15 daily fee/pet. Designated rooms, service with restrictions, supervision.

Oak Tree Inn H
(432) 445-1628. **$90-$115**. 22 N Frontage Rd 79772. I-20 exit 42, just w; on north frontage road. Int corridors. **Pets:** Accepted.

PERRYTON

BEST WESTERN Perryton Inn H 🐾
(806) 434-2850. **$129, 3 day notice**. 3505 S Main St (US 83) 79070. US 83, 2.2 mi s. Int corridors. **Pets:** Other species. $20 daily fee/pet. Designated rooms, service with restrictions, crate.

PHARR

La Quinta Inn & Suites North H
(956) 782-8832. **$84-$215**. 4607 N Cage Blvd 78577. US 281 exit Nolana Loop, just w. Int corridors. **Pets:** Large, other species. Service with restrictions.

◈◈◈◈ **La Quinta Inn & Suites Pharr** H

(956) 787-2900. **$84-$215.** 4603 N Cage Blvd 78577. US 281 exit Nolana Loop, just w. Int corridors. **Pets:** Large, other species. Service with restrictions. 🅼 ➠ 🛜 ✕ 🔌 💻

PLAINVIEW

◈◈◈◈ **Holiday Inn Express Hotel & Suites** H

(806) 296-9900. **Call for rates.** 4213 W 13th St 79072. I-27 exit 49 northbound, 0.5 mi nw; exit 50 southbound, 0.5 mi sw. Int corridors. **Pets:** Accepted. 🅼 ➠ 🛜 ✕ 🔌 💻

PLANO

◈◈◈ ◈◈◈◈ **Aloft Plano** H ❄

(214) 474-2520. **$84-$259.** 6853 N Dallas Pkwy 75024. Dallas North Tollway exit Spring Creek Pkwy/Tennyson Pkwy, just s of Tennyson Pkwy; on frontage road. Int corridors. **Pets:** Small, dogs only. Designated rooms, service with restrictions, supervision.

SAVE 🅼 ➠ 🛜 ✕ 🔌 💻

◈◈◈ ◈◈◈ **BEST WESTERN Park Suites Hotel** H

(972) 578-2243. **$105-$110.** 640 Park Blvd E 75074. US 75 exit 29A northbound, just e, then 0.5 mi s on frontage road; exit 29 southbound, just e on 15th St, then 0.5 mi n on frontage road. Int corridors. **Pets:** Medium, dogs only. $20 daily fee/pet. Designated rooms, service with restrictions. SAVE 🅼 ➠ 🛜 ✕ 🔌 💻

◈◈◈ **Candlewood Suites-Plano** H

(972) 618-5446. **$60-$160, 3 day notice.** 4701 Legacy Dr 75024. Jct SR 289 (Preston Rd) and Legacy Dr, just e. Int corridors. **Pets:** Accepted. 🛜 🔌 💻

◈◈◈ **Homewood Suites by Hilton** H

(972) 758-8800. **$109-$169.** 4705 Old Shepard Pl 75093. Jct Plano Pkwy and SR 289 (Preston Rd), 0.4 mi n, then just e. Int corridors. **Pets:** Accepted. 🅼 ➠ 🛜 🔌 💻

◈◈◈ ◈◈◈◈ **Hyatt Place Dallas/Plano** H ❄

(972) 378-3997. **$79-$239.** 3100 Dallas Pkwy 75093. Dallas Pkwy exit Park Blvd northbound; exit Parker Rd southbound; on northbound frontage road. Int corridors. **Pets:** Medium, dogs only. $75 one-time fee/room. Service with restrictions, supervision.

SAVE 🅼 ➠ 🛜 ✕ 🔌 💻

◈◈◈◈ **La Quinta Inn & Suites Dallas Plano West** H

(972) 599-0700. **$75-$214.** 4800 W Plano Pkwy 75093. Just e of jct SR 289 (Preston Rd). Int corridors. **Pets:** Large, other species. Service with restrictions. 🅼 ➠ 🛜 🔌 💻

◈◈◈ **NYLO Plano at Legacy** H

(972) 624-6990. **$99-$399.** 8201 Preston Rd 75024. Just s of jct SR 121. Int corridors. **Pets:** Accepted. 🍴 ➠ 🛜 ✕ 🔌 💻

◈◈◈ ◈◈◈ **Southfork Hotel** H

(972) 578-8555. **$89-$119.** 1600 N Central Expwy 75074. US 75 exit 29A northbound; exit 29 southbound; on northbound frontage road. Int corridors. **Pets:** Accepted. SAVE 🍴 ➠ 🛜 ✕ 🔌 💻

◈◈◈ ◈◈◈◈ **Staybridge Suites Plano/Richardson** H

(972) 612-8180. **$129-$139, 3 day notice.** 301 Silverglen Dr 75075. George Bush Toll Rd exit Coit Rd, n to Mapleshade Ln, just e, then just s. Int corridors. **Pets:** Medium, other species. $75 one-time fee/pet. Designated rooms, service with restrictions, crate.

SAVE 🅼 ➠ 🛜 ✕ 🔌 💻

◈◈◈ **Super 8-Plano** H

(972) 423-8300. **$55-$90.** 1704 N Central Expwy 75074. US 75 exit 29A (Park Blvd) northbound, just e; exit 29 southbound, 0.5 mi s on frontage road, just e on 15th St, then just n on frontage road. Int corridors. **Pets:** Accepted. 🅼 🛜 🔌 💻

◈◈◈ **TownePlace Suites by Marriott** H

(972) 943-8200. **$89-$149.** 5005 Whitestone Ln 75024. Dallas North Tollway exit Spring Creek Pkwy, 1.9 mi e, just n on SR 289 (Preston Rd) to Whitestone Ln, then just w. Int corridors. **Pets:** Accepted. 🅼 ➠ 🛜 ✕ 🔌 💻

PORT ARANSAS

◈◈◈ **Beachgate CondoSuites & Motel** CO

(361) 749-5900. **$60-$220, 30 day notice.** 2000 On the Beach Dr 78373. Between beach markers 8 and 9; street access on Anchor Rd off 11th St. Ext/int corridors. **Pets:** Accepted. ➠ 🛜 ✕ 🔌 💻

◈◈◈ **Island Hotel Port Aransas** M

(361) 749-8200. **Call for rates.** 2607 Hwy 361 78373. Just n of Paradise Dr. Ext corridors. **Pets:** Accepted. 🛜 ✕ 🔌 💻

◈◈◈ ◈◈◈ **Plantation Suites & Conference Center** M 🐾

(361) 749-3866. **Call for rates.** 1909 Hwy 361 78373. On SR 361, 0.4 mi s; on Mustang Island. Ext corridors. **Pets:** Other species. $100 deposit/room, $50 one-time fee/room. Service with restrictions, crate. SAVE ➠ 🛜 ✕ 🔌 💻

PORT LAVACA

◈◈◈ ◈◈◈ **BEST WESTERN Port Lavaca Inn** H 🐾

(361) 553-6800. **$109-$139.** 2202 N Hwy 35 77979. Jct US 87 and SR 35, 2.5 mi e. Int corridors. **Pets:** Large, other species. $20 daily fee/pet. Designated rooms, no service. SAVE ➠ 🛜 🔌 💻

◈◈◈ ◈◈◈ **La Quinta Inn & Suites Port Lavaca** H

(361) 552-8800. **$84-$294.** 910 Hwy 35 N 77979. Jct US 87 and SR 35, 2 mi e. Int corridors. **Pets:** Large, other species. Service with restrictions. SAVE 🅼 ➠ 🛜 ✕ 🔌 💻

POST

◈◈◈ ◈◈◈ **BEST WESTERN Post Inn** H

(806) 495-9933. **Call for rates.** 1011 N Broadway 79356. 1 mi n on US 84. Int corridors. **Pets:** Medium. $20 daily fee/pet. Designated rooms, service with restrictions, supervision. SAVE ➠ 🛜 🔌 💻

RANCHO VIEJO

◈◈◈ **Rancho Viejo Resort & Country Club** H

(956) 350-4000. **Call for rates.** 1 Rancho Viejo Dr 78575. US 77/83 exit Rancho Viejo. Ext corridors. **Pets:** Accepted. 🍴 ➠ ✕ 🛜 ✕ 🔌 💻

RAYMONDVILLE

◈◈◈ **La Quinta Inn & Suites Raymondville** H

(956) 689-4000. **$80-$217.** 128 N Expwy 77 78580. US 77, jct FM 186; on southbound access road. Int corridors. **Pets:** Large, other species. Service with restrictions. 🅼 ➠ 🛜 ✕ 🔌 💻

RICHARDSON

◈◈◈ ◈◈◈ **HYATT house Dallas/Richardson** H

(972) 671-8080. **$69-$199.** 2301 N Central Expwy 75080. US 75 exit 26 (Campbell Rd), 0.5 mi w to Collins Blvd, then 0.6 mi n. Int corridors. **Pets:** Medium. $150 one-time fee/pet. Service with restrictions, supervision. SAVE 🅼 ➠ 🛜 ✕ 🔌 💻

◈◈◈ ◈◈◈ **Hyatt Regency North Dallas/Richardson** H 🐾

(972) 619-1234. **$89-$249.** 701 E Campbell Rd 75081. US 75 exit 26 (Campbell Rd) southbound; exit northbound; on frontage road. Int corridors. **Pets:** Large, dogs only. $100 one-time fee/pet. Designated rooms, service with restrictions, supervision.

SAVE 🍴 🅼 ➠ 📶 ✕ 🔌 💻

◈◈◈ ◈◈◈◈ **Renaissance Dallas-Richardson Hotel** H 🐾

(972) 367-2000. **$75-$285.** 900 E Lookout Dr 75082. US 75 exit 27A (Gallatin Pkwy/Renner Rd) northbound; exit 26 (Gallatin Pkwy/Campbell Rd) southbound, just e. Int corridors. **Pets:** Large. $75 one-time fee/room. Service with restrictions.

SAVE 🍴 ➠ ✕ 📶 ✕ 🔌 💻

 Residence Inn by Marriott Richardson 🏨
(972) 669-5888. **$79-$209.** 1040 Waterwood Dr 75082. US 75 exit 26
(Campbell Rd), just e to Greenville Ave, 0.4 mi n to Glenville Rd, then
just w. Int corridors. **Pets:** Accepted.

[SAVE] [ECO] 🏊 🛜 ✕ ⛽ 💻

RICHLAND HILLS

🔷🔷 La Quinta Inn & Suites Fort Worth NE Mall 🏨
(817) 595-4442. **$89-$259.** 653 NE Loop 820 76118. I-820 exit 23, just
s of Glenview Dr. Int corridors. **Pets:** Large, other species. Service with
restrictions. 🅼 🏊 🛜 ✕ ⛽ 💻

ROANOKE

🔷🔷 Comfort Suites Near Alliance 🏨
(817) 490-1455. **$85-$125.** 801 W Byron Nelson Blvd 76262. I-35 exit
70 (SR 114), 2 mi e. Int corridors. **Pets:** Medium. $10 daily fee/pet.
Service with restrictions, crate. 🅼 🏊 🛜 ✕ ⛽ 💻

ROBSTOWN

🔷🔷🔷 Days Inn Ⓜ
(361) 387-8600. **$90-$143.** 650 Hwy 77 S 78380. Just n of jct CR 892
(Lincoln Ave) and US 77. Ext corridors. **Pets:** Accepted.

🏊 🛜 ⛽ 💻

ROCKPORT

🔷🔷 Days Inn Ⓜ
(361) 729-6379. **$65-$105.** 1212 Laurel St 78382. Jct Laurel St and
Business Rt SR 35; center. Ext corridors. **Pets:** Medium, dogs only. $15
daily fee/pet. Service with restrictions, supervision. 🏊 🛜 ⛽ 💻

ROCKWALL

 BEST WESTERN PLUS Rockwall Inn &
Suites 🏨
(972) 722-3265. **$90-$150.** 996 E I-30 75087. I-30 exit 68; on westbound frontage road. Int corridors. **Pets:** Medium, other species. $50
deposit/room, $10 daily fee/pet. Designated rooms, service with restric-
tions, supervision. [SAVE] 🅼 🏊 🛜 ✕ ⛽ 💻

🔷🔷 La Quinta Inn & Suites Rockwall 🏨
(972) 771-1685. **$79-$404.** 689 E I-30 75087. I-30 exit 67 (Ridge Rd)
westbound; exit 67B (Horizon Rd) eastbound; on eastbound frontage
road. Int corridors. **Pets:** Large, other species. Service with restrictions.

🅼 🏊 🛜 ⛽ 💻

ROSENBERG

🔷🔷 La Quinta Inn & Suites Rosenberg 🏨
(832) 595-6111. **$85-$255.** 28332 Southwest Frwy 77471. Jct US 59
and SR 36; on southbound frontage road. Int corridors. **Pets:** Large,
other species. Service with restrictions. 🏊 🛜 ✕ ⛽ 💻

ROUND ROCK *(Restaurants p. 642)*

🔷🔷🔷 BEST WESTERN Executive Inn 🏨
(512) 255-3222. **$79-$199.** 1851 N I-35 78664. I-35 exit 253 northbound; exit 253A southbound, U-turn. Ext corridors. **Pets:** Large, other
species. $5 daily fee/pet. Service with restrictions.

[SAVE] 🅼 🏊 🛜 ⛽ 💻

🔷🔷🔷 Candlewood Suites 🏨
(512) 828-0899. **Call for rates.** 521 S I-35 78664. I-35 exit 252A, just
n; on northbound frontage road. Int corridors. **Pets:** Accepted.

🛜 ⛽ 💻

🔷🔷🔷 Hampton Inn Austin-Round Rock 🏨
(512) 248-9100. **$119-$199.** 110 Dell Way 78664. I-35 exit 251; on east
frontage road. Int corridors. **Pets:** Medium. Service with restrictions,
supervision. 🅼 🏊 🛜 ✕ ⛽ 💻

🔷🔷🔷 Homewood Suites by Hilton 🏨
(512) 341-9200. **$129-$299.** 2201 S Mays St 78664. I-35 exit 251, just
n on east frontage road to Hesters Crossing, then just e. Int corridors.
Pets: Other species. $75 one-time fee/room. Service with restrictions,
crate. 🅼 🏊 🛜 ✕ ⛽ 💻

🔷🔷🔷 Residence Inn by Marriott Austin Round
Rock 🏨
(512) 733-2400. **$100-$300.** 2505 S I-35 78664. I-35 exit 250 southbound; exit 251 northbound; on east frontage road. Int corridors.
Pets: Accepted. [SAVE] 🅼 🏊 🛜 ✕ ⛽ 💻

🔷🔷🔷 SpringHill Suites by Marriott 🏨
(512) 733-6700. **$99-$169.** 2960 Hoppe Tr 78681. I-35 exit 256 southbound; exit 254 northbound; on west frontage road. Int corridors.
Pets: Accepted. 🅼 🏊 🛜 ✕ ⛽ 💻

🔷🔷🔷 Staybridge Suites Austin-Round Rock 🏨
(512) 733-0942. **$104-$189.** 520 I-35 S 78681. I-35 exit 252B northbound; exit 252AB southbound; on west frontage road. Int corridors.
Pets: Accepted. 🅼 🏊 🛜 ✕ ⛽ 💻

ROWLETT

🔷🔷🔷 Comfort Suites Lake Ray Hubbard 🏨
(972) 463-9595. **$79-$109.** 8701 E I-30 75088. I-30 exit 64 (Dalrock
Rd). Int corridors. **Pets:** Accepted. 🅼 🏊 🛜 ✕ ⛽ 💻

SAN ANGELO

🔷🔷🔷 BEST WESTERN San Angelo 🏨
(325) 223-1273. **$150-$225.** 3017 W Loop 306 76904. Loop 306 exit
College Hills Blvd, just s. Ext corridors. **Pets:** Accepted.

[SAVE] 🏊 🛜 ⛽ 💻

🔷🔷 Quality Inn 🏨
(325) 658-6594. **$160-$190.** 4613 S Jackson St 76903. Jct US 87 and
Jackson St. Ext corridors. **Pets:** $25 daily fee/pet. Designated rooms,
service with restrictions, crate. [SAVE] 🍽 🏊 🛜 ⛽ 💻

🔷🔷 Rodeway Inn 🏨
(325) 944-2578. **$165-$185.** 2502 Loop 306 76904. Loop 306 exit
Knickerbocker Rd. Ext corridors. **Pets:** Accepted.

🍽 🏊 🛜 ⛽ 💻

🔷🔷🔷 Staybridge Suites 🏨
(325) 653-1500. **Call for rates.** 1355 Knickerbocker Rd 76904. US 87
S, 1 mi w. Int corridors. **Pets:** Accepted. 🏊 🛜 ✕ ⛽ 💻

SAN ANTONIO

🔷🔷 Alamo Inn Ⓜ
(210) 227-2203. **$45-$120.** 2203 E Commerce St 78203. I-37 exit 141A,
1.2 mi e at Commerce St and New Braunfels Ave. Ext corridors.
Pets: Small. $10 daily fee/pet. Designated rooms, service with restric-
tions, crate. [SAVE] 🛜 ⛽ 💻

🔷🔷🔷 Aloft San Antonio Airport 🏨
(210) 541-8881. **$109-$169.** 838 NW Loop 410 78216. I-410 exit
Blanco Rd, just s. Int corridors. **Pets:** Accepted.

[SAVE] 🏊 🛜 ✕ 💻

🔷🔷🔷 Arbor House Suites Bed & Breakfast [BB]
(210) 472-2005. **$129-$207, 14 day notice.** 109 Arciniega St 78205.
Just s of E Nueva St; between S Presa and S St. Mary's sts; near La
Villita Historic District; in King William Historic District. Ext/int corridors.
Pets: Small, other species. $25 daily fee/pet. Service with restrictions,
supervision. [SAVE] 🛜 ✕ 💻

🔷🔷🔷 BEST WESTERN PLUS Posada Ana-Medical
Center 🏨
(210) 691-9550. **$90-$115.** 9411 Wurzbach Rd 78240. I-10 exit 561
(Wurzbach Rd); on eastbound access road. Int corridors.
Pets: Accepted. [SAVE] 🅼 🏊 🛜 ⛽ 💻

🔷🔷🔷 BEST WESTERN PLUS San Antonio East
Inn & Suites 🏨
(210) 661-8669. **$90-$190.** 8669 I-10 E 78219. I-10 exit 585 (Converse
Rd); on westbound frontage road. Int corridors. **Pets:** Accepted.

[SAVE] 🅼 🏊 🛜 ⛽ 💻

AAA ▼▼▼ **BEST WESTERN Posada Ana Inn-Airport** H

(210) 342-1400. **$90-$120.** 8600 Jones Maltsberger Rd 78216. Loop 410 exit 21A (Jones Maltsberger Rd), just s. Int corridors. **Pets:** Small. $10 daily fee/pet. Service with restrictions, crate.

 SAVE 🛏 📶 ⊗ 🖥 🖵

▼▼▼▼ **Candlewood Suites Hotel** H

(210) 615-0550. **$109-$199.** 9350 I-10 W 78230. I-10 W exit 561 (Wurzbach Rd); between Wurzbach Rd and Medical Dr; on eastbound access road. Int corridors. **Pets:** Large, other species. $10 one-time fee/room, $15 daily fee/room. Service with restrictions, crate.

🚹M 🛏 📶 🖥 🖵

▼▼▼▼ **Candlewood Suites San Antonio Downtown** H

(210) 226-7700. **Call for rates.** 1024 S Laredo St 78204. I-10/35 exit Laredo St; on frontage road. Int corridors. **Pets:** Accepted.

🛏 📶 ⊗ 🖥 🖵

▼▼▼ **Candlewood Suites San Antonio NW SeaWorld Area** H

(210) 523-7666. **Call for rates.** 9502 Amelia Pass 78254. Loop 1604 at Braun Rd; on northbound frontage road. Int corridors. **Pets:** Accepted.

🛏 📶 🖥 🖵

▼▼▼▼ **Candlewood Suites Stone Oak Area** H

(210) 545-2477. **Call for rates.** 21103 Encino Commons Blvd 78259. US 281 exit Evans Rd; on northbound frontage road. Int corridors. **Pets:** Accepted. 🛏 📶 ⊗ 🖥 🖵

▼▼▼ **Comfort Inn & Suites** H

(210) 733-8080. **Call for rates.** 6039 IH-10 W 78201. I-10 exit 565B eastbound; exit 565C (Vance Jackson Rd) westbound on westbound frontage rd. Int corridors. **Pets:** Accepted. 🛏 📶 ⊗ 🖥 🖵

AAA ▼▼▼▼ **Comfort Inn & Suites Airport** H

(210) 249-2000. **$80-$170.** 8640 Crownhill Blvd 78209. I-410 exit Airport Blvd, just off eastbound frontage road; just e of Broadway Ave. Int corridors. **Pets:** Small, other species. $25 one-time fee/pet. Service with restrictions, crate. SAVE 🚹M 🛏 📶 🖥 🖵

▼▼ **Comfort Inn-Fiesta** M

(210) 696-4766. **$70-$110.** 6755 N Loop 1604 W 78249. I-10 exit CR 1604 W, 0.5 mi w of La Cantera Pkwy. Int corridors. **Pets:** Accepted.

🚹M 🛏 📶 🖥 🖵

AAA ▼▼▼▼ **Crockett Hotel** H 🐾

(210) 225-6500. **$99-$295.** 320 Bonham St 78205. Center. Int corridors. **Pets:** Large, other species. $60 one-time fee/pet. Service with restrictions, supervision. SAVE 🛏 📶 ⊗ 🖥 🖵

▼▼▼▼ **Drury Inn & Suites Northeast** H

(210) 657-1107. **$120-$174.** 4900 Crestwind Dr 78239. I-35 exit 165 (Walzem Rd); on northbound access road. Int corridors. **Pets:** $10 daily fee/room. Service with restrictions, supervision.

🚹M 🛏 📶 🖥 🖵

▼▼▼▼ **Drury Inn & Suites-San Antonio Airport** H

(210) 308-8100. **$120-$209.** 95 NE Loop 410 78216. I-410 exit 21A (Jones Maltsberger Rd), 1.8 mi w of airport. Int corridors. **Pets:** $10 daily fee/room. Service with restrictions, supervision.

🚹M 🛏 📶 🖥 🖵

▼▼▼▼ **Drury Inn & Suites San Antonio-La Cantera** H

(210) 696-0800. **$135-$224.** 15806 IH-10 W 78249. I-10 exit Loop 1604; on eastbound access road. Int corridors. **Pets:** $10 daily fee/room. Service with restrictions, supervision. 🛏 📶 ⊗ 🖥 🖵

▼▼▼▼ **Drury Inn & Suites-San Antonio North** H

(210) 404-1600. **$110-$194.** 801 N Loop 1604 E 78232. Jct Loop 1604 and US 281, just w. Int corridors. **Pets:** $10 daily fee/room. Service with restrictions, supervision. 🛏 📶 🖥 🖵

▼▼▼▼ **Drury Inn & Suites-San Antonio Northwest** H

(210) 561-2510. **$130-$299.** 9806 I-10 W 78230. I-10 exit 561 (Wurzbach Rd); on southeast corner. Int corridors. **Pets:** $10 daily fee/room. Service with restrictions, supervision. 🛏 📶 ⊗ 🖥 🖵

▼▼▼▼ **Drury Inn & Suites-San Antonio Riverwalk** H

(210) 212-5200. **$160-$239.** 201 N St. Mary's St 78205. Just s of College St. Int corridors. **Pets:** $10 daily fee/room. Service with restrictions, supervision. 🍴 🚹M 🛏 📶 🖥 🖵

▼▼▼▼ **Drury Plaza Hotel-San Antonio Riverwalk** H

(210) 270-7799. **$165-$294.** 105 S St. Mary's St 78205. Jct Commerce, St. Mary's and Market sts. Int corridors. **Pets:** $10 daily fee/room. Service with restrictions, supervision. 🚹M 🛏 📶 ⊗ 🖥 🖵

▼▼▼▼ **Drury Plaza San Antonio North** H

(210) 494-2420. **$125-$219.** 823 N Loop 1604 E 78232. Jct Loop 1604 and US 281, just w. Int corridors. **Pets:** $10 daily fee/room. Service with restrictions, supervision. 🚹M 🛏 📶 ⊗ 🖥 🖵

AAA ▼▼▼ **Econo Lodge Downtown South** H

(210) 927-4800. **$49-$199.** 606 Division Ave 78214. I-35 exit 152A (Division Ave); on northbound frontage road. Ext corridors. **Pets:** Medium. $25 one-time fee/pet. Service with restrictions, supervision.

SAVE 🛏 📶 🖥 🖵

▼▼▼ **Econo Lodge Inn & Suites Downtown Northeast** M

(210) 229-9220. **$50-$250.** 2755 N PanAm Expwy 78208. I-35 exit 159 (Coliseum); on southbound access road. Ext corridors. **Pets:** Medium, dogs only. $25 daily fee/pet. Designated rooms, service with restrictions, crate. 🛏 📶 🖥 🖵

AAA ▼▼▼▼ **Econo Lodge Inn & Suites Fiesta Park** M

(210) 690-5500. **$50-$155.** 13575 I-10 W 78249. I-10 exit 557 westbound; exit 558 eastbound; on westbound access road. Ext corridors. **Pets:** Accepted. SAVE 🛏 🖥 🖵

AAA ▼▼▼▼ **Eilan Hotel Resort and Spa, Autograph Collection** H

(210) 598-2900. **$169-$399.** 17103 La Cantera Pkwy 78256. I-10 exit 554 (La Cantera Pkwy), just w; in Eilan office/shopping complex. Int corridors. **Pets:** Accepted. SAVE 🍴 📶 ⊗ 🖵

▼▼▼ **El Tropicano Riverwalk** H

(210) 223-9461. **$129-$169.** 110 Lexington Ave 78205. 0.3 mi s of jct Lexington Ave and I-35. Int corridors. **Pets:** Accepted.

🍴 🛏 📶 ⊗ 🖥 🖵

AAA ▼▼▼▼ **Emily Morgan Hotel-DoubleTree by Hilton** H

(210) 225-8486. **$119-$209.** 705 E Houston St 78205. Just n of Bonham St. Int corridors. **Pets:** Accepted.

SAVE 🍴 🚹M 🛏 📶 ⊗ 🖵

▼▼▼ **Extended Stay America-San Antonio-Colonnade** H

(210) 694-1229. **Call for rates.** 4331 Spectrum One 78230. I-10 exit 561 (Wurzbach Rd), just nw. Int corridors. **Pets:** Other species. $25 daily fee/pet. Service with restrictions, supervision. 🛏 📶 🖥 🖵

▼▼▼ **The Fairmount Hotel** H

(210) 224-8800. **Call for rates.** 401 S Alamo St 78205. Opposite convention center and Hemisfair Plaza. Ext/int corridors. **Pets:** Accepted. 🍴 ⊠ 📶 ⊗ 🖵

AAA ▼▼▼▼ **Grand Hyatt San Antonio** H

(210) 224-1234. **$99-$359.** 600 E Market St 78205. I-37 exit 141A (Market St); between S Alamo St and I-37. Int corridors. **Pets:** Accepted.

SAVE ECO 🍴 🚹M 🛏 💰 ⊗ 🖥 🖵

◆◆ **Hawthorn Suites by Wyndham** 🄷
(210) 561-9660. **$99-$199.** 4041 Bluemel Rd 78240. I-10 exit 561 (Wurzbach Rd), 0.3 mi w on eastbound access road; set back from interstate. Ext corridors. **Pets:** Accepted. 🐾 📶 ⊠ 🛢 🖵

◆◆◆ **Hilton Hill Country Hotel & Spa** 🄷
(210) 509-9800. **$119-$169.** 9800 Westover Hills Blvd 78251. Between Loop 410 and 1604, just off CR 151. Int corridors. **Pets:** Small. $50 one-time fee/room. Service with restrictions, crate.
🍴 🄼 🐾 ⊠ 📶 ⊠ 🛢

◆◆◆ **The Historic Menger Hotel** 🄷
(210) 223-4361. **$119-$299.** 204 Alamo Plaza 78205. Just s of the Alamo. Int corridors. **Pets:** Medium, dogs only. $125 one-time fee/pet. Designated rooms, service with restrictions, supervision.
[SAVE] 🍴 🐾 ⊠ 📶 ⊠ 🛢

◆◆ **Holiday Inn Express-San Antonio Airport** 🄷
(210) 308-6700. **$99-$129.** 91 NE Loop 410 78216. Loop 410 exit 21A (Jones Maltsberger Rd) eastbound; exit 20B westbound; between San Pedro Ave and Jones Maltsberger Rd; on westbound access road. Int corridors. **Pets:** Accepted. 🄼 🐾 📶 🛢 🖵

◆◆◆ **Holiday Inn Northwest-SeaWorld** 🄷
(210) 520-2508. **Call for rates.** 10135 State Hwy 151 78251. I-410 exit SR 151, 3 mi n on northbound access road. Int corridors.
Pets: Accepted. [SAVE] 🍴 🄼 🐾 📶 ⊠ 🛢 🖵

◆◆◆ **Holiday Inn San Antonio International Airport** 🄷
(210) 349-9900. **Call for rates.** 77 NE Loop 410 78216. I-410 exit 20B (McCullough St); on westbound access road. Int corridors.
Pets: Accepted. [SAVE] 🍴 🐾 📶 🛢 🖵

◆◆◆ **Home2 Suites by Hilton San Antonio Downtown-Riverwalk** 🄷
(210) 354-4366. **$109-$189.** 603 Navarro St 78205. Jct E Houston St. Int corridors. **Pets:** Accepted. 🐾 📶 🛢 🖵

◆◆◆ **Hotel Contessa** 🄷
(210) 229-9222. **Call for rates.** 306 W Market St 78205. At St. Mary's St. Int corridors. **Pets:** Accepted.
[SAVE] 🍴 🐾 ⊠ 📶 ⊠ 🛢 🖵

◆◆◆ **Hotel Havana** 🄲🄸
(210) 222-2008. **Call for rates.** 1015 Navarro St 78205. Just s of N St. Mary's St. Int corridors. **Pets:** Accepted. 🍴 🐾 📶 ⊠ 🛢

◆◆◆ **Hotel Indigo at the Alamo** 🄷
(210) 933-2000. **$130-$300.** 105 N Alamo Plaza 78205. I-37 exit 141 (Commerce St), just s. Int corridors. **Pets:** Accepted.
🍴 📶 ⊠ 🖵

◆◆◆ **Hotel Indigo Riverwalk** 🄷
(210) 527-1900. **$99-$179.** 830 N St. Mary's St 78205. Just n of Navarro St. Int corridors. **Pets:** Other species. $25 one-time fee/pet. No service, crate. 🍴 🐾 📶 ⊠ 🛢 🖵

◆◆◆ **Hyatt Place San Antonio Airport/Quarry Market** 🄷
(210) 930-2333. **$79-$209.** 7615 Jones Maltsberger Rd 78216. US 281 exit Jones Maltsberger Rd; on Loop 410. Int corridors. **Pets:** Medium, dogs only. $75 one-time fee/room. Designated rooms, service with restrictions, crate. [SAVE] 🐾 📶 ⊠ 🛢 🖵

◆◆◆ **Hyatt Place San Antonio North Stone Oak** 🄷
(210) 545-2810. **$79-$189.** 1610 E Sonterra Blvd 78258. US 281 exit Sonterra Blvd, just w. Int corridors. **Pets:** Accepted.
[SAVE] 🐾 📶 ⊠ 🛢 🖵

◆◆◆ **Hyatt Place San Antonio-Northwest/Medical Center** 🄷
(210) 561-0099. **$69-$179.** 4303 Hyatt Place Dr 78230. I-10 exit 561 (Wurzbach Rd), 0.5 mi on westbound access road. Int corridors.
Pets: Accepted. [SAVE] 🄼 🐾 📶 ⊠ 🛢 🖵

◆◆◆ **Hyatt Place San Antonio/Riverwalk** 🄷
(210) 227-6854. **$89-$249.** 601 S St. Mary's St 78205. I-35 exit 155B (Cesar E Chavez Blvd), 0.9 mi e. Int corridors. **Pets:** Accepted.
[SAVE] 🐾 📶 ⊠ 🛢 🖵

◆◆◆ **Hyatt Regency Hill Country Resort and Spa** 🄷
(210) 647-1234. **$149-$439, 3 day notice.** 9800 Hyatt Resort Dr 78251. Between Loop 410 and 1604, just off CR 151 exit Hyatt Resort Dr. Int corridors. **Pets:** Accepted.
[SAVE] [ECO] 🍴 🄼 🐾 ⊠ 📶 🛢 🖵

◆◆◆ **Hyatt Regency San Antonio** 🄷
(210) 222-1234. **$99-$359.** 123 Losoya St 78205. Between College and Crockett sts. Int corridors. **Pets:** Accepted.
[SAVE] [ECO] 🍴 🐾 📶 ⊠ 🛢 🖵

◆◆ **Inn on the Riverwalk** 🄱🄱
(210) 225-6333. **Call for rates.** 129 Woodward Pl 78204. Just n of W Cesar E Chavez Blvd. Ext/int corridors. **Pets:** Accepted.
📶 ⊠ 🛢 🖵

◆◆◆ **La Quinta Inn & Suites** 🄷
(210) 447-8000. **$65-$244.** 11155 W Loop 1604 N 78023. Just w of Bandera Rd. Int corridors. **Pets:** Large, other species. Service with restrictions. 🄼 🐾 📶 ⊠ 🛢 🖵

◆◆◆ **La Quinta Inn & Suites Dominion** 🄷
(210) 564-6700. **$69-$249.** 25042 IH-10 W 78257. I-10 exit 550 (Ralph Fair Rd), just e; on westbound access road. Int corridors. **Pets:** Large, other species. Service with restrictions. 🐾 📶 ⊠ 🛢 🖵

◆◆◆ **La Quinta Inn & Suites San Antonio Airport** 🄷
(210) 342-3738. **$79-$234.** 850 Halm Blvd 78216. I-410 exit 21A (Jones Maltsberger Rd); on eastbound frontage road. Int corridors. **Pets:** Large, other species. Service with restrictions. 🄼 🐾 📶 🛢 🖵

◆◆◆ **La Quinta Inn & Suites San Antonio Convention Center** 🄷
(210) 222-9181. **$129-$389.** 303 Blum St 78202. 0.5 mi ne. Ext/int corridors. **Pets:** Large, other species. Service with restrictions.
🐾 📶 🛢 🖵

◆◆◆ **La Quinta Inn & Suites San Antonio Downtown** 🄷
(210) 212-5400. **$109-$389.** 100 Cesar E Chavez Blvd 78204. I-10/35 exit 155B (Cesar E Chavez Blvd), 3 blks e of jct E Flores St. Int corridors. **Pets:** Large, other species. Service with restrictions.
🄼 🐾 📶 🛢 🖵

◆◆◆ **La Quinta Inn & Suites San Antonio North Stone Oak** 🄷
(210) 497-0506. **$79-$329.** 18502 Hardy Oak Blvd 78258. Jct Loop 1604 and US 281, just w. Int corridors. **Pets:** Large, other species. Service with restrictions. 🄼 🐾 📶 ⊠ 🛢 🖵

◆◆◆ **La Quinta Inn San Antonio AlamoDome South** 🄷
(210) 337-7171. **$99-$199.** 3180 Goliad Rd 78223. I-37 exit 135 (Brooks City Base/SE Military Dr), just w of interstate. Int corridors. **Pets:** Large, other species. Service with restrictions.
[SAVE] 🐾 📶 ⊠ 🛢 🖵

◆◆ **La Quinta Inn San Antonio I-35 North At Rittiman Rd** 🄷
(210) 653-6619. **$65-$229.** 6410 I-35 78218. I-35 exit 164A (Rittiman Rd); on northbound frontage road. Ext corridors. **Pets:** Large, other species. Service with restrictions. 🐾 📶 🖵

▼▼ **La Quinta Inn San Antonio Lackland** �H
(210) 674-3200. **$89-$229.** 6511 Military Dr W 78227. Sw of jct US 90 and Military Dr W. Ext corridors. **Pets:** Large, other species. Service with restrictions. 🔁 📶 🛗 🖥️

▼▼ **La Quinta Inn San Antonio Market Square** �H
(210) 271-0001. **$82-$469.** 900 Dolorosa St 78207. I-10/35 exit 155B (Cesar E Chavez Blvd), just n on Santa Rosa St, then just w on Nueva St. Ext corridors. **Pets:** Large, other species. Service with restrictions. 🔁 🛗 📶 🖥️

▼▼ **La Quinta Inn San Antonio SeaWorld/Ingram Park** �H
(210) 680-8883. **$65-$259.** 7134 NW Loop 410 78238. I-410 exit 10 (Culebra Rd); on eastbound access road. Ext corridors. **Pets:** Large, other species. Service with restrictions. 🔁 📶 🛗 🖥️

🅐🅐🅐 ▼▼▼ **Marriott Plaza San Antonio** �H
(210) 229-1000. **$125-$339.** 555 S Alamo St 78205. Opposite convention center and Hemisfair Plaza. Int corridors. **Pets:** Accepted.
[SAVE] 🍴 🛗 🔁 ✖️ 📶 ✖️ 🛗 🖥️

🅐🅐🅐 ▼▼▼ **Mokara Hotel & Spa** �H
(210) 396-5800. **$279-$499.** 212 W Crockett St 78205. Between St. Mary's and Navarro sts; on River Walk. Int corridors. **Pets:** Accepted.
[SAVE] 🍴 🛗 🔁 ✖️ 📶 ✖️ 🖥️

▼ **Motel 6-#1122** Ⓜ
(210) 225-1111. **$55-$165.** 211 N Pecos St 78207. I-10/35 exit 155B (Pecos St); on southbound frontage road. Ext corridors. **Pets:** Other species. Service with restrictions, crate. 🔁 📶 🛗

▼▼ **Motel 6-#4341** �H
(210) 447-9000. **Call for rates.** 126 Kenley Pl 78232. US 281 exit Brook Hollow Blvd, just n on northbound frontage road. Int corridors. **Pets:** Other species. Service with restrictions, crate. 🔁 📶 🛗

▼ **Motel 6 - #651** Ⓜ
(210) 673-9020. **$49-$85.** 2185 SW Loop 410 78227. I-410 exit 7 (Marbach Rd), 0.7 mi w; on westbound access road. Ext corridors. **Pets:** Other species. Service with restrictions, crate. 🔁 📶 🛗

▼ **Motel 6 - Medical Center South - #4429** �H
(210) 616-0030. **Call for rates.** 7500 Louis Pasteur Dr 78229. I-410 exit 14C (Babcock Rd), 1 mi nw, then 0.5 mi n. Int corridors. **Pets:** Other species. Service with restrictions, crate. 🛗 📶 ✖️ 🛗

🅐🅐🅐 ▼▼▼▼ **Omni La Mansión del Rio** �H 🐾
(210) 518-1000. **$179-$339.** 112 College St 78205. Just s on River Walk. Ext/int corridors. **Pets:** Small, other species. $50 one-time fee/room. Designated rooms, service with restrictions.
[SAVE] 🍴 🔁 📶 ✖️ 🛗 🖥️

🅐🅐🅐 ▼▼▼▼ **Omni San Antonio Hotel at the Colonnade** �H 🐾
(210) 691-8888. **$119-$219.** 9821 Colonnade Blvd 78230. I-10 exit 561 (Wurzbach Rd); on westbound frontage road. Int corridors. **Pets:** Small, other species. $50 one-time fee/room. Service with restrictions, crate.
[SAVE] 🍴 🔁 ✖️ 📶 ✖️ 🖥️

▼▼▼ **Pear Tree Inn by Drury-San Antonio Northeast** �H
(210) 654-1144. **$90-$159.** 8300 I-35 N 78239. I-35 exit 165 (Walzem Rd); on northbound access road. Ext/int corridors. **Pets:** $10 daily fee/room. Service with restrictions, supervision. 🔁 📶 🛗 🖥️

🅐🅐🅐 ▼▼ **Red Roof Inn-San Antonio Airport** �H
(210) 340-4055. **$50-$124.** 333 Wolfe Rd 78216. Just s of US 281 at Isom Rd; on southbound frontage road. Ext/int corridors. **Pets:** Large, other species. Service with restrictions, supervision.
[SAVE] 📶 ✖️ 🛗 🖥️

🅐🅐🅐 ▼▼▼ **Red Roof Inn San Antonio Lackland** �H
(210) 675-4120. **$60-$160.** 6861 Hwy 90 W 78227. Ne of jct US 90 and Military Dr W; access via Renwick St, off Military Dr, just n of jct US 90. Ext corridors. **Pets:** Large, other species. Service with restrictions, supervision. [SAVE] 🔁 📶 ✖️ 🛗 🖥️

🅐🅐🅐 ▼▼▼ **Red Roof Inn San Antonio (NW-SeaWorld)** �H
(210) 509-3434. **$49-$189.** 6880 NW Loop 410 78238. I-410 exit 11 (Alamo Downs Pkwy); on eastbound frontage road. Ext/int corridors. **Pets:** Large, other species. Service with restrictions, supervision.
[SAVE] 🛗 🔁 📶 🛗 🖥️

🅐🅐🅐 ▼▼▼ **Red Roof Plus+ San Antonio Downtown - Riverwalk** �H
(210) 229-9973. **$69-$240.** 1011 E Houston St 78205. I-37 exit 141 (Commerce St) northbound; exit 141B southbound. Int corridors. **Pets:** Large, other species. Service with restrictions, supervision.
[SAVE] 🔁 📶 ✖️ 🛗 🖥️

▼▼▼ **Residence Inn by Marriott Alamo Plaza** �H
(210) 212-5555. **$139-$189.** 425 Bonham St 78205. I-37 and US 281 exit Commerce St, just w to Bowie St, then 4 blks n. Int corridors. **Pets:** Accepted. 🔁 📶 ✖️ 🛗 🖥️

▼▼▼ **Residence Inn by Marriott North San Antonio** �H
(210) 490-1333. **$79-$189.** 1115 N SR 1604 E 78232. Loop 1604, just w of US 281; on eastbound frontage road. Int corridors. **Pets:** $100 one-time fee/room. Service with restrictions, crate.
🛗 🔁 📶 ✖️ 🛗 🖥️

▼▼▼ **Residence Inn by Marriott San Antonio-Airport** �H
(210) 805-8118. **$109-$299.** 1014 NE Loop 410 78209. Loop 410 exit Broadway St, 0.4 mi e; on eastbound access road. Ext corridors. **Pets:** Other species. $100 one-time fee/room. Designated rooms, service with restrictions, crate. [ECO] 🔁 ✖️ 📶 ✖️ 🛗 🖥️

🅐🅐🅐 ▼▼▼ **Residence Inn by Marriott San Antonio Downtown/Market Square** �H
(210) 231-6000. **$170-$199.** 628 S Santa Rosa Blvd 78204. I-10/35 exit 155B (Cesar E Chavez Blvd), 0.5 mi e. Int corridors. **Pets:** Accepted.
[SAVE] 🔁 📶 ✖️ 🛗 🖥️

▼▼▼ **Residence Inn by Marriott San Antonio Northwest at The RIM** �H
(210) 561-0200. **$99-$209.** 5707 Rim Pass Dr 78257. I-10 exit 556B (La Cantera Pkwy); on westbound access road; in The Rim Shopping Complex. Int corridors. **Pets:** Large, other species. $100 one-time fee/room. Service with restrictions. 🛗 🔁 📶 ✖️ 🛗 🖥️

▼▼▼ **Residence Inn by Marriott SeaWorld/Lackland AFB** �H
(210) 509-3100. **$99-$189.** 2838 Cinema Ridge 78238. I-410 exit 10 (Ingram Rd); on eastbound frontage road. Int corridors. **Pets:** Accepted.
🛗 🔁 📶 ✖️ 🛗 🖥️

🅐🅐🅐 ▼▼▼ **Sheraton Gunter** �H
(210) 227-3241. **$149-$269.** 205 E Houston St 78205. Center. Int corridors. **Pets:** Accepted. [SAVE] 🍴 🔁 📶 ✖️ 🖥️

▼▼ **Sleep Inn San Antonio** �H
(210) 344-5400. **$59-$109.** 8318 I-10 W 78230. I-10 exit 561 (Callaghan Rd); on eastbound frontage road. Int corridors. **Pets:** Accepted.
🔁 📶 🛗 🖥️

▼▼▼ **Staybridge Suites Downtown Convention Center** �H
(210) 444-2700. **Call for rates.** 123 Hoefgen Ave 78205. In Historic Sunset Station. Int corridors. **Pets:** Accepted. 🔁 📶 🛗 🖥️

▼▼▼▼ Staybridge Suites NW Near Six Flags Fiesta ⓗ
(210) 691-3443. **Call for rates.** 6919 N Loop 1604 W 78249. Loop 1604 exit La Cantera Pkwy; on westbound frontage road. Int corridors.
Pets: Accepted. 🅿 🛜 ✕ 🛏 ▣

▼▼▼▼ Staybridge Suites San Antonio-Airport ⓗ
(210) 341-3220. **Call for rates.** 66 NE Loop 410 78216. I-410 exit 20B (McCullough St); on eastbound access road. Int corridors.
Pets: Accepted. 🅿 🛜 🛏 ▣

▼▼▼▼ Staybridge Suites San Antonio NW-Colonnade ⓗ
(210) 558-9009. **Call for rates.** 4320 Spectrum One 78230. I-10 exit 561 (Wurzbach Rd), 0.3 mi w; off westbound access road. Int corridors.
Pets: Accepted. 🅿 🛜 🛏 ▣

▼▼▼▼ Staybridge Suites San Antonio-Stone Oak ⓗ
(210) 497-0100. **Call for rates.** 808 N Loop 1604 E 78232. On Loop 1604, 0.4 mi w of US 281. Int corridors. **Pets:** Accepted.
🅼 🅿 🛜 ✕ 🛏 ▣

▼▼▼▼ Staybridge Suites-SeaWorld San Antonio ⓗ
(210) 767-1100. **Call for rates.** 10919 Town Center Dr 78251. SR 151 exit Westover Hills, just off northbound access road. Int corridors.
Pets: Accepted. 🅿 🛜 🛏 ▣

ⒶⒶⒶ ▼▼▼ Super 8 ⓗ
(210) 265-8888. **$69-$100.** 723 Hot Wells Blvd 78223. I-37 exit 137 (Hot Wells Blvd); on southbound access road. Int corridors.
Pets: Accepted. 〔SAVE〕 🅿 🛜 🛏 ▣

▼▼ Super 8 on Roland ⓗ
(210) 798-5500. **$79-$160.** 302 Roland Ave 78210. I-10 exit 577 (Roland Ave); on eastbound access road. Ext corridors. **Pets:** Accepted.
🅿 🛜 🛏 ▣

▼▼ Super 8-Six Flags Fiesta ⓗ
(210) 696-6916. **$60-$100.** 5319 Casa Bella 78249. I-10 exit 557 westbound; exit 558 eastbound; on westbound frontage road. Int corridors.
Pets: Accepted. 🅿 🛜 🛏 ▣

▼▼▼▼ TownePlace Suites Airport by Marriott ⓗ
(210) 308-5510. **$99-$139.** 214 NE Loop 410 78216. I-410 exit 21A (Jones Maltsberger Rd); on eastbound frontage road. Int corridors.
Pets: Accepted. 🛜 ✕ 🛏 ▣

▼▼▼▼ TownePlace Suites by Marriott San Antonio Downtown ⓗ
(210) 271-3444. **$99-$189.** 409 E Houston St 78205. 1 blk w of Broadway St. Int corridors. **Pets:** Accepted. 🅿 🛜 ✕ 🛏 ▣

▼▼▼▼ TownePlace Suites by Marriott San Antonio Northwest ⓗ
(210) 694-5100. **$89-$139.** 5014 Prue Rd 78240. I-10 exit 560 (Huebner Rd) westbound; exit 559 eastbound, 1 blk sw to Fredericksburg Rd, then just n. Int corridors. **Pets:** Accepted.
🅼 🅿 🛜 ✕ 🛏 ▣

ⒶⒶⒶ ▼▼▼▼ The Westin Riverwalk, San Antonio ⓗ
(210) 224-6500. **$129-$459.** 420 W Market St 78205. 2 blks w of Navarro St. Int corridors. **Pets:** Accepted.
〔SAVE〕 🍽 🅼 🅿 🛜 ✕ ▣

ⒶⒶⒶ ▼▼▼▼ Wyndham Garden River Walk Museum Reach ⓗ
(210) 515-4555. **Call for rates.** 103 9th St 78215. Jct 9th and N St. Mary's sts. Int corridors. **Pets:** Accepted.
〔SAVE〕 🍽 🅼 🛜 ✕ 🛏 ▣

SAN MARCOS

▼▼▼▼ Embassy Suites-San Marcos Hotel, Spa and Conference Center ⓗ
(512) 392-6450. **$149-$219.** 1001 E McCarty Ln 78666. I-35 exit 201; on east frontage road. Int corridors. **Pets:** Accepted.
🍽 🅼 🅿 ✕ 🛜 ✕ 🛏 ▣

▼▼▼ La Quinta Inn San Marcos ⓗ
(512) 392-8800. **$72-$349.** 1619 I-35 N 78666. I-35 exit 206 southbound, 0.5 mi s; on west frontage road; exit northbound, 1 mi n to turnaround to west frontage road, then 1.5 mi s. Ext/int corridors.
Pets: Large, other species. Service with restrictions.
🅼 🅿 🛜 🛏 ▣

ⒶⒶⒶ ▼▼▼ Ramada Limited ⓗ
(512) 395-8000. **$60-$160.** 1701 I-35 N 78666. I-35 exit 206 southbound, 0.4 mi s on west frontage road; exit northbound, 1 mi n to turnaround for west frontage road, then 1.4 mi s. Ext corridors. **Pets:** Small, dogs only. $20 daily fee/pet. Designated rooms, no service, crate.
〔SAVE〕 🅿 🛜 🛏 ▣

SCHERTZ

▼▼▼▼ Fairfield Inn & Suites by Marriott ⓗ
(210) 658-1466. **$99-$169.** 5008 Corridor Loop Rd 78154. I-35 exit 175 (Natural Bridge Cavern Rd); just off northbound frontage road. Int corridors. **Pets:** Accepted. 🅿 🛜 ✕ 🛏 ▣

▼▼▼ La Quinta Inn & Suites ⓗ
(210) 655-2700. **$94-$249.** 17650 Four Oaks Ln 78154. I-35 exit 175 CR 3009 (Natural Bridge Cavern Rd); just w. Int corridors. **Pets:** Large, other species. Service with restrictions. 🛜 ✕ 🛏 ▣

SCHULENBURG

ⒶⒶⒶ ▼▼▼▼ BEST WESTERN PLUS Schulenburg Inn & Suites ⓗ
(979) 743-2030. **$100-$190.** 101 Huser Blvd 78956. I-10 exit 674, just s. Int corridors. **Pets:** Medium, other species. $10 daily fee/pet. Service with restrictions, supervision. 〔SAVE〕 🅼 🅿 🛜 ✕ 🛏 ▣

SEABROOK

ⒶⒶⒶ ▼▼▼▼ BEST WESTERN PLUS Seabrook Suites ⓗ
(281) 291-9090. **Call for rates.** 5755 Bayport Blvd 77586. 1.5 mi n on SR 146. Int corridors. **Pets:** Medium, other species. $50 one-time fee/pet. Designated rooms, service with restrictions, crate.
〔SAVE〕 🅿 🛜 ✕ 🛏 ▣

SEALY

ⒶⒶⒶ ▼▼▼ Americas Best Value Inn of Sealy ⓗ
(979) 885-3707. **$70-$95, 3 day notice.** 2107 Hwy 36 S 77474. I-10 exit 720. Ext corridors. **Pets:** Accepted. 〔SAVE〕 🅿 🛜 ▣

SEGUIN

▼▼▼▼ La Quinta Inn & Suites Seguin ⓗ
(830) 372-0567. **$109-$219.** 1501 Hwy 46 N 78155. I-10 exit 607 (SR 46), just off westbound frontage road. Int corridors. **Pets:** Large, other species. Service with restrictions. 🅼 🅿 🛜 ✕ 🛏 ▣

▼▼ Super 8 of Seguin ⓗ
(830) 379-6888. **$69-$190.** 1525 N Hwy 46 78155. I-10 exit 607 (SR 46); on eastbound frontage road. Ext corridors. **Pets:** Accepted.
🛜 🛏 ▣

SELMA

▼▼▼ Comfort Inn & Suites ⓗ
(210) 447-2305. **Call for rates.** 15771 IH 35 N 78154. I-35 exit 174A (Selma Shertz CR 1518); on southbound frontage road. Int corridors.
Pets: Accepted. 🅿 🛜 ✕ 🛏 ▣

SEMINOLE

BEST WESTERN PLUS Seminole Hotel & Suites H
(432) 955-6200. **$130-$160.** 308 S Main St (US 385) 79360. Just s of jct US 62/180. Int corridors. **Pets:** Medium. $150 deposit/room, $15 daily fee/pet. Designated rooms, service with restrictions, supervision.
SAVE ⓜ 🛜 ✕ 🛏 🖵

Seminole Inn M
(432) 758-9881. **Call for rates.** 2200 Hobbs Hwy 79360. 1.5 mi w on US 62/180. Ext corridors. **Pets:** Accepted. SAVE 🛜 🛏 🖵

SHAMROCK

BEST WESTERN PLUS Shamrock Inn & Suites H
(806) 256-1001. **$110-$120.** 1802 N Main St 79079. I-40 exit 163, just n. Int corridors. **Pets:** Large, other species. $10 daily fee/pet. Designated rooms, service with restrictions, supervision.
SAVE ⓜ ⌁ 🛜 ✕ 🛏 🖵

Western Motel M
(806) 256-3244. **$59-$169.** 104 E 12th St 79079. I-40 exit 163, 0.4 mi s. Ext corridors. **Pets:** Medium. $15 daily fee/pet. Designated rooms, service with restrictions, supervision. SAVE 🛜 🛏 🖵

SHERMAN

Comfort Suites of Sherman H
(903) 893-0499. **$79-$109.** 2900 US Hwy 75 N 75090. US 75 exit 63, 0.3 mi s of jct US 82. Int corridors. **Pets:** Small, other species. $20 one-time fee/room. Designated rooms, service with restrictions, supervision. ⌁ 🛜 ✕ 🛏 🖵

La Quinta Inn & Suites Sherman H
(903) 870-1122. **$65-$187.** 2912 US 75 N 75090. US 75 exit 63; on southbound frontage road. Int corridors. **Pets:** Large, other species. Service with restrictions. ⌁ 🛜 🛏 🖵

SINTON

BEST WESTERN Sinton M
(361) 364-2882. **$100-$130.** 8108 US Hwy 77 78387. 0.5 mi s of SR 188. Ext corridors. **Pets:** Accepted. SAVE ⌁ 🛜 🛏 🖵

SONORA

BEST WESTERN Sonora Inn H
(325) 387-9111. **$108-$132.** 270 Hwy 277 N 76950. I-10 exit 400, just s. Ext corridors. **Pets:** Medium. $10 daily fee/pet. Designated rooms, service with restrictions, supervision. SAVE ⌁ 🛜 ✕ 🛏 🖵

SOUTH PADRE ISLAND

The Inn at South Padre H ☙
(956) 761-5658. **Call for rates.** 1709 Padre Blvd 78597. 0.9 mi n of Queen Isabella Cswy; corner of W Palm St. Int corridors. **Pets:** Large, other species. $25 one-time fee/room. Service with restrictions.
ⓜ ⌁ 🛜 ✕ 🛏 🖵

Isla Grand Beach Resort H
(956) 761-6511. **$99-$625, 3 day notice.** 500 Padre Blvd 78597. 0.3 mi n of Queen Isabella Cswy. Ext/int corridors. **Pets:** Accepted.
🍽 ⌁ ✕ 🛜 ✕ 🛏 🖵

La Copa Inn Beach Hotel H
(956) 761-6000. **Call for rates.** 350 Padre Blvd 78597. Just s of Queen Isabella Cswy. Int corridors. **Pets:** Accepted.
🍽 ⌁ 🛜 ✕ 🛏 🖵

La Quinta Inn & Suites South Padre Beach H
(956) 772-7000. **$80-$500.** 7000 Padre Blvd 78597. 3 mi n of Queen Isabella Cswy. Int corridors. **Pets:** Large, other species. Service with restrictions. ⓜ ⌁ 🛜 ✕ 🛏 🖵

Super 8 H
(956) 761-6300. **$69-$299.** 4205 Padre Blvd 78597. 2.7 mi n of Queen Isabella Cswy. Ext corridors. **Pets:** Accepted.
SAVE ⌁ 🛜 ✕ 🛏 🖵

Travelodge H
(956) 761-4744. **$60-$310.** 6200 Padre Blvd 78597. 3 mi n of Queen Isabella Cswy. Ext corridors. **Pets:** Medium. $10 daily fee/pet. Service with restrictions. SAVE ⓜ ⌁ 🛜 🛏 🖵

STAFFORD

Residence Inn by Marriott Houston/Sugar Land H
(281) 277-0770. **Call for rates.** 12703 Southwest Frwy 77477. US 59 exit Corporate Dr southbound; exit Airport Blvd/Kirkwood Rd northbound; on northbound service road. Int corridors. **Pets:** Accepted.
SAVE ⌁ 🛜 ✕ 🛏 🖵

Staybridge Suites Stafford H
(281) 302-6535. **Call for rates.** 11101 Fountain Lake Dr 77477. US 59 exit Kirkwood Rd, just nw. Int corridors. **Pets:** Accepted.
ⓜ 🛜 ✕ 🛏 🖵

STANTON

Comfort Inn H
(432) 756-1100. **$149-$209.** 3414 W I-20 79782. I-20 exit 156, just se. Int corridors. **Pets:** Small. $25 daily fee/pet. Designated rooms, service with restrictions, supervision. ⌁ 🛜 ✕ 🛏 🖵

STEPHENVILLE

La Quinta Inn & Suites Stephenville H
(254) 918-2444. **$82-$209.** 105 Christy Plaza 76401. US 67/377 S, 5 mi s of jct US 281. Int corridors. **Pets:** Large, other species. Service with restrictions. ⓜ ⌁ 🛜 ✕ 🛏 🖵

SUGAR LAND

Drury Inn & Suites-Houston/Sugar Land H
(281) 277-9700. **$113-$189.** 13770 Southwest Frwy 77478. US 59 exit Dairy Ashford Rd/Sugar Creek Blvd; on north frontage road. Int corridors. **Pets:** $10 daily fee/room. Service with restrictions, supervision.
⌁ 🛜 🛏 🖵

Hyatt Place Houston/Sugar Land H
(281) 491-0300. **$79-$269.** 16730 Creek Bend Dr 77478. Jct US 59 and SR 6, just n on SR 6 to Fluor Daniel Dr, just e. Int corridors. **Pets:** Medium, dogs only. $75 one-time fee/room. Service with restrictions. SAVE ⓜ ⌁ 🛜 🛏 🖵

SWEETWATER

BEST WESTERN PLUS Sweetwater Inn & Suites H
(325) 236-6512. **$108-$135.** 300 NW Georgia Ave 79556. I-20 exit 244; on north service road. Int corridors. **Pets:** Accepted.
SAVE ⓜ ⌁ 🛜 🛏 🖵

TERRELL

BEST WESTERN Country Inn H
(972) 563-1521. **$72-$100.** 1604 Hwy 34 S 75160. I-20 exit 501 (SR 34), just n. Int corridors. **Pets:** Accepted. SAVE ⌁ 🛜 🛏 🖵

TEXARKANA

Fairfield Inn & Suites by Marriott H
(903) 838-1000. **$69-$139.** 4209 Mall Dr 75501. I-30 exit 219; on eastbound frontage road. Int corridors. **Pets:** Other species. $50 one-time fee/room. Service with restrictions, supervision.
ⓜ ⌁ 🛜 ✕ 🛏 🖵

TownePlace Suites by Marriott H
(903) 334-8800. **$87-$123.** 5020 N Cowhorn Creek Loop 75503. I-30 exit 222 (Summerhill Rd), w on frontage road, then just n. Int corridors. **Pets:** Accepted. ⌁ 🛜 ✕ 🛏 🖵

THE COLONY

⚜️ ▼▼▼ Comfort Suites 🏨

(972) 668-5555. **$80-$300.** 4796 Memorial Dr 75056. SR 121 exit Blair Oaks southbound; exit Main St northbound, just n to Memorial Dr, then just e. Int corridors. **Pets:** $35 daily fee/pet. Designated rooms, service with restrictions, supervision. [SAVE] 🛗 🛏️ 📶 ✖️ 🅿️

▼▼▼ Residence Inn by Marriott-Plano/Frisco/The Colony 🏨

(214) 469-1155. **$99-$199.** 6600 Cascades Ct 75056. SR 121 exit Spring Creek Pkwy; on southwest frontage road. Int corridors.
Pets: Accepted. 🔌 🛏️ 📶 ✖️ 🅿️ 🖥️

THE WOODLANDS

⚜️ ▼▼▼ BEST WESTERN PLUS The Woodlands 🏨

(936) 271-2378. **$109-$129.** 17081 I-45 S 77385. I-45 exit 79 (College Park Dr/Needham Rd) northbound; northeast corner of SR 242; on northbound frontage road. Int corridors. **Pets:** $20 daily fee/room. Designated rooms, service with restrictions, supervision.
[SAVE] 🛏️ 📶 ✖️ 🅿️ 🖥️

▼▼▼ Drury Inn & Suites-Houston/The Woodlands 🏨

(281) 362-7222. **$110-$199.** 28099 I-45 N 77380. I-45 exit 77 (Research Forest Dr/Tamina Rd) southbound; on southbound frontage road. Int corridors. **Pets:** $10 daily fee/room. Service with restrictions, supervision. 🛗 🛏️ 📶 ✖️ 🅿️ 🖥️

⚜️ ▼▼▼ Hyatt Place Houston/The Woodlands 🏨

(281) 298-4600. **$119-$399.** 1909 Research Forest Dr 77380. I-45 exit 77 (Research Forest Dr), 0.8 mi w. Int corridors. **Pets:** Accepted.
[SAVE] 📶 ✖️ 🅿️ 🖥️

▼▼▼ Residence Inn by Marriott Lake Front 🏨

(281) 292-3252. **$110-$310.** 1040 Lake Front Cir 77380. I-45 exit 79 (College Park Dr/Needham Rd) northbound; exit 77 (Research Forest Dr/Tamina Rd) southbound; just off southbound frontage road. Int corridors. **Pets:** Accepted. 🛏️ 📶 ✖️ 🅿️ 🖥️

⚜️ ▼▼▼▼ The Woodlands Waterway Marriott Hotel & Convention Center 🏨

(281) 367-9797. **$199-$329.** 1601 Lake Robbins Dr 77380. I-45 76B (Woodlands Pkwy) northbound, 1.6 mi w to Six Pines, then just n; exit 77 (Research Forest Dr/Tamina Rd) southbound, 0.5 mi w. Int corridors.
Pets: Accepted. [SAVE] [ECO] 🍴 🛗 🛏️ ✖️ 📶 ✖️ 🅿️ 🖥️

THREE RIVERS

⚜️ ▼▼▼ BEST WESTERN Inn-Three Rivers 🏨

(361) 786-2000. **$160-$165.** 900 N Harborth Ave 78071. I-37 exit 72 (US 281), 1.8 mi s; jct US 281 and SR 72. Ext corridors.
Pets: Accepted. [SAVE] 🛏️ 📶 🅿️ 🖥️

TYLER

⚜️ ▼▼▼▼ BEST WESTERN PLUS Southpark Inn & Suites 🏨

(903) 534-8800. **$100-$120.** 120 W Rieck Rd 75703. Jct US 69 and W Rieck Rd, just w. Int corridors. **Pets:** Accepted.
[SAVE] 🛏️ 📶 🅿️ 🖥️

▼▼▼ Candlewood Suites 🏨

(903) 509-4131. **Call for rates.** 315 E Rieck Rd 75703. 1.1 mi s of jct Loop 323 and US 69 to Rieck Rd, just e. Int corridors. **Pets:** $150 one-time fee/room. Crate. 🛗 📶 ✖️ 🅿️ 🖥️

▼▼▼ Holiday Inn South Broadway 🏨

(903) 561-5800. **Call for rates.** 5701 S Broadway Ave 75703. 1.1 mi s of jct Loop 323 and US 69. Int corridors. **Pets:** Accepted.
🍴 🛏️ 📶 ✖️ 🅿️ 🖥️

UNIVERSAL CITY

▼▼▼▼ Hawthorn Suites by Wyndham 🏨

(210) 655-9491. **$89-$149, 3 day notice.** 13101 E Loop 1604 N 78233. Loop 1604 at Pat Booker Rd; 0.8 mi e of I-35. Ext corridors.
Pets: Accepted. 🛏️ 📶 ✖️ 🅿️ 🖥️

UNIVERSITY PARK

⚜️ ▼▼▼ The Lumen 🏨

(214) 219-2400. **Call for rates.** 6101 Hillcrest Ave 75205. Just n of jct Mockingbird Ln and Hillcrest Ave. Int corridors. **Pets:** Accepted.
[SAVE] [ECO] 🍴 🛏️ 📶 ✖️ 🅿️

VAN HORN

⚜️ ▼▼▼ Econo Lodge 🏨

(432) 283-2211. **$69-$93.** 1601 W Broadway St 79855. I-10 exit 138, 0.5 mi e on Business Rt I-10. Ext corridors. **Pets:** Accepted.
[SAVE] 🛏️ 📶 🅿️

▼▼ Economy Inn 🅜

(432) 283-2754. **Call for rates.** 1500 W Broadway St 79855. I-10 exit 138, 0.5 mi e on US 80. Ext corridors. **Pets:** Accepted. 📶 🅿️

▼▼▼ Hampton Inn 🏨 🐾

(432) 283-0088. **$109-$149.** 1921 SW Frontage Rd 79855. I-10 exit 138, just w on S Frontage Rd. Int corridors. **Pets:** Other species. $10 one-time fee/pet. Designated rooms, service with restrictions, crate.
🛗 🛏️ 📶 ✖️ 🅿️ 🖥️

VEGA

⚜️ ▼▼▼ Americas Best Value Inn & Suites Country Inn 🅜

(806) 267-2131. **$80-$100.** 1800 W Vega Blvd 79092. 0.5 mi w on US 40 business loop. Ext corridors. **Pets:** Large. $10 daily fee/pet. Designated rooms, service with restrictions, supervision.
[SAVE] 🛏️ 📶 🅿️ 🖥️

VERNON

⚜️ ▼▼▼ BEST WESTERN Village Inn 🏨

(940) 552-5417. **$70-$85.** 1615 US Hwy 287 E 76384. Jct Main St, just e. Ext/int corridors. **Pets:** Accepted. [SAVE] 🛏️ 📶 🅿️ 🖥️

▼▼▼ Hampton Inn 🏨

(940) 552-2100. **$109.** 4131 Western Trail Dr 76384. Jct US 287 and 70; on W Frontage Rd. Int corridors. **Pets:** Accepted.
🛗 🛏️ 📶 ✖️ 🅿️ 🖥️

▼▼▼ Holiday Inn Express Hotel & Suites 🏨

(940) 552-0200. **$99-$114.** 700 Hillcrest Dr 76384. Jct US 287 and 70; on W Frontage Rd. Int corridors. **Pets:** Accepted.
🛗 🛏️ 📶 🅿️ 🖥️

VICTORIA

⚜️ ▼▼▼▼ BEST WESTERN PLUS Victoria Inn & Suites 🏨

(361) 485-2300. **$150-$160.** 8106 NE Zac Lenz Pkwy 77904. Jct Zac Lenz Pkwy and Invitational Dr. Int corridors. **Pets:** Accepted.
[SAVE] 🛏️ 📶 ✖️ 🅿️ 🖥️

▼▼▼ Candlewood Suites 🏨

(361) 578-0236. **$89-$164.** 7103 N Navarro St 77904. Jct US 77 and Navarro St, just s. Int corridors. **Pets:** Medium. $50 one-time fee/pet. Service with restrictions, crate. 🛏️ 📶 ✖️ 🅿️ 🖥️

▼▼▼ Comfort Inn & Suites 🏨

(361) 894-6480. **$90-$120.** 6603 NE Zac Lentz Pkwy 77904. Jct NE Zac Lentz Pkwy and US 77. Int corridors. **Pets:** $15 daily fee/pet. Service with restrictions, supervision. 🛗 📶 ✖️ 🅿️ 🖥️

▼▼ Knights Inn Victoria East 🏨

(361) 578-2030. **Call for rates.** 3112 E Houston Hwy (Business Rt 59) 77901. On Business Rt US 59, 2 mi ne. Ext corridors. **Pets:** Medium. $50 daily fee/pet. Designated rooms, service with restrictions, supervision. 🛏️ 📶 🅿️ 🖥️

▼▼ La Quinta Inn Victoria 🏨

(361) 572-3585. **$99-$234.** 7603 N Navarro St (US 77 N) 77904. 4 mi n; at Loop 463. Ext corridors. **Pets:** Large, other species. Service with restrictions. 🛏️ 📶 🅿️ 🖥️

◎◎◎ **▼▼▼** Lone Star Inn & Suites 🏠
(361) 579-0225. **$90-$170.** 1907 US 59 N 77905. US 59 exit Bloomington (SR 185); on northeast corner. Ext corridors. **Pets:** Medium. $15
daily fee/pet. No service, supervision. [SAVE] 🔁 🛰 🛢 🖵

WACO
▼▼▼▼ Hilton-Waco 🏠
(254) 754-8484. **$99-$169.** 113 S University Parks Dr 76701. I-35 exit
335B, 0.5 mi w. Int corridors. **Pets:** Accepted.
🍴 🔁 🛰 ✕ 🛢 🖵

▼▼ La Quinta Inn Waco University 🏠
(254) 752-9741. **$69-$279.** 1110 S 9th St 76706. I-35 exit 334 (17th St)
southbound; exit 334A (18th St) northbound; just n; on northbound
frontage road. Ext corridors. **Pets:** Large, other species. Service with
restrictions. 🔁 🛰 🛢 🖵

▼▼▼ Residence Inn by Marriott 🏠
(254) 714-1386. **$150-$230.** 501 S University Parks Dr 76706. I-35 exit
335B, 0.3 mi w. Int corridors. **Pets:** Accepted. 🔁 🛰 ✕ 🛢 🖵

▼▼ Super 8-Waco 🏠
(254) 754-1023. **$49-$109.** 1320 S Jack Kultgen Frwy 76706. I-35 exit
334 (17th St), just n; on east frontage road. Int corridors.
Pets: Accepted. 🛰 🛢 🖵

◎◎◎ **▼▼▼** Super 8 Waco Mall 🏠
(254) 776-3194. **$55-$109.** 6624 Woodway Dr (Hwy 84 W) 76712. Jct
US 84 and SR 6; on southwest corner. Ext corridors. **Pets:** Medium.
$10 daily fee/pet. Service with restrictions, supervision.
[SAVE] 🔁 🛰 🛢 🖵

WASHINGTON
◎◎◎ **▼▼▼▼** The Inn at Dos Brisas 🆑
(979) 277-7750. **$400-$1400, 30 day notice.** 10000 Champion Dr
77880. US 290 exit Chapel Hill to FM 1155, 6.5 mi n. Ext corridors.
Pets: Accepted. [SAVE] 🍴 🔁 🛰 ✕ 🛢 🖵

WAXAHACHIE
◎◎◎ **▼▼▼** BEST WESTERN PLUS Waxahachie Inn &
Suites 🏠
(972) 938-1600. **$85-$95.** 1701 US Hwy 77 N 75165. US 287 exit US
77, just n. Int corridors. **Pets:** Accepted. [SAVE] 🔁 🛰 🛢 🖵

▼▼ Super 8 🏠
(972) 938-9088. **$55-$125.** 400 N I-35 E 75165. I-35E exit 401B. Int
corridors. **Pets:** Accepted. 🔁 🛰 🛢 🖵

WEATHERFORD
◎◎◎ **▼▼▼▼** BEST WESTERN PLUS Cutting Horse Inn &
Suites 🏠
(817) 599-3300. **$115-$195.** 210 Alford Dr 76086. I-20 exit 408, just s
on SR 171, then just w. Int corridors. **Pets:** Accepted.
[SAVE] 🛰 🔁 🛰 🛢 🖵

▼▼▼ Hampton Inn 🏠
(817) 599-4800. **$94-$169.** 2524 S Main St 76087. I-20 exit 408. Int
corridors. **Pets:** Small. $15 daily fee/pet. Designated rooms, service with
restrictions, supervision. 🔁 🛰 🛢 🖵

▼▼ Quality Inn & Suites 🏠
(817) 599-3700. **$75-$119.** 2500 S Main St 76087. I-20 exit 408, just s.
Ext/int corridors. **Pets:** Accepted. 🛰 🔁 🛰 🛢 🖵

▼▼▼ Weatherford Heritage Inn 🏠
(817) 594-7401. **Call for rates.** 1927 Santa Fe Dr 76086. I-20 exit 409
(Clear Lake Rd/FM 2552), 0.3 mi nw. Ext corridors. **Pets:** Accepted.
🔁 🛰 🛢 🖵

WEBSTER
◎◎◎ **▼▼▼** Comfort Suites 🏠
(281) 554-5400. **$108-$117.** 16931 N Texas Ave 77598. I-45 exit 26
(Bay Area Blvd), 0.5 mi e to Texas Ave, then just s. Int corridors.
Pets: Medium, dogs only. $25 daily fee/pet. Designated rooms, service
with restrictions, crate. [SAVE] 🛰 🔁 🛰 ✕ 🛢 🖵

▼▼▼ Staybridge Suites Houston/Clear Lake 🏠
(281) 338-0900. **$139-$199, 3 day notice.** 501 W Texas Ave 77598.
I-45 exit 26 (Bay Area Blvd), right, then left at 3rd light. Int corridors.
Pets: Accepted. 🛰 🔁 🛰 ✕ 🛢 🖵

WICHITA FALLS
▼▼ Baymont Inn & Suites Wichita Falls 🏠
(940) 691-7500. **$52-$91.** 4510 Kell Blvd 76309. US 82/277 exit McNeil
Ave, just w. Int corridors. **Pets:** Accepted. 🛰 🛢 🖵

◎◎◎ **▼▼▼▼** BEST WESTERN PLUS University Inn &
Suites 🏠
(940) 687-2025. **$75-$125.** 4540 Maplewood Ave 76308. Jct Southwest
Pkwy (CR 369), just n. Int corridors. **Pets:** Accepted.
[SAVE] 🛰 🔁 🛰 ✕ 🛢 🖵

▼▼▼ Hotel at Wichita Falls 🏠
(940) 761-6000. **Call for rates.** 100 Central Frwy 76306. I-44 exit 1C;
on west side access road. Int corridors. **Pets:** Accepted.
🛰 🔁 🛰 🛢 🖵

▼▼ La Quinta Inn Event Center North 🏠
(940) 322-6971. **$59-$224.** 1128 Central Frwy N 76306. I-44 exit 2
(Maurine St), just w. Ext corridors. **Pets:** Large, other species. Service
with restrictions. 🔁 🛰 🛢 🖵

◎◎◎ **▼▼▼** Red Roof Inn-Witchita Falls 🏠
(940) 766-6881. **$50-$80.** 1032 Central Frwy 76306. I-44 exit 2 (Maurine St), just w. Ext corridors. **Pets:** Large, other species. Service with
restrictions, supervision. [SAVE] 🔁 🛰 🛢 🖵

▼▼ Super 8-Wichita Falls 🏠
(940) 322-8880. **$50-$80.** 1307 Kenley Ave 76306. I-44 exit 2 (Maurine
St), just w. Int corridors. **Pets:** Accepted. 🛰 🛢 🖵

WINNIE
▼▼▼ Comfort Inn & Suites 🏠
(409) 296-6200. **$80-$94.** 338 Spur 5 77665. I-10 exit 829, just s. Int
corridors. **Pets:** Accepted. 🔁 🛰 ✕ 🛢 🖵

▼▼ Days Inn & Suites 🏠
(409) 296-2866. **$69-$114.** 14932 FM 1663 77665. I-10 exit 829, just n.
Ext corridors. **Pets:** Medium. $20 daily fee/pet. Service with restrictions,
supervision. 🛰 🛰 🛢 🖵

ZAPATA
◎◎◎ **▼▼** BEST WESTERN Inn by the Lake 🏠
(956) 765-8403. **$85-$106.** 1896 S US Hwy 83 78076. On US 83, 0.5
mi se. Ext corridors. **Pets:** Accepted. [SAVE] 🔁 🛰 🛢 🖵

AMERICAN FORK

◈ ◈◈◈ **Holiday Inn Express & Suites American Fork-North Provo** 🅷

(801) 763-8500. **$89-$169, 3 day notice.** 712 S Utah Valley Dr 84003. I-15 exit 276, 0.3 mi n on S 500 E, just e on E 620 S, then 0.3 mi s. Int corridors. **Pets:** Accepted. 🆂🅰🆅🅴 🍽 🛡🅼 🔊 🛰 ✖ 🛄 🖵

BEAVER

◈ ◈◈◈ **BEST WESTERN Butch Cassidy Inn** 🅼

(435) 438-2438. **Call for rates.** 161 S Main St 84713. I-15 exit 109, 1.8 mi e. Ext corridors. **Pets:** Accepted.
🆂🅰🆅🅴 🍽 🔊 🛰 ✖ 🛄 🖵

◈ ◈◈◈ **BEST WESTERN Paradise Inn** 🅷

(435) 438-2455. **$80-$140.** 314 W 1425 N 84713. I-15 exit 112, just e. Ext corridors. **Pets:** Medium, other species. $9 daily fee/room. Designated rooms, service with restrictions, supervision.
🆂🅰🆅🅴 🍽 🔊 🛰 ✖ 🛄 🖵

◈◈◈ **Quality Inn** 🅷

(435) 438-5426. **$65-$90.** 781 W 1800 S 84713. I-15 exit 109, just w. Int corridors. **Pets:** Accepted. 🔊 🛰 🛄 🖵

BICKNELL

◈◈◈ **Aquarius Motel & Restaurant** 🅼

(435) 425-3835. **Call for rates.** 240 W Main St 84715. 0.4 mi w of center on SR 24. Ext/int corridors. **Pets:** Accepted.
🍽 🔊 ✖ 🛰 ✖ 🛄 🖵

BLANDING

◈◈◈ **Super 8** 🅼

(435) 678-3880. **$60-$200.** 755 S Main St 84511. On US 191 (Main St). Int corridors. **Pets:** Accepted. 🛰 ✖ 🛄 🖵

BLUFF

◈◈◈ **Kokopelli Inn** 🅼

(435) 672-2322. **$86-$104, 3 day notice.** 160 E Main St 84512. On US 191 (Main St). Int corridors. **Pets:** Accepted. 🛰 ✖ 🛄 🖵

BOULDER

◈◈◈ **Boulder Mountain Lodge** 🅷

(435) 335-7460. **$85-$295, 30 day notice.** 20 N Hwy 12 84716. Just s. Ext/int corridors. **Pets:** Dogs only. $15 daily fee/pet. Designated rooms, service with restrictions, supervision. 🍽 🛰 ✖ 🛄 🖵

BRIAN HEAD

◈◈◈◈ **Grand Lodge at Brian Head** 🅷

(435) 677-9000. **$109-$379, 3 day notice.** 314 Hunter Ridge Dr 84719. On SR 143. Int corridors. **Pets:** Accepted.
🍽 🛡🅼 🛰 ✖ 🛰 ✖ 🛄 🖵

BRIGHAM CITY

◈◈◈ **Crystal Inn** 🅷

(435) 723-0440. **$96-$229.** 480 Westland Dr 84302. I-15 exit 362, 1 mi e to S 500 W, then just n. Int corridors. **Pets:** Accepted.
🛡🅼 🛰 🔊 ✖ 🛄 🖵

BRYCE CANYON CITY

◈◈◈ ◈◈◈ **BEST WESTERN PLUS Ruby's Inn** 🅷

(435) 834-5341. **$70-$145.** 26 S Main St 84764. On SR 63, 1 mi s of SR 12. Ext/int corridors. **Pets:** Accepted.
🆂🅰🆅🅴 🍽 🛰 ✖ 🔊 ✖ 🛄 🖵

◈◈◈ **Bryce View Lodge** 🅼

(435) 834-5180. **$60-$120.** 105 E Center St 84764. 1 mi s of SR 12. Ext corridors. **Pets:** Accepted. 🆂🅰🆅🅴 ✖ 🔊 ✖ 🛄 🖵

CAINEVILLE

◈◈◈ **Rodeway Inn Capitol Reef** 🅼

(435) 456-9900. **$80-$120.** 25 E SR 24 84775. West end of town. Ext corridors. **Pets:** Accepted. 🆂🅰🆅🅴 🍽 🛰 🔊 ✖ 🛄 🖵

CEDAR CITY

◈◈◈ **Americas Best Value Inn** 🅷

(435) 867-4700. **$43-$95.** 333 N 1100 W 84720. I-15 exit 59, just e. Int corridors. **Pets:** Medium, other species. $10 daily fee/room. Service with restrictions, crate. 🛰 🔊 ✖ 🛄 🖵

◈◈◈ ◈◈◈ **BEST WESTERN El Rey Inn & Suites** 🅷

(435) 586-6518. **$59-$199.** 80 S Main St 84720. I-15 exit 57, 2 mi n; center. Ext corridors. **Pets:** Large. $20 one-time fee/room. Designated rooms, service with restrictions, supervision.
🆂🅰🆅🅴 🍽 🛰 🔊 ✖ 🛄 🖵

◈◈◈ **Comfort Inn & Suites** 🅷

(435) 865-0003. **$79-$169.** 1288 S Main St 84720. I-15 exit 57, just e, then just n. Int corridors. **Pets:** Accepted.
🍽 🛡🅼 🛰 🔊 ✖ 🛄 🖵

◈◈◈ **Crystal Inn Cedar City** 🅷

(435) 586-8888. **$81-$190.** 1575 W 200 N 84720. I-15 exit 59, just w. Ext/int corridors. **Pets:** Accepted. 🍽 🛰 ✖ 🔊 🛄 🖵

◈◈◈ **Days Inn** 🅼

(435) 867-8877. **$54-$84.** 1204 S Main St 84720. I-15 exit 57, 0.4 mi ne. Ext corridors. **Pets:** Accepted. 🍽 🛰 🔊 🛄 🖵

◈◈◈ **Holiday Inn Express Hotel & Suites** 🅷

(435) 865-7799. **Call for rates.** 1555 S Old Hwy 91 84720. I-15 exit 57, just e, then s. Int corridors. **Pets:** Accepted.
🍽 🛡🅼 🛰 🔊 ✖ 🛄 🖵

◈◈◈ **Motel 6 of Cedar City - 4041** 🅼

(435) 586-9200. **Call for rates.** 1620 W 200 N 84720. I-15 exit 59, just w. Int corridors. **Pets:** Other species. Service with restrictions, crate. 🛡🅼 🔊 🛄

◈◈◈ **Quality Inn** 🅼

(435) 586-2082. **$50-$129.** 250 N 1100 W 84720. I-15 exit 59, just e. Ext corridors. **Pets:** Accepted. 🛰 🔊 ✖ 🛄 🖵

CIRCLEVILLE

◈◈◈ **Butch Cassidy's Hideout** 🅼

(435) 577-2008. **$60-$90.** 339 S Hwy 89 84723. Just s of center. Ext corridors. **Pets:** $10 daily fee/pet. Service with restrictions, supervision.
🍽 🔊 ✖ 🔳 🛄 🖵

COALVILLE

◈◈◈ ◈◈◈ **BEST WESTERN Holiday Hills** 🅷

(435) 336-4444. **$89-$99.** 500 W 120 S 84017. I-80 exit 162, just w. Int corridors. **Pets:** $20 daily fee/room. Designated rooms, service with restrictions, supervision. 🆂🅰🆅🅴 🍽 🛰 🔊 🛄 🖵

COTTONWOOD HEIGHTS

◈◈◈ ◈◈◈ **Hawthorn Suites by Wyndham Salt Lake City Fort Union**

(801) 567-0111. **$60-$150.** 6990 S Park Centre Dr 84121. I-15 exit 297 (7200 S), 2.4 mi e on 7200 S (Fort Union Blvd) to 1300 E, continue just e to Park Centre Dr, then just s. Int corridors. **Pets:** Small. $75 one-time fee/room. Service with restrictions, crate.
🆂🅰🆅🅴 🔊 ✖ 🛄 🖵

DELTA

◈◈◈ **Days Inn** 🅼

(435) 864-3882. **$80-$90.** 527 E Topaz Blvd 84624. Jct US 6 and 50. Ext corridors. **Pets:** $15 one-time fee/room. Designated rooms, service with restrictions, supervision. 🛰 🔊 🛄 🖵

ESCALANTE

▽▽ ▽▽ Rainbow Country Bed & Breakfast BB

(435) 826-4567. **$84-$114, 3 day notice.** 585 E 300 S 84726. Just s of SR 12; east end of town. Int corridors. **Pets:** $10 daily fee/pet. Service with restrictions, supervision. ⊞ 🏝 ⊗ 🛒 🗷

FILLMORE

◈◈◈ ▽▽▽ BEST WESTERN Paradise Inn & Resort Ⓜ

(435) 743-6895. **Call for rates.** 905 N Main St 84631. I-15 exit 167, just e. Ext corridors. **Pets:** Other species. Designated rooms, service with restrictions, supervision. ⟨SAVE⟩ ⊞ 🏝 🛜 🛏 🖵

GLENDALE

▽▽ ▽▽ Historic Smith Hotel Bed & Breakfast BB

(435) 648-2156. **$60-$108, 4 day notice.** 295 N Main St 84729. US 89; north end of town. Int corridors. **Pets:** Other species. Designated rooms, no service, supervision. 🛜 ⊗ 🗷

GREEN RIVER

▽▽▽ Holiday Inn Express Ⓗ

(435) 564-4439. **Call for rates.** 1845 E Main St 84525. I-70 exit 164, 1.7 mi nw. Int corridors. **Pets:** Accepted. 🏝 🛜 ⊗ 🛏 🖵

▽▽ Super 8 Ⓜ

(435) 564-8888. **$75-$90.** 1248 E Main St 84525. I-70 exit 164, 1.3 mi n. Int corridors. **Pets:** Accepted. ⊞ 🏝 🛜 🛏 🖵

HATCH

▽▽ ▽▽ Mountain Ridge Motel Ⓜ

(435) 735-4300. **Call for rates.** 106 S Main St 84735. On US 89; center. Ext corridors. **Pets:** Accepted. 🛜 ⊗ 🗷 🛏 🖵

HEBER CITY

◈◈◈ ▽▽▽ Swiss Alps Inn Ⓜ

(435) 654-0722. **$70-$120.** 167 S Main St 84032. I-80 exit 146 (US 40), 15 mi s. Ext corridors. **Pets:** Other species. $10 daily fee/room. Designated rooms, service with restrictions, supervision.

⟨SAVE⟩ 🏝 ⊗ 🛜 ⊗ 🛏 🖵

HOLLADAY

◈◈◈ ▽▽▽▽ Hyatt Place Salt Lake City/Cottonwood Ⓗ

(801) 890-1280. **$84-$199.** 3090 E 6200 S 84121. I-215 exit 6 (6200 S), 0.3 mi s; at base of Big Cottonwood Canyon. Int corridors. **Pets:** Medium, dogs only. $75 one-time fee/pet. Service with restrictions, supervision. ⟨SAVE⟩ ⊞ 🅼 🛜 ⊗ 🛏 🖵

HUNTSVILLE

▽▽▽ Jackson Fork Inn Ⓒ

(801) 745-0051. **$90-$160, 3 day notice.** 7345 E 900 S 84317. I-15 exit 344 (12th St), 12 mi e. Int corridors. **Pets:** $20 one-time fee/room. Designated rooms, service with restrictions, supervision.

⊞ 🛜 ⊗ 🗷

KANAB

◈◈◈ ▽▽▽ BEST WESTERN Red Hills Ⓜ

(435) 644-2675. **$57-$101.** 125 W Center St 84741. Center. Ext/int corridors. **Pets:** Medium. $15 daily fee/room. Designated rooms, service with restrictions, supervision. ⟨SAVE⟩ 🏝 🛜 ⊗ 🛏 🖵

▽▽ ▽▽ Days Inn & Suites Ⓗ

(435) 644-2562. **$54-$97.** 296 W 100 N 84741. On US 89; n of downtown. Int corridors. **Pets:** Dogs only. Designated rooms, service with restrictions, supervision. ⊞ 🏝 🛜 ⊗ 🛏 🖵

▽▽▽ Holiday Inn Express Hotel & Suites Ⓗ

(435) 644-3100. **Call for rates.** 217 S 100 E 84741. On US 89; jct 200 S. Int corridors. **Pets:** Accepted. 🏝 🛜 ⊗ 🛏 🖵

Parry Lodge Ⓜ

▽▽

(435) 644-2601. **$55-$120.** 89 E Center St 84741. On US 89; corner of 100 E; center. Ext/int corridors. **Pets:** Accepted.

⊞ 🏝 🛜 ⊗ 🛏 🖵

LAYTON

◈◈◈ ▽▽▽▽ Comfort Inn Ⓗ

(801) 544-5577. **$69-$129.** 877 N 400 W 84041. I-15 exit 331, just e. Int corridors. **Pets:** Accepted. ⟨SAVE⟩ 🅼 🏝 🛜 🛏 🖵

▽▽▽ Hampton Inn Ⓗ

(801) 775-8800. **$99-$159.** 1700 N Woodland Park Dr 84041. I-15 exit 332 (Antelope Dr), 0.3 mi e, then just s. Int corridors. **Pets:** Accepted. 🅼 🛜 🛏 🖵

▽▽▽ Home2 Suites by Hilton Ⓗ

(801) 820-9222. **$99-$139.** 803 W Heritage Park Blvd 84041. I-15 exit 332 (Antelope Dr), 0.6 mi e to 700 W, then 0.5 mi s. Int corridors. **Pets:** Accepted. 🅼 🏝 🛜 🛏 🖵

▽▽▽ La Quinta Inn & Suites Salt Lake City Layton Ⓗ

(801) 776-6700. **$75-$274.** 1965 N 1200 W 84041. I-15 exit 332 (Antelope Dr), just e. Int corridors. **Pets:** Large, other species. Service with restrictions. 🏝 🛜 🛏 🖵

▽▽▽ TownePlace Suites by Marriott Ⓗ

(801) 779-2422. **$111-$183.** 1743 Woodland Park Dr 84041. I-15 exit 332 (Antelope Dr), 0.3 mi se. Int corridors. **Pets:** Accepted.

🏝 🛜 ⊗ 🛏 🖵

LEHI

◈◈◈ ▽▽▽ BEST WESTERN Timpanogos Inn Ⓗ

(801) 768-1400. **Call for rates.** 195 S 850 E 84043. I-15 exit 279, just w, then just s. Int corridors. **Pets:** Accepted.

⟨SAVE⟩ 🏝 🛜 ⊗ 🛏 🖵

▽▽▽ Home2 Suites by Hilton Lehi-Thanksgiving Point Ⓗ

(801) 753-5430. **$89-$169.** 3051 W Club House Dr 84043. I-15 exit 284, 0.5 mi w. Int corridors. **Pets:** Accepted. 🅼 🛜 ⊗ 🛏 🖵

LOGAN

◈◈◈ ▽▽▽ BEST WESTERN Baugh Motel Ⓜ

(435) 752-5220. **$90-$170.** 153 S Main St 84321. Just s of center. Ext corridors. **Pets:** Accepted. ⟨SAVE⟩ 🏝 🛜 🛏 🖵

◈◈◈ ▽▽▽▽ BEST WESTERN PLUS Weston Inn Ⓜ

(435) 752-5700. **$119-$175, 3 day notice.** 250 N Main St 84321. 0.3 mi n of center. Ext corridors. **Pets:** $15 daily fee/room. Designated rooms, service with restrictions, supervision.

⟨SAVE⟩ ECO 🅼 🏝 ⊗ 🛜 🛏 🖵

▽▽▽ Crystal Inn Ⓗ

(435) 752-0707. **$92-$229.** 853 S Hwy 89 and 91 84321. 2 mi s of center. Int corridors. **Pets:** Accepted. 🅼 🏝 🛜 ⊗ 🛏 🖵

▽▽▽ Holiday Inn Express & Suites Ⓗ

(435) 752-3444. **$89-$199.** 2235 N Main St 84341. 2.8 mi n of center. Int corridors. **Pets:** Accepted. ⊞ 🅼 🏝 🛜 🛏 🖵

MANTI

▽▽ ▽▽ Manti Country Village Motel Ⓜ

(435) 835-9300. **$69-$99.** 145 N Main St 84642. On US 89 (Main St), just n of center. Ext corridors. **Pets:** Medium, dogs only. $75 deposit/pet. Designated rooms, service with restrictions, crate. 🛜 ⊗ 🛏

MIDVALE

◈◈◈ ▽▽▽▽ BEST WESTERN PLUS Midvale Inn Ⓗ

(801) 566-4141. **$59-$159.** 280 W 7200 S 84047. I-15 exit 297 (7200 S), just e. Int corridors. **Pets:** Accepted.

⟨SAVE⟩ 🅼 🏝 🛜 ⊗ 🛏 🖵

◆◆◆ **Staybridge Suites Midvale** **H**

(801) 871-0871. **$100-$250.** 747 W Blue Vista Ln 84047. I-15 exit 297 (7200 S), 0.4 mi w, then just s. Int corridors. **Pets:** Accepted.

🍴 ♿ 📶 🚭 🧊 📺

◆◆ **Super 8** **H**

(801) 255-5559. **$95-$152.** 7048 S 900 E 84047. I-15 exit 297 (7200 S), 2.4 mi e via 7200 S (Fort Union Blvd) to 900 E, then just n. Int corridors. **Pets:** Accepted. 📶 🚭 🧊 📺

MIDWAY

AAA ◆◆◆ **Homestead Resort** **H**

(435) 654-1102. **$99-$219.** 700 N Homestead Dr 84049. I-80 exit 146 (US 40), 13 mi s to River Rd traffic light, 2.9 mi w to roundabout, 1.2 mi w, follow signs to Homestead Dr, then 0.4 mi s. Ext/int corridors. **Pets:** Accepted. SAVE 🍴 ♿ 🏊 🏋 📶 🚭 🧊 📺

MOAB *(Restaurants p. 642)*

AAA ◆◆ **Big Horn Lodge** **M** 🐾

(435) 259-6171. **$50-$140.** 550 S Main St 84532. 0.5 mi s. Ext corridors. **Pets:** Large, other species. $5 daily fee/pet. Designated rooms, service with restrictions, supervision.

SAVE 🍴 🏊 📶 🚭 🧊 📺

AAA ◆◆ **Bowen Motel** **M**

(435) 259-7132. **$59-$149, 3 day notice.** 169 N Main St 84532. Downtown. Ext corridors. **Pets:** Small. $10 daily fee/room. Designated rooms, service with restrictions, crate. SAVE 🏊 📶 🚭 🧊 📺

AAA ◆◆◆ **The Gonzo Inn** **H**

(435) 259-2515. **$169-$349.** 100 W 200 S 84532. Just w of 200 S and S Main St. Ext/int corridors. **Pets:** Other species. $30 daily fee/room. Service with restrictions. SAVE 🏊 📶 🚭 🧊 📺

AAA ◆◆◆ **La Quinta Inn Moab** **H**

(435) 259-8700. **$74-$334.** 815 S Main St 84532. 0.8 mi s. Int corridors. **Pets:** Large, other species. Service with restrictions.

SAVE 🏊 📶 🚭 🧊 📺

◆ **Motel 6 Moab #4119** **M**

(435) 259-6686. **$59-$199.** 1089 N Main St 84532. 1.5 mi n. Int corridors. **Pets:** Other species. Service with restrictions, crate.

🍴 🏊 📶 🚭

AAA ◆◆◆ **Red Cliffs Lodge - Moab's Adventure Headquarters** **RA**

(435) 259-2002. **$99-$340, 30 day notice.** Milepost 14 Hwy 128 84532. 2.3 mi n to jct US 191 and SR 128, 14 mi e to MM 14. Ext corridors. **Pets:** $20 daily fee/pet. Designated rooms, service with restrictions, supervision. SAVE 🍴 🏊 🏋 📶 🚭 🧊 📺

AAA ◆ **Red Stone Inn** **M** 🐾

(435) 259-3500. **$59-$140.** 535 S Main St 84532. 0.5 mi s. Int corridors. **Pets:** Medium. $5 daily fee/room. Designated rooms, service with restrictions, supervision. SAVE 📶 🚭 🧊 📺

AAA ◆◆ **River Canyon Lodge, An Extended Stay Inn & Suites** **M**

(435) 259-8838. **$49-$199.** 71 W 200 N 84532. Just w of 200 N and Main St. Int corridors. **Pets:** $25 one-time fee/pet. Designated rooms, service with restrictions, supervision. SAVE 🏊 📶 🚭 🧊 📺

AAA ◆ **Silver Sage Inn** **M**

(435) 259-4420. **$40-$110.** 840 S Main St 84532. 0.9 mi s of the center. Int corridors. **Pets:** Accepted. SAVE 📶 🚭 🧊 📺

◆◆◆◆ **Sorrel River Ranch Resort & Spa** **H**

(435) 259-4642. **Call for rates.** Hwy 128 at MM 17 84532. 17 mi e of jct US 191 and SR 128; at MM 17. Ext corridors. **Pets:** Accepted.

🍴 🏊 🏋 📶 🚭 🧊 📺

MONUMENT VALLEY

AAA ◆◆ **Goulding's Lodge & Tours** **H**

(435) 727-3231. **$89-$250, 3 day notice.** 1000 Main St 84536. 2 mi w of US 163; 0.5 mi n of Arizona border. Ext corridors. **Pets:** Accepted.

SAVE 🍴 🏊 📶 🚭 🧊 📺

MURRAY

◆◆◆ **Residence Inn by Marriott Salt Lake City Murray** **H**

(801) 262-4200. **$125-$206.** 171 E 5300 S 84107. I-15 exit 300 (5300 S), 0.8 mi e. Int corridors. **Pets:** Accepted.

🍴 ♿ 📶 🚭 🧊 📺

NEPHI

AAA ◆◆ **BEST WESTERN Paradise Inn of Nephi** **M**

(435) 623-0624. **Call for rates.** 1025 S Main St 84648. I-15 exit 222, 0.5 mi n. Ext corridors. **Pets:** Accepted. SAVE 🏊 📶 🚭 🧊 📺

NORTH SALT LAKE

AAA ◆◆◆ **BEST WESTERN PLUS CottonTree Inn** **H**

(801) 292-7666. **$99-$149.** 1030 N 400 E 84054. I-15 exit 315 (Woods Cross), just e to Onion St, then just s. Int corridors. **Pets:** Accepted.

SAVE ♿ 🏊 📶 🚭 🧊 📺

OGDEN

AAA ◆◆◆ **BEST WESTERN PLUS High Country Inn** **H** 🐾

(801) 394-9474. **$89-$150.** 1335 W 12th St 84404. I-15 exit 344 (12th St), just e. Ext/int corridors. **Pets:** Medium. $10 daily fee/room. Service with restrictions, crate. SAVE 🍴 🏊 📶 🧊 📺

AAA ◆◆◆ **Comfort Suites** **H**

(801) 621-2545. **$89-$125.** 2250 S 1200 W 84401. I-15 exit 343 (21st St), 0.3 mi e. Int corridors. **Pets:** $25 one-time fee/pet. Service with restrictions, supervision. SAVE 🍴 ♿ 🏊 📶 🚭 🧊 📺

◆◆◆ **Holiday Inn Express & Suites** **H**

(801) 392-5000. **$89-$199.** 2245 S 1200 W 84401. I-15 exit 343 (21st St), 0.3 mi e. Int corridors. **Pets:** Other species. $25 one-time fee/room. Designated rooms, service with restrictions, supervision.

♿ 🏊 📶 🚭 🧊 📺

AAA ◆◆ **Sleep Inn** **H**

(801) 731-6500. **$68-$82.** 1155 S 1700 W 84404. I-15 exit 344 (12th St), just w. Int corridors. **Pets:** Accepted. SAVE 📶 🧊 📺

OREM

◆◆◆ **Holiday Inn Express & Suites Orem-North Provo** **H**

(801) 655-1515. **Call for rates.** 1290 W University Pkwy 84058. I-15 exit 269 (University Pkwy), 0.5 mi w. Int corridors. **Pets:** Accepted.

🍴 ♿ 🏊 🏋 📶 🧊 📺

◆◆◆ **La Quinta Inn & Suites Orem University Parkway** **H**

(801) 226-0440. **$79-$260.** 521 W University Pkwy 84058. I-15 exit 269 (University Pkwy), 0.4 mi e. Int corridors. **Pets:** Large, other species. Service with restrictions. ♿ 🏊 📶 🚭 🧊 📺

◆◆◆ **TownePlace Suites by Marriott Orem-North Provo** **H**

(801) 225-4477. **$111-$183.** 873 N 1200 W 84057. I-15 exit 272 (800 N), just e. Int corridors. **Pets:** Accepted. ♿ 🏊 📶 🚭 🧊 📺

PARK CITY *(Restaurants p. 642)*

AAA ◆◆ **BEST WESTERN PLUS Landmark Inn & Pancake House** **H**

(435) 649-7300. **$79-$239.** 6560 N Landmark Dr 84098. I-80 exit 145 (Kimball Jct), 0.3 mi s, then 0.3 mi nw. Int corridors. **Pets:** Accepted.

SAVE 🍴 🏊 🏋 📶 🚭 🧊 📺

▼▼▼▼ Holiday Inn Express Hotel & Suites H

(435) 658-1600. **Call for rates.** 1501 W Ute Blvd 84098. I-80 exit 145 (Kimball Jct), just s to Ute Blvd, then 0.3 mi e. Int corridors.
Pets: Accepted. ᕦM ➨ ☒ 🛜 ☒ 🛆 🛢 ▣

◉◉◉ ▼▼▼ ▼▼▼ Hyatt Escala Lodge at Park City H ❀

(435) 940-1234. **$139-$799, 7 day notice.** 3551 N Escala Ct 84098. I-80 exit 145 (Kimball Jct), 3 mi sw on SR 224 (Park Ave), then 0.8 mi w; at Canyons. Int corridors. **Pets:** $150 one-time fee/room. Service with restrictions. SAVE ECO ❙❙ ᕦM ➨ ☒ 🛜 🛆 🛢 ▣

◉◉◉ ▼▼▼ ▼▼▼ Montage Deer Valley H ❀

(435) 604-1300. **Call for rates.** 9100 Marsac Ave 84060. I-80 exit 145 (Kimball Jct), at roundabout, take Marsac Ave exit, 2 mi s to Guardsman Connection, then 2 mi sw. Int corridors. **Pets:** Medium. $100 one-time fee/room. Service with restrictions, supervision.

SAVE ❙❙ ᕦM ➨ ☒ 🛜 ☒ 🛆 🛢 ▣

◉◉◉ ▼▼▼ ▼▼▼ St. Regis Deer Valley H

(435) 940-5700. **$269-$2400, 7 day notice.** 2300 Deer Valley Dr E 84060. I-80 exit 145 (Kimball Jct), 6 mi s to Deer Valley Dr, 1 mi se to roundabout, take third exit (Deer Valley Dr), then 1.2 mi se. Int corridors. **Pets:** Accepted. SAVE ❙❙ ᕦM ➨ ☒ 🛜 🛆 🛢 ▣

▼▼▼▼ Washington School House H

(435) 649-3800. **Call for rates.** 543 Park Ave 84060. I-80 exit 145 (Kimball Jct), 6 mi se to Kearns Blvd and SR 224 (Park Ave), then 1.2 mi s; downtown. Int corridors. **Pets:** Accepted. ➨ 🛜 ☒

PAROWAN

▼▼ Days Inn Parowan M

(435) 477-3326. **$55-$80.** 625 W 200 S 84761. I-15 exit 75, 1.5 mi e. Ext corridors. **Pets:** Accepted. ❙❙ ➨ 🛜 🛢 ▣

PRICE

▼▼ Ramada Price H

(435) 637-8880. **$81-$115.** 838 Westwood Blvd 84501. US 6 exit 240 (Business Loop), just e. Int corridors. **Pets:** Accepted.

❙❙ ➨ 🛜 ☒ 🛢 ▣

PROVO

▼▼ Baymont Inn & Suites Provo River H ❀

(801) 373-7044. **$79-$139.** 2230 N University Pkwy 84604. I-15 exit 269 (University Pkwy), 3.2 mi e, then just n; in CottonTree Square. Int corridors. **Pets:** Large. $25 one-time fee/room. Service with restrictions, supervision. ➨ 🛜 ☒ 🛢 ▣

▼ Econo Lodge M

(801) 373-0099. **$50-$90.** 1625 W Center St 84601. I-15 exit 265 (Center St), just w. Ext corridors. **Pets:** Accepted. ❙❙ 🛜 🛢 ▣

▼▼▼ Hampton Inn Provo H

(801) 377-6396. **$109-$249.** 1511 S 40 E 84601. I-15 exit 263 (University Ave), just e. Int corridors. **Pets:** Accepted.
ᕦM ➨ 🛜 ☒ 🛢 ▣

▼▼ La Quinta Inn Provo Town Center H

(801) 374-9750. **$75-$179.** 1460 S University Ave 84601. I-15 exit 263 (University Ave), 0.5 mi e. Int corridors. **Pets:** Large, other species. Service with restrictions. ❙❙ ᕦM ➨ 🛜 ☒ 🛢 ▣

▼▼▼ Residence Inn by Marriott H

(801) 374-1000. **$97-$160.** 252 W 2230 N 84604. I-15 exit 269 (University Pkwy), 3.2 mi e to W 2230 N, then 0.3 mi e. Int corridors.
Pets: Accepted. ᕦM ➨ 🛜 ☒ 🛢 ▣

▼▼ Sleep Inn H

(801) 377-6597. **$60-$150.** 1505 S 40 E 84606. I-15 exit 263 (University Ave), just e. Int corridors. **Pets:** Accepted.
➨ 🛜 ☒ 🛢 ▣

RICHFIELD

◉◉◉ ▼▼▼ BEST WESTERN Richfield Inn H

(435) 893-0100. **$90-$100.** 1275 N Main St 84701. I-70 exit 40, just s. Int corridors. **Pets:** $15 daily fee/pet. Designated rooms, service with restrictions, supervision. SAVE ➨ 🛜 ☒ 🛢 ▣

▼▼▼ Comfort Inn H

(435) 893-0119. **$80-$130.** 1070 W 1250 S 84701. I-70 exit 37, just e. Int corridors. **Pets:** Accepted. ➨ 🛜 ☒ 🛢 ▣

▼▼▼▼ Holiday Inn Express & Suites H

(435) 896-8552. **Call for rates.** 20 W 1400 N 84701. I-70 exit 40, just s. Int corridors. **Pets:** Accepted.
⊟ ❙❙ ᕦM ➨ 🛜 ☒ 🛢 ▣

▼ Super 8 M

(435) 896-9204. **$55-$86, 3 day notice.** 1377 N Main St 84701. I-70 exit 40, just s. Ext/int corridors. **Pets:** Accepted. 🛜 🛢 ▣

ROOSEVELT

▼▼ Americas Best Value Inn M

(435) 722-4644. **Call for rates.** 2203 E Hwy 40 84066. 1 mi e of center. Ext corridors. **Pets:** Accepted. ❙❙ 🛜 🛢 ▣

ST. GEORGE

▼▼▼ America's Best Inn & Suites M

(435) 652-3030. **Call for rates.** 245 N Red Cliffs Dr 84790. I-15 exit 8, just e. Ext corridors. **Pets:** Accepted. ➨ 🛜 🛢 ▣

▼▼▼ Comfort Inn H

(435) 628-8544. **$75-$136, 3 day notice.** 138 E Riverside Dr 84790. I-15 exit 6 (Bluff St), just e. Int corridors. **Pets:** Accepted.
ᕦM ➨ 🛜 ☒ 🛢 ▣

▼▼ Crystal Inn St. George H

(435) 688-7477. **$84-$209.** 1450 S Hilton Dr 84770. I-15 exit 6 (Bluff St), just w. Int corridors. **Pets:** Other species. $25 one-time fee/room. Designated rooms, service with restrictions, supervision.

❙❙ ➨ ☒ 🛜 ☒ 🛢 ▣

▼▼▼ Green Gate Village Historic Inn BB

(435) 628-6999. **$99-$239, 7 day notice.** 76 W Tabernacle St 84770. I-15 exit 8, 2 mi w to Main St, just left, then just right. Ext/int corridors. **Pets:** Accepted. ➨ 🛜 ☒ 🛢 ▣

◉◉◉ ▼▼▼ ▼▼▼ Green Valley Boutique Hotel and Spa H

(435) 628-8060. **$129-$179.** 1871 W Canyon View Dr 84770. Jct Bluff and S Main sts, 4 mi sw via Hilton Dr to Dixie Dr, then just w to Canyon View Dr. Ext corridors. **Pets:** Medium, other species. $500 deposit/pet, $5 daily fee/pet. Designated rooms, service with restrictions, crate.

SAVE ❙❙ ᕦM ➨ ☒ 🛜 ☒ 🛢 ▣

◉◉◉ ▼▼▼ Howard Johnson Inn M

(435) 628-8000. **$49-$200.** 1040 S Main St 84770. I-15 exit 6 (Bluff St), just w, then just e. Ext corridors. **Pets:** Dogs only. $15 daily fee/pet. Service with restrictions, supervision.
SAVE ᕦM ➨ 🛜 ☒ 🛢 ▣

▼ The Inn at St. George M

(435) 673-4666. **Call for rates.** 60 W St. George Blvd 84770. 1 blk w of Main St; downtown. Ext corridors. **Pets:** Accepted.
➨ 🛜 ☒ 🛢

▼▼▼ La Quinta Inn & Suites - St. George H

(435) 674-2664. **$79-$299.** 91 E 2680 S 84790. I-15 exit 4, just e on Brigham Rd. Int corridors. **Pets:** Large, other species. Service with restrictions. ❙❙ ᕦM ➨ 🛜 ☒ 🛢 ▣

◉◉◉ ▼▼▼ Quality Inn St. George H

(435) 628-4481. **$99-$199.** 1165 S Bluff St 84770. I-15 exit 6 (Bluff St), just w. Ext corridors. **Pets:** Accepted. SAVE ➨ 🛜 ☒ 🛢 ▣

▼▼ **Ramada St. George** H
(435) 628-2828. **$71-$189.** 1440 E St. George Blvd 84790. I-15 exit 8, just e. Int corridors. **Pets:** Accepted. 🛲 🛜 ✖️ 📶 📺

▼▼ **St. George Inn & Suites** H
(435) 673-6661. **$69-$129.** 1221 S Main St 84770. I-15 exit 6 (Bluff St), just w. Ext corridors. **Pets:** Small, other species. $15 daily fee/room. Designated rooms, service with restrictions, supervision.
🛲 ✖️ 🛜 📶 📺

▼▼▼ **Seven Wives Inn** BB
(435) 628-3737. **Call for rates.** 217 N 100 W 84770. I-15 exit 8, 2.1 mi w, then n. Ext/int corridors. **Pets:** $20 one-time fee/pet. Designated rooms, service with restrictions, crate. 🛲 🛜 ✖️ 📶

♨♨ ▼▼▼ **TownePlace Suites by Marriott** H
(435) 986-9955. **$104-$171.** 251 S 1470 E 84790. I-15 exit 8, just e. Int corridors. **Pets:** Other species. $100 daily fee/room. Designated rooms, service with restrictions, supervision.
SAVE Ⓜ 🛲 🛜 ✖️ 📶 📺

SALINA

♨♨ ▼▼ **Scenic Hills Super 8** M
(435) 529-7483. **$60-$100.** 375 E 1620 S 84654. I-70 exit 56, just n. Ext corridors. **Pets:** Medium. $15 daily fee/room. Designated rooms, service with restrictions, supervision. SAVE 🛲 🛜 📶 📺

SALT LAKE CITY

▼▼ **Candlewood Suites Airport East** H
(801) 359-7500. **Call for rates.** 2170 W North Temple 84116. 3 mi w of Temple Square. Int corridors. **Pets:** Accepted. 🛜 ✖️ 📶 📺

▼▼▼ **Crystal Inn Downtown** H
(801) 328-4466. **$79-$209.** 230 W 500 S 84101. Cross streets 500 S and 200 W. Int corridors. **Pets:** Accepted.
Ⓜ 🛲 ✖️ 🛜 📶 📺

♨♨ ▼▼▼ **DoubleTree by Hilton Salt Lake City Airport** H
(801) 539-1515. **$105-$129.** 5151 Wiley Post Way 84116. I-80 exit 114 (Wright Brothers Dr), just n off ramp, then 0.4 mi w. Int corridors.
Pets: Accepted. SAVE 🍽 Ⓜ 🛲 🛜 ✖️ 📺

♨♨ ▼▼▼ **Hilton Salt Lake City Center** H
(801) 328-2000. **$104-$249.** 255 S West Temple 84101. Just s of cross streets 200 S and S West Temple. Int corridors. **Pets:** Large. $25 daily fee/pet. Service with restrictions.
SAVE 🍽 Ⓜ 🛲 🛜 ✖️ 📶 📺

▼▼▼ **Holiday Inn & Suites Salt Lake City Airport** H
(801) 741-1800. **$85-$359, 3 day notice.** 5001 W Wiley Post Way 84116. I-80 exit 114 (Wright Brothers Dr), just n off ramp, then 0.4 mi w. Int corridors. **Pets:** Accepted. 🍽 Ⓜ 🛲 🛜 ✖️ 📶 📺

▼▼▼ **Holiday Inn Express & Suites Airport East** H
(801) 741-1500. **$89-$189.** 200 N 2100 W 84116. 3 mi w of Temple Square. Int corridors. **Pets:** Accepted. Ⓜ 🛲 🛜 📶 📺

♨♨ ▼▼▼ **Hotel Monaco** H 🐾
(801) 595-0000. **$149-$359, 3 day notice.** 15 W 200 S 84101. Cross streets 200 S and Main St. Int corridors. **Pets:** Other species. Service with restrictions, crate. SAVE ECO 🍽 Ⓜ ✖️ 🛜 ✖️

♨♨ ▼▼▼ **Hyatt Place Salt Lake City Airport** H
(801) 363-1400. **$70-$210.** 52 N Tommy Thompson Rd 84116. I-80 exit 114 (Wright Brothers Dr), just n off ramp, just e, then just se. Int corridors. **Pets:** Accepted. SAVE 🍽 Ⓜ 🛲 🛜 ✖️ 📶 📺

♨♨ ▼▼▼ **Hyatt Place Salt Lake City Downtown/The Gateway** H
(801) 456-6300. **$79-$499.** 55 N 400 W 84101. 0.5 mi w of Temple Square via W South Temple to 400 W, then just n. Int corridors.
Pets: Accepted. SAVE 🍽 🛲 🛜 ✖️ 📶 📺

▼▼▼ **Radisson Hotel Salt Lake City Downtown** H
(801) 531-7500. **Call for rates.** 215 W South Temple 84101. Cross streets 200 S and W South Temple. Int corridors. **Pets:** Accepted.
ECO 🍽 Ⓜ 🛲 ✖️ 🛜 ✖️ 📶 📺

▼▼▼ **Red Lion Hotel Salt Lake Downtown** H
(801) 521-7373. **$80-$170.** 161 W 600 S 84101. Cross streets S West Temple and 600 S. Int corridors. **Pets:** Accepted.
🍽 🛲 🛜 ✖️ 📶 📺

▼▼▼ **Residence Inn by Marriott Salt Lake City Airport** H 🐾
(801) 532-4101. **$139-$229.** 4883 W Douglas Corrigan Way 84116. I-80 exit 114 (Wright Brothers Dr), just n off ramp. Int corridors. **Pets:** $75 one-time fee/room. Service with restrictions, crate.
Ⓜ 🛲 🛜 ✖️ 📶 📺

▼▼▼ **Residence Inn Salt Lake City Center** H
(801) 355-3300. **$153-$252.** 285 W Broadway (300 S) 84101. At 300 W and 300 S. Int corridors. **Pets:** Other species. $100 one-time fee/room. Service with restrictions. Ⓜ 🛲 🛜 ✖️ 📶 📺

♨♨ ▼▼▼ **Sheraton Salt Lake City Hotel** H 🐾
(801) 401-2000. **$99-$369.** 150 W 500 S 84101. Cross streets 200 W and 500 S. Int corridors. **Pets:** Dogs only. Service with restrictions, supervision. SAVE 🍽 Ⓜ 🛲 🛜 ✖️ 📶 📺

SANDY

♨♨ ▼▼▼ **BEST WESTERN PLUS CottonTree Inn** H
(801) 523-8484. **$124-$134.** 10695 S Auto Mall Dr 84070. I-15 exit 293 (10600 S), 0.3 mi e, then just s. Int corridors. **Pets:** Accepted.
SAVE Ⓜ 🛲 🛜 ✖️ 📶 📺

♨♨ ▼▼▼ **Holiday Inn Express & Suites** H 🐾
(801) 495-1317. **$99-$189.** 10680 S Auto Mall Dr 84070. I-15 exit 293 (10600 S), 0.3 mi e, then just s. Int corridors. **Pets:** Medium, other species. $25 daily fee/room. Designated rooms, service with restrictions, supervision. SAVE Ⓜ 🛲 🛜 ✖️ 📶 📺

♨♨ ▼▼▼ **HYATT house Salt Lake City-Sandy** H
(801) 304-5700. **$94-$249.** 9685 S Monroe St 84070. I-15 exit 295 (9000 S), 0.3 mi e to Frontage Rd, then 1 mi s. Int corridors. **Pets:** Medium. $75 one-time fee/pet. Service with restrictions, supervision. SAVE 🍽 Ⓜ 🛲 🛜 ✖️ 📶 📺

▼▼▼ **Residence Inn by Marriott** H
(801) 561-5005. **$125-$206.** 270 W 10000 S 84070. I-15 exit 293 (10600 S), 0.4 mi e to State St, 0.7 mi n to 10000 S, then 0.3 mi w. Int corridors. **Pets:** Accepted. 🍽 Ⓜ 🛲 🛜 ✖️ 📶 📺

SPANISH FORK

♨♨ ▼▼ **Western Inn** H
(801) 798-9400. **$50-$82.** 632 Kirby Ln 84660. I-15 exit 257B, on US 6. Int corridors. **Pets:** Other species. $6 daily fee/pet. Designated rooms, service with restrictions, supervision. SAVE 🛜 ✖️

SPRINGDALE (Restaurants p. 642)

♨♨ ▼▼▼ **BEST WESTERN Zion Park Inn** H
(435) 772-3200. **Call for rates.** 1215 Zion Park Blvd 84767. 2 mi s of Zion National Park entrance. Int corridors. **Pets:** Accepted.
SAVE 🍽 🛲 🛜 ✖️ 📶 📺

▼▼ **Canyon Ranch Motel** M
(435) 772-3357. **Call for rates.** 668 Zion Park Blvd 84767. SR 9, just s of south gate to Zion National Park. Ext corridors. **Pets:** Accepted.
🛲 🛜 ✖️ 📶 📺

▼▼▼ **Hampton Inn & Suites Springdale Zion National Park** H
(435) 627-9191. **$159-$249.** 1127 Zion Park Blvd 84767. 2 mi s of Zion National Park entrance. Int corridors. **Pets:** $25 one-time fee/pet. Service with restrictions, supervision. 🛜 ✖️ 📶 📺

SPRINGVILLE

🔺 ▼▼▼ BEST WESTERN Mountain View Inn 🅷 ❄️

(801) 489-3641. **$80-$200.** 1455 N 1750 W 84663. I-15 exit 261, just e. Int corridors. **Pets:** Medium, other species. $20 daily fee/room. Designated rooms, service with restrictions, supervision.

[SAVE] [🐾] [📶] [✖] [🛁] [📺]

▼▼ Days Inn 🅷

(801) 491-0300. **$60-$129.** 520 S 2000 W 84663. I-15 exit 260, just w. Int corridors. **Pets:** Accepted. [🐾] [📶] [✖] [🛁] [📺]

TOOELE

▼▼▼ Comfort Inn & Suites 🅷 ❄️

(801) 250-3600. **$105-$209.** 8580 N Hwy 36 84074. I-80 exit 99, just s. Int corridors. **Pets:** Medium, dogs only. $40 one-time fee/room. Designated rooms, service with restrictions, supervision.

[🍴] [🐾] [📶] [✖] [🛁] [📺]

TORREY

▼▼ Affordable Inn of Capital Reef 🅷

(435) 425-3866. **$89-$109.** 877 N SR 24 84775. 1.5 mi ne of jct SR 12 and 24. Ext corridors. **Pets:** Accepted. [📶] [✖] [🛁] [📺]

▼ Red Sands Hotel 🅷

(435) 425-3688. **Call for rates.** 670 E SR 24 84775. 0.3 mi w of jct SR 12 and 24. Int corridors. **Pets:** Medium, dogs only. $10 daily fee/pet. Designated rooms, service with restrictions, supervision.

[♿M] [🐾] [📶] [✖] [🛁]

▼ The Rim Rock Inn & Restaurants 🅼 ❄️

(435) 425-3398. **$54-$84.** 2523 E Hwy 24 84775. 2.5 mi ne of jct SR 12 and 24. Ext corridors. **Pets:** Other species. $10 one-time fee/pet. Designated rooms, service with restrictions, supervision. [🍴] [📶] [✖]

TREMONTON

▼▼▼ Hampton Inn 🅷

(435) 257-6000. **$105-$129.** 2145 W Main St 84337. I-84 exit 40, 0.4 mi e. Int corridors. **Pets:** Accepted. [🍴] [♿M] [🐾] [📶] [✖] [🛁] [📺]

🔺 ▼ Western Inn 🅷 ❄️

(435) 257-3399. **$67-$85.** 2301 W Main St 84337. I-84 exit 40, just e. Int corridors. **Pets:** Dogs only. $15 daily fee/pet. Designated rooms, service with restrictions, supervision. [SAVE] [🍴] [📶] [✖] [🛁]

VERNAL

▼▼▼ TownePlace Suites by Marriott 🅷

(435) 789-8050. **$132-$240.** 1219 W Hwy 40 84078. 1.3 mi w of center. Int corridors. **Pets:** Accepted. [🍴] [♿M] [🐾] [📶] [✖] [🛁] [📺]

WASHINGTON

▼▼▼ Holiday Inn Express & Suites 🅷

(435) 986-1313. **$89-$179.** 2450 N Town Center Dr 84780. I-15 exit 16, just e. Int corridors. **Pets:** Other species. $35 one-time fee/room. Designated rooms, service with restrictions, crate.

[🍴] [🐾] [📶] [✖] [🛁] [📺]

WENDOVER

🔺 ▼▼▼ BEST WESTERN PLUS Wendover Inn 🅷

(435) 665-2215. **$90-$140.** 685 E Wendover Blvd 84083. I-80 exit 2. Int corridors. **Pets:** Accepted. [SAVE] [🐾] [📶] [✖] [🛁] [📺]

▼▼ Super 8 Wendover 🅼

(435) 665-7811. **$69-$99.** 935 E Wendover Blvd 84083. I-80 exit 2, 2 mi w. Ext corridors. **Pets:** $10 daily fee/pet. Designated rooms, service with restrictions, supervision. [🐾] [📶] [🛁] [📺]

WEST VALLEY CITY

▼▼▼ Holiday Inn Express & Suites Water Park West Valley City 🅷

(801) 517-4000. **Call for rates.** 3036 S Decker Lake Dr 84119. I-215 exit 18A (3500 S), just e, 0.6 mi n, then just w. Int corridors. **Pets:** Accepted. [🍴] [♿M] [🐾] [✖] [📶] [🛁] [📺]

▼▼▼ Home2 Suites by Hilton - Salt Lake City/West Valley City 🅷

(801) 679-8222. **$99-$299.** 4028 Parkway Blvd 84120. I-15 exit 305A (West Valley/2100 S), 4.2 mi w on CR 201 exit 13 (Bangerter Hwy), 1.2 mi s to Parkway Blvd, then 0.3 mi w. Int corridors. **Pets:** Accepted.

[🍴] [♿M] [🐾] [📶] [🛁] [📺]

▼▼ La Quinta Inn Salt Lake City West 🅷

(801) 954-9292. **$69-$329.** 3540 S 2200 W 84119. I-215 exit 18 (3500 S), just e, then just s. Int corridors. **Pets:** Large, other species. Service with restrictions. [🐾] [📶] [🛁] [📺]

▼▼▼ Staybridge Suites West Valley City 🅷

(801) 746-8400. **Call for rates.** 3038 S Decker Lake Dr 84119. I-215 exit 18A (3500 S), just e, 0.6 mi n, then just w. Int corridors. **Pets:** Accepted. [🍴] [♿M] [🐾] [✖] [📶] [🛁] [📺]

WOODS CROSS

▼▼▼ Hampton Inn - Salt Lake City North/Woods Cross 🅷

(801) 296-1211. **$99-$179.** 2393 S 800 W 84087. I-15 exit 315, just w, then just n. Int corridors. **Pets:** Accepted.

[♿M] [🐾] [📶] [✖] [🛁] [📺]

VERMONT

ALBURG

▼▼ Ransom Bay Inn & Restaurant 🅱🅱

(802) 796-3399. **Call for rates.** 4 Center Bay Rd 05440. Jct SR 78, 0.5 mi s on US 2, then just e. Int corridors. **Pets:** Accepted.

[🍴] [📶] [✖] [🎞] [🚭]

ARLINGTON

🔺 ▼ Candlelight Motel 🅼

(802) 375-6647. **$59-$115, 14 day notice.** 4893 SR 7A 05250. Historic SR 7A, 1 mi n. Ext corridors. **Pets:** Medium, dogs only. $10 daily fee/pet. Designated rooms, service with restrictions, supervision.

[SAVE] [🍴] [🐾] [📶] [🛁]

BENNINGTON

▼ Bennington Motor Inn 🅼

(802) 442-5479. **$69-$179, 3 day notice.** 143 W Main St 05201. Jct US 7, 0.4 mi w on SR 9. Ext corridors. **Pets:** Medium. $15 daily fee/pet. Designated rooms, service with restrictions, supervision.

[🍴] [📶] [✖] [🛁] [📺]

▼ Harwood Hill Motel 🅼

(802) 442-6278. **Call for rates.** 864 Harwood Hill Rd (SR 7A) 05201. Jct SR 9, 1.2 mi n on US 7, then 1.7 mi n on Historic SR 7A. Ext corridors. **Pets:** Accepted. [🍴] [📶] [✖] [🛁] [📺]

▼ Knotty Pine Motel 🅼

(802) 442-5487. **$87-$115.** 130 Northside Dr 05201. Jct SR 9, 1.2 mi n on US 7, then just n on Historic SR 7A. Ext corridors. **Pets:** Designated rooms, service with restrictions, supervision. [🐾] [📶] [✖] [🛁] [📺]

BRANDON

▼▼ **Brandon Motor Lodge** M

(802) 247-9594. **Call for rates.** 2095 Franklin St 05733. 2 mi s on US 7. Ext corridors. **Pets:** Accepted. ⬛ 🍽 🛍 📶 ❌ 🔋 💻

▼▼◆ **The Lilac Inn** CI

(802) 247-5463. **Call for rates.** 53 Park St 05733. Just e on SR 73. Int corridors. **Pets:** Dogs only. $35 one-time fee/room. Service with restrictions, supervision. ⬛ 🍽 📶 ❌ 🐾

BRATTLEBORO

▼▼ **Econo Lodge** M

(802) 254-2360. **$60-$140.** 515 Canal St 05301. I-91 exit 1, 0.3 mi n on US 5. Ext/int corridors. **Pets:** Accepted. 🛍 📶 🔋 💻

BURLINGTON

🆔 ▼▼◆ **Hilton Burlington** H

(802) 658-6500. **$189-$309.** 60 Battery St 05401. At Battery and College sts; just n of ferry terminal; center. Int corridors. **Pets:** Accepted. 🅂🅰🅅🄴 🍽 🍴 🛍 📶 ❌ 🔋 💻

▼▼◆ **Hotel Vermont** H 🐾

(802) 651-0080. **Call for rates.** 41 Cherry St 05401. Just e of Battery St. Int corridors. **Pets:** Medium, dogs only. $35 daily fee/pet. Designated rooms, service with restrictions, supervision. 🍽 ❌ 📶 ❌ 🔋

CAVENDISH

▼▼◆ **The Pointe at Castle Hill Resort & Spa** H

(802) 226-7688. **Call for rates.** 2940 SR 103 05142. On SR 103, just n of jct SR 131. Int corridors. **Pets:** Accepted.
🍽 🛍 ❌ 📶 ❌ 🔋 💻

COLCHESTER

▼▼ **Days Inn Colchester** H

(802) 655-0900. **$70-$175.** 124 College Pkwy 05446. I-89 exit 15 northbound, just e on SR 15; exit 16 southbound, 1.1 mi s on US 7, then 1 mi e on SR 15. Int corridors. **Pets:** Dogs only. $10 daily fee/pet. Service with restrictions, crate. 🍽 🍴 🛍 📶 ❌ 💻

▼▼◆ **Hampton Inn & Event Center** H

(802) 655-6177. **$139-$269.** 42 Lower Mountain View Dr 05446. I-89 exit 16, just n on US 7. Int corridors. **Pets:** Other species. Designated rooms, service with restrictions, supervision.
⬛ 🍽 🍴 🛍 📶 ❌ 🔋 💻

▼▼ **Motel 6 #1407** H

(802) 654-6860. **Call for rates.** 74 S Park Dr 05446. I-89 exit 16, just s on US 7. Int corridors. **Pets:** Other species. Service with restrictions, crate. 🛍 🆂🆂

▼◆▼◆ **Residence Inn by Marriott, Burlington-Colchester** H 🐾

(802) 655-3100. **$104-$217.** 71 Rathe Rd 05446. I-89 exit 16, 0.6 mi n on US 2 W/7 N, then just w. Int corridors. **Pets:** Other species. $100 one-time fee/room. Service with restrictions, crate.
🍽 🍴 🛍 📶 ❌ 🔋 💻

ESSEX JUNCTION

▼◆▼◆ **The Essex Resort & Spa** H 🐾

(802) 878-1100. **$169-$349.** 70 Essex Way 05452. SR 289 exit 10, 0.3 mi s. Int corridors. **Pets:** $45 daily fee/room. Designated rooms, service with restrictions. ⬛ 🍽 🍴 🛍 ❌ 📶 ❌ 🔋 💻

▼▼ **Handy Suites-Essex** H

(802) 872-5200. **$89-$249.** 27 Susie Wilson Rd 05452. I-89 exit 15 northbound, 2 mi e, then just n. Int corridors. **Pets:** Accepted.
🍽 🍴 🛍 📶 🔋 💻

FLETCHER

▼▼ **The Inn at Buck Hollow Farm** BB

(802) 849-2400. **$125-$145, 14 day notice.** 2150 Buck Hollow Rd 05454. 6 mi n of jct SR 104 via Buck Hollow Rd. Int corridors. **Pets:** $20 daily fee/pet. Service with restrictions, crate.
🍽 🛍 📶 ❌ 🆉

JAMAICA

▼▼ **Three Mountain Inn** CI

(802) 874-4140. **Call for rates.** 3732 Main St/Rt 100/30 05343. On SR 30; center. Ext/int corridors. **Pets:** Accepted. 🍽 🛍 📶 ❌

KILLINGTON

🆔 ▼▼◆ **The Cascades Lodge** H

(802) 422-3731. **$115-$329, 21 day notice.** 58 Old Mill Rd 05751. 3.6 mi s on Killington Rd from jct SR 100/US 4, then just e. Int corridors. **Pets:** Small, dogs only. $50 daily fee/pet. Designated rooms, service with restrictions, crate. 🅂🄰🅅🄴 🍽 🛍 ❌ 📶 ❌ 🔋 💻

LONDONDERRY

▼ **Snowdon Motel** M

(802) 824-6047. **Call for rates.** 4071 VT Rt 11 05148. Jct SR 100, 2 mi e. Ext corridors. **Pets:** Accepted. 🍽 📶 ❌ 🆉 🔋

LUDLOW

▼▼ **Andrie Rose Inn** BB

(802) 228-4846. **Call for rates.** 13 Pleasant St 05149. Corner of Depot St; center. Int corridors. **Pets:** Accepted. 🍽 📶 ❌ 🆉 🔋

MANCHESTER CENTER

▼▼ **Casablanca Motel** CA 🐾

(802) 362-2145. **$75-$160, 14 day notice.** 5927 Main St (Rt 7A) 05255. Jct SR 11/30, 1 mi n on Historic SR 7A. Ext corridors. **Pets:** Dogs only. $15 daily fee/pet. Designated rooms, service with restrictions.
⬛ 🍽 📶 ❌ 🆉 🔋 💻

🆔 ▼▼◆ **Manchester View Fine Lodging** M 🐾

(802) 362-2739. **$85-$350, 14 day notice.** 77 High Meadows Way 05255. On Historic SR 7A, 2 mi n of jct SR 11/30 N, then just e. Ext/int corridors. **Pets:** Small. $20 daily fee/pet. Designated rooms, service with restrictions, supervision. 🅂🄰🅅🄴 🍽 🛍 📶 ❌ 🔋 💻

▼▼ **Weathervane Motel** M

(802) 362-2444. **Call for rates.** 2212 Main St (Historic SR 7A) 05255. Jct SR 11/30, 2.3 mi s. Ext corridors. **Pets:** Accepted.
🍽 🛍 📶 ❌ 🔋 💻

MANCHESTER VILLAGE
(Restaurants p. 642)

🆔 ▼▼◆▼ **The Equinox, a Luxury Collection Golf Resort & Spa** H

(802) 362-4700. **$199-$699, 21 day notice.** 3567 Main St 05254. 1.3 mi s on Historic SR 7A, from jct SR 11/30. Int corridors. **Pets:** Accepted. 🅂🄰🅅🄴 ⬛ 🍽 🍴 🛍 ❌ 📶 ❌

🆔 ▼▼◆ **The Inns at Equinox** H

(802) 362-4700. **Call for rates.** 3567 Main St 05254. Jct SR 11/30, 1.3 mi s on Historic SR 7A; at The Equinox, a Luxury Collection Golf Resort & Spa. Ext/int corridors. **Pets:** Accepted.
🅂🄰🅅🄴 🍽 🍴 ❌ 📶 🔋

MIDDLEBURY

▼▼ **The Middlebury Inn** H 🐾

(802) 388-4961. **$139-$309, 3 day notice.** 14 Court Square 05753. On US 7; center. Ext/int corridors. **Pets:** Other species. $35 one-time fee/room. Designated rooms, service with restrictions, supervision. ⬛ 🍽 📶 🔋 💻

▼▼◆ **Swift House Inn** CI

(802) 388-9925. **$139-$299, 7 day notice.** 25 Stewart Ln 05753. 0.3 mi n on US 7 from jct SR 125 W. Ext/int corridors. **Pets:** Accepted.
⬛ 🍽 📶 ❌ 💻

MORRISVILLE

🛆 ▼▼ Sunset Motor Inn **M**
(802) 888-4956. **$85-$142, 7 day notice.** 160 SR 15 W 05661. Jct SR 100, just w. Ext/int corridors. **Pets:** Dogs only. $50 deposit/pet. Designated rooms, service with restrictions, crate.

〔SAVE〕 ⑪ 〔&M〕 ⊇ ⌘ 🖥 🖵

NORTH HERO

▼▼▼ Shore Acres Inn **CI**
(802) 372-8722. **$130-$253, 21 day notice.** 237 Shore Acres Dr 05474. 0.5 mi s on US 2. Ext/int corridors. **Pets:** Dogs only. $20 one-time fee/ pet, $5 daily fee/pet. Service with restrictions, supervision.

⑪ ⊠ ⌘ ⊠ 🗲 🖥

RANDOLPH

🛆 ▼▼▼ Three Stallion Inn **BB** ❀
(802) 728-5575. **$98-$170, 15 day notice.** 665 Stock Farm Rd 05060. I-89 exit 4 (SR 66), 2 mi w; jct SR 12, just e on SR 66, then just s. Ext/int corridors. **Pets:** Other species. $25 deposit/pet. Designated rooms, service with restrictions, crate.

〔SAVE〕 ⑪ ⊇ ⊠ ⌘ ⊠

RUTLAND

▼▼ Days Inn **H**
(802) 775-4303. **$72-$185.** 401 US Hwy 7 S 05701. 0.8 mi s on US 7 and 4. Int corridors. **Pets:** Accepted. ⊇ ⌘ 🖥 🖵

▼▼▼ Holiday Inn Rutland/Killington **H**
(802) 775-1911. **Call for rates.** 476 Holiday Dr 05701. 2.4 mi s on US 7 from US 4 W; 0.4 mi n on US 7 from US 4 E. Int corridors.
Pets: Accepted. ⑪ 〔&M〕 ⊇ ⊠ ⌘ ⊠ 🖥 🖵

ST. ALBANS

▼▼ La Quinta Inn & Suites St. Albans **H**
(802) 524-3300. **$105-$295.** 813 Fairfax Rd 05478. I-89 exit 19, just w on Interstate Access Rd, then just s. Int corridors. **Pets:** Large, other species. Service with restrictions. ⑪ 〔&M〕 ⊇ ⌘ 🖥 🖵

ST. JOHNSBURY

▼▼ Fairbanks Inn **M**
(802) 748-5666. **Call for rates.** 401 Western Ave 05819. I-91 exit 21, 0.8 mi e on US 2. Ext corridors. **Pets:** Accepted.

⑪ ⊇ ⌘ ⊠ 🖥

SHAFTSBURY

▼ Serenity Motel **CA**
(802) 442-6490. **$75-$95.** 4379 Rt 7A 05262. Jct SR 67, 3.3 mi n on Historic SR 7A. Ext corridors. **Pets:** Accepted.

⑪ ⌘ ⊠ 🖥 🖵

SOUTH BURLINGTON

🛆 ▼▼▼ BEST WESTERN PLUS Windjammer Inn & Conference Center **H**
(802) 863-1125. **$110-$250.** 1076 Williston Rd 05403. I-89 exit 14E, 0.3 mi e on US 2. Int corridors. **Pets:** Accepted.

〔SAVE〕 〔ECO〕 ⑪ 〔&M〕 ⊇ ⌘ ⊠ 🖥 🖵

🛆 ▼▼▼ DoubleTree by Hilton Hotel Burlington **H**
(802) 658-0250. **$169-$279.** 1117 Williston Rd 05403. I-89 exit 14E, just e on US 2. Int corridors. **Pets:** Other species. $75 deposit/pet. Service with restrictions, supervision.

〔SAVE〕 〔ECO〕 ⑪ 〔&M〕 ⊇ ⌘ ⊠ 🖥 🖵

▼▼▼ Green Mountain Suites Hotel **H**
(802) 860-1212. **$149-$489, 3 day notice.** 401 Dorset St 05403. I-89 exit 14E, just e on US 2, then 0.8 mi s. Int corridors. **Pets:** Medium, dogs only. $50 daily fee/room. Designated rooms, service with restrictions, supervision. 〔ECO〕 〔&M〕 ⊇ ⌘ ⊠ 🖥 🖵

▼▼ La Quinta Inn & Suites South Burlington **H**
(802) 865-3400. **$92-$309.** 1285 Williston Rd 05403. I-89 exit 14E, 0.5 mi e on US 2. Int corridors. **Pets:** Large, other species. Service with restrictions. 〔&M〕 ⊇ ⌘ 🖥 🖵

🛆 ▼▼▼ Sheraton Burlington Hotel & Conference Center **H**
(802) 865-6600. **$89-$299.** 870 Williston Rd 05403. I-89 exit 14W, just w on US 2. Int corridors. **Pets:** Accepted.

〔SAVE〕 〔ECO〕 ⑪ ⊇ 🍽 ⊠ 🖥 🖵

SOUTH WOODSTOCK

▼▼▼ Kedron Valley Inn **CI**
(802) 457-1473. **Call for rates.** 4778 South Rd 05071. Jct US 4, 5 mi s. Ext/int corridors. **Pets:** Accepted. ⑪ ⌘ ⊠ 🗲 🖥

SPRINGFIELD

▼▼▼ Holiday Inn Express **H**
(802) 885-4516. **Call for rates.** 818 Charlestown Rd 05156. I-91 exit 7, just w on SR 11 (Charlestown Rd). Int corridors. **Pets:** Accepted.

⑪ 〔&M〕 ⊇ ⌘ ⊠ 🖥 🖵

STOWE

▼▼ Commodores Inn **H**
(802) 253-7131. **$98-$198, 3 day notice.** 823 S Main St 05672. Jct SR 108, 0.8 mi s on SR 100. Int corridors. **Pets:** Other species. $10 daily fee/room. Designated rooms. ⑪ ⊇ ⊠ ⌘ ⊠ 🖥

▼▼▼ Edson Hill Manor **CI**
(802) 253-7371. **Call for rates.** 1500 Edson Hill Rd 05672. Jct SR 100, 3.4 mi w on SR 108, 1.3 mi n. Ext/int corridors. **Pets:** Accepted.

⑪ ⊇ ⌘ ⊠

🛆 ▼▼▼ Golden Eagle Resort **M**
(802) 253-4811. **$99-$299, 7 day notice.** 511 Mountain Rd 05672. Jct SR 100, 0.5 mi w on SR 108. Ext corridors. **Pets:** Accepted.

〔SAVE〕 〔ECO〕 ⑪ ⊇ ⊠ ⌘ ⊠ 🖥 🖵

▼▼ Hob Knob Inn & Restaurant **M**
(802) 253-8549. **$90-$160, 15 day notice.** 2364 Mountain Rd 05672. Jct SR 100, 2.5 mi w on SR 108. Ext/int corridors. **Pets:** Dogs only. $20 daily fee/pet. Designated rooms, service with restrictions, crate.

〔ECO〕 ⑪ ⊇ ⌘ ⊠ 🖥 🖵

▼▼▼ The Mountain Road Resort at Stowe **M**
(802) 253-4566. **Call for rates.** 1007 Mountain Rd 05672. Jct SR 100, 1 mi w on SR 108. Ext corridors. **Pets:** Accepted.

⊇ ⊠ ⌘ ⊠ 🖥 🖵

▼▼▼ The Snowdrift Motel **M**
(802) 253-7629. **$90-$190, 7 day notice.** 2135 Mountain Rd 05672. Jct SR 100, 2.1 mi w on SR 108. Ext/int corridors. **Pets:** Dogs only. $12 daily fee/pet. Designated rooms, service with restrictions, crate.

⊇ ⊠ ⌘ ⊠ 🖥 🖵

🛆 ▼▼▼ Stoweflake Mountain Resort & Spa **H** ❀
(802) 253-7355. **$199-$559, 15 day notice.** 1746 Mountain Rd 05672. Jct SR 100, 1.4 mi w on SR 108. Int corridors. **Pets:** Large, dogs only. $40 daily fee/room. Designated rooms, service with restrictions, crate.

〔SAVE〕 ⑪ ⊇ ⊠ ⌘ ⊠ 🖥 🖵

🛆 ▼▼▼ Stowe Mountain Lodge **H**
(802) 760-4755. **$199-$829, 14 day notice.** 7412 Mountain Rd 05672. Jct SR 100, 7.3 mi w on SR 108. Int corridors. **Pets:** Accepted.

〔SAVE〕 〔ECO〕 ⑪ ⊇ ⊠ ⌘ ⊠ 🖥 🖵

🛆 ▼▼▼ Sun & Ski Inn and Suites **M**
(802) 253-7159. **Call for rates.** 1613 Mountain Rd 05672. Jct SR 100, 1.7 mi w on SR 108. Ext corridors. **Pets:** Accepted.

〔SAVE〕 ⑪ ⊇ ⊠ ⌘ ⊠ 🖥 🖵

Topnotch Resort H
(802) 253-8585. **Call for rates.** 4000 Mountain Rd 05672. Jct SR 100, 4.2 mi w on SR 108. Ext/int corridors. **Pets:** Accepted.

Trapp Family Lodge H ❖
(802) 253-8511. **Call for rates.** 700 Trapp Hill Rd 05672. Jct SR 100, 2.1 mi w on SR 108, 1.4 mi s on Luce Hill Rd, follow signs. Int corridors. **Pets:** Medium, dogs only. $50 daily fee/pet. Designated rooms, service with restrictions, crate.

SWANTON

Swanton Motel M
(802) 868-4284. **Call for rates.** 112 Grand Ave (US 7) 05488. I-89 exit 21, 0.8 mi w on SR 78, then 0.5 mi s. Ext corridors. **Pets:** Accepted.

VERGENNES

Strong House Inn CI
(802) 877-3337. **$140-$340, 14 day notice.** 94 W Main St 05491. 0.6 mi s on SR 22A. Int corridors. **Pets:** Medium, dogs only. $35 daily fee/room. Designated rooms, service with restrictions, crate.

WARREN

The Pitcher Inn CI
(802) 496-6350. **$350-$800, 30 day notice.** 275 Main St 05674. Center. Ext/int corridors. **Pets:** Large, dogs only. $75 one-time fee/room. Designated rooms, service with restrictions, crate.

WATERBURY

The Old Stagecoach Inn BB
(802) 244-5056. **Call for rates.** 18 N Main St 05676. I-89 exit 10, just s on SR 100, then just e. Ext/int corridors. **Pets:** Other species. $20 daily fee/room. Designated rooms, service with restrictions, supervision.

WEST DOVER

The Hermitage Inn CI
(802) 464-3511. **Call for rates.** 25 Handle Rd 05356. Jct SR 9, 3 mi n on SR 100, 3 mi w on Coldbrook Rd. Ext/int corridors. **Pets:** Accepted.

WESTMORE

WilloughVale Inn on Lake Willoughby CI
(802) 525-4123. **Call for rates.** 793 SR 5A 05860. Jct SR 16 and 5A, just s. Ext/int corridors. **Pets:** Accepted.

WHITE RIVER JUNCTION

The White River Inn and Suites H
(802) 295-3015. **Call for rates.** 91 Ballardvale Dr 05001. I-91 exit 11, just s on US 5. Int corridors. **Pets:** Accepted.

WILLISTON

Residence Inn by Marriott Burlington Williston H
(802) 878-2001. **$111-$240.** 35 Hurricane Ln 05495. I-89 exit 12, just s on SR 2A, then just e. Ext corridors. **Pets:** Accepted.

TownePlace Suites by Marriott Burlington Williston H
(802) 872-5900. **$97-$217.** 66 Zephyr Rd 05495. I-89 exit 12, 1.1 mi n on SR 2A. Int corridors. **Pets:** Accepted.

WOODSTOCK

The Shire Riverview Inn M
(802) 457-2211. **Call for rates.** 46 Pleasant St 05091. 0.4 mi e on US 4; downtown. Ext/int corridors. **Pets:** Accepted.

VIRGINIA

ABINGDON

Holiday Inn Express H
(276) 676-2829. **$109-$169.** 940 E Main St 24210. I-81 exit 19 (US 11), just w. Int corridors. **Pets:** Accepted.

ALEXANDRIA *(Restaurants p. 642)*

Candlewood Suites Alexandria-Ft. Belvoir H
(703) 780-1111. **Call for rates.** 8847 Richmond Hwy 22309. I-95/495 exit 177A, 7.2 mi s on US 1. Int corridors. **Pets:** Accepted.

Comfort Inn & Suites Alexandria H ❖
(703) 922-9200. **$99-$199.** 5716 S Van Dorn St 22310. I-95/495 exit 173, 2 mi e of jct I-395 and 495. Int corridors. **Pets:** Small. $25 daily fee/pet. Designated rooms, service with restrictions, supervision.

Comfort Inn Landmark H ❖
(703) 642-3422. **Call for rates.** 6254 Duke St 22312. I-395 exit 3B, just w. Int corridors. **Pets:** Small, other species. $25 one-time fee/pet. Designated rooms, service with restrictions, crate.

Extended Stay America-Washington DC-Alexandria-Eisenhower Ave H
(703) 329-3399. **Call for rates.** 200 Bluestone Rd 22304. I-95/495 exit 176B, 1 mi s on Eisenhower Ave. Int corridors. **Pets:** Other species. $25 daily fee/pet. Service with restrictions, supervision.

Extended Stay America-Washington DC-Alexandria-Landmark H
(703) 941-9440. **Call for rates.** 205 N Breckinridge Pl 22312. I-395 exit 3B, 0.3 mi w on SR 236, 0.4 mi ne on Beauregard St, just e on Gloucester Rd, then just s. Int corridors. **Pets:** Other species. $25 daily fee/pet. Service with restrictions, supervision.

Hilton Alexandria Mark Center H
(703) 845-1010. **$199-$229.** 5000 Seminary Rd 22311. I-395 exit 4, just w. Int corridors. **Pets:** Accepted.

Holiday Inn Hotel & Suites-Historic District Alexandria H
(703) 548-6300. **$89-$329.** 625 First St 22314. George Washington Memorial Pkwy, just e of jct First and Washington sts. Int corridors. **Pets:** Accepted.

Hotel Monaco Alexandria-A Kimpton Hotel H ❖
(703) 549-6080. **$149-$309.** 480 King St 22314. On SR 7; between S Pitt and S Royal sts; just sw of City Hall. Int corridors. **Pets:** Accepted.

Lorien Hotel & Spa-A Kimpton Hotel H
(703) 894-3434. **$149-$339.** 1600 King St 22314. Between Harvard and Peyton sts. Int corridors. **Pets:** Accepted.

Morrison House-A Kimpton Hotel H ❖

(703) 838-8000. **$125-$500.** 116 S Alfred St 22314. Jct King and S Alfred sts, just s. Int corridors. **Pets:** Other species. Service with restrictions. SAVE ECO ⛔ 🛜 ✕ 🖥

Red Roof Plus+ Washington DC-Alexandria H

(703) 960-5200. **$70-$130.** 5975 Richmond Hwy 22303. I-95/495 exit 177A, 0.5 mi s on US 1. Ext corridors. **Pets:** Large, other species. Service with restrictions, supervision. SAVE ⛔M 🛜 ✕ 🖥 💻

Residence Inn by Marriott Alexandria-Old Town/Duke St. H

(703) 548-5474. **$89-$359.** 1456 Duke St 22314. I-95/495 exit 176B, 0.5 mi n on SR 241, then 0.7 mi e on SR 236. Int corridors. **Pets:** Medium, other species. $150 one-time fee/room, $15 daily fee/room. Service with restrictions. SAVE ⛔M 🏊 🛜 ✕ 🖥 💻

Residence Inn by Marriott Alexandria Old Town South at Carlyle H

(703) 549-1155. **$99-$289.** 2345 Mill Rd 22314. I-95/495 exit 176B, 0.3 mi n on Eisenhower Ave, then just w. Int corridors. **Pets:** Accepted. ECO ⛔M 🛜 ✕ 🖥 💻

Sheraton Suites Old Town Alexandria H

(703) 836-4700. **$99-$429.** 801 N St. Asaph St 22314. Just e of Washington St. Int corridors. **Pets:** Accepted. SAVE ECO ⛔ ⛔M 🏊 🛜 ✕ 🖥 💻

The Westin Alexandria H ❖

(703) 253-8600. **Call for rates.** 400 Courthouse Square 22314. I-95/495 exit 176B, just n on Telegraph Rd (SR 241 N), 0.4 mi e on SR 236, then just s on Dulany St. Int corridors. **Pets:** Large, dogs only. Designated rooms, supervision. SAVE ⛔ ⛔M 🏊 ✕🛜 ✕ 🖥 💻

ALTAVISTA

Comfort Inn H

(434) 369-4000. **$67-$199.** 1558 Main St 24517. US 29 business route, jct US 29. Int corridors. **Pets:** Accepted. 🏊 🛜 🖥 💻

Days Inn H

(434) 369-4070. **$75-$100.** 1557 Main St 24517. US 29 business route, jct US 29. Int corridors. **Pets:** Accepted. ⛔M 🛜 🖥 💻

APPOMATTOX

Super 8 M

(434) 352-2339. **$65-$200.** 7571 Richmond Hwy 24522. US 460, just w of jct US 26. Int corridors. **Pets:** Accepted. 🛜 🖥 💻

ARLINGTON (Restaurants p. 642)

Arlington Court Suites Hotel, A Clarion Collection H

(703) 524-4000. **$89-$429.** 1200 N Courthouse Rd 22201. 1.5 mi sw of Theodore Roosevelt Bridge off US 50. Int corridors. **Pets:** $75 one-time fee/room. Service with restrictions, crate. SAVE ⛔M 🛜 ✕ 🖥 💻

Hyatt Regency Crystal City at Reagan National Airport H

(703) 418-1234. **$84-$459.** 2799 Jefferson Davis Hwy 22202. 2 mi s of 14th St Bridge on US 1, jct SR 233; entrance just e of US 1 on Clark St. Int corridors. **Pets:** Accepted. SAVE ⛔ 🏊 🛜 ✕ 🖥 💻

Le Méridien Arlington H ❖

(703) 351-9170. **Call for rates.** 1121 N 19th St 22209. I-66 exit 73, just sw of Key Bridge. Int corridors. **Pets:** Medium. Service with restrictions, supervision. SAVE ⛔ ⛔M 🛜 ✕

Residence Inn by Marriott Arlington Ballston H

(703) 310-1999. **$129-$309.** 650 N Quincy St 22203. I-66 exit 71, 0.9 mi s on N Glebe Rd (SR 120), then just n. Int corridors. **Pets:** Accepted. ⛔ ⛔M 🛜 ✕ 🖥 💻

Residence Inn by Marriott Arlington Capital View H

(703) 415-1300. **$79-$349.** 2850 S Potomac Ave 22202. 2 mi s of 14th St Bridge on US 1; just s of jct SR 233. Int corridors. **Pets:** Accepted. SAVE ⛔M 🏊 🛜 ✕ 🖥 💻

Residence Inn by Marriott Arlington Courthouse H

(703) 312-2100. **$119-$319.** 1401 N Adams St 22201. Jct Clarendon Blvd and N Adams St. Int corridors. **Pets:** Accepted. ECO ⛔M 🏊 🛜 ✕ 🖥 💻

Residence Inn by Marriott Arlington Rosslyn H ❖

(703) 812-8400. **$109-$339.** 1651 N Oak St 22209. I-66 exit 73, 0.3 mi s on Fort Myer Dr, 0.3 mi w on Wilson Blvd to N Pierce St, then 2 blks e on Clarendon Blvd. Int corridors. **Pets:** Medium, other species. $100 one-time fee/pet. Service with restrictions, crate. SAVE 🛜 ✕ 🖥 💻

Residence Inn by Marriott-Pentagon City H

(703) 413-6630. **$89-$356.** 550 Army Navy Dr 22202. I-395 exit 8C, 1 mi s of 14th St Bridge. Int corridors. **Pets:** Accepted. SAVE ECO ⛔M 🏊 🛜 ✕ 🖥 💻

Sheraton Pentagon City Hotel H ❖

(703) 521-1900. **$89-$499.** 900 S Orme St 22204. I-395 exit 8A, at SR 27 and 244; 1.3 mi s of 14th St Bridge. Int corridors. **Pets:** Medium, dogs only. Service with restrictions, supervision. SAVE ⛔ 🏊🛜 ✕

The Westin Arlington Gateway H

(703) 717-6200. **Call for rates.** 801 N Glebe Rd 22203. I-66 exit 71, just e on Fairfax Dr to Vermont Ave; just n of jct N Glebe Rd (SR 120) and Wilson Blvd. Int corridors. **Pets:** Accepted. SAVE ECO ⛔ ⛔M 🏊 🛜 ✕ 🖥 💻

ASHBURN (Restaurants p. 643)

Aloft Dulles Airport North H

(703) 723-6969. **Call for rates.** 22390 Flagstaff Plaza 20148. On Loudoun County Pkwy (CR 607), just s of jct SR 267 (Toll Rd) exit 7. Int corridors. **Pets:** Accepted. SAVE ECO ⛔M 🏊 🛜 ✕ 🖥 💻

Homewood Suites by Hilton/Dulles North H

(703) 723-7500. **$99-$259.** 44620 Waxpool Rd 20147. 1.7 mi w of jct SR 28 and Waxpool Rd (CR 625); SR 7, 3.4 mi s on Loudoun County Pkwy (CR 607), 0.3 mi w. Int corridors. **Pets:** Accepted. SAVE ⛔M 🏊 🛜 🖥 💻

BEDFORD

Super 8 H

(540) 587-0100. **$65-$240.** 842 Sword Beach Ln 24523. 1.5 mi w on US 221 and 460. Int corridors. **Pets:** $10 daily fee/pet. Designated rooms, no service, supervision. ⛔M 🛜 🖥 💻

BIG STONE GAP

Country Inn Motel M

(276) 523-0374. **Call for rates.** 627 Gilley Ave 24219. US 23, 1 mi w on US 23 business route and 58A. Ext corridors. **Pets:** Other species. $3 daily fee/pet. Service with restrictions, supervision. 🛜 🖥

BLACKSBURG

Comfort Inn Blacksburg H ❖

(540) 951-1500. **$89-$117.** 3705 S Main St 24060. 3.5 mi s on US 460; jct US 460 Bypass. Int corridors. **Pets:** Other species. Service with restrictions, crate. SAVE 🏊 🛜 🖥 💻

☆☆☆ Days Inn Blacksburg ⊞
(540) 951-1330. **$75-$334.** 3503 Holiday Ln 24060. 3.8 mi s on US 460; jct US 460 Bypass. Ext corridors. **Pets:** Accepted.
〔SAVE〕🐾 🛜 🛄 🖵

BRISTOL

☆☆☆ Baymont Inn & Suites ⊞
(276) 669-9353. **$58-$75.** 1014 Old Airport Rd 24201. I-81 exit 7, just e. Ext corridors. **Pets:** Accepted. 🅼 🐾 🛜 🛄 🖵

☆☆☆ Holiday Inn Hotel & Suites ⊞
(276) 466-4100. **$109-$139.** 3005 Linden Dr 24202. I-81 exit 7, just w. Int corridors. **Pets:** Large, other species. $50 one-time fee/room. Designated rooms, service with restrictions, supervision.
〔ECO〕🍴 🅼 🐾 🛜 ✕ 🛄 🖵

☆☆ Motel 6 #4125 Ⓜ
(276) 466-6060. **$55-$200.** 21561 Clear Creek Rd 24202. I-81 exit 7, 0.3 mi w. Int corridors. **Pets:** Other species. Service with restrictions, crate. 🅼 🛜 🛄

☆☆☆ Quality Inn ⊞
(276) 669-8164. **Call for rates.** 131 Bristol East Rd 24202. I-81 exit 7 northbound, just w. Int corridors. **Pets:** Accepted.
🐾 🛜 ✕ 🛄 🖵

BUCHANAN

☆☆☆ Wattstull Inn Ⓜ
(540) 254-1551. **$60-$75, 7 day notice.** 130 Arcadia Rd 24066. I-81 exit 168, just e on SR 614. Ext corridors. **Pets:** $10 one-time fee/room. Designated rooms, service with restrictions, supervision.
〔SAVE〕🍴 🐾 🛜 🛄 🖵

CAPE CHARLES *(Restaurants p. 643)*

☆☆ Shore Stay Suites Ⓜ
(757) 331-4090. **$129.** 26406 Lankford Hwy 23310. On US 13. Ext corridors. **Pets:** Large. $50 one-time fee/pet. Service with restrictions, crate. 〔ECO〕🅼 🛜 ✕ 🛡 🛄 🖵

CENTREVILLE

☆☆ Extended Stay America-Washington DC-Centreville/Manassas ⊞
(703) 988-9955. **Call for rates.** 5920 Fort Dr 20121. I-66 exit 53, 0.9 mi s on SR 28; off SR 28, 0.3 mi s of jct US 29. Int corridors. **Pets:** Other species. $25 daily fee/pet. Service with restrictions, supervision.
🅼 🛜 🛄 🖵

CHANTILLY *(Restaurants p. 643)*

☆☆ Extended Stay America Washington DC-Chantilly-Airport ⊞
(703) 263-7200. **Call for rates.** 4506 Brookfield Corporate Dr 20151. I-66 exit 53, 3 mi n on SR 28; jct US 50, 1 mi s of SR 28. Int corridors. **Pets:** Other species. $25 daily fee/pet. Service with restrictions, supervision. 🅼 🐾 🛜 🛄 🖵

☆☆☆ Hampton Inn Washington Dulles International Airport South ⊞ 🐾
(703) 818-8200. **$79-$169.** 4050 Westfax Dr 20151. Jct SR 28, 1 mi w on US 50. Int corridors. **Pets:** Designated rooms, service with restrictions, supervision. 〔ECO〕🅼 🐾 🛜 ✕ 🛄 🖵

☆☆☆ Holiday Inn Chantilly-Dulles Expo Center ⊞
(703) 815-6060. **$69-$209.** 4335 Chantilly Shopping Center 20151. I-66 exit 53, 3 mi n or SR 28; 1 mi s of jct US 50 and SR 28. Int corridors. **Pets:** Accepted. 🍴 🅼 🐾 🛜 ✕ 🛄 🖵

☆☆☆ Hyatt Place Chantilly/Dulles Airport-South ⊞
(703) 961-8160. **$64-$199.** 4994 Westone Plaza Dr 20151. I-66 exit 53, 2 mi n on SR 28, then just w on Westfields Blvd; 1.7 mi s of jct SR 28 and US 50. Int corridors. **Pets:** Accepted.
〔SAVE〕🅼 🐾 🛜 ✕ 🛄 🖵

☆☆☆ Residence Inn by Marriott Chantilly Dulles South ⊞
(703) 263-7900. **$84-$239.** 14440 Chantilly Crossing Ln 20151. Jct SR 28, just w on US 50. Int corridors. **Pets:** Accepted.
〔ECO〕🅼 🐾 🛜 ✕ 🛄 🖵

☆☆☆ Staybridge Suites Hotel Chantilly/Dulles International Airport ⊞
(703) 435-8090. **$99-$299.** 3860 Centerview Dr 20151. Jct SR 28, just e on US 50. Int corridors. **Pets:** Accepted. 〔ECO〕🅼 🛜 🛄 🖵

☆☆ TownePlace Suites by Marriott-Chantilly Dulles South ⊞
(703) 709-0453. **$79-$175.** 14036 Thunderbolt Pl 20151. Jct SR 28, just e on US 50. Int corridors. **Pets:** Accepted.
〔ECO〕🐾 🛜 ✕ 🛄 🖵

☆☆☆ Wingate by Wyndham Dulles Airport-Chantilly ⊞
(571) 203-0999. **$79-$259.** 3940 Centerview Dr 20151. Jct SR 28, just e on US 50. Int corridors. **Pets:** Accepted.
〔SAVE〕🅼 🐾 🛜 ✕ 🛄 🖵

CHARLES CITY *(Restaurants p. 643)*

☆☆☆ Edgewood Plantation Bed & Breakfast 🅱🅱
(804) 829-2962. **Call for rates.** 4800 John Tyler Memorial Hwy 23030. Jct SR 609, just e on SR 5. Ext/int corridors. **Pets:** Accepted.
🐾 🛜 ✕ 🛡 🛄 🖵

CHARLOTTESVILLE

☆☆☆ The Cavalier Inn at the University ⊞ 🐾
(434) 296-8111. **$85-$650.** 105 N Emmet St 22903. Jct US 29 (Emmet St) and 250 Bypass, 1.3 mi s on US 29 business route. Ext/int corridors. **Pets:** $25 one-time fee/pet. Service with restrictions.
〔SAVE〕〔ECO〕🐾 🛜 ✕ 🛄 🖵

☆☆☆ Comfort Inn University ⊞
(434) 293-6188. **$124-$289.** 1803 Emmet St 22901. Jct US 250 Bypass, just n on US 29 (Emmet St). Int corridors. **Pets:** Accepted.
〔SAVE〕🐾 🛜 🛄 🖵

☆☆☆ DoubleTree by Hilton Hotel Charlottesville ⊞ 🐾
(434) 973-2121. **$129-$239.** 990 Hilton Heights Rd 22901. I-64 exit 118B (US 29/Emmet St), 4 mi n of jct US 250 Bypass. Int corridors. **Pets:** Medium. $35 one-time fee/pet. Designated rooms, service with restrictions, crate. 〔SAVE〕〔ECO〕🍴 🐾 🛜 🛄 🖵

☆☆☆ Fairfield Inn by Marriott ⊞
(434) 964-9411. **$129-$142.** 577 Branchlands Blvd 22901. US 29 (Emmet St), 1.3 mi n of US 250 Bypass. Int corridors. **Pets:** Accepted.
🐾 🛜 ✕ 🛄 🖵

☆☆☆ Holiday Inn-Monticello/Charlottesville ⊞
(434) 977-5100. **$89-$289.** 1200 5th St SW 22902. I-64 exit 120, just n on SR 631. Int corridors. **Pets:** Accepted. 🍴 🐾 🛜 🛄 🖵

☆☆☆ Omni Charlottesville Hotel ⊞ 🐾
(434) 971-5500. **$159-$329.** 212 Ridge McIntire Rd 22903. I-64 exit 120, 2.3 mi n on SR 631; downtown. Int corridors. **Pets:** Small. $50 one-time fee/pet. Service with restrictions.
〔SAVE〕〔ECO〕🍴 🐾 🗙 🛜 ✕ 🛄 🖵

☆☆ Red Roof Inn Charlottesville- University of Virginia ⊞
(434) 295-4333. **$70-$249.** 1309 W Main St 22903. US 29 (Emmet St), 1 mi e on US 250 (University Ave). Int corridors. **Pets:** Large, other species. Service with restrictions, supervision. 🛜 🛄 🖵

☆☆☆ Residence Inn by Marriott ⊞
(434) 923-0300. **$174-$194.** 1111 Millmont St 22903. I-64 exit 118B (US 29/Emmet St), 2.5 mi n on US 29/250 E, just s on Barracks Rd, then just se. Int corridors. **Pets:** Accepted.
〔ECO〕🐾 🗙 🛜 ✕ 🛄 🖵

CHESAPEAKE

△△△ ▼▼▼▼ **Aloft Chesapeake** 🄷
(757) 410-9562. **Call for rates.** 1454 Crossways Blvd 23320. I-64 exit 289B (Greenbrier Pkwy), just s to Jarman Rd (at Crossways Center) to Crossways Blvd, then 0.7 mi n. Int corridors. **Pets:** Accepted.

🆂🅰🆅🅴 🄴🄲🄾 🅗🄼 ⛌ 🛜 ✖ 🔋 🖵

△△△ ▼▼▼▼ **BEST WESTERN PLUS**
Portsmouth-Chesapeake Hotel 🄷 🐾
(757) 484-5800. **$69-$119.** 3235 Western Branch Blvd 23321. I-664 exit 9B northbound; exit 8B southbound, 1 mi s on US 17. Int corridors. **Pets:** Large, other species. $20 daily fee/pet. Service with restrictions.

🆂🅰🆅🅴 🅗🄼 🛜 🔋 🖵

▼▼▼▼ **Candlewood Suites** 🄷
(757) 405-3030. **$79-$89.** 4809 Market Pl 23321. I-664 exit 11A (SR 337 W). Int corridors. **Pets:** Accepted. 🄴🄲🄾 🅗🄼 🛜 🔋 🖵

▼▼▼▼ **Comfort Inn & Suites** 🄷
(757) 673-8585. **$59-$249.** 3355 S Military Hwy 23323. I-64 exit 296A, just n on George Washington Memorial Hwy N (US 17 Bypass), then just e on US 460 and 13. Int corridors. **Pets:** Medium, dogs only. $35 daily fee/pet. Designated rooms, service with restrictions, supervision.

🅗🄼 🛜 ✖ 🖵

▼▼▼▼ **Hampton Inn & Suites** 🄷
(757) 819-5230. **$89-$249.** 1421 N Battlefield Blvd 23320. I-64 exit 290B, just s; jct Coastal Way. Int corridors. **Pets:** Accepted.

♿🄼 ⛌ 🛜 ✖ 🔋 🖵

▼▼▼▼ **Hampton Inn Chesapeake/Greenbrier** 🄷
(757) 420-1550. **$89-$239.** 701A Woodlake Dr 23320. I-64 exit 289A (Greenbrier Pkwy), just n. Int corridors. **Pets:** Accepted.

⛌ 🛜 🔋 🖵

△△△ ▼▼▼▼ **Hyatt**
Place-Chesapeake/Greenbrier 🄷 🐾
(757) 312-0020. **$89-$189.** 709 Eden Way N 23320. I-64 exit 289B (Greenbrier Pkwy), 1 mi s; in Towne Place at Greenbrier. Int corridors. **Pets:** Medium, other species. $75 one-time fee/pet. Service with restrictions, crate. 🆂🅰🆅🅴 🄴🄲🄾 🅗🄼 ⛌ 🛜 ✖ 🔋 🖵

△△△ ▼▼▼▼ **Red Roof Inn Chesapeake Conference**
Center 🄷
(757) 523-0123. **$50-$120.** 724 Woodlake Dr 23320. I-64 exit 289A (Greenbrier Pkwy), just n to Woodlake Dr, then just e. Ext corridors. **Pets:** Large, other species. Service with restrictions, supervision.

🆂🅰🆅🅴 🅗🄼 🛜 ✖ 🔋 🖵

▼▼▼▼ **Residence Inn by Marriott,**
Chesapeake-Greenbrier 🄷
(757) 502-7300. **$79-$179.** 1500 Crossways Blvd 23320. I-64 exit 289B (Greenbrier Pkwy), just s to Jarman Rd (at Crossways Center) to Crossways Blvd, then 0.6 mi n. Int corridors. **Pets:** Accepted.

🄴🄲🄾 ⛌ 🛜 ✖ 🔋 🖵

▼▼▼▼ **Staybridge Suites Greenbrier** 🄷
(757) 420-2525. **Call for rates.** 709 Woodlake Dr 23320. I-64 exit 289A (Greenbrier Pkwy), just n. Int corridors. **Pets:** Medium. $75 one-time fee/pet. Service with restrictions, crate. 🅗🄼 ⛌ 🛜 🔋 🖵

CHESTER

△△△ ▼▼▼▼ **Fairfield Inn by Marriott** 🄷
(804) 778-7500. **$89-$129.** 12400 Redwater Creek Rd 23831. I-95 exit 61B, just w of jct SR 10. Int corridors. **Pets:** Very small. $75 one-time fee/pet. Designated rooms, service with restrictions, supervision.

🆂🅰🆅🅴 🅗🄼 ⛌ 🛜 ✖ 🔋 🖵

△△△ ▼▼▼▼ **Hyatt Place Richmond/Chester** 🄷
(804) 530-4600. **$69-$169.** 13148 Kingston Ave 23836. I-295 exit 15B, just w; I-95 exit 61A, 4.5 mi e; in River's Bend. Int corridors. **Pets:** Medium, dogs only. $75 one-time fee/pet. Service with restrictions, supervision. 🆂🅰🆅🅴 🍽 🅗🄼 ⛌ 🛜 ✖ 🔋 🖵

▼▼▼▼ **Residence Inn by Marriott** 🄷
(804) 530-5501.' **$159-$175.** 800 Bermuda Hundred Rd 23836. I-295 exit 15, just w; in River's Bend. Int corridors. **Pets:** Accepted.

🄴🄲🄾 🅗🄼 ⛌ 🛜 ✖ 🔋 🖵

CHESTERFIELD

△△△ ▼▼▼▼ **La Quinta Inn Richmond South** 🄷
(804) 743-0770. **$69-$209.** 9040 Pams Ave 23237. I-95 exit 64, just w. Int corridors. **Pets:** Large, other species. Service with restrictions.

🆂🅰🆅🅴 🅗🄼 🛜 🔋 🖵

△△△ ▼▼▼▼ **Sleep Inn Richmond** 🄷
(804) 275-8800. **$84-$149.** 2321 Willis Rd 23237. I-95 exit 64, just w. Int corridors. **Pets:** Accepted. 🆂🅰🆅🅴 🅗🄼 🛜 🔋 🖵

CHINCOTEAGUE

△△△ ▼▼▼ **Americas Best Value Inn & Suites** Ⓜ
(757) 336-6562. **$50-$210, 10 day notice.** 6151 Maddox Blvd 23336. Just e. Ext corridors. **Pets:** Dogs only. $10 daily fee/pet. Designated rooms, no service, crate. 🆂🅰🆅🅴 ⛌ 🛜 🔋 🖵

△△△ ▼▼▼ **Rodeway Inn Chincoteague** 🄷
(757) 336-6565. **$45-$300.** 6273 Maddox Blvd 23336. Just e of jct Main St. Ext corridors. **Pets:** Medium, dogs only. $15 daily fee/pet. Designated rooms, service with restrictions, supervision.

🅗🄼 ⛌ 🛜 🔋 🖵

CHRISTIANSBURG

△△△ ▼▼ **Econo Lodge** Ⓜ
(540) 382-6161. **$50-$200.** 2430 Roanoke St 24073. I-81 exit 118, just w on US 11/460. Ext corridors. **Pets:** Accepted.

🆂🅰🆅🅴 🅗🄼 ⛌ 🛜 🔋 🖵

▼▼▼▼ **Hampton Inn Christiansburg/Blacksburg** 🄷 🐾
(540) 381-5874. **$129-$149.** 380 Arbor Dr 24073. I-81 exit 118B, 4 mi w on US 460 Bypass, just n on Peppers Ferry Rd, then just w. Int corridors. **Pets:** Other species. Service with restrictions.

⛌ 🛜 🔋 🖵

△△△ ▼▼▼▼ **Quality Inn** Ⓜ 🐾
(540) 382-2055. **$75-$200.** 50 Hampton Blvd 24073. I-81 exit 118C, just e. Ext corridors. **Pets:** Other species. $10 daily fee/room. Service with restrictions. 🆂🅰🆅🅴 ⛌ 🛜 🔋 🖵

CLARKSVILLE

△△△ ▼▼ **Magnuson Hotel On The Lake**
Clarksville 🄷
(434) 374-5023. **$90-$130, 3 day notice.** 103 Second St 23927. US 58 business route, just n; downtown. Int corridors. **Pets:** Other species. $100 deposit/pet, $20 daily fee/pet. Designated rooms, service with restrictions, crate. 🆂🅰🆅🅴 🅗🄼 ⛌ 🛜 🔋 🖵

COLLINSVILLE

▼▼ **Quality Inn-Dutch Inn Hotel & Convention**
Center 🄷
(276) 647-3721. **$75-$99.** 2360 Virginia Ave 24078. Jct US 58, 3 mi n on US 220 business route. Ext corridors. **Pets:** Accepted.

🍽 ⛌ 🛜 🔋 🖵

COLONIAL HEIGHTS

▼▼▼▼ **Candlewood Suites** 🄷
(804) 526-0111. **$99-$129.** 15820 Woods Edge Rd 23834. I-95 exit 58 northbound; exit 58B southbound, just w. Int corridors. **Pets:** Medium, other species. $75 one-time fee/pet. Service with restrictions, crate.

🅗🄼 🛜 🔋 🖵

COVINGTON

△△△ ▼▼ **BEST WESTERN Mountain View** 🄷
(540) 962-4951. **$115.** 820 E Madison St 24426. I-64 exit 16, just n. Ext corridors. **Pets:** Accepted. 🆂🅰🆅🅴 🍽 ⛌ 🛜 🔋 🖵

CULPEPER

▼▼ Comfort Inn-Culpeper
(540) 825-4900. **$80-$120.** 890 Willis Ln 22701. 2 mi s on Main St (US 29 business route); jct US 29, just e. Ext corridors. **Pets:** Accepted.

DANVILLE

▼▼ Comfort Inn & Suites 🅷
(434) 793-2000. **$100-$139.** 100 Tower Dr 24540. Jct US 29 business route/SR 86, just w on US 58 business route. Int corridors.
Pets: Accepted.

▼▼ Courtyard by Marriott 🅷
(434) 791-2661. **$139-$159.** 2136 Riverside Dr 24540. Jct US 29 business route/SR 86, 0.5 mi e on US 58 business route. Int corridors.
Pets: Accepted.

▼▼ Innkeeper Danville North 🅼
(434) 836-1700. **Call for rates.** 1030 Piney Forest Rd 24540. Jct US 58 business route, 2 mi n on US 29 business route/SR 86. Ext corridors. **Pets:** Accepted.

🅐🅐🅐 ▼▼ Super 8 🅼
(434) 799-5845. **$65-$194, 3 day notice.** 2385 Riverside Dr 24541. Jct US 29 business route/SR 86, just e on US 58 business route. Int corridors. **Pets:** Accepted.

DOSWELL

🅐🅐🅐 ▼▼ BEST WESTERN Kings Quarters 🅷
(804) 876-3321. **$70-$179, 3 day notice.** 16102 Theme Park Way 23047. I-95 exit 98, just e on SR 30; entrance to theme park. Ext corridors. **Pets:** Accepted.

▼▼ Days Inn Kings Dominion 🅷
(804) 612-8680. **$46-$130.** 16220 International St 23047. I-95 exit 98, just e on SR 30. Int corridors. **Pets:** Other species. $15 daily fee/pet. Designated rooms, service with restrictions, supervision.

🅐🅐🅐 ▼▼▼ La Quinta Inn & Suites Doswell - Kings Dominion 🅷
(804) 876-6900. **$59-$299.** 16280 International St 23047. I-95 exit 98, just e on SR 30. Int corridors. **Pets:** Large, other species. Service with restrictions.

DUBLIN

▼▼▼ Holiday Inn Express 🅷
(540) 674-1600. **$109-$150.** 4428 Cleburne Blvd 24084. I-81 exit 98, just e. Int corridors. **Pets:** Accepted.

EMPORIA

🅐🅐🅐 ▼▼ BEST WESTERN Emporia 🅷
(434) 634-3200. **$75-$85.** 1100 W Atlantic St 23847. I-95 exit 11B, just w on US 58. Ext corridors. **Pets:** Accepted.

▼▼▼ Country Inn & Suites By Carlson Emporia 🅷
(434) 336-0001. **Call for rates.** 107 Sadler Ln 23847. I-95 exit 11A, just e on US 58. Int corridors. **Pets:** Accepted.

🅐🅐🅐 ▼▼ Days Inn-Emporia 🅷
(434) 634-9481. **$60-$70.** 921 W Atlantic St 23847. I-95 exit 11B, just w on US 58. Ext corridors. **Pets:** $10 daily fee/pet. Designated rooms, service with restrictions, supervision.

▼▼▼ Hampton Inn 🅷
(434) 634-9200. **$89-$159.** 898 Wiggins Rd 23847. I-95 exit 11B, just w on US 58. Int corridors. **Pets:** Accepted.

🅐🅐🅐 ▼▼▼ Sleep Inn 🅷
(434) 348-3900. **$76-$119.** 899 Wiggins Rd 23847. I-95 exit 11B, just e on US 58, then just s. Int corridors. **Pets:** Accepted.

EXMORE

▼▼▼ Holiday Inn Express & Suites 🅷
(757) 442-5522. **Call for rates.** 3446 Lankford Hwy 23350. On US 13. Int corridors. **Pets:** Accepted.

FAIRFAX *(Restaurants p. 643)*

▼▼ Candlewood Suites Fairfax-Washington, D.C. 🅷
(703) 359-4490. **$71-$209.** 11400 Random Hills Rd 22030. I-66 exit 57A, 0.5 mi e on US 50, just s on Waples Mill Rd, then 0.4 mi w. Int corridors. **Pets:** Accepted.

▼▼ Comfort Inn University Center 🅷
(703) 591-5900. **$69-$190.** 11180 Fairfax Blvd 22030. I-66 exit 57A, 0.8 mi se on US 50; 0.5 mi nw of jct US 29 and US 50. Int corridors.
Pets: Accepted.

▼▼ Extended Stay America Washington DC-Fairfax 🅷
(703) 359-5000. **Call for rates.** 3997 Fair Ridge Dr 22033. I-66 exit 57B, 1.2 mi w on US 50. Int corridors. **Pets:** Other species. $25 daily fee/pet. Service with restrictions, supervision.

▼▼ Extended Stay America-Washington DC-Fairfax-Fair Oaks 🅼
(703) 273-3444. **Call for rates.** 12104 Monument Dr 22033. I-66 exit 57B, 0.8 mi w on US 50, 0.3 mi s on SR 620 (W Ox Rd), then just se. Ext corridors. **Pets:** Other species. $25 daily fee/pet. Service with restrictions, supervision.

▼▼ Extended Stay America Washington DC-Falls Church-Merrifield 🅷
(703) 204-0088. **Call for rates.** 8281 Willow Oaks Corporate Dr 22031. I-495 exit 50A, just w on US 50 to Gallows Rd, then just s. Ext corridors. **Pets:** Other species. $25 daily fee/pet. Service with restrictions, supervision.

🅐🅐🅐 ▼▼▼ Hyatt Fairfax at Fair Lakes 🅷
(703) 818-1234. **$69-$259.** 12777 Fair Lakes Cir 22033. I-66 exit 55 (SR 286/Fairfax County Pkwy N), just w, then just s. Int corridors.
Pets: Accepted.

🅐🅐🅐 ▼▼▼ HYATT house Falls Church/Merrifield 🅷
(571) 327-2277. **$84-$269.** 8296 Glass Alley 22031. I-495 exit 50A, just w to SR 650, 0.5 mi n on SR 650, then just w on US 29. Int corridors.
Pets: Accepted.

🅐🅐🅐 ▼▼▼ Residence Inn by Marriott Fairfax City 🅷
(703) 267-2525. **$77-$285.** 3565 Chain Bridge Rd 22030. I-66 exit 60, 0.5 mi s on SR 123; jct US 29/50. Int corridors. **Pets:** Accepted.

🅐🅐🅐 ▼▼▼ Residence Inn by Marriott-Fair Lakes 🅷
(703) 266-4900. **$71-$241.** 12815 Fair Lakes Pkwy 22033. I-66 exit 55 (SR 286/Fairfax County Pkwy N), just w. Int corridors. **Pets:** Large. $150 one-time fee/room. Service with restrictions, supervision.

FALLS CHURCH *(Restaurants p. 643)*

▼▼ Comfort Inn Arlington Boulevard 🅷 🐾
(703) 534-9100. **$89-$189.** 6111 Arlington Blvd 22044. 0.8 mi e of jct SR 7. Int corridors. **Pets:** Small. $25 daily fee/pet. Designated rooms, service with restrictions, supervision.

▼▼▼ **Homewood Suites by Hilton-Falls Church** �H

(703) 560-6644. **$129-$249.** 8130 Porter Rd 22042. I-495 exit 50A, just w to SR 650, then 0.4 mi n on SR 650. Int corridors. **Pets:** Medium, dogs only. $100 deposit/pet. Service with restrictions, crate.

🔲 🛏 🛜 ✕ 🔋 🖥

▼▼▼ **Residence Inn by Marriott Fairfax-Merrifield** �H

(703) 573-5200. **$89-$265.** 8125 Gatehouse Rd 22042. I-495 exit 50A, just w to SR 650 N. Int corridors. **Pets:** Large, other species. $150 one-time fee/room. Service with restrictions.

(SAVE) 🔲 🛏 🛜 ✕ 🔋 🖥

▼▼ **TownePlace Suites by Marriott-Falls Church** �H

(703) 237-6172. **$75-$259.** 205 Hillwood Ave 22046. I-495 exit 50B, 2.5 mi e on US 50, 0.6 mi o on Annandale Rd (CR 649), then e; just s of US 29. Int corridors. **Pets:** Accepted.

🔲ECO 🔲 🛏 🛜 ✕ 🔋 🖥

▼▼▼ **The Westin Tysons Corner** �H

(703) 893-1340. **$89-$399.** 7801 Leesburg Pike 22043. I-495 exit 47B, just e on SR 7. Int corridors. **Pets:** Accepted.

(SAVE) ECO 🍴 🔲 🛏 s🛜 ✕ 🔋 🖥

FANCY GAP

▼▼ **Doe Run Lodging at Groundhog Mountain** CO

(276) 398-4099. **Call for rates.** 27 Buck Hollar Rd 24328. Blue Ridge Parkway at milepost 189.2; 10 mi n from US 52. Ext corridors. **Pets:** Accepted. 🍴 🛜 🔋 🖥

FARMVILLE

▼▼ **Comfort Inn-Farmville** �H 🐾

(434) 392-8163. **$81-$129.** 2108 S Main St 23901. Jct US 460 Bypass and US 15. Int corridors. **Pets:** Medium, other species. $25 one-time fee/pet. Designated rooms, service with restrictions, supervision.

🛏 🛜 🔋 🖥

FLOYD

▼▼ **Hotel Floyd** M

(540) 745-6080. **$79-$169.** 120 Wilson St 24091. Just e; center. Ext corridors. **Pets:** Accepted. 🍴 🛜 ✕ 🔋 🖥

FREDERICKSBURG *(Restaurants p. 643)*

▼▼▼ **BEST WESTERN Central Plaza** M

(540) 786-7404. **$69-$89.** 3000 Plank Rd 22401. I-95 exit 130B (SR 3). Ext corridors. **Pets:** Large, other species. $10 daily fee/pet. Service with restrictions, supervision. (SAVE) ECO 🔲 🛜 🔋 🖥

▼▼▼ **BEST WESTERN Fredericksburg** �H 🐾

(540) 371-5050. **$89-$110.** 2205 Plank Rd 22401. I-95 exit 130A (SR 3), 0.3 mi e. Ext corridors. **Pets:** $10 daily fee/pet. Service with restrictions. (SAVE) ECO 🔲 🛏 🛜 🔋 🖥

▼▼▼ **Candlewood Suites** �H 🐾

(540) 376-7244. **Call for rates.** 4821 Crossings Ct 22407. I-95 exit 126B northbound; exit 126 southbound, just s on US 1/17 (Jefferson Davis Hwy). Int corridors. **Pets:** Other species. $25 daily fee/pet. Service with restrictions. (SAVE) 🔲 🛜 🔋 🖥

▼▼▼ **Clarion Inn Fredericksburg** �H

(540) 371-5550. **$68-$90.** 564 Warrenton Rd 22406. I-95 exit 133, nw on US 17. Ext corridors. **Pets:** Medium. Designated rooms, service with restrictions, supervision. (SAVE) 🍴 🛏 🛜 🔋 🖥

▼▼▼ **Country Inn & Suites By Carlson, Fredericksburg South** �H

(540) 898-1800. **$89-$179.** 5327 Jefferson Davis Hwy 22408. I-95 exit 126 southbound; exit 126A northbound; just n on US 1. **Pets:** Accepted. 🛏 🛜 ✕ 🔋 🖥

▼▼▼ **Fredericksburg Hospitality House Hotel & Conference Center** �H

(540) 786-8321. **$79-$169.** 2801 Plank Rd 22401. I-95 exit 130B (SR 3). Int corridors. **Pets:** Accepted.

(SAVE) 🍴 🔲 🛏 🛜 ✕ 🔋 🖥

▼▼▼ **Homewood Suites by Hilton at Celebrate Virginia** �H

(540) 786-9700. **$129-$179.** 1040 Hospitality Ln 22401. I-95 exit 130B (SR 3), just w to Carl D Silver Pkwy, then 2 mi n. Int corridors. **Pets:** Accepted. (SAVE) 🔲 🛏 🛜 🔋 🖥

▼▼▼ **Hyatt Place Fredericksburg at Mary Washington** �H

(540) 654-3333. **$79-$269.** 1241 Jefferson Davis Hwy 22401. On US 1/17; jct College Ave; in Eagle Village. Int corridors. **Pets:** Accepted.

(SAVE) 🛜 ✕ 🔋 🖥

▼▼ **Quality Inn Fredericksburg** M 🐾

(540) 373-0000. **$45-$79.** 543 Warrenton Rd 22406. I-95 exit 133, just n on US 17. Ext corridors. **Pets:** $15 one-time fee/room. Designated rooms, service with restrictions, crate. 🛜 ✕ 🔋 🖥

▼▼ **Residence Inn by Marriott** �H

(540) 786-9222. **$129-$186.** 60 Town Centre Blvd 22407. I-95 exit 130B (SR 3), just w to Mall Dr, then just s. Int corridors. **Pets:** Accepted.

🔲 🛏 ✕ 🛜 ✕ 🔋 🖥

▼▼▼ **TownePlace Suites by Marriott** �H

(540) 891-0775. **$109-$120.** 4700 Market St 22408. I-95 exit 126 southbound; exit 126A northbound, just n on US 1 (Jefferson Davis Hwy), then just e. Int corridors. **Pets:** Accepted.

(SAVE) 🔲 🛏 🛜 ✕ 🔋 🖥

FRONT ROYAL

▼ **Budget Inn** M

(540) 635-2196. **$46-$70.** 1122 N Royal Ave 22630. I-66 exit 6, 2.2 mi s on US 340/522 and SR 55. Ext corridors. **Pets:** Medium. $8 daily fee/pet. Designated rooms, no service, supervision. 🛜 🔋

GLADE SPRING

▼ **Econo Lodge Glade Spring** M

(276) 429-5191. **$60-$175.** 33361 Lee Hwy 24340. I-81 exit 29, just e. Ext corridors. **Pets:** Accepted. 🛜 🔋

GLEN ALLEN

▼▼▼ **Aloft Richmond West** �H

(804) 433-1888. **$129-$189.** 3939 Duckling Dr 23060. I-64 exit 178B, just w on W Broad St; in West Broad Village. Int corridors.

Pets: Accepted. (SAVE) 🛏 🛜 ✕ 🔋 🖥

▼▼▼ **BEST WESTERN PLUS Glen Allen Inn** �H

(804) 266-3500. **$79-$189.** 8507 Brook Rd 23060. I-95 exit 83B, 0.5 mi w to Brook Rd, then just n. Int corridors. **Pets:** Accepted.

(SAVE) 🔲 🛏 🛜 🔋 🖥

▼▼ **Candlewood Suites Richmond-West** �H

(804) 364-2000. **Call for rates.** 4120 Brookriver Dr 23060. I-64 exit 178, just w on W Broad St. Int corridors. **Pets:** Accepted.

🔲 🛜 🔋 🖥

▼▼▼ **Candlewood Suites Virginia Center Commons** �H

(804) 262-2240. **$85-$200, 3 day notice.** 10609 Telegraph Rd 23059. I-295 exit 43C, 1.7 mi n to JEB Stuart Pkwy, then just w; I-95 exit 86B (SR 656/Elmont), just w, then 1 mi s. Int corridors. **Pets:** Medium. $25 deposit/pet, $75 one-time fee/pet. Service with restrictions, supervision. 🔲 🛜 🔋 🖥

▼▼▼ Comfort Suites-Innsbrook 🅗 🐾

(804) 217-9200. **$90-$139.** 4051 Innslake Dr 23060. I-64 exit 178B, just e on W Broad St to Cox Rd, then just n. Int corridors. **Pets:** Medium. $25 daily fee/room. Service with restrictions.

[ECO] [🛁M] [🏊] [📶] [✕] [🛏] [📺]

◈◈◈ ▼▼▼ Hyatt Place Richmond/Innsbrook 🅗

(804) 747-9644. **$79-$179.** 4100 Cox Rd 23060. I-64 exit 178B, 0.5 mi e to Dominion Blvd, then just n. Int corridors. **Pets:** Accepted.

[SAVE] [ECO] [🛁M] [🏊] [📶] [✕] [🛏] [📺]

◈◈◈ ▼▼▼ TownePlace Suites by Marriott 🅗

(804) 747-5253. **$58-$109.** 4231 Park Place Ct 23060. I-64 exit 178B, just e on W Broad St to Cox Rd, then just n to Innslake Dr. Int corridors. **Pets:** Accepted. [SAVE] [ECO] [🛁M] [🏊] [📶] [✕] [🛏] [📺]

▼▼▼ ▼▼▼ Wyndham Virginia Crossings Hotel & Conference Center 🅗

(804) 727-1400. **$99-$205.** 1000 Virginia Center Pkwy 23059. I-295 exit 43C, just n on US 1, then 1 mi e. Int corridors. **Pets:** Accepted.

[🍴] [🛁M] [🏊] [✕] [📶] [✕] [🛏] [📺]

GLOUCESTER

▼▼▼ Comfort Inn Gloucester 🅗 🐾

(804) 696-1900. **$99-$140.** 6639 Forest Hill Ave 23061. US 17, just s. Int corridors. **Pets:** Large, other species. $25 daily fee/pet. Service with restrictions, crate. [🏊] [📶] [🛏] [📺]

GRETNA

▼▼▼ Hampton Inn Gretna/Altavista/Chatham 🅗 🐾

(434) 656-9000. **$129-$175.** 200 McBride Ln 24557. US 29, just e on SR 40. Int corridors. **Pets:** Small, other species. Service with restrictions. [🛁M] [🏊] [📶] [🛏] [📺]

GRUNDY

▼▼▼ Comfort Inn 🅗

(276) 935-5050. **$99-$144.** 22006 Riverside Dr 24614. On US 460 business route, 0.5 mi e. Int corridors. **Pets:** Accepted. [🛁M] [📶] [🛏] [📺]

HAMPTON (Restaurants p. 643)

▼▼▼ Candlewood Suites 🅗

(757) 766-8976. **Call for rates.** 401 Butler Farm Rd 23666. I-64 exit 261B (Hampton Roads Center Pkwy) eastbound; exit 262B (Magruder Blvd) westbound, just n. Int corridors. **Pets:** Accepted.

[ECO] [🛁M] [📶] [✕] [🛏] [📺]

HARRISONBURG

▼▼ Candlewood Suites Harrisonburg 🅗

(540) 437-1400. **Call for rates.** 1560 Country Club Rd 22802. I-81 exit 247, just e. Int corridors. **Pets:** Accepted. [ECO] [📶] [🛏] [📺]

▼▼▼ Comfort Inn 🅗

(540) 433-6066. **$84-$129.** 1440 E Market St 22801. I-81 exit 247A, just e. Int corridors. **Pets:** Other species. $15 daily fee/room. Service with restrictions, supervision. [ECO] [🏊] [📶] [🛏] [📺]

◈◈◈ ▼◈▼ Days Inn Harrisonburg Ⓜ

(540) 433-9353. **$68-$214.** 1131 Forest Hill Rd 22801. I-81 exit 245, just e. Int corridors. **Pets:** Small. $15 daily fee/pet. Designated rooms, service with restrictions, supervision. [SAVE] [🏊] [📶] [🛏] [📺]

▼▼ Harrisonburg Econo Lodge Ⓜ

(540) 433-2576. **$60-$200.** 1703 E Market St 22801. I-81 exit 247A, 0.5 mi e on US 33. Ext/int corridors. **Pets:** Accepted. [🏊] [📶] [🛏] [📺]

▼▼ Microtel Inn & Suites by Wyndham 🅗

(540) 437-3777. **$69-$250.** 85 Pleasant Valley Rd 22801. I-81 exit 243, just w. Int corridors. **Pets:** Accepted. [🍴] [📶] [✕] [🛏] [📺]

▼▼ Ramada 🅗

(540) 434-9981. **$74-$129.** 91 Pleasant Valley Rd 22801. I-81 exit 243, just w, then just n on US 11. Ext corridors. **Pets:** Accepted.

[🏊] [📶] [🛏] [📺]

◈◈◈ ▼◈▼ Residence Inn by Marriott Harrisonburg 🅗

(540) 437-7426. **$149-$175.** 1945 Deyerle Ave 22801. I-81 exit 245, just e. Int corridors. **Pets:** Other species. $100 one-time fee/room. Service with restrictions, supervision. [SAVE] [🏊] [📶] [✕] [🛏] [📺]

◈◈◈ ▼◈▼ Sleep Inn & Suites 🅗

(540) 433-7100. **$84-$125.** 1891 Evelyn Byrd Ave 22801. I-81 exit 247A, 0.5 mi e on US 33 to University Blvd, 0.3 mi s to Evelyn Byrd Ave, then just w. Int corridors. **Pets:** Medium. $15 daily fee/pet. Designated rooms, service with restrictions, crate. [SAVE] [ECO] [📶] [🛏] [📺]

◈◈◈ ▼▼▼ Super 8 Ⓜ

(540) 433-8888. **$60-$220, 3 day notice.** 3330 S Main St 22801. I-81 exit 243, just e, then just s on US 11. Int corridors. **Pets:** Small. $10 daily fee/pet. Designated rooms, service with restrictions, supervision.

[SAVE] [📶]

◈◈◈ ▼▼▼ The Village Inn 🅗

(540) 434-7355. **$79-$95.** 4979 S Valley Pike 22801. I-81 exit 240 southbound, 0.6 mi w on SR 257, then 1.5 mi n on US 11; exit 243 northbound, just w to US 11, then 1.7 mi s. Ext corridors. **Pets:** Other species. $12 daily fee/pet. Service with restrictions, crate.

[SAVE] [ECO] [🍴] [🏊] [📶] [🛏] [📺]

HERNDON (Restaurants p. 643)

▼▼▼ Candlewood Suites Washington Dulles-Herndon 🅗

(703) 793-7100. **$79-$179.** 13845 Sunrise Valley Dr 20171. SR 267 (Dulles Toll Rd) exit 9A, 1.1 m s on SR 28, 0.3 mi e on Frying Pan Rd (CR 608), then 0.6 mi nw. Int corridors. **Pets:** Accepted.

[🛁M] [📶] [✕] [🛏] [📺]

◈◈◈ ▼▼▼ Hilton Washington Dulles Airport 🅗

(703) 478-2900. **Call for rates.** 13869 Park Center Rd 20171. SR 267 (Dulles Toll Rd) exit 9, 3 mi s on SR 28; at McLearen Blvd (SR 668). Int corridors. **Pets:** Accepted.

[SAVE] [ECO] [🍴] [🛁M] [🏊] [✕] [📶] [✕] [🛏] [📺]

◈◈◈ ▼▼▼ Hyatt Dulles 🅗

(703) 713-1234. **$65-$319.** 2300 Dulles Corner Blvd 20171. Jct SR 657 and 267 (Dulles Toll Rd) exit 10, 0.5 mi s on Centreville Rd (SR 657), 1.1 mi w on Sunrise Valley Dr. Int corridors. **Pets:** Medium. $50 one-time fee/pet. Designated rooms, service with restrictions, supervision.

[SAVE] [ECO] [🍴] [🛁M] [🏊] [📶] [✕] [🛏] [📺]

◈◈◈ ▼▼▼ HYATT house Herndon 🅗

(703) 437-5000. **$69-$269.** 467 Herndon Pkwy 20170. SR 267 (Dulles Toll Rd) exit 11 (SR 286/Fairfax County Pkwy), just n to Spring St exit, just s to CR 606 (Herndon Pkwy), then just w. Int corridors.

Pets: Accepted. [SAVE] [🛁M] [🏊] [📶] [✕] [🛏] [📺]

◈◈◈ ▼▼▼ Hyatt Place Herndon/Dulles Airport-East 🅗

(571) 643-0905. **$70-$239.** 13711 Sayward Blvd 20171. SR 267 (Dulles Toll Rd) exit 9A, 1.1 mi s on SR 28, 0.3 mi e on Frying Pan Rd (CR 608), then 1.2 mi nw on Sunrise Valley Dr. Int corridors.

Pets: Accepted. [SAVE] [🛁M] [🏊] [📶] [✕] [🛏] [📺]

▼▼▼ Residence Inn by Marriott-Herndon/Reston 🅗

(703) 435-0044. **$89-$274.** 315 Elden St 20170. 0.4 mi w on CR 606 (Herndon Pkwy) from jct SR 286 (Fairfax County Pkwy). Int corridors.

Pets: Accepted. [🛁M] [🏊] [📶] [✕] [🛏] [📺]

◈◈◈ ▼▼▼ Sheraton Herndon Dulles Airport Hotel 🅗

(571) 643-0950. **Call for rates.** 13715 Sayward Blvd 20171. SR 267 (Dulles Toll Rd) exit 9A, 1.1 mi s on SR 28, 0.3 mi e on Frying Pan Rd (CR 608), then 1.2 mi nw on Sunrise Valley Dr. Int corridors.

Pets: Accepted. [SAVE] [🍴] [🛁M] [🏊] [📶] [✕] [📺]

▼▼▼ Staybridge Suites Herndon Dulles **H**

(703) 713-6800. **Call for rates.** 13700 Coppermine Rd 20171. SR 267 (Dulles Toll Rd) exit 9A, 1.1 mi s on SR 28, 0.3 mi e on Frying Pan Rd (CR 608), 0.7 mi nw on Sunrise Valley Dr, then just e. Ext corridors. **Pets:** Accepted. 🐾 📶 ⊗ 🛢 💻

AAA ▼▼▼▼ The Westin Washington Dulles Airport **H**

(703) 793-3366. **$89-$269.** 2520 Wasser Terrace 20171. SR 28, 0.4 mi e on Frying Pan Rd, 0.8 mi nw. Int corridors. **Pets:** Accepted. 🅂🄰🅅🄴 🄴🄲🄾 🍴 🕭 🐾 📶 ⊗ 🛢 💻

HILLSVILLE

AAA ▼▼▼ BEST WESTERN Four Seasons South **M** 🐾

(276) 728-4136. **$71-$91.** 57 Airport Rd 24343. I-77 exit 14, just w on US 58 and 221. **Pets:** Other species. $13 deposit/room, $13 one-time fee/room. Designated rooms, crate.

🅂🄰🅅🄴 🐾 📶 🛢 💻

▼▼▼▼ Quality Inn **H**

(276) 728-2120. **$79-$179.** 85 Airport Rd 24343. I-77 exit 14, just w on US 58 and 221. Ext corridors. **Pets:** Accepted.

🕭 🐾 📶 🛢 💻

HOPEWELL

▼▼▼ Candlewood Suites **H**

(804) 541-0200. **Call for rates.** 5113 Plaza Dr 23860. I-295 exit 9B (SR 36), just w. Int corridors. **Pets:** Other species. $30 one-time fee/pet. Service with restrictions, crate. 🕭 📶 🛢 💻

▼▼▼▼ Fairfield Inn & Suites by Marriott **H**

(804) 458-2600. **$89-$129.** 3952 Courthouse Rd 23860. I-295 exit 9A (SR 36), just e. Int corridors. **Pets:** Accepted.

🕭 🐾 📶 ⊗ 🛢 💻

▼▼▼▼ Stay Over Suites **H**

(804) 452-1377. **Call for rates.** 4115 Old Woodlawn St 23860. I-295 exit 9A (SR 36), just e, then just n. Int corridors. **Pets:** Accepted.

📶 ⊗ 🛢 💻

HUDDLESTON

▼▼▼▼ Mariners Landing **CO**

(540) 297-4900. **Call for rates.** 1217 Graves Harbor Tr 24104. On SR 626; on Smith Mountain Lake. Ext/int corridors. **Pets:** Accepted.

🍴 🕭 🐾 ⊗ 📶 ⊗ 🛢 💻

IRVINGTON

AAA ▼▼▼▼ The Tides Inn **H**

(804) 438-5000. **$210-$395, 7 day notice.** 480 King Carter Dr 22480. 0.3 mi w of SR 200. Ext/int corridors. **Pets:** Accepted.

🅂🄰🅅🄴 🄴🄲🄾 🍴 🕭 🐾 ⊗ 📶 ⊗ 🛢 💻

KESWICK

AAA ▼▼▼▼ Keswick Hall **H**

(434) 979-3440. **$249-$1500, 7 day notice.** 701 Club Dr 22947. I-64 exit 129, just n. Int corridors. **Pets:** Accepted.

🅂🄰🅅🄴 🍴 🕭 🐾 ⊗ 📶 ⊗

KILMARNOCK

▼▼▼ Kilmarnock Inn **CI**

(804) 435-0034. **Call for rates.** 34 E Church St 22482. SR 3 to town. Ext/int corridors. **Pets:** Accepted. 🍴 🕭 📶 ⊗ 🎦 🛢 💻

LEBANON

▼▼ Lebanon Super 8 **M**

(276) 889-1800. **$64-$246.** 71 Townview Dr 24266. Just e on SR 654 from US 19 Bypass. Int corridors. **Pets:** Accepted. 🕭 📶 🛢 💻

LEESBURG (*Restaurants p. 643*)

AAA ▼▼▼ BEST WESTERN Leesburg Hotel & Conference Center **H**

(703) 777-9400. **$99-$149.** 726 E Market St 20176. Off SR 7 business route, just w of jct US 15. Int corridors. **Pets:** Medium, dogs only. $10 daily fee/pet. Service with restrictions, supervision.

🅂🄰🅅🄴 🕭 🐾 📶 🛢 💻

▼▼▼▼ Homewood Suites by Hilton Leesburg **H**

(571) 258-1068. **$139-$189.** 115 Fort Evans Rd NE 20176. Off SR 7 business route, just w of jct US 15, just n. Int corridors.
Pets: Accepted. 🕭 🐾 📶 🛢 💻

AAA ▼▼▼ ▼▼ Lansdowne Resort **H** 🐾

(703) 729-8400. **$129-$309, 3 day notice.** 44050 Woodridge Pkwy 20176. SR 7, 3.6 mi w of jct SR 28; 4.4 mi e of jct US 15. Int corridors. **Pets:** Large, dogs only. $100 one-time fee/room. Designated rooms, service with restrictions, crate.

🅂🄰🅅🄴 🍴 🕭 🐾 ⊗ 📶 ⊗ 🛢 💻

LEXINGTON

AAA ▼▼▼ BEST WESTERN Lexington Inn **M**

(540) 458-3020. **$70-$200.** 850 N Lee Hwy 24450. I-64 exit 55, just s on US 11; I-81 exit 191, 1.6 mi w. Ext corridors. **Pets:** $20 one-time fee/room. Service with restrictions, crate. 🅂🄰🅅🄴 📶 🛢 💻

AAA ▼▼▼ BEST WESTERN PLUS Inn at Hunt Ridge **H**

(540) 464-1500. **$114-$149.** 25 Willow Spring Rd 24450. I-64 exit 55, just n on US 11 to SR 39; I-81 exit 191, 0.6 mi w. Int corridors.
Pets: Accepted. 🅂🄰🅅🄴 🍴 🕭 🐾 📶 ⊗ 🛢 💻

▼▼▼▼ Comfort Inn-Virginia Horse Center **H**

(540) 463-7311. **$81-$189.** 62 Comfort Way 24450. I-64 exit 55, just s on US 11; I-81 exit 191, 0.6 mi w. Int corridors. **Pets:** Accepted.

🐾 📶 🛢 💻

▼▼▼▼ Holiday Inn Express **H**

(540) 463-7351. **Call for rates.** 880 N Lee Hwy 24450. I-64 exit 55, just s on US 11; I-81 exit 191, 1 mi w. Int corridors. **Pets:** Accepted.

📶 ⊗ 🛢 💻

▼▼▼ Howard Johnson Inn **H** 🐾

(540) 463-9181. **$69-$109.** 2836 N Lee Hwy 24450. I-81 exit 195, just s on US 11. Int corridors. **Pets:** Other species. $14 daily fee/pet. Designated rooms, service with restrictions, supervision. 🐾 📶 🛢 💻

▼▼ Motel 6 **M**

(540) 463-7371. **Call for rates.** 65 Econo Ln 24450. I-81 exit 191, just s on US 11. Ext corridors. **Pets:** Other species. Service with restrictions, crate. 📶 🛢

AAA ▼▼▼ Quality Inn & Suites **H**

(540) 463-6400. **$71-$149.** 2814 N Lee Hwy 24450. I-81 exit 195, just sw on US 11. Int corridors. **Pets:** Medium. $10 daily fee/pet. Designated rooms, service with restrictions, supervision.

🅂🄰🅅🄴 🐾 📶 🛢 💻

AAA ▼▼▼ Sleep Inn & Suites **H**

(540) 463-6000. **$75-$249.** 95 Maury River Rd 24450. I-64 exit 55, just n. Int corridors. **Pets:** Medium. $15 daily fee/pet. Service with restrictions, supervision. 🅂🄰🅅🄴 🐾 📶 ⊗ 🛢 💻

AAA ▼▼▼ Super 8 Lexington **M**

(540) 463-7858. **$75-$90.** 1139 N Lee Hwy 24450. I-64 exit 55, just n. Int corridors. **Pets:** Medium. $10 daily fee/pet. Designated rooms, service with restrictions, supervision. 🅂🄰🅅🄴 📶 🛢 💻

LORTON

▼▼▼ Comfort Inn Gunston Corner **H**

(703) 643-3100. **$89-$189.** 8180 Silverbrook Rd 22079. I-95 exit 163, just w. Int corridors. **Pets:** Small. $25 one-time fee/room. Service with restrictions, supervision. 🐾 📶 ⊗ 🛢 💻

LOW MOOR

▼▼▼ Oak Tree Inn M

(540) 965-0090. **$79-$89.** 123 Westvaco Rd 24457. I-64 exit 21, just s. Int corridors. **Pets:** Accepted. 🛜 ✕ 📋 💻

LURAY

🔷🔷 ▼▼▼ BEST WESTERN Intown of Luray M

(540) 743-6511. **$75-$150.** 410 W Main St 22835. 0.3 mi w on US 211 business route. Ext corridors. **Pets:** Medium. $20 daily fee/pet. Service with restrictions, crate. 〔SAVE〕 ⁑ ⌘ 🛜 📋 💻

▼▼ Days Inn-Luray M

(540) 743-4521. **$80-$290.** 138 Whispering Hill Rd 22835. US 211 Bypass, 1.7 mi e of jct US 340. Ext/int corridors. **Pets:** Accepted. ⌘ 🛜 📋 💻

LYNCHBURG

🔷🔷 ▼▼▼ BEST WESTERN of Lynchburg M ❖

(434) 237-2986. **$80-$120.** 2815 Candlers Mountain Rd 24502. Jct US 29 and 460. Ext corridors. **Pets:** Medium. $15 daily fee/room. Designated rooms, service with restrictions, supervision. 〔SAVE〕 ⌘ 🛜 📋 💻

🔷🔷 ▼▼▼ The Craddock Terry Hotel and Event Center H

(434) 455-1500. **$149-$299.** 1312 Commerce St 24504. US 29 business route exit 1A (Main St), just w. Int corridors. **Pets:** Accepted. 〔SAVE〕 〔ECO〕 🛜 ✕ 📋 💻

▼▼▼ Extended Stay America - Lynchburg - University Blvd M

(434) 239-8863. **Call for rates.** 1910 University Blvd 24502. US 460 exit Candlers Mountain Rd/University Blvd. Int corridors. **Pets:** Other species. $25 daily fee/pet. Service with restrictions, supervision. ♿ 🛜 ✕ 📋 💻

▼▼▼ Holiday Inn Downtown Lynchburg H

(434) 528-2500. **$92-$139.** 601 Main St 24504. US 29 business route exit 1A (Main St), 0.7 mi w. Int corridors. **Pets:** Accepted. ⁑ ♿ ⌘ 🛜 ✕ 📋 💻

▼▼▼ Holiday Inn Express H

(434) 237-7771. **Call for rates.** 5600 Seminole Ave 24502. US 460 exit Candlers Mountain Rd, 0.3 mi w; US 29 business route exit Candlers Mountain Rd. Int corridors. **Pets:** Accepted. ⌘ 🛜 ✕ 📋 💻

▼▼▼ La Quinta Inn & Suites Lynchburg at Liberty University H

(434) 847-8655. **Call for rates.** 3320 Candlers Mountain Rd 24502. US 29 exit US 501, just e. Int corridors. **Pets:** Accepted. ⌘ 🛜 ✕ 📋 💻

▼▼▼ Microtel & Suites by Wyndham Lynchburg H

(434) 239-2300. **Call for rates.** 5704 Seminole Ave 24502. US 460 exit Candlers Mountain Rd, 0.3 mi w; US 29 business route exit Candlers Mountain Rd. **Pets:** Accepted. 🛜 ✕ 📋 💻

🔷 ▼▼▼ Sleep Inn Lynchburg H

(434) 846-6900. **$110-$250.** 3620 Candlers Mountain Rd 24502. US 29 exit 8B. Int corridors. **Pets:** Accepted. 〔SAVE〕 ♿ 🛜 ✕ 📋 💻

MANASSAS (Restaurants p. 643)

🔷 ▼▼▼ BEST WESTERN Battlefield Inn H ❖

(703) 361-8000. **$109-$200, 30 day notice.** 10820 Balls Ford Rd 20109. I-66 exit 47A westbound; exit 47 eastbound, just s on SR 234 business route. Ext corridors. **Pets:** Other species. $10 daily fee/pet. Service with restrictions. 〔SAVE〕 ⁑ ⌘ 🛜 📋 💻

▼▼▼ Candlewood Suites Manassas H

(703) 530-0550. **$99-$129.** 11220 Balls Ford Rd 20109. I-66 exit 47A westbound; exit 47 eastbound, just s on SR 234 business route, then 0.7 mi w. Int corridors. **Pets:** Accepted. ♿ 🛜 📋 💻

▼▼▼ Comfort Suites Manassas H

(703) 686-1100. **$99-$139.** 7350 Williamson Blvd 20109. I-66 exit 47A westbound; exit 47 eastbound, 0.5 mi s on SR 234 business route, then just e. Int corridors. **Pets:** Large. $50 one-time fee/pet. Designated rooms, service with restrictions. ⌘ ✕ 🛜 ✕ 📋 💻

🔷 ▼▼▼ Red Roof Plus+ Washington DC-Manassas M

(703) 335-9333. **$69-$99.** 10610 Automotive Dr 20109. I-66 exit 47A westbound; exit 47 eastbound, just s on SR 234 business route, then just e on Balls Ford Rd. Ext corridors. **Pets:** Large, other species. Service with restrictions, supervision. 〔SAVE〕 ♿ 🛜 ✕ 📋 💻

🔷 ▼▼▼ Residence Inn by Marriott Manassas Battlefield Park H 🐾

(703) 330-8808. **$109-$189.** 7345 Williamson Blvd 20109. I-66 exit 47A westbound; exit 47 eastbound, 0.5 mi s on SR 234 business route, then just e. Int corridors. **Pets:** Small. $100 one-time fee/room. Service with restrictions, crate. 〔SAVE〕 ♿ ⌘ 🛜 ✕ 📋 💻

MARTINSVILLE

▼▼▼ Baymont Inn & Suites Martinsville H

(276) 638-0479. **$49-$101.** 378 Commonwealth Blvd W 24112. Jct US 220 business route, just e. Int corridors. **Pets:** Accepted. ♿ 🛜 📋 💻

▼▼▼ Comfort Inn Martinsville H

(276) 666-6835. **$95-$135.** 1895 Virginia Ave 24112. Jct US 58, 2.4 mi n on US 220 business route. Int corridors. **Pets:** Accepted. ⌘ 🛜 📋 💻

▼▼▼ Econo Lodge H

(276) 632-5611. **$60-$225.** US 220 Business Rt S 24112. Jct US 58, 2.3 mi n. Ext corridors. **Pets:** Accepted. ⁑ ⌘ 🛜 📋 💻

▼▼▼ Hampton Inn H

(276) 647-4700. **$149-$159.** 50 Hampton Dr 24112. Jct US 58, 2.5 mi n on US 220 business route. Int corridors. **Pets:** Accepted. ⌘ 🛜 📋 💻

MAX MEADOWS

▼▼▼ Super 8 M

(276) 637-4141. **$55-$125.** 194 Ft. Chiswell Rd 24360. I-77/81 exit 80, just e. Ext corridors. **Pets:** Accepted. 🛜 📋 💻

MECHANICSVILLE

▼▼▼ Hampton Inn H

(804) 559-0559. **$125-$139.** 7433 Bell Creek Rd 23111. I-295 exit 37A (US 360 E) to Bell Creek Rd, just n. Int corridors. **Pets:** Accepted. ♿ ⌘ 🛜 📋 💻

▼▼▼ Holiday Inn Express-Richmond-Mechanicsville H

(804) 559-0022. **$109-$149.** 7441 Bell Creek Rd 23111. I-295 exit 37A (US 360 E) to Bell Creek Rd, just n. Int corridors. **Pets:** Accepted. ♿ ⌘ 🛜 📋 💻

MIDLOTHIAN

▼▼▼ La Quinta Inn & Suites - Richmond-Chesterfield H

(804) 794-4999. **$92-$240.** 1301 Huguenot Rd 23113. Just n of jct US 60 and SR 147; adjacent to Chesterfield Town Center. Int corridors. **Pets:** Large, other species. Service with restrictions. ♿ 🛜 ✕ 📋 💻

MINT SPRING

▼▼ Days Inn-Staunton M

(540) 337-3031. **$70-$180.** 372 White Hill Rd 24401. I-81 exit 217, just e on SR 654. Ext corridors. **Pets:** Large, other species. $10 daily fee/pet. Service with restrictions, supervision. ⌘ 🛜 📋 💻

MOUNTAIN LAKE

▼▼▼ Mountain Lake Lodge 🏨

(540) 626-7121. **$145-$375, 7 day notice.** 115 Hotel Cir 24136. Jct US 460, 6.6 mi n on SR 700; caution, steep narrow paved mountain road. Ext/int corridors. **Pets:** Large, dogs only. $75 one-time fee/pet. Designated rooms, service with restrictions, crate.

🍴 ➰ ⌧ 📶 ⌧ 🎾 🛏 🖥

MOUNT JACKSON

▼▼ Super 8 - Mt. Jackson Ⓜ

(540) 477-2911. **$66-$76.** 250 Conicville Blvd 22842. I-81 exit 273, just e. Ext corridors. **Pets:** Accepted. ➰ 📶 🛏 🖥

▼▼▼ The Widow Kip's 🅱🅱 ❀

(540) 477-2400. **$120-$145, 5 day notice.** 355 Orchard Dr 22842. I-81 exit 273, 1.5 mi s on US 11, just w on SR 263, then just sw on SR 698. Int corridors. **Pets:** Other species. $20 daily fee/pet. Designated rooms, no service. 🌿 ➰ 📶 ⌧ 🛏 🖥

MCLEAN

Ⓐ ▼▼▼ Staybridge Suites-McLean-Tysons Corner (Washington, DC area) 🏨

(703) 448-5400. **$109-$369.** 6845 Old Dominion Dr 22101. I-495 exit 46B, 2 mi n on SR 123, then 0.3 mi e on SR 309. Int corridors. **Pets:** Accepted. 🆂🅰🆅🅴 🔥 ➰ 📶 ⌧ 🛏 🖥

NEW CHURCH

▼▼▼ The Garden & The Sea Inn 🅱🅱 ❀

(757) 894-9097. **$110-$250, 10 day notice.** 4188 Nelson Rd 23415. US 13, 0.3 mi n, just w on CR 710 (Nelson Rd). Int corridors. **Pets:** Other species. $25 one-time fee/room. 🌿 ➰ 📶 ⌧ 🎾 🛏 🖥

NEW MARKET

Ⓐ ▼▼▼ Quality Inn Shenandoah Valley 🏨

(540) 740-3141. **$60-$119.** 162 W Old Cross Rd 22844. I-81 exit 264, just e on US 11/211, then just n. Ext/int corridors. **Pets:** Accepted.

🆂🅰🆅🅴 🍴 ➰ 📶 🛏 🖥

NEWPORT NEWS *(Restaurants p. 643)*

Ⓐ ▼▼▼ Comfort Inn 🏨

(757) 249-0200. **$81-$117.** 12330 Jefferson Ave 23602. I-64 exit 255A, just s on Clarie Ln. Int corridors. **Pets:** Accepted.

🆂🅰🆅🅴 🔥 ➰ 📶 🛏 🖥

▼▼ Crestwood Suites Ⓜ

(757) 951-1017. **$50-$75.** 11 Old Oyster Point Rd 23602. I-64 exit 256A, just s on Oyster Point Rd to Canon Blvd, just e, then just n. Int corridors. **Pets:** Accepted. 📶 🛏 🖥

▼▼ Extended Stay America-Newport News - I-64 - Jefferson Ave 🏨

(757) 882-8847. **Call for rates.** 12359 Hornsby Ln 23602. I-64 exit 255A, just s on Jefferson Ave. Int corridors. **Pets:** Other species. $25 daily fee/pet. Service with restrictions, supervision.

🔥 ➰ 📶 🛏 🖥

▼▼ Jameson Inn & Suites Newport News 🏨

(757) 951-1177. **Call for rates.** 21 Old Oyster Point Rd 23602. I-64 exit 256A, just s on Oyster Point Rd to Canon Blvd, just e, then just n. Int corridors. **Pets:** Accepted. 🔥 ➰ 📶 🛏 🖥

▼▼▼ Mulberry Inn 🏨

(757) 887-3000. **Call for rates.** 16890 Warwick Blvd 23603. I-64 exit 250A (SR 105/Ft Eustis Blvd S), s to US 60, then 0.3 mi w. Ext/int corridors. **Pets:** Medium. $50 deposit/room, $15 daily fee/pet. Designated rooms, service with restrictions, crate. 🌿 🔥 ➰ 📶 🛏 🖥

▼▼ Point Plaza-Suites at City Center 🏨

(757) 599-4460. **$69-$159.** 950 J Clyde Morris Blvd 23601. I-64 exit 258B (US 17), just n. Ext/int corridors. **Pets:** Accepted.

🌿 ➰ 📶 🛏 🖥

▼▼▼ Residence Inn by Marriott Newport News Airport 🏨

(757) 842-6214. **$99-$189.** 531 St. Johns Rd 23602. I-64 exit 255A, just s on Jefferson Ave to Freedom Way, then just nw. Int corridors. **Pets:** Accepted. 🔥 ➰ 📶 ⌧ 🛏 🖥

NORFOLK *(Restaurants p. 643)*

Ⓐ ▼▼▼ BEST WESTERN PLUS Holiday Sands Inn & Suites 🏨

(757) 583-2621. **$89-$224.** 1330 E Ocean View Ave 23503. US 60, 4 mi e of Hampton Roads Bridge Tunnel. Ext corridors. **Pets:** Large, dogs only. $50 deposit/room, $20 daily fee/room. Designated rooms, service with restrictions, supervision. 🆂🅰🆅🅴 🌿 ➰ 📶 ⌧ 🛏 🖥

▼▼▼ Candlewood Suites Norfolk Airport 🏨

(757) 605-4001. **Call for rates.** 5600 Lowery Rd 23502. I-264 exit 13B (US 13/Military Hwy), 1.3 mi n, then just w. Int corridors. **Pets:** Accepted. 🔥 ➰ 📶 🛏 🖥

▼▼▼ DoubleTree Hotel Norfolk Airport 🏨

(757) 466-8000. **$89-$249.** 1500 N Military Hwy 23502. I-64 exit 281 (Military Hwy), just s; jct US 13 and SR 165. Int corridors. **Pets:** Accepted. 🌿 🍴 🔥 ➰ 📶 ⌧ 🛏 🖥

Ⓐ ▼▼▼ La Quinta Inn & Suites Norfolk Airport 🏨

(757) 466-7001. **$72-$269.** 1387 N Military Hwy 23502. I-64 exit 281 (Military Hwy), just s. Int corridors. **Pets:** Large, other species. Service with restrictions. 🆂🅰🆅🅴 🔥 ➰ 📶 ⌧ 🛏 🖥

Ⓐ ▼▼▼ Page House Inn Bed & Breakfast 🅱🅱

(757) 625-5033. **$145-$230, 7 day notice.** 323 Fairfax Ave 23507. I-264 exit 9, 1.4 mi n on Waterside Dr to Olney Rd, just w to Mowbray Arch, then just s; in Ghent Historic District. Int corridors. **Pets:** Accepted.

🆂🅰🆅🅴 📶 ⌧ 🛏

Ⓐ ▼▼▼ Quality Suites Lake Wright 🏨 🐾

(757) 461-6251. **$89-$144.** 6280 Northampton Blvd 23502. I-64 exit 282, just w on US 13. Int corridors. **Pets:** Other species. $35 one-time fee/room. Designated rooms, service with restrictions, crate.

🆂🅰🆅🅴 🌿 🍴 🔥 ➰ 📶 🛏 🖥

▼▼▼ Residence Inn by Marriott Downtown 🏨

(757) 842-6216. **$89-$199.** 227 W Brambleton Ave 23510. Jct Duke St; downtown. Int corridors. **Pets:** Accepted.

🌿 🔥 ➰ 📶 ⌧ 🛏 🖥

▼▼▼ Residence Inn by Marriott Norfolk Airport 🏨

(757) 333-3000. **$89-$179.** 1590 N Military Hwy 23502. I-64 exit 281B (Military Hwy); jct Lake Wright Dr. Int corridors. **Pets:** Accepted. 🌿 🔥 ➰ 📶 ⌧ 🛏 🖥

Ⓐ ▼▼▼ Sheraton Norfolk Waterside Hotel 🏨

(757) 622-6664. **$99-$299.** 777 Waterside Dr 23510. I-264 exit 9 (Waterside Dr); downtown. Int corridors. **Pets:** Accepted. 🆂🅰🆅🅴 🌿 🍴 ➰ 📶 ⌧ 🛏 🖥

▼▼ Sleep Inn Lake Wright 🏨 🐾

(757) 461-1133. **$74-$94.** 6280 Northampton Blvd 23502. I-64 exit 282, just w on US 13. **Pets:** Other species. $25 one-time fee/room. Designated rooms, service with restrictions, crate.

🌿 🍴 🔥 ➰ 📶 🛏 🖥

Ⓐ ▼▼ Tazewell Hotel Downtown, an Ascend Hotel Collection Member 🏨

(757) 623-6200. **$89-$139.** 245 Granby St 23510. Jct Tazewell St; downtown. Int corridors. **Pets:** Small. $25 daily fee/pet. Service with restrictions, crate. 🆂🅰🆅🅴 📶 🛏 🖥

Ⓐ ▼▼▼ Wyndham Garden Norfolk Downtown 🏨

(757) 627-5555. **$79-$259.** 700 Monticello Ave 23510. Jct Brambleton Ave and St Pauls Blvd; downtown. Int corridors. **Pets:** Medium. $100 one-time fee/room. Designated rooms, service with restrictions, crate.

🆂🅰🆅🅴 🍴 🔥 ➰ 📶 ⌧ 🛏 🖥

NORTON

🙞🙞 Super 8-Norton Ⓜ

(276) 679-0893. **$57-$123.** 425 Wharton Ln 24273. Jct US 58 and 23. Int corridors. **Pets:** Accepted. 📶 🖥 💻

ONANCOCK *(Restaurants p. 643)*

🙞🙞 1890 Spinning Wheel Bed & Breakfast 🅱🅱 🐾

(757) 787-7311. **$99-$125, 5 day notice.** 31 North St 23417. Just n of jct Market (SR 179) and North sts. Int corridors. **Pets:** Other species. $15 daily fee/pet. Designated rooms, supervision.
🅴🅲🅾 📶 ❌ 🄿 💈

PETERSBURG *(Restaurants p. 644)*

🙞🙞 Comfort Inn-Petersburg South 🄷

(804) 732-2000. **$67-$81.** 12001 S Crater Rd 23805. I-95 exit 45, just n on US 301. Int corridors. **Pets:** Accepted. 🅼 🙠 📶 🖥 💻

PORTSMOUTH *(Restaurants p. 644)*

🅰🅰🅰 🙞🙞🙞 Governor Dinwiddie Hotel Old Towne, an Ascend Hotel Collection Member 🄷

(757) 392-1330. **$79-$129.** 506 Dinwiddie St 23704. Jct High St. Int corridors. **Pets:** Accepted. 🆂🅰🆅🅴 🍽 📶 ❌ 🖥 💻

POUNDING MILL

🙞🙞🙞 Claypool Hill Holiday Inn Express Hotel & Suites 🄷

(276) 596-9880. **Call for rates.** 180 Clay Dr 24637. 0.5 mi e of US 19/460. Int corridors. **Pets:** Accepted. 🙠 📶 🖥 💻

🙞 Claypool Hill Super 8 Ⓜ

(276) 964-9888. **$63-$165.** 12367 Governor GC Peery Hwy 24637. 0.3 mi w on US 19/460. Int corridors. **Pets:** Small. $10 daily fee/pet. Designated rooms, service with restrictions, supervision. 📶 ❌ 🖥 💻

PRINCE GEORGE

🅰🅰🅰 🙞🙞 Baymont Inn & Suites Prince George 🄷

(804) 452-0022. **$69-$139.** 5380 Oaklawn Blvd 23875. I-295 exit 9B (SR 36), just w. Int corridors. **Pets:** Small. $15 one-time fee/room. Service with restrictions, crate. 🆂🅰🆅🅴 🍽 🅼 🙠 📶 🖥 💻

RADFORD

🅰🅰🅰 🙞🙞🙞 BEST WESTERN Radford Inn 🄷

(540) 639-3000. **$69-$209.** 1501 Tyler Ave 24141. I-81 exit 109, 2.7 mi nw on SR 177. Int corridors. **Pets:** Medium. $10 daily fee/room. Designated rooms, service with restrictions, crate.
🆂🅰🆅🅴 🍽 🙠 ❌ 📶 🖥 💻

🙞🙞🙞 Comfort Inn & Suites 🄷

(540) 639-3333. **$60-$350.** 2331 Tyler Rd 24073. I-81 exit 109, just w. Int corridors. **Pets:** Medium. $15 daily fee/pet. Designated rooms, service with restrictions, supervision. 🅼 🙠 📶 ❌ 🖥 💻

🅰🅰🅰 🙞🙞🙞 La Quinta Inn Radford Ⓜ

(540) 633-6800. **$69-$299.** 1450 Tyler Ave 24141. I-81 exit 109, 2.6 mi w on SR 177. Int corridors. **Pets:** Large, other species. Service with restrictions. 🆂🅰🆅🅴 🍽 📶 ❌ 🖥 💻

🙞 Super 8-Radford Ⓜ

(540) 731-9355. **$59-$114.** 1600 Tyler Ave 24141. I-81 exit 109, just w. Int corridors. **Pets:** Accepted. 📶 🖥 💻

RAPHINE

🅰🅰🅰 🙞🙞 Comfort Inn & Suites Ⓜ

(540) 377-2604. **Call for rates.** 584 Oakland Cir 24472. I-81 exit 205, just sw. Int corridors. **Pets:** Medium. $10 daily fee/pet. Designated rooms, service with restrictions, supervision. 🆂🅰🆅🅴 🙠 📶 🖥

RESTON

🙞🙞 Extended Stay America Washington DC-Reston Ⓜ

(703) 707-9700. **Call for rates.** 12190 Sunset Hills Rd 20190. SR 267 (Dulles Toll Rd) exit 12 (Reston Pkwy), just n, then just w. Ext corridors. **Pets:** Other species. $25 daily fee/pet. Service with restrictions, supervision. 📶 🖥 💻

🅰🅰🅰 🙞🙞 🙞🙞 Hyatt Regency Reston 🄷

(703) 709-1234. **$129-$399.** 1800 Presidents St 20190. SR 267 (Dulles Toll Rd) exit 12 (Reston Pkwy); center. Int corridors. **Pets:** Accepted.
🆂🅰🆅🅴 🅴🅲🅾 🍽 🅼 🙠 ❌ 📡 ❌ 🖥 💻

🅰🅰🅰 🙞🙞 💎 Sheraton Reston Hotel 🄷

(703) 620-9000. **Call for rates.** 11810 Sunrise Valley Dr 20191. SR 267 (Dulles Toll Rd) exit 12 (Reston Pkwy), just s. Int corridors. **Pets:** Accepted. 🆂🅰🆅🅴 🍽 🅼 🙠 📡 ❌ 🖥 💻

🅰🅰🅰 🙞🙞 The Westin Reston Heights 🄷

(703) 391-9000. **Call for rates.** 11750 Sunrise Valley Dr 20191. SR 267 (Dulles Toll Rd) exit 12 (Reston Pkwy), just s. Int corridors. **Pets:** Accepted. 🆂🅰🆅🅴 🄲 🍽 🅼 🙠 📡 ❌ 💻

RICHMOND *(Restaurants p. 644)*

🅰🅰🅰 🙞🙞🙞 The Berkeley Hotel 🄷 🐾

(804) 780-1300. **$149-$269.** 1200 E Cary St 23219. Just s of state Capitol; jct 12th St. Int corridors. **Pets:** Small. $50 one-time fee/pet. Designated rooms, service with restrictions.
🆂🅰🆅🅴 🍽 📶 ❌ 🖥 💻

🅰🅰🅰 🙞🙞🙞 BEST WESTERN PLUS Governor's Inn 🄷

(804) 323-0007. **$84-$169.** 9826 Midlothian Tpke 23235. 1.5 mi w of jct Powhite Pkwy (SR 76). Int corridors. **Pets:** Accepted.
🆂🅰🆅🅴 🅼 🙠 📶 🖥 💻

🙞🙞 Candlewood Suites 🄷

(804) 271-0016. **Call for rates.** 4301 Commerce Rd 23234. I-95 exit 69, just n. Int corridors. **Pets:** Accepted. 🅼 📶 🖥 💻

🅰🅰🅰 🙞🙞 Commonwealth Park Suites 🄷

(804) 343-7300. **$139-$159.** 901 Bank St 23219. Jct 9th and Bank sts. Int corridors. **Pets:** Medium. $50 daily fee/pet. Designated rooms, service with restrictions, crate. 🆂🅰🆅🅴 🅴🅲🅾 🍽 📶 🖥 💻

🙞🙞 Econo Lodge North-Parham Rd Ⓜ

(804) 262-7070. **$55-$120.** 8350 Brook Rd 23227. I-95 exit 83B, 0.5 mi w. Ext corridors. **Pets:** Accepted. 🅼 📶 🖥

🙞🙞 Extended Stay America North Chesterfield Arboretum 🄷

(804) 272-1800. **Call for rates.** 241 Arboretum Pl 23236. Jct Powhite Pkwy (SR 76) and Midlothian Tpke (US 60), just w. Int corridors. **Pets:** Other species. $25 daily fee/pet. Service with restrictions, supervision. 🅼 📶 🖥 💻

🙞🙞 Extended Stay America Richmond-Glenside North 🄷

(804) 285-7050. **Call for rates.** 6807 Paragon Pl 23230. I-64 exit 183C (W Broad St), just w to Glenside Dr, then just n. Int corridors. **Pets:** Other species. $25 daily fee/pet. Service with restrictions, supervision. 🅼 🙠 📶 🖥 💻

🙞🙞🙞 Fairfield Inn & Suites by Marriott Northwest 🄷

(804) 545-4200. **$79-$139.** 9937 Mayland Dr 23233. I-64 exit 180B, just n on Gaskins Rd. Int corridors. **Pets:** Medium, other species. $50 one-time fee/room. Designated rooms, service with restrictions, supervision. 🅼 🙠 📶 ❌ 🖥 💻

🅰🅰🅰 🙞🙞🙞 Four Points by Sheraton Richmond 🄷

(804) 323-1144. **$99-$309.** 9901 Midlothian Tpke 23235. 1 mi w of Powhite Pkwy (SR 76). Int corridors. **Pets:** Accepted. 🆂🅰🆅🅴 🅴🅲🅾 🍽 🅼 🙠 📶 ❌ 🖥 💻

AAA ▽▽▽▽ **Four Points by Sheraton Richmond Airport** H

(804) 226-4300. **Call for rates.** 4700 S Laburnum Ave 23231. I-64 exit 195, 0.5 mi s. Int corridors. **Pets:** Accepted.

[SAVE] [ECO] [⊞] [≈] [🖥] [✕] [📶] [☕]

AAA ▽▽▽ ▽▽▽ **Hilton Richmond Hotel & Spa/Short Pump** H

(804) 364-3600. **$129-$219.** 12042 W Broad St 23233. I-64 exit 178, 2 mi w. Int corridors. **Pets:** Accepted.

[SAVE] [ECO] [⊞] [🅼] [≈] [🖥] [✕] [📶] [☕]

▽▽▽▽ **Holiday Inn Express** H

(804) 934-9300. **$89-$169.** 9933 Mayland Dr 23233. I-64 exit 180B, just n to Mayland Dr, then just w. Int corridors. **Pets:** Medium, other species. $50 daily fee/pet. Designated rooms, supervision.

[🅼] [≈] [≈] [📶] [☕]

AAA ▽▽▽▽ **Holiday Inn Express Midlothian Turnpike** H

(804) 320-8900. **Call for rates.** 8710 Midlothian Tpke 23235. Jct Powhite Pkwy (SR 76) and Midlothian Tpke (US 60), just e. Int corridors.

Pets: Accepted. [SAVE] [🅼] [≈] [≈] [✕] [📶] [☕]

▽▽▽ **Holiday Inn South - Bells Road** H

(804) 592-2900. **Call for rates.** 4303 Commerce Rd 23234. I-95 exit 69 (Bells Rd), just n. Int corridors. **Pets:** Accepted.

[⊞] [🅼] [≈] [≈] [📶] [☕]

AAA ▽▽▽▽ **Hyatt Place Richmond Airport** H

(804) 549-4865. **$84-$249.** 4401 S Laburnum Ave 23231. I-64 exit 195, just s; in White Oak Village. Int corridors. **Pets:** Accepted.

[SAVE] [🅼] [≈] [≈] [✕] [📶] [☕]

AAA ▽▽▽▽ **Hyatt Place Richmond/Arboretum** H

(804) 560-1566. **$69-$159.** 201 Arboretum Pl 23236. Jct Powhite Pkwy (SR 76) and Midlothian Tpke (US 60), just w. Int corridors.

Pets: Accepted. [SAVE] [🅼] [≈] [≈] [✕] [📶] [☕]

▽▽▽▽ **Omni Richmond Hotel** H

(804) 344-7000. **Call for rates.** 100 S 12th St 23219. I-95 exit 74A (I-195) exit Canal St; in James Center. Int corridors. **Pets:** Accepted.

[ECO] [⊡] [⊞] [🅼] [≈] [≈] [✕] [📶] [☕]

▽▽ **Quality Inn West End** H

(804) 346-0000. **$69-$109.** 8008 W Broad St 23294. I-64 exit 183C (W Broad St) westbound; exit 183 eastbound, 1.5 mi w. Int corridors.

Pets: Accepted. [≈] [≈] [📶] [☕]

AAA ▽▽▽ **Red Roof Inn-Richmond South** M

(804) 271-7240. **$50-$100.** 4350 Commerce Rd 23234. I-95 exit 69. Ext corridors. **Pets:** Large, other species. Service with restrictions, supervision. [SAVE] [≈] [✕] [📶] [☕]

AAA ▽ **Super 8** M

(804) 262-8880. **$44-$160.** 5615 Chamberlayne Rd 23227. I-95 exit 82. Int corridors. **Pets:** Accepted. [SAVE] [≈] [📶] [☕]

AAA ▽▽▽ ▽▽▽ **The Westin Richmond** H 🐾

(804) 282-8444. **$144-$299.** 6631 W Broad St 23230. I-64 exit 183 eastbound; exit 183B westbound; in Reynolds Crossing. Int corridors. **Pets:** Medium, dogs only. Designated rooms, service with restrictions, supervision. [SAVE] [ECO] [⊞] [🅼] [≈] [✕] [≈] [✕] [📶] [☕]

ROANOKE

AAA ▽▽▽▽ **BEST WESTERN PLUS Inn at Valley View** H

(540) 362-2400. **$80-$180.** 5050 Valley View Blvd 24012. I-581 exit 3E, just e, then just s via shopping center exit. Int corridors.

Pets: Accepted. [SAVE] [🅼] [≈] [≈] [✕] [📶] [☕]

▽▽▽ **Comfort Inn Airport** H 🐾

(540) 527-2020. **$90-$180.** 5070 Valley View Blvd 24012. I-81 exit 143 to I-581 exit 3, e to Hershberger Rd. Int corridors. **Pets:** Other species. $25 one-time fee/room. Designated rooms, service with restrictions, supervision. [≈] [≈] [✕] [📶] [☕]

AAA ▽▽▽ **Days Inn** M

(540) 366-0341. **$70-$110.** 8118 Plantation Rd 24019. I-81 exit 146, just e on SR 115. Ext/int corridors. **Pets:** Medium. $15 one-time fee/room. Designated rooms, service with restrictions, supervision.

[SAVE] [≈] [≈] [📶] [☕]

▽ **Econo Lodge Civic Center** M

(540) 343-2413. **$56-$60.** 308 Orange Ave 24016. I-581 exit 4E, just e on US 460. Ext corridors. **Pets:** Other species. $10 daily fee/pet. Service with restrictions, supervision. [≈] [📶] [☕]

▽▽▽ **Fairfield Inn & Suites by Marriott Roanoke North** H

(540) 362-4200. **$99-$159.** 7944 Plantation Rd 24019. I-81 exit 146, just e. Int corridors. **Pets:** Accepted. [≈] [≈] [✕] [📶] [☕]

▽▽▽ **Holiday Inn Roanoke Valley View** H 🐾

(540) 362-4500. **$89-$149.** 3315 Ordway Dr 24017. I-581 exit 3W, just w to Ordway Dr, then 0.6 mi n via service road. Int corridors. **Pets:** $25 one-time fee/room, $10 daily fee/room. Designated rooms, service with restrictions, crate. [ECO] [⊞] [≈] [≈] [📶] [☕]

AAA ▽▽▽ ▽▽▽ **Holiday Inn Tanglewood/Roanoke** H

(540) 774-4400. **$99-$149, 15 day notice.** 4468 Starkey Rd 24018. I-581 exit US 220 (Franklin Rd/Salem), 0.8 mi s on SR 419 (Electric Rd). Int corridors. **Pets:** $35 one-time fee/room. Designated rooms, service with restrictions, crate. [SAVE] [ECO] [⊞] [≈] [≈] [📶] [☕]

AAA ▽▽▽▽ **Hyatt Place Roanoke Airport/Valley View Mall** H

(540) 366-4700. **$74-$199.** 5040 Valley View Blvd 24012. I-581 exit 3E, just e, then just s via shopping center exit. Int corridors.

Pets: Accepted. [SAVE] [🅼] [≈] [≈] [✕] [📶] [☕]

▽▽▽ **MainStay Suites Roanoke Airport** H

(540) 527-3030. **$99-$140.** 5080 Valley View Blvd 24012. I-581 exit 3E, just n. Int corridors. **Pets:** Large, dogs only. $40 deposit/pet. Service with restrictions, supervision. [≈] [📶] [☕]

AAA ▽▽▽ **Quality Inn/Tanglewood** M

(540) 989-4000. **$59-$159.** 3816 Franklin Rd SW 24014. I-581 exit US 220 (Franklin Rd/Salem), just n on US 220 business route, then w on Frontage Rd. Ext corridors. **Pets:** Accepted. [SAVE] [🅼] [≈] [📶] [☕]

▽▽▽▽ **Residence Inn by Marriott Roanoke Airport** H

(540) 265-1119. **$109-$239.** 3305 Ordway Dr NW 24017. I-581 exit 3W, just s. Int corridors. **Pets:** Accepted. [🅼] [≈] [≈] [📶] [☕]

AAA ▽▽▽▽ **Sheraton Roanoke Hotel & Conference Center** H

(540) 563-9300. **Call for rates.** 2801 Hershberger Rd 24017. I-581 exit 3W, just w to Ordway Dr, then just n via service road. Int corridors.

Pets: Accepted. [SAVE] [ECO] [⊞] [🅼] [≈] [✕] [≈] [✕] [📶] [☕]

AAA ▽ **Super 8** M

(540) 563-8888. **$58-$90, 3 day notice.** 6616 Thirlane Rd 24019. I-581 exit 25, s on SR 117 (Peters Creek Rd), then just w. Int corridors. **Pets:** Medium. $10 daily fee/pet. Designated rooms, service with restrictions, supervision. [SAVE] [≈] [📶] [☕]

ROCKY MOUNT

▽▽ **Comfort Inn-Rocky Mount** H

(540) 489-4000. **$72-$92.** 1730 N Main St 24151. 1.5 mi n on US 220 business route. Int corridors. **Pets:** Medium, other species. $25 one-time fee/pet. Service with restrictions, supervision. [≈] [≈] [📶] [☕]

▼▼▼▼ Holiday Inn Express Hotel & Suites �H

(540) 489-5001. **Call for rates.** 395 Old Franklin Tpke 24151. US 220 S, just e on SR 40. Int corridors. **Pets:** Accepted.
🛁 🤶 ✕ 🛏 🖃

SALEM

▼▼▼▼ Comfort Suites Inn at Ridgewood Farm �H

(540) 375-4800. **$75-$115.** 2898 Keagy Rd 24153. I-81 exit 141, 4.7 mi s on SR 419, then just w. Int corridors. **Pets:** Other species. $15 daily fee/pet. Designated rooms, service with restrictions, crate.
🛁 🤶 ✕ 🛏 🖃

 ▼▼▼ Days Inn Ⓜ

(540) 986-1000. **$65-$251.** 1535 E Main St 24153. I-81 exit 141, 2 mi s on SR 419, then just w on US 460. Ext/int corridors. **Pets:** Medium. $15 one-time fee/room. Designated rooms, service with restrictions, supervision. [SAVE] 🤶 🛏 🖃

▼▼▼ La Quinta Inn Roanoke Salem �H

(540) 562-2717. **$82-$314.** 140 Sheraton Dr 24153. I-81 exit 141, 0.5 mi se on SR 419. Int corridors. **Pets:** Large, other species. Service with restrictions. 🛁 🤶 ✕ 🛏 🖃

▼▼▼ Quality Inn Ⓜ

(540) 387-1600. **$65-$190.** 151 Wildwood Rd 24153. I-81 exit 137, 0.3 mi e on SR 112. Ext corridors. **Pets:** Accepted. 🛁 🤶 🛏 🖃

SANDSTON

▼▼▼▼ Candlewood Suites Richmond Airport �H

(804) 652-1888. **$79-$139.** 5400 Audubon Dr 23231. I-64 exit 197A (Sandston-RIC Airport), 1 mi w. Int corridors. **Pets:** Large, other species. $150 one-time fee/room. Service with restrictions, crate.
[ECO] [&M] 🤶 ✕ 🛏 🖃

▼▼▼▼ Holiday Inn Express �H

(804) 222-1499. **$99-$189.** 491 International Center Dr 23150. I-64 exit 197A (Sandston-RIC Airport), just s to Audubon Dr, then just n. Int corridors. **Pets:** Accepted. [&M] 🛁 🤶 🛏 🖃

SOUTH BOSTON

▼▼▼▼ The Berry Hill Resort and Conference Center �H

(434) 517-7000. **Call for rates.** 3105 River Rd S 24592. Jct US 58, 1.2 mi n on US 501, 0.6 mi w on Edmunds St, 2.3 mi nw on Berry Hill Rd, then 1 mi s. Ext/int corridors. **Pets:** Accepted.
[ｉↀ] 🛁 ⊠ 🤶 ✕ 🛏 🖃

▼▼▼▼ Holiday Inn Express �H

(434) 575-4000. **Call for rates.** 1074 Bill Tuck Hwy 24592. Jct US 501, just e on US 58. Int corridors. **Pets:** Accepted.
[&M] 🛁 🤶 🛏 🖃

SOUTH HILL

 ▼▼▼ Comfort Inn & Suites �H

(434) 447-2200. **$79-$109.** 250 Thompson St 23970. I-85 exit 12A, just n. Int corridors. **Pets:** Medium. $20 daily fee/pet. Service with restrictions. [SAVE] [&M] 🤶 🛏 🖃

▼▼▼▼ Fairfield Inn & Suites by Marriott South Hill I-85 �H

(434) 447-6800. **$94-$144.** 150 Arnold Dr 23970. I-85 exit 12A, just e on US 58. Int corridors. **Pets:** Other species. $75 one-time fee/room. Service with restrictions, crate. [ECO] [&M] 🛁 🤶 ✕ 🛏 🖃

 ▼▼▼ Quality Inn �H

(434) 447-2600. **$63-$70.** 918 E Atlantic St 23970. I-85 exit 12B, just w. Ext corridors. **Pets:** Accepted. [SAVE] 🤶 🛏 🖃

SPRINGFIELD *(Restaurants p. 644)*

▼▼▼ Comfort Inn Washington DC/Springfield �H

(703) 922-9000. **$89-$139.** 6560 Loisdale Ct 22150. I-95 exit 169A, just e on SR 644 E; jct I-395 and 495, 0.8 mi s. Int corridors.
Pets: Accepted. 🤶 🛏 🖃

▼▼▼ Hampton Inn Washington DC/Springfield �H

(703) 924-9444. **$89-$129.** 6550 Loisdale Ct 22150. I-95 exit 169A, just e on SR 644 E; jct I-395 and 495, 0.8 mi s. Int corridors.
Pets: Medium. $25 daily fee/room. Designated rooms, service with restrictions, supervision. [&M] 🛁 🤶 🛏 🖃

▼▼▼ Homewood Suites by Hilton Springfield �H

(703) 866-6045. **$189-$219.** 7010 Old Keene Mill Rd 22150. I-95 exit 169A, just nw of SR 644; jct I-395 and 495, 0.8 mi s. Int corridors.
Pets: Accepted. [&M] 🤶 ✕ 🛏 🖃

▼▼▼ Residence Inn by Marriott Springfield Old Keene Mill �H

(703) 644-0020. **$79-$263.** 6412 Backlick Rd 22150. I-95 exit 169A, just nw of SR 644; jct I-395 and 495, 0.8 mi s. Int corridors.
Pets: Accepted. [&M] 🛁 🤶 ✕ 🛏 🖃

▼▼▼ TownePlace Suites by Marriott Springfield �H

(703) 569-8060. **$80-$206.** 6245 Brandon Ave 22150. I-95 exit 169B, just nw of SR 644; jct I-395 and 495, 0.8 mi s. Int corridors.
Pets: Other species. $100 one-time fee/room. Service with restrictions, crate. [&M] 🤶 ✕ 🛏 🖃

STAFFORD *(Restaurants p. 644)*

 ▼▼▼ BEST WESTERN Aquia/Quantico Inn �H

(540) 659-0022. **$70-$99.** 2868 Jefferson Davis Hwy 22554. I-95 exit 143A, jct US 1 and SR 610. Ext corridors. **Pets:** Medium, other species. $20 daily fee/pet. Designated rooms, service with restrictions, crate. [SAVE] 🛁 🤶 🛏 🖃

 ▼▼▼ Country Inn By Carlson �H

(540) 659-4330. **$89-$179.** 153 Garrisonville Rd 22554. I-95 exit 143B, just w. Int corridors. **Pets:** Medium. $25 one-time fee/pet. Designated rooms, service with restrictions, supervision.
[SAVE] [&M] 🤶 ✕ 🛏 🖃

▼▼▼ Quality Inn & Suites �H 🐾

(540) 657-5566. **$85-$110.** 28 Greenspring Dr 22554. I-95 exit 143B, just w on Garrisonville Rd. Int corridors. **Pets:** Other species. $20 daily fee/pet. Service with restrictions, crate. 🤶 🛏 🖃

▼▼▼▼ Staybridge Suites Stafford/Quantico �H

(540) 720-2111. **Call for rates.** 2996 Jefferson Davis Hwy 22554. I-95 exit 143A, just n on US 1. Int corridors. **Pets:** Large. $75 one-time fee/pet. Service with restrictions, crate. [&M] 🛁 🤶 🛏 🖃

 ▼▼▼▼ TownePlace Suites by Marriott Quantico-Stafford �H 🐾

(540) 657-1990. **$99-$199.** 2772 Jefferson Davis Hwy 22554. I-95 exit 143A, just s on US 1. Int corridors. **Pets:** Other species. $15 daily fee/pet. Service with restrictions. [SAVE] [&M] 🛁 🤶 🛏 🖃

STAUNTON

 ▼▼▼ BEST WESTERN Staunton Inn �H 🐾

(540) 885-1112. **$84-$145.** 92 Rowe Rd 24401. I-81 exit 222, just e on US 250. Int corridors. **Pets:** Large, other species. Service with restrictions, supervision. [SAVE] [ECO] 🛁 🤶 ✕ 🛏 🖃

 ▼▼▼ Comfort Inn �H

(540) 886-5000. **$90-$140.** 1302 Richmond Ave 24401. I-81 exit 222, just w on US 250. Int corridors. **Pets:** Other species. $10 daily fee/pet. Service with restrictions, supervision. [SAVE] 🛁 🤶 🛏 🖃

 ▼▼▼▼ Econo Lodge Staunton Ⓜ

(540) 885-5158. **$72-$99.** 1031 Richmond Ave 24401. I-81 exit 222, 0.7 mi w on US 250. Ext/int corridors. **Pets:** Accepted.
[SAVE] 🤶 ✕ 🛏 🖃

 ▼▼▼▼ Holiday Inn Staunton Conference Center �H

(540) 248-6020. **Call for rates.** 152 Fairway Ln 24401. I-81 exit 225, 0.3 mi w on SR 262. Int corridors. **Pets:** Accepted.
[SAVE] [ｉↀ] 🛁 🤶 ✕ 🛏 🖃

◆◆ **Red Roof Inn-Staunton** Ⓜ
(540) 885-3117. **$69-$110.** 42 Sangers Ln 24401. I-81 exit 222, just e on US 250. Ext corridors. **Pets:** Large, other species. Service with restrictions, supervision. 🛜 🛎 💻

◆◆ **Sleep Inn** Ⓗ ❀
(540) 887-6500. **$84-$145.** 222 Jefferson Hwy 24401. I-81 exit 222, just e on US 250. Int corridors. **Pets:** Small, other species. Designated rooms, service with restrictions, crate. 🛜 ✕ 🛎 💻

⟐⟐ ◆◆◆◆ **Stonewall Jackson Hotel & Conference Center** Ⓗ
(540) 885-4848. **$109-$249.** 24 S Market St 24401. Between Beverley and Johnson sts; downtown. Int corridors. **Pets:** Accepted.
[SAVE] [ECO] 🍴 ➜ ✕ 🛜 ✕ 💻

STEPHENS CITY
⟐⟐ ◆◆ **Comfort Inn-Stephens City** Ⓗ
(540) 869-6500. **$71-$113.** 167 Town Run Ln 22655. I-81 exit 307, just se. Int corridors. **Pets:** Accepted. [SAVE] ➜ 🛜 🛎 💻

STERLING
⟐⟐ ◆◆ **BEST WESTERN Dulles Airport Inn** Ⓜ
(703) 471-8300. **$69-$139.** 45440 Holiday Dr 20166. 1.7 mi n on SR 28 from jct SR 267 (Dulles Toll Rd), just e on SR 846, just s on Shaw Rd. Ext corridors. **Pets:** Accepted. [SAVE] [ECO] 🛜 🛎 💻

◆◆ **Candlewood Suites Washington Dulles/Sterling** Ⓗ
(703) 674-2288. **Call for rates.** 45520 Severn Way 20166. 1.3 mi s on SR 28 from jct SR 7, 0.3 mi e on Nokes Blvd, 0.4 mi s on Atlantic Blvd. Int corridors. **Pets:** Accepted. ♿ 🛜 ✕ 🛎 💻

◆◆◆◆ **Hampton Inn-Dulles/Cascades** Ⓗ
(703) 450-9595. **$139-$169.** 46331 McClellan Way 20165. 1.7 mi e on SR 7 from jct SR 28, 0.5 mi n on SR 1794 (Cascades Pkwy) to Pali-sade Pkwy, just e, then 0.4 mi s on Whitfield Pl. Int corridors. **Pets:** Accepted. [ECO] ♿ ➜ 🛜 ✕ 🛎 💻

◆◆◆◆ **Holiday Inn Washington Dulles International Airport** Ⓗ
(703) 471-7411. **Call for rates.** 45425 Holiday Dr 20166. 1.7 mi n on SR 28 from jct SR 267 (Dulles Toll Rd), just e on SR 846, just s on Shaw Rd. Int corridors. **Pets:** Accepted.
[ECO] 🍴 ♿ ➜ ✕ 🛜 🛎 💻

⟐⟐ ◆◆◆◆ **HYATT house Sterling/Dulles Airport-North** Ⓗ
(703) 435-9002. **$74-$199.** 45520 Dulles Plaza 20166. 1 mi n on SR 28 from jct SR 267 (Dulles Toll Rd), just e on CR 606. Int corridors. **Pets:** Accepted. [SAVE] ♿ ➜ 🛜 ✕ 🛎 💻

⟐⟐ ◆◆◆◆ **Hyatt Place Sterling/Dulles Airport-North** Ⓗ
(703) 444-3909. **$69-$199.** 21481 Ridgetop Cir 20166. 1.3 mi e on SR 7 from jct SR 28. Int corridors. **Pets:** Accepted.
[SAVE] ♿ ➜ 🛜 ✕ 🛎 💻

⟐⟐ ◆◆◆◆ **Residence Inn by Marriott Dulles Airport @ Dulles 28 Centre** Ⓗ
(703) 421-2000. **$209-$250.** 45250 Monterey Pl 20166. SR 28 exit CR 625 (Waxpool Rd), just w, just n on Pacific Blvd, then just e on Com-mercial Dr. Int corridors. **Pets:** Accepted.
[SAVE] ♿ ➜ 🛜 ✕ 🛎 💻

◆◆ **Suburban Extended Stay Hotel Washington-Dulles/Sterling** Ⓗ
(703) 674-2299. **$79-$119.** 45510 E Severn Way 20166. 1.3 mi s on SR 28 from jct SR 7, 0.3 mi e on Nokes Blvd, then 0.4 mi s on Atlantic Blvd. Int corridors. **Pets:** $75 one-time fee/room. Service with restric-tions. 🛜 🛎 💻

◆◆ **TownePlace Suites by Marriott at Dulles Airport** Ⓗ
(703) 707-2017. **$79-$184.** 22744 Holiday Park Dr 20166. 1.7 mi n on SR 28 from jct SR 267 (Dulles Toll Rd), just e on SR 846, just s on Shaw Rd. Int corridors. **Pets:** Accepted. [ECO] 🛜 ✕ 🛎 💻

◆◆ **TownePlace Suites by Marriott Dulles North** Ⓗ
(703) 421-1090. **Call for rates.** 21123 Whitfield Pl 20165. 1.7 mi e on SR 7 from jct SR 28, 0.5 mi n on SR 1794 (Cascades Pkwy) to Pali-sades Pkwy, just e, then just s. Int corridors. **Pets:** Accepted.
➜ 🛜 ✕ 🛎 💻

STONY CREEK
◆◆◆ **Hampton Inn-Stony Creek** Ⓗ
(434) 246-5500. **$99-$159.** 10476 Blue Star Hwy 23882. I-95 exit 33, 0.3 mi s on SR 301. Int corridors. **Pets:** Accepted.
♿ ➜ 🛜 ✕ 🛎 💻

◆◆◆ **Sleep Inn & Suites** Ⓗ
(434) 246-5100. **$109-$169.** 11019 Blue Star Hwy 23882. I-95 exit 33, 0.3 mi s on SR 301. Int corridors. **Pets:** Accepted. ➜ 🛜 🛎 💻

STRASBURG
◆◆◆ **Hotel Strasburg** Ⓒ
(540) 465-9191. **Call for rates.** 213 S Holliday St 22657. I-81 exit 298, 2.2 mi s on US 11, then just s. Int corridors. **Pets:** Accepted. 🍴 🛜

◆◆ **Ramada** Ⓗ
(540) 465-2444. **$75-$139.** 21 Signal Knob Dr 22657. I-81 exit 298, just e. Int corridors. **Pets:** Small. $10 daily fee/pet. Designated rooms, ser-vice with restrictions, crate. 🍴 ➜ ✕ 🛜 🛎 💻

SUFFOLK
◆◆◆ **TownePlace Suites by Marriott** Ⓗ
(757) 483-5177. **$89-$169.** 8050 Harbour View Blvd 23435. I-664 exit 8A (College Dr), just n. Int corridors. **Pets:** Accepted.
[ECO] ♿ ➜ 🛜 ✕ 🛎 💻

TAPPAHANNOCK
◆◆◆ **The Essex Inn** 🅱🅱
(804) 443-9900. **$175-$205, 7 day notice.** 203 Duke St 22560. 0.3 mi s on US 17, then just e. Ext/int corridors. **Pets:** Accepted.
[ECO] 🛜 ✕ 🛎 💻

◆ **Super 8** Ⓜ
(804) 443-3888. **$63-$86.** 1800 Tappahannock Blvd 22560. 1.2 mi s on US 17/360. Int corridors. **Pets:** Accepted. ♿ 🛜 🛎 💻

TROUTVILLE
◆◆ **Comfort Inn** Ⓗ
(540) 992-5600. **$109-$159.** 2545 Lee Hwy S 24175. I-81 exit 150A, just s on US 11. Int corridors. **Pets:** Medium, other species. $25 one-time fee/room. Service with restrictions, supervision.
➜ 🛜 🛎 💻

◆◆ **Quality Inn** Ⓗ
(540) 992-5335. **$64-$94.** 3139 Lee Hwy S 24175. I-81 exit 150A, just ne on US 11. Ext/int corridors. **Pets:** Medium. $25 one-time fee/room. Service with restrictions, crate. ➜ 🛜 🛎 💻

TYSONS CORNER
⟐⟐ ◆◆ **Comfort Inn Tysons Corner** Ⓜ
(703) 448-8020. **$89-$119.** 1587 Spring Hill Rd 22182. I-495 exit 47A, 1.8 mi w on SR 7, then just s; just e of jct SR 267 (Dulles Toll Rd). Ext corridors. **Pets:** Small. $25 daily fee/pet. Service with restrictions, super-vision. [SAVE] ➜ 🛜 🛎 💻

◆◆◆ **Crowne Plaza Tysons Corner** Ⓗ ❀
(703) 893-2100. **Call for rates.** 1960 Chain Bridge Rd 22102. I-495 exit 46A, 0.5 mi s on SR 123, just nw on International Dr, then just sw on Greensboro Dr. Int corridors. **Pets:** Medium, other species. $75 one-time fee/room. Designated rooms, service with restrictions, crate.
[ECO] 🍴 ♿ ➜ 🛜 ✕ 🛎 💻

▼▼ **Extended Stay America-Washington, DC-Tysons Corner** �H

(703) 356-6300. **Call for rates.** 8201 Old Courthouse Rd 22182. I-495 exit 47A, 0.6 mi w on SR 7, then just s on Gallows Rd. Int corridors. **Pets:** Other species. $25 daily fee/pet. Service with restrictions, supervision. 🅵ᴹ 📶

AAA ▼▼▼▼ **Residence Inn by Marriott-Tysons Corner** �H

(703) 893-0120. **$75-$399.** 8616 Westwood Center Dr 22182. I-495 exit 47A, 1.9 mi w on SR 7, then just s. Ext corridors. **Pets:** $125 one-time fee/room. Service with restrictions. 🆂🅰🆅🅴 🔁 📶 ✕ 🔋 💻

▼▼▼ **Residence Inn by Marriott Tysons Corner Mall** �H

(703) 917-0800. **$129-$241.** 8400 Old Courthouse Rd 22182. I-495 exit 46A, 1.1 mi s on SR 123; 0.3 mi s of jct SR 7 and 123. Int corridors. **Pets:** Accepted. 🅵ᴹ 🔁 📶 ✕ 🔋 💻

AAA ▼▼▼▼ **The Ritz-Carlton, Tysons Corner** �H

(703) 506-4300. **Call for rates.** 1700 Tysons Blvd 22102. I-495 exit 46A, 0.3 mi sw on SR 123, then just nw; I-495 Express Lanes exit Jones Branch Dr. Int corridors. **Pets:** Accepted. 🆂🅰🆅🅴 🄴🄲🄾 🔌 🍽 🅵ᴹ 🔁 ✕ 💻

AAA ▼▼▼▼ **Sheraton Tysons Hotel** �H

(703) 448-1234. **$89-$409.** 8661 Leesburg Pike 22182. SR 7, just e of jct SR 267 (Dulles Toll Rd). Int corridors. **Pets:** Accepted. 🆂🅰🆅🅴 🄴🄲🄾 🔌 🍽 🅵ᴹ 🔁 ✕ 💻

VIRGINIA BEACH (Restaurants p. 644)

▼▼▼ **Candlewood Suites** �H 🐾

(757) 213-1500. **$59-$249.** 4437 Bonney Rd 23462. I-264 exit 17B (Independence Blvd/Pembroke area), just n to Bonney Rd, then just e. Int corridors. **Pets:** Medium, other species. $75 one-time fee/pet. Service with restrictions, crate. 🄴🄲🄾 🅵ᴹ 📶 🔋 💻

AAA ▼▼▼▼ **Clarion Inn & Suites** �H

(757) 961-8190. **$59-$249.** 2604 Atlantic Ave 23451. I-264 0.5 mi n of terminus; jct Atlantic Ave and 26th St. Int corridors. **Pets:** Small, dogs only. $15 daily fee/room. Designated rooms, service with restrictions, crate. 🆂🅰🆅🅴 🅵ᴹ 🔁 💻

AAA ▼▼▼▼ **Comfort Suites at the Beach** �H

(757) 491-2400. **$109-$329.** 2321 Atlantic Ave 23451. I-264 terminus, just n. Ext corridors. **Pets:** Accepted. 🆂🅰🆅🅴 🅵ᴹ 🔁 📶 ✕ 🔋

AAA ▼▼▼▼ **DoubleTree by Hilton Hotel Virginia Beach** �H

(757) 422-8900. **$69-$269.** 1900 Pavilion Dr 23451. I-264 exit 22 (Birdneck Rd), just e. Int corridors. **Pets:** Accepted. 🆂🅰🆅🅴 🄴🄲🄾 🍽 🔁 📶 ✕ 🔋 💻

AAA ▼▼▼▼ **The Founders Inn and Spa** �H

(757) 424-5511. **$99-$259, 3 day notice.** 5641 Indian River Rd 23464. I-64 exit 286B, just e; on campus of Christian Broadcasting Network & Regent University. Int corridors. **Pets:** Accepted. 🆂🅰🆅🅴 🄴🄲🄾 🍽 🔁 ✕ 📶 ✕ 🔋 💻

▼▼▼ **Homewood Suites by Hilton** �H

(757) 552-0080. **$129-$399.** 5733 Cleveland St 23462. I-264 exit 15 (Newtown Rd N), just n. Int corridors. **Pets:** Accepted. 🄴🄲🄾 🅵ᴹ 🔁 📶 🔋 💻

▼▼▼ **La Quinta Inn & Suites Virginia Beach** �H

(757) 428-2203. **$72-$375.** 2800 Pacific Ave 23451. I-264 0.5 mi n of terminus. Int corridors. **Pets:** Large, other species. Service with restrictions. 🅵ᴹ 🔁 📶 🔋 💻

▼▼ **La Quinta Inn Norfolk/Town Center** �H

(757) 497-6620. **$65-$209.** 192 Newtown Rd 23462. I-264 exit 284B to I-264 exit Newtown Rd S. Int corridors. **Pets:** Large, other species. Service with restrictions. 🅵ᴹ 🔁 📶 🔋 💻

AAA ▼▼▼ **Quality Inn** Ⓜ

(757) 460-5566. **$69-$139.** 5189 Shore Dr 23455. Just w of Independence Blvd (SR 225); at Gate 5 of the Naval Amphibious Base. Ext corridors. **Pets:** Small, other species. $25 one-time fee/pet. Designated rooms, service with restrictions, supervision. 🆂🅰🆅🅴 🔁 📶 🔋 💻

▼▼▼▼ **Residence Inn by Marriott Virginia Beach Oceanfront** �H 🐾

(757) 425-1141. **$129-$409, 3 day notice.** 3217 Atlantic Ave 23451. I-264 1.5 mi n of terminus; jct 33rd St. Int corridors. **Pets:** Other species. $100 one-time fee/room. Service with restrictions. 🄴🄲🄾 🅵ᴹ 🔁 📶 ✕ 🔋 💻

AAA ▼▼▼▼ **Sheraton Virginia Beach Oceanfront Hotel** �H 🐾

(757) 425-9000. **$89-$275.** 3501 Atlantic Ave 23451. I-264 1 mi n of terminus; jct 36th St. Int corridors. **Pets:** Medium, dogs only. Designated rooms, service with restrictions, crate. 🆂🅰🆅🅴 🄴🄲🄾 🍽 🅵ᴹ 🔁 ✕ 📶 ✕ 🔋 💻

AAA ▼▼▼ **TownePlace Suites by Marriott** �H 🐾

(757) 490-9367. **$99-$189.** 5757 Cleveland St 23462. I-64 exit 284B to I-264 exit Newtown Rd N. Int corridors. **Pets:** Medium. $100 one-time fee/room. Service with restrictions, supervision. 🆂🅰🆅🅴 🄴🄲🄾 🅵ᴹ 🔁 📶 ✕ 🔋 💻

AAA ▼▼▼▼ **The Westin Virginia Beach Town Center** �H 🐾

(757) 557-0550. **$119-$369.** 4535 Commerce St 23462. I-264 exit 17B (Independence Blvd), just n, then just e. Int corridors. **Pets:** Medium, dogs only. Service with restrictions, supervision. 🆂🅰🆅🅴 🄴🄲🄾 🍽 🔁 📶 ✕ 🔋 💻

▼▼▼ **Wyndham Virginia Beach Oceanfront** �H

(757) 428-7025. **$69-$299, 3 day notice.** 5700 Atlantic Ave 23451. I-264 2.2 mi n of terminus. Int corridors. **Pets:** Accepted. 🄴🄲🄾 🍽 🅵ᴹ 🔁 ✕ 📶 ✕ 🔋 💻

WARRENTON (Restaurants p. 644)

▼▼▼ **Holiday Inn Express Hotel & Suites** �H

(540) 341-3461. **Call for rates.** 410 Holiday Ct 20186. US 15/29 and 17 exit Meetze Rd (SR 643), just w, then 0.8 mi n on Walker Rd. Int corridors. **Pets:** $35 daily fee/pet. Designated rooms, service with restrictions, supervision. 🅵ᴹ 🔁 📶 ✕ 🔋 💻

WASHINGTON

AAA ▼▼▼▼ **Middleton Inn** 🅱🅱

(540) 675-2020. **$325-$575, 14 day notice.** 176 Main St 22747. 0.5 mi w on US 211 business route. Ext/int corridors. **Pets:** Accepted. 🆂🅰🆅🅴 📶 ✕ 🔋 💻

WAYNESBORO

AAA ▼▼▼▼ **BEST WESTERN PLUS Waynesboro Inn & Suites Conference Center** �H

(540) 942-1100. **$109-$199.** 109 Apple Tree Ln 22980. I-64 exit 94, just n. Int corridors. **Pets:** Accepted. 🆂🅰🆅🅴 🄴🄲🄾 🔁 📶 ✕ 🔋 💻

▼▼▼ **Comfort Inn Waynesboro** �H

(540) 932-3060. **$94-$116.** 15 Windigrove Dr 22980. I-64 exit 94, 0.5 mi n on US 340, then just e. Int corridors. **Pets:** Accepted. 🔁 📶 🔋 💻

AAA ▼▼ **Days Inn Waynesboro** Ⓜ

(540) 943-1101. **$70-$105.** 2060 Rosser Ave 22980. I-64 exit 94, 0.5 mi n on US 340. Ext corridors. **Pets:** Other species. $10 one-time fee/room. Service with restrictions, supervision. 🆂🅰🆅🅴 🔁 📶 🔋 💻

▼▼▼ **The Iris Inn & Cabins** 🅱🅱

(540) 943-1991. **$149-$339, 7 day notice.** 191 Chinquapin Dr 22980. I-64 exit 96, just s on SR 624, then just e. Ext/int corridors. **Pets:** Accepted. 🄴🄲🄾 📶 ✕ 🐾 🔋 💻

AAA ▽▽▽ **Quality Inn Waynesboro** M
(540) 942-1171. **$60-$120.** 640 W Broad St 22980. I-64 exit 96, 3 mi w on SR 624; jct US 250 and 340. Ext/int corridors. **Pets:** Accepted.
SAVE ⌑ 🛜 🍴 💻

▽▽▽ **Residence Inn by Marriott Waynesboro** H
(540) 943-7426. **$139-$279.** 44 Windigrove Dr 22980. I-64 exit 94, 0.5 mi n on US 340, then just e. Int corridors. **Pets:** Medium. $100 one-time fee/room. Service with restrictions, supervision.
⌑ 🛜 ✖ 🍴 💻

▽▽▽ **Super 8 Waynesboro** M
(540) 943-3888. **$54-$95.** 2045 Rosser Ave 22980. I-64 exit 94, n on US 340 to Lew Dewitt Blvd, then just w to Apple Tree Ln. Int corridors. **Pets:** $10 daily fee/pet. Designated rooms, service with restrictions, supervision. 🛜 🍴 💻

WILLIAMSBURG *(Restaurants p. 644)*

AAA ▽▽▽▽ **Clarion Hotel Historic District** H ❁
(757) 229-4100. **$59-$129.** 351 York St 23185. US 60 E, 0.3 mi se of jct SR 5 and 31. Int corridors. **Pets:** Other species. $25 one-time fee/pet. Designated rooms, service with restrictions, crate.
SAVE 🍴 ♿ ⌑ 🛜 ✖ 🍴 💻

AAA ▽▽▽ **Fort Magruder Hotel & Conference Center** H
(757) 220-2250. **Call for rates.** 6945 Pocahontas Tr 23185. US 60, 0.8 mi e of jct SR 5 and 31. Int corridors. **Pets:** Accepted.
SAVE ECO 🍴 ⌑ ✖ 🛜 ✖ 🍴 💻

▽▽ **Holiday Inn Patriot-Williamsburg** H
(757) 565-2600. **$104-$149.** 3032 Richmond Rd 23185. I-64 exit 234 (SR 199 E) to US 60, 2.5 mi e. Int corridors. **Pets:** Small. $25 daily fee/room. Designated rooms, service with restrictions, supervision.
🍴 ⌑ 🛜 🍴 💻

▽▽ **Quality Inn & Suites** H
(757) 645-3636. **$59-$109.** 5351 Richmond Rd 23188. 1.6 mi w from jct Bypass Rd. Ext/int corridors. **Pets:** Accepted.
🍴 ♿ ⌑ 🛜 🍴 💻

AAA ▽▽▽ **Residence Inn by Marriott Williamsburg** H
(757) 941-2000. **$79-$189.** 1648 Richmond Rd 23185. US 60, just w of jct Bypass Rd. Int corridors. **Pets:** Accepted.
SAVE ♿ ⌑ 🛜 ✖ 🍴 💻

AAA ▽▽▽ **Super 8-Williamsburg/Historic Area** M
(757) 229-0500. **$40-$95.** 304 2nd St 23185. I-64 exit 242 (SR 199 W), 0.6 mi w to SR 143, 1.6 mi w to SR 162, then just w. Ext corridors. **Pets:** Medium, dogs only. $20 daily fee/pet. No service, supervision.
SAVE ⌑ 🛜 🍴 💻

AAA ▽▽▽▽ **Westgate Historic Williamsburg** H
(757) 229-6220. **Call for rates.** 1324 Richmond Rd 23185. Jct Richmond and Bypass rds, just e. Ext/int corridors. **Pets:** Large. $100 deposit/room, $170 one-time fee/room. Designated rooms, service with restrictions. SAVE ECO ♿ ⌑ ✖ 🛜 ✖ 🍴 💻

▽▽▽▽ **Williamsburg Inn** H
(757) 220-7978. **$335-$799, 3 day notice.** 136 E Francis St 23185. In Colonial Williamsburg restored area. Int corridors. **Pets:** Accepted.
🍴 ♿ ⌑ ✖ 🛜 ✖

WINCHESTER

AAA ▽▽▽▽ **Aloft Winchester** H
(540) 678-8899. **$69-$135.** 1055 Millwood Pike 22602. I-81 exit 313, just e. Int corridors. **Pets:** Accepted.
SAVE ECO ⌑ 🛜 ✖ 🍴 💻

AAA ▽▽▽ **BEST WESTERN Lee-Jackson Inn & Conference Center** H
(540) 662-4154. **$74.** 711 Millwood Ave 22601. I-81 exit 313B, just nw on US 17/50/522. Ext corridors. **Pets:** Other species. $5 daily fee/pet. Designated rooms, service with restrictions, crate.
SAVE 🍴 ⌑ 🛜 🍴 💻

▽▽▽ **Candlewood Suites** H
(540) 667-8323. **Call for rates.** 1135 Millwood Pike 22602. I-81 exit 313 northbound; exit 313A southbound, just se. Int corridors.
Pets: Accepted. ECO 🛜 🍴 💻

▽▽▽ **Country Inn & Suites By Carlson** H
(540) 869-7657. **Call for rates.** 141 Kernstown Commons Blvd 22602. I-81 exit 310, just w. Int corridors. **Pets:** Accepted.
⌑ 🛜 ✖ 🍴 💻

AAA ▽▽▽ **Econo Lodge North** M
(540) 662-4700. **$63-$87.** 1593 Martinsburg Pike 22603. I-81 exit 317, 0.3 mi sw on US 11. Int corridors. **Pets:** Accepted. SAVE 🛜 🍴 💻

AAA ▽▽▽ **Red Roof Inn - Winchester** M
(540) 667-5000. **$50-$80.** 991 Millwood Pike 22602. I-81 exit 313 northbound; exit 313A southbound, just se on US 50/17. Ext corridors.
Pets: Large, other species. Service with restrictions, supervision.
SAVE 🛜 🍴

▽▽▽ **TownePlace Suites by Marriott Winchester** H
(540) 722-2722. **$109-$120.** 170 Getty Ln 22602. I-81 exit 315, just e. Int corridors. **Pets:** Medium, other species. $75 one-time fee/room. Service with restrictions, crate. ⌑ 🛜 ✖ 🍴 💻

WOODBRIDGE

▽▽▽ **Residence Inn by Marriott Potomac Mills** H
(703) 490-4020. **$139-$193.** 14301 Crossing Pl 22192. I-95 exit 158B (Prince William Pkwy), 0.5 mi sw. Int corridors. **Pets:** Accepted.
♿ ⌑ 🛜 ✖ 🍴 💻

WOODSTOCK

AAA ▽▽▽▽ **Comfort Inn Woodstock** H
(540) 459-7600. **$89-$169.** 1011 Motel Dr 22664. I-81 exit 283, just e. Int corridors. **Pets:** Other species. $10 daily fee/pet. Service with restrictions, supervision. SAVE ⌑ 🛜 🍴 💻

WYTHEVILLE

AAA ▽▽▽ **BEST WESTERN Wytheville Inn** H
(276) 228-7300. **$75-$109.** 355 Nye Rd 24382. I-77 exit 41, just e. Int corridors. **Pets:** Accepted. SAVE ⌑ 🛜 ✖ 🍴 💻

▽▽▽ **Comfort Inn** H
(276) 637-4281. **$100-$200.** 2594 E Lee Hwy 24382. I-77/81 exit 80, just w. Int corridors. **Pets:** Accepted. ♿ ⌑ 🛜 🍴 💻

▽▽ **Days Inn** M
(276) 228-5500. **$58-$69.** 150 Malin Dr 24382. I-77/81 exit 73, just w. Ext corridors. **Pets:** Medium, other species. $15 daily fee/room. Service with restrictions, supervision. 🛜 🍴 💻

▽▽▽ **La Quinta Inn Wytheville** H
(276) 228-7400. **$87-$217.** 1800 E Main 24382. I-77/81 exit 73, just w. Int corridors. **Pets:** Large, other species. Service with restrictions.
⌑ 🛜 ✖ 🍴 💻

▽▽▽ **Red Roof Inn & Suites- Wytheville** M
(276) 223-1700. **$50-$149.** 1900 E Main St 24382. I-77/81 exit 73, just w. Ext corridors. **Pets:** Large, other species. Service with restrictions, supervision. ⌑ 🛜 🍴 💻

YORKTOWN

▽▽▽ **Candlewood Suites-Yorktown** H
(757) 952-1120. **Call for rates.** 329 Commonwealth Dr 23693. I-64 exit 256B, just n, then just e. Int corridors. **Pets:** Accepted.
♿ ⌑ 🛜 🍴 💻

▼▼▼ Comfort Inn 🅷

(757) 283-1111. **Call for rates.** 4531 George Washington Memorial Hwy 23692. I-64 exit 256B, 0.8 mi ne on Victory Blvd (SR 171), then 2.4 mi n on US 17. Int corridors. **Pets:** Accepted. 🐾 🛜 🛢 💻

▼▼▼▼ Staybridge Suites 🅷

(757) 251-6644. **Call for rates.** 401 Commonwealth Dr 23693. I-64 exit 256B, just n, then just e. Int corridors. **Pets:** Medium. $75 one-time fee/pet. Designated rooms, service with restrictions, crate.

🅴🅲🅾 ♿ᴹ 🐾 🛜 🛢 💻

⟨ᴬᴬᴬ⟩ ▼▼▼ TownePlace Suites by Marriott 🅷

(757) 874-8884. **$99-$219.** 200 Cybernetics Way 23693. I-64 exit 256B, e to Kiln Creek Pkwy. Int corridors. **Pets:** Accepted.

🆂🅰🆅🅴 🅴🅲🅾 ♿ᴹ 🐾 🛜 ✕ 🛢 💻

WASHINGTON

AIRWAY HEIGHTS

▼▼ Days Inn & Suites 🅷

(509) 244-0222. **$78-$148.** 1215 S Garfield Rd 99001. I-90/US 2 exit 277 to US 2, 4 mi w. Int corridors. **Pets:** Dogs only. $10 daily fee/pet. Designated rooms, no service, supervision. ♿ᴹ 🛜 🛢 💻

ANACORTES

▼▼ Anacortes Ship Harbor Inn 🅼

(360) 293-5177. **$89-$219, 3 day notice.** 5316 Ferry Terminal Rd 98221. 0.3 mi s of ferry landing. Ext corridors. **Pets:** Dogs only. $30 one-time fee/pet. Designated rooms, service with restrictions, supervision. 🛜 ✕ 🅰 🛢 💻

▼▼ Fidalgo Country Inn 🅷

(360) 293-3494. **$89-$149, 3 day notice.** 7645 SR 20 98221. Jct Fidalgo Bay Rd. Ext/int corridors. **Pets:** $20 one-time fee/pet. Designated rooms, service with restrictions, supervision.

♿ᴹ 🐾 🛜 🛢 💻

▼▼ Islands Inn 🅼

(360) 293-4644. **$69-$159.** 3401 Commercial Ave 98221. Just s of downtown. Ext corridors. **Pets:** Dogs only. $10 daily fee/pet. Designated rooms, service with restrictions, supervision. 🍽 🐾 🛜 🛢 💻

⟨ᴬᴬᴬ⟩ ▼▼▼ Majestic Inn & Spa 🅷

(360) 299-1400. **$119-$399, 3 day notice.** 419 Commercial Ave 98221. At 5th Ave; downtown. Int corridors. **Pets:** Small, dogs only. $50 one-time fee/pet. Designated rooms, service with restrictions, supervision.

🆂🅰🆅🅴 🍽 🛜 ✕ 🛢 💻

ARLINGTON

⟨ᴬᴬᴬ⟩ ▼▼▼ BEST WESTERN PLUS
Arlington/Marysville 🅷

(360) 363-4321. **$119-$189.** 3721 172nd St NE 98223. I-5 exit 206, 0.4 mi e. Int corridors. **Pets:** Accepted. 🆂🅰🆅🅴 ♿ᴹ 🛜 ✕ 🛢 💻

AUBURN

▼▼ Auburn GuestHouse Inn 🅷

(253) 735-9600. **$69-$139.** 9 14th St NW 98001. SR 167 exit 15th St NW, 0.8 mi e, just s on A St NE, then just w. Int corridors. **Pets:** Accepted. 🛜 ✕ 🛢 💻

⟨ᴬᴬᴬ⟩ ▼▼▼ BEST WESTERN PLUS Peppertree Auburn Inn 🅷 ✿

(253) 887-7600. **$99-$599.** 401 8th St SW 98001. SR 18 exit C St, just s, then just w. Int corridors. **Pets:** Dogs only. Designated rooms, service with restrictions, supervision. 🆂🅰🆅🅴 🐾 ✕ 🛜 ✕ 🛢 💻

▼▼ Comfort Inn-Auburn 🅷

(253) 333-8888. **$79-$169.** 1 16th St NE 98002. SR 167 exit 15th St NW, 0.8 mi e, then just n on A St NE. Int corridors. **Pets:** Accepted.

🐾 🛜 🛢 💻

ZION CROSSROADS

⟨ᴬᴬᴬ⟩ ▼▼▼ BEST WESTERN PLUS Crossroads Inn & Suites 🅷 ✿

(540) 832-1700. **$220-$240, 90 day notice.** 135 Wood Ridge Terr 22942. I-64 exit 136, just n. Int corridors. **Pets:** Other species. $20 daily fee/room. Designated rooms, service with restrictions, crate.

🆂🅰🆅🅴 🅴🅲🅾 ♿ᴹ 🐾 🛜 ✕ 🛢 💻

▼▼▼▼ La Quinta Inn & Suites Auburn 🅷

(253) 804-9999. **$105-$334.** 225 6th St SE 98002. SR 18 exit Auburn Way N, just sw. Int corridors. **Pets:** Large, other species. Service with restrictions. 🐾 🛜 ✕ 🛢 💻

BAINBRIDGE ISLAND

⟨ᴬᴬᴬ⟩ ▼▼▼ BEST WESTERN PLUS Bainbridge Island Suites 🅷 ✿

(206) 855-9666. **$140-$180.** 350 NE High School Rd 98110. 0.8 mi n of ferry dock on SR 305, just w. Int corridors. **Pets:** Medium, dogs only. $20 daily fee/pet. Designated rooms, service with restrictions, supervision. 🆂🅰🆅🅴 🛜 ✕ 🛢 💻

BELLEVUE (Restaurants p. 644)

▼▼▼ Embassy Suites Hotel Bellevue 🅷

(425) 644-2500. **$132-$246.** 3225 158th Ave SE 98008. I-90 exit 11 westbound; exit 11A (SE Eastgate Way/156th Ave SE) eastbound, just ne. Int corridors. **Pets:** Accepted. 🍽 ♿ᴹ 🐾 ✕ 🔊 🛢 💻

▼▼ Extended Stay
America-Seattle-Bellevue-Downtown 🅷

(425) 453-8186. **Call for rates.** 11400 Main St 98004. I-405 exit 13A, just se. Int corridors. **Pets:** Other species. $25 daily fee/pet. Service with restrictions, supervision. ♿ᴹ 🛜 ✕ 🛢 💻

⟨ᴬᴬᴬ⟩ ▼▼▼▼ Fairfield Inn & Suites by Marriott Seattle Bellevue/Redmond 🅷

(425) 869-6548. **$99-$285.** 14595 NE 29th Pl 98007. I-405 exit 14 (SR 520), 2.3 mi e to 148th Ave NE (north exit), then just nw. Int corridors. **Pets:** $50 one-time fee/room. Designated rooms, service with restrictions, supervision. 🆂🅰🆅🅴 ♿ᴹ 🛜 ✕ 🛢 💻

▼▼▼▼ Hotel Bellevue 🅷

(425) 454-4424. **$225-$2150.** 11200 SE 6th St 98004. I-405 exit 12, 0.4 mi nw. Int corridors. **Pets:** Accepted.

🆂🅰🆅🅴 🍽 ♿ᴹ 🐾 ✕ 🛜 ✕

⟨ᴬᴬᴬ⟩ ▼▼▼▼ HYATT house Seattle/Bellevue 🅷

(425) 747-2705. **$99-$299.** 3244 139th Ave SE 98005. I-90 exit 11 westbound, 0.9 mi w, just n; exit 10B eastbound, just n, 0.7 mi e, then just n. Int corridors. **Pets:** Accepted.

🆂🅰🆅🅴 🍽 ♿ᴹ 🐾 🛜 ✕ 🛢 💻

⟨ᴬᴬᴬ⟩ ▼▼▼▼ Hyatt Regency Bellevue 🅷 ✿

(425) 462-1234. **$139-$379.** 900 Bellevue Way NE 98004. I-405 exit 13B, 1.5 mi w on NE 8th St. Int corridors. **Pets:** Medium, dogs only. $100 one-time fee/room. Service with restrictions.

🆂🅰🆅🅴 🅴🅲🅾 🍽 ♿ᴹ 🐾 🔊 ✕ 🛢 💻

⟨ᴬᴬᴬ⟩ ▼▼▼▼ La Residence Suite Hotel 🅷

(425) 455-1475. **$129-$199.** 475 100th Ave NE 98004. I-405 exit 13B, 0.9 mi w on NE 8th St, then just s. Int corridors. **Pets:** Other species. $15 daily fee/pet. Service with restrictions. 🆂🅰🆅🅴 🛜 ✕ 🛢 💻

◈ ▼▼▼▼ **Larkspur Landing Bellevue** H

(425) 373-1212. **Call for rates.** 15805 SE 37th St 98006. I-90 exit 11 westbound; exit 11A (SE Eastgate Way/156th Ave SE) eastbound, 0.9 mi se on south frontage road. Int corridors. **Pets:** Accepted.

[SAVE] [&M] [📶] [✕] [🛏] [💻]

◈ ▼▼▼▼ **Red Lion Hotel Bellevue** H

(425) 455-5240. **$99-$229.** 11211 Main St 98004. I-405 exit 12, 0.4 mi n on 114th St. Int corridors. **Pets:** Accepted.

[SAVE] [🍴] [🏊] [📶] [✕] [🛏] [💻]

▼▼▼▼ **Residence Inn by Marriott Seattle Bellevue** H

(425) 882-1222. **$299-$395.** 14455 NE 29th Pl 98007. I-405 exit 14 (SR 520), 2.3 mi e to 148th Ave NE (north exit), then just nw. Ext corridors. **Pets:** Accepted. [&M] [🏊] [📶] [✕] [🛏] [💻]

▼▼▼▼ **Residence Inn by Marriott Seattle Bellevue/Downtown** H

(425) 637-8500. **$89-$319.** 605 114th Ave SE 98004. I-405 exit 12, just nw. Int corridors. **Pets:** Accepted. [&M] [🏊] [📶] [✕] [🛏] [💻]

◈ ▼▼▼▼ **Sheraton Bellevue Hotel** H

(425) 455-3330. **$99-$359.** 100 112th Ave NE 98004. I-405 exit 12 northbound; exit 13 southbound, just s. Int corridors. **Pets:** Accepted.

[SAVE] [🍴] [&M] [🏊] [✕] [💻]

◈ ▼▼▼▼ **The Westin Bellevue** H ❀

(425) 638-1000. **$169-$399.** 600 Bellevue Way NE 98004. I-405 exit 13B, 1.5 mi w on NE 8th St, then just s. Int corridors. **Pets:** Small, dogs only. $75 deposit/pet. Designated rooms, no service, supervision.

[SAVE] [🍴] [&M] [🏊] [🏊] [✕] [🛏] [💻]

BELLINGHAM *(Restaurants p. 644)*

◈ ▼▼▼▼ **Baymont Inn & Suites** H ❀

(360) 671-6200. **$79-$139.** 125 E Kellogg Rd 98226. I-5 exit 256A, 1 mi ne via Meridian St. Int corridors. **Pets:** Service with restrictions, supervision. [SAVE] [&M] [🏊] [📶] [✕] [🛏] [💻]

◈ ▼▼▼▼ **BEST WESTERN PLUS Heritage Inn** H ❀

(360) 647-1912. **$110-$250.** 151 E McLeod Rd 98226. I-5 exit 256A, just se. Int corridors. **Pets:** $20 daily fee/room. Designated rooms, service with restrictions, supervision.

[SAVE] [🔌] [&M] [🏊] [📶] [✕] [🛏] [💻]

◈ ▼▼▼ **BEST WESTERN PLUS Lakeway Inn** H ❀

(360) 671-1011. **$129-$269.** 714 Lakeway Dr 98229. I-5 exit 253 (Lakeway Dr), just se. Int corridors. **Pets:** Large, other species. $20 one-time fee/pet. Designated rooms, service with restrictions, supervision.

[SAVE] [🍴] [🏊] [✕] [📶] [✕] [🛏] [💻]

◈ ▼▼▼▼ **The Chrysalis Inn & Spa** H

(360) 756-1005. **$199-$355.** 804 10th St 98225. I-5 exit 250, 1.3 mi nw on Old Fairhaven Pkwy, 0.6 mi n via 12th and 11th sts, just w on Taylor Ave, then just n. Int corridors. **Pets:** Accepted.

[SAVE] [🍴] [&M] [📶] [✕] [🛏] [💻]

◈ ▼▼▼▼ **Econo Lodge Inn & Suites** H

(360) 671-4600. **$64-$159.** 3750 Meridian St 98225. I-5 exit 256A, just sw. Ext corridors. **Pets:** Dogs only. $10 daily fee/pet. Designated rooms, service with restrictions, supervision. [SAVE] [&M] [🏊] [📶] [🛏] [💻]

▼▼▼ **GuestHouse Intl Inn-Bellingham** H

(360) 671-9600. **$79-$115.** 805 Lakeway Dr 98229. I-5 exit 253 (Lakeway Dr), just ne. Int corridors. **Pets:** Accepted.

[&M] [📶] [✕] [🛏] [💻]

◈ ▼▼▼▼ **Holiday Inn Express-Bellingham** H

(360) 671-4800. **$98-$168.** 4160 Meridian St 98226. I-5 exit 256A, 0.7 mi e. Int corridors. **Pets:** Accepted. [SAVE] [&M] [🏊] [📶] [✕] [🛏] [💻]

▼▼▼▼ **Hotel Bellwether** H

(360) 392-3100. **$189-$590.** One Bellwether Way 98225. I-5 exit 253 (Lakeway Dr), 0.9 mi nw via Lakeway Dr and E Holly St, just w on Bay St, 0.6 mi n via W Chestnut St and Roeder Ave, then just w. Int corridors. **Pets:** Accepted. [🍴] [&M] [📶] [✕] [🛏] [💻]

◈ ▼▼▼▼ **SpringHill Suites by Marriott Bellingham** H ❀

(360) 714-9600. **$99-$269.** 4040 Northwest Ave 98226. I-5 exit 257, just n. Int corridors. **Pets:** Medium, dogs only. $75 one-time fee/room. Service with restrictions, crate. [SAVE] [&M] [📶] [✕] [🛏] [💻]

BLAINE

◈ ▼▼▼▼ **Semiahmoo Resort Golf & Spa** H ❀

(360) 318-2000. **$129-$299, 3 day notice.** 9565 Semiahmoo Pkwy 98230. I-5 exit 270, 9.5 mi nw on Semiahmoo Spit. Int corridors. **Pets:** Small, dogs only. $25 daily fee/room. Designated rooms, service with restrictions, supervision.

[SAVE] [🍴] [&M] [🏊] [✕] [📶] [✕] [🛏] [💻]

BOTHELL

▼▼ **Country Inn & Suites By Carlson** H

(425) 485-5557. **$89-$225.** 19333 N Creek Pkwy 98011. I-405 exit 24, just e. Int corridors. **Pets:** Accepted. [ECO] [&M] [🏊] [📶] [🛏] [💻]

▼▼ **Extended Stay America-Seattle-Bothell-West** H

(425) 402-4252. **Call for rates.** 923 228th St SE 98021. I-405 exit 26, just sw. Int corridors. **Pets:** Other species. $25 daily fee/pet. Service with restrictions, supervision. [&M] [📶] [🛏]

▼▼▼ **Residence Inn by Marriott Seattle NE** H

(425) 485-3030. **$109-$249.** 11920 NE 195th St 98011. I-405 exit 24, 0.4 mi ne. Ext corridors. **Pets:** Large, other species. $75 one-time fee/pet. Service with restrictions, crate. [&M] [🏊] [📶] [✕] [🛏] [💻]

BREMERTON

▼▼▼ **Super 8-Bremerton** H

(360) 377-8881. **$70-$80.** 5068 Kitsap Way 98312. SR 3 exit Kitsap Way, just ne; 4.2 mi w of ferry terminal. Int corridors. **Pets:** $10 daily fee/pet. Designated rooms, service with restrictions, crate.

[&M] [📶] [🛏] [💻]

BURLINGTON

▼▼▼ **Candlewood Suites-Burlington** H

(360) 755-3300. **Call for rates.** 1866 S Burlington Blvd 98233. I-5 exit 229, just e on George Hopper Dr, then just s. Int corridors. **Pets:** Accepted. [&M] [📶] [✕] [🛏] [💻]

CAMAS

◈ ▼▼▼ **Camas Hotel** H

(360) 834-5722. **$89-$172, 7 day notice.** 405 NE 4th Ave 98607. Jct NE Cedar St; downtown. Int corridors. **Pets:** Accepted.

[SAVE] [🍴] [📶] [✕] [🛏] [💻]

CASHMERE

◈ ▼ **Village Inn Motel** M

(509) 782-3522. **$59-$94, 7 day notice.** 229 Cottage Ave 98815. On Business Rt US 2 and 97; downtown. Ext corridors. **Pets:** $10 daily fee/pet. Service with restrictions, supervision. [SAVE] [📶] [🛏]

CASTLE ROCK

◈ ▼▼▼ **Timberland Inn & Suites** M

(360) 274-6002. **$60-$200.** 1271 Mount St. Helens Way 98611. I-5 exit 49, just ne. Ext corridors. **Pets:** Very small, dogs only. $15 daily fee/pet. Designated rooms, service with restrictions, supervision.

[SAVE] [📶] [🛏] [💻]

CENTRALIA

▼ **Motel 6 - #394** M

(360) 330-2057. **$51-$65.** 1310 Belmont Ave 98531. I-5 exit 82, just w on Harrison Ave, then just n. Ext corridors. **Pets:** Other species. Service with restrictions, crate. [🏊] [🏊] [🛏]

Peppermill Empress Inn H
(360) 330-9441. **$67-$95.** 1233 Alder St 98531. I-5 exit 81 (Mellen St), just se. Int corridors. **Pets:** Accepted. 🆂🅰🆅🅴 ⏪ 🛜 ⬛ ⬛ ⬛

CHEHALIS

BEST WESTERN PLUS Park Place Inn & Suites H 🐾
(360) 748-4040. **$105-$155.** 201 SW Interstate Ave 98532. I-5 exit 76, just se. Int corridors. **Pets:** Medium, dogs only. $20 daily fee/room. Designated rooms, service with restrictions, supervision.
🆂🅰🆅🅴 🅟Ⓜ ⏪ 🛜 ❌ ⬛ ⬛

Holiday Inn Express & Suites Chehalis H
(360) 740-1800. **$109-$199.** 730 NW Liberty Pl 98532. I-5 exit 77, just ne. Int corridors. **Pets:** Accepted. ⏪ 🛜 ❌ ⬛ ⬛

CHELAN

Lakeside Lodge & Suites H
(509) 682-4396. **$99-$329, 7 day notice.** 2312 W Woodin Ave 98816. West end of town. Ext corridors. **Pets:** Accepted.
🆂🅰🆅🅴 ⏪ 🛜 ❌ ⬛ ⬛

CHEWELAH

Nordlig Motel M
(509) 935-6704. **$61-$66, 3 day notice.** 101 W Grant Ave 99109. North edge of town on US 395. Ext corridors. **Pets:** Dogs only. $10 one-time fee/room. Designated rooms, service with restrictions, supervision.
🆂🅰🆅🅴 🛜 ⬛

CLARKSTON

BEST WESTERN RiverTree Inn M
(509) 758-9551. **$108-$149.** 1257 Bridge St 99403. 0.9 mi w of Snake River Bridge on US 12. Ext corridors. **Pets:** Accepted.
🆂🅰🆅🅴 🅟Ⓜ ⏪ ❌ 🛜 ❌ ⬛ ⬛

Quality Inn & Suites Conference Center H
(509) 758-9500. **$100-$235.** 700 Port Dr 99403. Just w of Snake River Bridge on US 12, then 0.3 mi n via 5th St. Int corridors.
Pets: Accepted. 🅣 🅟Ⓜ ⏪ 🛜 ❌ ⬛ ⬛

CLE ELUM

Suncadia Resort H
(509) 649-6460. **$129-$359, 7 day notice.** 3600 Suncadia Tr 98922. I-90 exit 80, 2 mi n, then 0.3 mi w. Int corridors. **Pets:** Accepted.
🆂🅰🆅🅴 🅒 🅣 🅟Ⓜ ⏪ ❌ 🛜 ❌ ⬛ ⬛

Timber Lodge Inn M
(509) 674-5966. **$72-$104.** 301 W 1st St 98922. I-90 exit 84 eastbound, 1 mi ne; exit westbound, just w; downtown. Int corridors.
Pets: Accepted. 🅟Ⓜ 🛜 ❌ ⬛

COLFAX

BEST WESTERN Wheatland Inn H
(509) 397-0397. **Call for rates.** 701 N Main St 99111. 0.6 mi n of downtown. Int corridors. **Pets:** Small, dogs only. $15 daily fee/pet. Service with restrictions, supervision.
🆂🅰🆅🅴 🅣 🅟Ⓜ ⏪ 🛜 ❌ ⬛ ⬛

CONCRETE

Ovenell's Heritage Inn and Log Cabins CA
(360) 853-8494. **$115-$250, 3 day notice.** 46276 Concrete Sauk Valley Rd 98237. 0.5 mi w of downtown on SR 20, 3 mi se. Ext corridors. **Pets:** Dogs only. $20 daily fee/pet. Designated rooms, service with restrictions, supervision. 🆂🅰🆅🅴 🛜 ❌ 🅩 ⬛ ⬛

DAYTON

BEST WESTERN PLUS Dayton Hotel & Suites H
(509) 382-4790. **$120-$160.** 507 E Main St 99328. Just e of downtown. Int corridors. **Pets:** Accepted. 🆂🅰🆅🅴 🅟Ⓜ 🛜 ❌ ⬛ ⬛

The Weinhard Hotel H
(509) 382-4032. **$125-$180, 7 day notice.** 235 E Main St 99328. Downtown. Int corridors. **Pets:** $20 one-time fee/pet. Supervision.
🛜 ❌ ⬛

DEER HARBOR

Deer Harbor Inn CI
(360) 376-4110. **Call for rates.** 33 Inn Ln 98243. In Deer Harbor; 7 mi sw of ferry landing; 3.5 mi sw of Westsound. Ext/int corridors.
Pets: Accepted. 🅣 🛜 ❌ 🅐🅒 🅩 ⬛ ⬛

EASTSOUND *(Restaurants p. 644)*

Eastsound Landmark Inn CO
(360) 376-2423. **$139-$289, 7 day notice.** 67 Main St 98245. In Eastsound; between N Beach and Orcas rds; downtown. Ext corridors. **Pets:** $25 daily fee/pet. Designated rooms, service with restrictions, supervision. 🆂🅰🆅🅴 🛜 ❌ 🅐🅒 ⬛ ⬛

Turtleback Farm Inn BB
(360) 376-4914. **$125-$260, 15 day notice.** 1981 Crow Valley Rd 98245. 4 mi sw of Eastsound on Orcas Rd. Int corridors. **Pets:** Dogs only. Designated rooms, service with restrictions, supervision.
🆂🅰🆅🅴 🛜 ❌ 🅐🅒 🅟 🅩 ⬛ ⬛

EAST WENATCHEE

Cedars Inn, East Wenatchee H
(509) 886-8000. **Call for rates.** 80 9th St NE 98802. Just e of SR 28. Int corridors. **Pets:** Accepted. 🅟Ⓜ ⏪ 🛜 ⬛ ⬛

EATONVILLE

Mill Village Motel M
(360) 832-3200. **$100-$120.** 210 Center St E 98328. Just e of jct SR 161. Ext corridors. **Pets:** Small, dogs only. $20 one-time fee/room. Supervision. 🆂🅰🆅🅴 🛜 ❌ ⬛ ⬛

EDMONDS *(Restaurants p. 644)*

BEST WESTERN PLUS Edmonds Harbor Inn H 🐾
(425) 771-5021. **$110-$190.** 130 W Dayton St 98020. Just s at Port of Edmonds. Ext/int corridors. **Pets:** Large. $20 daily fee/room. Designated rooms, service with restrictions, supervision.
🆂🅰🆅🅴 🅟Ⓜ ⏪ ❌ 🛜 ❌ ⬛ ⬛

ELLENSBURG

BEST WESTERN PLUS Lincoln Inn & Suites H
(509) 925-4244. **$90-$220.** 211 W Umptanum Rd 98926. I-90 exit 109, just n, then just w. Int corridors. **Pets:** Large, dogs only. $17 daily fee/pet. Service with restrictions, supervision.
🆂🅰🆅🅴 🅟Ⓜ ⏪ 🛜 ❌ ⬛ ⬛

Days Inn H
(509) 933-1500. **$70-$123.** 901 Berry Rd 98926. I-90 exit 109, just s. Int corridors. **Pets:** Other species. $15 daily fee/pet. Supervision.
🆂🅰🆅🅴 🅟Ⓜ ⏪ 🛜 ❌ ⬛ ⬛

Econo Lodge M
(509) 925-9844. **$60-$100.** 1390 N Dollarway Rd 98926. I-90 exit 106, just n. Ext corridors. **Pets:** Medium, dogs only. $15 daily fee/pet. Designated rooms, supervision. 🛜 ⬛

Ellensburg Comfort Inn H
(509) 925-7037. **$90-$215.** 1722 Canyon Rd 98926. I-90 exit 109, just n. Int corridors. **Pets:** Accepted. ⏪ 🛜 ⬛ ⬛

Holiday Inn Express H
(509) 962-9400. **Call for rates.** 1620 Canyon Rd 98926. I-90 exit 109, just n. Int corridors. **Pets:** Accepted. 🅒 ⏪ 🛜 ❌ ⬛ ⬛

ELMA

▽▽▽ **GuestHouse Inn & Suites** 🅷
(360) 482-6868. **Call for rates.** 800 E Main St 98541. Just ne of jct US 12 and SR 8. Int corridors. **Pets:** Accepted. 🤍 ✖ 🎁 🖥

EPHRATA

△△△ ▽▽▽ **BEST WESTERN Rama Inn** 🅷 ✿
(509) 754-7111. **$89-$139.** 1818 Basin St SW 98823. On SR 28; west end of town. Int corridors. **Pets:** Large, other species. $20 one-time fee/room. Designated rooms, service with restrictions, supervision.
🆂🅰🆅🅴 🕭ᴹ 🙩 🤍 🎁 🖥

EVERETT *(Restaurants p. 644)*

△△△ ▽▽▽ **BEST WESTERN Cascadia Inn** 🅷
(425) 258-4141. **$89-$139.** 2800 Pacific Ave 98201. I-5 exit 193 northbound; exit 194 southbound, just w. Int corridors. **Pets:** Accepted.
🆂🅰🆅🅴 🕭ᴹ 🙩 🤍 ✖ 🎁 🖥

△△△ ▽▽▽ **BEST WESTERN PLUS Navigator Inn & Suites** 🅷 ✿
(425) 347-2555. **$129-$169.** 10210 Evergreen Way 98204. I-5 exit 189, 1 mi w on SR 526 to Evergreen Way, then 1.6 mi s. Int corridors. **Pets:** Dogs only. $20 daily fee/room. Designated rooms, service with restrictions, supervision. 🆂🅰🆅🅴 🕭ᴹ 🙩 🤍 ✖ 🎁 🖥

▽▽▽ **Extended Stay America-Seattle-Everett-Silverlake** 🅷
(425) 337-1341. **Call for rates.** 1431 112th St SE 98208. I-5 exit 189, 1.5 mi se on 19th Ave SE, then 0.3 mi w. Int corridors. **Pets:** Other species. $25 daily fee/pet. Service with restrictions, supervision.
🕭ᴹ 🤍 ✖ 🎁 🖥

▽▽▽ **Holiday Inn Downtown Everett** 🅷
(425) 339-2000. **$109-$179, 3 day notice.** 3105 Pine St 98201. I-5 exit 193 northbound; exit 194 southbound, just sw. Int corridors.
Pets: Accepted. 🍴 🕭ᴹ 🙩 🤍 ✖ 🎁 🖥

△△△ ▽▽▽ **Inn at Port Gardner** 🅷
(425) 252-6779. **$119-$249.** 1700 W Marine View Dr 98201. I-5 exit 193 northbound, 1.2 mi w on Pacific Ave, then 1.2 mi n; exit 194 southbound, 1.2 mi w on Everett Ave, then 1 mi n; in Everett Marina Village. Int corridors. **Pets:** Dogs only. $25 one-time fee/pet. Service with restrictions, supervision. 🆂🅰🆅🅴 🕭ᴹ 🤍 ✖ 🎁 🖥

△△△ ▽▽▽ **La Quinta Inn Everett** 🅷
(425) 347-9099. **$74-$194.** 12619 4th Ave W 98204. I-5 exit 186, just nw. Int corridors. **Pets:** Large, other species. Service with restrictions.
🆂🅰🆅🅴 🕭ᴹ 🙩 🤍 ✖ 🎁 🖥

▽▽▽ **Quality Inn & Suites** 🅷
(425) 609-4550. **$100-$175.** 101 128th St SE 98208. I-5 exit 186, just ne. Int corridors. **Pets:** Accepted. 🕭ᴹ 🤍 ✖ 🎁 🖥

FEDERAL WAY

△△△ ▽▽▽▽ **BEST WESTERN PLUS Evergreen Inn & Suites** 🅷 ✿
(253) 529-4000. **$99-$139.** 32124 25th Ave S 98003. I-5 exit 143, just sw. Int corridors. **Pets:** Medium, other species. $50 deposit/room, $20 daily fee/room. Designated rooms, service with restrictions, supervision.
🆂🅰🆅🅴 🍴 🙩 🤍 ✖ 🎁 🖥

△△△ ▽▽▽ **Clarion Hotel Federal Way** 🅷
(253) 941-6000. **$92-$199.** 31611 20th Ave S 98003. I-5 exit 143, 0.5 mi w on 320th St, then just n. Int corridors. **Pets:** Accepted.
🆂🅰🆅🅴 🍴 🙩 🤍 ✖ 🎁 🖥

FERNDALE

△△△ ▽▽▽▽ **Silver Reef Hotel Casino Spa** 🅷 ✿
(360) 383-0777. **$116-$299.** 4876 Haxton Way 98248. I-5 exit 260, 3.6 mi w on Slater Rd. Int corridors. **Pets:** Small, other species. $15 one-time fee/pet. Designated rooms, service with restrictions.
🆂🅰🆅🅴 🍴 🕭ᴹ 🙩 ✖ 🤍 🎁 🖥

▽▽▽ **Super 8 Ferndale** 🅷
(360) 384-8881. **$80-$105.** 5788 Barrett Rd 98248. I-5 exit 262, just ne. Int corridors. **Pets:** Accepted. 🕭ᴹ 🙩 🤍 ✖ 🎁 🖥

FIFE

△△△ ▽▽▽▽ **Emerald Queen Hotel & Casino** 🅷
(253) 922-2000. **$89-$129.** 5700 Pacific Hwy E 98424. I-5 exit 137, just ne. Int corridors. **Pets:** Medium, dogs only. $25 one-time fee/room. Designated rooms, service with restrictions, supervision.
🆂🅰🆅🅴 🍴 🕭ᴹ 🙩 🤍 🎁 🖥

▽▽▽ **Extended Stay America-Tacoma-Fife** 🅷
(253) 926-6316. **Call for rates.** 2820 Pacific Hwy E 98424. I-5 exit 136B northbound; exit 136 southbound, just nw. Int corridors.
Pets: Other species. $25 daily fee/pet. Service with restrictions, supervision. 🤍 🎁 🖥

FORKS

▽▽ **Manitou Lodge** 🅱🅱
(360) 374-6295. **Call for rates.** 813 Kilmer Rd 98331. 7.7 mi sw on SR 110 (LaPush Rd), 0.7 mi w on Mora Rd, then 0.8 mi n. Ext/int corridors. **Pets:** Accepted. 🤍 ✖ 🐾 🐾 🎁 🖥

▽▽ **Miller Tree Inn Bed & Breakfast** 🅱🅱
(360) 374-6806. **$110-$235, 7 day notice.** 654 E Division St 98331. 0.3 mi e of US 101 (S Forks Ave). Ext/int corridors. **Pets:** $10 daily fee/pet. Designated rooms, service with restrictions. 🤍 ✖ 🐾 🎁 🖥

▽▽ **Olympic Suites Inn** 🅼
(360) 374-5400. **$49-$139.** 800 Olympic Dr 98331. North end of town; just ne off US 101 (S Forks Ave). Ext corridors. **Pets:** Accepted.
🤍 ✖ 🐾 🎁 🖥

FRIDAY HARBOR

▽▽▽ **Argyle House Bed & Breakfast** 🅱🅱 ✿
(360) 378-4084. **$110-$280, 14 day notice.** 685 Argyle Ave 98250. In Friday Harbor; 0.3 mi e of jct Spring St. Ext/int corridors. **Pets:** Dogs only. $25 one-time fee/room. Crate. 🤍 ✖ 🐾 🐾 🎁 🖥

▽▽▽ **Earthbox Inn & Spa** 🅷 ✿
(360) 378-4000. **$89-$409.** 410 Spring St 98250. In Friday Harbor; 0.5 mi w of ferry dock. Ext corridors. **Pets:** Dogs only. $15 daily fee/pet. Designated rooms, service with restrictions, supervision. 🙩 ✖ 🤍 ✖ 🎁 🖥

▽▽▽ **Friday Harbor House** 🅷
(360) 378-8455. **$169-$409, 14 day notice.** 130 West St 98250. In Friday Harbor; just w of Spring St. Ext/int corridors. **Pets:** Accepted.
🍴 🤍 ✖ 🐾 🎁 🖥

△△△ ▽▽▽ **Friday Harbor Suites** 🅷
(360) 378-3031. **$140-$390, 7 day notice.** 680 Spring St 98250. In Friday Harbor; 0.7 mi w of ferry dock. Int corridors. **Pets:** $20 daily fee/room. Designated rooms, service with restrictions, supervision.
🆂🅰🆅🅴 🍴 🕭ᴹ 🤍 ✖ 🐾 🎁 🖥

▽▽▽ **Lakedale Resort at Three Lakes** 🅷
(360) 378-2350. **$295-$439, 14 day notice.** 4313 Roche Harbor Rd 98250. In Friday Harbor; 4 mi n via Second St, Guard St and Tucker Ave. Ext/int corridors. **Pets:** Accepted. 🤍 ✖ 🐾 🎁 🖥

GIG HARBOR

△△△ ▽▽▽▽ **BEST WESTERN PLUS Wesley Inn & Suites** 🅷
(253) 858-9690. **Call for rates.** 6575 Kimball Dr 98335. SR 16 exit City Center, just e on Pioneer Way, then 0.3 mi s. Int corridors.
Pets: Accepted. 🆂🅰🆅🅴 🕭ᴹ 🙩 🤍 ✖ 🎁 🖥

▽▽▽ **The Inn at Gig Harbor** 🅷
(253) 858-1111. **Call for rates.** 3211 56th St NW 98335. SR 16 exit Olympic Dr, just w, then 0.4 mi n. Int corridors. **Pets:** Accepted.
🍴 🕭ᴹ ✖ 🤍 ✖ 🎁 🖥

GOLDENDALE

▼▼ Quality Inn & Suites ⬚
(509) 773-5881. $81-$99. 808 E Simcoe Dr 98620. US 97 exit Simcoe Dr, just sw. Ext corridors. Pets: Accepted. 🛥 📶 🛢 💻

HOODSPORT

▼▼ Glen Ayr Hood Canal Waterfront Resort ⬚
(360) 877-9522. $85-$199, 7 day notice. 25381 N US 101 98548. 1.5 mi n. Ext corridors. Pets: Medium, other species. $15 daily fee/pet. Designated rooms, service with restrictions, supervision.
❌ 📶 ❌ 🐾 📷 🛢 💻

ILWACO

▼ Heidi's Inn Ilwaco Ⓜ
(360) 642-2387. $49-$115. 126 E Spruce St 98624. Downtown. Ext corridors. Pets: Accepted. 📶 🐾 🛢 💻

KALALOCH

🅐🅐🅐 ▼▼ Kalaloch Lodge Ⓒ🅐
(360) 962-2271. Call for rates. 157151 Hwy 101 98331. In Kalaloch; at MM 157. Ext/int corridors. Pets: Accepted.
[SAVE] 🍴 📶 ❌ 🐾 📺 📷 🛢 💻

KELSO

🅐🅐🅐 ▼▼ BEST WESTERN Aladdin Inn ⬚
(360) 425-9660. $99-$159. 310 Long Ave 98626. I-5 exit 39, 1.1 mi w via Allen and W Main sts, then just n on 5th Ave NW. Int corridors.
Pets: Accepted. [SAVE] 🛥 📶 ❌ 🛢 💻

▼▼ GuestHouse Inn & Suites ⬚
(360) 414-5953. Call for rates. 501 Three Rivers Dr 98626. I-5 exit 39, 0.3 mi w on Allen St, then 0.3 mi s; behind Safeway. Int corridors.
Pets: Accepted. 🛥 📶 🛢 💻

▼ Motel 6 - #43 Ⓜ
(360) 425-3229. $49-$75. 106 Minor Rd 98626. I-5 exit 39, just ne. Ext corridors. Pets: Other species. Service with restrictions, crate.
🛥 🔵 🛢

▼▼▼ Red Lion Hotel & Conference Center Kelso/Longview ⬚
(360) 636-4400. $99-$265. 510 Kelso Dr 98626. I-5 exit 39, 0.3 mi se. Int corridors. Pets: Accepted. 🍴 🛥 📶 ❌ 🛢 💻

▼▼ Super 8 ⬚
(360) 423-8880. $73-$106. 250 Kelso Dr 98626. I-5 exit 39, just se. Int corridors. Pets: Accepted. 🅼 🛥 📶 🛢 💻

KENNEWICK

🅐🅐🅐 ▼▼▼ BEST WESTERN PLUS Kennewick Inn ⬚ 🌣
(509) 586-1332. $120-$170. 4001 W 27th Ave 99337. I-82 exit 113 (US 395), 0.8 mi n. Int corridors. Pets: Large. $15 one-time fee/room. Service with restrictions, supervision.
[SAVE] 🅼 🛥 ❌ 📶 ❌ 🛢 💻

▼▼ Clover Island Inn ⬚ 🌣
(509) 586-0541. $79-$349. 435 Clover Island Dr 99336. US 395 exit Port of Kennewick, 1 mi e on Columbia Dr, then 0.7 mi n. Int corridors. Pets: Other species. $10 one-time fee/pet. Designated rooms, service with restrictions, supervision. 🍴 🛥 ❌ 📶 ❌ 🛢 💻

▼▼ Comfort Inn ⬚
(509) 783-8396. $84-$144. 7801 W Quinault Ave 99336. 0.5 mi s on N Columbia Center Blvd from SR 240. Int corridors. Pets: Accepted.
🍴 🛥 📶 ❌ 🛢 💻

▼▼▼ Fairfield Inn by Marriott ⬚
(509) 783-2164. $159-$191. 7809 W Quinault Ave 99336. 0.5 mi s on N Columbia Center Blvd from SR 240. Int corridors. Pets: Other species. $15 daily fee/pet. Service with restrictions, crate.
🍴 🅼 🛥 📶 ❌ 🛢 💻

🅐🅐🅐 ▼▼ Kennewick Super 8 ⬚
(509) 736-6888. $65-$85, 3 day notice. 626 N Columbia Center Blvd 99336. 1.1 mi s of SR 240. Int corridors. Pets: Other species. $10 daily fee/room. Designated rooms, service with restrictions, supervision.
[SAVE] 🅼 🛥 📶 ❌ 🛢 💻

▼▼▼ La Quinta Inn & Suites Kennewick ⬚
(509) 736-3656. $89-$249. 2600 S Quillan Pl 99338. I-82 exit 113 (US 395), 0.8 mi n. Int corridors. Pets: Large, other species. Service with restrictions. 🛥 📶 ❌ 🛢 💻

▼▼ Quality Inn Kennewick ⬚
(509) 735-6100. $71-$109. 7901 W Quinault Ave 99336. 0.5 mi s on Columbia Center Blvd from SR 240. Int corridors. Pets: Accepted.
🍴 🅼 🛥 📶 ❌ 🛢 💻

▼▼▼ Red Lion Hotel Columbia Center - Kennewick ⬚
(509) 783-0611. $89-$149. 1101 N Columbia Center Blvd 99336. SR 240, 0.5 mi s. Int corridors. Pets: Accepted.
🅼 🛥 📶 ❌ 🛢 💻

🅐🅐🅐 ▼▼▼ Red Lion Inn & Suites Kennewick ⬚
(509) 396-9979. Call for rates. 602 N Young St 99336. 1 mi s of SR 240 on N Columbia Center Blvd, just e. Int corridors. Pets: Accepted.
[SAVE] 🍴 🅼 🛥 📶 ❌ 🛢 💻

KENT

▼▼ Comfort Inn Kent ⬚
(253) 872-2211. $70-$199. 22311 84th Ave S 98032. SR 167 exit 84th Ave S, just n. Int corridors. Pets: Large, dogs only. $20 daily fee/room. Designated rooms, service with restrictions, supervision.
🛥 📶 ❌ 🛢 💻

🅐🅐🅐 ▼▼ Red Lion Inn & Suites Kent ⬚
(253) 520-6670. $179-$299, 3 day notice. 25100 74th Ave S 98032. I-5 exit 149, 2.5 mi se via Kent Des Moines Rd (SR 516) to 74th Ave S.
Int corridors. Pets: Accepted. [SAVE] 🅼 🛥 ❌ 📶 ❌ 🛢 💻

▼▼▼ TownePlace Suites by Marriott-Seattle Southcenter ⬚
(253) 796-6000. $89-$285. 18123 72nd Ave S 98032. I-405 exit 1 (SR 181), 1.6 mi s on W Valley Hwy, just e on S 180th St, then just s. Ext corridors. Pets: Accepted. 🅼 🛥 📶 ❌ 🛢 💻

KIRKLAND

▼▼ Comfort Inn-Kirkland ⬚
(425) 821-8300. $92-$280. 12204 NE 124th St 98034. I-405 exit 20B northbound; exit 20 southbound, just e. Int corridors. Pets: Accepted.
🅼 🛥 📶 ❌ 🛢 💻

🅐🅐🅐 ▼▼ ▼▼ The Heathman Hotel ⬚ 🌣
(425) 284-5800. $199-$349, 30 day notice. 220 Kirkland Ave 98033. I-405 exit 18 (NE 85th St), 1 mi w, just s on 3rd St, then just w. Int corridors. Pets: Other species. Service with restrictions.
[SAVE] 🍴 🅼 📶 ❌ 💻

▼▼ La Quinta Inn & Suites Seattle Bellevue/Kirkland ⬚
(425) 828-6585. $85-$281. 10530 NE Northup Way 98033. I-405 exit 14 (SR 520 W) via exit 108th Ave, just n, then just w. Int corridors.
Pets: Large, other species. Service with restrictions.
🅼 🛥 📶 ❌ 🛢 💻

🅐🅐🅐 ▼▼ ▼▼ Woodmark Hotel & Still Spa ⬚
(425) 822-3700. $199-$329. 1200 Carillon Point 98033. On Lake Washington Blvd, 1 mi n of SR 520. Int corridors. Pets: Accepted.
[SAVE] 🍴 🅼 📶 ❌ 💻

LACEY

🅐🅐🅐 ▼▼▼▼ BEST WESTERN PLUS Lacey Inn & Suites 🄷 ❀

(360) 456-5655. **$110-$135.** 8326 Quinault Dr NE 98516. I-5 exit 111 (Marvin Rd), just ne. Int corridors. **Pets:** Small, dogs only. $20 daily fee/pet. Designated rooms, service with restrictions, supervision.

SAVE 🔜 🛜 ✖ 🄿 💻

▼▼▼▼ Candlewood Suites 🄷

(360) 491-1698. **$140-$299.** 4440 3rd Ave SE 98503. I-5 exit 108 northbound, just n; exit 109 southbound, just s on Martin Ave E, just e on College Way, then just s. Int corridors. **Pets:** Large, other species. $150 one-time fee/room. Service with restrictions. 🛜 🄿 💻

LA CONNER

▼▼▼ La Conner Country Inn 🄷

(360) 466-3101. **Call for rates.** 107 S 2nd St 98257. Jct 2nd and Morris sts; downtown. Ext/int corridors. **Pets:** Accepted.

🛜 ✖ 🄿 💻

LANGLEY *(Restaurants p. 644)*

▼▼▼▼ The Inn at Langley 🄷 ❀

(360) 221-3033. **Call for rates.** 400 1st St 98260. Between Anthes and Park aves. Ext corridors. **Pets:** Dogs only. $50 one-time fee/pet. Designated rooms, supervision. 🍴 🔜 🛜 ✖ 🄺

LEAVENWORTH

▼▼ Alpine Rivers Inn 🄷

(509) 548-8888. **$105-$135, 7 day notice.** 1505 Alpensee Strasse 98826. US 2, just n. Ext corridors. **Pets:** Accepted.

🔜 🛜 ✖ 🄿 💻

🅐🅐🅐 ▼▼▼▼ BEST WESTERN PLUS Icicle Inn 🄷

(509) 548-7000. **$129-$329, 14 day notice.** 505 W US 2 98826. West side of town. Int corridors. **Pets:** Accepted.

SAVE 🍴 🔜 ✖ 🛜 ✖ 🄿 💻

🅐🅐🅐 ▼▼▼ Der Ritterhof Motor Inn 🄷

(509) 548-5845. **$80-$125.** 190 US 2 98826. 0.3 mi w; downtown. Ext corridors. **Pets:** Accepted. SAVE 🔜 🔜 🛜 ✖ 🄿 💻

▼▼ Obertal Inn 🄼 ❀

(509) 548-5204. **$99-$299, 3 day notice.** 922 Commercial St 98826. From US 2, just s on 9th St, just nw. Ext corridors. **Pets:** Other species. $18 daily fee/pet. Service with restrictions, crate.

🛜 ✖ 🄿 💻

LIBERTY LAKE

🅐🅐🅐 ▼▼▼▼ BEST WESTERN PLUS Peppertree Liberty Lake Inn 🄷

(509) 755-1111. **$99-$299.** 1816 N Pepper Ln 99019. I-90 exit 296 (Liberty Lake), just n. Int corridors. **Pets:** Accepted.

SAVE 🔜 🔜 🛜 ✖ 🄿 💻

LONG BEACH

▼▼▼ Anchorage Cottages 🄲🄰 ❀

(360) 642-2351. **$80-$147, 14 day notice.** 2209 Boulevard N 98631. Just w of SR 103; north end of downtown. Ext corridors. **Pets:** Other species. $10 daily fee/pet. Designated rooms, no service, supervision.

🛜 ✖ 🄺 🔜 🄿 💻

🅐🅐🅐 ▼▼▼ The Breakers 🄲🄾 ❀

(360) 642-4414. **$78-$328, 20 day notice.** 210 26th St NW 98631. Just w of SR 103; north end of downtown. Ext corridors. **Pets:** $15 daily fee/room. Service with restrictions, supervision.

SAVE 🔜 ✖ 🛜 ✖ 🄺 🄿 💻

▼▼▼ Rodeway Inn & Suites 🄼

(360) 642-3714. **$60-$200.** 115 3rd St SW 98631. Just off SR 103; downtown. Ext corridors. **Pets:** Accepted. 🔜 🛜 🄺 🄿 💻

▼▼▼ Super 8 🄷

(360) 642-8988. **$79-$199.** 500 Ocean Beach Blvd 98631. On SR 103; downtown. Int corridors. **Pets:** Accepted.

SAVE 🔜M 🛜 ✖ 🄺 🄿 💻

LONGVIEW

▼▼▼ Hudson Manor Inn & Suites 🄼

(360) 425-1100. **Call for rates.** 1616 Hudson St 98632. Downtown. Ext corridors. **Pets:** Accepted. 🛜 ✖ 🄿 💻

LYNNWOOD

🅐🅐🅐 ▼▼▼ BEST WESTERN Alderwood 🄷

(425) 775-7600. **$80-$121.** 19332 36th Ave W 98036. I-5 exit 181B northbound, just w on 196th St SW, then just n; exit 181 (SR 524 W) southbound, just nw. Int corridors. **Pets:** Medium, dogs only. $25 one-time fee/pet. Designated rooms, service with restrictions, supervision.

SAVE 🔜M 🔜 🛜 🄿 💻

▼▼▼▼ Embassy Suites Hotel Seattle North/Lynnwood 🄷

(425) 775-2500. **$119-$219.** 20610 44th Ave W 98036. I-5 exit 181A northbound, just se; exit 181 (SR 524 W) southbound, 0.5 mi w on 196th St SW, then 0.6 mi s. Int corridors. **Pets:** Accepted.

🍴 🔜M 🔜 ✖ 🛜 🄿 💻

🅐🅐🅐 ▼▼▼▼ Hampton Inn & Suites 🄷

(425) 771-1888. **$119-$229.** 19324 Alderwood Mall Pkwy 98036. I-5 exit 181B northbound, 0.6 mi n; exit 181 (SR 524 E) southbound, 0.5 mi e on 196th St SE, then just n. Int corridors. **Pets:** Accepted.

SAVE 🔜M 🔜 🛜 ✖ 🄿 💻

▼▼▼▼ Homewood Suites by Hilton Seattle/Lynnwood 🄷

(425) 670-8943. **$149-$229.** 18123 Alderwood Mall Pkwy 98037. I-5 exit 183, 0.4 mi w on 164th St SW, then 1.2 mi se. Int corridors.

Pets: Accepted. 🔜M ✖ 🛜 🄿 💻

🅐🅐🅐 ▼▼▼ La Quinta Inn Lynnwood 🄷

(425) 775-7447. **$79-$259.** 4300 Alderwood Mall Blvd 98036. I-5 exit 181A northbound, just w; exit 181 (SR 524 W) southbound, 0.5 mi w on 196th St SW, just s on 44th Ave SW, then just e. Int corridors. **Pets:** Large, other species. Service with restrictions.

SAVE 🔜 🛜 ✖ 🄿 💻

▼▼▼▼ Residence Inn by Marriott-Seattle North/Lynnwood 🄷

(425) 771-1100. **$159-$219.** 18200 Alderwood Mall Pkwy 98037. I-5 exit 183, 0.4 mi w on 164th St SW, then 1.2 mi se. Ext corridors. **Pets:** Other species. $75 daily fee/room. Service with restrictions.

🔜M 🔜 🛜 ✖ 🄿 💻

MARYSVILLE

▼▼▼▼ Holiday Inn Express Hotel & Suites-Marysville 🄷 ❀

(360) 530-1234. **$119-$209.** 8606 36th Ave NE 98270. I-5 exit 200, just se. Int corridors. **Pets:** Other species. $40 one-time fee/room. Service with restrictions, crate. 🔜M 🔜 🛜 ✖ 🄿 💻

MOCLIPS

🅐🅐🅐 ▼▼▼ Ocean Crest Resort 🄷 ❀

(360) 276-4465. **$75-$225, 4 day notice.** 4651 SR 109 98562. South edge of town. Ext corridors. **Pets:** Other species. $15 daily fee/pet. Designated rooms, service with restrictions, supervision.

SAVE 🍴 🔜 ✖ 🛜 ✖ 🄺 🄿 💻

MONROE

🅐🅐🅐 ▼▼▼ BEST WESTERN Sky Valley Inn 🄷

(360) 794-3111. **$109-$199.** 19233 SR 2 98272. West end of town. Int corridors. **Pets:** Dogs only. $20 daily fee/pet. Service with restrictions, supervision. SAVE 🔜M 🔜 🛜 ✖ 🄿 💻

WWW GuestHouse International Inn & Suites H

(360) 863-1900. **$119-$199.** 19103 SR 2 98272. West end of town. Int corridors. **Pets:** Dogs only. $20 daily fee/room. Service with restrictions, crate. (SAVE) (占M) ⌂ 🕿 ✕ 📶 🖵

MORTON

WWW Seasons Motel M

(360) 496-6835. **$100-$130.** 200 Westlake Ave 98356. Corner of US 12 and SR 7. Ext corridors. **Pets:** Small, dogs only. $20 one-time fee/pet. Supervision. (SAVE) 🕿 ✕ 📶 🖵

MOSES LAKE

WW AmeriStay Inn & Suites H

(509) 764-7500. **$89-$249.** 1157 N Stratford Rd 98837. I-90 exit 179, 1 mi n to SR 17, 2.8 mi nw; exit Stratford Rd, just e. Int corridors. **Pets:** Other species. $25 one-time fee/room. Service with restrictions. (占M) ⌂ 📶 🖵

WW BEST WESTERN PLUS Lake Front Hotel H

(509) 765-9211. **$100-$126.** 3000 Marina Dr 98837. I-90 exit 176, just nw. Int corridors. **Pets:** Small. $20 deposit/pet, $20 daily fee/pet. Designated rooms, no service, supervision.

(SAVE) (ᵀ¶) (占M) ⌂ ✕ 🕿 ✕ 📶 🖵

WWW Comfort Suites Moses Lake H

(509) 765-3731. **$90-$220.** 1700 E Kittleson Rd 98837. I-90 exit 179, just nw. Int corridors. **Pets:** Small, dogs only. $25 daily fee/pet. Designated rooms, supervision. (SAVE) (占M) ⌂ 🕿 ✕ 📶 🖵

WW Inn at Moses Lake H

(509) 766-7000. **$80-$120.** 1741 E Kittleson Rd 98837. I-90 exit 179, just nw. Int corridors. **Pets:** Accepted. 🕿 ✕ 📶 🖵

WWW Moses Lake Super 8 H

(509) 765-8886. **$61-$141.** 449 Melva Ln 98837. I-90 exit 176, just n. Int corridors. **Pets:** Accepted. (SAVE) ⌂ 🕿 📶 🖵

WWW Ramada Moses Lake H 🌿

(509) 766-1000. **$38-$96.** 1745 E Kittleson Rd 98837. I-90 exit 179, just n. Int corridors. **Pets:** Other species. $10 daily fee/pet. Service with restrictions, supervision. 🕿 ✕ 📶 🖵

MOUNT RAINIER NATIONAL PARK

WWWW Alta Crystal Resort at Mt Rainier H

(360) 663-2500. **$179-$339, 30 day notice.** 68317 SR 410 E 98022. 2 mi outside northeast entrance. Ext corridors. **Pets:** Accepted.

(SAVE) ⌂ ✕ 🕿 ✕ 🎾 📶 🖵

MOUNT VERNON

WWW BEST WESTERN College Way Inn H

(360) 424-4287. **$85-$195.** 300 W College Way 98273. I-5 exit 227, just w. Ext corridors. **Pets:** $20 daily fee/room. Designated rooms, service with restrictions, supervision. (SAVE) (占M) ⌂ 🕿 ✕ 📶 🖵

WWW Quality Inn-Mount Vernon H

(360) 428-7020. **$63-$113.** 1910 Freeway Dr 98273. I-5 exit 227, just w on College Way, then just n. Ext corridors. **Pets:** Accepted.

(SAVE) (占M) ⌂ 🕿 📶 🖵

WWW Tulip Inn M

(360) 428-5969. **$69-$109.** 2200 Freeway Dr 98273. I-5 exit 227, just w on College Way, then just n. Ext corridors. **Pets:** Accepted.

(SAVE) (占M) 🕿 ✕ 📶 🖵

MUKILTEO

WWWW Staybridge Suites Seattle North-Everett H

(425) 493-9500. **Call for rates.** 9600 Harbour Pl 98275. Jct Paine Field Blvd and SR 525 (Mukilteo Speedway). Int corridors. **Pets:** Accepted.

(SAVE) (占M) ⌂ 🕿 ✕ 📶 🖵

WWW TownePlace Suites by Marriott-Mukilteo H

(425) 551-5900. **$89-$199.** 8521 Mukilteo Speedway 98275. Just se of jct 84th St SW and SR 525 (Mukilteo Speedway). Ext corridors. **Pets:** Accepted. (占M) ⌂ 🕿 ✕ 📶 🖵

OAK HARBOR (Restaurants p. 644)

WWW BEST WESTERN PLUS Harbor Plaza & Conference Center H

(360) 679-4567. **$109-$179.** 33175 SR 20 98277. Just n of town. Int corridors. **Pets:** Accepted. (SAVE) (占M) ⌂ 🕿 ✕ 📶 🖵

WWWW Candlewood Suites-Oak Harbor H 🌿

(360) 279-2222. **Call for rates.** 33221 SR 20 98277. Just n of town. Int corridors. **Pets:** Other species. $75 deposit/pet, $10 daily fee/pet. Service with restrictions, crate. (占M) 🕿 ✕ 📶 🖵

WWW Coachman Inn H

(360) 675-0727. **$94-$209.** 32959 SR 20 98277. Jct Goldie Rd and Midway Blvd. Ext corridors. **Pets:** Medium. $8 daily fee/pet. Designated rooms, service with restrictions, supervision.

(SAVE) ⌂ ✕ 🕿 ✕ 📶 🖵

OCEAN PARK

WWW Ocean Park Resort M

(360) 665-4585. **Call for rates.** 25904 R St 98640. Just e of SR 103; downtown. Ext corridors. **Pets:** Small, other species. $7 daily fee/pet. Service with restrictions, supervision.

⌂ 🕿 ✕ 🎾 🔲 📶 🖵

OCEAN SHORES

WWW BEST WESTERN Lighthouse Suites Inn H 🌿

(360) 289-2311. **$89-$189.** 491 Damon Rd NW 98569. Just w of main entrance to town; north end of downtown. Int corridors. **Pets:** Large, dogs only. $20 daily fee/room. Designated rooms, service with restrictions, supervision. (SAVE) (ᵀ¶) ⌂ ✕ 🕿 ✕ 🎾 📶 🖵

WWW The Canterbury Inn CO 🌿

(360) 289-3317. **$86-$214.** 643 Ocean Shores Blvd NW 98569. 0.3 mi s of Chance A La Mer Blvd. Int corridors. **Pets:** Large, dogs only. $150 deposit/room, $15 daily fee/pet. Service with restrictions, supervision.

⌂ 🕿 ✕ 🎾 📶 🖵

WWW The Polynesian Condominium Resort CO

(360) 289-3361. **Call for rates.** 615 Ocean Shores Blvd NW 98569. 0.3 mi s of Chance A La Mer Blvd. Ext/int corridors. **Pets:** Accepted.

(SAVE) (ᵀ¶) ⌂ ✕ 🕿 ✕ 🎾 📶 🖵

WWW Shilo Inn Suites Hotel - Ocean Shores H

(360) 289-4600. **Call for rates.** 707 Ocean Shores Blvd NW 98569. Northwest corner of Chance A La Mer and Ocean Shores blvds NW. Int corridors. **Pets:** Accepted. (ᵀ¶) (占M) ⌂ ✕ 🕿 ✕ 📶 🖵

OKANOGAN

WWW Okanogan Inn H

(509) 422-6431. **$67-$70.** 11B Apple Way 98840. SR 97 exit SR 20, just w. Int corridors. **Pets:** Medium. $10 daily fee/pet. Designated rooms, service with restrictions, supervision. (SAVE) (ᵀ¶) ⌂ 🕿 📶

OLYMPIA

WWW Red Lion Hotel Olympia H

(360) 943-4000. **Call for rates.** 2300 Evergreen Park Dr SW 98502. I-5 exit 104, 0.7 mi w on US 101, just n on Cooper Point Rd N, 0.7 mi e on S Evergreen Park Dr SW, then just n on Lakeridge Way SW. Int corridors. **Pets:** Accepted. (ᵀ¶) (占M) ⌂ 🕿 ✕ 📶 🖵

OMAK

WWWW BEST WESTERN PLUS Peppertree Inn at Omak H

(509) 422-2088. **$99-$299.** 820 Koala Dr 98841. US 97, just n of Riverside Dr. Int corridors. **Pets:** Accepted.

(SAVE) (占M) ⌂ 🕿 ✕ 📶 🖵

AAA ▼▼ **Omak Inn LLC** H
(509) 826-3822. **Call for rates.** 912 Koala Dr 98841. On US 97, just n of Riverside Dr. Int corridors. **Pets:** Other species. $25 one-time fee/room. Designated rooms, service with restrictions, crate.
[SAVE] [symbols]

OTHELLO
AAA ▼▼ **Quality Inn** H
(509) 488-5671. **$100-$130.** 1020 E Cedar St 99344. Just off Main St; jct 10th St. Int corridors. **Pets:** Accepted. [SAVE] [symbols]

PACIFIC
AAA ▼▼ **Quality Inn & Suites** H
(253) 288-1916. **$79-$139.** 415 Ellingson Rd 98047. SR 167 exit Algona/Pacific, just se. Int corridors. **Pets:** Accepted.
[SAVE] [symbols]

PACKWOOD
▼▼ **Cowlitz River Lodge** M
(360) 494-4444. **$65-$100, 3 day notice.** 13069 US 12 98361. East end of town. Ext corridors. **Pets:** Dogs only. $20 one-time fee/pet. Designated rooms, supervision. [symbols]

AAA ▼▼ **Crest Trail Lodge** H
(360) 494-4944. **$100-$130.** 12729 US 12 98361. West end of town. Int corridors. **Pets:** Small, dogs only. $20 one-time fee/pet. Supervision.
[SAVE] [symbols]

PASCO
AAA ▼▼▼ **BEST WESTERN PLUS Pasco Inn & Suites** H
(509) 543-7722. **$130-$180.** 2811 N 20th Ave 99301. I-182 exit 12B, just n. Int corridors. **Pets:** Accepted.
[SAVE] [symbols]

▼▼▼ **Holiday Inn Express Pasco at TRAC** H
(509) 543-7000. **$120-$300.** 4525 Convention Pl 99301. I-182 exit 9 (Rd 68), just n, then just e. Int corridors. **Pets:** Small, dogs only. $20 daily fee/pet. Designated rooms, service with restrictions, supervision.
[symbols]

▼▼▼ **Red Lion Hotel Pasco** H
(509) 547-0701. **Call for rates.** 2525 N 20th Ave 99301. I-182 exit 12B, just n. Int corridors. **Pets:** Accepted.
[symbols]

▼▼ **Sleep Inn** H
(509) 545-9554. **$95-$175.** 9930 Bedford St 99301. I-182 exit 7, just ne. Int corridors. **Pets:** Accepted. [symbols]

PORT ANGELES
▼▼ **Days Inn** H
(360) 452-4015. **$69-$122.** 1510 E Front St 98362. Jct Alder St; on east side. Ext corridors. **Pets:** Accepted. [symbols]

▼▼▼ **Red Lion Hotel Port Angeles** H
(360) 452-9215. **Call for rates.** 221 N Lincoln St 98362. On US 101 westbound; at ferry landing. Ext/int corridors. **Pets:** Accepted.
[symbols]

▼▼ **Super 8 Port Angeles** M
(360) 452-8401. **$56-$150.** 2104 E 1st St 98362. 1.8 mi e of downtown, just s of US 101; jct Del Guzzi Dr. Int corridors. **Pets:** Large, other species. $15 daily fee/room. Service with restrictions, crate.
[symbols]

PORT ORCHARD
AAA ▼▼ **Comfort Inn Port Orchard** M
(360) 895-2666. **$90-$125.** 1121 Bay St 98366. SR 16 exit Tremont St, 0.9 mi e to Sidney Ave, 1.2 mi n to Bay St, then just e. Ext corridors.
Pets: Accepted. [SAVE] [symbols]

PORT TOWNSEND
▼▼▼ **Ann Starrett Mansion** H
(360) 385-3205. **$89-$129, 14 day notice.** 744 Clay St 98368. Jct of Adams St; on bluff. Ext/int corridors. **Pets:** Accepted.
[symbols]

AAA ▼▼▼ **Bishop Victorian Hotel** H ❀
(360) 385-6122. **$120-$275, 3 day notice.** 714 Washington St 98368. Corner of Washington and Quincy sts. Int corridors. **Pets:** Dogs only. $20 daily fee/pet. Designated rooms, supervision.
[SAVE] [symbols]

▼▼ **Harborside Inn** H
(360) 385-7909. **Call for rates.** 330 Benedict St 98368. Just s of SR 20; between Jefferson and Washington sts. Ext corridors.
Pets: Accepted. [symbols]

▼▼▼ **Old Consulate Inn** BB ❀
(360) 385-6753. **$110-$220, 7 day notice.** 313 Walker St 98368. Jct Washington St; on the bluff. Int corridors. **Pets:** Dogs only. $25 one-time fee/room. Designated rooms, service with restrictions, crate.
[symbols]

AAA ▼▼ **The Swan Hotel** M ❀
(360) 385-1718. **$100-$325, 3 day notice.** 222 Monroe St 98368. Jct Water St; downtown. Ext corridors. **Pets:** Dogs only. $20 daily fee/pet. Designated rooms, service with restrictions, supervision.
[SAVE] [symbols]

POULSBO
▼▼ **GuestHouse International Inn & Suites** H ❀
(360) 697-4400. **$89-$179.** 19801 7th Ave NE 98370. SR 3, 1.4 mi e on SR 305, then just s; just n from jct NE Liberty Rd. Int corridors. **Pets:** $30 daily fee/pet. Service with restrictions, supervision.
[symbols]

AAA ▼▼ **Poulsbo Inn & Suites** M
(360) 779-3921. **$89-$130, 7 day notice.** 18680 SR 305 NE 98370. SR 3, 2.3 mi e. Ext corridors. **Pets:** Small. $15 daily fee/pet. Designated rooms, service with restrictions, supervision.
[SAVE] [symbols]

PROSSER
AAA ▼▼▼ **BEST WESTERN PLUS The Inn at Horse Heaven** H
(509) 786-7977. **$105-$158.** 259 Merlot Dr 99350. I-82 exit 80, just s. Int corridors. **Pets:** Dogs only. $10 daily fee/pet. Designated rooms, service with restrictions, supervision.
[SAVE] [symbols]

PULLMAN
▼▼▼ **Holiday Inn Express & Suites Pullman** H ❀
(509) 334-4437. **$129-$229.** 1190 SE Bishop Blvd 99163. Jct US 195 business route, 0.5 mi s, 1 mi e on SR 270. Int corridors.
Pets: Medium, dogs only. $20 daily fee/pet. Designated rooms, service with restrictions, supervision. [symbols]

AAA ▼▼▼ **Residence Inn by Marriott Pullman** H
(509) 332-4400. **$139-$349.** 1255 NE North Fairway Rd 99163. Jct Grand Ave and NE Stadium Way, 1 mi se, 0.8 mi ne. Int corridors.
Pets: $100 one-time fee/room. Service with restrictions, supervision.
[SAVE] [symbols]

PUYALLUP
AAA ▼▼▼ **BEST WESTERN PREMIER Plaza Hotel & Conference Center** H ❀
(253) 848-1500. **$139-$169.** 620 S Hill Park Dr 98373. SR 512 exit S Hill Park Dr southbound; exit 9th St SW northbound, just w. Int corridors. **Pets:** Dogs only. $20 daily fee/room. Designated rooms, service with restrictions, supervision. [SAVE] [symbols]

▼▼▼ **Holiday Inn Express Hotel & Suites** 🅷 🐾
(253) 848-4900. **Call for rates.** 812 S Hill Park Dr 98373. SR 512 exit S Hill Park Dr southbound; exit 9th St SW northbound, just w. Int corridors. **Pets:** Dogs only. $20 daily fee/room. Service with restrictions, crate. 🔲 🔲 🔲 🔲 🔲

QUINAULT

▼▼ **Lake Quinault Lodge** 🅷
(360) 288-2900. **$99-$350, 3 day notice.** 345 S Shore Rd 98575. 2.2 mi ne of US 101 and S Shore Rd. Ext/int corridors. **Pets:** Dogs only. $25 one-time fee/room. Designated rooms, service with restrictions, crate. 🔲 🔲 🔲 🔲 🔲 🔲 🔲 🔲

REDMOND

🔷🔷 ▼▼▼ **HYATT house Seattle/Redmond** 🅷
(425) 497-2000. **$99-$409.** 15785 Bear Creek Pkwy NE 98052. I-405 exit 14 (SR 520), 4.5 mi e to W Lake Sammamish Pkwy, just n to Leary Way, just e to Bear Creek Pkwy, then just n. Int corridors. **Pets:** Accepted. 🔲 🔲 🔲 🔲 🔲 🔲 🔲 🔲

🔷 ▼▼▼ **Redmond Marriott Town Center** 🅷
(425) 498-4000. **$107-$319.** 7401 164th Ave NE 98052. I-405 exit 14 (SR 520), 4.5 mi e to W Lake Sammamish Pkwy, just n to Leary Way, just e to Bear Creek Pkwy, just s to NE 74th Ave, then just w. Int corridors. **Pets:** Accepted. 🔲 🔲 🔲 🔲 🔲 🔲 🔲 🔲 🔲

▼▼▼ **Residence Inn by Marriott Seattle East / Redmond** 🅷
(425) 497-9226. **$99-$260.** 7575 164th Ave NE 98052. I-405 exit 14 (SR 520), 4.5 mi e to W Lake Sammamish Pkwy, just n to Leary Way, just e to Bear Creek Pkwy, just s to NE 74th Ave, just w to 164th Ave NE, then just n; center. Int corridors. **Pets:** Accepted.
🔲 🔲 🔲 🔲 🔲 🔲 🔲

RENTON *(Restaurants p. 644)*

🔷🔷 ▼▼▼ **Larkspur Landing Renton** 🅷
(425) 235-1212. **Call for rates.** 1701 E Valley Rd 98057. SR 167 exit E Valley Rd, 1 mi nw. Int corridors. **Pets:** Accepted.
🔲 🔲 🔲 🔲 🔲

▼▼ **Quality Inn Renton** 🅷
(425) 226-7600. **$99-$159.** 1850 SE Maple Valley Hwy 98057. I-405 exit 4 (Bronson Way) northbound, follow Maple Valley Hwy; exit southbound, 0.6 mi s to 2nd light, then just e. Int corridors. **Pets:** Accepted.
🔲 🔲 🔲

▼▼ **TownePlace Suites by Marriott Seattle South/Renton** 🅷
(425) 917-2000. **$159-$230.** 300 SW 19th St 98057. SR 167 exit E Valley Rd, 1 mi nw, then just w. Int corridors. **Pets:** Accepted.
🔲 🔲 🔲 🔲 🔲 🔲

REPUBLIC

🔷🔷 ▼ **Prospector Inn** 🅷
(509) 775-3361. **$51-$150, 4 day notice.** 979 S Clark Ave 99166. Downtown. Int corridors. **Pets:** $12 daily fee/pet. Service with restrictions, supervision. 🔲 🔲 🔲 🔲 🔲 🔲

RICHLAND

▼▼▼ **Holiday Inn Express & Suites** 🅷
(509) 737-8000. **$119-$179.** 1970 Center Pkwy 99352. Just s on Columbia Center Blvd from SR 240, then just w. Int corridors. **Pets:** Accepted. 🔲 🔲 🔲 🔲 🔲 🔲 🔲

▼▼▼ **Red Lion Hotel Richland - Hanford House** 🅷
(509) 946-7611. **Call for rates.** 802 George Washington Way 99352. I-182 exit 5B, 1.3 mi n on SR 240 business route. Int corridors. **Pets:** Accepted. 🔲 🔲 🔲 🔲 🔲 🔲

🔷🔷 ▼▼▼ **TownePlace Suites by Marriott - Richland/ Columbia Point** 🅷
(509) 943-9800. **$130-$154.** 591 Columbia Point Dr 99352. I-182 exit 5B, just n to Columbia Point Dr, then 0.8 mi e. Int corridors. **Pets:** Accepted. 🔲 🔲 🔲 🔲 🔲 🔲 🔲

RITZVILLE

🔷🔷 ▼▼▼ **BEST WESTERN PLUS Bronco Inn** 🅷
(509) 659-5000. **$94-$149.** 105 W Galbreath Way 99169. I-90 exit 221, cross overpass, then second left. Int corridors. **Pets:** $20 one-time fee/pet. Designated rooms, service with restrictions, supervision.
🔲 🔲 🔲 🔲 🔲 🔲

🔷🔷 ▼▼ **Cedars Inn & Suites Ritzville** 🅷
(509) 659-1007. **Call for rates.** 1513 Smitty's Blvd 99169. I-90 exit 221, just n. Int corridors. **Pets:** Medium, other species. $10 one-time fee/room. Service with restrictions, supervision. 🔲 🔲 🔲 🔲 🔲

SEATAC

▼▼ **Clarion Hotel** 🅷
(206) 242-0200. **$97-$263.** 3000 S 176th St 98188. Jct SR 518, 1.2 mi s on International Blvd (SR 99) then just e. Int corridors. **Pets:** Small. $20 daily fee/pet. Service with restrictions, supervision.
🔲 🔲 🔲 🔲 🔲 🔲 🔲

▼▼▼ **DoubleTree by Hilton Hotel Seattle Airport** 🅷
(206) 246-8600. **$89-$349.** 18740 International Blvd (SR 99) 98188. Jct SR 518, 1.7 mi s. Int corridors. **Pets:** Accepted.
🔲 🔲 🔲 🔲 🔲 🔲 🔲

▼▼▼ **Hilton Seattle Airport & Conference Center** 🅷
(206) 244-4800. **$99-$399.** 17620 International Blvd 98188. Jct SR 518, 1.3 mi s. Int corridors. **Pets:** Accepted.
🔲 🔲 🔲 🔲 🔲 🔲 🔲

▼▼▼ **Holiday Inn Express Hotel & Suites-Seattle Sea-Tac Airport** 🅷
(206) 824-3200. **Call for rates.** 19621 International Blvd (SR 99) 98188. Jct SR 518, 2.5 mi s. Int corridors. **Pets:** Accepted. 🔲 🔲 🔲

▼▼▼ **Radisson Hotel Seattle Airport** 🅷
(206) 244-6666. **Call for rates.** 18118 International Blvd (SR 99) 98188. Jct SR 518, 1.5 mi s. Int corridors. **Pets:** Accepted.
🔲 🔲 🔲 🔲 🔲 🔲 🔲

🔷🔷 ▼▼▼ **Red Lion Hotel Seattle Airport** 🅷
(206) 246-5535. **$89-$279.** 18220 International Blvd (SR 99) 98188. Jct SR 518, 1.6 mi s. Int corridors. **Pets:** Accepted.
🔲 🔲 🔲 🔲 🔲 🔲

🔷🔷 ▼▼▼ **Red Roof Inn Seattle Airport-SeaTac** 🅷
(206) 248-0901. **$54-$169.** 16838 International Blvd (SR 99) 98188. Jct SR 518, 0.8 mi s. Int corridors. **Pets:** Large, other species. Service with restrictions, supervision. 🔲 🔲 🔲 🔲 🔲

▼▼ **Super 8 Sea-Tac** 🅷
(206) 433-8188. **$67-$83.** 3100 S 192nd St 98188. Jct SR 518, 2.2 mi s on International Blvd (SR 99) then just e. Int corridors. **Pets:** Large. $10 daily fee/pet. Service with restrictions, supervision. 🔲 🔲 🔲

SEATTLE *(Restaurants p. 645)*

🔷🔷 ▼▼▼▼ **Alexis Hotel-A Kimpton Hotel** 🅷
(206) 624-4844. **Call for rates.** 1007 1st Ave 98104. Corner of Madison St and 1st Ave. Int corridors. **Pets:** Accepted.
🔲 🔲 🔲 🔲 🔲 🔲 🔲 🔲

🔷🔷 ▼▼ ◇ **Comfort Inn & Suites Seattle** 🅷
(206) 361-3700. **$90-$450.** 13700 Aurora Ave N 98133. I-5 exit 175, 1.1 mi w on NE 145th St, then 0.3 mi s. Int corridors. **Pets:** Accepted.
🔲 🔲 🔲 🔲

🔷🔷 ▼▼ ◇ **Crowne Plaza Seattle-Downtown** 🅷
(206) 464-1980. **$149-$309, 3 day notice.** 1113 6th Ave 98101. Corner of 6th Ave and Seneca St. Int corridors. **Pets:** Accepted.
🔲 🔲 🔲 🔲 🔲 🔲 🔲

AAA ▽▽▽ ▽▽▽ **The Edgewater** H
(206) 728-7000. **$179-$549, 3 day notice.** 2411 Alaskan Way, Pier 67
98121. On waterfront at Pier 67; at base of Wall St. Int corridors.
Pets: Accepted. SAVE ⫽ 🛜 ✕ 🛏 💻

AAA ▽▽▽ ▽▽▽ **The Fairmont Olympic Hotel** H
(206) 621-1700. **$199-$449.** 411 University St 98101. Corner of 4th Ave
and University St. Int corridors. **Pets:** Accepted.
SAVE ECO ⫽ 🏊 ✕ 🛰 ✕ 🛏 💻

AAA ▽▽▽ ▽▽▽ **Four Seasons Hotel Seattle** H 🐾
(206) 749-7000. **Call for rates.** 99 Union St 98101. Southwest corner
of 1st Ave and Union St. Int corridors. **Pets:** Small, dogs only. Service
with restrictions, supervision. SAVE ⫽ 🛒M 🏊 ✕ ✕

AAA ▽▽▽ ▽▽▽ **Grand Hyatt Seattle** H 🐾
(206) 774-1234. **$179-$419, 3 day notice.** 721 Pine St 98101. Corner
of 7th Ave and Pine St. Int corridors. **Pets:** Medium, dogs only. $100
one-time fee/room. Designated rooms, service with restrictions, supervision. SAVE ECO ⫽ ✕ 🛰 🛏 💻

AAA ▽▽▽ ▽▽▽ **Homewood Suites by Hilton Seattle**
                    Convention Center/Pike Street H
(206) 682-8282. **$159-$399.** 1011 Pike St 98101. I-5 exit 165 northbound to Pike St via 6th Ave; exit Union St southbound to Pike St. Int
corridors. **Pets:** Medium, dogs only. $75 one-time fee/room. Service
with restrictions, crate. SAVE 🛒M 🏊 ✕ 🛜 🛏 💻

▽▽▽ **Homewood Suites by Hilton-Seattle**
        Downtown H
(206) 281-9393. **$119-$379.** 206 Western Ave W 98119. I-5 exit 167
(Mercer St), 0.3 mi w, 0.5 mi s on Fairview Ave, 1.2 mi w on Denny
Way, then just n. Int corridors. **Pets:** Accepted. 🛜 ✕ 🛏 💻

AAA ▽▽▽ ▽▽▽ **Hotel 1000** H
(206) 957-1000. **$249-$599.** 1000 1st Ave 98104. Northeast corner of
1st Ave and Madison St. Int corridors. **Pets:** Accepted.
SAVE ⫽ 🛜 ✕ 💻

AAA ▽▽▽ ▽▽▽ **Hotel Max** H 🐾
(206) 728-6299. **$129-$409.** 620 Stewart St 98101. Corner of 7th Ave
and Stewart St. Int corridors. **Pets:** $45 one-time fee/room. Designated
rooms, service with restrictions, supervision.
SAVE ⫽ 🛒M 🛰 ✕ 🛏 💻

AAA ▽▽▽ ▽▽▽ **Hotel Monaco Seattle-A Kimpton**
                    Hotel H
(206) 621-1770. **Call for rates.** 1101 4th Ave 98101. Corner of 4th Ave
and Spring St. Int corridors. **Pets:** Accepted.
SAVE ECO ⊟ ⫽ ✕ 🛰 ✕

AAA ▽▽▽ ▽▽ **Hotel Nexus Seattle** H
(206) 365-0700. **$109-$289.** 2140 N Northgate Way 98133. I-5 exit 173,
just nw. Ext corridors. **Pets:** Small, dogs only. $15 daily fee/room. Des-
ignated rooms, service with restrictions, supervision.
SAVE 🛒M 🏊 🛜 ✕ 🛏 💻

AAA ▽▽▽ ▽▽▽ **Hotel Vintage-A Kimpton Hotel** H
(206) 624-8000. **Call for rates.** 1100 5th Ave 98101. Corner of Spring
St and 5th Ave. Int corridors. **Pets:** Accepted.
SAVE ECO ⊟ ⫽ ✕ 🛰 ✕

AAA ▽▽▽ ▽▽▽ **Hyatt at Olive 8** H
(206) 695-1234. **$159-$419.** 1635 8th Ave 98101. Between Olive Way
and Pine St. Int corridors. **Pets:** Accepted.
SAVE ECO ⫽ 🏊 ✕ 🛰 ✕ 🛏 💻

▽▽▽ **La Quinta Inn & Suites Seattle Downtown** H
(206) 624-6820. **$99-$309.** 2224 8th Ave 98121. Corner of 8th Ave and
Blanchard St. Int corridors. **Pets:** Large, other species. Service with
restrictions. 🛜 ✕ 🛏 💻

▽▽▽ **The Maxwell Hotel** H
(206) 286-0629. **Call for rates.** 300 Roy St 98109. Corner of Roy St
and 3rd Ave N. Int corridors. **Pets:** Accepted.
⫽ 🛒M 🏊 🛜 ✕ 🛏 💻

AAA ▽▽▽ ▽▽▽ **Motif Seattle** H
(206) 971-8000. **Call for rates.** 1415 5th Ave 98101. Between Pike and
Union sts. Int corridors. **Pets:** Accepted. SAVE ⫽ 🛜 ✕ 🛏 💻

AAA ▽▽▽ ▽▽▽ **Pan Pacific Hotel Seattle** H
(206) 264-8111. **$225-$525.** 2125 Terry Ave 98121. Just s of jct E
Denny Way. Int corridors. **Pets:** Accepted.
SAVE ⫽ ✕ 🛜 ✕ 💻

AAA ▽▽▽ ▽▽▽ **Renaissance Seattle Hotel** H
(206) 583-0300. **$159-$369.** 515 Madison St 98104. Corner of Madison
St and 6th Ave. Int corridors. **Pets:** $50 one-time fee/room. Service with
restrictions, supervision. SAVE ⫽ 🛒M 🛰 ✕ 🛏 💻

▽▽▽ **Residence Inn by Marriott Seattle Downtown/Lake**
        Union H 🐾
(206) 624-6000. **$149-$389.** 800 Fairview Ave N 98109. I-5 exit 167
(Mercer St), just nw; south end of Lake Union. Int corridors.
Pets: Other species. $20 daily fee/room. Service with restrictions, crate.
🏊 ✕ 🛜 ✕ 🛏 💻

AAA ▽▽▽ ▽▽ **The Roosevelt, A Coast Hotel** H
(206) 621-1200. **Call for rates.** 1531 7th Ave 98101. Corner of 7th Ave
and Pine St. Int corridors. **Pets:** Accepted. SAVE 🛜 ✕ 🛏 💻

AAA ▽▽▽ ▽▽▽ **Sheraton Seattle Hotel** H
(206) 621-9000. **$199-$399.** 1400 6th Ave 98101. Between Pike and
Union sts. Int corridors. **Pets:** Accepted.
SAVE ECO ⫽ 🛒M 🏊 🛰 ✕ 💻

▽▽▽ ▽▽▽ **Sorrento Hotel** H
(206) 622-6400. **Call for rates.** 900 Madison St 98104. I-5 exit Madison
St, just e; jct 9th Ave. Int corridors. **Pets:** Accepted.
⫽ 🛒M 🛜 ✕ 💻

▽▽ **University Inn** H
(206) 632-5055. **Call for rates.** 4140 Roosevelt Way NE 98105. I-5 exit
169, just e on NE 45th St, then just s. Int corridors. **Pets:** Accepted.
⫽ 🏊 🛜 ✕ 🛏 💻

AAA ▽▽▽ ▽▽▽ **The Westin Seattle** H
(206) 728-1000. **$169-$569.** 1900 5th Ave 98101. Corner of 5th Ave
and Stewart St. Int corridors. **Pets:** Accepted.
SAVE ECO ⫽ 🛒M 🏊 🛰 ✕ 💻

AAA ▽▽▽ ▽▽▽ **W Seattle** H 🐾
(206) 264-6000. **$199-$698.** 1112 4th Ave 98101. Corner of 4th Ave
and Seneca St. Int corridors. **Pets:** Large. $100 one-time fee/room.
Service with restrictions, supervision.
SAVE ECO ⊟ ⫽ 🛒M 🛰 ✕

SEQUIM
▽▽▽ **Juan de Fuca Cottages** CA
(360) 683-4433. **$110-$275, 14 day notice.** 182 Marine Dr 98382. US
101 exit Sequim Ave, 4.9 mi nw on Sequim/Dungeness Ave, 0.7 mi nw
on E Anderson Rd, then 1.3 mi nw. Ext corridors. **Pets:** Accepted.
🛜 ✕ 🎖 🎁 🛏 💻

▽▽ ▽▽ **Quality Inn & Suites - Sequim** H 🐾
(360) 683-2800. **$109-$189.** 134 River Rd 98382. US 101 exit River
Rd, just nw. Int corridors. **Pets:** Medium, dogs only. $10 daily fee/room.
Designated rooms, service with restrictions, supervision.
ECO 🏊 🛜 ✕ 🛏 💻

AAA ▽▽ **Sequim West Inn** M
(360) 683-4144. **$59-$149, 3 day notice.** 740 W Washington St 98382.
US 101 exit River Rd, 0.9 mi ne via River Rd and W Washington St.
Ext corridors. **Pets:** Small, dogs only. $15 daily fee/pet. Designated
rooms, service with restrictions, supervision. SAVE 🛜 🛏 💻

SHELTON

Little Creek Casino Resort 🅷
(360) 427-7711. **$59-$299.** 91 W SR 108 98584. Jct US 101 and SR 108. Int corridors. **Pets:** Other species. $50 one-time fee/room. Designated rooms, service with restrictions, supervision.

[SAVE] [🍴] [&M] [🛂] [🗙] [📶] [🛢] [💻]

Super 8 of Shelton Ⓜ
(360) 426-1654. **$61-$74.** 2943 Northview Cir 98584. US 101 exit Wallace-Kneeland Blvd, just se. Int corridors. **Pets:** Dogs only. $25 daily fee/pet. Designated rooms, service with restrictions, supervision.

[📶] [🛢] [💻]

SILVERDALE

BEST WESTERN PLUS Silverdale Beach Hotel 🅷 ❖
(360) 698-1000. **$89-$109.** 3073 NW Bucklin Hill Rd 98383. SR 3 exit Newberry Hill Rd, just e, 1 mi n on Silverdale Way, then just e. Int corridors. **Pets:** Other species. $20 daily fee/pet. Designated rooms, service with restrictions. [SAVE] [🍴] [🛂] [🗙] [📶] [🗙] [🛢] [💻]

Oxford Inn Silverdale 🅷
(360) 692-7777. **$79-$119, 3 day notice.** 9734 NW Silverdale Way 98383. SR 3 exit Newberry Hill Rd, just e, then 1.2 mi n. Int corridors. **Pets:** Accepted. [SAVE] [📶] [🛢] [💻]

Oxford Suites Silverdale 🅷 ❖
(360) 698-9550. **$125-$199, 3 day notice.** 9550 NW Silverdale Way 98383. SR 3 exit Newberry Hill Rd, just e, then 1 mi n. Int corridors. **Pets:** Small. $25 one-time fee/pet. Designated rooms, service with restrictions, crate. [SAVE] [🍴] [🛂] [🗙] [📶] [🗙] [🛢] [💻]

SNOHOMISH

Inn At Snohomish Ⓜ
(360) 568-2208. **$76-$167.** 323 2nd St 98290. Just e, corner of Pine St. Ext corridors. **Pets:** Other species. $50 deposit/room. Service with restrictions, supervision. [SAVE] [&M] [📶] [🛢] [💻]

SNOQUALMIE

Salish Lodge & Spa 🅷 ❖
(425) 888-2556. **$199-$439, 7 day notice.** 6501 Railroad Ave SE 98065. I-90 exit 25 eastbound, 3.6 mi n on Snoqualmie Pkwy, then 0.4 mi n; exit 31 westbound, 7 mi nw via SR 202. Int corridors. **Pets:** Dogs only. $65 one-time fee/pet. Designated rooms, service with restrictions, supervision. [🍴] [🗙] [📶] [🗙] [🛢] [💻]

SOAP LAKE

Inn at Soap Lake Ⓜ
(509) 246-1132. **$62-$140, 7 day notice.** 226 E Main Ave 98851. Just w of SR 17. Ext/int corridors. **Pets:** Other species. $10 daily fee/pet. Designated rooms, service with restrictions, supervision.

[📶] [🗙] [🛢] [💻]

Notaras Lodge Ⓜ
(509) 246-0462. **$85-$145.** 236 E Main Ave 98851. Just w of SR 17. Ext corridors. **Pets:** Accepted. [📶] [🗙] [🛢] [💻]

SPOKANE *(Restaurants p. 645)*

Apple Tree Inn Ⓜ
(509) 466-3020. **$44-$79.** 9508 N Division St 99218. Jct US 2 and 395, just n. Ext/int corridors. **Pets:** Small, dogs only. $10 daily fee/pet. Designated rooms, service with restrictions, crate. [SAVE] [🛂] [📶] [🛢]

BEST WESTERN PLUS City Center 🅷 ❖
(509) 623-9727. **$79-$230.** W 33 Spokane Falls Blvd 99201. I-90 exit 281 (Division St), 0.5 mi n, then just w. Int corridors. **Pets:** Dogs only. $15 daily fee/pet. Designated rooms, service with restrictions, crate. [SAVE] [&M] [📶] [🗙] [🛢] [💻]

BEST WESTERN PLUS Peppertree Airport Inn 🅷 ❖
(509) 624-4655. **$99-$220.** 3711 S Geiger Blvd 99224. I-90 exit 276 (Geiger Field), 1.3 mi n, 0.8 mi s, 0.4 mi e, then just s. Int corridors. **Pets:** Dogs only. Designated rooms, service with restrictions, supervision. [SAVE] [&M] [🛂] [📶] [🗙] [🛢] [💻]

Comfort Inn North 🅷
(509) 467-7111. **$95-$125.** 7111 N Division St 99208. I-90 exit 281 (Division St), 4.4 mi n. Int corridors. **Pets:** Accepted.
[&M] [🛂] [🗙] [📶] [🛢] [💻]

The Davenport Tower, Autograph Collection 🅷 ❖
(509) 455-8888. **Call for rates.** 111 S Post St 99201. Center. Int corridors. **Pets:** Dogs only. $50 one-time fee/pet. Designated rooms, supervision. [SAVE] [🍴] [&M] [📶] [🗙] [🛢] [💻]

DoubleTree by Hilton Spokane City Center 🅷 ❖
(509) 455-9600. **$109-$239.** 322 N Spokane Falls Ct 99201. I-90 exit 281 (Division St), just n; downtown. Int corridors. **Pets:** Large. $25 one-time fee/pet. Service with restrictions, supervision. [SAVE] [ECO] [🍴] [&M] [🛂] [📶] [🗙] [🛢] [💻]

Fairbridge Inn Express 🅷
(509) 838-6630. **Call for rates.** 211 S Division St 99202. I-90 exit 281 (Division St), just n. Int corridors. **Pets:** Accepted. [&M] [📶] [🛢] [💻]

The Historic Davenport, Autograph Collection 🅷 ❖
(509) 455-8888. **$145-$199.** 10 S Post St 99201. Downtown. Int corridors. **Pets:** Dogs only. $50 one-time fee/pet. Designated rooms, supervision. [SAVE] [ECO] [🍴] [&M] [🛂] [🗙] [📶] [🛢]

Holiday Inn Express-Downtown 🅷 ❖
(509) 328-8505. **Call for rates.** 801 N Division St 99202. I-90 exit 281 (Division St), 0.8 mi n. Ext/int corridors. **Pets:** Dogs only. Designated rooms, service with restrictions, supervision. [&M] [📶] [🗙] [🛢] [💻]

Howard Johnson Inn North Ⓜ
(509) 326-5500. **$54-$105.** 3033 N Division St 99207. I-90 exit 281 (Division St), 2.5 mi n on US 2 and 395. Int corridors. **Pets:** $10 daily fee/room. Designated rooms, service with restrictions, supervision.
[&M] [🛂] [📶] [🗙] [🛢] [💻]

The Madison Inn by Riversage 🅷
(509) 474-4200. **$78-$95, 3 day notice.** 15 W Rockwood Blvd 99204. I-90 exit 281 (Division St) eastbound, just e to Cowley St, 0.4 mi s, then just w; exit westbound, just n to 2nd Ave, just w to Browne St, 0.5 mi s to 9th Ave, then just e. Int corridors. **Pets:** Other species. $12 daily fee/pet. Designated rooms, service with restrictions, crate.
[SAVE] [&M] [📶] [🛢] [💻]

Montvale Hotel 🅷
(509) 747-1919. **$99-$299.** 1005 W First Ave 99201. At Monroe St; downtown. Int corridors. **Pets:** Dogs only. $25 daily fee/room. Service with restrictions, supervision. [🍴] [&M] [📶] [🗙]

Oxford Suites-Downtown Spokane 🅷 ❖
(509) 353-9000. **$119-$309.** 115 W North River Dr 99201. I-90 exit 281 (Division St), 1 mi n, then just n. Int corridors. **Pets:** Medium. $25 one-time fee/pet. Designated rooms, service with restrictions, supervision.
[SAVE] [🍴] [🛂] [🗙] [📶] [🗙] [🛢] [💻]

Quality Inn Oakwood 🅷 ❖
(509) 467-4900. **$89-$149.** 7919 N Division St 99208. I-90 exit 281 (Division St), 6.5 mi n. Int corridors. **Pets:** $30 one-time fee/room. Designated rooms, service with restrictions, crate.
[SAVE] [&M] [🛂] [📶] [🗙] [🛢] [💻]

▼▼ Ramada at Spokane Airport �H

(509) 838-5211. **$100-$226.** 8909 Airport Dr 99224. I-90 exit 277B eastbound; exit 277 westbound, 3.4 mi n. Int corridors. **Pets:** $10 daily fee/pet. Designated rooms, service with restrictions, supervision.

🍴 🏊 📶 ✖ 🔌 💻

▼▼▼▼ Red Lion Hotel at the Park-Spokane �H

(509) 326-8000. **$99-$249.** 303 W North River Dr 99201. I-90 exit 281 (Division St), 1.5 mi n on US 195, then just w. Int corridors. **Pets:** Accepted. 🍴 🏊 📶 ✖ 🔌 💻

▼▼ Red Lion River Inn-Spokane �H

(509) 326-5577. **Call for rates.** 700 N Division St 99202. I-90 exit 281 (Division St), 1 mi n; downtown. Int corridors. **Pets:** Accepted. 🍴 ♿M 🏊 📶 ✖ 🔌 💻

▼▼ Super 8 Airport West M

(509) 838-8800. **$70-$90.** 11102 W Westbow Blvd 99224. I-90 exit 272 (Medical Lake Rd), just s. Int corridors. **Pets:** $5 deposit/pet. Designated rooms, crate. ♿M 🏊 📶 🔌 💻

▼▼▼▼ Wingate by Wyndham Spokane Airport �H

(509) 838-3226. **$101-$152.** 2726 S Flint Rd 99201. I-90 exit 277B eastbound; exit 277 westbound, 3 mi w, then just s. Int corridors. **Pets:** Other species. $10 daily fee/room. Service with restrictions, supervision. ♿M 🏊 📶 ✖ 🔌 💻

SPOKANE VALLEY *(Restaurants p. 645)*

AAA ▼▼▼▼ Comfort Inn & Suites at Spokane Valley �H

(509) 926-7432. **$109-$309.** 12415 E Mission Ave 99216. I-90 exit 289 (N Pines Rd), just se. Int corridors. **Pets:** Accepted.
SAVE ♿M 🏊 📶 ✖ 🔌 💻

▼▼▼▼ Holiday Inn Express-Valley �H 🐾

(509) 927-7100. **$119-$209.** 9220 E Mission Ave 99206. I-90 exit 287, just s. Ext/int corridors. **Pets:** Other species. Designated rooms, service with restrictions, supervision. ♿M 🏊 📶 ✖ 🔌 💻

▼▼▼ La Quinta Inn & Suites Spokane �H

(509) 893-0955. **$69-$239.** 3808 N Sullivan Rd 99216. I-90 exit 291B, 1.5 mi n. Int corridors. **Pets:** Large, other species. Service with restrictions. ♿M 🏊 📶 ✖ 🔌 💻

AAA ▼▼▼▼ Mirabeau Park Hotel & Convention Center �H 🐾

(509) 924-9000. **$89-$159.** 1100 N Sullivan Rd 99037. I-90 exit 291B, just s. Int corridors. **Pets:** Large. $30 one-time fee/room. Service with restrictions. SAVE 🍴 🏊 ✖ 📶 🔌 💻

AAA ▼▼▼▼ Oxford Suites Spokane Valley �H

(509) 847-1000. **$99-$195.** 15015 E Indiana Ave 99216. I-90 exit 291A eastbound; exit 291B westbound, just nw. Int corridors. **Pets:** Accepted. SAVE 🍴 ♿M 🏊 ✖ 📶 🔌 💻

▼▼▼▼ Quality Inn Valley Suites �H

(509) 928-5218. **$110-$190.** 8923 E Mission Ave 99212. I-90 exit 287. Int corridors. **Pets:** Accepted. ♿M 🏊 ✖ 📶 ✖ 🔌 💻

▼▼▼▼ Residence Inn by Marriott �H

(509) 892-9300. **$139-$199.** 15915 E Indiana Ave 99216. I-90 exit 291 westbound, just e; exit 291B eastbound, just n, then just e. Int corridors. **Pets:** Accepted. ♿M 🏊 ✖ 📶 🔌 💻

▼▼ Super 8 M

(509) 928-4888. **$58-$157.** 2020 N Argonne Rd 99212. I-90 exit 287, just n. Int corridors. **Pets:** Other species. $50 deposit/room, $15 one-time fee/room. Designated rooms, service with restrictions, supervision. 🏊 📶 🔌 💻

STEVENSON

AAA ▼▼▼▼ Skamania Lodge �H

(509) 427-7700. **$159-$359, 6 day notice.** 1131 SW Skamania Lodge Way 98648. 1 mi w on SR 14, just n on Rock Creek Dr, then just w. Int corridors. **Pets:** Accepted. SAVE 🍴 🏊 ✖ 📶 ✖ 🔌 💻

SULTAN *(Restaurants p. 645)*

AAA ▼▼ Dutch Cup Motel M

(360) 793-2215. **$83-$110, 3 day notice.** 819 Main St 98294. Jct US 2 and Main St. Ext corridors. **Pets:** Medium, other species. $9 daily fee/pet. Designated rooms, service with restrictions, supervision. SAVE 📶 🔌 💻

SUMNER *(Restaurants p. 645)*

▼▼▼▼ Holiday Inn Express Sumner �H

(253) 299-0205. **Call for rates.** 2500 136th Ave Ct E 98390. SR 167 exit 24th St, just se. Int corridors. **Pets:** Accepted. ♿M 🏊 📶 ✖ 🔌 💻

SUNNYSIDE

AAA ▼▼▼▼ BEST WESTERN PLUS Grapevine Inn �H

(509) 839-6070. **$90-$140.** 1849 Quail Ln 98944. I-82 exit 69, just n, then just w. Int corridors. **Pets:** Accepted. SAVE ♿M 🏊 📶 ✖ 🔌 💻

SUQUAMISH

▼▼▼ Suquamish Clearwater Casino Resort �H 🐾

(360) 598-8700. **$99-$259.** 15347 Suquamish Way 98392. SR 3 exit SR 305, 6.2 mi se. Ext/int corridors. **Pets:** Other species. $20 daily fee/pet. Crate. 🍴 🏊 ✖ 📶 🔌 💻

TACOMA

AAA ▼▼▼▼ BEST WESTERN PLUS Tacoma Dome Hotel �H

(253) 272-7737. **$99-$199.** 2611 East E St 98421. I-5 exit 133 (City Center), follow E 26th St/Tacoma Dome lanes, just n on E 26th St, then just e. Int corridors. **Pets:** Accepted. SAVE 🍴 ♿M 🏊 ✖ 📶 ✖ 🔌 💻

▼▼▼▼ Holiday Inn Express & Suites - Tacoma Downtown �H

(253) 272-2434. **$129-$139.** 2102 S C St 98402. I-5 exit 133 (City Center) to I-705 N exit S 21st St (SR 509), just w, then just s; downtown. Int corridors. **Pets:** $50 one-time fee/room. Designated rooms, service with restrictions. ♿M 🏊 ✖ 📶 🔌 💻

AAA ▼▼▼▼ Hotel Murano �H 🐾

(253) 238-8000. **$189-$269.** 1320 Broadway Plaza 98402. I-5 exit 133 (City Center) to I-705 N exit A St, just w on 11th St, then just s; downtown. Int corridors. **Pets:** Medium, dogs only. $45 one-time fee/room, $20 daily fee/room. Designated rooms, service with restrictions, supervision. SAVE 🍴 📶 ✖ 🔌 💻

▼▼▼▼ La Quinta Inn & Suites Tacoma Seattle �H

(253) 383-0146. **$89-$364.** 1425 E 27th St 98421. I-5 exit 135 southbound; exit 134 northbound, just n. Int corridors. **Pets:** Large, other species. Service with restrictions. 🍴 🏊 ✖ 📶 🔌 💻

AAA ▼▼▼ Red Lion Hotel Tacoma �H

(253) 548-1212. **$109-$149.** 8402 S Hosmer St 98444. I-5 exit 128 northbound, just ne; exit 129 southbound, just e on 72nd St, then 1 mi s. Int corridors. **Pets:** Accepted. SAVE 🏊 📶 🔌 💻

▼▼▼ Shilo Inn & Suites - Tacoma �H

(253) 475-4020. **Call for rates.** 7414 S Hosmer St 98408. I-5 exit 129, just se. Int corridors. **Pets:** Accepted. 🏊 ✖ 📶 ✖ 🔌 💻

TUKWILA

▼▼▼▼ Embassy Suites Hotel �H 🐾

(425) 227-8844. **$99-$419.** 15920 W Valley Hwy 98188. I-405 exit 1 (SR 181), just s. Int corridors. **Pets:** Other species. $75 one-time fee/room. Designated rooms, service with restrictions, supervision.
🍴 🏊 📶 🔌 💻

▼▼▼ **Extended Stay America-Seattle-Tukwila** H
(206) 244-2537. **Call for rates.** 15451 53rd Ave S 98188. I-5 exit 153 northbound, just n on Southcenter Pkwy, just n on 61st St, just w on Southcenter Blvd, then just sw; exit 154B (Southcenter Mall) southbound, just sw. Ext corridors. **Pets:** Other species. $25 daily fee/pet. Service with restrictions, supervision. 🛰 🖥 💻

▼▼▼ **Homewood Suites by Hilton Seattle Airport - Tukwila** H
(206) 433-8000. **$139-$209.** 6955 Fort Dent Way 98188. I-405 exit 1 (SR 181), just ne. Ext/int corridors. **Pets:** Accepted.
🔄 🛰 🖥 💻

▼▼▼ **Ramada Limited Sea-Tac Airport** H
(206) 244-8800. **$55-$109.** 13900 Tukwila International Blvd (SR 99) 98168. Jct SR 518, 1 mi n. Int corridors. **Pets:** Accepted.
🛰 🖥 💻

▼▼▼ **Residence Inn by Marriott-Seattle South** H
(425) 226-5500. **$189-$389.** 16201 W Valley Hwy 98188. I-405 exit 1 (SR 181), just s. Ext corridors. **Pets:** Accepted.
🔳 🔄 🛰 🗙 🖥 💻

TUMWATER

▼▼▼ **Comfort Inn Conference Center** H
(360) 352-0691. **$89-$119.** 1620 74th Ave SW 98501. I-5 exit 101, just se. Int corridors. **Pets:** Other species. $15 daily fee/pet. Designated rooms, service with restrictions, crate. 🔄 🛰 🗙 🖥 💻

▼▼▼ **Extended Stay America - Olympia/Tumwater** H
(360) 754-6063. **Call for rates.** 1675 Mottman Rd SW 98512. I-5 exit 104, 0.6 mi nw on US 101, just s on Crosby Blvd, then just se. Int corridors. **Pets:** Other species. $25 daily fee/pet. Service with restrictions, supervision. 🛰 🖥 💻

▼▼ ▼ **GuestHouse Inn & Suites** H
(360) 943-5040. **$79-$139.** 1600 74th Ave SW 98501. I-5 exit 101, just se. Int corridors. **Pets:** Other species. $15 daily fee/pet. Designated rooms, service with restrictions, crate. 🔳 🔄 🛰 🖥 💻

UNION

▼▼▼▼ **Alderbrook Resort & Spa** H
(360) 898-2200. **Call for rates.** 7101 E SR 106 98592. Just e of town. Ext/int corridors. **Pets:** Accepted. 🍴 🔄 🗙 🛰 🗙 🖥 💻

UNION GAP

ⓐⓐⓐ ▼▼▼ **BEST WESTERN PLUS Ahtanum Inn** H
(509) 248-9700. **$80-$130.** 2408 Rudkin Rd 98903. I-82 exit 36, just n. Ext/int corridors. **Pets:** Accepted. 🅢🅐🅥🅔 🔄 🛰 🖥 💻

ⓐⓐⓐ ▼ **Super 8** H
(509) 248-8880. **$71-$116.** 2605 Rudkin Rd 98903. I-82 exit 36, just s. Int corridors. **Pets:** Accepted. 🅢🅐🅥🅔 🔄 🛰 🖥 💻

VANCOUVER (Restaurants p. 645)

ⓐⓐⓐ ▼▼▼ **BEST WESTERN PLUS Vancouver Mall Dr Hotel & Suites** H
(360) 256-0707. **$100-$160.** 9420 NE Vancouver Mall Dr 98662. I-205 exit 30A northbound, 0.5 mi e on SR 500, just n on NE Gher Rd, then 0.7 mi sw on NE Fourth Plain Blvd; exit 30 (Vancouver Mall Dr) southbound, just ne on NE Fourth Plain Blvd. Int corridors. **Pets:** Accepted.
🅢🅐🅥🅔 🔄 🗙 🛰 🗙 🖥 💻

▼▼ **Comfort Inn & Suites Downtown Vancouver** H
(360) 696-0411. **$99-$209.** 401 E 13th St 98660. I-5 exit 1C (E Mill Plain Blvd), just w, just s on C St, then just e. Int corridors.
Pets: Accepted. 🔳 🔄 🗙 🛰 🗙 🖥 💻

▼▼ **Comfort Suites** H
(360) 253-3100. **$89-$199.** 4714 NE 94th Ave 98662. I-205 exit 30 (SR 500 W), 0.6 mi w to Thurston Way, just n to Vancouver Mall Dr, then 0.5 mi e; southeast edge of Westfield Shopping Center. Int corridors.
Pets: Accepted. 🔄 🛰 🗙 🖥 💻

ⓐⓐⓐ ▼▼▼ **DoubleTree by Hilton - Vancouver** H
(360) 891-9777. **$129-$189.** 12712 SE 2nd Cir 98684. I-205 exit 28 (E Mill Plain Blvd), 0.8 mi e, then just n on SE 126th Ave. Int corridors.
Pets: Accepted. 🅢🅐🅥🅔 🔄 🛰 🗙 🖥 💻

ⓐⓐⓐ ▼▼▼ **Hilton Vancouver Washington** H
(360) 993-4500. **$99-$219.** 301 W 6th St 98660. I-5 exit 1C (E Mill Plain Blvd) southbound, 0.3 mi w, then 0.3 mi s on W Columbia St; exit 1B northbound, 0.5 mi sw, follow signs to City Center/6th St. Int corridors. **Pets:** Large. $35 one-time fee/room. Service with restrictions.
🅢🅐🅥🅔 🄴🄲🄾 🍴 🔳 🔄 🛰 🗙 🖥 💻

▼▼▼ **Homewood Suites by Hilton** H
(360) 750-1100. **$129-$219.** 701 SE Columbia Shores Blvd 98661. SR 14 exit 1, just s. Ext/int corridors. **Pets:** Medium, other species. $75 one-time fee/pet. Supervision. 🔄 🛰 🖥 💻

ⓐⓐⓐ ▼▼▼ **Quality Inn & Suites** H 🐾
(360) 696-0516. **$72-$137.** 7001 NE Hwy 99 98665. I-5 exit 4, 0.5 mi se. Int corridors. **Pets:** Large, other species. $10 daily fee/room. Service with restrictions, supervision. 🅢🅐🅥🅔 🔄 🛰 🗙 🖥 💻

▼▼▼ **Quality Inn & Suites** H
(360) 574-6000. **Call for rates.** 13207 NE 20th Ave 98686. I-5 exit 7, just e; I-205 exit 36, just w. Int corridors. **Pets:** Accepted.
🔄 🛰 🗙 🖥 💻

▼▼ **Red Lion Hotel Vancouver at the Quay** H
(360) 694-8341. **Call for rates.** 100 Columbia St 98660. 0.5 mi s of dock at foot of Columbia St. Int corridors. **Pets:** Accepted.
🍴 🔳 🔄 🛰 🗙 🖥 💻

▼▼▼ **Residence Inn by Marriott Portland North - Vancouver** H 🐾
(360) 253-4800. **$169-$209.** 8005 NE Parkway Dr 98662. I-205 exit 30 (SR 500 W), 0.5 mi w to Thurston Way, just n to NE Parkway Dr, then just w. Ext corridors. **Pets:** Other species. $75 one-time fee/room. Service with restrictions. 🔳 🔄 🛰 🗙 🖥 💻

▼▼ **Shilo Inn & Suites-Salmon Creek** H
(360) 573-0511. **Call for rates.** 13206 Hwy 99 98686. I-5 exit 7, just e; I-205 exit 36, just w. Int corridors. **Pets:** Accepted.
🔄 🗙 🛰 🗙 🖥 💻

▼▼▼ **Staybridge Suites Vancouver-Portland** H
(360) 891-8282. **Call for rates.** 7301 NE 41st St 98662. I-205 exit 30 (SR 500 W), 1.5 mi w to NE Andresen Rd, just n to NE 40th St, just e to NE 72nd St, just n to NE 41st St, then just e. Int corridors.
Pets: Accepted. 🔳 🔄 🛰 🗙 🖥 💻

VASHON

▼ **The Swallow's Nest Guest Cottages** 🄲🄰
(206) 463-2646. **$125-$330, 90 day notice.** 6030 SW 248th St 98070. North end Ferry Landing, 7.8 mi s on Vashon Hwy; south end (Tahlequah) Ferry Landing, 5.8 mi n on Vashon Hwy, 1.4 mi e on Quartermaster Dr, 1.5 mi s on Dockton Rd, 0.4 mi s on 75th Ave, then 1 mi e. Ext corridors. **Pets:** Other species. $20 daily fee/pet. Designated rooms, service with restrictions, supervision. 🛰 🗙 🄺 🖥 💻

WALLA WALLA (Restaurants p. 645)

ⓐⓐⓐ ▼▼▼▼ **BEST WESTERN PLUS Walla Walla Suites Inn** H
(509) 525-4700. **$93-$136.** 7 E Oak St 99362. US 12 exit 2nd Ave, just s. Int corridors. **Pets:** Dogs only. $10 daily fee/pet. Service with restrictions, supervision. 🅢🅐🅥🅔 🔳 🔄 🛰 🗙 🖥 💻

ⓐⓐⓐ ▼▼▼ **Holiday Inn Express** H
(509) 525-6200. **$90-$220, 3 day notice.** 1433 W Pine St 99362. US 12 exit Pendleton/Prescott. Int corridors. **Pets:** Other species. $20 daily fee/pet. Designated rooms, service with restrictions, supervision.
🅢🅐🅥🅔 🔳 🔄 🛰 🗙 🖥 💻

▼▼ La Quinta Inn Walla Walla 🏠

(509) 525-2522. **$79-$289.** 520 N 2nd Ave 99362. US 12 exit 2nd Ave, 0.3 mi s. Int corridors. **Pets:** Large, other species. Service with restrictions. 🐾 🛜 ✕ 🛋 💻

🆎 ▼▼▼ Marcus Whitman Hotel & Conference Center 🏠

(509) 525-2200. **$129-$349.** 6 W Rose St 99362. At N 2nd Ave and W Rose St; downtown. Int corridors. **Pets:** Accepted.

🆂🅰🆅🅴 🍴 🛜 ✕ 🛋 💻

WENATCHEE

🆎 ▼▼▼ Coast Wenatchee Center Hotel 🏠 🐾

(509) 662-1234. **$79-$185.** 201 N Wenatchee Ave 98801. Jct 2nd St; downtown. Int corridors. **Pets:** $10 one-time fee/room. Designated rooms, service with restrictions, supervision.

🆂🅰🆅🅴 🍴 🐾 🛜 🛋 💻

🆎 ▼▼▼ Comfort Inn Downtown 🏠

(509) 662-1700. **$69-$169.** 815 N Wenatchee Ave 98801. Downtown. Int corridors. **Pets:** Accepted. 🆂🅰🆅🅴 🐾 🛜 🛋 💻

▼▼▼▼ Holiday Inn Express 🏠

(509) 663-6355. **$109-$169.** 1921 N Wenatchee Ave 98801. Northwest side of town. Int corridors. **Pets:** Accepted.

🅼 🐾 🛜 ✕ 🛋 💻

▼▼ La Quinta Inn & Suites Wenatchee 🏠

(509) 664-6565. **$69-$264.** 1905 N Wenatchee Ave 98801. Northwest side of town. Int corridors. **Pets:** Large, other species. Service with restrictions. 🅼 🐾 ✕ 🛜 ✕ 🛋 💻

▼▼▼▼ Red Lion Hotel Wenatchee 🏠

(509) 663-0711. **Call for rates.** 1225 N Wenatchee Ave 98801. Just nw of downtown. Int corridors. **Pets:** Accepted.

🍴 🐾 🛜 ✕ 🛋 💻

🆎 ▼▼ Super 8 Wenatchee 🏠

(509) 662-3443. **$55-$125.** 1401 N Miller St 98801. 1.5 mi n on US 2. Int corridors. **Pets:** Accepted. 🆂🅰🆅🅴 🐾 🛜 🛋 💻

🆎 ▼▼▼ Travelodge-Wenatchee 🅼

(509) 662-8165. **$55-$160.** 1004 N Wenatchee Ave 98801. Downtown. Ext corridors. **Pets:** Accepted. 🆂🅰🆅🅴 🅼 🐾 🛜 🛋 💻

WESTPORT

▼▼ Chateau Westport Resort 🏠

(360) 268-9101. **Call for rates.** 710 W Hancock St 98595. Just w of SR 105 Spur N; 1.5 mi n of Twin Harbors State Park. Int corridors. **Pets:** Accepted. 🐾 ✕ 🛜 ✕ 🆊 🛋 💻

WINTHROP

▼▼ River Run Inn 🅼

(509) 996-2173. **$85-$175, 7 day notice.** 27 Rader Rd 98862. 0.5 mi w on SR 20. Ext corridors. **Pets:** Other species. $15 daily fee/pet. Service with restrictions, supervision. 🅼 🐾 🛜 ✕ 🛋 💻

🆎 ▼▼ Winthrop Inn 🅼 🐾

(509) 996-2217. **$88-$140, 7 day notice.** 960 Hwy 20 98862. 0.9 mi e. Int corridors. **Pets:** Dogs only. $10 daily fee/pet. Designated rooms, supervision. 🆂🅰🆅🅴 🐾 🛜 ✕ 🛋

WOODINVILLE

▼▼▼ ▼▼▼ Willows Lodge 🏠 🐾

(425) 424-3900. **$209-$699, 3 day notice.** 14580 NE 145th St 98072. I-405 exit 20B (NE 124th St), 0.7 mi e, 1.2 mi n on 132nd Ave NE, 0.6 mi e on NE 143rd Pl, then just e. Int corridors. **Pets:** $35 one-time fee/room. Designated rooms, crate.

🆊 🍴 ✕ 🛜 ✕ 🛋 💻

WOODLAND

▼▼ Lewis River Inn 🅼

(360) 225-6257. **Call for rates.** 1100 Lewis River Rd 98674. I-5 exit 21, just e. Ext corridors. **Pets:** Accepted. 🛜 🛋 💻

YAKIMA

🆎 ▼▼▼ BEST WESTERN PLUS Lincoln Inn 🏠 🐾

(509) 453-8898. **$90-$220.** 1614 N 1st St 98901. I-82 exit 31, just s. Int corridors. **Pets:** Medium, dogs only. $20 daily fee/room. Designated rooms, service with restrictions, supervision.

🆂🅰🆅🅴 🐾 🛜 ✕ 🛋 💻

🆎 ▼▼▼ Fairfield Inn & Suites by Marriott 🏠

(509) 452-3100. **$119-$179.** 137 N Fair Ave 98901. I-82 exit 33A eastbound, just s; exit 33 westbound, just w to 9th St, just n to B St, then just e. Int corridors. **Pets:** $25 daily fee/room. Supervision.

🆂🅰🆅🅴 🅼 🐾 🛜 ✕ 🛋 💻

▼▼▼▼ Holiday Inn Downtown Yakima 🏠 🐾

(509) 494-7000. **$129-$189.** 802 E Yakima Ave 98901. I-82 exit 33 westbound; exit 33B eastbound, 0.7 mi w. Int corridors. **Pets:** Other species. $20 one-time fee/room. Designated rooms, service with restrictions, crate. 🍴 🐾 🛜 ✕ 🛋 💻

▼▼▼▼ Holiday Inn Express Yakima 🏠

(509) 249-1000. **$119-$169.** 1001 Staff Sgt Pendleton Way 98901. I-82 exit 33B eastbound; exit 33 westbound, just w to 9th St, just n to A St, then just e. Int corridors. **Pets:** Accepted.

🅼 🐾 🛜 ✕ 🛋 💻

▼▼▼▼ Howard Johnson Plaza Yakima 🏠

(509) 452-6511. **$99-$269.** 9 N 9th St 98901. I-82 exit 33 westbound; exit 33B eastbound, just s. Int corridors. **Pets:** Accepted.

🅼 🐾 🛜 ✕ 🛋 💻

🆎 ▼▼▼ Oxford Inn Yakima 🏠

(509) 457-4444. **$85-$109, 3 day notice.** 1603 E Yakima Ave 98901. I-82 exit 33 westbound, just e; exit 33B eastbound. Int corridors. **Pets:** Accepted. 🆂🅰🆅🅴 🅼 🐾 🛜 🛋 💻

🆎 ▼▼▼ Oxford Suites Yakima 🏠 🐾

(509) 457-9000. **$105-$159, 3 day notice.** 1701 E Yakima Ave 98901. I-82 exit 33 westbound; exit 33B eastbound. Int corridors. **Pets:** Medium. $25 one-time fee/room. Designated rooms, service with restrictions, crate. 🆂🅰🆅🅴 🅼 🐾 ✕ 🛜 ✕ 🛋 💻

▼▼▼▼ Red Lion Hotel Yakima Center 🏠

(509) 248-5900. **Call for rates.** 607 E Yakima Ave 98901. I-82 exit 33 westbound; exit 33B eastbound, 0.8 mi w. Ext/int corridors. **Pets:** Accepted. 🍴 🐾 🛜 ✕ 🛋 💻

WEST VIRGINIA

BARBOURSVILLE

▼▼▼▼ Barboursville Holiday Inn & Suites 🏠 🐾

(304) 733-3338. **$99-$129.** 3551 Rt 60 E 25504. I-64 exit 20, just s. Int corridors. **Pets:** Medium. $25 daily fee/pet. Designated rooms, service with restrictions, supervision. 🍴 🛜 ✕ 🛋 💻

🆎 ▼▼▼ BEST WESTERN Huntington Mall Inn 🅼

(304) 736-9772. **$90-$110.** 3441 US 60 E 25504. I-64 exit 20A eastbound; exit 20 westbound, 0.3 mi s. Int corridors. **Pets:** $15 one-time fee/room. Service with restrictions, crate. 🆂🅰🆅🅴 🐾 🛜 🛋 💻

▼▼▼▼ **Comfort Inn by Choice Hotels** �H
(304) 733-2122. **$85-$115.** 249 Mall Rd 25504. I-64 exit 20, 0.4 mi n.
Int corridors. **Pets:** $25 one-time fee/room. Designated rooms, service
with restrictions. 🚭Ⓜ 🛋 🛜 🍴 🖵

BECKLEY
▼▼▼▼ **Country Inn & Suites By Carlson** �H
(304) 252-5100. **$99-$199, 7 day notice.** 2120 Harper Rd 25801.
I-64/77 exit 44, just w on SR 3. Int corridors. **Pets:** Other species. $30
one-time fee/room. Designated rooms, service with restrictions, supervision. 🚭Ⓜ 🛋 🗙 🛜 🍴 🖵

▼▼ **Econo Lodge** Ⓜ ❀
(304) 255-2161. **$64-$94.** 1909 Harper Rd 25801. I-64/77 exit 44, 0.3
mi e on SR 3. Ext/int corridors. **Pets:** Designated rooms, service with
restrictions, supervision. 🛜 🍴 🖵

AAA ▼▼▼▼ **Fairfield Inn & Suites by Marriott** �H
(304) 252-8661. **$97-$160.** 125 Hylton Ln 25801. I-64/77 exit 44, just e.
Int corridors. **Pets:** Large. $30 one-time fee/room. Designated rooms,
service with restrictions, supervision. 🆂🅰🆅🅴 🛋 🛜 🗙 🍴 🖵

AAA ▼▼▼ **Travelodge** Ⓜ
(304) 252-0671. **$53-$70.** 1939 Harper Rd 25801. I-64/77 exit 44, just e
on SR 3. Ext/int corridors. **Pets:** Accepted. 🆂🅰🆅🅴 🛜 🖵

BERKELEY SPRINGS
AAA ▼▼▼▼ **BEST WESTERN Berkeley Springs Inn** Ⓜ
(304) 258-9400. **$80-$95.** 1776 Valley Rd 25411. 1.1 mi s on US 522.
Int corridors. **Pets:** Medium. $20 daily fee/room. Designated rooms,
service with restrictions, supervision. 🆂🅰🆅🅴 🛋 🛜 🗙 🍴 🖵

BRADLEY
AAA ▼▼▼ **Days Inn** Ⓜ
(304) 877-6455. **$69-$99.** 127 Ontario Dr 25880. I-64/77 exit 48, 1 mi
ne on US 19. Int corridors. **Pets:** Small, dogs only. $15 daily fee/pet.
Designated rooms, service with restrictions, supervision.
🆂🅰🆅🅴 🛋 🛜 🍴 🖵

BRIDGEPORT
AAA ▼▼▼▼ **BEST WESTERN PLUS Bridgeport**
Inn �H
(304) 842-5411. **$140.** 100 Lodgeville Rd 26330. I-79 exit 119, just e on
US 50. Int corridors. **Pets:** Medium, other species. $20 daily fee/pet.
Service with restrictions, crate. 🆂🅰🆅🅴 🍴 🚭Ⓜ 🛋 🍴 🖵

▼▼▼▼ **TownePlace Suites by Marriott-Bridgeport**
Clarksburg �H
(304) 842-3600. **$125-$206.** 101 Platinum Dr 26330. I-79 exit 119, just
w on US 50. Int corridors. **Pets:** Accepted.
🚭Ⓜ 🛋 🛜 🗙 🍴 🖵

BRUCETON MILLS
▼▼ **Microtel Inn & Suites by Wyndham**
Hazelton Ⓜ ❀
(304) 379-7900. **$74-$125.** 886 Casteel Rd 26525. I-68 exit 29 (Hazelton), just n. Int corridors. **Pets:** $15 daily fee/pet. Designated rooms,
service with restrictions, crate. 🛜 🗙 🍴 🖵

BUCKHANNON
▼▼ **Microtel Inn & Suites by Wyndham,**
Buckhannon �H
(304) 460-2525. **$91-$135.** 2 Northridge Dr 26201. US 19, just n. Int
corridors. **Pets:** Dogs only. $25 daily fee/room. Service with restrictions,
crate. 🛜 🍴 🖵

CHARLESTON
AAA ▼▼▼ **BEST WESTERN Charleston Plaza**
Hotel �H
(304) 345-9779. **Call for rates.** 1010 Washington St E 25301. I-64/77
exit 100, 0.3 mi w. Int corridors. **Pets:** Accepted.
🆂🅰🆅🅴 🛋 🛜 🍴 🖵

AAA ▼▼▼▼ **Charleston Residence Inn by Marriott** �H
(304) 345-4200. **$132-$217.** 200 Hotel Cir 25311. I-64/77 exit 99, just e.
Int corridors. **Pets:** Accepted. 🆂🅰🆅🅴 🛋 🛜 🗙 🍴 🖵

AAA ▼▼ **Red Roof Inn Charleston - Kanawha City,**
WV Ⓜ
(304) 925-6953. **$64-$89.** 6305 SE MacCorkle Ave 25304. I-77 exit 95,
just s on SR 61. Ext corridors. **Pets:** Large, other species. Service with
restrictions, supervision. 🆂🅰🆅🅴 🛜 🗙 🍴

COMFORT
▼▼ **Oak Tree Inn** Ⓜ
(304) 837-3377. **Call for rates.** 129 Deanna Ave 25049. 1 mi s on SR
3; entrance at V-Mart. Int corridors. **Pets:** Accepted.
🛜 🗙 🍴 🖵

CROSS LANES
▼▼ **Comfort Inn Charleston West** Ⓜ
(304) 776-8070. **$99-$109.** 102 Racer Dr 25313. I-64 exit 47, just s. Int
corridors. **Pets:** Accepted. 🛋 🛜 🍴 🖵

DANIELS
AAA ▼▼▼▼ **The Resort at Glade Springs** �H
(304) 763-2000. **$79-$194, 7 day notice.** 255 Resort Dr 25832. I-64
exit 125, 1.5 mi w on SR 307, then 2.8 mi w on US 19. Ext/int corridors. **Pets:** Accepted. 🆂🅰🆅🅴 🍴 🛋 🗙 🛜 🍴 🖵

DAVIS
▼▼ **Black Bear Resort** 🅲🅰
(304) 866-4391. **$100-$560, 14 day notice.** 247 Lodge Dr 26260. 4.5
mi s on SR 32. Ext corridors. **Pets:** Accepted.
🛋 🗙 🛜 🍴 🖵

EDRAY
AAA ▼▼▼ **Marlinton Motor Inn** Ⓜ
(304) 799-4711. **$65-$140, 3 day notice.** 21507 Seneca Tr N 24954.
Center. Ext corridors. **Pets:** Small, dogs only. $15 daily fee/pet. Desig-
nated rooms, service with restrictions, supervision.
🆂🅰🆅🅴 🍴 🛋 🛜 🍴 🖵

FAIRMONT
AAA ▼▼▼ **Clarion Inn Fairmont** �H
(304) 366-5500. **$110-$225.** 930 E Grafton Rd 26554. I-79 exit 137, just
e. Int corridors. **Pets:** Medium, other species. $25 one-time fee/pet.
Service with restrictions, crate.
🆂🅰🆅🅴 🍴 🚭Ⓜ 🛋 🛜 🗙 🍴 🖵

AAA ▼▼▼ **Red Roof Inn Fairmont** �H
(304) 366-6800. **$84-$110.** 42 Spencer Dr 26554. I-79 exit 132, 0.3 mi
s on US 250, just w, then just s. Ext corridors. **Pets:** Large, other species. Service with restrictions, supervision. 🆂🅰🆅🅴 🛜 🗙 🍴 🖵

▼▼▼ **Super 8** Ⓜ
(304) 363-1488. **$72-$89.** 2208 Pleasant Valley Rd 26554. I-79 exit
133, just e. Int corridors. **Pets:** Accepted. 🚭Ⓜ 🛜 🍴 🖵

FALLING WATERS
▼▼▼▼ **Quality Inn Spring Mills - Martinsburg North** �H
(304) 274-6100. **Call for rates.** 1220 TJ Jackson Dr 25419. I-81 exit
20, just w. Int corridors. **Pets:** Accepted. 🛋 🛜 🗙 🍴 🖵

FROST
▼▼▼ **The Inn at Mountain Quest** 🅲🅸
(304) 799-7267. **Call for rates.** 303 Mountain Quest Ln 24954. On SR
92, 0.4 mi n. Ext corridors. **Pets:** Accepted. 🗙 🛜 🗙

GASSAWAY

▼▼ Microtel Inn & Suites by Wyndham Gassaway/Sutton **M** ❖

(304) 364-6100. **$59-$89.** 115 Reston Pl 26624. I-79 exit 62, just w. Int corridors. **Pets:** Dogs only. $20 daily fee/pet. Designated rooms, service with restrictions, crate. 🖚 ⊠ 🛏 💻

HARPERS FERRY

⚑ ▼▼ Quality Hotel Conference Center **H**

(304) 535-6302. **$83-$139.** 4328 William L Wilson Frwy 25425. Just w on US 340. Int corridors. **Pets:** Large. Designated rooms, service with restrictions. 🆂🅰🆅🅴 ¶¶ 🖚 🛏 💻

HUNTINGTON

▼▼▼ Holiday Inn Hotel & Suites **H** ❖

(304) 523-8880. **$109-$149.** 800 3rd Ave 25701. I-64 exit 11, 3 mi n on SR 10, then 0.9 mi w; downtown. Int corridors. **Pets:** Medium. $25 daily fee/pet. Designated rooms, service with restrictions, supervision.

¶¶ 🅼 🖚 🖚 ⊠ 🛏 💻

▼▼▼ Ramada Limited Huntington **H**

(304) 523-4242. **$89-$109.** 3094 16th Street Rd 25701. I-64 exit 11, just n. Int corridors. **Pets:** $20 daily fee/pet. Designated rooms, supervision. 🖚 ⊠ 🖚 🛏 💻

⚑ ▼▼ Red Roof Inn Huntington **H**

(304) 733-3737. **$60-$90.** 5190 US Rt 60 E 25705. I-64 exit 15, just s. Ext corridors. **Pets:** Large, other species. Service with restrictions, supervision. 🆂🅰🆅🅴 🖚 ⊠ 🛏

▼▼ Super 8 **H**

(304) 525-1410. **$83-$103.** 3090 16th Street Rd 25701. I-64 exit 11, just n. Int corridors. **Pets:** Accepted. 🖚 ⊠ 🖚 🛏 💻

▼▼▼ TownePlace Suites by Marriott Huntington **H**

(304) 525-4877. **$125-$206.** 157 Kinetic Dr 25701. I-64 exit 11, just n. Int corridors. **Pets:** Accepted. 🖚 🖚 ⊠ 🛏 💻

HURRICANE

⚑ ▼▼▼ Red Roof Inn Charleston West-Hurricane, WV **H**

(304) 757-6392. **$55-$80.** 500 Putnam Village Dr 25526. I-64 exit 39, just n on SR 34, then just e. Ext corridors. **Pets:** Large, other species. Service with restrictions, supervision. 🆂🅰🆅🅴 🖚 ⊠ 🛏 💻

KEYSER

⚑ ▼▼▼ Keyser Inn **M**

(304) 788-0913. **$64-$87.** 51 Josie Dr 26726. On US 220, 2.3 mi s. Int corridors. **Pets:** Small. $27 one-time fee/room. Service with restrictions, supervision. 🆂🅰🆅🅴 🖚 ⊠ 🛏

▼▼ Microtel Inn & Suites by Wyndham Keyser **H**

(304) 597-1400. **$90-$120, 3 day notice.** 70 N Tornado Way 26726. On US 220, 2.1 mi s. Int corridors. **Pets:** Accepted. 🖚 ⊠ 🛏 💻

LEWISBURG

▼▼▼ Lewisburg Holiday Inn Express Hotel & Suites **H**

(304) 645-5750. **Call for rates.** 222 Hunter Ln 24901. I-64 exit 169, just s. Int corridors. **Pets:** Small. $25 daily fee/pet. Designated rooms, service with restrictions, supervision. 🖚 🖚 ⊠ 🛏 💻

⚑ ▼▼💎 Quality Inn Lewisburg Conference Center **H**

(304) 645-7722. **$84-$140.** 540 N Jefferson St 24901. I-64 exit 169, just s on US 219. Ext corridors. **Pets:** Accepted.

🆂🅰🆅🅴 ¶¶ 🖚 🖚 🛏 💻

▼▼ Super 8 **M**

(304) 647-3188. **$68-$94.** 550 N Jefferson St 24901. I-64 exit 169, just s on US 219. Int corridors. **Pets:** $10 daily fee/pet. Designated rooms, service with restrictions, supervision. 🖚 ⊠ 🛏 💻

MARTINSBURG

▼▼▼ Holiday Inn Martinsburg **H**

(304) 267-5500. **$109-$169.** 301 Foxcroft Ave 25401. I-81 exit 13, just e on W King St (CR 15). Int corridors. **Pets:** Accepted.

¶¶ 🖚 🖚 ⊠ 🛏 💻

▼▼ Knights Inn-Martinsburg **M**

(304) 267-2211. **$55-$150.** 1997 Edwin Miller Blvd 25404. I-81 exit 16E, 0.4 mi e on SR 9. Ext corridors. **Pets:** Accepted. 🖚 ⊠ 🛏

MINERAL WELLS

⚑ ▼▼💎 Comfort Suites Parkersburg South **H** ❖

(304) 489-9600. **$99-$139.** 167 Elizabeth Pike 26150. I-77 exit 170, 0.3 mi se. Ext/int corridors. **Pets:** Other species. $10 one-time fee/room. Crate. 🆂🅰🆅🅴 🖚 🖚 ⊠ 🛏 💻

▼▼▼ Holiday Inn Express Hotel & Suites Parkersburg/ Mineral Wells **H**

(304) 489-4111. **Call for rates.** 80 Old Nicholette Rd 26150. I-77 exit 170. Int corridors. **Pets:** Small. $35 daily fee/room. Designated rooms, no service, crate. 🖚 🖚 ⊠ 🛏 💻

MORGANTOWN

▼▼ Comfort Inn-Morgantown **M** ❖

(304) 296-9364. **$79-$139.** 225 Comfort Inn Dr 26508. I-68 exit 1, 0.3 mi n on US 119. Int corridors. **Pets:** Medium. $25 one-time fee/pet. Designated rooms, service with restrictions, supervision.

🖚 🖚 ⊠ 🛏 💻

▼▼ Microtel Inn & Suites by Wyndham, Morgantown **H** ❖

(304) 292-0055. **$80-$130.** 15 Lawless Rd 26505. I-79 exit 152, just w. Int corridors. **Pets:** Dogs only. $25 daily fee/pet. Designated rooms, service with restrictions, supervision. 🖚 ⊠ 🛏 💻

▼▼▼ Ramada Conference Center **H**

(304) 296-3431. **$89-$169.** 20 Scott Ave 26508. I-68 exit 1, 0.3 mi n. Int corridors. **Pets:** Accepted. ¶¶ 🅼 🖚 🖚 ⊠ 🛏 💻

▼▼▼ Residence Inn by Marriott Morgantown **H**

(304) 599-0237. **$111-$183.** 1046 Willowdale Rd 26505. I-79 exit 155, 2 mi s on US 19, then 0.9 mi e on SR 705. Int corridors. **Pets:** Accepted. 🅼 🖚 🖚 ⊠ 🛏 💻

▼▼ Super 8 Morgantown **H**

(304) 296-4000. **$61-$99.** 603 Venture Dr 26508. I-68 exit 7, just n. Int corridors. **Pets:** Accepted. 🖚 ⊠ 🛏 💻

OAK HILL

⚑ ▼▼▼ Holiday Lodge Hotel and Conference Center **H** ❖

(304) 465-0571. **$70-$165.** 340 Oyler Ave 25901. US 19 exit Oyler Ave, just w. Int corridors. **Pets:** Medium, dogs only. $25 daily fee/room. Service with restrictions, crate. 🆂🅰🆅🅴 ¶¶ 🅼 🖚 🖚 🛏 💻

PARKERSBURG

▼▼▼ The Blennerhassett **H**

(304) 422-3131. **$125-$242, 3 day notice.** 320 Market St 26101. Between 4th and 5th sts; downtown. Int corridors. **Pets:** Accepted.

¶¶ 🖚 ⊠ 🛏 💻

▼▼ Red Roof Inn Parkersburg **M**

(304) 485-1741. **$64-$99.** 3714 E 7th St 26104. I-77 exit 176, just w on US 50. Ext corridors. **Pets:** Large, other species. Service with restrictions, supervision. 🖚 ⊠ 🛏 💻

PHILIPPI

⚑ ▼▼ Mountaineer Inn **M**

(304) 457-5888. **$65-$125.** 14928 Barbour County Hwy 26416. 2.5 mi s on US 250. Int corridors. **Pets:** Accepted. 🆂🅰🆅🅴 🅼 🖚 🛏

PRINCETON

◆◆ Comfort Inn-Princeton Ⓜ ☼

(304) 487-6101. $79-$109. 136 Ambrose Ln 24740. I-77 exit 9, 0.3 mi w on US 460. Int corridors. Pets: Medium, other species. $25 one-time fee/pet. Service with restrictions, supervision. 📶 🛏 💻

🔷 ◆◆ Days Inn Ⓜ

(304) 425-8100. $65-$150, 3 day notice. 347 Meadowfield Ln 24740. I-77 exit 9, 0.3 mi w on US 460, just s on Ambrose Ln, then just e. Ext corridors. Pets: Medium. $20 daily fee/pet. Designated rooms, service with restrictions, supervision. SAVE 🛏 📶 🛏 💻

🔷 ◆◆◆ Holiday Inn Express Princeton Ⓗ ☼

(304) 425-8156. $85-$180. 805 Oakvale Rd 24740. I-77 exit 9, just w. Int corridors. Pets: $20 daily fee/pet. Designated rooms, service with restrictions, supervision. SAVE 🛏 📶 🛏 💻

◆◆ Sleep Inn & Suites Ⓗ ☼

(304) 431-2800. $84-$114. 1015 Oakvale Rd 24740. I-77 exit 9, just w on US 460, then just n via service road. Int corridors. Pets: $15 daily fee/room. Service with restrictions, supervision. 🛏 📶 🛏 💻

RIPLEY

◆◆◆ Holiday Inn Express & Suites Ripley Ⓗ

(304) 372-4444. $125-$250, 3 day notice. 110 Memorial Dr 25271. I-77 exit 138, e on US 33, then s on New Stone Ridge Rd. Int corridors. Pets: $25 daily fee/pet. Service with restrictions, supervision.

🛏 📶 🛏 💻

🔷 ◆◆◆ Quality Inn Ⓗ

(304) 372-5000. $96-$169. 1 Hospitality Dr 25271. I-77 exit 138, just w on US 33, then 0.3 mi n. Ext/int corridors. Pets: Accepted.

SAVE 📶 🛏 💻

◆ Ripley Super 8 Ⓜ

(304) 372-8880. $64-$87. 102 Duke Dr 25271. I-77 exit 138, just e on US 33. Int corridors. Pets: Accepted. 📶 🛏 💻

ROANOKE

🔷 ◆◆◆ Stonewall Resort Ⓗ

(304) 269-7400. $159-$269, 3 day notice. 940 Resort Dr 26447. I-79 exit 91, just e. Ext/int corridors. Pets: Small. $150 deposit/room. Designated rooms, service with restrictions, crate.

SAVE 🍴 🛏 ✕ 📶 🛏 💻

SHEPHERDSTOWN

◆◆ Comfort Inn Shepherdstown Ⓜ

(304) 876-3160. $89-$109. 70 Maddex Square Dr 25443. Just w on SR 45; center. Int corridors. Pets: Accepted. 📶 🛏 💻

SOUTH CHARLESTON

🔷 ◆◆◆ Holiday Inn & Suites Charleston West Ⓗ ☼

(304) 744-4641. Call for rates. 400 2nd Ave SW 25303. I-64 exit 56, just nw. Int corridors. Pets: $25 daily fee/pet. Designated rooms, service with restrictions, supervision. SAVE 🍴 🛏 📶 🛏 💻

SUMMERSVILLE

🔷 ◆◆◆ Baymont Inn & Suites Ⓜ

(304) 872-6500. $59-$119. 903 Industrial Dr N 26651. US 19, 1.9 mi n of jct SR 39. Int corridors. Pets: Accepted.

SAVE 🛏 ✕ 📶 🛏 💻

◆◆ Econo Lodge Ⓗ

(304) 872-6900. $60-$80. 1203 S Broad St 26651. US 19 and Broad St; 0.6 mi s of jct SR 39. Ext corridors. Pets: Other species. $15 daily fee/pet. Designated rooms, service with restrictions, supervision.

📶 🛏 💻

◆◆◆◆ Hampton Inn Ⓗ

(304) 872-7100. $90-$95. 5400 Webster Rd 26651. Just s on SR 41 from US 19. Int corridors. Pets: Small, other species. Service with restrictions, supervision. 🛏M 🛏 📶 🛏 💻

◆◆◆◆ La Quinta Inn & Suites Ⓗ

(304) 872-0555. $76-$231. 106 Merchants Walk 26651. US 19, just w. Int corridors. Pets: Large, other species. Service with restrictions.

🛏 🛏 ✕ 🛏 💻

🔷 ◆◆◆ Sleep Inn of Summersville Ⓜ

(304) 872-4500. Call for rates. 701 Professional Park Dr 26651. US 19, 1.7 mi n of jct SR 39. Int corridors. Pets: Accepted.

SAVE 🛏 📶 🛏 💻

◆ Super 8-Summersville Ⓜ

(304) 872-4888. $65-$79. 306 Merchants Walk 26651. US 19, just n. Int corridors. Pets: Accepted. 📶 🛏

TRIADELPHIA

◆◆ Econo Lodge Inn & Suites Conference Center Wheeling East Ⓜ

(304) 547-1380. $120-$150. 87 Jenkins Ln 26059. I-70 exit 11, 0.3 mi w on CR 41. Int corridors. Pets: Small. $25 daily fee/pet. Designated rooms, service with restrictions, supervision. 🛏 📶 🛏 💻

◆◆◆ Holiday Inn Express & Suites Ⓗ

(304) 907-4470. Call for rates. 45 Wayfarer Dr 26059. I-70 exit 10 (Cabela Dr), just w. Int corridors. Pets: Accepted.

🛏M 📶 ✕ 🛏 💻

◆◆◆ Suburban Ⓗ ☼

(304) 547-1037. Call for rates. 40 Robinson Dr 26059. I-70 exit 10 (Cabela Dr), just w. Int corridors. Pets: $25 one-time fee/pet. Service with restrictions. 🛏M 📶 ✕ 🛏 💻

VIENNA

◆◆◆ Wingate by Wyndham Ⓗ

(304) 295-5501. $115-$136. 1502 Grand Central Ave 26105. I-77 exit 179, 3.9 mi w on SR 68. Int corridors. Pets: Accepted.

🛏 📶 ✕ 🛏 💻

WEIRTON

◆◆◆ Holiday Inn Ⓗ

(304) 723-5522. $139-$169, 3 day notice. 350 Three Springs Dr 26062. 4.5 mi e on US 22 exit Three Springs Dr. Int corridors. Pets: Accepted.

🍴 🛏M 🛏 📶 🛏 💻

WESTON

◆◆◆ Holiday Inn Express Hotel & Suites Ⓗ

(304) 269-3550. $120-$130. 215 Staunton Dr 26452. I-79 exit 99, just e. Int corridors. Pets: Small. $25 daily fee/pet. Service with restrictions, crate. 🛏 📶 ✕ 🛏 💻

🔷 ◆◆◆ Quality Inn Ⓗ

(304) 269-7000. $89-$185. 2906 US Hwy 33 E 26452. I-79 exit 99, just e. Ext corridors. Pets: Medium. $15 daily fee/pet. Designated rooms, service with restrictions, crate. SAVE 🛏 📶 ✕ 🛏 💻

◆◆ Weston Super 8 Ⓗ

(304) 269-1086. $67-$75. 100 Market Place Mall, Suite 12 26452. I-79 exit 99, just e. Int corridors. Pets: Accepted. 📶 ✕ 🛏 💻

WHEELING

🔷 ◆◆◆ Wheeling Super 8 Ⓜ

(304) 243-9400. $79-$130. 2400 National Rd 26003. I-70 exit 5, just e. Int corridors. Pets: Accepted. SAVE 📶 🛏 💻

WISCONSIN

ABBOTSFORD
▼▼ Rodeway Inn 🅷

(715) 223-3337. **$70-$95.** 300 E Elderberry Rd 54405. SR 29 exit 132 (SR 13), just se. Int corridors. **Pets:** Accepted.
🍴 ⓜ ⌲ 🛜 ✕ 🛏 💻

ADAMS
▼▼ Adams Inn Hotel 🅷

(608) 339-6088. **Call for rates.** 2188 SR 13 53910. Just s. Int corridors. **Pets:** Accepted. 🍴 🛜 ✕ 🛏

ALGOMA
▼ Algoma Beach Motel Ⓜ

(920) 487-2828. **$59-$329, 3 day notice.** 1500 Lake St 54201. Jct SR 54, 0.4 mi s on SR 42. Ext/int corridors. **Pets:** Accepted.
🍴 ⓜ 🛜 ✕ 🛏

▼ Scenic Shore Inn Ⓜ 🐾

(920) 487-3214. **$55-$75, 3 day notice.** 2221 Lake St 54201. Jct SR 54, 0.8 mi s on SR 42. Ext corridors. **Pets:** Dogs only. $5 daily fee/pet. Designated rooms, service with restrictions, supervision.
🍴 🛜 ✕ 🛏

ANTIGO
▼▼ America's Best Inn & Suites 🅷

(715) 623-0506. **Call for rates.** 525 Memory Ln 54409. 0.4 mi n of jct SR 64 E and US 45, just w. Int corridors. **Pets:** Accepted.
⌲ 🛜 ✕ 🛏 💻

▼▼▼ Holiday Inn Express & Suites Antigo 🅷

(715) 627-7500. **$79-$99.** 2407 Neva Rd 54409. Just n of jct SR 64 E and US 45, just e. Int corridors. **Pets:** Dogs only. $15 daily fee/pet. Designated rooms, service with restrictions, supervision.
ⓜ ⌲ ✕ 🛜 ✕ 🛏 💻

▼▼ Super 8-Antigo 🅷

(715) 623-4188. **$74-$106.** 535 Century Ave 54409. On US 45 at SR 64 E. Int corridors. **Pets:** Dogs only. $15 daily fee/pet. Designated rooms, service with restrictions, supervision.
ⓜ ⌲ 🛜 ✕ 🛏 💻

APPLETON *(Restaurants p. 645)*
🆑🆑 ▼▼ BEST WESTERN Fox Valley Inn 🅷

(920) 731-4141. **$61-$160, 3 day notice.** 3033 W College Ave 54914. US 41 exit 137 (SR 125), 0.5 mi e. Int corridors. **Pets:** Medium, dogs only. $20 daily fee/pet. Designated rooms, no service, supervision.
🆂🅰🆅🅴 🛜 ✕ 🛏 💻

▼▼ Candlewood Suites 🅷 🐾

(920) 739-8000. **$59-$139.** 4525 W College Ave 54914. US 41 exit 137 (SR 125), just w. Int corridors. **Pets:** Large, other species. $15 daily fee/room. Service with restrictions, crate. ⓜ 🛜 ✕ 🛏 💻

▼▼ Country Inn & Suites By Carlson 🅷

(920) 830-3240. **Call for rates.** 355 Fox River Dr 54913. US 41 exit 137 (SR 125), just nw. Int corridors. **Pets:** Accepted.
⌲ 🛜 ✕ 🛏 💻

▼▼ Extended Stay America-Appleton-Fox Cities 🅷

(920) 830-9596. **$54-$199.** 4141 Boardwalk Ct 54915. US 41 exit 137 (SR 125), just w on College Ave, then just s on Nicolet Rd. Int corridors. **Pets:** Other species. $25 daily fee/pet. Service with restrictions, supervision. ⓜ 🛜 ✕ 🛏 💻

▼▼ Fairfield Inn by Marriott 🅷

(920) 954-0202. **$90-$160.** 132 N Mall Dr 54913. US 41 exit 137 (SR 125), just nw. Int corridors. **Pets:** Accepted. ⌲ 🛜 ✕ 🛏 💻

▼▼ La Quinta Inn & Suites Appleton College Avenue 🅷

(920) 734-7777. **$85-$359.** 3800 W College Ave 54914. US 41 exit 137 (SR 125), just e. Int corridors. **Pets:** Large, other species. Service with restrictions. ⓜ ⌲ ✕ 🛜 ✕ 🛏 💻

▼▼ La Quinta Inn Appleton Fox River Mall Area Ⓜ

(920) 734-6070. **$59-$259.** 3920 W College Ave 54914. US 41 exit 137 (SR 125), just e. Ext/int corridors. **Pets:** Large, other species. Service with restrictions. ⌲ 🛜 ✕ 🛏 💻

▼▼ Microtel Inn & Suites by Wyndham Appleton 🅷

(920) 997-3121. **$50-$200.** 321 Metro Dr 54913. US 41 exit 137 (SR 125), just nw. Int corridors. **Pets:** Dogs only. $10 daily fee/pet. Service with restrictions, supervision. 🛜 ✕ 🛏 💻

▼ Motel 6 Appleton #4957 🅷

(920) 733-5551. **$50-$134.** 210 Westhill Blvd 54914. US 41 exit 137 (SR 125), just e. Int corridors. **Pets:** Accepted. 🛜 ✕ 🛏 💻

▼▼▼ Residence Inn by Marriott 🅷 🐾

(920) 954-0570. **$139-$229.** 310 Metro Dr 54913. US 41 exit 137 (SR 125), just nw on Mall Dr. Int corridors. **Pets:** Other species. $100 one-time fee/room. Service with restrictions. ⌲ 🛜 ✕ 🛏 💻

ARKDALE
▼▼▼ Northern Bay Resort & Castle Course 🆒

(608) 339-2090. **$104-$445, 14 day notice.** 1844 20th Ave 54613. 2.9 mi w on SR 21, 3 mi s on CR Z, 0.9 mi w on Czech Ave, then 0.4 mi se. Int corridors. **Pets:** Medium. $25 daily fee/pet. Designated rooms, no service, crate. 🍴 ⌲ ✕ 🛜 ✕ 🛏 💻

ASHLAND
▼▼ AmericInn of Ashland 🅷

(715) 682-9950. **Call for rates.** 3009 Lake Shore Dr E 54806. On US 2, 2.3 mi e of jct SR 13 S. Int corridors. **Pets:** Accepted.
🍴 ⓜ ⌲ ✕ 🛜 ✕ 🛏 💻

🆀🆀🆀 ▼▼ Ashland Lake Superior Lodge 🅷

(715) 682-5235. **Call for rates.** 30600 US Hwy 2 54806. On US 2, 2.5 mi w of jct SR 13 S. Ext/int corridors. **Pets:** $25 daily fee/pet. Designated rooms, service with restrictions, supervision.
🆂🅰🆅🅴 🍴 ⓜ ⌲ 🛜 🛏 💻

BALDWIN
▼▼ AmericInn Lodge & Suites of Baldwin Ⓜ

(715) 684-5888. **Call for rates.** 500 Baldwin Plaza Dr 54002. I-94 exit 19 (US 63), just ne. Int corridors. **Pets:** Accepted.
ⓜ ⌲ 🛜 ✕ 🛏 💻

▼▼ Super 8 🅷

(715) 684-2700. **$64-$119.** 805 Energy St 54002. I-94 exit 19 (US 63), just se. Int corridors. **Pets:** Medium, other species. $15 daily fee/pet. Designated rooms, service with restrictions, supervision.
⌲ 🛜 ✕ 🛏 💻

BARABOO
▼▼ Clarion Hotel & Convention Center 🅷

(608) 356-6422. **$64-$159.** 626 W Pine St 53913. On US 12, 0.3 mi n of SR 33. Int corridors. **Pets:** Accepted.
🍴 ⓜ ⌲ 🛜 ✕ 🛏 💻

BEAVER DAM
▼▼▼ AmericInn Lodge & Suites of Beaver Dam 🅷 🐾

(920) 356-9000. **$90-$150.** 325 Seippel Blvd 53916. US 151 exit 134 (CR B/Industrial Dr). Int corridors. **Pets:** Small, dogs only. $10 daily fee/room. Designated rooms, service with restrictions, supervision.
ⓜ ⌲ 🛜 ✕ 🛏 💻

▼▼ ▼▼ Super 8 🅗

(920) 887-8880. **$64-$89.** 711 Park Ave 53916. US 151 exit 132 (SR 33), just w. Int corridors. **Pets:** Accepted. 🛜 ⊠ 🔌 🖵

BELOIT

▼▼▼▼ Fairfield Inn & Suites by Marriott 🅗

(608) 365-2200. **$97-$160.** 2784 Milwaukee Rd 53511. I-90 exit 185A, just sw; at I-43 and SR 81. Int corridors. **Pets:** Accepted.

🕭 ⌫ 🛜 ⊠ 🔌 🖵

◈◈◈ ▼▼▼▼ Ironworks Hotel 🅗 ❦

(608) 362-5500. **$149-$289.** 500 Pleasant St 53511. Downtown. Int corridors. **Pets:** Dogs only. $20 daily fee/pet. Service with restrictions.

(SAVE) 🍴 🛜 ⊠ 🔌 🖵

▼▼▼▼ Quality Inn of Beloit 🅗

(608) 362-2666. **$70-$160.** 2786 Milwaukee Rd 53511. I-90 exit 185A, just w; at I-43 and SR 81. Int corridors. **Pets:** Accepted.

⌫ 🛜 ⊠ 🔌 🖵

◈◈◈ ▼▼▼ Rodeway Inn Ⓜ

(608) 364-4000. **$57-$80.** 2956 Milwaukee Rd 53511. I-90 exit 185A, 0.3 mi w. Ext/int corridors. **Pets:** Accepted.

(SAVE) 🍴 🕭 🛜 ⊠ 🔌 🖵

BERLIN

▼▼▼ Countryside Lodge Ⓜ

(920) 361-4411. **$71-$159.** 227 Ripon Rd 54923. On SR 49; at CR F. Int corridors. **Pets:** Small, dogs only. $10 one-time fee/pet. Designated rooms, service with restrictions, supervision. 🛜 ⊠ 🔌 🖵

BIRCHWOOD

▼▼▼ Cobblestone Bed & Breakfast 🅱🅱 ❦

(715) 354-3494. **$119-$185, 8 day notice.** 319 S Main St 54817. 0.8 mi e of SR 48; center. Int corridors. **Pets:** Large, other species. Supervision. 🛜 ⊠ 🗲

BLACK RIVER FALLS

◈◈◈ ▼▼ ▼▼ BEST WESTERN Arrowhead Lodge & Suites 🅗

(715) 284-9471. **$85-$95.** 600 Oasis Rd 54615. I-94 exit 116 (SR 54), just ne. Int corridors. **Pets:** Medium, dogs only. $100 deposit/room, $25 daily fee/pet. Designated rooms, service with restrictions, supervision.

(SAVE) 🍴 🕭 🕭 ⌫ 🛜 ⊠ 🔌 🖵

▼▼▼▼ Comfort Inn & Suites 🅗

(715) 284-0888. **$83-$175.** W10170 Hwy 54 E 54615. I-94 exit 116 (SR 54), just nw. Int corridors. **Pets:** Medium, other species. $15 daily fee/pet. Designated rooms, service with restrictions, supervision.

🍴 🕭 ⌫ 🛜 ⊠ 🔌 🖵

▼▼▼ Days Inn 🅗

(715) 284-4333. **$60-$133.** 919 Hwy 54 E 54615. I-94 exit 116 (SR 54), just w. Int corridors. **Pets:** Accepted.

🕭 ⌫ ⊠ 🛜 ⊠ 🔌 🖵

BROOKFIELD

◈◈◈ ▼▼▼ Brookfield Suites Hotel & Convention Center 🅗 ❦

(262) 782-2900. **Call for rates.** 1200 S Moorland Rd 53005. I-94 exit 301A (Moorland Rd), just s. Int corridors. **Pets:** Dogs only. $25 one-time fee/room. Designated rooms, service with restrictions, crate.

(SAVE) 🍴 🕭 ⌫ ⊠ 🛜 ⊠ 🔌 🖵

◈◈◈ ▼▼▼▼ Country Inn & Suites By Carlson, Milwaukee-West 🅗

(262) 782-1400. **$99-$269.** 1250 S Moorland Rd 53005. I-94 exit 301A (Moorland Rd), just se. Int corridors. **Pets:** Medium. $75 one-time fee/room. Designated rooms, service with restrictions, crate.

(SAVE) 🍴 🕭 ⌫ 🛜 ⊠ 🔌 🖵

▼▼▼ Extended Stay America-Milwaukee/Brookfield 🅗

(262) 782-9300. **$69-$119.** 325 N Brookfield Rd 53045. I-94 exit 297, 1.1 mi e on US 18, then just e. Int corridors. **Pets:** Other species. $25 daily fee/pet. Service with restrictions, supervision.

🕭 🛜 ⊠ 🔌 🖵

▼▼▼ La Quinta Inn Milwaukee West-Brookfield 🅗

(262) 782-9100. **$65-$185.** 20391 W Bluemound Rd 53045. I-94 exit 297, just e on US 18. Int corridors. **Pets:** Large, other species. Service with restrictions. 🕭 🛜 ⊠ 🔌 🖵

◈◈◈ ▼▼▼ Midway Hotel & Suites Brookfield 🅗

(262) 786-9540. **$99-$199.** 1005 S Moorland Rd 53005. I-94 exit 301A (Moorland Rd), just s. Int corridors. **Pets:** Medium, dogs only. $25 daily fee/pet. Designated rooms, service with restrictions, supervision.

(SAVE) 🍴 ⌫ ⊠ 🛜 ⊠ 🔌 🖵

◈◈◈ ▼▼▼ Quality Inn-Milwaukee/Brookfield 🅗 ❦

(262) 785-0500. **$80-$110.** 20150 W Bluemound Rd 53045. I-94 exit 297, just e on US 18. Ext/int corridors. **Pets:** Medium. $10 one-time fee/pet. Designated rooms, service with restrictions.

(SAVE) ⌫ 🛜 ⊠ 🔌 🖵

◈◈◈ ▼▼▼▼ Residence Inn by Marriott Milwaukee-Brookfield 🅗

(262) 782-5990. **$108-$252.** 950 S Pinehurst Ct 53005. I-94 exit 301A (Moorland Rd), just s. Ext corridors. **Pets:** $100 one-time fee/room. Service with restrictions, crate.

(SAVE) 🍴 🕭 ⌫ 🛜 ⊠ 🔌 🖵

◈◈◈ ▼▼▼▼ Sheraton Milwaukee Brookfield 🅗 ❦

(262) 364-1100. **$89-$229.** 375 S Moorland Rd 53005. I-94 exit 301B (Moorland Rd), just n. Int corridors. **Pets:** Medium, dogs only. Service with restrictions, supervision. (SAVE) 🍴 🕭 ⌫ 🛜 ⊠ 🔌 🖵

▼▼▼ TownePlace Suites by Marriott 🅗

(262) 784-8450. **$122-$229.** 600 N Calhoun Rd 53005. I-94 exit 297 eastbound, 2.1 mi e on US 18; exit 301B (Moorland Rd) westbound, 1.5 mi n, then 0.4 mi w on US 18. Int corridors. **Pets:** Accepted.

⌫ 🛜 ⊠ 🔌 🖵

BROWN DEER

▼▼▼ Candlewood Suites Milwaukee North 🅗

(414) 355-3939. **$95-$144.** 4483 W Schroeder Dr 53223. Just nw of jct SR 100 and 57. Int corridors. **Pets:** Large, other species. $25 daily fee/pet. Service with restrictions, crate. 🕭 🛜 ⊠ 🔌 🖵

CADOTT

◈◈◈ ▼▼▼ Countryside Motel Ⓜ

(715) 289-4000. **$65-$120.** 545 Lavorata Rd 54727. SR 29 just e 91 (SR 27), just s. Int corridors. **Pets:** Small, dogs only. $5 daily fee/pet. Designated rooms, service with restrictions, supervision. (SAVE) 🕭 🛜 ⊠

CHIPPEWA FALLS

▼▼▼ AmericInn Motel & Suites of Chippewa Falls Ⓜ

(715) 723-5711. **Call for rates.** 11 W South Ave 54729. 2 mi s on SR 124. Int corridors. **Pets:** Accepted. 🍴 🕭 ⌫ 🛜 ⊠ 🔌 🖵

CLINTONVILLE

▼▼▼ Cobblestone Inn & Suites 🅗

(715) 823-2000. **Call for rates.** 175 Waupaca St 54929. Jct US 45 and CR C. Int corridors. **Pets:** Accepted. 🍴 🕭 🛜 ⊠ 🔌 🖵

COLUMBUS

▼▼ ▼▼ Super 8-Columbus 🅗

(920) 623-8800. **$68-$119.** 219 Industrial Dr 53925. US 151 exit 118 (SR 16/60), just ne. Int corridors. **Pets:** Accepted.

🕭 ⌫ 🛜 ⊠ 🔌 🖵

CRANDON

BEST WESTERN Crandon Inn & Suites 🄷

(715) 478-4000. **$80-$120.** 9075 E Pioneer St 54520. 0.5 mi e on US 8 and SR 32. Int corridors. **Pets:** Accepted.

Four Seasons Motel Ⓜ

(715) 478-3377. **Call for rates.** 304 W Glen St 54520. 0.5 mi w on US 8. Ext/int corridors. **Pets:** Medium. $20 deposit/pet. Designated rooms, service with restrictions, supervision.

DE FOREST

Comfort Inn & Suites 🄷

(608) 846-9100. **$79-$129.** 5025 County Rd V 53532. I-90/94 exit 126 (CR V), just w. Int corridors. **Pets:** Medium. $20 one-time fee/pet. Designated rooms, service with restrictions, crate.

Holiday Inn Express 🄷

(608) 846-8686. **$104-$209.** 7184 Morrisonville Rd 53532. I-90/94 exit 126 (CR V), just e. Int corridors. **Pets:** Accepted.

DELAFIELD *(Restaurants p. 645)*

The Delafield Hotel 🄷 🐾

(262) 646-1600. **$209, 3 day notice.** 415 Genesee St 53018. I-94 exit 285, 0.4 mi n on CR C (Genesee St). Int corridors. **Pets:** $35 one-time fee/room. Service with restrictions, crate.

La Quinta Inn & Suites Milwaukee Delafield 🄷

(262) 395-1162. **$75-$195.** 2801 Hillside Dr 53018. I-94 exit 287, just s on SR 83, then just e. Int corridors. **Pets:** Large, other species. Service with restrictions.

DE PERE

Kress Inn, an Ascend Hotel Collection Member 🄷

(920) 403-5100. **$79-$109.** 300 Grant St 54115. US 41 exit 163 (Main Ave), 1 mi e, then just s on 3rd St. Int corridors. **Pets:** Accepted.

DODGEVILLE

BEST WESTERN Quiet House & Suites 🄷

(608) 935-7739. **$90-$160.** 1130 N Johns St 53533. On US 18, just e of jct SR 23. Int corridors. **Pets:** Small, dogs only. $15 deposit/pet. Designated rooms, service with restrictions, supervision.

Super 8 of Dodgeville 🄷

(608) 935-3888. **$60-$121, 3 day notice.** 1308 Johns St 53533. Just n of US 18. Int corridors. **Pets:** $50 deposit/pet. Service with restrictions, supervision.

EAGLE RIVER

Days Inn 🄷

(715) 479-5151. **$72-$196.** 844 Railroad St N 54521. On US 45, 0.5 mi n. Int corridors. **Pets:** Large, dogs only. $15 daily fee/pet. Designated rooms, service with restrictions, supervision.

Super 8 🄷

(715) 477-0888. **$68-$165.** 200 W Pine St 54521. On SR 70; center. Int corridors. **Pets:** Accepted.

EAU CLAIRE *(Restaurants p. 645)*

AmericInn Motel & Suites of Eau Claire 🄷

(715) 874-4900. **Call for rates.** 6200 Texaco Dr 54703. I-94 exit 59, jct US 12. Int corridors. **Pets:** Accepted.

BEST WESTERN PLUS Trail Lodge Hotel & Suites 🄷

(715) 838-9989. **$105-$140.** 3340 Mondovi Rd 54701. I-94 exit 65, just n. Int corridors. **Pets:** Medium, dogs only. $20 daily fee/pet. Designated rooms, service with restrictions, supervision.

Clarion Hotel Campus Area 🄷

(715) 835-2211. **Call for rates.** 2703 Craig Rd 54701. I-94 exit 65, 1.3 mi n on SR 37; just w of jct US 12. Int corridors. **Pets:** Accepted.

Econo Lodge 🄷

(715) 833-8818. **$60-$120.** 4608 Royal Dr 54701. I-94 exit 68, just n on SR 93, just w on Golf Rd, then just s. Int corridors. **Pets:** Accepted.

Motel 6 🄷

(715) 834-3193. **$61-$66.** 2305 Craig Rd 54701. I-94 exit 65, 1.3 mi n on SR 37; just w of jct US 12. Int corridors. **Pets:** Other species. Service with restrictions, crate.

Sleep Inn & Suites Conference Center 🄷

(715) 874-2900. **$84-$134.** 5872 N 33rd Ave 54703. SR 29 exit 69 (CR T), just sw. Int corridors. **Pets:** Medium. $10 daily fee/room. Service with restrictions, crate.

EGG HARBOR

The Shallows Resort Ⓜ

(920) 868-3458. **$85-$450, 30 day notice.** 7353 Horseshoe Bay Rd 54209. On CR G, 2.5 mi s. Ext corridors. **Pets:** Small, dogs only. $20 daily fee/pet. Service with restrictions, supervision.

ELKHORN

AmericInn Lodge & Suites of Elkhorn 🄷

(262) 723-7799. **$82-$189.** 210 E Commerce Ct 53121. I-43 exit 25, just s. Int corridors. **Pets:** $25 daily fee/pet. Designated rooms, service with restrictions, supervision.

EPHRAIM

Trollhaugen Lodge Inn, Motel & Log Cabin Ⓜ 🐾

(920) 854-2713. **$79-$169, 7 day notice.** 10176 Hwy 42 54211. 0.6 mi n of Village Hall. Ext/int corridors. **Pets:** Other species. $25 one-time fee/room. Designated rooms, supervision.

FISH CREEK

Julie's Park Cafe & Motel Ⓜ

(920) 868-2999. **Call for rates.** 4020 Hwy 42 54212. On SR 42, 0.3 mi n. Ext corridors. **Pets:** Accepted.

FITCHBURG

Candlewood Suites 🄷

(608) 271-3400. **Call for rates.** 5421 Caddis Bend 53711. US 12/18 exit 260 (Fish Hatchery/CR D), 1.5 mi s. Int corridors. **Pets:** Accepted.

Wyndham Garden 🄷

(608) 274-7200. **$104-$169.** 2969 Cahill Main 53711. US 12/18 exit 260 (Fish Hatchery/CR D), 1.5 mi s at CR PD (McKee Rd). Int corridors. **Pets:** Accepted.

FOND DU LAC

Comfort Inn by Choice Hotels Fond du Lac 🄷

(920) 921-4000. **$79-$149.** 77 Holiday Ln 54937. US 41 exit 97 (Military Rd), just sw. Int corridors. **Pets:** Large, other species. Service with restrictions, supervision.

Executive Lodge Fond du Lac 🄷

(920) 923-2020. **$49-$89.** 649 W Johnson St 54935. US 41 exit 99 (SR 23/Johnson St), 0.3 mi e. Int corridors. **Pets:** Other species. $5 daily fee/pet. Designated rooms, service with restrictions, supervision.

▼▼▼ Holiday Inn 🅷

(920) 923-1440. $109-$409. 625 W Rolling Meadows Dr 54937. US 41 exit 97 (Military Rd), just sw. Int corridors. **Pets:** Other species. Service with restrictions, supervision.

ECO ⚫ 📶 &M ☜ ☒ 🖐 ☒ 🖐 ☒

▼▼ Super 8-FOND DU LAC 🅷

(920) 922-1088. $55-$215, 3 day notice. 391 N Pioneer Rd 54935. US 41 exit 99 (SR 23/Johnson St), just n on east frontage road (CR VV). Int corridors. **Pets:** Accepted. &M ☜ ☒ 🖐 ☒

FORT ATKINSON

▼▼▼ Holiday Inn Express Hotel & Suites 🅷

(920) 563-3600. $114-$199. 1680 Madison Ave 53538. Jct SR 26 Bypass and US 12. Int corridors. **Pets:** Small. $30 one-time fee/room. Designated rooms, service with restrictions, crate.

&M ☜ ☒ 🖐 ☒ 🖐 ☒

FRANKLIN

🆎 ▼▼▼ Staybridge Suites Milwaukee Airport South 🅷

(414) 761-3800. $99-$159. 9575 S 27th St 53132. I-94 exit 322 (Ryan Rd), 0.6 mi w; jct 27th St. Int corridors. **Pets:** Accepted.

SAVE ECO &M ☜ ☒ 🖐 ☒ 🖐 ☒

GERMANTOWN

▼▼▼ Holiday Inn Express Milwaukee NW-Germantown 🅷

(262) 255-1100. Call for rates. W177 N9675 Riversbend Ln 53022. US 41 and 45 exit CR Q (County Line Rd), just w. Int corridors.

Pets: Accepted. &M ☜ ☜ ☒ 🖐 ☒

🆎 ▼▼▼ Super 8-Germantown/Milwaukee 🅷

(262) 255-0880. $69-$184. N96 W17490 County Line Rd 53022. US 41 and 45 exit CR Q (County Line Rd), just w. Int corridors. **Pets:** $10 daily fee/pet. Service with restrictions, supervision.

SAVE ☜ ☜ ☒ 🖐 ☒

GLENDALE

▼▼▼ La Quinta Inn & Suites Milwaukee Bayshore Area 🅷

(414) 962-6767. $95-$224. 5423 N Port Washington Rd 53217. I-43 exit 78A (Silver Spring Dr), just se. Int corridors. **Pets:** Large, other species. Service with restrictions. ☜ ☜ ☒ 🖐 ☒

▼▼ La Quinta Inn Milwaukee Glendale Hampton Ave 🅷

(414) 964-8484. $65-$186. 5110 N Port Washington Rd 53217. I-43 exit 78A (Silver Spring Dr), 0.4 mi se. Int corridors. **Pets:** Large, other species. Service with restrictions. ☜ ☒ 🖐 ☒

▼▼▼ Residence Inn by Marriott Milwaukee/Glendale 🅷

(414) 352-0070. $111-$206. 7275 N Port Washington Rd 53217. I-43 exit 80 (Good Hope Rd), just e. Ext corridors. **Pets:** Large. $100 one-time fee/room. Service with restrictions, crate.

⚫ ☜ ☜ ☒ 🖐 ☒

GRAFTON

🆎 ▼▼▼ Comfort Inn & Suites Milwaukee-Grafton 🅷

(262) 387-1180. $84-$139. 1415 N Port Washington Rd 53024. I-43 exit 92 (SR 60), just w, then just s. Int corridors. **Pets:** Accepted.

SAVE ⚫ &M ☜ ☜ ☒ 🖐 ☒

GREEN BAY

🆎 ▼▼▼ Aloft Green Bay 🅷 🐾

(920) 884-0800. $99-$309. 465 Pilgrim Way 54304. US 41 exit 163B, just e. Int corridors. **Pets:** Medium, dogs only. Designated rooms, service with restrictions, supervision.

SAVE ⚫ &M ☜ ☜ ☒ 🖐 ☒

🆎 ▼▼▼ AmericInn Lodge & Suites Green Bay East 🅷

(920) 964-0177. $75-$155. 2628 Manitowoc Rd 54311. I-43 exit 181, just w. Int corridors. **Pets:** Dogs only. $20 one-time fee/pet. Designated rooms, service with restrictions, crate.

SAVE &M ☜ ☜ ☒ 🖐 ☒

▼▼ AmericInn Lodge of Green Bay West 🅷 🐾

(920) 434-9790. Call for rates. 2032 Velp Ave 54303. US 41 exit 170, 0.3 mi w. Int corridors. **Pets:** $15 daily fee/pet. Designated rooms, service with restrictions, crate. ☜ ☜ ☒ 🖐 ☒

▼▼ Baymont Inn-Green Bay 🅷

(920) 494-7887. $59-$229. 2840 S Oneida St 54304. US 41 exit 164 (Oneida St), just e. Int corridors. **Pets:** Accepted. ☜ ☒ 🖐 ☒

🆎 ▼ Bay Motel Ⓜ

(920) 494-3441. $55-$85. 1301 S Military Ave 54304. US 41 exit 167 (Lombardi Ave), 0.4 mi e to Marlee Ln, then 0.6 mi n. Ext corridors. **Pets:** Accepted. SAVE ⚫ ☜ ☒ 🖐 ☒

🆎 ▼▼ BEST WESTERN Green Bay Inn Conference Center 🅷

(920) 499-3161. $89-$349. 780 Armed Forces Dr 54304. US 41 exit 167 (Lombardi Ave), 1.4 mi e to Holmgren Way, then just s. Int corridors. **Pets:** Accepted. SAVE ⚫ ☜ ☜ ☒ 🖐 ☒

▼▼▼ Country Inn & Suites By Carlson Green Bay North 🅷

(920) 884-2000. $89-$299. 2308 Lineville Rd 54313. US 41 exit Lineville Rd, 1 mi w. Int corridors. **Pets:** Medium, other species. $30 one-time fee/room. Designated rooms, service with restrictions, supervision.

&M ☜ ☒ 🖐 ☒

▼▼ Country Inn & Suites By Carlson Green Bay-Stadium District 🅷

(920) 336-6600. $129-$175, 3 day notice. 2945 Allied St 54304. US 41 exit 164 (Oneida St), just nw. Int corridors. **Pets:** Small. $15 daily fee/room. Designated rooms, service with restrictions, supervision.

☜ ☜ ☒ 🖐 ☒

▼▼ Extended Stay Airport 🅷

(920) 499-3600. $60-$225. 1639 Commanche Ave 54313. US 41 exit 165, 1 mi w on SR 172, then just s. Int corridors. **Pets:** Dogs only. $75 one-time fee/pet. Service with restrictions, crate. ☜ ☒ 🖐 ☒

▼▼ Hawthorn Suites by Wyndham Green Bay 🅷

(920) 435-2222. $69-$139. 335 W St. Joseph St 54301. SR 172 exit Riverside Dr, 1.1 mi n on SR 57, then just e. Ext corridors. **Pets:** Other species. $150 one-time fee/room. Service with restrictions.

☜ ☜ ☒ 🖐 ☒

▼ Motel 6 Green Bay – Lambeau #4954 🅷

(920) 499-3599. $59-$299. 2870 Ramada Way 54304. US 41 exit 164 (Oneida St), just e. Int corridors. **Pets:** Other species. Service with restrictions, crate. ☜ ☒ 🖐 ☒

▼▼ Quality Inn & Suites Downtown 🅷

(920) 437-8771. $79-$199. 321 S Washington St 54301-4214. On east side of Fox River, just s of Walnut St (SR 29); downtown. Int corridors. **Pets:** Accepted. ☜ ☒ ☜ ☒ 🖐 ☒

🆎 ▼▼ Ramada Plaza Hotel 🅷

(920) 499-0631. $89-$269. 2750 Ramada Way 54304. US 41 exit 164 (Oneida St), just e. Int corridors. **Pets:** Accepted.

SAVE ⚫ &M ☜ ☒ ☜ ☒ 🖐 ☒

▼ Super 8-Airport Stadium 🅷

(920) 494-2042. $68-$195. 2868 S Oneida St 54304. US 41 exit 164 (Oneida St), just e. Int corridors. **Pets:** Accepted. ☜ ☒ 🖐 ☒

HAYWARD

▼▼▼ **AmericInn of Hayward** ⊞
(715) 634-2700. **$110-$195, 3 day notice.** 15601 US Hwy 63 N 54843. Just n of jct SR 77. Int corridors. **Pets:** Small, dogs only. $10 daily fee/pet. Designated rooms, service with restrictions, supervision.
🏋M ➡ 🛜 ✕ 🛢 🖵

▼▼▼ **Comfort Suites** ⊞
(715) 634-0700. **$88-$329.** 15586 CR B 54843. 0.5 mi s of jct SR 27. Int corridors. **Pets:** Other species. $15 daily fee/room. Designated rooms, service with restrictions. 🏋M ➡ ✕ 🛜 ✕ 🛢 🖵

⚠ ▼▼▼ **The Flat Creek Inn & Suites** ⊞
(715) 634-4100. **$85-$165.** 10290 Hwy 27 S 54843. 0.7 mi s of jct US 63. Int corridors. **Pets:** Dogs only. $15 daily fee/room. Designated rooms, service with restrictions, supervision.
SAVE ▮¶ 🏋M ➡ 🛜 ✕ 🛢 🖵

▼▼ **Ross' Teal Lake Lodge and Teal Wing Golf Club** 🆑 ❀
(715) 462-3631. **$152-$282, 21 day notice.** 12425 N Ross Rd 54843. On SR 77, 20 mi ne of jct US 63. Ext corridors. **Pets:** Other species. $10 daily fee/pet. Service with restrictions.
▮¶ ➡ ✕ 🛜 ✕ 🗲 🛢 🖵

HILLSBORO

⚠ ▼▼▼ **Hotel Hillsboro** ⊞
(608) 489-3000. **$75-$125.** 1235 Water Ave (SR 33) 54634. Jct SR 80/82 and 33, just n. Int corridors. **Pets:** Large. $15 one-time fee/room. Designated rooms, service with restrictions, crate.
SAVE ▮¶ 🏋M ➡ 🛜 ✕ 🖵

HUDSON

▼▼▼ **Fairfield Inn by Marriott** ⊞
(715) 386-6688. **$76-$137.** 2400 Center Dr 54016. I-94 exit 2 (CR F), 0.3 mi s. Int corridors. **Pets:** Medium, other species. $20 one-time fee/room. Designated rooms, service with restrictions, crate.
🏋M ➡ 🛜 ✕ 🛢 🖵

▼▼▼ **Hudson House Grand Hotel** ⊞
(715) 386-2394. **$80-$100, 3 day notice.** 1616 Crest View Dr 54016. I-94 exit 2 (CR F), 0.7 mi w on south frontage road. Int corridors. **Pets:** Accepted. ▮¶ ➡ ✕ 🛜 ✕ 🛢 🖵

▼▼▼ **Quality Inn** ⊞
(715) 386-6355. **$85-$130.** 811 Dominion Dr 54016. I-94 exit 2 (CR F), 1 mi w on south frontage road (Crest View Dr). Int corridors. **Pets:** Accepted. ➡ 🛜 ✕ 🛢 🖵

HURLEY

⚠ ▼▼▼ **Days Inn of Hurley** ⊞
(715) 561-3500. **$79-$145.** 13355 N US Hwy 51 54534. Jct US 2 and 51, 0.4 mi s on US 51. Int corridors. **Pets:** $20 daily fee/room. Service with restrictions, supervision. SAVE ▮¶ ➡ ✕ 🛜 ✕ 🛢 🖵

JACKSON

▼▼▼ **Comfort Inn & Suites of Jackson** ⊞
(262) 677-1133. **$89-$299.** N W227 16890 Tillie Lake Ct 53037. US 41 exit 64 (SR 60), 2.9 mi e, jct US 45. Int corridors. **Pets:** Medium, dogs only. $15 daily fee/pet. Designated rooms, service with restrictions, supervision. 🏋M ➡ 🛜 ✕ 🛢 🖵

JANESVILLE

▼▼▼ **Baymont Inn & Suites** ⊞ ❀
(608) 758-4545. **$69-$109.** 616 Midland Rd 53546. I-90 exit 175B (SR 11), just ne. Int corridors. **Pets:** Other species. $10 daily fee/pet. Designated rooms, service with restrictions, crate. ➡ 🛜 ✕ 🖵

▼▼ **Econo Lodge-Janesville** ⊞
(608) 754-0251. **$56-$119.** 3520 Milton Ave 53545. I-90 exit 171A, just sw via Frontage Rd. Int corridors. **Pets:** Accepted. 🛜 ✕ 🛢 🖵

JOHNSON CREEK

▼▼▼ **Comfort Suites by Choice Hotels-Johnson Creek** ⊞
(920) 699-2800. **$95-$170.** 725 Paradise Ln 53038. I-94 exit 267 (SR 26), 1.4 mi n, 1.6 mi w on River Dr, 0.8 mi s on CR Y, then just w. Int corridors. **Pets:** Medium, dogs only. $15 daily fee/pet. Service with restrictions, supervision. ▮¶ 🏋M ➡ 🛜 ✕ 🛢 🖵

KENOSHA

⚠ ▼▼▼ **BEST WESTERN Harborside Inn & Kenosha Conference Ctr** ⊞
(262) 658-3281. **$160-$200.** 5125 6th Ave 53140. Just ne of jct SR 32 and 158; downtown. Int corridors. **Pets:** Accepted.
SAVE 🏋M ➡ 🛜 ✕ 🛢 🖵

▼▼▼ **Candlewood Suites** ⊞
(262) 842-5000. **Call for rates.** 10200 74th St 53142. SR 50 exit 104th Ave, just n. Int corridors. **Pets:** Accepted. 🏋M 🛜 ✕ 🛢 🖵

▼▼▼ **Comfort Inn & Suites** ⊞
(262) 857-3450. **$79-$145.** 7206 122nd Ave 53142. I-94 exit 344 (SR 50), just nw. Int corridors. **Pets:** Accepted.
🏋M ➡ 🛜 ✕ 🛢 🖵

KOHLER

⚠ ▼▼▼▼ **Inn on Woodlake** ⊞ ❀
(920) 452-7800. **$112-$299, 7 day notice.** 705 Woodlake Rd 53044. I-43 exit 126, 0.5 mi w on SR 23, 0.5 mi s on CR Y and Highland Dr; in Woodlake Shopping Center. Int corridors. **Pets:** Medium, dogs only. Designated rooms, service with restrictions, supervision.
SAVE 🛜 ✕ 🖵

LA CROSSE

⚠ ▼▼▼▼ **BEST WESTERN Riverfront Hotel** ⊞
(608) 781-7000. **$100-$200.** 1835 Rose St 54603. I-90 exit 3, 1 mi s on US 53. Int corridors. **Pets:** Accepted.
SAVE ▮¶ 🏋M ➡ ✕ 🛜 ✕ 🛢 🖵

▼▼▼▼ **Candlewood Suites** ⊞ ❀
(608) 785-1110. **Call for rates.** 56 Copeland Ave 54603. I-90 exit 3, 2 mi s on US 53. Int corridors. **Pets:** Large, other species. $75 one-time fee/room. Service with restrictions, crate. 🏋M 🛜 ✕ 🛢 🖵

⚠ ▼▼▼ **Days Inn Hotel & Conference Center** ⊞
(608) 783-1000. **$69-$179.** 101 Sky Harbour Dr 54603. I-90 exit 2, just sw; on French Island. Int corridors. **Pets:** Dogs only. $15 daily fee/room. Service with restrictions, crate.
SAVE ▮¶ ➡ 🛜 ✕ 🛢 🖵

⚠ ▼▼▼ **Econo Lodge** ⊞
(608) 781-0200. **$55-$160.** 1906 Rose St 54603. I-90 exit 3, 0.9 mi s on US 53. Int corridors. **Pets:** Accepted.
SAVE ▮¶ 🏋M 🛜 ✕ 🛢 🖵

▼▼▼ **GrandStay Residential Suites Hotel of La Crosse** ⊞
(608) 796-1615. **$90-$229.** 525 Front St N 54601. I-90 exit 3; downtown. Int corridors. **Pets:** Medium. $200 deposit/room, $10 daily fee/pet. Designated rooms, service with restrictions.
🏋M ➡ ✕ 🛜 ✕ 🛢 🖵

▼▼▼ **Holiday Inn Hotel & Suites** ⊞
(608) 784-4444. **Call for rates.** 200 Pearl St 54601. Downtown. Int corridors. **Pets:** Accepted. ▮¶ 🏋M ➡ 🛜 ✕ 🛢 🖵

▼▼▼ **Motel 6 - La Crosse, WI #4962** ⊞
(608) 781-0400. **$49-$279.** 2150 Rose St 54603. I-90 exit 3, 0.8 mi s on US 53. Int corridors. **Pets:** Other species. Service with restrictions, crate. 🛜 ✕ 🛢 🖵

▼▼▼▼ **Radisson Hotel La Crosse** ⊞
(608) 784-6680. **$129-$399.** 200 Harborview Plaza 54601. Just w of US 53; downtown. Int corridors. **Pets:** Accepted.
▮¶ 🏋M ➡ 🛜 ✕ 🛢 🖵

▼▼ ▼▼ **Settle Inn** 🅷

(608) 781-5100. **$60-$125.** 2110 Rose St 54603. I-90 exit 3, 0.9 mi s on US 53. Int corridors. **Pets:** Small, dogs only. $15 daily fee/pet. Service with restrictions, supervision. 🔥M 🏊 🛜 ✖ 📠 💻

LADYSMITH

▼▼ ▼▼ **Ladysmith Motel & Suites** Ⓜ

(715) 532-6650. **$90-$110, 3 day notice.** 800 W College Ave 54848. On SR 27, 0.5 mi s of US 8. Int corridors. **Pets:** Medium. $15 daily fee/pet. Designated rooms, service with restrictions, supervision.

🔥M 🏊 🛜 ✖ 📠 💻

LAKE GENEVA

ⒶⒶⒶ ▼▼▼▼ **Grand Geneva Resort & Spa** 🅷 🐾

(262) 248-8811. **$159-$449, 3 day notice.** 7036 Grand Geneva Way 53147. On SR 50, just e of jct US 12. Int corridors. **Pets:** Small, dogs only. $35 daily fee/pet. Service with restrictions, crate.

SAVE ECO 🔌 🍴 🔥M 🏊 🛜 ✖ 📠 💻

LAND O'LAKES

▼▼ ▼▼ **Sunrise Lodge** 🅲🅰

(715) 547-3684. **$89-$235, 21 day notice.** 5894 W Shore Dr 54540. 2 mi s on US 45, 2.8 mi e on CR E, then 1 mi n. Ext corridors. **Pets:** Other species. Service with restrictions, supervision.

🍴 🏊 🛜 📻 📠 💻

LODI

▼▼ ▼▼ **Quality Inn & Suites** 🅷

(608) 592-1450. **$60-$160.** W 9250 Prospect Dr 53555. I-90/94 exit 119, just w. Int corridors. **Pets:** Accepted.

🍴 🔥M 🏊 🛜 ✖ 📠 💻

MADISON

ⒶⒶⒶ ▼▼▼▼ **AmericInn Madison West** 🅷

(608) 662-1990. **$69-$299.** 516 Grand Canyon Dr 53719. US 12 and 14 exit 255 (Gammon Rd), just n, then 0.5 mi e on Odana Rd. Int corridors. **Pets:** $20 daily fee/pet. Designated rooms, service with restrictions, supervision. SAVE 🔥M 🏊 🛜 ✖ 📠 💻

▼▼ ▼▼ **Baymont Inn & Suites Madison West** 🅷

(608) 831-7711. **$75-$105.** 8102 Excelsior Dr 53717. US 12 and 14 exit 253 (Old Sauk Rd), just w, then 0.4 mi n. Int corridors. **Pets:** Accepted. 🔥M 🏊 🛜 ✖ 📠 💻

ⒶⒶⒶ ▼▼▼▼ **BEST WESTERN East Towne Suites** 🅷

(608) 244-2020. **$79-$189.** 4801 Annamark Dr 53704. I-90/94 exit 135A (US 151) southbound; exit 135C (US 151/High Crossing Blvd) northbound, just sw. Int corridors. **Pets:** Other species. $20 daily fee/pet. Service with restrictions, crate. SAVE 🏊 🛜 ✖ 📠 💻

ⒶⒶⒶ ▼▼▼▼ **BEST WESTERN West Towne Suites** 🅷 🐾

(608) 833-4200. **$90-$180.** 650 Grand Canyon Dr 53719. US 12 and 14 exit 255 (Gammon Rd), just e on Odana Rd, then just sw. Int corridors. **Pets:** Medium. $50 deposit/pet, $15 daily fee/room. Designated rooms, service with restrictions, supervision.

SAVE 🍴 🔥M 🛜 ✖ 📠 💻

▼▼ ▼▼ **Clarion Suites Madison at the Alliant Energy Center** 🅷 🐾

(608) 284-1234. **$99-$199.** 2110 Rimrock Rd 53713. US 12 and 18 exit 262 (Rimrock Rd), just nw. Int corridors. **Pets:** Large. $25 daily fee/pet. Designated rooms, service with restrictions, crate.

🍴 🔥M 🏊 🛜 ✖ 📠 💻

▼▼▼▼ **Comfort Suites-Madison** 🅷

(608) 836-3033. **$88-$329.** 1253 John Q Hammons Dr 53717. US 12 and 14 exit 252 (Greenway Blvd), just sw. Int corridors. **Pets:** Accepted.

ECO 🔥M 🏊 🛜 ✖ 📠 💻

ⒶⒶⒶ ▼▼▼▼ **Crowne Plaza Hotel Madison** 🅷

(608) 244-4703. **$109-$369.** 4402 E Washington Ave 53704. I-90/94 exit 135A (US 151), 0.4 mi w. Int corridors. **Pets:** Accepted.

SAVE ECO 🍴 🔥M 🏊 🏊 🛜 ✖ 📠 💻

ⒶⒶⒶ ▼▼ ▼▼ **Days Inn & Suites** 🅷

(608) 223-1800. **$72-$169.** 4402 E Broadway Service Rd 53716. US 12 and 18 exit 266 (US 51), just ne. Int corridors. **Pets:** Medium, dogs only. $50 deposit/room, $10 daily fee/pet. Designated rooms, service with restrictions, supervision. SAVE ECO 🔥M 🏊 🛜 ✖ 📠 💻

ⒶⒶⒶ ▼▼▼▼ **Econo Lodge of Madison** 🅷

(608) 241-4171. **$54-$200.** 4726 E Washington Ave 53704. I-90/94 exit 135A (US 151), just w. Int corridors. **Pets:** Accepted.

SAVE 🔥M 🛜 ✖ 📠 💻

▼▼▼▼ **Extended Stay America Old Sauk Rd** 🅷

(608) 833-2121. **$79-$299.** 45 Junction Ct 53717. US 12 and 14 exit 253 (Old Sauk Rd), just w. Int corridors. **Pets:** Other species. $25 daily fee/pet. Service with restrictions, supervision.

🔥M 🏊 🛜 ✖ 📠 💻

▼▼▼▼ **GrandStay Residential Suites Hotel** 🅷

(608) 241-2500. **Call for rates.** 5317 High Crossing Blvd 53718. I-90/94 exit 135C (US 151/High Crossing Blvd), 0.5 mi e. Int corridors. **Pets:** Accepted. 🍴 🔥M 🏊 🏊 🛜 ✖ 📠 💻

ⒶⒶⒶ ▼▼▼▼ **Hilton Madison Monona Terrace** 🅷

(608) 255-5100. **$149-$399.** 9 E Wilson St 53703. 2 blks e of Capitol Square; downtown. Int corridors. **Pets:** Accepted.

SAVE ECO 🍴 🔥M 🏊 🛜 ✖ 📠 💻

ⒶⒶⒶ ▼▼▼▼ **HotelRED** 🅷

(608) 819-8228. **Call for rates.** 1501 Monroe St 53711. Downtown. Int corridors. **Pets:** Accepted. SAVE 🍴 🔥M 🛜 ✖ 📠 💻

ⒶⒶⒶ ▼▼▼▼ **Hyatt Place Madison** 🅷

(608) 257-2700. **$99-$499.** 333 W Washington Ave 53703. 2 1/2 blks sw of Capitol Square; downtown. Int corridors. **Pets:** Medium, dogs only. $75 one-time fee/pet. Service with restrictions, supervision.

SAVE ECO 🍴 🔥M 🏊 🛜 ✖ 📠 💻

▼▼ ▼▼ **La Quinta Inn & Suites Madison American Center** 🅷

(608) 245-0123. **$72-$259.** 5217 E Terrace Dr 53718. US 151 exit 98B (American Pkwy), just sw. Int corridors. **Pets:** Large, other species. Service with restrictions. 🍴 🔥M 🏊 🛜 ✖ 📠 💻

▼▼ ▼▼ **Motel 6 Madison East, WI #4961** 🅷

(608) 241-3861. **$49-$81.** 4202 E Towne Blvd 53704. I-90/94 exit 135A (US 151), 0.5 mi w. Int corridors. **Pets:** Other species. Service with restrictions, crate. 🛜 ✖ 📠 💻

ⒶⒶⒶ ▼▼ ▼▼ **Red Roof Inn Madison, WI** Ⓜ

(608) 241-1787. **$59-$94.** 4830 Hayes Rd 53704. I-90/94 exit 135A (US 151), just sw. Ext corridors. **Pets:** Large, other species. Service with restrictions, supervision. SAVE 🔥M 🛜 ✖ 📠 💻

▼▼▼▼ **Residence Inn by Marriott Madison East** 🅷

(608) 244-5047. **$104-$217.** 4862 Hayes Rd 53704. I-90/94 exit 135A (US 151), just sw to Hayes Rd, then just ne. Int corridors. **Pets:** Accepted. 🔥M 🏊 🛜 ✖ 📠 💻

ⒶⒶⒶ ▼▼▼▼ **Sheraton Madison Hotel** 🅷 🐾

(608) 251-2300. **Call for rates.** 706 John Nolen Dr 53713. US 12 and 18 exit 263 (John Nolen Dr), just n. Int corridors. **Pets:** $25 one-time fee/pet. Designated rooms, service with restrictions, supervision.

SAVE ECO 🍴 🔥M 🏊 🛜 ✖ 📠 💻

▼▼▼▼ **Sleep Inn & Suites** 🅷

(608) 221-8100. **$99-$149.** 4802 Tradewinds Pkwy 53718. US 12 and 18 exit 266 (US 51), 0.5 mi se, then 0.6 mi on Dutch Mill Rd. Int corridors. **Pets:** Other species. $10 daily fee/pet. Service with restrictions, crate. 🍴 🔥M 🏊 🏊 🛜 ✖ 📠 💻

▼▼▼▼ **Staybridge Suites** 🅷

(608) 241-2300. **$119-$299, 3 day notice.** 3301 City View Dr 53718. I-90/94 exit 135C (US 151/High Crossing Blvd), just e. Int corridors. **Pets:** Accepted. 🍴 🔥M 🏊 🛜 ✖ 📠 💻

WW Super 8-Madison **H**
(608) 258-8882. **$60-$150.** 1602 W Beltline Hwy 53713. US 12 and 18 exit 260B (CR D), just w on N Frontage Rd. Int corridors. **Pets:** Medium, other species. $10 daily fee/room. Designated rooms, service with restrictions, crate. 🌊 🛜 ✖ 🛏 📺

MANITOWOC

WW AmericInn Lodge & Suites of Manitowoc **H** ❀
(920) 684-3344. **Call for rates.** 5020 Hecker Rd 54220. I-43 exit 149, just sw. Int corridors. **Pets:** Other species. $15 daily fee/pet. Service with restrictions, crate. 🍽 🌊 🛜 ✖ 🛏 📺

WW 💎💎 BEST WESTERN Lakefront Hotel **H**
(920) 682-7000. **$79-$199.** 101 Maritime Dr 54220. I-43 exit 152, 4.2 mi e on SR 42 N, then 1 mi s. Int corridors. **Pets:** Dogs only. $20 daily fee/room. Designated rooms, service with restrictions, crate.
[SAVE] 🍽 🌊 🛜 ✖ 🛏 📺

W Econo Lodge **H**
(920) 682-8271. **$60-$120.** 908 Washington St 54220. On US 151 business route; downtown. Int corridors. **Pets:** Accepted.
🍽 🛜 ✖ 🛏 📺

WWW Holiday Inn Manitowoc **H**
(920) 682-6000. **$129-$189.** 4601 Calumet Ave 54220. I-43 exit 149, just e. Int corridors. **Pets:** Other species. $150 deposit/room. Service with restrictions, crate. 🍽 ♿M 🌊 🛜 ✖ 🛏 📺

WW Quality Inn by Choice Hotels **H**
(920) 683-0220. **$70-$100.** 2200 S 44th St 54220. I-43 exit 149, just e. Int corridors. **Pets:** Medium. $25 one-time fee/pet. Designated rooms, service with restrictions, supervision. ♿M 🛜 ✖ 🛏 📺

MARINETTE

WWW Country Inn & Suites By Carlson **H**
(715) 732-3400. **Call for rates.** 2020 Old Peshtigo Ct 54143. Jct Cleveland Ave, 1 mi s of downtown. Int corridors. **Pets:** Dogs only. $20 daily fee/room. Designated rooms, service with restrictions, supervision.
🌊 🛜 ✖ 🛏 📺

MARSHFIELD

WW Baymont Inn & Suites-Marshfield **H**
(715) 384-5240. **$79-$129.** 2107 N Central Ave 54449. On SR 97; 1.6 mi n of SR 13. Int corridors. **Pets:** Medium, other species. $10 daily fee/room. Designated rooms, service with restrictions, supervision.
♿M 🌊 🛜 ✖ 🛏 📺

AAA **WWW** Hotel Marshfield **H** ❀
(715) 387-2700. **$119-$169.** 2700 S Central Ave 54449. Jct US 10 and SR 13, 1.3 mi n. Int corridors. **Pets:** Other species. $100 deposit/room, $20 daily fee/room. Designated rooms, service with restrictions, supervision. [SAVE] 🍽 ♿M ✖ 🛜 ✖ 🛏 📺

MAUSTON

AAA **WWWW** BEST WESTERN Park Oasis Inn **H**
(608) 847-6255. **$90-$160.** 1006 SR 82 E 53948. I-90/94 exit 69, just se. Int corridors. **Pets:** Other species. $50 deposit/room, $5 daily fee/pet. Designated rooms, service with restrictions, supervision.
[SAVE] 🍽 🌊 🛜 ✖ 🛏 📺

WW Quality Inn **H**
(608) 847-5959. **$74-$169.** 1001 SR 82 53948. I-90/94 exit 69, just ne. Int corridors. **Pets:** Accepted. 🌊 🛜 ✖ 🛏 📺

WW Super 8 **M**
(608) 847-2300. **$74-$160.** 1001A Hwy 82 E 53948. I-90/94 exit 69, just ne. Int corridors. **Pets:** $10 daily fee/pet. Service with restrictions, supervision. ♿M 🌊 🛜 ✖ 🛏 📺

MEDFORD

WW Boarders Inn & Suites **H**
(715) 748-2330. **$74-$120.** 435 S 8th St 54451. On SR 13, 0.5 mi s of jct SR 64. Int corridors. **Pets:** $30 one-time fee/room. Designated rooms, service with restrictions, supervision.
♿M 🌊 🛜 ✖ 🛏 📺

WW Woodlands Inn & Suites **M**
(715) 748-3995. **$69-$124.** 854 N 8th St 54451. On SR 13, 0.6 mi n of jct SR 64. Int corridors. **Pets:** Accepted. 🌊 🛜 ✖ 🛏 📺

MENOMONIE

WW Menomonie Motel 6 #4109 **H**
(715) 235-6901. **$51-$75.** 2100 Stout St 54751. I-94 exit 41 (SR 25), just se. Int corridors. **Pets:** Other species. Service with restrictions, crate. 🛜 ✖ 🛏

WW Super 8-Menomonie **H**
(715) 235-8889. **$69-$79.** 1622 N Broadway St 54751. I-94 exit 41 (SR 25), just s. Int corridors. **Pets:** Other species. $10 one-time fee/room. Service with restrictions, crate. 🌊 🛜 ✖ 🛏 📺

MEQUON

AAA **WWW** Baymont Inn & Suites **H**
(262) 241-3677. **$89-$179.** 10330 N Port Washington Rd 53092. I-43 exit 85 (Mequon Rd), just w on SR 167, then 1 mi s. Int corridors. **Pets:** Accepted. [SAVE] ♿M 🌊 🛜 ✖ 🛏 📺

MERRILL

WW America's Best Inn Badger Hotel **H**
(715) 536-6880. **Call for rates.** 3209 E Main St 54452. US 51 exit 208, 0.5 mi w on SR 64. Int corridors. **Pets:** Accepted.
♿M 🌊 🛜 ✖ 🛏 📺

WW AmericInn Lodge & Suites of Merrill **H**
(715) 536-7979. **$89-$149.** 3300 E Main St 54452. US 51 exit 208, 0.5 mi w on SR 64. Int corridors. **Pets:** Other species. $30 daily fee/pet. Service with restrictions, supervision. ♿M 🌊 🛜 ✖ 🛏 📺

MIDDLETON

WWW Residence Inn by Marriott-Madison West/Middleton **H**
(608) 662-1100. **$132-$217.** 8400 Market St 53562. US 12/14 exit 252 (Greenway Blvd), just w, then just n; in Greenway Station. Int corridors. **Pets:** $75 one-time fee/room. Service with restrictions.
♿M 🌊 🛜 ✖ 🛏 📺

WWW Staybridge Suites **H**
(608) 664-5888. **$99-$500, 3 day notice.** 7790 Elmwood Ave 53562. US 12/14 exit 251 (University Ave), just nw. Int corridors. **Pets:** Medium, dogs only. $150 one-time fee/room. Service with restrictions, crate. ♿M 🌊 🛜 ✖ 🛏 📺

MILWAUKEE

AAA **WWW** Aloft Milwaukee Downtown **H**
(414) 226-0122. **$70-$599.** 1230 N Old World 3rd St 53212. I-43 exit 73A, just se. Int corridors. **Pets:** Accepted.
[SAVE] 🍽 ♿M 🌊 🛜 ✖ 🛏 📺

WWW Ambassador Hotel **H**
(414) 345-5000. **$119-$399.** 2308 W Wisconsin Ave 53233. I-94 exit 308 (US 41), just n to Wisconsin Ave (US 18) exit, then 1.5 mi e; jct N 24th St. Int corridors. **Pets:** Accepted. 🍽 ♿M 🛜 ✖ 🛏

WWWW Comfort Suites at Park Place **H**
(414) 979-0250. **$99-$349.** 10831 W Park Pl 53224. US 41/45 exit 47B (Good Hope Rd), just e. Int corridors. **Pets:** Other species. $50 deposit/room. Crate. ♿M 🌊 🛜 ✖ 🛏 📺

AAA **WWWWW** Hilton Milwaukee City Center **H**
(414) 271-7250. **$89-$319.** 509 W Wisconsin Ave 53203. Jct 5th St. Int corridors. **Pets:** Accepted. [SAVE] [ECO] 🍽 ♿M 📶 ✖ 🛏 📺

WWWW Holiday Inn & Suites Milwaukee Airport **H**
(414) 482-4444. **$99-$149, 3 day notice.** 545 W Layton Ave 53207. I-94 exit 317, 1.3 mi e. Int corridors. **Pets:** Accepted.
🍽 ♿M 🌊 ✖ 🛜 ✖ 🛏 📺

▼▼▼ **Holiday Inn Express & Suites Milwaukee Airport** H
(414) 563-4000. **Call for rates.** 1400 W Zellman Ct 53221. I-94 exit 319 (College Ave/CR ZZ), 0.4 mi e to S 13th St, then just s. Int corridors. **Pets:** Accepted. 🌿 �ᴹ ⊷ ⊠ 🛜 ✕ ▤ ▣

▼▼▼ **Hotel Metro** H ❀
(414) 272-1937. **$199-$389.** 411 E Mason St 53202. Jct Milwaukee St. Int corridors. **Pets:** Large, dogs only. $100 one-time fee/pet. Designated rooms, service with restrictions, crate.
🌿 ⑪ �ᴹ ⊠ 🛜 ✕ ▣

⨭ ▼▼▼▼ **Hyatt Place Milwaukee Airport** H
(414) 744-3600. **$87-$225.** 200 W Grange Ave 53207. I-94 exit 318 (Airport), 1.1 mi e, just n on Howell Ave (SR 38), then just w. Int corridors. **Pets:** Accepted. 🆂🅰🆅🅴 �ᴹ ⊷ 🛜 ✕ ▤ ▣

⨭ ▼▼▼▼ **Hyatt Place Milwaukee-West** H
(414) 462-3500. **$87-$225.** 11777 W Silver Spring Dr 53225. US 45 exit 46 (Silver Spring Dr), just w. Int corridors. **Pets:** Medium, dogs only. $75 one-time fee/room. Service with restrictions, crate.
🆂🅰🆅🅴 ⑪ �ᴹ ⊷ 🛜 ✕ ▤ ▣

⨭ ▼▼▼▼▼ **The Iron Horse Hotel** H
(414) 374-4766. **$159-$509.** 500 W Florida St 53204. Jct 6th St. Int corridors. **Pets:** Accepted. 🆂🅰🆅🅴 ⑪ �ᴹ ⊷ 🛜 ✕ ▤ ▣

▼▼▼ **La Quinta Inn Milwaukee Northwest** H
(414) 535-1300. **$62-$194.** 5442 N Lovers Lane Rd 53225. US 45 exit 46 (Silver Spring Dr), just se. Int corridors. **Pets:** Large, other species. Service with restrictions. 🛜 ✕ ▤ ▣

⨭ ▼▼▼ **The Pfister Hotel** H ❀
(414) 273-8222. **Call for rates.** 424 E Wisconsin Ave 53202. Corner of E Wisconsin Ave and Jefferson St. Int corridors. **Pets:** $100 one-time fee/room. Service with restrictions, supervision.
🆂🅰🆅🅴 🌿 ⑪ �ᴹ ⊷ 📡 ✕ ▤ ▣

⨭ ▼▼▼ **The Plaza Hotel Milwaukee** H
(414) 276-2101. **$249.** 1007 N Cass St 53202. Jct E State St. Int corridors. **Pets:** $50 one-time fee/pet. Designated rooms, service with restrictions, supervision. 🆂🅰🆅🅴 ⑪ ⊷ ✕ ▤ ▣

▼▼▼ **Sleep Inn & Suites Milwaukee Airport** H
(414) 831-2000. **$69-$129.** 4600 S 6th St 53221. I-94/US 41 exit 317 (Layton Ave), 1.5 mi e. Int corridors. **Pets:** Accepted.
ᴹ ⊷ 🛜 ✕ ▤ ▣

MINOCQUA
▼▼ **AmericInn of Minocqua** H
(715) 356-3730. **Call for rates.** 700 Hwy 51 54548. On US 51; downtown. Int corridors. **Pets:** $10 daily fee/room. Service with restrictions, supervision. 🌿 ᴹ ⊷ ⊠ 🛜 ✕ ▤ ▣

⨭ ▼▼▼ **BEST WESTERN PLUS Concord Inn** H
(715) 356-1800. **$90-$186.** 320 Front St 54548. On US 51; downtown. Int corridors. **Pets:** Dogs only. $10 daily fee/pet. Designated rooms, service with restrictions, supervision.
🆂🅰🆅🅴 ᴹ ⊷ 🛜 ✕ ▤ ▣

▼▼ **Quality Inn** H
(715) 358-2588. **$79-$154.** 8729 Hwy 51 N 54548. On US 51; at SR 70 W. Int corridors. **Pets:** Accepted. ⊷ 🛜 ✕ ▤ ▣

▼▼ **The Waters of Minocqua** H
(715) 358-4000. **$80-$406, 5 day notice.** 8116 Hwy 51 S 54548. On US 51, 1 mi s. Int corridors. **Pets:** Accepted.
🌿 ⑪ ᴹ ⊷ ⊠ 🛜 ✕ ▤ ▣

MONONA
▼▼ **AmericInn of Madison South/Monona** H
(608) 222-8601. **$90-$140.** 101 W Broadway 53716. US 12/18 exit 265 (Monona Dr), just nw. Int corridors. **Pets:** Accepted.
ᴹ ⊷ 🛜 ✕ ▤ ▣

MONROE
⨭ ▼▼▼ **Super 8 of Monroe** H
(608) 325-1500. **$73-$108.** 500 6th St 53566. On SR 69 S, 0.5 mi s of jct SR 81/11. Int corridors. **Pets:** Medium, dogs only. $5 one-time fee/pet, $5 daily fee/pet. Designated rooms, service with restrictions, supervision. 🆂🅰🆅🅴 🌿 ⊷ 🛜 ✕ ▤ ▣

NEILLSVILLE
▼▼ **Super 8-Neillsville** H
(715) 743-8080. **$80-$118.** 1000 E Division St 54456. On US 10; jct Boon Blvd and Division St. Int corridors. **Pets:** Accepted.
ᴹ ⊷ 🛜 ✕ ▤ ▣

NEW BERLIN
▼▼▼ **La Quinta Inn & Suites Milwaukee SW New Berlin** H
(262) 717-0900. **$82-$245.** 15300 W Rock Ridge Rd 53151. I-43 exit 57 (Moorland Rd), just se. Int corridors. **Pets:** Large, other species. Service with restrictions. ᴹ ⊷ 🛜 ✕ ▤ ▣

NEW GLARUS
⨭ ▼▼▼ **Chalet Landhaus Inn** H
(608) 527-5234. **$85-$239.** 801 SR 69 53574. On SR 69. Int corridors. **Pets:** Other species. $35 daily fee/pet. Service with restrictions, supervision. 🆂🅰🆅🅴 ⑪ ⊷ ⊠ 🛜 ✕ ▤ ▣

▼▼ **Swiss Aire Motel** H
(608) 527-2138. **$75-$115.** 1200 SR 69 53574. Just s of jct SR 39/69. Ext/int corridors. **Pets:** Accepted. 🛜 ✕ ▤ ▣

NEW LONDON
▼▼▼ **AmericInn Lodge & Suites of New London** H
(920) 982-5700. **$69-$200.** 1404 N Shawano St 54961. US 45 exit US 54, just n. Int corridors. **Pets:** Medium. $20 one-time fee/room. Designated rooms, service with restrictions, supervision.
ᴹ ⊷ 🛜 ✕ ▤ ▣

NEW RICHMOND
▼▼ **AmericInn Hotel** H
(715) 246-3993. **Call for rates.** 1020 S Knowles Ave 54017. Just s on SR 65. Int corridors. **Pets:** Accepted. ᴹ ⊷ 🛜 ✕ ▤ ▣

OAK CREEK
▼▼▼ **Comfort Suites Milwaukee Airport** H
(414) 570-1111. **$94-$249.** 6362 S 13th St 53154. I-94 exit 319 (College Ave), just e on CR 22, then just s. Int corridors. **Pets:** Accepted.
🌿 ᴹ ⊷ ⊠ 🛜 ✕ ▤ ▣

▼▼ **La Quinta Inn Milwaukee Airport / Oak Creek** H
(414) 762-2266. **$65-$195.** 7141 S 13th St 53154. I-94 exit 320 (Rawson Ave), just se. Int corridors. **Pets:** Large, other species. Service with restrictions. 🛜 ✕ ▤ ▣

▼▼ **MainStay Suites Oak Creek** H
(414) 571-8800. **$79-$109.** 1001 W College Ave 53154. I-94 exit 319 (College Ave), just e. Int corridors. **Pets:** Accepted.
ᴹ 🛜 ✕ ▤ ▣

▼▼ **Motel 6 Oak Creek #4959** H
(414) 764-1776. **$54-$149.** 1201 W College Ave 53154. I-94 exit 319 (College Ave), just e. Int corridors. **Pets:** Designated rooms, service with restrictions, supervision. ᴹ 🛜 ✕ ▤ ▣

OCONOMOWOC
▼▼▼ **Staybridge Suites Milwaukee West** H
(262) 200-2900. **Call for rates.** 1141 Blue Ribbon Dr 53066. I-94 exit 282 (SR 67), just s. Int corridors. **Pets:** Accepted.
⑪ ᴹ ⊷ 🛜 ✕ ▤ ▣

ONALASKA

▼▼▼▼ Holiday Inn Express 🏠
(608) 783-6555. **$109-$149.** 9409 Hwy 16 54650. I-90 exit 5, 1 mi e.
Int corridors. **Pets:** Service with restrictions, supervision.
♿M 🛏 📶 ✕ 🛢 🖃

▼▼ Microtel Inn by Wyndham 🏠
(608) 783-0833. **$55-$160.** 3240 N Kinney Coulee Rd 54650. I-90 exit
5, just ne. Int corridors. **Pets:** Accepted. 📶 ✕ 🛢 🖃

▼▼▼▼ Stoney Creek Hotel & Conference Center 🏠
(608) 781-3060. **$89-$129.** 3060 S Kinney Coulee Rd 54650. I-90 exit
5, just se. Int corridors. **Pets:** Accepted.
♿M 🛏 🗙 📶 ✕ 🛢 🖃

OSCEOLA

▼▼ River Valley Inn & Suites 🏠
(715) 294-4060. **Call for rates.** 1030 Cascade St 54020. Just n on SR
35. Int corridors. **Pets:** Accepted. 🛏 📶 ✕ 🛢 🖃

OSHKOSH

▼▼▼ AmericInn Lodge & Suites Oshkosh 🏠
(920) 232-0300. **$70-$300.** 1495 W South Park Ave 54902. US 41 exit
116 (SR 44), 0.4 mi e. Int corridors. **Pets:** Medium, dogs only. $15 daily
fee/room. Service with restrictions, supervision.
🛏 📶 ✕ 🛢 🖃

**▼▼▼▼ Comfort Suites by Choice Hotels at
Oshkosh** 🏠
(920) 230-7378. **$105-$160.** 400 S Koeller St 54902. US 41 exit 117
(9th Ave), just e. Int corridors. **Pets:** Accepted.
♿M 🛏 🗙 📶 ✕ 🛢 🖃

▼▼ Fairfield Inn by Marriott 🏠
(920) 233-8504. **$97-$160.** 1800 S Koeller St 54902. US 41 exit 117
(9th Ave), 0.8 mi s on east frontage road. Int corridors. **Pets:** Accepted.
♿M 🛏 📶 ✕ 🛢 🖃

▼▼▼▼ Holiday Inn Express & Suites 🏠
(920) 303-1300. **Call for rates.** 2251 Westowne Ave 54904. US 41 exit
119, 0.4 mi w of jct SR 21. Int corridors. **Pets:** Accepted.
🅴🅲🅾 ♿M 🛏 📶 ✕ 🛢 🖃

▼▼ La Quinta Inn Oshkosh 🏠
(920) 233-4190. **$69-$369.** 1886 Rath Ln 54902. US 41 exit 119, jct SR
21. Int corridors. **Pets:** Large, other species. Service with restrictions.
♿M 📶 ✕ 🛢 🖃

PLATTEVILLE

▼▼ Mound View Inn 🏠
(608) 348-9518. **$65-$199, 3 day notice.** 1755 E Business Hwy 151
53818. On US 151 exit 21, just w. Int corridors. **Pets:** Small. $10 daily
fee/pet. Designated rooms, service with restrictions, supervision.
🗙 📶 ✕ 🛢

▼▼ Super 8 🏠
(608) 348-8800. **$62-$152.** 100 Hwy 80/81 S 53818. Jct US 151 and
SR 80. Int corridors. **Pets:** Large, other species. $10 daily fee/pet. Ser-
vice with restrictions. ♿M 📶 ✕ 🛢 🖃

PLEASANT PRAIRIE

▼▼ La Quinta Inn Pleasant Prairie Kenosha 🏠
(262) 857-7911. **$62-$175.** 7540 118th Ave 53158. I-94 exit 344 (SR
50), just e. Int corridors. **Pets:** Large, other species. Service with
restrictions. 🍴 ♿M 📶 ✕ 🛢 🖃

PLOVER

▼▼ AmericInn of Plover/Stevens Point 🏠
(715) 342-1244. **Call for rates.** 1501 American Dr 54467. I-39 exit 153
(CR B), just nw. Int corridors. **Pets:** Accepted.
♿M 🛏 🗙 📶 ✕ 🛢 🖃

PORTAGE

AAA▼ ▼▼▼ Comfort Suites 🏠
(608) 745-4717. **$80-$175.** N5780 Kinney Rd 53901. I-90/94 exit 108A
(SR 78). Int corridors. **Pets:** Accepted.
🆂🅰🆅🅴 ♿M 🛏 🗙 📶 ✕ 🛢 🖃

▼▼ Super 8-Portage 🏠
(608) 742-8330. **$59-$72.** 3000 New Pinery Rd 53901. I-39 exit 92, just
s. Int corridors. **Pets:** Other species. $11 daily fee/room. Service with
restrictions, supervision. 📶 ✕ 🛢 🖃

PORT WASHINGTON

▼▼ Holiday Inn Harborview 🏠
(262) 284-9461. **Call for rates.** 135 E Grand Ave 53074. On SR 33; on
waterfront of Lake Michigan; downtown. Int corridors. **Pets:** Accepted.
🍴 ♿M 🛏 🗙 📶 ✕ 🛢 🖃

PRAIRIE DU CHIEN

▼▼ Super 8-Prairie Du Chien 🏠
(608) 326-8777. **$52-$110.** 1930 S Marquette Rd 53821. On US 18, 1.9
mi e of jct SR 27 N. Ext/int corridors. **Pets:** Accepted.
♿M 📶 ✕ 🛢 🖃

RACINE

▼▼▼▼ Racine Marriott Hotel 🏠
(262) 886-6100. **$125-$206.** 7111 Washington Ave 53406. I-94 exit 333,
4 mi e on SR 20. Int corridors. **Pets:** Accepted.
🍴 ♿M 🛏 📶 ✕ 🛢 🖃

RHINELANDER

▼▼ Comfort Inn 🏠
(715) 369-1100. **$111-$146.** 1490 Lincoln St 54501. On Business Rt US
8, 2.6 mi e of jct SR 47. Int corridors. **Pets:** Accepted.
🍴 ♿M 🛏 📶 ✕ 🛢 🖃

▼▼ Days Inn & Suites 🏠
(715) 362-7100. **$77-$125.** 70 N Stevens St 54501. Between Davenport
and Rives sts; downtown. Int corridors. **Pets:** Accepted.
🍴 ♿M 🗙 📶 ✕ 🛢 🖃

RICE LAKE

▼▼ Microtel Inn & Suites by Wyndham Rice Lake 🏠
(715) 736-2010. **$72-$109.** 2771 Decker Dr 54868. US 53 exit 140 (CR
O), just ne. Int corridors. **Pets:** Other species. $10 one-time fee/room.
Designated rooms, service with restrictions, supervision.
🍴 📶 ✕ 🛢 🖃

RICHLAND CENTER

▼▼ The Center Lodge 🏠
(608) 647-8988. **$70-$90, 10 day notice.** 100 Foundry Dr 53581. 0.9 mi
e on US 14. Int corridors. **Pets:** Other species. $50 deposit/pet. Service
with restrictions, supervision. ♿M 🛏 📶 🛢 🖃

RIVER FALLS

AAA▼ ▼▼▼ BEST WESTERN PLUS Campus Inn 🏠
(715) 425-1045. **$90-$150.** 100 Spring St 54022. Downtown. Int corridors. **Pets:** Accepted. 🆂🅰🆅🅴 🍴 ♿M 🛏 📶 ✕ 🛢 🖃

▼▼ Country Inn River Falls 🏠
(715) 425-9500. **Call for rates.** 1525 Commerce Ct 54022. Just n of jct
SR 65 and 35. Int corridors. **Pets:** Medium, dogs only. $200 deposit/
room, $10 daily fee/pet. Designated rooms, service with restrictions,
crate. 🍴 ♿M 🛏 📶 ✕ 🛢 🖃

▼▼ Econo Lodge 🏠
(715) 425-8388. **Call for rates.** 1207 St. Croix St 54022. On SR 65,
0.5 mi w jct SR 35. Int corridors. **Pets:** Accepted.
♿M 🛏 📶 ✕ 🛢 🖃

ROTHSCHILD

BEST WESTERN PLUS Wausau/Rothschild Hotel H

(715) 355-8900. **Call for rates.** 803 Industrial Park Ave 54474. I-39 exit 185 (Business Rt US 51), just se. Int corridors. **Pets:** Medium. $20 daily fee/pet. Designated rooms, service with restrictions, crate.

SAVE &M ⊗ ⊠ ⊟ ⊑

Grand Lodge by Stoney Creek H

(715) 241-6300. **Call for rates.** 805 Creske Ave 54474. I-39 exit 185 (Business Rt US 51), just se. Int corridors. **Pets:** Accepted.

⊮ &M ⊗ ⊠ ⊟ ⊑

Holiday Inn Hotel & Suites H

(715) 355-1111. **$99-$149, 3 day notice.** 1000 Imperial Ave 54474. I-39 exit 185 (Business Rt US 51), just se. Int corridors. **Pets:** Accepted.

⊮ &M ➔ ⊠ ⊗ ⊠ ⊟ ⊑

Stoney Creek Inn H

(715) 355-6858. **Call for rates.** 1100 Imperial Ave 54474. I-39 exit 185 (Business Rt US 51), just e. Int corridors. **Pets:** Accepted.

&M ➔ ⊠ ⊗ ⊠ ⊟ ⊑

SAUKVILLE

Super 8-Saukville H

(262) 284-9399. **$68-$88.** 180 S Foster Rd 53080. I-43 exit 96, just s. Int corridors. **Pets:** Accepted. SAVE &M ⊗ ⊠ ⊟ ⊑

SHAWANO

Super 8-Shawano M

(715) 526-6688. **$70-$109.** 211 Waukechon St 54166. SR 29 exit 227, 1.8 mi n, then 1.1 mi w. Int corridors. **Pets:** Accepted.

⊗ ⊠ ⊟ ⊑

SHEBOYGAN

GrandStay Residential Suites Hotel H

(920) 208-8000. **Call for rates.** 708 Niagara Ave 53081. Jct N 7th St; downtown. Int corridors. **Pets:** $250 deposit/pet, $10 daily fee/pet. Service with restrictions, crate. &M ➔ ⊗ ⊠ ⊟ ⊑

La Quinta Inn Sheboygan H

(920) 457-2321. **$65-$304.** 2932 Kohler Memorial Dr 53081. I-43 exit 126, 1 mi e on SR 23. Int corridors. **Pets:** Large, other species. Service with restrictions. ⊗ ⊠ ⊟ ⊑

Quality Inn H

(920) 457-7724. **$89-$299.** 4332 N 40th St 53083. I-43 exit 128, 0.3 mi e on Business Rt SR 42. Int corridors. **Pets:** Large, other species. $10 daily fee/pet. Designated rooms, service with restrictions, crate.

&M ➔ ⊗ ⊠ ⊟ ⊑

SHEBOYGAN FALLS

The Rochester Inn, A Historic Hotel BB

(920) 467-3123. **Call for rates.** 504 Water St 53085. Just e of downtown via CR PP. Int corridors. **Pets:** Accepted. ⊗ ⊠ ⊟ ⊑

SIREN

BEST WESTERN Northwoods Lodge H

(715) 349-7800. **Call for rates.** 23986 SR 35 S 54872. On SR 35; at SR 70 W and CR B E. Int corridors. **Pets:** Accepted.

SAVE &M ➔ ⊗ ⊠ ⊟ ⊑

The Lodge at Crooked Lake H

(715) 349-2500. **$89-$275.** 24271 SR 35 N 54872. On SR 35, 0.5 mi n of jct SR 70. Int corridors. **Pets:** Accepted.

SAVE ➔ ⊠ ⊗ ⊠ ⊟ ⊑

SISTER BAY *(Restaurants p. 645)*

Country House Resort M ☘

(920) 854-4551. **$78-$185, 14 day notice.** 2468 Sunnyside Rd 54234. Jct SR 42 and 57, 0.3 mi s on SR 42 to Highland Ave, then just w. Ext corridors. **Pets:** Large, dogs only. $20 daily fee/pet. Designated rooms, service with restrictions, supervision.

SAVE ECO ⊮ ➔ ⊠ ⊗ ⊠ ⊟ ⊑

SPARTA

BEST WESTERN PLUS Sparta Trail Lodge H

(608) 269-2664. **Call for rates.** 4445 Theatre Rd 54656. I-90 exit 28 (SR 16), just w. Int corridors. **Pets:** Accepted.

SAVE ⊮ &M ➔ ⊠ ⊗ ⊠ ⊟ ⊑

Country Inn & Suites By Carlson H ☘

(608) 269-3110. **$83-$185.** 737 Avon Rd 54656. I-90 exit 25 (SR 27), just n. Int corridors. **Pets:** Other species. $10 daily fee/pet. Service with restrictions, supervision. &M ➔ ⊗ ⊠ ⊟ ⊑

Super 8 Sparta H

(608) 269-8489. **$79-$146.** 716 Avon Rd 54656. I-90 exit 25 (SR 27), just n. Int corridors. **Pets:** Accepted. ➔ ⊗ ⊠ ⊟ ⊑

SPOONER

BEST WESTERN American Heritage Inn H ☘

(715) 635-9770. **$85-$190.** 101 W Maple St 54801. On SR 70, just e of US 63, then 1.5 mi w of US 53. Int corridors. **Pets:** Other species. $15 daily fee/room. Designated rooms, service with restrictions, supervision.

SAVE ➔ ⊠ ⊗ ⊠ ⊟ ⊑

Country House Motel & RV Park M

(715) 635-8721. **Call for rates.** 717 S River St 54801. On US 63, 0.5 mi s of jct SR 70. Ext/int corridors. **Pets:** Accepted.

&M ➔ ⊗ ⊠ ⊟ ⊑

STEVENS POINT

Country Inn & Suites By Carlson H

(715) 345-7000. **$109-$144.** 301 Division St N 54481. I-39 exit 161 (US 51 business route), 0.6 mi s. Int corridors. **Pets:** Accepted.

&M ➔ ⊗ ⊠ ⊟ ⊑

Fairfield Inn & Suites by Marriott Stevens Point H

(715) 342-9300. **$84-$138.** 5317 Hwy 10 E 54482. I-39 exit 158A (US 10), just se. Int corridors. **Pets:** Accepted.

&M ➔ ⊗ ⊠ ⊟ ⊑

Holiday Inn Express H

(715) 344-0000. **$89-$139.** 1100 Amber Ave 54482. I-39 exit 158 (US 10), 1 mi e, then just n. Int corridors. **Pets:** Accepted.

SAVE &M ➔ ⊗ ⊠ ⊟ ⊑

La Quinta Inn & Suites Stevens Point H

(715) 344-1900. **$69-$235.** 4917 Main St 54481. I-39 exit 158B (US 10), just sw. Int corridors. **Pets:** Large, other species. Service with restrictions. &M ➔ ⊗ ⊠ ⊟ ⊑

STURGEON BAY

BEST WESTERN Maritime Inn H

(920) 743-7231. **Call for rates.** 1001 N 14th Ave 54235. 1 mi n on Business Rt SR 42/57; jct N 14th Ave. Int corridors. **Pets:** Medium, dogs only. $15 one-time fee/room. Designated rooms, service with restrictions, crate. SAVE &M ➔ ⊗ ⊠ ⊟ ⊑

SUN PRAIRIE

Quality Inn & Suites-Sun Prairie H

(608) 834-9889. **$80-$180.** 105 Business Park Dr 53590. US 151 exit 103 (CR N), just n. Int corridors. **Pets:** Accepted.

SAVE ⊮ &M ➔ ⊗ ⊠ ⊟ ⊑

SUPERIOR

BEST WESTERN Bridgeview Motor Inn H
(715) 392-8174. **$65-$189.** 415 Hammond Ave 54880. 0.8 mi n at south end of Blatnik Bridge. Int corridors. **Pets:** Accepted.

TOMAH

AmericInn Lodge & Suites of Tomah H
(608) 372-4100. **$80-$200.** 750 Vandervort St 54660. I-94 exit 143 (SR 21), just e. Int corridors. **Pets:** Accepted.

BEST WESTERN Tomah Hotel H ❖
(608) 372-3211. **$99-$219.** 1017 E McCoy Blvd 54660. I-94 exit 143 (SR 21), just e. Int corridors. **Pets:** Other species. $10 daily fee/pet. Service with restrictions, supervision.

Econo Lodge H
(608) 372-9100. **$70-$185.** 2005 N Superior Ave 54660. I-94 exit 143 (SR 21), just w. Ext/int corridors. **Pets:** Accepted.

Lark Inn M
(608) 372-5981. **$60-$129.** 229 N Superior Ave 54660. I-94 exit 143 (SR 21), 1.5 mi s on US 12; 1-90 exit 41, 2 mi n on US 12. Ext/int corridors. **Pets:** Accepted.

Quality Inn Tomah H
(608) 372-6600. **$59-$184.** 305 Wittig Rd 54660. I-94 exit 143 (SR 21), just w. Int corridors. **Pets:** Accepted.

Super 8-Tomah H
(608) 372-3901. **$66-$100.** 1008 E McCoy Blvd 54660. I-94 exit 143 (SR 21), just e. Int corridors. **Pets:** Accepted.

TOMAHAWK

Rodeway Inn & Suites H
(715) 453-8900. **$80-$220.** 1738 Comfort Dr 54487. US 51 exit 229, just nw. Int corridors. **Pets:** Accepted.

Super 8-Tomahawk H
(715) 453-5210. **$75-$105.** 108 W Mohawk Dr 54487. US 51 exit 231, 1.4 mi w, then 0.6 mi s on 4th St. Int corridors. **Pets:** Accepted.

TWO RIVERS

Lighthouse Inn on Lake Michigan H
(920) 793-4524. **Call for rates.** 1515 Memorial Dr 54241. 0.3 mi s on SR 42. Int corridors. **Pets:** Accepted.

VERONA

Holiday Inn Express Hotel & Suites Madison-Verona H
(608) 497-4500. **$120-$400.** 515 W Verona Ave 53593. US 18 and 151 exit 76, 0.6 mi ne. Int corridors. **Pets:** Medium, other species. $25 daily fee/pet. Designated rooms, service with restrictions, supervision.

VIROQUA

Hickory Hill Motel M
(608) 637-3104. **Call for rates.** S 5539 US 14 54665. On US 61/US 14/SR 27/SR 82, 2.1 mi se of downtown. Ext corridors. **Pets:** Accepted.

WATERFORD

Baymont Inn & Suites-Waterford H
(262) 534-4100. **$69-$139.** 750 Fox Ln 53185. On SR 36, 1 mi s of jct SR 164. Int corridors. **Pets:** Accepted.

WAUKESHA

BEST WESTERN Waukesha Grand H
(262) 524-9300. **$80-$130.** 2840 N Grandview Blvd 53072. I-94 exit 293, just s on CR T. Int corridors. **Pets:** Accepted.

Ramada Waukesha H
(262) 547-7770. **$69-$129.** 2111 E Moreland Blvd 53186. I-94 exit 297, 0.9 mi sw on US 18 (E Moreland Ave). Int corridors. **Pets:** Medium. $10 daily fee/pet. Designated rooms, service with restrictions, supervision.

Super 8-Waukesha H
(262) 786-6015. **$66-$126.** 2510 Plaza Ct 53186. I-94 exit 297, just w on CR JJ (Bluemound Rd). Int corridors. **Pets:** Medium. $10 daily fee/pet. Designated rooms, service with restrictions, supervision.

WAUPACA

BEST WESTERN PLUS Grand Seasons Hotel H
(715) 258-9212. **Call for rates.** 110 Grand Seasons Dr 54981. Jct US 10/SR 49/54 and CR QQ, just w. Int corridors. **Pets:** Accepted.

Comfort Suites at Foxfire H
(715) 942-0500. **$109-$259.** 199 Foxfire Dr 54981. Jct US 10/SR 49/54 and CR QQ, 0.7 mi sw. Int corridors. **Pets:** Accepted.

WAUPUN

Inn Town Motel M
(920) 324-4211. **Call for rates.** 27 S State St 53963. US 151 exit 146 (SR 49), 1 mi w on Main St, then just s. Ext corridors. **Pets:** Accepted.

WAUSAU

Jefferson Street Inn H ❖
(715) 845-6500. **$119-$325, 3 day notice.** 201 Jefferson St 54403. Just w of jct 2nd St; center. Int corridors. **Pets:** $30 daily fee/pet. Service with restrictions, crate.

Quality Inn H
(715) 842-1616. **$74-$159.** 2901 Hummingbird Rd 54401. US 51 exit 190 (CR NN), just sw. Int corridors. **Pets:** Accepted.

Super 8 Wausau H
(715) 848-2888. **$47-$75.** 2006 Stewart Ave W 54401. I-39 exit 192, just se. Int corridors. **Pets:** Medium, dogs only. $10 daily fee/pet. Designated rooms, service with restrictions, crate.

WAUTOMA

Super 8-Wautoma H
(920) 787-4811. **$73-$108.** W7607 SR 21/73 54982. On SR 21 and 73, 1.5 mi e. Int corridors. **Pets:** $10 one-time fee/pet. Designated rooms, service with restrictions, supervision.

WAUWATOSA

Extended Stay America-Milwaukee-Wauwatosa H
(414) 443-1909. **$64-$109.** 11121 W North Ave 53226. US 45 exit 42A, just n. Int corridors. **Pets:** Other species. $25 daily fee/pet. Service with restrictions, supervision.

Holiday Inn Express Milwaukee West-Medical Center H
(414) 778-0333. **Call for rates.** 11111 W North Ave 53226. US 45 exit 42A, just n on SR 100, then just w. Int corridors. **Pets:** Medium, other species. $35 one-time fee/room. Service with restrictions, crate.

WISCONSIN DELLS

▼▼ Americas Best Value Day's End Motel Ⓜ
(608) 254-8171. **$55-$130, 3 day notice.** N 604 Hwy 12-16 53965.
I-90/94 exit 85 (US 12), 0.8 mi nw. Ext corridors. **Pets:** Accepted.
🌊 🛜 ☒ 🛏 🖵

▼▼ Baker's Sunset Bay Resort 🅷 🐾
(608) 254-8406. **Call for rates.** 921 Canyon Rd 53965. I-90/94 exit 92
(US 12), 0.5 mi w, just e on Adams St, then 0.8 mi n. Ext/int corridors.
Pets: $10 daily fee/pet. Designated rooms, service with restrictions.
🍴 🌊 ☒ 🛜 ☒ 🛏 🖵

▼▼ Super 8-Wisconsin Dells 🅷
(608) 254-6464. **$48-$99.** 800 CR H 53965. I-90/94 exit 87 (SR 13),
just e. Int corridors. **Pets:** Accepted. 🌊 🛜 ☒ 🛏 🖵

WISCONSIN RAPIDS

▼▼▼ Quality Inn 🅷
(715) 423-5506. **$70-$100.** 3120 8th St S 54494. 1.5 mi s on SR 13.
Int corridors. **Pets:** Accepted. 🌊 🛜 ☒ 🛏 🖵

▼▼ Sleep Inn & Suites 🅷
(715) 424-6800. **$79-$150.** 4221 8th St S 54494. 1.3 mi s on SR 13
from jct SR 54. Int corridors. **Pets:** Accepted.
🅼 🌊 🛜 ☒ 🛏 🖵

WITTENBERG

⒜ ▼▼▼ BEST WESTERN Wittenberg Inn 🅷
(715) 253-3755. **$75-$99.** W17267 Red Oak Ln 54499. SR 29 exit 198,
just se. Int corridors. **Pets:** Other species. $20 one-time fee/room. Des-
ignated rooms, service with restrictions.
🆂🅰🆅🅴 🅼 🌊 🛜 ☒ 🛏 🖵

WYOMING

AFTON

▼ Lazy B Motel Ⓜ
(307) 885-3187. **$82-$110.** 219 S Washington St (US 89) 83110. On
US 89; center. Ext corridors. **Pets:** Large, dogs only. Supervision.
🌊 🛜 ☒ 🛏 🖵

BUFFALO

⒜ ▼▼ Comfort Inn 🅷
(307) 684-9564. **$89-$169.** 65 US Hwy 16 E 82834. I-25 exit 299 (US
16), just e; I-90 exit 58, 1.3 mi w. Ext/int corridors. **Pets:** Large, other
species. $10 daily fee/pet. Designated rooms, service with restrictions,
supervision. 🆂🅰🆅🅴 🅼 🌊 🛜 ☒ 🛏 🖵

⒜ ▼▼▼ The Occidental Hotel 🅷
(307) 684-0451. **$75-$285, 14 day notice.** 10 N Main St 82834. Center.
Int corridors. **Pets:** Accepted. 🆂🅰🆅🅴 🍴 🛜 ☒ 🅩 🛏 🖵

⒜ ▼ Rodeway Inn Ⓜ
(307) 684-5505. **Call for rates.** 610 E Hart St 82834. I-25 exit 299 (US
16), just w; I-90 exit 58, 1.3 mi w. Ext corridors. **Pets:** Accepted.
🆂🅰🆅🅴 🌊 🛜 🛏 🖵

CASPER *(Restaurants p. 645)*

⒜ ▼▼▼ BEST WESTERN Ramkota Hotel 🅷 🐾
(307) 266-6000. **$110-$130.** 800 N Poplar St 82601. I-25 exit 188B (N
Poplar St), just ne. Int corridors. **Pets:** Other species. $20 one-time
fee/room. Designated rooms, service with restrictions, supervision.
🆂🅰🆅🅴 🍴 🅼 🌊 🛜 🛜 ☒ 🛏 🖵

▼▼ Days Inn Casper 🅷
(307) 234-1159. **$90-$175, 3 day notice.** 301 E 'E' St 82601. I-25 exit
188A (Center St), just s, then just e. Int corridors. **Pets:** Accepted.
🌊 🛜 🛏 🖵

▼▼ Quality Inn & Suites Casper 🅷
(307) 266-2400. **$86-$185.** 821 N Poplar St 82601. I-25 exit 188B (N
Poplar St), just e. Int corridors. **Pets:** Accepted. 🛜 ☒ 🛏 🖵

▼▼ Super 8 Casper West 🅷
(307) 266-3480. **$95-$145.** 3838 CY Ave 82604. I-25 exit 188B (N Poplar St), 1.5 mi s to CY Ave, then 1.7 mi w. Int corridors.
Pets: Accepted. 🛜 🛏 🖵

CHEYENNE

**⒜ ▼▼▼ BEST WESTERN PLUS Frontier
Inn** 🅷 🐾
(307) 638-8891. **$109-$315.** 8101 Hutchins Dr 82007. I-80 exit 367, just
w. Int corridors. **Pets:** Other species. $20 daily fee/pet. Service with
restrictions, supervision. 🆂🅰🆅🅴 🅼 🌊 🛜 ☒ 🛏 🖵

▼▼▼ Candlewood Suites 🅷
(307) 634-6622. **$109-$160.** 2335 Tura Pkwy 82001. I-25 exit 9, just e
on I-80 business loop/US 30, then just n. Int corridors. **Pets:** Accepted.
🅼 🛜 ☒ 🛏 🖵

▼▼ Cheyenne My Place Hotel 🅷
(307) 634-1400. **$109.** 1920 W Lincolnway 82001. I-25 exit 9, 0.6 mi e.
Int corridors. **Pets:** Accepted. 🅼 🛜 ☒ 🛏 🖵

▼▼▼ Days Inn Cheyenne 🅷
(307) 778-8877. **$90-$160.** 2360 W Lincolnway 82001. I-25 exit 9, just
e. Int corridors. **Pets:** $5 daily fee/pet. Designated rooms, service with
restrictions, supervision. 🌊 🛜 ☒ 🛏 🖵

▼▼ La Quinta Inn Cheyenne 🅷
(307) 632-7117. **$79-$366.** 2410 W Lincolnway 82009. I-25 exit 9, just
e. Int corridors. **Pets:** Large, other species. Service with restrictions.
🌊 🛜 🛏 🖵

⒜ ▼▼▼ Nagle Warren Mansion B & B 🅱🅱 🐾
(307) 637-3333. **$158-$192, 3 day notice.** 222 E 17th St 82001. I-80
exit 362, 1.2 mi n on I-25 business loop/US 85/87 business route, then
just e; jct House St; downtown. Int corridors. **Pets:** Medium. $25 daily
fee/pet. Designated rooms, service with restrictions, supervision.
🆂🅰🆅🅴 🅼 ☒ 🛜 ☒

▼▼ Oak Tree Inn Cheyenne 🅷
(307) 778-6620. **Call for rates.** 1625 Stillwater Ave 82009. I-25 exit 12,
0.8 mi se to Yellowstone Rd, 0.3 mi n to Dell Range Blvd, 1.2 mi e,
then just se. Ext/int corridors. **Pets:** Accepted.
🍴 🛜 ☒ 🛏 🖵

▼▼ Quality Inn of Cheyenne 🅷
(307) 638-7202. **$87-$119.** 2245 Etchepare Dr 82007. I-25 exit 7, just
w. Int corridors. **Pets:** Accepted. 🅼 🌊 🛜 ☒ 🛏 🖵

▼▼ Super 8 Cheyenne Ⓜ
(307) 635-8741. **$69-$179.** 1900 W Lincolnway 82001. I-25 exit 9, 0.7
mi e. Int corridors. **Pets:** Accepted. 🅼 🛜 🛏 🖵

⒜ ▼▼▼ TownePlace Suites Cheyenne WY 🅷
(307) 634-0400. **$199-$252.** 1710 W Lincolnway 82001. I-25 exit 9, 0.3
mi se, then 0.8 mi ne. Int corridors. **Pets:** Accepted.
🆂🅰🆅🅴 🅼 🛜 ☒ 🛏 🖵

▼▼▼ Windy Hills Guest House 🅱🅱
(307) 632-6423. **$159-$295.** 393 Happy Jack Rd 82009. I-25 exit 10B,
22 mi w on SR 210 (Happy Jack Rd), then 1 mi s on private gravel
road. Ext corridors. **Pets:** Dogs only. $25 one-time fee/pet. Designated
rooms, service with restrictions, crate.
☒ 🛜 ☒ 🅺 🅩 🛏 🖵

CODY

◇◇◇ ▽▽▽ BEST WESTERN Sunset Motor Inn M
(307) 587-4265. **$105-$175.** 1601 8th St 82414. 0.8 mi w on US 14/16/20. Ext corridors. **Pets:** Medium. $25 one-time fee/pet. Designated rooms, service with restrictions, supervision.
🅂🄰🅅🄴 ⌷⌷ ⊇ ⊗ 🛜 ⊗ 🔲 💻

▽▽▽ The Cody H
(307) 587-5915. **Call for rates.** 232 W Yellowstone Ave 82414. 2 mi w on US 14/16/20. Int corridors. **Pets:** Accepted.
🄼 ⊇ ⊗ 🛜 ⊗ 🔲 💻

◇◇◇ ▽ Cody Motor Lodge M
(307) 527-6291. **Call for rates.** 1455 Sheridan Ave 82414. Just w on US 14/16/20 and SR 120. Int corridors. **Pets:** Accepted.
🅂🄰🅅🄴 🛜 🔲 💻

DOUGLAS

◇◇◇ ▽▽▽ Holiday Inn Express & Suites H
(307) 358-4500. **$159-$209.** 900 W Yellowstone Hwy 82633. I-25 exit 140, 1 mi e. Int corridors. **Pets:** Accepted.
🅂🄰🅅🄴 🄼 ⊇ 🛜 ⊗ 🔲 💻

◇◇◇ ▽▽▽ Sleep Inn & Suites H
(307) 358-2777. **$119-$187.** 508 Cortez Dr 82633. I-25 exit 140, 0.5 mi e. Int corridors. **Pets:** Accepted. 🅂🄰🅅🄴 🄼 ⊇ 🛜 ⊗ 🔲 💻

DUBOIS

◇◇◇ ▽▽▽ The Longhorn Ranch Lodge and RV Resort M ❄
(307) 455-2337. **$79-$149, 3 day notice.** 5810 US Hwy 26 82513. 3 mi e on US 26 and 287. Ext corridors. **Pets:** Other species. $10 daily fee/room. Service with restrictions, supervision.
🅂🄰🅅🄴 🛜 ⊗ 🏊 🔲 💻

▽ Rocky Mountain Lodge M
(307) 455-2844. **Call for rates.** 1349 W Ramshorn St 82513. 1.6 mi w on US 26 and 287. Ext corridors. **Pets:** Other species. $5 daily fee/pet. Service with restrictions, supervision. 🛜 ⊗ 🏊 🔲 💻

◇◇◇ ▽▽▽ Stagecoach Motor Inn M
(307) 455-2303. **$65-$119, 3 day notice.** 103 Ramshorn St 82513. On US 26 and 287; downtown. Ext corridors. **Pets:** Medium. $10 daily fee/pet. Designated rooms, service with restrictions, supervision.
🅂🄰🅅🄴 ⊇ ⊗ 🛜 🔲 💻

EVANSTON

◇◇◇ ▽▽ BEST WESTERN Dunmar Inn M ❄
(307) 789-3770. **$110-$130.** 1601 Harrison Dr 82930. I-80 exit 3 (Harrison Dr), 0.3 mi n. Ext corridors. **Pets:** Small. Designated rooms, service with restrictions, supervision. 🅂🄰🅅🄴 ⌷⌷ ⊇ ⊗ 🛜 🔲 💻

▽▽ Comfort Inn H
(307) 789-7799. **$85-$150.** 1931 Harrison Dr 82930. I-80 exit 3 (Harrison Dr), just n. Int corridors. **Pets:** Accepted. ⊇ 🛜 🔲 💻

EVANSVILLE

▽▽ Comfort Inn H ❄
(307) 237-8100. **Call for rates.** 269 Miracle St 82636. I-25 exit 185, just n to Lathrop Rd, then just e. Int corridors. **Pets:** Other species. $15 daily fee/room. Designated rooms, service with restrictions, supervision.
🄼 ⊇ 🛜 🔲 💻

▽▽▽ Sleep Inn & Suites Casper East H
(307) 235-3100. **$85-$115.** 6733 Bonanza Rd 82636. I-25 exit 182, just n on Hat Six Rd. Int corridors. **Pets:** Accepted.
⊇ 🛜 ⊗ 🔲 💻

GILLETTE

▽▽ Arbuckle Lodge H ❄
(307) 685-6363. **$139-$279.** 1400 S Garner Lake Rd 82718. I-90 exit 129, just e. Int corridors. **Pets:** Small. $20 daily fee/pet. Service with restrictions, supervision. 🄼 🛜 ⊗ 🔲 💻

▽▽▽ Candlewood Suites H
(307) 682-6100. **Call for rates.** 904 Country Club Rd 82718. I-90 exit 126, 0.5 mi s, then just e. Int corridors. **Pets:** Accepted. 🛜 🔲 💻

◇◇◇ ▽▽▽ Comfort Inn & Suites of Gillette H
(307) 685-2223. **$139-$220.** 1607 W 2nd Ave 82716. I-90 exit 124, 0.3 mi ne, then just se. Int corridors. **Pets:** Accepted.
🅂🄰🅅🄴 🄼 ⊇ 🛜 ⊗ 🔲 💻

▽▽▽ Holiday Inn Express & Suites H ❄
(307) 686-9576. **$149-$299.** 1908 Cliff Davis Dr 82718. I-90 exit 126, just s to Boxelder Rd, then just e to Cliff Davis Dr. Int corridors. **Pets:** Medium. $25 one-time fee/pet. Designated rooms, service with restrictions, supervision. ⊇ 🛜 ⊗ 🔲 💻

GRAND TETON NATIONAL PARK

▽▽ Headwaters Lodge & Cabins at Flagg Ranch H
(307) 543-2861. **Call for rates.** Hwy 89 83013. 25 mi n of jct US 89/191; 2.5 mi s of Yellowstone National Park south entrance. Ext corridors. **Pets:** Accepted. ⌷⌷ 🛜 ⊗ 🏊 🎾 🔲 💻

▽▽▽ Jackson Lake Lodge H
(307) 543-2811. **Call for rates.** US Hwy 89 83013. 5 mi nw of jct US 89/191. Ext/int corridors. **Pets:** Accepted.
🄴🄲🄾 ⌷⌷ 🄼 ⊇ 🛜 ⊗ 🏊 🎾 🔲 💻

▽▽ Signal Mountain Lodge H
(307) 543-2831. **$169-$363, 7 day notice.** 1 Inner Park Rd 83013. Jct US 89/191/287, 2 mi s on Teton Park Rd. Ext corridors. **Pets:** Other species. $20 daily fee/room. Designated rooms, service with restrictions, crate. 🄴🄲🄾 ⌷⌷ ⊗ 🛜 ⊗ 🎾 🔲 💻

▽▽ Togwotee Mountain Lodge H
(307) 543-2847. **Call for rates.** 27655 Hwy US 26 & 287 83013. Jct US 26/287, 16.5 mi e of Moran. Ext/int corridors. **Pets:** Accepted.
⌷⌷ ⊗ 🛜 ⊗ 🔲 💻

GREEN RIVER

▽▽▽ Hampton Inn & Suites H ❄
(307) 875-5300. **$99-$169.** 1055 Wild Horse Canyon Rd 82935. I-80 exit 89, 0.4 mi s to Wild Horse Canyon Rd, then 0.5 mi n. Int corridors. **Pets:** Small. $100 deposit/room. Service with restrictions, supervision.
🄼 ⊇ 🛜 ⊗ 🔲 💻

HULETT

◇◇◇ ▽ Hulett Motel M
(307) 467-5220. **$97-$130.** 202 Main St 82720. On SR 24 (Main St), north end of town. Ext corridors. **Pets:** Small, dogs only. $30 one-time fee/room. Designated rooms, service with restrictions, supervision.
🅂🄰🅅🄴 ⌷⌷ 🛜 ⊗ 🔲 💻

JACKSON

◇◇◇ ▽▽ Antler Inn M
(307) 733-2535. **$86-$275, 4 day notice.** 43 W Pearl St 83001. Just s of town square. Ext/int corridors. **Pets:** Dogs only. Service with restrictions, supervision. 🅂🄰🅅🄴 ⊗ 🛜 ⊗ 🔲 💻

◇◇◇ ▽▽ Cowboy Village Resort CA
(307) 733-3121. **$94-$284.** 120 S Flat Creek Dr 83001. 0.4 mi w of town square, just s. Ext corridors. **Pets:** Dogs only. Supervision.
🅂🄰🅅🄴 ⊇ 🛜 ⊗ 🔲 💻

◇◇◇ ▽▽ Elk Country Inn M
(307) 733-2364. **$76-$268, 14 day notice.** 480 W Pearl St 83001. 0.4 mi w of town square, then just e. Ext/int corridors. **Pets:** Accepted.
🅂🄰🅅🄴 🄼 ⊗ 🛜 ⊗ 🔲 💻

▽▽▽ Homewood Suites by Hilton H
(307) 739-0808. **$139-$389.** 260 N Millward St 83001. Just nw of town square, n on Millward St or w on Mercill Ave, from US 26/89/191. Int corridors. **Pets:** Accepted. 🄼 ⊗ 🛜 🔲 💻

Painted Buffalo Inn M

(307) 733-4340. **$90-$245.** 400 W Broadway 83001. Just w of town square. Ext corridors. **Pets:** Other species. $20 one-time fee/pet. Service with restrictions, supervision. [SAVE] [&M] [≥] [≈] [⛁] [⚎]

Snow King Resort Hotel H

(307) 733-5200. **$125-$325, 14 day notice.** 400 E Snow King Ave 83001. 0.4 mi s of E Broadway. Ext/int corridors. **Pets:** Dogs only. $50 one-time fee/pet. Designated rooms, service with restrictions.
[⚑] [&M] [≥] [✕] [≈] [✕] [⛁] [⚎]

KEMMERER

BEST WESTERN PLUS Fossil Country Inn & Suites H

(307) 877-3388. **$98-$110.** 760 US 30/189 83101. Jct US 30 and 189. Int corridors. **Pets:** Medium. $10 daily fee/room. Designated rooms, service with restrictions, supervision.
[SAVE] [&M] [≥] [≈] [✕] [⛁] [⚎]

LANDER

Holiday Inn Express & Suites Lander H

(307) 332-4005. **$99-$159.** 1002 11th St 82520. 1 mi w on US 287, just w on Lincoln St. Int corridors. **Pets:** $25 one-time fee/room. Designated rooms, service with restrictions, supervision.
[&M] [≥] [≈] [✕] [⛁] [⚎]

Holiday Lodge, Lander M

(307) 332-2511. **$70-$95, 3 day notice.** 210 McFarlane Dr 82520. Jct US 287 and SR 789. Ext corridors. **Pets:** Accepted. [≈] [⛁]

The Inn at Lander H

(307) 332-2847. **$90-$130.** 260 Grand View Dr 82520. Jct US 287 and SR 789. Int corridors. **Pets:** Accepted. [SAVE] [≥] [≈] [✕] [⛁] [⚎]

Rodeway Inn & Suites Pronghorn Lodge M

(307) 332-3940. **$74-$125.** 150 E Main St 82520. Just n of jct US 287 and SR 789. Ext corridors. **Pets:** Accepted. [SAVE] [†↑] [≈] [⛁] [⚎]

LARAMIE

AmericInn Lodge & Suites of Laramie H

(307) 745-0777. **$90-$229.** 4712 E Grand Ave 82070. I-80 exit 316 (Grand Ave), just n. Int corridors. **Pets:** Accepted.
[&M] [≥] [≈] [✕] [⛁] [⚎]

BEST WESTERN Laramie Inn & Suites H

(307) 745-5700. **$100-$170.** 1767 N Banner Rd 82072. I-80 exit 310 (Curtis St), just n. Int corridors. **Pets:** Medium. $20 daily fee/pet. Designated rooms, service with restrictions, supervision.
[SAVE] [≥] [≈] [✕] [⛁] [⚎]

Days Inn H

(307) 745-5678. **$91-$151.** 1368 N McCue St 82072. I-80 exit 310 (Curtis St), 0.3 mi e, then just s. Int corridors. **Pets:** Accepted.
[≥] [≈] [⛁] [⚎]

Hampton Inn H

(307) 742-0125. **$90-$199.** 3715 E Grand Ave 82070. I-80 exit 316 (Grand Ave), 2.2 mi nw to Boulder Dr. Int corridors. **Pets:** Accepted.
[&M] [≥] [≈] [⛁] [⚎]

Holiday Inn H ❀

(307) 721-9000. **$129-$199, 14 day notice.** 204 S 30th St 82070. I-80 exit 316 (Grand Ave), 2.5 mi w to 30th St. Int corridors. **Pets:** $25 one-time fee/pet. Designated rooms, service with restrictions, supervision.
[†↑] [&M] [≥] [≈] [✕] [⛁] [⚎]

Quality Inn & Suites H

(307) 742-6665. **$80-$159.** 1655 Centennial Dr 82070. I-80 exit 310 (Curtis St), just w, then just s. Int corridors. **Pets:** Other species. $15 daily fee/pet. Designated rooms, service with restrictions, crate.
[&M] [≥] [≈] [✕] [⛁] [⚎]

LITTLE AMERICA

Little America Hotel M ❀

(307) 875-2400. **$69-$109.** I-80, exit 68 82929. I-80 exit 68, just n. Ext/int corridors. **Pets:** Other species. $10 one-time fee/room. Designated rooms, service with restrictions, supervision.
[SAVE] [≥] [≈] [✕] [⛁] [⚎]

LUSK

BEST WESTERN Pioneer M

(307) 334-2640. **$109-$189.** 731 S Main St 82225. Just n of jct US 20/85. Ext corridors. **Pets:** $20 daily fee/room. Designated rooms, service with restrictions. [SAVE] [≥] [≈] [⛁] [⚎]

PAINTER

Hunter Peak Ranch RA

(307) 587-3711. **$215, 91 day notice.** 4027 Crandall Rd 82414. SR 296, 5 mi s of US 212; 40 mi n of SR 120. Ext corridors. **Pets:** Dogs only. $20 daily fee/pet. No service, supervision.
[≈] [✕] [✕] [✕] [✕] [⛁] [⚎]

PINEDALE

Baymont Inn & Suites H

(307) 367-8300. **$59-$109.** 1424 W Pine St 82941. 1 mi n on US 191. Int corridors. **Pets:** Medium. $25 daily fee/room. Service with restrictions, supervision. [SAVE] [&M] [≥] [≈] [✕] [⛁] [⚎]

BEST WESTERN Pinedale Inn H

(307) 367-6869. **$90-$160.** 864 W Pine St 82941. 0.5 mi n on US 191. Int corridors. **Pets:** Accepted. [SAVE] [≥] [≈] [✕] [⛁] [⚎]

POWELL

Americas Best Value Inn M

(307) 754-5117. **$90-$175.** 777 E 2nd St 82435. 0.3 mi e on US 14A. Ext corridors. **Pets:** $10 daily fee/pet. Designated rooms, service with restrictions, crate. [SAVE] [≥] [≈] [⛁] [⚎]

RAWLINS

BEST WESTERN CottonTree Inn H

(307) 324-2737. **$119-$179.** 2221 W Spruce St 82301. I-80 exit 211, just n. Ext/int corridors. **Pets:** $20 daily fee/room. Designated rooms, service with restrictions, supervision.
[SAVE] [†↑] [&M] [≥] [≈] [✕] [⛁] [⚎]

Comfort Inn & Suites H

(307) 324-3663. **$100-$150.** 2366 E Cedar St 82301. I-80 exit 215 (Cedar St), 0.3 mi w. Int corridors. **Pets:** Small. $30 one-time fee/room. Designated rooms, service with restrictions, supervision.
[SAVE] [≥] [≈] [✕] [⛁] [⚎]

Pronghorn Inn & Suites H

(307) 324-5588. **$109-$180.** 812 Locust St 82301. I-80 exit 214, 0.4 mi n on Higley Blvd, then just e. Int corridors. **Pets:** Accepted.
[SAVE] [≈] [⛁] [⚎]

RIVERTON

Comfort Inn & Suites H ❀

(307) 856-8900. **$99-$169.** 2020 N Federal Blvd 82501. 1.5 mi ne on US 26/SR 789. Int corridors. **Pets:** Large. Service with restrictions, supervision. [&M] [≥] [≈] [⛁] [⚎]

Days Inn M

(307) 856-9677. **$80-$105.** 909 W Main St 82501. 0.5 mi nw on US 26. Ext corridors. **Pets:** Accepted. [≈] [⛁] [⚎]

Hampton Inn & Suites Riverton H

(307) 856-3500. **$119-$159.** 2500 N Federal Blvd (US 26) 82501. 2 mi ne on US 26/SR 789. Int corridors. **Pets:** Accepted.
[&M] [≥] [≈] [✕] [⛁] [⚎]

Super 8 M

(307) 857-2400. **$65-$99, 3 day notice.** 1040 N Federal Blvd 82501. 1 mi ne on US 26/SR 789. Int corridors. **Pets:** Medium. $15 daily fee/pet. Designated rooms, service with restrictions, supervision. [≈] [⛁] [⚎]

AAA ▼▼▼▼ **Wind River Hotel & Casino** H

(307) 856-3964. **$80-$149.** 10269 Hwy 789 82501. 2 mi s from jct US 26. Int corridors. **Pets:** Dogs only. $25 daily fee/room. Designated rooms, service with restrictions, crate.

[SAVE] [♦♦] [♿M] [♋] [✕] [♦] [▣]

ROCK SPRINGS

▼▼▼▼ **Hampton Inn** H

(307) 382-9222. **$109-$209.** 1901 Dewar Dr 82901. I-80 exit 102 (Dewar Dr), 0.5 mi se. Int corridors. **Pets:** Accepted.

[♿M] [♋] [♋] [✕] [♦] [▣]

▼▼▼▼ **Holiday Inn** H ❀

(307) 382-9200. **$129-$200.** 1675 Sunset Dr 82901. I-80 exit 102 (Dewar Dr), just e, then 0.7 mi sw. Ext/int corridors. **Pets:** Other species. $10 daily fee/room. Designated rooms, service with restrictions, supervision. [♦♦] [♿M] [♋] [✕] [♦] [▣]

▼▼▼▼ **Holiday Inn Express & Suites** H

(307) 362-9200. **$150-$180, 10 day notice.** 1660 Sunset Dr 82901. I-80 exit 102 (Dewar Dr), just e, then 0.5 mi sw. Int corridors. **Pets:** Accepted. [♿M] [♋] [♋] [✕] [♦] [▣]

▼▼ **La Quinta Inn Rock Springs** H

(307) 362-1770. **$84-$204.** 2717 Dewar Dr 82901. I-80 exit 102 (Dewar Dr), just n. Int corridors. **Pets:** Large, other species. Service with restrictions. [♿M] [♋] [♋] [♦] [▣]

▼▼ **Quality Inn** M

(307) 382-9490. **$80-$146.** 1670 Sunset Dr 82901. I-80 exit 102 (Dewar Dr), just e, then 0.5 mi sw. Ext corridors. **Pets:** Accepted.

[♋] [♋] [♦] [▣]

SHERIDAN *(Restaurants p. 645)*

▼ **Americas Best Value Inn** M ❀

(307) 672-9757. **$69-$119.** 580 E 5th St 82801. I-90 exit 23 (5th St), 0.4 mi w. Ext corridors. **Pets:** Other species. Designated rooms, service with restrictions, supervision. [♋] [♦] [▣]

AAA ▼▼▼ **BEST WESTERN Sheridan Center** M 🐾

(307) 674-7421. **$90-$169.** 612 N Main St 82801. I-90 exit 23 (5th St), 1 mi w, then just s. Ext/int corridors. **Pets:** Other species. $25 one-time fee/room. Designated rooms, service with restrictions, supervision.

[SAVE] [♦♦] [♋] [♋] [✕] [♦] [▣]

▼▼▼▼ **Candlewood Suites** H

(307) 675-2100. **$109-$139.** 1709 Sugarland Dr 82801. I-90 exit 25, just w, then just n. Int corridors. **Pets:** Other species. $25 one-time fee/room. Service with restrictions. [♿M] [♋] [♦] [▣]

AAA ▼▼▼▼ **Holiday Inn Atrium & Convention Center** H

(307) 672-8931. **$109-$159.** 1809 Sugarland Dr 82801. I-90 exit 25, 0.3 mi nw. Int corridors. **Pets:** Accepted.

[SAVE] [♦♦] [♿M] [♋] [✕] [♋] [✕] [♦] [▣]

▼▼ **Mill Inn** M

(307) 672-6401. **Call for rates.** 2161 Coffeen Ave 82801. I-90 exit 25, 0.3 mi w. Ext/int corridors. **Pets:** Accepted. [♋] [♦] [▣]

▼ **Super 8 Sheridan** M

(307) 672-9725. **$52-$97.** 2435 N Main St 82801. I-90 exit 20, 0.7 mi n. Int corridors. **Pets:** Other species. $15 one-time fee/pet. Service with restrictions, supervision. [♋] [♦] [▣]

SUNDANCE

AAA ▼▼▼ **BEST WESTERN Inn at Sundance** H

(307) 283-2800. **$80-$210.** 2719 E Cleveland St 82729. I-90 exit 189, just n, then just w; 1.5 mi ne of SR 585. Int corridors. **Pets:** Large, other species. $15 daily fee/pet. No service, supervision.

[SAVE] [♿M] [♋] [♋] [✕] [♦] [▣]

TETON VILLAGE

AAA ▼▼▼▼▼ **Four Seasons Resort & Residences Jackson Hole** H ❀

(307) 732-5000. **$375-$1600, 30 day notice.** 7680 Granite Loop Rd 83025. At base of Jackson Hole Mountain Resort; Upper Village. Int corridors. **Pets:** Small, dogs only. Service with restrictions, supervision.

[SAVE] [♦♦] [♿M] [♋] [✕] [♋] [✕] [♦] [▣]

AAA ▼▼▼▼ **Teton Mountain Lodge & Spa** H

(307) 734-7111. **$139-$3200, 30 day notice.** 3385 W Cody Ln 83025. Upper Village. Int corridors. **Pets:** Dogs only. $25 daily fee/room. Designated rooms, no service, supervision.

[SAVE] [♦♦] [♿M] [♋] [✕] [♋] [✕] [♦] [▣]

THERMOPOLIS

▼▼▼ **Days Inn Hot Springs Convention Center** H

(307) 864-3131. **$77-$159.** 115 E Park St 82443. In Hot Springs State Park. Ext/int corridors. **Pets:** Accepted. [♦♦] [♋] [✕] [♋] [♦] [▣]

TORRINGTON

▼▼ **Americas Best Value Inn** M

(307) 532-7118. **Call for rates.** 1548 S Main St 82240. Just s of jct US 26 (W Valley Rd) and 85 (Main St). Int corridors. **Pets:** Accepted.

[♋] [♋] [♦] [▣]

▼▼▼ **Holiday Inn Express & Suites** H

(307) 532-7600. **Call for rates.** 1700 E Valley Rd 82240. On US 26 (E Valley Rd), 0.4 mi e of US 85 (Main St). Int corridors. **Pets:** Dogs only. $20 daily fee/pet. Designated rooms, service with restrictions, supervision. [♿M] [♋] [♋] [✕] [♦] [▣]

UCROSS

▼▼▼▼ **The Ranch at Ucross** RA

(307) 737-2281. **Call for rates.** 2673 US Hwy 14 E 82835. Jct US 14/16, 0.5 mi w. Ext/int corridors. **Pets:** Accepted.

[♦♦] [♋] [✕] [♋] [✕] [𝒲]

WHEATLAND

AAA ▼▼▼ **BEST WESTERN Torchlite Motor Inn** M 🐾

(307) 322-4070. **$130-$150, 30 day notice.** 1809 N 16th St 82201. I-25 exit 80, just e, then 0.6 mi s. Ext corridors. **Pets:** Other species. $10 daily fee/pet. Designated rooms, service with restrictions, crate.

[SAVE] [♋] [♋] [♦] [▣]

WRIGHT

▼▼▼ **Wright Hotel** H

(307) 464-6060. **$129-$139, 3 day notice.** 300 Reata Dr 82732. Just w of jct SR 59 and 387. Int corridors. **Pets:** $25 daily fee/pet. Designated rooms, service with restrictions, supervision.

[♦♦] [♿M] [♋] [✕] [♦] [▣]

YELLOWSTONE NATIONAL PARK

AAA ▼▼▼ **Elephant Head Lodge** CA

(307) 587-3980. **$150-$350, 30 day notice.** 1170 Yellowstone Hwy 82414. 11.7 mi e of Yellowstone National Park east gate on US 14/16/20. Ext corridors. **Pets:** Other species. $25 one-time fee/pet. Designated rooms, service with restrictions, supervision.

[SAVE] [♦♦] [♋] [♋] [✕] [𝒦] [𝒲] [♦] [▣]

▼▼ **Shoshone Lodge** CA

(307) 587-4044. **$140-$330, 30 day notice.** 349 North Fork Hwy 82190. 3.5 mi e of Yellowstone National Park east gate on US 14/16/20. Ext corridors. **Pets:** Accepted. [♦♦] [♋] [𝒦] [🎫] [♦] [▣]

Canadian Hotels

AIRDRIE

Ⓐ ◈◈ **BEST WESTERN Airdrie** 🅷

(403) 948-3838. **$134-$179.** 121 Edmonton Tr SE T4B 1S2. Hwy 2 exit Airdrie/Irricana, just w, then 0.5 mi (0.9 km) s. Ext/int corridors. **Pets:** Accepted. 🆂🅰🆅🅴 ⊞ 🛜 ⊠ 🛡 📇

Ⓐ ◈◈◈ **Comfort Inn & Suites Airdrie** 🅷 🐾

(403) 948-3411. **$153-$170.** 133 Sierra Springs Dr SE T4B 3G7. Hwy 2 exit 282 (Yankee Valley Blvd), just w. Int corridors. **Pets:** Medium, dogs only. $20 daily fee/pet. Designated rooms, service with restrictions, supervision. 🆂🅰🆅🅴 🅻🅼 ⇀ 🛜 ⊠ 🛡 📇

◈◈◈◈ **Holiday Inn Express & Suites Airdrie-Calgary North** 🅷

(403) 912-1952. **Call for rates.** 64 E Lake Ave NE T4A 2G8. Hwy 2 exit E Airdrie, 0.8 mi (1.3 km) n. Int corridors. **Pets:** Accepted.
🅴🅲🅾 🅻🅼 ⇀ 🛜 ⊠ 🛡 📇

◈◈ **Super 8 Airdrie** 🅷

(403) 948-4188. **$120-$135.** 815 E Lake Blvd T4A 2G4. Hwy 2 exit E Airdrie, just e. Int corridors. **Pets:** Accepted. 🛜 ⊠ 🛡 📇

ATHABASCA

◈◈◈◈ **Days Inn Athabasca** 🅷

(780) 675-7020. **$139-$179.** 2805 48th Ave T9S 0A4. Jct Hwy 2 and 55, 1.6 mi (2.7 km) e; east end of town. Int corridors. **Pets:** Accepted.
🛜 🛡 📇

BANFF *(Restaurants p. 646)*

◈◈ **Banff Ptarmigan Inn** 🅷 🐾

(403) 762-2207. **$99-$229, 3 day notice.** 337 Banff Ave T1L 1B1. Between Moose and Elk sts. Int corridors. **Pets:** Medium, other species. $25 one-time fee/pet. Designated rooms, service with restrictions, supervision. 🍽 ⊠ 🛜 ⊠ 🅰🅲 🛡 📇

◈◈◈ **Banff Rocky Mountain Resort** 🅲🅾 🐾

(403) 762-5531. **Call for rates.** 1029 Banff Ave T1L 1A2. Jct Banff Ave and Tunnel Mountain Rd; just s of Trans-Canada Hwy 1. Ext corridors. **Pets:** $25 daily fee/pet. Designated rooms, service with restrictions, supervision. 🍽 ⇀ ⊠ ⊠ 🅰🅲 🛡 📇

Ⓐ ◈◈◈ **BEST WESTERN PLUS Siding 29 Lodge** 🅷

(403) 762-5575. **$100-$400.** 453 Marten St T1L 1B3. 0.6 mi (1 km) ne, just off Banff Ave. Int corridors. **Pets:** $15 daily fee/pet. Service with restrictions, supervision. 🆂🅰🆅🅴 ⊞ ⇀ 🛜 ⊠ 🛡 📇

◈◈ **Castle Mountain Chalets** 🅲🅰 🐾

(403) 762-3868. **$149-$359, 7 day notice.** Bow Valley Pkwy (Hwy 1A) & Hwy 93 S T1L 1B5. 20 mi (32 km) w on Trans-Canada Hwy 1 to jct Castle Mountain, 0.6 mi (1 km) ne on Hwy 1A (Bow Valley Pkwy). Ext corridors. **Pets:** Dogs only. $25 daily fee/pet. Designated rooms, service with restrictions, supervision. ⊠ 🅰🅵 ⊠ 🅰🅲 🛅 🛡 📇

Ⓐ ◈◈◈ **Douglas Fir Resort & Chalets** 🅲🅾 🐾

(403) 762-5591. **$142-$610, 14 day notice.** 525 Tunnel Mountain Rd T1L 1B2. Jct Banff Ave and Wolf St, 1 mi (1.6 km) ne. Ext/int corridors. **Pets:** Dogs only. $23 daily fee/pet. Designated rooms, service with restrictions, supervision. 🆂🅰🆅🅴 ⇀ ⊠ 🛜 ⊠ 🛡 📇

Ⓐ ◈◈◈◈ **The Fairmont Banff Springs** 🅷

(403) 762-2211. **$319-$679, 3 day notice.** 405 Spray Ave T1L 1J4. Just s on Banff Ave over the bridge, 0.3 mi (0.5 km) e. Int corridors. **Pets:** Accepted. 🆂🅰🆅🅴 🅴🅲🅾 ⊞ 🍽 ⇀ ⊠ 🛜 ⊠ 🛡 📇

◈◈◈◈ **Hidden Ridge Resort** 🅲🅾

(403) 762-3544. **$119-$299, 3 day notice.** 901 Hidden Ridge Way T1L 1B7. Jct Banff Ave and Wolf St, 1 mi (1.6 km) ne. Ext corridors. **Pets:** Accepted. ⊠ 🛜 ⊠ 🛡 📇

◈◈ **Irwin's Mountain Inn** 🅷

(403) 762-4566. **$169-$209.** 429 Banff Ave T1L 1B2. N of Rabbit St. Int corridors. **Pets:** Other species. $20 daily fee/pet. Designated rooms, service with restrictions, crate. 🍽 ⊠ 🛜 ⊠ 🛡 📇

Ⓐ ◈◈◈ **Johnston Canyon Resort** 🅲🅰

(403) 762-2971. **$149-$345, 7 day notice.** Hwy 1A T1L 1A9. 15 mi (24 km) nw on Hwy 1A (Bow Valley Pkwy). Ext corridors. **Pets:** Accepted.
🆂🅰🆅🅴 🅴🅲🅾 🍽 🅰🅵 ⊠ 🅰🅲 🛅 🛡 📇

◈◈ **Red Carpet Inn** 🅷

(403) 762-4184. **$89-$219.** 425 Banff Ave T1L 1B6. Between Beaver and Rabbit sts. Ext/int corridors. **Pets:** Accepted. 🛜 ⊠ 🛡 📇

Ⓐ ◈◈◈◈ **The Rimrock Resort Hotel** 🅷 🐾

(403) 762-3356. **$178-$428, 3 day notice.** 300 Mountain Ave T1L 1J2. 2.4 mi (4 km) s via Sulphur Mountain Rd; adjacent to Upper Hot Springs Pool. Int corridors. **Pets:** Other species. $40 daily fee/pet. Designated rooms, service with restrictions, crate. 🆂🅰🆅🅴 🍽 🅻🅼 ⇀ ⊠ 🛜 ⊠ 🛡 📇

BONNYVILLE

Ⓐ ◈◈◈ **BEST WESTERN Bonnyville Inn & Suites** 🅷 🐾

(780) 826-6226. **$170-$190.** 5401 43rd St T9N 0H3. Hwy 28, just n at 44th St. Int corridors. **Pets:** Small, dogs only. $25 daily fee/room. Designated rooms, service with restrictions, supervision. 🆂🅰🆅🅴 🅻🅼 🛜 ⊠ 🛡 📇

BROOKS

◈◈ **Canalta Hotel** 🅷

(403) 363-0080. **$120-$200.** 115 15th Ave W T1R 1C4. Just s off Trans-Canada Hwy 1. Ext/int corridors. **Pets:** Accepted.
🅴🅲🅾 ⇀ 🛜 ⊠ 🛡 📇

◈◈ **Heritage Inn Hotel & Convention Centre Brooks** 🅷

(403) 362-6666. **$119-$180.** 1217 2nd St W T1R 1P7. Trans-Canada Hwy 1 exit Hwy 873, 0.5 mi (0.8 km) s. Int corridors. **Pets:** Medium, dogs only. $20 daily fee/pet. Designated rooms, service with restrictions, crate. 🍽 🛜 🛡 📇

◈◈ **Lakeview Inns & Suites** 🅷

(403) 362-7440. **Call for rates.** 1307 2nd St W T1R 1P7. Trans-Canada Hwy 1 exit Hwy 873, 0.5 mi (0.8 km) s. Int corridors. **Pets:** Accepted.
⇀ 🛜 🛡 📇

Ⓐ ◈◈◈ **Ramada Brooks** 🅷

(403) 362-6440. **$140-$200.** 1319 2nd St W T1R 1P7. Trans-Canada Hwy 1 exit Hwy 873, 0.5 mi (0.8 km) s. Ext/int corridors. **Pets:** Accepted. 🆂🅰🆅🅴 🅴🅲🅾 ⊞ ⇀ ⊠ 🛜 ⊠ 🛡 📇

CALGARY *(Restaurants p. 646)*

Ⓐ ◈◈◈◈ **Calgary Marriott Downtown** 🅷

(403) 266-7331. **$139-$749.** 110 9th Ave SE T2G 5A6. Jct 9th Ave and Centre St; adjacent to TELUS Convention Centre. Int corridors. **Pets:** Accepted. 🆂🅰🆅🅴 🅴🅲🅾 ⇀ 🛜 ⊠ 🛡 📇

◈◈◈ **Calgary Westways Guest House** 🅱🅱 🐾

(403) 229-1758. **$130-$189, 4 day notice.** 216 25th Ave SW T2S 0L1. 1.1 mi (1.7 km) s on Hwy 2A (Macleod Tr), just w. Int corridors. **Pets:** Other species. $10 daily fee/pet. 🛜 🛡 📇

Ⓐ ◈◈◈ **Carriage House Inn** 🅷 🐾

(403) 253-1101. **$145-$285.** 9030 Macleod Tr S T2H 0M4. On Hwy 2A (Macleod Tr); corner of 90th Ave SW. Int corridors. **Pets:** Medium. $20 daily fee/pet. Designated rooms, service with restrictions, supervision. 🆂🅰🆅🅴 🅴🅲🅾 🍽 ⇀ ⊠ 🛜 ⊠ 🛡 📇

◆◆◆ **Clarion Hotel & Conference Centre Calgary Airport** 🅷

(403) 291-4666. **$119-$139.** 2120 16th Ave NE T2E 1L4. Just e of jct Hwy 2 (Deerfoot Tr) and 16th Ave NE (Trans-Canada Hwy 1). Int corridors. **Pets:** Other species. $25 one-time fee/pet. Designated rooms, service with restrictions, crate.

[ECO] 🍴 🛗 ⊇ 🛜 ✕ 🔋 🖥

◆◆ **Coast Plaza Hotel & Conference Centre** 🅷 🐾

(403) 248-8888. **$109-$289, 3 day notice.** 1316 33rd St NE T2A 6B6. Just s of jct 16th Ave (Trans-Canada Hwy 1) and 36th St NE, just w on 12th Ave NE. Int corridors. **Pets:** $20 daily fee/pet. Designated rooms, service with restrictions. [ECO] 🍴 ⊇ 🛜 ✕ 🔋 🖥

◆◆ **Delta Bow Valley** 🅷 🐾

(403) 266-1980. **$109-$599.** 209 4th Ave SE T2G 0C6. Jct 1st St SE and 4th Ave SE. Int corridors. **Pets:** Large, other species. $35 one-time fee/pet. Designated rooms, service with restrictions, supervision.

[ECO] 🍴 🛗 ⊇ ✕ 🛜 ✕ 🔋 🖥

(CAA) ◆◆ **Delta Calgary Airport** 🅷

(403) 291-2600. **$149-$409.** 2001 Airport Rd NE T2E 6Z8. At Calgary International Airport. Int corridors. **Pets:** Accepted.

[SAVE] [ECO] 🍴 🛗 ⊇ 🛜 ✕ 🔋 🖥

◆◆ **Delta Calgary South** 🅷

(403) 278-5050. **$109-$429.** 135 Southland Dr SE T2J 5X5. On Hwy 2A (Macleod Tr); corner of Southland Dr. Int corridors. **Pets:** Accepted.

[ECO] 🍴 🛗 ⊇ ✕ 🔋 🖥

◆◆ **Econo Lodge Motel Village** 🅜

(403) 289-2561. **$79-$149.** 2440 16th Ave NW T2M 0M5. Jct 16th Ave NW (Trans-Canada Hwy 1) and Banff Tr NW. Ext/int corridors. **Pets:** Medium. $10 daily fee/pet. Designated rooms, service with restrictions, supervision. 🛜 🔋 🖥

(CAA) ◆◆◆ **Econo Lodge South** 🅜

(403) 252-4401. **$99-$129.** 7505 Macleod Tr SW T2H 0L8. Corner of Hwy 2A (Macleod Tr) and 75th Ave SW. Ext/int corridors.
Pets: Accepted. [SAVE] [ECO] ⊇ 🛜 🔋 🖥

◆◆◆ **Executive Royal Hotel North Calgary** 🅷 🐾

(403) 291-2003. **$104-$235.** 2828 23rd St NE T2E 8T4. Barlow Tr NE, just w; at 27th Ave NE. Int corridors. **Pets:** Large, other species. $25 one-time fee/room. Service with restrictions, crate.

[ECO] 🍴 🛗 🛜 ✕ 🔋 🖥

(CAA) ◆◆◆◆ **The Fairmont Palliser** 🅷

(403) 262-1234. **$129-$649, 3 day notice.** 133 9th Ave SW T2P 2M3. Jct 9th Ave SW and 1st St SW. Int corridors. **Pets:** Accepted.

[SAVE] [ECO] 🍴 🛗 ⊇ ✕ 🛜 ✕

(CAA) ◆◆◆ **Holiday Inn Calgary-Airport** 🅷

(403) 230-1999. **$160-$170, 4 day notice.** 1250 McKinnon Dr NE T2E 7T7. 0.6 mi (1 km) e of jct Hwy 2 (Deerfoot Tr) and 16th Ave NE (Trans-Canada Hwy 1). Int corridors. **Pets:** Accepted.

[SAVE] 🍴 🛗 ⊇ 🛜 🔋 🖥

(CAA) ◆◆◆ **Holiday Inn Calgary-Macleod Trail South** 🅷

(403) 287-2700. **Call for rates.** 4206 Macleod Tr S T2G 2R7. Corner of 42nd Ave SW and Macleod Tr S. Int corridors. **Pets:** $20 one-time fee/room. Designated rooms, service with restrictions, supervision.

[SAVE] [ECO] 🍴 🛗 ⊇ 🛜 ✕ 🔋 🖥

◆◆◆ **Holiday Inn Express Hotel & Suites Calgary-South** 🅷

(403) 225-3000. **$139-$300, 7 day notice.** 12025 Lake Fraser Dr SE (Macleod Tr S) T2J 7G5. Hwy 2 (Deerfoot Tr) exit Anderson Rd W, just s on Macleod Tr, just e on Lake Fraser Gate, then 0.4 mi (0.7 km) n. Int corridors. **Pets:** Medium. $20 one-time fee/pet. Designated rooms, service with restrictions. ⊇ 🛜 🔋 🖥

◆◆◆ **Homewood Suites Calgary Airport** 🅷 🐾

(403) 453-7888. **$129-$259.** 1000 2021 100th Ave NE T3J 0R3. Hwy 2 (Deerfoot Tr) exit 266, 1.1 mi (1.8 km) e on Airport Tr NE, then just n on 19th St NE. Int corridors. **Pets:** Small, cats only. $75 one-time fee/room. Designated rooms, service with restrictions, supervision.

🛗 🛜 ✕ 🔋 🖥

◆◆◆ **Hotel Arts** 🅷

(403) 266-4611. **$139-$469.** 119 12th Ave SW T2R 0G8. At 1st St SW; center. Int corridors. **Pets:** $60 one-time fee/room. Designated rooms, service with restrictions, supervision.

🍴 🛗 ⊇ 🔊 ✕ 🔋 🖥

◆◆◆ **Hotel Blackfoot** 🅷

(403) 252-2253. **$139-$329.** 5940 Blackfoot Tr SE T2H 2B5. At 58th Ave SE. Int corridors. **Pets:** Accepted.

[ECO] ◀ 🍴 🛗 ⊇ ✕ 🛜 ✕ 🔋 🖥

◆◆◆ **Hotel Le Germain Calgary** 🅷 🐾

(403) 264-8990. **Call for rates.** 899 Centre St SW T2G 1B8. Corner of 1st St SW and 9th Ave SW; center. Int corridors. **Pets:** $30 daily fee/room. Service with restrictions, crate. 🍴 ✕ 🛜 ✕ 🖥

(CAA) ◆◆◆ **Hyatt Regency Calgary** 🅷 🐾

(403) 717-1234. **$139-$689.** 700 Centre St SE T2G 5P6. Corner of Centre St and 7th Ave SW. Int corridors. **Pets:** Small. $100 one-time fee/room. Service with restrictions, supervision.

[SAVE] 🍴 ⊇ ✕ 🛜 🔋 🖥

◆◆◆ **Lakeview Signature Inn** 🅷

(403) 735-3336. **$140-$310, 3 day notice.** 2622 39th Ave NE T1Y 7J9. Barlow Tr NE, just e. Int corridors. **Pets:** Accepted.

[ECO] 🛗 ⊇ 🛜 ✕ 🔋 🖥

(CAA) ◆◆◆ **Residence Inn by Marriott Calgary Airport** 🅷

(403) 278-1000. **$139-$359.** 2530 48th Ave NE T3J 4V8. Just n of jct Barlow Tr NE and McKnight Blvd NE. Int corridors. **Pets:** $100 one-time fee/room. Designated rooms, service with restrictions, supervision.

[SAVE] 🍴 🛗 ⊇ 🛜 ✕ 🔋 🖥

◆◆ **Sandman Hotel Downtown Calgary** 🅷

(403) 237-8626. **Call for rates.** 888 7th Ave SW T2P 3J3. Corner of 7th Ave SW and 8th St SW. Int corridors. **Pets:** Accepted.

[ECO] 🍴 ⊇ 🛜 ✕ 🔋 🖥

◆◆ **Sandman Hotel Suites & Spa Calgary Airport** 🅷

(403) 219-2475. **$129-$224.** 25 Hopewell Way NE T3J 4V7. Just n of jct Barlow Tr and McKnight Blvd. Int corridors. **Pets:** Accepted.

[ECO] 🍴 🛗 ⊇ 🛜 ✕ 🔋 🖥

◆◆◆ **Service Plus Inn & Suites Calgary** 🅷

(403) 256-5352. **$139-$159.** 3503 114th Ave SE T2Z 3X2. South end of Barlow Tr, just w. Int corridors. **Pets:** Accepted.

[SAVE] 🛗 ⊇ ✕ 🔋 🖥

(CAA) ◆◆◆ **Sheraton Cavalier Hotel** 🅷 🐾

(403) 291-0107. **$139-$409.** 2620 32nd Ave NE T1Y 6B8. Barlow Tr at 32nd Ave NE. Int corridors. **Pets:** Other species. Service with restrictions, crate. [SAVE] [ECO] 🍴 ⊇ ✕ 🛜 ✕ 🖥

(CAA) ◆◆◆◆ **Sheraton Suites Calgary Eau Claire** 🅷

(403) 266-7200. **$129-$389.** 255 Barclay Parade SW T2P 5C2. At 3rd St SW and 2nd Ave SW. Int corridors. **Pets:** Accepted.

[SAVE] [ECO] 🍴 ⊇ ✕ 🔊 ✕ 🔋 🖥

(CAA) ◆◆◆ **Staybridge Suites Calgary Airport** 🅷

(403) 204-7829. **$169-$269.** 2825 Sunridge Way NE T1Y 7K7. Trans-Canada Hwy 1 exit Barlow Tr NE, just n, then just e. Int corridors.
Pets: Accepted. [SAVE] 🛗 ⊇ 🛜 ✕ 🔋 🖥

ⒶⒶ ◈◈ **Travelodge Calgary University** H

(403) 289-6600. **$109-$199.** 2227 Banff Tr NW T2M 4L2. 16th Ave NW (Trans-Canada Hwy 1) and Banff Tr NW. Int corridors. **Pets:** Other species. $10 one-time fee/room. Designated rooms, service with restrictions, supervision. SAVE ECO ⊅ 🛜 🗐 💻

ⒶⒶ ◈◈◈ **The Westin Calgary** H

(403) 266-1611. **$159-$539.** 320 4th Ave SW T2P 2S6. Corner of 4th Ave SW and 3rd St. Int corridors. **Pets:** Accepted.
SAVE 🍴 🕭 ⊅ ✕ 🛜 ✕ 🗐 💻

◈◈◈ **Wingate by Wyndham Calgary** H ❀

(403) 514-0099. **$139-$309.** 400 Midpark Way SE T2X 3S4. Hwy 2A (Macleod Tr), 0.3 mi (0.5 km) e on Sun Valley Blvd SE, just n on Midpark Blvd SE, then just s. Int corridors. **Pets:** $100 daily fee/pet. Service with restrictions, supervision. ECO 🕭 ⊅ 🛜 ✕ 🗐 💻

CAMROSE

ⒶⒶ ◈◈◈ **BEST WESTERN PLUS Camrose Resort & Casino** H

(780) 679-2376. **$127-$134.** 3201 48th Ave T4V 0K9. Hwy 13 (48th Ave), just s of Correction Line Rd; eastern approach to city. Int corridors. **Pets:** Accepted. SAVE 🍴 🕭 ⊅ ✕ 🛜 ✕ 🗐 💻

◈◈ **Norsemen Inn** H

(780) 672-9171. **Call for rates.** 6505 48th Ave T4V 3K3. Hwy 13 (48th Ave) at 65th St; west end of town. Int corridors. **Pets:** $20 daily fee/room. Service with restrictions, crate. 🍴 🛜 ✕ 🗐 💻

◈◈ **Super 8 Camrose** H

(780) 672-7303. **$135-$245.** 4710 73rd St T4V 0E5. Hwy 13 (48th Ave), just s. Int corridors. **Pets:** Accepted. ⊅ 🛜 ✕ 🗐 💻

CANMORE *(Restaurants p. 646)*

ⒶⒶ ◈◈◈ **Banff Boundary Lodge** CO

(403) 678-9555. **Call for rates.** 1000 Harvie Heights Rd T1W 2W2. Trans-Canada Hwy 1 exit 86, just n. Ext corridors. **Pets:** Accepted.
SAVE 🛜 ✕ 🎿 🗐 💻

ⒶⒶ ◈◈◈ **BEST WESTERN PLUS Pocaterra Inn** H

(403) 678-4334. **$110-$305.** 1725 Mountain Ave T1W 2W1. Trans-Canada Hwy 1 exit 86, 1.3 mi (2.1 km) e. Int corridors. **Pets:** Accepted.
SAVE 🕭 ⊅ ✕ 🛜 ✕ 🗐 💻

◈◈ **Bow Valley Motel** M

(403) 678-5085. **Call for rates.** 610 8th St T1W 2B5. Trans-Canada Hwy 1 exit 89, 1.1 mi (1.8 km) se. Ext corridors. **Pets:** Accepted.
🛜 ✕ 🗐 💻

ⒶⒶ ◈◈◈ **Canadian Rockies Chalets** CO

(403) 678-3799. **$104-$269, 3 day notice.** 1206 Bow Valley Tr T1W 1N6. Trans-Canada Hwy 1 exit 89, 0.9 mi (1.5 km) se. Ext corridors. **Pets:** Medium, other species. $20 daily fee/pet. Designated rooms, no service, crate. SAVE 🛜 ✕ 🎿 🗐 💻

ⒶⒶ ◈◈◈ **Coast Canmore Hotel & Conference Centre** H

(403) 678-3625. **$99-$299, 3 day notice.** 511 Bow Valley Tr T1W 1N7. Trans-Canada Hwy 1 exit 89, 1.4 mi (2.2 km) s. Int corridors. **Pets:** Accepted. SAVE ECO 🍴 🕭 ⊅ 🛜 ✕ 🗐 💻

ⒶⒶ ◈◈◈ **Econo Lodge Canmore** H

(403) 678-5488. **$75-$190.** 1602 2nd Ave T1W 1M8. Trans-Canada Hwy 1 exit 89, 1.3 mi (2.1 km) e. Int corridors. **Pets:** Accepted.
SAVE 🍴 🛜 ✕ 🗐 💻

◈◈◈ **Fire Mountain Lodge** CO

(403) 609-9949. **$199-$350.** 121 Kananaskis Way T1W 2X2. Trans-Canada Hwy 1 exit 89, 1 mi (1.6 km) s. Ext corridors. **Pets:** Medium. $25 daily fee/pet. Designated rooms, no service, crate.
🛜 ✕ 🗐 💻

◈◈◈ **Mystic Springs Chalets & Hot Pools** CO ❀

(403) 609-0333. **Call for rates.** 140 Kananaskis Way T1W 2X2. Trans-Canada Hwy 1 exit 89, 1.1 mi (1.8 km) s. Ext corridors. **Pets:** Medium. $25 daily fee/pet. Designated rooms, no service, crate.
ECO ⊅ ✕ 🛜 ✕ 🗐 💻

ⒶⒶ ◈◈◈ **Quality Resort-Chateau Canmore** H

(403) 678-6699. **$99-$189.** 1720 Bow Valley Tr T1W 2X3. Trans-Canada Hwy 1 exit 86, 0.5 mi (0.8 km) s. Int corridors. **Pets:** Accepted.
SAVE 🍴 ⊅ ✕ 🛜 ✕ 🗐 💻

◈◈ **Ramada Inn & Suites Canmore** H

(403) 609-4656. **$89-$260.** 1402 Bow Valley Tr T1W 1N5. Trans-Canada Hwy 1 exit 89, 1 mi (1.6 km) se. Int corridors. **Pets:** Accepted.
🕭 ⊅ 🛜 ✕ 🗐 💻

ⒶⒶ ◈◈◈ **Rocky Mountain Ski Lodge** M

(403) 678-5445. **$129-$209.** 1711 Bow Valley Tr T1W 2T8. Trans-Canada Hwy 1 exit 86, 0.5 mi (0.8 km) s. Ext corridors. **Pets:** Medium. $10 daily fee/pet. Designated rooms, service with restrictions, supervision. SAVE ECO ✕ 🛜 ✕ 🗐 💻

◈◈◈ **Solara Resort & Spa** CO

(403) 609-3600. **$159-$309, 7 day notice.** 187 Kananaskis Way T1W 0A3. Trans-Canada Hwy 1 exit 89, 1.2 mi (2 km) s. Int corridors. **Pets:** Accepted. ✕ ⊅ ✕ 🗐 💻

CLARESHOLM

◈◈ **Bluebird Motel** M

(403) 625-3395. **Call for rates.** 5505 1st St W T0L 0T0. 0.3 mi (0.5 km) n on Hwy 2. Ext corridors. **Pets:** Accepted. 🛜 ✕ 🗐 💻

◈◈ **Motel 6 Claresholm** H

(403) 625-4646. **Call for rates.** 11 Alberta Rd (Hwy 2) T0L 0T0. North end of town. Int corridors. **Pets:** Other species. Service with restrictions, crate. 🕭 🛜 🗐

COCHRANE

◈◈ **Days Inn & Suites Cochrane** H

(403) 932-5588. **$99-$190.** 5 West Side Dr T4C 1M1. Jct Hwy 1A and 22, 0.4 mi (0.6 km) s, just e on Quigley Dr, then just s. Int corridors. **Pets:** $10 daily fee/pet. Service with restrictions, supervision.
⊅ 🛜 🗐 💻

ⒶⒶ ◈◈ **Super 8 Cochrane** H

(403) 932-1410. **$120-$244.** 11 West Side Dr T4C 1M1. Jct Hwy 1A and 22, 0.4 mi (0.6 km) s, just e on Quigley Dr, then just s. Ext/int corridors. **Pets:** Large. $15 daily fee/pet. Designated rooms.
SAVE ✕ 🛜 ✕ 🗐 💻

DEAD MAN'S FLATS

◈◈◈ **Copperstone Resort Hotel** CO ❀

(403) 678-0303. **Call for rates.** 250 2nd Ave T1W 2W4. Trans-Canada Hwy 1 exit 98, just n on 2nd St, then just e. Int corridors. **Pets:** $20 daily fee/room. Designated rooms, service with restrictions, supervision.
🛜 ✕ 🗐 💻

DRAYTON VALLEY

◈◈ **Lakeview Inn & Suites** H

(780) 542-3200. **Call for rates.** 4302 50th St T7A 1M4. Hwy 22 exit Drayton Valley, 1.5 mi (2.4 km) n. Int corridors. **Pets:** Accepted.
🍴 🛜 🗐 💻

◈◈◈ **Ramada Drayton Valley** H

(780) 514-7861. **$140-$200.** 2051 50th St T7A 1S5. Just n on Hwy 39; south end of town. Ext/int corridors. **Pets:** Accepted.
ECO 🕭 ⊅ 🛜 ✕ 🗐 💻

DRUMHELLER

ⒶⒶ ◈◈◈ **Canalta Jurassic Hotel** H

(403) 823-7700. **Call for rates.** 1103 Hwy 9 S T0J 0Y0. Hwy 9, southeast access to town. Ext/int corridors. **Pets:** Accepted.
SAVE ECO 🛜 ✕ 🗐 💻

▼▼▼ Inn and Spa at Heartwood 🆑

(403) 823-6495. **$129-$305, 3 day notice.** 320 N Railway Ave E T0J 0Y4. Jct Hwy 9 and 575 (S Railway Ave SE), just n, just e. Ext/int corridors. **Pets:** Accepted. 🛜 ✕ 🗄 💻

▼▼◆ Ramada Inn & Suites 🏨

(403) 823-2028. **$160-$250.** 680 2nd St SE T0J 0Y0. Jct Hwy 9 and 575 (S Railway Ave SE), just ne. Ext/int corridors. **Pets:** Accepted.

🌿 🛗 🛜 ✕ 🗄 💻

▼▼ Super 8 🏨

(403) 823-8887. **$140-$266.** 600-680 2nd St SE T0J 0Y0. Jct Hwy 9 and 575 (S Railway Ave SE), just ne. Ext/int corridors. **Pets:** Accepted.

🌿 🛗 🛜 ✕ 🗄 💻

EDMONTON

🅐 ▼▼▼ BEST WESTERN Cedar Park Inn 🏨

(780) 434-7411. **$96-$149.** 5116 Gateway Blvd T6H 2H4. Hwy 2 (Gateway Blvd) at 51st Ave. Int corridors. **Pets:** Accepted.

SAVE 🍴 🛗 🛗 🛜 ✕ 🗄 💻

🅐 ▼▼▼ BEST WESTERN PLUS Westwood Inn 🏨

(780) 483-7770. **$109-$139.** 18035 Stony Plain Rd T5S 1B2. Hwy 16A (Stony Plain Rd) at 180th St. Int corridors. **Pets:** Accepted.

SAVE 🍴 🛗 🛜 ✕ 🗄 💻

🅐 ▼▼▼ Comfort Inn West 🏨

(780) 484-4415. **$120-$150.** 17610 100th Ave T5S 1S9. At 176th St. Int corridors. **Pets:** Small. $20 daily fee/pet. Service with restrictions, supervision. SAVE 🌿 🍴 🛗 🛜 🗄 💻

▼▼ Continental Inn 🏨

(780) 484-7751. **$110-$145, 6 day notice.** 16625 Stony Plain Rd T5P 4A8. On Hwy 16A (Stony Plain Rd) at 166th St. Int corridors. **Pets:** Accepted. 🍴 🛜 🗄 💻

▼▼▼ Courtyard by Marriott Edmonton Downtown 🏨

(780) 423-9999. **$189-$245.** 1 Thornton Ct T5J 2E7. Just off Jasper Ave; between 99th and 97th sts. Int corridors. **Pets:** Accepted.

🍴 🛗 🛜 ✕ 🗄 💻

▼▼◆▼ Delta Edmonton Centre Suite Hotel 🏨

(780) 429-3900. **$109-$389.** 10222 102nd St NW T5J 4C5. At 102nd St NW and 103rd Ave NW. Int corridors. **Pets:** Accepted.

🌿 🍴 🛗 🗙 🛜 ✕ 🗄 💻

🅐 ▼▼◆▼ Delta Edmonton South Hotel and Conference Centre 🏨 🐾

(780) 434-6415. **Call for rates.** 4404 Gateway Blvd T6H 5C2. Jct Hwy 2 (Gateway Blvd) and Whitemud Dr. Int corridors. **Pets:** Other species. $35 daily fee/room. Service with restrictions, crate.

SAVE 🌿 🍴 🛗 🛜 ✕ 🗄 💻

▼▼▼ DoubleTree by Hilton West Edmonton 🏨

(780) 484-0821. **$149-$209.** 16615 109th Ave T5P 4K8. 1 mi (1.6 km) n of jct Hwy 2 (170th St) and 16A (Stony Plain Rd). Int corridors. **Pets:** Accepted. 🌿 🍴 🛗 🛗 🛜 ✕ 🗄 💻

▼▼▼ Executive Royal Inn West Edmonton 🏨

(780) 484-6000. **$124-$200, 7 day notice.** 10010 178th St T5S 1T3. Corner of 178th St and 100th Ave. Int corridors. **Pets:** Accepted.

🌿 🍴 🛜 ✕ 🗄 💻

🅐 ▼▼◆▼ The Fairmont Hotel Macdonald 🏨 🐾

(780) 424-5181. **$189-$489, 7 day notice.** 10065 100th St T5J 0N6. Just s of Jasper Ave. Int corridors. **Pets:** Medium, other species. $25 daily fee/pet. Designated rooms.

SAVE 🌿 🍴 🛗 🛗 🗙 🛜 ✕ 💻

🅐 ▼▼◆ Fantasyland Hotel 🏨

(780) 444-3000. **$178-$498, 3 day notice.** 17700 87th Ave T5T 4V4. At 178th St; in West Edmonton Mall, at southwest end. Int corridors. **Pets:** Accepted. SAVE 🌿 🍴 🛗 🛜 ✕ 🗄 💻

🅐 ▼▼▼ Four Points by Sheraton Edmonton South 🏨

(780) 465-7931. **$125-$225.** 7230 Argyll Rd T6C 4A6. Hwy 2 (Gateway Blvd), 2.3 mi (3.7 km) e at 63rd Ave (which becomes Argyll Rd); at 75th St. Int corridors. **Pets:** Other species. $25 daily fee/pet. Designated rooms, service with restrictions, crate.

SAVE 🍴 🛗 🗙 🛜 ✕ 🗄 💻

▼▼◆ Holiday Inn Express & Suites Edmonton South 🏨

(780) 440-5000. **$129-$159.** 2440 Calgary Tr NW T6J 5J6. Hwy 2 (Gateway Blvd), just w at 31st Ave, 0.5 mi (0.8 km) s on 104th St; Hwy 2 (Gateway Blvd) northbound, just w at 23rd Ave, just n. Int corridors. **Pets:** Other species. $20 daily fee/room. Designated rooms, service with restrictions, supervision. 🛗 🛗 🛜 ✕ 🗄 💻

🅐 ▼▼◆ Holiday Inn Express Edmonton Downtown 🏨

(780) 423-2450. **$139-$209.** 10010 104th St T5J 0Z1. Corner of 100th Ave; center. Int corridors. **Pets:** Accepted.

SAVE 🌿 🛗 🛗 🗙 🛜 ✕ 🗄 💻

▼▼▼ Metterra Hotel on Whyte 🏨

(780) 465-8150. **$144-$225.** 10454 82nd Ave (Whyte Ave) T6E 4Z7. Just e of 105th St. Int corridors. **Pets:** Accepted.

🛗 🛜 ✕ 🗄 💻

▼▼▼ Quality Inn West Harvest 🏨 🐾

(780) 484-8000. **$114-$144.** 17803 Stony Plain Rd NW T5S 1B4. Jct Hwy 16A (Stony Plain Rd) and 178th St. Int corridors. **Pets:** Medium, other species. $20 daily fee/pet. Designated rooms, service with restrictions, supervision. 🍴 🛜 ✕ 🗄 💻

🅐 ▼▼◆▼ Radisson Hotel and Convention Centre 🏨

(780) 468-5400. **$169-$299, 7 day notice.** 4520 76th Ave T6B 0A5. Hwy 14, just s via 50th St exit, just e. Int corridors. **Pets:** Accepted.

SAVE 🍴 🛗 🗙 🛜 🗄 💻

▼▼◆▼ Radisson Hotel Edmonton South 🏨 🐾

(780) 437-6010. **Call for rates.** 4440 Gateway Blvd NW T6H 5C2. Between Whitemud Dr and 45th Ave. Int corridors. **Pets:** Other species. $10 daily fee/pet. Designated rooms, service with restrictions, supervision. 🌿 🍴 🛗 🗙 🛜 ✕ 🗄 💻

🅐 ▼▼▼ Sands Inn & Suites 🅜

(780) 474-5476. **$109-$119.** 12340 Fort Rd T5B 4H5. Hwy 16 (Yellowhead Tr) exit 392, just s. Int corridors. **Pets:** Medium, dogs only. $100 deposit/room, $20 daily fee/pet. Designated rooms, service with restrictions. SAVE 🍴 🛗 🛜 🗄 💻

🅐 ▼▼▼ Sawridge Inn Edmonton South 🏨

(780) 438-1222. **$109-$189.** 4235 Gateway Blvd T6J 5H2. Just s of Whitemud Dr. Int corridors. **Pets:** Accepted.

SAVE 🌿 🍴 🛗 ✕ 🗄 💻

▼▼ Super 8 Edmonton South 🏨

(780) 433-8688. **$120-$200.** 3610 Gateway Blvd T6J 7H8. Jct 36th Ave. Int corridors. **Pets:** Accepted. 🛗 🛗 🛜 ✕ 🗄 💻

▼▼▼ The Sutton Place Hotel Edmonton 🏨

(780) 428-7111. **Call for rates.** 10235 101st St T5J 3E9. Jct 102nd Ave and 101st St. Int corridors. **Pets:** Accepted.

🌿 🍴 🛗 🗙 🛜 ✕ 🗄 💻

🅐 ▼▼▼ Travelodge Edmonton East 🏨

(780) 474-0456. **$92-$104.** 3414 118th Ave T5W 0Z4. 5 mi (8 km) e of Capilano Dr, 0.6 mi (1 km) s from W Hwy 16 (Yellowhead Tr) exit Victoria Tr. Int corridors. **Pets:** Small, dogs only. $300 deposit/room, $35 one-time fee/room. Designated rooms, service with restrictions, supervision. SAVE 🌿 🍴 🛜 🗄 💻

▼▼▼ Varscona Hotel on Whyte 🏨

(780) 434-6111. **$126-$207.** 8208 106th St T6E 6R9. Corner of 82nd Ave (Whyte Ave) and 106th St. Int corridors. **Pets:** Accepted.

🌿 🍴 🛜 ✕ 🗄 💻

ⒸⒶ ♦♦ West Edmonton Mall Inn H

(780) 444-9378. $129-$199, 3 day notice. 17504 90th Ave T5T 6L6. From Whitemud Dr exit 170th St N, just w. Int corridors.
Pets: Accepted. [SAVE] [&M] [≋] [✕] [🛏] [💻]

ⒸⒶ ♦♦♦ The Westin Edmonton H ☺

(780) 426-3636. $119-$550. 10135 100th St T5J 0N7. Jct 101st Ave. Int corridors. Pets: Designated rooms, service with restrictions, supervision.
[SAVE] [ECO] [❢] [≋] [✕] [≋] [✕] [🛏] [💻]

♦♦♦ Wingate Inn Edmonton West H

(780) 443-1000. $136-$239. 18220 100th Ave T5S 2V2. From Anthony Henday Dr, 0.9 mi (1.5 km) e; at 182nd St. Int corridors.
Pets: Accepted. [❢] [≋] [≋] [✕] [🛏] [💻]

EDSON

ⒸⒶ ♦♦ BEST WESTERN High Road Inn H

(780) 712-2378. $146-$166. 300 52nd St T7E 1V8. On 2nd Ave; center. Int corridors. Pets: Accepted. [SAVE] [⬛] [❢] [&M] [≋] [≋] [🛏] [💻]

♦♦♦ Lakeview Inn & Suites Edson Airport West H

(780) 723-7508. Call for rates. 528 63rd St T7E 1M1. Hwy 16, west end of town. Int corridors. Pets: Accepted.
[ECO] [&M] [≋] [✕] [🛏] [💻]

ⒸⒶ ♦♦♦ Ramada Edson H

(780) 723-9797. $74-$134. 4536 2nd Ave T7E 1C3. 0.6 mi (1 km) e on Hwy 16. Int corridors. Pets: Small, other species. $10 daily fee/pet. Designated rooms, service with restrictions, crate. [SAVE] [≋] [🛏] [💻]

FORT MACLEOD

ⒸⒶ ♦ Sunset Motel M

(403) 553-4448. $78-$88. 104 Hwy 3 W T0L 0Z0. 0.6 mi (1 km) w on Hwy 2 and 3. Ext corridors. Pets: Accepted. [SAVE] [≋] [🛏] [💻]

FORT MCMURRAY

♦♦♦ Clearwater Suite Hotel H

(780) 799-7676. Call for rates. 4 Haineault St T9H 1L6. Hwy 63 (Sakitawaw Tr) exit Hardin St, just n, just e on Franklin Ave, then just s. Int corridors. Pets: Small, dogs only. $500 deposit/room, $25 daily fee/room. Designated rooms, service with restrictions, crate.
[ECO] [✕] [≋] [✕] [🛏] [💻]

♦♦♦ Vantage Inn & Suites H

(780) 713-4111. Call for rates. 200 Parent Way T9H 5E6. 3.1 mi (5 km) s on Hwy 63 (Sakitawaw Tr). Int corridors. Pets: Other species. $20 daily fee/pet. Designated rooms, service with restrictions, crate.
[ECO] [≋] [🛏] [💻]

FORT SASKATCHEWAN

♦♦♦ The Kanata H

(780) 998-2770. Call for rates. 9820 86th Ave T8L 4P4. Just sw of jct Hwy 15/21 and 101st St. Int corridors. Pets: Accepted.
[&M] [≋] [✕] [🛏] [💻]

♦♦♦ Lakeview Inns & Suites H

(780) 998-7888. Call for rates. 10115 88th Ave T8L 2T1. Just w of jct Hwy 15/21 and 101st St. Int corridors. Pets: Accepted.
[ECO] [❢] [≋] [🛏] [💻]

♦♦♦ Super 8 Hotel-Fort Saskatchewan H

(780) 998-2898. $118-$194. 8750 84th St T8L 4P5. Just e of jct Hwy 15/21. Int corridors. Pets: Accepted. [❢] [≋] [≋] [🛏] [💻]

GRANDE PRAIRIE

ⒸⒶ ♦♦♦ BEST WESTERN Grande Prairie Hotel & Suites H ☺

(780) 402-2378. $150-$190. 10745 117th Ave T8V 7N6. Corner of Hwy 43 (100th Ave) and 117th Ave. Int corridors. Pets: Medium. $35 one-time fee/room. Designated rooms, service with restrictions, supervision.
[SAVE] [ECO] [❢] [≋] [≋] [🛏] [💻]

♦♦♦ Holiday Inn Hotel & Suites H

(780) 402-6886. $149-$209. 9816 107th St T8V 8E7. Jct Hwy 43 (100th Ave) and 40 (108th St). Int corridors. Pets: $30 daily fee/room. Designated rooms, service with restrictions, supervision.
[ECO] [❢] [&M] [≋] [✕] [≋] [🛏] [💻]

♦♦♦ Motel 6 Grande Prairie #5709 H

(780) 830-7744. Call for rates. 15402 101st St T8V 0P7. Jct Hwy 2 and 43 (100th Ave), just s. Int corridors. Pets: Other species. Service with restrictions, crate. [ECO] [&M] [≋] [🛏] [💻]

♦♦♦ Paradise Inn & Conference Centre Grande Prairie Airport H

(780) 539-6000. Call for rates. 11201 100th Ave T8V 5M6. 1.8 mi (2.9 km) w on Hwy 2. Int corridors. Pets: Accepted.
[ECO] [❢] [≋] [🛏] [💻]

♦♦♦ Podollan Inn & Spa H

(780) 830-2000. $189-$239, 3 day notice. 10612 99th Ave T8V 8E8. Jct Hwy 43 (100th Ave) and 40 (108th St), just e. Int corridors.
Pets: Accepted. [❢] [≋] [✕] [🛏] [💻]

♦♦♦ Pomeroy Hotel H

(780) 532-5221. $149-$179. 11633 100th St T8V 3Y4. Jct Hwy 43 (100th Ave) and 116th Ave. Int corridors. Pets: Accepted.
[ECO] [❢] [&M] [≋] [✕] [≋] [🛏] [💻]

♦♦♦ Pomeroy Inn & Suites, Grande Prairie H

(780) 831-2999. $161-$185. 11710 102nd St T8V 7S7. 102nd St at 117th Ave. Int corridors. Pets: Accepted. [ECO] [&M] [≋] [≋] [🛏] [💻]

♦♦ Service Plus Inns and Suites H

(780) 538-3900. $139-$305. 10810 107A Ave T8V 7A9. 1.4 mi (2.2 km) w on Hwy 2, just n. Int corridors. Pets: Accepted. [≋] [≋] [🛏] [💻]

♦ Stanford Inn H

(780) 539-5678. Call for rates. 11401 100th Ave T8V 5M6. Jct Hwy 2 and 43 (100th Ave), just e of 116th St. Ext/int corridors. Pets: Medium. $10 daily fee/pet. Designated rooms, service with restrictions, crate.
[ECO] [❢] [≋] [🛏] [💻]

♦♦ Stonebridge Hotel H

(780) 539-5561. Call for rates. 12102 100th St T8V 5P1. 100th St at 121st Ave. Int corridors. Pets: Accepted. [❢] [≋] [🛏] [💻]

♦♦ Super 8 H

(780) 532-8288. $137-$190. 10050 116th Ave T8V 4K5. 102nd St at 117th Ave. Int corridors. Pets: Accepted. [ECO] [≋] [≋] [🛏] [💻]

GRIMSHAW

ⒸⒶ ♦♦♦ Pomeroy Inn & Suites H

(780) 332-2000. Call for rates. 4311 51st St T0H 1W0. On Hwy 2; south end of town. Int corridors. Pets: Accepted.
[SAVE] [ECO] [≋] [≋] [🛏] [💻]

HIGH LEVEL

ⒸⒶ ♦♦♦ BEST WESTERN PLUS Mirage Hotel & Resort H

(780) 821-1000. $170-$220. 9616 Hwy 58 T0H 1Z0. Jct Hwy 35 and 58; north end of town. Ext/int corridors. Pets: Accepted.
[SAVE] [❢] [≋] [≋] [🛏] [💻]

♦♦ Super 8 High Level H

(780) 841-3448. $135-$179. 9502 114th Ave T0H 1Z0. Hwy 35, just se; south end of town. Ext/int corridors. Pets: Accepted.
[ECO] [&M] [≋] [≋] [🛏] [💻]

HIGH PRAIRIE

♦♦ Peavine Inn & Suites H

(780) 523-2398. Call for rates. 3905 51st Ave T0G 1E0. Hwy 2, just n; east end of town. Ext/int corridors. Pets: Accepted.
[❢] [≋] [≋] [🛏] [💻]

HIGH RIVER

▼▼ ▼▼ Heritage Inn Hotel & Convention Centre H

(403) 652-3834. **$132-$188.** 1104 11th Ave SE T1V 1M4. Hwy 2 exit 194B, 0.5 mi (0.8 km) w. Int corridors. **Pets:** Medium, dogs only. $20 daily fee/pet. Designated rooms, service with restrictions, crate.

▼▼▼▼ Ramada Inn & Suites High River H

(403) 603-3183. **Call for rates.** 1512 13th Ave SE T1V 2B1. Hwy 2 exit 194B, just w. Int corridors. **Pets:** Accepted.

▼▼ ▼▼ Super 8 H

(403) 652-4448. **$125-$160.** 1601 13th Ave SE T1V 2B1. Hwy 2 exit 194B, just w. Int corridors. **Pets:** Accepted.

HINTON

ⓐ ▼▼ ▼▼ BEST WESTERN White Wolf Inn H

(780) 865-7777. **$135-$155, 7 day notice.** 828 Carmichael Ln T7V 1T1. At west end of town; just off Hwy 16. Ext corridors. **Pets:** Accepted.

▼▼ ▼▼ Lakeview Inns & Suites H

(780) 865-2575. **Call for rates.** 500 Smith St T7V 2A1. 1.1 mi (1.7 km) e on Hwy 16. Ext/int corridors. **Pets:** Accepted.

▼▼ Overlander Mountain Lodge CI

(780) 866-2330. **Call for rates.** 27010 Hwy 16 T7V 1X5. Hwy 16, 15 mi (24 km) w; just outside Jasper National Park gates. Ext/int corridors. **Pets:** Accepted.

INNISFAIL

ⓐ ▼▼▼▼ BEST WESTERN Innisfail Inn H

(403) 227-4405. **$140-$150.** 5010 40th Ave T4G 1Z1. Hwy 2 exit Hwy 54 (Innisfail/Caroline), just w. Int corridors. **Pets:** Medium, dogs only. $20 daily fee/pet. Designated rooms, service with restrictions, supervision.

JASPER

ⓐ ▼▼▼▼ BEST WESTERN Jasper Inn & Suites H

(780) 852-4461. **$120-$253, 3 day notice.** 98 Geikie St T0E 1E0. Corner of Geikie and Bonhomme sts. Ext/int corridors. **Pets:** Accepted.

▼▼ ▼▼ Chateau Jasper H ❧

(780) 852-5644. **$137-$278.** 96 Geikie St T0E 1E0. Corner of Juniper and Geikie sts. Int corridors. **Pets:** Large, other species. $15 daily fee/room. Designated rooms, service with restrictions, crate.

ⓐ ▼▼▼▼ The Fairmont Jasper Park Lodge H

(780) 852-3301. **Call for rates.** 1 Old Lodge Rd T0E 1E0. 3 mi (4.8 km) ne via Hwy 16, 2 mi (3.2 km) se off highway via Maligne Rd, follow signs. Ext corridors. **Pets:** Accepted.

▼▼ ▼▼ Lobstick Lodge H ❧

(780) 852-4431. **$127-$283.** 94 Geikie St T0E 1E0. Corner of Geikie and Juniper sts. Int corridors. **Pets:** Large, other species. $15 daily fee/room. Designated rooms, service with restrictions, crate.

▼▼ ▼▼ Marmot Lodge M ❧

(780) 852-4471. **Call for rates.** 86 Connaught Dr T0E 1E0. 1 mi (1.6 km) ne. Ext corridors. **Pets:** Large, other species. $15 daily fee/room. Designated rooms, service with restrictions, crate.

▼▼ ▼▼ Patricia Lake Bungalows CA

(780) 852-3560. **$99-$329, 7 day notice.** Pyramid Lake Rd T0E 1E0. 3 mi (4.8 km) nw via Pyramid Lake Rd. Ext corridors. **Pets:** Medium, dogs only. $12 daily fee/pet. Designated rooms, service with restrictions, supervision.

▼▼▼▼ Pyramid Lake Resort H ❧

(780) 852-4900. **Call for rates.** Pyramid Lake Rd T0E 1E0. From Connaught Dr, 3.8 mi (6 km) nw. Ext corridors. **Pets:** Large, other species. $15 daily fee/room. Designated rooms, service with restrictions, crate.

ⓐ ▼▼▼▼ Sawridge Inn & Conference Centre Jasper H ❧

(780) 852-5111. **$98-$409, 3 day notice.** 76 Connaught Dr T0E 1E0. 1.1 mi (1.7 km) e. Int corridors. **Pets:** Dogs only. $20 daily fee/pet. Designated rooms, service with restrictions, supervision.

▼▼ ▼▼ Sunwapta Falls Rocky Mountain Lodge CA

(780) 852-4852. **$119-$479, 3 day notice.** Hwy 93 T0E 1E0. 34.7 mi (55 km) s on Icefields Pkwy (Hwy 93). Ext corridors. **Pets:** Accepted.

▼▼ ▼▼ Tonquin Inn M ❧

(780) 852-4987. **$135-$275.** 100 Juniper St T0E 1E0. Corner of Juniper and Geikie sts. Ext corridors. **Pets:** Medium. $25 one-time fee/pet. Designated rooms, service with restrictions, crate.

KANANASKIS

▼▼▼▼ Delta Lodge at Kananaskis H

(403) 591-7711. **$179-$699, 3 day notice.** Kananaskis Village T0L 2H0. Trans-Canada Hwy 1, 14.7 mi (23.5 km) s on Hwy 40 (Kananaskis Tr), 1.8 mi (3 km) on Kananaskis Village access road, follow signs. Int corridors. **Pets:** Accepted.

LAKE LOUISE

ⓐ ▼▼▼▼ The Fairmont Chateau Lake Louise H

(403) 522-3511. **$299-$599, 3 day notice.** 111 Lake Louise Dr T0L 1E0. 1.8 mi (3 km) up the hill from the village. Int corridors. **Pets:** Accepted.

▼▼ ▼▼ Lake Louise Inn H

(403) 522-3791. **Call for rates.** 210 Village Rd T0L 1E0. Just w of 4-way stop. Ext/int corridors. **Pets:** Medium, dogs only. $50 one-time fee/room. Designated rooms, service with restrictions, supervision.

LEDUC

▼▼ ▼▼ Days Inn Edmonton Airport H

(780) 986-6550. **Call for rates.** 5705 50th St T9E 6Z8. 1.2 mi (2 km) ne of jct Hwy 2 and 39. Int corridors. **Pets:** Accepted.

LETHBRIDGE

ⓐ ▼▼▼▼ Coast Lethbridge Hotel & Conference Centre H

(403) 327-5701. **Call for rates.** 526 Mayor Magrath Dr S T1J 3M2. Hwy 3 (Crowsnest Tr) exit Mayor Magrath Dr S, just s. Int corridors. **Pets:** Medium. $15 daily fee/pet. Designated rooms, service with restrictions, supervision.

▼▼ ▼▼ Comfort Inn H

(403) 320-8874. **$109-$179.** 3226 Fairway Plaza Rd S T1K 7T5. Hwy 3 (Crowsnest Tr) exit Mayor Magrath Dr S, 1.8 mi (3 km) s, then just e on 24th Ave. Int corridors. **Pets:** Accepted.

▼▼ ▼▼ Days Inn Lethbridge H

(403) 327-6000. **$103-$150.** 100 3rd Ave S T1J 4L2. Corner of 3rd Ave and Scenic Dr; center. Ext/int corridors. **Pets:** Medium. $10 daily fee/pet. Designated rooms, service with restrictions, supervision.

▼▼▼▼ Holiday Inn Express Hotel & Suites Lethbridge H

(403) 394-9292. **$133-$181.** 120 Stafford Dr S T1J 4W4. Hwy 3 (Crowsnest Tr) exit Stafford Dr, just s; downtown. Int corridors. **Pets:** Other species. $25 one-time fee/room. Designated rooms, supervision.

▼▼▼ **Holiday Inn Hotel Lethbridge** 🄷

(403) 380-5050. **$139-$199.** 2375 Mayor Magrath Dr S T1K 7M1. Hwy 3 (Crowsnest Tr) exit Mayor Magrath Dr S, 1.8 mi (3 km) s, then just e on 22nd St. Int corridors. **Pets:** Accepted.

⬛ 🍴 ⊇ ✕ 📶 ✕ 🔋 💻

Ⓐ ▼▼▼ **Lethbridge Lodge Hotel and Conference Centre** 🄷

(403) 328-1123. **$99-$179.** 320 Scenic Dr T1J 4B4. Jct 4th Ave S; center. Int corridors. **Pets:** Other species. $15 daily fee/pet. Designated rooms, service with restrictions, supervision.

⬛ ⬛ 🍴 ⊇ 📶 ✕ 🔋 💻

▼▼ **Quality Inn & Suites** 🄷

(403) 331-6440. **$119-$218.** 4070 2nd Ave S T1J 3Z2. Hwy 3 (Crowsnest Tr), just s on WT Hill Blvd, just e. Int corridors. **Pets:** Accepted. 🚶 ⊇ 📶 🔋 💻

▼▼ **Sandman Hotel Lethbridge** 🄷

(403) 328-1111. **$99-$149.** 421 Mayor Magrath Dr S T1J 3L8. Hwy 3 (Crowsnest Tr) exit Mayor Magrath Dr S, just s. Int corridors. **Pets:** Accepted. ⬛ 🍴 ⊇ 📶 ✕ 🔋 💻

LLOYDMINSTER

▼▼ **Days Hotel & Suites Lloydminster** 🄷

(780) 875-4404. **$160-$240.** 5411 44th St T9V 0A9. 0.5 mi (0.8 km) w on Hwy 16 from jct Hwy 17. Int corridors. **Pets:** Accepted.

🍴 ⊇ 📶 🔋 💻

MEDICINE HAT

Ⓐ ▼▼▼ **BEST WESTERN PLUS Sun Country** 🄷

(403) 527-3700. **$120-$190.** 722 Redcliff Dr T1A 5E3. On Trans-Canada Hwy 1, 0.3 mi (0.4 km) w of jct Hwy 3; access on 7th St SW. Ext/int corridors. **Pets:** Accepted.

⬛ ⬛ 🚶 ⊇ ✕ 📶 ✕ 🔋 💻

Ⓐ ▼▼ **Comfort Inn & Suites** 🄷 🐾

(403) 504-1700. **$105-$225.** 2317 Trans-Canada Way SE T1B 4E9. Trans-Canada Hwy 1, just n on Dunmore Rd, just w. Int corridors. **Pets:** Large, other species. $25 daily fee/room. Designated rooms, service with restrictions, crate. ⬛ ⬛ ⊇ 📶 ✕ 🔋 💻

▼▼▼ **Holiday Inn Express Hotel & Suites** 🄷

(403) 504-5151. **Call for rates.** 9 Strachan Bay SE T1B 4Y2. Trans-Canada Hwy 1, just s on Dunmore Rd, just e; east end of city. Int corridors. **Pets:** Accepted. ⬛ 🚶 ⊇ 📶 ✕ 🔋 💻

▼▼▼ **Medicine Hat Lodge Resort, Casino & Spa** 🄷

(403) 529-2222. **$127-$131.** 1051 Ross Glen Dr SE T1B 3T8. Trans-Canada Hwy 1, just n on Dunmore Rd. Int corridors. **Pets:** Accepted.

🍴 🚶 ⊇ ✕ 📶 🔋 💻

▼ **Motel 6 Medicine Hat** 🄷

(403) 527-1749. **$95-$110, 3 day notice.** 20 Strachan Ct SE T1B 4R7. Trans-Canada Hwy 1, just s on Dunmore Rd, just w; southeast end of city. Int corridors. **Pets:** Other species. Service with restrictions, crate.

⬛ 🚶 📶 🔋

MORLEY

▼▼▼ **Stoney Nakoda Resort & Casino** 🄷

(403) 881-2830. **$89-$169.** Jct Trans-Canada Hwy 1 and Hwy 40 T0L 1N0. Jct Hwy 40, just s. Int corridors. **Pets:** Medium. $10 daily fee/pet. Designated rooms, service with restrictions, crate.

🍴 ⊇ 📶 🔋 💻

NISKU

Ⓐ ▼▼▼ **Four Points by Sheraton Edmonton International Airport** 🄷

(780) 770-9099. **$129-$189.** 403 11th Ave T9E 7N2. Hwy 2 exit Edmonton International Airport/Nisku Business Park (10th Ave), 0.5 mi (0.9 km) e. Int corridors. **Pets:** Accepted. ⬛ 🍴 🚶 📶 ✕ 🔋 💻

OKOTOKS

Ⓐ ▼▼▼ **BEST WESTERN PLUS Okotoks Inn & Suites** 🄷

(403) 995-6262. **Call for rates.** 100 Southbank Rd T1S 0N3. Hwy 2 exit 209 (Hwy 7), 2.7 mi (4.5 km) w. Int corridors. **Pets:** Accepted.

⬛ 📶 ✕ 🔋 💻

▼▼ **Lakeview Inn & Suites** 🄷

(403) 938-7400. **$114-$134, 14 day notice.** 22 Southridge Dr T1S 1N1. Hwy 2 exit 222 (Hwy 2A), 2.4 mi (4 km) s to Southridge Dr. Int corridors. **Pets:** Accepted. ⬛ 📶 🔋 💻

OLDS

▼▼▼ **Ramada Olds** 🄷

(403) 507-8349. **$130-$150.** 500 6700 46th St T4H 0A2. Hwy 2 exit 340B (Hwy 27), 4.2 mi (7 km) w. Int corridors. **Pets:** Accepted.

🚶 ✕ 📶 ✕ 🔋 💻

PINCHER CREEK

▼▼ **Heritage Inn & Hotel Convention Centre Pincher Creek** 🄷

(403) 627-5000. **$125-$269.** 919 Waterton Ave (Hwy 6) T0K 1W0. Jct Hwy 785, just s. Int corridors. **Pets:** Medium, dogs only. $20 daily fee/pet. Designated rooms, service with restrictions, crate.

🍴 🚶 📶 ✕ 🔋 💻

▼▼▼ **Ramada Inn & Suites** 🄷

(403) 627-3777. **$140-$250.** 1132 Table Mountain St T0K 1W0. Hwy 3 (Crowsnest Tr), 1.3 mi (2.1 km) s on Hwy 6. Ext/int corridors. **Pets:** Accepted. ⬛ 🚶 📶 ✕ 🔋 💻

RED DEER *(Restaurants p. 646)*

Ⓐ ▼▼▼ **BEST WESTERN PLUS Red Deer Inn & Suites** 🄷 🐾

(403) 346-3555. **$134-$149.** 6839 66th St T4P 3T5. Hwy 2 exit 401 (67th St), just e. Int corridors. **Pets:** Other species. $20 daily fee/room. Designated rooms, service with restrictions, supervision.

⬛ ⬛ 🚶 ⊇ 📶 ✕ 🔋 💻

▼▼▼ **Comfort Inn & Suites** 🄷

(403) 348-0025. **$135-$210.** 6846 66th St T4P 3T5. Hwy 2 exit 401 (67th St), just e. Int corridors. **Pets:** Accepted. 🚶 📶 🔋 💻

▼ **Motel 6 Red Deer** 🄷

(403) 340-1749. **$91-$109, 7 day notice.** 900-5001 19th St T4R 3R1. Hwy 2 exit 394 (Gaetz Ave), just w; in Southpointe Common Shopping District. Int corridors. **Pets:** Other species. Service with restrictions, crate. ⬛ 📶 🔋 💻

Ⓐ ▼▼▼ **Quality Inn North Hill** 🄷

(403) 343-8800. **$116-$139.** 7150 50th Ave T4N 6A5. Hwy 2 exit 401 (67th St), 1.7 mi (2.9 km) e, then 0.5 mi (0.8 km) n. Int corridors. **Pets:** Dogs only. $10 daily fee/room. Designated rooms, service with restrictions, crate. ⬛ 🍴 🚶 📶 ✕ 🔋 💻

Ⓐ ▼▼▼ **Ramada Red Deer Hotel & Suites** 🄷

(403) 342-4445. **$118-$142.** 6853 66th St T4P 3T5. Hwy 2 exit 401 (67th St), just e. Int corridors. **Pets:** Accepted.

⬛ 🚶 📶 🔋 💻

Ⓐ ▼▼▼ **Red Deer Lodge Hotel and Conference Centre** 🄷

(403) 346-8841. **Call for rates.** 4311 49th Ave T4N 5Y7. Hwy 2 exit 394 (Gaetz Ave), 2.6 mi (4.2 km) n. Int corridors. **Pets:** Accepted.

⬛ ⬛ ✚ 🍴 🚶 ✕ 📶 🔋 💻

▼▼▼ **Sandman Hotel Red Deer** 🄷

(403) 343-7400. **$119-$189.** 2818 Gaetz Ave T4R 1M4. 1 mi (1.6 km) n on Hwy 2A (Gaetz Ave). Int corridors. **Pets:** Other species. $10 daily fee/pet. Designated rooms, service with restrictions.

⬛ 🍴 🚶 📶 🔋 💻

△△ ▼▼▼▼ Sheraton Red Deer Hotel 🄷

(403) 346-2091. **$159-$299.** 3310 50th Ave T4N 3X9. 1.3 mi (2 km) n on Hwy 2A (Gaetz Ave). Int corridors. **Pets:** Accepted.

[SAVE] 🍴 🏊 ⊠ 📶 ⊠ 🛗 🖥 🖵

RIMBEY

△△ ▼▼▼▼ BEST WESTERN Rimstone Ridge Hotel 🄷 🐾

(403) 843-2999. **$145-$150.** 5501 50th Ave T0C 2J0. Hwy 20, 1.2 mi (2 km) e. Int corridors. **Pets:** Medium, dogs only. $20 daily fee/pet. Designated rooms, service with restrictions, crate.

[SAVE] 🍴 🏊 📶 ⊠ 🛗 🖵

ROCKY MOUNTAIN HOUSE

△△ ▼▼▼ BEST WESTERN Rocky Mountain House Inn & Suites 🄷 🐾

(403) 844-3100. **$160.** 4407 41st Ave T4T 1A5. Hwy 11 and 22, just w on 42nd Ave, just s; east end of town. **Pets:** $20 daily fee/pet. Service with restrictions, crate. [SAVE] [ECO] 🏊 📶 🛗 🖵

▼▼▼ Rocky Mountain House Canalta 🄷

(403) 846-0088. **Call for rates.** 4406 41st Ave T4T 1J6. Hwy 11 and 22, just w on 42nd Ave, just s; east end of town. Ext/int corridors. **Pets:** Accepted. [ECO] [&M] 🏊 📶 ⊠ 🛗 🖵

ST. ALBERT

△△ ▼▼▼▼ BEST WESTERN PLUS The Inn at St. Albert 🄷

(780) 470-3800. **$150-$230.** 460 St. Albert Tr T8N 5J9. Hwy 2 (St. Albert Tr), just w at Lennox Dr. Int corridors. **Pets:** Accepted.

[SAVE] 🏊 📶 ⊠ 🛗 🖵

SHERWOOD PARK

▼▼ Franklin's Inn 🄷

(780) 467-1234. **Call for rates.** 2016 Sherwood Dr T8A 3X3. At Granada Blvd. Int corridors. **Pets:** Accepted. 🍴 📶 🛗 🖵

▼▼▼ MainStay Suites East Edmonton/Sherwood Park 🄷

(780) 570-8080. **$129-$174.** 201 Palisades Way T8H 0N3. Hwy 16 exit 403 (Sherwood Dr), 0.9 mi (1.5 km) s. Int corridors. **Pets:** Accepted. [&M] 📶 🛗 🖵

▼▼ Ramada Limited-Edmonton East/Sherwood Park 🄷

(780) 467-6727. **$125-$175.** 30 Broadway Blvd T8H 2A2. Hwy 16 exit Broadmoor Blvd, 1.2 mi (2 km) s. Int corridors. **Pets:** Accepted. 📶 ⊠ 🛗 🖵

SLAVE LAKE

▼▼▼ Lakeview Inns & Suites 🄷

(780) 849-9500. **$108-$148.** 1550 Holmes Tr SE T0G 2A3. Hwy 2, just n; east end of town. Int corridors. **Pets:** Accepted. [ECO] 📶 🛗 🖵

STETTLER

△△ ▼▼▼ Ramada Inn & Suites 🄷

(403) 742-6555. **$50-$149.** 6711 49th Ave T0C 2L1. Jct Hwy 56 and 11, 0.7 mi (1.2 km) w. Int corridors. **Pets:** Accepted.

[SAVE] [&M] 📶 ⊠ 🛗 🖵

STONY PLAIN

△△ ▼▼▼▼ BEST WESTERN Sunrise Inn & Suites 🄷

(780) 968-1716. **$142-$157.** 3101 43rd Ave T7Z 1L1. Hwy 16A (Township Rd 530), just s at S Park Dr, just e. Int corridors. **Pets:** Accepted. [SAVE] 🏊 ⊠ 📶 ⊠ 🛗 🖵

▼▼ Motel 6 Stony Plain 🄷

(780) 968-5123. **Call for rates.** 66 Boulder Blvd T7Z 1V7. Just off Hwy 16A (Township Rd 530). Int corridors. **Pets:** Other species. Service with restrictions, crate. [ECO] 📶 ⊠ 🛗 🖵

▼▼ Ramada Inn & Suites 🄷

(780) 963-0222. **$120-$189.** 3301 43rd Ave T7Z 1L1. Hwy 16A (Township Rd 530), just s on S Park Dr, just e. Ext/int corridors. **Pets:** Accepted. 🍴 🏊 📶 🛗 🖵

STRATHMORE

△△ ▼▼▼ BEST WESTERN Strathmore Inn 🄷

(403) 934-5777. **$120-$230.** 550 Hwy 1 T1P 1M6. Jct Trans-Canada Hwy 1 and 817; center. Int corridors. **Pets:** Medium. $15 daily fee/room. Designated rooms, service with restrictions, supervision.

[SAVE] 🏊 📶 ⊠ 🛗 🖵

△△ ▼▼▼ Days Inn & Suites 🄷

(403) 934-1134. **$140-$175.** 400 Ranch Market T1P 0B2. Trans-Canada Hwy 1, just n at Lakeside Blvd (Centre St). Int corridors. **Pets:** Accepted. [SAVE] [&M] 🏊 📶 ⊠ 🛗 🖵

▼▼▼ Travelodge Strathmore 🄷 🐾

(403) 901-0000. **$139-$259.** 350 Ridge Rd T1P 1B5. Just n of Trans-Canada Hwy 1. Int corridors. **Pets:** Other species. $15 daily fee/room. Designated rooms, service with restrictions, supervision.

🏊 📶 🛗 🖵

SYLVAN LAKE

△△ ▼▼▼▼ BEST WESTERN PLUS Chateau Inn Sylvan Lake 🄷

(403) 887-7788. **$140-$220.** 5027 Lakeshore Dr T4S 1R3. Jct Hwy 11 and 781 (50th St), 1.9 mi (3.1 km) n, just e. Int corridors. **Pets:** Other species. $20 daily fee/pet. Designated rooms, service with restrictions.

[SAVE] 🏊 📶 ⊠ 🛗 🖵

TABER

▼▼ Heritage Inn Hotel & Convention Centre Taber 🄷

(403) 223-4424. **$103-$163.** 4830 46th Ave T1G 2A4. Jct Hwy 3 and 36 S, 1.5 mi (2.5 km) se. Int corridors. **Pets:** Medium, dogs only. $20 daily fee/pet. Designated rooms, service with restrictions, crate.

🍴 ⊠ 📶 ⊠ 🛗 🖵

THREE HILLS

△△ ▼▼▼▼ BEST WESTERN Diamond Inn 🄷 🐾

(403) 443-7889. **$119-$125.** 351 7th Ave N T0M 2A0. Jct Hwy 21/27 and 583, 1.1 mi (1.9 km) w. Int corridors. **Pets:** Other species. $50 deposit/room, $20 one-time fee/room. Designated rooms, service with restrictions, supervision. [SAVE] 📶 🛗 🖵

▼▼ Super 8 Three Hills 🄷

(403) 443-8888. **$82-$116.** 208 18th Ave N T0M 2A0. Jct Hwy 21 and 583. Int corridors. **Pets:** Medium. $100 deposit/room, $20 daily fee/pet. Designated rooms, service with restrictions, supervision.

📶 ⊠ 🛗 🖵

VALLEYVIEW

△△ ▼▼▼ Western Valley Inn 🄼

(780) 524-4000. **$130-$170, 3 day notice.** 5402 Highway St T0H 3N0. Just w of jct Hwy 43 and 49. Ext corridors. **Pets:** Accepted. [SAVE] 🍴 📶 🛗 🖵

WAINWRIGHT

△△ ▼▼▼ BEST WESTERN Wainwright Inn & Suites 🄷

(780) 845-9934. **$170-$190.** 1209 27th St T9W 0A2. Jct Hwy 14 and 41, just e. Int corridors. **Pets:** Accepted. [SAVE] [&M] 🏊 📶 🛗 🖵

▼▼▼ Ramada Wainwright 🄷

(780) 842-5010. **$99-$142.** 1510 27th St T9W 0A4. 0.3 mi (0.5 km) nw of jct Hwy 14 and 41. Ext/int corridors. **Pets:** Accepted.

📶 ⊠ 🛗 🖵

WATERTON PARK

△△ ▼▼▼ Aspen Village Inn 🄼

(403) 859-2255. **$99-$259.** 111 Windflower Ave T0K 2M0. Center. Ext corridors. **Pets:** Accepted. [SAVE] 📶 ⊠ 🐾 🛗 🖵

(AA) ▼▼▼ **Bayshore Inn Resort & Spa** [M]
(403) 859-2211. **$134-$294, 3 day notice.** 111 Waterton Ave T0K 2M0. Center. Ext/int corridors. **Pets:** Accepted.
[SAVE] [¶] [&M] [📶] [✕] [⊟] [▣]

(AA) ▼▼▼ **Waterton Lakes Resort** [H]
(403) 859-2150. **$99-$289.** 101 Clematis Ave T0K 2M0. Center. Ext/int corridors. **Pets:** Accepted. [SAVE] [¶] [⊸] [✕] [📶] [✕] [⊟] [▣]

WESTEROSE
▼▼▼ **Village Creek Country Inn** [H]
(780) 586-0006. **$129-$199, 3 day notice.** 15 Village Dr, RR 2 T0C 2V0. Hwy 2 exit 482, 17.5 mi (28 km) w on Hwy 13; in Village at Pigeon Lake. Ext/int corridors. **Pets:** Accepted.
[¶] [📶] [✕] [⊟] [▣]

WESTLOCK
(AA) ▼▼▼ **BEST WESTERN Westlock** [H]
(780) 349-4102. **$96.** 10520 100th St T7P 2C6. Jct Hwy 18 and 44, just e. Ext/int corridors. **Pets:** $20 one-time fee/room. Designated rooms, service with restrictions, crate. [SAVE] [¶] [📶] [⊟] [▣]

WETASKIWIN
(AA) ▼▼▼ **BEST WESTERN Wayside Inn** [H]
(780) 312-7300. **$130-$150.** 4103 56th St T9A 1V2. On Hwy 2A, just n of jct Hwy 13 W. Int corridors. **Pets:** Accepted.
[SAVE] [¶] [📶] [✕] [⊟] [▣]

▼▼▼ **Super 8 Wetaskiwin** [H] ❀
(780) 361-3808. **$125-$160.** 3820 56th St T9A 2B2. On Hwy 2A, just s of jct Hwy 13 W. Ext/int corridors. **Pets:** Medium, other species. $5 deposit/pet. Designated rooms, service with restrictions, crate.
[📶] [⊟] [▣]

WHITECOURT
▼▼▼ **Super 8** [H]
(780) 778-8908. **$140-$176.** 4121 Kepler St T7S 0A3. On Hwy 43, just e of Hwy 32. Int corridors. **Pets:** Accepted. [ECO] [📶] [⊟] [▣]

BRITISH COLUMBIA

100 MILE HOUSE
▼▼▼ **Super 8 100 Mile House** [M]
(250) 395-8888. **$89-$139.** 989 Alder Ave V0K 2E0. 0.6 mi (1 km) s on Hwy 97. Ext corridors. **Pets:** Accepted. [&M] [📶] [✕] [⊟] [▣]

ABBOTSFORD
(AA) ▼▼▼ **BEST WESTERN Bakerview Inn** [M] ❀
(604) 859-1341. **$99-$139.** 1821 Sumas Way V2S 4L5. Trans-Canada Hwy 1 exit 92 (Town Centre), just n on Hwy 11. Ext corridors. **Pets:** Medium. $15 one-time fee/room. Service with restrictions, crate.
[SAVE] [ECO] [⊸] [📶] [⊟] [▣]

ALDERGROVE
(AA) ▼▼▼ **BEST WESTERN PLUS Country Meadows Inn** [H]
(604) 856-9880. **$90-$259.** 3070 264th St V4W 3E1. Trans-Canada Hwy 1 exit 73 (264th St/Aldergrove), 3.1 mi (5 km) s on 264th St (Hwy 13). Int corridors. **Pets:** Medium, dogs only. $15 one-time fee/pet. Designated rooms, supervision.
[SAVE] [ECO] [¶] [&M] [⊸] [📶] [✕] [⊟] [▣]

BARRIERE
▼▼▼ **Mountain Springs Motel & RV Park** [M]
(250) 672-0090. **Call for rates.** 4253 Yellowhead Hwy V0E 1E0. 0.6 mi (1 km) s on Hwy 5 (Yellowhead Hwy). Ext corridors. **Pets:** Accepted.
[&M] [📶] [✕] [⊟] [▣]

BRENTWOOD BAY
(AA) ▼▼▼▼ **Brentwood Bay Resort & Spa** [H] ❀
(250) 544-2079. **$199-$599, 7 day notice.** 849 Verdier Ave V8M 1C5. Hwy 17 exit 18 (Brentwood Bay), 1.8 mi (3 km) w on Keating Rd, 0.9 mi (1.5 km) n on W Saanich Rd, then 0.6 mi (1 km) w to Mill Bay Ferry. Ext corridors. **Pets:** Small. $30 daily fee/room. Designated rooms, service with restrictions, crate.
[SAVE] [ECO] [¶] [&M] [⊸] [✕] [📶] [✕] [⊟] [▣]

BURNABY
▼▼▼ **Accent Inns** [H]
(604) 473-5000. **$109-$179.** 3777 Henning Dr V5C 6N5. Trans-Canada Hwy 1 exit 28 (Grandview Hwy), just n on Boundary Rd. Ext corridors. **Pets:** Accepted. [ECO] [¶] [&M] [✕] [📶] [✕] [⊟] [▣]

(AA) ▼▼▼ **BEST WESTERN PLUS Kings Inn & Conference Center** [H]
(604) 438-1383. **$119-$139.** 5411 Kingsway V5H 2G1. Trans-Canada Hwy 1 exit 29 (Willingdon Ave), 1.9 mi (3 km) s to Kingsway, then 1.2 mi (2 km) e. Ext corridors. **Pets:** Accepted.
[SAVE] [&M] [⊸] [📶] [⊟] [▣]

(AA) ▼▼▼▼ **Delta Burnaby Hotel and Conference Centre** [H] ❀
(604) 453-0750. **$139-$299.** 4331 Dominion St V5G 1B2. Trans-Canada Hwy 1 exit 29 (Willingdon Ave), just w on Canada Way, then n on Sumner St. Int corridors. **Pets:** Large. $35 deposit/pet. Service with restrictions. [SAVE] [ECO] [¶] [&M] [✕] [📶] [✕] [⊟] [▣]

▼▼▼▼ **Hilton Vancouver Metrotown** [H] ❀
(604) 438-1200. **$189-$259.** 6083 McKay Ave V5H 2W7. Trans-Canada Hwy 1 exit 29 (Willingdon Ave), 1.8 mi (3 km) s to Kingsway, then just e. Int corridors. **Pets:** Large. $49 one-time fee/room. Designated rooms, service with restrictions, supervision.
[ECO] [¶] [&M] [⊸] [📶] [✕] [⊟] [▣]

▼▼▼ **Holiday Inn Express Metrotown** [H] ❀
(604) 438-1881. **$129-$249.** 4405 Central Blvd V5H 4M3. Trans-Canada Hwy 1 exit 29 (Willingdon Ave), 3.1 mi (5 km) s to Central Blvd, then just e. Int corridors. **Pets:** Medium. $25 one-time fee/room. Designated rooms, service with restrictions, crate.
[ECO] [&M] [⊸] [📶] [✕] [⊟] [▣]

CACHE CREEK
▼▼▼ **Bonaparte Motel** [M]
(250) 457-9693. **Call for rates.** 1395 Hwy 97 N V0K 1H0. Just n of jct Trans-Canada Hwy 1. Ext corridors. **Pets:** Accepted.
[⊸] [📶] [✕] [⊟] [▣]

CAMPBELL RIVER
(AA) ▼▼▼ **BEST WESTERN PLUS Austrian Chalet** [H]
(250) 923-4231. **$115-$170.** 462 S Island Hwy V9W 1A5. 2 mi (3.2 km) s on Island Hwy 19A. Ext/int corridors. **Pets:** $250 deposit/room, $20 one-time fee/room. Designated rooms, service with restrictions, supervision. [SAVE] [&M] [⊸] [✕] [📶] [✕] [⊟] [▣]

▼▼▼ **Ocean Resort** [M]
(250) 923-4281. **Call for rates.** 4384 S Island Hwy V9H 1E8. 11 mi (18 km) s on Island Hwy 19A. Int corridors. **Pets:** Accepted.
[✕] [📶] [✕] [Ⱥ℃] [⊟] [▣]

Town Centre Inn M

(250) 287-8866. **Call for rates.** 1500 Dogwood St V9W 3A6. Follow Island Hwy 19A through town, follow signs, just e; corner of 16th Ave. Ext corridors. **Pets:** Accepted.

CASTLEGAR

Quality Inn Castlegar H

(250) 365-2177. **$94-$126.** 1935 Columbia Ave V1N 2W8. Jct Hwy 3A and 3B, just s. Ext/int corridors. **Pets:** Other species. $10 daily fee/pet. Designated rooms, service with restrictions, crate.

Super 8-Castlegar H

(250) 365-2700. **$125-$299.** 651 18th St V1N 2N1. Jct Hwy 3, just n on Hwy 22. Int corridors. **Pets:** Accepted.

CHASE

Chase Country Inn Motel M

(250) 679-3333. **$69-$109.** 576 Coburn St V0E 1M0. Jct Trans-Canada Hwy 1 and Coburn St. Ext corridors. **Pets:** Accepted.

Quaaout Lodge & Spa, Talking Rock Golf H

(250) 679-3090. **Call for rates.** 1663 Little Shuswap Lake Rd V0E 1M0. Trans-Canada Hwy 1 exit Squilax Bridge, 1.5 mi (2.5 km) w. Int corridors. **Pets:** Large. $15 daily fee/room. Designated rooms, service with restrictions, supervision.

CHEMAINUS

BEST WESTERN PLUS Chemainus Inn H

(250) 246-4181. **$137-$169.** 9573 Chemainus Rd V0R 1K5. Trans-Canada Hwy 1 exit Henry Rd, 0.9 mi (1.4 km) e. Int corridors. **Pets:** Large, dogs only. $20 daily fee/room. Designated rooms, service with restrictions, supervision.

CHETWYND

Lakeview Inns & Suites H

(250) 788-3000. **$132, 3 day notice.** 4820 N Access Rd V0C 1J0. Hwy 29 and 97, just n on 48th St, just e. Int corridors. **Pets:** Accepted.

Pomeroy Inn & Suites H

(250) 788-4800. **Call for rates.** 5200 N Access Rd V0C 1J0. Hwy 29 and 97, just n on 52nd St. Int corridors. **Pets:** Other species. $20 one-time fee/pet, $5 daily fee/pet. Designated rooms, service with restrictions, crate.

CHILLIWACK

BEST WESTERN Rainbow Country Inn H

(604) 795-3828. **$109-$149.** 43971 Industrial Way V2R 3A4. Trans-Canada Hwy 1 exit 116 (Lickman Rd). Int corridors. **Pets:** Accepted.

The Coast Chilliwack Hotel H

(604) 792-5552. **$109-$164.** 45920 First Ave V2P 7K1. Trans-Canada Hwy 1 exit 119, 1.8 mi (2.9 km) n on Vedder Rd, then just e. Int corridors. **Pets:** Accepted.

Comfort Inn M

(604) 858-0636. **$99-$159.** 45405 Luckakuck Way V2R 3C7. Trans-Canada Hwy 1 exit 119, s on Vedder Rd, then 0.6 mi (1 km) w. Int corridors. **Pets:** Small. $10 daily fee/pet. Designated rooms, service with restrictions, crate.

Travelodge Hotel Chilliwack H

(604) 792-4240. **$69-$219, 3 day notice.** 45466 Yale Rd W V2R 3Z8. Trans-Canada Hwy 1 exit 119, just n. Int corridors. **Pets:** Medium. $250 deposit/room, $10 daily fee/pet. Designated rooms, service with restrictions, supervision.

CHRISTINA LAKE

New Horizon Motel M

(250) 447-9312. **$85-$175, 14 day notice.** 2037 Hunter Frontage Rd (Hwy 3) V0H 1E2. Just e on Hwy 3. Ext corridors. **Pets:** Accepted.

CLEARWATER

Clearwater Valley Resort & KOA Kampground CA

(250) 674-3909. **Call for rates.** 373 Clearwater Valley Rd V0E 1N1. Jct Hwy 5 (Yellowhead Hwy) and Clearwater Valley Rd. Ext corridors. **Pets:** Medium. $10 daily fee/pet. Designated rooms, service with restrictions, supervision.

COMOX

Port Augusta Inn & Suites M

(250) 339-2277. **$70-$110.** 2082 Comox Ave V9M 1P8. Hwy 19A (Cliffe Ave), follow signs to Comox Ave, 2.5 mi (4 km) e. Ext/int corridors. **Pets:** Medium. $10 daily fee/room. Designated rooms, service with restrictions, supervision.

COURTENAY

Anco Inn M

(250) 334-2451. **Call for rates.** 1885 Cliffe Ave V9N 2K9. Just s of Hwy 19A Connector. Ext corridors. **Pets:** Dogs only. $10 daily fee/pet. Designated rooms, service with restrictions, supervision.

BEST WESTERN PLUS The Westerly Hotel & Convention Centre H

(250) 338-7741. **$120-$150.** 1590 Cliffe Ave V9N 2K4. Corner of Cliffe Ave and Island Hwy 19A N. Int corridors. **Pets:** Large. $15 daily fee/pet. Designated rooms, service with restrictions, supervision.

Crown Isle Resort & Golf Community H

(250) 703-5050. **$139-$279, 7 day notice.** 399 Clubhouse Dr V9N 9G3. Island Hwy 19A N, 0.9 mi (1.5 km) n on Comox Ave, 1.6 mi (2.5 km) ne on Ryan Rd to Crowne Isle Dr, then e, follow signs. Ext corridors. **Pets:** Accepted.

Holiday Inn Express & Suites Comox Valley H

(778) 225-0010. **$125-$160.** 2200 Cliffe Ave V9N 2L4. 0.6 mi (1.1 km) s on Island Hwy 19A S. Int corridors. **Pets:** Other species. $15 daily fee/room. Designated rooms, service with restrictions, supervision.

Kingfisher Oceanside Resort & Spa H

(250) 338-1323. **Call for rates.** 4330 S Island Hwy V9N 9R9. 3.8 mi (6 km) s on Island Hwy 19A S, follow signs. Ext corridors. **Pets:** $25 daily fee/room. Designated rooms, service with restrictions.

Travelodge Courtenay M

(250) 334-4491. **$93-$123.** 2605 Cliffe Ave V9N 2L8. 0.8 mi (1.2 km) s on Island Hwy 19A S. Ext corridors. **Pets:** Other species. $13 daily fee/pet. Designated rooms, service with restrictions, supervision.

CRANBROOK

BEST WESTERN Cranbrook Hotel H

(250) 417-4002. **$156-$200.** 1019 Cranbrook St N V1C 3S4. Hwy 3 and 95; center. Int corridors. **Pets:** Accepted.

Days Inn Cranbrook H

(250) 426-6683. **$109-$160.** 600 Cranbrook St N V1C 3R7. Corner of 6th St and Cranbrook St N. Int corridors. **Pets:** Accepted.

▼▼ ▼▼ Heritage Inn Hotel & Convention Centre
Cranbrook **H**

(250) 489-4301. **$114-$222.** 803 Cranbrook St N V1C 3S2. Hwy 3 and 95, just n of 6th St N. Int corridors. **Pets:** Medium, dogs only. $20 daily fee/pet. Designated rooms, service with restrictions, crate.

🏨 🛗 ⊶ 🛜 🛎 🖵

(CAA) ▼▼▼▼ St. Eugene Golf Resort & Casino **H**

(250) 420-2000. **Call for rates.** 7731 Mission Rd V1C 7E5. Hwy 3 exit Kimberley/Airport (Hwy 95A) to Mission Rd, 2.8 mi (4.5 km) n. Int corridors. **Pets:** Other species. $25 daily fee/room. Designated rooms, service with restrictions, crate.

[SAVE] [ECO] 🏨 ⊶ 🗙 🛜 🗙 🛎 🖵

CRESTON

(CAA) ▼▼ ▼▼ Skimmerhorn Inn **M**

(250) 428-4009. **Call for rates.** 2711 Hwy 3 V0B 1G0. 0.8 mi (1.3 km) e. Ext corridors. **Pets:** Dogs only. $10 daily fee/pet. Designated rooms, service with restrictions, crate. [SAVE] ⊶ 🛜 🗙 🛎 🖵

DAWSON CREEK

(CAA) ▼▼ ▼▼ Dawson Creek Super 8 **H**

(250) 782-8899. **$146-$192.** 1440 Alaska Ave V1G 1Z5. Jct Hwy 2 and 49, 0.5 mi (0.8 km) ne. Int corridors. **Pets:** Accepted.

[SAVE] 🏨 🛜 🗙 🛎 🖵

▼▼▼▼ Pomeroy Inn & Suites **H**

(250) 782-3700. **$170-$330.** 540 Hwy 2 V1G 0A4. Jct Hwy 49, 1.6 mi (2.6 km) s on 8th St (Hwy 2), just e; south end of town. Int corridors. **Pets:** Accepted. 🛗 ⊶ 🛜 🛎 🖵

(CAA) ▼▼▼▼ Stonebridge Hotel Dawson Creek **H**

(250) 782-6226. **$179-$199.** 500 Hwy 2 V1G 0A4. Jct Hwy 49, 1.6 mi (2.6 km) s on 8th St (Hwy 2), just e; south end of town. Int corridors. **Pets:** Accepted. [SAVE] [ECO] 🏨 🛗 ⊶ 🛜 🛎 🖵

DELTA

(CAA) ▼▼▼▼ The Coast Tsawwassen Inn **H** ❀

(604) 943-8221. **$113-$235.** 1665 56th St V4L 2B2. Hwy 99 exit 28 (Tsawwassen Ferries), 5 mi (8 km) s, then 0.7 mi (1.1 km) s; from Tsawwassen Ferry Terminal, 3.5 mi (5.9 km) ne, 0.7 mi (1.1 km) s. Int corridors. **Pets:** Other species. $15 daily fee/pet. Service with restrictions, supervision. [SAVE] [ECO] 🏨 🛗 ⊶ 🗙 🛜 🗙 🛎 🖵

DUNCAN

(CAA) ▼▼ ▼▼ BEST WESTERN Cowichan Valley Inn **H**

(250) 748-2722. **$129-$169.** 6474 Trans-Canada Hwy V9L 6C6. 1.8 mi (3 km) n. Int corridors. **Pets:** Medium, dogs only. $20 one-time fee/ room. Designated rooms, service with restrictions, supervision.

[SAVE] 🏨 ⊶ 🛜 🗙 🛎 🖵

FAIRMONT HOT SPRINGS

(CAA) ▼▼ ▼▼ Fairmont Hot Springs Resort **H**

(250) 345-6070. **$119-$239, 3 day notice.** 5225 Fairmont Resort Rd V0B 1L1. 1 mi (1.6 km) e off Hwy 93 and 95. Ext/int corridors. **Pets:** Accepted. [SAVE] [ECO] 🏨 ⊶ 🗙 🛜 🗙 🛎 🖵

FERNIE

(CAA) ▼▼▼▼ BEST WESTERN PLUS Fernie Mountain
Lodge **H** ❀

(250) 423-5500. **$176-$246.** 1622 7th Ave V0B 1M0. Jct Hwy 3 and 7th Ave; east end of town. Int corridors. **Pets:** Other species. $20 one-time fee/room. Designated rooms, service with restrictions, supervision.

[SAVE] [ECO] 🏨 ⊶ 🗙 🛜 🗙 🛎 🖵

▼▼▼▼ Park Place Lodge **H**

(250) 423-6871. **$148-$268.** 742 Hwy 3 V0B 1M0. At 7th St. Int corridors. **Pets:** Designated rooms, service with restrictions, supervision.

🏨 ⊶ 🗙 🛜 🗙 🛎 🖵

FORT NELSON

▼▼ ▼▼ Lakeview Inn & Suites **H**

(250) 233-5001. **$137-$147.** 4507 50th Ave S V0C 1R0. Just off Hwy 97 (Alaska Hwy); at 44th St. Int corridors. **Pets:** Accepted.

[ECO] 🗙 🛜 🛎 🖵

FORT ST. JOHN

▼▼ ▼▼ Lakeview Inns & Suites **H**

(250) 787-0779. **$130-$180.** 10103 98th Ave V1J 1P8. Corner of 100th Ave; center of downtown. Int corridors. **Pets:** Accepted.

[ECO] 🏨 🛜 🛎 🖵

(CAA) ▼▼▼▼ Pomeroy Hotel **H**

(250) 262-3233. **$179-$249, 14 day notice.** 11308 Alaska Rd V1J 5T5. Just w on Hwy 97 (Alaska Hwy). Int corridors. **Pets:** Accepted.

[SAVE] 🏨 🛗 ⊶ 🛜 🗙 🛎 🖵

▼▼ ▼▼ Pomeroy Inn & Suites **H**

(250) 262-3030. **Call for rates.** 9320 Alaska Rd V1J 6L5. Just s on Hwy 97 (Alaska Hwy). Int corridors. **Pets:** Accepted. 🛜 🛎 🖵

▼▼▼▼ Quality Inn Northern Grand **H**

(250) 787-0521. **$129-$209.** 9830 100th Ave V1J 1Y5. Center. Int corridors. **Pets:** Accepted. [ECO] 🏨 🛗 ⊶ 🗙 🛜 🛎 🖵

(CAA) ▼▼ ▼▼ Super 8-Fort St. John **H**

(250) 785-7588. **$159-$179.** 9500 W Alaska Rd V1J 6L5. Just s on Hwy 97 (Alaska Hwy). Int corridors. **Pets:** Medium. $50 one-time fee/ room, $25 daily fee/pet. Designated rooms, service with restrictions, supervision. [SAVE] [ECO] 🛗 ⊶ 🛜 🛎 🖵

FORT STEELE

▼▼▼▼ Bull River Guest Ranch **RA**

(250) 429-3760. **Call for rates.** 2975 Bull River Rd V1C 4H7. Hwy 93 and 95, 12.9 mi (21.4 km) se of town on Ft Steele-Wardner Rd, 7.2 mi (12 km) ne on gravel road; Hwy 3 and 93, 24.6 mi (41 km) e of Cranbrook, 5 mi (8.2 km) n on Ft Steele-Wardner Rd, 7.2 mi (12 km) ne on gravel road. Ext corridors. **Pets:** Accepted.

🗙 🛜 🗙 🐾 📺 🌀 🛎 🖵

GALIANO ISLAND

▼▼▼▼ Galiano Oceanfront Inn & Spa **H** ❀

(250) 539-3388. **$199-$399, 7 day notice.** 134 Madrona Dr V0N 1P0. From Sturdies Bay Ferry Terminal, just ne on Sturdies Bay Rd. Ext/int corridors. **Pets:** Other species. $50 one-time fee/room. Designated rooms, service with restrictions, crate.

🏨 🛗 🗙 🛜 🗙 🐾 🛎 🖵

GOLD BRIDGE

▼▼▼▼ Tyax Wilderness Resort & Spa **H**

(250) 238-2221. **Call for rates.** 1 Tyaughton Lake Rd V0K 1P0. 5 mi (8 km) n from Tyaughton Lake turnoff, follow signs. Int corridors. **Pets:** Accepted. 🏨 🛗 🗙 🛜 🗙 🐾

GOLDEN *(Restaurants p. 646)*

(CAA) ▼▼ ▼▼ BEST WESTERN Mountainview Inn **H** ❀

(250) 344-2333. **$110-$190.** 1024 11th St N V0A 1H2. Just w of jct Hwy 95 and Trans-Canada Hwy 1; on S Service Rd. Int corridors. **Pets:** Dogs only. $20 daily fee/pet. Designated rooms, service with restrictions, supervision. [SAVE] ⊶ 🛜 🗙 🛎 🖵

▼▼ ▼▼ Days Inn Golden **M**

(250) 344-2216. **$89-$155.** 1416 Golden View Rd V0A 1H1. On Trans-Canada Hwy 1, 1 mi (1.6 km) e of jct Hwy 95. Ext corridors. **Pets:** Small, other species. $20 daily fee/pet. Designated rooms, supervision. 🛗 ⊶ 🛜 🗙 🛎 🖵

GRAND FORKS

(CAA) ▼▼ ▼▼ Western Traveller Motel **M**

(250) 442-5566. **$74-$139, 3 day notice.** 1591 Central Ave V0H 1H0. West end of town on Hwy 3. Ext corridors. **Pets:** Medium, dogs only. $10 daily fee/pet. Designated rooms, no service, supervision.

[SAVE] 🛗 🛜 🛎 🖵

HARRISON HOT SPRINGS

⚅ ◈◈◈◈ Harrison Beach Hotel H ☀

(604) 796-1111. **$99-$269, 3 day notice.** 160 Esplanade Ave V0M 1K0. Just w. Int corridors. **Pets:** Other species. $25 daily fee/room. Designated rooms, service with restrictions, crate.

⬛ ⬛ ⬛ ⬛ ⬛ ⬛ ⬛ ⬛ ⬛

⚅ ◈◈◈ Harrison Hot Springs Resort & Spa H

(604) 796-2244. **$119-$289, 3 day notice.** 100 Esplanade Ave V0M 1K0. Just w; on lakefront. Int corridors. **Pets:** Accepted.

⬛ ⬛ ⬛ ⬛ ⬛ ⬛ ⬛ ⬛ ⬛

HOPE

⚅ ◈◈◈ Alpine Motel M

(604) 869-9931. **$85-$125.** 505 Old Hope-Princeton Way V0X 1L0. Trans-Canada Hwy 1 exit 173 westbound; exit 170 eastbound, just n from lights. Ext corridors. **Pets:** Small. $50 deposit/room, $10 daily fee/room. No service, supervision. ⬛ ⬛ ⬛

⚅ ◈◈◈ Best Continental Motel M

(604) 869-9726. **Call for rates.** 860 Fraser Ave V0X 1L0. Trans-Canada Hwy 1 exit 170 to downtown; at Fort St. Ext corridors. **Pets:** Dogs only. $7 daily fee/pet. Designated rooms, no service, supervision.

⬛ ⬛ ⬛ ⬛

⚅ ◈◈◈ Heritage Inn M

(604) 869-7166. **$78-$119.** 570 Old Hope-Princeton Way V0X 1L0. Trans-Canada Hwy 1 exit 173 westbound; exit 170 eastbound, just n from lights. Ext corridors. **Pets:** $10 daily fee/pet. Designated rooms, service with restrictions, supervision. ⬛ ⬛ ⬛ ⬛ ⬛ ⬛

⚅ ◈◈◈ Travelodge Hope M

(604) 869-9951. **$90-$145.** 350 Old Hope-Princeton Way V0X 1L0. Trans-Canada Hwy 1 exit 173 westbound; exit 170 eastbound, just n from lights. Int corridors. **Pets:** Medium. Service with restrictions, supervision. ⬛ ⬛ ⬛ ⬛ ⬛ ⬛ ⬛

HUDSON'S HOPE

◈◈◈ Sigma Inn & Suites H

(250) 783-2300. **Call for rates.** 9006 Clark Ave V0C 1V0. Hwy 29, north end of town. Int corridors. **Pets:** Accepted.

⬛ ⬛ ⬛ ⬛ ⬛ ⬛

INVERMERE

⚅ ◈◈◈ BEST WESTERN Invermere Inn H

(250) 342-9246. **$120-$160.** 1310 7th Ave V0A 1K0. Hwy 93 and 95 exit Invermere, 1.8 mi (3 km) w; center. Int corridors. **Pets:** Accepted.

⬛ ⬛ ⬛ ⬛ ⬛ ⬛

◈◈◈ Copperpoint Resort H

(250) 341-4000. **Call for rates.** 760 Cooper Rd V0A 1K2. Hwy 93 and 95, just w. Int corridors. **Pets:** Accepted.

⬛ ⬛ ⬛ ⬛ ⬛ ⬛ ⬛

KAMLOOPS

◈◈ Accent Inns M

(250) 374-8877. **$99-$179.** 1325 Columbia St W V2C 6P4. Trans-Canada Hwy 1 exit 370 (Summit Dr) westbound; exit 369 (Columbia St) eastbound, at Notre Dame Dr. Ext corridors. **Pets:** Accepted.

⬛ ⬛ ⬛ ⬛ ⬛ ⬛ ⬛ ⬛

⚅ ◈◈◈ BEST WESTERN PLUS Kamloops Hotel H ☀

(250) 374-7878. **$140-$250.** 660 Columbia St W V2C 1L1. Trans-Canada Hwy 1 exit 369 (Columbia St) eastbound; exit 370 (Summit Dr) westbound to Columbia St via City Centre, 1.1 mi (1.8 km) n. Int corridors. **Pets:** Medium, other species. $20 one-time fee/room. Designated rooms, service with restrictions, supervision.

⬛ ⬛ ⬛ ⬛ ⬛ ⬛ ⬛ ⬛

◈◈ Canadas Best Value Inn and Suites M

(250) 374-8100. **$69-$199.** 1200 Rogers Way V1S 1N5. Trans-Canada Hwy 1 exit 368 (Hillside Ave), just s. Ext corridors. **Pets:** $10 daily fee/pet. Designated rooms, service with restrictions, supervision.

⬛ ⬛ ⬛ ⬛ ⬛

◈◈◈ The Coast Kamloops Hotel & Conference Centre H

(250) 828-6660. **Call for rates.** 1250 Rogers Way V1S 1N5. Trans-Canada Hwy 1 exit 368 (Hillside Ave), just s. Int corridors. **Pets:** Dogs only. $200 deposit/room, $20 daily fee/room. Designated rooms, service with restrictions. ⬛ ⬛ ⬛ ⬛ ⬛ ⬛ ⬛ ⬛

◈◈◈ Comfort Inn & Suites H

(250) 372-0987. **$89-$199.** 1810 Rogers Pl V1S 1T7. Trans-Canada Hwy 1 exit 368 (Hillside Ave), just s. Int corridors. **Pets:** Medium, dogs only. $20 daily fee/room. Designated rooms, service with restrictions, supervision. ⬛ ⬛ ⬛ ⬛ ⬛ ⬛

◈◈◈ DoubleTree by Hilton Kamloops H

(250) 851-0026. **Call for rates.** 339 St. Paul St V2C 2J5. Between 3rd and 4th aves; downtown. Int corridors. **Pets:** Accepted.

⬛ ⬛ ⬛ ⬛ ⬛ ⬛

◈◈◈ Hampton Inn by Hilton H ☀

(250) 571-7897. **$115-$135.** 1245 Rogers Way V1S 1R9. Trans-Canada Hwy 1 exit 368 (Hillside Ave), just s via Hillside Way. Int corridors. **Pets:** Dogs only. $20 daily fee/room. Designated rooms, service with restrictions, supervision. ⬛ ⬛ ⬛ ⬛ ⬛ ⬛

◈◈◈ Holiday Inn & Suites H ☀

(250) 376-8288. **Call for rates.** 675 Tranquille Rd V2B 3H7. Trans-Canada Hwy 1 exit 374 (Jasper Ave), 2.5 mi (4 km) w on Halston Connector Rd, 1.8 mi (3 km) s on 8th St to Fortune Dr, then just s. Int corridors. **Pets:** Medium, dogs only. $20 daily fee/pet. Designated rooms, service with restrictions, supervision.

⬛ ⬛ ⬛ ⬛ ⬛ ⬛ ⬛ ⬛ ⬛

◈◈◈ Holiday Inn Express Kamloops H

(250) 372-3474. **$130-$230.** 1550 Versatile Dr V1S 1X4. Trans-Canada Hwy 1 exit 367 (Pacific Way), just w. Int corridors. **Pets:** Accepted.

⬛ ⬛ ⬛ ⬛ ⬛

◈◈ Pacific Host Inn & Suites H

(250) 372-0952. **$99-$189.** 1820 Rogers Pl V1S 1T7. Trans-Canada Hwy 1 exit 368 (Hillside Ave), just w. Int corridors. **Pets:** Dogs only. $20 daily fee/room. Service with restrictions, supervision.

⬛ ⬛ ⬛ ⬛ ⬛ ⬛ ⬛

◈◈ Quality Inn M

(250) 851-0111. **$92-$139.** 1860 Rogers Pl V1S 1T7. Trans-Canada Hwy 1 exit 368 (Hillside Ave). Int corridors. **Pets:** Accepted.

⬛ ⬛ ⬛ ⬛ ⬛

◈ Ranchland Inn M

(250) 828-8787. **$79-$125.** 2357 Trans-Canada Hwy 1 E V2C 4A8. 2.8 mi (4.5 km) e on Trans-Canada Hwy 1 exit River Rd, just w on service access road. Ext corridors. **Pets:** Medium. $20 daily fee/pet. Designated rooms, service with restrictions, supervision. ⬛ ⬛ ⬛ ⬛

⚅ ◈◈◈ Scott's Inn & Restaurant M ☀

(250) 372-8221. **$80-$130, 3 day notice.** 551 11th Ave V2C 3Y1. Trans-Canada Hwy 1 exit City Center (from eastern approach), 0.5 mi (0.9 km) w on Battle St, then just s. Ext corridors. **Pets:** Dogs only. $10 daily fee/pet. Designated rooms, service with restrictions, crate.

⬛ ⬛ ⬛ ⬛ ⬛ ⬛ ⬛ ⬛

⚅ ◈◈◈ The Thompson Hotel & Conference Centre H

(250) 374-1999. **$99-$209.** 650 Victoria St V2C 2B4. Between 6th and 7th aves; downtown. Int corridors. **Pets:** Accepted.

⬛ ⬛ ⬛ ⬛ ⬛ ⬛ ⬛ ⬛

KELOWNA

◈◈ Accent Inns H

(250) 862-8888. **Call for rates.** 1140 Harvey Ave V1Y 6E7. Corner of Hwy 97 N (Harvey Ave) and Gordon Dr. Ext corridors. **Pets:** Accepted.

BEST WESTERN PLUS Kelowna Hotel & Suites H ❀

(250) 860-1212. **$139-$230.** 2402 Hwy 97 N V1X 4J1. 0.6 mi (1 km) s of jct Hwy 97 N (Harvey Ave) and 33; corner of Leckie Rd. Int corridors. **Pets:** $20 daily fee/pet. Designated rooms, service with restrictions, crate. SAVE ECO ⊞ ⌘ 丩 & M ➷ ⊠ 🛈 ⊠ ✚ ⚏

Comfort Suites H ❀

(250) 861-1110. **$130-$220.** 2656 Hwy 97 N V1X 4J4. Jct Hwy 97 N (Harvey Ave) and 33, 0.5 mi (0.9 km) n. Int corridors. **Pets:** Large. $25 daily fee/pet. Designated rooms, service with restrictions, supervision. SAVE ECO & M ➷ 🛈 ⊠ ✚ ⚏

Delta Grand Okanagan Resort & Conference Centre H ❀

(250) 763-4500. **$159-$499, 3 day notice.** 1310 Water St V1Y 9P3. Hwy 97 (Harvey Ave), 0.6 mi (1 km) w along Water St. Int corridors. **Pets:** Medium. $35 one-time fee/room. Designated rooms, service with restrictions. ECO 丩 & M ➷ ⊠ 🛈 ⊠ ✚ ⚏

Econo Lodge M

(250) 762-3221. **$84-$254.** 1780 Gordon Dr V1Y 3H2. Hwy 97 N (Harvey Ave), just s. Ext corridors. **Pets:** Accepted. SAVE ➷ 🛈 ⊠ ✚ ⚏

Fairfield Inn & Suites by Marriott Kelowna H ❀

(250) 763-2800. **$129-$229.** 1655 Powick Rd V1X 4L1. Just s of jct Hwy 97 N (Harvey Ave) and 33. Int corridors. **Pets:** Other species. $15 daily fee/pet. Designated rooms, service with restrictions. ECO & M ➷ 🛈 ⊠ ✚ ⚏

Four Points by Sheraton Kelowna Airport H

(250) 807-2000. **$129-$269.** 5505 Airport Way V1V 3C3. Hwy 97 (Harvey Ave), just w. Int corridors. **Pets:** Accepted. SAVE 丩 & M 🛈 ⊠ ✚ ⚏

Holiday Inn Express Kelowna Conference Centre H

(250) 763-0500. **$129-$199, 3 day notice.** 2429 Hwy 97 N V1X 4J2. 0.6 mi (1 km) w of jct Hwy 97 N (Harvey Ave) and 33. Int corridors. **Pets:** Accepted. ECO & M ➷ 🛈 ⊠ ✚ ⚏

Kelowna Inn & Suites M

(250) 762-2533. **Call for rates.** 1070 Harvey Ave V1Y 8S4. Corner of Hwy 97 N (Harvey Ave) and Gordon Dr. Ext/int corridors. **Pets:** Small, dogs only. $15 daily fee/pet. Designated rooms, service with restrictions, supervision. ECO 丩 & M 🛈 ⊠ ✚ ⚏

Lake Okanagan Resort H

(250) 769-3511. **$119-$299, 14 day notice.** 2751 Westside Rd V1Z 3T1. From Floating Bridge, 1.5 mi (2.5 km) sw on Hwy 97 (Harvey Ave), 10.6 mi (17 km) nw on Westside Rd (narrow winding road), follow signs. Ext corridors. **Pets:** Accepted. 丩 & M ➷ ⊠ 🛈 ⊠ ✚ ⚏

Ramada Hotel & Conference Centre H ❀

(250) 860-9711. **$119-$220.** 2170 Harvey Ave V1Y 6G8. Hwy 97 N (Harvey Ave) at Dilworth Dr. Ext/int corridors. **Pets:** Other species. $15 daily fee/room. Designated rooms, service with restrictions, supervision. 丩 & M ➷ ⊠ ✚ ⚏

Recreation Inn & Suites M

(250) 860-3982. **$69-$129.** 1891 Parkinson Way V1Y 7V6. Hwy 97 (Harvey Ave), just n on Spall Rd. Ext corridors. **Pets:** Accepted. ➷ 🛈 ⊠ ✚ ⚏

The Royal Anne Hotel H ❀

(250) 763-2277. **$89-$219, 3 day notice.** 348 Bernard Ave V1Y 6N5. Between Pandosy and Water sts; downtown. Int corridors. **Pets:** Large. $20 daily fee/room. Designated rooms, service with restrictions, crate. SAVE 🛈 ⊠ ✚ ⚏

KIMBERLEY

Trickle Creek Lodge H

(250) 427-5175. **$99-$329.** 500 Stemwinder Dr V1A 2Y6. From Gerry Sorensen Way, follow signs. Int corridors. **Pets:** Accepted. SAVE ➷ ⊠ 🛈 ⊠ ✚ ⚏

LANGLEY

BEST WESTERN PLUS Langley Inn H

(604) 530-9311. **$129-$159.** 5978 Glover Rd V3A 4H9. Trans-Canada Hwy 1 exit 66 (232nd St), 3.6 mi (6 km) se on Hwy 10, follow signs. Int corridors. **Pets:** Medium, dogs only. $15 daily fee/pet. Designated rooms, service with restrictions, supervision. SAVE 丩 & M ➷ 🛈 ⊠ ✚ ⚏

Coast Hotel & Convention Centre H

(604) 530-1500. **$112-$149, 3 day notice.** 20393 Fraser Hwy V3A 7N2. Trans-Canada Hwy 1 exit 58 (200th St/Langley City), 3.9 mi (6.3 km) s on 200th St, then just e. Int corridors. **Pets:** Accepted. SAVE ECO 丩 & M 🛈 ⊠ ✚ ⚏

Days Inn & Suites Langley H

(604) 539-0100. **$99-$169.** 20250 Logan Ave V3A 4L6. Trans-Canada Hwy 1 exit 58 (200th St/Langley City), 3.9 mi (6.3 km) s on 200th St, then just e. **Pets:** Dogs only. $15 daily fee/room. Designated rooms, service with restrictions, crate. SAVE ECO & M 🛈 ⊠ ✚ ⚏

Holiday Inn Express Hotel & Suites Langley H ❀

(604) 882-2000. **$109-$169.** 8750 204th St V1M 2Y5. Trans-Canada Hwy 1 exit 58 (200th St/Langley City), just e on 88th Ave. Int corridors. **Pets:** Small. $10 daily fee/pet. Designated rooms, service with restrictions, supervision. SAVE ECO & M ➷ ⊠ 🛈 ⊠ ✚ ⚏

Quality Hotel & Suites H

(604) 534-5110. **$79-$94.** 6465 201st St V2Y 0G8. Trans Canada Hwy 1 exit 58, 1.8 mi (3 km) s on 200th St, just e on 64 Ave, then just s. Int corridors. **Pets:** Accepted. SAVE 丩 & M 🛈 ⊠ ✚ ⚏

Sandman Hotel Langley H

(604) 888-7263. **Call for rates.** 8855 202nd St V1M 2N9. Trans-Canada Hwy 1 exit 58 (200th St/Langley City), just e on 88th Ave. Int corridors. **Pets:** Accepted. ECO 丩 & M 🛈 ✚ ⚏

Westward Inn & Suites M

(604) 534-9238. **$59-$99.** 19682 Fraser Hwy V3A 4C7. Trans-Canada Hwy 1 exit 58 (200th St/Langley City), 3.1 mi (5 km) s on 200th St, 0.6 mi (1 km) w on Hwy 10, then just w. Ext corridors. **Pets:** Other species. $200 deposit/room, $10 daily fee/pet. Designated rooms, service with restrictions, supervision. 🛈 ✚ ⚏

MADEIRA PARK

Painted Boat Resort Spa & Marina CO

(604) 883-2456. **Call for rates.** 12849 Lagoon Rd V0N 2H0. Hwy 101, just w on Gonzales Rd, just s, follow signs. Ext corridors. **Pets:** $25 daily fee/pet. Designated rooms, service with restrictions. 丩 ➷ ⊠ 🛈 ⊠ ✚ ⚏

Sunshine Coast Resort & Marina H

(604) 883-9177. **$119-$219, 21 day notice.** 12695 Sunshine Coast Hwy V0N 2H0. Just n of Madeira Park Rd, follow signs. Ext/int corridors. **Pets:** Accepted. & M ⊠ 🛈 ⊠ ✚ ⚏

MAPLE RIDGE

BEST WESTERN Maple Ridge M

(604) 467-1511. **$90-$100.** 21650 Lougheed Hwy V2X 2S1. 1.2 mi (2 km) w on Lougheed Hwy (Hwy 7). Int corridors. **Pets:** Dogs only. $100 deposit/pet, $20 daily fee/pet. Service with restrictions, supervision. SAVE ➷ 🛈 ⊠ ✚ ⚏

Quality Inn H

(604) 463-5111. **$79-$139.** 21735 Lougheed Hwy V2X 2S2. 1.2 mi (2 km) w on Lougheed Hwy (Hwy 7). Ext corridors. **Pets:** Medium, other species. $10 daily fee/pet. Designated rooms, service with restrictions, crate. SAVE 丩 & M 🛈 ✚ ⚏

MCBRIDE

▼▼ North Country Lodge Ⓜ

(250) 569-0001. **Call for rates.** 868 N Frontage Rd V0J 2E0. Just w of village main exit; on Hwy 16 north service road. Ext corridors. **Pets:** Small. $10 daily fee/pet. Service with restrictions, crate.

🛜 🖨 💻

MERRITT

Ⓐ ▼▼▼ Quality Inn Merritt Ⓜ ☙

(250) 378-4253. **$117-$157.** 4025 Walters St V1K 1K1. Hwy 5 exit 290, 0.6 mi (1 km) w. Ext corridors. **Pets:** Small. $10 daily fee/pet. Designated rooms, supervision. SAVE 🍴 🔥M 🏊 🛜 ✕ 🖨 💻

Ⓐ ▼▼▼ Ramada Limited Ⓜ

(250) 378-3567. **$90-$149.** 3571 Voght St V1K 1C5. Hwy 5 exit 290, just w. Ext corridors. **Pets:** Small. $10 daily fee/pet. Designated rooms, service with restrictions, supervision. SAVE 🏊 ✕ 🛜 🖨 💻

▼▼ Super 8 Merritt Ⓜ

(250) 378-9422. **$75-$105.** 3561 Voght St V1K 1C5. Hwy 5 exit 290, just w. Ext corridors. **Pets:** Accepted. 🍴 🔥M 🏊 🛜 🖨 💻

MISSION

Ⓐ ▼▼▼ BEST WESTERN PLUS Mission City Lodge 🎃

(604) 820-5500. **$109-$130.** 32281 Lougheed Hwy V2V 1A3. Just w of Hwy 11; corner of Lougheed Hwy (Hwy 7) and Hurd St. Int corridors. **Pets:** Accepted. SAVE 🍴 ♿ 🏊 ✕ 🛜 ✕ 🖨 💻

NANAIMO

Ⓐ ▼▼▼ BEST WESTERN Dorchester Hotel 🎃 ☙

(250) 754-6835. **$129-$169.** 70 Church St V9R 5H4. Hwy 19A (Island Hwy) to Comox Rd; downtown. Int corridors. **Pets:** Medium. $25 daily fee/pet. Designated rooms, service with restrictions, supervision.

SAVE ECO 🍴 🛜 ✕ 🖨 💻

Ⓐ ▼▼▼ BEST WESTERN Northgate Inn 🎃

(250) 390-2222. **$120-$220.** 6450 Metral Dr V9T 2L8. Hwy 19A (Island Hwy), just w on Aulds Rd, just s. Int corridors. **Pets:** Accepted.

SAVE ✕ 🛜 ✕ 🖨 💻

▼▼ Days Inn Nanaimo Harbourview 🎃

(250) 754-8171. **$100-$190.** 809 Island Hwy S V9R 5K1. Hwy 19A (Island Hwy), 1.3 mi (2 km) s. Int corridors. **Pets:** Medium. $15 daily fee/pet. Designated rooms, service with restrictions, supervision.

🍴 🔥M 🏊 🛜 ✕ 🖨 💻

Ⓐ ▼▼▼ Inn on Long Lake 🎃 ☙

(250) 758-1144. **$125-$300, 3 day notice.** 4700 Island Hwy N V9T 1W6. 3.1 mi (5 km) n on Hwy 19A (Island Hwy) from Departure Bay Ferry Terminal. Ext corridors. **Pets:** $20 one-time fee/room. Designated rooms, service with restrictions, supervision.

SAVE ECO 🔥M ✕ 🛜 🖨 💻

Ⓐ ▼▼▼ Travelodge Nanaimo 🎃 ☙

(250) 754-6355. **$89-$189.** 96 Terminal Ave N V9S 4J2. Between Terminal Ave N and Stewart Ave. Int corridors. **Pets:** $15 daily fee/pet. Designated rooms, service with restrictions, supervision.

SAVE ECO 🛜 ✕ 🖨 💻

NELSON

Ⓐ ▼▼▼ BEST WESTERN PLUS Baker Street Inn & Convention Centre 🎃 ☙

(250) 352-3525. **$130-$180.** 153 Baker St V1L 4H1. Jct Hwy 3A and 6. Int corridors. **Pets:** Medium. $20 daily fee/pet. Designated rooms, service with restrictions, supervision.

SAVE ECO 🍴 🔥M 🛜 ✕ 🖨 💻

▼ North Shore Inn Ⓜ

(250) 352-6606. **$68-$94, 3 day notice.** 687 Hwy 3A V1L 5P7. 1.9 mi (3 km) n on Hwy 3A via Nelson Bridge. Int corridors. **Pets:** Accepted. 🛜 ✕ 🖨

NORTH VANCOUVER

Ⓐ ▼▼▼ Holiday Inn & Suites North Vancouver 🎃 ☙

(604) 985-3111. **$139-$189.** 700 Old Lillooet Rd V7J 2H5. Trans-Canada Hwy 1 exit 22 (Mount Seymour Pkwy), follow signs. Int corridors. **Pets:** Medium, dogs only. $200 deposit/room, $25 daily fee/pet. Designated rooms, service with restrictions, supervision.

SAVE ECO 🍴 🔥M 🏊 ✕ 🛜 ✕ 🖨 💻

Ⓐ ▼▼▼ North Vancouver Hotel Ⓜ ☙

(604) 987-4461. **$79-$149.** 1800 Capilano Rd V7P 3B6. Trans-Canada Hwy 1 exit 14 (Capilano Rd), 0.9 mi (1.5 km) s; from north end of Lions Gate Bridge, 0.6 mi (1 km) e on Marine Dr, just n. Ext corridors. **Pets:** Medium. $20 daily fee/room. Designated rooms, service with restrictions, supervision. SAVE 🔥M 🏊 🛜 ✕ 🖨 💻

▼▼ Pinnacle Hotel at the Pier 🎃

(604) 986-7437. **$139-$289.** 138 Victory Ship Way V7L 0B1. Corner of Esplanade St and Lonsdale Ave. Int corridors. **Pets:** Accepted.

ECO 🍴 🔥M 🏊 ✕ 🛜 ✕ 🖨 💻

▼▼ Travelodge Vancouver Lionsgate Ⓜ

(604) 985-5311. **$59-$149.** 2060 Marine Dr V7P 1V7. Trans-Canada Hwy 1 exit 14 (Capilano Rd), 0.9 mi (1.5 km) s, then just w; from north end of Lions Gate Bridge, just e. Ext corridors. **Pets:** Accepted.

🛜 🖨 💻

OSOYOOS

Ⓐ ▼▼▼ BEST WESTERN PLUS Sunrise Inn 🎃

(250) 495-4000. **$169-$250.** 5506 Main St V0H 1V0. Jct Hwy 97, 1.9 mi (3 km) on Hwy 3 (Main St). Int corridors. **Pets:** Accepted.

SAVE ECO 🍴 🔥M 🏊 🛜 ✕ 🖨 💻

Ⓐ ▼▼▼ The Coast Osoyoos Beach Hotel Ⓜ

(250) 495-6525. **$79-$299, 14 day notice.** 7702 Main St V0H 1V0. Jct Hwy 97, 1.2 mi (2 km) e. Ext/int corridors. **Pets:** Accepted.

SAVE ECO 🏊 🛜 ✕ 🖨 💻

▼▼▼ Spirit Ridge Vineyard Resort & Spa CO

(250) 495-5445. **$99-$479, 14 day notice.** 1200 Rancher Creek Rd V0H 1V6. Hwy 97 S, e on Hwy 3 (Main St), cross bridge, left on 45th St, then 0.9 mi (1.5 km) e. Ext/int corridors. **Pets:** Accepted.

ECO 🍴 🔥M 🏊 ✕ 🛜 ✕ 🖨 💻

▼▼▼ Watermark Beach Resort CO

(250) 495-5500. **$99-$699.** 15 Park Pl V0H 1V0. Corner of Park Pl and Main St; downtown. Ext/int corridors. **Pets:** Accepted.

ECO 🍴 🔥M 🏊 🛜 ✕ 🖨 💻

PARKSVILLE

▼▼ Arbutus Grove Motel Ⓜ

(250) 248-6422. **$69-$149.** 1182 E Island Hwy V9P 1W3. Island Hwy 19 exit 46 (Parksville), 1 mi (1.6 km) n on Hwy 19A. Ext corridors. **Pets:** Accepted. 🛜 ✕ 🖨 💻

▼▼▼ Oceanside Village Resort CA

(250) 248-8961. **$120-$310, 30 day notice.** 1080 Resort Dr V9P 2E3. Island Hwy 19 exit 46 (Parksville), 1.8 mi (2.5 km) n on Hwy 19A. Ext corridors. **Pets:** Other species. $20 daily fee/pet. Designated rooms, no service, crate. 🏊 🛜 ✕ 🖨 💻

Ⓐ ▼▼▼ Quality Resort Bayside 🎃

(250) 248-8333. **$89-$161.** 240 Dogwood St V9P 2H5. Island Hwy 19 exit 51 (Parksville/Coombs), 1.3 mi (2 km) e, then 0.6 mi (1 km) n on Hwy 19A. Int corridors. **Pets:** Medium, dogs only. $15 daily fee/pet. Designated rooms, service with restrictions, crate.

SAVE 🍴 🔥M 🏊 ✕ 💻

▼▼ Tigh-Na-Mara Seaside Spa Resort & Conference Centre 🎃

(250) 248-2072. **$123-$213, 5 day notice.** 1155 Resort Dr V9P 2E3. Island Hwy 19 exit 46 (Parksville), 1.3 mi (2 km) n on Hwy 19A. Ext corridors. **Pets:** Accepted. 🍴 🏊 ✕ 🛜 🐾 🖨 💻

▼▼ **Travelodge Parksville** 🄷

(250) 248-2232. **$89-$169.** 424 W Island Hwy V9P 1K8. Island Hwy 19 exit 51 (Parksville/Coombs), 1.3 mi (2 km) e, then just n on Hwy 19A. Int corridors. **Pets:** Accepted. 🄴🄲🄾 ⓖᴹ 🛏 📶 ✕ 🔋 📺

▼ **V.I.P. Motel** Ⓜ

(250) 248-3244. **Call for rates.** 414 W Island Hwy V9P 1K8. Island Hwy 19 exit 51 (Parksville/Coombs), 1.3 mi (2 km) e, then just n on Hwy 19A. Ext corridors. **Pets:** Accepted. 📶 ✕ 🔋 📺

PEMBERTON
▼▼▼ **Pemberton Valley Lodge** 🄷 🐾

(604) 894-2000. **$139-$419, 7 day notice.** 1490 Sea to Sky Hwy V0N 2L1. Just e on Hwy 99 from Pioneer Junction. Int corridors. **Pets:** Large, dogs only. $45 one-time fee/room. Designated rooms.

PENDER ISLANDS
▼▼▼ **Poets Cove Resort & Spa** 🄷

(250) 629-2100. **Call for rates.** 9801 Spalding Rd V0N 2M3. From Otter Bay Ferry Terminal, follow signs to South Pender Island, 10 mi (16 km) s; Otter Bay Rd to Bidwell Harbour Rd to Canal Rd. Ext/int corridors. **Pets:** Accepted.

PENTICTON
Ⓒ⒜ ▼▼▼ **BEST WESTERN Inn at Penticton** 🄷

(250) 493-0311. **$89-$209.** 3180 Skaha Lake Rd V2A 6G4. From downtown, 2.5 mi (4 km) s. Ext corridors. **Pets:** Accepted.

Ⓒ⒜ ▼▼▼ **Coast Penticton Hotel** 🄷

(250) 492-0225. **$89-$269, 7 day notice.** 950 Westminster Ave W V2A 1L2. Hwy 97 (Eckhardt Ave W), just n to Westminster Ave W, just e. Ext/int corridors. **Pets:** $10 daily fee/pet. Designated rooms, service with restrictions, supervision. (SAVE) 🍴 🛏 📶 ✕ 🔋 📺

▼▼ **Days Inn & Conference Centre Penticton** 🄷

(250) 493-6616. **$104-$214.** 152 Riverside Dr V2A 5Y4. Hwy 97, just n. Int corridors. **Pets:** Accepted.
🄴🄲🄾 🍴 ⓖᴹ 🛏 ✕ 📶 ✕ 🔋 📺

Ⓒ⒜ ▼▼▼▼ **Penticton Lakeside Resort, Convention Centre & Casino** 🄷

(250) 493-8221. **$131-$251.** 21 Lakeshore Dr W V2A 7M5. Main St at Lakeshore Dr W. Int corridors. **Pets:** Accepted.
(SAVE) 🄴🄲🄾 🍴 ⓖᴹ 🏊 🛏 ✕ 📶 ✕ 🔋 📺

Ⓒ⒜ ▼▼▼ **Ramada Inn & Suites** 🄷 🐾

(250) 492-8926. **$99-$350.** 1050 Eckhardt Ave W V2A 2C3. 0.8 mi (1.2 km) w on Hwy 97. Ext/int corridors. **Pets:** Other species. $15 daily fee/pet. Supervision. (SAVE) 🄴🄲🄾 🍴 ⓖᴹ 🛏 ✕ 📶 ✕ 🔋 📺

Ⓒ⒜ ▼ **Spanish Villa Resort** Ⓜ

(250) 492-2922. **$68-$350, 14 day notice.** 890 Lakeshore Dr W V2A 1C1. Corner of Power St and Lakeshore Dr W. Ext corridors. **Pets:** Accepted. (SAVE) 🛏 📶 ✕ 🔋 📺

▼▼ **Super 8 Penticton** Ⓜ

(250) 492-3829. **$95-$350.** 1706 Main St V2A 5G8. Jct Main St and Industrial Ave. Ext/int corridors. **Pets:** Accepted.
🛏 📶 ✕ 🔋 📺

PORT ALBERNI
Ⓒ⒜ ▼▼▼ **BEST WESTERN PLUS Barclay Hotel** 🄷

(250) 724-7171. **$140-$150.** 4277 Stamp Ave V9Y 7X8. Johnston Rd (Hwy 4), just s on Gertrude St. Int corridors. **Pets:** Accepted.
(SAVE) 🍴 🛏 ✕ 📶 ✕ 🔋 📺

Ⓒ⒜ ▼▼▼ **The Hospitality Inn** 🄷 🐾

(250) 723-8111. **$99-$149.** 3835 Redford St V9Y 3S2. 2 mi (3.2 km) sw of jct Hwy 4 via City Centre/Port Alberni south route. Int corridors. **Pets:** $10 daily fee/pet. Service with restrictions, crate.
(SAVE) 🄴🄲🄾 ⊟ 🍴 🛏 📶 🔋 📺

▼▼ **Riverside Motel** Ⓜ

(250) 724-9916. **Call for rates.** 5065 Roger St V9Y 3Y9. Johnston Rd (Hwy 4), just s on Gertrude St, just w. Ext corridors. **Pets:** Accepted.
📶 ✕ 🔋 📺

▼▼▼ **Somass Motel and RV** Ⓜ

(250) 724-3236. **Call for rates.** 5279 River Rd V9Y 6Z3. 0.5 mi (0.8 km) nw on River Rd from jct Johnston Rd (Hwy 4). Ext corridors. **Pets:** Accepted. 🛏 📶 ✕ 🔋 📺

PORT HARDY
▼ **Airport Inn** 🄷

(250) 949-9434. **Call for rates.** 4030 Byng Rd V0N 2P0. Hwy 19, 3.1 mi (5 km) ne, follow signs. Int corridors. **Pets:** Accepted.
🍴 📶 ✕ Ⓚ 🔋 📺

▼▼ **Quarterdeck Inn & Marina** 🄷

(250) 902-0455. **$110-$165.** 6555 Hardy Bay Rd V0N 2P0. Hwy 19, 0.9 mi (1.5 km) n. Int corridors. **Pets:** Accepted.
🍴 ⓖᴹ 📶 ✕ Ⓚ 🔋 📺

PORT MCNEILL
▼ **Haida-Way Motor Inn** Ⓜ

(250) 956-3373. **Call for rates.** 1817 Campbell Way V0N 2R0. Hwy 19, 1.3 mi (2 km) e. Int corridors. **Pets:** Accepted.
🍴 📶 Ⓚ 🔋 📺

POWELL RIVER
▼▼ **Powell River Town Centre Hotel** 🄷

(604) 485-3000. **Call for rates.** 4660 Joyce Ave V8A 3B6. 0.5 mi (0.8 km) e on Duncan St (Westview-Powell Ferry Terminal), 0.6 mi (1 km) n. Int corridors. **Pets:** Accepted. 🍴 ⓖᴹ 📶 ✕ 🔋 📺

PRINCE GEORGE
▼▼ **Econo Lodge City Centre Inn** Ⓜ

(250) 563-1267. **$109-$139.** 910 Victoria St V2L 2K8. Just n of Victoria St (Hwy 16) and Patricia Blvd; downtown. Ext corridors. **Pets:** Accepted. 🍴 🛏 📶 🔋 📺

▼▼▼ **Sandman Signature Hotel & Suites Prince George** 🄷

(250) 645-7263. **Call for rates.** 2990 Recreation Place Dr V2N 0B2. Hwy 16, just w on Ferry Ave, just s. Int corridors. **Pets:** Accepted.
🍴 ⓖᴹ 📶 ✕ 🔋 📺

PRINCE RUPERT
▼▼ **Inn on the Harbour** 🄷

(250) 624-9107. **Call for rates.** 720 1st Ave W V8J 3V6. Corner of 6th St. Int corridors. **Pets:** Accepted. ⓖᴹ 📶 ✕ 🔋 📺

PRINCETON
Ⓒ⒜ ▼▼ **Canadas Best Value Princeton Inn & Suites** 🄷

(250) 295-3537. **$110-$150.** 169 Hwy 3 V0X 1W0. Hwy 3, just n on Vermilion Ave. Ext corridors. **Pets:** Accepted.
(SAVE) ⓖᴹ 🛏 📶 🔋 📺

QUADRA ISLAND
▼▼ **Taku Resort & Marina** Ⓜ

(250) 285-3031. **Call for rates.** 616 Taku Rd V0P 1H0. From Campbell River Ferry Terminal, 4.1 mi (6.6 km) n on West Rd, just e on Heriot Bay Rd, follow signs to Heriot Bay. Ext corridors. **Pets:** Accepted.
✕ 📶 ✕ Ⓚ 🎬 🔋 📺

▼▼ **Tsa-Kwa-Luten Lodge** 🄷

(250) 285-2042. **$110-$380, 3 day notice.** 1 Lighthouse Rd V0P 1N0. From Campbell River Ferry Terminal, just se on Green Rd, 0.6 mi (1 km) e on Noble Rd, 1.8 mi (2.9 km) se on Cape Mudge Rd to Joyce Rd, 0.6 mi (1 km) sw, then 1.4 mi (2.2 km) s. Ext/int corridors. **Pets:** Accepted. 🄴🄲🄾 🍴 ⓖᴹ ✕ 🎬 ✕ Ⓚ ⓦ 🔋 📺

QUESNEL

ⓐ ▼▼ ▼▼ BEST WESTERN PLUS Tower Inn 🅷

(250) 992-2201. **$125.** 500 Reid St V2J 2M9. Hwy 97, just e on Shepherd Ave; downtown. Int corridors. **Pets:** Accepted.

[SAVE] [C] [¶] [&M] [📶] [✕] [📦] [🖥]

ⓐ ▼▼ ▼▼ Quality Inn & Suites 🅼

(250) 992-7247. **$89-$119.** 753 Front St V2J 2L2. Hwy 97, 0.6 mi (1 km) n of Carson Ave. Int corridors. **Pets:** Small. $10 daily fee/pet. Designated rooms, service with restrictions, supervision.

[SAVE] [&M] [📶] [✕] [📦] [🖥]

ⓐ ▼▼ ▼▼ Travelodge Quesnel 🅼

(250) 992-7071. **$80-$110.** 524 Front St V2J 2K6. Hwy 97, 0.5 mi (0.8 km) n of Carson Ave. Ext corridors. **Pets:** Medium. $15 daily fee/pet. Designated rooms, service with restrictions, supervision.

[SAVE] [ECO] [&M] [🏊] [📶] [📦] [🖥]

RADIUM HOT SPRINGS

ⓐ ▼▼▼▼ BEST WESTERN PLUS Prestige Inn Radium Hot Springs 🅷

(250) 347-2300. **$140-$220.** 7493 Main St W V0A 1M0. Jct Hwy 93 and 95. Int corridors. **Pets:** Accepted.

[SAVE] [¶] [🏊] [✕] [📶] [✕] [📦] [🖥]

ⓐ ▼▼ Bighorn Motel 🅼

(250) 347-9111. **$70-$80.** 4881 St. Mary's St E V0A 1M0. Jct Hwy 93 and 95, just s on Main St W, just w. Ext corridors. **Pets:** Accepted.

[SAVE] [📶] [✕] [🟦] [📦] [🖥]

REVELSTOKE

ⓐ ▼▼▼▼ BEST WESTERN PLUS Revelstoke 🅷 🐾

(250) 837-2043. **$165-$220.** 1925 Laforme Blvd V0E 2S0. Trans-Canada Hwy 1, just n. Int corridors. **Pets:** Medium. $20 daily fee/pet. Designated rooms, service with restrictions, supervision.

[SAVE] [C] [&M] [🏊] [✕] [📶] [✕] [📦] [🖥]

ⓐ ▼▼▼▼ Coast Hillcrest Hotel 🅷 🐾

(250) 837-3322. **$138-$199, 3 day notice.** 2100 Oak Dr V0E 2S0. 2.7 mi (4.3 km) e on Trans-Canada Hwy 1, 0.6 mi (1 km) sw. Int corridors. **Pets:** Other species. $15 one-time fee/room. Designated rooms, supervision. [SAVE] [ECO] [¶] [&M] [✕] [📶] [✕] [📦] [🖥]

RICHMOND

▼▼ ▼▼ Accent Inns 🅷

(604) 273-3311. **Call for rates.** 10551 St Edwards Dr V6X 3L8. Hwy 99 exit 39 (Bridgeport Rd/Airport) northbound; exit 39A (Richmond/Airport) southbound to St Edwards Dr. Ext corridors. **Pets:** Accepted.

[ECO] [¶] [&M] [📶] [✕] [📦] [🖥]

ⓐ ▼▼▼▼ BEST WESTERN PLUS Abercorn Inn 🅷

(604) 270-7576. **$130-$220.** 9260 Bridgeport Rd V6X 1S1. Hwy 99 exit 39 (Bridgeport Rd/Airport) northbound; exit 39A (Richmond/Airport) southbound. Int corridors. **Pets:** Accepted.

[SAVE] [ECO] [¶] [&M] [📶] [✕] [📦] [🖥]

ⓐ ▼▼▼ ▼ The Fairmont Vancouver Airport 🅷

(604) 207-5200. **$239-$429.** 3111 Grant McConachie Way V7B 0A6. In Vancouver International Airport. Int corridors. **Pets:** Accepted.

[SAVE] [ECO] [¶] [&M] [🏊] [✕] [📶] [✕] [🖥]

ⓐ ▼▼▼ Hilton Vancouver Airport 🅷

(604) 273-6336. **$229-$329.** 5911 Minoru Blvd V6X 4C7. Corner of Minoru Blvd and Westminster Hwy. Int corridors. **Pets:** Accepted.

[SAVE] [ECO] [¶] [&M] [🏊] [📶] [✕] [📦] [🖥]

▼▼▼▼ Holiday Inn Express Vancouver-Airport 🅷

(604) 273-8080. **$105-$300.** 9351 Bridgeport Rd V6X 1S3. Hwy 99 exit 39 (Bridgeport Rd/Airport) northbound; exit 39A (Richmond/Airport) southbound. Int corridors. **Pets:** Accepted.

[ECO] [&M] [📶] [✕] [📦] [🖥]

▼▼▼▼ Holiday Inn Vancouver Airport-Richmond 🅷

(604) 821-1818. **$105-$300.** 10720 Cambie Rd V6X 1K8. Hwy 99 exit 39A (Bridgeport Rd/Airport) northbound to St Edwards Dr, 0.6 mi (1 km) n; exit 39B (No. 4 Rd) southbound, just e. Int corridors. **Pets:** Accepted.

[ECO] [¶] [&M] [📶] [✕] [📦] [🖥]

▼▼▼▼ Hotel at River Rock 🅷

(604) 247-8900. **$269-$319.** 8888 River Rd V6X 3P8. Hwy 99 exit 39 (Bridgeport Rd/Airport) northbound; exit 39A (Richmond/Airport) southbound; just w on Bridgeport Rd, then just n on Great Canadian Way. Int corridors. **Pets:** Large. $25 daily fee/room. Service with restrictions.

[¶] [&M] [📶] [✕] [📦] [🖥]

ⓐ ▼▼▼▼ Pacific Gateway Hotel 🅷

(604) 278-1241. **$149-$329.** 3500 Cessna Dr V7B 1C7. Just s of island airport interchange; at Russ Baker Way. Int corridors. **Pets:** $35 daily fee/room. Service with restrictions.

[SAVE] [ECO] [¶] [&M] [🏊] [📶] [✕] [📦] [🖥]

ⓐ ▼▼▼▼▼ River Rock Casino Resort 🅷 🐾

(604) 247-8900. **$152-$224.** 8811 River Rd V6X 3P8. Hwy 99 exit 39 (Bridgeport Rd/Airport) northbound; exit 39A (Richmond/Airport) southbound, just w on Bridgeport Rd, then just n on Great Canadian Way. Int corridors. **Pets:** Large. $25 daily fee/room. Service with restrictions.

[SAVE] [¶] [&M] [🏊] [✕] [📶] [✕] [📦] [🖥]

▼▼ ▼▼ Sandman Hotel Vancouver Airport 🅷

(604) 303-8888. **Call for rates.** 3233 St Edwards Dr V6X 3K4. Hwy 99 exit 39 (Bridgeport Rd/Airport) northbound; exit 39A (Richmond/Airport) southbound to St Edwards Dr. Int corridors. **Pets:** Accepted.

[ECO] [¶] [&M] [📶] [📦] [🖥]

ⓐ ▼▼▼▼ Sheraton Vancouver Airport Hotel 🅷 🐾

(604) 273-7878. **$139-$369.** 7551 Westminster Hwy V6X 1A3. Corner of Minoru Blvd and Westminster Hwy. Int corridors. **Pets:** $20 daily fee/room. Service with restrictions, supervision.

[SAVE] [ECO] [¶] [&M] [🏊] [📶] [✕] [📦] [🖥]

ⓐ ▼▼▼▼ Vancouver Airport Marriott 🅷

(604) 276-2112. **$279-$340.** 7571 Westminster Hwy V6X 1A3. Corner of Minoru Blvd and Westminster Hwy. Int corridors. **Pets:** Accepted.

[SAVE] [¶] [&M] [🏊] [📶] [✕] [📦] [🖥]

ⓐ ▼▼▼▼ The Westin Wall Centre Vancouver Airport 🅷

(604) 303-6565. **Call for rates.** 3099 Corvette Way V6X 4K3. Hwy 99 exit 39 (Bridgeport Rd/Airport) northbound; exit 39A (Richmond/Airport) southbound, just w to No. 3 Rd. Int corridors. **Pets:** Accepted.

[SAVE] [¶] [&M] [🏊] [📶] [✕] [🖥]

ROSSLAND

▼▼ Casa Alpina 🅼

(250) 362-7364. **Call for rates.** 1199 Nancy Greene Hwy V0G 1Y0. 0.6 mi (1 km) w on Hwy 3B; jct Hwy 22. Ext corridors. **Pets:** Accepted.

[📶] [📦] [🖥]

SALMON ARM

▼▼▼ Comfort Inn & Suites 🅷 🐾

(250) 832-7711. **$123-$300.** 1090 22nd St NE V1E 2V5. Trans-Canada Hwy 1, access via 30th St NE, just w on 11th Ave NE. Int corridors. **Pets:** Other species. $15 daily fee/pet. Designated rooms, service with restrictions, supervision. [ECO] [&M] [🏊] [📶] [📦] [🖥]

▼▼ ▼▼ Podollan Inn 🅷

(250) 832-6025. **Call for rates.** 1460 Trans-Canada Hwy NE V1E 4N1. At 14th St and 9th Ave NE. Ext/int corridors. **Pets:** Accepted.

[¶] [&M] [🏊] [📶] [✕] [📦] [🖥]

▼▼ ▼▼ Super 8 Salmon Arm 🅼

(250) 832-8812. **$85-$190.** 2901 10th Ave NE V1E 2S3. Trans-Canada Hwy 1, access via 30th St NE. Int corridors. **Pets:** Accepted.

[&M] [📶] [✕] [📦] [🖥]

SALT SPRING ISLAND

▼▼▼ Harbour House Hotel 🅷

(250) 537-5571. **Call for rates.** 121 Upper Ganges Rd V8K 2S2. 0.6 mi (1 km) n on Lower Ganges Rd, just e, towards Long Harbour Ferry Terminal. Ext/int corridors. **Pets:** Accepted.

🌐 🍴 &M 🛜 ✕ 📆 💻

▼▼▼ Salt Springs Spa Resort 🆑

(250) 537-4111. **Call for rates.** 1460 N Beach Rd V8K 1J4. From Ganges Township, 4.9 mi (8 km) n on North End Rd, 0.6 mi (1 km) ne on Fernwood Rd, then 6.8 mi (10.8 km) nw. Ext corridors. **Pets:** Accepted.

🛜 ✕ 🅺 🅿 🅕 📆 💻

SICAMOUS

ⒶⒶ ▼▼▼▼ BEST WESTERN Sicamous Inn 🅼 🐾

(250) 836-4117. **$129-$175.** 806 Trans-Canada Hwy 1 V0E 2V0. Jct Trans-Canada Hwy 1 and 97; at east end of town. Ext/int corridors. **Pets:** Large, dogs only. $20 daily fee/room. Designated rooms, service with restrictions, supervision. 🆂🅰🆅🅴 🔛 &M 🛆 🛜 ✕ 📆 💻

SIDNEY

ⒶⒶ ▼▼▼ BEST WESTERN PLUS Emerald Isle Motor Inn 🅷 🐾

(250) 656-4441. **$139-$175.** 2306 Beacon Ave V8L 1X2. Hwy 17 exit 28 (Sidney), just e. Int corridors. **Pets:** $15 daily fee/pet. Designated rooms, service with restrictions, supervision.

🆂🅰🆅🅴 🌐 🔛 🍴 &M 🛆 🛜 ✕ 📆 💻

▼▼ The Cedarwood Inn & Suites 🅷

(250) 656-5551. **Call for rates.** 9522 Lochside Dr V8L 1N8. Hwy 17 exit 26, just e on McTavish Rd, then 0.8 mi (1.4 km) n. Ext corridors. **Pets:** $20 one-time fee/pet. Service with restrictions, supervision.

&M 🛜 ✕ 🅺 📆 💻

ⒶⒶ ▼▼▼▼ The Sidney Pier Hotel & Spa 🅷 🐾

(250) 655-9445. **$139-$369.** 9805 Seaport Pl V8L 4X3. Hwy 17 exit 28 (Beacon Ave), 0.6 mi (1 km) e. Int corridors. **Pets:** Medium, dogs only. $50 one-time fee/pet. Designated rooms, supervision.

🆂🅰🆅🅴 🌐 🍴 &M 🛆 🛜 ✕ 📆 💻

▼▼ Victoria Airport Travelodge Sidney 🅷

(250) 656-1176. **$99-$149.** 2280 Beacon Ave V8L 1X1. Hwy 17 exit 28 (Beacon Ave), just e. Int corridors. **Pets:** Medium, other species. $15 daily fee/room. Designated rooms, service with restrictions, supervision.

🍴 &M 🛆 🛜 📆 💻

SMITHERS

▼▼ Aspen Inn & Suites 🅼

(250) 847-4551. **Call for rates.** 4628 Yellowhead Hwy V0J 2N0. 0.9 mi (1.5 km) w on Hwy 16. Ext corridors. **Pets:** Accepted.

🍴 &M 🛆 🛜 ✕ 📆 💻

SOOKE

ⒶⒶ ▼▼▼▼ BEST WESTERN PREMIER Prestige Oceanfront Resort 🅷 🐾

(250) 642-0805. **$140-$200.** 6929 W Coast Rd V9Z 0V1. 1 mi (1.6 km) w on Hwy 14. Int corridors. **Pets:** Large, dogs only. $20 daily fee/pet. Designated rooms, supervision.

🆂🅰🆅🅴 🔛 🍴 &M 🛆 🛜 ✕ 📆 💻

◆▼ Ocean Wilderness Inn 🆐

(250) 646-2116. **$95-$165, 7 day notice.** 9171 W Coast Rd V9Z 1G3. 8.6 mi (14 km) w on Hwy 14. Ext/int corridors. **Pets:** Accepted.

🛜 ✕ 🅺 🅿 🅕 📆

ⒶⒶ ▼▼▼▼ Sooke Harbour Resort and Marina 🅒🅞

(250) 642-3236. **$199-$249, 3 day notice.** 6971 W Coast Rd V9Z 0V1. 1 mi (1.6 km) w on Hwy 14. Ext corridors. **Pets:** Accepted.

🆂🅰🆅🅴 🛜 ✕ 🅺 📆 💻

SQUAMISH

ⒶⒶ ▼▼▼▼ BEST WESTERN Mountain Retreat Hotel 🅷

(604) 815-0883. **$90-$170.** 38922 Progress Way V8B 0K5. 0.9 mi (1.5 km) n on Hwy 99; at Industrial Way. Int corridors. **Pets:** $20 daily fee/room. Designated rooms, service with restrictions, supervision.

🆂🅰🆅🅴 🍴 &M 🛜 📆 💻

ⒶⒶ ▼▼▼ Executive Suites Hotel & Resort 🅷

(604) 815-0048. **Call for rates.** 40900 Tantalus Rd V8B 0R3. Hwy 99, just e on Garibaldi Way, 0.6 mi (1 km) n. Int corridors. **Pets:** Accepted.

🆂🅰🆅🅴 🍴 &M 🛆 🛜 ✕ 📆 💻

SUMMERLAND

▼▼ Summerland Motel 🅼

(250) 494-4444. **$69-$159, 10 day notice.** 2107 Tait St V0H 1Z4. 3.1 mi (5 km) s on Hwy 97 (32nd St). Ext corridors. **Pets:** Accepted.

🛆 🛜 ✕ 📆 💻

SUN PEAKS

▼▼ Coast Sundance Lodge 🅷

(250) 578-0200. **$89-$161.** 3160 Creekside Way V0E 5N0. Hwy 5, 19.5 mi (31 km) ne on Todd Mountain Rd, follow signs to village. Int corridors. **Pets:** Other species. $20 daily fee/room. Service with restrictions.

🌐 🍴 &M 🛆 🛜 ✕ 🅺 📆 💻

▼▼ Hearthstone Lodge 🅷

(250) 578-6969. **Call for rates.** 3170 Creekside Way V0E 5N0. Hwy 5, 19.4 mi (31 km) ne on Todd Mountain Rd, follow signs to village. Int corridors. **Pets:** Dogs only. $15 daily fee/pet. Designated rooms, service with restrictions. 🌐 🍴 &M 🛆 🛜 ✕ 🅺 📆 💻

▼▼ Heffley Boutique Inn 🅷

(250) 578-8343. **$89-$425, 30 day notice.** 3185 Creekside Way V0E 5N0. Hwy 5, 19.4 mi (31 km) ne on Todd Mountain Rd, follow signs to village. Int corridors. **Pets:** Very small. $150 deposit/pet, $20 daily fee/pet. Service with restrictions, supervision.

&M 🛆 📠 ✕ 🅺 📆 💻

▼▼▼ The Sun Peaks Grand Hotel & Conference Center 🅷

(250) 578-6000. **$89-$599, 3 day notice.** 3240 Village Way V0E 5N0. Hwy 5, 19.4 mi (31 km) ne on Todd Mountain Rd, follow signs to village. Int corridors. **Pets:** Medium. $35 one-time fee/pet. Designated rooms, service with restrictions, supervision.

🌐 🍴 &M 🛆 🛆 🛜 ✕ 📆 💻

SURREY

ⒶⒶ ▼▼▼ BEST WESTERN Peace Arch Inn 🅼

(604) 541-8100. **$125-$155, 3 day notice.** 2293 King George Blvd V4A 5A4. Hwy 99 exit 10 southbound, 2.8 mi (4.5 km) s; exit 2 northbound, 2.1 mi (3.5 km) n. Int corridors. **Pets:** $10 deposit/pet. Designated rooms, supervision. 🆂🅰🆅🅴 🌐 &M 🛆 🛆 🛜 ✕ 📆 💻

ⒶⒶ ▼▼▼ Coast Surrey Guildford Hotel 🅷

(604) 930-4700. **$89-$129, 3 day notice.** 10410 158th St V4N 5C2. Trans-Canada Hwy 1 exit 50 (160th St), just w on 104th Ave. Int corridors. **Pets:** Accepted. 🆂🅰🆅🅴 🍴 &M 🛆 🛆 🛜 ✕ 📆 💻

▼▼▼ Comfort Inn & Suites Surrey 🅷

(604) 576-8888. **$89-$109.** 8255 166th St V4N 5R8. Trans-Canada Hwy 1 exit 53 (176th St/Hwy 15), 2.9 mi (4.8 km) s to Fraser Hwy (Hwy 1A), then 1.6 mi (2.6 km) nw. Int corridors. **Pets:** Medium. $15 daily fee/pet. Designated rooms, service with restrictions, crate.

&M 🛜 ✕ 📆 💻

ⒶⒶ ▼▼▼ Ramada Langley-Surrey 🅷 🐾

(604) 576-8388. **$99-$179.** 19225 Hwy 10 (56 Ave) V3S 8V9. Trans-Canada Hwy 1 exit 58 (200th St/Langley City), 3.1 mi (5 km) s on 200th St, then 1.2 mi (2 km) w on Hwy 10 (56th Ave); corner of 192nd St and Hwy 10. Int corridors. **Pets:** Dogs only. $15 daily fee/pet. Designated rooms, service with restrictions, supervision.

🆂🅰🆅🅴 🍴 &M 🛆 🛜 ✕ 📆 💻

Sheraton Vancouver Guildford Hotel

(604) 582-9288. **Call for rates.** 15269 104th Ave V3R 1N5. Trans-Canada Hwy 1 exit 48 eastbound, 0.6 mi (1 km) s on 152nd St, then just e; exit 50 westbound, just w. Int corridors. **Pets:** Medium, dogs only. Service with restrictions, supervision.

TOFINO

BEST WESTERN Tin Wis Resort Lodge

(250) 725-4445. **Call for rates.** 1119 Pacific Rim Hwy V0R 2Z0. 1.8 mi (3.5 km) s on Hwy 4. Ext corridors. **Pets:** Accepted.

Long Beach Lodge Resort

(250) 725-2442. **$199-$639, 7 day notice.** 1441 Pacific Rim Hwy V0R 2Z0. 4.7 mi (7.5 km) s on Hwy 4. Ext/int corridors. **Pets:** Other species. $50 one-time fee/room. Designated rooms.

Pacific Sands Beach Resort

(250) 725-3322. **$195-$790, 7 day notice.** 1421 Pacific Rim Hwy V0R 2Z0. 4.7 mi (7.5 km) s on Hwy 4. Ext corridors. **Pets:** Accepted.

Tofino Motel

(250) 725-2055. **$85-$215.** 542 Campbell St V0R 2Z0. Jct Campbell and 4th sts; downtown. Ext corridors. **Pets:** Medium, dogs only. $25 one-time fee/pet. Designated rooms, no service, supervision.

Wickaninnish Inn

(250) 725-3100. **$300-$580, 14 day notice.** 500 Osprey Ln at Chesterman Beach V0R 2Z0. 2.7 mi (4.3 km) e on Hwy 4. Int corridors. **Pets:** Other species. $40 daily fee/pet. Designated rooms, service with restrictions, crate.

TUMBLER RIDGE

Trend Mountain Hotel & Conference Center

(250) 242-2000. **$116-$250.** 375 Southgate St V0C 2W0. Hwy 29, just n on Monkman Way, 0.5 mi (0.9 km) ne. Int corridors. **Pets:** Accepted.

UCLUELET

Black Rock Oceanfront Resort

(250) 726-4800. **Call for rates.** 596 Marine Dr V0R 3A0. 1 mi (1.6 km) e on Peninsula Rd, just s on Matterson Rd, just w. Ext/int corridors. **Pets:** Accepted.

VALEMOUNT

BEST WESTERN PLUS Valemount Inn & Suites

(250) 566-0086. **$124-$166, 3 day notice.** 1950 Hwy 5 S V0E 2Z0. 0.9 mi (1.5 km) s on Hwy 5 (Yellowhead Hwy). Int corridors. **Pets:** Other species. $20 one-time fee/room. Designated rooms, service with restrictions.

VANCOUVER *(Restaurants p. 646)*

2400 Motel

(604) 434-2464. **$72-$189.** 2400 Kingsway V5R 5G9. 4.5 mi (7.2 km) se on Hwy 1A and 99A (Kingsway and 33rd Ave). Ext corridors. **Pets:** Other species. $15 daily fee/room. Designated rooms, service with restrictions, supervision.

BEST WESTERN PLUS Downtown Vancouver

(604) 669-9888. **$109-$229.** 718 Drake St V6Z 2W6. Between Howe and Granville sts. Int corridors. **Pets:** Accepted.

BEST WESTERN PLUS Sands

(604) 682-1831. **$110-$359.** 1755 Davie St V6G 1W5. Between Bidwell and Denman sts. Int corridors. **Pets:** Accepted.

The Burrard

(604) 681-2331. **Call for rates.** 1100 Burrard St V6Z 1Y7. Between Helmcken and Davie sts. Ext corridors. **Pets:** Medium. $25 daily fee/pet. Designated rooms, service with restrictions.

The Coast Coal Harbour Hotel

(604) 697-0202. **$159-$449.** 1180 W Hastings St V6E 4R5. Between Thurlow and Bute sts. Int corridors. **Pets:** $25 daily fee/pet. Designated rooms, service with restrictions, supervision.

Delta Vancouver Suites

(604) 689-8188. **$159-$399.** 550 W Hastings St V6B 1L6. Between Seymour and Richards sts; entrance in alley way. Int corridors. **Pets:** Accepted.

Executive Hotel Le Soleil

(604) 632-3000. **$169-$499.** 567 Hornby St V6C 2E8. Between Dunsmuir and Pender sts. Int corridors. **Pets:** Accepted.

The Fairmont Hotel Vancouver

(604) 684-3131. **$199-$449.** 900 W Georgia St V6C 2W6. Corner of Burrard at W Georgia St; enter from Hornby St. Int corridors. **Pets:** Accepted.

Fairmont Pacific Rim

(604) 695-5300. **$269-$639, 3 day notice.** 1038 Canada Place V6C 0B9. Between Burrard and Thurlow sts. **Pets:** Accepted.

The Fairmont Waterfront

(604) 691-1991. **$199-$539, 7 day notice.** 900 Canada Place Way V6C 3L5. Between Howe and Burrard sts. Int corridors. **Pets:** Accepted.

Four Seasons Hotel Vancouver

(604) 689-9333. **Call for rates.** 791 W Georgia St V6C 2T4. Between Howe and Granville sts. Int corridors. **Pets:** Other species. Service with restrictions, supervision.

Georgian Court Hotel

(604) 682-5555. **$159-$399.** 773 Beatty St V6B 2M4. Between Georgia and Robson sts. Int corridors. **Pets:** Large, other species. $20 daily fee/pet. Designated rooms, service with restrictions, crate.

Granville Island Hotel

(604) 683-7373. **$189-$550.** 1253 Johnston St V6H 3R9. Granville Island; below the bridge, follow signs. Int corridors. **Pets:** Large. $30 daily fee/room. Designated rooms, service with restrictions, supervision.

Holiday Inn Express Vancouver

(604) 254-1000. **$119-$309.** 2889 E Hastings St V5K 2A1. Between Renfrew and Kaslo sts. Int corridors. **Pets:** Accepted.

Hyatt Regency Vancouver

(604) 683-1234. **$139-$439.** 655 Burrard St V6C 2R7. Between W Georgia and Melville sts. Int corridors. **Pets:** Medium, dogs only. $100 one-time fee/room. Designated rooms, service with restrictions, supervision.

L'Hermitage Hotel

(778) 327-4100. **$200-$650.** 788 Richards St V6B 3A4. Between Robson and W Georgia sts. Int corridors. **Pets:** Accepted.

(CAA) ▼▼ ▼▼ **Pan Pacific Vancouver** H ❀

(604) 662-8111. **$199-$419.** 300-999 Canada Pl V6C 3B5. Between Howe and Burrard sts. Int corridors. **Pets:** Medium. $30 daily fee/room. Service with restrictions, supervision.

[SAVE] [ECO] [icons]

▼▼▼ **Pinnacle Vancouver Harbourfront Hotel** H

(604) 689-9211. **$149-$429.** 1133 W Hastings St V6E 3T3. Between Thurlow and Bute sts. Int corridors. **Pets:** Other species. $25 one-time fee/room. Service with restrictions, crate.

[ECO] [icons]

▼▼ **Quality Hotel Downtown-The Inn at False Creek** H

(604) 682-0229. **$199-$259.** 1335 Howe St V6Z 1R7. Between Drake and Pacific sts. Int corridors. **Pets:** Accepted.

[ECO] [icons]

(CAA) ▼▼▼ **Ramada Vancouver Downtown** H

(604) 685-1111. **$79-$299.** 1221 Granville St V6Z 1M6. Between Davie and Drake sts. Int corridors. **Pets:** Accepted.

[SAVE] [ECO] [icons]

(CAA) ▼▼▼ **Residence Inn by Marriott Vancouver Downtown** H

(604) 688-1234. **$135-$399.** 1234 Hornby St V6Z 1W2. Between Drake and Davie sts. Int corridors. **Pets:** Accepted.

[SAVE] [ECO] [icons]

(CAA) ▼▼▼▼ **Rosewood Hotel Georgia** H

(604) 682-5566. **$260-$475.** 801 W Georgia St V6C 1P7. Between Hornby and Howe sts, entrance on Howe St. Int corridors.
Pets: Accepted. [SAVE] [icons]

(CAA) ▼▼▼▼ **Shangri-La Hotel Vancouver** H

(604) 689-1120. **$225-$525.** 1128 W Georgia St V6E 0A8. Between Thurlow and Bute sts. Int corridors. **Pets:** Accepted.

[SAVE] [ECO] [icons]

(CAA) ▼▼▼ ▼▼ **Sheraton Vancouver Wall Centre Hotel** H

(604) 331-1000. **Call for rates.** 1088 Burrard St V6Z 2R9. Between Helmcken and Nelson sts. Int corridors. **Pets:** Accepted.

[SAVE] [ECO] [icons]

(CAA) ▼▼▼ ▼▼ **The Sutton Place Hotel** H

(604) 682-5511. **Call for rates.** 845 Burrard St V6Z 2K6. Between Smithe and Robson sts. Int corridors. **Pets:** Accepted.

[SAVE] [ECO] [icons]

▼▼ **Sylvia Hotel** H ❀

(604) 681-9321. **$100-$400.** 1154 Gilford St V6G 2P6. Between Pendrell St and Beach Ave. Int corridors. **Pets:** Other species. Service with restrictions, supervision. [icons]

(CAA) ▼▼ ▼▼ **Vancouver Marriott Pinnacle Downtown** H

(604) 684-1128. **$149-$429.** 1128 W Hastings St V6E 4R5. Between Thurlow and Bute sts. Int corridors. **Pets:** Accepted.

[SAVE] [ECO] [icons]

(CAA) ▼▼▼ ▼▼ **The Westin Bayshore Vancouver** H

(604) 682-3377. **$199-$510.** 1601 Bayshore Dr V6G 2V4. Jct W Georgia and Cardero sts. Int corridors. **Pets:** Accepted.

[SAVE] [ECO] [icons]

(CAA) ▼▼▼ ▼▼ **The Westin Grand, Vancouver** H

(604) 602-1999. **$199-$479.** 433 Robson St V6B 6L9. Between Homer and Richards sts. Int corridors. **Pets:** Accepted.

[SAVE] [ECO] [icons]

VERNON

(CAA) ▼▼▼ **BEST WESTERN PLUS Vernon Lodge & Conference Centre** H ❀

(250) 545-3385. **$130-$300, 3 day notice.** 3914 32nd St V1T 5P1. 1 mi (1.6 km) n on Hwy 97 (32nd St). Int corridors. **Pets:** Other species. $15 deposit/room, $100 daily fee/pet. Designated rooms, service with restrictions, supervision. [SAVE] [icons]

(CAA) ▼▼▼ **Days Inn Vernon** M

(250) 549-2224. **$85-$140.** 5121 26th St V1T 8G4. Hwy 97 (32nd St), 0.4 mi (0.7 km) e, just n on 27th St. Ext corridors. **Pets:** $15 daily fee/room. Designated rooms, service with restrictions, supervision.

[SAVE] [icons]

(CAA) ▼▼▼ **Holiday Inn Express Hotel & Suites Vernon** H

(250) 550-7777. **$130-$200.** 4716 34th St V1T 5Y9. Hwy 97 (32nd St); corner of 48th Ave. Int corridors. **Pets:** Accepted.

[SAVE] [icons]

(CAA) ▼▼▼ ▼▼ **Pacific Inn & Suites** H

(250) 558-1800. **Call for rates.** 4790 34th St V1T 5Y9. Hwy 97 (32nd St); corner of 48th Ave. Int corridors. **Pets:** $20 daily fee/room. Designated rooms, service with restrictions, supervision.

[SAVE] [icons]

(CAA) ▼▼▼ ▼▼ ▼▼ **Sparkling Hill Resort** H

(250) 275-1556. **$240-$580, 3 day notice.** 888 Sparkling Pl V1H 2K7. 6 mi (10 km) s on Hwy 97, 1.1 mi (1.9 km) n on Bailey Rd, 2.4 mi (4 km) nw on Commonage Rd, then 1.8 mi (3 km) w on Predator Ridge Dr, follow signs. Int corridors. **Pets:** Accepted.

[SAVE] [icons]

(CAA) ▼▼▼ **Super 8 Vernon** H

(250) 542-4434. **$79-$150.** 4204 32nd St V1T 5P4. Hwy 97 (32nd St); jct 43rd Ave. Int corridors. **Pets:** Accepted.

[SAVE] [icons]

(CAA) ▼▼▼ **Village Green Hotel** H

(250) 542-3321. **$102-$152, 5 day notice.** 4801 27th St V1T 4Z1. Hwy 97 (32nd St), 0.4 mi (0.7 km) e on 48th Ave. Int corridors. **Pets:** Medium. $10 daily fee/room. Designated rooms, supervision.

[SAVE] [icons]

VICTORIA

▼▼ ▼▼ **Accent Inns** H

(250) 475-7500. **$89-$179.** 3233 Maple St V8X 4Y9. 1.9 mi (3 km) n on Blanshard St (Hwy 17); corner of Blanshard St and Cloverdale Ave. Ext corridors. **Pets:** Accepted. [ECO] [icons]

▼▼ ▼▼ **Chateau Victoria Hotel and Suites** H

(250) 382-4221. **$99-$239, 3 day notice.** 740 Burdett Ave V8W 1B2. Between Douglas and Blanshard (Hwy 17) sts. Int corridors.
Pets: Accepted. [ECO] [icons]

(CAA) ▼▼▼ **Comfort Inn & Suites Victoria** H ❀

(250) 382-4400. **$99-$189.** 3020 Blanshard St V8T 5C7. 1.6 mi (2.6 km) n on Hwy 17 (Blanshard St), just s of Finlayson St. Ext/int corridors. **Pets:** $20 daily fee/pet. Designated rooms, supervision.

[SAVE] [ECO] [icons]

(CAA) ▼▼▼ **Days Inn Victoria on the Harbour** H ❀

(250) 386-3451. **$93-$203.** 427 Belleville St V8V 1X3. Between Oswego and Menzies sts. Int corridors. **Pets:** Other species. $15 daily fee/room. Designated rooms, service with restrictions, crate.

[SAVE] [ECO] [icons]

(CAA) ▼▼▼ ▼▼ **Delta Victoria Ocean Pointe Resort and Spa** H ❀

(250) 360-2999. **$129-$399.** 45 Songhees Rd V9A 6T3. Just w of Johnson St Bridge; jct Esquimalt and Tyee rds. Int corridors. **Pets:** Medium. $35 one-time fee/room. Designated rooms, service with restrictions, crate. [SAVE] [ECO] [icons]

ⒶⒶ ▼▼ **Econo Lodge Inn & Suites** 🅜 ❀

(250) 388-7861. **$67-$125.** 101 Island Hwy V9B 1E8. Douglas St, 3.1 mi (5 km) w on Gorge Rd, just s on Admirals Rd. Ext/int corridors. **Pets:** Medium, dogs only. $15 daily fee/pet. Designated rooms, service with restrictions, crate. 〔SAVE〕 🛄 🛜 🚪 🖵

▼▼ **Embassy Inn** 🄷 ❀

(250) 382-8161. **$89-$370.** 520 Menzies St V8V 2H4. Corner of Quebec St. Ext/int corridors. **Pets:** Medium. $20 daily fee/pet. Service with restrictions, supervision. 〔¶〕 〔�575M〕 🛄 🛜 🚫 🚪 🖵

ⒶⒶ ▼▼▼ **The Fairmont Empress** 🄷

(250) 384-8111. **$199-$499, 3 day notice.** 721 Government St V8W 1W5. Between Belleville and Humboldt sts. Int corridors. **Pets:** Accepted.
〔SAVE〕〔ECO〕〔¶〕〔ㄅM〕 🛄 🚫 🛰 🚫 🄺 🚪 🖵

ⒶⒶ ▼▼▼ **Harbour Towers Hotel & Suites** 🄷

(250) 385-2405. **$100-$450.** 345 Quebec St V8V 1W4. Between Oswego and Pendray sts. Int corridors. **Pets:** $35 one-time fee/pet. Designated rooms, service with restrictions.
〔SAVE〕〔ECO〕〔¶〕〔ㄅM〕 🛄 🚫 🛜 🚫 🄺 🚪 🖵

▼▼▼ **Hotel Zed** 🄷

(250) 388-4345. **Call for rates.** 3110 Douglas St V8Z 3K4. Between Finlayson St and Speed Ave. Ext corridors. **Pets:** Accepted.
〔ECO〕〔¶〕 🛄 🛜 🚫 🄺 🚪 🖵

ⒶⒶ ▼▼▼ **Huntingdon Manor** 🄷

(250) 381-3456. **$99-$275, 7 day notice.** 330 Quebec St V8V 1W3. Between Oswego and Pendray sts. Int corridors. **Pets:** Accepted.
〔SAVE〕〔¶〕 🛜 🚫 🚪 🖵

ⒶⒶ ▼▼▼▼ **The Magnolia Hotel & Spa** 🄷

(250) 381-0999. **Call for rates.** 623 Courtney St V8W 1B8. Corner of Courtney and Gordon sts. Int corridors. **Pets:** Accepted.
〔SAVE〕〔ECO〕〔¶〕 🛄 🛜 🚫 🚪 🖵

ⒶⒶ ▼▼ **Quality Inn Downtown Inner Harbour Victoria** 🄷

(250) 385-6787. **$69-$199.** 850 Blanshard St V8W 2H2. Between Courtney St and Burdett St. Int corridors. **Pets:** Medium, dogs only. $20 daily fee/room. Designated rooms, service with restrictions.
〔SAVE〕〔ECO〕 🛄 🛜 🚫 🄺 🚪 🖵

▼▼ **Robin Hood Motel** 🅜

(250) 388-4302. **$65-$149.** 136 Gorge Rd E V9A 1L4. From Douglas St, 1.2 mi (2 km) w. Ext corridors. **Pets:** Dogs only. $5 daily fee/pet. Designated rooms, service with restrictions, supervision. 🛜 🚪 🖵

ⒶⒶ ▼▼▼ **Royal Scot Hotel & Suites** 🄷

(250) 388-5463. **$399.** 425 Quebec St V8V 1W7. Between Menzies and Oswego sts. Int corridors. **Pets:** Dogs only. $50 one-time fee/pet. Designated rooms, service with restrictions, supervision.
〔SAVE〕〔ECO〕〔¶〕 🛄 🚫 🛜 🚫 🄺 🚪 🖵

▼▼▼ **Spinnakers Gastro Brewpub & Guesthouses** 🄱🄱

(250) 386-2739. **$149-$299, 7 day notice.** 308 Catherine St V9A 3S8. 1.3 mi (2 km) nw over Esquimalt Rd from jct Johnson St Bridge, just s. Ext/int corridors. **Pets:** $50 one-time fee/room. Designated rooms, service with restrictions.
〔¶〕 🛜 🚫 🄺 🚪 🖵

▼▼▼ **Swans Suite Hotel** 🄷

(250) 361-3310. **$149-$359.** 506 Pandora Ave V8W 1N6. Corner of Pandora Ave and Store St. Int corridors. **Pets:** Accepted.
〔¶〕 🛜 🚫 🄺 🚪 🖵

ⒶⒶ ▼▼▼ **Travelodge Victoria** 🄷 ❀

(250) 388-6611. **$65-$230.** 229 Gorge Rd E V9A 1L1. From Douglas St, 1.2 mi (2 km) w at Washington Ave. Ext corridors. **Pets:** $10 daily fee/pet. Service with restrictions, supervision.
〔SAVE〕〔ECO〕〔¶〕 🛄 🚪 🖵

ⒶⒶ ▼▼▼ ▼▼▼ **Victoria Marriott Inner Harbour** 🄷

(250) 480-3800. **$132-$361.** 728 Humboldt St V8W 3Z5. Between Blanshard (Hwy 17) and Douglas sts. Int corridors. **Pets:** Accepted.
〔SAVE〕〔¶〕〔ㄅM〕 🛄 🚫 🛜 🚫 🚪 🖵

ⒶⒶ ▼▼▼ ▼▼▼ **Westin Bear Mountain Golf Resort & Spa** 🄷 ❀

(250) 391-7160. **$109-$399.** 1999 Country Club Way V9B 6R3. Trans-Canada Hwy 1 exit 14 (Langford/Highlands), 1.1 mi (1.7 km) n on Millstream Rd, then 1.9 mi (3 km) ne on Bear Mountain Pkwy, follow signs. Int corridors. **Pets:** Small, dogs only. $20 daily fee/room. Designated rooms, service with restrictions, supervision.
〔SAVE〕〔ECO〕〔¶〕〔ㄅM〕 🛄 🚫 🛜 🚪 🖵

WEST KELOWNA

ⒶⒶ ▼▼▼▼ **BEST WESTERN PLUS Wine Country Hotel & Suites** 🄷 ❀

(250) 707-1637. **Call for rates.** 3460 Carrington Rd V4T 3C1. Hwy 97 (Okanagan Hwy), just e on Elk Rd. Int corridors. **Pets:** Medium. $20 daily fee/room. Designated rooms, service with restrictions, supervision.
〔SAVE〕〔ECO〕〔ㄅM〕 🛄 🛜 🚪 🖵

▼▼▼ **The Cove Lakeside Resort** 🄷 ❀

(250) 707-1800. **$159-$989, 7 day notice.** 4205 Gellatly Rd V4T 2K2. Hwy 97 (Okanagan Hwy), 1.5 mi (2.5 km) s, follow signs. Int corridors. **Pets:** Other species. $20 daily fee/pet. Designated rooms, service with restrictions, crate. 〔ECO〕〔¶〕〔ㄅM〕 🛄 🚫 🛜 🚫 🚪 🖵

▼▼ **Super 8 West Kelowna Hotel** 🄷

(250) 769-2355. **$90-$230.** 1655 Westgate Rd V1Z 3P1. Jct Hwy 97 (Okanagan Hwy) and Bartley Rd, s to Ross Rd. Int corridors. **Pets:** Accepted. 〔ㄅM〕 🛄 🛜 🚫 🖵

WHISTLER

▼▼▼ **Aava Whistler Hotel** 🄷

(604) 932-2522. **$101-$450, 14 day notice.** 4005 Whistler Way V0N 1B4. Hwy 99, just e on Village Gate Blvd, just s. Int corridors. **Pets:** Accepted. 〔ㄅM〕 🛄 🚫 🛜 🚫 🚪 🖵

▼▼▼ **The Coast Blackcomb Suites at Whistler** 🄲🄾

(604) 905-3400. **Call for rates.** 4899 Painted Cliff Rd V0N 1B4. Hwy 99, 0.6 mi (1 km) e on Lorimer Rd (Upper Village), just ne on Blackcomb Way, then just s, follow road to terminus. Int corridors.
Pets: Accepted. 〔ECO〕🔌〔ㄅM〕 🛄 🚫 🛜 🚫 🄺 🚪 🖵

▼▼▼ **Crystal Lodge & Suites** 🄷

(604) 932-2221. **$99-$373, 30 day notice.** 4154 Village Green V0N 1B4. Hwy 99, just e on Village Gate Blvd, just s on Whistler Way then just e. Int corridors. **Pets:** Accepted.
〔ECO〕〔¶〕〔ㄅM〕 🛄 🚫 🛜 🚫 🚪 🖵

▼▼▼▼ **Delta Whistler Village Suites** 🄷 ❀

(604) 905-3987. **$139-$649, 30 day notice.** 4308 Main St V0N 1B4. Hwy 99, just e on Village Gate Blvd, nw on Northlands Blvd, then just e. **Pets:** Medium. $35 one-time fee/room. Designated rooms, service with restrictions, supervision.
〔ECO〕〔ㄅM〕 🛄 🚫 🛜 🚫 🚪 🖵

ⒶⒶ ▼▼▼ **Edgewater Lodge** 🄷

(604) 932-0688. **$135-$339, 14 day notice.** 8020 Alpine Way V0N 1B0. 2.5 mi (4 km) n of Whistler Village via Hwy 99, just e. Ext corridors.
Pets: Accepted. 〔SAVE〕〔¶〕 🚫 🛜 🚫 🄺 🚪

ⒶⒶ ▼▼▼ ▼▼▼ **The Fairmont Chateau Whistler** 🄷 ❀

(604) 938-8000. **$179-$999, 3 day notice.** 4599 Chateau Blvd V0N 1B4. Hwy 99, 0.6 mi (1 km) e on Lorimer Rd (Upper Village), just s on Blackcomb Way, then just e. Int corridors. **Pets:** Other species. $50 daily fee/room. Service with restrictions, supervision.
〔SAVE〕〔ECO〕〔¶〕〔ㄅM〕 🛄 🚫 🛰 🚫 🚪 🖵

ⒶⒶ ▼▼▼ ▼▼▼ **Four Seasons Resort and Residences Whistler** 🄷

(604) 935-3400. **Call for rates.** 4591 Blackcomb Way V0N 1B4. Hwy 99, 0.6 mi (1 km) e on Lorimer Rd (Upper Village), just n. Int corridors.
Pets: Accepted. 〔SAVE〕〔¶〕〔ㄅM〕 🛄 🚫 🛜 🚫 🚪 🖵

ⓒⒶ ▼▼▼ **Hilton Whistler Resort & Spa** 🏨

(604) 932-1982. **$159-$447.** 4050 Whistler Way V0N 1B4. Hwy 99, just e on Village Gate Blvd, just s. Int corridors. **Pets:** Accepted.

⟦SAVE⟧ ⟦ECO⟧ 🍴 🅼 ⤳ ✕ 📶 ✕ ▮ 🖵

▼▼ **The Listel Hotel Whistler** 🏨

(604) 932-1133. **$89-$499, 14 day notice.** 4121 Village Green V0N 1B4. Hwy 99, just e on Village Gate Blvd, just s on Whistler Way, then just e. Int corridors. **Pets:** Accepted. 🍴 🅼 📶 ✕ ▮ 🖵

ⓒⒶ ▼▼ ▼▼ **Nita Lake Lodge** 🏨

(604) 966-5700. **$149-$650, 14 day notice.** 2131 Lake Placid Rd V0N 1B2. 1.8 mi (3 km) s on Hwy 99, just w. Int corridors. **Pets:** Accepted.

⟦SAVE⟧ ⟦ECO⟧ 🍴 🅼 ⤳ ✕ 📶 ✕ ▮ 🖵

▼▼▼ **Pan Pacific Whistler Village Centre** 🏨

(604) 966-5500. **$149-$959, 30 day notice.** 4299 Blackcomb Way V0N 1B4. Hwy 99, just e on Village Gate Blvd, just s. Int corridors.

Pets: Accepted. ⟦ECO⟧ 🅼 ⤳ ✕ 📶 ✕ ▮ 🖵

▼▼▼ **Summit Lodge & Spa** 🏨 ❀

(604) 932-2778. **Call for rates.** 4359 Main St V0N 1B4. Hwy 99, just e on Village Gate Blvd, just n on Northlands Blvd, then just e. Int corridors. **Pets:** Other species. Designated rooms, service with restrictions, supervision. ⟦ECO⟧ 🍴 🅼 ⤳ ✕ 📶 ✕ ▮ 🖵

▼▼ **Tantalus Resort Lodge** 🆑

(604) 932-4146. **$139-$599.** 4200 Whistler Way V0N 1B4. Hwy 99, just e on Village Gate Blvd, follow Whistler Way to terminus. Int corridors. **Pets:** Medium. $35 one-time fee/pet. Service with restrictions, crate.

⟦ECO⟧ ⤳ ✕ 📶 ✕ 🐾 ▮ 🖵

ⓒⒶ ▼▼ ▼▼ **The Westin Resort & Spa, Whistler** 🏨

(604) 905-5000. **Call for rates.** 4090 Whistler Way V0N 1B4. Hwy 99, just e on Village Gate Blvd, just s. Int corridors. **Pets:** Accepted.

⟦SAVE⟧ ⟦ECO⟧ 🍴 🅼 ⤳ ✕ 📶 ✕ ▮ 🖵

▼▼ **Whistler Pinnacle Hotel** 🏨

(604) 938-3218. **$129-$348, 30 day notice.** 4319 Main St V0N 1B4. Hwy 99, just e on Village Gate Blvd, just n on Northlands Blvd, then just e. Int corridors. **Pets:** Accepted.

🍴 🅼 ⤳ 📶 ✕ ▮ 🖵

▼▼ **Whistler Village Inn + Suites** 🏨

(604) 932-4004. **Call for rates.** 4429 Sundial Pl V0N 1B4. Hwy 99, just e on Village Gate Blvd, just s on Blackcomb Way. Int corridors.

Pets: Accepted. 🅼 ⤳ ✕ 📶 ✕ ▮ 🖵

WHITE ROCK

▼▼▼ **Ocean Promenade Hotel** 🏨

(604) 542-0102. **Call for rates.** 15611 Marine Dr V4B 1E1. Hwy 99 exit 2B southbound; exit 2 (White Rock/8th Ave) northbound, 1.3 mi (2 km) w. Ext/int corridors. **Pets:** Accepted. 🅼 📶 ✕ ▮ 🖵

WILLIAMS LAKE

ⓒⒶ ▼▼▼ **BEST WESTERN Williams Lake Hotel** 🏨

(778) 412-9000. **$129-$250.** 1850 S Broadway Ave V2G 5G8. 1.3 mi (2.1 km) s on Hwy 97. Int corridors. **Pets:** Accepted.

⟦SAVE⟧ 📶 ✕ ▮ 🖵

▼▼ **Ramada Williams Lake** 🏨

(250) 392-3321. **$102-$132.** 1118 Lakeview Cres V2G 1A3. Jct Hwy 97 and 20, just e. Int corridors. **Pets:** Other species. $15 daily fee/pet. Designated rooms, service with restrictions, supervision.

🍴 📶 ✕ ▮ 🖵

ⓒⒶ ▼▼ ▼▼ **Super 8 Williams Lake** Ⓜ

(250) 398-8884. **$87-$168.** 1712 Broadway Ave S V2G 2W4. 1.2 mi (2 km) s on Hwy 97. Int corridors. **Pets:** Medium, other species. $10 daily fee/pet. Designated rooms, crate. ⟦SAVE⟧ 🅼 📶 ✕ ▮ 🖵

MANITOBA

BRANDON

ⓒⒶ ▼▼ **Canad Inns Destination Centre Brandon** 🏨

(204) 727-1422. **$120-$250, 3 day notice.** 1125 18th St R7A 7C5. On Hwy 10 (18th St); jct Brandon Ave. Int corridors. **Pets:** Accepted.

⟦SAVE⟧ ⟦ECO⟧ 🍴 🅼 ⤳ 📶 ✕ ▮ 🖵

ⓒⒶ ▼▼ **Comfort Inn Brandon** Ⓜ ❀

(204) 727-6232. **$129-$219.** 925 Middleton Ave R7C 1A8. Trans-Canada Hwy 1; between Hwy 10 (18th St) N and 10 S; on north side of service road. Int corridors. **Pets:** Other species. $20 one-time fee/room. Service with restrictions, supervision.

⟦SAVE⟧ ⟦ECO⟧ ⟳ 🅼 📶 ✕ ▮ 🖵

▼▼ **Days Inn & Suites Brandon** 🏨

(204) 727-3600. **$89-$170.** 2130 Currie Blvd R7B 4E7. Jct Trans-Canada Hwy 1, 4.9 mi (7.9 km) s on Hwy 10 (18th St). Int corridors. **Pets:** $15 daily fee/pet. Designated rooms, service with restrictions, supervision. ⟦ECO⟧ 🅼 ⤳ 📶 ✕ ▮ 🖵

CHURCHILL

▼▼ **The Tundra Inn** 🏨

(204) 675-8831. **$135-$255, 30 day notice.** 34 Franklin St R0B 0E0. Just n on Kelsey Blvd, just e; center. Int corridors. **Pets:** Accepted.

🍴 🅼 📶 ✕ ⓐ ▮ 🖵

HEADINGLEY

▼▼▼ **BEST WESTERN PLUS Winnipeg West** 🏨

(204) 594-2200. **Call for rates.** 4140 Portage Ave R4H 1C5. Hwy 1(Portage Ave), east side of town. Int corridors. **Pets:** Accepted.

⟳ 🅼 📶 ✕ ▮ 🖵

HECLA

▼▼▼ **Lakeview Hecla Resort** 🏨

(204) 279-2041. **Call for rates.** Hwy 8 R0C 2R0. 3.7 mi (6 km) ne. Int corridors. **Pets:** Accepted. 🍴 ⤳ ✕ 📶 ✕ ▮ 🖵

RUSSELL

▼▼ **The Russell Inn Hotel & Conference Centre** 🏨 ❀

(204) 773-2186. **$89-$196, 14 day notice.** Hwy 16 R0J 1W0. 0.8 mi (1.2 km) se on Hwy 16 and 83. Ext/int corridors. **Pets:** Other species. Designated rooms, service with restrictions, crate.

🍴 ⤳ ✕ 📶 ✕ ▮ 🖵

STEINBACH

▼▼ **Days Inn** 🏨

(204) 320-9200. **$110-$120.** 75 Hwy 12 N R5G 1T3. 0.5 mi (0.8 km) n of jct Hwy 52. Int corridors. **Pets:** Accepted.

🅼 ⤳ 📶 ✕ ▮ 🖵

SWAN RIVER

▼▼ **Swan Valley Super 8** 🏨

(204) 734-7888. **$109-$144.** 115 Kelsey Tr R0L 1Z0. Corner of Hwy 10 and 83. Int corridors. **Pets:** Other species. $10 daily fee/room. Designated rooms, service with restrictions, supervision.

⟦ECO⟧ 🅼 📶 ▮ 🖵

THE PAS

▼▼ **Kikiwak Inn** 🏨

(204) 623-1800. **$115-$125.** Hwy 10 N R0B 2J0. On Hwy 10, 0.4 mi (0.6 km) n. Int corridors. **Pets:** Accepted.

🍴 🅼 ⤳ 📶 ✕ ▮ 🖵

▼▼ Super 8 **H**

(204) 623-1888. **$120-$130.** 1717 Gordon Ave R9A 1K3. At southern approach to town. Int corridors. **Pets:** Accepted.

🛆ᴹ 🚮 🛜 ✖ 🔋 🖵

THOMPSON

▼▼ Lakeview Inn & Suites **H**

(204) 778-8879. **$121, 3 day notice.** 70 Thompson Dr N R8N 1Y8. Just w of Hwy 6. Int corridors. **Pets:** $25 one-time fee/room. Service with restrictions, supervision. 🅴🅲🅾 🛆ᴹ ✖ 🛜 ✖ 🔋 🖵

WINNIPEG

ⒸⒶⒶ ▼▼▼▼ BEST WESTERN PLUS Pembina Inn & Suites **H** 🐾

(204) 269-8888. **$160-$238.** 1714 Pembina Hwy R3T 2G2. 0.6 mi (1 km) n of jct Bishop Grandin Blvd. Int corridors. **Pets:** $12 daily fee/pet. Designated rooms, supervision.

[SAVE] 🅴🅲🅾 🛆ᴹ 🚮 🛜 ✖ 🔋 🖵

ⒸⒶⒶ ▼▼▼▼ BEST WESTERN PLUS Winnipeg Airport Hotel **H**

(204) 775-9889. **$124-$149.** 1715 Wellington Ave R3H 0G1. At Century St. Int corridors. **Pets:** Large, other species. $50 deposit/pet. Designated rooms, service with restrictions, supervision.

[SAVE] 🅴🅲🅾 🍽 🛆ᴹ 🚮 🛜 🔋 🖵

ⒸⒶⒶ ▼▼ Canad Inns Destination Centre Polo Park **H** 🐾

(204) 775-8791. **$115-$259, 3 day notice.** 1405 St. Matthews Ave R3G 0K5. Just e of St James St. Int corridors. **Pets:** Designated rooms, service with restrictions, supervision.

[SAVE] 🅴🅲🅾 🍽 🛆ᴹ 🚮 🛜 ✖ 🔋 🖵

ⒸⒶⒶ ▼▼ Comfort Inn Airport **M**

(204) 783-5627. **$108-$142.** 1770 Sargent Ave R3H 0C8. At King Edward St. Int corridors. **Pets:** Large, other species. $15 daily fee/pet. Designated rooms, service with restrictions, crate.

[SAVE] 🅴🅲🅾 🛆ᴹ 🛜 ✖ 🔋 🖵

ⒸⒶⒶ ▼▼ Comfort Inn Winnipeg South **M**

(204) 269-7390. **$126-$160.** 3109 Pembina Hwy R3T 4R6. Just n of jct Perimeter Hwy 100 and 75. Int corridors. **Pets:** Medium. $15 daily fee/room. Designated rooms, service with restrictions, supervision.

[SAVE] 🅴🅲🅾 🛆ᴹ 🛜 ✖ 🔋 🖵

▼▼▼ Courtyard by Marriott Winnipeg Airport **H**

(204) 505-8600. **Call for rates.** 780 Powerhouse Rd R3H 1C7. At Winnipeg James Armstrong Richardson International Airport. Int corridors. **Pets:** Accepted. 🍽 🛜 ✖ 🔋 🖵

▼▼▼ Delta Winnipeg **H** 🐾

(204) 942-0551. **$109-$399, 7 day notice.** 350 St. Mary Ave R3C 3J2. At Hargrave St. Int corridors. **Pets:** Medium. $35 one-time fee/room. Service with restrictions, crate.

🅴🅲🅾 🍽 🛆ᴹ 🚮 🛜 ✖ 🔋 🖵

▼▼▼ Fairfield Inn & Suites by Marriott **H**

(204) 783-7900. **$139-$279.** 1301 Ellice Ave R3G 0N5. Between Empress and Strathcona sts. Int corridors. **Pets:** Accepted.

🚮 🛜 ✖ 🔋 🖵

▼▼▼ The Fairmont Winnipeg **H** 🐾

(204) 957-1350. **Call for rates.** 2 Lombard Pl R3B 0Y3. Just e of Portage Ave and Main St. Int corridors. **Pets:** $25 daily fee/pet. Service with restrictions. 🅴🅲🅾 🍽 🛆ᴹ 🚮 ✖ 🥓 ✖ 🖵

ⒸⒶⒶ ▼▼▼▼ Four Points by Sheraton Hotel Winnipeg Airport **H**

(204) 775-5222. **$119-$153.** 1999 Wellington Ave R3H 1H5. At Winnipeg James Armstrong Richardson International Airport. Int corridors. **Pets:** Accepted. [SAVE] 🅴🅲🅾 🍽 🛜 ✖ 🔋 🖵

▼▼▼▼ Hilton Winnipeg Airport Suites **H** 🐾

(204) 783-1700. **$120-$180.** 1800 Wellington Ave R3H 1B2. At Berry St. Int corridors. **Pets:** Medium, other species. Service with restrictions, crate. 🅴🅲🅾 🔗 🍽 🛆ᴹ 🚮 ✖ 🛜 ✖ 🔋 🖵

▼▼▼▼ Holiday Inn Winnipeg South **H**

(204) 452-4747. **Call for rates.** 1330 Pembina Hwy R3T 2B4. At McGillivray Blvd. Int corridors. **Pets:** Accepted.

🅴🅲🅾 🍽 🛆ᴹ 🚮 🛜 🔋 🖵

▼▼▼▼ Homewood Suites by Hilton Winnipeg Airport-Polo Park **H**

(204) 515-2126. **Call for rates.** 1295 Ellice Ave R3G 0N5. Between Empress and Strathcona sts. Int corridors. **Pets:** Accepted.

🛜 ✖ 🔋 🖵

ⒸⒶⒶ ▼▼▼▼ MainStay Suites Winnipeg **H**

(204) 594-0500. **$90-$160.** 670 King Edward St R3H 0P2. Between Sargent and Ellice aves. Int corridors. **Pets:** Accepted.

[SAVE] 🛆ᴹ ✖ 🛜 ✖ 🔋 🖵

▼▼▼▼ Mere Hotel **H**

(204) 594-0333. **Call for rates.** 333 Waterfront Dr R3C 0A2. Between Pacific and Bannatyne aves; downtown. Int corridors. **Pets:** Accepted.

🍽 🛆ᴹ 🛜 ✖ 🔋 🖵

ⒸⒶⒶ ▼▼▼ Quality Inn & Suites **H** 🐾

(204) 453-8247. **$89-$299.** 635 Pembina Hwy R3M 2L4. Just s of Grant Ave. Int corridors. **Pets:** Other species. $15 daily fee/pet. Service with restrictions. [SAVE] 🍽 🛜 🔋 🖵

ⒸⒶⒶ ▼▼▼ Radisson Hotel Winnipeg Downtown **H**

(204) 956-0410. **$160-$265, 3 day notice.** 288 Portage Ave R3C 0B8. At Smith St. Int corridors. **Pets:** Accepted.

[SAVE] 🅴🅲🅾 🍽 🛜 ✖ 🔋 🖵

▼▼▼▼ Sandman Hotel & Suites Winnipeg Airport **H**

(204) 775-7263. **$151.** 1750 Sargent Ave R3H 0C7. Between King Edward and Century sts. Int corridors. **Pets:** Accepted.

🅴🅲🅾 🍽 🛆ᴹ 🚮 🛜 ✖ 🔋 🖵

▼▼ Super 8 Winnipeg **M**

(204) 253-1935. **Call for rates.** 1485 Niakwa Rd E R2J 3T3. Jct Fermor Ave (Hwy 135) and Lagimodiere Blvd (Hwy 20), just e. Int corridors. **Pets:** Accepted. 🛜 ✖ 🔋 🖵

▼▼ Travelodge Winnipeg East **M**

(204) 255-6000. **$104-$164.** 20 Alpine Ave R2M 0Y5. Just e of jct Fermor Ave and St. Anne's Rd. Int corridors. **Pets:** Accepted.

🅴🅲🅾 🍽 🛆ᴹ 🚮 ✖ 🛜 ✖ 🔋 🖵

ⒸⒶⒶ ▼▼▼ Viscount Gort Hotel **H** 🐾

(204) 775-0451. **$117-$145.** 1670 Portage Ave R3J 0C9. Jct Rt 90. Int corridors. **Pets:** Medium. $10 daily fee/room. Designated rooms, service with restrictions, crate. [SAVE] 🍽 🛆ᴹ 🚮 🛜 ✖ 🔋 🖵

BATHURST

▼▼▼ Atlantic Host Hotel 🅷
(506) 548-3335. **$129-$225.** 1450 Vanier Blvd E2A 4H7. Rt 11 exit 310 (Vanier Blvd). Int corridors. **Pets:** Accepted.
🍴 ⓜ ➤ ✕ 🤝 🛄 ▣

▼▼ Comfort Inn 🅷
(506) 547-8000. **$89-$149.** 1170 St. Peter Ave E2A 2Z9. 2.1 mi (3.4 km) n on Rt 134 (St. Peter Ave). Int corridors. **Pets:** Accepted.
ⓜ 🤝 ✕ 🛄 ▣

▼▼ Danny's Inn & Conference Centre 🅷
(506) 546-6621. **$92-$159, 3 day notice.** 1223 rue Principale E2A 3Z2. Rt 11 exit 310 (Vanier Blvd) northbound to Rt 134 (St. Peter Ave), 2.3 mi (3.7 km) n; exit 318 southbound to Rt 134 (St. Peter Ave), 2.3 mi (3.7 km) s. Ext/int corridors. **Pets:** Designated rooms, service with restrictions, supervision. 🍴 ➤ 🤝 ✕ 🛄 ▣

BOUCTOUCHE

▼▼ Auberge Bouctouche Inn & Suites 🅷
(506) 743-5003. **$85-$165.** 50 Industrielle St E4S 3H9. Rt 11 exit 32A/B. Int corridors. **Pets:** $10 daily fee/pet. Designated rooms, service with restrictions, supervision. ⓜ 🤝 ✕ 🛄 ▣

CAMPBELLTON

▼▼ Comfort Inn 🅷
(506) 753-4121. **$105-$160.** 111 chemin Val D'Amour Rd E3N 5B9. Hwy 11 exit 415, 0.6 mi (1 km) e on Sugarloaf St W. Ext/int corridors. **Pets:** Accepted. 🅴🅒🅞 🤝 🛄 ▣

⒜ ▼▼ Quality Hotel & Conference Centre 🅷
(506) 753-4133. **$99-$127.** 157 Water St E3N 3H2. Hwy 134; in City Centre Complex. Int corridors. **Pets:** Accepted.
🆂🅰🆅🅴 🍴 ⓜ 🤝 ✕ 🛄 ▣

▼▼ Super 8-Campbellton 🅷
(506) 753-8080. **$100-$180.** 26 Duke St E3N 2K3. Just s of Roseberry St; jct George and Duke sts; downtown. Ext/int corridors. **Pets:** $20 daily fee/pet. Designated rooms, service with restrictions, supervision.
🅴🅒🅞 ⓜ ➤ ✕ 🤝 ✕ 🛄 ▣

CARAQUET

▼▼ Super 8 🅷
(506) 727-0888. **$115-$175.** 9 Carrefour Ave E1W 1B6. Just e of jct Rt 11 and St. Pierre Blvd E. Int corridors. **Pets:** Accepted.
ⓜ ➤ 🤝 ✕ 🛄 ▣

COCAGNE

▼ Cocagne Motel 🅼
(506) 576-6657. **Call for rates.** 1718 Rt 535 E4R 1N6. Rt 11 exit 15, 0.6 mi (1 km) n. Ext corridors. **Pets:** Accepted. 🤝 🛄 ▣

DALHOUSIE

⒜ ▼▼ Days Inn Dalhousie 🅷
(506) 684-5681. **$90-$99.** 385 Adelaide St E8C 1B4. At Brunswick St; center. Int corridors. **Pets:** Accepted.
🆂🅰🆅🅴 🍴 ⓜ 🤝 ✕ 🛄 ▣

DIEPPE

⒜ ▼▼▼ Coastal Inn 🅷
(506) 857-9686. **Call for rates.** 502 Kennedy St E1A 5Y7. At Paul St. Ext/int corridors. **Pets:** Other species. Designated rooms, service with restrictions, supervision. 🆂🅰🆅🅴 🅴🅒🅞 🍴 ➤ 🤝 🛄 ▣

⒜ ▼▼▼ Super 8 Moncton/Dieppe 🅷
(506) 858-8880. **$100-$140.** 370 Dieppe Blvd E1A 8H4. Hwy 15 exit 16, 0.6 mi (1 km) s. Int corridors. **Pets:** Accepted.
🆂🅰🆅🅴 🅴🅒🅞 ⓜ ➤ 🤝 ✕ 🛄 ▣

DOAKTOWN

▼▼▼▼ The Ledges Inn 🅒🅘
(506) 365-1820. **Call for rates.** 30 Ledges Inn Ln E9C 1A7. On Rt 8; just w of center. Ext corridors. **Pets:** Accepted. 🍴 🤝 ✕

EDMUNDSTON

⒜ ▼▼▼▼ BEST WESTERN PLUS Edmundston Hotel 🅷
(506) 739-0000. **$155-$375.** 280 Hebert Blvd E3V 0A3. Trans-Canada Hwy 2 exit 18 (Hebert Blvd). Ext/int corridors. **Pets:** Accepted.
🆂🅰🆅🅴 🅴🅒🅞 🄲🄴 ⓜ ➤ 🤝 ✕ 🛄 ▣

⒜ ▼▼▼ Comfort Inn 🅷
(506) 739-8361. **$108-$161.** 5 Bateman Ave E3V 3L1. Trans-Canada Hwy 2 exit 18 (Hebert Blvd). Ext/int corridors. **Pets:** Service with restrictions, supervision. 🆂🅰🆅🅴 🅴🅒🅞 🤝 ✕ 🛄 ▣

▼▼ Days Inn Edmundston 🅷
(506) 263-0000. **$75-$156.** 10 rue Mathieu E7C 3E1. Trans-Canada Hwy 2 exit 26. Ext/int corridors. **Pets:** Accepted. 🍴 🤝 🛄 ▣

⒜ ▼▼▼ Four Points by Sheraton Edmundston 🅷 ❀
(506) 739-7321. **$99-$295.** 100 rue Rice E3V 1T4. Trans-Canada Hwy 2 exit 18 (Hebert Blvd), 1 mi (1.6 km) sw, then just w on Church Rd. Int corridors. **Pets:** Medium. Designated rooms, service with restrictions, supervision. 🆂🅰🆅🅴 🍴 ⓜ ➤ 🤝 ✕ 🛄 ▣

▼▼ Quality Inn 🅷
(506) 735-5525. **$97-$175.** 919 chemin Canada Rd E3V 3X2. Trans-Canada Hwy 2 exit 13A-B. Ext/int corridors. **Pets:** Accepted.
🍴 ⓜ ➤ ✕ 🤝 🛄 ▣

FLORENCEVILLE-BRISTOL

▼▼ Florenceville Inn 🅼
(506) 392-6053. **$116-$146.** 239 Burnham Rd E7L 1Z1. Trans-Canada Hwy 2 exit 153, 2.5 mi (4 km) e on Rt 110 to Rt 130, 2 mi (3.7 km) s. Ext/int corridors. **Pets:** Accepted. 🍴 ➤ 🤝 ✕ 🛄 ▣

FREDERICTON

⒜ ▼▼▼▼ BEST WESTERN PLUS Fredericton Hotel & Suites 🅷
(506) 455-8448. **$135-$155.** 333 Bishop Dr E3C 2M6. Rt 8 exit 6A eastbound; exit 6B westbound, just w of Regent Mall. Int corridors. **Pets:** Accepted. 🆂🅰🆅🅴 🍴 ⓜ ➤ 🤝 ✕ 🛄 ▣

▼▼ City Motel 🅷
(506) 450-9900. **$85-$100.** 1216 Regent St E3B 3Z4. Trans-Canada Hwy 2 exit 285A eastbound; exit 285B westbound, 2 mi (3.3 km) n on Rt 101 (Regent St). Int corridors. **Pets:** $150 deposit/room. Crate.
🍴 🤝 🛄 ▣

⒜ ▼▼ Comfort Inn 🅷 ❀
(506) 453-0800. **$104-$160.** 797 Prospect St E3B 5Y4. Trans-Canada Hwy 2 exit 281, 2.5 mi (4 km) ne on Rt 640 (Hanwell Rd), then right. Int corridors. **Pets:** Other species. Service with restrictions.
🆂🅰🆅🅴 🅴🅒🅞 ⓜ 🤝 ✕ 🛄 ▣

▼▼▼ Crowne Plaza Fredericton Lord Beaverbrook 🅷 ❀
(506) 455-3371. **$140-$260.** 659 Queen St E3B 1C3. Corner of Regent St. Int corridors. **Pets:** Designated rooms, service with restrictions, crate. 🅴🅒🅞 🄲🄴 🍴 ➤ ✕ 🤝 ✕ 🛄 ▣

⒜ ▼▼▼▼ Delta Fredericton 🅷 ❀
(506) 457-7000. **$149-$259.** 225 Woodstock Rd E3B 2H8. 1 mi (1.6 km) n on Rt 102; downtown. Int corridors. **Pets:** Medium, other species. $35 one-time fee/room. Service with restrictions, supervision.
🆂🅰🆅🅴 🅴🅒🅞 🍴 ⓜ ➤ 🤝 ✕ 🛄 ▣

Ⓐ ▼▼ **Fredericton Inn** 🅷

(506) 455-1430. **$109-$159.** 1315 Regent St E3C 1A1. Trans-Canada Hwy 2 exit 285A eastbound; exit 285B. Ext/int corridors. **Pets:** Accepted. 🆂🅰🆅🅴 🍽 🛜 ✖ 🔒 💻

▼▼▼ **Holiday Inn Express & Suites** 🅷

(506) 459-0035. **$135-$219.** 665 Prospect St E3B 6B8. Rt 8 exit 3 (Hanwell Rd) eastbound; exit 5 (Smythe St) westbound. Int corridors. **Pets:** Accepted. 🅴🅲🅾 🛜 ✖ 🔒 💻

▼▼ **Knights Inn** 🅼

(506) 458-8784. **$46-$87.** 1214 Lincoln Rd E3B 8C8. 1.2 mi (2 km) n on Rt 102 from airport. Ext corridors. **Pets:** Accepted. 🍽 🛜 ✖ 🔒

▼▼ **Ramada Hotel Fredericton** 🅷

(506) 460-5500. **$89-$159.** 480 Riverside Dr E3A 8C2. On Rt 105; at north end of Princess Margaret Bridge. Int corridors. **Pets:** Accepted. 🅴🅲🅾 🍽 🏊 ✖ 🛜 ✖ 🔒 💻

GRAND FALLS

Ⓐ ▼▼▼ **BEST WESTERN PLUS Grand-Sault Hotel & Suites** 🅷

(506) 473-6200. **$135-$155.** 187 Ouellette St E3Z 3E8. Trans-Canada Hwy 2 exit 79. Int corridors. **Pets:** Accepted. 🆂🅰🆅🅴 🅴🅲🅾 🍽 🛜 🏊 🛜 ✖ 🔒 💻

▼▼ **Quality Inn Grand Falls** 🅷

(506) 473-1300. **$135-$185.** 10039 Rt 144 E3Y 3H5. Trans-Canada Hwy 2 exit 75, just w. Ext/int corridors. **Pets:** Very small. $15 one-time fee/room. Designated rooms, service with restrictions, supervision. 🍽 🛜 🏊 ✖ 🛜 🔒 💻

MIRAMICHI

▼ **Camping Miramichi Cottages** 🅲🅰

(506) 773-6252. **Call for rates.** 116 N Black River Rd E1N 5S4. 6 mi (10 km) s on Hwy 11, 0.6 mi (1 km) e. Int corridors. **Pets:** Accepted. 🍽 🏊 🛜 🐾 🔒 💻

▼▼ **Days Inn** 🅷

(506) 622-1215. **$89-$149.** 475 King George Hwy E1V 7G2. 0.6 mi (1 km) w of center. Int corridors. **Pets:** Large. $10 daily fee/pet. Designated rooms, service with restrictions, supervision. 🅴🅲🅾 🛜 🔒 💻

▼▼ **Howard Johnson Inn & Suites Miramichi** 🅷

(506) 622-0302. **$88-$119.** 1 Jane St E1V 2S6. Just s off King George Hwy. Int corridors. **Pets:** Accepted. 🍽 🏊 🛜 ✖ 🔒 💻

▼▼ **Lakeview Inns & Suites** 🅷

(506) 627-1999. **Call for rates.** 333 King George Hwy E1V 1L2. 1.1 mi (1.8 km) w from center. Int corridors. **Pets:** Accepted. 🅴🅲🅾 🛜 🔒 💻

▼▼▼ **Rodd Miramichi River-A Rodd Signature Hotel** 🅷 🐾

(506) 773-3111. **$115-$199.** 1809 Water St E1N 1B2. Hwy 11 exit 120, 1 mi (1.6 km) e. Int corridors. **Pets:** Designated rooms, service with restrictions, crate. 🅴🅲🅾 🍽 🛜 🏊 ✖ 🛜 ✖ 🔒 💻

MONCTON

Ⓐ ▼▼▼▼ **Casino New Brunswick** 🅷 🐾

(506) 861-4661. **$149-$999.** 21 Casino Dr E1G 0R7. Trans-Canada Hwy 2 exit 450. Int corridors. **Pets:** $30 one-time fee/room. Designated rooms, service with restrictions, crate.
🆂🅰🆅🅴 🍽 🛜 🏊 ✖ 🛜 ✖ 🔒 💻

Ⓐ ▼▼ **Comfort Inn** 🅷

(506) 384-3175. **$105-$156.** 2495 Mountain Rd E1G 2W4. Trans-Canada Hwy 2 exit 450. Int corridors. **Pets:** Large, other species. Service with restrictions, supervision. 🆂🅰🆅🅴 🅴🅲🅾 🛜 ✖ 🔒 💻

Ⓐ ▼▼ **Comfort Inn** 🅷

(506) 859-6868. **$99-$169.** 20 Maplewood Dr E1A 6P9. Trans-Canada Hwy 2 exit 459A on Hwy 115 S, left on Rt 134 E (Lewisville Rd). Int corridors. **Pets:** Large, other species. Service with restrictions, supervision. 🆂🅰🆅🅴 🅴🅲🅾 🛜 ✖ 🔒 💻

Ⓐ ▼▼▼ **Crowne Plaza Moncton Downtown** 🅷

(506) 854-6340. **$119-$159.** 1005 Main St E1C 1G9. At Highfield and Main sts; downtown. Int corridors. **Pets:** Accepted. 🆂🅰🆅🅴 🅴🅲🅾 🍽 🏊 ✖ 🛜 ✖ 🔒 💻

▼▼▼ **Delta Beausejour** 🅷 🐾

(506) 854-4344. **$129-$329.** 750 Main St E1C 1E6. Jct Main St and Sommet Ln; downtown. Int corridors. **Pets:** Other species. $35 one-time fee/room. Service with restrictions, supervision. 🅴🅲🅾 ♿ 🍽 🏊 ✖ 🛜 ✖ 🔒 💻

Ⓐ ▼▼▼ **Four Points by Sheraton Moncton** 🅷

(506) 852-9600. **$119-$189.** 40 Lady Ada Blvd E1G 0E3. Trans-Canada Hwy 2 exit 454. Int corridors. **Pets:** Accepted. 🆂🅰🆅🅴 🍽 🛜 🛜 ✖ 🔒 💻

Ⓐ ▼▼▼ **Hampton Inn & Suites Moncton** 🅷

(506) 855-4819. **$139-$170.** 700 Mapleton Rd E1G 0L7. Trans-Canada Hwy 2 exit 454. Int corridors. **Pets:** Accepted. 🆂🅰🆅🅴 🍽 🛜 🏊 🛜 ✖ 🔒 💻

Ⓐ ▼▼▼ **Holiday Inn Express Hotel & Suites Moncton** 🅷

(506) 384-1050. **$109-$159.** 2515 Mountain Rd E1G 2W4. Trans-Canada Hwy 2 exit 450. Ext/int corridors. **Pets:** Accepted. 🆂🅰🆅🅴 🅴🅲🅾 🛜 🏊 ✖ 🛜 ✖ 🔒 💻

▼▼▼ **Hotel St. James** 🅷

(506) 388-4283. **Call for rates.** 14 Church St E1C 4Y9. Corner of Main and Church sts. Int corridors. **Pets:** Accepted. 🍽 🛜 ✖ 🔒

Ⓐ ▼▼ **Quality Inn** 🅷

(506) 386-6749. **Call for rates.** 2530 Mountain Rd E1G 1B4. Trans-Canada Hwy 2 exit 450. Int corridors. **Pets:** Other species. Service with restrictions, crate. 🆂🅰🆅🅴 🛜 🏊 🛜 ✖ 🔒

Ⓐ ▼▼▼ **Residence Inn by Marriott Moncton** 🅷 🐾

(506) 854-7100. **$125-$206.** 600 Main St E1C 0M6. At Assomption Blvd. Int corridors. **Pets:** Other species. $75 one-time fee/room. Designated rooms, service with restrictions, supervision. 🆂🅰🆅🅴 🅴🅲🅾 🍽 🛜 🏊 🛜 ✖ 🔒 💻

▼▼ **Rodd Moncton** 🅷

(506) 382-1664. **$99-$159.** 434 Main St E1C 1B9. On Rt 106 (Main St) at King St. Ext/int corridors. **Pets:** Accepted. 🅴🅲🅾 🏊 🛜 ✖ 🔒 💻

Ⓐ ▼▼▼ **Travelodge Suites Moncton** 🅷 🐾

(506) 852-7000. **$89-$249.** 2475 Mountain Rd E1G 2J5. Trans-Canada Hwy 2 exit 450. Int corridors. **Pets:** $10 one-time fee/room. Service with restrictions, crate. 🆂🅰🆅🅴 🅴🅲🅾 🛜 🔒 💻

▼▼ **V Hotel & Suites** 🅷

(506) 382-3395. **$89-$130.** 42 Highfield St E1C 5N3. Center; 1 blk n of Main St. Ext/int corridors. **Pets:** Accepted. 🍽 🏊 🛜 ✖ 🔒 💻

OROMOCTO

Ⓐ ▼▼▼ **Days Inn & Conference Centre Oromocto** 🅷

(506) 357-5657. **$105-$221.** 60 Brayson Blvd E2V 4T9. Trans-Canada Hwy 2 exit 301 eastbound; exit 303 westbound, just s to Pioneer Ave, then 1 mi (1.6 km) w. Int corridors. **Pets:** Large, other species. $15 daily fee/pet. Designated rooms, service with restrictions, supervision. 🆂🅰🆅🅴 🅴🅲🅾 🍽 🛜 🏊 🛜 ✖ 🔒 💻

PERTH-ANDOVER

Ⓐ ▼▼▼▼ **The Castle Inn** CI
(506) 273-9495. **$119-$229.** 21 Brentwood Dr E7H 1P1. Trans-Canada Hwy 2 exit 115, follow signs over Saint John River, then s on Station Rd. Int corridors. **Pets:** Accepted.
SAVE ⊡ ⊡ ⊡ ⊡ ⊡ ⊡ ⊡

POINTE-VERTE

▼▼▼▼ **Gite Toutes Saisons Bed & Breakfast** BB
(506) 783-3122. **Call for rates.** 10 rue des Oiseaux E8J 2V6. Rt 11 exit 333 to Rt 134, 0.8 mi (1.3 km) nw. Int corridors. **Pets:** Dogs only. $25 one-time fee/pet. Designated rooms, service with restrictions, supervision. ⊡ ⊡ ⊡ ⊡ ⊡ ⊡ ⊡

SACKVILLE

▼▼ ▼▼ **Coastal Inn Sackville** H
(506) 536-0000. **$99-$155.** 15 Wright St E4L 4P8. Trans-Canada Hwy 2 exit 504. Int corridors. **Pets:** Designated rooms, service with restrictions, supervision. ⊡ ⊡ ⊡ ⊡ ⊡

Ⓐ ▼▼▼▼ **Marshlands Inn** CI
(506) 536-0170. **$94-$225.** 55 Bridge St E4L 3N8. On Hwy 106; center. Int corridors. **Pets:** Accepted. SAVE ⊡ ⊡ ⊡

ST. ANDREWS

Ⓐ ▼▼▼▼▼ **The Algonquin Resort, Autograph Collection** H ❀
(506) 529-8823. **$97-$229, 3 day notice.** 184 Adolphus St E5B 1T7. Off Hwy 127. Int corridors. **Pets:** Other species. $35 one-time fee/room. Designated rooms, service with restrictions, supervision.
SAVE ⊡ ⊡ ⊡ ⊡ ⊡ ⊡ ⊡ ⊡

Ⓐ ▼▼▼▼ **Tara Manor Inn** M ❀
(506) 529-3304. **$99-$169, 3 day notice.** 559 Mowat Dr E5B 2P2. 1.7 mi (2.8 km) n on Hwy 127. Ext corridors. **Pets:** Medium, dogs only. $25 one-time fee/pet. Designated rooms, service with restrictions, supervision. SAVE ⊡ ⊡ ⊡ ⊡ ⊡

ST-JACQUES

▼▼ ▼▼ **Auberge Les Jardins Inn** H
(506) 739-5514. **$89-$179.** 60 Principale St E7B 1V7. Trans-Canada Hwy 2 exit 8, just e. Ext/int corridors. **Pets:** Accepted.
⊡ ⊡ ⊡ ⊡

SAINT JOHN *(Restaurants p. 646)*

Ⓐ ▼▼▼▼ **BEST WESTERN PLUS Saint John Hotel & Suites** H ❀
(506) 657-9966. **$109-$149.** 55 Majors Brook Dr E2J 0B2. Hwy 1 exit 129 westbound, 1 mi (1.6 km) s on Rt 100 (Rothesay Ave) to McAllister Dr, just e; exit 128 eastbound, 1 mi (1.6 km) n on Rt 100 (Rothesay Ave), just n to McAllister Dr, just e. Int corridors. **Pets:** Medium. $15 daily fee/pet. Designated rooms, service with restrictions, supervision.
SAVE ⊡ ⊡ ⊡ ⊡ ⊡ ⊡

Ⓐ ▼▼▼ **Comfort Inn** H ❀
(506) 674-1873. **$100-$145.** 1155 Fairville Blvd E2M 5T9. Hwy 1 exit 117 westbound; exit 119 eastbound, then left. Int corridors. **Pets:** Large. Service with restrictions. SAVE ⊡ ⊡ ⊡ ⊡

Ⓐ ▼▼▼▼ **Delta Brunswick** H
(506) 648-1981. **$90-$234.** 39 King St E2L 4W3. Center of downtown; in Brunswick Square Mall. Int corridors. **Pets:** Accepted.
SAVE ⊡ ⊡ ⊡ ⊡ ⊡ ⊡ ⊡ ⊡

Ⓐ ▼▼▼▼ **Hampton Inn & Suites** H
(506) 657-4600. **$119-$199.** 51 Fashion Dr E2J 0A7. Hwy 1 exit 129, 1.5 mi (2.4 km) s on Rothesay Ave to Retail Dr; behind Home Depot. Int corridors. **Pets:** Accepted. SAVE ⊡ ⊡ ⊡ ⊡ ⊡ ⊡

Ⓐ ▼▼▼▼ **Hilton Saint John** H ❀
(506) 693-8484. **$99-$159.** 1 Market Square E2L 4Z6. Hwy 1 exit 122; at Market Square. Int corridors. **Pets:** Other species. Service with restrictions, crate. SAVE ⊡ ⊡ ⊡ ⊡ ⊡ ⊡ ⊡

Ⓐ ▼▼▼▼ **Holiday Inn Express & Suites** H
(506) 642-2622. **$119-$159.** 400 Main St/Chesley Dr E2K 4N5. 0.6 mi (1 km) w on Hwy 1; north end of Chesley Dr exit 121; off Harbour Bridge. Int corridors. **Pets:** Accepted.
SAVE ⊡ ⊡ ⊡ ⊡ ⊡ ⊡

▼▼▼▼ **Homeport Historic Inn Circa 1858** BB ❀
(506) 672-7255. **$109-$175, 4 day notice.** 80 Douglas Ave E2K 1E4. Hwy 1 exit 121 eastbound; exit 123 westbound. Int corridors. **Pets:** Dogs only. Supervision. ⊡ ⊡ ⊡ ⊡

▼▼ ▼▼ **Howard Johnson Fort Howe Plaza & Convention Center** H
(506) 657-7320. **$124-$149.** 10 Portland St E2K 4H8. Hwy 1 exit 123 westbound; exit 121 eastbound off Harbour Bridge. Int corridors. **Pets:** Accepted. ⊡ ⊡ ⊡ ⊡ ⊡ ⊡

▼▼ ▼▼ **Travelodge Suites Saint John** H
(506) 635-0400. **$95-$114.** 1011 Fairville Blvd E2M 5T9. Hwy 1 exit 119A westbound; exit 119B eastbound, left on Catherwood Dr, then left at lights. Int corridors. **Pets:** Accepted. ⊡ ⊡ ⊡ ⊡

ST-LEONARD

Ⓐ ▼▼ ▼▼ **Daigle's Motel** M
(506) 423-6351. **$89-$129, 3 day notice.** 68 rue DuPont E7E 1Y1. Hwy 17, 0.6 mi (1 km) s of Trans-Canada Hwy 2 exit 58. Ext corridors.
Pets: Accepted. SAVE ⊡ ⊡ ⊡ ⊡ ⊡ ⊡ ⊡

ST. MARTINS

▼▼ ▼▼ **Weslan Inn** BB ❀
(506) 833-2351. **Call for rates.** 45 Main St E5R 1B4. Just e off Rt 111. Int corridors. **Pets:** Medium, dogs only. Designated rooms, no service, supervision. ⊡ ⊡ ⊡ ⊡ ⊡

ST. STEPHEN

▼▼ **St. Stephen Inn** M
(506) 466-1814. **Call for rates.** 99 King St E3L 2C6. Just n of Prince William St; center. Ext/int corridors. **Pets:** Medium. $10 daily fee/pet. Service with restrictions, supervision. ⊡ ⊡

Ⓐ ▼▼▼ **Winsome Inn** M
(506) 466-2130. **$92-$130, 3 day notice.** 198 King St E3L 2E2. Hwy 1 exit King St, just s on Rt 3. Ext corridors. **Pets:** Other species. $10 daily fee/room. Designated rooms, service with restrictions, supervision.
SAVE ⊡ ⊡ ⊡ ⊡ ⊡

SHEDIAC

▼▼ **Gaudet Chalets & Motel** M
(506) 533-8877. **Call for rates.** 14 Bellevue Heights E4P 1H2. On Rt 133, 1.4 mi (2.4 km) w of Rt 15 exit 37. Ext corridors. **Pets:** Accepted.
⊡ ⊡ ⊡

Ⓐ ▼▼▼▼ **Hotel Shediac** H
(506) 532-6100. **$139-$209.** 222 Belliveau St E4P 0M2. Rt 133 at Weldon St, just n. Int corridors. **Pets:** Accepted.
SAVE ⊡ ⊡ ⊡ ⊡ ⊡ ⊡

▼▼ ▼▼ **Seely's Motel** M
(506) 532-6193. **$79-$179, 3 day notice.** 21 Bellevue Heights E4P 1G9. On Rt 133, 1.5 mi (2.4 km) w of Rt 15 exit 37. Ext corridors.
Pets: Accepted. ⊡ ⊡ ⊡ ⊡ ⊡

SUSSEX

All Seasons Inn M

(506) 433-2220. **$69-$149, 3 day notice.** 1015 Main St E4E 2M6. Hwy 1 exit 192 eastbound; exit 198 westbound, left towards Sussex Corner; center. Ext corridors. **Pets:** Accepted.

Fairway Inn H

(506) 433-3470. **$135-$185, 3 day notice.** 216 Roachville Rd E4E 5L6. Hwy 1 exit 193. Ext/int corridors. **Pets:** Medium. $10 daily fee/pet. Designated rooms, service with restrictions, supervision.

WAASIS

Travelodge Fredericton M

(506) 446-9077. **Call for rates.** 42 Chaperral Rd E3B 0G9. Trans-Canada Hwy 2 exit 297. Ext/int corridors. **Pets:** Accepted.

WOODSTOCK

BEST WESTERN PLUS Woodstock Hotel & Conference Centre H

(506) 328-2378. **$140-$170.** 123 Gallop Ct E7M 3P7. Trans-Canada Hwy 2 exit 185. Int corridors. **Pets:** Medium. $20 one-time fee/room. Designated rooms, service with restrictions, supervision.

Canadas Best Value Inn & Suites H

(506) 328-8876. **$70-$120.** 168 Houlton Rd (Rt 555) E7M 6B5. Trans-Canada Hwy 2 exit 188 (Houlton Rd). Ext/int corridors. **Pets:** Accepted.

Howard Johnson Inn M

(506) 328-3315. **$85-$139.** 159 Rt 555 exit 188 TCH E7M 6B5. Trans-Canada Hwy 2 exit 188 (Houlton Rd). Ext/int corridors. **Pets:** Designated rooms, service with restrictions, supervision.

NEWFOUNDLAND AND LABRADOR

CHANNEL-PORT AUX BASQUES

Hotel Port Aux Basques H

(709) 695-2171. **$115, 3 day notice.** 1 Grand Bay Rd A0M 1C0. Jct Trans-Canada Hwy 1. Int corridors. **Pets:** Accepted.

St. Christopher's Hotel H

(709) 695-7034. **Call for rates.** 146 Caribou Rd A0M 1C0. Trans-Canada Hwy 1 exit Port aux Basques, follow signs 1.2 mi (2 km); downtown. Int corridors. **Pets:** Accepted.

CLARENVILLE

St. Jude Hotel H

(709) 466-1717. **$113-$134.** 247 Trans-Canada Hwy A5A 1Y4. Center. Int corridors. **Pets:** Medium, other species. $25 one-time fee/room. Designated rooms, service with restrictions, supervision.

CORNER BROOK

Comfort Inn H ❀

(709) 639-1980. **$129-$152.** 41 Maple Valley Rd A2H 6T2. Trans-Canada Hwy 1 exit 5 eastbound; exit 6 westbound, via Confederation Ave. Int corridors. **Pets:** Designated rooms, service with restrictions, supervision.

Glynmill Inn H

(709) 634-5181. **$118-$204, 3 day notice.** 1B Cobb Ln A2H 2V3. Just w of W Valley Rd; center. Int corridors. **Pets:** $250 deposit/room. Designated rooms, service with restrictions, supervision.

COW HEAD

Shallow Bay Motel & Cabins H

(709) 243-2471. **$125-$139, 3 day notice.** Rt 430, The Viking Tr A0K 2A0. Hwy 430, 2.5 mi (4 km) w towards the ocean, follow signs. Ext/int corridors. **Pets:** Other species. $15 daily fee/pet. Designated rooms, service with restrictions, supervision.

DEER LAKE

Holiday Inn Express H

(709) 635-3232. **Call for rates.** 38 Bennett Ave A8A 1A9. Trans-Canada Hwy 1 exit 15, just n on Nicholsville Rd, then just s. Int corridors. **Pets:** Accepted.

GANDER

Albatross Hotel H

(709) 256-3956. **Call for rates.** 114 Trans-Canada Hwy A1V 1W8. On Trans-Canada Hwy 1. Ext/int corridors. **Pets:** Other species. Designated rooms, service with restrictions, crate.

Comfort Inn H

(709) 256-3535. **$135-$175.** 112 Trans-Canada Hwy 1 A1V 1P8. Center. Ext/int corridors. **Pets:** Accepted.

Sinbad's Hotel & Suites H

(709) 651-2678. **$138-$299.** 133 Bennett Dr A1V 1W8. Center; opposite Gander Mall. Ext corridors. **Pets:** Medium, other species. Designated rooms, service with restrictions, crate.

GRAND FALLS-WINDSOR

Mount Peyton Hotel H

(709) 489-2251. **$115-$125.** 214 Lincoln Rd A2A 1P8. 0.6 mi (1 km) ne on Trans-Canada Hwy 1. Ext/int corridors. **Pets:** Accepted.

PORT BLANDFORD

Terra Nova Golf Resort H

(709) 543-2525. **Call for rates.** Trans-Canada Hwy 1 A0C 2G0. Center. Int corridors. **Pets:** Accepted.

ROCKY HARBOUR

Fisherman's Landing Inn H

(709) 458-2711. **$109-$189.** 21-29 W Link Rd A0K 4N0. Rt 430; first entrance to Rocky Harbour. Ext/int corridors. **Pets:** Small, dogs only. $25 one-time fee/pet. Service with restrictions, supervision.

Ocean View Hotel H

(709) 458-2730. **Call for rates.** 38-42 Main St A0K 4N0. Rt 430, just s on W Link Rd, just w on Pond Rd, then just n. Ext/int corridors. **Pets:** Accepted.

ST. JOHN'S

Capital Hotel H

(709) 738-4480. **$141-$151.** 208 Kenmount Rd A1B 3P9. Trans-Canada Hwy 1 exit 45, 4 mi (6.4 km) s on Team Gushue Hwy to Kenmount Rd. Int corridors. **Pets:** Medium, other species. Designated rooms, service with restrictions, crate.

Comfort Inn Airport H ❀

(709) 753-3500. **$120-$190.** 106 Airport Rd A1A 4Y3. Trans-Canada Hwy 1 exit 47A, 0.6 mi (1 km) n on Rt 40 (Portugal Cove Rd). Int corridors. **Pets:** $35 one-time fee/room. Service with restrictions, crate.

Delta St. John's Hotel and Conference Centre H

(709) 739-6404. **Call for rates.** 120 New Gower St A1C 6K4. At Barter's Hill Rd; center. Int corridors. **Pets:** Medium, dogs only. $35 one-time fee/pet. Designated rooms, service with restrictions, supervision.

▼▼▼ **Extended Stay Canada** 🏠
(709) 754-7888. **Call for rates.** 222 LeMarchant Rd A1C 2H9. Corner of Pleasant St. Int corridors. **Pets:** Other species. $25 daily fee/pet. Service with restrictions, supervision. ♿ 📶 ✖ 🔋 💻

▼▼ **The Guv'nor Inn** 🏠
(709) 726-0092. **$120-$230.** 389 Elizabeth Ave A1B 1V1. 2 blks n of Freshwater Rd. Ext/int corridors. **Pets:** Accepted. 🍴 📶 🔋 💻

▼▼▼▼ **Holiday Inn St. John's-Govt Centre** 🏠
(709) 722-0506. **$169-$229.** 180 Portugal Cove Rd A1B 2N2. Trans-Canada Hwy 1 exit 47A, 0.9 mi (1.4 km) s. Ext/int corridors. **Pets:** Accepted. 🅴🅲🅾 🍴 ♿ ⇌ 📶 🔋 💻

🅐🅐 ▼▼▼▼ **Quality Hotel-Harbourview** 🏠
(709) 754-7788. **$122-$153.** 2 Hill O' Chips St A1C 6B1. At Cavendish Square; center. Int corridors. **Pets:** $30 daily fee/pet. Service with restrictions, crate. 🆂🅰🆅🅴 🅴🅲🅾 🍴 📶 ✖ 🔋 💻

🅐🅐 ▼▼▼▼ **Sheraton Hotel Newfoundland** 🏠
(709) 726-4980. **Call for rates.** 115 Cavendish Square A1C 3K2. At Duckworth and Ordnance sts. Int corridors. **Pets:** Accepted.
🆂🅰🆅🅴 🅴🅲🅾 🍴 ⇌ ✖ 📶 ✖ 🔋 💻

▼▼ **Super 8** 🏠 ❀
(709) 739-8888. **$126-$229.** 175 Higgins Line A1B 4N4. Trans-Canada Hwy 1 exit 47A, just s on Rt 40 (Portugal Cove Rd). Int corridors. **Pets:** $20 one-time fee/room. Designated rooms, service with restrictions, supervision. 🅴🅲🅾 ♿ ⇌ 📶 ✖ 🔋 💻

STEPHENVILLE

▼▼ **Days Inn Stephenville** 🏠 ❀
(709) 643-6666. **$106-$138.** 44 Queen St A2N 2M5. Center. Int corridors. **Pets:** Other species. $10 one-time fee/room. Designated rooms, service with restrictions, crate. 🅴🅲🅾 🍴 📶 ✖ 🔋 💻

NORTHWEST TERRITORIES

YELLOWKNIFE

🅐🅐 ▼▼▼ **Coast Fraser Tower** 🏠
(867) 873-8700. **$170-$197.** 5303 52nd St X1A 1V1. Corner of 52nd St and 53rd Ave. Int corridors. **Pets:** Medium. $15 daily fee/pet. Designated rooms, service with restrictions, crate.
🆂🅰🆅🅴 🅴🅲🅾 📶 ♿ 🔋 💻

▼▼▼ **Days Inn & Suites Yellowknife** 🏠
(867) 873-9700. **$170-$210.** 4401 50th Ave X1A 2N2. Downtown. Int corridors. **Pets:** Accepted. 🍴 📶 ✖ 🔋 💻

▼▼▼ **The Explorer Hotel** 🏠
(867) 873-3531. **Call for rates.** 4825 49th Ave X1A 2R3. Downtown. Int corridors. **Pets:** Accepted. 🍴 📶 ✖ 🔋 💻

▼▼▼ **Super 8 Yellowknife** Ⓜ
(867) 669-8888. **$188-$224.** 308 Old Airport Rd X1A 3G3. 1.2 mi (2 km) s on Franklin Ave, 0.6 mi (1 km) w; in Walmart Plaza. Int corridors. **Pets:** Accepted. 🅴🅲🅾 📶 ✖ 🔋 💻

NOVA SCOTIA

AMHERST

▼▼ **Amherst Wandlyn Meeting & Convention Hotel** 🏠 ❀
(902) 667-3331. **$115-$155.** 1539 Southampton Rd B4H 3Y4. Trans-Canada Hwy 104 exit 3, 0.6 mi (1 km) w. Ext/int corridors. **Pets:** $10 one-time fee/pet. Designated rooms, service with restrictions, crate.
🍴 ⇌ 📶 🔋 💻

▼▼ **Super 8** 🏠
(902) 660-8888. **$101-$159.** 40 Lord Amherst Dr B4H 4W6. Trans-Canada Hwy 104 exit 4. Int corridors. **Pets:** Medium, other species. $15 daily fee/pet. Service with restrictions, supervision.
🅴🅲🅾 ♿ ⇌ 📶 🔋 💻

ANNAPOLIS ROYAL

▼▼ **Annapolis Royal Inn** Ⓜ
(902) 532-2323. **$89-$150, 30 day notice.** 3924 Hwy 1 B0S 1A0. 0.6 mi (1 km) w. Ext corridors. **Pets:** Accepted. 🍴 📶 ✖ 🔋 💻

▼▼▼ **The Garrison House Inn** 🅶🅸 ❀
(902) 532-5750. **Call for rates.** 350 St George St B0S 1A0. Jct Rt 1 and 8. Int corridors. **Pets:** Medium, dogs only. $25 daily fee/room. Designated rooms, service with restrictions. 🍴 📶 ✖ 🆉

▼▼▼ **Hillsdale House Inn** 🅱🅱 ❀
(902) 532-2345. **Call for rates.** 519 St. George St B0S 1A0. Just e of Rt 1; center. Int corridors. **Pets:** Large. $25 one-time fee/room. Designated rooms, service with restrictions. 📶 ✖

▼▼▼ **The King George Inn** 🅱🅱
(902) 532-5286. **Call for rates.** 548 Upper St. George St B0S 1A0. Jct Rt 1 and 8, just e on Rt 8. Int corridors. **Pets:** Accepted.
📶 ✖ 🆉 💻

ANTIGONISH

▼▼ **Maritime Inn Antigonish** 🏠
(902) 863-4001. **$123-$200.** 158 Main St B2G 2B7. Between St. Mary's and Court sts; center. Ext/int corridors. **Pets:** Designated rooms, service with restrictions, supervision. 🍴 ♿ 📶 ✖ 🔋 💻

AULD'S COVE

▼▼ **Cove Motel & Restaurant/Gift Shop** Ⓜ
(902) 747-2700. **$99-$135.** 227 D-31 Rd B0H 1P0. Trans-Canada Hwy 104, opposite exit 39; 1.9 mi (3 km) w of Canso Cswy. Ext corridors. **Pets:** Accepted. 🍴 📶 ✖ 🔋 💻

BADDECK

▼▼ **Hunter's Mountain Chalets** 🅲🅰
(902) 295-3392. **$88-$138, 4 day notice.** 562 Cabot Tr B0E 1B0. Trans-Canada Hwy 105 exit 7, 1.6 mi (2.6 km) n. Ext corridors. **Pets:** Dogs only. $10 daily fee/pet. No service, supervision.
🍴 ♿ 📶 ✖ ♿ 🆉 💻

🅐🅐 ▼▼▼ **Inverary Resort on Baddeck Bay** 🏠
(902) 295-3500. **$99-$159, 3 day notice.** 368 Shore Rd B0E 1B0. Trans-Canada Hwy 105 exit 8, 1 mi (1.6 km) e on Rt 205 (Shore Rd). Ext/int corridors. **Pets:** Accepted.
🆂🅰🆅🅴 🍴 ♿ ⇌ ✖ 📶 ✖ 🔋 💻

▼▼ **McIntyre's Housekeeping Cottages** 🅲🅰
(902) 295-1133. **$80-$350, 4 day notice.** 8908 Hwy 105 B0E 1B0. Trans-Canada Hwy 105, 3 mi (5 km) w. Ext corridors. **Pets:** Other species. $20 daily fee/pet. Designated rooms, service with restrictions.
🍴 ♿ 📶 ✖ 🔋 💻

▼▼ **Silver Dart Lodge & MacNeil House Suites** 🏠
(902) 295-2340. **$110-$185.** 257 Shore Rd B0E 1B0. Trans-Canada Hwy 105 exit 8, 0.6 mi (1 km) e on Rt 205 (Shore Rd). Ext/int corridors. **Pets:** Accepted. 🍴 ♿ ⇌ ✖ 📶 ✖ 🔋 💻

BRIDGETOWN

▼▼ Bridgetown Motor Inn Ⓜ

(902) 665-4403. **Call for rates.** 396 Granville St B0S 1C0. Hwy 101 exit 20, 0.6 mi (1 km) w on Rt 1. Ext corridors. **Pets:** Accepted.

BRIDGEWATER

Ⓐ ▼▼▼▼ BEST WESTERN PLUS Bridgewater Hotel & Convention Centre Ⓗ ❀

(902) 530-0101. **$120-$140.** 527 Hwy 10 B4V 7P4. Hwy 103 exit 12, just n. Int corridors. **Pets:** Dogs only. $20 daily fee/room. Designated rooms, service with restrictions, supervision.

SAVE ⊞ ⊞ ⊠ ⊠ ⊠ ⊠ ⊠ ⊠

▼▼ Comfort Inn Ⓗ

(902) 543-1498. **$105-$149.** 49 North St B4V 2V7. Hwy 103 exit 12, 1.1 mi (1.8 km) s on Rt 10. Ext/int corridors. **Pets:** Other species. $10 one-time fee/room. Supervision. ECO ⊠ ⊠ ⊠ ⊠

▼▼ Days Inn & Conference Centre Bridgewater Ⓗ

(902) 543-7101. **$86-$205.** 50 North St B4V 2V6. Hwy 103 exit 12, 1.1 mi (1.8 km) s on Rt 10. Int corridors. **Pets:** Accepted.

⊠ ⊠ ⊠ ⊠ ⊠ ⊠

CHARLOS COVE

▼▼▼ Seawind Landing Country Inn Ⓒ ❀

(902) 525-2108. **$99-$169.** 159 Wharf Rd B0H 1T0. Rt 316, 0.5 mi (0.8 km) se on gravel road. Ext/int corridors. **Pets:** Designated rooms, service with restrictions, supervision. ⊠ ⊠ ⊠ ⊠ ⊠

CHESTER

▼ Windjammer Motel Ⓜ

(902) 275-3567. **Call for rates.** 4070 Rt 3 B0J 1J0. 0.6 mi (1 km) w. Ext corridors. **Pets:** Designated rooms, supervision. ⊠ ⊠

CHÉTICAMP

▼▼ Cabot Trail Sea & Golf Chalets Ⓒ

(902) 224-1777. **$139-$179, 7 day notice.** 71 Fraser Doucet Ln B0E 1H0. Center. Ext corridors. **Pets:** Dogs only. $15 daily fee/pet. Service with restrictions, crate. ⊠ ⊠ ⊠ ⊠ ⊠ ⊠ ⊠

▼▼ Laurie's Motor Inn Ⓗ

(902) 224-2400. **$99-$164.** 15456 Laurie Rd B0E 1H0. Center. Ext/int corridors. **Pets:** Medium. $15 one-time fee/room. Designated rooms, service with restrictions, crate. ⊠ ⊠ ⊠ ⊠ ⊠ ⊠

DARTMOUTH

▼▼ Comfort Inn Ⓗ

(902) 463-9900. **$93-$132.** 456 Windmill Rd B3A 1J7. Hwy 111 exit Shannon Park. Int corridors. **Pets:** Accepted. ECO ⊠ ⊠ ⊠

Ⓐ ▼▼▼▼ Hampton Inn & Suites by Hilton-Halifax/Dartmouth Ⓗ ❀

(902) 406-7700. **Call for rates.** 65 Cromarty Dr B3B 0G2. Hwy 118 (Lakeview Dr) exit Wright Ave; in Dartmouth Crossing Outlet Mall. Int corridors. **Pets:** Other species. Designated rooms.

SAVE ECO ⊠ ⊠ ⊠ ⊠ ⊠ ⊠

Ⓐ ▼▼▼▼ Hearthstone Inn Dartmouth/Halifax Ⓗ

(902) 469-5850. **$99-$119.** 313 Prince Albert Rd B2Y 1N3. Hwy 111 exit 6A, 1 blk s. Int corridors. **Pets:** Accepted.

SAVE ⊠ ⊠ ⊠ ⊠ ⊠

Ⓐ ▼▼▼▼ Holiday Inn Halifax-Harbourview Ⓗ

(902) 463-1100. **$104-$149.** 101 Wyse Rd B3A 1L9. Adjacent to Angus L MacDonald Bridge. Int corridors. **Pets:** Accepted.

SAVE ECO ⊠ ⊠ ⊠ ⊠ ⊠ ⊠

Ⓐ ▼▼▼▼ Park Place Hotel & Conference Centre Ramada Plaza Ⓗ

(902) 468-8888. **$106-$199.** 240 Brownlow Ave B3B 1X6. From A. Murray MacKay Bridge, 0.7 mi (1.2 km) n on Hwy 111 exit 3 (Burnside Dr). Int corridors. **Pets:** Accepted.

SAVE ECO ⊠ ⊠ ⊠ ⊠ ⊠ ⊠ ⊠

▼▼ Travelodge Suites Dartmouth Ⓗ ❀

(902) 465-4000. **$95-$210.** 101 Yorkshire Ave Ext B3A 0C5. Hwy 111 exit Princess Margaret Blvd; at toll booth for A. Murray MacKay Bridge. Int corridors. **Pets:** $10 one-time fee/room. Designated rooms, service with restrictions, supervision. ECO ⊠ ⊠ ⊠

DIGBY

Ⓐ ▼▼▼ Admiral Digby Inn & Cottages Ⓗ

(902) 245-2531. **$99-$129.** 441 Shore Rd B0V 1A0. Hwy 101 exit 26, 1.5 mi (2.5 km) n, follow Saint John Ferry signs, 3 mi (5 km) w on Victoria Rd; just e of ferry terminal. Ext corridors. **Pets:** Dogs only. $20 daily fee/room. Designated rooms, service with restrictions, supervision.

SAVE ⊠ ⊠ ⊠ ⊠ ⊠

Ⓐ ▼▼▼▼ Digby Pines Golf Resort and Spa Ⓗ ❀

(902) 245-2511. **$182-$338, 3 day notice.** 103 Shore Rd B0V 1A0. Hwy 101 exit 26, 1.5 mi (2.5 km) n, follow Saint John Ferry signs, 1.5 mi (2.5 km) w on Victoria Rd, follow signs; 1.2 mi (2 km) e of ferry terminal. Ext/int corridors. **Pets:** $25 one-time fee/pet. Designated rooms, service with restrictions.

SAVE ECO ⊠ ⊠ ⊠ ⊠ ⊠ ⊠ ⊠

▼▼▼ Dockside Suites Ⓗ

(902) 245-4950. **$89-$169.** 34 Water St B0V 1A0. Center; in Fundy Complex. Ext/int corridors. **Pets:** Accepted. ⊠ ⊠ ⊠ ⊠ ⊠

ENFIELD

▼▼▼▼ ALT Hotel-Halifax Airport Ⓗ

(902) 334-0136. **Call for rates.** 40 Silver Dart Dr B2T 1K2. 1 mi (1.6 km) e of Hwy 102, exit 6; opposite the Halifax Stanfield International Airport terminal. Int corridors. **Pets:** Accepted.

⊠ ⊠ ⊠ ⊠ ⊠ ⊠

▼▼▼▼ Holiday Inn Express Hotel & Suites Halifax Airport Ⓗ ❀

(902) 576-7600. **$139-$229.** 180 Pratt & Whitney Dr B2T 0C8. Hwy 102 exit 5A, 0.8 mi (1.2 km) e, then just n. Int corridors. **Pets:** Large. Service with restrictions, supervision. ⊠ ⊠ ⊠ ⊠ ⊠

HALIFAX

Ⓐ ▼▼▼▼ Atlantica Hotel Halifax Ⓗ ❀

(902) 423-1161. **$119-$260.** 1980 Robie St B3H 3G5. Jct Quinpool St. Int corridors. **Pets:** Medium. Service with restrictions, supervision.

SAVE ECO ⊠ ⊠ ⊠ ⊠ ⊠ ⊠

Ⓐ ▼▼▼▼ BEST WESTERN PLUS Chocolate Lake Hotel Ⓗ ❀

(902) 477-5611. **$129-$169, 14 day notice.** 20 St. Margaret's Bay Rd B3N 1J4. 0.4 mi (0.7 km) e of Armdale Rotary. Ext/int corridors. **Pets:** Large. Designated rooms, supervision.

SAVE ECO ⊠ ⊠ ⊠ ⊠ ⊠ ⊠ ⊠

Ⓐ ▼▼▼▼ Cambridge Suites Hotel Ⓗ

(902) 420-0555. **$139-$214.** 1583 Brunswick St B3J 3P5. Corner of Brunswick and Sackville sts. Int corridors. **Pets:** Accepted.

SAVE ECO ⊠ ⊠ ⊠ ⊠ ⊠ ⊠

Ⓐ ▼▼▼▼ Château Bedford Hotel & Suites Ⓗ

(902) 445-1100. **Call for rates.** 133 Kearney Lake Rd B3M 4P3. Hwy 102 exit 2, just e. Int corridors. **Pets:** Accepted.

SAVE ECO ⊠ ⊠ ⊠ ⊠ ⊠

▼▼ Chebucto Inn Ⓜ

(902) 453-4330. **$85-$145.** 6151 Lady Hammond Rd B3K 2R9. Jct Hwy 111 and Rt 2 (Bedford Hwy), 0.4 mi (0.7 km) e. Ext corridors. **Pets:** Medium, dogs only. $10 one-time fee/room. Designated rooms, service with restrictions, supervision. ⊠ ⊠ ⊠

ⓐ 🔷🔷 **Coastal Inn Halifax** 🅷
(902) 450-3020. **$99-$159.** 98 Chain Lake Dr B3S 1A2. Hwy 102 exit 2A eastbound; Hwy 103 exit 2. Ext/int corridors. **Pets:** Accepted.
SAVE ECO ♿ 🏊 📶 ✕ 🖥 ☕

ⓐ 🔷🔷 **Comfort Inn Halifax** 🅷
(902) 443-0303. **$99-$169.** 560 Bedford Hwy B3M 2L8. On Rt 2 (Bedford Hwy), 6 mi (9.6 km) w. Ext/int corridors. **Pets:** Medium. $20 one-time fee/pet. Designated rooms, service with restrictions, supervision.
SAVE ♿ 🏊 📶 ✕ 🖥 ☕

🔷🔷 **Delta Barrington** 🅷
(902) 429-7410. **$139-$239.** 1875 Barrington St B3J 3L6. Between Cogswell and Duke sts. Int corridors. **Pets:** Accepted.
ECO 🍽 🏊 📶 ✕ 🖥 ☕

🔷🔷 **Delta Halifax** 🅷
(902) 425-6700. **Call for rates.** 1990 Barrington St B3J 1P2. Corner of Cogswell and Barrington sts. Int corridors. **Pets:** Accepted.
ECO 🍽 ♿ 🏊 ✕ 📶 🖥 ☕

ⓐ 🔷 **Esquire Motel** Ⓜ
(902) 835-3367. **$80-$100.** 771 Bedford Hwy B4A 1A1. Hwy 102 exit 4A, 3.3 mi (5.3 km) e on Rt 2 (Bedford Hwy). Ext corridors.
Pets: Accepted. SAVE 🏊 📶 🖥 ☕

ⓐ 🔷🔷 **Four Points by Sheraton Halifax** 🅷
(902) 423-4444. **$110-$230.** 1496 Hollis St B3J 3Z1. Between Salter and Bishop sts. Int corridors. **Pets:** Accepted.
SAVE ECO 🍽 ♿ 🏊 📶 ✕ 🖥 ☕

🔷 🔷 **Future Inns Halifax Hotel & Conference Centre** 🅷 🐾
(902) 443-4333. **$112-$185.** 30 Fairfax Dr B3S 1P1. Hwy 102 exit 2A. Int corridors. **Pets:** Other species. Designated rooms.
🍽 ♿ 📶 ✕ 🖥 ☕

ⓐ 🔷🔷🔷 **Halifax Marriott Harbourfront** 🅷
(902) 421-1700. **$153-$321.** 1919 Upper Water St B3J 3J5. Adjacent to historic properties and Casino Nova Scotia. Int corridors. **Pets:** Other species. $50 one-time fee/room. Service with restrictions, supervision.
SAVE ECO 🍽 ♿ 🏊 ✕ 📶 ✕ 🖥 ☕

ⓐ 🔷🔷🔷 **Hampton Inn by Hilton Halifax-Downtown** 🅷 🐾
(902) 422-1391. **Call for rates.** 1960 Brunswick St B3J 2G7. Between Cogswell St and Rainnie Dr. Int corridors. **Pets:** Medium. $35 one-time fee/room. Designated rooms, service with restrictions, supervision.
SAVE ♿ 📶 ✕ ☕

ⓐ 🔷🔷🔷 **Homewood Suites by Hilton Halifax-Downtown** 🅷 🐾
(902) 429-6620. **Call for rates.** 1960 Brunswick St B3J 2G7. Between Cogswell St and Rainnie Dr. Int corridors. **Pets:** Medium. $35 one-time fee/room. Designated rooms, service with restrictions, supervision.
SAVE ♿ 📶 ✕ 🖥 ☕

🔷🔷🔷 **Inn on the Lake, an Ascend Hotel Collection Member** 🅷
(902) 861-3480. **$139-$169.** 3009 Hwy 2 B2T 1J5. Hwy 102 exit 5, right off exit ramp. Int corridors. **Pets:** Designated rooms, service with restrictions, supervision. 🍽 🏊 📶 ✕ 🖥 ☕

ⓐ 🔷🔷🔷 **The Lord Nelson Hotel & Suites** 🅷 🐾
(902) 423-6331. **$129-$189, 3 day notice.** 1515 S Park St B3J 2L2. Corner of Park St and Spring Garden Rd. Int corridors. **Pets:** Other species. $35 one-time fee/room. Designated rooms, service with restrictions, supervision. SAVE ECO 🍽 ♿ 📶 ✕ 🖥 ☕

ⓐ 🔷🔷🔷 **The Prince George Hotel** 🅷
(902) 425-1986. **Call for rates.** 1725 Market St B3J 3N9. Between Prince and Carmichael sts. Int corridors. **Pets:** Accepted.
SAVE ECO 🍽 ♿ 🏊 ✕ 📶 ✕ 🖥 ☕

ⓐ 🔷🔷 **Quality Inn & Suites Halifax** 🅷
(902) 444-6700. **$100-$160.** 980 Parkland Dr B3M 4Y7. Hwy 102 exit 2, just e on Kearney Lake Rd, then just s. Int corridors.
Pets: Accepted. SAVE ECO ♿ 🏊 ✕ 📶 ✕ 🖥 ☕

ⓐ 🔷🔷 **Quality Inn Halifax Airport** 🅷
(902) 873-3000. **$109-$169.** 60 Sky Blvd B2T 1K3. Hwy 102 exit 6, just s. Int corridors. **Pets:** Large, other species. Service with restrictions, supervision. SAVE ECO 🍽 🏊 📶 ✕ 🖥 ☕

ⓐ 🔷🔷 **Residence Inn by Marriott Halifax Downtown** 🅷 🐾
(902) 422-0493. **$118-$240.** 1599 Grafton St B3J 2C3. Corner of Sackville St. Int corridors. **Pets:** Other species. $100 one-time fee/room. Service with restrictions. SAVE ECO ♿ 📶 ✕ 🖥 ☕

ⓐ 🔷🔷🔷 **The Westin Nova Scotian** 🅷
(902) 421-1000. **$129-$249.** 1181 Hollis St B3H 2P6. Between Barrington and Lower Water sts. Int corridors. **Pets:** Accepted.
SAVE ECO 🍽 ♿ 🏊 ✕ 📶 ✕ 🖥 ☕

INGONISH BEACH

ⓐ 🔷🔷🔷 **Keltic Lodge Resort & Spa** 🅷
(902) 285-2880. **$160-$691, 3 day notice.** 383 Keltic In Rd B0C 1L0. In Cape Breton Highlands National Park; off Cabot Tr. Ext/int corridors.
Pets: Accepted. SAVE 🍽 ♿ 🏊 📶 ✕ 🖥 ☕

KEMPTVILLE

🔷🔷 **Trout Point Lodge** 🅲🅸
(902) 761-2142. **$199-$459, 21 day notice.** 189 Trout Point Rd B0W 1Y0. 6.6 mi (11 km) e on Rt 203, 2.1 mi (3.5 km) n on gravel entry road. Ext corridors. **Pets:** Accepted.
🍽 ✕ 📶 ✕ ⓦ 🖥 ☕

KENTVILLE

🔷🔷 **Sun Valley Motel** Ⓜ
(902) 678-7368. **Call for rates.** 843 Park St B4N 3V7. Hwy 101 exit 14, 0.5 mi (0.8 km) e on Rt 1. Ext corridors. **Pets:** Accepted.
🍽 📶 🐾 🚫 🖥

KINGSTON

ⓐ 🔷🔷 **BEST WESTERN Aurora Inn** 🅷
(902) 765-3306. **$140-$145.** 831 Main St B0P 1R0. Hwy 101 exit 17 to Rt 1, follow signs. Ext corridors. **Pets:** $10 one-time fee/room. Service with restrictions, supervision. SAVE 🍽 📶 ✕ 🖥 ☕

LISCOMB

ⓐ 🔷🔷 **Liscombe Lodge Resort & Conference Centre** 🅷
(902) 779-2307. **$140-$210, 3 day notice.** 2884 Hwy 7 B0J 2A0. On Hwy 7. Ext/int corridors. **Pets:** Large, other species. Designated rooms, service with restrictions. SAVE 🍽 ♿ 🏊 ✕ 📶 ✕ 🖥 ☕

LIVERPOOL

ⓐ 🔷🔷🔷 **BEST WESTERN PLUS Liverpool Hotel & Conference Centre** 🅷
(902) 354-2377. **$130-$140.** 63 Queens Place Dr B0T 1K0. Hwy 103 exit 19, just e. Int corridors. **Pets:** Accepted.
SAVE ECO ♿ 🏊 📶 ✕ 🖥 ☕

LOWER ARGYLE

ⓐ 🔷🔷🔷 **Argyler Lodge** 🅲🅸
(902) 643-2500. **$100-$215, 3 day notice.** Rt 3, 52 Ye Olde Argyler Rd B0W 1W0. Hwy 103 exit 32, 4.5 mi (7.5 km) e. Int corridors.
Pets: Accepted. SAVE 🍽 📶 ✕ 🖥

LUNENBURG

🔷🔷 **The Homeport Motel** Ⓜ
(902) 634-8234. **Call for rates.** 167 Victoria Rd B0J 2C0. 0.6 mi (1 km) w on Rt 3. Ext corridors. **Pets:** $15 daily fee/room. Designated rooms, service with restrictions, crate. 📶 ✕ 🚫 🖥 ☕

▼▼▼▼ **Lunenburg Arms Hotel & Spa** 🅷

(902) 640-4040. **Call for rates.** 94 Pelham St B0J 2C0. Corner of Pelham and Duke sts; center. Int corridors. **Pets:** Accepted.

🍽 🛬ᴹ 🛜 ⊠ 🛏 💻

MAHONE BAY
▼▼▼▼ **Bayview Pines Country Inn** 🅱🅱

(902) 624-9970. **$110-$145, 5 day notice.** 678 Oakland Rd B0J 2E0. Hwy 103 exit 10, 1.2 mi (2 km) w on Rt 3 to Kedy's Landing, then 3.6 mi (6 km) e of Mahone Bay. Ext/int corridors. **Pets:** Accepted.

🍽 🗙 🛜 ⊠ 🐾 🗾 🛏 💻

NEW GLASGOW
▼▼ **Comfort Inn** 🅷 🐾

(902) 755-6450. **$99-$159.** 740 Westville Rd B2H 2J8. On Hwy 289, just e of jct Trans-Canada Hwy 104 exit 23. Int corridors. **Pets:** $10 one-time fee/pet. Service with restrictions, supervision.

🅴🅲🅾 🛜 ⊠ 🛏 💻

▼▼ **Travelodge Suites** 🅷

(902) 928-1333. **$90-$150.** 700 Westville Rd B2H 2J8. On Hwy 289, just e of jct Trans-Canada Hwy 104 exit 23. Int corridors. **Pets:** Other species. $10 daily fee/room. Service with restrictions, supervision.

🅴🅲🅾 🛜 🛏 💻

NEW HARBOUR
▼▼▼ **Lonely Rock Seaside Bungalows** 🅲🅰

(902) 387-2668. **$90-$230, 14 day notice.** 150 New Harbour Rd B0H 1T0. Rt 316, 0.4 mi (0.7 km) s. Ext corridors. **Pets:** Dogs only. $10 daily fee/pet. Designated rooms, no service, supervision.

🍽 🛬ᴹ 🛜 ⊠ 🐾 🛏 💻

NORTH SYDNEY
🅰 ▼▼▼ **Clansman Motel** 🅼

(902) 794-7226. **$95-$125.** 9 Baird St B2A 0A9. Hwy 125 exit 2, just e on King St. Ext/int corridors. **Pets:** $5 one-time fee/room. Designated rooms, service with restrictions. 🆂🅰🆅🅴 🍽 🛬ᴹ 🛬 🛜 🛏 💻

PARRSBORO
▼▼▼ **Gillespie House Inn** 🅱🅱

(902) 254-3196. **Call for rates.** 358 Main St B0M 1S0. On Rt 2; center. Int corridors. **Pets:** Accepted. 🛬ᴹ 🛜 ⊠ 🐾 🆆 🗾

▼▼ **The Sunshine Inn** 🅼

(902) 254-3135. **Call for rates.** 4487 Hwy 2 N B0M 1S0. 2 mi (3.2 km) n. Ext corridors. **Pets:** Accepted. 🍽 🛜 🗾 🛏

PICTOU
▼▼ **Caribou River Cottage** 🅲🅰

(902) 485-6352. **Call for rates.** 1308 Shore Rd B0K 1H0. From PEI ferry terminal, 2.7 mi (4.5 km) w on Three Brooks Rd to Shore Rd. Ext corridors. **Pets:** Accepted. 🍽 🛜 ⊠ 🐾 🗾 🛏 💻

▼▼ **Pictou Lodge Beach Resort** 🅷

(902) 485-4322. **$140-$383, 3 day notice.** 172 Lodge Rd B0K 1H0. 4.3 mi (7 km) nw on Braeshore Rd; midway between Pictou and PEI ferry terminal at Caribou. Ext corridors. **Pets:** Accepted.

🍽 🛬 🗙 🛜 ⊠ 🛏 💻

▼▼ **Willow House Inn** 🅱🅱

(902) 485-5740. **Call for rates.** 11 Willow St B0K 1H0. Corner of Willow and Church sts; center. Int corridors. **Pets:** Medium, dogs only. Crate.

🛜 ⊠

PORT DUFFERIN
▼▼ **Marquis of Dufferin Seaside Inn** 🅼

(902) 654-2696. **Call for rates.** 25658 Hwy 7, RR 1 B0J 2R0. On Hwy 7. Ext corridors. **Pets:** Accepted. 🍽 🗙 🛜 ⊠ 🐾 🗾 💻

PORT HASTINGS
▼▼▼ **Canadas Best Value Inn-Port Hawkesbury/Port Hastings** 🅼

(902) 625-0621. **Call for rates.** 373 Hwy 4 B9A 1M8. 1 mi (1.6 km) n; 1 mi (1.6 km) s of Canso Cswy. Ext corridors. **Pets:** Accepted.

🛬ᴹ 🛬 🛜 ⊠ 🛏 💻

PORT HAWKESBURY
▼▼▼ **Maritime Inn Port Hawkesbury** 🅷

(902) 625-0320. **$117-$180.** 717 Reeves St B9A 2S2. 4.2 mi (6.4 km) e of Canso Cswy on Hwy 4. Ext/int corridors. **Pets:** Service with restrictions, supervision. 🍽 🛬 🛜 ⊠ 🛏 💻

PORT HOOD
▼▼▼ **Haus Treuburg Country Inn & Cottages** 🅲🅸

(902) 787-2116. **$109-$210, 14 day notice.** 175 Main St B0E 2W0. Center. Ext/int corridors. **Pets:** Accepted.

🍽 🛜 ⊠ 🐾 🛏 💻

ST. PETER'S
▼▼▼ **Bras d'Or Lakes Inn** 🅷

(902) 535-2200. **$125-$144, 3 day notice.** 10095 Greenville St B0E 3B0. Rt 104, just w of St. Peter's Bay Bridge. Int corridors. **Pets:** $25 daily fee/pet. Designated rooms, service with restrictions, supervision.

🍽 🗙 🛜 ⊠ 🛏 💻

SHELBURNE
▼▼ **Wildwood Motel** 🅼 🐾

(902) 875-2964. **Call for rates.** 242 Minto St B0T 1W0. Hwy 103 exit 26, 1.1 mi (1.8 km) e on Rt 3. Ext corridors. **Pets:** Large, other species. $10 one-time fee/room. Designated rooms, supervision.

🍽 🛜 ⊠ 🛏 💻

SMITHS COVE
▼▼▼ **Harbourview Inn** 🅱🅱 🐾

(902) 245-5686. **$124-$179, 7 day notice.** 25 Harbourview Rd B0S 1S0. Hwy 101 exit 25 eastbound; exit 24 westbound. Ext/int corridors. **Pets:** Medium, dogs only. $10 one-time fee/room. Service with restrictions, supervision. 🍽 🛬 🛜 ⊠ 🛏 💻

▼▼ **Hedley House Inn By The Sea** 🅼

(902) 245-2500. **Call for rates.** RR 1 B0S 1S0. Hwy 101 exit 25 eastbound; exit 24 westbound. Ext corridors. **Pets:** Accepted.

🍽 🛜 ⊠ 🗾 🛏 💻

STELLARTON
▼▼▼ **Holiday Inn Express Stellarton-New Glasgow** 🅷

(902) 755-1020. **$129-$154.** 86 Lawrence Blvd B0K 1S0. Hwy 104 exit 24, just s, then 0.6 mi (1 km) w. Int corridors. **Pets:** Accepted.

🍽 🛬ᴹ 🛬 🛜 ⊠ 🛏 💻

SYDNEY
▼▼▼ **Cambridge Suites Hotel** 🅷 🐾

(902) 562-6500. **$109-$204.** 380 Esplanade B1P 1B1. Hwy 4, 3.1 mi (5 km) e of jct Hwy 125 exit 6E; downtown. Int corridors. **Pets:** Other species. $25 one-time fee/pet. Designated rooms, service with restrictions, supervision. 🅴🅲🅾 🍽 🗙 🛜 ⊠ 🛏 💻

▼▼ **Comfort Inn** 🅷 🐾

(902) 562-0200. **$115-$145.** 368 Kings Rd B1S 1A8. Hwy 4, 2.1 mi (3.5 km) e of jct Hwy 125 exit 6E. Int corridors. **Pets:** $10 one-time fee/room. Designated rooms, service with restrictions, crate.

🅴🅲🅾 🍽 🛜 🛏 💻

🅰 ▼▼▼ **Hampton by Hilton Sydney** 🅷 🐾

(902) 564-6555. **Call for rates.** 60 Maillard St B1S 3W3. Hwy 125 exit 7, 1.2 mi (2 km) n on Rt 327 to Membertou St, then just s. Int corridors. **Pets:** Designated rooms, service with restrictions, supervision.

🆂🅰🆅🅴 🛬ᴹ 🛬 🛜 ⊠ 🛏 💻

▼▼▼ **Holiday Inn Sydney - Waterfront** ⊞
(902) 562-7500. **Call for rates.** 300 Esplanade B1P 1A7. At Prince St; center. Int corridors. **Pets:** Medium. $35 one-time fee/room. Designated rooms, service with restrictions, crate.

〔ECO〕〔�␣〕🍴 ⊸ 🛜 ✕ 🔌 🖵

TRURO
▼▼ **Comfort Inn** ⊞ ✿
(902) 893-0330. **$117-$156.** 12 Meadow Dr B2N 5V4. Hwy 102 exit 14. Int corridors. **Pets:** Service with restrictions, supervision.

〔ECO〕🛜 🔌 🖵

▼▼▼ **Holiday Inn Hotel & Conference Centre Truro** ⊞
(902) 895-1651. **$129-$139.** 437 Prince St B2N 1E6. Just e of Willow St; center. Int corridors. **Pets:** $25 one-time fee/room. Designated rooms, service with restrictions, crate.

〔ECO〕🍴 〔ᵯ〕⊸ 🛜 ✕ 🔌 🖵

▼▼ **Super 8** ⊞
(902) 895-8884. **$130-$150.** 85 Treaty Tr B2N 5A9. Hwy 102 exit 13A. Int corridors. **Pets:** Accepted. 〔ECO〕〔ᵯ〕⊸ 🛜 🔌 🖵

WESTERN SHORE
Ⓐ ▼▼▼ **Atlantica Oak Island Resort and Conference Centre** ⊞
(902) 627-2600. **$99-$189, 3 day notice.** 36 Treasure Dr B0J 3M0. Hwy 103 exit 9 or 10, follow signs on Rt 3; 6 mi (10 km) e of Mahone Bay. Int corridors. **Pets:** Accepted.

〔SAVE〕〔ECO〕🍴 〔ᵯ〕⊸ 🗙 🛜 ✕ 🔌 🖵

WHITE POINT
▼▼▼ **White Point Beach Resort** ⊞ ✿
(902) 354-2711. **$145-$525, 3 day notice.** 75 White Point Beach Resort Rd B0T 1G0. Hwy 103 exit 20A westbound, 5 mi (8 km) w on Rt 3; exit 20 eastbound, 6 mi (10 km) e on Rt 3. Ext/int corridors. **Pets:** Other species. $25 one-time fee/room. Designated rooms.

〔ECO〕🍴 ⊸ 🗙 🛜 ✕ 🔌 🖵

WHYCOCOMAGH
▼▼▼ **Keltic Quay Bayfront Lodge & Cottages** Ⓒ
(902) 756-1122. **Call for rates.** 90 Main St B0E 3M0. Just se off Trans-Canada Hwy 105; center. Ext corridors. **Pets:** Accepted.

〔ᵯ〕🛜 ✕ 🔌 🖵

WINDSOR
▼▼ **Super 8** ⊞
(902) 792-8888. **$120-$140.** 63 Cole Dr B0N 2T0. Hwy 101 exit 5A, just s. Int corridors. **Pets:** Accepted. 〔ECO〕⊸ 🛜 ✕ 🔌 🖵

WOLFVILLE
▼▼▼ **Tattingstone Inn** 〔BB〕
(902) 542-7696. **$106-$150.** 620 Main St B4P 1E8. 0.4 mi (0.6 km) w on Rt 1. Ext/int corridors. **Pets:** Medium. Designated rooms, service with restrictions, supervision. ⊸ 🛜 ✕

YARMOUTH
Ⓐ ▼▼▼ **BEST WESTERN Mermaid Yarmouth** Ⓜ
(902) 742-7821. **$106-$150.** 545 Main St B5A 1J6. Corner of Main St and Starrs Rd. Ext corridors. **Pets:** Accepted. 〔SAVE〕⊸ 🛜 🔌 🖵

Ⓐ ▼▼ **Comfort Inn** ⊞
(902) 742-1119. **$113-$145.** 96 Starrs Rd B5A 2T5. Jct Hwy 101 E and 3. Int corridors. **Pets:** Other species. $10 one-time fee/room. Designated rooms, service with restrictions, supervision.

〔SAVE〕〔ECO〕🛜 🔌 🖵

▼▼ **Rodd Grand Yarmouth** ⊞
(902) 742-2446. **$95-$149.** 417 Main St B5A 4B2. Corner of Grand St. Int corridors. **Pets:** Accepted. 〔ECO〕🍴 ⊸ 🗙 🛜 ✕ 🔌 🖵

▼▼ **Voyageur Motel** Ⓜ
(902) 742-7157. **$89-$189, 3 day notice.** 518 Hwy 1 B5A 4A5. 3 mi (4.8 km) ne on Hwy 1. Ext corridors. **Pets:** Accepted.

🍴 🛜 〔ᴋ〕🔌

ONTARIO

AJAX
▼▼ **Super 8-Ajax** ⊞
(905) 428-6884. **$99-$114.** 210 Westney Rd S L1S 7P9. Hwy 401 exit Westney Rd, 0.6 mi (1 km) s; jct Bayly St. Int corridors. **Pets:** Accepted. ⊸ 🛜 ✕ 🔌 🖵

ALGONQUIN PROVINCIAL PARK
Ⓐ ▼▼▼ **Killarney Lodge** Ⓒ
(705) 633-5551. **$398-$788, 3 day notice.** Hwy 60-Lake of Two Rivers-Algonquin P1H 2G9. 21 mi (33 km) into park from west gate; 14 mi (23 km) from east gate. Ext corridors. **Pets:** Large, dogs only. $25 daily fee/pet. Designated rooms, service with restrictions, crate.

〔SAVE〕🍴 🗙 🛜 ✕ 〔ᴋ〕〔ᵂ〕〔ᵤ〕

ALLISTON
Ⓐ ▼▼ **Red Pine Inn & Conference Centre** Ⓜ
(705) 435-4381. **$125.** 497 Victoria St E L9R 1T9. 1.8 mi (3 km) e of King St. Ext/int corridors. **Pets:** Accepted.

〔SAVE〕🍴 ⊸ 🛜 🔌 🖵

ALTON
Ⓐ ▼▼ ▼▼ **Millcroft Inn & Spa** Ⓒ
(519) 941-8111. **$170-$350, 3 day notice.** 55 John St L7K 0C4. 2.5 mi (4 km) n off Hwy 136 from Hwy 24, 0.6 mi (1 km) w on Queen St E, then just n. Ext/int corridors. **Pets:** Small, dogs only. $35 daily fee/pet. Designated rooms, service with restrictions, supervision.

〔SAVE〕🍴 ⊸ 🗙 🛜 ✕ 🔌 🖵

ARNPRIOR
▼▼ **Country Squire Motel** Ⓜ
(613) 623-6556. **$69-$135, 3 day notice.** 111 Staye Court Dr K7S 0E8. Hwy 17 exit White Lake Rd, just n to Staye Court Dr, then just w. Ext corridors. **Pets:** Small, dogs only. $15 daily fee/pet. Designated rooms, service with restrictions, supervision. 🛜 🔌 🖵

Ⓐ ▼▼ **Quality Inn** ⊞
(613) 623-7991. **$120-$175.** 70 Madawaska Blvd K7S 1S5. Hwy 417 exit 180, 0.4 mi (0.7 km) n on CR 29, then 1.4 mi (2.3 km) w. Int corridors. **Pets:** Other species. $10 daily fee/room. Service with restrictions, crate. 〔SAVE〕🍴 🛜 ✕ 🔌 🖵

BANCROFT
Ⓐ ▼▼▼ **BEST WESTERN Sword Motor Inn** Ⓜ
(613) 332-2474. **$160-$165.** 146 Hastings St K0L 1C0. On Hwy 62 N; center. Ext/int corridors. **Pets:** Accepted.

〔SAVE〕🍴 ⊸ 🗙 🛜 🔌 🖵

BARRIE
Ⓐ ▼▼ **Comfort Inn** ⊞
(705) 722-3600. **$90-$180.** 75 Hart Dr L4N 5M3. Hwy 400 exit 96A (Dunlop St E). Int corridors. **Pets:** Large, other species. $10 daily fee/room. Service with restrictions. 〔SAVE〕〔ECO〕🍴 🛜 🔌 🖵

Ⓐ ▼▼ **Comfort Inn & Suites** ⊞
(705) 721-1122. **$82-$175.** 210 Essa Rd L4N 3L1. Hwy 400 exit 94 (Essa Rd), just e. Int corridors. **Pets:** Medium. Designated rooms, service with restrictions, supervision. 〔SAVE〕〔ECO〕🛜 🔌 🖵

▼▼▼ **Days Inn Barrie** 🄷
(705) 733-8989. **$106-$220.** 60 Bryne Dr L4N 9Y4. Hwy 400 exit 94 (Essa Rd), just s, then just e. Int corridors. **Pets:** Accepted.
ECO 🍴 ⊇ 📶 🛢 ▣

CAA ▼▼▼ **Holiday Inn Barrie-Hotel & Conference Centre** 🄷
(705) 728-6191. **$140-$200.** 20 Fairview Rd L4N 4P3. Hwy 400 exit 94 (Essa Rd), just e. Int corridors. **Pets:** Large. $10 daily fee/room. Designated rooms, service with restrictions, crate.
SAVE ECO 🍴 ⤴M ⊇ 🗙 📶 🛢 ▣

CAA ▼▼▼ **Holiday Inn Express Hotel & Suites Barrie** 🄷
(705) 725-1002. **$115-$189.** 506 Bryne Dr L4N 9P6. Hwy 400 exit 90 (Mapleview Dr), just sw. Int corridors. **Pets:** Small. $15 one-time fee/room. Designated rooms, service with restrictions, supervision.
SAVE 🍴 ⊇ 📶 🗙 🛢 ▣

CAA ▼▼▼ **Horseshoe Resort** 🄷 🌸
(705) 835-2790. **$99-$349, 8 day notice.** 1101 Horseshoe Valley Rd W L4M 4Y8. Hwy 400 exit 117 (Horseshoe Valley Rd), 3.8 mi (6 km) e. Int corridors. **Pets:** Dogs only. $35 one-time fee/pet. Service with restrictions, supervision. SAVE 🍴 ⊇ 🗙 📶 🗙 🛢 ▣

▼▼ **Quality Inn** 🄷 🌸
(705) 734-9500. **$69-$200.** 55 Hart Dr L4N 5M3. Hwy 400 exit 96A (Dunlop St E). Int corridors. **Pets:** Other species. $100 deposit/room. Designated rooms, service with restrictions.
ECO 🍴 ⊇ 📶 🗙 🛢 ▣

▼▼ **Super 8 Barrie** 🄷
(705) 814-8888. **$100-$180.** 441 Bryne Dr L4N 6C8. Hwy 400 exit 90 (Mapleview Dr), just nw. Int corridors. **Pets:** Accepted.
ECO ⊇ 📶 🗙 🛢 ▣

BARRY'S BAY
▼ **Mountain View Motel** Ⓜ
(613) 756-2757. **Call for rates.** 18508 Hwy 60 E K0J 1B0. 2.5 mi (4 km) e of town. Ext corridors. **Pets:** Accepted. 🍴 📶 🗙 🛢 ▣

BAYFIELD *(Restaurants p. 646)*
CAA ▼▼▼▼ **The Little Inn of Bayfield** 🄲🄸 🌸
(519) 565-2611. **Call for rates.** 26 Main St N0M 1G0. Hwy 21 exit Main St; jct Catherine St. Int corridors. **Pets:** $25 one-time fee/room. Designated rooms, service with restrictions. SAVE 🍴 📶 🗙 🛢 ▣

BELLEVILLE
CAA ▼▼▼ **BEST WESTERN Belleville** 🄷
(613) 969-1112. **$135-$200.** 387 N Front St K8P 3C8. Hwy 401 exit 543A, 0.3 mi (0.5 km) s on Hwy 62. Int corridors. **Pets:** Other species. Designated rooms, service with restrictions, supervision.
SAVE ECO ⊜ ⊇ 📶 🗙 🛢 ▣

CAA ▼▼ **Comfort Inn** 🄷
(613) 966-7703. **$107-$142.** 200 N Park St K8P 2Y9. Hwy 401 exit 543A, 0.6 mi (1 km) s on Hwy 62. Int corridors. **Pets:** $10 daily fee/pet. Service with restrictions, supervision. SAVE 📶 🛢 ▣

CAA ▼▼ **Travelodge Hotel Belleville** 🄷
(613) 968-3411. **$99-$169.** 11 Bay Bridge Rd K8P 3P6. 0.3 mi (0.5 km) s of Hwy 2 (Dundas St). Int corridors. **Pets:** Accepted.
SAVE ECO 🍴 ⊇ 🗙 📶 🗙 🛢 ▣

BLIND RIVER
▼▼ **Lakeview Inn** Ⓜ
(705) 356-0800. **Call for rates.** 143 Causley St P0R 1B0. On Hwy 17, just e of Hwy 557. Ext corridors. **Pets:** Accepted.
🍴 📶 🗙 🛢 ▣

BLUE MOUNTAINS
CAA ▼▼▼ ▼▼ **The Westin Trillium House, Blue Mountain** 🄷 🌸
(705) 443-8080. **$149-$389, 7 day notice.** 220 Gord Canning Dr L9Y 0V9. Jct Hwy 26 and Mountain Rd, 6.3 mi (10 km) w on Mountain Rd, just w on Jozo Weider Blvd, then just w. Int corridors. **Pets:** Medium, dogs only. Designated rooms, no service, supervision.
SAVE 🍴 ⊇ 🗙 $📶 🗙 🛢 ▣

BOWMANVILLE
▼▼▼ **Holiday Inn Express & Suites Bowmanville** 🄷
(905) 697-8089. **$129-$169.** 37 Spicer Square L1C 5M2. Jct Hwy 401 and Waverly Rd N. Int corridors. **Pets:** $25 daily fee/pet. Designated rooms, service with restrictions, crate.
🍴 ⤴M ⊇ 📶 🗙 🛢 ▣

BRACEBRIDGE
▼▼ **Sleep Inn Muskoka** Ⓜ
(705) 645-2519. **$90-$200.** 510 Hwy 118 W P1L 1W8. Just e of Manitoba St. Int corridors. **Pets:** Small, dogs only. $15 daily fee/pet. Service with restrictions, crate. 📶 🗙 🛢 ▣

CAA ▼▼ **Travelodge Bracebridge** Ⓜ 🌸
(705) 645-2235. **$99-$169.** 320 Taylor Rd P1L 1K1. Hwy 11 exit 189 (Hwy 42/Taylor Rd), 0.6 mi (1 km) w. Ext corridors. **Pets:** Dogs only. $50 deposit/pet, $10 daily fee/pet. Designated rooms, service with restrictions, supervision. SAVE 🍴 ⊇ 📶 🛢 ▣

BRAMPTON
▼▼ **Motel 6 Brampton #1902** 🄷
(905) 451-3313. **Call for rates.** 160 Steelwell Rd L6T 5T3. Hwy 410 exit Steeles Ave E, s on Tomken Rd, then just w. Int corridors. **Pets:** Other species. Service with restrictions, crate.
ECO 🍴 📶 🛢

BRANTFORD
CAA ▼▼▼ **BEST WESTERN PLUS Brant Park Inn & Conference Centre** 🄷 🌸
(519) 753-8651. **$125-$145.** 19 Holiday Dr N3R 7J4. Jct Hwy 403 and Wayne Gretzky Pkwy. Int corridors. **Pets:** Large, other species. $20 daily fee/room. Designated rooms, service with restrictions, crate.
SAVE ECO ⊜ 🍴 ⤴M ⊇ 🗙 📶 🗙 🛢 ▣

CAA ▼▼ **Comfort Inn** 🄷 🌸
(519) 753-3100. **$95-$125.** 58 King George Rd N3R 5K4. Just s of jct Hwy 403 and 24. Int corridors. **Pets:** Other species. Service with restrictions, supervision. SAVE 🍴 📶 🛢 ▣

▼▼ **Days Inn** 🄷
(519) 759-2700. **$80-$230.** 460 Fairview Dr N3R 7A9. Hwy 403 exit Wayne Gretzky Pkwy, 0.5 mi (0.8 km) n. Int corridors. **Pets:** Accepted.
ECO 📶 🗙 🛢 ▣

BRIGHTON
CAA ▼▼▼ **Timber House Country Inn** 🄲🄸
(613) 475-3304. **Call for rates.** 116 Cedardale Rd K0K 1H0. Jct Hwy 2 and 64, just w over swing bridge, follow signs. Int corridors. **Pets:** Accepted. SAVE 🍴 ⊇ 📶 🗙

BROCKVILLE
CAA ▼▼ **Comfort Inn** 🄷
(613) 345-0042. **$130-$250.** 7777 Kent Blvd K6V 6N7. Hwy 401 exit 696, just nw. Int corridors. **Pets:** $15 daily fee/pet. Designated rooms, service with restrictions, supervision. SAVE 📶 🛢 ▣

CAA ▼▼▼ **Super 8 Brockville** Ⓜ 🌸
(613) 345-1622. **$89-$99.** 1843 Hwy 2 E K6V 5T1. Hwy 401 exit 698, 1.2 mi (1.9 km) s on N Augusta Rd, then 0.9 mi (1.5 km) e. Ext corridors. **Pets:** Small, dogs only. $100 deposit/room, $15 one-time fee/pet, $15 daily fee/pet. Designated rooms, service with restrictions, supervision. SAVE ⊇ 📶 ▣

BURLINGTON

ⒶⒶ ▼▼▼▼ **Admiral Inn** 🄷

(905) 639-4780. **$95-$105.** 3500 Billings Ct L7N 3N6. QEW exit Walkers Line westbound, just s to Harvester Rd, then just w to S Service Rd; exit Guelph Line Rd eastbound, just s to Harvester Rd, then just e to S Service Rd. Int corridors. **Pets:** Accepted.

🆂🅰🆅🅴 🍽 🛏 ✕ 🔌 🖵

ⒶⒶ ▼▼▼ **Comfort Inn** 🄷

(905) 639-1700. **Call for rates.** 3290 S Service Rd L7N 3M6. QEW exit Walkers Line westbound, just s to Harvester Rd, then just w; exit Guelph Line Rd eastbound, just s to Harvester Rd, then just e. Int corridors. **Pets:** $25 daily fee/pet. Designated rooms, service with restrictions. 🆂🅰🆅🅴 🄴🄲🄾 ⏿ 🛜 🔌 🖵

ⒶⒶ ▼▼▼▼ **Homewood Suites by Hilton** 🄷 ❀

(905) 631-8300. **$129-$209.** 975 Syscon Rd L7L 5S3. QEW exit Burloak Dr, s to Harvester Rd, then w. Int corridors. **Pets:** Medium. $75 one-time fee/pet. Designated rooms, service with restrictions, crate.

🆂🅰🆅🅴 🍽 🛥 🛜 🔌 🖵

▼▼ **Motel 6 Burlington #1900** 🄷

(905) 331-1955. **Call for rates.** 4345 N Service Rd L7L 4X7. QEW exit Walkers Line N to N Service Rd, 0.9 mi (1.4 km) e. Int corridors. **Pets:** Other species. Service with restrictions, crate.

🄴🄲🄾 🍽 🛜 🔌

▼▼▼▼ **Quality Hotel Burlington** 🄷

(905) 639-9290. **$99-$149.** 950 Walkers Line L7N 2G2. QEW exit Walkers Line, just s. Int corridors. **Pets:** Small, other species. $25 daily fee/pet. Designated rooms, service with restrictions, crate.

🄴🄲🄾 🍽 🛥 🔌 🖵

ⒶⒶ ▼▼▼▼ **Waterfront Hotel - Downtown Burlington** 🄷 ❀

(905) 681-5400. **$149-$199.** 2020 Lakeshore Rd L7R 4G8. Corner of Brant St; downtown. Int corridors. **Pets:** Medium. $15 one-time fee/room. Designated rooms, service with restrictions, crate.

🆂🅰🆅🅴 🄴🄲🄾 🍽 🛥 🛜 ✕ 🔌 🖵

CAMBRIDGE

ⒶⒶ ▼▼▼▼ **Cambridge Hotel Conference Centre** 🄷

(519) 622-1505. **$105-$140, 30 day notice.** 700 Hespeler Rd N3H 5L8. Hwy 401 exit 282, just s. Int corridors. **Pets:** Small. $50 one-time fee/room. Designated rooms, service with restrictions, supervision.

🆂🅰🆅🅴 🍽 🛜 ✕ 🔌 🖵

ⒶⒶ ▼▼▼ **Comfort Inn** 🄷 🐾

(519) 658-1100. **$100-$120.** 220 Holiday Inn Dr N3C 1Z4. Hwy 401 exit 282, just n to Groh Ave. Int corridors. **Pets:** Other species. $20 one-time fee/room. Service with restrictions. 🆂🅰🆅🅴 🄴🄲🄾 🛜 ✕ 🔌 🖵

▼▼▼ **Holiday Inn Cambridge** 🄷

(519) 658-4601. **Call for rates.** 200 Holiday Inn Dr N3C 1Z4. Hwy 401 exit 282, just n to Groh Ave. Int corridors. **Pets:** Medium, dogs only. $25 daily fee/pet. Designated rooms, service with restrictions, crate.

🄴🄲🄾 🍽 🛥 🅇 🛜 🔌 🖵

▼▼▼ **Homewood Suites by Hilton Cambridge/Waterloo** 🄷

(519) 651-2888. **$144-$209.** 800 Jamieson Pkwy N3C 4N6. Hwy 401 exit 286 (Townline Rd), just n. Int corridors. **Pets:** Medium, other species. $75 one-time fee/room. Service with restrictions, supervision.

🛥🄼 🛥 🛜 🔌 🖵

ⒶⒶ ▼▼▼▼▼ **Langdon Hall Country House Hotel & Spa** 🄲🄸

(519) 740-2100. **Call for rates.** 1 Langdon Dr N3H 4R8. Hwy 401 exit 275, 0.8 mi (1.3 km) se on Fountain St, 0.6 mi (1 km) s on Blair Rd, follow signs. Ext/int corridors. **Pets:** Accepted.

🆂🅰🆅🅴 🍽 🛥 🅇 🛜 ✕ 🔌 🖵

▼▼▼ **Super 8 Cambridge** 🄷

(519) 622-1070. **$90-$120.** 650 Hespeler Rd N1R 6J8. Hwy 401 exit 282, 0.6 mi (1 km) s. Int corridors. **Pets:** Accepted.

🍽 🛥 🛜 🔌 🖵

CHATHAM

▼▼ ▼▼ **Comfort Inn** 🄷

(519) 352-5500. **$80-$130.** 1100 Richmond St N7M 5J5. Hwy 401 exit 81 (Bloomfield Rd), 3.1 mi (5 km) n. Int corridors. **Pets:** Medium, other species. Service with restrictions, supervision. 🄴🄲🄾 🛜 ✕ 🔌 🖵

▼▼▼▼ **Holiday Inn Express & Suites** 🄷

(519) 351-1100. **Call for rates.** 575 Richmond St N7M 1R2. Hwy 401 exit 81 (Bloomfield Rd) to jct Hwy 2, 0.9 mi (1.5 km) e, then 0.9 mi (1.5 km) w. Int corridors. **Pets:** Accepted.

🛥🄼 🛥 🛜 ✕ 🔌 🖵

CHATSWORTH

▼▼ ▼▼ **Key Motel** 🄼

(519) 794-2350. **Call for rates.** 317051 Hwy 6/10 N0H 1G0. On SR 6 and 10. Ext/int corridors. **Pets:** Designated rooms, service with restrictions, supervision. 🍽 🛥 🛜 🔌

COBOURG

ⒶⒶ ▼▼▼▼ **BEST WESTERN PLUS Cobourg Inn & Convention Centre** 🄷

(905) 372-2105. **$149-$309.** 930 Burnham St K9A 2X9. Hwy 401 exit 472 (Burnham St S). Int corridors. **Pets:** Accepted.

🆂🅰🆅🅴 🄴🄲🄾 ⏿ 🍽 🛥 🛜 🔌 🖵

▼▼ ▼▼ **Comfort Inn** 🄷

(905) 372-7007. **$89-$135.** 121 Densmore Rd K9A 4J9. Hwy 401 exit 474, just se. Int corridors. **Pets:** Other species. Designated rooms, service with restrictions, crate. 🄴🄲🄾 🍽 🛜 🔌 🖵

COLLINGWOOD

ⒶⒶ ▼▼ ▼▼ **Cranberry Golf Resort & Conference Centre** 🄷

(705) 445-6600. **$89-$539.** 19 Keith Ave (RR 4) L9Y 4T9. Jct Hwy 26. Int corridors. **Pets:** Dogs only. $50 one-time fee/room. Designated rooms, service with restrictions, supervision.

🆂🅰🆅🅴 🍽 🛥 🅇 🛜 ✕ 🔌 🖵

CORNWALL *(Restaurants p. 646)*

ⒶⒶ ▼▼▼▼ **BEST WESTERN PLUS Parkway Inn & Conference Centre** 🄷

(613) 932-0451. **$140-$260.** 1515 Vincent Massey Dr K6H 5R6. Hwy 401 exit 789 (Brookdale Ave), 1.8 mi (2.8 km) s, then just w. Int corridors. **Pets:** Service with restrictions, supervision.

🆂🅰🆅🅴 🄴🄲🄾 ⏿ 🍽 🛥 🅇 ✕ 🔌 🖵

▼▼ ▼▼ **Comfort Inn-Cornwall** 🄷

(613) 937-0111. **$99-$175.** 1625 Vincent Massey Dr K6H 5R6. Hwy 401 exit 789 (Brookdale Ave), 1.8 mi (2.8 km) s, then 0.4 mi (0.7 km) w. Int corridors. **Pets:** Medium. $20 one-time fee/room. Designated rooms, service with restrictions, crate. 🛥 🛜 🔌 🖵

DRYDEN

ⒶⒶ ▼▼▼▼ **BEST WESTERN PLUS Dryden Hotel & Conference Centre** 🄷 ❀

(807) 223-3201. **$120-$145.** 349 Government St P8N 2P4. On Hwy 17. Int corridors. **Pets:** Medium. $20 deposit/room. Designated rooms, service with restrictions, supervision.

🆂🅰🆅🅴 ⏿ 🍽 🛥 🅇 🛜 ✕ 🔌 🖵

▼▼ ▼▼ **Comfort Inn** 🄼 ❀

(807) 223-3893. **$119-$169.** 522 Government St P8N 2P7. On Hwy 17. Int corridors. **Pets:** Other species. $10 daily fee/pet. Designated rooms, service with restrictions, supervision. 🄴🄲🄾 🛜 ✕ 🔌 🖵

FONTHILL

▼▼ **Hipwell's Motel** 🄼

(905) 892-3588. **$45-$75.** 299 Reg Rd 20 W L0S 1E0. 1 mi (1.6 km) w; center. Ext corridors. **Pets:** Dogs only. $5 daily fee/pet. Service with restrictions, supervision. 🍽 🛜 🔌

FORT ERIE

CAA ◆◆◆ **Clarion Hotel & Conference Centre** [H]
(905) 871-8333. **$100-$210.** 1485 Garrison Rd L2A 1P8. QEW exit Gilmore Rd. Int corridors. **Pets:** Accepted.
[SAVE] [ECO] 🍴 🏊 🏋 📶 🚭 🧊 📺

FORT FRANCES

CAA ◆◆ **La Place Rendez-Vous** [H]
(807) 274-9811. **$109-$119.** 1201 Idylwild Dr, B2-RR 2 P9A 3M3. Hwy 11, just e on Lake Rd; east end of town. Int corridors. **Pets:** $10 one-time fee/room. Designated rooms, service with restrictions, crate.
[SAVE] 🍴 📶 🚭 🧊 📺

◆◆ **Super 8** [H]
(807) 274-4945. **$106-$190.** 810 Kings Hwy P9A 2X4. On Hwy 11. Int corridors. **Pets:** Accepted. ♿ 🏊 📶 🧊 📺

GANANOQUE

CAA ◆◆◆ **BEST WESTERN Country Squire Resort** [H]
(613) 382-3511. **$69-$149.** 715 King St E K7G 1H4. Hwy 401 exit 647 eastbound; exit 648 westbound, 0.6 mi (1 km) w on Hwy 2 (King St). Ext/int corridors. **Pets:** Accepted.
[SAVE] 🍴 🏊 🏋 📶 🚭 🧊 📺

CAA ◆◆◆ **Comfort Inn & Suites Thousand Islands Harbour District** [H]
(613) 382-7272. **Call for rates.** 22 Main St K7G 2L7. Corner of Hwy 2 (King St); center. Int corridors. **Pets:** Accepted.
[SAVE] 🏊 📶 🧊 📺

CAA ◆◆◆ **Holiday Inn Express & Suites 1000 Islands** [H]
(613) 382-8338. **$99-$299.** 777 King St E K7G 1H4. Just w of jct Hwy 2 (King St), 401 and 1000 Islands Pkwy. Int corridors. **Pets:** Accepted.
[SAVE] [ECO] ♿ 🏊 📶 🚭 🧊 📺

CAA ◆◆ **Quality Inn & Suites 1000 Islands** [M]
(613) 382-1453. **$79-$199.** 650 King St E K7G 1H3. Hwy 401 exit 647 eastbound; exit 648 westbound, 0.6 mi (1 km) w on Hwy 2 (King St). Ext corridors. **Pets:** Small, dogs only. $10 daily fee/pet. Designated rooms, service with restrictions, supervision.
[SAVE] 🍴 🏊 📶 🧊 📺

◆◆ **Ramada Provincial Inn** [M]
(613) 382-2038. **$99-$179.** 846 King St E K7G 1H3. Hwy 401 exit 647 eastbound; exit 648 westbound, 0.3 mi (0.5 km) w on Hwy 2 (King St). Ext corridors. **Pets:** Accepted. 🍴 🏊 📶 🚭 🧊 📺

CAA ◆◆ **Travelodge 1000 Islands** [M]
(613) 382-4728. **$67-$250.** 785 King St E K7G 1H4. Hwy 401 exit 647 eastbound; exit 648 westbound, 0.3 mi (0.5 km) w on Hwy 2 (King St). Ext/int corridors. **Pets:** Accepted. [SAVE] 🏊 📶 🚭 🧊 📺

◆◆◆ **Trinity House Inn** [CI]
(613) 382-8383. **$99-$250, 7 day notice.** 90 Stone St S K7G 1Z8. Corner of Pine St; center. Int corridors. **Pets:** Designated rooms, service with restrictions, crate. 🍴 📶 🚭 📵 🧊 📺

GEORGETOWN

CAA ◆◆ **BEST WESTERN Inn On The Hill** [H]
(905) 877-6986. **$99-$149.** 365 Guelph St (Hwy 7) L7G 4B6. At Delrex Blvd. Ext corridors. **Pets:** Medium. $25 daily fee/pet. Designated rooms, service with restrictions, supervision. [SAVE] 📶 🧊 📺

GRAVENHURST

CAA ◆◆◆ **Residence Inn by Marriott Gravenhurst Muskoka Wharf** [H] 🐾
(705) 687-6600. **$111-$304.** 285 Steamship Bay Rd P1P 1Z9. Hwy 11 exit 169 (Bethune Dr); at Muskoka Wharf, follow signs. Int corridors. **Pets:** $100 one-time fee/room. Service with restrictions, supervision.
[SAVE] ♿ 🏊 📶 🚭 🧊 📺

GRIMSBY

CAA ◆◆ **Super 8-Grimsby** [H]
(905) 309-8800. **$106-$126.** 11 Windward Dr L3M 4E9. QEW exit 74 (Casablanca Blvd N). Int corridors. **Pets:** Medium, other species. $10 daily fee/pet. Service with restrictions, crate.
[SAVE] 🏊 📶 🚭 🧊 📺

GUELPH

CAA ◆◆◆ **Comfort Inn Guelph** [H] 🐾
(519) 763-1900. **$90-$190.** 480 Silvercreek Pkwy N1H 7R5. Jct Hwy 6 and 7. Int corridors. **Pets:** Dogs only. $15 daily fee/pet. Service with restrictions, crate. [SAVE] [ECO] 📶 🧊 📺

CAA ◆◆ **Days Inn-Guelph** [H]
(519) 822-9112. **$92-$160.** 785 Gordon St N1G 1Y8. Hwy 401 exit 299 (Brock Rd), 7 mi (11.5 km) n. Int corridors. **Pets:** Accepted.
[SAVE] [ECO] 🍴 📶 🚭 🧊 📺

◆◆◆ **Delta Guelph Hotel and Conference Centre** [H]
(519) 780-3700. **$139-$219.** 50 Stone Rd W N1G 0A9. Jct Gordon St. Int corridors. **Pets:** Accepted. [ECO] 🍴 ♿ 📶 🚭 🧊 📺

CAA ◆◆◆ **Holiday Inn Guelph Hotel & Conference Centre** [H]
(519) 836-0231. **$99-$169.** 601 Scottsdale Dr N1G 3E7. Jct Hwy 6 N and Stone Rd E; 5 mi (8 km) n of jct Hwy 401. Int corridors. **Pets:** Accepted. [SAVE] [ECO] 🍴 🏊 🏋 📶 🧊 📺

CAA ◆◆◆ **Staybridge Suites** [H]
(519) 767-3300. **Call for rates.** 11 Corporate Ct N1G 5G5. Jct Hwy 6 and Laird St, just e. Int corridors. **Pets:** Accepted.
[SAVE] [ECO] 🍴 ♿ 🏊 📶 🧊 📺

HALIBURTON

◆ **Lakeview Motel** [M]
(705) 457-1027. **$152-$300, 5 day notice.** 4951 CR 21 K0M 1S0. Jct Hwy 118, 1.6 mi (2.5 km) w. Ext corridors. **Pets:** Medium, other species. $12 daily fee/pet. Designated rooms, service with restrictions.
🍴 🏊 📶 🚭 🧊 📺

CAA ◆◆◆ **Pinestone Resort, Conference Centre, Spa & Golf Course** [H]
(705) 457-1800. **$129-$249, 3 day notice.** 4252 CR 21 K0M 1S0. 3.8 mi (6 km) s of town. Ext/int corridors. **Pets:** Medium, dogs only. $50 one-time fee/room. Service with restrictions, supervision.
[SAVE] [ECO] 🍴 🏊 🏋 📶 🚭 🧊 📺

HAMILTON

CAA ◆◆ **Comfort Inn** [H]
(905) 560-4500. **$110-$154.** 183 Centennial Pkwy N L8E 1H8. QEW exit 88 (Hwy 20), 0.6 mi (1 km) s. Int corridors. **Pets:** Large. $15 daily fee/room. Designated rooms, service with restrictions, crate.
[SAVE] [ECO] 📶 🚭 🧊 📺

CAA ◆◆◆ **Homewood Suites by Hilton Hamilton** [H]
(905) 667-1200. **$169-$209.** 40 Bay St S L8P 0B3. Jct George St; downtown. Int corridors. **Pets:** Accepted. [SAVE] ♿ 📶 🚭 🧊 📺

CAA ◆◆◆ **Sheraton Hamilton Hotel** [H]
(905) 529-5515. **Call for rates.** 116 King St W L8P 4V3. Between Bay and James sts; downtown. Int corridors. **Pets:** Accepted.
[SAVE] 🍴 ♿ 🏊 📶 🚭 🧊 📺

CAA ◆◆◆ **Staybridge Suites - Hamilton Downtown** [H]
(905) 527-1001. **Call for rates.** 20 Caroline St S L8P 0B1. Between Main and King sts. Int corridors. **Pets:** Accepted.
[SAVE] 🏊 📶 🚭 🧊 📺

◆◆ **Super 8-Hamilton Airport/Mount Hope** [H]
(905) 679-3355. **$95-$136.** 2975 Homestead Dr L0R 1W0. Jct Hwy 6 S (Upper James St) and Homestead Dr. Int corridors. **Pets:** Accepted.
📶 🚭 🧊 📺

HUNTSVILLE

▼▼ ▼▼ Comfort Inn 🅷
(705) 789-1701. **$88-$228.** 86 King William St P1H 1E4. Jct Hwy 60. Int corridors. **Pets:** Medium, other species. Designated rooms, service with restrictions, supervision. 🅔🅒🅞 📶 🛅 🖵

ⒶⒶ ▼▼▼▼ Deerhurst Resort 🅷
(705) 789-6411. **$119-$379, 7 day notice.** 1235 Deerhurst Dr P1H 2E8. Jct Hwy 11, 4.3 mi (7 km) e on Hwy 60 to Deerhurst Canal Rd (CR 23), then 1.2 mi (2 km), follow signs. Ext/int corridors. **Pets:** $50 one-time fee/room. Designated rooms, service with restrictions, supervision.
🆂🅰🆅🅴 🅔🅒🅞 🍴 ⊶ 🗙 📶 🗙 🛅 🖵

▼▼▼ Hidden Valley Resort, an Ascend Hotel Collection Member 🅷
(705) 789-2301. **$99-$349, 3 day notice.** 1755 Valley Rd P1H 1Z8. Jct Hwy 11, 4 mi (6.5 km) e on Hwy 60 to Canal Rd, follow signs. Int corridors. **Pets:** Small, dogs only. $35 one-time fee/room. Designated rooms, service with restrictions, crate.
🍴 🗄🅼 ⊶ 🗙 📶 🗙 🛅 🖵

ⒶⒶ ▼▼▼▼ Holiday Inn Express Hotel & Suites 🅷
(705) 788-9500. **$129-$259.** 100 Howland Dr P1H 2P9. Jct Hwy 11 and 60, just se. Int corridors. **Pets:** Accepted.
🆂🅰🆅🅴 ⊶ 📶 🗙 🛅 🖵

▼▼ ▼▼ Motel 6-Huntsville 🅷
(705) 787-0118. **Call for rates.** 70 Howland Dr P1H 2P9. Jct Hwy 11 and 60, just se. Int corridors. **Pets:** Other species. Service with restrictions, crate. 🅔🅒🅞 ⊶ 📶 🛅

▼▼ Tulip Inn 🅜
(705) 789-4001. **$69-$140, 3 day notice.** 211 Arrowhead Park Rd P1H 2J4. Hwy 11 exit 226 (Muskoka Rd 3), follow signs for Arrowhead Park. Ext corridors. **Pets:** Service with restrictions, crate. 🍴 📶 🛅 🖵

IGNACE

ⒶⒶ ▼▼ ▼ Trading Post Motel 🅜
(807) 934-2386. **$65-$79.** 1001 Main St, Hwy 17 E P0T 1T0. On Hwy 17, east end of town. Ext corridors. **Pets:** Other species. $8 daily fee/pet. Service with restrictions, supervision.
🆂🅰🆅🅴 🍴 ⊶ 📶 🛅 🖵

INGERSOLL

▼▼▼ Comfort Inn & Suites 🅷
(519) 425-1100. **$108-$148.** 20 Samnah Cres N5C 3J7. Hwy 401 exit 216 (Culloden Rd). Int corridors. **Pets:** Other species. $10 one-time fee/room. Crate. 🗙 🍴 ⊶ 📶 🛅 🖵

JACKSONS POINT

ⒶⒶ ▼▼▼▼ The Briars Resort and Spa 🅷
(905) 722-3271. **$159-$479, 21 day notice.** 55 Hedge Rd, RR 1 L0E 1L0. Hwy 48, through Sutton to Jacksons Point, 0.6 mi (1 km) e. Ext/int corridors. **Pets:** Medium, dogs only. $25 daily fee/pet. Designated rooms, service with restrictions.
🆂🅰🆅🅴 🍴 ⊶ 🗙 📶 🗙 🛅 🖵

KANATA

ⒶⒶ ▼▼ ▼▼ Brookstreet Hotel 🅷
(613) 271-1800. **$139-$499.** 525 Legget Dr K2K 2W2. Hwy 417 exit 138 (March Rd), 2.3 mi (3.7 km) n, just e on Solandt Dr to Legget Dr, then just n. Int corridors. **Pets:** $250 deposit/room, $25 daily fee/room. Service with restrictions, crate.
🆂🅰🆅🅴 🅔🅒🅞 🍴 ⊶ 🗙 📶 🛅 🖵

ⒶⒶ ▼▼ ▼ Comfort Inn Ottawa West Kanata 🅷
(613) 592-2200. **$99-$179.** 222 Hearst Way K2L 3A2. Hwy 417 exit 138 (Eagleson Rd), 0.4 mi (0.6 km) s, just w on Katimavik Rd, then 0.5 mi (0.8 km) n. Int corridors. **Pets:** Accepted.
🆂🅰🆅🅴 🅔🅒🅞 📶 🗙 🛅 🖵

KAPUSKASING

ⒶⒶ ▼▼ ▼▼ Comfort Inn 🅷
(705) 335-8583. **$115-$150.** 172 Government Rd E P5N 2W9. Hwy 11; corner of Brunelle Rd. Int corridors. **Pets:** Other species. $10 one-time fee/room. Service with restrictions, crate.
🆂🅰🆅🅴 🅔🅒🅞 📶 🗙 🛅 🖵

ⒶⒶ ▼▼▼▼ Super 8 🅷
(705) 335-8887. **$120-$142.** 430 Government Rd P5N 2X7. Hwy 11. Int corridors. **Pets:** Medium. $10 one-time fee/room. Designated rooms, service with restrictions, supervision.
🆂🅰🆅🅴 ⊶ 🗙 📶 🗙 🛅 🖵

KENORA

ⒶⒶ ▼▼ ▼ BEST WESTERN Lakeside Inn & Conference Centre 🅷 🐾
(807) 468-5521. **$137-$157.** 470 1st Ave S P9N 1W5. Just s on 4th Ave S from jct Hwy 17. Int corridors. **Pets:** $15 daily fee/room. Designated rooms, service with restrictions, supervision.
🆂🅰🆅🅴 🅔🅒🅞 🗙 🍴 ⊶ 📶 🗙 🛅 🖵

▼▼ ▼▼ Comfort Inn 🅜 🐾
(807) 468-8845. **$119-$179.** 1230 Hwy 17 E P9N 1L9. 0.9 mi (1.5 km) e of town. Int corridors. **Pets:** Other species. $15 one-time fee/pet. Designated rooms, service with restrictions, crate. 🍴 📶 🗙 🛅 🖵

KILLALOE

▼▼▼▼ Annie's Inn Bed & Breakfast 🅱🅱
(613) 757-0950. **$90-$225, 7 day notice.** 67 Roche St K0J 2A0. Hwy 60 exit Maple St, 1 blk to Roche St, then w; driveway entrance is at the end of the street. Int corridors. **Pets:** Supervision.
🍴 📶 🗙 🗙 🛅 🖵

KINCARDINE

ⒶⒶ ▼▼▼▼ BEST WESTERN PLUS Governor's Inn 🅷 🐾
(519) 396-8242. **$160-$180.** 791 Durham St N2Z 1M4. Jct Hwy 21. Int corridors. **Pets:** Large, dogs only. $20 daily fee/room. Designated rooms, service with restrictions, supervision.
🆂🅰🆅🅴 🍴 🗙 📶 🗙 🛅 🖵

▼▼▼▼ Holiday Inn Express and Suites-Kincardine 🅷
(519) 395-3545. **$165-$195.** 2 Millenium Way N2Z 0B5. Jct Hwy 21. Int corridors. **Pets:** Accepted. 🗄🅼 ⊶ 📶 🗙 🛅 🖵

KINGSTON

ⒶⒶ ▼▼▼▼ BEST WESTERN Fireside Inn 🅷 🐾
(613) 549-2211. **$129-$189.** 1217 Princess St K7M 3E1. Hwy 401 exit 615 (Sir John A MacDonald Blvd), 2.5 mi (4 km) sw. Int corridors. **Pets:** $10 daily fee/room. Designated rooms, service with restrictions, supervision. 🆂🅰🆅🅴 🗙 🍴 ⊶ 📶 🗙 🛅 🖵

ⒶⒶ ▼▼ ▼▼ Comfort Inn Hwy 401 🅷
(613) 546-9500. **$95-$210.** 55 Warne Cres K7K 6Z5. Hwy 401 exit 617 (Division St), just s to Dalton Ave. Int corridors. **Pets:** Large. $10 daily fee/room. Service with restrictions, crate.
🆂🅰🆅🅴 🅔🅒🅞 📶 🗙 🛅 🖵

▼▼ ▼▼ Comfort Inn Midtown 🅷
(613) 549-5550. **$95-$116.** 1454 Princess St K7M 3E5. Hwy 401 exit 613 (Sydenham Rd), 2.5 mi (4 km) se. Int corridors. **Pets:** Other species. Service with restrictions, supervision. 🅔🅒🅞 📶 🛅 🖵

▼▼ ▼▼ Confederation Place Hotel 🅷
(613) 549-6300. **$89-$189.** 237 Ontario St K7L 2Z4. Center of downtown. Int corridors. **Pets:** Other species. $15 daily fee/pet. Designated rooms, service with restrictions, supervision. ⊶ 📶 🗙 🛅 🖵

ⒶⒶ ▼▼▼▼ Delta Kingston Waterfront Hotel 🅷
(613) 549-8100. **Call for rates.** 1 Johnson St K7L 5H7. At foot of Johnson St; downtown. Int corridors. **Pets:** Accepted.
🆂🅰🆅🅴 🅔🅒🅞 🍴 ⊶ 📶 🗙 🛅 🖵

▼▼▼ The Executive Inn & Suites M
(613) 549-1620. **$99-$149, 3 day notice.** 794 Hwy 2 E K7L 4V1. Hwy 401 exit 623, 5 mi (8 km) s, then 1.3 mi (2 km) e. Ext corridors.
Pets: Accepted. 🍴 ⇔ 🛰 ✕ 🛏 💻

(AAA) ▼▼▼ Green Acres Inn M
(613) 546-1796. **$119-$179.** 2480 Princess St K7M 3G4. Hwy 401 exit 611 (Hwy 38), 1.9 mi (3 km) s, then 0.3 mi (0.5 km) e. Ext corridors. **Pets:** Dogs only. $400 deposit/room. Designated rooms, service with restrictions, crate. [SAVE] ⇔ 🛰 ✕ 🛏 💻

(AAA) ▼▼▼ Holiday Inn Kingston-Waterfront H
(613) 549-8400. **$129-$249.** 2 Princess St K7L 1A2. Corner of Ontario St; center of downtown. Int corridors. **Pets:** Other species. $35 daily fee/room. Designated rooms, service with restrictions, supervision.
[SAVE] [ECO] 🍴 ⚒ ⇔ 🛰 ✕ 🛏 💻

▼▼ Motel 6 Kingston H
(613) 507-6666. **Call for rates.** 1542 Robinson Ct K7L 4V2. Hwy 401 exit 611, just s. Int corridors. **Pets:** Other species. Service with restrictions, crate. [ECO] 🍴 ⚒ 🛰 ✕ 🛏

▼▼ Peachtree Inn H
(613) 546-4411. **Call for rates.** 1187 Princess St K7M 3E1. Hwy 401 exit 615 (Sir John A MacDonald Blvd), 2.5 mi (4 km) sw. Int corridors. **Pets:** Accepted. 🛰 ✕ 🛏 💻

▼▼▼ Residence Inn by Marriott Kingston Water's Edge H
(613) 544-4888. **$146-$298.** 7 Earl St K7L 0A4. Hwy 401 exit 617 (Division St) to Princess St, right on King St, then left, 2 blks w of city hall. Int corridors. **Pets:** Accepted. 🍴 ⚒ ⇔ 🛰 ✕ 🛏 💻

KIRKLAND LAKE
▼▼ Comfort Inn H
(705) 567-4909. **$135-$210.** 455 Government Rd W P0K 1A0. On Hwy 66. Int corridors. **Pets:** Other species. Service with restrictions.
[ECO] 🛰 ✕ 🛏 💻

KITCHENER
(AAA) ▼▼▼ Crowne Plaza Kitchener-Waterloo H
(519) 744-4141. **$144-$349, 30 day notice.** 105 King St E N2G 2K8. Corner of King and Benton sts; downtown. Int corridors.
Pets: Accepted. [SAVE] [ECO] 🍴 ⇔ 🛰 ✕ 🛏 💻

(AAA) ▼▼▼ Radisson Hotel Kitchener Waterloo H
(519) 894-9500. **Call for rates.** 2960 King St E N2A 1A9. Hwy 401 exit 278, 3.8 mi (6 km) w on Hwy 8 exit Weber St. Int corridors.
Pets: Accepted. [SAVE] [ECO] 🍴 ⇔ 🛰 ✕ 🛏 💻

▼▼▼▼ The Walper Hotel H
(519) 745-4321. **Call for rates.** 20 Queen St S N2G 1V6. Corner of King and Queen sts; downtown. Int corridors. **Pets:** Accepted.
🍴 🛰 ✕ 🛏 💻

LEAMINGTON
▼▼ Comfort Inn H
(519) 326-9071. **$110-$160.** 279 Erie St S N8H 3C4. 0.6 mi (1 km) s of jct Talbot and Erie sts; on direct route to Point Pelee National Park. Int corridors. **Pets:** Accepted. [ECO] 🛰 ✕ 🛏 💻

▼▼ Days Inn Leamington H
(519) 325-0260. **$100-$250, 3 day notice.** 201 Erie St N N8H 3A5. 0.6 mi (1 km) n of Talbot St. Int corridors. **Pets:** Accepted.
[ECO] ⇔ ✕ 🛰 🛏 💻

LINCOLN
▼▼▼▼ Inn on the Twenty CI
(905) 562-5336. **$159-$389, 7 day notice.** 3845 Main St L0R 1S0. QEW exit 57 (Victoria Ave/Reg Rd 24), 1.9 mi (3 km) s, 1.9 mi (3 km) e on Reg Rd 81, then just n. Ext/int corridors. **Pets:** Accepted.
🍴 🛰 ✕ 🛏 💻

▼▼ Ramada Jordan Beacon Harbourside Hotel & Suites H
(905) 562-4155. **$69-$179.** 2793 Beacon Blvd L0R 1S0. QEW exit 55. Int corridors. **Pets:** Accepted. 🍴 ⇔ ✕ 🛰 ✕ 🛏 💻

LONDON
(AAA) ▼▼▼ BEST WESTERN PLUS Lamplighter Inn & Conference Centre H
(519) 681-7151. **$129-$209.** 591 Wellington Rd S N6C 4R3. Hwy 401 exit 186 (Wellington Rd), 2.3 mi (3.7 km) n. Int corridors.
Pets: Accepted. [SAVE] [ECO] 🍴 ⇔ ✕ 🛰 ✕ 🛏 💻

▼▼ Comfort Inn H
(519) 685-9300. **$89-$124.** 1156 Wellington Rd N6E 1M3. Hwy 401 exit 186B (Wellington Rd), just n. Int corridors. **Pets:** Accepted.
[ECO] 🛰 🛏 💻

(AAA) ▼▼▼ Delta London Armouries H
(519) 679-6111. **$125-$161.** 325 Dundas St N6B 1T9. Between Wellington and Waterloo sts. Int corridors. **Pets:** Accepted.
[SAVE] [ECO] 🍴 ⇔ ✕ 🛰 ✕ 🛏 💻

(AAA) ▼▼▼ Hilton London Ontario H
(519) 439-1661. **$109-$115.** 300 King St N6B 1S2. Jct King St and Wellington Rd. Int corridors. **Pets:** Accepted.
[SAVE] [ECO] 🍴 ⚒ ⇔ 🛰 🛏 💻

(AAA) ▼▼▼ Holiday Inn Hotel & Suites London H
(519) 668-7900. **Call for rates.** 855 Wellington Rd S N6E 3N5. Jct Wellington and Southdale rds. Int corridors. **Pets:** Accepted.
[SAVE] [ECO] 🍴 ⇔ 🛰 ✕ 🛏 💻

▼▼▼ Homewood Suites by Hilton London H
(519) 686-7700. **$119-$199.** 45 Bessemer Rd N6E 0A2. Hwy 401 exit 186B (Wellington Rd), just n. Int corridors. **Pets:** Accepted.
⚒ ⇔ 🛰 🛏 💻

▼▼▼ Hotel Metro-London H
(519) 518-9000. **$129-$199.** 32 Covent Market Pl N6A 1E8. Jct Talbot St. Int corridors. **Pets:** Accepted. 🍴 🛰 ✕ 🛏 💻

(AAA) ▼▼ London Airport Inn & Suites H
(519) 457-1200. **$89-$149, 7 day notice.** 2230 Dundas St E N5V 1R5. Hwy 401 exit Veteran's Memorial Pkwy, 4.8 mi (7.7 km) n; corner of Airport Rd and Dundas St E. Int corridors. **Pets:** Accepted.
[SAVE] 🍴 🛰 🛏 💻

▼▼ Motel 6 London #5703 H
(519) 680-0900. **Call for rates.** 810 Exeter Rd N6E 1L5. Hwy 401 exit 186 (Wellington Rd), just n. Int corridors. **Pets:** Other species. Service with restrictions, crate. [ECO] ⚒ ⇔ 🛰 🛏

▼▼ Quality Suites H
(519) 680-1024. **$89-$125.** 1120 Dearness Dr N6E 1N9. Hwy 401 exit 186B (Wellington Rd), 1 mi (1.6 km) n. Int corridors. **Pets:** Accepted.
[ECO] 🛰 🛏 💻

▼▼ Ramada London H
(519) 681-4900. **$79-$139.** 817 Exeter Rd N6E 1W1. Hwy 401 exit 186B (Wellington Rd), just n. Int corridors. **Pets:** Accepted.
🍴 ⇔ 🛰 🛏 💻

(AAA) ▼▼▼ Residence Inn by Marriott London H 🐾
(519) 433-7222. **$125-$206.** 383 Colborne St N6B 3P5. Jct King St. Int corridors. **Pets:** Other species. $75 one-time fee/pet. Designated rooms, service with restrictions, crate. [SAVE] [ECO] 🛰 ✕ 🛏 💻

(AAA) ▼▼▼ StationPark All Suite Hotel H 🐾
(519) 642-4444. **$139-$229.** 242 Pall Mall St N6A 5P6. Hwy 401 exit 186B (Wellington Rd), 5.6 mi (9 km) n. Int corridors. **Pets:** Large. Designated rooms, service with restrictions, crate.
[SAVE] ✕ 🛰 ✕ 🛏 💻

Ⓐ ▽▽/▽ **Staybridge Suites** 🅷

(519) 649-4500. **Call for rates.** 824 Exeter Rd N6E 1L5. Hwy 401 exit 186B (Wellington Rd), just n. Int corridors. **Pets:** Other species. $40 one-time fee/room. Service with restrictions, supervision.

[SAVE] [ECO] [¶] [&M] [🛏] [🛜] [📦] [💻]

Ⓐ ▽▽/▽ **TownePlace Suites by Marriott** 🅷

(519) 681-1200. **$68-$81.** 800 Exeter Rd N6E 1L5. Hwy 401 exit 186B (Wellington Rd), just n. Int corridors. **Pets:** Accepted.

[SAVE] [ECO] [🛜] [✕] [📦] [💻]

MAGNETAWAN

▽▽ **Ahmic Lake-Woodland Echoes Resort** 🅒🅐

(705) 387-3866. **Call for rates.** 3 Victoria St P0A 1P0. Hwy 11 exit Burks Falls/Ontario St to Hwy 520 W, then 12.5 mi (20 km) w. Ext corridors. **Pets:** Accepted. [¶] [✕] [🛜] [✕] [☒] [📦] [💻]

MARKHAM

▽▽/▽ **Comfort Inn** 🅷

(905) 477-6077. **$94-$129.** 8330 Woodbine Ave L3R 2N8. Hwy 401 exit 375, 5.6 mi (9 km) n; Hwy 404 exit Hwy 7, just e, then s. Int corridors. **Pets:** Accepted. [🛏] [✕] [🛜] [📦] [💻]

▽▽/▽ **Courtyard by Marriott Toronto Northeast/Markham** 🅷

(905) 474-0444. **$126-$164.** 7095 Woodbine Ave L3R 1A3. Hwy 404 exit Steeles Ave, just n. Int corridors. **Pets:** Accepted.

[¶] [&M] [🞲] [✕] [📦] [💻]

▽▽/▽ **Delta Markham** 🅷

(905) 477-2010. **$99-$179.** 50 E Valhalla Dr L3R 0A3. Hwy 404 exit Hwy 7, just e. Int corridors. **Pets:** Medium, other species. $35 one-time fee/room. Service with restrictions, crate.

[ECO] [¶] [🛏] [✕] [🛜] [📦] [💻]

Ⓐ ▽▽/▽▽ **Hilton Toronto/Markham Suites Conference Centre & Spa** 🅷

(905) 470-8500. **$125-$239.** 8500 Warden Ave L6G 1A5. Hwy 404 exit Hwy 7, 2 mi (3.2 km) e. Int corridors. **Pets:** Accepted.

[SAVE] [ECO] [¶] [🛏] [✕] [🛜] [📦] [💻]

▽▽/▽ **Homewood Suites by Hilton Toronto/Markham** 🅷

(905) 477-4663. **$179-$189.** 50 Bodrington Ct L6G 0A9. Hwy 407 exit 84 (Woodbine Ave), just ne. Int corridors. **Pets:** Small. $30 daily fee/room. Designated rooms, service with restrictions, supervision.

[&M] [🛏] [🛜] [📦] [💻]

▽▽/▽ **Residence Inn by Marriott Toronto-Markham** 🅷

(905) 707-7933. **$125-$206.** 55 Minthorn Blvd L3T 7Y9. Hwy 404 exit Hwy 7, 0.7 mi (1.1 km) w. Int corridors. **Pets:** Accepted.

[🛏] [🛜] [✕] [📦] [💻]

▽▽/▽ **Staybridge Suites Toronto-Markham** 🅷

(905) 771-9333. **$122-$189.** 355 S Park Rd L3T 7W2. Hwy 404 exit Hwy 7, 0.9 mi (1.4 km) w, 0.3 mi (0.5 km) s on Commerce Valley Dr W, then just e. Int corridors. **Pets:** Accepted.

[¶] [🛏] [🛜] [✕] [📦] [💻]

▽▽/▽ **TownePlace Suites by Marriott Toronto Northeast/Markham** 🅷

(905) 752-0446. **$135-$175.** 7095 Woodbine Ave L3R 1A3. Hwy 404, exit Steeles Ave, just n. Int corridors. **Pets:** Accepted.

[¶] [&M] [🛜] [✕] [📦] [💻]

MASSEY

▽ **Mohawk Motel Inc** 🅼

(705) 865-2722. **Call for rates.** 335 Sable St P0P 1P0. Center. Ext/int corridors. **Pets:** Accepted. [🛜] [✕] [📦] [💻]

MIDLAND

Ⓐ ▽▽/▽▽ **BEST WESTERN PLUS Highland Inn & Conference Centre** 🅷

(705) 526-9307. **$110-$200.** 924 King St L4R 0B8. Jct Hwy 12 and King St. Ext/int corridors. **Pets:** Small. $20 daily fee/pet. Designated rooms, service with restrictions, supervision.

[SAVE] [¶] [🛏] [✕] [🛜] [📦] [💻]

▽▽/▽ **Comfort Inn** 🅷 🐾

(705) 526-2090. **$85-$190.** 980 King St L4R 4K3. Jct Hwy 12 and King St. Int corridors. **Pets:** Large, dogs only. $15 daily fee/pet. Designated rooms, supervision. [ECO] [🛜] [✕] [📦] [💻]

▽▽/▽ **Super 8 Midland** 🅷

(705) 526-8288. **$110-$190.** 1144 Hugel Ave L4R 0B1. Jct Hwy 93 N. Int corridors. **Pets:** Accepted. [🛏] [🛜] [✕] [📦] [💻]

MILTON

Ⓐ ▽▽/▽▽ **BEST WESTERN PLUS Milton** 🅷

(905) 875-3818. **$129-$179.** 161 Chisholm Dr L9T 4A6. Jct Hwy 401 and 25 S. Int corridors. **Pets:** Accepted.

[SAVE] [📶] [¶] [🛏] [🛜] [✕] [📦] [💻]

MINDEMOYA

▽ **Mindemoya Motel** 🅼

(705) 377-4779. **Call for rates.** 6375 Hwy 542 P0P 1S0. In Mindemoya; 0.6 mi (1 km) w of jct Hwy 551 and 542. Ext corridors. **Pets:** Accepted.

[¶] [🛜] [📦] [💻]

MISSISSAUGA

▽▽/▽ **Admiral Inn & Suites Mississauga** 🅷

(905) 403-9777. **Call for rates.** 2161 N Sheridan Way L5K 1A3. QEW exit Erin Mills Pkwy, just n to N Sheridan Way, then just w. Int corridors. **Pets:** Accepted. [¶] [&M] [🛏] [✕] [🛜] [✕] [📦] [💻]

▽▽/▽ **Alt Toronto Airport** 🅷 🐾

(905) 362-4337. **Call for rates.** 6080 Viscount Rd L4V 0A1. Just s of Airport Rd; connected to Toronto Pearson International Airport by monorail. Int corridors. **Pets:** $30 one-time fee/room. Service with restrictions, crate. [📶] [¶] [🛜] [✕] [💻]

▽▽/▽ **Comfort Inn Airport West** 🅷

(905) 624-6900. **$88-$199.** 1500 Matheson Blvd L4W 3Z4. Hwy 401 exit Dixie Rd, then s. Int corridors. **Pets:** Accepted.

[ECO] [¶] [🛜] [📦] [💻]

Ⓐ ▽▽/▽ **Comfort Inn Toronto Airport** 🅷

(905) 677-7331. **$94-$144.** 6355 Airport Rd L4V 1E4. 1.3 mi (2 km) s of Derry Rd. Int corridors. **Pets:** Accepted.

[SAVE] [¶] [🛜] [✕] [📦] [💻]

Ⓐ ▽▽/▽ **Delta Meadowvale Hotel and Conference Centre** 🅷

(905) 821-1981. **$99-$249.** 6750 Mississauga Rd L5N 2L3. Hwy 401 W exit 336 (Mississauga Rd), just s. Int corridors. **Pets:** $35 one-time fee/room. Supervision. [SAVE] [ECO] [¶] [&M] [🛏] [✕] [🛜] [✕] [📦] [💻]

Ⓐ ▽▽/▽ **Four Points by Sheraton Mississauga Meadowvale** 🅷

(905) 858-2424. **$90-$180.** 2501 Argentia Rd L5N 4G8. Hwy 401 exit 336 (Mississauga Rd), just s on Erin Mills Pkwy, then 1 mi (1.6 km) w. Int corridors. **Pets:** Medium. $25 daily fee/pet. Designated rooms, service with restrictions, crate.

[SAVE] [ECO] [¶] [&M] [🛏] [🛜] [✕] [📦] [💻]

▽▽/▽ **Holiday Inn Mississauga Toronto West** 🅷

(905) 890-5700. **Call for rates.** 100 Britannia Rd E L4Z 2G1. Hwy 401 exit Hwy 10 S (Hurontario St). Int corridors. **Pets:** Accepted.

[ECO] [¶] [🛏] [🛜] [📦] [💻]

▼▼▼ Holiday Inn Toronto-Mississauga 🏨

(905) 855-2000. **$89-$159, 3 day notice.** 2125 N Sheridan Way L5K 1A3. QEW exit Erin Mills Pkwy. Int corridors. **Pets:** $35 one-time fee/pet. Designated rooms, service with restrictions, crate.

🍴 ♿M 🏊 🛜 🔌 🖥️

▼▼ Motel 6 Mississauga #1910 🏨

(905) 814-1664. **Call for rates.** 2935 Argentia Rd L5N 8G6. Hwy 401 exit 333 (Winston Churchill Blvd), just s. Int corridors. **Pets:** Other species. Service with restrictions, crate. 🌿 🍴 ♿M 🛜 🔌

CAA ▼▼▼▼ Novotel Toronto Mississauga Centre 🏨

(905) 896-1000. **$109-$249.** 3670 Hurontario St L5B 1P3. Hwy 403 exit 344, 0.8 mi (1.2 km) s on Hwy 10 (Hurontario St); at Burnhamthorpe Rd. Int corridors. **Pets:** Accepted.

SAVE 🌿 🍴 🏊 🛜 ✖️ 🔌 🖥️

▼▼▼▼ Residence Inn by Marriott Mississauga Airport Corporate Centre West 🏨

(905) 602-7777. **$174-$344.** 5070 Creekbank Rd L4W 5R2. Hwy 401 W exit Dixie Rd S, 0.9 mi (1.5 km) e to Eglinton Ave, then 0.6 mi (1 km). Int corridors. **Pets:** Other species. $100 one-time fee/room. Service with restrictions, supervision. 🍴 🏊 ✖️ 🛜 ✖️ 🔌 🖥️

▼▼▼▼ Residence Inn by Marriott Toronto-Mississauga/Meadowvale 🏨

(905) 567-2577. **$153-$309.** 7005 Century Ave L5N 7K2. Hwy 401 exit Erin Mills Pkwy/Mississauga Rd, s to Argentia Rd. Int corridors. **Pets:** Accepted. ♿M 🏊 🛜 ✖️ 🔌 🖥️

CAA ▼▼▼ Sheraton Gateway Hotel in Toronto International Airport 🏨

(905) 672-7000. **$139-$429.** Terminal 3, Toronto AMF L5P 1C4. In Toronto Pearson International Airport. Int corridors. **Pets:** Accepted.

SAVE 🍴 ♿M 🏊 ✖️ 🛜 ✖️ 🔌 🖥️

▼▼▼▼ Staybridge Suites Mississauga 🏨

(905) 564-6892. **Call for rates.** 6791 Hurontario St L5T 2W1. Hwy 401 W exit Hwy 10 (Hurontario St), 0.9 mi (1.5 km) n; just s of Derry Rd. Int corridors. **Pets:** Accepted. 🍴 🏊 🛜 🔌 🖥️

▼▼▼▼ SW Hotel Toronto Airport 🏨

(905) 238-0159. **$139-$299.** 5400 Dixie Rd L4W 4T4. Hwy 401 exit 346 (S Dixie Rd), 0.6 mi (1 km) s. Int corridors. **Pets:** Accepted.

🍴 🏊 ✖️ 🛜 🔌 🖥️

▼▼▼▼ Toronto Airport West Hotel 🏨

(905) 624-1144. **$99-$219.** 5444 Dixie Rd L4W 2L2. 0.6 mi (1 km) s of jct Hwy 401 and Dixie Rd. Int corridors. **Pets:** Medium. $7 daily fee/room. Service with restrictions.

🌿 🍴 🏊 ✖️ 🛜 ✖️ 🔌 🖥️

CAA ▼▼▼▼ TownePlace Suites by Marriott Mississauga - Airport Corporate Centre 🏨

(905) 238-9600. **$118-$194.** 5050 Orbitor Dr L4W 4X2. Jct Eglinton Ave and Renforth Dr, 1.4 mi (2.3 km) w on Eglinton Ave. Int corridors. **Pets:** Accepted. SAVE 🌿 🍴 🏊 🛜 ✖️ 🔌 🖥️

▼▼▼ The Waterside Inn 🏨

(905) 891-7770. **Call for rates.** 15 Stavebank Rd S L5G 2T2. QEW exit Hwy 10 S (Hurontario St S), just w on Lakeshore Blvd. Int corridors. **Pets:** Accepted. 🍴 🛜 ✖️ 🔌 🖥️

MONETVILLE

▼▼ Memquisit Lodge 🅲🅰

(705) 898-2355. **Call for rates.** 506 Memquisit Rd P0M 2K0. 13 mi (20.8 km) ne on west arm of Lake Nipissing, on Hwy 64 and Memquisit Lodge Rd; 23 mi (36.8 km) sw off Hwy 17, on Hwy 64. Ext corridors. **Pets:** Other species. $54 deposit/pet. Service with restrictions, supervision. 🍴 ✖️ 🛜 🎣 🚣 🚳 🔌 🖥️

MORRISBURG

CAA ▼▼▼ The McIntosh Country Inn & Conference Centre 🏨

(613) 543-3788. **$99-$209.** 12495 Hwy 2 E K0C 1X0. Hwy 401 exit 750, 1.2 mi (2 km) s on Rt 31, then 0.6 mi (1 km) e. Int corridors. **Pets:** Medium, dogs only. $20 daily fee/pet. Designated rooms, service with restrictions, supervision. SAVE 🍴 🏊 ✖️ 🛜 🔌 🖥️

NEWMARKET

CAA ▼▼▼ Comfort Inn 🏨 🐾

(905) 895-3355. **$100-$145.** 1230 Journey's End Cir L3Y 8Z6. Hwy 404 exit 51 (Davis Dr), just w, then just n on Harry Walker Pkwy. Int corridors. **Pets:** Medium, dogs only. $40 daily fee/room. Designated rooms, service with restrictions, supervision.

SAVE 🌿 🍴 🛜 ✖️ 🔌 🖥️

NIAGARA FALLS

CAA ▼▼▼ BEST WESTERN Fallsview 🏨

(905) 356-0551. **$59-$350, 3 day notice.** 6289 Fallsview Blvd L2G 3V7. Jct Niagara River Pkwy, just n on Murray St. Ext/int corridors. **Pets:** Accepted. SAVE 🌿 🍴 🏊 🛜 ✖️ 🖥️

CAA ▼▼ Crystal Inn 🅼

(905) 354-9444. **Call for rates.** 4267 River Rd L2E 3E7. 1.8 mi (2.8 km) n of the falls on Niagara River Pkwy. Ext corridors. **Pets:** Accepted.

SAVE 🍴 🏊 🛜 ✖️ 🔌 🖥️

▼▼ Days Inn Clifton Hill Casino 🏨

(905) 356-2461. **$59-$329.** 5657 Victoria Ave L2G 3L5. Just e on Hwy 20. Ext/int corridors. **Pets:** Accepted.

🍴 🏊 ✖️ 🛜 ✖️ 🔌 🖥️

▼▼ Days Inn Fallsview 🏨

(905) 356-1722. **$53-$389.** 6519 Stanley Ave L2G 7L2. Corner of Dixon Ave; 2 blks from Konica Minolta Tower. Int corridors. **Pets:** Accepted.

🍴 🏊 🛜 ✖️ 🔌 🖥️

CAA ▼▼▼ Falls Manor Resort & Restaurant 🅼

(905) 358-3211. **$49-$149.** 7104 Lundy's Ln L2G 1W2. On Hwy 20, 2.1 mi (3.4 km) w. Ext corridors. **Pets:** Large, dogs only. $100 deposit/room, $20 daily fee/pet. Designated rooms, service with restrictions, supervision. SAVE 🍴 🏊 🛜 ✖️ 🔌

CAA ▼▼▼ Howard Johnson Hotel by the Falls 🏨

(905) 357-4040. **$68-$380.** 5905 Victoria Ave L2G 3L8. On Hwy 20; 0.4 mi (0.6 km) from the falls. Int corridors. **Pets:** Small, dogs only. $30 daily fee/pet. Designated rooms, service with restrictions.

SAVE 🌿 🍴 ♿M 🏊 ✖️ 🛜 ✖️ 🔌 🖥️

CAA ▼▼▼▼ Peninsula Inn & Resort 🏨

(905) 354-8812. **$59-$339, 3 day notice.** 7373 Niagara Square Dr L2E 6S5. QEW exit McLeod Rd, just w. Int corridors. **Pets:** Small, other species. $10 daily fee/pet. Designated rooms, service with restrictions, supervision. SAVE 🍴 ♿M 🏊 ✖️ 🎣 🔌 🖥️

NIAGARA-ON-THE-LAKE
(Restaurants p. 646)

CAA ▼▼▼ BEST WESTERN Colonel Butler Inn 🏨 🐾

(905) 468-3251. **$99-$299.** 278 Mary St L0S 1J0. Jct Hwy 55 (Mississauga St). Int corridors. **Pets:** Dogs only. $20 daily fee/room. Designated rooms, service with restrictions, supervision.

SAVE 🛜 ✖️ 🔌 🖥️

CAA ▼▼▼▼ Harbour House Hotel 🏨

(905) 468-4683. **Call for rates.** 85 Melville St L0S 1J0. Jct Ricardo St. Int corridors. **Pets:** Accepted. SAVE 🛜 ✖️ 🔌 🖥️

CAA ▼▼▼▼ The Oban Inn, Spa and Restaurant 🏨 🐾

(905) 468-2165. **$150-$495, 7 day notice.** 160 Front St L0S 1J0. Jct Gate St. Ext/int corridors. **Pets:** Dogs only. $25 daily fee/room. Designated rooms, service with restrictions, crate.

SAVE 🍴 🏊 ✖️ 🛜 ✖️ 🖥️

(AA) ▽▽▽▽ **Pillar and Post Hotel** **CI** ❈
(905) 468-2123. **$200-$600, 3 day notice.** 48 John St L0S 1J0. Just n
on Hwy 55 (Mississauga St), just e; 13 mi (20.8 km) from QEW. Ext/int
corridors. **Pets:** Small, dogs only. $35 daily fee/pet. Designated rooms,
service with restrictions. (SAVE) 〔❙〕 🏊 ✕ 📶 ✕ 🔌 💻

(AA) ▽▽▽▽ **Prince of Wales Hotel & Spa** **H** ❈
(905) 468-3246. **$220-$700, 3 day notice.** 6 Picton St L0S 1J0. Jct
Picton and King sts; 9 mi (14.4 km) e of jct QEW and Hwy 55 (Mississauga St), via Hwy 55. Ext/int corridors. **Pets:** Small, dogs only. $35
daily fee/pet. Designated rooms, service with restrictions.
(SAVE) 〔❙〕 🏊 ✕ 📶 ✕ 🔌 💻

▽▽▽▽ **Shaw Club Hotel and Spa** **H**
(905) 468-5711. **Call for rates.** 92 Picton St L0S 1J0. Jct Wellington St.
Int corridors. **Pets:** Accepted. 〔❙〕 ✕ 📶 ✕ 🔌 💻

NORTH BAY

(AA) ▽▽▽▽ **BEST WESTERN North Bay Hotel &**
Conference Centre **H** ❈
(705) 474-5800. **$132-$190.** 700 Lakeshore Dr P1A 2G4. Hwy 11 exit
338, 2.5 mi (4 km) w. Int corridors. **Pets:** Medium, other species. Service with restrictions. (SAVE) (ECO) 〔❙〕 🏊 ✕ 📶 ✕ 🔌 💻

(AA) ▽▽▽▽ **Clarion Resort Pinewood Park** **H**
(705) 472-0810. **$80-$159.** 201 Pinewood Park Dr P1B 8Z4. Hwy 11
exit 338, just w on Lakeshore Dr, then 0.4 mi (0.7 km) s. Int corridors.
Pets: Other species. Service with restrictions, crate.
(SAVE) 〔❙〕 🏊 ✕ 📶 ✕ 🔌 💻

(AA) ▽▽▽ **Comfort Inn-Airport** **H** ❈
(705) 476-5400. **$80-$145.** 1200 O'Brien St P1B 9B3. On Hwy 11/17;
jct O'Brien St. Int corridors. **Pets:** Other species. Designated rooms,
service with restrictions, crate. (SAVE) 📶 🔌 💻

(AA) ▽▽▽ **Holiday Inn Express Hotel & Suites** **H**
(705) 476-7700. **$129-$189.** 1325 Seymour St P1B 9V6. Jct Hwy 11/17.
Int corridors. **Pets:** Accepted. (SAVE) (ECO) 🏊 📶 ✕ 🔌 💻

(AA) ▽▽ **Super 8 North Bay** **H**
(705) 495-4551. **$100-$110.** 570 Lakeshore Dr P1A 2E6. Hwy 11 exit
338, 2.8 mi (4.5 km) w. Int corridors. **Pets:** $10 one-time fee/room.
Designated rooms, service with restrictions, supervision.
(SAVE) 📶 🔌 💻

(AA) ▽▽ **Travelodge Airport North Bay** **H**
(705) 495-1133. **$110-$200.** 1525 Seymour St P1B 8G4. Jct Hwy 11/17.
Int corridors. **Pets:** Medium. Service with restrictions, supervision.
(SAVE) (ECO) 🏊 📶 🔌 💻

(AA) ▽▽ **Travelodge Lakeshore** **H**
(705) 472-7171. **$110-$200.** 718 Lakeshore Dr P1A 2G4. Hwy 11 exit
338, 2.5 mi (4 km) w. Int corridors. **Pets:** Accepted.
(SAVE) (ECO) 📶 🔌 💻

OAKVILLE

▽▽▽ **Holiday Inn Oakville Centre** **H**
(905) 842-5000. **Call for rates.** 590 Argus Rd L6J 3J3. QEW exit 118
(Trafalgar Rd), just s. Int corridors. **Pets:** Other species. $35 one-time
fee/room. Service with restrictions, crate.
(ECO) 〔❙〕 ♿M 🏊 📶 ✕ 🔌 💻

(AA) ▽▽▽ **Staybridge Suites Oakville Burlington** **H**
(905) 847-2600. **$140-$260.** 2511 Wyecroft Rd L6L 6P8. QEW exit 111
(Bronte Rd/Hwy 25), 0.3 mi (0.5 km) s, then just e. Int corridors.
Pets: Large. $75 one-time fee/room. Designated rooms, service with
restrictions. (SAVE) ♿M 🏊 📶 🔌 💻

ORILLIA

(AA) ▽▽▽▽ **BEST WESTERN PLUS Couchiching Inn** **H**
(705) 325-6505. **$134-$219.** 440 Couchiching Point Rd L3V 6P8. Jct
Hwy 12 S and Couchiching Point Rd. Int corridors. **Pets:** Accepted.
(SAVE) (ECO) 〔❙〕 ✕ 📶 🔌 💻

(AA) ▽▽▽▽ **BEST WESTERN PLUS Mariposa Inn &**
Conference Centre **H** ❈
(705) 325-9511. **$121-$199.** 400 Memorial Ave L3V 6J3. Jct Hwy 12
and Memorial Ave, just s. Int corridors. **Pets:** Small. $20 daily fee/room.
Designated rooms, service with restrictions, supervision.
(SAVE) (ECO) 🔲 〔❙〕 🏊 ✕ 📶 🔌 💻

(AA) ▽▽▽ **Comfort Inn** **H**
(705) 327-7744. **$121-$151.** 75 Progress Dr L3V 6H1. Hwy 11 N exit
Hwy 12, just s on Memorial Ave; corner of Progress Dr and Memorial
Ave. Int corridors. **Pets:** $15 daily fee/room. Designated rooms, service
with restrictions, crate. (SAVE) (ECO) 📶 🔌 💻

(AA) ▽▽▽ **Highwayman Inn & Conference Centre** **H**
(705) 326-7343. **Call for rates.** 201 Woodside Dr L3V 6T4. Hwy 11 exit
Hwy 12 (Coldwater Rd), just e, then just s. Int corridors.
Pets: Accepted. (SAVE) 〔❙〕 🏊 ✕ 📶 ✕ 🔌 💻

(AA) ▽▽▽ **Rodeway Inn Champlain Waterfront** **H**
(705) 325-0770. **$60-$140.** 2 Front St N L3V 4R5. Jct Mississaga St;
downtown. Int corridors. **Pets:** Accepted. (SAVE) 📶 🔌 💻

OSHAWA

▽▽▽ **Comfort Inn** **H**
(905) 434-5000. **$89-$239.** 605 Bloor St W L1J 5Y6. Hwy 401 exit 415
(Stevenson Rd), s to Bloor St, then 0.5 mi (0.8 km) w. Int corridors.
Pets: Accepted. (ECO) 〔❙〕 📶 🔌 💻

(AA) ▽▽▽ **Quality Hotel & Conference Centre Oshawa**
Whitby **H**
(905) 576-5101. **$109-$149.** 1011 Bloor St E L1H 7K6. Hwy 401 exit
419 (Harmony Rd). Int corridors. **Pets:** Small. $15 daily fee/pet. Desig-
nated rooms, service with restrictions, crate.
(SAVE) 〔❙〕 🏊 ✕ 📶 🔌 💻

▽▽▽ **Travelodge Oshawa** **H**
(905) 436-9500. **$99-$159.** 940 Champlain Ave L1J 7A6. Hwy 401 exit
412 (Thickson Rd N). Int corridors. **Pets:** Accepted.
(ECO) 〔❙〕 🏊 📶 🔌 💻

OTTAWA *(Restaurants p. 646)*

(AA) ▽▽▽ **ARC The.Hotel** **H**
(613) 238-2888. **Call for rates.** 140 Slater St K1P 5H6. Between Metcalfe and O'Connor sts. Int corridors. **Pets:** Accepted.
(SAVE) (ECO) 〔❙〕 📶 🔌 💻

(AA) ▽▽▽▽ **BEST WESTERN PLUS Ottawa/Kanata Hotel &**
Conference Centre **H**
(613) 828-2741. **$120-$190, 30 day notice.** 1876 Robertson Rd K2H
5B8. Hwy 417 exit 130, 1.8 mi (2.9 km) s. Int corridors. **Pets:** Other
species. $20 daily fee/room. Designated rooms, service with restrictions,
crate. (SAVE) 🔲 〔❙〕 🏊 ✕ 📶 ✕ 🔌 💻

▽▽▽ **Cartier Place Suite Hotel** **H**
(613) 236-5000. **$149-$199.** 180 Cooper St K2P 2L5. Between Elgin
and Cartier sts. Int corridors. **Pets:** Accepted.
〔❙〕 🏊 ✕ 📶 🔌 💻

(AA) ▽▽▽ **Comfort Inn** **H**
(613) 744-2900. **$99-$150.** 1252 Michael St K1J 7T1. Hwy 417 exit 115
(St. Laurent Blvd), just ne. Int corridors. **Pets:** Service with restrictions,
supervision. (SAVE) (ECO) 📶 ✕ 🔌 💻

(AA) ▽▽▽ **Days Inn-Downtown Ottawa** **H**
(613) 789-5555. **$100-$180.** 319 Rideau St K1N 5Y4. Between Nelson
St and King Edward Ave. Ext/int corridors. **Pets:** Small, other species.
Designated rooms, service with restrictions, supervision.
(SAVE) (ECO) 〔❙〕 📶 🔌 💻

ⓐ ♦♦ **Days Inn Ottawa West** 🅗
(613) 726-1717. **$130-$170.** 350 Moodie Dr K2H 8G3. Hwy 417 exit 134, 0.9 mi (1.5 km) s. Int corridors. **Pets:** $10 deposit/room, $10 daily fee/room. Designated rooms, service with restrictions, supervision.
SAVE 🍴 📶 ✕ 🛏 💻

ⓐ ♦♦♦ **Delta Ottawa City Centre** 🅗
(613) 237-3600. **$149-$309.** 101 Lyon St K1R 5T9. Entrance at corner of Albert St. Int corridors. **Pets:** Accepted.
SAVE ECO 🍴 ➰ 📶 ✕ 🛏 💻

♦♦♦ **Extended Stay Canada - Ottawa Downtown** 🅗
(613) 236-7500. **Call for rates.** 141 Cooper St K2P 0E8. Between Elgin and Cartier sts. Int corridors. **Pets:** Other species. $25 daily fee/pet. Service with restrictions, supervision. 🍴 📶 ✕ 🛏 💻

ⓐ ♦♦♦ **Fairmont Château Laurier** 🅗
(613) 241-1414. **$189-$369.** 1 Rideau St K1N 8S7. Just e of Parliament Buildings. Int corridors. **Pets:** Very small. $25 daily fee/room. Service with restrictions, supervision.
SAVE ECO 🍴 ♿ ➰ ✕ 📶 ✕ 🛏 💻

♦♦♦ **Hotel Indigo Ottawa** 🅗
(613) 231-6555. **Call for rates.** 123 Metcalfe St K1P 5L9. Corner of Laurier Ave W. Int corridors. **Pets:** Accepted.
ECO 🍴 ➰ ✕ 📶 ✕ 🛏 💻

ⓐ ♦♦♦ **Les Suites Hotel Ottawa** 🅗 🐾
(613) 232-2000. **Call for rates.** 130 Besserer St K1N 9M9. Between Nicholas and Waller sts. Int corridors. **Pets:** $45 one-time fee/pet. Service with restrictions, crate.
SAVE ECO 🍴 ♿ ➰ ✕ 📶 ✕ 🛏 💻

♦♦♦ **Lord Elgin Hotel** 🅗
(613) 235-3333. **$119-$399.** 100 Elgin St K1P 5K8. Between Laurier Ave and Slater St. Int corridors. **Pets:** Accepted.
ECO 🍴 ➰ ✕ 📶 ✕ 🛏 💻

ⓐ ♦♦♦ **Marriott Ottawa Hotel** 🅗
(613) 238-1122. **$209-$344.** 100 Kent St K1P 5R7. Corner of Queen St. Int corridors. **Pets:** Accepted.
SAVE ECO 🍴 ➰ ✕ 📶 ✕ 🛏 💻

♦♦♦ **Novotel Ottawa Hotel** 🅗
(613) 230-3033. **Call for rates.** 33 Nicholas St K1N 9M7. Corner of Daly Ave. Int corridors. **Pets:** Accepted.
ECO 🍴 ➰ ✕ 📶 🛏 💻

ⓐ ♦♦♦ **Radisson Hotel Ottawa Parliament Hill** 🅗
(613) 236-1133. **$109-$299.** 402 Queen St K1R 5A7. Corner of Bay and Queen sts. Int corridors. **Pets:** $25 one-time fee/pet. Designated rooms, service with restrictions, crate. SAVE 🍴 📶 ✕ 🛏 💻

♦♦♦ **Ramada Ottawa On The Rideau** 🅗
(613) 288-3500. **Call for rates.** 2259 Prince of Wales Dr K2E 6Z8. 0.5 mi (0.8 km) s of Hunt Club Rd. Ext corridors. **Pets:** Accepted.
ECO 🍴 ➰ ✕ 📶 ✕ 🛏 💻

♦♦♦ **Residence Inn by Marriott Ottawa Downtown** 🅗
(613) 231-2020. **$186-$306.** 161 Laurier Ave W K1P 5J2. Corner of Elgin St. Int corridors. **Pets:** Accepted.
ECO ➰ ✕ 📶 ✕ 🛏 💻

ⓐ ♦♦♦ **Rideau Heights Inn** Ⓜ
(613) 226-4152. **$99-$129.** 72 Rideau Heights Dr K2E 7A6. Hwy 16 (Prince of Wales Dr), 0.3 mi (0.5 km) n of Hunt Club Rd. Ext corridors. **Pets:** Small. $10 daily fee/pet. Designated rooms, service with restrictions, supervision. SAVE 🍴 📶 ✕ 🛏 💻

ⓐ ♦♦♦♦ **Sheraton Ottawa Hotel** 🅗 🐾
(613) 238-1500. **$169-$299.** 150 Albert St K1P 5G2. Corner of O'Connor St. Int corridors. **Pets:** Dogs only. $50 deposit/pet. Designated rooms, service with restrictions, supervision.
SAVE ECO 🍴 ➰ 📶 ✕ 🛏 💻

ⓐ ♦♦♦ **Southway Hotel** 🅗
(613) 737-0811. **Call for rates.** 2431 Bank St K1V 8R9. On Hwy 31; jct Hunt Club Rd. Int corridors. **Pets:** Accepted.
SAVE 🍴 ➰ ✕ 📶 ✕ 🛏 💻

ⓐ ♦♦♦ **Travelodge Ottawa East** 🅗 🐾
(613) 745-1133. **$105-$165.** 1486 Innes Rd K1B 3V5. Hwy 417 exit 112 (Innes Rd), just e. Int corridors. **Pets:** Other species. $10 one-time fee/ room. Designated rooms, service with restrictions, crate.
SAVE ECO 🍴 ➰ 📶 🛏 💻

♦♦♦ **Travelodge Ottawa Hotel & Conference
          Centre** 🅗
(613) 722-7600. **$110-$180.** 1376 Carling Ave K1Z 7L5. Hwy 417 exit 124, just s. Int corridors. **Pets:** Accepted.
ECO 🍴 ➰ 📶 ✕ 🛏 💻

ⓐ ♦♦ **Webb's Motel** Ⓜ
(613) 728-1881. **$85-$125.** 1705 Carling Ave K2A 1C8. Hwy 417 exit 126, 0.3 mi (0.5 km) n on Maitland Ave, then 0.3 mi (0.5 km) e. Ext/int corridors. **Pets:** Accepted. SAVE 🍴 📶 🛏 💻

ⓐ ♦♦ **WelcomINNS** 🅗
(613) 748-7800. **$115-$150.** 1220 Michael St K1J 7T1. Just ne off Hwy 417; just e of St. Laurent Blvd. Int corridors. **Pets:** Small. $20 daily fee/pet. Designated rooms, service with restrictions, crate.
SAVE ECO 📶 ✕ 🛏 💻

ⓐ ♦♦ ♦♦ **The Westin Ottawa** 🅗
(613) 560-7000. **$129-$409.** 11 Colonel By Dr K1N 9H4. Corner of Rideau St. Int corridors. **Pets:** Accepted.
SAVE ECO 🍴 ➰ ✕ 📶 ✕ 🛏 💻

OWEN SOUND *(Restaurants p. 646)*

ⓐ ♦♦♦ **BEST WESTERN Inn On The Bay &
               Conference Centre** 🅗
(519) 371-9200. **$150-$190.** 1800 2nd Ave E N4K 5R1. 1 mi (1.5 km) n of 10th St E. Int corridors. **Pets:** Accepted.
SAVE ECO ⏏ 🍴 ✕ 📶 ✕ 🛏 💻

♦♦ **Comfort Inn** 🅗
(519) 371-5500. **$110-$150.** 955 9th Ave E N4K 6N4. Jct Hwy 6, 10, 21 and 26. Int corridors. **Pets:** Accepted. ECO 🍴 📶 ✕ 🛏 💻

ⓐ ♦♦♦ **Days Inn & Conference Centre** 🅗
(519) 376-1551. **$109-$299.** 950 6th St E N4K 1H1. Just off Hwy 6 and 10. Int corridors. **Pets:** Accepted.
SAVE ECO 🍴 ➰ ✕ 📶 🛏 💻

PARRY SOUND
♦♦ **Comfort Inn** 🅗
(705) 746-6221. **$125-$200.** 120 Bowes St P2A 2L7. Hwy 69 exit 224 (Bowes St), just w. Int corridors. **Pets:** Service with restrictions, supervision. ECO 📶 ✕ 🛏 💻

♦♦ **Microtel Inn & Suites by Wyndham** 🅗
(705) 746-2700. **$94-$137.** 292 Louisa St P2A 0A1. Hwy 69 exit 224 (Bowes St), just w. Int corridors. **Pets:** Accepted.
🍴 📶 ✕ 🛏 💻

PEMBROKE
♦♦ **Colonial Fireside Inn** Ⓜ
(613) 732-3623. **Call for rates.** 1350 Pembroke St W K8A 7A3. 2.7 mi (4.3 km) n on Forest Lea Rd (CR 42) from jct Hwy 17, just e. Ext corridors. **Pets:** Small, dogs only. $10 daily fee/pet. Service with restrictions, supervision. ➰ 📶 🛏 💻

ⓐ ♦♦ **Comfort Inn** 🅗
(613) 735-1057. **$120-$150.** 959 Pembroke St E K8A 3M3. 1 mi (1.6 km) e of town center. Int corridors. **Pets:** Large. $15 daily fee/room. Designated rooms, service with restrictions, supervision.
SAVE ECO 📶 🛏 💻

PETAWAWA

Petawawa River Inn & Suites 🏨
(613) 687-4686. **Call for rates.** 3520 Petawawa Blvd K8H 1W9. Hwy 17 exit Paquette Rd, 1.5 mi (2.4 km) e, then just s. Int corridors. **Pets:** Accepted. 🍴 📶 ⬛ 💻

Quality Inn & Suites Petawawa 🏨
(613) 687-2855. **$139-$205.** 3119-B Petawawa Blvd K8H 1X9. Hwy 17 exit Murphy Rd (Hwy 37), 1.8 mi (3 km) ne. Int corridors. **Pets:** Accepted. SAVE 🗲M ➳ ✕ 📶 ✕ ⬛ 💻

PETERBOROUGH

Comfort Hotel & Suites 🏨
(705) 740-7000. **$90-$136.** 1209 Lansdowne St W K9J 7M2. 0.4 mi (0.6 km) w of jct Hwy 28. Int corridors. **Pets:** Other species. Designated rooms, service with restrictions, supervision.
SAVE ECO 🍴 ➳ 📶 ✕ ⬛ 💻

King Bethune House, Guest House & Spa BB ✿
(705) 743-4101. **Call for rates.** 270 King St K9J 2S2. From Charlotte and George sts (clock tower), 1 blk s on George St to King St, then just w. Int corridors. **Pets:** Other species. $25 daily fee/pet. Service with restrictions, supervision. 🍴 📶 ✕ ⬛ 💻

Motel 6 - Peterborough 🏨
(705) 748-0550. **Call for rates.** 133 Landsdowne St E K9J 7P7. 1.6 mi (2.6 km) e of The Parkway. Int corridors. **Pets:** Other species. Service with restrictions, crate. ECO 📶 ✕ ⬛

Quality Inn 🏨 ✿
(705) 748-6801. **$110-$130.** 1074 Lansdowne St W K9J 1Z9. 1.9 mi (3 km) from jct Hwy 115. Int corridors. **Pets:** Medium. Designated rooms, service with restrictions, crate. ECO 📶 ✕ ⬛ 💻

Super 8 Peterborough 🏨 ✿
(705) 876-8898. **$89-$161.** 1257 Lansdowne St W K9J 7M2. 0.3 mi (0.5 km) e from jct Hwy 28. Int corridors. **Pets:** Medium, other species. $25 one-time fee/room. Designated rooms, service with restrictions.
ECO ➳ 📶 ✕ ⬛ 💻

PICKERING

Comfort Inn 🏨
(905) 831-6200. **$99-$189.** 533 Kingston Rd L1V 3N7. Hwy 401 exit 394N (Whites Rd) to Hwy 2, 0.3 mi (0.5 km) w. Int corridors. **Pets:** $10 one-time fee/pet. Designated rooms, service with restrictions.
SAVE ECO 📶 ⬛ 💻

PLANTAGENET

Motel de Champlain 🅼
(613) 673-5220. **Call for rates.** 5999 Hwy 17 K0B 1L0. Jct CR 9. Ext/int corridors. **Pets:** Large, other species. $20 daily fee/room. Service with restrictions, crate. 🍴 📶 ✕ ⬛

PORT COLBORNE

Canadas Best Value Inn 🅼
(905) 835-5202. **Call for rates.** 10134 Hwy 3 W L3K 5V4. 0.6 mi (1 km) w of jct Rt 58 and 3. Ext/int corridors. **Pets:** Accepted.
🍴 ➳ 📶 ⬛ 💻

PORT HOPE

Comfort Inn 🏨
(905) 885-7000. **$89-$109.** 2211 County Rd 28 L1A 3V6. Hwy 401 exit 464 (Hwy 28), just n. Int corridors. **Pets:** Medium. Service with restrictions, supervision. 📶 ⬛ 💻

PROVIDENCE BAY

Aux Huron Sands Motel 🅼
(705) 377-4616. **$80-$160, 3 day notice.** 5216 Hwy 551 P0P 1T0. In Providence Bay; center. Ext corridors. **Pets:** Accepted.
📶 ☎ ⬛ 💻

RENFREW

BEST WESTERN Renfrew Inn & Conference Centre 🏨
(613) 432-8109. **$122-$129.** 760 Gibbons Rd K7V 0B7. Hwy 17 exit O'Brien Rd, just s to Wrangler Rd, then just w. Int corridors. **Pets:** Other species. $20 daily fee/pet. Designated rooms, service with restrictions, supervision. SAVE 🍴 ➳ 📶 ⬛ 💻

The Rocky Mountain Lodge 🅼
(613) 432-5801. **Call for rates.** 409 Stewart St N K7V 1Y4. Hwy 17 exit Bruce St, 1.9 mi (3.1 km) s, then just w. Ext corridors. **Pets:** Accepted. 🍴 📶 ⬛ 💻

RICHMOND HILL

Holiday Inn Express & Suites Toronto-Markham 🏨
(905) 695-5990. **Call for rates.** 10 E Pearce St L4B 0A8. Just n of jct Leslie St and Hwy 7. Int corridors. **Pets:** Accepted.
SAVE ECO 🍴 🗲M ➳ 📶 ✕ ⬛ 💻

Sheraton Parkway Toronto North Hotel and Suites 🏨
(905) 881-2121. **Call for rates.** 600 Hwy 7 E L4B 1B2. Hwy 404 exit 27, 0.6 mi (1 km) w. Int corridors. **Pets:** Accepted.
SAVE ECO 🍴 ➳ ✕ 📶 ✕ ⬛ 💻

ST. CATHARINES

BEST WESTERN St. Catharines Hotel & Conference Centre 🏨
(905) 934-8000. **$119-$299.** 2 N Service Rd L2N 4G9. QEW exit 46 (Lake St), just e. Int corridors. **Pets:** Accepted.
SAVE 🍴 ➳ ✕ 📶 ✕ ⬛ 💻

Comfort Inn 🏨 ✿
(905) 687-8890. **$90-$145.** 2 Dunlop Dr L2R 1A2. QEW exit 46 (Lake St); between Lake and Geneva sts. Int corridors. **Pets:** Large. Designated rooms, service with restrictions. ECO 🍴 🗲M 📶 ⬛ 💻

Days Inn St. Catharines Niagara 🏨
(905) 934-5400. **$119-$209.** 89 Meadowvale Dr L2N 3Z8. QEW exit 46 (Lake St). Int corridors. **Pets:** Other species. $15 daily fee/pet. Designated rooms, service with restrictions, supervision.
SAVE 🍴 ➳ 📶 ✕ ⬛ 💻

Holiday Inn & Suites Parkway Conference Center 🏨 ✿
(905) 688-2324. **Call for rates.** 327 Ontario St L2R 5L3. QEW exit 47 (Ontario St), 0.5 mi (0.8 km) s. Int corridors. **Pets:** $15 daily fee/pet. Designated rooms, service with restrictions, crate.
SAVE 🍴 🗲M ➳ ✕ 📶 ✕ ⬛ 💻

ST. THOMAS

Cardinal Court Motel 🅼
(519) 633-0740. **$79-$91.** 10401 Sunset Rd, RR 7 N5P 3T2. Hwy 4, 4.1 mi (6.5 km) s of jct Hwy 4 and 401 exit 177A. Ext corridors. **Pets:** Small, dogs only. $5 daily fee/room. Service with restrictions, supervision. SAVE 🍴 📶 ✕ ⬛ 💻

Comfort Inn 🏨 ✿
(519) 633-4082. **$80-$175.** 100 Centennial Ave N5R 5B2. On Hwy 3, 4.1 mi (6.5 km) e. Int corridors. **Pets:** Medium, other species. $25 one-time fee/room. Designated rooms, service with restrictions, supervision. 🍴 📶 ✕ ⬛ 💻

SARNIA

BEST WESTERN PLUS Guildwood Inn 🏨 ✿
(519) 337-7577. **$124-$134.** 1400 Venetian Blvd N7T 7W6. 0.6 mi (1 km) e of Bluewater Bridge. Ext/int corridors. **Pets:** Small. $15 daily fee/pet. Service with restrictions, supervision.
SAVE 🍴 ➳ 📶 ⬛ 💻

▼▼ **Comfort Inn** 🅗 ❀

(519) 383-6767. **$95-$125.** 815 Mara St N7V 0A2. Jct Church St. Int corridors. **Pets:** Small. $20 one-time fee/room. Designated rooms, service with restrictions, supervision. 🛜 🍴 🛏 💻

▼▼ **Super 8-Sarnia** 🅗

(519) 337-3767. **$80-$130.** 420 Christina St N N7T 5W1. Between Exmouth St and London Rd. Ext/int corridors. **Pets:** Accepted. 🅰🆖 🛜 🛏 💻

SAULT STE. MARIE

▼ **Adams Motel** 🅜

(705) 254-4345. **$69-$99.** 647 Great Northern Rd (Hwy 17) P6B 5A1. Hwy 17, 2.8 mi (4.4 km) n. Ext corridors. **Pets:** Accepted. 🛜 🛏 💻

🅐🅐 ▼▼▼ **Algoma's Water Tower Inn & Suites** 🅗

(705) 949-8111. **$119-$179, 7 day notice.** 360 Great Northern Rd P6B 4Z7. Jct Hwy 17 and Second Line. Int corridors. **Pets:** Small. $25 one-time fee/room. Designated rooms, service with restrictions, supervision. 🆂🅰🆅🅴 🅴🅲🅾 🍴 🔜 ⊠ 🛜 ⊗ 🛏 💻

▼ **Ambassador Motel** 🅜

(705) 759-6199. **$69-$99.** 1275 Great Northern Rd P6B 0B9. 4 mi (6.4 km) n on Hwy 17. Ext corridors. **Pets:** Other species. $10 daily fee/pet. Designated rooms, service with restrictions, crate. 🔜 🛜 🛏 💻

🅐🅐 ▼ **Catalina Motel** 🅜

(705) 945-9260. **$89-$125.** 259 Great Northern Rd P6B 4Z2. 2 mi (3.2 km) n on Hwy 17. Ext corridors. **Pets:** $100 one-time fee/room. Designated rooms, no service, crate. 🆂🅰🆅🅴 🛜 ⊗ 🛏 💻

🅐🅐 ▼▼ **Comfort Inn** 🅗

(705) 759-8000. **$90-$170.** 333 Great Northern Rd P6B 4Z8. 2.3 mi (3.6 km) n on Hwy 17. Int corridors. **Pets:** Medium. $15 daily fee/pet. Designated rooms, service with restrictions, supervision. 🆂🅰🆅🅴 🅴🅲🅾 🛜 🛏 💻

🅐🅐 ▼▼ **Days Inn & Suites** 🅗

(705) 759-1400. **$110-$175.** 332 Bay St P6A 1X1. Between Elgin and Bruce sts; downtown; opposite Station Mall. Int corridors. **Pets:** Accepted. 🆂🅰🆅🅴 🅴🅲🅾 🍴 🛜 🛏 💻

▼▼▼ **Delta Sault Ste. Marie Waterfront Hotel and Conference Centre** 🅗

(705) 949-0611. **$129-$189, 14 day notice.** 208 St. Marys River Dr P6A 5V4. Just sw of Bay St. Int corridors. **Pets:** Accepted. 🅴🅲🅾 🔌 🍴 🔜 ⊠ 🛜 ⊗ 🛏 💻

▼▼ **Glenview Cottages** 🅲🅰

(705) 759-3436. **$129-$199.** 2611 Great Northern Rd P6A 5K7. 6 mi (9.6 km) n on Hwy 17. Ext corridors. **Pets:** Medium, dogs only. $10 daily fee/pet. Designated rooms, service with restrictions, crate. 🅴🅲🅾 🍴 🏊 ⊗ 🛜 🛏 💻

▼ **Holiday Motel** 🅜

(705) 759-8608. **$60-$90.** 435 Trunk Rd P6A 3T1. On Hwy 17, just e of jct Hwy 17B. Ext corridors. **Pets:** Accepted. 🛜 🛏 💻

▼ **Northlander Motel** 🅜

(705) 254-6452. **Call for rates.** 243 Great Northern Rd P6B 4Z2. 1.9 mi (2 km) n on Hwy 17. Ext corridors. **Pets:** Accepted. 🛜 🛏 💻

🅐🅐 ▼ **Skyline Motel** 🅜

(705) 942-1240. **$69-$85, 5 day notice.** 232 Great Northern Rd P6B 4Z5. 1.9 mi (3 km) n on Hwy 17. Ext corridors. **Pets:** $5 daily fee/pet. Designated rooms, no service, supervision. 🆂🅰🆅🅴 🛜 🛏 💻

▼▼ **Sleep Inn** 🅗

(705) 253-7533. **$119-$139.** 727 Bay St P6A 6Y3. Between East and Church sts; downtown. Int corridors. **Pets:** Accepted. 🛜 ⊗ 🛏 💻

▼▼ **Super 8** 🅗

(705) 254-6441. **$95-$150.** 184 Great Northern Rd P6B 4Z3. 1.3 mi (2 km) n on Hwy 17. Int corridors. **Pets:** Accepted. 🛜 🛏 💻

SIMCOE

🅐🅐 ▼▼▼ **BEST WESTERN Little River Inn** 🅗

(519) 426-2125. **$111-$141.** 203 Queensway W (Hwy 3) N3Y 2M9. Jct Hwy 24, just w on Hwy 3. Int corridors. **Pets:** Medium. Designated rooms, service with restrictions, supervision. 🆂🅰🆅🅴 🍴 🔜 🛜 🛏 💻

▼▼ **Comfort Inn** 🅗

(519) 426-2611. **$105-$135.** 85 Queensway E N3Y 4M5. 0.3 mi (0.5 km) e on Hwy 3. Int corridors. **Pets:** Other species. $10 one-time fee/room. Designated rooms, service with restrictions. 🅴🅲🅾 🍴 🛜 ⊠ 🛏 💻

SMITHS FALLS

🅐🅐 ▼▼▼ **BEST WESTERN Colonel By Inn** 🅗

(613) 426-2111. **$90-$150.** 88 Lombard St K7A 4G5. On Hwy 15, just w of jct Hwy 29. Int corridors. **Pets:** Small, dogs only. $10 daily fee/pet. Designated rooms, no service, supervision. 🆂🅰🆅🅴 🔜 🛜 ⊠ 🛏 💻

SOUTH BAYMOUTH

🅐🅐 ▼ **Huron Motor Lodge** 🅜

(705) 859-3131. **Call for rates.** 24 Water St N P0P 1Z0. In South Baymouth; center. Ext corridors. **Pets:** Medium. $10 daily fee/pet. Designated rooms, service with restrictions, supervision. 🆂🅰🆅🅴 🔜 🖼 ⊠ 🎦 ♻ 🛏

STRATFORD (Restaurants p. 646)

▼▼▼ **Arden Park Hotel** 🅗

(519) 275-2936. **$99-$199, 3 day notice.** 552 Ontario St (Hwy 7 & 8) N5A 3J3. Jct Romeo St. Int corridors. **Pets:** Medium. $35 one-time fee/room. Service with restrictions, crate. 🍴 🅰🆖 🔜 🛜 ⊠ 🛏 💻

STURGEON FALLS

▼▼▼ **Comfort Inn** 🅗

(705) 753-5665. **$109-$149.** 11 Front St P2B 3L3. On Hwy 17 at western approach to town. Int corridors. **Pets:** Accepted. 🍴 🔜 🛜 ⊠ 🛏 💻

SUDBURY

🅐🅐 ▼▼▼ **BEST WESTERN Downtown Sudbury Centreville** 🅗

(705) 673-7801. **$110-$130.** 151 Larch St P3E 1C3. Just w of Paris St; center. Int corridors. **Pets:** $20 daily fee/pet. Designated rooms, service with restrictions, supervision. 🆂🅰🆅🅴 🍴 🛜 ⊠ 🛏 💻

🅐🅐 ▼▼ **Comfort Inn** 🅗

(705) 522-1101. **$89-$183.** 2171 Regent St P3E 5V3. Trans-Canada Hwy 17 exit Hwy 69/RR 46, 1.8 mi (2.8 km) n. Int corridors. **Pets:** Medium. $15 one-time fee/room. Designated rooms, service with restrictions, supervision. 🆂🅰🆅🅴 🅴🅲🅾 🛜 ⊠ 🛏 💻

🅐🅐 ▼▼ **Comfort Inn East** 🅗

(705) 560-4502. **$120-$190.** 440 2nd Ave N P3B 4A4. Just s of Kingsway Rd. Int corridors. **Pets:** Other species. $15 daily fee/pet. Designated rooms, service with restrictions, crate. 🆂🅰🆅🅴 🅴🅲🅾 🅰🆖 🛜 ⊠ 🛏 💻

▼▼ **Days Inn-Sudbury** 🅗 ❀

(705) 674-7517. **$116-$156.** 117 Elm St P3C 1T3. Corner of Lorne St; downtown. Int corridors. **Pets:** Medium. $20 daily fee/pet. Designated rooms, service with restrictions, supervision. 🍴 🔜 🛜 ⊠ 🛏 💻

🅐🅐 ▼▼▼ **Holiday Inn Hotel Sudbury** 🅗

(705) 522-3000. **Call for rates.** 1696 Regent St P3E 3Z8. Trans-Canada Hwy 17 exit Hwy 69/RR 46, 2.4 mi (3.9 km) n. Int corridors. **Pets:** Accepted. 🆂🅰🆅🅴 🍴 🔜 🖼 🛜 ⊠ 🛏 💻

(CAA) ▼▼▼ **Homewood Suites by Hilton Sudbury** H

(705) 523-8100. **$109-$269.** 2270 Regent St P3E 0B4. Trans-Canada Hwy 17 exit Hwy 69/RR 46, 1.6 mi (2.5 km) n. Int corridors. **Pets:** Other species. $50 one-time fee/room. Service with restrictions.

[SAVE] [&M] [≈] [📶] [🔒] [💻]

▼▼ **Quality Inn & Conference Centre** H 🐾

(705) 675-1273. **$109-$229.** 390 Elgin St S P3B 1B1. 0.6 mi (0.9 km) s on Paris St from jct Kingsway Rd and Elm St. Int corridors. **Pets:** Other species. $10 daily fee/room. Designated rooms, service with restrictions, crate. [ECO] [🛢] [¶] [≈] [📶] [✕] [🔒] [💻]

(CAA) ▼▼▼ **Radisson Hotel Sudbury Downtown** H

(705) 675-1123. **$109-$299.** 85 Ste. Anne Rd P3E 4S4. Jct Notre Dame Ave; downtown. Int corridors. **Pets:** Medium. $30 one-time fee/pet. Designated rooms, service with restrictions, crate.

[SAVE] [¶] [≈] [📶] [✕] [🔒] [💻]

▼▼▼ **TownePlace Suites by Marriott Sudbury** H

(705) 525-7700. **$119-$196.** 1710 Kingsway Rd P3B 0E4. Just e of jct Falconbridge Rd. Int corridors. **Pets:** Accepted.

[♿M] [≈] [📶] [✕] [🔒] [💻]

(CAA) ▼▼▼ **Travelodge Hotel Sudbury** H

(705) 522-1100. **$119-$120.** 1401 Paris St P3E 3B6. Trans-Canada Hwy 17 exit Hwy 69/RR 46, 2 mi (3.2 km) n on Regent St, then 0.9 mi (1.5 km) e. Int corridors. **Pets:** Other species. $25 one-time fee/room. Designated rooms, service with restrictions, supervision.

[SAVE] [ECO] [¶] [≈] [📶] [✕] [🔒] [💻]

THESSALON

(CAA) ▼▼▼ **Carolyn Beach Motor Inn** M

(705) 842-3330. **$100-$145.** 1 Lakeside Dr P0R 1L0. On Hwy 17B, just s of jct Hwy 17. Ext corridors. **Pets:** Accepted.

[SAVE] [¶] [📶] [✕] [🔒] [💻]

THOROLD

(CAA) ▼▼▼ **Four Points by Sheraton St. Catharines Niagara Suites** H

(905) 984-8484. **Call for rates.** 3530 Schmon Pkwy L2V 4Y6. Hwy 406 exit St. David's Rd W; just s of Brock University. Int corridors. **Pets:** Accepted. [SAVE] [🛢] [¶] [&M] [≈] [✕] [📶] [✕] [🔒] [💻]

THUNDER BAY

(CAA) ▼▼▼ **BEST WESTERN Crossroads Motor Inn** H 🐾

(807) 577-4241. **$125-$139.** 655 W Arthur St P7E 5R6. Just e of Hwy 61. Ext/int corridors. **Pets:** Small. $15 daily fee/room. Designated rooms, service with restrictions, supervision. [SAVE] [📶] [✕] [🔒] [💻]

(CAA) ▼▼▼ **BEST WESTERN PLUS Nor'Wester Hotel & Conference Centre** H

(807) 473-9123. **$132-$152, 30 day notice.** 2080 Hwy 61 P7J 1B8. On Hwy 61 at Loch Lomond Rd. Int corridors. **Pets:** Dogs only. $20 one-time fee/room. Designated rooms, service with restrictions, crate.

[SAVE] [🛢] [¶] [&M] [≈] [✕] [📶] [✕] [🔒] [💻]

(CAA) ▼▼ **Comfort Inn** M 🐾

(807) 475-3155. **$109-$179.** 660 W Arthur St P7E 5R8. Just e of Hwy 61. Int corridors. **Pets:** Very small, other species. $20 daily fee/pet. Service with restrictions, supervision. [SAVE] [ECO] [≈] [✕] [🔒] [💻]

(CAA) ▼▼ **Econo Lodge** H

(807) 344-6688. **$80-$100.** 686 Memorial Ave P7B 3Z5. 0.6 mi (1 km) e of Harbour Expwy. Int corridors. **Pets:** Accepted.

[SAVE] [¶] [≈] [✕] [🔒] [💻]

▼▼ **Victoria Inn Hotel & Convention Centre** H

(807) 577-8481. **$122-$158.** 555 W Arthur St P7E 5R5. 0.5 mi (0.8 km) e of Hwy 61. Int corridors. **Pets:** Accepted.

[¶] [≈] [📶] [✕] [🔒] [💻]

TILLSONBURG

▼▼ **Howard Johnson/Tillsonburg** H

(519) 842-7366. **$99-$110.** 92 Simcoe St N4G 2J1. Hwy 19, just e. Int corridors. **Pets:** $10 daily fee/pet. Service with restrictions, supervision.

[ECO] [¶] [📶] [✕] [🔒] [💻]

TIMMINS

(CAA) ▼▼▼ **Comfort Inn** H 🐾

(705) 264-9474. **$129-$189.** 939 Algonquin Blvd E P4N 7J5. Hwy 101, 0.3 mi (0.5 km) e of Hwy 655. Int corridors. **Pets:** Other species. $15 one-time fee/pet. Designated rooms, service with restrictions, crate.

[SAVE] [ECO] [📶] [✕] [🔒] [💻]

(CAA) ▼▼▼ **Holiday Inn Express & Suites Timmins** H

(705) 531-4000. **$139-$299.** 30 Algonquin Blvd W P4N 2R3. Hwy 101; jct Mountjoy St. Int corridors. **Pets:** Accepted.

[SAVE] [&M] [≈] [📶] [✕] [🔒] [💻]

▼▼▼ **Microtel Inn & Suites by Wyndham Timmins** H 🐾

(705) 264-1477. **$99-$159.** 1960 Riverside Dr P4R 0A2. Hwy 101, just e of Government Rd N. Int corridors. **Pets:** $10 one-time fee/room. Designated rooms. [&M] [≈] [✕] [📶] [✕] [🔒] [💻]

TOBERMORY

▼▼ **Coach House Inn** M

(519) 596-2361. **Call for rates.** 7189 Hwy 6 N0H 2R0. 1.2 mi (2 km) s of ferry docks. Ext corridors. **Pets:** Accepted.

[¶] [≈] [📶] [✕] [🖼] [🔒]

TORONTO *(Restaurants p. 646)*

(CAA) ▼▼▼ **BEST WESTERN Roehampton Hotel & Suites** H

(416) 487-5101. **$145-$250.** 808 Mt. Pleasant Rd M4P 2L2. Just n of Eglinton Ave. Int corridors. **Pets:** Small. $50 daily fee/pet. Service with restrictions, supervision. [SAVE] [ECO] [≈] [🔒] [💻]

(CAA) ▼▼ **Comfort Inn** H

(416) 736-4700. **$85-$105.** 66 Norfinch Dr M3N 1X1. Hwy 400 exit Finch Ave E, just n. Int corridors. **Pets:** Medium. $15 daily fee/pet. Service with restrictions, crate. [SAVE] [ECO] [≈] [🔒] [💻]

▼▼ **Comfort Inn** H

(416) 967-6781. **$119-$299.** 321 Jarvis St M5B 2C2. Just s of Gerrard St. Int corridors. **Pets:** Accepted. [≈] [✕] [🔒] [💻]

(CAA) ▼▼▼ **Comfort Inn Toronto East** H

(416) 269-7400. **$90-$109.** 3306 Kingston Rd M1M 1P8. Hwy 401 exit 383 (Markham Rd), 3.1 mi (5 km) s to Hwy 2 (Kingston Rd), then 0.6 mi (1 km) w. Int corridors. **Pets:** Medium. $15 daily fee/pet. Designated rooms, service with restrictions, supervision. [SAVE] [¶] [≈] [🔒] [💻]

(CAA) ▼▼▼ **Cosmopolitan Hotel Toronto** H

(416) 350-2000. **Call for rates.** 8 Colborne St M5E 1E1. Between King and Wellington sts. Int corridors. **Pets:** Accepted.

[SAVE] [¶] [✕] [≈] [✕] [🔒] [💻]

(CAA) ▼▼▼ **Crowne Plaza Toronto Airport** H

(416) 675-1234. **Call for rates.** 33 Carlson Ct M9W 6H5. Just w of jct Hwy 27, just n of Dixon Rd. Int corridors. **Pets:** Accepted.

[SAVE] [ECO] [¶] [≈] [✕] [≈] [✕] [🔒] [💻]

(CAA) ▼▼▼ **Delta Toronto East** H

(416) 299-1500. **$119-$299.** 2035 Kennedy Rd M1T 3G2. Hwy 401 exit 379 (Kennedy Rd), just ne. Int corridors. **Pets:** Medium, other species. $35 one-time fee/room. Designated rooms, service with restrictions, supervision. [SAVE] [ECO] [¶] [≈] [✕] [≈] [✕] [🔒] [💻]

(CAA) ▼▼▼ **Eaton Chelsea, Toronto** H 🐾

(416) 595-1975. **$130-$323.** 33 Gerrard St W M5G 1Z4. Just w of Yonge St; just s of College St. Int corridors. **Pets:** Medium. $35 one-time fee/room. Service with restrictions.

[SAVE] [ECO] [🛢] [¶] [≈] [✕] [≈] [✕] [🔒] [💻]

(AA) ▼▼▼ ▼▼▼ **The Fairmont Royal York** 🅷
(416) 368-2511. **Call for rates.** 100 Front St W M5J 1E3. QEW/
Gardiner Expwy, exit n on York or Bay sts; entrance on Wellington St.
Int corridors. **Pets:** Accepted.
[SAVE] [ECO] [†|] [&M] [⇌] [✕] [s🐾] [♦] [▭]

(AA) ▼▼▼▼▼ **Four Seasons Hotel Toronto** 🅷
(416) 964-0411. **$445-$770.** 60 Yorkville Ave M4W 0A4. Jct Bay St. Int
corridors. **Pets:** Accepted.
[SAVE] [†|] [&M] [⇌] [✕] [🛜] [✕] [♦] [▭]

▼▼▼ ▼ **The Grand Hotel & Suites Toronto** 🅷
(416) 863-9000. **Call for rates.** 225 Jarvis St M5B 2C1. Jct Dundas St.
Int corridors. **Pets:** Accepted. [†|] [⇌] [✕] [🛜] [♦] [▭]

(AA) ▼▼ ▼ **Holiday Inn Express Toronto Downtown** 🅷
(416) 367-5555. **$129-$179.** 111 Lombard St M5C 2T9. Gardiner Expwy
exit Jarvis St, 0.6 mi (1 km) n, then just w; between Adelaide and Richmond sts. Int corridors. **Pets:** Accepted. [SAVE] [ECO] [🛜] [✕] [♦] [▭]

(AA) ▼▼▼▼ **Holiday Inn Express Toronto-North York** 🅷
(416) 665-3500. **$109-$149.** 30 Norfinch Dr M3N 1X1. Hwy 400 exit
Finch Ave E. Int corridors. **Pets:** $25 daily fee/pet. Designated rooms,
service with restrictions, crate. [SAVE] [&M] [🛜] [♦] [▭]

(AA) ▼▼▼▼ **Holiday Inn Toronto Airport East** 🅷
(416) 240-7511. **Call for rates.** 600 Dixon Rd M9W 1J1. East of jct
Hwy 27 N and Dixon Rd; w of jct Hwy 401 and Dixon Rd. Int corridors.
Pets: Accepted. [SAVE] [ECO] [†|] [⇌] [🛜] [✕] [♦] [▭]

(AA) ▼▼ ▼ **Hotel Carlingview Toronto Airport** 🅷
(416) 675-3303. **$99-$129.** 221 Carlingview Dr M9W 5E8. QEW exit
Hwy 427 N to Dixon Rd E, 0.6 mi (1 km) to Carlingview Dr, then just s.
Ext/int corridors. **Pets:** Accepted. [SAVE] [ECO] [†|] [🛜] [♦] [▭]

(AA) ▼▼ ▼ **Hotel Indigo Toronto Airport** 🅷 🐾
(416) 637-7000. **Call for rates.** 135 Carlingview Dr M9W 5E7. Just n of
Dixon Rd. Int corridors. **Pets:** Medium. $250 deposit/room, $35 daily
fee/pet. Service with restrictions, supervision.
[SAVE] [†|] [⇌] [✕] [🛜] [✕] [♦] [▭]

▼▼▼ ▼▼▼ **Hotel Le Germain Maple Leaf Square** 🅷
(416) 649-7575. **Call for rates.** 75 Bremner Blvd M5J 0A1. Jct York St,
just w of Air Canada Centre. Int corridors. **Pets:** Accepted.
[†|] [🛜] [✕] [♦] [▭]

▼▼▼ ▼▼▼ **Hotel Le Germain Toronto** 🅷
(416) 345-9500. **Call for rates.** 30 Mercer St M5V 1H3. Between John
St and Blue Jays Way. Int corridors. **Pets:** Accepted.
[†|] [&M] [🛜] [✕] [♦] [▭]

(AA) ▼▼▼ ▼▼▼ **Hyatt Regency Toronto on King** 🅷
(416) 343-1234. **$99-$499.** 370 King St W M5V 1J9. Between Spadina
Ave and Peter St. Int corridors. **Pets:** Accepted.
[SAVE] [†|] [⇌] [✕] [s🐾] [♦] [▭]

(AA) ▼▼▼ ▼▼▼ **InterContinental Toronto Centre** 🅷
(416) 597-1400. **Call for rates.** 225 Front St W M5V 2X3. Between
Spadina and University aves. Int corridors. **Pets:** Accepted.
[SAVE] [ECO] [†|] [⇌] [✕] [s🐾] [♦] [▭]

(AA) ▼▼▼ ▼▼▼ **InterContinental Toronto Yorkville** 🅷
(416) 960-5200. **$195-$405.** 220 Bloor St W M5S 1T8. Just w of
Avenue Rd. Int corridors. **Pets:** Accepted.
[SAVE] [ECO] [†|] [⇌] [✕] [s🐾] [✕] [♦] [▭]

(AA) ▼▼▼ ▼ **International Plaza Hotel and Conference
Centre Toronto Airport** 🅷
(416) 244-1711. **$99-$199.** 655 Dixon Rd M9W 1J3. Jct Hwy 27 N, just
w of jct Hwy 401. Int corridors. **Pets:** Medium. $35 one-time fee/room.
Service with restrictions, supervision.
[SAVE] [ECO] [†|] [&M] [⇌] [✕] [🛜] [✕] [♦] [▭]

(AA) ▼▼▼ ▼▼▼ **Novotel Toronto Centre** 🅷 🐾
(416) 367-8900. **$159-$295.** 45 The Esplanade M5E 1W2. Just ne of
Gardiner Expwy via Yonge St. Int corridors. **Pets:** Service with restric-
tions, crate. [SAVE] [ECO] [†|] [⇌] [✕] [🛜] [▭]

(AA) ▼▼▼ ▼▼▼ **Novotel Toronto North York** 🅷
(416) 733-2929. **Call for rates.** 3 Park Home Ave M2N 6L3. Hwy 401
exit Yonge St, 1.1 mi (1.7 km) n, then just w. Int corridors.
Pets: Accepted. [SAVE] [ECO] [†|] [⇌] [🛜] [✕] [♦] [▭]

▼▼▼ ▼▼▼ **The Omni King Edward Hotel** 🅷
(416) 863-9700. **$189-$439.** 37 King St E M5C 1E9. Just e of Yonge
St. Int corridors. **Pets:** Accepted. [†|] [s🐾] [✕] [♦] [▭]

(AA) ▼▼▼ ▼▼▼ **Pantages Hotel Toronto Centre** 🅷
(416) 362-1777. **$179-$399.** 200 Victoria St M5B 1V8. Jct Shuter St. Int
corridors. **Pets:** Accepted. [SAVE] [†|] [✕] [🛜] [✕] [♦] [▭]

(AA) ▼▼▼ ▼▼▼ **Park Hyatt Toronto** 🅷
(416) 925-1234. **$229-$459, 3 day notice.** 4 Avenue Rd M5R 2E8. Corner of Bloor St W. Int corridors. **Pets:** Accepted.
[SAVE] [†|] [&M] [✕] [🛜] [✕] [♦] [▭]

(AA) ▼▼▼ ▼▼▼ **Quality Hotel & Suites Toronto Airport
East** 🅷
(416) 240-9090. **$89-$169.** 2180 Islington Ave M9P 3P1. Hwy 401 exit
356, just s. Int corridors. **Pets:** Medium. $15 daily fee/pet. Designated
rooms, service with restrictions, crate.
[SAVE] [ECO] [†|] [🛜] [✕] [♦] [▭]

(AA) ▼▼▼ ▼ **Quality Suites Toronto Airport** 🅷
(416) 674-8442. **$99-$159.** 262 Carlingview Dr M9W 5G1. 0.6 mi (1
km) w of jct Hwy 27 N and Dixon Rd. Int corridors. **Pets:** Other species. $10 daily fee/pet. Designated rooms, service with restrictions,
crate. [SAVE] [ECO] [†|] [🛜] [♦] [▭]

(AA) ▼▼▼▼ **Radisson Suite Hotel Toronto Airport** 🅷
(416) 242-7400. **Call for rates.** 640 Dixon Rd M9W 1J1. Just e of jct
Hwy 27; just w of jct Hwy 401. Int corridors. **Pets:** Accepted.
[SAVE] [ECO] [†|] [🛜] [♦] [▭]

(AA) ▼▼▼ ▼▼▼ **Renaissance Toronto Downtown
Hotel** 🅷
(416) 341-7100. **$209-$344.** 1 Blue Jays Way M5V 1J4. Jct Front St.
Int corridors. **Pets:** Large, dogs only. $50 one-time fee/room. Service
with restrictions, crate. [SAVE] [ECO] [†|] [⇌] [✕] [🛜] [✕] [♦] [▭]

(AA) ▼▼▼ ▼ **Residence Inn by Marriott Toronto
Airport** 🅷
(416) 798-2900. **$125-$206.** 17 Reading Ct M9W 7K7. Just w of jct
Hwy 27 and Dixon Rd. Int corridors. **Pets:** Medium. $100 one-time fee/
room. Designated rooms, service with restrictions, supervision.
[SAVE] [ECO] [†|] [&M] [⇌] [🛜] [✕] [♦] [▭]

▼▼▼ ▼ **Residence Inn by Marriott Toronto Downtown/
Entertainment District** 🅷
(416) 581-1800. **$216-$355.** 255 Wellington St W M5V 3P9. Jct Blue
Jays Way. Int corridors. **Pets:** Medium. $100 one-time fee/room. Service
with restrictions, crate. [ECO] [⇌] [🛜] [✕] [♦] [▭]

(AA) ▼▼▼ ▼▼▼ **The Ritz-Carlton, Toronto** 🅷
(416) 585-2500. **$450-$625.** 181 Wellington St W M5V 3G7. Between
Simcoe and John sts. Int corridors. **Pets:** Accepted.
[SAVE] [†|] [&M] [⇌] [✕] [s🐾] [✕] [♦] [▭]

(AA) ▼▼▼ ▼▼▼ **Shangri-La Hotel Toronto** 🅷
(647) 788-8888. **Call for rates.** 188 University Ave M5H 0A3. Between
Adelaide and Richmond sts. Int corridors. **Pets:** Accepted.
[SAVE] [†|] [⇌] [✕] [🛜] [✕] [▭]

(CAA) ▼▼▼▼ **Sheraton Centre Toronto Hotel** H
(416) 361-1000. **$159-$600.** 123 Queen St W M5H 2M9. Opposite Toronto Civic Centre and City Hall. Int corridors. **Pets:** Accepted.
SAVE ECO ⊟ ¶¶ 🛁 ➹ ✕ 🔊 ✕ ❚ 💻

(CAA) ▼▼▼ ▼▼▼ **Sheraton Toronto Airport Hotel & Conference Centre** H
(416) 675-6100. **Call for rates.** 801 Dixon Rd M9W 1J5. Jct Hwy 27 N and Dixon Rd. Int corridors. **Pets:** Accepted.
SAVE ECO ¶¶ 🛁 ➹ ✕ ❚ 💻

(CAA) ▼▼▼ ▼▼▼ **SoHo Metropolitan Hotel** H
(416) 599-8800. **$250-$895.** 318 Wellington St W M5V 3T4. Jct Blue Jays Way. Int corridors. **Pets:** Accepted.
SAVE ¶¶ 🛁 ✕ ➹ ❚ 💻

(CAA) ▼▼▼ **Super 8 Downtown Toronto** H
(647) 426-8118. **$88-$259.** 222 Spadina Ave M5T 3B3. At Dundas St; at Chinatown Centre. Int corridors. **Pets:** Accepted.
SAVE ECO ¶¶ ➹ ✕ ❚ 💻

▼▼▼ ▼▼▼ **Thompson Hotel Toronto** H
(416) 640-7778. **$295-$495, 3 day notice.** 550 Wellington St W M5V 2V4. Jct Bathurst St. Int corridors. **Pets:** Accepted.
¶¶ 🛁 🔊 ✕ ❚ 💻

(CAA) ▼▼▼▼ **Toronto Don Valley Hotel & Suites** H ☙
(416) 449-4111. **Call for rates.** 175 Wynford Dr M3C 1J3. Don Valley Pkwy exit 375 (Wynford Dr); jct Don Valley Pkwy and Eglinton Ave E. Int corridors. **Pets:** Very small. $15 daily fee/pet. Designated rooms, service with restrictions, supervision.
SAVE ECO ¶¶ 🛁 ✕ ➹ ✕ ❚ 💻

(CAA) ▼▼▼ ▼▼▼ **Toronto Marriott Bloor Yorkville** H
(416) 961-8000. **$181-$355.** 90 Bloor St E M4W 1A7. Just e of Yonge St. Int corridors. **Pets:** Accepted.
SAVE ECO ¶¶ 🛁M ➹ ✕ ❚ 💻

(CAA) ▼▼▼ **Travelodge Hotel Toronto Airport** H
(416) 674-2222. **$89-$359.** 925 Dixon Rd M9W 1J8. Corner of Carlingview Dr. Int corridors. **Pets:** $25 one-time fee/pet. Designated rooms, service with restrictions, crate.
SAVE ECO ¶¶ 🛁 ➹ ❚ 💻

▼▼▼ **Travelodge Toronto East** H
(416) 299-9500. **$111-$149.** 20 Milner Business Ct M1B 3C6. Jct Hwy 401 exit 383 (Markham Rd), just n. Int corridors. **Pets:** Accepted.
ECO ¶¶ 🛁 ➹ ❚ 💻

(CAA) ▼▼▼ ▼▼▼ **Trump International Hotel and Tower Toronto®** H
(416) 306-5800. **$395-$950.** 325 Bay St M5H 4G3. Jct Adelaide St. Int corridors. **Pets:** Accepted.
SAVE ¶¶ 🛁M 🛁 ✕ ➹ ✕ ❚ 💻

(CAA) ▼▼▼ ▼▼▼ **The Westin Bristol Place Toronto Airport** H
(416) 675-9444. **$95-$329.** 950 Dixon Rd M9W 5N4. 1.6 mi (2.6 km) w of jct Hwy 401. Int corridors. **Pets:** Accepted.
SAVE ¶¶ 🛁 🔊 ✕ ❚ 💻

(CAA) ▼▼▼ ▼▼▼ **The Westin Harbour Castle** H
(416) 869-1600. **$159-$600.** One Harbour Sq M5J 1A6. At the foot of Bay St. Int corridors. **Pets:** Accepted.
SAVE ECO ¶¶ 🛁M 🛁 ✕ 🔊 ✕ ❚ 💻

(CAA) ▼▼▼ ▼▼▼ **The Westin Prince Toronto** H ☙
(416) 444-2511. **$119-$459.** 900 York Mills Rd M3B 3H2. Just s of Hwy 401 via Leslie St exit to York Mills Rd E. Int corridors. **Pets:** Medium, dogs only. Designated rooms, service with restrictions, supervision.
SAVE ¶¶ 🛁M 🛁 ✕ ➹ ❚ 💻

▼▼▼ ▼▼▼ **Windsor Arms Hotel** H
(416) 971-9666. **Call for rates.** 18 St. Thomas St M5S 3E7. Just s of Bloor St. Int corridors. **Pets:** Accepted.
¶¶ 🛁 ✕ ➹ ✕ ❚ 💻

TRENTON

▼▼▼ **Comfort Inn** H
(613) 965-6660. **$103-$190.** 68 Monogram Pl K8V 6S3. Hwy 401 exit 526 (Glen Miller Rd), just s, then just e. Int corridors. **Pets:** Accepted.
ECO 🛁M ➹ ❚ 💻

(CAA) ▼▼▼ **Ramada Trenton Hotel** H
(613) 394-4855. **$99-$149.** 99 Glen Miller Rd K8V 5P8. Hwy 401 exit 526 (Glen Miller Rd), just s. Int corridors. **Pets:** Accepted.
SAVE ECO ¶¶ 🛁 ✕ ➹ ❚ 💻

(CAA) ▼▼▼ **Travelodge Trenton** H
(613) 965-6789. **$89-$125.** 598 Old Hwy 2 K8V 5P5. Hwy 401 exit 538, 1.3 mi (2 km) s to Old Hwy 2, then 3.8 mi (6 km) w; 3.1 mi (4.9 km) e of jct Hwy 33. Int corridors. **Pets:** Service with restrictions, crate.
SAVE ECO ¶¶ ➹ ✕ ❚ 💻

TWEED

▼▼▼ **Park Place Motel** M
(613) 478-3134. **Call for rates.** 43 Victoria St S K0K 3J0. Hwy 37, 0.3 mi (0.5 km) s of center. Ext corridors. **Pets:** Medium, dogs only. $10 daily fee/pet. Designated rooms, service with restrictions, supervision.
¶¶ ➹ ✕ ❚ 💻

VAUGHAN

(CAA) ▼▼▼ ▼▼▼ **Aloft Vaughan Mills** H ☙
(905) 695-0500. **Call for rates.** 151 Bass Pro Mills Dr L4K 0E6. Hwy 400 exit 33 (Rutherford Rd) southbound; exit 32 (Bass Pro Mills Dr) northbound. Int corridors. **Pets:** Small, dogs only. Service with restrictions, supervision. SAVE ¶¶ 🛁M 🛁 ➹ ✕ ❚ 💻

(CAA) ▼▼▼ **Element Vaughan Southwest** H
(905) 264-6474. **$169-$229.** 6170 Hwy 7 L4H 0R2. Jct Hwy 27. Int corridors. **Pets:** Accepted. SAVE ⊟ 🛁M ➹ ✕ ❚ 💻

▼▼▼ ▼▼▼ **Holiday Inn Express & Suites Vaughan-Southwest** H
(905) 851-1510. **Call for rates.** 6100 Hwy 7 L4H 0R2. Jct Hwy 27. Int corridors. **Pets:** Accepted. ECO 🛁 ➹ ✕ ❚ 💻

(CAA) ▼▼▼ ▼▼▼ **Novotel Toronto Vaughan Centre** H
(905) 660-0212. **$99-$399, 3 day notice.** 200 Bass Pro Mills Dr L4K 0B9. Hwy 400 S exit 33 (Rutherford Rd); Hwy 400 N exit 32 (Bass Pro Mills Dr). Int corridors. **Pets:** Accepted.
SAVE ECO ¶¶ 🛁M 🛁 ➹ ✕ ❚ 💻

▼▼▼ ▼▼▼ **Residence Inn by Marriott Toronto/Vaughan** H
(905) 695-4002. **$174-$344.** 11 Interchange Way L4K 5W3. Hwy 400 exit 29 (Hwy 7), 0.6 mi (1 km) e. Int corridors. **Pets:** Accepted.
🛁M 🛁 ➹ ✕ ❚ 💻

WATERLOO

(CAA) ▼▼▼ **Comfort Inn** H
(519) 747-9400. **$115-$150.** 190 Weber St N N2J 3H4. Jct University Ave, just s. Int corridors. **Pets:** Large, other species. $35 one-time fee/room. Designated rooms, service with restrictions, crate.
SAVE ECO ¶¶ ➹ ❚ 💻

(CAA) ▼▼▼ ▼▼▼ **Delta Waterloo** H
(519) 514-0404. **$149-$249.** 110 Erb St W N2L 0C6. At Father David Bauer Dr. Int corridors. **Pets:** Accepted. SAVE ¶¶ ➹ ✕ ❚ 💻

▼▼▼ ▼▼▼ **Les Diplomates B & B (Executive Guest House)** BB
(519) 725-3184. **$138-$156, 3 day notice.** 100 Blythwood Rd N2L 4A2. Hwy 85 N exit King St, s to Columbia St, w to Hazel St, then just n. Ext/int corridors. **Pets:** Accepted. ¶¶ ➹ ✕ ❚ 💻

▼▼▼ **The Waterloo Inn Conference Hotel** 🏨
(519) 884-0220. **$154-$204.** 475 King St N N2J 2Z5. 1.9 mi (3 km) n on King St, jct Hwy 85. Int corridors. **Pets:** Accepted.
🍴 👤M 🛏 ✂ 🛜 ✕ 📱 💻

WAWA *(Restaurants p. 646)*

▼▼ **Best Northern Motel & Restaurant** Ⓜ
(705) 856-7302. **$89-$135.** 150 Hwy 17 S P0S 1K0. On Hwy 17, 3.3 mi (5.3 km) s of jct Hwy 101. Ext corridors. **Pets:** Other species. $15 daily fee/pet. Designated rooms, service with restrictions, supervision.
🍴 🛜 ✕ 🖊 📱 💻

Ⓒ ▼▼ **Parkway Motel** Ⓜ
(705) 856-7020. **$89-$129.** 232 Hwy 17 S P0S 1K0. On Hwy 17, 2.5 mi (4 km) s of jct Hwy 101. Ext corridors. **Pets:** Accepted.
SAVE 🍴 🛜 ✕ 🖊 📱 💻

WELLAND

▼▼ **Comfort Inn-Niagara/Welland** 🏨
(905) 732-4811. **$85-$350.** 870 Niagara St L3C 1M3. 1.5 mi (2.5 km) n. Int corridors. **Pets:** Accepted. 🛜 📱 💻

WHITBY

▼▼ **Canadiana Inn** Ⓜ
(905) 668-3686. **Call for rates.** 732 Dundas St E (Hwy 2) L1N 2J7. Hwy 401 exit 410 (Brock St/Hwy 12), 1 mi (1.6 km) n to Dundas St, then 0.6 mi (1 km) e. Ext corridors. **Pets:** Accepted.
🛏 🛜 📱 💻

▼▼ **Motel 6 Whitby #1907** 🏨
(905) 665-8883. **Call for rates.** 165 Consumers Dr L1N 1C4. Hwy 401 exit 410 (Brock St/Hwy 12), just ne. Int corridors. **Pets:** Other species. Service with restrictions, crate. ECO 🛜 📱

Ⓒ ▼▼ **Quality Suites** 🏨
(905) 432-8800. **$130-$200.** 1700 Champlain Ave L1N 6A7. Hwy 401 exit 412 (Thickson Rd), 0.3 mi (0.5 km) n to Champlain Ave, then 0.6 mi (1 km) e. Int corridors. **Pets:** Large. $20 daily fee/room. Designated rooms, service with restrictions. SAVE ECO 🍴 🛜 📱 💻

▼▼▼ **Residence Inn by Marriott Whitby** 🏨
(905) 444-9756. **$111-$183.** 160 Consumers Dr L1N 9S3. Hwy 401 exit 410 (Brock St/Hwy 12). Int corridors. **Pets:** Medium, other species. $75 one-time fee/room. Service with restrictions, crate.
👤M 🛏 🛜 ✕ 📱 💻

WINDSOR

Ⓒ ▼▼▼ **BEST WESTERN PLUS Waterfront Hotel** 🏨
(519) 973-5555. **$115-$199.** 277 Riverside Dr W N9A 5K4. 0.6 mi (1 km) w of Detroit-Windsor Tunnel; 0.6 mi (1 km) e of Ambassador Bridge; downtown. Int corridors. **Pets:** Accepted.
SAVE ECO 🍴 🛏 ✂ 🛜 ✕ 📱 💻

▼▼ **Cadillac Inn** Ⓜ
(519) 969-9340. **$79-$109, 7 day notice.** 2498 Dougall Ave N8X 1T2. 2.5 mi (4 km) s on Hwy 3B from Detroit-Windsor Tunnel, just w on Eugenie St, then just n. Ext corridors. **Pets:** Accepted.
🍴 🛏 🛜 📱

Ⓒ ▼▼ **Comfort Inn** 🏨
(519) 966-7800. **$105-$155.** 2955 Dougall Ave N9E 1S1. 3.3 mi (5.3 km) s on Hwy 3B, off Hwy 401 via Detroit-Windsor Tunnel exit. Int corridors. **Pets:** Accepted. SAVE ECO 🍴 🛜 📱 💻

Ⓒ ▼▼ **Comfort Inn & Suites Ambassador Bridge** 🏨 🐾
(519) 972-1100. **$130-$186.** 2330 Huron Church Rd N9E 3S6. North of EC Row Expwy. Int corridors. **Pets:** Large, other species. $20 one-time fee/room. Service with restrictions, supervision.
SAVE 🍴 🛏 🛜 ✕ 📱 💻

▼▼▼ **Hampton Inn & Suites by Hilton Windsor** 🏨
(519) 972-0770. **$139-$169.** 1840 Huron Church Rd N9C 2L5. 0.9 mi (1.5 km) n of EC Row Expwy. Int corridors. **Pets:** Accepted.
👤M 🛏 🛜 ✕ 📱 💻

▼▼▼ **Holiday Inn & Suites Windsor (Ambassador Bridge)** 🏨
(519) 966-1200. **Call for rates.** 1855 Huron Church Rd N9C 2L6. Jct Huron Church and Malden rds; 0.9 mi (1.5 km) n of EC Row Expwy. Int corridors. **Pets:** Accepted. ECO 🍴 🛏 ✂ 🛜 ✕ 📱 💻

Ⓒ ▼▼▼ **Holiday Inn Downtown Windsor** 🏨 🐾
(519) 256-4656. **$139-$249.** 430 Ouellette Ave N9A 1B2. 0.3 mi (0.5 km) s of Riverside Dr at Park St W. Int corridors. **Pets:** $30 deposit/room, $30 one-time fee/room. Service with restrictions.
SAVE 🍴 👤M 🛏 🛜 ✕ 📱 💻

▼▼ **Howard Johnson Plaza Hotel - Windsor Central** 🏨
(519) 966-1860. **$60-$220.** 2530 Ouellette Ave N8X 1L7. Jct Eugenie St. Int corridors. **Pets:** Accepted. 🍴 🛜 📱 💻

▼▼ **Ivy Rose Motor Inn** Ⓜ
(519) 966-1700. **$74-$150.** 2885 Howard Ave N8X 3Y4. 3 mi (4.8 km) s of downtown; just n of Devonshire Mall. Ext corridors. **Pets:** Accepted.
🍴 🛏 🛜 📱

▼▼ **Quality Suites Windsor** 🏨
(519) 977-9707. **Call for rates.** 250 Dougall Ave N9A 7C6. Jct Chatham St; downtown. Int corridors. **Pets:** Accepted.
ECO 🍴 👤M 🛜 📱 💻

Ⓒ ▼▼▼ **Travelodge Hotel Downtown Windsor** 🏨
(519) 258-7774. **$95-$159.** 33 Riverside Dr E N9A 2S4. Jct Ouellette Ave; downtown. Int corridors. **Pets:** Small. $100 deposit/room. Service with restrictions, supervision. SAVE ECO 🍴 🛏 🛜 📱 💻

WOODSTOCK

▼▼ **Days Inn** 🏨
(519) 421-4588. **$70-$110.** 560 Norwich Ave N4V 1C6. Hwy 401 exit 232, just n; w of Hwy 59. Int corridors. **Pets:** Accepted. 🛜 📱 💻

Ⓒ ▼▼▼ **Quality Hotel and Suites** 🏨
(519) 537-5586. **$120-$130.** 580 Bruin Blvd N4V 1E5. Hwy 401 exit 232, just n; w of Hwy 59. Int corridors. **Pets:** Other species. $25 deposit/room. Designated rooms, service with restrictions, crate.
SAVE ECO 🍴 🛏 ✕ 🛜 📱 💻

PRINCE EDWARD ISLAND

ALBERTON

Briarwood Inn, Cottages & Lodge M
(902) 853-2518. **$65-$150, 7 day notice.** 253 Matthews Ln C0B 1B0. 1.9 mi (3 km) e on Rt 12. Ext/int corridors. **Pets:** Accepted.

CAVENDISH

Bay Vista Motel M
(902) 963-2225. **$69-$135.** 9517 Cavendish Rd W C0A 1E0. Jct Rt 13, 2.8 mi (4.8 km) w on Rt 6. Ext corridors. **Pets:** Medium. Designated rooms, service with restrictions, supervision.

Cavendish Bosom Buddies Cottages & Suites CA
(902) 963-3449. **Call for rates.** 84 MacCoubrey Ln C0A 1N0. Jct Rt 6 and 13, 0.4 mi (0.7 km) e on Rt 6. Ext corridors. **Pets:** Accepted.

Sundance Cottages CA
(902) 963-2149. **$90-$375, 14 day notice.** 34 MacCoubrey Ln C0A 1N0. Jct Rt 13, 0.4 mi (0.6 km) e on Rt 6. Ext corridors. **Pets:** Other species. $10 daily fee/pet. Service with restrictions, crate.

CHARLOTTETOWN

BEST WESTERN Charlottetown H
(902) 892-2461. **$124-$184.** 238 Grafton St C1A 1L5. Between Hillsborough and Weymouth sts; center. Int corridors. **Pets:** Accepted.

Comfort Inn H
(902) 566-4424. **$120-$140.** 112 Capital Dr C1E 1E7. Trans-Canada Hwy 1, 2.8 mi (4.5 km) w. Int corridors. **Pets:** Service with restrictions, crate.

Delta Prince Edward H
(902) 566-2222. **$129-$319.** 18 Queen St C1A 4A1. At Water and Queen sts. Int corridors. **Pets:** Accepted.

Holiday Inn Express & Suites Charlottetown H
(902) 892-1201. **$129-$189.** 200 Capital Dr C1E 2E8. On Trans-Canada Hwy 1, 3 mi (5 km) w. Int corridors. **Pets:** Other species. Designated rooms, service with restrictions, supervision.

The Holman Grand Hotel H
(902) 367-7777. **$164-$355.** 123 Grafton St C1A 1K9. Between University Ave and Queen St. Int corridors. **Pets:** Medium, other species.

Quality Inn & Suites Downtown H
(902) 894-8572. **$99-$199.** 150 Euston St C1A 1W5. Just e of University Ave. Int corridors. **Pets:** Other species. Designated rooms, service with restrictions, crate.

Rodd Charlottetown H
(902) 894-7371. **$125-$259.** 75 Kent St C1A 7K4. Corner of Kent and Pownal sts. Int corridors. **Pets:** Accepted.

Rodd Royalty H
(902) 894-8566. **$99-$195.** 1 Capital Dr C1A 8C2. 2.5 mi (4 km) w on Trans-Canada Hwy 1. Ext/int corridors. **Pets:** Accepted.

CORNWALL

Howard Johnson Dutch Inn H
(902) 566-2211. **$80-$135.** 100 Trans-Canada Hwy C0A 1H0. On Hwy 1, 4.3 mi (7 km) w of Charlottetown. Ext/int corridors. **Pets:** Accepted.

Super 8 H
(902) 892-7900. **$99-$159.** 15 York Point Rd C0A 1H0. On Hwy 1, 3.7 mi (6 km) w of Charlottetown. Int corridors. **Pets:** Accepted.

DALVAY BEACH

Dalvay by-the-Sea Heritage Inn CI
(902) 672-2048. **$199-$299, 3 day notice.** 16 Cottage Cres PEI National Pkwy C0A 1P0. Off Rt 6; at east end of PEI National Park. Ext/int corridors. **Pets:** Accepted.

FRENCH RIVER

The Beach House Inn BB
(902) 886-2145. **$89-$199, 14 day notice.** 712 Cape Rd C0B 1M0. 0.8 mi n on River Rd, 0.9 mi e. Ext/int corridors. **Pets:** Dogs only. $10 daily fee/pet. Designated rooms, service with restrictions, crate.

MAYFIELD

Cavendish Gateway Resort H
(902) 963-2213. **$100-$300, 7 day notice.** 6596 Rt 13 C0A 1N0. On Rt 13, 3.6 mi (6 km) w of Cavendish; center. Ext/int corridors. **Pets:** Accepted.

MORELL

Rodd Crowbush Golf & Beach Resort H
(902) 961-5600. **$159-$246.** 632 Rt 350 Lakeside C0A 1S0. 3 mi (5 km) w on Rt 2, follow signs. Ext/int corridors. **Pets:** Accepted.

ROSENEATH

Brudenell Chalets CA
(902) 652-2900. **Call for rates.** 1068 Georgetown Rd C0A 1L0. Jct Rt 4 and 3, 4 mi (6.4 km) e on Rt 3. Ext corridors. **Pets:** Accepted.

Rodd Brudenell River Resort H
(902) 652-2332. **$123-$214.** 86 Dewars Ln, Rt 3 C0A 1L0. Jct Rt 4, 3.3 mi (5.5 km) e; in Brudenell River Provincial Park. Ext/int corridors. **Pets:** Accepted.

ST. PETERS

The Inn at St. Peters CI
(902) 961-2135. **$175-$270, 7 day notice.** 1668 Greenwich Rd C0A 2A0. Jct Rt 16 and 313, 0.6 mi (1 km) w on Rt 313. Ext corridors. **Pets:** Large. $10 daily fee/room. Designated rooms, service with restrictions.

STANLEY BRIDGE

Inn at the Pier CI
(902) 886-3126. **$115-$249, 14 day notice.** 9796 Cavendish Rd C0A 1E0. Rt 6, 3.6 mi (6 km) w of Cavendish; center. Ext/int corridors. **Pets:** Accepted.

SUMMERSIDE

Quality Inn & Suites H
(902) 436-2295. **$109-$169.** 618 Water St E C1N 2V5. 1 mi (1.6 km) e on Hwy 11. Ext/int corridors. **Pets:** Other species. $10 one-time fee/pet. Designated rooms, service with restrictions, supervision.

(A) ▼▼▼ **Slemon Park Hotel & Conference Centre** H
(902) 432-1780. **$89-$109.** 12 Redwood Ave C0B 1T0. On Rt 2, 3 mi
(5 km) w at Summerside Airport. Int corridors. **Pets:** Accepted.
SAVE [T] &M 🖥 ✕ 📦 ▣

WOODSTOCK
▼▼ **Rodd Mill River Resort** H
(902) 859-3555. **$110-$161.** 180 Mill River Resort Rd, Rt 136 C0B 1V0.
On Rt 136, just e of jct Rt 2; in Mill River Provincial Park. Int corridors.
Pets: Accepted. [T] 🖥 ✕ 🖥 ✕ 📦 ▣

QUEBEC

ALMA
▼▼ **Comfort Inn** H
(418) 668-9221. **Call for rates.** 870 ave du Pont S G8B 2V8. On Hwy
169; center. Int corridors. **Pets:** Medium, other species. $25 daily fee/
pet. No service, crate. 🖥 ✕ 📦 ▣

AMOS
▼▼ **Amosphere Complexe Hotelier** H
(819) 732-7777. **$95-$190.** 1031 Rt 111 est J9T 1N2. Center. Ext/int
corridors. **Pets:** Other species. Supervision.
🔌 [T] ✕ 🖥 📦 ▣

ANJOU
(A) ▼▼▼ **Quality Hotel East** H
(514) 493-6363. 8100 ave Neuville H1J 2T2. Hwy 40 exit 78,
just n on boul Langelier, 0.4 mi (0.7 km) e on rue Jarry, then s. Int
corridors. **Pets:** Other species. $35 one-time fee/room. Designated
rooms, service with restrictions, supervision.
SAVE ECO [T] 🖥 📦 ▣

BAIE-COMEAU
▼▼ **Comfort Inn** H
(418) 589-8252. **$143-$165.** 745 boul Lafleche G5C 1C6. On Rt 138.
Int corridors. **Pets:** Other species. $25 one-time fee/room. Service with
restrictions, supervision. ECO 🖥 ✕ 📦 ▣

▼▼▼ **Hotel Le Manoir** H
(418) 296-3391. **Call for rates.** 8 ave Cabot G4Z 1L8. Jct Rt 138 and
boul Lasalle, 2.6 mi (4.4 km) e, follow signs. Int corridors.
Pets: Accepted. [T] ✕ 🖥 ✕ 📦 ▣

BELOEIL
(A) ▼▼▼▼ **Hotel Rive Gauche** H
(450) 467-4477. **$130.** 1810 boul Richelieu J3G 4S4. Hwy 20 exit 112,
0.6 mi (1 km) s on rue Serge-Pepin, just sw on Rt 223, follow signs. Int
corridors. **Pets:** Accepted. SAVE [T] 🖥 ✕ 📦 ▣

BOISCHATEL
(A) ▼▼▼ **Econo Lodge Montmorency** H
(418) 822-4777. **$80-$140.** 5490 boul Ste-Anne G0A 1H0. On Hwy 138.
Int corridors. **Pets:** Accepted. SAVE 🖥 📦

BOUCHERVILLE
(A) ▼▼▼ **Comfort Inn** M
(450) 641-2880. **$121-$140.** 96 boul de Mortagne J4B 5M7. Hwy 20
exit 92, just n. Int corridors. **Pets:** Very small. $30 daily fee/pet. Desig-
nated rooms, service with restrictions, supervision.
SAVE ECO 🖥 ✕ 📦 ▣

BROMONT
▼▼▼ **Le St-Martin Bromont Hotel & Suites** H
(450) 534-0044. **Call for rates.** 111 boul du Carrefour J2L 3L1. Hwy 10,
exit 78, just s on boul de Bromont, then just w. Int corridors.
Pets: Accepted. 🖥 🖥 ✕ 📦 ▣

BROSSARD
▼▼▼ **Alt Hotel Quartier Dix 30** H
(450) 443-1030. **$154-$194.** 6500 boul de Rome J4Y 0B6. Jct Hwy 10
and 30, just w on Hwy 30 exit boul de Rome; in Quartier Dix 30 Mall.
Int corridors. **Pets:** Accepted. ECO 🖥 ✕ ▣

(A) ▼▼▼▼ **BEST WESTERN Hotel Brossard** H
(450) 466-6756. **$142-$146.** 7746 boul Taschereau J4X 1C2. Rt 134 0.8
mi (1.3 km) w of Hwy 10 exit boul Taschereau ouest. Ext/int corridors.
Pets: Accepted. SAVE ECO 🖥 🖥 ✕ 📦 ▣

▼▼ **Comfort Inn** H
(450) 678-9350. **$109-$147.** 7863 boul Taschereau J4Y 1A4. Rt 134,
0.9 mi (1.5 km) w of Hwy 10 exit boul Taschereau. Int corridors.
Pets: $25 one-time fee/pet. Service with restrictions, crate.
ECO 🖥 📦 ▣

CHICOUTIMI
▼▼ **Comfort Inn** H
(418) 693-8686. **Call for rates.** 1595 boul Talbot G7H 4C3. Jct Rt 170,
1.8 mi (2.8 km) n. Int corridors. **Pets:** Very small. $25 daily fee/pet.
Designated rooms, no service, supervision. 🖥 ✕ 📦 ▣

DORVAL
(A) ▼▼▼▼ **Aloft Montréal Airport** H ❀
(514) 633-0900. **$109-$229.** 500 ave McMillan H9P 0A2. Just n of Hwy
520 on north side service road at airport entrance. Int corridors.
Pets: Small. Designated rooms, service with restrictions, supervision.
SAVE [T] &M 🖥 🖥 ✕ 📦 ▣

(A) ▼▼▼ **Comfort Inn Dorval** H
(514) 636-3391. **$92-$130.** 340 ave Michel-Jasmin H9P 1C1. Hwy 520
exit 2 eastbound; exit 1 westbound, just e along service road to ave
Marshall, follow to ave Michel-Jasmin. Int corridors. **Pets:** Large, other
species. $25 daily fee/room. Designated rooms, crate.
SAVE ECO 🖥 📦 ▣

(A) ▼▼▼▼ **Hampton Inn & Suites by Hilton Montreal**
(Dorval) H
(514) 633-8243. **$135-$230.** 1900 Rt Transcanadienne (Hwy 40) H9P
2N4. Hwy 40 exit 55, 0.5 mi (0.8 km) e of boul des Sources; on south
side service road. Int corridors. **Pets:** Medium. $50 one-time fee/pet.
Designated rooms, service with restrictions, supervision.
SAVE [T] &M 🖥 🖥 📦 ▣

(A) ▼▼▼▼▼ **Sheraton Montreal Airport Hotel** H
(514) 631-2411. **$119-$225.** 555 McMillan Blvd H9P 1B7. Just n of Hwy
520 on north side service road; at airport entrance. Int corridors.
Pets: Accepted. SAVE [T] &M 🖥 ✕ 🖥 ✕ 📦 ▣

DRUMMONDVILLE
(A) ▼▼▼▼ **BEST WESTERN PLUS Hotel Universel**
Drummondville H
(819) 478-4971. **$119-$359.** 915 rue Hains J2C 3A1. Hwy 20 exit 177,
just s on boul St-Joseph, then just e. Int corridors. **Pets:** Accepted.
SAVE [T] 🖥 🖥 ✕ 📦 ▣

(A) ▼▼▼ **Comfort Inn** H
(819) 477-4000. **$99-$139.** 1055 rue Hains J2C 6G6. Hwy 20 exit 177,
0.3 mi (0.5 km) s on boul St-Joseph, then just n. Int corridors.
Pets: Medium, other species. $25 one-time fee/pet. Service with restric-
tions, supervision. SAVE ECO 🖥 ✕ 📦 ▣

▼▼▼ **Hotel & Suites Le Dauphin** H ❀
(819) 478-4141. **$99-$150, 30 day notice.** 600 boul St-Joseph J2C
2C1. Hwy 20 exit 177, 0.8 mi (1.3 km) s. Ext/int corridors. **Pets:** $15
daily fee/room. Designated rooms, service with restrictions, supervision.
ECO [T] 🖥 🖥 ✕ 📦 ▣

(CAA) ▼▼▼ **Hotel-Motel Drummond** 🅼

(819) 478-4614. **$65-$135.** 105 boul St-Joseph ouest J2E 1A4. Hwy 20 exit 177, just n on boul St-Joseph, then just w on rue St-Roch. Ext corridors. **Pets:** $12 one-time fee/pet. Designated rooms, service with restrictions, supervision. 🆂 🕃 🍴 ⊠ 🛜 🔌 💻

▼▼▼▼ **Quality Suites** 🅷 🐾

(819) 472-2700. **$99-$159.** 2125 rue Canadien J2C 7V8. Hwy 20 exit 175, just s. Int corridors. **Pets:** Medium. $25 one-time fee/room. Designated rooms, service with restrictions, supervision.
🄴🄲🄾 🕃 🛜 ⊠ 🔌 💻

FORESTVILLE
▼▼ **Econo Lodge** 🅼

(418) 587-2278. **$100-$130.** 5 Rt 138 est G0T 1E0. Center. Ext/int corridors. **Pets:** $10 daily fee/room. Designated rooms, service with restrictions, supervision. 🍴 🛜 🔌 💻

GATINEAU
(CAA) ▼▼▼ **Comfort Inn Gatineau** 🅷

(819) 243-6010. **$100-$150.** 630 boul La Gappe J8T 7S8. Hwy 50 exit 140, 1.1 mi (1.9 km) e; in Hull sector. Int corridors. **Pets:** Large, other species. $15 daily fee/pet. Service with restrictions, supervision.
🆂 🄴🄲🄾 ⊠ 🔌 💻

▼▼▼▼ **Crowne Plaza Gatineau-Ottawa** 🅷

(819) 778-3880. **Call for rates.** 2 rue Montcalm J8X 4B4. 0.5 mi (0.8 km) w of Portage Bridge at Rt 148 and rue Montcalm; in Hull sector. Int corridors. **Pets:** Other species. $50 one-time fee/room. Designated rooms, service with restrictions. 🍴 🕃 ⊠ 🛜 ⊠ 🔌 💻

(CAA) ▼▼▼▼ **Four Points by Sheraton Hotel & Conference Centre Gatineau-Ottawa** 🅷

(819) 778-6111. **$109-$209.** 35 rue Laurier J8X 4E9. Corner of rue Victoria; across from Canadian Museum of Civilization; in Hull sector. Int corridors. **Pets:** Accepted. 🆂 🄴🄲🄾 🍴 🕃 🛜 ⊠ 💻

(CAA) ▼▼▼ ▼▼▼ **Hilton Lac-Leamy** 🅷

(819) 790-6444. **$189-$439.** 3 boul du Casino J8Y 6X4. In Casino du Lac Leamy; in Hull sector. Int corridors. **Pets:** Accepted.
🆂 🄴🄲🄾 🍴 🕃 🕃 ⊠ 🛜 🔌 💻

ISLE-AUX-COUDRES
▼▼ **Hotel Motel La Roche Pleureuse** 🅷

(418) 438-2734. **Call for rates.** 2901 chemin des Coudriers G0A 2A0. On Ile aux Coudres, 4.8 mi (8 km) e of ferry dock, follow signs; in la Baleine sector; access by ferry boat. Ext/int corridors. **Pets:** Accepted.
🍴 🕃 ⊠ 🛜 ⊠

JONQUIÈRE
▼▼▼ **Delta Saguenay Hotel** 🅷

(418) 548-3124. **Call for rates.** 2675 boul du Royaume G7S 5B8. Hwy 70 exit 39, just ne, follow signs. Int corridors. **Pets:** Accepted.
🍴 🕃 ⊠ 🛜 ⊠ 🔌 💻

LAC-BROME (KNOWLTON)
▼▼ **Auberge Knowlton** 🅲🅸

(450) 242-6886. **Call for rates.** 286 chemin Knowlton J0E 1V0. Corner of Hwy 104 and Rt 243; center. Int corridors. **Pets:** Accepted.
🍴 🛜 ⊠

LA MALBAIE
(CAA) ▼▼▼ ▼▼▼ **Fairmont Le Manoir Richelieu** 🅷

(418) 665-3703. **$149-$299, 3 day notice.** 181 rue Richelieu G5A 1X7. On Rt 362, 2.6 mi (4.1 km) w of jct Rt 138. Int corridors. **Pets:** $25 daily fee/room. Service with restrictions, supervision.
🆂 🄴🄲🄾 🕃 🍴 🕃 ⊠ 🛜 🔌 💻

▼▼▼ ▼▼▼ **La Pinsonnière** 🅲🅸

(418) 665-4431. **Call for rates.** 124 rue St-Raphael G5A 1X9. Just off Rt 138, follow signs; in Cap-a-L'Aigle sector. Int corridors.
Pets: Accepted. 🍴 🕃 ⊠ 🛜 ⊠ 🔌 💻

L'ANCIENNE-LORETTE
▼▼▼ **Comfort Inn** 🅷

(418) 872-5900. **$95-$150.** 1255 boul Duplessis G2G 2B4. Jct boul Duplessis and Wilfrid-Hamel (Hwy 138). Int corridors. **Pets:** Medium, other species. $25 one-time fee/pet. Designated rooms, service with restrictions, crate. 🄴🄲🄾 🛜 ⊠ 🔌 💻

LAVAL
(CAA) ▼▼▼▼ **BEST WESTERN PLUS Laval-Montreal** 🅷

(450) 681-9000. **$124-$134.** 3655 Autoroute des Laurentides H7L 3H7. Hwy 15 exit 10, just n on east side service road. Int corridors. **Pets:** Medium, other species. $10 daily fee/pet. Designated rooms, service with restrictions, supervision. 🆂 🍴 🕃 🛜 ⊠ 🔌 💻

(CAA) ▼▼▼ **Comfort Inn** 🅷

(450) 686-0600. **$125-$135.** 2055 Autoroute des Laurentides H7S 1Z6. Hwy 15 exit 8 (boul St-Martin), e on boul St-Martin, 0.4 mi (0.7 km) n on boul Le Corbusier, then just w on boul Tessier. Int corridors. **Pets:** Medium. $25 one-time fee/pet. Service with restrictions, supervision. 🆂 🄴🄲🄾 🍴 🛜 🔌 💻

▼▼▼ **Econo Lodge** 🅷

(450) 681-6411. **$75-$125.** 1981 boul Cure-Labelle H7T 1L4. Hwy 15 exit 8 (boul St-Martin) northbound; exit 10 southbound 1.3 mi (2 km) w on boul St-Martin ouest, then 0.3 mi (0.5 km) n. Ext/int corridors. **Pets:** Medium. Service with restrictions, supervision.
🕃 🛜 🔌 💻

(CAA) ▼▼▼ **Quality Suites Laval** 🅷

(450) 686-6777. **$132-$142.** 2035 Autoroute des Laurentides H7S 1Z6. Hwy 15 exit 8 (boul St-Martin), n 0.4 mi (0.7 km) n on boul Tessier, then just w on boul Tessier. Int corridors. **Pets:** Medium. $25 one-time fee/pet. Designated rooms, service with restrictions, supervision.
🆂 🄴🄲🄾 🛜 ⊠ 🔌 💻

LÉVIS
▼▼▼▼ **Comfort Inn & Suites Rive-Sud Québec** 🅷

(418) 836-3336. **$123-$152.** 495 Rt du Pont G7A 2N9. Hwy 20 exit 311, just ne on Rt 116; in St-Nicolas sector. Int corridors.
Pets: Accepted. 🕃 🛜 ⊠ 🔌 💻

▼▼▼ **Comfort Inn Levis** 🅷

(418) 835-5605. **$95-$200.** 10 du Vallon est G6V 9J3. Hwy 20 exit 325S eastbound; exit 325 westbound. Int corridors. **Pets:** Accepted.
🄴🄲🄾 🛜 🔌 💻

(CAA) ▼▼▼ **Hotel-Motel Hospitalite** 🅼

(418) 837-6664. **$70-$130.** 3500 Blvd De La Rive sud G6W 6N7. Jct chemin des Iles, just s. Ext corridors. **Pets:** Accepted.
🆂 🍴 🛜 💻

LOUISEVILLE
▼▼ **Gite du Carrefour et Maison historique J.L.L. Hamelin** 🅱🅱

(819) 228-4932. **$65-$95, 15 day notice.** 11 ave St-Laurent ouest J5V 1J3. On Rt 138; Hwy 40 exit 174 westbound; exit 166 eastbound; center. Int corridors. **Pets:** No service, supervision.
🍴 🛜 ⊠ 🅰 🆆 🆉 💻

MONTEBELLO
(CAA) ▼▼▼ ▼▼▼ **Fairmont Le Château Montebello** 🅷 🐾

(819) 423-6341. **$179-$559, 3 day notice.** 392 rue Notre-Dame J0V 1L0. On Rt 148, just w of Rt 323. Int corridors. **Pets:** Dogs only. $39 daily fee/pet. Designated rooms, service with restrictions, crate.
🆂 🄴🄲🄾 🍴 🕃 ⊠ 🕃 ⊠ 🔌 💻

MONT-LAURIER
(CAA) ▼▼▼▼ **BEST WESTERN PLUS Mont-Laurier** 🅷

(819) 623-5252. **$121.** 1231 boul Albiny-Paquette J9L 1M6. On Rt 117; center. Ext/int corridors. **Pets:** Accepted.
🆂 🕃 🍴 🕃 🛜 🔌 💻

▼▼▼ **Comfort Inn** 🅷
(819) 623-6465. **$122-$137.** 700 boul Albiny-Paquette J9L 1L4. On Rt 117; center. Ext/int corridors. **Pets:** Small. $25 one-time fee/room. Designated rooms, service with restrictions, supervision.

🔳 🍴 ⊠ 📶 ✕ 🛗 🖥

⑭ ▼▼▼ **Quality Inn Mont-Laurier** 🅷
(819) 623-3555. **$120-$142.** 111 boul Albiny-Paquette J9L 1J2. On Rt 117; center. Ext/int corridors. **Pets:** Accepted.

SAVE 🍴 ⊇ ⊠ 📶 🛗 🖥

MONTRÉAL *(Restaurants p. 647)*

⑭ ▼▼▼▼ **Chateau Versailles Hotel** 🅷
(514) 933-3611. **Call for rates.** 1659 rue Sherbrooke ouest H3H 1E3. Corner of rue St-Mathieu. Int corridors. **Pets:** Accepted.

SAVE 📶 ✕ 🖥

⑭ ▼▼▼▼ **Delta Montreal** 🅷 🐾
(514) 286-1986. **$159-$399.** 475 ave du President-Kennedy H3A 1J7. Corner of rue City Councillors. Int corridors. **Pets:** Small, other species. $35 one-time fee/pet. Designated rooms, supervision.

SAVE ECO 🍴 ⊇ ⊠ 📶 ✕ 🛗 🖥

⑭ ▼▼▼▼ **Fairmont The Queen Elizabeth** 🅷 🐾
(514) 861-3511. **$169-$359.** 900 boul Rene-Levesque ouest H3B 4A5. Between rues University and Mansfield. Int corridors. **Pets:** Other species. $25 daily fee/room. Supervision.

SAVE ECO 🔳 🍴 ⊾ᴹ ⊇ ⊠ 📡 🛗 🖥

⑭ ▼▼▼ **Holiday Inn Express Hotel & Suites Montreal Centre-Ville** 🅷
(514) 448-7100. **$109-$209.** 155 boul Rene-Levesque est H2X 3Z8. Corner of rue de Bullion. Int corridors. **Pets:** Accepted.

SAVE ECO 📶 🛗 🖥

⑭ ▼▼▼ **Hotel 10 Montreal** 🅷
(514) 843-6000. **$149-$549.** 10 rue Sherbrooke ouest H2X 4C9. Corner of boul St-Laurent. Int corridors. **Pets:** Other species. $50 one-time fee/pet. Service with restrictions, crate. SAVE 🍴 📶 ✕ 🛗 🖥

⑭ ▼▼▼▼ **Hotel Bonaventure Montreal** 🅷
(514) 878-2332. **$199-$699.** 900 rue de la Gauchetiere ouest H5A 1E4. Corner of rue Mansfield. Int corridors. **Pets:** $50 one-time fee/room. Designated rooms, service with restrictions, crate.

SAVE ECO 🍴 ⊾ᴹ 📶 🛗 🖥

▼▼▼ **Hôtel Espresso Montréal Centre-Ville/Downtown** 🅷
(514) 938-4611. **Call for rates.** 1005 rue Guy H3H 2K4. Just s of boul Rene-Levesque. Int corridors. **Pets:** Accepted.

🍴 ⊇ ⊠ 📶 ✕ 🛗 🖥

⑭ ▼▼▼▼ **Hotel Gault** 🅷
(514) 904-1616. **$240-$720, 3 day notice.** 449 rue Ste-Helene H2Y 2K9. Just s of rue Notre-Dame. Int corridors. **Pets:** Accepted.

SAVE 🍴 📶 ✕ 🛗 🖥

⑭ ▼▼▼▼ **Hotel Gouverneur Place Dupuis** 🅷
(514) 842-4881. **$109-$399.** 1415 rue St-Hubert H2L 3Y9. Between boul de Maisonneuve and rue Ste-Catherine. Int corridors.
Pets: Accepted. SAVE ECO 🍴 ⊇ 📶 ✕ 🛗 🖥

⑭ ▼▼▼▼ **Hôtel Le Crystal** 🅷 🐾
(514) 861-5550. **Call for rates.** 1100 rue de la Montagne H3G 0A1. Corner of boul Rene-Levesque. Int corridors. **Pets:** Medium. $75 one-time fee/room. Service with restrictions, crate.

SAVE ECO 🍴 ⊾ᴹ ⊇ ⊠ 📶 ✕ 🛗 🖥

▼▼ ▼▼ **Hôtel Le Germain Montréal** 🅷
(514) 849-2050. **$229-$319.** 2050 rue Mansfield H3A 1Y9. Corner of ave du President-Kennedy. Int corridors. **Pets:** Accepted.

🍴 📶 ✕ 🛗 🖥

⑭ ▼▼▼ **Hôtel Le St-James** 🅷
(514) 841-3111. **$400-$975.** 355 rue St-Jacques H2Y 1N9. Corner of rue St-Pierre. Int corridors. **Pets:** Accepted.

SAVE 🍴 ⊠ 📶 🛗 🖥

⑭ ▼▼▼▼ **Hôtel Omni Mont-Royal** 🅷 🐾
(514) 284-1110. **$169-$279.** 1050 rue Sherbrooke ouest H3A 2R6. Corner of rue Peel. Int corridors. **Pets:** Small, dogs only. $50 one-time fee/room. Designated rooms, service with restrictions, supervision.

SAVE 🍴 ⊇ ⊠ 📶 ✕ 🛗 🖥

▼▼▼ **Hotel St-Paul** 🅷
(514) 380-2222. **$179-$299.** 355 rue McGill H2Y 2E8. Corner of rue St-Paul. Int corridors. **Pets:** Accepted. 🍴 📶 ✕ 🖥

⑭ ▼▼▼ **Hotel Travelodge Montreal Centre** 🅷
(514) 874-9090. **$84-$139.** 50 boul Rene-Levesque ouest H2Z 1A2. Between rues Clark and St-Urbain. Int corridors. **Pets:** Accepted.

SAVE ECO 📶 ✕ 🛗 🖥

⑭ ▼▼▼▼ **Hyatt Regency Montreal** 🅷
(514) 982-1234. **$89-$419.** 1255 rue Jeanne-Mance H5B 1E5. Corner of rue Ste-Catherine. Int corridors. **Pets:** Accepted.

SAVE 🍴 ⊾ᴹ ⊇ ⊠ 📡 🛗 🖥

⑭ ▼▼▼▼ **InterContinental Montréal** 🅷
(514) 987-9900. **$159-$990.** 360 rue St-Antoine ouest H2Y 3X4. Corner of rue St-Pierre. Int corridors. **Pets:** Accepted.

SAVE ECO 🍴 ⊇ ⊠ 📡 ✕ 🛗 🖥

⑭ ▼▼▼ **L'Appartement Hotel** 🅷
(514) 284-3634. **$134-$234.** 455 rue Sherbrooke ouest H3A 1B7. Corner of rue Durocher. Int corridors. **Pets:** Service with restrictions, supervision. SAVE ECO ⊇ 📶 ✕ 🛗 🖥

⑭ ▼▼▼▼ **Le Centre Sheraton** 🅷 🐾
(514) 878-2000. **$189-$759.** 1201 boul Rene-Levesque ouest H3B 2L7. Between rues Drummond and Stanley. Int corridors. **Pets:** Medium. Service with restrictions, supervision.

SAVE ECO 🔳 🍴 ⊇ ⊠ 📡 ✕ 🛗 🖥

⑭ ▼▼▼▼ **Le Meridien Versailles-Montreal** 🅷
(514) 933-8111. **Call for rates.** 1808 rue Sherbrooke ouest H3H 1E5. Corner of rue St-Mathieu. Int corridors. **Pets:** Accepted.

SAVE 🍴 📶 ✕ 🛗 🖥

⑭ ▼▼▼▼ **Le Saint-Sulpice Hôtel & Suites Montréal** 🅷
(514) 288-1000. **$189-$539.** 414 rue St-Sulpice H2Y 2V5. Just n of rue St-Paul. Int corridors. **Pets:** Accepted. SAVE 🍴 📶 ✕ 🛗 🖥

⑭ ▼▼▼▼ **Le Square Phillips Hotel & Suites** 🅷
(514) 393-1193. **$149-$399.** 1193 Place Phillips H3B 3C9. Between rue Ste-Catherine and boul Rene-Levesque. Int corridors. **Pets:** Service with restrictions. SAVE ECO 🍴 ⊇ 📶 ✕ 🛗 🖥

⑭ ▼▼▼▼ **Le Westin Montréal** 🅷
(514) 380-3333. **Call for rates.** 270 rue St-Antoine ouest H2Y 0A3. Corner of rue Jeanne-Mance. Int corridors. **Pets:** Accepted.

SAVE 🍴 ⊾ᴹ ⊇ ⊠ 📶 ✕ 🛗 🖥

⑭ ▼▼▼▼ **Loews Hôtel Vogue** 🅷
(514) 285-5555. **$169-$899.** 1425 rue de la Montagne H3G 1Z3. Between rue Ste-Catherine and boul de Maisonneuve. Int corridors. **Pets:** Accepted. SAVE 🍴 📶 ✕ 🛗 🖥

▼▼ ▼▼ **Novotel Montreal Centre** 🅷
(514) 861-6000. **$119-$499.** 1180 rue de la Montagne H3G 1Z1. Between rue Ste-Catherine and boul Rene-Levesque. Int corridors. **Pets:** Medium. $35 one-time fee/room. Designated rooms, service with restrictions, supervision. ECO 🍴 📶 🛗 🖥

▼▼▼▼ **Parc Suites Hotel** �H

(514) 985-5656. **$99-$199, 3 day notice.** 3463 ave du Parc H2X 2H6. Between rues Sherbrooke and Milton. Int corridors. **Pets:** $20 daily fee/pet. Service with restrictions. 🛜 ✕ 📠 💻

▼▼▼▼ **Residence Inn by Marriott Montreal Airport** �H

(514) 336-9333. **$146-$240.** 6500 Place Robert-Joncas H4M 2Z5. Hwy 40 exit 64 (boul Cavendish), 0.3 mi (0.5 km) w on north side service road, then just n on rue Beaulac. Int corridors. **Pets:** Accepted.

🅔🅒🅞 🍽 ⅙ᴹ 🏊 ✕ 🛜 ✕ 📠 💻

🅐🅐 ▼▼▼▼ **Residence Inn by Marriott Montreal-Downtown** �H

(514) 982-6064. **$139-$298.** 2045 rue Peel H3A 1T6. Between rue Sherbrooke and boul de Maisonneuve. Int corridors. **Pets:** Other species. $100 one-time fee/room. Service with restrictions, crate.

🅢🅐🅥🅔 🅔🅒🅞 🛜 ✕ 📠 💻

🅐🅐 ▼▼▼▼ **Residence Inn by Marriott Montreal Westmount** �H

(514) 935-9224. **$108-$223.** 2170 ave Lincoln H3H 2N5. Just e of rue Atwater. Int corridors. **Pets:** Accepted.

🅢🅐🅥🅔 🅔🅒🅞 ⅙ᴹ 🏊 🛜 ✕ 📠 💻

🅐🅐 ▼▼▼▼▼ **The Ritz-Carlton Montréal** �H 🐾

(514) 842-4212. **$505-$695.** 1228 rue Sherbrooke ouest H3G 1H6. Corner of rue de la Montagne. Int corridors. **Pets:** Small. $300 one-time fee/room. Service with restrictions, supervision.

🅢🅐🅥🅔 🍽 ⅙ᴹ 🏊 ✕ 🛜 ✕ 📠 💻

🅐🅐 ▼▼▼▼ ▼▼▼▼ **Sofitel Montréal Le Carré Doré** �H 🐾

(514) 285-9000. **$209-$600, 3 day notice.** 1155 rue Sherbrooke ouest H3A 2N3. Corner of rue Stanley. Int corridors. **Pets:** Other species. Designated rooms, supervision.

🅢🅐🅥🅔 🅔🅒🅞 🍽 ✕ 🛜 ✕ 📠 💻

🅐🅐 ▼▼▼▼ ▼▼▼▼ **W Montréal** �H 🐾

(514) 395-3100. **$239-$659.** 901 Square Victoria H2Z 1R1. Corner of rue St-Antoine. Int corridors. **Pets:** Medium, other species. $100 one-time fee/room, $25 daily fee/pet. Service with restrictions.

🅢🅐🅥🅔 🍽 ⅙ᴹ 🏊 ✕ 📠 💻

MONT-TREMBLANT

🅐🅐 ▼▼▼▼ ▼▼▼▼ **Fairmont Tremblant** �H

(819) 681-7000. **$199-$599, 7 day notice.** 3045 chemin de la Chapelle J8E 1E1. In Mont-Tremblant Resort Centre. Int corridors. **Pets:** Dogs only. $35 daily fee/pet. Designated rooms, supervision.

🅢🅐🅥🅔 🅔🅒🅞 ⊟ 🍽 🏊 ⅙ᴹ ✕ 🛜 ✕ 📠 💻

▼▼▼▼ **Le Grand Lodge Mont-Tremblant** �H

(819) 425-2734. **$147-$327.** 2396 rue Labelle J8E 1T8. On Rt 327, 0.3 mi (0.4 km) s of Montee Ryan. Int corridors. **Pets:** Accepted.

🍽 🏊 ✕ 🛜 ✕ 📠 💻

🅐🅐 ▼▼▼▼ ▼▼▼▼ **Le Westin Resort & Spa, Tremblant** �H

(819) 681-8000. **Call for rates.** 100 chemin Kandahar J8E 1E2. Hwy 117 N exit 119 (Montee Ryan), 6 mi (10 km) e, follow signs. Int corridors. **Pets:** Accepted. 🅢🅐🅥🅔 🍽 🏊 ✕ 🛜 ✕ 📠 💻

ORFORD

▼▼▼▼ **Hotel Cheribourg** �H

(819) 843-3308. **$120-$260.** 2603 chemin du Parc J1X 8C8. Hwy 10 exit 118, 1.9 mi (3 km) n on Hwy 141. Ext/int corridors. **Pets:** Accepted.

🍽 🏊 ✕ 🛜 ✕ 📠 💻

PERCÉ

▼ **Au Pic de l'Aurore** 🅜

(418) 782-2151. **$78-$220, 3 day notice.** 1 Rt 132 W G0C 2L0. 1.2 mi (2 km) w from village. Ext corridors. **Pets:** Large, dogs only. $25 one-time fee/pet. Designated rooms, service with restrictions, supervision.

🍽 🛜 ✕ 📠 💻

▼▼▼▼ **Hotel La Normandie** �H

(418) 782-2112. **$79-$259.** 221 Rt 132 ouest G0C 2L0. Center. Int corridors. **Pets:** Small. $30 one-time fee/pet. Designated rooms, service with restrictions, crate. 🍽 🛜 ✕ 🎦 📠

▼▼▼▼ **Hotel/Motel Le Mirage** 🅜

(418) 782-5151. **$89-$198.** 288 Rt 132 ouest G0C 2L0. On Rt 132. Ext corridors. **Pets:** Small, dogs only. $15 daily fee/pet. Designated rooms, supervision. 🍽 🏊 🛜 ✕ 📠

▼▼▼▼ **Hotel • Motel Manoir de Percé** �H

(418) 782-2022. **$79-$185, 3 day notice.** 212 Rt 132 G0C 2L0. Center. Ext/int corridors. **Pets:** Dogs only. $25 one-time fee/room. Service with restrictions, supervision. 🍽 🛜 ✕ 📠

POINTE-CLAIRE

🅐🅐 ▼▼▼▼ **Quality Suites Montreal Aeroport, Pointe-Claire** �H

(514) 426-5060. **$129-$185.** 6300 Rt Transcanadienne H9R 1B9. Hwy 40 exit 52 eastbound, south side service road; exit westbound, follow signs for boul St-Jean sud and Hwy 40 est to access south side service road. Int corridors. **Pets:** Medium. $25 daily fee/room. Designated rooms, service with restrictions, supervision.

🅢🅐🅥🅔 🅔🅒🅞 🍽 ⅙ᴹ 🛜 📠 💻

QUÉBEC *(Restaurants p. 647)*

▼▼▼▼ **ALT Hotel-Québec** �H 🐾

(418) 658-1224. **$149-$189.** 1200 ave Germain-des-Pres G1V 3M7. Just n of boul Laurier; facing Laurie Québec. Int corridors. **Pets:** $30 daily fee/room. Designated rooms, service with restrictions, supervision.

🍽 🛜 ✕ 📠 💻

▼▼▼▼ **Appartements La Pergola** 🅒🅞

(418) 809-8814. **Call for rates.** 405 boul Rene-Levesque ouest G1S 1S2. Between aves Moncton and des Erables. Int corridors. **Pets:** Accepted. 🍽 🛜 ✕ 📠 💻

▼▼▼▼ **Auberge Place d'Armes** �H

(418) 694-9485. **Call for rates.** 24 rue Ste-Anne G1R 3X3. Just w of rue du Trésor. Int corridors. **Pets:** Accepted. 🍽 🛜 ✕ 📠 💻

🅐🅐 ▼▼▼▼ **BEST WESTERN PLUS City Centre/Centre-Ville** �H

(418) 649-1919. **$110-$500.** 330 rue de la Couronne G1K 6E6. Corner of rue du Roi. Int corridors. **Pets:** Large. $15 daily fee/room. Service with restrictions, crate. 🅢🅐🅥🅔 ⊟ 🍽 🏊 🛜 ✕ 📠 💻

▼▼▼▼ **Delta Quebec** �H

(418) 647-1717. **$144-$364.** 690 boul Rene-Levesque est G1R 5A8. Just w of boul Honore-Mercier. Int corridors. **Pets:** Accepted.

🅔🅒🅞 🍽 🏊 🛜 ✕ 📠 💻

🅐🅐 ▼▼▼▼ ▼▼▼▼ **Fairmont Le Château Frontenac** �H

(418) 692-3861. **$199-$489, 3 day notice.** 1 rue des Carrieres G1R 4P5. In Old Québec. Int corridors. **Pets:** Accepted.

🅢🅐🅥🅔 🅔🅒🅞 🍽 🏊 ✕ 🎦 ✕ 📠 💻

🅐🅐 ▼▼▼▼ ▼▼▼▼ **Hilton Québec** �H

(418) 647-2411. **$199-$359.** 1100 boul Rene-Levesque est G1R 4P3. Corner of ave Honore-Mercier. Int corridors. **Pets:** Accepted.

🅢🅐🅥🅔 🍽 🏊 ✕ 🎦 📠 💻

▼▼▼ **Hotel & Suites Normandin** �H

(418) 622-1611. **$116-$249.** 4700 boul Pierre-Bertrand G2J 1A4. Hwy 40 exit 312N eastbound to boul Pierre-Bertrand, then n to rue Bouvier; exit westbound, just w. Int corridors. **Pets:** Accepted.

🍽 ⅙ᴹ 🛜 ✕ 📠 💻

▼▼▼▼ **Hotel Champlain Vieux-Québec** �H

(418) 694-0106. **Call for rates.** 115 rue Ste-Anne G1R 3X6. Between rue Ste-Angele and St-Stanislas. Int corridors. **Pets:** Accepted.

🛜 ✕ 📠

▼▼ **Hôtel Citadelle** H
(418) 871-3938. **Call for rates.** 4800 boul Wilfrid-Hamel G1P 2J9. Just e of Hwy 73. Ext/int corridors. **Pets:** Accepted. 🛰 🛗 💻

(CAA) ▼▼ **Hotel Clarion Québec** H
(418) 653-4901. **$89-$184.** 3125 boul Hochelaga G1V 4A8. Hwy 73 exit 136 (boul Hochelaga ouest). Int corridors. **Pets:** Other species. $15 daily fee/room. Designated rooms, service with restrictions, crate.
[SAVE] 🍴 ⤳ 🗙 🛰 🗙 🛗 💻

▼▼▼ **Hotel Dauphin Québec City** H
(418) 688-3888. **$99-$259.** 400 rue du Marais G1M 3R1. Hwy 40 exit 312S (Pierre-Bertrand sud), just w of Rt 358. Int corridors.
Pets: Accepted. [ECO] 🛗M 🛰 🗙 🛗 💻

▼▼▼▼ **Hôtel Le Germain Dominion** H
(418) 692-2224. **$189-$415, 3 day notice.** 126 rue St-Pierre G1K 4A8. Corner of rue St-Paul. Int corridors. **Pets:** Accepted. 🛰 🗙 💻

▼▼▼ **Hotel Super 8 Québec Ste-Foy** H
(418) 877-6888. **$80-$168.** 7286 boul Wilfred-Hamel G2G 1C1. Hwy 138, 0.7 mi (1.1 km) w of Hwy 540 (Autoroute Duplessis). Int corridors.
Pets: Medium. $20 daily fee/pet. Designated rooms, service with restrictions, supervision. [ECO] ⤳ 🛰 🗙 🛗 💻

(CAA) ▼▼▼ **Le Bonne Entente** H
(418) 653-5221. **$159-$499.** 3400 chemin Ste-Foy G1X 1S6. Hwy 540 (Autoroute Duplessis) exit chemin Ste-Foy, just w. Int corridors.
Pets: Accepted. [SAVE] 🍴 ♿ ⤳ 🗙 🛰 🗙 💻

▼▼▼ **Le Port-Royal Hotel & Suites** H
(418) 692-2777. **Call for rates.** 144 rue St-Pierre G1K 8N8. In Old Port district of Old Québec. Int corridors. **Pets:** Accepted.
🍴 🛰 🗙 🛗 💻

(CAA) ▼▼▼ **L'Hotel du Capitole** H
(418) 694-4040. **$135-$335.** 972 rue St-Jean G1R 1R5. Corner of des Glacis. Int corridors. **Pets:** $50 daily fee/pet. Service with restrictions, supervision. [SAVE] 🍴 🛰 🗙 🛗 💻

▼▼▼ **L'Hôtel du Vieux-Québec** H
(418) 692-1850. **Call for rates.** 1190 rue St-Jean G1R 1S6. Corner of rue de l'Hotel-Dieu. Int corridors. **Pets:** Accepted.
[ECO] 🍴 🛰 🗙 🛗 💻

▼▼ **N Hôtel** H
(418) 666-1226. **$89-$159.** 3390 boul Ste-Anne G1E 3L7. Hwy 440 exit Francois-de-Laval. Int corridors. **Pets:** Accepted. 🛰 🗙 🛗

(CAA) ▼▼ ▼▼ **Relais & Châteaux Auberge Saint-Antoine** H 🐾
(418) 692-2211. **$209-$1500, 3 day notice.** 8 rue St-Antoine G1K 4C9. Corner of rue Dalhousie. Int corridors. **Pets:** $30 daily fee/room. Crate.
[SAVE] 🍴 🗙 🛰 🗙 🛗 💻

(CAA) ▼▼▼▼ **TRYP Wyndham Hotel PUR** H
(418) 647-2611. **$105-$189.** 395 rue de la Couronne G1K 7X4. Corner of rue St-Joseph est. Int corridors. **Pets:** Medium, dogs only. $25 daily fee/room. Supervision. [SAVE] 🍴 🛗M ⤳ 🛰 🗙 🛗

RIGAUD
▼▼ **Howard Johnson** H
(450) 458-7779. **$89-$119.** 93 Montee Lavigne (Rt 201) J0P 1P0. Hwy 40 exit 17, just ne. Int corridors. **Pets:** Accepted. 🛰 🗙 🛗 💻

RIMOUSKI
▼▼ **Comfort Inn** H
(418) 724-2500. **$120-$140.** 455 boul St-Germain ouest G5L 3P2. On Rt 132. Int corridors. **Pets:** Dogs only. $30 one-time fee/pet. No service, supervision. [ECO] 🍴 🛰 🗙 🛗 💻

(CAA) ▼▼ **Hotel Gouverneur Rimouski** H
(418) 723-4422. **$89-$169.** 155 boul Rene-Lepage E G5L 1P2. On Rt 132. Int corridors. **Pets:** Large. $25 one-time fee/room. Designated rooms, service with restrictions, supervision.
[SAVE] 🍴 ⤳ 🛰 🛗 💻

▼▼ **Hotel L'Empress** H
(418) 723-6944. **Call for rates.** 360 Montee Industrielle & Commerciale G5M 1X1. Hwy 20 exit 614, 2.1 mi (3.4 km) n. Int corridors.
Pets: Dogs only. $20 daily fee/room. Designated rooms, service with restrictions. 🗙 🍴 🛰 🛗 💻

RIVIÈRE-DU-LOUP
▼▼ **Comfort Inn** H
(418) 867-4162. **$100-$130.** 85 boul Cartier G5R 4X4. Hwy 20 exit 507, just se; Hwy 85 exit 96 (Fraserville), follow signs. Int corridors.
Pets: Other species. $25 one-time fee/pet. Service with restrictions, supervision. [ECO] 🛰 🛗 💻

(CAA) ▼▼▼ **Hotel Universel Riviere-du-Loup** H
(418) 862-9520. **$119-$199.** 311 boul Hotel-de-Ville G5R 5S4. At Hwy 132. Ext/int corridors. **Pets:** Other species. $35 one-time fee/room. Designated rooms, supervision. [SAVE] 🍴 🛗M 🛰 🛗 💻

(CAA) ▼▼▼ **Motel Au Vieux Piloteux** M
(418) 867-2635. **$79-$150.** 185 rue Fraser G5R 1E2. Hwy 20 exit 503, 0.6 mi (1 km) e on Rt 132. Ext corridors. **Pets:** Small, dogs only. $10 deposit/room. Designated rooms, no service, supervision.
[SAVE] ⤳ 🗙 🛰 🛗 💻

ROUYN-NORANDA
(CAA) ▼▼▼ **BEST WESTERN PLUS Albert Centre-Ville** H
(819) 762-3545. **$130-$150.** 84 Ave Principale J9X 4P2. Center. Int corridors. **Pets:** Accepted. [SAVE] 🗙 🍴 🗙 🛰 🗙 🛗 💻

▼▼ **Comfort Inn** H
(819) 797-1313. **$121-$151.** 1295 ave Lariviere J9X 6M6. On Rt 117, 2.5 mi (4 km) s from town center. Int corridors. **Pets:** Other species. $25 one-time fee/pet. Service with restrictions, supervision.
[ECO] 🛰 🗙 🛗 💻

▼▼▼ **Hôtel Gouverneur le Noranda** H
(819) 762-2341. **$112-$132.** 41 6ieme rue J9X 1Y8. Corner of rue Murdoch; center. Ext/int corridors. **Pets:** Accepted.
🍴 🗙 🛰 🗙 🛗 💻

ST-APOLLINAIRE
▼▼ **Econo Lodge** H
(418) 881-3335. **$85-$160.** 372 rue Laurier G0S 2E0. Hwy 20 exit 291, just ne. Ext/int corridors. **Pets:** Small. Designated rooms, no service, supervision. 🍴 🛰 🛗 💻

ST-FAUSTIN-LAC-CARRÉ
▼ **Motel Tremblant** M
(819) 688-2102. **Call for rates.** 357 Rt 117 J0T 1J2. On Rt 117, 2.5 mi (4 km) e of exit for city. Ext/int corridors. **Pets:** Accepted.
🍴 ⤳ 🛰 🗙 🛗 💻

ST-HYACINTHE
▼▼▼ **Holiday Inn Express & Suites** H
(450) 251-1111. **$129-$279, 5 day notice.** 1500 rue Johnson est J2S 8W5. Hwy 20 exit 133, just sw on boul Casavant est. Int corridors.
Pets: Medium, other species. $30 one-time fee/room. Service with restrictions, supervision. 🗙 🛗M ⤳ 🛰 🗙 🛗 💻

ST-JEAN-PORT-JOLI
▼▼ **Auberge Du Faubourg** M
(418) 598-6455. **$80-$450, 10 day notice.** 280 ave de Gaspe ouest (Rt 132) G0R 3G0. 1.4 mi (2.4 km) w from jct Rt 204; Hwy 20 exit 414. Ext corridors. **Pets:** Accepted. 🍴 ⤳ 🛰 🗙 🗙 🛗 💻

ST-JEAN-SUR-RICHELIEU

CAA ▼▼▼▼ **Holiday Inn Express** 🅗 ❧

(450) 359-4466. **$110-$209.** 700 rue Gadbois J3A 1V1. Hwy 35 exit 45, e on rue Pierre-Caisse. Int corridors. **Pets:** Medium. $15 daily fee/room. Designated rooms, service with restrictions.

SAVE ⬛ 🛏 📶 ✕ 🅗 🖥

ST-JÉRÔME

▼▼ **Super 8 St-Jerome** 🅗

(450) 438-4388. **$99-$159.** 3 boul J. F. Kennedy J7Y 4B4. Hwy 15 exit 41 southbound, just n; on west side of autoroute. Int corridors. **Pets:** Accepted. 🍴 ⬛ 🛏 📶 ✕ 🅗 🖥

ST-LAURENT

▼▼▼ **Crowne Plaza Montréal Airport** 🅗

(514) 344-1999. **$99-$250.** 6600 Côte de Liesse Expwy H4T 1E3. Hwy 520 exit 3E eastbound on south side service road; exit westbound to rue Ness, follow signs for rue Hickmore and Hwy 520 E. Int corridors. **Pets:** Accepted. 🍴 🛏 📶 ✕ 🅗 🖥

▼▼ **Holiday Inn Montreal-Airport** 🅗

(514) 739-3391. **$109-$209.** 6500 Côte-de-Liesse H4T 1E3. Hwy 520 exit 5 eastbound on south side service road; exit westbound to rue Ness, follow signs for rue Hickmore and Hwy 520 E. Ext/int corridors. **Pets:** Accepted. 🍴 ⬛ 🛏 ✕ 📶 ✕ 🅗 🖥

▼▼▼ **Novotel Montreal Airport** 🅗

(514) 337-3222. **$129-$329.** 2599 boul Alfred-Nobel H4S 2G1. Hwy 40 exit 60 (boul Alfred-Nobel); in St-Laurent Technoparc, just s of south side service road. Int corridors. **Pets:** Accepted.

ECO 🍴 🛏 📶 ✕ 🅗 🖥

STE-AGATHE-DES-MONTS

▼▼ **Super 8 Ste-Agathe** 🅗

(819) 324-8880. **$89-$196.** 500 rue Leonard J8C 0A3. Hwy 15 exit 86, just w on Rt 117 to rue Leonard, 0.3 mi (0.5 km) s. Int corridors. **Pets:** $15 daily fee/pet. Designated rooms, service with restrictions, supervision. ECO 🍴 🛏 📶 ✕ 🅗 🖥

STE-ANNE-DE-BEAUPRÉ

CAA ▼▼▼ **Quality Suites Mont Sainte-Anne** 🅗

(418) 827-1570. **$106-$120.** 9800 boul Ste-Anne G0A 3C0. On Hwy 138. Int corridors. **Pets:** Accepted. SAVE 📶 ✕ 🅗 🖥

STE-EULALIE

▼▼ **Motel Marie-Dan** Ⓜ

(819) 225-4604. **$69-$89.** 311 rue des Bouleaux (Rt 161) G0Z 1E0. Hwy 20 exit 210, follow signs to Rt 161, just s. Ext corridors. **Pets:** Accepted. 🛏 📶 🅗

SEPT-ÎLES

▼▼ **Comfort Inn** 🅗

(418) 968-6005. **$150-$180.** 854 boul Laure G4R 1Y7. 2.8 mi (4.5 km) w on Rt 138. Int corridors. **Pets:** Other species. $25 one-time fee/room. Service with restrictions, supervision. ECO 📶 ✕ 🅗 🖥

SHAWINIGAN

▼▼ **Auberge Escapade Inn** 🅗

(819) 539-6911. **Call for rates.** 3383 rue Garnier G9N 6R4. Hwy 55 exit 217, 0.3 mi (0.5 km) n on Rt 351. Ext/int corridors. **Pets:** Accepted. 🍴 📶 ✕ 🅗

▼▼▼ **Auberge Gouverneur & Centre de Congrès Shawinigan** 🅗

(819) 537-6000. **$84-$285.** 1100 Promenade-du-St-Maurice G9N 1L8. Hwy 55 N exit 211, 2.8 mi (4.4 km) n on Hwy 153, follow signs. Int corridors. **Pets:** Accepted. 🍴 🛏 ✕ 📶 ✕ 🅗 🖥

▼▼▼ **Comfort Inn & Suites** 🅗

(819) 536-2000. **$88-$143.** 500 boul du Capitaine G9P 5J6. Hwy 55 N exit 211, 2.8 mi (4.4 km) n on Hwy 153, then 1.3 mi (2 km) s on Rt 157. Int corridors. **Pets:** Other species. $25 one-time fee/room. Designated rooms, service with restrictions, crate.

ECO 🍴 📶 ✕ 🅗 🖥

SHERBROOKE

▼▼ **Comfort Inn** 🅗 ❧

(819) 564-4400. **$105-$140.** 4295 boul Bourque J1N 1S4. Hwy 410 exit 4W, 0.9 mi (1.5 km) w on Rt 112. Ext/int corridors. **Pets:** Small. $30 one-time fee/pet. Designated rooms, service with restrictions, supervision. ECO 📶 ✕ 🅗 🖥

▼▼▼ **Delta Sherbrooke Hotel and Conference Centre** 🅗

(819) 822-1989. **Call for rates.** 2685 rue King ouest J1L 1C1. Hwy 410 exit 4W, 0.6 mi (1 km) e on Rt 112. Int corridors. **Pets:** Accepted.

ECO 🍴 🛏 ✕ 📶 ✕ 🅗 🖥

TERREBONNE

▼▼ **Super 8 Hotel Lachenaie Terrebonne** 🅗

(450) 582-8288. **$180-$220.** 1155 ave Yves-Blais J6V 0A9. Hwy 640 exit 50, just s on Montee des Pionniers, then just e; in Lachenaie sector. Int corridors. **Pets:** Accepted. ECO 🛏 📶 ✕ 🅗 🖥

THETFORD MINES

▼▼ **Hotel Comfort Inn Thetford Mines** 🅗

(418) 338-0171. **$113-$153.** 123 boul Frontenac ouest G6G 7S7. On Rt 112. Int corridors. **Pets:** $25 daily fee/room. Designated rooms, crate.

ECO 🍴 📶 ✕ 🅗 🖥

TROIS-RIVIÈRES

▼▼ **Comfort Inn** 🅗

(819) 371-3566. **$99-$139.** 6255 rue Corbeil G8Z 4P9. Hwy 55 exit 183 (boul Jean XXIII); 1.3 mi (2 km) n of Laviolette Bridge, 0.3 mi (0.5 km) e. Int corridors. **Pets:** Small. $25 one-time fee/pet. Service with restrictions, supervision. ECO 📶 🅗 🖥

CAA ▼▼▼ **Delta Trois-Rivieres Hotel and Conference Centre** 🅗

(819) 376-1991. **$119-$286, 3 day notice.** 1620 rue Notre-Dame Centre G9A 6E5. Corner of rue St-Roch; center. Int corridors. **Pets:** Accepted.

SAVE ECO 🍴 🛏 ✕ 📶 ✕ 🅗 🖥

CAA ▼▼▼ **Hotel Gouverneur Trois-Rivieres** 🅗

(819) 379-4550. **Call for rates.** 975 rue Hart G9A 4S3. Jct rue Laviolette; center. Int corridors. **Pets:** Medium. $25 one-time fee/room. Designated rooms, service with restrictions, supervision.

SAVE 🍴 🛏 📶 📺 🖥

▼▼▼ **Super 8 Trois-Rivieres** 🅗

(819) 377-5881. **$110-$190.** 3185 boul St-Jean G9B 2M4. Hwy 55 exit 183 (boul Jean XXIII), just nw. Int corridors. **Pets:** Accepted.

ECO 🛏 📶 ✕ 🅗 🖥

VAL-D'OR

▼▼ **Comfort Inn** 🅗

(819) 825-9360. **$119-$155.** 1665 3ieme Ave J9P 1V9. In town center. Int corridors. **Pets:** Small, dogs only. $25 one-time fee/room. Service with restrictions, supervision. ECO 📶 ✕ 🅗 🖥

▼▼▼ **L'Escale Hotel Suites** 🅗

(819) 824-2711. **$130-$165.** 1100 rue L'Escale J9P 4G8. In town center. Ext/int corridors. **Pets:** Designated rooms, service with restrictions, supervision. 🍴 📶 ✕ 🅗 🖥

VICTORIAVILLE

▼▼▼ **Quality Inn & Suites Victoriaville** 🅗

(819) 330-8888. **$117-$160.** 1 boul Arthabaska est G6T 0S4. Jct Rue Notre-Dame Est. Int corridors. **Pets:** Accepted.

🛏 ✕ 📶 ✕ 🅗 🖥

WAKEFIELD

▼▼▼▼ Moulin Wakefield Mill Hotel & Spa 🅗

(819) 459-1838. **$179-$219, 7 day notice.** 60 chemin Mill J0X 3G0. 0.6 mi (1 km) w of Riverside Dr; center. Int corridors. **Pets:** Accepted.

🔲 ⏸ 🏊 ⊠ 🛜 ⊠ 🔲

WEST BROME

▼▼ ▼▼ Auberge & Spa West Brome 🅗

(450) 266-7552. **Call for rates.** 128 Rt 139 J0E 2P0. Jct Rt 104, 1.3 mi (2.1 km) s. Int corridors. **Pets:** Accepted.

🔲 🔌 ⏸ 🏊 ⊠ 🛜 ⊠ 🔲 🔲

SASKATCHEWAN

ESTEVAN

🅐 ▼▼▼▼ BEST WESTERN PLUS Estevan Inn & Suites 🅗 ❀

(306) 634-7447. **Call for rates.** 92 King St S4A 2T5. Hwy 39, 1 mi (1.6 km) n at Kensington Ave. Int corridors. **Pets:** Medium. $20 daily fee/pet. Designated rooms, no service, supervision. (SAVE) ⏩ 🛜 🔲 🔲

▼▼ ▼▼ Microtel Inn & Suites by Wyndham Estevan 🅗

(306) 634-7474. **$133-$142.** 120 King St S4A 2T5. Hwy 39, 1 mi (1.7 km) n at Kensington Ave, just w. Int corridors. **Pets:** Small. $15 daily fee/pet. Designated rooms, service with restrictions, supervision.

🛜 ⊠ 🔲 🔲

▼▼ Motel 6 Estevan 🅜

(306) 634-8666. **Call for rates.** 88 King St E S4A 2A4. Hwy 39, 1 mi (1.7 km) n at Kensington Ave, just e. Int corridors. **Pets:** Other species. Service with restrictions, crate. 🔲ᴹ 🛜 🔲

MOOSE JAW

▼▼ ▼▼ Comfort Inn 🅗

(306) 692-2100. **$125-$187.** 155 Thatcher Dr W S6J 1M1. 0.8 mi (1.2 km) s on Hwy 2 from jct Trans-Canada Hwy 1, just w. Int corridors. **Pets:** Other species. $15 one-time fee/room. Designated rooms, service with restrictions, supervision. 🛜 🔲 🔲

▼▼ ▼▼ Heritage Inn Hotel & Convention Centre 🅗

(306) 693-7550. **$130-$255.** 1590 Main St N S6J 1L3. On Hwy 2, 0.9 mi (1.4 km) s of jct Trans-Canada Hwy 1. Int corridors. **Pets:** Medium, dogs only. $20 daily fee/pet. Designated rooms, service with restrictions, crate. ⏸ ⏩ 🛜 ⊠ 🔲 🔲

▼▼ ▼▼ Prairie Oasis Motel 🅜

(306) 692-4894. **$86-$91.** 955 Thatcher Dr E S6H 4N9. Just s of jct Trans-Canada Hwy 1. Ext corridors. **Pets:** Dogs only. Designated rooms, service with restrictions, crate. ⏩ 🛜 🔲 🔲

▼▼ ▼▼ Super 8-Moose Jaw 🅗

(306) 692-8888. **$117-$142.** 1706 Main St N S6J 1L4. On Hwy 2, 0.7 mi (1.1 km) s of jct Trans-Canada Hwy 1. Int corridors. **Pets:** Other species. $15 daily fee/pet. Designated rooms, service with restrictions, crate. 🛜 🔲 🔲

NORTH BATTLEFORD

▼▼ ▼▼ Super 8 🅗

(306) 446-8888. **$95-$165.** 1006 Hwy 16 S9A 3W2. 0.3 mi (0.5 km) nw of jct Hwy 16 (Yellowhead Hwy). Int corridors. **Pets:** Other species. $25 one-time fee/room. Designated rooms, service with restrictions, supervision. 🛜 🔲 🔲

PRINCE ALBERT

🅐 ▼▼ ▼▼ BEST WESTERN Marquis Inn & Suites 🅗 ❀

(306) 922-9595. **$109-$125, 3 day notice.** 602 Marquis Rd E S6V 7P2. Jct Hwy 3 (6th Ave E). Int corridors. **Pets:** Medium. Service with restrictions, supervision. (SAVE) ⏸ 🛜 ⊠ 🔲 🔲

🅐 ▼▼ ▼▼ Comfort Inn Prince Albert 🅗

(306) 763-4466. **$120-$175.** 3863 2nd Ave W S6W 1A1. On Hwy 2, 1.6 mi (2.6 km) s. Int corridors. **Pets:** Large, other species. $10 daily fee/pet. Service with restrictions, crate. (SAVE) 🔲 🔲ᴹ 🛜 ⊠ 🔲 🔲

▼▼ ▼▼ Super 8-Prince Albert 🅗

(306) 953-0088. **$119-$144.** 4444 2nd Ave W S6V 5R7. On Hwy 2, 1.7 mi (2.7 km) s. Int corridors. **Pets:** Small. $10 daily fee/room. Designated rooms, service with restrictions, supervision.

🔲ᴹ 🛜 ⊠ 🔲 🔲

▼▼ ▼▼ Travelodge Prince Albert 🅜

(306) 764-6441. **$104-$123.** 3551 2nd Ave W S6V 5G1. On Hwy 2, 1.4 mi (2.2 km) s. Ext/int corridors. **Pets:** Accepted.

🔲 ⏸ 🛜 🔲 🔲

REGINA *(Restaurants p. 647)*

🅐 ▼▼▼▼ BEST WESTERN PLUS Eastgate Inn & Suites 🅗

(306) 352-7587. **$148-$214.** 3840 Eastgate Dr S4Z 1A5. Trans-Canada Hwy 1, 1.5 mi (2.4 km) e of Ring Rd, just n. Int corridors. **Pets:** Accepted. (SAVE) 🔲ᴹ 🛜 ⊠ 🔲 🔲

🅐 ▼▼ ▼▼ BEST WESTERN Seven Oaks Inn 🅗

(306) 757-0121. **$160-$225.** 777 Albert St S4R 2P6. On Hwy 6; jct 2nd Ave. Int corridors. **Pets:** Large, other species. $11 daily fee/room. No service, supervision. (SAVE) 🔌 ⏸ 🔲ᴹ ⏩ 🛜 ⊠ 🔲 🔲

🅐 ▼▼ ▼▼ Comfort Inn 🅗

(306) 789-5522. **$114-$189.** 3221 E Eastgate Dr S4Z 1A4. Trans-Canada Hwy 1, 1.3 mi (2 km) e of Ring Rd; at eastern approach to city. Int corridors. **Pets:** $20 daily fee/room. Designated rooms, service with restrictions, crate. (SAVE) 🔲 🛜 🔲 🔲

▼▼ ▼▼ Country Inn & Suites By Carlson 🅗

(306) 789-9117. **$115-$199, 3 day notice.** 3321 Eastgate Bay S4Z 1A4. Trans-Canada Hwy 1, 1.2 mi (2 km) e of Ring Rd; at eastern approach to city. **Pets:** Other species. $25 one-time fee/room. Designated rooms, service with restrictions, crate. 🔲 🛜 ⊠ 🔲 🔲

▼▼ ▼▼ Delta Regina 🅗

(306) 525-5255. **$165-$300.** 1919 Saskatchewan Dr S4P 4H2. At Rose St; center. Int corridors. **Pets:** Accepted.

🔲 🔌 ⏸ ⏩ ⊠ 🛜 🔲 🔲

🅐 ▼▼▼▼ Executive Royal Hotel & Resort Regina 🅗 ❀

(306) 586-6755. **$130.** 4025 Albert St S S4S 3R6. On Hwy 6, 1.2 mi (2 km) n of jct Trans-Canada Hwy 1. Int corridors. **Pets:** Other species. $22 daily fee/room. Designated rooms, service with restrictions, crate.

(SAVE) ⏸ 🛜 ⊠ 🔲 🔲

🅐 ▼▼ ▼▼ Quality Hotel 🅗

(306) 569-4656. **$104-$189.** 1717 Victoria Ave S4P 0P9. Just e of Broad St; downtown. Int corridors. **Pets:** $15 daily fee/pet. Service with restrictions, supervision. (SAVE) 🔲 ⏸ 🛜 🔲 🔲

🅐 ▼▼▼▼ ▼▼ Radisson Plaza Hotel Saskatchewan 🅗

(306) 522-7691. **$160-$500.** 2125 Victoria Ave S4P 0S3. At Scarth St; center. Int corridors. **Pets:** Accepted.

(SAVE) 🔲 ⏸ ⊠ 🛜 ⊠ 🔲 🔲

▼▼▼▼ Sandman Hotel Suites & Spa Regina 🅗

(306) 757-2444. **Call for rates.** 1800 Victoria Ave E S4N 7K3. On Trans-Canada Hwy 1, just e of Ring Rd. Int corridors. **Pets:** Accepted.

🔲 ⏸ 🔲ᴹ ⏩ 🛜 🔲 🔲

▼▼ Super 8 Regina H

(306) 789-8833. **$127-$143.** 2730 Victoria Ave E S4N 6M5. On Trans-Canada Hwy 1, 1 mi (1.6 km) e of Ring Rd; at eastern approach to city. Int corridors. **Pets:** Accepted. 🛜 🔲 🖿

▼▼▼ Wingate by Wyndham H

(306) 584-7400. **$149-$329.** 1700 Broad St S4P 1X4. Jct Saskatchewan Dr; center. Int corridors. **Pets:** Accepted.

ECO 🍴 ♿M 🗙 🔲 🖿

SASKATOON *(Restaurants p. 647)*

CAA ▼▼▼▼ BEST WESTERN PLUS Blairmore H ✿

(306) 242-2299. **$160-$188.** 306 Shillington Cres S7M 1L7. Jct Hwy 7 and 14. Int corridors. **Pets:** Medium, other species. $20 daily fee/room. Designated rooms, service with restrictions, crate.

SAVE 🌊 🛜 🗙 🔲 🖿

CAA ▼▼▼ BEST WESTERN Royal Hotel H ✿

(306) 244-5552. **$140-$156.** 1715 Idylwyld Dr N S7L 1B4. On Hwy 11 (Idylwyld Dr), 0.4 mi (0.7 km) s of jct Circle Dr. Int corridors. **Pets:** Large, other species. $15 daily fee/room. Designated rooms, service with restrictions, crate. SAVE ECO 🍴 ♿M 🛜 🗙 🔲 🖿

CAA ▼▼▼ Colonial Square Inn & Suites H

(306) 343-1676. **$119-$149.** 1301 8th St E S7H 0S7. 1.5 mi (2.4 km) e of jct Hwy 11 (Idylwyld Dr S); 1.4 mi (2.3 km) w of jct Circle Dr. Int corridors. **Pets:** Small, dogs only. $20 daily fee/pet. Designated rooms, service with restrictions, supervision. SAVE 🍴 🛜 🗙 🔲 🖿

CAA ▼▼▼ Comfort Inn M ✿

(306) 934-1122. **$139-$179.** 2155 Northridge Dr S7L 6X6. Just ne of jct Hwy 11 (Idylwyld Dr N) and Circle Dr. Int corridors. **Pets:** Medium. $15 daily fee/room. Designated rooms, service with restrictions, supervision.

SAVE ECO ♿M 🛜 🔲 🖿

▼▼ Country Inn & Suites By Carlson H

(306) 934-3900. **$120-$170.** 617 Cynthia St S7L 6B7. Just w on Circle Dr from jct Hwy 11 (Idylwyld Dr N), just n on Ave CN. Int corridors. **Pets:** Large, other species. $25 one-time fee/room. Designated rooms, service with restrictions, crate. ECO 🛜 🗙 🔲 🖿

CAA ▼▼▼▼ Delta Bessborough H

(306) 244-5521. **$149-$399.** 601 Spadina Cres E S7K 3G8. Jct 21st St E; center. Int corridors. **Pets:** Medium, other species. $35 one-time fee/pet. Service with restrictions, supervision.

SAVE ECO 🔌 🍴 🌊 🗙 🗙 🔲 🖿

▼▼▼ Hilton Garden Inn Saskatoon Downtown H

(306) 244-2311. **$154-$229.** 90 22nd St E S7K 3X6. Just e of jct Hwy 11 (Idylwyld Dr N); at 1st Ave. Int corridors. **Pets:** Accepted.

ECO 🍴 🌊 🛜 🗙 🔲 🖿

▼▼▼ Holiday Inn Express Hotel & Suites Saskatoon H

(306) 384-8844. **$149-$189.** 315 Idylwyld Dr N S7L 0Z1. On Hwy 11 (Idylwyld Dr), just n of jct 23rd St. Int corridors. **Pets:** Accepted.

ECO ♿M 🌊 🛜 🗙 🔲 🖿

▼▼▼ Motel 6 Saskatoon H

(306) 665-6688. **Call for rates.** 231 Marquis Dr S7R 1B7. Just e of jct Trans-Canada Hwy 16; 0.4 mi (0.7 km) w of Hwy 11 (Idylwyld Dr N). Int corridors. **Pets:** Other species. Service with restrictions, crate.

♿M 🌊 🛜 🗙 🔲 🖿

CAA ▼▼▼▼ Radisson Hotel Saskatoon H ✿

(306) 665-3322. **$169-$249, 3 day notice.** 405 20th St E S7K 6X6. At 4th Ave S; center. Int corridors. **Pets:** Designated rooms, service with restrictions, supervision. SAVE ECO 🍴 ♿M 🌊 🛜 🗙 🔲 🖿

CAA ▼▼▼ Ramada Hotel-Saskatoon H

(306) 665-6500. **$140-$280.** 806 Idylwyld Dr N S7L 0Z6. On Hwy 11 (Idylwyld Dr), 2.5 mi (4 km) s of jct Circle Dr. Int corridors. **Pets:** Accepted. SAVE ECO 🍴 🌊 🛜 🔲 🖿

▼▼▼ Sandman Hotel Saskatoon H

(306) 477-4844. **Call for rates.** 310 Circle Dr W S7L 2Y5. Just w of Hwy 11 (Idylwyld Dr). Int corridors. **Pets:** Accepted.

ECO 🍴 ♿M 🌊 🛜 🗙 🔲 🖿

CAA ▼▼▼▼ Sheraton Cavalier Saskatoon Hotel H

(306) 652-6770. **Call for rates.** 612 Spadina Cres E S7K 3G9. Jct 21st St E; center. Int corridors. **Pets:** Accepted.

SAVE ECO 🍴 🌊 🛜 🗙 🔲 🖿

▼▼ Super 8-Saskatoon H

(306) 384-8989. **$127-$150.** 706 Circle Dr E S7K 3T7. 1.3 mi (2 km) e of jct Hwy 11 (Idylwyld Dr N). Ext/int corridors. **Pets:** Accepted.

♿M 🛜 🗙 🔲 🖿

SWIFT CURRENT

CAA ▼▼▼ Comfort Inn Swift Current H

(306) 778-3994. **$125-$130.** 1510 S Service Rd E S9H 3X6. Trans-Canada Hwy 1, just w of 22nd Ave NE. Int corridors. **Pets:** Other species. $20 daily fee/pet. Service with restrictions, supervision.

SAVE ECO 🛜 🗙 🔲 🖿

▼▼ Motel 6 Swift Current H

(306) 778-6060. **$90-$110.** 1185 5th Ave NE S9H 5N7. Trans-Canada Hwy 1, just e of Central Ave N, on N Service Rd W, then just n. Int corridors. **Pets:** Other species. Service with restrictions, crate.

🛜 🗙 🔲

UNITY

▼▼ Prairie Moon Inn & Suites H

(306) 228-3333. **Call for rates.** 103 2nd Ave S S0K 4L0. On Hwy 14, just w. Int corridors. **Pets:** Very small, dogs only. $10 daily fee/room. Designated rooms, service with restrictions, supervision.

🛜 🗙 🔲 🖿

WEYBURN

▼▼▼ Canalta Hotel H

(306) 842-8000. **Call for rates.** 1360 Sims Ave S4H 3N9. On Hwy 39, just w of Hwy 35. Ext/int corridors. **Pets:** $15 daily fee/room. Designated rooms, service with restrictions, supervision.

ECO ♿M 🗙 🛜 🗙 🔲 🖿

CAA ▼ Perfect Inns & Suites M

(306) 842-2691. **$99-$250.** 238 Sims Ave S4H 2J8. 0.3 mi (0.5 km) w of jct Hwy 35 and 39. Ext/int corridors. **Pets:** Accepted.

SAVE 🛜 🗙 🔲

CAA ▼▼▼ Ramada Inn & Suites H

(306) 842-4994. **$139-$249.** 1420 Sims Ave S4H 3N9. On Hwy 39, just w of Hwy 35. Ext/int corridors. **Pets:** $15 daily fee/room. Designated rooms, service with restrictions, supervision.

SAVE ECO 🌊 🛜 🗙 🔲 🖿

▼▼ Travelodge Hotel Weyburn M

(306) 842-1411. **Call for rates.** 53 Government Rd S S4H 2A2. Jct Simms Ave. Ext/int corridors. **Pets:** Accepted. ECO 🍴 🛜 🔲 🖿

YORKTON

▼▼▼ Days Inn & Suites Yorkton H

(306) 782-3112. **Call for rates.** 1-275 Broadway St E S3N 0N5. Just w of jct Hwy 9, 10 and 16 (Yellowhead Hwy). Int corridors. **Pets:** Accepted. ♿M 🛜 🗙 🔲 🖿

YUKON

DAWSON CITY

▼▼ Klondike Kate's Cabins CA
(867) 993-6527. **$140-$200.** 1102 3rd Ave Y0B 1G0. Corner of 3rd Ave and King St; center. Ext corridors. **Pets:** Accepted.

🍴 &M 🛜 ✕ 🆊 🔌 💻

▼▼ Westmark Inn Dawson City H
(867) 993-5542. **$119-$179.** 813 5th Ave Y0B 1G0. At Harper St. Int corridors. **Pets:** Accepted. 🍴 &M 🛜 ✕ 💻

WHITEHORSE

CAA ▼▼▼ BEST WESTERN Gold Rush Inn H
(867) 668-4500. **$145-$180.** 411 Main St Y1A 2B6. Between 4th and 5th aves; center. Int corridors. **Pets:** Medium, other species. $20 daily fee/pet. Designated rooms, service with restrictions, crate.

SAVE ECO 🛜 ✕ 🆊 💻

CAA ▼▼ Coast High Country Inn H
(867) 667-4471. **$145-$185, 3 day notice.** 4051 4th Ave Y1A 1H1. 0.4 mi (0.6 km) e of Main St. Int corridors. **Pets:** Medium. $15 daily fee/pet. Designated rooms, service with restrictions, crate.

SAVE ECO 🍴 🛜 ✕ 🆊 💻

▼▼ Westmark Whitehorse Hotel & Conference Center H
(867) 393-9700. **$129-$169.** 201 Wood St Y1A 2E4. At 2nd Ave; center. Int corridors. **Pets:** Designated rooms, service with restrictions, supervision. 🍴 &M 📞 ✕ 🆊 🔌 💻

Pet-Friendly Restaurants

United States
Canada

United States

Alabama

BIRMINGHAM

▼▼ **Cosmo's Pizza**
(205) 930-9971. Pizza. Casual Dining. **$3-$24.** 2012 Magnolia Ave 35205. Corner of 20th St S and Magnolia Ave; across from Highlands United Methodist Church; in Five Points South. L D

▼▼▼ **FLIP burger Boutique**
(205) 968-2000. New American. Casual Dining. **$7-$21.** 220 Summit Blvd, Suite 140 35243. Just n of jct US 280 and I-459; in The Summit shopping center. L D M

▼▼▼ **Fuego Cantina and Saloon**
(205) 933-1544. Tex-Mex. Casual Dining. **$8-$18.** 1101 20th St S 35205. Jct 20th St S and 11th Ave S; just se of University Blvd; in Five Points South. L D LATE M N

▼▼▼ **Little Savannah**
(205) 591-1119. Southern Natural/Organic. Casual Dining. **$13-$38.** 3811 Clairmont Ave 35222. Between 38th and 39th sts S; near Highland Golf Course. D

CULLMAN

▼▼ **Rumors Deli & Coffee House**
(256) 737-0911. Sandwiches. Quick Serve. **$5-$9.** 105 1st Ave NE 35055. Across from Clark St NE; downtown. B L

DECATUR

▼▼ **Simp McGhee's**
(256) 353-6284. American. Casual Dining. **$18-$36.** 725 Bank St 35601. Between Vine and Lafayette sts NE; in historic downtown. D

DOTHAN

▼▼ **District Restaurant & Ultra Lounge**
(334) 673-2623. Burgers. Gastropub. **$6-$15.** 158 N Foster St 36303. Between W Main and Troy sts; downtown. D LATE M

EUFAULA

▼▼ **The Cajun Corner**
(334) 616-0816. Cajun. Casual Dining. **$8-$23.** 114 N Eufaula Ave 36027. Corner of W Broad St and US 431; in historic downtown area. L D

FAIRHOPE

▼ **Mary Ann's**
(251) 928-3663. Deli. Casual Dining. **$6-$17.** 85 N Bancroft St 36532. Corner of Equality St; downtown; in Windmill Market. L

HOMEWOOD

▼ **Dave's Pizza**
(205) 871-3283. Pizza. Casual Dining. **$8-$35.** 1819 29th Ave S 35209. Jct US 31, just w. L D

▼▼▼ **DoDiYo's**
(205) 453-9300. Mediterranean. Casual Dining. **$8-$26.** 1831 28th Ave S, Suite 110 35209. Between 18th and 19th sts; downtown; in SoHo Square, behind City Hall. L D M

▼▼ **Nabeel's Cafe and Market**
(205) 879-9292. Greek. Casual Dining. **$7-$19.** 1706 Oxmoor Rd 35209. Jct Central Ave and Oxmoor Rd. L D

HUNTSVILLE

🔺 ▼▼ **Cantina Laredo**
(256) 327-8580. Mexican. Casual Dining. **$12-$26.** 300 The Bridge St NW, Suite 110 35806. I-565 exit 14A, 0.5 mi n on SR 255 (Research Park Blvd), then w on Old Madison Pike; in Bridge Street Town Centre. L D M

▼ **Main St Cafe & Bakery**
(256) 881-0044. Sandwiches Desserts. Quick Serve. **$6-$8.** 7500 S Memorial Pkwy 35802. I-565 exit 19A, 5 mi s on US 231/431/Memorial Pkwy. B L

🔺 ▼▼ **Pane e Vino Pizzeria**
(256) 533-1180. Italian Pizza. Casual Dining. **$7-$15.** 300 Church St 35801. Corner of Williams Ave; downtown. L D M

▼▼▼ **Sage Grille**
(256) 428-5424. Mediterranean. Fine Dining. **$9-$30.** 6800 Governors West NW 35806. I-565 exit 14A, 0.5 mi n on SR 255 (Research Park Blvd), just w on Old Madison Pike, then 0.5 mi n; in The Westin Huntsville. B L D M

▼▼ **Sam & Greg's Pizzeria - Gelateria**
(256) 533-9030. Pizza. Casual Dining. **$6-$25.** 119 North Side Square 35801. Between Jefferson and Washington sts; downtown; across from courthouse. L D

IRONDALE

▼ **Hamburger Heaven**
(205) 951-3570. Burgers. Quick Serve. **$2-$7.** 1703 Crestwood Blvd 35210. I-20 exit 132B, just s on Montevallo Rd, then 0.5 mi e. L D M

MOBILE

▼▼ **Jerusalem Cafe**
(251) 304-1155. Middle Eastern. Casual Dining. **$6-$17.** 4715 Airport Blvd, Suite 330 36608. I-65 exit 3 (Airport Blvd), 3 mi w; in Regency Square Shopping Center; behind Applebee's. L D

MONTGOMERY

▼▼ **Chappy's Deli**
(334) 279-1226. Deli Sandwiches. Casual Dining. **$5-$8.** 8141 Vaughn Rd 36116. I-85 exit 9 (Taylor Rd), 1.5 mi s, then just e; in Peppertree Shopping Center. B L D M

▼▼▼ **Michael's Table**
(334) 272-2500. International. Casual Dining. **$10-$30.** 2960 Zelda Rd, Suite A 36106. I-85 exit 3, 0.8 mi se. L D

▼▼ **Sinclair's Cloverdale**
(334) 834-7462. American. Casual Dining. **$8-$26.** 1051 E Fairview Ave 36106. I-65 exit 170, 1.7 mi e; corner of Boultier Ave. L D

MOUNTAIN BROOK

▼▼ **La Paz Restaurant**
(205) 879-2225. Mexican. Casual Dining. **$7-$17.** 99 Euclid Ave 35213. Just w of Church St. L D

ORANGE BEACH

▼▼ **Cosmo's Restaurant**
(251) 948-9663. Seafood. Casual Dining. **$8-$28.** 25753 Canal Rd 36561. On SR 180, just w of jct SR 161. L D M

PRATTVILLE

◊◊ ◊◊ **Chappy's Deli**
(334) 290-3313. Sandwiches. Family Dining. **$5-$8.** 585 Pinnacle Pl 36066. I-65 exit 179, just w. [B] [L] [D] [&M] [◣]

◊◊ **Fanci Free Boutique & Garden Cafe**
(334) 358-1524. Sandwiches. Casual Dining. **$3-$10.** 146 W Main St 36067. Between Chestnut and Bridge sts; downtown. [L]

TROY

◊◊◊ **Country's Barbecue**
(334) 566-9940. Barbecue. Casual Dining. **$6-$14.** 100 Southland Village, US Hwy 231 36079. Jct US 231/167; in Southland Village. [L] [D]

TUSCALOOSA

◊◊◊◊ **Epiphany Farm-to-Fork**
(205) 344-5583. Southern American. Fine Dining. **$14-$25.** 519 Greensboro Ave 35401. Between University Blvd and 6th St; downtown. [D]

VESTAVIA HILLS

◊◊ ◊◊ **Diplomat Deli**
(205) 979-1515. Sandwiches Deli. Quick Serve. **$6-$20.** 1425 Montgomery Hwy 35216. I-65 exit 252, 1 mi n; in Park South Plaza. [L] [D] [&M]

◊◊ ◊◊ **Mudtown Eat & Drink**
(205) 967-3300. American. Casual Dining. **$9-$29.** 3144 Green Valley Rd 35243. Just e of US 280. [L] [D]

Arizona

CHANDLER

◊◊◊◊ **La Stalla**
(480) 855-9990. Italian. Casual Dining. **$7-$23.** 68 W Buffalo St 85225. Jct Chandler Blvd, just s on Arizona Ave, just w. [L] [D]

CORNVILLE

◊◊ ◊◊ **The Manzanita Restaurant**
(928) 634-8851. Continental. Fine Dining. **$9-$27.** 11425 E Cornville Rd 86325. 4.5 mi e of jct SR 89A. [L] [D]

FLAGSTAFF

◬◞ ◊◊◊◊ **Cottage Place Restaurant**
(928) 774-8431. Continental. Fine Dining. **$21-$37.** 126 W Cottage Ave 86001. Just s of downtown; just w of Beaver St. [D]

◬◞ ◊◊◊◊ **Josephine's**
(928) 779-3400. American. Fine Dining. **$10-$27.** 503 N Humphrey's St 86001. Just n of jct Old Route 66. [L] [D]

GOLD CANYON

◊◊◊◊ **Kokopelli's**
(480) 671-5517. American. Fine Dining. **$8-$33.** 6100 S Kings Ranch Rd 85219. US 60 exit Kings Ranch Rd, 1 mi n; in Gold Canyon Golf Resort. [B] [L] [D]

GRAND CANYON NATIONAL PARK (SOUTH RIM)

◬◞ ◊◊ **We Cook Pizza & Pasta**
(928) 638-2278. Pizza. Quick Serve. **$10-$29.** 605 N Hwy 64 86023. 2 mi s of South Rim entrance. [L] [D]

LAKE HAVASU CITY

◊◊ ◊◊ **The Turtle Grill**
(928) 855-1897. American. Casual Dining. **$9-$35.** 1000 McCulloch Blvd N 86403. 1.4 mi w of London Bridge, follow signs; in The Nautical Beachfront Resort. [B] [L] [D]

PHOENIX

◊◊◊ **Alexi's Grill**
(602) 279-0982. Northern Italian. Casual Dining. **$9-$29.** 3550 N Central Ave 85012. Just n of Osborn Rd. [L] [D]

◊◊◊ **The Arrogant Butcher**
(602) 324-8502. American. Gastropub. **$12-$34.** 2 E Jefferson St, #150 85004. Northwest corner of Jefferson and 1st sts; in CityScape. [L] [D]

◊◊ ◊◊ **Aunt Chilada's Hideaway**
(602) 944-1286. Mexican. Casual Dining. **$6-$18.** 7330 N Dreamy Draw Dr 85020. SR 51 exit 5 (Glendale Ave), 0.4 mi w to 16th St, 0.6 mi to Morten Ave, then just e. [L] [D]

◊◊◊◊ **Cibo Urban Pizzeria Cafe**
(602) 441-2697. Italian. Casual Dining. **$9-$15.** 603 N 5th Ave 85003. Corner of Fillmore St; center. [L] [D]

◊◊◊◊ **North Italian Farmhouse**
(602) 324-5600. Italian. Casual Dining. **$10-$33.** 4925 N 40th St 85018. Jct Camelback Rd, just s. [L] [D]

◊◊◊◊ **Phoenix City Grille**
(602) 266-3001. American. Casual Dining. **$10-$31.** 5816 N 16th St 85016. 0.8 mi n of Camelback Rd. [L] [D]

PINETOP-LAKESIDE

◊◊ **Village Grill**
(928) 368-2424. Burgers. Quick Serve. **$4-$12.** 1477 W White Mountain Blvd, Suite 4 85929. Jct Woodland Rd; in Lakeside. [L] [D]

PRESCOTT

◊◊ ◊◊ **Firehouse Kitchen**
(928) 776-4566. American. Casual Dining. **$8-$34.** 218 W Goodwin St, Suite 101 86303. Just w of Montezuma St. [L] [D]

RIO RICO

◊◊◊ **San Cayetano**
(520) 281-1901. Regional American. Casual Dining. **$9-$25.** 1069 Camino Caralampi 85648. I-19 exit 17 (Rio Rico Dr), just w to Camino Caralampi, then just s; in Esplendor Resort at Rio Rico. [B] [L] [D]

SCOTTSDALE

◊◊◊◊ **The Herb Box**
(480) 289-6160. American. Casual Dining. **$15-$32.** 7134 E Stetson Dr 85251. Jct Scottsdale Rd, just w; in Southbridge District. [L] [D]

◊◊◊◊ **NoRTH**
(480) 948-2055. New Italian. Casual Dining. **$8-$28.** 15024 N Scottsdale Rd, #160 85254. Just w on Greenway Pkwy; in Kierland Commons. [L] [D]

◊◊◊◊ **Persian Room**
(480) 614-1414. Middle Eastern. Fine Dining. **$9-$35.** 17040 N Scottsdale Rd 85255. Jct Bell Rd, just n. [L] [D]

◊◊◊◊ **Stingray Sushi**
(480) 427-2011. Sushi. Casual Dining. **$9-$30.** 15027 N Scottsdale Rd 85260. SR 101 exit 34 (Scottsdale Rd), 2.2 mi s; in Scottsdale Quarter. [L] [D] [LATE]

◊◊◊◊ **Tommy V's Urban Kitchen and Bar**
(480) 427-2264. Italian. Casual Dining. **$15-$26.** 7303 E Indian School Rd 85251. Jct Scottsdale Rd, just e. [L] [D]

▼▼▼ **Zinc Bistro**
(480) 603-0922. French. Casual Dining. **$10-$36.** 15034 N Scottsdale Rd, Suite 140 85254. Just w of jct N Scottsdale Rd and Greenway-Hayden Loop; in Kierland Commons. [L] [D]

SEDONA

▼▼▼ **The Heartline Cafe**
(928) 282-0785. American. Fine Dining. **$8-$30.** 1600 W Hwy 89A 86336. On SR 89A, 1.5 mi s of jct SR 179. [B] [L] [D]

▼▼ **Judi's Restaurant**
(928) 282-4449. American. Casual Dining. **$11-$31.** 40 Soldier's Pass Rd 86336. Jct SR 179, 1 mi w on SR 89A; northeast corner. [L] [D]

▼▼ **Mesa Grill**
(928) 282-2400. Italian. Casual Dining. **$10-$29.** 1185 Airport Rd 86336. Jct SR 179, 1 mi w on SR 89A, 1 mi s. [B] [L] [D] [&M]

🚗 ▼▼▼ **Rene At Tlaquepaque**
(928) 282-9225. Continental. Fine Dining. **$9-$42.** 336 Hwy 179, B-118 86336. SR 89A, 0.3 mi s; in Tlaquepaque Arts & Crafts Village. [L] [D]

▼▼▼ **Shugrue's Hillside Grill**
(928) 282-5300. Seafood. Fine Dining. **$11-$36.** 671 Hwy 179, Suite D 86336. Jct SR 89A, 0.8 mi s; in Hillside Courtyard and Marketplace, Building D, upper level. [L] [D]

▼▼ **Spoke & Wheel Tavern and Eatery**
(928) 203-5334. American. Casual Dining. **$12-$26.** 160 Portal Ln 86336. Jct SR 89A, just s on SR 179, then just w; in Los Abrigados Resort & Spa. [B] [L] [D]

▼▼ **Szechuan Chinese Restaurant & Sushi Bar**
(928) 282-9288. Asian. Casual Dining. **$10-$20.** 1350 W Hwy 89A, Suite 21 86336. Jct SR 179, 1.3 mi w. [L] [D]

SELIGMAN

▼ **Delgadillos Snow Cap Drive-In**
(928) 422-3291. Burgers Desserts. Quick Serve. **$2-$8.** 301 W Chino Ave 86337. I-40 exit 121, 1 mi n, then 0.7 mi e. [L] [AC]

TEMPE

▼▼ **Pita Jungle**
(480) 804-0234. Mediterranean. Casual Dining. **$6-$15.** 1250 E Apache Blvd, Suite 113 85282. 0.4 mi e of jct Rural Rd and Apache Blvd. [L] [D]

TUCSON

▼▼▼ **Dakota Bar & Grill**
(520) 298-7188. American. Casual Dining. **$10-$24.** 6541 E Tanque Verde Rd 85715. Jct Campbell Ave, 5.6 mi e on Grant Rd, just s. [B] [L] [D]

▼▼ **Ghini's French Caffe**
(520) 326-9095. French. Casual Dining. **$7-$13.** 1803 E Prince Rd 85719. Just w of Campbell Ave. [B] [L]

▼▼▼ **McMahon's Steakhouse**
(520) 327-7463. Steak. Casual Dining. **$11-$45.** 2959 N Swan Rd 85712. I-10 exit 256 (Grant Rd), 5.6 mi e, then 0.7 mi n. [L] [D] [&M]

▼▼▼ **NoRTH**
(520) 299-1600. New Italian. Casual Dining. **$9-$29.** 2995 E Skyline Dr 85718. Jct Campbell Ave; northwest corner; in La Encantada Plaza. [L] [D]

▼▼ **Pasco Kitchen & Lounge**
(520) 882-8013. New American. Casual Dining. **$9-$20.** 820 E University Blvd 85719. I-10 exit 257 (Speedway Blvd), 1.5 mi e, 0.3 mi s on Euclid Ave, then just e. [L] [D]

▼▼ **Sullivan's Steakhouse**
(520) 299-4275. Steak. Fine Dining. **$20-$65.** 1785 E River Rd 85718. Just w of Campbell Ave. [L] [D]

WILLIAMS

▼▼ **Cruiser's Route 66 Bar & Grill**
(928) 635-2445. American. Gastropub. **$8-$20.** 233 W Route 66 86046. Jct Route 66 and 3rd St. [L] [D]

▼▼ **Pancho McGillicuddy's**
(928) 635-4150. Mexican. Casual Dining. **$10-$18.** 141 W Railroad Ave 86046. I-40 exit 163, 0.5 mi s. [L] [D] [AC] [➲]

🚗 ▼▼ **Western View Steakhouse**
(928) 635-4400. Steak. Casual Dining. **$17-$30.** 2600 W Route 66 86046. I-40 exit 161, just e; in BEST WESTERN PLUS Inn of Williams. [D] [&M]

Arkansas

EUREKA SPRINGS

▼▼▼ **Rogue's Manor at Sweet Spring**
(479) 253-4911. American. Fine Dining. **$14-$70.** 124 Spring St 72632. Jct US 62, 0.5 mi n on US 62B Historic Loop; in historic district. [D]

California

AGOURA HILLS

▼▼▼ **Padri Cucina Italiana & Martini Bar**
(818) 865-3700. Italian. Fine Dining. **$11-$35.** 29008 Agoura Rd 91301. US 101 exit 36 (Kanan Rd), 0.3 mi w, then just s. [L] [D]

ALISO VIEJO

▼▼ **Cosmo's Italian Kitchen**
(949) 448-9040. Italian. Casual Dining. **$10-$19.** 23411 Aliso Viejo Pkwy, Suite A 92656. I-5 exit 90 (Alicia Pkwy), 1 mi w, 0.4 mi n on Paseo de Valencia, then 1.4 mi w on Laguna Hills Dr (which becomes Aliso Viejo Pkwy); in Aliso Viejo Creek Marketplace. [L] [D] [➲]

AVILA BEACH

▼▼▼ **The Gardens of Avila**
(805) 595-7302. American. Casual Dining. **$10-$34.** 1215 Avila Beach Dr 93405. US 101 exit 195 (Avila Beach Dr), 1 mi w; in Sycamore Mineral Springs. [B] [L] [D] [AC]

▼▼ **The Old Custom House**
(805) 595-7555. American. Casual Dining. **$10-$38.** 404 Front St 93424. US 101 exit 195 (Avila Beach Dr), 3 mi w, then just s. [B] [L] [D]

AZUSA

▼▼▼ **Tulipano Ristorante Italiano**
(626) 967-6670. Italian. Casual Dining. **$9-$22.** 530 S Citrus Ave 91702. I-210 exit 41 (Citrus Ave), 0.4 mi s. [L] [D]

BENICIA

▼▼ **First St Cafe & Catering**
(707) 745-1400. American. Casual Dining. **$9-$25.** 440 First St 94510. I-780 exit 2nd St/Downtown Benicia W, just n on Military St, then 0.5 mi w; jct East E St. [B] [L] [D] [&M]

BERKELEY

🚗 ▼▼▼ **Bistro Liaison**
(510) 849-2155. French. Fine Dining. **$10-$32.** 1849 Shattuck Ave 94709. I-80 exit 11 (University Ave), 2 mi e, then just n at Hearst Ave. [L] [D] [AC]

BEVERLY HILLS

Bouchon
(310) 271-9910. French. Fine Dining. **$18-$49.** 235 N Canon Dr 90210. I-10 exit 7A (La Cienega Blvd), 0.6 mi w, 2 mi n, 1.2 mi w on Wilshire Blvd, then just n. ⎡L⎤ ⎡D⎤

BIG BEAR LAKE

Cowboy Express Steak House
(909) 866-1486. Steak. Casual Dining. **$7-$30.** 40433 Lakeview Dr 92315. 0.5 mi w of Pine Knot Ave, just n of SR 18. ⎡L⎤ ⎡D⎤ ⎡&M⎤

BISHOP

Upper Crust Pizza Company
(760) 872-8153. Pizza. Casual Dining. **$7-$29.** 1180 N Main St 93514. On US 395. ⎡L⎤ ⎡D⎤ ⎡◣⎤

BLYTHE

Rosita's
(760) 922-4090. Mexican. Family Dining. **$6-$16.** 611 W Hobsonway 92225. I-10 exit 239 (Lovekin Blvd), just n, then just e. ⎡B⎤ ⎡L⎤ ⎡D⎤ ⎡◣⎤

CALABASAS

King's Fish House
(818) 225-1979. Seafood. Casual Dining. **$13-$45.** 4798 Commons Way 91302. US 101 exit 30 (Pkwy Calabasas), just s, just e, then just s. ⎡L⎤ ⎡D⎤

CALISTOGA

Barolo
(707) 942-9900. Southern Italian. Casual Dining. **$14-$24.** 1457 Lincoln Ave 94515. On SR 29; center; in Mount View Hotel & Spa. ⎡D⎤ ⎡&M⎤

CAMARILLO

Bistro 13
(805) 383-3388. Italian. Casual Dining. **$12-$26.** 4910 Verdugo Way 93010. US 101 exit 52 (Pleasant Valley Rd/Santa Rosa Rd), just n; in Pardee Plaza. ⎡L⎤ ⎡D⎤

CAMBRIA

Old Stone Station
(805) 927-4229. American. Casual Dining. **$8-$36.** 713 Main St 93428. SR 1 exit Main St northbound, 2 mi ne; exit Cambria Dr southbound, just se. ⎡L⎤ ⎡D⎤

Robin's
(805) 927-5007. International. Casual Dining. **$18-$32.** 4095 Burton Dr 93428. SR 1 exit Burton Dr, 1 mi ne. ⎡L⎤ ⎡D⎤ ⎡AC⎤

Wild Ginger
(805) 927-1001. Asian. Casual Dining. **$14-$19.** 2380 Main St 93428. SR 1 exit Main St northbound, 1.5 mi nw; in East Village area. ⎡L⎤ ⎡D⎤ ⎡AC⎤

CARLSBAD

Bellefleur Restaurant
(760) 603-1919. California. Casual Dining. **$9-$35.** 5610 Paseo Del Norte, Suite 100B 92008. I-5 exit 47 (Palomar Airport Rd), just e, 0.5 mi n on Paseo Del Norte, then just e. ⎡L⎤ ⎡D⎤ ⎡&M⎤

Bistro West
(760) 930-8008. American. Casual Dining. **$11-$29.** 4960 Avenida Encinas 92008. I-5 exit 48 (Cannon Rd), just w, then just n; next to West Inn & Suites. ⎡L⎤ ⎡D⎤ ⎡&M⎤

Broken Yolk Cafe
(760) 943-8182. American. Casual Dining. **$6-$13.** 7670 El Camino Real 92009. I-5 exit 44 (La Costa Ave), 1.8 mi e. ⎡B⎤ ⎡L⎤

Fresco Trattoria & Bar
(760) 720-3737. Mediterranean. Casual Dining. **$8-$30.** 264 Carlsbad Village Dr 92008. I-5 exit 50 (Carlsbad Village Dr), 0.9 mi w. ⎡L⎤ ⎡D⎤ ⎡&M⎤

CARMEL-BY-THE-SEA

Casanova
(831) 625-0501. French. Fine Dining. **$14-$52.** 5th Ave between Mission St & San Carlos St 93922. Just n of Ocean Ave. ⎡L⎤ ⎡D⎤ ⎡&M⎤

CATALINA ISLAND

Ristorante Villa Portofino
(310) 510-2009. Italian. Fine Dining. **$16-$36.** 101 Crescent Ave 90704. In Avalon; between Whittley and Marilla aves; in Hotel Villa Portofino. ⎡D⎤

CATHEDRAL CITY

Don & Sweet Sue's Cafe
(760) 770-2760. American. Family Dining. **$8-$16.** 68-955 Ramon Rd 92234. I-10 exit 126 (Date Palm Dr), 2.2 mi s, then just w. ⎡B⎤ ⎡L⎤ ⎡D⎤ ⎡◣⎤

CORONA

Hunny's Cafe
(951) 735-7020. American. Family Dining. **$7-$18.** 402 S Corona Mall 92879. SR 91 exit 50B (S Main St) eastbound; exit 50 westbound, just s, then just e. ⎡B⎤ ⎡L⎤ ⎡D⎤ ⎡◣⎤

CORONADO

Chez Loma French Bistro
(619) 435-0661. French. Casual Dining. **$10-$33.** 1132 Loma Ave 92118. I-5 exit 14A (Coronado Bridge), 2.4 mi nw, 1 mi sw on Orange Ave, then just n. ⎡L⎤ ⎡D⎤ ⎡◣⎤

COSTA MESA

Nello Cucina
(714) 540-3365. Italian. Casual Dining. **$11-$28.** 3333 Bear St, Suite 118 92626. SR 73 exit 17B (Bear St), 0.5 mi n. ⎡L⎤ ⎡D⎤ ⎡◣⎤

DEL MAR

Pacifica Del Mar
(858) 792-0476. Seafood. Casual Dining. **$12-$36.** 1555 Camino Del Mar, Suite 321 92014. I-5 exit 34 (Del Mar Heights Rd), 1 mi w, then 1 mi. ⎡L⎤ ⎡D⎤ ⎡&M⎤

Sbicca
(858) 481-1001. California. Casual Dining. **$9-$34.** 215 15th St 92014. I-5 exit 34 (Del Mar Heights Rd), 1 mi w, 1 mi n, then just w. ⎡L⎤ ⎡D⎤ ⎡AC⎤

EL SEGUNDO

Marmalade Cafe
(310) 648-7200. American. Casual Dining. **$10-$25.** 2014 Park Pl 90245. I-405 exit 43 (Rosecrans Ave), 1.5 mi w, then just n; in Plaza El Segundo. ⎡B⎤ ⎡L⎤ ⎡D⎤ ⎡&M⎤

ESCONDIDO

Vincent's
(760) 745-3835. French. Casual Dining. **$10-$36.** 113 W Grand Ave 92025. I-15 exit 31 (Valley Pkwy), 0.6 mi se, then 0.5 mi e. ⎡D⎤

FALLBROOK

Aqua Terra
(760) 728-5881. American. Casual Dining. **$8-$38.** 2001 Old Hwy 395 92028. I-15 exit 46 (SR 76/Pala Rd/Oceanside), just w, then 2 mi n; in Pala Mesa Resort. ⎡B⎤ ⎡L⎤ ⎡D⎤ ⎡◣⎤

La Caseta Fine Mexican Food
(760) 728-9737. Mexican. Family Dining. **$9-$16.** 111 N Vine St 92028. I-15 exit 51 (Mission Rd), 4.9 mi w, then just s. ⎡L⎤ ⎡D⎤ ⎡◣⎤

FOLSOM

◆◆ **Karen's Bakery Cafe & Catering**
(916) 985-2665. Breads/Pastries Sandwiches. Quick Serve. **$9-$15.** 705 Gold Lake Dr, Suite 340 95630. Jct Leidesdorf St; downtown; near American River Bridge. B L ♿M

FOOTHILL RANCH

◆ **California Fish Grill**
(949) 470-9600. Seafood. Quick Serve. **$7-$14.** 41 Auto Center Dr, Suite 113 92610. I-5 exit 92A (Lake Forest Dr) northbound exit 92 (Bake Pkwy/Lake Forest Dr); southbound, 5 mi e on Lake Forest Dr, just n on Towne Center, then just e. L D ◈

FORESTVILLE

◆ **Russian River Pub**
(707) 887-7932. Burgers Sandwiches. Casual Dining. **$8-$14.** 11829 River Rd 95436. 7 mi w of jct SR 101. L D

FREMONT

◆ **Falafel, Etc.**
(510) 795-7170. Middle Eastern. Quick Serve. **$7-$14.** 39200 Fremont Blvd 94538. I-880 exit Mowry Ave, 1.5 mi e, then just s at Beacon Ave; in Gas Light Square. L D ♿M

GARBERVILLE

𝒜𝒜𝒜◈ ◆◆◆◆ **Benbow Inn Restaurant**
(707) 923-2124. Regional California. Fine Dining. **$21-$45.** 445 Lake Benbow Dr 95542. US 101 exit 636 (Benbow Lake Rd), just w; in Benbow Inn. B D

GEYSERVILLE

◆◆◆ **Diavola Pizzeria & Salumeria**
(707) 814-0111. Italian. Casual Dining. **$14-$25.** 21021 Geyserville Ave 95441. US 101 exit Geyserville Ave/SR 128, 0.5 mi s. L D

HALF MOON BAY

◆◆ **Half Moon Bay Brewing Company**
(650) 728-2739. American. Casual Dining. **$14-$23.** 390 Capistrano Rd 94018. SR 1, just w. L D 𝒜𝒞

HEALDSBURG

◆◆◆ **Bistro Ralph**
(707) 433-1380. California. Fine Dining. **$13-$36.** 109 Plaza St 95448. Downtown. L D ♿M

◆◆◆ **Spoonbar**
(707) 433-7222. Mediterranean. Casual Dining. **$11-$24.** 219 Healdsburg Ave 95448. Between Matheson and Mill sts; in H2 Hotel. D

HEMET

◆◆ **Sweet Baby Jane's BBQ Bar & Grill**
(951) 652-4227. Barbecue Steak. Casual Dining. **$7-$24.** 124 S Harvard St 92543. SR 74, just e of State St, just s. L D ◈

HESPERIA

◆◆ **Cancun Mexican Seafood Restaurant**
(760) 956-7720. Mexican Seafood. Casual Dining. **$7-$18.** 15550 Main St, Suite A-1 92345. I-15 exit 143 (Hesperia/Main St), 3.4 mi e; in The Plaza on Main Street Shopping Center. L D ◈

HIGHLAND

◆◆ **Mi Cocina Restaurant**
(909) 425-0393. Mexican. Family Dining. **$6-$19.** 27961 Highland Ave 92346. SR 330 exit Highland Ave, just w; in San Manuel Village. L D

IDYLLWILD

◆◆ **Gastrognome Restaurant**
(951) 659-5055. American. Casual Dining. **$8-$32.** 54381 Ridgeview Dr 92549. Just e of SR 243; in Village Center. B L D

INDIAN WELLS

◆◆◆ **The Nest**
(760) 346-2314. Continental. Casual Dining. **$13-$38.** 75-188 Hwy 111 92210. I-10 exit 134 (Cook St), 4.4 mi s, then just e. D ♿M ◈

INDUSTRY

◆◆◆ **Red**
(626) 854-2509. California. Casual Dining. **$20-$42.** One Industry Hills Pkwy 91744. SR 60 exit 18 (Azusa Ave), 1.3 mi n, then 0.5 mi w; in Pacific Palms Resort. L D LATE

IRVINE

◆◆◆ **Gulliver's**
(949) 833-8411. American. Gastropub. **$10-$50.** 18482 MacArthur Blvd 92612. I-405 exit 8 (MacArthur Blvd/John Wayne Airport), just sw. L D ◈

JULIAN

◆◆ **Julian Grille**
(760) 765-0173. American. Casual Dining. **$8-$32.** 2224 Main St 92036. Just w of SR 78 and 79. L D

◆◆ **Romano's Restaurant**
(760) 765-1003. Italian. Casual Dining. **$8-$25.** 2718 B St 92036. Just s of SR 78 and 79. L D 𝒜𝒞 ◈

JUNE LAKE

◆◆ **Carson Peak Inn**
(760) 648-7575. Traditional American. Casual Dining. **$18-$35.** Hwy 158, Boulder Dr 93529. 2 mi w of village. D

KERNVILLE

◆ **Cheryl's Diner**
(760) 376-6131. American. Casual Dining. **$6-$20.** 11030 Kernville Rd 93238. Center; across from Circle Park. B L D ◈

LAGUNA BEACH

◆◆ **Ristorante Rumari**
(949) 494-0400. Italian. Casual Dining. **$16-$46.** 1826 S Coast Hwy 92651. SR 133, 1 mi s on SR 1. D

LA HABRA

◆◆ **El Cholo Cafe**
(562) 691-4618. Mexican. Casual Dining. **$8-$18.** 840 E Whittier Blvd 90631. 1.5 mi e of SR 39 (Beach Blvd). L D ◈

LA JOLLA

◆◆◆ **Cafe Japengo**
(858) 450-3355. Pacific Rim. Casual Dining. **$16-$42.** 8960 University Center Ln 92122. I-5 exit 28 (La Jolla Village Dr), just e; across from Hyatt Regency La Jolla. L D ♿M ◈

◆◆◆ **Nine-Ten**
(858) 964-5400. California. Fine Dining. **$12-$39.** 910 Prospect St 92037. I-5 exit 28 (La Jolla Village Dr) southbound, 0.7 mi w to Torrey Pines Rd, 2.5 mi sw to Prospect St, then 0.6 mi w; exit 26A (La Jolla Pkwy) northbound, 1.5 mi n to Torrey Pines Rd, 1 mi sw, then 0.6 mi w; in The Grande Colonial. B L D ◈

▼▼▼ Tapenade
(858) 551-7500. French. Fine Dining. **$14-$38.** 7612 Fay Ave 92037. I-5 exit 28 (La Jolla Village Dr) southbound; 1 mi w to Torrey Pines Rd, 2.5 mi sw to Prospect St, 1 mi sw, then 0.3 mi se; exit 26A (La Jolla Pkwy) northbound, 1.5 mi n to Torrey Pines Rd, 1.2 mi w to Prospect St, 1 mi sw, then 0.3 mi se. ⓛ ⓓ ⓜ Ⓝ

LAKE ELSINORE

▼▼▼ Vincenzo's Olive Tree
(951) 674-8941. Southern Italian. Family Dining. **$8-$25.** 31712 Casino Dr, Suite 3B 92530. I-15 exit 73 (Diamond Dr/Railroad Canyon Rd), just w, then just s. ⓛ ⓓ Ⓝ

LAKE FOREST

▼▼ The Original Peppino's Italian Family Restaurant
(949) 951-2611. Traditional Italian Pizza. Family Dining. **$8-$23.** 23600 Rockfield Blvd 92630. I-5 exit 92A (Lake Forest Dr) northbound; exit 92 (Bake Pkwy/Lake Forest Dr) southbound, 0.5 mi e, then just n.
ⓛ ⓓ Ⓝ

LA MESA

▼▼ Anthony's Fish Grotto
(619) 463-0368. Seafood. Casual Dining. **$9-$50.** 9530 Murray Dr 91942. I-8 exit 14C (Severin Dr), just n. ⓛ ⓓ ⓜ

LARKSPUR

▼▼▼ Left Bank
(415) 927-3331. French. Casual Dining. **$10-$32.** 507 Magnolia Ave 94939. At Ward St; downtown. ⓛ ⓓ

LEE VINING

▼ Whoa Nellie Deli
(760) 647-1088. American. Casual Dining. **$9-$25.** 22 Vista Point Dr 93541. Jct US 395, at SR 120; in Tioga Mobil Gas Mart.
Ⓑ ⓛ ⓓ Ⓚ

LITTLE RIVER

▼▼ Little River Inn Restaurant
(707) 937-5942. California. Fine Dining. **$13-$31.** 7901 N SR 1 95456. On SR 1, just s of Van Damme State Park entrance; in Little River Inn.
Ⓑ ⓓ

LIVERMORE

▼▼▼ Uncle Yu's at the Vineyard
(925) 449-7000. Chinese. Fine Dining. **$10-$25.** 39 S Livermore Ave, Suite 125 94550. I-580 exit N Livermore Ave, 1.5 mi s. ⓛ ⓓ ⓜ

LONG BEACH

▼▼ The Attic
(562) 433-0153. Southern American. Casual Dining. **$10-$28.** 3441 E Broadway 90803. Jct Ocean Blvd and Newport Ave, 0.7 mi n.
Ⓑ ⓛ ⓓ

LOS ANGELES

▼▼▼ Ca' Brea Italian Country Cuisine
(323) 938-2863. Northern Italian. Fine Dining. **$13-$26.** 346 S La Brea Ave 90036. I-10 exit 8 (La Brea Ave), 2.6 mi n. Ⓑ ⓛ ⓓ Ⓝ

▼▼▼ Chaya Brasserie
(310) 859-8833. Continental. Casual Dining. **$18-$35.** 8741 Alden Dr 90048. I-10 exit 7A (La Cienega Blvd), 2.2 mi n to San Vincentes Blvd, just ne, then just w. ⓛ ⓓ

▼▼ Napa Valley Grille
(310) 824-3322. American. Fine Dining. **$14-$44.** 1100 Glendon Ave 90024. I-405 exit 55B (Wilshire Blvd), 0.6 mi e, then just n; in Westwood Village. ⓛ ⓓ

▼▼ Pizzicotto
(310) 442-7188. Italian. Casual Dining. **$11-$18.** 11758 San Vicente Blvd 90049. I-405 exit 55A (Wilshire Blvd), 0.6 mi w, then 0.6 mi nw; in Brentwood area. ⓛ ⓓ

▼▼ Rockwell Table & Stage
(323) 661-6163. California. Casual Dining. **$18-$36.** 1714 N Vermont Ave 90027. US 101 exit 6A (Vermont Ave), 1.5 mi n; in Los Felix area.
ⓛ ⓓ Ⓝ

▼▼ Tanino Ristorante
(310) 208-0444. Italian. Casual Dining. **$13-$40.** 1043 Westwood Blvd 90024. I-405 exit 55B (Wilshire Blvd), 0.5 mi e, then just n; in Westwood Village. ⓛ ⓓ

MAMMOTH LAKES

▼▼ Base Camp
(760) 934-3900. American. Casual Dining. **$9-$18.** 3325 Main St 93546. On SR 203, 0.3 mi w of Sierra Park Rd. Ⓑ ⓛ ⓓ Ⓚ

MARINA DEL REY

▼▼ The Warehouse Restaurant
(310) 823-5451. Seafood Steak. Casual Dining. **$19-$39.** 4499 Admiralty Way 90292. SR 90 (Marina Frwy) exit Lincoln Blvd (SR 1), just s, then just w on Bali Way. ⓛ ⓓ ⓜ

MARYSVILLE

▼ The Brick Coffee House Cafe
(530) 743-5283. American. Quick Serve. **$7-$10.** 316 D St 95901. Between 3rd and 4th sts; center; in historic downtown. Ⓑ ⓛ

MENDOCINO

ⒶⒶⒶ ▼▼▼ The Ravens'
(707) 937-5615. Vegetarian. Fine Dining. **$16-$27.** 44850 Comptche-Ukiah Rd 95460. SR 1 exit Comptche-Ukiah Rd, just e; in Stanford Inn by the Sea Eco-Lodge. ⊟ Ⓑ ⓓ Ⓚ

MONTEREY

ⒶⒶⒶ ▼▼▼ Cafe Fina
(831) 372-5200. Seafood. Fine Dining. **$10-$30.** 47 Fisherman's Wharf 93940. On Fisherman's Wharf. ⓛ ⓓ

▼▼▼ The C Restaurant + Bar
(831) 375-4800. California Seafood. Casual Dining. **$14-$45.** 750 Cannery Row 93940. Between Prescott and David aves; in InterContinental The Clement Monterey. Ⓑ ⓛ ⓓ ⓜ

▼▼▼ Tarpy's Roadhouse
(831) 647-1444. Regional American. Fine Dining. **$9-$47.** 2999 Monterey Salinas Hwy 93940. On SR 68, 2.5 mi e of jct SR 1.
ⓛ ⓓ ⓜ Ⓚ

MONTROSE

▼▼▼ New Moon Restaurant
(818) 249-4393. Chinese. Casual Dining. **$10-$16.** 2138 Verdugo Blvd 91020. I-210 exit 18 (Oceanview Blvd), just s to Honolulu Ave, just e, then just ne. ⓛ ⓓ

▼▼ Oceanview Restaurant
(818) 248-2722. American. Casual Dining. **$8-$30.** 3826 Oceanview Blvd 91020. I-210 exit 18 (Oceanview Blvd), 0.4 mi s. Ⓑ ⓛ ⓓ Ⓝ

MORRO BAY

▼▼ Harbor Hut Restaurant
(805) 772-2255. Seafood. Casual Dining. **$9-$35.** 1205 Embarcadero 93442. From Main St, just w on Harbor Dr. ⓛ ⓓ Ⓚ

MOSS BEACH

◢◣◢ ▼▼▼ **Moss Beach Distillery**
(650) 728-5595. Seafood. Casual Dining. **$13-$39.** 140 Beach Way 94038. SR 1 exit Cypress St, 6 mi n of jct SR 92. ⌑L⌑ ⌑D⌑

MOUNTAIN VIEW

▼▼▼ **Cascal**
(650) 940-9500. Latin American Small Plates. Casual Dining. **$13-$29.** 400 Castro St 94041. Corner of Castro and California sts; downtown.
⌑L⌑ ⌑D⌑

NATIONAL CITY

▼▼ **Buster's**
(619) 336-1783. California. Casual Dining. **$6-$20.** 740 Bay Marina Dr 91950. I-5 exit 10 (Bay Marina Dr), just w. ⌑B⌑ ⌑L⌑ ⌑D⌑ ⌑◥⌑

NEEDLES

▼▼▼ **Juicy's Famous River Cafe**
(760) 326-2233. American. Family Dining. **$10-$20.** 2411 W Broadway 92363. I-40 exit 141 (W Broadway/River Rd), just se; on Business Loop I-40. ⌑B⌑ ⌑L⌑ ⌑D⌑

▼▼ **River City Pizza Co.**
(760) 326-9191. Italian Pizza. Family Dining. **$6-$12.** 1901 Needles Hwy 92363. I-40 exit 141 (W Broadway/River Rd), 0.7 mi se on Business Loop I-40. ⌑L⌑ ⌑D⌑ ⌑◥⌑

NEWPORT BEACH

▼▼▼ **Bayside Restaurant**
(949) 721-1222. American. Casual Dining. **$14-$36.** 900 Bayside Dr 92660. SR 73 exit 15 (Jamboree Rd), 3.5 mi s to Pacific Coast Hwy, then just nw. ⌑L⌑ ⌑D⌑

NOVATO

▼▼▼ **Moylan's Brewery & Restaurant**
(415) 898-4677. American. Casual Dining. **$10-$20.** 15 Rowland Way 94945. US 101 exit Rowland Way, just e. ⌑L⌑ ⌑D⌑ ⌑⅚M⌑

OCEANO

▼▼ **Old Juan's Cantina**
(805) 489-5680. Mexican. Casual Dining. **$8-$18.** 649 Pier Ave 93445. SR 1, just w. ⌑L⌑ ⌑D⌑

▼▼ **Rock & Roll Diner**
(805) 473-2040. American. Family Dining. **$6-$18.** 1300 Railroad St 93445. On SR 1; jct Mendel Dr. ⌑B⌑ ⌑L⌑ ⌑D⌑ ⌑◥⌑

OCEANSIDE

▼▼▼ **Fratelli's Italian Kitchen**
(760) 696-9007. Italian. Family Dining. **$10-$27.** 3915 Mission Ave, Suite 12 92058. I-5 exit 53 (Mission Ave), 3.5 mi e; in Mission Douglas Plaza.
⌑L⌑ ⌑D⌑

OJAI

▼▼ **The Deer Lodge**
(805) 646-4256. Steak. Casual Dining. **$10-$28.** 2261 Maricopa Hwy 93023. SR 33, 1 mi n. ⌑L⌑ ⌑D⌑ ⌑LATE⌑ ⌑◥⌑

PALM DESERT

▼▼ **Cafe Des Beaux Arts**
(760) 346-0669. Provincial French. Casual Dining. **$13-$30.** 73-640 El Paseo 92260. Just s of SR 111; corner of Larkspur Ln.
⌑B⌑ ⌑L⌑ ⌑D⌑ ⌑⅚M⌑

▼▼▼ **Cuistot**
(760) 340-1000. French. Fine Dining. **$15-$45.** 72-595 El Paseo 92260. I-10 exit 131 (Monterey Ave), 5.7 mi s, then 0.6 mi w. ⌑L⌑ ⌑D⌑ ⌑◥⌑

▼▼ **Daily Grill**
(760) 779-9911. American. Casual Dining. **$9-$33.** 73061 El Paseo 92260. On SR 74, just s of SR 111, just e. ⌑L⌑ ⌑D⌑ ⌑⅚M⌑

▼▼ **Fisherman's Market & Grill**
(760) 776-6533. Seafood. Quick Serve. **$8-$24.** 44-250 Town Center Way, Suite C-2 92260. I-10 exit 131 (Monterey Ave), 5.7 mi s, 0.4 mi w on SR 111, then 0.3 mi n on Village Center Dr. ⌑L⌑ ⌑D⌑ ⌑⅚M⌑ ⌑◥⌑

▼▼ **Roc's Firehouse Grille**
(760) 340-3222. American. Casual Dining. **$9-$35.** 36-891 Cook St, Suite 10 92211. I-10 exit 134 (Cook St), just s; in The Village at University Park. ⌑L⌑ ⌑D⌑ ⌑LATE⌑ ⌑◥⌑

PALM SPRINGS

▼▼ **Blue Coyote Bar & Grill**
(760) 327-1196. Southwestern. Casual Dining. **$9-$25.** 445 N Palm Canyon Dr 92262. 0.4 mi n of Tahquitz Canyon Way; downtown.
⌑L⌑ ⌑D⌑ ⌑⅚M⌑ ⌑◥⌑

▼▼ **El Mirasol at Los Arboles**
(760) 459-3136. Regional Mexican. Family Dining. **$10-$18.** 784 N Indian Canyon Dr 92262. 0.6 mi n of Tahquitz Canyon Way.
⌑B⌑ ⌑L⌑ ⌑D⌑ ⌑⅚M⌑

◢◣◢ ▼▼▼▼ **Europa Restaurant at the Villa Royale Inn**
(760) 327-2314. Continental. Fine Dining. **$25-$39.** 1620 S Indian Tr 92264. 2 mi se of Tahquitz Canyon Way on Palm Canyon Dr, just n; in Villa Royale Inn. ⌑D⌑

▼▼ **Fisherman's Market & Grill**
(760) 327-1766. Seafood. Quick Serve. **$9-$30.** 235 S Indian Canyon Dr 92262. From Tahquitz Canyon Way, just s; downtown.
⌑L⌑ ⌑D⌑ ⌑⅚M⌑ ⌑◥⌑

▼▼▼ **Sherman's Deli & Bakery**
(760) 325-1199. Deli Sandwiches. Family Dining. **$8-$15.** 401 E Tahquitz Canyon Way 92262. Just e of downtown. ⌑B⌑ ⌑L⌑ ⌑D⌑

▼▼▼ **Spencer's Restaurant**
(760) 327-3446. American. Fine Dining. **$8-$55.** 701 W Baristo Rd 92262. Just s of Tahquitz Canyon Way; just w of Palm Canyon Dr; at west end of Baristo Rd. ⌑B⌑ ⌑L⌑ ⌑D⌑

PASADENA

▼▼▼ **Bistro 45**
(626) 795-2478. French. Fine Dining. **$17-$40.** 45 S Mentor Ave 91106. I-210 exit 26B (Lake Ave), 0.5 mi s to Colorado Blvd, just e, then just s.
⌑L⌑ ⌑D⌑

▼▼ **Mi Piace**
(626) 795-3131. Italian. Casual Dining. **$15-$40.** 25 E Colorado Blvd 91105. I-210 exit 25A (Fair Oaks Ave), just s, then just w; exit Colorado Blvd eastbound, 0.5 mi e; in Old Town. ⌑B⌑ ⌑L⌑ ⌑D⌑ ⌑LATE⌑

PETALUMA

▼▼ **Sugo Trattoria**
(707) 782-9298. Italian. Casual Dining. **$10-$24.** 5 Petaluma Blvd S 94952. Jct B St; downtown. ⌑L⌑ ⌑D⌑ ⌑⅚M⌑

PISMO BEACH

▼▼ **Spyglass Inn Restaurant**
(805) 773-1222. Seafood. Casual Dining. **$8-$40.** 2703 Spyglass Dr 93449. US 101 exit 193 (Spyglass Dr) northbound; exit 193 (Shell Beach Rd) southbound, just w, then just n; in Spyglass Inn. ⌑B⌑ ⌑L⌑ ⌑D⌑

RANCHO CUCAMONGA

▼▼▼ **P.F. Chang's China Bistro**
(909) 463-4095. Chinese. Fine Dining. **$10-$25.** 7870 Monticello Ave 91739. I-15 exit 112 (Foothill Blvd), just w to Dry Creek Blvd, just n to Victoria Park Ln, just e, then just n. ⌑L⌑ ⌑D⌑

RANCHO MIRAGE

▼▼ ▼▼ Babe's Bar-B-Que Grill & Brewhouse
(760) 346-8738. Barbecue. Casual Dining. **$8-$33.** 71-800 Hwy 111, Bldg A176 92270. I-10 exit 130 (Bob Hope Dr), 5.9 mi s, then just w; at west end of The River Shopping/Dining Center. L D &M

RANCHO SANTA FE

▼▼▼▼ Delicias
(858) 756-8000. Continental. Casual Dining. **$12-$42.** 6106 Paseo Delicias 92067. I-5 exit 37 (Lomas Santa Fe Dr), 4 mi e on CR S-8; in Village area. L D &M

▼▼▼▼ Mille Fleurs
(858) 756-3085. French. Fine Dining. **$12-$50.** 6009 Paseo Delicias 92067. I-5 exit 37 (Lomas Santa Fe Dr), 4 mi e on CR S-8; in Village area. L D &M

REDDING

▼▼ The Habit Burger Grill
(530) 223-1027. Burgers. Quick Serve. **$5-$10.** 1020 E Cypress Ave 96002. I-5 exit 677 (Cypress Ave), just e. L D &M

RIVERSIDE

▼▼▼▼ Mario's Place
(951) 684-7755. Northern Italian. Fine Dining. **$12-$36.** 3646 Mission Inn Ave 92501. SR 91 exit 64 (University Ave) eastbound; exit 64 (Mission Inn Ave) westbound, just w. D

ROCKLIN

▼▼ ▼▼ Lucille's Smokehouse Bar-B-Que & Catering
(916) 780-7427. Barbecue. Casual Dining. **$10-$31.** 6628 Lonetree Blvd 95765. SR 65 exit Blue Oaks Blvd, just e, then just n; in Blue Oaks Town Center. L D

SACRAMENTO

▼▼ ▼▼ Pizza Rock
(916) 737-5777. Pizza. Casual Dining. **$11-$30.** 1020 K St 95814. Between 10th and 11th sts. L D LATE &M

▼▼ ▼▼ Selland's Market - Cafe
(916) 736-3333. American. Casual Dining. **$5-$23.** 5340 H St 95819. Business Rt I-80 (Capital City Frwy) exit J St, 1.7 mi e, then just n on El Dorado Way; jct El Dorado Way. L D &M

ST. HELENA

▼▼ Gott's Roadside
(707) 963-3486. American. Quick Serve. **$8-$15.** 933 Main St 94574. On SR 29; between Mitchell Dr and McCorkle Ave. B L D 𝒜

▼▼ ▼▼ Himalayan Sherpa Kitchen
(707) 963-4439. Indian. Casual Dining. **$12-$25.** 1148 Main St 94574. On SR 29; center. L D

▼▼▼▼ Tra Vigne
(707) 963-4444. Italian. Fine Dining. **$18-$30.** 1050 Charter Oak Ave 94574. 0.5 mi s on SR 29. L D

SAN CARLOS

▼▼▼▼ Locanda Positano
(650) 591-5700. Italian. Casual Dining. **$13-$28.** 617 Laurel St 94070. US 101 exit Holly St, 0.3 mi w, then just s. L D

▼▼▼▼ Piacere Ristorante
(650) 592-3536. Italian. Casual Dining. **$12-$39.** 727 Laurel St 94070. SR 82, just w on San Carlos Ave, 0.3 mi s. L D

SAN DIEGO

▼▼ ▼▼ Edgewater Grill
(619) 232-7581. Seafood. Casual Dining. **$12-$36.** 861 W Harbor Dr 92101. I-5 exit 16B (6th Ave/Downtown) northbound, just n, then 2.5 mi w on Market St; exit 17 (Front St/Civic Center) southbound, 1.5 mi s, then 5 mi w on Market St; in Seaport Village. B L D &M

𝔸𝔸𝔸 ▼▼ ▼▼ Grant Grill
(619) 744-2077. California. Fine Dining. **$20-$50.** 326 Broadway 92101. I-5 exit 17 (Front St/Civic Center) southbound, 0.9 mi s to Broadway, then just e; exit 16B (6th Ave/Downtown) northbound, 0.6 mi s, then just w; in The US Grant, A Luxury Collection Hotel. ⊞ B L D &M ⬚

▼▼ ▼▼ King's Fish House
(619) 574-1230. Seafood. Casual Dining. **$12-$45.** 825 Camino de La Reina 92108. I-8 exit 5 (Mission Center Rd), just n; in Mission Valley West Center. L D

▼▼▼▼ The Prado At Balboa Park
(619) 557-9441. California. Casual Dining. **$10-$35.** 1549 El Prado 92101. I-5 exit 15B (Pershing Dr/Civic Center) northbound, just e, just n on Florida St, just w on Zoo St, just s on Park Blvd, just e on Presidents Way, just n on Pan American Rd, then just e; SR 163 exit 1B (Via de San Ysidro Blvd) southbound, just n, just w on Presidents Way, just n on Pan American Rd, then just e. L D

▼▼ ▼▼ Restaurant Vallarta Mexican & Seafood
(619) 661-1826. Mexican. Family Dining. **$8-$20.** 2335 Roll Dr, Suite 11 92154. I-905 exit 9 (Siempre Viva), just e, then just s; in Roll Drive Center, just n of Otay Mesa International Border Crossing. L D ⬚

▼▼▼▼ Sally's Seafood on the Water
(619) 358-6740. Seafood. Fine Dining. **$15-$40.** 1 Market Pl 92101. I-5 exit 17 (Front St/Civic Center), 1.3 mi s, then just w; in Manchester Grand Hyatt San Diego. L D ⬚

▼▼ ▼▼ Stish
(619) 543-9000. California. Casual Dining. **$8-$29.** 901 Camino del Rio S 92108. I-8 exit 5 (Mission Center Rd), just s, then just w; in Hilton San Diego Mission Valley Zoo/SeaWorld Area. B L D &M

SAN FRANCISCO

▼▼▼▼ 54 Mint
(415) 543-5100. Italian. Casual Dining. **$16-$28.** 16 Mint Plaza 94103. On the Plaza; enter on 5th or Mission sts. L D 𝒜

▼▼ ▼▼ Baker Street Bistro
(415) 931-1475. French. Casual Dining. **$10-$26.** 2953 Baker St 94123. Between Green and Lombard sts. L D

▼▼ ▼▼ Boulettes Larder
(415) 399-1155. Natural/Organic. Casual Dining. **$10-$30.** 1 Ferry Building Marketplace 94111. In northeast corner of Ferry Building Marketplace. B L D

▼▼ ▼▼ hops & hominy
(415) 373-6341. Southern. Casual Dining. **$10-$28.** 1 Tillman Pl 94108. At Sutter St. L D 𝒜

▼▼ ▼▼ La Mediterranee
(415) 921-2956. Mediterranean. Casual Dining. **$12-$17.** 2210 Fillmore St 94115. Between Sacramento and Clay sts. L D 𝒜

𝔸𝔸𝔸 ▼▼▼▼ North Beach Restaurant
(415) 392-1700. Italian. Fine Dining. **$19-$35.** 1512 Stockton St 94133. At Columbus Ave. L D

𝔸𝔸𝔸 ▼▼ ▼▼ Oriental Pearl Restaurant
(415) 433-1817. Chinese. Casual Dining. **$11-$55.** 778 Clay St 94108. Jct Grant St; 2nd Floor; in Chinatown. L D

▼▼ ▼▼ Padrecito
(415) 742-5505. Mexican Small Plates. Casual Dining. **$12-$16.** 901 Cole St 94117. At Carl St. D 𝒜

▼▼▼▼ **Piperade**
(415) 391-2555. French. Fine Dining. **$14-$32.** 1015 Battery St 94111.
At Green St. ⌊L⌋ ⌊D⌋

🅐🅐🅐✎ ▼▼▼ **Pompei's Grotto**
(415) 776-9265. Seafood. Casual Dining. **$11-$30.** 340 Jefferson St
94133. At Fisherman's Wharf. ⌊L⌋ ⌊D⌋ ⌊𝓐𝓒⌋

▼▼▼▼ **Rose Pistola**
(415) 399-0499. Italian. Casual Dining. **$12-$38.** 532 Columbus Ave
94133. Between Green and Union sts. ⌊L⌋ ⌊D⌋

▼▼▼ **Rose's Cafe**
(415) 775-2200. Italian. Casual Dining. **$12-$27.** 2298 Union St 94123.
At Steiner St. ⌊B⌋ ⌊L⌋ ⌊D⌋

▼▼▼▼ **Sociale Caffe & Wine Bar**
(415) 921-3200. Italian. Casual Dining. **$13-$32.** 3665 Sacramento St
94118. Just w of jct Locust St; in Laurel Heights. ⌊L⌋ ⌊D⌋ ⌊♿M⌋

▼▼ **Tal-Y-Tara Tea & Polo Shoppe**
(415) 751-9275. Specialty. Casual Dining. **$8-$12.** 6439 California St
94121. Between 26th and 27th aves. ⌊L⌋ ⌊𝓐𝓒⌋

▼▼ **Universal Cafe**
(415) 821-4608. California. Casual Dining. **$18-$28.** 2814 19th St 94110.
Between Bryant and Florida sts. ⌊L⌋ ⌊D⌋ ⌊𝓐𝓒⌋

▼▼▼ **The Waterfront Restaurant**
(415) 391-2696. California Seafood. Fine Dining. **$16-$35.** Pier 7 94111.
Just n of the Ferry Building; on The Embarcadero at Broadway St.
⌊L⌋ ⌊D⌋ ⌊♿M⌋

▼ **Wise Sons Deli**
(415) 787-3354. Deli. Quick Serve. **$9-$13.** 3150 24th St 94110. At
Shotwell St. ⌊B⌋ ⌊L⌋ ⌊𝓐𝓒⌋

SAN JOSE

▼▼▼ **The Grill on the Alley**
(408) 294-2244. Steak. Fine Dining. **$15-$52.** 172 S Market St 95113. At
Fairmont Plaza; in The Fairmont San Jose. ⌊L⌋ ⌊D⌋ ⌊♿M⌋

▼▼ **Habana Cuba**
(408) 998-2822. Cuban. Casual Dining. **$10-$32.** 238 Race St 95126.
I-280 exit Race St, just n; at San Carlos St. ⌊L⌋ ⌊D⌋ ⌊♿M⌋

▼▼▼▼ **Three Flames Restaurant**
(408) 269-3133. Continental. Fine Dining. **$15-$30.** 1547 Meridian Ave
95125. Just n of Hamilton Ave; in Carriage Square Shopping Center.
⌊L⌋ ⌊D⌋ ⌊♿M⌋

SAN JUAN CAPISTRANO

▼▼ **Cafe Mozart**
(949) 496-0212. Continental. Casual Dining. **$9-$33.** 31952 Camino
Capistrano, Suite A1 92675. I-5 exit 82 (SR 74/Ortega Hwy), 0.3 mi s,
then just s; in Mercado Village. ⌊L⌋ ⌊D⌋ ⌊◥⌋

▼▼▼▼ **Cedar Creek Inn**
(949) 240-2229. American. Casual Dining. **$10-$31.** 26860 Ortega Hwy
92675. I-5 exit 82 (SR 74/Ortega Hwy), 0.5 mi w; in Mission Promenade.
⌊L⌋ ⌊D⌋

▼▼▼▼ **Sundried Tomato Cafe**
(949) 661-1167. American. Casual Dining. **$12-$28.** 31781 Camino
Capistrano 92675. I-5 exit 82 (SR 74/Ortega Hwy), 0.3 mi w, then just s.
⌊L⌋ ⌊D⌋

▼▼ **The Tea House on Los Rios**
(949) 443-3914. English Coffee/Tea Breads/Pastries. Casual Dining.
$15-$18. 31731 Los Rios St 92675. I-5 exit 82 (SR 74/Ortega Hwy), just
w, 0.4 mi sw on Del Obispo St, then just n. ⌊L⌋

SAN LUIS OBISPO

▼▼▼ **Luna Red Restaurant**
(805) 540-5243. Small Plates Wild Game. Fine Dining. **$8-$26.** 1023
Chorro St 93401. US 101 exit 202 (Broad St), nw on Palm St, then just e;
next to Mission Church. ⌊B⌋ ⌊L⌋ ⌊D⌋ ⌊LATE⌋

SAN MATEO

▼▼▼ **Spiedo Ristorante**
(650) 375-0818. Italian. Casual Dining. **$10-$30.** 223 E 4th Ave 94401.
US 101 exit E 3rd Ave, 0.5 mi w. ⌊L⌋ ⌊D⌋ ⌊♿M⌋

SANTA ANA

▼▼▼ **Darya**
(714) 557-6600. Persian. Casual Dining. **$13-$20.** 3800 S Plaza Dr
92704. I-405 exit 9B (Bristol St), just n to Sunflower Ave, just w, then just
n; in South Coast Plaza Village. ⌊L⌋ ⌊D⌋

SANTA BARBARA

▼▼▼▼ **Carlito's Cafe y Cantina**
(805) 962-7117. Mexican. Casual Dining. **$11-$19.** 1324 State St 93101.
US 101 exit 98 (Carrillo St), 0.5 mi e, then just n. ⌊L⌋ ⌊D⌋

▼▼ **C'est Cheese**
(805) 965-0318. Sandwiches Breads/Pastries. Casual Dining. **$6-$20.**
825 Santa Barbara St 93101. US 101 exit (Garden St), 0.3 mi e, then just
s. ⌊B⌋ ⌊L⌋ ⌊♿M⌋ ⌊𝓐𝓒⌋

▼ **Madam Lu Chinese Restaurant**
(805) 898-9289. Chinese. Family Dining. **$9-$20.** 3524 State St 93105.
US 101 exit 101A (La Cumbre Rd/Hope Ave) northbound, just n, then 0.4
mi w; exit 101B (State St) southbound, 0.6 mi w. ⌊L⌋ ⌊D⌋

▼▼ **Pascucci**
(805) 963-8123. Italian. Casual Dining. **$8-$16.** 729 State St 93101. US
101 exit 98 (Carrillo St), just e, then 0.5 mi s; in Paseo Nuevo.
⌊L⌋ ⌊D⌋ ⌊𝓐𝓒⌋

▼▼ **Via Maestra 42**
(805) 569-6522. Italian. Casual Dining. **$8-$32.** 3343 State St 93105. US
101 exit 100 (Las Positas Rd), 0.8 mi n to State St, then just w.
⌊B⌋ ⌊L⌋ ⌊D⌋ ⌊◥⌋

SANTA CLARA

▼ **Old Ironsides Cafe**
(408) 727-5147. Mediterranean Deli. Quick Serve. **$6-$10.** 4655 Old
Ironsides Dr, Suite 150 95054. US 101 exit Great America Pkwy/Bowers
Ave, 1 mi n, just w on Patrick Henry Dr, then just n; in Marriott Business
Park. ⌊B⌋ ⌊L⌋ ⌊♿M⌋

SANTA MARIA

▼▼▼ **Garden Room at Historic Santa Maria Inn**
(805) 346-7908. American. Fine Dining. **$12-$39.** 801 S Broadway
93454. US 101 exit 171 (Main St), 1 mi w, then 0.5 mi s; in Historic Santa
Maria Inn. ⌊B⌋ ⌊L⌋ ⌊D⌋

SANTA ROSA

▼▼ **Flavor Bistro**
(707) 573-9600. California. Casual Dining. **$10-$27.** 96 Old Courthouse
Square 95404. US 101 exit downtown Santa Rosa/3rd St, 0.3 mi e on 3rd
St, then just n. ⌊B⌋ ⌊L⌋ ⌊D⌋ ⌊♿M⌋

▼▼ **Third Street AleWorks**
(707) 523-3060. American. Casual Dining. **$9-$18.** 610 3rd St 95404.
Between D St and Mendocino Ave. ⌊L⌋ ⌊D⌋ ⌊LATE⌋ ⌊♿M⌋

SANTEE

▼▼ **Oggi's Pizza & Brewing Co.**
(619) 449-6441. American. Gastropub. **$8-$14.** 9828 Mission Gorge Rd,
Suite A 92071. SR 52 exit 17 (Cuyamaca St), 0.4 mi n, then 0.3 mi e; at
Trolley Square at Santee Town Center. ⌊L⌋ ⌊D⌋

SAN YSIDRO

◆◆ Achiote Sabor Mexicano
(619) 690-1494. Mexican. Family Dining. **$6-$20.** 4419 Camino de la Plaza 92173. I-5 exit 2 (Dairy Mart Rd), just w, then 2 mi s; 0.5 mi n of Mexico border; next to Las Americanas Premium Outlet.
B L D ⅃M ◯

SAUSALITO

◆◆◆ Poggio
(415) 332-7771. Italian. Casual Dining. **$14-$69.** 777 Bridgeway 94965. US 101 exit Alexander Ave, 1.5 mi e; in Casa Madrona Hotel & Spa.
B L D

SEAL BEACH

◆◆◆ Spaghettini Grill & Jazz Club
(562) 596-2199. Northern Italian. Casual Dining. **$14-$45.** 3005 Old Ranch Pkwy 90740. I-405 exit 22 (Seal Beach Blvd/Los Alamitos), just n.
L D ◯

SHERMAN OAKS

◆◆ Cafe Cordiale
(818) 789-1985. American. Casual Dining. **$7-$30.** 14015 Ventura Blvd 91423. US 101 exit 16 (Woodman Ave), 0.5 mi s, then 0.4 mi w.
L D

◆◆◆ P.F. Chang's China Bistro
(818) 784-1694. Chinese. Fine Dining. **$10-$25.** 15301 Ventura Blvd, Suite P-22 91403. US 101 exit 18 (Sepulveda Blvd) northbound, just s, then just w; exit 19B (Haskell Ave) southbound, just s, then just w; in Sherman Oaks Galleria. L D

SOLANA BEACH

◆◆ Parioli Italian Bistro
(858) 755-2525. Italian. Casual Dining. **$9-$28.** 647 S Hwy 101 92075. I-5 exit 36 (Via de la Valle), 1 mi w, then just n. L D ⅃M

SOLVANG

◆◆ Chomp
(805) 688-7733. Burgers. Family Dining. **$7-$10.** 1693 Mission Dr 93463. SR 154 exit 246 (Mission Dr) northwest, just w. L D

◆ Greenhouse Cafe
(805) 688-8408. American. Casual Dining. **$8-$14.** 487 Atterdag Rd 93463. SR 246, just s. B L D ◯

◆ Mandarin Touch
(805) 686-0222. Mandarin. Casual Dining. **$8-$29.** 1635 Mission Dr 93463. On SR 246. L D LATE ◯

SONOMA

◆ Crisp Bake Shop
(707) 933-9999. American. Quick Serve. **$7-$9.** 720 W Napa St 95476. Between 5th St W and Sonoma Hwy. B L

◆◆◆ the girl & the fig
(707) 938-3634. French. Casual Dining. **$12-$24.** 110 W Spain St 95476. In historic Sonoma Plaza; in Sonoma Hotel. L D

◆◆ HopMonk Tavern Sonoma
(707) 935-9100. American. Casual Dining. **$11-$23.** 691 Broadway St 95476. SR 12, just s. L D

◆◆◆ LaSalette Restaurant
(707) 938-1927. Portuguese. Casual Dining. **$11-$28.** 452-H 1st St E 95476. In Sonoma Plaza. L D ⅃M

◆◆ Swiss Hotel Restaurant
(707) 938-2884. Swiss. Casual Dining. **$9-$30.** 18 W Spain St 95476. In Sonoma Plaza. L D

SOUTH LAKE TAHOE

◆◆◆ Nepheles
(530) 544-8130. California. Casual Dining. **$22-$37.** 1169 Ski Run Blvd 96150. 1.1 mi s of casino area to Ski Run Blvd, 0.3 mi w. D 🎟

TAHOE CITY

◆◆ Dockside 700 Wine Bar & Grill
(530) 581-0303. American. Casual Dining. **$8-$32.** 700 N Lake Tahoe Blvd 96145. Jct SR 89 and 28 (N Lake Blvd), just ne; at Tahoe City Marina. L D ⅃M

TEHACHAPI

◆◆◆ Jake's Steakhouse
(661) 822-6015. Steak. Casual Dining. **$9-$26.** 213 S Curry St 93561. SR 58 exit 149 (Mill St), s on H St, then just e on Tehachapi Blvd; downtown. L D

TEMECULA

◆◆◆ Cafe Champagne
(951) 699-0088. California. Casual Dining. **$17-$39.** 32575 Rancho California Rd 92591. I-15 exit 59 (Rancho California Rd), 4 mi e; at Thornton Winery. L D

◆◆◆ Pinnacle Restaurant
(951) 676-8231. Mediterranean. Casual Dining. **$15-$22.** 40620 Calle Contento 92591. I-15 exit 59 (Rancho California Rd), 5 mi e, then 0.3 mi n; at Falkner Winery. L

◆◆◆ Texas Lil's Mesquite Grill
(951) 699-5457. Barbecue Steak. Casual Dining. **$9-$27.** 28495 Old Town Front St 92590. I-15 exit 59 (Rancho California Rd), just w, then 0.5 mi s. L D ◯

THOUSAND OAKS

◆◆◆ Lazy Dog Restaurant and Bar
(805) 449-5206. American. Casual Dining. **$9-$18.** 172 W Hillcrest Dr 91360. US 101 exit 44 (Moorpark Rd), just n on Hillcrest; next to Thousand Oaks Mall. L D LATE ⅃M

THREE RIVERS

◆◆◆ Gateway Restaurant
(559) 561-4133. American. Casual Dining. **$12-$41.** 45978 Sierra Dr 93271. SR 198, 6 mi ne of town center; 0.5 mi sw of entrance to Sequoia National Park; in Gateway Lodge. L D ◯

TORRANCE

◆◆◆ Restaurant Christine
(310) 373-1952. Continental. Casual Dining. **$11-$33.** 24530 Hawthorne Blvd 90505. I-405 exit 42A (Hawthorne Blvd), 6.1 mi s; s of Pacific Coast Hwy; in Hillside Village. L D

TUSTIN

◆◆◆ Quinn's Old Town Grill
(714) 731-2263. Irish. Gastropub. **$14-$30.** 405 El Camino Real 92780. I-5 exit 102 (Newport Ave), just ne on Newport Ave, then just e.
B L D

TWENTYNINE PALMS

◆◆ The Rib Co.
(760) 367-1663. Barbecue. Casual Dining. **$9-$32.** 72183 Twentynine Palms Hwy 92277. SR 62, 1.8 mi w of Adobe Rd. L D ◯

UPPER LAKE

◆◆ Blue Wing Saloon Restaurant
(707) 275-2233. American. Gastropub. **$11-$26.** 9520 Main St 95485. Just n of SR 20; downtown. L D

VENTURA

▼▼ 71 Palm Restaurant
(805) 653-7222. French. Casual Dining. **$10-$30.** 71 N Palm St 93001. US 101 exit 70A (California St), just n to Main St, just w, then just n.
[L] [D]

▼▼ Greek at the Harbor
(805) 650-5350. Greek. Casual Dining. **$12-$30.** 1583 Spinnaker Dr, Suite 101 93001. US 101 exit 68 (Seaward Ave), just w, 1.8 mi sw on Harbor Blvd, then 0.8 mi w; in Ventura Harbor Village.
[B] [L] [D] [AC]

▼ Spinnaker Steak & Seafood Broiler
(805) 658-6220. Steak Seafood. Casual Dining. **$10-$40.** 1583 Spinnaker Dr, Suite 109 93001. US 101 exit 68 (Seaward Ave), 1.8 mi sw on Harbor Blvd, then 0.8 mi w; in Ventura Harbor Village. [L] [D]

VISALIA

▼▼▼ The Vintage Press
(559) 733-3033. California. Fine Dining. **$12-$38.** 216 N Willis St 93291. SR 198 exit 105A (Central Visalia), just n to Center St, then just w; downtown. [L] [D]

WESTLAKE VILLAGE

▼▼▼ Marmalade Cafe
(805) 370-1331. American. Casual Dining. **$11-$23.** 140 Promenade Way, Suite 1 91362. US 101 exit 40 (Westlake Blvd), just n; in Westlake Promenade. [B] [L] [D]

▼▼▼ Mediterraneo
(818) 889-9105. Mediterranean. Fine Dining. **$15-$35.** 32037 Agoura Rd 91361. US 101 exit 40 (Westlake Blvd), 1.3 mi se; in Westlake Village Inn. [B] [L] [D] [✎]

▼▼▼ Tuscany II Ristorante
(805) 495-2768. Italian. Fine Dining. **$12-$35.** 968 S Westlake Blvd 91361. US 101 exit 40 (Westlake Blvd), 0.3 mi w; in Westlake Plaza Shopping Center. [L] [D]

WOODLAND HILLS

▼▼ Jerry's Famous Deli and Restaurant
(818) 340-0830. Deli. Casual Dining. **$10-$19.** 21857 Ventura Blvd 91307. US 101 exit 26 (Ventura Blvd), just n. [B] [L] [D] [LATE]

YERMO

⚡ ▼ Peggy Sue's Diner
(760) 254-3370. American. Family Dining. **$7-$13.** 35654 Yermo Rd 92398. I-15 exit 191 (Ghost Town Rd), just ne. [B] [L] [D] [✎]

Colorado

BOULDER

▼▼▼ The Greenbriar Inn
(303) 440-7979. American. Fine Dining. **$22-$39.** 8735 N Foothills Hwy 80302. North of town on US 36 (28th St), west side of highway. [D]

BROOMFIELD

▼▼▼ Village Tavern
(720) 887-6900. American. Casual Dining. **$9-$30.** 100 W Flatiron Crossing Dr 80021. US 36 (Boulder Tpke) exit Interlocken Loop/Storagetek Dr; in Flatiron Shopping District. [L] [D]

CARBONDALE

▼▼ Village Smithy Restaurant
(970) 963-9990. American. Casual Dining. **$5-$18.** 26 S 3rd St 81623. At 3rd and Main sts; downtown. [B] [L]

CRESTED BUTTE

▼▼▼ Django's Restaurant & Wine Bar
(970) 349-7574. Small Plates. Fine Dining. **$11-$25.** 620 Gothic Rd 81225. 2.6 mi n of Elk Ave; in Mountaineer Square Courtyard; at Mt. Crested Butte. [D]

DENVER

▼▼▼ Bistro Vendome
(303) 825-3232. French. Casual Dining. **$16-$25.** 1420 Larimer St 80202. Between 14th and 15th sts. [D]

DURANGO

⚡ ▼▼▼ Guido's Favorite Foods
(970) 259-5028. Italian. Casual Dining. **$12-$26.** 1201 Main Ave 81301. Corner of 12th St and Main Ave. [L] [D]

HESPERUS

▼▼▼ Kennebec Cafe
(970) 247-5674. Mediterranean. Casual Dining. **$12-$36.** 4 CR 124 81326. 10 mi w on US 160 (north side). [L] [D]

PUEBLO

▼▼ Magpies
(719) 542-5522. American. Casual Dining. **$7-$23.** 229 S Union Ave 81003. I-25 exit 98B, 0.3 mi w, then 0.5 mi sw; downtown. [L]

VAIL

▼▼▼ Bol Vail
(970) 476-5300. American. Casual Dining. **$16-$36.** 141 E Meadow Dr 81657. I-70 exit 176, just s, 3rd exit at roundabout, 0.3 mi e to Vail Center Rd, just s, then just w; in Solaris Residences. [D]

Connecticut

CHESTER

▼▼▼ Restaurant L & E
(860) 526-5301. French. Fine Dining. **$17-$36.** 59 Main St 06412. Jct SR 148, just se; center. [D]

HARTFORD

▼▼▼ Trumbull Kitchen
(860) 493-7417. International. Fine Dining. **$11-$30.** 150 Trumbull St 06103. Between Asylum and Pearl sts; downtown. [L] [D]

MANCHESTER

▼▼▼ Cavey's Restaurant-Italian
(860) 643-2751. Northern Italian. Fine Dining. **$9-$44.** 45 E Center St 06040. On US 6 and 44, just e of jct SR 83; downtown. [D]

MYSTIC

▼▼▼ Anthony J's Bistro
(860) 536-0448. New Italian. Casual Dining. **$9-$32.** 6 Holmes St 06355. I-95 exit 90, 1.1 mi s on SR 27, then just w. [L] [D]

NEW CANAAN

▼▼▼ The Roger Sherman Inn
(203) 966-4541. Continental. Casual Dining. **$14-$46.** 195 Oenoke Ridge 06840. Merritt Pkwy exit 37, 3 mi n on SR 124. [L] [D]

▼▼▼ Solé
(203) 972-8887. Italian. Fine Dining. **$12-$38.** 105 Elm St 06840. Between Park St and South Ave; downtown. [L] [D]

NEW HAVEN

▼▼▼▼ John Davenport's at the Top of the Park
(203) 772-6664. New England. Fine Dining. $13-$34. 155 Temple St 06510. Between Chapel and Crown sts; downtown; in Omni New Haven Hotel at Yale. [B] [L] [D]

SOUTH NORWALK

▼▼▼▼ Match
(203) 852-1088. New American. Casual Dining. $21-$38. 98 Washington St 06854. I-95 exit 14 northbound, 0.3 mi nw on Fairfield Ave, then just e; exit 16 southbound, 0.4 mi se on East Ave, then 0.7 mi w to SR 136. [D]

▼▼▼▼ Strada 18
(203) 853-4546. Italian. Casual Dining. $11-$26. 122 Washington St 06854. I-95 exit 14 northbound, 0.3 mi nw on Fairfield Ave, then just e; exit 16 southbound, 0.4 mi se on East Ave, then 0.7 mi w to SR 136. [L] [D]

STAMFORD

▼▼▼▼ Barcelona Restaurant and Wine Bar
(203) 348-4800. Spanish Small Plates. Casual Dining. $6-$26. 222 Summer St 06901. Between Broad and Main sts; downtown. [L] [D] [&M]

STONINGTON

▼▼ Dog Watch Cafe
(860) 415-4510. American. Casual Dining. $10-$26. 194 Water St 06378. Jct US 1A, just sw on Alpha Ave, then just n. [L] [D] [&M]

WEST HARTFORD

▼▼▼▼ Max's Oyster Bar
(860) 236-6299. Seafood. Fine Dining. $15-$35. 964 Farmington Ave 06107. On SR 4; between S Main St and Lasalle Rd; center. [L] [D] [&M]

WESTPORT

▼ Shake Shack
(203) 682-6570. Burgers Hot Dogs. Quick Serve. $3-$9. 1849 Post Rd E 06880. I-95 exit 19, just e on US 1. [L] [D] [&M]

WOODSTOCK

🔺🔺🔺 ▼▼▼▼ Inn at Woodstock Hill
(860) 928-0528. Continental. Fine Dining. $10-$50. 94 Plaine Hill Rd 06281. 0.8 mi n on SR 169. [L] [D]

Delaware

LEWES

▼▼▼ The Buttery
(302) 645-7755. American. Fine Dining. $12-$38. 102 2nd St 19958. Jct 2nd St and Savannah Rd (US 9 business route). [L] [D]

REHOBOTH BEACH

🔺🔺🔺 ▼▼▼ Victoria's
(302) 227-0615. American. Fine Dining. $10-$36. 2 Olive Ave 19971. Just n of Rehoboth Ave; in Boardwalk Plaza Hotel. [B] [L] [D]

District of Columbia

WASHINGTON, D.C.

▼▼▼ 14K Restaurant & Lounge
(202) 218-7575. American. Casual Dining. $8-$36. 1001 14th St NW 20005. At 14th and K sts NW; in Hamilton Crowne Plaza, Washington DC. [B] [L] [D] [&M]

▼▼▼▼ Acadiana
(202) 408-8848. Southern American. Fine Dining. $13-$35. 901 New York Ave NW 20001. Between 9th and 10th sts. [L] [D]

▼▼▼ Art and Soul
(202) 393-7777. Regional American. Casual Dining. $15-$39. 415 New Jersey Ave NW 20001. On Capitol Hill, just n of Capitol grounds; in The Liaison Capitol Hill, An Affinia Hotel. [B] [L] [D] [&M]

▼▼▼ Blue Duck Tavern
(202) 419-6755. American. Fine Dining. $14-$45. 1201 24th St NW 20037. 24th and M sts NW; in Park Hyatt Washington, D.C. [B] [L] [D] [&M]

▼▼▼ Bobby Van's Grill
(202) 589-1504. Steak. Fine Dining. $12-$50. 1201 New York Ave NW 20005. 12th St and New York Ave NW. [L] [D] [&M]

▼▼▼ Bourbon Steak
(202) 944-2026. American. Fine Dining. $19-$65. 2800 Pennsylvania Ave NW 20007. Jct M St NW and Pennsylvania Ave NW; in Four Seasons Hotel Washington, D.C. [L] [D] [&M]

▼▼▼ Brasserie Beck
(202) 408-1717. Belgian. Casual Dining. $12-$36. 1101 K St NW 20005. Jct K and 11th sts NW. [L] [D] [LATE]

▼▼▼ Cafe du Parc
(202) 942-7000. French. Casual Dining. $15-$32. 1401 Pennsylvania Ave NW 20004. Just e of the White House; jct 14th St NW; in The Willard InterContinental. [B] [L] [D] [&M]

▼▼▼ Cafe Milano
(202) 333-6183. Italian. Casual Dining. $16-$56. 3251 Prospect St NW 20007. Off Wisconsin Ave; just n of M St NW. [L] [D]

▼▼ Café Olé
(202) 244-1330. Mediterranean Small Plates. Casual Dining. $5-$16. 4000 Wisconsin Ave NW 20016. Jct Upton St; in Tenleytown area. [L] [D]

▼▼▼ Cashion's Eat Place
(202) 797-1819. American. Fine Dining. $22-$32. 1819 Columbia Rd NW 20009. Between 18th St and Belmont Rd NW; in Adams Morgan area. [D]

▼▼▼ Central Michel Richard
(202) 626-0015. American. Fine Dining. $15-$35. 1001 Pennsylvania Ave NW 20004. Jct 11th St NW and Pennsylvania Ave NW. [L] [D] [&M]

▼▼▼ Charlie Palmer Steak
(202) 547-8100. Steak. Fine Dining. $18-$49. 101 Constitution Ave NW 20001. On Capitol Hill; jct 1st St and Constitution Ave NW. [L] [D] [&M]

▼▼▼ Doi Moi
(202) 733-5131. Asian Small Plates. Casual Dining. $14-$25. 1800 14th St NW 20009. At 14th and S sts NW. [D] [&M]

▼▼ The Grill from Ipanema
(202) 986-0757. Brazilian. Casual Dining. $15-$25. 1858 Columbia Rd NW 20009. Between 18th St and Belmont Rd; in Adam's Morgan area. [D]

▼▼ Lauriol Plaza
(202) 387-0035. Latin American. Casual Dining. $9-$22. 1835 18th St NW 20009. Jct 18th and T sts NW. [L] [D]

▼▼ Mai Thai of Georgetown
(202) 337-2424. Thai. Casual Dining. $10-$35. 3251 Prospect St NW 20007. Between 33rd St and Wisconsin Ave; in Georgetown. [L] [D]

▼▼ Meiwah Restaurant
(202) 833-2888. Chinese. Casual Dining. $10-$32. 1200 New Hampshire Ave NW 20036. Jct M St and New Hampshire Ave NW. [L] [D] [&M]

▼ Menomale
(202) 248-3946. Pizza. Casual Dining. $11-$19. 2711 12th St NE 20018. Just n of Rhode Island Ave NE. [L] [D] [&M]

▼▼▼ New Heights

(202) 234-4110. New American. Fine Dining. **$18-$34.** 2317 Calvert St NW 20008. Just w of Connecticut Ave NW; opposite Rock Creek Park. [D] [&M]

▼▼ Petits Plats

(202) 518-0018. French. Casual Dining. **$13-$29.** 2653 Connecticut Ave NW 20008. At Calvert St. [L] [D]

▼▼▼ Robert's Restaurant

(202) 756-5300. American. Fine Dining. **$14-$46.** 2500 Calvert St NW 20008. Just w of Connecticut Ave; in Omni Shoreham Hotel. [B] [L] [D]

▼▼▼▼ Westend Bistro

(202) 974-4900. New American. Fine Dining. **$12-$36.** 1150 22nd St NW 20037. At 22nd and M sts NW; in The Ritz-Carlton, Washington, D.C. [L] [D] [&M]

Florida

BOCA RATON

▼▼▼ Rocco's Tacos & Tequila Bar

(561) 416-2131. Mexican. Fine Dining. **$3-$24.** 5250 Town Center Cir 33486. I-95 exit 44 (Palmetto Park Rd), 0.7 mi w to Military Tr, then 1.1 mi n; in The Shops at Boca Center. [L] [D] [LATE] [&M] [🌙]

▼▼▼ Uncle Tai's

(561) 368-8806. Chinese. Fine Dining. **$12-$49.** 5250 Town Center Cir 33486. I-95 exit 44 (Palmetto Park Rd), 0.3 mi w, then 1 mi n on Military Tr; in The Shops at Boca Center. [L] [D] [🌙]

BONITA SPRINGS

▼▼ Big Al's City Grill

(239) 948-7444. American. Casual Dining. **$6-$20.** 25101 S Tamiami Tr 34135. I-75 exit 116, 3.5 mi w to US 41 (Tamiami Tr), then 3.1 mi n; in The Prado at Spring Creek Plaza. [L] [D] [LATE] [&M]

BOYNTON BEACH

▼▼ Hurricane Alley Raw Bar & Restaurant

(561) 364-4008. American. Casual Dining. **$8-$18.** 529 E Ocean Ave 33435. I-95 exit 57 (Boynton Beach Blvd), 1 mi e to US 1 (Federal Hwy), just s to Ocean Ave, then just w. [L] [D] [🌙]

CAPE CORAL

▼ New England Moorings Seafood & Moor

(239) 851-9141. Seafood. Casual Dining. **$9-$18.** 1326 SE 16th Pl 33990. Just e of jct S Del Prado Blvd on SE 14th St, just n. [D]

CAPE HAZE

▼▼ Johnny Leverock's Seafood House

(941) 698-6900. Seafood. Casual Dining. **$7-$30.** 7092 Placida Rd 33946. Jct CR 771/775/776, 5 mi s to Panama Blvd, just w to Ferry Landing (Gulf Blvd), then 1.1 mi w. [L] [D]

CAPTIVA

▼▼ The Green Flash Bayside Restaurant

(239) 472-3337. Seafood. Casual Dining. **$7-$47.** 15183 Captiva Dr 33924. Jct Murmond Ln. [L] [D]

▼▼ The Mucky Duck

(239) 472-3434. Seafood. Casual Dining. **$8-$39.** 11546 Andy Rosse Ln 33924. Just w of jct Captiva Dr. [L] [D]

▼▼ R C Otter's Island Eats

(239) 395-1142. American. Casual Dining. **$7-$29.** 11506 Andy Rosse Ln 33924. Jct Captiva Dr. [B] [L] [D]

CELEBRATION

▼▼ Market Street Cafe

(407) 566-1144. American. Casual Dining. **$8-$18.** 701 Front St 34747. SR 417 exit 2 (Celebration Ave), 0.6 mi sw to Mulberry Ave, then just se to Front St, then just sw; downtown. [B] [L] [D]

CLEARWATER

▼▼ Pickles Plus Deli

(727) 725-3325. Sandwiches Breakfast. Casual Dining. **$7-$11.** 2530 N McMullen Booth Rd 33761. On CR 611 at Enterprise Rd; in Northwood Plaza. [B] [L] [D]

COCONUT GROVE

▼▼ Berries in the Grove

(305) 448-2111. International. Casual Dining. **$11-$25.** 2884 SW 27th Ave 33133. Just e of US 1. [L] [D]

▼▼▼ Calamari Restaurant

(305) 441-0219. Italian. Casual Dining. **$12-$36.** 3540 Main Hwy 33133. Between Franklin and Charles aves; downtown. [L] [D]

CORAL GABLES

▼▼ Angelique Euro Cafe

(305) 529-9922. International. Casual Dining. **$8-$38.** 117 Miracle Mile 33134. Between Ponce de Leon Blvd and Galiano St; downtown. [L] [D]

▼▼◆ Caffe Abbracci

(305) 441-0700. Northern Italian. Casual Dining. **$17-$26.** 318 Aragon Ave 33134. At Aragon Ave and Salzedo St; just e of SR 953 (LeJeune Rd); downtown. [L] [D] [🌙]

▼▼▼ Ortanique Cuisine of the Sun

(305) 446-7710. New Caribbean. Casual Dining. **$12-$55.** 278 Miracle Mile 33134. Between SR 953 (LeJeune Rd) and Ponce de Leon Blvd; next to theater. [L] [D] [&M]

▼▼▼ Sawa Restaurant and Lounge

(305) 447-6555. International Fusion. Casual Dining. **$12-$29.** 360 San Lorenzo Ave, Suite 1500 33146. In Village of Merrick Park. [L] [D] [&M]

▼▼ Spritz of Coral Gables

(305) 444-3388. Italian. Casual Dining. **$11-$22.** 2305 Ponce de Leon Blvd 33134. Just s of Giralda Ave; between Aragon and Giralda aves. [L] [D] [&M]

▼▼ Tarpon Bend Raw Bar & Grill

(305) 444-3210. Seafood. Casual Dining. **$12-$37.** 65 Miracle Mile 33134. On Miracle Mile; just w of Douglas Rd; between Galiano St and S Douglas Rd. [L] [D] [&M]

CORAL SPRINGS

▼▼◆ Big Bear Brewing Company

(954) 341-5545. American. Gastropub. **$9-$30.** 1800 N University Dr 33065. From SR 814 (Atlantic Blvd), 0.9 mi n. [L] [D] [&M] [🌙]

▼▼◆ Runyon's

(954) 752-2333. Continental. Fine Dining. **$10-$49.** 9810 W Sample Rd 33065. Florida Tpke exit 69 (SR 834), 5.7 mi w. [L] [D] [🌙]

CRESTVIEW

▼▼▼ The Wild Olive

(850) 682-4455. American. Casual Dining. **$9-$29.** 797 N Pearl St 32536. Corner of Hickory Ave; downtown. [L] [D] [&M]

DAVIE

▼ Char-Hut 84

(954) 474-9312. American. Quick Serve. **$4-$20.** 9000 W SR 84 33324. I-595 exit 4, just w; in Pine Island Ridge Plaza. [L] [D] [&M]

DELRAY BEACH

▼▼▼▼ 32 East
(561) 276-7868. New American. Fine Dining. **$24-$45.** 32 E Atlantic Ave 33444. I-95 exit 52 (Atlantic Ave), 1.1 mi e; just e of Swinton Ave.
[D] [&M]

▼▼ Boston's on the Beach
(561) 278-3364. American. Casual Dining. **$7-$34.** 40 S Ocean Blvd 33483. I-95 exit 52 (Atlantic Ave), 2 mi e to SR A1A (Ocean Blvd), then just s. [L] [D] [LATE]

DESTIN

▼▼ Graffiti
(850) 424-7514. Mediterranean. Casual Dining. **$9-$29.** 707 Harbor Blvd 32541. On US 98, 2.9 mi w of bridge. [D]

▼▼ Hog's Breath Saloon & Cafe
(850) 837-5991. American. Casual Dining. **$7-$22.** 541 Harbor Blvd 32541. On US 98, 1 mi e of Destin Bridge. [L] [D]

FORT LAUDERDALE

▼▼▼ Big City Tavern Restaurant & Bar
(954) 727-0307. American. Casual Dining. **$12-$35.** 609 E Las Olas Blvd 33301. I-95 exit 27 (Broward Blvd), 2.4 mi e to US 1, just s to Las Olas Blvd, then just e; downtown. [L] [D] [LATE]

▼▼▼ Bimini Boatyard Bar & Grill
(954) 525-7400. Caribbean. Casual Dining. **$11-$32.** 1555 SE 17th St 33316. I-95 exit 25 (SR 84), 2 mi e to SE 6th Ave (US 1), 0.5 mi n to SE 17th St, then 0.6 mi e. [L] [D] [&M] [\]

▼▼ Johnny V Restaurant & Lounge
(954) 761-7920. Regional Continental. Casual Dining. **$9-$42.** 625 E Las Olas Blvd 33301. Just e of US 1 (Federal Hwy); downtown. [L] [D]

▼▼▼ Sunfish Grill
(954) 788-2434. New American. Fine Dining. **$14-$39.** 2775 E Oakland Park Blvd 33306. I-95 exit 31A (Oakland Park Blvd), 3.3 mi e. [D] [&M]

▼▼▼ Thai Spice
(954) 771-4535. Thai. Fine Dining. **$12-$85.** 1514 E Commercial Blvd 33334. I-95 exit 32 (Commercial Blvd), 1.5 mi e. [L] [D]

FORT MYERS

▼▼ The Prawnbroker Restaurant & Fish Market
(239) 489-2226. Seafood. Casual Dining. **$12-$25.** 13451-16 McGregor Blvd 33919. 0.7 mi s of jct College Pkwy at Cypress Lake Dr; in Cypress Square. [D]

GULF BREEZE

▼▼ Aegean Breeze
(850) 916-0430. Greek. Casual Dining. **$7-$25.** 913 Gulf Breeze Pkwy, Unit 20 32561. Just e of jct SR 399; in Harbour Town Village Plaza. [L] [D]

HIGHLAND BEACH

▼▼▼ Latitudes Ocean Grill
(561) 278-6241. American. Casual Dining. **$10-$35.** 2809 S Ocean Blvd 33487. I-95 exit 51 (Linton Blvd), 1.7 mi e to Ocean Blvd (SR A1A), then 1.1 mi s; in Delray Sands Resort on Highland Beach.
[B] [L] [D] [&M] [\]

HOLLYWOOD

▼ The Le Tub Saloon
(954) 921-9425. American. Casual Dining. **$9-$21.** 1100 N Ocean Dr 33019. I-95 exit 21 (Sheridan St), 3 mi e to Ocean Dr (SR A1A), then 1.1 mi s; on Intracoastal Waterway. [L] [D] [LATE] [AC] [\]

INLET BEACH

▼▼ Spicy Noodle
(850) 231-0955. Italian. Casual Dining. **$7-$18.** 13667 E Emerald Coast Pkwy 32413. 1 mi e of Rosemary Beach, just w of Phillips Inlet Bridge.
[L] [D]

ISLAMORADA

▼▼ Marker 88 Restaurant
(305) 852-9315. Seafood. Casual Dining. **$10-$38.** 88000 Overseas Hwy 33036. US 1 at MM 88. [L] [D] [\]

JACKSONVILLE

▼▼ Seven Bridges Grille & Brewery
(904) 997-1999. International. Casual Dining. **$10-$27.** 9735 Gate Pkwy N 32246. I-95 exit 344 (SR 202), 2.5 mi e on J Turner Butler Blvd, 0.8 mi n on SR 115, then just e. [L] [D] [&M]

JACKSONVILLE BEACH

▼▼ Metro Diner
(904) 853-6817. American. Casual Dining. **$8-$14.** 1534 3rd St N 32250. On SR A1A/3rd St, between 14th and 15th aves N. [B] [L]

JUNO BEACH

▼▼ Juno Beach Fish House
(561) 626-2636. Seafood. Casual Dining. **$8-$29.** 13980 US Hwy 1 33408. I-95 exit 83 (Donald Ross Rd), 4.2 mi e to US 1; jct US 1 and Donald Ross Rd. [L] [D] [&M]

KEY BISCAYNE

▼▼ Sushi Siam
(305) 361-7768. Asian. Casual Dining. **$13-$33.** 632 Crandon Blvd 33149. Just s of jct Crandon Blvd and McIntyre St. [L] [D]

KEY LARGO

▼▼ Ballyhoo's Historic Seafood Grille
(305) 852-0822. Seafood. Casual Dining. **$9-$36.** 97860 Overseas Hwy 33037. US 1 at MM 97.8; in median. [L] [D]

◢◣◢ ▼▼ The Fish House Restaurant & Seafood Market
(305) 451-4665. Seafood. Casual Dining. **$11-$32.** 102401 Overseas Hwy 33037. US 1 at MM 102.4. [L] [D]

KEY WEST

▼ Amigo's
(305) 292-2009. Mexican. Quick Serve. **$6-$17.** 425 Greene St 33040. Between Duval St and Telegraph Ln. [B] [L] [D]

▼▼▼ Blackfin Bistro
(305) 509-7408. International. Casual Dining. **$12-$32.** 918 Duval St 33040. Between Truman and Olivia sts. [L] [D]

▼▼ Blue Heaven
(305) 296-8666. Caribbean. Casual Dining. **$8-$35.** 729 Thomas St 33040. Just s of Duval St; corner of Petronia and Thomas sts.
[B] [L] [D] [AC] [\]

▼ Half Shell Raw Bar
(305) 294-7496. American. Casual Dining. **$7-$22.** 231 Margaret St 33040. West end of Margaret St; at Lands End Village in Historic Seaport District; at Key West Bight Ferry Terminal. [L] [D] [&M] [AC]

▼ Harpoon Harry's
(305) 294-8744. Comfort Food. Casual Dining. **$7-$13.** 832 Caroline St 33040. Corner of Margaret and Caroline sts; across from Key West Historic Seaport. [B] [L] [D]

Lobo's Mixed Grill
(305) 296-5303. Burgers Sandwiches. Quick Serve. **$9-$12.** 5 Key Lime Square 33040. Between Southland and Angela sts; just off Duval St.
L D Ⓐ

Louie's Backyard
(305) 294-1061. Regional American. Casual Dining. **$12-$40.** 700 Waddell Ave 33040. Just s of Truman Ave via Simonton St to South St, just e to Vernon, then s. L D &M

Pepe's Cafe
(305) 294-7192. American. Casual Dining. **$12-$31.** 806 Caroline St 33040. Between Margaret and William sts; just e of Duval St.
B L D

Prime Steakhouse
(305) 296-4000. Steak Seafood. Casual Dining. **$24-$45.** 951 Caroline St 33040. Between Grinnel and Margaret sts; in Conch Harbor Marina in Old Town; above Dante's Key West Bar & Pool. D

SHOR American Seafood Grill
(305) 809-4000. American. Casual Dining. **$13-$46.** 601 Front St 33040. Corner of Simonton and Front sts; just n of Mallory Square; in Old Town; in Hyatt Key West Resort & Spa. B L D

Square One Restaurant
(305) 296-4300. American. Fine Dining. **$8-$35.** 1075 Duval St 33040. At Duval Square, just e of Truman Ave. D &M

LAKE MARY

Liam Fitzpatrick's Irish Restaurant & Pub
(407) 936-3782. Irish. Gastropub. **$10-$26.** 951 Market Promenade, Suite 1115 32746. I-4 exit 101A, just w; in Colonial TownPark.
L D LATE

LAKE WORTH

Brogues Down Under
(561) 585-1885. Irish. Casual Dining. **$12-$22.** 621 Lake Ave 33460. I-95 exit 64 (10th Ave), 0.7 mi e to US 1 (Dixie Hwy), 0.8 mi s to Lake Ave, then just e; downtown. L D LATE ✎

Dave's Last Resort & Raw Bar
(561) 588-5208. American. Casual Dining. **$6-$20.** 632 Lake Ave 33460. Jct K St and Lake Ave; downtown. L D ✎

Havana Hideout
(561) 585-8444. Latin American. Casual Dining. **$5-$12.** 509 Lake Ave 33460. i-95 exit 64 (10th Ave), 0.7 mi e to US 1 (Dixie Hwy), 0.8 mi s to Lake Ave, then just e; downtown. L D Ⓐ ✎

MARCO ISLAND

CJ's on the Bay
(239) 389-4511. International. Casual Dining. **$10-$36.** 740 N Collier Blvd 34145. Jct SR 951 (N Collier Blvd) and W Elkcam Cir; in Esplanade Complex; on Smokehouse Bay. L D

MELBOURNE

El Chico
(321) 722-4622. Tex-Mex. Casual Dining. **$7-$16.** 1751 Evans Rd 32904. I-95 exit 180 (US 192/New Haven Ave), 3.2 mi e to Evans Rd, then just n; in front of Melbourne Square Mall. L D &M ✎

MIAMI

Buena Vista Bistro
(305) 456-5909. International. Casual Dining. **$10-$33.** 4582 NE 2nd Ave 33137. I-195 exit 2B, just w to NE 2nd Ave, then 0.5 mi n.
L D LATE ✎

Burger & Beer Joint
(305) 523-2244. Burgers. Casual Dining. **$10-$32.** 900 S Miami Ave, Suite 130 33130. Corner of SW 9th St and S Miami Ave; in The Shops at Mary Brickell Village. L D LATE

Fratelli Milano
(305) 373-2300. Italian. Casual Dining. **$10-$28.** 213 SE 1st St 33131. Between SE 3rd and NE 2nd aves; in Ingraham Building. L D

Mercadito
(786) 369-0430. Mexican Small Plates. Casual Dining. **$8-$24.** 3252 NE 1st Ave 33137. I-195 exit 2A (N Miami Ave), just s to NE 34th St, just e to NE 1st Ave, then just s. L D LATE &M

Morgan's
(305) 573-9678. International. Casual Dining. **$14-$27.** 28 NE 29th St 33132. Corner of N Miami Ave and NE 29th St. B L D &M

Soyka
(305) 759-3117. New American. Casual Dining. **$10-$34.** 5556 NE 4th Ct 33137. I-95 exit 6A (NW 62nd St), 1.2 mi e to NE 4th Ct, then 0.4 mi s.
L D &M

Tobacco Road
(305) 374-1198. American. Casual Dining. **$8-$15.** 626 S Miami Ave 33130. Just n of jct 7th St SW. L D LATE

MIAMI BEACH

Alta Mare
(305) 532-3061. International. Casual Dining. **$19-$42.** 1233 Lincoln Rd 33139. Between Alton Rd and Alton Ct; far west end of Lincoln Road Mall.
D &M

Aura
(305) 695-1100. International. Casual Dining. **$12-$36.** 613 Lincoln Rd 33139. Between Pennsylvania and Euclid aves. L D ✎

Balans
(305) 534-9191. International. Casual Dining. **$9-$30.** 1022 Lincoln Rd 33139. Between Michigan and Lenox aves. B L D ✎

Big Pink
(305) 532-4700. American. Casual Dining. **$10-$23.** 157 Collins Ave 33139. Jct 2nd St. B L D LATE

The Cafe at Books and Books
(305) 695-8898. International. Casual Dining. **$10-$23.** 933 Lincoln Rd 33139. Between Michigan and Jefferson aves; in Lincoln Road Mall.
L D &M Ⓐ

Doraku
(305) 695-8383. Japanese. Casual Dining. **$7-$30.** 1104 Lincoln Rd 33139. Between Lenox and Alton rds; in Lincoln Road Mall.
L D &M

Huahua's Taqueria
(305) 534-8226. Mexican. Quick Serve. **$7-$9.** 1211 Lincoln Rd 33139. Between Alton Rd and Alton Ct. L D LATE

News Cafe
(305) 538-6397. International. Casual Dining. **$11-$20.** 800 Ocean Dr 33139. Corner of 8th St and Ocean Dr. B L D 24 ✎

Nexxt Cafe
(305) 532-6643. International. Casual Dining. **$8-$27.** 700 Lincoln Rd 33139. Between Euclid and Meridian aves; in Lincoln Road Mall area.
B L D &M ✎

Pelican Restcafé
(305) 673-3373. International. Casual Dining. **$11-$46.** 826 Ocean Dr 33139. Between 8th and 9th sts; just e of SR A1A (Collins Ave).
B L D LATE

Prime 112
(305) 532-8112. Steak. Fine Dining. **$15-$56.** 112 Ocean Dr 33139. Just e of SR A1A (Collins Ave), jct 1st St and Ocean Dr; in The Browns Hotel.
L D ✎

♦♦♦ Sardinia Ristorante
(305) 531-2228. Italian. Fine Dining. **$15-$40.** 1801 Purdy Ave 33139. Corner of Purdy Ave and 18th St; across from Island View Park.
[L] [D] [LATE] [&M]

♦ Shake Shack
(305) 434-7787. Hot Dogs Burgers. Quick Serve. **$3-$9.** 1111 Lincoln Rd 33139. Between Alton Rd and Lenox Ave. [L] [D]

♦♦♦ Sushi Samba Dromo
(305) 673-5337. Asian. Casual Dining. **$15-$39.** 600 Lincoln Rd 33139. Corner of Pennsylvania Ave; in Lincoln Road Mall. [L] [D] [LATE] [&M]

♦♦♦ Tongue and Cheek
(305) 704-2900. New American. Casual Dining. **$16-$42.** 431 Washington Ave 33139. Corner of Washington Ave and 5th St. [L] [D]

MILTON

♦♦ Blackwater Bistro
(850) 623-1105. American. Casual Dining. **$9-$24.** 5147 Elmira St 32570. Jct US 90 (Caroline St), just s; in historic downtown district.
[L] [D] [&M]

MOUNT DORA

♦ One Flight Up Café
(407) 758-9818. Sandwiches. Quick Serve. **$9-$10.** 440 Donnelly St 32757. Jct 5th Ave, just s; downtown. [B] [L] [D] [LATE]

NAPLES

♦♦♦ M Waterfront Grille
(239) 263-4421. New Continental. Fine Dining. **$13-$39.** 4300 Gulf Shore Blvd 34103. 1.2 miles w of US 41 (9th St N); corner of Park Shore Dr and Gulf Shore Blvd; in The Village on Venetian Bay.
[L] [D] [LATE] [&M]

♦♦♦ Noodles Italian Cafe & Sushi Bar
(239) 592-0050. Italian Noodles Sushi. Casual Dining. **$9-$29.** 1585 Pine Ridge Rd, Suite 5 34109. I-75 exit 107, 3 mi w on Pine Ridge Rd (CR 896); in Mission Square. [L] [D]

♦♦♦ Sea Salt
(239) 434-7258. New Seafood. Fine Dining. **$16-$38.** 1186 3rd St S 34102. Downtown; in Old Naples. [L] [D] [&M]

♦♦♦ Yabba Island Grill
(239) 262-5787. Caribbean. Casual Dining. **$15-$32.** 711 5th Ave S 34102. Just w of US 41 (Tamiami Tr); downtown. [D] [&M]

NEW SMYRNA BEACH

♦ Cafe Heavenly
(386) 427-7475. American. Quick Serve. **$8-$21.** 115 Flagler Ave 32169. East end of North Causeway Bridge. [L] [D] [↘]

♦♦♦ Gnarly Surf Bar & Grill
(386) 957-3844. Fusion. Casual Dining. **$9-$22.** 114 Flagler Ave 32169. Jct Flagler and N Peninsula aves; at base of draw bridge. [L] [D]

NORTH BAY VILLAGE

♦♦♦ Oggi Ristorante Italiano
(305) 866-1238. Italian. Casual Dining. **$14-$31.** 1666 79th St Cswy, Suite 102 33141. 2 mi w of SR A1A (Collins Ave). [L] [D]

ORLANDO

♦♦♦ 310 Lakeside
(407) 373-0310. New American. Fine Dining. **$10-$30.** 301 E Pine St 32801. Jct Rosalind and Central aves, just e. [L] [D] [LATE]

♦ Christo's Cafe
(407) 425-8136. American. Casual Dining. **$4-$12.** 1815 Edgewater Dr 32804. I-4 exit 85, 1 mi w, then just s. [B] [L] [D] [↘]

♦♦ Dandelion Communitea Cafe
(407) 362-1864. Vegetarian. Casual Dining. **$8-$10.** 618 N Thornton Ave 32803. Jct SR 50 (Colonial Dr) and Thornton Ave, just s. [L] [D]

♦ Graffiti Junktion
(407) 426-9503. American. Casual Dining. **$9-$13.** 900 E Washington Ave 32801. Jct E Washington and S Hyer aves. [L] [D] [LATE]

♦♦♦ K Restaurant & Wine Bar
(407) 872-2332. Continental. Fine Dining. **$12-$26.** 1710 Edgewater Dr 32804. I-4 exit 85, 1 mi w, then just w. [L] [D]

PALM BEACH

♦♦♦ Polo Steaks & Seafood
(561) 655-5430. Steak Seafood. Fine Dining. **$10-$45.** 155 Hammon Ave 33480. 1 blk s of Worth Ave; between S County Rd and SR A1A (Ocean Blvd); in The Colony Palm Beach. [B] [L] [D]

⬙⬙⬙ ♦♦ Testa's Palm Beach
(561) 832-0992. International. Casual Dining. **$12-$39.** 221 Royal Pociana Way 33480. 0.3 mi e of Flagler Memorial Bridge. [B] [L] [D]

PALM BEACH GARDENS

♦♦♦ Cafe Chardonnay
(561) 627-2662. Continental. Fine Dining. **$11-$36.** 4533 PGA Blvd 33418. I-95 exit 79B (PGA Blvd), 0.3 mi w; jct PGA Blvd and Military Tr; in Garden Square Shoppes. [L] [D] [↘]

♦♦♦ The Capital Grille
(561) 630-4994. Steak. Fine Dining. **$17-$49.** 11365 Legacy Ave 33410. I-95 exit 79A (PGA Blvd), 0.7 mi e to Legacy Ave, then just s. [L] [D]

♦ Chuck Burger Joint
(561) 629-5191. Burgers. Quick Serve. **$6-$12.** 4665 PGA Blvd 33418. I-95 exit 79B (PGA Blvd), 0.7 mi w; on Mainstreet at Midtown.
[L] [D] [↘]

PALM BEACH SHORES

♦♦ Johnny Longboats Tropical Grill on the Beach
(561) 249-2795. Caribbean. Casual Dining. **$10-$26.** 2401 N Ocean Dr 33404. On Singer Island; just s of SR A1A. [B] [L] [D] [&M] [↘]

♦♦ Sailfish Waterfront Dining
(561) 842-8449. Seafood. Casual Dining. **$10-$35.** 98 Lake Dr 33404. I-95 exit 76 (Blue Heron Blvd), 4 mi e to Lake Dr, then 0.4 mi s; in Sailfish Marina & Resort. [B] [L] [D] [↘]

PALM HARBOR

♦♦ East Lake Cafe
(727) 772-0707. Breakfast Sandwiches. Casual Dining. **$8-$12.** 3430 E Lake Rd 34685. 1.9 mi e of jct US 19 on Tampa Rd (CR 752); in East Lake Woodlands Shopping Center. [B] [L]

♦♦ Thirsty Marlin Grill & Bar
(727) 784-3469. Seafood. Casual Dining. **$8-$26.** 1023 Florida Ave 34683. Just e of jct US 19. [L] [D] [LATE]

PANAMA CITY BEACH

♦♦ Hofbrau Beer Garden
(850) 235-4632. German. Casual Dining. **$8-$18.** 701 Pier Park Dr, Suite 155 32413. 1.2 mi e of jct SR 79 and 30, just n. [L] [D] [&M]

♦♦ Triple "J" Steak & Seafood
(850) 233-9514. Steak Seafood. Casual Dining. **$7-$32.** 2218 Thomas Dr 32408. 1 mi s of US 98. [L] [D]

PENSACOLA

▼▼▼ Angus

(850) 432-0539. Steak Seafood. Casual Dining. **$10-$39.** 1101 Scenic Hwy 32503. On US 90; between E Moreno and E Blount sts. ⟨D⟩ ⟨✕⟩

▼▼▼ The Oar House on Bayou Chico

(850) 549-4444. American. Casual Dining. **$8-$23.** 1000 S Pace Blvd 32502. I-110 exit 4, 1.1 mi w on SR 295 (Fairfield Dr), then 3 mi s on SR 292. ⟨L⟩ ⟨D⟩ ⟨LATE⟩ ⟨&M⟩ ⟨AC⟩

▼▼▼ O'Briens Bistro

(850) 477-9120. American. Casual Dining. **$9-$25.** 4350 Bayou Blvd, Suite 8 32503. Jct N 12th Ave and SR 296, just n. ⟨L⟩ ⟨D⟩ ⟨&M⟩

PENSACOLA BEACH

▼▼ Hemingway's Island Grill

(850) 934-4747. American. Casual Dining. **$8-$34.** 400 Quietwater Beach, Suite 16 32561. On Quietwater Beach boardwalk. ⟨L⟩ ⟨D⟩

PLANTATION

▼▼ Mustard Seed Bistro & Market

(954) 533-9326. Continental. Casual Dining. **$12-$34.** 256 S University Dr 33324. I-595 exit 5 (University Dr), 1.2 mi w to University Dr, then 1.2 mi n; in Plantation Community Plaza. ⟨B⟩ ⟨L⟩ ⟨D⟩

PORT CHARLOTTE

▼▼ K's Family Pizzeria & Restaurant

(941) 625-6989. Italian. Casual Dining. **$5-$19.** 2000 Rio De Janiero Ave 33954. I-75 exit 170, just n on CR 769 (Kings Hwy), 2.1 mi se on Sandhill Blvd, then 1.1 mi s; jct Rampart Blvd; in Deep Creek Plaza. ⟨L⟩ ⟨D⟩

PUNTA GORDA

▼▼ Porto Bello at Latitudes

(941) 639-3650. American. Casual Dining. **$11-$23.** 3200 Matecumbe Key Rd 33955. On CR 768/765 (Burnt Store Rd); in Burnt Store Marina and Country Club. ⟨L⟩ ⟨D⟩ ⟨&M⟩

QUINCY

▼▼ The Whip Waterfront Pub & Grub

(850) 875-2605. Seafood Steak. Casual Dining. **$8-$24.** 3129 Cooks Landing Rd 32351. 3 mi se of jct SR 267. ⟨L⟩ ⟨D⟩

ST. PETE BEACH

▼▼ Sea Critters Cafe

(727) 360-3706. Seafood. Casual Dining. **$8-$25.** 2007 Pass-A-Grille Way 33706. On SR 699, 0.8 mi s of Pinellas Bayway, jct 21st Ave; in Historic Pass-A-Grille. ⟨L⟩ ⟨D⟩

ST. PETERSBURG

▼▼ Babalu Restaurant & Bar

(727) 576-7414. Comfort Food. Casual Dining. **$4-$18.** 9246 4th St N 33702. Jct 92nd Ave N. ⟨L⟩ ⟨D⟩

SANTA ROSA BEACH

▼ Miss Lucille's Gossip Parlor

(850) 267-2522. American. Quick Serve. **$3-$10.** 45 Town Center Loop, Suite C7 32459. Jct CR 393, 3 mi e of US 98, on CR 30A; in Gulf Place Shopping Village. ⟨B⟩ ⟨L⟩

SARASOTA

▼▼ Mattison's City Grille

(941) 330-0440. Continental. Casual Dining. **$8-$25.** 1 N Lemon Ave 34236. Jct Main St; downtown. ⟨L⟩ ⟨D⟩ ⟨LATE⟩ ⟨AC⟩

SIESTA KEY

▼▼ The Old Salty Dog

(941) 349-0158. American. Casual Dining. **$4-$29.** 5023 Ocean Blvd 34242. Just n; in Siesta Village. ⟨L⟩ ⟨D⟩ ⟨LATE⟩

▼▼ Village Cafe

(941) 349-2822. Breakfast Sandwiches. Casual Dining. **$5-$10.** 5133 Ocean Blvd 34242. Jct Avenida Madera; center; in Siesta Village. ⟨B⟩ ⟨L⟩

SOUTH MIAMI

▼▼ Blu by Best Friends

(305) 666-9285. Italian Pizza. Casual Dining. **$8-$16.** 7201 SW 59th Ave 33143. Just se of US 1 exit Sunset Dr. ⟨L⟩ ⟨D⟩

▼ Khoury's Restaurant

(305) 662-7707. Mediterranean. Casual Dining. **$8-$25.** 5887 SW 73rd St 33143. Just e off US 1. ⟨L⟩ ⟨D⟩

▼▼ Trattoria Sole

(305) 666-9392. Italian. Casual Dining. **$12-$30.** 5894 Sunset Dr 33143. Just se of US 1. ⟨L⟩ ⟨D⟩

TALLAHASSEE

▼▼ Avenue Eat and Drink

(850) 224-0115. Southern Fusion. Casual Dining. **$8-$46.** 115 E Park Ave 32301. Jct Adams St and Park Ave; downtown. ⟨L⟩ ⟨D⟩

🆔 ▼▼ Barnacle Bill's

(850) 385-8734. Seafood. Casual Dining. **$8-$19.** 1830 N Monroe St 32303. I-10 exit 199, 2 mi s. ⟨D⟩ ⟨&M⟩

▼ The Black Bean Cuban Cafe

(850) 656-7848. Cuban. Family Dining. **$5-$10.** 2205 Apalachee Pkwy 32301. 1 mi se on US 27. ⟨L⟩ ⟨D⟩

▼▼ Midtown Filling Station

(850) 329-7981. American. Gastropub. **$6-$12.** 1122 Thomasville Rd 32303. Between E 5th and Williams sts; downtown. ⟨L⟩ ⟨D⟩

▼▼▼ The Mockingbird Cafe

(850) 222-4956. American. Casual Dining. **$7-$25.** 1225 N Monroe St 32303. Just n of downtown. ⟨L⟩ ⟨D⟩ ⟨LATE⟩

▼▼▼ Rummy's Pizza, Pasta & Grill

(850) 878-8669. Pizza. Casual Dining. **$7-$19.** 2887 Kerry Forest Pkwy 32312. 3 mi n on Thomasville Rd. ⟨L⟩ ⟨D⟩ ⟨&M⟩

TAMPA

▼▼ SQUARE 1 Burgers & Bar

(813) 414-0101. Burgers. Casual Dining. **$8-$15.** 3701 Henderson Blvd 33609. I-275 exit 41A, 1.4 mi s on N Dale Mabry Hwy (US 92), then just e. ⟨L⟩ ⟨D⟩ ⟨&M⟩

WEST PALM BEACH

▼▼ Howley's Restaurant

(561) 833-5691. American. Casual Dining. **$7-$22.** 4700 S Dixie Hwy 33405. I-95 exit 68 (Southern Blvd), 1 mi e to US 1 (Dixie Hwy), then 0.4 mi s. ⟨B⟩ ⟨L⟩ ⟨D⟩ ⟨LATE⟩ ⟨✕⟩

▼ Relish

(561) 629-5377. Burgers. Quick Serve. **$10-$17.** 401 Northwood Rd 33407. I-95 exit 71 (Palm Beach Lakes Blvd), 2.3 mi e to US 1 (Dixie Hwy), then 0.7 mi n; in Northwood Village. ⟨L⟩ ⟨D⟩ ⟨✕⟩

WINTER PARK

▼▼▼ 310 Park South
(407) 647-7277. American. Casual Dining. **$10-$33.** 310 S Park Ave 32789. Between E Lyman and E New England aves. ⌊L⌋ ⌊D⌋

▼▼ Bosphorous Turkish Cuisine
(407) 644-8609. Turkish. Fine Dining. **$9-$28.** 108 S Park Ave 32789. Just s of Morse Blvd. ⌊L⌋ ⌊D⌋ ⌊◣⌋

▼▼ The Briarpatch
(407) 628-8651. American. Casual Dining. **$8-$15.** 252 N Park Ave 32789. I-4 exit 87 (Fairbanks Ave), 2 mi e, then 0.5 mi n. ⌊B⌋ ⌊L⌋ ⌊◣⌋

▼ Bubbalou's Bodacious Bar-B-Que
(407) 628-1212. Barbecue. Family Dining. **$5-$16.** 1471 Lee Rd 32789. On SR 423, just w of jct US 17-92. ⌊L⌋ ⌊D⌋ ⌊◣⌋

▼ BurgerFi
(407) 622-2010. Burgers Hot Dogs. Quick Serve. **$5-$9.** 538 S Park Ave 32789. Jct S Park and Fairbanks aves. ⌊L⌋ ⌊D⌋ ⌊LATE⌋

▼▼▼ Cafe De France
(407) 647-1869. French. Fine Dining. **$9-$34.** 526 S Park Ave 32789. I-4 exit 87, 1.9 mi e, then just n. ⌊L⌋ ⌊D⌋ ⌊◣⌋

▼▼▼ Dexter's of Winter Park
(407) 629-1150. New American. Casual Dining. **$7-$25.** 558 W New England Ave 32789. I-4 exit 87 (Fairbanks Ave), 0.7 mi e, 0.3 mi n to Morse Blvd, just e to Pennsylvania Ave, then just s. ⌊L⌋ ⌊D⌋ ⌊◣⌋

Georgia

ATHENS

▼▼▼ DePalma's Italian Cafe
(706) 552-1237. Italian. Casual Dining. **$6-$20.** 2080 Timothy Rd 30606. SR 8/10 Loop exit US 78 business route (Broad St), just e. ⌊L⌋ ⌊D⌋ ⌊◣⌋

▼▼▼ East West Bistro
(706) 546-4240. International. Fine Dining. **$8-$28.** 351 E Broad St 30605. Downtown. ⌊L⌋ ⌊D⌋

▼▼▼ Hilltop Grille
(706) 353-7667. American. Casual Dining. **$7-$31.** 2310 W Broad St 30606. Jct SR 10 Loop and US 78 business route (Broad St), 2.9 mi ne on US 78 business route (Broad St). ⌊L⌋ ⌊D⌋ ⌊◣⌋

▼ Marti's at Midday
(706) 543-3541. Deli. Quick Serve. **$5-$10.** 1280 Prince Ave 30606. SR 10 Loop exit 7 (Prince Ave), 0.7 mi se. ⌊B⌋ ⌊L⌋

▼▼▼ The National
(706) 549-3450. European. Fine Dining. **$10-$26.** 232 W Hancock Ave 30601. Just w of center; downtown. ⌊L⌋ ⌊D⌋

ATLANTA

▼ Alon's Bakery & Market
(404) 872-6000. Deli. Quick Serve. **$6-$12.** 1394 N Highland Ave 30306. Jct Virginia and Highland aves, 1.5 mi n. ⌊B⌋ ⌊L⌋ ⌊D⌋

▼▼▼▼ C & S Seafood & Oyster Bar
(770) 272-0999. Seafood. Fine Dining. **$10-$40.** 3240 Cobb Pkwy 30339. I-285 exit 20 westbound; exit 19 eastbound, 1.3 mi s; in Riverview Village. ⌊L⌋ ⌊D⌋ ⌊◣⌋

▼▼ Cowtippers
(404) 874-3751. Steak. Casual Dining. **$6-$23.** 1600 Piedmont Ave NE 30324. Jct Monroe Dr NE, just s. ⌊L⌋ ⌊D⌋

▼▼ Five Season's Brewing Company
(404) 255-5911. New American. Gastropub. **$8-$27.** 5600 Roswell Rd, Suite 21 30342. I-285 exit 27, just s; in The Prado. ⌊L⌋ ⌊D⌋

▼▼▼ Food 101
(404) 497-9700. New American. Fine Dining. **$12-$29.** 4969 Roswell Rd, Suite 200 30342. I-285 exit 25, 1.5 mi s; in Belle Isle Shopping Center. ⌊L⌋ ⌊D⌋ ⌊◣⌋

▼ Grindhouse Killer Burgers
(404) 254-2223. Burgers. Quick Serve. **$3-$9.** 1842 Piedmont Ave NE 30324. I-85 exit 86 northbound, just n to Monroe Dr, just e to Piedmont Rd NE, then just s; exit 88 southbound, just e to Lenox Rd, just e to Cheshire Bridge Rd, 1.5 mi e to Piedmont Rd, then just w. ⌊L⌋ ⌊D⌋ ⌊◣⌋

▼ J. Christopher's
(404) 917-0350. Breakfast. Casual Dining. **$5-$11.** 3050 Peachtree Rd NW 30305. Jct Peachtree and W Paces Ferry rds, just s. ⌊B⌋ ⌊L⌋ ⌊◣⌋

◈◈▼▼▼ Max Lager's Wood-Fired Grill & Brewery
(404) 525-4400. American. Casual Dining. **$9-$32.** 320 Peachtree St NW 30308. I-75/85 exit 249A to Baker St, 0.3 mi w to Peachtree St, then just n. ⌊L⌋ ⌊D⌋

▼ Pig-N-Chik
(404) 255-6368. Barbecue. Quick Serve. **$6-$24.** 4920 Roswell Rd NE 30342. I-285 exit 25, 1.5 mi s; in Fountain Oaks Shopping Center. ⌊L⌋ ⌊D⌋

▼▼▼ Starfish Restaurant
(404) 350-0799. Japanese. Fine Dining. **$7-$30.** 2255 Peachtree Rd NE 30309. Between Collier Rd and 26th St. ⌊L⌋ ⌊D⌋ ⌊◣⌋

▼▼▼ Violette
(404) 633-3363. French. Casual Dining. **$9-$25.** 2948 Clairmont Rd 30329. I-85 exit 91, just w. ⌊L⌋ ⌊D⌋

AUGUSTA

▼▼▼ French Market Grille
(706) 737-4865. Cajun. Casual Dining. **$7-$30.** 425 Highland Ave 30909. Jct SR 28 (Washington Rd), 1.8 mi s on Berckmans Rd; in Surrey Center. ⌊L⌋ ⌊D⌋

▼▼▼ Oliviana's Pizzeria & Grill
(706) 723-1242. Northern Italian. Fine Dining. **$9-$21.** 399 Highland Ave, Suite A 30909. Jct SR 28 (Washington Rd), 1.8 mi s on Berckmans Rd; in Surrey Center. ⌊L⌋ ⌊D⌋ ⌊◣⌋

▼▼ Somewhere in Augusta Bar & Grill
(706) 739-0002. American. Casual Dining. **$7-$15.** 2820 Washington Rd 30909. I-20 exit 199 (Washington Rd), 0.6 mi e. ⌊L⌋ ⌊D⌋ ⌊LATE⌋ ⌊◣⌋

CANTON

▼ Casey's Home Cooking
(770) 720-0017. Southern. Quick Serve. **$5-$7.** 140 Keith Dr 30114. I-575 exit 20, just e, then just s. ⌊L⌋ ⌊D⌋

COLUMBUS

▼▼ Ben's ChopHouse Steak & Seafood
(706) 256-0466. Steak Seafood. Casual Dining. **$15-$49.** 5300 Sidney Simons Blvd 31904. I-185 exit 8, just w to Sidney Simons Blvd, then just s. ⌊L⌋ ⌊D⌋ ⌊◣⌋

▼▼ Cannon Brewpub
(706) 653-2337. American. Gastropub. **$10-$28.** 1041 Broadway 31901. In historic uptown district. ⌊L⌋ ⌊D⌋

DULUTH

▼▼▼ Kurt's Euro Bistro
(770) 623-4128. European. Fine Dining. **$12-$38.** 3305 Peachtree Industrial Blvd, Suite 100 30096. Jct River Green Pkwy; in The Village at River Green. ⌊D⌋

EAST POINT

♦ UBar
(404) 349-2301. American. Casual Dining. **$6-$26.** 3515 Camp Creek Pkwy, Suites 50-70 30344. I-285 exit 2, just w; in Camp Creek Pointe. ⌑L⌑ ⌑D⌑ ⌑LATE⌑ ⌑♿⌑

FORT VALLEY

♦ Peachtree Café
(478) 825-3592. American. Family Dining. **$5-$12.** 50 Lane Rd 31030. I-75 exit 142 (SR 96), 4.9 mi w; in Lane Southern Orchard. ⌑D⌑

HELEN

♦♦ Cafe International
(706) 878-3102. Continental. Casual Dining. **$6-$18.** 8546 Main St 30545. Downtown. ⌑L⌑ ⌑D⌑

JEKYLL ISLAND

♦♦ Latitude 31
(912) 635-3800. American. Casual Dining. **$9-$35.** 370 Riverview Dr 31527. 1 mi n from Jekyll Island Bridge. ⌑L⌑ ⌑D⌑

KENNESAW

♦♦ Kuroshio Sushi Bar & Grille
(770) 499-7160. Japanese. Casual Dining. **$9-$46.** 840 Ernest Barrett Pkwy NW, Suite 500 30144. I-75 exit 69, 0.3 mi w. ⌑L⌑ ⌑D⌑ ⌑♿⌑

MACON

♦♦ Molly's Cafe
(478) 744-9898. Sandwiches. Casual Dining. **$6-$12.** 402 Cherry St 31201. I-16 exit 2, 0.5 mi s on Martin Luther King Jr Blvd, then just w; downtown. ⌑L⌑

♦♦ The Rookery
(478) 746-8658. American. Casual Dining. **$8-$17.** 543 Cherry St 31201. I-16 exit 2, 0.5 mi s on Martin Luther King Jr Blvd, then just w; downtown. ⌑L⌑ ⌑D⌑

MADISON

♦♦ Madison Chophouse Grille
(706) 342-0910. American. Casual Dining. **$8-$25.** 202 S Main St 30650. I-20 exit 114, 3 mi n on US 441; Historic Town Square. ⌑L⌑ ⌑D⌑

MARIETTA

♦♦♦ Chicken And The Egg
(678) 388-8813. American. Casual Dining. **$9-$18.** 800 Whitlock Ave, Suite 124 30064. 0.8 mi w of Historic Marietta Square. ⌑L⌑ ⌑D⌑ ⌑♿⌑

♦ Jack's New Yorker Deli
(770) 424-1402. Sandwiches. Quick Serve. **$5-$12.** 168 Roswell St 30060. Just off Historic Marietta Square; downtown. ⌑B⌑ ⌑L⌑ ⌑♿⌑

♦♦ Willie Rae's
(770) 792-9995. Cajun. Casual Dining. **$8-$19.** 25 N Park Square 30060. On Historic Marietta Square; downtown. ⌑L⌑ ⌑D⌑

PLAINS

♦ Buffalo Cafe at The Old Bank
(229) 824-4520. American. Casual Dining. **$4-$10.** 118 Main St 31780. Center. ⌑L⌑ ⌑D⌑

PORT WENTWORTH

♦♦ El Ranchito
(912) 965-0270. Mexican. Casual Dining. **$6-$15.** 7306 Hwy 21, Suite 201 31407. I-95 exit 109 (SR 21), 0.5 mi n to SR 30, then just e; in shopping center. ⌑L⌑ ⌑D⌑ ⌑♿⌑

ROSWELL

♦♦♦ Brookwood Grill
(770) 587-0102. New American. Fine Dining. **$10-$27.** 880A Holcomb Bridge Rd 30076. SR 400 exit 7B, 0.8 mi w. ⌑L⌑ ⌑D⌑

♦♦ Pastis
(770) 640-3870. French. Fine Dining. **$10-$30.** 928 Canton St 30075. Downtown. ⌑L⌑ ⌑D⌑

ST. SIMONS ISLAND

♦♦ Barbara Jean's Restaurants
(912) 634-6500. Regional Comfort Food. Family Dining. **$8-$24.** 214 Mallery St 31522. Between Beachview Dr and Lord Ave; on south side of island. ⌑L⌑ ⌑D⌑

SAVANNAH

♦♦ Cilantro's Grill & Cantina
(912) 232-7070. Mexican. Casual Dining. **$6-$19.** 135 W Bay St 31401. Between Whitaker and Barnard sts. ⌑L⌑ ⌑D⌑ ⌑♿⌑

♦ Clary's Cafe
(912) 233-0402. Breakfast Sandwiches. Casual Dining. **$7-$13.** 404 Abercorn St 31401. Jct Jones St. ⌑B⌑ ⌑L⌑

♦♦♦ Corleone's
(912) 232-2720. Italian. Casual Dining. **$6-$30.** 44 Martin Luther King Jr Blvd 31401. Jct W Congress Ln. ⌑L⌑ ⌑D⌑

♦♦ The Distillery
(912) 236-1772. American. Casual Dining. **$7-$15.** 416 W Liberty St 31401. Jct W Broad St. ⌑L⌑ ⌑D⌑ ⌑LATE⌑ ⌑♿⌑

♦♦ Firefly Cafe
(912) 234-1971. American. Casual Dining. **$9-$25.** 321 Habersham St 31401. S of E Liberty St; at Harris St; on Troup Square. ⌑L⌑ ⌑D⌑

♦♦ Huey's New Orleans Cafe
(912) 234-7385. Creole. Casual Dining. **$8-$32.** 115 E River St 31401. On historic riverfront; under River Street Inn. ⌑B⌑ ⌑L⌑ ⌑D⌑

♦♦ Love's Seafood Restaurant
(912) 925-3616. Seafood. Casual Dining. **$11-$30.** 6817 Chief O.F. Love Rd 31419. I-95 exit 94 (SR 204/Abercorn St), 1.9 mi e to US 17 S, 2.8 mi sw to Basin Rd; just ne of Ogeechee River at Kings Ferry Bridge. ⌑D⌑ ⌑♿⌑

♦♦♦ Moon River Brewing Company
(912) 447-0943. American. Gastropub. **$6-$26.** 21 W Bay St 31401. Between Bull and Whitaker sts. ⌑L⌑ ⌑D⌑

♦♦♦ The Olde Pink House
(912) 232-4286. Regional Seafood. Fine Dining. **$12-$36.** 23 Abercorn St 31401. Between E Bryan and E Saint Julian sts; facing Reynolds Square. ⌑L⌑ ⌑D⌑

♦♦♦ River House Seafood & Bakery
(912) 234-1900. Seafood. Casual Dining. **$10-$36.** 125 W River St 31401. On historic riverfront. ⌑B⌑ ⌑L⌑ ⌑D⌑

♦♦♦ Sam Snead's Oak Grill & Tavern
(912) 963-0797. American. Fine Dining. **$10-$30.** 7 Sylvester C. Formey Dr 31408. I-95 exit 104, just se to Crossroads Pkwy, then just sw. ⌑L⌑ ⌑D⌑ ⌑♿⌑

♦♦♦ Vic's on the River Restaurant & Bar
(912) 721-1000. New American. Fine Dining. **$8-$32.** 26 E Bay St 31401. On historic riverfront; alternate entrance at 15 E River St. ⌑L⌑ ⌑D⌑ ⌑♿⌑

STATESBORO

♦♦ Gnats Landing
(912) 489-8291. American. Casual Dining. **$6-$18.** 470 S Main St 30458. Jct US 301/25 and SR 67, just s. ⌑L⌑ ⌑D⌑ ⌑LATE⌑

THOMASVILLE

▼ Granddaddy's Barbeque
(229) 225-9500. Barbecue. Casual Dining. **$7-$15.** 2128 Smith Ave 31792. Jct US 19 and 84. [B] [L] [D]

TIFTON

▼ ▼ El Cazador Mexican Restaurant
(229) 386-2126. Mexican. Casual Dining. **$5-$19.** 1021 W 2nd St 31794. I-75 exit 63B, just e. [L] [D]

VALDOSTA

▼▼▼ 306 North
(229) 249-5333. American. Casual Dining. **$7-$26.** 306 N Patterson St 31601. Downtown. [L] [D]

WOODSTOCK

▼ Burger Inn
(770) 926-1308. Sandwiches. Quick Serve. **$2-$8.** 9680 Main St 30188. I-575 exit 7, 0.9 mi e to Main St (Canton Rd), then just s. [B] [L]

▼▼▼ Century House Tavern
(770) 693-4552. New American. Fine Dining. **$15-$23.** 125 E Main St 30188. I-575 exit 8, 0.5 mi e to Main St, then just s; downtown. [L] [D] [&M]

▼ Hot Dog Heaven
(770) 591-5605. Hot Dogs. Quick Serve. **$3-$8.** 8558 Main St 30188. I-575 exit 8, 0.5 mi e; downtown. [L]

▼▼ TownLake Diner
(770) 675-3390. American. Casual Dining. **$6-$15.** 2990 Eagle Dr, Suite 100 30189. I-575 exit 8, 2 mi w. [B] [L] [D] [&M]

Idaho

GLENNS FERRY

▼▼ Carmela Vineyards Restaurant
(208) 366-2313. American. Casual Dining. **$7-$25.** 1289 W Madison Ave 83623. I-84 exit 120, 0.5 mi s to Bannock St, 0.4 mi e to Commercial St, 0.5 mi s to Madison Ave, then 0.7 mi w. [L] [D]

MCCALL

▼ Bistro 45 Wine Bar & Cafe
(208) 634-4515. American. Quick Serve. **$6-$13.** 1101 N 3rd St 83638. Downtown. [B] [L] [D]

WALLACE

ⒶⒶⒶ ▼▼ 1313 Club
(208) 752-9391. American. Casual Dining. **$6-$23.** 608 Bank St 83873. Downtown. [B] [L] [D]

Indiana

CARMEL

▼▼ Petite Chou
(317) 566-0765. French. Casual Dining. **$8-$29.** 14360 Clay Terrace Blvd 46032. I-465 exit 31, 6 mi n on US 31, then 0.4 mi w. [B] [L] [D] [&M]

INDIANAPOLIS

▼▼ The Barking Dog Cafe
(317) 924-2233. American. Casual Dining. **$7-$16.** 115 E 49th St 46205. I-65 exit 113, 4 mi n on Meridian St, then just e. [L] [D]

▼▼ Fire by the Monon
(317) 602-8590. American. Casual Dining. **$10-$17.** 6523 Ferguson St 46220. Jct N College Ave and 66th St, just s. [L] [D]

▼▼ Indianapolis Colts Grille
(317) 631-2007. American. Casual Dining. **$9-$36.** 110 W Washington St 46204. Jct Washington and Illinois sts. [L] [D] [LATE] [&M]

▼▼ The Milano Inn
(317) 264-3585. Italian. Casual Dining. **$8-$23.** 231 S College Ave 46202. Between Louisiana and Georgia sts. [L] [D] [&M]

▼▼ Monon Food Company
(317) 722-0176. American. Casual Dining. **$7-$15.** 6420 Cornell Ave 46220. Jct N College Ave and 64th St, just n on Cornell Ave; in a residential area. [L] [D] [&M]

▼▼ Patachou on the Park
(317) 632-0765. Breakfast Sandwiches. Casual Dining. **$8-$18.** 225 W Washington St 46204. Jct Washington St and Capitol Ave. [B] [L] [&M]

▼▼ Petite Chou
(317) 259-0765. French. Casual Dining. **$8-$29.** 823 Westfield Blvd 46220. I-465 exit 31, 4.7 mi s on Meridian St, then 1 mi e. [B] [L] [D]

▼▼ Sabbatical
(317) 273-5252. Small Plates. Casual Dining. **$3-$10.** 921 Broad Ripple Ave 46220. Jct Guilford Ave, just w. [L] [D] [LATE]

NASHVILLE

▼▼ Big Woods Brewing Company
(812) 988-6000. American. Casual Dining. **$8-$18.** 60 Molly Ln 47448. Jct SR 135 and Main St, just w to Molly Ln, then just n. [L] [D]

ZIONSVILLE

▼▼▼ Noah Grant's Grill House & Oyster Bar
(317) 732-2233. Steak Seafood. Casual Dining. **$8-$44.** 65 S 1st St 46077. Jct W Oak St. [D] [&M]

Kansas

COTTONWOOD FALLS

ⒶⒶⒶ ▼▼ Grand Central Grill
(620) 273-6763. American. Casual Dining. **$8-$35.** 215 Broadway 66845. US 177, just w on Main St, then just s; center of downtown; in Grand Central Hotel. [L] [D]

Kentucky

BOWLING GREEN

▼▼ Chaney's Dairy Barn & Restaurant
(270) 843-5567. Desserts Chicken. Quick Serve. **$6-$10.** 9191 Nashville Rd 42101. I-65 exit 20B (Natcher Pkwy), 3 mi nw to exit 6, then 4.8 mi s on SR 31 W. [L] [D] [&M]

▼▼ Griffs Deli
(270) 904-4743. Sandwiches Deli. Quick Serve. **$5-$9.** 1640 Scottsville Rd 42104. I-65 exit 22 (Scottsville Rd), 2.7 mi w. [L] [D] [&M]

CAVE CITY

▼▼ El Mazatlan
(270) 773-7448. Mexican. Casual Dining. **$7-$20.** 105 Gardner Ln 42127. I-65 exit 53, just e. [L] [D] [&M] [◣]

GRAND RIVERS

▼▼ Lite Side Cafe & Bakery
(270) 362-4586. Breakfast Burgers. Quick Serve. **$6-$8.** 2115 Dover Rd 42045. I-24/69 exit 31 (SR 453), 3.5 mi s. [B] [L]

PADUCAH

▼▼▼ Max's Brick Oven Cafe
(270) 575-3473. Mediterranean. Casual Dining. **$10-$25.** 112 Market House Square 42001. Between Broadway St and Kentucky Ave, on 2nd St; in historic downtown. [D] [◣]

▼▼ Tribeca Mexican Cuisine
(270) 444-3960. Mexican. Casual Dining. **$7-$15.** 127 Market House Square 42001. Between Kentucky Ave and Broadway St, on 2nd St; in historic downtown. [L] [D]

▼▼ Whaler's Catch
(270) 444-7701. Seafood. Casual Dining. **$10-$40.** 123 N 2nd St 42001. Downtown. [L] [D]

Louisiana

ABITA SPRINGS

▼▼ Abita Brew Pub
(985) 892-5837. Regional American. Casual Dining. **$9-$23.** 72011 Holly St 70420. Center; just w of traffic circle. [L] [D]

BATON ROUGE

▼ Red Zeppelin Pizza
(225) 302-7153. Pizza. Casual Dining. **$8-$20.** 4395 Perkins Rd 70808. Just w of College Rd. [L] [D]

COVINGTON

▼▼▼ Del Porto Ristorante
(985) 875-1006. Italian. Fine Dining. **$12-$36.** 501 E Boston St 70433. Jct New Hampshire St; downtown. [L] [D] [&M]

HAMMOND

▼▼ Tope la'
(985) 542-7600. Regional American. Casual Dining. **$9-$30.** 104 N Cate St 70401. I-12 exit 40 (US 51), 1.9 mi n, just e on W Morris St, then just n. [L] [D]

LAFAYETTE

▼▼▼ Blue Dog Cafe
(337) 237-0005. Cajun. Casual Dining. **$8-$32.** 1211 W Pinhook Rd 70503. SR 182, 1.1 mi w of jct US 90 (Evangeline Thruway). [L] [D]

NEW ORLEANS

▼ Cafe Beignet
(504) 525-2611. American. Quick Serve. **$5-$13.** 311 Bourbon St 70130. Between Bienville and Conti sts. [B] [L] [AC] [◣]

▼▼▼ Green Goddess
(504) 301-3347. New International. Casual Dining. **$12-$23.** 307 Exchange Pl 70130. Between Bienville and Conti sts, just sw of Supreme Court Building. [L] [D]

▼▼▼ The Marigny Brasserie
(504) 945-4472. Regional American. Casual Dining. **$12-$24.** 640 Frenchmen St 70116. Jct Royal St. [L] [D]

▼▼▼ Palace Cafe
(504) 523-1661. Creole. Fine Dining. **$12-$42.** 605 Canal St 70130. Between Royal and Chartres sts. [L] [D]

▼ Voo Doo BBQ & Grill
(504) 522-4647. Barbecue. Quick Serve. **$6-$25.** 1501 St. Charles Ave 70130. Between Melpomene Ave and Terpsichore St. [L] [D]

Maine

BAR HARBOR

▼▼▼ Cafe This Way
(207) 288-4483. American. Casual Dining. **$8-$26.** 14 Mt Desert St 04609. Between School and Main sts. [B] [D] [AC]

▼▼ Fish House Grill & Oyster Bar
(207) 288-3070. Seafood. Casual Dining. **$12-$40.** 1 West St 04609. Center; at Town Pier. [L] [D] [AC]

▼▼ Jack Russell's Steakhouse & Brewery
(207) 288-5214. American. Casual Dining. **$15-$28.** 102 Eden St 04609. 1.8 mi w on SR 3. [L] [D] [AC]

AAA ▼▼▼ The Looking Glass Restaurant
(207) 288-5663. American. Casual Dining. **$12-$39.** 50 Eden St 04609. 0.5 mi w on SR 3; in A Wonder View Inn. [B] [D]

▼▼▼ McKay's Public House
(207) 288-2002. American. Casual Dining. **$9-$26.** 231 Main St 04609. Just s of Newton Way; center. [D]

CAPE ELIZABETH

▼▼ Sea Glass
(207) 799-3134. Seafood. Fine Dining. **$12-$38.** 40 Bowery Beach Rd 04107. On SR 77, 7 mi s; in Inn by the Sea. [B] [L] [D] [&M]

KENNEBUNKPORT

▼▼▼ The Marine Room
(207) 967-3331. American. Casual Dining. **$10-$27.** 140 Ocean Ave 04046. From Dock Square, 1 mi s; in The Colony Hotel. [L] [D] [&M]

Maryland

ANNAPOLIS

AAA ▼▼ Buddy's Crabs & Ribs
(410) 626-1100. Seafood. Family Dining. **$8-$25.** 100 Main St 21401. Just nw of State Circle. [L] [D]

▼▼▼ Harry Browne's
(410) 263-4332. Continental. Fine Dining. **$10-$35.** 66 State Circle 21401. In historic district facing the State Capitol. [L] [D]

▼▼▼ Maria's Sicilian Ristorante & Cafe
(410) 268-2112. Italian. Casual Dining. **$10-$45.** 12 Market Space 21401. In historic district at city dock. [L] [D]

▼▼ Pusser's
(410) 626-0004. International. Casual Dining. **$10-$29.** 80 Compromise St 21401. At the city dock; in Annapolis Marriott Waterfront Hotel. [B] [L] [D]

BALTIMORE

▼▼▼ Ambassador Dining Room
(410) 366-1484. Indian Vegetarian. Fine Dining. **$13-$27.** 3811 Canterbury Rd 21218. Jct Canterbury Rd and 39th St; 1 blk from Johns Hopkins University Homewood Campus; in Ambassador Apartments. [L] [D]

▼▼ Amicci's
(410) 528-1096. Italian. Casual Dining. **$8-$19.** 231 S High St 21202. In Little Italy area. [L] [D]

▼▼▼ b-A Bolton Hill Bistro
(410) 383-8600. American. Casual Dining. **$13-$33.** 1501 Bolton St 21217. Jct Bolton and Mosher sts; in Bolton Hill area. [D]

▼▼▼ Germano's Piattini
(410) 752-4515. Regional Italian Small Plates. Casual Dining. **$6-$18.** 300 S High St 21202. At S High and Fawn sts; in Little Italy area. [L] [D]

BETHESDA

◈◈ Cesco Osteria
(301) 654-8333. Northern Italian. Fine Dining. **$11-$29.** 7401 Woodmont Ave 20814. Jct Montgomery Ln; 2 blks w of Wisconsin Ave. [L] [D]

◈◈ Uncle Julio's
(301) 656-2981. Mexican. Casual Dining. **$9-$24.** 4870 Bethesda Ave 20814. 2 blks w of SR 355; downtown. [L] [D]

CATONSVILLE

◈ Chef Paolino Cafe
(410) 747-4949. Italian. Family Dining. **$6-$19.** 726 Frederick Rd 21228. I-695 exit 13, 0.4 mi w; just n of jct Bloomsbury Ave. [L] [D]

CHESAPEAKE BEACH

◈◈ Rod 'N' Reel Restaurant
(301) 855-8351. Seafood. Casual Dining. **$10-$35.** 4160 Mears Ave 20732. Jct SR 261 and Mears Ave; in Chesapeake Beach Resort and Spa. [L] [D] [&M]

COLUMBIA

◈◈ The Tomato Palace
(410) 715-0211. Italian. Casual Dining. **$10-$27.** 10221 Wincopin Cir 21044. Off SR 175 (Little Patuxent Pkwy), 1.5 mi w of jct US 29; center. [L] [D]

FREDERICK

◈◈◈ Isabella's Taverna & Tapas Bar
(301) 698-8922. Spanish Small Plates. Casual Dining. **$11-$23.** 44 N Market St 21701. Between Church and Patrick sts; in historic district. [L] [D] [&M]

GLEN BURNIE

◈ Mission BBQ
(410) 773-9888. Barbecue. Casual Dining. **$7-$19.** 7748 Ritchie Hwy 21061. I-695 exit 3B eastbound; exit 2 westbound, 4.3 mi s on SR 2; in Harundale Plaza. [L] [D] [&M]

HANOVER

◈◈◈ Grillfire
(410) 799-2883. American. Casual Dining. **$11-$34.** 7793-A Arundel Mills Blvd 21076. SR 295 (Baltimore-Washington Pkwy) exit Arundel Mills Blvd, just e; in The Hotel at Arundel Preserve. [B] [L] [D] [&M]

◈◈ Rangoli
(410) 799-5650. Indian. Casual Dining. **$12-$27.** 7791-C Arundel Mills Blvd 21076. SR 295 (Baltimore-Washington Pkwy) exit Arundel Mills Blvd, just e. [L] [D] [&M]

LA PLATA

◈◈◈ The Crossing at Casey Jones
(301) 392-5116. American. Casual Dining. **$10-$30.** 417 E Charles St 20646. Just e of US 301. [L] [D]

LEONARDTOWN

◈◈◈ Cafe des Artistes
(301) 997-0500. French. Fine Dining. **$8-$39.** 41655 Fenwick St 20650. 0.4 mi w on Business Rt SR 5 from jct SR 5; on square. [L] [D]

NATIONAL HARBOR

◈◈ Fiorella Italian Kitchen & Pizzeria
(301) 839-1811. Italian Pizza. Casual Dining. **$12-$25.** 152 National Plaza 20745. I-95/495 exit 2A, 0.5 mi e. [L] [D]

NORTH EAST

◈◈◈◈ ◈◈ Woody's Crab House
(410) 287-3541. Seafood. Casual Dining. **$9-$35.** 29 S Main St 21901. I-95 exit 100, 2 mi e on SR 272. [L] [D]

OCEAN CITY

◈◈ The Blue Ox Bar & Grill
(410) 250-6440. American. Casual Dining. **$7-$26.** 12601 Coastal Hwy 21842. At 127th St. [B] [L] [D] [&M]

◈◈ Hooked
(410) 723-4665. American. Casual Dining. **$9-$25.** 8003 Coastal Hwy 21842. Jct 80th St. [L] [D] [&M]

◈◈ Malia's Cafe
(443) 664-2420. Breakfast Sandwiches. Casual Dining. **$5-$12.** 1800 N Baltimore Ave 21842. Jct 18th St. [B] [L]

◈◈◈ Sunset Grille
(410) 213-8110. Seafood. Casual Dining. **$10-$33.** 12933 Sunset Ave 21842. In West Ocean City; 0.6 mi s on Golf Course Rd from jct US 50, just e; at Sunset Marina. [L] [D] [&M]

POTOMAC

◈◈◈ Old Angler's Inn
(301) 365-2425. American. Fine Dining. **$10-$34.** 10801 MacArthur Blvd 20854. I-495 exit 41, 3 mi w via Clara Barton Pkwy and MacArthur Blvd. [L] [D]

ROCKVILLE

◈◈ Mykonos Grill
(301) 770-5999. Greek. Casual Dining. **$8-$31.** 121 Congressional Ln 20852. Jct SR 28, 2 mi s on SR 355; in Congressional Shopping Plaza. [L] [D]

◈◈◈ Nick's Chophouse
(301) 926-8869. Steak Seafood. Fine Dining. **$8-$46.** 700 King Farm Blvd 20850. I-270 exit 8 (Shady Grove Rd), 0.5 mi e, then 0.6 mi s on Gaither Rd. [L] [D]

SYKESVILLE

◈◈◈ Baldwin's Station
(410) 795-1041. American. Casual Dining. **$8-$36.** 7618 Main St 21784. I-70 exit 80 (SR 32), 7.6 mi n. [L] [D]

WESTMINSTER

◈◈◈ Liberatore's Ristorante
(410) 876-2121. Italian. Casual Dining. **$8-$29.** 521 Jermor Ln 21157. Jct SR 140 and 97; in 140 Village Shopping Center. [L] [D] [&M]

WHITE MARSH

◈◈ Red Brick Station
(410) 931-7827. American. Gastropub. **$7-$30.** 8149 Honeygo Blvd 21236. I-95 exit 67, 0.5 mi w on SR 43 (White Marsh Blvd), then 0.6 mi s; in The Avenue at White Marsh. [L] [D] [&M]

Massachusetts

BOSTON

◈◈◈ Masa
(617) 338-8884. Southwestern. Casual Dining. **$8-$30.** 439 Tremont St 02116. Between Arlington and E Berkeley sts. [D]

◈◈◈ Oak Long Bar & Kitchen
(617) 267-5300. American. Fine Dining. **$15-$40.** 138 St. James Ave 02116. At Copley Square; in The Fairmont Copley Plaza Boston. [B] [L] [D]

CAMBRIDGE

◈◈◈ Henrietta's Table
(617) 661-5005. Regional American. Casual Dining. **$7-$37.** 1 Bennett St 02138. Just s of Harvard Square; at Eliot St; in The Charles Hotel, Harvard Square. [◁] [B] [L] [D] [&M]

CHELMSFORD

▼▼▼ **moonstones**
(978) 256-7777. Mediterranean. Casual Dining. **$8-$36.** 185 Chelmsford Rd 01824. I-495 exit 34, just s on SR 110. [L] [D] [&M]

HYANNIS

▼▼▼ **Alberto's Ristorante**
(508) 778-1770. Northern Italian. Casual Dining. **$8-$36.** 360 Main St 02601. Just w of jct Barnstable Rd; downtown. [L] [D]

WELLESLEY

▼▼▼ **Blue Ginger, an East-West Bistro**
(781) 283-5790. Pacific Rim. Casual Dining. **$11-$41.** 583 Washington St 02482. SR 16, just se of SR 135. [L] [D] [&M]

WELLFLEET

▼▼▼ **Winslow's Tavern**
(508) 349-6450. New American. Casual Dining. **$13-$28.** 316 Main St 02667. US 6 exit Wellfleet Center, just e to town center. [D]

Michigan

ANN ARBOR

▼▼▼ **Real Seafood Co.**
(734) 769-7738. Seafood. Casual Dining. **$10-$36.** 341 S Main St 48104. Jct Huron St, just s; downtown. [L] [D]

BAY CITY

▼ **BJay's Pizza & Coneys**
(989) 686-2499. Pizza Hot Dogs. Quick Serve. **$6-$18.** 363 State Park Dr 48706. I-75 exit 164 (Wilder Rd), 1.5 mi e to N Euclid, then 3 mi n. [L] [D] [&M] [ℳ]

GRAND RAPIDS

▼▼ **HopCat**
(616) 451-4677. American. Casual Dining. **$8-$11.** 25 Ionia Ave NW 49503. Jct Weston St SW; downtown. [L] [D] [LATE]

PETOSKEY

▼▼▼ **Chandler's - A Restaurant**
(231) 347-2981. American. Fine Dining. **$10-$42.** 215 1/2 Howard St 49770. Jct E Lake St; downtown. [L] [D]

SUTTONS BAY

▼▼▼ **Martha's Leelanau Table Cafe**
(231) 271-2344. Regional American. Casual Dining. **$17-$30.** 413 N St. Joseph St 49682. Downtown. [B] [L] [D] [LATE] [&M]

Minnesota

MINNEAPOLIS

▼▼ **Birchwood Cafe**
(612) 722-4474. Natural/Organic. Casual Dining. **$6-$20.** 3311 E 25th St 55406. Jct S 33rd Ave. [B] [L] [D]

▼▼▼ **Cafe Lurcat-Bar Lurcat**
(612) 486-5500. New American. Fine Dining. **$19-$38.** 1624 Harmon Pl 55403. Just sw of Hennepin Ave. [D] [LATE]

▼▼▼ **Masa**
(612) 338-6272. New Mexican. Fine Dining. **$11-$33.** 1070 Nicollet Mall 55403. At 11th St. [L] [D]

▼▼▼ **Sanctuary**
(612) 339-5058. New American. Fine Dining. **$18-$32.** 903 Washington Ave S 55432. At 9th St. [D]

▼▼ **Sea Salt Eatery**
(612) 721-8990. Seafood Vegetarian. Casual Dining. **$6-$19.** 4801 Minnehaha Ave 55417. In Refectory Building; in Minnehaha Park. [L] [D]

MINNETONKA

▼▼▼ **Bacio**
(952) 544-7000. Italian. Fine Dining. **$9-$40.** 1571 S Plymouth Rd 55305. I-394 exit 1C (Ridgedale Dr), northeast corner of Bonaventure Shopping Center. [L] [D]

Mississippi

COLUMBUS

▼▼▼ **Jackson Square Grill**
(662) 328-8656. American. Casual Dining. **$8-$20.** 1927 Hwy 45 N 39705. On US 45, 0.9 mi n of jct US 82; in Jackson Square. [L] [D] [&M]

▼ **Sweet Peppers Deli**
(662) 328-6889. Sandwiches Soup. Quick Serve. **$6-$14.** 2017 Hwy 45 N 39705. On US 45, 0.9 mi n of jct US 82; in Jackson Square. [L] [D] [&M]

TUPELO

▼ **Crossroads Rib Shack**
(662) 840-1700. Barbecue. Casual Dining. **$5-$18.** 3061 Tupelo Commons 38804. US 45 exit Barnes Crossing, 0.5 mi sw, then 1 mi e; behind BEST WESTERN PLUS Tupelo Inn & Suites. [L] [D] [&M]

Missouri

KANSAS CITY

▼▼▼ **Bristol Seafood Grill**
(816) 448-6007. Seafood. Casual Dining. **$10-$39.** 51 E 14th St 64106. Jct 14th and Main sts. [L] [D] [&M]

ST. LOUIS

▼▼ **Bar Italia Ristorante**
(314) 361-7010. Italian. Casual Dining. **$7-$30.** 13 Maryland Plaza 63108. I-64/US 40 exit 36A (Kingshighway Blvd), 1 mi n, then just e. [L] [D]

▼▼ **Boathouse Forest Park**
(314) 367-2224. American. Family Dining. **$8-$11.** 6101 Government Dr 63110. I-64/US 40 exit 34D (Hampton Ave), just n, just w on Wells Dr, then just n; in Forest Park. [L] [D]

Montana

BOZEMAN

▼▼ **Cafe Francais Des Arts**
(406) 209-7490. French. Casual Dining. **$5-$10.** 24 S Tracy Ave 59715. Between Main and Babcock sts; downtown. [B] [L] [&M]

Nebraska

OMAHA

🔺🔺🔺 ▼▼ **Black Oak Grill**
(402) 341-0622. American. Casual Dining. **$8-$22.** 220 S 31st Ave, Suite 3107 68131. I-480 exit 2B westbound; exit 2A northbound, just w; in Midtown Crossing. [L] [D] [&M]

▼▼ **McFoster's Natural Kind Cafe**
(402) 345-7477. Natural/Organic Vegetarian. Casual Dining. **$9-$22.** 302 S 38th St 68131. I-480 exit 2B westbound; exit 2A northbound, 0.6 mi w on Dodge St, then just s. [L] [D]

Nevada

BEATTY

◆◆ **KC's Outpost Saloon & Eatery**
(775) 553-9175. Sandwiches. Quick Serve. **$4-$8.** 100 E Main St 89003.
Center. Ⓛ Ⓓ ◣

BOULDER CITY

◆◆ **The Dillinger**
(702) 293-4001. Burgers Sandwiches. Gastropub. **$8-$12.** 1224 Arizona
St 89005. Center. Ⓛ Ⓓ

◆ **Milo's Cellar**
(702) 293-9540. Sandwiches. Gastropub. **$9-$13.** 538 Nevada Way
89005. Downtown. Ⓛ Ⓓ

CARSON CITY

ⒶⒶⒶ ◆◆◆ **Cafe at Adele's**
(775) 882-3353. Continental. Fine Dining. **$7-$47.** 1112 N Carson St
89701. Jct US 395 and 50. Ⓑ Ⓛ Ⓓ

◆◆◆ **Glen Eagles**
(775) 884-4414. Italian Steak Seafood. Casual Dining. **$9-$38.** 3700 N
Carson St 89701. US 395; north end of town. Ⓛ Ⓓ

HENDERSON

◆ **Rachel's Kitchen**
(702) 522-7887. Sandwiches. Quick Serve. **$8-$12.** 2265 Village Walk
Dr 89052. I-215 exit 5 (Green Valley Pkwy), just s; in The District Shopping
Center. Ⓑ Ⓛ

LAS VEGAS

◆◆◆ **ADDICTION Restaurant & RUMOR Bar**
(702) 369-5400. American. Casual Dining. **$18-$29.** 455 E Harmon Ave
89169. Jct Paradise Rd, just w; in RUMOR. Ⓑ Ⓛ Ⓓ

◆◆◆ **Grape Street Cafe**
(702) 228-9463. Italian. Fine Dining. **$16-$35.** 7501 W Lake Mead Blvd,
Suite 120 89128. US 95 exit 82 (W Lake Mead Blvd), 0.5 mi w. Ⓛ Ⓓ

◆◆ **John Cutter**
(702) 309-6200. American. Casual Dining. **$12-$32.** 11770 W Charleston
Blvd 89135. I-215 exit 26 (Charleston Blvd), 0.7 mi w. Ⓛ Ⓓ ⓁⒶⓉⒺ

◆◆ **Market Grille Cafe**
(702) 396-0070. Greek. Family Dining. **$7-$13.** 7070 N Durango Dr
89149. US 95 exit 93 (Durango Dr), 1 mi w. Ⓛ Ⓓ

◆◆ **Satay Asian Bistro & Bar**
(702) 369-8788. Asian. Casual Dining. **$7-$26.** 3900 Paradise Rd, Suite
N 89169. Just n of jct Flamingo and Paradise rds; between Twain Ave and
Flamingo Rd. Ⓛ Ⓓ

RENO

◆◆◆ **Rapscallion Seafood House & Bar**
(775) 323-1211. Seafood. Casual Dining. **$16-$60.** 1555 S Wells Ave
89502. I-80 exit Wells Ave, 1 mi s. Ⓛ Ⓓ

New Hampshire

CAMPTON

◆◆ **The Country Cow Restaurant at Blair Bridge**
(603) 536-1331. American. Casual Dining. **$9-$25.** 57 Blair Rd 03223.
I-93 exit 27, just ne. Ⓛ Ⓓ ♿Ⓜ

HANCOCK

◆◆◆ **The Hancock Inn**
(603) 525-3318. American. Casual Dining. **$14-$33.** 33 Main St 03449.
Jct SR 123 and 137; center. Ⓓ

MANCHESTER

◆◆◆ **XO on Elm**
(603) 560-7998. Northern American. Casual Dining. **$11-$31.** 827 Elm St
03101. At Manchester St; downtown. Ⓓ

New Jersey

HOBOKEN

◆◆◆ **The Brass Rail Restaurant & Bar**
(201) 659-7074. Continental. Fine Dining. **$10-$32.** 135 Washington St
07030. Corner of Washington and 2nd sts; downtown. Ⓛ Ⓓ

NORTH BERGEN

◆◆◆ **Sabor Latin Bistro**
(201) 943-6366. Latin American. Casual Dining. **$10-$36.** 8809 River Rd
07047. I-95 exit 16E (Lincoln Tunnel) to SR 495, 1.2 mi e to Weehawken/
Hoboken exit, 1.5 mi n on JFK Blvd, just e on Hillside Rd (CR 505), then
1.6 mi n. Ⓛ Ⓓ

PISCATAWAY

◆◆◆ **Al Dente**
(732) 985-8220. Italian. Casual Dining. **$16-$30.** 1665 Stelton Rd 08854.
I-287 exit 5, 1.7 mi s; jct US 1 and Plainfield Ave, 3 mi nw. Ⓛ Ⓓ

New Mexico

ALAMOGORDO

◆◆ **Sunset Run**
(575) 434-9000. Barbecue. Casual Dining. **$8-$18.** 54 McDonald Rd
88310. Just w of jct 10th St and US 54. Ⓛ Ⓓ

ALBUQUERQUE

◆◆ **Flying Star Cafe**
(505) 275-8311. American. Family Dining. **$9-$13.** 4501 Juan Tabo Blvd
NE 87111. Just n of jct Montgomery Blvd. Ⓑ Ⓛ Ⓓ

◆◆◆ **Marcello's Chophouse**
(505) 837-2467. Steak. Fine Dining. **$8-$65.** 2201 Q St, Suite B 87110.
I-40 exit 162, 0.5 mi n; in Uptown Center. Ⓛ Ⓓ ♿Ⓜ

◆◆◆ **Nob Hill Bar & Grill**
(505) 266-4455. American. Casual Dining. **$11-$25.** 3128 Central Ave
SE 87106. Jct Girard Blvd, southwest corner. Ⓛ Ⓓ

◆◆◆ **Pars Cuisine**
(505) 345-5156. Mediterranean. Casual Dining. **$10-$28.** 4320 The 25
Way NE, Suite 100 87109. I-25 exit 229 (Jefferson St), just e. Ⓛ Ⓓ

◆◆ **Ragin' Shrimp**
(505) 254-1544. Cajun. Casual Dining. **$10-$20.** 3624 Central Ave SE
87108. I-40 exit 160, 1.7 mi s on Carlisle Blvd, then just e at Copper Ave;
in Nob Hill. Ⓛ Ⓓ

◆◆◆ **Savoy Bar & Grill**
(505) 294-9463. American. Fine Dining. **$9-$38.** 10601 Montgomery Blvd
NE 87111. Between Juan Tabo Blvd and Morris St. Ⓛ Ⓓ

◆◆◆ **Tucanos Brazilian Grill**
(505) 246-9900. Brazilian. Casual Dining. **$16-$23.** 110 Central Ave SW
87102. Jct 1st St. Ⓛ Ⓓ

BERNALILLO

◆◆ **Flying Star Cafe**
(505) 404-2100. American. Casual Dining. **$6-$16.** 200 S Camino del
Pueblo 87004. I-25 exit 242, just s; jct Camino del Pueblo and US 550.
Ⓑ Ⓛ Ⓓ

CHIMAYÓ

▼▼ **Rancho de Chimayo**
(505) 351-4444. Regional Mexican. Casual Dining. **$7-$21.** 300 CR 98
87522. 0.6 mi s on CR 98 from jct SR 76. Ⓛ Ⓓ

CLOUDCROFT

◈◈◈ ▼▼▼ **Rebecca's**
(575) 682-2566. American. Casual Dining. **$8-$38.** 601 Corona Pl
88317. US 82, 0.3 mi s on Curlew Pl/Corona Pl; in The Lodge Resort.
Ⓑ Ⓛ Ⓓ

DEMING

▼▼ **Palma's Italian Grill**
(575) 544-3100. Italian. Family Dining. **$10-$30.** 110 S Silver Ave 88030.
Jct Silver Ave and Pine St; center. Ⓛ Ⓓ

ESPAÑOLA

▼▼ **La Cocina Restaurant & Cantina**
(505) 753-3016. Mexican. Casual Dining. **$7-$14.** 415 Santa Clara
Bridge Rd 87532. Just e of jct SR 30 and US 84. Ⓑ Ⓛ Ⓓ

LAS CRUCES

◈◈◈ ▼▼▼ **De La Vega's Pecan Grill & Brewery**
(575) 521-1099. American. Casual Dining. **$7-$25.** 500 S Telshor Blvd
88011. I-25 exit 3 (Lohman Ave), just e. Ⓛ Ⓓ Ⓛᴬᵀᴱ ⓖᴹ

▼▼ **St. Clair Winery & Bistro**
(575) 524-0390. American. Casual Dining. **$7-$20.** 1720 Avenida de
Mesilla 88004. I-10 exit 135, just w. Ⓛ Ⓓ ⓖᴹ

LOS ALAMOS

▼▼ **The Blue Window Bistro**
(505) 662-6305. International. Casual Dining. **$9-$28.** 813 Central Ave
87544. 0.5 mi w of jct SR 502 and Central Ave. Ⓛ Ⓓ

MESILLA

▼▼▼ **Savoy de Mesilla**
(575) 527-2869. International. Casual Dining. **$8-$26.** 1800 Avenida de
Mesilla 88005. I-10 exit 140, 1 mi sw on SR 28. Ⓛ Ⓓ

RUIDOSO

▼▼ **Grill Caliente**
(575) 630-0224. Mexican. Casual Dining. **$8-$28.** 2800 Sudderth Dr
88345. Just e of Mechem Dr; downtown. Ⓛ Ⓓ

▼▼ **The Village Buttery**
(575) 257-9251. Sandwiches Soup. Quick Serve. **$6-$9.** 2107 Sudderth
Dr 88345. Center. Ⓛ

SANTA FE

▼▼▼ **Cafe Cafe**
(505) 466-1391. Italian. Casual Dining. **$9-$28.** 500 Sandoval St 87501.
Jct Sandoval and Manhattan sts; center. Ⓛ Ⓓ

◈◈◈ ▼▼▼ **Fuego**
(505) 954-9670. International. Fine Dining. **$15-$36.** 330 E Palace Ave
87501. Jct Paseo de Peralta and E Palace Ave; in La Posada de Santa
Fe Resort & Spa. Ⓑ Ⓛ Ⓓ

▼▼▼ **Restaurant Martin**
(505) 820-0919. New American. Fine Dining. **$10-$36.** 526 Galisteo St
87501. Jct Paseo de Peralta and Galisteo St; center. Ⓛ Ⓓ

▼▼▼ **Santa Fe Capitol Grill**
(505) 471-6800. International. Casual Dining. **$8-$27.** 3462 Zafarano Dr
87507. Northwest of jct Cerrillos Rd; in San Isidro Plaza. Ⓛ Ⓓ

▼▼ **Saveur**
(505) 989-4200. French. Casual Dining. **$6-$16.** 204 Montezuma Ave
87501. Jct Galisteo St, Cerrillos Rd and Montezuma Ave; downtown.
Ⓑ Ⓛ

▼▼ **Vinaigrette**
(505) 820-9205. Natural/Organic. Casual Dining. **$10-$19.** 709 Don
Cubero Alley 87505. Just e of jct Cerrillos Rd and Guadalupe St, just w of
jct Cerrillos Rd and Paseo de Peralta. Ⓛ Ⓓ ⓖᴹ

TAOS

▼▼▼▼ **El Meze Restaurant**
(575) 751-3337. Regional Spanish. Casual Dining. **$16-$28.** 1017 Paseo
del Pueblo Norte 87571. 1.2 mi n of plaza. Ⓓ

TRUTH OR CONSEQUENCES

▼▼▼▼ **Cafe BellaLuca**
(575) 894-9866. Italian. Casual Dining. **$8-$38.** 303 Jones St 87901.
Center. Ⓛ Ⓓ

New York

ALBANY

▼ **Bountiful Bread**
(518) 438-3540. Sandwiches. Quick Serve. **$7-$11.** 1475 Western Ave
12203. Jct US 20 (Western Ave); in Stuyvesant Plaza.
Ⓑ Ⓛ Ⓓ ⓖᴹ

CARLE PLACE

▼▼▼ **West End Cafe**
(516) 294-5608. New American. Casual Dining. **$10-$34.** 187 Glen Cove
Rd 11514. Meadow Brook Pkwy exit 31, 0.5 mi s; in shopping center.
Ⓛ Ⓓ

EAST HAMPTON

▼▼▼▼ **The Living Room Restaurant**
(631) 324-5006. Natural/Organic. Fine Dining. **$20-$45.** 207 Main St
11937. Jct SR 114, just s on SR 27; in c/o The Maidstone. Ⓑ Ⓛ Ⓓ

FLY CREEK

▼▼▼ **Portabello's**
(607) 547-5145. American. Casual Dining. **$17-$34.** 6207 State Hwy 28
13337. Center. Ⓓ

ITHACA

▼▼▼ **Madeline's Patisserie**
(607) 277-2253. New Fusion. Casual Dining. **$17-$28.** 215 E State St,
Suite 10 14850. Downtown; on The Commons. Ⓓ

LIBERTY

▼▼▼ **Piccolo Paese**
(845) 292-7210. Northern Italian. Fine Dining. **$19-$36.** 2071 SR 52
12754. SR 17 exit 100 westbound, just n; exit eastbound, just s. Ⓛ Ⓓ

MIDDLETOWN

▼▼▼ **Nina**
(845) 344-6800. American. Fine Dining. **$8-$33.** 27 W Main St 10940.
Just w of North St; downtown. Ⓛ Ⓓ

MOUNT KISCO

▼▼▼ **Cafe of Love**
(914) 242-1002. French. Casual Dining. **$15-$42.** 38 E Main St 10549.
Jct SR 117, just nw on SR 133. Ⓛ Ⓓ

NEW YORK

▼▼▼ Circo

(212) 265-3636. Italian. Casual Dining. **$17-$60.** 120 W 55th St 10019. Between 6th (Ave of the Americas) and 7th aves. ⓛ ⓓ

▼▼▼▼ Da Nico Ristorante

(212) 343-1212. Italian. Fine Dining. **$9-$40.** 164 Mulberry St 10013. In Little Italy; between Broome and Grand sts. ⓛ ⓓ

ROMULUS

▼▼ Knapp Winery & Vineyard Restaurant

(607) 869-9271. Continental. Casual Dining. **$8-$14.** 2770 Ernsberger Rd 14541. Off SR 414, just e on CR 128 (Ernsberger Rd). ⓛ

SLINGERLANDS

▼▼▼ Mangia

(518) 439-5555. Italian. Casual Dining. **$9-$22.** 1562 New Scotland Rd 12159. I-90 exit 4; center of village; on US 85. ⓛ ⓓ ⓶ⓜ

SYRACUSE

▼ The Blue Tusk Pub & Wine Bar

(315) 472-1934. American. Casual Dining. **$8-$18.** 165 Walton St 13202. Center; in Armory Square. ⓛ ⓓ

TANNERSVILLE

▼▼ Last Chance Antiques & Cheese Cafe

(518) 589-6424. American. Casual Dining. **$6-$20.** 6009 Main St 12485. Center. ⓛ ⓓ

North Carolina

ASHEVILLE

▼▼ Plant

(828) 258-7500. Vegan. Casual Dining. **$15-$21.** 165 Merrimon Ave 28801. I-240 exit 5A (Merrimon Ave), just n. ⓓ

▼ Westville Pub

(828) 225-9782. American. Casual Dining. **$8-$15.** 777 Haywood Rd 28806. I-240 eastbound, exit 3A; westbound exit straight onto US 19/23, then 1 mi w, just s on Louisiana Ave, just w on Pruett St, just s on Mildred Ave, then just e on US 19 business route. ⓛ ⓓ ⓛⓐⓣⓔ

BLOWING ROCK

▼▼▼ Bistro Roca

(828) 295-4008. American. Fine Dining. **$7-$28.** 143 Wonderland Tr 28605. Just s on Laurel Ln, bear right, then just w; center. ⓛ ⓓ ⓶ⓜ

CAROLINA BEACH

▼▼ Michael's Seafood Restaurant & Catering

(910) 458-7761. Seafood. Casual Dining. **$10-$36.** 1206 N Lake Park Blvd 28428. From Snow's Cut Bridge, just e; in Cross Bridge Shopping Center. ⓛ ⓓ

CARRBORO

▼▼ Spotted Dog Restaurant & Bar

(919) 933-1117. American. Casual Dining. **$7-$13.** 111 E Main St 27510. Just e; center. ⓛ ⓓ

CASHIERS

▼▼ Cornucopia Restaurant

(828) 743-3750. American. Casual Dining. **$8-$28.** Hwy 107 S 28717. Jct SR 64, 0.5 mi s. ⓛ ⓓ ⓶ⓜ

GREENSBORO

▼▼ Europa Bar & Cafe

(336) 389-1010. European. Casual Dining. **$8-$15.** 200 N Davie St 27401. Jct Friendly Ave, just n; downtown. ⓛ ⓓ

HIGH POINT

▼▼ J Butler's Bar & Grille

(336) 861-5758. American. Casual Dining. **$6-$18.** 3030 S Main St 27263. I-85 exit 111, 1.5 mi n on US 311; in Archdale Commons Shopping Center. ⓛ ⓓ

WAYNESVILLE

▼▼ Pasquale's Italian Restaurant

(828) 454-5002. Italian. Casual Dining. **$7-$23.** 1863 S Main St 28786. 2 mi s on US 23 business route. ⓛ ⓓ

Oklahoma

MOORE

ⒶⒶ ▼▼ Royal Bavaria Restaurant & Brewery

(405) 799-7666. German. Casual Dining. **$12-$28.** 3401 S Sooner Rd 73165. I-240 exit 8, 6 mi s. ⓓ

TULSA

▼▼▼ The Bistro At Seville

(918) 296-3000. American. Fine Dining. **$7-$29.** 10021 S Yale Ave 74145. Jct 101st St. ⓛ ⓓ

Oregon

ASTORIA

▼▼▼ Baked Alaska Restaurant, Lounge & Pizzeria

(503) 325-7414. Regional Seafood. Casual Dining. **$8-$28.** 1 12th St, Suite 1 97103. On waterfront; downtown. ⓛ ⓓ ⓚ

▼▼ Rogue Ales Public House

(503) 325-5964. American. Casual Dining. **$10-$28.** 100 39th St, Pier 39 97103. 3 mi e of Astoria Bridge on US 30. ⓛ ⓓ ⓚ

▼▼ Wet Dog Cafe & Astoria Brewing Co.

(503) 325-6975. American. Casual Dining. **$10-$21.** 144 11th St 97103. Corner of 11th and Astor sts; downtown. ⓛ ⓓ ⓚ

BEND

▼▼ Cascade Lakes Lodge Brewing Company

(541) 388-4998. American. Casual Dining. **$9-$16.** 1441 SW Chandler Ave, Suite 100 97702. US 97 exit 138 (Downtown/Mt Bachelor Dr), 1.7 mi sw on NW Colorado Ave, then just w. ⓛ ⓓ

▼▼ McKay Cottage Restaurant

(541) 383-2697. American. Casual Dining. **$8-$13.** 62910 OB Riley Rd 97701. Just n of 3rd Ave and Butler Market Rd. ⓑ ⓛ ⓚ

ENTERPRISE

▼ Terminal Gravity Brew Pub

(541) 426-0158. American. Casual Dining. **$7-$15.** 803 SE School St 97828. 0.7 mi se of jct North and River sts (SR 82), just s, follow signs. ⓛ ⓓ ⓚ

EUGENE

▼▼ Studio One Cafe

(541) 342-8596. Breakfast. Casual Dining. **$7-$13.** 1473 E 19th Ave 97403. 0.6 mi e from jct SR 99 and 126 (Franklin Blvd), 0.5 mi s on Agate St, just w. ⓑ ⓛ

GEARHART

▼▼ McMenamins Sand Trap

(503) 717-8150. American. Casual Dining. **$10-$20.** 1157 N Marion Ave 97138. US 101 exit City Center, 1 mi w; in Gearhart By The Sea. ⓑ ⓛ ⓓ ⓶ⓜ

GRANTS PASS

▼▼ Wild River Brewing & Pizza Co.
(541) 471-7487. American. Casual Dining. **$7-$26.** 595 NE E St 97526.
I-5 exit 58, 1.7 mi s on SR 99, then 0.4 mi e on NE F St. [L] [D]

MEDFORD

▼▼ Downtown Market Co
(541) 973-2233. American. Casual Dining. **$9-$13.** 231 E Main St
97501. Jct E Main St and S Bartlett St; downtown. [L]

▼▼ Misoya Bistro
(541) 772-4120. Asian Fusion Sushi. Casual Dining. **$8-$17.** 235 Theater Alley 97501. At Central St and Theater Alley; downtown.
[L] [D] [&M]

MCMINNVILLE

▼▼ ▼▼ McMenamins Hotel Oregon Pub
(503) 472-8427. American. Casual Dining. **$9-$27.** 310 NE Evans St
97128. At NE 3rd and Evans sts; downtown; in McMenamins Hotel
Oregon. [B] [L] [D] [LATE] [&M]

NEWPORT

AAA ▼▼ ▼▼ Canyon Way Restaurant & Bookstore
(541) 265-8319. American. Casual Dining. **$8-$16.** 1216 SW Canyon
Way 97365. 4 blks e of jct US 101 and SW Hurbert St; 1 blk from bayfront. [L] [Æ]

▼▼ ▼▼ Chowder Bowl at Nye Beach
(541) 265-7477. Seafood. Casual Dining. **$8-$21.** 728 NW Beach Dr
97365. Jct US 20, just n on US 101, 0.4 mi w on W 3rd St, just n on NW
Coast St, then just w. [L] [D] [Æ]

PORTLAND

▼▼ ▼▼ McMenamins Kennedy School Courtyard Restaurant
(503) 288-2192. American. Casual Dining. **$5-$29.** 5736 NE 33rd Ave
97211. I-84 exit 33rd Ave eastbound, 2 mi n; exit 43rd Ave westbound,
follow signs to Broadway, 1 mi w on Broadway, then 2 mi n.
[B] [L] [D] [LATE]

▼▼ ▼▼ McMenamins Mall 205
(503) 254-5411. American. Casual Dining. **$9-$14.** 9710 SE Washington
St 97216. I-205 exit 21A southbound; exit 20 northbound, just e on Washington St, then just s. [L] [D] [LATE]

▼▼ ▼▼ McMenamins Market Street Pub
(503) 497-0160. American. Casual Dining. **$7-$13.** 1526 SW 10th Ave
97201. Corner of SW 10th Ave and Market St. [L] [D] [LATE]

▼▼ ▼▼ McMenamins White Eagle Cafe & Saloon
(503) 282-6810. American. Casual Dining. **$9-$14.** 836 N Russell St
97227. Just e of N Interstate Ave. [L] [D] [LATE]

REEDSPORT

▼▼ ▼▼ Schooner Cafe
(541) 271-3945. Sandwiches. Casual Dining. **$8-$12.** 423 Riverfront Way
97467. Jct US 101/SR 38, just e on SR 38, just n on 3rd St (at post
office), just e on Water Ave, then just nw; adjacent to Umpqua Discovery
Center. [L] [&M] [◥]

ROSEBURG

▼▼ ▼▼ McMenamins Roseburg Station Pub & Brewery
(541) 672-1934. American. Casual Dining. **$5-$18.** 700 SE Sheridan St
97470. I-5 exit 124, 0.5 mi e, then just s; in Village Station.
[L] [D] [LATE]

SALEM

▼▼ ▼▼ McMenamins Boon's Treasury
(503) 399-9062. American. Casual Dining. **$8-$15.** 888 Liberty St NE
97301. I-5 exit 256, 2 mi w on Market St NE, then just s; 0.6 mi n of
downtown. [L] [D] [LATE]

WILSONVILLE

▼▼ ▼▼ McMenamins Old Church & Pub
(503) 427-2500. American. Casual Dining. **$10-$20.** 30340 SW Boones
Ferry Rd 97070. I-5 exit 283, just sw. [B] [L] [D] [LATE] [&M]

Pennsylvania

CHAMBERSBURG

▼▼▼▼ Bistro 71 Restaurant & Bar
(717) 261-0007. American. Casual Dining. **$16-$29.** 71 N Main St
17201. I-81 exit 16, 1.5 mi w on US 30 (Lincoln Way); downtown.
[D] [&M]

HARRISBURG

▼▼▼▼ Zia's Trattoria At Red Door
(717) 920-0330. Italian. Fine Dining. **$8-$29.** 110 N 2nd St 17101.
Between Locust and Walnut sts; downtown. [L] [D]

PHILADELPHIA

▼▼▼▼ a.kitchen
(215) 825-7030. American. Casual Dining. **$8-$26.** 135 S 18th St 19103.
Between Walnut and Sansom sts. [L] [D]

AAA ▼▼▼▼ City Tavern
(215) 413-1443. American. Casual Dining. **$9-$27.** 138 S 2nd St 19106.
Corner of 2nd and Walnut sts. [L] [D]

▼▼▼▼ The Plough and The Stars Irish Restaurant & Bar
(215) 733-0300. Continental. Fine Dining. **$8-$24.** 123 Chestnut St
19106. Just n of jct 2nd and Chestnut sts; entrance on 2nd St.
[L] [D] [&M]

▼▼▼▼ Pub and Kitchen
(215) 545-0350. American. Gastropub. **$9-$26.** 1946 Lombard St 19146.
Corner of Lombard and 20th sts. [D] [LATE]

▼▼▼▼ Serafina Rittenhouse
(215) 977-7755. Italian. Casual Dining. **$9-$29.** 130 S 18th St 19103. At
18th and Samson sts. [L] [D]

WEST CHESTER

▼▼▼▼ Limoncello
(610) 436-6230. Italian. Fine Dining. **$8-$30.** 9 N Walnut St 19380.
Between E Market and E Gay sts; downtown. [L] [D]

▼▼▼▼ Pietro's Prime
(484) 760-6100. Steak Seafood. Fine Dining. **$10-$48.** 125 W Market St
19382. Between Church and Darlington sts; downtown. [L] [D] [&M]

Rhode Island

NEWPORT

▼▼▼▼ Bouchard Restaurant & Inn
(401) 846-0123. French. Fine Dining. **$20-$38.** 505 Thames St 02840.
Jct SR 138A, 0.5 mi s. [D]

PROVIDENCE

▼▼▼▼ Red Stripe
(401) 437-6950. French. Casual Dining. **$10-$25.** 465 Angell St 02906.
Between Wayland and Elmgrove aves. [L] [D] [&M]

▼▼▼▼ Trattoria Zooma
(401) 383-2002. Southern Italian. Casual Dining. **$10-$34.** 245 Atwells
Ave 02903. I-95 exit 21, 0.3 mi w. [L] [D]

WARWICK

🛇🛇🛇 Eleven Forty Nine
(401) 884-1149. New American. Fine Dining. **$7-$30.** 1149 Division St 02818. On SR 401, just e of jct SR 2. [L] [D] [&M]

South Carolina

BLUFFTON

🛇🛇 Okatie Ale House
(843) 706-2584. American. Casual Dining. **$9-$20.** 25 William Pope Ct 29909. I-95 exit 8 (US 278), 7.2 mi e, then just s; adjacent to Sun City.
[L] [D] [&M] [🛇]

CHARLESTON

🛇🛇 Brown Dog Deli
(843) 853-8081. Deli. Quick Serve. **$8-$14.** 40 Broad St 29401. Between Church and State sts. [L] [D]

🛇🛇 Molly Darcy's
(843) 737-4085. American. Gastropub. **$8-$20.** 235 E Bay St 29401. Jct N Market St, just n. [L] [D] [&M] [🛇]

🛇🛇 The Mustard Seed
(843) 762-0072. Regional American. Casual Dining. **$9-$20.** 1970 Maybank Hwy 29412. Jct SR 171 (Folly Rd), 0.7 mi w; on James Island.
[L] [D] [&M]

🛇🛇 Triangle Char & Bar
(843) 377-1300. Burgers Sandwiches. Casual Dining. **$9-$16.** 828 Savannah Hwy 29407. Jct US 17/SR 171 (Folly Rd), 0.7 mi w on US 17; in West Ashley. [L] [D] [LATE]

COLUMBIA

🛇🛇🛇 Hampton Street Vineyard
(803) 252-0850. American. Fine Dining. **$7-$28.** 1201 Hampton St 29201. Between Main and Sumter sts; downtown. [L] [D]

🛇🛇 Villa Tronco
(803) 256-7677. Traditional Italian. Casual Dining. **$9-$25.** 1213 Blanding St 29201. Between Sumter and Main sts; downtown. [L] [D] [&M]

🛇🛇 Yesterdays Restaurant & Tavern
(803) 799-0196. American. Casual Dining. **$7-$15.** 2030 Devine St 29205. Corner of Devine and Harden sts; in Five Points. [L] [D] [LATE]

FOLLY BEACH

🛇 Taco Boy
(843) 588-9761. Mexican. Casual Dining. **$4-$16.** 13 Center St 29439. Center. [L] [D]

GEORGETOWN

🛇🛇 Rice Paddy Restaurant
(843) 546-2021. Regional American. Casual Dining. **$8-$35.** 732 Front St 29440. Between Broad and Screven sts. [L] [D]

GREENVILLE

🛇🛇🛇 Soby's
(864) 232-7007. New Southern. Casual Dining. **$16-$28.** 207 S Main St 29601. Corner of E Court St; downtown. [D] [&M]

HILTON HEAD ISLAND

🛇 Amigos Café y Cantina
(843) 785-8226. Mexican. Quick Serve. **$4-$10.** 70 Pope Ave 29928. Sea Pines Cir, 0.8 mi se; in The Circle Center. [L] [D]

🛇🛇 Bella Italia Bistro & Pizzeria
(843) 689-5560. Italian. Casual Dining. **$10-$16.** 95 Matthews Dr, Suite D-13 29928. 5 mi e of J Wilton Graves Bridge on US 278 business route; in Port Royal Plaza. [L] [D]

🛇🛇🛇 Giuseppi's Pizza & Pasta
(843) 785-4144. Italian. Casual Dining. **$7-$12.** 32 D Shelter Cove Ln 29928. 8.2 mi e of J Wilton Graves Bridge on US 278 business route; in Plaza at Shelter Cove. [L] [D] [&M]

🛇🛇🛇 HogsHead Kitchen & Wine Bar
(843) 837-4647. Regional Southern. Fine Dining. **$9-$24.** 1555 Fording Island Rd, Suite D 29926. 0.9 mi nw of J Wilton Graves Bridge on US 278; on the mainland; in Moss Creek Village. [L] [D]

🛇🛇 Kenny B's Cajun Seafood Hut
(843) 785-3315. Cajun. Casual Dining. **$9-$17.** 70 A Pope Ave, Circle Bi-Lo Center 29928. Jct Coligny Cir and Pope Ave, just nw on Pope Ave to Nassau St, just sw. [B] [L] [D]

🛇🛇 Main Street Café and Pub
(843) 689-3999. American. Casual Dining. **$8-$25.** 1411 Main St 29928. 3.5 mi e of J Wilton Graves Bridge on US 278 business route, just n; in Main Street Village. [L] [D] [&M]

🛇🛇 Reilley's Grill & Bar
(843) 842-4414. American. Gastropub. **$9-$26.** 7D Greenwood Dr 29928. Jct Sea Pines Cir, just w; in Hilton Head Plaza. [L] [D] [&M]

🛇🛇 The Salty Dog Cafe
(843) 671-5199. Regional Seafood. Casual Dining. **$9-$30.** 232 S Sea Pines Dr 29928. Coligny Plaza, 5.2 mi sw on S Forest Beach/Sea Pines drs; at South Beach Marina; in The Sea Pines Resort. [L] [D]

🛇🛇 San Miguel's - Mexican Cafe
(843) 842-4555. Mexican. Casual Dining. **$7-$17.** 9 Shelter Cove Ln 29928. 8.5 mi from J Wilton Graves Bridge on US 278 business route to Shelter Cove Ln, just w; in Harbourside II; at Shelter Cove. [L] [D]

ISLE OF PALMS

🛇🛇🛇 The Boathouse at Breach Inlet
(843) 886-8000. Seafood. Casual Dining. **$16-$33.** 101 Palm Blvd (SR 703) 29451. At south end of island; at Breach Inlet Bridge. [D] [&M]

🛇🛇🛇 Morgan Creek Grill
(843) 886-8980. American. Casual Dining. **$10-$26.** 80 41st Ave 29451. Jct SR 517 (Isle of Palms Connector)/703 (Palm Blvd), 1.8 mi ne of SR 703 (Palm Blvd), just n; in Isle of Palms Marina. [L] [D] [&M]

JOHNS ISLAND

🛇🛇 King Street Grille
(843) 768-5444. American. Casual Dining. **$11-$25.** 679 Freshfields Dr 29455. Jct Kiawah Island Pkwy, Seabrook Island Rd and Betsy Kerrison Pkwy; in Freshfields Village. [L] [D] [LATE] [&M]

MOUNT PLEASANT

🛇🛇 Charleston's Cafe
(843) 856-7796. Regional Breakfast Sandwiches. Casual Dining. **$5-$11.** 1039 Johnnie Dodds Blvd 29464. 2.2 mi ne of Arthur Ravenel Jr Bridge on US 17 (Johnnie Dodds Blvd); in Anna Knapp Plaza. [B] [L] [&M]

🛇🛇🛇 Crave Kitchen & Cocktails
(843) 884-1177. New American. Fine Dining. **$10-$30.** 1968 Riviera Dr, Suite O 29464. I-526 exit 29 (Georgetown/US 17 N), 1.4 mi ne on US 17 to jct SR 517 (Isle of Palms Connector), then 1 mi se on SR 517; in Seaside Farms. [L] [D] [&M]

🛇🛇 The Dog & Duck
(843) 881-3056. Sandwiches Wings. Gastropub. **$7-$11.** 624-A Long Point Rd 29464. I-526 exit 28 (Long Point Rd), just ne; in Belle Hall Shopping Center. [L] [D] [&M]

🛇🛇 Juanita Greenberg's Nacho Royale
(843) 329-6224. Mexican. Casual Dining. **$7-$10.** 410 W Coleman Blvd 29464. 1 mi e of Arthur Ravenel Jr Bridge on SR 703 (Coleman Blvd).
[L] [D] [&M] [🛇]

▼▼▼ **Southerly Restaurant & Patio**

(843) 416-5960. Regional Southern. Fine Dining. **$11-$25.** 730 Coleman Blvd 29464. 1.9 mi se of Arthur Ravenel Jr Bridge on US 701 (Coleman Blvd). [B] [L] [D] [&M]

▼▼▼ **Stack's Evening Eats**

(843) 388-6968. New Southern. Casual Dining. **$16-$25.** 1440 Ben Sawyer Blvd, Suite 1107 29464. Jct US 17 business/701/SR 703, just e on SR 703 (Ben Sawyer Blvd); in Mount Pleasant Square Shopping Center. [D] [&M]

MYRTLE BEACH

▼▼▼ **Banditos Restaurant & Cantina**

(843) 808-9800. Mexican. Casual Dining. **$4-$19.** 1410 N Ocean Blvd 29577. Jct 14th Ave N. [L] [D] [&M]

▼▼ **Beach House Bar & Grill**

(843) 839-4705. American. Casual Dining. **$9-$29.** 1205 N Ocean Blvd 29572. Jct 12th Ave N. [L] [D] [LATE] [&M] [⬍]

▼▼ **Capriccio**

(843) 445-7100. Italian Pizza. Casual Dining. **$8-$22.** 1285 38th Ave N 29577. Jct US 17; in Plantation Point Plaza. [L] [D] [&M]

NORTH CHARLESTON

▼▼ **Coosaw Creek Crab Shack**

(843) 552-7171. Regional Seafood. Casual Dining. **$7-$25.** 8486 Dorchester Rd 29420. Jct Ashley Phosphate and Dorchester rds, just nw. [L] [D] [&M]

NORTH MYRTLE BEACH

▼▼ **Midtown Bistro**

(843) 427-4720. Italian. Casual Dining. **$9-$25.** 2004 Hwy 17 S 29582. Jct 20th Ave S. [L] [D] [&M]

RIDGELAND

▼▼ **Jasper's Porch Lakefront Dining**

(843) 726-9521. Regional Southern. Casual Dining. **$8-$19.** 100 James F. Taylor Dr 29936. I-95 exit 21 (US 336), just w to W Frontage Rd, then just n. [B] [L] [D]

SIMPSONVILLE

▼▼ **Arizona Steakhouse**

(864) 962-1700. Regional American. Casual Dining. **$8-$25.** 3952 Grandview Dr 29680. I-385 exit 27, just s on Fairview Rd, then just se on Service Rd. [L] [D] [&M]

SULLIVAN'S ISLAND

▼▼ **Sullivan's**

(843) 883-3222. Seafood. Casual Dining. **$9-$25.** 2019 Middle St 29482. Just sw of center. [D]

▼▼ **Taco Mamacita**

(843) 789-4107. Mexican. Casual Dining. **$4-$13.** 2213-B Middle St 29482. Just sw of center. [L] [D]

SUMMERVILLE

▼▼ **The Continental Corner**

(843) 871-1160. Greek. Casual Dining. **$7-$20.** 123 W Richardson Ave 29483. Jct US 17 alternate route, just nw; downtown. [L] [D]

Tennessee

BRENTWOOD

▼▼▼ **Fulin's Asian Cuisine**

(615) 377-9788. Asian. Casual Dining. **$8-$22.** 782 Old Hickory Blvd, Suite 115 37027. I-65 exit 74A (SR 254 E), just e; in Target shopping plaza. [L] [D] [&M]

▼ **Mediterranean Cuisine**

(615) 661-4100. Greek. Quick Serve. **$5-$13.** 214 Ward Cir 37027. I-65 exit 74B, 0.3 mi s on Franklin Rd (US 31), 0.5 mi w on Maryland Way. [L] [D]

CHATTANOOGA

▼▼ **Aretha Frankensteins**

(423) 265-7685. Breakfast. Casual Dining. **$5-$10.** 518 Tremont St 37405. Jct Frazier St, 0.5 mi e to Tremont St, 0.5 mi n; on north shore. [B] [L] [D] [LATE]

▼▼▼ **Chato Brasserie**

(423) 305-1352. New American. Fine Dining. **$17-$32.** 200 Manufacturers Rd, Suite 101 37405. Jct Cherokee St, just w; on north shore. [D] [&M]

▼▼▼ **FoodWorks**

(423) 752-7487. American. Fine Dining. **$8-$25.** 205 Manufacturers Rd, Suite C 37421. Jct Cherokee St, just w; in Knitting Mill. [L] [D] [&M]

▼▼▼ **Hennen's**

(423) 634-5160. New American. Casual Dining. **$9-$32.** 193 Chestnut St 37401. Center. [L] [D] [&M]

▼▼ **The Terminal Brewhouse**

(423) 752-8090. American. Casual Dining. **$7-$14.** 6 E 14th St 37408. I-24 exit 178 (Broad St) eastbound; exit Market St westbound, 0.5 mi n. [L] [D] [LATE]

▼▼ **Tony's Pasta Shop and Trattoria**

(423) 265-5033. Italian. Casual Dining. **$4-$15.** 212 High St 37403. US 27 exit 1C (4th St), 1 mi e, then just n; in Bluff View Arts District. [L] [D]

COLUMBIA

▼▼ **Puckett's Gro. & Restaurant**

(931) 490-4550. Southern Barbecue. Casual Dining. **$7-$25.** 15 Public Square 38401. In historic downtown. [B] [L] [D] [&M]

▼▼▼ **Square Market & Cafe**

(931) 840-3636. American. Casual Dining. **$5-$11.** 36 Public Square 38401. In historic downtown; northwest corner behind courthouse. [B] [L] [D] [&M]

COUNCE

▼▼ **Freddy T's**

(731) 689-3099. American. Casual Dining. **$11-$27.** 12750 Hwy 57 S 38326. SR 57, 4.3 mi se of jct SR 128; at Pickwick Dam. [L] [D]

FRANKLIN

▼▼▼ **Cajun Steamer - Bar & Grill**

(615) 435-3074. Cajun. Casual Dining. **$9-$24.** 1175 Meridian Blvd, Suite 108 37067. I-65 exit 68A, just e on Cool Springs Blvd, then just n on Carothers Pkwy. [L] [D] [&M]

JACKSON

▼▼ **Old Town Spaghetti Store**

(731) 668-4937. Italian. Casual Dining. **$6-$33.** 550 Carriage House Dr 38305. I-40 exit 80A, just s on US 45 Bypass, then just e. [L] [D] [&M]

JOHNSON CITY

▼▼ **Alta Cucina Italian Restaurant**

(423) 928-2092. Italian. Casual Dining. **$10-$35.** 1200 N Roan St 37601. I-26 exit 22, just s on W Unalaka Ave, then just w. [L] [D]

KNOXVILLE

▼▼ **Chesapeake's**

(865) 673-3433. Seafood. Casual Dining. **$9-$40.** 500 Henley St 37902. I-40 exit 388, 1 mi s, then just e. [▣] [L] [D]

MEMPHIS

▽▽▽ Capriccio Grill
(901) 529-4199. Italian. Fine Dining. **$12-$42.** 149 Union Ave 38103. Jct 2nd St; in Peabody Memphis. [◧] [B] [L] [D] [&M]

▽ Central BBQ in Memphis
(901) 272-9377. Barbecue. Quick Serve. **$4-$20.** 2249 Central Ave 38104. Between S Cooper St and E Parkway S. [L] [D]

▽▽▽ Napa Cafe
(901) 683-0441. Continental. Fine Dining. **$13-$32.** 5101 Sanderlin Ave, Suite 122 38117. I-240 exit 15 (Poplar Ave), 1 mi w, 0.5 mi n on White Station Rd, then just w; in Sanderlin Centre. [L] [D] [&M]

▽▽▽ SOB - South of Beale
(901) 526-0388. American. Gastropub. **$9-$21.** 361 S Main St 38103. Jct Beale St, just s. [L] [D] [LATE]

NASHVILLE

▽ Hog Heaven
(615) 329-1234. Barbecue. Quick Serve. **$4-$11.** 115 27th Ave N 37203. I-440 exit West End Ave, 3 mi e; across from Centennial Park. [L] [D]

PIGEON FORGE

▽ Blue Moose Burgers & Wings
(865) 286-0364. Wings Burgers. Casual Dining. **$6-$10.** 2430 Teaster Ln 37863. US 441, just e of traffic light 2; in Teaster Center.
[L] [D] [LATE] [&M]

SWEETWATER

▽▽ Bradley's Pit BBQ & Grill
(423) 351-7190. American. Casual Dining. **$5-$20.** 517 New Hwy 68 37874. I-75 exit 60, 1.2 mi e. [L] [D]

Texas

ADDISON

▽▽ The Londoner
(972) 458-2444. English. Casual Dining. **$8-$12.** 14930 Midway Rd 75001. Just s of jct Midway and Belt Line rds. [L] [D] [LATE] [N]

AUSTIN

▽▽ Apothecary Cafe and Wine Bar
(512) 371-1600. Small Plates. Casual Dining. **$9-$20.** 4800 Burnet Rd, Suite 450 78757. I-35 exit 237A (Airport Blvd), 1.7 mi w, then just n; in Roseville Village Center. [D] [N]

▽▽ Daily Grill
(512) 836-4200. American. Casual Dining. **$12-$31.** 11506 Century Oaks Terr 78758. Jct Loop 1 (Mo-Pac Expwy) and Braker Ln; in The Domain. [L] [D] [&M]

▽▽▽ Kona Grill
(512) 835-5900. Pacific Rim Fusion. Casual Dining. **$11-$30.** 11410 Century Oaks Terr 78758. Loop 1 (Mo-Pac Expwy) and Braker Ln, just n; in The Domain. [L] [D] [&M]

▽▽ Moonshine Patio Bar & Grill
(512) 236-9599. American. Casual Dining. **$11-$23.** 303 Red River St 78701. Jct E 3rd and Red River sts. [L] [D]

▽▽▽ North by Northwest Restaurant and Brewery
(512) 467-6969. American. Gastropub. **$9-$24.** 10010 Capital of Texas Hwy N 78759. US 183 N to Capital of Texas Hwy (SR 360), 2 blks e; on northeast corner. [L] [D] [&M]

COLUMBUS

▽▽ Nancy's Steakhouse
(979) 732-9700. Steak. Casual Dining. **$8-$25.** 2536 Hwy 71 S 78934. I-10 exit 696 (SR 71), just s. [L] [D] [N]

DALLAS

▽▽ Bread Winners Cafe & Bakery
(214) 754-4940. American. Casual Dining. **$8-$30.** 3301 McKinney Ave 75204. Corner of Hall St; uptown. [B] [L] [D]

▽▽ Gloria's Latin Cuisine
(214) 942-1831. Latin American. Casual Dining. **$11-$21.** 600 N Bishop Ave 75208. I-35 E exit 425A (Zang), 0.8 mi n, then just w. [L] [D]

▽▽ Green Papaya
(214) 521-4811. Vietnamese. Casual Dining. **$6-$17.** 3211 Oak Lawn Ave, Suite B 75219. I-35 exit 430A (Oak Lawn Ave), 0.9 mi e.
[L] [D] [N]

▽▽ Ziziki's Restaurant
(214) 521-2233. Mediterranean. Casual Dining. **$11-$26.** 4514 Travis St, Suite 122 75205. US 75 exit Knox St/Henderson Ave, just w to Travis St, then just s; in Travis Walk Shopping Complex. [L] [D]

FRISCO

▽▽ The Londoner
(214) 618-5025. English. Casual Dining. **$9-$15.** 5454 Main St, Suite 123 75034. George Bush Tpke exit Main St; on northeast corner.
[L] [D] [&M] [N]

GEORGETOWN

▽▽ Milano Trattoria Pizza & Pasta
(512) 869-0444. Italian. Casual Dining. **$8-$21.** 1015 W University Ave, Suite 420 78628. I-35 exit 261, just w; in southeast section of Wolf Ranch Shopping Center. [L] [D] [&M]

GRAPEVINE

▽▽ Cozymel's Coastal Mex
(972) 724-0277. Tex-Mex. Casual Dining. **$9-$20.** 2655 Grapevine Mills Cir 76051. SR 121 W exit Bass Pro Dr; in Grapevine Mills Mall Circle.
[L] [D]

HIGHLAND PARK

▽▽▽ Cafe Pacific
(214) 526-1170. Seafood. Fine Dining. **$12-$45.** 24 Highland Park Shopping Village 75205. Just sw of jct Mockingbird Ln and Preston Rd.
[L] [D]

HOUSTON

▽ Amazon Grill
(713) 522-5888. Latin American. Quick Serve. **$10-$27.** 5114 Kirby Dr 77098. US 59 (Southwest Frwy) exit Kirby Dr, just s. [L] [D]

▽▽ Brasserie Max & Julie
(713) 524-0070. French. Casual Dining. **$13-$32.** 4315 Montrose Blvd 77006. At Richmond Ave. [L] [D]

▽▽ BRC Gastropub
(713) 861-2233. American. Gastropub. **$12-$27.** 519 Shepherd Dr 77007. 0.3 mi n of jct Memorial Dr. [L] [D] [&M]

▽▽▽ Cafe Mezza & Grille
(713) 334-2000. Mediterranean. Casual Dining. **$11-$32.** 6100 Westheimer Rd, Suite 154 77057. Between Fountain View Dr and Voss Rd.
[L] [D] [&M]

▽▽▽ Churrascos
(713) 527-8300. Latin American. Fine Dining. **$11-$56.** 2055 Westheimer Rd 77098. At Shepherd Dr; in Shepherd Square Shopping Center.
[L] [D]

▽▽ Chuy's
(281) 970-0341. Tex-Mex. Casual Dining. **$6-$12.** 19827 Northwest Frwy 77065. Jct US 290 and FM 1960; off southbound frontage road. [L] [D]

🏆🏆🏆 **The Grove**

(713) 337-7321. American. Fine Dining. **$14-$43.** 1611 Lamar St 77010. In Discovery Green Park. [L] [D] [&M]

🏆🏆🏆 **Hugo's**

(713) 524-7744. Regional Mexican. Casual Dining. **$15-$30.** 1600 Westheimer Rd 77006. Between Dunlavy St and Montrose Blvd. [L] [D]

🏆🏆 **Mi Luna Tapas Restaurant & Bar**

(713) 520-5025. Small Plates. Casual Dining. **$8-$22.** 2441 University Blvd 77005. US 59 exit Kirby Dr, 1.1 mi s. [L] [D]

🏆🏆 **Mockingbird Bistro**

(713) 533-0200. American. Fine Dining. **$22-$46.** 1985 Welch St 77019. US 59 (Southwest Frwy) exit Shepherd Dr, 0.8 mi n to Westheimer Rd, just e to McDuffie St, then 0.4 mi n. [L] [D]

🏆🏆 **Tila's Restaurante & Bar**

(713) 522-7654. Mexican. Casual Dining. **$12-$29.** 1111 S Shepherd Dr 77019. I-10 exit 765B (Shepherd Dr), 1.5 mi s. [L] [D]

🏆🏆🏆 **Zelko Bistro**

(713) 880-8691. American. Casual Dining. **$14-$28.** 705 E 11th St 77008. 1 mi n of I-10 on Studewood St, just w; in Houston Heights. [L] [D]

LA GRANGE

🏆🏆 **Bistro 108**

(979) 968-9108. American. Casual Dining. **$7-$35.** 108 S Main St 78945. Downtown. [L] [D]

LAKE JACKSON

🏆🏆 **Wurst Haus**

(979) 297-3003. German. Casual Dining. **$9-$29.** 102 This Way 77566. Jct SR 288 and This Way St, 2 blks e. [B] [L] [D]

LAKEWAY

🏆🏆🏆 **The Grille At Rough Hollow**

(512) 261-3444. Steak Seafood. Casual Dining. **$12-$40.** 103 Yacht Club Cove 78738. Jct SR 620 and Lakeway Blvd, 2.4 mi n to Highlands Blvd, 0.7 mi w to Rough Hollow Dr, 1.1 mi n to Rough Hollow Yacht Club, then 0.4 mi w. [L] [D]

ROUND ROCK

🏆🏆 **The Salt Lick Bar-B-Que**

(512) 386-1044. Barbecue. Casual Dining. **$10-$23.** 3350 Palm Valley Blvd 78665. US 79, 2 mi e; at The Dell Diamond. [L] [D] [&M]

SALADO

🏆🏆 **The Shed**

(254) 913-8699. American. Casual Dining. **$7-$15.** 220 Royal St 76571. I-35 exit 284, 2 blks e; downtown. [L] [D]

Utah

MOAB

🏆🏆🏆 **Sorrel River Grill**

(435) 259-4642. American. Fine Dining. **$14-$39.** Hwy 128, MM 17 84532. 17 mi e of jct US 191 and SR 128; at MM 17; in Sorrel River Ranch Resort & Spa. [B] [L] [D]

PARK CITY

🏆🏆🏆 **Silver Star Cafe**

(435) 655-3456. Regional American. Casual Dining. **$10-$27.** 1825 Three Kings Dr 84060. Just n of SR 224 and Park City Golf Club. [L] [D]

SPRINGDALE

🏆🏆 **Cafe Oscar's**

(435) 772-3232. Mexican. Casual Dining. **$5-$22.** 948 Zion Park Blvd 84767. Jct Winderland Dr. [B] [L] [D]

Vermont

BROOKFIELD

🏆🏆🏆 **Ariel's Restaurant**

(802) 276-3939. American. Fine Dining. **$18-$28.** 29 Stone Rd 05036. Center. [D] [🐾]

EAST MIDDLEBURY

🏆🏆🏆 **Waybury Inn Dining Room**

(802) 388-4015. American. Fine Dining. **$13-$30.** 457 Main St (SR 125) 05740. On SR 125; 1.3 mi e of jct US 7. [L] [D]

MANCHESTER VILLAGE

🏆🏆🏆 **The Marsh Tavern at The Equinox**

(802) 362-7833. American. Casual Dining. **$12-$38.** 3567 Main St 05254. Jct SR 11/30, 1.3 mi s on Historic SR 7A; at The Equinox, a Luxury Collection Golf Resort & Spa; in The Inns at Equinox. [L] [D]

Virginia

ALEXANDRIA

🏆🏆🏆 **Brabo**

(703) 894-3440. French. Fine Dining. **$26-$38.** 1600 King St 22314. Between Harvard and Peyton sts; in Old Town; in Lorien Hotel & Spa-A Kimpton Hotel. [☎] [B] [D] [&M]

🏆🏆 **Chez Andree**

(703) 836-1404. French. Casual Dining. **$8-$27.** 10 E Glebe Rd 22305. 0.4 mi w of US 1. [L] [D]

🏆🏆 **Clyde's of Mark Center**

(703) 820-8300. American. Casual Dining. **$13-$26.** 1700 N Beauregard St 22311. I-395 exit 4, 0.3 mi w on Seminary Rd, then 0.3 mi s. [L] [D] [LATE] [&M]

🏆 **Holy Cow**

(703) 666-8616. Burgers. Quick Serve. **$6-$13.** 2312 Mt. Vernon Ave 22301. Jct E Oxford Ave; in Del Ray area. [L] [D] [&M]

🏆 **Pork Barrel BBQ**

(703) 822-5699. Barbecue. Quick Serve. **$7-$23.** 2312 Mt. Vernon Ave 22301. Jct E Oxford Ave; in Del Ray area. [L] [D]

🏆🏆 **Southside 815**

(703) 836-6222. Regional American. Casual Dining. **$7-$21.** 815 S Washington St 22314. 0.6 mi s of jct King St. [L] [D]

🏆🏆🏆 **Warehouse Bar & Grill**

(703) 683-6868. Regional American. Fine Dining. **$8-$33.** 214 King St 22314. Between Fairfax and Lee sts; in Old Town. [L] [D]

ARLINGTON

🏆🏆 **Luna Grill and Diner**

(703) 379-7173. American. Casual Dining. **$8-$20.** 4024 Campbell Ave 22306. I-395 exit 6 northbound; exit 7 southbound, just w; in The Village at Shirlington. [B] [L] [D]

🏆🏆 **Mele Bistro**

(703) 522-0284. Continental. Casual Dining. **$11-$39.** 1723 Wilson Blvd 22209. I-66 exit 73, just s on Fort Myer Dr, then 0.4 mi w; in shopping plaza. [L] [D]

🏆🏆 **Thaiphoon**

(703) 413-8200. Thai. Casual Dining. **$9-$15.** 1301 S Joyce St, Suite D4 22202. I-395 exit 8C, just s on Army Navy Dr; in Pentagon Row. [L] [D]

ASHBURN

◈◈ **The V Eatery & Brew House**
(703) 723-6500. American. Gastropub. **$9-$18.** 44630 Waxpool Rd 20147. Just w of jct Loudoun County Pkwy (CR 607); from SR 28, 1.3 mi w. L D LATE ♿M

CAPE CHARLES

◈◈◈ **Aqua**
(757) 331-8660. Seafood. Fine Dining. **$8-$29.** 900 Marina Village Cir 23310. At Kings Creek Resort Marina. L D ♿M

◈◈ **The Shanty**
(757) 695-3853. Seafood. Casual Dining. **$8-$25.** 33 Marina Rd 23310. SR 184 (Mason Ave), just s on Old Cape Charles Rd, just w on Bayshore Rd, then just n; just s of downtown. L D ♿M ⓚ

CHANTILLY

◈◈ **Anita's**
(703) 378-1717. Mexican. Casual Dining. **$8-$15.** 13921 Lee Jackson Memorial Hwy 20151. US 50, 0.4 mi e of jct SR 28. B L D ♿M

CHARLES CITY

◈◈◈ **Charles City Tavern**
(804) 829-5004. Regional American. Casual Dining. **$10-$29.** 9220 John Tyler Memorial Hwy 23030. On SR 5. L D

DUMFRIES

◈◈ **Giorgio's Family Restaurant**
(703) 580-8500. Italian. Family Dining. **$8-$22.** 4394 Kevin Walker Dr 22025. I-95 exit 152B, 2 mi n on SR 234; in Montclair Shopping Plaza. L D ♿M

FAIRFAX

◈◈ **Anita's**
(703) 385-2965. Mexican. Casual Dining. **$8-$15.** 10880 Lee Hwy 22030. I-66 exit 60, 0.7 mi s on SR 123, then 0.7 mi w on US 50/29. B L D

◈◈ **Blue Iguana**
(703) 502-8108. American. Casual Dining. **$6-$21.** 12727 Shoppes Ln 22033. I-66 exit 55 (Fairfax County Pkwy N), 0.3 mi n, then just w; in The Shops at Fair Lakes. L D

◈◈ **Cantina D'Italia**
(703) 631-2752. Italian. Casual Dining. **$9-$30.** 13015 Fair Lakes Shopping Center 22033. I-66 exit 55 (Fairfax County Pkwy N), 0.3 mi n, then 0.5 mi w on Fair Lakes Pkwy; in Fair Lakes Shopping Center. L D ♿M

◈ **Red Apron**
(703) 676-3550. Sandwiches Hot Dogs. Quick Serve. **$5-$10.** 8298 Glass Alley 22031. I-495 exit 50A, just w to SR 650, 0.5 mi n on Gallows Rd; in Mosaic District. L D ♿M

FALLS CHURCH

◈◈ **Four Sisters Restaurant**
(703) 539-8566. Vietnamese. Casual Dining. **$10-$25.** 8190 Strawberry Ln, Suite 1 22042. I-495 exit 50A, just w to SR 650, then 0.4 mi n on Gallows Rd: in Mosaic District. L D ♿M

◈◈◈ **Sea Pearl**
(703) 372-5161. Seafood Sushi. Casual Dining. **$10-$30.** 8191 Strawberry Ln, Suite 2 Ln 22042. I-495 exit 50A, just w to SR 650, then 0.4 mi n on Gallows. Rd: in Mosaic District. L D ♿M

FREDERICKSBURG

◈◈◈ **The Bavarian Chef**
(540) 656-2101. German. Fine Dining. **$8-$36.** 200 Lafayette Blvd 22401. Between Caroline and Princess Anne sts; in Olde Towne; in Amtrak station. L D ♿M

◈◈◈ **Bistro Bethem**
(540) 371-9999. American. Fine Dining. **$7-$28.** 309 William St 22401. Jct Caroline St; in Olde Towne. L D

HAMPTON

◈◈◈ **The Point at Phoebus**
(757) 224-9299. American. Gastropub. **$10-$30.** 30 E Mellen St 23663. I-64 exit 268 (E Mallory St), just n to E Mellen St; in downtown Phoebus. L D

HERNDON

◈◈ **TurCuisine**
(571) 323-3330. Turkish. Casual Dining. **$9-$25.** 13029 Worldgate Dr 20170. Jct SR 657 and 267 (Dulles Toll Rd) exit 10; in Worldgate Centre. L D ♿M

LEESBURG

◈◈◈ **Lightfoot**
(703) 771-2233. American. Fine Dining. **$7-$34.** 11 N King St 20176. Just n of jct E Market St (SR 7 business route). L D

◈ **MELT gourmet cheeseburgers**
(703) 443-2105. Burgers. Quick Serve. **$7-$15.** 525 E Market St, Suite J 20176. On SR 7 business route, 0.4 mi w from jct US 15; in Bellwood Commons Shopping Center. L D ♿M

◈◈ **Vintage 50 Restaurant and Brew Lounge**
(703) 777-2169. American. Casual Dining. **$8-$20.** 50 Catoctin Cir NE, Suite 100 20176. 0.6 mi w on SR 7 business route from jct US 15, just n. D ♿M

MANASSAS

◈◈ **City Square Cafe**
(703) 369-6022. International. Casual Dining. **$10-$30.** 9428 Battle St 20110. I-66 exit 47; in Historic Old Town; opposite train station. L D

◈◈ **Okra's Cajun Creole**
(703) 330-2729. Regional American. Casual Dining. **$10-$25.** 9110 Center St 20110. Jct Battle St; in Historic Old Town. L D

NASSAWADOX

◈◈ **The Great Machipongo Clam Shack**
(757) 442-3800. Seafood. Casual Dining. **$6-$24.** 6468 Lankford Hwy 23413. 0.8 mi n on US 13. L D ♿M

NEWPORT NEWS

◈ **Aromas**
(757) 240-4650. Coffee/Tea. Casual Dining. **$5-$11.** 706 Town Center Dr, Suite 104 23606. I-64 exit 255A, 2.5 mi s to Thimble Shoals Dr E; in City Center of Oyster Point. B L D

NORFOLK

◈◈◈ **219 American Bistro**
(757) 416-6219. New American. Casual Dining. **$7-$28.** 219 Granby St 23510. Jct Brooke Ave; downtown. L D

◈◈ **Bite Restaurant & Catering**
(757) 486-0035. American. Casual Dining. **$8-$12.** 440 Monticello Ave 23510. Jct Charlotte St; downtown; in Wells Fargo Center. B L

◈◈ **Capt. Groovy's Grill & Raw Bar**
(757) 965-4667. Seafood. Casual Dining. **$8-$25.** 8101 Shore Dr 23518. Just n of jct Little Creek Rd; in East Ocean View. L D ♿M

ONANCOCK

◈◈ **Bizzotto's Gallery-Caffe**
(757) 787-3103. Continental. Fine Dining. **$7-$34.** 41 Market St 23417. 1 mi w of US 13; center. L D

PETERSBURG

◆◆◆ **Dixie Restaurant**
(804) 732-7425. Southern Breakfast Comfort Food. Casual Dining.
$5-$10. 250 N Sycamore St 23803. Jct W Bank St; in Olde Towne Historic District. B L

PORTSMOUTH

◆◆ **Cafe Europa**
(757) 399-6652. Continental. Fine Dining. **$10-$18.** 319 High St 23704.
Just s of Crawford Pkwy; center. L D

RICHMOND

◆◆◆ **Bistro 27**
(804) 780-0086. American. Fine Dining. **$6-$23.** 27 W Broad St 23219.
Jct Adams St. L D

◆ **Fresca...on Addison**
(804) 359-8638. Vegetarian. Casual Dining. **$8-$12.** 22 S Addison St
23220. Jct W Main St; in Historic Fan District. L D

◆◆◆ **Rowland**
(804) 257-9885. American. Fine Dining. **$10-$23.** 2132 W Main St
23220. Jct Shields St; in Historic Fan District. D

◆ **Super Stars Gourmet Pizza**
(804) 673-3663. Pizza Sandwiches. Quick Serve. **$5-$17.** 5700 Patterson Ave 23226. Jct Libbie Ave and Willow Lawn Rd. L D

SPRINGFIELD

◆ **BGR-The Burger Joint**
(703) 451-4651. Burgers. Quick Serve. **$7-$15.** 8420 Old Keene Mill Rd
22152. I-95 exit 169B, 3 mi w on SR 644; jct Rolling Rd; in Old Keene Mill
Center. L D

STAFFORD

◆◆◆ **Zibibbo 73 Trattoria & Bar**
(540) 288-3349. Italian. Casual Dining. **$9-$30.** 2757 Jefferson Davis
Hwy 22554. I-95 exit 143A, just s on US 1; in Aquia Park Shopping Center. L D ♿M

VIRGINIA BEACH

◆◆◆ **Eurasia Cafe & Wine Bar**
(757) 422-0184. New American. Fine Dining. **$10-$30.** 960 Laskin Rd
23451. 1 mi w of oceanfront on 31st St (Laskin Rd/US 58); in Linkhorn
Shops. L D ♿M

◆◆◆ **Thirty-Seven North Restaurant and Bar**
(757) 412-0203. American. Fine Dining. **$18-$28.** 2105 W Great Neck
Rd, #101 23451. Just s of US 60/Shore Dr; in Long Bay Pointe Boating
Resort. D ♿M

WARRENTON

◆◆ **Black Bear Bistro**
(540) 428-1005. American. Casual Dining. **$7-$24.** 32 Main St 20186.
Between Culpepper and 2nd sts; in Old Town area. L D

WILLIAMSBURG

◆◆◆ **Berret's Seafood Restaurant and Taphouse Grill**
(757) 253-1847. Seafood. Casual Dining. **$8-$30.** 199 S Boundary St
23185. Center; in Merchants Square. L D

◆◆◆ **Blue Talon Bistro**
(757) 476-2583. French. Casual Dining. **$7-$30.** 420 Prince George St
23185. Center; in Merchants Square. B L D

Washington

BELLEVUE

◆◆◆ **Bis On Main**
(425) 455-2033. International. Casual Dining. **$12-$60.** 10213 Main St
98004. I-405 exit 13B, 0.8 mi w. L D

BELLINGHAM

◆◆◆ ◆◆◆ **Dirty Dan Harris Steakhouse**
(360) 676-1011. Steak. Casual Dining. **$18-$37.** 1211 11th St 98225. I-5
exit 250, 1.5 mi nw; in Fairhaven Historic District. D

COUPEVILLE

◆◆◆ **Christopher's on Whidbey**
(360) 678-5480. Seafood. Casual Dining. **$8-$28.** 103 NW Coveland St
98239. Downtown. L D

EASTSOUND

◆◆◆ **Rose's Bakery & Cafe**
(360) 376-5805. American. Casual Dining. **$9-$20.** 382 Prune Alley
98245. In Eastsound; downtown. B L

EDMONDS

◆◆◆ ◆◆◆ **Chanterelle**
(425) 774-0650. American. Casual Dining. **$7-$25.** 316 Main St 98020.
Between 3rd and 4th sts; downtown. B L D ♿M

EVERETT

◆◆◆ **Anthony's Restaurant**
(425) 252-3333. Seafood. Casual Dining. **$15-$35.** 1726 W Marine View
Dr 98201. I-5 exit 193 northbound, 1.2 mi w on Pacific Ave, then 1.4 mi n;
exit 194 southbound, 1.2 mi w on Everett Ave, then 1 mi n; in Everett
Marina Village. L D

KALAMA

◆◆ **Kalama Burger Bar**
(360) 673-2091. American. Quick Serve. **$2-$7.** 49 Ivy St 98625. I-5 exit
30, 0.4 mi n; exit southbound, just e, then 0.4 mi s. B L D ♿M

LANGLEY

◆◆ **The Braeburn**
(360) 221-3211. American. Casual Dining. **$7-$13.** 197 D 2nd St 98260.
South end of town center. B L ♿

MILL CREEK

◆◆ **McMenamins Mill Creek**
(425) 316-0520. American. Casual Dining. **$8-$16.** 13300 Bothell Everett
Hwy, Suite 304 98012. I-5 exit 186, 1 mi e, then just s. L D LATE

OAK HARBOR

◆◆◆ **Frasers Gourmet Hideaway**
(360) 279-1231. International. Casual Dining. **$24-$39.** 1191 SE Dock St
98277. Jct SR 20, 0.6 mi e on Barrington Dr, just s. D

RENTON

◆◆ **Plum Delicious**
(425) 255-8510. American. Casual Dining. **$9-$23.** 3212 NE Sunset Blvd
98056. I-405 exit 5, 1.3 mi e. B L D

SEATTLE

▼▼▼▼ Barolo Ristorante
(206) 770-9000. Italian. Casual Dining. **$13-$35.** 1940 Westlake Ave 98101. Corner of Westlake Ave and Virginia St. [L] [D]

▼▼▼ Barrio
(206) 588-8105. Mexican. Casual Dining. **$11-$22.** 1420 12th Ave 98122. Just n of Madison Ave, between E Pike and E Union sts. [L] [D] [LATE] [&M]

▼▼▼▼ Cuoco
(206) 971-0710. Northern Italian. Casual Dining. **$10-$24.** 310 Terry Ave N 98109. Jct Harrison St, just s. [L] [D] [&M]

▼▼▼▼ Serafina
(206) 323-0807. Italian. Casual Dining. **$18-$27.** 2043 Eastlake Ave E 98102. Corner of Boston St and Eastlake Ave. [L] [D] [AC]

▼▼▼▼ Stumbling Goat Bistro
(206) 784-3535. American. Casual Dining. **$20-$29.** 6722 Greenwood Ave N 98103. I-5 exit 172, 1.3 mi w on 85th St, then 1 mi s. [D]

▼▼▼▼ Szmania's
(206) 284-7305. Regional Continental. Fine Dining. **$12-$34.** 3321 W McGraw St 98199. 3.5 mi nw of Space Needle via Elliott Way; over Magnolia Bridge. [D]

AAA ▼▼▼▼ Tulio Ristorante
(206) 624-5500. Regional Italian. Casual Dining. **$8-$38.** 1100 5th Ave 98101. Corner of Spring St and 5th Ave; in Hotel Vintage-A Kimpton Hotel. [⊟] [B] [L] [D]

SPOKANE

▼▼▼▼ Latah Bistro
(509) 838-8338. Regional American. Casual Dining. **$9-$28.** 4241 S Cheney-Spokane Rd, Suite C 99224. I-90 exit 279 (US 195 S), 2.4 mi s, then 0.4 mi w. [L] [D] [&M]

▼▼▼▼ Santé Restaurant & Charcuterie
(509) 315-4613. Continental. Casual Dining. **$6-$29.** 404 W Main Ave 99201. Between N Washington and N Stevens sts; downtown. [B] [L] [D]

SPOKANE VALLEY

▼▼▼▼ Ambrosia Bistro & Wine Bar
(509) 928-3222. International. Casual Dining. **$11-$27.** 9211 E Montgomery Ave 99206. I-90 exit 287 (Argonne Rd), 0.4 mi n on Mullan Rd/Argonne Rd, then just e. [L] [D] [&M]

SULTAN

▼ Sultan Bakery
(360) 793-7996. American. Quick Serve. **$4-$12.** 711 W Stevens Ave 98294. Just e on SR 2. [B] [L] [D]

SUMNER

▼▼▼ Al Lago Ristorante Italiano
(253) 863-8636. Italian. Casual Dining. **$8-$29.** 3110 Sumner Tapps Hwy E 98390. Jct W Tapps Dr E. [L] [D]

VANCOUVER

▼▼▼ The Grant House Restaurant
(360) 906-1101. American. Casual Dining. **$8-$27.** 1101 Officers Row 98661. I-5 exit 1C (E Mill Plain Blvd), just e, just s on Fort Vancouver Way, then just e. [L] [D]

▼▼ McMenamins East Vancouver
(360) 254-3950. American. Casual Dining. **$7-$14.** 1900 NE 162nd Ave, Suite B-107 98684. SR 14 exit 8, 2.5 mi n via 164th and 162nd aves. [L] [D] [LATE] [&M]

WALLA WALLA

▼▼▼ T. Maccarone's
(509) 522-4776. Italian. Casual Dining. **$14-$44.** 4 N Colville St 99362. Jct 4th and Colville sts; downtown. [L] [D]

Wisconsin

APPLETON

▼▼ GingeRootz Asian Grille
(920) 738-9688. Asian. Casual Dining. **$8-$32.** 2920 N Ballard Rd 54911. US 41 exit 144 (Ballard Rd), 0.6 mi s. [L] [D]

CABLE

AAA ▼▼▼ Rookery Pub Fine Dining
(715) 794-2062. American. Casual Dining. **$15-$45.** 20100 County Hwy M 54821. 7 mi e of jct US 63. [D]

DELAFIELD

▼▼▼ Seven Seas on Nagawicka Lake
(262) 367-3903. International. Fine Dining. **$6-$58.** 1807 Nagawicka Rd 53029. I-94 exit 287, 1.2 mi n on SR 83, then 0.7 mi w. [D] [&M]

EAU CLAIRE

▼▼ Mike's Smokehouse
(715) 834-8153. Barbecue. Family Dining. **$5-$16.** 2235 N Clairemont Ave 54703. 1 mi s of jct US 12 and 312. [L] [D]

SISTER BAY

▼▼▼ Inn at Kristopher's
(920) 854-9419. American. Fine Dining. **$21-$44.** 734 Bay Shore Dr 54234. On SR 42; downtown. [D]

▼▼ Mission Grille
(920) 854-9070. American. Casual Dining. **$12-$44.** 10627 N Bay Shore Dr 54234. Jct SR 42 and 57. [L] [D]

Wyoming

CASPER

▼▼ Bosco's Italian Restaurante
(307) 265-9658. Italian. Casual Dining. **$6-$24.** 847 E 'A' St 82601. I-25 exit 188A (Center St), 0.4 mi s to E 'A' St, then 0.5 mi e. [L] [D]

SHERIDAN

▼ Java Moon
(307) 673-5991. Coffee/Tea. Casual Dining. **$6-$15.** 170 N Main St 82801. Center. [B] [L] [AC]

Canada

Alberta

BANFF

♦♦ **Coyotes Deli & Grill**
(403) 762-3963. New Southwestern. Casual Dining. **$8-$29.** 206 Caribou St T1L 1A2. Just w of Banff Ave; center. [B] [L] [D]

CALGARY

♦♦♦ **Big Fish**
(403) 277-3403. Seafood. Casual Dining. **$23-$31.** 1112 Edmonton Tr NE T2E 3K4. Jct Memorial Dr, 0.8 mi (1.3 km) n. [L] [D]

CANMORE

♦♦♦ **O Bistro**
(403) 678-3313. French. Casual Dining. **$13-$32.** 626 Main St, #2 T1W 2B5. Downtown. [L] [D] [&M]

RED DEER

♦♦ **Moxie's Classic Grill**
(403) 340-0111. American. Casual Dining. **$11-$30.** 2828 Gaetz Ave T4R 1M4. 1 mi (1.6 km) n on Hwy 2A (Gaetz Ave); in Sandman Hotel Red Deer. [B] [L] [D] [LATE] [&M]

British Columbia

GIBSONS

♦♦ **Molly's Reach Restaurant**
(604) 886-9710. American. Casual Dining. **$7-$16.** 647 School Rd V0N 1V0. Jct School Rd and Gibsons Way; on waterfront.
[B] [L] [D] [&M] [X]

GOLDEN

♦♦♦ **The Island Restaurant**
(250) 344-2400. New Canadian. Casual Dining. **$11-$33.** 101 Gould's Island, 10th Ave V0A 1H0. Just between the bridges; downtown.
[B] [L] [D] [&M]

VANCOUVER

♦♦♦ **Abigail's Party**
(604) 739-4677. Comfort Food. Casual Dining. **$11-$25.** 1685 Yew St V6K 3E6. Between Cornwall and 1st aves; in Kitsilano District. [D] [LATE]

New Brunswick

SAINT JOHN

♦♦ **Billy's Seafood Restaurant**
(506) 672-3474. Seafood. Casual Dining. **$13-$55.** 49-51 Charlotte St E2L 2H8. Center; in City Market. [L] [D]

♦♦♦ **Bourbon Quarter & Magnolia Cafe**
(506) 642-1885. Creole. Fine Dining. **$8-$28.** 112 Prince William St E2L 2B3. Corner of Princess St. [B] [L] [D]

Ontario

BAYFIELD

♦♦♦ **The Red Pump Restaurant & Inn**
(519) 565-2576. International. Fine Dining. **$14-$38.** 21 Main St N0M 1G0. Hwy 21 exit Main St; between Charles and Catherine sts. [L] [D]

CORNWALL

♦♦♦ **Peppermill's Grill & Bakery**
(613) 932-0451. Canadian. Casual Dining. **$9-$35.** 1515 Vincent Massey Dr K6H 5R6. Hwy 401 exit 789 (Brookdale Ave), 1.8 mi (2.8 km) s, then just w; in BEST WESTERN PLUS Parkway Inn & Conference Centre.
[C] [B] [L] [D]

KLEINBURG

♦♦♦ **The Doctor's House Restaurant**
(905) 893-1615. International. Fine Dining. **$15-$68.** 21 Nashville Rd L0J 1C0. Just w at Islington Ave (CR 17). [L] [D]

NIAGARA-ON-THE-LAKE

(CAA) ♦♦♦ **The Epicurean**
(905) 468-3408. International. Fine Dining. **$9-$35.** 84 Queen St L0S 1J0. Center. [L] [D]

OTTAWA

♦♦♦ **Mamma Teresa Ristorante**
(613) 236-3023. Italian. Casual Dining. **$10-$35.** 300 Somerset St W K2P 0J6. Corner of O'Connor St. [L] [D]

♦♦♦ **Métropolitain Brasserie - Restaurant**
(613) 562-1160. French Seafood. Casual Dining. **$14-$38.** 700 Sussex Dr K1N 1K4. Corner Rideau St. [B] [L] [D] [LATE]

OWEN SOUND

♦♦♦ **Norma Jean's**
(519) 376-2232. International. Casual Dining. **$10-$29.** 243 8th St E N4K 1L2. Between 2nd and 3rd aves. [L] [D]

STRATFORD

♦♦♦ **Keystone Alley Cafe**
(519) 271-5645. International. Casual Dining. **$10-$33.** 34 Brunswick St N5A 3L8. Between Downie and Waterloo sts. [L] [D]

TORONTO

♦♦♦ **Bodega Restaurant**
(416) 977-1287. French. Fine Dining. **$11-$30.** 30 Baldwin St M5T 1L3. Between McCaul and Beverley sts. [L] [D]

♦♦♦ **Dynasty Chinese Cuisine**
(416) 923-3323. Chinese. Casual Dining. **$17-$78.** 69 Yorkville Ave M5R 1B3. Just w of Bay St. [L] [D]

WAWA

♦♦ **Kinniwabi Pines Restaurant**
(705) 856-7226. Continental. Casual Dining. **$7-$34.** 136 Hwy 17 S P0S 1K0. 3.3 mi (5.3 km) s of jct Hwy 101. [B] [L] [D]

Prince Edward Island

BRACKLEY BEACH

♦♦♦ **The Dunes Cafe & Studio Gallery**
(902) 672-1883. Canadian. Casual Dining. **$15-$38.** Rt 15 C1E 1Z3. Jct Rt 6 and 15, 0.6 mi (1 km) n. [L] [D] [&M] [X]

NORTH RUSTICO

♦♦♦ **The Pearl & Eclectic Eatery**
(902) 963-2111. Canadian. Casual Dining. **$25-$40.** 7792 Cavendish Rd C0A 1X0. 2 mi (3.2 km) w on Rt 6. [D] [&M] [X]

Quebec

MONTRÉAL

◆◆◆ Le Pois Penché Brasserie Parisienne
(514) 667-5050. French. Casual Dining. **$16-$48.** 1230 boul de Maison-neuve ouest H3G 1M2. Corner of rue Drummond. [L] [D]

QUÉBEC

(CAA) ◆◆◆ Savini resto-bar/vinotheque
(418) 647-4747. Italian. Casual Dining. **$13-$33.** 680 Grande-Allee est G1R 2K5. Between rue d'Artigny and La Chevrotiere. [L] [D]

◆◆◆ Trattoria La Scala
(418) 529-8457. Italian. Casual Dining. **$11-$40.** 31 boul Rene-Levesque ouest G1R 2A3. Between rue Cartier and de Salaberry. [L] [D]

WESTMOUNT

◆◆◆ Vago Cucina Italiana
(514) 846-1414. Italian. Casual Dining. **$18-$42.** 1336 ave Greene H3Z 2B1. Just s of rue Sherbrooke. [L] [D]

Saskatchewan

REGINA

◆◆◆ Creek In Cathedral Bistro
(306) 352-4448. American. Casual Dining. **$13-$31.** 3414 13th Ave S4T 1P7. Just e of Elphinstone St. [L] [D]

SASKATOON

◆◆◆ Calories Bakery & Restaurant
(306) 665-7991. International Desserts. Casual Dining. **$13-$32.** 721 Broadway Ave S7N 1B3. Just s of Broadway Bridge. [L] [D] [&M]

Pet-Friendly Campgrounds

United States
Canada

United States

Camping information provided by Woodall's®

Alabama

ELBERTA — **LAKE OSPREY RV RESORT.** (251) 986-3800.
$40-$55. 12054 Gateway Dr 36530. From Jct of I-10 & Exit 44 (SR-59), S 18.7 mi to US 98, E 8.2 mi to CR-95, S 1.2 mi (L). RV type restrictions: No travel trailers 🏕️ 🛶 ✕

FOLEY — **ANCHORS AWEIGH RV RESORT.** (251) 971-6644.
$36-$39. 19814 County Rd 20 S 36535. From Jct of SR-59 & CR-20 South, W 0.25 mi on CR-20 South (L) Note: S-bnd on SR-59 2nd CR20S after Cracker Barrel 🏕️ 🛶 ✕

FOLEY — **BELLA TERRA OF GULF SHORES.** (866) 417-2416.
$50-$75. 101 Via Bella Terra 36535. From Jct of I-10 & Hwy 59 (Exit 44) S 15 mi on SR-59 to Foley Beach Expressway SE 10 mi to Brinks Willis Rd, W 0.25 mi (L) Note: Class A only 🏕️ 🛶 ✕

FOLEY — **JOHNNY'S LAKESIDE RV RESORT.** (251) 970-3773.
$29-$35. 15810 State Hwy 59 North 36535. N-bnd: From Jct of Hwy 98 & Hwy 59 (in Foley), N 3.4 mi on Hwy 59 (R); or S-bnd: From Jct of I-10 & Hwy 59 (exit 44), S 15 mi on Hwy 59 (L) 🏕️ 🛶 ✕

GULF SHORES — **SUGAR SANDS RV RESORT.** (251) 968-2223. **$48.** 5343 Roscoe Rd 36542. From Jct of US. 98 & Foley Beach Expressway S. 6mi on Foley Beach Expressway to Rosco Rd rt 1.9 mi on Roscoe Rd (R). (under construction opening early spring 2014)

GUNTERSVILLE — **BLUE HERON RV RESORT.** (256) 571-7527. **$50.** 1727 Convict Camp Rd 35976. From Jct of large river bridge (Guntersville) & Hwy 431, N 3 mi on Hwy 431 to Hwy 79, N on Hwy 79 2.5 mi (L) 🏕️ 🛶 ✕

LANGSTON — **WINDEMERE COVE RV RESORT.** (256) 228-3010. **$24-$49.** 10174 County Rd 67 35755. From Jct of US 431 & Hwy 227 (Guntersville), go 12 mi E on Hwy 227, then at Jct of Hwy 227 & S. Sauty Rd (CR-67) continue going E 8 mi on CR-67 (R) Please note: RV's 26' or more - 2001 or newer 🏕️ 🛶 ✕

MONTGOMERY — **CAPITAL CITY RV PARK.** (877) 271-8026. **$30-$35.** 4655 Old Wetumpka Hwy 36110. From Jct of I-85 & East Blvd (Exit 6), NW 4.4 mi on East Blvd to Hwy 231, N 2.6 mi to Old Wetumpka Hwy (CR-111), E 0.1 mi (R) From NW of Montgomery or From Jct of I-65 & Hwy 152 (Northern Blvd) Exit 173, NE 6.5 mi on Hwy 152 to Hwy 231N, N 2.8 mi on Hwy 231 to Old Wetumpka Hwy (CR-111), E 0.1 mi (R) 🏕️ ✕

ORANGE BEACH — **HERITAGE MOTORCOACH RESORT & MARINA.** (800) 730-7032. **$75-$150.** 28888 Canal Rd. 36561. From Jct of I-10 & AL 59 (Exit 44), S 15.3 mi on AL 59 to Foley Beach Expy, E 14 mi on Foley Beach Expy to AL 180 (Canal Rd), E 5.8 mi on AL 180 (Canal Rd) (R). Note: Class A Motorhomes only 🏕️ 🛶 ✕

TROY — **DEER RUN RV PARK.** (334) 566-6517. **$29.** 25629 Us Hwy 231 36081. (In Montgomery) From Jct of I 85 & Hwy 271 (Taylor Rd) S 4.9 mi on Hwy 271 to Jct of Hwy 271 (Taylor Rd) & Hwy 231 S 31.8 mi on Hwy 231 to CR 1124 W .01 mi (R)(From Troy) Jct of Hwy 231 & Hwy 29, N 6.3 mi on Hwy 231 to CR 1124, W .01 mi on CR1124 (R) 🏕️ 🛶 ✕

Alaska

PALMER — **BIG BEAR RV PARK.** (907) 745-7445. **$25-$36.** 2010 S Church St 99645. From Jct of Parks Hwy (SR-3) & Trunk Rd, S 500 ft on Trunk Rd to E Fireweed Rd, W 0.8 mi to Church St, SW 0.1 mi (R) ✕

TOK — **TOK RV VILLAGE & CABINS.** ⒶⒶⒶ (907) 883-5877. **$33-$53.** 1313.4 Mile Alaska Hwy 99780. N-bnd on AK Hwy at MP-1313.4 (R) ✕

Arizona

AMADO — **DE ANZA RV RESORT.** (520) 398-8628. **$36-$44.** 2869 E Frontage Rd 85645. S-bnd: From Jct of I-19 & Arivaca Rd (Exit 48), S 1.5 mi on East Frontage Rd (L); N-bnd: From Jct of I-19 & Agualinda Rd (Exit 42), N 2 mi on East Frontage Rd (R) 🏕️ 🛶 ✕

APACHE JUNCTION — **ARIZONIAN RV RESORT.** (520) 463-2978. **$38.** 15976 East Us Hwy 60 85118. From Jct of US Hwy 60 & Goldfield Rd (Exit 198), E 9.2 mi on Hwy 60 (L) 🏕️ 🛶 ✕

APACHE JUNCTION — **LA HACIENDA RV RESORT.** (480) 982-2808. **$42.** 1797 W 28th Ave 85120. From Jct of US Hwy 60 & Ironwood Dr (exit 195), N 200 yds on Ironwood Dr to 28th, W 250 ft (L) 🏕️ 🛶 ✕

APACHE JUNCTION — **MERIDIAN RV RESORT.** (866) 770-0080. **$47.** 1901 S Meridian 85120. From Jct of US-60 & Signal Butte Rd, (exit 193), N 0.5 mi on Signal Butte Rd to Southern Ave, E 1 mi to Meridian, N 0.2 mi (R) 🏕️ 🛶 ✕

APACHE JUNCTION — **SHIPROCK RV RESORT.** (480) 505-1300. **$50.** 1700 W Shiprock St 85120. From jct Fwy 202 Loop & US 60 (Superstition Fwy): Go 5 mi E on US 60 (exit 195/Ironwood Dr), then 2-3/4 mi N on Ironwood Dr, then 300 ft W on Shiprock St. 🏕️ 🛶 ✕

APACHE JUNCTION — **SUNRISE RV RESORT.** (480) 983-2500. **$35.** 1403 W Broadway Ave 85120. From Jct of US Hwy 60 & Ironwood Dr (exit 195), N 1.4 mi on Ironwood Dr to Broadway, E 0.1 mi (R) 🏕️ 🛶 ✕

APACHE JUNCTION — **SUPERSTITION LOOKOUT RV RESORT.** (480) 982-2008. **$35.** 1371 E 4th Ave 85119. From Jct of US Hwy 60 & Tomahawk Rd (exit 197), N 1.6 mi on Tomahawk Rd to 4th Ave, W 600 ft (L) 🏕️ 🛶 ✕

APACHE JUNCTION — **SUPERSTITION SUNRISE RV RESORT.** (800) 624-7027. **$30-$50. (no credit cards).** 702 S Meridian Rd 85120. From Jct of US Hwy 60 & Ironwood Dr (exit 195), N 0.5 mi on Ironwood Dr to Southern Ave, W 1 mi to Meridian Rd, N 0.6 mi (L) 🏕️ 🛶 ✕

APACHE JUNCTION — **WEAVER'S NEEDLE RV RESORT.** (480) 982-3683. **$38.** 250 So Tomahawk Rd 85119. From Jct of US Hwy 60 & Tomahawk Rd (exit 197), N 1.7 mi on Tomahawk Rd (L) 🏕️ 🛶 ✕

ARIZONA CITY — QUAIL RUN RV RESORT. (800) 301-8114. **$40-$45.** 14010 S Amado Blvd 85123. From Jct of I-10 & Sunland Gin Rd (exit 200): Go south 3.6 mi on Sunland Gin Rd to Santa Cruz Blvd, W 0.7 mi to Park (R) Santa Cruz changes to Amado Blvd. Call for GPS directions (Monthly reservations only) 🏕️ 🚐 🗙

BENSON — BUTTERFIELD RV RESORT. 🔺 (800) 863-8160. **$38.** 251 S Ocotillo Ave 85602. From Jct of I-10 & Ocotillo Ave (exit 304), go S 0.6 mi on Ocotillo Ave/past Safeway shopping center to 3rd entrance on (L) 🏕️ 🚐 🗙

BENSON — COCHISE TERRACE RV RESORT. (520) 720-0911. **$27-$35.** 1030 S Barrel Cactus Ridge 85602. From Jct of I-10 & Hwy 90 (exit 302), S 0.9 mi on Hwy 90 (R) 🏕️ 🚐 🗙

BLACK CANYON CITY — BLACK CANYON RANCH RV RESORT. (623) 374-9800. **$40.** 33900 S. Old Black Canyon Hwy 85324. N-bnd: From Jct of I-17 & Exit 242 (W over Fwy to Old Black Canyon Hwy), N 1.3 mi (L); or S-bnd: From Jct of I-17 & Exit 244, S 1 mi on S Old Black Canyon Hwy (R) 🏕️ 🚐 🗙

BUCKEYE — LEAF VERDE RV RESORT. (623) 386-3132. **$34.** 1500 S Apache Rd 85326. E-bnd: From Jct of I-10 & Exit 114 (Miller Rd), S 0.3 mi to Durango St, E 1.4 mi (Durango St becomes Yuma Rd) to Apache Rd, S 0.3 mi on Apache Rd (R); or W-bnd: From Jct of I-10 & Exit 117 (Watson Rd), S 0.6 mi on Watson Rd to Yuma Rd, W 1 mi to Apache Rd, S 0.3 mi (R) note: Do not follow GPS 🏕️ 🚐 🗙

BULLHEAD CITY — COLORADO RIVER OASIS RESORT. (928) 763-4385. **$35-$55.** 1641 Highway 95 86442. From Jct of Hwy 95 & Bullhead City Pkwy (Laughlin Bridge), S 3.4 mi on Hwy 95 (R) 🏕️ 🚐 🗙

CAMP VERDE — DISTANT DRUMS RV RESORT. (928) 554-8000. **$36-$42.** 583 W Middle Verde Rd 86322. From Jct of I-17 & exit 289 (Montezuma Castle), NW 200 yards on Montezuma Castle Rd (L) 🏕️ 🚐 🗙

CASA GRANDE — CASA GRANDE RV RESORT & COTTAGES. (520) 421-0401. **$28.** 195 W Rodeo Rd 85122. From Jct of I-10 and Pinal Rd (Exit 185) S 5 mi on Pinal Rd to Rodeo Rd, E 300ft (R) 🏕️ 🚐 🗙

CASA GRANDE — CASITA VERDE RV RESORT. (520) 836-9031. **$43.** 2200 N Trekell Rd 85122. From Jct of I-10 & McCartney Rd (exit 190), W 2.1 mi on McCartney Rd to Trekell Rd, S 1.5 mi (L) 🏕️ 🚐 🗙

CASA GRANDE — PALM CREEK GOLF & RV RESORT. 🔺 (888) 551-9407. **$34-$58.** 1110 N Henness Rd 85122. From Jct of I-10 & Florence Blvd (exit 194), W 0.5 mi on Florence Blvd to Henness Rd, N 0.2 mi (R) 🏕️ 🚐 🗙

CASA GRANDE — SUNDANCE 1 RV RESORT. (520) 426-9662. **$25-$39.** 1703 N Thornton Rd 85122. From Jct of I-10 & Pinal Ave (exit 185), S 7.3 mi on Pinal Ave to Cottonwood, W 1 mi to Thornton Rd, N 0.2 mi (L); or From Jct of I-8 & Thornton Rd (Exit 172), N 5 mi on Thornton Rd (L) 🏕️ 🚐 🗙

CASA GRANDE — SUNSCAPE ESTATES RV RESORT. (520) 723-9533. **$25-$37.** 1083 E Sunscape Way 85194. From Jct of I-10 & exit 194 (SR 287/Florence Blvd), E 6.9 mi on SR 287 to Eleven Mile Corner Rd, S 1.3 mi to Sunscape Way, E 0.9 mi (R) Gated property reservations required. 🏕️ 🚐 🗙

DEWEY-HUMBOLDT — ORCHARD RANCH RV RESORT. (928) 772-8266. **$35.** 11250 E Hwy 69 86327. From Jct of I-17 & Hwy 169 (Exit 278), W 15.1 mi on Hwy 169 to SR 69 (in Dewey), NW 3.2 mi (R) 🏕️ 🚐 🗙

EHRENBERG — ARIZONA OASIS RV RESORT. (928) 923-8230. **$40-$55.** 50238 Ehrenberg/Parker Hwy 85334. From Jct of I-10 & Exit 1 (Parker/Ehrenberg), N 0.25 mi on Poston Rd to Ehrenberg/Parker Hwy, W 0.3 mi (R) 🚐 🗙

EHRENBERG — RIVER BREEZE RV PARK & OHV RESORT. (928) 923-7483. **$42-$52.** 50202 Ehrenberg Parker Hwy 85334. From Jct of I-10 & Exit 1, N 0.25 mi on Access Rd to Ehrenberg/Parker Hwy, W 600 ft (R) 🚐 🗙

EL MIRAGE — PUEBLO EL MIRAGE GOLF & RV RESORT. (800) 445-4115. **$27-$61.** 11201 N El Mirage Rd 85335. From Jct of I-10 & Dysart Rd (Exit 129), N 6.9 mi on Dysart Rd to Olive Ave, E 1 mi to El Mirage Rd, N 1.5 mi (R); or From Jct of I-10 & Loop 101 (Exit 133), N 9 mi on Loop 101 to Olive Ave (Exit 9), W 3.8 mi to El Mirage Rd, N 1.5 mi (R). Note: 26' min length 🏕️ 🚐 🗙

ELOY — DESERT VALLEY RV PARK. (866) 502-4700. **$34.** 4555 W Tonto Rd 85131. From Jct of I-10 & Toltec Rd (exit 203): Go N for .5 mi on Toltec Rd, turn W on Tonto Rd for .5 mi in to Park 🏕️ 🚐

ELOY — LAS COLINAS RV PARK. 🔺 (520) 836-5050. **$39. (no credit cards).** 7136 Sunland Gin Rd 85131. From Jct of I-10 & Exit 200 (Sunland Gin Rd): Go N on Sunland Gin Rd for .5 mi to Redd Rd (First St), turn W on Redd Rd, go 300 ft (L) 🏕️ 🚐 🗙

FLAGSTAFF — J & H RV PARK. (928) 526-1829. **$48.** 7901 North Us Hwy 89 86004. From Jct of I-40 & Exit 201 (Page-Grand Cyn exit), go N 0.25 mi on exit rd to N Hwy 89, turn NE 3 mi on US 89 (R) No motorcycles. 🏕️ 🗙

FLORENCE — DESERT GARDENS RV PARK. (520) 868-3800. **$36-$40. (no credit cards).** 9668 N Hwy 79 85132. From Jct of Hwy 79 & SR-287, S 4.2 mi on Hwy 79 (R) Note: No popups or Pickup campers 🏕️ 🚐 🗙

FLORENCE — RANCHO SONORA RV PARK. (520) 868-8900. **$36.** 9160 N Hwy 79 85132. From Jct of Hwy 79 & SR-287 (on S side of town), S 4.3 mi on Hwy 79 (R). MP 128 🏕️ 🚐 🗙

FORT MCDOWELL — EAGLE VIEW RV RESORT AT FORT MCDOWELL. (480) 789-5310. **$44-$49.** 9605 N Fort Mcdowell Rd 85264. From Jct of SR-87 (Beeline Hwy) & N Fort McDowell Rd, S 0.4 mi on N Fort McDowell Rd (E) 🏕️ 🚐 🗙

GOLD CANYON — CANYON VISTAS RV RESORT & SUPERSTITION VIEWS RESORT. (888) 940-8989. **$47.** 6601 E Us Hwy 60 85118. From Jct Hwy 88 & US 60: Go E 4.9 mi on US 60 for 4.9 mi. 🏕️ 🚐 🗙

GOLD CANYON — GOLD CANYON RV & GOLF RESORT. (877) 465-3226. **$32-$45. (no credit cards).** 7151 E Us Hwy 60 85118. From Jct of E US Hwy 60 & Goldfield exit (end of freeway), E 3.4 mi on Hwy 60 at mm 202 (R) 🏕️ 🚐 🗙

GOLD CANYON — SUPERSTITION VIEWS RESORT & CANYON VISTAS RV RESORT. (888) 940-8989. **$47.** 6601 E Us Hwy 60 85218. From Jct Hwy 88 & US 60: Go E 4.9 mi on US 60 for 4.9 mi.

GOODYEAR — **COTTON LANE RV & GOLF RESORT.** (888) 907-7223. **$34.** 17506 W. Van Buren 85338. From Jct of I-10 & Cotton Ln (exit 125), S 0.7 mi on N Citrus Rd to Van Buren St, E 0.5 mi (L) 🖼 🛶 🗙

GOODYEAR — **DESTINY PHOENIX RV RESORTS.** (888) 667-2454. **$27-$43.** 416 N Citrus Rd 85338. E-bnd: From Jct of I-10 & Exit 123, S 0.7 mi on N Citrus Rd (R), or W-bnd: From Jct of I-10 & Exit 125, S 0.8 mi on Sarival Rd to Van Buren, W 2 mi to N Citrus Rd, N 0.1 mi (L) 🖼 🛶 🗙

KINGMAN — **BLAKE RANCH RV PARK.** (928) 757-3336. **$24-$28.** 9315 E Blake Ranch Rd 86401. From Jct of I-40 & Blake Ranch Rd (exit 66), N 0.2 mi on Blake Ranch Rd (E). Note: Do Not Use GPS 🖼 🗙

LAKE HAVASU CITY — **HAVASU FALLS RV RESORT.** (928) 764-0050. **$40-$44.** 3493 Hwy 95 N 86404. N-bnd: From Jct of Hwy 95 (London Bridge Overpass),′ N 4.4 mi on Hwy 95 (L); or S-bnd: From Jct of I-40 & Hwy 95 (exit 9), S 15.1 mi on Hwy 95 (R) 🖼 🛶

LAKE HAVASU CITY — **ISLANDER RV RESORT.** (928) 680-2000. **$56-$106.** 751 Beachcomber Blvd 86403. From Jct of Hwy 95 & Mesquite Ave, E 0.1 mi on Mesquite Ave to Lake Havasu Ave, S 0.1 mi to McCulloch Blvd (becomes Beachcomber), W 1.8 mi across London Bridge (L) 🖼 🛶 🗙

LAKE HAVASU CITY — **THE REFUGE GOLF & COUNTRY CLUB.** (928) 764-1404. **$89-$109.** 3103 London Bridge Rd 86404. From Jct of US-95 & Palo Verde Blvd (north of town), W 1 mi on Palo Verde Blvd to London Bridge Rd, N 1.6 mi on London Bridge Rd (L) 🛶 🗙

MARANA — **VALLEY OF THE SUN RV RESORT.** (520) 682-3434. **$30-$34.** 13377 N Sandario Rd 85653. From Jct of I-10 & Marana Rd (exit 236), S 0.7 mi on Sandario Rd (R) 🖼 🛶 🗙

MESA — **APACHE WELLS RV RESORT.** (888) 940-8989. **$23-$46.** 2656 N 56th St 85215. From Jct of Loop 202 & Higley Rd, S 1 mi on Higley Rd to Mc Dowell Rd, E 0.5 mi to N 56th St, S 200 ft (R) 🖼 🛶 🗙

MESA — **ARIZONA COWBOY RV PARK.** (480) 986-3333. **$30-$40.** 139 S Crismon Rd 85208. From Jct of US Hwy 60 & Crismon Rd (exit 192), N 1.7 mi (R) 🖼 🗙

MESA — **AZTEC RV PARK LLC.** (855) 832-2700. **$45.** 4220 E Main St 85205. From Jct of US Hwy 60 & Greenfield Rd (exit 185), N 2 mi on Greenfield Rd to Main St, W 0.2 mi (R) 🖼 🛶 🗙

MESA — **GOOD LIFE RV RESORT.** (888) 940-8989. **$23-$45.** 3403 E Main St 85213. From Jct of US Hwy 60 & Val Vista Rd (exit 184), N 2 mi on Val Vista Rd to Main St, W 0.2 mi (L) 🖼 🛶 🗙

MESA — **MESA REGAL RV RESORT.** (800) 845-4752. **$39.** 4700 E Main 85205. From Jct of US Hwy 60 (Superstition Fwy) & Greenfield Rd (exit 185), N 2 mi on Greenfield Rd to Main St, E 0.4 mi (L) 🖼 🛶 🗙

MESA — **MESA SPIRIT RV RESORT.** 🆎 (877) 924-6709. **$49-$61.** 3020 E Main St 85213. From Jct of Superstition Fwy (US Hwy 60) & Gilbert Rd (182), N 2 mi on Gilbert Rd to Main St, E 1.25 mi (L) 🖼 🛶 🗙

MESA — **MONTE VISTA VILLAGE RESORT.** (800) 435-7128. **$51.** 8865 E Baseline Rd 85209. From Jct of US-60 & Ellsworth Rd (Exit 191), S 0.5 mi on Ellsworth Rd to Baseline Rd, W 0.25 mi (L). Limited pet sites available 🖼 🛶 🗙

MESA — **PALM GARDENS MHC & RV PARK.** (480) 832-0290. **$40. (no credit cards).** 2929 E. Main St 85213. From Jct of US-60 & Gibbert St (Exit 132): Go N on Gilbert St for 2 mi, turn E onto E. Main for 1.1 mi to Park on right 🖼 🛶 🗙

MESA — **SILVERIDGE RV RESORT.** (800) 354-0054. **$50.** 8265 E Southern Ave 85209. From Jct of US Hwy 60 & Ellsworth (Exit 191), N 0.4 mi on Ellsworth Rd to Southern Ave, W 1.1 mi (L) 🖼 🛶 🗙

MESA — **SUN LIFE RV RESORT.** (888) 940-8989. **$23-$45.** 5055 E University Dr 85205. From Jct of Hwy 60 & Higley Rd (exit 186), N 2.5 mi on Higley Rd to University Dr, W 0.2 mi (L) 🖼 🛶 🗙

MESA — **THE RESORT.** (866) 386-1101. **$50.** 1101 S Ellsworth Rd 85208. From Jct of US Hwy 60 & Ellsworth Rd (Exit 191), N 0.6 mi on Ellsworth Rd (R) 🖼 🛶 🗙

MESA — **TOWERPOINT RESORT.** (888) 940-8989. **Call for rates.** 4860 E Main St 85205. From Jct of US Hwy 60 & Higley Rd (exit 186), N 2 mi on Higley Rd to Main St, W 0.4 mi (R) 🖼 🛶 🗙

MESA — **VAL VISTA VILLAGE RV RESORT.** 🆎 (888) 940-8989. **$41-$75.** 233 N Val Vista Dr 85213. From Jct of US Hwy 60 & Val Vista Dr (exit 184), N 2.3 mi on Val Vista Dr (R). Note: No Pickup campers 🖼 🛶 🗙

MESA — **VALLE DEL ORO RV RESORT.** (888) 940-8989. **$49.** 1452 S Ellsworth Rd 85209. From Jct of US Hwy 60 & Ellsworth Rd (exit 191), N 0.1 mi on Ellsworth Rd (L) 🖼 🛶 🗙

MESA — **VIEWPOINT RV & GOLF RESORT.** (480) 373-8700. **$64.** 8700 E University Dr 85207. From Jct of US Hwy 60 & AZ 202N (Exit 190A), N 2.5 mi on AZ 202N to University Dr, W 0.4 mi (R) 🖼 🛶 🗙

MOHAVE VALLEY — **MOON RIVER RV RESORT.** 🆎 (928) 788-6666. **$33-$36.** 1325 Boundary Cone Rd 86440. From Jct of Hwy 95 & Boundary Cone Rd, W 200 yds on Boundary Cone Rd (R); or From SR 68 & Hwy 95, (Laughlin Bridge), S 15.2 mi on Hwy 95 to Boundary Cone Rd, W 200 yds (R). Note: GPS users please call. 🖼 🛶

MUNDS PARK — **MUNDS PARK RV RESORT.** (928) 286-1309. **$31-$35.** 17550 Munds Ranch Rd. 86017. From Jct of I-17 & Exit 322 (Pinewood-Munds Park), go N 0.25 mi on Munds Ranch Rd (L) 🖼 🛶 🗙 .

PAYSON — **PAYSON CAMPGROUND AND RV RESORT.** 🆎 (928) 472-2267. **$35-$40.** 808 E Hwy 260 85541. From Jct of Hwy 87 & Hwy 260, go E 0.7 mi on Hwy 260 (L) 🛶 🗙

PEORIA — **PLEASANT HARBOR RV RESORT.** (800) 475-3272. **$28-$51.** 8708 W Harbor Blvd 85383. From Jct of I-17 & Carefree Hwy (Exit 223B), W 8 mi on Carefree Hwy to 87th Ave, N 1.8 mi (L) 🛶 🗙

PHOENIX — **DESERT SHADOWS RV RESORT.** (800) 595-7290. **$37-$69.** 19203 N 29th Ave 85027. N-bnd: From Jct of I-17 & Union Hills Dr (Exit 214 A & B), W 0.4 mi on Union Hills Dr to 29th Ave, N 0.4 mi (R); or S-bnd: From Jct of I-17 & Union Hills Dr/Yorkshire (Exit 214 A & B), S 0.6 mi on N Black Canyon Hwy/Frontage Rt to Union Hills Dr, W 0.4 mi to 29th Ave, N 0.4 mi (R) 🖼 🛶 🗙

PHOENIX — DESERT'S EDGE RV-THE PURPLE PARK. (623) 587-0940. **$30-$75.** 2398 W Williams Dr 85027. S-bnd: From Jct of I-17 & Deer Valley Rd/Exit 215B (N side of Phoenix), E 0.1 mi on Deer Valley to 23rd Ave, N 0.4 mi on 23rd Ave to Williams Dr, W 0.1 mi (R); or N-bnd: I-17 & Deer Valley/Rose Garden (Exit 215A), E 0.1 mi on Rose Garden to 23rd Ave, N 0.9 mi to Williams Dr, W 0.1 mi (R) 🏕️ 🛶 📶

PHOENIX — PHOENIX METRO RV PARK. (623) 582-0390. **$37-$75.** 22701 N. Black Canyon Hwy 85027. From Jct of 101 & I-17, N 1 mi on I-17 to Deer Valley Rd/Rose Garden (Exit 215), N 0.7 mi on N Black Canyon Hwy/E Frontage Rd (R). Call If using GPS 🏕️ 🛶 📶

PHOENIX — ROYAL PALM RV RESORT/MHC. (602) 943-5833. **$32.** 2050 West Dunlap Ave 85021. From Jct of I-10 & I-17, N 6.5 mi on I-17 (Exit 207) to Dunlap Ave, E 0.8 mi (L) 🏕️ 🛶 📶

PICACHO — PICACHO PEAK RV RESORT. ⓐ (520) 466-7841. **$31.** 17065 E Peak Lane 85141. From Jct of I-10 & exit 219, exit to S Frontage Rd., SE 0.5 mi (R) 🏕️ 🛶 📶

QUEEN VALLEY — QUEEN VALLEY RV RESORT. (520) 463-2300. **$39.** 50 West Oro Viejo Dr 85118. From Jct of US Hwy 60 & Idaho Rd (in Apache Jct), E 17.6 mi on US-60, past Hwy 60/79 Jct, to Queen Valley Rd (M 214), NW 5.4 mi, follow signs (R) or From Jct of US 60 & Hwy 79 (Florence Jct), E 2 mi on US 60 to Queen Valley Rd (M 214), NW 5.4 mi (follow signs) (R) Follow written directions only. 🏕️ 🛶 📶

SAFFORD — LEXINGTON PINES RESORT LLC. (928) 428-7570. **$26.** 1535 Thatcher Blvd 85546. W-bnd: From Jct of US-191 & US-70, W 1.2 mi on US-70 (L); or E-bnd: From Jct of Hwy 70 & 20th St, E .01 mi on Hwy 70 (R). Note: Behind Auto Zone 🏕️ 📶

SALOME — BLACK ROCK RV VILLAGE. (928) 927-4206. **$31-$39.** 46751 E Hwy 60 85348. From Jct of I-10 & Hwy 60 (exit 31), NE 4 mi on Hwy 60 (L) 🏕️ 🛶 📶

SALOME — DESERT GOLD RV RESORT. (800) 927-2101. **$32.** 46628 E Hwy 60 85348. From Jct of I-10 & Hwy 60 E (exit 31), NE 4 mi on Hwy 60 E (R); or W-bnd: From Jct of I-10 & Exit 45 (Vicksburg Rd), N 7 mi on Vicksburg Rd to Hwy 60, SW 10 mi (L) 🏕️ 🛶 📶

SALOME — DESERT PALMS RV RESORT. (928) 859-2000. **$35.** 39258 Harquahala Rd 85348. E-bnd: From Jct of I-10 & US Hwy 60 (Exit 31) NE 25 mi to Salome Rd, S 0.3 mi on Salome Rd to Harquahala Rd, SW 0.75 mi (R); or W-bnd: From Jct of I-10 W & Salome Rd (Exit 81), NW 30 mi on Salome Rd to Harquahala Rd, SW 0.75 (R) 🏕️ 🛶 📶

SURPRISE — SUNFLOWER RV RESORT. (623) 583-0100. **$25-$55.** 16501 N. El Mirage Rd 85378. N-bnd: From Jct of I-10 & 101 Loop (Exit 133), N 12.5 mi on the 101 Loop to Bell Rd (Exit 14), W 5.6 mi on Bell Rd to N El Mirage Rd, S 0.3 mi (L); or S-bnd: From Jct of I-17 & 101 Loop (Exit 285), W 8 mi on 101 Loop to Bell Rd (Exit 14), W 5.6 mi on to El Mirage Rd, S 0.3 mi (L). Min. length 22 ft 🏕️ 🛶 📶

TOMBSTONE — TOMBSTONE TERRITORIES RV PARK. (520) 457-2584. **$20-$35.** 2111 E Hwy 82 85616. From Jct of I-10 & AZ Hwy 90 (Exit 302), go S on AZ-90 for 19 mi to AZ-82, turn E on to AZ-82, go 7.8 mi (L) 🏕️ 🛶 📶

TONOPAH — SADDLE MOUNTAIN RV PARK. (623) 386-3892. **$32.** 40902 W Osborn Rd 85354. From Jct of I-10 & Exit 94 (Tonopah), S 0.7 mi on N 411th Ave to Osborn, E 0.2 mi (L) Note: Limited free WiFi 🏕️ 🛶 📶

TUCSON — FAR HORIZONS TUCSON VILLAGE RV RESORT. (800) 480-3488. **$29-$49.** 555 N Pantano Rd 85710. From Jct of I-10 & Kolb Rd (Exit 270), N 9 mi on Kolb Rd to Speedway, E 1 mi to Pantano Rd, S 0.5 mi (R) 🏕️ 🛶 📶

TUCSON — MISSION VIEW RV RESORT. (800) 444-8439. **$25-$38. (no credit cards).** 31 West Los Reales 85756. From Jct of I-10 & I-19 (Exit 260), S 8.5 mi on I-19 to San Xavier Loop Rd (Exit 92), E 1.4 mi on San Xavier Loop Rd (L). Note: No tent trailers 🏕️ 🛶 📶

TUCSON — PRINCE OF TUCSON RV PARK. (800) 955-3501. **$29.** 3501 N Freeway 85705. From Jct of I-10 & Prince Rd (Exit 254), Go SW 0.2 mi on Prince Rd, then E 0.1 mi on Business Center Dr, then N 0.1 mi on Frontage Rd (R) 🏕️ 🛶 📶

TUCSON — RINCON COUNTRY EAST RV RESORT. ⓐ (520) 886-8431. **$45-$49.** 8989 E Escalante Rd 85730. From Jct of I-10 & Kolb Rd (exit 270), N 5 mi on Kolb Rd to Escalante Rd, E 2.5 mi (L) 🏕️ 🛶 📶

TUCSON — RINCON COUNTRY WEST RV RESORT. ⓐ (520) 294-5608. **$49-$55.** 4555 S Mission Rd 85746. From Jct of I-10 & I-19 (exit 260), S 1.5 mi on I-19 to Ajo Way (exit 99), W 1 mi to Mission Rd, S 0.5 mi (L) 🏕️ 🛶 📶

TUCSON — TUCSON LAZYDAYS KOA. (520) 799-3701. **$30-$35.** 5151 S Country Club Rd 85706. E Bnd: From Jct of I-10 & Irvington (Exit 264 B), W 0.7 on Irvington (L). W Bnd: From Jct of I-10 & Irvington (Exit 264), N 0.1 mi on Palo Verde Rd (Left lane) to Irvington Rd., W 0.1 mi (L). If using GPS use 3200 E Irvington Rd 🏕️ 🛶 📶

TUCSON — VOYAGER RV RESORT. (800) 405-6188. **$25-$54.** 8701 S Kolb Rd 85756. From Jct of I-10 & Kolb Rd (exit 270), S 0.5 mi on Kolb Rd (L) 🏕️ 🛶 📶

TUCSON — WESTERN WAY RV RESORT. (800) 292-8616. **$52.** 3100 S Kinney Rd 85713. From Jct of I-19 & I-10 (Exit 260), S 1.5 mi on I-19 to Ajo Way (Exit 99), W 5 mi on Ajo Way to Kinney Rd, N 1.5 mi to Western Way Cir, SW 500 ft (R) 🏕️ 🛶 📶

WICKENBURG — HORSPITALITY RV PARK. (928) 684-2519. **$28-$38.** 51802 Us Hwy 60-89 85390. From Jct of US-60/89 & SR-93, SE 2 mi on Hwys 60/89/93, between MP-112 & 113 (R) 📶

WILLOW BEACH — WILLOW BEACH MARINA & RV PARK. (928) 767-4747. **$35.** 25804 N Willow Beach Rd 86445. From Jct of US 93 & Willow Beach Rd (between Mile Marker 14 & 15), NW 4.2 mi on Willow Beach Rd (E) 📶

WINSLOW — METEOR CRATER RV PARK. ⓐ (800) 478-4002. **$30-$35.** I-40 Exit 233 86047. From Jct of I-40 & Meteor Crater Rd (exit 233), go S 100 yds on Meteor Crater Rd (R). (Do not use GPS)

YUMA — ARIZONA WEST RV PARK. (928) 726-1481. **$30.** 6825 E 32nd Street 85365. From Jct of I-8 & Araby Rd (Exit 7), S 0.4 mi on Araby Rd to E 32nd St, E 0.3 mi (R) 🏕️ 🛶 📶

YUMA — ARABY ACRES RV RESORT. (800) 405-6188. **$51.** 6649 E 32nd St 85365. From Jct of I-8 & Araby Rd (exit 7), S 0.5 mi on Araby Rd to 32nd St (Bus 8), E 500 ft (R) 🏕️ 🛶 📶

YUMA — BONITA MESA RV RESORT. ⓐ (928) 342-2999. **$38.** 9400 N Frontage Rd 85365. From Jct of I-8 & exit 12 (Fortuna Rd), N on Fortuna Rd to Frntg rd, W 1.5 mi (R) 🏕️ 🛶 📶

YUMA — **CARAVAN OASIS RV RESORT.** (928) 342-1480. **$42.** 10500 N Frontage Rd 85365. From Jct of I-8 & Exit 12 (Fortuna Rd), N on Fortuna Rd to Frntg Rd, W 0.2 mi (R) 🏕️ 🛶 ⊠

YUMA — **COCOPAH BEND RV & GOLF RESORT.** (800) 537-7901. **$43.** 6800 S Strand Ave 85364. From Jct of I-8 & Winterhaven/ 4th Ave (CA Exit 172), Go S 1/2 mi on 4th Ave (I-8 Bus Loop) then Go W 2-1/4 mi on 1st St, then Go S 1/4 mi on Ave C, then go W 1-1/2 mi on Riverside Dr, then go N 3/4 mi on Strand Ave, (E) 🏕️ 🛶 ⊠

YUMA — **DEL PUEBLO RV PARK AND TENNIS RESORT.** (928) 341-2100. **$49.** 14794 S. Ave 3e 85365. Jct of I-8 & Ave 3E (exit 3), S 5.2 mi on Ave 3E (R) 🏕️ 🛶 ⊠

YUMA — **DESERT HOLIDAY RV RESORT.** (928) 344-4680. **$30-$40.** 3601 S 4th Ave 85365. From Jct of I-8 & 4th Ave (Exit 172 in CA), S 4 mi on 4th Ave to 4th Ave Extension, S 0.6 mi (L) 🏕️ 🛶 ⊠

YUMA — **FRIENDLY ACRES RV PARK.** (928) 783-8414. **$27.** 2779 W 8th St 85364. From Jct of I-8 & 4th Ave (Exit 172 in CA), go S 1-1/4 mi on 4th Ave to 8th St, then go W 1-1/2 mi on 8th St (L) 🏕️ 🛶 ⊠

YUMA — **FORTUNA DE ORO RV RESORT.** (928) 342-5051. **$40.** 13650 N Frntg Rd 85367. From Jct of I-8 & Foothills Blvd (exit 14), N 50 ft on Foothills Blvd to N frntg rd, E 0.6 mi (L) 🏕️ 🛶 ⊠

YUMA — **LAS QUINTAS OASIS RV RESORT.** (928) 305-9005. **$40.** 10442 N Frontage Rd 85365. From Jct of I-8 & Exit 12 (Fortuna Rd), N on Fortuna Rd to Frntg Rd, W 0.6 mi (R) Do not use GPS 🏕️ 🛶 ⊠

YUMA — **SHANGRI-LA RV RESORT.** (928) 342-9123. **$38-$46.** 10498 N Frontage Rd 85365. From Jct of I-8 & Exit 12 (Fortuna Rd), N on Fortuna Rd to frntg rd, W 0.4 mi (R). Note: Do not use GPS 🏕️ 🛶 ⊠

YUMA — **SUN VISTA RV RESORT.** ⒶⒶⒶ (800) 423-8382. **$47.** 7201 E 32nd St 85365. W-bnd: From Jct of I-8 & Exit 9 (Ave 8 1/2 E), W 0.7 mi on N Frontage Rd to 32nd St (Bus 8), W 0.9 mi (L); or E-bnd: From Jct of I-8 & Araby Rd (exit 7), S 0.5 mi on Araby Rd to 32nd St (Bus 8), E 0.6 mi (R) 🏕️ 🛶 ⊠

YUMA — **VILLA ALAMEDA RV RESORT.** (928) 344-8081. **$33. (no credit cards).** 3547 S Ave 5 E 85365. From Jct of I-8 & Ave 3E (exit 3), Go 1-1/4 mi S on Ave 3E, then 2 mi E on 32nd St (Bus 8), then 1/2 mi S on Ave 5E (L); or From Jct of I-8 & Araby Rd (Exit 7), Go 1/2 mi S on Araby Rd, then 1-1/2 mi W on 32nd St (Bus 8), then 1/2 mi S on Ave 5E (L) 🏕️ 🛶 ⊠

YUMA — **WESTWIND RV & GOLF RESORT.** ⒶⒶⒶ (928) 342-2992. **$22-$50.** 9797 E 32nd St 85365. From Jct of I-8 & Fortuna Rd (exit 12), S 50 ft on Fortuna Rd to S Frontage Rd, W 1 mi (L) Do not use GPS 🏕️ 🛶 ⊠

Arkansas

EUREKA SPRINGS — **WANDERLUST RV PARK, LLC.** (479) 253-7385. **$32.** 468 Passion Play Rd 72632. From Jct of US-62 & SR-23S, E 2 mi on US-62 to Passion Play Rd, N 0.5 mi (L) 🛶

HARRISON — **HARRISON VILLAGE CAMPGROUND & RV PARK.** (870) 743-3388. **$24-$30.** 2364 Hwy 65 S 72601. From Jct of US-65 & 7 (in town), S 3.5 mi on US-65 (R); or E-bnd: From Jct of US-412 & US-62, E 7 mi on 412/62 to US-65, S 9 mi (R); or N-bnd: From Jct of US 412/62 & US-65, N 1.5 mi on US 65 (L) 🛶 ⊠

HARRISON — **PARKERS RV PARK.** (870) 743-2267. **$24-$27.** 3629 Hwy 65 N 72601. From Jct of US-62/US-412 & US-65 (N of Harrison), S 1.3 mi on US-65 (R) 🏕️ ⊠

HOT SPRINGS — **CATHERINE'S LANDING AT HOT SPRINGS.** (501) 262-2550. **$29-$42.** 1700 Shady Grove Rd 71901. From Jct of US 270 & AR 128 (Exit 7), W 0.3 mi on AR 128 (Carpenter Dam Rd) to Shady Grove Rd, SE 1.7 mi (R) 🏕️ 🛶 ⊠

MAGNOLIA — **MAGNOLIA RV PARK, LLC.** (870) 562-2908. **$35-$50. (no credit cards).** 1399 W University 71753. S-Bnd: Jct of US-82 & US-371, S .5 mi on US-371 to W University, R .5 mi (R) N-Bnd: Jct of US-371 & US-82B, N 1.6 mi on US-371 to W University, L .5 mi (R) 🏕️ ⊠

MOUNTAIN VIEW — **OZARK RV PARK.** (870) 269-2542. **$24-$28.** 1022 Park Ave 72560. N-bnd: Jct of SR-5/9/14, N 0.5 mi on SR14 to E Webb, W 0.7 mi to Park Ave, N 0.4 mi (L); S-bnd: Jct of SR-5/9/14, N of town, S 5 mi on SR9 to SR382, W 0.2 mi to Roper, SW 0.5 mi to Park Ave, N 0.1 mi (L); E-bnd: Jct of 65/66, E 27 mi on 66 to Peabody, N 500' to Webb, E 150' to Park Ave, N 0.4 mi (L) ⊠

OAK GROVE — **OZARKS RV RESORT ON TABLE ROCK LAKE.** (888) 749-7396. **$45-$65.** 1229 Cr 663 72660. From Jct of US-65 & SR-86, W 11.6 mi on SR-86 to SR-13/21, S 1.1 mi to SR-311 (straight thru Blue Eye), E 4.9 mi to entrance sign, E 1.2 mi (R). Call for RV restrictions 🏕️ 🛶 ⊠

TEXARKANA — **SUNRISE RV PARK.** (870) 772-0751. **$35.** 8225 Camper Lane 71854. From Jct of I-30 & Rte 108 (exit 7), W 0.1 mi on Rte 108 to Service Rd, NE 0.2 mi (L) 🛶 ⊠

California

ACTON — **THE CALIFORNIAN RV RESORT.** ⒶⒶⒶ (888) 787-8386. **$42.** 1535 W. Sierra Hwy 93510. N-bnd: From Jct of Hwy 14 N & Exit Santiago (L), right at stop sign, 1 mi (L); or S-bnd: From Jct of Hwy 14 S, Exit #27 Soledad Canyon Rd, right at stop sign (L) 🏕️ 🛶 ⊠

ANGELS CAMP — **ANGELS CAMP RV & CAMPING RESORT.** ⒶⒶⒶ (209) 736-0404. **$37-$53.** 3069 Highway 49 South 95222. From Jct of Hwy 49 & Hwy 4, S 2.6 mi on Hwy 49 (L) 🛶 ⊠

ARCATA — **MAD RIVER RAPIDS RV PARK.** ⒶⒶⒶ (800) 822-7776. **$37-$47.** 3501 Janes Rd 95521. From Jct of US-101 & SR-299, N 0.2 mi on US-101 to Giuntoli Ln/Janes Rd Exit 716B, W 0.3 mi on Janes Rd (L) 🏕️ 🛶 ⊠

BAKERSFIELD — **A COUNTRY RV PARK.** (866) 787-2750. **$36.** 622 S Fairfax Rd 93307. From Jct of Hwy 99 & Hwy 58: Go 6 mi E on Hwy 58 to Fairfax Rd, then 1/4 mi S on Fairfax Rd (R) 🏕️ 🛶 ⊠

BAKERSFIELD — **BAKERSFIELD RIVER RUN RV PARK.** ⒶⒶⒶ (888) 748-7786. **$33-$59.** 3715 Burr St 93308. From Jct of Hwy 99 & Hwy 58 W/Rosedale Hwy (Exit 26): Go 1/2 mi W on Hwy 58 to Gibson St, then 1/4 mi S on Gibson St to Burr St, then 1/4 mi E on Burr St (E) 🏕️ 🛶 ⊠

BAKERSFIELD — **BAKERSFIELD RV RESORT.** (661) 833-9998. **$44.** 5025 Wible Rd 93313. From Jct of Hwy 99 & White Lane (exit 21): Go 100 ft W on White Lane to Wible Road, then 1/2 mi S on Wible Rd (R) 🏕️ 🛶 ⊠

BAKERSFIELD — ORANGE GROVE RV PARK. ⚠️ (661) 366-4662. **$30-$42.** 1452 S Edison Rd 93307. From Jct of Hwy 99 & Hwy 58E (exit 24): Go 8 mi E on Hwy 58 to S Edison Rd (exit 119), then 1/8 mi S on S Edison Rd (R) 🏔️ ➰ ✖️

BORREGO SPRINGS — THE SPRINGS AT BORREGO RV RESORT & GOLF COURSE. (866) 330-0003. **$29-$104.** 2255 Digiorgio Road 92004. From Jct of Hwys S-3 & S-22 (in town), E 0.5 mi on Hwy S-22 to Di Giorgio Rd, N 0.6 mi (R) 🏔️ ➰ ✖️

BUELLTON — FLYING FLAGS RV RESORT & CAMP-GROUND. ⚠️ (805) 688-3716. **$32-$98.** 180 Avenue Of Flags 93427. From jct of US 101 & Rte 246 (Exit 140): Go 1/4 mi W on Rte 246 to Ave of the Flags, then 1/4 mi S on Ave of the Flags (L) ➰ ✖️

CATHEDRAL CITY — OUTDOOR RESORT PALM SPRINGS. (800) 843-3131. **$41-$84.** 69-411 Ramon Rd 92234. From Jct of I-10 & Bob Hope Dr (Exit 130), S 0.3 mi on Bob Hope Dr to Ramon Rd, W 2.1 mi (L) 🏔️ ➰ ✖️

CHICO — ALMOND TREE RV PARK. ⚠️ (530) 899-1271. **$39-$43.** 3124 Esplanade 95973. From Jct of SR-99 & SR-32 (SE of town/ Exit 389), N 3.7 mi on SR-99 to Eaton Rd, SW 0.2 mi to Esplanade, SE 0.4 mi (L) 🏔️ ➰ ✖️

CHOWCHILLA — THE LAKES RV & GOLF RESORT. (866) 665-6980. **$40-$60.** 5001 E Robertson 93610. From Jct of Hwy 99 & E Robertson Blvd (Exit 170): Go 1-1/4 mi E on Robertson Blvd (R) (No tent trailers) 🏔️ ➰ ✖️

CHULA VISTA — CHULA VISTA RV RESORT AND MARINA. ⚠️ (800) 770-2878. **$50-$75.** 460 Sandpiper Way 91910. From Jct of I-5 & J St (exit 7B), W 500 ft on J St (becomes Marina Pkwy), continue 0.5 mi on Marina Pkwy to Sandpiper Way, W 0.2 mi (L) 🏔️ ➰ ✖️

CLIO — CLIO'S RIVERS EDGE RV PARK. (530) 836-2375. **$36-$50.** 3754 Hwy 89 96106. From Jct of SR-89 & SR-70, S 4.2 mi on SR-89 (L) 🏔️ ✖️

DESERT HOT SPRINGS — CALIENTE SPRINGS RESORT. (888) 894-7727. **$50-$59.** 70-200 Dillon Rd 92241. E-bnd: From Jct of I-10 & Palm Dr (Exit 123), N 3.1 mi on Palm Dr to Dillon Rd, E 3.7 mi (L) 🏔️ ➰ ✖️

DESERT HOT SPRINGS — SANDS RV & GOLF RESORT. (760) 251-1030. **$42-$49.** 16400 Bubbling Wells Rd 92240. From Jct of I-10 & Palm Dr (Exit 123), N 3 mi on Palm Dr to Dillon Rd, E 1 mi to Bubbling Wells Rd, N 0.2 mi (R) 🏔️ ➰ ✖️

DESERT HOT SPRINGS — SKY VALLEY RESORT. (888) 893-7727. **$50-$59.** 74-711 Dillon Rd 92241. E-bnd: From Jct of I-10 & Palm Dr (Exit 123), N 3.1 mi on Palm Dr to Dillon Rd, E 8.5 mi (R); W-bnd: From Jct of I-10 & Dillon Rd, NW 18.6 mi on Dillon Rd (L) 🏔️ ➰ ✖️

EL CENTRO — RIO BEND RV & GOLF RESORT. ⚠️ (760) 352-7061. **$38-$70.** 1589 Drew Rd 92243. From Jct of I-8 & Hwy 86 (Imperial Ave), W 8 mi on I-8 to Drew Rd (Exit 107), S 0.4 mi (R) 🏔️ ➰ ✖️

FORTUNA — RIVERWALK RV PARK & CAMPGROUND. (707) 725-3359. **$38-$48.** 2189 Riverwalk Dr 95540. From Jct of US-101 & Kenmar Rd/Riverwalk Dr (Exit 687), W 0.2 mi on Riverwalk Dr (R) ➰ ✖️

GARBERVILLE — BENBOW KOA. (707) 923-2777. **$35-$90.** 7000 Benbow Dr 95542. From Jct of Hwy 101 & Exit 636 (Benbow Dr), N 0.2 mi on Benbow Dr (L) ➰ ✖️

GOLETA — OCEAN MESA AT EL CAPITAN. ⚠️ (866) 410-5783. **$75-$95.** 100 El Capitan Terrace Lane 93117. S-bnd: From Jct of Hwy 101 & El Capitan State Beach Rd (Exit 117), N 0.2 mi on El Capitan State Beach Rd (under freeway) to Calle Real, S 0.4 mi (R); or N-bnd: From Jct of Hwy 101 & El Capitan State Beach Rd (Exit 117), S 0.6 mi on Calle Real (R) ➰ ✖️

GREENFIELD — YANKS RV RESORT. (855) 926-5778. **$44-$64.** 305 Yanks Way 93927. From jct Hwy 101 & Thorne Rd (Exit 295): Go 0.1 mi E on Livingston Rd (E) ➰ ✖️

HEMET — GOLDEN VILLAGE PALMS RV RESORT - SUN-LAND. ⚠️ (866) 225-6320. **$45-$90.** 3600 W Florida Ave 92545. From Jct of Hwys 74/79 (Florida Ave) & Sanderson Ave, W 0.2 mi on Florida Ave (R) 🏔️ ➰ ✖️

INDIO — INDIAN WATERS RV RESORT & COTTAGES. (760) 342-8100. **$36-$61.** 47-202 Jackson St. 92201. From Jct of I-10 & Golf Center Pky (Exit 144): Go SW 0.9 mi on Golf Center Pkwy to Hwy 111, then W 0.3 mi to Jackson St, then S 0.7 mi (L) 🏔️ ➰ ✖️

INDIO — INDIAN WELLS CAREFREE RV RESORTS. (760) 347-0895. **$46-$90.** 47-340 Jefferson St 92201. From Jct of I-10 & Jefferson St (Exit 139), S 2.7 mi on Jefferson St (L) 🏔️ ➰ ✖️

INDIO — MOTORCOACH COUNTRY CLUB. (888) 277-0789. **$90-$184.** 80-501 Avenue 48 92201. From Jct of I-10 & Jefferson St (Exit 139), S 3 mi on Jefferson St to Ave 48, E 0.5 mi (R). Note: Class A motorcoach, min. 30 ft only. 🏔️ ➰ ✖️

INDIO — OUTDOOR RESORT INDIO. (800) 892-2992. **$60-$110.** 80-394 Avenue 48 92201. From Jct of I-10 & Jefferson St (Exit 139), S 3 mi on Jefferson St to Ave 48, E 0.3 mi (L). Class A Motor-homes only - Minimum 34 ft. Note: Minimum length of stay may apply. 🏔️ ➰ ✖️

INDIO — SHADOW HILLS RV RESORT. (760) 360-4040. **$38-$63.** 40 655 Jefferson Street 92203. From Jct of I-10 & Jefferson St (Exit 139), N 0.25 mi on Jefferson St (L) ➰ ✖️

JACKSON — JACKSON RANCHERIA RV PARK. (800) 822-WINN. **$45-$55.** 11407 Dalton Rd 95642. From Jct of Hwy 49 & Hwy 88 (in Jackson), E 2.5 mi on Hwy 88 to Dalton Rd, N 0.9 mi (L) 🏔️ ➰ ✖️

LAKESIDE — RANCHO LOS COCHES RV PARK. (800) 630-0448. **$39-$48.** 13468 Hwy 8 Bus 92040. From Jct of I-8 & Los Coches Rd (Exit 22), N 0.5 mi on Los Coches Rd to Hwy 8 Bus, E 0.4 mi (L) ➰ ✖️

LODI — FLAG CITY RV RESORT. ⚠️ (866) 371-4855. **$54.** 6120 W Banner Rd 95242. From Jct of I-5 & SR 12, E 0.2 mi on SR 12 to Star St, S 500 ft to Banner St, E 0.1 mi (R) 🏔️ ➰

LONE PINE — BOULDER CREEK RV RESORT. ⚠️ (760) 876-4243. **$40.** 2550 S Hwy 395 93545. From Jct of US-395 & SR-136: Go 2.6 mi S on US-395 (L) ➰ ✖️

MANCHESTER — MANCHESTER BEACH/MENDOCINO COAST KOA. (800) 562-4188. **$45-$65.** 44300 Kinney Rd 95459. From town, N 0.7 mi on SR-1 to Kinney Rd, W 0.3 mi (R) ➰ ✖️

MANTECA — FRENCH CAMP RV PARK RESORT & GOLF COURSE. (209) 234-1544. **$41-$50.** 3919 E French Camp Rd 95336. From Jct of Hwy 99 & Exit 246 (French Camp), W 0.1 mi on French Camp Rd (R); or From Jct of I-5 & French Camp exit, E 4.3 mi on French Camp Rd (L) 🏕 🚣

NEEDLES — PALMS RIVER RESORT. (760) 326-0333. **$30-$40.** 4170 Needles Hwy 92363. From Jct of I 40 & W. Broadway (Exit 141), N 3 mi on Needles Hwy/River Rd (R). Note: No pop-up trailers. 🏕 🚣 ⊠

NEWPORT BEACH — NEWPORT DUNES WATERFRONT RESORT & MARINA. (800) 765-7661. **$64-$350.** 1131 Back Bay Dr 92660. From Jct of Pacific Coast Hwy (Hwy 1) & Jamboree Rd exit, N 0.2 mi on Jamboree Rd to Back Bay Dr, W 0.1 mi (L); or From Jct of I-405 & Jamboree Rd exit (in Irvine), S 5 mi on Jamboree Rd to Back Bay Dr, W 0.1 mi (L) 🚣 ⊠

NILAND — FOUNTAIN OF YOUTH SPA RV RESORT. (760) 354-1340. **$35-$49.** 1500 Spa Rd 92257. From Jct of Hwy 111 & Hot Mineral Spa Rd (14 mi N of Niland), E 1.5 mi to Spa Rd, SE 1 mi (L) 🚣 ⊠

NOVATO — NOVATO RV PARK. ⒶⒶⒶ (800) 733-6787. **$65.** 1530 Armstrong Ave 94945. From Jct of US-101 & Atherton Ave/San Marin Dr exit, E 300 ft on Atherton Ave to Armstrong Ave, S 0.1 mi (L) 🏕 🚣 ⊠

OCEANO — PISMO SANDS RV PARK. (800) 404-7004. **$50-$59.** 2220 Cienaga St 93445. N-bnd: From Jct of US-101 & Grand Ave (Hwy 227) exit, W 0.5 mi on Grand Ave to Halcyon Rd, S 1.4 mi to Cienaga St (Hwy 1), W 0.8 mi (L); or S-bnd: From Jct of US-101 & Halcyon Rd exit, S 1.6 mi on Halcyon Rd to Cienaga St (Hwy 1), W 0.8 mi (L) 🏕 🚣 ⊠

ORLAND — THE PARKWAY RV RESORT & CAMPGROUND. (530) 865-9188. **$34-$37.** 6330 County Road 200 95963. From Jct of I-5 & SR-32, Exit 619 (Orland/Chico), W 0.5 mi on Rd 200 (Newville Rd) (R) 🚣 ⊠

OROVILLE — FEATHER FALLS KOA & CASINO. (800) 562-5079. **$37-$75.** 3 Alverda Drive 95966. From Jct of Hwy 70 & Ophir Rd, E 3.3 mi on Ophir Rd (L) 🏕 🚣 ⊠

PALM DESERT — EMERALD DESERT RV RESORT - SUN-LAND. ⒶⒶⒶ (866) 226-9001. **$98.** 76-000 Frank Sinatra Dr 92211. From Jct of I-10 & Cook St (Exit 134), S 0.9 mi on Cook St to Frank Sinatra Dr, E 1 mi to El Dorado (L) 🏕 🚣 ⊠

PASO ROBLES — WINE COUNTRY RV RESORT. (888) 713-0819. **$44-$85.** 2500 Airport Rd 93446. From Jct of Hwy 101 & Hwy 46E, E 2.2 mi on Hwy 46E to Airport Rd, N 0.2 mi (R) 🏕 🚣 ⊠

PETALUMA — SAN FRANCISCO NORTH/PETALUMA KOA. (800) 992-2267. **$30-$77.** 20 Rainsville Rd 94952. From Jct of US-101 & SR-116E, N 3.8 mi on US-101 to Old Redwood Hwy/Penngrove exit (34 mi N of Golden Gate Bridge), exit to W side of fwy, W 300 ft to Stony Point Rd, N 0.4 mi to Rainsville Rd, W 300 ft (R) 🚣 ⊠

PISMO BEACH — PISMO COAST VILLAGE RV RESORT. (888) 782-3224. **$46-$62.** 165 S Dolliver St 93449. N-bnd: From Jct of US-101 & Price St, N 75 ft on Price St to Ocean View Rd, W 0.1 mi to Dolliver St (SR-1), S 0.5 mi (R); or S-bnd: From Jct of US-101 & Pismo Beach exit (Hwy 1 Dolliver St), S 0.9 mi on Dolliver St (R) 🏕 🚣 ⊠

PLYMOUTH — FAR HORIZONS 49ER VILLAGE RV RESORT. (800) 339-6981. **Call for rates.** 18265 Hwy 49 95669. From Sacramento: From Jct of Hwy 50 & Hwy 16 (Jackson Rd) :Go 30 miles SE on Hwy 16 (Jackson Rd) (to intersection Hwy 16 & Hwy 49)-(which turns into Hwy 49) continue E 1.8 mi on Hwy 49 (L) 🏕 🚣 ⊠

QUINCY — PIONEER RV PARK. (530) 283-0769. **$36.** 1326 Pioneer Rd. 95971. E-bnd: From Jct SR-70/SR-89 & Fairground Rd (in town), N 0.1 mi on Fairground Rd to Pioneer Rd, E 0.1 mi (E) 🏕 ⊠

RED BLUFF — DURANGO RV RESORT. ⒶⒶⒶ (866) 770-7001. **$43-$58.** 100 Lake Ave 96080. From Jct of I-5 & Antelope Blvd (Exit 649), W 0.1 mi on Antelope Blvd to Belle Mill Rd, N 0.1 mi to East Ave, NE 0.1 mi (L) 🏕 🚣 ⊠

REDDING — JGW RV PARK. (530) 365-7965. **$35-$47.** 6612 Riverland Dr. 96002. From Jct of I-5 & Knighton Rd exit 673 (6 mi S of town), exit to W side of I-5 to Riverland Dr (Frntg Rd), S 2 mi (R) 🏕 🚣 ⊠

REDDING — MOUNTAIN GATE RV PARK. (800) 404-6040. **$28-$40.** 14161 Holiday Rd 96003. From Jct of I-5 & SR-44/SR-299E, N 6.5 mi on I-5 to Mountain Gate/Wonderland Blvd (Old Oregon Trail) exit 687, E 100 ft on Old Oregon Trail (unmarked rd) to Holiday Rd, S 0.4 mi (L) 🏕 🚣 ⊠

REDDING — REDDING PREMIER RV RESORT. (888) 710-8450. **$38-$48.** 280 N Boulder Dr 96003. From Jct of I-5 & Exit 680 (SR-299E/Lake Blvd/Burney-Alturas), W 0.2 mi on Lake Blvd to N Boulder Dr, N 0.1 mi (L) 🚣 ⊠

REDDING — REDDING RV PARK. (530) 241-0707. **$28-$33.** 11075 Campers Ct 96003. From Jct of I-5 & SR-299E (Exit 680), W 0.2 mi on Lake Blvd to Black Marble/Boulder (second stoplight W of I-5, get in inside lane), S 50 ft to Boulder Dr, SE 0.2 mi on Frontage Rd (Boulder Dr) to Campers Ct, S 0.2 mi (L) 🏕 🚣 ⊠

SAN DIEGO — CAMPLAND ON THE BAY. (800) 422-9386. **$39-$397.** 2211 Pacific Beach Dr 92109. N-bnd: Jct of I-5 & Grand/Garnet exit 23A (becomes Mission Bay Dr), N 0.2 mi on Mission Bay Dr to Grand Ave, W 0.8 mi to Olney, S 0.2 mi to Pacific Beach Dr, E 0.2 mi (E); or S-bnd: Jct of I-5 & Balboa/Garnet St (Mission Bay Dr), S 0.5 mi on Mission Bay Dr to Grand Ave, follow N-bnd directions (E) 🚣 ⊠

SAN JOSE — COYOTE VALLEY RV RESORT. ⒶⒶⒶ (866) 376-5500. **$60-$77.** 9750 Monterey Rd 95113-2008. From Jct of Hwy 101 & Cochrane Rd (Exit 367): Go 3/4 mi W on Cochrane Rd to Monterey Rd, then 4 mi N on Monterey Rd (R) 🏕 🚣 ⊠

SAN JUAN BAUTISTA — BETABEL RV PARK. ⒶⒶⒶ (800) 278-7275. **$45.** 9664 Betabel Rd 95045. From Jct of US-101 & Hwy 156: Go N 2 mi on US-101 to Betabel Rd (Exit 349), Cross over US-101, S on Betabel Rd 0.2 mi (R) 🏕 🚣 ⊠

SHINGLETOWN — MT LASSEN/SHINGLETOWN KOA. (530) 474-3133. **$42-$64.** 7749 Koa Rd 96088. From center of town, NE 4.4 mi on SR-44 (R) 🚣 ⊠

SUSANVILLE — SUSANVILLE RV PARK. ⒶⒶⒶ (877) 686-7878. **$42.** 3075 Johnstonville Rd 96130. E-bnd: From Jct of SR-36 & SR-139, SE 1.1 mi on SR-36 to E Riverside Dr, NE (left turn) 0.1 mi to Johnstonville Rd (1st left turn), NW 0.1 mi (R); or W-bnd: From Jct of SR-36 & US-395, NW 2.9 mi on SR-36 to E Riverside Dr, NE (right turn) 0.1 mi to Johnstonville Rd (1st left turn), NW 0.1 mi (R) 🏕 ⊠

TEMECULA — **PECHANGA RV RESORT.** (AAA) (951) 770-2656. **$45-$99.** 45000 Pechanga Pkwy 92592. From Jct of I-15 & Hwy 79S/Temecula Pkwy), E 0.8 mi on Hwy 79S/Temecula Pkwy) to Pechanga Pkwy, SE 2.1 mi to Pechanga Resort Dr, S 0.25 mi (L)

VACAVILLE — **VINEYARD RV PARK.** (AAA) (866) 447-8797. **$52-$55.** 4985 Midway Rd 95688. From Jct of I-80 & I-505, N 3.3 mi to Midway Rd, E 0.4 mi (L) or From Jct of I-80 & Midway Rd exit, W 0.1 mi to Midway Rd, W 3 mi (R)

WILLITS — **WILLITS KOA.** (800) 562-8542. **$45-$75.** 1600 Hwy 20 95490. From Jct of US-101 & SR-20, W 1.5 mi on SR-20 (R)

Colorado

BAYFIELD — **BAYFIELD RIVERSIDE RV PARK.** (970) 884-2475. 41743 Us Hwy 160 81122. From Jct of US 160 & CR-501 (West edge of town), W 0.25 mi on US 160 between milepost 102 and 103 (R) (Onsite) No Fishing License Required

BRECKENRIDGE — **TIGER RUN RV RESORT.** (800) 895-9594. **$55-$100.** 85 Revett Dr 80424. From Jct of I-70 & SR-9 (Exit 203), S 6.3 mi on SR-9 (L)

CAÑON CITY — **ROYAL VIEW @ ROYAL GORGE CAMP-GROUND.** (719) 275-1900. **$31-$55.** 43590 Us Hwy 50 W 81212. E-bnd: From Jct of US-50 & SR-9, E 500 ft on US-50, between MP-269 & 270 (R); or W-bnd: From Jct of US-50 & Royal Gorge Rd, W 1 mi on US-50 (L)

COLORADO SPRINGS — **GARDEN OF THE GODS RV RESORT.** (800) 248-9451. **$42-$64.** 3704 W Colorado Ave 80904. From Jct of I-25 & US-24 (exit 141), W 2.7 mi on US-24 to 31st St, N 0.1 mi to Colorado Ave, W 0.7 mi (R)

CORTEZ — **SUNDANCE RV PARK LLC.** (800) 880-9413. **$36.** 815 E Main 81321. E-Bnd: From Jct of US-160 & US-491, E 1 mi on US-160 (R); or W-Bnd: From Jct of US-160 & SR-145, W 1.3 mi on US-160 (L)

CREEDE — **MOUNTAIN VIEWS AT RIVERS EDGE RV RESORT.** (719) 658-2710. **$28-$39.** 539 Airport Rd 81130. From town, W 0.5 mi on Hwy 149 to Airport Rd, S 0.3 mi (L)

ESTES PARK — **SPRUCE LAKE RV PARK.** (970) 586-2889. **$50-$60.** 1050 Mary'S Lake Rd 80517. From W Jct of Bus US 34 & US 36 (Elkhorn Ave), W 0.3 mi on Elkhorn Ave to Moraine Ave (US 36W), SW 0.8 mi to Mary's Lake Rd, S 0.1 mi (L) NOTE: DO NOT follow GPS

FORT COLLINS — **FORT COLLINS KOA LAKESIDE.** (800) 562-9168. **$39-$91.** 1910 Lakeside Resort Ln. 80524. From Jct of I-25 & SR-14, W 3.3 mi on SR-14 to Riverside Ave, NW 1 mi to College Ave (US-287), N 4.1 mi to CR 54G (toward LaPorte) to Taft Hill Rd (CR 19), S 0.08 mi (L)

FOUNTAIN — **COLORADO SPRINGS KOA.** (AAA) (719) 382-7575. **$34-$54.** 8100 Bandley Dr 80817. From Jct of I-25 & Exit 132, exit E to Bandley Dr (Frontage Rd), S 1 mi (L)

GOLDEN — **DAKOTA RIDGE RV RESORT.** (303) 279-1625. **$48-$56.** 17800 W Colfax Ave 80401. E-bnd: From Jct of I-70 & US-40 (exit 259), NE 1.5 mi on US-40/Colfax Ave (R); or W-bnd: From Jct of I-70 & US-40 (exit 262), W 1.7 mi on US-40/Colfax Ave (L)

GRAND JUNCTION — **CRUISE INN - JUNCTION WEST RV PARK.** (970) 245-8531. **$35-$39.** 793 22 Rd 81505. From Jct of I-70 & US-6 (exit 26), W 0.2 mi on US-6/US-50 to 22 Rd, N 0.5 mi (L)

GRAND JUNCTION — **GRAND JUNCTION KOA.** (AAA) (800) 562-1510. **$35-$50.** 2819 Hwy 50 81503. E-bnd: From Jct of I-70 & US-50 (exit 26), SE 9 mi on US-50 (R); or W-bnd: From Jct of I-70 & Bus I-70 (exit 37), SW 0.8 mi on Bus I-70 to SR-141 (turn left), S 5.4 mi to US-50, N 3.3 mi (L)

IGNACIO — **SKY UTE CASINO RV PARK.** (970) 563-7777. **$30.** 14324 Hwy 172n 81137. From Jct of US 160 & US 550 (E edge of Durango), E 2 mi on US 160 to SR-172, S 17 mi (L) Check in at hotel lobby in casino.

MANCOS — **MESA VERDE RV RESORT.** (AAA) (800) 776-7421. **$36-$45.** 35303 Hwy 160 81328. From Jct of US-160 & SR-184 (in Mancos), W 6.5 mi on US-160 (R); or From Jct of US-160 & Mesa Verde Nat'l Park exit, E 0.75 mi on US-160 (L)

MONTROSE — **CEDAR CREEK RV PARK.** (877) 425-3884. **$31-$37.** 126 Rose Ln 81401. From Jct of US-50 & 550, E 1.5 mi on US-50 to Hillcrest Dr, S 0.1 mi to Alley Way, W 0.1 mi (W)

PAGOSA SPRINGS — **WOLF CREEK RUN MOTOR COACH RESORT.** (970) 264-0365. **$55-$75.** 1742 E Hwy 160 81147. From Jct of US 160 & Hwy 84, E 0.4 mi on US 160 (L) Class A Only

PUEBLO — **PUEBLO SOUTH/COLORADO CITY KOA.** (888) 676-3370. **$40-$45.** 9040 I-25 S Exit 74 81004. From Jct of I-25 & (Exit 74), E .01 mi on exit rd to frntg rd, S 0.25 mi (L)

WELLINGTON — **FORT COLLINS NORTH/WELLINGTON KOA.** (800) 562-8142. **$34-$45.** 4821 E Cr 70 80549. From Jct of I-25 (exit 281) & Owl Canyon Rd, E 0.3 mi on Owl Canyon Rd (R)

Connecticut

BOZRAH — **ODETAH CAMPING RESORT.** (860) 889-4144. **$52-$73.** 38 Bozrah St. Ext. 06334. From Jct of Rte-2 & Hwy 163 (Exit 23), to Bozrah St, E 0.5 mi (R)

BRISTOL — **BEAR CREEK CAMPGROUND AT LAKE COMPOUNCE.** (860) 583-3300. **$40-$60.** 186 Enterprise Drive 06010. From Jct I-84 and Rte 229 (exit 31) N 2 mi on Rte 229 and follow signs.

EAST LYME — **ACES HIGH RV PARK.** (877) 785-8478. **$54-$59.** 301 Chesterfield Road 06333. From Jct of I-95 & SR-161 (exit 74), N 3 mi on SR-161 (R)

OLD MYSTIC — **SEAPORT RV RESORT & CAMPGROUND.** (AAA) (888) 472-4189. **$52-$71.** 45 Campground Rd 06372. From Jct of I-95 & Allyn St/Cow Hill Rd (Exit 89), N 1.3 mi on Allyn St/Cow Hill Rd to Gold Star Rd/SR-184, E (Rt turn) 1.5 mi (L)

PRESTON — **HIDDEN ACRES FAMILY CAMPGROUND.** (860) 887-9633. **$48-$58.** 47 River Rd 06365. From Jct of I-395 & Hwy 164 (Exit 85), S 0.9 mi on Hwy 164 (rt turn) to Palmer Rd (River Ridge Golf Course), SW 1.6 mi to River Rd, W 1.4 mi (R).

Delaware

LINCOLN — YOGI BEAR'S JELLYSTONE PARK AT DELAWARE BEACH. (302) 491-6614. **$40-$85.** 8295 Brick Granary Rd 19960. From Jct of US 113 & SR-1 (E of Lincoln), S 6.5 mi on SR-1 (towards beaches) to Brick Granary Rd, Right 0.2 mi (L) 🏕️ 🛒

MILLSBORO — LEISURE POINT RESORT. (302) 945-2000. **$70.** 25491 Dogwood Ln 19966. From Jct of RT-113 & RT-24, E 8 mi on RT-24 to Longneck Rd, S 2 mi on Longneck Rd to Dogwood Lane (L) 🏕️ 🛒 🍽️

REHOBOTH BEACH — BIG OAKS FAMILY CAMPGROUND. (302) 645-6838. **$59-$67. (no credit cards).** 35567 Big Oaks Lane 19971. S-bnd: From Jct of SR-1 & SR-24 (John Williams Hwy), S 0.7 mi on SR-1 to Munchy Branch Rd (CR 270A), E 1.1 mi to Wolf Neck Rd, N 0.1 mi (L); or N-bnd: From Jct of SR-1 & CR-270 (Wolf Neck Rd), E 0.5 mi on CR-270 (L) 🏕️ 🛒

Florida

ARCADIA — CROSS CREEK RV RESORT. (863) 494-7300. **$55.** 6837 Ne Cubitis Ave 34266. From Jct of SR-70 & US-17, N 4.9 mi on US-17 to CR-660, W (L) 100 yds to NE Cubitis Ave, N (R) 0.9 mi (L) 🏕️ 🛒 🍽️

ARCADIA — RIVERSIDE RV RESORT & CAMPGROUND. 🅰🅰🅰 (800) 795-9733. **$42-$58.** 9770 Sw Cr-769 Kings Hwy 34269. From Jct of I-75 & CR-769 (Exit 170), NE 4.5 mi on CR-769/Kings Hwy (R) 🛒 🍽️

BEVERLY HILLS — SANDY OAKS RV RESORT. (352) 465-7233. **$34-$40.** 6760 N Lecanto Hwy (Cr-491) 34465. From Jct of US 41 & CR 491, S 0.7 mi on CR 491 (R) 🏕️ 🛒 🍽️

BOWLING GREEN — TORREY OAKS RV & GOLF RESORT. (863) 773-3157. **$40.** 2908 Country Club Dr. 33834. From jct of Hwy 62 & US-17: Go N 0.5 mi on US-17, then W 0.3 mi on Bostick Rd. (R). Class A & 5th Wheels only 🏕️ 🛒 🍽️

CARRABELLE BEACH — CARRABELLE BEACH RV RESORT. (850) 697-2638. **$43.** 1843 Hwy 98 W 32322. From town Bus Dist, W 1.5 mi on US-98 (R) 🏕️ 🛒 🍽️

CEDAR KEY — CEDAR KEY RV RESORT. (352) 543-5097. **$30.** 11980 Sw Shiloh Rd 32625. From Jct of Hwy 19/98 & SR-24 (Otter Creek), W 15 mi on Hwy 24 to Shiloh Rd, N .01 mi (L) 🏕️ 🛒

CHOKOLOSKEE — OUTDOOR RESORTS/CHOKOLOSKEE ISLAND. (239) 695-3788. **$69-$89.** 150 Smallwood Dr, Hwy 29 S 34138. From jct US-41 & Hwy-29 (CR 29): Go 8 mi S on CR 29 (L) 🏕️ 🛒 🍽️

CITRA — GRAND LAKE RV & GOLF RESORT. 🅰🅰🅰 (888) 842-9219. **$25-$35.** 18545 Nw 45th Avenue Rd 32113. From Jct of I-75 (exit 368) & Hwy 318, E 2.9 mi on Hwy 318, cross over Hwy 441 (L) 🏕️ 🛒 🍽️

CLERMONT — OUTDOOR RESORTS AT ORLANDO, INC. (800) 531-3033. **$33.** 9000 Us Hwy 192 #1000 34714. From Jct of US-27 & US-192: Go E 0.8 mi on US-192 (R) 🏕️ 🛒 🍽️

CORTEZ — HOLIDAY COVE RV RESORT. (941) 792-1111. **$74-$115.** 11900 Cortez Rd W 34215. From Jct of I-75 (Exit 217) & SR-70: Go W 12 mi on SR-70, then N 1 mi on 75 St., then W 2.8 mi on Cortez Rd (SR-684) (R) 🏕️ 🛒 🍽️

CRYSTAL RIVER — ROCK CRUSHER CANYON RV PARK LLC. (352) 564-9350. **$34-$42.** 237 S Rock Crusher Rd 34429. From Jct of US-19 & SR-44, E 3.4 mi on SR-44 to Rock Crusher Rd, S 1.6 mi (L); or From Jct of I-75 & SR-44 (exit 329), W 22 mi to CR-490, SW 3.5 mi to Rock Crusher Rd, N 2.1 mi (R) 🏕️ 🛒 🍽️

CUDJOE KEY — VENTURE OUT RESORT. (305) 414-8936. **$40-$85.** 701 Spanish Main Dr 33042. From jct US-1 & Spanish Main Dr (MM23), S 1 mi on Spanish Main Dr (L) 🏕️ 🛒 🍽️

DESTIN — CAMP GULF. (877) 226-7485. **$55-$165.** 10005 W Emerald Coast Pkwy 32550. From Jct of Mid Bay Bridge (SR-293) & US-98, E 5 mi on US-98 (R); or From Jct of Hwy 331 & Hwy 98, W 9 mi on Hwy 98 (L) 🛒 🍽️

DUNEDIN — DUNEDIN CAREFREE RV RESORT & THE BLUE MOON INN. (727) 784-3719. **$60.** 2920 Bay Shore Blvd 34698. From Jct of Alt US-19 & SR-586 (Curlew Rd): Go N 0.5 mi on Alt US-19 (R) 🏕️ 🛒 🍽️

EASTPOINT — COASTLINE RV RESORT. (850) 799-1016. **$60.** P.O. Box 1064 32328. From the jct of SR 65 and US98, W .3 mi on US 98 (L) 🛒 🍽️

EVERGLADES CITY — EVERGLADES ISLE MOTORCOACH RETREAT & MARINA. (239) 695-2600. **$89-$149.** 803 N. Collier Ave 34139. From Jct of US 41 & SR-29, S 3 mi on SR-29 (R). Note: Class A's Only 🏕️ 🛒 🍽️

FORT MYERS — CYPRESS WOODS RV RESORT. (888) 299-6637. **$40-$80.** 5551 Luckett Rd 33905. From jct Hwy 82 & I-75: Go 1-1/2 mi N on I-75 (exit 139), then 1/2 mi E on Luckett Rd. (L) 🏕️ 🛒 🍽️

FORT MYERS — CYPRESS TRAIL RV RESORT. (239) 333-3249. **$40-$80.** 5468 Tice Street 33905. From Jct of I-75: Go 1-1/2 mi N on I-75(exit 139), then 1/4 mi E on Luckett Rd, then 1 mi N on Country Lakes Dr, then 1/4 mi E on Tice St. (R) 🏕️ 🛒 🍽️

FORT MYERS — GROVES RV RESORT. 🅰🅰🅰 (877) 540-1931. **$31-$48.** 16175 John Morris Rd 33908. From Jct of I-75 & Daniels Pkwy (exit 131), W 5.5 mi on Daniels Pkwy/Cypress Lake Dr to Summerlin Rd, SW 7.2 mi to John Morris Rd, N 0.8 mi (R) 🛒 🍽️

FORT MYERS — ORANGE HARBOR CO-OP & RV RESORT. 🅰🅰🅰 (239) 694-3707. **$27-$60.** 5749 Palm Beach Blvd 33905. From Jct I-75 (exit 141) & SR-80/Palm Beach Blvd: Go E 1 mi (L) 🛒 🍽️

FORT MYERS — WOODSMOKE CAMPING RESORT. 🅰🅰🅰 (800) 231-5053. **$50-$81.** 19551 S Tamiami Trail (Us 41s) 33908. From Jct of I-75 & Corkscrew Rd (exit 123), W 2 mi on Corkscrew Rd to US-41, N 2 mi (R) 🛒 🍽️

FORT MYERS BEACH — GULF WATERS RV RESORT. 🅰🅰🅰 (239) 437-5888. **$46-$84.** 11301 Summerlin Sq. Dr 33931. From Hwy 82 & I-75: Go 6 mi S on I-75 (exit 131), then 5-3/4 mi W on Daniels Rd/Cypress Lake Dr, then 5-1/2 mi S on Summerlin Rd, then 100 feet E on Pine Ridge Rd, then 500 feet S on Summerlin Sq Dr (L) 🏕️ 🍽️

FORT PIERCE — ROAD RUNNER TRAVEL RESORT. 🅰🅰🅰 (800) 833-7108. **$40.** 5500 St Lucie Blvd 34946. From Jct of FL Tpke & SR-713 (exit 152), N 5 mi on SR-713 to CR-608, E 1.2 mi (L); or From Jct of I-95 & Indrio Rd (exit 138), E 3.2 mi on Indrio Rd to SR-713, S 2.5 mi to CR-608 (St Lucie Blvd), E 1.2 mi (L) 🛒 🍽️

FORT PIERCE — TREASURE COAST RV RESORT. (772) 468-2099. **$42-$50.** 2550 Crossroads Parkway 34945. From Jct of I-95 & exit 129 (Okeechobee Rd/SR 70), W 0.1 mi on Okeechobee Rd/SR 70 to Peters Rd/Crossroads Pkwy, N 0.25 mi (R); or From Jct of FL Tpke & exit 152 (Okeechobee Rd/SR 70), E 0.2 mi on Okeechobee Rd/SR 70 to Peters Rd/Crossroads Pkwy, N 0.25 mi (R) ⚔ ⤳

FORT WALTON BEACH — DESTIN WEST RV RESORT. (850) 200-4533. **$97.** 1310 Miracle Strip Pkwy Se 32548. From Jct of US 98 & Santa Rosa Blvd, E 0.3 mi on US 98 (L) ⚔ ⤳ ⊠

FREEPORT — LIVE OAK LANDING. ⓐⓐ (877) 436-5063. **$40-$45.** 229 Pitts Ave 32439. From Jct of US 331 & CR-3280, E 1.2 mi on CR-3280 to McDaniels Fish Camp Rd, S 0.8 mi (L) ⚔ ⤳ ⊠

FROSTPROOF — RAINBOW RV RESORT. ⓐⓐ (888) 650-8189. **$50.** 700 Cr-630a 33843. From Jct of US 27 & SR-60: Go S 10.2 mi on US 27, then E 0.8 mi on CR-630A (L) ⚔ ⤳ ⊠

JACKSONVILLE — FLAMINGO LAKE RV RESORT. ⓐⓐ (800) 782-4323. **$44.** 3640 Newcomb Rd 32218. From Jct of I-295 & Lem Turner Rd exit 32, W 0.1 mi on Lem Turner Rd to Newcomb Rd, S 100 yds (E) ⚔ ⤳ ⊠

JACKSONVILLE — PECAN PARK RV RESORT. (904) 751-6770. **$44.** 650 Pecan Park Rd 32218. From Jct of I-95 & Pecan Park Rd Exit 366, W 0.1 mi on Pecan Park Rd (L) ⚔ ⤳ ⊠

JUNO BEACH — JUNO OCEAN WALK RV RESORT. (561) 622-7500. **$35-$78.** 900 Juno Ocean Walk 33408. From Jct of I-95 & Exit 83, Donald Ross Rd, E 4.4 mi on Donald Ross Rd to US 1, N 0.8 mi to Juno Ocean Walk, W 0.2 mi (R) ⚔ ⤳ ⊠

KEY LARGO — POINT OF VIEW KEY LARGO RV RESORT. (305) 451-5578. **$65-$140.** 99010 Overseas Hwy 33037. S-Bound: On US-1 at MM 99 (R) ⚔ ⤳ ⊠

KEY WEST — BLUEWATER KEY RV RESORT. ⓐⓐ (305) 745-2494. **$76-$155.** 2950 Us Hwy 1 33040. S-bnd: On US-1 at MP-14.5 (L) ⚔ ⤳ ⊠

KISSIMMEE — TROPICAL PALMS RESORT & CAMP-GROUND. (800) 647-2567. **$30-$85.** 2650 Holiday Trail 34746. From Jct of I-4 (exit 64) & US-192: Go E 1.5 mi on US-192, then S 0.5 mi on Holiday Trail (E) ⤳ ⊠

LABELLE — RIVERBEND MOTORCOACH RESORT. (866) 787-4837. **$90-$112.** 5800 West Sr-80 33935. From Jct of I-75 & SR-80 (exit 141 in Ft Myers), E 16.5 mi on SR-80 (L). Note: Class A Motorhomes only ⚔ ⤳ ⊠

LABELLE — WHISPER CREEK RV RESORT. (863) 675-6888. **$35-$40.** 1887 North State Rd 29 33935. From Jct of SR-80 & SR-29, N 1.8 mi on SR-29 (L) ⚔ ⤳ ⊠

LADY LAKE — RECREATION PLANTATION. (800) 448-5646. **$48.** 609 Hwy 466 32159. From Jct of US-27/441 & SR-466, W 1 mi on SR-466 (R) ⤳ ⊠

LADY LAKE — THE GRAND OAKS RV RESORT. (352) 750-6300. **$45-$55.** 3525 Griffin Ave 32159. From the jct of US 441/27 (in Lady Lake) & Griffin Ave, E 2.5 mi on Griffin Ave (L) ⊠

LAKE BUENA VISTA — DISNEY'S FORT WILDERNESS RESORT & CAMPGROUND. (407) 939-2267. **$48-$132.** 4510 N. Fort Wilderness Trail 32830. From Jct of I-4 (exit 64) & US-192: Go W 0.75 mi on US-192, then N 1 mi on World Dr (R) ⤳ ⊠

LAKE PLACID — CAMP FLORIDA RESORT. (863) 699-1991. **$35-$45.** 100 Shoreline Dr 33852. From Jct of US-27 & SR-70: Go N 4 mi on US-27 (R) ⚔ ⤳ ⊠

LAKE WALES — LAKE WALES RV & CAMPSITES. (863) 638-9011. **$38.** 15898 Hwy 27 33859. From Jct of US-27 & SR-60: Go S 3.3 mi on US-27 (R) ⤳ ⊠

LOXAHATCHEE — LION COUNTRY SAFARI KOA. (561) 793-9797. **$65-$70.** 2000 Lion Country Safari Rd 33470. From Jct of I-95 & Southern Blvd (exit 68/SR-80), W 15.5 mi on Southern Blvd to Lion Country Safari Rd, N (right) 2 mi (E). Note: Max 40 ft ⤳ ⊠

MADISON — YOGI BEAR JELLYSTONE CAMP RESORTS. ⓐⓐ (850) 973-8269. **$40-$55.** 1051 Sw Old St. Augustine Rd 32340. From Jct of I-10 (exit 258) & SR-53, S 0.2 mi on SR-53 to St. Augustine Rd, W 0.5 mi (L) ⤳ ⊠

MALABAR — CAMELOT RV PARK, INC. (321) 724-5396. **$34-$40.** 1600 Us-1 32950. From Jct of I-95 (exit 173) & SR-514 (Malabar Rd): Go E 4.2 mi on Malabar Rd, then S 0.3 mi on US-1 (R) ⚔ ⤳ ⊠

MARATHON — MARATHON MARINA & RV RESORT. (305) 743-6575. **$119-$200.** 1021 11th St Ocean 33050. From US-1 at mile marker 47 1/2: Go 1/4 mi S on 11th St Ocean E (L) ⚔ ⤳ ⊠

MARGATE — AZTEC RV RESORT. (888) 493-2856. **$59-$81.** 1a Aztec Blvd 33068. From Jct of I-95 & Exit 36 (SR-814, W. Atlantic Blvd), W 5 mi on SR-814 (W. Atlantic Blvd) to US 441 (SR-7), S 0.6 mi to Aztec Blvd, E 0.4 mi (E); or From Jct of Florida Turnpike & Exit 62 (SR-870, NW 56th St), E 0.5 mi on SR-870 (NW 56th St) to US 441 (SR-7), N 2.7 mi to Aztec Blvd, E 0.4 mi (E) ⚔ ⤳ ⊠

MILTON — GULF PINES KOA. ⓐⓐ (888) 562-4258. **$44-$57.** 8700 Gulf Pines Dr 32583. From Jct of I-10 & Hwy 87 (exit 31), N 0.1 mi on Hwy 87 to Gulf Pines Dr, E 300 yds ⤳ ⊠

MOORE HAVEN — NORTH LAKE ESTATES RV RESORT. ⓐⓐ (877) 417-6193. **$34-$40.** 12044 East State Rd 78 33471. From Jct of US-27 & SR-78 (1 mi N of Moore Haven), NE 11 mi on SR-78 (R); or From Jct of SR-70 & US-441/98 (Okeechobee), S 3 mi on US-441/98 to SR-78, SW 23 mi (L) ⚔ ⤳ ⊠

NAPLES — CRYSTAL LAKE RV RESORT. (239) 348-0017. **$35-$90.** 14960 Collier Blvd 34119. From Jct of I-75 & CR-846 (exit 111/Immokalee Rd), E 3.2 mi on CR-846 to CR-951/Collier Blvd, S 0.5 mi (L) Note: RVs cannot enter after office hours unless prior arrangements are made. Minimum 25' RV length ⚔ ⤳ ⊠

NAPLES — NAPLES MOTORCOACH RESORT. (866) 942-2942. **$39-$124.** 13300 Tamiami Trail E 34114. From Jct of I-75 & Collier Blvd (CR-951/Exit 101), S 7 mi on Collier Blvd/CR-951 to US 41, SE 0.7 mi (R) ⚔ ⤳ ⊠

NAPLES — PELICAN LAKE MOTORCOACH RESORT. (800) 835-4389. **$60-$135.** 4555 Southern Breeze Dr 34114. From Jct of I-75 & Collier Blvd (exit 101), S 9.2 mi on Collier Blvd (CR-951) (L) Note: Class A motorhomes 26 ft or larger only ⚔ ⤳ ⊠

NAPLES — ROCK CREEK RV RESORT. (239) 643-3100. **$38-$66.** 3100 North Rd 34104. From Jct of I-75 & Golden Gate Pkwy (Exit 105), W 2 mi on Golden Gate Pkwy to Hwy 31/Airport Pulling Rd, S 2.4 mi to North Rd, W 100 yds on North Rd (L) ⚔ ⤳ ⊠

NAPLES — SILVER LAKES RV RESORT & GOLF CLUB. (800) 843-2836. **$45-$85.** 1001 Silver Lakes Blvd 34114. From Jct of I-75 & Collier Blvd (CR-951/Exit 101), S 9 mi on Collier Blvd (CR-951) (L) Note: 25' minimum length RV. ⚔ ⤳ ⊠

NAVARRE — EMERALD BEACH RV PARK. (866) 939-3431. **$49-$75.** 8885 Navarre Pkwy 32566. E-bnd: From the Jct of US 87 & US 98, E 1 mi on US 98 (R); W-bnd: From entrance to Hurlburt Field (US Army Installation) & US 98, W 9 mi on US 98 (past park entrance) to Navarre Sound Circle, U-turn if possible or S onto Navarre Sound Circle & back to Hwy 98, E 0.1 mi (R) 🏕 🚐 🗶

NAVARRE — NAVARRE BEACH CAMPGROUND. 🔺🔺🔺 (888) 639-2188. **$49-$85.** 9201 Navarre Pkwy 32566. From Jct of Hwy 87 & US-98, E 2 mi on US-98 (R) 🚐 🗶

NAVARRE — ST ROSA SOUND RV RESORT. (888) 936-4791. **$45-$95. (no credit cards).** 8315 Navarre Pkwy 32566. From the Jct of IH & SR-87, go S 16 mi on SR-87 to dead end at Hwy 98, W 0.1 mi (L) 🏕 🚐 🗶

NEW SMYRNA BEACH — NEW SMYRNA BEACH RV PARK. (800) 928-9962. **$35-$43.** 1300 Old Mission Rd 32168. S-bnd: From Jct of I-95 & SR-44 (exit 249A), E 3 mi on SR-44 to Mission Drive (becomes Old Mission Rd), S 1.3 mi (R); or N-bnd: From Jct of I-95 & CR-442 (exit 244), E 0.9 mi on CR-442 to Old Mission Rd, N 3 mi (L) 🚐 🗶

NOKOMIS — ROYAL COACHMAN RV RESORT. (800) 405-6188. **$40-$85.** 1070 Laurel Rd E 34275. From Jct of I-75 (exit 195) & Laurel Rd: Go W 2 mi on Laurel Rd, then S 0.25 mi on Terra Cove Rd (E) 🏕 🚐 🗶

NORTH FORT MYERS — RAINTREE RV RESORT. (239) 731-1441. **$60-$72.** 19250 N Tamiami Tr 33903. S-bnd: From Jct of I-75 & Tuckers Grade Rd (exit 158), W 1 mi on Tuckers Grade Rd to US-41, S 9 mi (L); or N-bnd: From Jct of I-75 & SR-78 (exit 143), W 5.3 mi on SR-78 to Bus US-41, N 2.4 mi to US-41, NW 2.3 mi (R) 🏕 🚐 🗶

NORTH FORT MYERS — UPRIVER RV RESORT. 🔺🔺🔺 (239) 543-3330. **$35-$77.** 17021 Upriver Dr 33917. From Jct of I-75 & SR-78 (exit 143/Bayshore Rd), E 1.6 mi on SR-78 (R) 🏕 🚐 🗶

OCALA — OCALA SUN RV RESORT. (352) 307-1100. **$34-$44.** 2559 Sw Hwy 484 34473. From Jct of I-75 & SR-484 (Exit 341), W 0.5 mi on SR-484 (R) 🏕 🚐 🗶

OKEECHOBEE — OKEECHOBEE KOA KAMPGROUND & GOLF COURSE. (863) 763-0231. **$45-$80.** 4276 Us Hwy 441 S 34974. From Jct of US-441 & SR-70, S 4 mi on US-441 (L) 🚐 🗶

OKEECHOBEE — SILVER PALMS RV RESORT. (888) 323-4833. **$38-$115.** 4143 Hwy 441 S 34974. From Jct of US-441 & SR 70, S 4 mi on US-441 (R) 🏕 🚐 🗶

OLD TOWN — LUCKY CHARM RV PARK. (352) 542-0033. **$32.** 4114 Ne Hwy 349 N 32680. From Jct of US 19/98 & SR-349, N 4 mi on SR-349 (R) 🚐 🗶

OLD TOWN — YELLOW JACKET RESORT. (352) 542-8365. **$34-$49.** 55 Se 503 Ave 32680. From Jct of US 19/98 & SR 349, S 10 mi on SR 349 to Yellow Jacket Rd, E 0.8 mi to SE 477 Ave, E 0.3 mi (R) 🚐 🗶

PANAMA CITY BEACH — EMERALD COAST RV BEACH RESORT. 🔺🔺🔺 (800) BEA-CHRV. **$65-$75.** 1957 Allison Ave 32407. From Hathaway Bridge, W 1.5 mi on US-98 (Panama City Beach Pkwy) to Alison Ave, S 0.25 mi (R) 🏕 🚐 🗶

PANAMA CITY BEACH — PANAMA CITY BEACH RV RESORT. (866) 637-3529. **$57-$74.** 4702 Thomas Dr. 32408. From Jct of US 98 & Thomas Rd, S 3.5 mi on Thomas Rd to CR 392, E 0.3 mi (L) 🏕 🚐

PENSACOLA — AVALON LANDING RV PARK. (866) 995-5898. **$37-$44.** 2444 Avalon Blvd 32598. From Jct of IH10 & SR 281 (Avalon Blvd Exit 22), S 0.4 mi on SR 281 (L) 🏕 🚐 🗶

PENSACOLA — PENSACOLA BEACH RV RESORT. (850) 438-1266. **$65-$125.** 17 Via De Luna Dr. 32598. From Jct of US 98 & Pensacola Beach Blvd, E 2.2 mi on Pensacola Beach Blvd (becomes Via De Luna Dr at Fort Pickens Rd) (L) 🏕 🚐 🗶

PENSACOLA — PERDIDO COVE RV RESORT & MARINA. 🔺🔺🔺 (877) 402-7873. **$57-$110.** 13770 River Rd. 32507. From Jct of IH 10 & Pine Forest Rd (Exit 7A), S 2.5 mi on Pine Forest to Blue Angel Pkwy, S 10.5 mi to Sorrento Rd (SR 292), W 6 mi across the Theo Barrs Bridge to Gongora Rd, E 100 ft to Don Carlos Dr, N 0.1 mi to River Rd, W 0.1 mi (R) 🏕 🚐 🗶

PORT CHARLOTTE — HARBOR LAKES RV RESORT. (800) 405-6188. **$35-$66.** 3737 El Jobean Rd 33953. From Jct of I-75 & North Port/Toledo Blade Blvd (Exit 179), S 6.3 mi on Toledo Blade Blvd to SR-776, W 3.5 mi (R) 🏕 🚐 🗶

PORT CHARLOTTE — MYAKKA RIVER MOTORCOACH RESORT. (941) 740-2599. **$60-$120.** 14100 Myakka Ave 33953. Go 5.5 mi W on SR-776, then 1/4 mi N on Kerrigan Circle, then 1/4 mi NW on Myakka Ave to end. 🏕 🚐 🗶

PORT ST. LUCIE — OUTDOOR RESORT ST. LUCIE WEST. (772) 336-1135. **$30-$88.** 800 Nw Peacock Blvd 34986. From Jct of I-95 & St Lucie Blvd (Exit 121), E 0.3 mi on St Lucie Blvd to NW Peacock Blvd, N 1.3 mi (L) Note: Class A Motorhomes only 🏕 🚐 🗶

SARASOTA — SUN-N-FUN RV RESORT. (941) 371-2505. **$46-$80.** 7125 Fruitville Rd 34240. From Jct of I-75 (exit 210) & SR-780: Go E 1.1 mi on SR-780/Fruitville Rd (L) 🚐 🗶

SEBASTIAN — VERO BEACH KAMP, INC. (877) 589-5643. **$38-$55.** 8850 N Us Hwy-1 32958. From Jct of I-95 (Exit 156) & CR-512: Go E 2.4 mi on CR-512, then S 5.8 mi on CR-510, then N 0.4 mi on US-1 (R) 🚐 🗶

SEBRING — BUTTONWOOD BAY RV RESORT & MANU-FACTURED HOME COMMUNITY. 🔺🔺🔺 (888) 469-1733. **$25-$54.** 10001 Us 27 S 33876. From Jct of US-27 & SR 98/66: Go S 1 mi on US-27 (R) 🏕 🚐 🗶

SEBRING — OUTBACK RV RESORT AT TANGLEWOOD. (863) 402-1501. **$39-$89.** 3000 Tanglewood Pkwy 33872. From Jct of US-27 & CR-634A: Go N 0.7 mi on US-27 (L) 🏕 🚐 🗶

SILVER SPRINGS — WHISPERING PINES RV PARK. (352) 625-1295. **$28.** 1700 Ne 115th Ave 34488. From Jct of Hwys 35 & 40, E 5.8 mi on Hwy 40 to NE 118th Ave, S 0.4 mi to NE 19th St, W 0.2 mi (end) to NE 115th Ave, S 0.1 mi (R) 🏕 🗶

SILVER SPRINGS — WILDERNESS RV RESORT AT SILVER SPRINGS. 🔺🔺🔺 (352) 625-1122. **$37-$40.** 2771 Ne 102nd Ave Rd 34488. From jct I-75 & Hwy 326 (Exit 358): Go E 9 mi on Hwy 326 to US 40, then E 3 mi (L) 🏕 🚐 🗶

SORRENTO — WEKIVA FALLS RESORT. (352) 383-8055. **$39-$49.** 30700 Wekiva River Rd 32776. From Jct of I-4 (exit 101C) & SR-46: Go W 5.5 mi on SR-46, then S 1.4 mi on Wekiva River Rd (L) 🚐 🗶

TALLAHASSEE — TALLAHASSEE RV PARK. 🔺🔺🔺 (850) 878-7641. **$46.** 6504 Mahan Dr 32308. From Jct of I-10 & US-90 (exit 209A) W 0.5 mi on US-90 (R) 🏕 🚐

TAMPA — BAY BAYOU RV RESORT. (813) 855-1000. **$41-$64.** 8492 Manatee Bay Dr 33635. From Jct of I-275 (exit 47) & SR-580/Hillsborough Ave: Go W 10.8 mi, then N 0.5 mi on Country Way Blvd, then W 0.75 mi on Memorial Hwy (L) 🏕 ⛵ ✗

TITUSVILLE — SEASONS IN THE SUN RV RESORT. ⨁ (877) 687-7275. **$33-$45.** 2400 Seasons In The Sun Blvd 32754. From Jct of I-95 (exit 223) & SR-46: Go W 0.4 mi on SR-46 (L) 🏕 ⛵ ✗

TITUSVILLE — THE GREAT OUTDOORS RV, NATURE & GOLF RESORT. (321) 269-5004. **$40-$55.** 125 Plantation Drive 32780. From Jct of I-95 (exit 215) & SR-50: Go W 0.5 mi on SR-50 (Cheney Hwy) to entrance rd (L) 🏕 ⛵ ✗

WEBSTER — FLORIDA GRANDE MOTORCOACH RESORT. (352) 569-1169. **$46.** 9675 Se 49th Terrace 33597. From Jct of CR-478 & CR-471: Go E 2 mi on CR-478 (L) 🏕 ⛵ ✗

WESLEY CHAPEL — QUAIL RUN RESORT. (800) 582-7084. **$38-$48.** 6946 Old Pasco Rd 33544. From Jct of I-75 (exit 279) & SR-54: Go W 0.5 mi on SR-54 then N 2 mi on Old Pasco Rd (R) 🏕 ⛵ ✗

WEST PALM BEACH — VACATION INN RESORT OF THE PALM BEACHES. (561) 848-6170. **$35-$66.** 6500 N Military Tr 33407. From Jct of US 98/80 (Southern Blvd) & I-95: Go 8 mi N on I-95 (Exit 76), then 1/2 mi W on Hwy 708 (Blue Heron Blvd), then 3/4 mi S on Hwy 809 (Military Rd) (L) 🏕 ⛵ ✗

WILDWOOD — THREE FLAGS RV RESORT. (800) 405-6188. **$35.** 1755 E Sr Road 44 34785. From Jct of I-75 (Exit 329) & US 44, E 1.4 mi on US 44 (R) ⛵ ✗

WILLISTON — WILLISTON CROSSINGS RV RESORT. ⨁ (877) 785-4405. **$34-$39.** 410 N.E. 5th St 32696. S-bnd: From Jct of I-75 & CR-121/Williston Rd (Exit 382), SW 15 mi on CR-121/Williston Rd to US 27/41, S 0.3 mi to US 27/Alt 27, SE 0.4 mi to NE 5th St, N 0.2 mi (R); or N-bnd: From Jct of I-75 & US 27 (Exit 354) NW 21 mi on US 27 to NE 5th St, N 0.2 mi (R) 🏕 ✗

Georgia

BRUNSWICK — COASTAL GEORGIA RV RESORT. (912) 264-3869. **$40.** 287 South Port Parkway 31523. From the Jct of I-95 (Exit 29) & US 17/US 82: W on US 17/US-82 0.6 mi to US 17 South, S 0.3 mi to Martin Palmer Dr, SE 0.6 mi on South Port Parkway (E) 🏕 ⛵ ✗

DILLARD — RIVER VISTA MOUNTAIN VILLAGE. (888) 850-7275. **$30-$60.** 20 River Vista Dr. 30537. From Jct of US-441 & SR-246, E 1 mi on SR-246 (R) 🏕 ⛵ ✗

HIAWASSEE — BALD MOUNTAIN CAMPING RESORT. (706) 896-8896. **$40.** 751 Gander Gap Rd 30546. From E Jct of US-76 & SR-288, SW 0.2 mi on SR-288 to Fodder Creek Rd, S 3.6 mi (L) ⛵ ✗

STATESBORO — PARKWOOD RV PARK & COTTAGES. (912) 681-3105. **$32-$33.** 12188 Us Hwy 301 S 30458. From Jct of I-16 & US-301 (Exit 116), N 8.75 mi on US-301 (R); or S-bnd: From Jct of US-301 & US 301 By-pass, SW 6 mi to US-301, S 0.25 mi (L) ⛵

WACO — YOGI BEARS JELLYSTONE PARK-CAMP RESORT. (404) 855-2778. **$34-$41.** 106 King St. 30182. From Jct of I-20 (Exit 9) & Waco Rd, N 1.1 mi on Waco Rd to US-78/SR-8, W 0.7 mi to King St, SW 0.3 mi (L) ⛵ ✗

Idaho

CALDWELL — AMBASSADOR RV RESORT. ⨁ (888) 877-8307. **$35.** 615 S Smeed Pkwy 83605. From Jct I-84 & US 20/26 (exit 29) : Go 3/4 mi E on US 20/26, then 1/8 mi N on Smeed Pkwy (R) 🏕 ⛵ ✗

CALDWELL — COUNTRY CORNERS RV PARK AND CAMP-GROUND. (877) 474-9826. **$28.** 17671 Oasis Rd 83607. From Jct I-84 & Oasis Rd (exit 17): Go 1/4 mi E Oasis on Rd (R)

COEUR D'ALENE — BLACKWELL ISLAND RV RESORT. (888) 571-2900. **$40-$58.** 800 S Marina Dr 83814. From Jct of I-90 & US 95 (exit 12) : Go 1 1/2 mi S on US 95, then 1/16 mi S on S Marina (L) 🏕 ✗

DECLO — VILLAGE OF TREES RV RESORT. ⨁ (800) 777-9121. **$32.** 274 Hwy 25 83323. From Jct I-84 & Rupert-Declo Rd (exit 216): Go 1/4 mi N on Rupert-Declo Rd (L) ⛵ ✗

MCCALL — MCCALL RV RESORT. ⨁ (208) 634-5646. **$39-$47.** 200 Scott Street 83638. From Jct US 95 & Hwy 55 / Payette River Scenic Byway : Go 13 mi S on Hwy 55, then 1/2 mi W on Dein-hard, then 1/4 mi S on Mission, then 1/8 mi W on Scott St (E) 🏕 ⛵ ✗

MONTPELIER — MONTPELIER CREEK KOA. (800) 562-7576. **$30-$59.** 28501 Us Hwy 89n 83254. From Jct US 30 & US 89: Go 2-1/4 mi N on US 89 (R) ⛵ ✗

MOUNTAIN HOME — MOUNTAIN HOME RV PARK. ⨁ (208) 580-1211. **$37.** 2295 American Legion Blvd 83647. From Jct I-84 & Hwy 51 / American Legion Blvd (Exit 95) : Go 1/2 mi S on Hwy 51 / American Legion Blvd (L) ✗

OROFINO — CLEARWATER CROSSING RV PARK. (208) 476-4800. **$25-$32.** 500 Riverfront Rd. 83544. From Jct US 12 & Hwy 7 / Michigan Ave : Go 1/8 mi N on Hwy 7 / Michigan Ave, then 1/16 mi NW on Hwy 7 / Riverfront Rd (L) Enter through hardware store parking lot. ✗

POST FALLS — COEUR D'ALENE RV RESORT. (208) 773-3527. **$41-$43.** 2652 E Mullan Ave 83854. From Jct I-90 & Hwy 41 (exit 7): Go 1/4 mi N on Hwy 41, then 1 mi W on E Mullan Ave (L) 🏕 ⛵ ✗

VICTOR — TETON VALLEY RV PARK. (208) 787-2647. **$48-$57.** 1208 Hwy 31 83455. From Jct Hwy 33 & Hwy 31 (in Victor): Go 3/4 mi SW on Hwy 31 (R) ⛵ ✗

Illinois

AMBOY — O'CONNELL'S YOGI BEAR JELLYSTONE PARK CAMP RESORT. (800) 405-6188. **$43-$59.** 970 Green Wing Rd. 61310. From Jct I-39 & US-30: Go W 13 mi on US-30 to Pine Hill Rd, then S 1 mi to Inlet Rd, then W 0.7 mi to Green Wing Rd, then S 1.5 mi (L); or From Jct US-30 & US-52: Go S 2 mi on US-52 to Main St, then E 1.2 mi to Shaw Rd, then SE 2.5 mi to Green Wing Rd, then N 1.2 mi (R) ⛵ ✗

CHATHAM — DOUBLE J CAMPGROUND & RV PARK. (217) 483-9998. **$40.** 9683 Palm Rd 62629. S-bnd: From Jct of I-55 & Exit 88, SW 2 mi on Frntg Rd (Palm Rd) (R); or N-bnd: From Jct of I-55 & Exit 83 (to stop sign), W 0.3 mi to Frntg Rd, N 2.5 mi (L). Do Not Use GPS. ⛵ ✗

EAST ST. LOUIS — CASINO QUEEN RV PARK. (800) 777-0777. **$53.** 200 South Front Street 62201. W-bnd: From Jct of I-55/70 & Exit 2A (3rd St), S 0.3 mi on 3rd St to River Park Dr, W 0.4 mi (L); or E-bnd: From Jct of I-55/64/70 (at bridge, on MO side), E 1.5 mi on I-55/64/70 over bridge to 4th St (bus exit), NE 0.4 mi on exit rd to River Park Dr, W 0.5 mi (L) 🏊 🍴

HILLSDALE — SUNSET LAKES RESORT. (800) 747-5253. **$39-$64.** 3333 290th St North 61257. From Jct of I-88 & SR-92 (Exit 6): Go E 1 mi on Hwy 92, then 1/2 mi S on 290th St (L) 🏊 🍴

KNOXVILLE — GALESBURG EAST CAMPGROUND. (309) 289-2267. **$32-$37.** 1081 Us Hwy 150 E 61448. From Jct I-74 & US-150 (Exit 54): Go E 1/2 mi on US-150 (L). Note: Do not use GPS, follow blue camping signs. 🏊 🍴

MARENGO — LEHMAN'S LAKESIDE RV RESORT. (815) 923-4533. **$38-$48.** 19609 Harmony Rd 60152. From Jct I-90 & US-20 (Marengo exit): Go N 1 mi on US-20, then W 3 mi on Harmony Rd (L) 🍴

MILLBROOK — YOGI BEAR'S JELLYSTONE PARK CAMP RESORT. ⚠ (800) 438-9644. **$41-$59.** 8574 Millbrook Rd 60536. From Jct SR-47 & SR-71: Go SW 6 mi on SR-71, then N 1.2 mi on Millbrook Rd (R) 🏊 🍴

MULBERRY GROVE — CEDARBROOK RV PARK & CAMPGROUND. ⚠ (618) 326-8865. **$34. (no credit cards).** 1109 Mulberry Grove Rd 62262. From Jct of I-70 & Mulberry Grove/Keyesport Rd (exit 52), S 1 mi on Mulberry Grove/Keyesport Rd (R) 🏊 🍴

ROCK ISLAND — ROCK ISLAND/QUAD CITIES KOA. (800) 787-0605. **$30-$60.** 2311 78th Ave W 61201. From Jct of I-280 & SR-92 (exit 11A): Go S 1-1/2 mi on SR-92, then E 500 ft on 78th Ave/SR-92 (Andalusia Rd Exit), then E 1 mi on 78th Ave (L). 🏊 🍴

SHELBYVILLE — ROBIN HOOD WOODS CAMPGROUND & RESORT. (217) 774-4222. **$30-$35.** Rr 4, Box 16a 62565. From Jct Hwy 128 & Hwy 16: Go 4-1/2 mi E on Hwy 16. 🏊 🍴

SHOREWOOD — LEISURE LAKE RESORT. (815) 741-9405. **$50.** 21900 Sw Frontage Rd 60404. S-bnd: From Jct I-55 & IL-59 (Exit 251): Go W 0.1 mi on Seil Rd, then S 2 mi on Frontage Rd (R) or N-bnd: From Jct I-55 & US 52 (Exit 253): Go W 0.5 mi on US 52 (Jefferson St), then S 1 mi on IL-59 (Cottage St), then W 0.1 mi on Seil Rd, then S 2 mi on Frontage Rd (R) 🏊 🍴

UTICA — HICKORY HOLLOW CAMPGROUND. (815) 667-4996. **$35-$38.** 757 N 3029 Rd 61373. From Jct I-80 & Hwy 178 (Utica exit 81): Go N 20 ft on Hwy 178, then W 1/2 mi on Frontage Rd (R) 🏊 🍴

WHITTINGTON — WHITTINGTON WOODS CAMPGROUND AT BENTON. (618) 435-3401. **$28-$37.** 14297 State Highway 37 62897. From Jct of I-57 & SR-154 (exit 77), E 0.25 mi on SR-154 to SR-37, S 0.25 mi (R) 🏊 🍴

Indiana

ANDERSON — TIMBERLINE VALLEY RV RESORT. (765) 378-5909. **$33-$41.** 3230 E Cr-75 N 46017. From Jct of I-69 & Hwy 32 (exit 234), W 2.8 mi on Hwy 32 to CR 300 E, N 0.5 mi to E CR-75 N, E 0.25 mi (L) Note: N-bnd exit 34, stay right, continue up ramp to the Jct of State Rd 32 🍴

BLOOMINGTON — JELLYSTONE PARK AT LAKE MONROE. (812) 824-3322. **$36-$69.** 9396 S Strain Ridge Rd 47401. From Jct of Hwy 37 & Harrodsburg/Lake Monroe exit, E 0.1 mi to East Monroe Dam Rd, E 0.8 mi to South Strain Ridge Rd, N 0.5 mi (L) 🏊 🍴

FLORENCE — FOLLOW THE RIVER RV RESORT. (812) 427-3330. **$38-$49.** 12273 Markland Town Rd 47020. From Jct of I-71 & (Kentucky SR 1039) Exit 55, N 6 mi on SR 1039, W 1 mi on (Indiana SR 156) (R) 🏊 🍴

SANTA CLAUS — LAKE RUDOLPH CAMPGROUND & RV RESORT. (888) 349-9733. **$30-$62.** 78 N Holiday Blvd 47579. From Jct of I-64 & SR-162 (exit 63), S 7.2 mi on SR-162 to SR 245 (Holiday Blvd.), N 0.2 mi (R) 🏊 🍴

Iowa

ADEL — DES MOINES WEST KOA. (515) 834-2729. **$34-$47.** 34308 L Ave 50003. From Jct of I-80 & Exit 106, N 1.5 mi on Dallas County P-58-L Ave (R). Use 3418 L Ave for GPS 🏊 🍴

CENTER POINT — LAZY ACRES RV PARK. (319) 443-4000. **$30-$34.** 5486 32nd Ave 52213. From Jct of I-380 & Exit 41 (N of Center Point), E 0.1 mi on 54th St Trail to 32nd Ave, N 0.1 mi (R). Don't rely on GPS. Call for directions 🍴

DAVENPORT — INTERSTATE RV PARK. (563) 386-7292. **$28-$40.** 8448 N. Fairmount St 52806. From Jct of I-80 & SR-130 (Exit 292), NW 0.6 mi on SR-130 to Fairmount St, W 0.1 mi (R). Don't rely on GPS 🏊 🍴

ELKADER — DEER RUN RESORT. (563) 245-3337. **$34-$40.** 501 High St Se 52043. From Jct of Hwy 128 & Hwy 13, S 3 mi on Hwy 13 to S High St, N 0.4 mi (R). Don't rely on GPS 🏊 🍴

NEWTON — NEWTON KOA. ⚠ (641) 792-2428. **$28-$42.** 1601 E 36th St S 50208. From Jct of I-80 & Newton exit (Exit 168), NW 0.7 mi on SE Speedway Dr to E 36th St S, (left) S 0.2 mi (E). Hard left turn between church and Barney's. Don't rely on GPS. Call for directions 🍴

ONAWA — ON-UR-WA RV PARK. (712) 423-1387. **$31-$35.** 1111 28th St 51040. From Jct of I-29 & SR-175 (exit 112), E 500 ft on SR-175 to 28th St, S 300 ft (L) 🏊 🍴

TIPTON — HUNT'S CEDAR RIVER CAMPGROUND. (563) 946-2431. **$28-$31.** 1231 306th St 52772. From Jct of I-80 & SR-38 (exit 267), N 0.2 mi on SR-38 to Frntg Rd, W 0.7 mi (E) 🏊 🍴

WAUKEE — TIMBERLINE CAMPGROUND. (515) 987-1714. **$37-$39.** 31635 Ashworth Rd 50263. From Jct of I-35 & I-80 (West Jct), W 5 mi on I-80 to CR-R22 (Exit 117), N 0.9 mi to CR-F64 (Ashworth Rd), E 0.4 mi (L). Don't rely on GPS. Call to verify GPS directions 🍴

Kansas

DODGE CITY — GUNSMOKE RV PARK, INC. (620) 227-8247. **$32-$34.** 11070 108 Rd 67801. E-bnd: (W of Town) 0.1 mi before Jct Bus US-50 (Wyatt Earp Blvd) & US-50 (L); or W-bnd: From Jct US-400 & US 56/283: Go .4 mi N on US-283, then 5 mi W on Bus 50 (Wyatt Earp Blvd) (R); or N-bnd: From Jct US-56 & US-283: Go 2 mi N on 2nd Ave, then 3 mi W on Bus US-50 (Wyatt Earp Blvd) (R) 🏊 🍴

LAWRENCE — KANSAS CITY JELLYSTONE PARK. (785) 842-3877. **$28-$50.** 1473 N. 1800 Rd/Hwy 24/40 66044. From jct I-70 (exit 204) & US-59: Go N 1/2 mi on US-59, then E 1/4 mi on US-24 (R) 🏊 🍴

MAYETTA — **PRAIRIE BAND CASINO RESORT RV PARK.** (877) 2RV-PARK. **$21-$32.** 12305 150th Rd 66509. From jct I-70 (exit 358a) & US-75: Go N 17-1/4 mi on US-75, then W 1-1/2 mi on 150th Rd. (L) 🅰️

TOPEKA — **DEER CREEK VALLEY RV PARK LLC.** (785) 357-8555. **$42.** 3140 Se 21st Street 66607. From jct I-70 (exit 364B) & Carnahan: Go S 1/4 mi on Carnahan, then E 1/4 mi on 21st St. (L) 🅰️ 🔁 ⊠

Kentucky

FRANKFORT — **ELKHORN CAMPGROUND.** (502) 695-9154. **$34.** 165 N Scruggs Ln 40601. From Jct of I-64 & US-60 (exit 58), NW 2.7 mi on US-60 to US-460, E 2.2 mi to N Scruggs Ln, S 0.1 mi (R). Note: N Scruggs Ln is narrow 🔁 ⊠

GEORGETOWN — **WHISPERING HILLS RV PARK.** (502) 863-2552. **$33.** 257 Rogers Gap Road 40324. From Jct of I-75 & Exit 129 (Cherry Blossom Way), W on Cherry Blossom Way 0.5 mi to US-25, N 1.7 mi to Hwy 620 (Rogers Gap Rd), E 0.6 mi (R) 🅰️ 🔁 ⊠

WALTON — **OAK CREEK CAMPGROUND.** ⟪AAA⟫ (859) 485-9131. **$31.** 13329 Oak Creek Rd 41094. From Jct of I-75 & SR-16 (Exit 171), SW 0.8 mi on SR-16 to Oak Creek Dr, NW 200 ft (L); or From Jct of I-71 & SR-14 (Exit 72), E 1.8 mi on SR-14 to SR-16, N 3.3 mi (L). Sharp left turn, swing wide 🔁 ⊠

Louisiana

BREAUX BRIDGE — **CAJUN PALMS RV RESORT.** (337) 667-7772. **$32-$74.** 1055 N Barn Road 70517. From Jct of I-10 (exit 115) & LA-347/Henderson: Go NE 1/2 mi on LA-347/ Grand Point Hwy, then E 1/4 mi on N Barn Rd. (L) 🅰️ 🔁 ⊠

CARENCRO — **BAYOU WILDERNESS RV RESORT.** (337) 896-0598. **$39-$42.** 600 North Wilderness Trail 70520. From Jct of I-10 & I-49/US 167 (Exit 103-B), N 2.5 mi on I-49/US 167 to Gloria Switch Rd (Exit 2), E 2.3 mi to N Wilderness Trail, N 0.7 mi (R) Note: Left turn 25 ft past bridge 🔁 ⊠

CONVENT — **POCHE PLANTATION RV RESORT.** (225) 715-9510. **$20-$35.** 6554 Louisiana Hwy 44 70723. E-bnd From Jct of I-10 & Exit 179, S 15.6 mi on LA44 (L) W-bnd From Jct of I-10 & Exit 194 (LA 641/3213), S 7 mi to LA 44, W 7.8 mi (R) 🅰️ 🔁 ⊠

KINDER — **RED SHOES PARK AT COUSHATTA CASINO RESORT.** (800) 584-7263. **$20-$65.** 711 Pow Wow Parkway 70648. From jct of I-10 & US-165 (exit 44): Go N 22-1/2 mi on US-165 (L); or from jct of I-49 & US-165 (exit 86): Go S 55 mi on US-165 (R) 🅰️ 🔁 ⊠

LIVINGSTON — **LAKESIDE RV PARK.** (225) 686-7676. **$35-$52.** 28370 S Frost Rd 70754. From Jct of I-12 (exit 22) & LA 63/Frost Rd, S 1 mi on Frost Rd (L) 🅰️ 🔁 ⊠

MARKSVILLE — **PARAGON CASINO RV RESORT.** (800) 946-1946. **$17-$32.** 124 Earl J Barbry Sr Blvd 71351. From jct of LA-1 & LA-115/107 (in Marksville): Go S 1-1/2 mi on LA-1 (L) 🅰️ 🔁 ⊠

NEW ORLEANS — **PONTCHARTRAIN LANDING.** (877) 376-7850. **$59-$179.** 6001 France Road 70126. E-bnd: From Jct of I-10 exit 239B, exit to Louisa St N, N 0.2 mi (lt) to Chef Menteur, E 0.4 mi (rt) to France Rd, N 1.1 mi (R) or W-bnd: From Jct of I-10 & exit 239, exit to Old Gentilly Hwy, E 200 ft (rt) to Desire, N 500 ft (lt) to Chef Menteur, E 0.3 mi (rt) to France Rd, N 1.1 mi (R) 🔁 ⊠

SULPHUR — **A+ MOTEL & RV PARK.** (337) 583-2631. **$33-$37.** 4631 Hwy 27 South 70665. From jct of I-10 & LA 27 (exit 20): Go S 2 mi on LA 27 (L) 🅰️ 🔁 ⊠

VIDALIA — **RIVER VIEW RV PARK AND RESORT.** ⟪AAA⟫ (888) 628-2430. **$30-$39.** 100 Riverview Parkway 71373. From Jct of US-65/US-84 & LA-131 (on the West side of Mississippi River Bridge), S 0.8 mi on LA-131 (also Martin Luther King Ave) (L) 🔁 ⊠

Maine

DURHAM — **FREEPORT DURHAM KOA.** (207) 688-4288. **$33-$48.** 82 Big Skye Ln 04222. From Jct of I-295 & Rte 136 (exit 22/old exit 20), N 3 mi on Rte 136 to Brown Rd, NW 2.6 mi to Rte 9, N 0.3 mi (R) 🔁 ⊠

KENNEBUNKPORT — **RED APPLE CAMPGROUND.** (207) 967-4927. **$53-$58. (no credit cards).** 111 Sinnott Rd 04046. From Jct of Rte & Rte 35 (exit 25), SE 1.8 mi on Rte 35 to US-1, N 1.5 mi to Old Post Rd, E (right) 0.7 mi to Sinnott Rd, E (continue straight) 1.5 mi (L) ⊠

NAPLES — **NAPLES KOA CAMPGROUND.** (207) 693-5267. **$30-$60.** 295 Sebago Rd (Route 114/11) 04055. From Jct of US-302 & Rte 11/114, S 1.4 mi on Rte 11/114 (R) 🅰️ 🔁 ⊠

OLD ORCHARD BEACH — **HID'N PINES FAMILY CAMP-GROUND.** ⟪AAA⟫ (207) 934-2352. **$35-$68.** 8 Cascade Rd 04064. From Jct of ME Tpke & I-195 (exit 36), E 1.2 mi on I-195 to Rte 1, NE 3 mi to Rte 98, S 2 mi (L) 🔁 ⊠

OLD ORCHARD BEACH — **OLD ORCHARD BEACH CAMPGROUND.** (207) 934-4477. **$50-$58.** 27 Ocean Park Rd 04064. From Jct I-95 (exit 36) & I-195: Go 2 mi E on I-195, then Rt 5 joins I-195, immediate R. 🔁 ⊠

OLD ORCHARD BEACH — **POWDER HORN FAMILY CAMPING RESORT.** ⟪AAA⟫ (207) 934-4733. **$35-$74.** 48 Cascade Rd 04064. From Jct of ME Tpke & I-195 (exit 36), E 1.2 mi on I-195 to US-1, N 3 mi to Rte 98, S 1.8 mi (L) 🔁 ⊠

OLD ORCHARD BEACH — **WILD ACRES RV RESORT & CAMPGROUND.** ⟪AAA⟫ (888) 451-3586. **$45-$83.** 179 Saco Ave 04064. From Jct of ME Tpke & I-195 (exit 36), E 2 mi on I-195 to Rte 5, E 1.5 mi (R) 🔁 ⊠

SCARBOROUGH — **BAYLEY'S CAMPING RESORT.** (207) 883-6043. **$35-$82.** 275 Old Pine Point Rd 04074. From Jct I-95 Maine Tpk (exit 42) & Scarborough (US-1): Go 1-1/2 mi S on US-1, then 3 mi E on Hwy 9 West to Pine Point. (R) 🔁 ⊠

TRENTON — **TIMBERLAND ACRES RV PARK.** (207) 667-3600. **$29-$47.** 57 Bar Harbor Rd 04605. From Jct of US-1 & SR-3 (in Ellsworth), S 2 mi on SR-3 (R) 🔁 ⊠

WELLS — **SEA-VU CAMPGROUND.** ⟪AAA⟫ (207) 646-7732. **$45-$65.** 1733 Post Rd 04090. From Jct of ME Tpke & Rte 109 (exit 19 Wells-Sanford), E 1.5 mi on Rte 109 to US-1, N 0.4 mi (R) 🔁 ⊠

WELLS — **SEA-VU WEST.** (207) 646-0785. **$45-$65.** 23 College Drive 04090. From Jct I 95 (exit 19) & Rte 109: Go 1/2 mi E on Rte. 109, then 1/2 mi SE on Chapel Rd, then 1/4 mi S on College Rd. (R) 🅰️ 🔁 ⊠

WELLS — **WELLS BEACH RESORT.** ⟪AAA⟫ (207) 646-7570. **$50-$90.** 1000 Post Rd - Us Rte 1 04090. From Jct of ME Tpke (I-95) & Rte 109 (exit 19, Wells-Sanford), E 1.5 mi on Rte 109 to US-1, S 1.4 mi (R) 🔁 ⊠

Maryland

ABINGDON — BAR HARBOR RV PARK & MARINA. 🆀
(800) 351-CAMP. **$55-$60.** 4228 Birch Ave 21009. From Jct of I-95 &
SR-543 (exit 80), S 1.4 mi on SR-543 to US-40, W 1.4 mi to Long Bar
Harbor Rd, SE 0.7 mi to Baker Ave, E 0.5 mi (E) 🔥 🍴 🗙

BERLIN — CASTAWAYS RV RESORT & CAMPGROUND.
(888) 693-0528. **$55-$124.** 12550 Eagles Nest Rd 21811. From Jct of
US-50 & SR-611, right (SW) 2.2 mi on SR-611 to Eagles Nest Rd, E
(left) 1.5 mi at Y in Rd, stay left (R) 🍴 🗙

COLLEGE PARK — CHERRY HILL PARK. 🆀 (301) 937-
7116. **$63-$73.** 9800 Cherry Hill Rd 20740. S-bnd: From Jct of I-95 &
SR-212/Powder Mill Rd (exit 29B Calverton), W 1.2 mi on SR-212/
Powder Mill Rd to Cherry Hill Rd, S (Lt turn) 1.1 mi (R); or From Belt-
way I-495/95 & US-1/ Baltimore Ave (exit 25), S 0.4 mi on US-1/Balt.
Ave to Cherry Hill Rd (Rt Turn) 1 mi (L) 🍴 🗙

FREELAND — MERRY MEADOWS RECREATION FARM.
🆀 (800) 643-7056. **$39-$56.** 1523 Freeland Rd 21053. From Jct of
I-83 & SR-439 (exit 36), W 0.2 mi on SR-439 to SR-45, N 1 mi to
Freeland Rd, W 3 mi (L) 🍴 🗙

OCEAN CITY — FRONTIER TOWN CAMPGROUND. (800)
228-5590. **$41-$111.** 8428 Stephen Decatur Hwy. 21843. From Jct of
US-50 & SR-611, SW 3.7 mi on SR-611 (L) 🍴 🗙

WHALEYVILLE — FORT WHALEY CAMPGROUND. (888)
322-7717. **$35-$89.** 11224 Dale Road 21872. From Jct of US-50 &
SR-528 (at S end of Ocean City), W 13.8 mi on US-50 to SR-610
(Whaleyville), entrance is on SE corner of intersection (L) 🍴 🗙

WILLIAMSPORT — YOGI BEAR'S JELLYSTONE PARK
CAMP-RESORT/HAGERSTOWN. (301) 223-7117. **$38-$127.** 16519
Lappans Rd 21795. From Jct of I-81 & SR-68 (exit 1), E 1.3 mi on
SR-68 (R); or From Jct of I-70 & SR-632 (exit 28), SW 2.7 mi on
SR-632 to SR-68W, W 0.8 mi (L) 🍴 🗙

WOODBINE — RAMBLIN' PINES FAMILY CAMPGROUND
& RV PARK. 🆀 (800) 550-8733. **$58.** 801 Hoods Mill Rd 21797.
E-bnd: From Jct of I-70 & SR-94 (exit 73), N 3.4 mi on SR-94 to
Hoods Mill Rd, E 2.3 mi (R); or W-bnd: From Jct of I-70 & SR-97 (exit
76), N 2.7 mi on SR-97 (left turn) onto Hoods Mill Rd, W 0.6 mi (L)
🍴 🗙

Massachusetts

BELLINGHAM — CIRCLE CG FARM CAMPGROUND. 🆀
(508) 966-1136. **$45-$55.** 131 N Main St 02019. From Jct of MA Pike
& I-495, S 12 mi on I-495 to Hwy 126 (exit 18), S 1 mi (L); or From Jct
of I-95 & I-495, N 13 mi on I-495 to Hwy 126 (exit 18), S 1 mi (L)
🍴 🗙

BOURNE — BAY VIEW CAMPGROUND. (508) 759-7610. **$45-
$65.** 260 Macarthur Blvd 02532. From Jct of I-195 & I-495/Rte 25, SE
9 mi on Rte 25 to Bourne bridge (over bridge to Rotary) to Rte 28S, S
1.2 mi (R) 🍴 🗙

EAST FALMOUTH — CAPE COD CAMPRESORT & CAB-
INS. (508) 548-1458. **$39-$95.** 176 Thomas B Landers Rd 02536.
From Jct of Rte 28S & Thomas B Landers Rd, E 2.5 mi on Thomas B
Landers Rd (R) 🍴 🗙

FOXBORO — NORMANDY FARMS FAMILY CAMPING
RESORT. (866) 673-2767. **$51-$84.** 72 West St 02035. From Jct of
I-95 & Rte 1 (exit 9), S 6.7 mi on Rte 1 to Thurston St, E 1.3 mi (R);
or From Jct of I-495 & Rte 1 (exit 14A), N 1 mi on Rte 1 to Thurston
St (2nd traffic light), E 1.3 mi (R) 🍴 🗙

LITTLETON — BOSTON MINUTEMAN CAMPGROUND. 🆀
(978) 772-0042. **$46-$57.** 264 Ayer Road 01460. From Jct of I-495 &
Rte 2A (exit 30), W 3 mi on Rte 2A (L) 🍴 🗙

MONSON — SUNSETVIEW FARM CAMPING AREA, INC.
🆀 (413) 267-9269. **$38-$56.** 57 Town Farm Rd 01057. E-bnd: From
Jct of MA Pike & Rte 32 (exit 8), S 2.5 mi on Rte 32 to Fenton Rd, E
0.5 mi to Town Farm Rd, S 1.5 mi (L); or N-bnd: From CT: From Jct
of I-84 & Rte 32 (exit 70), N 17 mi on Rte 32 to Brimfield Rd (in town),
E 2 mi to Town Farm Rd, N 0.5 mi (R) 🍴 🗙

OAKHAM — PINE ACRES FAMILY CAMPING RESORT.
(508) 882-9509. **$38-$75.** 203 Bechan Rd 01068. From Jct of Hwy 122
& Hwy 148, SW 2 mi on Rte 148 to Spencer Rd, S 0.1 mi to Bechan
Rd, E 0.4 mi (L) 🍴 🗙

PHILLIPSTON — LAMB CITY CAMPGROUND. (800) 292-
5262. **$31-$44.** 85 Royalston Rd 01331. E-bnd: From Jct of Rtes 2 &
2A (Exit 19), N 0.1 mi on Rte 2A to Royalston Rd, W 0.5 mi (L); or
W-bnd: From Jct of Rtes 2 & 2A (Exit 19), W 300 ft on Rte 2A to Royalston Rd, W 0.5 mi (L) 🍴 🗙

SALISBURY — BEACH ROSE RV PARK. (800) 382-2230.
$40-$60. 147 Beach Rd 01952. N-Bnd: From Jct of I-495 & Rte 110/
exit 55, E 3.5 mi on Rte 110 to Rte 1, N 500 ft to Rte 1A, E 1.3 mi (L);
OR S-Bnd: From Jct of I-95 & Rte 110/exit 58, E 2.4 mi on Rte 110 to
Rte 1, N 500 ft to Rte 1A, E 1.3 mi (L) 🔥 🍴 🗙

SALISBURY — BLACK BEAR CAMPGROUND. (978) 462-
3183. **$45-$55.** 54 Main St 01952. N-bnd: From Jct of I-495 & I-95, N
0.5 mi on I-95 to Exit 60 to 1st set of lights (Main St), E 0.1 mi (L); or
S-bnd: From Jct of I-95 & Exit 60, exit rd to 1st set of lights (Main St),
E 0.1 mi (L) 🍴 🗙

SANDWICH — PETERS POND RV RESORT. 🆀 (888) 543-
7951. **$49-$99.** 185 Cotuit Rd 02563. From Jct of Rte 6 & Hwy 130
(exit 2), S 3 mi on Hwy 130 to Quaker Meeting House Rd, E 0.8 mi to
Cotuit Rd, S 0.7 mi (R) 🍴 🗙

SHELBURNE FALLS — COUNTRY AIRE CAMPGROUND.
(413) 625-2996. **$35-$40.** 1753 Mohawk Trail 01370. From Jct of I-91
& Rte 2 (exit 26), W 13 mi on Rte 2 (R) 🍴 🗙

WEBSTER — INDIAN RANCH. (508) 943-3871. **$45-$85.** 200
Gore Rd 01570. From Jct of I 395 & Rte 16 (Exit 2), E 1.3 mi on Rte
16 (R) 🔥 🍴 🗙

WESTHAMPTON — NORTHAMPTON - SPRINGFIELD
KOA. (413) 527-9862. **$35-$52.** 139 South Rd 01027. S-bnd: From Jct
of I-91 & Rte 5 (exit 18), NW 0.8 mi on Rte 5 to Rte 66, W (left turn)
8 mi to South Rd, N 0.1 mi (L); or N-bnd: From Jct of I-90 & I-91, N
4 mi on I-91 (exit 17B) to Hwy 141, W 4.7 mi to Rte 10, SW 0.5 mi
(first right) to Glendale, N 4 mi to Rte 66, W 2 mi to South Rd, N 0.2
mi (L) 🍴 🗙

Michigan

BALDWIN — PERE MARQUETTE OAKS CONDOMINIUM RV
PARK. (231) 898-2665. **$40. (no credit cards).** 6150 W 76th St.
49304. From South Jct of M-37 & US-10, S 3.6 mi on M-37 to 76th St,
W 3.5 mi (R) Note: Minimum length for RV is 22 feet. No tents or pop
ups. 🔥 🍴 🗙

BUCKLEY — TRAVERSE CITY KOA. (800) 249-3203. **$25-$55.**
9700 S M 37 49620. From Jct. of US 31 & M-37, S. on M-37, 9.6 mi
(R) 🍴 🗙

CEDAR SPRINGS — **LAKESIDE CAMP PARK.** (616) 696-1735. **$32-$36.** 13677 White Creek Ave 49319. From Jct of US-131 & M-46 (17 Mile Rd exit 104), E 0.1 mi on 17 Mile Rd to White Creek Ave, S 0.25 mi (R) ⊠

COVERT — **COVERT/SOUTH HAVEN KOA.** (269) 764-0818. **$34-$65.** 39397 M-140 Highway 49043. From Jct of I-196 & M-140 (Exit 18) S 6.2 mi on M-140 (L) From Jct of I 94 & M-140 (Exit 41), N 7.3 mi on M-140 (R) ⊠ ⊠

DORR — **HUNGRY HORSE CAMPGROUND.** (616) 681-9843. **$35-$40.** 2016 142nd Avenue 49323. From Jct of US-131 & 142nd Ave (exit 68), W 3.5 mi on 142nd Ave (L) ⊠ ⊠

FRANKENMUTH — **YOGI BEAR'S JELLYSTONE PARK CAMP-RESORT.** ⒶⒶⒶ (989) 652-6668. **$42-$72.** 1339 Weiss St 48734. N-bnd: From Jct of I-75 & M-83 (Exit 136), E 2 mi on M-83 (Birch Run Rd) to M-83 (Gera Rd), N 5 mi to Weiss St, NE .01 mi (R) ⊠ ⊠

GAYLORD — **GAYLORD KOA RESORT.** (800) 562-4146. **$28-$59.** 5101 Campfires Parkway 49735. From Jct of I-75 & Old US-27 (exit 279), S 2 mi on Old US-27 to Charles Brink Rd, E 1.0 mi (R) ⊠ ⊠ ⊠

HILLSDALE — **GATEWAY PARK CAMPGROUND.** (517) 437-7005. **$39-$53.** 4111 W Hallett Rd 49242. From Jct of US-12 & M-99S (in Jonesville), S 1.4 mi on M-99S to Lake Wilson Rd, SW 3.4 mi to Hallett Rd, W 1.1 mi (L) ⊠ ⊠ ⊠

HOLLAND — **OAK GROVE RESORT.** (616) 399-9230. **$40-$54.** 2011 Ottawa Beach Rd 49424. From Jct of US-31 & Lakewood Blvd, W 1.2 mi on Lakewood Blvd to Douglas Ave/Ottawa Beach Rd, SW 4.8 mi (R) ⊠ ⊠ ⊠

HOPKINS — **HIDDEN RIDGE RV RESORT.** ⒶⒶⒶ (888) 451-2180. **$42-$53.** 2306 12th St 49328. From Jct of US 131 & 124th Ave (exit 59), W 0.1 mi on 124th Ave to 12th St, S 0.3 mi (R). Note: Minimum RV length 22' - no pop-ups. ⊠ ⊠ ⊠

HOWELL — **LAKE CHEMUNG OUTDOOR RESORT.** (517) 546-6361. **$40. (no credit cards).** 320 S Hughes Rd 48843. From Jct of I-96 & Exit 145 (Grand River Ave), NW on Grand River Ave, 3 mi to Hugh Rd, N .2 mi (R) ⊠ ⊠ ⊠

IONIA — **ALICE SPRINGS RV PARK & CAMPGROUND.** (616) 527-1608. **$39.** 5087 Alice Court 48846. From Jct I-96 & M-66 (Exit 67), N 2 mi on M-66 (R) ⊠ ⊠

JACKSON — **GREENWOOD ACRES FAMILY CAMPGROUND.** ⒶⒶⒶ (517) 522-8600. **$38-$44.** 2401 Hilton Rd 49201. From Jct of I-94 & Race Rd (exit 147), S 0.2 mi on Race Rd to Ann Arbor Rd, W 0.8 mi to Portage Rd, S 1.25 mi to Greenwood Rd, E 0.4 mi to Hilton Rd (L) ⊠ ⊠

LAKE LEELANAU — **LAKE LEELANAU RV PARK.** (231) 256-7236. **$59-$79.** 3101 Lake Shore Dr 49653. From Jct of M-204 & CR-643 (in Lake Leelanau), S 3.5 mi on CR-643 (L) ⊠

LUDINGTON — **PONCHO'S POND.** (888) 308-6602. **$50-$53.** 5335 W Wallace Road 49431. From W Jct of US-31 & US-10, W 1.5 mi on US-10 to Pere Marquette Rd, S 0.1 mi (L) ⊠ ⊠

LUDINGTON — **VACATION STATION RV RESORT.** (800) 499-1060. **$35-$65.** 4895 W Us-10 49431. From W Jct of US 31 & US 10, W 1 mi on US 10 (L) ⊠ ⊠

MANISTEE — **LITTLE RIVER CASINO RV PARK.** (866) 572-4386. **$33-$45.** 2700 Orchard Hwy 49660. From Jct of US 31 & M-55, N 3.1 mi on US 31 to M-22, W 0.1 mi (L). Follow signs to RV Park ⊠ ⊠ ⊠

MARSHALL — **CAMP TURKEYVILLE RV RESORT.** (269) 781-4293. **$45.** 18935 15 1/2 Mile Rd 49068. From Jct of I-69 & Exit 42 (N Dr & Turkeyville Rd), W 0.9 mi on Turkeyville Rd (L) Note : Pull into Turkeyville main lot. Park drive is on the west side of the main lot. ⊠ ⊠ ⊠

MICHIGAMME — **MICHIGAMME SHORES CAMPGROUND RESORT.** ⒶⒶⒶ (906) 339-2116. **$37-$43.** Hwy 41 W 49861. From Jct of US-41 & M-95, W 5 mi on US-41 (L) ⊠

MONROE — **HARBORTOWN RV RESORT.** (734) 384-4700. **$40-$52.** 14931 Laplaisance Rd 48161. From Jct of I-75 & La Plaisance Rd (exit 11), W 0.6 mi on La Plaisance Rd (L) ⊠ ⊠

MOUNT PLEASANT — **SOARING EAGLE HIDEAWAY RV PARK.** (989) 817-4803. **$49-$72.** 5514 E Airport Rd 48858. From the Jct of US-127 & Exit 143 (Pickard Rd), E .2 mi on Pickard Rd (L) ⊠ ⊠ ⊠

MUSKEGON — **DUCK CREEK RV RESORT.** (231) 766-3646. **$40-$60.** 1155 W Riley Thompson Rd 49445. From Jct of US-31 & Russell Rd (Exit 121), N 1 mi to Riley Thompson Rd, W 1.5 mi (L) ⊠ ⊠ ⊠

PETOSKEY — **HEARTHSIDE GROVE MOTORCOACH RESORT.** (888) 476-8388. **$90-$120.** 2400 Us 31 North 49770. From Jct of US 31 N & M119, NE 2.5 mi on US 31 N (R) ⊠ ⊠ ⊠

PETOSKEY — **PETOSKEY KOA RV & CABIN RESORT.** (800) 562-0253. **$41-$70.** 1800 Us-31 North 49770. From Jct of US-31N & M-119 (E of town), N 1 mi on US-31N (R) ⊠ ⊠ ⊠

PETOSKEY — **PETOSKEY RV RESORT.** (888) 517-2341. **$59-$99.** 5505 Charlevoix Ave 49770. From Jct of US 131 & US 31, S 5 mi on US 31 (L) ⊠ ⊠ ⊠

SILVER LAKE — **SILVER CREEK RV RESORT.** (866) 832-7601. **$25-$60.** 1441 N. 34th Ave 49436. From Jct of US-31 & Polk Rd (Hart/Mears exit), W 1.2 mi on Polk Rd to 56th St, S 0.5 mi to Fox Rd, W 2.7 mi to 34th Ave, S 0.7 mi (R) ⊠ ⊠ ⊠

SOUTH HAVEN — **SOUTH HAVEN SUNNY BROOK RV RESORT.** (888) 499-5253. **$48-$64.** 68300 Cr 388 Phoenix Rd 49090. From Jct of I-196 & CR 388 (Phoenix Rd Exit 20), E 2.2 mi on CR 388/ Phoenix Rd (L) ⊠ ⊠ ⊠

SOUTH HAVEN — **YOGI BEAR'S JELLYSTONE PARK CAMP-RESORT.** (269) 637-6153. **$30-$75.** 03403 64th Street 49090. From Jct of I-196 & CR 388, Exit 20 (Phoenix Rd), E 4.2 mi to 64th St, N 0.4 mi (R) ⊠ ⊠

STANWOOD — **RIVER RIDGE RV RESORT & MARINA.** (877) 287-4837. **$38-$55.** 22265 8 Mile Road 49346. From Jct of US 131 & M-20 (Exit 131), W 2 mi on M-20 (8 Mile Road) to Elder Rd, S 0.2 mi (L) ⊠ ⊠ ⊠

TRAVERSE CITY — **HOLIDAY PARK CAMPGROUND.** (231) 943-4410. **$45-$57.** 4860 Us-31s 49685. From SW Jct of M-37 & US-31, SW 1 mi on US-31 (R). Note: No Motorcycles. ⊠

WILLIAMSBURG — TRAVERSE BAY RV RESORT. (231) 938-5800. **$60-$85.** 5555 M-72 East 49690. From N Jct of US 31N & Hwy 72, E 1.5 mi on Hwy 72 (L). Note: RVs restricted to Class "A" & "C" Motorhomes & Fifth Wheels 10 years or approval and minimum 28'. 🏕 🛶 ⊗

Minnesota

CASS LAKE — STONY POINT RESORT RV PARK & CAMP-GROUND. ⚫️ (218) 335-6311. **$32-$40.** 5510 Us 2 Nw 56633. From Jct of US 2 & SR-371, E 1.8 mi on US 2 - between MP 131 & 132 (L) ⊗

DETROIT LAKES — COUNTRY CAMPGROUND. (218) 847-9621. **$35.** 13639 260th Av 56501. N-bnd: From Jct of I-94 (Exit 50) & US-59, N 35 mi on US-59 to CR-22 (R), .05 mi to 130th St (R), 1 mi to 260th Ave.(L), .7 mi (R). S-bnd: From Jct of US-10 & US-59, S 4.7 mi on US-59 to CR-22 (L), .05 mi to 130th St (R), 1 mi to 260th Ave.(L), .7 mi (R) ⊗

DETROIT LAKES — FOREST HILLS RV & GOLF RESORT. (800) 482-3441. **$60.** 22931 185th St 56501. From Jct of US-59 & US-10, W 3.3 mi on US-10 (L) 🏕 🛶 ⊗

FARIBAULT — CAMP FARIBO. (507) 332-8453. **$37-$39.** 21851 Bagley Ave 55021. From Jct of I-35 & SR-60 (exit 56), E 0.3 mi on SR-60 to Western/Bagley Ave, S 1.5 mi (L) 🛶 ⊗

GRANITE FALLS — PRAIRIE VIEW RV PARK & CAMP-GROUND. (866) 293-2121. **$16-$24.** 5616 Prairies Edge Lane 56241. From Jct of Hwy 23 & Hwy 212 (in town) S. 2.2 mi on Hwy 23 to Hwy 274, S 0.4 mi on Hwy 274 to Prairies Edge Lane E 0.8 mi (L). Note: Don't use GPS coordinates 🛶 ⊗

HINCKLEY — GRAND CASINO HINCKLEY RV RESORT. (800) 472-6321. **$27-$35.** 1326 Fire Monument Rd 55037. From Jct of I-35 & SR-48 (Exit 183), E 1 mi on SR-48 (R) 🏕 🛶 ⊗

ORTONVILLE — LAKESHORE RV PARK INC. (800) 9FO-RFUN. **$35.** 39445 Lakeshore Rv Park Rd 56278. From Jct of US-12 & SR-7W (in town), NW 2.7 mi on SR-7W (L) 🛶 ⊗

PEQUOT LAKES — RV RESORT VILLAGE AT THE PRE-SERVE. (218) 568-8009. **$39-$65.** 28668 Hurtig Rd 56472. From the center of Nisswa, N 4 mi on Hwy 371 to CR-168, W 0.2 mi to Hurtig Rd, S 0.2 mi (L) 🏕 🛶

PIPESTONE — PIPESTONE RV CAMPGROUND. ⚫️ (507) 825-2455. **$29-$34.** 919 N Hiawatha Ave 56164. From Jct of US-75 & SR-23 (N side of town), N 0.4 mi on US-75 to NE 9th St (CR-22), W 0.6 mi (R); or From Jct of I-90 & SR-23 (exit 1), N 28 mi on SR-23 to Hiawatha Ave, N 1.4 mi (R) 🛶 ⊗

PRIOR LAKE — DAKOTAH MEADOWS RV PARK. (800) 653-CAMP. **$23-$33.** 2341 Park Place N.W. 55372. From Jct of I-35 & 185th St. W (Exit 84), W 1.2 mi on 185th St (185th St becomes CR-21) to CR-21, then NW 7.2 mi on CR-21 to CR-82/154th St, W 1.8 mi to Mystic Lake Blvd, N 0.2 mi (R) 🏕 🛶 ⊗

RED WING — TREASURE ISLAND RV PARK. (800) 222-7077. **$25-$35.** 5630 Sturgeon Lake Rd 55089. From Jct of US-61 & CR-18 (NW of town), N 2.5 mi on CR-18 to Sturgeon Lake Rd, E 1.3 mi (L) 🛶 ⊗

ROCHESTER — KOA ROCHESTER/MARION. (507) 288-0785. **$26-$40.** 5232 65th Ave Se 55904. From Jct of I-90 & US-52, S 0.6 mi on US-52 to 54 SE St, E 0.1 mi to 65th Ave SE, (L). 🛶 ⊗

ST. CLOUD — ST CLOUD CAMPGROUND & RV PARK. (320) 251-4463. **$34-$38.** 2491 2nd St Se 56304. From Jct of US-10 & SR-23, E 0.1 mi on SR-23 to CR-8 (14th Ave SE), S 0.1 mi on CR-8, E 1 mi on CR-8 (L) S-bnd: From Jct of SR-23 & CR-8, E 1 mi on CR-8 to 2nd St SE, S 1 mi on 2nd St SE (R) 🛶 ⊗

WALKER — TRAILS RV PARK. (877) 280-0322. **$44-$49.** 9424 State 371 Nw 56484. From Jct of SR 200/371 & SR 34 (in Walker), N 4.1 mi on SR 371 (R). 🏕 🛶 ⊗

WASECA — KIESLER'S CAMPGROUND AND RV RESORT. (507) 835-3179. **$43-$70.** 14360 Hwy 14 East 56093. From Jct of SR-13 & US-14, E 1.5 mi on US-14 (R) 🛶 ⊗

WATERVILLE — KAMP DELS. (507) 362-8616. **$47-$69.** 14842 Sakatah Lake Rd 56096. From Jct of US-60 & SR 13, N 0.9 mi on SR 13 to CR-131, E 0.5 mi (L) 🛶 ⊗

Mississippi

BAY ST. LOUIS — BAY HIDE AWAY RV PARK & CAMP-GROUND. (228) 466-0959. **$25-$50.** 8360 Lakeshore Rd 39520. E-bnd: From Jct of I-10 (exit 2 Welcome Center) & Hwy 607/US-90, SE 8.6 mi on Hwy 607/US-90 to Lakeshore Rd, S 0.5 mi (L); or W-bnd: From Jct of I-10 (exit 13) & Hwys 43/603, S 5.2 mi on Hwys 43/603 to US-90, W 4.7 mi to Lakeshore Rd, S 0.5 mi (L) 🏕 🛶 ⊗

BAY ST. LOUIS — HOLLYWOOD CASINO RV PARK-GULF COAST. (866) 758-2591. **$35-$45.** 711 Hollywood Blvd 39520. E-Bnd: From Jct of I-10 & SR-607 (exit 2), SE 7 mi on SR-607 to US-90, E 9 mi to Blue Meadow Rd, N 0.6 mi to Hollywood Blvd, E 1.3 mi (E); or W-Bnd: From Jct of I-10 & SR-603 (exit 13), SE 5.2 mi on SR-603 to US-90, E 3.5 mi to Blue Meadow Rd, N 0.6 mi to Hollywood Blvd, E 1.3 mi (E) 🏕 🛶 ⊗

BILOXI — MAJESTIC OAKS RV RESORT. (228) 436-4200. **$39-$44.** 1750 Pass Road 39531. From Jct of I-10 & I-110 (Exit 46A), S 4.2 mi on I-110 to US-90, W 3.1 mi to Rodenberg Ave, N 0.6 mi to Pass Rd, W 0.2 mi (R) 🏕 🛶

HORN LAKE — MEMPHIS JELLYSTONE CAMP RESORT. (662) 280-8282. **$45-$55.** 1400 Audubon Point Drive 38637. From Jct of I-55 & Church Rd (exit 287), W 1.0 mi on Church Rd to US-51, N 0.8 mi to Audubon Point Dr, E 500 ft (E) 🛶

PELAHATCHIE — YOGI ON THE LAKE. ⚫️ (601) 854-6621. **$26-$55.** 143 Campground Rd 39145. From Jct of I 20 (exit 68) & Hwy 43, N 2.2 mi on Hwy 43 to Lake Rd, W 1.1 mi to Campground Rd, N 0.2 mi (E) 🛶 ⊗

PICAYUNE — SUN ROAMERS RV RESORT. (601) 798-5818. **$30-$36.** 41 Mississippi Pines Blvd 39466. From Jct of I-59 & SR 43 S (exit 4), E 0.8 mi on SR 43S to Stafford Rd, S 0.6 mi to Mississippi Pines Blvd, W 500 ft (E) 🛶 ⊗

SOUTHAVEN — EZ DAZE RV PARK. (662) 342-7720. **$40.** 536 W.E. Ross Pkwy 38671. From Jct of I-55 & Church Rd (Exit 287), W 0.2 mi on Church Rd to Pepper Chase Dr, N 0.5 mi to W E Ross Pkwy, W 0.2 mi (R) 🏕 🛶 ⊗

Missouri

ANNAPOLIS — BIG CREEK RV PARK. (573) 598-1064. **$33.** 47247 Hwy 49 63620. From Jct K & Hwy 49N: Go 4.8 mi N on Hwy 49N. From St. Louis: Take I-55S to US 67 Exit (3.5 mi), Go S on US 67 34 mi to Hwy 221, turn W on Hwy 221 to Hwy 21 9 mi, turn L on Hwy 21 to Hwy 49 (9 mi) Go 4 mi to Big Creek RV Park (L) 🏕 🛶 ⊗

BRANSON — AMERICA'S BEST CAMPGROUND. (800) 671-4399. **$37.** 499 Buena Vista Rd 65616. From Jct of US 65 & SR-248, W 1.7 mi on SR-248 (move to right turning lane), continue N 1.3 mi on SR-248 to Buena Vista Rd, W 0.3 mi (L). Use these directions, do not use GPS 🛥 🛒

BRANSON — BLUE MOUNTAIN CAMPGROUND. (417) 338-2114. **$23. (no credit cards).** 8766 State Hwy 76 65737. From Jct of Hwy 65 & Hwy 465/Ozark Mtn Highroad, S 7.0 mi on Hwy 465 to Hwy 76, W 1.9 mi (L) 🛥

BRANSON — BRANSON KOA & CONVENTION CENTER. (800) 562-4177. **$31-$51.** 397 Animal Safari Rd 65616. From Jct of US-65 & SR-76, W 3.3 mi on SR-76 to SR-165 (Gretna Rd), S 0.7 mi to Animal Safari Rd, W 0.1 mi (L) 🛥 🛒

BRANSON — COOPER CREEK CAMPGROUND & RESORT. (417) 334-4871. **$30-$38.** 471 Cooper Creek Rd 65616. From Jct of US-65 & SR-76, W 1 mi on SR-76 to Fall Creek Rd, 1.6 mi on Fall Creek Rd, L on River Ln, then .1 mi to L on Cooper Creek Rd. 🛥 🛒

BRANSON — MUSICLAND RV PARK, LLC. (888) 248-9080. **$27-$39.** 116 Gretna Rd 65616. From Jct of US-65 & Hwy-248, W 1.9 mi on Hwy-248 to Gretna Rd. (stay in left lane, continue straight ahead) 3.1 mi (L) 🛥 🛒

BRANSON — TALL PINES CAMPGROUND. 🄰🄰🄰 (800) 425-2300. **$30-$36.** 5558 St Hwy 265 65616. From Jct of Hwy 65 & Hwy 465/Ozark Mountain Highroad, (North of town), S 7 mi on Hwy 465 to Hwy 76, W 0.5 mi on Hwy 76 to Hwy 265, S 0.1 mi (L) 🛥 🛒

CAPE GIRARDEAU — CAPE CAMPING & RV PARK. (573) 332-8888. **$35.** 1900 N Kings Hwy 63701. From Jct of I-55 & Exit 99, E 1.5 mi on Hwy 61/Kings Highway (L) 🛥 🛒

CAPE GIRARDEAU — THE LANDING POINT RV PARK. (573) 334-7878. **$35.** 3020 Boutin Dr 63701. From Jct of I-55 and LaSalle Ave (Exit 102), E 2.2 mi on LaSalle Ave to Route W, S 1.8 mi on Route W, continue S on Route W 0.2 mi (L)

COLUMBIA — COTTONWOODS RV PARK. 🄰🄰🄰 (573) 474-2747. **$25-$37.** 5170 Oakland Gravel Rd 65202. From Jct of I-70 & US-63 (exit 128A), N 3 mi on US-63 to Oakland Gravel Rd (paved), NE 0.25 mi (R); or S-bnd: From Jct of US-63 & Prathersville Rd, E 0.2 mi to Oakland Gravel Rd (paved), S 0.25 mi (L) 🛥 🛒

DANVILLE — LAZY DAY CAMPGROUND. (573) 564-2949. **$33-$35.** 214 Hwy J 63361. From Jct of I-70 & Hwy J (Exit 170), S 1.4 mi on Hwy J (L). Use these directions, do not use GPS . 🛥 🛒

FORSYTH — JELLYSTONE CAMP RESORT. (417) 546-3000. **$43-$75.** 11020 E State Hwy 76 65653. From Jct of US 65 & US 160, E 12 mi (thru Forsyth) to St Hwy 76, S 1.2 mi on US 160 (L) 🛥 🛒

GRAIN VALLEY — TRAILSIDE RV PARK & STORE. (800) 748-7729. **$34-$36.** 1000 R.D. Mize Rd 64029. From Jct of I-70 & CR-AA (Grain Valley Exit 24), S 80 ft on CR-AA to US 40 West, W 0.3 mi to OOIDA Dr, N 0.1 mi to R.D. Mize, W 0.3 mi (R) Note: Do not use GPS, call park. 🛥 🛒

LAKE OZARK — RIVERVIEW RV PARK. (573) 365-1122. **$32.** 398 Woodriver Rd 65049. N-bound: From Jct US-54 & Bus 54 (S of town): Go E 1 mi on US-54, then N 100 yards on Woodriver Rd (watch carefully for small sign on R) (R); OR S-bound: From North Jct Bus US-54 & US-54: Go W 2.3 mi on US-54, then S immediately after Osage River Bridge on Woodriver Rd (L). 🛥 🛒

MONROE CITY — MARK TWAIN LANDING. 🄰🄰🄰 (573) 735-9422. **$42-$59.** 42819 Landing Ln 63456. From Jct of US-36 & CR-J, S 7.7 mi on CR-J (R) 🛥 🛒

NEVADA — OSAGE PRAIRIE RV PARK. (417) 667-2267. **$33.** 1501 N Osage Blvd 64772. N-bnd: From Jct of I-49 (US 71) & US 54, N 1 mi on US-71 to Exit 103 (Highland Av), W (over hwy) to N Osage/W Outer Rd, S 0.5 mi (R); or S-Bnd: From Jct 71 & Exit 103 (Highland Ave), W 100 yds on Highland Ave to W Outer Rd, S 0.5 mi (R) 🛥 🛒

OAK GROVE (JACKSON COUNTY) — KOA KANSAS CITY EAST. (816) 690-6660. **$33-$40.** 303 NE 3rd St 64075. From Jct of I-70 & CR-H (Oak Grove exit 28), N 200 ft on CR-H to 3rd St, E 200 ft (R) 🛥

OSAGE BEACH — OSAGE BEACH RV PARK. (573) 348-3445. **$29-$33.** 3949 Campground Ln 65065. From Jct US 54 Expressway & SR-42/Osage Beach Parkway North Exit: W (over hwy) to SR-42,then E 1/4 mi on watch for sign on right) to Access Road (watch for sign on R), then S 1/10 mi to office (R) 🏍 🛥 🛒

OWENSVILLE — LOST VALLEY LAKE RESORT. (573) 764-2129. **Call for rates.** 2334 Hwy Zz 65066. From jct I-44 & US 50 (Exit 247): Go W 25 mi on US 50, then N 3-1/2 mi on Hwy Y, then W 6 mi on Hwy ZZ (R).

PLATTE CITY — BASSWOOD RESORT. 🄰🄰🄰 (800) 242-2775. **$37-$51.** 15880 Interurban Rd 64079. From Jct of I-29 & SR-92 (exit 18), E 3.4 mi on SR-92 to N Winan Rd, N 1.7 mi to Interurban Rd, NW 0.3 mi (L) 🛥 🛒

SPRINGFIELD — SPRINGFIELD/RT 66 KOA. (417) 831-3645. **$35-$65.** 5775 W Farm Rd 140 65802. From Jct of I-44 & Exit 70 (MM), S 0.1 mi on CR-MM to Farm Road 140, E 1 mi (L); or N-bnd: From Jct of Hwy 65 & Hwy 60, W 12 mi on Hwy 60 to Hwy 360, 2 mi on Hwy 360 to MM Exit, N 2 mi to Farm Road-140, E 1 mi (L) 🛥

STRAFFORD — PARADISE IN THE WOODS RV PARK & CAMPGROUND. (417) 859-2175. **$25.** 2481 Grier Branch Rd 65757. W-bnd: From Jct I-44 (Exit 96) & Evergreen: Go 2 1/4 mi W on N service rd, then 1 block N on Grier Branch Rd. Turn (R). E-bnd: From Jct I-84 (Exit 88), turn L, returning over Hwy 44, then R (East) on Evergreen Rd 4.5 mi, L on Grier Branch Rd. 🛥 🛒

WEST PLAINS — CHIPMUNK CROSSING RV PARK. (417) 256-0788. **$28-$32. (no credit cards).** 11738 State Rte 17 65775. From Jct of US-63 & SR-17 (S of West Plains), S 8 mi on SR-17 (L) 🛥 🛒

Montana

BILLINGS — YELLOWSTONE RIVER RV PARK & CAMPGROUND. (406) 259-0878. **$39-$68.** 309 Garden Ave. 59101. W-bnd: From Jct I-90 & Hwy 3 / 27th St (exit 450): Go 1/8 mi S on 27th St, then 1/4 mi SW on Garden Ave (L) or E-bnd: From Jct I-90 & S Billings Blvd (exit 447): Go 1/4 mi S on S Billings Blvd, then 3 mi E on S Frontage Rd/Garden Ave (R) 🛥 🛒

MISSOULA — JELLYSTONE RV PARK. (800) 318-9644. **$36-$42.** 9900 Jellystone Dr 59808. From Jct of I-90 & US 93 (exit 96): Go 1/2 mi N on US 93 (L) 🛥 🛒

POLSON — EAGLE NEST RV RESORT. (406) 883-5904. **$31-$48.** 35800 Eagle Nest Dr (Mt 35) 59860. From Jct US 93 & Hwy 35: Go 1/4 mi E on Hwy 35 (L) 🛥 🛒

POLSON — **POLSON MOTORCOACH & RV RESORT.** (406) 883-2333. **$45-$95.** 200 Irvine Flats Rd 59860. From Jct US 93 & Hwy 35 : Go 3 mi N on US 93, then 1/4 mi W on Irvine Flats Rd (R) (MP-62) 🏍 ➰ ⊠

POLSON — **POLSON/FLATHEAD LAKE KOA.** (406) 883-2151. **$27-$58.** 200 Irvine Flats Rd 59860. From Jct US 93 & Hwy 35 : Go 3 mi N on US 93, then 1/4 mi W on Irvine Flats Rd (R) (MP-62) 🏍 ➰ ⊠

ST. REGIS — **NUGGET RV PARK.** (888) 800-0125. **$36-$38.** 1037 Old Highway 10 East 59866. From Jct I-90 & Hwy 135 (St Regis, exit 33): Go 1/8 mi N on Hwy 135, then 1 mi E on Mullan Rd (L) ➰ ⊠

WEST YELLOWSTONE — **YELLOWSTONE PARK / WEST GATE KOA.** 🅐🅐🅐 (800) 562-7591. **$44-$77.** 3305 Targhee Pass/Us 20 59758. From Jct of US 20/191 & US 287: Go W 6 mi on US 20 (R) ➰ ⊠

Nebraska

DONIPHAN — **GRAND ISLAND KOA.** (800) 562-0850. **$30-$45.** 904 South B Rd 68832. From Jct of I-80 & NE 2 (exit 318): Go 1/4 mi S on unmarked rd (L) ➰ ⊠

GREENWOOD — **PINE GROVE RV PARK.** 🅐🅐🅐 (402) 944-3550. **$32-$48.** 23403 Mynard Rd 68366. W Bnd: From Jct I-80 & NE 63 (exit 420): Go 100 ft N on NE 63; then 1/2 mi W on Mynard Rd (L) or; E Bnd: From Jct I-80 & NE 63 (exit 420): On NE 63 go N over I-80; continue past ramps another 100'; then 1/2 mi W on Mynard Rd (L) ➰ ⊠

LINCOLN — **CAMP A WAY.** 🅐🅐🅐 (402) 476-2282. **$37-$48.** 200 Campers Circle 68521. From Jct of I-80 (Downtown Exit) (exit 401/401A) & I-80/Hwy 34 E: Go 1/4 mi S on Hwy 34 E, then 1/4 mi W on Superior St (exit 1), then 1/4 mi N on Campers Circle (E) ➰ ⊠

Nevada

CARSON CITY — **COMSTOCK COUNTRY RV RESORT.** 🅐🅐🅐 (775) 882-2445. **$34-$40.** 5400 S Carson St 89701. From Jct of US 395 (Carson St) & US 50 W: Go 1600 ft S on NV 395, then 750 ft W on Old Clear Creek Rd (R) ➰ ⊠

ELKO — **IRON HORSE RV RESORT.** 🅐🅐🅐 (800) 782-3556. **$32-$47.** 3400 East Idaho St 89801. From Jct of I-80 & Exit 303 (Jennings Way): Go 500 ft S on Jennings Way (not marked), then 1/4 mi E on East Idaho St (R) 🏍 ➰ ⊠

LAS VEGAS — **ARIZONA CHARLIE'S BOULDER RV PARK.** (800) 970-7280. **$32.** 4445 Boulder Hwy 89121. From Jct of I-515 (US 93/95 Expwy) & Boulder Hwy (exit 70): Go 2 mi S on Boulder Hwy (L) 🏍 ➰ ⊠

LAS VEGAS — **HITCHIN' POST RV PARK.** 🅐🅐🅐 (888) 433-8402. **$33.** 3640 Las Vegas Blvd North 89115. S-bnd: From Jct of I-15 & Exit 50 (Lamb): Go 2 mi S on Lamb, then 500 ft S on Las Vegas Blvd (L) or N-bnd: From Jct of I-15 & Craig Rd (exit 48): Go 1-1/4 mi E on Craig Rd, then 1 mi SE on Lamb Blvd, then 500 ft on Las Vegas Blvd (L) Note: Call for updated directions 🏍 ➰ ⊠

LAS VEGAS — **LAS VEGAS RV RESORT.** (702) 451-8005. **$29-$45.** 3890 S Nellis Blvd 89121. From Jct of Boulder Hwy & Nellis Blvd: Go 1/4 mi N on Nellis Blvd (R) 🏍 ➰ ⊠

LAS VEGAS — **LVM RESORT.** (866) 897-9300. **$59-$99.** 8175 Arville St 89139. From Jct of & I-215 & I-15: Go 3/4 mi S on I-15 (Exit 33), then 1 mi SW on Blue Diamond West (SR160), then 1/4 mi N on Arville St (L) 🏍 ➰ ⊠

LAS VEGAS — **OASIS LAS VEGAS RV RESORT.** (800) 566-4707. **$43-$70.** 2711 W Windmill Lane 89123. From Jct of I-15 & Blue Diamond Rd (Exit 33): Go 1/4 mi E on Blue Diamond Rd (R) Note: S-bnd, move immediately to right lane from exit ramp. 🏍 ➰ ⊠

MESQUITE — **DESERT SKIES RV RESORT.** (928) 347-6000. **$35-$49.** 350 E. Hwy 91 89024. From Jct of I-15 & Sandhill Blvd (Exit 122): Go 200 ft S on Sandhill Blvd, then 1-1/2 mi E on Hillside Dr (Hwy 91) (R) 🏍 ➰ ⊠

MINDEN — **SILVER CITY RV RESORT.** 🅐🅐🅐 (800) 997-6393. **$40.** 3165 Hwy 395 N 89423. From Jct of NV 88 & US 395: Go 7-1/4 mi N on US 395 (R) ➰ ⊠

PAHRUMP — **LAKESIDE CASINO & RV RESORT.** (888) 558-5253. **$30-$50.** 5870 S Homestead Rd 89048. From Jct of Hwy 160 & Homestead Rd (S end of town): Go S 3-3/4 mi on Homestead Rd, then W 100 ft on Thousandaire Rd (R) 🏍 ➰ ⊠

PAHRUMP — **NEVADA TREASURE RV RESORT.** 🅐🅐🅐 (800) 429-6665. **$40-$60.** 301 West Leslie St. 89060. From Jct of SR-372 & SR-160: Go N 7-1/2 mi on SR-160, then go 500 ft on Leslie St (L) 🏍 ➰ ⊠

PAHRUMP — **PREFERRED RV RESORT.** (800) 445-7840. **$33.** 1801 E Crawford Way 89048. From Jct of SR-160 & Crawford Way: Go NE 1/4 mi on Crawford Way (R). 🏍 ➰ ⊠

PAHRUMP — **WINE RIDGE RV RESORT & COTTAGES.** (775) 751-7805. **$23.** 3800 Winery Road 89048. From Jct of SR-160 & Winery Rd: Go 3/4 mi on Winery Rd (L) 🏍 ➰ ⊠

RENO — **BORDERTOWN CASINO & RV RESORT.** (800) 218-9339. **$31-$38.** 19575 Hwy 395 N 89508. From Jct of US-395 & Exit 83: Go 1/4 mi NW on Frontage Rd (L) 🏍

RENO — **SHAMROCK RV PARK.** (775) 329-5222. **$33-$37.** 260 Parr Blvd 89512. From Jct of I-80 & US-395 (Exit 15): Go 3 mi N on US-395 (Exit 71), then 1 mi W on Parr Blvd (L) 🏍 ➰

SPARKS — **SPARKS MARINA RV PARK.** 🅐🅐🅐 (775) 851-8888. **$23-$49.** 1200 E Lincoln Way 89434. From Jct of I-80 & Exit 20 (Sparks Blvd): Go 1/4 min N on Sparks Blvd, then 1/2 mi W on E Lincoln Way (R) 🏍 ➰ ⊠

SPARKS — **VICTORIAN RV PARK.** (800) 955-6405. **$34-$42.** 205 Nichols Blvd 89431. From Jct of Hwy 395 & I-80 (Exit 19): Go 1/4 mi N on McCarren Blvd, then 1/4 mi W on Nichols Blvd (L) 🏍 ➰ ⊠

VERDI — **GOLD RANCH CASINO & RV RESORT.** 🅐🅐🅐 (877) 914-6789. **$29-$35.** 320 Gold Ranch Road 89439. From Jct of I-80 & NV 40 (Gold Ranch Rd): Go 500 ft S on Gold Ranch Rd (R) 🏍 ➰

WINNEMUCCA — **HI-DESERT RV.** 🅐🅐🅐 (775) 623-4513. **$19-$38.** 5575 E Winnemucca Blvd 89445. From Jct of I-80 & Exit 180 (East Winnemucca Blvd): Go 3/4 mi E on East Winnemucca Blvd (R) ➰ ⊠

New Hampshire

ASHLAND — AMES BROOK CAMPGROUND. **AAA** (603) 968-7998. **$37-$43.** 104 Winona Rd 03217. From Jct of I-93 & Exit 24 (Rtes 3 & 25), S 0.75 mi on Rte 3 & 25 to Rte 132, S 0.25 mi to Winona Rd, S 0.5 mi (R) (Avoid S end of Winona Rd, low bridge) 🏊 ✕

FREEDOM — DANFORTH BAY CAMPING & RV RESORT. (603) 539-2069. **$44-$80.** 196 Shawtown Rd 03836. From Jct of Rte 16 & Rte 41 (in West Ossipee), E 0.5 mi on Rte 41 to Ossipee Lake Rd, SE 4.8 mi to Shawtown Rd, NE 1 mi (R) 🏊 ✕

FREEDOM — THE BLUFFS RV RESORT. (603) 539-2069. **$46-$54.** 196 Shawtown Rd 03836. From Jct of Rte 16 & Rte 41 (in West Ossipee), E 0.5 mi on Rte 41 to Ossipee Lake Rd, SE 4.8 mi to Shawtown Rd, NE 1 mi (R). One week minimum stay, age 50 and older. 🎿 🏊 ✕

LANCASTER — MOUNTAIN LAKE CAMPGROUND RV PARK & LOG CABINS. (603) 788-4509. **$49-$63.** 485 Prospect St 03584. From Jct of US-3 & US-2 (in town), S 4.5 mi on US-3 (R) 🏊 ✕

MEREDITH — HARBOR HILL CAMPING AREA. (603) 279-6910. **$42-$45.** 189 Nh Rte 25 03253. From Jct of US-3 & Rte 25, NE 1.5 mi on Rte 25 (R); or From Jct of I-93 & Rte 104 (exit 23), E 11 mi on Rte 104 to Rte 3, N 1 mi to Rte 25, NE 1.5 mi (R) 🏊 ✕

MEREDITH — MEREDITH WOODS 4 SEASON CAMPING AREA. (603) 279-5449. **$32-$50.** 551 Nh Rte 104 03253. From Jct of I-93 & Rte 104 (exit 23), E 3 mi on Rte 104 (L) 🏊 ✕

NEW BOSTON — FRIENDLY BEAVER CAMPGROUND. (603) 487-5570. **$40-$46.** 98 Cochran Hill Rd 03070. From Jct of Rtes 77 & 136 & 13 (in town), S 100 ft on Rte 13 to Old Coach Rd, W 2 mi (R) 🏊 ✕

STRAFFORD — CROWN POINT CAMPGROUND. **AAA** (603) 332-0405. **$49-$68.** 79 First Crown Point Rd 03884. From Jct of Spaulding Tpke exit 14 & Ten Rod Road, S 0.2 mi to Rte 11/Main St, E 0.1 mi to Twombly St, SW 0.3 mi to Rte 202A, W 4 mi to First Crown Point Rd, N 0.3 mi (L) 🏊 ✕

TAMWORTH — CHOCORUA CAMPING VILLAGE KOA. (888) 237-8642. **$40-$84.** 893 White Mountain Hwy 03886. From Northern Jct of Hwy 16 & Rte 25W, N 3 mi on Hwy 16 (R). Do not use GPS. Call for directions. 🏊 ✕

WEARE — COLD SPRINGS CAMP RESORT. (603) 529-2528. **$58-$62.** 62 Barnard Hill Rd 03281. From S Jct of I-93 & I-293, W 3 mi on I-293 to Rte 101, W 1.5 mi to Rte 114, NW 12 mi to Barnard Hill Rd, N 0.2 mi (R) 🏊 ✕

New Jersey

CAPE MAY — HOLLY SHORES CAMPGROUND & RV RESORT. **AAA** (877) 494-6559. **$43-$76.** 491 Rte 9 08204. From Jct of Garden State Pkwy & SR-47 (exit 4A), W 0.5 mi on SR-47 to US-9, S 1 mi (L) 🏊 ✕

CAPE MAY — SEASHORE CAMPSITES & RV RESORT. **AAA** (888) 478-8799. **$30-$70.** 720 Seashore Rd 08204. From Jct of Garden State Pkwy & SR-47 (exit 4A), N 0.9 mi on SR-47 to SR-626 (Railroad Ave), S 2.7 mi (R); or From Cape May-Lewes Ferry, E 1.9 mi on US-9N to SR-626 N (Seashore Rd), N 1.2 mi (L) 🏊 ✕

CAPE MAY COURT HOUSE — BIG TIMBER LAKE RV AND CAMPING RESORT. **AAA** (888) 306-2853. **$49-$80.** 116 Swainton-Goshen Rd 08210. From Jct of Garden State Pkwy & Rte 601 (exit 13), W 0.5 mi on Rte 601 to US-9, S 0.8 mi to CR-646, W 1 mi (R); or From Dennisville, S 1.7 mi on SR-47 to Rte 657, S 3 mi to Rte 646, E 0.8 mi (L) 🏊 ✕

CAPE MAY COURT HOUSE — DRIFTWOOD TOO CAMPING RESORT. (609) 624-9015. **$62-$68.** 1142 Rte 83 08210. From Jct of Garden State Pkwy & CR-625 (exit 17), W 0.25 mi on CR-625 to US-9, S 3 mi to SR-83, W 0.5 mi (R) 🏊 ✕

CLARKSBORO — TIMBERLANE CAMPGROUND. **AAA** (856) 423-6677. **$46-$49.** 117 Timberlane Rd 08020. S-bnd: From Jct of I-295 & Rte 667 (Exit 18), SE 1 mi on Rte 667 to Friendship Rd, W 0.3 mi to Timber Ln, N 200 ft (L); or N-bnd: From Jct of I-295 & Timber Lane Rd (Exit 18), E 0.8 mi (R) 🏊 ✕

CLERMONT — DRIFTWOOD CAMPING RESORT. (888) 363-2901. **$62-$67.** 1955 Rte 9 North 08210. From Jct of US 9 & SR-83, S 0.1 mi on US 9 (R) 🏊 ✕

DOROTHY — COUNTRY OAKS CAMPGROUND. (609) 476-2143. **$50-$55.** 13 S Jersey Ave 08317. From Jct of Rte 50 & Rte 40 (in May's Landing), S 1.1 mi on Rte 50 to Rte 669 (11th Ave), SW 5.5 mi to S Jersey (turn before RR tracks), NW 1.2 mi (R) 🏊 ✕

GALLOWAY — POMONA RV PARK. (609) 965-2123. **$50-$55.** 536 S. Pomona Rd 08205. S-bnd: From Jct of Garden State Pkwy & CR-575 (exit 44), S 5 mi on CR-575 (L) E-bnd: From Jct of Atlantic City Expressway & CR-575 (exit 12), N 3 mi on CR 575 (R) 🏊 ✕

GALLOWAY — SHADY PINES CAMPING RESORT. (609) 652-1516. **$42.** 443 S 6th Ave 08205. From Jct of US-9 & US-30, W 1.2 mi on US-30 to 6th Ave, N 1.5 mi (L) 🎿 🏊 ✕

MARMORA — WHIPPOORWILL CAMPGROUND. (609) 390-3458. **$60.** 810 S Shore Rd 08223. From Jct of Garden State Pkwy & CR-623 (Exit 25), W 0.25 mi on CR-623 to US 9, S 1.5 mi (R) 🏊 ✕

OCEAN VIEW — OCEAN VIEW RESORT CAMPGROUND. **AAA** (609) 624-1675. **$39-$88.** 2555 Rte 9 08230. From Jct of Garden State Pkwy & CR-625 (exit 17), W 0.4 mi on CR-625 to US-9, N 0.3 mi (L) 🏊 ✕

TUCKERTON — ATLANTIC CITY NORTH FAMILY CAMPGROUND. **AAA** (609) 296-9163. **$60-$68.** 450 Ishmael Rd 08087. From Jct of Garden State Pkwy & CR-539 (exit 58), E 0.1 mi on CR-539 to Poormans Pkwy(frontage rd), S 4.2 mi to Stage Rd, E 0.7 mi to access rd, SW 0.5 mi (E) 🏊 ✕

WEST CREEK — SEA PIRATE CAMPGROUND. **AAA** (609) 296-7400. **$63-$66.** 148 Main St. 08092. From Jct of Garden State Pkwy & SR-72 (exit 63), SE 1 mi on SR-72 to US-9, S 4.9 mi (L) 🏊 ✕

WILLIAMSTOWN — HOSPITALITY CREEK CAMPGROUND. (856) 629-5140. **$56-$75.** 117 Coles Mill Rd 08094. From Jct of Atlantic City Expwy & Rte 54 (exit 28), S 1.9 mi on Rte 54 to Rte 332, NW 4.5 mi to Rte 538 (Coles Mill Rd), W 0.2 mi (R) 🏊 ✕

New Mexico

CARLSBAD — CARLSBAD KOA. (575) 457-2000. **$48-$68.** # 2 Manthei Rd 88220. From Carlsbad: Go 15 mi N on Hwy 285 to Skyward Dr, (between MP 51 & MP 52) on Hwy 285, then 1/3 mi E (R) 🏊 ✕

ELEPHANT BUTTE — **ELEPHANT BUTTE LAKE RV RESORT.** (AAA) (575) 744-5996. **$34-$44.** 402 Hwy 195 87935. From Jct of I-25 & Hwy 181 (exit 83), SE 0.1 mi on Hwy 181 to Hwy 195 (follow signs for Elephant Butte State Park), SE 3.25 mi (R) 🏊 🚣 ⌧

GALLUP — **USA RV PARK.** (505) 863-5021. **$30-$36.** 2925 W Hwy 66 87301. From jct of I-40 & exit 16 (Historic Route 66/W US Hwy 66/Hwy 118/Bus Loop 40): Go 1 mi E on W US Hwy 66/Hwy 118/Bus Loop 40 (R) (don't rely solely on GPS) 🚣 ⌧

RIO RANCHO — **STAGECOACH STOP RV PARK.** (505) 867-1000. **$39-$44.** 3650 State Hwy 528 Ne 87144. From jct of I-25 & Exit 242 (Hwy 550): Go W 2.4mi on Hwy 550 to Hwy 528, S 0.6 mi to Montoya, E 0.1 mi on Montoya to Christopher Way (behind McDonalds),N 0.1 mi to Gabby Way, E 0.1 mi (R) 🏊 🚣 ⌧

SANTA FE — **THE TRAILER RANCH RV RESORT & 55+ COMMUNITY.** (505) 471-9970. **$37-$45.** 3471 Cerrillos Rd 87507. From Jct of I-25 & Cerrillos Rd (exit 278 or 278B): Go 3-1/2 mi NE on Cerrillos Rd (L) or (S bnd) From (North of Santa Fe) US-285/St Francis Dr to Cerrillos Rd, then 3-1/2 mi SW (R) 🏊 🚣

New York

BAINBRIDGE — **TALL PINES CAMPGROUND & CANOEING.** (607) 563-8271. **$32-$52.** Anderson Lane 13733. From Jct of I-88 & SR-8 (exit 9), N 3.5 mi on SR 8 to CR 35 (at Blinker), E 0.1 mi (L) (For GPS: Anderson Ln, Bainbridge NY 13733) 🚣 ⌧

BATH — **HICKORY HILL FAMILY CAMPING RESORT.** (607) 776-4345. **$44-$68.** 7531 County Route 13 14810. From Jct of I-86 & SR-54 (Exit 38), N 1.4 mi on SR-54 to the Y intersection, left at Y, on to Haverling St. (CR-13), N 2.0 mi (L). Note: Minimum 3 day stay on holiday weekends 🚣 ⌧

BYRON — **SOUTHWOODS RV RESORT.** (585) 548-9002. **$32-$40.** 6749 Townline Rd 14422. W-bnd: From Jct of I-90 & SR-19 (exit 47), N 3.2 mi on SR-19 to SR-262, W 4.6 mi (L); or E bnd: From Jct of I-90 & SR-98 (exit 48), N 3.5 mi on SR-98 to SR-262, E 7.8 mi (R) Note: Min 3 day stay on holiday weekends 🚣 ⌧

CANANDAIGUA — **KOA CANANDAIGUA/ROCHESTER KAMPGROUND.** (585) 398-3582. **$38-$48.** 5374 Canandaigua Farmington Town Line Rd 14425. From Jct of I-90 & SR-332 (exit 44), SE 3 mi on SR-332 to Canandaigua/Farmington Townline Rd, E 1.3 mi (L); or From Jct of I-90 & SR-21 (exit 43) S on SR 21, 0.2 mi, NW 2.5 mi on SR-96 to CR-28, S 1.5 mi to Townline Rd, W 1.5 mi (R) 🚣 ⌧

CLAYTON — **MERRY KNOLL 1000 ISLANDS CAMPGROUND.** (315) 686-3055. **$34-$41. (no credit cards).** 38115 Rt 12e 13624. From Jct of SR-12 & SR-12E, S 2.5 mi on SR-12E (R) 🚣 ⌧

CONESUS — **CONESUS LAKE CAMPGROUND.** (585) 346-CAMP. **$38-$43.** 5609 E Lake Rd 14435. From Jct of I-390 & SR-20A (exit 8), E 2 mi on SR-20A to East Lake Rd (traffic light), S 6 mi (L). Note: 3 day minimum stay on holiday weekends, maximum length 35 ft. 🚣 ⌧

COOPERSTOWN — **COOPERSTOWN-SHADOW BROOK CAMPGROUND.** (607) 264-8431. **$35-$51.** 2149 County Hwy 31 13326. From Jct of SR-80E & Main St, SE 0.75 mi on Main St (becomes CR-31), N 10 mi on CR-31 (L); or From Jct of US-20 & CR-31 (in E Springfield), S 1 mi on CR-31 (R) 🚣 ⌧

COPAKE — **COPAKE KOA.** (518) 329-2811. **$56-$76.** 2236 County Route 7 12516. From Jct of SR-22 & SR-23, S 2.9 mi on SR-22 to Farm Rd (CR-7/7A), SW 3 mi (L) 🚣 ⌧

DEWITTVILLE — **CHAUTAUQUA LAKE KOA.** (716) 386-3804. **$38-$60.** 5652 Thum Rd 14728. From Jct of I-86/SR-17 & SR-430 (exit 10), W 6 mi on SR-430 to Thum Rd, E 0.5 mi (L) Note: Min 3 day stay on holiday weekends 🚣 ⌧

FLORIDA — **BLACK BEAR CAMPGROUND INC.** (845) 651-7717. **$60-$70.** 197 Wheeler Rd 10921. From Jct of SR-17 & SR-94 (exit 126), SW 4.7 mi on SR-94 to Bridge St, W 2 blks to CR 41, 1.5 mi (L) 🏊 🚣 ⌧

FRANKLINVILLE — **TRIPLE R CAMPING RESORT & TRAILER SALES.** (716) 676-3856. **$44.** 3491 Bryant Hill Rd 14737. S-bnd: From Jct of SR-98 & SR-16, S 1.9 mi on SR-16 to Elm St (traffic light), W 1.5 mi to Bryant Hill Rd, W 0.3 mi (L); or N-bnd: From Jct of I-86 (SR-17) & SR-16 (Exit 27), N 12 mi on SR-16 to Elm St (traffic light), W 1.5 mi to Bryant Hill Rd, W 0.3 mi (L) 🚣 ⌧

GARDINER — **YOGI BEAR'S JELLYSTONE PARK AT LAZY RIVER.** (845) 255-5193. **$42-$70.** 50 Bevier Rd 12525. From Jct of US-44/55 & SR-32, W 4 mi on US-44/55 to Albany Post Rd, S 0.2 mi (across bridge) to Bevier Rd, E 0.5 mi (L) 🚣 ⌧

GRAND ISLAND — **BRANCHES OF NIAGARA CAMPGROUND & RESORT.** (877) 321-2267. **$48-$99.** 2659 Whitehaven Rd 14072. From Jct of I-190 & Whitehaven Rd (Exit 19), E 0.75 mi on Whitehaven Rd (R) 🚣 ⌧

GREENFIELD PARK — **JELLYSTONE PARK AT BIRCHWOOD ACRES.** (888) 726-4073. **$70-$75.** 85 Martinfeld Road 12435. From Jct of SR-209 & SR-52 (in Ellenville), W 8.5 mi on SR-52 to Martinfeld Rd, S 1 mi (L) 🚣 ⌧

GREENFIELD PARK — **SKYWAY CAMPING RESORT INC.** (800) 447-5992. **$65.** 99 Mountaindale Rd. 12435. From Jct of SR-52 & US-209 (in Ellenville), W 5 mi on SR-52 to Mountaindale Rd., SW 1.2 mi (L) 🚣 ⌧

HARPURSVILLE — **BELDEN HILL CAMPGROUND LLC.** (607) 693-1645. **$30-$38.** 1843 State Rt 7 13787. From Jct of I-88 & Martin Hill Rd (exit 5), N 0.6 mi on Martin Hill Rd to SR-7, E 0.30 mi (L) ⌧

HENDERSON — **KOA 1000 ISLANDS AT ASSOCIATION ISLAND.** (800) 393-4189. **$35-$80.** 15530 Snowshoe Rd 13650. From Jct of I-81 & Rt 178 (Exit 41), W 9 mi on Rt 178 to Snowshoe Rd, NW 2.5 mi to end, cross causeway to island (E) CAUTION: Registration and security gate closed at 8:00pm. Note: Min 3 day stay on holiday weekends 🚣 ⌧

HERKIMER — **HERKIMER DIAMOND CAMPGROUND KOA.** (315) 891-7355. **$34-$69.** 4626 Sr 28n 13350. From Jct of I-90 & SR-28 (exit 30), N 8.7 mi on SR-28 (R) 🚣 ⌧

LAKE GEORGE — **KING PHILLIPS CAMPGROUND.** (518) 668-5763. **$40-$57.** 14 Bloody Pond Rd 12845. From Jct of I-87 & US-9N (exit 21), N 0.2 mi on US-9N to US-9, S 0.8 mi to Bloody Pond Rd, E 0.1 mi (R) 🚣 ⌧

LAKE GEORGE — **LAKE GEORGE RV PARK.** (AAA) (518) 792-3775. **$62-$89.** 74 Sr-149 12845. From Jct of I-87 & US-9 (exit 20), N 0.5 mi on US-9 to SR-149, E 0.5 mi (R) Note: 3 night minimum on holiday weekends 🏊 🚣 ⌧

MILFORD — HARTWICK HIGHLANDS CAMPGROUND. (607) 547-1996. **$47.** 131 Burke Hill Rd 13807. S-bnd: From Jct of SR-28 & SR-80 (in Cooperstown), S 4 mi on SR-28 to Seminary Rd, NW 1.5 mi (R); or N-bnd: From Jct of I-88 & SR-28 (Exit 17), N 12.5 mi on SR-28 to Seminary Rd, NW 1.5 mi (R). Do not use GPS ▣ ▣

MOUNT VISION — MEADOW-VALE CAMPSITES. (607) 293-8802. **$38-$42.** 505 Gilbert Lake Rd 13810. From Jct of I 88 & SR 205 (exit 13), N 11 mi on SR 205 to CR 11B in Mt Vision, W 0.25 mi on CR 11B and then follow campground signs for 6 mi (R) ▣ ▣

NORTH HUDSON — YOGI BEAR'S JELLYSTONE PARK AT PARADISE PINES CAMPING RESORT. (518) 532-7493. **$52-$63.** 4035 Blue Ridge Rd 12855. From Jct of I-87 & Blue Ridge Rd (exit 29), E 0.1 mi on Blue Ridge Rd (L) ▣ ▣

NORTH JAVA — JELLYSTONE PARK OF WESTERN NEW YORK. ▣ (877) 469-7590. **$32-$94.** 5204 Youngers Rd 14113. From Jct of SR-78/SR-98 & Peedee Rd, E 1.6 mi on Peedee Rd to Youngers Rd, S 0.7 mi (R) Note: Min 3 day min. stay on holiday weekends. ▣ ▣

PHELPS — JUNIUS PONDS CABINS & CAMPGROUND LLC. (315) 781-5120. **$34-$37.** 1475 W Townline Rd 14532. From Jct of I-90 & SR-318 (Exit 42), E 0.7 mi on SR-318 to Townline Rd, N 0.3 mi (E).Caution: Follow these directions, GPS not always reliable. ▣ ▣

PLATTEKILL — NEW YORK CITY NORTH/NEWBURGH KOA. (845) 564-2836. **$49-$67.** 119 Freetown Highway 12568. From Jct of I-84 & SR-300 (Exit 7B), or Jct of I-87 & SR-300 (Exit 17), N 3 mi on SR-300 to SR-32, N 6 mi to Freetown Hwy, NE 0.5 mi (L) ▣ ▣

RANDOLPH — POPE HAVEN CAMPGROUND. (716) 358-4900. **$28-$42.** 11948 Pope Rd 14772. From Jct of I-86 & SR 394 (Main St) (exit 16), E 1.4 mi (thru town) on SR-394 (Main St.) to SR-241, N 3.5 mi to Pope Rd, E 100 ft (L) ▣ ▣

RHINEBECK — INTERLAKE RV PARK & SALES. (845) 266-5387. **$47-$55.** 428 Lake Dr 12572. From Jct of US 9 & SR-9G (N of town), S 3.5 mi on SR-9G to Slate Quarry Rd (CR-19), E 3.5 mi on CR-19 to Lake Dr, S 0.3 mi (L) ▣ ▣

SPRINGWATER — HOLIDAY HILL CAMPGROUND. (800) 719-2267. **$40-$45.** 7818 Marvin Hill Rd 14560. From Jct of I-390 & Rte 15 (exit 3) N 3.9 mi to Walker Rd, E 0.6 mi to Strutt St, N 3.6 mi, follow signs (L) Caution: if towing do not use Marvin Hill Rd. Enter on (L) ▣ ▣

STOW — CAMP CHAUTAUQUA CAMPING RESORT. (716) 789-3435. **$30-$60.** 3900 W. Lake Rd 14785. From Jct of I-86/SR-17 & SR-394 (exit 8), N 2 mi on SR-394 (R) ▣ ▣

VERONA — THE VILLAGES AT TURNING STONE. (315) 361-7275. **$40-$55.** 5065 Sr 365 13478. From Jct of I-90 (exit 33) & SR-365, W 1 mi on SR-365 (R) ▣ ▣ ▣

WATKINS GLEN — WATKINS GLEN/CORNING KOA CAMPING RESORT. (800) 562-7430. **$52-$74.** 1710 Route 414 S 14891. From Jct of I-86 (SR-17) & SR-414 (Exit 46), N 15.3 mi on SR-414 (R). GPS use 1710 KOA Dr ▣ ▣

WILMINGTON — NORTH POLE RESORTS. ▣ (518) 946-7733. **$46-$48.** 5644 Rte 86 12997. N-bnd: From Jct of I-87 & SR-73 (Exit 30), NW 16 mi on SR-73 to SR-9N, 10 mi N on SR-9N to SR-86, W 5 mi on SR-86 to Jct 431, continue on SR-86 W 0.2 mi (L); or S-bnd: From Jct of I-87 & SR-9N (Exit 34), S 16 mi on SR-9N to SR-86, W 5 mi on SR-86 to Jct 431, continue on SR-86 W 0.2 mi (L) ▣ ▣

WINDSOR — LAKESIDE CAMPGROUND. ▣ (607) 655-2694. **$40-$43.** 336 Hargrave Rd 13865. From Jct of I-86 (Rt 17) & SR-79 (Exit 79), S 4 mi on SR-79 to Edson Rd, W 3.5 mi (L); or From Jct of I-81 & PA-171 (PA Exit 230), E 1.5 mi on PA-171 to PA-1027, NE 4.5 mi to W Judd Rd, NW 0.6 mi to Hargrave Rd, NE 0.8 mi (R). Note: Re GPS; call ahead ▣

North Carolina

ASHEBORO — ZOOLAND FAMILY CAMPGROUND, LLC. (336) 381-3422. **$27-$32.** 3671 Pisgah Covered Bridge Rd 27205. From Jct of US 64 & US 220 (Bypass), S 4.7 mi on US 220 (Bypass) to exit 68 (Ulah-Troy), W 1.2 mi on Dawson-Miller Rd to Pisgah Covered Bridge Rd, SW 1.4 mi (L) ▣ ▣

ASHEVILLE — ASHEVILLE BEAR CREEK RV PARK. ▣ (800) 833-0798. **$40-$45.** 81 S Bear Creek Rd 28806. W-bnd: From Jct of I-40 & NC-191 (exit 47), cross NC-191 to S Bear Creek Rd, W 0.6 mi (L); or E-bnd: From Jct of I-40 & NC-191 (exit 47), N 0.1 mi on NC-191 to S Bear Creek Rd, W 0.6 mi (L); or From Jct of I-26 & NC-191 (exit 31), N 1.1 mi on NC-191 to S Bear Creek Rd, W 0.6 mi (L) ▣ ▣ ▣

CANDLER — ASHEVILLE-WEST KOA. (800) 562-9015. **$35-$43.** 309 Wiggins Rd 28715. From Jct of I-40 & US-19/23 (exit 37), S 200 ft on unmarked rd to US-19/23, W 0.4 mi to Wiggins Rd, N 0.2 mi (R) ▣ ▣

CEDAR MOUNTAIN — BLACK FOREST FAMILY CAMPING RESORT. (828) 884-2267. **$33-$42.** 280 Summer Rd 28718. N-bnd: From Jct of I-85 & Exit 48/Hwy 276, NW 36.3 mi on Hwy 276 to Caesars Head St Pk, con't 3 mi to Summer Rd, E 0.4 mi (R); or S-bnd: From Jct of US-64 & US-276 (in downtown Brevard), SE 12.6 mi on US-276 to Summer Rd, E 0.4 mi (R) ▣ ▣

CHEROKEE — HAPPY HOLIDAY CAMPGROUND. (828) 497-9204. **$37-$49.** 1553 Wolfetown Rd (Us-19) 28719. From W Jct of US 74 & US 441N, N 3.8 mi on US 441N to Bus-441N, NE 0.8 mi to US 19N, N 3.3 mi (L); or From Jct of Blue Ridge Pkwy (MP-455.5) & US 19, SW 7.6 mi on US 19S (R) ▣ ▣

CHEROKEE — YOGI IN THE SMOKIES. ▣ (828) 497-9151. **$40-$68.** 317 Galamore Bridge Rd 28719. From W Jct of US-19 & US-441, N 2.2 mi on US-441 to Big Cove Rd, NE 7.7 mi (R) ▣ ▣

EMERALD ISLE — HOLIDAY TRAV-L-PARK RESORT FOR CAMPERS. (252) 354-2250. **$50-$110.** 9102 Coast Guard Rd 28594. From Jct of NC-24 & NC-58, S 2 mi on NC-58 to Coast Guard Rd (traffic light), S 200 ft (L) ▣ ▣

FLAT ROCK — LAKEWOOD RV RESORT. (888) 819-4200. **$40-$45.** 15 Timmie Lane 28731. From Jct of I-26 & Upward Rd (exit 53), E 0.2 mi on Upward Rd (unmarked) to Ballenger Rd (Left), NE 0.2 mi (Right) to main entrance (R) ▣ ▣ ▣

FLETCHER — RUTLEDGE LAKE RV RESORT. ▣ (828) 654-7873. **$40-$76.** 170 Rutledge Rd 28732. From Jct of I-26 & NC-280 (exit 40), E 1 mi on NC-280 (Airport Rd) to Rutledge Rd, S 1 mi (L) ▣ ▣

FOUR OAKS — RALEIGH OAKS RV RESORT & COT-TAGES. (919) 934-3181. **$30-$40.** 497 Us 701s 27524. From Jct of I-95 & US-701 (exit 90), S 0.4 mi on US-701 (L) 🛒 ⊠

FRANKLIN — THE GREAT OUTDOORS RV RESORT. (828) 349-0412. **$37-$40.** 321 Thumpers Trail 28734. N-bnd: From Jct of US 64 & US 441/23: Go N 6.2 mi on US 441 to Echo Valley Rd, W 200 ft (R); or S-bnd: From Jct of US 74 & US 23/441 (Exit 81A): Go S 13.8 mi on US 23/441 to Echo Valley Rd, W 200 ft (R) 🎿 🛒 ⊠

HENDERSONVILLE — JAYMAR TRAVEL PARK. (828) 685-3771. **$28-$33. (no credit cards).** 140 Jaymar Park Dr 28792. From Jct of I-26 & US-64 (exit 49A), E 2.7 mi on US-64 (L) 🎿 ⊠

LAKE TOXAWAY — MOUNTAIN FALLS LUXURY MOTOR-COACH RESORT. (828) 966-9350. **$55-$65.** 20 Resorts Blvd 28747. E-bnd: From Jct of US-64 & NC-281 (S), E 1.9 mi on US-64 (R); or W-bnd: From Jct of US-64 & NC-281, W 0.8 mi on US-64 (L) Class A Motorhomes only 🎿 🛒 ⊠

NEW BERN — NEW BERN KOA. (800) 562-3341. **$40-$75.** 1565 B St 28560. N-bnd: From SE Jct of US 70 & US 17 (exit 417), N 4.8 mi on US 17 (toward Washington) (L) 🛒 ⊠

NEWPORT — WHISPERING PINES RV PARK. (252) 726-4902. **$60.** 25 Whispering Pines 28570. From jct US 70 & Hwy 24: Go 8 mi W on Hwy 24 (L) 🎿 🛒 ⊠

ROANOKE RAPIDS — THE RV RESORT AT CAROLINA CROSSROADS. (252) 538-9776. **$30-$43.** 415 Wallace Fork Road 27870. From Jct of I-95 & Hwy 125 (exit 171), S 0.2 mi on Hwy 125 to Carolina Crossroads Blvd, (main entrance to Carolina Crossroads), N 0.9 mi (R) 🎿 🛒 ⊠

SHAWBORO — NORTH RIVER CAMPGROUND & RV PARK. (252) 336-4414. **$42.** 256 Garrington Island Rd 27973. From Jct of NC 168 & NC 34: Go SW 3.5 mi on SC 34 to Indian Town Rd, S 8.2 to Garrington Island Rd, E 1.5 mi (R) 🛒 ⊠

SHERRILLS FORD — LAKE NORMAN RV RESORT. (877) 489-6033. **$40-$68.** 6738 East Nc Hwy 150 28673. E-bnd: From Jct of I-85 & US 321 (Exit 17), N 14 mi on US 321 to NC 150 (Exit 24 Lincolnton), E 14 mi on NC 150 (L); or W-bnd: From Jct of I-77 & NC-150 (exit 36), W 10.3 mi on NC-150 (R) 🎿 ⊠

STATESVILLE — MIDWAY CAMPGROUND RESORT. (855) 882-7999. **$39-$49.** 114 Midway Dr 28625. E-bnd: From Jct of I-77 & I-40, E 9.6 mi on I-40 to Exit 162/Cool Springs/ US-64, W (right) 0.1 mi on US-64 to Campground Rd, E (left) 0.2 mi (L); or W-bnd: From Jct of I-40 & Exit 162/Cool Springs/US-64, W (left) 0.2 mi on US-64 to Campground Rd, E (left) 0.2 mi (L) 🛒 ⊠

STELLA — WHITE OAK SHORES CAMPING & RV RESORT. (252) 393-3244. **$55-$75.** 400 Wetherington Landing Rd 28582. From Jct of NC 24 & NC 58, NW 8.5 mi on NC 58 to Morristown Rd, S 1 mi to Wetherington Landing Rd, N 0.7 mi (L) 🛒 ⊠

SUNSET BEACH — BRUNSWICK BEACHES CAMPING RESORT. (855) 579-2267. **$40-$65.** 7200 Koa Dr 28468. From Jct of NC 17 & NC 904, E 0.7 mi on NC 904 (R) 🛒 ⊠

TABOR CITY — CARROLL WOODS RV PARK AT GRAPE-FULL SISTERS VINEYARD. (910) 653-5538. **$37-$45.** 4903 Ramsey Ford Rd 28463. From Jct of US 17 & SC 9, NW 12.4 mi on SC 9, to Camp Swamp Church Rd, N 2.3 mi to Dothan, E 0.2 mi to Ramsey Ford Rd, NE 2.5 mi (R) 🛒

TABOR CITY — YOGI BEARS JELLYSTONE PARK AT DADDY JOE'S. (877) 668-8586. **$28-$70.** 626 Richard Wright Rd 28463. From Jct of SC-9 & US 701, N 5.8 mi on US 701 (Bypass) to Richard Wright Rd, E 0.3 mi (R); or S-bnd: From Jct of I-95 & NC-74 (exit 14), E 26 mi on NC-74 to NC-410, SE 15 mi to NC-701, S 0.5 mi to Richard Wright Rd, E 0.3 mi (R) 🛒 ⊠

WADE — FAYETTEVILLE RV RESORT & COTTAGES. (910) 484-5500. **$46-$54.** 6250 Wade-Stedman Rd 28395. From Jct of I-95 & Exit 61 (Wade-Stedman Rd), E 0.3 mi on Wade-Stedman Rd (L) 🎿 🛒 ⊠

WASHINGTON — TRANTER'S CREEK RESORT & CAMP-GROUND. (252) 948-0850. **$35-$48.** 6573 Clarks Neck Rd 27889. From Jct of US-17 & US-264, W 1.5 mi on 264 to Clarks Neck Rd, SW 1.6 mi (R) 🛒 ⊠

WAVES — CAMP HATTERAS. (252) 987-2777. **$48-$102.** 24798 Hwy 12, Mile Post 40.5 27968. S-bnd: From Jct of US-158/64/264 & NC-12, S 24.7 mi on NC-12 (L); or N-bnd: From Jct of Ocracoke/ Hatteras Ferry & NC-12, N 34.3 mi on NC-12 (R) (Mile Post 40.5) 🛒 ⊠

WILMINGTON — WILMINGTON KOA. (888) 562-5699. **$49-$125.** 7415 Market St 28411. From Jct of I-40 & Hwy 17 (exit 416B), E 4.8 mi on Hwy 17 to 17 Bus South, S 2.3 mi (R) 🛒

North Dakota

BISMARCK — BISMARCK KOA KAMPGROUND. (701) 222-2662. **$39-$49.** 3720 Centennial Rd 58503. From Jct of I-94 & Bismarck Expressway (exit 161): Go 1 mi N on Centennial Rd (L) 🛒 ⊠

Ohio

BROOKVILLE — DAYTON TALL TIMBERS RESORT KOA. (800) 562-3317. **$45-$59.** 7796 Wellbaum Rd 45309. W-bnd: From W Jct of I-70 & SR-49 (Exit 24), N 0.5 mi on SR-49 to Pleasant Plain Rd, W 0.6 mi to Wellbaum Rd, S 0.2 mi (L); or E-bnd: From Jct of I-70 & Brookville/Salem Rd (Exit 24), SW 0.3 mi on Brookville/Salem Rd to Wellbaum Rd, N 0.3 mi (R) 🛒 ⊠

DELAWARE — CROSS CREEK CAMPING RESORT. 🅐🅐🅐 (800) 988-2267. **$42-$60.** 3190 S Old State Rd 43015. From Jct of I-71 (Exit 131) & SR-36/37: Go 3 mi W on SR-36/37, then 3 mi S on Lackey (Old State Rd). 🛒 ⊠

DUNDEE — EVERGREEN PARK RV RESORT. (888) 359-6429. **$53.** 16359 Dover Rd 44624. E-bnd: From Jct of US-250 & SR 241, S 0.4 mi on US-250 (R); or From Jct of I-77 & US-250, NW 12.6 mi on US-250 (L) 🛒 ⊠

EAST SPARTA — BEAR CREEK RESORT RANCH KOA. (330) 484-3901. **$44-$76.** 3232 Downing St Sw 44626. S-bnd: From Jct of I-77 & Fohl Rd (Exit 99), W 0.5 mi on Fohl Rd to Sherman Church Ave SW, S 2.4 mi to Haut St, E 1.2 mi (R); or N-bnd: From Jct of I-77 & Zoar Bolivar Rd (Exit 93), W 0.1 mi to CR-102, N 3 mi to Haut St, E 1 mi (R) 🛒 ⊠

GRANVILLE — LAZY RIVER AT GRANVILLE. 🅐🅐🅐 (740) 366-4385. **$35-$60.** 2340 Dry Creek Rd Ne 43023. From Jct of I-70 & SR-37 (exit 126), N 8 mi on SR-37 to SR-661 (Granville), N 4.5 mi to Dry Creek Rd, E 1.2 mi (R) 🛒 ⊠

LOUISVILLE — CUTTY'S SUNSET CAMPING RESORT. (800) 533-7965. **$43.** 8050 Edison St Ne 44641. From Jct of State Route, OH 43 & State Route OH 619, go E 5 mi on OH 619 (Maple St/Edison St) (R) 🛒 ⊠

NEW PARIS — **ARROWHEAD CAMPGROUND.** (937) 996-6203. **$49.** 1361 Thomas Rd 45347. From Jct of I-70 West & US 127 (exit 10): Go N 6.8 mi to OH 722,W 6.4 mi to OH 121, N 2 mi to Thomas Rd, W on Thomas 1mi (L) or From Jct of I-70 East & US 40(exit 156B INDIANA): Go E 1.1 mi on US 40 to OH 320 N 1.5 mi to OH 121, N 8 mi to Thomas Rd W 1 mi (L) 📖 ⊠

NEW PHILADELPHIA — **WOOD'S TALL TIMBER RESORT.** ⏺ (330) 602-4000. **$38-$46.** 1921 Tall Timber Rd. Ne 44663. From Jct of I-77 & US 250, SR 39 (Exit 81), E 5.8 mi on SR 39 (Exit 81) to Tall Timber Rd, N 1 mi (R) ⊠

OREGONIA — **OLIVE BRANCH CAMPGROUND.** (513) 932-CAMP. **$35-$40.** 6985 Wilmington Rd 45054. From Jct of I-71 & Wilmington Rd (exit 36), E 0.3 mi on Wilmington Rd (R) 📖 ⊠

SUNBURY — **AUTUMN LAKES.** (740) 625-6600. **$41-$60.** 8644 Porter Central Rd 43074. From Jct of I-71 & SR-37 (Exit 131 towards Sunbury), N 0.2 mi on Wilson Rd/SR-656, N 8.5 mi to Porter Central, S 0.2 mi (L) 📖 ⊠

VAN BUREN — **PLEASANT VIEW RECREATION.** (419) 299-3897. **$30-$38.** 12611 Allen Township Rd 218 45889. From Jct of I-75 & SR-613 (exit 164): Go E 0.7 mi on SR-613 to Twp Rt-218, S 0.5 mi (R) ⊠

WAYNESVILLE — **FRONTIER CAMPGROUND.** (937) 488-1127. **$32-$48.** 9580 Collett Rd 45068. From Jct of I-71 & SR-73 (Exit 45): Go E 0.2 mi on SR-73 to SR-380, N 6.6 mi to Roxanna-New Burlington Rd, W 2.5 mi to Pence Jones Rd, SW 0.7 mi to Collett Rd, W 0.2 mi (L) 📖 ⊠

ZANESVILLE — **WOLFIES CAMPGROUND.** (740) 454-0925. **$36.** 101 Buckeye Dr 43701. From Jct of I-70 & SR-146 W (Exit 155, Eastbound must turn left at bottom of the ramp onto Elberon), W 0.25 mi on SR-146, N 0.75 mi on OH-666, N 0.75 mi on Lewis Dr (OH-666), first right past Riverside Park, (Buckeye Dr), E 0.2 mi on Buckeye Dr (L) 📖 ⊠

Oklahoma

CHOCTAW — **OKLAHOMA CITY EAST KOA.** (800) 562-5076. **$44-$69.** 6200 S Choctaw Rd 73020. From jct of I-40 & Choctaw Rd (exit 166): Go N 1/2 mi on Choctaw Rd (R) 📖 ⊠

DURANT — **CHOCTAW CASINO RESORT KOA.** (800) 562-6073. **$40-$50.** 3650 Enterprise Blvd. 74701. From Jct of US-70 & US-69: Go S 3-1/2 mi on US-69 to Choctaw Road, then E 1/4 mi to Enterprise Dr, then N 1 block. (R) 📖 ⊠

EUFAULA — **LITTLE TURTLE RV & STORAGE.** (918) 618-2140. **$39.** 114161 Highway 69 74432. From jct of I-40 (exit 264) & US-69: Go S 6-1/2 mi on US-69, then E 300 yds OK-150/Texanna Rd, then S 300 yds Old US-69. (L)

GORE — **MARVAL RESORT.** ⏺ (800) 340-4280. **$37-$59.** 445104 E 1011 Rd 74435. From jct of I-40 & Hwy 100 (Exit 287): Go N 6 mi on Hwy 100 to 4450 Rd, then E 1/4 mi to 1011 Rd, then N 1/2 mi. (E) 📖 ⊠

THACKERVILLE — **WINSTAR RV PARK.** (580) 276-8900. **$40-$50.** 21902 Merle Wolfe Rd 73459. From Jct of I-35 (exit 1) & US-77 N: Go NE 1-1/2 mi on Casino Ave, then E 1/2 mi on Vegas Rd, then N 1 blk on Merle Wolfe Rd. (L) 📖 ⊠

WYANDOTTE — **WHISPERING WOODS RV PARK.** (918) 666-9200. **$10.** 70220 East Highway 60 74370. From jct OK-10 & US-60: Go NE 4-3/4 mi on US-60 (R) 📖

Oregon

ALBANY — **BLUE OX RV PARK.** (541) 926-2886. **$38-$41.** 4000 Blue Ox Dr Se 97322. From Jct of I-5 & Hwy 20 (exit 233): Go E 0.2 mi on Hwy 20 to Price Rd, then N 0.1 mi (R) Note: Use GPS coord. or call park for precise directions 📖 📖

BAKER CITY — **MT VIEW RV.** ⏺ (541) 523-4824. **$32-$34.** 2845 Hughes Ln 97814. From Jct of I-84 & Campbell St (exit 304), W 1.5 mi on Campbell St to 10th St, N 1 mi to Hughes Ln, E 1000 ft (R) 📖 ⊠

BEND — **BEND/SISTERS GARDEN RV RESORT.** (888) 503-3588. **$44-$65.** 67667 Hwy 20 97701. From Jct of US-20 & Hwy 126 (E edge of Sisters), SE 4 mi on US-20 (R) 📖 📖 ⊠

BEND — **CROWN VILLA RV RESORT.** (541) 388-1131. **$36-$84.** 60801 Brosterhous Rd 97702. N-bnd & S-bnd: From Jct of Business-97/3rd St & Murphy Rd (S of town), E 1.2 mi on Murphy Rd to Brosterhous Rd, S 0.1 mi (R) 📖 ⊠

CANYONVILLE — **SEVEN FEATHERS RV RESORT.** ⏺ (877) 839-3599. **$41-$49.** 325 Quintioosa Blvd 97417. S-Bnd: From Jct of I-5 (exit 99) to Quintioosa Blvd (R); N-Bnd: From Jct of I-5 & exit 99, Go N on Frontage Rd, then under freeway 0.2 mi to Quintioosa Blvd (L) 📖 📖 ⊠

COBURG — **PREMIER RV RESORTS - EUGENE.** (541) 686-3152. **$42-$49.** 33022 Van Duyn Rd 97408. From Jct of I-5 & Van Duyn Rd (exit 199): Go E 300 ft on Van Duyn Rd (R) 📖 📖 ⊠

COOS BAY — **AAA MIDWAY RV PARK.** (541) 888-9300. **$30-$70.** 92478 Cape Arago Hwy 97420. From Jct of US 101 & Newmark (at casino): Go W 2.9 mi on Newmark to Empire (Cape Arago Hwy), S 1.2 mi (L) 📖 ⊠

DAYTON — **WILLAMETTE WINE COUNTRY RV PARK.** (503) 864-2233. **$40.** 16205 Se Kreder Rd 97114. From Jct of US-99W & Hwy 18/SE Dayton Bypass: Go SW 0.9 mi on Hwy 18 (L) 📖 📖 ⊠

FAIRVIEW — **PORTLAND FAIRVIEW RV PARK.** (877) 777-1047. **$42.** 21401 Ne Sandy Blvd 97024. From Jct of I-84 & 207th Ave N (exit 14): Go N 0.1 mi on 207th Ave to NE Sandy Blvd, then E 0.3 mi (L) 📖 📖 ⊠

FLORENCE — **PACIFIC PINES RV PARK & STORAGE, INC.** (541) 997-1434. **$30-$33.** 4044 Hwy 101 97439. From Jct of US-101 & Hwy 126 (in town): Go N 2 mi on US-101 to 42nd St, then E 0.1 mi (R) 📖 ⊠

FLORENCE — **WOAHINK LAKE RV RESORT.** ⏺ (541) 997-6454. **$36-$40.** 83570 Hwy 101 S 97439. From Jct of Hwy 126 & US-101 (in town): Go S 5.1 mi on US-101 (R) (MP-195.5) 📖 ⊠

FOSTER — **FOSTER LAKE RV RESORT.** (541) 367-5629. **$42-$44.** 6191 Hwy 20 East 97345. From Jct of US-228 & US-20: Go E 3.8 mi on US-20 (R) 📖 ⊠

HARRISBURG — **RIVER LIFE RESORT.** (541) 995-9995. **$29-$35.** 23650 Peoria Rd 97446. From Jct of Hwy 99 & Peoria Rd (N of town): Go N 0.5 mi on Peoria Rd (L) 📖

LA GRANDE — **EAGLES HOT LAKE RV PARK.** ⏺ (541) 963-5253. **$34.** 65182 Hot Lake Ln 97850. From Jct of I-84 & Hwy 203 (exit 265): Go SE 4.5 mi on Hwy 203 to Hot Lake Ln, then W 0.3 mi (L) 📖 ⊠

LEBANON — MALLARD CREEK GOLF & RV RESORT. (866) 632-9133. **$43.** 31958 Bellinger Scale Rd 97355. From the Jct of Hwy 20 & Waterloo Rd 4.5 mi E (SW of Lebanon): Go NE 2.3 mi on Waterloo Rd to Berlin Rd, then E 0.3 mi to Bellinger Scale Rd, then N 0.4 mi (L) 🅰️ 🔤

LINCOLN CITY — DEVILS LAKE RV PARK. 🅰🅰🅰 (541) 994-3400. **$35-$38.** 4041 Ne West Devils Lake Rd 97367. From Jct of Hwy 101 & W Devils Lake Rd (N of town): Go E 0.2 mi on W Devils Lake Rd (R) 🔤

LINCOLN CITY — PREMIER RV RESORTS - LINCOLN CITY. (877) 871-0663. **$47-$55.** 4100 Se Hwy 101 97367. N-Bnd: From Jct of Hwy 101 & 51st St (S of town): Go N 0.2 mi on Hwy 101 (R); or S-Bnd: From Jct of Hwy 101 & E Devils Lake Rd (outlet mall): Go S 2.5 mi on Hwy 101 (L) 🅰️ 🔤

MCMINNVILLE — OLDE STONE VILLAGE RV PARK. (877) 472-4315. **$35.** 4155 Ne Three Mile Ln 97128. From Jct of Hwy 99W & E Hwy 18 bypass (S of McMinnville): Go NE 4.2 mi on Hwy 18 bypass to MP-48.25 (L) 🅰️ 🔤

NEWPORT — PACIFIC SHORES MOTORCOACH RESORT. (541) 265-3750. **$60-$90.** 6225 N Coast Hwy 101 97365. From Jct of US 20 & N Hwy 101: Go N 3.5 mi (L) NOTE: A & C Class Motorhomes ONLY 🔤

PACIFIC CITY — CAPE KIWANDA RV RESORT & MARKET PLACE. (503) 965-6230. **$35-$48.** 33305 Cape Kiwanda Dr 97135. From Jct of US-101 & Brooten Rd/Pacific City Jct (MP-90.3 N of Lincoln City): Go NW 3 mi on Brooten Rd to Pacific Ave (blinking light in town), then W 0.2 mi to Kiwanda Dr, then N 1 mi (R). Note: Some GPS require Cloverdale, OR as city 🔤

PENDLETON — WILDHORSE RV RESORT. (800) 654-9453. **$28-$40.** 46510 Wildhorse Blvd 97801. From Jct of I-84 & Hwy 331 (exit 216), N 0.8 mi on Hwy 331 (R) 🔤

PORTLAND — JANTZEN BEACH RV PARK. 🅰🅰🅰 (800) 443-7248. **$32.** 1503 N Hayden Island Dr 97217. From Jct of I-5 & Jantzen Beach (exit 308/N of Portland), take exit rd to N Hayden Island Dr, W 0.3 mi (R) 🅰️ 🔤

SALEM — HEE HEE ILLAHEE RV RESORT. 🅰🅰🅰 (877) 564-7295. **$40.** 4751 Astoria Street N.E. 97305. From Jct of I-5 & Hwy 99E/Portland Rd (Exit 258): Go N 1/4 mi on Hwy 99E/Portland Rd to Astoria St, then NW 1/4 mi (L) 🅰️ 🔤

SALEM — PHOENIX RV PARK. 🅰🅰🅰 (503) 581-2497. **Call for rates.** 4130 Silverton Rd Ne 97305. S-bnd: From Jct of I-5 & Market St (Exit 256): Go E 0.3 mi on Market to Lancaster Dr, then N 1.5 mi to Silverton Rd, then E 0.1 mi (R); or N-bnd: From Jct of I-5 & Market St (exit 256): Go E 0.3 mi on Market to Lancaster Dr, then N 1.5 mi to Silverton Rd, then E 0.1 mi (R) 🔤

SALEM — PREMIER RV RESORTS - SALEM. (877) 364-9990. **$46-$52.** 4700 Salem-Dallas Hwy 22 97304. N bnd: From Jct of I-5 & SR-22/99E Bus/Mission St (exit 253): Go W 3.8 mi on SR-22/99E Bus, then 4.3 mi on SR-22 (L) NOTE: Stay on SR-22 at Marion St. OR S bnd: From Jct of I-5 Salem Parkway/99E (exit260A): Go SW 4.5 mi on Salem Pkwy/Commercial St/99E to Marion St/22W, then W 4.3 mi (L) 🔤

TROUTDALE — SANDY RIVERFRONT RV RESORT, LLC. (503) 665-6722. **$33-$37.** 1097 E Historic Columbia River Hwy 97060. From Jct of I-84 & Exit 17: Go E 0.3 mi on Frontage Rd to Graham (Loves), then S 0.3 mi to Historic Columbia River Hwy, then E & S 0.6 mi (L) 🅰️ 🔤

TUALATIN — ROAMER'S REST RV PARK LLC. (503) 692-6350. **$42.** 17585 Sw Pacific Hwy 97062. S-bnd: From Jct of Hwys 217 & 99W: Go S 3.5 mi on Hwy 99W/MP 12.5 (R); or N-bnd: From Jct of I-5 & Nyberg Rd. (Exit 289, stay left at fork): Go W 2.8 mi on Nyber/Tualatin-Sherwood Rd to 124th, then NW 1.3 mi to Pacific Hwy (Hwy 99) West (stay in left lane), N 0.3 mi (L) 🅰️

WESTFIR — CASEY'S RIVERSIDE RV PARK. (541) 782-1906. **$38-$42.** 46443 Westfir Rd 97492. E-bnd: From Jct of I-5 & Hwy 58 (exit 188A): Go E 31.3 mi on Hwy 58 to Westfir Rd (Old Willamette Hwy), then SE 0.4 mi (L); or W-bnd: From Jct of Hwy 97 & Hwy 58: Go W 55 mi on Hwy 58 to Westfir Rd (MP-31 1/4), then NE 0.4 mi (L) 🅰️ 🔄 🔤

WILSONVILLE — PHEASANT RIDGE RV RESORT. (503) 682-7829. **$44-$57.** 8275 Sw Ellisgen Rd 97070. From Jct of I-5 & SW Elligsen Rd/N Wilsonville (exit 286): Go E 0.5 mi on SW Elligsen Rd (L) 🅰️ 🔄 🔤

YACHATS — SEA PERCH RV RESORT. (541) 547-3505. **$55-$85.** 95480 Hwy 101 S - Mp 171 97498. From Jct of Hwy 126 & US 101 (in Florence): Go N 17 mi on US 101 to MP-171 (L) 🅰️ 🔤

Pennsylvania

BEDFORD — FRIENDSHIP VILLAGE CAMPGROUND & RV PARK. 🅰🅰🅰 (814) 623-1677. **$33-$46.** 348 Friendship Village Rd 15522. From Jct I-76(exit 146) & US 220: Go 300 yds N on Bus US 220, then 1-1/2 mi S on US 220, then 1-1/2 mi NW on US 30, then 1/2 mi NE on Friendship Village Rd(E) 🔄 🔤

BELLEFONTE — BELLEFONTE/STATE COLLEGE KOA. (800) 562-8127. **$30-$90.** 2481 Jacksonville Rd 16823. From Jct I-80 (exit 161) & Hwy 26: Go 2-1/2 mi N on Hwy 26 (L) 🔄 🔤

CHARLEROI — PINE COVE BEACH CLUB & RV RESORT. (724) 239-2900. **$55-$65.** 1495 Rte 481 15022. From Jct of I-70 & Rte 481 (exit 35): Go 1/4 mi N on Rte 481 (L) 🅰️ 🔄 🔤

EAST STROUDSBURG — DELAWARE WATER GAP/POCONO MOUNTAIN KOA. (570) 223-8000. **$49-$69.** 227 Hollow Rd 18302. From Jct I-80(exit 309) & US-209: Go 6-1/4 mi NE on US 209, then 1 mi E on Hollow Rd (L) 🔄 🔤

EAST STROUDSBURG — MOUNTAIN VISTA CAMP-GROUND. (570) 223-0111. **$40-$60.** 415 Taylor Drive 18301. From Jct I-80 & US 209(exit 309): Go 3 mi N on US 209/Seven Bridges Rd, then enter roundabout, take 2nd exit follow signs for US 209 to Marshalls Creek, then 1/2 mi N on Seven Bridges Rd, then 1/2 mi W on Bus US 209, then 1 mi N on Craigs Meadow Rd, then 1/2 block W on Taylor Dr(R) 🔄 🔤

EAST STROUDSBURG — OTTER LAKE CAMP-RESORT. 🅰🅰🅰 (570) 223-0123. **$44-$74.** 1639 Marshalls Creek Rd 18302. From Jct I-80 & US-209(exit 309): Go 3 mi N on US 209/Seven Bridges Rd, then enter roundabout, (take 2nd exit, follow signs for Bus US-209), then 1/2 mi N on Hwy 1019/Seven Bridges Rd, then 1 blk E on Bus US 209, then 7-1/2 mi NW on Marshalls Creek Rd (L) 🔄 🔤

ELIZABETHTOWN — ELIZABETHTOWN/HERSHEY KOA. 🅰🅰🅰 (800) 562-4774. **$45-$84.** 1980 Turnpike Rd 17022. From Jct Hwy 283 & Hwy 743 (Elizabethtown/Hershey exit): Go 1-1/2 mi S on Hwy 743, then 1/2 mi E on Hwy 230 (Market St), then 1/2 mi W on W High St, then 2-1/4 mi N on Turnpike Rd(L) 🔄 🔤

EMLENTON — GASLIGHT CAMPGROUND. (724) 867-6981. **$34-$40.** 6297 Emlenton Clintonville Rd 16373. From Jct I-80(exit 42) & Hwy 38: Go 500 ft N on Hwy 38, then 1/4 mi W on Hwy 208/Emlenton Clintonville Rd(R) 🔄 🔤

GETTYSBURG — **DRUMMER BOY CAMPING RESORT.** (800) 293-2808. **$50-$69.** 1300 Hanover Rd 17325. From Jct of US 15 (Bypass) & Hwy 116: Go 150 ft E on Hwy 116. (L) 🛶 ⊠

GETTYSBURG — **GETTYSBURG CAMPGROUND.** 🅐🅐🅐 (717) 334-3304. **$37-$66.** 2030 Fairfield Rd 17325. From Jct of US 30 & Bus US 15 S (Lincoln Square in Gettysburg): Go 1 blk S on Bus US 15, then 3 mi W on Hwy 116/Middle St. (L) 🛶 ⊠

GETTYSBURG — **ROUND TOP CAMPGROUND.** (717) 334-9565. **$39-$74.** 180 Knight Rd 17325. From Jct of US 15 & Hwy 134 (Taneytown exit): Go 100 ft N on Hwy 134, then 1/4 mi W on Knight Rd. (L) 🛶 ⊠

HARRISVILLE — **JELLYSTONE PARK AT KOZY REST.** (724) 735-2417. **$44-$58.** 449 Campground Rd 16038. From Jct I-80 (exit 29) & Hwy 8: Go 5 mi S on Hwy 8, then 1/2 mi E on Hwy 58, then 2 mi N on Campground Rd (L); or From Jct of I-79 (exit 113) & Hwy 208: Go 4 mi E on Hwy 208, then 4-3/4 mi SE on Hwy 58, then 2 mi N on Campground Rd (L) 🛶 ⊠

HUMMELSTOWN — **HERSHEYPARK CAMPING RESORT.** (717) 534-8999. **$35-$65.** 1200 Sweet Street 17036. E-bnd: From Jct of US 322/422 & Hwy 39W (Hershey Park Dr): Go 1/2 mi N on Hwy 39W (Hershey Park Dr) (L) W-bnd: From Jct of I-81 & Hwy 39E (exit 77): Go 6 mi W on Hwy 39E, then 1 mi W on Hershey Park Dr (R) 🛶 ⊠

LEHIGHTON — **STONEYBROOK CAMPGROUND.** (570) 386-4088. **$40-$45.** 1435 Germans Rd 18235. From Jct Hwy 309 & Hwy 895(in Snyders): Go 7 mi E on Hwy 895, then 1 mi S on Lauchnor Rd, then 500 ft NE on Germans Rd(R) 🏕 🛶 ⊠

LEWISTOWN — **WATERSIDE CAMPGROUND & RV PARK.** (717) 248-3974. **$40-$53.** 475 Locust Rd 17044. From Jct Hwy 103 (in Lewistown) & US 22: Go 2-1/2 mi SW on US 22(W 4th St), then 2 mi SE on Loop Rd, then 1/2 mi S on Locust Rd (E) 🛶 ⊠

LOYSVILLE — **PARADISE STREAM FAMILY CAMP-GROUND.** (717) 789-2117. **$45-$59.** 693 Paradise Stream Rd 17047. From Jct of Hwy 850 & Hwy 274 (in Loysville): Go 4-1/2 mi W on Hwy 274, then 1/4 mi S on Rt 3008 (Couchtown Rd), then 1/2 mi SW on Paradise Stream Rd (R) Note: No GPS after Loysville 🛶 ⊠

MANHEIM — **PINCH POND FAMILY CAMPGROUND.** 🅐🅐🅐 (800) 659-7640. **$41-$46.** 3075 Pinch Rd 17545. From Jct of I-76 & Hwy 72 (exit 266): Go 1 mi S on Hwy 72, then 1/2 mi W on Cider Press Rd, then 1 mi N on Pinch Rd(R) 🛶 ⊠

MEADVILLE — **MEADVILLE KOA.** (814) 789-3251. **$38-$61.** 25164 Hwy 27 16335. From Jct I-79(exit 147A) & US 6/19: Go 1-1/5 mi NE on US 6/19, the 1/2 mi N on Park Ave, then 6 mi E on SR 27/North St(L) 🛶 ⊠

MILL RUN — **MILL RUN YOGI BEAR'S JELLYSTONE CAMP RESORT.** (800) 439-9644. **$31-$85.** 839 Mill Run Rd 15464. From Jct I-70/76/Pa Tpk(exit 91) & Hwy 31: Go 2 mi E on Hwy 31, then 10 mi S on Hwy 711/Hwy 381, then 3 mi S on Hwy 381(R) Note: Bridge with height restrictions. Call for instructions. 🛶 ⊠

MOUNT POCONO — **MOUNT POCONO CAMPGROUND.** 🅐🅐🅐 (570) 839-8950. **$45-$55.** 30 Edgewood Rd 18344. From Jct I-380 & Hwy 940 (exit 3): Go 2-1/2 mi NE on Hwy 940, then 1/2 mi N on Hwy 196, then 1/2 mi E mi on Edgewood (R) 🛶 ⊠

MUNCY VALLEY — **PIONEER CAMPGROUND.** 🅐🅐🅐 (570) 946-9971. **$38-$48.** 307 Pioneer Trail 17758. From Jct US 220 & Hwy 42(in La Porte): Go S 2 mi on US 220(R) 🛶 ⊠

NARVON — **LAKE-IN-WOOD RESORT.** 🅐🅐🅐 (877) 790-1516. **$45-$68.** 576 Yellow Hill Rd 17555. From Jct of Hwy 23 & Hwy 625: Go 4-1/2 mi N on Hwy 625, then 1 mi E on Oaklyn Dr, then 1-1/2 mi NE on Yellow Hill Rd(R) 🛶 ⊠

NEW TRIPOLI — **ALLENTOWN-LEHIGH VALLEY KOA.** (610) 298-2160. **$41-$60.** 6750 Koa Dr 18066. From Jct I-476(PA Tpk) & I-78/US22: Go 3 mi W on I-78/US-22(exit 49B), then 6-1/2 mi N on Hwy 100, then 1/4 mi W on Narris Rd(L) GPS Incorrect 🛶 ⊠

PINE GROVE — **TWIN GROVE RV RESORT & COTTAGES.** (717) 865-4602. **$35-$70.** 1445 Suedburg Rd 17963. From Jct I-81 & Hwy 443 (exit 100): Go 5 mi W on Hwy 443(R) 🛶 ⊠

PORTERSVILLE — **BEAR RUN CAMPGROUND.** 🅐🅐🅐 (888) 737-2605. **$35-$57.** 184 Badger Hill Rd 16051. From Jct I-79(exit 96) & Hwy 488: Go 50 yds E on Hwy 488, then 1/2 mi N on Badger Hill Rd(R) 🛶 ⊠

SOMERSET — **PIONEER PARK CAMPGROUND.** (814) 445-6348. **$32-$54.** 273 Trent Rd 15501. E-bnd: From Jct of I-70/76/PA Tpk(exit 110) & Hwy 601: Go 1/2 mi S on Hwy 601, then 7 mi W on Hwy 31, then 1/4 mi S on Trent Rd(R) W-bnd: From Jct I-70/76/PA Tpk(exit 91)& Hwy 31: Go 12 mi E on Hwy 31, then 1/4 mi S on Trent Rd(R) 🛶 ⊠

TRANSFER — **SHENANGO VALLEY RV PARK.** (724) 962-9800. **$52-$59.** 559 E Crestview Drive 16154. From Jct I-80(exit 4B) & Hwy 18: Go 13 mi N on Hwy 18, then 1/2 mi E on Reynolds Industrial Rd, then 1 mi SE on Crestview Dr, stay left at Y, continue 1 mi SE on Crestview Dr (L) 🏕 🛶 ⊠

WAYMART — **KEEN LAKE CAMPING & COTTAGE RESORT.** (570) 488-5522. **$42-$61.** 155 Keen Lake Rd 18472. From Jct of US 6 & Hwy 296: Go 1-1/2 mi E on US 6(R) 🛶 ⊠

Rhode Island

WEST KINGSTON — **WAWALOAM CAMPGROUND.** (401) 294-3039. **$46-$58.** 510 Gardiner Rd 02892. From Jct of I-95 & Rte 102 (exit 5A), SE 2.5 mi on Rte 102 to Town Hall Rd, S 0.6 mi to Ten Rod Rd, W 0.1 mi to Gardiner Rd, SW 1.5 mi (R) 🏕 🛶 ⊠

South Carolina

ANDERSON — **ANDERSON/LAKE HARTWELL KOA.** (800) 562-5804. **$30-$40.** 200 Wham Rd 29625. From Jct of I-85 & SC-187 (exit 14), SW 0.9 mi on SC-187 (L) 🛶

CHARLESTON — **OAK PLANTATION CAMPGROUND, LP.** (843) 766-5936. **$42-$50.** 3540 Savannah Hwy 29455. From W Jct of I-526 & US-17, S 4.4 mi on US-17 (R) or From Jct of I-95 & Hwy 17, N on Hwy 17 (N) 53 mi (L) Note: Do not take 17A. 🏕 🛶 ⊠

GAFFNEY — **SPARTANBURG NORTHEAST/GAFFNEY KOA.** (800) 562-0362. **$29-$44.** 160 Sarratt School Rd 29341. From Jct I-85 (exit 87) & Hwy 39: Go to I-85 N-Bnd on-ramp, take ramp 250 ft to Overbrook Dr, then E 1 mi on Overbrook Dr, then S 1/4 mi on Sarratt School Rd (R) 🛶 ⊠

HARDEEVILLE — **CAMP LAKE JASPER RV RESORT.** (843) 784-5200. **$31-$47.** 44 Camp Lake Drive 29927. From Jct. of I-95 (exit 8) and Hwy 278: Go E .01 mi on Hwy 278 then 1.1 mi N on Medical Center Drive then E 1.1 mi. on Red Dam Rd (R) 🏕 🛶 ⊠

HILTON HEAD ISLAND — **HILTON HEAD HARBOR RV RESORT & MARINA.** (843) 681-3256. **$54-$69.** 43-A Jenkins Rd 29926. From Jct of I-95 & US-278 (exit 8), E 19 mi on US-278 to Jenkins Rd, N 0.4 mi (L) 🏕 🛶 ⊠

HILTON HEAD ISLAND — HILTON HEAD ISLAND MOTORCOACH RESORT/OUTDOOR RESORTS. (800) 722-2365. **$60-$80.** 133 Arrow Rd 29928. From Jct of I-95 & US-278 (exit 8), E 20.4 mi on US-278 to Cross Island Expwy (toll road - becomes Palmetto Bay Rd), S 5.4 mi on Expwy to Target Rd, N 0.1 mi to Arrow Rd, E 500 ft (L) Class A & C motorhomes only 🏍 🛁 ⊠

KINARDS — MAGNOLIA RV PARK & CAMPGROUND. (864) 697-1214. **$26-$32.** 567 Fairview Church Rd 29355. From Jct of I-26 & SC-66 (exit 60), SW 0.1 mi on SC-66 to Fairview Church Rd, SE 0.6 mi (L) 🛁 ⊠

LONGS — WILLOWTREE RV RESORT & CAMPGROUND. (866) 207-2267. **$31-$93.** 520 Southern Sights Drive 29568. From Jct of SC-9 & SC-905, N 1.8 mi on SC-905 to Old Buck Creek Rd, N 1.5 mi (R) 🏍 🛁 ⊠

MOUNT PLEASANT — MT PLEASANT/CHARLESTON KOA. (843) 849-5177. **$40-$69.** 3157 Hwy 17 29466. From E Jct of I-526 & US-17 Exit 29 (N-bnd), NE 5 mi on US-17 (R) 🛁 ⊠

MYRTLE BEACH — BRIARCLIFFE RV RESORT. (843) 272-2730. **$40-$61.** 10495 N Kings Hwy 29572. From Jct of US 501 & SC 22, E 28 mi on SC 22 to North Myrtle Beach Exit (US 17/N. Kings Hwy) N 1.2 mi (L) 🏍 🛁 ⊠

MYRTLE BEACH — CYPRESS CAMPING RESORT. (843) 293-0300. **$30-$65.** 101 Cypress Rv Way 29588. From the Jct of US-31 & US-544: Go 1 mi E on US-544, then 1/4 mi N on US-707, then 1/4 mi W on River Rd (L) 🛁 ⊠

MYRTLE BEACH — LAKEWOOD CAMPING RESORT. ⚠ (877) 525-3966. **$27-$75.** 5901 S Kings Hwy 29575. From Jct of US-501 & SC 544, SE 14.5 mi to Bus US-17, NE 0.4 mi (R) 🛁 ⊠

MYRTLE BEACH — MYRTLE BEACH TRAVEL PARK. ⚠ (800) 255-3568. **$40-$73.** 10108 Kings Rd 29572. From Jct of US-501 & SC 22, E 28 mi on SC 22 to Kings Rd Exit, E 0.6 mi (L) 🛁 ⊠

MYRTLE BEACH — MYRTLE BEACH KOA. (800) 562-7790. **$31-$79.** 613 5th Ave S 29577. From Jct of US-501 & US-17, E 1 mi on US-501 to 3rd Ave S, SE 1 mi to Bus US-17 (Kings Hwy), S 0.2 mi to 5th Ave S, NW 0.2 mi (L) 🛁 ⊠

MYRTLE BEACH — OCEAN LAKES FAMILY CAMPGROUND. ⚠ (800) 341-6659. **$29-$76.** 6001 S Kings Hwy 29575. From Jct of US-501 & SC 544, SE 14.5 mi to Kings Hwy US 17 Bus (E) 🛁 ⊠

MYRTLE BEACH — PIRATELAND FAMILY CAMPING RESORT. (800) 443-2267. **$32-$80.** 5401 S Kings Hwy 29575. From Jct of US-501 & SC 544, SE 13.5 mi to Bus US-17, NE 1.2 mi (R) 🛁 ⊠

ROEBUCK — PINE RIDGE CAMPGROUND. (864) 576-0302. **$30-$32.** 199 Pine Ridge Campground Rd 29376. From Jct of I-26 (exit 28) & US 221, NE 0.2 mi to Stillhouse Rd., SE 1 mi to Otts Shoals Rd, N 1.5 mi on Otts Shoals Rd to Pine Ridge Campground Rd. (R) 🏍 🛁 ⊠

SWANSEA — YOGI BEAR'S JELLYSTONE PARK AT RIVER BOTTOM FARMS. (803) 568-4182. **$36.** 357 Cedar Creek Rd 29160. S-bnd: From Jct of I-77 & US 321 S (Exit 71), S 15 mi on US 321 to SC3, SW 6.5 mi on SC-3 to SC-178, NW 0.5 mi on 178 to Cedar Creek Rd, W 0.7 mi (L); N-bnd: From Jct of US-321 & SC 178 (S of Swansea), W 6.3 mi on SC 178 to Cedar Creek Rd, W 0.7 mi (L) 🛁 ⊠

TOWNVILLE — LAKE HARTWELL CAMPING & CABINS. (864) 287-3223. **$27-$35.** 400 Ponderosa Point 29689. From Jct of I-85 (exit 11) & SC-24, NW 2.6 mi on SC-24 to O'Neal Ferry Rd, NE 0.3 mi to Ponderosa Point Rd, E 0.5 mi (E) 🛁 ⊠

WEST UNION — CROOKED CREEK RV PARK. (864) 882-5040. **$30-$40.** 777 Arvee Ln 29696. S-bnd: From Jct of I-85/US 76/US 28 (exit 19B), W 21.4 mi on SC 28 to SC 188, NE 3.3 mi to Ebenezer Rd, NW 1.6 mi to Arvee Ln (R). Call for directions 🛁 ⊠

South Dakota

ABERDEEN — WYLIE PARK & STORYBOOK LAND. ⚠ (888) 326-9693. **$30-$31.** 2300 24th Ave Nw 57401. From Jct US-12 & US-281: Go 2 1/4 mi N on US-281, then 1/4 mi W on Seratoma Pkwy (L) Don't rely on GPS - Call for directions ⊠

BRANDON — SIOUX FALLS YOGI BEAR. (605) 332-2233. **$25-$45.** 26014 478th Ave 57005. From Jct of I-29 & I-90: Go 6 mi E on I-90 (Exit 402), then 1 block N on CR-121. (R) 🛁 ⊠

CUSTER CITY — BEAVER LAKE CAMPGROUND. ⚠ (800) 346-4383. **$36-$45.** 12005 W Hwy 16 57730. From Jct US 385 & US 16 (in town): Go 3.5 mi W on US 16 (L). Note: can also call for directions 🛁 ⊠

DEADWOOD — WHISTLER GULCH RV PARK & CAMPGROUND. (800) 704-7139. **$35-$48.** 235 Cliff St (Hwy 85 S) 57732. From Jct US 85 & US 14A: Go 3 mi S on US 85 (L); or From Jct US 385 & US 85: Go .5 mi E on US 85 (R). Note: Don't use GPS - Call for directions 🛁 ⊠

HILL CITY — HORSE THIEF CAMPGROUND AND RESORT INC. (800) 657-5802. **$35-$45.** 24391 Sd Hwy 87 57745. From south city limits of Hill City: Go 3 1/2 mi S on US-16/385, then 2 mi S & E on Hwy 87 (R) 🛁 ⊠

HILL CITY — RAFTER J BAR RANCH CAMPING RESORT. (605) 574-2527. **$35-$54.** 12325 Rafter J Rd 57745. From south city limits of Hill City: Go 3.0 mi S on US-16/385 (R) 🛁 ⊠

INTERIOR — BADLANDS/WHITE RIVER KOA. (800) KOA-3897. **$30-$46.** 20720 Sd Hwy 44 57750. From Jct I-90 (Exit 131) & SR-240: go 8 1/4 mi S on SR-240, then 2 1/4 mi S on SR-377 (towards interior), then 4 mi E on SR-44 (L) 🛁 ⊠

MITCHELL — DAKOTA CAMPGROUND. (605) 996-9432. **$23-$25.** 1800 W Spruce 57301. From Jct of I-90 & Exit 330, S 0.2 mi on 408th Ave/Ohlman St to Spruce St, W 0.1 mi on Spruce St (R) Don't rely on GPS. Call. 🛁 ⊠

MITCHELL — FAMIL-E-FUN CAMPGROUND & RV PARK. (605) 996-8983. **$29-$30.** 25473 403rd Avenue 57301. From Jct of I-90 & Exit 325 (Betts Rd), S 0.2 mi on Betts Rd (R). Don't use GPS 🛁 ⊠

RAPID CITY — HART RANCH CAMPING RESORT CLUB. ⚠ (800) 605-4278. **$15-$50.** 23756 Arena Drive 57702. From Jct I-90 (Exit 61) & US-16 Truck Rte/Hwy 79: Go 5-1/4 mi S on US-16 Truck Rte/Hwy 79 (N Elk Vale Rd), then 6 mi S on Hwy 79, then 2 mi W on Spring Creek Rd (L) 🛁 ⊠

RAPID CITY — MYSTERY MOUNTAIN RESORT. (605) 342-5368. **$32-$38.** 13752 S Hwy 16 West 57702. From Jct of I-90 & US-16W (Exit 61): Go 13.5 mi S on US-16W (R) 🛁 ⊠

RAPID CITY — RUSHMORE SHADOWS RESORT. Ⓐ (800) 231-0425. **$35-$62.** 23680 Busted Five Court 57702. From Jct I-90 (Exit 61) & US-16 Truck/Hwy 79: Go 9 mi S & W on US-16 Truck, then 6-1/2 mi W on US-16 W (R) 🔜 ⊠

SALEM — CAMP AMERICA CAMPGROUND. (605) 425-9085. **$29-$38.** 25495 Us-81 57058. From Jct of I-90 (Exit 364) & US-81: Go 1.25 mi N on US-81 (L). Do not rely on GPS. 🔜 ⊠

SPEARFISH — CHRIS' CAMP. Ⓐ (800) 350-2239. **$33-$35. (no credit cards).** 701 Christensen Dr 57783. From Jct US-85 N & I-90: Go 4 mi E on I-90 (Exit 14), then 1/2 mi W on Bus I-90, then 3/4 mi S on Christensen Dr (R) 🔜 ⊠

SPEARFISH — ELKHORN RIDGE RV RESORT & GOLF CLUB. Ⓐ (877) 722-1800. **$40-$56.** 20189 Us Hwy 85 57783. From Jct I-90 & US 85 (Exit 17): Go .6 mi SE on US 85 (R) 🔜 ⊠

STURGIS — RUSH NO MORE RV RESORT & CAMP-GROUND. (605) 347-2916. **$37-$52.** 21137 Brimstone Pl 57785. From Jct US-14A & I-90: Go 5 mi SE on I-90 (Exit 37), then 3/4 mi W on Pleasant Valley Rd, then 1/4 mi S on Brimstone Pl (R) 🔜 ⊠

YANKTON — YANKTON/MISSOURI RIVER KOA. (605) 260-1010. **$36-$44.** 807 Bill Baggs Rd 57078. From Jct Hwy 81 & Hwy 50E: Go approx. 2 mi E on Hwy 50E, then 600 ft S on Bill Baggs Rd (R) 🔜 ⊠

Tennessee

BLOUNTVILLE — ROCKY TOP CAMPGROUND & RV PARK. (800) 452-6456. **$42.** 496 Pearl Lane 37617. From Jct of I-81 & Exit 63 (Airport Pkwy), NW 0.4 mi on Airport Pkwy/Browder Rd to Pearl Ln, W 0.6 mi (R) ⊠

CHATTANOOGA — BEST HOLIDAY TRAV-L-PARK. (800) 693-2877. **$37-$41.** 1709 Mack Smith Rd 37412. N-bnd: From Jct of I-75 & US-41N (exit 1B, North US-41), W 0.5 mi on US-41N to Mack Smith Rd, S 0.7 mi (R); or S-bnd: From Jct of I-75 & US-41N (exit 1), W 0.25 mi on US-41N to Mack Smith Rd, S 0.7 mi (R) 🔜 ⊠

CLARKSVILLE — CLARKSVILLE RV PARK LLC. (931) 648-8638. **$34-$37.** 1270 Tylertown Rd 37040. From Jct of I-24 & Hwy-48 (exit 1), N 0.1 mi on Hwy-48 to Tylertown Rd, W 0.3 mi (L) 🔜 ⊠

CROSSVILLE — DEER RUN RV RESORT. (931) 484-3333. **$36.** 3609 Peavine Firetower Rd 38571. From Jct of I 40 & Hwy 101 (Exit 322), NE 1.9 mi on Hwy 101 to Peavine Fire Tower Rd, N 3.6 mi (L) 🔜 ⊠

DANDRIDGE — ANCHOR DOWN RV RESORT. (877) 784-4446. **$49-$69.** 1703 Highway 139 37725. From Jct of I 40 & Deep Springs (Exit 412), S 3.0 mi on Deep Springs to SR 139, W 0.9 mi on SR 139 (L)

GATLINBURG — CAMP LECONTE LUXURY OUTDOOR RESORT. Ⓐ (865) 436-8831. **$49-$59.** 1739 East Parkway 37738. From Jct of US-441 & US-321N (traffic light #3 in downtown Gatlinburg), E 4 mi on US-321N/East Parkway (L) 🔜

GATLINBURG — GREAT SMOKY JELLYSTONE CAMP-RESORT. (800) 210-2119. **$33-$62.** 4946 Hooper Hwy 37722. E-bnd: From Jct of I-40 & US-321S (exit 435): Go S 14 mi on US-321S (L); or W-bnd on I-40: From Jct of I-40 & Hwy 73 (exit 440): Go W 2 mi on Hwy 73 to US-321S, S 10 mi (L); or E-bnd From Gatlinburg: From Jct of US-441 & US-321N, E 15 mi on US-321N (R) 🔜 ⊠

GATLINBURG — OUTDOOR RESORTS/GATLINBURG. (800) 677-5861. **$35-$45.** 4229 E Pkwy (Hwy 321n) 37738. From Jct of US-441 & US-321N/SR-73E, E 11 mi on US-321N/SR-73E (L) (40' Max Length) 🏕 🔜 ⊠

GATLINBURG — SMOKY BEAR CAMPGROUND. (865) 436-8372. **$33-$48.** 4857 East Parkway 37738. E-bnd: From Jct of I-40 & US 321S (exit 435), S 17.2 mi on US 321S (R); or W-bnd: From Jct of I-40 & US 73S (Exit 440), S 2.3 mi on US 73S to US 321S, S 11.6 mi (R) 🔜 ⊠

GATLINBURG — TWIN CREEK RV RESORT. (800) 252-8077. **$50-$58.** 1202 E Parkway 37738. From Jct of US-441 & US-321N (traffic light #3 in downtown Gatlinburg), E 2 mi on US-321N/East Parkway (R) 🏕 🔜 ⊠

HARRIMAN — CANEY CREEK RV RESORT & MARINA. (865) 882-4042. **$49-$65.** 3615 Roane State Hwy 37748. From Jct of I-40 & SR 29 (Exit 350), S 0.5 mi on SR 29 to US-70, W 3 mi (L) Entrance just past county park 🏕 🔜 ⊠

HERMITAGE — NASHVILLE SHORES RV PARK. Ⓐ (615) 889-7050. **$45-$60.** 4001 Bell Rd 37076. From Jct of I-40 & Old Hickory Blvd (Exit 221 & 221B), S 0.5 mi on Old Hickory Blvd to Bell Rd, W 0.5 mi (L) ⊠

MANCHESTER — MANCHESTER KOA. (800) 562-7785. **$42-$65.** 586 Campground Rd 37355. From Jct of I-24 & US-41 (exit 114), SE 300 ft on US-41 to Campground Rd, N 0.5 mi (R) 🔜 ⊠

NASHVILLE — NASHVILLE KOA. (800) 562-7789. **$64-$73.** 2626 Music Valley Dr 37214. From Jct of I-65 & Briley Pkwy (exit 90B S-bnd; exit 90B N-bnd), E 4.5 mi on Briley Pkwy to (exit 12), W 0.2 mi to Music Valley Dr, N 2 mi (L); or W-bnd: From Jct of I-40 & Briley Pkwy (exit 215), N 5.3 mi on Briley Pkwy to (Exit 12), W 0.2 mi to Music Valley Dr, N 2 mi (L) 🔜 ⊠

PIGEON FORGE — BEAR COVE VILLAGE. (865) 453-8117. **$40-$57.** 3404 Whaley Dr 37863. From Jct of Hwy 66 & Hwy 441, NE 1.4 mi on Hwy 441 to Veterans Blvd, E 5.3 mi to Whaley Dr, NE 100 ft (L) 🔜

PIGEON FORGE — CREEKSIDE RV PARK. (865) 428-4801. **$28-$42.** 2475 Henderson Springs Rd 37863. From Jct of US-441 & US-321, SW 0.7 mi on US-321 to Henderson Springs Rd, NW 0.2 mi (R) (2nd campground on right) 🏕 🔜

PIGEON FORGE — PINE MOUNTAIN RV PARK. (877) 753-9994. **$35-$58.** 411 Pine Mountain Road 37863. From Jct of US-441 & Pine Mountain Rd (traffic light #6 in Pigeon Forge), SE 0.4 mi on Pine Mountain Rd (L) 🏕 🔜

PIGEON FORGE — PIGEON FORGE/GATLINBURG KOA. (865) 453-7903. **$42-$81.** 3122 Veterans Blvd 37863. From Jct of US-441 & Wears Valley Rd (US-321S), S 2.1 mi on US-441 to Dollywood Ln (stop light #8), E 0.3 mi to Veterans Blvd, N 1000 ft (L) 🔜 ⊠

SEVIERVILLE — RIVERSIDE RV PARK & RESORT. (800) 341-7534. **$36-$38.** 4280 Boyds Creek Hwy 37876. From Jct of I-40 & Hwy 66 (exit 407): Go S 4 mi on Hwy 66 to Boyds Creek Rd, W 500 ft (R) 🏕 🔜 ⊠

SEVIERVILLE — TWO RIVERS LANDING RV RESORT. (866) 727-5781. **$55-$65.** 2328 Business Center Circle 37876. From Jct of I 40 & Hwy 66 (Exit 407), S 3 mi on Hwy 66 to Knife Works Ln, W 0.1 mi to Business Center Circle (R) 🏕 🔜 ⊠

SWEETWATER — **SWEETWATER VALLEY KOA.** (800) 562-9224. **$36-$55.** 269 Murrays Chapel Rd 37874. From Jct of I-75 & Hwy 322 (exit 62), W 0.8 mi on Hwy 322 to Murray's Chapel Rd, S 0.4 mi (L) 🏕 🚐 ⊠

TOWNSEND — **BIG MEADOW FAMILY CAMPGROUND.** (888) 497-0625. **$45-$55.** 8215 Cedar Creek Road 37882. From Jct of US-321 & Hwy 73, NE 0.2 mi on US-321 to Cedar Creek Rd, W 300 ft (R) 🏕 ⊠

Texas

ALAMO — **ALAMO PALMS RV RESORT.** (800) 405-6188. **$35-$38.** 1341 W Bus Hwy 83 78516. From Jct of US-83 (Expwy) & Cesar Chavez Rd exit, S 0.5 mi on Cesar Chavez Rd to Bus 83, E 0.3 mi (R) 🏕 🚐 ⊠

ALEDO — **COWTOWN RV PARK.** (817) 441-7878. **$33.** 7000 I-20 East 76008. From Jct I-20 (exit 418) & Ranch House Rd: Go 1 mi E on S Frontage Rd. (R) 🏕 🚐 ⊠

ALPINE — **LOST ALASKAN RV RESORT.** (432) 837-1136. **$34-$45.** 2401 N Hwy 118 79830. From Jct of US-90 & Hwy 118: Go 1-1/2 mi N on Hwy 118 (L) 🚐 ⊠

AMARILLO — **AMARILLO RANCH RV PARK.** ⨁ (806) 373-4962. **$37.** 1414 Sunrise Dr 79104. From Jct of I-40 (exit 74) & Whitaker Rd: Go 1/2 mi W on N Service Rd (R) 🚐 ⊠

AMARILLO — **FORT AMARILLO RV RESORT.** (806) 331-1700. **$39.** 10101 Amarillo Blvd W 79124. From jct I-40 (exit 64) & Loop 335: Go 1/4 mi N on W Loop 335, then 1-1/4 W on Rt 66/Amarillo Blvd W (L) 🏕 🚐 ⊠

AMARILLO — **OASIS RV RESORT.** (888) 789-9697. **$25-$37.** 2715 Arnot Rd 79124. From Jct of I-40 (Exit 60) & Arnot Rd: Go 1/2 mi S on Arnot Rd. (L) 🏕 🚐 ⊠

AMARILLO — **OVERNITE RV PARK.** (800) 554-5305. **$33.** 900 S Lakeside Dr 79118. From Jct of I-40 (Exit 75) & Lakeside Dr: Go 1/4 mi N on Lakeside Dr (Loop 335) (L) 🏕 🚐

ARANSAS PASS — **ARANSAS BAY RV RESORT.** (830) 423-4322. **$35-$45.** 501 N Avenue A 78336. From jct of 188 & 35 bypass: Go 4 miles west to Aransas Pass exit, then right on North Avenue A (L) 🏕 🚐

ARANSAS PASS — **RANSOM ROAD RV PARK.** (361) 758-2715. **$37-$42.** 240 Ransom Road 78336. From Jct of Bus 35 & Commercial St (S Loop 90), SW 1.6 mi on Commercial St to Ransom Rd, E 0.1 mi (L) 🏕 ⊠

ATHENS — **TEXAN RV PARK.** (903) 677-3326. **$30.** 9024 Us Hwy 175 W 75751. From Jct of Loop 7 & US 175: Go 4 mi N on US 175. (R) 🚐 ⊠

AUBREY — **SHADY CREEK RV PARK AND STORAGE.** (972) 347-5384. **$30. (no credit cards).** 1893 Fm 1385 76227. From E jct US 377 & US 380: Go 6-1/4 mi E on US 380, then 1 mi N on FM 1385 (L) 🚐 ⊠

AUSTIN — **LA HACIENDA RV RESORT.** (512) 266-8001. **$48-$57.** 5220 Hudson Bend Rd 78734. S-Bnd: From Jct of I-35 & FM-620, S 18.7 mi on FM-620 to Hudson Bend Rd, W 1.5 mi (L); N-Bnd: From Jct of I-35 & (Exit 230) Hwy 290/71, W 7.7 mi on US 290 to TX 71, NW 7.1 mi to Ranch Road 620, N 7.9 mi to Hudson Bend Rd, NW 1.4 mi (L) 🏕 🚐 ⊠

AUSTIN — **OAK FOREST RV PARK.** (512) 926-8984. **$45.** 8207 Canoga Ave 78724. From Jct of I-35 (Exit 238B) & Hwy 290: Go E 6.5 mi E on Hwy 290, then 4 mi S on Decker Ln (FM 3177), then 500 ft W on Canoga (L) 🏕 🚐 ⊠

BASTROP — **BASTROP/COLORADO RIVER/KOA.** (512) 321-7500. **$45-$55.** 98 Hwy 71 W 78602. W-Bnd: From Jct of Hwys W 21/71 & Hasler Blvd Exit, cross under freeway, E 0.3 mi on S frntg rd move to & stay in right lane (R) E-Bnd: From Jct of US 71 & Hasler/Childress Exit, E 1.3 mi on S frntg rd (move to & stay in right lane) (R) 🚐 ⊠

BEAUMONT — **GULF COAST RV RESORT.** (866) 410-7801. **$40.** 5175 Brooks Rd 77705. W-bnd: From Jct of I-10 & Exit 847 (Brooks Rd/Major Dr), S 0.1 mi on Brooks Rd (R); or E-bnd: From Jct of I-10 & Exit 845 (Major Dr/Brooks Rd), E 1.6 mi on frontg rd to Brooks Rd, S 0.1 mi (R) 🏕 🚐 ⊠

BOERNE — **TOP OF THE HILL RV RESORT.** (830) 537-3666. **$38-$50.** 12 Green Cedar Rd 78006. From Jct I-10 & Exit 533, (FM-289/Welfare) (W of Boerne): Go NW 0.8 mi on FM-289 to Green Cedar Rd (L) 🚐 ⊠

BROOKSHIRE — **HOUSTON WEST RV PARK.** ⨁ (281) 375-5678. **$37-$39.** 35303 Cooper Rd 77423. From Jct of I-10 & FM-1489 (exit 731), N 0.2 mi on FM-1489 to Cooper Rd, W 0.2 mi (L) 🏕 🚐 ⊠

BULLARD — **K.E. BUSHMAN'S CAMP.** (903) 894-8221. **$21-$32.** 51152 S. Us Hwy 69n 75757. From Jct of FM 344 & US 69: Go 1-1/2 mi S on US 69. (L) 🚐 ⊠

CADDO MILLS — **DALLAS NE CAMPGROUND.** (903) 527-3615. **$39-$42.** 4268 Fm 36 S 75135. From Jct I-30 (Exit 85) & FM-36: Go 1/4 mi N on FM-36 (L) 🚐 ⊠

CANTON — **MILL CREEK RANCH RESORT.** (866) 599-7275. **$37-$66.** 2102 N. Trade Days Blvd 75103. From Jct I-20 (Exit 527) & Hwy 19 (Trade Days Blvd): Go 1/4 mi S on Hwy 19 (L) 🏕 🚐 ⊠

CASTROVILLE — **ALSATIAN RESORT & GOLF CLUB.** (830) 931-9190. **$35-$85.** 1581 County Road 4516 78009. From Jct Hwy 90 & CR 4516: Go 2.5 mi on CR 4516 (R) 🚐 ⊠

CORPUS CHRISTI — **COLONIA DEL REY RV PARK.** (361) 937-2435. **$32-$40.** 1717 Waldron Rd 78418. From Jct of I-37 & Hwy 358 (Padre Island Dr), SE 15.7 mi on Hwy 358 to Waldron Rd exit, S 0.8 mi (L) 🏕 🚐 ⊠

DALE — **LAKE FALLING STAR RV RESORT.** (512) 398-7827. **$37-$47.** 7355 Fm 713 78616. From Jct of FM 713 & TX 86 (in McMahan), NE 1 mi on FM 713 (L) 🏕 🚐 ⊠

DENTON — **DESTINY RV RESORTS-DALLAS.** (888) 238-1532. **$32-$41.** 7100 S I-35e 76210. From Jct of I-35E & Exit 460: Go 1 mi S on W Service Rd. (R) 🏕 🚐 ⊠

FORT STOCKTON — **FORT STOCKTON RV PARK.** (432) 395-2494. **$33-$35.** 3604 Koa Road 79735. From Jct I-10 & Warnock Rd (exit 264), 400 yards Ni on Warnock Rd (R) 🚐 ⊠

FREDERICKSBURG — **FREDERICKSBURG RV PARK.** (866) 324-7275. **$40.** 305 E Highway St 78624. From Jct of US 290 & S US 87 (Washington St): Go 3/4 mi SE on Hwy 87, then 1/2 block W on Highway St (L) 🏕 ⊠

GALVESTON — JAMAICA BEACH RV PARK. (409) 632-0200. **$43-$54.** 17200 San Luis Rd 77554. From Jct of I-45 & 61st St. exit (1A), S 1.7 mi to Seawall Blvd (FM-3005), W 11 mi (R)

GALVESTON — SANDPIPER RV RESORT. (409) 765-9431. **$45-$100.** 201 Seawall Blvd 77550. From I-45 in Galveston (Broadway St), continue S .5 mi on Broadway St to Seawall Blvd (curve left), E 0.3 mi on Seawall Blvd (R)

GARLAND — HOUSTON EAST RV RESORT. (281) 383-3618. **$39.** 310 East Interstate 30, Suite 320 75043. W-bnd: From Jct of I-10 & Hwy 146 (Exit 798): Go E 1.4 mi on S Frntg Rd (R) or E-bnd: From Jct of I-10 & Exit 797, E 1.5 mi on S. Frntg Rd (R)

GEORGETOWN — NEW LIFE RV PARK. (512) 931-2073. **$29-$33. (no credit cards).** 1200 County Rd 152 78626. S: Jct of I-35 & exit 264, cross over to Austin Ave, N 0.8 mi on Austin Ave (keep rt) to Frntg Rd for S130 Toll Rd (stay on Frntg Rd), SE 0.7 mi to CR 152, NE 0.3 mi (R); N: Jct of I-35 & exit 265/Austin Ave (keep rt) to Frntg Rd for S130 Toll Rd (stay on Frntg Rd), SE 0.7 mi to CR 152, NE 0.3 mi (R)

GLADEWATER — SHALLOW CREEK RV RESORT. (888) 984-4513. **$33.** 5261 Hwy 135 N 75647. From Jct of I-20 (exit 583) & SR 135: Go 1-1/2 mi N on SR 135 (R)

HARLINGEN — PARK PLACE ESTATES & RV RESORT MHP. (956) 428-4414. **$36.** 5401 W Bus 83 78552. From Jct of US-83/77 (Expwy) & Bus 83 exit, W 1.8 mi on Bus 83 (L)

HIGHLANDS — SAN JACINTO RIVERFRONT RV PARK. (281) 426-6919. **$45.** 540 S. Main 77562. From Jct of I-10 & Exit 787 Highlands/Crosby-Lynchburg Rd (S. Main), N 1 mi on Crosby-Lynchburg/S. Main (L)

HOUSTON — ADVANCED RV RESORT. (713) 433-6950. **$50-$55.** 2850 S Sam Houston Pkwy E. 77047. From Jct of I-610 & Hwy 288, S 5.5 mi on US 288 to Beltway 8 exit, SE 0.5 mi on Beltway 8 Frontage Rd (R)

HOUSTON — ALLSTAR RV RESORT. (713) 981-6814. **$35-$54.** 10650 Sw Plaza Ct 77074. S-bnd: From Jct of US-59 (southside of Houston) & Beltway 8 Frntg Rd exit, stay on Frntg Rd S. to U-turn under fwy, N 0.4 mi on Frntg Rd to SW Plaza Dr, E 0.1 mi (R); or N-bnd: From Jct of US-59 & Murphy Rd/Wilcrest Dr exit stay on Frontage Rd N 1.6 mi to SW Plaza Dr (R)

HOUSTON — EASTLAKE RV RESORT. (832) 243-6919. **$42-$81.** 18102 Lockwood Rd 77044. From Jct N Lake Houston Parkway & Lockwood Rd: Go N 2.1 mi (R)

HOUSTON — LAKEVIEW RV RESORT. (800) 385-9122. **$38-$51.** 11991 S Main St 77035. From S Jct of I-610 & US-90A (South Main St): Go SW 1.9 mi on S Main St to Holmes Rd/Hiram Clark exit, E uturn under bridge to frontage rd, NE .01 (R)

HOUSTON — NORTHLAKE RV RESORT. (281) 209-1770. **$43-$65.** 1919 Humble-Westfield Road 77073. From Jct I-45 & FM 1960: Go 2 mi E on FM 1960, then go .05 mi S on Humble-Westfield Rd (R)

HOUSTON — TRADERS VILLAGE RV PARK. (281) 890-5500. **$30-$33.** 7979 N Eldridge Rd 77041. From Jct of I-10 & Eldridge Rd (exit 753A), N 7.8 mi on Eldridge Rd (L); or From N Jct of I-45 & Beltway 8/Sam Houston Tollway (exit 60), W 12.6 mi on Beltway 8/Sam Houston Tollway to US-290, NW 2.2 mi to Eldridge Rd, S 0.6 mi (R)

HOUSTON — WESTLAKE RV RESORT. (281) 463-8566. **$43-$68.** 18602 Clay Rd 77084. From Jct of I-10 & Barker Cypress Rd exit: Go N 3 mi on Barker Cypress Rd to Clay Rd, W 0.2 mi (R)

INGRAM — JOHNSON CREEK RV RESORT & PARK. (830) 367-3300. **$40-$48.** 4279 Junction Hwy 78025. From Jct of Hwy 39 & Hwy 27, NW 4.7 mi on Hwy 27 (L); or From Jct of I-10 & Exit 488 (Hwy 27), SE 9 mi on Hwy 27 (R)

JUNCTION — JUNCTION NORTH LLANO RIVER RV PARK. (877) 446-3138. **$36-$39.** 2145 Main St 76849. From Jct of I-10 & US-377 (exit 456), S 0.5 mi on US-377 (R)

KEMAH — MARINA BAY RV RESORT. (281) 334-9944. **$58-$89.** 925 Fm 2094 77565. From Jct of I-45 & exit 23 (FM-518), E 2.7 mi on FM-518 to FM-2094, E 3.5 mi (R)

KERRVILLE — BUCKHORN LAKE RESORT. (830) 895-0007. **$42-$52.** 2885 Goat Creek Rd 78028. From Jct of I-10 & Exit 501 (FM-1338/Goat Creek Rd) - on the NW corner of N access rd & Goat Creek Rd, N 50 yds on Goat Creek Rd (L)

KERRVILLE — GUADALUPE RIVER RV RESORT. (830) 367-5676. **$39-$43.** 2605 Junction Hwy 78028. From Jct of I-10 & exit 505 (Harper Rd), S 2.4 mi on Harper Rd to Hwy 27, W 2.6 mi (L)

KINGSVILLE — NATURE'S OWN RV RESORT. (361) 221-2928. **$40. (no credit cards).** 5151 S Us Hwy 77 78363. From Jct of US-77 & FM-1356 (Gen Cavazos Rd), S 1.9 mi on US-77 (R)

LA GRANGE — COLORADO LANDING RV RESORT. (979) 968-9465. **$38.** 64 East Bluffview 78945. From Jct of US-77 & Bus SR-71 (downtown La Grange), S 0.4 mi on US-77 to Cedar St, W 0.1 mi (E)

LEANDER — LEANDER/NW AUSTIN KOA. (512) 259-7200. **$39-$45.** 2689 Hero Way 78641. From Jct I-35 (Exit 260) & FM 2243: Go 8 mi W on FM 2243, then 1/2 mi N on Ronald Regan Blvd, then 1 mi W on CR 269. (L)

LIBERTY HILL — RIO BONITO RV & CABIN. (512) 922-1383. **$35.** 1095 Cr 256 78642. From Jct Hwy 29 & US 183: Go 3-3/4 mi N on US 183, then 1/4 mi E on FM 3405, then 1/2 mi S on CR 257, then 1/4 mi SE on CR 256 (R)

LONGVIEW — FERNBROOK PARK. (903) 643-8888. **$35-$40.** 2073 Fm 2011 75603. From Jct of I-20 (exit 591) & FM 2011: Go 2 mi SE on FM 2011. (L)

MANSFIELD — TEXAN RV RANCH. (817) 473-1666. **$35.** 1961 Lone Star Rd 76063. From Jct of I-20 & US-287: Go 10 1/2 mi S on US-287, then 1/4 mi SW on Lone Star Rd (FM 157) (R)

MARBLE FALLS — SUNSET POINT ON LAKE LBJ. (830) 798-8199. **$48-$90.** 2322 N Wirtz Dam Rd 78654. From Jct of US 281 & FM 1431 (in Marble Falls): Go 3 1/4 mi W on FM 1431, then 2 1/4 mi S on Wirtz Dam Rd (R)

MEDINA — MEDINA HIGHPOINT RESORT. (800) 225-0991. **$45-$50.** 23195 Hwy 16 N 78055. From Kerrville, S 16 mi on Hwy 173 to Hwy 2828, W 7 mi to Hwy 16, NW 11.3 mi (L)

MERCEDES — **LLANO GRANDE LAKE PARK RESORT & COUNTRY CLUB MHP.** (956) 565-2638. **$30-$50.** 2215 East West Blvd 78570. From Jct of Expwy 83 & Mile 2 W Rd exit, S 1.5 mi on Mile 2 W Rd (R) 🏕 ➤ ⊠

MERCEDES — **PARADISE SOUTH RV RESORT.** (800) 405-6188. **$35.** 9099 N. Mile 2 West Rd 78570. From Jct of US-83 (Expwy) & Mile 2 W Rd exit, N 0.2 mi on Mile 2 W Rd (L) 🏕 ➤ ⊠

MISSION — **BENTSEN GROVE RESORT MHP.** (956) 585-7011. **$28-$39. (no credit cards).** 810 Bentsen Palm Drive 78572. W-bnd: From Jct of US-83 (Expwy) & Hwy 364/La Homa Rd/Bentsen Palm Dr exit, W 1.5 mi on N Frntg Rd to Bentsen Palm Dr (second light), S 0.9 mi on Bentsen Palm Dr (L); E-bnd: From Jct of US Expwy 83 & Bentsen Palm Dr, S 0.9 mi on Bentsen Palm Dr (L) 🏕 ➤ ⊠

MISSION — **BENTSEN PALM VILLAGE RV RESORT.** (877) 247-3727. **$40-$56.** 2500 S Bentsen Palm Dr 78572. E-bnd: From Jct of US-83 Expwy & Bentsen Palm Dr, S 3.1 mi on Bentsen Palm Dr (L); W-bnd: From Jct of US-83 Expwy & Hwy 364/La Homa/Bentsen Palm Dr exit, W 1.5 mi on N Frntg Rd to Bentsen Palm Dr (second light), S 3.1 mi on Bentsen Palm Dr (L) 🏕 ➤ ⊠

MISSION — **SPLIT RAIL RV PARK.** (956) 585-8135. **$38. (no credit cards).** 513 N Los Ebanos 78572. E-bnd: From Jct of US-83 (Expwy) & HWY 281, exit Los Ebanos Rd exit, N 0.1 mi on Los Ebanos (L) 🏕 ➤ ⊠

NEW BRAUNFELS — **HILL COUNTRY COTTAGE AND RV RESORT.** (830) 625-1919. **$44-$52.** 131 Rueckle Rd 78130. From Jct of I-35 & Ruekle Rd (exit 184): Go E 0.1 mi on Ruekle Rd (L) 🏕 ➤ ⊠

NEW CANEY — **FOREST RETREAT RV PARK.** (281) 354-9888. **$45-$55.** 21711 Mccleskey Rd 77357. From Jct of Hwy 59 & FM 1485 (New Caney exit): Go S 1 mi on Frontage Rd to McCleskey Rd, W 0.75 mi (R) 🏕 ➤ ⊠

NEWTON — **WHISPERING CREEK LODGING AND RV PARK.** (409) 379-8400. **$25-$29.** 3713 Hwy 190e 75966. From Jct of SR 87 & US 190, SE 3.2 mi on US 190 (L) ➤ ⊠

NORTHLAKE — **NORTHLAKE VILLAGE RV PARK.** ⏺ (817) 430-3303. **$35-$37.** 13001 Cleveland-Gibbs Rd #79 76262. From Jct I-35W (exit 70) & Hwy 114: Go 1 mi E on Hwy 114, then 1/4 mi N on Cleveland-Gibbs Rd (E) 🏕 ⊠

ONALASKA — **LAKE LIVINGSTON/ONALASKA KOA.** (936) 646-3824. **$32-$50.** 15152 Us Hwy 190 West 77360. E-bnd: From Jct of US 190 & FM-356 (in Onalaska), W 0.7 mi on US 190 (L); or W-bnd: From Jct of US 59 & US 190 (west of Livingston), W 12 mi on US 190 (R) ➤ ⊠

ONALASKA — **NORTHSHORE RV RESORT.** (936) 646-3124. **$35-$55.** 168 Butler 77360. E-bnd: From Jct of US 190 & FM 356 (in Onalaska), E 1.5 mi on US-190 (R); W-bnd: From Jct of US 59 & US 190 (West of Livingston), W 11.4 mi on US-190 (L) 🏕 ➤ ⊠

PHARR — **TEXAS TRAILS RV RESORT.** (956) 787-6538. **$36.** 501 W Owassa Rd 78577. S-bnd: US-281 & Bus 281 (Owassa Rd exit), W 0.3 mi on Owassa Rd (L) or N-bnd: US-83 & US-281, N 1.8 mi on US-281 to Edinburgh (Owassa Rd exit), N 0.8 mi on E Frntg Rd to Owassa Rd, W 0.3 mi (L) 🏕 ➤ ⊠

PORT ARANSAS — **PIONEER BEACH RESORT.** (361) 749-6248. **$42-$49.** 120 Gulfwind Dr 78373. From Jct of ferry landing & Hwy 361 (Cutoff Rd), SE 1 mi on Hwy 361 to first light, SW 3.4 mi on Hwy 361 (L); or From Jct of Park Rd 22 (Hwy 358) & Hwy 361, N 13.7 mi on Hwy 361 (R) 🏕 ➤ ⊠

PORTLAND — **SEA BREEZE RV PARK.** (361) 643-0744. **$34-$39.** 1026 Seabreeze Lane 78374. From Jct of US-181 & FM-893/Moore Ave exit, NW 1 mi on FM-893/Moore Ave to Marriott St, SW 0.5 mi to Doyle, S 0.2 mi (R) 🏕 ➤ ⊠

PORT LAVACA — **TEXAS LAKESIDE RV RESORT.** (361) 551-2267. **$40-$55.** 2499 W Austin St 77979. From Jct Hwy 87 & I-35: Go S .05 mi on Hwy 35, then go E 1 mi on County Road 101 ➤ ⊠

ROCKPORT — **ANCIENT OAKS RV PARK.** (361) 729-5051. **$32-$40.** 1222 Bus Hwy 35 S 78382. From Jct of Bus Hwy 35 & FM-1069, SW 0.7 mi on Bus Hwy 35 (L) ➤ ⊠

SAN ANTONIO — **ADMIRALTY RV RESORT.** (210) 647-7878. **$40-$60.** 1485 N Ellison Dr 78251. From Jct of Loop 410 & Hwy 151, Sea World (Exit 9A), NW 2.7 mi on Hwy 151 to W. Military Dr, W 0.3 mi to Ellison S .02 mi (R) 🏕 ➤ ⊠

SAN ANTONIO — **BLAZING STAR LUXURY RV RESORT.** ⏺ (888) 838-7186. **$44-$73.** 1120 W Loop 1604 N 78251. (W Bnd from Houston) East Jct of I-10 & Loop 410, W 8.3 mi on I-10 to Hwy 90, W 11.7 mi on Hwy 90 to Loop 1604, N 4.5 mi (R) Located between Potranco Rd & Military Dr W (E Bnd from El Paso) W Jct of I-10 & Loop 1604, SW 14 mi on Loop 1604 to Potranco Rd. Turn around & go back 0.6 mi on Loop 1604 (R) 🏕 ➤ ⊠

SAN ANTONIO — **GREENTREE VILLAGE RV PARK MHP.** (210) 655-3331. **$45.** 12015 O'Connor Rd 78233. From NE Jct of I-410 Loop & I-35, N 2.2 mi on I-35 to Wurzbach Pkwy/O'Connor Rd (exit 169), W 0.5 mi on O'Connor Rd, then NW 0.1 mi on O'Connor Rd (L) 🏕 ➤ ⊠

SAN ANTONIO — **TRAVELER'S WORLD RV RESORT.** (210) 532-8310. **$42-$47.** 2617 Roosevelt Ave 78214. From Jct of I-37S & Military Dr W (exit 135), W 3.1 mi on Military Dr to Roosevelt, N 1.3 mi (L); or From Jct of I-35S & Military Dr (exit 150B), E 2.7 mi on Military Dr to Roosevelt, N 1.3 mi (L) Do NOT follow GPS 🏕 ➤ ⊠

SAN MARCOS — **CANYON TRAIL RV RESORT.** (512) 805-9988. **$35-$37.** 6050 I-H 35 S 78666. From jct Hwy 80 & I-35: Go 6 mi S on I-35 (Exit 199), then 1 mi S on W Frontage Rd (R) 🏕

SAN MARCOS — **PECAN PARK RIVERSIDE RV & CABINS.** (512) 396-0070. **$39-$55.** 50 Squirrel Run 78666. From Jct I-35 (exit 205) & Hwy 80: Go 2 mi SE on Hwy 80 (1 mi past Blanco River Bridge), then 1 block S on Old Bastrop Hwy, then 1/2 mi E on Martindale Rd. (R) 🏕 ➤ ⊠

SANTO — **COFFEE CREEK RV RESORT & CABINS.** (940) 769-2277. **$30-$38.** 13429 S Hwy 281 76472. From Jct of I-20 & Exit 386 (US 281): Go 1/2 mi N on US 281 (R) 🏕 ➤ ⊠

SOUTH PADRE ISLAND — **SOUTH PADRE KOA.** (800) 562-9724. **$46-$80.** 1 Padre Blvd 78597. From Jct of Queen Isabella Causeway & Padre Blvd (Park Rd 100), S 0.3 mi on Padre Blvd (R) 🏕 ➤ ⊠

SPRING — RAYFORD CROSSING RV RESORT. (281) 298-8008. **$49-$68.** 29321 S. Plum Creek Dr 77386. From Jct I-45 & Rayford Rd (Exit 73), Go 1.5 mi E on Rayford Rd then 1/2 mi S on Geneva Rd to dead end, then 1/4 mi E on N Plum Creek Dr (L) NOTE: No Pop up trailers 🏕 ⛵ 🍴

TERRELL — BLUEBONNET RIDGE RV PARK & COTTAGES. (972) 524-9600. **$40.** 16543 Fm 429 75161. From Jct of I-20 (exit 506) & FM-429: Go 1/2 mi N on FM-429 (L) 🏕 ⛵ 🍴

TEXARKANA — SHADY PINES RV PARK. (903) 832-1268. **$30.** 10010 W 7th St 75501. From Jct of US 59 & US 67 (W side of Texarkana): Go 6 mi W on US 67 (R) 🏕 🍴

VICTORIA — LAZY LONGHORN RV PARK. (361) 485-1598. **$30. (no credit cards).** 1402 S Laurent St 77901. From Jct of US-59 & Hwy 185, NW 1 mi on Hwy 185 (Laurent St) (R) or From Jct of Bus Hwy 59 & Laurent St (Hwy 185), SE 2 mi on Laurent St (L) 🏕 ⛵ 🍴

VICTORIA — VICTORIA COLETO CREEK LAKE KOA. **$43-$51.** 500 Coleto Park Road 77905. From jct US Hwy 59 & Coleto Park Rd, go W .5 mi (L) ⛵

WALLER — LONESTAR YOGI. 🅰🅰🅰 (979) 826-4111. **$34-$58.** 34843 Betka Rd 77484. From Jct of US 290 & FM-1098 (E of Hempstead): Go S 4.1 mi on FM-1098 (E) ⛵ 🍴

WEATHERFORD — OAK CREEK RV PARK. (817) 594-0200. **$35.** 7652 W I-20 76088. From Jct FM 1189 & I-20 (Exit 397): Go 1/2 mi W on N Service Rd (R) 🏕 ⛵ 🍴

WICHITA FALLS — WICHITA FALLS RV PARK. 🅰🅰🅰 (800) 252-1532. **$30-$38.** 2944 Seymour Hwy 76301. N-bnd: From Jct of US 287 & Broad St exit: Go 3/4 mi N (stay right at split), then 1-1/4 mi W on 5th St/Seymour Hwy. (R) S-bnd: From Jct of US 287 & exit 1A: Go 1-1/4 mi SW on Bus 277 (5th/Seymour Hwy). (R) 🏕 ⛵ 🍴

WILLS POINT — CANTON I-20 RV PARK. (903) 873-8561. **$35.** 24481 Ih-20 75169. From Jct of I-20 & Exit 519, E 0.25 mi on South access rd (R) ⛵ 🍴

WOLFFORTH — MESA VERDE RV PARK. (806) 773-3135. **$33.** 503 E Hwy 62/82 79382. From Jct W Loop 289 & US 62/82 (Lubbock): Go 5 mi SW on US 62/82 (Exit FM 179), then 1-1/4 mi N on E Service Rd (R) 🏕 ⛵

Utah

FILLMORE — FILLMORE KOA. (435) 743-4420. **$35-$40.** 905 South Hwy 99 84631. From Jct of I-15 & exit 163 (bus loop), N 0.3 mi on bus loop to 900 S St, E 0.5 mi (E) ⛵ 🍴

HEBER CITY — MOUNTAIN VALLEY RV RESORT. (435) 657-6100. **$35-$45.** 2120 South Hwy 40 84032. From Jct of SR 40 & SR 189 (in town), S 1.0 mi on SR 40 (R) (Park is under construction-targeted opening date Oct 2013) ⛵ 🍴

HURRICANE — WILLOWWIND RV PARK. (435) 635-4154. **$33-$43. (no credit cards).** 80 S 1150 W 84737. E-bnd: From Jct of I-15 & Hwy 9 (Exit 16), E 8 mi on Hwy 9 to 1150 West, S 0.1 mi (L); or W-bnd: From Jct of SR-9 & SR-17, 3.8 mi on SR-9 to S 1150 W, L 0.1 mi on S 1150 W (L)

MONUMENT VALLEY — GOULDING'S MONUMENT VALLEY & RV PARK CAMPGROUND. 🅰🅰🅰 (435) 727-3235. **$49.** 2000 Main St 84536. From Kayenta, AZ, N 22 mi on US-163 to Monument Valley Rd, W 2 mi (R); or From Mexican Hat town center, SW 21 mi on US-163 to Monument Valley Rd, W 2 mi (R) ⛵

PROVO — LAKESIDE RV CAMPGROUND. 🅰🅰🅰 (801) 373-5267. **$30-$33.** 4000 West Center St 84601. S-bnd: From Jct of I-15 & Center St (exit 265), W 2.2 mi on Center St (R); or N-bnd: From Jct of I-15 & Center St (exit 265), W 2.2 mi on Center St (R) ⛵ 🍴

ST. GEORGE — MCARTHUR'S TEMPLE VIEW RV RESORT. 🅰🅰🅰 (800) 510-6765. **$42.** 975 S Main St 84770. From Jct of I-15 & Bluff St (exit 6), N 0.2 mi on Bluff St to Main St, NE 0.3 mi (R) ⛵ 🍴

SALT LAKE CITY — SALT LAKE CITY KOA. 🅰🅰🅰 (801) 328-0224. **$47-$55.** 1400 W N Temple 84116. W-bnd: From Jct of I-15 & I-80 (exit 308), W 1.7 mi on I-80 to Redwood Rd exit (exit 118), N 0.3 mi on Redwood Rd to N Temple, E 0.3 mi to 1460 West, N on 1460 West 100 ft. (R) E-bnd: From Jct of I-80 & exit 115 (N Temple), E 3 mi on N Temple (follow signs) to 1460 West, N on 1460 West 100 ft (R) ⛵ 🍴

VIRGIN — ZION RIVER RESORT. (888) 466-8594. **$49-$62.** 551 E Hwy 9 84779. N-bnd: From Jct of I-15 & Hwy 9 (exit 16), E 18.9 mi on Hwy 9 to MP 19 (R); or S-bnd: From Jct of I-15 & Hwy 17 (exit 27), S 6 mi on Hwy 17 to Hwy 9, E 6.3 mi to MP 19 (R) ⛵ 🍴

Vermont

DANVILLE — SUGAR RIDGE RV VILLAGE & CAMPGROUND INC. (802) 684-2550. **$40-$42.** 24 Old Stagecoach Rd 05828. From Jct of I-91 & Rte 2 (exit 21), W 4.5 mi on Rte 2 (L) ⛵ 🍴

Virginia

ASHLAND — AMERICAMPS RV RESORT. (804) 798-5298. **$35-$49.** 11322 Air Park Rd 23005. From Jct of I-95 & I-295, N 4 mi on I-95 to Jct of exit 89 (Lewistown Rd/Rte 802) & Rte 802, E 0.1 mi on Rte 802 to Air Park Rd, S 0.75 mi (L) ⛵ 🍴

CAPE CHARLES — CHERRYSTONE FAMILY CAMPING RESORT. 🅰🅰🅰 (757) 331-3063. **$17-$71.** 1511 Townfield Dr 23310. From Jct of Chesapeake Bay Bridge Tunnel (N end) & US-13, N 11.1 mi on US-13 to SR-680, W 1.5 mi (E) ⛵ 🍴

CHARLOTTESVILLE — CHARLOTTESVILLE KOA. (434) 296-9881. **$30-$48.** 3825 Red Hill Rd 22903. From Jct of I-64 & SR20 (exit 121A), S 8.5 mi on SR20 to SR-708 (Red Hill Rd), W 1.5 mi (R) ⛵ 🍴

DOSWELL — KINGS DOMINION CAMP WILDERNESS. (804) 876-3006. **$38-$75.** 10061 Kings Dominion Blvd 23047. From Jct of I-95 (exit 98/Doswell/Kings Dominion) & SR-30, E 0.6 mi on SR-30 (R) ⛵ 🍴

FANCY GAP — FANCY GAP / BLUE RIDGE PARKWAY KOA. (800) 562-1876. **$32-$55.** 47 Fox Trail Loop 24328. From Jct of I-77 & SR-148/Chance Creek Rd (Exit 8) W 0.1 mi on SR-148 to Pottery Dr, SW 0.3 mi to Frog Spur Rd, E 0.9 mi (R) ⛵ 🍴

FREDERICKSBURG — FREDERICKSBURG-WASH, DC KOA. (800) 562-1889. **$33-$51.** 7400 Brookside Ln 22408. S-bnd: Jct I-95 & US-1 (exit 126/Spotsylvania), S 4 mi on US-1 to SR-607, E 2.5 mi (R); or N-bnd: Jct I-95 & Rte 606 (exit 118/Thornburg), W 0.2 mi on Rte 606 to US-1, N 4 mi to SR-607, E 2.5 mi (R) ⛵ 🍴

GORDONSVILLE — SHENANDOAH CROSSING. (540) 832-9400. **$50.** 174 Horseshoe Cir 22942. From Jct I-64 (Exit 135) & Hwy 15, N 10.1 mi on Hwy 5 to Hwy 33, E 3.6 mi on Hwy 33 to Rte 749 (Forest Hill Rd), S 1.7 mi on Rte 749 to Horseshoe Circle, W 0.2 mi on Horseshoe Circle (E) ⛵ 🍴

GREENWOOD — MISTY MOUNTAIN CAMP RESORT. ⬭
(888) 647-8900. **$35-$46.** 56 Misty Mountain Rd 22943. From Jct of
I-64 (exit 107/Crozet) & US-250 (13 mi W of Charlottesville), W 0.7 mi
on US-250 (L) 🔁 🔀

HAYES — YOGI BEAR'S JELLYSTONE PARK CAMP-
RESORT AT GLOUCESTER POINT. (800) 332-4316. **$39-$69.**
3149 Campground Rd 23072. N-bnd: From Jct US-17 & SR 216, E 0.9
mi on SR-216 to SR-641, N 1.5 mi to SR-655, E 0.35 mi to SR-714, N
0.2 mi (R); or S-bnd: From Jct US-17 & SR-636, E 0.5 mi on SR-636
to SR-656, SE 1.4 mi to SR-641,S 0.8 mi to SR-655, E 0.35 mi to
SR-714, N 0.2 mi (R) 🔁 🔀

LURAY — LURAY KOA. (800) 562-2790. **$44-$69.** 3402 Kimball
Rd 22835. From Jct of US 211 & US 340 (in Luray), N 2.3 mi on US
340 to SR-658/Kimball Rd, E 0.25 mi (L); or From Jct of I-66 & US 340
(Exit 6), S 23 mi on US 340 to SR-658/Kimball Rd, E 0.25 mi (L)
🔁 🔀

MADISON — SHENANDOAH HILLS CAMPGROUND. ⬭
(540) 948-4186. **$35-$51.** 110 Campground Lane 22727. From Jct of
I-64 & US 29 (Exit 118), N 28 mi on US 29 (L) 🏊 🔀

MAX MEADOWS — FORT CHISWELL RV PARK. (276)
637-6868. **$32-$36.** 312 Ft Chiswell Rd 24360. From Jct of I-81/77 &
US-52 (exit 80), S 0.5 mi on US-52 (L) 🎿 🔁 🔀

MOUNT JACKSON — SHENANDOAH VALLEY CAMP-
GROUND. (540) 477-3080. **$35-$47.** 168 Industrial Park Road 22842.
N- Bnd: From Jct of I-81 & Exit 269 (Shenandoah Caverns) W on
Caverns Rd., continue right onto Caverns Rd (SR 730 before high
school.) W 0.8 mi to Industrial Park Rd, NE 0.2 mi (R) S-bnd: from Jct:
of I-81 & Exit 269 (Shenandoah Caverns) W on Caverns follow N-Bnd
directions 🔁 🔀

NATURAL BRIDGE — NATURAL BRIDGE-LEXINGTON
KOA. ⬭ (540) 291-2770. **$34-$72.** 214 Kildeer Lane 24578. S-bnd:
From Jct of I-81 (Fancy Hill) & US-11 (exit 180B), cross US-11 to
entrance rd (E); or N-bnd: From Jct of I-81 & US-11 (exit 180), NE .6
mi (under I-81) to entrance rd (L) 🔁 🔀

STAUNTON — STAUNTON / WALNUT HILLS KOA. (800)
699-2568. **$34-$65.** 484 Walnut Hills Rd 24401. N-bnd: From Jct of
I-81 & US-11 (Exit 213), S (R) 0.2 mi on US-11 to US-340/Stuarts
Draft Hwy, NE (L) 2.5 mi to SR-655/Walnut Hills Rd, N (L) 03. mi; or
S-bnd: From Jct of I-81 & White Hill Rd (Exit 217), W (R) 0.4 mi on
White Hill Rd to US-11, S (L) 1.5 mi to SR-655/Walnut Hills Rd, E (L)
1 mi (L) 🔁 🔀

TEMPERANCEVILLE — TALL PINES HARBOR WATER-
FRONT CAMPGROUND. (757) 824-0777. **$34-$71.** 8107 Tall Pines
Ln 23442. From Jct of SR-695 and US-13 in Temperanceville, W 6.5
mi on SR-695 to Entrance Rd (R) 🔁 🔀

TOPPING — GREY'S POINT CAMP. (804) 758-2485. **$40-$75.**
3601 Greys Point Rd 23169. From Jct of US 17 & SR-33 (in Saluda),
E 8 mi on SR-33 to SR-3, NW approx 5 mi (L) 🎿 🔁 🔀

URBANNA — BETHPAGE CAMP RESORT. (804) 758-4349.
$40-$85. 679 Brown'S Lane 23175. From Jct of US-17 & SR-33 (in
Saluda), NW 1 mi on US-17 to Rte 616, E 2 mi to Rte 602, NW 0.1 mi
to Rte 684, N 0.5 mi to entrance rd (R) 🎿 🔁 🔀

VIRGINIA BEACH — INDIAN COVE RESORT. (757) 426-
2601. **Call for rates.** 1053 Sandbridge Rd 23456. From Jct I-64 &
Indian River Rd (Exit 286): E 1.5 mi on Indian River Rd to Ferrell
Pkwy, E 2.5 mi on Ferrell Pkwy to Princess Anne Rd, SE 7.8 mi on
Princess Anne Pkwy to Sandbridge Rd, SE 4 mi on Sandbridge Rd (R)

VIRGINIA BEACH — OUTDOOR RESORTS-VIRGINIA
BEACH. (800) 333-7515. **$82-$92.** 3665 S Sandpiper Rd 23456. From
Jct of General Booth Blvd & Princess Anne Rd, SE 0.8 mi on Princess
Anne Rd to Sandbridge Rd, SE 5 mi to Sandpiper Rd, S 3.5 mi (R)
🎿 🔁 🔀

WAYNESBORO — WAYNESBORO NORTH 340 CAMP-
GROUND. (540) 943-9573. **$36.** 1125 Eastside Hwy (Us-340) 22980.
From Jct of I-64 & US-340 (exit 96), N 7 mi on US-340 (R); or From
Jct of I-81 & SR-612 (exit 227), E 9.6 mi on SR-612 to US-340, S 2 mi
(L) 🔁 🔀

WILLIAMSBURG — AMERICAN HERITAGE RV PARK.
⬭ (888) 530-2267. **$46-$70.** 146 Maxton Lane 23188. From Jct of
I-64 & Rte 607 (exit 231A), SW 0.5 mi on Rte 607 to Maxton Ln on
left, S 0.2 mi (L) 🔁 🔀

WILLIAMSBURG — ANVIL CAMPGROUND. (757) 565-
2300. **$35-$65.** 5243 Mooretown Rd 23188. From Jct of I-64 & Rte 143
(Camp Peary-exit 238), S 0.1 mi on Rte 143 to Rochambeau Dr, NW
1.4 mi to Rte 645 (Airport Rd), SW 1.8 mi to Rte 603 (Mooretown Rd),
SE 0.3 mi (R); or From Jct of US-60 & Rte 645, NE 0.1 mi on Rte 645
to Rte 603, SE 0.3 mi (R) 🔁 🔀

WILLIAMSBURG — COLONIAL CENTRAL KOA. (800) 562-
1733. **$35-$68.** 4000 Newman Rd 23188. E-bnd: From Jct of I-64 (exit
234) & Rte 646 (Newman Rd), NE 1 mi on Rte 646 (R); or W-bnd:
From Jct of I-64 (exit 234B) & Rte 646 (Newman Rd), NE 1 mi on Rte
646 (R) 🔁 🔀

WILLIAMSBURG — WILLIAMSBURG KOA. ⬭ (800) 562-
1733. **$35-$68.** 5210 Newman Rd 23188. E-bnd: From Jct of I-64 &
Rte 646 (exit 234/Newman Rd)lt turn, NE 1.5 mi on Rte 646 (R); or
W-bnd: From Jct of I-64 & Rte 646 (exit 234B), NE 1.5 mi on Rte 646
(R) 🔁 🔀

Washington

BOTHELL — LAKE PLEASANT RV PARK. (425) 487-1785.
$44. 24025 Bothell Everett Hwy Se 98021. S-bnd: From Jct of I-5 (Exit
182) & I-405: Go 3 mi S on I-405 to Bothell Hwy (Exit 26), then 1-1/8
mi S on Bothell Hwy to 242nd St (L). N-bnd: From Jct of I-5 & I-405:
Go 26 mi N on I-405 to Bothell Hwy (Exit 26), then 1-1/8 mi S on Bothell Hwy to 242nd St (L). 🎿

CASTLE ROCK — TOUTLE RIVER RV RESORT. (360) 274-
8373. **$42.** 150 Happy Trails 98611. From Jct of I-5 (Exit 52) & Barnes
Rd: Go 1/8 mi on Barnes Rd to Happy Trails Rd (L) 🔁 🔀

CENTRALIA — MIDWAY RV PARK. (800) 600-3204. **$39.** 3200
Galvin Rd 98531. From Jct of I-5 & Harrison Ave (exit 82), W 0.8 mi
on Harrison Ave to Galvin Rd, S 0.3 mi (L) 🎿

CHENEY — PONDEROSA FALLS RV RESORT. (800) 494-
7275. **$37-$42.** 7520 S Thomas Mallen Rd 99004. From Jct of I-90 &
Medical Lake exit (Exit 272/Medical Lake): Go 1-1/8 mi S on Aero Rd
to Thomas Mallen Rd, then 1/4 mi S on Thomas Mallen Rd (R)
🔁 🔀

CLARKSTON — GRANITE LAKE PREMIER RV RESORT.
(800) 989-4578. **$42-$49.** 306 Granite Lake Dr 99403. From Jct of
Hwy 12 & 5th St (in town): Go 1/4 mi N on 5th St (L) 🎿 🔀

CLARKSTON — **HELLS CANYON RV RESORT & MARINA.**
(509) 758-6963. **$32-$42.** 1550 Port Drive 99403. From Jct of SR-12 &
SR 193 (15th St, W-side of town): Go 1/8 mi N on SR-193 to Port Dr,
then W on Port Dr (L) ⌁ ⌧

DEER PARK — **SPOKANE RV RESORT AT DEER PARK**
GOLF CLUB. (877) 276-1555. **$37.** 1205 Country Club Dr 99006.
From Jct of US-395 & Crawford St (between MP 180 & 181): Go 1-3/4
mi E on W Crawford St to N Country Club Dr, then 1 mi N on Country Club Dr (R) ⌁ ⌁ ⌧

EVERETT — **LAKESIDE RV PARK.** ⏣ (800) 468-7275. **$39.**
12321 Hwy 99 S 98204. From Jct I-5 N & WA-525 (Exit 182), merge
onto WA-525 toward WA-99: Go 3 mi N on WA-525, then merge onto
Hwy 99 N toward Everett, then 1-1/2 mi N on Hwy 99 (R) ⌧

FERNDALE — **THE CEDARS RV RESORT.** (360) 384-2622.
$40-$47. 6335 Portal Way 98248. From Jct of I-5 & Portal Way (exit
263): Go 1 mi N on Portal Way (L) ⌁ ⌧

GIG HARBOR — **GIG HARBOR RV RESORT.** (253) 858-
8138. **$30-$42.** 9515 Burnham Dr Nw 98332. From Jct of I-5 & SR-16
(exit 132): Go 12-1/2 mi W on SR-16 to Burnham Dr exit, then at traffic
circle east of freeway take first exit onto Burnham Dr, then 1.2 mi E on
Burnham Dr (L). ⌁

KELSO — **BROOKHOLLOW RV PARK.** (800) 867-0453. **$35.**
2506 Allen St 98626. From Jct of I-5 & Allen St (exit 39): Go 1 mi E
on Allen St (just past mobile home park look for white RV park sign)
(R) ⌁ ⌧

KENNEWICK — **COLUMBIA SUN RV RESORT.** ⏣ (509)
420-4880. **$45-$55.** 103907 E Wiser Parkway 99338. From Jct US 395
& I-82: Go 3-1/2 mi NW on I-82 to Badger Rd (Exit 109), then 1/2 mi
SW on Badger Rd to Wiser Pkwy, then 3/4 mi W on Wiser Pkwy (L).
⌁ ⌧

LEAVENWORTH — **ICICLE RIVER RV RESORT.** ⏣ (509)
548-5420. **$35-$44.** 7305 Icicle Rd 98826. From Jct of US-2 & Icicle
Rd exit (W end of town): Go 3 mi SW on Icicle Rd (L) ⌁ ⌧

MEAD — **ALDERWOOD RV RESORT.** (888) 847-0500. **$30-$45.**
14007 N Newport Hwy 99021. From Jct of I-90 & Argonne Rd. (Exit
287): Go 8-1/4 mi N on Argonne Rd to US-206, then 2-1/4 mi W on
US 206 to US-2, then 1/8 mi S on US 2 (R), or S-Bnd: From Jct of
US-2 & US-206: Go 1/8 mi S on US-2 (R) ⌁ ⌧

MOSES LAKE — **SUNCREST RESORT.** (509) 765-0355. **$33-
$40.** 303 Hansen Rd 98837. From Jct of I-90 & Hansen Rd (exit 174):
Go 1/4 mi N on Hansen Rd (R) ⌁ ⌁ ⌧

PORT ANGELES — **ELWHA DAM RV PARK.** (877) 435-9421.
$36. 47 Lower Dam Rd 98363. From Jct of US 101 & Lincoln St (in
town): Go 5-1/2 mi W on US 101 to SR-112, then 3/4 mi W on SR-112
to Lower Dam Rd, then 1/8 mi S on Dam Rd (L) ⌧

REPUBLIC — **WINCHESTER RV PARK.** (509) 775-1039. **$33-
$36. (no credit cards).** 8 West Curlew Lake Rd 99166. From Jct of
US-20 & US-21N: Go 2-1/2 mi N on US-21N to W Curlew Lake Rd,
then 1/8 mi W on Curlew Lake Rd (R) ⌧

RICHLAND — **HORN RAPIDS RV RESORT.** (866) 557-9637.
$36. 2640 Kingsgate Way 99354. From Jct of I-182 & Hwy 240W (exit
4): go 4 mi NE on Hwy 240W, then 2 mi NW on Hwy 240W to Kingsgate Wy, then 1/8 mi NE on Kingsgate Wy (R). ⌁ ⌁ ⌧

SHELTON — **LITTLE CREEK CASINO RESORT RV PARK.**
(800) 667-7711. **$29-$45.** 91 W State Route 108 98584. From Jct US
101 & Hwy 108: Go 1/8 mi W on Hwy 108 (L)

SHELTON — **THE WATERFRONT AT POTLATCH.** (360) 877-
9422. **$40-$50.** 21660 North Us Hwy 101 98584. From Jct of US 101
& SR-119/N Lake Cushman Rd (in town): Go 2.7 mi S on US Hwy
101, between MP 334 & 335 (L) ⌁ ⌧

STANWOOD — **CEDAR GROVE SHORES RV PARK.** (866)
342-4981. **$30-$35. (no credit cards).** 16529 West Lake Goodwin Rd
98292. From Jct of I-5 & 172nd St (exit 206), W 2.2 mi on 172nd St to
Lakewood Rd (SR-531), W 3.2 mi to West Lake Goodwin Rd, S 0.7 mi
(L) ⌁ ⌧

TOPPENISH — **YAKAMA NATION RV RESORT.** ⏣ (800)
874-3087. **$40-$45.** 280 Buster Rd 98948. From Jct of I-82 & US 97:
Go 13.8 mi SE on Hwy 97 to Buster Rd, then 1/8 mi SW on Buster Rd
(R); or From Jct of I-82 & Toppenish/SR-22E (exit 50): Go 3 mi S on
SR-22E to W First Ave, then 1/2 mi W on W First Ave to US-97 (no
street sign), then 3/4 mi NW to Buster Rd, then 1/8 mi SW on Buster
(R). ⌁ ⌧

WOODLAND — **COLUMBIA RIVERFRONT RV PARK.** ⏣
(800) 845-9842. **$38-$46.** 1881 Dike Rd 98674. From Jct of I-5 & Exit
22: Go 1-1/2 mi W on Dike Access Rd to Dike Rd, then 1 mi S on
Dike Rd (R). ⌁ ⌁ ⌧

Wisconsin

ALMA CENTER — **KOA HIXTON/ALMA CENTER LLC.**
(800) 562-2680. **$30-$53.** N 9657 State Hwy 95 54611. From Jct of
I-94 & Hwy 95 (exit 105), E 3.5 mi on Hwy 95 (L) ⌁ ⌧

BAILEYS HARBOR — **BAILEYS GROVE CAMPGROUND.**
(920) 839-2559. **$35-$39.** 2552 County Road F 54202. From Jct of
Hwy 57 & CR-F, W 0.7 mi on CR-F (R) ⌁ ⌧

BARABOO — **DELL BOO FAMILY CAMPGROUND.** ⏣
(608) 356-5898. **$43-$51.** E 10562 Shady Lane Rd 53913. From Jct of
I-90/94 & US-12 (exit 92), L to Baraboo, then take exit 214 L to stop
light, then L on Business 12 Cty Trunk BD 1mi, then L on Shady Lane
Rd, then go 3/4 mi (R) ⌁ ⌧

DE FOREST — **MADISON KOA.** (800) 562-5784. **$39-$55.** 4859
County Road V 53532. From Jct of I-90/94 & CR-V (exit 126), E 0.25
mi on CR-V (R) ⌁ ⌧

GLENBEULAH — **WESTWARD HO RV RESORT & CAMP-
GROUND.** ⏣ (888) 712-9617. **$31-$57.** N5456 Division Rd 53023.
From Jct US-41 & Hwy 23: Go 16 mi E on Hwy 23, then 3 mi S on
CR-G, then 1/2 mi E on CR-T & follow signs. ⌁ ⌧

MILTON — **HIDDEN VALLEY RV RESORT & CAMP-
GROUND.** (800) 469-5515. **$38-$72.** 872 E State Road 59 53563.
From Jct of I-90 & Hwy 59E (exit 163): Go E 1/2 mi on State Rd 59E
(R) ⌁ ⌧

OSSEO — **STONEY CREEK RV RESORT.** (888) 349-6399. **$37-
$52.** 50483 Oak Grove Rd 54758. From Jct of Hwy 10 & I-94 (exit 88),
E 0.1 mi on Hwy 10 to Oak Grove Rd, S 0.4 mi (R) ⌁ ⌧

PARDEEVILLE — **PRIDE OF AMERICA CAMPING RESORT.**
(800) 236-6395. **$45-$65.** W7520 West Bush Rd 53954. From Jct of
Hwys 33 & 51/16, SE 3 mi on Hwy 51/16 to CR-P, E 1.6 mi to CR-G,
E 0.25 mi to W Bush Rd, N 0.2 mi (L) ⌁ ⌧

RIO — **SILVER SPRINGS CAMPSITES.** (920) 992-3537. **$35-$54.**
N5048 Ludwig Rd 53960. From Jct of Hwy 16 & CR-B, N 0.5 mi on
CR-B into RIO, E 3.3 mi on Cty B to Ludwig Rd, N 1 mi (R) ⌁ ⌧

SPRING GREEN — **WISCONSIN RIVERSIDE RESORT.** (608) 588-2826. **$36-$55.** S13220 Shifflet Rd 53588. From Jct of Hwy 23 & Hwy 14, S 0.8 mi on Hwy 23 to Madison St, W 0.7 mi on Madison St to Shifflet Rd, S 0.75 mi (E) 🛶 ⊠

WATERTOWN — **RIVER BEND RV RESORT.** (920) 261-7505. **$30-$90.** W 6940 Rubidell Rd 53094. From Jct of 26 & 19, W 6 mi on 19 to Q St, S 1 mi to Hubbleton Rd, W 1 mi to Riverbend Rd, S 1 mi to Rubidell, W 0.7 mi (R) ⊠

WEST SALEM — **NESHONOC LAKESIDE CAMP-RESORT.** (608) 786-1792. **$49-$77.** N 5334 Neshonoc Rd 54669. From Jct of I-90 & C (West Salem Exit 12), N 1 mi on C to Hwy 16, E 1.5 mi (R) (ADA pool lifts available in both pools) 🛶 ⊠

WILD ROSE — **EVERGREEN CAMPSITES & RESORT.** ⓐⓐⓐ (866) 450-2267. **$49-$64.** W 5449 Archer Lane 54984. From Jct of SR-22 & CRs-G & H, E 3 mi on CR-H to Archer Ln, E 1.75 mi (R) 🛶 ⊠

WISCONSIN DELLS — **CHRISTMAS MOUNTAIN VILLAGE CAMPGROUND.** (608) 253-1000. **$55.** S944 Christmas Mtn Rd 53965. From Jct I-90/94 (Exit 87) & Hwy 13: Go 1/2 mi E on Hwy 13, then 4 mi NW on CR-H, then 1/2 mi S on Lyndon Rd. 🛶 ⊠

WISCONSIN DELLS — **SHERWOOD FOREST CAMPING & RV PARK.** (877) 474-3796. **$32-$57.** 2852 Wisconsin Dells Parkway 53965. From Jct of I-90/94 & SR-13 (exit 87), E 0.25 mi on SR-13 to US-12/SR-16, NW 0.4 mi (R) 🛶 ⊠

WISCONSIN DELLS — **WISCONSIN DELLS KOA.** (800) 254-4177. **$39-$67.** S 235 A Stand Rock Rd 53965. From Jct of I-90/94 & Hwy 13N (Exit 87): Go E 1 mi on Hwy 13N to Standrock Rd (3rd stoplight), then N 3/4 mi (L); or From Jct of I-90/94 & Hwy 12/16 (Exit 85): Go E 1/4 mi on Hwy 12/16 to Hwy A, then N 1/2 mi on Hwy A to Stand Rock Rd, then S 1/3 mi (R) 🛶 ⊠

WISCONSIN DELLS — **YOGI BEAR'S JELLYSTONE PARK CAMP-RESORT.** ⓐⓐⓐ (800) 462-9644. **$39-$119.** S1915 Ishnala Rd 53965. From Jct of I-90/94 & US-12 (exit 92), NW 0.5 mi on US-12 to Gasser Rd, W 1 mi to Ishnala Rd, S 100 ft (R) 🛶 ⊠

WOODRUFF — **HIAWATHA TRAILER RESORT.** (888) 429-2842. **$34-$39.** 1077 Old Hwy 51s 54568. From Jct of Hwys 51 & 47, E 0.3 mi on Hwy 47 to Old Hwy 51 (Balsam St), N 0.5 mi (L) 🚐 ⊠

WOODRUFF — **INDIAN SHORES RV & COTTAGE RESORT.** (715) 356-5552. **$35-$77.** 7750 Indian Shores Rd 54568. From Jct of Hwys 51 & 47, SE 4.5 mi on Hwy 47 (R) 🛶 ⊠

Wyoming

BUFFALO — **BUFFALO KOA.** (307) 684-5423. **$38-$48.** 87 Us Hwy 16e 82834. From Jct of I-90 & US-16 (exit 58), W 1 mi on US-16 (L); or From Jct of I-25 & US-16 (exit 299), E 0.3 mi on US-16 (R) 🛶 ⊠

BUFFALO — **DEER PARK.** ⓐⓐⓐ (307) 684-5722. **$32-$42.** 146 Us Hwy 16e Deer Park Rd 82834. From Jct of I-90 & US-16 (exit 58), W 0.7 mi on US-16 (R); or From Jct of I-25 & US-16 (exit 299), E 0.7 mi on US-16 (L) 🛶 ⊠

GREYBULL — **GREYBULL KOA.** ⓐⓐⓐ (800) 562-7508. **$39-$55.** 399 N 2nd St 82426. From Jct of US-14 (Greybull Ave) & US-16/14 (6th St), N 0.4 mi on 6th St to 4th Ave, E 0.4 mi (E) 🛶 ⊠

Canada

Camping information provided by Woodall's®

Alberta

HINTON — **HINTON/JASPER KOA.** ⓐⓐ (888) 562-4714. **$35-$50.** 50409b Hwy 16 T7V 1X3. From Jct of Hwy 40N & Hwy 16, W 0.7mi/1.1km (L); or From Jasper Natl Park East Gate, E 11.2 mi (18 km) on Hwy 16 (R) ⊠

SPRUCE GROVE — **DIAMOND GROVE RV CAMPGROUND.** (780) 962-8003. **$45-$55.** 41 Century Close T7X 3B3. From Jct of Hwy 16A & Hwy 60, W 8km/5 mi on Hwy16A to Century Rd, S 1.3km/0.8 mi to Century Close, W 316 yds/ 288 m (L) 🚐 ⊠

British Columbia

ALDERGROVE — **EAGLE WIND RV PARK.** (604) 856-6674. **$37-$52.** 26920 52nd Ave V4W 1N6. From Hwy 1 (TCH) & 264th St (Exit 73) S 0.2km/0.1 mi to 52nd Ave, E 1km/0.6 mi (R) 🛶

BLACK CREEK — **PACIFIC PLAYGROUNDS RV PARK COTTAGES MARINA.** (877) 239-5600. **$33-$50.** 9082 Clarkson Ave V9J 1B3. From Jct of Hwy 19 & Hamm Rd (exit 144), E 5km/3.2 mi on Hamm Rd to Hwy 19A, N 1.6km/1 mi to Regent Rd, E 0.4 km/0.3 mi to Saratoga Rd (which becomes Henderson Ave.), S 0.6km/0.4 mi to Eyre St, E 0.2km/0.1 mi to Clarkson Dr, N 0.6km/0.4 mi (E) 🛶 ⊠

BURNABY — **BURNABY CARIBOO RV PARK AND CAMPGROUND.** ⓐⓐ (604) 420-1722. **$62-$68.** 8765 Cariboo Place V3N 4T2. From Jct of Hwy 1 & Gaglardi Way (exit 37) W 9.6km/6 mi (W of Port Mann Bridge), N 91m/300 ft to traffic light, E 91m/300 ft on Cariboo Rd, N 0.3km/0.2 mi on Cariboo Rd (under overpass) to Cariboo Pl (E) 🛶 ⊠

CAMPBELL RIVER — **RIPPLE ROCK RV PARK AT BROWN'S BAY RESORT.** (877) 361-7847. **$40-$45.** P.O.Box 285 V9W 5B1. From Jct of Hwy 19 & Hwy 28, N 19.2km/12 mi on Hwy 19 to park sign at Browns Bay Rd, E 4.8km/3.2 mi (R)-5kms gravel rd at entrance. 🛶 ⊠

CAMPBELL RIVER — **SALMON POINT RESORT RV PARK & MARINA.** (866) 246-6605. **$36-$50.** 2176 Salmon Point Rd V9H 1E5. N-bnd: From Jct of Hwy 19 & Hamm Rd (exit 144), E 5.1km/3.2 mi on Hamm Rd to Hwy 19A, N 4.1km/2.6 mi to Salmon Pt Rd, E 0.6km/0.4 mi (L) 🛶 ⊠

COMOX — **CAPE LAZO CAMPGROUND & RV.** (888) 558-3946. **$26-$45.** 685 Lazo Rd V9M 3X2. From Jct of Hwy 19 & Ryan Rd (Ferry/NE end of Courtenay), E 3.2km/2 mi on Ryan Rd to Anderton Rd, S 2.9km/1.8 mi to Guthrie Rd, E 2.9km/1.8 mi to Lazo Rd, N 1km/0.6 mi (R)

FAIRMONT HOT SPRINGS — FAIRMONT HOT SPRINGS RESORT LTD. (AA) (800) 663-4979. **$40-$65.** 5225 Fairmont Resort Rd. V0B 1L1. From Jct of Hwy 93/95 & Fairmont Resort Rd, E 0.8kms/ 0.5 mi on Fairmont Resort Rd (E) 🏍 ⊠

HOPE — SUNSHINE VALLEY RV RESORT & CAMPING CABINS. (604) 869-0066. **$40-$69.** 14850 Alpine Blvd V0X 1L5. From Jct of Hwy 1 (Exit 170) & Hwy 3, E 20.6km/12.9 mi on Hwy 3 to Branch Bend, S 30m/100 ft to Cedar Blvd (becomes Alpine Blvd), E 0.3km/0.2 mi on Cedar Blvd/Alpine Blvd 0.3km/0.2 mi (L) ⊅ ⊠

KELOWNA — HOLIDAY PARK RESORT. (250) 766-4255. **$45-$70.** I-415 Commonwealth Rd V4V 1P4. From Jct Hwy 97 & Commonwealth Rd, 0.6km/0.4 mi on Commonwealth Rd (L) 🏍 ⊅ ⊠

NANAIMO — LIVING FOREST OCEANSIDE CAMPGROUND & RV PARK. (250) 755-1755. **$25-$49.** 6 Maki Rd V9R 6N7. From Jct of Hwy 19 & Hwy 1 (exit 9): Go N 0.7km/0.5 mi on Hwy 1 to Maki Rd, E 0.6km/0.4 mi (E) ⊠

OSOYOOS — NK'MIP CAMPGROUND & RV PARK. (250) 495-7279. **$40-$52.** 8000 45th St V0H 1V6. From Jct of Hwy 3 & 45th St, N 0.8 mi on 45th St (E) ⊅ ⊠

OSOYOOS — WALTON'S LAKEFRONT RESORT. (AA) (800) 964-1148. **$35-$80.** 3207 Lakeshore Drive V0H 1V6. From Jct of Hwy 3 & Lakeshore Dr, S 0.5 mi on Lakeshore Dr (L) 🏍 ⊅ ⊠

PARKSVILLE — SURFSIDE RV RESORT. (866) 642-2001. **$35-$65.** 200 N Corfield St V9P 2H5. From Jct of Hwy 19 & Hwy 4A (Parksville/Coombs exit 51), E 2km/1.2 mi on Hwy 4A to Hwy 19A, S 0.5km/0.3 mi to N Corfield St, E 0.2 km/0.1 mi (E) 🏍 ⊅ ⊠

RADIUM HOT SPRINGS — RADIUM VALLEY VACATION RESORT. (250) 347-9715. **$59-$74.** 7274 Radium Valley Rd V0A 1M0. From Jct of Hwy 93 & Hwy 95, N 0.7 mi on Hwy 95 to Radium Valley Vacation Resort Rd (L) 🏍 ⊅ ⊠

ROSEDALE — CAMPERLAND BRIDAL FALLS. (604) 794-7361. **$40-$62.** 53730 Bridal Falls Rd V0X 1X1. From Jct of Hwy 1 & Hwy 9 (exit 135), S 0.2km/0.1 mi on Hwy 9 to Bridal Falls Rd, E 1.6km/1 mi on Bridal Falls Rd (R) ⊅ ⊠

SAANICHTON — OCEANSIDE RV RESORT. (250) 544-0508. **$34-$54.** 3000 Stautw Rd V8M 2K5. From Jct of Hwy 17 & Mt Newton X Rd, E 0.5km/0.3 mi on Mt Newton X Rd to Stautw Rd, E 1.1km/0.7 mi (R)

SURREY — HAZELMERE RV PARK & CAMPGROUND. (AA) (604) 538-1167. **$36-$43.** 18843-8th Ave V3S 9R9. From Jct Pacific Hwy (Hwy 15) & 8th Ave, E 2.4km/1.5mi on 8th Ave (L) ⊅ ⊠

VERNON — SWAN LAKE RV RESORT. (250) 558-1116. **$38-$48.** 8000 Highland Rd, Box 1010 V1B 3W5. From Jct of Hwy 97A & Hwy 97 (Kamloops exit), N 0.2km/0.1 mi on Hwy 97 to Highland Rd, S 0.3km/0.2 mi (R) 🏍 ⊅

New Brunswick

CARAQUET — CAMPING COLIBRI. (506) 727-2222. **$32-$45.** 913 Boul Des Acadiens Rte 11 E1W 0C6. At W-end of town on Rte 11 (L) ⊅ ⊠

FREDERICTON — HARTT ISLAND RV RESORT. (506) 462-9400. **$50-$60.** 2475 Woodstock Rd Rte 102 E3C 1P6. W-bnd:From Jct of TCH-2 & Exit 294 (Hwy 7 to Hwy 8), N 6 mi on Hwy 7 to Edmundston-Mactaquac exit (Hwy 8-S), S 2 mi to exit 3 (Hanwell/Rte 102), N 3 mi (R); or E-bnd:From Jct of TCH-2 & Exit 280 (Hwy 8), N 2 mi on Hwy 8 to Exit 3, (Fredericton Centre), N 0.2 mi to Prospect St/Rte 102, N 3 mi (R) ⊅ ⊠

MONCTON — CAMPER'S CITY RV RESORT. (877) 512-7868. **$31-$42.** 138 Queensway Dr E1G 2L2. From Jct of TCH-2 & Exit 454 (Mapleton Rd), N 500 ft on Mapleton Rd to Queensway Dr, E 0.25 mi (L) ⊅ ⊠

PETIT-ROCHER-NORD — CAMPING MURRAYWOOD PARK LTD. (506) 783-2137. **$26-$39.** 281 Route 134 E8J 2E5. From Jct of Hwy 11 & Exit 326 (Rte 315), E 2.4 mi on Rte 315 to Rte 134, N 1.8 mi (R) ⊅ ⊠

POKEMOUCHE — CAMPING POKEMOUCHE. (AA) (506) 727-6090. **$35-$39.** 11220, Rte 11 E8P 1H9. From Jct of Hwy 11 & 113, S 1.5 mi (L) ⊅ ⊠

WOODSTOCK — YOGI BEAR'S JELLYSTONE PARK. (506) 328-6287. **$42-$45.** Po Box 9004 E7M 6B5. From Jct of TCH-2 & Exit 191 (Beardsley Rd/Woodstock Direction), N 0.25 mi on Beardsley Rd to Hemlock St, W 0.25 mi, follow signs (E) ⊅ ⊠

Nova Scotia

BADDECK — BADDECK CABOT TRAIL CAMPGROUND. (AA) (902) 295-2288. **$34-$46.** 9584 Hwy 105 B0E 1B0. W-bnd: From town, W 5 mi on TCH-105 (R); or E-bnd: From Jct of TCH-105 & Exit 7 (Cabot Trail Entrance), E 0.5 mi on TCH-105 (L) ⊅ ⊠

BADDECK — BRAS D'OR LAKES CAMPGROUND. (AA) (902) 295-2329. **$32-$53.** Box 595, 8885 Hwy 105 B0E 1B0. From town, W 3 mi on TCH-105 (L) Between Exit 7 & 8, MM 80 ⊅ ⊠

DEBERT — ELM RIVER RV PARK LTD. (AA) (888) 356-4356. **$39-$42.** Rr 1, 85 Elm River Parkway B0M 1G0. From Jct of Hwy 104 & Exit 12 (Rtes 2 & 4), W 0.6 mi on Rte 4 (R) ⊅ ⊠

GRANVILLE FERRY — DUNROMIN CAMPSITE. (902) 532-2808. **$32-$45.** 4618 Hwy 1 B0S 1K0. From Jct of Hwy 101 & Exit 22 (Rtes 8 & 1), N 3.8 mi on Rte 8 to Rte 1, E 1.4 mi (R) ⊅ ⊠

LOWER FIVE ISLANDS — FIVE ISLAND OCEAN RESORT. (902) 254-2824. **$30-$50.** 482 Hwy 2 B0M 1N0. From Jct of TCH-104 & Exit 12 (Rte 4), E 1 mi on Rte 4 to Rt 2, N 30 mi (L) ⊅ ⊠

Ontario

BRIGHTON — BRIGHTON KOA. (800) 562-0906. **$40-$58.** 15051 Telephone Rd. K0K 1H0. From Jct of Hwy 401 & CR-30 (Exit 509), N 0.16 km (0.1 mi) on CR 30 to Telephone Rd (runs adjacent to Hwy 401), W 1.2 km (0.75 mi) (L) ⊅ ⊠

CARRYING PLACE — NORTH SHORE RV PARK. (613) 475-2036. **$42-$51.** 1675 County Rd 64 K0K 1L0. From Jct of Hwy 401 & Hwy 30 (Exit 509), S 4.8 km (3 mi) on Hwy 30 to CR-64, E 10 km (6.3 mi) to Shoreline Rd, S 0.8 km (0.5 mi) (E). W-bnd; From Jct of Hwy 40 (Wooler Rd, exit 522) go S till no. 40 ends at Hwy 33, turn right until you cross the Murray Canal, turn on CR 64, 4 km (2.8 mi) ⊅ ⊠

CHERRY VALLEY — QUINTE'S ISLE CAMPARK. (613) 476-6310. **$43-$66.** 237 Salmon Pt Rd K0K 1P0. From Jct of Hwys 401 & 62 (Exit 543A), S 46.6 km (29 mi) on Hwy 62 to Hwy 33, E 9.6 km (6 mi) to CR-10 (Lake St, in Picton), S 8 km (5 mi) to CR-18, SW 8 km (5 mi) to Salmon Pt Rd, S 2 km (1.25 mi) (L). Note: 3 night minimum stay on holiday weekends 🛶 🏊

COOKSTOWN — TORONTO NORTH/COOKSTOWN KOA. (800) 562-2691. **$40-$75.** 139 Reive Blvd L0L 1L0. S-Bnd: From Jct of Hwys 400 & 89 (Exit 75), E 64 m (70 yds) on Hwy 89 to Reive Blvd, N 0.6 km (0.4 mi) (R); or N-bnd: From Jct of Hwys 400 & 89 (Exit 75), continue directly across Hwy 89 to Reive Blvd, N 0.6 km (0.4 mi) (R). Min 3 night stay on holiday weekends 🛶 🏊

ESSEX — WILDWOOD GOLF & RV RESORT. (866) 994-9699. **$44.** 11112 11th Concession Rd N8M 0A7. From Jct of Hwy 401 & CR-19 (Manning Rd) Exit 21, S 4.7 km (2.9 mi) on CR-19 to Hwy 3, SE 4.8 km (3 mi) to N. Malden Rd, SW 9.2 km (5.7 mi) to 11th Conc Rd, W 0.6 km (0.4 mi) (R) 🏌 🛶 🏊

KAKABEKA FALLS — HAPPY LAND RV PARK. ⒶⒶ (866) 473-9003. **$37-$47.** I-4650 Hwy 11-17 P7K 0J1. From Jct of Hwys 61 and 11/17 (in town), go W 24.8 km (15.4 mi) on Hwy 11/17 (R) 🛶 🏊

KINCARDINE — FISHERMAN'S COVE TENT & TRAILER PARK. (519) 395-2757. **$49-$59.** 13 Southline Ave, Rr4 N2Z 2X5. From Jct of Hwys 21 & 9, E 18 km (11.25 mi) on Hwy 9 to Bruce CR-1, S 2 km (1.3 mi) to Southline, SE 0.8 km (0.5 mi) (E). Note: Min 3 ngt stay on holiday weekends 🏌 🛶 🏊

LANSDOWNE — 1000 ISLANDS IVY LEA KOA. (800) 562-2471. **$30-$90.** 514-1000 Islands Parkway K0E 1L0. From Jct of Hwy 401 and Reynolds Rd (Exit 659), S 2.4 km (1.5 mi) on Reynolds Rd to 1000 Island Pkwy, W 3.2 km (2 mi) (R). Note: Min. 3 night stay on holiday weekends and 2 nights on event weekends 🛶 🏊

MILLER LAKE — SUMMER HOUSE PARK. (519) 795-7712. **$35-$55.** 197 Miller Lake Shore Rd N0H 1Z0. From Jct of Hwy 6 & Miller Lake Rd, E 3.2 km (2 mi) on Miller Lake Rd (L). Min 3-5 nights stay on holiday weekends. 🏊

NIAGARA FALLS — CAMPARK RESORTS. ⒶⒶ (877) CAM-PARK. **$42-$58.** 9387 Lundy'S Lane L2E 6S4. S-bnd: Jct of QEW & Exit 30B, W 0.16 km (0.1 mi) to Montrose Rd, S 0.8 km (0.5 mi) to Lundy's Ln, W 2.6 km (1.6 mi) (R); N-bnd: Jct of QEW & McLeod Rd (Exit 27), W 0.5 km (0.3 mi) on McLeod Rd to Montrose Rd, N 2 km (1.3 mi) to Lundy's Ln, W 2.6 km (1.6 mi) (R). Min. 2 ngts stay holiday weekends 🛶 🏊

NIAGARA FALLS — NIAGARA FALLS KOA. (800) KOA-MIST. **$44-$100.** 8625 Lundy'S Lane L2H 1H5. S-bnd: From jct of QEW & Exit 30B, W 0.16 km (0.1 mi) to Montrose Rd, S 0.8 km (0.5 mi) to Lundy's Lane, W 1.6 km (1 mi) (R); or N-bnd: From Jct of QEW & McLeod Rd (Exit 27), W 0.48 km (0.3 mi) on McLeod Rd to Montrose Rd, N 2.1 km (1.3 mi) to Lundy's Lane, W 1.6 km (1 mi) (R) 🛶 🏊

NIAGARA FALLS — YOGI BEAR'S JELLYSTONE PARK CAMP-RESORT. (800) 263-2570. **$43-$68.** 8676 Oakwood Dr L2E 6S5. From Jct of QEW & McLeod Rd (Exit 27), E 182 m (200 yds) on McLeod Rd to Oakwood Dr, S 2.4 km (1.5 mi) (L). NOTE: Min. 3 day stay on summer holiday weekends 🛶 🏊

OTTAWA — CAMP HITHER HILLS. (613) 822-0509. **$32-$43.** 5227 Bank St K2P 0S5. E-bnd: From Jct of Hwy 417 & 416S (Exit 131), S 17.7 km (11 mi) on Hwy 416S to Bankfield Rd (Exit 57), E 4.5 km (2.8 mi) to Manotick Main St, SE 0.3 km (0.2 mi) to Bridge St, NE 11 km (6.8 mi) to Bank St, NW 1.3 km (0.8 mi) (R). Min 3 ngts stay on July 1 weekend 🛶 🏊

PARRY SOUND — PARRY SOUND KOA. (800) 562-2681. **$40-$56.** 276 Rankin Lake Rd P2A 2W8. From Jct of Hwy 400 & Seguin Trail Rd/Horseshoe Lake Rd (Exit 214), S 1.4 km (0.9 mi) on Horseshoe Lake Rd to Black Rd, W 1 km (0.6 mi) to Rankin Lake Rd, W 1 km (0.6 mi) (R). Note: Min 3 day stay on holiday weekends 🛶 🏊

PUSLINCH — EMERALD LAKE TRAILER RESORT & WATERPARK. (905) 659-7923. **$70-$80.** 7248 Gore Rd, Rr # 2 N0B 2J0. From Jct of Hwy 401 & Hwy 6S, (Exit 299), S 4.8 km (3 mi) on Hwy 6S to Flamborough Conc 11 West (then becomes Gore Rd), W 4.8 km (3 mi) (R) 🛶 🏊

RIDGEVILLE — BISSELL'S HIDEAWAY RESORT. (888) 236-0619. **$40-$90.** 205 Metler Rd L0S 1M0. From Jct of QEW & RR 24 (Exit 57), S 13.8 km (8.6 mi) on RR 24 (Victoria Ave) to Metler Rd, E 6.9 km (4.3 mi) on Metler Rd (L). Note: Min 3 night stay on holiday weekends 🛶 🏊

SAUBLE BEACH — CARSONS' CAMP LIMITED. (519) 422-1143. **$45-$52.** 110 Southampton Pkwy N0H 2G0. From Jct of CR-8 & CR-13 (Southampton Pkwy), S 0.8 km (0.5 mi) on CR-13 (Southampton Pkwy) (R). Note: Min 7 nights stay-July & August. No access to the park after hours unless by prior reservation 🛶 🏊

SAUBLE BEACH — WOODLAND PARK. (519) 422-1161. **$32-$55.** 47 Sauble Falls Parkway N0H 2G0. From Jct of CR-8 & CR-13 (Sauble Falls Pkwy), N 0.4 km (0.25 mi) on CR-13/Sauble Falls Pkwy (R) Note: Min. 3 nights stay on holiday weekends. 🛶 🏊

THUNDER BAY — THUNDER BAY KOA. (800) 562-4162. **$36-$49.** 162 Spruce River Road P7B 5E4. From Jct of Hwy 11/17 & Hwy 527 (Spruce River Rd) at E city limits, S 0.4 km (0.25 mi) on Spruce River Rd (L) 🛶 🏊

VINELAND — N.E.T. CAMPING RESORT. (866) 490-4745. **$36-$55.** 2325 Rr 24 L0R 2C0. W-bnd: From Jct of QEW & N Service Rd, NW 0.16 km (0.1 mi) on N Service Rd to Victoria Ave (RR24), S 11.6 km (7.2 mi) (L); or E-bnd: From Jct of QEW & S Service Rd (Exit 57), W 0.16 km (0.1 mi) on S Service Rd to Victoria Ave (RR 24) S 11.3 km (7 mi) (L). Min. 3 day stay on holiday weekends 🛶 🏊

WYOMING — COUNTRY VIEW MOTEL & CAMPING RESORT. (519) 845-3394. **$34-$42.** Rr1 4569 London Line/Hwy 22 N0N 1T0. From Jct of Hwy 402 & Hwy 21 (Exit 25), S 1.2 km (0.75 mi) on Hwy 21 to CR-22 (London Line), E 91 m (300 ft) (R) 🛶 🏊

Prince Edward Island

BORDEN-CARLETON — BORDEN-CARLETON KOA. (902) 855-3492. **$32-$44.** 23714 Tch-1 C0B 1X0. From town, NE 1.25 mi on Hwy 1 (L) 🏊

CORNWALL — CORNWALL KOA. (902) 566-2421. **$35-$63.** 208 Ferry Rd. C0A 1H0. E-bnd: From Jct of TCH-1 & Rte 248 (Ferry Rd), E 1 mi on Rte 248 to park entrance (R); or W-bnd: From Jct of TCH-1 & Rte 248 (York Point Rd), S 2.2 mi on Rte 248 to Ferry Rd, W 1.3 mi to park entrance (L) 🛶 🏊

HUNTER RIVER — CAVENDISH KOA. ⒶⒶ (800) 562-1879. **$34-$68.** 198 Forest Hill Lane C0A 1N0. From Jct of Rtes 6 & 13, W 0.8 mi on Rte 6 (L) 🛶 🏊

HUNTER RIVER — MARCO POLO LAND INC. ⒶⒶ (902) 963-2352. **$36-$43.** 7406 Route 13 C0A 1N0. From Jct of Rtes 6 & 13, S 0.5 mi on Rte 13 (L) 🛶 🏊

KENSINGTON — TWIN SHORES CAMPING AREA. (877) 734-2267. **$39-$55.** 702 Lower Darnley Rd. C0B 1M0. In Kensington; From Jct of Hwy 2 & Rte 20, N 10 mi on Rte 20 to Lower Darnley Rd, W 2.5 mi (E) 🏊

Québec

COMPTON — CAMPING DE COMPTON. (800) 563-5277. **$30-$45.** 24 Chemin De La Station J0B 1L0. From jct Hwy 208 W & Hwy 147: Go 65 meters/215 ft N on Hwy 147, then 0.3 km/1/4 mi W on Rue de la Station. 🛶 🏊

GRANBY — CAMPING L'ESTRIVAL. (450) 378-9410. **$43-$46.** 1680 Rue Principale (Rte 112) J2J 0M6. From Jct of Hwy 10 & Exit 68 (Rte 139), N 5 mi on Rte 139 to Rte 112, W 2.8 mi (L) 🛶 🏊

LA BAIE — CAMPING AU JARDIN DE MON PERE. (418) 544-6486. **$29-$40.** 3736 Chemin St Louis G7B 4M8. From Jct of Rtes 170 & 381 (in town), S 1 mi on Rte 381, follow signs (R) 🛶 🏊

LÉVIS — CAMPING TRANSIT. (418) 838-0948. **$30-$45.** 600 Chemin St. Roch G6V 6N4. E-bnd: From Jct of Hwy 20 & Exit 330 (Rte Lallemand/Chemin St-Roch), E 2.5 mi on Chemin St-Roch, follow signs (L); or W-bnd: From Jct of Hwy 20 & Exit 337 (Rte 279), S 0.5 mi on Rte 279 to Chemin St-Roch Rd, W 2 mi (R) 🛶 🏊

MONTMAGNY — CAMPING POINTE AUX OIES. (418) 248-9710. **Call for rates.** 45 Bassin Nord Avenue G5V 4E5. From Jct of Hwy 20 & exit 378 (Rte 283), N 1.75 mi on Rte 283 to Rte 132. Follow signs (E) 🛶 🏊

NOTRE-DAME-DE-LA-SALETTE — ROYAL PAPINEAU (PARKBRIDGE). (819) 766-2826. **$38-$50.** 237 Chemin Du Golf J0X 2L0. From Rte 309 (in town), N 8 mi on Thomas Rd S (E) 🛶 🏊

NOTRE-DAME-DES-PINS — CAMPING LA ROCHE D'OR (PARKBRIDGE). (418) 774-9191. **$42.** 3005 Route 173 G0M 1K0. From St-Georges De Beauce, N 5 mi on Rte 173 (R) 🛶 🏊

ST-ANTONIN — CAMPING CHEZ JEAN. (418) 862-3081. **$26-$33.** 434 Principale G0L 2J0. From Jct of Rte 185 & St Antonin exit, W 2.3 mi on Rue Principale (R) Follow signs 🛶 🏊

ST-APOLLINAIRE — DOMAINE DE LA CHUTE (PARKBRIDGE). Ⓒ (418) 831-1311. **$39-$44.** 74 Chemin De La Chute G0S 2E0. E-bnd: From Jct of Hwy 20 & Exit 296 (Rte Du Cap), S 0.7 mi on Rte Du Cap to Chemin de la Chute, E 1.5 mi, follow signs (E) 🛶 🏊

ST-MATHIEU-DE-BELOEIL — CAMPING ALOUETTE (PARKBRIDGE). Ⓒ (450) 464-1661. **$44-$52.** 3449 De L'Industrie J3G 4S5. From Jct of TCH 20 & Exit 105, E 1 mi on N service rd (De L'Industrie St) (L) 🛶 🏊

ST-MATHIEU-DE-RIOUX — KOA BAS-ST-LAURENT CAMPGROUND. Ⓒ (800) 562-2482. **$50.** 109 Chemin Du Lac Sud G0L 3T0. From Rt 132 in St Simonde Rimouski, go NE toward Rue d'Anjou 0.9 mi on Rt 132. R (SE) on Route de Saint Simon Saint Mathieu 2.7 mi. R at stop sign go SW 0.4 mi. On 3e Rang 0. L (SE) on Chemin Du Lac Sud 1.6 mi. Follow KOA sign. 🏊

ST-PHILIPPE — CAMPING LA CLE DES CHAMPS RV RESORT. (450) 659-3389. **$46-$53.** 415 Montee St-Claude J0L 2K0. From Jct of Hwy 30 & Exit 104 (Rte 104), E 1.7 mi on Rte 104 to Rang St-Raphael, S 2 mi to Montee St-Claude, W 0.5 mi (R) 🏌 🛶 🏊

ST-RAPHAEL-DE-BELLECHASSE — CAMPING LA JOLIE ROCHELLE. (418) 243-1320. **$52.** 135 Petite Troisieme G0R 4C0. From jct Hwy 20 & 348: Go 19 km S on 281, then .5 km W on Rang, then 2.4 km S on God Bout. 🛶 🏊

ST-VALLIER — CAMPING LE DOMAINE CHAMPETRE. (418) 884-2270. **$33-$55.** 888 Montee De La Station G0R 4J0. From Jct of Hwy 20 & exit 356 (Montee De La Station), E 400 m. on Chemin D'Azur (exit Rd) to Montée De La Station, S 2.7 km (L) 🛶 🏊

Saskatchewan

INDIAN HEAD — INDIAN HEAD CAMPGROUND. (855) 695-3635. **$34-$41.** 1100 Mckay St S0G 2K0. From Jct of Hwy 1 & East Entrance to Indian Head, N (across railway tracks) 0.3km/0.2 mi (L) 🛶 🏊

MAPLE CREEK — EAGLE VALLEY PARK CAMPGROUND LTD. (306) 662-2788. **$34-$36.** Sw Q-8 Of 12 Of 26 W 3rd. S0N 1N0. From Jct of Trans Cda Hwy 1 & Hwy 21, W 3 mi (4 km) on Trans Cda Hwy 1 (L) - 88kms/54.7 mi E of Medicine Hat. 🏊

AAA PetBook Reader Questionnaire

We "paws-itively" want to hear from you! Your comments, opinions and suggestions are important to AAA. Please help us to improve the AAA PetBook® by taking a few minutes to complete this simple questionnaire.

> Please mail your completed questionnaire to: AAA PetBook, Mail Stop 64, 1000 AAA Drive, Heathrow, FL 32746-5063
>
> Or, email us your comments at PetBookFeedback@national.aaa.com

1. Where did you purchase the AAA PetBook®?
   - ☐ AAA Club _____ (club name)
   - ☐ Bookstore _____ (name of bookstore)
   - ☐ Online _____ (web site)

2. What specific pet-related information contained in the AAA PetBook is important to you when planning to travel with your pet? (Please check all that apply)
   - ☐ Hotels
   - ☐ Restaurants
   - ☐ Campgrounds
   - ☐ National Public Lands
   - ☐ Attractions
   - ☐ DogParks
   - ☐ Emergency Animal Clinics
   - ☐ U.S. / Canada Border Crossing Procedures
   - ☐ Traveling by Car
   - ☐ Traveling by Air
   - ☐ Traveling with Disabilities

3. When traveling with your pet, what additional information would be helpful?
   _____

4. How well does the AAA PetBook® meet your expectations?
   - ☐ Exceeds
   - ☐ Meets all
   - ☐ Meets most
   - ☐ Falls below

5. Are you familiar with the annual photo contest at AAA.com/PetBook? ☐ Yes ☐ No

Additional feedback or comments about the AAA PetBook:
   _____
   _____

Which age group are you in? ☐ Under 25 ☐ 25-34 ☐ 35-44 ☐ 45-54 ☐ 55-64 ☐ 65 +

On average, how many overnight leisure trips do you take a year?
   ☐ None ☐ One ☐ Two ☐ Three or more

How many trips/outings a year include traveling with your pet? _____

What is the average distance traveled? _____

In addition to the AAA PetBook, did you buy any other pet-travel or general travel guides for your trip? ☐ Yes ☐ No

If yes, which ones?
   _____
   _____

Optional:

Name (Mr/Mrs/Ms) _____

Address _____

City _____ State _____ Zip _____

Are you a AAA member? ☐ Yes ☐ No, If yes, name of AAA club: _____

Thank you for taking the time to complete this questionnaire. We appreciate your feedback.

17th edition

🐾 Pet-Friendly Travel Notes 🐾